Oxford Dictionary of National Biography

IN ASSOCIATION WITH
The British Academy

From the earliest times to the year 2000

Edited by
H. C. G. Matthew
and
Brian Harrison

Volume 8
Brown–Burstow

OXFORD
UNIVERSITY PRESS

OXFORD
UNIVERSITY PRESS

Great Clarendon Street, Oxford OX2 6DP

Oxford University Press is a department of the University of Oxford.
It furthers the University's objective of excellence in research, scholarship,
and education by publishing worldwide in

Oxford New York

Auckland Bangkok Buenos Aires Cape Town
Chennai Dar es Salaam Delhi Hong Kong Istanbul Karachi
Kolkata Kuala Lumpur Madrid Melbourne Mexico City Mumbai Nairobi
São Paulo Shanghai Taipei Tokyo Toronto

Oxford is a registered trade mark of Oxford University Press
in the UK and in certain other countries

Published in the United States
by Oxford University Press Inc., New York

© Oxford University Press 2004

Illustrations © individual copyright holders as listed in
'Picture credits', and reproduced with permission

Database right Oxford University Press (maker)

First published 2004

British Library Cataloguing in Publication Data
Data available

Library of Congress Cataloging in Publication Data
Data available: for details see volume 1, p. iv

ISBN 0-19-861358-X (this volume)
ISBN 0-19-861411-X (set of sixty volumes)

Text captured by Alliance Phototypesetters, Pondicherry
Illustrations reproduced and archived by
Alliance Graphics Ltd, UK
Typeset in OUP Swift by Interactive Sciences Limited, Gloucester
Printed in Great Britain on acid-free paper by
Butler and Tanner Ltd,
Frome, Somerset

LIST OF ABBREVIATIONS

1 *General abbreviations*

AB	bachelor of arts	BCnL	bachelor of canon law
ABC	Australian Broadcasting Corporation	BCom	bachelor of commerce
ABC TV	ABC Television	BD	bachelor of divinity
act.	active	BEd	bachelor of education
A$	Australian dollar	BEng	bachelor of engineering
AD	*anno domini*	bk *pl.* bks	book(s)
AFC	Air Force Cross	BL	bachelor of law / letters / literature
AIDS	acquired immune deficiency syndrome	BLitt	bachelor of letters
AK	Alaska	BM	bachelor of medicine
AL	Alabama	BMus	bachelor of music
A level	advanced level [examination]	BP	before present
ALS	associate of the Linnean Society	BP	British Petroleum
AM	master of arts	Bros.	Brothers
AMICE	associate member of the Institution of Civil Engineers	BS	(1) bachelor of science; (2) bachelor of surgery; (3) British standard
ANZAC	Australian and New Zealand Army Corps	BSc	bachelor of science
appx *pl.* appxs	appendix(es)	BSc (Econ.)	bachelor of science (economics)
AR	Arkansas	BSc (Eng.)	bachelor of science (engineering)
ARA	associate of the Royal Academy	bt	baronet
ARCA	associate of the Royal College of Art	BTh	bachelor of theology
ARCM	associate of the Royal College of Music	*bur.*	buried
ARCO	associate of the Royal College of Organists	C.	command [identifier for published parliamentary papers]
ARIBA	associate of the Royal Institute of British Architects	*c.*	*circa*
ARP	air-raid precautions	c.	*capitulum pl. capitula*: chapter(s)
ARRC	associate of the Royal Red Cross	CA	California
ARSA	associate of the Royal Scottish Academy	Cantab.	Cantabrigiensis
art.	article / item	cap.	*capitulum pl. capitula*: chapter(s)
ASC	Army Service Corps	CB	companion of the Bath
Asch	Austrian Schilling	CBE	commander of the Order of the British Empire
ASDIC	Antisubmarine Detection Investigation Committee	CBS	Columbia Broadcasting System
ATS	Auxiliary Territorial Service	cc	cubic centimetres
ATV	Associated Television	C$	Canadian dollar
Aug	August	CD	compact disc
AZ	Arizona	Cd	command [identifier for published parliamentary papers]
b.	born	CE	Common (*or* Christian) Era
BA	bachelor of arts	cent.	century
BA (Admin.)	bachelor of arts (administration)	cf.	compare
BAFTA	British Academy of Film and Television Arts	CH	Companion of Honour
BAO	bachelor of arts in obstetrics	chap.	chapter
bap.	baptized	ChB	bachelor of surgery
BBC	British Broadcasting Corporation / Company	CI	Imperial Order of the Crown of India
BC	before Christ	CIA	Central Intelligence Agency
BCE	before the common (*or* Christian) era	CID	Criminal Investigation Department
BCE	bachelor of civil engineering	CIE	companion of the Order of the Indian Empire
BCG	bacillus of Calmette and Guérin [inoculation against tuberculosis]	Cie	Compagnie
BCh	bachelor of surgery	CLit	companion of literature
BChir	bachelor of surgery	CM	master of surgery
BCL	bachelor of civil law	cm	centimetre(s)

Cmd	command [identifier for published parliamentary papers]
CMG	companion of the Order of St Michael and St George
Cmnd	command [identifier for published parliamentary papers]
CO	Colorado
Co.	company
co.	county
col. *pl.* cols.	column(s)
Corp.	corporation
CSE	certificate of secondary education
CSI	companion of the Order of the Star of India
CT	Connecticut
CVO	commander of the Royal Victorian Order
cwt	hundredweight
$	(American) dollar
d.	(1) penny (pence); (2) died
DBE	dame commander of the Order of the British Empire
DCH	diploma in child health
DCh	doctor of surgery
DCL	doctor of civil law
DCnL	doctor of canon law
DCVO	dame commander of the Royal Victorian Order
DD	doctor of divinity
DE	Delaware
Dec	December
dem.	demolished
DEng	doctor of engineering
des.	destroyed
DFC	Distinguished Flying Cross
DipEd	diploma in education
DipPsych	diploma in psychiatry
diss.	dissertation
DL	deputy lieutenant
DLitt	doctor of letters
DLittCelt	doctor of Celtic letters
DM	(1) Deutschmark; (2) doctor of medicine; (3) doctor of musical arts
DMus	doctor of music
DNA	dioxyribonucleic acid
doc.	document
DOL	doctor of oriental learning
DPH	diploma in public health
DPhil	doctor of philosophy
DPM	diploma in psychological medicine
DSC	Distinguished Service Cross
DSc	doctor of science
DSc (Econ.)	doctor of science (economics)
DSc (Eng.)	doctor of science (engineering)
DSM	Distinguished Service Medal
DSO	companion of the Distinguished Service Order
DSocSc	doctor of social science
DTech	doctor of technology
DTh	doctor of theology
DTM	diploma in tropical medicine
DTMH	diploma in tropical medicine and hygiene
DU	doctor of the university
DUniv	doctor of the university
dwt	pennyweight
EC	European Community
ed. *pl.* eds.	edited / edited by / editor(s)
Edin.	Edinburgh
edn	edition
EEC	European Economic Community
EFTA	European Free Trade Association
EICS	East India Company Service
EMI	Electrical and Musical Industries (Ltd)
Eng.	English
enl.	enlarged
ENSA	Entertainments National Service Association
ep. *pl.* epp.	*epistola(e)*
ESP	extra-sensory perception
esp.	especially
esq.	esquire
est.	estimate / estimated
EU	European Union
ex	sold by (*lit.* out of)
excl.	excludes / excluding
exh.	exhibited
exh. cat.	exhibition catalogue
f. *pl.* ff.	following [pages]
FA	Football Association
FACP	fellow of the American College of Physicians
facs.	facsimile
FANY	First Aid Nursing Yeomanry
FBA	fellow of the British Academy
FBI	Federation of British Industries
FCS	fellow of the Chemical Society
Feb	February
FEng	fellow of the Fellowship of Engineering
FFCM	fellow of the Faculty of Community Medicine
FGS	fellow of the Geological Society
fig.	figure
FIMechE	fellow of the Institution of Mechanical Engineers
FL	Florida
fl.	*floruit*
FLS	fellow of the Linnean Society
FM	frequency modulation
fol. *pl.* fols.	folio(s)
Fr	French francs
Fr.	French
FRAeS	fellow of the Royal Aeronautical Society
FRAI	fellow of the Royal Anthropological Institute
FRAM	fellow of the Royal Academy of Music
FRAS	(1) fellow of the Royal Asiatic Society; (2) fellow of the Royal Astronomical Society
FRCM	fellow of the Royal College of Music
FRCO	fellow of the Royal College of Organists
FRCOG	fellow of the Royal College of Obstetricians and Gynaecologists
FRCP(C)	fellow of the Royal College of Physicians of Canada
FRCP (Edin.)	fellow of the Royal College of Physicians of Edinburgh
FRCP (Lond.)	fellow of the Royal College of Physicians of London
FRCPath	fellow of the Royal College of Pathologists
FRCPsych	fellow of the Royal College of Psychiatrists
FRCS	fellow of the Royal College of Surgeons
FRGS	fellow of the Royal Geographical Society
FRIBA	fellow of the Royal Institute of British Architects
FRICS	fellow of the Royal Institute of Chartered Surveyors
FRS	fellow of the Royal Society
FRSA	fellow of the Royal Society of Arts

FRSCM	fellow of the Royal School of Church Music
FRSE	fellow of the Royal Society of Edinburgh
FRSL	fellow of the Royal Society of Literature
FSA	fellow of the Society of Antiquaries
ft	foot *pl.* feet
FTCL	fellow of Trinity College of Music, London
ft-lb per min.	foot-pounds per minute [unit of horsepower]
FZS	fellow of the Zoological Society
GA	Georgia
GBE	knight or dame grand cross of the Order of the British Empire
GCB	knight grand cross of the Order of the Bath
GCE	general certificate of education
GCH	knight grand cross of the Royal Guelphic Order
GCHQ	government communications headquarters
GCIE	knight grand commander of the Order of the Indian Empire
GCMG	knight or dame grand cross of the Order of St Michael and St George
GCSE	general certificate of secondary education
GCSI	knight grand commander of the Order of the Star of India
GCStJ	bailiff or dame grand cross of the order of St John of Jerusalem
GCVO	knight or dame grand cross of the Royal Victorian Order
GEC	General Electric Company
Ger.	German
GI	government (*or* general) issue
GMT	Greenwich mean time
GP	general practitioner
GPU	[Soviet special police unit]
GSO	general staff officer
Heb.	Hebrew
HEICS	Honourable East India Company Service
HI	Hawaii
HIV	human immunodeficiency virus
HK$	Hong Kong dollar
HM	his / her majesty('s)
HMAS	his / her majesty's Australian ship
HMNZS	his / her majesty's New Zealand ship
HMS	his / her majesty's ship
HMSO	His / Her Majesty's Stationery Office
HMV	His Master's Voice
Hon.	Honourable
hp	horsepower
hr	hour(s)
HRH	his / her royal highness
HTV	Harlech Television
IA	Iowa
ibid.	*ibidem*: in the same place
ICI	Imperial Chemical Industries (Ltd)
ID	Idaho
IL	Illinois
illus.	illustration
illustr.	illustrated
IN	Indiana
in.	inch(es)
Inc.	Incorporated
incl.	includes / including
IOU	I owe you
IQ	intelligence quotient
Ir£	Irish pound
IRA	Irish Republican Army
ISO	companion of the Imperial Service Order
It.	Italian
ITA	Independent Television Authority
ITV	Independent Television
Jan	January
JP	justice of the peace
jun.	junior
KB	knight of the Order of the Bath
KBE	knight commander of the Order of the British Empire
KC	king's counsel
kcal	kilocalorie
KCB	knight commander of the Order of the Bath
KCH	knight commander of the Royal Guelphic Order
KCIE	knight commander of the Order of the Indian Empire
KCMG	knight commander of the Order of St Michael and St George
KCSI	knight commander of the Order of the Star of India
KCVO	knight commander of the Royal Victorian Order
keV	kilo-electron-volt
KG	knight of the Order of the Garter
KGB	[Soviet committee of state security]
KH	knight of the Royal Guelphic Order
KLM	Koninklijke Luchtvaart Maatschappij (Royal Dutch Air Lines)
km	kilometre(s)
KP	knight of the Order of St Patrick
KS	Kansas
KT	knight of the Order of the Thistle
kt	knight
KY	Kentucky
£	pound(s) sterling
£E	Egyptian pound
L	lira *pl.* lire
l. *pl.* ll.	line(s)
LA	Lousiana
LAA	light anti-aircraft
LAH	licentiate of the Apothecaries' Hall, Dublin
Lat.	Latin
lb	pound(s), unit of weight
LDS	licence in dental surgery
lit.	literally
LittB	bachelor of letters
LittD	doctor of letters
LKQCPI	licentiate of the King and Queen's College of Physicians, Ireland
LLA	lady literate in arts
LLB	bachelor of laws
LLD	doctor of laws
LLM	master of laws
LM	licentiate in midwifery
LP	long-playing record
LRAM	licentiate of the Royal Academy of Music
LRCP	licentiate of the Royal College of Physicians
LRCPS (Glasgow)	licentiate of the Royal College of Physicians and Surgeons of Glasgow
LRCS	licentiate of the Royal College of Surgeons
LSA	licentiate of the Society of Apothecaries
LSD	lysergic acid diethylamide
LVO	lieutenant of the Royal Victorian Order
M. *pl.* MM.	Monsieur *pl.* Messieurs
m	metre(s)

m. *pl.* mm.	membrane(s)
MA	(1) Massachusetts; (2) master of arts
MAI	master of engineering
MB	bachelor of medicine
MBA	master of business administration
MBE	member of the Order of the British Empire
MC	Military Cross
MCC	Marylebone Cricket Club
MCh	master of surgery
MChir	master of surgery
MCom	master of commerce
MD	(1) doctor of medicine; (2) Maryland
MDMA	methylenedioxymethamphetamine
ME	Maine
MEd	master of education
MEng	master of engineering
MEP	member of the European parliament
MG	Morris Garages
MGM	Metro-Goldwyn-Mayer
Mgr	Monsignor
MI	(1) Michigan; (2) military intelligence
MI1c	[secret intelligence department]
MI5	[military intelligence department]
MI6	[secret intelligence department]
MI9	[secret escape service]
MICE	member of the Institution of Civil Engineers
MIEE	member of the Institution of Electrical Engineers
min.	minute(s)
Mk	mark
ML	(1) licentiate of medicine; (2) master of laws
MLitt	master of letters
Mlle	Mademoiselle
mm	millimetre(s)
Mme	Madame
MN	Minnesota
MO	Missouri
MOH	medical officer of health
MP	member of parliament
m.p.h.	miles per hour
MPhil	master of philosophy
MRCP	member of the Royal College of Physicians
MRCS	member of the Royal College of Surgeons
MRCVS	member of the Royal College of Veterinary Surgeons
MRIA	member of the Royal Irish Academy
MS	(1) master of science; (2) Mississippi
MS *pl.* MSS	manuscript(s)
MSc	master of science
MSc (Econ.)	master of science (economics)
MT	Montana
MusB	bachelor of music
MusBac	bachelor of music
MusD	doctor of music
MV	motor vessel
MVO	member of the Royal Victorian Order
n. *pl.* nn.	note(s)
NAAFI	Navy, Army, and Air Force Institutes
NASA	National Aeronautics and Space Administration
NATO	North Atlantic Treaty Organization
NBC	National Broadcasting Corporation
NC	North Carolina
NCO	non-commissioned officer
ND	North Dakota
n.d.	no date
NE	Nebraska
nem. con.	*nemine contradicente*: unanimously
new ser.	new series
NH	New Hampshire
NHS	National Health Service
NJ	New Jersey
NKVD	[Soviet people's commissariat for internal affairs]
NM	New Mexico
nm	nanometre(s)
no. *pl.* nos.	number(s)
Nov	November
n.p.	no place [of publication]
NS	new style
NV	Nevada
NY	New York
NZBS	New Zealand Broadcasting Service
OBE	officer of the Order of the British Empire
obit.	obituary
Oct	October
OCTU	officer cadets training unit
OECD	Organization for Economic Co-operation and Development
OEEC	Organization for European Economic Co-operation
OFM	order of Friars Minor [Franciscans]
OFMCap	Ordine Frati Minori Cappucini: member of the Capuchin order
OH	Ohio
OK	Oklahoma
O level	ordinary level [examination]
OM	Order of Merit
OP	order of Preachers [Dominicans]
op. *pl.* opp.	opus *pl.* opera
OPEC	Organization of Petroleum Exporting Countries
OR	Oregon
orig.	original
OS	old style
OSB	Order of St Benedict
OTC	Officers' Training Corps
OWS	Old Watercolour Society
Oxon.	Oxoniensis
p. *pl.* pp.	page(s)
PA	Pennsylvania
p.a.	per annum
para.	paragraph
PAYE	pay as you earn
pbk *pl.* pbks	paperback(s)
per.	[during the] period
PhD	doctor of philosophy
pl.	(1) plate(s); (2) plural
priv. coll.	private collection
pt *pl.* pts	part(s)
pubd	published
PVC	polyvinyl chloride
q. *pl.* qq.	(1) question(s); (2) quire(s)
QC	queen's counsel
R	rand
R.	Rex / Regina
r	recto
r.	reigned / ruled
RA	Royal Academy / Royal Academician

RAC	Royal Automobile Club
RAF	Royal Air Force
RAFVR	Royal Air Force Volunteer Reserve
RAM	[member of the] Royal Academy of Music
RAMC	Royal Army Medical Corps
RCA	Royal College of Art
RCNC	Royal Corps of Naval Constructors
RCOG	Royal College of Obstetricians and Gynaecologists
RDI	royal designer for industry
RE	Royal Engineers
repr. *pl.* reprs.	reprint(s) / reprinted
repro.	reproduced
rev.	revised / revised by / reviser / revision
Revd	Reverend
RHA	Royal Hibernian Academy
RI	(1) Rhode Island; (2) Royal Institute of Painters in Water-Colours
RIBA	Royal Institute of British Architects
RIN	Royal Indian Navy
RM	Reichsmark
RMS	Royal Mail steamer
RN	Royal Navy
RNA	ribonucleic acid
RNAS	Royal Naval Air Service
RNR	Royal Naval Reserve
RNVR	Royal Naval Volunteer Reserve
RO	Record Office
r.p.m.	revolutions per minute
RRS	royal research ship
Rs	rupees
RSA	(1) Royal Scottish Academician; (2) Royal Society of Arts
RSPCA	Royal Society for the Prevention of Cruelty to Animals
Rt Hon.	Right Honourable
Rt Revd	Right Reverend
RUC	Royal Ulster Constabulary
Russ.	Russian
RWS	Royal Watercolour Society
S4C	Sianel Pedwar Cymru
s.	shilling(s)
s.a.	*sub anno*: under the year
SABC	South African Broadcasting Corporation
SAS	Special Air Service
SC	South Carolina
ScD	doctor of science
S$	Singapore dollar
SD	South Dakota
sec.	second(s)
sel.	selected
sen.	senior
Sept	September
ser.	series
SHAPE	supreme headquarters allied powers, Europe
SIDRO	Société Internationale d'Énergie Hydro-Électrique
sig. *pl.* sigs.	signature(s)
sing.	singular
SIS	Secret Intelligence Service
SJ	Society of Jesus
Skr	Swedish krona
Span.	Spanish
SPCK	Society for Promoting Christian Knowledge
SS	(1) Santissimi; (2) Schutzstaffel; (3) steam ship
STB	bachelor of theology
STD	doctor of theology
STM	master of theology
STP	doctor of theology
supp.	supposedly
suppl. *pl.* suppls.	supplement(s)
s.v.	*sub verbo* / *sub voce*: under the word / heading
SY	steam yacht
TA	Territorial Army
TASS	[Soviet news agency]
TB	tuberculosis (*lit.* tubercle bacillus)
TD	(1) *teachtaí dála* (member of the Dáil); (2) territorial decoration
TN	Tennessee
TNT	trinitrotoluene
trans.	translated / translated by / translation / translator
TT	tourist trophy
TUC	Trades Union Congress
TX	Texas
U-boat	*Unterseeboot*: submarine
Ufa	Universum-Film AG
UMIST	University of Manchester Institute of Science and Technology
UN	United Nations
UNESCO	United Nations Educational, Scientific, and Cultural Organization
UNICEF	United Nations International Children's Emergency Fund
unpubd	unpublished
USS	United States ship
UT	Utah
v	verso
v.	versus
VA	Virginia
VAD	Voluntary Aid Detachment
VC	Victoria Cross
VE-day	victory in Europe day
Ven.	Venerable
VJ-day	victory over Japan day
vol. *pl.* vols.	volume(s)
VT	Vermont
WA	Washington [state]
WAAC	Women's Auxiliary Army Corps
WAAF	Women's Auxiliary Air Force
WEA	Workers' Educational Association
WHO	World Health Organization
WI	Wisconsin
WRAF	Women's Royal Air Force
WRNS	Women's Royal Naval Service
WV	West Virginia
WVS	Women's Voluntary Service
WY	Wyoming
¥	yen
YMCA	Young Men's Christian Association
YWCA	Young Women's Christian Association

2 Institution abbreviations

All Souls Oxf.	All Souls College, Oxford
AM Oxf.	Ashmolean Museum, Oxford
Balliol Oxf.	Balliol College, Oxford
BBC WAC	BBC Written Archives Centre, Reading
Beds. & Luton ARS	Bedfordshire and Luton Archives and Record Service, Bedford
Berks. RO	Berkshire Record Office, Reading
BFI	British Film Institute, London
BFI NFTVA	British Film Institute, London, National Film and Television Archive
BGS	British Geological Survey, Keyworth, Nottingham
Birm. CA	Birmingham Central Library, Birmingham City Archives
Birm. CL	Birmingham Central Library
BL	British Library, London
BL NSA	British Library, London, National Sound Archive
BL OIOC	British Library, London, Oriental and India Office Collections
BLPES	London School of Economics and Political Science, British Library of Political and Economic Science
BM	British Museum, London
Bodl. Oxf.	Bodleian Library, Oxford
Bodl. RH	Bodleian Library of Commonwealth and African Studies at Rhodes House, Oxford
Borth. Inst.	Borthwick Institute of Historical Research, University of York
Boston PL	Boston Public Library, Massachusetts
Bristol RO	Bristol Record Office
Bucks. RLSS	Buckinghamshire Records and Local Studies Service, Aylesbury
CAC Cam.	Churchill College, Cambridge, Churchill Archives Centre
Cambs. AS	Cambridgeshire Archive Service
CCC Cam.	Corpus Christi College, Cambridge
CCC Oxf.	Corpus Christi College, Oxford
Ches. & Chester ALSS	Cheshire and Chester Archives and Local Studies Service
Christ Church Oxf.	Christ Church, Oxford
Christies	Christies, London
City Westm. AC	City of Westminster Archives Centre, London
CKS	Centre for Kentish Studies, Maidstone
CLRO	Corporation of London Records Office
Coll. Arms	College of Arms, London
Col. U.	Columbia University, New York
Cornwall RO	Cornwall Record Office, Truro
Courtauld Inst.	Courtauld Institute of Art, London
CUL	Cambridge University Library
Cumbria AS	Cumbria Archive Service
Derbys. RO	Derbyshire Record Office, Matlock
Devon RO	Devon Record Office, Exeter
Dorset RO	Dorset Record Office, Dorchester
Duke U.	Duke University, Durham, North Carolina
Duke U., Perkins L.	Duke University, Durham, North Carolina, William R. Perkins Library
Durham Cath. CL	Durham Cathedral, chapter library
Durham RO	Durham Record Office
DWL	Dr Williams's Library, London
Essex RO	Essex Record Office
E. Sussex RO	East Sussex Record Office, Lewes
Eton	Eton College, Berkshire
FM Cam.	Fitzwilliam Museum, Cambridge
Folger	Folger Shakespeare Library, Washington, DC
Garr. Club	Garrick Club, London
Girton Cam.	Girton College, Cambridge
GL	Guildhall Library, London
Glos. RO	Gloucestershire Record Office, Gloucester
Gon. & Caius Cam.	Gonville and Caius College, Cambridge
Gov. Art Coll.	Government Art Collection
GS Lond.	Geological Society of London
Hants. RO	Hampshire Record Office, Winchester
Harris Man. Oxf.	Harris Manchester College, Oxford
Harvard TC	Harvard Theatre Collection, Harvard University, Cambridge, Massachusetts, Nathan Marsh Pusey Library
Harvard U.	Harvard University, Cambridge, Massachusetts
Harvard U., Houghton L.	Harvard University, Cambridge, Massachusetts, Houghton Library
Herefs. RO	Herefordshire Record Office, Hereford
Herts. ALS	Hertfordshire Archives and Local Studies, Hertford
Hist. Soc. Penn.	Historical Society of Pennsylvania, Philadelphia
HLRO	House of Lords Record Office, London
Hult. Arch.	Hulton Archive, London and New York
Hunt. L.	Huntington Library, San Marino, California
ICL	Imperial College, London
Inst. CE	Institution of Civil Engineers, London
Inst. EE	Institution of Electrical Engineers, London
IWM	Imperial War Museum, London
IWM FVA	Imperial War Museum, London, Film and Video Archive
IWM SA	Imperial War Museum, London, Sound Archive
JRL	John Rylands University Library of Manchester
King's AC Cam.	King's College Archives Centre, Cambridge
King's Cam.	King's College, Cambridge
King's Lond.	King's College, London
King's Lond., Liddell Hart C.	King's College, London, Liddell Hart Centre for Military Archives
Lancs. RO	Lancashire Record Office, Preston
L. Cong.	Library of Congress, Washington, DC
Leics. RO	Leicestershire, Leicester, and Rutland Record Office, Leicester
Lincs. Arch.	Lincolnshire Archives, Lincoln
Linn. Soc.	Linnean Society of London
LMA	London Metropolitan Archives
LPL	Lambeth Palace, London
Lpool RO	Liverpool Record Office and Local Studies Service
LUL	London University Library
Magd. Cam.	Magdalene College, Cambridge
Magd. Oxf.	Magdalen College, Oxford
Man. City Gall.	Manchester City Galleries
Man. CL	Manchester Central Library
Mass. Hist. Soc.	Massachusetts Historical Society, Boston
Merton Oxf.	Merton College, Oxford
MHS Oxf.	Museum of the History of Science, Oxford
Mitchell L., Glas.	Mitchell Library, Glasgow
Mitchell L., NSW	State Library of New South Wales, Sydney, Mitchell Library
Morgan L.	Pierpont Morgan Library, New York
NA Canada	National Archives of Canada, Ottawa
NA Ire.	National Archives of Ireland, Dublin
NAM	National Army Museum, London
NA Scot.	National Archives of Scotland, Edinburgh
News Int. RO	News International Record Office, London
NG Ire.	National Gallery of Ireland, Dublin

NG Scot.	National Gallery of Scotland, Edinburgh
NHM	Natural History Museum, London
NL Aus.	National Library of Australia, Canberra
NL Ire.	National Library of Ireland, Dublin
NL NZ	National Library of New Zealand, Wellington
NL NZ, Turnbull L.	National Library of New Zealand, Wellington, Alexander Turnbull Library
NL Scot.	National Library of Scotland, Edinburgh
NL Wales	National Library of Wales, Aberystwyth
NMG Wales	National Museum and Gallery of Wales, Cardiff
NMM	National Maritime Museum, London
Norfolk RO	Norfolk Record Office, Norwich
Northants. RO	Northamptonshire Record Office, Northampton
Northumbd RO	Northumberland Record Office
Notts. Arch.	Nottinghamshire Archives, Nottingham
NPG	National Portrait Gallery, London
NRA	National Archives, London, Historical Manuscripts Commission, National Register of Archives
Nuffield Oxf.	Nuffield College, Oxford
N. Yorks. CRO	North Yorkshire County Record Office, Northallerton
NYPL	New York Public Library
Oxf. UA	Oxford University Archives
Oxf. U. Mus. NH	Oxford University Museum of Natural History
Oxon. RO	Oxfordshire Record Office, Oxford
Pembroke Cam.	Pembroke College, Cambridge
PRO	National Archives, London, Public Record Office
PRO NIre.	Public Record Office for Northern Ireland, Belfast
Pusey Oxf.	Pusey House, Oxford
RA	Royal Academy of Arts, London
Ransom HRC	Harry Ransom Humanities Research Center, University of Texas, Austin
RAS	Royal Astronomical Society, London
RBG Kew	Royal Botanic Gardens, Kew, London
RCP Lond.	Royal College of Physicians of London
RCS Eng.	Royal College of Surgeons of England, London
RGS	Royal Geographical Society, London
RIBA	Royal Institute of British Architects, London
RIBA BAL	Royal Institute of British Architects, London, British Architectural Library
Royal Arch.	Royal Archives, Windsor Castle, Berkshire [by gracious permission of her majesty the queen]
Royal Irish Acad.	Royal Irish Academy, Dublin
Royal Scot. Acad.	Royal Scottish Academy, Edinburgh
RS	Royal Society, London
RSA	Royal Society of Arts, London
RS Friends, Lond.	Religious Society of Friends, London
St Ant. Oxf.	St Antony's College, Oxford
St John Cam.	St John's College, Cambridge
S. Antiquaries, Lond.	Society of Antiquaries of London
Sci. Mus.	Science Museum, London
Scot. NPG	Scottish National Portrait Gallery, Edinburgh
Scott Polar RI	University of Cambridge, Scott Polar Research Institute
Sheff. Arch.	Sheffield Archives
Shrops. RRC	Shropshire Records and Research Centre, Shrewsbury
SOAS	School of Oriental and African Studies, London
Som. ARS	Somerset Archive and Record Service, Taunton
Staffs. RO	Staffordshire Record Office, Stafford
Suffolk RO	Suffolk Record Office
Surrey HC	Surrey History Centre, Woking
TCD	Trinity College, Dublin
Trinity Cam.	Trinity College, Cambridge
U. Aberdeen	University of Aberdeen
U. Birm.	University of Birmingham
U. Birm. L.	University of Birmingham Library
U. Cal.	University of California
U. Cam.	University of Cambridge
UCL	University College, London
U. Durham	University of Durham
U. Durham L.	University of Durham Library
U. Edin.	University of Edinburgh
U. Edin., New Coll.	University of Edinburgh, New College
U. Edin., New Coll. L.	University of Edinburgh, New College Library
U. Edin. L.	University of Edinburgh Library
U. Glas.	University of Glasgow
U. Glas. L.	University of Glasgow Library
U. Hull	University of Hull
U. Hull, Brynmor Jones L.	University of Hull, Brynmor Jones Library
U. Leeds	University of Leeds
U. Leeds, Brotherton L.	University of Leeds, Brotherton Library
U. Lond.	University of London
U. Lpool	University of Liverpool
U. Lpool L.	University of Liverpool Library
U. Mich.	University of Michigan, Ann Arbor
U. Mich., Clements L.	University of Michigan, Ann Arbor, William L. Clements Library
U. Newcastle	University of Newcastle upon Tyne
U. Newcastle, Robinson L.	University of Newcastle upon Tyne, Robinson Library
U. Nott.	University of Nottingham
U. Nott. L.	University of Nottingham Library
U. Oxf.	University of Oxford
U. Reading	University of Reading
U. Reading L.	University of Reading Library
U. St Andr.	University of St Andrews
U. St Andr. L.	University of St Andrews Library
U. Southampton	University of Southampton
U. Southampton L.	University of Southampton Library
U. Sussex	University of Sussex, Brighton
U. Texas	University of Texas, Austin
U. Wales	University of Wales
U. Warwick Mod. RC	University of Warwick, Coventry, Modern Records Centre
V&A	Victoria and Albert Museum, London
V&A NAL	Victoria and Albert Museum, London, National Art Library
Warks. CRO	Warwickshire County Record Office, Warwick
Wellcome L.	Wellcome Library for the History and Understanding of Medicine, London
Westm. DA	Westminster Diocesan Archives, London
Wilts. & Swindon RO	Wiltshire and Swindon Record Office, Trowbridge
Worcs. RO	Worcestershire Record Office, Worcester
W. Sussex RO	West Sussex Record Office, Chichester
W. Yorks. AS	West Yorkshire Archive Service
Yale U.	Yale University, New Haven, Connecticut
Yale U., Beinecke L.	Yale University, New Haven, Connecticut, Beinecke Rare Book and Manuscript Library
Yale U. CBA	Yale University, New Haven, Connecticut, Yale Center for British Art

3 Bibliographic abbreviations

Adams, *Drama* — W. D. Adams, *A dictionary of the drama*, 1: *A–G* (1904); 2: *H–Z* (1956) [vol. 2 microfilm only]

AFM — J O'Donovan, ed. and trans., *Annala rioghachta Eireann | Annals of the kingdom of Ireland by the four masters*, 7 vols. (1848–51); 2nd edn (1856); 3rd edn (1990)

Allibone, *Dict.* — S. A. Allibone, *A critical dictionary of English literature and British and American authors*, 3 vols. (1859–71); suppl. by J. F. Kirk, 2 vols. (1891)

ANB — J. A. Garraty and M. C. Carnes, eds., *American national biography*, 24 vols. (1999)

Anderson, *Scot. nat.* — W. Anderson, *The Scottish nation, or, The surnames, families, literature, honours, and biographical history of the people of Scotland*, 3 vols. (1859–63)

Ann. mon. — H. R. Luard, ed., *Annales monastici*, 5 vols., Rolls Series, 36 (1864–9)

Ann. Ulster — S. Mac Airt and G. Mac Niocaill, eds., *Annals of Ulster (to AD 1131)* (1983)

APC — *Acts of the privy council of England*, new ser., 46 vols. (1890–1964)

APS — *The acts of the parliaments of Scotland*, 12 vols. in 13 (1814–75)

Arber, *Regs. Stationers* — F. Arber, ed., *A transcript of the registers of the Company of Stationers of London, 1554–1640 AD*, 5 vols. (1875–94)

ArchR — *Architectural Review*

ASC — D. Whitelock, D. C. Douglas, and S. I. Tucker, ed. and trans., *The Anglo-Saxon Chronicle: a revised translation* (1961)

AS chart. — P. H. Sawyer, *Anglo-Saxon charters: an annotated list and bibliography*, Royal Historical Society Guides and Handbooks (1968)

AusDB — D. Pike and others, eds., *Australian dictionary of biography*, 16 vols. (1966–2002)

Baker, *Serjeants* — J. H. Baker, *The order of serjeants at law*, SeldS, suppl. ser., 5 (1984)

Bale, *Cat.* — J. Bale, *Scriptorum illustrium Maioris Brytannie, quam nunc Angliam et Scotiam vocant: catalogus*, 2 vols. in 1 (Basel, 1557–9); facs. edn (1971)

Bale, *Index* — J. Bale, *Index Britanniae scriptorum*, ed. R. L. Poole and M. Bateson (1902); facs. edn (1990)

BBCS — *Bulletin of the Board of Celtic Studies*

BDMBR — J. O. Baylen and N. J. Gossman, eds., *Biographical dictionary of modern British radicals*, 3 vols. in 4 (1979–88)

Bede, *Hist. eccl.* — *Bede's Ecclesiastical history of the English people*, ed. and trans. B. Colgrave and R. A. B. Mynors, OMT (1969); repr. (1991)

Bénézit, *Dict.* — E. Bénézit, *Dictionnaire critique et documentaire des peintres, sculpteurs, dessinateurs et graveurs*, 3 vols. (Paris, 1911–23); new edn, 8 vols. (1948–66), repr. (1966); 3rd edn, rev. and enl., 10 vols. (1976); 4th edn, 14 vols. (1999)

BIHR — *Bulletin of the Institute of Historical Research*

Birch, *Seals* — W. de Birch, *Catalogue of seals in the department of manuscripts in the British Museum*, 6 vols. (1887–1900)

Bishop Burnet's History — *Bishop Burnet's History of his own time*, ed. M. J. Routh, 2nd edn, 6 vols. (1833)

Blackwood — *Blackwood's [Edinburgh] Magazine*, 328 vols. (1817–1980)

Blain, Clements & Grundy, *Feminist comp.* — V. Blain, P. Clements, and I. Grundy, eds., *The feminist companion to literature in English* (1990)

BL cat. — *The British Library general catalogue of printed books* [in 360 vols. with suppls., also CD-ROM and online]

BMJ — *British Medical Journal*

Boase & Courtney, *Bibl. Corn.* — G. C. Boase and W. P. Courtney, *Bibliotheca Cornubiensis: a catalogue of the writings … of Cornishmen*, 3 vols. (1874–82)

Boase, *Mod. Eng. biog.* — F. Boase, *Modern English biography: containing many thousand concise memoirs of persons who have died since the year 1850*, 6 vols. (privately printed, Truro, 1892–1921); repr. (1965)

Boswell, *Life* — *Boswell's Life of Johnson: together with Journal of a tour to the Hebrides and Johnson's Diary of a journey into north Wales*, ed. G. B. Hill, enl. edn, rev. L. F. Powell, 6 vols. (1934–50); 2nd edn (1964); repr. (1971)

Brown & Stratton, *Brit. mus.* — J. D. Brown and S. S. Stratton, *British musical biography* (1897)

Bryan, *Painters* — M. Bryan, *A biographical and critical dictionary of painters and engravers*, 2 vols. (1816); new edn, ed. G. Stanley (1849); new edn, ed. R. E. Graves and W. Armstrong, 2 vols. (1886–9); [4th edn], ed. G. C. Williamson, 5 vols. (1903–5) [various reprs.]

Burke, *Gen. GB* — J. Burke, *A genealogical and heraldic history of the commoners of Great Britain and Ireland*, 4 vols. (1833–8); new edn as *A genealogical and heraldic dictionary of the landed gentry of Great Britain and Ireland*, 3 vols. [1843–9] [many later edns]

Burke, *Gen. Ire.* — J. B. Burke, *A genealogical and heraldic history of the landed gentry of Ireland* (1899); 2nd edn (1904); 3rd edn (1912); 4th edn (1958); 5th edn as *Burke's Irish family records* (1976)

Burke, *Peerage* — J. Burke, *A general [later edns A genealogical] and heraldic dictionary of the peerage and baronetage of the United Kingdom [later edns the British empire]* (1829–)

Burney, *Hist. mus.* — C. Burney, *A general history of music, from the earliest ages to the present period*, 4 vols. (1776–89)

Burtchaell & Sadleir, *Alum. Dubl.* — G. D. Burtchaell and T. U. Sadleir, *Alumni Dublinenses: a register of the students, graduates, and provosts of Trinity College* (1924); [2nd edn], with suppl., in 2 pts (1935)

Calamy rev. — A. G. Matthews, *Calamy revised* (1934); repr. (1988)

CCI — *Calendar of confirmations and inventories granted and given up in the several commissariots of Scotland* (1876–)

CClR — *Calendar of the close rolls preserved in the Public Record Office*, 47 vols. (1892–1963)

CDS — J. Bain, ed., *Calendar of documents relating to Scotland*, 4 vols., PRO (1881–8); suppl. vol. 5, ed. G. G. Simpson and J. D. Galbraith [1986]

CEPR letters — W. H. Bliss, C. Johnson, and J. Twemlow, eds., *Calendar of entries in the papal registers relating to Great Britain and Ireland: papal letters* (1893–)

CGPLA — *Calendars of the grants of probate and letters of administration* [in 4 ser.: *England & Wales, Northern Ireland, Ireland,* and *Éire*]

Chambers, *Scots.* — R. Chambers, ed., *A biographical dictionary of eminent Scotsmen*, 4 vols. (1832–5)

Chancery records — chancery records pubd by the PRO

Chancery records (RC) — chancery records pubd by the Record Commissions

CIPM	*Calendar of inquisitions post mortem*, [20 vols.], PRO (1904–); also *Henry VII*, 3 vols. (1898–1955)
Clarendon, *Hist. rebellion*	E. Hyde, earl of Clarendon, *The history of the rebellion and civil wars in England*, 6 vols. (1888); repr. (1958) and (1992)
Cobbett, *Parl. hist.*	W. Cobbett and J. Wright, eds., *Cobbett's Parliamentary history of England*, 36 vols. (1806–1820)
Colvin, *Archs.*	H. Colvin, *A biographical dictionary of British architects, 1600–1840*, 3rd edn (1995)
Cooper, *Ath. Cantab.*	C. H. Cooper and T. Cooper, *Athenae Cantabrigienses*, 3 vols. (1858–1913); repr. (1967)
CPR	*Calendar of the patent rolls preserved in the Public Record Office* (1891–)
Crockford	*Crockford's Clerical Directory*
CS	Camden Society
CSP	*Calendar of state papers* [in 11 ser.: domestic, Scotland, Scottish series, Ireland, colonial, Commonwealth, foreign, Spain [at Simancas], Rome, Milan, and Venice]
CYS	Canterbury and York Society
DAB	*Dictionary of American biography*, 21 vols. (1928–36), repr. in 11 vols. (1964); 10 suppls. (1944–96)
DBB	D. J. Jeremy, ed., *Dictionary of business biography*, 5 vols. (1984–6)
DCB	G. W. Brown and others, *Dictionary of Canadian biography*, [14 vols.] (1966–)
Debrett's Peerage	*Debrett's Peerage* (1803–) [sometimes *Debrett's Illustrated peerage*]
Desmond, *Botanists*	R. Desmond, *Dictionary of British and Irish botanists and horticulturists* (1977); rev. edn (1994)
Dir. Brit. archs.	A. Felstead, J. Franklin, and L. Pinfield, eds., *Directory of British architects, 1834–1900* (1993); 2nd edn, ed. A. Brodie and others, 2 vols. (2001)
DLB	J. M. Bellamy and J. Saville, eds., *Dictionary of labour biography*, [10 vols.] (1972–)
DLitB	Dictionary of Literary Biography
DNB	*Dictionary of national biography*, 63 vols. (1885–1900), suppl., 3 vols. (1901); repr. in 22 vols. (1908–9); 10 further suppls. (1912–96); *Missing persons* (1993)
DNZB	W. H. Oliver and C. Orange, eds., *The dictionary of New Zealand biography*, 5 vols. (1990–2000)
DSAB	W. J. de Kock and others, eds., *Dictionary of South African biography*, 5 vols. (1968–87)
DSB	C. C. Gillispie and F. L. Holmes, eds., *Dictionary of scientific biography*, 16 vols. (1970–80); repr. in 8 vols. (1981); 2 vol. suppl. (1990)
DSBB	A. Slaven and S. Checkland, eds., *Dictionary of Scottish business biography, 1860–1960*, 2 vols. (1986–90)
DSCHT	N. M. de S. Cameron and others, eds., *Dictionary of Scottish church history and theology* (1993)
Dugdale, *Monasticon*	W. Dugdale, *Monasticon Anglicanum*, 3 vols. (1655–72); 2nd edn, 3 vols. (1661–82); new edn, ed. J. Caley, J. Ellis, and B. Bandinel, 6 vols. in 8 pts (1817–30); repr. (1846) and (1970)
DWB	J. E. Lloyd and others, eds., *Dictionary of Welsh biography down to 1940* (1959) [Eng. trans. of *Y bywgraffiadur Cymreig hyd 1940*, 2nd edn (1954)]
EdinR	*Edinburgh Review, or, Critical Journal*
EETS	Early English Text Society
Emden, *Cam.*	A. B. Emden, *A biographical register of the University of Cambridge to 1500* (1963)
Emden, *Oxf.*	A. B. Emden, *A biographical register of the University of Oxford to AD 1500*, 3 vols. (1957–9); also *A biographical register of the University of Oxford, AD 1501 to 1540* (1974)
EngHR	*English Historical Review*
Engraved Brit. ports.	F. M. O'Donoghue and H. M. Hake, *Catalogue of engraved British portraits preserved in the department of prints and drawings in the British Museum*, 6 vols. (1908–25)
ER	The English Reports, 178 vols. (1900–32)
ESTC	*English short title catalogue, 1475–1800* [CD-ROM and online]
Evelyn, *Diary*	*The diary of John Evelyn*, ed. E. S. De Beer, 6 vols. (1955); repr. (2000)
Farington, *Diary*	*The diary of Joseph Farington*, ed. K. Garlick and others, 17 vols. (1978–98)
Fasti Angl. (Hardy)	J. Le Neve, *Fasti ecclesiae Anglicanae*, ed. T. D. Hardy, 3 vols. (1854)
Fasti Angl., 1066–1300	[J. Le Neve], *Fasti ecclesiae Anglicanae, 1066–1300*, ed. D. E. Greenway and J. S. Barrow, [8 vols.] (1968–)
Fasti Angl., 1300–1541	[J. Le Neve], *Fasti ecclesiae Anglicanae, 1300–1541*, 12 vols. (1962–7)
Fasti Angl., 1541–1857	[J. Le Neve], *Fasti ecclesiae Anglicanae, 1541–1857*, ed. J. M. Horn, D. M. Smith, and D. S. Bailey, [9 vols.] (1969–)
Fasti Scot.	H. Scott, *Fasti ecclesiae Scoticanae*, 3 vols. in 6 (1871); new edn, [11 vols.] (1915–)
FO List	*Foreign Office List*
Fortescue, *Brit. army*	J. W. Fortescue, *A history of the British army*, 13 vols. (1899–1930)
Foss, *Judges*	E. Foss, *The judges of England*, 9 vols. (1848–64); repr. (1966)
Foster, *Alum. Oxon.*	J. Foster, ed., *Alumni Oxonienses: the members of the University of Oxford, 1715–1886*, 4 vols. (1887–8); later edn (1891); also *Alumni Oxonienses … 1500–1714*, 4 vols. (1891–2); 8 vol. repr. (1968) and (2000)
Fuller, *Worthies*	T. Fuller, *The history of the worthies of England*, 4 pts (1662); new edn, 2 vols., ed. J. Nichols (1811); new edn, 3 vols., ed. P. A. Nuttall (1840); repr. (1965)
GEC, *Baronetage*	G. E. Cokayne, *Complete baronetage*, 6 vols. (1900–09); repr. (1983) [microprint]
GEC, *Peerage*	G. E. C. [G. E. Cokayne], *The complete peerage of England, Scotland, Ireland, Great Britain, and the United Kingdom*, 8 vols. (1887–98); new edn, ed. V. Gibbs and others, 14 vols. in 15 (1910–98); microprint repr. (1982) and (1987)
Genest, *Eng. stage*	J. Genest, *Some account of the English stage from the Restoration in 1660 to 1830*, 10 vols. (1832); repr. [New York, 1965]
Gillow, *Lit. biog. hist.*	J. Gillow, *A literary and biographical history or bibliographical dictionary of the English Catholics, from the breach with Rome, in 1534, to the present time*, 5 vols. [1885–1902]; repr. (1961); repr. with preface by C. Gillow (1999)
Gir. Camb. opera	*Giraldi Cambrensis opera*, ed. J. S. Brewer, J. F. Dimock, and G. F. Warner, 8 vols., Rolls Series, 21 (1861–91)
GJ	*Geographical Journal*

Gladstone, *Diaries* — *The Gladstone diaries: with cabinet minutes and prime-ministerial correspondence*, ed. M. R. D. Foot and H. C. G. Matthew, 14 vols. (1968–94)

GM — *Gentleman's Magazine*

Graves, *Artists* — A. Graves, ed., *A dictionary of artists who have exhibited works in the principal London exhibitions of oil paintings from 1760 to 1880* (1884); new edn (1895); 3rd edn (1901); facs. edn (1969); repr. [1970], (1973), and (1984)

Graves, *Brit. Inst.* — A. Graves, *The British Institution, 1806–1867: a complete dictionary of contributors and their work from the foundation of the institution* (1875); facs. edn (1908); repr. (1969)

Graves, *RA exhibitors* — A. Graves, *The Royal Academy of Arts: a complete dictionary of contributors and their work from its foundation in 1769 to 1904*, 8 vols. (1905–6); repr. in 4 vols. (1970) and (1972)

Graves, *Soc. Artists* — A. Graves, *The Society of Artists of Great Britain, 1760–1791, the Free Society of Artists, 1761–1783: a complete dictionary* (1907); facs. edn (1969)

Greaves & Zaller, *BDBR* — R. L. Greaves and R. Zaller, eds., *Biographical dictionary of British radicals in the seventeenth century*, 3 vols. (1982–4)

Grove, *Dict. mus.* — G. Grove, ed., *A dictionary of music and musicians*, 5 vols. (1878–90); 2nd edn, ed. J. A. Fuller Maitland (1904–10); 3rd edn, ed. H. C. Colles (1927); 4th edn with suppl. (1940); 5th edn, ed. E. Blom, 9 vols. (1954); suppl. (1961) [see also *New Grove*]

Hall, *Dramatic ports.* — L. A. Hall, *Catalogue of dramatic portraits in the theatre collection of the Harvard College library*, 4 vols. (1930–34)

Hansard — *Hansard's parliamentary debates*, ser. 1–5 (1803–)

Highfill, Burnim & Langhans, *BDA* — P. H. Highfill, K. A. Burnim, and E. A. Langhans, *A biographical dictionary of actors, actresses, musicians, dancers, managers, and other stage personnel in London, 1660–1800*, 16 vols. (1973–93)

Hist. U. Oxf. — T. H. Aston, ed., *The history of the University of Oxford*, 8 vols. (1984–2000) [1: *The early Oxford schools*, ed. J. I. Catto (1984); 2: *Late medieval Oxford*, ed. J. I. Catto and R. Evans (1992); 3: *The collegiate university*, ed. J. McConica (1986); 4: *Seventeenth-century Oxford*, ed. N. Tyacke (1997); 5: *The eighteenth century*, ed. L. S. Sutherland and L. G. Mitchell (1986); 6–7: *Nineteenth-century Oxford*, ed. M. G. Brock and M. C. Curthoys (1997–2000); 8: *The twentieth century*, ed. B. Harrison (2000)]

HJ — *Historical Journal*

HMC — Historical Manuscripts Commission

Holdsworth, *Eng. law* — W. S. Holdsworth, *A history of English law*, ed. A. L. Goodhart and H. L. Hanbury, 17 vols. (1903–72)

HoP, *Commons* — *The history of parliament: the House of Commons* [1386–1421, ed. J. S. Roskell, L. Clark, and C. Rawcliffe, 4 vols. (1992); 1509–1558, ed. S. T. Bindoff, 3 vols. (1982); 1558–1603, ed. P. W. Hasler, 3 vols. (1981); 1660–1690, ed. B. D. Henning, 3 vols. (1983); 1690–1715, ed. D. W. Hayton, E. Cruickshanks, and S. Handley, 5 vols. (2002); 1715–1754, ed. R. Sedgwick, 2 vols. (1970); 1754–1790, ed. L. Namier and J. Brooke, 3 vols. (1964), repr. (1985); 1790–1820, ed. R. G. Thorne, 5 vols. (1986); in draft (used with permission): 1422–1504, 1604–1629, 1640–1660, and 1820–1832]

IGI — *International Genealogical Index*, Church of Jesus Christ of the Latterday Saints

ILN — *Illustrated London News*

IMC — Irish Manuscripts Commission

Irving, *Scots.* — J. Irving, ed., *The book of Scotsmen eminent for achievements in arms and arts, church and state, law, legislation and literature, commerce, science, travel and philanthropy* (1881)

JCS — *Journal of the Chemical Society*

JHC — *Journals of the House of Commons*

JHL — *Journals of the House of Lords*

John of Worcester, *Chron.* — *The chronicle of John of Worcester*, ed. R. R. Darlington and P. McGurk, trans. J. Bray and P. McGurk, 3 vols., OMT (1995–) [vol. 1 forthcoming]

Keeler, *Long Parliament* — M. F. Keeler, *The Long Parliament, 1640–1641: a biographical study of its members* (1954)

Kelly, *Handbk* — *The upper ten thousand: an alphabetical list of all members of noble families*, 3 vols. (1875–7); continued as *Kelly's handbook of the upper ten thousand for 1878* [1879], 2 vols. (1878–9); continued as *Kelly's handbook to the titled, landed and official classes*, 94 vols. (1880–1973)

LondG — *London Gazette*

LP Henry VIII — J. S. Brewer, J. Gairdner, and R. H. Brodie, eds., *Letters and papers, foreign and domestic, of the reign of Henry VIII*, 23 vols. in 38 (1862–1932); repr. (1965)

Mallalieu, *Watercolour artists* — H. L. Mallalieu, *The dictionary of British watercolour artists up to 1820*, 3 vols. (1976–90); vol. 1, 2nd edn (1986)

Memoirs FRS — *Biographical Memoirs of Fellows of the Royal Society*

MGH — Monumenta Germaniae Historica

MT — *Musical Times*

Munk, *Roll* — W. Munk, *The roll of the Royal College of Physicians of London*, 2 vols. (1861); 2nd edn, 3 vols. (1878)

N&Q — *Notes and Queries*

New Grove — S. Sadie, ed., *The new Grove dictionary of music and musicians*, 20 vols. (1980); 2nd edn, 29 vols. (2001) [also online edn; see also Grove, *Dict. mus.*]

Nichols, *Illustrations* — J. Nichols and J. B. Nichols, *Illustrations of the literary history of the eighteenth century*, 8 vols. (1817–58)

Nichols, *Lit. anecdotes* — J. Nichols, *Literary anecdotes of the eighteenth century*, 9 vols. (1812–16); facs. edn (1966)

Obits. FRS — *Obituary Notices of Fellows of the Royal Society*

O'Byrne, *Naval biog. dict.* — W. R. O'Byrne, *A naval biographical dictionary* (1849); repr. (1990); [2nd edn], 2 vols. (1861)

OHS — Oxford Historical Society

Old Westminsters — *The record of Old Westminsters*, 1–2, ed. G. F. R. Barker and A. H. Stenning (1928); suppl. 1, ed. J. B. Whitmore and G. R. Y. Radcliffe [1938]; 3, ed. J. B. Whitmore, G. R. Y. Radcliffe, and D. C. Simpson (1963); suppl. 2, ed. F. E. Pagan (1978); 4, ed. F. E. Pagan and H. E. Pagan (1992)

OMT — Oxford Medieval Texts

Ordericus Vitalis, *Eccl. hist.* — *The ecclesiastical history of Orderic Vitalis*, ed. and trans. M. Chibnall, 6 vols., OMT (1969–80); repr. (1990)

Paris, *Chron.* — *Matthaei Parisiensis, monachi sancti Albani, chronica majora*, ed. H. R. Luard, Rolls Series, 7 vols. (1872–83)

Parl. papers — *Parliamentary papers* (1801–)

PBA — *Proceedings of the British Academy*

Pepys, *Diary*	*The diary of Samuel Pepys*, ed. R. Latham and W. Matthews, 11 vols. (1970–83); repr. (1995) and (2000)
Pevsner	N. Pevsner and others, Buildings of England series
PICE	*Proceedings of the Institution of Civil Engineers*
Pipe rolls	*The great roll of the pipe for . . .*, PRSoc. (1884–)
PRO	Public Record Office
PRS	*Proceedings of the Royal Society of London*
PRSoc.	Pipe Roll Society
PTRS	*Philosophical Transactions of the Royal Society*
QR	*Quarterly Review*
RC	Record Commissions
Redgrave, *Artists*	S. Redgrave, *A dictionary of artists of the English school* (1874); rev. edn (1878); repr. (1970)
Reg. Oxf.	C. W. Boase and A. Clark, eds., *Register of the University of Oxford*, 5 vols., OHS, 1, 10–12, 14 (1885–9)
Reg. PCS	J. H. Burton and others, eds., *The register of the privy council of Scotland*, 1st ser., 14 vols. (1877–98); 2nd ser., 8 vols. (1899–1908); 3rd ser., [16 vols.] (1908–70)
Reg. RAN	H. W. C. Davis and others, eds., *Regesta regum Anglo-Normannorum, 1066–1154*, 4 vols. (1913–69)
RIBA Journal	*Journal of the Royal Institute of British Architects* [later *RIBA Journal*]
RotP	J. Strachey, ed., *Rotuli parliamentorum ut et petitiones, et placita in parliamento*, 6 vols. (1767–77)
RotS	D. Macpherson, J. Caley, and W. Illingworth, eds., *Rotuli Scotiae in Turri Londinensi et in domo capitulari Westmonasteriensi asservati*, 2 vols., RC, 14 (1814–19)
RS	Record(s) Society
Rymer, *Foedera*	T. Rymer and R. Sanderson, eds., *Foedera, conventiones, literae et cuiuscunque generis acta publica inter reges Angliae et alios quosvis imperatores, reges, pontifices, principes, vel communitates*, 20 vols. (1704–35); 2nd edn, 20 vols. (1726–35); 3rd edn, 10 vols. (1739–45); facs. edn (1967); new edn, ed. A. Clarke, J. Caley, and F. Holbrooke, 4 vols., RC, 50 (1816–30)
Sainty, *Judges*	J. Sainty, ed., *The judges of England, 1272–1990*, SeldS, suppl. ser., 10 (1993)
Sainty, *King's counsel*	J. Sainty, ed., *A list of English law officers and king's counsel*, SeldS, suppl. ser., 7 (1987)
SCH	Studies in Church History
Scots peerage	J. B. Paul, ed. *The Scots peerage, founded on Wood's edition of Sir Robert Douglas's Peerage of Scotland, containing an historical and genealogical account of the nobility of that kingdom*, 9 vols. (1904–14)
SeldS	Selden Society
SHR	*Scottish Historical Review*
State trials	T. B. Howell and T. J. Howell, eds., *Cobbett's Complete collection of state trials*, 34 vols. (1809–28)
STC, 1475–1640	A. W. Pollard, G. R. Redgrave, and others, eds., *A short-title catalogue of . . . English books . . . 1475–1640* (1926); 2nd edn, ed. W. A. Jackson, F. S. Ferguson, and K. F. Pantzer, 3 vols. (1976–91) [see also Wing, *STC*]
STS	Scottish Text Society
SurtS	Surtees Society
Symeon of Durham, *Opera*	*Symeonis monachi opera omnia*, ed. T. Arnold, 2 vols., Rolls Series, 75 (1882–5); repr. (1965)
Tanner, *Bibl. Brit.-Hib.*	T. Tanner, *Bibliotheca Britannico-Hibernica*, ed. D. Wilkins (1748); repr. (1963)
Thieme & Becker, *Allgemeines Lexikon*	U. Thieme, F. Becker, and H. Vollmer, eds., *Allgemeines Lexikon der bildenden Künstler von der Antike bis zur Gegenwart*, 37 vols. (Leipzig, 1907–50); repr. (1961–5), (1983), and (1992)
Thurloe, *State papers*	*A collection of the state papers of John Thurloe*, ed. T. Birch, 7 vols. (1742)
TLS	*Times Literary Supplement*
Tout, *Admin. hist.*	T. F. Tout, *Chapters in the administrative history of mediaeval England: the wardrobe, the chamber, and the small seals*, 6 vols. (1920–33); repr. (1967)
TRHS	*Transactions of the Royal Historical Society*
VCH	H. A. Doubleday and others, eds., *The Victoria history of the counties of England*, [88 vols.] (1900–)
Venn, *Alum. Cant.*	J. Venn and J. A. Venn, *Alumni Cantabrigienses: a biographical list of all known students, graduates, and holders of office at the University of Cambridge, from the earliest times to 1900*, 10 vols. (1922–54); repr. in 2 vols. (1974–8)
Vertue, *Note books*	[G. Vertue], *Note books*, ed. K. Esdaile, earl of Ilchester, and H. M. Hake, 6 vols., Walpole Society, 18, 20, 22, 24, 26, 30 (1930–55)
VF	*Vanity Fair*
Walford, *County families*	E. Walford, *The county families of the United Kingdom, or, Royal manual of the titled and untitled aristocracy of Great Britain and Ireland* (1860)
Walker rev.	A. G. Matthews, *Walker revised: being a revision of John Walker's Sufferings of the clergy during the grand rebellion, 1642–60* (1948); repr. (1988)
Walpole, *Corr.*	*The Yale edition of Horace Walpole's correspondence*, ed. W. S. Lewis, 48 vols. (1937–83)
Ward, *Men of the reign*	T. H. Ward, ed., *Men of the reign: a biographical dictionary of eminent persons of British and colonial birth who have died during the reign of Queen Victoria* (1885); repr. (Graz, 1968)
Waterhouse, *18c painters*	E. Waterhouse, *The dictionary of 18th century painters in oils and crayons* (1981); repr. as *British 18th century painters in oils and crayons* (1991), vol. 2 of *Dictionary of British art*
Watt, *Bibl. Brit.*	R. Watt, *Bibliotheca Britannica, or, A general index to British and foreign literature*, 4 vols. (1824) [many reprs.]
Wellesley index	W. E. Houghton, ed., *The Wellesley index to Victorian periodicals, 1824–1900*, 5 vols. (1966–89); new edn (1999) [CD-ROM]
Wing, *STC*	D. Wing, ed., *Short-title catalogue of . . . English books . . . 1641–1700*, 3 vols. (1945–51); 2nd edn (1972–88); rev. and enl. edn, ed. J. J. Morrison, C. W. Nelson, and M. Seccombe, 4 vols. (1994–8) [see also *STC, 1475–1640*]
Wisden	*John Wisden's Cricketer's Almanack*
Wood, *Ath. Oxon.*	A. Wood, *Athenae Oxonienses . . . to which are added the Fasti*, 2 vols. (1691–2); 2nd edn (1721); new edn, 4 vols., ed. P. Bliss (1813–20); repr. (1967) and (1969)
Wood, *Vic. painters*	C. Wood, *Dictionary of Victorian painters* (1971); 2nd edn (1978); 3rd edn as *Victorian painters*, 2 vols. (1995), vol. 4 of *Dictionary of British art*
WW	*Who's who* (1849–)
WWBMP	M. Stenton and S. Lees, eds., *Who's who of British members of parliament*, 4 vols. (1976–81)
WWW	*Who was who* (1929–)

Brown. *See also* Broun, Browne.

Brown, Agnes Henderson [Nannie] (1866–1943), suffragist, was born at 125 Princes Street, Edinburgh, on 12 April 1866, the youngest child of William Brown, master fruiterer, and his wife, Jessie Henderson. She was generally known as Nannie Brown, and had two brothers and one sister, Jessie, who was also an active suffragette and involved in many of the same activities as Nannie. Nannie's father, who was the proprietor of a number of fruiterer shops in Edinburgh, was sympathetic to the suffrage movement. He was a leading figure in the opposition to annuity tax, part of the suffrage struggle, as it opposed taxation on women so long as they were not considered 'persons'—that is, did not have the vote. William Brown was jailed for his part in that campaign, wrote a book about his experiences in prison, and is said to have passed on his public-spiritedness to his two daughters. Nannie was later to refer to her father as the last political prisoner in the old Calton prison for making this stand.

Nannie Brown's early public activities were associated with the suffrage movement and the Women's Freedom League. She was one of only six women who participated in the historic march of the 'Brown Women' from Edinburgh to London. The march, which was organized by the Women's Freedom League in 1912, lasted for five weeks. The women, dressed in the tailor-made coats and skirts of russet brown which gained them their name, and wearing white blouses and light green scarves and hats, collected signatures on the way and sometimes held as many as four meetings a day. Given her father's support for the suffrage movement, it is unsurprising that Nannie Brown favoured admitting men to the Women's Freedom League, and in 1913 she became the honorary secretary of the Northern Men's Federation for Women's Suffrage.

From 1917 Nannie Brown was associated with the Scottish Women's Rural Institutes (SWRI), playing a leading role in organizing the movement on a Scotland-wide level. When the SWRI was included in the work of the board of agriculture for Scotland, she served as a member of the board's staff. After the SWRI division was cut out of the board's work, she continued to work for the south-eastern area. However, ill health forced her to retire from this work in 1928, although she continued as honorary adviser to the area. She was also, in 1918, one of the fourteen founder members of the Scottish Council of Women's Citizens' Associations whose aim was to promote civic awareness among women and to gain greater representation of women in public affairs and equality of treatment with men.

However, Nannie Brown's activities were not confined to the endless round of meetings associated with formal organizations; she was a prodigious writer of articles, stories, lectures, and plays, an active participant in and promoter of amateur dramatics in Edinburgh, and, with her sister, a leading member of the Edinburgh Dickens Fellowship. She was also a keen walker and traveller. She once spent two separate holidays walking from John o' Groats to London and some of her travel experiences in France, Corsica, Russia, and Germany found expression in articles which she contributed to the *Weekly Scotsman*. Her pioneering spirit was also manifested in other areas; according to one of her obituaries, she was one of the first women who learned to type and, with her sister, Jessie, among the first women to be seen riding a bicycle in Scotland.

Although Nannie Brown was described as 'thoroughly stern in outlook' (*The Scotsman*, 3 Dec 1943), there are countless references to her vivid personality and lively sense of humour. When in later years she became too frail to venture far afield, her house in Castle Terrace, Edinburgh, became a centre where any and every SWRI member could find advice and hospitality. Indeed, the home which she shared with Jessie in Castle Terrace became something of a cultural centre after the First World War. They would hold 'Scots evenings' or 'Dickens evenings', at which stories, songs, and sketches were performed.

Nannie Brown died on 1 December 1943 at 3 Blackford Road, Edinburgh. The words spoken at her burial service (she was buried in Edinburgh) perhaps best sum up her life: 'Look up not down, Look out not in, And lend a hand' (private information).   ELEANOR GORDON

Sources L. Leneman, *A guid cause: the women's suffrage movement in Scotland* (1991) · S. Livingstone, *Bonny fechters* (1996) · private information (2004) · *The Scotsman* (3 Dec 1943) · *Common Cause* (1917–18) · b. cert. · d. cert.

Wealth at death £921 6s. 2d.: confirmation, 2 Feb 1944, *CCI*

Brown, Albert Richard (1839–1913), shipping agent and consul for Japan, was born on 29 August 1839 at Ringwood, in Hampshire, the son of Richard Brown, wine merchant and clerk to the Ringwood board of guardians, and his wife, Mary Ann, *née* Pritchard. In 1853 he went to sea as a cabin-boy on the brig *Industrious*, leaving the vessel four years later as an able seaman. In 1860 he obtained his second mate's certificate, and the following year joined the *Malta*, of the Peninsular and Oriental Steamship Company (P. & O.), as fourth officer. He obtained a first mate's certificate in 1866, and joined the P. & O.'s *Malacca* as first officer. He married on 19 May 1866 Louisa, *née* Pyne (*b*. 1840/41). His only son, Edward Albert, was born in 1867.

The voyages of the *Malacca* took Brown to the Far East, and he obtained his master's certificate in Hong Kong. In February 1869 Richard H. Brunton (1841–1901), the engineer supervising the construction of a network of lighthouses on the Japanese coast (and who had sailed to Japan on Brown's ship), advised the lighthouse section of Japan's department of public works to engage Brown as the master of the lighthouse-tender *Tomio Maru*. The steamer transported supplies and equipment to lighthouse sites, and Brown assisted on numerous survey expeditions around the coast of Japan and in the investigation of potential sites for lighthouses and beacons— work which was vital in the development of Japan's coastal and foreign trade. In March 1870 Brown took command of a new ship, the *Thabor*. His seamanship impressed the Japanese authorities, and in 1871 he was asked to train Japanese students in the skills of navigation. His pupils went on to form the core of the country's mercantile marine service.

In 1874 the Japanese government launched an expedition to Formosa (Taiwan) to punish the Botan population for atrocities committed on shipwrecked Japanese sailors. The American and British governments refused to permit the chartering of ships for the expedition, and there was a danger that, as the Japanese did not have suitable transports to carry men and material, the expedition would result in humiliating failure. The *Thabor* was requisitioned as a transport, and Brown was asked to purchase and fit out five other ships for the purpose. He personally commanded one, the former P. & O. steamer *Delta* (renamed *Takasago Maru*), and carried General Saigo and 1500 men to a landing at Lingkiao Bay. The expedition was successful, and the grateful Japanese government announced that Brown would be rewarded with the payment of 3000 yen and invested with the order of the Rising Sun, fourth class. Although the British government initially refused to give its approval, he was finally permitted to accept the honour in April 1881.

In late August 1874 Brown was commanded to return to Britain to take delivery of a new lighthouse-tender, *Meiji Maru*, from Robert Napier & Sons' shipyard in Glasgow. While in Britain he received instructions to purchase two more steamers for the shipping company Mitsubishi Shokai. He returned to Japan in 1875, and was invited to help form a marine bureau and to take charge of its shipbuilding and mercantile marine activities. While holding this government office he continued to act for Mitsubishi, and returned to Britain in 1877 to supervise the construction of new ships for the company. In 1883 he returned again to supervise the construction of ships for the Kiodo Unyu Kaisha (the 'National transportation company'), and another for Mitsubishi.

In 1885 Kiodo Unyu Kaisha and Mitsubishi merged to form the Nippon Yusen Kaisha (the 'Japanese mail steamship company') (NYK), Japan's leading shipping line. Brown was appointed general manager, and travelled extensively in the Far East in 1886 to investigate the company's existing services and the potential for expansion. The following year he returned to Britain to supervise the construction of ships for NYK, and in March 1889 he resigned as NYK's general manager in order to stay in Britain to supervise the company's building programme and other business affairs there. Before he left, in the summer, he was awarded the order of the Rising Sun, third class, and appointed consul for Japan in Glasgow.

In 1889 Brown formed his own company, A. R. Brown, to handle his agency work for the Japanese and to trade as Japan merchants and consulting engineers. In 1899 his son joined him as a partner in A. R. Brown & Co., and in 1900 they formed a private limited liability company, A. R. Brown, McFarlane & Co. Ltd, in partnership with George McFarlane, a consulting engineer and naval architect. The firm designed, placed contracts for, and supervised the construction of most of the warships and merchant vessels built in Britain for Japanese customers prior to the First World War.

As Japan's consul in Glasgow, Brown was responsible for the welfare of Japanese students who visited the city, and his young charges included the sons of some of Japan's leading families. In 1909 he was awarded the order of the Sacred Treasure, second class.

Brown was a keen yachtsman and a member of the Royal Clyde and Clyde Corinthian yacht clubs. His Scottish home, Summerhill, was in the village of Shandon, on the Gareloch, and he was a member of the executive—and from 1909 until his death the chairman—of the Clyde training ship for boys, the *Empress*. The Browns had a home, Furlong House, in Ringwood, Hampshire, and also spent long holidays in Bournemouth.

Albert Brown died at Parkstone, Dorset, on 7 March 1913, and was buried five days later at Ringwood. He was survived by his wife and son. He is remembered in Japan as a pioneer of that country's steam navigation, a hero of the Formosa expedition, and one of the founders of the Japanese mercantile marine. IAIN F. RUSSELL

Sources L. Bush, *The life and times of the illustrious Captain Brown* (1970) · R. H. Brunton, 'Pioneer engineering in Japan', U. Glas., Archives and Business Records Centre, UGD 172/5/7/4 · *Paddington, Kensington and Bayswater Chronicle* (22 March 1913) · O. Checkland, *Britain's encounter with Meiji Japan, 1868–1912* (1989) · *Glasgow Herald* (8 March 1913), 9 · b. cert. · m. cert. · CCI (1914)
Archives U. Glas., A. R. Brown, McFarlane & Co. Ltd, UGD 172 · U. Glas. L.
Likenesses photograph (of the *Meiji Maru* with inset picture of A. R. Brown), U. Glas., archives, UGD 172/4/2/28
Wealth at death £45,891 10s. 8d.: confirmation, 14 April 1913, CCI · £4804 16s. 7d.: additional estate, 10 Jan 1914, CCI · £1809 10s.: additional estate, 21 Nov 1914, CCI

Brown, Alexander (1764–1834), merchant and banker, was born on 17 November 1764 in Ballymena, co. Antrim, the son of William Brown (b. 1715) and Margaret Davison. There may have been as many as thirteen children in the family, but only four—three sons, of whom Alexander was the second, and one daughter—survived to maturity. Both his parents came from Scots-Irish and Presbyterian stock.

There is very little information about Brown's early years. He married Grace Davison on 17 November 1783 and they had seven children, of whom four boys, William, George, John, and James, survived. His wife was a woman of great character and indomitable courage, and 'no great issue, no problem, no crisis arose without it being shared with her' (Ellis, 6). By the early 1790s Brown was auctioning linen in Belfast, and in 1796 he consigned linen to his younger brother Stewart in the firm of Falls and Brown of Philadelphia and Baltimore. He was sufficiently wealthy to send his sons to be educated in Yorkshire. In the late 1790s he had to hide during the Irish troubles. These experiences probably account for his emigration to Baltimore with his eldest son, William *Brown (1784–1864), in 1800. His wife and the other boys followed in 1802. He was also probably lured by Baltimore's prosperity at this time.

Brown soon established himself as a successful linen importer. By 1810 he was worth $122,000. The French wars, the American embargoes, and the Anglo-American War of 1812–14 disrupted Baltimore's trade, but although these misfortunes broke many American merchants, the best informed and most decisive could prosper. Alexander Brown was a careful risk-taker, and his letter-books reveal the quality of his information and commercial analysis. He sent William to Liverpool in 1809, and all through the war at least one of his sons was in Britain. William and John married daughters of his main linen suppliers in Ireland, Andrew Gihon and John Patrick. In these difficult conditions he traded in whatever staples would safely turn a profit, and he bought his first ship, the *Armata*, in 1812. By 1815 he was worth $396,000. The Baltimore house, starting as Alexander Brown, had also, within seven years, become Alexander Brown & Sons.

The disturbed conditions during the post-war boom and slump of 1815–17 provided Brown with further chances to increase his fortune, and by 1820 he was worth nearly $1 million. However, in the early 1820s New York increasingly began to dominate transatlantic trade at the expense of Baltimore and Philadelphia. Simultaneously the margin on Brown's main import, Irish linen, and on many other dry goods, fell disastrously; hence he sent John to Philadelphia in 1818 and James to New York in 1825. His letter-books show he kept his sons on a tight rein—even William, the most independent, was firmly directed at times. To his sons he was the 'dear father' to whose judgement they all 'gave up' as long as he lived (Kouwenhoven, 25).

Brown also formed an effective commercial network in the American south, at first composed of fellow Ulstermen such as James Adger in Charleston, John Cumming in Savannah, John Hagan in Mobile, and Johnston McClanahan in New Orleans. Cumming and McClanahan were relations. Brown's letters reveal that he was loyal to good agents, but harsh on defaulters. Most large transatlantic firms attempted to create similar networks, but Brown's was especially well organized. This network could be conveniently managed from Baltimore, but did not rely on the city's immediate prosperity.

Brown depended on William to develop his contacts in England. In the early 1820s he received very large cotton orders from the leading Liverpool brokers, which he transferred to Baltimore. His father then executed them through the southern agents, surmounting considerable problems in providing sufficient funds in the American south and in matching the exact staples required. The size of the orders, the lack of instant communications, and the variability of prices made transactions extremely hazardous. This put the brokers in a very strong position, but by the mid-1820s the Browns and other merchants had resumed their traditional leadership. In the late 1820s Alexander Brown was usually able to ensure that William received the most cotton in Liverpool—in 1827 the huge amount of 65,000 bales. Access to finance was critical.

During the commercial crisis of 1825, when many Liverpool merchants failed, Brown sent large sums to William to ensure he could meet all demands. Such large imports were mostly financed by advances to southern factors, but he also transferred to William large quantities of stock of the Bank of the United States, to enable him to raise money cheaply in England. Although William was himself a dominant character, his father controlled the whole enterprise, preventing William and his other sons from embarking on over-speculative enterprises and making sure that cotton sales were kept moving.

After the Anglo-American War of 1812–14 Alexander Brown also built up a small fleet of ships usually named after the family—the *Alexander*, the *Grace Brown*, and the *William Brown*, for instance. These were first-class vessels, often built by Henry Eckford of New York. They were used mainly to transport cotton from the American south and British goods to America. Generally Brown was able to insist that merchants and planters who needed credit should employ the ships, but if cargoes were scarce he sometimes filled spare space with bales on his own account. Occasionally he used the ships to rush a speculative cargo to Liverpool entirely on his own account. Possession of the ships often cushioned him from commercial shocks: if a huge harvest forced prices down, the additional cargoes could raise freight rates sufficiently high to compensate. Brown also used the ships in the high-quality packet lines, sailing between the east coast and Liverpool. New York merchants had established the first packets in 1818, and Baltimore and Philadelphia merchants soon demanded similar services. In Philadelphia, Brown co-operated with Thomas Cope to provide from 1822 the city's only long-lasting packet line. In Baltimore, which had few return goods to send to Liverpool, Brown promised to provide regular ships if the importers would give him the preference. However, trade still slipped away to New York, and William and James participated in the New York–Liverpool packet lines after the New York branch was established in 1825.

Relatively cheap capital and easy entry into transatlantic commerce produced such intense competition that by the mid-1820s Alexander Brown was finding it very hard to make consistent profits in trading staples. Hence he increasingly adopted the role of merchant banker by giving advances to planters or manufacturers rather than buying goods himself. Even making advances could be dangerous if the value of the goods fell below the level of the advance. Brown also entered the market in foreign exchange. During the season each Atlantic port was awash with sterling or dollar bills of exchange drawn by junior partners or agents on prominent international merchants, or on their home branches, to raise funds to buy cotton or raw manufactures. Such bills often circulated through many hands before presentation for final payment. Brown and his sons were very well informed about the merchants in each major port and were expert at buying and selling bills. Their own name was so well known they could normally issue their own bills at high prices. By the late 1820s Brown had become the leading trader in transatlantic bills. The firm's letter-books show he understood the likely seasonal rhythms and was expert at predicting and exploiting probable interlocking shifts in commodity prices, freight rates, and the sterling–dollar exchange rates.

The Bank of the United States was the leading dealer in domestic bills in the 1820s and 1830s, and Alexander Brown had become a large stockholder when the bank was floated in 1816. He became a director of the Baltimore branch and enabled his son John to join the board of directors in Philadelphia, and his southern correspondents to become directors of the branches in Charleston, Savannah, Mobile, and New Orleans. He helped to oppose the inflationary policy of its president William Jones in 1818, and to secure the election of Langdon Cheves in 1819. In the 1820s under Nicholas Biddle the bank opened branches in all the main trading centres of the Union, and it controlled the American domestic bill market. Sterling accumulated in the southern states as British firms purchased cotton, but it was short in the north as Americans ordered British goods. The bank organized the equalizing flows. Brown was able to time his own purchases of bills to coincide with the bank's. When Nicholas Biddle took over in 1822 he first co-operated with the Browns, but he then became suspicious that they were exploiting their privileged position as directors. When the bank finally failed in the early 1840s, Brown's sons took over a large part of its internal exchange business.

Alexander Brown and his sons helped to transfer British railway technology to the USA and to build the first large American railroad, the Baltimore and Ohio. Simultaneously their agent in Charleston, James Adger, helped to establish the South Carolina Railway. Later their associate in Philadelphia, Thomas Cope, organized the Pennsylvania railroad. As early as March 1825 Brown had commented to William on the widespread interest in railways. In early 1827 Brown wrote that a railroad might resuscitate Baltimore and make her the first city in the Union, and asked William for information about the Liverpool and Manchester Railway. Later Brown sent American engineers via William to study English railways and to visit George Stephenson. George Brown held in his house the organizing meeting of the Baltimore and Ohio railroad, and the Brown family helped to raise the $4.2m required to float the venture. Brown also secured capital in England and sent orders for railroad iron to William for execution. When work began Brown reported to William that 'our AB and GB have had to direct the work at every point.' For a time the letter-books contained many engineering sketches, and Alexander and George Brown were to ride in the first carriage pulled by steam in the USA.

By 1830 Alexander had established a well-diversified merchant house worth about $2.8m. He was by far the richest merchant in Baltimore, and possibly the richest active merchant in the United States. He no longer imported linen and dry goods, but the cotton trade had grown enormously. He regularly gave the largest factors and private bankers in the south, such as Reynolds Byrne

of New Orleans or Yeatman Woods of Nashville, credits of £40,000–£50,000—an immense amount—which generated large flows of cotton and exchange. He maintained his interest in ships and just a few months before his death was considering establishing a Charleston–Liverpool packet with James Adger. His interest in railways was leading to investment banking. He sold Maryland stocks in England and was importing railroad iron. Finally in the 'panic' of 1834, he promised during a meeting at the merchants' exchange that no solvent Baltimore merchant would be allowed to fail.

It was at this meeting that Alexander Brown caught the pneumonia from which he died, at Baltimore, on 4 April 1834. At his death his firm was worth about $4.6m. Following his passing, a prominent merchant from New York wrote in his diary that Brown had been one of 'the royal merchants of America, as the Medici of old were of Italy' (Kouwenhoven, 25). Another commended him as 'an Irish gentleman "who knew" when to go in, how long to stay in, and when to get out. He coined money' (ibid., 25). A shrewd but decisive man of business, Brown nevertheless adhered to Presbyterian standards of honour. Brown's death shocked his sons: 'the head that thought for us is gone' wrote George (Kouwenhoven, 25). Nevertheless, during the mid-1830s boom the firm's business expanded as never before. By the early 1840s, however, chastened by crises in the late 1830s, Brown's sons had completed a change of direction for the firm: away from diversified commerce, and towards specialized banking.

J. R. KILLICK

Sources L. Cong., manuscript division, Alexander Brown & Sons MSS · J. C. Brown, *A hundred years of merchant banking: a history of Brown Brothers and Company, Brown Shipley and Company and the allied firms* (privately printed, New York, 1909) · G. L. Browne, 'Business innovation and social change: the career of Alexander Brown after the war of 1812', *Maryland Historical Magazine*, 69 (1974), 243–5 · A. Ellis, *Heir of adventure: the story of Brown, Shipley & Co., merchant bankers* (privately printed, London, 1960) · F. R. Kent, *The story of Alexander Brown & Sons* (1925) · J. R. Killick, 'Risk, specialization and profit in the mercantile sector of the nineteenth century cotton trade: Alexander Brown & Sons, 1820–80', *Business History*, 16 (1974), 1–16 · J. R. Killick, 'The cotton operations of Alexander Brown and Sons in the deep south, 1820–1860', *Journal of Southern History*, 43 (1977), 169–94 · J. A. Kouwenhoven, *Partners in banking: an historical portrait of a great private bank, Brown Brothers, Harriman & Co., 1818–1968* (1968) · E. J. Perkins, *Financing Anglo-American trade: the house of Brown, 1800–1880* (1975)
Archives L. Cong. · New York Historical Society
Likenesses S. Peale?, group portrait, *c.*1832 (with four sons), repro. in Kouwenhoven, *Partners in banking*, 25
Wealth at death $913,020—agreed by sons: Alexander Brown & Sons MSS, L. Cong. · $4,610,321—value of the Brown companies: Perkins, *Financing Anglo-American trade*, 238

Brown, Alexander [Sandy] (1929–1975), band leader and acoustic architect, was born on 25 February 1929 in Izatnagar, near Bareilly in India, the second son of John Brown, a railway engineer who died about 1936, and his wife, Minnie Henderson (d. 1975). His parents were Scottish and Presbyterian, although Sandy sometimes said his mother was Indian. His robust medium build, hooked nose, bushy black beard, and sallow complexion did give him something of the look of a Sikh. The family moved back to Scotland in the early 1930s, and lived at Wishaw, near Glasgow, later moving to 4 Abercorn Crescent, Edinburgh.

When he was twelve Brown taught himself to play the clarinet, this absence of formal training being crucial to his unique approach to the instrument. His strident sound and percussive style was reminiscent of his early model, the New Orleans clarinettist Johnny Dodds. His technique was remarkable because he had lost his front teeth, and removed his false teeth when playing, enabling him to put more pressure on the mouthpiece than a normal player. In 1943 he formed his first band with fellow schoolmates from the Royal High School, Edinburgh, including Al Fairweather (trombone, later trumpet) and Stan Greig (piano and drums), with whom he was to record some of his best work. He did national service with the Royal Army Ordnance Corps. On demobilization in 1949 he reformed his band, and was apprenticed to an architect. At the same time he studied architecture and acoustic engineering at Edinburgh College of Art, where he obtained a diploma in architecture.

Brown and his band played at the local Oddfellows Hall, where the 'bouncer' was Tom Connery, who later became famous as the actor Sean Connery. They made their first records in 1949 for S. & M. (Swarbrick and Mossman), and these led to a historic concert at the Usher Hall in Edinburgh in 1952, where they shared the bill with Big Bill Broonzy, the American blues singer and guitarist. There followed a broadcast for the BBC in 1953, the first of many. In July the band went to London to play a National Jazz Federation concert at the Royal Festival Hall, and made some recordings for Esquire which became their first recordings on national release. Trumpeter Fairweather remained in London when the band returned to Edinburgh, and was replaced by Alex Welsh (1929–1982). Later that year Brown and Fairweather recorded two numbers with Humphrey Lyttelton.

On 29 September 1954 Brown married legal secretary Florence Armstrong (b. 1927), known as Flo, and was appointed acoustic architect at the BBC, moving permanently to London. There he formed a new band with Fairweather and made a series of recordings for Tempo, including his own composition *African Queen*. He also recorded several sides for Decca, duetting with Wally Fawkes, clarinettist with the Humphrey Lyttelton band, otherwise known as the cartoonist Trog. Then came an LP for Nixa entitled *McJazz*. This was a collection of original compositions with an African 'high life' feel by Brown, Fairweather, and Greig, long recognized as the outstanding British jazz recording of the decade. A series of LPs followed for Columbia, *Al & Sandy*, *Doctor McJazz*, and *The Incredible McJazz*, but one of the finest recordings of his later career was with the American blues pianist Sammy Price. *Hair at its Hairiest*, recorded in 1968 with an all-star band, including George Chisholm on trombone and Kenny Wheeler on trumpet, was less successful. Perhaps the best of his recordings was that made with the Brian Lemon trio in 1971, *In the Evening*. Here he shows all the passion and improvisatory invention of a true jazz master.

As the BBC's chief acoustics architect Brown was involved with all major BBC radio and television projects throughout the UK. His collaboration with the BBC research department resulted in the first modular acoustic absorbers, a mobile, stacking acoustic screen used in all BBC and commercial recording studios, and the innovative use of refrigerator magnetic seals in acoustic doors. He left in 1969 to set up his own consultancy practice, and in six years of independent practice as Sandy Brown Associates he raised the acoustic design of commercial sound recording studios to an internationally known product, and built studios for the Beatles, Eric Clapton, the Rolling Stones, and others. In 1972 he was invited as acoustic consultant to the Edinburgh opera house project, using a one-eighth-scale physical acoustic model. This technique had been developed by his colleagues at the BBC, subsequently his partners, and this was the first time it had been used in the design of an auditorium. Sandy Brown Associates was the first major UK buildings acoustics consultancy, and remains so to this day. Sandy's work, and that of the practice that survives him, has had a major influence on the development of building acoustics both in the UK and throughout the world.

Sandy Brown was also a witty and widely read writer; in particular he contributed a series of articles in *The Listener* (1968–73), which was reprinted in *The McJazz Manuscripts* (1979), a collection of his writings published in his memory. He also contributed an important piece on Johnny Dodds to *Storyville* magazine.

Brown died of malignant hypertension on 15 March 1975 at his London home, 122 Green Croft Gardens, West Hampstead, while watching Scotland lose to England at rugby, a glass of Scotch by his side. He was forty-six. He was cremated at Golders Green crematorium, and was survived by his wife and two children. Bronze plaques honouring him and Fairweather, paid for by public subscription, were later put up in the Royal High School and the 100 Club, and another was planned for the Usher Hall. To many he was the greatest jazz musician that Britain had produced.   A. J. H. LATHAM

Sources S. Brown, *The McJazz manuscripts: a collection of the writings of Sandy Brown* (1979) · G. Bielderman and J. Latham, *Sandy Brown discography*, 4th edn (1997) · J. Chilton, *Who's who of British jazz*, 2nd edn (1998) · B. Kernfeld, ed., *The new Grove dictionary of jazz* (1994) · J. Latham, 'Sandy Brown: in retrospect', *Jazz Journal International* (June 1994), 10–11 · J. Latham, 'The Royal High School Gang', *Jazz Journal International* (May 1996), 10 · J. Latham, 'Stan Greig: action man', *Jazz Rag* (Nov–Dec 1998), 19 · J. Latham, 'Al Fairweather', *Jazz Journal International* (Jan 1993), 16–17 · S. Race, 'Great records of our time', *Melody Maker* (31 Jan 1959), 9 · S. Brown, 'Johnny Dodds', *Storyville*, 1/3 (Feb 1966), 11–14 · private information (2004) [F. Brown, widow]

Likenesses photographs, priv. coll.

Wealth at death £46,874: probate, 19 Aug 1975, *CGPLA Eng. & Wales*

Brown, Alexander Crum (1838–1922), chemist, was born in Edinburgh on 26 March 1838, the only son of a United

Alexander Crum Brown (1838–1922), by Andrew Swan Watson

Presbyterian minister, John *Brown (1784–1858), and his second wife, Margaret Fisher Crum (*d.* 1841), sister of the chemist Walter Crum FRS (1796–1867) and a descendant of Ebenezer Erskine. His half-brother, John *Brown MD (1810–1882), was famed as an author; their grandfather was John *Brown of Whitburn (1754–1832), and their great-grandfather was John Brown of Haddington. Crum Brown, as he was generally known, spent five years at the Royal High School, Edinburgh, then went to Mill Hill School, Middlesex. He entered the University of Edinburgh in 1854 to study arts, but changed to medicine, and was a gold medallist in chemistry and natural philosophy. He graduated MA in 1858 and MD in 1861. He simultaneously studied science at London University where he gained his DSc in 1862. In the following year he went to Germany to study chemistry, under Bunsen at Heidelberg and Kolbe at Marburg. He returned to Edinburgh to teach medical students, as extramural lecturer in chemistry in 1863 and professor from 1869 to his retirement in 1908. He obtained his FRCP (Edin.) in 1865. In 1866 he married Jane Bailie (*d.* 1910), daughter of the Revd James Porter of Drumlee, co. Down. There were no children.

In keeping with his medico-chemical interests, Crum Brown's Edinburgh MD thesis, 'On the theory of chemical combination' (1861), proposed a new way to represent chemical constitution: each atom was to be indicated by the chemical symbol for the element concerned, bonds between atoms being symbolized by lines. Essentially this

was the system of notation later employed universally. For clarifying atomic relationships within a molecule, according to the new valency theories of Edward Frankland and Kekulé, this simple device was of untold value and greatly facilitated the emergence of the theory of structure upon which later chemistry was predicated. It transformed the teaching of organic chemistry, particularly in the hands of Frankland, becoming known, somewhat unfairly, as 'Frankland's notation'. The system was introduced to a wider audience at a lecture on chemical constitution and its relation to physiological action, reported in *Chemical News* complete with the new 'graphic formulae'. His name is remembered now chiefly for the Crum Brown–Gibson rule, enunciated with his assistant J. Gibson (1855–1914) in 1892, concerning substitution in a benzene molecule.

Though his most enduring concern was the establishment of a truly mathematical theory of chemistry (in which he was unsuccessful) Crum Brown also worked on optical activity, organo-sulphur compounds, and electrolytic synthesis of half-esters. He wrote on the physiology of the inner ear, where he correctly related vertigo to the motion of fluid in channels of the inner ear. He was proficient in Japanese, and an expert in systems of knitting. His other interests included the university senate, the Royal Society of Edinburgh, and the synod of his church. He was the first holder of a London DSc (1862), received honorary degrees from all four Scottish universities, and became FRSE in 1863 and FRS in 1879. He was president of the Chemical Society from 1891 to 1893. Crum Brown died on 28 October 1922 at his home, 8 Belgrave Crescent, Edinburgh.   COLIN A. RUSSELL, *rev.*

Sources J. W., *JCS*, 123 (1923), 3422–31 · *DSB* · *The Times* (31 Oct 1922) · 'Alexander Crum Brown, 1838–1922', A. Boyle, *The Royal Society of Edinburgh: scientific and engineering fellows elected, 1784–1876*, ed. F. Bennet (1984), vol. 5 of *Scotland's cultural heritage* (1981–4), 11–12 · J. Walker, *Proceedings of the Royal Society of Edinburgh*, 43 (1922–3), 268–76 · *CGPLA Eng. & Wales* (1923)

Archives BL · CUL, letters to Sir George Stokes · NL Scot. · Open University, Milton Keynes, E. Frankland archive · U. Edin. · U. St Andr.

Likenesses E. A. Walton, portrait, 1910, Royal Society of Edinburgh · A. Swan Watson, photograph, Wellcome L. [*see illus.*] · photograph, repro. in J. D. Comrie, *History of Scottish medicine* (1934) · photograph, repro. in 'Alexander Crum Brown' · photograph, Royal Society of Chemistry · print, repro. in W. Hole, *Quasicursores* (1884)

Wealth at death see confirmation, 1923, *CGPLA Eng. & Wales*

Brown, Alfred Reginald Radcliffe- (1881–1955), social anthropologist, was born Alfred Reginald Brown on 17 January 1881 at 39 Farm Road, Aston, Warwickshire, the second son and last of three children of Alfred Brown (1834–1886), manufacturer's clerk, and his second wife, Hannah (*c.*1845–1925), daughter of Owen Radcliffe, engineer, and his wife, Susan Smith. By 1917 he was adding Radcliffe to his name, following the lead of his brother Herbert whose middle name it was, and began assuming the hyphenated form by 1923. He was educated at the Commercial Travellers' School, Pinner, Middlesex, from 1890 to 1896; at King Edward VI School, Birmingham, from 1896 to 1898, where he was a foundation scholar; and at Trinity

College, Cambridge, from 1902 to 1906, to which he won an exhibition in 1901. There he read for the mental and moral science tripos, and obtained a second class (division 1) in part one (1904) and a first in part two (1905); he was trained in anthropology by A. C. Haddon and W. H. R. Rivers. He married Winifred Marie Lyon (b. 1880), daughter of Algernon Jasper Lyon, a Cambridge solicitor, and his wife, Mary Elizabeth Mason, on 19 April 1910. They had one child, Mary Cynthia Lyon Radcliffe. Radcliffe-Brown and his wife had become estranged by about 1926, but did not divorce.

Seemingly possessed by a wanderlust, Radcliffe-Brown spent well over half his adult life outside England. He was a fellow of Trinity College from 1908 to 1914, a master at the Sydney Church of England grammar school from 1915 to 1917, and director of education in the kingdom of Tonga from 1918 to 1919, and was the first professor of anthropology at the universities of Cape Town from 1921 to 1925, Sydney from 1926 to 1931, and Oxford from 1937 to 1946. He held chairs at Chicago from 1931 to 1937, and Alexandria from 1947 to 1949, and was also a visiting professor at Yenching (Yanjing) University in China, from 1935 to 1936, the University of São Paulo in Brazil from 1942 to 1944, and Rhodes University in South Africa in 1952. If his career was brilliant, his childhood circumstances had been difficult, and he was fortunate to have been admitted to the Commercial Travellers' School, founded in 1845 to provide for 'the destitute Orphans of deceased and the Children of necessitous Commercial Travellers.' School records show that his family had neither property nor expectations.

A pioneer of social anthropology Although he did not achieve the standards later set by Bronislaw Malinowski, in which emphasis is placed on long-term participant observation of a limited area, Radcliffe-Brown was one of the first British anthropologists to undertake fieldwork on his own, principally in the Andaman Islands from 1906 to 1908, and Western Australia from 1910 to 1912, with shorter periods in several states of Australia between 1914 and 1930. Some uncertainty surrounds the circumstances of his main research, especially in the Andamans, about the deficiencies of which he had no illusions, but he did not—as is sometimes claimed—depend there or in Australia on the inmates of gaols and hospitals. He travelled extensively in his Australian fieldwork, obtaining information especially on kinship, social organization, and totemism, thus laying a foundation for the comparative and analytical studies for which he had a natural talent and with which his name is especially associated.

Radcliffe-Brown's role in creating the academic discipline of social anthropology in English-speaking countries was 'immense' (Pocock, 54) and is unmatched even by Malinowski. Effectively it began with his Cape Town appointment, though he had lectured in Cambridge, London, and Birmingham before the First World War. The courses he developed at Cape Town and subsequently at Sydney drew the attention of undergraduates to the nature of African and Australian societies, the comparative method, and the theories of the French sociological school. He conveyed a clear and comprehensive view of the scope and method of anthropology and a sense that new ground was being broken and obsolete theories overthrown. The difficulty in both countries of instituting and maintaining an adequately funded programme of research was all the more disappointing because he was confident that his type of anthropology could solve ethnographic problems, discover laws of society, and provide enlightened guidance to governments and the public.

In South Africa and Australia anthropology had been developed by amateur scholars, some of whom achieved much in spite of their isolation. In the United States, where the discipline was already well established in universities, Radcliffe-Brown's approach stimulated a number of anthropologists 'to reconsider the whole matter of method, to scrutinize their objectives, and to attend to new problems and new ways of looking at problems' (Redfield, ix). In particular, he staked a claim for anthropology, or comparative sociology as he also called it, to be the basis of a possible unified natural science of society, and sought to undermine counter-claims by economics and psychology to provide models for this science. Once again, however, he remained for only a few years before leaving for another country. Whatever hopes he brought to Oxford came to little owing to the suspension of anthropology during the Second World War and his retirement, which he is said to have resisted, shortly afterwards. Later he regretted having left Chicago (Stocking, 'Yours affectionately, Rex', 4–5, 8).

Radcliffe-Brown conceived of anthropology as an 'investigation of the nature of human society by the systematic comparison of societies of diverse type' (Radcliffe-Brown, *Method*, 133). He attached great importance to the study of primitive societies (though he also encouraged studies of communities in China, India, and Japan and was appreciative of W. L. Warner's Yankee City series), partly because of their differences from Western civilization and partly because they were changing or being destroyed so rapidly. Investigation involved a series of steps: carrying out intensive field research; demonstrating how institutions such as kinship, religion, politics, and economics are interconnected; and analysis in terms of the concepts of social structure and social function (the concept of social value was important to him in principle, but less salient in practice). Social structure, not culture, was the linchpin in this scheme of inquiry. Thus unlike Malinowski, who understood function as essentially biological, Radcliffe-Brown defined it as the contribution a belief or custom made to the maintenance of the social structure. Although the stress in his work, as in that of the anthropologists most influenced by him, was on synchronic rather than diachronic studies, he held that all societies resulted from a process of evolution which explained the great variety among them.

Radcliffe-Brown has been taxed with ignoring conflict and assuming that customs and institutions work smoothly together to serve a larger purpose—hence the comment that 'a dose of Marx or Adam Ferguson would have done Radcliffe-Brown the world of good' (E. E. Evans-Pritchard, 'Fifty years of British anthropology', *TLS*, 6 July

1973, 763). In fact, he never supposed that simple solidarity was the only characteristic of human life. His early opinion that opposition 'is of the utmost importance to inquiry', is expressed in war and between the sexes, and 'is as fundamentally necessary to human society as solidarity', was further developed in lectures to Sydney students on 'social opposition' or 'socially regulated antagonism' (Maddock, 11, 15). It was also conveyed to a wider audience in his Huxley memorial lecture (1951), when he argued that the 'Heraclitean union of opposites' has been often used 'not only in the establishment of systems of cosmology but also in organising social structures' (Radcliffe-Brown, *Structure*, 115). True, his writings do not convey the impression that 'social arrangements are transient creations based on domination, and ever liable to challenge from a new social movement' (N. McInnes, *The Western Marxists*, 1972, 23–4). But societies of the kind in which Radcliffe-Brown was most interested were not characterized by class conflicts or challenged by revolutionary or reform movements developing from within. Their transformation, as he knew from his Andamanese, Australian, and African experience, arose from contact and collision with alien societies.

Speculation about the sources of Radcliffe-Brown's anthropology has often derived it mainly from one preeminent figure, usually Rivers or Emile Durkheim. In fact, he placed himself in 'a cultural tradition of two hundred years' (Radcliffe-Brown, *Structure*, 14) originating with eighteenth-century thinkers, mostly from France or Scotland, who included Montesquieu, Lafiteau, and Adam Ferguson—and further developed by some of the pioneering sociologists and anthropologists of the nineteenth century. As he did not engage in scholarly exegesis of the work of others it can be difficult to discern their precise significance in his thought. A number of influences can, however, be identified with some confidence. For example, his interest in natural science (and art) began as a schoolboy, his first reported lecture being on zinc mines in Cumberland to the Natural History Society at King Edward VI School on 21 February 1898 (not long after his brother, who became a mine surveyor in South Africa, had graduated in engineering science from King's College, London). His interest in anthropology and in French sociology also predates Cambridge, having been awakened by Peter Kropotkin and Havelock Ellis respectively. To these sources he added Herbert Spencer's hypothesis of social evolution, the methodology of the French sociologists, and the ideas of Heraclitus and Chinese philosophy on social and cosmic dualism. Rivers and Durkheim may have been the most important influences, but he criticized aspects of their thought and it would be wrong to see him as a disciple—discipleship, as opposed to influence or inspiration, would have conflicted with his scientific outlook.

Radcliffe-Brown wrote with 'crystalline clarity' (J. G. Peristiany, 'Obituary', *Nature*, 17 Dec 1955, 1149) and had the gift of enthusing students, 'with whom he was always ready to discuss the problems of their science, not only in the lecture room but at any time and in any place. He numbered these students all over the world' (Evans-Pritchard, 200). Yet he published relatively little and wrote slowly, confessing to Winifred Hoernlé that he could spend a week over one or two sentences. His difficulty was not shortage of ideas. As Raymond Firth wrote to Camilla Wedgwood on 22 September 1929, 'R. B. has many projects; I should like to see some of them mature' (Wedgwood papers, NL Aus., MS 483, box 1). The only book he completed was *The Andaman Islanders* (1922), based on his first fieldwork. Other planned works, including a collaborative study of African religion and social structure with Winifred Hoernlé, his 1937 Chicago seminar on a natural science of society, his Josiah Mason lectures at the University of Birmingham on primitive cosmology (1951), and an introduction to social anthropology, were never finished, though a stenographic version of the original Chicago seminar circulated during his lifetime and was published after his death.

Appearance, personality, and interests Radcliffe-Brown's appearance and manners fascinated contemporaries. The biologist and novelist E. L. Grant Watson, who knew him from Cambridge and accompanied him in Western Australia, described him as a man of dramatic personality and inventive genius, 'beautiful to behold' as he expounded anthropology (*But to what Purpose*, 83–4). The educationist Professor D. D. T. Jabavu, who attended his vacation school lectures in Cape Town, reported him to be 'tall of stature, with the typical flowing hair of the carefree genius' and to possess 'a sense of humour and joie de vivre in his subject' (*Cape Times*, 24 March 1924). According to a popular Australian magazine, his 'aesthetic appearance has earned for him the sobriquet of "the Valentino of the 'Varsity". This versatile professor of anthropology is equally at home in discoursing on the latest movements of modern art as he is in determining the age of paleolithic relics' (*The Home*, 1 Oct 1928). Student songs captured his flamboyance. In one he is bad, mad, and faddy, frequents gas-bagging bohemian circles, is the idol of Sydney's younger set, and is pally with Government House (*Sydney University Song Book*, 1928).

Outside anthropology Radcliffe-Brown had an astonishing range of interests on which he addressed university and other audiences. He opened art exhibitions, spoke on music, debated the authorship of Shakespeare's plays and championed both modernism and the League of Nations. He spoke with few or no notes and with a few exceptions (including articles for *Art in Australia* on the painters Lionel Lindsay and Margaret Preston) did not develop his views in writing. His circle of acquaintances also extended beyond academe to embrace artists, writers, and bohemians. In Sydney, for example, they included Lionel and Norman Lindsay, Aletta Lewis, Ethel Anderson, George Lambert, and Christopher Brennan. Perhaps he would have achieved more in anthropology had he concentrated his energy, but his versatility and personal qualities attracted students of the new discipline and helped recruit some who would take leading positions in it. Moreover, his thoughts out of class were of a piece with his approach to anthropology and help throw light on it. For example, what he admired in modern art was its scientific spirit and love of clarity, its appeal to intellect and hatred of sentimentality—even the brutality of modern German painters, he told the Society of Artists, could be commended as 'a good antidote to the over-sentimental' (*Sydney Morning Herald*, 19 Sept 1929). Addressing a conference on international affairs, he stated that antagonism is 'as necessary to the life of society as solidarity' and cannot be eliminated (*Sydney University Union Recorder*, 2 Oct 1930, 250).

Nicknamed 'Anarchy Brown', he was an anarchist as a student, but 'not of the violent bomb-throwing type, though he had known several of these' (Watson, 'To this end', 90). He came to see the anarchist ideal, unlike socialism, as unrealizable, but saw the latter as having a dangerous tendency to glorify the state. His later views might be described as libertarian in a non-doctrinal sense, characterized by freedom from convention and sympathy for 'unpopular but intellectually defensible causes' (Firth, 296). An atheist from at least his student years, he became an honorary associate of the Rationalist Press Association in 1952. An Oxford student remembered him as 'somewhat assertive in his arguments against religion' (C. Fuller, 'An interview with M. N. Srinivas', *Anthropology Today*, 15/5, 1999, 5), but the nearest he came to showing it in print was the suggestion that religion is a source of 'fears and anxieties from which [men] would otherwise be free—the fear of black magic or of spirits, fear of God, of the Devil, of Hell' (Radcliffe-Brown, *Structure*, 149). In the Josiah Mason lectures founded by the Rationalist Press Association, he denied that the secret ceremonies of Australia and New Guinea are based on 'sham and fraud', insisting that the old men in charge used secrecy as a method of conveying their sense of the world as a mysterious place. In general he avoided intruding his personal values into anthropology, holding that the anthropologist's job is to investigate beliefs as part of social reality, not to determine whether they are true or ethical or logical. His restraint may have sprung from an austere conception of science or from the functionalist fear that destroying a people's beliefs will undermine their social system.

Radcliffe-Brown died on 24 October 1955 at University College Hospital, St Pancras, London, and was cremated at Golders Green.   KENNETH MADDOCK

Sources R. Firth, 'Arthur Reginald Radcliffe-Brown, 1881–1955', *PBA*, 42 (1956), 287–302 • A. R. Radcliffe-Brown, *Structure and function in primitive society* (1952) • A. R. Radcliffe-Brown, *Method in social anthropology*, ed. M. N. Srinivas (1958) • K. Maddock, 'Affinities and missed opportunities: John Anderson and A. R. Radcliffe-Brown in Sydney', *Australian Journal of Anthropology*, 3 (1992), 3–18 • A. Barnard, 'Through Radcliffe-Brown's spectacles: reflections on the history of anthropology', *History of the Human Sciences*, 5/4 (1992), 1–20 • G. W. Stocking, *After Tylor: British social anthropology, 1888–1951* (1996) • E. L. G. Watson, *But to what purpose* (1946) • E. L. G. Watson, 'To this end', [n.d.], NL Aus., MS 4950, box 1 • D. F. Pocock, *Social anthropology* (1961) • E. E. Evans-Pritchard, *A history of anthropological thought* (1981) • R. Redfield, 'Preface', *Social anthropology of North American tribes*, ed. F. Eggan (1937), ix–xiv • G. W. Stocking, '"Yours affectionately, Rex": Radcliffe-Brown during and after World War II', *History of Anthropology Newsletter*, 12/2 (1985), 3–11 • *Nature* (17 Dec 1955) • *The Times* (27 Oct 1955) • *American Anthropologist*, 58 [1956], 544–7 • *Oceania*, 31 [1955–6], 239–51 • b. cert.

Archives U. Oxf., Institute of Social and Cultural Anthropology, corresp. • University of Sydney, archives | Bodl. Oxf., corresp. with J. L. Myres • CUL, corresp. with Meyer Forbes

Likenesses N. Lindsay, pencil, *c.*1917, priv. coll. • photographs, U. Oxf., Institute of Social and Cultural Anthropology

Wealth at death £1795 3*s.* 10*d.*: administration, 13 Jan 1956, *CGPLA Eng. & Wales*

Brown, Ann Dudin (1822–1917), benefactor, was born on 2 January 1822, the only child of John Dudin Brown (1795–1855), Thames wharfinger, and his wife, Ann, *née* Round (1798–1855). She spent her childhood and early adult years in the affluent surroundings of her parents' house in Sydenham. Her father, a freeman of the Company of Watermen and Lightermen of London, made notable donations in land and money to the almshouses and adjacent church of St John the Evangelist erected by the company in the nearby hamlet of Penge, and when both her parents died, within a few months of each other in 1855, she felt compelled to devote her inherited wealth to the support of charitable and evangelistic enterprises.

Deciding for whatever reason against setting up a home for herself (she never married), Ann Dudin Brown resided for the remainder of her long life in London hotels, latterly the Norfolk Hotel in South Kensington, attaching herself to churches where the preaching and parochial life were in harmony with her evangelical standpoint and where missionary interests were strong. Penge, and the spiritual needs of its rapidly increasing population, were not forgotten: St John's was enlarged with her help in 1860 and a new church, Holy Trinity, received a handsome donation in 1872. Through small but timely gifts she alleviated the distress of innumerable private applicants, former governesses in particular.

Hearing when she was nearly sixty of Mary Lyon's pioneering work at Mount Holyoke, USA, the college where American women missionaries of the type she most admired received their early education, Miss Dudin Brown resolved to found a college on the same model—which featured household along with school work—in England. In the event, however, Westfield College in Hampstead (opened October 1882) was modelled on the first women's colleges in Cambridge and Oxford and was geared to the preparation of its students for London degrees. The change of plan, due in part to the persuasiveness of two young women, Mary Petrie, one of the first to graduate from University College, London, and Constance Maynard, certificated student of Girton, did not diminish Ann Dudin Brown's generosity towards the college, and her capital endowment of £10,000 was still forthcoming. Even so, the preoccupation at Westfield with 'these hard exams' continued to irk the 'foundress' (as she was called in Westfield council minutes), who would remark with a sigh, 'It was not what I intended' (Maynard, 6).

What did not change was Miss Dudin Brown's vision, shared by Constance Maynard, the first mistress, of a college founded and governed on Christian principles. With this aim in view, membership of the council was formally restricted to Anglicans, and in practice to those on the evangelical wing. Miss Dudin Brown's own life membership—which endured for more than thirty years—ensured that no decisions, on small matters as well as large, were taken without her consent. In 1890 she demonstrated her faith in Westfield's future by agreeing to the release, in stages, of her capital endowment for the purchase and extension of Kidderpore Hall as Westfield's permanent home; two later benefactions in aid of buildings brought the total up to £15,000. She also funded a scholarship and gave private help to students in financial need. In 1913, taking note of the many forms of missionary activity in which Westfield graduates were engaged, she confessed: 'of all my enterprises, Westfield has proved the most satisfactory' (Maynard, 8). In small doses, she enjoyed the students' company as a respite from her solitary life and even resided for short spells in the college, in rooms, for which she paid, set aside for her use.

Ann Dudin Brown died at the Norfolk Hotel, Harrington Road, South Kensington, London, on 30 June 1917. Her funeral was held in St Luke's, the church alongside Westfield which she had helped to build. She was buried in Hampstead cemetery on 4 July. Westfield, left a legacy of £10,000, was the largest single beneficiary under her will; thirty-three charitable organizations and almost as many private persons also benefited.   JANET SONDHEIMER

Sir Arthur Whitten Brown (1886–1948), by Sir John Lavery

Sources C. L. Maynard, *Ann Dudin Brown, foundress of Westfield College* (1917) · J. Sondheimer, *Castle Adamant in Hampstead: a history of Westfield College, 1882–1982* (1983) · Queen Mary College, London, Westfield College Archives · gravestone, Hampstead cemetery · d. cert.
Likenesses drawing?, Queen Mary College, London
Wealth at death £62,347 17s. 8d.: probate, 28 July 1917, *CGPLA Eng. & Wales*

Brown, Sir Arthur Whitten (1886–1948), air navigator and engineer, was born in Glasgow on 23 July 1886, the only child of American parents, Arthur George Brown, an electrical engineer, and his wife, Emma Whitten. Arthur was still an infant when his parents moved their home to Ellerslie, 6 Oswald Road, Chorlton-cum-Hardy, and from here he received his first education at the central high school, Manchester, where he proved a thoughtful pupil, painstaking and shy. Like his father, Whitten Brown became an electrical engineer. He served an apprenticeship with the British Westinghouse Electric and Manufacturing Company (later known as the Metropolitan-Vickers Electrical Company Ltd) at Trafford Park, Manchester, studying at the Municipal School of Technology in Manchester in his spare time; subsequently the company sent him to South Africa. He returned to England in the summer of 1914, took up British nationality (he was born a US citizen), and joined one of the universities and public schools battalions. In January 1915 he gained a commission in the Manchester regiment and took part in the second battle of Ypres before being transferred to the Royal Flying Corps and trained as an observer. In November 1915 he was shot down over Valenciennes in France, in enemy territory, permanently injuring one leg, and he remained a prisoner of war of the Germans until he was repatriated

in September 1917. He worked in the aircraft production department of the Ministry of Munitions until the end of the war. While working at the ministry he met and became engaged to his future wife, Marguerite Kathleen (*b*. 1895/6), daughter of Major David Henry Kennedy OBE of the Royal Air Force.

In 1919 Brown, who had obtained his private pilot's licence in the previous year, was out of work and looking for employment. He visited Vickers of Weybridge seeking a post, shortly after the firm had decided to make an attempt on the first direct flight across the Atlantic for the prize of £10,000 offered by the *Daily Mail*. John Alcock had already been taken on as pilot and Brown's evident knowledge of long-distance navigation convinced the firm's managers and Alcock that he should be employed as navigator for the flight.

A modified Vickers Vimy two-engine bomber was made available and sent to Newfoundland, where other aircraft and aspirants had already assembled; and something like a race ensued to get ready first. In May 1919 a United States flying-boat made the first crossing of the Atlantic, in eleven days, taking the Azores route to Portugal, with an interval between each hop. At 16.13 Greenwich mean time (GMT) on 14 June 1919 the Vimy, heavily loaded with fuel, just managed to take off from the short grass runway at St John's. The flight was completed in 16 hours 27 minutes, the aeroplane landing at 08.40 GMT the following day, in what looked like a grass field but proved to be a bog, at Clifden, in Galway. A wing was damaged, but the occupants were unhurt. In the course of their flight they were mostly in or below clouds. For part of the journey the airspeed indicator was out of action, its Pitot tube probably blocked by ice, so that Whitten Brown, as navigator, had to make his own estimate of the speed for the purposes of dead reckoning. Only on four occasions (and only once during the hours of darkness) was he able to take his bearings and make a more accurate plot of the aircraft's position. Meanwhile the formation of ice on the aircraft was beginning to affect the performance of the motors, which were now covered, even obstructing the vital fuel sight-gauges so that Brown was prompted to perform an astonishing act of bravery: despite his leg injury, on five occasions he climbed out onto the ice-covered struts in the freezing blast at over 8000 feet to hack the instruments' faces clear with a pocket knife and to remove the snow. Making a landfall in Galway, not far from their intended landing place and after only sixteen hours' flying, was therefore an excellent piece of navigation on a 1900 mile journey in an aeroplane which cruised at about 90 miles an hour, even though it was helped by an average tailwind of about 30 miles an hour. The achievement was acknowledged as outstanding. Alcock and Whitten Brown were fêted on their arrival in London and appointed KBE a few days later. Eight years were to pass before the next non-stop aeroplane flight was made across the Atlantic.

A few weeks after the flight, on 29 July 1919, Whitten Brown married Marguerite Kennedy, with whom he had one son. For a while he worked with Vickers Ltd, the makers of the Vimy bomber. Then he returned to his original employers, Metropolitan-Vickers. In 1923 he was appointed the company's chief representative at Swansea, a centre from which he covered a wide area. During the Second World War he returned to the Royal Air Force in order to train pilots in navigation and engineering, though he never flew again after Alcock's death in 1919 and was heartbroken by the loss of his son, Arthur, who was killed in action as a flight lieutenant of the Royal Air Force on D-day 1944 at the age of twenty-two. In the post-war years few noted the lonely figure who returned annually to view the Vimy, which was preserved in the Science Museum, Kensington, to muse under its wings on the anniversary of the epic flight. He died at his home, 24 Belgrave Court, Uplands, Swansea, on 4 October 1948 from an accidental overdose of veronal, and was buried later that month in Swansea.

A memorial to Alcock and Whitten Brown was erected in 1952, near the field from which they took off at St John's, by the Historic Sites and Monuments Board of Canada. A memorial by William McMillan was erected at London Heathrow airport.

E. C. SHEPHERD, rev. PETER G. COOKSLEY

Sources *The Times* (16 June 1919) · *The Times* (5 Oct 1948), 4, 6 · *The Times* (20 Oct 1948), 2 · *Journal of the Institution of Electrical Engineers*, 95/1 (1948), 558 · G. Wallace, *The flight of Alcock and Brown* (1955) · private information (1959) · *The story of Alcock and Brown*, City of Manchester publicity office (1969) · *Flight International* (12 July 1969), 959–61 · *CGPLA Eng. & Wales* (1948) · m. cert. · d. cert.
Archives British Aerospace (Vickers), Weybridge, Surrey, aircraft compass, navigation log and (believed) navigational instruments | British aerospace (Vickers), Weybridge, Surrey, toy stuffed cat (black) mascot, Twinkletoes [taken as good luck mascot] | FILM BFI NFTVA, documentary footage · BFI NFTVA, news footage · IWM FVA, actuality footage · IWM FVA, documentary footage
Likenesses photographs, 1919, Hult. Arch. · J. Lavery, oils, Royal Air Force Museum, Hendon [*see illus.*] · double portrait, plaque (with Alcock), Manchester town hall · double portraits, photographs (with Alcock), Marconi Wireless Telegraph Co. Ltd · memorial, Heathrow airport · photographs, Royal Aeronautical Society, London · photographs, British Aerospace, photographic and audiovisual department · photographs, Kemsley Newspapers · photographs, Manchester City Archives Department
Wealth at death £5002 0s. 3d.: probate, 16 Dec 1948, *CGPLA Eng. & Wales*

Brown, Dame Beryl Paston (1909–1997), educationist, was born at 78 Ribblesdale Road, Streatham, London, on 7 March 1909, the only daughter and elder child of Paston Charles Brown, bank clerk, and his wife, Florence May, *née* Henson. Her father claimed descent from the Pastons of the Paston letters. Her mother was related to Herbert Hensley Henson, bishop of Durham. Beryl was a pupil at Streatham Hill high school and felt privileged all her life to have had a suburban childhood with access to art galleries, concerts, and, most important, the Old Vic. She became a scholar of Newnham College, Cambridge, in 1929, and was awarded firsts in both parts of the English tripos. She then trained as a teacher at the London Day Training College (later the London Institute of Education).

Paston Brown's first teaching appointment, in 1933, was at Portsmouth Training College, where she divided her time between teaching students and teaching in schools. In 1937 she became a member of the English department of Goldsmiths' College, London, and remained there until 1952 with a two-year interval (1944–6) as a temporary assistant lecturer in her old college, Newnham. After Goldsmiths' she became principal of the Leicester City Training College. Her last appointment was in 1961 when she was offered the post of principal of Homerton College, Cambridge, where she remained until her retirement in 1971.

Homerton had already a well-established academic tradition, and under Paston Brown's leadership developed this further, first with the new three-year course and then with the introduction of the four-year BEd course. Cambridge University was at first reluctant to recognize this development, and Homerton's first degree students secured their BEds from the University of London. By 1971, however, with patient diplomacy and the help of friends in the university, particularly from Newnham, the foundations of a Cambridge degree in education had been laid. Alongside all this Paston Brown's policy of consultation, delegation, and open communication transformed Homerton's fairly authoritarian culture (common among many training colleges) into one of collegiality among both staff and students. She created a representative and effective academic board in the college several years before this became a required element in all college constitutions, and students were encouraged to create a college culture comparable with that in other Cambridge colleges.

Paston Brown was also a significant figure in the Association of Teachers in Colleges and Departments of Education (ATCDE). She was a lively editor (1948–54) of its journal, *Education for Teaching*, transforming it from an in-house journal into one of wider interest concerned with issues of educational policy and research. She was chairman of the principals' panel in 1960–61, and was an influential voice in preparing the association's evidence to the Robbins committee on higher education. She was later appointed a member of the Newsom committee whose report, *Half our Future*, was published in 1963. This dealt with the education of secondary-school youngsters of average and below average ability, and echoed the ATCDE policy on the value of the concurrent course for the training of teachers in this field. Beryl herself was a strong advocate of this concept of combining in the one course academic study, professional skills, and school experience, particularly for primary school teachers and some areas of secondary teaching. She was elected chairman of the association for 1965–6 and in the following year became a dame of the British empire, the first from the world of teacher training colleges to be so honoured.

In 1971 Paston Brown retired with her Siamese cat to a small eighteenth-century house in Keere Street, Lewes, Sussex, and until her last illness greatly enjoyed her life there. She made many new friends and entered fully into the life of the community, particularly its musical and literary life, enlivened as it was by the new and neighbouring University of Sussex. She did work for Age Concern and became an enthusiastic tutor for the Open University. She was awarded an honorary degree by the Open University in 1978; this gave her great pleasure, especially as she found herself sitting next to Sir John Gielgud (a lifetime's hero) at lunch. She was an attractive, scholarly woman. Children loved her and she had great concern for them. She was a good listener, and old students and former colleagues, from the Portsmouth days and onwards, kept in touch and clearly regarded her with gratitude and affection. She died at her home, 21 Keere Street, Lewes, following a series of strokes, on 25 July 1997, and was cremated at Brighton crematorium on 5 August. She never married. Her younger brother died on active service with the RAF during the Second World War, and following the death of her father in the 1950s she was the only surviving member of her family.   JOYCE SKINNER

Sources personal knowledge (2004) · J. D. Browne, *Teachers of teachers* (1979) · B. P. Brown, 'Education for teaching', *Journal of the A.T.C.D.E.*, 69 (Feb 1966), 2–19 · *WWW* · Open University records · *The Times* (30 Aug 1997) · *The Independent* (6 Aug 1997) · b. cert.
Likenesses E. Vellacott, pencil, 1971, Homerton College, Cambridge · R. Cook, portrait, 1986, Homerton College, Cambridge · photograph, repro. in *The Independent*
Wealth at death £249,740: probate, 1997, *CGPLA Eng. & Wales*

Brown, Capability. *See* Brown, Lancelot (*bap.* 1716, *d.* 1783).

Brown, Catherine Emily Madox (1850–1927). *See under* Pre-Raphaelite women artists (*act.* 1848–1870s).

Brown, Charles (1678/9–1753), naval officer, whose place of birth and parentage are unknown, entered the navy about 1693 and, aged twenty-one, passed his lieutenant's examination on 3 February 1700. After service in the *Content*, *Ranelagh*, and *Barfleur*, he was appointed master and commander of the yacht *Queenborough* on 23 June 1708 by Sir George Byng. Brown was stationed in the channel, escorting convoys and intercepting small French privateers which operated out of Nieuport. On 18 March 1709 he achieved post rank as captain of the fifth rate *Strombolo* (28 guns), a converted fireship. Brown continued his service in the channel in the *Strombolo* and his subsequent command, the *Medway Prize* (10 June 1709). On 23 May 1710 he was appointed to command the *Chester*, which was stationed in New England, but he appears to have been captured on his way to join the vessel and returned home through Brest and St Malo; reports of these events he sent to the Admiralty.

On 24 January 1711 Brown was appointed captain of the *Dover* and resumed his duties in the channel. On 11 November he was given command of the *Reserve*, in which he convoyed trade to New England and the West Indies. At the end of the war he returned to England, where he was given a succession of commands—the *Hampshire* (29 October 1715), the *York* (11 February 1716), the *Antelope* (11 March 1719), and the *Preston* (21 June 1720)—all of which kept him in the channel and Soundings. On 24 December 1720 Brown was appointed to command the *Feversham* and was sent to the West Indies to protect trade and cruise against pirates. He returned home in 1723. By now Brown was looking for command of a larger battleship, but he was given the *Advice* (50 guns) during 1726. At last, in February 1727, he was appointed to the *Orford* (70 guns), but he moved to another 50-gun ship, the *Romney*, on 16 July 1728. After service in the Mediterranean Brown was appointed to the *Buckingham* (70 guns) on 7 June 1731, which he commanded until she was paid off in July 1736. During this time Brown served with Admiral Sir John Norris's squadron at Lisbon (1735–6).

By the end of 1737 Brown had accumulated substantial experience in different roles and different parts of the world. As the dispute with Spain worsened over Spanish coastguard activity in the West Indies, Brown was appointed commodore at Jamaica, with his pennant on the *Hampton Court* (9 December 1737). He used his small squadron to cruise off Cuba and protect trade, until superseded by Vice-Admiral Edward Vernon in October 1739. Vernon was determined to attack Porto Bello, on the Isthmus of Panama, and Brown was ordered to lead the British line into the harbour. On 21 November Brown led the approach, but light winds prevented the force penetrating as far as intended and Brown anchored the *Hampton Court* alongside the Iron Castle, the most immediate point in the harbour defences. He pounded it with a fierce cannonade until other vessels came up. When the fort surrendered, the Spanish commander presented his sword to Brown, who refused to accept it as he was only second in command. When, in Vernon's presence, the Spaniard again insisted that he surrender his sword to Brown, Vernon took it and presented it to Brown as a memento.

During the early part of 1740 Brown commanded at

Jamaica while Vernon carried out attacks upon the Spanish main, but Brown's health gradually deteriorated. He was sent home and arrived in England in October. On 10 January 1741 he was given command of the *Duke* (90 guns), from which he exchanged to the *Sandwich* on 9 June. During this time he was periodically senior officer commanding in the Thames, in the Medway, and at the Nore. On 27 March 1742 he left sea service to take up the post of resident commissioner of the Navy Board at the Chatham Dockyard. He carried out the role effectively until his death on 23 March 1753. He was buried in the churchyard of St Mary's, Chatham, on 27 March. One of his two daughters, Lucy, became the wife of Admiral William Parry, and her daughter married Captain Locker, under whom Nelson served in his early days. RICHARD HARDING

Sources PRO, ADM 1/1469 (1708–9); ADM 1/1470 (1710–11); ADM 1/1471 (1712–16); ADM 1/1472 (1717–23); ADM 1/1473 (1724–7); ADM 1/1474 (1728–30); ADM 1/1475 (1731–4); ADM 1/1476 (1735–8); ADM 1/1477 (1740) · fleet disposition lists, PRO, ADM 8/18 to ADM 8/21 · warrants and commission registers, PRO, ADM 6/6, 138; ADM 6/7, 110; ADM 6/8, 119; ADM 6/9, 172; ADM 6/10, 46, 69; ADM 6/11, 46, 99, 176; ADM 6/12, 55, 88, 157, 204, 225; ADM 6/13, 96, 133, 209; ADM 6/14, 76, 81; ADM 6/15, 85, 367, 395, 426, 438 · passing certificates, PRO, ADM 107/1, 187 · parish register, St Mary's, Chatham, 1753 · *The Vernon papers*, ed. B. McL. Ranft, Navy RS, 99 (1958) · seniority list, PRO, ADM 6/424
Archives PRO, ADM 1/1469–1477 · PRO, ADM 8/18–8/21 · PRO, ADM 6/6–6/15 · PRO, ADM 6/424
Likenesses J. Faber jun., mezzotint, 1740 (after oils, 1740), BM, NPG · oils, 1740, NMM · medals, BM
Wealth at death properties in parish of Christchurch (Isle of Sheppey), Greenhithe in Kent, Gordon Street in Gillingham, and parish of Upchurch, Kent: will, 3 Oct 1752, PRO, PROB 11/801, sig. 129

Brown, Charles. *See* Speckman, Charles (1734?–1763).

Brown, Charles Armitage (1787–1842), writer, was born on 14 April 1787 at Grey's Walk, Lambeth, London, the sixth of seven children of William Brown (*d.* 1816), stockbroker from a Hebridean family, and his wife, Jane, daughter of John Armitage (probably), of whom little is known except that she married Joseph Rennock Browne after William's death. Nothing is known of his schooling, but tradition has it that at school Brown formed an association with Charles Wentworth Dilke, who was to become another in the Keats circle. Evidence of Charles's early career is not reliable, but he seems after an apprenticeship as a merchant to have joined his brother John in the Russian trade, travelling at the age of about eighteen to represent the firm in St Petersburg. They initially prospered and accumulated 'some £20,000 of capital' (Carlino Brown to F. Holland Day, 12 July 1890, quoted in *The Keats Circle*, lv), but then they 'invested largely beyond their means in bristles', and the business failed (ibid.). Brown left Russia almost penniless just before he reached the age of twenty-two. He officially became bankrupt in 1809, and for four years lived in dignified penury, vowing never to put his legs under a lord's table (a vow he later broke to dine with Byron). On his return from Russia he wrote a comic opera on a Russian theme, *Narensky, or, The Road to Yaroslaf*, which was produced at Drury Lane in January 1814, bringing him

£300 and contacts in the theatre world. About 1813 he joined his brother James's East Indian company as the London representative. When James died in October 1815 he left Charles 'the sum of Ten thousand pounds sterling' (which shrank to £3000 by the time the assets were finalized) and an estate in Lambeth, 'the competence', writes his son Carlino, 'which allowed him to lead a life of literary leisure afterwards' (*Keats Circle*, lv–lvi).

After the death of James, Brown in association with Dilke began building Wentworth Place in semi-rural Hampstead, later to become Keats's home and now named Keats House. It was completed by May 1816 while Brown may have been on a walking tour of the Welsh mountains. By this time, the orphaned Keats family had moved to 1 Well Walk in Hampstead. Apparently Brown and Keats were introduced to each other by Reynolds, and by September 1817 Keats was a regular visitor to Wentworth Place and 'very thick' with Brown (*Letters of John Keats*, 1.237). They went on and wrote about a walking tour of the north of England and Scotland from June 1818 to late September or October when Keats returned through illness while Brown stayed in Edinburgh. At this time, Brown was 'a convivial, corpulent, bearded, balding gentleman of property and leisure, an epicure, and something of a ladies' man' (*Letters*, ed. Stillinger, 1). After the death of Tom Keats on 1 December 1818, Keats turned to Brown for support and within a matter of days was given lodging in Wentworth Place. For the next seventeen months they lodged together and collaborated on the play *Otho the Great*, which was never staged. Brown transcribed some of Keats's poems and claims to have rescued from oblivion the Nightingale ode and other pieces, 'fugitive pieces … used as a mark to a book, or thrust any where aside' (Brown, *Life of Keats*, 63, 54). In some cases Brown's transcripts are the only surviving manuscript sources. Keats described Brown as 'always one's friend in a disaster' and spoke fulsomely of his generosity and 'disinterested character' (*Letters of John Keats*, 2.78, 279).

In July 1819, when Brown rented out his house for the summer, Keats accompanied James Rice to the Isle of Wight and then Brown to Winchester. Brown nursed him through a haemorrhage on 3 February 1820, and often paid his bills and lent him money. The only rift between them was over Fanny Brawne, Keats's fiancée, with whom Keats morbidly suspected Brown of flirting. In May 1820 Brown, as was his custom, rented out the house for the summer, ensured that Keats was lodged in Kentish Town, and sailed for Scotland on holiday. While he was away Keats took his last journey to Italy and died of tuberculosis in the company of Joseph Severn on 23 February 1821. It seems clear that Brown underestimated the seriousness of Keats's illness, thinking it imaginary in nature and exacerbated by hostile reviews, a view which Keats's own doctors encouraged. Brown acted like an executor in distributing Keats's books among eighteen friends and Fanny Keats, conspicuously omitting George Keats and Benjamin Haydon. Later, in the face of legal action threatened by Dilke over copyright, Brown published in the *New*

Monthly Magazine and the *Plymouth and Devonport Weekly Journal* many of the manuscript poems by Keats which he had in his possession.

Dilke, who became increasingly estranged from Brown, reproached him for not going to Italy until mid-1822. By this time Brown had a son, Charles, known as Carlino, whose mother, Brown's Irish housekeeper Abigail Donhaugh, he married about August 1819, apparently with a ceremony of dubious legality. Carlino was born on 16 July 1820 while Brown was in Scotland, and Brown had custody of his son from March 1822, since by then he and his wife were permanently estranged. Brown sold his half of Wentworth Place and in August 1822 moved to Italy with Carlino, where they lived for thirteen years. Here Brown travelled between Rome, Pisa, Milan, Florence, Naples, and Venice, and kept company with other English expatriate writers and visitors such as Leigh Hunt, Joseph Severn, Byron, Walter Savage Landor, and Edward John Trelawny. He published articles in English periodicals, the best-known essays being 'La Bella Tabaccia' and 'Shakespeare's Fools' (both 1823). Brown and Severn ensured that a headstone was placed on Keats's grave in 1823, and Brown insisted on complying with Keats's request that the poet's name be omitted from the inscription, and that the phrase 'Here lies One Whose Name was writ in Water' be included. Brown had promised to write a biography of Keats, but could not bring himself to until 1837 by which time he had returned to live in Plymouth (1835–41). The memoir was not published until 1937. Although important because of Brown's close friendship with Keats, it adds little to knowledge of Keats because Brown had already generously supplied facts to Keats's earliest biographer, Richard Monckton Milnes. Brown spent many years engaged in proving his suspicions that Keats's brother George had unfairly impoverished the poet. In a letter to Brown on 10 April 1824, George with dignity and in detail defended his handling of the family's finances. Dilke in 1848 was to describe Brown's personality as a mixture of generosity and meanness, and wrote, 'He was the most scrupulously honest man I ever knew—but wanted nobleness to lift this honesty out of the commercial kennel …' (Dilke, hand-written notes in copy of Milnes's *Life … John Keats*, 1848).

Brown published in 1838 *Shakespeare's Autobiographical Poems* on the sonnets, a modest set of essays described by a hostile Dilke in *The Athenaeum* (21 July 1838) as a 'holiday pastime', although other reviewers were kinder. For much of his adult life he was engaged in writing his own semi-autobiographical novel, *Walter Hazlebourn*, which was never completed. Brown tried assiduously but without success to gain Carlino an entrance into the world of commercial engineering, and in 1841 they emigrated in separate boats to New Zealand in the hopes of establishing a sawmill company in the New Plymouth company settlement in the Taranaki district. The sawmill company failed dismally through loss of equipment in the sea, and Brown, dogged by ill health, made himself thoroughly disliked by all officials in the New Zealand company through his constant complaints. He died in Taranaki of an apoplectic stroke, aged fifty-five, on 5 June 1842 and was buried as he wished on unsanctified ground outside the churchyard, Marsland Hill, on the 7th. The grave was grown over and eventually relocated in 1921, and was marked by a stone inscribed 'Charles Armitage Brown. The Friend of Keats'.   R. S. WHITE

Sources E. H. McCormick, *The friend of Keats: a life of Charles Armitage Brown* (1989) · *The letters of Charles Armitage Brown*, ed. J. Stillinger (1966) · H. E. Rollins, ed., *The Keats circle: letters and papers and more letters and poems of the Keats circle*, 2 vols. (1965) · *The letters of John Keats, 1814–1821*, ed. H. E. Rollins, 2 vols. (1958) · C. A. Brown, *Life of John Keats*, ed. D. H. Bodurtha and W. B. Pope (1937) · parish register, Lambeth, St Mary-at-Lambeth, 25 Aug 1787 [baptism] **Archives** CAC Cam. · Harvard U., Houghton L. · Keats House, Hampstead, London, corresp. and papers · NL NZ, Turnbull L. · Taranaki Museum, New Plymouth, New Zealand | BL, letters to Leigh Hunt, Add. MSS 38108–38109 · Bodl. Oxf., letters to Robert Finch · Christchurch, New Zealand, H. T. Hartley collection **Likenesses** bust, 1830, Keats House, Hampstead, London

Brown, Charles Philip (1798–1884), Telugu scholar and Indologist, was born on 10 November 1798 in Calcutta. He was the son of David *Brown (1762–1812), East India Company chaplain and provost of the College of Fort William, Calcutta, and his second wife, Frances, daughter of Hannah *Cowley, Tiverton dramatist and poet, and her husband, Thomas Cowley. In 1814 he enrolled in East India College, Haileybury, before entering the Madras civil service in 1817. Following further training at the College of Fort St George, Madras, he was employed from 1820 until 1835 in revenue, magisterial, and judicial duties in the predominantly Telugu-speaking region of south India (modern Andhra Pradesh). In addition to a knowledge of Persian, Sanskrit, Urdu, and other south Asian languages, he acquired particular expertise in Telugu language and literature. Following a three-year leave in England, Brown returned to Madras. In 1838 he was appointed Persian translator, and in 1846 postmaster-general and Telugu translator to the Madras government. He also held unpaid positions as a member of the council of education, a government director of the Madras Bank, and curator of manuscripts in the college library.

Brown's principal works were his dictionaries of Telugu–English (Madras, 1852; rev. 2nd edn, 1903) and English–Telugu (Madras, 1852). These dictionaries remain in print and continue to be of great value and utility. His other publications included a grammar, a reader, and a book of exercises for those wishing to learn Telugu, writings on Sanskrit and Telugu prosody, translations from Telugu, and a translation of St Luke into Telugu. He also published two works detailing Hindu and Islamic methods of reckoning time. Different versions of his autobiography were printed for private circulation in 1855, 1866 and 1872. He frequently contributed articles on Telugu language and literature, the Virasaiva sect, and other aspects of south Indian history and culture to the *Madras Journal of Literature and Science* and other scholarly journals. Some of his works were translated into Tamil, Kannada, and Urdu.

On his resignation in 1855, Brown returned to England

and in 1865 he was appointed professor of Telugu at University College, London. He died, apparently unmarried, on 12 December 1884 at his home, 22 Kildare Gardens, Westbourne Grove, London, and was buried in Kensal Green cemetery.

One of Brown's chief claims to fame is the fine collection of manuscripts, including over 2000 Sanskrit and Telugu works, which he presented in 1845 to the Madras Literary Society and which became part of the Government Oriental Manuscripts Library, Madras. The extensive collection of Telugu manuscripts resulted from Brown's quest to gather all existing Telugu literature. Under his direction and sponsorship, many works of Telugu literature were critically edited and underwent initial publication. Consequently, Brown is credited with fostering a revival of Telugu language and literature.

PETER L. SCHMITTHENNER

Sources P. Schmitthenner, *Telugu resurgence: C. P. Brown and cultural consolidation in nineteenth-century south India* (2001) • C. P. Brown, *Literary autobiography of C. P. Brown*, ed. G. N. Reddy and Bangorey (1978) • K. Veerabhadra Rao, *C. P. Brown*, 2nd edn (1988) [in Telugu] • C. P. Brown, *Narrative of the literary life of Charles Philip Brown* (privately printed, Madras, 1855); repr. as *Some account of the literary life of Charles Philip Brown* (1866); repr. (1872) • *The Times* (20 Dec 1884) • R. M. MacDonald, *The Athenaeum* (3 Jan 1885), 14 • *Journal of the Royal Asiatic Society of Great Britain and Ireland*, new ser., 17 (1885), xv–xx • d. cert. • records, Kensal Green cemetery
Archives BL OIOC, papers, MSS Eur. A 23–24, B 53–64, 66, C 50–67, D 285–298, 301–303, 867, E 122, F 44 • Government Oriental MSS Library, Madras | BL OIOC, letters to H. H. Wilson, MSS Eur. E 301
Wealth at death £2336 16s. 5d.: probate, 4 Feb 1885, *CGPLA Eng. & Wales*

Christy Brown (1932–1981), by unknown photographer

Brown, Christy (1932–1981), writer and painter, was born on 5 June 1932 at the Rotunda Hospital, Dublin, the son of Patrick Brown (d. 1955), a Catholic bricklayer active in the trade union, and his wife, Bridget Fagan (d. 1968). There were seventeen children in all, thirteen of whom survived into adulthood; Christy was the tenth. Shortly after his birth it became clear that he was suffering from a severe physical disability, later diagnosed as cerebral palsy. This made both movement and speech difficult for him throughout his life as he strove to control wayward movements of his body, and to overcome the physical and psychological inhibitions on achieving self-expression. The family was told he was a 'mental defective'—a label mockingly referred to by Brown in the working title of his autobiography, 'Reminiscences of a mental defective'—but his indefatigable mother devoted much of her considerable energy to proving the authorities wrong. She became in effect his private tutor since there was then no possibility of formal education. The breakthrough occurred when Christy was six and was watching his older brothers and sisters working on their lessons with chalk and slate. Grabbing hold of both with the only part of his body he could actively direct—his left foot—and with the coaxing of his mother, he wrote a shaky but identifiable letter 'A'. As he remarks in his poem on Helen Keller, 'that kind of triumph is seldom won', a temporary liberation

from the 'deafmute world' in which he seemed condemned to live. Christy's mother went on to teach him all the letters of the alphabet and, armed with that, he soon began to write. The primary medium of communication throughout his growing years was painting, and it offered temporary release from the torment that words themselves brought. He painted throughout his life and had a number of exhibitions; the artistic life offered a more gregarious world than the solitary life of the writer.

When Christy's mother was seriously ill with her last baby, the Rotunda Hospital sent a social worker, Katrina Delahunt, to the Brown household. She immediately took an interest in Christy and his burgeoning artistic potential. In his autobiography he writes of the romantic yearnings stirred in him by the arrival of this beautiful young woman and of the jealousy he suffered when she showed up one day with an engagement ring. This pattern—of romantic longing for the women who entered his world, most often in a caring capacity—repeated itself throughout his life. His waning faith was bolstered by a visit to Lourdes in 1950, and his hopes were raised by the arrival of the paediatrician Dr Robert Collis. Collis wished to develop the study and treatment of cerebral palsy in Ireland and nurtured literary ambitions himself. He judged the nascent autobiography that Christy was writing to be the most promising of his literary productions so far, but was critical of certain stylistic excesses, urging him to use 'a short word rather than a long one'. When the autobiography appeared, certain people held it to be the work of Collis; Christy was aware of the charge and countered it by acknowledging the editorial role which Collis had performed and, while they remained friends, by determining to write subsequent works without his input. Collis sent Christy to his sister Dr Eirene Collis, who had established a clinic for children with cerebral palsy at Queen Mary's Hospital, Carshalton. She, like her brother, thought he was treatable, but insisted he give up working with his left foot, and instead develop his whole body equally. The treatment continued back in Dublin, where separate quarters were constructed for Christy in the garden of his family home, becoming a kind of artist's studio. It emphasized his growing independence.

In 1954 the London firm of Secker and Warburg, under the editorship of David Ferrer, published Brown's autobiography *My Left Foot* to immediate success. It comprises a series of short, vivid chapters covering his growing up, first with his family, then with a series of social workers, doctors, and carers. The heart of the book is the watchful, loving care of his mother (to whom the book is dedicated), and the close bond between them. It is also the story of Brown's developing relationship with himself, as he struggles to come to terms with his condition, and the highs and lows he experiences. This heightened sense of Brown's determination to follow his own path is frequently at odds with the more conventional narrative of progress that his later novel depicts. Nowhere is this better illustrated than in Brown's decision to overthrow Eirene Collis's advice and to return to writing with his left foot.

The question of how to follow the success of an autobiography published in his early twenties dogged Brown for more than a decade. At first he considered writing a sequel, taking the story up through the years of his success. Instead he wrote something more like a novel, more deliberately literary in its treatment and broadening the social canvas beyond his own life story. *Down All the Days* did not appear until 1970, but when it did, it was praised for its novelistic skills, and made more acceptable the notion of Christy Brown as a writer. It revisits the terrain of the autobiography, but is much franker in its treatment of the young man's sexual urges; these form a central part of the ordeal to which his body subjects him. While his father in *My Left Foot* remained in the background, the novel is dominated by the hulking figure of the frequently alcoholic bricklayer, alternating between brooding and outbursts of graphically depicted violence, and his baffled relationship with the daughter who defies him. The closing account of the father's death and burial is clearly based on the sudden death of Patrick Brown in 1955. But these realistic scenes are preceded by an impressionistic account of the father's last walk home, which recalls Gypo Nolan in Liam O'Flaherty's *The Informer*. His mother is here the one relegated to the background. She is replaced by the Rabelaisian figure of a blowsy, drunken, big-breasted widow, whose gossipy scenes with two other old women form a break with literal autobiography. Bridget Brown, who continued to work despite increasing ill health, died in 1968. Christy's care passed to his married sister Ann Jones.

When *Down All the Days* was published in 1970 its worldwide success provided Brown with financial security for the rest of his life. He now occupied the niche vacated by Brendan Behan, writing with the same 'sad hilarity' (as his poem on Behan puts it) about working-class Dublin. But the combination of fame and drink induced the same downward spiral. In the remaining eleven years of his life, Brown wrote three more novels, *A Shadow on Summer* (1974), *Wild Grow the Lilies* (1976), and *A Promising Career* (1982), but none achieved the financial success or literary acclaim of his first two books. A more lasting legacy was provided by three volumes of poetry, *Come Softly to my Wake* (1971), *Background Music* (1973), and *Of Snails and Skylarks* (1977), where the poetic form imposes a discipline increasingly lacking in his prose, and where the various lyrical, satirical, and philosophical aspects of his personality achieve expression.

At Easter 1972 Brown became engaged to Mary Carr (b. 1945), a dental hygienist from co. Kerry living in London, daughter of Marie Cecilia Carr. Because she was divorced, they married, on 5 October 1972, in the Dublin register office. In the following year they went to live in Ballyheigue in north Kerry; the poems in *Of Snails and Skylarks* speak of increasing depression and solitary drinking amid the natural splendour of north Kerry. The couple moved to Parbrook in Somerset in 1980. Christy Brown died at his home there, Longacre, 2 Withial Lane, on 6 September 1981 after choking on some food. His body was returned to Dublin and buried at Glasnevin cemetery along with his parents. He was survived by his wife.

Brown's funeral was described by his fellow Dubliner Noel Pearson as 'probably the most colorful funeral I was ever at'. Ever since meeting Christy at an art exhibition in the early 1970s, Pearson had been fascinated by him—'because of Christy's absolute determination to be normal'—and tried to make a film of *Down All the Days*. When the rights to that proved unavailable, Pearson acquired those to *My Left Foot*. The final screenplay, by the novelist–actor–playwright Shane Connaughton and the theatre director Jim Sheridan, drew on extra material from the novel and brought the life up to his marriage. The film *My Left Foot* was produced by Pearson and directed by Sheridan in 1989, a first work for both men and a labour of love. Daniel Day-Lewis was cast as Christy and won an Oscar for his role, as did Brenda Fricker for hers as Bridget Brown. The film was a worldwide success, exploring Christy and his life with understanding, sympathy, and a complete lack of condescension. His story remains extraordinary. The autobiographical, fictional, and filmic versions of it have earned him what he always hoped for: enduring literary fame. ANTHONY ROCHE

Sources A. Jordan, *Christy Brown's women: a biography* (Dublin, [n.d.]) · private information (2004) [Noel Pearson] · R. Hogan, ed., *Dictionary of Irish literature*, 2nd edn (Westport, CT, 1996) · J. Powell, ed., *The Annual Obituary* (1982) [New York] · b. cert. · m. cert.

Likenesses photograph, Rex Features Ltd, London [*see illus.*]

Brown, David (*b. c.*1755, *d.* in or after **1797**), landscape painter, started his career painting signboards. From the age of thirty-five, and having sold his former business, he apprenticed himself to George Morland, with whose work he had become infatuated, and was an assiduous copyist and imitator of the latter's pictures. Some of his copies are said to have been sold as originals. He bought some of his master's works and sold them at inflated prices. He left London and obtained employment in the country as a drawing-master. The date of his death is unknown, but he exhibited ten landscapes and rustic genre pictures at the Royal Academy between 1792 and 1797.

L. A. FAGAN, *rev.* R. J. LAMBERT

Sources Waterhouse, *18c painters* · Bryan, *Painters* (1903–5) · M. H. Grant, *A dictionary of British landscape painters, from the 16th century to the early 20th century* (1952) · M. Rosenthal, 'Morland, George', *The dictionary of art*, ed. J. Turner (1996)

Brown, David (1762–1812), East India Company chaplain, was the son of Francis Brown, a prosperous farmer of Driffield Greets, Yorkshire. He was educated privately at Scarborough and then at Hull grammar school and Magdalene College, Cambridge. In February 1785, his studies incomplete, he accepted the post of superintendent of the Bengal Military Orphan Asylum. Before sailing he was ordained deacon and on 4 March 1785 married a Miss Robinson (*d.* 1794), of Hull.

The couple arrived in Calcutta in June 1786. A son had been born to them on the voyage, but they now acquired the care of a further 500 boys at the orphanage and Brown was additionally appointed garrison chaplain. He learned Bengali and opened a boarding-school for Hindu famine-orphans, and he also volunteered to serve the pastorless congregation of John Kiernander's old mission church. So highly did he rate this latter duty that in 1788 he accepted dismissal from the orphanage rather than give it up. Although an East India Company chaplain, Brown was passionately interested in missionary work and, with like-minded company servants, including Charles Grant, he petitioned clergy in Britain to establish a mission in Bengal. This agitation was received warmly by the influential Cambridge evangelical Charles Simeon, and resulted in the formation of the Church Missionary Society.

In 1794, the year of his first wife's death, Brown was appointed presidency chaplain and began to preach also in the new church of St John. He was not a natural preacher, but he was a tall, handsome man, with a straightforward, persuasive manner, and under his stewardship the congregation swelled. Brown's second marriage, on 9 July 1796, was to Frances, daughter of Thomas Cowley and his wife, Hannah *Cowley, playwright and poet. In 1800, impressed by the sobering influence Brown had exercised on Calcutta's English population, Lord Wellesley appointed him provost of Fort William College, his educational experiment to reform the morals and intellect of the company's new recruits. In 1806, however, after Wellesley's fall from grace, the position was abolished.

Brown offered to continue the students' moral education gratis, but the company declined his offer.

In February 1811 Brown became the first secretary of the Calcutta branch of the British and Foreign Bible Society. In 1812 he had just managed to get the first report of the society through the press when his health collapsed through overwork. He ventured on a restorative sea voyage to Madras, but his ship was grounded on a sandbar in the bay and he was brought back to Calcutta, where he died at the house of J. H. Harington, Chowringhee, on 14 June 1812. He was buried the next day in the South Park Street cemetery, Calcutta. His wife survived him with nine children. They were poor, as Brown had spent most of his considerable income in charity, but public sympathy and a memorial volume, edited by Charles Simeon and published in 1816, raised a comfortable sum for them. Jane, Brown's only surviving child from his first marriage, married Robert Merttins Bird, a rising evangelical civilian. A son, Charles Philip *Brown (1798–1884), became a leading Telugu scholar.   A. J. ARBUTHNOT, *rev.* KATHERINE PRIOR

Sources C. Simeon, *Memorial sketches of the Rev. David Brown* (1816) · S. Neill, *A history of Christianity in India, 1707–1858* (1985) · *Calcutta Gazette* (18 June 1812) [suppl.] · Venn, *Alum. Cant.* · M. E. Gibbs, *The Anglican church in India, 1600–1970* (1972) · E. Chatterton, *A history of the Church of England in India* (1924) · ecclesiastical records, BL OIOC · accountant-general's records, BL OIOC, L/AG/34/29/24, fols. 225–8 · 'Memoir of the Rev. David Brown', *Asiatic Journal*, 8 (1819), 1–8, 105–12, 217–19, 417–20

Archives LPL, petition to archbishop of Canterbury, 10 Sept 1787, urging church to undertake missionary work in Calcutta

Wealth at death exact value unknown; all property left to widow: will, BL OIOC, L/AG/34/29/24, fols. 225–8

Brown, Sir David (1904–1993), industrialist, was born on 10 May 1904 at 8 Princess Street, Huddersfield, Yorkshire, the younger son of Francis (Frank) Edwin Brown (*d.* 1941), joint managing director of David Brown & Sons, gear manufacturers, of Huddersfield, and his wife, Caroline (Carrie), formerly Brook. He was educated at King James's School, Almondbury, and Rossall School, and joined the family business, founded by his grandfather in 1860, as an engineering apprentice in 1921, attending classes at Huddersfield Technical College. He married Daisie Muriel Firth in 1926: they had a son and a daughter. Divorced in 1955, Brown made two further marriages: in 1955 he married Marjorie Deans, and following their divorce in 1980 he married his former personal assistant, Paula Benton Stone (*b. c.*1951).

Brown's early experience in the business included running the small Keighley Gear Company which the firm had acquired, and in 1928 he was sent to the United States, South Africa, and continental Europe to study new methods of gear manufacture. He was made a director in 1929, and in 1932 managing director, following the death of his uncle and his father's decision to confine himself to the chairmanship of the company. One of Brown's first decisions as managing director was in 1934 to buy a site at Penistone for a new foundry, and David Brown Foundries began making high grade steel, and steel castings, the following year. David Brown Tractors was formed in 1935, initially in partnership with Harry Ferguson, who later took his design to the Ford Motor Company. Working with a new designer, Brown launched his first tractor in 1939 at the Royal Agricultural Show, and moved the tractor company to a disued mill at Meltham to begin production.

During the Second World War the Park works in Huddersfield made gears for all types of machines and vehicles, and began to make aircraft gears for the Rolls-Royce Merlin engine. The aero-gear division moved to Meltham in 1940, supplying gears for the Hercules engines of the Bristol Aeroplane Company, and for Spitfires: at one point during the battle of Britain, Meltham was the only factory making Spitfire gears. Brown established a tank gearbox division at Meltham, at Penistone produced armour plating for Churchill and Cromwell tanks, and steel casing for the blockbuster high-explosive bomb, developed an aircraft foundry at Penistone to make castings for aero-engines, and made cables for the oil pipeline system for the Normandy landings.

The company continued to expand. In 1944 Brown bought the Muir Machine Tool Company of Manchester and moved the machine tool division there, where it made gear cutting and gear finishing tools which were exported all over the world. In the early 1950s David Brown Construction Equipment Ltd was formed to make industrial and earth-moving equipment. In 1951 all the businesses were brought into the new David Brown Corporation, with Brown as chairman and managing director and its headquarters in Huddersfield. A number of overseas subsidiaries were formed after the war, beginning in South Africa, where he set up David Brown S. A. (Proprietary) Ltd to import gears, and in 1955 David Brown Tractors (South Africa) Ltd to import and assemble David Brown tractors. He also set up companies in Ireland, Canada, and Australia, and in 1959 bought an interest in Foote Brothers of Chicago, a leading American gear manufacturer. There was another major reorganization in 1960 when ownership of the gear, foundry, and tool divisions was transferred to a new company, David Brown & Sons (Huddersfield) Ltd.

David Brown bought Aston Martin for £20,000 in 1947, after he saw an advertisement in *The Times* for the sale of an unnamed sports car company. A few months later he bought Lagonda, because he wanted the new 2.3 litre engine, designed by W. O. Bentley, Lagonda's technical director, for the Aston Martin chassis. Aston Martin Lagonda Ltd was founded at Hanworth Air Park, near Feltham, Middlesex, and the Aston Martin DB2, with a 2.6 litre version of the Lagonda engine, was launched in 1949. For a time the company continued to produce Lagondas but in 1958 it was decided to concentrate on selling one range of high-performance sports cars, the Aston Martin DB series, and the production of Lagondas ceased. Although the marque was revived from 1961 to 1965 with the new 4 litre Lagonda Rapide, it was never as popular as the Aston Martin DB4, launched in 1958, the first British car capable of speeds of up to 140 m.p.h. Brown bought Tickford Ltd, of Newport Pagnell, Buckinghamshire, a bodybuilding plant, in 1954, and in 1957 all Aston Martin

Lagonda car production was moved there, and the other departments in 1964.

A win at the 1948 twenty-four hour sports car race at Spa, in Belgium, led David Brown to enter the motor racing world in earnest in 1950, when he appointed John Wyer as racing team manager, with the ambition of winning the Mille Miglia, and the Le Mans twenty-four hour race. While racing successes undoubtedly brought prestige for the whole David Brown group—from 1955 the cars were advertised as 'David Brown Aston Martins'—racing also gave the designers and engineers the opportunity to test new cars and obtain technical information. However, during the 1950s racing cars became less and less like the models available to the public, until to compete at all it was necessary to develop and build a totally different car. In 1955 Wyer created separate design offices for the competition and road cars, and the DBR1 was built especially for racing. The Aston Martin team, led by Stirling Moss, won at Le Mans in 1959, and went on to win the World Sports Car Championship the same year, the first British car manufacturer to do so. Even so, following these wins Brown decided to withdraw from sports car racing and concentrate on the development and manufacture of production cars, and in 1960 he pulled out of grand prix racing as well. Despite the enormous publicity surrounding the use of an Aston Martin DB5 in the James Bond film *Goldfinger* in 1964, with special features such as a passenger ejector seat and chariot scythes, the company was unable to reap the benefits as the factory was only able to make eleven of the hand-assembled cars a week. Brown always claimed that he had bought Aston Martin as a hobby, and it never made a profit.

David Brown was knighted in 1968, but by the early 1970s the David Brown Corporation was in severe financial difficulties. In 1971 he was removed from executive control for a year by the bankers supporting the corporation, and in 1972 he sold David Brown Tractors, following a drop in worldwide tractor sales, and then Aston Martin, saddled with £5 million debts. After his shipbuilding company, Vosper Thorneycroft, was nationalized in 1978, he resigned from the chairmanship of the David Brown Corporation and moved to Monte Carlo. He died on 3 September 1993 in Monte Carlo, Monaco, and was survived by his third wife.   ANNE PIMLOTT BAKER

Sources D. Donnelly, *David Brown's: the story of a family business, 1860–1960* (1960) · A. Davey and A. May, *Lagonda: a history of the marque* (1978), 467–9 · J. Wyer, *Racing with the David Brown Aston Martins*, 2 vols. (1980) · J. Wood, *Aston Martin DB4, DB5, and DB6* (1992) · *The Times* (7 Sept 1993) · *The Independent* (8 Sept 1993) · b. cert.
Likenesses photograph, c.1980, Hult. Arch. · C. Inaz?, drawing, repro. in Donnelly, *David Brown's*, frontispiece · photograph, repro. in *The Times*

Brown, Douglas Clifton, Viscount Ruffside (1879–1958), speaker of the House of Commons, was born on 16 August 1879 at Holmbush, Horsham, Sussex, the fourth of five sons in the nine children of Colonel James Clifton Brown (1841–1917), Liberal member of parliament for Horsham (1876–80), and his wife, Amelia (d. 1922), daughter of Charles Rowe of Elm House, Liverpool. Educated at

Cheam School, Eton College, and Trinity College, Cambridge, where he graduated in 1901, he was commissioned into the Lancashire Royal Garrison Artillery in 1900, transferred to the 1st King's dragoon guards (1902), became captain (1908), transferred to the special reserve (1910), served in France and Belgium (1914–18), and was promoted major (1919). In 1907 he married Violet Cicely Kathleen (*d.* 1969), daughter of Frederick Eustace Arbuthnott Wollaston of Shenton Hall, Nuneaton, Warwickshire. They had one daughter.

In December 1910 Clifton Brown unsuccessfully contested the constituency of St George-in-the-East, London, but in the general election of 1918 he was returned as a coalition Unionist for the Hexham division of Northumberland. With the exception of the period November 1923 to October 1924 he held this seat as a Unionist or as speaker until he retired from the House of Commons in 1951. He continued in the yeomanry, commanding the Northumberland hussars in 1925–9. In 1920–22 he was parliamentary private secretary to Ian Macpherson, then minister of pensions.

In 1937 Clifton Brown was nominated a member of the chairmen's panel, presiding over standing committees and serving from time to time as temporary chairman of committees of the whole house. On 9 November 1938 he was elected deputy chairman of ways and means. In 1941 he was sworn of the privy council and in January 1943 was elected chairman of ways and means. Following the death in office of the speaker, E. A. FitzRoy, Clifton Brown was elected speaker on 9 March 1943. The House of Commons had then been in existence for nearly eight years under Mr Speaker FitzRoy's somewhat authoritarian sway and as, so long as the war continued, domestic politics were in abeyance, procedural problems did not trouble the new speaker. The assault by V 1 and V 2 bombs raised fresh questions of safety with which Clifton Brown was well fitted to deal, for since 1941 he had been chairman of the defence committee of the Palace of Westminster.

With the war in Europe over, party politics were resumed and in the general election of 1945 the Labour Party was returned with a huge majority. Following the precedents of 1895 and 1906 Clifton Brown was unanimously re-elected speaker on 1 August 1945. Conditions were very different from those in the previous house: there were many new members, party political warfare had been resumed with great bitterness, and, smarting from an unexpected defeat, the opposition were in no mood to accept in silence rulings contrary to their views. To reimpose the sort of discipline which had existed under FitzRoy would have meant a struggle in which it was by no means certain that the speaker would have commanded the support of the house and which would have been quite contrary to Clifton Brown's temperament. So where his predecessors had relied upon authority Brown relied on good humour, patience, and his patent wish to help members to the utmost of his ability. Although successful to a point, the speaker's willingness to listen to representations on his rulings was often much abused and the time of the house wasted. Lord Winterton

later wrote that Clifton Brown was not equal to the task. His youthful, usually smiling, countenance gave 'the impression of a happy boy at school', a disadvantage, in Winterton's view, for a speaker, who needed to be 'grim and formidable' to impose authority. Neither did Clifton Brown have 'the command of the English language possessed by his predecessor or successor. It was sometimes difficult to follow the meaning of his observations and rulings' (Winterton, 294).

Still, that Clifton Brown was unanimously elected for the third time in the parliament which met on 1 March 1950 was a tribute to his popularity. With the government's majority of only six the political struggle was sterner than at any time since 1914. Inevitably these conditions imposed a heavy burden on the speaker, with long hours of sitting and perpetual procedural wrangles. Although Clifton Brown continued to act with the most conscientious impartiality, the circumstances were peculiarly distasteful to a man of his peace-loving temperament and moderate views, and it was no surprise when in 1951 he announced that he would not seek re-election at the coming general election.

During his time as speaker, Clifton Brown's personal qualities were perhaps used to best effect when he formally represented the house at functions in Britain and overseas. He paid formal visits abroad: to Caen on the anniversary of D-day; to Nuremberg during the war criminals' trial; to Paris as the guest of M. Herriot, then president of the French national assembly, who had previously been officially entertained at Westminster; to Rome, and to Copenhagen; in Britain he visited the general assembly in Edinburgh. There were also occasions of more domestic interest. Colleagues noted that his proudest moments were when he relit the lantern in Big Ben after the war and then gave a moving speech; when he led the Commons to St Margaret's to return thanks for victory in Europe; and when he first took his seat in the chair of the rebuilt House of Commons and subsequently led a procession of the speakers of the Commonwealth into Westminster Hall to present an address to the king.

Clifton Brown held honorary degrees from Durham, Cambridge, and Caen, received the grand cross of the Légion d'honneur, and was created Viscount Ruffside of Hexham in 1951. He died at the Mount Vernon Hospital, Northwood, Middlesex, on 5 May 1958. He left no male heir and the title became extinct. His daughter, Audrey Pellew Clifton Brown (*b.* 1908), married Sir Harry Hylton-Foster, speaker of the House of Commons from 1959 to 1965, and was created a life peer in 1965 after her husband's death.   E. A. FELLOWES, *rev.* MARC BRODIE

Sources *JHC* · P. A. C. Laundy, *The office of speaker* (1964) · personal knowledge (1971) · private information (1971) · *CGPLA Eng. & Wales* (1958) · *The Times* (6 May 1958) · Burke, *Peerage* · E. T. Winterton, *Orders of the day* (1953) · S. Lloyd, *Mr Speaker, sir* (1976) · *WWW* · Venn, *Alum. Cant.*
Archives FILM BFI NFTVA, news footage
Likenesses W. Stoneman, photograph, 1947, NPG · W. O. Hutchison, oils, 1953, Palace of Westminster, London · photograph, repro. in *The Times*

Wealth at death £138,167 16s. 4d.: probate, 25 July 1958, *CGPLA Eng. & Wales*

Brown, Dame Edith Mary (1864–1956), medical missionary and founder of the North India School of Medicine for Christian Women, was born on 24 March 1864 at Bank Buildings, 10A Coats Lane, Whitehaven, Cumberland. One of six children, she was the second of three daughters born to George Wightman Brown (1814?–1871), a bank manager, and his second wife, Mary, *née* Walther.

A well-educated girl, Edith was taught first at Manchester High School for Girls and then, from 1875, at the Croydon High School for Girls. In 1882 she won a scholarship to Girton College, Cambridge. Her future career was already determined, for her childhood ambition was to become a missionary in India, an aim fostered by her family's devotion to Christianity. In adulthood she decided that the best way to give practical expression to her Christian faith was to become a medical missionary, for this would enable her to help relieve the suffering of Indian women, some of whom were denied access to the benefits of western medicine because of the rigid rules of caste, creed, and purdah.

After taking second-class honours in the natural sciences tripos at Girton in 1885 Edith began teaching science at Exeter High School for Girls as she was unable to afford medical training. Fortunately, within a year, she was offered financial support by missionary friends in Bristol who worked for the zenana (women's) branch of the Baptist Mission Society. Edith, who later remarked 'I felt the Lord had sent the money and I rejoiced' (Reynolds, 57), was more than willing to agree to go to India as a pioneering doctor for the mission once she qualified. She completed her studies at the London School of Medicine for Women and qualified LRCP (Edin.) and LRCS (Edin.), LRFPS (Glas.), MA (Dublin) and MD (Brux.). Within weeks, in November 1891, she left England as one of the first two women missionary doctors to be sent to India by the Baptist Mission Society.

Life was never easy for Edith, and in India she rapidly discovered that as a single-handed doctor she could never hope to help the thousands of women who desperately needed medical attention. What she knew she needed, but which was not available, was skilled assistance. Her solution was to set about establishing a medical school where suitable Indian Christian women could train as doctors and nurses. Against all the odds, later dismissed by Edith as preliminary difficulties, the North India School of Medicine for Christian Women, the first women's medical college in south-east Asia, opened in Ludhiana, Punjab, in October 1894 with four pupils, a borrowed hospital, rented schoolhouse, £50, and Edith Brown as founder and principal. Over the next fifty years, which were regularly punctuated by financial uncertainty, opposition, and grave political instability—in 1919, for example, the students had to be evacuated during the riots in the Punjab—Edith Brown's undertaking developed into a modern hospital and medical school. When the jubilee of her arrival in India was celebrated in 1941

the college had awarded diplomas to 411 doctors, 143 nurses, 168 dispensers, and more than 1000 midwives.

Edith's courage, determination, and strength came from her unwavering faith in God, and she lived by her motto, 'My work is for a king'. Her appearance—plainly dressed in very long skirts, her hair plaited around her head—reflected her Victorian upbringing. She was a reserved, quietly dignified woman, and a strict but fair disciplinarian who expected her fellow workers to adhere to the same high religious, spiritual, and medical standards that she maintained. A gifted surgeon and a tireless and devoted worker, she also found time to involve herself with innumerable medical councils and faculties in north India. Her handbook, *Daigiri Ke Asul* (n.d., Mission Press, Allahabad), written in Urdu, Hindi, and Punjabi, all languages she had mastered, became the 'bible' of Indian Christian midwives. In recognition of her outstanding service to India, Edith Brown was awarded the silver kaisar-i-Hind medal in 1911, the gold in 1922, and in 1932 she was created dame commander in the Order of the British Empire, the first missionary to be so honoured.

Retirement was an agonizing decision for Edith, and she was persuaded, very reluctantly, to step down as principal in 1942. The next few years were difficult for all concerned: Edith, now principal emeritus and honorary treasurer, remained in Ludhiana, unable to detach herself from her beloved college, but her continued presence adversely affected its development and intensified the friction which existed between her and the governing body. She finally moved to Kashmir in 1948, where she continued her missionary work. This included opening a Christian Reading Room near her houseboat, establishing a Bible correspondence course and recording teaching tapes in Kashmiri. Her other interests included writing poetry, gardening, and reading. Dame Edith Brown died on her houseboat, *Water Music*, Island Ghat, Srinagar, Kashmir, on 6 December 1956, and was buried at Srinagar cemetery six days later. She is remembered in Whitehaven by a memorial plaque, unveiled in July 1995, which marks the house where she was born.

SUSAN L. COHEN

Sources F. L. French, *Miss Brown's hospital: the story of the Ludhiana Medical College and Dame Edith Brown, O.B.E., its founder* (1954) • E. M. Brown, 'A medical college in the Punjab', *Girton Review*, Lent term (1939), 8–14 • C. Reynolds, *Punjab pioneer* (1968) • *My work is for a king* (1994) [Ludhiana Medical College and Hospital, Ludhiana, centenary souvenir, 1894–1994] • C. Tinling, *India's womanhood: forty years' work at Ludhiana* (1935) • Royal Free Hospital, London • K. T. Butler and H. I. McMorran, eds., *Girton College register, 1869–1946* (1948) • d. cert. • *BMJ* (22 Dec 1956), 1490–91 • *Conquest by Healing*, 33/1 (March 1957), 2–10 • private information (2004) • b. cert. • M. Lal, 'The politics of gender and medicine in colonial India: the Countess of Dufferin's Fund', *Bulletin of the History of Medicine*, 68 (1994), 29–66
Archives BBC WAC, transcripts of two live talks for BBC radio; 'Missionary Talk: India's women doctors', 'Empire exchange: missionary doctors in India' • Ludhiana Medical College, Ludhiana, Punjab, India • Royal Free Hospital, London
Likenesses photographs, Royal Free Hospital, London • portrait, repro. in *Conquest by Healing*, 1
Wealth at death £1359 6s. 4d. effects in England: probate, 20 May 1957, *CGPLA Eng. & Wales*

Brown, Elizabeth (1830–1899), astronomer and meteorologist, was born on 6 August 1830 at Further Barton, Hampton Road, Cirencester, Gloucestershire, the elder of the two daughters of Thomas Crowther Brown (1772?–1883), a wine merchant and amateur meteorologist, and his wife, Jemimah. The family was comfortably off and Elizabeth was taught at home by a governess; later she studied extensively and persistently on her own, reading both science and literature. Her mother died when she was still a child and she was very close to her father, who taught her how to watch the sky for meteorological information and use a small hand telescope that allowed her to see Saturn's rings and Jupiter's satellites. From 1871 it was she who carried out the daily rainfall recording for the Royal Meteorological Society previously done for many years by her father. For a time she also recorded temperature, deep-well measurements, and thunderstorm activity. She was elected a fellow of the society in 1893, an honour few women had received and one she greatly prized. Beginning about 1881 a number of her meteorological notes appeared at intervals, often in *Nature*.

Shortly after the death of her father, whom she looked after in his last years, Brown began to take part publicly in astronomical work, and in 1883 presented a paper on sunspots to the then very active Liverpool Astronomical Society. Unlike the Royal Astronomical Society, this group accepted women members; Brown became director of its recently organized solar section, making observations herself and collecting and reporting data of others. Her own work was done in one of two observatories (the other housed meteorological instruments) built at Further Barton. She made two long, somewhat arduous, expeditions, with the charge of presenting reports to the Liverpool Society, to observe solar eclipses. The first was to Russia (1887) and the second to Trinidad (1889). Only the latter was successful scientifically, but Brown wrote lively accounts of both. *In Pursuit of a Shadow* (1888) described her journey, with a woman friend, across northern Europe to Kineshma, some 200 miles north-east of Moscow, where she was a guest at the dacha ('a delightful, romantic house') of a Russian astronomer. *Caught in the Tropics*, describing her Trinidad trip, appeared in 1890.

Following the decline of the Liverpool society, Brown became very active in a move to organize a metropolitan-based amateur group, which became the British Astronomical Association (BAA). On its founding in 1890 she accepted the directorship of its solar section, thus becoming, *ex officio*, a member of council. From then on she was increasingly absorbed in the work her post entailed, although she also helped in other sections and occasionally made observations of the moon and of variable and coloured stars. Her chief interest remained the daily registering of sunspots—demanding work, requiring accuracy in observation and artistic skill. Her reports appeared in more than twenty papers in the BAA's *Journal* throughout the 1890s and in seven lengthy annual reports of the solar section (BAA *Memoirs*, 1891–9). The latter were major contributions, widely recognized; each included a detailed

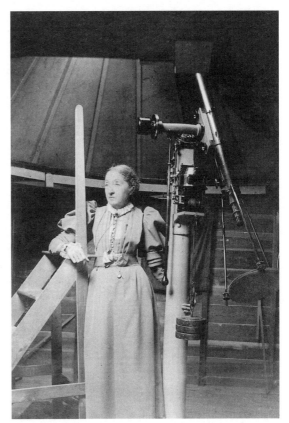

Elizabeth Brown (1830–1899), by F. Mortimer Savory

pictorial calendar of sunspots and faculae and a life history 'ledger' for each spot. They earned her a distinguished place among amateur astronomers of her time. Brown held memberships in the Astronomical Society of the Pacific, the Astronomical Society of France, and the Astronomical Society of Wales. Although proposed (1892) for fellowship in the Royal Astronomical Society (whose meetings she frequently attended) she was not elected.

Calm, gentle, and unassuming by nature, a member of the Society of Friends and a regular attender of meetings, Brown spent a quiet life in the country. She never married, and after the death of her father her only companion was her sister, Jemima. In general she avoided interruptions to her routine of observing, drawing, writing, and rainfall recording, but she had an active correspondence with astronomers and other friends in many countries. In addition to her eclipse expeditions (the third and last of which was to northern Norway in 1896), she went to the Montreal meeting of the British Association in 1884 and afterwards travelled in Canada and the United States. Shorter journeys took her to Scotland, Ireland, and Spain. She recorded landscapes and wild flowers, a special interest, in colour sketches, and described her experiences in vivid letters to her sister.

Never very robust, Brown died suddenly, of cardiac thrombosis, at Further Barton, her lifelong home, on 5 March 1899, after a week of bronchial illness and in the midst of preparing for a fourth eclipse expedition. She was interred in the Friends' meeting-house burial-ground, Cirencester. She left her astronomical observatory, its contents, and £1000 to the British Astronomical Association.　　　　　　　　　　　MARY R. S. CREESE

Sources *The Observatory*, 22 (1899), 171–2 · *Journal of the British Astronomical Association*, 9 (1898–9), 214–15 · *Quarterly Journal of the Royal Meteorological Society*, 26 (1900), 214–15 · *The Times* (16 March 1899) · *Leopoldina*, 35 (1899), 134–5 · *Wiltshire and Gloucestershire Standard* (11 March 1899) · *ILN* (25 March 1899) · *The Friend*, new ser., 39 (1899), 172 · *Friends' Quarterly Examiner*, 33 (1899), 383 · 'Dictionary of Quaker biography', RS Friends, Lond. [card index] · private information (2004) · d. cert. · K. Weitzenhoffer, 'A forgotten astronomer', *Astronomy*, 20 (1992), 13–14 · M. Creese, 'Elizabeth Brown (1830–1899), solar astronomer', *Journal of the British Astronomical Association*, 108 (1998), 193–7

Likenesses F. M. Savory, photograph, RAS [*see illus.*] · Savory of Cirencester, photograph, repro. in *ILN* · photograph, repro. in *Journal of the British Astronomical Association*

Wealth at death £37,007 6s. 4d.: resworn probate, Nov 1899, *CGPLA Eng. & Wales*

Brown, (Alfred) Ernest (1881–1962), politician, was born at 2 Marine Cottages, Waldron Steps, Torquay, Devon, on 27 August 1881, the eldest son of William Henry Brown, fisherman, and his wife, Anna Badcock. His father was a prominent Baptist and he was involved from an early age in his father's religious work, taking easily to preaching with the benefit of 'a tremendous and far-reaching platform voice' (*The Times*, 16 Feb 1962, 18) and a particular aptitude for public speaking. He also used his skills to assist the local Liberal Party, becoming a much sought-after political orator at a time when loudspeakers had not yet been invented.

Brown was educated locally and became a clerk. On 8 June 1907 he married Isabel Eva (b. 1879/80), daughter of Richard Bonstow Narracott, master plumber, of Torquay; they had no children. In 1914 he joined the sportsmen's battalion, and in 1916 he was commissioned in the Somerset light infantry. He won the Military Medal as a private, and the Military Cross and the Italian silver star for valour as an officer. After the war he made unsuccessful attempts in 1918 and in 1922 to be elected as Liberal member for Salisbury, and he failed again, at Mitcham, in February 1923. He was elected for the Rugby constituency in November of the same year but was defeated in 1924. Three years later he gained Leith for the Liberals and held this seat until 1945. But, dissatisfied with the support given by his party to the Labour government after 1929, from which he believed they should 'stand entirely aloof' (Wilson, 365), he joined Sir John Simon and Sir Robert Hutchison in 1931 and became a Liberal National.

In the National and coalition governments between 1931 and the end of the war Brown held a number of ministerial posts. In 1931–2 he was parliamentary secretary to the Ministry of Health and also chairman of the select committee on procedure. Next he moved to the mines department, where he was forced to defend the actions of his department regarding the Gresford mine disaster. He was appointed minister of labour in 1935 and had charge of the Unemployment Insurance (Agriculture) Act of 1936, which brought in nearly all workers in agriculture,

horticulture, and forestry. He often noted with pride the 1937 Trades Union Congress resolution, passed without opposition, that thanked him for the part that he had played in organizing the workers in the distributive trades. The growing need to prepare for war occupied much of Brown's time in this position, and in 1939 the Ministry of National Service was added to his responsibilities.

When Churchill formed his cabinet in May 1940 Brown became—an unusual figure—an English secretary of state for Scotland. While in that office he visited the highlands, concerned himself with hill sheep farming, and secured a subsidy for breeding ewes. In this period Brown also became leader of the now much reduced Liberal National Party and attempted to 'bring about a reunion' (*The Times*, 16 Feb 1962, 18) between it and the Liberal Party, now led by Sir Archibald Sinclair. Negotiations continued for some time but were ultimately unsuccessful.

Early in 1941 Brown took over the Ministry of Health, a transfer which made him responsible for evacuating people to safer areas and finding accommodation for workers at a period of severe housing shortage. He was attacked for failures in this area, and in mid-1943 motions were unsuccessfully moved in the House of Commons declaring a lack of confidence in his capacity for the job. Later that year he was replaced as minister and was appointed chancellor of the duchy of Lancaster, and then from May to July 1945 minister of aircraft production in Churchill's caretaker government before the general election. During 1944 and the early part of 1945 he acted as chairman of the European committee of the United Nations Relief and Rehabilitation Administration.

Brown was president of the Baptist Union of Great Britain and Ireland in 1948–9 and a leader in the Baptist Men's Movement. He went as a delegate in 1948 to the Amsterdam assembly of the World Council of Churches and served from 1948 to 1954 as a member of its central committee, visiting India in 1952–3 for its meetings in Lucknow. In 1950–51 he toured Australia as guest of the federal government and addressed religious meetings throughout the country. For many years he was an officer of the Free Church Federal Council; he was also a dedicated temperance worker. His youthful enthusiasm for rugby football was kept up long after he had ceased to play and he was a keen yachtsman. The large and wide-ranging library that he collected was a main source of his leisure. In his later years he suffered from the effects of a stroke.

The ebullience which made Brown a more than life-size figure in parliament sometimes led to his being a target for affectionate amusement. Baldwin is said to have remarked, on seeing him in a House of Commons callbox, that he never knew that Brown needed a telephone to speak to his constituents in Leith. He was sworn of the privy council in 1935 and ten years later appointed CH. He died at St Pancras Hospital, London, on 16 February 1962 and was cremated at Golders Green on 21 February.

A. P. RYAN, *rev.* MARC BRODIE

Sources *The Times* (16 Feb 1962) · *The Times* (17 Feb 1962) · T. Wilson, *The downfall of the liberal party, 1914–1935* (1966) · R. Douglas, *The* *history of the liberal party, 1895–1970* (1971) • *WWBMP* • S. Koss, *Non-conformity in modern British politics* (1975) • b. cert. • m. cert. • d. cert. • *CGPLA Eng. & Wales* (1962)

Archives HLRO, corresp. with J. C. C. Davidson
Likenesses double portrait, photograph, 1936 (with J. W. Phillips), Hult. Arch. • D. Berwin, photograph, 1937, Hult. Arch. • F. Morley, photograph, 1938, Hult. Arch. • W. Stoneman, photograph, 1941, NPG • L. McCombe, photograph, 1943, Hult. Arch. • H. Coster, photographs, NPG • D. Low, caricature, pencil drawing, NPG • photograph, repro. in *The Times* (16 Feb 1962), 18
Wealth at death £2258 13s. 5d.: administration with will, 22 March 1962, *CGPLA Eng. & Wales*

Brown, Ernest William (1866–1938), mathematician and astronomer, was born on 29 November 1866 at Hull, the second child and elder son of William Brown, farmer, and later a lumber merchant of Hull, and his wife, Emma Martin. Educated at the Hull and East Riding College, he entered Christ's College, Cambridge, as a scholar in 1884. He was sixth wrangler in the mathematical tripos of 1887 and was elected a fellow of Christ's in 1889. At the suggestion of George Darwin he took up in 1888 the study of the American astronomer George William Hill's papers on the lunar theory. This led him to what was to prove his life's work: for the next twenty years he gave little thought to other research and it remained his favourite subject during the thirty years that came after. In 1891 he went to the United States of America as professor of applied mathematics at Haverford College, Pennsylvania; in 1907 he was appointed professor of mathematics at Yale University, retiring in 1932, on account of ill health, with the title of emeritus professor. He retained his connection with Cambridge and with Christ's College, spending a part of almost every summer there. He was elected an honorary fellow of Christ's in 1911.

In 1896 Brown published *An Introductory Treatise on the Lunar Theory*, containing a critical examination of the various methods of predicting the motion of the moon. His own theory was a development of Hill's method. The main results were published in five parts in the *Memoirs of the Royal Astronomical Society* between 1897 and 1908. For an essay on the direct planetary perturbations of the moon he was awarded, in 1907, the Adams prize of the University of Cambridge. The heavy task of reducing the theory to tables was begun in 1908, the numerical values of the constants used in the tables being obtained from comparison of the theory with the Greenwich observations of the moon (some 20,000 in number) from 1750 to 1900. His monumental *Tables of the Motion of the Moon* in three volumes were published in 1919, and were for many years employed to calculate the moon's place in the *Nautical Almanac*.

The completeness and accuracy of Brown's theory enabled one of the most pressing problems in gravitational astronomy to be decided. Comparison between the moon's observed positions and the earlier theory of Petrus Andreas Hansen had shown large fluctuations, which could not be explained by any known gravitational cause but which might have arisen from errors or incompleteness in the theory. Comparison with Brown's *Tables* soon showed that the moon's observed positions were not accurately represented by the theory. Brown suggested that the cause was a variable rate of rotation of the earth and obtained evidence in support of this view, which has since been conclusively established. In order to improve the observed positions of the moon, he organized a worldwide programme for the observation and reduction of occultations of stars by the moon. In his later years he made significant contributions to various problems in celestial mechanics, mainly concerned with planetary theory.

Brown was elected FRS in 1898. He was awarded the gold medal of the Royal Astronomical Society in 1907; the Pontecoulant prize of the Paris Academy of Sciences in 1909; a royal medal of the Royal Society in 1914; the Bruce medal of the Astronomical Society of the Pacific in 1920; and the Watson medal of the National Academy of Sciences, Washington, in 1937. He received honorary degrees from the universities of Adelaide (1914), Yale (1933), Columbia (1934), and McGill (1936). He never married. He died at Yale observatory, New Haven, Connecticut, on 22 July 1938. H. SPENCER JONES, *rev.* ISOBEL FALCONER

Sources C. G. Darwin, *Obits. FRS*, 3 (1939–41), 19–22 • private information (1949) • personal knowledge (1949) • election certificate, RS • *CGPLA Eng. & Wales* (1938)
Likenesses Moull & Fox, photograph, RS • Phillips, photograph, RS • photograph, repro. in Darwin, *Obits. FRS*, facing p. 19
Wealth at death £787 13s. 0d.: administration with will, 20 Dec 1938, *CGPLA Eng. & Wales*

Brown, Ford Madox (1821–1893), painter and designer, was born at Calais, France, on 16 April 1821, the son of Ford Brown (d. 1842) and his wife, Caroline (d. 1839), the daughter of Tristram Maries Madox, of an old Kent yeoman family. Ford Madox Brown's unorthodox and anti-establishment leanings were prefigured by those of his grandfather John Brown (bap. 1735, d. 1788), the son of a Scottish labourer, whose career as an innovative medical doctor was marked by hostility to social superiors and professional peers. The doctor's second son, Ford Brown (named after Dr Ford, a favourite pupil), at one time purser on the *Arethusa*, retired after the Napoleonic wars. Financial stringencies forced Ford and Caroline Brown to seek inexpensive lodgings in Calais, and it was these reduced circumstances which marked Ford Madox Brown's boyhood.

Education and early career Frequent travel between France and Britain dominated a childhood in which Brown acquired only a patchy education. A juvenile talent for drawing was nurtured through copying a hanging of *Pizarro's Conquest of Peru* in the *hôtel garni* where his parents lived; an Italian drawing-master, engaged when he was seven, set him copying prints by Raphael, Correggio, and Bartolozzi. Despite initial misgivings, and an unsuccessful attempt to place his son in the navy, Brown's father moved the family to Bruges in 1835 in order to facilitate the already accomplished youngster's artistic education. At the age of fourteen he began his studies under Aelbert Gregorius, a student of David, at the Bruges Academy; a year later, in 1836, he transferred to the academy at Ghent, where he studied under another pupil of David, Pierre Van

Ford Madox Brown (1821–1893), self-portrait, 1877

Hanselaer. These early masters offered Brown a rather hard-edged neo-classicism with which he never seems to have been entirely at ease. At this time Brown began to sell paintings, mainly portraits and small genre scenes; the finest surviving work from this period is an accomplished portrait of his father, a querulous figure with a shock of white hair (c.1837; Tate collection). A move to Antwerp in 1837 to study at the academy with Gustaf, Baron Wappers, was decisive for Brown's artistic development. His parents returned to London, allowing Brown to enjoy a bohemian lifestyle at the Pot d'Etain lodging house, where he struck up a friendship with the Irish artist Daniel Casey. Brown acquired from Wappers a technical accomplishment and intellectual rigour far in advance of that available to his contemporaries at the Royal Academy Schools in London. Wappers's Rubensian painterliness affected Brown less than his belief that history painting should engage with contemporary moral and political issues. The death of his mother on 2 September 1839 left Brown and his sister an annuity allowing him to continue his work at the Antwerp Academy.

In 1840 Brown's painting from Byron The Giaour's Confession (destroyed), begun at Antwerp, was exhibited at the Royal Academy in London; next he embarked upon a major history painting, The Execution of Mary, Queen of Scots (small version, Whitworth Art Gallery, Manchester), completed in March. Containing passages of fine naturalism but also several rather histrionic figures, it indicates a considerable but as yet immature talent. His cousin Elisabeth Bromley (1818/19–1847) (the daughter of his mother's sister Mary), who in 1840 joined the Brown family in Antwerp after finishing school in Germany, modelled for the swooning attendant in The Execution. They grieved together for Brown's sister Eliza, known as Lyly, who died suddenly in June 1840. Nineteen and doubly bereaved, Brown fell in love with Elisabeth, his kindly, sophisticated, somewhat older cousin, and on 3 April 1841 they were married at her home parish church in Meopham, Kent. Standing at the altar, slight (at 5 feet 7 inches), with flowing light brown hair, Brown looked so young that the vicar asked where the bridegroom might be.

The summer of 1841 saw the couple take lodgings in Montmartre, accompanied by Brown's invalid father. Like his friend Casey, Brown went to Paris in the hope of benefiting from the French state's lavish patronage of the arts. Elisabeth, genteel and elegant, cut an impressive figure in Paris, and he long recalled this period as an idyll of domestic happiness. The first of three subjects from Byron painted at this time, Manfred on the Jungfrau (1840–41; Manchester City Galleries), though melodramatic in composition, reflects a new interest in natural lighting. Personal tragedy intervened when the death of his father in the summer of 1842 was followed by that in November of Brown's own first child. Emma Lucy [see Rossetti, (Emma) Lucy Madox Brown], their only surviving child, was born in July 1843.

In 1843 the announcement of an annual competition to select designs for frescoes to decorate the new palace of Westminster indicated a rare source of patronage for history painting in England. In 1844 Brown submitted a large cartoon of The Body of Harold Brought before William, which survives in fragments (Camberwell College of Art). Its sardonic portrayal of the Normans—possibly intended as a critique of the aristocracy—may have offended the jury; a more likely cause for its failure, however, was its refusal to conform to pictorial orthodoxy, essaying instead an exaggerated Michelangelesque style similar to that of the German painter Peter Cornelius. Another competition, seeking an altarpiece for St James's Church in Bermondsey, south London, heightened Brown's enthusiasm for public art. His opulently coloured study The Ascension (1844; Forbes Magazine Collection, New York) was also unsuccessful. The prospect of further competitions brought Brown back to England; after spending the summer of 1844 with family in Kent, where his wife remained, in November Brown settled in at Charles Lucy's studios at Tudor Lodge, London. By the next summer he had completed a boldly drawn cartoon of The Abstract Spirit of Justice (surviving study of 1845; Manchester City Galleries), which once more was unsuccessful in the Westminster competition.

In 1845 Brown and Elisabeth travelled to Rome in search of a cure for her failing health. On the journey Brown was impressed by the Holbeins at Basel, and in Rome he admired not only the Renaissance masters but also contemporary work by the German 'Nazarenes'. Possibly on the advice of his friend William Cave Thomas, he sought out Johann Friedrich Overbeck and Peter Cornelius, who became key influences in his subsequent works such as Wycliffe (1847–8; Cartwright Hall, Bradford), which appeared at the 'Free' exhibition of 1848. Elisabeth grew weaker on the trip and died of consumption on the return journey, at Paris on 5 June 1847; she was buried at Highgate cemetery. After a period of grief Brown was able to return to a triptych he had begun in Rome, originally intended for the Westminster competitions, *Seeds and Fruits of English Poetry* (small version, 1845–53; AM Oxf.). Only the large central panel was completed, as *Chaucer at the Court of Edward III* (1846–51; Art Gallery of New South Wales, Sydney), an elaborate multi-figure composition which was displayed at the Royal Academy six years after its conception in 1851.

Brown and the Pre-Raphaelite Brotherhood In the intervening period Brown had met and befriended the artists of the Pre-Raphaelite Brotherhood, among whom the main figures, several years his junior, were discontented students of the Royal Academy Schools. Dante Gabriel Rossetti approached Brown for lessons in 1848, in a letter whose extravagance the touchy Brown took as satirical, setting off with a 'stout stick' (Watkinson and Newman, 39) to rebuke the perpetrator. Although only briefly a pupil, Rossetti became a lifelong friend, and his early works markedly show Brown's influence. Although Brown did not become a member of the brotherhood (accounts differ as to whether he was ever asked to join), he published in the Pre-Raphaelite journal, *The Germ*, in 1850, and adopted the brilliant palette and intense realism pioneered by William Holman Hunt, whom he greatly admired, and John Everett Millais. He had reworked *Chaucer* in this vein by 1851; it was followed by *Jesus Washes Peter's Feet* (c.1851–1856; Tate collection), a history painting in which passages of striking realism, painted in the Pre-Raphaelites' wet-in-white technique, inflect a conventionally heroic composition. As with much of Brown's output, his practice of retouching works later in his career makes the precise dating of this painting difficult.

From 1848 onwards one of Brown's most frequent models was Emma Hill (1829–1890). She soon became Brown's mistress, and in 1848 she moved with him to 17 Newman Street, London, close to Rossetti's studio, though the relationship remained a secret from all but his closest friends. The social distance separating the two was great. Emma, who was born Matilda, was a daughter of Thomas Hill, a bricklayer: illiterate, she sometimes worked as a domestic servant. In November 1850 Emma gave birth to a daughter, Catherine Emily, and in June 1851 the family moved to Stockwell in south London. Nearby, on Clapham Common, Brown painted *The Pretty Baa-Lambs* (1851; Birmingham Museums and Art Gallery), with his wife and child modelling for the central figures; lambs and sheep were brought each morning in a truck, and, in an advance on previous Pre-Raphaelite practice, the entire work was painted outside. It is a brilliant exercise in Pre-Raphaelite realism which represents a sunlit landscape with glowing colour and precision.

During 1852 Brown lived in Hampstead, while Emma and her daughter moved from lodgings in Hendon to Highgate. By this time Brown had taught Emma to read and write, and she seems to have attended a school for young ladies to acquire the accomplishments necessary

for a middle-class wife of the period. They were married at St Dunstan-in-the-West, London, on 5 April 1853, in the presence only of Rossetti and another artist friend, Thomas Seddon. Only gradually was Emma introduced to the wider circle of Brown's acquaintance. Her features, however, may be seen in his works of the period, many of which dwell on domestic themes verging on the autobiographical: in the striking *Take your Son, Sir!* (1851, retouched 1856–7; Tate collection) a new-born child is handed from mother to a father seen reflected in a convex mirror, based on Jan van Eyck's *Arnolfini Marriage* (1434; National Gallery, London). In *An English Fireside of 1854–5* (1851–5; Walker Art Gallery, Liverpool) Emma cradles an infant on her knee in the glow of a fire.

Three works conceived by Brown in 1852 and slowly completed in later years stand among the most brilliant achievements of the Pre-Raphaelite circle, carrying its realist tenets to the limits. Brown's life at this time, illuminated by the survival of his diary, was marked by intense periods of depression; his work failed to sell and he declared himself to be 'intensely miserable very hard up & a little mad' (*Diary*, 78). There is an autobiographical element to *The Last of England* (1852–5; Birmingham Museums and Art Gallery), which memorializes the period of emigration to the colonies in the years before the Crimean War. Based on the departure for Australia in 1852 of the Pre-Raphaelite brother Thomas Woolner, the anxious couple seen leaving from Dover bear the features of Ford and Emma Brown themselves. At his most desperate, Brown had himself considered leaving for India. The composition is a tondo recalling Renaissance images of the holy family. As Sidney Colvin noted in 1870, in *The Last of England* 'the most rigid minuteness of photographic detail is combined with the utmost pregnancy of associated suggestion' (Colvin, 85). Brown recorded that 'the madder ribbons of the bonnet took me 4 weeks to paint' (*Diary*, 80). Sittings took place in the garden of 33 High Street, Hampstead, in which Brown's painting room stood above the china shop of a Mrs Coates. From the rear of the house could be seen the panoramic vista he recorded in *An English Autumn Afternoon* (1852–5; Birmingham Museums and Art Gallery), an oval painting providing a 'literal transcript' (*An Exhibition of Work*) of the quotidian north London landscape observed with extraordinary intensity. A disagreement in 1855 about the merits of this painting with John Ruskin, for whom it depicted 'such a very ugly subject' (*Diary*, 144), came at the culmination of a long antagonism. This lost Brown any chance of support from the most influential Victorian art critic. Landscape paintings from nature form a small but significant element in Brown's output. As well as early efforts at naturalism, such as *Windermere* (1848; Lady Lever Art Gallery, Port Sunlight), he completed in the 1850s several small landscapes which record with striking fidelity his experience of the countryside near Hendon, where Emma lived for a while in 1852 (for example, *Carrying Corn*, 1854–5; Tate collection).

Brown found solace from his psychological torments in periods of extended and visionary labour, devoted mainly to a painting entitled *Work* (Manchester City Galleries), also begun in Hampstead in 1852 but completed only in 1863. This most complex and sophisticated British modern-life painting of the nineteenth century includes portraits of two intellectuals, the Revd F. D. Maurice and Thomas Carlyle, with whose ideas the artist was deeply engaged. He taught a class of artisans at the working men's college, founded by Maurice, from 1858 to 1860 with great success, and *Work* makes many references to Carlyle's texts, such as *Past and Present* (1843). Although *Work* ostensibly records an everyday scene in which navvies are installing a new water main in Heath Street, Hampstead, its numerous dramatis personae, subtle social analysis, and elaborate visual language required an extensive written explanation in the catalogue of Brown's solo exhibition in London in 1865. The image has spawned numerous subsequent interpretations, for example, Boime (1981) and Curtis (1992). Critical of the idle, rich and poor, it lauds the manual labourer 'in the pride of manly health and beauty' (*An Exhibition of Work*), while acknowledging the influence of intellectual work. A perceptive critic of the day noted that the fantastic elaboration of the painting itself 'may be admitted as one accepted example of the dignity of labour' (*The Builder*, 18 March 1865). Brown failed to persuade the dealer Ernest Gambart to commission an engraving of *Work*, preventing the hoped-for spreading of its gospel into homes and institutions across the country.

Brown was never financially successful, but in the late 1850s he found a number of patrons in the north of England. Thomas E. Plint, an evangelical stockbroker from Leeds, commissioned Brown to bring the canvas of *Work* to completion, demanding some changes in the composition, but died before it was finished. George Rae of Birkenhead, John Miller of Liverpool, and James Leathart, a Newcastle lead manufacturer, also commissioned and purchased works by Brown. In the late 1850s, angered by the refusal of some of his works and the poor hanging of others, Brown abandoned the Royal Academy and rebuffed Millais's offer to support his candidacy for associate membership. He continued, however, to exhibit in Liverpool, where he won £50 prizes in 1856 and 1858. Brown himself organized a Pre-Raphaelite exhibition at Russell Place in 1857, and his work featured in a similar show in New York, Philadelphia, and Boston that same year. Brown's enthusiasm for the art of William Hogarth—like himself, fiercely independent and committed to the representation of modern life—led directly to the founding in 1858 of the Hogarth Club. Intended as an alternative to the Royal Academy, it was an exhibiting forum where artists and patrons could meet informally. Key figures in the club were Rossetti and two young followers of his who first met Brown in 1856. They were William Morris, who immediately purchased Brown's *The Hayfield* (1855–6; Tate collection), and Edward Burne-Jones, for whom Brown was 'wisest and kindest of friends' (Watkinson and Newman, 115). The club began well, with a membership of thirty-eight in 1858, rising to eighty-eight in 1860. It attracted established academicians as well as aspirants such

as Frederic Leighton, but collapsed amid controversy in 1861.

Later career Brown's sudden resignation from the Hogarth Club, another example of his notable touchiness, came when the hanging committee refused to include his designs for furniture in the 1860 exhibition. Brown was foreshadowing the move towards greater integration of fine and decorative arts, which characterized the aesthetic movement of the later 1860s, pioneered by Morris. From 1855 to 1865 Brown lived at 13 Fortess Terrace in Kentish Town—the outlook is recorded in *Hampstead from my Window* (1857; Delaware Art Museum, Wilmington)—and designed new tables and chairs for his home. By the 1860s he had become an accomplished designer of both furniture and stained glass. A partner in Morris, Marshall, Faulkener & Co. from its foundation in 1861, Brown contributed many designs for production by the firm. Among them were the *Egyptian Chair* (1860s; V&A) and an impressively simple and workmanlike set of bedroom furniture, made for Morris himself, which, indebted to earlier work by Pugin, prefigured the arts and crafts style of the 1880s and 1890s. For the firm he made almost 130 subject and single-figure designs for stained glass, retaining copyright of the images for their reuse in paintings. Often, however, his vigorous designs presented insuperable technical problems for the glass makers. He transferred many of his designs from one medium to another: *King René's Honeymoon* began as a design for a painted wooden chest by J. P. Seddon (1861–2; V&A), but emerged also as a stained-glass window, and as a watercolour (1864; Tate collection). The dissolution of the firm in 1874 and its reconfiguration as Morris & Co. caused Brown to feel considerable bitterness, and he severed all connections with Morris for some time. In 1890 Brown contributed to the arts and crafts exhibition, where he was accorded some recognition as a pioneer, only to grumble at 'the risk of being mistaken for an upholsterer and decorator' (Bendiner, 79). He also designed elaborate carved and gilded picture frames for his works. Brown's explorations of another medium, wood-engraved book illustration, demonstrate similar flair: his designs for Dalziel's *Bible Gallery* (London, 1863–4) rival the celebrated contributions of Leighton and Millais. In 1865 Brown mounted an exhibition at 191 Piccadilly, intended as a retrospective of his career to date, with *Work* as the climax. He included furniture and designs as well as a substantial proportion of his major works, providing in the accompanying pamphlet an idiosyncratic *catalogue raisonné* which remains a keynote for the interpretation of his work. Press notices were favourable, notably William Michael Rossetti's eloquent response in *Fraser's Magazine*.

Despite their own lack of resources, Ford and Emma Brown constantly provided help to people less fortunate than themselves, even opening a soup kitchen during the hard winter of 1860. They repeatedly played host both to the exploitative D. G. Rossetti and to his ailing lover, and from 1860 his wife, Elizabeth Siddal. Domesticity was also disrupted by Emma's frequent—perhaps epileptic—fits and her alcoholism. Their beloved child Arthur, vividly portrayed in the foreground of *Work*, died in infancy in

1857. Both Brown's daughters, Lucy and Emma, became capable artists under his direction, and his pupil Albert Goodwin began a successful professional career. Further disruption was caused by Brown's passionate but evidently unconsummated desire for his student from 1864 to 1872, the Anglo-Greek painter Marie Spartali (later Stillman). The special destiny of Brown's elder boy, Oliver Madox *Brown (1855–1874), was already marked out in the regal, Holbeinesque portrait *The English Boy* (1860; Manchester City Galleries). Nurturing the talents of Nolly, as he was known, became a major preoccupation of Brown in the later 1860s. Oliver's juvenile precocity in drawing and poetry, some of it published during his short lifetime, convinced Brown that his son was a 'perfect genius' (Hueffer, 238). Oliver's work was exhibited, alongside that of his two sisters, at the Dudley Gallery as early as 1869.

The years about 1870 found Brown for once relatively prosperous and content; his house at Fitzroy Square became the centre of a talented literary and artistic circle. In 1872–3 he was confident enough to apply, albeit unsuccessfully, for the Slade professorship at Cambridge, claiming that a practising artist, rather than a connoisseur, should hold this post. In 1874, the year in which Brown's daughter Lucy was married to William Michael Rossetti, Oliver died of blood poisoning. This was undoubtedly the greatest catastrophe of Brown's life: he became a virtual recluse and maintained 'Nolly's room', a shrine containing the boy's books and papers, in each subsequent house he lived in. The wide circle of friends, which had made gatherings at Fitzroy Square glittering occasions, diminished, and once again the spectre of financial hardship haunted the artist. In 1877 Brown painted a self-portrait (Harvard U., Fogg Art Museum) showing his characteristic flowing beard and greying hair parted in the centre: despite the golden lustre of the decorative leather screen which forms the background, the artist's physiognomy speaks of melancholy and resignation.

In his later work Brown abandoned the heightened realism of the 1850s for more dramatic effects; contemporaries noted a certain grotesqueness attaching to his figure compositions. *The Death of Sir Tristram* (1864; Birmingham City Art Gallery), originally designed for a stained-glass panel in 1862, features attenuated figures with grimacing features, though the ingenious geometry of the composition allows for a striking display of medieval fabrics. Typical of the emotionalism of this later work is the watercolour *The Entombment* (1870–71; National Gallery of Victoria, Melbourne), richly coloured and marked by a swooping, decorative sense of line. *Don Juan Found by Haidée* (1870–73; Birmingham Museums and Art Gallery) exhibits a new sensuousness and perhaps a wish to emulate painters of the nude such as Leighton. However, *Cromwell on his Farm* (Lady Lever Art Gallery, Port Sunlight), completed in 1874 on the basis of a drawing dating back to 1853, presents a Carlylean image of the puritan, Bible in hand, preoccupied with his higher destiny and ignoring the chaos of everyday life. Teeming with Hogarthian details, this work reverts to both the style and the concerns of the 1850s.

The Manchester painter Frederic Shields and the collector Charles Rowley were largely responsible for gaining Brown the major public commission which had eluded him hitherto. In 1878 he was asked to provide wall paintings for the great hall of Alfred Waterhouse's Gothic town hall in Manchester. The subjects, drawn from the history of Manchester, were selected by a committee (although Brown's own suggestions—such as the politically charged *Peterloo Massacre, 1819*—were rejected). Anxious to avoid the technical flaws which had plagued the earlier Westminster frescoes, Brown visited Antwerp in 1875 and 1877 to examine Baron Leys's celebrated works in the medium. For the first seven of the twelve panels he used Thomas Gambier-Parry's spirit fresco technique, but the final five were painted in oils on canvas in the studio, then attached to the wall. Exaggerated posture and gesture characterize this triumphantly inventive though somewhat uneven series of compositions. For much of the period from 1879 to 1887 Brown lived in Manchester, where, in addition to work on the frescoes, his interest in social issues grew. Horrified by the suffering caused by unemployment, he formed a labour bureau in 1886. In addition he employed Joe Waddington, an out-of-work joiner, who made up Brown's design for a workman's chest of drawers, exhibited at the Manchester Jubilee Exhibition of 1887, on the stand of the architect and social reformer Arthur Mackmurdo. Brown also made designs for the massive images of labouring figures which adorned the exhibition building.

Final years and death On his return to London in 1887 Brown rented 1 St Edmund's Terrace, Primrose Hill, which with Mackmurdo he decorated in the latest aesthetic style. Here, in declining health, he painted the last three of the Manchester wall paintings, completing *Bradshaw's Defence of Manchester* (1893; Manchester town hall) just before he died. His granddaughter recalled Brown at work in his last years as an imposing but genial figure with long silver hair parted in the centre, pince-nez, and a blue cloth tam-o'-shanter. The death of his wife on 11 October 1890 troubled him greatly. Brown himself died at his home of podagra (gout) on 6 October 1893 and was buried at St Pancras and Islington cemetery, East Finchley, on 11 October. His obituarists were polite rather than enthusiastic in their appreciation of his *œuvre*. A memoir by his grandson Ford Madox Hueffer (later Ford Madox Ford), published in 1896, provides a loyal family portrait. A major retrospective exhibition in Liverpool in 1964 rescued his work from neglect; later, the Tate Gallery's revelatory exhibition 'The Pre-Raphaelites' of 1984 rightly emphasized Brown's central contribution to that movement. Recent critical opinion has discerned in Brown a painter and designer of the highest originality, who ranks among the most significant of British artists.   TIM BARRINGER

Sources F. M. Hueffer, *Ford Madox Brown: a record of his life and works* (1896) • T. Newman and R. Watkinson, *Ford Madox Brown and the Pre-Raphaelite circle* (1991) • *The diary of Ford Madox Brown*, ed. V. Surtees (New Haven, 1981) • M. Bennett, *Ford Madox Brown, 1821–1893* (1964) [exhibition catalogue, Walker Art Gallery, Liverpool, full catalogue entries for large no. of works] • L. Parris, ed., *The Pre-*

Raphaelites (1984) [exhibition catalogue, Tate Gallery, London, catalogue entries for major works] · K. Bendiner, *The art of Ford Madox Brown* (University Park, Pennsylvania, 1998) · A. Staley, *The Pre-Raphaelite landscape* (1973) · W. M. Rossetti, 'Ford Madox Brown's pictures', *Fraser's Magazine* (May 1865), 598–606 · W. M. Rossetti, 'Ford Madox Brown: characteristics', *Century Guild Hobby Horse*, 1 (1886), 48–54 · S. Colvin, 'English painters of the present day, VIII: Ford Madox Brown', *The Portfolio* (1870), 81–6 · F. M. Brown, 'On the mechanism of a historical picture', *The Germ*, 2 (1850), 70–73 · [F. M. Brown], *An exhibition of Work and other paintings by Ford Madox Brown at the Gallery, 191 Piccadilly (opposite Sackville Street)* (1865) [exhibition catalogue] · [F. M. Brown], *The Slade professorship: address to the very rev., the vice-chancellor of the University of Cambridge* (1872) · F. M. Brown, *Particulars relating to the Manchester town hall and description of the mural paintings in the great hall by Ford Madox Brown* [n.d., c.1893] · H. M. M. Rossetti, *Ford Madox Brown* (1901) [exhibition catalogue, Whitechapel Art Gallery, London, 1901] · E. M. Tait, 'The pioneer of art furniture: Madox Brown's furniture designs', *The Furnisher: A Journal of Eight Trades* (Oct 1900), 61–3 · A. Boime, 'Ford Madox Brown: meaning and mystification of work in the nineteenth century', *Arts Magazine*, 56 (1981), 116–25 · G. Curtis, 'Ford Madox Brown's *Work*: an iconographic analysis', *Art Bulletin*, 74/4 (1992), 623–36 · J. Treuherz, 'Ford Madox Brown and the Manchester murals', *Art and architecture in Victorian Manchester*, ed. J. H. G. Archer (1985), 162–207 · W. D. Paden, 'The ancestry and families of Ford Madox Brown', *Bulletin of the John Rylands Library of Manchester*, 50 (1967–8), 124–35 · L. Rabin, *Ford Madox Brown and the Pre-Raphaelite history picture* (1978) · J. Soskice, *Chapters from childhood: reminiscences of an artist's granddaughter* (1921) · W. E. Fredeman, *Pre-Raphaelitism: a bibliocritical study* (Cambridge, Massachusetts, 1965) [with full bibliography of works up to 1965] · m. cert. [Elisabeth Bromley] · m. cert. [Emma Hill] · d. cert. · *IGI* [Matilda Hill]

Archives AM Oxf., diaries · Hunt. L., corresp. · Morgan L., diary · Princeton University, New Jersey, papers · V&A NAL, papers | BL, corresp. with T. G. Hake, Add. MS 49469, *passim* · Bodl. Oxf., letters to John Payne · Bodl. Oxf., letters to Dante Gabriel Rossetti · Bodl. Oxf., letters to Charles Rowley · Bodl. Oxf., letters to F. G. Stephens · JRL, letters to M. H. Spielmann · U. Leeds, Brotherton L., letters to Watts-Duncan · University of British Columbia Library, letters to James Leathart

Likenesses F. M. Brown, self-portrait, pencil and chalk, 1850, Birmingham Museums and Art Gallery · D. G. Rossetti, pencil drawing, 1852, NPG · D. G. Rossetti, pencil drawing, 1852, NPG, V&A · F. M. Brown, self-portrait, 1852–5, Birmingham Museums and Art Gallery · photograph, 1860–69, Westminster Central Library; repro. in Watkinson and Newman, *Ford Madox Brown*, pl. 136 · F. M. Brown, self-portrait, oils, 1877, Fogg Art Museum, Cambridge, Massachusetts [*see illus.*] · W. Hodgson, pencil and watercolour sketch, 1892, NPG · W. & D. Downey, carte-de-visite, NPG · C. Dressler, plaster bust, Man. City Gall. · Elliott & Fry, carte-de-visite, NPG · J. M. Johnstone, woodcut (aged fifty-five; after F. M. Brown), BM · F. J. Shields, chalk drawing (after drawing of death mask), Man. City Gall.

Wealth at death £2943 7s. 8d.: probate, Oct 1894, *CGPLA Eng. & Wales*

Brown, Francis Charles Claypon Yeats- (1886–1944), soldier and author, was born on 15 August 1886 in Genoa, Italy, the third son of Montagu Yeats-Brown (1834–1921), who was British consul-general in Genoa, and his wife, Agnes Matilda, *née* Bellingham. He was educated at Harrow School and the Royal Military College, Sandhurst. In 1904 he joined the King's Royal Rifle Corps and was posted in 1906 to Bareilly, India, as a second lieutenant. In 1906 he was gazetted to the Bengal lancers and stationed in Bannu in the North-West Frontier Province. While he enjoyed the danger of skirmishes with the tribesmen and the camaraderie of regimental life, he was fascinated by India

itself. He saw it as 'avid for life and colour and gaiety, yet preserving always a sense of a world unseen' (Yeats-Brown, *Indian Pageant*, 290), and he began a search for teachers who could give him an understanding of Hinduism's spiritual practices and beliefs.

In 1907 Yeats-Brown was posted to the 17th cavalry of the Indian army and made adjutant in 1913. He went on leave to England in 1914, joined the 5th Royal Irish Lancers, and served for six months in France before being sent to Mesopotamia, where he was transferred to the Royal Flying Corps with the rank of captain. He was captured by the Turks in 1915 near Baghdad, and after a number of attempts to escape, one time disguising himself as a woman, he finally got away in 1918. His first book, *Caught by the Turks* (1919) was a light-hearted, but graphic, account of the miseries of Turkish prisons. Surrounded by 'dirt and drunkenness, savagery and stupidity', he used yogic practice to become 'poised and relaxed and completely in my body' (Yeats-Brown, *Bengal Lancer*, 197–9). Awarded the DFC, he returned to India as a major, and retired from the army in 1924.

From 1925 to 1928, Yeats-Brown was assistant editor of *The Spectator*, but what brought him literary fame was the publication in 1930 of *Bengal Lancer*, which went through many editions in both Great Britain and the United States, and won the James Tait Black memorial prize. Much of the book consists of episodes and anecdotes about Yeats-Brown's life in the Bengal lancers, interspersed with colourful descriptions of the author's travels throughout India. What attracted many readers, however, was the quality that led Rabindranath Tagore to describe it as unmatched as 'a genuine psychological record of an intimate touch of a western mind with the mind of the east' (*Book Review Digest*, 1930, 1153). Some reviewers, however, while praising his accounts of army life and the Indian scene, were displeased with what seemed fulsome praise of Indian spirituality: 'if the triumph of man's spiritual achievement be the perception that all is one, that god and man are confounded in a cosmic process, to some this will seem a dismal triumph' (*TLS*). The Hollywood film company Paramount bought the rights to the book before it was published; but the very popular film that was made (in 1935), using the book's American title *The Lives of a Bengal Lancer*, with such famous actors as Gary Cooper and C. Aubrey Smith, was not really based on the book. The success of the book led Yeats-Brown to revise *Caught by the Turks*, with new background on the last decade of Ottoman rule; he published it in 1932 as *Golden Horn* and in the United States as *Bloody Years*. In 1934 he turned his attention to the issue of Britain's military preparedness. Angered by the success of Beverly Nichols's pacifist book, *Cry Havoc!* (1933), which he felt showed the failure of the British to see the dangers of pacifism, he wrote a reply called *The Dogs of War!* in 1934. Some of its themes were expanded in *European Jungle* in 1939 but its antisemitism, coupled with arguments in support of Hitler and Mussolini, brought deserved criticism from reviewers in both Britain and the United States.

Yeats-Brown continued to explore Indian themes in *Lancer at Large*, published in 1937, which covered much of the same ground as *Bengal Lancer*. But his comments on Indian politics show little awareness of the forces that were to challenge his belief that British rule would continue in India. In the same year he published *Yoga Explained*, one of the earliest attempts to popularize yoga in the West as beneficial to both physical and spiritual health. It has pictures of him standing on his head and in other yogic poses. He lectured in Europe and the United States on India, yoga, and religion.

Yeats-Brown remained single until 1938 when he married Olga, widow of Denzil Phillips, and daughter of Colonel Apollon Zoueff. During and after the Second World War, he collaborated with E. W. Sheppard in compiling five volumes with texts and pictures on the record of the British army from 1939 to 1942 (published 1943–7). He continued to write on India, and *Indian Pageant*, published in 1942, emphasizes the splendour of India's spiritual and intellectual achievements. He appeared on BBC radio programmes on Indian themes, notably a series in 1941 called *Gods, Saints, and Heroes of Hindustan*. *Martial India* (1945), his last book, published posthumously, is an affectionate picture of the Indian army, but has little historical depth. While generally well reviewed none of those books on India achieved the popularity of *Bengal Lancer*.

Yeats-Brown died of heart failure at 38 Cheriston Gardens, Kensington, London, on 19 December 1944, his wife surviving him. His funeral was at Golders Green crematorium on 23 December, and a memorial service was held at Grosvenor Chapel on 28 December, where he was praised for his patriotism, courage, and love of India. While his reputation was diminished by his political views, his books remain very readable and provide interesting insights into British attitudes between the two world wars.   AINSLIE T. EMBREE

Sources F. Yeats-Brown, *Bengal lancer* (1930) · F. Yeats-Brown, *Caught by the Turks* (1919) · F. Yeats-Brown, *Lancer at large* (1936) · F. Yeats-Brown, *Yoga explained* (1937) · D. Bank and others, eds., *British biographical archive* (1984–98) [microfiche; with index, 2nd edn, 1998] · WW [CD-ROM] · *India List, and India Office List* (1906); *India Office List* (1907–24) · *Book review digest* (New York, 1920–45) · *TLS* (24 July 1930), 604 · S. A. Moseley, *Who's who in broadcasting* (1933) · *The Times* (20 Dec 1944), 7; (23 Dec 1944), 7; (28 Dec 1944), 6 · F. Yeats-Brown, *Indian pageant* (1942) · d. cert.
Likenesses portraits, repro. in F. Yeats-Brown, *Golden Horn* (1932) · portraits, repro. in Yeats-Brown, *Yoga explained*

Brown, Frederick (1851–1941), university professor, was born at Chelmsford on 14 March 1851, the third child and second son of the seven children of William Brown, an artist who did armorial painting on carriages and taught drawing, and his wife, Susan Brewster. He was educated at King Edward VI Grammar School, Chelmsford, and in 1868 entered the National Art Training School (later the Royal College of Art), South Kensington, to study design. He was critical of the teaching methods at South Kensington and the Royal Academy, where drawing was taught by copying casts of ancient sculptures, but he spent eight years there, before the appointment of Edward Poynter as director in 1875 improved the situation. Both Alphonse

Legros, the new head of etching, and Frank Moody, the new head of the design school, were important influences on Brown.

In 1877 Brown was appointed head of the Westminster School of Art, at that time an evening class for working men, held at the Royal Architectural Museum in Tufton Street. After spending the winter of 1883–4 studying in Paris, Brown began to reform the teaching of art, and by the end of the 1880s the Westminster School of Art was regarded as the most progressive art school in London. Among his pupils were Aubrey Beardsley and Henry Tonks.

In 1892 Brown succeeded Legros as Slade professor of fine art at University College, London. Continuing the teaching and liberal outlook of Poynter and Legros, he built up the school of drawing, and tried to develop the individuality of his pupils, while encouraging them to study form by means of an analytical rather than an imitative approach to draughtsmanship, returning to the methods of masters such as Ingres. He attracted a strong teaching staff, establishing the principle that all teachers should be practising artists, and his earliest appointments included Henry Tonks, who became his assistant in 1894, and his close friend Philip Wilson Steer, with whom he spent every summer holiday from 1888 to 1909 landscape painting in Yorkshire. Later appointments included Walter Russell, Ambrose McEvoy, J. Havard Thomas, and Derwent Lees. A succession of brilliant artists, including Augustus John and William Orpen, trained at the Slade. Brown retired in 1917, although he continued to teach at the Slade until 1920, helping Tonks, his successor, in the early years of his professorship.

Brown was one of the founders of the New English Art Club in 1886, a group of British artists who had trained in Paris and felt their work was neglected by the Royal Academy. Early exhibitors included Wilson Steer, Sickert, and Whistler. Brown drew up the constitution, sat on all the committees and juries, and encouraged his Slade students to exhibit there. Although at first Brown himself painted popular pictures such as *Rural England* (exh. RA, 1885) and *Hard Times* (1886; Walker Art Gallery, Liverpool), and exhibited thirteen paintings at the Royal Academy between 1879 and 1891, by the 1890s his style had changed under the influence of the French impressionists and he became very opposed to the Royal Academy. Several of his paintings, including *The Storm* (1914), a self-portrait (1920), and *The Garden* (1937), are in the Tate collection. Brown died, unmarried, in the Royal Hospital, Richmond, Surrey, on 8 January 1941. He was cremated on 10 January at Mortlake crematorium.   ANNE PIMLOTT BAKER

Sources F. Brown, 'Recollections', *Artwork*, 6 (1930), 149–60, 269–78 · R. Schwabe, 'Three teachers: Brown, Tonks and Steer', *Burlington Magazine*, 82 (1943), 141–6 · D. S. MacColl, 'Professor Brown: teacher and painter', *Magazine of Art*, 17 (1893–4), 403–9 · D. S. MacColl, *Philip Wilson Steer* (1945) · J. Hone, *The life of Henry Tonks* (1939) · *The Times* (9 Jan 1941) · *The Times* (10 Jan 1941) · Graves, *RA exhibitors* · d. cert. · S. C. Hutchison, *The history of the Royal Academy, 1768–1986*, 2nd edn (1986) · S. Chaplin, *A Slade School of Fine Art archive reader: a compendium of documents, 1868–1975*, 1 (1998)

Archives Slade School of Fine Art, London, archives, MSS | RA, letters to George Clausen · U. Glas. L., letters to D. S. MacColl
Likenesses A. Beardsley, pencil-and-ink drawing, c.1892, Tate collection · P. W. Steer, chalk drawing, 1894, NPG · C. G. Beresford, photograph, 1904, NPG · F. Brown, self-portrait, 1911, UCL · F. Brown, self-portrait, 1920, Tate collection; repro. in *Artwork*, 150 · F. Brown, self-portrait, 1926, Ferens Art Gallery, Kingston upon Hull · F. Brown, self-portrait, 1932, Tate collection · C. G. Beresford, sepia print, NPG · D. G. Maclaren, group portrait, watercolour (*Some members of the New English Art Club*), NPG · W. Orpen, group portrait, oils (*The selecting jury of the New English Art Club, 1909*), NPG · W. Sickert, drawing, repro. in *Magazine of Art*, 403 · E. Walker, oils, Bradford City Art Gallery · photogravure (after portrait), NPG
Wealth at death £19,539 16s. 1d.: probate, 10 March 1941, *CGPLA Eng. & Wales*

Brown, Frederick Richard (1910–1991), cricketer, was born at Lima, Peru, on 16 December 1910, the son of Roger Grounds Brown, who had strong business interests in South America, and his wife, Inez Anita Milne. He attended St Peter's preparatory school, Vina del Mar, Valparaiso, until the age of ten, when he was brought to Britain. He was coached at St Piran's School, Maidenhead, by the famous South African G. A. Faulkner, founder of the first indoor cricket school. At the Leys School, Cambridge, already able to bowl the googly, he was brought on by N. J. Holloway and the Nottinghamshire professional Albert Iremonger. After four years in the eleven, two as captain, he emerged a ready-made all-rounder, tall, broad-chested, and powerful, a formidable striker of the ball and a strong wrist spinner.

As a Cambridge freshman (1930) Brown headed the bowling averages; in the next season he headed the batting and at the age of twenty won his first England caps against New Zealand. In 1931, after two years reading economics, he went down from St John's College, Cambridge, to take up a position in a firm of Lloyd's insurance brokers, which allowed him to continue to play cricket. In 1932 with Surrey he did the double of 1000 runs (1135) and 100 wickets (120), nearly all on the perfect Oval pitches. He also played one of the most memorable innings in county history, 168 in 2 hours 10 minutes against Kent at Blackheath. Then, with seven sixes in an innings of 212 lasting 3 hours 20 minutes, he lambasted Middlesex at the Oval.

Brown was a natural choice to tour Australia in 1932–3, though his brand of cricket formed no part of the bodyline scheme of his captain, D. R. Jardine. In the remaining pre-war years he alternated between county and club cricket to the benefit of both. Commissioned into the Royal Army Service Corps in 1939, he was taken prisoner at Tobruk in June 1942 and lost 4 stone in captivity at Chieti, Italy. On his return to Britain he married, on 9 June 1945, Marjorie Elizabeth Palmer (b. 1910), the daughter of Ernest Cecil Nottage Palmer, deputy chairman of Huntley and Palmers, biscuit manufacturers. They had three sons and one daughter. Business claims, meanwhile, seemed to have put a finish to a career of rich promise, largely unfulfilled.

However, in 1949 came an opportunity which combined a profitable job with the leadership of Northamptonshire, a county apparently destined to be permanent holders of the wooden spoon. Brown not only transformed them, 'doing the double' in that season as he had done for Surrey seventeen years before, but was chosen again for England, and as a result of an admirable 122 out of 131 in under two hours for Gentlemen against Players at Lord's the following year was chosen to take MCC to Australia in 1950–51.

Though England were beaten in the rubber, as in the two previous ones, Brown's all-round cricket and cheerful personality greatly endeared him to the Australian public. After four defeats England won the fifth test, the captain, bowling now chiefly at medium pace, taking in the match eight for 81. In 1951 he led England to a 3–1 victory over South Africa, and became a selector. Nor was that the swansong. In June 1953 his fellow selectors persuaded him to turn out once more against Australia, and in a highly dramatic drawn match at Lord's he played a full part with 50 runs and in 52 overs six wickets. After a gallant stand of 163 for the fifth wicket in the England second innings between Watson and Bailey, when Australia seemed to be coasting to victory, Brown added 28 to enable England to hold the fort.

Brown's qualities, surprising to say, did not adapt happily to the managership of overseas tours, when he took MCC sides to South Africa (1956–7) and Australia (1958–9). Press relations, amiable enough during his captaincy, were never cordial afterwards. Still to come, however, was long service in the governance of cricket, as chairman of selectors, president of MCC (1971–2), chairman of the Cricket Council, and first chairman and then president of the National Cricket Association (1974–90), where he was active in the encouragement of youth cricket. In the transfer between the loose control of the game by MCC and the more democratic structures dating from 1968 he played a leading part. For a few years he was in his element as a BBC commentator. He was raised from MBE to CBE in 1980. Brown died at his home, 13 Isles Court, Ramsbury, Marlborough, Wiltshire, on 24 July 1991.   E. W. SWANTON

Sources *The Times* (25 July 1991) · D. Hodgson, *The Independent* (26 July 1991) · *Daily Telegraph* (25 July 1991) · F. R. Brown, *Cricket musketeer* (1954) · 'Cricketers of the year', *Wisden* (1933) · *Wisden* (1992) · J. Fingleton, *Brown and company* (1951) · E. W. Swanton, *Elusive victory* (1951) · St John Cam. · m. cert. · d. cert.
Archives FILM BFI NFTVA, sports footage
Likenesses D. Glass, photograph, repro. in Brown, *Cricket musketeer*, frontispiece · photograph, repro. in *The Times* · photographs, repro. in Brown, *Cricket musketeer*
Wealth at death approx. £125,000: administration with will, 12 Sept 1991, *CGPLA Eng. & Wales*

Brown, George [*name in religion* Gregory] (d. 1618), prior of St Laurence, Dieulouard, was born in Essex and educated for two years (1602–4) at the English College, Douai, which he left to join the Benedictines in Spain. He was professed at the abbey of Santa Maria, Obarnes, in 1605, and took the name Gregory in religion. He was prior of the English monastery of St Laurence at Dieulouard in Lorraine from 1609 to 1610. He was 'a diligent promoter' of the developing English Benedictine residencies in France and the Low Countries (Allanson, 1.18). The translation of the *Life of St Mary Magdalen de 'Pazzi* (1619), dedicated to Lady Mary Percy, abbess of the English Benedictine monastery at

Brussels, was attributed to Brown by George Oliver on a mistaken inference from the Brussels convent chronicle that Brown was chaplain at Brussels. Tobie Matthew seems a more likely translator (Allison and Rogers, 2.106–7). Brown died on 21 October 1618 at the French Benedictine convent of nuns at Chelles, near Paris, where he had been since 1613. DOMINIC AIDAN BELLENGER

Sources A. Allanson, 'Biography of the English Benedictines', 1850, Downside Abbey [2 vols.], vol. 1 • A. F. Allison and D. M. Rogers, eds., *The contemporary printed literature of the English Counter-Reformation between 1558 and 1640*, 1 (1989) • D. Lunn, *The English Benedictines, 1540–1688* (1980) • Y. Chaussy, *Les bénédictins anglais réfugiés en France au XVIIᵉ siècle (1611–1669)* (Paris, 1967) • DNB

Brown, George (*c*.1650–1730), arithmetician and minister of religion, may be identifiable with the George Brown who attended the University of Aberdeen from 1664, graduating MA in 1668. He married Elspeth Anderson in Edinburgh on 13 January 1674, when he was described as a mathematician. Some time between 1682 and 1684 he became minister at Stranraer, and in 1685 he was appointed to Kilmaurs in Ayrshire, where covenanters were particularly active. When the revolution of 1688 replaced episcopacy with presbyterianism, he was forcibly ejected from the parish, returning to Edinburgh in 1689 with his wife and family. In 1692, refusing to pray publicly for William and Mary as monarchs, he was banished from Edinburgh. Some of the following years were spent at Stirling, where he taught mathematics. He returned to Edinburgh in 1698. His wife died some time after that, and in or before 1705 Katherine Livingstone, widow of Archibald Menzies of Culdares, became his second wife.

While at Stirling (*c*.1697) Brown invented the 'rotula arithmetica', an instrument 'to teach those of very ordinary capacity who can but read figures, to Add, Subtract, multiply and divide … tho' they are not otherways able readily to condescend whether seven and four be eleven or twelve'. The device was also

> useful, if not necessary for the ablest accomptants. There being nothing yet found comparable to it, not only for dispatch and certainty, but for freeing the mind from all that rack of intortion to which it is obliged in long additions. (NA Scot., PC.1. 1 Dec 1698)

A Scottish patent was granted for this device. It was mechanically cumbersome and arithmetically naïve, useful as an initial teaching aid, but of little assistance to the numerate. In his *Account of the Rotula Arithmetica* (1700), Brown sought to increase the usefulness of his machine by applying it to the calculation of decimals, especially the conversion of sums of money into decimal quantities. To assist this he had engraved (1700) a decimal ready reckoner, *A specie book, … to turne any pure number … of pieces of silver current in this kingdom to pounds Scots or sterling*, and a table (1701) for use at the Edinburgh mint giving the decimal value 'pr grain, drop, ounce, pound and stone weight of Bullion'. He also published *A Compendious, but a Compleat System of Decimal Arithmetick* (1701). Although the rotula had limited impact, subsequent writers acknowledged a debt to the *Decimal Arithmetick*, which advocated the use of decimals in practical arithmetic.

By *c*.1712 Brown had acted on an earlier intention 'to goe for London and try his fortune there' (BL, Sloane MS 4037, fol. 175). Here he published by subscription a decimal ready reckoner entitled *Arithmetica infinita* (1718), in which he gave decimal equivalents for sums of money from 1 farthing to 19*s*. 11¾*d*., proceeding in farthing steps, and giving decimals of a pound to seven places. This work replaced his earlier *Specie book*, of which the only recorded extant copy is held by the National Museums of Scotland. In a letter published in the second and third impressions of the book (1718), John Keill commended *Arithmetica infinita*, the tables being 'exceedingly advantageous to all Shop-keepers and Traders'. Augustus De Morgan wrote 'it will certainly be re-printed as soon as decimals of the pound gain their proper footing' (De Morgan, 65). However, Brown's emphasis on decimals was before its time. Arithmetical operations as such were simplified, but decimal fractions were too much of an abstraction. Users preferred to undertake arithmetical operations with familiar aliquot parts, fractions that represented the physical coins, weights, and measures in daily use. Brown died, probably in London, on 11 February 1630.

D. J. BRYDEN

Sources D. J. Bryden, 'George Brown, author of the rotula', *Annals of Science*, 28 (1972), 1–29 • A. De Morgan, *Arithmetical books from the invention of printing to the present time* (1847) • NA Scot., PC.1.51, 1 Dec 1698 • *The historical register*, 15 (1730), 11 Feb 1730 • H. Paton, ed., *The register of marriages for the parish of Edinburgh, 1595–1700*, Scottish RS, old ser., 27 (1905)
Archives National Museums of Scotland, Edinburgh • Sci. Mus. • Tankerness House Museum, Kirkwall, Orkney
Likenesses G. Vertue, line engraving (after drawing by E. Wright), BM, NPG; repro. in G. Brown, *Arithmetica infinita*, 2nd impression (1718)

Brown, Sir George (1790–1865), army officer, third son of George Brown, provost of Elgin, and his wife, the daughter of Lord Provost Clark of Aberdeen, was born at Linkwood, near Elgin, on 3 July 1790, into a family with 'many military heroes since the days of James I' (Ryan, 58). Brown's brothers were Peter and James (1797–1812), the latter an artillery officer, and he had two sisters: one the wife of a Mr Innes and the other, Mary, married to Lieutenant-Colonel Patrick Stuart.

Early years Brown attended Elgin Academy, but in 1803 his uncle, Lieutenant-Colonel (later Major-General) John Brown (*d*. 1816), suggested placing him at the military college where he would obtain a fine education for £90 per annum. Possibly he attended the junior department of the Royal Military College, Marlow. Through his uncle's influence he became an ensign without purchase on 23 January 1806 in the 43rd light infantry, part of the force centred on Shorncliffe to deter a French invasion. Having advanced to lieutenant on 18 September 1806, he sailed with the regiment's 1st battalion on 1 August 1807 in the expedition to Denmark. Before re-embarking for England on 20 October Brown saw action in a skirmish at Kioge, near Copenhagen. After dining with his nephew as he prepared to sail with his regiment for the Peninsula in July 1808 Colonel John Brown assured his brother that his son George

Sir George Brown (1790–1865), by Roger Fenton, 1855

looked forward enthusiastically to the impending campaign and that he was highly regarded by his fellow officers.

Peninsula and America Lieutenant George Brown fought with the 2nd battalion of the 43rd at the battle of Vimeiro (21 August 1808). In October 1808, two months after the convention of Cintra had ended hostilities in Portugal, the battalion marched into Spain under Lieutenant-General Sir John Moore, leaving Brown behind in charge of 213 sick or wounded. He therefore escaped the traumatic retreat to Corunna, and his ad hoc company independently became part of the force led by Lieutenant-General Sir Arthur Wellesley (later Viscount Wellington), which advanced northwards from Lisbon in 1809. Brown took part in the crossing of the Douro River and capture of Oporto (12 May 1809), and during the battle of Talavera (27–28 July 1809) was wounded in both thighs as his company repelled an assault with bayonets. Shortly afterwards the 1st battalion of the 43rd arrived from England. Having recovered from his wounds, Brown fought with it in the action at Almeida (24 July 1810) which denied the enemy passage of a critical bridge over the Coa River, and the battle of Busaco (27 September 1810) before retirement into winter quarters behind the lines of Torres Vedras. In letters to his father Brown showed a firm grasp of strategy and tactics. From Aruda he praised the strength of the British defensive position and explained that with the main French army static before it, Portuguese militia were busily attacking its lines of communication.

When Wellington's army advanced to drive the French out of Portugal the following spring, Brown was engaged in skirmishes at Redinha (12 March 1811), Cazal Novo (14 March), and Foz d'Aronce (15 March), and the battles of Sabugal (3 April 1811) and Fuentes d'Oñoro (5 May 1811). He secured a captaincy in the 3rd garrison battalion on 20 June 1811, returned to England, and attended the senior department of the Royal Military College, High Wycombe, from 2 February 1812 until 12 January 1813. Meanwhile he had exchanged into the 85th foot (after 1821 light infantry) on 2 July 1812, heeding his uncle's advice to choose a regiment with one battalion. In May 1813, after travelling via Sweden with the duke of Cumberland, he commented from Stralsund on troop dispositions in northern Germany and the implications of Napoleon's triumph against Prussia and Russia at the battle of Bautzen. Two months later he once more found himself in the Peninsula and was soon engaged in the siege of San Sebastian (July–August 1813), where he distinguished himself on the night of 25–6 August during the capture of an important island redoubt. He took part in the battles of the Nivelle (10 November) and the Nive (9–13 December) and the siege of Bayonne (winter 1813–14). For his services during these years he was awarded the silver military general service medal with seven clasps for Vimeiro, Talavera, Busaco, Fuentes d'Oñoro, San Sebastian, the Nivelle, and the Nive. The Peninsular War over, Brown purchased a majority in the 85th on 26 May 1814, and the following month went with his new regiment in General Robert Ross's expedition to the east coast of the United States. At Bladensburg, close to Washington, on 24 August 1814 he was 'slightly wounded in the head and very severely in the left groin' (*Army List*). He did not, therefore, take part in the capture of Washington and was left in Bladensburg with other wounded when Ross's army re-embarked.

Command, marriage, and the Horse Guards Brown became a brevet lieutenant-colonel on 29 September 1814, according to his uncle a promotion thoroughly deserved and achieved entirely through his own merit. Major-General Brown believed that his nephew now had an excellent chance of rising to high rank. The influence of his uncle, the deputy quartermaster-general, seems likely to have brought him appointment as assistant quartermaster-general at the Horse Guards on 11 May 1815. Brown certainly remained in that post until 1819, but his military career from then until 1841 is obscure. He left the 85th by purchasing a half-pay lieutenant-colonelcy on 17 July 1823, before exchanging into the rifle brigade on 5 February 1824. According to the *Gentleman's Magazine*, while serving as assistant quartermaster-general in Malta in 1826 he married Maria Macdonell, third daughter of Hugh Macdonell, consul-general in Algiers. However, his obituary in *The Times* gave 1831 as the marriage year, and one regimental historian records that he conscientiously commanded the 2nd battalion, the rifle brigade, from 1824, never going anywhere 'without his Scotch terriers' (Bryant, 454). Brown was promoted colonel on 6 May 1831, simultaneously becoming aide-de-camp to the king; and he was to be retained as aide-de-camp to Queen Victoria on her accession in 1837. In 1831 he was made a KH, and on 19 July 1838 a CB. He may have been appointed assistant adjutant-general at the Horse Guards in 1828, and he undoubtedly did become deputy adjutant-general there with the rank of major-general on 23 November 1841.

Brown succeeded Lieutenant-General Sir John Macdonald as adjutant-general after the latter's death on 8 April 1850. J. H. Stocqueler, in his study of the Horse Guards, condemned Brown for his inflexibility and rudeness: 'Brusque in his manner to applicants for small favours, almost boorish in his rebukes, and obstinately wedded to Regulations' (Stocqueler, 207). Brown allegedly terrorized or humiliated both junior and senior officers. He also 'derided' proposals to change equipment, like the knapsack and smooth-bore musket. 'Useful as a deputy adjutant-general, general Brown was quite beyond himself in a more responsible position' (ibid., 208), Stocqueler caustically concluded. There is ample evidence, though, that during Macdonald's last years much of his work devolved on Brown, and he therefore exercised considerable responsibility for the discipline and efficiency of the British army. Even Stocqueler acknowledged caring personal qualities. 'He [Brown] had a heart that could feel for misfortune and poverty, but did not allow his sympathies to extend to his military duties' (ibid., 207). Brown would no doubt have argued that private feelings should never influence professional judgement. In September 1852 FitzRoy Somerset (later Lord Raglan) reassured Brown that there was no 'organized conspiracy' against him (Sweetman, 161), after the third Earl Grey, former secretary of state for war and the colonies, had complained that he relayed the content of their conversation to the commander-in-chief. Similarly, the duke of Cambridge objected to correspondence between them being divulged. Brown was indeed sensitive to apparent slights and soon displayed unease that the more progressive Lord Hardinge had succeeded Wellington as commander-in-chief. On 24 January 1853 he submitted his resignation, which Somerset persuaded him to withdraw. The truce proved short-lived, and his renewed resignation took effect on 12 December. Meanwhile Brown had become colonel of the 77th foot on 11 April 1851, and lieutenant-general on 11 November 1851; he was appointed KCB on 7 April 1852 and attended Wellington's funeral at St Paul's Cathedral on 18 November 1852.

Crimean War In February 1854, when war with Russia appeared imminent, an expeditionary force to the eastern Mediterranean was mooted; Brown offered to serve under Raglan, its commander, and was appointed to lead the light division. Colonel Richard Airey, who had known Brown at the Horse Guards, turned down a staff appointment with Raglan to lead one of Brown's brigades. On 23 March Brown left England for Paris, where he met the commander of the allied French force, Marshal St Arnaud, thinking him 'a strange flighty fellow and one it will not do to take at his word' (Hibbert, 22), as Raglan would discover. Leaving Paris, Brown travelled overland to Marseille and by sea to Malta. At the head of the advance party, he was the first British general to reach the Gallipoli peninsula on 6 April. He found a French camp well established, making his task of preparing for the main force complicated by lack of provisions, water, and shelter.

Nevertheless, after Raglan visited him *en route* for Constantinople on 28 April, he reported Brown to be 'going famously' (Sweetman, 182), energetically tackling administrative shortcomings. Brown led the first regiments to reach Bulgaria in June 1854 and, before Raglan's arrival later that month, acted as local commander. Within the light division Brown gained the reputation of a martinet, insisting on 'pipe-claying, close-shaving and tight-stocking' (*DNB*) even in high temperatures to the disapproval of *The Times*'s correspondent W. H. Russell. Raglan's aide-de-camp, Captain Nigel Kingscote, thought him 'very unpopular' (Sweetman, 194), but the division was undoubtedly well disciplined and supplies of bread, for example, were 'excellent' (ibid., 205).

Opposition within the cabinet, based on Hardinge's advice, had prevented Brown from being appointed Raglan's second-in-command and, unknown to him, another divisional commander (Lieutenant-General Sir George Cathcart) had been given a dormant commission to take Raglan's place in an emergency. None the less the British commander constantly consulted Brown. Initially the allied armies gathered in Bulgaria to prevent a Russian advance through the Balkans to Constantinople. When the enemy retired north of the Danube and this danger receded, the British government ordered Raglan to capture the Crimean naval port of Sevastopol. Aware of inadequate intelligence about Russian strength on the Peninsula, Raglan asked Brown's opinion. Brown replied that they should think what 'the Great Duke' (Wellington) would have done under the circumstances, concluding that he would have obeyed the government. So preparations for the invasion went ahead. On 21 July 1854 Brown represented Raglan when an allied party reconnoitred the western Crimean coastline from HMS *Fury* and chose the mouth of the Kacha River, 7 miles north of Sevastopol, for the landing beach. Seven days later he attended a conference at which the French expressed doubts about attacking the Crimea so late in the year, and on his arrival in the theatre of war the veteran engineer Lieutenant-General Sir John Burgoyne dismissed the Kacha beach as too narrow, open, and close to Sevastopol. Thus on 9 September, when the allied armada was already at sea, Raglan personally undertook a second reconnaissance, accompanied by Brown, and selected Calamita Bay, 30 miles north of Sevastopol.

On 14 September 1854 Brown, aged sixty-four, was almost captured by Cossacks shortly after landing in possibly the first boat ashore. As the allied British, French, and Turkish armies marched south towards Sevastopol, Brown was present at the skirmish on the Bulganek Stream (19 September), and at the battle of the Alma River the following day. There the light division formed the extreme left of the allied line east of the village of Burlyuk and attacked over the river uphill against the Great Redoubt containing 12 cannon. Urging on his men, Brown had a horse shot from under him. Later he would criticize A. W. Kinglake for depicting him 'with plumes in my cocked hat and appalling the Russians by my sanctified appearance'. He never wore plumes in the Crimea, and 'as for the Russians, they showed their respect and consideration for me by hitting my horse in five places' (Thomas, 224). Major W. S. Norcott recorded Brown 'riding fearlessly at the head of the [rifle] brigade urging them on' (Bryant, 134). In his dispatch Raglan wrote: 'The mode in which Lieutenant-General Sir George Brown conducted his division, under the most trying circumstances, demands my warmest approbation' (Ryan, 60). Once the enemy had been defeated the allies continued their advance to skirt Sevastopol to the east and occupy southern upland, from which the Russian port could be besieged. Brown's able performance at the Alma prompted the rescinding of Cathcart's dormant commission on 13 October.

When strong Russian cavalry and infantry units threatened the British supply port of Balaklava on 25 October, Brown held his division in reserve on the upland, ready to combat a simultaneous sortie by the Sevastopol garrison. Stationed in the area of Victoria Ridge on 5 November, the light division was only slightly involved in the battle of Inkerman, when Russian troops did emerge along the adjacent Careenage Ravine. However, against another enemy concentration on the Inkerman heights further east Brown himself saw action, possibly leading French Zouaves after earlier that morning reputedly declining their assistance: 'Our reserves are sufficient to take care of all eventualities' (Hibbert, 168). He was shot through the arm and in the chest so seriously that he temporarily surrendered command of his division while refusing to leave the front. During the destructive hurricane of 14 November he showed considerable coolness and courage. Brown began a brief period as colonel of the 7th foot on 22 December 1854, and on 18 January 1855 he became colonel commandant of the 2nd battalion, the rifle brigade, which he had previously commanded. Having resumed command of his division, Brown attended allied councils of war on 4 and 6 March 1855 to determine future tactics, and on 15 March he received a worrying private communication from Lord Panmure, the secretary of state for war. Claiming that he did not want Raglan replaced, Panmure nevertheless held that the commander's 'lack of communication' (Sweetman, 292) in dispatches made it difficult for ministers in London to defend him. Presumably Panmure hoped that Brown would intercede with Raglan, but it was a strange letter from a minister who had once declared that 'he never knew a man [Brown] who so cordially hated all change' (Hibbert, 14).

Brown showed his compassion when writing to Raglan's elder daughter Charlotte about her father's health and incidentally revealing that he remained the commander's confidant. 'He [Raglan] tells me that they [worries] keep him from rest at night … Never was any poor man so unreasonably or unjustly assailed by calumny as he has been by those vile newspapers' (Sweetman, 294). On 14 and 15 April 1855 Brown once more represented Raglan at allied conferences. Concern had long been expressed about the ability of the Russians to bring supplies across the Peninsula from the Sea of Azov, whose entrance was dominated by the defences of Azov. On 3 May an Anglo-French force of 8500 men under Brown's

command sailed eastwards before the French contingent was recalled. Brown sensibly declined to press on with the remaining 3000 British troops in the light of estimates that between 9000 and 27,000 Russian troops lay ahead. The operation was remounted on 22 May, the allied numbers having been increased to 15,000 including Turks. Raglan declared the enterprise 'a complete success' (Sweetman, 307), but in truth Azov and nearby Yenikale were disgracefully pillaged after their capture. Mounting regular cavalry patrols, Brown tried in vain to prevent the outrages by ill-disciplined Turkish troops and local Tartars.

On 18 June 1855 a massive allied assault was planned on the eastern defences of Sevastopol, with the French attacking the Mamelon and Malakhov bastions on the right, the British the Great Redan on the left. Owing to a misunderstanding the French attacked prematurely and Brown, who was in overall charge of the British contingent, under orders from Raglan launched his three columns over open ground without a preliminary bombardment. The predictable outcome was heavy loss and failure, but Brown considered Raglan had no alternative. Three days later Brown was sick in his tent when Raglan visited him. 'This was the last intercourse with my dear friend and much respected commander', Brown recalled (Sweetman, 317). Precisely one week later Raglan died and on that same day a medical board invalided Brown home. He was appointed GCB on 5 July and promoted general on 7 September 1855, subsequently receiving the Turkish order of the Mejidiye (first class) and grand cross (first class) of the French Légion d'honneur. When Raglan was buried at Badminton, on 28 July, Brown was a pall-bearer.

Later years On 1 April 1860 Brown was appointed general commanding the troops and a member of the privy council in Ireland. He became colonel of the 32nd foot on 1 April 1863, and seventeen days later colonel-in-chief of the rifle brigade. After resigning through ill-health he formally left the Irish command on 1 July 1865. He was a generous contributor to the Drummond Institute for soldiers' daughters. Brown resided at his brother's house at Linkwood, near Elgin, where he had been born, and there he died on 27 August 1865. Five veteran riflemen bore his coffin to the burial-ground of Elgin Cathedral on 31 August.

Brown left 'behind him a memory endeared by many acts of kindness, a name of unsullied honour, and a reputation of spotless integrity' (*The Times*). Clean-shaven, with thick white hair in later years, he had a slight stoop that belied his height of 5 feet 9 inches. In Bulgaria he was described as 'broad-shouldered, narrow-waisted … well mounted and well seated on a regulation height charger, with his handsome face well set in his stock' (*The Times*). George Ryan thought him 'a studious, careworn-looking man', quite unlike the 'fire eating soldier' seen in battle (Ryan, 58). He never lost his Scottish accent. Brown was survived by his wife, but no male heir. According to the *Gentleman's Magazine* obituary 'much of his roughness was merely assumed, under the idea of supporting discipline' (*GM*, 644), and according to the *Annual Register* 'Like many good-hearted men, he disliked his own good-nature, and covered it in with a cloak of asperity ... and created unfavourable impressions which a closer acquaintance would have removed' (*Annual Register*, 187).

JOHN SWEETMAN

Sources *Army List* · NRA, priv. coll., report 17577 · *The Times* (29 Aug 1865) · G. Ryan, *Our heroes of the Crimea* (1855) · *Annual Register* (1865) · E. H. Nolan, *The illustrated history of the war against Russia*, 2 vols. (1855–7) · *Dod's Peerage* (1858) · C. R. B. Barrett, ed., *The 85th king's light infantry* (1913) · *GM*, 3rd ser., 19 (1865), 643–4 · D. Thomas, *Cardigan: the hero of Balaclava* (1987) · C. Hibbert, *The destruction of Lord Raglan* [1961] · A. Bryant, *Jackets of green* (1972) · S. David, *The homicidal earl, the life of Lord Cardigan* (1997) · A. W. Kinglake, *The invasion of the Crimea*, [new edn], 9 vols. (1877–88), vols. 2–8 · R. G. A. Levinge, *Historical records of the forty-third regiment, Monmouthshire light infantry* (1868) · J. Sweetman, *Raglan: from the Peninsula to the Crimea* (1993) · J. H. Stocqueler, *A personal view of the horse guards, 1750–1872* (1873) · A. F. Mockler-Ferryman, *Regimental war tales, 1741–1919* (1942) · W. Cope, *The history of the rifle brigade* (1877) · DNB

Archives NL Scot., corresp. and papers · NRA Scotland, priv. coll., letters to his family · Royal Green Jackets Museum, Winchester, corresp. and papers | Bodl. Oxf., corresp. with Lord Kimberley · Bodl. Oxf., letters to Sir William Napier and Lady Caroline Napier · NAM, corresp. with Lord Raglan · NL Wales, letters to Louisa Lloyd · NL Wales, letters to William Lloyd · NRA Scotland, Leslie of Kininvie papers · U. Nott. L., corresp. with the duke of Newcastle · W. Sussex RO, letters to the duke of Richmond

Likenesses M. Alophe, lithograph, 1854 (*Les défenseurs du droit et de la liberté de l'Europe*), BM · R. Fenton, photograph, 1855, NPG [*see illus.*] · D. J. Pound, print, NPG · mezzotint, NPG · portrait, repro. in Barrett, ed., *The 85th king's light infantry*, facing p. 467

Wealth at death £20,532 18s. 8d.: confirmation, 3 Nov 1865, NA Scot., SC 26/39/9, 711–13

Brown, George (1818–1880), politician and journalist in Canada, was born at Alloa, Scotland, on 29 November 1818. His father, **Peter Brown** (1784–1863), also a journalist in Canada, born in Edinburgh on 29 June 1784, the son of James Brown, a builder and general commissioner of police, was originally a merchant. Following financial difficulties he emigrated in 1837 to New York, where in July 1842 he founded the *British Chronicle*, a weekly newspaper especially intended for Scottish emigrants. Free Kirk sympathizers in Canada encouraged the relocation of the *British Chronicle* to Toronto. This inducement, combined with the competition in New York of *The Albion*, which represented general British interests, led in 1843 to the removal of the Brown family to Toronto, where the newspaper was renamed *The Banner*. While in New York in 1842 Brown published, under the pseudonym Libertas, *The Fame and Glory of England Vindicated*, which was a reply to C. E. Lester's *The Glory and Shame of England* (1841). In 1813 he married Marianne (d. 1862), the only daughter of George Mackenzie of Stornoway on the island of Lewis in the Hebrides. They had two surviving sons and four daughters. He died in Toronto on 30 June 1863.

George, the third child and elder son, was educated in Edinburgh at the high school and at the Southern Academy. He accompanied his father to New York in 1837, where the rest of the family joined them in 1838. He became publisher and business manager of the *British Chronicle*. During the visit to Toronto which resulted in the *Chronicle* and Brown's family moving to that town, his ability attracted the attention of the leaders of the Reform

Party and of Free Kirk sympathizers in Canada. Brown was a strong supporter of the Free Kirk movement following the Great Disruption in the Presbyterian Church of Scotland in 1843. His deeply felt evangelical protestantism was a guiding light throughout his life, both in his personal and in his political behaviour.

In 1844 Brown founded *The Globe* to support the Reform Party. This political journal, originally published weekly, soon became one of the leading Canadian papers. In 1853 it began to be issued daily. During Brown's lifetime it was distinguished by its vigorous editorial style and its effective partisan stance on public issues.

In 1848 Brown was secretary of a commission to investigate alleged abuses in Kingston penitentiary and drafted the report which brought about substantial reforms in the prison system.

Brown strongly supported the Reform Party in its struggle with Sir Charles Theophilus Metcalfe (afterwards Baron Metcalfe) on the question of responsible government. In 1851, however, he severed himself from the party, which was then in power under the Baldwin–LaFontaine ministry. His main dispute with the party concerned state subsidies for religion, as he, like most evangelicals, firmly believed that churches should be supported voluntarily by their own members. He also robustly opposed state support for separate schools and was increasingly heated in his denunciation of the political influence of the Roman Catholic church, whose vigorous reorganization under Pope Pius IX was causing much concern in Britain and elsewhere. Opposition to Roman Catholicism also underlay Brown's condemnation of equal representation in the legislature of the predominantly French and Catholic Lower Canada with the overwhelmingly protestant and more rapidly growing Upper Canada.

In December 1851 Brown entered the Canadian legislative assembly as an independent Liberal for the county of Kent. In the legislature of the united province of Canada he worked with the 'Clear Grits', radical Reformers in Upper Canada whose newspaper *North American* he purchased in 1855. He differed from the Clear Grits in a number of respects, however, notably in his belief in the superiority of the British parliamentary model over that of the United States. He sought to unify the Reform movement of Upper Canada by focusing on the issue of French-Canadian and Catholic domination of the united province of Canada, and he urged the creation of a system of representation by population as a means of redressing the balance. In the election of 1854 he was returned for Lambton county and in 1857 for Toronto. He dominated the Reform convention of 1857 which united the various strands of the party with a platform of representation by population, non-sectarian education, free trade, and the annexation of the north-west, the vast territory beyond the Great Lakes.

On 31 July 1858, on the defeat of the government of John A. Macdonald and G. E. Cartier, Brown undertook to form a ministry. He succeeded in patching up a heterogeneous cabinet with A. A. Dorion, the leader of the Liberals of Lower Canada (*rouges*), but it held office for only a few days.

In 1859, having failed to persuade the assembly to adopt representation by population, Brown urged the Reform convention to adopt a federal union of the two Canadas as party policy. Some more moderate Reformers led by John Sandfield Macdonald were unconvinced, and in 1862 they formed an alliance with Dorion and the *rouges* committed to preserving the constitutional status quo. In 1861 Brown's health collapsed and he was defeated in the general election of that year.

On 27 November 1862, during a visit to Britain, Brown married, at Edinburgh, Anne (*d.* 1906), the eldest daughter of Thomas *Nelson and his wife, Margaret, of Abden House, Edinburgh [*see under* Nelson family]. They had several children. After returning to Canada, Brown was successful in a by-election in March 1863 and supported the Sandfield Macdonald–Dorion ministry in July of that year, when he was re-elected for South Oxford. The election left the Reformers and Conservatives almost equal, and Brown was appointed to chair a select committee to find a solution to the political deadlock. He recommended an immediate federal union of British North America or, if that proved impossible, a federal union of the two Canadas to which the other colonies might later be admitted. Brown's initiative proved critical in breaking the political deadlock and making possible a coalition in June 1864 between Brown and the majority of Upper Canada Reformers and the Conservatives led by John A. Macdonald and Cartier. Brown became president of the council in the 'Great Coalition' which was the driving force behind the confederation movement. He played a major role in the 1864 Quebec and Charlottetown conferences where a scheme of union was worked out between Canada and the maritime provinces. In 1864 and again the following year he travelled to London to get British support for the measure.

Brown was a member of the confederate council that sat in Quebec in September 1865 to negotiate commercial treaties, but he resigned office in December because he disapproved of the proposed terms for reciprocity with the United States. After the establishment of confederation in 1867 he failed to win a seat in the federal elections of that year.

Brown retired from public life and devoted himself to his family, *The Globe*, and his stock farm near Brantford, Ontario. *The Globe* remained the most important Liberal organ in Canada, and Brown was regularly consulted by both the Ontario Liberal Party and the federal Liberal opposition led by his former election agent, Alexander Mackenzie. In late 1873 Mackenzie came to power and appointed Brown to the senate. In 1874 Brown undertook a mission to the United States to negotiate a new reciprocity treaty. He was successful in this, but the treaty was never approved by the American senate. Thereafter Brown played a declining part in politics. In 1875 he refused the lieutenant-governorship of Ontario and in 1879 the offer of a knighthood (KCMG). On 25 March 1880 he was shot at the *Globe* office by George Bennett, a discharged employee, and died at his home, Lambton Lodge,

Beverley Street, Toronto, from the effects of the injury on 9 May. He was buried in the necropolis cemetery, Toronto, on 12 May. A. ST LEGER

Sources J. M. S. Careless, *Brown of The Globe*, 2 vols. (1959–63) · D. G. Creighton, *John A. Macdonald*, 2 vols. (Toronto, 1952–5) · W. L. Morton, *The critical years: the union of British North America, 1857–1873* (1964) · J. Lewis, *George Brown*, The Makers of Canada Series, 7 (1926) · D. C. Thomson, *Alexander Mackenzie: clear grit* (1960) · J. M. S. Careless, ed., *The pre-confederation premiers: Ontario government leaders, 1841–1867* (1980)
Archives NA Canada | NA Canada, John A. Macdonald MSS · Queen's University archives, Kingston, Ontario, Alexander Mackenzie MSS
Likenesses W. Brodie, statue, 1880, Toronto · Notman and Fraser, photograph, repro. in Careless, *Brown of the Globe*, vol. 1 · engraving, National Archives of Canada; repro. in *The Globe* · photograph, National Archives of Canada · photograph, Metropolitan Toronto Reference Library · wood-engraving (after photograph by Ellisson & Co.), NPG; repro. in *ILN* (12 Nov 1864)

Brown, George Alfred, Baron George-Brown (1914–1985), politician, was born on 2 September 1914 at Flat 22, I Block, Peabody Buildings, Duke Street, Lambeth, London, the elder son of the four children of George Brown, a grocer's packer who later worked as a driver, and his wife, Rosina (Rose) Harriett, née Mason. His paternal grandfather, John Brown, was a carter, while his maternal grandfather was an asphalter. For a career in Labour politics, George Brown had impeccable working-class credentials.

Making of a trade union organizer More than that, George Brown saw himself as having been born into and later married into the labour movement. His father had worked in a London dock warehouse and been a member of the Dock, Wharf and Riverside Workers' Union before becoming a car, van, and lorry driver, with his union forming part of the Transport and General Workers' Union (TGWU). After the First World War his father graduated from branch secretary to a member of the union's executive committee. The young George Brown experienced hard times after his father was sacked for actively supporting the general strike in 1926.

Brown grew up in a poor working-class community in Southwark. After his birth his parents had left the small flat which they shared with his grandmother Anne Mason in Lambeth for their own accommodation at another Peabody Trust block at Peabody Square, Blackfriars Road, Southwark, near Waterloo station. He attended Gray Street elementary school, then West Square central school, both close to his home. While still at elementary school he became a choirboy and a committed Christian, much influenced by Father John Sankey of the City of London church of St Andrew by the Wardrobe. He was a keen Labour Party supporter, even at school. He later claimed, probably accurately, to have leafleted for Labour in 1922. He left school at fifteen, but attended evening classes run by the London county council near by, near the Elephant and Castle, then Workers' Educational Association and National Council of Labour Colleges courses.

George Brown gained his first two jobs through an

George Alfred Brown, Baron George-Brown (1914–1985), by Paul Joyce, 1976

agency which helped promising boys from his and other similar schools. He spent a year as a clerk in a Cheapside merchant firm, then worked in retailing as a fur salesman for the John Lewis Partnership at its Oxford Street store. He worked there until he was twenty-two. He pursued his political interests by seeking a job in his father's trade union. He failed to secure a post as a trade union officer but instead returned to being a clerk in the TGWU ledger room. After two years he applied successfully to be a district organizer based in Watford, where he organized agricultural, brickyard, building, and other workers in the small towns of the area. With the coming of the Second World War he became involved in organizing within war industries, serving on industrial committees and trade boards and also on the war agricultural executive. He volunteered for the RAF but Ernest Bevin, the minister of labour, kept Brown and other trade union officials in their civilian jobs.

Labour party activist, MP, and minister Brown's main ambition lay in politics, not in trade unionism. While living in Streatham, at Mountearl Gardens, he was active in his local Labour Party. In 1932, at the nadir of the Labour Party's fortunes, he became vice-president of the Streatham constituency Labour Party and a member of the national advisory committee of the Labour league of youth. He also became an avid participant in Clarion events sponsored by Sir Stafford Cripps, and enjoyed spending weekends at conferences and schools at the Clarion youth hostel at Hoddesdon. It was through this group that at the age of eighteen he met his future wife,

Sophie Levene (1911–1990), like her father, a bookbinder. In marrying her, he married into a very committed Labour Party family: her father, Solomon Levene JP, was a founder member of the Mile End Labour Party and, with his wife, Kate, a lifelong Labour Party activist. They married at Stepney register office on 27 April 1937 and bought a house at 59 Lakeside Crescent, East Barnet, before moving during the war to Potters Bar. In Barnet he quickly became secretary of the St Albans divisional Labour Party, unsuccessfully stood for the East Barnet urban district council in 1938, and went as the constituency delegate to the Labour Party conference in 1939.

Brown's speech on 29 May 1939 at the Labour Party conference, supporting the expulsion of Sir Stafford Cripps from party membership, first established him as a tough spokesperson for the moderate wing of the Labour Party. In it he struck what were to be characteristic stances. He stated that his constituency party was 'entitled to some greater consideration … than the views of those centres of revolutionary activity in the centre of London which have been sending us such long-winded circulars on the subject'. As well as deploring the distraction Cripps caused from campaigning, he also denounced 'a small, noisy section of intellectuals and the middle class' in his own constituency for trying to tell others what to do. He ended with a call for Cripps and his associates to 'forget to be a leader for a little while and work as a rank and file member' (*Report of the 38th Annual Conference, 1939*, 235–6). This speech won the support of that year's party chairman, George Dallas, who had had a long career in the Workers' Union and was a former member of St Albans Labour Party. Dallas helped to secure Brown the nomination as prospective parliamentary candidate for Belper, Derbyshire, a seat with a Conservative majority of only 828 to overturn. Belper was one of several east midlands constituencies whose Labour Party was predominantly working class and loyal to the moderate leadership of the Labour Party. Brown, sponsored by the TGWU, was elected with a majority of 8881 in the general election of 1945, and held the seat until 1970. From 1945 until 1964 the Browns lived at 77 Court Lane, Dulwich, then in 1964 moved to 103 Portsea Hall, Marble Arch.

In parliament Brown almost immediately became parliamentary private secretary to George Isaacs, the minister of labour. He accompanied Isaacs to Canada and the USA for the annual meeting of the International Labour Organization, and met the big figures in American trade unionism. In 1947 he became parliamentary private secretary to Hugh Dalton, chancellor of the exchequer. While in this role Brown was a conspicuous plotter to replace Attlee as prime minister with Bevin, an activity deplored by Bevin. Attlee, nevertheless, appointed him undersecretary of state for agriculture, a post he held from 7 October 1947 until 26 April 1951. Brown then attained ministerial rank and membership of the privy council, but not membership of the cabinet, as minister of works, a post he held until the fall of the government in October 1951.

In opposition: champion of the Labour right However, now accustomed to a ministerial salary, Brown, faced with a great drop in income, seriously considered leaving parliament and returning to trade union work. He was kept in politics by a £500 a year (later £1250 a year) retainer from Cecil King to advise the *Daily Mirror*, then the biggest mass circulation newspaper.

Brown emerged from office as a combative anti-Bevanite. Shortly after the general election defeat Dalton reported in his diary that 'Brown thinks it ought to be war to the knife with the Bevanites' (Dalton, 567–8). George Brown actively organized opposition to Aneurin Bevan and the left-wingers loosely associated with him, the Bevanites. In March 1954 he secured a power base. Tony Benn wrote in his diary of this that 'After fifteen years of pleasant slumber the Trade Union Group [of Labour MPs] have been seized in a most unscrupulous *coup d'état*' and he described Brown as 'thrusting, ambitious, unscrupulous' (Benn, *Years of Hope*, 178). One of several south London working-class Labour MPs, Brown followed in the footsteps of Bevin, his former trade union boss, and Herbert Morrison, the leading south London Labour politician. He supported Herbert Morrison for a period, but Attlee's continued tenure of the leadership of the Labour Party led Brown by 1955 to become a supporter of Hugh Gaitskell. While Brown fitted in badly with many of Gaitskell's intellectual supporters (including the so-called 'Hampstead set'), with Gaitskell complaining in his diary on 9 November 1954 that Brown was 'a difficult person, and at times has an irritating chip on his shoulder' (*The Diary of Hugh Gaitskell, 1945–1956*, ed. P. M. Williams, 1983, 348), his abilities and his trade union credentials were welcome. Brown also reinforced his anti-left-wing credentials when, at a dinner in honour of the Soviet leaders Nikita Khrushchov and Marshal Bulganin in 1956, he objected to Khrushchov's critical comments on Britain's war efforts and condemned the Soviet pact with Ribbentrop, thereby causing a substantial row with the Russians.

This probably did no harm to Brown's attempt to succeed Hugh Gaitskell, the new party leader, as party treasurer. However, the hitherto reliable 'loyalist' trade union block vote was divided by an upsurge of support for Bevan in some trade unions and by the candidature of two other 'moderate' trade union-supported candidates. Most areas of the National Union of Miners backed Bevan, as did the railway workers' and shopworkers' unions. In October 1956 Bevan beat Brown by a small margin, 3,029,000 to 2,755,000 votes. Brown won the deputy leadership of the Labour Party in 1960, winning the support of most of the trade union group and also most of the Gaitskellites. In the first ballot he polled 118 to Fred Lee's 73 and James Callaghan's 55 votes; in the second round he gained 148 to Lee's 83.

This was a high-water mark for Brown within the party. In opposition he increasingly eased stress with alcohol. Ironically, given his ultra-sensitivity to middle-class intellectuals in the Labour Party, his heavy drinking was tolerated by Hugh Gaitskell and Harold Wilson; a contrast to some earlier working-class temperance figures such as Arthur Henderson, who had acted firmly against alcoholism in party officials. Even such supporters as Hugh Dalton were concerned by 1960 about his volatility: Dalton noted in his diary that Brown was the best candidate, even 'though very awkward, vain, sensitive and fundamentally self-seeking and unfaithful' (Dalton, 700). Nevertheless, Brown was respected for his sharp intellect, his position as the ablest trade union MP, and his considerable skills as a speaker in the House of Commons and on public platforms. He was one of the twentieth century's great performers in general elections, an excellent knock-about open-air speaker who dealt brilliantly with hecklers.

However, Brown's dependence on alcohol and his general volatility undermined his bid to succeed Hugh Gaitskell as the Labour Party leader in 1963. The eminent Liberal Lady Violet Bonham Carter noted in her diary after appearing on the radio programme *Any Questions* with Brown in October 1954, 'I have never before—in the course of an unsheltered life …—met anyone so completely un-house-trained' (*Daring to Hope*, 140). When it came to the leadership contest she expressed views widely held at the time: 'Brown v. Wilson presents a harsh choice between an often (though not always) drunken boor—rude, clumsy, devoid of finesse or subtlety, but an honest & loyal man—& a *very* able, clever, experienced but universally distrusted one, of proven disloyalty' (ibid., 264). The candidature of James Callaghan provided opponents of Wilson with a less volatile alternative than Brown. In February 1963 Wilson polled 115, Brown 88, and Callaghan 41 votes in the first round; Wilson defeated Brown by 144 to 103 votes in the second round.

Brown was mortified by his defeat. Far from being magnanimous, he withdrew for five days and was not contactable. He asked to be shadow foreign secretary, a post Wilson refused to give him. Brown's drinking remained a problem and he was often unpredictable. Of the many embarrassing incidents, the best remembered was an emotional but drunken tribute to President John F. Kennedy after his assassination; later, early in 1967, the satirical magazine *Private Eye* coined the euphemism for inebriation 'tired and emotional' in relation to Brown (P. Marnham, *The Private Eye Story*, 1982, 117, cited in Paterson, 8).

The Wilson government: economic affairs and Foreign Office With Labour's victory in the general election of 1964 George Brown became first secretary of state and secretary of state for economic affairs, posts he held from 16 October 1964 until 11 August 1966. The Department of Economic Affairs was intended to be the powerhouse of modernizing and reconstructing British industry. It was responsible for economic planning, increasing productivity, and securing competitiveness in external and internal markets. George Brown and his planning department drew up a long-term economic plan, the national plan, published on 13 September 1965. Harold Wilson later described it as 'a remarkable and thorough piece of work' (Wilson, 137). A controversial part of the planning was carried out by the prices and incomes department of Brown's ministry, which Brown appointed the former Conservative minister Aubrey Jones to head. Brown was also behind the establishment of the Industrial Reorganization Corporation, which assisted industrial mergers in an attempt to create larger, more efficient units which could compete with industry in the USA and elsewhere. In 1966, faced with a serious balance of payments crisis, the government's determination not to devalue led to the July deflationary measures, which undercut Brown's work. Brown, who by this time accepted the need for devaluation, was dissuaded from resignation by an appeal from over 100 Labour MPs. Staying on in office, he had to argue (against his own views) in favour of a statutory incomes policy.

On 11 August 1966 Brown achieved one of his aspirations by becoming foreign secretary. He was a successor to Bevin, whom he much admired. Perhaps he also admired Palmerston, for he replaced a portrait of George III with one of Palmerston in his Foreign Office room. He ran the Foreign Office in a highly controversial way, laying great stress on his aim to break down the class prejudice there, and getting the office run more informally (a synonym for his notorious rudeness to civil servants). He continually complained about 'the old, protocol-ridden regime' (*Sunday Times* 7 April 1968, 50).

Always pro-American, Brown joined Wilson in trying to secure an honourable basis for American withdrawal from Vietnam, but he was less optimistic than the prime minister. Brown was an enthusiastic advocate of British entry into the Common Market. His statement of the British case for EEC entry at the meeting of the Western European Union in July 1967 was impressively argued, and came to be recognized as a state paper of major importance (*The Times*, 1 July 1970, 11). Although he refused to be daunted by General de Gaulle's second veto of 27 November 1967, and kept Britain's application for entry active, the failure to be admitted was a major disappointment for him as foreign secretary. Brown succeeded in restoring diplomatic relations with Egypt, and with the help of Hugh Mackintosh Foot, Baron Caradon, British ambassador to the United Nations, he was involved in drafting the Security Council resolution 242 (22 November 1967), which sought to achieve a basis for peace between Israel and the Arab states following the Six-Day War.

Brown, highly sensitive about his political status after losing the leadership contest in 1960, was increasingly suspicious and resentful of Harold Wilson's preference for dealing with his 'kitchen cabinet' of favoured associates rather than carefully consulting Brown and other ministers. His repeated threats to resign became legendary. Brown had legitimate cause for complaint when Wilson's associates briefed the media that Brown favoured resumption of arms sales to South Africa. What was probably an inevitable breach between the two men came in March 1968, when Brown was outraged that Wilson failed to prioritize seeking out Brown to consult him over the closure of the London gold market and the declaration of a special bank holiday. Brown resigned on 15 March 1968, never to return to office.

Life peer Brown soon regretted resigning. He later saw Wilson, but Wilson made it clear that he would not remove Michael Stewart so Brown could return as foreign secretary and Brown would accept no lesser post. Wilson, according to Richard Crossman, considered giving Brown a leading role at Transport House, the then Labour Party headquarters. Brown addressed some 200 meetings during the general election campaign of 1970, dynamic and impressive performances. However, boundary changes had always made it likely that he would lose Belper, which he did by 2424 votes. In the dissolution honours announced in August 1970 he was made a life peer, taking the title Lord George-Brown of Jevington in the county of Sussex (the location of his weekend cottage), after a lengthy tussle over his title with the Garter king of arms.

Brown had taken his defeat badly for the Labour Party leadership in 1960 and he took his departure from office in 1968 and the loss of his seat (and thereby the post of deputy leader) even worse. He very soon made clear his differences with the Labour Party in the introduction (finished in December 1970) to his autobiography *In my Way* (1971). During 1970–75 Labour's repudiation of the EEC was an important component of his alienation from the party. He emphasized the idealism that lay behind the idea of creating the EEC in the 1950s and believed that the idea of entry was too important to be influenced by party-political considerations. Moreover, the former political voice of the trade unions became increasingly their vigorous opponent, writing hostile pieces for the *News of the World* and, by the early 1980s, for the *Daily Express* and *Sunday Express*.

Labour's failure to assert itself against the trade unions had previously caused Brown to consider the possibility of a centre party, and in March 1976 he moved from the Labour benches to the cross-benches of the House of Lords after opposing a government bill to restore certain forms of legal rights to trade union 'closed shops'. His resignation was accompanied by degrading press photographs of him falling over beside his car and being helped to his feet by journalists. 'One is torn between pity and loathing for a man who is ruined', Tony Benn recorded (A. Benn, *Against the Tide: Diaries, 1973–76*, 1989, 526). Benn saw Brown as 'a fallen angel. He was one of the high-flying leaders of the Party and now earns his living attacking it' (A. Benn, *Conflicts of Interest: Diaries, 1977–80*, 1990, 508). He became president of the Social Democratic Alliance in January 1981 and was a signatory to the 'Limehouse declaration' in February 1981, but delayed actually joining the Social Democratic Party for four years.

Brown's private life ended equally unpredictably. His family had appeared the epitome of the close-knit London working-class family. Sophie Brown loyally backed him. They had two daughters, Frieda and Pat, and were proud grandparents by the time he entered the cabinet. He also received loyal political support from his brother Ronald William Brown (1921–2002), MP for Shoreditch and Finsbury and assistant whip in 1966–7. While his political dedication and his alcoholism put strains on the marriage from the 1960s, there was general surprise when he walked out of his home on Christmas eve 1982 and thereafter lived in Sussex, then Cornwall, with Margaret Rosalinde Mary (Maggie) Haimes (*b.* 1947), his secretary. As his health deteriorated he also turned his back on his Anglo-

Catholic religious beliefs and converted to the Roman Catholic church. He died of liver complaints on 2 June 1985 at the Duchy Hospital, Truro, Cornwall. He was cremated at Golders Green crematorium. He was survived by his wife and by Maggie Haimes.   CHRIS WRIGLEY

Sources G. Brown, *In my way: the political memoirs of Lord George-Brown* (1971) · P. Paterson, *Tired and emotional: the life of Lord George-Brown* (1993) · *DNB* · *The political diary of Hugh Dalton, 1918–1940, 1945–1960*, ed. B. Pimlott (1986) · *The Castle diaries, 1964–1970* (1984) · R. H. S. Crossman, *The diaries of a cabinet minister*, 3 vols. (1975–7) · *The backbench diaries of Richard Crossman*, ed. J. Morgan (1981) · H. Wilson, *The labour government, 1964–70* (1971) · A. Benn, *Years of hope: diaries, 1940–62* (1994) · T. Benn, *Out of the wilderness: diaries, 1963–67* (1987) · A. Benn, *Office without power: diaries, 1968–72* (1988) · *Daring to hope: the diaries and letters of Violet Bonham Carter, 1946–1969*, ed. M. Pottle (2000) · b. cert. · m. cert. [Sophie Levene] · d. cert.
Archives Bodl. Oxf., papers · Bodl. RH, corresp. relating to colonial issues | HLRO, corresp. with Lord Beaverbrook · King's Lond., Liddell Hart C., corresp. with Sir B. H. Liddell Hart · NL Wales, letters to Desmond Donnelly · U. Warwick Mod. RC, Richard Crossman diaries · U. Warwick Mod. RC, Transport and General Workers' Union papers
Likenesses P. Joyce, photograph, 1976, NPG [*see illus.*]
Wealth at death £81,436: probate, 24 Sept 1985, *CGPLA Eng. & Wales*

Brown, George Clifford (1879–1944), headmaster, was born in the High Street, Sandown, Isle of Wight, on 29 May 1879, the son of Dr George Brown, a chemist, and his wife, Lucy Anne Hallett. He was educated at Solent College, Lymington, and the University of London, before spending two years as a research student at the London School of Economics and Political Science, as well as doing research in medieval history. After teaching in various schools he became, at the age of twenty-six, headmaster of Tollington School, London, and during his time there the school achieved notable academic, athletic, and chess distinctions.

On 23 April 1902 Brown married Catherine Harvey Robertson Smith (*d.* 1930), the daughter of William Charles Ernest Smith, civil engineer. They had three sons and a daughter. The health of one of his children obliged him to leave London. He had almost decided to go to Guatemala but, after some persuasion from his wife, he decided to accept the headmastership of Worcester College for the Blind, from January 1913, with pupil numbers in single figures, despite some notable achievements by former pupils since its foundation in 1866.

Despite financial constraints that dogged the school for most of Brown's headship and, unhappily, were in some instances reflected in the quality of the staff, pupil numbers steadily increased. By 1919 they had reached twenty-four and eventually nearly fifty.

After an inspection in 1915 the school was recognized as efficient by the Board of Education, and in 1918 the board agreed to make an annual grant to the school. In that year Canon William Haighton Chappel, headmaster of the King's School, Worcester, made an inspection and wrote of Brown: 'He is ubiquitous, and the impress of his originality and energy are everywhere apparent' (Bell, 51).

Brown was intent on integrating his boys and his school. With his keenness on sport and other recreations and his flair for publicity he sought the interest and help of those whose names would get the school into the headlines. The celebrated oarsman Guy Nikalls raised money for a swimming pool and later, as a governor, for a substantial endowment. A rowing crew sent to Henley in 1927 lost to the winners of the Thames cup. Capablanca, soon to become world chess champion, resigned to a Worcester boy in a forty board simultaneous match. In 1934 Lord Burghley, the Olympic athlete, opened the school running track.

Another preoccupation of Brown's was the employment of boys leaving Worcester; this meant for some finding anything at all or only something well below their abilities. Few professions were open to them—mainly the church, the law, and what was then called massage. To help the boys to acquire employable skills Brown instituted a strong modern side, himself developing a book-keeping Braille frame.

A close friend wrote that Brown, to a greater or lesser degree, formed the boys in his own image. 'He insisted that blindness was not a barrier, nor even a handicap, but just a nuisance to be overcome' (Bell, 64).

In 1932 Brown was elected to the Headmasters' Conference. It was the ultimate accolade, and a unique distinction for so small a school. But two years earlier his wife had died, and although all his children were involved in the school in various ways he was not the man he had been. He was never a master of day-to-day administration (letters were answered at once or not at all) and notably unpunctual, so his last years in office, not helped by his health problems, left a good deal to be desired. In 1936 the then National Institute for the Blind undertook 'financial responsibility and guiding control' (Bell, 62), and Brown retired in 1938. In retirement he lived with close friends at Hawford House, North Claines, Worcestershire, where he died rather suddenly on 16 July 1944. He was buried in Whittington churchyard, near the school.

Except in mathematics Brown was not an outstanding teacher, but when senior boys gathered at the foot of the main stairs in the evening his exchanges with them were in the nature of Socratic dialogues. In one public address he said that his preferred designation was pedagogue. He had many of the characteristics of a headmaster. He was tall, well built, and upright, with a decided presence, but friendly and in no way condescending. The devotion of his old boys, not least the most distinguished among them, was lifelong and unwavering. One of them made permanent provision for the upkeep of his grave, and the old boys' union installed a memorial chiming clock.

KENNETH R. WHITTON

Sources M. G. Thomas, *The first seventy years: Worcester College for the Blind, 1866–1936* (1937) · D. Bell, ed., *An experiment in education: the history of Worcester College for the Blind, 1866–1966* (1967) · personal knowledge (2004) · private information (2004) · *WWW* · m. cert. · b. cert.
Likenesses photograph, repro. in Thomas, *First seventy years*, facing p. 78 · photograph, repro. in Bell, *Experiment in education*, facing p. 3
Wealth at death £148 8s. 5d.: administration, 4 Sept 1944, *CGPLA Eng. & Wales*

Brown, George Douglas (1869–1902), writer, was born at Ochiltree, Ayrshire, on 26 January 1869, the son of George Douglas Brown (1813–1897), a farmer of Muirsmudden, and Sarah Gemmell (1832/3–1895), a farm servant. Brown was illegitimate, a fact that plagued him throughout his life. He was devoted to his mother, who was thirty-six when he was born. The Brown family prevented her marrying Brown's father, and she moved around, taking various jobs to support her son. The young boy was often taunted by village gossips, who referred to him as 'Smudden's bastard'.

Brown attended local schools at Ochiltree and Colyton and passed the sixth standard of the Scottish education department in 1881. However, lack of money forced him to become a pithead boy at Trabboch, where he sifted detritus from the coal. Then in 1884 a former teacher, Mr Maybin, provided money for Brown to attend Ayr Academy, and his mother moved to a cottage at Crofthead, Ayr. In 1887, having won the Cowan bursary especially reserved for Ayr Academy boys, Brown matriculated at the University of Glasgow. One of his professors, Gilbert Murray, encouraged the young undergraduate, who suffered from bouts of depression, impatience, and laziness, yet was 'marked by a remarkable vigour of mind' (Lennox, 73). He graduated MA, with first-class honours, in 1890 and won the Cowan gold medal for excellence in Greek. In 1891 he won the Luke history prize, but relinquished his Eglinton fellowship after winning the Snell exhibition to study at Balliol College, Oxford. He matriculated there on 20 October 1891 and took a first in classical moderations in 1893. Yet Brown was never really comfortable or happy in Oxford. He was older than most of his contemporaries, had little money, and became increasingly bored with his studies. Gilbert Murray commented that 'he wanted to be at real work, to give out or create' (ibid., 85). When his mother became seriously ill, early in 1895, he returned to Scotland to nurse her. Her death, in March, was a great blow to him and he returned to Oxford to achieve only a third in Greats later in that year.

Brown left Oxford in summer 1895 and settled in London, where he became a hack writer and private tutor, determined to devote himself to literature. He rejected the efforts of his friends to find him regular employment, preferring to have the freedom to write when and how he chose. As a freelance writer he wrote poetry, reviews, and short stories, anonymously and pseudonymously, for a number of periodicals, including *Chapman's Magazine*, *Realm*, *The Speaker*, and the *Illustrated London News*. His article on Robert Burns appeared in *Blackwood's Magazine* in August 1896, and he helped D. S. Meldrum to edit John Galt's novels for Blackwood.

Since 1892 Brown had known and been in love with Isabella MacLennan, and at about this time decided to propose to her. He imagined himself as a 'successful writer and she the lovely, witty hostess' (Lennox, 106). Discovering that Isabella and her family were visiting Paris, Brown impetuously travelled there and asked her to marry him. She refused, realizing that she could not reciprocate his feelings. Bitterly disappointed, but with no animosity towards Isabella, he returned to London and his literary work. In 1899 he became sub-editor as well as contributor to *Sandow's Magazine*, for which he wrote articles on the American poet Walt Whitman and on 'The strong man in Dumas's fiction'. Brown also published potboilers and historical books for boys; *Love and a Sword: a Tale of the Afridi War* (1899) was published under the pseudonym Kennedy King, while for *Famous Fighting Regiments* (1900) he used the pen-name George Hood.

At the same time Brown was working on his novel *The House with the Green Shutters*, which was published in autumn 1901 in both Britain and the United States under the pseudonym George Douglas. Far from being the cosy, heartwarming world of J. M. Barrie, Ian Maclaren, or S. R. Crockett—writers of the kailyard school—Brown's vision of Scottish life 'is grim and vindictive' (C. Craig, introduction, in G. Douglas, *The House with the Green Shutters*, 1996, vi). Set in the rural town of Barbie, the novel has as its central character John Gourlay, the domineering man who owns the house with the green shutters. He rejects the coming industrialization of Barbie and is financially ruined by the inventive and ambitious Wilson. Gourlay sends his son John, who is emotionally weak and no match for his father's brutality, to Edinburgh University in order that he may learn a trade to re-establish the family's fortunes. But young John descends into alcoholism and returns in disgrace. After a quarrel, and egged on in part by the village gossips, he murders his father in a fit of drunken rage. Then, with his mother and sister, he commits suicide. The tragedy of *The House with the Green Shutters* was no mere counterblast to kailyard fiction. Brown utilized the genre's very distinctive elements—the pretty rural village, the characters who populate it, the theme of impending change resisted—and showed how 'the kailyard world … subverts itself from within' (I. Campbell, 'George Douglas Brown's kailyard novel', *Studies in Scottish Literature*, 12, 1974–5, 69). On the surface Barbie is attractive, but 'it is no rustic paradise; Barbie is rotten to the core' (ibid., 70). The village folk, who in kailyard stories are the decent, Christian voices of the community, are malevolent 'bodies'. They

> became not only the chorus to Gourlay's tragedy, buzzing it abroad and discussing his downfall; they became also, merely by their maddening tattle, a villain of the piece and an active cause of the catastrophe … There was a pretty hell-broth brewing in the little town. (G. Douglas, *The House with the Green Shutters*, 1901, 104)

Acclaimed by critics, this 'black terrible story' (Lennox, 144) in its tragedy and determinism has been described as a turning point in Scottish writing. Edwin Muir judged the novel 'full of genius and style' (Muir, 31) and Scottish modernists such as Hugh MacDiarmid, Lewis Grassic Gibbon, and Neil Gunn hailed its stark realism. By the time of its fifth edition it had sold 12,000 copies and was still in demand. Brown, however, received no royalties.

Late in 1901 Brown set about writing what he intended to be his second novel, set in Cromwellian times. It was to be a love story, and he endeavoured 'to put the tender side of his nature' into it (Lennox, 168), but it was never completed. He also had ideas for the plot of a third novel, 'The Incompatibles', along the lines of *The House with the Green Shutters*. After a peripatetic existence in London he moved to Beacon Hill Cottage at Penn, Buckinghamshire, with fragments of other work in progress, including a study of *Hamlet*. He became engaged to Lizzie MacLennan, Isabella's younger sister, early in 1902. They set their wedding date for 16 October, but while on holiday in Scotland Brown had a premonition that they would never be husband and wife.

With a heavy brow and 'somewhat pensive and melancholy cast to his features' (Lennox, 14), Brown had always suffered from liver problems and periods of lethargy that he tried to fight off by doggedly continuing his routine: 'he walked, smoked and worked as usual' (Lennox, 178). In June he moved to Briar Cottage at Haslemere, Surrey, but further attacks forced him in August to consult a physician in London, who seems to have brushed aside the seriousness of his illness. He went to stay at 45 Onslow Gardens, Muswell Hill Road, Hornsey, Middlesex—the home of his friend the publisher Andrew Melrose—his state continuing to deteriorate. On the morning of his third day there, 28 August 1902, George Douglas Brown died. The cause of death is recorded as laryngitis, congestion of the lungs, and heart failure, but a post-mortem, which would have given a more specific conclusion, was ruled out 'in deference to the feelings of his fiancée' (Lennox, 183). He was buried on 1 September at Holmston cemetery, Ayr, with his mother. JANE POTTER

Sources C. Lennox, *George Douglas Brown: a biographical memoir* (1903) · J. Veitch, *George Douglas Brown* (1952) · A. Melrose, 'George Douglas Brown: reminiscences of a friendship, and a notable novel', *The Bookman* (Oct 1902), 12–19 · E. Muir, *Latitudes* (1924) · *DNB* · d. cert. · www.slainte.org.uk/scotauth/browndsw.htm, 7 Feb 2002
Archives NL Scot., notebooks · NRA, corresp. and literary papers | NL Scot., letters, mainly to Tom Smith
Likenesses R. Bryden, etching, repro. in Veitch, *George Douglas Brown*

Brown, George Hilary (1786–1856), vicar apostolic of the Lancashire district and Roman Catholic bishop of Liverpool, born on 13 January 1786 in Clifton, near Lytham, Lancashire, was the son of William Brown and his wife, Helen (*née* Gradwell). In 1799 he entered the seminary at Crook Hall in co. Durham, which in 1808 moved to Ushaw and became St Cuthbert's College; he was ordained priest in 1810 and became vice-president and professor of theology at the college. He left in 1819 to become missioner at St Peter's, Lancaster. On the partition of the northern district he was appointed vicar apostolic of the Lancashire district by Pope Gregory XVI, and was consecrated at Liverpool on 24 August 1840 with the title of bishop of Bugia 'in partibus infidelium', changed to the title of bishop of Tloa in 1842. On the restoration of the hierarchy by Pius IX in 1850 he was translated to the newly created see of Liverpool, where he died on 25 January 1856. Brown presided over an expanding community on which he imposed a new ecclesiastical discipline, abolishing lay control of the local missions. THOMPSON COOPER, *rev.* J. A. HILTON

Sources W. M. Brady, *Annals of the Catholic hierarchy in England and Scotland* (1877), 417 · R. N. Billington and J. Brownbill, *St Peter's, Lancaster: a history* (1910), 93–4 · T. Burke, *Catholic history of Liverpool* (1910), 65–123 · B. Plumb, *Arundel to Zabi: a biographical dictionary of the Catholic bishops of England and Wales (deceased), 1623–1987* (privately printed, Warrington, [1987]) · J. A. Hilton, *Catholic Lancashire: from Reformation to renewal, 1559–1991* (1994), 84–6 · P. Doyle, '"A tangled skein of confusion": the administration of George Hilary Brown, bishop of Liverpool, 1850–1856', *Recusant History*, 25 (2000–01), 294–303
Archives Lancs. RO, Liverpool diocesan archive, corresp. and papers | Ushaw College, Durham, letters to Charles Newsham; letters to E. Winstanley; letters to Nicholas Wiseman · Westm. DA, letters to N. Wiseman
Likenesses portrait, Metropolitan Cathedral, Liverpool

Brown, George Mackay (1921–1996), poet and writer, was born on 17 October 1921 in Victoria Street, Stromness, on mainland Orkney, the last of six children of John Brown (1875–1940), tailor and postman, and his wife, Mhairi (Mary Jane; 1891–1967), daughter of Hugh Mackay of Strathy, Sutherland, and his wife, Georgina. His parents were both Scottish, although Brown, like most Orcadians, always stressed the cultural gulf between the islanders and their neighbours on the Scottish mainland. His mother was a native Gaelic speaker.

The formal education Brown received in local schools was ultimately less important to him than the reading discoveries he made for himself as a young man. The stories told by his elder sister Ruby were formative, and as he himself wrote, 'literature entered the mind stealthily, like a thief; only it was a good thief, like Robin Hood or Brecht's Asdak, and left treasures instead of taking them' (Brown, *For the Islands I Sing*, 41). His lifelong tendency to poor health began with a bad attack of measles during his mid-teens, though his smoking from the age of twelve may not have helped, as he freely acknowledged. Brown's father died suddenly in 1940, leaving his youngest son living with his mother but unable to earn an adult wage. Pulmonary tuberculosis confined him to a sanatorium in Kirkwall for six months in 1941, after which he began to write verse and to contribute articles and reviews to a local newspaper, the *Orkney Herald*. Journalism provided an important and congenial outlet for his writing throughout his life. He extended his knowledge of literature, music, and history, and made friends with local artists and intellectuals. He was later encouraged to apply for a place at the newly established Newbattle Abbey College (at Dalkeith, south of Edinburgh), an adult education college under the wardenship of the poet Edwin Muir. A meeting with Muir and his wife Willa, in summer 1951, secured Brown a place for the 1951–2 session: 'Newbattle stimulated me, and gave me a sense of purpose and direction' (ibid., 93). He published his first poetry collection, *The Storm, and other Poems*, in 1954 at his own expense. Muir provided an introduction.

Further illness preceded a second brief spell at Newbattle in 1956. This in turn encouraged Brown to enter Edinburgh University as an undergraduate (1956–60). At Muir's instigation the Hogarth Press issued Brown's next collection, *Loaves and Fishes*, in 1959. Thereafter, a brief taste of teacher training convinced him that teaching was not an appropriate career; in any case, his health broke down once more and he spent winter 1960–61 in Tor-Na-Dee sanatorium west of Aberdeen. After his recovery Brown became a Roman Catholic in 1961. Never satisfied by the Calvinism in which he was brought up, he had been drawn to Roman Catholicism since his teens, especially after reading Lytton Strachey's essay on Cardinal Manning. Whatever Strachey's intention, this account allowed Brown to glimpse something of the strength and durability of the Catholic faith. As with the other values on which his life was founded, literary expression was central to his commitment to it: 'In the end it was literature that broke down my last defences. There are many ways of entering a fold; it was the beauty of words that opened the door to me' (Brown, *For the Islands I Sing*, 53).

During a further two years of postgraduate work in Edinburgh, Brown studied Hopkins, a poet he had long loved but whom he claimed to have chosen for this purpose because 'Hopkins' collected poems are probably the fewest in English literature' (Brown, *For the Islands I Sing*, 149). He gained no second degree, however. His years in Edinburgh were important for the contacts and friendships he made among the poets and literati there, including Norman MacCaig, Sydney Goodsir Smith, and Hugh MacDiarmid. Smith's *Kynd Kittock's Land* (1965) gives a glimpse of Brown in their convivial company:

While lean MacCaig stauns snuffin the Western seas
And Brown leads wi his Viking chin
And winna be rebukit.

In all Brown published thirty-one books of poetry, many of which are limited editions, or collaborations with artists. Fourteen, however, are substantial collections. His poems, characteristically, are impersonal and avoid autobiographical confession. Many tell stories, however briefly; many, also, illustrate his instinct for pattern and order. All demonstrate his care as a craftsman and his sensual responsiveness to the sounds of words.

Like his mentor Edwin Muir, Brown strove in his verse 'to express universal insights' (Bold, 19). Whereas Muir's means of achieving this, however, often involved his turning to regions of dream and archetype, Brown habitually draws on Orkney life, on history, and on religious ritual.

Brown's origins were as humble and geographically obscure as the role of 'lad o' pairts' usually demands, but where an immense talent might have been expected to elevate its possessor above his origins Brown defied the pattern and continued living unpretentiously in Stromness for most of his life. His achievement as a writer did not propel him into the wider world; rather, it brought the world to him and to Orkney. This was not only literally true, though his fame eventually drew many visitors and scholars. It was also true in the sense that the world has accepted Brown's vision of Orkney as valid and enriching, a place created in literature like Joyce's Dublin and Dickens's London.

Brown's first collection of short stories, *A Calendar of Love and other Stories*, appeared in 1967. In all, twelve volumes of stories were published during his lifetime and for many readers it is for his prose stories that he is best

remembered and most valued. They share many of the characteristic features of his poems, especially as regards subject matter and approach to structure. As he said himself during an interview:

Lots of my poems are sort of compressed stories and you could expand them and make a short story of them. Maybe a novel if you wanted to go to town. And also lots of the stories could be compressed a good bit into a poem, you know, with all the inessentials left out. (Murray, 51)

His five novels, like his poems and short stories, reflect Orkney past and present, sometimes realistically, sometimes in fable. Many readers find the first, *Greenvoe* (1972), to be the most appealing: it is a portrait of a modern Orkney island snuffed out by a sinister government conspiracy but with the possibility of resurgence thanks to the spiritual strength of the indigenous inhabitants and their rituals.

The destruction of the fictional Greenvoe by the bureaucratic project Black Star (read by some as a foreshadowing of the impact of the oil industry on Orkney, but later described by Brown as a project of 'preparations for a third world war, much more hideous than its two predecessors'; Brown, *For the Islands I Sing*, 173) is one of many instances in which he made clear his opposition to the doctrine of progress. That opposition was memorably spelt out in *An Orkney Tapestry* (1969):

There is a new religion, Progress, in which we all devoutly believe, and it is concerned only with material things in the present and in a vague golden-handed future. It is a rootless utilitarian faith, without beauty or mystery; a kind of blind unquestioning belief that men and their material circumstances will go on improving until some kind of nirvana is reached and everyone will be rich, free, fulfilled, well-informed, masterful. … I feel that this religion is in great part a delusion, and will peter out in the marsh. A community like Orkney dare not cut itself off from its roots and sources. (Brown, *Orkney Tapestry*, 20–21)

Against this trend he emphasized the simplicity of traditional Orkney life, the interpenetration of past and present, and the ceremonies of Catholicism. In his later years he softened his vehemence against progress (even eventually owning a black and white television) but insisted on the necessity to 'keep people in touch with their roots and sources' (Murray, 42).

Brown's last novel, *Beside the Ocean of Time* (1994), won the Saltire Scottish Book of the Year award and was shortlisted for the 1994 Booker prize. All his novels are deeply characteristic of their author, as are his plays; nevertheless, it is as a short-story writer that his finest achievement outside his verse lies. His plays, by his own acknowledgement lacking true theatrical vitality, contain much excellent writing: 'I think they're probably better read than seen on the stage' (Murray, 34–5). He was a natural taleteller, however, and his large body of short stories is a significant contribution to twentieth-century literature.

Brown was awarded an OBE in 1974 and became a fellow of the Royal Society of Literature in 1977. He was awarded honorary degrees by the Open University (MA, 1976), the

University of Dundee (LLD, 1977), and the University of Glasgow (DLitt, 1985).

Just as, by and large, he felt no call to move beyond Orkney in his quest for things to write about, so in real life Brown seems to have disliked travelling outside his familiar northern landscape. Despite the happiness of his time at Newbattle and Edinburgh, a city he came to love, Orkney was his only possible home. His sense of values and also his sense of Orkney were steeped in his response to the islands' past. That past, in which a simple way of life founded on farming and fishing changed little, as he saw it, over the millennia, was characterized by a striking historical narrative, especially in the viking period, and also by a religious richness and strength which reached a peak of holiness in the martyrdom of St Magnus on the island of Egilsay on Easter Monday 1117. The figure of Magnus was a potent one for Brown throughout his life, and one whose story he retold several times, most notably in *The Martyrdom of St Magnus*, an opera written in collaboration with his friend the composer Peter Maxwell Davies. Closely associated with Brown from the time of his first visit to Orkney in 1970, Davies set many of Brown's works and with Brown's help founded the St Magnus Festival in 1977. Imaginative and spiritual elements were further bound together for Brown in the distinctive literary achievement of *Orkneyinga Saga* (written early in the thirteenth century), a work which not only provided him with much literary inspiration, but also helped him discern a significance in his obscure corner of the globe which he communicated to the rest of the world through his writing.

After his mother's death Brown lived in a council flat at 3 Mayburn Court, Stromness; his writing desk was the kitchen table and he wrote at it every morning with the self-discipline of a craftsman. He had a weekly column in *The Orcadian* newspaper, which he continued to write up until the last week of his life. All who knew him stress his gentleness, his shyness, his reticence, though those close to him also recall his strong sense of humour. He never married.

Brown's features were striking, often described as 'craggy'. Photographs from his final years show how severe his health problems had become. An operation for cataract in 1988 was followed by one for cancer in 1990. His death certificate lists several problems, including kidney and heart failure possibly brought about by the onset of bronchitis. He died in Balfour Hospital, Kirkwall, on 13 April 1996. Peter Maxwell Davies's sixth symphony, completed on the day of Brown's death, is dedicated to him. George Mackay Brown was buried in Stromness kirkyard on 16 April, St Magnus's day.   DAVID ROBB

Sources G. M. Brown, *For the islands I sing: an autobiography* (1997) · H. Spear, ed., *George Mackay Brown: a survey of his work and a full bibliography* (2000) · A. Bold, *George Mackay Brown* (1978) · I. Murray, ed., *Scottish writers talking* (1996) · G. M. Brown, 'An autobiographical essay', *As I remember: ten Scottish authors recall how writing began for them*, ed. M. Lindsay (1979), 9–21 · G. M. Brown, *An Orkney tapestry* (1969) · b. cert. · d. cert.
Archives NL Scot., corresp. and literary MSS · NL Scot., papers · Orkney Archives, Kirkwall, corresp. and literary MSS · U. Edin. L., corresp. and literary MSS | NL Scot., corresp. with R. Glen · Shetland Archives, Lerwick, letters to P. Jamieson · U. Edin. L., letters to C. Senior; letters to D. Swinley
Likenesses G. Wright, photograph, 1979; copy, NL Scot. · A. Moffat, group portrait, oils, 1980 (*Poet's pub*), Scot. NPG · E. Hoffmann, tempera, 1988, Aberdeen Art Gallery · A. Catlin, photograph, repro. in A. Catlin, *Natural light: portraits of Scottish writers* (1985)

Brown, Sir **George Thomas** (1827–1906), veterinary surgeon, born in London on 30 December 1827, was the elder son of Thomas Brown of Notting Hill Terrace, London, and his wife, Grace Bryant. Colonel Sir William James Brown KCB (1832–1918), was his younger brother. After being educated privately George entered the Royal Veterinary College in 1846. He obtained his diploma on 15 May 1847 and commenced veterinary practice in London. In 1850, when only twenty-three, he was appointed professor of veterinary science at the Royal Agricultural College at Cirencester, where he remained for thirteen years. He married Margaret, daughter of James Smith of Stroud, in 1860, and they had two sons and three daughters.

A change in the administration of the college brought Brown back to London in 1863, though he continued his association with the college as honorary professor until 1906. In June 1865 the great cattle plague broke out in London. It was an epidemic of rinderpest, a highly contagious, virulent disease which had been imported with a cargo of live cattle from Russia. It spread rapidly through the country and killed most of the animals that became infected. There were no established means for controlling it, and it fell to the Privy Council Office to take action. Its veterinary adviser was James Beart Simonds of the Royal Veterinary College and Brown was appointed as chief inspector to work under Simonds. Thus began a career in government service which lasted for twenty-eight years, until Brown retired in 1893.

Brown was a skilled administrator and highly regarded for his professional advice. He was firm in the opinion that contagious diseases of animals, some of which also caused disease in humans, could only be effectively controlled by direct action from central government and that it was pointless to give permissive powers to local authorities. In the course of his career his reports covered foot-and-mouth disease, rabies, anthrax, bovine pleuro-pneumonia, glanders, swine fever, and tuberculosis. Brown was made CB in 1887, at Queen Victoria's jubilee, and he was knighted at Osborne on 23 January 1898.

In addition to his official duties, Brown served as lecturer on physiology, therapeutics, and pharmacy at the Royal Veterinary College from 1872 until 1881, when he became professor of cattle pathology. In 1887 he was appointed principal, a position he held until 1894. He also served the Royal College of Veterinary Surgeons as an examiner, as member of the council, and as president in 1873–4. He was a consultant to the Royal Agricultural Society and to the Bath and West of England Agricultural Society, and he was veterinary editor of *The Field*. He was said to be a fluent public speaker, but his reserved manner and doleful expression did not inspire the students. He wrote or edited several books and pamphlets, but his major contribution was through his official reports and the work he did in establishing a state veterinary service. It was his groundwork that led to the Diseases of Animals Act 1894, a powerful, comprehensive piece of legislation that remained virtually unchanged for more than fifty years.

After his retirement from the Board of Agriculture Brown lived at Orme Lodge, Stanmore, Middlesex, where he died on 20 June 1906; he was buried at Stanmore.

ERNEST CLARKE, rev. SHERWIN A. HALL

Sources *The Veterinarian*, 67 (1894), 730–35 · *Veterinary Record* (23 June 1906) · E. Cotchin, *The Royal Veterinary College, London: a bicentenary history* (1990), 109–115 · personal knowledge (1912) · private information (1912) · *Journal of the Royal Agricultural Society of England*, 67 (1906), 215 · d. cert.
Likenesses Messrs Ball, photograph, repro. in *The Veterinarian* · H. Speed, oils, posthumous, Royal College of Veterinary Surgeons, London
Wealth at death £14,500 10s. 8d.: probate, 17 July 1906, CGPLA Eng. & Wales

Brown, Gerard Baldwin (1849–1932), art historian, was born on 31 October 1849 at 10 Hoxley Road, Kennington, London, the only son of James Baldwin *Brown (1820–1884), minister of Brixton Independent Chapel, and his wife, Elizabeth, daughter of William Gerard Leifchild of Moorgate Street and Wanstead and sister of the sculptor Henry *Leifchild (1823–1884). Brown was educated at Uppingham School when Edward Thring was headmaster, and won a scholarship to Oriel College, Oxford, in 1869. He was awarded a second in classical moderations in 1871, and a first in *literae humaniores* in 1873. In 1874 he was elected to a fellowship at Brasenose College, where one of his colleagues was Walter Pater; he won the chancellor's prize for an English essay entitled 'The short periods during which art has remained at its zenith in various countries'. He remained at Brasenose until 1877, when he decided that he wanted to become an artist, and went to study painting at the National Art Training School in South Kensington (later the Royal College of Art).

In 1880 Brown was appointed to the new Watson Gordon chair of fine art at Edinburgh University, the first chair in fine art to be established in the British Isles. He later formed the intention of retiring early to devote the rest of his life to writing, and rented a flat near the British Museum, but changed his mind on the outbreak of the First World War, and remained in the post until 1930. On 25 April 1882 he married Maude Annie (d. 1931), daughter of Robert Hull Terrell of Exeter; she illustrated many of his books. The couple had no children.

Although his first lectures at Edinburgh were mainly on Greek art, Brown's first book was *From schola to cathedral: a study of early Christian architecture and its relation to the life of the church* (1886). His most important work was the six-volume *Arts in Early England* (1903–37): he was working on the final volume at the time of his death, and it was completed by Eric Hyde (Lord Sexton), in 1937. Brown's other publications include *The Fine Arts* (1891; 4th edn, 1916), *William Hogarth* (1905), *Rembrandt* (1907), *The Arts and Crafts of our Teutonic Forefathers* (1910), and *The Art of the Cave Dweller*

(1928). He also contributed a number of papers to academic journals; these included 'The origin of Roman imperial architecture', a paper read before the Royal Institute of British Architects in 1889.

Brown's approach to art history was a transitional one. He combined a connoisseur's interest in the individual work of art with an appreciation of the craftsmanship involved and attention to the connection between art and its social background. His perspective on his subject contrasted with the theoretical approach which dominated art historical studies by the time of his death. His approach was reflected in his concern for the preservation of ancient monuments. It was after reading Brown's work *The Care of Ancient Monuments* (1905) that the secretary of state for Scotland in 1908 set up a royal commission to compile an inventory of ancient Scottish monuments; naturally, Brown was appointed a member of this commission.

Brown was awarded the honorary degrees of LLD and DLitt at Edinburgh University, and was elected to an honorary fellowship at Oriel College, Oxford (1923) and to a fellowship of the British Academy (1924). Very fit and active, he loved cycling and climbing mountains, and visited cave paintings in France and Spain when he was nearly eighty. He died at his home, 18 Atholl Crescent, Edinburgh, on 12 July 1932, and was cremated at Warriston, Edinburgh, on 16 July.

D. T. RICE, rev. ANNE PIMLOTT BAKER

Sources G. Macdonald, 'Gerard Baldwin Brown, 1849–1932', *PBA*, 21 (1935), 375–84 · Foster, *Alum. Oxon.* · *Oxford University Calendar* (1874) · *Oxford University Calendar* (1875) · *The Times* (14 July 1932) · b. cert. · m. cert. · d. cert. · personal knowledge (1949) · private information (1949)
Archives U. Edin. L., corresp. and papers
Likenesses C. d'O. P. Jackson, bronze bust, 1930, U. Edin. · W. Hole, etching, NPG; repro. in W. B. Hole, *Quasi cursores: portraits of the high officers and professors of the University of Edinburgh at its tercentenary festival* (1884)
Wealth at death £9482 7s. 9d.: Scottish confirmation sealed in London, 16 Sept 1932, CGPLA Eng. & Wales

Brown, Gilbert (d. 1612), abbot of Sweetheart and Roman Catholic priest, was the son of Richard Brown (d. in or after 1546) and his wife, Elizabeth Lindsay (d. in or after 1577), of Carsluith. He was professed as a Cistercian monk at Sweetheart (New Abbey) near Dumfries under Abbot John Brown, his cousin, and signed community documents between July 1559 and March 1560. After the Reformation Parliament in 1560 put an end to the public manifestation of monastic life and prevented further recruitment, Brown matriculated at St Andrews in 1562 and graduated in arts in 1565. At St Andrews he accepted protestantism and took the protestant sacrament. On 23 May 1565 he received a crown gift of Sweetheart, resigned by John Brown, who retained the revenues. He signed the bond supporting Queen Mary in March 1568, was forfeited by parliament in August, but attended parliament in 1571 and 1573. He was restored to possession of Sweetheart in April 1573. In January 1576, John Brown having died, he succeeded to the Sweetheart revenues.

Brown now began to figure as an adversary of protestantism. In 1578 Lord Herries's son was causing trouble, he and his family being influenced by Brown's papist counsel, and in 1579 the general assembly laid censures on Brown for his apostasy in enticing people round Dumfries to popery and for having a high altar still standing in Sweetheart. In September 1585 he was denounced in the privy council for not appearing in court to answer charges, no doubt concerning the activity of Jesuit priests in his area, and he was deprived of Sweetheart. Also in 1585 he entered the Scots College in Lorraine (later at Douai), and on 28 March 1587 he was ordained priest in Paris and set out for Rome. By November he was back in Scotland.

From 1588 on Brown was frequently denounced for his recusant activities and for a time he was outlawed. The English warden of the west marches, alarmed by his harbouring of Englishmen and his suspected dealings with Spain and Ireland, planned a raid to capture him. Brown's fortunes prospered, however. His successor at Sweetheart sold him the abbey, and his reputation was enhanced by his reported casting out of a devil from a young girl. The authorities considered he had corrupted the whole district with Roman Catholicism.

In 1605 Brown was captured by force of arms and warded in Edinburgh Castle, but the kirk was then outraged by the benign treatment he received: the king paid his expenses, his religious gear was restored, and after saying mass he departed for France—he seemingly had influential friends in high places as well as in the south-west. By spring 1608 he was again operating in south-west Scotland, but in June, bedridden with an infected leg, he was arrested and his gear was later publicly burnt. From October 1609 he was in Paris, aged, unwell, and poor, and he died on 13 or 14 May 1612. His career had included very varied religious commitment and, almost certainly before 1585, he fathered three illegitimate children. His only surviving literary work is a refutation of an attack on Roman Catholicism by John Welsch, a local minister, and a further rebuttal of Welsch's published reply of 1602.

MARK DILWORTH

Sources M. Dilworth, 'Abbot Gilbert Brown: a sketch of his career', *Innes Review*, 40 (1989), 153–8 • F. J. Stewart and R. C. Reid, 'The early Browns in Newabbey', *Transactions of the Dumfriesshire and Galloway Natural History and Antiquarian Society*, 3rd ser., 38 (1961), 93–110 • J. M. Anderson, ed., *Early records of the University of St Andrews*, Scottish History Society, 3rd ser., 8 (1926) • T. Thomson, ed., *A diurnal of remarkable occurrents that have passed within the country of Scotland*, Bannatyne Club, 43 (1833), 331
Wealth at death very little: Dilworth, 'Abbot Gilbert Brown', 156

Brown, (Arthur) Godfrey Kilner (1915–1995), athlete and schoolmaster, was born on 21 February 1915 in Bankura, Bengal, India, the fourth child and third son of the Revd Arthur E. Brown, principal of Bankura College, Bengal, and his wife, Gertrude Parsons. His parents met at Cambridge, where his father took a first in mathematics before embarking on missionary work in India and passing on his enthusiasm for athletics to his children, of whom Godfrey was the best of a very talented family. Godfrey Brown was an exceptionally versatile runner from his

days at Warwick School, and ran all distances from 100 to 880 yards. He went to Peterhouse, Cambridge, to read history in 1935 and won a blue in his first year. He made his first international appearance against Germany the same year at Munich, then returned to Berlin the following year in the British Olympic team. Like most of the athletes, he was too preoccupied with his event to take much interest in the wider political and racial aspects of the 1936 games. 'Keeping politics out of sport' was at the core of the amateur credo of which he was a prime exponent.

Not doing much in the way of training was another tenet of the English amateur. Brown, however, did rather more than most, and worked out his own routine of 'miles and miles of slow jogging' for an hour and a half a day, relying on the Olympic heats to bring him to top form for the 400 metres final. Despite drawing the difficult outside lane, he ran a marvellous race: he almost beat Archie Williams of the United States to the gold medal, set a new European record, and knocked a full second off his best previous time. In fact, his time was even better than he knew, since he lost by only 0.02 of a second and not 0.2, as officially reported, 'so as not to injure the vanity of the hand time-keepers', as Norris McWhirter discovered much later.

Brown was a shy, reserved figure, 'never an aggressively competitive person but he had a quiet determination', as his sister recalled. 'Although he never spoke of it', she continued, 'I always felt he was very disappointed with himself for not winning the Gold Medal' (private information). His greatest moment, however, followed hard upon his greatest disappointment. Brown was chosen to run the final leg of the 4 × 400 metres relay against strong American and German teams. Alongside Brown the British team consisted of Freddie Wolff, Bill Roberts, a powerful quarter-miler who had just missed a bronze in the 400 metres individual event, and Godfrey Rampling, an army officer and relay silver medallist from the 1932 Olympics. Preparation for the race was wonderfully unscientific. Duncanson and Collins recall Rampling saying, 'Look here chaps, we really ought to practise some baton-changing', but adding 'we soon got bored and packed it in'. Brown, however, was less casual. He had watched the Americans and was convinced the British team had the talent to win. Wolff ran an indifferent first leg but Rampling ran a great second lap, making up the deficit and giving Roberts a slight lead which he extended, leaving Brown to bring home the title in style by a margin of about 15 metres.

It was Britain's only track gold medal of the games and brought Brown to the attention of the general public. He was still only twenty-one and ran successfully in 1937 and in 1938, clocking a personal best for the 880 yards in America in 1937 and remaining unbeaten in 1938. By then he had left Cambridge and started a career as a schoolmaster. Lack of time for training told in his relatively poor form in 1939. Extreme short-sightedness—he always ran with glasses—meant he spent the war as a schoolmaster and he never recovered his pre-war form. On 15 April 1939 he married Mary Denholm Armstrong (1915/16–1993), the daughter of a railway manager, with whom he had four children, three daughters and a son. He kept up his links with athletics through summer coaching schemes, acted as an official at meetings, and even built a cinder running track with the help of a few volunteers at Cheltenham College, where he taught from 1943 to 1950. From 1950 until 1978 he was headmaster of Worcester Royal Grammar School, where he taught sixth-form history and set up a development fund which enabled a major building programme to be completed, including a new science wing. Despite poor sight he was a good rugby player and cricketer and was active within the local community, prominent in getting the Swan Theatre built in Worcester, and playing the French horn in the local orchestra.

Brown always set great store by his family's remarkable athletic achievements. His sister Audrey won a silver medal in the 100 metres relay in the 1936 Olympics, while his elder brother Ralph was an Amateur Athletics Association champion hurdler (and a future High Court judge). But for injury, Ralph would have joined his brother and sister at Berlin in 1936 in a unique triumph for 'muscular Christianity' and for the Achilles club, of which the brothers were both members.

Brown retired to Clifton-on-Theme and then to Sussex. His wife died in 1993 and he died two years later, on 4 February 1995, shortly before his eightieth birthday, in Crawley Hospital, Sussex.   RICHARD HOLT

Sources N. Duncanson and P. Collins, *Tales of gold* (1988) · I. Buchanan, *British Olympians* (1991) · private information (2004) [Sir Ralph Kilner Brown (brother); Mrs Audrey Court (sister); Professor John M. Brown (son)] · *Daily Telegraph* (7 Feb 1995) · m. cert. · d. cert. · *Evening News* [Worcester] (6 March 1995)
Likenesses group photograph, repro. in N. McWhirter, ed., *The Olympics, 1896–1972* (1972)
Wealth at death £125,000: probate, 30 March 1995, *CGPLA Eng. & Wales*

Brown, Sir (Ernest) Henry Phelps (1906–1994), economist, was born in the High Street, Calne, Wiltshire, on 10 February 1906, the second child of Edgar Brown, who kept an ironmonger's shop in Calne, and his wife, Ada, *née* Bibbing. His mother died when he was two years old, and his father married her elder sister. Ernest, as he was called until he was eighteen, when he was persuaded to use his second name, Henry, referred to his stepmother and father as his parents. They were Baptists, and attended the local chapel, to which they took the young Ernest every Sunday, twice. He, however, gradually lost faith, and was never baptized. He had learned to read by the age of three and early became a voracious reader. He won a scholarship to Taunton School, and in 1924 a history scholarship to Wadham College, Oxford. He enjoyed an active undergraduate life, joining play-reading, political, and debating societies (he was secretary of the Oxford Union Society in 1928), and engaging in cross-country running for his college and university. A first-class degree in modern history in 1927 was followed two years later by a first in politics, philosophy, and economics (one of his tutors being Lionel Robbins). Elected to a fellowship at New College, Oxford,

Sir (Ernest) Henry Phelps Brown (1906–1994), by unknown photographer [detail]

in 1930, he felt his training as an economist to be inadequate and in 1930–31 he took a Rockefeller travelling fellowship to the United States, where he encountered leading American economists and attended the class in mathematical economics and statistics of Henry Schultz.

On 14 March 1932 Phelps Brown married (Dorothy) Evelyn Mostyn Bowlby (*b*. 1910), the third daughter of Sir Anthony Alfred *Bowlby, baronet (1855–1929), the eminent surgeon, and sister of (Edward) John Mostyn *Bowlby (1907–1990), who became a pioneer in child psychology and influenced Henry's sociological approach to economics. With George Shackle as assistant, he wrote papers on monetary circulation and real turnover. He participated in the newly established Institute of Statistics at Oxford, and wrote *The Framework of the Pricing System* (1936), which explained the principles of the Walrasian general equilibrium model for students with little training in mathematics. The Munich settlement convinced him that war was likely and he joined a Territorial Army antiaircraft battery. When war came he joined a regular Royal Artillery regiment in France in November 1939, before returning from Dunkirk in June 1940. He served through the London blitz, and was later given command of a mobile battery going to north Africa in 1943, and on to Italy. He was demobilized with the rank of lieutenant-colonel and appointed MBE. His experience in France formed the background of a novel, *The Balloon* (1953). On returning to Oxford he resumed teaching, but found tutorials no more congenial than before, and in 1947 he accepted an invitation to take a new chair in the economics of labour at the London School of Economics.

There Phelps Brown's main preoccupation was with the research division. He resumed his pre-war practice of acquiring a talented research assistant, of whom there was to be a remarkable succession, and produced a stream of journal articles. The best-known were probably a group of five, written with Sheila Hopkins, on 'wages through the ages'. The most striking results were that British real wages appeared to have been higher towards the end of the fifteenth century than at any time before the second half of the nineteenth century, and, equally remarkable, that between 1413 and 1914 the ratio of the pay rates of building craftsmen to those of labourers barely changed. Phelps Brown regarded his field of study as wider than, but still including, the conventional subject of industrial relations. *The Growth of Industrial Relations* (1959) was the first of two books studying the role of trade unions in the labour market. Unlike those of most developed countries, British trade unions had been able to steer clear of the law, and in his conclusions Phelps Brown was inclined to approve the voluntary tradition in British collective bargaining. But when he returned to the subject later in *The Origins of Trade Union Power* (1983), he could no longer give his approval, since he believed that the industrial and political power of trade unions had become too great. The year after he retired from the London School of Economics he spent in Australia, and was favourably impressed by the Australian arrangements for conciliation and arbitration. The questions of distribution and inequality were tackled in two other books, *The Inequality of Pay* (1977) and *Egalitarianism and the Generation of Inequality* (1988). The former dealt with differences in earnings of different kinds of labour as a major source of the inequality of incomes. Of particular interest was the connection between pay and the social rank of different occupations. Supply and demand were dominant, but their forces did not work with precision, leaving a wide band of indeterminacy within which there was room for the independent influence of status. *Egalitarianism* extended the scope to include non-labour incomes and wealth. A magisterial survey of the evolution of ideas about inequality from the ancient Greeks to modern times was followed by the presentation of statistical data on income and wealth distribution in a number of countries. The last part of the book sought to establish a philosophical basis for contemporary egalitarianism.

As his reputation as a scholar grew, Phelps Brown not only received recognition from his academic peers—he was elected a fellow of the British Academy in 1960—but was also called upon for a variety of forms of public service. In 1959 he succeeded Sir Dennis Robertson on the Council on Prices, Productivity and Incomes ('the three wise men'), and he shifted the emphasis from demand inflation to cost inflation, with its implication for 'incomes policy'. The council was wound up in 1961, but Phelps Brown was immediately transferred to the newly formed National Economic Development Council. His most substantial public work came a little later, when he was appointed a member of the royal commission on the distribution of income and wealth, under the chairmanship of Lord Diamond, in 1974. In its short life the commission undertook and published a wide range of reports, and it was natural that Phelps Brown should play a major role in the research programme, for which he was

knighted in 1976. A dapper man with a rather military-looking moustache, Phelps Brown was a keen walker throughout his life and took pride in mountaineering.

Throughout his working life Phelps Brown believed that the purpose of economics was to explain the real world, and on occasion he gave public expression to his concern at the direction being taken in economics. The most notable of such occasions was his presidential address to the Royal Economic Society in 1971. The boundaries between economics and other social sciences should be removed; economic studies should be field-determined and not discipline-determined. The economist was not trained if he was not numerate, but neither was he trained if he was not conversant with history. Two years after *Egalitarianism* was published Phelps Brown suffered a serious stroke which, while leaving his mind unimpaired, ruled out further writing. He died at his home, 16 Bradmore Road, Oxford, on 15 December 1994. His body was cremated at Oxford crematorium on 21 December. He was survived by his wife and three children, Juliet (*b.* 1934), Nicholas (*b.* 1936), and Thomas (*b.* 1948).   G. D. N. WORSWICK

Sources *Review of Political Economy*, 8/2 (April 1996) [memorial no., incl. autobiographical notes] • D. Worswick, 'Ernest Henry Phelps Brown, 1906–1994', *PBA*, 90 (1996), 319–44 • K. Hancock and J. E. Isaac, *Economic Journal*, 108 (1998), 25ff. • *The Times* (4 Jan 1995) • *The Independent* (21 Dec 1994) • *WWW* • Burke, *Peerage* • private information (2004) • personal knowledge (2004)
Archives BLPES, corresp. relating to Royal Economic Society and the *Economic Journal* • BLPES, papers relating to economics and public work | BLPES, corresp. with J. E. Meade | SOUND BL NSA, oral history interviews
Likenesses photograph, repro. in *The Times* [*see illus.*]

Brown, Henton (1697/8–1775), Quaker minister and banker, of unknown parentage, was born in London. He was educated by Friends, and in 1718 he married Sarah, of whom further details are unknown, in an Anglican ceremony, contrary to the beliefs of the society. The couple repented this action and their acknowledgement of wrongdoing was accepted by the society on 20 January 1720. The couple had eleven children, many of whom died in infancy.

When he was twenty-five Brown made his first public testimony of his faith and was 'measurably preserved in faithfulness' (Testimonies, 3.97). On 28 November 1731 he was accepted as a minister of the society, following a recommendation by the Horsleydown meeting, Southwark. Brown's ministry was nevertheless commented upon by William Gibson in his *Saul's Errand to Damascus* (1728), in which he criticized Brown's reflections upon 'Inward and Spiritual Grace' (Gibson, 11). Between 1726 and 1735 Brown wrote several treatises defending the Society of Friends from attacks by William Bromfield and by William Notcutt, notably *An Examination of William Bromfield's Principles* (1726) and *A Vindication of Robert Barclay's Apology … Against the Attempts of William Notcut* (1732). In 1727 a manuscript written by Brown against Bromfield was submitted to the morning meeting but, on 16 October 1727, was rejected by Friends who thought it more prudent to stay out of the argument. This presumably was Brown's *The Divine and Human Natures United in the Person of Jesus*

Christ (1727). In 1735 Brown again attacked Bromfield in *An Examination of William Notcutt's Reply to H.B.'s Vindication*. In this period Brown, along with other Friends, warmly congratulated the prince of Orange on his marriage to the princess royal. Between 1743 and 1763 Brown wrote several addresses to the crown, including commentaries on the Jacobite rising, the accession of George III, the king's marriage to Queen Charlotte and the royal birth, and on the negotiation of peace with France in 1763. Brown was also interested in issues which affected the Quaker community and was an influential member of the yearly meeting and meeting for sufferings.

In 1744 Brown travelled, as a Quaker minister, through Essex, Suffolk, and Norfolk, visiting Friends, where, 'being a man of strong natural parts, and having acquired reputation on this account, he became acquainted with several persons of considerable rank, and gradually fell into much business, and a variety of worldly engagements' (Testimonies, 3.97; 'Dictionary of Quaker biography'). By 1748 Brown, with his son James (1721–1781), had established his own bank, Henton Brown & Son. Benjamin Franklin became an important client during his first visit to Britain as a provincial agent for Pennsylvania. Later Thomas Collinson (1727–1803), the husband of Brown's youngest daughter, Sarah, became a partner, and the bank changed its name to Brown and Collinson in 1770. His grandson John Henton Tritton (1753–1833), the son of his second daughter, Anna Maria, and her husband, Thomas Tritton (1717–1786), was left a partnership in the bank in Brown's will. Tritton's right to a quarter share of the business was nevertheless conditional on his completion of an apprenticeship and his reaching his majority.

Brown also participated in a lively correspondence with John Fothergill (1712–1780) and the Philadelphian James Pemberton (1723–1809) on the issues affecting the society in America. In May 1754 Brown waited on the new governor of Pennsylvania, Robert Hunter Morris, and on 21 March 1755, along with Fothergill, David Barclay, Silvanus Bevan, and Capel Hanbury, he became a committee member appointed by the meeting for sufferings to examine Friends' needs in the state. On 8 April 1766, with John Fothergill, he also wrote a formal attestation on behalf of Benjamin Franklin, to reassure the German community in Pennsylvania of Franklin's 'loyalty to the colonial cause' (Corner and Booth, 262).

By May 1750 Brown had obtained permission from Friends at the Horsleydown monthly meeting to move, with his family, to the monthly meeting at Gracechurch Street, London. This action was presumably taken in order to be nearer to his bank on Lombard Street. By 1754, however, Brown had also become prosperous enough to own the leasehold of a country house on Clapham Common, near Mount Pond. His good fortune clearly troubled his conscience, as he complained to a friend, in 1764, that he had spent too much time acquiring material wealth, commenting, 'What end will it answer, what end will it answer? It may possibly find wings for my children to fly from the blessed truth' (Testimonies, 3.98; 'Dictionary of Quaker biography'). Although Brown was a 'pretty

constant attender of … [Wandsworth] meeting, as well as a benefactor to it' ('Dictionary of Quaker biography'), he retained his membership of the Gracechurch Street meeting, and it is possible that he may have attended the London two weeks meeting for Gracechurch Street. It is further known that as a member of the Horsleydown monthly meeting between 1728 and 1743 he was on the committee concerned with the Friends' workhouse, and he attended London yearly meeting in 1735, 1754, and 1759. He may well have attended more meetings than this, for in 1775, in spite of ill health and the need to be supported by two other Friends, he is noted as having attended yearly meeting.

Henton Brown died of dropsy at his country residence, near Mount Pond, Clapham Common, on 23 September 1775 aged seventy-seven, after a long illness, and was interred at the Quaker burial-ground at Long Lane, Southwark, on 1 October 1775. His will, which was proved on 23 October 1775, included a £100 bequest for building a new meeting-house at Wandsworth, but this was cancelled by the addition of a codicil, written in 1774, which acknowledged that Brown had paid £40 towards the repairs of the old meeting-house. Brown's total bequests were in excess of £30,000 (excluding properties) and he bequeathed £100 for the Friends' workhouse at Clerkenwell, and £50 and £20 respectively for poor members at the Gracechurch Street and Wandsworth meetings.

RICHARD C. ALLEN

Sources Testimonies concerning ministers deceased, 1774–91, RS Friends, Lond., 97–100 • 'Dictionary of Quaker biography', RS Friends, Lond. [card index] [Brown, Henton] • will, proved, Oct 1775, PRO, PROB 11/1011 • Horsleydown monthly meeting, 5, 1713–1721, minutes, 30 July 1719; 28 Aug 1719; 7, 1728–1743/4, 154, 522; 8, 1743/4–1758, 285, 294, RS Friends, Lond. • Southwark monthly meeting, Henton and Sarah Brown letter of repentance, 20 Nov 1719, RS Friends, Lond., MS4/63 • J. H. Tritton, *Tritton: the place and the family* (1907), 123–6, 129–30, 137, 141–2, 173, 282 • births and burials digest, London and Middlesex quarterly meeting, RS Friends, Lond. • digest registers (marriages), RS Friends, Lond. [Sussex and Surrey quarterly meeting] • book of disorderly walkers, Horsleydown monthly meeting, 1, 1728–83, RS Friends, Lond., 49 [certificate for travel in the ministry, 18 Feb 1744] • J. J. Green, ed., *Souvenir of the address to King Edward VII* (1901), 46–51 • *Universal Weekly Pamphlet*, 1734, RS Friends, Lond., Tract vol. 00/139, 465–6 • index of yearly meeting representatives, RS Friends, Lond. [typescript] • London yearly meeting, minutes, 15, 1774–7, RS Friends, Lond., 352 [answers to the queries, dated 5 May 1776 (5th query)] • meeting for sufferings, 29 1747–56, 355, 357, 424; 31, 1761–6, 54, 62, RS Friends, Lond. • morning meeting minutes, 4, 1711–34, RS Friends, Lond., 371 • London two weeks meeting, copies of certificates, vol. A, 1716–1767, *passim*; copies of certificates, vol. 1, 1767–85, *passim*, RS Friends, Lond. • Wandsworth monthly meeting, RS Friends, Lond., MS 3/86 • *Chain of friendship: selected letters of Dr John Fothergill of London, 1735–1780*, ed. B. C. Corner and C. C. Booth (1971), 252–62 • P. W. Matthews, *History of Barclays Bank Limited*, ed. A. W. Tuke (1926), 16–19, 22–3, 38 • F. G. Hilton Price, *A handbook of London bankers*, enl. edn (1890–91), 24 • A. T. Gary, 'The political and economic relations of English and American Quakers (1750–1785)', DPhil diss., U. Oxf., 1935, appx A, 124–5, 133, 456–7 • T. Thayer, 'The library [of the *Historical Society of Pennsylvania*]: the Pemberton papers', *Pennsylvania Magazine of History and Biography*, 67 (1943), 280–86 • G. S. Eddy, ed., 'Account book of Benjamin Franklin', *Pennsylvania Magazine of History and Biography*, 55 (1931), 97–133 • 'Notes and queries', *Pennsylvania Magazine of History and Biography*, 42 (1918), 285–6

Wealth at death over £30,000; plus property; annuities and bequests to family and friends; £40 to Wandsworth Quaker Meeting House for repairs; apprenticeships to grandsons: will, proved, Oct 1775, PRO, PROB 11/1011

Brown, Horatio Robert Forbes (1854–1926), historian, the elder son of Hugh Horatio Brown, of Newhall House, Carlops, Midlothian, and his wife, Giulielmina Forbes, sixth daughter of Alexander Ranaldson *Macdonell, last chief of Glengarry, was born at Nice, then part of the kingdom of Sardinia, on 16 February 1854. Mrs Brown, who was considerably younger than her husband, after his death took a house at Clifton, Bristol, to be near her two sons, Horatio and Allan. The boys had been entered at Clifton College, then under the headmastership of Dr John Percival, in 1864. While at school Horatio Brown made the acquaintance of John Addington Symonds, who gave lectures on the Greek poets to the Clifton College boys. Thus began one of the closest and most formative friendships of Brown's life. Symonds replaced the father that Brown had lost, and Brown took the place of the son that Symonds never had. Symonds appointed Brown his literary executor, and on Symonds's death in 1893 Brown inherited all his private papers. Because of its homosexual content, Brown made only very discreet use of this material in his two books on Symonds, *John Addington Symonds, a Biography* (1895) and *Letters and Papers of John Addington Symonds* (1923), and in his will he left instructions that all papers in his possession were to be destroyed. The only exception was Symonds's autobiography, which he bequeathed to the London Library with an embargo against publication of fifty years.

From Clifton, Brown proceeded to New College, Oxford, with an exhibition which he forfeited owing to two failures to pass responsions. He was, however, encouraged to read for *literae humaniores*, in which he obtained a second class in 1877. He did not proceed to a degree, and consequently in the course of time became senior commoner of New College, a position which he used to say nothing but death or bankruptcy could take from him. He thought, however, that he would have made a good fellow of All Souls. He spoke French, Italian, and German, and read Greek fluently. The books which he knew he absorbed; to write verse, he said, was the greatest pleasure in life; he had a tenderness for minor poets, saying that 'they were more like us' (such as T. E. Brown, his Clifton master, to whose works he contributed an introduction in 1908). Contemporaries remembered him as 'pleasant and sociable … having artistic tastes which he could afford to indulge', and as 'a fair-haired, breezy out-of-doors person with a crisp Highland-Scottish speech' (*DNB*).

In 1877 the family finances deteriorated, and Allan Brown emigrated to New South Wales, where he was killed in an accident in 1901. Newhall House was let, and Brown's circumstances never allowed him to live there again. In the same year the Symonds family moved to Davos. It may have been this example which decided Brown and his mother to settle at Venice. This they did,

Horatio Robert Forbes Brown (1854–1926), by unknown photographer

after trying Florence (where Mrs Brown's relatives, the Misses Forbes, lived), in 1879. The Browns first took an apartment on the Grand Canal, in the Palazzo Balbi-Valier. In 1885, however, they bought a tenement block on the Zattere, adjacent to the Ponte dei Incurabili, and converted it into a single residence. It was a high, narrow building, something like a ship, which commanded the Giudecca Canal and the Giudecca itself opposite. Brown, who never married, became devoted to a gondolier, Antonio Salin, whom he now installed with his wife and family in the back parts of his house. This he called Cà Torresella, from the name of the side canal as given on an old map.

In 1883 Rawdon Lubbock Brown died. He had been commissioned by the British government to calendar the Venetian state papers, preserved at the Frari, which concerned British history. His calendars, chiefly of the reports sent home by the Venetian ambassadors in London, had reached the year 1558 and were brought down to 1580 by his executor, G. Cavendish-Bentinck. Through the influence of Sir Henry Layard, head of the Anglo-American colony in Venice, Horatio Brown (he was no connection) was appointed to succeed him, and between 1889 and 1905 he compiled calendars covering the years 1581 to 1613. He occupied his mornings with transcription and epitomization, and more or less liked the work. He would return home for lunch, and then set out on the *solito giro* in the *Fisolo* (his sandolo) with Antonio to the Lido, then a nearly deserted sandbank. His Monday receptions were attended by Venetians as well as by members of the somewhat miscellaneous English colony, and were described with satirical bite by Frederick Rolfe in *The Desire and Pursuit of the Whole* (1934). He was fond of climbing, belonged to the Venetian Alpine Club, and scaled peaks in Switzerland, the Tyrol, and the Friulan Alps.

Brown's appointment at the Frari had the result of turning his attention from literature to history. Sir Richard Lodge said of him:

> My impression is that Brown's original tastes and interests were literary rather than historical. His work in the archives compelled him to turn to history and to become a very competent historian. He had no academic training in modern history, and he never had to teach it. The result was that in his historical writings there was always a little of what some people would call 'amateurishness', but which was really the freshness and vigour of one who was exploring hitherto rather unfamiliar fields—refreshing in contrast to the rather blasé treatment of most academic historians. *(DNB)*

Brown produced *Venetian Studies* (1887), a collection of articles on historical subjects; a formal history, *Venice, an Historical Sketch* (1893; compressed as the *Venetian Republic*, 1902, which Edward Armstrong declared was his best book); some chapters in the Cambridge Modern History (vol. 1, 1902, and vol. 4, 1905); and *Studies in the History of Venice* (2 vols., 1907), his most substantial work. Towards the end of his life he wrote a chapter for the Cambridge Medieval History (vol. 4, 1923). His interest was in politics and political theory, as, for instance, the relations between the Serene Republic and the Holy See, and he projected a book on Paolo Sarpi, on whom he delivered the Taylorian lecture at Oxford in 1900. As a recognition the University of Edinburgh conferred on him the degree of LLD, and this was followed by a gold medal from the British Academy and the rank of *cavaliere* from the Italian crown.

Brown's researches at the Frari had another result. He discovered the registers of printed books, the laws of the republic dealing with publishing, and other documents relating to the book trade—all unpublished. He had these transcribed, and prefixed to them chapters on the early printers and their production in *The Venetian Printing Press* (1891). The experts in possession of this field were not cordial to the newcomer, and Symonds disapproved of his spending time over bibliography. The value of the documents, however, was acknowledged.

During his first years in Venice Brown led something of a double life. This donnish *littérateur*, pillar of the Anglo-American colony, churchwarden of St George's Church, president of the Cosmopolitan Hospital, and treasurer of the Sailors' Institute, cultivated contacts and friendships among the gondoliers and fishermen, whose battles he helped to fight and whose world he described in one of his earliest and most popular books, *Life on the Lagoons* (1884). Like many British expatriates in Italy, he undoubtedly sought and found homosexual encounters. However, he was not by nature promiscuous, and he flinched from the unbridled sexual heresy of Symonds. He published a few mildly homoerotic poems in his collection *Drift* (1900); but thereafter made no further excursions into the territory

of 'pagan' literature. The early works of Gide left him somewhat aghast, and he was apt to be scathing about the Uranian circle of poets and writers whose centre was Edward Carpenter. Because of his failure to publish the truth about Symonds, they regarded him as pusillanimous and a hindrance to the cause of homosexual emancipation. This accusation was endorsed by the Bloomsbury circle, to whom Brown was 'an old pussycat'; but it was with justice resented by Brown, who had in fact been willing to divulge far more than Symonds's family would permit.

After the death of his formidable mother, in 1909, Venice, now invaded by American millionaires, became less congenial, and Brown felt increasingly out of sympathy with the new spirit of imperialistic hubris in Italian public life. He began to return regularly to Britain and spent every summer in Midlothian, where he either stayed at the village inn of Penicuik or enjoyed the hospitality of his friend and neighbour Lord Rosebery. The First World War put paid to his plans to exploit the shale deposits at Newhall, and hastened his decision to sell the estate. He remained in Venice during the first part of the war, opening his house as a refuge to the poor of the quarter when a bombardment was threatened, 'My duty', he said, 'is to appear at the top of the stairs and say *calma, calma*'. As there are no Venetian cellars, the shelter was illusory. When the capture of Venice seemed imminent he said he could not face an Austrian prison, and went first to Florence and then to Scotland, where he lived among the military at the New Club in Edinburgh or in his own village of Carlops.

Brown returned to Venice in 1919, destined not to see Scotland again. Venetian society was even less agreeable after the war; his sight had deteriorated, despite an operation for cataracts at Zürich; and his income had diminished. Newhall was without a purchaser, and he had to sell Cà Torresella, retaining the *mezzanino*. He assisted in the arrangements for the visit of George V to the Asiago battlefields in 1923. In March 1925 Brown had a severe heart attack, from which he recovered, thanks to the skill of his doctor and the devotion of his servants. His estate had been sold, and he spent his last year serenely, dying of heart failure on 19 August 1926 at his doctor's house at Belluno, where he had gone to escape the heat. His body, like that of his mother, was cremated on the Venetian cemetery island of San Michele. A monument was put up to him in St George's Church, campo San Vio, Venice.

JOHN PEMBLE

Sources *The letters of John Addington Symonds*, ed. H. M. Schueller and R. L. Peters, 3 vols. (1967–9) · University of Bristol Library, Symonds MSS · NL Scot., Rosebery MSS · U. Leeds, Brotherton L., Gosse MSS · HLRO, Strachey MSS · *The Times* (21 Aug 1926) · *The Scotsman* (22 Aug 1926) · J. Pemble, *Venice rediscovered* (1995) · *CCI* (1926)
Archives Bodl. Oxf., notes relating to Italian history · LUL | BL, letters to E. W. Gosse, Ashley MS 5739 · BL, letters to Sir A. H. Layard, Add. MSS 39037–39100, *passim* · HLRO, corresp. with John St Loe Strachey · NL Scot., corresp. with Lord Rosebery · U. Leeds, Brotherton L., Gosse MSS · U. Reading L., letters to Macmillan & Co. Ltd · University of Bristol Library, letters to Madge Symonds

Likenesses H. S. Tuke, portrait, 1899, priv. coll. · monument, St George's Church, campo San Vio, Venice · photograph, University of Bristol [*see illus.*]
Wealth at death £6117 0s. 8d.: confirmation, 1926, CCI

Brown, Hugh Stowell (1823–1886), Baptist minister, was born on 10 August 1823 at Douglas, Isle of Man, the second son of Robert Brown, a Church of England priest, and his wife, Dorothy, daughter of John Thomson, a gardener. He had three sisters and five brothers, including the poet Thomas Edward *Brown (1830–1897).

His father, **Robert Brown** (*c*.1792–1846), was chaplain of St Matthew's Chapel in Douglas. An evangelical with low views of churchmanship, he never read the Athanasian creed and refused to have his children confirmed. In 1832 he became curate of Kirk Braddan, Isle of Man, succeeding as vicar in 1836. The family relied heavily on tithes to survive, and it was one of the duties of Robert Brown's sons to collect them. Hugh spent about a year at St Matthew's Grammar School, but his chief education between the ages of eleven and sixteen consisted in reading for four or five hours a day to his father, who had become almost blind. Robert Brown was found dead by the roadside on 28 November 1846, having gone out to dissuade one of his sons from sailing for Liverpool during a storm. Twenty-two of his sermons were published as *Sermons on Various Subjects* (1818) and his *Poems, Principally Sacred* appeared in 1826.

Having expressed a desire to see the world, in 1839 Hugh Brown was apprenticed to a land surveyor, and was employed in tithe commutation and ordnance surveys in Cheshire, Shrewsbury, Birmingham, and York. In 1840 he entered the London and Birmingham Railway Company's works at Wolverton, Buckinghamshire. There he received his first lessons in Greek from the Revd George Weight, the eager student chalking his first exercises on a locomotive firebox. At this time he became a teetotaller, and with some like-minded friends ran a Sunday school for the children of the works. After three years he returned home and entered King William's College at Castletown to study for the ministry of the Church of England. However, doubts about confirmation and baptism led him to abandon the idea, and he left Castletown in August 1846, again attempting to find work in England. In Manchester he embraced Baptist principles, and was baptized by a friend from his railway days in November 1846. He had planned to attend the Baptist college at Bristol, but his father's death brought him back to the Isle of Man. The family moved to Castletown; there Brown attended and preached at the Independent church. In March 1847 he unexpectedly received an invitation to come as a supply preacher to Myrtle Street Baptist Chapel in Liverpool. Despite a disastrous first sermon, of which he later remarked, 'I have often wondered since that the chapel was not all in a titter, nay that there were not even bursts of laughter' (Caine, 74), he was invited to stay on as a probationer, and was later accepted as a minister.

Early in his ministerial career, Brown spoke frequently to large audiences of working men, instituting Sunday afternoon lectures in 1854 in the Congress Hall, Liverpool.

The addresses, which were spiced with humour, were the foundation of his nationwide fame. Later in life he came to oppose the separation of religious services along class lines. During Brown's pastorate the church increased in numbers and the building had to be enlarged. Several smaller chapels affiliated to Myrtle Street as branches, and the church was active in local missions. In 1873 he realized a lifelong ambition by visiting Canada and the United States.

Brown was president of the Baptist Union in 1878. His addresses to the union were an appeal for a better educated nonconformist ministry. He was in favour of abandoning denominational colleges and letting the students take their degrees at existing universities. He was an active member of the Baptist Missionary Society, and for many years president of the Liverpool Peace Society and chairman of the Seaman's Friend Association. His lectures to working men were printed both singly and in collections, and he contributed a series of 'Sunday readings' to the monthly magazine *Good Words*.

Brown was married twice. His first wife, whom he married in 1848, was Alice Chibnall Sirett (*d.* 1863), with whom he had several children. His second wife, whom he married in 1865, was Phoebe Caine (*d.* 1884): she was the sister of William Sproston *Caine MP, who had married Brown's eldest daughter Alice, and who was to edit Brown's autobiography (1887). The second marriage was childless.

In 1880 Brown attempted to resign his long pastorate, but his congregation prevailed upon him to remain. He died after suffering a stroke on 24 February 1886 at his home, 29 Falkner Square, Liverpool, and was buried in the city's West Derby Road cemetery.

CHARLOTTE FELL-SMITH, *rev.* L. E. LAUER

Sources E. C. Starr, ed., *A Baptist bibliography*, 3 (1953), 192–4 · J. W., 'Memoirs of deceased ministers', *Baptist Hand-Book* (1887), 96–9 · *Hugh Stowell Brown: his autobiography, his commonplace book and extracts from his sermons and addresses*, ed. W. S. Caine (1887) · *Letters of Thomas Edward Brown*, ed. S. I. Irwin, 1 (1900), 118 · *Liverpool Mercury* (25 Feb 1886) · *Liverpool Mercury* (27 Feb 1886) · *Liverpool Mercury* (1 March 1886) · *CGPLA Eng. & Wales* (1886) · GM, 2nd ser., 27 (1847), 325
Likenesses E. Long, portrait, 1872 · Brown, Barnes & Bell, photograph, Regent's Park College, Oxford
Wealth at death £8915 10s. 11d.: probate, 11 June 1886, CGPLA Eng. & Wales

Brown, Ignatius. *See* Browne, Ignatius (1630–1679).

Brown, Isaac Baker (1811–1873), surgical gynaecologist, was born at Colne Engaine, Essex, the second son of Isaac Baker Brown (*b.* 1786), gentleman farmer, and Catherine, daughter of the Revd James Boyer, master of the Blue Coat School. Baker Brown was educated at Halstead in Essex and began his career as an apprentice to Mr Gibson, principal surgeon of the county. In 1831 he became a student at Guy's Hospital, London, distinguishing himself in midwifery and diseases of women. On 18 June 1833 he married Anne Rusher Barron at St Mary the Virgin (at the Walls),

Colchester. In 1834 he became a member of the Royal College of Surgeons and opened a general practice in Connaught Square, London. Subsequently he achieved a considerable reputation as an accoucheur and 'woman's surgeon', eventually limiting his practice to gynaecological disease.

In 1848, after becoming a fellow of the Royal College of Surgeons and a founding member of St Mary's Hospital, Baker Brown enthusiastically adopted the emerging surgical model for gynaecology. His faith in the ultimate efficacy of ovariotomy, for example, was so strong that he performed his fourth ovariotomy on his own sister in 1852, even though each of his first three patients died as a result of the surgery. Fortunately his sister recovered, encouraging his pursuit of dramatic new cures by surgical means.

During the nineteenth century obstetrics and gynaecology were separate fields of medical practice. Given his training in obstetrics, why did Isaac Baker Brown choose to limit his practice to gynaecological disease? The answer is suggested by his relatively modest origins. Baker Brown's obituaries identify his father simply as a 'gentleman farmer', while his mother received only slightly more recognition as the daughter of a school headmaster. He was educated locally and served an apprenticeship with a county surgeon. Even though he distinguished himself during his hospital appointment, his background was provincial. He also lacked the key requirement for entry to the medical élite, a university degree. As an ambitious young man, therefore, Baker Brown needed other avenues to higher professional and social status.

The new field of surgical gynaecology offered Baker Brown just such possibilities. There is always more scope for advancement in an emerging field than in an older one and by the 1840s obstetrics was well established, with its own hierarchy of practitioners. After the introduction of anaesthesia in 1847, surgical innovation and experimentation expanded. Along with a number of British and American surgeons in the 1850s, Baker Brown saw the possibilities in developing supposedly fast, painless, and complete surgical treatments for 'female complaints' as an alternative to lengthy, painful, and often ineffective medical therapies.

Another British pioneer in gynaecological surgery, Thomas Spencer Wells, served as colleague, supporter, and role model for Baker Brown in the early years of his career. Baker Brown may have been even more inspired, however, by the entrepreneurial spirit of American gynaecologist J. Marion Sims. Sims spent considerable time in London during the American Civil War and demonstrated his operation for vesico-vaginal fistula to Baker Brown. Both men shared somewhat humble origins and a penchant for self-promotion in the non-medical press.

Baker Brown achieved prominence as a pioneering surgical gynaecologist, establishing a reputation for surgical dexterity and daring. In 1854 he published *On some Diseases of Women Admitting of Surgical Treatment* and four years later opened the London Surgical Home where he could devote himself to refining and expanding surgical procedures.

He reached the zenith of his career in 1865 with his election as president of the Medical Society of London. His career ended in disgrace, however, when his promotion of clitoridectomy as a cure for numerous female 'nervous complaints' precipitated professional controversy and a public scandal.

In his attempts to apply surgical therapeutics to every aspect of women's health Baker Brown singled out 'nervous disease' in women and treated many such patients at his London Surgical Home. In 1866 Baker Brown published his theories and the 'successful' results of their application in *On the Curability of Certain Forms of Insanity, Epilepsy, Catalepsy, and Hysteria in Females*. Baker Brown identified the cause of these diseases as peripheral excitement of the pudic nerve centring on the clitoris, that is masturbation. The cure was simple. By removing the site of irritation, 'unnatural practices' stopped, and the woman regained her health. The extensive list of conditions he included required a greatly expanded estimate of female auto-eroticism.

Baker Brown appealed directly to the lay public, especially women, through speeches and newspaper articles in order to popularize his 'special treatment'. Baker Brown carefully presented his new therapy in the most favourable light, neglecting to mention the more negative aspects of clitoridectomy. Reports surfaced that he frequently operated on women ignorant of the nature of the operation or even without their prior consent. Some colleagues welcomed this new cure-all operation, but the majority of the medical community castigated Baker Brown for his publicity seeking and the shocking nature of his claims.

The gynaecological profession as a whole feared a backlash from female patients and their families. The most disturbing repercussion of clitoridectomy was the slur on a respectable woman's moral character. Many practitioners of the day believed in a link between masturbation and physical and mental disease but identified it as a male problem. If Baker Brown was right, thousands of Englishwomen stood accused of 'unnatural' vice. Eventually, gynaecologists worried, no respectable woman would consult them for fear of being branded immoral. Numerous physicians rushed to defend female honour and condemn Baker Brown for speaking openly on such a subject.

The final blow to Baker Brown came when the London commissioners for lunacy discovered he had illegally performed clitoridectomy on institutionalized women without the specific consent of family members. At this point, to quell growing public furore, the Obstetrical Society of London decided to hold a hearing on the question of Baker Brown and clitoridectomy. The 'trial' of Isaac Baker Brown took place on 3 April 1867 and resulted in his expulsion from the society.

Baker Brown's practice declined rapidly after his repudiation and he never regained his professional standing. His health failed and he was subject to what *The Lancet* described as paralytic seizures, becoming a total invalid for the last year of his life. He died at 88 Albany Street,

Regent's Park, London, on 3 February 1873. He was survived by his second wife, Catherine Read, whom he married on 21 May 1863 after the death of his first wife, and three young children.   JUDITH M. ROY

Sources 'The debate at the Obstetrical Society', *BMJ* (1867), 387–410 · V. G. Plarr, *Plarr's Lives of the fellows of the Royal College of Surgeons of England*, rev. D'A. Power, 2 vols. (1930) · *BMJ* (28 April 1866), 438–40 · *The Lancet* (5 May 1866), 485–6 · review, *Medical Times and Gazette* (5 May 1866), 479–80 · *BMJ* (8 Feb 1873), 158–9 · *The Lancet* (8 Feb 1873), 222–3 · *The Times* (15 Dec 1866) · *The Times* (24 Jan 1867) · 'A gloomy rite!', *Medical Times and Gazette* (15 Dec 1866), 641–2 · IGI · A. Dally, *Women under the knife* (1991) · Boase, *Mod. Eng. biog.* · m. cert. · d. cert.

Likenesses portrait, repro. in M. J. O'Dowd and E. E. Philipp, *History of obstetrics and gynaecology* (1994), 407

Brown, Ivor John Carnegie (1891–1974), theatre critic and writer, was born on 25 April 1891 in Penang, Malaya, the younger of the two sons of Dr William Carnegie Brown of Aberdeen, and his first wife, Jean Carnegie. His father, a graduate of Aberdeen University and an expert in tropical diseases, had a practice in the Federated Malay States, and Brown was sent to England to be educated at Suffolk Hall preparatory school and then, from 1902 to 1907, at Cheltenham College. After a year's private tuition by a crammer, he headed the scholarship list at Balliol College at Oxford and took a double first in classical honour moderations (1911) and *literae humaniores* (1913). He passed sixth into the civil service and was sent to the Home Office. There his career lasted two days, still a strong candidate for a Whitehall record. His first assignment was to minute an application by Staffordshire police for an increased provision of water-closets. He wrote his comments and walked out, thereafter to earn his living as a freelance writing about more interesting matters.

During the First World War Brown was a conscientious objector, and he hotly engaged in progressive politics. He lectured for the Oxford tutorial classes committee, published two ephemeral books of political theory and three novels, and wrote iconoclastic articles for the *New Age*. His versatile, profuse, and very fast pen fitted him exceptionally for journalism—so in 1919 he joined the London office of the *Manchester Guardian*. There he wrote everything from editorials to colour pieces about sport; but particularly he wrote about the theatre, which became the master passion of his life. On 4 January 1916 he married Irene Gladys (*b.* 1891/2), the elder daughter of Bertha Posener and Carl Hentschel, a photo-engraver who made blocks for Fleet Street newspapers. She was a professional actress who became a successful director of plays, and her knowledge of the far side of the footlights enriched her husband's criticism. There were no children of the marriage.

Brown was drama critic for the *Saturday Review* from 1923 to 1930. In 1926 he was appointed Shute lecturer on the art of the theatre at Liverpool University. In 1929 he became theatre critic of *The Observer* and for the next thirty years, during a brilliant period of change and experiment on the London stage, he was the most influential and perceptive voice in British dramatic criticism. In 1939 he was made professor of drama to the Royal Society of Literature. When the Council for the Encouragement of

Ivor John Carnegie Brown (1891–1974), by Howard Coster, 1940

Music and the Arts (CEMA; later the Arts Council) was set up during the Second World War, Brown was the obvious choice for its director of drama, a position he held in 1940–42.

When J. L. Garvin retired from the editorship of *The Observer* in 1942, Brown was appointed to the post. He carried on as chief drama critic and managed also to make time to write regular leading and feature articles and, when the muse struck, elegant satiric verses. As editor he led *The Observer* with a light and liberal hand through the difficult wartime shortages of staff and newsprint. He put news on the front page, introduced new blood, broadened the paper's interests, changed its typography, and made it exceptionally well written. But as his own writing was the element in which he preferred to live, he resigned his editorship of the paper in 1948. He continued as drama critic until 1954, but after that devoted himself entirely to his own books.

Brown was among the most prolific and versatile writers of his generation, publishing more than seventy-five books, including novels, essays, biography, autobiography, criticism, coffee-table books, and even a light (and not very good) play. As well as using the English language expertly, he was one of those logophiles, such as F. G. Fowler, H. W. Fowler, and Eric Partridge, who are fascinated by language itself. He became famous for his books about words, agreeable rambles around correct usage and philology, enlivened by literary allusion, quotation, wit, and personal anecdote. He wrote thirteen of these in all, collecting words as others collect porcelain. In the first, *A Word in your Ear* (1942), he observed how gargantuan journalese was ruining such good old words as 'epic', 'odyssey', and 'tragedy'. In *A Charm of Names* (1972) he explored the history of Christian or given names, from Abigail to Zuleika—of course not forgetting his own name, Ivor. He was the most good-humoured of prescriptivists, but was still incorrigibly convinced that there existed such a thing as correct English, and that it was to be preferred to the other kind.

Shakespeare was another lifelong enthusiasm. Brown wrote a number of books about him full of amateur common sense and expert theatrical and linguistic wisdom. He was a very professional master of the English language and literature, happiest when writing, which he did very quickly while chewing the end of his handkerchief on the rare occasions when he was stuck for a word or an idea. He was a big, burly, shy man, full of Aberdonian *gravitas*, who could suddenly spark with a flash of frivolity or frolic.

Brown was chairman of the British Drama League from 1954 to 1965 and a fellow of the Royal Society of Literature, and was awarded the honorary degrees of LLD at St Andrews and Aberdeen universities (1950). After the war he lectured much in Denmark, which conferred on him a knighthood of the order of Dannebrog. In 1957 he was appointed CBE. Ivor Brown died in London on 22 April 1974.   PHILIP HOWARD

Sources *The Times* (23 April 1974) · J. B. Priestley, *The Observer* (28 April 1974) · I. Brown, *The way of my world* (1954) · m. cert. · *CGPLA Eng. & Wales* (1974)
Archives Boston University, literary MSS and papers | JRL, letters to the *Manchester Guardian* · JRL, letters to Allan Monkhouse · NL Scot., letters to Mrs Ray Mitchell · Royal Society of Literature, London, letters to the Royal Society of Literature
Likenesses K. Hutton, photograph, 5 Nov 1938, Hult. Arch. · H. Coster, photograph, 1940, NPG [*see illus.*] · A. McBean, photograph, *c.*1950, NPG · H. Coster, photographs, NPG
Wealth at death £132,010: probate, 29 Aug 1974, *CGPLA Eng. & Wales*

Brown [Browne], **James** (*b.* 1615/16), General Baptist minister, was born in Mangotsfield, Gloucestershire, the son of Thomas Brown; the identity of his mother is not known. He matriculated at Oriel College, Oxford, on 24 April 1635 aged nineteen and graduated BA on 7 April 1638. He was ordained and served as the vicar of Tenbury, Worcestershire. Although his activities during the 1640s are unrecorded, it seems likely that he joined the parliamentarian army, probably as a chaplain. He reappears in the record by 1652 when he was a Baptist minister, signing a petition to Cromwell as of Bridgnorth, Shropshire, in February, and preaching to troops of the army at Oadby and Mountsorrel in Leicestershire in March. His preaching that Christ died for all and against infant baptism provoked controversy with William Troughton, minister at Wanlip, Leicestershire, and led to the publication in 1653 of Brown's *Scripture Redemption Freed from Mens Restrictions*. As chaplain to Colonel Charles Fairfax's regiment of foot in Scotland in 1652 and 1653, Brown rebaptized several of the regiment and took part in a public debate with James Wood at Cupar. By 1655 Brown had left Fairfax's regiment

and on 30 April 1656 was a moderator in a public debate between Henry Haggar and Thomas Porter at Ellesmere, Shropshire, on infant baptism. Brown also criticized the Quakers and Ranters and so earned a rebuke from George Fox in a tract of 1659. In 1665 Brown disputed the 'light within' with Quakers in Leicester gaol. The date of his death is unknown. The erroneous suggestion that Brown conformed to the restored Church of England can be traced to Anthony Wood who misread Brown's *Scripture Redemption* principally because he misdated it to 1673, a mistake repeated by several subsequent authorities.

JOHN SPURR

Sources A. Laurence, *Parliamentary army chaplains, 1642–1651*, Royal Historical Society Studies in History, 59 (1990), 103–4 · Foster, *Alum. Oxon.* · Wood, *Ath. Oxon.*, new edn, 4.504 · Wood, *Ath. Oxon.: Fasti* (1815), 500 · J. Brown, *Scripture redemption freed from mens restrictions* (1653) · *A true and faithful narrative (for substance) of a public dispute between Mr Tho. Porter, and Mr Hen. Haggar* (1656)

Brown, James (1709–1788), traveller and scholar, was born at Kelso, Roxburghshire, on 23 May 1709, the son of James Brown, physician, of Kelso. Nothing is known of his family background but it seems to have involved an early move to London, since he was educated at Westminster School, 'where he was well instructed in the Latin and Greek classics' (Lysons, 3.301). He appears to have left school at thirteen, however, because in 1722 he accompanied his father to Constantinople, perhaps in connection with the Levant Company. In the three years of his stay in the Levant, 'having a great natural aptitude for the learning of languages' (ibid.), he learned Turkish, modern Greek, and Italian—all much in use in the cosmopolitan Ottoman capital. In 1725 he returned to London and learned Spanish. About 1732 he had the idea of publishing a *Directory of the Principal Traders in London*, although a similar directory had already been published in London, albeit some time previously, in 1677. Somewhat deterred by his failure to find a publisher he passed it to the printer Henry Kent of Finch Lane, Cornhill, who not only published it but also made money on it.

The possibility of developing trade with Persia and even India via Russia and the Caspian Sea was much discussed in London's commercial circles in the early 1740s, stimulated a few years earlier by an Anglo-Russian commercial agreement signed in 1734. In 1741 an act of parliament sanctioned just such a commercial project by the merchant adventurer Captain John Elton. It was also approved by the Russian government. Brown was caught up in the enthusiasm for such a trade route. Encouraged by support from twenty-four leading London merchants, members of the (British) Russia Company that had also approved Elton's scheme, and taking a letter from George II to the Persian ruler, Nadir Shah, he sailed for Riga in September 1741, down the Volga to Astrakhan, and across the Caspian to Resht in Persia, where he established a trading house along with several other British merchants. No details of their activities appear in Jonas Hanway's *Historical Account of the British Trade over the Caspian Sea* (1754), although Hanway gives a lengthy account of their contemporary

Elton. After four years, however, discouraged by the disorder in northern Persia at the time but also by the hostility of the Russian government to the trade as well as to Persian activity on the Caspian previously monopolized by Russian shipping, Brown resigned and returned to London on 25 December 1746.

In the following year, after the assassination of Nadir Shah, Brown's establishment was looted and the trans-Caspian trade with Persia came to an end. However, Brown had acquired such a proficiency in Persian during his stay that on his return he compiled 'a copious Persian dictionary and grammar', which sadly was never published. Daniel Lysons states that Brown was also the author of a translation of two orations of Isocrates, published anonymously (Lysons, 3.302). He died of a stroke on 30 November 1788, at home in Stoke Newington, where he had owned a house since 1734. He was buried in the parish church of St Mary. G. V. BENSON, *rev.* S. SEARIGHT

Sources D. Lysons, *The environs of London*, 4 vols. (1792–6) · L. Lockhart, *Nadir Shah* (1938) · D. Reading, *The Anglo-Russian commercial treaty of 1734* (1938) · W. E. Minchinton, *English overseas trade* (1969) · J. B. Fraser, *Travels and adventures in Persia* (1826) · *GM*, 1st ser., 58 (1788), 1128

Brown, James (1812–1881), Roman Catholic bishop of Shrewsbury, the son of James and Winifred Brown, was born on 11 January 1812 in Wolverhampton. He was educated at Sedgley Park School (1821–6) and Oscott College (1826–37), and was ordained priest by Bishop Walsh on 18 February 1837. His reserved manner and proficiency in classics marked him out for a career in teaching; after ordination, he joined the staff at Oscott, subsequently returned to Sedgley Park in 1845 as vice-president, then, in 1848, became president. In 1851 Brown was unexpectedly appointed bishop of the new diocese of Shrewsbury, and hurried into office in the face of the Ecclesiastical Titles Bill, an attempt to prevent the new Roman Catholic bishops from assuming territorial titles. He was consecrated by Cardinal Wiseman in St George's Cathedral, Southwark, on 27 July 1851.

Cardinal Manning was later to sum Brown up as a man 'completely retiring and self-concealing' (*The Tablet*, 22 Oct 1881, 675), but Brown worked hard to combine parts of three former, somewhat disparate, vicariates into a new administrative structure: his few extant letters reveal his struggle to assert claims on finances belonging to the old vicariates as well as his desire to preserve an interest in the seminaries which had served them. The diocesan chapter was installed temporarily in St Alban's Church, Macclesfield, being the only church of any size in the diocese, and a series of diocesan synods followed. Brown was responsible for about 20,000 people and had the assistance of only thirty-three priests. One of his first pastoral letters draws a vivid picture of the task which faced him: 'The Holy Sacrifice is offered in some of our congregations in a room of a public tavern, in one in a loft over a stable, in another over a common blacksmith's shop' (Phillips, 'A Catholic community', 382). Things were bad enough in Shropshire and Cheshire, but far worse in Wales: 'there are two counties in our Diocese in which there is only one

Chapel, and three in which there is neither Station, nor Chapel, nor Priest' (ibid.). By the time of Brown's death in 1881, however, the number of priests in the diocese had risen from thirty-three to ninety-eight and the number of churches and chapels from thirty-one to eighty-four.

On becoming bishop, Brown resided at Salter's Hall, Newport, Shropshire, although letters to Augustus Welby Pugin suggest that he considered moving to Chester, which was far more central to the diocese. Later he considered building the cathedral for the diocese in Birkenhead, in response to the needs of its urban population. The cathedral was eventually opened in Shrewsbury in 1856, the first major work of the architect Edward Welby Pugin. Bishop Brown moved from Newport to the clergy house, adjoining the cathedral, in September 1868. The following autumn he was scheduled to attend the First Vatican Council but a serious fall delayed the journey until February 1870, and he returned to England the following May suffering from sunstroke. This resulted in his absence from the council at the time of its proclamation of papal infallibility. Bishop Brown's health continued to deteriorate but he was able to celebrate his silver jubilee in 1876: Gerard Manley Hopkins, at this time resident in the Jesuit house of St Beuno, north Wales, contributed some occasional verses to mark the event. Brown lived on quietly in Shrewsbury but, after the appointment of Edmund Knight as auxiliary bishop in 1879, he moved into semi-retirement at St Mary's Grange, an estate just outside Shrewsbury, purchased in 1876 as the site for a possible future minor seminary. Here he died on 14 October 1881 and, after a funeral service in the cathedral, presided over by Cardinal Manning, Brown was buried in the Franciscan cemetery at Pantasaph, north Wales.

PETER PHILLIPS

Sources *The Times* (15 Oct 1881) · *The Tablet* (22 Oct 1881), 674–5 · *Weekly Register* (22 Oct 1881) · E. M. Abbott, *History of the diocese of Shrewsbury* (1986), 11–12 · P. Phillips, 'A Catholic community: Shrewsbury. Part II: 1850–1920', *Recusant History*, 20 (1990–91), 380–402 · P. Phillips, 'James Brown, first bishop of Shrewsbury', *Shrewsbury: millennium essays for a Catholic diocese*, ed. J. Marmion (2000), 151–78 · P. Phillips, '"Or else we shall be bound hand and foot": James Brown and the oversight of seminaries', *Recusant History*, 25 (2000–01), 237–348 · W. M. Brady, *The episcopal succession in England, Scotland, and Ireland, AD 1400 to 1875*, 3 vols. (1876–7) · F. J. Cwiekowski, *The English bishops and the First Vatican Council* (1971) · *DNB* · d. cert.
Archives Shrewsbury diocesan archives | CUL, Acton MSS · Westm. DA
Wealth at death £2085 14*s.* 8*d.*: probate, 6 March 1882, *CGPLA Eng. & Wales*

Brown, James (1815–1881), journalist and political reformer, was born in Liverpool on 2 August 1815. His father, James Brown, also known as Cato, was a black Nova Scotian, probably from the loyalist community which had settled there in consequence of the American War of Independence, and had served in the Royal Navy before becoming a foundry worker. Nothing is known of his mother; according to family tradition, she was white and connected with a family of Liverpool merchants named Gough. James Brown attended the Liverpool Bluecoat

School, before becoming a printers' compositor on the *Liverpool Mercury*. He married Eleanor Jane McKenzie (*d.* 1864), daughter of a Scottish builder in Liverpool and the Isle of Man and a Manx woman. Their eldest son, John Archibald Brown, was born in 1839, and was apparently followed by at least six daughters and another son.

In 1846 Brown moved to the Isle of Man, where there was a flourishing printing industry. Under Manx law there were no taxes on newspapers (duties were payable in the rest of Britain), while a loophole allowed them to be sent free of charge through the post to subscribers on the mainland. 'Single cause' publications, including some supporting Chartism and other radical movements, were produced on the Isle of Man and dispatched in vast quantities, their editors safely beyond the jurisdiction of the English law. The Chartist leader Bronterre O'Brien was among them, as well as William Shirrefs, and Brown worked for Shirrefs and Russell's Steam Press, where he may have acquired his interest in political reform. An act of parliament in 1848 imposed punitive postage rates on such publications and the printing boom collapsed, leaving Brown to survive as a jobbing printer and publisher of free advertising circulars.

In 1861 Brown founded his own newspaper, the *Isle of Man Times*, and used it to campaign for democratic reform of the House of Keys. This body, the Manx equivalent of the House of Commons, was self-elected and unrepresentative of what Brown's editorials called 'the source of all power—the people themselves'. In 1864 the Keys contemptuously rejected a petition for by-laws which would facilitate improvements to the growing seaside resort of Douglas; a member of the assembly had remarked that the elected Douglas town commissioners were fit only to take control of the donkeys on the beach. This comment, said Brown, had 'elicited marks of approval from the donkeys around him', and he castigated them as despotic rulers. The Keys, claiming ancient right, summoned him for libel and contempt, and sentenced him to six months in prison. From prison he continued to publish defiant editorials in support of freedom of the press and democracy, likening the Keys to the Star Chamber and the inquisition. His journalist son, John Archibald Brown, orchestrated support in the English press and organized an application to the court of queen's bench which ruled that the House of Keys had no power to try or sentence Brown, and he was released after serving seven weeks of his sentence. Brown had great popular support, and sued the members of the House of Keys for wrongful imprisonment and was awarded £519 in damages by a Manx jury. Two years later the unelected House of Keys, under pressure from Westminster (which held out fiscal carrots and sticks), voted for democratic elections. Brown's activities had played a part in influencing popular opinion in favour of the reforms.

Eleanor Brown died in August 1864, and in the following year, on 13 February, Brown married Isabella Anne Bromley (*d.* 1912). Brown's business flourished; according to his will it was worth £7000 in 1877 when he assigned it to his elder son, John, in return for 5 per cent annual interest on that sum. James Brown was an active freemason from about 1858, serving as secretary of the Irish lodge (no. 123), of the Royal Isle of Man lodge, and he initiated his son into the lodge on his coming of age. He died at Douglas on 12 March 1881 and was buried on 15 March in Kirk Braddan cemetery. At the time of the 1881 census his widow was living at their home, 18 Prospect Terrace, Douglas, with her two unmarried step-daughters.

Under John Archibald Brown (1839–1925), who continued to run the family business, the firm was contracted to print government publications and officially to report the proceedings of the legislature, but his newspaper remained critical of authority. The *Isle of Man Times* came to dominate local readership and remained in family hands until 1958, and *Brown's Isle of Man Directory* (1881), produced by the firm, is an invaluable source for historians.

John Archibald Brown was a speculative property developer who contributed to the rise of Manx mass tourism, was a justice of the peace, and an officer of the freemasons. His brother, James William Ross Brown, had a successful career at the English bar. There was no black community on the Isle of Man, but race seems to have been no barrier to the Browns' social acceptance and material success.   MARTIN FARAGHER

Sources M. Faragher, 'The Browns of the *Times*', *North West Labour History*, 20 (1995–6), 2, 44–9 • private information (2004) • *Brown's directory of the Isle of Man* (1894) • J. C. Belcham, 'Radical entrepreneur — Wm. Shirrefs and the Manx free press', *Proceedings of Isle of Man Natural History and Antiquarian Society*, 10/1 (1989–91) • *Isle of Man Times* (19 March 1881) [Manx Museum Library, Douglas (microfilm N7)] • will, Manx Museum Library, Douglas [archidiaconal wills: microfilm BM 242] • *IGI* • census returns, 1881 • *Isle of Man Weekly Times* (26 Sept 1925)
Likenesses J. Swynnerton, marble effigy, Manx Museum, Douglas, Isle of Man • two photographs, Manx Museum, Douglas, Isle of Man
Wealth at death see will, Manx Museum Library (archidiaconal wills: microfilm BM 242)

Brown, James (1862–1939), trade unionist and politician, was born on 16 December 1862, at Whitletts, Ayr, the third child, but first to survive infancy, of James Brown, a weaver turned miner, and his wife, Christine MacMillan, *née* O'Hara. His mother was of protestant Irish and Scottish highland descent. Brown himself narrowly survived smallpox, which mildly marked him for life. The family moved to the nearby mining village of Annbank, where he went to elementary school. He left aged twelve to 'go down the pit', despite offers to keep him as a monitor and pupil teacher. He worked first with pit ponies and then hewed at the coalface for more than twenty years. However, he had four years' night school and developed a taste for self-education, especially in literature, rooted in Bible knowledge but ranging from piety to poetry.

On 17 August 1888 Brown married Catherine MacGregor Steel (*c.*1860–1942), a finisher in a paper mill, of Kilbarchan, Renfrewshire. Her father, Matthew Steel, was a shoemaker. They had four sons, the youngest being killed in the First World War, and a daughter; of these the daughter and a son died in infancy.

Brown joined the Ayrshire miners' union, serving on a local committee from the age of sixteen, and became Ayrshire president, a lay office, in 1895, the year after the Scottish miners' strike. He ceased to work as a miner on his appointment as an Ayrshire miners' agent in 1904. He became general secretary of the Ayrshire miners in 1908, and secretary of the National Union of Scottish Mineworkers in 1917. Standing as a Labour candidate, he unsuccessfully fought North Ayrshire in the general elections of 1906 and January 1910. However, in December 1918 he won the mining and agricultural seat of South Ayrshire, formerly held by the Liberals, and, apart from 1931–5, retained the seat until his death. His political career was combined with a continuing involvement in Scottish mining unionism, and he continued to hold office as secretary of the Scottish miners until 1936.

Like his mentor Keir Hardie, an Ayrshireman by adoption, Brown thought of himself as an 'advanced' Liberal, but became a Christian socialist. He was also, like Hardie, a temperance campaigner, and was active in the Independent Order of Good Templars. However, unlike him, and most Scottish radicals, he belonged to the 'Establishment', the Church of Scotland which survived the Disruption of 1843. He was an elder of Annbank church and, for more than forty years, a Sunday school superintendent. He also undertook lay preaching, less common in the Scottish kirk than in English nonconformity.

These credentials prompted the first Labour prime minister, Ramsay MacDonald, to choose Brown for what would later be described as 'gesture politics'. In 1924, on the suggestion of the secretary of state for Scotland, the Baptist ex-miner William Adamson, MacDonald nominated Brown as lord high commissioner (the personal representative of the sovereign) to the general assembly of the Church of Scotland, which entailed a temporary move from a two-room-and-kitchen miner's cottage to the palace of Holyroodhouse. MacDonald repeated the nomination in 1930 and 1931, the first ordinary general assemblies of the kirk after the reunion of the Presbyterian churches (the United Free Church and the Church of Scotland) in 1929. Brown contributed to this as a member of the union committee and by his parliamentary advocacy of the necessary legislation. His role as lord high commissioner—almost viceroy for a fortnight—seemed startling at the time, as Brown was the first commoner since the seventeenth century to hold the ceremonial but symbolic post. The appointment, made possible by a £2000 allowance, drew mixed reactions, with ribaldry and criticism on the left, initial distrust among social and ecclesiastical conservatives, and considerable popular enthusiasm. Brown's dignity, sincerity, and experience as an assembly member made it a success, though he was more at ease during his later terms than in 1924. Then the novelty seemed to make him, in a phrase used in the church's magazine but at odds with Presbyterian principles, 'the central figure of the Assembly'. He bridled what could be a sharp tongue and did not make public his view that a

prominent Labour critic, Churchill's future Scottish secretary Tom Johnston, was 'a dirty beggar', or a similar less decorous phrase (Galbraith, 95).

Brown's role in the Church of Scotland contributed to the acceptance of Labour as a lasting force in Scottish politics that made conciliation and co-operation inevitable. It helped to confirm that the main elements of the labour movement were ready to work with existing institutions. Brown also argued for the church as an instrument of social reform.

Brown epitomized Victorian virtues, including the belief that social and moral improvement should go together. A good influence rather than a great power in politics, able to appear forceful yet forbearing, he was out of sympathy and temperamentally at odds with some mid-twentieth-century trends in his party and the far-left influences which came to dominate the leadership of the Scottish miners. He was one of the established Scottish miners' leaders challenged vigorously by the communists and their allies in the late 1920s, though the communists were less strong in the Ayrshire coalfield than in Fife and Lanarkshire. In wider labour politics he was 'always a moderate but moved more to the right in the years after the First World War' (Knox, 70).

Brown was made OBE in 1917 for wartime services—he served on tribunals in Ayrshire—and a privy councillor in 1930. He was a freeman of Ayr (1930), and Girvan (1931), deputy lieutenant of Ayrshire, and doctor of laws of Glasgow University (1931). He died in an Ayr nursing home on 21 March 1939 and was buried in Annbank on 23 March.

R. D. KERNOHAN

Sources A. Gammie, *From pit to palace: the life of the Right Hon. James Brown MP* (1931) · J. H. Gillespie, *James Brown: a king o'men* (1939) · W. Knox, ed., *Scottish labour leaders, 1918–39: a biographical dictionary* (1984) · *DLB* · *DSCHT* · W. P. Livingstone, 'The lord high commissioner', *Life and Work* (1930), 195–7 · E. Kyle, 'Mrs James Brown', *Life and Work* (1931), 189–90 · A. G. Stewart, 'Right Hon. James Brown', *Life and Work* (1939), 201 · R. Galbraith, *Without quarter: a biography of Tom Johnston, 'the uncrowned king of Scotland'* (1995) · parish church records, Annbank, Ayrshire · private information (2004) [family] · records of the Ayrshire miners' union and Ayrshire region of the National Union of Mineworkers, NL Scot., Dep. 258 · Brown–Glasier correspondence, U. Lpool L., special collections and archives, Bruce Glasier papers · A. Campbell, *The Scottish miners, 1874–1939*, 2 vols. (2000)

Archives NL Scot., Ayrshire miners' union records, Dep. 258 · U. Lpool L., corresp. with J. Bruce Glasier and K. Bruce Glasier

Likenesses W. P. Livingstone, photographs, 1930, repro. in Livingstone, 'The lord high commissioner', 196–7 · W. P. Livingstone, photographs, 1930, repro. in Kyle, 'Mrs James Brown', 189 · D. Young, photograph, 1930 · photograph, Annbank church, Ayrshire

Wealth at death £2309 1s. 1d.: confirmation, Scotland, 1939

Brown, James (1921–1993), petroleum engineer, was born on 13 March 1921 at 151 Cartvale Road, Glasgow, the son of William Brown, engineer's toolmaker, and his wife, Margaret-Ann, formerly Cameron. Brown was educated at Queen's Park secondary school, Glasgow, then became a tax officer, an experience which stood him in good stead when he joined Shell. The Second World War changed his life. Enlisted in the Argyll and Sutherland Highlanders, he underwent tough commando training in Lochaber, and volunteered—the youngest to be accepted—for the hazardous raid on the U-boat pens of St Nazaire in 1942. Along with other members of no. 5 commando, Brown protected HMS *Campbelltown*, which, disguised as a German ship, rammed the dock gates with explosive; inevitably, he was captured. He was dispatched to Stalag 8B, 60 miles east of Breslau. An ever-determined escaper, his first attempt ended in tragi-comedy. He managed to dye his overcoat and scarf with polish. Alas, with sweat, the polish began to run on to his neck and skin, presenting a most remarkable spectacle. So he dived into a public lavatory in the town of Opeln, only to find that five minutes later the door was forced open by two members of the Gestapo. They frogmarched him, and made him sit between them on a tramcar on the way back to camp. Nothing daunted, when the conductor came along, Brown said sweetly: 'A penny half to Sauchiehall Street, Missus!' Even the Gestapo, one of whom had been in Britain before the war, did not suppress a smirk. After further unsuccessful attempts to escape, it was 'Fifth Time Lucky', the title of his memoirs, and a dramatic escape to Switzerland, where he worked on an English-language publication until the autumn of 1944, when the American army reached the Franco-Swiss border. Brown was awarded the Military Medal.

On demobilization Brown became a miner in Auchengeoch colliery, near Glasgow. A grant from the commandos gave him entrance to the mining engineering course at the Royal Technical College in Glasgow, and subsequently Glasgow University. On 18 June 1948 he married Catherine Ann MacDonald (1923–1990), a clerk, and from 1948 until 1975, he worked for Shell in Trinidad, Turkey, Kuwait, and Venezuela, but frequently returned to London and the Netherlands to participate in Shell's most advanced training courses.

Brown had a global understanding of the oil industry. Briefing government officials and ministers on legislation on North Sea oil in the period 1975–90, he would insist: 'If you do things purely for the advantage of Britain in UK legislation, just remember that there is a tit-for-tat effect.'

At fifty-four Brown was recruited as the first professor of petroleum engineering at Heriot-Watt. This Edinburgh engineering and science-based university had by 1975 an internationally formidable reputation in offshore engineering, and now needed to develop the expertise needed to get the reserves out of the sea-bed. He also brought to Heriot-Watt immense and important goodwill: Royal Dutch Shell crucially lent him the services of a clever young Dutchman, Bau van Ort. Brown was uniquely placed to get money out of the oil companies for the young department and gathered around him a talented and subsequently distinguished staff who were united in their respect for the blunt and genial professor.

Brown and his ever supportive wife entertained many overseas students at their house at Dundarroch on Loch Ard, near Aberfoyle. Incalculable goodwill towards Britain remained with many of those who shared these beautiful surroundings, and subsequently attained important posts in their own country's oil industry. After Brown retired in 1981 he worked for Britoil, and set up a company: Edinburgh Petroleum Services. His wife died suddenly in Tenerife, where they had gone for health reasons in 1990. Brown moved to Hampshire, where his son William Allan Brown was living, and he died at Frimley Park Hospital, Surrey, on 5 December 1993.   TAM DALYELL

Sources *The Independent* (13 Dec 1993) · personal knowledge (2004) · private information (2004) · b. cert. · m. cert. · d. cert.
Likenesses photograph, repro. in *The Independent*

Brown, James Baldwin, the elder (1785–1843), judge and legal writer, was called to the bar at the Inner Temple in 1816, and practised on the northern circuit and at the Lancashire quarter sessions. He was appointed judge of the Oldham court of requests in 1840. He married a sister of the nonconformist minister Thomas Raffles, Mary (d. 1858), and was father of James Baldwin *Brown the younger.

In 1818 Brown published his memoirs of John Howard, which he dedicated to William Wilberforce. He also wrote two books on the subject of ecclesiastical law and, with Thomas Raffles and Jeremiah Holmes Wiffen, a collection of poems. He died in November 1843.

THOMPSON COOPER, rev. JONATHAN HARRIS

Sources *GM*, 2nd ser., 21 (1844), 93–4 · [J. Watkins and F. Shoberl], *A biographical dictionary of the living authors of Great Britain and Ireland* (1816) · T. S. Raffles, *Memoirs of the life and ministry of the Rev. Thomas Raffles, D.D., LL.B.* (1864), 374
Likenesses C. Penny, stipple, NPG · engraving, repro. in E. Evans, *Catalogue of a collection of engraved portraits*, 1 (1836), 42

Brown, James Baldwin, the younger (1820–1884), Congregational minister, was born on 19 August 1820 at 10 Harcourt Buildings, Inner Temple, London, the son of Dr James Baldwin *Brown the elder (1785–1843), barrister, and his wife Mary (d. 1858), who was the sister of the Independent minister Thomas *Raffles. He had one brother, William Raffles Brown, an architect in London and Dublin. Baldwin Brown was educated at a school connected with the University of London. He graduated in arts from the University of London in 1839, and then entered the Inner Temple, but in 1841 he decided to abandon the law. He took this step as a result of reading Carlyle's *Sartor Resartus*, and under the influence of John Leifchild (1780–1862), whose ministry at Craven Chapel, Bayswater, the church attended by his family, had commenced in 1831. Baldwin Brown entered Highbury College as a candidate for the ministry, and in 1843 he became pastor of a new Congregational church at London Road, Derby. In November of that year he married Elizabeth, daughter of William Gerard Leifchild, surveyor, the niece of John Leifchild and sister of the sculptor Henry Stormonth Leifchild. In 1846 he moved to Claylands Chapel, Clapham Road, Clapham, Surrey, and in 1870 a new church was opened for his congregation at Brixton at a cost of £13,000; he ministered there for the rest of his life.

Baldwin Brown was a controversial figure because he embraced liberal theological views in opposition to the

Calvinism that prevailed at that time among Congregationalists. Thus he found himself embroiled in the rivulet controversy. In November 1855 Thomas Toke Lynch published *Hymns for Heart and Voice; the Rivulet*. It was severely criticized for its lack of evangelical piety by the *Morning Advertiser* but was defended from that attack by fifteen distinguished ministers, including Baldwin Brown. John Campbell (1794–1867), a militant advocate of orthodoxy and editor of the *British Banner*, retaliated by publishing a furious condemnation of Lynch and his defenders. Baldwin Brown contributed to the ensuing controversy in *The Way of Peace for the Congregational Union* (1857). Uneasiness about Baldwin Brown's theological stance deepened with the publication of his book, *The Divine Life in Man*, in 1859. It made the fatherhood of God the central motif of his thinking to such an extent that his critics were dismayed by his apparent lack of emphasis on the other divine attributes. As a result he became isolated from his fellow ministers, an isolation that caused him much pain. His critics were quite right in assuming that he was departing from Calvinism. He opposed it as a hindrance to the benign influence of Christ on the hearts of human beings, but it is an exaggeration to assert that he was mainly responsible for the decline of Calvinism among Congregationalists. His theological liberalism was expressed also in his belief that Christ died for all humanity, not for the elect alone. His opposition to the concept of conditional immortality was based on this conviction, and he set out his belief on this matter in his *Doctrine of Annihilation* (1875). With the spread of liberal views, Baldwin Brown's isolation from his colleagues lessened and he became chairman of the Congregational Union in 1877. But that office plunged him into a new controversy. The union had discussed a resolution to assert an orthodox evangelical declaration of its theology. A conference held at Leicester in October 1877 had resolved that religious communion should be based on religious feeling rather than credal uniformity. Naturally Baldwin Brown, in his chairman's address on 7 May 1878, came down on the side of the liberals, and sought to persuade the assembly to support the demand of the Leicester conference. But to no avail: the assembly rejected his plea. In these ways Baldwin Brown contributed to the decline of evangelical orthodoxy among Congregationalists.

Baldwin Brown was a sharp critic of revivalism but an enthusiast for social action, as befitted one whose stress on the fatherhood of God led him to promote 'Christian Brotherhood as manifested in the Son of Man'. In 1859 he initiated social gatherings for the poor in connection with his church, and these paved the way for the founding of the Moffat Institute at Lambeth to support large-scale social work among the poor. His interest in the Lancashire cotton famine as well as in international conflicts was animated by the same concern for the sufferers. His publications reveal his convictions about morality and the relationship between Christianity and the capitalist system. A rather unexpected aspect of his moral stance was that, although he supported temperance, he was opposed to

total abstinence. His uneasiness about the social consequences of capitalism are discussed in *Competition, the Labour Market, and Christianity* (1851) and in *Buying and Selling and Getting Gain* (1871). His eagerness to contribute towards the enrichment of spirituality finds expression in *Aids to the Development of the Divine Life* (1861) and *The Divine Mysteries* (1869). The concern for personal and social morality are the themes of *The Christian Policy of Life* (1870) and *Our Morals and Manners* (1872). The bibliography in Elizabeth Baldwin Brown's *In Memoriam* (1884) lists twenty titles by Baldwin Brown, but mistakenly attributes two of his father's books to him.

Baldwin Brown died of a stroke at Coombe House, Kingston Hill, Surrey, on 23 June 1884. Twin daughters had died soon after he moved to London, but he was survived by his son, Gerard Baldwin *Brown, the art historian, and his wife, whose memoir of her husband was published in 1884.   R. TUDUR JONES

Sources E. B. Brown, ed., *In memoriam: James Baldwin Brown* (1884) · *Congregational Year Book* (1885), 181–4 · A. Peel, *The Congregational two hundred, 1530–1948* (1948) · *The Times* (24 June 1884) · R. Tudur Jones, *Congregationalism in England, 1662–1962* (1962) · M. T. E. Hopkins, 'Baptists, Congregationalists and theological change: some late nineteenth century leaders and controversies', DPhil diss., U. Oxf., 1988, chap. 1 · m. cert.
Likenesses G. B. Brown, chalk drawing (after portrait), repro. in Brown, ed., *In memoriam*
Wealth at death £1205 3s. 10d.: probate, 8 Sept 1884, *CGPLA Eng. & Wales*

Brown, James Duff (1862–1914), librarian and compiler of music reference books, was born on 6 November 1862 at 3 Reid Terrace, Stockbridge, Edinburgh, the second of seven children of James Brown of St Fergus, Aberdeenshire, a bookkeeper, and his wife, Margaret Douglas of Aberdeen (both *fl.* 1840–1880). Family legend maintained that his grandmother, Elizabeth Smith, was descended from Rob Roy Macgregor, following a son's judicious change of name. Brown attended the Church of Scotland normal school in Edinburgh from 1871 until 1875, when he was apprenticed to a bookseller and publisher. His family moved to Glasgow in 1876, where he joined the bookselling business of W. R. McPhun. Finding his position uncongenial and the manager frequently drunk, he successfully applied for the post of library assistant at the new Mitchell Library.

Brown took up his appointment on Christmas day 1876 and was surprised to find the library closed (because the librarian, F. T. Barrett, was English, he reasoned). Working in a rapidly expanding library was an exciting experience, despite long hours, and Brown did not waste the opportunity for self-education. He rose early to pursue musical interests. In 1884 he became Glasgow correspondent to the *Musical Standard* and in 1886 published his important *Biographical Dictionary of Musicians*, later praised by George Grove. He edited George Chalmers's *Caledonia* (8 vols., 1887–1902). On 1 September 1887 he married his cousin, Annie Watt of Waterbeck; three daughters survived.

In 1888 the Library Association of the United Kingdom

met in Glasgow, when Brown spoke on dictionary catalogues, his first, timely, contact with members of his profession. The post of librarian at the newly established public library in Clerkenwell had been advertised, and Brown was appointed with a salary of £150 per annum. Public libraries in London were the responsibility of vestries, and Brown was fortunate to influence from the start the planning of the service, including the design of a building. He employed female library assistants, a controversial rarity, but was always supported by his library committee, and especially by Henry W. Fincham, local antiquary and close friend.

Brown produced in 1889 a dictionary catalogue with an innovatory classified arrangement following the model of Edward Edwards at Manchester Public Library in the 1850s. From 1890 Brown was encouraged by John MacAlister, editor of the Library Association's journal *The Library*, to contribute regular columns on administration. He was the first public librarian since Edwards in his *Memoirs of Libraries* (1859) to concern himself with the minutiae of organization. He contributed to Thomas Greenwood's influential *Public Libraries* (3rd and 4th edns, 1890–91), published *A Handbook of Library Appliances* (1892), and produced a stream of booklists, including one for J. F. Rowbotham's *Private Lives of the Great Composers* (1892). He published *Guide to the Formation of a Music Library* (1893), *British Musical Biography* (1897), and *Characteristic Songs and Dances of All Nations* (1901).

The most controversial innovation was sparked by visiting the American Library Association's conference in Chicago in 1893. Many American public libraries allowed access to the shelves; in Britain, borrowers ordered books from a catalogue after checking an indicator. On 1 May 1894 Clerkenwell became the first library in the country to adopt 'safe-guarded open-access'. For several years a bitter, occasionally humorous, war raged in journals and pamphlets. Virulent opposition came from Alfred Cotgreave (1849–1911), fellow librarian and patentee and manufacturer of the best-known library indicator. Brown ultimately won the day, and Clerkenwell became a mecca for librarians visiting London.

Brown issued a regular bulletin listing new accessions, another first, and supported classified lists of books over dictionary catalogues. He devised a classification scheme, after Edwards's example, which became the 'adjustable' classification, described in his *Manual of Library Classification and Shelf Arrangement* (1898). Such was Brown's enthusiasm for librarianship as a science that in 1898 he founded the *Library World* (which became the *New Library World* in 1969). Brown could indulge his humour and opinions with like-minded contributors, such as L. S. Jast, and reported, with considerable licence, the doings of a librarians' social club, The Pseudonyms; he was Rob Roy.

In 1900 Clerkenwell was absorbed into the metropolitan borough of Finsbury; Brown became borough librarian. The year 1903 saw the publication of *Manual of Library Economy*, the first textbook of public library practice since Edwards's *Memoirs* (the final, seventh, edition, appeared in 1961). In 1904 Islington established a public library, using

Brown's *Manual* as a model, and in 1905 he was appointed its first borough librarian, moving his family to 15 Canonbury Park South. Brown developed his classification scheme, published as the *Subject Classification* (1906), adopted by many libraries in preference to the Dewey system.

Work was an uphill struggle, for in 1906, despite a Liberal national government, most councils in London passed from Liberal to Conservative hands. The new council's support for public libraries was unenthusiastic, but they grudgingly admired Islington's new open-access central library, opened in 1907. In the same year Brown published *The Small Library*, a practical guide for domestic, church, or workplace libraries. Though Brown's book-buying budgets were severely cut, the classified catalogue of 1910 proved another model for other libraries.

Brown had been a stalwart of the Library Association, but resigned in 1911 because he disagreed with their policies. He advocated structural reform, but particularly opposed a professional register, believing that librarianship should be open to all. By now unwell, he handed the editorship of *Library World* to his nephew, James D. Stewart (1885–1965), then working at Islington Library. In 1912 Brown, described as small, frail, and unobtrusive (Jast, 248), suffered heart attacks, probably attributable to Bright's disease. He did little work but published a guide-book, *A British Library Itinerary* (1913). He died at home in Canonbury Park on 26 February 1914 and was buried at the Great Northern London cemetery, Southgate. His *Manual* and *Subject Classification* were continued by his nephew, Stewart. K. A. MANLEY

Sources W. A. Munford, *James Duff Brown, 1862–1914* (1968) · L. S. Jast and others, *Library Association Record*, 16 (1914), 239–62
Likenesses two photographs, 1899–*c*.1910, Islington Public Libraries, London; repro. in Munford, *James Duff Brown*
Wealth at death £177 6s. 10d.: probate, 28 March 1914, *CGPLA Eng. & Wales*

Brown, James Jackson (1882–1953), general practitioner and cricketer, was born on 9 October 1882 in Jamaica, one of nine children of Thomas Brown, sugar planter. Both parents died when he was young, but their estate in St Thomas, managed by a man named Hamilton, provided financial support for Brown and his siblings. He attended York Castle high school and Jamaica College, then went to Canada to study medicine. Disliking the style of the tuition, he moved to London, where in September 1905 his Canadian qualifications were recognized and he was admitted as a student at the London Hospital. A need to wear spectacles because of snow blindness was a result of his Canadian sojourn. He completed the first part of his training in April 1906 and the second in 1907, but did not sit his finals until 1911. He qualified MRCS (England) and LRCP (London) in 1914. The factors contributing to his delayed success included his marriage, a family, participation in the London Hospital cricket team, changing finances, and the impact of the assassination of Sir William Curzon Wyllie by Madan Lal Dhingra in London in 1909, when, as Brown was to tell his younger son, 'Every coloured person had a hell of a time', and he failed the oral section of his anatomy examination (private information, son). He married Amelia (Milly) Green (1886/7–1936), daughter of Solomon Green, a compositor on the *Jewish World* and his landlord in Hackney, on 12 November 1906. She was given an adverse report by another Jamaican, so Brown's handsome allowance stopped. They had two sons, Gerald R. Hamilton Brown (*b.* 1907) and Leslie S. Hamilton Brown (*b.* 1909).

Brown worked at the London Hospital as a dresser for Sir Jonathan Hutchinson in 1909 and as clinical clerk to Bertrand Dawson in 1910. Both eminent surgeons graded him as 'good' (private information, London Hospital). After qualifying, he set up as a general practitioner. By 1921 his practice was in a substantial house at 63 Lauriston Road, Hackney, with a surgery in the grounds. About half his patients were Jewish: he encouraged their custom by having his price list in both English and Hebrew characters. He charged more than other local practitioners, and had a higher reputation. He also worked for the local private maternity home; his brass plate proclaimed him to be an 'obstetrician and accoucheur'. The medical practice suffered from his inability to organize paperwork, pay bills, and collect fees.

A well-spoken fool asked Brown, at a London Hospital cricket match, 'Why don't you find more than one or two Niggers together?', to which Brown responded: 'Eleven will come and play you' (private information). Brown wrote to colleges, hospitals, and institutions in the London area where there might be cricket enthusiasts like himself, and he duly formed the Tropics team. It included Indians; by 1919 it was composed entirely of players of African and Caribbean descent and called the Africs. In picking team members Brown included social refinement as a qualification. The British Guianan barrister Samuel S. A. Cambridge was secretary. Brown's team took on whites at their own game, and beat them; and at the same time reduced the ignorance of the British about black people.

The cricket team, always playing away as it lacked grounds, occupied one weekday and Saturdays. Several West Indian future doctors, barristers, and accountants, and at least one judge played for the Africs. So did Africans, including the Dulwich College-educated barrister Archie Casely-Hayford, who took Brown's son Leslie with him to Ghana in 1934, believing his motor engineering skills would be useful. Brown purchased equipment, made loans, and paid expenses for the Africs. His home became an informal centre for black students, residents, and visitors, including the future prime minister of Trinidad Eric Williams and the Nobel prize-winning economist Arthur Lewis. Milly Brown fed them; in winter there were bridge sessions and an annual dance in central London. The neat and polite style of the men was recalled fifty years later. Brown was kept informed of events in the Caribbean and elsewhere in the black world. It is not surprising that his son Leslie regarded himself as a 'London-born West Indian' (private information, son).

Brown was an opinionated man, who knew that British society was racist. In the First World War the military refused to accept him as an officer in the Royal Army Medical Corps (doctors were always officers) because he was black. He had little time for Dr Harold Moody and his League of Coloured Peoples, with its spirit of co-operation. A tall and dark man, he was a dominating figure. In his home nobody else was allowed to use his cup or saucer. His self-assurance led to an appearance before the General Medical Council, at which he was so confident that he did not consult a brother-in-law who was a solicitor. He had issued a certificate so that a man with substantial family commitments could evade military service. This sympathetic gesture might have been tolerated, but Brown's dogmatic approach—he was a professional and he was correct—was a disaster. In February 1943 he was struck off, and he never worked as a doctor again, although wartime work for the St John Ambulance Brigade used his expertise. He busied himself in freemasonry, becoming a lodge master. The Lauriston Road practice was run by his son Gerald (who qualified in 1937) and then, into the 1990s, by the Barbadian Colin Franklin. Leslie Brown worked in the wartime aviation industry, then in business. Milly Brown had died in 1936, and Brown subsequently married one of his patients. He died at 63 Lauriston Road, Hackney, of bronchopneumonia and heart failure on 18 October 1953; on 21 October the *Hackney Gazette* reported, 'Popular Hackney Doctor Dies'. He was survived by his second wife, the two sons of his first marriage, and four grandchildren. The name Hamilton continued among the males of the family, forming a link to the Jamaica that Brown had left a half-century before his death.   JEFFREY GREEN

Sources J. Green, 'West Indian doctors in London: John Alcindor (1873–1924) and James Jackson Brown (1882–1953)', *Journal of Caribbean History*, 20/1 (June 1986), 49–77 · *Hackney Gazette* (21 Oct 1953) · *Who's who in Jamaica, 1941–46* · private information (2004) [son; nephew; London Hospital] · m. cert. · d. cert.
Likenesses photographs (after print), repro. in A. Ali, ed., *Third world impact*, 8th edn (1988), 237 · photographs, repro. in J. Green, *Black Edwardians* (1998), 195 · print, priv. coll.

Brown, John. See Browne, John (*fl. c.*1480–*c.*1505); Browne, John (*d.* 1735).

Brown, John (*d.* 1532), painter, of unknown parents, was appointed painter to King Henry VIII by a patent issued on 20 December 1511 and held the position until his death. According to his will he married, first, Alice, with whom he had two daughters—one married to Richard Colard, probably the painter–stainer of that name, and the other to Edmund Lee—and, second, Anne, with whom he also had two daughters, Elizabeth and Isabel.

Brown is first recorded in 1502 as a supplier of heraldic painting for the funeral of Prince Arthur, the son of King Henry VII. From 1511, as king's painter, he was responsible for the supply of decorative and heraldic painting for use in court ceremonial and at war. His salary was 2*d.* a day (£3 0*s.* 10*d.* a year), plus a livery of 4 ells of woollen cloth at 6*s.* 8*d.* a yard each Christmas. On 12 March 1527 this salary was raised to £10 a year and the title changed to that of serjeant painter, though the responsibilities appear to have been unchanged. The records of Henry VIII's accounts show that Brown was responsible for a variety of work, from the supply of flags for the *Great Harry* and other ships to heraldic surcoats, banners, and standards for the army sent into France under the duke of Suffolk in 1523, as well as decorative work for the Field of Cloth of Gold in 1520, cloths painted with antique work for a court entertainment in 1524, and decorations for the banqueting house at Greenwich in 1527. He also supplied painted work for funerals, in liaison with the heralds. Brown's role may often have put him at one remove from the business of painting and gilding. At Greenwich he was the supplier of much gold leaf, and he appears there to have acted as a supervisor. He was probably also responsible for engaging other painters to work on royal projects, often members of the London Painter–Stainers' Company, of which Brown was warden. However, there is little doubt that he also possessed the practical skills of the painter: his will mentions the patterns which were necessary to carry out his trade, as well as his grindstones, colours, gold, and silks. There is no need to suppose that Brown produced the portraits or subject pictures which were the province of other painters employed at court such as Holbein; no payment for such work has been found, nor any pictures signed by him.

Brown was a wealthy citizen of London, as his assessment for the subsidy in 1523 at a worth of £1000 shows. He owned several properties in and close to the city, including a house in the village of Kingsland and land in nearby Hackney, as well as a brewhouse called the Swan on the Hope in the Strand and another house in Little Trinity Lane, which he had acquired in 1504. In a deed of 21 September 1532 he conveyed the last-named house to the London Company of Painter–Stainers, and it became their hall (the hall was destroyed in the great fire of 1666 and rebuilt on the same site). Brown was also a member of the Haberdashers' Company. He was elected an alderman of London in 1522, was sworn sheriff on 16 May 1523, and sat on the commission of the peace in Essex and Middlesex during the last years of his life. He died, probably in London, between 17 September 1532 (when he made his will) and 2 December 1532, the date his will was proved, and was buried in St Vedast, Foster Lane. A portrait in the Painter–Stainers' Hall appears to be a copy made after 1666 of a portrait of Brown dated 1504, but whether or not this goes back to a contemporary likeness must be regarded as uncertain.   SUSAN FOISTER

Sources London Painter–Stainers' Company records, GL, MS 5670, nos. 13 and 14 • will, PRO, PROB 11/24 • Greenwich revels accounts, PRO, E 36/227, treasury of the receipt, miscellaneous books (LP 1V (2) 3104) • BL, Lansdowne MS 858 • accounts of the great wardrobe, PRO, LC 2/1 • *LP Henry VIII*, 1.1044 (8) [John Brown's patent]; 5.1139 (30) [his change of title] • E. Auerbach, *Tudor artists* (1954) • H. M. Colvin and others, eds., *The history of the king's works*, 3 (1975) • J. G. Nicholas, 'Notices of the contemporaries and successors of Holbein', *Archaeologia*, 39 (1863), 19–46 • A. B. Chamberlain, *Hans Holbein the younger*, 2 vols. (1913) • A. Payne, 'Sir Thomas Wriothesley and his heraldic artists', *Illuminating the book … essays in honour of Janet Backhouse*, ed. M. P. Brown and S. McKendrick (1998), 143–62
Likenesses oils, Painter–Stainers' Hall, London

Brown, John (*c*.1610–1679), Church of Scotland minister, was probably born at Kirkcudbright and may have been the son of James and Jean Brown referred to in the letters of Samuel Rutherford. He graduated at the University of Edinburgh on 24 July 1630 and was a protester in the religious disputes of the 1650s. It seems to have been 1655 before he was ordained, in the parish of Wamphray, Dumfriesshire. During the period prior to the Restoration he was a diligent minister and was remembered with affection by his parishioners when he met with harder times later in life.

In 1662 he was one of the ministers deprived of his living and arrested for refusing to accept the restoration of episcopacy. He was banished in December that year and in March 1663 arrived in Rotterdam, where he was an influential early member of the exile community that evolved in the Netherlands during Charles II's reign. Although he did not take up a charge in one of the Scottish congregations he did continue to preach and minister both in the pulpit and in private meeting-houses. Brown and his great friend Robert McWard also developed close links with the great Dutch theologians of the day, including Spanheim in Leiden, and Leydecker and the famous Voetius in Utrecht. Several of Brown's publications were translated into Dutch.

Brown and McWard, though in exile, remained particularly influential in persuading many against the indulgences, a series of measures introduced in Scotland in the 1660s and 1670s with the aim of tempting moderate presbyterians back to the established church. Brown was especially militant, and succeeded only in offending the indulged and moderate non-indulged. This offence was increased by his agreement shortly before his death in September 1679 to take part in the ordination of the young extremist Richard Cameron at Rotterdam, when he commented on the deplorable state of Scotland through the text 'Israel deserves to be punished' (Jeremiah 2: 35).

Brown's published criticisms of prelates and the indulged included *An Apologeticall Relation* (1665) and *The History of the Indulgence* (1678). His stance caused problems in the Rotterdam congregation, as one of the incumbents, Robert Fleming, was a moderate and published a tract to refute Brown's views in 1681. Brown also disliked the Quakers and after the arrival in the Netherlands of four influential British Quakers in 1677 Brown published *Quakerisme the Path-Way to Paganisme* (1678). A number of sermons, lectures, and theological treatises were also published between the 1670s and 1790s.

Brown may have been involved in minor political intrigue: he was in correspondence with the spy William Carstares in 1674 and later seems to have received money from the Dutch government. But it was his and McWard's continuing attacks on Erastianism and the indulgences which made them a threat to the Scottish government and which persuaded Charles II in 1676 to urge the Dutch states general to banish them. Although a banishment order was passed in February 1677, ultimately it was not enforced. Brown himself was ill and, with evidence from his physician, was permitted to stay in the Netherlands.

Brown died in Rotterdam in September 1679. Like many of the exiles, he entrusted much of the business relating to his will to the much respected Rotterdam merchant Andrew Russell. His will left express instructions about the disposal of his worldly goods, including his money and the book that was in the process of being printed. Exiles who benefited included his old friend McWard and he also left money to the poor of the Rotterdam congregation. The cost of Brown's funeral and burial in the kirk was more than 300 guilders and the total outlay from the estate reached more than 3000 guilders. The money was balanced out by a variety of means, including (as instructed in the will), the proceeds of an auction of Brown's library.

Brown was respected by several theologians of his day: as early as 1637 Rutherford noted that he 'saw Christ in [Brown] more than in his brethren' (*DSCHT*, 98). Robert Wodrow referred to him as a man of 'very great learning, warm zeal, and remarkable piety' (Wodrow, 1.304).

GINNY GARDNER

Sources *Fasti Scot.*, new edn, 2.224–5 • R. Wodrow, *The history of the sufferings of the Church of Scotland from the Restauration to the revolution*, 2 vols. (1721–2) • *DSCHT* • T. Lockerby, *A sketch of the life of the Rev. John Brown* (1839) • NA Scot., Andrew Russell papers, RH 15/106 • G. Gardner, 'The Scottish exile community in the United Provinces, 1660–1690', DPhil diss., U. Oxf., 1998 • I. B. Cowan, *The Scottish covenanters, 1660–1688* (1976) • W. Steven, *The history of the Scottish church, Rotterdam* (1832, 1833) • *DNB*
Archives NA Scot., Andrew Russell papers, RH 15/106 • NL Scot., Wodrow papers, corresp., esp. fols. 58–9
Wealth at death over 3000 guilders outlay from estate: NA Scot., Andrew Russell papers

Brown, John [*called* the Christian Carrier] (**1626/7–1685**), covenanter, lived near Priesthill Farm in the parish of Muirkirk in Ayrshire, an important location for the Cameronians or society people who opposed the crown's episcopalian policies during the 'killing times' of the 1680s. Nothing is known of his early life. Brown had risen in arms at the battle of Bothwell Brig in 1679 and associated with field preachers, one of whom, Alexander Peden, conducted his marriage, in 1682, to his second wife, Marion (sometimes recorded as Isobel) Weir. Peden is said to have foretold Brown's early and violent end, advising his wife to 'prize his company, and keep linen by you to be his winding sheet' (Walker, 1.61).

It was his execution by John Graham of Claverhouse and his dragoons on 1 May 1685 which ensured Brown's place among Scottish covenanting martyrology. According to Patrick Walker's account Peden had spent the preceding night in Brown's house and left only on the approach of Claverhouse. Claverhouse pursued John Brown and his nephew, John Browning, apprehending them near Brown's house, which upon investigation was found to contain arms and ammunition as well as treasonable documents. Brown refused to take the abjuration oath (issued by the government to counter James Renwick's *Apologetical Declaration*) 'nor would he swear not to ryse in armes against the King, but said he kneu no King' (*Buccleuch MSS*, 292). After further searching the troops discovered an underground chamber containing swords and

pistols; there, according to his nephew, Brown had been hiding since Bothwell Brig.

Several accounts survive of Brown's execution, which reportedly took place in front of one of his children and his pregnant wife. According to Claverhouse's own account, written to the duke of Queensberry on 3 May, he apprehended Brown and his nephew, searched his house and 'there being found bullets and match in his house and treasonable peapers, I caused shoot him dead, which he suffered very inconcernedly' (*Buccleuch MSS*, 292). Robert Wodrow claimed that Brown's prayers so moved the soldiers that Claverhouse 'was forced to turn executioner himself, and in a fret, shot him with his own hand' (Wodrow, 4.245). According to Patrick Walker's account, however, the execution was not carried out by Claverhouse but by the dragoons. Walker's description of events was supplied by Brown's widow 'sitting upon her husbands grave'. According to this account Claverhouse asked Weir 'What thinkest thou of thy husband now, woman?' to which she replied 'I thought ever so much good of him, and as much now as ever' (Walker, 1.85).

Brown was buried on open moorland about a mile from Priesthill. His grave was marked by a stone bearing a verse acrostic and the inscription:

> Here lies the body of JOHN BROWN martyr who was murdered in this place by Graham of Claverhouse for his testimony to the Covenanted work of Reformation Because he durst not own the authority of the Then Tyrant destroying the Same, who died the first day of May AD 1685 and of his age 58.

Questioned following the execution Brown's nephew confessed to his own involvement in the rescue of covenanting prisoners at Newmilns and named several local covenanters and frequenters of conventicles. Browning was hanged at Mauchline on 6 May 1685.

SHARON ADAMS

Sources J. Thomson, *The martyr graves of Scotland* (1903) • P. Walker, *Six saints of the covenant*, ed. D. H. Fleming, 2 vols. (1901) • R. Wodrow, *The history of the sufferings of the Church of Scotland from the Restoration to the revolution*, ed. R. Burns, 4 vols. (1828–30) • J. Thomson, ed., *A cloud of witnesses* (1871) • *DNB* • *The manuscripts of his grace the duke of Buccleuch and Queensberry … preserved at Drumlanrig Castle*, 2 vols., HMC, 44 (1897–1903), vol. 1

Brown, John (**1715–1766**), author and moralist, was born on 5 November 1715 in Rothbury, Northumberland, the son of the Revd John Brown (1677–1763), from Cockburnspath in Berwickshire, and his wife, Eleanor Troutbeck, *née* Potts (*c.*1679–1758), the widow of Anthony Troutbeck (*d.* 1710). For generations the Brown family had lived in Colstown, near Haddington. Brown's father came from a family of Episcopalians and had been ordained by a nonjuring Scottish bishop. It was said he was 'a gentleman of a human, charitable disposition, and universally respected by his neighbours and acquaintance' (*Newcastle Courant*, 17 March 1763). His mother's first marriage produced a son in 1710, also named John, who survived only a few months. His parents married in August 1712, and their first child, Margaret (*d.* 1722), was born in 1713. Shortly after John's birth his father was presented with the living of Wigton in Cumberland. Brown was educated at the local grammar school, and on 8 May 1732 was admitted as a sizar to St John's College, Cambridge, where he matriculated on 18 December, and from where he graduated BA in 1735, MA in 1739, and DD in 1755. He was probably acquainted with Francis Blackburne at Cambridge, and may also have met there John Gay, Soame Jenyns, Edmund Law, David Hartley, Daniel Waterland, and John Jortin. After a brief return to Wigton as his father's curate, he took oaths as minor canon at the cathedral church, Carlisle, on 28 April 1738, and on 23 June 1739 was nominated to a lectureship in the cathedral. On 23 December 1739 he was ordained priest by Sir George Fleming, bishop of Carlisle, and on 6 June 1743 inducted vicar of Morland in Westmorland.

At the siege of Carlisle in 1745 Brown served as aide-de-camp to the militia commandant and was present at the recapture of the city. The two assize sermons he gave in September 1746, entitled 'The mutual connexion between religious truth and civil freedom', established his reputation as a popular preacher of protestant principles. They also brought him to the attention of Bishop Osbaldeston of Carlisle, who appointed him one of his chaplains in 1747. When censured by the dean for omitting, probably deliberately, the Athanasian creed from a service, Brown asserted his orthodoxy by reading the creed the following Sunday, then resigned his minor canonry. In 1752 he was appointed vicar of Lazonby in Cumberland and in 1756 the earl of Hardwicke, on the recommendation of William Warburton, bishop of Gloucester, presented him with the living of Great Horkesley, near Colchester, Essex. He resigned from Morland and from Lazonby, the latter in favour of his father (who retained the living until his death), and on 14 November 1757 he relinquished his cathedral lectureship in Carlisle.

It was Brown's *An Essay on Satire Occasion'd by the Death of Mr Pope* (1745) which had brought him to the attention of Warburton, who requested permission to include the poem in his edition of Pope (1751). Brown and Warburton became acquainted through Robert Dodsley, the editor of *A Collection of Poems by Several Hands* and publisher of Brown's poems and sermons during these years. Dodsley included Brown's first published poem, 'Honour' (1743), with *An Essay on Satire* in his popular poetical anthology. Brown was introduced to Warburton's circle, and probably met Richard Hurd, William Mason, Thomas Balguy, Thomas Gray, and Charles Yorke, the brother of Philip, earl of Hardwicke. *An Essay on Satire* contained criticisms of Shaftesbury, and Warburton suggested that Brown expand the remarks into a general critique. *Essays on the Characteristics of the Earl of Shaftesbury* (1751) is a sure-footed and crisp repudiation of Shaftesbury's deism and 'moral sense' philosophy. The second of the three essays expounds a well-reasoned moral theory founded on the principle of utility and belief in God's benevolent will, which was later praised by J. S. Mill in his critical essay, 'Bentham' (1838). *Essays on the Characteristics* was extensively reviewed in the *Monthly Review* (5, 1751, 44–65) and the *Gentleman's Magazine* (21, 1751, 215–18, 249–52), and it provoked several responses, the most virulent of which were two pamphlets by Charles Bulkley, *A Vindication of my*

Lord Shaftesbury (1751, 1752). Warburton's praise of the finished work was tempered by doubts about the cogency of Brown's moral theory.

Brown showed his versatility with the pen by writing two plays. On 17 December 1754 *Barbarossa* was performed at Drury Lane Theatre with considerable success. The less impressive *Athelstan*, dedicated to the duke of Devonshire, was performed at Covent Garden on 27 February 1756. Colley Cibber and David Garrick acted in both plays, and Garrick wrote the prologue and epilogue to the first and the epilogue to the second. Johnson, in disbelief, declared that Brown 'would no more suffer Garrick to write a line in his play, than he would suffer him to mount his pulpit' (Boswell, *Life*, 2.131). Neither of the plays has retained literary interest. Warburton let it be known he was annoyed by Brown's neglect of his clerical duties 'to make connexions with Players' (Warburton, 182).

In 1760, when Osbaldeston, now bishop of London, presented Brown to the more substantial living of St Nicholas, Newcastle upon Tyne, he resigned from Great Horkesley. It is doubtful whether the dispute which attended the resignation had its source in political differences. Rather it stemmed from Brown's desire to retain Great Horkesley and its tithes *in absentia*, which Lord Royston would not permit. However, the stir produced by Brown's popular success with *An Estimate of the Manners and Principles of the Times* (1757) did little to gain him political favour. It is a vigorous attack on the '*vain, luxurious* and *selfish* EFFEMINACY' of England's higher ranks, in the wake of the loss of Minorca to the French at the opening of the Seven Years' War. Brown rehearsed the usual complaints of corruption under Walpole and argued that public virtue had been undermined by a preoccupation with luxury and commerce. Garrick is mentioned as an exception to the general decay in the arts, Warburton is appreciated as the intellectual 'colossus' of the age, and Pitt is hailed as 'the Great Minister' to whom England should turn for salvation. Printed seven times within the year, the book earned for its author the sobriquet Estimate Brown. Macaulay attributed the book's success to England's morbid interest in its own decline. 'The inestimable estimate of Brown', wrote Cowper in 'Table Talk', 'Rose like a paper kite and charmed the town'. It was a temporary elevation, for 'Victory refuted all he said' (*The Poems of William Cowper*, 3 vols., 1980, 1.251 ll.384–9). A chorus of adversaries responded with counter-estimates. Boswell remarked in verse on the affair,

> exulting to behold
> Minerva's birds engage, a dunghill cock.
> (Boswell, 'On the contest', 2.74)

Brown affected indifference to his critics in a second volume of the *Estimate* (1758), but in *An Explanatory Defence of the Estimate* (1758) he defended his position and claimed it was the prospect of military failure that prompted him to do 'service to his country' by pointing out 'the fundamental *latent causes* of this ill success' (J. Brown, *An Explanatory Defence of the Estimate*, 5–7). He acknowledged only the Edinburgh divine Robert Wallace as a 'decent and candid adversary' (ibid., 35).

Warburton, no stranger to controversy, betrayed his jealousy of his protégé, commenting to Richard Hurd that in the *Estimate* Brown was 'rather perter than ordinary, but no wiser' (Warburton, 256). This, together with the displeasure aroused by Brown's foray into drama, caused the Warburton circle in general to turn against him. Thereafter he became uneasy about his ties to the bishop. In *Letter to the Rev. Dr. Lowth* (1766) he denied the imputation that he was Warburton's 'obsequious deputy'. Francis Blackburne, writing after Brown's death in the *St James Chronicle* (16 October 1766), blamed the difficulties of his final days on those who had led him into intimacy with Warburton. Brown also managed to irritate Hume by a remark in the *Estimate* accusing him of seeking financial gain by disgracing religion. Hume professed himself puzzled at the attack.

Brown's years at St Nicholas's, where he remained until his death, were among the busiest of his life. In 1760 he published *An Additional Dialogue of the Dead* in defence of Pitt against the insinuations of George Lyttleton. In March 1761 he printed his inaugural sermon at St Nicholas's, 'On the natural duty of a personal service', occasioned by a 'late dangerous Insurrection at Hexham' against the imposition of militia service. In the same year Osbaldeston seems to have used his influence to make Brown a royal chaplain. In March 1763 he preached at St Paul's in support of an appeal for funds to establish colleges in Philadelphia and New York. The sermon, 'On religious liberty', was printed in the *London Chronicle* and praised in the *Monthly Review*. 'The Cure of Saul: a Sacred Ode', a poem on the healing powers of music and nature, was also published in 1763, set to music as an oratorio, and staged at Covent Garden twice that year, and again in 1767. The poem was reprinted with Brown's *A dissertation on the rise, union, and power, the progressions, separations and corruptions of poetry and music* (1763), a pioneering work of conjectural history reminiscent of the *Scienza nuova*, though it is doubtful that Brown was familiar with Vico's work. An abridged version (omitting the parts on music) appeared as *A History of the Rise and Progress of Poetry* in 1764, and in the same year he published *Sermons on Various Subjects*. Sermons 1–3, 'On the first principles of education', constitute the first English response to the educational prescriptions of Rousseau's *Émile*. In May 1765 Brown separately published a sermon, 'On the female character and education', together with an appendix advocating a national system of Christian education. Around the same time he became embroiled in a dispute with the Newcastle Quakers in the local press over their refusal, on religious principle, to pay the tithes that were his due. He claimed he took the Quakers to court 'at the request of the Quakers themselves' and that he always regarded the sect as 'an honest and conscientious body of men', but the acrimony created in the city did him no good (Roberts, 59). The same year Brown published *Thoughts on Civil Liberty, on Licentiousness and Faction*, extolling the virtues of Sparta in support of the argument for a state-sponsored code of education. This caught the eye of Priestley, whose objections appeared in *An Essay*

on a Course of Liberal Education* (1765) and *An Essay on the First Principles of Government* (1768).

In July 1765 Brown's views on a Russian school system were solicited by the educationist Daniel Dumaresq on behalf of the Empress Catherine. In reply, on 1 October 1765, he set down the principles upon which education reform in Russia should proceed, and grandly confided in a letter of 19 January 1766 to Garrick: 'I have lately been invited to assist in the civilization of a great empire' (*The Private Correspondence of David Garrick*, 2 vols., 1831, 1.220). An invitation to St Petersburg followed (31 January 1766), and Brown vowed to Garrick that, if he failed to use the opportunity to construct 'a general and connected plan of legislation, may I be knouted to death by the Metropolitan of Novgorod or Moscow' (ibid., 1.154). The empress forwarded £1000 through her London ambassador M. de Moussin Pouschkin to facilitate Brown's journey (3 June 1766). However, William Stevens, Brown's former curate at Great Horkesley, persuaded him to abandon the idea, arguing his health would not be equal to the task (30 July 1766). Brown suffered from gout and rheumatism, and experienced renewed attacks at this time. Reluctantly, he wrote to Pouschkin and the empress on 8 and 28 August 1766, accounting for his expenses, explaining his situation, and proposing an elaborate scheme for sending young Russians to be educated in England. Brown's Russian plans were known among London's literati and roundly satirized by Mason in 'Ode to the legislator elect of Russia on his being prevented from entering on his high office of civilization by a fit of the gout'. Brown's ambition is captured in the lines

> dread Empress! I to thee
> Will Solon, will Lycurgus be,
> And Montesquieu also.
> (Mason)

Concerns about Brown's health were well founded. He had for long been subject to depression and fits of 'frenzy' (Kippis, 2.673). In a later letter to William Cole, Horace Walpole could not resist his usual criticisms of Brown, 'that mountebank, who for a little time made as much noise by his *Estimate*, as ever quack did by nostrum', but added 'poor Dr. Brown was mad; and therefore might be in earnest, whether he played the Fool or the Reformer' (Walpole, *Corr.*, 2.187). On 23 September 1766, in his apartments in Pall Mall, Brown committed suicide by cutting his throat, and on 1 October was interred in a vault at St James's Church in Piccadilly, London. He never married, and his character was marred by an over-zealous ambition which made ease in friendship difficult to attain.

Brown was a stylish and skilful writer, a moralist who set utility together with God at the centre of his theory, a political polemicist and forthright defender of orthodox Christianity, an original and perceptive historian of aesthetics, and a minor poet worth recalling in the literary history of the times. His political ideas were a synthesis of elements of Machiavelli, Locke, Bolingbroke, and Montesquieu, and he made serious criticisms of the thought of Shaftesbury, Mandeville, Hume, and Rousseau. His views on education were designed to support the established

Christian and political principles, but were none the less progressive for the times. His early appreciation of the dramatic scenery of the Lake District led a contemporary to acclaim him 'the Columbus of Keswick', and his miscellaneous writings include 'A description of the lake at Keswick and the adjacent country in Cumberland' (*London Chronicle*, April 1766). Modern commentators have described Brown as an aesthetic progenitor of Wordsworth, an affinity Wordsworth recognized himself when he included the Keswick poem in his *Guide to the Lakes* (1835). Brown is also thought to have written 'A Fragment on Rhapsody' and the brief panegyric 'The Jesuits' (undated). In 1764 he promised the speedy publication of a work in eight volumes entitled 'On the Principles of Christian Legislation', the manuscripts for which were left to his cousin William Hall. The work was deemed too fragmentary and incomplete to be published, and the manuscripts have since been lost.   JAMES E. CRIMMINS

Sources D. D. Eddy, *A bibliography of John Brown* (1971) · W. G. Roberts, *A dawn of imaginative feeling: the contribution of John Brown (1715–66) to eighteenth-century thought and literature* (1996) · A. Kippis and others, eds., *Biographia Britannica, or, The lives of the most eminent persons who have flourished in Great Britain and Ireland*, 2nd edn, 2 (1780), 658–74 · P. M. Horsley, 'Dr John Brown (1715–1766)', *Transactions of the Cumberland and Westmorland Antiquarian and Archaeological Society*, new ser., 69 (1969), 240–74 · Nichols, *Lit. anecdotes*, 3.715–18 · [W. Warburton], *Letters from a late eminent prelate to one of his friends*, ed. R. Hurd, 2nd edn (1809) · R. Anderson, *A complete edition of the poets of Great Britain*, 13 vols. (1792–5), vol. 10 [incl. poems by Brown and a short life] · T. Hollis, 'Character of the late Dr Brown, vicar of Newcastle', in F. Blackburne, *Memoirs of Thomas Hollis*, 2 vols. (1780), 2.717 · J. E. Crimmins, 'The political ideas of the Rev. Dr John Brown (1715–1766)', MA diss., U. Wales, Swansea, 1980 · N. Hans, 'Dumaresq, Brown and some early educational projects of Catherine II', *Slavonic and East European Review*, 40 (1961–2), 229–35 · D. D. Eddy, 'John Brown: "the Columbus of Keswick"', *Modern Philology*, 73 (1975–6), S74–S84 · *GM*, 1st ser., 24–48 (1754–78) · A. W. Evans, *Warburton and the Warburtonians: a study in some eighteenth-century controversies* (1932) · H. Walpole, *Memoirs of the reign of King George the Third*, ed. G. F. R. Barker, 4 vols (1894); repr. (1971) · Walpole, *Corr.* · W. D. Templeman, 'Warburton and Brown continue the battle over ridicule', *Huntington Library Quarterly*, 17 (1953–4), 17–36 · W. Mason, 'Ode to the legislator elect of Russia', in *Correspondence of Thomas Gray*, ed. P. Toynbee and L. Whibley, 3 (1935), appx R, 1248–50 · W. Hutchinson, *The history of the county of Cumberland*, 2 vols. (1794); facs. edn (1974) · J. Boswell, 'On the contest between the author of an estimate of the manners and principles of the times, and the writers in opposition to him', *A collection of original poems by the Revd Mr Blacklock and other Scotch gentlemen*, 2 (1760), 74 · *The letters of David Hume*, ed. J. Y. T. Greig, 2 vols. (1932) · E. C. Mossner, *The life of David Hume* (1954) · Boswell, *Life* · T. B. Macaulay, 'William Pitt, earl of Chatham', *Critical and historical essays* (1880) [1834] · IGI

Archives BL, 'An essay on satire' and corresp. · TCD, annotations and marginalia in Brown's hand, vol. 1 of *Estimate* (1757), TCD 1448 | Bodl. Oxf., letters to Robert Dodsley, MS Toynbee d.19 · Bodl. Oxf., letters to William Gilpin, MS Eng. misc. c.389, fols. 58–88 · St John Cam., letter to Catherine the Great · V&A NAL, Forster Library, letters to David Garrick

Likenesses P. Kahn, charcoal and chalk (after portrait), repro. in Eddy, *A bibliography of John Brown*, frontispiece · oils, Wigton vicarage · portrait; formerly at St Nicholas, Newcastle, 1894

Wealth at death approx. £500; incl. £400 bequeathed to friends and relatives; £100 from sale of furniture and other goods: will, PRO, PROB 11/923

Brown, John [*known as* John Brown of Haddington] (1722–1787), minister of the Secession church and theologian, was one of four children born to John Brown (*d. c.*1733), weaver and salmon fisher, and Catherine, *née* Millie (*d. c.*1735), in the now abandoned hamlet of Carpow, near Abernethy, Perthshire. His parents' lowly means and their deaths when he was entering teenage years afforded Brown little formal education, only a few months at Abernethy elementary school, of which one month, without his parents' permission, he devoted to Latin. Their godliness and a religious seriousness induced by his own grave illness after his mother's death inclined him towards an earnest and methodical piety along lines indicated by Joseph Alleine's *An Alarm to Unconverted Sinners* (1672). He found work as a herdsman with John Ogilvie, an illiterate sheep farmer and elder of Alexander Moncrieff's Abernethy congregation, who got Brown to read to him. Brown used every spare moment to advance his own education, becoming proficiently self-taught in Latin, Greek, and Hebrew. He acquired the elements of Greek unaided, by working back from Latin and the English New Testament. He then made a rapid 50 mile round hike to St Andrews to buy a Greek Testament with hard won savings, but made such an impression on a professor in the bookshop that he was given it free. Brown would go on to learn Syriac, Persian, Ethiopic, and Arabic, as well as the main modern European languages. Nor was his passion for knowledge limited to languages, for he had the makings—and even the aspirations—of a universal scholar.

Brown's learning while still a shepherd was so exceptional that he became the object of malign suspicion instead of wonderment. The allegation that he was in league with the devil he had to live down, but such hostility may have induced him to gain employment as a travelling salesman—a chapman—in Fife, Kinross-shire, and the Lothians. His consuming interest in books, however, including religious works he found in the homes he called at, displaced the business of selling, and he was given up as 'fit for nothing else but for being a scholar' (Mackenzie, 49).

In the Jacobite rising of 1745 Brown immediately volunteered for the Fife regiment on the government side, and was sent to defend Blackness Castle on the Forth, and then Edinburgh Castle. He then turned to schoolteaching, first at Gairney Bridge, near Kinross (1747–8) and for a year and a half at the Spittal, near Penicuik, south of Edinburgh. His self-education had continued unabated, which secured him acceptance, in lieu of a university degree, for theological training for the ministry of the Associate Synod church. Brown had early sided with the Secession from the Church of Scotland in 1733 led by Ebenezer and Ralph Erskine, Alexander Moncrieff of Abernethy, and others, whose decisive conference took place at Gairney Bridge. When 'the breach' split the Secession in 1747 over the wording of the burgess oath—did it or did it not entail approval of the established kirk?—Brown followed the less rigid Erskines (but not his home minister Moncrieff, who in any case paid excessive heed to murmuring

John Brown [of Haddington] (1722–1787), by William Home Lizars

against Brown) into the Associate Synod. It was under the synod's professors of theology, first Ebenezer Erskine at Stirling and then James Fisher at Glasgow, that Brown studied philosophy and divinity during school vacations (1748–50).

Brown was licensed by the Associate Presbytery of Edinburgh on 14 November 1750. On 4 July of the following year he was ordained to Haddington, Haddingtonshire, where he served until his death in 1787. (He disapproved of ministers flitting from charge to charge.) In visitation, catechizing, and examination, in prayer and spiritual conference with elders, in admitting new communicants, and above all in Sunday duty, Brown was a tirelessly faithful pastor. For eight months of the year he delivered a lecture, two sermons, and an exercise each Sunday. Yet he blamed the multiplicity of services accompanying the annual observance of the Lord's supper—the communion season—for obscuring its apostolic simplicity and militating against greater frequency. In 1756 he introduced twice yearly celebration, justifying his action in *Apology for the More Frequent Administration of the Lord's Supper* (posthumously published, 1804). If, as his detractors claimed, infrequency safeguarded solemnity, he reasoned, then why not preach and pray infrequently also? Brown also encouraged the presence, but not participation, of children at communion.

In addition, from 1767 to the end of his life Brown served as the Associate Synod's theological professor (without additional salary). This meant that during August and September each year about thirty students attended his classes in Haddington. About 160 hours were crammed in annually over a four- or five-year course, with Brown teaching all the subjects of the curriculum. Spiritual formation, preaching skills, and academic disciplines were equally his concern, as he shaped a whole generation of Associate Synod ministers.

Brown was also a prolific writer, displaying his exhaustive knowledge of the Bible and the riches of his well-stocked mind. Series of letters entitled *Gospel Preaching, Behaviour of Ministers, The Christian, the Student, and the Pastor Exemplified in the Lives of Nine Eminent Ministers* (1782), and *Practical Piety Exemplified in the Lives of Thirteen Eminent Christians* (1783) illustrate his directly pedagogic bent. *A General History of the Christian Church* (1771), *A Compendious History of the British Churches* (1784), *A Historical Account of the Secession* (1766), and *A Compendious View of Natural and Revealed Religion* (his systematics, 1782) all embodied and supported his teaching. Some works were apologetic or polemical, such as *Thoughts on the Travelling of the Mail on the Lord's Day* (1785) and *The absurdity and perfidy of all authoritative toleration of gross heresy, blasphemy, idolatry, and popery in Britain* (1780). Even *An Help for the Ignorant*, his first publication (1758), intended to provide 'an Easy Explication' of the Westminster confession and catechisms for children, ran to 400 pages. What he said in it about the relationship between the righteousness of Christ and of Christian believers attracted criticism, but he defended his stance in *A Brief Dissertation on Christ's Righteousness* (1759). Explicit theological controversy made little demand on Brown's labours.

None of the works mentioned above is now of more than historical interest. Perhaps Brown's ablest work was the 1784 *History of the British Churches*, with the second volume devoted to Scotland. But he listed his authorities without furnishing references at particular points. It was for *The Self-Interpreting Bible* (1778) and *A Dictionary of the Holy Bible* (1769) that Brown enjoyed greatest recognition as an author. The latter, unlike modern counterparts, explained ordinary words, such as 'Finally, Find, Finish, Firm, Fit', even 'To' and 'That'. It supplied much general knowledge, on geography, history, and the natural world, often to quaint effect. The frog, we are told, has 'four legs for leaping with' and is 'much given to croaking' (J. Brown, *A Dictionary of the Holy Bible*, 1797 edn, 467). Though the elm tree is mentioned only once in scripture (Hosea, 4: 13), Brown gives various details, including the fact that one elm in a hundred years will on average yield 33 million seeds. Yet the dictionary is an excellent pioneer in the field, of exemplary directness, clarity, and accuracy in explaining key terms and concepts. Theology and church controversies scarcely intrude. A century later it was still highly regarded for popular use.

The Self-Interpreting Bible remained in print until the twentieth century, in much revised form. Brown transferred lists, tables, and other such aids from his dictionary. The *Bible* was a far more substantial work, which did not prevent its becoming, as Robert Burns bore out, as familiar in Presbyterian households as John Bunyan's *Pilgrim's Progress* and Thomas Boston's *Human Nature in its Fourfold State*. Brown's text was furnished with a battery of cross-references, minor marginal notes, short introductions to each book, a summary of contents at the head of each chapter, 'reflections' on each chapter—in effect applying its message to readers—and explanatory footnotes. A lengthy introduction deals with the Bible's authority and inspiration, its interpretation, and biblical history from creation. All were intended, as the title made clear, to make the Bible accessible to the humblest reader, unlike much biblical scholarship today.

In 1779 Brown met a request from the countess of Huntingdon for a copy of his theological lectures by writing them out in full himself. They were for delivery at the countess's college at Trefeca in Wales. But it was much more the *Bible* and the dictionary that made Brown widely known overseas, where some of his former students had journeyed as missionaries or migrants. In 1784 he declined an invitation to a chair in the Dutch Reformed church's new college in New York. In Scotland he was the most voluminous religious writer of his day, and almost a household name. Unlikely hearers recognized the force of his preaching, which he never allowed to carry too heavy a weight of learning. Attributed to David Hume is a comparison of an aspiring young minister with Brown: 'The first preacher spoke as if he did not believe what he said; the latter as if he were conscious that the Son of God stood at his elbow' (Mackenzie, 100). Brown favoured Archbishop Ussher's guidance: 'It will take all our learning to make things plain' (Mackenzie, 101).

In September 1753 Brown had married Janet Thomson (1732/3–1771), daughter of a Musselburgh merchant; the couple had several children, two of whom, John *Brown (1754–1832) and Ebenezer, survived childhood. Both followed their father as ministers respectively of Whitburn, Linlithgowshire (1777–1832), and Inverkeithing, Fife (1780–1836). Following his wife's death, aged thirty-eight, on 10 May 1771, Brown married Violet Croumbie (1744/5–1822), daughter of a merchant in Stenton, Haddingtonshire, on 19 January 1773. They had nine children, five of whom survived childhood, including Thomas (b. 1776), who served as minister of Dalkeith from 1799 to his death in 1828, Samuel (1779–1839), a pioneer of itinerating libraries, and William (1783–1863), who was secretary of the Scottish Missionary Society and author of the weighty *History of Missions*. John Brown died at the Associate Synod manse, Haddington, on 19 June 1787 after a long period of growing debility. He was buried four days later in Haddington churchyard. The deep and wide impact of his ministries by word and pen has always seemed enhanced by the unpromising beginnings of this 'lad o' pairts'. In theology he espoused an unremarkable federal Calvinism in the Westminster mould, which he grounded profusely in scripture and directed towards a warm Christ-centred devotion. Some sentiments from a letter to the countess of Huntingdon in 1779 show the heart and mind of the man:

> But, dropping the superficial chat concerning my poor books, let us have a word concerning that great, that glorious, that truly original *Book of God*—GOD MADE MANIFEST IN THE FLESH. Blessed be God for our English

translation of His oracles, and for our easy access to peruse them. Blessed be God for the Hebrew and Greek originals of the Testament of our Lord Jesus Christ. And blessed be above all blessings, and praised be God for that Original Bible, Jesus Christ, of which He Himself hath *engraved the engraving*. (Mackenzie, 220)

One of Brown's descendants, one of many namesakes, who was the grandson of John of Whitburn, a doctor and author of *Horae subsecivae* (1861), said of John Brown of Haddington, 'He was our King, the founder of our dynasty; we dated from him' (Mackenzie, 307). When Robert Mackenzie's life was written (1918), the dynasty had expanded to more than 400. Several edited memoirs and remains of Brown or produced new editions of the dictionary and *Bible*. They have marked anniversaries and retain a sense of shared identity. When the present writer preached in Haddington on the bicentenary of Brown's death on 21 June 1987, some had travelled from the USA to be present. Their ranks have included, besides numerous ministers, eminent scientists, literary figures, and activists in public life.   D. F. WRIGHT

Sources R. Mackenzie, *John Brown of Haddington* (1918) · Chambers, *Scots.*, rev. T. Thomson (1875), 1/1.176–80 · *Memoir and select remains of the Rev John Brown*, ed. W. Brown (1856) · J. Brown, ed., *Memoir* (1828) · J. Cairns, *Memoir of John Brown: including a letter to Dr Cairns from John Brown* (1860) · J. C. Brown, ed., *Centenary memorial … of John Brown of Haddington: a family record* (1887) · D. F. Wright, 'Brown, John', *DSCHT*
Archives Wellcome L., notes on lectures
Likenesses Kinnerley, stipple, pubd 1813 (after an unknown artist), NPG · stipple, pubd 1832 (after an unknown artist), NPG · stipple and line engraving, pubd 1832, BM; NPG · G. Inglis, oils, Scot. NPG · J. Kay, oils, Scot. NPG; repro. in Mackenzie, *John Brown*, frontispiece · Kinnerley, two oil paintings, Scot. NPG · W. H. Lizars, mixed method engraving (after an unknown artist), NPG [see illus.] · W. H. Lizars, oils, Scot. NPG · R. Scott, two oil paintings, Scot. NPG · A. Wilson, stipple, NPG · oils, repro. in Mackenzie, *John Brown*, facing p. 270 · pencil drawing, NPG

Brown, John (*bap.* 1735, *d.* 1788), physician, the son of Archibald Brown, a weaver at Lintlaws, was baptized in the parish church of Bunckle, Berwickshire, Scotland, on 17 May 1735. His father died when Brown was young and his mother remarried. At the age of five Brown was sent to the parish school of Duns and was apparently taught by an unusually good Latinist named Cruickshank. The school was attended by boys who were generally Brown's social superiors. He was, according to his son William Cullen Brown, a child prodigy who by the age of five had read the whole of the Old Testament (*Works*, 1.xix). By the age of ten he was head of his school but he was taken away and apprenticed to a weaver. Apparently Cruickshank persuaded the parents to let him return free of charge, and by thirteen Brown had become a pupil teacher. Brown had a reputation for great physical and mental strength as a youth, and Thomas Beddoes observed that 'he had vigour of body with vigour of mind and exerted both' (*Elements*, xli). He was among the foremost at boxing, wrestling, and football, and also reputedly had great powers of memory; on one occasion, after going through two pages of Cicero with the class, he closed the book and repeated the passage word for word.

John Brown (*bap.* 1735, *d.* 1788), self-portrait, *c.*1780

At the age of eighteen Brown became a tutor in a laird's household, soon after which he went to Edinburgh where he attended lectures in philosophy and divinity, and supported himself by private tuition. After a few years he returned to Duns as usher in the school. Twelve months later, aged twenty-four, he returned to Edinburgh and applied, unsuccessfully, for a mastership in the high school. Brown's biographers, whose accounts of the details of his life are often markedly different, agree that in Edinburgh he turned to the study of medicine and was admitted free by the professors to their lectures, that he taught Latin, and that he became a 'grinder' or extramural coach and composer of theses. He also opened a boarding house, in 1765, and in the same year married the daughter of an Edinburgh citizen named Lamond; they had four daughters and four sons, one of whom was Ford Brown, father of the artist Ford Madox Brown.

By this time, according to Brown's son William, 'the pleasures of the table and the unconstrained hilarity he enjoyed at the convivial meetings of ... [his] companions, were by nature sufficiently agreeable to one of his vivacity of disposition and strong passions' (*Works*, lii). Beddoes, however, suggested that Brown had acquired a taste for alcohol and opium. Moreover, during these years, William Brown relates that his father, in consequence of his menial position, had to render himself 'agreeable to those on whom his livelihood depended' (ibid., liii). One of these

was the popular and well-connected professor of medicine, William Cullen, who had employed Brown as tutor to his children. Brown's son represented Cullen as the exploiter of his father's talents. He wrote that 'Dr Cullen, who was extremely deficient in classical erudition, conceived the idea of turning his pupil's intimate knowledge of Latin to his own permanent advantage' (ibid., lv). Beddoes took a similar view. John Thomson, however, observed that this was 'entirely a piece of invention. The only capacity in which Dr Cullen employed Mr John Brown was as tutor or private teacher to his children, to assist them in the preparation of their lessons and their Latin exercises' (Thomson, 2.711). Thomson further expressed surprise that Beddoes could possibly think that a man as great as Cullen would employ, as an amanuensis, a man who was little more than an adept at the art of 'low buffoonery' (ibid., 2.713).

The events following Brown's association with Cullen are the subject of striking differences of interpretation among the biographers. According to Brown's son William, Cullen had promised to exert his interest on Brown's behalf for the first vacant university chair and, accordingly, in 1776 Brown put himself forward for the chair of the Institutes of Medicine. Beddoes, who also stated that Cullen had made such a promise, contended that Cullen, on being shown the name of Brown in the list of candidates, is said to have exclaimed in the 'vulgar dialect' of the country 'Why sure this can never be our Jock!' (*Elements*, lviii), the suggestion being that the urbane Cullen stigmatized Brown as a rustic and thus wholly unfitted to aspire to an Edinburgh chair and the polite social world to which it gave entry. Thomson, however, denied the suggestion that Cullen had ever encouraged Brown and, indeed, claimed that the town council records showed that Brown had never been a candidate for the chair. Following this episode there was at least one further serious disagreement between Cullen and Brown. Brown put his name forward for election to the prestigious Edinburgh Philosophical Society and was blackballed. According to Thomson, Cullen had advised Brown, for his own good, to withdraw his application. William Brown, however, held that his father's rejection was negotiated by Cullen, who was jealous of Brown's originality and was 'dreading the shock, which his own favourite opinions ... would sustain ... from a rival' (*Works*, lxiv). The result, Beddoes stated, was that 'Cullen estranged the mind of his Latin secretary' (*Elements*, lviii), or, as Thomson observed, 'Cullen ceased to hold any communication with him; it is said even to mention his name' (Thomson, 2.715).

Following the breach between the two men, Brown began to teach his own system of medicine in Edinburgh in opposition to that of Cullen. He received his degree of MD from St Andrews in 1779. Around these years he was popular and influential at the students' Royal Medical Society, where he had been made president in 1776 and again in 1780. He began a course of public lectures on the practice of physic in 1778. Brown used contemporary ideas of irritability and sensibility as the basis for a dualist theory of disease and a radically simplified therapeutics.

He taught that excitability, a property of the nervous system, was the fundamental feature of living bodies. It was activated by environmental stimuli to produce excitement, the life force. Brown's system, known as Brunonianism, was thus important in its claim that living bodies could not be understood simply through knowledge of mathematical or physical laws, a view that prevailed during the first half of the eighteenth century. For Brown, health was an equilibrium between stimulus and excitability. Insufficient stimulation caused asthenic diseases, with a deficit of excitement and a surfeit of unused excitability. Treatment for these diseases, by far the most common, was by stimulation, notably by the ingestion of opium and alcohol, a therapy Brown applied liberally for his own gout. Indeed a severe attack of this disease in 1771 was said by Brown to have been the origin of his system. Consulting an unnamed medical worthy (possibly Cullen) for his attack, Brown was told to abstain from meat and alcohol. Receiving no relief he treated the disorder as a debilitating and not as a plethoric one. Brown resumed convivial drinking and hearty Scottish fare and was rewarded with six gout-free years. The opposite of asthenic diseases were the less frequent sthenic disorders which required mild depletion. By eighteenth-century standards Brunonianism was sparing in its use of bloodletting and purging. The influence of Brunonianism in this respect is difficult to gauge, since fever therapy in general was moving away from depletives at the end of the eighteenth century.

Opposed to the orthodoxies of Cullen in particular and of Edinburgh medicine in general, Brown's system of medicine appears to have been popular in Edinburgh among outsiders in the medical profession and was supported by those seeking wider political reform in the city. Indeed it seems to have had its greatest popularity elsewhere in Britain, among political radicals, such as Beddoes, or among more humble practitioners and military and naval surgeons. In 1780 Brown published the *Elementa medicinae* and, anonymously in 1787, *Observations on the Principle of the Old System of Physic*. Another Brunonian work, *An Inquiry into the State of Medicine*, was published in 1781 under the name of Robert Jones, an Edinburgh physician who was a close friend of Brown. However, William Brown stated that the work was written by his father since it was a 'moral certainty' (*Works*, clxviii) that it could not have been the production of Jones. Nevertheless, Jones probably was the author. Contemporaries and biographers were in marked disagreement as to how much Brown's teaching differed from Cullen's. Some authors, such as Beddoes, found Brown's work strikingly original, while others, such as Thomson, a Cullen disciple, found it entirely derivative. It was, however, a typical Edinburgh product, in so far as his ideas were enshrined in a system.

Popular though Brown was among the students, he gained little practice in Edinburgh. He had serious money troubles and at one time was imprisoned for debt. Nearly all authors, including the hostile Thomson, took the view that Brown's character, or perhaps his charisma, was the foundation of the attraction of his teachings, both for students and for others. They also concur in the opinion that this charisma was fuelled by the consumption of large amounts of brandy and opium. The charisma, however, was not universally effective. Beddoes recorded that, after encountering Brown in 1782, 'I never desired his conversation a second time'. He spoke, said Beddoes, with a Doric dialect which 'had nothing prepossessing to an English ear. It was so broad as to leave me often uncertain of what he said' (*Elements*, lxxx). Beddoes also gave an equally unsympathetic account of a Brunonian evening:

> One of his pupils informs me that when he found himself languid, he sometimes placed a bottle of whisky in one hand, and a phial of laudanum on the other; and that, before he began his lecture, he would take forty or fifty drops of laudanum in a glass of whisky; repeating the dose four or five times during the lecture. Between the effects of these stimulants and voluntary exertion, he soon waxed warm, and by degrees his imagination was exalted into phrenzy. (*Elements*, lxxxvii)

His son denied the charges of gross indulgence and claimed that his father's 'intemperate excesses' were 'egregiously exaggerated', and that 'many ridiculous stories of the frolics committed by him in a state of ebriety have been circulated at his expense' (*Works*, cxxxiii). However, he admitted that his father was rather free in his religious sentiments and that he also had unconventional political allegiances. Beddoes recorded that 'Brown was the first person I ever saw absurd enough to profess himself a Jacobite' (*Elements*, lxxxi). The remainder of Brown's life in Edinburgh was as colourful as his early career. In 1784 or 1785 he established a masonic institution, the Lodge of the Roman Eagle, with the noble intention of preventing the decline of Roman language and literature.

In 1786 Brown moved with his family to London and lived in a house in Golden Square. As in Edinburgh he was unable to establish a successful practice, although men of letters, including Dr Samuel Parr, were said to visit him socially. There was also, apparently, an invitation from Frederick the Great for Brown to settle at the court of Berlin. For reasons unknown the offer miscarried or was withdrawn. Through debt Brown found himself in the king's bench prison for a time. He began to write a great deal and made an English translation of his *Elementa medicinae*, completing it in twenty-one days. He contracted with a publisher for £500 to produce a treatise on the gout, and he had other literary projects which would occupy him, he said, for ten years to come. His professional prospects improved. He had several families to attend and patient numbers were increasing, when he was struck down by apoplexy. He died on 17 October 1788. Beddoes ungenerously recorded that 'he died, if I am not misinformed, in the night, having swallowed as he went to bed a very large dose of laudanum; a species of dram to which he had long been addicted' (*Elements*, xciii). Brown was buried in the churchyard of St James's, Piccadilly. His sons and daughters were provided for by the generosity of his friends, notably Dr Parr. His eldest son, William Cullen Brown, subsequently studied medicine at Edinburgh where, apparently, he was received with much kindness by James Gregory and other professors, and admitted to their lectures without fee. Like his father he became president of the Royal Medical Society, and he brought out an edition of his father's works.

The Brunonian doctrine occupied a considerable space in medical literature, after the death of its author. The English version of the *Elementa* was republished at Philadelphia in 1790 by Benjamin Rush. The Latin edition appeared from Hildburghausen in 1794. A German translation of it was made at Frankfurt in 1795, and a second edition appeared in 1798. A German translation also appeared from Copenhagen in 1798, and by 1804 a third edition had been published there. An exposition of the system was published by Christoph Girtanner, at Göttingen, in 1797. There was also a French translation in 1805 which was said to have been laid before the national convention and honourably commended. An account of the doctrines was published by Giovanni Rasori, at Pavia, in 1792. In the same year the *Elementa* was reprinted in Milan. Jones's *Inquiry* was brought out in Italian by Joseph Frank, at Pavia, in 1795.

As practised, Brunonianism probably enjoyed its greatest success in Germany, where it gained a supporter in Friedrich Schelling. Brunonian doctrines were debated in the context of Romantic debates on the nature of life, and Brunonian practices were adopted by civil and military practitioners. It is said that in 1802 the University of Göttingen was convulsed by a controversy between Brunonian and anti-Brunonian factions to the extent that a physical combat in the streets had to be dispersed by troops. Brown's ideas were expanded, successfully, by Joseph Frank, son of Johann Peter Frank, at the universities of Pavia, Vienna, and Vilna. In Austria, Brunonianism seemed 'to offer a progressive and systematic approach to therapeutics' (Bynum and Porter, ix). Brown's system made additional headway in Italy through the teaching and translations of Professor Rasori, also at Pavia. Brunonianism was adopted by a number of French doctors (mainly military surgeons) after several abridgements from Italian sources appeared in 1797 and 1798. The professors at the Paris medical school, however, were hostile to it.   CHRISTOPHER LAWRENCE

Sources J. Brown, *The elements of medicine: a new edition, revised and corrected with a biographical preface by Thomas Beddoes MD* (1795), vol. 1 • *The works of Dr John Brown*, ed. W. C. Brown, 3 vols. (1804), vol. 1 • J. Thomson, *An account of the life, lectures and writings of William Cullen*, 2 (1859) • W. F. Bynum and R. Porter, eds., *Brunonianism in Britain and Europe* (1988) • G. B. Risse, 'The history of John Brown's medical system in Germany during the years 1790–1806', PhD diss., University of Chicago, 1971 • E. Rossi, 'Giovanni Rasori (1766–1837) or Italian medicine in transition', *Bulletin of the History of Medicine*, 29 (1955), 116–33 • G. B. Risse, 'The quest for certainty in medicine: John Brown's system of medicine in France', *Bulletin of the History of Medicine*, 45 (1971), 1–12 • *DNB* • parish register (baptism), Bunckle and Preston, Bunckle church, 17 May 1735
Likenesses J. Brown, self-portrait, drawing, c.1780, National Museums of Scotland [*see illus.*] • J. Kay, etchings, 1786–1819, NPG, Wellcome L. • J. Bogle, miniature, 1788, NG Scot. • W. Blake, stipple, pubd 1795 (after J. Donaldson), BM, NPG • line engraving, 1795 (after W. Blake), Wellcome L. • J. Caldwall, line print, pubd 1799 (after J. Donaldson), BM, NPG • J. Heath, line print, pubd 1799 (after J. Donaldson), BM • J. Adam, line engraving (after J. Cagnoni), Wellcome L. • J. Brown, pencil drawing, NPG • J. Caldwall, line engraving (after J. Donaldson), Wellcome L. • J. Cary, aquatint, Wellcome L. • J. Heath, line engraving (after J. Donaldson), Wellcome L. • J. Thomson, stipple (after J. Donaldson), Wellcome L. • line engraving, Wellcome L.

Brown, John (1736–1803), merchant and politician in the United States of America, was born on 27 January 1736 in Providence, Rhode Island, the third son of James Brown (1698–1739) merchant and shipowner, and Hope Power (1702–1792). John Brown was a member of a distinguished Providence family whose history over numerous generations has been involved with the business, cultural, philanthropic, and educational past and present of Rhode Island. His eldest brother James (1724–1756) was lost early in life at sea, but his other brothers, Nicholas (1729–1791), Joseph (1733–1785), and Moses (1738–1836) were all prominent and energetic figures, active in the business, politics, and educational growth of Rhode Island. John Brown married on 27 November 1760 Sarah, daughter of Daniel Smith and Dorcas Harris; they had six children, James, Benjamin, Abigail, Abby, Sally or Sarah, and Alice.

Early in his career Brown, 'a man of magnificent projects and extraordinary enterprise', was in a partnership with his three brothers in the family business, Nicholas Brown & Co.; a man of nearly 300 pounds, his size and stature were noteworthy. A promoter, with his brothers, of the Hope Furnace in Cranston in 1765 (which manufactured cannon for use in the American army during the American War of Independence), John withdrew from his family business in 1771 to venture off on his own in more adventurous and risk-taking business enterprises. During the war and the years leading up to its outbreak, John was an active American patriot. He participated fully in the fierce political struggles that characterized Rhode Island during this period. Allying himself with Governor Samuel Ward and Joseph Wanton, Brown adamantly opposed British attempts to tax internally the American colonists, even going so far as to lead the party that burned the British customs schooner *Gaspee* that ran aground in Narragansett Bay on 9 June 1772.

Throughout the American War of Independence Brown and his brother Nicholas helped the American cause by supplying weapons, clothing, and munitions to the continental army and congress. After the war he supported the new constitution as a staunch federalist and was elected twice to congress, in 1784 and 1785 (but did not participate). He later served in the house of representatives (1799–1801).

When the war ended Brown went into partnership with his son-in-law, John Francis (the husband of Abby Brown), and formed Brown and Francis. They established the first venture by a Providence vessel to engage in the East India and China trade. In December 1787 the *George Washington* inaugurated the East India trade in Providence, and took a cargo composed of anchors, cordage, sail cloth, cannon, bar iron, sheet copper, steel, spars, liquors, cheese, and spermaceti candles (total value of $26,348), and returned eighteen months later with tea, silks, china, cotton goods, lacquered ware, and cloves (total value of $99,848). Although John had joined the society formed in June 1790 for the promotion of the abolition of slavery in the United States and for improving the condition of the African race, during 1800 he was one of the opponents of a bill in Rhode Island prohibiting the slave trade in the United States to any foreign place or country, because he thought that the trade was financially beneficial to the United States, and that there should not be any interference by the government with free enterprise in business.

The Brown brothers were instrumental in the establishment of educational institutions in Rhode Island. On 14 May 1770 John Brown laid the cornerstone of the first building of the College of Rhode Island, now known as University Hall, on the home lot of his ancestor, Chad Browne. The land had previously been sold by the family, but was repurchased and presented to the corporation of the college. Brown was treasurer of the College of Rhode Island for twenty years (1775–95) before it was renamed Brown University in 1804. John also supported the Baptist church throughout his life and created a permanent fund for the Baptist Society. In the life of the city he helped to secure the construction of the Washington Bridge across the Seekonk River, and built one of the most beautiful remaining late eighteenth-century colonial homes on Power Street, which is managed by the Rhode Island Historical Society. Brown died in Providence on 20 September 1803 and was buried at the north burial-ground.

MURNEY GERLACH

Sources J. B. Hedges, *The colonial years* (1968), vol. 1 of *The Browns of Providence plantations* · A. B. Bulkley, *The Chad Browne memorial, consisting of genealogical memoirs of a portion of the descendants of Chad and Elizabeth Browne, 1638–1888* (1888) · J. B. Hedges, 'The Brown papers: the record of a Rhode Island business family', *Proceedings of the American Antiquarian Society*, 51 (1942), 21–36 · W. G. Roelker, 'The Browns and Brown University', *Brown Alumni Monthly*, 49/4 (Dec 1948), 3–7 · E. Donnan, ed., *Documents illustrative of the history of the slave trade to America*, 4 (1930–35); repr. (1965) · H. S. Taft, 'John Brown's mansion house on the hill', *Rhode Island Historical Society Collections*, 34 (1941), 107–12 · *Providence Gazette* (24 Sept 1803) · D. D. Wax, 'The Browns of Providence and the slave voyage of the brig *Sally*, 1764–1765', *American Neptune*, 32 (1972), 171–9 · G. S. Kimball, *Providence in colonial times* (1912) · R. A. Guild, *History of Brown University* (1867) · W. B. Weeden, 'Early oriental commerce in Providence', *Proceedings of the Massachusetts Historical Society*, 3rd ser., 1 (1906–8), 236 · *Collections of the Massachusetts Historical Society*, 7th ser., 9–10 (1914–15) [*Commerce of Rhode Island, 1726–1800*] · 'The founding of the Providence Bank (October 3, 1791)', *Rhode Island Historical Society Collections*, 34 (1941), 113–28 · M. Thompson, *Moses Brown: reluctant reformer* (1962)

Archives Brown University, Rhode Island, John Carter Brown Library, Brown family business papers · Brown University, Rhode Island, John Nicholas Brown Center · Rhode Island Historical Society | Rhode Island Historical Society, Moses Brown papers

Likenesses E. G. Malbone, miniature, 1794, New York Historical Society

Brown, John (1749–1787), miniature painter and draughtsman, was born on 18 June 1749 in Edinburgh, the eldest of five children of Samuel Brown (1722–1787), and his wife and cousin, Agnes Fyfe Scoular (1716–1787). His father was a watchmaker and deacon of the Hammermen of Edinburgh and a free burgess of Peebles and Edinburgh, and his uncle James Scoular was a musical instrument maker; his cousin James Scoular or Scouler (1740–1812) was also a miniaturist. John Brown studied at the Trustees' Academy, Edinburgh, probably under William Delacour and then Charles Pavillon. By 1769 he was in London, where he ordered a camera obscura, an instrument which he regarded as 'useful and even necessary to a landscape painter' (Pressly, 55). On 15 October 1769 he was ready to set sail from Falmouth for Italy in the company of David Erskine, who was well connected in Rome.

Brown was fortunate in not only having connections to Roman society through Erskine's cousin, Charles, later Cardinal Erskine, but also to its artistic circle through friendship with his fellow Scot Alexander Runciman, who was there from 1767 and who was part of the circle of artists around Henry Fuseli. By spring 1772 Brown was travelling as draughtsman to the antiquary and collector Charles Townley and his companion William Young. Their extensive tour of the lesser-known parts of southern Italy, Sicily, and Malta was documented by Young in his *Journal of a summer's excursion by the road of Montecasino to Naples, and from there over all the southern parts of Italy, Sicily and Malta, in the year 1772* ([1773?]), and by Townley, in his personal papers. However, neither Young nor Townley provides a record of Brown's activities and few of the drawings of antiquities made on this tour survive. It was during this tour that Brown contracted malaria.

Townley and Brown enjoyed a warm relationship, and Brown was far from intellectually inferior to his more privileged companions. He was later described by John Burnett, Lord Monboddo, as 'more learned in the Italian arts of painting, sculpture, music and poetry than any man I ever conversed with' (Brown, iii). On his return to Rome in 1773 Brown, probably through Runciman, became involved with Fuseli and his circle; his intellectual interests no doubt found resonance with the Swiss artist's. In Rome, Brown made numerous studies of Roman life as well as sensitive portraits. He worked in pencil, and pen and ink, and like other members of the circle developed 'a more emotionally expressive and dramatic approach' which evolved into 'a homogeneous style' through artistic exchange (Pressly, ix). *The Stiletto Merchant* (c.1775–80; Pierpont Morgan Library, New York), a scene of sinister dramatically illuminated nightlife, and carefully observed character, is one of Brown's most potent images. The same threatening atmosphere is also found in *Woman Standing among Friars* (Cleveland Museum of Art), which employs similar dramatic techniques of strongly contrasting dark and light, forcefully observed character bordering on caricature, and a sinuous line in drawing, typical of Fuseli's circle. Brown also drew the antiquities and landscape of Rome, including *A View of the Coliseum at Rome*, which he exhibited at the Royal Academy in 1774, and *The Basilica of Maxentius* [*and Constantine*] (c.1774–6; NG Scot.), and continued to work for Townley, producing drawings of antique sculpture.

Brown was in Florence by 31 August 1776, where he drew

in the Uffizi: its director described him as 'esatto e diligente, modesto, quiete' (Ingamells, 138). Thomas Jones met him at the English Hotel in November 1776, and with Christopher Ebden, the architect, the artists visited the collection of Lord Cowper. Brown seems to have remained in Florence for the rest of his time in Italy, continuing to work for Townley and visiting Venice in 1779.

Brown was probably in London by March 1780 and thereafter returned to Scotland. His most important commission there was for a group of thirty-one small-scale portrait drawings (Scot. NPG) of the members of the Society of Antiquaries, commissioned by David Steuart Erskine, eleventh earl of Buchan, between 1780 and 1781 at the cost of 1 guinea each. He may have visited London shortly after this date but was certainly in Edinburgh in 1784 when he sat for a remarkably animated double portrait with and by Runciman (Scot. NPG), for Erskine. He married Mary, daughter of Charles Esplin, variously described as a merchant, painter, and limner, of New Kirk parish, Edinburgh, on 2 February 1786; they had one son, Charles. In that same year he travelled to London; however, the malaria he contracted in Italy forced him to return home, and after making the voyage by sea he died at Leith on 5 September 1787. He was buried on 6 September at Greyfriars burial-ground, Edinburgh. In 1789 his *Letters upon the Poetry and Music of the Italian Opera; Addressed to a Friend* were published by their recipient Lord Monboddo, who in the introduction acclaimed Brown as 'one of the greatest artists that ever was in Scotland' who, on the subject of this work, was 'more learned … than any man in Great Britain' (Brown, iii). DEBORAH GRAHAM-VERNON

Sources N. L. Pressly, *The Fuseli circle in Rome: early Romantic art of the 1770s* (New Haven, CT, 1979) [exhibition catalogue, Yale U. CBA, 12 Sept – 11 Nov 1979] · J. Ingamells, ed., *A dictionary of British and Irish travellers in Italy, 1701–1800* (1997) · D. Irwin and F. Irwin, *Scottish painters at home and abroad, 1700–1900* (1975) · D. Foskett, *Miniatures: dictionary and guide* (1987) · private information (2004) · B. Skinner, 'John Brown and the antiquarians', *Country Life* (12 Aug 1971), 392–6 · J. Brown, *Letters upon the poetry and music of the Italian opera; addressed to a friend* (1789) · G. Vaughan, 'The collecting of classical antiquities in England in the 18th century: a study of Charles Townley (1737–1805) and his circle', DPhil diss., U. Oxf., 1988 · A. P. Oppé, ed., 'Memoirs of Thomas Jones, Penkerrig, Radnorshire', *Walpole Society*, 32 (1946–8) [whole issue], esp. 51 · parish register, Edinburgh, New Kirk, 2 Feb 1786 [marriage]
Archives NRA Scotland, priv. coll., letters to his father
Likenesses A. Runciman, double portrait, oils (with Runciman), Scot. NPG

Brown, John [*known as* John Brown of Whitburn] (1754–1832), minister of the Secession church, was born at Haddington, Haddingtonshire, on 24 July 1754, the eldest son of John *Brown of Haddington (1722–1787), Secession church minister and theologian, and his first wife, Janet (1732/3–1771), daughter of John Thomson, a Musselburgh merchant. Brown's piety was evident from an early age: according to his brother Ebenezer, later minister at Inverkeithing, Fife, John engaged boys of his own age not in sports but 'religious conversation and prayer' (M'Kerrow, 908). He entered Edinburgh University aged about fourteen and later studied under his father, who was then professor of theology at the Associate (Burgher) Synod. On 21

John Brown [of Whitburn] (1754–1832), by John Pairman, in or before 1813

May 1776 he was licensed to preach by the Associate Presbytery at Edinburgh and was called to Whitburn, Linlithgowshire, where he was ordained on 22 May of the following year, and where he remained for the rest of his life. Like his celebrated father, Brown was notable for his plain and direct mode of address: 'As a preacher, he was characterized by the simplicity and seriousness of his manner, and by that highly evangelical tone of his sentiments, his preaching being "peculiarly savoury to the pious"' (ibid.). Also remarkable was his habit of chanting sermons, Brown being one of the last ministers to adopt this form.

In addition to his duties at Whitburn, Brown also took a particular interest in communicating the Associate Synod's teachings to highland communities, visiting Perthshire in 1818 and providing Gaelic translations of works by his father and Thomas Boston. Four years previously he had travelled to London, a city he very much enjoyed, and he wrote warmly of the work of the Bible Society. During a previous visit to the capital, prior to his ordination at Whitburn, Brown had administered for six months to the Revd Archibald Hall's congregation. It was here that he met his first wife, Isabella Cranston (d. 1795), with whom he had eight children, including John *Brown (1784–1858), theologian and minister of the United Presbyterian church. Brown was also director of the London Missionary Society.

Brown was a prolific author. His works include compendia of eighteenth-century English sermons (*The Evangelical Preacher*, 1802–6), studies for the young (*A Collection of Letters … Suited to Children and Youth*, 1815), records of his travels (*A Brief Account of a Tour in the Highlands of Perthshire*,

1818), guides to theological works (*A Descriptive List of Religious Books in the English Language*, 1827), biographies (*Memoirs of the Life and Character of the Late Rev James Hervey*, 1806, and *A Memoir of Rev Thomas Bradbury*, 1831), and histories (*Memorials of the Nonconformist Ministers of the Seventeenth Century*, his last work, published in 1832). Brown also published a five-volume collection of the sermons of Thomas Boston, whose work on the Marrow controversy he had read in his youth. Again the practical and didactic tone of such works—'unaffected piety' (M'Kerrow, 908)—followed the example set by his father (whose *Select Remains* he published in 1789), to whom Brown was, perhaps unfairly, often compared. According to the mid-nineteenth-century churchman John Cairns, Brown lacked the 'mental powers of his father', though he had possessed a 'laborious diligence' which 'raised him, in his own day, to considerable influence in religion' (Cairns, 11). Worn down by his diligence, Brown suffered protracted ill health before his death at Whitburn on 10 February 1832. His *Letters on Sanctification* appeared posthumously in 1834, along with a memoir by the Revd David Smith. Brown was survived by his second wife, details of whom are unknown.   PHILIP CARTER

Sources *DNB* · S. Isbell, 'Brown, John', *DSCHT* · J. M'Kerrow, *History of the Secession church*, rev. edn (1841) · R. Mackenzie, *John Brown of Haddington* (1918) · D. Smith, 'Memoir', in J. Brown, *Letters of sanctification* (1834) · J. Cairns, *Memoir of John Brown: including a letter to Dr Cairns from John Brown* (1860)
Archives NL Scot., papers
Likenesses Blood, stipple, pubd 1813 (after J. Pairman), NPG · J. Pairman, miniature, watercolour on ivory, in or before 1813, Scot. NPG [*see illus.*]

Brown, John (*bap.* 1756?, *d.* 1816), military engineer and artist, was the second son of George Brown, an Aberdeenshire land surveyor, and Barbara, *née* May. He was probably baptized in Perth on 20 November 1756. Nothing is known of his education or early life; but he must have trained as a surveyor. He went at an early age to Tobago, where he settled as a planter. By 1781 he had been appointed chief surveyor and assistant engineer of the island, and was also serving in the militia. In that year he fathered a child with a mixed-race slave: the boy was called Charly Stewart (*b.* 1781), although no Jacobite leanings on Brown's part are to be assumed. Times were hard in Tobago, 'this damn'd country', as Brown called it, and only problems with his land and slaves prevented him from moving to St Lucia and joining the army. His aim had been to 'make as much money in this place as enable me to go anywhere else like a Gentleman, or perish in the attempt' (NL Scot., MS 2835, fols. 2, 4v). He had no desire to return immediately to the life of a surveyor in Scotland.

Brown was taken prisoner at the French conquest of Tobago, but was released and went to St Lucia. Here he indeed became a regular soldier, being commissioned into the 27th (Inniskilling) regiment of foot. His regimental duties were augmented by staff appointments as assistant adjutant-general, military surveyor and draughtsman to the army, and subsequently assistant engineer. Having served in Antigua, Grenada, and Barbados, Brown

returned to Britain with his regiment and did duty in England, Scotland, and, for a considerable period, in Ireland. Here he transferred to the corps of Royal Irish engineers, having been advised to reject the offer of an Indian posting. By 1801, when he petitioned Lord Cornwallis (NL Scot., MS 3258, fols. 75–6), he could look back on twenty-seven years of varied military service. Being anxious to join the Royal Engineers, in which the Irish engineers were incorporated at the union of 1801, he argued forcefully that his lack of a Woolwich education should not be allowed to stand in his way, and that his training and experience should be deemed sufficient. Since 1789 he had worked on surveys throughout Ireland but particularly in the south, and on building defences at Cork harbour and Bantry Bay. Having spent a year on the staff of the commander-in-chief he was appointed, in 1796, commanding engineer in the southern district with the rank of major. He recorded his work in a meticulous series of small drawings in private notebooks. In 1799 he took part in the Helder expedition as an assistant quartermaster-general, and was promoted lieutenant-colonel on 1 January 1800.

Brown was an able and resourceful officer but perhaps not an easy man to deal with. He was certainly confident of his abilities, and when he fell out with Major-General Charles Vallancey, chief engineer in Ireland, he petitioned the master-general of the ordnance in defence of his professional reputation. His temperament showed itself again when he was serving in the south of England, first as assistant quartermaster-general at the Horse Guards, where he worked on the defences of London, and then from May 1802 as lieutenant-colonel commanding, Royal Staff Corps. It was Brown who, in 1804, conceived the idea of the Royal Military Canal as the principal element of the coastal defence of Kent and Sussex and as an alternative to the potentially devastating inundation of Romney Marsh and Pevensey Level. This work, carried on under Brown's direction, brought him into conflict with John Rennie, the civil engineer engaged on the project. Brown's private journal records their disputes, and also details his vehement opposition to the scheme of Martello tower defence, which he branded 'expensive and diabolical'. Brown attended a conference at Rochester on 21 October at which were present William Pitt, the duke of York, the master-general of the ordnance, and all the military officers responsible for the defences as a whole. He could barely conceal his contempt for Pitt and the others who acceded to the arguments in favour of 'Tower, Tower, Tower' (NL Scot., MS 2868, fol. 2). His divergent opinions notwithstanding, Brown was praised for his 'extraordinary exertions and intelligent direction' of the canal, and received £3000 for his services between 1805 and 1808 (NL Scot., MS 2835, fol. 43).

From his early days in the West Indies, Brown had exercised his artistic talents. He recorded in watercolour painting even the actual French landing on Tobago. He continued to paint in St Lucia, and when the 27th foot returned to England Brown recorded the scenery in

Hampshire and the Isle of Wight. Although he drew figures and portrait sketches, topography was his forte. Among his most important works is a useful record of Lord Bute's Highcliffe House, sometimes attributed to Robert Adam, before its demolition in 1794. On periods of leave in Scotland in 1785 and 1791 he drew scenes in the highlands and lowlands, and recorded the ruins of medieval buildings in Moray, where his brother George lived. He displayed considerable understanding and appreciation of Gothic architecture. In Ireland he sketched country houses and parks (Emo in particular), and views of the harbours and shipping, coastal scenery, and lakes and mountains of the south. Brown's sketches are typically executed in pencil, pen and ink, or ink with a wash, either monochrome or more usually full colour. His small notebooks contain many finely detailed examples of military draughtsmanship: plans of fortifications, ordnance, engineering drawings, inventions, and the like. His professional and private interest in engineering and mechanics was matched by ability as an inventor, and in 1811 he designed a surveying compass.

Brown knew many of the distinguished watercolour painters of the day. He made minute and copious notes on the palette and technique of John Varley (from whom he bought much work), John Laporte, 'Warwick' Smith, Nicholas Pocock, Paul Sandby, and W. S. Gilpin. Laporte in particular was his chosen master, and he noted his methods in the media of watercolour, body-colour, aquatint, etching, and his treatment of subjects such as harbours and townscapes.

In 1810 Brown was appointed colonel of the Royal Staff Corps, and on 19 July 1811 deputy quartermaster-general of the forces. On 4 June 1813 he was promoted major-general. Unmarried and without a legitimate heir, he took an interest in the military careers of his two nephews; one of them became General Sir George *Brown of Crimea fame. George, then a lieutenant-colonel, was the principal beneficiary of his uncle's estate which, at his death at home on 20 March 1816, proved considerable. Besides his house at 82 Sloane Street, Chelsea (left to his nieces), there were substantial funds in cash and stock, and George also inherited an extensive library and collections of maps, mathematical and scientific instruments, and lathes. John Brown, ever combative, had disputes with the makers of these instruments, but his older brother George could nevertheless refer to him as 'so valuable and respectable a kind brother … a thin, slender-made man, most sober in living, both in eating and drinking and as unlikely to be carried off by apoplexy as most men' (NL Scot., MS 2835, fol. 166).   IAIN GORDON BROWN

Sources MSS and sketchbooks of John Brown, NL Scot. · S. G. P. Ward, 'Defence works in Britain, 1803–1805', *Journal of the Society for Army Historical Research*, 27 (1949), 18–37 · I. MacKenzie, 'Major-General John Brown, 1756–1816', MA diss., U. Leeds, 1982 · M. R. Dobie, 'Military manuscripts in the National Library of Scotland', *Journal of the Society for Army Historical Research*, 27 (1949), 118–20 · Mallalieu, *Watercolour artists*, 2nd edn, 1.55 · *West India Committee Circular*, 42/758 (20 Oct 1927), 418 · *The Times* (22 March 1816) · *GM*, 1st ser., 86/1 (1816), 375

Archives NL Scot., MSS 1847, 2835, 2863–2868, 3258, 3262, 3265–3270, 8026; Ch. 1442–1446, 2478–2490 | priv. coll.
Likenesses H. Hone, miniature, 1795, priv. coll.
Wealth at death approx. £19,665; £1200 house and furniture: NL Scot., MS 3258, fol. 153; MS 2835, fol. 172

Brown, John (d. 1826?), writer, became a resident of Bolton in Lancashire in the early 1820s. Very little is known about his early life, except that he travelled widely in northern Europe and mixed in European politics. Drawing on his experiences, he wrote several works on international law, including *Mysteries of Neutralization* (1806). He showed a keen interest in European monarchs, and published *Anecdotes and Characters of the House of Brunswick* (1821) and *Northern Courts* (1818). He also compiled and edited *The Historical Gallery of Criminal Portraitures, Foreign and Domestic* (1823). After settling in Bolton, he began to write a history of the town, of which seventeen numbers were published in 1824–5. About this time he became friendly with the inventor Samuel Crompton, also a Bolton man, and, laying his *History of Bolton* aside, began to support Crompton's claims to a second remuneration from parliament for his invention of the spinning mule. In 1825 he wrote a pamphlet on the subject, and shortly afterwards moved to London, where he prepared a memorial (1825) addressed to the lords of the Treasury and a petition (1826) to the House of Commons. He was, however, completely unsuccessful, owing, as he wrote to Crompton, to secret opposition on the part of 'your primitive enemy', as he called the elder Sir Robert Peel. Brown's life in the metropolis was in all ways a failure, and in despair he committed suicide in his London lodgings, probably in 1826.

Brown's most memorable work was published posthumously and was a biography elucidating the horrors of child labour in the cotton mills, entitled *A Memoir of Robert Blincoe*. First published as a serial in Richard Carlile's *The Lion* in 1828, it was reprinted as a pamphlet later that year. In 1832 it was published as a book by the radical publisher John Doherty in Manchester. The publicity given to Blincoe's case later led to an invitation to him to give evidence at the 1833 royal commission on the employment of children.   FRANCIS WATT, rev. ZOË LAWSON

Sources G. J. French, *The life and times of Samuel Crompton*, 2nd edn (1860) · F. Leary, 'Robert Blincoe, the parish apprentice', *Manchester Notes and Queries* (14 July 1888), 222 · *The Lion*, 1 (1828) [publisher's preface to Blincoe's memoir], 145–6 · 'Preface', J. Brown, *A memoir of Robert Blincoe* (1977)

Brown, John (1778–1848), Free Church of Scotland minister and theological writer, was born at Glasgow, the only son of Thomas Brown, a shoemaker. He was educated in the Associate Burgher Hall at Selkirk, but joined the Church of Scotland. He was licensed by the presbytery of Glasgow on 8 June 1803 and ordained minister of Gartmore in 1805. He was translated to Langton, Berwickshire, in 1810. About this time, he married Marjory, the daughter of George Graham of Duniverag; they had four sons and eleven daughters. He received the degree of DD from the University of Glasgow in November 1815.

Brown was one of the earliest promoters of evangelical views in the Church of Scotland, and a contributor to the

Edinburgh Christian Instructor, edited by Andrew Mitchell Thomson (1779–1831). He was author of two books which attained some popularity: *The Vindication of the Form of Presbyterian Church Government, in Reply to the Independents* (1805), which was considered the standard treatise on its subject; and *The Exclusive Claims of Puseyite Episcopalians to the Christian Ministry Indefensible* (1842). In 1843 he joined the Free Church. Brown died at Langton on 25 June 1848. His wife outlived him, dying in October 1863.

W. G. BLAIKIE, rev. ROSEMARY MITCHELL

Sources *Fasti Scot.* · private information (1886)
Archives U. Edin. L., corresp. and papers · U. Edin., New Coll. L., family corresp. | U. Edin., New Coll. L., letters to Thomas Chalmers
Wealth at death £1458 1s. 7d.: inventory, 1848, Lauder, Scotland

Brown, John (1780x85–1859), geologist and fossil collector, was born at Braintree, Essex. He was apprenticed to a stonemason in Braintree before moving to Colchester as a master mason about 1805. He married first Jane Byford and in 1820, after her death, Elizabeth Eagle, a widow; there were no children from either marriage. He moved to a farm at Stanway, just outside Colchester, about 1830 and became interested in the local geology, particularly the nearby Pleistocene deposits at Copford, Clacton, and Walton on the Naze. He was elected a fellow of the Geological Society in 1836, and began to correspond with and meet many of the leading geologists of the day. Richard Owen of the Royal College of Surgeons visited him at Stanway several times, and borrowed fossil bones and teeth of rhinoceros, mammoth, and other mammals for description in his monographs.

Brown published his first paper in the *Magazine of Natural History* in 1834, and contributed thirty-four papers on the fossils of East Anglia to this and other periodicals. Although not a great traveller, he visited London for scientific meetings, attended meetings of the British Association for the Advancement of Science, and collected fossils in Kent and Wiltshire. He gave specimens from his collection to the Geological Society, to the British Museum, and to museums in Ipswich, Oxford, and elsewhere, as well as to his friends T. R. Jones and W. Whitaker. In his will he bequeathed all his remaining books, philosophical instruments, and specimens to Richard Owen, who subsequently passed the specimens to the British Museum. Brown died at Stanway on 28 November 1859; according to his death certificate he was seventy-nine, though the 1851 census returns state that he was then sixty-six. He was buried at Stanway on 16 December 1859. The value of his geological work was credited by the Geological Survey in their official memoirs, *Geology of the Eastern End of Essex* (1877) and *Geology of the Neighbourhood of Colchester* (1880).

JOHN C. THACKRAY

Sources A. P. Wire, 'Memoir of the late John Brown, FGS, of Stanway', *Essex Naturalist*, 4 (1890), 158–68 · *Quarterly Journal of the Geological Society*, 16 (1860), xxvii–xxviii · R. Owen, *A history of British fossil mammals and birds* (1844–6) · census returns, 1851 · *CGPLA Eng. & Wales* (1860) · parish register (marriage), 1820, St James, Colchester · d. cert. · *Chelmsford Chronicle* (16 Dec 1859)
Archives GS Lond. · NHM, corresp., notes, and lists | NHM, corresp. with Richard Owen and William Clift

Likenesses photograph, 1856, repro. in *Essex Naturalist*
Wealth at death under £7000: probate, 26 Jan 1860, *CGPLA Eng. & Wales*

Brown, John (1784–1858), minister of the United Presbyterian church and theologian, was born at Burnhead, Whitburn, Linlithgowshire, on 12 July 1784, the third child and eldest son of the Secession minister John *Brown of Whitburn (1754–1832) and his first wife, Isabella Cranston (d. 1795), and grandson of John *Brown of Haddington (1722–1787), editor of *The Self-Interpreting Bible*. After education at the local school, he attended sessions at Edinburgh University between 1797 and 1800. Thereafter, with a guinea to start him off in life, he supported himself through teaching at Elie in Fife, while for two months of the year he attended the Associate Synod Divinity Hall at Selkirk, under George Lawson, between 1800 and 1804.

Licensed by the presbytery of Stirling and Falkirk on 12 February 1805, Brown was called to congregations in Stirling and Biggar, Lanarkshire. As was then the practice, the synod had the power to choose which of the calls to accept and they favoured the Biggar congregation, following a plea on their behalf by Brown's father. He was ordained on 6 February 1806. In August 1807 he married Jane Nimmo (d. 1816), with whom he had two daughters and two sons; the elder son was John *Brown (1810–1882), physician and author. Brown became a preacher of sufficient repute to attract occasional hearers from the established church. He emerged as a controversialist with his *Strictures on Mr Yates's Vindication of Unitarianism* (1815), which grew from a review for the *Edinburgh Christian Instructor*. From 1816 he was editor of the *Christian Repository and Religious Register*, the theological organ of the Burgher church. This later merged to form the *Christian Monitor*, which Brown edited until 1826.

Inevitably, Brown attracted interest from larger congregations, and although an overture from North Leith was rejected in 1817 he was translated to Rose Street Church in Edinburgh, where he was inducted on 4 June 1822. He remained there for seven years before transferring to Broughton Place Church. This was a sensitive move, given that the church was a prosperous offshoot of the Rose Street congregation, but it was accomplished without acrimony, albeit at the second attempt and with a transfer of several hundred members from Rose Street. In 1830 Brown received the degree of DD from Jefferson College, Pennsylvania.

Brown was an avid reader, most at home in his study and with a personal theological library which ultimately numbered 9000 volumes. In 1834, following Dr Dick's death and the reorganization of his church's theological training, he was appointed to the chair of exegetical theology. It was, however, a duty that had to be discharged in addition to the demands of his large congregation. On 23 June 1835 he married Margaret Fisher Crum (d. 1841), with whom he had a further three children, among them Alexander Crum *Brown, chemist. Her untimely death occurred at a period when Brown had himself suffered ill health and acknowledged the necessity of the appointment of a colleague at Broughton Place. It also coincided with the early stages of the most vexatious of the controversies in which he was involved.

Brown was not shy of conflict on issues of principle and he had been actively involved in the Apocrypha controversy, over the inclusion of the Apocrypha in missionary Bibles. In the voluntary controversy he had taken his opposition to church establishments to the extent of refusing to pay the annuity tax levied for the stipends of ministers of the established church in Edinburgh, and had suffered distraint of his goods. In the atonement controversy, occasioned by the expulsion of James Morison from the United Secession church in 1841 for arguing a universalist position, Brown found himself at the very centre of the debate. His sympathy for Morison, a favourite pupil, caused a fellow minister, Andrew Marshall, to pursue a campaign against him and his fellow professor Robert Balmer, believing them to be the source of Morison's views. The issue was finally forced, and resolved, when Brown demanded a formal libel be brought against him by Marshall, who had largely conducted his campaign in print. A meeting of the synod in July 1845 cleared Brown on every count (Balmer having died in 1844) and confounded Marshall, but it had been a gruelling experience.

Brown could not stand apart from any of the religious movements of the day, and on the day of the Disruption in 1843 he waited in the Tanfield Hall in Edinburgh to greet the ministers who had left the established church. He also took a prominent role in the foundation of the Evangelical Alliance in 1847. The final years of his life were largely given over to the publication of a number of commentaries, eleven volumes of which appeared between 1848 and 1857. In the autumn of 1857 he discharged his duties as a professor for the last time; thereafter he declined in health before dying at his home, Arthur Lodge, Newington, Edinburgh, on 13 October 1858. His funeral, a week later, was one of the largest ever seen in Edinburgh and was attended by clergymen of all denominations. He was buried in the new Calton cemetery.

A tall, lean figure, whose baldness merely emphasized his finely sculptured features, Brown appeared venerable before he was truly old, his remaining locks being so silvery. Though plain in dress, he none the less contrived to appear neat and stylish. His son remembered 'a face almost too beautiful for a man's' (Cairns, 430), though even within his family he was taciturn and reserved. A streak of melancholy was often evident, an understandable consequence of the premature loss of his mother and his two wives. In his youth he was an able horseman, on one occasion swimming his horse across a swollen river in order to keep an open-air preaching engagement. One of the leading figures in Edinburgh of his time, his preaching had a power and intensity likened to that of Chalmers. 'There is the same uncouth, unmodulated, and earnest voice—the same hastening, pauselessly onward—the same breathless attention commanded. Brown is Chalmers chained' (Smith, 279). He further compelled his hearers' attention with the emphatic stamp of his foot, though as a concession to age he read his sermons latterly. An

expositor of exemplary clearness and a scholar of great erudition, Brown was also a very liberal churchman who successfully moved his church away from its excessive adherence to the standards laid down by the Westminster assembly of divines. LIONEL ALEXANDER RITCHIE

Sources *The Scotsman* (14 Oct 1858) • *The Scotsman* (21 Oct 1858) • 'Death of the Rev. Dr Brown', *United Presbyterian Magazine*, new ser., 2 (1858), 528 • J. Cairns, *Memoir of John Brown: including a letter to Dr Cairns from John Brown* (1860) • 'Dr Brown's life and works', *North British Review*, 33 (1860), 21–56 • W. Hunter, *Biggar and the house of Fleming* (1867), 266–72 • *On the deaths of Rev. John M'Gilchrist, John Brown DD, James Henderson DD* (1860), 7–16 • R. Small, *History of the congregations of the United Presbyterian church from 1733 to 1900*, 1 (1904), 438, 456; 2 (1904), 407–8 • J. Smith, *Our Scottish clergy*, 1st ser. (1848), 272–80 • J. Nicholls, 'Brown, John', *DSCHT* • *DNB* • *IGI*
Archives U. Edin. L., sermon notebooks | U. Edin. L., sermons and other papers
Likenesses W. H. Egleton, stipple (after H. Anelay), NPG • S. Freeman, stipple, BM; repro. in *Evangelical Magazine* (1821) • A. Haehnisch, lithograph (after W. Trautschold), NPG • J. Pairman, line print, NPG • L. Stocks, line print, NPG • engraving (aged seventy-three; after photograph), repro. in Cairns, *Memoir of John Brown*, frontispiece
Wealth at death £4430 2s. 11d.: inventory, 27 April 1859, NA Scot., SC 70/1/100/711

Brown, John (1797–1861), geographer, was born at Dover on 2 August 1797 into an old Kentish family. From 1811 to 1815 he was a midshipman in the service of the East India Company and sailed to China and the spice islands. He then took other appointments at sea until, in March 1818, he was forced to change his career because of a defect in his sight. After trying various alternative occupations, including that of assistant to a surgeon, he set up as a wholesale goldsmith and diamond merchant in London, at which trade he made a fortune. While continuing in business he used his wealth to develop his interest in exploration, particularly of the poles, and became the centre of a scientific circle of polar explorers and their supporters. In 1839 he presented the Royal Geographical Society, of which he had been elected fellow in 1837, with a portrait of his friend James Weddell, explorer of the Antarctic, with a letter advocating further expeditions. In 1843 he persuaded Sir Robert Peel to grant a pension to Weddell's widow and to find employment for Weddell's son. Brown was an energetic advocate of expeditions in search of Sir John Franklin. Working on the assumption that Franklin would have followed his orders, and using his own knowledge of prevailing sea currents, Brown defined the area which the expedition was ultimately found to have reached, but his advice was ignored. In 1858 he published *The North-West Passage and the Plans for the Search for Sir John Franklin: a Review*, of which a second edition appeared in 1860. Alexander von Humboldt complimented Brown on this work which summarized the current state of knowledge of the Arctic and pressed for further searches for Franklin.

Brown was a founder of the Ethnological Society in 1843, was a collector of memorabilia of Arctic exploration, and was keenly interested in archaeological and antiquarian research. He married in 1828; his wife, of whom nothing more is known, died in 1859. Brown himself died on 7 February 1861 at his home, Scaleby Lodge, Camden Road, Islington, London, leaving three sons and two daughters. On his death he was still described as a 'manufacturing goldsmith', a business into which he was followed by his son John Allen Brown. He died a wealthy man: his will was proved at under £30,000.

ELIZABETH BAIGENT

Sources Boase, *Mod. Eng. biog.* · *Journal of the Royal Geographical Society*, 31 (1861), 116–17 · *CGPLA Eng. & Wales* (1861) · *GM*, 3rd ser., 10 (1861), 571–3
Archives BL, corresp., Add. MSS 42712–42713 · RGS, letters to Royal Geographical Society · Scott Polar RI, corresp. and papers relating to biography of James Weddell
Wealth at death under £30,000: administration, 6 March 1861, *CGPLA Eng. & Wales*

Brown, John (1810–1882), physician and author, was born in the Secession manse, Biggar, Lanarkshire, on 22 September 1810, the elder son of John *Brown (1784–1858), minister of the Secession church there, and his wife, Jane (*d.* 1816), daughter of William Nimmo, a Glasgow surgeon. His mother died while he was still a child, and in 1822 his father moved to Edinburgh, ministering successively to two important congregations and also becoming a distinguished teacher of theology. Most of the boy's early education took place at home, under his father; but in October 1824 he joined the rector's class in the city's high school, where he proved himself a good scholar. Two years later Brown entered Edinburgh University, and after a year in arts he began the study of medicine in May 1827. At the same time he became a pupil and apprentice of the eminent surgeon James Syme. In 1829 Syme founded his own Surgical Hospital and Dispensary in Minto House, George Square; and there John served as dispenser, dresser, clerk, and assistant—incidentally witnessing the scenes to be graphically described in 'Rab and his friends'. Despite his admiration and affection for Syme, John opted for the life of a physician rather than a surgeon, and in 1831 he was appointed assistant to a Scottish doctor in Chatham. There he remained some two years, earning Charles Dickens's admiration for his faithful attendance on cholera victims. On his return to Edinburgh he graduated MD and set himself up in general practice. On 4 June 1840 he married Catherine (Kitty) Scott (1819–1864), daughter of James McKay, merchant, and Helen Scott. The Browns went on to have one son and two daughters.

In the 1840s, while building up a select and devoted medical clientele in Edinburgh, Brown also made his literary début. Already known as a charming correspondent, he began contributing short articles and reviews to *The Scotsman* and other periodicals, and in 1846 Hugh Miller commissioned his 'Notes on art' for the *Witness* newspaper. In the next year, the *North British Review* published his appreciation of Ruskin's *Modern Painters*, an early testimony to its genius; and before the end of the decade his deeply researched 'Locke and Sydenham' won him the admiration and friendship of that great arbiter of taste

John Brown (1810–1882), by Sir George Reid, 1881

Lord Jeffrey. There followed a modest stream of essays on various subjects, philosophical, artistic, literary, biographical, and autobiographical. The scenery and history of Scotland ('Minchmoor' and the 'Letter to John Cairns, D.D.'), his favourite artists (Raeburn, Leech, Wilkie, and others), the writings of Thackeray, the theory and practice of medicine ('Our Gideon Grays' and 'Plain words on health'), notable characters ('Dr. Chalmers', 'Marjorie Fleming', and 'The duke of Athole'), humble folk ('Jeems the doorkeeper' and 'Her last half-crown'), and of course his canine friends ('Our dogs' and the incomparable 'Rab'): all were handled in a fascinatingly distinctive style of which the blend of learning and personal idiosyncrasy is reminiscent of Charles Lamb. It is as if, in conversation with friends, he rises at times from his chair to consult a favourite volume and read from it, occasionally interrupts himself to recall a long-past but treasured incident, and quite often concludes with some pious words of adjuration and a pertinent phrase from the Bible or the classics.

Individual papers—'Rab' above all—were frequently republished in various guises; but Brown's work as a whole was made conveniently accessible in three comprehensive volumes, each issued during his lifetime under the title *Horae subsecivae* (translated by him as 'By-hours'). The first series appeared in 1858, the second in 1861, and the third shortly before his death in 1882. From the outset, his writings were enthusiastically received. The Victorian public delighted in his penchant for the quaint and the pathetic, his unpretentious erudition, his whimsical, gently Puckish humour, his uncanny insight into doggish ways, his lively sympathy with the human condition, his lucid and musical prose. Nor were they alienated by his basic solemnity (verging at times on sententiousness and sermonizing), and his proud indebtedness to the Christian faith of his Seceding forefathers. That, as a close relative observed, 'was *in* him, and he could no more leave it behind than he could leave his body behind' (introductory note by A. C. Brown in McLaren, vi). And he himself once remarked: 'I am so glad I was grounded in historic Christianity in my youth, and am almost mechanically secured against these fellows ["Renan and all his crew"]' (Peddie, 157).

FRCP (1847) and FRSE (1859), rector's assessor on Edinburgh University court (1861–2) and LLD (Edinburgh, 1874), Brown was awarded a royal pension in 1876 'for distinguished literary eminence'. His reputation has since been severely eclipsed, though it is likely to rise again as Scottish writing of the period undergoes an extensive revaluation by critics. The qualities which made Brown a fine doctor and a much-admired writer were also evident in his personal relationships. His correspondence reveals that, despite long and devastating attacks of depression, he made and kept a host of friends—artists such as Sir George Harvey and Sir George Reid, writers such as Thackeray, Ruskin, and O. W. Holmes, theologians such as R. H. Hutton and Dean Stanley, and academics such as Benjamin Jowett and Principal Shairp. One of them affectionately recalled 'his large and beautifully formed head and forehead, his silver locks, penetrating yet soft and sympathetic spectacled eyes; his firm but sweetly sensitive mouth, and his singularly genial and attractive manners' (Peddie, 22). But Andrew Lang's memorial tribute perhaps gives the most persuasive explanation of his enduring attractiveness:

> From everything that was beautiful and good—from a summer day on the Tweed, or from the eyes of a child, or from the humorous saying of a friend, or from the treasured memories of old Scottish worthies, from recollections of his own childhood, from experience of the stoical heroism of the poor—he seemed to extract matter for pleasant thoughts of men and the world, and nourishment for his own great and gentle nature. I have never known any man to whom other men were so dear—men dead and men living. (Brown, 64)

On his death, Mark Twain remarked that 'He was the most extensive slave-holder of his time, and the kindest, and yet he died without setting one of his bondsmen free' (Peddie, 164).

Brown perhaps never fully recovered from a nervous breakdown brought on by his wife's death, after a long and distressing mental illness, in 1864. He died of pneumonia at his home, 23 Rutland Street, Edinburgh, on 11 May 1882, and was buried five days later beside his father, his wife, and his infant daughter in the new Calton cemetery.   A. C. CHEYNE

Sources A. Peddie, *Recollections of Dr John Brown, author of 'Rab and his friends', etc., with a selection from his correspondence* (1893) • *Letters of Dr John Brown: with letters from Ruskin, Thackeray, and others*, ed. J. Brown and D. W. Forrest (1907) • J. T. Brown, *Dr. John Brown: a biography and criticism, edited with a short sketch of the biographer by W. B.*

Dunlop, M.A. (1903) • E. T. McLaren, *Dr. John Brown and his sisters Isabella and Jane*, 6th edn (1901) [with introductory note by A. C. Brown] • T. D. Johnstone, 'Dr Brown and John Ruskin', PhD diss., U. Edin., 1979 [uses archival material in the NL Scot.] • bap. reg. Scot. • d. cert. • m. reg. Scot.

Archives Hunt. L., letters • NL Scot., corresp. and papers | BL, letters to W. E. Gladstone, Add MSS 44373–44463, *passim* • CUL, letters to Lady Anderson • Mitchell L., Glas., Glasgow City Archives, letters to Sir William Stirling-Maxwell • NL Scot., letters to Abercromby family; letters to J. S. Blackie; letters to Blackwoods; letters to John Hill Burton; corresp. with George Combe • letters to *The Scotsman*

Likenesses Caldesi, photograph, 1859, repro. in McLaren, *Dr. John Brown and his sisters* • R. Cauer, marble bust, 1862, Scot. NPG • Fergus, Large, photograph, 1871, repro. in Peddie, *Recollections of Dr. John Brown* • J. R. Swinton, chalk drawing, 1874, Scot. NPG • H. von Angeli, oils, 1875, Osborne House, Isle of Wight • G. Reid, oils, 1881, Scot. NPG [*see illus.*] • C. Sohn, oils on wood panel, 1889, Osborne House, Isle of Wight • W. Fettes, oils, Scot. NPG • J. W. Gordon, pencil drawing, Scot. NPG • J. Moffat, carte-de-visite, NPG • C. O. Murray, etching (after calotype by D. O. Hill), repro. in Brown, *Dr. John Brown*, frontispiece • T. Rodger, carte photograph, NPG • carte-de-visite, NPG • pencil drawing, NPG

Wealth at death £9974 4s. 2d.: confirmation, 18 July 1882, *CCI*

Brown, Sir John (1816–1896), steel maker, was born on 6 December 1816 in Favell's Yard, Fargate, in Sheffield, the second son of Samuel Brown, a slater, and his wife, Anne. Though his education in a garret-school was modest, his family was able to provide the £500 capital needed to allow Brown in 1837 to become a partner in the local tool and cutlery merchants of Earl, Horton & Co. (to whom he had been apprenticed at the age of fourteen). Brown's success as a traveller enabled him in 1844 to relinquish merchanting and expand into steelmaking.

There were three decisive steps in Brown's career. First, in 1848 he exploited the railway boom by inventing and manufacturing a highly successful conical steel spring buffer for railway wagons. In 1855 he was able to abandon his furnaces and workshops in central Sheffield and follow other big steelmakers, such as Charles Cammell (1810–1879) and Mark Firth (1819–1880), in concentrating his operations on a greenfield site in the Don valley. This was the Atlas works on Savile Street, where Brown began his second important move: the utilization of new steel technologies. In 1858 he pioneered in Sheffield the manufacture of 'puddled' steel, which he used in railway materials and armour-plate. More significantly, in 1860 he became the first Sheffield steel maker to adopt Henry Bessemer's pneumatic steel-making process, which allowed Brown to become one of the foremost UK manufacturers of Bessemer steel, especially for rail manufacture. By 1865 Brown was producing about half of UK rail requirements and was the largest rail maker in the world.

Brown's third major step occurred in 1859, when he pioneered the production of rolled iron armour-plate. By 1867, when the Atlas works was rolling the world's largest armour-plates, it was reported that three-quarters of British navy ironclads were protected by Brown's armour. The arms trade, combined with demand from the railways and engineering, brought unprecedented growth. By 1870

John Brown & Co. Ltd, founded almost as a one-man business, covered a 21 acre site, and had some 4000 workers and a turnover of nearly £1 million.

Brown became Sheffield's most prominent industrialist in the early 1860s. He married Mary, the eldest daughter of Benjamin Schofield, a local auctioneer, on 4 September 1839; they remained childless. A Conservative and churchman, he was elected to the town council in 1856, became an alderman three years later, mayor in 1861 and 1862, and was master cutler in 1865 and 1866. The significance of his work for state security, which brought him personal visits from Lord Palmerston and the lords of the Admiralty and a knighthood in 1867, also meant that he was one of the few Sheffield steel makers known nationally. But by 1870 the 'heroic' phase of Brown's career had ended. The Atlas works had become (alongside Cammells) the largest steelworks in Sheffield, but the price was Brown's loss of personal control. In 1859, he became a partner with two Birmingham industrialists, William Bragge and J. D. Ellis; and his influence was further reduced in 1864, when the firm embraced limited liability. Brown was chairman and held £125,000 of the £750,000 capital, but his shareholding was matched by several Manchester industrialists led by Henry Davis Pochin (d. 1895) and Benjamin Whitworth, who became unhappy at Brown's massive expenditure on armour-plate plant. Unable to work with these 'outside' shareholders, after 1865 Brown increasingly absented himself from business and left the company entirely in 1871.

Brown's subsequent ventures, such as his involvement in the founding of the Sheffield steel firm of Brown, Bayley, and Dixon, and his investments in Spanish iron ore mines, were unsuccessful. After the death in 1881 (28 November) of his wife, Mary, and with his own health declining, Brown withdrew from public life. In 1892 he left Sheffield for good and his mansion, Endcliffe Hall, was sold. While his old company prospered as one of the most famous names in British engineering, Brown died in obscurity, as a result of a cerebral haemorrhage on 27 December 1896 at Nervion, Shortlands, Beckenham, Kent. His fortune largely gone (his will was proved at £27,221), he left no children, and was interred on 31 December alongside his wife at All Saints' parish church, Ecclesall, near Sheffield.   GEOFFREY TWEEDALE

Sources R. H. Dunbar, 'Eminent manufacturers - IV: Sir John Brown of Sheffield', *Great industries of Great Britain*, 1 (1886), 286–91 · *Sheffield Daily Telegraph* (28 Dec 1896) · G. Tweedale, *Giants of Sheffield steel* (1986) · A. J. Grant, *Steel and ships: the history of John Brown's* (1950) · W. Odom, *Hallamshire worthies* (1926) · J. H. Stainton, *The making of Sheffield, 1865–1914* (1924) · C. J. Erickson, *British industrialists: steel and hosiery, 1850–1950* (1959) · P. L. Payne, *Rubber and railways in the nineteenth century: a study of the Spencer papers* (1961) · E. Mensforth, *Family engineers* (1981) · G. Tweedale, *Steel city: entrepreneurship, strategy, and technology in Sheffield, 1743–1993* (1995) · K. C. Barraclough, *Steelmaking, 1850–1900* (1990) · H. Bessemer, *Sir Henry Bessemer, FRS: an autobiography* (1905) · J. Goddard, 'Endcliffe Hall: the residence of a gentleman industrialist', *Aspects of Sheffield*, ed. M. Jones, 1 (1997) · d. cert.

Archives John Brown plc, 20 Eastbourne Terrace, London

Likenesses R. Smith, portrait, 1863, Cutlers' Hall, Sheffield · double portrait, oils (with his wife, Mary), John Brown plc, London; repro. in Mensforth, *Family engineers* · engraving (after photograph by E. H. Cox), repro. in Dunbar, 'Eminent manufacturers' · photograph (after photograph, Hadfield papers, Sheffield Central Library), repro. in Tweedale, *Giants of Sheffield steel*

Wealth at death £27,221: *DBB* · £16,784 11s. 9d.: probate, 10 March 1897, *CGPLA Eng. & Wales*

Brown, John (1826–1883), servant to Queen Victoria, was born on 8 December 1826 at Crathienaird in the parish of Crathie, Aberdeenshire, the second among the nine sons and two daughters of John Brown (1790–1875), a tenant farmer, and his wife, Margaret Leys (1799–1876). In 1831 the family moved to the Bush Farm, Crathie, where Brown spent his childhood. He had some formal education (in English and Gaelic) at Crathie school, and became a voracious reader, but the traditional skills of the highlander—deerstalking, fishing, shooting, riding, mountain walking, and natural history—he learned outside the schoolroom. At the age of fourteen he became a stable-boy, and eventually found work in the stables at Balmoral, which was then leased by Sir Robert Gordon. He became a gillie, and was kept on in that position when Queen Victoria and Prince Albert took over the tenancy of the estate in 1848 after Gordon's death.

Queen Victoria first mentioned Brown by name in her journal for 11 September 1849, when she noted him as one of the gillies attending the royal party on an expedition to Loch Dhu. He made himself useful and prominent, assisted by his rugged good looks, and in 1851 he was taken into the permanent royal establishment and began leading the queen's pony while she was out riding. In 1858 he was selected by Prince Albert to be the queen's personal servant in Scotland, which gave him considerable authority in the servants' quarters. Johnny Brown was soon a great favourite with the queen, who described him time and again as 'discreet, careful, intelligent, attentive … handy and willing to do everything and anything, and to overcome every difficulty' (*Leaves*, 201). When the duke of Atholl offered to lead her pony on a royal jaunt up Glen Tilt, the queen replied 'laughingly, "Oh, no, only I like best being led by the person I am accustomed to"' (ibid., 232). Brown was a fixture in the highlands.

When the queen went into her prolonged mourning and seclusion after the death of the prince consort in December 1861, fears were entertained for her health, and it was as a medical precaution that John Brown and her favourite pony, Lochnagar, were brought from Balmoral to Osborne, to enable the queen to take more exercise. He rapidly became indispensable. In April 1865 the queen wrote an account of his duties to her eldest daughter: he was taken 'entirely and permanently as my personal servant for out of doors—besides cleaning my things and doing odd "jobs"'. She found it convenient to deal only with one person, who went 'to my room after breakfast and luncheon to get his orders—and everything is always right' (Fulford, 3.21–2). He was given the title the queen's highland servant, and in the deeply hierarchical and class-segregated royal household he answered only to the queen. But Brown's utility to the queen rested in more than the details of his constant daily service (he took no

John Brown (1826–1883), by W. & D. Downey, 1868 [with Queen Victoria]

leave). Victoria needed to be of the first importance to somebody: with her husband and mother dead, her older children marrying and developing new emotional ties, her younger children as yet too immature to receive her confidences, and with no possibility of genuine friendship with the aristocratic women of her household—who were still her subjects—she found herself profoundly isolated. As she said after Albert's death, 'There is no-one to call me Victoria now' (M. Charlot, *The Young Queen*, 1991, 425). Brown could not call her Victoria (although it was not beyond him to call her 'Wumman'), but he was genuinely devoted to her: his 'only object and interest is my service', Victoria told her daughter. 'God knows, how I want so much to be taken care of' (Fulford, 3.22).

Inevitably, rumours about the nature of the relationship between Brown and the queen began to flourish. By 1866 provincial Scottish newspapers were publishing scandal about Brown, and on 7 July 1866 *Punch* printed its famous spoof 'court circular': 'Mr John Brown walked on the Slopes. He subsequently partook of a haggis. In the evening Mr John Brown was pleased to listen to a bag-pipe. Mr John Brown retired early.' This apparently innocuous paragraph summed up the ill feeling which was beginning to swirl around the reclusive queen and her court, suggesting the overthrow of the social order, and an inappropriate relationship between the queen and her servant. Moreover, the very dullness of the activities denoted—which resembled the more usual, genuine 'The queen drove out in the afternoon'—emphasized the failure of the queen herself to resume her place as the social,

political, and ceremonial head of the country. The privacy Victoria sought to nurse her grief left her vulnerable to suspicion, and the scandal flourished, virtually unchecked. The queen, it was said, had secretly borne a child by Brown, whom she had married morganatically; other rumours made Brown her medium in attempts to contact the dead Prince Albert, while still others suggested that the queen had lost her mind and that Brown was her keeper. The public scandal escalated between 1865 and 1871, fuelled both by the queen's invisibility and by her one attempt to offer a substitute for her actual presence. She published *Leaves from a Journal of our Life in the Highlands* (1868) as a memorial to her life with Albert, and to set (especially to the upper classes) an example of pure family life and 'kind and proper feeling towards the poor and the servants' (Fulford, 3.172). It was this latter that caused further difficulties, for the text was littered with references to servants, including Brown, with regular footnotes outlining their careers and characters, which fuelled speculation. No plausible evidence or proof of a sexual relationship between Brown and the queen was ever offered (nor was it likely that it should be), but the balance of probabilities makes such a relationship extremely unlikely: while Victoria was no prude, her deep moral and religious convictions would have inhibited a sexual relationship outside marriage, while her immovable sense of her own position would make marriage with a domestic servant unthinkable. And Albert, she knew, would be watching her from heaven.

The queen would hear no word spoken against Brown. Outspoken, arrogant, increasingly confident of his position with the queen, Brown made enemies at court. Many courtiers—and all of Victoria's children—found him intolerable: he was brusque and rude to them, often drunk, and his familiar, bullying manner towards the queen was viewed as unforgivable *lèse-majesté*. They were more put out by the way he acted as gatekeeper to the queen: no one could see her without Brown's permission. The queen's private secretary, Sir Henry Ponsonby, almost alone maintained a sense of perspective: she could have chosen many more dangerous intimates than Brown. He had no political axe to grind, had no thoughts of being the power behind the throne (*Punch* cartoons such as 'A Brown study!' from 1867 notwithstanding). Ponsonby knew the limits of Brown's position, and, as one of the prince of Wales's courtiers observed after Brown's death:

> his successor might do a great deal more harm than Brown, who after all ... confined his interference chiefly to the stables, shooting and the servants. But if he had been an ambitious man ... he might have meddled in more important matters. (Ponsonby, 128)

Moreover, Brown was 'the only person who could fight and make the Queen do what she did not wish' (ibid.). He could also prevent her from doing things he did not like: he disliked foreigners and felt uncomfortable out of his usual environment, and when obliged to travel abroad with the queen he rigidly imposed the routine to which he was accustomed at home, which greatly curtailed the queen's pleasure in new places.

When Victoria reluctantly resumed a fuller programme of public commitments in 1872, the public scandal about Brown waned. He continued to be a source of tension at court and in the queen's family, but his place on the queen's carriage came to be seen as inevitable. At a time when little attention was given to Victoria's personal safety, he took it upon himself to patrol the grounds around the queen's rooms every evening, and he slept with a revolver under his pillow to defend her against possible assassins. His fears were not groundless: on five previous occasions she had been attacked, and on 29 February 1872 it was Brown who apprehended Arthur O'Connor, who was approaching the queen with a pistol to make her sign a petition. For this she awarded him a faithful service medal and an annuity, together with a specially instituted devoted service medal (which was never awarded to anyone else). No one took Brown's place with the queen, and at Balmoral in particular he continued to reign supreme, but once her interest in politics was stimulated again and she began to look outwards, his position as sole confidant had less significance: Disraeli became from 1874 until his death in 1881 the most important man in her life. Besides, Victoria was no longer a young widow, and so was a less likely target for salacious gossip.

On 18 March 1883 the queen sent Brown to gather evidence about an alleged attack on Lady Florence Dixie in Windsor Great Park. He caught a severe cold and, although he continued to attend to his duties, his condition declined. By 25 March he was suffering badly from erysipelas and a high fever, and in the evening he lapsed into delirium tremens. On 27 March he sank into a coma, and he died later that evening in his rooms at Windsor Castle. After funeral services at Windsor, his body was taken to Crathie cemetery and buried on 5 April. The queen, suffering badly from rheumatism, was distraught, and her tributes to Brown's memory revived speculation about the nature of their relationship. The tombstone she ordered bore the inscription: 'In affectionate and grateful memory of John Brown, personal attendant and beloved friend of Queen Victoria in whose service he had been for 34 years' (Lamont-Brown, 144). If the love and affection caught the eye of the prurient, it was the service that was most important to Victoria.

Brown's influence continued to be felt for years after his death. Victoria marked his anniversaries and dedicated the second volume of her highland diary, *More Leaves from the Journal of a Life in the Highlands* (1884), 'To my loyal Highlanders and especially to the memory of my devoted personal attendant and faithful friend John Brown'. The prominence given to Brown in the journal (in itself surely indicative of the innocence of the relationship) once again caused unfavourable comment, and when the queen sought to follow it up with a memoir of Brown, her horrified courtiers passed the manuscript to Randall Davidson, the dean of Windsor, who took his career in his hands and told the queen he thought it unwise. Eventually she decided to drop the idea, and the manuscript, and Brown's diaries, were apparently burnt. After her own death in 1901, and in accordance with her instructions, a picture of Brown, a lock of his hair, and various mementoes of Brown and his family were secretly placed in her coffin by her doctor, Sir James Reid. Soon after the funeral the new king (who had always loathed Brown) ordered a mass destruction and dispersal of all his mother's artefacts, pictures, and papers relating to Brown. But he could not obliterate the public memory of Brown, or the continuing fascination of his relationship with Queen Victoria. Twentieth-century commentators determined to expose the 'hypocrisy' of the Victorians seized on the business with glee: the byword for prudery, sexual repression, and stern morality caught with her crinoline disarranged. Periodically it is suggested that a cache of papers exists which will 'expose' their relationship once and for all; if they exist, they have yet to see the light of day. Cinema has been more circumspect in its portrayal of the relationship, emphasizing Brown's drinking rather than possible sexual scandal: Gordon McLeod played him opposite Anna Neagle in *Victoria the Great* (1937) and *Sixty Glorious Years* (1938), and opposite Fay Compton in *The Prime Minister* (1941); Findlay Currie played him in *The Mudlark* (1950); while a sympathetic, allusive account of the relationship is given in *Mrs Brown* (1998), with Billy Connolly playing opposite Dame Judi Dench.

The Victorians found it hard to understand or appreciate John Brown's place at their queen's court. The role of the jester had long fallen into abeyance, but, dressed in his own kind of highland motley, Brown had the licence of the fool, albeit a peculiarly Victorian fool. Surrounded by courtiers and children cowed by her rank and afraid of her anger, after Albert's death Victoria needed one person who would tell her the truth about herself, who was not intimidated by her position or alarmed about her mental health, but who was also genuinely solicitous of her welfare and uninterested in wielding political power. In 1840 the queen had put up a tombstone to her childhood companion, a King Charles spaniel, Dash. It read:

> Here lies Dash the favourite spaniel of Her Majesty Queen Victoria in his 10th year. His attachment was without selfishness, his playfulness without malice, his fidelity without deceit. Reader, If you would be beloved and die regretted profit by the example of Dash.

John Brown shared, in human form, many of Dash's virtues, and was similarly beloved. In John Brown, Victoria found her perfect fool; he had no successor.

K. D. REYNOLDS

Sources R. Lamont-Brown, *John Brown: Queen Victoria's highland servant* (2000) · E. Longford, *Victoria RI* (1964) · H. Ponsonby, ed., *Sir Henry Ponsonby: his life from his letters* (1942) · *Dearest child: letters between Queen Victoria and the princess royal, 1858–1861*, ed. R. Fulford (1964) · *Dearest mama: letters between Queen Victoria and the crown princess of Prussia, 1861–1864*, ed. R. Fulford (1968) · *Your dear letter: private correspondence of Queen Victoria and the crown princess of Prussia, 1865–1871*, ed. R. Fulford (1971) · *Darling child: private correspondence of Queen Victoria and the crown princess of Prussia, 1871–1878*, ed. R. Fulford (1976) · *Beloved mama: private correspondence of Queen Victoria and the German crown princess, 1878–1885*, ed. R. Fulford (1981) · *The letters of Queen Victoria*, ed. A. C. Benson, Lord Esher [R. B. Brett], and G. E. Buckle, 9 vols. (1907–32) · S. Weintraub, *Victoria* (1987) · Queen Victoria, *Leaves from the journal of our life in the highlands*, ed. A. Helps

(1868) · Queen Victoria, *More leaves from the journal of a life in the high-lands, from 1862 to 1882* (1884) · T. Cullen, *The Empress Brown* (1969) · E. E. P. Tisdall, *Queen Victoria's John Brown* (1938)

Archives Aberdeen Libraries · priv. coll. · Royal Arch.

Likenesses W. & D. Downey, group photograph, 1861–9, NPG · R. Hill & J. Saunders, photograph, *c*.1863, NPG; repro. in Lamont-Brown, *John Brown* · G. W. Wilson, double portrait, photograph, *c*.1863 (with Queen Victoria), Scot. NPG; repro. in Lamont-Brown, *John Brown* · portraits, 1863–83, repro. in Lamont-Brown, *John Brown* · E. Landseer, oils, 1865, Osborne House, Isle of Wight · E. Landseer, group portrait, oils, 1866, Royal Collection · W. & D. Downey, photograph, 1868, NPG [*see illus.*] · W. & D. Downey, two photographs, 1868, NPG · E. Boehm, bust, 1869, repro. in Longford, *Victoria R.I.* · H. von Angeli, oils, 1875, Osborne House, Isle of Wight · C. Burton Barber, oils, 1883 (posthumous), Osborne House, Isle of Wight · C. R. Sohn, oils, 1883 (posthumous), Scottish Tartans Society, Comrie, Ayrshire; repro. in Lamont-Brown, *John Brown* · C. R. Sohn, oils, 1883 (posthumous), Osborne House, Isle of Wight · W. H. Emmett, lithograph, BM · J. Hughes, albumen print, NPG · chromolithograph (after photograph), BM · prints, Royal Collection · wood-engraving (after photograph by W. & D. Downey), NPG; repro. in *ILN* (7 April 1883)

Wealth at death £7198: Lamont-Brown, *John Brown*

Brown, Sir John (1880–1958), architect and army officer, was born in Northampton on 10 February 1880, the elder son of John Brown, a clicker, later a licensed victualler and an alderman, of Abington, Northampton, and his wife, Kate Davis (*née* Allen). He was educated at Magdalen College School, Brackley, Northamptonshire, and qualified as associate of the Royal Institute of British Architects in 1921 (fellow 1930). For many years he was in practice in Northampton and London in partnership with A. E. Henson. But his distinction as an architect was much exceeded by his career as a territorial soldier. On 31 May 1904 Brown married Annie Maria (Nancy), third daughter of Francis Tonsley, confectioner and alderman, of Northampton; they had two sons.

Brown entered the 1st volunteer battalion, later the 4th (territorial) battalion, the Northamptonshire regiment, in 1901, and with it went to the Dardanelles in 1915 where he took part in the August landings at Suvla Bay. He served with the battalion in the Palestine campaign and subsequently commanded (DSO 1918).

Brown made such a mark that in 1924 he was given command of the 162nd (East Midland) infantry brigade, which soon became the best-known territorial formation and distinguished itself in the 1925 army manoeuvres. Brown became the foremost figure and most dynamic leader in the Territorial Army (TA) during years when its strength and efficiency were declining, and he created a local territorial revival.

Exceptionally 'John Brown's brigade' brought 85 per cent of brigade members to annual camp. Its outstanding battalion was the 4th Northamptons, which repeatedly brought more than 600 (90 per cent). Brown promised them no easy time but real training for war, and made it interesting and exciting.

Many of the officers and NCOs attended as many as thirty weekend trainings a year. In camp, petty restrictions, 'bull', and fatigues were cut to a minimum. The men were kept so active during the day and so well entertained in the evenings that few wanted to leave camp. The standard of tactical training was higher than in many regular battalions and some regular officers brought their NCOs to watch. There was a waiting list to join and in Northampton crowds cheered as the local battalion set out for camp. Brown had long criticized the power of the county territorial associations, and in 1926 he opposed reduction of the TA training grant. He corresponded with Captain Basil Liddell Hart.

The divisional commander, Sir John Duncan, a regular soldier and tactical enthusiast, recommended Brown as his successor. This would have fulfilled Haldane's 1907 promise that territorial officers should be eligible for general officers' appointments. But the recommendation was turned down as it would have diminished the number of major-generals' posts available for regulars. So Brown's services were lost to the army in 1928.

From 1930 to 1934 Brown was British Legion chairman, implementing reforms and dealing effectively and tactfully with awkward internal problems. He had a way of talking bluntly as plain John Brown, with frequent dropping of aitches, and was shrewdly skilled in handling all kinds of men.

In 1937 Leslie Hore-Belisha became secretary of state for war and his reforms included the belated fulfilment of Haldane's promise. Brown, too old for active command, was made deputy director-general of the TA, the first territorial major-general and the first with a high position in the War Office and the chance to guide policy on the TA. Hore-Belisha arranged that Brown, though never a full member, attended Army Council meetings and expressed his views there. Brown got on well with the senior regular officers and in 1939, after the war began, was promoted lieutenant-general and made deputy adjutant-general (TA). In 1940 he became director-general of the TA and inspector-general, welfare and education, in the War Office—dual posts which he held until retirement in 1941.

Brown had been appointed CBE (1923), CB (1926), and KCB (1934). He was twice master (1942–4 and 1950–51) of the worshipful company of Pattenmakers, and an honorary freeman of Northampton (1934). Brown died at his home, 30A Billing Road, Northampton, on 4 April 1958.

B. H. L. HART, *rev.* ROGER T. STEARN

Sources private information (1971) · personal knowledge (1971) · *WWW* · Burke, *Peerage* (1949) · P. Dennis, *The Territorial Army, 1906–1940*, Royal Historical Society Studies in History, 51 (1987) · B. Bond, *British military policy between the two world wars* (1980) · I. F. W. Beckett, *The amateur military tradition, 1558–1945* (1991) · R. J. Minney, *The private papers of Hore-Belisha* (1960) · *CGPLA Eng. & Wales* (1958)

Archives IWM, letter-book

Likenesses W. Stoneman, photograph, 1934, NPG

Wealth at death £17,948 19*s.* 4*d.*: administration with will, 19 June 1958, *CGPLA Eng. & Wales*

Brown, John Alexander Harvie-, of Dunipace (1844–1916), naturalist, was born on 27 August 1844 in Edinburgh, the only son of John Harvie (*d.* 1880), landowner, and Elizabeth Spottiswoode, the daughter and heir of Thomas Spottiswoode of Dunipace, near Stirling. His father assumed the additional surname of Brown under the terms of the will of Alexander Brown of Quarter, Stirlingshire. Harvie-Brown was educated at Merchiston School and subsequently at Edinburgh and Cambridge universities (although he appears not to have graduated from either). At Cambridge he formed a friendship with Professor Alfred Newton, the ornithologist, a friendship that encouraged Harvie-Brown's interest in natural history. A man of independent means, Harvie-Brown was able to devote his life to the traditional highland laird pursuits with rod and gun and to ornithology.

In the 1880s there was considerable interest in bird migration and Harvie-Brown initiated a scheme, developed by the British Association, to use records of migrating birds collected by lighthouse keepers. Much of Harvie-Brown's life was spent in producing a series of volumes on the vertebrate fauna of Scotland, his most important works. The first volume, co-authored with J. E. Buckley, was published in 1887, the *Vertebrate Fauna of Sutherland, Caithness, and West Cromarty*; it was followed, over the next twenty-five years, by volumes on the Outer Hebrides, the Orkneys, Argyll and the Inner Hebrides, the Moray basin, the Shetlands, the north-west Highlands and Skye, the Tay basin and Strathmore, and the Tweed area. The books describe the distribution and abundance of the vertebrate fauna of each area, and have information on geology, topography, and climate.

Harvie-Brown travelled widely in Scotland and in 1887 he built his own yacht, *Shiantelle*, to visit the islands and sea lochs of the west coast. He also travelled widely in Europe, especially in northern Scandinavia and Russia, and in 1905 he published a two-volume account of his experiences in *Travels of a Naturalist in Northern Europe*. He was a prolific writer and was the founder, owner, and joint editor for twenty-five years of *The Annals of Scottish Natural History*, later to become the *Scottish Naturalist*. He was a fellow of the Zoological Society and of the Royal Society of Edinburgh and an honorary life member of the American Ornithologists' Union. In 1912 he was awarded an honorary LLD by the University of Aberdeen.

Harvie-Brown was a short, thickset, powerfully built man. As the laird of Dunipace estate, he was regarded with affection by his tenants, employees, and neighbours. He became seriously ill with influenza in 1899 and his health never fully recovered. He also suffered from asthma, and from a constant battle with his weight which rose to 25 stones. For the last few years of his life he was more or less confined to a ground floor study bedroom in his house, from where he kept up a continuous flow of correspondence. He died at his home, Dunipace House, Larbert, after a short final illness, on 26 July 1916 and was buried in the family graveyard at Dunipace, in front of the house. He never married.   ROBERT RALPH

Sources J. McNaughton, 'John Alexander Harvie-Brown, LL.D., F.R.S.E., of Quarter and Dunipace, naturalist and sportsman', *Transactions of the Stirling Natural History and Archaeology Society*, 58 (1935–6), 50–63 • Venn, *Alum. Cant.* • *WWW* • Burke, *Gen. GB* **Archives** NL Scot., corresp. and papers • Royal Scottish Museum, Chamber's Street, Edinburgh, corresp. and papers • U. Edin. L.,

notes | CUL, letters to Alfred Newton • NHM, letters to Sir Norman Kinnear • NHM, letters to Mrs Ratcliff on the papers of Sir William Jardine, her father **Likenesses** J. Peddar, watercolour, Scot. NPG • photographs, Royal Scottish Museum **Wealth at death** £28,660 15*s*. 3*d*.: confirmation, 29 March 1917, *CCI*

Brown, John Crawford (1805–1867), landscape painter, the son of John Brown, a grain merchant, and his wife, Elizabeth Crawford, was born in Glasgow and studied art there. After travelling round the Netherlands, Flanders, and Spain, he lived in London for some time before returning to his native city and then settling in Edinburgh, initially at Viewforth Cottage, South Leith. He exhibited at the Royal Scottish Academy from 1830 until 1865, and posthumously in 1880. He painted landscapes, genre, and historical paintings, including *Catching Birds with Nets* (1836) and *Fugitives after the Battle of Culloden* (1844). Individual works were shown in London at the Royal Academy, the British Institution, the Society of British Artists, and the New Watercolour Society. He became an Associate of the Royal Scottish Academy in 1843. Brown was married to Margaret Strang, and they had at least one son. He died at his home, 10 St Vincent Street, Edinburgh, on 8 May 1867; his wife survived him.

L. A. FAGAN, *rev.* EMILY M. WEEKS

Sources Redgrave, *Artists* • Wood, *Vic. painters*, 3rd edn • d. cert., Scotland **Wealth at death** £311 12*s*. 0*d*.: 'confirmation not required', 1867, Scotland

Brown, John Wright (1836–1863), botanist, was born on 19 December 1836, probably in Glasgow, the second of the eleven children of Charles John Brown (1806–1884), clergyman and religious writer, and his wife, Jane Bannatyne Wright (*d.* 1895). His father, the son of a lord provost of Aberdeen, transferred to New North Parish, Edinburgh, in 1837, and joined the Free Church on the disruption in 1843. Brown had a great love for plants, and, at the age of sixteen, was placed in one of the Edinburgh nurseries. He was of a delicate constitution, and the exposure connected with garden work proved too much for his health. John Hutton Balfour appointed him to an assistantship in the herbarium connected with the Royal Botanic Garden, Edinburgh, where he became well acquainted with botany. He was much interested in the Scottish flora, and contributed a list of the plants of Elie, Fife, to the Botanical Society of Edinburgh, of which he was an associate (*Transactions*, 7, 1863, 430). He died at his home, 39 St George Square, Edinburgh, on 23 March 1863.

JAMES BRITTEN, *rev.* ALEXANDER GOLDBLOOM

Sources Desmond, *Botanists*, rev. edn • *Transactions of the Botanical Society* [Edinburgh], 7 (1863), 430, 519 • *Fasti Scot.* • Boase, *Mod. Eng. biog.*

Brown, Joseph (1784–1868), physician, was born at North Shields in September 1784, the son of a respected member of the Society of Friends. He studied medicine at Edinburgh and also in London, and though brought up as a Quaker he entered the Army Medical Service. He was attached to Wellington's staff in the Peninsular War, and was present at Busaco, Albuera, Vitoria, the Pyrenees, and Nivelle, gaining high commendation for his service. After Waterloo, Brown remained with the army of occupation in France.

On his return to Britain, Brown again studied at Edinburgh, and he graduated MD in 1819. He married, and settled at Sunderland, where he took a leading part in local philanthropy and politics. For many years he acted as physician to the Sunderland and Bishopwearmouth Infirmary. He was also an active borough magistrate and was once mayor of Sunderland. He was deeply sympathetic to the poor. Brown died at his home, 15 Villiers Street, Sunderland, on 19 November 1868, having taken ill while visiting his dispensary patients.

Besides numerous contributions to medical reviews, and several articles in Sir J. Forbes's *Cyclopaedia of Practical Medicine*, in 1828 Brown published a study of fever and inflammation, which was followed in 1865 by a work on food and diet. He also published on subjects of religious and social interest including, in 1851, *A Defence of Revealed Religion* and, in 1863, *Memories of the Past and Thoughts on the Present Age*.　　　G. T. BETTANY, rev. CLAIRE E. J. HERRICK

Sources The Lancet (5 Dec 1868) · Sunderland Herald (20 Nov 1868) · BMJ (28 Nov 1868), 583 · CGPLA Eng. & Wales (1868)
Archives Tyne and Wear Archives Service, Newcastle upon Tyne, letters from him mainly relating to the Peninsular War [copies]
Wealth at death under £1500: probate, 10 Dec 1868, CGPLA Eng. & Wales

Brown, Joseph (1809–1902), barrister, born at Walworth, Surrey, on 4 April 1809, was the second son of Joseph Brown, wine merchant, of the Cumberland family of Scales, near Kirk Oswald. Educated by his uncle, the Revd John Whitridge, of Carlisle, at Camberwell grammar school, and at a private school at Wimbledon, he entered, at eighteen, the office of Armstrong & Co., a London firm of West India merchants. Two years later he started to study law with Peter Turner, a solicitor in the City of London. Meanwhile he matriculated at Queens' College, Cambridge, where he graduated BA in 1830 and proceeded MA in 1833. He was admitted to Middle Temple, London, on 12 January 1832, and under Sir William Henry Watson and Sir John Bayley he learnt the art of special pleading, becoming a pleader under the bar in 1834. On 24 August 1840 he married Mary Smith (1807/8–1891), daughter of Thomas Smith, of Winchcombe, Gloucestershire. There were five children of the marriage, three sons and two daughters.

Called to the bar on 7 November 1845, Brown soon acquired a large commercial practice and was engaged in several important cases, including the trial of the Royal British Bank directors before Lord Campbell in 1858. In 1865 he took silk and was made a bencher of the Middle Temple, of which he was treasurer from 1878 to 1879. Brown played a prominent part in the steps taken to replace the old law reports, then produced privately and by no means comprehensively. He was largely responsible for the preparation and publication in 1865 of the new series of the *Law Reports*. He was chosen to represent the Middle Temple on the Council of Law Reporting in 1872, and from 1875 to 1892 was chairman of the council. Created CB

on his retirement in 1893, he largely contributed by his energy and practical ability to the success of the council's publications.

Brown had a wide-ranging intellect and interests. He was a fellow of the Geological Society of London and a skilled numismatist and antiquary. He contributed to the *Proceedings* of the Social Science Congress, and wrote several pamphlets, including two urging reform of the system of trial by jury. In 1870 he published a paper on the evils of unlimited liability for accidents on railways. He brought his eldest son, Harold (1844–1910), into the congress too. Harold Brown became well known as an authority on company law, having been educated at Highgate School and articled in the City to James Linklater in 1861; he was admitted a solicitor in 1866 and became a partner in 1870. In that year too his elder sister, Marianne, married Joseph Addison, already a partner in the firm known as Linklaters. The children of these two marriages—and in turn their children and grandchildren—were to be involved in running the firm, one of a small number of leading City law firms, well into the second half of the twentieth century. Joseph Brown died at his residence, 54 Avenue Road, Regent's Park, London, on 9 June 1902.　　　C. E. A. BEDWELL, rev. JUDY SLINN

Sources J. Slinn, Linklaters and Paines (1987) · The Times (10 June 1902) · Law Journal (14 June 1902) · WW (1901) · CGPLA Eng. & Wales (1902) · m. cert.
Wealth at death £85,126 7s. 11d.: resworn probate, Nov 1902, CGPLA Eng. & Wales

Brown, Lancelot [known as Capability Brown] (bap. **1716**, d. **1783**), landscape gardener and architect, was baptized on 30 August 1716 at Kirkharle, Northumberland, the fifth of the six children of William Brown, a yeoman farmer; his mother's name is not known. Two of their other children, John and George, married into the gentry—the Fenwick and Loraine families respectively; the former became the agent at Kirkharle, the latter the mason and architect at the neighbouring estate of Wallington.

Education and early career Brown was educated at the village school in nearby Cambo and then began work for Sir William Loraine, who had extensive formal gardens west of his house at Kirkharle. Brown's plan for remodelling this landscape survives, but may have been drawn for a later campaign. He left Kirkharle in 1739, but his movements over the next two years remain unclear. He may have worked for Bennet Langton in December 1739 on the enclosure of Mareham in Lincolnshire, close to Tumby, the home of Bridget Wayet (d. 1786), whom he was to marry in 1744. John Penn later asserted of this period that 'the first piece of water that he formed was at Lady Mostyn's [Kiddington] in Oxfordshire' (Penn, 33), and it seems likely that his work there attracted the notice of Lord Cobham.

Following the departure in March 1741 of William Love, the head gardener at Stowe, Buckinghamshire, Brown was employed by Lord Cobham, and rapidly assumed responsibility for the execution of both architectural and landscaping works under the supervision of Lord Cobham himself and his designers, principally William Kent and

Lancelot Brown [Capability Brown] (*bap.* **1716**, *d.* **1783**), by Nathaniel Dance, *c.*1773

James Gibbs. In addition to presiding over the buildings of the 1740s, particularly the Grecian temple, the queen's temple, and the Cobham monument, Brown's work at Stowe included the south lawn (which replaced the parterre off the south front of the house), alterations to the lakes, the excavation of the Grecian valley, and the transplantation of trees to turn avenues into more irregular vistas, as well as planting on a prodigious scale.

While at Stowe, Brown established himself as an independent designer and contractor with a number of major landscaping commissions, including Croome Court, Worcestershire (from 1750); Packington Hall, Warwickshire (from *c.*1750); Petworth, Sussex (from *c.*1750); Wakefield Lodge, Northamptonshire (*c.*1748); Warwick Castle (from 1749); and Wotton, Buckinghamshire (from 1750). In the autumn of 1751, shortly after Lord Cobham's death, Brown left Stowe and moved with his family to the Mall, Hammersmith.

In the decade to 1760 Brown undertook more than forty large commissions. His turnover, as recorded by his account at Drummond's Bank, rose to an average of over £8000 per year, with over £10,000 in 1759. His reputation was already such as to make current his nickname, Capability, first given him for his habit of referring to the capabilities of the places at which he was consulted. However, an attempt by several of his clients to obtain a royal appointment for him at Kensington in 1758 was unsuccessful, and it was not until 1764 that a second application secured his appointment as master gardener at Hampton Court and Richmond, and gardener at St James's. From 1764 he lived at his official residence, Wilderness House at Hampton Court.

In the 1760s Brown undertook more than sixty-five commissions; these included Blenheim, Oxfordshire

(from 1764), which is generally regarded as his masterpiece. Although he had a number of emulators by this time, among them Richard Woods (1715/16–1793) and William Emes (1729–1803), he had no real rivals, and indeed Brown seems to have been content to let his foremen, such as Thomas White the elder (1736–1811) and Nathaniel Richmond (1723/4–1784), set up on their own account. During this decade his turnover at Drummond's fluctuated considerably, but still averaged over £15,000 per annum. Although the number of his large new commissions fell to about fifty in the 1770s, giving him an average turnover of £9000 per annum, there is no evidence that his style had fallen out of fashion.

Brown's landscape business Brown offered a number of different services to his clients: for a round number of guineas he could provide a survey and plans for buildings and landscaping and leave his client to execute his proposal, as at Howsham, Yorkshire (*c.*1770); more frequently he provided a foreman to oversee the work, which was carried out by labour recruited from the estate. Even in 1753, when he opened his account with Drummond's Bank, Brown was employing four foremen, and by the end of the decade he had more than twenty on his books. Finally he could oversee the work himself, usually by means of visits for a certain number of days each year, as seems to have happened at King's Weston, Bristol (*c.*1771).

Brown was famous for the speed at which he worked. As François de la Rochefoucauld recorded, 'after an hour on horse-back he conceived the design for an entire park, and … after that, half-a-day was enough for him to mark it out on the ground' (Scarfe, 36). These methods were in marked contrast to those of William Kent, who hated travelling and preferred to design in London.

Many of Brown's foremen were highly skilled and traded in their own right. They were recruited, some from Northumberland and presumably known to Brown in his youth (William Ireland and perhaps Nathaniel Richmond), some from other gardens and from related trades (James Clarke may have been a nurseryman). Some were specialists: John Spyers was a surveyor, Lapidge had both surveyed and carried out waterworks at Cassiobury, Hertfordshire, before joining Brown, Benjamin Read was another lake-maker, John Hobcroft and Henry Holland the elder were builders. Others, such as George Bowstreed and John Midgely, had general skills. Despite this degree of delegation, stylistic distinctions between the work of the different foremen cannot be made save where, as with Nathaniel Richmond and Thomas White the elder, they became designers in their own right. Furthermore, the cartographic style that Brown adopted was used by all his draughtsmen, including Richmond and White, and it is difficult to tell their hands apart: Brown's style was imposed on everything that he did, and this is a testimony both to the strength of his design and to his managerial skills.

Brown also worked as an architect. His earliest surviving architectural drawings are for a Kentian grotto and cascade at Packington Hall, although Henry Holland the younger attributed several buildings at Stowe to him. During the 1750s he designed large country houses, for example, Croome Court, and carried out extensive remodelling at Newnham Paddox, Warwickshire (from 1745), and Burghley House, Northamptonshire (from 1754). William Mason later attributed Brown's adventures in architecture to the 'great difficulty … in forming a picturesque whole where the previous building had been ill-placed or of improper dimensions' (Repton, 14). Like his master William Kent, and his contemporary Thomas Wright, Brown seems to have been prepared to try every kind of design, though his architecture may have lacked their originality, being usually a rather austere classical, perhaps derived from Sanderson Miller (Croome Court), or a Strawberry Hill Gothic, of the kind advocated by Batty Langley and Richard Bentley (the lodge at Rothley, c.1765). Notwithstanding Humphry Repton's comment 'the many good houses built under his direction, prove him to have been no mean proficient in an art, the practice of which he had found, from experience, to be inseparable from landscape gardening' (Loudon, 266), Brown's architecture played a secondary part in his 'place-making'.

Brown worked with other designers, in particular with Robert Adam at Harewood House, Yorkshire (from 1758), William Mason at Nuneham Courtenay, Oxfordshire (from 1778), Sanderson Miller at Lacock Abbey, Wiltshire (from 1754), Thomas Wright at Wrest, Bedfordshire (from 1758), and Henry Holland the elder and his son Henry, the last of whom he took into an informal partnership in 1770, and who married his elder daughter, Bridget, in 1773. In several cases, of which Sanderson Miller's ruined castle at Wimpole, Cambridgeshire, is the best-known example (designed 1752, erected 1770), he was happy to construct what others had designed. In addition he frequently stepped in to help clients whose zeal for improvement threatened to overwhelm their executive ability, as is implied in the correspondence on Belhus, Essex (from 1754).

Style Brown's style was derived from the two practical principles of comfort and elegance. First, there was a determination that everything should work, and that a landscape should provide for every need of a great house, an aspect of Brown's work that was influenced by the tradition of the *ferme ornée*, of ornamental walks around working fields. It was a tradition that Brown himself did much to popularize, and which he had learned from working at Stowe and from Philip Southcote's Woburn Farm. Indeed, had he never designed a building or planted a tree, Brown might still be known for his agricultural improvements. As Lord Coventry recalled after Brown's death, 'Croome … was entirely his creation, and, I believe, originally as hopeless a spot as any in the island'. Second, his landscapes had to cohere, and hence read as naturally and unaffectedly elegant. While his designs have great variety, they also appear seamless. In pursuit of the former, and in spite of his devotion to agricultural improvement, he would often leave commons unenclosed and wasteland of little agricultural value in sight of the house, as at Chatsworth (Derbyshire) and Croome Court and Longleat (Wiltshire),

allowing the landscape to drift imperceptibly up to this rough ground, over lakes and trees, becoming less polished as it did so. In fact Laleham, Middlesex (from 1778), and Mareham, Lincolnshire, are the only places where he was explicitly employed on an enclosure.

Brown is also associated with deer parks, but only about 30 per cent of the landscapes on which he worked had parks, and these were often some way away from the house, on poor ground. Indeed there is little in his work to suggest that he recommended the conspicuous wasting of good ground, as has sometimes been suggested.

Although often associated with setting a house in a grass field, Brown regularly designed large complex pleasure grounds that led off from the house and which consisted of numerous different types of planting, such as the arboretum, the wilderness, the flower garden, the evergreen shrubbery, and the greenhouse shrubbery at Croome. Sudden transitions were allowed, by means of screens of planting, but contrasting scenes were never visible together. Further evidence of his range and use of rough scenery is found in his quarry gardens, for example at Clandon, Surrey (from 1781), and the many ruins that he landscaped, of which Roche Abbey, Yorkshire (from 1766), is the best-known.

The fierce attacks made posthumously on Brown's reputation in the 'picturesque controversy', led by Richard Payne Knight and Uvedale Price in the 1790s, established an interpretation of his work that has not been questioned since. Price and Knight claimed that Brown's style was formulaic, that his plans were sent down from London, and that he had no regard for the *genius loci*. Further, they maintained that he had no understanding of pictorial composition, that his houses were isolated on extensive lawns, that his landscapes were too uniform, too smooth, and too bland, and consisted only of lakes, grass, and scattered trees. Despite its general acceptance, this interpretation is, however, wrong in every respect.

Brown's style is formulaic only in the sense that his clients had broadly similar needs for forestry, agriculture, and sport. His landscapes ranged from town houses to palaces, and about 25 per cent of them were villas. He was employed on the whole range of English topography, from the sublime uplands of Chatsworth, Derbyshire (from 1760), to the extensive levels of Burton Constable and Rise, Yorkshire (from 1759 and 1775 respectively). While he is regarded as a leader of the informal English landscape tradition, he usually retained elements of earlier formal designs, whether parkland avenues, as at Charlton, Wiltshire (from 1767), and Charlecote, Warwickshire (from 1757); water, as with the moats at Ditton, Berkshire (from 1768); or parterres, such as those at Wotton, Buckinghamshire, and Hampton Court, Middlesex. Furthermore he designed numerous formal gardens, usually strung along a serpentine walk, as at Brocklesby, Lincolnshire (from 1771), Tottenham, Wiltshire (from 1763), and Syon House, Middlesex (from 1760). Far from isolating the house, he frequently took care to bring a public road through its parkland so as to animate the view, and his lawns, so often described as 'bare and bald', were in fact hay meadows and brought the central, socially levelling episode of the agricultural year right into the heart of the estate. Few of his landscapes were surrounded by belts of trees, and his parklands were never isolated from the surrounding countryside. No one who has visited his late masterpiece at Berrington, Herefordshire, and seen the view from the dining-room at the end of a late September's afternoon will deny his ability to compose a Claudian image out of the least Claudian of settings; his instincts were sound, even if he had no formal training in the composition of pictures.

The principal device through which Brown achieved the effortless coherence of his designs was the sunk fence or ha-ha, and he used this with a sophistication that has never been matched. His ha-has used a range of construction techniques to confuse the eye into believing that different pieces of parkland, though managed and stocked quite differently, were one (as at Corsham, Wiltshire, from 1760); that lakes, at different levels and unconnected, formed a single body of water (for example at Swynnerton, Staffordshire); and that the parkland itself could run on indefinitely across, for example, the counties of Sussex, in the case of Cowdray (from 1768), and Hertfordshire, in the case of Youngsbury.

This coherence is taken for granted today with a complacency that was predicted in Brown's obituary: 'Such, however, was the effect of his genius that when he was the happiest man he will be least remembered, so closely did he copy Nature that his works will be mistaken' (Stroud, 202). Brown's success can be measured only against the few surviving incoherent landscapes that survive from his time. For example, in 1758 at Buckland, Oxfordshire, Richard Woods laid out an improbable set of lakes on the side of a hill, planted scraps of avenue, dug insignificant valleys, bedded roses, and popped incongruous buildings about the place in order to achieve some superb views, particularly from the windows of the pavilions of John Wood the younger's house, at the expense of any sense of unity.

Brown never published, and wrote only one paragraph about his intentions as a designer. This was sent in 1775 with a plan to France and was intended as an introduction to his style: 'Gardening and Place-Making', he wrote:

> when rightly understood will supply all the elegance and all the comforts which Mankind wants in the Country and (I will add) if right, be exactly fit for the owner, the Poet and the Painter. To produce these effects there wants a good plan, good execution, a perfect knowledge of the country and the objects in it, whether natural or artificial, and infinite delicacy in the planting etc., so much Beauty depending on the size of the trees and the colour of their leaves to produce the effect of light and shade so very essential to the perfecting a good plan: as also the hideing what is disagreeable and shewing what is beautifull, getting shade from the large trees and sweets from the smaller sorts of shrubbs etc. (Stroud, 157)

Character Brown had detractors among his contemporaries, of whom the most notable was the architect Sir William Chambers, his rival and colleague on a number of projects from Ingress Abbey (from 1756) to Milton Abbey,

Dorset (from 1763). He was attacked both for his lack of education and for his background, though his family had a greater standing than his detractors claimed. Brown himself rose higher than many of the gentry for whom he worked. In 1772 he served as high sheriff of Huntingdonshire, and he had the friendship of a series of prime ministers (William Pitt, his rival Lord Bute, George Grenville, and Lord North) and the ear of George III. Among his clients only Lord Shelburne at Bowood and Sir John Griffin Griffin at Audley End are known to have objected to him, either as a man or as a designer; both were themselves impossible clients, and it is telling that the architect James Paine entirely revised his negative opinions after he had met and started working with Brown.

To judge from the surviving correspondence, Brown's marriage was a happy one. He and his wife, Bridget, had two daughters and three sons, one of whom, Lancelot Brown (1748–1802), served as MP for Totnes (1780–84), Huntingdon (1784), and Huntingdonshire (1792–4), while John (1751–1808) joined the navy and rose to the rank of an admiral of the blue. Brown's dry wit made him 'an agreeable, pleasant companion', as Elizabeth Montague wrote, and William Mason's epitaph 'Christian, Husband, Father, Friend' expressed a widely felt sentiment (Stroud, 195, 203).

Death and posthumous reputation From the time of his move to Hammersmith in 1751 Brown suffered from asthma, and his habit of constant travel, together with his practice of not always charging for work (he would sometimes allow his client to determine the value of what he had done, and seems frequently to have submitted plans and surveys without a bill), affected both his health and his finances towards the end of his life. He continued to work and travel, however, until his sudden collapse on 6 February 1783 after a visit to Lord Coventry. He died on the same day at Wilderness House and was buried at Fenstanton, the estate that he had acquired in Huntingdonshire in 1767. He wrote his will in 1779, making bequests amounting to over £10,000. The residue of the estate was put into trust, and Samuel Lapidge was given the uncompleted contracts.

Capability Brown is rightly regarded as the classic English gardener—classic in the sense that so much early eighteenth-century design is epitomized by him, classic too in that, although his work is continually reassessed, every landscape gardener since, both in Britain and across the developed world, has been influenced in one way or another by him. While more than 30 per cent of the landscapes attributed to him were relatively small (120 hectares or less), he was capable of working on an immense scale, not only constructing gardens and parkland, but planting woods and building farms linked by carriage drives, or 'ridings', that ran many miles from the main house (as at Heveningham, Suffolk, from 1781), and it is for these very large landscapes that he is best remembered. The images that he created are as deeply embedded in the English character as the paintings of Turner and the poetry of Wordsworth.   JOHN PHIBBS

Sources D. Stroud, *Capability Brown* (1950); rev. edn (1957); pbk edn (1984) · P. Willis, 'Capability Brown's account with Drummond's Bank, 1753–1783', *Architectural History*, 27 (1984), 382–91 · J. C. Loudon, ed., *Landscape gardening and landscape architecture of the late Humphry Repton* (1841) · D. Jacques, *Georgian gardens: the reign of nature* (1983) · Colvin, *Archs.* · P. Willis, 'Capability Brown in Northumberland', *Garden History*, 9/2 (1981), 157–83 · J. Penn, *An historical and descriptive account of Stowe Park in Buckinghamshire* (1813) · T. R. Leach, *Lincolnshire country houses and their families* (1990), pt 1 · H. Repton, *Sketches and hints on landscape gardening* (1794) · J. Paine, *Plans, elevations, and sections of noblemen and gentlemen's houses*, 2 (1783) · N. Scarfe, 'A Frenchman's year in Suffolk', *Suffolk Records Society*, 30 (1988) · *Capability Brown and the northern landscape* (1983) [exhibition catalogue, Tyne and Wear County Council Museums]
Archives BL, corresp., Add. MS 69795 · priv. coll., corresp. and papers, incl. plan relating to Petworth · Royal Horticultural Society, London, account book | priv. coll., letters to eighth earl of Northampton relating to Fenstanton · PRO, letters to first earl of Chatham, PRO 30/8 · Staffs. RO, agreements relating to work at Weston Park, Staffordshire · Wilts. & Swindon RO, letters to Methuen family relating to Corsham Court
Likenesses N. Dance, oils, *c*.1773, NPG [*see illus.*] · attrib. R. Cosway, oils, priv. coll. · R. Cosway, pencil drawing, priv. coll. · N. Dance, oils, Burghley House, Peterborough
Wealth at death over £10,000: will, 1779

Brown, Levinius (1671–1764), Jesuit, born in Norfolk on 19 September 1671, was the son of Richard Brown and his wife, Mary. He was educated at the English colleges at St Omer and at Rome (1691–8). He was ordained on 16 June 1696 and entered the Society of Jesus in 1698. In 1701 he first became a missioner at Ladyholt, the seat of the Caryll family in Sussex. He was rector of the English College at Rome from 1723 to 1731, and was then appointed rector at Watten. Chosen provincial of his order in 1733, he continued in that office until 1737, and then moved to the rectorship of Liège College. After 1740 he spent the last years of his life in the college of St Omer, and witnessed the forcible expulsion of the English Jesuits from that institution by the parliament of Paris in 1762. Being too old and infirm to be removed, he was allowed to remain in the house until his death on 7 November 1764.

Brown was a friend of Alexander Pope's, and it is probable that during his residence as missioner of Ladyholt he induced the poet to compose his beautiful version of St Francis Xavier's hymn 'O Deus, ego amo te'. He published a two-volume translation of Bossuet's *History of the Variations of the Protestant Churches* (1742).

THOMPSON COOPER, *rev.* ROBERT BROWN

Sources Gillow, *Lit. biog. hist.* · G. Holt, *The English Jesuits, 1650–1829: a biographical dictionary*, Catholic RS, 70 (1984) · H. Foley, ed., *Records of the English province of the Society of Jesus*, 7 vols. in 8 (1875–83) · G. Oliver, *Collections towards illustrating the biography of the Scotch, English and Irish members of the Society of Jesus* (1835)

Brown, Sir (George) Lindor (1903–1971), physiologist, was born in Liverpool on 9 February 1903, the only son and younger child of George William Arthur Brown, schoolmaster in Warrington, and his wife, Helen Wharram, of Yorkshire. He attended first his father's school and then the Boteler grammar school in Warrington. At eighteen he won a scholarship to the University of Manchester, following his sister, Kathleen, and read medicine rather than chemistry as he had originally intended. He did well in

Sir (George) Lindor Brown (1903–1971), by Walter Stoneman, 1946

pre-clinical studies, and his physiology teachers, A. V. Hill, H. S. Raper, and B. A. McSwiney, influenced him towards a research career. Encouraged by McSwiney, he took an honours BSc in physiology (1924); after winning the Platt physiological scholarship, he spent a further year doing research in McSwiney's laboratory towards an MSc (1925). He qualified in medicine in 1928 (MB ChB Manch.), winning the Bradley prize and medal for operative surgery.

McSwiney had moved in 1926 to the physiology chair in Leeds, and in 1928 Brown joined him there as lecturer in physiology, working for some years on the nervous control of the motility of gastric muscle. In 1930 he married Jane Rosamond (*d.* 1975), daughter of Charles Herbert Lees, professor of physics in the University of London, and vice-principal of Queen Mary College. They had met five years earlier in clinical school. There were four children: Helen, who graduated in medicine; Christopher, an engineer; Stephen, an airline pilot; and Humphrey, a biomedical engineer.

In 1932 Brown took advantage of six months' leave to work in the laboratory of Sir C. S. Sherrington at Oxford, collaborating with J. C. Eccles in an electrophysiological analysis of vagal action on the heart. On returning to Leeds he began his own first fully independent research on ganglionic transmission, with kindred methods. In giving papers to the Physiological Society, he attracted the attention of Sir Henry H. Dale, who offered him a job at the National Institute for Medical Research in Hampstead. Brown took up the appointment in March 1934, joining John H. Gaddum and W. S. Feldberg in Dale's department of biochemistry and pharmacology.

There followed 'anni mirabiles', during which the cholinergic theory of chemical transmission was established: namely that excitation is transmitted from particular types of nerves to their target structures not by electric currents, but by the release of a chemical transmitter, acetylcholine. Brown and Feldberg's work on the transmission of impulses and release of acetylcholine by the superior cervical ganglion led them to study acetylcholine metabolism in the ganglion, and they were the first to estimate the turnover rate of a transmitter. Working also with Marthe Vogt and Dale, Brown and Feldberg showed that acetylcholine acted as a transmitter at the junction between a motor nerve and voluntary muscle. This was important, not only for general physiology, but also because of the possibility of a chemical link being susceptible to pharmacological manipulation for therapeutic purposes (as has proved to be the case). Brown brought to the group electrophysiological methods, a beautiful experimental technique, and an insight into the physiology of excitable tissues that was vital at the time. He also became increasingly influential in the Physiological Society; he served as honorary secretary from 1941 to 1949; as foreign secretary from 1949 to 1961; and as editor of the *Journal of Physiology* from 1940 to 1947.

With the advent of the Second World War, the institute turned to new activities. Brown, who also became a private in the Home Guard, first engaged in research on motion sickness, body armour, and tank design. Then in 1942 the royal naval personnel research committee (RNPRC) was set up jointly by the Medical Research Council and the chief executive. First to be formed was an underwater subcommittee, in which Brown brought together scientists (including J. B. S. Haldane) and naval officers involved with diving and submarine operations, in an exceptionally fruitful co-operation. He had a flair for removing barriers, and commanded the confidence of his naval colleagues to a remarkable degree. The Hampstead Physiology Laboratory, under Brown's direction after Dale's retirement in 1942, turned to the study of underwater breathing, the effects of excess of oxygen or carbon dioxide on humans (using themselves and colleagues as subjects), and the design of diving apparatus. Other committees, on clothing, gunnery, habitability, and visual problems, followed. Brown remained secretary of the RNPRC until 1949, and was then its chairman for nearly another twenty years.

With the end of the war the laboratory returned to its previous work, but Brown was now a prominent figure. He was elected FRS in 1946 and appointed CBE in 1947. In 1949 he accepted the Jodrell chair of physiology at University College, London. He was happy and successful there, much strengthening both the physiology department and

that of biophysics under Bernard Katz, and developing with J. S. Gillespie important work on adrenergic transmission. They established the relationship between impulse frequency and transmitter release, and clearly distinguished between that release and overflow of transmitter into the circulation. Despite giving up the secretaryship of the RNPRC and of the Physiological Society in 1949, he was carrying many outside activities and a sudden gastric haemorrhage in 1952 made him shed some of these. But new demands appeared, and having served on various Royal Society committees he became its biological secretary from 1955 to 1963.

In 1960, after advising the electors to the Waynflete chair of physiology in Oxford, Brown was himself offered the post, and accepted. He became a fellow of Magdalen College. Three years later he became a member of hebdomadal council, and also of the Franks commission of inquiry into the working of Oxford University. In 1967 he was elected principal of Hertford College. He resigned his chair, but his research group continued in the pharmacology department. He inaugurated the college's major appeal, negotiated two senior research fellowships, and dealt with student unrest with a light touch.

Brown was knighted in 1957 and made FRCP in 1958. At various times he served on the Medical Research Council, the Council for Scientific and Industrial Research, and the governing body of the Lister Institute, latterly as chairman. He was president of the Institute of Information Scientists and of the International Union of Physiological Sciences. He was Feldberg prize lecturer in 1961 and Royal Society Croonian lecturer in 1964. He held honorary doctorates at the universities of St Andrews (1958), Brazil (1958), Liège (1959), Leicester (1968), and Monash (1969), and was a member of the Danish and Brazilian academies of science, and an officer of the Order of the Southern Cross of Brazil (1959). The Physiological Society, which had made him an honorary member in 1970, established in his name the G. L. Brown lecture, given in a number of physiology departments every year.

Brown had a friendly, invigorating, light-hearted but determined personality. He was an excellent judge of talent and character, a stimulating and supportive head of department, devoted to laboratory work despite all his outside activities, and best and happiest in the company of the young. His recreations included workshop practice, making woodcuts and engravings, playing the flute, and writing topical ballades.

Early in 1970 Brown was immobilized by a stroke, and though he made a good recovery, he was struck by biliary obstruction in December. The primary tumour was rapidly operated on, but subsequently renal failure set in and he died in the Radcliffe Infirmary, Oxford, on 22 February 1971.   W. D. M. PATON, *rev.* E. M. TANSEY

Sources F. C. MacIntosh and W. D. M. Paton, *Memoirs FRS*, 20 (1974), 41–73 · personal knowledge (1986) · private information (2004) · Wellcome L., Physiological Society archives, CMAC · J. H. Gaddum, *Vasodilator substances of the tissues*, revised edn, retranslated from 1936 edn (1986)

Archives Hertford College, Oxford · National Institute for Medical Research, London · RS | Wellcome L., Physiological Society

archives, CMAC | FILM British Medical Association, Physiological Society collection
Likenesses W. Stoneman, photograph, 1946, NPG [*see illus.*] • photograph, National Institute for Medical Research, London • photographs, RS • photographs, Wellcome L. • photographs, U. Oxf., laboratory of physiology
Wealth at death £1516: probate, 22 July 1971, *CGPLA Eng. & Wales*

Brown, Sir (George) Malcolm (1925–1997), geologist, was born on 5 October 1925 at 21 Southampton Street, Redcar, Yorkshire, the second of the three children of George Arthur Brown (1891–1937), legal clerk, and his wife, Anne, *née* Fellowes (1900–1986). He attended the Church of England elementary school at Wensley in the Yorkshire dales (where he first developed an interest in natural history) before passing on to Sir William Turner's (Coatham) School at Redcar on his family's return there in 1937. After joining the Royal Air Force in 1944 he underwent aircrew training, but hostilities ceased before he saw active service. He remained with the RAF until 1947. After entering Durham University in that year he chose to specialize in geology, graduating with first-class honours in 1950. Much influenced by the teaching and research activities of Professor Lawrence Rickard (Bill) Wager, Brown migrated to Oxford on Wager's assumption of the chair there in 1950, beginning a close scientific collaboration and personal friendship which was to last until Wager's death in 1965.

Brown's first researches comprised a superb field and laboratory study of the layered ultrabasic igneous rocks of the island of Rum, for which he was awarded the DPhil degree, and which remains a classic contribution. Awarded a Commonwealth Fund (Harkness) fellowship in 1954, Brown went to Princeton University (where he made the acquaintance of Albert Einstein) to work with Professor Harry H. Hess on the chemical, optical, and crystallographic properties of pyroxene minerals in the rocks of the Skaergaard layered basic intrusion. Brown had visited the intrusion as a member of the east Greenland geological expedition led by Wager and W. A. Deer in the summer of 1953, further deepening the interest in layered igneous masses which was to last the rest of his life, culminating in the publication, with Wager, of the definitive monograph *Layered Igneous Rocks*, in 1968.

On his return from America in 1955 Brown was appointed university lecturer in petrology at Oxford, continuing vigorously in research, and expanding his interests to encompass major studies of the volcanic island arc of the West Indies and the petrogenesis of granitic rocks in the Tertiary volcanic districts of north-west Scotland, particularly Skye and Rum. Melting experiments carried out in the laboratory materially aided his conclusion that these latter acid igneous rocks arose from the partial fusion at depth of pre-Cambrian (Lewisian) basement rocks. On 24 August 1963 he married Valerie Jane Gale. There were no children of the marriage, which was dissolved in 1977. Brown's second visit to America, in 1966–7, as a Carnegie senior fellow at the world-renowned geophysical laboratory in Washington, produced further important researches into the pyroxene group of minerals as well as

a series of synthetic experimental studies relevant to igneous petrogenesis.

In 1967 Brown was appointed to the chair of geology at his old university, Durham, in succession to Kingsley Dunham. He inherited one of the best geological departments in the country, its international reputation becoming further enhanced during the next twelve years under Brown's leadership. Not only was he an inspiring teacher, but he soon proved himself an able, willing, and unusually popular administrator, filling for a time the office of pro-vice-chancellor, in 1979. Brown's major scientific contributions during his years at Durham centred upon his part in the study of the first samples of rock from the moon, returned to earth by the Apollo 11 astronauts in 1968. With the help of four able and enthusiastic collaborators (C. H. Emeleus, J. G. Holland, A. Peckett, and R. Phillips) Brown produced a steady stream of scientific results of the highest quality which, with the depth of his experience in petrology coupled with a bold yet rational scientific imagination, he used to interpret aspects of the evolution and origin of the moon, using the limited data available to him to the very best advantage. His hypothesis, that the moon must in its early history have passed through a stage when it was essentially molten and behaved rather like a vast layered intrusion, at first met with some scepticism, but, with some modifications, steadily gained wide acceptance. Lunar research at the time was dominated by the efforts of the well-equipped, sophisticated American laboratories, but with resources exceedingly modest by comparison Brown and his small team made contributions of disproportionate significance.

Brown's career culminated in 1979 in his appointment as director of the Institute of Geological Sciences (the much expanded successor to the original Geological Survey of Great Britain, founded in 1835). This post, which was commonly regarded as the most prestigious in British geology, carried with it the directorship of the Geological Museum, and of the Geological Survey of Northern Ireland. Although he had a marked taste for organizing and running things, Brown found the institute a daunting task. Several factors conspired to place the new director in a straitjacket: severe financial constraints; unfamiliarity with the Machiavellian ways of the civil service; the implementation of Lord Rothschild's 'customer–contractor' principle; and the interference of the parent Natural Environment Research Council in many details of the institute's work. Nevertheless, Brown achieved much by putting science first, particularly encouraging his younger and more active staff, who greatly admired him. In addition to the successful move of the institute's base from London to Keyworth, near Nottingham, he instigated major internal reorganizations. However, these were only partially achieved due to inadequate funds. He had clear visions of what the institute (renamed at his insistence the British Geological Survey, in 1984) needed in the late twentieth century and what its role should be, both as a scientific institution and as a government service. Given more support—moral as well as material—he could have achieved even more in the way of reform. All in all, his years with the Geological Survey carried frustrations, and cannot be counted among his happiest or most satisfying, but on his retirement in 1985 he left the organization in good heart and much better equipped to face the future.

Brown was one of the most brilliant scientists of the generation that immediately followed the Second World War, a leading authority on the petrology of igneous rocks and on the composition, structure, and origin of the moon. He became a leading figure in the international geological world. His extensive published work, his complete integrity, and the soundness of his judgement led him to be sought after by many organizations in his retirement, and he led an active professional life right up to his untimely death. He received many honours, including fellowship of the Royal Society (1975), fellowship of the Royal Society of Edinburgh (1966), the Wollaston Fund (1963) and Murchison medal (1981) of the Geological Society, and honorary degrees from the University of Leicester (1985) and the Open University (1990). He received a knighthood in the birthday honours in 1985.

In appearance Brown was well built, with handsome features and dark hair. His quiet voice retained traces of his native Yorkshire accent. His personality displayed contrasts: he was at the same time self-confident yet curiously diffident; preternaturally serious and then suddenly completely relaxed. He was capable of enormous feats of concentration and worked extremely efficiently. Outside his science his interests ranged widely, encompassing politics, literature, and especially poetry, for which he had had a passion since boyhood. His character was marked by a constant concern and care for others, yet, with a wide circle of acquaintances, he appeared to have rather few close personal friends. But he was a lovable and stimulating companion, and he never behaved selfishly. He enjoyed a good party, dashing sports cars, and elegant, intelligent female company; he was for a time as a young man friendly with the third of the well-known Beverley sisters.

Brown married, on 26 July 1985, Sally Jane Marston, *née* Spencer (b. 1945), secretary. This marriage proved most happy and successful. Through his wife Brown acquired a family of two stepdaughters of whom he was very fond. In retirement he and his wife lived in various houses near Oxford. He died of pancreatic cancer on 27 March 1997 at the Acland Hospital, Oxford, after a short illness and was buried in Headington cemetery on 10 April. He was survived by his second wife and her two daughters.

E. A. VINCENT

Sources E. A. Vincent, *Memoirs FRS*, 44 (1998), 65–76 · *The Independent* (4 April 1997) · *Daily Telegraph* (7 April 1997) · *The Times* (9 April 1997) · *The Guardian* (10 April 1997) · *WWW* · personal knowledge (2004) · private information (2004) · b. cert. · d. cert. · *CGPLA Eng. & Wales* (1997)
Archives priv. coll. · RS
Likenesses Godfrey Argent Studio, photograph, 1975, repro. in *Memoirs FRS*, 64 · photograph, repro. in *The Independent* · photograph, repro. in *Daily Telegraph* · photograph, repro. in *The Times* · photograph, repro. in *The Guardian* · photographs, priv. coll.

Brown [*née* Solomon]**, Mary** (1847–1935), social reformer, was born at Sea Point, Cape Town, Cape Colony, on 20 July 1847, one of the eleven children of Henry Solomon (b. 1816), a Jewish convert to Christianity, and his wife, Julia Middleton, the daughter of a Yorkshire doctor. Henry Solomon's British-born parents had moved to the Cape, where their family became prominent and influential. Mary Brown's childhood was happy, with more freedom than was usual for girls of her time. In adult life she had striking features, with deep-set eyes and dark curly hair. She went to a small dame-school in Cape Town, and, showing great intellectual promise, joined the first classes for women at Cape Town University when she was seventeen.

At the age of nineteen Mary Solomon met Dr John Brown (1842–1929), the son of a London Missionary Society missionary, the Revd J. C. Brown. He had been educated in Scotland, returning to South Africa in 1864 as a newly qualified doctor. His advanced views on freedom and the education of women attracted Mary. When they were engaged he sent her to Scotland on a six-month visit to his parents and to see London and Paris. They were married in Cape Town on 22 June 1869. Her husband was practising in Fraserburg, and after a short honeymoon at the Cape they travelled there by Cape-cart, a journey taking nearly a week.

It was an isolated life. John Brown had books sent out from England, including John Stuart Mill's *Liberty* and *The Subjection of Women*, and read aloud to his wife most evenings. A son was born in 1870, followed by a daughter, Rachel, in 1872, and another son, John, in 1874, who died in infancy. In 1876 John Brown gave up his practice and returned to Edinburgh with his family to study. Three years later they moved to Burnley in Lancashire, where Mary Brown began the social work for which she became well known. She was the first woman to be elected a poor-law guardian, and it was due to her that the cruel practice of separating elderly married couples when they entered the workhouse was ended. Seeing the trouble caused by alcohol she 'took the pledge' and founded the Burnley branch of the Women's Temperance Movement.

A close friend in South Africa was Olive Schreiner; Mary Brown persuaded Chapman and Hall to publish *The Story of an African Farm* (1883), and the two women remained close until Schreiner's death in 1920. Mary Brown joined the Burnley Co-operative Society and became a leader of the Women's Co-operative Movement. She supported the Labour Party from its foundation, and she and her husband were staunch friends of Keir Hardie. An excellent public speaker, she was also a competent chair of meetings and committees.

Confirmed in the Anglican church in 1880, Mary Brown was deeply religious but never sectarian. Although she was in sympathy with the socialism of her day she could not always agree with its methods, putting her Christian faith first and politics second. During the great Burnley coal strike she organized soup kitchens for the men and their families. 'Moral and social hygiene' engrossed her: she helped found a rescue home for girls, becoming its secretary and treasurer, and sometimes took desperate pregnant girls into her own home. When General Booth visited Burnley she added the Salvationists to the causes she supported. She joined in the fight for women's suffrage, though was never a militant.

When John Brown retired in 1898 he and his wife spent a year travelling in South Africa. She met President Kruger in Pretoria and President Steyn in Bloemfontein. The stupidity of the Jameson raid of 1895 had angered her and she was certain war was near. It broke out after their return to England: regarding it as an unnecessary war, she supported self-government for South Africa.

The Browns returned to South Africa in 1905 and spent the rest of their lives there. Although nearly sixty Mary entered the battle to bring social reform to her country. Elected a member of the Women's Christian Temperance Union of Cape Colony, in 1907 she became the superintendent of its department for social purity and moral education. After the Union of South Africa was created in 1910 this post led to her dealing with social welfare throughout South Africa, being particularly involved with work for the 'feeble minded'. She also founded the first Mothers' Union in the Cape and worked for women's suffrage. She went to Johannesburg to help start a moral welfare campaign there and about 1908–9 was involved in a parliamentary commission of inquiry into 'the Colour Question', which meant the prevention of venereal disease. In 1912 she led a deputation to the minister of justice demanding that the age of consent be raised to a uniform sixteen throughout the country. It was strongly opposed, but she was ultimately successful. With the help of a Jesuit priest she organized special meetings for men, and together they opened a 'home for rescuing girl children from evil surroundings'.

Brown died on 8 May 1929. Mary Brown, in her last years, suffered badly from arthritis and was nearly blind. She died in her sleep on 16 January 1935 at her home, Avondrust, Rosebank, Cape Town.   VIVIEN ALLEN

Sources A. James and N. Hills, eds., *Mrs John Brown* (1937)
Likenesses photograph, *c.*1890, repro. in James and Hills, eds., *Mrs John Brown*, frontispiece

Brown, Mary. *See* Leigh, Mary (*b.* 1885, *d.* in or after 1965).

Brown, Meredith Jemima (1845/6–1908), social reformer, was the youngest daughter of the Very Revd David Brown, principal of the Free Church college, Aberdeen, and one of the revisers of the New Testament. She moved to London in the 1880s and became interested in the impoverished lives led by the factory girls living and working in the East End. Realizing that west London factory girls were in a similar position, she decided to try to improve their lives. She began by setting up a place where they could meet in their free time. A wish to learn more about their lives led Meredith Brown and a friend of hers to disguise themselves as factory girls and visit the West End slums. She described their experiences in a book, *Only a Factory Girl*, 18,000 copies of which were printed. The publication brought in £2000, which she used to buy an old house at 16 Union Street, Lisson Grove. She named it the Shaftesbury

Institute and opened a night shelter for women and a crèche for babies there. Meredith Brown extended her mission work by establishing Bible classes and visiting the homes and lodging-houses of the West End slums. The success of these ventures encouraged her to set up a training home for girls in Clarendon Road, Maida Vale, London, and a men's labour home in Bell Street, Lisson Grove.

Meredith Brown lived at Lisson Grove and 'practically managed the whole work' (*The Times*, 10 Nov 1908), though she had many valued assistants. The expenses of the institute, of which she was superintendent and honorary president, were met from charitable subscriptions. In 1904 the county council issued instructions for the building in which the Shaftesbury Institute was housed to be altered to conform to new regulations. In view of the expenses involved, it was decided that the house should be demolished and replaced by a modern, well-equipped building on the same site. The cost of this was estimated to be over £6000 and many regarded the scheme as too ambitious. The council agreed to license a temporary building in the meantime, so Meredith Brown closed the men's labour home in Bell Street and had it converted to a home for working women. This was opened in 1906 by Lady Kilmorey. Meredith Brown's fund-raising efforts for the rebuilding of the Shaftesbury Institute meant that by 1907, although the cost had risen to £9000, only £400 was outstanding. On 29 February the new building, designed by Theodore Fyfe, was opened by Princess Louise Augusta, on behalf of her mother, the Princess Christian. The building was called Portman House, by permission of Lord Portman, a generous donor to the funds. On the day of the opening Princess Louise Augusta accepted the office of president of the institute.

Meredith Brown was judged by her contemporaries to be extremely successful in reforming the characters and habits of the poor of the West End of London:

> The influence of many years has told on the factory girls and the working women of the neighbourhood in a way that outsiders would hardly believe. The whole tone is altered, and the class aimed at is so changed in elevation, in habits, in ideas, that those who knew the neighbourhood when Miss Brown first settled among them would hardly know it now. (*The Times*, 10 Nov 1908)

She was considered to be:

> A very remarkable woman, full of faith and of consequent zeal, in the noble cause of benefiting her poor and degraded sisters, of untiring energy and perseverance, of a strong will and of unique will over her assistants, and especially over the class to the raising of which she devoted her life.   (ibid.)

She died, unmarried, on 5 November 1908 at the Shaftesbury Institute.   SERENA KELLY

Sources *The Times* (10 Nov 1908) · *WWW* · d. cert.
Wealth at death £1391 16s. 5d.: probate, 8 Jan 1909, *CGPLA Eng. & Wales*

Brown, Myra Eleanor Sadd [*née* Myra Eleanor Sadd] (1872–1938), women's rights activist and internationalist, was born on 3 October 1872 in Maldon, Essex, the tenth of eleven children of John Granger Sadd and Mary Ann Price. The family ran a firm of timber merchants and processors in Maldon, and were noted for their innovative ideas: the firm owned what is believed to be the first traction engine in Essex, which caused some local controversy, with fears of damage to bridges and frightening livestock. They also built an electric power station to supply the factory, and eventually the town.

Myra Sadd was educated privately at a school in Colchester. One of her interests was cycling; through this she met Ernest Brown (1868–1931), a co-founder of a firm supplying bicycle parts, whom she married on 21 July 1896. An interesting feature of the wedding was the colour scheme of purple, white, and green, twelve years later to become the suffragette colours, which might be seen as foretelling the future of Myra Sadd Brown (like many couples of progressive convictions at this time, Myra and Ernest combined their surnames). The couple moved to London, first to Finsbury Park, then to Hampstead. They had three daughters and one son. The firm of Brown Brothers rapidly met with success and diversified into electrical appliances and motor car manufacture, assuring Myra Sadd Brown of a degree of independence.

Myra Sadd Brown came from a progressive and independent-minded Congregationalist background; later in life she became a Christian Scientist. She had a keen interest in artistic matters. She was an enthusiastic follower of George Bernard Shaw's plays, and had a number of artistic acquaintances, including William Somerville, Henry Holliday, and Jessie Mothersole; she was even described as keeping a salon. However, her most enduring mark has been as a women's rights activist. Her convictions date back before her marriage; she is believed to have bought a small cottage in order to claim the vote as a ratepayer. She also became a poor-law guardian for Hackney. She was very active in the women's suffrage movement; she became a member of the militant Women's Social and Political Union, being arrested and imprisoned in 1912, on which occasion she went on hunger strike and was forcibly fed. She was a keen propagandist for the suffrage cause, her letters appearing in such periodicals as the *Christian Commonwealth*. Later, she was associated with Sylvia Pankhurst's East London Federation of Suffragettes; her eldest daughter, Myra Stedman, recollected being recruited to stand on street corners selling the *Woman's Dreadnought*. She would invite bus loads of east London women to visit her house near Maldon.

Myra Sadd Brown was also genuinely interested in other cultures and other countries. She regretted her lack of knowledge of foreign languages, and insisted on her children learning French and German. On several occasions she went with her husband, whose heart had been weakened by rheumatic fever in childhood, to winter in Italy and Egypt. After the First World War she became an active member of the International Woman Suffrage Alliance (later the International Alliance of Women). She travelled widely in Europe to conferences, usually accompanied by her eldest daughter.

Another major interest was the evolving Commonwealth. As early as 1923 Myra Sadd Brown had been involved in meetings which in 1925 led to the formation of the British Commonwealth League (later the Commonwealth Countries League), a feminist organization devoted to the upholding of women's rights in Commonwealth countries. She became treasurer of the league, less because of her skill at double entry bookkeeping than because of her ability to use her funds to guarantee the lease on the league's premises.

Myra Sadd Brown's husband died of rheumatic heart disease in 1931. In 1937 she went on an extended visit to south-east Asia, to be present at the birth of her second grandchild, and extended the tour to visit Angkor Wat and Malaya. She continued the journey to Hong Kong, planning to return via the Trans-Siberian Railway, but suffered a stroke on the way, and died in Kowloon Hospital, Hong Kong, on 13 April 1938. She was cremated the following day at the Hindoo crematory, Happy Valley, Hong Kong.

As a memorial, the British Commonwealth League established the Sadd Brown Library of material on women in the Commonwealth as part of the then Women's Service Library (now the Women's Library). Her active interest in the Commonwealth Countries League, and the International Alliance of Women, has been maintained first by her daughter Myra Stedman, and subsequently by her granddaughter, Diana Dollery, both of whom have been closely involved in the development of the Sadd Brown Library.   DAVID DOUGHAN

Sources private information (2004) · b. cert. · m. cert. · d. cert. · Women's Library, London, Myra Sadd Brown MSS
Archives Women's Library, London, autograph letter collection
Likenesses photographs, priv. coll.
Wealth at death £17,262 6s. 3d.: probate, 18 July 1938, *CGPLA Eng. & Wales*

Brown, Nessie Stewart [*née* Nessie Muspratt] (1864–1958), local politician, was born on 5 September 1864 at Seaforth Hall, Litherland, near Liverpool, the second of eight surviving children of the chemical industrialist Dr Edmund Knowles *Muspratt (1833–1923) and his wife, Frances Jane Baines, daughter of the editor of the *Liverpool Times*. The Muspratts were active Liberals and nonconformists who assured their place among Liverpool's foremost radicals when they supported the northern side in the American civil war. They also believed strongly in the education of girls, and Nessie and her sisters were encouraged to continue their education beyond secondary school. Nessie was educated at Cheltenham Ladies' College, Liverpool University, Paris, and Leipzig—her father having academic contacts in Germany.

On 13 September 1888 Nessie married Egerton Stewart Brown MA (*b.* 1862), a local barrister from an equally wealthy family, the son of Stewart Henry Brown, a merchant. Together they set up house at 16 Ullet Road, on the fringes of Liverpool's fashionable Sefton Park. Egerton was also a keen Liberal, and actively supported his wife as she became increasingly involved in public life. She became honorary secretary of the ladies' branch of the Liverpool Royal Society for the Prevention of Cruelty to Animals, which led her into broader philanthropic concerns. At the same time she was becoming increasingly active in Liberal politics. She joined the Women's Liberal

Federation (WLF) and worked hard to build the organization in her own city, forming branches at West Derby and Wavertree and serving as president for West Toxteth branch. The local WLF was dominated by Muspratt women at this time: Nessie was joined in her work by her mother, her aunt Mrs Sheridan Muspratt, her sisters Julia (Mrs Herbert Solly) and Stella (Mrs William Permewan), and her sister-in-law Helena. Nessie was not content to remain a leading light in Liverpool Liberal circles, and in 1892 she successfully stood for a position on the WLF national executive.

Much of Nessie's local work for the WLF involved canvassing on behalf of male candidates in municipal and local elections. In this she was an eager participant, often berating other women for not taking as active a role as herself. At this stage she believed that Liberalism was more important than other causes, a position which led her to become a vigorous opponent nationally of the 'test' question, a measure suggested by some women Liberals as a means of ensuring that WLF members would only undertake electoral work on behalf of candidates who supported women's suffrage. However, she was no anti-suffragist. Indeed, she began speaking for women's suffrage in 1891, and became increasingly involved with the local branch of the National Union of Women's Suffrage Societies (NUWSS) and served as its chairman. Until 1913 she maintained a phenomenal level of activity in both institutions, with her beliefs about each cause informing her work with the other. Much of her dislike of suffrage militancy, for example, stemmed from the fact that it was mainly directed against the Liberal Party. She also opposed NUWSS's election fighting fund which she saw as a move to link constitutional suffrage and socialism. She responded by joining Eleanor Rathbone in establishing a network of Women's Citizens' Associations in Liverpool's municipal wards in 1911. These had no socialist connections so did not compromise her Liberal activism. Nevertheless, her commitment to women's suffrage was strong, and by June 1913 she had lost patience with the Liberal Party's procrastination to such an extent that she resigned her presidency of the Lancashire and Cheshire Union of WLFs in protest.

The outbreak of the First World War suspended many of her immediate suffrage concerns, but gave Nessie no opportunity to rest from public life. Instead she devoted her not inconsiderable energies to several local organizations involved in relief work. Predictably, she selected bodies with a feminist agenda, notably the Scottish Women's Hospitals' Association, of which she was on the executive committee, and the Liverpool branch of the National Union of Women Workers, of whose women's patrols committee she was honorary secretary. More controversially she also became involved in attempts to promote Anglo-German conciliation. Her efforts in this direction were understandably tentative during the war years, and aimed at helping German women and English-born wives of Germans classified as 'enemy aliens'. Much of her motivation came from family connections, tempered by

personal experience—she and her husband were in Germany at the outbreak of war, where Egerton was interned for several months. After the war she continued her efforts, and worked more overtly for reconciliation between the two nations. She became chairman of the Women's International League's Liverpool branch, and was on the executive of Liverpool's League of Nations Union branch.

The partial enfranchisement of women in 1918 gave Nessie the vote and freed her from suffrage work. She was now able to return to the Liberal Party, and was elected city councillor on their behalf in 1920, resigning her seat in 1922 when she was selected as Liberal candidate for the parliamentary seat of Waterloo. Despite a hard-fought campaign in which she reduced the sitting Conservative's majority by 16 per cent, she failed, and perhaps this safe Conservative seat was not the best vehicle for the talents of a woman *The Vote* described as 'one of our most able politicians'. Although she did not break with the party, this marked the end of her electoral ambitions as a Liberal.

Electoral failure did not signal the end of Nessie's public life. She had continued her work for the Women's Citizens' Associations, and also for the women's patrols committee, and was among the leadership of the Liverpool Women's Council, a post-war body aimed at furthering feminist interests in civic life. This work, and her earlier track record in civic life, made her an ideal candidate for the magistracy, and in 1924 she became one of the first women elected to the Liverpool bench. She served diligently in this capacity until her retirement, taking a special interest in work with children which arose from her earlier work with the patrols.

Nessie Stewart Brown left Liverpool for a house at Beaumaris, Anglesey, overlooking the Menai Strait. She died at Lleiniog Penmon, Llangoed, on 7 April 1958.

Nessie's husband predeceased her. Her longevity in many ways served to obscure her achievements—at the time of her death even the *Women's Liberal Federation News* acknowledged that, despite her achievements, few readers would remain who remembered her. She was, in many ways, the last of her kind.　　KRISTA COWMAN

Sources S. Tooley, 'Ladies of Liverpool', *c*.1895, Lpool RO [photocopy of unidentified magazine piece] · E. K. Muspratt, *My life and work* (1917) · 'Liverpool's women magistrates', *The Liverpolitan* (June 1933) · *The Times* (28 April 1958) · W. T. Pike, *Liverpool and Birkenhead in the twentieth century: contemporary biographies* (1911) · K. Cowman, 'Engendering citizenship: women in Merseyside politics, 1890–1920', PhD diss., University of York, 1994 · V. Webster, 'What women are doing in Liverpool', *Womanhood*, 3 (1900), 279–81, 353–6 · b. cert. · m. cert. · d. cert.

Archives Lpool RO, Legge MSS · Lpool RO, Muspratt MSS · Lpool RO, Women's Citizens' Association MSS · University of Bristol, Women's Liberal Federation MSS · Women's Library, London, National Union of Women's Suffrage Society MSS

Likenesses photograph, Lpool RO; repro. in Tooley, 'Ladies of Liverpool' · photograph, repro. in 'Liverpool's women magistrates'

Wealth at death £51,873 5*s*. 5*d*.: probate, 27 June 1958, *CGPLA Eng. & Wales*

Brown, Oliver Frank Gustave (1885–1966), art dealer, was born at Dulwich on 4 October 1885, the only son and elder child of Ernest George Brown (*d.* 1915), fine art dealer, and his wife, Elsie Taylor. Leaving St Paul's School in 1902, he spent six months in Tours learning French. Brown's father, who had been managing the exhibitions at the Fine Art Society, Bond Street, for some twenty-five years, was an old friend of Lawrence B. Phillips, inventor and artist, whose sons Wilfred and Cecil Phillips had opened the Leicester Galleries, Leicester Square, in 1902, and in 1903 Ernest Brown joined the new firm, which became Ernest Brown and Phillips.

In the autumn of 1903 Oliver Brown joined the Leicester Galleries, where he was to spend most of the rest of his life. In his father's lifetime Brown appears to have been dominated by his taste and interests. During this period the galleries displayed the Mortimer Menpes collections of the prints of James Abbott McNeil Whistler and mounted exhibitions of works by Charles Conder, J. F. Millet, William Holman Hunt, Ford Madox Brown, and the illustrators Philip William (Phil) May, (Edward) Gordon Craig, Arthur Rackham, Edmund Dulac, and Max Beerbohm.

Brown frequently visited art schools, observing developments and enjoying social occasions, especially at the Slade. However, in 1912, rheumatic fever seriously affected his heart and caused a deafness which was to burden him for the rest of his life and which barred him from enlistment in the forces during the First World War. After a year's absence he returned to work in 1913, and became a partner in the firm in 1914 when his father became ill. His father died in 1915. During the war Brown and his partners supported many young artists, adding new names to the galleries' repertoire. Among them were Henri Gaudier-Brzeska, Jacob Epstein, and three official war artists—C. R. W. Nevinson, Paul Nash, and Eric Kennington. In 1918 Brown married Monica Mary (Mona), daughter of Dr Charles MacCormack, medical inspector of the Prisons Board of Ireland. They had two sons and one daughter. The eldest son, Nicholas, became a director of the Leicester Galleries in 1946.

Between the wars Brown and Cecil Phillips mounted a series of important shows by foreign artists. These included the first one-man exhibition in England of Henri Matisse (1919), Camille Pissarro (1920), Picasso (1921), the whole of the sculpture of Degas (1923), Vincent Van Gogh (1923), Paul Gauguin (1924), Paul Cézanne (1925), P. A. Renoir (1926), and Marc Chagall (1935). They also arranged monumental displays of sculpture by Epstein, Rodin, and Henry Moore. Brown wanted to revive interest in nineteenth-century artists who had painted pictures of their own times, rather than historical pictures, and bought many paintings by James Tissot: this led to an exhibition of Tissot's work in 1933. In 1937, to mark the centenary of Queen Victoria's accession, Brown put on 'Victorian Life', a large exhibition of Victorian art.

Brown was interested in all the arts, except perhaps music. His main associates were painters, sculptors, and writers, and he was at his happiest in their company—at the Café Royal, the pubs and haunts they frequented, the Alhambra, the 'old' Empire, or in the studios of Hampstead, Chelsea, or Fitzrovia. His encouragement to newcomers was unstinting, and, however preoccupied he was, he always aimed to examine their work. He was a close friend of Walter Sickert, with whom he shared a love of music-hall, and his many other friends included William Nicholson, Paul Nash, C. R. W. Nevinson, Osbert Sitwell, Ethelbert White, Henry Moore, and Reginald Wilenski.

Brown had an obsessional interest in mounting exhibitions, often as many as three a month, and the Leicester Galleries became the chief exhibition gallery in London. His experience made him invaluable to the Arts Council in its earlier days. He was on the arts panel for two periods of three years, from January 1949 to December 1954. In 1960 he was appointed an OBE. Brown's last visits to the continent were in 1951—to Paris to acquire paintings by Sickert from the heirs of André Gide, and to Rapallo to see Sir Max Beerbohm. A comprehensive exhibition of Beerbohm's work, 'Max in Retrospect', was mounted in 1952.

After living in London for most of his life, Brown moved to Rye in 1960, but continued to visit London several times a week. In Rye he began to write his memoirs (published in 1968 as *Exhibition*) which were completed shortly before his death, which occurred on 20 December 1966 in Rye Memorial Hospital. His wife survived him.

P. L. PHILLIPS, *rev.* ANNE PIMLOTT BAKER

Sources O. Brown, *Exhibition* (1968) · *The Times* (21 Dec 1966) · *The Times* (23 Dec 1966) · personal knowledge (1981) · private information (1981) · *CGPLA Eng. & Wales* (1967)
Likenesses W. Roberts, pencil drawing, 1924; known to be in family possession in 1981 · B. Dunstan, oils, 1957 (*Oliver Brown in the Leicester Galleries*), repro. in Brown, *Exhibition* (1968) · L. Toynbee, oils, 1967; known to be in family possession in 1981
Wealth at death £22,362: probate, 26 June 1967, *CGPLA Eng. & Wales*

Brown, Oliver Madox (1855–1874), author and artist, born at Finchley, Middlesex, on 20 January 1855, was the second child and only son of Ford Madox *Brown (1821–1893), already a distinguished painter, and his second wife, Emma Hill (1829–1890), daughter of a bricklayer. Ford Madox Brown was the son of a ship's purser from Berwickshire and his Kentish wife, who lived and worked out of Calais and Antwerp.

A precocious child, Oliver (known as Nolly) was enrolled in the junior school at University College, London, but removed after two years because of his chronic untidiness, unfitness for academic discipline, and artistic promise, which his master explained to Oliver's father might flower under instruction at home. (Dante Gabriel Rossetti would pen a limerick about Nolly, 'Whose habits, tho' dirty, were jolly' (Ford, 261). In December 1865, when Ford Madox Brown moved with his young family (including a second daughter) to 37 Fitzroy Square, he became his son's tutor. Nolly had no further formal education, though in 1871 he studied art briefly outside his father's studio, attending life classes in the atelier of Victor Barthé in Chelsea, where he received a prize in a drawing competition judged by George Frederic Watts. At the same time

Brown's friend the diplomat Jules Andrieu instructed Nolly in Latin and French.

The first watercolour that Oliver was known to have done was *Centaurs Hunting*, at the age of eight. At eleven he painted *Queen Margaret and the Robbers*, which he considered finished enough to present to Rossetti, who praised it on 10 May 1867 as 'very beautiful both in design and colour, and a first effort of which you need never be ashamed, however much you may advance as an artist' (*Letters of Dante Gabriel Rossetti*, 2.620). He reported showing the picture to Whistler, who 'admired it very much indeed' (ibid., 621). Rossetti advised nevertheless, when sending Oliver painting materials, that 'hard study and application' were 'not to be dispensed with' (ibid., 620).

To his brother William Michael Rossetti, Dante Gabriel reported on Oliver's firm fatherly tutelage that he was working 'on the strict Praeraphaelite system', almost exclusively in watercolours. It was in this medium that Oliver exhibited a picture in public, *The Infant Jason Delivered to the Centaur*, at the Dudley Gallery in London in 1869, its concept drawn from William Morris's writings. In 1870 he exhibited two horse-and-rider seashore paintings, *Exercize* at the Royal Academy and *Obstinacy* at the Dudley Gallery; he was fifteen. At the same time, for the Moxon Popular Poets series he produced two illustrations for *The Poetical Works of Byron*, edited by William Michael Rossetti and otherwise illustrated by Ford Madox Brown. His *Mazeppa* and *The Deformed Transformed* were then replicated in oils, and *Mazeppa* was exhibited at the British Institution in 1871. (The companion picture was never completed.)

The failure to finish the second painting was indicative of Oliver's turning towards writing, though he continued to draw and paint. Problems with his vision may have been involved; at thirteen he had begun wearing glasses. Furthermore, he would not be competing with his famous father. At fourteen he showed a group of sonnets to his family, which surprised them as they did not realize that he even knew what a sonnet was. Several of them escaped being destroyed, one because he had produced it to be mounted in gilt on the frame of a painting by Marie Spartali. Written at thirteen, it began, 'Leaning against the window, rapt in thought' (Ingram, 24), a Pre-Raphaelite image suggesting 'The Blessed Damozel'. Another described a 'withered' survivor from an imagined 'past world' and concluded, Rossetti-like, that the 'great Dante knew thee not'. A third would later be attached to the manuscript of his novel *The Black Swan*. In it, 'death's obliteration' is like the disappearance of 'wind-tossed sea's foam'.

During the winter of 1871–2, when Oliver was sixteen, he began *The Black Swan*, published posthumously in the *Literary Remains*. (Its bowdlerized version became *Gabriel Denver*.) '[Ford Madox] Brown called', William Michael Rossetti wrote in his diary on 18 March 1872. 'He says Nolly has, to the astonishment of everybody, & without consulting anybody, written a prose tale of passion, of extraordinary power' (*Diary of William Michael Rossetti*, 179–80).

Secluded in his fireless room, Oliver had imagined an Australian colonist, Gabriel Denver, who in 1824 leaves with his wife, Dorothy, for England to claim a legacy. Aboard the *Black Swan*, his passion for his wife long spent, he is attracted to a young woman, Laura, who is accompanied by a devoted servant. The aged escort soon dies, and Gabriel and the two women remain the only passengers. Dorothy observes her husband becoming mesmerized by Laura, and watches them caressing in the shadows. During the long voyage all three are wretched, but Dorothy is silent until one evening six weeks into the sailing Denver passionately clasps the woman waiting for him in the darkness and discovers that it is his wife. She dares him to throw her overboard and he almost yields to the taunt, when Laura's voice is heard, singing of her love. Still distant from Cape Town, the ship is wracked by fire and the crew perishes. The three passengers drift in a lifeboat (as Nolly had once done, off Southend, his rowlocks broken) for four days, during which Dorothy, desperate with thirst, drinks sea water and dies raving that she had torched the *Black Swan*. After the two survivors are picked up by a passing vessel, Laura, weakened by hunger, thirst, and exposure, dies. Denver, seizing her body in his arms, leaps overboard.

When Smith Williams, Smith and Elder's cautious editor, demanded drastic expurgations, Oliver, compelled to relinquish the strongest elements of the novel so that it could be published, rewrote some of it and mutilated what remained, conceding even his flashback narrative scheme. His 'ugly duckling' (Ingram, 76), as he ruefully called it, was published as *Gabriel Denver*. Dante Gabriel Rossetti (on 10 November 1873) professed himself 'much astonished and impressed' (*Letters of Dante Gabriel Rossetti*, 3.1230). Publication was, however, a bitter baptism into authorship. Oliver had been encouraged by his father on the grounds that publication was worth all the prudish compromises. He received £50 for the copyright, and Williams, who had emasculated the text, expressed hope to the author 'that your first book will make so strong an impression on novel readers as to establish your popularity as a writer of romance' (Ingram, 78). Four major notices did appear, in *The Academy*, *The Athenaeum*, *The Spectator*, and the *Saturday Review*, the last of which (apparently by Leslie Stephen) Oliver found 'slashing' (Fredeman, 45). However, to be noticed in such papers was authentic recognition, and he pressed ahead with a new novel, *The Dwale Bluth* ('deadly nightshade'). By July 1874 he had completed twenty-two chapters, which Williams suggested might be offered first to the *Cornhill Magazine* for serial prepublication. Unfortunately, Stephen was the *Cornhill*'s reader. Oliver reluctantly made the proposed revisions, but Stephen again returned the manuscript.

By then Oliver was gravely ill with peritonitis aggravated by septicaemia. In late September he was dying. From his bed he continued to write, then to dictate, beginning a third novel, *Hebditch's Legacy*, several short fictions, and further verses. Although he had smoked since sixteen, wasted now by fever he recoiled from the odour of tobacco that hung about his father. 'Very well, my dear,' said Ford Madox Brown, 'I will never smoke again until you get up to smoke with me' (Ford, 296).

Oliver Madox Brown died at his home, 37 Fitzroy Square, London, on 5 November 1874, the first anniversary of the publication of *Gabriel Denver*. In anguish, his father drew a deathbed portrait, which showed his son's clipped brown beard flecked with gold, and penned a sonnet about 'broken promises that showed so fair' (Ford, 297). A family friend, the liberal minister Moncure Conway, conducted a non-denominational service over the open grave at St Pancras and Islington cemetery, East Finchley, London, on 12 November. At the age of nineteen Oliver Madox Brown's finished achievement inevitably was small. As Dante Gabriel Rossetti wrote, in moving memorial verses, Nolly was 'All things to come' (Ingram, 2).   STANLEY WEINTRAUB

Sources W. E. Fredeman, 'Pre-Raphaelite novelist manqué: Oliver Madox Brown', *Bulletin of the John Rylands University Library*, 51 (1968–9), 27–72 · J. H. Ingram, *Oliver Madox Brown: a biographical sketch* (1883) · F. M. Hueffer [F. M. Ford], *Ford Madox Brown: a record of his life and work* (1896) · *The diary of William Michael Rossetti, 1870–1873*, ed. O. Bornand (1977) · introduction, *The dwale bluth, Hebditch's legacy, and other literary remains by Oliver Madox Brown*, ed. W. M. Rossetti and F. Hueffer, 2 vols. (1876) · H. R. Angeli, *Dante Gabriel Rossetti: his friends and enemies* (1949) · *Letters of Dante Gabriel Rossetti*, ed. O. Doughty and J. R. Wahl, 4 vols. (1965–7), vols. 2–3 · W. M. Rossetti, ed., *Rossetti papers, 1862–1870* (1903), 329 [William Michael Rossetti's diary] · T. Newman and R. Watkinson, *Ford Madox Brown and the Pre-Raphaelite circle* (1991) · *IGI* [Matilda Hill]
Archives JRL, MSS | L. Cong., letters to Marston · Ransom HRC, Rossetti MSS · University of British Columbia Library, Helen Rossetti Angeli MSS
Likenesses F. M. Brown, oils, 1860 (*The English boy*), Man. City Gall. · F. M. Brown, pastel drawing, 1874, repro. in Hueffer, *Ford Madox Brown* · F. M. Brown, pastel drawing, 1883, repro. in Ingram, *Oliver Madox Brown* · F. M. Brown, chalk drawing, AM Oxf.

Brown, Pamela Mary (1917–1975), actress, was born at 45 Howitt Road, Hampstead, London, on 8 July 1917, the daughter of George Edward Brown, a journalist, and his wife, Helen Blanche Ellerton. She was educated at St Mary's Convent, Ascot, and subsequently studied at the Royal Academy of Dramatic Art (1935–6). Pamela Brown made her stage début at Stratford upon Avon, in the 1936 season, playing Juliet, The Widow in *The Taming of the Shrew*, and 'a delicious' Cressida, which she played lisping, drawing critical attention to herself (Trewin, 112). Her London début came in November 1936 at the Little Theatre, in *The King and Mistress Shore*. Between 1937 and 1941 she played seasons in repertory in Oxford with occasional forays into the West End. Her work in Oxford established her as an actress to be reckoned with—in such parts as Hedda Gabler, Lady Teazle, Bella Manningham in *Gaslight* by Patrick Hamilton, Sadie Thompson in *Rain* by J. Cotton and C. Randolph, and Nina in *The Seagull* by Anton Chekhov. An early marriage to the actor Peter Copley ended in divorce in February 1953.

The intelligence of Pamela Brown's work and her remarkable incandescent personality and striking good looks began to be recognized during the early years of the Second World War. Michael Powell, the film director, recalled how at that time she was 'a spectacular young

Pamela Mary Brown (1917–1975), by Anthony Buckley, 1949

actress with resplendent chestnut hair to her shoulders, and great liquid eyes full of disdain, that could dart a glance backward like a nervous thoroughbred. She was tall, with a long back and lovely legs' (Powell, 478). She played Ophelia in 1944 to Robert Helpmann's Hamlet and in 1946 she was Cordelia to Laurence Olivier's King Lear. She was by then an accepted star actress, the favourite of James Agate, the most influential critic of his time. He praised her 'superb performance' in the eponymous role in Jean-Jacques Bernard's *Madeleine* (1944), adding that 'I shall be content to echo a colleague's "She stands higher than any of her generation for flashes of revealing fire"' (Agate, 92).

Pamela Brown made her New York début at the Royale Theater in 1947 as Gwendolen Fairfax in Oscar Wilde's *The Importance of being Earnest*, and in 1949 had an outstanding success in the play with which she has been closely associated, *The Lady's not for Burning*, in the role of Jennet Jourdemayne, specially written for her by Christopher Fry. 'Miss Pamela Brown glides, sidles, darts and twists with a wonderful grace and flash, and she matches Mr Gielgud's delivery. Technically, it is all dazzling' (Worsley, 83). After London, the play was taken to New York and Washington, and Pamela Brown continued her alternation of West End hits and the major classic roles. For John Gielgud's season at the Lyric, Hammersmith, she played Mrs Millamant in *The Way of the World* by William Congreve and Aquilina in *Venice Preserv'd* by Thomas Otway.

From the early 1950s illness was beginning to make playing on the stage difficult: owing to an arthritic condition, which began when Pamela Brown was aged only fifteen, her mobility was restricted and she was in great pain, kept at bay by drugs. Nevertheless, in December 1953, she appeared in Wynyard Browne's *A Question of Fact*, opposite Paul Scofield. According to one reviewer, 'Pam Brown brought to a part that didn't have all the character that it might have had, enormous character' (Duff, 86). Despite her health problems, Brown continued to appear in films down to the early 1970s. These included appearances in *Lust for Life* (1956) with Kirk Douglas, the Richard Burton and Elizabeth Taylor *Cleopatra* (1963), and remakes of *Wuthering Heights* (1970) and *Dracula* (1974) with Jack Palance as Dracula. By and large her films were not as distinctive as her stage work, but her physical presence had a luminous quality which drew attention to her, enabling her stillness to leave impressions which lasted well after the film had run its course. Of her appearance as Jane Shore in Olivier's film of *Richard III* (1955), an obituarist noted that although this was a non-speaking part, 'in her hands [it was] an eloquent symbol of clandestine love and conspiracy' (*The Times*, 20 Sept 1975). Her appearance as Nicklaus, in *The Tales of Hoffman* (1951), a silent, mocking smile playing around her lips, her eyes eloquently commenting on the folly and rashness of her master, lingers in the memory.

Pamela Brown lived for many years with the film director, Michael Latham *Powell (1905–1990). She died from cancer on 19 September 1975 at 4 Lee Cottages, Avening, Gloucestershire, and was buried in Holy Cross churchyard, Avening. Because of the fading away of her career, Pamela Brown's passing received scant notice in obituaries. Her memorial remains in *The Tales of Hoffman*, the masterpiece of Michael Powell, whose great love and muse she was. As Amy Greenfield has written, 'Allusions to Brown's situation and Powell's relationship to her are scattered throughout the film' (Greenfield).

CLIVE BARKER

Sources *The Times* (20 Sept 1975) · F. Gaye, ed., *Who's who in the theatre*, 14th edn (1967) · A. Greenfield, 'The tales of Hoffman', *Film Comment* (13 March 1995) · C. Duff, *The lost summer* (1995) · T. C. Worsley, *The fugitive art* (1952) · S. Morley, *The great stage stars* (1986) · J. Agate, *The contemporary theatre, 1944–45* (1946) · A. Williamson, *Theatre of two decades* (1951) · M. Powell, *A life in movies* (2000) · *CGPLA Eng. & Wales* (1976) · b. cert. · d. cert. · J. C. Trewin, *The turbulent thirties* (1960)

Archives FILM BFI NFTVA, documentary and performance footage | SOUND BL NSA, performance recordings

Likenesses A. Buckley, photograph, 1949, NPG [*see illus.*]

Wealth at death £19,595: probate, 26 Feb 1976, *CGPLA Eng. & Wales*

Brown, Peter (1784–1863). *See under* Brown, George (1818–1880).

Brown, Peter Hume (1849–1918), historian, was born on 17 December 1849 at Tranent, East Lothian, Scotland. His father died in 1852, and his mother moved to Prestonpans, where he was sent in 1857 to the Free Church school. Although his mother died in 1866, he remained at the school as a pupil teacher until 1869. He then moved south, teaching as far afield as Wales; but it was from Newcastle upon Tyne that he returned to Edinburgh in 1872, matriculating at the university with the intention of becoming a minister. Persistent doubts about this vocation led to his

Peter Hume Brown (1849–1918), by James Russell & Sons

withdrawal after two years, a decision he marked by the sale of his theological books and purchase of Montaigne's *Essays*. While at the university, however, he had met R. B. Haldane, whose friendship, along with that of his mother and sister, was to provide Hume Brown with personal and intellectual bearings for the rest of his life. Through Mrs Haldane he secured a tutorship in Weston-super-Mare, with the expectation of travel abroad. Ill health cut off this prospect, and he returned to Edinburgh University in 1875, taking his MA in 1878: while he later acknowledged debts to David Masson and Alexander Campbell Fraser among the professors, it was the breadth and seriousness of his own reading which impressed contemporaries. Following graduation he opened a private school in Edinburgh, and in 1879 he married. But his wife died in May 1882, prompting him to leave the school and devote himself to literary and historical scholarship, sustained by a little tutoring and the Haldanes' friendship.

It was a courageous course, since the continued predominance of philosophy in the traditional 'general degree' of the Scottish universities meant that there were no academic openings for historians. Lodgings above those of David Patrick, editor of *Chambers's Encyclopaedia*, led to articles for that work; meanwhile Hume Brown undertook the research for his first book, *George Buchanan, Humanist and Reformer*, published in 1890. This was quickly followed by editions of *Early Travellers in Scotland* (1891), Buchanan's *Vernacular Writings* (1892), and *Scotland before 1700, from Contemporary Documents* (1893). A companion biography, *John Knox*, appeared in 1895: like that of Buchanan, it paid close attention to the formative continental years of its subject's career. His scholarly reputation established, Hume Brown was commissioned by Cambridge University Press to write a new *History of Scotland*, which was published in three volumes, appearing successively in 1898, 1902, and 1909. Accompanying these were abridgements for schools of both the *History* and the biographies of Buchanan and Knox.

Following the 1892 university reforms, Hume Brown was a candidate for the new chair of history at Edinburgh in 1894; but it went to G. W. Prothero. Recognition and financial security were at last forthcoming in 1898, when he succeeded David Masson as editor of the *Register of the Privy Council of Scotland*: method and application enabled him to publish a volume a year until 1915, and gave him a thorough command of a major source for the writing of his Scottish history. From 1901 he combined the position with an academic career, being appointed the first holder of the Sir William Fraser professorship of ancient (Scottish) history and palaeography at Edinburgh University. His Scottish history course ran from the origins to 1500, and was at first for honours only; but the appointment in 1909 of H. W. Meikle as a lecturer in Scottish history enabled him to add a further course from the Reformation until the close of the 18th century, and to offer the two courses for the ordinary degree. Hume Brown was diffident of his lecturing ability, but he developed a conversational style suited to his initially small classes; and his obvious integrity earned him the respect of his students, whose careers he was conscientious in supporting. Outside Edinburgh he gave the Rhind lectures at St Andrews in 1903, on *Scotland in the Time of Queen Mary* (1904), and the Ford lectures at Oxford in 1914, on *The Legislative Union of England and Scotland* (1914). He also succeeded Masson as historiographer-royal for Scotland in 1908. He lived alone with his dog at the foot of the Braid Hills, where his friends were entertained by the range and charm of his conversation. But he was also a frequent visitor of the Haldanes (and their dogs) at Cloan, and from 1898 until 1912 the high point of the year was the 'pilgrimage' which he and Richard Haldane undertook each spring to Weimar and Ilmenau. Behind the visit, and their friendship, was a deep mutual affection for Germany, and for Goethe in particular; politics were secondary to philosophy and literature, and Hume Brown's own liberalism never took an active form.

As a historian, Hume Brown's achievement was to establish the academic respectability of Scottish history. Committed to the evidence, studiously moderate in judgement, he wrote in a style regarded even by contemporaries as 'lacking somewhat in forcibility'. Nevertheless Hume Brown believed that Scottish history bore witness to Scotland's nationhood, and he offered a sympathetic defence of those episodes which had done most to discredit Scottish history in the eyes of Enlightenment historians. Comparing the Scottish nobility with their counterparts elsewhere in Europe, he rehabilitated their commitment to constitutional liberty in the face of royal ambition. He celebrated the Reformation through the characters of Buchanan and Knox, in the belief that it had created a national consciousness among all Scots, as well as laying a foundation, through shared protestantism, for future union with the English. For that to be realized, secular interests had had to override divisions between protestants: but once that occurred, the Union of 1707 had enabled Scotland to make its great contribution to the modern world. On these terms Hume Brown's conception of national history was by no means exclusive: he consistently advocated the study of Scottish history alongside that of other countries. It was the Scots' contribution to Europe, rather than to the empire, which interested him: he was unusually well informed about the influence of Scottish upon German thought. He was also deeply committed to combining the study of history with literature, in which his interests were again European: Montaigne, Sainte-Beuve, and, above all, Goethe were his greatest inspirations. A life of Goethe was his last major project: the *Youth of Goethe* appeared in 1913, and he continued to work on the poet's later years during the First World War.

Hume Brown suffered a cerebral haemorrhage on the evening of 30 November 1918, and died shortly after midnight on 1 December 1918 at his home, 20 Corrennie Gardens, Edinburgh. Viscount Haldane collected a number of his individual lectures into *Surveys of Scottish History* (1919); and in 1920 he and his sister Elizabeth fulfilled Hume Brown's wish that they should complete and publish his *Life of Goethe*.   JOHN ROBERTSON

Sources C. H. Firth, 'In memoriam: Peter Hume Brown', *SHR*, 16 (1918–19), 153–61 [incl. bibliography] · G. Macdonald, 'P. Hume Brown, 1849–1918', *PBA*, [8] (1917–18), 591–6 · Viscount Haldane and P. Hume Brown, *Surveys of Scottish history* (1919) · Viscount Haldane and P. Hume Brown, *Life of Goethe*, 2 vols. (1920) · NL Scot., Haldane MSS · *The Gambolier: the student's magazine, Edinburgh University*, 4/4 (1911), 50–51 · *Edinburgh University calendar* (1902–3) · *Edinburgh University calendar* (1910–11) · *Edinburgh University calendar* (1917–18) · *DNB* · *CCI* (1919)
Archives NL Scot., corresp. with Lord Haldane · U. Edin. L., corresp. with Charles Sarolea
Likenesses J. Russell & Sons, photograph, repro. in Firth, 'In memoriam' [*see illus.*] · photograph, U. Edin. L.; repro. in *The Gambolier*
Wealth at death £14,187 7s. 2d.: confirmation, 7 Jan 1919, *CCI*

Brown, Philip (*d.* 1779), botanist, was a doctor of medicine, practising in Manchester. Towards the close of his life he became interested in botany, establishing an extensive garden with a greenhouse and stove. He procured seeds from various parts of the world through his connections with merchants and ship captains. At his death, which occurred in Manchester in 1779, a catalogue of the collections was drawn up for sale. Many of the entries are identified only as 'a new Plant' and were supposed to be unique in England. Brown's is the first British example of a stock of living plants being sold after the collector's death.

B. D. JACKSON, *rev.* P. E. KELL

Sources *A catalogue of very curious plants, collected by the late Philip Brown* (1779) · B. Henrey, *British botanical and horticultural literature before 1800*, 2 (1975)

Brown, Rawdon Lubbock (1806–1883), historian and antiquary, was born in London, the son of Hugh William

Rawdon Lubbock Brown (1806–1883), by G. & L. Fratelli Vianelli, 1883

Brown and Anne Elizabeth Lubbock, sister of Sir John Lubbock, bt. He was a boarder at Charterhouse School, 1820–21, and appears to have studied at Oxford; but the record is uncertain until his arrival in Venice in 1833, on a whimsical mission to find the grave of Thomas Mowbray, the 'banish'd Norfolk' of Shakespeare's *Richard II*. He made his home in Venice, where he bought the Palazzo Dario in 1838 for £480. Financial problems, apparently connected with an estrangement from his family, caused him to sell the *palazzo* in 1842, and move into an apartment—first in the Palazzo Businello, and then, in 1852, in the Palazzo Gussoni-Grimani della Vida. His attachment to the city was profound. 'I never wake in the morning,' he told Charles Eliot Norton, 'but I thank God that he has let me pass my days in Venice.' Browning wrote a sonnet about the legendary occasion when Brown was about to leave on a trip to England, took a last look at the Grand Canal from his window, and decided that he could not tear himself away ('Sonnet to Rawdon Brown', 1883).

Brown never married, and he acquired a reputation for misanthropy and cantankerousness; yet he acted as host and cicerone to a crowd of eminent visitors—to Ruskin most notably, whom he assisted in the researches for *The Stones of Venice*. During the difficult period preceding the annulment of the Ruskins' marriage, Brown's sympathies were firmly with Effie; but subsequently the breach with John was healed. He acquired a unique knowledge of the history and antiquities of Venice, and spent most of his life in studying its archives. After publishing some original investigations into the life and works of the Venetian historian Marino Sanuto the younger, *Ragguagli sulla vita e sulle opere di Marino Sanuto* (1837), he discovered and edited contemporary copies (the originals had been destroyed) of the dispatches of Sebastian Giustinian, the Venetian ambassador in London at the beginning of the reign of Henry VIII; these were published in 1854 under the title *Four Years at the Court of Henry VIII*. The new light which this book threw on the relation of the Venetian archives to English history induced Lord Palmerston, at the instance of Sir Henry Layard, to commission Brown in 1862 to calendar those Venetian state papers which dealt with English history. This work engaged all Brown's attention for the rest of his life. He published five volumes of the *Calendar of state papers and manuscripts relating to English affairs existing in the archives and collections of Venice, and in other libraries of northern Italy* (1864–81), and a sixth was completed and published in the year after his death by his executor G. Cavendish-Bentinck.

Brown bequeathed to the Public Record Office the 126 volumes of his transcripts from the Venetian archives, dating from early times to 1797. Among his other works is *Avviso di Londra*, an account of newsletters sent from London to Venice during the first half of the seventeenth century, published in volume 4 of the Philobiblon Society's *Bibliographical and Historical Miscellanies* (1854). Brown died on 25 August 1883 at Casa della Vida in Venice; he had hoped to be buried in the old protestant cemetery of San Nicolò, on the Lido, where he had bought a plot and prepared a grave. But the authorities withheld permission, and he was interred in the protestant section of the cemetery island of San Michele.

SIDNEY LEE, *rev.* JOHN PEMBLE

Sources *Effie in Venice: unpublished letters of Mrs John Ruskin written from Venice between 1849–1852*, ed. M. Lutyens (1965) · P. Kaufman, 'Rawdon Brown and his adventures in Venetian archives', *English Miscellany*, 18 (1967), 283–302 · P. Kaufman, 'John Ruskin and Rawdon Brown: the unpublished correspondence of an Anglo-Venetian friendship', *North American Review*, 222 (1925–6), 112–20, 311–20 · D. Sutton, 'Two historians in Venice', *Apollo*, 110 (1979), 364–73 · *The Times* (29 Aug 1883) · *The Times* (8 Sept 1883) · *The Athenaeum* (8 Sept 1883), 307

Archives CUL · PRO · U. Nott. L., corresp. and papers | BL, letters to Sir Austin Layard, Add. MSS 38987–39120

Likenesses G. & L. Fratelli Vianelli, photograph, 1883, Archivio di Stato, Venice [*see illus.*]

Wealth at death £5339 0s. 8d.: probate, 17 Nov 1883, *CGPLA Eng. & Wales*

Brown, Sir Raymond Frederick (1920–1991), industrialist, was born on 19 July 1920 at 4 Nettleton Road, Greenwich, London, the son of Frederick Brown, then working as a dock labourer but later a small shopkeeper, and his wife, Susie Evelyn, *née* Hutchins. After leaving Morden Terrace London county council school at the age of fourteen he joined Broadcast and Relay Services (later Rediffusion) as an engineering apprentice, continuing his education at evening classes at South East London Technical College and Morley College. He spent the war years on secondment from Rediffusion installing radio navigation beacons for the RAF, and after the war he helped to install mobile transmitters in Germany to enable the British army of the Rhine to receive broadcasts from the British Forces Broadcasting Service. He married Eva Constance Hugh (*b.* 1921/2), daughter of Henry Hugh Jennings, engineer gauge maker, on 13 September 1942; they had one daughter but were divorced in 1949. On 19 June 1953 he married Carol Jacqueline Elizabeth (*b.* 1931/2), daughter of

Henry Robert James Spinks, company director. They had two sons and one daughter.

Brown worked as sales manager in the communications division of Plessey Ltd from 1949 to 1950 when he left to found Racal Ltd jointly with Wing Commander (George) Calder (Jock) Cunningham: the name Racal—pronounced 'Ray-call'—came from a combination of RAY-mond and CAL-der. Based in north London, it began as a consultancy for the planning of radio communications systems but in 1951 they formed Racal Electronics Ltd as a private company, to manufacture radio equipment for the major communications companies. The company moved from its original small factory in Isleworth to larger premises built to its requirements in Bracknell New Town, Berkshire, in 1954, and continued to expand in the field of radio communications, concentrating on high frequency equipment. Racal was the first British company to sell proprietary radio communications equipment, rather than entering into contracts with customers to supply to their individual specifications. Among its most successful products in the early years were the RA 17 high frequency radio receiver, first manufactured in 1957, and the Harness B intercommunication units for tanks and military vehicles. Cunningham died in 1958 but the company continued to grow, with the volume of business quadrupling between 1957 and 1962. In 1961, when it was floated as a public company with Brown as chairman and managing director, Racal had a workforce of 825, with 50 per cent of its sales to British government departments, while international customers included NATO, SHAPE, and governments throughout the world. When Brown left the company in 1966, 62 per cent of its orders were for exports. Since 1956 he had spent some six months in every year selling Racal products abroad, negotiating licensing agreements for the overseas manufacture of equipment designed by Racal, and acquiring licences for it to make equipment developed elsewhere. Several overseas subsidiary companies were formed, starting with Racal (Australia) Pty Ltd in 1961. An installation section of the company was developed, which undertook major projects abroad.

Brown was appointed head of the new department of defence sales at the Ministry of Defence in 1966 and spent three years there working to increase Britain's share of the world market in defence equipment. He was knighted in 1969 and appointed adviser on commercial policy and exports to the Department of Health and Social Security, where he remained until 1972. He subsequently served as an adviser to the National Economic Development Office. He joined Muirhead, another leading electronics company, as chief executive and managing director in 1970, holding these positions until 1982, when he was elected chairman. He was one of the first to realize the possibilities of the facsimile machine, and was responsible for its development at Muirhead. When he left in 1985 he became an executive director of STC (formerly Standard Telephones and Cables Ltd). He retired in 1990.

A horse lover and keen polo player, Brown not only kept horses and a string of polo ponies, but was also chairman of Racecourse Technical Services from 1970 to 1984. At his country estate in Witley, near Godalming, Surrey, he had a prize-winning herd of Hereford cattle, and he enjoyed golf and shooting. He had a warm and exuberant personality, and was enthusiastic about anything that he did. He held no strong political views, and was happy to serve under any political party: it was coincidental that most of his government work was done while the Labour government was in power. He devoted much time to charitable causes, including the Ronald Raven Chair of Clinical Oncology Trust, and muscular dystrophy. He died of cancer at his home, Witley Park House, Surrey, on 3 September 1991 and was buried in the churchyard at Witley on 11 September. He was survived by his second wife and their three children, his daughter by his first marriage having predeceased him. A memorial service was held at St Martin-in-the-Fields on 2 November 1991.

ANNE PIMLOTT BAKER

Sources R. Brown, *Racal: a story of expansion* (1962) · private information (2004) [Racal Electronics plc] · *The Times* (16 Sept 1991) · *The Independent* (13 Sept 1991) · *The Times* (4 Sept 1991) · *The Times* (11 Oct 1991) · *WWW*, 1991–5 · b. cert. · m. certs. · d. cert.
Likenesses photograph, repro. in *The Times* (16 Sept 1991) · photograph, repro. in *The Independent*
Wealth at death £13,605,121: probate, 1991, *CGPLA Eng. & Wales*

Brown, Richard (1736–1816), stonemason and manufacturer of decorative stone, was born in Derby and baptized at the collegiate church of All Saints on 25 July 1736, son of **Richard Browne** [Richard [i] Brown] (1700–1756), mason, and his second wife, Ann, *née* Twigg (*d.* 1738). Richard [i], son of an earlier Richard and his wife Mary, *née* Frost, was the founder of the most important Derbyshire stoneworking firm; at the end of the eighteenth century it was one of the chief tourist attractions in Derbyshire.

Richard [i] was elected parish clerk of All Saints in 1727, the year when he was paid for masonry work in its churchyard. He married Sarah Ford on 20 October 1729 but she died the following month. On 15 April 1734 he married Ann Twigg, and in 1735 he advertised 'monuments or chimney pieces &c performed in Marble or Alabaster, likewise Grave Stones' (*Derby Mercury*, 17 April 1735). Ann was buried on 20 November 1738 and by 1745, when he made his will, he had married, third, Mary (*d.* 1785), probably from Draycot, Wilne. Richard [i] died in Derby of a violent fever on 3 January 1756 and was buried at All Saints three days later.

His son Richard [ii] Brown was immediately appointed parish clerk (despite much dispute, as he was still under age). Richard [ii] soon expanded the family business. His first recorded work was paving the floor of All Saints in 1759, which he renewed in 1782. On 7 January 1761 he married Ann Hind (*bap.* 23 Sept 1740) at Newtown Linford, Leicester, with whom he had six children, including **Richard** [iii] **Brown** (1765–1848). In 1759 work had started on Kedleston Hall, the most splendid Georgian house in Derbyshire, with which two generations of Browns were involved. By 1765 Richard [ii] was working in Blue John fluorspar, making the fine purple obelisks which survive there. He was now using as his workshop the 'Old Shop', part of the famous Old Derby Silk Mill. In 1768 Matthew Boulton wrote to John Whitehurst that only 'one person in Derby has it' (Craven, 77), referring to Brown's early domination of Blue John working.

Richard [ii] also worked Ashford black marble, selling this from at least 1772, and later his firm ran these works at Ashford. The antiquary William Bray reported in 1777 and 1783 on the marbles, spars, and petrifactions with which Brown worked in Derby, noting their ability to take a fine polish and to be shaped into beautiful vases, urns, pillars, columns, ornaments, and chimney pieces. From the 1780s Richard [ii] also traded in minerals, including among his customers Thomas Beddoes, Erasmus Darwin—who called him the 'fossil-philosopher of Derby' (*Letters*, 174)—Philip Rashleigh, Barthelmy Faujas de St Fond, Josiah Wedgwood, and other collectors of these popular curiosities. In his only known publication, *Catalogue of Minerals for Sale* (*c*.1797), Richard [ii] lists a wide variety of such materials. In April 1782 he was assigned a mortgage on Derby property through the offices of Samuel Mawe senior. In 1783 he witnessed the marriage of Mawe's son, Samuel junior, whose brother John he soon took into partnership.

The French geologist Faujas de St Fond confirmed that in 1784, when Richard [ii] was elected a member of the London-based Society for Promoting Natural History, his products were better worked, more finely polished, and sold at more reasonable prices than those made elsewhere in Derbyshire. By April 1785 Brown was in contact with his fellow mason White Watson (1760–1835), who soon started making inlaid tablets showing Derbyshire minerals in their correct stratigraphic order (as had been revealed by John Whitehurst in 1778). Both firms—Watson's, and Brown, Son, and Mawe—later made many such tablets, the latter in Derby 'from actual surveys by John Mawe' (Mawe, 14, 45). But not all visitors to Derby were impressed. John Byng (1742–1813) noted in 1789 that Brown, a 'pedantic puppy, keeps a spar-shop of useless ornaments' (Andrews, 2.62). By this date Brown was manufacturing large quantities of Derbyshire and foreign marble, and local alabaster (gypsum) and spar, making vases, obelisks, and ornaments for chimney pieces. His works then employed between eighty and ninety people, helped from the 1780s by a London showroom shared with William Duesbury, a Derby porcelain-maker. In 1796 Brown, Son, and Mawe opened a new alabaster quarry on the earl of Harrington's estate at Elvaston, near Shardlow, to better work the material which had earlier been used so effectively at Kedleston.

From 1787 to 1794 the firm was named Richard Brown & Son, Petrefactioners. Richard [iii] had by then joined the company, and in 1788 a cousin, John Tatlow (1757–1824), noted that the firm was expanding sales to Ireland. In 1793 Richard [ii] leased property at Old St Helens, Derby, and soon moved his manufacturing here. Late in 1794 the firm became Brown, Son, and Mawe, proprietors and manufacturers of Derbyshire spar ornaments. John Mawe (1766–1829), briefly apprenticed to the firm, married Richard

[ii]'s daughter Sarah (1767–1846) in 1794, and was immediately taken into partnership to run their London showroom and warehouse at 5 Tavistock Street, Covent Garden.

Charles Hatchett had in 1796 noted the 'novel, simple and ingenious machinery' for sawing and polishing marbles which Richard [ii] had introduced in Derby (Warner, 116). It was powered by a water-wheel 30 feet in diameter, using water from the River Derwent to turn one set of saws, two sets of polishing machines, and six or eight lathes. With such mechanization, the workforce had reduced to forty by 1802. Further works at Castleton had been established in 1800, and in 1802 Brown's lease on his part of the Silk Mill ended and he moved his Derby works to new premises at Old St Helen's House, King Street, with a separate warehouse. Here he erected spacious workshops, now powered by a 6 hp steam engine. In 1812 the firm's marble-polishing machinery was described in detail, the Browns having 'justly attained great celebrity as workers of spar and marble' (Rees).

In 1810 Richard [ii] Brown became part owner of the Heights of Abraham at Matlock, where he opened a commercial museum. In September 1815, however, he moved the greater part of his firm's machinery to locations elsewhere in Derbyshire, and put the Derby steam engine up for sale, while announcing that the chimney piece and ornamental trade there would continue. Richard [ii] was now nearly eighty. His will of April 1815 left all the estates to his eldest son, Richard [iii]. Richard [ii] died on 22 August 1816 at St Helens Street, and was buried at All Saints' Church on 26 August; his wife had predeceased him.

Richard [iii] Brown continued to improve the working of marble. He too served as parish clerk at All Saints until his resignation in 1795. He married Mary Cooper of Buxton at Bakewell on 12 December 1798; she died in September 1802 and on 27 May 1806 he married Sarah Eley of St Alkmund's, Derby, with whom he had a daughter. Grand Duke Nicholas Pavlovich of Russia visited the works in 1816, followed in 1818 by his brother Michael. In 1820 work started on the great north wing at Chatsworth, with Richard [iii] as the master mason. To aid this Richard purchased the Ashford black marble works, which he owned until 1831.

In 1828 Richard [iii] began to dispose of his assets. In March he auctioned thirty-seven Italian marble chimney pieces and in 1829 he sold his last scagliola items to Chatsworth. In 1832 the Derby marble works and its stock were offered at auction, Richard [iii] having 'decided to retire immediately' (*Derby Mercury*, 30 May and 13 June 1832). This nearly ended the family's direct connection with the century-old firm, but in 1832 Joseph Hall (1789–*c*.1850), husband of Ann, granddaughter of Richard [ii], a sculptor and mineralist who was then working for John Mawe in London and who had opened his own works in Derby, took over the Brown works, and he continued to run them until 1881.

Richard [iii] Brown died on 24 June 1848 at his house in St Helens Street, Derby, and was buried at All Saints on 1

July. When the will of his sister Sarah (Mawe) was proved in 1846, she was found to have left nearly £25,000, indicating the profits to be made, mostly in London, from the Derbyshire marble and spar trade. Conversely, Richard [iii], whose industry underpinned this trade, left less than £600.   H. S. TORRENS

Sources M. Craven, *John Whitehurst of Derby: clockmaker and scientist, 1713–88* (1996) • H. S. Torrens, 'Under royal patronage, the early work of John Mawe, 1766–1829, in geology and the background of his travel in Brazil, 1807–1810', *O conhecimento geologico na America Latina: trabalhos do I coloquio Brasileiro de histoira e teoria do conhecimento geologico* [Campinas 1988], ed. M. M. Lopes and S. F. de M. Figueira (1990), 103–13 • B. Faujas de St Fond, *A journey through England and Scotland … in 1784*, ed. A. Geikie, 2 vols. (1907) • J. Mawe, *The mineralogy of Derbyshire* (1802) • R. Warner, *A tour through the northern counties* (1802), 1.115–16 • J. Britton and others, *The beauties of England and Wales*, 3 (1802) • *The letters of Erasmus Darwin*, ed. D. King-Hele (1981) • C. B. Andrews, ed., *The Torrington diaries … between 1781 and 1794*, 2 (1935) • 'Marble, polishing of', A. Rees and others, *The cyclopaedia, or, Universal dictionary of arts, sciences, and literature*, 22 (1819) [2 pp. and pl.] • J. Gilpin, correspondence and diaries, Hist. Soc. Penn., Gilpin papers • J. M. Hedinger, *Description of Castleton*, 4th edn (1800) • J. C. Cox and W. H. S. Hope, *The chronicles of the collegiate church or free chapel of All Saints, Derby* (1881) • R. Gunnis, *Dictionary of British sculptors, 1660–1851*, new edn (1968) • S. Glover, *History of the county of Derby*, 2 vols. (1829–33), 1.597 • *Derby Mercury* (17 April 1735), notices; (9 Jan 1756); (29 Aug 1816); (30 May 1832); (13 June 1832); (28 June 1848) • furnishing account, 1821–39, Chatsworth House, Derbyshire • W. Adam, *The gem of the Peak*, 4th edn (1845); 5th edn (1851) • parish register, 5 June 1765, All Saints, Derby; 18 Feb 1700 [births]; 25 July 1736 [births]
Archives Chatsworth House, Derbyshire, letters • Kedleston Hall, Derbyshire, letters • Keele University, Wedgwood Archive, letters
Wealth at death under £1000: will • under £600—Richard [iii] Brown

Brown, Richard (1765–1848). *See under* Brown, Richard (1736–1816).

Brown, Robert. *See* Browne, Robert (*bap.* 1672, *d.* 1753).

Brown, Sir Robert, first baronet (*d.* 1760), politician and diplomatist, was the first son of William Brown, a London merchant, and his wife, Grisel Brice. As a young man he is said to have gone out to Venice with no other capital than a large second-hand wig, which he sold for £5. At Venice he amassed a fortune by successful trading, and for some years he held the office of British resident in the republic. He received a baronetcy from George II in March 1732. Writing to the earl of Essex, then ambassador at Turin, in May 1734, he said that he was about to be returned to parliament, that he was glad to say that his election would entail little expense or trouble on him, though he did not know for what place he would be put up.

Brown returned to England, and was elected one of the members for Ilchester, Somerset, on 30 August 1734; he retained his seat during that parliament and the succeeding one summoned in 1741. He was a loyal supporter of the whig government; Lord Egmont described him as 'a very devoted man to Sir Robert Walpole'. From 1741 to July 1742 he held office as paymaster of the king's works. He continued to support the whig government after Walpole's fall, and left the Commons at the 1747 election.

Brown married Margaret Cecil, the granddaughter of

Sir Robert Brown, first baronet (*d.* 1760), attrib. Jonathan Richardson the elder, 1730s

the third earl of Salisbury and the daughter of Robert Cecil MP, with whom he had two, or, according to Horace Walpole, three, daughters who died before their parents. Lady Brown had a reputation for being a woman of wit and fashion. According to Charles Burney:

> Lady Brown gave the first private concerts under the direction of the Count of Germain; she held them on Sunday evenings, at the risk of her windows. She was an enemy of Handel and a patroness of the Italian style.

Walpole records a bitter retort she made on Lady Townshend (*Memoirs*, 2.58, n. 5), and sneers at her 'Sunday nights' as 'the great mart for all travelling and travelled calves' (*Correspondence*, 9.15, 18.66, 30.84). Sir Robert's reputation was more for avarice, a characteristic seen, according to Walpole, in his treatment of his eldest daughter. When she was ordered to ride for the benefit of her health, Brown drew a map marking all the by-lanes, so as to avoid the turnpikes on which tolls were levied. When she was dying, he bargained with the undertaker about her funeral, urging the man to name a low sum by claiming that she might recover. He died on 5 October 1760, leaving everything, even, Walpole believed, his avarice, to his widow. Lady Brown died in 1782.

WILLIAM HUNT, *rev.* PHILIP CARTER

Sources S. Matthews, 'Brown, Sir Robert', HoP, *Commons* • Walpole, *Corr.* • Burney, *Hist. mus.*, vol. 4 • H. Walpole, *Memoirs of King George II*, ed. J. Brooke, 3 (1985)
Likenesses attrib. J. Richardson the elder, portrait, 1730–39, Hatfield House, Hertfordshire [*see illus.*]

Brown, Robert (1757–1831), writer on agriculture, was born on 27 August 1757 in East Linton, Haddingtonshire, Scotland. He entered into business in East Linton but soon turned to farming, which he carried on first at West Fortune and afterwards at Markle, where he conducted several important experiments. He was a close friend of George Rennie. He published *A General View of the Agriculture of the West Riding of Yorkshire* (1799), with Rennie and John Shirreff, and *A Treatise on Rural Affairs* (1811), dedicated to Sir John Sinclair, president of the board of agriculture, with whom he corresponded for many years. In this he advocated ploughing all uncultivated fields to keep the soil clean and rich. He wrote many articles under the name of Verus in the Edinburgh *Farmer's Magazine*, a quarterly journal of which he was the first editor (1800–14). Some of these articles were translated into French and German. A collection of his newspaper articles was reprinted in *Letters on the Distressed State of Agriculturalists* (1816). He also contributed to the *Edinburgh Encyclopaedia*. Brown died at Drylaw, East Lothian on 14 February 1831, and was buried in the churchyard at East Linton.

WILLIAM HUNT, *rev.* ANNE PIMLOTT BAKER

Sources GM, 1st ser., 101/2 (1831), 647 · Anderson, *Scot. nat.* · W. F. Gray and J. H. Jamieson, *East Lothian biographies* (1941)

Brown, Robert (1773–1858), botanist, was born at Montrose on 21 December 1773, second and only surviving son of the Revd James Brown (1734?–1791), an Episcopalian, and his wife, Helen, daughter of Robert Taylor, a Presbyterian minister. After beginning his education at home, Brown attended the grammar school (subsequently Montrose Academy) and, from 1787 to 1790, Marischal College, Aberdeen, where he was awarded an annual Ramsay bursary three times. He initially studied philosophy, and in 1788–9 mathematics, and he probably also attended botany lecturers given by unofficial lecturers in the college, which had a strong tradition in the subject.

Without taking a degree, Brown moved with his parents to Edinburgh where his father became pastor of the dissenters and, in an apparently illegal action, was consecrated bishop by Bishop Rose at Down. Brown studied medicine at Edinburgh University from 1790 but also attended the natural history lectures of John Walker, and assembled a herbarium of Scottish plants. In August 1791 he accompanied George Don (1764–1814) on one of Don's highland expeditions to collect plants. The expedition led to his presenting a paper on the flora of Angus to the Edinburgh Natural History Society: in its preparation he corresponded with William Withering, who acknowledged Brown's findings in print. The paper (unpublished until 1871) showed remarkable insights, with suggestions for physiological experiments as well as discussing taxonomic issues. Brown made several more highland journeys and began drawing up descriptions of plants both wild and cultivated, two activities which were to stand him in good stead in his botanical career.

Brown discontinued his medical studies in 1793 and, after his highland journey of the following year, enlisted in the Fife fencibles, being appointed surgeon's mate in June 1795 and posted to Ireland. Between his apparently rather leisurely duties there he botanized and corresponded with Withering. Visiting Withering while on

Robert Brown (1773–1858), by Henry William Pickersgill, *c.*1835

leave, Brown was provided with an introduction to the Portuguese botanist José Francisco Correia de Serra, who was then working in the herbarium of Sir Joseph Banks.

About 1798 Banks was planning to send Mungo Park, a schoolfriend of Brown, to Port Jackson, New South Wales, to lead a scientific expedition to the interior. Park eventually declined the appointment because he wished to marry and stay in Britain and so, in October 1798, Correia wrote to Banks on Brown's behalf, proposing that Brown be Park's replacement. In the event, Brown was sent to England to lead a recruiting party for the fencibles. However, the posting did allow him to meet Banks in London.

Returning to Ireland in 1799, Brown continued his self-education over a wide range of scientific and literary topics. He trained himself in microscopy as well as continuing botanical fieldwork (discovering a number of mosses new to science), meeting the Irish botanical establishment, and corresponding with James Dickson, Park's brother-in-law. Brown's (unacknowledged) manuscript descriptions of cryptogams were published in Dickson's *Fasciculi plantarum cryptogamicarum Britanniae* (1801) and Dickson commemorated him in the name of a minute moss, now called *Tetrodontium brownianum*.

Australian travels In 1800 the Admiralty learned that the French were mounting an expedition to the south Pacific and Matthew Flinders persuaded Banks that this would give the opportunity to send a British expedition to ascertain whether New Holland was one or several islands. The French sailed in October and the Admiralty approved Banks's plan to survey the Australian coast. In December

Banks offered Brown the position of naturalist on a voyage to be commanded by Flinders: Brown accepted by return of post and reached Banks's house on Christmas day 1800. After some negotiation Brown was able to retain his fencibles commission and was to receive, additionally, £420. Brown was to oversee collecting of animals, rocks, and plants, supported by the artist Ferdinand Bauer, the gardener Peter Good, and a miner, John Allen.

Flinders's ship, HMS *Investigator*, now with a prefabricated plant house on board, was delayed at Portsmouth and Brown began working on a herbarium of Australian plants he had made from Banks's collections. The ship finally left on 18 July 1801 but within a few days was leaking. At Madeira, their first port of call, Brown prepared a list of local plants. Though they visited Bujio in the Desertas by cutter, their Madeira visit was marred by lack of proper guides and the loss of most of their collections. They revictualled at the Cape of Good Hope, where Brown and his team collected many plants, insects, and minerals, and ascended Table Mountain. They left on 4 November and sighted Australia some two months later; during the voyage Brown was able to build up a set of some 6000 plant descriptions. With the *Investigator* anchored in King George Sound, western Australia, the scientific party collected some 500 plant species (almost all new to science) in three weeks. At this first anchorage, Brown made notes of the Aborigines' language, which he was to do at later sites too, while Good was set to collecting live plants for Kew Gardens.

The *Investigator* next surveyed Australia's south coast, calling at Lucky Bay and the Recherche archipelago; the tally of plant species climbed to some 700 before it reached New South Wales. The expedition was the first in south Australia, with Brown reaching the top of what was subsequently named Mount Brown in the Flinders ranges near Port Augusta. On 8 April 1802 they met the French expedition with the botanist Jean Leschenault de la Tour at Encounter Bay near present-day Adelaide. Continuing eastwards, Brown was the first botanist to reach Victoria, and King Island gave him more species than any other visited. Flinders now knew that there was no strait dividing Australia and he pressed on to Port Jackson, New South Wales, which was reached on 9 May 1802. Collecting continued there but the original plan to circumnavigate Australia clockwise was now reversed. The prefabricated plant house was erected on the quarter-deck, but was cut down to two-thirds of its planned size because of the weight of earth, the living plants already collected being planted in the governor's garden.

The *Investigator*, together with the *Lady Nelson*, left Port Jackson on 21 July 1802, to explore the Queensland coast. As they picked their way to Torres Strait the *Investigator*'s leakiness increased and the *Lady Nelson* was sent back. The Gulf of Carpentaria was virgin botanizing for Brown but, though noting the red cliffs at Pera Head, he missed the greatest bauxite deposits in Queensland as no minerals were collected there. The ship was by now leaking badly but, rather than retrace his route, Flinders pressed on. Brown made florulae of the islands visited in the gulf, but

the health of the crew began to deteriorate. Flinders reached Timor in March 1803 and the dash back to Port Jackson began on 8 April. When they arrived in June the ship was condemned. Flinders was to go to England on the *Porpoise* and return with a fresh ship to complete the survey. Brown and Bauer successfully petitioned him to let them stay in New South Wales. The plant house was erected on the *Porpoise*, and the top set of Brown's specimens was also transferred to her. However, on 10 August the vessel was wrecked on a reef off the Queensland coast and the specimens were lost. (Flinders returned to Sydney to sail in the *Cumberland* to England but he was detained by the French in Mauritius and did not finally get home until October 1810.) Brown sent his second set of specimens to England on the *Calcutta*—they arrived there in July 1804. Meanwhile, Brown collected in the Kent group and Van Diemen's Land, which he visited twice and where he made detailed observations of the Aborigines and found 300 plant species. Brown was with the governor when the colony was moved to what is now Hobart. He ascended Mount Wellington ten times and carried out much original exploration on the island, where he is commemorated in the name of Browns River near Hobart. He collected 540 plant species in Van Diemen's Land, about a hundred of which were new to science. A number of these were subsequently successfully introduced to Britain, via Kew. Brown later based himself in Kingstown, New South Wales, from where he undertook botanical exploration of the Hunter River basin.

Brown left Australia with Bauer on 24 May 1805 aboard the refitted *Investigator* carrying the 1200 plant gatherings made since Flinders's departure, the seeds, and all the mineral and animal collections, but leaving the living plants in the care of George Caley (1770–1829). On the voyage Brown worked on a study set of specimens; he reached Liverpool on 13 October 1805. The expedition had collected some 3600 plant gatherings (3200 different) from Australia and 200 from Timor. The zoological collections included a live wombat, but only the birds and insects were subsequently worked on systematically. The botanical collections were to occupy Brown throughout his career and provided the touchstone for major advances in cytology and palynology as well as in systematics and biogeography.

The Linnean Society On 17 December 1805 Brown was appointed clerk, librarian, and housekeeper to the Linnean Society of London, at a salary of £100. His duties were very light and, through Banks's influence, he also continued to receive a salary (£378 in 1808) from the Admiralty to continue working up the expedition materials for publication. By 6 January 1810, Brown had described 2200 plant species, more than 1700 of them new. Influenced by the work of Adanson and Gaertner, and particularly Correia, Brown espoused the natural system of classification, though he had used the artificial Linnaean one as a convenient filing system for plants as they were gathered on the voyage.

The first paper to result from the Australian expedition was Brown's magisterial paper on Proteaceae (1810), which was prompted by William Townsend Aiton's wish to use Brown's new names in a new edition of *Hortus Kewensis* (1810–13). Brown's monograph drew on his knowledge of almost 200 species of Proteaceae in the field and his microscopic skill in investigating features of the ovules and pollen (while stressing the significance of developmental studies); together with his other publications of March to April 1810 it confirmed him as a brilliant botanist. Some of the taxonomic work was pre-empted by Richard Salisbury who had been working on Proteaceae for some years and amended his work to take account of Brown's findings before those were published; this led to their falling out and a lifelong bitterness.

It had generally been agreed that work on Australian plants would not be published in Britain until Brown's work was ready; a prodromus (to get priority over the French) was distributed at the end of March 1810. Using the natural system, the *Prodromus florae Novae Hollandiae et Insulae Van Diemen* covered ferns, monocotyledons, and thirty-seven families of dicotyledons, plus the cycads. In it Brown established many new families and covered 464 genera (187 new) and about 1000 species. It was ecstatically received by European botanists and for fifty years was considered 'the greatest botanical work that has ever appeared' (Joseph Hooker, 1859). There were only 250 copies printed; it was a small unfinished, unillustrated, unindexed, and, at 18*s*., expensive volume, on bad paper and poorly printed: Brown distributed it himself and booksellers' sales were derisory. Despite the good reception of the *Prodromus*, neither the rest of the book (one of two volumes in Latin originally planned) nor the projected illustrated flora was ever published, though much original work on Australian plants, particularly Leguminosae, appeared in Brown's contributions to Aiton's *Hortus Kewensis*. Apparently now without Banks's support for further work, Brown toyed with emigrating but Banks's librarian, Jonas Dryander (1748–1810), died and Brown not only took over the editing of Aiton's *Hortus Kewensis* from him but also became librarian at a salary of £200 (in addition to his Linnean salary of £100 for only eight hours' attendance over two days a week). He was elected FRS in 1811 but even so seems to have considered resuming a medical career in 1812.

Brown's 'General remarks' appeared in the appendix to Flinders's account of the *Investigator* voyage (1814). It was a pioneering work in plant geography as well as providing interpretations of the flowers in *Euphorbia* and *Eucalyptus*. Increasingly sympathetic to the French school, Brown took up work on the *Prodromus* again; he met Alexander von Humboldt in Paris in 1816 and later provided him with phytogeographical facts. A major paper on Compositae (1817), based largely on his Australian experiences, and another (1818) on seeds, stressing the significance of developmental anatomy, confirmed his pre-eminence as the country's greatest botanical practitioner. As custodian of Banks's herbarium he saw all new plant collections, and he published an important account of the flora of the Congo in 1818—its phytogeographical observations were much to influence Charles Darwin's thought—as well as

papers on materials collected in Ethiopia (Salt, 1814), China (Abel, 1818), and the Arctic regions (Ross, Scoresby, Franklin, and Parry, 1819–23).

In 1819 Brown was encouraged to accept the chair of botany at Edinburgh University, which offered to bend every regulation to secure his services at £1200 a year for three months' residence, but he was made Banks's legatee and consequently declined. He also declined the chair at Glasgow, so making way for William Jackson Hooker. When Banks died the Banksian collections were bequeathed to the trustees of the British Museum but with a life interest for Brown, who was also to have a £200 annuity (not always received). He gave up the clerk and housekeeper parts of his Linnean duties but remained librarian, with undiminished salary. The society subleased part of Banks's house, Brown receiving rent and remaining in the Dean Street side: he lived on the ground floor at no. 17 in what had been the coach house and stables under Banks's library and study. He resigned as Linnean librarian in 1822 and declined the post of honorary secretary in 1825. However, he now had under one roof the greatest herbarium in the world and Banks's unrivalled library of books and drawings. He also had the collaboration of Ferdinand Bauer's brother, Franz (1758–1840), at Kew, to which Banks had intended Brown to be (in effect) botanical consultant.

Further research and the post-Banks years Brown received many honours including the silver Banksian medal of the Horticultural Society (1821), honorary membership of the Royal Society of Edinburgh (1825), membership of the Royal Swedish Academy of Sciences, and the Royal Society of Denmark. He was the centre of a network of correspondence ranging all over Europe and oversaw plant collections pouring in from South America, China, and the Pacific. His research continued unabated and in an important work (1821) on the sensational parasitic *Rafflesia* of Sumatra he discusses the homology of floral parts and alludes to the fact that what are now called gymnosperms do not enclose the ovules before fertilization. This was followed up by work on new material from Australia appended to which, as was his wont, were two fundamental contributions on the development of ovules and especially the distinction between angiosperms and gymnosperms. This was extended in a further paper on *Rafflesia*, read in 1834, where the nature of gymnospermy was set out. Brown's work was most respected on the continent and a reprint of his works, including the *Prodromus*, was published in Germany (1825–34); Brown himself undertook many continental journeys in the summer, botanizing, distributing his publications, and sightseeing. At home, however, his increasingly obsessive perfectionism led to frustration from editors and compilers of travel works in which many of his most original findings were published.

Brown's financial uncertainty after Banks's death may have been the stimulus for him to enter into negotiations with the trustees of the British Museum over the future of the Banksian herbarium and library. At the same time, the University of London was being founded and Brown was offered the chair of botany, but accepting that post would have ended his annuity. Driving a hard bargain with the trustees, Brown was appointed to the new post of under-librarian with a salary of £200 for attendance of two days a week and up to £150 for up to two more with a fourteen-week summer vacation. He had exclusive control of the botanical collections (the Banksian department) and access to the library, permission to continue collaboration with Kew, and £150 salary for an assistant (John Joseph Bennett) to attend five days a week. Thus was established for the first time in Britain a nationally owned botanical collection of world importance, available to the public, albeit under conditions extremely favourable to Brown; the collections were moved to the museum at Montagu House in the winter of 1827–8.

Microscopical discoveries At the height of the negoti-ations, Brown was making microscopical discoveries, finding moving bodies (about 1 micrometre in diameter) in the pollen grains of *Clarkia*, which he at first associated with the 'vital force' in fertilization. However, after observing the bodies in dried material, he assumed they were the elementary particles of organic matter, but he later also saw them in glass and metals. By contrast with his tardily produced floristic papers, his findings were announced in a rapidly printed, privately circulated pamphlet (1828), which caused sufficient stir so as to be mentioned in George Eliot's *Middlemarch*. Brown demon-strated the phenomenon to the Deutscher Naturforscher Versammlung at Heidelberg in 1829. The bodies were in fact artefacts and had been noted (obscurely) by Ingen Housz in 1784, but Brown's careful extended work dis-pelled the animist view of the construction of organic material. However, the true significance of what became known as Brunonian or Brownian motion or movement was not realized until long afterwards by physicists and mathematicians.

Continuing to incorporate his findings, as they occurred, in otherwise pedestrian papers, often on the plants collected on Flinders's voyage, Brown developed his ideas on pollination and fertilization, the presence of a nucleus in each cell, and the phenomenon of cytoplasmic streaming, but again published his most pregnant find-ings in a pamphlet (1831). He traced pollen tubes to the micropyle of the ovule in orchids and asclepiads and in *Cypripedium* noted the ubiquity of the nucleus (a term he coined) in plant cells (a phenomenon not confirmed in animals until much later). In *Tradescantia*, he described what is now called meiosis, as well as cytoplasmic stream-ing in its staminal hairs. All these observations were made using simple microscopes. He demonstrated streaming to Charles Darwin who went to sit with him for training in microscopy and who much later was to build on Brown's pioneering work on pollination and fertilization. Brown, again using his simple microscopes, also helped James Paget to investigate trichinosis.

Recognition and later life In 1827 Brown was appointed vice-president of the Linnean Society. He was a member of the Raleigh Club which drew up a constitution for what

became the Geographical Society; he served on the soci-ety's first council. Brown was cited by David Brewster, reviewing Charles Babbage's *Reflections on the Decline of Sci-ence* (1830), as an example of eminent but underhonoured scientists in Britain. He was with the radicals supporting Herschel in the contested presidency of the Royal Society that year and was on the council of the British Association for the Advancement of Science. At the association's Oxford meeting of 1832 Brown, together with Dalton, Brewster, and Faraday, was given an honorary DCL. He was elected foreign associate of the Academy of Sciences of the Institute of France in March 1833, beating Faraday, Herschel, and Oersted among others, and by the 1840s almost all the scientific societies in Europe had honoured him. He was awarded the Copley medal of the Royal Soci-ety for his work on fertilization and embryology, given the honorary degree of LLB at Glasgow (1834), and the free-dom of the cities of Edinburgh and Glasgow.

With advancing age Brown's output slowed, to the increasing frustration of collaborators. In 1837 the find-ings of a select committee on the museum led to the ban-ning of the holding of external posts, so that Brown lost any possibility of gaining control of Kew Gardens. In 1840 another committee examined Kew as part of a review of royal expenses and in 1847 commissioners were appoin-ted to look once more into the museum. Brown had had the herbarium, the last of Banks's legacy at Kew, moved to the museum in 1840 and he now resisted amalgamation of his department with Kew, citing the inadequacy of the lib-rary there. By the time of Brown's death, even the protag-onists of amalgamation realized Brown was right to oppose them.

Meantime Brown's scientific interests turned increas-ingly to palaeobotany; in 1836 he made a fossil-hunting expedition to Burgundy. He also received many fossils including, from Darwin, gymnospermous wood from Val-paraiso. His caution, however, led to his publishing very little on fossils. His most important contribution was his paper on what became known as 'Brown's cone' (1847)—the strobilus of *Lepidodendron brownii*. His interests remained broad, for he was carrying out experiments on the viability of seeds and writing on the Sargasso Sea; by 1856 he was entertaining the notion of some form of grad-ual evolution.

Brown declined to be nominated as president of the Royal Society and, repeatedly, the Linnean, but eventually acceded to presidency of the latter in 1849. The society took a lease of Soho Square in 1851 and Brown now sublet. He declined a civil-list pension of £200 and until his death occupied Banks's old sitting-room, crowded with books and specimens, still carrying out his duties at the museum at the age of eighty-four. In the spring of 1858 he suc-cumbed to bronchitis and, declining further medication, died on the morning of 10 June 1858. He was buried at Kensal Green cemetery on 15 June.

Brown's death led to an extra meeting of the Linnean Society at which the papers by Darwin and Wallace on evo-lution were presented, precipitating Darwin into publish-ing his long-delayed work as the *Origin of Species* (1859).

Brown left estate worth £12,000 and, after bequests to his former housekeeper, Louisa Harris, and to Sylvia, the daughter of John Porter, his servant on the *Investigator*, the bulk went to his assistant at the museum, Bennett, who published an almost comprehensive collection of Brown's writings (1866-8). On Bennett's death in 1876, Brown's herbarium was incorporated in that of the Natural History Museum and duplicates sent to institutions all over Europe, though his fossil collection and drawings by Ferdinand Bauer had already gone directly to the museum. Much of his library and miscellaneous specimens were sold, the lots often for trifling amounts. As well as in geographical features in Australia, Brown is commemorated in Mount Brown in the Rockies and in scores of names of plants and animals, mostly from Australia.

Character Brown was a little spare man with high principles but a retiring disposition. When old he had a heavy lower lip and jaw, dressed in dingy black clothes, and walked with his head down. When sure of his company he was generous and witty, though often sarcastic, but had a deep distrust of politicians and was a religious sceptic. Brown's wide interests included painting and music and his knowledge of scientific literature was prodigious, but he jealously guarded his scientific findings and was frustratingly cautious in publishing them, wishing never to make a mistake in print. His procrastination may have been due to the perfectionism of an obsessional personality and his 'constitutional idleness' perhaps an illness during periods of stress, possibly a psychoneurosis. With advancing age he was increasingly out of sympathy with much of the botanical establishment which was by then absorbed in supplying scientific expertise for colonial expansion and popular horticulture. To the end he maintained a strong interest in all technological advances including photography, railways, telegraphs, and the displays, particularly Australian, at the great exhibitions. Although shy with women there is evidence that Brown proposed to Frances Leonora (Fanny) Macleay about 1815, an attachment not acceptable to her mother Eliza; Fanny left England with her father, Alexander Macleay, when he was appointed colonial secretary in New South Wales. In later life Brown was much attached to Louisa Harris of Islington. Joseph Hooker considered him a miser but, when old, Brown supported John Porter and read aloud to him daily.

Brown was concerned perhaps largely for his own well-being, but the result was part of the professionalization of science, as his work ensured the setting up for the first time of a department of botanists in the state's employ. He saw no division between experimental and descriptive botany and was praised first in France, then in Germany, many of his advances being due to his unparalleled use of the microscope. His failure to complete an Australian flora was at odds with the colonial cataloguing favoured by his former protégés, but through his profound insights he had a greater influence on the advance of plant science in the broad sense than did any other nineteenth-century British botanist.   D. J. MABBERLEY

Sources D. J. Mabberley, *Jupiter botanicus: Robert Brown of the British Museum* (1985) • T. G. Vallance, 'Jupiter Botanicus in the bush: Robert Brown's Australian field-work, 1801-1805', *Proceedings of the Linnean Society of New South Wales*, 112 (1990), 49-86 • D. J. Mabberley, 'Robert Brown on *Pterocymbium*', *Archives of Natural History*, 13 (1986), 307-12 • E. Windschuttle, *Taste and science: the women of the MacLeay family, 1790-1850* (1988) • B. G. Gardiner, 'The homes of the Linnean Society', *The Linnean*, 4/2 (1988), 23-33 • M. F. Brown, 'Robert Brown', *The Linnean*, 4/3 (1988), 38-43 • R. Desmond, *Kew: the history of the Royal Botanic Gardens* (1995)

Archives BL, corresp. and papers, Add. MSS 32439-32441, 33227 • NHM, diaries and papers | Linn. Soc., letters to Sir James E. Smith • NHM, letters to members of the Sowerby family • Oxf. U. Mus. NH, letters to J. O. Westwood • RBG Kew, letters to Sir William Hooker

Likenesses H. W. Pickersgill, oils, *c*.1835, Linn. Soc., NPG [*see illus.*] • W. Brockedon, chalk drawing, 1849, NPG • T. H. Maguire, lithograph, 1851, BM, NPG • R. C. Lucas, wax medallion, 1852, RBG Kew • S. Pearce, oils, *c*.1856, RBG Kew • Polyblank, photograph, 1857, repro. in Mabberley, *Jupiter Botanicus*, fig. 61 • P. Slater, marble bust, 1859, Linn. Soc. • H. W. Pickersgill, oils, copy, NG Ire. • J. F. Skill, J. Gilbert, and E. Walker, group portrait, pencil and wash (*Men of science living in 1807-08*), NPG • marble bust, Montrose; copy, Aberdeen • oils (Brown as a young man?), NHM

Wealth at death under £12,000: probate, 30 June 1858, *CGPLA Eng. & Wales*

Brown, Robert (*c*.1792-1846). *See under* Brown, Hugh Stowell (1823-1886).

Brown, Robert (1842-1895), geographer, the only son of Thomas Brown of Campster, Caithness, was born at Campster on 23 March 1842. He is sometimes known humorously as Robert Brown 'Campsterianus' to distinguish him from the other geographer and botanist Robert Brown (1773-1858). He was educated at the University of Edinburgh, where he graduated BA in 1860, and afterwards at Leiden, Copenhagen, and Rostock, where he gained the honorary degree of PhD in 1870. In 1861 he visited Svalbard, Greenland, and Baffin Bay, and in the next two years he visited the Pacific and travelled in North and South America. He was botanist to the British Columbia expedition in 1863 and led the Vancouver Island exploration of 1864, when the interior of the island was charted for the first time under his supervision. His report on Vancouver was published in 1865.

With the mountaineer Edward Whymper, he visited Greenland in 1867 to investigate its natural history and glaciers. His views on the glacial origins of fjords (described in the *Journal of the Royal Geographical Society*, 39, 1859, 121-31; 41, 1861, 348-60) were substantially correct, but aroused opposition at the time. Through his detailed empirical observations and a refusal to align himself dogmatically with either catastrophists or uniformitarians he made a useful contribution to glaciology.

After travelling in north-west Africa, he settled at Edinburgh in 1869 and became lecturer in natural history at the School of Arts, later called Heriot-Watt College. He was also lecturer at the university in medicine, botany, and geology, and published memoirs on botany and geography in the *Transactions* of the Linnean and Royal Geographical societies. In 1873 he failed to secure the chair of botany at the University of Edinburgh; this failure depressed him and led him to turn from serious science to popular literature and journalism.

He wrote for various reference works and for the *Academy* and *Scotsman*. In 1876 he moved to London to take up a post with the *Echo*. In 1879 he became a leader writer for the *Standard*, a post which he kept until his death. His popular works included *The Races of Mankind* (4 vols., 1873–6), *The Countries of the World* (6 vols., 1876–81), *Science for All* (5 vols., 1877–82), *Our Earth and its Story* (2 vols., 1887–8, based on Alfred Kirchhoff's *Unser Wissen von der Erde: allgemeine Erdkunde*), and *The Story of Africa and its Explorers* (4 vols., 1892–5). These were mostly issued in weekly or monthly parts and, with their numerous illustrations, proved popular. Brown's more serious works included *A Manual of Botany* (1874), a compilation of his papers previously published in the journals of learned societies, and his translations and editions of works by H. J. Rink—*Tales and Traditions of the Eskimo* (1875) and *Danish Greenland* (1877); the latter has a scholarly botanical appendix by Brown. He also published works on Morocco, where he travelled in his later years.

Brown died suddenly at his home, Fersley, Rydale Road, Streatham, on 26 October 1895 and was buried at Norwood cemetery on 30 October. He left a widow, Augusta, of whom nothing more is known. He was for nearly thirty years fellow of the Royal Geographical Society and served on its council. He was also president of the Royal Physical Society of Edinburgh, vice-president of the Institute of Journalists, and fellow of many other learned societies. He is commemorated by Brown's Range, Mount Brown, and Brown's River in Vancouver Island, and by Cape Brown in Svalbard and Brown Island north of Novaya Zemlya, as well as by two flowering plants, two lichens, and a fossil plant. Despite these lasting testimonies, his promising early work, and his familiarity with German scientific advances, Brown's contribution to the new geography, then just being established in Britain, was slight. By turning to popular writing he achieved immediate success at the price of lasting fame. His obituarist in the *Geographical Journal* described him as genial and kindly, and remarked that he retained to the end his love of botany and geography, which circumstance did not allow him fully to develop.

THOMAS SECCOMBE, *rev.* ELIZABETH BAIGENT

Sources *GJ*, 6 (1895), 577–8 · RGS · *The Times* (29 Oct 1895) · Boase, *Mod. Eng. biog.* · J. Jewitt, *The adventures of John Jewitt* (1896) · *CGPLA Eng. & Wales* (1896)
Archives British Columbia Archives and Records, Canada, corresp., journal, and papers · RGS · Scott Polar RI, corresp. and journals
Likenesses portrait, repro. in Jewitt, *Adventures of John Jewitt*
Wealth at death £4438 2s. 2d.: probate, 2 Jan 1896, *CGPLA Eng. & Wales*

Brown, Robert Urquhart (1906–1972), piper, piobaireachd player, and teacher, was born on 1 May 1906 in Strachan, Kincardineshire, son of Francis Farquharson Brown (1875–1955?) head keeper of Blackhall estate, and his wife, Margaret Dunbar (1871–1937). He was educated at Banchory Academy. He started piping at the age of eleven, and

soon showed a love for piobaireachd, the classical music of the highland bagpipe. His early tutors were Jonathan Ewing, Peter Ewen, and George S. Allan. In 1925 Brown was invited by Douglas Ramsay, factor of the Balmoral estate, to enter royal service as a piper and gamekeeper. Apart from four years in Fairburn, Ross-shire, after his marriage on 15 November 1928 to Annie Fairlie Abercrombie (*b.* 1907), housekeeper, and service in the Second World War as pipe major in the Gordon Highlanders (seeing action at the battle of El Alamein and in Normandy), he remained at Balmoral for the rest of his life.

Brown's enthusiasm for piobaireachd was nurtured at Balmoral. George V wanted his pipers to have the best tuition, so Brown and his lifelong friend and colleague Robert Nicol were sent to the foremost authority, John MacDonald of Inverness. Each year, from 1928 to 1939, they went for up to eight weeks of intensive study with MacDonald. They each took different tunes, so that when they returned home they could teach one another, so maximizing their repertory. MacDonald influenced Brown hugely, and Brown was to have a similar effect on his own pupils, thus contributing to the continuity and spread of piobaireachd. Bob Brown's gift was to bring piobaireachd alive. Straightforward tunes, such as the 'Lament for Mary MacLeod', 'Tulloch Ard', or 'The Gathering of Clan Chattan', sang out from his clear, sweet-sounding pipe, and complex pieces like 'The King's Taxes', 'Lament for Patrick Og MacCrimmon', or 'The Unjust Incarceration' became yet more powerful thanks to his sure touch, fluency, and definition of melody and phrase. He won all the major piobaireachd prizes, including both Highland Society of London gold medals (Inverness, 1928; Oban, 1931), the clasp (Inverness, 1947, 1951), and the Gillies cup in London eleven times. He was made MBE in 1968.

From the 1950s Brown became an inspirational and generous teacher, attracting pipers from around the world to his home, Garbh Allt Shiel. He believed that the music of piobaireachd could remain pure only if it was sung from teacher to pupil down the generations, and so he taught as he had been taught, by singing. He insisted that the pupil concentrate on 'the song', using the written music only as a guide. He talked of contrast, balance, 'scansion', and playing from the heart. In this way he made the complex idiom that is piobaireachd seem more simple. He broadcast frequently, made three records and many informal recordings; the best have been reissued on compact disc.

Brown was a warm and unassuming man, with a deep love and understanding of nature. He had two daughters and a son; the latter was also a piper. After he retired, Brown gave masterclasses and recitals in the USA, Canada, South Africa, New Zealand, and Australia. He died at his home, Riverside Cottage, Balmoral, on 24 April 1972. At his burial in Crathie churchyard Robert Nicol played 'Lament for Donald Ban MacCrimmon'.

JACK LORIMER TAYLOR

Sources [P. Graham and B. MacRae], eds., *The Gordon highlanders pipe music collection*, 2 (1985) · private information (2004) · personal knowledge (2004) · J. MacFadyen, 'The glen is mine: a tribute to R. U. Brown', BBC Scotland, June 1972 [radio programme] ·

J. Pincet, *Highland bagpipe music from Brittany, Scotland, Ireland*, 2 [n.d.] • m. cert. • disc notes, *Bagpipe memories: the cairn on the hill. Piping by P/M R. U. Brown* (Frontrow, 1972) [LP recording] • disc notes, *Robert U. Brown and Robert B. Nicol* (Greentrax, 1998), vol. 1 of *Masters of piobaireachd* [CDTRAX153, LP recording]

Archives SOUND priv. coll.

Likenesses photographs, repro. in Gordon highlanders, *Pipe music collection*, pp. xxv–xxviii • photographs, repro. in *Masters of piobaireachd* [CD-ROM sleeve notes]

Brown, Rosalind Mabel Haig (1872–1964). *See under* Brown, William Haig (1823–1907).

Brown, Samuel. *See* Browne, Samuel (d. 1698).

Brown, Sir Samuel (1776–1852), civil engineer and naval officer, was born in London, the eldest son of William Brown of Borland, Galloway, and his wife, a daughter of the Revd Robert Hogg, of Roxburgh. Brown entered the navy as an able seaman in June 1795, serving with distinction during the Napoleonic wars from that year. He was commissioned in 1800 and, as lieutenant on the *Phoenix* in 1806, was involved in a furious engagement, culminating in the surrender of the frigate *Le Didon*. He was promoted commander in 1811, a rank he held until his retirement as captain in 1842. On 14 August 1822 he married Mary, daughter of John Horne of Edinburgh, writer to the signet. In January 1835 he was made a knight of the Royal Guelphic Order (3rd class) and became a knight bachelor in 1838.

Brown's naval career ran concurrently with his engineering interests. In 1816 he installed a machine in his own workshops for the testing of chain cables, the first of its kind. Cables for the steamship *Great Eastern* were made at his works in Pontypridd. He took out patents relating to iron chains and cables, and his work led to the introduction of chain cables into the navy. Brown's prototype bridge of 105 foot span, incorporating innovative eye-bar links for a suspension bridge of 1000 foot span, so impressed Telford that he modified his design for the Menai Bridge accordingly. Brown's concept was used on the Union Bridge across the Tweed near Berwick, completed in 1820, the first major construction of a suspension bridge of this type. A picture of this bridge by Alexander Nasmyth is in the possession of the Royal Society of Arts. Overambitious technically, Brown's design for the Runcorn project embodied stresses double those of Telford's and led to disagreements over the form of the project.

Brown was involved in the erection of a pier at Newhaven, near Edinburgh; a bridge at West Boat, near Hexham, and the supply of ironwork for Hammersmith Bridge. In 1823 he constructed the chain pier at Brighton in the conventional catenary form. On 5 December 1896 it was destroyed in a storm. In 1824–5 he prepared specifications for a suspension bridge over the River Esk at Montrose, and a patent wrought-iron suspension bridge over the Thames, just below the Tower, which was not built. Brown died on 13 March 1852 at Vanburgh Lodge, Blackheath, Kent, leaving a widow but no children.

B. P. CRONIN

Sources engineers' notebooks, Inst. CE, John James collection • E. C. Smith, 'Joshua Field's diary of a tour in 1821 through the provinces, pt II', *Transactions* [Newcomen Society], 13 (1932–3), 15–50 • R. A. Paxton and M. I. Mun, 'Menai Bridge (1818–1826) and its influence on suspension bridge development', *Transactions* [Newcomen Society], 49 (1977–8), 87–110 • E. C. Ruddock, 'The building of the North Bridge, Edinburgh, 1763–1775', *Transactions* [Newcomen Society], 47 (1974–6), 9–33 • *Monthly Magazine*, 26 (1808), 329–45 • patents, 1808–50 • J. G. Bishop, *The Brighton chain pier: in memoriam. Its history from 1823 to 1896* (1897) • S. Brown, *Reports and observations on the patent iron cables* (1815) • S. Brown, *Specification of a bridge of suspension over the River Esk at Montrose* (1824–5) • S. Brown, *Description of the trinity pier of suspension at Newhaven* (1822) • S. Brown, engineer's notebook, North Eastern railways; Stockton and Darlington railways, 1829 • *Navy List* (1843) • *DNB* • *GM*, 2nd ser., 37 (1852), 519–20 • parish register (marriage), Edinburgh, 4/8/1822

Archives NA Scot., corresp. and papers | BL, Lieven MSS, Add. MS 47292 • BL, Liverpool MSS, Add. MS 38370 • BL, O'Byrne MSS, Add. MS 38044 • BL, Peel MSS, Add. MS 40499 • Inst. CE, John James collection

Brown, Samuel (1810–1875), actuary and statistician, entered the office of the Equitable Life in 1829 as a junior, but nothing else is known about his early years. He was subsequently appointed actuary of the Mutual Life Office in 1850, and of the Guardian Insurance Company in 1855, succeeding Griffith Davies (1788–1855), doyen of the actuarial profession. Brown contributed numerous papers to the *Assurance Magazine*, and also to the *Journal of the Statistical Society*. He took a very prominent part in the decimal coinage movement, and several times discussed the question before the International Statistical Congress. He also advocated uniform weights and measures throughout the commercial world.

Brown took an active part in founding the Institute of Actuaries in 1848, and became its president in 1867, holding the office for three consecutive years. He was also joint editor of the *Journal of the Institute of Actuaries*. In 1868 he was president of the economic section of the British Association at Norwich. He instituted the Brown prize at the Institute of Actuaries, and the first award under the terms of the endowment—50 guineas for the best essay on the history of life insurance—was made in 1884. He gave evidence on insurance and kindred topics before various parliamentary committees, including that on assurance associations in 1853. Brown died of chronic bronchitis on 20 March 1875 at his home, The Elms, 42 Larkhall Rise, Clapham, London.

CORNELIUS WALFORD, *rev.* ROBERT BROWN

Sources C. Walford, *The insurance cyclopaedia*, 6 vols. (1871–80) • Boase, *Mod. Eng. biog.* • *CGPLA Eng. & Wales* (1875) • d. cert.

Wealth at death under £7000: administration with will, 21 May 1875, *CGPLA Eng. & Wales*

Brown, Samuel (1817–1856), chemist, was born at Haddington, Scotland, on 23 February 1817, fourth son of Samuel Brown, founder of 'itinerating libraries' and grandson of John Brown, theological writer and author of *The Self-Interpreting Bible* (1778). He attended the grammar school at Haddington, the high school at Edinburgh, and then from 1832 the University of Edinburgh where he graduated MD in 1839 with a thesis on chemistry. In 1837 he spent some time in Russia; he planned also to visit Berlin and see the eminent crystallographer E. Mitscherlich, but at St Petersburg he fell ill with typhus fever and dysentery, which permanently affected his health, and had to return directly to Edinburgh. There in 1841 he gave a course of lectures on the philosophy of the sciences with Edward Forbes, later distinguished as a natural historian; Brown lectured on dynamical science. Contemporaries saw a brilliant future before him.

By then chemistry was Brown's passion, and he seems to have pursued it with the intensity of the young Frankenstein, writing, like an alchemist, poetry about his laboratory:

> It has been my shifting tent,
> Here to-day, to-morrow there,
> Where my impassioned life is spent
> Still in burning hope and prayer.
> (*North British Review*, 395)

He hoped to discover the fundamental constitution of matter. He could not accept John Dalton's belief that each chemical element had a distinct kind of atom; arguing that the world could not be made of so many different kinds of building-blocks. He experimented with 'paracynogen', previously investigated by J. F. W. Johnston, who had shown that it had the same components in the same proportions as cyanogen. Brown's experiments, done in somewhat improvised laboratories, seemed to indicate that when heated this substance turned into silica. He believed that he had induced four carbon atoms to coalesce into one of silicon, and that this was an indication that the chemical elements were stable arrangements, like radicals, of simpler ultimate particles. The atomic arrangements inferred by J. J. Berzelius and by Mitscherlich were the basis of Brown's conjectures, and his experiments; he believed that chemical reaction was a true synthesis, rather than a mere juxtaposition of dissimilar particles.

Brown lived secluded at Rosebank, Portobello (near Edinburgh), where he and assistants turned night into day to accommodate prolonged and elaborate processes, sustained by a diet of tea, sugar, salt fish, and ship's biscuit. Although he saw in nature the Creator at work, he became impatient of formal embodiments of religion in creeds and churches. In 1843 he gave a series of four lectures on the atomic theory in chemistry to a highly intellectual Edinburgh audience, including the logician Sir William Hamilton and Humphry Davy's brother John. Distinguishing various kinds of atomic theory, all of them being inadequate, he proposed a theory of matter in which the various chemical elements were very stable, not because they were composed of solid billiard-ball particles, but because their components were identical particles or groups which could not be polarized. Thus in paracyanogen the two cyanogens were rotating about each other in a fixed orbit; and thus boron and silicon were composed of carbon.

Such speculations were not uncommon in the nineteenth century, and Brown's qualified respect for the alchemists was shared, for example, by Michael Faraday.

But chemistry was a highly empirical science, and a claim of a transmutation by a serious man of science required confirmation; it would make or break a tremendous reputation. In 1841 Brown had published his transformation of carbon into silicon, communicated to the Royal Society of Edinburgh by his friend Robert Christison. When in the autumn of 1843 T. C. Hope, professor of chemistry at Edinburgh, retired, Brown declared himself a candidate, and saw the verification of this claim as essential to his success. George Wilson in Edinburgh, and Robert Kane in Dublin, tried to repeat the experiments, but could not do so: Brown was denounced by rivals as a charlatan and withdrew his application for the professorship. The chair went by only a narrow margin to William Gregory, translator and protégé of Justus Liebig (who dismissed Brown as incompetent). Brown was unheard of as a chemist thereafter.

Despite this disappointment, Brown continued his researches and published many reviews and essays concerned with both science and literature. In his rather flowery writings, there is apparent something of the power which had impressed Thomas Chalmers, Thomas Carlyle, Robert Chambers, Hamilton, and Forbes. He was well aware of the ideas of Auguste Comte, and in writing on the history of science (1846) discussed Comte's three stages: the theological, the metaphysical, and the positive. But he disagreed with Comte that the third was the final one, and looked forward to an emerging fourth stage, where faith was the first condition of science, facts its object, and reason its lawgiver. An era of faith was imminent. This idea was elaborated in two 'lay sermons' delivered in 1841–2, and reprinted in the posthumous *Lectures on the Atomic Theory and Essays Scientific and Literary* of 1858. There he described faith as the ground of everything, and like S. T. Coleridge denounced the school of natural theology associated with William Paley. Other essays discussed George Herbert's poetry and David Scott's painting; more curious and entertaining are those on vegetarianism and other health crazes, as he saw them, of the day, on mesmerism, and on ghosts. These discussed the fringe medicine of the 1840s and 1850s (he was a keen phrenologist, and friend of George Combe), and miracles, and reported on wraiths such as those subsequently investigated by the Society for Psychical Research. The essays show wide reading, and some wit.

In June 1849 Brown married his cousin, Helen Littlejohn; they had a daughter, Spring (*b*. 1851), and a son, Samuel (*b*. 1854). At the time of his marriage he was already in declining health; after a long battle against disease, he left Haddington for Edinburgh in June 1856, and died there on 20 September of the same year.   DAVID KNIGHT

Sources *North British Review*, 26 (1856–7), 376–406 · D. M. Knight, *The transcendental part of chemistry* (1978) · S. T. Hall, *Biographical sketches of remarkable people* (1873), 49–71 · R. Cooter, *The cultural meaning of popular science: phrenology and the organization of consent in nineteenth-century Britain* (1984)
Archives NL Scot., corresp. and papers | NL Scot., letters to J. S. Blackie · NL Scot., corresp. with George Combe · NL Scot., letters to Alexander Campbell Fraser

Likenesses D. O. Hill & R. Adamson, double portrait, photograph, 1844 (with George Gilfillan), U. Texas, Gernsheim collection · D. Scott, oils, NG Scot.

Brown, Sir Samuel Harold (1903–1965), lawyer, was born on 28 December 1903 at 16 Norfolk Square, London, the son of Harold George Brown (1876–1949), a solicitor, and his wife, Dorothy, *née* Beale, who was through her mother descended from the family of Oliver Cromwell. Brown was born into a family of impeccable legal tradition. His great-grandfather Joseph Brown QC was a member of Middle Temple, and his grandfather Harold Brown (1844–1910) was a solicitor and formed a partnership with James Linklater, William Hackwood, and Joseph Addison, becoming joint senior partner in 1895. His son Harold George Brown (Samuel Harold Brown's father) was made a junior partner in the firm in 1902 and established a reputation for himself in company law matters. Harold Brown was appointed senior partner in July 1933 but retired the following October, though he continued his interest in corporate matters by serving as a member of the boards of the BBC and the British Overseas Airways Corporation.

Samuel Brown was educated at Rugby School, and maintained his links with the school throughout his life, later serving as a governor. As his father had done before him he went up to Trinity College, Cambridge, and graduated BA before returning to London to be articled to his cousin Gerald Lacy Addison at Linklaters and Paines, as the partnership was called from 1920. Brown was admitted as a solicitor in 1928, and in the same year he was made a junior partner. On 27 April 1929 he married Barbara Compton, daughter of Alfred Cordeux Hays, a music publisher. They had one son and one daughter.

Brown practised as a solicitor with Linklaters from 1928 until his retirement in 1961, although he remained a senior adviser to the firm until his death. His service was interrupted by the Second World War, in which he was actively engaged, first as a principal in the Ministry of Economic Warfare (1940), and then as principal assistant secretary (1940–43) and under-secretary (1943–5) to the Ministry of Aircraft Production. He returned to legal practice in August 1945 and was knighted in 1946.

Brown's area of expertise within Linklaters was company law, and this led to his appointment to a large number of corporations. He was chairman of Sangamo Weston and was appointed as an additional director of Vickers Ltd. He was also a director of the Debenture Corporation Ltd, Clerical Medical and General Life Insurance Society, Merchants Marine Insurance Co. Ltd, and Northern and Employers Assurance Co. Ltd, and was a member of the local London board of the Bank of Scotland. In 1963 his vast experience led to his becoming one of two members appointed to a commission to create a new national industrial organization to replace the Federation of British Industries, the British Employers' Confederation, and the National Association of British Manufacturers. The commission's final report led to the establishment of the Confederation of British Industry.

Brown became senior partner at Linklaters in 1956, after the death of Gerald Addison, and he remained in that post until his retirement in 1961. He died of a cerebral haemorrhage at Hurstwood Park Hospital, Haywards Heath, Sussex, on 17 December 1965. A leading figure both in the legal profession and within the engineering and allied industries, Brown was one of the last examples of the family domination of the large city law firms characteristic of the solicitors' branch of the profession from mid-Victorian times to the 1970s.   MARK LUNNEY

Sources J. Slinn, *Linklaters & Paines: the first one hundred and fifty years* (1987) · *The Times* (20 Dec 1965) · *Law Society's Gazette*, 63 (Jan 1966), 85 · *WWW*, 1961–70 · b. cert. · m. cert. · d. cert.
Wealth at death £106,314: probate, 1 Feb 1966, *CGPLA Eng. & Wales*

Brown, Sarah Benedict (1817/18–1902), benefactor, was the eldest child of James Brown (1791–1877) of Philadelphia, merchant, and his first wife, Louisa Kirkland Benedict. Her paternal grandfather, Alexander *Brown (1764–1834), linen merchant of co. Antrim, had emigrated to the USA with his family in 1800 and settled in Baltimore, where he successfully expanded his business, eventually involving his four sons in family undertakings which straddled the Atlantic. Sarah Benedict Brown presumably spent her childhood partly in Philadelphia, where her father was the local manager of Brown Brothers & Co., and partly in New York, to which he moved in 1825; here he added banking to the firm's activities and became a noted philanthropist, contributing in particular to the founding in 1838 of the Union Theological Seminary. In December 1838 she married her first cousin, Alexander Brown (1817–1849), whose father, Sir William *Brown (1784–1864), directed from his base in Liverpool the worldwide operations of Brown, Shipley & Co., in which Alexander Brown was a partner. Thereafter she lived permanently in England, at first at Beilby Grange, Yorkshire, where in 1849 her husband died prematurely, leaving her with three sons (and possibly more children) to bring up.

How and when Sarah Benedict Brown came to be acquainted with Ann Dudin Brown, and so to lend her support to the foundation in 1882 of Westfield College, a college in Hampstead preparing women for London University degrees, is not clear. They were not related, but both were living at the time in Westminster, Sarah Benedict Brown in her own house in Grosvenor Gardens, Ann Dudin Brown in the Buckingham Palace Hotel; quite possibly they had met at the nearby church, St Michael's, Chester Square, where Ann Dudin Brown is known to have worshipped. Sarah Benedict Brown was appointed a founder member of the Westfield College council (with two other women and four men), on which she served until her death in 1902. For the first eighteen months she held the office of treasurer: at her insistence the accounts were submitted to outside audit and were pronounced satisfactory. She did not expect, or probably even wish, to continue in the position when the duties attached became more onerous. Her successor, like all future treasurers down to 1939, was a man. Her numerous benefactions to the college were well timed and imaginative, starting with two high-quality Brussels carpets which added a touch of luxury to Westfield's first home. Quick to see that Ann Dudin Brown's capital endowment would require supplementation from a building fund, she made a pump-priming donation in 1887, following it with more substantial sums as the need arose. She bought and presented to the college a piece of land vital to its development which could not otherwise have been afforded; she also founded a scholarship. The unaffordability argument, when applied to publicizing the college, she found hard to understand, but generously paid for the advertising of scholarships, 'rather more largely than the Council had directed'. She was a frequent and welcome visitor to the college; on at least one occasion, perhaps again with an eye on publicity, she brought some American friends—the only hint in Westfield sources at her transatlantic origins. The portrait in oils (artist unknown) that on her instructions came to the college after her death shows an imposing, almost regal figure, a benefactor *par excellence*, but scarcely conveys the grandmotherly warmth of her affection for the college, and especially for the students, whose later careers she followed with keen interest.

Sarah Benedict Brown died, aged eighty-four, on 19 August 1902 at Bearehurst, Holmwood, Surrey, near the country house of her third son, Sir Alexander Hargreaves Brown, MP for the Wellington division of Shropshire. In 1903 her daughter-in-law, Lady Hargreaves Brown, was appointed to serve on the Westfield College council.

JANET SONDHEIMER

Sources J. Sondheimer, *Castle Adamant in Hampstead: a history of Westfield College, 1882–1982* (1983) · Burke, *Peerage* [Brown] · d. cert.
Likenesses oils, 1900, Queen Mary College, London
Wealth at death £231,755 1s. 9d.: probate, 15 Oct 1902, CGPLA Eng. & Wales

Brown, Sidney George (1873–1948), electrical engineer and inventor, was born in Chicago, USA, on 6 July 1873, the eldest son of English parents, Sidney Brown and his wife, Clara, née Napier. The family returned to England in 1879, and Brown attended a private school in Parkstone, near Bournemouth. He was subsequently educated at Harrogate College, Yorkshire, and, in 1894–6, at University College, London. From 1892 to 1897 he was a paying pupil at Crompton's electrical engineering works in Chelmsford. After completing his pupillage, he was employed for a further six months by Cromptons; his father's illness then obliged him to return to the family business in Bournemouth. He continued to work at his electrical interests and in 1899 he patented the first of many inventions for improving telegraph cables. At about the same time he was assisting Sir Henry Hozier, secretary of Lloyds, to develop a radio telegraph system. He formed the Telegraph Condenser Company in 1906 to manufacture and market his inventions.

Brown married Alice Mary Herbert Russell, only daughter of the Revd Charles John Stower, of Sudbury, Suffolk, on 15 January 1908. She took a keen interest in his work. In later years she was largely responsible for the administration and financial control of his companies. He formed a new company, S. G. Brown Ltd, in 1911, to manufacture telephone equipment. With his wife's assistance, he designed a telephone relay, an improved receiver, and an effective loudspeaker (the Browns being first to use this name for the device). By 1914 his businesses had expanded to employ over a thousand people. Already a member of the Institution of Electrical Engineers and a fellow of the Institute of Physics, he was elected a fellow of the Royal Society in 1916.

At the outbreak of war in 1914 there was no British manufacturer of gyro compasses, which had been imported from Germany. Brown set out to remedy the deficiency. During this work, he also devised a new method—called 'liquid ballistic control'—of damping the oscillation set up in a compass by a change in course. He supplied two compasses to the Admiralty for tests in 1916; the time taken to evaluate and put them into production meant they were not available for service during the war. However, his compasses were later adopted for use in both ships and aircraft. Brown also served as a member of the Admiralty's inventions board during the First World War.

Despite the severe depression of the inter-war years, there was still a lucrative market for electrical equipment. The electrical power network was spreading out over the country; the BBC had started its radio broadcasting service. Brown's companies provided components for both power and radio applications, as well as for their established telegraph and telephone businesses. There appears to have been little difficulty in raising new capital to expand the Telegraph Condenser Company in 1933, which involved turning the organization from a private into a public company; Alice Brown made sure that she and her husband retained full financial and managerial control. During the Second World War the Admiralty took charge of S. G. Brown Ltd, replacing the Browns with its nominated directors. Brown retired in 1943. He sold his interest in the Telegraph Condenser Company to a syndicate, and S. G. Brown Ltd, including all gyro compass and radio telegraphy rights, to the Admiralty. In retirement, he devoted time mainly to cultivating orchids.

Brown's professional and business success was offset by tragedy in his private life; he and Alice had three children, but they all died young. He was a modest man, interested mainly in his electrical studies. Where possible, he preferred experimenting, lecturing, and writing technical papers to business administration. He depended largely on his wife to ensure that he had an adequate income to pursue these more congenial activities. He died at his home, Brownlands, Salcombe Regis, Sidmouth, Devon, on 7 August 1948, survived by his wife.

ROWLAND F. POCOCK

Sources *The Times* (9 Aug 1948) · C. Shaw, 'Brown, Sidney George', *DBB* · m. cert. · d. cert.
Wealth at death £140,761 10s. 4d.: probate, 25 Nov 1948, CGPLA Eng. & Wales

Brown, Spencer Curtis (1906–1980), literary agent, was born at 4 St John's Wood Park, London, on 20 January 1906, the younger son and youngest of three children of Albert Curtis Brown, who founded a literary agency, and his wife, Caroline, née Lord. He was educated at Harrow School, and at Magdalene College, Cambridge, where he was an exhibitioner. He obtained a second class (second division) in part one of the history tripos in 1926 and a third in part two of the English tripos (1927).

In 1927 Spencer Curtis Brown went down from Cambridge and joined the firm which still bears his father's name to run the drama department. In 1928 he married Jean, daughter of William Watson DD, a Presbyterian minister; they had one daughter. By that time the Curtis Brown agency was well abreast of its rivals, J. B. Pinker and A. P. Watt. Michael Joseph, who was manager of the agency, went on in 1935 to found his own publishing house. He was succeeded as manager by Spencer Curtis Brown in 1936.

The occasional news-sheet of Curtis Brown Ltd of 1930 gives an indication of the business in which Spencer Curtis Brown found himself as a young man:

> Reproduction of Mr Milne's world-famous Winnie the Pooh and other characters has been arranged for in various forms … Arrangements have been made for a series of twelve monthly articles to be written for a group of newspapers by the Rt. Hon. Winston Churchill … In the last six months we have made play deals … for (inter alia) Noël Coward, John Galsworthy, Maurice Maeterlinck, A. A. Milne, R. C. Sheriff … We have even made a contract for performances of 'Journey's End' in the Dutch East Indies!

In addition to this the agency's New York branch had already been set up at 130 West 42nd Street, and there was also a branch in Leipzig. The magazine department was thriving under the direction of Nancy Pearn; the agency was selling English language rights on behalf of continental publishers; short stories were being sold to continental publishers at a loss, but such sales were winning authors a new audience. Curtis Brown was acting for thirty-one American publishers on their British rights and for a further sixteen on their European rights. Volume translation rights were at last making a profit for the agency and first novels had been placed with British publishers for Nancy Mitford, R. C. Hutchinson, and Daphne Du Maurier; and non-fiction titles placed for Ivor Brown, G. D. H. Cole, Sir J. R. Shane Leslie, D. B. Wyndham Lewis, Herbert E. Read, Edith Sitwell, Ethel Mannin, and Major F. Yeats-Brown.

Just before the Second World War, Nancy Pearn, Lawrence Pollinger, and David Higham left Curtis Brown, not without bitterness, to set up their own agency, D. H. Lawrence and Dorothy L. Sayers going with them. But such was the power of the Curtis Brown agency that those defections only temporarily created a disturbance. With the outbreak of war the agency's links with Europe were severed, causing Curtis Brown to sell the New York branch to Alan Collins, while maintaining a reciprocal trading relationship. During the war, after a short spell in the British army, Spencer Curtis Brown worked from 1941 to 1943 for the Polish forces in exile as personal adviser to the Polish prime minister, General Sikorski. He then joined the intelligence corps (special services).

In 1945 Curtis Brown assisted in reorganizing the book trade in liberated countries and became chairman of Curtis Brown. The agency's American book department was never more active and successful, helping to establish the reputation of writers such as John Steinbeck, William Faulkner, and Norman Mailer in Britain and the Commonwealth. Spencer Curtis Brown was acting for C. P. Snow, Angus Wilson, Lawrence Durrell, Gerald Durrell, Kingsley Amis, Alan Bullock, J. H. Plumb, and Isaiah Berlin. All remained with Curtis Brown except for Amis and Plumb. He quarrelled with C. P. Snow, but the relationship continued none the less. Colin Wilson was turned away on the evidence of *The Outsider* (1956), but there were few writers of importance who were not Curtis Brown clients at some point in their careers. Curtis Brown also made important choices in non-fiction, both trade and academic.

Colleagues included Peter Janson-Smith, who left Curtis Brown to set up on his own; Ronald Barker, who became secretary to the Publishers' Association (1958–76); and two celebrated theatre personalities, Kitty Black and John Barber. Curtis Brown had an ambition to set up a branch in Australia—during the appropriate test match year. He used to discuss this with his friend and client Richard Gordon (Dr Gordon Ostlere), with whom he shared a fondness for cricket, but it was left to his colleague and successor Graham Watson to fulfil this particular dream.

Shortly before his retirement Spencer Curtis Brown and Alan Collins quarrelled, and the link with Curtis Brown New York was severed. After a brief flirtation with the William Morris agency, he founded a new American office, John Cushman Associates New York. He retired in 1968, having sold Curtis Brown to Industrial Finance Investments Ltd (later Dawnay Day). To the end of his life he maintained a personal and professional interest in the works of certain of his authors. He was the executor of A. A. Milne with his widow, and literary executor to W. Somerset Maugham. He held the same position for Elizabeth Bowen, and wrote the biographical introduction to her *Pictures and Conversations* (1975). He remained life president of Curtis Brown. An undated memorandum, addressed to his staff, contains the following words of wisdom: 'You have many authors, but each author has only one agent'.

In a period of great personalities in the publishing world, Curtis Brown was a larger-than-life figure. He was a complex man, capable of inspiring great affection and great animosity. Clever, shrewd, with a sardonic sense of humour, he was interested in people. His *Who's Who* entry listed his hobby as 'listening to other people'. He had a genuine dislike of display and snobbery. Frequently his companion at Lord's was ex-Sergeant Gerrard, who packed the parcels in the office. With his ability to recognize quality in literature of all kinds, and his relish for the tussle of negotiation, he stimulated his staff to give of their best. He could be charming, particularly to women. Irascible, he did not easily forgive those whom he felt had let him down. Tall, leonine in appearance, he preferred casual to formal dress. Although a Londoner for most of his life, he had a deep attachment to Monks Hall, his seventeenth-century house in Suffolk, and it was there that he spent his retirement. Curtis Brown died suddenly

and peacefully in University College Hospital, Camden, London, on 16 January 1980. He was reading a book at the time.   ANDREW BEST and ELIZABETH STEVENS, *rev.*
                                                    CLARE L. TAYLOR

Sources J. G. Hepburn, *The author's empty purse and the rise of the literary agent* (1968) · office memoranda, Curtis Brown Ltd · private information (1986) · *The Bookseller* (26 Jan 1980) · *WW* · *CGPLA Eng. & Wales* (1980) · b. cert. · d. cert.
Archives CUL, corresp. with W. A. Gerhardie
Wealth at death £203,420: probate, 2 April 1980, *CGPLA Eng. & Wales*

Brown, Stephen (*d.* after **1420**), bishop of Ross, was a Carmelite friar and appears to have studied theology at Oxford. On 24 April 1399 he was appointed bishop of Ross, in Ireland, but there were difficulties with rival claimants, and Brown was not granted the temporalities of the diocese until 6 May 1402. This did not resolve matters, and he had to be provided to the see again on 25 June 1403. Brown is not known to have ever visited his diocese, and he acted as a suffragan in a number of English sees in the west of England. He is recorded as assisting in St David's, Wales, in 1409, in Bath and Wells in 1410–11, Hereford in 1418, and Worcester in 1420. Conrad Tremonius, a German Carmelite, attributes to him collections of sermons and of lectures; none has survived. Nothing is known about Brown's early life, and John Bale has confused the issue by claiming that he was born in Scotland, but this is possibly because he thought that Brown was bishop of Ross in Scotland instead of Ireland. In addition Bale, Dempster, and others include Brown in the group of Scottish Carmelites sent by Edward I to study at Oxford *c.*1300, which is chronologically impossible.   RICHARD COPSEY

Sources J. Bale, Bodl. Oxf., MS Bodley 73 (SC 27635), fol. 137*v* · J. Bale, Bodl. Oxf., MS Selden supra 41, fol. 166*v* · J. Bale, BL, Harley MS 3838, fol. 31*v* · Bale, *Cat.*, 2.215–6 · C. Eubel and others, eds., *Hierarchia Catholica medii et recentioris aevi*, 2nd edn, 1 (Münster, 1913), 425, 550–1 · Emden, *Oxf.*, 1.285–6 · *The whole works of Sir James Ware concerning Ireland*, ed. and trans. W. Harris, rev. edn, 1 (1764), 587 · T. Dempster, *Historia ecclesiastica gentis Scotorum* (Bologna, 1627), 107 · C. de S. E. de Villiers, ed., *Bibliotheca Carmelitana*, 2 vols. (Orléans, 1752), vol. 2, pp. 767–8, 970

Brown, Thomas (*d.* **1180**), officer of the exchequer, was possibly one of the Brown family, members of which had served as officials for Henry I. After that king's death, like others of his countrymen, Brown went to Norman Sicily. In two royal charters of Roger II, king of Sicily (1130–54), dated 1143 and 1147, he appears in a prominent position as *magister* Thomas. He may also have been both *capellanus regis* ('king's chaplain') and datary of royal documents, although only spurious documents now survive as evidence for his tenure of these offices, so no precise dating can be given; it was probably while Robert of Selby, his fellow countryman, was Sicilian royal chancellor in 1139–52. That he was already *magister* in Sicily suggests some experience and seniority before his exile. The death of Selby in 1152 and the rise of Maio di Bari to be all-powerful minister under Roger II's son and successor, William I (1154–66), probably clouded Brown's prospects of further advancement. Richard fitz Nigel, the bishop of London,

who knew him well, says in the *Dialogus de Scaccario* that he had held a high place in the councils of the king of Sicily until 'a king arose who knew him not'; eventually, therefore, in response to repeated invitations from Henry II, Brown returned to England.

For two years from 1157 Brown's nephew Ralph was paid as a royal clerk at the rate of 4*d.* a day; Thomas Brown himself received £42 14*s.* from the king in 1160 and an annual stipend of £7 12*s.* 1*d.* (5*d.* a day) for the next twenty years while he held an important position in the royal exchequer. The king was so confident of his loyalty and discretion that Brown was made responsible for keeping a special roll on which he recorded the laws of the realm and the *secreta* of the king. It has been supposed that there was a deliberate word play here on the Greek word *secreton*, used of the Sicilian financial office, but there is no evidence for Brown's employment in Sicily on the financial affairs of the crown—a consideration that removes the principal reason for believing in the reciprocal influence of the Sicilian and English royal financial institutions. Although Madox conjectured that the special duties assigned to Brown were the basis of the later office of chancellor of the exchequer, Poole argued that his functions were more like those of the thirteenth-century remembrancers. Between 1164 and 1175 he was also described as the king's almoner, and during this period he has been credited with the responsibility for revising the Domesday information about Herefordshire, the county from whose farm his stipend was drawn. He had property of his own in both Hereford and Winchester. He died after Easter in 1180.   D. J. A. MATTHEW

Sources R. Fitz Nigel [R. Fitzneale], *Dialogus de scaccario / The course of the exchequer*, ed. and trans. C. Johnson (1950), xxxiv, 18, 35–6 · R. L. Poole, *The exchequer in the twelfth century* (1912), 118–22 · C. R. Brühl, ed., *Rogerii II regis diplomata latina* (1987) · 'Magister Thomas Brunus, Beamter Rogers von Sicilien and Heinrichs II von England', R. Pauli, *Nachrichten von der königlichen Gesellschaft der Wissenschaft und der Georg-Augusts Universität zu Göttingen*, suppl. (1878), 523–40 · C. H. Haskins, 'England and Sicily in the twelfth century', *EngHR*, 26 (1911), 433–47, 641–65, esp. 438–43 · V. H. Galbraith and J. Tait, eds., *Herefordshire domesday, circa 1160–1170*, PRSoc., 63, new ser., 25 (1950), xxii–xxiv · G. Stollberg, *Die soziale Stellung der intellektualen Oberschichten in England des 12. Jahrhunderts* (1973), 110–11 · J. A. Green, *The government of England under Henry I* (1986), 236–7 · *Pipe rolls*, 4–26 Henry II · T. Madox, *The history and antiquities of the exchequer of the kings of England* (1711), 9, 17

Brown, Thomas. *See* Brouns, Thomas (*d.* 1445).

Brown, Thomas (*fl.* **1570**), translator, was a member of Lincoln's Inn. He was either the Thomas Brown admitted on 13 October 1562, or Thomas Brown of London, admitted on 6 August 1565. The second of these could have been 'Thomas Browne of London', admitted to the Inner Temple in November 1575. He was not one of the myriad Thomas Browns in the university lists. Brown translated Johannes Sturm's *Ad Werteres fratres nobilitas literata* (1549) into English under the title *A Ritch Storehouse, or, Treasurie for Nobilitye and Gentlemen* in 1570. Sturm (1507–1589) was a leading evangelical educator, a friend of Roger Ascham, and an ardent Ciceronian whose work served as a model for sixteenth-century school statutes, both protestant and

Catholic. Brown's dedication to the fourteen-year-old Lord Philip Howard refers ambiguously to his services to the Howards, but his 'To the reader' would indicate he was a puritan. Brown has puritan sensitivies to linguistic purity, but 'coynes new words, the auncient already being employed on lewde and peradventure wicked matters', and he abhors those who 'utter rather than in unseasonable time painted words and smooth Rhetoricke, then matter good and precious'. He may have had some experience as a schoolmaster. His concern with the education of the gentleman suggests he was the Thomas Browne who signed verses prefaced to Robert Peterson's *Galateo*. His careful translation of Sturm's approach to dialectic through rhetoric would indicate that he was interested in Peter Ramus's ideas on education, but not convinced by them. L. G. KELLY

Sources W. P. Baildon, ed., *The records of the Honorable Society of Lincoln's Inn: admissions*, 1 (1896), 69, 73 · T. Brown, *A ritch storehouse, or, Treasurie for nobilitye and gentlemen* (1570)

Brown, Thomas (*bap.* 1663, *d.* 1704), writer, was baptized on 1 January 1663 at St Nicholas's Church, Newport, Shropshire, the son of William Brown (1619–1671), a local farmer, and his wife, Dorothy. He was educated at Newport grammar school, where he is said to have 'attained considerable distinction as a linguist' (Bates, 316). He then entered Christ Church, Oxford, matriculating on 4 July 1678, where he was 'equally distinguished by ability and dissipation' (ibid.). His ability during these undergraduate years is highly praised in the preface to the posthumous *Works* (1707) by James Drake, who refers to 'his extraordinary genius, which he signaliz'd ... by diverse odes, and copies of excellent Latin verses', some of which he wrote for others at the university, since 'fortune obliged him to prefer money to reputation' (*Works*, 1.vii). On the other hand his undisciplined life led, it is said, to a threat of expulsion by the then dean of Christ Church, Dr John Fell, who withdrew the threat on condition that Brown produce an apology and an extempore translation of Martial's epigram 1.32 ('*Non amo, te, Sabidi*'). Brown's mischievous response:

I do not love thee Dr Fell
The reason why I cannot tell;
But this I know and know full well,
I do not love thee, Dr Fell

achieved a lasting minor notoriety, but on the dean's death in 1686 he wrote a respectful epitaph. After graduating BA on 20 March 1684 he sought his fortune in London, but after some time was driven by poverty to take a post as master of the free school at Kingston upon Thames, Surrey. He returned to London about 1687 to attempt a career as a professional writer.

Brown remained in London and was throughout his life dependent on his pen for his living; he 'wrote for his bread and wrote much' (Solly, 210). The result is a large corpus of literary productions, variable in quality and ranging from squibs and epigrams to serious prose works and full-length drama. His earliest publication was probably in *The Miscellany, Poems and Translations by Oxford Hands* (1685), one poem being dated '1682'. In 1688 he published the first of the satires which brought him notice: *Reason of Mr Bayes*

Changing his Religion, a fierce though entertaining and witty anti-Dryden pamphlet. He returned to attack Dryden, under the pseudonym Dudley Tomkinson, in subsequently published parts to this work, and on many other occasions. His satire was typically directed at a handful of targets, whom he attacked repeatedly, often in epigrams. After Dryden:

Traitor to God, and rebel to the pen,
Priest-ridden poet, perjur'd son of Ben
('To Mr Dryden on his Conversion')

the most frequent was Sir Richard Blackmore:

Thine is the only muse in British ground
Whose *satire* tickles and whose *praises* wound.
('To Sir R—d B—e')

He took great delight in regularly baiting Blackmore, author of the epic *Prince Arthur*, with squibs such as 'On Seeing a Man Light a Pipe of Tobacco in a Coffee-House with a Leaf of King Arthur'. The style adopted by satirists of omitting the vowels from the names of objects of satires 'when they would be more satirical than usual ... and fall unmercifully upon the consonants' is attributed by Addison, in his essay entitled 'Mystery and innuendo', to Brown 'of facetious memory' (Addison, 42). His reputation for playful satire led to the misattribution to Brown for many years of Ned Ward's *The London-Spy*.

Brown drew on his natural abilities as a linguist to write many translations from languages which included, as well as Latin and Greek, French, Italian, and Spanish.

His stile was strong and clear, and if he was not so nice in the choice of his authors as might be expected from a man of his taste, he must be excused; because doing those things for his subsistence he did not consult his own liking as much as his bookseller's ... prudence directed him to prefer the drudgery of most gain. (*Works*, 1.xii)

He was the author of three stage plays: *Physic Lies a Bleeding, or, The Apothecary Turned Doctor* (1697), *The Stage Beaux Toss'd in a Blanket* (1704), and *The Dispensary* (1697, published 1707). He wrote many humorous verse and prose sketches of low life in London, for example: 'A Letter to a Gentleman wherein is Describ'd the Humours of a Drunken Encounter' (*Works*, 1.314). They are witty and entertaining, drawing on his innate satirical impulse and manifestly informed by personal experience. In 1692 Brown and some friends launched a bi-weekly journal, *The Lacedemonian Mercury*, as a skittish riposte to what they saw as the excessive solemnity of John Dunton's whig publication the *Athenian Gazette*. Brown's journal ended at the end of May, but not before it had enraged Dunton with its irreverence. Among Brown's non-satirical serious works are a translation of Baron Maurier's *Mémoires pour servir à l'histoire de Hollande* (*Lives of the Princes of Orange*, published with Brown's *The Life of King William III from his Birth to his Landing in England*, 1693), *Letters from the Dead to the Living* (1702), a long series of essays in imitation of Lucian's *Dialogues*, and literary essays such as 'On the satire of the ancients'.

Brown's attractive and learned personality tended to save him from the consequences of his satirical attacks, but one piece, *A Satyr upon the French King on the Peace of*

Reswick (1697), resulted in his imprisonment. He claims to have recovered his liberty by a witty 'Petition to the lords in council by which he received his enlargement from prison' which includes the following lines:

> For if poets are punish'd for libelling trash,
> *John Dryden*, tho' Sixty may yet fear the Lash,
> No Pension nor Praise,
> Much *Birch* without Bays,
> These are not right ways,
> Our Fancy to raise
> To the writing of Plays …

James Drake comments on this incident: 'that person must have been of a very agreeable sense, that could soften and unbend the temper of King William' (*Works*, 1.v). Among his very many miscellaneous works the best are characterized by a mixture of an acerbic wit, learning, and in his poetry a highly developed facility for rhyme. His writing was heavily influenced by the classical authors he knew and admired, and many of his poems are imitations or translations of, for example, Horace, Martial, and Juvenal. His *Miscellany Poems* (1699) was the only collection of poetry published in his lifetime.

Brown is alleged to have lived a very licentious life, with an extensive knowledge of the taverns of London, and 'as of his mistresses, he was very negligent in the choice of his companions, who were sometimes mean and despicable' (Baker, 1.48). On the other hand there was something bookish about him; he had 'less the spirit of a gentleman than the rest of the wits, and more of a scholar' (ibid.). He was undoubtedly popular, and after his death affectionately scurrilous epitaphs were circulated. Among his close friends was Aphra Behn, whom he had met early in his London career, perhaps at a twelfth night party in 1684, and on whom he made a powerful first impression as 'a God in Wit, tho man in look' (Todd, 313). Brown assisted her in literary compositions, and may have written some of her satirical pieces. They were to remain lifelong friends; the poetry of both hints at a greater intimacy. After her death he included in *Letters from the Dead to the Living* a witty and immodest exchange between Behn and the actress Anne Bracegirdle. Although Brown is commonly remembered as a 'facetious writer, who is the delight of such as admire low humour' (Baker, 1.48) in fact a substantial proportion of his voluminous writings comprises serious prose essays.

Brown died at Aldersgate Street, London, on 16 June 1704 and was buried on 22 June in the east cloister of Westminster Abbey, next to the grave of Behn. His *Works* were published in two volumes in 1707; a third volume was added the same year, and a fourth in 1711.

WILLIAM R. JONES

Sources B. Boyce, *Tom Brown of facetious memory: Grub Street in the age of Dryden* (1939) · *DNB* · W. Bates, 'Tom Brown', *N&Q*, 6th ser., 1 (1880), 316–17, 337–8 · E. Solly, 'Tom Brown', *N&Q*, 6th ser., 2 (1880), 210 · J. Drake, preface, in J. Drake, *The works of Mr Thomas Brown*, 1 (1707) · D. E. Baker, *Biographia dramatica, or, A companion to the playhouse*, rev. I. Reed, new edn, 1 (1782), 48 · Foster, *Alum. Oxon.* · Wood, *Ath. Oxon.*, new edn, 4.662–4 · R. Shiels, *The lives of the poets of Great Britain and Ireland*, ed. T. Cibber, 3 (1753), 204–17 · J. Todd, *The secret life of Aphra Behn* (1996) · J. L. Chester, ed., *The marriage, baptismal, and burial registers of the collegiate church or abbey of St Peter, Westminster*, Harleian Society, 10 (1876), 254 · T. Brown, *A collection of miscellany poems, letters etc.* (1699) · J. Addison, 'Mystery and innuendo', *The Spectator*, 8 (1715), 42

Likenesses E. K., caricature, line engraving, NPG · J. Tuck, line engraving, BM; repro. in J. Caulfield, *Portraits, memoirs and characters of remarkable persons from the Revolution in 1688 to the end of the reign of George II*, 4 vols. (1819–20) · etching, BM

Brown, Thomas (1778–1820), philosopher and poet, was born on 9 January 1778 at the manse of Kirkmabreck, Kirkcudbrightshire, the youngest of thirteen children of the Revd Samuel Brown (1724–1779), minister of Kirkmabreck and Kirkdale, and of Margaret Smith (1735–1817), daughter of John Smith, of Wigton. Early deprived of paternal guidance, the young Brown was eventually taken in hand by his maternal uncle, Captain Smith, who, recognizing the openness and perspicacity of his mind, sent him successively to various schools in Camberwell, Chiswick, Bromley, and Kensington. The year 1792 saw him again in Edinburgh, where he immediately engaged the attention first of James Finlayson, who held the chair of logic, then, in the following year, of Dugald Stewart, whose lectures in moral philosophy were drawing enthusiastic audiences.

Metaphysics, Hume, and poetry The warm reception given by Stewart (though it was later to cool) and the analytic tenor of his *Elements of the Philosophy of the Human Mind* (1792) encouraged Brown to further his studies in metaphysics. The oft-cited episode of the young student challenging his professor over a curious feature of dream recollection (how does a conscious act take hold of supposedly unconscious materials?) is less significant than the fact that Brown pursued the matter through his subsequent medical training, which culminated in a dissertation on the intricate structures of both willed and unwilled (or 'mechanical') movement (*De somno*, 1803). That same fascination with the physiological as well as 'metaphysical' (or conceptual) functions of memory and attention is evident in Brown's David-and-Goliath challenge to the materialist assumptions of Erasmus Darwin's *Zoonomia*. His *Observations* on this work (1798) drew one reviewer's apt comment that 'If he be inferior to Dr Darwin in brilliancy of imagination, or in elegance of expression, he exhibits much logical acuteness and general information … [moreover] he appears to be always an honourable and candid antagonist' (*Monthly Review*, June 1799). Darwin was less appreciative, as eventually was the teacher who had urged him to transcribe his scribbled notes into a full and 'candid' rebuttal.

The issue of 'the nature of causation' had also arisen in Darwin's 'materialist system', and Brown returned to that subject during the political furore over the candidature of John Leslie, a whiggish layman, for the chair of mathematics at Edinburgh. While the 'moderates' in the general assembly were successful in thwarting Leslie, whom they accused of heterodoxy, they met their eventual match in Brown's book-length defence of the real target of their ire, namely Hume's views on causality, which

Thomas Brown (1778–1820), by Henry Cousins, pubd 1845 (after George Watson, 1806)

had much influenced Leslie's treatise on heat. Brown both disarmed their fears and set out to recast the sceptic's argument in a language of 'suggestion' which later became something of a trademark. Before his death two editions under the original title had been published (in 1805 and 1806), and a third was newly cast (as *Inquiry into the Relation of Cause and Effect*, 1818), with a new preface, and fresh form and direction. Now largely regarded, and reprinted, as only a mediocre response to Hume, the work's value lies in its exploration of both the physical and conceptual ramifications of muscular exertion or 'will-power'. It marked too Brown's growing alienation from the tenets of Thomas Reid and Stewart, and his closer affinity with such French thinkers as Maine de Biran.

Meanwhile the refined sensibility of Brown, which Cockburn thought replete with 'affectation' (Cockburn, 1872 edn, 317), his friend Erskine 'too delicate', and Mackintosh 'both grand and melancholy' (Mackintosh) was making bold to commit its 'effusions', said one reviewer, to the 'preservation of the press' (*Imperial Review*, 3, 1804, 451–6). From his first collection of poems, in 1804, until his final separate volume, *Emily*, in 1819 (the same year in which his sister Margaret published her own collection) Brown made seven attempts to render philosophical insight and 'the spirit of love' into the charm of verse. He aspired to be an Akenside; his friends found him an embarrassment. Dr James Gregory, with whom he entered into medical practice in 1806, regarded his amalgam of verse with philosophy as badly conceived. A four-volume compilation, *Poetical Works*, was published in the year of Brown's death.

The *Edinburgh Review*: Brown's critics A rising star and recording secretary of Edinburgh's Academy of Physics, Brown was a founder member of the *Edinburgh Review*. His only substantial philosophic entry for the *Review* was an article on Kant based on a review by a French emigrant, Charles Villers, intended to effect the 'mutual correction of the errors of Condillac and Kant' (*Edinburgh Review*, 2, 1803). But he desperately wanted to review, and himself to be remembered through reviews, as a literary figure (in the first instance, appraising the dramatist Joanna Baillie). Whether as a well-meaning friend or as a foe, the *Review*'s editor, Francis Jeffrey, would ultimately deny him that. Between the latter's 1804 review of Stewart's *Account of the Life and Writings of Thomas Reid* and his 1810 review of the Edinburgh professor's *Philosophical Essays* (the latter coinciding with Brown's ascendancy to the lecture stage at Edinburgh), the perhaps innocent clash of literary tastes turned deeply philosophical. Jeffrey now questioned the 'analytical' persuasion of the entire Scottish school. Brown, like Macvey Napier, fought back through his lectures but, as late as 1838–9, in a profound series in *Blackwood's Magazine*, J. F. Ferrier chided him as an 'analytic poulterer'.

Brown's 'French' tastes, which showed themselves as early as 1800 through his involvement (with Horner, Reddie, Erskine, Murray, and Webb Seymour) in a projected translation of Turgot's collected writings, were clearly too 'fine' (as Cockburn said of his poetry). Moreover, as his (mis)reading of Kant through the French translation of Charles Villers revealed, he was ever prone to tip the scale of German transcendentalism in the direction of the French 'sensationalism' of Condillac; and the disparaging tone of the *Review* article probably retarded the study of Kant's ideas in Britain. An anonymous writer in the *North American Review* (1815) observed how Brown, along with Alison and Mackenzie, pitted Voltaire against Jeffrey's Shakespeare, in a gesture that was both politically and critically charged.

In 1808/9 ill health had forced Stewart to arrange for Brown to teach his moral philosophy classes. The following year, he assumed even fuller duties and, by 1810/11, when it became clear that Stewart must withdraw altogether, he formally co-occupied with him the chair of moral philosophy. Students, including many from North America who wrote glowing reports home, were captivated by his eloquence, though Cockburn found it 'peculiar' (*Memorials*). Brown's biographer, the Revd David Welsh, popularized the tale that Brown composed his entire lecture series *ex nihilo* in virtually a single session. Yet his extant lecture notes, penned first in 1810–12, reveal extensive and continuous revision, the product of a tireless mind.

Four insistent charges both sustained and, affirmed one memorialist, made Brown's reputation seem antiquated. First, Brown was accused (by his French detractors and their Scottish ally, Sir William Hamilton) of metaphysical '*infidélité*' towards Reid and Stewart. Second, along with his Glaswegian counterpart, James Mylne, he was denounced for preferring the genetic accounts of French sensationalists and *idéologues* (Condillac and Destutt de Tracy, primarily) over the constitutive depictions of the human mind consistently advanced in Scotland after Hutcheson. Third, and insidiously (Welsh being the unlikely culprit), Brown was bracketed with such phrenologists as the brothers Andrew and George Combe, not to mention Welsh himself, because he could see no immediate contradiction in the idea of a connection between the activities of mind and brain. Moreover, consistent with the original policies of the short-lived Academy of Physics, Brown had conducted analyses under the headings of 'intellectual physics' and 'physiology'. Welsh mistook a line of inquiry which, in Brown's words, 'reduces to simpler elements, some complex feeling that seems to us virtually to involve them' for one which transformed all 'mental' into 'materialist' principles. Finally, Brown's philosophical legacy has been cast among those who espouse phenomenalism (more flatteringly, by allying Brown with Berkeleian idealism) and his psychological one among the Hartleian forebears of associationalist theories of mental activity.

Brown's rejoinders and his apologists In view of the strenuous debates surrounding each of the above charges, Victor Cousin's slur on the supposed *timidité* of Scottish 'metaphysical' thought as a whole appears misplaced. Of the charge that he had betrayed the principles of Reid and Stewart, Brown was at once the victim and perpetrator. Even as Scottish philosophy was settling itself into a 'school', Brown chose to stoke the fires of open and critical discussion—both publicly in the lecture hall and eventually in his *Sketch of a System of the Philosophy of the Human Mind* (April 1820), and in the *Lectures on the Philosophy of the Human Mind* (assembled posthumously the same year). To his friend William Erskine, who steered the *Lectures* through a second 'corrected' edition, Brown confessed that every opinion voiced against the views of Reid, 'in which Mr Stewart perhaps coincided', resulted for him in 'the most unpleasant circumstances attending my situation'. Even while Brown was inscribing *Agnes; a Poem* to Stewart in 1818 'with best regards', his mentor was scarcely able to restrain his ire at the liberties which his pupil now took of his philosophy. The manuscript evidence suggests, however, that Brown strove to raise the argument beyond names to a broader, more 'profound' empirical analysis of mental phenomena. Ironically the gradual substitution in his lecture notes of 'simple' and 'relative suggestion' for the old 'faculties' of conception and judgement served only to exacerbate the sensitive issue of names. Infidelity extended to concepts as well as to persons.

The allegation that Brown conspired with *les idéologues* likewise followed his reputation well beyond the grave. Hamilton snarled darkly about Brown's 'doctrine of *Generalizations*' as deriving from views 'commonly taught by philosophers not Scottish' (*Edinburgh Review*, 52, 1830, 158–207). The notion from Locke, thence Condillac, that higher mental operations might arise out of a 'succession

of feelings' which just happen to occur to the mind was anathema to the Scottish view of a fully constituted mind, active in its own self-cultivation. The stakes were high; for Scottish thinkers they were moral, too.

Brown countered that sensationalists after Condillac had grossly oversimplified their account of the mind. But Reid, he argued, had gone to the opposite extreme of an '*excessive amplification*' of the mind's powers. Where the former group failed to recognize that the mind's 'susceptibility' to be affected by experience was a thing altogether distinct from the 'sensation itself', Reid and his followers had 'given up [the] labour too soon'. Consequently, they had fallen back on a plethora of 'different' powers. Both thinkers had erred in classification as well as in theory. Brown repeatedly testified that he had no 'eagerness to innovate', and denied strenuously that his views were expressed 'after any particular School'. Above all he sincerely hoped that, the 'principle of [his] arrangement' being in time understood, the knowledge of these 'general laws or tendencies of succession' would furnish the basis for the 'intellectual and moral history of our future life'.

This hope would later be fulfilled by another student of Stewart, W. P. Alison, who reiterated the two 'leading principles' of the Scottish school. The first, and Baconian, affirms that the mind is and can only be known by a direct and attentive observation which discloses the constitution and powers of the mind, before generalizing these 'by the process of induction' into 'laws of nature'. The second appeals to 'certain fundamental laws of belief', whose authority is 'immediate' and 'irresistible', in Brown's own words, and beyond which no inquiry can or should proceed. Such a limiting principle impedes the onset of scepticism, guides analysis, and ultimately leaves the mind whole. Unlike the phrenologists, and contrary to Jeffrey's 'argumentative levities' (*Memorials*), Alison fully appreciated Brown's adherence to the school's philosophical Calvinism (Alison).

Sir James Mackintosh best sums up Brown's stormy reputation. Hamilton wanted to put Brown 'upon his proper level': the 'gentle' Mackintosh (in Cockburn's depiction) did just that. Stewart sought revenge in his 'Note' tucked inside the 1827 edition of his *Elements*, accusing Brown of '[im]*patient thinking*', not to mention 'very loose and inaccurate use of language', and turned even more fiercely upon the 'solicitous' and 'shallow' Welsh. His parting shot was that 'when [Brown] got to the end of his soundingline … he [fancied he had] reached the bottom of the ocean'. Mackintosh, alluding to the poet as well as the thinker, owned that Brown had more in common with 'the lonely visionary', who observes the human condition and the 'wider world, with the eye of a metaphysician'. Brown himself imagined his work to be a 'Georgics' of the mind, a culturing of its very science. This higher art raises us up:

> from the dust, where we slept or trembled, in sluggish, yet ferocious ignorance, the victims of each other, and of every element around us, to be the sharers and diffusers of the blessings of social polity, the measurers of the earth and of

the skies, and the rational worshippers of that eternal Being by whom they and we were created. (T. Brown, *Lectures on the Philosophy of the Human Mind*, 1820, lecture 34)

This was scarcely the voice of *timidité*. Neither does it indicate, as Mackintosh feared, that the 'love of speculative philosophy' had already 'expired in Scotland'. Between 1810 and 1820 Brown regularly demonstrated that passion upon the lecture stage. Never one to rest, his mind sought frequent outlets in verse or in the preparation of the second, and more 'physiological', phase of his 'philosophy of the human mind'. When necessary, it might find refuge in the family hearth of his beloved mother and sisters, where it was known to travel in the warmest companionship. His mind knew little comfort even here, however, for the name 'antagonist' continued to stalk his speculations.

Brown was medium height, with a 'manner and address' said by one later writer to have been 'somewhat too fastidious, not to say finical and feminine, for a philosopher' (J. McCosh, *The Scottish Philosophy*, 322). Emotionally high-strung, subject to anxiety attacks, arrhythmias, and light-headedness, and so devoted to his students that he refused blood letting during the Christmas recess of 1819 lest he delay the resumption of classes, he had to call upon a substitute early in 1820 (John Stewart, who himself died that year). After voyaging south to London, Brown expired in Brompton on 2 April. At his request, he was laid to rest beside his parents in the tiny churchyard of Kirkmabreck. J.C. STEWART-ROBERTSON

Sources D. Welsh, *Account of the life and writings of Thomas Brown, MD* (1825) · D. Welsh, 'Sketch of the philosophy of the human mind. Part first. Comprehending the physiology of the mind. By Thomas Brown ...', *Edinburgh Christian Instructor*, 119 (June 1820), 349–360 · *Memorials of his time, by Henry Cockburn*, another edn, ed. H. A. Cockburn (1910) · J. Mackintosh, 'Dissertation on the progress of ethical philosophy, chiefly during the seventeenth and eighteenth centuries', *The miscellaneous works of the Rt Hon. Sir James Mackintosh*, ed. R. J. Mackintosh (1848), 170–84 [orig. prefixed to *Encyclopaedia Britannica*, 7th edn] · [Clarke], *The Georgian era: memoirs of the most eminent persons*, 3 (1834), 503–4 · W. P. Alison, 'Observations on the speculations of Dr Brown and other recent metaphysicians regarding the exercise of the senses', *Transactions of the Royal Society of Edinburgh*, 20 (1853), 513–40 · 'Character and writings of Dr Brown', *North American Review*, 21 (1825), 19–51 · W. Hamilton, 'Brown's writings, and philosophy of perception', *EdinR*, 52 (1830–31), 158–207 · L. Hedge, ed., *A treatise on the philosophy of the human mind; being the lectures of the late Thomas Brown. Abridged, and distributed according to the natural divisions of the subject* (1827) [reviewed in *North American Review*, 24 (1827), 480–82] · 'Letters from Edinburgh', *North American Review*, 1 (1815), 338–50 · 'Poems by Thomas Brown, MD', *Imperial Review*, 3 (1804), 451–6 · J. G. Wilson, ed., *The poets and poetry of Scotland*, 2 (1877), 28–30 · J. McCosh, 'Scottish metaphysicians', *North British Review*, 27 (1857), 402–34 · *The statistical account of the Stewartry of Kirkcudbright by the ministers of the respective parishes* (1845), 325, 328–31 · *Fasti Scot.*, new edn, 2.367–8 · *Pre-1855 gravestone inscriptions: an index for the Stewartry of Kirkcudbright*, 6 (1993), 6–7 · Chambers, *Scots.* (1855)
Archives U. Edin. L., lecture notes for the moral philosophy class at Edinburgh, entitled 'Brown's lectures on the philosophy of the human mind' | NL Scot., Academy of Physics minute book · NL Scot., letters to Robert Lundie · NL Scot., letters to James Reddie · NL Scot., letters to Reddie concerning Brown, MS 3704 · U. Edin.,

students' notes of Brown's lectures · U. Edin. L., letters to John Playfair, letters to James Reddie
Likenesses G. Watson, oils, 1806, U. Edin. · W. Walker, engraving, 1825 (after G. Watson) · H. Cousins, engraving, pubd 1845 (after G. Watson, 1806), NPG [*see illus.*] · W. H. Lizars, engraving, 1846 (after G. Watson, 1806)
Wealth at death total unknown; two £5 sterling certificates of deposit in his possession at the time of death came to 'ten pounds Sterling' (£120 Scots): NA Scot., CC 8/8/147 fols. 144 r–146r

Brown, Thomas [*name in religion* Joseph] (1798–1880), Roman Catholic bishop of Newport and Menevia, was born at Bath, the son of Thomas and Catherine Brown, on 2 May 1798. From 1807 to 1814 he was educated at Acton Burnell, near Shrewsbury, where the English Benedictines recently expelled from Douai in France had established a small college. There on 19 April 1813, aged only fifteen, he received the Benedictine habit and took the name Joseph. In 1814 he migrated with the rest of the community to their new house at Downside, near Bath, where he was to remain until 1840. He owed his monastic formation to Dom Martin Joseph Leveaux, a Maurist, and his ecclesiastical education, which left him a lifelong Gallican, to Dr Jean François Elloi, a former professor of the Sorbonne, both émigrés residing at Downside.

Ordained priest on 7 April 1823 Brown began teaching theology to the young monks as well as engaging in frequent debate with protestant controversialists, most notably in 1830 in the riding school at Cheltenham, where for five days he parried the attacks of representatives of the Protestant Reformation Society before an audience of 4000 people until the proceedings degenerated into a riot. In 1834 he engaged in a similar marathon at Downside itself. These early philippics reveal him as he was to remain—articulate, combative, relentless. Not surprisingly, Brown's published works are almost entirely polemical: they include *Catholic Truth Vindicated Against the Misconceptions and Calumnies of 'Popery Unmasked'* (1834) and *Downside Discussion* (1836). In 1829 he also revealed a talent for business and diplomacy. He was sent to Rome to contest the claims of Bishop Baines, then vicar apostolic of the western district in which Downside was situated, to override the community's traditional freedom from episcopal intervention. Not only did Brown ensure the continued existence of the monastery at Downside, he also made a deep impression on Cardinal Cappellari, the future Pope Gregory XVI. His brethren evidently appreciated his capabilities, and in 1834 elected him prior of Downside. The general chapter, the supreme legislative body of the English Benedictine congregation, also honoured him with the title 'cathedral prior of Winchester' and with one of the three doctorates of divinity which the Holy See allowed it to confer.

In 1840 the vicars apostolic in England were increased from four to eight. Wales was detached from the western district and made into a separate vicariate, and as there had developed a tradition that one of the vicars apostolic should always be a regular, Brown as a Benedictine, in spite of his total lack of pastoral experience, was nominated its first bishop with the title bishop of Apollonia *in partibus infidelium.* He was consecrated by Bishop Griffiths in St John's Chapel, Bath, on 28 October 1840.

The newly created vicariate, though it embraced not only the twelve counties of Wales, but also Herefordshire and Monmouthshire, contained only nineteen chapels, eleven of which were in the two border counties where there was a sprinkling of Catholic squires. But for the many thousands of Irish immigrants in the industrial regions, mass had to be said in private rooms, public houses, and even in a slaughterhouse. Brown's greatest achievement was to leave to his successor, in the much reduced diocese of Newport and Menevia (which emerged in 1850 when the six northern counties of Wales were transferred to the diocese of Shrewsbury), fifty-eight churches and sixty-two priests. Brown was also the chief force behind the foundation in 1854 of Belmont Priory, Hereford, which served as his cathedral. In 1858 he obtained permission from the Holy See that the cathedral chapter might be composed exclusively of Benedictine monks, thereby reviving a widespread practice in England before the Reformation. Later, though a Benedictine himself, Brown aligned himself with Cardinal Manning and the other English bishops in their fight at Rome to bring under closer episcopal control the parishes run by the religious orders, which had previously enjoyed virtual independence of the local bishop.

In 1859 Brown was responsible for a clumsy intervention which had a prolonged baneful effect on the standing of John Henry Newman with the Roman authorities. Newman had published an article in *The Rambler* (July 1859), 'On consulting the faithful in matters of doctrine', in which he pointed out that there had been times during the Arian disputes when most of the bishops were heterodox, while the true faith was preserved by the laity, a situation which he called 'a temporary suspense of the Church's infallible authority'. Brown was so outraged that he delated Newman to Rome, and because Cardinal Wiseman was too negligent to transmit to the right quarters Newman's explanation of his phraseology, Newman remained under a cloud at Rome for many years. Brown had acted with characteristic precipitation, neither asking Newman directly to explain himself, nor writing in the first instance to Newman's bishop. However, Brown soon came to discover that he and Newman were in agreement in their general ecclesiological views: Brown applauded Newman's reply to Pusey's *Eirenicon* (1865); supported the project for an oratory at Oxford; and aligned himself with Newman's letter to Ullathorne in 1870, deploring the proposed definition of infallibility as the work of 'an aggressive insolent faction'. He wrote four times to invite Newman to accompany him to the First Vatican Council as his theologian, but without avail. In 1874 he coaxed Newman to reply to Gladstone's *Vatican Decrees* which declared the Catholic faith to be incompatible with civil liberty. The result was Newman's famous letter to the duke of Norfolk.

In 1873 Brown, by now the most senior of the English bishops, was granted the assistance of an auxiliary bishop, his fellow Benedictine John Cuthbert Hedley, who became his successor. Bishop Brown died at his residence at Manor House, Lower Bullingham, in Herefordshire on 12 April 1880, and was buried at Belmont Priory.

DAVID DANIEL REES

Sources 'Memoir of the late Bishop Brown', *Downside Review*, 1 (1880), 4–15 · B. Whelan, *The history of Belmont Abbey* (1959) · C. Butler, *The life and times of Bishop Ullathorne, 1806–1889* (1926) · T. B. Snow, *Obit book of the English Benedictines from 1600 to 1912*, rev. H. N. Birt (privately printed, Edinburgh, 1913) · H. N. Birt, *Downside, the history of St Gregory's school from its commencement at Douay* (1902) · *The letters and diaries of John Henry Newman*, ed. C. S. Dessain and others, [31 vols.] (1961–), vol. 24, pp. 361–2 · F. J. Cwiekowski, *The English bishops and the First Vatican Council* (1971) · B. Whelan, *Annals of the English congregation of the black monks of St Benedict, 1850–1900* (1971) · J. A. Harding, 'Dr William Clifford, third bishop of Clifton (1857–1893)', PhD diss., University of Bristol, 1970
Archives Cardiff Roman Catholic Archdiocesan Archives, corresp. and papers · Downside Abbey, near Bath, archives | Westm. DA, letters to Archbishop Wiseman
Likenesses portrait, Downside Abbey
Wealth at death under £6000: probate, 2 Sept 1880, *CGPLA Eng. & Wales*

Brown, Thomas Edward (1830–1897), poet, was born at Douglas, Isle of Man, on 5 May 1830, the fourth son and sixth of the nine children of Robert *Brown (c.1792–1846) [see under Brown, Hugh Stowell], vicar of Kirk Braddan in the Isle of Man, a poet and preacher of some repute, and his wife, Dorothy Thomson. He was born at Douglas on 5 May 1830. Hugh Stowell *Brown (1823–1886), the well-known Baptist minister of Myrtle Street, Liverpool, was an elder brother. Thomas was educated at the village school in Port-e-Slee and introduced to Latin and the English classics by his father. After passing through King William's College, Isle of Man (1845–9), he obtained a servitorship at Christ Church, Oxford, matriculating on 17 October 1849. Though he took a double first in classics and law and history in 1853, Oxford proved to be a humiliating and unhappy experience, as servitors were treated very differently from commoners. Brown later related his experiences in 'Christ-Church servitors in 1852' (*Macmillan's Magazine*, 1868). He nevertheless obtained a fellowship at Oriel in 1854, when a fellowship there was still the highest distinction Oxford could confer, and graduated MA in 1856. It was also there that he was influenced by Newman's Oxford Movement and, as the rigorous sacramentalism associated with this movement was regarded with suspicion by the Manx church, he could never fulfil his original plan of becoming a priest in the Isle of Man, though he was ordained in 1855.

Instead, Brown took a mastership at King William's College and was vice-principal from 1858 to 1861. In 1858 he married his cousin Amelia (d. 1888), daughter of Dr Thomas Stowell of Ramsey, with whom he was to have three sons and four daughters. He also became closely involved with life on the island. From September 1861 for a little over two years he was headmaster of the Crypt School, Gloucester (where he taught W. E. Henley). In September 1863 Dr Percival persuaded him to accept the post of second master (and head of the modern side) at Clifton College, Bristol, where he remained, a very powerful factor in the success of the school, for nearly thirty years. He was much admired and idolized by his students, one of whom described him as having 'an aspect not sentimental; rapid, decisive motion and speech; great power of command, and of supporting that command by missiles of humour and scorn aimed at the disobedient; a large and generous heart' (Mozley, 15).

Brown had written poetry as a student in Oxford but seems to have abandoned writing until 1868. His tales in verse, 'Betsy Lee' and 'Christmas Rose', were privately printed, after which 'Betsy Lee' was revised for publication in *Macmillan's Magazine*. It was praised and admired by George Eliot and Mrs Tennyson, wife of the poet laureate. Yet when the collected volume of these Manx narrative poems, *Fo'c'sle Yarns*, was published in 1889, Brown was compelled by Macmillan to censor its bawdier aspects. In the originals he swears, describes prostitutes, and asks if his shipmates ever felt attraction for a boy. Other Manx tales followed: *The Doctor and other Poems* in 1887 and *The Manx Witch and other Poems* in 1889. A second edition of the *Yarns* was also published in 1889.

In addition to his scholastic post Brown was curate of St Barnabas, Bristol, from 1884 to 1893. He took priestly orders in 1885. Troubled by health problems and deeply grieved by his wife's death in 1888, he gave up teaching in 1892 and returned to his old home in Ramsey in 1893.

From 1890 Brown contributed occasional lyrics to the *Scots* (*Afterwards National*) *Observer* and to the *New Review* under the direction of his former pupil, Henley, and many of these pieces were republished in the volume entitled *Old John* (1893). He immersed himself in life on the island once more. He gave sermons and public lectures on Manx life. In May 1895 he recommended as a genuine 'Mona Bouquet' a little book, *Manx Tales*, by a young friend, Egbert Rydings. In 1894 he was offered but refused the archdeaconry of the Isle of Man, as he had done in 1886. He retained to the end his early ideal of mirroring the old Manx life and speech before it was submerged. T. E. Brown died suddenly from a brain haemorrhage at Clifton College while giving an address to the boys, on 29 October 1897. He was buried at Redland Green, Bristol. A collected edition of his poems, edited by Henley, H. F. Brown, and H. G. Dakyns, was published in 1900 by Macmillan (reprinted 1952) as well as a collected edition of his letters. The poems were reprinted in 1952 with one additional piece, 'The Manx Litany'. An uncensored edition of *Fo'c'sle Yarns* was published in 1998. His contribution to the preservation of the Manx dialect is unsurpassed.

THOMAS SECCOMBE, rev. SAYONI BASU

Sources A. Quiller-Couch, 'Memoir', *Thomas Edward Brown: a memorial volume, 1830–1930* (1930) • S. T. Irwin, 'Memoir', *The letters of T. E. Brown*, 2 vols. (1900) • *The Times* (1 Nov 1897) • *The Academy* (13 Nov 1897), 404 • *New Review* (Dec 1897) • review, *QR*, 187 (1898), 384–99 • *Monthly Review* (Oct 1900) • *Macmillan's Magazine*, 82 (1900), 401–10 • *Macmillan's Magazine*, 83 (1900–01), 212–16 • S. H. W. Hughes-Games, 'The Reverend Thomas Edward Brown: poet', *Fortnightly Review*, 74 (1900), 765–77 • A. H. Miles, ed., *The poets and the poetry of the nineteenth century*, 5 (1906) • d. cert. • J. R. Mozley, *Clifton memories* (1927)

Archives BL, corresp. with Macmillans, Add. MS 55006

Likenesses photograph, 1897?, repro. in Quiller-Couch, *Thomas Edward Brown*, frontispiece • W. Richmond, oils, Clifton College, Bristol • photograph, repro. in T. E. Brown, *Collected poems* (1900), frontispiece

Wealth at death £13,597 14*s.* 10*d.*: probate, 15 Jan 1898, *CGPLA Eng. & Wales*

Brown, Thomas Graham (1882–1965), neurophysiologist and mountaineer, was born on 27 March 1882 in Edinburgh, the eldest child of the three sons and one daughter of John James Graham Brown, sometime president of the Royal College of Physicians of Edinburgh, and his wife, Jane Pasley Hay Thorburn. He was educated at the Edinburgh Academy and the University of Edinburgh, where he studied medicine; his fellow students appointed him president of the Royal Medical Society. He gained a BSc *summa cum laude* in 1903, and graduated with honours in medicine in 1906. Awarded a travelling scholarship, he went to Strasbourg to work in Professor Ewald's laboratory, and on his return in 1907 he determined to make physiology his career.

Graham Brown was Muirhead demonstrator in physiology at the University of Glasgow until 1910, when he was awarded a Carnegie fellowship to work on neurophysiology with Charles Sherrington at the University of Liverpool. During the busy and productive period which followed he published a series of papers on aspects of 'experimental epilepsy' in guinea-pigs, and a further series dealing with general aspects of the reflex activity of the central nervous system and with factors influencing that reflex activity, topics which were at that time the chief concern of Sherrington's laboratory. In 1912 he was awarded an MD and a gold medal, and in 1914 a DSc.

In 1913 Graham Brown became a lecturer in experimental physiology at the University of Manchester, but left in 1915 to join the Royal Army Medical Corps, with which, from 1916 onwards, he served on the Salonika front. There he diverted himself with imaginative day-dreams of direct routes on alpine faces of which he had read but which he did not yet know, the faces of Mont Blanc, on which he was later to make his reputation as a mountaineer.

Graham Brown's health suffered in Salonika, but it was not until November 1919 that he was demobilized. In 1920 he was appointed professor of physiology in the University of Wales, a chair tenable at University College, Cardiff, and one which he occupied until his retirement. He was burdened, in the difficult post-war years, with the task of building up his department; nevertheless he continued to research actively. He was a skilful and tireless experimenter, but one whose work was at that time rather outside the main stream of advance in neurophysiology. He became MRCP (Edinburgh) in 1921 and was elected FRS in 1927.

An independent and determined man, Graham Brown was not averse, when he thought it in the interest of his department, to crossing swords with the university and college authorities. He never married, and at Cardiff he lived a rather solitary life, lodging in a hotel. After his retirement in 1947 he continued to occupy his old laboratory, a large room filled with stacks of books, periodicals, and papers, some of them physiological, most of them alpine. Behind the stacks his camp bed and his belongings were invisible, and he himself (for he was short of stature) hardly to be seen until a visitor came close to him.

In early middle life Graham Brown's attention moved more and more to mountaineering and to his dream of a new route on the Brenva face of Mont Blanc, which he first saw in 1926. In 1927, with F. S. Smythe, he made his first route on the face, the Sentinelle route, and a year later, again with Smythe, climbed the more demanding Route Major; five years later his long obsession with the Brenva face culminated in the climbing of the via della Pera, the last of the great routes described in his book *Brenva*, published in 1944. His companions now were the guides Alexander Graven and Adolf Aufdenblatten. The Brenva climbs were joint achievements, and Graham Brown's contribution probably lay chiefly in the imaginative conception, in the calm appraisal of risks, and in meticulous planning and timing. He may be regarded as the last representative of an earlier epoch when the amateur planned the expedition and guides supplied much of the technical expertise.

Graham Brown's mountaineering extended far beyond the Alps: to Alaska (Mt Foraker), to the Himalayas (Nanda Devi), and to the Karakoram (Masherbrum); but his chief interest was alpine, and in the 1930s he was one of the few British mountaineers whose alpine reputation was internationally recognized as outstanding.

In the series of Graham Brown's alpine seasons one was remarkable by any standards: 1933. That year, in addition to eight major expeditions in other parts of the Alps, he climbed Mont Blanc by six separate routes: the Chamonix face, the Bionnassay Ridge (descending by Mont Maudit and Mont Blanc du Tacul), the Brouillard Ridge, the Innominata, Route Major, and the Pear (first ascent).

On Graham Brown's last visit to the Alps in 1952, in his seventieth year, he made his only ascent of the Matterhorn—by the Hörnli Ridge, an expedition put off in earlier years; his hopes of climbing the mountain by the more elegant Zmutt or Italian ridge were thwarted by weather.

From 1949 to 1953 Graham Brown was editor of the *Alpine Journal* and he retained into his seventies his keen interest in mountaineering. He became, however, physically less active, and turned to an old love, the sea. He bought and converted the former Cromer lifeboat, which had taken part in the Dunkirk evacuation, and named her *Thekla*; in her he cruised widely in Scottish and Norwegian waters, one year going as far north as Tromsø.

As well as *Brenva*, Graham Brown wrote numerous scholarly articles on mountaineering subjects and in 1957, jointly with Sir Gavin de Beer, published *The First Ascent of Mont Blanc*.

Graham Brown returned to Edinburgh for the last years of his life, 20 Manor Place being his last address. He died on 28 October 1965, leaving to the National Library of Scotland his rare and valuable library of alpine books.

CHARLES EVANS, rev.

Sources Lord Adrian, *Memoirs FRS*, 12 (1966), 23–33 · *CGPLA Eng. & Wales* (1965)

Archives NL Scot., corresp. and papers relating to mountaineering
Wealth at death £128,162 17s.: confirmation, 17 Dec 1965, NA Scot., SC 70/1/1609/225-33 · £2363 5s.: additional estate, 17 Dec 1965, NA Scot., SC 70/1/1609/225-33 · £834 14s.: additional estate, 17 Dec 1965, NA Scot., SC 70/1/1609/225-33

Brown, Timothy (1743/4–1820), banker and radical, details of whose parentage and upbringing are unknown, was by 1778 residing at St Mary Hill, London, and working as a hop merchant. By this time he had probably married the woman named Sarah with whom he had six daughters and three sons, and on 11 September 1778 he was made free of the Worshipful Company of Brewers by redemption and admitted to the livery. Over the years Brown maintained a distinguished association with the Brewers' Company, being elected assistant to the court on 11 December 1801, renter warden on 12 August 1814, middle warden on 16 August 1815, and upper warden on 12 August 1816, and ultimately serving as master of the company from his election on 10 October 1817. At some stage Brown became a partner in the banking firm of Bowles, Brown, Ogden, Cobb, and Stokes in Lombard Street, London, and in 1799 he joined Samuel Whitbread, Jacob Yallowley, and Robert Sangster as a managing partner in the brewery at Chiswell Street, London. Brown's initial stake in the brewery was valued at £99,999, but the following year he sold a third of his share to another banker, Sir Benjamin Hobhouse, of Bath. By 1802 the relationship between Brown and his partners showed signs of deterioration. Brown was disgruntled about the level of his salary, the managerial skills of Yallowley and Sangster, and the refusal of Whitbread to transfer the brewery's cash account to Brown's Lombard Street bank. He was clearly disillusioned with the business and on 25 October 1802 declared in a letter to Whitbread: 'I have it loudly hinted how little influence I had in the Brewery, that it was my Money only was wanted, and now I feel it' (Mathias, 306). Within four years the situation had worsened, and in October 1806 Brown appealed to Whitbread to 'find some person to take my place in whom you have more confidence and of whom you have a better opinion, and permit me to retire in quietness' (ibid.).

Amid rumours that Brown's banking firm was failing, his attitude became less passionate and he decided to stay on at the brewery; but by 1809, with continued doubts about his solvency, his partners were eager for him to sell his share in the business to Hobhouse's banking partner, Daniel Clutterbuck. Initially Brown refused to leave, but after protracted legal negotiations he sold his portion in the brewery business in July 1810. Sangster could hardly disguise his enthusiasm for Brown's departure, declaring to Whitbread that 'I hope you will have growing reason to rejoice in the exchange of persons' and claiming that Brown was 'flourishing away with his money in a very ridiculous manner' (Mathias, 307). Despite the unsettled nature of his business relationships and the alleged near collapse of his banking firm, Brown nevertheless amassed a considerable fortune from his ventures, including a country estate near the Isle of Wight and a house, Peckham Lodge, in Rye Lane, Camberwell, Surrey.

Brown's wealth made him an important ally for political radicals during the late eighteenth and early nineteenth centuries, and he earned further credibility in radical circles through John Horne Tooke, who 'entertained a high opinion of the character and integrity' of Brown (Stephens, 326). Brown was Horne Tooke's banker for many years, and the two men fraternized regularly with other radicals at Tooke's Wimbledon home. Although not known to have been a member of the London Corresponding Society, Brown donated to a subscription raised in 1798 to assist the society's members then under arrest, and in 1802 he was a supporter of Sir Francis Burdett's election campaign to gain the seat of Middlesex, declaring to Whitbread that 'Burdett will stand the poll and I hope turn out the [government] ... of the Bastille' (Mathias, 301). Sentiments like these brought Brown under the surveillance of the authorities in 1802–3, and his receipt of foreign newspapers did nothing to mitigate the government's suspicions. He continued to play an active role in London radicalism, among other activities participating in a committee, which included Robert Waithman, William Frend, William Cobbett, and Major John Cartwright, organized to raise funds in support of Gwyllym Lloyd Wardle after successive legal engagements in 1809–10; and in 1812 he was one of the founding members of Cartwright's Union for Parliamentary Reform. While his prominence as a political reformer saw him dubbed Equality Brown, he also acquired a particular taste for religious controversy in these years. In 1807 he edited Edward Evanson's *A New Testament*, and by 1812 Peckham Lodge was the rendezvous of such London radical and freethinking talent as James Baverstock, Joseph Webb, and Cobbett. Brown financed part of the publication by Daniel Isaac Eaton in 1812 of part 3 of Thomas Paine's *The Age of Reason*, and the following year he was active in the financing and promotion of Eaton's publication of Baron d'Holbach's *Ecce homo, or, A Critical Inquiry into the History of Jesus Christ* (1813), which had been brought to London by a young radical journalist from Scotland, George Houston. Two years later, when George Cannon published the *Theological Inquirer*, Brown's circle provided the core of the contributors, and Brown himself submitted a number of articles to the periodical. In 1820 he tried organizing a meeting of Camberwell residents in the parish church in support of Queen Caroline, but the churchwardens did not allow the church to be used for political meetings. Nevertheless, Brown had an address drawn up in sympathy with Queen Caroline, but when at Peckham Lodge on 4 September 1820, aged seventy-six, he reportedly 'dropped down suddenly whilst his servant was bringing him a change of apparel in which he was to go up with an address to Her Majesty' (*Annual Register*). He bequeathed a significant fortune of £40,000 to his nine children and was buried in the grounds of the parish church of Camberwell.

MICHAEL T. DAVIS

Sources I. McCalman, *Radical underworld: prophets, revolutionaries, and pornographers in London, 1795–1840* (1988) · J. A. Hone, *For the cause of truth: radicalism in London, 1796–1821* (1982) · P. Mathias, *The brewing industry in England, 1700–1830* (1959) · D. Allport, *Collections illustrative of the geology, history, antiquities and associations of Camberwell and the neighbourhood* (1841) · A. Stephens, *Memoirs of John Horne Tooke* (1813) · *Annual Register* (1820), 581 · will, PRO, PROB 6/196, fol. 111r · death duties on estate of Timothy Brown, PRO, IR 26/212, fols. 126v–127r

Likenesses F. Chantrey, marble bust, 1814, Whitbread Brewery PLC

Wealth at death £40,000: PRO, death duty registers, IR 26/212, fols. 126v–127r · will, PRO, PROB 6/196, fol. 111r

Brown, Ulysses Maximilian von. *See* Browne, Maximilian Ulysses von, Jacobite third earl of Browne, and Count von Browne in the nobility of the Holy Roman empire (1705–1757).

Brown, Sir Walter Langdon- (1870–1946), physician, was born at Dame Alice Street, Bedford, on 13 August 1870, the eldest son of the Revd Dr John Brown, pastor of the Bunyan Meeting, and his wife, Ada Haydon, daughter of the Revd David Everard Ford, a Congregational minister of Lymington. Brown was educated at Bedford School and after a term at University College, London, obtained a sizarship at St John's College, Cambridge. He spent the two intervening terms at Owens College, Manchester, where an enthusiasm for biology was awakened by Arthur Milnes Marshall. At Cambridge he responded eagerly to the stimulus of such teachers as Michael Foster and W. H. Gaskell, his indebtedness to whom he was always delighted to acknowledge. He was elected a scholar and was placed in the first class in both parts of the natural sciences tripos (1892, 1893).

Brown won an open scholarship in science at St Bartholomew's Hospital, which he entered in 1894. In 1897 he qualified and became house physician to S. J. Gee, who also greatly influenced him. In 1900 Brown went to Pretoria as senior physician in charge of the Imperial Yeomanry Hospital. He returned at the end of the year to his post as casualty physician at St Bartholomew's Hospital and in the next year he won the Raymond Horton-Smith prize for his Cambridge MD thesis on pylephlebitis. He became medical registrar to the hospital in 1906, but he was forty-three before he was appointed assistant physician in 1913 and he did not become full physician until 1924. He was also in post at the Metropolitan Hospital as assistant physician (1900–06) and full physician (1906–22), and in 1902 he married a nursing sister at the hospital, Eileen Presland (d. 1931). Unfortunately, their marriage was marred by her mental illness.

Brown's reputation extended far beyond the walls of St Bartholomew's. In 1908 he published *Physiological Principles in Treatment*, a timely book which inspired and informed his generation and showed that the new and powerful resources of physiology and pharmacology were ready to be used in the treatment of disease. His was the first textbook of applied physiology and the forerunner of many others. He was elected FRCP in 1908 and became a distinguished servant of the college. He gave the Croonian lectures in 1918, on the sympathetic nervous system in disease, in which he emphasized that it was by the autonomic pathways that emotional disturbances produced disorders of bodily function. He was one of the first English physicians to relate the work of Freud, Jung, and Adler to the practice of clinical medicine, and he showed some courage, in a mechanistic age, in defending concepts of disease which did not admit of quantitative assessment. 'Scientific humanism' is a just description of his medical philosophy, and his explanations of personality disorders were the more readily accepted since he spoke with unimpeachable scientific authority. He became senior censor to the college in 1934 and in 1936 he delivered the Harveian oration, 'The background to Harvey'. This lecture was reprinted in *Thus we are Men* (1938), a volume of beautifully written essays which revealed the range of Brown's interests and the quality of his intellect.

After his retirement in 1930 from the staff of St Bartholomew's, Brown continued his busy consulting practice and this, with examining, lecturing, and travelling, for a time filled his days. In 1931, following the death of his first wife, Brown married Winifred Marion (*d.* 1953), daughter of Henry Bishop Hurry, of Eye, Northamptonshire. There were no children from either marriage. In 1932 Brown was appointed regius professor of physic at Cambridge and was elected a professorial fellow of Corpus Christi College. He retired from his chair in 1935, but in a short time had made a permanent impression on the medical life of the university. It was a period of great happiness for him and, stimulated by the academic life he loved, his intellectual powers reached their zenith. He was the true 'scholar–physician', widely read in the classics, English literature, poetry, and history. He was also interested in painting and had a remarkable knowledge of Italian art. A large and somewhat formidable figure with bushy eyebrows, Brown had a host of friends whom he entertained with good conversation, food and wine, and endless anecdote.

Brown was knighted in 1935, when he changed his name to Langdon-Brown. Many academic honours were conferred upon him, including the honorary degrees of LLD from Dalhousie University and the National University of Ireland (1938), and DSc from Oxford (1936). He was an honorary fellow of the Royal College of Physicians of Ireland and of the Royal Society of Medicine. He was also president of the Medical Society of Individual Psychology, and chairman of the Langdon-Brown committee on postgraduate training in psychological medicine, which reported in 1943. After the outbreak of war in 1939 he returned to live in Cambridge, where he delivered the Linacre lecture in 1941. In the last year of his life he wrote *Some Chapters in Cambridge Medical History* (1946), much of which was dictated to his second wife, who acted as secretary owing to Langdon-Brown's increasing incapacity in a long and difficult illness. He died at 12 Madingley Road, Cambridge, on 3 October 1946.

D. V. HUBBLE, *rev.* MICHAEL BEVAN

Sources *The Lancet* (12 Oct 1946) · *BMJ* (12 Oct 1946), 556–7 · 'Thus we are men', *BMJ* (26 Jan 1952), 206 · *St Bartholomew's Hospital Journal*, 50 (1946–7), 147–9 · M. Hynes, *The Eagle*, 53 (1948–9), 62–4 · L. Whitby, *Cambridge Review* (12 Oct 1946) · personal knowledge (1954) · b. cert. · d. cert.

Likenesses W. Stoneman, photograph, 1940, NPG · W. Stoye, pencil drawing, 1959, priv. coll.
Wealth at death £24,104 14s. 7d.: probate, 24 May 1947, *CGPLA Eng. & Wales*

Brown, William (*fl.* 1671–1705), legal writer, is very difficult to identify. In dedicating his *The Entering Clerk's Vade Mecum* (1678) to Thomas Robinson (later first baronet), chief protonotary of the court of common pleas, Brown referred to 'my sixteen years experience (as clerk of your office)'. Thus it would appear that Brown began his service shortly after the Restoration. As late as his *Privilegia parliamentaria* (1704) he was described as 'a clerk of the court of Common Pleas'. It seems likely from this fact that he was of insufficient status to be identified with any of his namesakes who were educated in the inns of court after the Restoration.

Brown's stock-in-trade consisted of books of tutorials for the aspiring clerk, books of precedents, and manuals for public officials such as justices of the peace. His first work appears to have been *Formulae bené placitandi: a Book of Entries, Containing Variety of Choice Precedents*, published in 1671, which had a second edition in 1675. *Modus intrandi placita generalia: the Entring Clerk's Introduction* followed in 1674, with a second edition in 1687. *The Entering Clerk's Vade Mecum* followed in 1678. Further guides and collections of precedents followed. After the revolution he appears to have branched out, publishing in 1705 *Astraeae abdicatae restauratio, or, Advice to Justices of the Peace*, but the method was the same, a compendium of information.

Brown was rarely an original writer. He edited works by William Sheppard, and the preface to Brown's *Methodus novissima intrandi placita generalia* (1699) revealed something of his method. He had waited thirty years to obtain the drafts of William Gardiner, late of Barnard's Inn, another clerk of the common pleas, which he now presented to the public.

Brown's date of death is unknown, but the will of a 'William Browne of the Middle Temple' was proved in October 1712. Writing on 20 April 1712, the author describes himself as 'gent', and refers to 'my circumstances being in not so good a condition as I could wish' (PRO, PROB 11/529, sig. 180), and to chambers in Fig Tree Court in the Temple, which he had purchased from Denham Pritherick for life, and now rented to Sam Provost. He himself lived in Brick Lane in the Temple, and left a wife, Elizabeth, and a brother, Robert.

STUART HANDLEY

Sources W. Brown, *The entering clerk's vade mecum* (1678) · W. Brown, *Privilegia parliamentaria* (1704) · W. Brown, *Methodus novissima intrandi placita generalia* (1699) · N. L. Matthews, *William Sheppard, Cromwell's law reformer* (1984), 93, 122 · will, PRO, PROB 11/529, sig. 180

Brown, William (1748–1825), gem-engraver, was trained in London, but of his origins and family circumstances nothing is known. He suffered an early set-back in his career when, aged fourteen, he competed for a Royal Society of Arts drawing prize but, with four others, was disqualified for cheating; he was consequently ruled ineligible when he tried for the premium for intaglio-engraving in 1763. Nevertheless, in 1766 he began exhibiting engraved gems annually, first at the Society of Artists, and from 1770 at the Royal Academy; his subjects were drawn mainly from classical history and contemporary portraiture. His brother Charles Brown (1749–1795), who joined him and shared his London workshops, also exhibited from 1771.

The brothers ceased exhibiting between 1786 and 1795, when most of their work was produced to commission for Catherine II of Russia. They may have visited Russia, and they certainly travelled to Paris at the invitation of the French court in 1788, returning early in the following year. Because much of their work went abroad, they seem not to have won the recognition in Britain that they deserved; few of their works are in British public collections, whereas the Russian commissions, some 200 gems, survive complete at the Hermitage Museum in St Petersburg. They include both intaglios, some of superlative quality, and cameos depicting subjects from the antique, animals, allegories of Russian contemporary events, such as *On Catherine's Recovery from an Illness* (1790), and portraits, including the series *Kings of England* and *Kings of France*. They are mostly signed simply 'BROWN'. Some were collaborative works, but around eighty gems have been identified as solely William's work (a few of these signed 'W. BROWN INVᵀ').

After his brother's death in 1795, William Brown continued supplying the Russian court intermittently but also resumed exhibiting his work, mostly contemporary portraits, at the Royal Academy. He died on 20 July 1825 at his home, 45 John Street, Fitzroy Square, London, aged seventy-seven.   CHRISTOPHER MARSDEN

Sources G. Meissner, ed., *Allgemeines Künstlerlexikon: die bildenden Künstler aller Zeiten und Völker*, [new edn, 34 vols.] (Leipzig and Munich, 1983–) · G. Seidmann, 'Brown', *The dictionary of art*, ed. J. Turner (1996) · J. O. Kagan, *Reznye kamni Vil'yama i Charlza Braunov* (1976) · V. Antonov, 'New documents about the Browns gems', *Burlington Magazine*, 120 (1978), 841–2 · J. Etkina, 'Russian themes in the work of the English gem cutters William and Charles Brown', *Burlington Magazine*, 107 (1965), 421–5 · Graves, *Soc. Artists* · Graves, *RA exhibitors* · G. Seidmann, '"A very ancient, useful and curious art": the society and the revival of gem-engraving in eighteenth-century England', *The virtuoso tribe of arts and sciences: studies in the eighteenth-century work and membership of the London Society of Arts*, ed. D. G. C. Allan and J. L. Abbott (1992), 120–31, 385–8 · *GM*, 1st ser., 95/2 (1825) · *Engraved in the memory: James Walker, engraver to the Empress Catherine the Great, and his Russian anecdotes*, ed. A. Cross (1993), 134 · will, 1795, PRO, PROB 11/1261 [Charles Brown]
Archives State Archive, St Petersburg, records of works commissioned in Russia · State Archive of Old Acts, Moscow, records of works commissioned in Russia
Likenesses W. Brown, self-portrait, engraved gem, intaglio, repro. in Kagan, *Reznye kamni Vil'yama i Charlza Braunov*; copy of impression, V&A

Brown, William (1764–1835), Church of Scotland minister and historical writer, was the son of William Brown, a stonemason in Peeblesshire, whose second wife was an aunt of Thomas Carlyle. Brown was licensed by the presbytery of Stirling in August 1791 and was presented to the parish of Eskdalemuir by Henry Scott, third duke of Buccleuch, in January 1792. There he fulfilled the duties of minister for forty-three years. On 28 April 1797 he married Mary Moffat; they had three sons and two daughters. He received the degree of DD from the University of Aberdeen in 1816.

In 1820 Brown published *The Antiquities of the Jews*, a work which contained a great deal of detail about Jewish customs and religious ceremonials, but barely touched upon their political history. It was favourably reviewed in the *Christian Remembrancer* in June of that year. He also wrote the description of Eskdalemuir for *The Statistical Account of Scotland*. Brown died at Eskdalemuir on 21 September 1835, and his wife in July 1855.

NEWCOMEN GROVES, *rev.* ROSEMARY MITCHELL

Sources *Fasti Scot.* · *GM*, 2nd ser., 4 (1835), 554 · Allibone, *Dict.*
Wealth at death £4667 6s. 4d.: inventory, 1836, Scotland

Brown, William (1777–1857), naval officer, the son of a small farmer, was born at Foxford, co. Mayo, Ireland. He accompanied his family to America in 1786 and, left destitute by his father's death, worked as cabin-boy on a merchant ship. In 1796 he was pressed into a British warship, and served for several years in the navy. Afterwards, having obtained the command of a British merchant ship, he came, in 1812, to Buenos Aires, where he settled with his family. In 1814 he accepted a naval command in the service of the Argentinian rebel republican government. He engaged a Spanish flotilla at the mouth of the Uruguay, and he fought another and more decisive action off Montevideo, capturing four of the Spanish vessels and dispersing the rest. He received the title of admiral, and fitted out a privateer, in which he cruised against the Spaniards in the Pacific. His ship was captured by a British warship, sent to Antigua, and there condemned, but was afterwards restored on appeal to the home government.

Brown lived in retirement at Buenos Aires until December 1825, when Brazil declared war against the republic and blockaded the River Plate. On 4 February 1826 Brown attacked the enemy, of more than four times his force, and drove them 24 miles down the coast. In February 1827 he almost totally destroyed a squadron of nineteen small vessels at the mouth of the Uruguay. On 9 April he put to sea with a few brigs, and was at once brought to action by a superior force of the enemy. Some of the brigs seem to have got back without much loss; Brown, though badly wounded, succeeded in running one ashore and setting fire to her; the other was reduced to a wreck and captured. The loss obliged the republic to enter negotiations, which resulted in peace.

In the civil war of 1842–5 Brown was again in command of the fleet of Buenos Aires, and with a very inefficient force kept up the blockade of Montevideo, notwithstanding an order from the British commodore to throw up his command. In 1845, when the British and French squadrons were directed to intervene and restore peace to the river, their first step was to take possession of Brown's ships, thus reducing him to compulsory inactivity. He had no further service, but passed the rest of his life on his small estate in the neighbourhood of Buenos Aires. He died at Barracas, near Buenos Aires, on 3 May 1857. He was married, but it is not known whether his wife survived him.   J. K. LAUGHTON, *rev.* ROGER MORRISS

Sources M. G. Mulhall, *The English in South America* (1878), 144 · F. S. Drake, *Dictionary of American biography, including men of the time*, new edn (1876) · J. Miller, *Memoirs of General Miller, in the service of the republic of Peru*, 2 vols. (1828) · J. Armitage, *History of Brazil*, 1 (1836) · M. Chevalier de Saint-Robert, *Le Général Rosas et la question de la Plata* (Paris, 1848), 27 · A. Mallalieu, *Buenos Ayres, Monte Video and affairs in the River Plate* (1844), 27 · Boase, *Mod. Eng. biog.*
Likenesses miniature, *c.*1820, National Gallery of Argentina, Buenos Aires · R. Del Villar, oils, 1931 (after miniature, *c.*1820), NMM

Brown, Sir William, first baronet (1784–1864), merchant and politician, was born on 30 May 1784 at Ballymena, co. Antrim, the eldest son of seven children of Alexander *Brown (1764–1834), merchant, and Grace, daughter of John Davison of Drumnasole.

Education and early years in America   There is little information about William's boyhood except that he was sent with his brothers, George (1787–1859), John (1788–1852), and James (1791–1877), to be educated at the school of the Revd J. Bradley in Catterick, North Riding of Yorkshire. Like them he initially learned slowly until his poor sight was corrected with glasses. Late in life he said he was too fond of playing at school, but his letters reveal a forceful, well-written style. His father, who at this time was a linen auctioneer in Belfast, was forced to hide during the Irish troubles of the late 1790s, and in 1800 he emigrated to Baltimore with William. Mrs Brown brought the other boys out with her in 1802. Alexander, George, James, and John then remained in America for the rest of their lives, but William sailed for Britain in late 1808 and visited America only twice thereafter.

William's return to Britain was due partly to his father's plan to establish branches at other major Atlantic ports. Alexander had rapidly become the leading linen importer in Baltimore. He made William a partner in 1805, and then in 1806 sent him to Philadelphia to establish a branch there. However, by 1808 it was obvious that the greater need was in Liverpool. The same family strategy sent John to Philadelphia in 1818 to found John A. Brown, and James to New York in 1825 to found Brown Brothers. George remained with his father in Baltimore to help in Alexander Brown & Sons. It is curious that William's first partnership in Liverpool was with his cousin, William A. Brown, and did not include his father and brothers. Possibly there were legal reasons in this troubled period, but William was the most determined of Alexander's sons and may have wished to escape his father's authority.

Settling in Britain, and marriage   William married, on 1 January 1810, Sarah (*d.* 1858), daughter of Andrew Gihon of Ballymena, Alexander's principal linen supplier. They had thirteen children, all of whom predeceased him. Sarah accompanied William to Baltimore in 1811, but they quickly left again for Britain after war was declared with the USA. George and John were also in Britain for part of

Sir William Brown, first baronet (1784–1864), by Sir John Watson-Gordon, 1857

the war, but left in 1814. In 1815 William formed a new partnership with his brothers, but not with his father, called William and James Brown (W. and J. Brown). William, however, was a partner in all of the family's American companies. The firms did well during the Anglo-American War of 1812–14. The net worth of the partnerships rose from $122,000 in 1810 (not including Liverpool) to $540,000 in 1815, and to $920,000 by 1821, with very large gains in the immediate post-war years when America restocked with British goods; there was only a 6 per cent reduction in the panic year of 1819. Few records of the Liverpool firm have survived, but William's activities can be inferred from the detailed letters written to him from Baltimore. They reveal that the firms speculated shrewdly in American staples and British goods as well as in commercial bills and government stocks.

After the war, trade from Britain to the USA grew more slowly than American exports, and that from New York and Philadelphia grew at the expense of Baltimore, from where Alexander continued to exercise authority. The new trade was mainly in raw cotton. Alexander established agents in Charleston, Savannah, Mobile, and New

Orleans, who consigned cotton to William. The commercial crisis of 1825 destroyed many of the older Liverpool houses, and in the late 1820s W. and J. Brown was regularly the largest cotton importer. In 1827 the Bank of England agent in Liverpool reported to London that the W. and J. Brown concerns were very large indeed: 'They have already this year had 70 ships from America consigned to them, and expect 30 more, and they hold at least 30,000— say thirty thousand—bags of cotton unsold' (Bank of England Liverpool agent to head office, 8 Sept 1827). That year William imported 65,000 bales of cotton, worth about $3 million, when total American exports to Britain were worth about $26 million.

Initially William entered the cotton trade by accepting orders from rich Liverpool and Manchester brokers which were then transferred to Alexander for execution by the southern agents. Later, Alexander made advances to large factors or planters in the south who accepted the speculative risk of holding the cotton. William's role was to sell the cotton to the best advantage of the firm's American clients. In a rapidly changing market precise instructions were usually soon out of date, and it was understood that William had considerable discretion. Alexander usually urged him to press on with sales even in a falling market. Occasionally Alexander ordered cotton on the Baltimore firm's own account, to fill his ships or to encourage joint purchases, and he then consigned it to W. and J. Brown for sale. William was successful because the family, despite occasional wilfulness, proved capable of managing these very complex arrangements and calculations.

William's capital grew from £36,000 in 1815 to £287,000 in 1830, and Alexander supplemented this when necessary with his own resources. William was therefore able to make very large advances in his own right to Liverpool merchants buying cotton or to British manufacturers exporting goods. Similarly his firm was well placed to negotiate bills of other merchants in Anglo-American trade. In 1827 the Bank of England agent reported:

> They act as agents for some of the American Banks so that a considerable portion of the Exchange business between the two Countries is effected through this House … [and they give credits to] … approved agents of American Houses who travel through the manufacturing districts and order goods at Manchester, Birmingham, Sheffield and other places and who pay for such goods by bills drawn upon this House, on which they receive a commission for which they get repaid by consignments of American produce.   (Bank of England Liverpool agent to head office, 8 Sept 1827)

In 1831 William became first chairman of the Bank of Liverpool, to aid his and other merchants' bill transactions.

Shipping interests The Browns owned a small fleet of ships from 1812 until the 1840s. They were registered in Baltimore, so they could legally participate in the American coastal as well as transatlantic trades, but they regularly visited Liverpool. It was said that William even regularly entertained—and gleaned the latest commercial gossip from—all the American packet-ship captains at the best hostelry in Liverpool, renowned for its turtle soup.

Besides managing their own ships, W. and J. Brown handled the cargoes of several American packet-ship lines. An example was the Cope Line. Thomas P. Cope was a Philadelphia merchant who established the first Philadelphia–Liverpool packet line in 1822. Initially his cargoes were consigned to fellow Quakers Rathbone Hodgson and Cropper Benson. When the Browns persuaded him to run his ships with theirs, Cope apologized to Cropper Benson. The Browns, he said, 'have acquired command of the shipping of a large proportion of Philadelphia goods … we saw should we decline [co-operation] we should encounter a most powerful and determined opposition' (Cope to Cropper Benson, 21 March 1822, Cope letter-books). Thereafter the Browns handled Cope's cargoes and ships for fifty years. They made similar arrangements with at least two New York–Liverpool packet lines as well as with 'regular ships' from Baltimore, thus ensuring the earliest information, and very profitable commissions on high-value freights.

Alexander Brown died in 1834, leaving William as the senior partner. However, distance and the partnership structure meant that although the brothers had to co-operate closely, in practice they had considerable discretion. George was severely shocked by Alexander's death and wished to specialize in finance. William's reaction is unknown. However, in the next few years the family firms expanded dramatically in the boom of the mid-1830s and they survived the panics of 1837–9. In 1830 financial flows between Liverpool and the Baltimore and New York branches were about $3.5 million, evenly divided between Baltimore and New York. By 1835 the joint flow had risen to $11 million compared to total American exports to Britain of $52 million. Similarly the capital of the firms as a whole had increased from $2.8 million in 1830 to $4.6 million when Alexander died. William's share of the assets in 1834 was about $1.7 million. By December 1836 total assets had risen to $5.9 million, but by late 1840, after John and George had withdrawn, the remaining capital had fallen to about $3 million.

The panic of 1837 severely tested the Liverpool firm. In late 1836 the Bank of England, afraid of gold outflows to the United States, had commenced restricting credits to the leading Anglo-American houses, including W. and J. Brown. By early 1837 the American houses had severely restrained their credits to their southern factors and others. In April 1837 the general pressure precipitated widespread panic in the United States, which soon affected Liverpool as bill and produce remittances depreciated, or failed to arrive. By May 1837 W. and J. Brown was in great difficulties and appealed to the Bank of England. As William was ill, Joseph Shipley, his junior partner, represented the firm. Supported by the Bank of Liverpool and the private bankers Denisons, Brown argued that the company was essentially sound, but that if they failed the consequences would be 'more felt than that of any other house in England … As no doubt a very large proportion of our acceptances are held by the Bank, we hope you will feel an interest and find an advantage in supporting us' (Ellis, 47). Thus while many other large houses failed, the Bank of England enabled W. and J. Brown to survive, through the very large loan of £2 million. Its magnitude can be assessed by comparison with the total British government expenditure in 1837 of £51 million and a total American expenditure of £8 million. This confidence proved justified, and by early 1838 the company had almost fully recovered; the bank loan was repaid, and the Liverpool firm, aided by the collapse of competitors, received more cotton than ever before. The company name was changed to Brown Shipley in 1839, in recognition of Shipley's role and his increasing importance in the firm.

Finance and banking In the mid-1830s Brown was running a very large, diversified merchant house. By 1850 Brown Shipley specialized in finance. There was a general but not universal trend towards specialization at this time as trade flows increased and the capital requirements of some activities such as shipowning grew. However, Brown Shipley shed many of its old interests for specific reasons. Alexander Brown's death and the panic of 1837 reduced George and John's enthusiasm for business and they retired in 1837 and 1839 respectively. Henceforth the Baltimore and Philadelphia offices took a marginal role. The demise of the Bank of the United States created a great opportunity for Brown Shipley and Brown Brothers to take over the bank's American domestic exchange business. The collapse of British exports to America finally ended Brown Shipley's role as export merchants. The Browns' interests in cotton lasted longer—in fact they opened branches in the south in the late 1830s to operate their exchange business and were forced, through their forfeiture on mortgages, to manage several bankrupt plantations. However, William Brown was increasingly sceptical of close connections with southern factors and planters: 'It is advances on plantations that has ruined most of the Old houses here' he wrote to James in 1846 (letter-book, 18 Oct 1847).

The Browns sold their sailing ships in the early 1840s, but in 1847 James Brown undertook to support the plan of Edward Knight Collins to create a steamship line to rival Cunard. William Brown's reaction was extremely hostile: 'I do not know when I was more surprised, astonished and mortified than … to find that you had become principals in Collins Steam Boat Scheme' (letter-book, 23 Jan 1848). He disliked the diversion of time and capital from the firms' existing business, and distrusted the new technology. Seeking to strike a deal with Cunard, he wrote to D. and C. McIver, Cunard's Liverpool agents in 1849, considering

> how unpleasant it would be for your vessels and those coming to us to be carrying on a war of mutual injuries … I have written to my Brother James … to see Mr Cunard … and if possible to make such arrangements as would prevent injury to either concerns.   (letter-book, 8 March 1849)

This led to the first effective steamship cartel. However, despite Brown's arrangements, and a generous federal subsidy, excessive costs and losses forced the Collins Line out of business in 1858.

By now, however, the Browns' central business concern was finance. In the early 1840s they took over the role of the Bank of the United States as the leading negotiator of

sterling and dollar bills of exchange, first in the cotton trade and then in all the leading transatlantic and American import trades. The growth of the business can be measured by the size of the firms' New York–Liverpool accounts. In 1845 the exchange flows stood at $16 million (against total American exports of $45 million); by 1855 these were $32 million (against $92 million), and by 1859 they were $45 million (against total American exports of $133 million). Meanwhile the firms' capital had increased from $3 million in 1840, to $5 million in 1850, and $6 million in 1860. A considerable portion of this was unfortunately locked up in the Collins Line and in southern plantations and other investments, and it was no wonder that William Brown was concerned, especially after panics, to free as much of the firms' capital as possible. In a letter to James he wrote:

> The more I think of it … the more I think it is desirable to get every shilling unlocked from fixed property. … When you think in our extensive Bill Business the very large amount of disappointments we must have even when we ultimately recover a large amount, it must be guarded against.   (letter-book, 18 Oct 1847)

Political campaigns By the early 1840s William Brown had delegated much of the detailed running of the business to able 'juniors' such as Joseph Shipley, Francis Hamilton, and Mark Collett, a future governor of the Bank of England. Instead he had become increasingly interested in politics. He had first entered Liverpool politics in the mid-1820s when he agitated for reform of the Liverpool docks, and he became a member of the important Liverpool dock committee in 1828. The Bank of England agent in Liverpool reported that the Brown partners 'are not men of much education and mix very little in the best society of the town' (Bank of England Liverpool agent to head office, 8 Sept 1827); nevertheless, William became an important figure behind the scenes, supporting the campaigns of free-trade allies such as John Denison, who was related to Brown's London bankers. Brown was a Liverpool alderman from 1835 to 1838 and a borough magistrate from 1833 to 1845, and he led the campaign against the corn laws in Liverpool in 1840. He became the Anti-Corn Law League's candidate for parliament in South Lancashire in 1844 but, although he lost, this election led to the re-organization of the electoral register. Hence when Lord Ellesmere resigned in 1846, Brown was returned unopposed to what he called the most commercial seat in Britain.

Brown was one of the leaders and financiers of the Liberal group of MPs who secured free trade. He reported his maiden speech to James:

> Lord George Bentinck had been promulgating … the most erroneous opinions … the spirit moved me … and up I got to attack this great protective Leviathan … before I had proceeded far the cheers became loud and long, so that the Reporters lost some of my argument. … When I had done … I received the congratulations of all the members around me and of the Ministerial bench.   (letter-book, 24 Jan 1847)

Nevertheless Brown was not a commanding speaker in parliament: his voice was too weak and he often chose dull commercial subjects. However, he lobbied effectively for Liverpool, Anglo-American, and international affairs. For instance, during the commercial crisis of late 1847 he represented the Liverpool merchants' interest to Sir Charles Wood, the chancellor of the exchequer. In February 1848 he wrote authoritatively to Wood that his colleagues Alexander Henry, Richard Cobden, John Bright, Joseph Brotherton, Thomas Thornley, and Joseph Hume wished to interview Wood and Lord John Russell. He also represented the Lancashire free-traders in the Brussels Congress of All Nations in 1847. He generally supported good international causes, had lobbied in favour of the penny post in Liverpool in 1838, and supported the extension of the uniform post principle to transatlantic mail in the late 1840s. He wrote regularly to prominent Americans, which included a widely published correspondence with W. M. Meredith, secretary of the US Treasury in 1849–50, opposing protection.

In the early 1850s Brown turned to his own preferred domestic reform, decimalization, and in April 1853 secured the appointment of a select committee on decimals which he chaired. Initially he hoped to introduce a comprehensive decimal system of weights and measures as well as currency but Gladstone persuaded him to attempt currency first. His proposed system included a sovereign worth 1000 farthings or mils, with the florin—the predecessor of the current 10 pence piece—worth 100. He wrote to Charles Wood in February 1852: 'I am glad that the mint is at work on the Florins—I wish they were at work on the copper coinage—a cent or a penny called five farthings, then our decimal coinage would be complete' (letter-book, 10 Feb 1852). Gladstone told him that although the government was in favour in principle, Brown must demonstrate public interest before it would act. Hence Brown wrote hundreds of letters to mayors, commercial associations, universities, and mechanics' institutes. For instance he wrote to Thomas Bazley:

> Master manufacturers might take the trouble of explaining to their intelligent Foremen the advantages of a Decimal System and ... a grand petition might be signed by all the adult hands in their mills, which would I think have great weight with the Chancellor. ... He is very timid and fears the masses would not be satisfied with the change—we must use a little pressure with him. (letter-book, 1 Dec 1853)

These methods secured favourable votes in the House of Commons, and between 150 and 200 MPs joined the Decimal Society. However, the conservative royal commission, appointed by the government in 1856, dispatched the proposal.

Fostering good Anglo-American relations Brown attempted to improve Anglo-American relations. He entertained or interviewed each American ambassador including Abbott Lawrence, James Buchanan, and Charles Francis Adams. Free trade itself was an obvious exercise in Anglo-American relations. Brown also mediated between Palmerston and George Mifflin Dallas, American minister in London, in the foreign recruitment issue in 1856 when the USA objected to Britain's attempts to recruit American volunteers for the Crimean War. He persuaded Palmerston that a rupture between Britain and the USA would

seriously affect British trade, and that American protests were probably motivated by domestic electoral rather than diplomatic concern and would therefore soon fade.

Brown also became directly involved in Anglo-American negotiations in Central America, where a rail route was required to link the shipping services between New York and San Francisco. Under the Clayton–Bulwer treaty of 1850 Britain and the USA had agreed not to seek exclusive control in Central America, leaving a confused power vacuum in which the Central American republics and American filibusters contended for control. Britain itself had interests in Honduras, the Mosquito Coast, and the Bay Islands. Brown reluctantly accepted a request in 1856 from the British government to form the Honduras Interoceanic Railway Company to build a railway across Honduras. He wrote to Charles Pelham Villiers MP that it had been made clear to him that 'the settlement of our affairs with the United States and Honduras was based upon carrying forward the railroad ... the importance of the adjustment of our American difficulties to our respective countries cannot be overrated'. Although New York and London boards were formed, the venture collapsed in the commercial panic of 1857. By this time rail and lake steamer routes, dominated by American interests, had been built across Panama and Nicaragua and the longer Honduras route was never exploited.

Last years, character, and appearance, 1859–1864 In the last years of his life Brown continued to sponsor Anglo-American projects such as the first (unsuccessful) transatlantic telegraph. However, his major interests were local. He gave £40,000 to Liverpool to build in 1857–60 the imposing Brown Picton Public Library, and he was rewarded with a baronetcy in 1863. The American consul, the novelist Nathaniel Hawthorne, who attended the dedication in 1857, wrote that among all the dignitaries William Brown 'was the plainest, and simplest man of all: an exceedingly unpretending old gentleman in black, small, withered, white haired, pale, quiet and respectable' (Kouwenhoven, 105). Brown also, in the spirit of the times, raised, equipped, and commanded the 1st brigade of Lancashire artillery volunteers.

Hawthorne's portrait of William Brown is somewhat qualified by Benjamin Orchard, the leading late-nineteenth-century Liverpool biographer. Orchard had no love for Brown, and in his sketch called him William Green. Like Hawthorne he noted that in the open air Brown seemed 'rather small of stature; at no time dignified or dashing in manner; with stooping shoulders, shrinking air and hesitating speech, in neat but unpretentious attire, few would have turned again to look at him.' Nevertheless, Orchard observes:

> But see him with his hat off, seated in his office chair, giving directions to a junior partner, or sedately chatting with one of his trade connections, and no intelligent observer would doubt that he had before him one of those remarkable men who seem specially formed by nature to become the great cornerstones of a nation's commerce. Whoever has examined the portraits of William and his brother George ... must have seen this; but exquisitely as they are painted, they do not tell all. There were about William Green an amplitude

of temple, a lofty and compact squareness of brow, a weight of character in each line round the mouth, an inscrutable keenness of eye, a mingling of calm power and enterprising shrewdness, so unusual and so impressive as to startle even the most stupid beholder.   (Orchard, 211–215)

Many of Orchard's comments are clearly biased or inaccurate, but these descriptions do help to explain the contrast between Brown's meek appearance and his dominating character, and his provincial background and his international success.

The American Civil War was potentially a great disaster for the Browns, especially if Britain had become involved. William visited Charles Francis Adams, the American ambassador, and wrote to the secretary of state, William Henry Seward, arguing that the belligerents should respect private property. When James was pressed to invest in federal bonds, William wrote firmly that the main responsibility of the partners was not to the north or to Britain, but to the future of the firm. In practice the firm did relatively well during the war, but its future was also threatened because, though William remained healthy into old age, all his children died before him, and his grandchildren were still young in 1860. He and James, most of whose children had also died, were forced to make complex settlements to protect the firm and their heirs. William died at his home, Richmond Hill, Walton, near Liverpool, on 3 March 1864. He had transferred some of his private capital to the firm before his death, and therefore left under £1 million. His eldest son, Alexander Brown, having died on 8 October 1849, his grandson, Lieutenant-Colonel William Richmond Brown, succeeded to the baronetcy. Obituaries acknowledged Brown's abilities and accomplishments, but concluded that despite his long public service to Liverpool, some element in his character denied him public affection.   J. R. KILLICK

Sources L. Cong., manuscript division, Alexander Brown and Sons MSS · NYPL, Humanities and Social Sciences Library, Brown Brothers & Company MSS, special collections · William Brown letter-books, Brown Shipley, London · letters of Liverpool agent to London office, Bank of England Archives, London · Hist. Soc. Penn., Cope MSS · Joseph Shipley MSS, Eleutherian Mills, Wilmington, Delaware, USA · J. C. Brown, *A hundred years of merchant banking: a history of Brown Brothers and Company, Brown Shipley and Company and the allied firms* (privately printed, New York, 1909) · G. Chandler, *Four centuries of banking*, 2 vols. (1964–8) · A. Ellis, *Heir of adventure: the story of Brown, Shipley & Co., merchant bankers* (privately printed, London, 1960) · H. R. Fox Bourne, *English merchants: memoirs in illustration of the progress of British commerce*, 2 vols. (1866) · J. R. Killick, 'Risk, specialization and profit in the mercantile sector of the nineteenth century cotton trade: Alexander Brown & Sons, 1820–80', *Business History*, 16 (1974), 1–16 · J. R. Killick, 'The cotton operations of Alexander Brown and Sons in the deep south, 1820–1860', *Journal of Southern History*, 43 (1977), 169–94 · *DNB* · d. cert. · J. A. Kouwenhoven, *Partners in banking: an historical portrait of a great private bank, Brown Brothers, Harriman & Co., 1818–1968* (1968) · B. G. Orchard, *Liverpool's legion of honour* (1893) · E. J. Perkins, *Financing Anglo-American trade: the house of Brown, 1800–1880* (1975) · Burke, *Peerage*

Archives Brown–Picton Library, Liverpool · GL · L. Cong. · New York Historical Society · NYPL | BL, corresp. with Sir Charles Wood, Add. MS 49552, *passim* · Borth. Inst., letters to Sir Charles Wood · Hist. Soc. Penn., Cope MSS

Likenesses J. Watson-Gordon, portrait, 1857, Walker Art Gallery, Liverpool [*see illus.*] · C. Baugniet, lithograph, 1858, BM · P. Macdowell, statue, 1858, St George's Hall, Liverpool · J. Stephenson, mezzotint (after portrait by C. Agar, *c.*1846), repro. in Kouwenhoven, *Partners in banking*, 26 · portrait, repro. in Brown, *A hundred years of merchant banking* · portrait (as lieutenant-colonel of the volunteers; with two sons), repro. in Brown, *A hundred years of merchant banking*, 130 · portraits, repro. in Kouwenhoven, *Partners in banking* · wood-engraving, repro. in *ILN* (12 July 1851) · wood-engraving, repro. in *ILN* (26 July 1851)

Wealth at death under £900,000: probate, 8 April 1864, *CGPLA Eng. & Wales*

Brown, William (1881–1952), psychologist and psychiatrist, was born on 5 December 1881 at the School House, Slinfold, Horsham, Sussex, the second son of William Brown, a schoolmaster of Northumbrian origins, and his wife, Kezia Harriett (*née* Evans). He attended Collyer's School in Horsham, winning a scholarship to Christ Church, Oxford, in 1899, where he took mathematical moderations in 1902 and final honours in natural science (physiology) in 1904. In the following year he added *literae humaniores* while studying psychology as a special subject under William McDougall. He spent some time in Germany as the 1906 John Locke scholar in mental philosophy before embarking on mathematical and medical studies in London. In 1910 Brown earned a DSc (and the Carpenter medal) from the University of London for pioneering work on applying Karl Pearson's statistical ideas to psychological measurement.

Meanwhile, Brown held a lectureship in psychology at King's College, University of London, from 1909, becoming reader in 1914 (when he also qualified in medicine at King's College Hospital). In 1921 Brown succeeded McDougall as Wilde reader in mental philosophy, remaining in Oxford until his retirement in 1946. It was largely through his efforts, and an endowment of £10,000 from one of his patients, Mrs Hugh Watts, that the Institute of Experimental Psychology, of which he was the first director (1936–45), was founded in 1936, and psychology at last gained honour school status in 1946.

However, serving as a Royal Army Medical Corps officer during the First World War, Brown joined a small band of fellow neuropsychologists (including McDougall, W. H. R. Rivers, and C. S. Myers) who were attempting to treat the war neuroses that afflicted large numbers of front-line troops. This experience had gradually transformed Brown from quantitative psychologist into the eclectic psychotherapist and psychiatrist of his later years. Already sympathetic to Freudian ideas, he became interested in the treatment of shell-shock by hypnotically induced abreaction while training at the Maghull Military Hospital. This technique was the bedrock of his work as neurologist to the British expeditionary force in France (1916–18), as commandant of the Craiglockhart Hospital for Neurasthenic Officers (where the poets Siegfried Sassoon and Wilfred Owen had earlier been patients of Rivers) between 1918 and 1919, and also at the Maudsley Hospital. Paralleling this evolution was his steady acquisition of medical qualifications: DM (Oxford) in 1918, then MRCP and FRCP in 1921 and 1930 respectively. But the war period also changed Brown's life in more immediate and personal ways by the death of his wife, whom he had married on 29 September 1906, May Leslie Rayment English (*b.* 1880/81), daughter of Edmund English, early in 1916 and his marriage, on 19 July 1917, to a military nurse, Dorothea Mary (*b.* 1889/90), daughter of PC Edwin Stone of the Somerset constabulary. There were three children from these marriages, a son from the first, then another son and a daughter from the second.

Although publishing widely on medical aspects of psychology from 1922 onwards, Brown's *The Essentials of Mental Measurement* (1911), based on his DSc thesis, had brought him to early prominence within the growing British psychological establishment, not least by sparking off a prolonged conflict with Charles Spearman. Indeed, Brown's attack on Spearman's notion of general intelligence was renewed (albeit with growing unease on Brown's part) in the later editions which were co-authored with Godfrey Thomson, an even more implacable opponent of Spearman's theories. To Spearman's public delight Brown defected to the general intelligence camp in 1932, when he published strong evidence supporting a key aspect of Spearman's theory of intelligence.

By the late 1920s, however, Brown was devoting less time to academic psychology than to administrative matters in Oxford and to his burgeoning clinical practice, which included appointments at King's College Hospital, London, and at the Bethlem Royal Hospital. His writings on psychiatry now focused on grander issues such as religion and war, and on the foundations of the discipline, in *Mind, Medicine and Metaphysics* (1936), for instance, rather than on the practical concerns of his earlier professional life.

Brown was active in many societies concerned with advancing psychological knowledge. He served as president of section J (psychology) of the British Association for the Advancement of Science in 1927, and of the Society for the Study of Addiction between 1935 and 1937. In the last year of his life the British Psychological Society, an organization with which he had been closely associated from as early as 1907, chose him as its president.

Brown died from a coronary thrombosis on 17 May 1952 at the Berystede Hotel, Sunninghill, near Windsor, Berkshire. He was survived by his wife.

P. LOVIE and A. D. LOVIE

Sources *The Lancet* (24 May 1952) · *British Journal of Medical Psychology*, 26 (1953), 120–22 · *British Journal of Psychology, Statistical Section*, 5 (1952), 137–8 · *The Times* (19 May 1952) · *WWW* · L. S. Hearnshaw, *A short history of British psychology, 1840–1940* (1964) · b. cert. · m. certs. · d. cert. · J. B. Morrell, 'The non-medical sciences, 1914–1939', *Hist. U. Oxf.* 8: *20th cent.*, 139–63 · *CGPLA Eng. & Wales* (1952)
Likenesses photogravure, 1915, repro. in W. H. R. Rivers, *Psychology and politics* (1923)
Wealth at death £13,529 0s. 1d.: probate, 3 July 1952, *CGPLA Eng. & Wales*

Brown, William (1888–1975), mycologist and plant pathologist, was born on 17 February 1888 at Middlebie, Dumfriesshire, the second son and child of Gavin Brown, small farmer and agricultural engineer, and his wife, Margaret Broatch. In 1900 he went to the Annan Academy as a day scholar, obtaining in 1904 a leaving certificate in mathematics, English, Latin, French, and German, and a bursary for Edinburgh University. In 1908 he took his MA degree, with first-class honours in mathematics, qualifying also in physics and other sciences. Until 1906 he had continued to study Latin (first prize and medal); for the rest of his life he read both Greek and Roman authors in their native texts. Following graduation he spent two more years at Edinburgh, qualifying in 1910 for a BSc in advanced botany and zoology. Over the six years of his studies he was awarded fourteen medals.

In 1912, after two years as a temporary lecturer in plant physiology in the Edinburgh botany department, Brown gained a two-year scholarship to the botany department of the Imperial College of Science and Technology. He became a research student under Vernon Blackman, and was awarded a London DSc in 1916. In 1923 he was appointed assistant professor on the college staff, and in 1928 was made professor of plant pathology in the University of London, the first such post to be established in Britain. In 1921 Brown had married Lucy Doris Allen (*d.* 1966), a graduate of London University (Bedford College) with first-class honours in botany; she was the daughter of a shipping agent and her mother was from a family of London clockmakers. They had a son and three daughters, one of whom, Lucy, taught at the London School of Economics.

Brown's experimental work on the physiology of fungal growth in culture and of infection of plant tissues was published in a series of eighteen papers (1915–28), and is regarded as a pioneering achievement in these twin subjects. He showed that soft-rot of plant tissues is mediated by fungal secretion of pectinase enzymes and that fungal infectivity is enhanced by nutrients diffusing through the thin cuticle of flower petals and young leaves. His studies of the growth of fungi of the genus *Fusarium* in culture revealed serious flaws in the taxonomic disposition of species within the genus, which was later revised accordingly. In his paper on combinations of gas and cold storage for control of fungal rots of apple fruits, which was published in the *Annals of Botany* in 1922, Brown concluded that the effect of fungistatic factors was greatest when the fungal energy of growth was least. This was Brown's major generalization; it led to the concept of fungal inoculum potential for colonization of plant tissues, both living and dead.

As a supervisor Brown was regarded with affection and respect by his research students. Although he may have appeared conventional in dress and behaviour, his approach to research was anything but so. In his lectures to undergraduates he disdained any tricks of oratory, and his lucid exposition, enlivened by flashes of dry humour, compelled close attention. These qualities are revealed by his lecture entitled 'Spontaneous generation', published in the Royal College of Science *Journal* in 1952.

In 1938 Brown was elected FRS. In the same year, he became head of the botany department and continued thus until his retirement in 1953, overseeing a difficult period of post-war reconstruction. As a young man Brown was quite athletic; he was a competent golfer and tennis player. After retirement his chief outdoor interest was gardening. He died in Manchester on 18 January 1975.

S. D. GARRETT, rev.

Sources S. D. Garrett, *Memoirs FRS*, 21 (1975), 155–74 · personal knowledge (1986) · *WWW, 1971–80* · *CGPLA Eng. & Wales* (1975)
Wealth at death £17,928: probate, 17 April 1975, *CGPLA Eng. & Wales*

Brown, William Beattie (1831–1909), landscape painter, was born in the parish of Haddington, near Edinburgh, on 9 November 1831, the son of Adam Brown, farmer, and his wife, Ann Beattie. When he was still young the family moved to Leith, then a separate burgh outside Edinburgh, and he was educated at Leith high school. He was then apprenticed as a glass-stainer to the firm of Messrs James Ballantine & Son in Edinburgh. Very soon he showed considerable artistic talent and before his apprenticeship was completed he was accepted as a student at the Trustees' Academy in Edinburgh under the directorship of Robert Scott Lauder. His skill and accuracy as a draughtsman led to his employment as an illustrator for medical works. Early in his career he was also employed as a picture restorer by Henry Doig, an Edinburgh art dealer, carver, and gilder. On 23 December 1858 he married his employer's daughter, Esther Love Doig (c.1838–1904); they had three sons and six daughters.

Beattie Brown first exhibited at the Royal Scottish Academy in 1852 and from then on became a regular and prolific exhibitor for the rest of his life. He also exhibited at the Royal Academy in London periodically from 1863 to 1899. In 1871 he was elected an associate of the Royal Scottish Academy and in 1884 a full academician. He specialized in landscape painting, in the early years particularly of the Edinburgh area, the lowlands, and the Scottish borders. Gradually he was increasingly drawn to the attractions of the wilder parts of Scotland further north, and it is by these works that he is best remembered. For example, his diploma work in the Royal Scottish Academy, *Coire-na-Faireamh* (1883), set in Applecross deer forest in Ross-shire, is a dramatic representation of one of the steepest passes in the north-west highlands. Painted remarkably freely in dark, heavy colours, and with strong contrasts of the highlights of light on water, it evokes very forcefully the idea of a remote and deserted wilderness. The directness of such paintings is a result of his fondness for working *en plein air*, a practice for which he was an early enthusiast. These works, often characterized by an overall brown tone, brought him much popularity in his lifetime.

Like many others of his contemporaries from the east of Scotland, Beattie Brown also studied in the Low Countries, working particularly in watercolour when away from home. In the late 1880s and early 1890s he exhibited a number of quieter landscapes of the scenery around Dordrecht in the Netherlands and further south in Belgium. He also produced a certain amount of work in the English home counties and Yorkshire. Towards the end of his life his colours became lighter and brighter, reflecting the influence of higher-keyed paintings by, for example, the Glasgow Boys and other younger artists. William Beattie Brown died at his home at 15 St Bernard's Crescent, Edinburgh, on 31 March 1909 and was buried in Warriston cemetery in that city on 3 April.

JOANNA SODEN

Sources *Annual Report of the Council of the Royal Scottish Academy of Painting, Sculpture, and Architecture*, 82 (1909), 16–17 · *The Scotsman* (1 April 1909) · *Art Journal*, new ser., 29 (1909), 180 · C. B. de Laperriere, ed., *The Royal Scottish Academy exhibitors, 1826–1990*, 4 vols. (1991), vol. 1, pp. 203–9 · Graves, *RA exhibitors*, 1 (1905), 315 · *DNB* · P. J. M. McEwan, *Dictionary of Scottish art and architecture* (1994), 94–5 · J. L. Caw, *Scottish painting past and present, 1620–1908* (1908), 298 · Wood, *Vic. painters*, 2nd edn · bap. reg. Scot. · m. cert. · d. cert. · Royal Scot. Acad.
Likenesses J. B. Abercromby, wash drawing, 1898, Scot. NPG · J. B. Abercromby, oils, Royal Scot. Acad. · photographs, Royal Scot. Acad.
Wealth at death £3134 17s. 1d.: confirmation, 28 April 1909, *CCI*

Brown, William Cheselden (c.1768–1814), naval officer, was the son of Suffield Brown, of Leesthorpe, near Melton Mowbray, Leicestershire. He passed his examination for lieutenant in the Royal Navy in February 1788 and further promotion soon followed. By 1792 he had advanced to the rank of commander and at the end of 1793 he was made a captain. By then he had seen service on the Mediterranean and on the home stations and in 1794 he joined the Channel Fleet under Lord Howe, in command of the frigate *Venus*. He was present at the battle of 1 June 1794, though he played no particularly distinguished role in the battle. He remained at sea on the home station and patrolling off the coast of Portugal, despite increasing ill health, until November 1797, when he was sent to hospital in Lisbon. On his recovery, in March 1798 he was sent to command the *Defence*, a line-of-battle ship, followed by another vessel, the *Santa Dorothea*, in January 1799. It was probably at some point after this, though it is impossible to be certain, that Brown married a daughter of John Travers, a director of the East India Company.

Brown's career is overshadowed by the events of 22 July 1805, when he was in command of the *Ajax*, under Sir Robert Calder. Vice-Admiral Calder's squadron, cruising off Ferrol, intercepted the Franco-Spanish fleet of Admiral Villeneuve, which was returning to Europe after sailing to the West Indies. The battle occurred on a foggy afternoon, when any control over the forces engaged was extremely difficult. Calder attempted to break the enemy line, but was unable to do so, mainly owing—so it was said at the time—to his timidity and to Brown's turning his ship away from the Franco-Spanish line to communicate with his admiral, which weakened the van of the British fleet at this critical moment. Calder broke off the action as darkness fell and Villeneuve's ships were able to slip into port, while Calder was summoned back to England to explain his conduct. More recently the overall outcome of the engagement has been seen as more favourable to the Royal Navy, Brown's role being overlooked or not regarded as specially significant. Whatever the case, Brown's career does not seem to have suffered unduly as a result. He missed the battle of Trafalgar because he was in Britain attending Calder's court martial at the request of the admiral, but Brown continued to hold active appointments ashore. He spent some time as commissioner at Malta and Sheerness dockyards, and was promoted rear-admiral in 1812. In June 1813 he was appointed commander-in-chief in Jamaica, and it was while holding this post that, in January 1814, he was taken ill. He died on the twentieth of the month, after an illness of five days, leaving a widow and nine children.

MICHAEL PARTRIDGE

Sources DNB · GM, 1st ser., 84/2 (1814), 611 · examination for lieutenant, PRO, ADM MS 106/11 · O'Byrne, Naval biog. dict. [Charles Foreman Brown and William Cheselden Brown] · R. Gardiner, ed., The campaign of Trafalgar (1997) · N. Tracy, 'Sir Robert Calder's action', Mariner's Mirror, 77 (1991), 259–70 · A. Schom, Trafalgar: countdown to battle (1990) · W. James, The naval history of Great Britain, from the declaration of war by France in 1793, to the accession of George IV, [5th edn], 6 vols. (1859–60), vol. 3, p. 361

Brown, William Francis (1862–1951), Roman Catholic bishop, was born in Park Place House, Dundee, on 3 May 1862, the third of the four sons and six children of Andrew Brown of Lochton House, Inchture, Perthshire, who was the grandson of James Brown of Cononsyth, pioneer of the flax spinning industry in Dundee. His mother was Fanny Mary, daughter of Major James Wemyss of Carriston, of the Royal Scots Greys, who was the central figure in the famous painting *Scotland for Ever!* by Lady Butler.

Brown attended the high school, Dundee, Trinity College, Glenalmond, and University College School, London. His parents were Episcopalians but within eight years of his mother's becoming a Roman Catholic in 1873 the entire family was of the same faith. Brown's own reception in 1880 turned his thoughts from the forestry service in India to the priesthood. He went to the short-lived Catholic University established in Kensington by Cardinal Manning, entered St Thomas's Seminary, Hammersmith, as a student for the diocese of Westminster in 1882, and, having changed to the diocese of Southwark, was ordained priest in 1886. He was appointed curate to the Sacred Heart Church, Camberwell, until in 1892 he became priest-in-charge of a new district formed by detaching part of the area between Lambeth Bridge and Battersea, Clapham, and Camberwell, until then served from St George's Cathedral. This was to become the parish of St Anne, Vauxhall, where Brown spent the rest of his life as parish priest, and from which the prospect of high ecclesiastical office in his native Scotland and still less the intensive bombing of the war years could not separate him. That was where his heart lay, and his unceasing perambulation of his parish made him one of the best-known personalities in south London, and inspired his zeal for social reform long before such a tendency ceased to be regarded as dangerous or at least eccentric.

To a parish priest for whom children were the apple of his eye, education became an all-consuming interest. In 1896 Brown became secretary of the diocesan association set up in Southwark to administer the grants to voluntary schools. He had already stood unsuccessfully in 1894 as a Catholic candidate for the London school board, to which he was elected in 1897. Two years later his motion that the

William Francis Brown (1862–1951), by Howard Coster, 1940s

board should seek powers to feed undernourished children was defeated, but in the end the necessary legislation was promoted and a start was made with what became an accepted part of the school system. By the time the board came to an end in 1904 Brown was recognized as an expert on educational questions who was frequently consulted by Robert Morant, permanent secretary of the Board of Education, over the act of 1902 and its implementation as well as the subsequent Liberal attempts to amend it. In recognition of his work he was appointed protonotary apostolic in 1907.

Ten years later he was the obvious choice of the Holy See as apostolic visitor to Scotland at a critical period in the history of the Catholic church in that country. The phenomenal growth of the Catholic population in the industrial areas had thrown an impossible burden on the financial resources of a church faced with the responsibility of providing both schools and teachers. A new education bill was mooted. One solution was to absorb Catholics into a national system of education without prejudice to their principles. The times were propitious. The Catholic population had done its bit in the war effort. The Irish nationalist party, from its peculiar point of vantage, came to the aid of its Catholic brethren, themselves mostly of Irish origin. By the exercise of Brown's consummate skill in controlling a team which at times made heavy demands on his reserves of patience and tact, and indeed his physical endurance, the bill became the historic Education (Scotland) Act, 1918. Brown refused the offer of a Scottish archbishopric, but it gave him enormous pleasure that, by a remarkably apt coincidence, the very house in which he was born eventually became part of the first Catholic junior secondary school in Dundee. In the diocese of Southwark he was consecrated auxiliary bishop (with the titular see of Pella) in 1924. He had been vicar-general since 1904 and provost of the chapter since 1916.

Brown was a stocky, virile figure with a rugged beetle-browed face. Tough, but by no means rough, he was very far from being the proud prelate so dear to the imagination of some of his fellow countrymen. Like so many of them, too, he was austere in his habits, and knew the value of money, especially when it was not his own. The fine church of St Anne which he built was cleared of debt in time to be consecrated in 1911 on the twenty-fifth anniversary of his ordination. He never lost his Scots accent and retained to his dying day the liveliest interest in men and affairs. He could have escaped notice at a meeting of the general assembly. Church House, the law courts, and even the Old Bailey were not unknown to him. His sole publication was a long contemplated volume of reminiscences, *Through Windows of Memory* (1946). This slim volume, introduced by Sir Shane Leslie, gave a rapid sketch of his life with its catholic interests and varied contacts. Brown died in Southwark on 16 December 1951.

J. D. SCANLAN, rev.

Sources *The Times* (18 Dec 1951) · W. F. Brown, *Through windows of memory* (1946) · Burke, *Gen. GB* (1952) · *The Tablet* (22 Dec 1951) · personal knowledge (1971) · *WWW* · *CGPLA Eng. & Wales* (1952)
Archives St George's Roman Catholic Cathedral, Southwark, London, Southwark Roman Catholic diocesan archives, papers, incl. material relating to education acts and Scotland | FILM BFI NFTVA, news footage
Likenesses H. Coster, photograph, 1940–49, NPG [*see illus.*] · H. Coster, photographs, NPG · photograph, repro. in Brown, *Through windows of memory*, frontispiece
Wealth at death £11,872 6s. 10d.: confirmation, 29 May 1952, *CCI* · £107 12s. 11d.: additional estate, 27 May 1952, *CCI*

Brown, William Haig (1823–1907), headmaster, was born at Bromley by Bow, Middlesex, on 3 December 1823, the third son of Thomas Brown of Edinburgh and his wife, Amelia, daughter of John Haig, of the family of 'Haig of Bemersyde'. In his tenth year he received a presentation to Christ's Hospital, where he remained, first in the junior school at Hertford, and later on in London, until 1842. He entered Pembroke College, Cambridge, graduating BA in 1846 as eighth junior optime in the mathematical and second in the first class in the classical tripos. He was briefly a schoolmaster at Edinburgh and Richmond, Yorkshire, publishing school editions of Sophocles (1847, 1848), before his election as a fellow of his college in October 1848 (MA 1849). He took holy orders (deacon 1852 and priest 1853), and was a college tutor until 1857, when his marriage to Annie Marion, eldest daughter of the Revd E. E. Rowsell, obliged him to vacate his fellowship. He became headmaster of Kensington proprietary school, a post he held until 1863, when he was appointed to the headmastership of Charterhouse, in spite of the long-established tradition that the schoolmaster (such was then his title) should have been educated at the school.

The following year Haig Brown proceeded LLD at Cambridge.

The position of Charterhouse was at this time critical. Placed in the heart of London, and with the new Smithfield market at its doors, its existence as a boarding-school was rapidly becoming impossible, and the report of the public schools' commission, issued early in 1864, definitely recommended its removal. Apart from the objections of radical politicians like A. S. Ayrton, who denounced the removal as an injury 'to twenty, thirty, or even 50,000 families in the metropolis' who had a claim to benefit by its endowments, a stubborn resistance was offered by the governors and their chairman, Archdeacon William Hale, the master of the hospital, whose authority was then superior to that of the schoolmaster. Haig Brown thereupon issued a circular to old Carthusians, laying the whole case before them, the result being that they voted in the proportion of ten to one for removal, while he also won over Lord Derby, an influential governor, who became prime minister in June 1866, and he secured the support of Gladstone, who had recently been made a governor. In May 1866 the governors decided on the removal, and a private bill, giving the necessary powers, was introduced in the House of Lords, passed the House of Commons on 16 August, and became law four days later.

The new and admirable site at Godalming, Surrey, was accidentally discovered by Haig Brown, who, when on a visit to his wife's father at his rectory of Hambledon in the neighbourhood, heard that the Deanery Farm estate was for sale, walked over the same day, and made up his mind. The governors, who had sold a large portion of their London estate to Merchant Taylors' School for a price far below its real value, refused, by what proved to be a very costly error, to purchase more than 55 acres, a large part of which was useless either for buildings or for playing fields, and made provision for the accommodation of only about 180 boys. But the main point was carried; the first sod was turned on Founder's day 1869, and on 18 June 1872 the new school was occupied by 117 old and 33 new boys. From that moment its progress was remarkable. The schoolmaster no longer occupied a position subordinate to the master of the hospital, but by the appointment of a 'new governing body of Charterhouse school' (distinct henceforth from the 'governors of Charterhouse'), in accordance with the Public Schools Act of 1868, he became a headmaster, with the considerable statutory powers which that act bestowed. Once Haig Brown held power he knew how to use it. Fearless himself, he inspired all around him with his own courage and confidence. Within a few years, in addition to the three houses originally built by the governors, eight others were erected by various masters entirely at their own expense, until by September 1876 the number of boys had grown to 500, the number to which it was then limited, though it afterwards crept up to 560. In 1874 the school chapel was consecrated, and from then for more than thirty years frequent additions were made to the school in the shape of classrooms, a hall, a museum, and new playing fields. When Haig

Brown retired in 1897 he was justly known everywhere as 'our second founder'.

In 1872 the future of Charterhouse was precarious; in 1897 it was secure, though the move had turned Charterhouse almost entirely into a boarding-school. The result was mainly due to the powerful, single-minded personality of the headmaster. Haig Brown was not a great teacher, certainly no theorist about education, no lover of exact rules, and rather one who allowed both boys and masters the largest measure of independence. Like the other three great schoolmasters of the century, Arnold, Thring, and Kennedy, he neither sought nor received ecclesiastical preferment. Though bold to make changes, he was loyal to the past, so that he became the living embodiment of 'the spirit of the school', both in its old and its new 'home'. A man 'of infinite jest', though he could be very stern, he was always very human, so that 'Old Bill', as he was called, was an object equally of awe and of affection. His published works on the school and its traditions showed his attachment to the institution. Three of his hymns were included in the service for founder's day.

On his retirement from the school in 1897 Haig Brown was appointed master of Charterhouse (in London). He took an active part in the government of the hospital, and remained an energetic member of the governing body of the school. He also maintained a close connection with Christ's Hospital as a member of the governing body, his experience being of especial service when the school was moved to Horsham in 1902. He was the author of the Christ's Hospital school song. Among other distinctions bestowed on him were those of honorary canon of Winchester in 1891, and honorary fellow of Pembroke, his old college at Cambridge, in 1899. He was also made officier de l'Académie in 1882, and officier de l'Instruction publique in 1900. He died at the master's lodge at the hospital on 11 January 1907, and was buried in the chapel at Charterhouse School.

Of Haig Brown's five sons and seven daughters, **Rosalind Mabel Haig Brown** (1872–1964) had a notable career as a headmistress. Born in London on 20 January 1872, she was educated at Guildford high school and, from 1893, at Girton College, Cambridge, where she obtained second-class honours in the first part of the mathematical tripos (1896) and third-class honours in the medieval and modern languages tripos (1897), graduating MA from Trinity College, Dublin, in 1906. An assistant mistress at Blackheath high school from 1897 to 1901, she was appointed headmistress of Oxford high school in 1902 at the age of twenty-nine. In a period when the value of an academic secondary education for girls was still under question, and the performance of girls' schools liable to be measured against boys' public schools, she set a high intellectual standard. Boarding-houses were opened during her headship, and she was noted for her school addresses on ethics, published as *Ad lucem* (1931). 'Haggles' as she was known at the school, was described as 'tall and dignified', usually wearing a dark dress (Stack, 39). She retired in 1932, devoting her leisure to work for voluntary associations, including the United Nations Association and particularly the

Oxford City Moral Welfare Association, whose casework among unmarried mothers recalled Victorian purity and rescue movements. Rosalind Haig Brown died, unmarried, at St Joseph's Nursing Home, Boars Hill, Oxford, on 7 September 1964, and was buried in St Andrew's churchyard, Oxford, on 3 October.

T. E. PAGE, *rev.* M. C. CURTHOYS

Sources H. E. H. Brown, ed., *William Haig Brown of Charterhouse* (1908) · A. Quick, *Charterhouse: a history of the school* (1990) · personal knowledge (1912) · *Oxford Times* (11 Sept 1964) [Rosalind Mabel Haig Brown] · *Oxford Times* (24 Feb 1956) [Rosalind Mabel Haig Brown] · V. E. Stack, ed., *Oxford high school … 1875–1960* (1963) [Rosalind Mabel Haig Brown] · register, Girton Cam. [Rosalind Mabel Haig Brown] · Venn, *Alum. Cant.*
Archives CUL, letters to Sir George Stokes
Likenesses F. Holl, oils, exh. RA 1886, Charterhouse School, Surrey · H. Bates, bronze statue, *c.*1899, Charterhouse School, Surrey · M. Beerbohm, caricature, Charterhouse School, Surrey · M. Beerbohm, caricature, U. Cal., Los Angeles, William Andrews Clark Memorial Library · F. H. von Herkomer, etching (after F. Holl) · photograph (Rosalind Mabel Haig Brown), repro. in *Oxford Times* (24 Feb 1956), 8 · portrait, repro. in H. Brown, *Carthusian memories and other verses of leisure* (1905)
Wealth at death £19,241 1s. 9d.: probate, 27 Feb 1907, CGPLA Eng. & Wales · £13,188—Rosalind Mabel Haig Brown: probate, 29 Oct 1964, CGPLA Eng. & Wales

Brown, William John (1894–1960), trade unionist and politician, was born on 13 September 1894 in Battersea, London, the second son of Joseph Morris Brown, a plumber, and his wife, Rosina (Rose) Spicer. He attended the Salmestone elementary school, Margate, until the age of eleven, whereupon he won a scholarship to Sir Roger Manwood's Grammar School, Sandwich. Brown left school at fourteen to live with his grandmother in Battersea, and in 1910 he entered the civil service. At this time most boy clerks were taken on only to be discarded a couple of years later after a further examination. In November 1912 Brown gave evidence to the MacDonnell commission on the civil service, having recruited almost his entire grade into his newly formed Boy Clerks' Association. He was an assured witness and, indeed, most of the boy clerks' demands were met when the commission reported.

Brown's political development was rapid. By 1914 he was secretary of the Clapham branch of the Independent Labour Party. He later attributed his conversion to socialism to the poverty he had endured and also to his Methodism, though at the age of eighteen he lost his religious faith. At the outbreak of war he was a clerk in the office of works, and shortly afterwards he was elected to the executive committee of the Civil Service Assistant Clerks' Association (CSACA). He was appointed secretary of the CSACA in 1917. In the same year he married Mabel Prickett, daughter of Harry Prickett, solicitors' clerk of Anerley; they had two sons and one daughter.

In January 1919 Brown demanded that the maximum salary of clerks be increased to £200, hinting that strike action would follow should the demand be rejected: the Treasury capitulated. Shortly afterwards, a mass meeting

William John Brown (1894–1960), by Howard Coster, 1934

of CSACA members pressed Brown to become general secretary. The executive committee agreed to raise a fund in lieu of a pension and to pay him a salary of £400 p.a., making him the first full-time civil service union official. From its inception in 1919 he was a member of the National Whitley Council for the civil service. The Whitley Council system, which began in 1919, prompted civil servants to join unions and encouraged amalgamations among staff associations. Membership of the CSACA rose from 623 at the end of the war to over 3500 in 1919. Brown's predatory approach ensured that numerous smaller staff associations were subsumed into his union during the period 1920–22, and under his leadership the renamed Civil Service Clerical Association (CSCA) became the largest and most powerful of the clerical civil service unions.

Brown was frequently in conflict with the Conservative government of 1922–3, which did not readily accept civil service trade unionism. Older civil service leaders believed that his confrontational approach was inimical to the ideals of the Whitley system, but the Southborough committee's recommendation of civil service higher starting salaries in June 1923 represented a successful climax to a campaign waged by Brown and his colleagues. In 1924 Civil Servant Holiday Camps Ltd, a private venture with Brown as the major shareholder, opened its first camp near Lowestoft. A second camp was subsequently established in Hampshire. Brown's role in the general strike of 1926 was controversial. At a meeting of union leaders on 1 May, Brown agreed to put the CSCA's membership and resources at the TUC's disposal. He later claimed that his positive answer had been qualified by circulars to the TUC from his union, which stated that there was no question of civil servants taking strike action. Nevertheless, he was forced on the defensive within the CSCA for a while.

In the following year, Brown travelled to the Soviet Union. He subsequently wrote a book, *Three Months in Russia* (1928), which pleaded for the Soviet system to evolve without outside interference. After standing unsuccessfully as Labour candidate for Uxbridge (1922) and West Wolverhampton (1923, 1924), he won the Wolverhampton West constituency at the general election of May 1929. While an MP he continued as the CSCA general secretary. In July 1929 he used the debate on the king's speech to attack the prevailing Treasury view on unemployment policy, and in 1930 he was elected secretary of the Independent Labour Party group of Labour MPs.

Brown became disillusioned with the MacDonald government, believing that it should either follow uncompromisingly socialist policies or form a reform-minded coalition with the Liberals. Instead, the government did neither. Brown's admiration for a fellow dissident, Oswald Mosley, led him to break with his ILP parliamentary colleagues. Brown was one of the authors of *A National Policy*, published in February 1931, which advocated a planned economy, a public works programme, and a national investment board, *inter alia*. This was the basis for Mosley's putative 'New Party'. Although he decided against joining the New Party, Brown resigned the Labour whip in March 1931. Standing as an independent Labour candidate, he lost his seat at the October 1931 general election.

Brown emerged from the 1929–31 parliament with a profound dislike of party caucuses. For the next few years his energies were largely consumed by union business: by 1934 the CSCA had over 35,000 members. He tried unsuccessfully to regain the Wolverhampton West constituency in the 1935 general election. Standing as the independent Labour candidate, he urged a public works programme, the abolition of capital punishment, and thoroughgoing nationalization. In addition, his manifesto included proposals for a national investments board and the creation of a special inner cabinet to direct economic reconstruction. He refused an offer from Lord Beaverbrook to finance his campaign, though he cultivated a somewhat obsequious friendship with the press baron.

In May 1936 Brown reached an agreement on behalf of the CSCA with the Treasury on clerical grading. Other civil service union leaders were critical of him, as the agreement involved a slight reduction in salaries for lower clerical officers. This criticism was less than fair. In fact, the new simplified grading structure encouraged departments to recruit clerical officers rather than the slightly cheaper alternative of clerical assistants. Brown's victory on behalf of the departmental clerks later that year was more clear cut, and their gradings were brought into line with the general Treasury scheme.

Brown's public support for rebel busmen in the aftermath of the London busmen's dispute of May 1937 provoked the fury of their union, the Transport and General Workers' Union (TGWU). He sympathized with the busmen and believed that the strike had been poorly handled. In his view, the decision of the TGWU general executive council to overrule the central bus committee and settle the strike epitomized the undemocratic nature of the TGWU. A rival non-political union, the National Passenger Workers' Union, was launched by Brown and rebel busmen in February 1938. The antipathy which ensued between Brown and the TUC undoubtedly harmed the cause of civil servants within the wider union movement.

In 1941 the Ministry of Information paid for Brown to visit America for a lecture tour on behalf of the British government, though he exploited dissatisfaction with the war effort when he won the Rugby by-election as an independent in April 1942. He relinquished the position of CSCA general secretary, which he had held since 1919, but the union allowed him to become its parliamentary officer on the understanding that he could resume the general secretary's duties at a later date. His politics at this time boiled down to a distinctive brand of individualism. In parliament he formed an alliance with Denis Kendall, the independent MP for Grantham, to promote a people's movement aimed at destroying the power of party caucuses. Like Brown, Kendall was one of a number of maverick figures who broke the wartime truce between the main political parties. Brown's autobiography, *So Far*, which was published in 1943, illustrated how far his politics had drifted to the right. His hatred of communism, which he frequently expressed in his later years, undoubtedly contributed to this process: he claimed to be a socialist only in a general sense, and warned that wholesale nationalization would produce an impersonal state machine, hostile to personal freedom.

Brown proved an effective champion of the civil service in parliament, his efforts bearing fruit in the form of the first Pensions (Increase) Act, 1944, which had its origin in an amendment moved by Brown to the king's speech in the previous December. He narrowly retained his seat as an independent MP at the 1945 general election, when both the Labour and Conservative parties ran candidates against him. Aside from the mines and the Bank of England, he opposed the government's programme of nationalization, and his attacks on the closed shop so embarrassed the CSCA that, by November 1946, Brown feared that his union would sack him as its parliamentary secretary. In 1947 he alleged to the committee of privileges that the CSCA was trying to exert improper pressure on him. The committee recommended that the arrangement between Brown and the CSCA be terminated. Though he had negotiated a generous gratuity from the union, the parting was not amicable. He also declared at the union's conference in 1948 that he was no longer a socialist. He lost his seat at Rugby in the 1950 general election, finishing bottom of the poll, and made an unsuccessful attempt to re-enter parliament, losing at West Fulham in 1951.

Brown was a flamboyant, loquacious character and a natural rebel whose combative temperament aroused strong, often hostile emotions. He became something of a media celebrity in his last decade, appearing on programmes such as *In the News*. An outstandingly able and aggressive union leader, his achievements were somewhat overshadowed by his bitter quarrels with the TUC and its affiliates. His political career never quite lived up to its early promise, when, along with Aneurin Bevan, he was considered to be one of Labour's brightest young stars. He was too much of an uncompromising individualist to achieve real influence. He died on 3 October 1960 at his country home, the Quarter House, Wittersham, Tenterden, Kent. His wife survived him.

RICHARD TEMPLE

Sources DNB · B. V. Humphreys, *Clerical unions in the civil service* (1958) · E. Wigham, *From humble petition to militant action* (1980) · W. J. Brown, *So far* (1943) · registry files, U. Warwick Mod. RC, TUC papers, MS 292 · U. Warwick Mod. RC, Transport and General Workers' Union archives, MS 126 · HLRO, Beaverbrook papers · *Red Tape* (1911–60) · N. Fishman, *The British communist party and the trade unions, 1933–45* (1995) · R. Skidelsky, *Oswald Mosley* (1975) · U. Warwick Mod. RC, Civil and Public Services Association papers, MS 48 · W. J. Brown, election addresses, U. Warwick Mod. RC, MS 21/1787 · K. Jeffreys, *The Churchill coalition and wartime politics, 1940–1945* (1991) · *The Labour who's who* (1927) · *WWW*, 1951–60 · D. Houghton, *Whitley Bulletin*, 40/10 (1960), 147–8

Archives U. Warwick Mod. RC, journals relating to his time as MP and as parliamentary secretary of the Civil Service Clerical Association, and trade unionist activities, election addresses, MS 21/1787 | HLRO, corresp. with Lord Beaverbrook · U. Warwick Mod. RC, Trades Union Congress registry files, MS 292 · U. Warwick Mod. RC, Transport and General Workers' Union archives, MS 126 · U. Warwick Mod. RC, Civil and Public Services Association MSS | FILM BFI NFTVA, documentary, news, and party political footage · IWM FVA, actuality footage

Likenesses H. Coster, photographs, 1930–39, NPG [*see illus.*] · photograph, 1942, Hult. Arch.; repro. in Wigham, *From humble petition to militant action*, 51 · W. Stoneman, photograph, 1948, NPG · photograph, Topham Picturepoint, London; repro. in Wigham, *From humble petition to militant action*, 122

Wealth at death £232,132 7s. 10d.: probate, 27 Oct 1960, CGPLA Eng. & Wales

Brown, William Laurence (1755–1830), Church of Scotland minister and university principal, was born in Utrecht on 7 January 1755, the second son of William Brown (1719–1791), minister of the Scots Kirk in Utrecht, and Janet Ogilvie (*bap.* 1724, *d.* 1813). In 1757 his father was appointed professor of ecclesiastical history at St Andrews; there young William attended first the grammar school and then the university, where he studied arts and divinity from 1767 to 1774; he graduated MA in 1772. He returned to Utrecht for further study, including civil law, under his uncle Robert Brown (1728–1777), now minister of the Scots Kirk. Elected to succeed him, William returned for a year to St Andrews, where he was licensed on 28 October 1777 and ordained on 7 January 1778.

Induction to the Utrecht charge on 22 March 1778 left Brown time to tutor private pupils, to travel in France, Germany, and Switzerland, and to win intellectual distinction. On 12 November 1783 he became St Andrews's youngest ever DD; he subsequently collected prizes, from the Stolpian Legacy of Leiden and from the Teylerian Society of Haarlem, for his essays *A Dissertation on the Folly of Scepticism* (1788) and *An Essay on the Natural Equality of Men* (1793), perhaps his most useful work.

On 29 May 1786 Brown married Anne Elizabeth (1764–1842), daughter of his uncle Robert Brown. They had five sons and four daughters, all of whom survived their father. Brown was unsettled by civil strife in the Netherlands but a change of government rewarded him with election to a new chair of ecclesiastical history and moral philosophy at Utrecht in December 1787; his inaugural *Oratio de religionis et philosophiae societate* was delivered on 14 February 1788. In 1790 he also became professor of natural law, and gave an inaugural lecture, *Oratio de imaginatione in vitae institutione regundae*. He was university rector in 1789–90. Of his three disciplines, church history was the poor relation.

An imminent French invasion led Brown to flee with his family to England in January 1795, when they survived a stormy crossing to Harwich in an open boat. In London the patronage of Lord Auckland, former ambassador in The Hague, and John Moore, archbishop of Canterbury, helped to secure him election, by Aberdeen city council on 15 June 1795, to the chair of divinity in Marischal College and the charge of Greyfriars (West) Church. He assumed both on 12 August 1795, and then the principalship of Marischal also, on 26 January 1796. His advancement without local support also served the interests of Henry Dundas, with whom he had corresponded about appointments since 1788. Brown in turn became a fount of patronage, as shown by his letters during 1804–27 to David Irving, writer and librarian of the Faculty of Advocates in Edinburgh.

Brown accumulated further offices, including some with emoluments to augment his inadequate stipend. The Gordon lectureship brought him £50 annually and his *Lectures on Practical Religion* was published in 1825. He was made a royal chaplain on 4 March 1800 and dean of the Thistle and of the Chapel Royal on 4 October 1803. His *Essay on the Existence of a Supreme Creator* (1816) won the £1250 Burnett prize.

Brown's wide range of publications included several tracts on religious, political, and social issues. His collected sermons (1803), dedicated to Archbishop Moore, gained an appreciative notice in the *Edinburgh Review* but his long rhyming prose poem on virtue, *Philemon* (1809), had little poetic sensibility. Of the numerous writings of his that were deemed weighty enough in his day, including *A Comparative View of Christianity and of the other Forms of Religion* (1826), none has enjoyed lasting merit.

Brown's reputation for humane learning, especially in languages, and for liberality of opinion in public affairs accompanied a somewhat superficial allegiance to the evangelicalism of the popular party in the Church of Scotland. He made some impact by his occasional contributions to general assembly debates. Respect for him rarely ran deep. Unusually for a principal of Marischal there is no record of a portrait of him. A contemporary described him as of medium height with a 'very intellectual countenance' (*Encyclopaedia Britannica*, 601). Brown died at his home in Aberdeen, of senile debility, on 11 May 1830 and was buried on 18 May in the churchyard of St Nicholas.

D. F. WRIGHT

Sources *Fasti Scot.*, new edn, 6.8; 7.360–61 · *Aberdeen Journal* (19 May 1830), 3, col. 3 · R. L. Emerson, *Professors, patronage, and politics: the Aberdeen universities in the eighteenth century* (1992) · J. M. Anderson, ed., *The matriculation roll of the University of St Andrews, 1747–1897* (1905) · P. J. Anderson and J. F. K. Johnstone, eds., *Fasti academiae Mariscallanae Aberdonensis: selections from the records of the Marischal College and University, MDXCIII–MDCCCLX*, 3 vols., New Spalding Club, 4, 18–19 (1889–98) · *Encyclopaedia Britannica*, 7th edn (1842) · *Album studiosorum academiae Rheno-Traiectinae MDCXXXVI–MDCCCLXXXVI: accedunt nomina curatorum et professorum per eadem secula* (Utrecht, 1886) · *EdinR*, 4 (1804), 190–97 · C. H. D. Grimes, *The early story of the English church at Utrecht* (1930) · A. M. Munro, 'Epitaphs and inscriptions in St Nicholas Church and churchyard', *Scottish Notes and Queries*, 1 (1887–8), 88 · private information (2004) · J. Martin, *Eminent divines in Aberdeen and the north* (1888) · W. Steven, *The history of the Scottish church, Rotterdam* (1832, 1833) · Chambers, *Scots.*, rev. T. Thomson (1875), 1.189–90 · *Nieuw Nederlandsch biografisch woordenboek*, 4 (1918), 321–2 · J. B. Salmond, *Veterum laudes: being a tribute to the achievements of the members of St Salvator's College* (1950) · *De Utrechtsche Academie, 1636–1815* (1936), vol. 1 of *De Utrechtsche Universiteit, 1636–1936*, 187–8 · *DNB* · *Scots Magazine*, 53 (Jan 1791)

Archives Mitchell L., Glas., Glasgow City Archives, letters | NRA Scotland, priv. coll., letters to Moncreiff family

Brown, William Michael Court (1918–1968), medical research worker, was born at Scotby, near Carlisle, on 17 April 1918, the only son of James Court Brown, market gardener, and his wife, Jessie Buchanan Hayes. He was educated at Fettes College, Edinburgh, and St Andrews University and soon showed that he had inherited his father's interest in chemistry. He graduated BSc in 1939 and completed his medical degree three years later. An interest in radiotherapy led him to take the diploma of medical radiology a year after he qualified and he went to join the department of radiotherapy at the Edinburgh Royal Infirmary. In 1946 Court Brown married Caroline, daughter of William Thom, of Edinburgh; they had a son and two daughters.

In 1950 Court Brown was elected a fellow of the Faculty of Radiologists and made deputy director of the department. By this time, however, he had developed an overriding interest in research; a career as a consultant radiotherapist no longer attracted him, and he resigned his clinical appointments to become a member of the scientific staff of the Medical Research Council in the department of medicine at the Postgraduate Medical School in London. In 1956 he was made director of the clinical effects of radiation research unit, which had been newly created by the Medical Research Council, and he and the group of people working with him moved to new laboratories in the Western General Hospital, Edinburgh, where he continued to work until his death.

Court Brown was one of the most productive medical research workers of his generation. Interested at first in the acute effects of radiation, he sought to find a biochemical explanation for the sickness and vomiting which was often a distressing complication of radiotherapy. This, however, was not a fruitful field and he soon began to study the long-term effects as well. Reports from the Atomic Bomb Casualty Commission provided evidence of an increased mortality from leukaemia among the survivors of the atomic bomb explosions at Hiroshima and Nagasaki and Court Brown showed that a similar increase followed the use of X-rays for the treatment of ankylosing spondylitis. At that time most scientists thought that the production of leukaemia and other forms of cancer required exposure to large amounts of radiation and that there was a minimum dose below which serious effects were not produced. There was, however, no real evidence that this was so, and it became increasingly important to be sure, as first one nation and then another added to the radioactivity of the environment by exploding hydrogen bombs. At the request of the Medical Research Council, he and Richard Doll tackled the problem as a matter of urgency. Information collected from 15,000 patients showed that the incidence of leukaemia was approximately proportional to the dose of radiation and a quantitative relationship was deduced which was used internationally as a basis for determining the acceptable levels of industrial and medical exposure.

Court Brown was not satisfied with this result, which depended on extrapolation from the effect of high doses, and he sought to confirm it by studying the effect of radiation on individual cells. Methods for displaying chromosomes were just being developed and he immediately introduced them into his unit, choosing as his colleague for this purpose Patricia Jacobs, a young zoologist from St Andrews. From then on discoveries followed one another with astonishing rapidity, the most notable being that Klinefelter's syndrome was due to the presence of three sex chromosomes in each cell (X, X, and Y) instead of two (X and X, or X and Y). This discovery showed for the first time that the Y chromosome was the determinant of maleness in mammals and that human disease could be due to an abnormal complement of chromosomes. In 1960, when it became possible to examine chromosomes from blood, the way was open for large-scale surveys. Court Brown saw that it would be necessary to determine the incidence of chromosomal abnormalities both in the new-born and in the general adult population in order to assess the significance of the findings obtained in selected groups, such as people mentally or congenitally handicapped, those who were infertile, or groups of people exposed to particular hazards. His work in this field established the study of human population cytogenetics on a firm basis and led to many discoveries, including the observation that a substantial proportion of males held in medical penal institutions had a 47,XYY chromosomal constitution, that chromosomal abnormalities increased in incidence with age, and that abnormalities in the circulating blood cells could be used to measure the extent of past irradiation down to levels experienced in the course of occupational exposure. His principal findings were presented and discussed critically in the short monograph *Chromosome Studies on Adults* (1966), in his book *Human Population Cytogenetics* (1967), and in a review in the *British Medical Bulletin* (25/1, 1969).

Court Brown saw medicine in the wider context of biology and was one of those rare people who could take an idea from one field and apply it in another. He had few interests outside science, and conversation with him was almost entirely limited to the subject of his current enthusiasm; but he was never dull. New ideas erupted continually; many of them led to early action. He did not suffer fools gladly, but was always ready to listen to criticism and, if presented with a good case, would set about building a new hypothesis on fresh foundations. He was unusually free from scientific jealousy and was delighted when his juniors were praised for work which had been his in origin. He was not always an easy taskmaster, but his standards of excellence and honesty, both scientific and personal, were impeccable. Among the circle of his immediate colleagues he inspired intense loyalty and affection.

Court Brown was appointed OBE in 1957 following his work on the leukaemogenic effects of radiation for the Medical Research Council's committee which produced the first white paper on the hazards to humans of nuclear and allied radiation; in the following year he was awarded (jointly) the Anderson-Berry prize of the Royal Society of Edinburgh for the same work. In 1965 he was elected FRCP Edin. and in 1967 the University of Edinburgh conferred on him the title of honorary professor. Court Brown expected to die young and cannot have been surprised when he had a serious coronary thrombosis in early 1968. He returned to work at the first opportunity but soon had a recurrence and died in Edinburgh on 16 December 1968.   RICHARD DOLL and PATRICIA JACOBS

Sources personal knowledge (2004) · private information (2004) · *The Times* (27 Dec 1968) · *BMJ* (4 Jan 1969) · *The Lancet* (4 Jan 1969) · *CCI* (1969)
Wealth at death £19,348: confirmation, 21 Jan 1969, *CCI*

Browne. For this title name *see* individual entries under Browne; *see also* Clinton, Elizabeth Fiennes de, countess of Lincoln [Elizabeth Fiennes Browne, Lady Browne] (1528?–1589).

Browne, Alexander (d. 1706), miniature painter and auctioneer, was also one of the first publishers of mezzotints. Of his parents and education nothing is known. In 1669 he wrote and published his *Ars Pictoria, or, An Academy Treating of Drawing, Painting, Limning and Etching*, one of the earliest such English treatises, which includes thirty-one plates by Arnold de Jode copied from earlier drawing-books. (A much simpler first version of the text had already appeared in 1660 as *The Whole Art of Drawing*.) Browne described himself on the title-page as 'practitioner in the art of limning'. It is in this role that he appears in the pages of Samuel Pepys's diary in 1665–6, giving lessons to Pepys's wife, somewhat to the diarist's discomfort as he suspected that the two were having an affair. In the second edition of his book in 1675 Browne stated that he had been supplying colours for limning for over fifteen years, and this places the beginning of his career in 1659. None of his miniatures, however, seems to have survived.

Browne published forty-three mezzotints from his address at the Blue Balcony in Little Queen Street near Lincoln's Inn Fields, London, thirty-seven after Lely and six after Van Dyck; they were probably made by Jan van Somer, Jan van der Vaart, and other as yet unidentified mezzotinters working to his commission. Other prints he published by Isaac Beckett, John Smith, and others were signed by their authors. On 29 February 1684 he was granted the protection of a royal licence for fourteen years; the original document (PRO SP 44/335, fols. 90–92) gives a complete list of the hundred or more plates which he had published. Most of them can be shown to have been made in 1680 or shortly thereafter, and to have been later than the similar series published by Richard Tompson. The two men jointly held the first regular auctions of paintings, drawings, and prints, between 1678 and 1686, and Browne subsequently continued alone from 1687 to 1692.

Browne died in 1706, and on 17 April his widow, whose name is unknown, auctioned his collection of ninety-seven paintings at his house in Gerrard Street, Soho, London, as well as his shells, agates, minerals, and medals. A remarkable contemporary album of his published mezzotints, formerly in the Brownlow family library at Belton House, Lincolnshire, is now in the National Portrait Gallery Archive, London.   ANTONY GRIFFITHS

Sources J. C. Smith, *British mezzotinto portraits*, 1 (1878), 105–23 · A. Griffiths, 'Early mezzotint publishing in England: Peter Lely, Tompson and Browne', *Print Quarterly*, 7 (1990), 130–45 · A. Griffiths and R. A. Gerard, *The print in Stuart Britain, 1603–1689* (1998), 216, 232–4 [exhibition catalogue, BM, 8 May – 20 Sept 1998]
Likenesses A. de Jode, line engraving, pubd 1684 (after J. Huysmans), BM, NPG, V&A; repro. in A. Browne, *Ars pictoria* (1669), frontispiece

Browne, Annie Leigh (1851–1936), educationist and suffragist, was born on 14 March 1851 at Fryern Street, Bridgwater, Somerset, the eldest daughter of Samuel Woolcott Browne (*d. c.*1870), merchant, and his wife, Thomazine Leigh Browne, formerly Carslake. Her parents were both from naval families and were of Unitarian and Liberal convictions. A second daughter, Thomazine Mary (1853–1943), became the second wife of Sir Norman Lockyer. The family settled in the Clifton district of Bristol. Annie and her sister had little formal schooling but received excellent tuition from visiting masters and governesses, while their home became a meeting place for men and women active in reformist politics. Both parents were involved in philanthropic and social work, and included among their friends the social reformers Mary Carpenter, Frances Power Cobbe, and Matthew Davenport Hill, all of whom were then living in the Clifton area.

In 1868 the family moved to London and the two girls went to Queen's College, Harley Street, although Annie attended as a regular student for only one year because she was needed at home. In that year, too, she attended her first women's suffrage meeting at the home of Dr John Beddoe and his wife (both associates of Mary Carpenter), and worked actively for the cause until 1918. She also helped her mother in the work of the Social Purity Alliance and the Moral Reform Union, and supported the efforts of two sisters, Maria Georgina Grey and Emily Anne Shirreff, to establish schools for academically oriented girls. To this end the National Union for the Improvement of the Education of Women of all Classes (generally known as the Women's Education Union) was established in 1871. On her father's death about 1870 Annie began a process of self-education, largely through the writings of Theodore Parker and the teachings of William Henry Channing and James Martineau. Four years later, mother and daughter accepted an invitation from Emma Paterson to promote the organization of women into trade unions and Annie continued to serve on the committee of the Women's Protective and Provident League until the early 1880s. At this time she became a friend of the working-class feminist Jeannette Wilkinson, who had worked as an upholsterer from the age of seventeen and in 1876 accepted an invitation to become a director of the Women's Printing Society, at a time when the trade excluded women.

From about 1880 Annie collaborated with her closest friend, Mary Stewart Kilgour (1851–1955), a Girton-educated maths lecturer who moved to London in 1877, in promoting the education of girls and women. Keenly aware of the lack of collegiate accommodation for women working at University College and the London school of medicine, during the winter of 1881 Miss Browne, her sister, and Miss Kilgour devoted their energies and their money to the establishment of a hostel for female students. Soon afterwards the women formed an organizing committee, of which Annie became honorary secretary, and by the autumn of 1882 College Hall was started in Byng Place, Gordon Square, with Miss Eleanor Grove and Miss Rosa Morison as its first principal and vice-principal, and two students. Subsequently the hall was enlarged by the addition of 2 Byng Place, and in March 1886 was established on a permanent basis when it was incorporated under the name of College Hall. In 1890 Annie resigned her position as honorary secretary to the council of College Hall and was succeeded by her sister; later came a much bigger achievement by the three women in the founding of College Hall, Malet Street, which Queen Mary opened in 1932. Two years later all three women assisted at the opening of an extension by Princess Alice in November 1934.

At the same time, Annie launched her personal crusade to promote women's work in local government when she brought together Mrs Amelia Charles, Mrs Evans, Caroline Biggs of the *Englishwomen's Review*, and Lucy Wilson of the Vigilance Association to form a Local Electors Association. The immediate objective was to secure female access to vestry politics, but the focus changed with the passing of the Local Government Act, 1888, which provided for the establishment of county councils. Early in November 1888 the Society for Promoting the Return of Women as County Councillors was formed, with the countess of Aberdeen (president of the executive of the

Women's Liberal Federation) as president, Mrs Eva McLaren (formerly Muller) as first honorary treasurer, and Mrs Louisa Temple Mallett (unsuccessful candidate for the London school board) and Annie Browne as joint secretaries of the committee. Renamed the Women's Local Government Society (WLGS) in 1893, the organization was established on a non-party basis for promoting the eligibility of women to elect to, and to serve on, all local governing bodies. Apart from Annie, Mary Kilgour, and Louisa Mallet, its inner circle also included Emma Cons (late alderman of the London county council), Emma Knox Maitland and Ellen McKee of the London school board, as well as Eva McLaren (a former Lambeth Guardian), who had helped form the Society for Promoting the Return of Women as Poor Law Guardians a few years earlier. The WLGS played a prominent part in the feminist campaign against the Education Acts of 1902 and 1903, under which the directly elected school boards on which women had been effective members since 1870 were replaced by local education authorities, on which women were disqualified from serving. Although as a concession to the agitation the new education committees included some co-opted women members who were chosen for their involvement in education, they lacked the authority or public support of elected members. Hence Annie Leigh Browne continued to organize and fund the campaign to secure access to local politics, and in 1907 her persistence was rewarded with the Qualification of Women (County and Borough Councils) Act.

A prominent Liberal in politics, in the early 1890s Annie became honorary secretary of the Paddington Women's Liberal Association. She was also an original member of the Albemarle Club, as well as being a strong opponent of vivisection. She lived at 58 Porchester Terrace, London. Annie Leigh Browne died of bronchitis and pneumonia at 55 Lancaster Gate, London, on 8 March 1936. Her close friend Mary Kilgour then moved to Sidmouth, where she lived in retirement in a house left to her for her lifetime by Annie Browne. Reluctantly agreeing to be interviewed by the feminist *Woman's Herald*, Annie herself declared that she 'did not think personal details are of general interest' (4 Feb 1893, 8).   JANE MARTIN

Sources A. M. Copping, *The story of College Hall* (1974) · 'Miss Browne', *Woman's Herald* (4 Feb 1893) · *The Times* (14 March 1936) · *Vaccination Inquirer and Health Review*, 38 (1936), 61 · P. Hollis, *Ladies elect: women in English local government, 1865–1914* (1987); pbk edn (1989) · b. cert. · d. cert.
Archives LMA, Women's Local Government Society MSS
Likenesses photograph, 1893, repro. in 'Miss Browne'
Wealth at death £55,685 13s. 0d.: probate, 29 June 1936, CGPLA Eng. & Wales

Browne, Sir Anthony (c.1500–1548), courtier, was the son of Sir Anthony Browne (d. 1506), a cadet of the Browne family of Betchworth, Surrey, and his wife, Lucy (d. 1534), widow of Sir Thomas Fitzwilliam of Aldwark, Yorkshire, and daughter and coheir of John Neville, Marquess Montagu. The elder Sir Anthony was Henry VII's standard-bearer and lieutenant of Calais Castle. His son probably grew up in Henry VIII's household, like his elder half-

Sir Anthony Browne (c.1500–1548), by unknown artist, c.1550

brother Sir William *Fitzwilliam, later earl of Southampton. Never as powerful as the king's great ministers, Browne nevertheless maintained an intimate friendship with Henry throughout the latter's reign. He was regularly at court when not engaged in diplomatic, military, or other official duties, and avoided the disgrace that befell many courtiers. His recorded royal service began in 1518, when he was about eighteen, when the king appointed him surveyor and master of hunting for the Yorkshire castles and lordships of Hatfield, Thorne, and Conisbrough and included him in an embassy to hand over Tournai to François I. Though recalled in 1519 for striking a fellow emissary, by October he had become a gentleman of the privy chamber and thus part of Henry's inner circle. In 1520 he demonstrated his prowess in a tournament at the Field of Cloth of Gold. Thomas Howard, earl of Surrey, knighted him on 1 July 1522 following the English raid on Morlaix, and Henry made him a knight of the body.

In 1525 Browne became lieutenant of the Isle of Man. He was ambassador to France in 1527, reporting home in a series of dispatches in which he showed himself increasingly hostile to all things French. By 1528 he had married Alice (d. 1540), daughter of Sir John Gage. They had seven sons—Anthony *Browne, Viscount Montagu (1528–1592), William, Henry, Francis, Thomas, George, and a second Henry—and three daughters, Mary, Mabel, and Lucy. Browne was royal standard-bearer jointly with Sir Edward Guildford in 1528–34, alone in 1534–46, and with his eldest son, Anthony, in 1546–8. From 1532 he was a JP for Surrey, where he, Fitzwilliam, and his cousin Sir Matthew Browne headed a locally powerful faction. In 1532 he was at Calais for Henry's meeting with François I concerning his divorce from Katherine of Aragon. Back in France with Thomas Howard, now third duke of Norfolk, in 1533, he was at Marseilles when Bishop Edmund Bonner presented Henry's appeal for a general council to Pope Clement VII.

Browne generally conformed to Henry's will during the upheavals of the early Reformation but remained at heart a religious conservative. In 1536 he and Fitzwilliam, with whom he habitually co-operated, assisted Cromwell in engineering Queen Anne Boleyn's downfall; Browne's sister Elizabeth, countess of Worcester, was reportedly the first to raise Henry's suspicions about her. Soon, though, Browne, Fitzwilliam, and others were themselves in trouble for allegedly supporting Princess Mary's restoration to the succession ahead of Princess Elizabeth. But, when questioned, Browne managed to allay the king's suspicions. He helped to suppress the Pilgrimage of Grace, leading his Surrey retinue and other cavalry from Ampthill to join the duke of Suffolk in Lincolnshire in October and proceeding thence to Yorkshire in November (Norfolk criticized him for taking more men than necessary). One of the delegation that negotiated with the rebels at Doncaster in December, he delivered commissions to the new deputy wardens of the northern marches in January 1537, and helped secure peace with Scotland in February and March.

Browne was present at Prince Edward's baptism on 15 October 1537. He was again in France in 1538, once more provoking controversy with complaints about his poor treatment and eliciting praise from Edmund Bonner and criticism from Thomas Cromwell. In 1539 Henry made him a privy councillor, master of the horse, and captain of the gentleman pensioners, and visited his house at Battle in Sussex. There was further trouble with Cromwell, who complained that Viscount Lisle was writing to Browne and others rather than to himself about sacramentaries at Calais. It was rumoured that Browne, Fitzwilliam, and Sir William Kingston wanted to replace Cromwell with Bishop Cuthbert Tunstall, and Browne was certainly on good terms with Gardiner, who was no friend to the chief minister. However, Cromwell apparently did not object to Fitzwilliam securing Browne's election as knight of the shire for Surrey in 1539. Active in that parliament, Browne was elected for Surrey again in 1542, 1545, and 1547. In the last two he arranged for his son Anthony to be returned as a burgess for Guildford. He also served on other local commissions from 1535 onwards. He was nominated for sheriff of Surrey and Sussex in November 1539, but lost out to Sir Christopher More of Loseley.

Henry selected Browne to meet Anne of Cleves in his stead at Rochester on new year's day 1540. The story that Browne had married her as the king's proxy is baseless (the proxy marriage was between Henry and Anne's procurator). Browne testified in July that Henry was unhappy with Anne's appearance at their first meeting and that he feared the king's anger with Fitzwilliam, who had praised her beauty. Meanwhile, Browne and Fitzwilliam were the only active councillors present on 5 March, when Henry upbraided the evangelical Robert Barnes at Hampton Court. Barnes was then engaged in theological controversy with Gardiner, whom Browne assisted in making a case against the 'heretic'. An increasingly influential figure at court, Browne became a knight of the Garter on 23 April. It is uncertain when he and Fitzwilliam broke completely with Cromwell, who lost power on 10 June, but it may have been in May, when Lisle was arrested. They drew closer to Norfolk thereafter, but not enough to suffer when Katherine Howard's infidelity came to light in November 1541; indeed, Henry in his despair turned to them first.

In 1542 the brothers served against the Scots under Norfolk, who this time praised Browne's work. Fitzwilliam died at Newcastle on 15 October, and Browne inherited his entailed lands, including Cowdray in Sussex, where he became a JP in 1544. By 1542 his pro-imperial reputation was such that the French ambassador Charles de Marillac regarded him as his country's greatest enemy, while the imperial ambassador Eustache Chapuys recommended that Charles V offer him a pension. In 1543 Browne became master of the king's harriers, and probably aided Gardiner in encouraging the prebendaries' plot against Archbishop Cranmer. He saw further meritorious military service in the Boulogne campaign of 1544, working closely with Suffolk and leading 300 horse and 500 foot. He, Suffolk, and Sir Thomas Wriothesley also secured loans for Henry in Antwerp. Browne served under Edward Seymour, earl of Hertford, defending the English coast in 1545–6, and was on muster commissions in several southern counties.

Browne's relationships with fellow courtiers fluctuated. Though friendly with Gardiner, Browne criticized his handling of the French war in 1544. Although he was often at odds with John, Baron Russell, who described him as 'moste unreasonable and … oone whose wordes and deedes do not agree togither' (Lehmberg, 202), Browne nevertheless referred to the special love and hearty affection he had for Russell when naming him an executor of his will. His relationship with the Howards was particularly changeable, and he was involved in the proceedings against Norfolk and his son Henry, earl of Surrey, in 1546–7. Browne tried unsuccessfully to persuade the dying Henry to include the conservative Gardiner among Edward VI's councillors, but was the first to accept the reformist Hertford (soon duke of Somerset) as protector. The two constants were Browne's loyalty to Fitzwilliam and to the king. It was Browne who early in 1547 informed Henry that he was near death. Henry left him £300 and made him an executor of his will and guardian of Edward and Elizabeth. Browne and Hertford subsequently informed the two children of their father's death, and Browne rode next to Edward in the formal procession from the Tower of London to Westminster Palace.

Browne died on 28 April 1548 at Byfleet, Surrey. On 12 December 1542 he had married Lady Elizabeth Fitzgerald (1528?–1589) [see Clinton, Elizabeth Fiennes de], the fifteen-year-old daughter of the ninth earl of Kildare. Acclaimed as the 'Fair Geraldine' in the verses of the earl of Surrey, she had two sons with Browne, Edward and

Thomas, who died in infancy. After her first husband's death she married Edward Fiennes de Clinton, from 1572 earl of Lincoln. Browne also had two illegitimate children, Charles and Anne. After a funeral procession from London, Browne was buried at Battle in a tomb with his first wife. His will of 22 April 1547 provided for 'masses and dirges to be donne for me … according to the anncient and laudable customs of the Churche of Englande', provided £20 for the poor to pray for his soul, and allowed up to £100 for his funeral (PRO, PROB 11/33/10). His executors were Gage, Russell, Baron St John, Baron Rich, Sir John Baker, and John Skinner of Reigate. He owned approximately 11,000 acres of land in Sussex worth £679 a year for those in his actual possession and £147 in reversion, as well as about 8500 acres in Surrey, worth almost half that amount and including the priory of St Mary Overie, which he obtained in 1544. Though most of his estate went to his heir, Anthony, he provided generously for his second wife, other children (legitimate and illegitimate), executors, and servants. A portrait of Browne survives in the National Portrait Gallery, London. Painted posthumously, about 1550, it shows him as a very young man, suggesting that it was based on a likeness made much earlier, possibly in France. The finery he wears helps explain Cromwell's exasperated description of him in 1538 as 'a vain old beau' (Starkey, *Henry VIII*, 119). Another portrait at Cowdray was destroyed by fire in 1793.

WILLIAM B. ROBISON

Sources HoP, *Commons, 1509–58*, 1.518–21 · W. B. Robison, 'The justices of the peace of Surrey in national and county politics, 1483–1570', PhD diss., Louisiana State University, 1983 · *LP Henry VIII*, vols. 1–21 · M. St C. Byrne, ed., *The Lisle letters*, 6 vols. (1981) · *VCH Sussex* · R. E. Brock, 'The courtier in early Tudor society', PhD diss., U. Lond., 1964 · Mrs. C. Roundell [J. A. E. Tollemache], *Cowdray: the history of a great English house* (1884) · E. W. Ives, 'Faction at the court of Henry VIII: the fall of Anne Boleyn', *History*, 57 (1972), 169–88 · S. E. Lehmberg, *The later parliaments of Henry VIII, 1536–1547* (1977) · G. Redworth, *In defence of the Church Catholic: the life of Stephen Gardiner* (1990) · D. R. Starkey, 'Intimacy and innovation: the rise of the privy chamber, 1485–1547', *The English court from the Wars of the Roses to the civil war*, ed. D. Starkey and others (1987), 71–118 · R. Warnicke, *The marrying of Anne of Cleves* (2000) · E. W. Ives, *Anne Boleyn* (1986) · S. J. Gunn, *Charles Brandon, duke of Suffolk, c.1484–1545* (1988) · D. Willen, *John Russell, first earl of Bedford: one of the King's men* (1981) · R. W. Hoyle, *The Pilgrimage of Grace and the politics of the 1530s* (2001) · A. F. Pollard, *England under Protector Somerset* (1900) · D. R. Starkey, *The reign of Henry VIII: personalities and politics* (1991) · will, prerogative court of Canterbury, PRO, PROB 11/33/10 · inquisition post mortem, PRO, C 142/88/79

Likenesses oil on panel, c.1550, NPG [*see illus.*] · line engraving, pubd 1777 (after effigy), BM · monumental effigy, Battle church, Sussex · portrait, Cowdray; destroyed by fire, 1793

Wealth at death almost 20,000 acres in Surrey and Sussex, value c.£1200 p.a.; total of specified bequests in money or goods to family, servants, and executors was £334 13s. 4d., plus 2300 marks, plus 20 nobles; also left annuities of £10, plus 240 marks; executors authorized to spend up to £100 on funeral, plus £20 to be dispersed to poor at funeral, and up to £20 for completion of tomb: will, 22 April 1547, PRO, PROB 11/33/10; PRO, C 142/88/79; HoP, *Commons*

Browne, Sir Anthony (1509/10–1567), judge, was born at Abbess Roding in Essex, a younger son of Sir Wistan Browne, who had been knighted by the king of Aragon, and Elizabeth, daughter of William Mordaunt of Turvey.

Three of his uncles were benchers of the Middle Temple. His paternal uncle Sir Humphrey *Browne was a justice of the common pleas. On his mother's side were Sir John Mordaunt (d. 1504), serjeant-at-law and chancellor of the duchy of Cornwall, and William Mordaunt (d. 1518), chief protonotary of the common pleas. It was therefore in keeping with family tradition that Anthony joined the Middle Temple and obtained a pupillage with John Jenour, the second protonotary; he was to acquire Mordaunt's great manuscript volume of precedents (now in the Library of Congress) from Mordaunt's son, and in the 1530s, perhaps while studying under Jenour, he practised for a few years as an attorney. It is possible that he contemplated a career on that side of the profession, because in 1538 he obtained the clerkship of assize on the home circuit from Sir John Spelman. Nevertheless, he became a member of parliament in 1545 and apparently flourished as a barrister. In 1554 he became a bencher of his inn, lecturing on a statute of 1542 concerning the effect of common recoveries on the king's feudal rights. The following year he was created serjeant-at-law, with the patronage of the earl of Oxford (on whose council he served) and Lord Rich, and was immediately appointed one of the queen's serjeants. He was obliged, as the junior serjeant-elect of his inn, to give a second reading; and on this occasion he drew on his expertise in pleading to expound the Statute of Jeofails of 1540. At an unknown date he married Jane, daughter and heir of William Farrington, and widow of Charles Booth and Henry Becconshall.

A month before the death of Queen Mary, Browne was chosen to succeed Sir Robert Broke as chief justice of the common pleas, and was appointed on 5 October 1558. The appointment was formally renewed by Elizabeth on 18 November, but the following January he was removed by the expedient of appointing him a puisne justice of the same court. The reason was doubtless religion. Although his demerits were not severe enough to require removal from the bench, it was thought impolitic to keep him in the post of chief justice. Following his demotion there was an unseemly contest over a valuable exigentership in the court, an appointment that normally belonged to the chief justice. Mary had granted it to a military man while the chief justiceship was vacant in 1558, but after Browne's appointment the judges rejected the grantee as unqualified and Browne thereupon appointed his nephew, Alexander Scrogges. The ensuing furore was resolved in 1561 in favour of Scrogges, though not before he had been illegally imprisoned and released by habeas corpus.

In 1563 it was rumoured that Browne was to replace Nicholas Bacon as lord keeper, and it was later supposed by Parsons that he had declined it on grounds of religious scruple; at any rate, Bacon remained in office. In 1565 he wrote a tract (preserved in BL, Harley MS 555) supporting Mary Stuart's claim to the throne, and this was substantially embodied in Bishop Leslie's more famous *Defense* of 1571. He is believed also to have encouraged Plowden to write his treatise on the same matter. It must be a matter of conjecture whether the queen knew these facts: if she did, it is an interesting comment on her views that she knighted Browne in February 1567. Browne remained a judge of the common pleas until his death, giving his last opinion in Easter term 1567 on the difference in law between crossing out and erasing words in a deed. He died at home, Weald Hall, South Weald, Essex, on 16 May 1567. His friend Plowden lamented his passing as a judge 'de profound ingeny et graund eloquence', inserting some laudatory Latin verses in his *Commentaries* (fols. 356, 376); while the Spanish ambassador noted his death as a great loss to the Catholics. He requested by will that his funeral be performed with such ceremonies as were used in 'the Catholike Churche of God', and that various friends, including Lord Rich, were to receive gold rings 'to be made like serjeantes ringes', engraved on the outside 'Wee dye' and on the inside 'Forgett nott'. He was buried in South Weald church. The tomb was largely destroyed when the church was restored in 1868, but there remains a headless brass figure in judicial robes and part of an inscription, which gives his age as fifty-seven.

Browne's marriage was childless, and his residuary estate was settled to pass after his wife's death to the issue of his brother George, with remainders to other relations (including Scrogges). His principal estate was in Essex, mostly in and around Brentwood and Dagenham, though he also had some property in Lancashire derived from his wife. The manor of South Weald (near Brentwood), where he settled at Weald Hall, was obtained from Lord Rich in 1548. He directed that, with the exception of some legal manuscripts, his library was to remain at South Weald for the use of its owners for the time being. His most lasting memorial is Brentwood School, which he founded in 1558 as 'The Grammar School of Anthony Browne, Serjeant at the Law, in Brentwood'.   J. H. BAKER

Sources HoP, *Commons, 1509–58*, 1.516–8 · Baker, *Serjeants*, 170, 434, 502 · C. H. Hopwood, ed., *Middle Temple records*, 1: *1501–1603* (1904) · Sainty, *Judges*, 48, 73 · will, PRO, PROB 11/49, sig. 20 · first reading, BL, Harley MS 51J6, fol. 35*v* · second reading, BL, Hargrave MS 199, fol. 2 · *Reports from the lost notebooks of Sir James Dyer*, ed. J. H. Baker, 1, SeldS, 109 (1994), xxv, xlix, lxxvii–lxxviii, 131 · *VCH Essex*, 8.80, 88 · M. Levine, *The early Elizabethan succession question, 1558–1568* (1966) · J. E. Neale, *Elizabeth I and her parliaments*, 1: *1559–1581* (1953), 130 · L. Abbott, 'Public office and private profit: the legal establishment in the reign of Mary Tudor', *The mid-Tudor polity, c.1540–1560*, ed. J. Loach and R. Tittler (1980), 137–58, esp. 137–8 · Emden, *Oxf.* · R. Doleman [R. Parsons], [W. Allen, F. Englefield, and others], *A conference about the next succession to the crowne of Ingland* ([Antwerp], 1594), pt 2, pp. 1–2 · W. C. Metcalfe, ed., *The visitations of Essex*, 1, Harleian Society, 13 (1878), 166 · *Les commentaries, ou, Les reportes de Edmunde Plowden* (1571) · monumental inscription, South Weald church

Likenesses brass effigy on monument, *c.*1567 (now headless), South Weald church, Essex

Browne, Anthony, first Viscount Montagu (1528–1592), nobleman and courtier, was born on 29 November 1528, the eldest of seven sons of Sir Anthony *Browne (*c.*1500–1548), courtier, of Cowdray Park, Sussex, and his first wife, Alice (*d.* 1540), daughter of Sir John *Gage (1479–1556), military administrator and courtier, of Firle, Sussex, and his wife, Philippa. He was Catholic like his parents but remained a trusted and active courtier during the reigns

Anthony Browne, first Viscount Montagu (1528–1592), by Hans Eworth, 1569

of Edward VI and Mary I. Sir Anthony Browne was one of Henry VIII's leading courtiers and privy councillors, amassing a great fortune worth at least £1177 12*s.* 2*d.* per annum in 1547, and paving the way for his heir's entrée at court. He had his son returned as MP for Guildford, Surrey, in 1545, and named joint standard-bearer of England with him in 1546, and used his position as master of the horse to obtain for him the position of equerry of the stable before 16 February 1547 and appointment as KB at Edward's coronation four days later.

About 1546 Anthony Browne the younger married Jane (1531/2–1552), daughter of Robert *Radcliffe, first earl of Sussex (1482/3–1542), and his second wife, Margaret. The couple had a son, Lord Anthony Browne (1552–1592), and a daughter, Mary (*d.* 1607), before Jane Browne's death on 22 July 1552. Browne's father died at Byfleet, Surrey, on 28 April 1548. Browne was removed from his position as standard-bearer on the grounds that he was too young, being restored only on his majority. He was conservative and made his opinions known, especially through his support of Princess Mary, which antagonized the regime. Despite this, he was re-elected for Guildford in 1547, allowed to purchase his wardship for £333 6*s.* 8*d.*, appointed sheriff of Surrey and Sussex from 1552 to 1553, and returned as MP for Petersfield, Hampshire, in March 1553. He was sheriff of Surrey and Sussex during the succession crisis and received a letter from the privy council in support of Lady Jane Grey on 8 July and a signet letter from her to the same effect on 10 July 1553. He appears to have done nothing.

Browne was re-elected for Petersfield in October 1553 and was knight of the shire for Surrey in April 1554. Nothing is known of his role in the House of Commons. He was keeper of Guildford Park from October 1553, steward of Hampton Court chase from June 1554, and JP for Surrey and Sussex from 1554. In April 1554 Browne was appointed master of the horse to Philip of Spain and given an annuity of £200. Philip dismissed Browne and other members of his English household and appointed Spaniards in their place in early September, causing some indignation among the English, who regarded the king as reneging on the understanding that he would not rely solely on his countrymen. Browne was elevated to the peerage as Viscount Montagu on 2 September on the occasion of Mary's official marriage to Philip at Hampton Court, and took his seat in the House of Lords on 12 November; he attended regularly. He was nominated to the Order of the Garter on 23 April and installed as knight on 17 October 1555. Montagu was sent as special ambassador with Thomas Thirlby, bishop of Ely, and Dr Edward Carne from 16 February to 24 August to treat regarding restoration of Catholicism in England, visiting Venice on the way. Later that year he was chief mourner and executor to Stephen Gardiner, bishop of Winchester. He was active in military actions at Calais and St Quentin, being named in 1557 lieutenant-general of the army in Picardy led by William Herbert, first earl of Pembroke, and performed his duties as lord lieutenant of Sussex from March to October 1558. His most prominent position was appointment to the privy council on 28 April 1557, but he attended fewer then a fifth of the meetings. In 1556 Montagu married Magdalen (1538–1608) [see Browne, Magdalen], daughter of William *Dacre, third Baron Dacre of Gilsland (1500–1563), and his wife, Elizabeth. The couple had five sons and three daughters. Also a Catholic, Magdalen Dacre walked in Mary's bridal procession in 1554 and attended her funeral in 1558, and that of Mary, queen of Scots, in 1587. Montagu was a patron of the Catholic restoration, founding two chantries in Sussex, one at Battle and the other at Midhurst.

Montagu was dropped from the privy council after Elizabeth I's accession. During the 1559 parliament his conscience required him to speak against the queen's religious policies. He voted against the bills for the dissolution of the religious houses restored by Mary, for the re-establishment of the royal supremacy, and for uniformity. During his speech against the Supremacy Bill, he made the astute observation that the lords 'be not noted thus often to chaunge your faith and religion, and with the prynce to burye your faithe', imploring them to remain true to Catholicism (Hartley, 1.11). Despite his religious convictions, Montagu was sent with Sir Thomas Chamberlain as special ambassador to Spain between 12 January and about 24 June 1560, with an allowance of £5 per day. They had an audience with Philip about 18 March. In 1563 Montagu spoke against the bill to extend the obligation to take the oath of supremacy. To his great surprise he was sent on a conference to the Low Countries to negotiate commercial treaties from 5 March 1565 to about 1 July 1566 (prorogued from 29 September 1565 to 15 April 1566).

On 19 February 1566 his daughter Mary married the Catholic Henry *Wriothesley, second earl of Southampton (bap. 1545, d. 1581).

Montagu was one of the wealthiest peers in Sussex, with an annual income in the 1560s of between £2000 and £3000. This local influence led to his inevitable reappointment as joint lord lieutenant of Sussex in November 1569, during the rising of the northern earls. However, in 1570 he was suspected of trying to flee abroad with Southampton and in 1571–2 he was implicated in the plot to marry Thomas Howard, fourth duke of Norfolk, to Mary, queen of Scots. In 1580 there were rumours that Montagu and Southampton would be arrested for contemplating rebellion but these seem to be unfounded. Montagu was removed from his lord lieutenancy on the outbreak of war with Spain in 1585. Perhaps to test his loyalty, he was among the peers commissioned in October 1586 to try Mary. He confirmed his loyalty to Elizabeth when he actively aided the defence against the Spanish Armada by leading a troop of horsemen with his son and grandson. In August 1591 the queen spent six days at Cowdray, where he entertained her lavishly, and she rewarded him by knighting his second son, George Browne, and his son-in-law, Robert Dormer.

Montagu died at his manor house of West Horsley, Surrey, on 19 October 1592 of a 'tedious, troublesome, and lingering kind of infirmity' (Smith, 20). He was buried at Midhurst on 6 December, under a splendid tomb of marble and alabaster, surmounted by a kneeling figure of himself and recumbent effigies of his two wives. That the monument was a replica of that at Titchfield, in style, dimensions, and materials is a testament to the closeness between Montagu and Southampton. Montagu's will, written on 19 July 1592 and proved 14 March 1593, named as his executors his wife, his son-in-law, Dormer, Edward Gage, Richard Lewknor, and Edmund Pelham. His grandson and heir, Anthony Maria Browne, second Viscount Montagu (1574–1629), inherited a fortune worth between £3600 and £5400 per annum. The dowager Viscountess Montagu died at Battle on 8 April 1608 from the effects of a stroke and was buried alongside her husband.

J. G. ELZINGA

Sources CSP dom., 1547–80 · CSP for., 1559–60; 1564–5 · CSP Spain, 1554; 1568–79 · GEC, Peerage · T. E. Hartley, ed., Proceedings in the parliaments of Elizabeth I, 3 vols. (1981–95) · HoP, Commons, 1558–1603, 1.513–6, 518–21 · JHL, 1 (1509–77) · R. B. Manning, 'Anthony Browne, 1st Viscount Montague: the influence in county politics of an Elizabethan Catholic nobleman', Sussex Archaeological Collections, 106 (1968), 103–12 · R. B. Manning, Religion and society in Elizabethan Sussex: a study of the enforcement of the religious settlement, 1558–1603 (1969) · DNB · will, PRO, PROB 11/81, sig. 22 · C. Roundell, Cowdray: the history of a great English house (1884) · R. Smith, An Elizabethan recusant house, comprising the life of the Lady Magdalen, Viscountess Montague, ed. A. C. Southern (1954) · The speeches and honourable entertainment given to the queen's majestie in progresse, at Cowdrey in Sussex, by the Right Honorable the Lord Monacute (1591)

Archives BL, household daybook, Add. MS 33508 · CUL, official letters on Spanish affairs · Hunt. L., Battle Abbey Muniments · Surrey HC, More of Loseley MSS | Folger, More of Loseley MSS · Hatfield House, Hertfordshire, Cecil papers

Likenesses H. Eworth, oils, 1569, NPG [see illus.] · G. P. Harding, watercolour drawing, 1848 (after L. de Heere), NPG · M. Gheeraerts

senior, etching (*Procession of garter knights* 1576), BM · L. de Heere, oils, Burghley House, Northamptonshire
Wealth at death see will, PRO, PROB 11/81, sig. 22

Browne, Arthur (1756?–1805), lawyer and politician, was born in Newport, Rhode Island, son of the Revd Marmaduke Browne (1731–1771) and his wife, Anne Franklin (*d.* 1767). Marmaduke Browne had been educated at Trinity College, Dublin; commissioned by the Society for the Propagation of the Gospel in Foreign Parts (SPG), and newly ordained, he arrived in Newport in 1755, where he was later rector of Trinity Church. Arthur Browne was educated at the Trinity parish school. His mother died in 1767, and his father died from fever after a long voyage from Europe to Newport in 1771. Orphaned at sixteen he had been entered at Harvard College, Cambridge, Massachusetts, but with the assistance of his father's parish, the SPG, and a legacy from his mother he entered Trinity College, Dublin, in 1772, where he was assisted by his father's friend the Revd Dr John Forsayeth, former senior fellow. At Trinity, Browne became a scholar in 1774, graduated BA in 1776, was elected junior fellow in 1777, and received his MA in 1779. He prepared for the English bar at Lincoln's Inn, in 1778, and was called to the bar in 1779. He completed his legal studies at Trinity College, Dublin, where he received an LLB in 1780 and an LLD in 1784, whereupon he became an advocate in the civil law courts.

Without the customary family connection Browne was elected to the Irish parliament from Trinity College in 1783, and re-elected in 1790 and in 1797; he was often with the Ponsonbys in opposition to Dublin Castle. He was devoted to civil liberties, to the reform of parliament, and to the relief of Roman Catholics from legal oppressions. A fierce opponent of military government he nevertheless defended tithes (he was the son, grandson, and great-grandson of priests) and the non-observance of the 1691 treaty of Limerick. A whig in politics he was one of the fraternal and convivial Knights of the Screw and a frequent contributor to the Royal Irish Academy but he was not a member of the United Irishmen. At the threat of French invasion in 1796 he organized and led a corps of Trinity students and fellows, having been unanimously elected by them, but his criticisms of government in 1798 led to a public rebuke. In 1799 he opposed the union of Ireland and Great Britain, yet changed his mind in 1800, a decision that tainted his reputation with former associates and cost him his seat in parliament.

Browne was appointed to the regius professorship of civil and canon law at Trinity College in 1785; his lectures were eventually published in Dublin as *A Compendious View of the Civil Law and of the Law of the Admiralty* (1797–9) and were republished in a second edition in London (1802–3). He also served as regius professor of Greek for three periods from 1792 to his death; he published several studies of classical Greek, one of which was republished in his two-volume *Miscellaneous Sketches* (1798), which in effect were commentaries on a very wide range of topics. Other publications included translations of poetry from several languages. In 1795 he was elected a senior fellow of Trinity College, and thus became a member of its governing body.

Arthur Browne (1756?–1805), by Hugh Douglas Hamilton, *c.*1795–1800

He continued to receive professional honours: he became a king's counsel in 1795, prime serjeant in 1802 (the last holder of the office), and a bencher of the King's Inns in 1803. He served as an assize judge and also acted as vicar-general of the Kildare diocese.

After the death of his first wife, Marianne, with whom he had a daughter, Browne remarried, and left five children at his death. He lived on Clare Street, Dublin, near the eastern end of the Trinity College yard, where he died on 8 June 1805, in his fiftieth year; he was buried three days later in the churchyard at St Ann's, Dawson Street, Dublin.   JOSEPH C. SWEENEY

Sources *DNB* · J. C. Sweeney, 'The admiralty law of Arthur Browne', *Journal of Maritime Law and Commerce*, 26 (1995), 58–132 · P. O'Higgins, 'Arthur Browne (1756–1805): an Irish civilian', *Northern Ireland Legal Quarterly*, 20 (1969), 255 · W. P. Baildon, ed., *The records of the Honorable Society of Lincoln's Inn: admissions*, 1 (1896) · J. R. Scott, *Review of the principal characters of the Irish House of Commons* (1789) · J. Porter, P. Byrne, and W. Porter, eds., *The parliamentary register, or, History of the proceedings and debates of the House of Commons of Ireland*, 1781–1797, 17 vols. (1784–1801) · W. E. Hume-Williams, *The Irish parliament from the year 1782 to 1800* (1892) · *Faulkner's Dublin Journal* (11–13 June 1805) · *Walker's Hibernian Magazine* (Oct 1805) · M. Rogers, *Glimpses of an old social capital* (1923)
Likenesses H. D. Hamilton, portrait, *c.*1795–1800, TCD [*see illus.*]

Browne, Sir Benjamin Chapman (1839–1917), engineer and shipbuilder, was born on 26 August 1839 at Stouts Hill, Uley, Gloucestershire, the youngest of the three sons of Colonel Benjamin Chapman Browne (*d. c.*1853) of the 9th lancers and later of the Gloucestershire yeomanry, and his wife, Mary Anne Lloyd, *née* Baker, of Hardwicke Court, Gloucestershire. He grew up in the Cotswolds, and went on to Westminster School. Although none of his family had any connection with engineering or business, he decided to study applied science and spent a year at King's College, London, before starting a mechanical engineering apprenticeship with William Armstrong at the Elswick works in Newcastle upon Tyne in 1856. In 1861 he married Annie Buddle, daughter of Robert Thomas Atkinson (1807–1845), a mining engineer, of High Cross House, Benwell, Newcastle. They had nine children, two of whom died in early childhood; three sons and four daughters survived him. His eldest son, Edward Granville *Browne (1862–1926), became professor of Arabic at the University of Cambridge in 1902.

For nearly ten years Browne worked as a civil engineer, first with James Abernoethy at Falmouth harbour, from 1861 to 1862, then with the Tyne Commission, working on the Tyne pier, from 1863 to 1865, and finally on the staff of Sir John Coode on the Isle of Man, where he was employed at the Port Erin works and also worked on the landing pier at Douglas.

In 1870, with the help of his friend Thomas Hodgkin, the Newcastle banker, of Hodgkin, Barnett & Co., Browne became senior partner in the group which bought the Forth Banks Engine works of R. and W. Hawthorn in Newcastle, set up in 1817. Intending to concentrate on the manufacture of marine engines, in 1871 the firm acquired the site of a former shipyard and built the St Peter's works, a new marine-engine works, while modernizing the antiquated Forth Banks works and installing new machinery, in order to continue to make locomotives, because of demand from the North Eastern Railway Company. The marine engineer Francis Carr Marshall (1831–1903) was in charge of the St Peter's works, and it was he who was responsible for the growing reputation of Hawthorns' marine engines. In 1874 orders for gunboat engines began to come in, and Hawthorns went on to supply engines to governments all over the world, including Austria, France, Italy, Chile, China, and Japan. Marine engines became increasingly important to the success of the business, and in 1882 the St Peter's works was enlarged: by 1885 marine engines accounted for more than 80 per cent of the firm's output. Browne was responsible for starting the manufacture of a steam tram at Forth Banks, which he described in a paper to the Institute of Mechanical Engineers in 1880: it was not a commercial success, and only eight trams were made.

In 1876 Browne became a trustee of his wife's family's estates, which included several large collieries, and in the early 1880s he considered withdrawing from Hawthorns in order to devote more time to their administration. But after the retirement of the iron shipbuilder Andrew Leslie from Andrew Leslie & Co., Leslie's partner, Arthur Coote, anxious to acquire a machine engine works, approached Hawthorns about the possibility of a merger and, despite Browne's opposition to the idea, in 1886 R. and W. Hawthorn amalgamated with Leslie & Co. to form R. and W. Hawthorn, Leslie & Co. Ltd. Browne agreed to become chairman of the new company, and remained until 1916. In the late 1880s the company began to build torpedo

boats and destroyers at the Hebburn yard, and under Herbert Rowell, shipyard manager from 1891, became a major supplier of marine engines, steam turbines, and destroyers to the Admiralty. It continued the strong links with Russia built up by Andrew Leslie from the 1860s, supplying naval ships for the Russian volunteer fleet. Hawthorn Leslie also built refrigerated ships, beginning its connection with the New Zealand frozen meat trade. The marine-engine works at St Peter's continued to prosper, and although the Forth Banks works was never as successful it continued to manufacture locomotives and also added water-tube boilers. By 1914 the total workforce was over 5250, and the annual turnover was more than £1.5 million. Browne's other business interests included the Newcastle and District Electric Light Company.

Browne was interested in economic and social questions, and was a member of the Newcastle Economic Society. His first experience of industrial unrest, the 20 week strike on Tyneside in 1871 in support of a nine-hour day, when the inflexibility of the employers prolonged the strike and led to victory for the workers, convinced him of the importance of good relations between employers and their employees. He joined the Iron Trades Employers' Association, and worked hard to improve his relations with his own workers. He publicly supported trade unionism, and as a member of the Engineering Employers' Federation, which he had helped to found in 1896, he played a crucial role in the great lockout of 1897, following the demand by the Amalgamated Society of Engineers for an eight-hour day. Although he was opposed to strike action, he was willing to compromise, and believed in personal contact with the trade-union leaders. Browne was regarded as an authority on industrial relations, and was often asked to give evidence to royal commissions, including the 1904 royal commission on trade disputes and trade combinations. He wrote articles in *The Times* and elsewhere on questions relating to capital and labour, and contributed a chapter, 'The relations between capital and labour: the standpoint of capital', to *After-War Problems* (1917), edited by William Harbutt Dawson.

A JP in Newcastle, Northumberland, and Gloucestershire, Browne was elected to Newcastle town council in 1879 and served as mayor of Newcastle from 1885 to 1887. He was responsible for the success of the Royal Jubilee Exhibition and the Royal Agricultural Show in Newcastle. He was knighted in 1887. He played an important part in the founding of the North East Coast Institution of Engineers and Shipbuilders, serving as president from 1898 to 1900, and he was closely involved in setting up the Durham College of Physical Science (later Armstrong College, which became part of the University of Newcastle in 1963). The University of Durham made him an honorary DCL in 1887.

Like his mother Browne was a devout member of the Church of England and a disciple of the Oxford Movement. He died on 1 March 1917 at Westacres, Benwell, Newcastle upon Tyne, his home since 1887.

ANNE PIMLOTT BAKER

Sources J. F. Clarke, *Power on land and sea: … a history of R. & W. Hawthorn Leslie & Co. Ltd* (1979) · 'Introduction', B. C. Browne, *Selected papers on social and economic questions*, ed. E. M. Browne and H. M. Browne (1918) · L. A. Ritchie, ed., *The shipbuilding industry: a guide to historical records* (1992) · E. Wigham, *The power to manage: a history of the Engineering Employers' Federation* (1973) · J. F. Clarke, 'Browne, Sir Benjamin Chapman', *DBB*, 1.481–3 · E. Allen and others, *The north-east engineers' strikes of 1871: the Nine Hours' League* (1971), chaps. 4 and 5, pp. 98–189 · census returns, 1881 · *WWW* · *Engineering* (9 March 1917), 234

Archives Tyne and Wear Archives Service, Newcastle upon Tyne, records of Leslie Hawthorn

Likenesses Elliott & Fry, photograph, repro. in *Engineering* (9 March 1917), 234 · photograph, repro. in Browne, *Selected papers on social and economic questions*, ed. Browne and Browne, frontispiece

Wealth at death £77,415: Clarke, 'Browne, Sir Benjamin Chapman'

Browne, Coral Edith (1913–1991), actress, was born Coral Edith Brown (she later added the 'e' to her surname for stage purposes) on 23 July 1913 in Melbourne, Australia, the only child of Leslie Clarence Brown, restaurateur, and his wife, Victoria Elizabeth Bennett. Her father ran a successful restaurant in Melbourne. She was educated at the Claremont Ladies' College there. Acting (at least for a well-brought-up young girl) was at the time unthinkable in one of Australia's most conservative communities. She had started to study costume design at an art school attached to the local repertory theatre when an actress fell suddenly ill and Browne was thrust on stage to play a woman living 'in sin' in Galsworthy's *Loyalties* (1931). She was never thereafter to leave the stage for long; at eighteen she was a notable Melbourne Hedda Gabler, and at twenty-one a widely experienced repertory actress.

For her twenty-first birthday Browne's father gave her £50 to visit London, on the condition that she would return home if the money ran out before she had made any kind of success. It duly ran out, but not before Browne had settled into the first of several liaisons, this one with the West End manager Firth Sheppard. 'Firth is my shepherd,' she once noted, 'I shall not want' (private information). It took her several years of understudying and minor role playing before she made her name in 1941, opposite Robert Morley, as the long-suffering secretary Maggie Cutler in *The Man who Came to Dinner* by Kaufman and Hart, which played in London and on tour almost throughout the Second World War. During this time she started an off-stage affair with the actor and singer Jack Buchanan (1890–1957) [see Buchanan, Walter John], with whom she shared a long run in *Castle in the Air* (1949).

By now thoroughly established as a comedienne of considerable elegance and a wicked wit, Browne decided as early as 1951 that she wished to be taken more seriously, even classically, on stage, and joined the Old Vic company in that year to play first Emilia to Douglas Campbell's Othello, and then Regan to Donald Wolfit's King Lear, an experience she likened to being 'a bit of fluff on the carpet at the approach of a vacuum cleaner in full thrust' (private information). Like Maggie Smith, whose career parallels Browne's in many ways, she became renowned for her

Coral Edith Browne (1913–1991), by Anthony Buckley, 1952

backstage commentaries; acting with Nigel Patrick in *The Remarkable Mr Pennypacker* (1955) was, she said, 'like working with two tons of condemned veal' (private information).

Browne's first truly classical success came in 1956, when (again at the Vic) she played a notable Lady Macbeth, and then Gertrude to the somewhat late-life Hamlet of Michael Redgrave; they subsequently took the latter production to Moscow, where Browne met with the spy Guy Burgess (who had been in love with Redgrave at Cambridge), an encounter which later became the subject of Alan Bennett's play *An Englishman Abroad*, in which Browne played her younger self for BBC television in 1983. Meanwhile Browne had married, on 26 June 1950, the actor and agent Philip Westrope Pearman (1910/11–1964), son of Albert Pearman, flour miller. The marriage 'was famously happy, perhaps *because of* rather than *despite* his ambiguous sexuality' (*The Independent*, 31 May 1991). Ten years after his death, and after a long affair with Michael Hordern [see Hordern, Sir Michael Murray (1911–1995)], she married the actor and art expert Vincent Price (1911–1993), whom she had met on a horror film, *Theatre of Blood* (1973). They decided to live in London and furnish a flat; told by a shop manager that the bed they wished to purchase for it had a five-week delivery delay, Coral pointed at her always-cadaverous new husband; 'Five weeks?' she asked, 'Have you seen Mr Price?' (private information).

In the 1960s Browne reverted to high comedy and seldom revisited the classics. Through the 1960s and 1970s she scored many London hits in such comedies as *The Right Honourable Gentleman* (1964–6) and *Lady Windermere's Fan*

(1966). Wilde and Lonsdale were always among her favourite dramatists, though she curiously missed out on Coward and Rattigan. In 1970 she joined the National Theatre for a notable Mrs Warren in *Mrs Warren's Profession*, her first return to Shaw since her early days in Melbourne, and later that decade she took on (with Vincent Price) two difficult Anouilhs, first *The Waltz of the Toreadors* (1974) and then *Ardèle* (1975).

Browne's film career was always intermittent, though she had notable successes as the tough, bitchy friend of the star in *Auntie Mame* (1958), the cynical procuress to Vivien Leigh in Tennessee Williams's *The Roman Spring of Mrs Stone* (1961), and the lesbian BBC administrator in *The Killing of Sister George* (1969). One of her last great appearances was as the elderly Mrs Alice Hargreaves, the original Alice in Wonderland, in *Dreamchild* (1985). By then she had settled in California as Mrs Vincent Price, though none too happily; Hollywood was altogether too artificial a culture for her tough Australian honesty. Told by a box office manager that she had rung far too late to secure tickets for a much vaunted *Macbeth* featuring Charlton Heston and Vanessa Redgrave that was opening at the local theatre, her response was 'Right then, I'll just have two tickets for after the interval' (private information).

Browne's friends sometimes wished she would more often take more challenging work. But that would be to overlook how good she was in what she did choose to do, and her courage was unquestionable, not least when she ventured into Joe Orton's *What the Butler Saw* (1969) at a time when few stars of her generation and elegance would even risk being seen in the audience. Like Edith Evans and Marie Tempest, but precious few others, she was often greater than her roles, and it is arguable that she was often funnier off-stage than on. She endured a long and painful terminal illness with characteristic grace, goodwill, and discretion before dying in Los Angeles on 29 May 1991. She was survived by her husband, Vincent Price. A mass of thanksgiving was celebrated at the church of the Immaculate Conception, Farm Street, London, on 5 September 1991. With her death the British theatre lost a certain style, made up equally of talent, courage, and arrogance, which it was already impossible truly to recapture in an age when directors, designers, and writers called the shots.   SHERIDAN MORLEY

Sources *The Times* (31 May 1991) · *The Independent* (31 May 1991) · *WWW*, 1991–5 · personal knowledge (2004) · private information (2004) · m. cert. [Philip Pearman] · V. Price, *Vincent Price: a daughter's biography* (1999)
Likenesses A. Buckley, photograph, 1952, NPG [*see illus.*] · G. Anthony, photograph, repro. in *The Independent* · photograph, repro. in *The Times*

Browne, David (*fl.* 1622–1638), writing-master and author, published some of the earliest English copybooks. Though little is known of his life it is likely that he was born in Scotland and his pride in this fact is evident in one surviving manuscript where he signed himself 'David Brown Scotus' (Harleian MS 5949). It is apparent again on the title-page of his first publication, *Calligraphia* (1622),

where he styled himself 'Master David Browne, His Majesties Scribe, Sainct Andrewes'. In this instance he also sought to promote the work by dedicating it to James I who had granted the book a 'licence and priviledge' (*Calligraphia*) and, according to Browne's assertion, the king had also seen and commended examples of his penmanship while at Holyroodhouse. While *Calligraphia* is a comprehensive text covering all aspects of the art of penmanship it differs from later copybooks as it was largely printed in letter press and incorporated hardly any examples of calligraphy. It did, however, provide blank spaces in which students could practise their own penmanship and, according to William Massey's *The Origins & Progress of Letters* (1763), in some copies these spaces were filled with examples of Browne's own autograph hand. *The introduction to the true understanding of the whole arte of expedition in teaching to write* (1638) was conceived along similar lines but its promise to teach writing in as little as six hours was somewhat grandiose. Equally, Browne's confidence was also manifest in this publication where he proclaimed his capacity by insisting that 'a Scotishman is more ingenious than one of another nation' (*The Introduction*).

Aside from writing didactic treatises on the art of penmanship Browne also taught students himself. At some point he moved from Scotland to London where he is found teaching at the Cat and Fiddle in Fleet Street and then, in 1638, from the sign of the Spectacles near his home at Jacob's Well, Kennington.

JOHN WESTBY-GIBSON, rev. LUCY PELTZ

Sources A. Heal, *The English writing-masters and their copy-books, 1570–1800* (1931) · W. Massey, *The origin and progress of letters: an essay in two parts* (1763) · G. Meissner, ed., *Allgemeines Künstlerlexikon: die bildenden Künstler aller Zeiten und Völker*, [new edn, 34 vols.] (Leipzig and Munich, 1983–)
Archives BL, Harley MS, calligraphic exercise, MS 5949

Browne, Sir Denis John Wolko (1892–1967), paediatric surgeon, was born on 28 April 1892 in Melbourne, Australia, the eldest in the family of four sons and two daughters of Sylvester Browne, explorer, gold prospector, and farmer, whose father had emigrated from Ireland in 1831, and his wife, Anne Catherine (Nancy), daughter of Sir William Jonas Foster *Stawell (1815–1889), chief justice of Victoria, Australia. He was nephew of the author Thomas Alexander Browne (Rolf Boldrewood) (1826–1915). Denis Browne was educated at King's School, Parramatta, Sydney, and Sydney University (MB, 1914). He joined the 13th light horse regiment and served in Gallipoli before being invalided home. He spent the last two years of the war in France as a major with Australian field ambulance units. Between 1922, when he gained his FRCS, and 1927, he was appointed successively house surgeon, registrar, and resident surgical officer at the Hospital for Sick Children, Great Ormond Street, London. He was also appointed consultant in congenital abnormalities to the London county council, working at Queen Mary's Hospital for Children, Carshalton. He was made consultant surgeon to the Hospital for Sick Children in 1928. He worked there until his retirement in 1957.

Browne was the first surgeon who operated exclusively on children and was the founder of modern paediatric surgery in England. He made outstanding contributions to all branches of children's surgery but his lifelong interest was the aetiology of malformations. From his great clinical experience he was able to postulate his 'mechanical theory', a conception of the fundamental part played by intra-uterine position and pressure on the production of congenital malformations. He was a magnificent surgical technician, a perfectionist who constantly improved his techniques, and ingenious in developing many new surgical instruments and splints. His methods of treatment were new and often revolutionary and were frequently attacked and criticized, but they worked.

Browne was Arris and Gale lecturer (1934 and 1954) and Hunterian professor (1947, 1949, 1950, and 1951) of the Royal College of Surgeons, and co-founder and first president of the British Association of Paediatric Surgeons in 1953. In 1957 he received the Dawson-Williams prize for services to paediatrics and the William E. Ladd medal in the USA for outstanding contributions to paediatric surgery. In 1961 he was appointed KCVO and a chevalier of the legion of honour. In 1965 he was made an honorary fellow of the Australasian College of Surgeons and became president of the International College of Surgeons. He was visiting professor at many universities in all five continents. Later, the Denis Browne gold medal became the highest honour the British Association of Paediatric Surgeons could bestow.

Browne was widely read, had a keen cynical sense of humour, and was intolerant of ignorance, illogicality, and conformity. He disliked committee procedures and bureaucracy. All his life he fought against prejudice, a struggle he greatly enjoyed. He was tall and elegant, a tennis player of a high standard, and an excellent shot.

In 1927 Browne married the novelist Helen de Guerry Simpson (1897–1940), daughter of Edward Percy Simpson, solicitor, of Sydney. They had one daughter. In 1945 he married Lady Moyra Blanche Madeleine, daughter of Vere Brabazon *Ponsonby, ninth earl of Bessborough, former governor-general of Canada. They had a son and a daughter. Browne died at his home, 16 Wilton Street, Grosvenor Place, London, on 9 January 1967. He was survived by his second wife.   P. P. RICKHAM, rev.

Sources J. P. Ross and W. R. Le Fanu, *Lives of the fellows of the Royal College of Surgeons of England, 1965–1973* (1981) · *BMJ* (21 Jan 1967), 178 · *BMJ* (25 Feb 1967), 508 · personal knowledge (1993) · private information (1993) · *CGPLA Eng. & Wales* (1967)
Archives Herts. ALS, letters to Lady Desborough, and letters to Monica, Lady Salmon
Likenesses Elliott & Fry, photograph, repro. in *BMJ* (21 Jan 1967)
Wealth at death £5251: probate, 8 March 1967, *CGPLA Eng. & Wales*

Browne, Edward (1644–1708), physician and traveller, was born in Norwich, the eldest of the eleven children of Sir Thomas *Browne (1605–1682), physician and author, and his wife, Dorothy Mileham (1621–1685). He was educated at Norwich grammar school and in 1657 was admitted a pensioner at Trinity College, Cambridge, where he graduated MB in 1663. He continued his medical studies with his father and, in 1664, with Christopher *Terne (1620/21–1673), physician to St Bartholomew's Hospital, London. In April of that year Browne left for the continent, where he widened his medical experience through visits to the Paris hospitals (April–August 1664), and rounded off his education as a gentleman by making a grand tour. *A Journal of a Visit to Paris in the Year 1664*, edited by G. Keynes, was published in 1923.

Browne returned home in October 1665, having seen Italy (Rome, Naples, Venice, Bologna, and Padua) and France (Arles, Montpellier, Toulouse, La Rochelle). The journey was also a social success, since Browne made the acquaintance of several distinguished people, including Sir William Trumbull, Sir Samuel Tuke, and Sir Christopher Wren. He now enrolled at Merton College, Oxford (19 June 1666), and on 4 July 1667 received his MD (incorporated at Cambridge in 1670). Since he had decided on a medical career in London, it was necessary for him to join the College of Physicians, and on 16 March 1668 he was accepted as a candidate.

However, Browne did not wish to begin a practice immediately, and persuaded his father to let him make another foreign journey. From August 1668 until Christmas 1669 he visited the Low Countries, Germany, Austria, Hungary, Serbia, Bulgaria, and northern Greece, where at Larissa he saw the court of the 'Grand Seigneur'. Browne had become a fellow of the Royal Society on 2 January 1668, and while abroad he sent letters to its secretary, Henry Oldenburg, containing, among other things, information on the gold, silver, and copper mines in Hungary, Transylvania, and Austria. In 1669–70 three letters were published in *Philosophical Transactions* (4, no. 54; 5, nos. 58, 59). Browne remained fairly active in the society until 1684, serving on its council in 1670, 1678, and 1683. His last foreign journey took place in the summer of 1673, when he and many other gentlemen joined Sir Joseph Williamson and Sir Leoline Jenkins on their mission as plenipotentiaries to the peace congress at Cologne. This allowed Browne to visit several cities in the Southern Netherlands and the mineral waters at Aix-la-Chapelle and Spa.

On 30 April 1672, two years after Browne had started building up his medical practice, he married Henrietta Susan (d. 1712), daughter of his former teacher Christopher Terne, at whose house in Lime Street, London, the couple lived until 1674, when they moved to Salisbury Court, Fleet Street. They had eleven children, only four of whom lived to adulthood. Browne worked hard at his profession; on 14 June 1675 he was chosen lecturer at Surgeons' Hall, and on 29 July 1675 he became a fellow of the College of Physicians, which he eventually served as treasurer (1694–1704) and president (1704–8). He had a large and lucrative medical practice, with many aristocratic patients; he was also consulted by King Charles II. On 7 September 1682 Browne became physician to St Bartholomew's Hospital.

Browne's literary output includes two translations: *A*

Discourse of … the Cossacks (1672), a translation of P. Chevalier's *Histoire de la guerre des Cosaques contre la Pologne* (Paris, 1663; 2nd edn, 1668); and the lives of Themistocles and Sertorius in John Dryden's *Plutarch's Lives* (1683–6). However, his reputation is based on *A brief account of some travels in Hungaria, Servia, Bulgaria, Macedonia, Thessaly, Austria, Styria, Carinthia, Carniola, and Friuli* (1673). It was translated into French (1674). An account of his journeys through the Low Countries and Germany (*An Account of Several Travels*) appeared in 1677. A collected edition with many illustrations and some new material, *A Brief Account of some Travels in Divers Parts of Europe*, was published in 1685 and was reprinted in 1687. John Harris adapted the text for his *Compleat Collection of Voyages and Travels* (1705). A Dutch edition, which was translated into German, appeared in 1682, followed by an enlarged and 'improved' version in 1696.

Numerous travellers used Browne as a vade-mecum, copying relevant passages into their own journals. William Nicholson asked Browne for permission to quote him for his volume of *The English Atlas* (1681). The critics were equally pleased with Browne's books. *Philosophical Transactions* (8, no. 94, 1673; 11, no. 130, 1676) published brief abstracts, but those in the Leipzig journal *Acta Eruditorum* (suppl., 1692, 337–46) and the Dutch *Boekzaal* (March–April 1697, 301–10) occupied a full ten pages each. In the introduction to A. Churchill's and J. Churchill's *A Collection of Voyages and Travels* (1704; 2nd edn, 1, 1732; xcii), John Locke called the book an 'ingenious piece, in which he has omitted nothing worthy the observation'; he particularly liked the account of the countries in central Europe 'which are not the common track of travellers'. Browne had 'composed a work of great use and benefit'.

Browne's international fame as author of travel books was partly due to his father, who urged him to adapt for publication the letters he had originally sent home. He advised Edward not to overemphasize the scientific descriptions, and to put in picturesque details about each country, suggesting relevant background reading as well. The result was a book written in a style very different from Browne's chatty letters and journals full of personal details. It is difficult to imagine his printed accounts as being real journeys: few dates are given and anecdotes involving the traveller are rare. They are in fact geographical treatises full of descriptions of foreign cities and customs, scientific experiments, and historical anecdotes: a factual and learned mixture of information on what was 'naturally, artificially, historically and topographically remarkable' (Browne, preface, *A Brief Account*). His approach does not substantially differ from that of other travelling scientists such as John Ray, Ellis Veryard, and William Northleigh.

Not surprisingly Browne's name found its way into reference works such as J. H. Zedler's *Grosses vollständiges Universal-Lexikon* (1733), C. G. Jöcher's *Allgemeines gelehrten Lexikon* (1750), and *Biographia Britannica* (1748), which devoted three and a half very complimentary pages to Browne. However, travel writing was changing. It became more personal and more specialized, and the second edition of *Biographia Britannica* (1780) quoted Samuel Johnson,

who in his 'Life of Sir Thomas Browne' (1756) wrote that Edward Browne's work might provide a naturalist with interesting data, but he could not 'recommend it as likely to give much pleasure to the common reader'. Browne exemplified the old-fashioned tourist, who had not sufficiently mingled 'pleasure with instruction', who made 'a show of knowledge', whereas modern readers preferred travellers who 'copied nature from the life', not from books.

Browne died, after a short illness, on 28 August 1708, in his country house at Northfleet in Kent. A long Latin inscription on the memorial stone over his grave in the local church pays tribute to him as an eminent physician, the author of travels, and a learned, kind-hearted, public-spirited man. He was survived by his wife. In January 1711, after the death of his son Thomas *Browne (*bap.* 1673, *d.* 1710), Edward Browne's library, which included his father's (about 2500 volumes in all), was sold by auction.

KEES VAN STRIEN

Sources *Sir Thomas Browne's works, including his life and correspondence*, ed. S. Wilkin, 4 vols. (1835–6) · *The works of Sir Thomas Browne*, ed. S. Wilkin, 3 (1852), 397–411 [incl. journal of Edward's studies at Norwich] · *The works of Sir Thomas Browne*, another edn, ed. G. Keynes, 6 vols. (1928–31) · Munk, *Roll* · C. D. van Strien, *British travellers in Holland during the Stuart period: Edward Browne and John Locke as tourists in the United Provinces* (1993), 237–97 · A. H. T. Robb-Smith, 'Cambridge medicine', *Medicine in seventeenth century England: a symposium held … in honor of C. D. O'Malley* [Berkeley 1974], ed. A. G. Debus (1974), 327–69 · *A journal of a visit to Paris in the year 1664*, ed. G. Keynes (1923) · J. Beckmann, *Litteratur der älteren Reisebeschreibungen*, 2 (1808–10), 238–63 · *The correspondence of Henry Oldenburg*, ed. and trans. A. R. Hall and M. B. Hall, 6–7 (1969–70) · M. Hunter, *The Royal Society and its fellows, 1660–1700: the morphology of an early scientific institution*, 2nd edn (1994) · J. S. Finch, *A catalogue of the libraries of Sir Thomas Browne and Dr Edward Browne, his son* (1986) · G. Wolstenholme and J. F. Kerslake, *The Royal College of Physicians of London: portraits catalogue II* (1977), 88–9 · Z. Levental, 'Edward Browne, 1642–1708', *The Barts Journal* (summer 1981), 22–9 · E. Browne, *A brief account of some travels* (1685)
Archives BL, corresp. and papers · RCP Lond. | Bodl. Oxf., Rawlinson MSS · RS, letters to Royal Society
Likenesses E. Harding, stipple, Wellcome L. · engraving (after oils, formerly priv. coll.?), RCP Lond., Wellcome L.; repro. in Keynes, ed., *Journal of a visit to Paris* · oils on panel, RCP Lond. · oils on panel, repro. in Levental, 'Edward Browne'; formerly priv. coll.?

Browne, Edward (*d.* 1730), merchant, was born in Cork, the son of James Browne. He later moved to Sunderland, where he served his apprenticeship and later became prosperous in overseas trade. In 1727 he built himself a substantial residence that was adjoined to several other houses for the captains of his ships and other persons in his employment. The building afterwards became the custom house for the port of Sunderland. Browne died at Cork on 27 August 1730. *Some Account of Edward Browne of Sunderland, with Copies of Manuscripts Respecting him* was printed for private circulation at Sunderland in 1821 and reprinted for sale in London in 1842.

THOMPSON COOPER, *rev.* PHILIP CARTER

Sources J. Smith, ed., *A descriptive catalogue of Friends' books*, 2 vols. (1867); suppl. (1893)

Browne, Edward Granville (1862–1926), Persian scholar, was born at Stouts Hill, Uley, Gloucestershire, the home of his grandfather Colonel Benjamin Chapman Browne, on 7 February 1862. He was the eldest son of the nine children of Sir Benjamin Chapman *Browne (1839–1917), civil engineer, and his wife, Annie, daughter of Robert Thomas Atkinson, of High Cross House, Newcastle upon Tyne. On his father's side he was descended from army officers and Gloucestershire landed gentry, in contrast to his mother's family of mining engineers and colliery managers. As the youngest son, his father trained as an engineer and soon became a partner in the civil engineering and ship-building firm of R. and W. Hawthorn, which he transformed into one of the most successful businesses in the north-east. He hoped that his eldest son would follow him into the family business, and with this in mind Edward was sent first to Trinity College, Glenalmond (1872–3), then a preparatory school, Burnside's, in Berkshire (1873–5), and Eton College (1876–7) where he stayed less than a year and a half, leaving abruptly a few weeks after his fifteenth birthday. He then attended the Newcastle College of Physical Science for two years (1877–9), before agreeing with his father that he should read for the natural sciences tripos at Pembroke College, Cambridge, with a view to a possible career in medicine.

It was while Browne was living and studying at Newcastle, shortly after his departure from Eton, that his sympathy with the Turks in their struggle against Russia led him to study Turkish. At Cambridge he continued his interest in oriental languages, studying Arabic with E. H. Palmer and William Wright, and Persian with E. B. Cowell. As a reward for successfully passing the natural sciences tripos in 1882, he spent the long vacation of 1882 in Constantinople where he deepened his knowledge of Ottoman, Persian classical poetry, and Sufism. The next two years he stayed on at Cambridge and took the Indian languages tripos in 1884, before resuming his medical studies at St Bartholomew's Hospital, London, qualifying as MB in 1887. Throughout these years in London, he continued his oriental interests by talking to Persians and reading Persian manuscripts and texts in the British Museum.

In 1887 Browne was elected to a fellowship at Pembroke College, and this enabled him to pay his first and, as it turned out, his only visit to Persia (October 1887 to September 1888); this country became thenceforth the central object of his studies and the absorbing interest of his life. He visited Tabriz, Tehran, Esfahan, Shiraz, Yazd, and Kerman, avoiding European society as much as possible, and throwing himself with ever-increasing interest into the company of Persians, mystics, dervishes, and Kalandars, whose friendship and confidence he gained to a degree hitherto unparalleled. During his year away in Persia he had in 1888 been appointed university lecturer in Persian at Cambridge. In 1902 he was elected Sir Thomas Adams's professor of Arabic. He lived in Pembroke, in the rooms once occupied by Thomas Gray and the younger Pitt. After his marriage in London on 20 June 1906 to Alice Caroline (1879–1925), daughter of Francis

Henry Blackburne Daniell, a barrister, he moved to Firwood, a large neo-Gothic house in Trumpington Road, where he spent the remainder of his life.

A year before his departure for Persia, Browne had happened to come across the writings of Count Gobineau, and the description which he found there of the rise of the Babi movement gave him a new object for his journey. He was spellbound by the story of the courage and devotion shown by the Bab and his faithful followers, and at once resolved to make a special study of this movement. As he himself said, whereas he had previously wished to visit Shiraz because it was the home of Hafiz and Sa'di, he now wished to see it because it was also the birthplace of Mirza Ali Muhammad, the Bab. He was eager to discover the nature of doctrines which could inspire so much heroism, and felt convinced that he would find among the Persians many still living who had known the Bab personally. The story down to 1852 had been adequately and eloquently told by Gobineau. It became Browne's object to continue the narrative from that date, and for some years after his return from Persia he contributed articles dealing with the Babis to the *Journal of the Royal Asiatic Society*. He published two translations of Babi histories, *A Traveller's Narrative, Written to Illustrate the Episode of the Bab* (1891) and *The New History of Mírzá 'Ali Muhammad, the Báb, Translated from the Persian* (1893). Both were enhanced by long introductions and important notes by Browne. He also published in 1893 *A Year amongst the Persians*, which, although it was later included among the foremost classics of travel in English literature, did not at the time attract the attention it deserved, and was not reprinted until 1926, after his death. It is remarkable for his sympathetic portrayal of aspects of Persian society which few, if any, Europeans had ever seen, including a frank account of the effects of opium.

Having made excellent use of the material gathered during his stay in Persia, Browne now turned his attention to the history of Persian literature and, in a number of important contributions to the *Journal of the Royal Asiatic Society*, he outlined his new approach, emphasizing the importance of publishing scholarly editions of classical texts, at first the *tazkirehs* (biographical dictionaries) and then unpublished *divans* and histories. These formed the basis of his great lifelong project, *A Literary History of Persia*, of which the first volume appeared in 1902, and subsequent volumes in 1906, 1920, and 1924. The work marks a turning point in the study of Persian history and literature, and at the close of the twentieth century had still not been completely superseded as the standard authority on the subject. Browne's greatest service lay in his exhaustive analysis of original sources. His knowledge of the Persian language was unrivalled, and his reading covered the whole field of Persian and Arabic literature, and much of Ottoman too. No man of his generation did more to enhance Britain's contribution in this field of scholarship.

Browne's early medical studies were often turned to good account in connection with his oriental researches. His FitzPatrick lectures, delivered at the Royal College of

Physicians in 1919 and 1920, and published in 1921 under the title *Arabian Medicine*, form the most notable product of his combined studies in these two subjects.

Apart from the many books and articles which bore his name, Browne also undertook as a labour of love the wearisome task of cataloguing the Islamic manuscripts in the Cambridge University Library and some of the college libraries, as well as two smaller collections at the India Office Library. He was also responsible for the publication of many Persian texts, several of which he produced at his own expense. Among the most valuable and onerous of the tasks which he undertook was the editing of *A History of Ottoman Poetry*, written by his friend Elias John Wilkinson Gibb. Of this important work only one volume had appeared when Gibb died in 1901. The task of seeing through the press the five remaining volumes was one upon which few men would have had the unselfishness to embark. The most arduous part was the verification and identification of the Turkish originals of the many poems translated in the course of the five volumes. In order to perpetuate the memory of her son, Jane Gibb left a sum of money to be used for the publication of texts and translations of Turkish, Arabic, and Persian books, and with this object in view Browne, with five other scholars, established in 1902 the E. J. W. Gibb memorial fund; he remained the moving spirit of the trust up to his death, by which time twenty-nine titles, in forty-four volumes, had been published, an enterprise which had put Browne at the centre of a scholarly network that included almost all the leading European orientalists of the period.

From the days when Browne's sympathies with the Turks were first aroused, down to the end of his life, politics continued, in the midst of his academic studies, to engross much of his time and thought. When the Persian revolution broke out in 1906 he followed events in Persia with the greatest interest and sympathy. He was instrumental in forming the Persia Committee, consisting of radical Liberal and socialist MPs, together with a few journalists and writers. For a period of over six years (1908–14) he conducted a tireless campaign in the national press and at public meetings in support of the Persian constitutionalists and against the policies of the foreign minister, Sir Edward Grey, particularly the Anglo-Russian agreement of 1907 and Grey's acquiescence in Russian activities in Persia. Ultimately the Persian constitutionalists were defeated, and Persia was overrun by foreign troops. With his spirit further crushed by the horror of the war in Europe, Browne withdrew from all political activity and devoted the rest of his life to scholarship, and his formidable expertise on Middle Eastern affairs was ignored in the redefinition of the area in the post-war era. But out of this period of intense political involvement there had come two major publications, *A History of the Persian Revolution of 1905–1909* (1910), and *The Press and Poetry of Modern Persia* (1914).

At Cambridge, as lecturer and professor, Browne quickly made his personality felt. He was able to achieve much for the promotion of oriental studies in the university, and was mainly responsible for the creation of a school of living oriental languages in Cambridge, in connection with the training of probationers for the Egyptian and Sudanese civil service and the Levant consular service. He was an inspiring teacher, and generations of Pembroke undergraduates and his own students, many of whom later held influential positions in the foreign or consular service, recalled with affection the hospitality, conversation, and warmth of their welcome in his college rooms or, after his marriage, at Firwood.

In middle life Browne gained considerable wealth, and was then able to give full play to his natural generosity, especially in the direction of helping indigent students, refugees, and war victims. He was without worldly ambition and was entirely absorbed in his work, though this did not prevent him from becoming a devoted husband and an affectionate father to his two sons, Patrick and Michael, who later became a High Court judge and a QC respectively.

Browne's capacity for mastering oriental languages was very remarkable, and he was among the very few Europeans who could write a correct letter with equal facility in Arabic, Persian, or Turkish. His memory was exceptional and his fund of quotation inexhaustible. A brilliant conversationalist himself, he also had the Boswellian gift of recalling whole conversations—a gift which contributed very largely to the value and interest of his *A Year amongst the Persians*. Persians themselves held him in the deepest affection and veneration; the name of the street called after him in Tehran remained unchanged even after the Islamic revolution of 1979. On his fifty-ninth birthday he received a number of remarkable tributes from leading men in Persia, and on his sixtieth birthday *A Volume of Oriental Studies*, edited by Sir T. W. Arnold and R. A. Nicholson, to which scholars of several countries contributed articles, was presented to him. The other honours bestowed on him were the Persian order of the Lion and Sun in 1900, and election as a fellow of the British Academy in 1903 and a fellow of the Royal College of Physicians in 1911.

In November 1924 Browne was suddenly stricken by a severe heart attack, which brought his intellectual activities to an end. In June 1925 his devoted wife, worn out with constant anxiety, suddenly collapsed and died. He never rallied from the blow, and survived her by only six months, dying at his home in Cambridge on 5 January 1926. He was buried in Elswick cemetery, Newcastle upon Tyne, Northumberland, on 8 January.

E. D. Ross, *rev.* John Gurney

Sources E. D. Ross, 'A memoir', in E. G. Browne, *A year amongst the Persians*, 2nd edn (1926), vii–xxii · R. A. Nicholson, introduction, *A descriptive catalogue of the oriental MSS belonging to the late E. G. Browne*, ed. R. A. Nicholson (1932), vi–xxii [incl. memoir and bibliography] · A. J. Arberry, 'The Persian: Edward Granville Browne', *Oriental essays: portraits of seven scholars* (1960), 160–96 · G. M. Wickens, 'Browne's life and academic career', *Encyclopaedia Iranica*, 4 (1990), 483–5 · J. Cole, 'Browne on Babism and Bahaism', *Encyclopaedia Iranica*, 4 (1990), 485–7 · K. Ekbal, 'Browne and the Persian constitutional movement', *Encyclopaedia Iranica*, 4 (1990), 487–8 · J. B. Atkins, introductory memoir, *A Persian anthology*, ed. E. D. Ross, trans. E. G. Browne (1927), 1–44 · M. Bonakdarian, 'Edward

G. Browne and the Iranian constitutional struggle: from academic orientalism to political activism', *Iranian Studies*, 26 (1993), 7–31 • M. Momen, *Selections from the writings of E. G. Browne on the Bábí and Bahá'í religions* (1987) • *Nāmehhā-yi 'Idvard Brawn beh Sayyid Hasan Taqīzādeh*, ed. A. Zaryāb and I. Afshār (Tehran, 1975) • H. M. Balyuzi, *Edward Granville Browne and the Bahá'í faith* (1970) • *The Times* (9 Jan 1926), 7c • d. cert. • m. cert.

Archives CUL, corresp. • Pembroke Cam., Persian journals | BL, corresp. with Sir Sydney Cockerell, Add. MS 52708 • BL OIOC, corresp. with Sir Frederic Goldsmid, MS Eur. F 134, no. 30 • CUL, corresp. with E. D. Ross • TCD, corresp. with John Dillon

Likenesses P. Clarke, photograph, *c.*1888, repro. in Ross, 'A memoir', frontispiece • P. Clarke, photograph, *c.*1888, repro. in Momen, ed., *Selections from the writings of E. G. Browne on the Bábí and Bahá'í religions*, frontispiece • C. Shannon, oils, 1912, Pembroke Cam. • W. Rothenstein, pencil sketch, 1917, priv. coll. • photographs, repro. in Zaryāb and Afshār, eds., *Nāmehhā-yi*, 203–4

Wealth at death £166,167 8*s.* 6*d.*: probate, 24 March 1926, *CGPLA Eng. & Wales*

Browne, Edward Harold (1811–1891), bishop of Winchester, was born on 6 March 1811 at Aylesbury, Buckinghamshire. He was the son of Colonel Robert Browne and Sarah Dorothea, daughter of Gabriel Steward of Nottington and Melcombe, Dorset. Sir Thomas Gore *Browne, army officer and colonial governor, was his elder brother. Browne was educated at Eton College, where his strongly Calvinistic views were challenged by exposure to the writings and ethos of the Caroline and high-church divines. He contrasted their accomplishments with a perceived lack of learning and knowledge of church order among the evangelicals. After entering Emmanuel College, Cambridge, at the age of seventeen, he graduated BA in 1832 as twenty-fourth wrangler, also taking a third in the classical tripos. This experience galvanized his theological studies. He won the Crosse theological scholarship in 1833, the Tyrwhitt Hebrew scholarship in 1834, and the Norrisian prize in 1835. He graduated MA in 1836 and later obtained his BD (1855) and DD (1864). He served as chaplain of Downing College and lectured at Emmanuel College. He became an enthusiastic supporter of the Tractarians. He was ordained deacon in 1836 and priest in 1837. He held a fellowship at Emmanuel College from 1837 to 1840 and was senior tutor in 1838.

In June 1840 Browne married Elizabeth Carlyon, daughter of Clement *Carlyon, MD, and was appointed curate of Holy Trinity, Stroud. In 1841 he became perpetual curate of St James's, Exeter, and in 1842 moved to St Sidwell's, Exeter. There Browne introduced the surplice during sermons, an unpopular decision, though typically Tractarian. His successor endured mob violence because of it. Partly as a result of the anti-Tractarian feeling in Exeter, Browne accepted the vice-principalship of St David's College, Lampeter, in 1843. He did a great deal of teaching and went some way to improving academic standards. He became disillusioned with the autocratic style of the principal, Llewelyn Lewellin, and the latter's erratic administration and financial management. In 1849 he was appointed incumbent of Kenwyn in Cornwall by the bishop of Exeter (Henry Phillpotts), and thereby prebend of Exeter Cathedral. Phillpotts appointed him his chaplain for Cornwall.

Edward Harold Browne (1811–1891), by George Frederic Watts, 1875–6

In May 1854 Browne was elected Norrisian professor of divinity at Cambridge. During Browne's time as professor, B. F. Westcott, J. B. Lightfoot, and F. J. A. Hort were all undergraduates. In 1855 he failed to be elected Lady Margaret professor, a position which would have increased his income considerably, by one vote in favour of his competitor, William Selwyn. He resigned Kenwyn in 1857 on his appointment by the dean and chapter to the vicarage of Heavitree, Exeter, with a canonry of Exeter. The bishop wanted him to be principal of a projected theological college and possibly also archdeacon, but this came to nothing.

Browne's generally conservative position led him to deplore many of the opinions inspired by liberal biblical criticism that appeared in *Essays and Reviews* (1860). He contributed to *Aids to Faith* (1861), a moderate response to the *Essays*, seeking to reassure those unsettled by the new thinking. In his article 'Inspiration', Browne criticized the essayists' approach to scripture, which he thought followed Coleridge's dictum 'whatever *finds* me bears witness to the procession of the Holy Spirit'. Browne held that the fathers, schoolmen, and the reformers saw a difference between what we know of ourselves and what is revealed. Browne's essay has been described as 'the most judicious and perhaps the most important' contribution to *Aids to Faith* (Altholz, 82). He later took part in Frederick Temple's consecration as bishop of Exeter in 1869, despite Temple's contribution to the 1860 volume, and never considered him heretical, although he did attempt to persuade him to repudiate *Essays and Reviews*. In 1863 Browne rebutted John William Colenso's views on the origin of the Pentateuch in *The Pentateuch and the Elohistic Psalms* (1863) but, as in Temple's case, he did not adopt an uncompromising position; he considered that Robert Gray's attempts to depose Colenso were excessive.

Browne was offered the see of Ely by Palmerston in February 1864 after the death of Thomas Turton. He was consecrated in Westminster Abbey on 29 March 1864. While bishop of Ely, Browne encouraged the work of societies such as the Additional Curates Society, but was less convinced of the wisdom of multiplying church buildings. He was central to the annual conferences of East Anglian bishops which began in 1866. The bishops of Lincoln, Norwich, Peterborough, and Rochester joined him to discuss matters of mutual concern. In his own diocese of Ely, Browne was an enthusiast for regular conferences between bishops, clergy, and laity. In 1865 he held the first meetings of rural deans and officials, and a more general meeting of clergy and laity. This sort of meeting soon spread to other dioceses. William Emery, archdeacon of Ely from 1864, encouraged similar discussions at archdeaconry and deanery level. What developed was a diocesan conference, based on the archdeaconries, to which clergy and churchwardens were invited. Discussion, always under Browne's clear leadership and control, ranged from the nature of the established church to lay work and church rates.

Gladstone offered Browne the see of Winchester in 1873, after the untimely death of Samuel Wilberforce. He was enthroned on 11 December of that year. At Winchester, Browne continued many of the policies he had followed at Ely. He sought to develop the ministry of suffragan bishops. He had appointed Bishop McDougall, formerly of Labuan and Sarawak, as archdeacon of Huntingdon in 1870, and McDougall became canon of Winchester (1873) and archdeacon of the Isle of Wight (1874). Browne was very keen to establish a suffragan see of Guildford and to provide more episcopal ministry in south London. Although a convinced high-churchman, he was opposed to the developing ritualism of the Anglo-Catholics and was known for his eirenic mediation between opposing church parties.

Browne had some hopes of being made archbishop of Canterbury after the death of Archibald Campbell Tait in 1882, and Gladstone, the prime minister, thought that Browne's claims were 'perhaps, the highest, with his long experience of the Bench' (Gladstone, 319). But Browne's age and ill health prevented Gladstone from pressing his case. In 1890 health problems forced Browne to resign the see, and on 18 December 1891 he died at his home in Shales, near Bitterne, Hampshire.   J. R. GARRARD

Sources G. W. Kitchin, *Edward Harold Browne* (1895) · Venn, *Alum. Cant.* · Boase, *Mod. Eng. biog.* · J. L. Altholz, *Anatomy of a controversy: the debate over 'Essays and Reviews', 1860–1864* (1994) · M. A. Crowther, *Church embattled: religious controversy in mid-Victorian England* (1970) · Gladstone, *Diaries* · DNB
Archives BL, letters to Lord Carnarvon, Add. MS 60836 · BL, corresp. with W. E. Gladstone, Add. MS 44115 · CUL, letters to Sir George Stokes · Durham Cath. CL, letters to J. B. Lightfoot · LPL, corresp. with Edward Benson · LPL, letters to Lord Selborne · LPL, corresp. with A. C. Tait · LPL, letters to Frederick Anthony White · LPL, corresp. with Christopher Wordsworth
Likenesses G. F. Watts, oils, 1875–6, Emmanuel College, Cambridge [*see illus.*] · Elliott & Fry, sepia photogravure, 1890, NPG · W. & D. Downey, carte-de-visite, NPG · Lock & Whitfield, woodburytype photograph, NPG; repro. in T. Cooper, *Men of mark: a gallery of contemporary portraits* (1876) · S. A. Walker & Sons, carte-de-visite, NPG · W. Walker & Sons, carte-de-visite, NPG · oils, St David's University College, Lampeter · portrait, repro. in S. A. Walker, *Dignitaries of the church* (1889) · portrait, repro. in ILN (26 Dec 1891), 823 · wood-engraving (after photograph by J. & C. Watkins), NPG; repro. in ILN (14 May 1864), 477
Wealth at death £36,562 12s. 0d.: resworn probate, May 1892, CGPLA Eng. & Wales

Browne, Frances (1816–1879), writer, was born on 16 January 1816 in Stranorlar, co. Donegal, the seventh of twelve children of Samuel Brown, the village postmaster. She lost her sight following smallpox at the age of eighteen months. The family was Presbyterian, and her conscious effort to acquire an education began at the age of six, when she heard a sermon she could not understand. From that time she adopted a plan for acquiring information through asking the meaning of every new word she heard. She also learned by listening to her siblings repeating their lessons. She had a thirst for facts and a tenacious memory, and bribed members of her family to read 'the drier, but more instructive books' which she latterly preferred, though in rural Ireland books of any kind were hard to come by.

Three early poems were published in the *Irish Penny Journal* (1840), and this volume was the first book Browne ever possessed. Encouraged, in 1841 she sent poems to *The Athenaeum*, and later to *Hood's Magazine* and to Marguerite, countess of Blessington, for *Keepsake*. A volume of poems, *The Star of Attéghei*, was published in 1844. With her literary earnings she paid for the education of a young sister, who became her amanuensis and moved to Edinburgh with her in 1847. In 1852 they moved to London.

Browne made what would seem to have been a precarious living as a journalist, contributing poetry, reviews, and articles on contemporary issues to the *Leisure Hour*, *Sunday at Home*, *Chambers's Journal*, *Tait's Magazine*, and other periodicals. Between 1860 and 1866 she made three successful applications for money from the Royal Literary Fund, whose archives give details. Early in her career Henry Petty-Fitzmaurice, third marquess of Lansdowne, had given her a generous sum; she also received grants from the Royal Bounty Fund and a pension from the civil list.

Browne wrote three three-volume novels: *My Share of the World* (1861), *The Castleford Case* (1862), and *The Hidden Sun* (1866). All were set in a wide range of localities, were powerful and dramatic, but lacked organization.

The handful of stories that Browne wrote for children were remarkable for their strong sense of place and feeling for landscapes she had never seen. *The Eriksons* (1852), for instance, described Norwegian life in great detail; 'Our Uncle's Story' (*Our Uncle the Traveller's Stories*, 1859) was set in the Black Forest, two others in the Lincolnshire fens and in southern Africa respectively. None of her books was reprinted in her lifetime, not even *Granny's Wonderful Chair* (1857), a collection of seven fairy-tales within a frame story, owing something to Grimm. It is for this book, her only attempt at fantasy, that she is remembered. Although it achieved classic status, it did not become generally known until the late Victorian period, when Frances Hodgson Burnett, who had read the book as a child, retold part of it from memory in *St Nicholas* in 1887, and the proper text was 'rediscovered'. Frances Browne died from apoplexy at her home, 19 St John's Grove, Richmond, Surrey, on 21 August 1879. She was unmarried.

GILLIAN AVERY

Sources D. Radford, in F. Browne, *Granny's wonderful chair* (1906) [Everyman edn] • F. Browne, *The star of Attéghei* (1844) [for memoir of early life] • Royal Literary Fund records • d. cert.
Wealth at death under £100: probate, 9 Sept 1879, *CGPLA Eng. & Wales*

Browne, (William Alexander) Francis Balfour- (1874–1967), entomologist, was born on 27 December 1874 at 16 Ebury Street, London, the eldest of the two sons and two daughters of John Hatton Balfour-Browne KC, later of Goldielea, Dumfries, and his wife, Caroline, daughter of Sir Robert *Lush, lord justice of appeal. He showed an early interest in natural history, but received little encouragement other than prizes for collections of birds' eggs and beetles while at St Paul's School, London. At Magdalen College, Oxford, he found that the first part of the botany course had been covered at school, so he obtained permission to spend a term at Edinburgh University, where the field botanical excursions left their mark. He represented Oxford against Cambridge at hockey in 1894 and 1895, and in the former year was also awarded a half-blue for cycling. In 1896 he gained a second-class honours degree in natural science (botany).

To satisfy his father, Balfour-Browne went on to study law at Middle Temple, London, being called to the bar in 1898. His briefs were by his reckoning largely awarded in order to ensure that his father, as a very busy leading counsel, would give extra attention to them. His first publications concerned railway law and the law of compensation, his father's specialities. After six months' experience and much to his father's regret, he returned to Oxford to take a course in zoology. His first post was at the Plymouth marine laboratory and his first scientific publication concerned the immature stages of bony fishes. In 1902 he became director of the Sutton Broad laboratory, the first freshwater research station in Britain. In the same year Balfour-Browne married Elizabeth Lochhead (d. 1947), daughter of the Revd William Henderson Carslaw, of Helensburgh, Dunbartonshire. They had one son (John, a water beetle enthusiast), and two daughters.

From 1906 Balfour-Browne taught biology at Queen's College, Belfast (from 1908 the Queen's University); in 1913 he went to Cambridge to teach entomology. During the First World War he served twice in France, initially as lieutenant in the sanitary company of the Royal Army Medical Corps, later as captain and staff lecturer in entomology. His first period of active service was terminated in 1916 by a shell-burst, which buried and deafened him.

He recuperated by surveying many remote Galloway lochs, thus generating a database of great value following concern over the effects of acidification ('acid rain'). He continued to teach at Cambridge, being greatly pleased with his ability to place students in work as economic entomologists in the Colonial Office. His teaching notes were later published as *A Text-Book of Practical Entomology* (1932), which became a standard text for many university courses in entomology. When in 1925 he tried to retire, he was persuaded instead to take the chair of entomology at Imperial College, London University, working on a part-time basis. He finally retired in 1930 in order to devote the rest of his life to the study of water beetles and their distribution.

Inspired by the works of A. R. Wallace, and encouraged by David Sharp, the most eminent British coleopterist, Balfour-Browne's Norfolk broads studies produced arguably the first intensive, community-based, survey of an insect group. In these studies he used the recording methods of his former Ulster colleague R. Lloyd Praeger—methods Balfour-Browne subsequently promoted for use in the British Isles as a whole. Balfour-Browne methodically amassed and critically appraised earlier records of water beetles, and thus became involved in taxonomy. Here his legal knowledge—in particular his adversarial skill—was brought to bear on the International Commission on Zoological Nomenclature, particularly with regard to implementation of the law of priority. Thus many of his 120 papers, written under the single forename Frank, contain extreme comments which perhaps failed to take into account the need for a common international language in naming the fauna, and also the need for diplomacy in dealing with some entomologists who were more used to being held in scientific regard than to being subjected to severe, though often justifiable, criticism.

Balfour-Browne's database was greatly extended, first by his own collecting across much of the British Isles, and second by his willingness to identify mundane material for others. Thus he was able to bring solid fact into a field where speculation had taken over. Theoreticians had assumed that water beetle distributions had not changed since the ice age, and had claimed the existence of land bridges not corroborated by geological knowledge. Balfour-Browne's data clearly indicated the dynamic nature of many distributions. Had he been aware of the postglacial climate pattern, with the early temperature optimum, Balfour-Browne might have been among the first to recognize that some of this dynamism resulted not from new invasions but from decline to relic status. However, his work did much to dispose of the land-bridging myth.

Balfour-Browne's spruce appearance, forthright comments, and genial personality wholly offset his small stature, and were familiar in many scientific societies. Widely known by the nickname B-B, he was a fellow of several learned societies, including the Royal Society of Edinburgh, and was a keen supporter of the British Association for the Advancement of Science. He was a life governor of the Freshwater Biological Association, and was associated with the Nature Conservancy at its inception. His generosity extended to not only his time but also financial support for many ventures.

Balfour-Browne's *magnum opus* was *British Water Beetles* (1940, 1950, 1958), written as three Ray Society monographs. These have spawned and enthused two generations of 'water beetlers'. This expansion in interest has led to an even more complete knowledge of the British fauna and also to the Balfour-Browne Club, an international group named in his honour, and founded in 1976. Balfour-Browne's last book, *Water Beetles and other Things* (1962), was partly autobiographical, and demonstrated his wit, clarity of thought, and pugnacity almost into his ninetieth year. After an illness in the winter of 1961–2, he gave his collections, notebooks, and card indexes to the Royal Museum of Scotland. Balfour-Browne died suddenly on 28 September 1967 while visiting Edinburgh from his home, Brocklehirst, Collin, Dumfries, and was cremated at Warriston crematorium, Edinburgh, on 30 September 1967.   G. N. FOSTER

Sources F. Balfour-Browne, *Water beetles and other things: half a century's work* (1962) · *Entomologist's Monthly Magazine*, 104 (1968), 286–8 · *DNB* · *The Scotsman* (29 Sept 1967) · 'Professor Balfour-Browne: a biography and a bibliography', *Balfour-Browne Club Newsletter*, 39 (1987), 12–19 · private information (2004)
Archives ICL, corresp. and papers · Royal Museum, Edinburgh, entomological notes and papers · U. Cam., department of zoology, lecture notes
Wealth at death £377,744 13s. 0d.: confirmation, 30 Oct 1967, NA Scot., SC 15/94/62/516

Browne, Geoffrey (c.1608–1668), lawyer and politician, was a son of Sir Dominick Browne (c.1588–1658), merchant and landowner, and Anastasia, daughter of James Rivagh D'Arcy; he belonged through both paternal and maternal descent to the 'tribes of Galway', the urban mercantile élite of the city. Some of the 'tribes', including the Brownes, acquired extensive landed interests in hitherto Gaelic areas throughout Connaught in the early seventeenth century. Entered at London's Middle Temple in 1627, and at Dublin's King's Inns in 1637, Browne earned a reputation as a lawyer in defending these interests, which were threatened by Wentworth's scheme to plant Connaught in the 1630s. Some time before 1633 he married Mary, daughter of Sir Henry Lynch, bt; they had five sons and a daughter.

Browne was active in the Irish parliamentary opposition to Wentworth and was among the most active and influential of the Catholic members in the 1640–41 parliament. He served as a member of the Irish parliamentary delegation to Charles I in December 1640, presenting the remonstrance demanding security of land tenure. In April 1641 Browne and another envoy took the king's letter of acquiescence to Ireland. The following month he returned to England, and in July that year he acted as an agent for the Spanish ambassador Cárdenas in hiring ships to transport troops recruited from Wentworth's disbanded army.

Following the 1641 rising, Browne served as a member of the supreme council of the confederate Catholics between 1642 and 1646. Identified with the influential minority peace or Ormondist faction, he was prepared to pare back Irish Catholic demands as the price of a definitive peace agreement with Charles I and Ormond, his lord lieutenant in Ireland. In July 1644 Browne was appointed a member of the 'committee of treaty' delegated by the general assembly, or legislature, to negotiate a definitive agreement with Ormond. As one of the inner circle of negotiators he, along with two other members of the committee, indicated privately to the king a willingness to compromise on religion, 'the principal thing insisted upon' (Ó Siochrú, 81), in return for other concessions. While Charles I was belatedly prepared to grant these concessions, Ormond proved an inflexible intermediary and negotiations stalled. A new general assembly convened in May 1645 wrested control of the negotiations from the committee, thereby reducing the possibility of speedy agreement.

On 28 January 1646 the supreme council ordered Browne and another lawyer to finalize an alternative agreement on the basis of promises made by a new royal negotiator, the earl of Glamorgan. In the following July three years of negotiations came to apparent fruition in a treaty with Ormond. However, the treaty was repudiated by the papal nuncio, Rinuccini, and subsequently by the general assembly. The newly installed clerical faction subsequently imprisoned Browne, and he was not released until later that year when the general assembly selected him as one of twelve members of a streamlined supreme council. This represented an unavailing attempt to heal divisions by including members from both factions on the supreme council.

Browne was one of three negotiators sent to Paris in February 1648 to conclude terms with the exiled Queen Henrietta Maria for a renewed royalist–confederate alliance. Whereas the committee in 1644–6 had tried to conclude a secret compromise deal, the committee on this occasion was not empowered to conclude a deal without reference to the general assembly. None the less, the royalists excluded the earl of Antrim from discussions even though he was nominally the confederates' chief negotiator. They preferred to deal with Muskerry and Browne in order to smooth the path for the return of the controversial earl of Ormond as the royal representative in Ireland. Ormond's return, together with other aspects of the reconstituted alliance, proved unacceptable to the clericalist faction. Browne was one of nine individuals blamed by the clericalists for the subsequent civil war within confederate Catholic ranks and for the 'ruin' of the Irish nation.

Browne served as one of a dozen commissioners of trust carrying on the former confederate Catholic government on behalf of Ormond. In July 1651 Clanricarde, by then leader of the faltering royalist resistance, sent Browne as one of three agents to solicit assistance from the duke of Lorraine at Brussels. Clanricarde criticized Browne—'you have in a high measure violated the trusts I reposed in you on his majesty's behalf' (Oranmore and Browne, 175)—for allowing Lorraine to encroach on royal prerogatives in return for aiding the Irish. Browne shrugged off the criticism; after the royalist defeat at Worcester (September 1651) he confessed that 'no aids we may expect … will be able to support the interests of that kingdom' (ibid., 176). Standing for Tuam, he was the only Catholic returned to the 1661 parliament but was unseated on a second election.

Regarded by clericalists as a 'venemous viper' (Gilbert), Browne was one of the hard core of the Ormondist faction on the confederate supreme council. Following the Restoration, Charles II directed that he should regain any lands confiscated by the Cromwellians because he 'was loyal to our cause throughout the war' (ibid.). It was not until after Browne's death on 14 January 1668 that the lands were finally regained by his heirs.

PÁDRAIG LENIHAN

Sources Lord Oranmore and Browne, 'The Brownes of Castlemacgarrett', *Journal of the Galway Archaeological and Historical Society*, 5 (1907–8), 165–77 • M. Perceval-Maxwell, *The outbreak of the Irish rebellion of 1641* (1994), 185 • M. Ó Siochrú, *Confederate Ireland, 1642–49: an historical and political analysis* (Dublin, 1999), 81, 99, 108, 114, 162, 164, 172, 185, 188, 223–4, 234, 245, 254, 266 • B. O'Ferrall and D. O'Connell, *Commentarius Rinuccinianus de sedis apostolicae legatione ad foederatos Hiberniae Catholicos per annos 1645–1649*, ed. J. Kavanagh, IMC, 3 (1939), 531, 414–15 • J. T. Gilbert, ed., *A contemporary history of affairs in Ireland from 1641 to 1652*, 1 (1879), 120 • TCD, MS 831, fols. 2–3 • B. McGrath, 'A biographical dictionary of the membership of the Irish House of Commons, 1640–1641', PhD diss., University of Dublin, 1997

Browne, George (*d.* in or after **1556**), Church of Ireland archbishop of Dublin, began his career in the early 1520s as an Augustinian friar. A member of the order's Oxford convent, he studied logic, philosophy, and theology for ten years before supplicating for his baccalaureate in theology at the university in July 1532. In the same year he was appointed prior of the friars' London house at Throckmorton, where on 6 October he obtained a royal licence to travel overseas. Although abroad for only a brief period he appears to have acquired his doctorate in theology from a foreign university, for which he was incorporated at Oxford on 20 July 1534 and at Cambridge in 1535–6.

Browne's appointment as prior of the Augustinian friars in London led directly to his involvement in the promotion of the early Reformation, for it was here that he came into contact with Thomas Cromwell, the motive force behind the king's emerging ecclesiastical revolution. Cromwell's London residence lay within the precincts of the convent, and he quickly entered into negotiations with Browne over the purchase of additional land for the purpose of building a more palatial abode. Through these business dealings Cromwell learned that the new prior was willing to lend his support to his plans for ending the legal impasse surrounding Henry VIII's divorce from Katherine of Aragon. Such support was particularly welcome because Browne was not merely a professional preacher, but one who had access to an important audience, given that Throckmorton was one of the most fashionable residential districts in London.

It was in the role of pulpit propagandist that Browne was initially recruited as an agent of the Henrician Reformation, and in the years 1533–5 he acted as a mouthpiece for Cromwell in promoting the official news and ideology of the new politico-religious order. On Easter Sunday 1533 he made the first public revelation, in a sermon at Paul's Cross, that the king had married Anne Boleyn; and in January 1535 he preached that the bishops derived their power of jurisdiction exclusively from the king as supreme head of the church. Yet Browne was also employed by Cromwell to put into practice what he preached, particularly in relation to securing obedience to the religious settlement from the mendicant friars. In this regard he was appointed provincial of his order in April 1534 by royal command, and he was joined in commission with John Hilsey, provincial of the Dominican friars, to carry out a general visitation of the mendicant orders, which included the administration of the first oath of succession.

Following the suppression of the Kildare uprising in the summer of 1535, Cromwell turned his attention to the task of introducing the Reformation in Ireland, and Browne's experience as an apologist and enforcer of the royal supremacy recommended him as a potential contributor. In particular he was identified as a suitable candidate to fill the see of Dublin, which had been vacant since July 1534 following the murder of John Alen by the Geraldine rebels. Browne was formally nominated for the position on 11 January 1536. On 19 March he received the pallium from Archbishop Cranmer and in the following July he landed at Dublin. From the outset it was intended that he would spearhead the enforcement of the Irish Reformation legislation, which was then being enacted by the 1536–7 parliament. Yet Browne displayed an initial reluctance to begin this task, primarily because of the legislative confusion that prevailed over the succession issue after Anne Boleyn's fall in May 1536. He thus deferred the enforcement campaign while awaiting further clarification of his duties, which earned him a fierce rebuke from an impatient king and Cromwell in September 1537. It was this rebuke, and the coincident enactment of two new statutes in the final session of parliament requiring the imposition of corporal oaths—the second Act of Succession and the act against the authority of the bishop of Rome—which finally moved him to bring the Henrician Reformation before his clergy and flock.

Beginning with a visitation of his own diocese and province in the winter of 1537–8, Browne worked diligently to enforce the new settlement over the next two years, particularly among the corporate clerical élite of the English pale, which he identified as a powerful and influential coterie within the church and society at large. However, his reformist measures—codified in a set of injunctions issued after the 1537–8 visitation—encountered very stiff resistance from this group, because they were perceived as undermining its traditional Roman Catholic ethos. Worse, his difficulties in overcoming this resistance were exacerbated by the poor relations he experienced with the king's deputy, Lord Leonard Grey. The aristocratic Grey, who disparagingly viewed Browne as a 'poll shorn knave friar' (*State Papers, Henry VIII*, 3.208–9), frequently undermined his authority by acts of public vilification and humiliation, and through interfering in his proceedings against the clergy. This was particularly marked in May

1538 when Grey released from the episcopal gaol one James Humphrey, a canon of St Patrick's Cathedral and the chief fomenter of clerical resistance in the diocese, whom Browne had had incarcerated for refusing to read 'The form of the bedes', the reformist bidding prayers which he had composed for use in the mass.

Browne thus made little headway in his efforts to reform his clergy in the late 1530s. The only aspect of the reform programme that can be truly said to have been a success was the campaign for the destruction of monasticism in the English pale in 1539–40, in which Browne participated as a royal commissioner. Yet even while this campaign progressed, his position was fatally weakened as the 'conservative reaction' in England—ushered in by the Act of Six Articles in 1539 and cemented by Cromwell's fall in the summer of 1540—took root in Ireland. The archbishop had married a local woman, Elizabeth Miagh, shortly after his arrival in Ireland, which transgressed one of the main provisions of the Act of Six Articles—the proscription of clerical marriage. His position, therefore, was untenable, and he felt he had no choice but to cast off his wife and to have her remarried to one of his lay servants, Robert Bathe, in the early 1540s. Further, in order to effect this settlement and to provide for the upkeep and education of his three young sons—Alexander, George, and Robert—he had to reach an accommodation with his erstwhile clerical enemies. Ironically these included James Humphrey, whom Browne placed at the head of a group of trustees charged with administering a fund for the maintenance of his sons until they reached the age of eighteen years.

The fall of his patron Cromwell and the arrangements he made for his family represented a major turning point in Browne's career as a reformer. He endeavoured thereafter to live in harmony with the local clergy and community, and took no part in any overtly reformist activity for the remainder of Henry VIII's reign. The succession of Edward VI in January 1547, and the reintroduction of a protestant religious settlement by his regime, caused Browne to flirt once again with the possibility of becoming an active reformer. However, his support for the Edwardian settlement, evinced in such actions as his proposal for the foundation of a university out of the revenues of the dissolved cathedral of St Patrick, were fitful and ambivalent. They were generally capable of being interpreted in a conservative light, as was the case with his university proposal, which was not only critical of the original dissolution of St Patrick's in Henry VIII's reign, but also sought to have the cathedral re-established in the guise of a university church. The ardent Edwardian reformer Bishop John Bale of Ossory was unimpressed by these efforts, and decried Browne as 'a dissembling proselyte' and as someone who had once prayed for Ireland's Reformation, but 'now … commandeth her to go a whoring again, and to follow the same devil that she followed before' (Bale, 56, 68).

The Browne of the 1540s and 1550s was a different creature from the Browne of the 1530s. A Cromwellian reformer by background and instinct, he had been forced by circumstance to abandon his reformist ideals and to throw in his lot with the indigenous clerical élite. This transformation was completed on the accession of Queen Mary in 1553. Although Browne was deprived of his archbishopric in the summer of 1554 because of his ill-fated marriage, he chose to become a full member of the local élite by securing from Cardinal Pole, on 13 March 1555, a pardon for his previous misdemeanours, and by accepting a prebend in the restored cathedral of St Patrick. It was here in Dublin, as prebendary of Clonmethan and as a fully reconciled member of the Roman Catholic church, that he died after 25 November 1556.   JAMES MURRAY

Sources B. Bradshaw, 'George Browne, first reformation archbishop of Dublin, 1536–1554', *Journal of Ecclesiastical History*, 21 (1970), 301–26 · J. Murray, 'Ecclesiastical justice and the enforcement of the reformation: the case of Archbishop Browne and the clergy of Dublin, 1536–1554', *As by law established: the Church of Ireland since the Reformation*, ed. A. Ford, J. McGuire, and K. Milne (1995), 33–51 · Emden, *Oxf.*, 4.76 · J. P. Collier, ed., *The Egerton papers*, CS, 12 (1840), 7–10 · J. Bale, *The Vocacyon of Johan Bale*, ed. P. Happé and J. N. King (1990) · *State papers published under … Henry VIII*, 11 vols. (1830–52), vols. 2–3
Archives LPL, Carew MSS

Browne, George von, Count von Browne in the nobility of the Holy Roman empire (1698–1792), army officer in the Russian service, was born in Limerick on 15 June 1698. He was apparently the illegitimate son of George Browne (*d.* 1729), who with his brother Ulysses Browne served in the imperial army; the elder George Browne was made a count of the Holy Roman empire in 1716 and earl of Browne in the Jacobite peerage in 1726. Although descended from an early settler family which could trace its lineage back to the time of the Conqueror, his immediate forebears were the Brownes of Camas, Limerick.

After being educated at Limerick diocesan school Browne, a Catholic and a Jacobite, followed the example of several of his relatives by travelling abroad to pursue a military career. In his twenty-seventh year he entered the service of the elector palatine and then passed in 1730 into Russian service. He distinguished himself in the Polish, French, and Turkish wars, and had risen to the rank of general, with the command of 30,000 men, when he was taken prisoner by the Turks. After being three times sold as a slave he obtained his freedom through the intervention of the French ambassador Villeneuve, who was acting on behalf of the Russian court. Browne remained for some time at Constantinople in his slave's costume and in this guise succeeded in discovering important state secrets, which he carried to St Petersburg. In recognition of this special service he was raised by Empress Anna to the rank of major-general, and in this capacity he accompanied General Peter Lacy on his first expedition to Finland.

On the outbreak of the Swedish war Browne's tactical skill was displayed to great advantage in checking Swedish attacks on Livonia. He was ennobled in Estonia in 1756. In the Seven Years' War he rendered important assistance as lieutenant-general under his cousin Field Marshal Maximilian Ulysses von *Browne (1705–1757). His fortunate diversion of the enemy's attacks at the battle of Kollin on 18 June 1757 contributed materially to the allied victory, and in token of her appreciation of his conduct Maria Theresa presented Browne with a snuff-box set with brilliants and adorned with her portrait. At Zorndorf on 25 August 1758 he again distinguished himself by his opportune assistance of the right wing at the most critical moment of the battle, which turned almost inevitable defeat into victory. He was named field marshal by Peter III and appointed to the chief command in the Danish war. However, he was deprived of his honours after addressing a remonstrance to the tsar in which he declared that the war was impolitic. He was commanded to leave the country, only to be recalled three days later by the repentant Peter, who appointed him governor of Livonia. He was confirmed in the office under Catherine II, and for more than thirty years to the close of his life he administered its affairs with remarkable practical sagacity. He was ennobled in Livonia (1780) and Courland (1784) and was made a count of the Holy Roman empire in 1773. He died in Livonia on 18 February 1792.

T. F. HENDERSON, rev. ROSEMARY RICHEY

Sources *Histoire de la vie de George de Browne, comte de Saint-Empire, gouverneur général de Livonie et d'Esthonie* (Riga, 1794) · J. S. Ersch and J. G. Gruber, *Allgemeine Encyclopädie der Wissenschaften und Künste, von Schriftstellern genannten*, section 1 (1818–89), 8.1, 112–13 · J. Ferrar, *An history of the city of Limerick* (1767)

Browne, George Forrest (1833–1930), bishop of Bristol, was born in York on 4 December 1833, the elder son of George Browne, proctor of the ecclesiastical court at York, and his wife, Anne, daughter of the Revd Robert Forrest, precentor of York. He attended St Peter's School, York, before matriculating at St Catharine's College, Cambridge, in 1852. There he came under the influence of the master, Henry Philpott, and was inspired by his capacity to combine learning with administrative responsibilities. In 1856 he graduated as thirtieth wrangler, and in the next year obtained a second class in the theological examination, which was not yet a tripos. He proceeded MA in 1863 and BD in 1880.

In 1857 Browne became a mathematics master at Trinity College, Glenalmond, and was ordained in the following year by Samuel Wilberforce. He returned to St Catharine's as fellow and assistant tutor in 1863, having refused a previous offer of a fellowship because he considered that Philpott's successor, Charles Henry Robinson, had acted dishonourably in the notorious election to the college mastership in 1861. He later, however, publicly defended Robinson's integrity. Browne vacated his college fellowship on his marriage (3 October 1865) to Mary Louisa (d. 1903), eldest daughter of Sir John Stewart Richardson, thirteenth baronet of Pitfour, Perthshire, with whom he had two sons and three daughters. He remained a dominant figure in his college as a bye-fellow from 1866, college chaplain, praelector, and tutor.

Browne was a leading Conservative in Cambridge politics both in the university and in the town, where he was elected a member of the town council and served on the magistrates' bench. In 1869 he was presented to the university living of Ashley-cum-Silverley as a political manoeuvre to block another candidate. For twenty years he

'was at the very centre of university affairs' (Roach, 165), holding office as proctor on three occasions (1867–9, 1877–9, and 1879–81), and as a member of the council of the senate (1874–8, 1880–92). For twenty-one years from its foundation in 1870 he was the first editor of the *Cambridge University Reporter*. By the casting vote of the vice-chancellor he was elected in March 1870 secretary of the Cambridge Local Examinations Syndicate, which organized examinations of schoolchildren, and took a leading part in the movement which associated the university more closely with the work of secondary schools. For two years, 1876–8, he was secretary to the Cambridge Local Lectures Syndicate, which pioneered extramural teaching. He promoted the higher education of women in Cambridge through examinations and local lectures, though he opposed their admission to Cambridge degrees, favouring instead independent development through a women's university. From 1877 to 1881 he was secretary to the commission set up to frame new statutes for the university and colleges. He was also a long-serving member of the council of Selwyn College, Cambridge, the Church of England foundation.

Browne found in scholarship and research a relief from the heavy demands of academic administration. In 1887 he was elected to the Disney professorship of archaeology at Cambridge. His interests were in the early history of the church in Britain: he published on Bede (1879) and pre-Augustine Christianity in the British Isles (1894). He made a special study of runic stones, and published *The Ilam Crosses* (1889) and *The Ancient Cross Shafts of Bewcastle and Ruthwell* (1917). He was the first chairman of the Church Historical Society (1894), vice-president of the Society of Antiquaries, a member of the Stonehenge Committee, and president of the Wiltshire Archaeological Society. He was also involved in the erection of the Caedmon cross at Whitby and the Bede cross at Jarrow. He was elected a fellow of the British Academy in 1903.

Browne relinquished his Cambridge chair and other university offices in 1892 when Lord Salisbury appointed him to a canonry of St Paul's Cathedral. He became examining chaplain to Frederick Temple and secretary to the London Diocesan Home Mission. In 1895 he was appointed, at Temple's suggestion, to the new suffragan bishopric of Stepney, and in 1897 he was translated to the diocese of Bristol. His handling of ritualist controversies was carefully balanced; he permitted the use of vestments to continue where it was already established, but made further innovations conditional upon his permission. He favoured compulsory confession for candidates for confirmation, and refused to ordain men who rejected verbal inspiration. He chaired committees of the upper house of convocation concerning the revision of rubrics and the Book of Common Prayer. Since the early 1860s he had found recreation in mountain climbing (see his article 'How we did Mont Blanc', *Contemporary Review*, June 1865), being president of the Alpine Club in 1905; he was also a keen fly-fisherman.

Browne resigned his bishopric in 1914. In retirement he published an entertaining autobiography, *The Recollections of a Bishop* (1915), which revealed his 'curious mixture of acuteness, warm-heartedness and self-importance' (Roach, 166). He died at the Wycombe Lodge Nursing Home, Bexhill, Sussex, on 1 June 1930, and was buried at Bexhill.   ELLIE CLEWLOW

Sources G. F. Browne, *The recollections of a bishop* (1915) · J. Roach, *Public examinations in England, 1850–1900* (1971) · *Men and women of the time* (1899) · Venn, *Alum. Cant.* · *Wellesley index* · D. A. Winstanley, *Later Victorian Cambridge* (1947) · E. E. Rich, ed., *St Catharine's College, Cambridge, 1473–1973: a volume of essays to commemorate the quincentenary of the foundation of the college* (1973) · *CGPLA Eng. & Wales* (1930)

Archives CUL, letters to Sir George Stokes · King's AC Cam., letters to Oscar Browning · LPL, corresp. with Frederick Temple · NRA, priv. coll., corresp. with S. H. Walpole

Likenesses Russell & Sons, cabinet photograph, *c.*1907, NPG · O. Eddis, photograph, 1912, repro. in Browne, *Recollections of a bishop* · E. Irby, photograph, repro. in Browne, *Recollections of a bishop* · L. Ward, cartoon, repro. in Browne, *Recollections of a bishop* · photograph, NPG

Wealth at death £4133 1*s.* 1*d.*: probate, 4 July 1930, *CGPLA Eng. & Wales*

Browne, Sir Granville St John Orde (1883–1947), army officer and colonial official, was born at Woolwich on 26 October 1883, the son of Captain Charles Orde Browne, soldier, and his wife, Annie Maria Michell. He was educated at Wellington College and at the Royal Military Academy, Woolwich, from where he was commissioned into the Royal Horse and Field Artillery in 1902. He was posted to South Africa and Mauritius from 1903 to 1907, serving in the 1906 Zulu rising. He returned briefly to Britain from 1907 to 1909, in which year he was seconded to the Colonial Office as an assistant district commissioner in the British East Africa Protectorate (later Kenya).

Orde Browne continued as an administrative officer until 1915 when he was recommissioned into the Royal Artillery. He then served throughout the German East Africa campaign being promoted to the rank of major, appointed CBE, and mentioned in dispatches four times. In view of his later career it is likely that the suffering of conscripted African labourers during the campaign, over 40,000 from the East Africa Protectorate alone dying from neglect or disease, left a lasting impression upon him.

The nature of British colonialism changed greatly after the war. Colonial governments were now seen as trustees for a dual mandate, formalized by Lord Lugard, of developing territories both for the world at large and also for their inhabitants. The mandate was reinforced by a new measure of accountability to the British parliament, which on occasions took a serious view of abuses of power, such as the harsh exploitation of labour in Kenya in the immediate post-war years.

To these wider perspectives of colonial administration Orde Browne returned, first as a senior commissioner in 1921 and then as labour commissioner in 1926, both posts in Tanganyika where the League of Nations mandate colonial government was additionally accountable to Geneva. He married Margaret Florence, daughter of the Revd H. Fearnley-Whittingstall, in 1923; they had three daughters. While serving as senior commissioner Orde Browne

was charged with the investigation of labour conditions in the territory and the task of making recommendations for the establishment of a labour department. He later produced an interesting anthropological study, *The Vanishing Tribes of Kenya* (1925). This work secured him a reputation outside Africa as a result of which, sponsored by the Institute of African Languages and Cultures, he wrote *The African Labourer* (1933), a seminal study from which all colonial territories were to benefit. The work falls into three parts, the first being a study of practices at the time, in particular housing, diet, wages, the contractual obligations of employer and employee, penal sanctions, recruitment, women, juvenile and child labour, migrant labour, and forced labour, set out together with immediate needs for improvement. The second part is an examination of labour legislation in all the European colonial territories in Africa, and the third and final part is concerned with international draft labour conventions and their application in Africa.

The work was published in 1933, two years after Orde Browne's retirement from the colonial service. In 1934 he became a consultant member of the International Labour Office's committee of experts on native labour. In the course of this work he visited the Belgian Congo, Portuguese East Africa, and later, in 1937, Northern Rhodesia. In 1938 he was appointed the first labour adviser to the secretary of state for the colonies, a post he held until his death in 1947. In this capacity he visited the West Indies in 1938, west Africa in 1939, and in 1941 Ceylon, Mauritius, and Malaya, and, after the war was over in 1945, east Africa. During each visit Orde Browne made a careful analysis of the local problems and in detailed reports, later published as command papers, offered practical suggestions usually, but not always, well received in colonial secretariats; among them was a recommendation for the establishment of labour advisory boards. In his time in office it became accepted that the British Trades Union Congress could offer advice to the Colonial Office on colonial labour issues, and in the case of the West Indies (later to be a precedent for other colonies), that emergent trade unions should be guided and assisted rather than discouraged. He also continually urged research into the social problems facing urban, mine, or plantation workers at work away from their traditional home areas.

Orde Browne's achievement was to provide an entirely new, constructive thinking about African labour, a subject generally ignored prior to his work, an achievement that before long resulted in the creation of specialist labour departments with trained staffs in all but the smallest of British colonies. These, as he foresaw, included both field inspectorates and technical staff for matters such as factory inspections, trade unions, workmen's compensation, and trade testing. These departments drew on his expertise and clarification of their functions. While labour conditions in British colonies could never approach the ideal, substantial improvements in conditions of work and wages, elimination of abuses, and compensation for injury were in large measure due to his inspiration. In

January 1947 he was knighted for his services. Orde Browne died on 12 May 1947 at the Middlesex Hospital, London. He was survived by his wife.

ANTHONY CLAYTON

Sources *The Times* (14 May 1947) · *WWW* · list of officers as at 6/1914, Royal Artillery Institution · B. C. Roberts, *Labour in the tropical territories of the Commonwealth* (1964) · G. St J. Orde Browne, *The African labourer* (1933) · A. Clayton and D. C. Savage, *Government and labour in Kenya, 1895–1963* (1974, [1975]) · *CGPLA Eng. & Wales* (1947)
Wealth at death £4439 14s. 11d.: probate, 27 Aug 1947, *CGPLA Eng. & Wales*

Browne, Hablot Knight [*pseud.* Phiz] (1815–1882), artist and illustrator, was born in Lower Kennington Lane, London, in June or July 1815 and baptized on 21 December 1815 at St Mary's, Lambeth; he was said to be the ninth son of William Loder Browne (1771–1855), a merchant, and his wife, Katherine, *née* Hunter (1774–1856).

Family and education William Loder Browne's father, Simon Browne, was a headmaster and writing teacher in Norwich, and his elegant decorations on invitations, banknotes, and the minutes of the mason's lodge to which he belonged adumbrate the talent which Phiz inherited. The family was descended from Huguenot refugees who Anglicized their French patronym, Bruneau. Browne, fourteenth in a family of fifteen children, was given the name Hablot in honour of Captain Nicolas Hablot, a cavalry officer in Napoleon's imperial guard, the fiancé of Browne's oldest sister, Kate. The family believed that Captain Hablot had died at the battle of Waterloo, but his service record indicates that he was seriously injured and retired to Carignan, Ardennes, where he married in 1816 and died in 1836. In the family's oral tradition, Browne is believed to have been illegitimate, a view based on evidence that at the time of his conception most of the family, except for William Loder Browne, were in France. It is therefore likely that he was the son of Kate Browne and Nicolas Hablot. The family retreated to England on Napoleon's return from Elba and thereafter lost touch with Captain Hablot. In 1822, when H. K. Browne was seven years old, William Loder Browne absconded to the United States, taking embezzled trust funds with him. (It is said his wife ran him into debt.) He changed his name to William L. Breton and sailed to Philadelphia, where he supported himself as an artist and drawing teacher until his death on 14 August 1855. His wife died in London a year later, having never mentioned his name after the day of his departure. To raise her children she relied to a great extent on the kindness of relatives and friends, in particular Thomas Moxon of Twickenham, who had married William Loder Browne's sister Ann.

H. K. Browne joined his older brothers Septimus and Octavius at boarding-school in Botesdale, Suffolk, where the Revd William Haddock was the first to encourage his artistic talent. Another supporter was the husband of Browne's sister Lucinda, Elhanan Bicknell (1788–1861), a wealthy collector of contemporary British paintings, especially those by J. M. W. Turner. Endeavouring to ensure that Browne could stand on his feet financially, Bicknell removed him from Botesdale and apprenticed

Hablot Knight Browne (1815–1882), by unknown engraver

him to the engravers William Finden (1787–1852) and Edward F. Finden (1791–1859). At the age of seventeen Browne won the silver Isis medal from the Society of Arts for the best illustration of a historical subject, and the next year he received another prize from the society for his large etching depicting John Gilpin's ride, a work that became his passport to fame. In a somewhat desultory fashion, because he did not care to draw from life, Browne attended the life school in St Martin's Lane, where William Etty and William Makepeace Thackeray were also students and where Browne preferred admiring Etty's nudes to drawing his own. When Bicknell later offered to pay for lessons with any master Browne cared to choose, the artist curtly turned him down. He grew so tired of slavishly copying others' works that he quit his apprenticeship prematurely and, with his fellow student Robert Young, set up a studio at no. 3 Furnival's Inn (across the court, as it chanced, from Dickens's lodgings at no. 13 and subsequently no. 15). While Browne excelled in design and translating his drawings onto metal, Young was talented at 'biting-in', burnishing, and printing etchings. The two often worked in partnership on the same plate, and their friendship continued until Browne's death. Young became so much a member of the Browne family that Phiz's children called him Uncle Bob and seemed unaware that he was not a blood relative.

Early career In spring 1836 the publishers Edward Chapman and William Hall asked Browne to illustrate their new monthly magazine, *Library of Fiction*, beginning in April, and also a polemical pamphlet directed against extreme sabbatarians, *Sunday under Three Heads*, in June.

Charles Dickens wrote the pamphlet under the pseudonym Timothy Sparks, and he also contributed two stories to the *Library of Fiction*. After Robert Seymour, the illustrator for Dickens's first serial fiction, *Pickwick Papers* (April 1836 – November 1837), committed suicide, and his successor, Robert W. Buss, failed to etch plates successfully, Dickens recommended Browne for the position. Though the author was an 'exacting' taskmaster (Forster, 2.316), Browne supplied everything Dickens needed in an illustrator. He was a skilled and rapid designer, co-operative, witty, and self-effacing, and, in the words of John Harvey, 'he possessed a talent of real originality, sensitivity, and liveliness, which unfolds with remarkable rapidity and brilliance' in Dickens's early fiction (Harvey, 103). For the next twenty-three years Browne was Dickens's foremost illustrator and first graphic interpreter. He produced nearly 740 original and duplicate plates, comprising around 570 steel etchings and approximately 170 wrappers and illustrations engraved into boxwood, plus preliminary designs for 866 wood-engravings inserted into the Household Edition (1871–9). Browne illustrated ten of the major novels: *Pickwick Papers* (1836–7), *Nicholas Nickleby* (1838–9), *The Old Curiosity Shop* (1840–41), *Barnaby Rudge* (1841), *Martin Chuzzlewit* (1843–4), *Dombey and Son* (1846–8), *David Copperfield* (1849–50), *Bleak House* (1851–3), *Little Dorrit* (1855–7), and *A Tale of Two Cities* (1859). He also provided plates for a number of ephemeral publications and reprints, and issued, with Dickens's approbation, portfolios of extra illustrations—portraits of some of the most popular characters. Browne and Dickens were good friends during the early days of their relationship and travelled together to France and Belgium (July 1837), to Yorkshire (in search of material for *Nicholas Nickleby* about the notorious boarding-schools there; February 1838), and to Wales and the midlands (autumn 1838) on a trip that included Manchester, where they met Daniel and William Grant, prototypes for the Cheeryble brothers.

On 28 March 1840 Browne married Susannah Reynolds (1824–1902), the daughter of a Baptist minister in Suffolk. Susannah was a cheerful Mrs Malaprop who afforded her husband much amusement. The Brownes were devoted to each other and to their many children. Out of a total of twelve, nine—five boys and four girls—grew to adulthood; all were artistically endowed. Two of the sons, Gordon Frederick (1858–1932) and Walter Robert Geoffrey (1845–1912), actually made their livings as illustrators. Charles Michael (1843–1900), also an accomplished artist, was a colonel in India; Edgar Athelstane (1842–1917), the eldest, became an eminent Liverpool eye surgeon; and Thomas Hablot (1854–1938) emigrated to Australia. All the daughters, Emma Grant (*b.* 1848), Eliza Mary (*b.* 1850), Mabel Anna (*b.* 1856), and Beatrice Alice (*b.* 1860), were artistic. Only Eliza married, and none of them had children. Together they took care of their parents and their nieces and nephews (regularly sent home from India), and ran a kindergarten in Brighton, which was attended by Eric Gill (1882–1940), later famous as a stone carver and designer of typefaces.

Book illustrations The early success of *Pickwick* ensured Browne's reputation. Having signed N.E.M.O. on his first two images for *Pickwick*, he changed his pseudonym to Phiz—more readily to harmonize, he said, with Dickens's Boz. His output was enormous—about 3660 images over his lifetime—and Phiz became a household familiar. While the early Dickens plates exhibit youthful buoyancy, inexperience, and a delight in portraying rumbustious crowds, Browne's art, nurtured in the Hogarthian tradition of verbal and visual satire, developed and deepened in time, setting a 'matchless standard for sustained collaboration' between artist and author (Cohen, 62). As G. K. Chesterton observes, 'no other illustrator ever created the true Dickens characters with the precise and correct quantum of exaggeration. No other illustrator ever breathed the true Dickens atmosphere, in which clerks are clerks and yet at the same time elves' (Chesterton, 74). Starting with Thomas Miller's *Godfrey Malvern* (1842), 'a turning point in Phiz's career' (Steig, 304), Browne began adding emblematic details that commented obliquely on the action and characters depicted; from 1847 he experimented with 'dark plates' scored with closely set parallel lines that printed in tones of grey and thus conveyed the drama of dark, light, and obscuring weather; and in the 1850s he explored the evocative potential of depopulated settings and designed more horizontal plates that were bound in at right angles to the letterpress.

Browne was soon 'besieged with clients' (E. Browne, 158). For the physician and novelist Charles Lever he designed nearly 500 etchings and many wood vignettes for seventeen titles, and on the whole 'succeeded brilliantly' in capturing Lever's rollicking stories (Muir, 97–8), especially in the early novels. When serving as doctor to the British community in Brussels, in the autumn of 1841 Lever invited Browne to join him and Samuel Lover for an extended visit. Overcoming Browne's 'natural shyness' (E. Browne, 41), Lever staged such a round of 'boisterous merriment' (Downey, 151) that the three friends consumed 108 bottles of champagne in sixteen days and became 'sworn allies' (Fitzpatrick, 152). Browne's work for Lever could sometimes grow slack, and Lever at least pretended to believe that his reputation for caricaturing the Irish was owing to Browne's not understanding the Irish physiognomy. Browne subsequently visited Lever in Ireland and enjoyed tearing across the Irish countryside on horseback with his genial host. Ireland obviously caught hold of his imagination, because he returned there with Robert Young in 1847, in the middle of the disastrous potato famine, and produced some thirty large elegant drawings of Irish scenes, which he had every intention of turning into etchings, but somehow never did.

The novelist (William) Harrison Ainsworth also benefited from Browne's artistry. Browne appreciated Ainsworth's 'out-of-the-way learning' (E. Browne, 194) and shared his fascination with crime. Though George Cruikshank supplied the plates for Ainsworth's big hits of the later 1830s and early 1840s, Browne supplanted the older artist by mid-decade, providing strikingly sinister experimental compositions for Ainsworth's *Auriol* (1844–5), a tale whose supernatural elements appealed to Browne's somewhat surprising fascination with otherworldly creatures and historical detritus. In all, Browne illuminated a half-dozen of Ainsworth's fictions; perhaps his best plates, twelve of the sixteen being 'dark' etchings, were executed for the interrupted monthly serial *Mervyn Clitheroe* (December 1851 – March 1852; December 1857 – June 1858). Among other authors for whom Browne designed plates were Edward Bulwer-Lytton, James Grant, Theodore Hook, Sheridan Le Fanu, Frank Smedley, Harriet Beecher Stowe, R. S. Surtees, Fanny Trollope, and Anthony Trollope. Occasionally Browne was offered the opportunity to illustrate classics by Sir Walter Scott (1842, Abbotsford Edition) and by Henry Fielding and Tobias Smollett (forty-eight wood-engravings for three novels by each, 1857). For much of his life he signed his work Phiz, but on occasion in prints, and often in other media, he identified himself by his real initials or name.

Browne's brilliance as an illustrator did not satisfy him. He never shed the idea that he was first and foremost a fine artist. He was a competent, spacious watercolourist and could always bring in guineas with his sporting scenes, but his lack of formal training in oils and his refusal to draw from life prevented him from achieving academic status. Undaunted by his lack of success in painting on a grand scale, Browne astonished the public in 1843 by entering, tongue in cheek, the contest for decorating the houses of parliament. He submitted two enormous cartoons, *A Foraging Party of Caesar's Forces Surprized by the Britons* (18 ft x 18 ft) and *Henry II Defied by a Welsh Mountaineer*. According to the family chroniclers, 'Nothing could have been funnier than the expression of the figures in these works' (Browne and Bicknell).

Personal life Browne moved house many times in London, and in the late 1840s he moved to Croydon for the sake of Susannah's well-being; her newborn baby had died in 1846, and another in 1847. They lived first at Thornton House, a rambling old place knocked together out of two cottages where Browne could stable a hack and a cob. The move was an unqualified success; Susannah soon recovered and Browne revelled in a change that made it possible for him to hunt. He was never satisfied with the second house, a new villa on Duppas Hill that lacked stabling, but a third home at Banstead, then in deep country, made him 'completely happy' (Thomson, 27).

In his middle years Browne was a handsome, sturdily built man with a long torso and relatively short arms and legs. Though of average height, he seemed shorter because of constantly bending over his work. He wore his medium brown, curly hair quite long, and grew a substantial beard darker than his hair by several shades. His eyes were hazel and his olive complexion clear. He ate sparingly and cared not a fig about the way he dressed. He loved most of all spending time with his family, and as he grew increasingly reclusive he spent his evenings drawing, scanning newspapers, or reading Shakespeare after a hard day's labour in the studio.

Browne remained prodigiously productive throughout the 1840s and 1850s, his greatest decades. Although he

entertained rather than worked on the sabbath, his weekday routine of drawing in the studio from breakfast to dinner enabled him to average more than one design every five days, or nearly eight images a month. From 1841 to 1850 he produced at least 567 etchings and 250 designs for wood-engravings, not counting duplicate steels for Dickens's serials. From March 1852 to September 1853 Browne executed 172 etchings for Dickens, Lever, Smedley, and Ainsworth. However, after more than ten years in the country, the Brownes returned to London in 1859, the year Phiz drew his last illustrations for a new Dickens title. The reason for the move was Browne's need to stimulate new commissions, a difficult task from Banstead, outside London's artistic loop. Sadly, etching was becoming unfashionable, and Browne's caricatural, intensely narrative style was at odds with the prevailing preference for academic drawing and 'realistic' images. After the illustrations to *A Tale of Two Cities*, which Browne's son thought showed 'a considerable declension in power, and even a languid attention' (E. Browne, 297), Dickens turned to more modern artists for his serials. Browne set to work doing watercolours, lithographs, woodcuts, and graphotypes (which he detested), and quickly re-established himself, though on a somewhat lower plane. From 1859 to 1867 he issued around 440 more images, but changes in the visual tastes of readers, in reproductive techniques for book illustration, and in the kind of books publishers issued (more cheap, unillustrated fiction) all worked against Browne's talent.

Starting in 1839, Browne also contributed to numerous illustrated periodicals, including *Ainsworth's Magazine*, the *Illuminated Magazine*, *Life*, *Once a Week*, the *Illustrated Gazette*, and *St James's Magazine*, and produced about 350 sketches, from July 1869 onwards, for *Judy*. He also indulged his love for drawing horses in sporting journals such as the *New Sporting Magazine*, the *Great Gun*, and the *Sporting Times*. In 1842 he designed the second cover for *Punch*, and he contributed occasional sketches to that magazine in 1842, 1844, and 1851, as well as three full-page cuts for *Punch*'s 1850 *Pocket-Book*. In the 1860s he produced still more cuts, for a total of more than sixty illustrations for *Punch*.

Browne was notoriously careless in business affairs and has been described as the sort of man it was no use to help. Although he must have been comfortably off during his prime, making from 5 to 15 guineas per drawing, the idea of saving never seems to have occurred to him. His brother Octavius, who made a small fortune during the Australian gold rush before returning to England, for many years bailed him out to the tune of £120 per annum.

Late career In 1867 Browne suffered a paralytic episode, variously referred to as a stroke, rheumatism, polio, and blood poisoning. While he himself always blamed his illness on having slept in a draught while staying at the seaside, a stroke was the most likely culprit. After five months of suffering, during which he was blind in one eye, he emerged from his room 'with white hair, pallid complexion, and a partial paralysis of the right arm and leg' (Thomson, 31). But he refused to give in. He trained himself to draw holding his pencil between his forefinger and middle finger, because he could not join his thumb to his fingers, and moving his whole body in a sweeping motion. From that point on his work became necessarily broader and less detailed; for shading, he resorted to housemaid's blacklead, which he could rub on and off with his otherwise useless thumb.

In spite of his affliction, Browne remained optimistic about the full recovery that never happened. Little by little commissions fell off until it became impossible for him to make ends meet. He tried oil painting again. The most ambitious was a canvas 8 feet long, *Les trois vifs et les trois morts*, and the most carefully finished was *Sintram and Death Descending into the Dark Valley*; in all, he completed some twenty-four oils. He also did a number of watercolours, especially of hunting and landscape scenes, and for private patrons he rendered in watercolour his previous images for Dickens and others. During the American Civil War he depicted in watercolour and grisaille two scenes 'dedicated to our American cousins': *Death's Revel* and *Death's Banquet* (E. Browne, 303–5).

In July 1878, at the urging of Luke Fildes, Browne applied for a government pension, telling Robert Young, 'If Dizzy is benign, I shall henceforth become his steady supporter and a true Conservative (of the pension) as long as I live' (Thomson, 33). Unfortunately, Disraeli was not benign. But, even in that worst of times, Browne's optimism never deserted him. He wrote again to Young, saying, 'my luck will turn sooner or later. Somehow, in spite of the black look of things, I have a sort of conviction that I shall die tolerably "*comfortable*." However, *faith* is a great thing, isn't it, my boy?' (ibid.). The following year he confessed that his 'occupation seems gone, extinct' (ibid., 32). But ultimately his luck did turn. In 1880, at the instigation of his friends Fildes and William Frith, the Royal Academy came to his rescue, granting him the small pension previously assigned to George Cruikshank. Browne was able to move to 8 Clarendon Villas, Hove, Sussex, where he spent his last two years surrounded by his wife, daughters, and grandchildren. He died at home on 8 July 1882 of progressive paralysis and stroke and was buried in the extramural cemetery, Lewes Road, Brighton, on 14 July. From January to March 1883 the Art Club in Liverpool staged an exhibition of 409 works in all media; 200 of these then were hung in the Bond Street rooms of the Fine Art Society, London, from October to December. Collections of prints, drawings, paintings, and books illustrated by Browne are held in Dickens House Museum, the Victoria and Albert Museum, and the British Museum, London; the Huntington Library, San Marino, California; the Free Library, Philadelphia; the Gimbel Collection, Yale University; the Houghton Library, Harvard University; the Pierpont Morgan Library, New York; and the Vanderpoel Collection, the University of Texas.

ROBERT L. PATTEN and VALERIE BROWNE LESTER

Sources C. G. Browne and A. S. Bicknell, 'Notes to assist the future authors of the history of the Huguenot family of Browne', 1903–29, priv. coll. • V. B. Lester, biography of H. K. Browne [forthcoming] • C. St Denys Moxon, 'History of the Browne family', 1877,

priv. coll. • E. Browne, *Phiz and Dickens* (1913) • D. C. Thomson, *The life and labours of Hablôt Knight Browne, 'Phiz'* (1884) • *The letters of Charles Dickens*, ed. M. House, G. Storey, and others, 12 vols. (1965–2002) • F. G. Kitton, *Dickens and his illustrators* (1899) • J. Forster, *The life of Charles Dickens*, 3 vols. (1872–4) • M. Steig, *Dickens and Phiz* (1978) • A. Johannsen, *Phiz: illustrations from the novels of Charles Dickens* (1956) • Boase, *Mod. Eng. biog.* • F. G. Kitton, *Phiz: a memoir* (1882) • G. K. Chesterton, *Charles Dickens: a critical study* (1906) • A. Allchin, 'An illustrator of Dickens: Hablot Knight Browne ("Phiz")', *Century Magazine*, 45 (1893), 386–94 • J. R. Cohen, *Charles Dickens and his original illustrators* (1980) • J. Buchanan-Brown, *Phiz! Illustrator of Dickens' world* (1978) • C. C. Sisson, *Hablot Knight Browne, 1815–1882: life, work, and methods* (1971) • A. Waugh, 'Charles Dickens and his illustrators', in C. Dickens, *Works* (1937) • W. J. Fitzpatrick, *The life of Charles Lever*, new edn [1884] • E. Downey, *Charles Lever: his life in his letters*, 2 vols. (1906) • L. Stevenson, *Dr Quicksilver: the life of Charles Lever* (1939) • S. M. Ellis, *William Harrison Ainsworth and his friends*, 2 vols. (1911) • G. J. Worth, *William Harrison Ainsworth* (1972) • R. Mitchell, *Picturing the past* (2000) • N. J. Hall, *Trollope and his illustrators* (1980) • J. R. Harvey, *Victorian novelists and their illustrators* (1970) • P. Muir, *Victorian illustrated books* (1971) • G. Everitt, *English caricaturists and graphic humourists of the nineteenth century* (1893) • *CGPLA Eng. & Wales* (1882)

Archives Harvard U. • Hunt. L., letters; illustrations to novels by Dickens | U. Texas, Vanderpoel Collection

Likenesses H. K. Browne, self-portrait, sketch, Morgan L. • W. Browne, portrait, repro. in Thomson, *Life and labours*, frontispiece • F. W. Pailthorpe, etching, NPG • engraving, Charles Dickens Museum, London [*see illus.*] • group portrait, wood-engravings (*Our artists—past and present*), BM, NPG; repro. in *ILN* (14 May 1892) • photograph, repro. in Browne, *Phiz and Dickens*, frontispiece • photograph, repro. in Browne, *Phiz and Dickens*, facing p. 306 • wood-engraving (after photograph by Dr Wallack), repro. in *The Graphic* (5 Aug 1882), 132 • wood-engraving, NPG; repro. in *ILN* (29 July 1882)

Wealth at death £750: administration, 19 Oct 1882, *CGPLA Eng. & Wales*

Browne, Henry (1804–1875), biblical scholar, was the son of the Revd John Henry Browne (*c*.1767–1843), rector of Crownthorpe, Norfolk. He was educated at Corpus Christi College, Cambridge, where he gained Bell's university scholarship in 1822; he graduated BA in 1826, and MA in 1830. He was vicar of Rudgwick, Sussex, from 1831 to 1833 and rector of Earnley, Sussex, from 1833 to 1854. He was assistant to Charles Marriott, whom he succeeded in 1841 as principal of the Theological College, Chichester. The college was criticized by the bishop of Chichester, A. T. Gilbert, and Browne attempted to defend its value as a diocesan institution. But the college declined and Browne resigned in November 1845. In 1842 he was collated to the prebendal stall of Waltham in Chichester Cathedral; from 1843 to 1870 he was examining chaplain to the bishop of Chichester. In 1854 he was preferred by the bishop to the prosperous rectory of Pevensey, Sussex. There he remained until his death on 19 June 1875. He left a widow, Octavia Hooker Irene.

Besides editions and translations of the classics, Browne applied himself chiefly to the elucidation of biblical chronology. The argument of his *Ordo saeclorum, a Treatise on the Chronology of Holy Scripture* (1844) was mainly on the same lines as the work of Henry Fynes Clinton, analysing biblical statements in the light of contemporary knowledge of oriental archaeology. The aim of his *Hierogrammata* (1848) was to show that recent discoveries in Egypt did not invalidate the Mosaic account in the Old Testament. In 1852 he published an attack on the conclusions of the biblical chronologist Edward Greswell. In collaboration with Charles Lewis Cornish (1809–1870) he translated for the Library of the Fathers seventeen short treatises of St Augustine and himself translated St Augustine's *Homilies on the Gospel According to St John* (1848). Browne contributed several volumes of Greek and Latin classics for Thomas Kerchever Arnold's School and College Series. He was also the author of several articles in the third edition (1862–70) of John Kitto's *Cyclopaedia of Biblical Literature*. ALFRED GOODWIN, rev. M. C. CURTHOYS

Sources *Men of the time* (1875) • Boase, *Mod. Eng. biog.* • Venn, *Alum. Cant.* • A. Haig, *The Victorian clergy* (1984)
Wealth at death under £5000: probate, 27 Sept 1875, *CGPLA Eng. & Wales*

Browne, Sir Humphrey (d. 1562), judge, was a younger son of Thomas Browne of Longhouse in Abbess Roding, Essex, and Mary, daughter of Thomas Charlton, perhaps Sir Thomas Charlton (d. 1465), speaker of the House of Commons. His elder brother, Wistan, was the father of Sir Anthony *Browne, who was for four years a fellow justice of the common pleas. He was admitted to the Middle Temple in the 1490s and gave his first reading in 1516. By this time he was already a justice of the peace for Northamptonshire and Essex. In 1521 he became a serjeant-at-law, and in 1530 one of the king's serjeants. He was removed from the office of king's serjeant in 1532, and imprisoned in the Tower, both for hunting in Waltham Forest and for advising felons on how to avoid forfeiture of their goods. The lawfulness of his imprisonment was discussed in the Star Chamber, a major constitutional debate reported briefly by Spelman. Browne was obliged to grant his land in Waltham to the crown, and having done this he sought his reinstatement in 1533, with the backing of the earl of Wiltshire and Lord Rochford; but he was not in the event restored until 1535.

By 1537 Browne was being actively considered for the next vacant judgeship, though he claimed not to be interested because it would cause him financial loss. In 1540, however, he was again removed from office and sent to the Tower, this time for advising on a method of feudal tax avoidance. The conveyancing device in question so worried the government that it was necessary to pass the Statute of Wills in 1540 to remove the threat. Such a double disgrace was unprecedented, and yet, once more, it proved merely temporary. In 1542 Browne was appointed one of the justices of the common pleas and served for twenty years. As a judge he transferred to the western circuit, having previously (as a serjeant) ridden on the northern, midland, and home in succession. By 1559, according to Plowden, he was 'so old that his senses were decayed and his voice could not be heard by the audience' (*Les commentaries*, fol. 190).

According to the 1559 pardon, Browne was also of Terling in Essex. His will mentions the rectory of Maldon and the manor of Manuden, both in Essex, and also manors in Gloucestershire and Middlesex. In 1516 he married Elizabeth, the widow of Nicholas Shelton (d. 1515), alderman of

London, from whom he apparently acquired his house in St Martin Orgar; she was still living in 1541. In 1531 the house was the subject of a burglary recorded in the king's bench files. He later built a mansion house in Cow Lane, London, on land formerly belonging to Watton Priory, Yorkshire, with six messuages in St Sepulchre's parish on the east side of his 'great gate'. His second wife (shown as the first in the visitation pedigrees) was Anne or Amy Mordaunt, daughter and coheir of Henry Vere of Addington. With his third wife, Agnes, a daughter of John *Hussey, Baron Hussey, and granddaughter of Chief Justice Sir William Hussey, he had three daughters: Mary, Christian, and Katherine. Christian was mother of the first earl of Thanet. Katherine was to marry as her second husband William Roper, chief clerk of the king's bench, biographer of Thomas More, and ancestor of the lords Teynham; by her first she was ancestor to the marquesses Townshend. Browne left one son and heir, George, who can hardly be the George Browne admitted to Lincoln's Inn in 1528.

Browne died on 5 December 1562, and was buried in the church of St Martin Orgar on 15 December. Agnes was his executor, and was sued in 1572 for diverting water to the house in Cow Lane through a conduit installed by her late husband. He bequeathed all his law books to Anthony Browne, his nephew and fellow judge, in return for assisting his widow as overseer of the will. J. H. BAKER

Sources Baker, *Serjeants* • *The reports of Sir John Spelman*, ed. J. H. Baker, 1, SeldS, 93 (1977), 1.183, 2.373–4, 388–9, 351 • *LP Henry VIII*, 6, no. 1635; 12/1, no. 42; 12/2, no. 805; 16, no. 304 • will, PRO, PROB 11/46, sig. 2 • E. W. Ives, *The common lawyers of pre-Reformation England* (1983), 58, 82, 387, 445, 469 • W. C. Metcalfe, ed., *The visitations of Essex*, 1, Harleian Society, 13 (1878), 166 • R. Hovenden, ed., *The visitation of Kent, taken in the years 1619–1621*, Harleian Society, 42 (1898), 118–19 • PRO, CP 40/1016, m. 605 • *Les commentaries, ou, Les reportes de Edmunde Plowden* (1571), fol. 190 • J. Dyer, *Cy ensuont ascuns nouel cases* (1585) • Foss, *Judges*, 5.469–70 • J. Stow, *A survay of London*, rev. edn (1603); repr. with introduction by C. L. Kingsford as *A survey of London*, 2 vols. (1908); repr. with addns (1971) • *CPR, 1558–60*, 212 • *The diary of Henry Machyn, citizen and merchant-taylor of London, from AD 1550 to AD 1563*, ed. J. G. Nichols, CS, 42 (1848)

Browne [Brown], **Ignatius** (1630–1679), Jesuit, was born in Waterford on either 1 or 9 November 1630; nothing is known about his parents and family. At some unspecified date in the late 1640s he studied philosophy at Compostella in Spain. On 27 June 1651 he entered the noviciate of the Jesuit province of Castile at Villagarcia, where he pronounced first vows on 29 June 1653. From the noviceship he was sent directly to theological studies in Valladolid. Ordained about 1658, he remained at Valladolid, where he held a chair of philosophy for an unspecified period. In the spring of 1663 he and another Jesuit, Andrew Sall (or Sale), set forth together for Ireland. Stationed at Waterford for eight years, Browne, reputedly a gifted preacher, travelled throughout south Munster, giving retreats and missions. After he was arrested in 1668 and sentenced to imprisonment, an unnamed Irish noble used his influence to gain Browne's release. On 15 August 1668 Browne pronounced his final vows. In 1671 he was transferred to Drogheda, where he remained until 1673. He was named superior of the Jesuit house in Dublin, but never assumed office because of ill health. Instead he received permission to retire to the continent for medical treatment. In the summer of 1673 he stopped at an unnamed English bath to take the hot waters. By November he was in Paris where, through the intercession of Father Jean Ferrier SJ, confessor to King Louis XIV, he gained approval for the foundation of an Irish college in Poitiers. Many Catholics, including Catherine of Braganza, queen of Charles II, contributed to its endowment. Browne was appointed the college's first rector. Unlike Irish colleges in Rome and Spain, which Jesuits administered only for the benefit of clerical students, this new college was specifically an Irish Jesuit house, combining a house of studies for Jesuits, a grammar school for students, and an infirmary/retirement home for elderly Irish Jesuits. Browne consistently benefited from his connections with élites in fund-raising but, unfortunately, nothing is known about the origin and nature of his contacts.

Andrew Sall, Browne's companion, abjured Catholicism in 1674 about the time the Irish College opened—according to Stephen Rice, then superior of Jesuits in Ireland, Sall was the first Irish Jesuit to abandon Catholicism (Oliver, 235n.). In a sermon at Christ Church, Dublin, on 5 July 1674 Sall explained the motivation for his repudiation of Catholicism: because of erroneous doctrines, including the most pernicious one of infallibility, salvation was impossible within the Roman church. Browne retaliated with *The Unerring and Unerrable Church* (1675): contrary to protestant claims of *sola scriptura*, scripture required an infallible interpreter, which was, for Browne, the Roman church. Moreover, Browne countered, since no branch of the protestant church was in any way part of the church of Christ, only 'invincible ignorance' could save a few protestants from damnation. Although Sall replied to all his critics with *True Catholic and Apostolic Faith* (1676), most of the work was directed against his principal critic, the author of *The Unerring and Unerrable Church*, whose identity was, apparently, unknown to Sall. The battle between former colleagues ended with Browne's *An Unerrable Church or none* (1678).

By this time Browne was not well. He stepped down as rector in early 1679; later that year he returned to Castile to serve as confessor to Marie Louise of Orléans, niece of Louis XIV, on her marriage to King Charles II of Spain. Browne died at Valladolid on his way to Madrid on 30 December 1679. Clancy and Oliver attribute *Pax vobis, or, Ghospell and Libertie Against Ancient and Modern Papists* (1679) to him. He left with English Jesuits, perhaps at Valladolid, the manuscript of this theological satire refuting protestant claims and pleading subtly for toleration for Catholics. Although generally not inclined to favour satires dealing with theological controversy, John Keynes, the provincial, submitted the manuscript to the scrutiny of censors who praised it highly. Thus he authorized publication; the work was reprinted six times in different editions during the reign of James II.   THOMAS M. MCCOOG

Sources T. H. Clancy, 'Pax vobis, 1679: its history and author', *Recusant History*, 23 (1996–7), 27–33 • H. Foley, ed., *Records of the English province of the Society of Jesus*, 7 vols. in 8 (1875–83) • L. McRedmond, *To the greater glory: a history of the Irish Jesuits* (1991) • F. O'Donoghue, 'The Jesuit mission in Ireland, 1598–1651', PhD diss., Catholic University of America, 1981 • P. Ó Fionnagáin, *Irish Jesuits, 1598–1773* (privately printed, [n.d.]) • G. Oliver, *Collections towards illustrating the biographies of the Scotch, English and Irish members of the Society of Jesus*, 2nd edn (1845)

Browne, Isaac Hawkins (1706–1760), poet, was born on 21 January 1706 at Burton upon Trent, the son of William Browne, minister of the parish, a man of private fortune and the holder of other ecclesiastical preferments, and his wife, Anne Hawkins. Receiving his first education at Lichfield, Browne passed to Westminster School, and thence on 12 September 1721 to Trinity College, Cambridge, where he obtained a scholarship and took the degree of MA. He was admitted to Lincoln's Inn on 5 June 1722, but though called to the bar in 1728 he did not seriously prosecute the practice of his profession. While at Lincoln's Inn he wrote 'On Design and Beauty', a verse epistle addressed to Highmore the painter. Published in 1734, the poem is a Platonic study of the power of genius in art.

On 10 February 1744 Browne married Jane Trimnell, daughter of Dr David Trimnell, archdeacon of Leicester. Through the influence of the Forester family he was twice returned (1744, 1748) to the House of Commons for the borough of Wenlock, Shropshire, near to which was his own estate. He was during his parliamentary career (1744–54) a supporter of Pelham's whig ministry.

Browne achieved popularity with *A Pipe of Tobacco*, a lively set of parodies of Ambrose Philips, Thomson, Young, Pope, Cibber, and Swift. They were printed in journals in 1735 and 1736, and published together in 1736. The parody of Philips was actually written by his friend John Hoadly, son of the bishop of Winchester, but was revised by Browne. He also published *Of Smoking* (1736), poems in praise of tobacco, and *The Fire Side* (1746), a satire on the inability of John Carteret, Earl Granville, to form a ministry. His principal work, published in 1754, was a Latin poem in two books (a third was intended, but only a fragment was completed) on the immortality of the soul—*De animi immortalitate*—which received high commendation from the scholars of his time. Of this there were several English translations, the best known of which is by Soame Jenyns.

Browne had little aptitude for professional or public life, but he was a man of lively talents. His parodies have continued to be read: they were praised by Byron (letters to Lord Holland, 30 Sept 1812, and John Murray, 17 Oct 1812), and reprinted by Blackwell in 1923. His works and character were commented on by some famous contemporaries. Warburton said of the poem on the soul that it 'gives me the more pleasure, as it seems to be a mark of the Author's growing serious' (Nichols, *Illustrations*). Mrs Piozzi reports Dr Johnson as saying of Browne that he was:

> of all conversers ... the most delightful with whom I ever was in company: his talk was at once so elegant, so apparently artless, so pure, and so pleasing, it seemed a perpetual stream of sentiment, enlivened by gaiety, and

sparkling with images.   (H. Piozzi, *Anecdotes of the Late Samuel Johnson*, 1786, 173)

Fifteen years after Browne's death Johnson thus illustrated the proposition that a man's powers are not to be judged by his capacity for public speech: 'Isaac Hawkins Browne, one of the first wits of this country, got into parliament, and never opened his mouth' (Boswell, *Life*, 2.339). In the 'Tour to the Hebrides', two years earlier, Boswell writes (5 September 1773):

Johnson told us that Isaac Hawkins Browne drank hard for thirty years, and that he wrote his poem, *De animi immortalitate*, in the last of these years. I listened to this with the eagerness of one who, conscious of being himself fond of wine, is glad to hear that a man of so much genius and good thinking as Browne had the same propensity.   (*Boswell's Journal*, 119)

If Browne was best known in his time as a witty conversationalist, his lasting fame is as one who 'holds a place of some honour' in the history of English parody (Brett-Smith, 1). After a lingering illness Browne died at his home in Great Russell Street, Bloomsbury Square, London, on 14 February 1760. An edition of his poems was published by his son, Isaac Hawkins *Browne, in 1768.

J. M. SCOTT, *rev.* W. B. HUTCHINGS

Sources A. Kippis and others, eds., *Biographia Britannica, or, The lives of the most eminent persons who have flourished in Great Britain and Ireland*, 2nd edn, 2 (1780), 647–53 · Venn, *Alum. Cant.* · D. F. Foxon, ed., *English verse, 1701–1750: a catalogue of separately printed poems with notes on contemporary collected editions*, 2 vols. (1975) · Nichols, *Illustrations*, 2.133 · Boswell, *Life* · *Boswell's journal of a tour to the Hebrides with Samuel Johnson*, ed. F. A. Pottle and C. H. Bennett (1963), vol. 9 of *The Yale editions of the private papers of James Boswell*, trade edn (1950–89) · H. B. F. Brett-Smith, 'Introduction', in I. H. Browne, *A pipe of tobacco* (1923), 1–23 · *Byron's letters and journals*, ed. L. A. Marchand, 2 (1973), 221, 228

Archives Trinity Cam., literary MSS and corresp. | BL, corresp. with Lord Hardwicke, Add. MSS 35593–35594, *passim* · Bodl. Oxf., corresp. with Thomas Edwards

Likenesses J. Highmore, oils, 1732, Trinity Cam. · J. Highmore, oils, 1744, Trinity Cam. · S. F. Ravenet, line engraving, 1768 (after J. Highmore), BM, NPG; repro. in I. H. Browne, *Poems upon various subjects* (1768) · J. Flaxman, relief medallion on monument, 1805, Trinity Cam.

Browne, Isaac Hawkins (1745–1818), politician and industrialist, the only son of Isaac Hawkins *Browne (1706–1760), poet and MP, and Jane Trimnell (*d. c.*1779), daughter and coheir of David Trimnell, archdeacon of Leicester, was born on 7 December 1745 and baptized on 16 December at St Andrew's, Holborn, London. He was educated at Westminster School and he matriculated at Hertford College, Oxford, in May 1763. He was a contemporary of Charles James Fox at college, but they formed no friendship, as 'their pursuits, indeed their habits, and connections, were of a widely different character' (*GM*, 179). Long after taking his MA in 1767, he kept his rooms at Oxford and frequently resided there; in 1773 he received the degree of DCL. In 1768 he edited his father's poems in two editions, the better of which, with plates by Laurence Sterne, was not for sale. This edition presumably contained the memoir of his father which he is said to have issued with the works as no memoir was included in the edition offered to the public.

After making a grand tour to France, Switzerland, Italy, and Germany in 1775–6, Browne settled on his property at Badger in Shropshire, and in 1783 served as sheriff for the county. He was a colliery owner and ironmaster and supported industrial interests in parliament where he represented Bridgnorth for twenty-eight years from 1784 to 1812. He was a supporter of William Pitt and later of the ministries of Henry Addington, the duke of Portland, and Spencer Perceval. Like his father, he seems to have had no gift for oratory but, according to one obituarist, when he spoke, 'his established reputation for superior knowledge and judgment secured to him that attention which might have been wanting to him on other accounts' (*GM*, 180). This assessment was confirmed by George Canning in 1794 who thought Browne 'a very sensible man, though queer in his manners—and a respectable though somewhat tiresome speaker' (*Letter-Journal*, 101). Bishop Thomas Newton had written of him as 'a very worthy good young man, possessed of many of his father's excellencies without his failings' (*Works*, 1.80).

Browne married twice: first on 12 May 1788 to Henrietta (*d.* 1802), daughter of the Hon. Edward Hay, son of the eighth earl of Kinnoull, and second on 13 December 1805 to Elizabeth, daughter of Thomas Boddington, a West India merchant of Clapton, Middlesex. Neither marriage produced any children. In 1815 Browne published anonymously *Essays, Religious and Moral*, which he afterwards acknowledged. His *Essays on Subjects of Important Inquiry in Metaphysics, Morals and Religion* (1822) was not published until after his death; if the seriousness of his mind is shown by the spirit of this volume, his exactness and capacity for taking pains are illustrated by the array of authorities by which the text is supported. Browne died at his house in South Audley Street, London, on 30 May 1818 and was buried in Badger.

J. M. SCOTT, *rev.* STEPHEN M. LEE

Sources J. Brooke, 'Browne, Isaac Hawkins', HoP, *Commons, 1754–90* · R. G. Thorne, 'Browne, Isaac Hawkins', HoP, *Commons, 1790–1820* · *GM*, 1st ser., 88/2 (1818), 179–82 · *The letter-journal of George Canning, 1793–1795*, ed. P. Jupp, CS, 4th ser., 41 (1991), 101 · *The works of … Thomas Newton*, 2nd edn, 1 (1787), 80 · A. Kippis and others, eds., *Biographia Britannica, or, The lives of the most eminent persons who have flourished in Great Britain and Ireland*, 2nd edn, 2 (1780), 647–53 · Foster, *Alum. Oxon.* · J. Ingamells, ed., *A dictionary of British and Irish travellers in Italy, 1701–1800* (1997), 141 · IGI

Archives JRL, corresp. · NA Scot., corresp. relating to fisheries | Birm. CA, letters to Boulton family · U. Edin. L., letters to G. J. Thorkelin

Likenesses F. Chantry, sculpture, relief?, St Giles's church, Badger, Shropshire · J. Fitter, line engraving, BM, NPG

Browne, James. *See* Brown, James (*b.* 1615/16).

Browne, James (1793–1841), newspaper editor and journalist, the son of a manufacturer at Coupar Angus, was born at Whitefield, Cargill, in Perthshire. He was educated for the ministry of the Church of Scotland at the University of St Andrews, where, after matriculating in 1806, he distinguished himself in classics. After being licensed to preach he spent some time on the continent as tutor in a family. On his return to Scotland he was assistant master at Perth Academy, and also assisted the minister of Kinnoull, Perthshire. Either because he found his work uncongenial, or because he saw little prospect of obtaining a parish, he resolved to study for the bar. He passed advocate in 1826, and received the degree of LLD from the University and King's College, Aberdeen.

Failing to obtain a practice, Browne gradually turned to a literary career, and in 1827 became editor of the *Caledonian Mercury*. It was mainly due to his articles in the paper that year that the murderer Burke was exposed. During his editorship he became involved in a dispute with Charles Maclaren, editor of *The Scotsman*, with the result that they fought a duel, in which neither was injured. In 1830 he temporarily resigned the editorship of the *Mercury* to start the *North Briton*, but the enterprise was short-lived. Subsequently he was appointed assistant editor of the seventh edition of the *Encyclopaedia Britannica*, to which he contributed many entries, including those on Petrarch and on the history of newspapers. His blustering manner was caricatured by James Hogg in an 1825 article in *Blackwood's Edinburgh Magazine* (vol. 18) entitled 'Some passages in the life of Colonel Cloud'. Some strictures on Hogg's autobiography were published by Browne in his pamphlet 'The life of the Ettrick Shepherd anatomized … by an old dissector' (1832). Browne was a contributor to the *Edinburgh Review* from 1824, and author of several works on Scottish history, the most successful of which was his *History of the Highlands and the Highland Clans* (4 vols., 1835–8). In his later years Browne became a convert to the Roman Catholic faith of his wife, a Stewart of Huntfield, and he wrote a tractate entitled *Examination of Sir Walter Scott's Opinions Regarding Popery*, which was published posthumously in 1845. Exhausted by overwork, he suffered a severe attack of paralysis, from which he made only a partial recovery. He died in April 1841 at his home, Woodbine Cottage, Trinity, Edinburgh, and was buried in Duddingston cemetery, Edinburgh. His eldest daughter married James Grant (1822–1887), a historical novelist and writer on Scottish and military subjects.

T. F. HENDERSON, *rev.* G. MARTIN MURPHY

Sources Anderson, *Scot. nat.*, 400–01 · Allibone, *Dict.* · *Caledonian Mercury* (10 April 1841) · *GM*, 2nd ser., 15 (1841), 662 · J. M. Anderson, ed., *The matriculation roll of the University of St Andrews, 1747–1897* (1905) · P. J. Anderson, ed., *Officers and graduates of University and King's College, Aberdeen, MVD–MDCCCLX*, New Spalding Club, 11 (1893) · D. L. Mack, *James Hogg: memoir of the author's life* (1972), 85 **Archives** NL Scot., corresp. | BL, letters to McVey Napier, Add. MSS 34613–34620, *passim*

Browne, Sir James Crichton- (1840–1938), physician and psychiatrist, was born in Edinburgh on 29 November 1840, the first of the eight children of William Alexander Francis *Browne (1805–1885) and his wife, Magdalene Howden Balfour, daughter of Dr Andrew Balfour of Edinburgh. The addition of Crichton to James's surname was derived from his godmother, Elizabeth Crichton, of Friars Carse, near Dumfries, whose family were instrumental in the financing of the Crichton Institution, Dumfries, where his father was medical superintendent. Crichton-Browne was educated at the Crichton Institution, then

Dumfries Academy and Trinity College, Glenalmond. He entered Edinburgh University in 1857. He was particularly favoured by the professor of physic, Thomas Laycock, one of a number of distinguished teachers. Crichton-Browne joined the Royal Medical Society in November 1858 and was elected as its senior president in 1861. He qualified for his licentiate at the College of Surgeons, Edinburgh, in 1861 and graduated MD with honours the following year. He then qualified LSA in London in 1863, before visiting a number of medical schools and asylums in Paris. Between then and 1865 he served as assistant medical officer in various asylums in the English provinces before becoming medical superintendent at the new borough asylum in Newcastle upon Tyne in 1865. It was in this year that he married Emily Halliday (d. 1903), daughter of John Halliday, surgeon, of Seacombe, Cheshire; they had a son and a daughter. A year later he was appointed medical director at the West Riding Lunatic Asylum at Wakefield in Yorkshire.

The ten years that Crichton-Browne spent at Wakefield secured him a national reputation within his profession as well as testifying to his energy and the range of his interests. He made new appointments (including that of a pathologist), he involved the local medical community, he organized the publication of medical reports, and he handled issues of asylum cleanliness, asylum drainage, and asylum social engagements. Much of his labour was based on the attempt to replicate some of his father's ideas on asylum government but Crichton-Browne added the dimension of a research institution to the more conventional business of custody. The asylum reports became famous, with contributions from David Ferrier, John Hughlings Jackson, Thomas Clifford Allbutt, and T. L. Brunton. Many of these articles previewed the separation of neurology from psychiatry and this logical progression was completed in 1878 when Crichton-Browne helped found and co-edit (with Jackson, Ferrier, and the psychiatrist J. C. Bucknill) the journal *Brain*.

In 1875 Crichton-Browne was appointed lord chancellor's visitor in lunacy and moved from Wakefield to London. He held the post until 1922, travelling the country to visit asylums and then reporting on chancery lunatics and their circumstances. From the mid-1870s through to the late 1890s there were about one thousand chancery lunatics to be visited by three visitors (two medical and one legal). Numbers dropped to between six hundred and five hundred in the period 1913–23. Patients in private quarters were seen quarterly and asylum patients annually. Care was taken of the lunatics' finances and provision was made for their treatment; the tasks of the visitors were famously laborious. However, Crichton-Browne profited from the forty-six years' experience the post gave him, fuelling his many pronouncements on mental health and public means to reduce the incidence of mental alienation.

Best known for his early encouragement of a physiological and neurological examination of asylum patients at Wakefield and elsewhere, Crichton-Browne in his later career synthesized a variety of approaches into one of the first versions of psychiatric paediatrics seen in Britain. He aimed these beliefs and these scientific judgements not just at his medical colleagues and medical students but at a wide book-buying and lecture-attending audience. A Scottish blend of dietary rules, strong emphasis on child-rearing patterns including sleep and educational practice, outdoor exercise, and overall temperance—all had as their focus the central image of the brain, the brain as the most vulnerable (in early life) and the most socially productive of all human organs. Indeed for Crichton-Browne the brain was the literal mediator for social health and advancing levels of practical and intellectual skills. If overworked in youth, or a product of bad heredity, or damaged by irresponsible parental behaviour, brains deteriorated and the overall strength and health of the social order were jeopardized.

Along with many of his British medical contemporaries, Crichton-Browne dismissed as dangerous any new therapies that substituted confessional forms of psychological analysis for older and trusted 'moral management'—work, sport, diversion. Hypnosis and Freudian psychoanalysis were the worst offenders. The vision of public mental hygiene endorsed by Crichton-Browne was not unlike the epic ideas of engineering prominent in the Victorian age: brains could be cleaned, restored, kept working, and free of contamination in the same way as drains. Parents, teachers, and doctors had to collaborate on the joint task of social responsibility for nurturing the infant brain because childhood insanities or mental deficiency would produce a deteriorating and immoral adult world. Lack of attention to the environment, regimen, or religious faith of the expectant mother and the young child would culminate in adult mental pathology and an increase in social misconduct, especially crime and intemperance. Many of the apparent advances in civilization, such as the motor car, were in fact wasteful, as were unhealthy fashions in diet and clothing. Over-intense educational examinations and competition could also be counter-productive in early life and the education of women at university level was inappropriate and dangerous. As he was at pains to stress, Crichton-Browne was not a secular pessimist as long as the nurturing mission that he felt so vital was actually understood and put into practice.

Elected FRS in 1883 (one of his proposers had been Charles Darwin), Crichton-Browne was knighted in 1886. He received a number of honorary degrees and was president of a variety of medical societies in the 1870s and 1880s. He married for the second time, on 16 January 1912; his wife was Audrey Emily Bulwer (b. 1865/6), daughter of General Sir Edward Earle Gascoyne *Bulwer (1829–1910). There were no children of the second marriage. During his later years Crichton-Browne published a number of popular reminiscences such as *Victorian Jottings* (1926), *What the Doctor Thought* (1930), *The Doctor's Second Thoughts* (1931), and *The Doctor's Afterthoughts* (1932).

The strong Scottish blend of natural science and moral vigilance was clearly in evidence in Crichton-Browne's criticisms of the writings of J. A. Froude on Thomas Carlyle. Froude's account of the private life of Carlyle and his marriage to Jane Welsh Carlyle was seen by Crichton-Browne as a betrayal and a disgrace, but the counter-attack on Froude was also a defence of Scottish ideals and Scottish genius, as embodied in Carlyle himself. All of Crichton-Browne's patriotism and moral ferocity were brought to bear in this case, with Froude seen as someone close to lunacy and Carlyle part of Crichton-Browne's own Scottish legacy. This defence of literary Scotland extended to a defence of Burns, claiming that he had not died from alcoholism. Crichton-Browne himself died at his home, Crindau, Dumfries, on 31 January 1938. He was survived by his second wife.   MICHAEL NEVE

Sources M. Neve and T. Turner, 'What the doctor thought and did: Sir James Crichton-Browne, 1840–1938', *Medical History*, 39 (1995), 399–432 · private information (2004) · *The Times* (1 Feb 1938) · *BMJ* (5 Feb 1938), 311 · *The Lancet* (12 Feb 1938), 906 · G. M. Holmes, *Obits. FRS*, 2 (1936–8), 519–21 · m. cert. [Audrey Emily Bulwer] · *CGPLA Eng. & Wales* (1938) · *DNB*
Archives BL, corresp. with Macmillans, Add. MS 55251
Likenesses W. Stoneman, photograph, 1917, NPG · Spy [L. Ward], cartoon, Wellcome L. · photograph, Wellcome L. · wood-engraving, NPG; repro. in *ILN* (30 Jan 1886)
Wealth at death £103,121 17s. 0d.: resworn probate, 2 April 1938, *CGPLA Eng. & Wales*

Browne, Sir James Frankfort Manners (1823–1910), army officer, was born in Dublin on 24 April 1823, the eldest son of the Hon. Henry Montague Browne (1799–1884), dean of Lismore, second son of James Caulfeild Browne, second Baron Kilmaine. His mother was the Hon. Catherine Penelope (d. 1858), daughter of Lodge Evans Morres, first Viscount Frankfort de Montmorency. Educated at Epsom and at Mr Millers's at Woolwich, he entered the Royal Military Academy, Woolwich, on 15 May 1838. On 1 January 1842 he was commissioned second lieutenant in the Royal Engineers. From 1842 to 1854 he served in England, Ireland, and Canada—including pioneering work in the Winnipeg area—and was promoted lieutenant in April 1845. On 24 April 1850 Browne married, at Quebec, Mary (d. 1888), daughter of James Hunt of Quebec, with whom he had two daughters. Promoted second captain on 7 February 1854, Browne commanded the 1st company of Royal Sappers and Miners at Chatham, and on 5 January 1855 embarked with it for the Crimea. It reached Balaklava on 5 February, and soon moved to the trenches of the British right attack on Sevastopol, remaining there until late August. On 22 March 1855, and again on 5 April, Browne took part in the repulse of Russian sorties. He was promoted first captain on 1 June and was the senior executive officer of engineers on 7 June, when he rendered conspicuous service in the successful attack on the quarry outworks covering the Redan. Captain Garnet Wolseley of the 90th foot was his assistant engineer, and Browne reported highly of his conduct. Browne was mentioned in dispatches, and on 17 July received a brevet majority.

When Lieutenant-Colonel Richard Tylden, RE, director of the right attack, was fatally wounded on 18 June 1855, his duties devolved on Browne. But on 24 August, Browne himself was severely wounded, and on 18 November was invalided home. He was created CB (military division) and a knight of the Légion d'honneur, and received the Mejidiye (fifth class), and a brevet lieutenant-colonelcy in December 1856. A pension of £200 a year, awarded him for three years, was afterwards made permanent.

On recovering his health at the end of 1856, Browne was stationed in Dublin until July 1859, then went to command the engineers in the Bombay presidency. In March 1860 he went to Mauritius as commanding royal engineer, and in August 1861 returned home to become superintendent of military discipline at Chatham, where he was second in command. He was promoted brevet colonel on 26 December 1864, and regimental lieutenant-colonel on 2 May 1865.

On 1 January 1866 Browne moved to the War Office, as assistant adjutant-general for Royal Engineers, on the staff of the commander-in-chief, and in 1871 was appointed deputy adjutant-general. In July 1870 he was a member of the committee on the pay of officers of the Royal Artillery and Royal Engineers, and in January 1873 on the admission of graduates to the scientific corps. He was awarded a distinguished service pension in October 1871.

On 1 January 1876 Browne was appointed colonel on the staff and commanding royal engineer of the south-eastern district, but his promotion to major-general on 2 October 1877 (afterwards antedated to 22 February 1870) placed him on the half-pay list. From 1880 to 1887 he was governor of the Royal Military Academy, Woolwich. He was promoted lieutenant-general on 13 August 1881, placed on the unemployed list in 1887, and promoted general on 12 February 1888.

Browne retired on a pension on 5 May 1888. On 6 April 1890 he was made a colonel-commandant of Royal Engineers, and on 26 May 1894 was created KCB. He died at his residence, 19 Roland Gardens, South Kensington, on 6 December 1910, and was buried in Brompton cemetery four days later. R. H. VETCH, rev. JAMES LUNT

Sources *The Times* (9 Dec 1910) · *Hart's Army List* · W. Porter, *History of the corps of royal engineers*, 2 (1889) · Royal Engineers' Records, Chatham · Royal Engineers' Records, PRO · WWW
Archives BL OIOC, MSS Eur. | BL, Durand collection, MSS Em. D. 727 · NAM, letters to Earl Roberts
Likenesses Bassano, photographs, 1898, NPG · C. Lutyens, oils, priv. coll. · attrib. B. Wigram, portrait, 38 engineer regiment, Ripon, North Yorkshire
Wealth at death £4290 17s. 7d.: resworn probate, 3 Feb 1911, *CGPLA Eng. & Wales* · £864: resealed probate, 27 Feb 1911, *CGPLA Ire.*

Browne, John (*fl. c.*1480–*c.*1505), composer, was in 1490 one of the chaplains of the household chapel of John de Vere, earl of Oxford; the identification is confirmed by a contemporary musical source in which the composer is named as 'Johannes Browne Oxoniensis'. No further information survives of the circumstances of his life, but that he was known also to royalty is suggested by the fact that his six-voice setting of *Stabat iuxta Christi crucem* was apparently written for Elizabeth of York following the untimely death of her son Prince Arthur in 1502. Musicians of this period in aristocratic employment commonly composed songs and devotional pieces to vernacular texts, as well as

church music; three compositions surviving in a songbook of 1501 attributed just to Browne, two to devotional texts and one to secular, may well be the work of this John Browne.

In the quality of his accomplishment Browne may be considered the greatest English composer of the period between John Dunstaple, who died in 1453, and John Taverner, who died in 1545. In the compilation (*c.*1502–5) of the Eton choirbook of sacred music his work was accorded pride of place. His fifteen compositions originally included there comprised eleven Marian antiphons and four settings of the Magnificat. Of these, nine survive in a state either complete or completable; most noteworthy among them are the eight-voice *O Maria salvatoris mater* and the three six-voice settings of texts derived from the sequence *Stabat mater*. Browne's polyphony is dense and endlessly resourceful. He is a master of cogency of overall planning, deploying *cantus firmus* technique and the alternation of reduced-voice and full scoring with an effortless artistry that wholly conceals the fact that several compositions stand upon an elaborately mathematical disposition of their successive and component proportions. He is representative of the English florid style of composition at not only its most assured, but also its most imaginative. Few closing periods approach in breadth and sweep the 'Salve' concluding Browne's five-voice *Salve regina*, or in poignancy the setting of 'gaudia' ending *Stabat iuxta Christi crucem* and, long before the contrivances of the madrigalists, he could create in his masterpiece, the six-voice *Stabat mater*, a mood of brooding, despairing introspection and melancholy that gathers an inexorable momentum and energy until its eruption into a startling and percussive outburst of 'Crucifige, crucifige!' ('Crucify, crucify!') that is articulated at the very top of the treble register and represents the work's greatest climax—an unforgettable piece of composition unequalled anywhere in the European music of its time. ROGER BOWERS

Sources F. L. Harrison, ed., *The Eton choirbook*, 2nd edn, 3 vols., Musica Britannica, 10–12 (1967–73) · F. Ll. Harrison, *Music in medieval Britain*, 2nd edn (1963), 307–29 · H. Benham, 'Prince Arthur (1486–1502), a carol and a cantus firmus', *Early Music*, 15 (1987), 463–7 · R. Bowers, 'University Library, MS Buxton 96', *Cambridge music manuscripts, 900–1700*, ed. I. A. Fenlon (1982), 114–17 · R. Bowers, 'Early Tudor courtly song: an evaluation of the Fayrfax Book', *The reign of Henry VII* [Harlaxton 1993], ed. B. Thompson (1995), 188–212 · *Household books of John, duke of Norfolk, and Thomas, earl of Surrey*, ed. J. P. Collier, Roxburghe Club, 61 (1844), 516

Browne, John (*c.*1590–1651), gun-founder, was born in Chiddingstone, Kent, the son of Thomas Browne, founder of iron ordnance to Elizabeth I and James I. He joined his father's thriving business, although not apprenticed in iron making, and took over Thomas's patent in 1615. The Brownes cast iron ordnance for both the crown and private merchants, and exported guns when permitted by the crown.

Browne supplied ordnance to the Dutch until 1619, at which time he employed 200 men at ironworks in Brenchley and Horsmonden, Kent. Half of his production was exported, and from 1618 to 1621 he also cast cannon for

Spain. In 1621 his domestic sales were cut sharply by a patent issued to Sir Sackville Crowe to supply ordnance to all English merchants. The rival patentees quarrelled for over a decade, taking the fight to parliament in 1624. Crowe subcontracted half his sales to Browne in 1626 and finally resigned his patent in 1635. From the mid-1620s Browne developed new, lighter, iron cannon. These 'turned' guns (or drakes) weighed a third less than conventional iron cannon and were intended to replace the costlier (but lighter) bronze guns on ships.

The tempo of Browne's gun-founding business followed the cycles of peace and war from the 1620s to the 1640s. A stagnant market and trade rivalries in the early 1620s were followed by expansion in the later 1620s (between 1625 and 1629 Browne's sales to the crown were over £4300 per annum), and then another slow period in the early 1630s. Renewed efforts to sell ordnance in the Netherlands, from 1629, met with intense competition from Swedish suppliers and resulted in substantial losses, including the £12,000 Browne paid the king for the licence. But within a few years Browne's fortunes were restored: he acquired monopolies of the manufacture and sales of both iron and bronze ordnance, as well as iron pots, kettles, chimney backs, and iron weights 'in the French manner'. The crown renewed purchases of bronze and iron naval guns, and the ordnance market expanded further with the Scottish rebellion of 1639–40 and the outbreak of civil war in 1642. Browne, the king's gun-founder, became parliament's gun-founder. His business grew as parliament gave him control of a number of ironworks, including the former royal ironworks in the Forest of Dean.

Browne's prosperity and monopolies were only once endangered, in 1645, when an intercepted letter named him as a royalist sympathizer. He and his son John protested their innocence to a parliamentary committee, and nothing could be proved against them. When, in 1651, the Rump ordered guns from a former employee of his, Browne delivered an emotional remonstrance to the House of Commons: the state's security, he claimed, depended upon a single gun-founder; his enterprise employed a 'stock' of £30,000, had overheads of at least £4000 per annum, and had to be kept busy.

Browne resided in Brenchley from about 1615 to 1635, then in Horsmonden. His stock in trade was valued at £16,000 c.1650. Browne married Martha, daughter of Henry Tilden, gentleman, in 1616. They had a daughter and three sons. After Martha's death in 1644 Browne married Elizabeth, daughter of Lancelot Bathurst, alderman of London. His will, made on 15 May 1651, included cash legacies totalling £14,000, and named his son George and his son-in-law Thomas Foley (1617–1677) as executors. He was buried in Horsmonden on 13 June 1651.

MICHAEL ZELL, rev.

Sources West Kent archives, Browne MSS · *CSP dom.*, 1615–51 · Brenchley and Horsmonden (Kent) parish registers · H. Cleere and D. Crossley, *The iron industry of the Weald* (1985) · will, 15 May 1651, PRO, PROB 11/217/108

Wealth at death £14,000: will, 15 May 1651, PRO, PROB 11/217/108

Browne, John (*c.*1608–1691), parliamentary official, was the only child of Thomas Browne (*d.* 1621), citizen and grocer of London, and his wife, Joan, whose surname may have been Wilson. He belonged to a family which originated at Bury St Edmunds. On his father's death in 1621 he was adopted by his uncle John Browne, a merchant tailor, from whom he eventually inherited a substantial fortune. He was admitted a student by the Middle Temple on 28 October 1628 but was not called to the bar. On 13 March 1638 he was appointed clerk of the parliaments. Parliament was then dissolved and he did not enter fully upon his duties as clerk of the House of Lords until the assembly of the Short Parliament in April 1640.

Browne was a firm adherent of the parliamentarian cause and following the final break between the king and parliament in 1642 he remained at Westminster to serve the House of Lords there. The abolition of the house in March 1649 deprived him of his employment until the Restoration. On 25 June 1650 the House of Commons ordered the records of the House of Lords in Browne's custody to be delivered to Henry Scobell, whom they had appointed their clerk and designated clerk of the parliaments. However, at the first meeting of the convention on 25 April 1660 the House of Lords ordered Scobell to return the records to Browne, who was reinstated as clerk of the parliaments, making a declaration of loyalty to Charles II on 30 May. He served the house for a further thirty years until his death.

Although not a profound scholar like some of his immediate predecessors Browne consolidated their work during his long term of office by bringing order and regularity to the procedure of the House of Lords. His reputation as a record-keeper has, however, suffered due to the loss through his agency of the Braye and Nalson manuscripts from the archives of the house. Browne was much interested in music and accumulated a large collection of musical manuscripts. He also acquired a considerable amount of property, mainly in Northamptonshire where his principal seat, Eydon, lay and possessed a house in Twickenham in addition to his official residence in the palace of Westminster.

Browne was twice married. His first wife was Temperance, third daughter of Sir Thomas Crew of Steane, Northamptonshire, speaker of the House of Commons in 1623 and 1625. They were childless and she died on 22 September 1634, aged twenty-five. His second wife, whom he married on 28 January 1636, was Elizabeth, daughter of John Packer of Shillingford, Berkshire, clerk of the privy seal and secretary to George Villiers, first duke of Buckingham; the marriage produced two daughters. Browne was buried at Eydon on 8 June 1691 and his second wife five days later.

J. C. SAINTY, rev.

Sources M. F. Bond, 'The formation of the archives of parliament, 1497–1691', *Journal of the Society of Archivists*, 1 (1955–9), 151–8 · *House of Lords Record Office memorandum*, 61 (1979), 13–14 · M. Edmond, notes on John Browne, HLRO · G. Baker, *The history and* *antiquities of the county of Northampton*, 2 vols. (1822–41) · *The manuscripts of the House of Lords*, new ser., 12 vols. (1900–77), vol. 11

Archives Bodl. Oxf., notebook · HLRO, journals, letters, state papers, etc.; official and personal papers · Yale U., Beinecke L., commonplace book

Browne, John (1642–1702/3?), surgeon, was probably born at Norwich, where his father, Joseph Browne, was a tailor and freeman of the city. His claim to being of a surgical family was through his uncle, William Cropp, a member of a well-established medical family in Norfolk. He does not appear to have been related to Sir Thomas Browne, although the latter wrote commendatory letters prefixed to two of his namesake's books.

When he was seventeen Browne went to London and in January 1660 was apprenticed to John Bishop, surgeon, for seven years. However, a contemporary maintained that he never served Bishop, a naval surgeon, but instead became a pupil of Thomas Hollyer, surgeon at St Thomas's Hospital, for whom he acted as skillet carrier. In 1663 Browne was appointed 'chirurgeon to one of His Majesty's ships'. He served in the Dutch war of 1665–7 and had his arm fractured by the wind of a cannon-ball. Shortly after this he left the navy and returned to surgical practice in Norwich, but by 1675 he was back in London. About this time he was appointed surgeon-in-ordinary to Charles II. Three years later his first two books were published: his treatise on tumours, dedicated to William Cropp, and the discourse on wounds, both dated 1678.

In 1683 a vacancy occurred for a surgeon at St Thomas's Hospital. The king recommended Browne for the appointment, and he was elected by the governors on 21 June. This was an unpopular decision for the next vacancy had been promised to an assistant surgeon, Edward Rice, who had taken charge of the hospital during the plague of 1665, when all the surgeons deserted their posts. To compensate for this injustice Rice was appointed supernumerary surgeon at a salary of £20 per annum, half that of Browne. A year before Browne's appointment a royal commission had visited the hospital and replaced many governors and staff with those more in sympathy with the king. Hence it was inevitable that Browne was appointed, despite Rice's strong claim. This was the beginning of a long and stormy relationship between Browne and the hospital. In January 1689 the work of the 1682 royal commission was overturned by act of parliament, whereupon most of the governors appointed since 1683 were dismissed and their predecessors reinstated. On 7 July 1691 Browne and the rest of the surgical staff were also dismissed on the grounds that they had not obeyed the regulations of the hospital, and had pretended that being appointed by royal mandamus they were not responsible to the governors. Browne and his colleagues petitioned the privy council, who threatened the hospital with another royal commission, but this was never acted upon. Browne lodged two further appeals in December 1691, one to the lords commissioners of the great seal, and another to the court of aldermen, to which the hospital governors sent a deputation to explain their actions. Meanwhile, another surgical post at St Thomas's fell vacant, for which Browne applied unsuccessfully in

January 1693. In March 1699 his final petition to the governors to be appointed supernumerary surgeon also failed.

Browne was a well-educated man, and a good surgeon for his time, although he was taken to court in 1687 by one Susanna Levine who claimed he had been negligent in the treatment of her fractured leg. The outcome of the case is unknown. His one original contribution to medicine is the first recorded description of cirrhosis of the liver, published in *Philosophical Transactions* in 1685 and based upon a post-mortem dissection of a St Thomas's patient. In *Adenochoiradelogia, or, An anatomick-chirurgical treatise of glandules … or king's evil swellings* (1684), Browne left the best surviving account of the ceremony of touching for the king's evil, which, as surgeon-in-ordinary, he would have attended. Browne's best-known work is *A Compleat Treatise of the Muscles*, published in 1681, but on which he had been working since 1675. After the second edition was published in 1683 the Plymouth surgeon James Yonge demonstrated that the text had been plagiarized from William Molins's *Muskotomia*, published in 1648, with the plates taken from the 1632 edition of Giulio Casserius' *Tabula anatomicae*. Despite this Browne's book was popular and appeared in ten editions.

Browne may have delivered the muscular lectures at Surgeons' Hall. The 1697 and 1698 editions of his muscle book refer to them, while about this time he signs himself 'Master of Anatomy'. No details of his private life have survived although he is thought to have been married, and while in London he is known to have lived near Charing Cross. The preface of his last book is dated 23 August 1702, but the second edition, 1703, is a reissue and, uncharacteristically, has an uncorrected preface date. It is assumed that he died some time between the publication of the two editions.   IAN LYLE

Sources K. F. Russell, 'John Browne, 1642–1702, a seventeenth-century surgeon, anatomist and plagiarist', *Bulletin of the History of Medicine*, 33 (1959), 393–414, 503–75 · K. F. Russell, 'A list of the works of John Browne, 1642–1702', *Bulletin of the Medical Library Association*, 50 (1962), 675–83 · Company of Barber–Surgeons, apprentice register 1657/8–1672, GL, MS 5266/1, fol. 27 · K. B. Roberts and J. D. W. Tomlinson, *The fabric of the body: European traditions of anatomical illustration* (1992) · J. Yonge, *Medicaster medicatus, or, A remedy for the itch of scribling* (1685) · H. Breun, 'A catalogue of engraved portraits of medical men, with additions and an index of painters and engravers', 1930, RCS Eng. · T. R. Forbes, 'The case of the casual chirurgeon', *Yale Journal of Biology and Medicine*, 51 (1978), 583–8 · DNB

Archives U. Glas. L., 'Anatomy of the eye'

Likenesses R. White, line engraving, 1681, Wellcome L. · H. Morland, engraving, repro. in *A compleat treatise of preternatural tumours* (1678), frontispiece · R. White, engraving, repro. in *A compleat treatise of the muscles* (1705), frontispiece · R. White, engraving, Wellcome L. · R. White, line engraving, BM, NPG; repro. in *A compleat discourse of wounds* (1678), frontispiece · R. White, line engraving (after H. Morland), Wellcome L. · R. White, line engraving (after J. Browne), Wellcome L. · R. White, print, BM · R. White, two line engravings, Wellcome L. · etching, BM; repro. in *Myographia nova* (1684), title-page

Browne [Brown], **John** (*d.* 1735), chemist, was probably born in London. He took his freedom in the Society of Apothecaries on 7 September 1697 by patrimony, his father being also John Browne, citizen and apothecary. He married Frances, daughter of Edward and Elizabeth Peck, at St Dunstan and All Saints, Stepney, on 28 February 1711; of their several children at least two sons and two daughters survived him.

Elected to the Royal Society on 30 November 1721, Browne took a lively interest in chemical matters, contributing several papers on the natures of Prussian blue (a dyestuff discovered in 1710), Epsom salts, camphor, and ambergris. His remarks, reported in the society's journal books, indicate that he often repeated the processes described by other speakers, and on occasion took issue with them at subsequent meetings. He served on the society's council in 1723–5. Browne was living at Old Fish Street, near St Paul's Cathedral, at the time of his death on 8 June 1735. In his will of 1729, proved on 19 June 1735, he named his widow sole executor and guardian of his children. His eldest son, John (b. 1714), and a younger son, William, had followed him in business and were to inherit their shares of his estate on reaching the age of twenty-one.   ANITA MCCONNELL

Sources M. B. Hall, *Promoting experimental learning* (1991), 128–9 · GL, MSS 8206, vol. 1, 8208, vol. 3 [Apothecaries' Company] · T. Thomson, *History of the Royal Society from its institution to the end of the eighteenth century* (1812) · will, PRO, PROB 11/671, sig. 116 · parish register, St Dunstan and All Saints, Stepney, 28 Feb 1711 [marriage] · parish register, 1714–, St Mary Magdalen, City of London [baptisms] · *GM*, 1st ser., 5 (1735), 332 · *London Magazine*, 4 (1735), 334 · *Historical Reg. Chronicle* (1735), 27 · L. Trengove, 'Chemistry at the Royal Society 1727–1800', PhD diss., 1957, London

Browne, John (1742–1801), engraver, was born in Finchingfield, Essex, where he was baptized on 16 April 1742, the posthumous son of the Revd John Browne (1715–1741/2) of Booton, Norfolk, and his wife, Mary (b. 1720), the daughter of George Paske, vicar of Finchingfield. He was educated at Mr Davy's school in Norwich and apprenticed from 1755 to John Tinney, an engraver in Fleet Street, London, who was also William Woollett's master. He remained with Tinney until 1761, whereupon he joined Woollett. Many of Woollett's plates were commenced by Browne, Woollett apparently always acknowledging his assistant's contribution, in spite of William Blake's comment: 'Wooletts best works … all that are Calld Wooletts were Etchd by Jack Browne' (*Blake's Writings*, 2.1037). Browne was elected a member of the Society of Artists in 1764, and a joint work with Woollett—*Celadon and Amelia*, after Richard Wilson—was shown at the society's exhibition in 1766, and again at its special exhibition in 1768. This work and *The Jocund Peasants*, after Cornelis Dusart, are among those on which Woollett publicly acknowledged Browne's contribution.

Once independent of Woollett, from the mid-1760s, Browne, a line engraver specializing in landscapes, achieved further recognition with notable works after old masters, including Salvator Rosa's *St John Preaching in the Wilderness* (the figures were engraved by John Hall); the etching was exhibited at the Society of Artists in 1767, the print in 1768. Browne was elected an associate of the Royal

Academy in 1770—one of the first engravers to be so honoured—and exhibited thirteen plates there between 1771 and 1801, among them *Going to Market* (after Peter Paul Rubens), *Banditti* (after Jan Both), and a landscape after Herman Van Swanevelt from the king's collection. Other outstanding works of Browne's included engravings after Claude Lorrain and those commissioned by John Boydell from the Houghton collection (*Africa*, after Paul Bril, *The Sportsman*, after Gaspar Poussin, *Europa*, after Bril, and *The Waggoner*, after Rubens). For Boydell's *Shakspeare* (1803) Browne engraved *Merchant of Venice, Act V, Scene i*, after William Hodges, for which he was paid £231. He also engraved four landscapes after his own designs—*Morning*, *Evening*, *After Sunset*, and *Moonlight*—the last two of which were exhibited at the Royal Academy in 1798.

Contemporaries held Browne to be a good-natured and generous individual, quiet, inoffensive, and with much personal integrity. He and his wife, Mary, had four children. Browne died after a long illness on 2 October 1801 at West Lane, Walworth, and was buried in St Saviour's churchyard, Southwark, on 8 October.

VIVIENNE W. PAINTING

Sources H. W. Lewer, 'John Browne of Finchingfield, engraver and etcher', *Essex Review*, 21 (1912), 174–91 · private information (2004) [John H. Shead] · Graves, *RA exhibitors* · Folger, Folger MS Y.d.369 · *GM*, 1st ser., 71 (1801), 1149 · *Annual Register* (1801) · William Blake's writings, ed. G. E. Bentley (1978), 2.1037 · Farington, *Diary*, 5.1669 · Venn, *Alum. Cant.* · IGI · Goldsmiths' Company, binding book, Goldsmiths' Company, Foster Lane, London, 7.222

Archives BL · Free Library of Philadelphia, Autograph of Engravers Collection, receipts · RA, receipts · Royal Arch. | Folger, list of payments made by J. Boydell to artists and engravers, Folger MS Y.d.369

Wealth at death leasehold of two houses, stock of copper plates and prints, two rings: Lewer, 'John Browne'

Browne, John (1823–1886), Congregational minister and historian, was born on 6 February 1823 at North Walsham, Norfolk, the elder son in the family of two sons and two daughters of James Browne (1781–1857), Congregational minister of North Walsham, and his first wife, Eliza (d. 1834), daughter of Richard Gedge of Honing. After Eliza's death, his father married Elizabeth Rayner of North Walsham. John was educated at University College, London, graduating BA in 1843 from London University, and at Coward College, Torrington Square, London, under Thomas William Jenkyn.

After leaving college in 1844, Browne ministered to the Congregational church at Lowestoft, Suffolk, and published a *Guide to Lowestoft* (1845). He left Lowestoft in 1846, and taught mathematics at Hall Collegiate School for a year before going to Wrentham, Suffolk, in September 1848, where he succeeded Andrew Ritchie (d. 26 Dec 1848) as minister of the Congregational church. He was ordained on 1 February 1849. In 1849 he married Mary Ann (d. 1899), eldest daughter of the Revd H. H. Cross of Bermuda; they had a son and five daughters.

From 1864 Browne was secretary of the Suffolk Congregational Union. At the end of 1877 he published his *History of Congregationalism and Memorials of the Churches of Norfolk and Suffolk*. He collected manuscripts, rare books, and portraits relevant to his subject, and the book, on which he had worked for five years, was meticulously researched. His other publications included *The Congregational Church at Wrentham [Suffolk] … its History and Biographies* (1854), *Dissent and the Church* (1870)—a reply to J. C. Ryle, later bishop of Liverpool—and *The History and Antiquities of Covehithe* (1874). Browne, who was short and stout, died on 4 April 1886 at Wrentham, and was buried in Wrentham cemetery on 9 April.

ALEXANDER GORDON, *rev.* ANNE PIMLOTT BAKER

Sources T. J. Hosken, *History of Congregationalism in Suffolk* (1920), 164 · J. Browne, *A history of Congregationalism and memorials of the churches in Norfolk and Suffolk* (1877), 321, 433, 532 · private information (1901) · personal knowledge (1901) · *Christian World* (8 April 1886) · *CGPLA Eng. & Wales* (1886)
Archives Norfolk RO, Colman Library, East Anglian dissenting history collections, corresp. and papers
Likenesses photograph, repro. in Hosken, *History of Congregationalism in Suffolk*, frontispiece
Wealth at death £4088 1s. 5d.: probate, 16 June 1886, *CGPLA Eng. & Wales*

Browne, John Collis (1819–1884), physician and manufacturer of patent medicine, was born on 18 June 1819 at Maidstone in Kent, and baptized at the church of All Saints with St Philip in that town. His parents were Captain William Browne of the 13th light dragoons and Clara (*née* Collis). 'Chlorodyne Browne', as he came to be known in later life—or 'J. C. B.' for short—was educated from 1834 to 1836 at Bromsgrove School in Worcestershire. With him were his two brothers, one of whom became dean of Worcester College, Oxford.

Browne began his career by 'walking the hospitals' in London, and in 1842 qualified as a member of the Royal College of Surgeons of England, while living at the new resort of Weston-super-Mare, Somerset. In 1845 he became an extra-licentiate of the Royal College of Physicians of London and then joined the Army Medical Service as an assistant surgeon. He was posted to the 98th regiment of foot, then stationed under Sir Colin Campbell at the port of Chushan in China. Soon after his arrival the 98th were transferred to Calcutta and in 1847 to Dinapore, near Patna, at a time when there was a 'desperate visitation of cholera'. They then marched north-westwards to Meerut (where the Sepoy mutiny began nine years later) and to Ambala on the confines of the Punjab. It was here, in 1848, that Browne 'realized' the compound of chloroform and morphine which, under the name of 'J. Collis Browne's mixture', was still being stocked in chemists' shops 150 years later (in a modified form) as a palliative for diarrhoea and other stomach disorders.

Following the end of the Second Anglo-Sikh War in 1849, the 98th moved against the Afridi tribesmen of the Kohat Pass, where two men were wounded. Browne, therefore, became one of the first regimental surgeons to practise his skills on the north-west frontier of India. In October 1851, he left for six months in Cape Colony as assistant staff surgeon, but then returned to England on half-pay. He was asked to go to the village of Trimdon in co. Durham to fight an outbreak of cholera. So successful

was he in treating his patients that the villagers presented him with a gold medal inscribed 'As a Testimonial to his Humanity, Skills and Ability, during the Visitation of Cholera, 1854'. Further praise came from the General Board of Health in London: 'we cannot too forcibly urge the necessity of generally adopting it [Browne's mixture] in all cases of cholera'; and from Earl Russell (addressing the College of Physicians in 1864): 'the only remedy of any service [in Manila] was "Chlorodyne"'. During the Crimean War, Browne returned to full pay at Fort Pitt, Chatham. In 1856 he left the army and went into partnership with John Thistlewood Davenport, chemist, of 33 Great Russell Street, Bloomsbury, whose firm was to manufacture Browne's remedy until the 1980s when the licence was released to another company.

Apart from medicine, which brought him a fortune, Browne had an inventive turn of mind in many other directions, as shown by patents he took out between 1852 and 1879. These ranged from improvements in building ships to magazines for storing explosives and 'means and apparatus for raising vessels and other sunken bodies'. He was also an advocate of beards for reasons of health, publishing a pamphlet on the subject and wearing one himself. Having retired to Ramsgate, Browne spent his remaining years as the proud owner of a 36 ton schooner, the *Kalafish*.

Browne died of hepatitis on 30 August 1884, at Mount Albion House, 22 Victoria Road, Ramsgate, and was interred at the church of St Laurence in Thanet.

Browne left his entire estate of £4789 to his widow, Harriet, with the request that his friend, Captain Berkeley, would 'aid and assist her in the development of my several patents'. He was also survived by a stepson, Ernest E. B. Skinner. In 1973 a mural tablet in his memory was erected on Mount Albion House. Although he was often referred to as Dr Browne, and the inscription on his gravestone included the letters MD, it is unlikely that he was so qualified.

J. P. J. ENTRACT

Sources J. P. Entract, 'Chlorodyne Browne', *London Hospital Gazette*, 73/4 (1970), 7–11 · letter from M. L. Walker, Royal College of Surgeons · C. D. Wilson, *A Victorian occasion: the unveiling of a plaque*, privately printed (1973) · RCP Lond., 'report of meeting of Elects', *College Annals*, 23 (1845) · W. Martindale, *The extra pharmacopoeia*, 27th edn, ed. A. Wade and others (1977); 29th edn, ed. J. E. F. Reynolds and others (1989) · school register, Bromsgrove School, Worcestershire · d. cert. · *CGPLA Eng. & Wales* (1884) · H. M. Chichester and G. Burges-Short, *The records and badges of every regiment and corps in the British army* (1895), 418 · U. St Andr. L., special collections department, muniments · Centurion Building, Gosport, Hampshire, Royal Marines Historical Records · *Medical Times and Gazette* (6 Sept 1884), 343
Archives priv. coll.
Likenesses portrait, 1883, repro. in Entract, 'Chlorodyne Browne'
Wealth at death £4789 14s. 11d.: probate, 21 Feb 1885, *CGPLA Eng. & Wales*

Browne, John Francis Archibald, sixth Baron Kilmaine (1902–1978), trust administrator, was born in Dublin on 22 September 1902, the eldest of three children and elder son of John Edward Deane Browne, fifth Baron Kilmaine (1878–1946), an Irish representative peer, and his wife,

Lady Aline Kennedy (d. 1957), daughter of Archibald, third marquess of Ailsa. The family lived in Gaulston in co. Mayo until 1925, when their last estates were sold and they moved to Kent.

John Browne was educated at Winchester College (where he won the English speech prize, was captain of the school shooting eight, and represented Ireland at rifle shooting) and at Magdalen College, Oxford. He passed moderations in modern history in 1922 and obtained third-class honours in philosophy, politics, and economics in 1925. He then spent four years (1925–9) with British Xylonite before moving to University College, Southampton, as administrative secretary in 1930. His very happy marriage, in that year, to Wilhelmina Phyllis, daughter of Scott Arnott, solicitor, of Brasted, Kent, produced two daughters and a son.

In 1933 the Oxford Society had been in existence for a year and was looking for a full-time professional secretary. John Browne was appointed and threw himself with characteristic energy and enthusiasm into the task of not only establishing the society as a worldwide organization but of allaying the suspicions of the colleges which in those days felt that a university society might subvert the loyalty of their old members. He launched the magazine *Oxford* and set up branches throughout the English-speaking world. In 1937 he organized the society's assistance to the university's appeal for the extension to the Bodleian Library and for the improvement of facilities for scientific research. By 1939 he was proposing to raise an endowment fund for the society when war came and he joined the Royal Army Service Corps. He served from 1940 to 1945, rose to the rank of lieutenant-colonel, served on the staff, and was twice mentioned in dispatches.

In 1945 Browne succeeded Thomas Jones as secretary of the Pilgrim Trust. He remained there for twenty-two years, during which time the scope of its benefactions widened enormously. His predecessor's interest had been mainly towards social welfare; Kilmaine (he succeeded to the title in 1946) directed the attention of the trustees towards a wider field of art, learning, and the preservation of the national heritage. He was active in persuading G. F. Fisher, the archbishop of Canterbury, to set up the Historic Churches' Preservation Trust, which the Pilgrim Trust then supported by annual block grants. He secured help for the 'little houses' scheme of the National Trust for Scotland, and his support for the conservation of vernacular housing round the old quay at Harwich was rewarded by his appointment as high steward of the borough (1966–76). He ensured the systematic listing and rescue of medieval wall paintings and was equally active in the preservation of medieval glass, arranging for the glaziers' workshops at York Minster to be converted into a national centre for its repair and preservation. He obtained charitable status for the workshops as the York Glaziers' Trust. He was one of the first to recognize and support the claims of industrial archaeology.

In 1953 Kilmaine, by then the recognized doyen of trust administrators, also took on the secretaryship of the newly-founded Dulverton Trust, which he retained until 1966. Meanwhile, in 1949, he had become chairman of the Oxford Society, to which he devoted much time and energy. When in 1957 several colleges approached the Pilgrim Trust for help with the restoration of their buildings, sadly neglected during the war years, John Kilmaine immediately saw not only the advantage of uniting them in a general appeal but also the necessity for a preliminary assessment of the total amount to be raised. Thus arose the highly successful Oxford Historic Buildings Appeal. His services to the nation were acknowledged by his appointment as CBE in 1956, and his services to Oxford by an honorary DCL in 1973, the year he retired from his chairmanship of the Oxford Society.

Kilmaine was a distinctive figure, tall, fair, formal in speech and manner. His capacity for work, attention to detail, unerring eye for accuracy, and clarity in summing up a problem were formidable. He could be tactless, and was not above an occasional, somewhat malicious amusement in cutting people down to size. Conscious of his heritage and background, he understandably regretted that events had deprived him of a seat in the House of Lords. If he expected deference, he also extended it to others, with a somewhat old-fashioned respect for position, though his warm sympathy with and interest in all he met (and perhaps his Irish upbringing) caused this to fall short of snobbery. Kilmaine died at Brasted on 26 July 1978. He was succeeded by his son, John David Henry Browne (b. 1948).

D. M. LENNIE, rev.

Sources personal knowledge (1986) · private information (1986) · *CGPLA Eng. & Wales* (1978) · *WWW* · Burke, *Peerage* (1980) · *The Times* (28 July 1978)
Wealth at death £87,312: probate, 30 Oct 1978, *CGPLA Eng. & Wales*

Browne, Joseph (*bap.* 1673, *d.* in or after 1721), physician and satirist, a younger son of Cuthbert Browne, cleric, who held livings first in Norfolk and then in Yorkshire, was born in Treeton, Yorkshire, and baptized in Sheffield on 20 May 1673. Joseph Browne matriculated at Lincoln College, Oxford, on 14 October 1689; two of his brothers, John, aged fourteen, and Richmond, aged eighteen, matriculated on the same day. Another brother, Obadiah, had entered Lincoln College some years earlier. However, on 15 October 1694 Joseph Browne transferred to Jesus College, Cambridge, where he graduated MB in 1695. It is not known which, if any, university awarded him a medical doctorate. For some time he practised as a physician in Rotherham, Yorkshire, where he provided a facility for cold bathing; most of his professional activities, however, took place in London. In 1706 he was twice convicted for libelling Queen Anne's administration. The first of these occasions, when he was fined 40 marks and ordered to stand in the pillory, was for the publication of *The country parson's honest advice to that judicious and worthy minister of state my lord keeper*. In a letter addressed to Robert Harley, 'occasioned by his late committment to Newgate', he denies the authorship of this pamphlet, of which at the same time he gives a professedly disinterested explanation. He also speaks of Harley as having 'not only treated him like a patriot, but given him friendly advice'. For thus acting as his own political interpreter he was again fined 40 marks and ordered to stand in the pillory twice. Later, he clashed with the Royal College of Physicians but, on that occasion, neither of the presentations brought against him was successful; he is described in the college annals as 'a notorious quack'. He has also been described as 'a mere tool of the booksellers and always needy' (Noble, 2.232).

Browne was an industrious writer, whose effrontery is discernible through an obscure and rambling style. Early in his career he damaged his credibility by lecturing and writing against Harvey's theory of the circulation of the blood. In the political sphere he continued the *Examiner* after it had been dropped by Mary de la Rivière Manley, who had succeeded Swift and others; 'consequently it became as inferior to what it had been as his abilities were to theirs'. He was importunate in seeking the patronage of the great and influential; for example, he dedicated *The Modern Practice of Physick Vindicated* (1703) to the duke of Leeds, without permission, for he was 'jealous it might be denied him', and his *Mayerui opera medica* (1700) has an impertinent dedication to William III. But not all his contributions should be judged harshly, for he made several important works accessible in English in translations from Latin and French. Thus, he translated Boerhaave's *Institutiones medicae* (1708), under the title *Institutions in Physick Collected of the most Eminent Physicians* (1714 and 1715). Though he omitted mention of Boerhaave in the title, he did acknowledge the source in the dedication. *A Compleat History of Druggs Written in French by Monsieur Pomet* (1712) was another important and widely used book he translated into English. In this instance he did not reveal his identity as translator, but did so in the publication in 1721 of *A Natural History of Worms*, his translation of a work by Daniel Le Clerc. His *Practical Treatise of the Plague* (1720) has a prefatory epistle to Dr Richard Mead, and his last known publication, also on the plague, was addressed to the president and members of the Royal College of Physicians, despite their recent antagonism. Beyond the date of this publication (1721) there is no trace of him.

D. D. GIBBS

Sources *A biographical history of England, from the revolution to the end of George I's reign: being a continuation of the Rev. J. Granger's work*, ed. M. Noble, 3 vols. (1806) • *N&Q*, 3rd ser., 1 (1862), 465 • *N&Q*, 3rd ser., 2 (1862), 13–14 • T. Short, *The history of mineral waters* (1734) • G. Clark and A. M. Cooke, *A history of the Royal College of Physicians of London*, 2 (1966) • Foster, *Alum. Oxon.* • Venn, *Alum. Cant.*
Likenesses W. Sherwin, engraving, repro. in J. Browne, *An essay towards the forming a true idea of fundamentals in physick, upon the mechanism of the blood* (1709), frontispiece • W. Sherwin, line engraving, Wellcome L.

Browne, Joseph (1700–1767), college head, was born at Tongue, in Watermillock, Cumberland, and baptized at Watermillock on 19 December 1700, the son of George Browne, of New Church, Cumberland, and Anne Troutbeck. He had a sister, Ann, who married Benjamin Grisdale. He was educated at Barton School, and matriculated commoner of Queen's College, Oxford, on 24 March 1716, aged fifteen, apparently funded by a private benefactor. He was elected taberdar of his college, graduated BA in

1721, and proceeded MA in 1724. Elected fellow on 1 April 1731, he served as chaplain and tutor and took the degrees of BD (1737) and DD (1743). In 1741 he was elected to the Sedleian chair of natural philosophy; he left little mark as professor. In 1746 he was presented with the college living of Bramshot, in Hampshire, and instituted prebendary of Hereford.

On 3 December 1756 Browne was elected provost of Queen's College. A tory in politics, he interested himself more in university than college affairs; he served as vice-chancellor from 1759 to 1765 and successfully supported the earl of Lichfield in his election as the new chancellor in 1762. Browne suffered a severe stroke on 25 March 1765, and died on 17 June 1767. His only known work was an edition of the poems of Urban VIII, which he published at Oxford in 1726.   WILLIAM HUNT, *rev.* S. J. SKEDD

Sources W. Hutchinson, *The history of the county of Cumberland*, 1 (1794), 426–7 • Foster, *Alum. Oxon.* • W. R. Ward, *Georgian Oxford* (1958) • *Hist. U. Oxf.* 5: *18th-cent. Oxf.* • will, PRO, PROB 11/931, sig. 297 • *IGI*
Archives Queen's College, Oxford, corresp. with J. Smith

Browne, Lancelot (*d.* 1605), physician, was a native of York; his parentage and date of birth have not been ascertained. He matriculated at St John's College, Cambridge, in May 1559, graduated BA in 1563, and MA in 1566. In the following year he was elected fellow of Pembroke College, receiving the university's licence to practise medicine in 1570. He actively opposed the new statutes of the university promulgated in 1572, and next year was made proctor.

Browne obtained his MD in 1576, in which year he sold his interest in lands in Baldersby, Yorkshire. Perhaps about this time he moved to London, where, on 10 June 1584, he was elected a fellow of the College of Physicians. Next year William Gilbert and Browne issued a certificate stating that a Mr Hungate needed to seek a warmer climate abroad for his health. Geoffrey Whitney addressed one of the pieces in *A Choice of Emblemes* (1586) 'Ad ornatiss. viros D. Ioannem Iames & Lancelottvm Browne, Medicos celeberrimos' ('to the most-splendid men, D(rs) John James and Lancelot Browne, distinguished physicians'; Whitney, 212). Sadly, the virtues expressed in the text are merely those applicable to many contemporary physicians. In his time Browne served the College of Physicians as censor (1587 and later occasions), an elect (1599), and a member of its council (1604–5). He was one of those appointed by the college in 1589 to prepare a pharmacopoeia, and again in 1594, but the work was stopped and not resumed until after Browne's death. No writings of his are known but a commendatory letter in Latin is prefixed to John Gerard's *Herball* (1597).

After George Talbot, sixth earl of Shrewsbury, had died in 1590 it was said that he had named Browne as an accessory to the scheming of his wife Elizabeth (Bess of Hardwick), and her daughter, Elizabeth Cavendish, regarding Arabella Stuart. Be that as it may, in late 1595 'honest Dr Browne' (*De L'Isle and Dudley MSS*, 2.188) was attending Lady Barbara Sidney during her pregnancy twice a day. By 1 December that year she was 'full of the measles' (ibid., 2.193), and he stayed the night there; at 9 p.m. she gave birth to a son (Robert), mother and child both surviving for many years. However, when 'the earl' (of Essex) was 'very sick', in October 1599, the queen refused to permit 'Dr Bruen' to attend him (ibid., 2.404).

In 1596 payment of £400 was due to Browne for his services as one of the queen's physicians-in-ordinary, which circumstance suggests that he had been acting in some capacity, unpaid, for several years. On 1 January 1600 he gave the queen a pot of green ginger and one of orange flowers, receiving in return gilt plate weighing 4⅞ ounces. In 1604 Martin Schoverus and Browne, physicians to James I and his queen, certified that the waters of Spa were beneficial for treating the ailments of Henry Jernegan sen., including 'the rheum, vertigo, convulsions, palsy, melancholia hypocondrica', and Jernegan was granted licence to travel there for a year's stay.

Browne's lease of Buckholt Farm, in Kent, for a period of twenty-one years from 1590, was extended in 1596. However, his home was in the large, extramural London parish of St Sepulchre: he had there in his tenure (as in April 1597) a messuage held of the city of London by Jane Baeshe, widow. On or after 24 November 1604 Browne's daughter Elizabeth, aged twenty-four, married the eminent physician William Harvey, at St Sepulchre's. (Harvey's only recorded reference to his wife, Elizabeth, concerns her pet parrot, on which he conducted a post-mortem.) On 17 July 1605 Browne wrote to Robert Cecil, stating that Roger Marbeck, another royal physician, was probably dying, and, although Dr Elvine was thought likely to succeed him, Browne gave reasons why his own son-in-law had a better claim:

> I did never in my life know any man anything near his years that was any way match with him in all points of good learning. … Being examined in the College three several times, … the whole company took very singular liking unto him.

Indeed, Browne was willing to 'dare life and limb for him' (*Salisbury MSS*, 17.324). On 22 July 1605 (not 1603, as calendared), Browne notified Cecil of Marbeck's death on the previous day, and continued to press Harvey's claim, unsuccessfully. Browne was admitted to Gray's Inn on 15 August 1605, doubtless *honoris causa*.

The dates of Browne's death and burial have not been found. It is known only that near his end, in 1605, he wrote an undated letter to Robert Cecil, telling him that he was 'dangerously ill', and asking him to befriend his family by having his royal pension continued, so as to relieve his widow of need, and afford the means of educating his children (*Salisbury MSS*, 24.38); letters of administration were granted to his widow, Joan, on 5 December 1605. Nothing further is known of his wife but their son Galen graduated MA at Trinity College, Cambridge (1608), was admitted an extra licentiate of the College of Physicians (1629), and was left an annuity of £20 by William Harvey.

JOHN BENNELL

Sources Cooper, *Ath. Cantab.*, 2.421 · Munk, *Roll* · *Report on the manuscripts of Lord De L'Isle and Dudley*, 2, HMC, 77 (1933), 188, 193–4, 404 · *Calendar of the manuscripts of the most hon. the marquess of Salisbury*, 17, HMC, 9 (1938), 324; 15 (1930), 206; 24 (1976), 38 · *CSP dom.*, 1581–90, p. 226, no. 41; p. 689, no. 73; 1595–7, p. 300; 1598–1600, no. 82; 1603–10, p. 99, no. 54; p. 102 · GL, MS 9168/16, fol. 17 · V. Robinson, *The story of medicine* (1943), 282 · *CPR, 1575–8*, no. 400 · E. A. Fry, ed., *Abstracts of inquisitiones post mortem relating to the City of London*, 3: 1577–1603, British RS, 36 (1908), 250, 252 · J. Nichols, *The progresses and public processions of Queen Elizabeth*, new edn, 3 (1823), 456, 465 · J. L. Chester and G. J. Armytage, eds., *Allegations for marriage licences issued by the bishop of London*, 1, Harleian Society, 25 (1887), 291 · J. Foster, *The register of admissions to Gray's Inn, 1521–1889, together with the register of marriages in Gray's Inn chapel, 1695–1754* (privately printed, London, 1889), 109 · G. Whitney, *A choice of emblemes* (1586); facs. edn, ed. H. Green (1866), 212, 391

Browne, Lyde (*d.* 1787), antiquary and banker, had one of the largest collections of classical antique objects in the eighteenth century. Well known to contemporaries, he is historically significant because his collection constitutes the major part of the collections of classical sculpture in both the Hermitage, St Petersburg, and the nearby Pavlovsk Palace. He married his wife, Margaret, whom he outlived, before 1752; they had six children, including Lyde *Browne (*bap.* 1759?, *d.* 1803), army officer.

In 1753–4 Browne travelled to Florence and Rome where in 1758, following the sculptor Simon Vierpyl and the Abbé William Wilkins, Thomas Jenkins became his buying agent. Jenkins sent Browne drawings of statues he had purchased which Browne often gave to the Society of Antiquaries, of which he was elected a fellow in 1752, resigning in 1772. Browne had a museum established in Rome; by 1762 this had been moved to his country house in Wimbledon. In 1768 he published a Latin catalogue of 130 objects in his collection, *Catalogus veteris aevi varii generis monumentorum quae cimeliarchio Lyde Browne … asservantur* ('Catalogue of the various ancient monuments in the museum of Lyde Browne'), with eighty detailed entries. In 1779, following a second journey to Italy in 1776–8—during which his eldest daughter, Frances, had her portrait painted by Pompeo Batoni—Browne published a catalogue in Italian entitled *Catologo [sic] dei piu scelti e preziosi marmi, che si conservano nella galleria del Sigr Lyde Browne* ('Catalogue of the choicest and most precious marbles in the gallery of Lyde Browne'), listing 260 items. Both catalogues detail the provenance of objects from well-known collections in Italy and from excavations near Rome. A series of drawings of pieces in Browne's collection by Giovanni Battista Cipriani, prepared for engraving, suggests that Browne intended to publish a third catalogue. Browne's collection changed constantly, and he sold many statues. In 1784 he sold his collection to Catherine II, empress of Russia, for £22,000. However, the bankruptcy of his agent in St Petersburg meant that Browne received only £10,000. Depressed, he died at his home in Foster Lane, Cheapside, London, of a stroke, on 10 September 1787.

Browne was a governor of the Bank of England from 1768 until his death, and lived in Foster Lane from 1752. The remainder of his collection, including terracotta models, paintings, prints, and drawings, was auctioned at Christies on 30 May 1788.

NICHOLAS GRINDLE

Sources J. Ingamells, ed., *A dictionary of British and Irish travellers in Italy, 1701–1800* (1997) · will, Family Record Centre, London, PROB.

11/1156.398 · *IGI* · *GM*, 1st ser., 57 (1787), 840 · O. Neverov, 'The Lyde Browne collection and the history of ancient sculpture at the Hermitage Museum', *American Journal of Archeology*, 88 (1984), 33–42 · A. M. Clark, *Pompeo Batoni: a complete catalogue of his works with an introductory text*, ed. E. P. Bowron (1985) · X. Gorbunova, 'Classical sculpture from the Lyde Browne collection', *Apollo*, 100 (1974), 460–67

Wealth at death over £12,000—three bequests of £4000 to sons; also many small gifts: will, PRO, PROB 11/1156.398

Browne, Lyde (*bap.* 1759?, *d.* 1803), army officer, was probably baptized on 3 May 1759 at St John Zachary, London, the son of Lyde *Browne (*d.* 1787), antiquary and banker, and his wife, Margaret (*d.* in or before 1787). He entered the army as cornet in the 3rd dragoons on 11 June 1777, and obtained his troop in the 20th light dragoons, a corps formed during the American War of Independence out of the light troops of other cavalry regiments. This was disbanded in 1783, when Browne was placed on half pay. He was brought on full pay in the 40th foot in May 1794, and served with that regiment in the West Indies; he became major in the 4th (Nicholl's) West India regiment in 1797. His later commissions were major in the 90th foot (1798), lieutenant-colonel in the 35th foot, with which he served at Malta (1800), lieutenant-colonel in the 85th foot (1801), and lieutenant-colonel in the 21st fusiliers (25 January 1802). The last regiment was stationed in Cork Street, Thomas Street, and Coombe barracks, Dublin, in July 1803. Browne was returning there to join his men at dusk on 23 July, the alarm having been raised concerning Robert Emmet's rising. He was shot dead by United Irishmen loyal to Emmet who immediately afterwards murdered Lord Kilwarden in an adjoining street.

H. M. CHICHESTER, rev. PHILIP CARTER

Sources *Army List* · R. Cannon, ed., *Historical record of the twenty-first regiment, or the royal north British fusiliers* (1849) · R. Trimen, ed., *An historical memoir of the 35th royal Sussex regiment of foot* (1873); repr. (1994) · *IGI*

Browne [*née* Dacre], **Magdalen**, **Viscountess Montagu** (1538–1608), patron of Roman Catholics, was the daughter of William *Dacre, third Baron Dacre of Gilsland (1500–1563), and his wife, Elizabeth (*d. c.*1559), fifth daughter of George Talbot, fourth earl of Shrewsbury. Her parents and her husband came from families with strong Catholic traditions and Lady Magdalen staunchly supported the Catholic faith throughout her life. She spent her childhood at her birthplace of Naworth Castle, her father's seat in Cumberland, where she lived under the care of her mother. Lady Magdalen's confessor and biographer, Richard Smith, later bishop of Chalcedon, praised her because as a child she remained 'in quiet repose at home' rather than 'hawking and hunting' with her sisters. At thirteen she was sent to live in the household of Anne, countess of Bedford, whom she attended 'in all virtue and piety' according to Smith (Southern, 9–10). In 1554 she was made a maid of honour to Mary Tudor and later that year walked in the bridal procession at the queen's marriage to Philip II of Spain.

In 1556 Magdalen Dacre married Anthony *Browne, first Viscount Montagu (1528–1592), as his second wife at a court wedding attended by the queen. After her marriage she spent most of her time at Battle Abbey or Cowdray House and Montague House, her husband's other homes in Sussex and Southwark. Viscount Montagu had previously been one of the three ambassadors chosen by Mary Tudor to negotiate the reconciliation of the Church of England with Rome, and his houses were all regarded as Catholic centres during the reigns of Elizabeth and James I. But although he was certainly the most important Catholic in Sussex and perhaps in England, he was no extremist and remained loyal to the crown. For these reasons Montagu was highly regarded by Elizabeth I, who was entertained at Cowdray for a week in 1591, the year before the viscount's death. After her husband's death, Lady Magdalen was scrupulous in avoiding any accusation of treason. In 1597, when her brother, the conspirator Francis Dacre, sent a messenger to Battle with letters for the earl of Essex, she handed the messenger and his letters to the nearest magistrate and personally informed the lord lieutenant, Lord Buckhurst.

During her widowhood Lady Magdalen maintained a household consisting of eighty people or more at Battle, almost all of whom were Catholics according to Smith. Not only did she pay her servants a competent wage and provide them with food and lodging, she also ensured that they could exercise their faith and were safe from persecution. She maintained three priests at Battle (which was called Little Rome by local protestants), including Thomas More, the great-grandson of the martyr, and Smith who became her confessor after 1603, when he returned to England having studied and taught at the Catholic colleges in Valladolid, Seville, and Douai. She built a chapel in her house at Battle where sometimes as many as 120 Catholics attended masses on feast days. Battle Abbey and Montague House also became important safe houses for Catholic priests travelling from overseas to London and elsewhere. Lady Magdalen's activities were largely ignored by the Sussex magistrates and ecclesiastical authorities, many of whom were themselves Catholics. Her position in the county was also reinforced by links with Lord Buckhurst, whose daughter had married her grandson Anthony, the second Viscount Montagu. Lady Magdalen came under suspicion in 1599, however, when her London home was unsuccessfully searched for gunpowder, arms, and armour by the Southwark JPs, and again after the Gunpowder Plot, when it was fruitlessly searched twice for priests.

Smith's *Life of the most Honourable and Vertuous Lady, the Lady Magdalen Viscountesse Montague* (St Omer, 1627) originated as a funeral sermon, and was published initially in Latin in Rome in 1609. The later English edition was translated by Cuthbert, alias John Fursdon, and was reprinted in full by Southern in 1954. In it Smith praises Lady Magdalen for her humility, chastity, patience, obedience, piety, and her zeal in preserving the Catholic faith in times of persecution. He records that she inculcated the Catholic faith in over thirty members of the next generation of her family in the persons of her children, her nephews, and her nieces. She was the mother of five sons and three daughters, four of whom predeceased her. Her surviving children were Sir George and Sir Henry Browne, Elizabeth, the wife of Sir Robert Dormer, and Jane, the wife of Sir Francis Lacon of Willey, Shropshire. Having suffered a stroke on 21 January 1608, she died at Battle on 8 April following and was buried at Midhurst. In her will, proved on 24 April that year, she made bequests to her children, grandchildren, other relatives, and servants. Among them was a silver and gold crucifix which her grandmother the countess of Shrewsbury had left her at her death. Lady Magdalen's importance to the Catholic faith and cause was summed up by the Archpriest George Birkhead in a letter to Smith, when he wrote that she was 'a great mother in Israel, and the priests everywhere did extol her as the worthy patroness of the holy faith and the singular ornament of the Catholic religion in England' (Southern, 65).   JACQUELINE EALES

Sources A. C. Southern, ed., *An Elizabethan recusant house: the life of the Lady Magdalen, Viscountess Montague* (1954) · will, PRO, PROB 11/111, fols. 230v–232v · GEC, *Peerage*, new edn, 9.97–9 · R. B. Manning, *Religion and society in Elizabethan Sussex* (1969)
Likenesses G. Johnson?, alabaster effigy, Easebourne church · photograph, repro. in Southern, ed., *An Elizabethan recusant house*, frontispiece

Browne, (Elliott) Martin (1900–1980), theatre director, was born at Zeals House, Zeals, Wiltshire, on 29 January 1900, the third son of Colonel Percival John Browne and his wife, Bernarda Gracia *née* Lees. He was educated at Eton College, and Christ Church, Oxford, where he took seconds in modern history (1921) and theology (1923). On graduating from Oxford he was appointed by Kent county council to be religious drama adviser for that county. On 20 December 1924 he married the actress Henzie Raeburn (Henzie Helena Flesch; 1896–1973), the daughter of Henry Charles Flesch, insurance broker. They had two sons. She supported his work and appeared in many of his productions. From 1924 to 1926 he was warden of an educational settlement in Doncaster. In 1927 he made a brief appearance in a Stage Society production at the Regent Theatre in London and immediately afterwards went to the United States as assistant professor of drama at the Carnegie Institute of Technology, Pittsburgh. For the following three years he played in various local 'stock' companies.

Back in England in 1930 Browne was appointed by George Bell, bishop of Chichester, to be director of religious drama for the diocese. One of Browne's early assignments was to organize a pageant, 'The Rock', to raise funds for the building of Anglican churches in the expanding suburbs of London. Through the good offices of Bishop Bell, T. S. Eliot was persuaded to write a series of choruses linking the loosely historical scenes of the pageant, which was played by amateurs and presented at Sadler's Wells Theatre from 28 May to 9 June 1934. On the strength of it, Bell invited Eliot and Browne to collaborate on a play to be presented at the Canterbury festival the following year. The text was to be written by Eliot and the production to be directed by Browne. Eliot gave to the play the title 'Fear in the way' but during rehearsals the title was changed. Some say the change was suggested by Henzie Raeburn, others that it was suggested by Bernard

Shaw. (The former seems the more likely candidate, in the circumstances.) The new title was *Murder in the Cathedral* and it was this production that established a working relationship of twenty years between Eliot as poet-playwright and Martin Browne as director. This first production of *Murder in the Cathedral*, with Robert Speaight as Becket, was staged in the chapter house (not in the cathedral itself) at Canterbury and was then taken to London, where it ran, astonishingly, for almost a year. It established Browne as the high priest of the then renascent 'poetic drama' movement. In February 1938, at the Ritz Theatre in New York, he directed the first American production of *Murder in the Cathedral*, playing the part of Fourth Tempter himself with Henzie Raeburn as the Chorus Leader.

In March 1939 Browne directed Eliot's second play, *The Family Reunion*, in London and in the same year, in association with the Arts Council, he launched a touring company which he called the Pilgrim Players (not to be confused with an earlier company—1906 to 1911—of the same name, run by Barry Jackson and John Drinkwater). The programme of Martin Browne's pilgrims, described in Henzie Raeburn's book, *Pilgrim Story* (1945), was dominated by the plays of Eliot and—to a lesser degree—of James Bridie (O. H. Mavor), the Scottish dramatist of rising reputation at that time. These tours continued until 1948.

Immediately after the Second World War, Browne took over the tiny Mercury Theatre in Notting Hill Gate and devoted it for the next three years entirely to the production of modern verse plays: first productions of plays by Christopher Fry, Ronald Duncan, Norman Nicholson, Anne Ridler, and Gilbert Horobin were staged, all directed by Martin Browne himself, together with revivals of already known plays by Bridie, Eliot, and others.

From 1948 to 1957 Browne was the director of the British Drama League, an organization devoted to giving assistance to the work of serious-minded amateur theatres. In 1951 he was responsible for the revival—the first since 1572—of the medieval cycle of York mystery plays, which he himself directed in the ruins of St Mary's Abbey, York, for the York festival (and in the year of the Festival of Britain). He repeated the production of the cycle at York in 1954, 1957, and 1966. Alongside these various activities in those years he continued his collaboration with T. S. Eliot, directing *The Cocktail Party* in 1949, *The Confidential Clerk* in 1953, and *The Elder Statesman* in 1958. And in 1969 he published *The Making of T. S. Eliot's Plays*. Various studies have pointed to Eliot's debt to Browne (for example F. B. Pinion, *A T. S. Eliot Companion*, 1986, and D. E. Jones, *The Plays of T. S. Eliot*, 1960).

For six months of each year from 1956 to 1962 Martin Browne served as visiting professor of religious drama at Union Theological College, New York, and from 1962 to 1965 he was drama adviser to Coventry Cathedral, directing the medieval mystery plays there in 1962 and 1964. In 1967 and 1968 he was directing at the Yvonne Arnaud Theatre in Guildford, the plays being *Murder in the Cathedral*, *The Family Reunion*, Thornton Wilder's *Our Town* and *The Long Christmas Dinner*, and the medieval morality play, *Everyman*.

Browne was a specialist of absolute integrity and of massive determination. Though his passion for theatre-as-art was intense and his work became, deservedly, well known on both sides of the Atlantic, he never showed any inclination to compromise his aesthetic ideals for the sake of popular acclamation or commercial appeal. It is true that his directorial style was perhaps 'caviare to the general', somewhat solemn and spare, on occasion. J. C. Trewin, the theatre critic, said of Browne's production of Laurie Lee's *Peasants' Priest* at the 1949 Canterbury festival: 'E. Martin Browne directed with some ingenuity … Ingenuity, yes: but where was the drama's kindling flare?' (Trewin, 120). And the same critic remarked, about the Mercury Theatre venture, 'Martin Browne, father-confessor of the new poet-dramatists, is a good actor and a director of talent. But I can only regret his choice of plays' (ibid., 90). But seen in its totality Browne's work added a unique and valuable dimension to the pattern of English mid-twentieth-century theatre. He was appointed CBE in 1952. Following the death of Henzie Raeburn, he married on 24 November 1974 Audrey Johnson, a medical social worker, the widow of John Rideout and daughter of Noel Johnson Tuck. He died in the Middlesex Hospital, Westminster, on 27 April 1980, survived by his second wife.

ERIC SALMON

Sources J. Parker, ed., *Who's who in the theatre*, 12th edn (1957) · *The Times* (29 April 1980) · J. C. Trewin, *We'll hear a play* (1949) · E. M. Browne, *The making of T. S. Eliot's plays* (1969) · R. Findlater, *The unholy trade* (1952) · *The Times* (30 Oct 1973) [obit. of Henzie Raeburn] · *CGPLA Eng. & Wales* (1980) · personal knowledge (2004) · b. cert. · d. cert. · m. certs.
Archives SOUND BL NSA, oral history interview · BL NSA, performance recording
Wealth at death £75,627: probate, 22 July 1980, *CGPLA Eng. & Wales*

Browne, Mary. *See* Evelyn, Mary (c.1635–1709).

Browne [*married name* Gray], **Mary Anne** (1812–1845), poet, was born near Maidenhead, Berkshire, on 24 September 1812, the eldest of the three children of a descendant of Sir Anthony Browne, a Kentish baronet, and Mary Anne Simmons, the only surviving child of Captain John Simmons of Liverpool and granddaughter of Thomas Briarly of Lancashire. Some sources erroneously claim Mary Anne Browne as the sister of Felicia Hemans. A child prodigy, she invented her own alphabet before being taught to write, and was soon producing verse, publishing from 1826 in the *Berkshire Chronicle*, whose editor (Mr Hanshall) became her first literary adviser. Her father, a man of literary tastes, taught her at home, and he also arranged publication of her first collection, *Mont Blanc and other Poems* (1827), when she was not yet fifteen. Then followed *Ada* (1828), *Repentance* (1829), *Coronal* (1833), and *Birthday Gift* (1834), the last much praised by Wordsworth. Many of her volumes went into second, even third, editions; they were widely reviewed, and her fame as a literary prodigy spread. Coleridge wanted to meet her; Letitia Elizabeth Landon, who became her friend, addressed a poem to her ('Stanzas to the author of "Mont Blanc", "Ada", &c.'); and Mary Russell Mitford, who met her at fourteen, registered

her true gift but admonished the proud parents not to spoil her (Mitford, 2.33).

In 1828 Mary Anne spent the summer in Wales, then moved with her family to a large house at Isleworth, close to London. From here she often visited London, her fame and soft attractiveness gaining her entrance to circles where she met many writers and artists, including William Jerdan, editor of the *Literary Gazette*, Allan Cunningham, and the painter John Martin. In 1832 she underwent a kind of religious conversion, bringing her from her own religion of the imagination into the fold of orthodoxy. In the same year she made the first of three annual summer trips to Ireland. About 1836 the family moved to Liverpool to further her younger brother's education in business, although he subsequently chose Dublin University and then ordination as the Revd Thomas Briarly Browne. Liverpool, meanwhile, was a disappointing literary environment, although she met among others the Chorley family and Dr Shelton Mackenzie, who encouraged her to contribute to the *Dublin University Magazine*, where she published extensively from 1839. She also learned German in order to read the literature. Her work achieved great popularity in America as well as at home, but, always self-critical, she had two 'great burnings' of her early work.

Late in 1842 Mary Anne Browne married James Gray, nephew of James Hogg and son of the Revd James Gray, one of the founders of *Blackwood's Edinburgh Magazine* and also a close friend of the poet Burns. She continued to write and publish after her marriage, but died of 'heart spasms' after giving birth to a son at her home at Sunday's Well, Cork, on 28 January 1845, and was buried in St Paul's Church, Cork. The *Dublin University Magazine* remained her major champion, publishing extensively from her poetical remains in 1845–6, as well as printing obituaries and recollections. Her pre-1832 volumes were diffused with a mixture of melancholy romanticism and a longing for intellectual expansion, while her later work was constrained by a sense of religious duty. Her last volume, however, *Sketches from the Antique* (1844), showed a new breadth and maturity. In all she published eight volumes of verse before her death at the age of thirty-two; material for several more might be gleaned from annuals and periodicals such as *Chambers's Edinburgh Journal*.

VIRGINIA H. BLAIN

Sources *Dublin University Magazine*, 25 (1845), 327–31 · [S. Hayman], 'Our portrait gallery, no. XLIII: the late Mrs James Gray', *Dublin University Magazine*, 29 (1847), 360–71 · M. R. Mitford, *Recollections of a literary life*, 3 vols. (1852)
Likenesses engraving, repro. in Hayman, 'The late Mrs James Gray', 360

Browne, Maurice (1555/6–1583), adventurer and courtier, was the fourth son of John Browne, merchant, of London, and his third wife, Christian, daughter of William Carkett of London. He was thirteen at the time of the visitation of London in 1568. John Browne died in September 1570, leaving Maurice's education to the care of his executors: Maurice had matriculated at Pembroke College, Cambridge, in 1569. His father had made a contract securing a little London property in Hart Street for him, probably from Maurice's mother's family. In 1576 Sir Thomas Smith referred to Maurice Browne as his servant and kinsman, and by 1580 he was apparently one of Sir Francis Walsingham's assistants. He was also the busy London agent for the Thynne family of Longleat, dealing with all kinds of tasks for them, domestic and political—he provided a lively commentary on the implications of court fortunes for the Thynne–Knyvet alliance. He negotiated with Walsingham and other court patrons for help against Thynne's enemies, especially Lord Stafford; and for John Thynne's appointment to Wiltshire offices. He informed Thynne in April 1580 that his ally Henry Knyvet would not gain the office of *custos rotulorum* of Wiltshire, because the earl of Leicester supported the earl of Pembroke for it. In May 1583 Browne described the rise to royal favour of Walter Ralegh, noting Ralegh's luxurious surroundings and sumptuous apparel. Since Thynne was at loggerheads with Ralegh's brother Carew, Browne thought Thynne should create a more dashing image when coming to court by investing in new clothes. Browne's advice was to cultivate Leicester, but also to approach a different patron, Sir Christopher Hatton. Browne also reported on family events in London such as the planned marriage of Thynne's widowed father-in-law, Sir Rowland Hayward, to the young daughter of Thomas (Customer) Smith.

In 1581 Browne went to Terceira in the Azores, probably sent by Walsingham as an agent for England's support of Don Antonio's claim to the Portuguese crown, against Spain. Browne returned about September 1581, with a Father John of the Holy Spirit, who was to serve as a 'living letter' (*CSP for.*, *1581–2*, nos. 366–7, 439), to report on the state of the island and its readiness for Don Antonio's defence.

Browne became interested in maps and cosmography, and in August 1582 Sir Humphrey Gilbert convinced him of the great riches expected in Gilbert's proposed colony in North America. Walsingham was a supporter of Gilbert's project, and encouraged Browne to go, and on his return to tell the queen of the colony's establishment, upon which news she had promised to send more shipping and men. During the long delays of late 1582 and early 1583 Browne spent much time with Gilbert. The little expedition departed in June 1583. Browne went as captain of the 40 ton *Swallow*, despite his lack of marine expertise; and he could not prevent the men from plundering a passing fishing ship. After Gilbert formally claimed possession of Newfoundland for England, Browne was appointed captain of the 120 ton *Delight* for the continuation of the voyage, leaving St John's on 20 August 1583. Allegedly, Gilbert insisted that the three ships sail a course towards Sable Island. On 28 August the men on the *Delight* were heard carousing with trumpets, drums, and fifes all night, but the crew did not keep proper watch as the wind rose, and the ship grounded next morning, with the loss of the supplies, and almost a hundred men. According to Edward Hayes's account, Browne nobly refused calls to save himself in the small boat in which sixteen men survived, instead going up to the highest deck to await imminent death. Browne had

been an assiduous and apparently charming courtier, on the fringe of the Walsingham–Gilbert–Hakluyt connection, and he impressed people: Walsingham and Gilbert gave him responsibilities, and Edward Hayes lamented the loss of a virtuous, honest, and discreet gentleman. However, enthusiasm could not compensate for inexperience (or Gilbert's misjudgements), and Browne could not adequately discipline the rough sailors. On 9 September Gilbert drowned too. This ambitious venture to colonize North America failed. Browne's untimely death on 29 August 1583 cut short his promising career and ended his lively reporting on the Elizabethan court.

ALISON WALL

Sources R. Cooke, *Visitation of London, 1568*, ed. H. Stanford London and S. W. Rawlins, [new edn], 2 vols. in one, Harleian Society, 109–10 (1963), 50 · R. Hakluyt, *The principall navigations voyages traffiques and discoveries of the English nation* (1599), vol. 3, pp. 143–67 · D. B. Quinn, *The voyages and colonising enterprises of Sir Humphrey Gilbert*, 2, Hakluyt Society, 2nd ser., 84 (1940), 380–446 · sixteen letters from Browne to John Thynne, Longleat House, Wiltshire, Marquess of Bath MSS, Thynne MSS [by permission of the late marquess of Bath], vol. 5 · *The new found land of Stephen Parmenius: the life and writings of a Hungarian poet, drowned on a voyage from Newfoundland, 1583*, ed. and trans. D. B. Quinn and N. M. Cheshire [1972], appx · A. Wall, 'Points of contact: court favourites and county faction in Elizabethan England', *Parergon*, new ser., 6 (1988), 215–26 · will, PRO, PROB 11/52, fols. 215r–216v [John Browne] · PRO, wards, 7/13/48

Browne, Maximilian Ulysses von, Jacobite third earl of Browne, and Count von Browne in the nobility of the Holy Roman empire (1705–1757), army officer in the imperial service, was born on 23 October 1705 at Basel, Switzerland, the only son of Ulysses Browne, Jacobite second earl of Browne and Count von Browne (1659–1731), an army officer, of Camas, co. Limerick, and his wife, Annabella (1677–1747), the daughter of James FitzGerald, of Knockany, co. Limerick. His father was a Jacobite military exile who left Ireland in 1690 and eventually became a major-general in the imperial army. At an early age Maximilian was sent to Ireland for a few years to be educated at the protestant diocesan grammar school in Limerick. He returned to Austria in 1715 to enter the regiment of his uncle George Browne, Jacobite first earl of Browne and Count von Browne (d. 1729), whose imperial and Jacobite titles he inherited through his father in 1731. His first campaigns were against the Turks and in Italy. From 1718 to 1723 it seems he studied at the Jesuit Clementinum University in Prague, completing a course in civil law before resuming his military career. On 25 August 1725 he married Maria Philippina Magdalena von Martinitz (1705–1760), the daughter and heir of Adam Ignaz, count von Martinitz (d. 1714), a former viceroy of Sicily. They had two sons, Philip George (1727–1803) and Joseph Ulysses (1728–1758).

Tall and lean in appearance, Browne was described as a gentle father, a staunch friend, and a sincere Catholic. He loved the comradeship and peripatetic character of army life, and his ability and connections soon marked him out for high command. A colonel at the age of twenty-four, he was promoted major-general in 1735, lieutenant-general and member of the imperial war council in 1739, full general in 1745, and field marshal in 1754. In 1736 he was made colonel-proprietor of the future 36th infantry regiment. He took part in the invasion of Corsica in 1731, the north Italian campaign of 1733–5, and the Banja Luka campaign against the Turks in 1737. In 1740 he had the first of many encounters with Frederick II and was forced to withdraw before superior Prussian strength in Silesia. He was wounded at the battle of Mollwitz. In 1742 he helped drive the French from Bohemia, and in 1743 he took part in the invasion of Bavaria. He was then assigned to liaise with the British at Hanau, where he made a favourable impression on George II. Posted to Italy in 1744, he captured Velletri from a garrison that included Hispano-Irish regiments, only to see it lost again to an enemy counter-attack. In 1745 he was wounded in the invasion of Bavaria, but recovered to participate in the last stages of the successful campaign which restored the Austrians on the Rhine and helped secure the imperial crown for Maria Theresa's consort, Francis Stephen. That same year he played a prominent role in the Austrian victory at Piacenza and the capture of Genoa, and in 1746–7 he led the invasion of Provence.

Subsequently, as peacetime commander in Transylvania and Bohemia, Browne implemented the new military reforms and oversaw improvements to fortifications, including those of Prague. In 1754 he was awarded the Polish order of the White Eagle and in 1756 the Habsburg order of the Golden Fleece. He was an imperial chamberlain and a member of the privy council of Bohemia, where he acquired the pleasant estate of Cerekwitz, near Königgrätz (now Hradec Králové). In 1756, following the outbreak of the Seven Years' War, his attempt to unite with the Saxon army was thwarted by Frederick at the battle of Lobositz. Browne was suffering from tuberculosis and clearly below his best in the campaign that followed Frederick's renewed offensive in Bohemia in 1757, in which he was subordinate to Prince Charles of Lorraine, the emperor's brother. At the battle to defend Prague on 6 May he was severely wounded in the leg while leading the Austrian grenadiers in a counter-attack. He was taken to the house of Prince Mansfeld in the city, where he died on 26 June, having made his confession and said farewell to his wife and sons. He was buried in the Capuchin church of St Joseph.

As a general Browne probably possessed the most comprehensive military talent of his time, utilizing every available technique and opportunity. He was a worthy opponent of Frederick the Great. His belief in bold, offensive warfare which favoured mobility and rapid action ran contrary to the cautious strategy of generals of the older generation, of whom he was openly critical. His younger son, Joseph, succeeded to the proprietorship of his regiment, but was killed at the battle of Hochkirch in 1758. His elder son, Philip, became a lieutenant-general and a founder member of the military order of Maria Theresa. The last of his line, he died childless in 1803.

HARMAN MURTAGH

Sources C. Duffy, *The wild goose and the eagle: a life of Field Marshal von Browne, 1705–1757* (1964) · *Neue deutsche Biographie*, [6 vols.] (Berlin, 1953–64), vol. 2, p. 640 · K. MacGrath, 'Count Maximilian Ulysses Browne (1705–57): an Irish field marshal in the Austrian service', *Irish Sword*, 1 (1949–53), 191–6 · 'Memoir of Field Marshal Count Brown', *Dublin University Magazine*, 44 (1854), 738–51 · GEC, *Peerage*, new edn, vol. 2 · W. Kavenagh, 'Irish colonel proprietors of imperial regiments', *Journal of the Royal Society of Antiquaries of Ireland*, 57 (1927), 120–21 · Browne pedigree, 1725, Genealogical Office of Dublin Pedigrees, vi, 160, fols. 106–8 · Brown pedigree, 1749, Royal Irish Acad., MS 3.D.7
Archives Österreichisches Staatsarchiv, Vienna, Kriegsarchiv, official reports
Likenesses engraving?, 1757, Heeresgeschichtliches Museum, Vienna, Austria · oils, Heeresgeschichtliches Museum, Vienna, Austria; repro. in MacGrath, 'Count Maximilian', pl. 11, facing p. 191 · oils, Military Academy, Wiener Neustadt, Austria · oils, Museum of Military History, Prague
Wealth at death substantial; owned estate at Cerekwitz, near Königgrätz in eastern Bohemia: Duffy, *The wild goose*, 14

Browne, Moses (1704–1787), poet and Church of England clergyman, was baptized on 17 December 1704 at Severn Stoke, Worcester, the son of John and Mary Brown. At the age of sixteen he addressed an ode celebrating the Hanoverian succession to his patron, the first Viscount Molesworth. While nothing is known of his early life, Browne probably owed his education to this Irish peer. The *Throne of Justice* (1721) was followed by a second ode, *The Richmond Beauties* (1722), and *Polidus, or, Distress'd Love*, a tragedy acted at a private theatre in London (1723). Molesworth died in 1725, leaving his young friend with neither place nor patron. His *Piscatory Eclogues* (1729) show unusual familiarity with Renaissance poetry and contain the first avowed imitation of Milton's 'Lycidas'. These strikingly naturalistic pastorals (the didactic portions are adapted from Izaak Walton's *Compleat Angler*) were reprinted as *Angling Sports* in 1773. Browne became a frequent contributor to the early numbers of the *Gentleman's Magazine*, which in 1736 awarded him a prize of £50 for the best poem on a theological subject.

On 3 June 1738 Browne married Ann Wibourne (1717/18–1783) at St James's, Clerkenwell. In the following year he published *Poems on Various Subjects*. Despite his respectable literary reputation (and fulsome dedications to prominent whigs), Browne was reduced to earning a living as a pen-cutter. Complaining that he, his wife, and seven children were in desperate straits, in 1745 he applied to Thomas Birch for a position as door-keeper to the Royal Society. While Browne received assistance and encouragement from Edward Cave of the *Gentleman's Magazine*, and from the countess of Hertford, it was a second series of publications appealing to the growing evangelical movement that mended his fortunes. In 1749 he published *Sunday Thoughts*, which introduced him to James Hervey, author of *Meditations among the Tombs*, and in 1750, at the canny suggestion of Dr Johnson, an updated and modernized edition of Walton and Cotton's *Compleat Angler*, last printed in 1676. This proved very successful, though Browne's editorial liberties involved him in controversy with Sir John Hawkins, who published a rival edition.

There followed a long georgic poem, *The Works and Rest of Creation* (1752).

Browne found new patrons, and at the suggestion of his new friend Hervey and with the assistance of his old friend Birch he entered into orders and in 1753 was given the living of Olney, Buckinghamshire, by Lord Dartmouth. About this time Hervey took up a collection to assist the rector and a family that now included thirteen children. In 1763 Browne was given the chaplaincy of Morden College, Blackheath; at a later date he was given the living of Sutton in Lincolnshire. He retained his Olney living *in absentia*: his curate there was John Newton, who with William Cowper published the *Olney Hymns* in 1779. After taking orders Browne largely confined himself to sermons, though *Percy Lodge*, a country-house poem written earlier for the countess of Hertford, was published in 1755. A translation, *The Excellency of the Knowledge of Jesus Christ* (1772), from the work by John Liborius Zimmerman, went through three editions.

Browne's wife died on 24 March 1783, aged sixty-five, and he himself died at Morden College on 13 September 1787; a tablet to his memory is in Olney church. An early admirer of Chaucer, Spenser, and Milton, Moses Browne was a deservedly popular minor poet. Though he did not find his way into the standard collections, both Nathan Drake and Robert Southey acknowledged Browne's early contribution to romantic naturalism.

DAVID HILL RADCLIFFE

Sources J. Hervey, *A collection of letters* (1760) · J. Hawkins, *The life of Samuel Johnson, LL.D.* (1787) · *GM*, 1st ser., 57 (1787), 840–41, 932 · N. Drake, 'On pastorals', *Literary Hours* (1799) · Nichols, *Lit. anecdotes* · *British Bibliographer*, 2 (1812), 357–60 · R. Southey, *Life and works of Cowper* (1835–7) · *DNB* · L. C. Carlson, *The first magazine* (1938) · H. M. Hall, *Idylls of fishermen* (1944) · B. H. Davis, 'The rival angler editors', *English writers of the eighteenth century*, ed. J. H. Middendorf (1971) · *IGI* · *The letters and prose writings of William Cowper*, ed. J. King and C. Ryskamp, 5 vols. (1979–86), vols. 1–2
Archives BL, letters to Thomas Birch, Add. MS 4301, fols. 329–44, 4323, fol. 11 · BL, corresp. with Edward Cave, 1734–9, Stowe MS 748
Likenesses C. Blackberd, stipple, pubd 1785, NPG · J. S. Müller, line engraving (after P. Brookes), BM; repro. in M. Browne, *Sunday thoughts* (1752) · line engraving, BM; repro. in *Gospel Magazine* (1778)

Browne, Patrick (*c*.1720–1790), physician and botanist, was probably born at Woodstock, near Claremorris, co. Mayo, Ireland, the fourth son of Edward Browne, a local gentleman. He received a good education locally, and in 1737 was sent to live with a relative in Antigua. The Caribbean climate did not suit him so he returned to Europe and studied medicine in Paris. He graduated MD on 1 December 1742 at the University of Rheims, and then moved to Leiden where he matriculated (21 February 1743) but did not graduate. After working as a physician in St Thomas's Hospital, London, he returned to the West Indies about 1746, eventually settling in Jamaica where he practised as a physician. In his spare time, he studied the island's natural history, collecting indigenous plants and animals.

Back in London, Browne published a map of Jamaica (1755), and *The Civil and Natural History of Jamaica* (1756),

illustrated with engravings of plants and animals based on drawings that Browne commissioned from Georg Ehret. His reputation as a botanist stems from the latter work because in it he became the first English-speaking author to use Linnaeus's system of classifying plants in print. He coined Latin names for over a hundred genera, some of which are still accepted. The second edition of the work (London, 1789), was augmented with indexes of Linnaean binomials, but the illustrations were crudely re-engraved and reversed because the original copper printing-plates were destroyed in the great fire in Cornhill, London, on 7 November 1765.

Browne's only other publication was a list of Linnaean binomials for Irish native birds and fishes (including marine mammals), though a number of his manuscripts survive in the Linnean Society, London, notably *Fa[s]ciculus plantarum Hiberniae*, two versions of a catalogue of Caribbean plants, an account of the vulcanology of Montserrat, and fragmentary medical notes, as well as his letters (1756–71) to Linnaeus. Ehret's original botanical drawings for the book on Jamaica also survive (London, Natural History Museum).

By 1757 Browne had returned again to the Caribbean and settled in St Croix. About 1758 he married a native of Antigua, but she was 'debauched' by Christian Juhl; embittered, Browne left her and moved to Montserrat about 1765. He retired to Ireland in 1770, but visited Antigua at least once again before his death. He died at Rushbrook, not far from his birthplace, on 29 August 1790, and was buried nearby, in his family's grave at All Saints' Church, Crossboyne. Nikolaus von Jacquin named *Brownea*, a genus of trees from tropical America belonging to the bean family, in his honour.

E. CHARLES NELSON

Sources R. O., 'The life of Patrick Browne, Esq. M.D. (author of History of Jamaica)', *Anthologia Hibernica*, 1 (Jan 1793), 2–5 · E. C. Nelson, 'Patrick Browne and the flowers of Mayo: a biographical essay', *The flowers of Mayo: Dr Patrick Browne's Fasciculus plantarum Hiberniae, 1788*, ed. E. C. Nelson (1995), 1–27 [incl. extensive footnotes and bibliography] · E. C. Nelson, 'Patrick Browne's *The civil and natural history of Jamaica* (1756, 1789)', *Archives of Natural History*, 24 (1997), 327–36
Archives L. Cong. | Linn. Soc., Linnaeus's herbarium, specimens · Linn. Soc., Linnaeus's MSS and other MSS · NHM, botany library

Browne, Peter (*d.* 1735), Church of Ireland bishop of Cork and Ross, was the son of Richard Browne; nothing more is known of his parentage or whether he came of a family long settled in Ireland. He was educated in Dublin, at St Patrick's Cathedral school and then at Trinity College, which he entered in 1682. He graduated BA in 1686 but his career was then interrupted by the Jacobite *revanche*. He moved to London, where in 1689 he was ordained. On his return to Ireland he proceeded to the degree of MA in 1691, and in the next year he was elected to a fellowship of his old college. Soon he was vice-provost, and feared as a disciplinarian. In 1699 he added to his degrees those of BD and DD. Meanwhile he officiated as lecturer at St Bride's Church, near the college, and in 1697 he was appointed rector of the newly created parish of St Mary. His talents within the university were recognized first by his being chosen to preach at the celebration of its centenary and then to refute the deist John Toland, whose *Christianity not Mysterious* had outraged the orthodox. Archbishop Francis Marsh of Dublin urged Browne to restate traditional teaching on revelation, which he did in 1697 with *A Letter in Answer to a Book Entitled Christianity not Mysterious*; Browne was thought by some to have marred his case with repetition and personal attacks on his opponent. He was also active within Dublin in the campaign to reform manners. Reward for his energetic services came with his selection as provost of Trinity in 1699.

Browne presided over a college that was already popular. Few innovations, whether in curriculum, discipline, or building, could be traced to him. Though he engaged in philosophical and theological debate his speculative cast did not lead him into the Dublin Society, either in the 1690s or during its brief revival in 1707. The controversies between whigs and tories resounded throughout the college. In handling incidents of alleged Jacobitism, Browne was accused of showing sympathy for the offenders. In convocation, where he represented the diocese of Killala as a proctor from 1703, he was also drawn into controversy. He chaired the committee for the reformation of manners, thus continuing the work with which he had been identified in the previous decade, and was active in other important business. In not pressing the demands of the clergy for greater official backing he was felt to have deferred too much to the administration. But his good standing with the executive, together with his sympathy for the now prevalent toryism, brought him the bishopric of Cork and Ross in 1710. His consecration on 2 April 1710 was interrupted by a protest against his unworthiness by Bishop John Pooley of Raphoe. The eccentric Pooley had in mind Browne's leniency towards the suspected Jacobites in the college and his supposed feebleness on behalf of clerical interests in convocation.

In Cork and Ross, Browne found a scattered diocese with problems of personnel, money, and materials. He was soon embroiled in an unseemly dispute with his dean, Rowland Davies, over the ordination of two candidates. Behind the ostensible issue lingered doubts about the bishop's political affiliations. These same concerns over Browne's supposed Jacobitism surfaced in the lengthy controversy over drinking healths to the dead. Although colleagues on the bench advised against it Browne published his objections and continued to air his opinions on the matter until 1722. He objected because such invocations mimicked the eucharist and were tantamount to sacrilege. His opponents felt that he was belittling the memory of William III, the subject of the toasts, and with him the principles of the 1688–9 revolution. Browne's case was answered by various pamphleteers, ranging from Bishop Edward Synge, future archbishop of Tuam, to incumbents in co. Cork. In print Browne also upheld the rites and ceremonies of the established church against those—notably Synge—who would have relaxed them in an effort to accommodate protestant dissenters. In insisting on severity Browne resembled other tory bishops who

seemed to regard protestant nonconformists as a greater menace to the established church than the Irish Catholics. Active in the parliaments at the end of Queen Anne's reign, he took no recorded part in the work of the Lords between 1717 and 1728 or after 1729.

Less controversially Browne encouraged the building or improvement of churches, donated communion plate to them, and supported philanthropy and education. He rebuilt the bishop's house in Cork and spent £2000 on a country residence intended for his successors. Shortly before his death he inaugurated the rebuilding of Cork Cathedral; he was also a generous benefactor to the city's public library. He continued to write on theological and philosophical questions. In order to refute the Arians and Socinians he argued that it was possible by analogy to apprehend God. His arguments were expounded copiously in *The Procedure, Extent and Limits of the Human Understanding* (1728) and *Things Divine and Supernatural Conceived by Analogy* (1732). These publications, modifying the earlier notions of Locke and Archbishop William King, drew dismissive ripostes from his former pupil George Berkeley, and were thought to have widened divisions among the orthodox rather than confuting the heterodox.

In addition to two topical sermons, published during his lifetime (1698 and 1716), two volumes of Browne's sermons were published posthumously in 1749. These treated fundamentals of faith. One former pupil revered Browne as an exemplar in preaching and practical charity; Patrick Delany contended that he had established 'true taste both in classical and sacred learning' (P. Delany, *Eighteen Discourses and Dissertations upon Various Very Important and Interesting Subjects*, 1766, xiii). A learned man with a library of at least 850 volumes, Browne retained the habits of the academic and was too readily tempted into print. Nevertheless he attended carefully to his diocese, but seemingly to the neglect of a larger public role in Dublin. He died in Cork on 25 August 1735 and was buried at Ballinaspig, co. Cork. He was reinterred in the new cathedral church of St Fin Barre in Cork in 1865.

TOBY BARNARD

Sources A. R. Winnett, *Peter Browne: provost, bishop, metaphysician* (1974) · journal of lower house of convocation, 1704–12, TCD, MS 668/1–3 · C. A. Webster, *The diocese of Cork* (1920) · W. M. Brady, *Clerical and parochial records of Cork, Cloyne, and Ross*, 3 (1864), 71 · LPL, MS 942/86 · J. Falvey, 'The Church of Ireland episcopate in the eighteenth century', MA diss., University College, Cork, 1995 · *DNB*
Archives Marsh's Library, Dublin, MSS · St Fin Barre's Cathedral, Cork, MSS · University of Newcastle, New South Wales, Australia, MSS | TCD, corresp. with William King
Likenesses H. Howard, oils, TCD

Browne, Sir Richard, first baronet (*c*.1602–1669), parliamentarian army officer and lord mayor of London, was born in London, the second son of John Browne (or Moses) of Wokingham, Berkshire, and London, and his wife, Anne, daughter of John Beard of Wokingham. Very little is known about Browne's early life and career. In 1622 he was admitted a member of the Honourable Artillery Company and about 1631 he married Bridget Bryan, daughter of Robert Bryan of Henley, Oxfordshire, mercer, with whom he had three sons and two daughters. He was also returned in the 1634 London heralds' visitation as of Far-ringdon Without, by which stage he had become free of the Woodmongers' Company. Acquiring his wealth as a merchant trading in coal and timber, by 1642 he was of sufficient substance to invest £600 in the Irish adventurers' scheme to finance the reconquest of Ireland. Yet royalist propagandists in the 1640s were to delight in sneering at Browne's social origins by continually referring to him as 'the woodmonger' or 'the faggot man' (Thomas, 1.426; 3.10, 221, 228). Browne was to translate to the more respectable Merchant Taylors' Company in December 1656. He made his initial mark on City politics in December 1641 when he was one of three radical inhabitants of St Dunstan-in-the-West returned, possibly for the first time, in controversial common-council elections. He served on five common-council committees in 1642–3, two of which drew upon his expertise in the Newcastle coal trade. Browne was again in radical company in July 1642 when he subscribed a petition of common councillors to the Lords complaining of Mayor Gurney's behaviour over the disposal of arms and ammunition from Hull.

However, Browne's chief contribution to the parliamentarian cause was as an energetic and successful military commander during the civil war. By spring 1642 he was the senior captain in the Orange regiment of the City trained bands and in the following September he helped to disarm Kent royalists. In December 1642 he served under Sir William Waller for the first time at the recapture of Winchester. Shortly afterwards he was active in London employing military force against peace petitioners, leading to a special royal demand that he and two other leading London parliamentarians be brought to justice. Having by now attained the rank of colonel, he was also one of the militia officers empowered to assist in levying distraints on London assessment defaulters. In July 1643 he was again sent into Kent to suppress a major royalist insurrection and achieved a notable victory at Tonbridge. His record in the field was recognized by parliament in December 1643 when they appointed him major-general of a brigade of trained bands and auxiliaries sent to reinforce Waller's army. Browne's forces helped Waller achieve victory at the battle of Cheriton in March 1644.

The next phase of Browne's military career began in June 1644 when he was appointed major-general of the forces raised for subduing Oxford and commander-in-chief of the forces of the associated counties of Berkshire, Buckinghamshire, and Oxfordshire. His headquarters were at Abingdon, where he served as governor until 1646. Browne put continuous pressure on Oxford and surrounding royalist territory, intercepting and plundering royalist supplies, capturing garrisons, and taking prisoners. In the summer of 1644, however, sharp differences arose between Browne and Waller over the extent of their respective commands; in September, faced with unpaid and hungry soldiers, a demoralized Browne requested to be called home from Abingdon. His complaints were being channelled at this point through Bulstrode Whitelocke, with whom he had entered into a close association.

Whitelocke and the parliamentarian leadership were also kept well informed of a lengthy deception practised by Browne on Lord Digby from September to December 1644. Digby was led to believe that Browne was ready to surrender Abingdon to the royalists in return for a baronetcy and other rewards. Yet Browne used the time to finish the defence works around Abingdon and acquire fresh provisions and men.

In May 1645 Browne was ordered to join forces with Oliver Cromwell and follow the movement of royalist forces out of Oxford but relations between the two commanders were apparently tense. After a quick visit to London to hasten supplies, Browne took part in the first siege of Oxford in June 1645. Yet he continued to take great offence at any perceived slights to his authority as royalist taunts about his humble origins perhaps hit home and, in an effort to mollify him, parliament in August 1645 voted him £760 of his arrears of pay. The following month Browne was elected recruiter MP for Chipping Wycombe, Buckinghamshire, but he was given leave to be absent from the house so that he could continue to take part in the final siege of Oxford. After the end of the war Browne was appointed one of the commissioners who were to receive the king from the Scots in January 1647 and he was with Charles at Holmby in the following June when the king was seized by Cornet Joyce. Browne vociferously opposed the seizure and, as both a religious and political presbyterian, he was soon using his extensive City influence to rally support for the king and to oppose the army and its Independent allies. He was elected alderman for Langbourn ward in June 1648, and sheriff in the following November, but after the army's advance on London in December 1648 he was one of those MPs accused of allying with the Scots for the invasion of England and was purged from the Commons and all his City offices. Five years of harsh imprisonment followed. Although returned by London in 1656 to the second protectorate parliament, Browne was excluded for refusing to take the oath recognizing the new regime. Yet he did sit in the third protectorate parliament of 1659 and was in the process of being restored to office, and having his substantial arrears paid, when he became implicated in Sir George Booth's rising and was forced into hiding in the City.

At the Restoration, Browne headed Charles's triumphal procession into London and was rewarded with a knighthood in May 1660, and a baronetcy in July. He was also restored to his aldermanry in September, and was elected lord mayor in October 1660. Appointed as president of Bethlem and Bridewell hospitals the same year, he had finally risen to the very top of the City's hierarchy. His military expertise and political reliability were acknowledged in April 1660 when he was made colonel of the London militia horse and, in the following July, major-general of the militia. Returned a London member to the Convention Parliament, Browne was moderately active in its deliberations. He defended his old ally Whitelocke during the debates on the indemnity bill but gave damning evidence of a private conversation with Colonel Adrian Scrope which led to Scrope's execution for regicide.

Arrears of pay totalling £2000 or more were granted to Browne, chargeable on the excise. He was also given a sinecure post on the board of appeals relating to the excise. Furthermore, vigorous action taken by Browne against Venner's Fifth-Monarchist rising in 1661 earned financial reward from the City. Returned as MP of Ludgershall, Buckinghamshire, in December 1661, he was a moderately active committeeman, mainly concerned with trade or London affairs. When the new Act of Uniformity came into force he urged toleration for presbyterian clergy, yet at the same time he served on a committee set up to prevent meetings of sectaries and demonstrated a strong personal animosity to Quakers. In 1662 he managed to purchase the manor of Debden in Essex, where he died intestate on 24 September 1669 and was buried on 12 October. Administration was granted in 1671 to his son and heir Sir Richard Browne (d. 1684).

KEITH LINDLEY

Sources GEC, *Baronetage*, 3.92, 354 · M. W. Helms and B. D. Henning, 'Browne, Richard', HoP, *Commons, 1660–90* · A. B. Beaven, ed., *The aldermen of the City of London, temp. Henry III–[1912]*, 2 (1913), 69, 182 · J. Rushworth, *Historical collections*, new edn, 5 (1721), 673–4, 754–62; 6 (1722), 34, 394, 513–17; 7 (1721), 802–3, 1037, 1179, 1354, 1361 · J. Vicars, *England's worthies* (1647), 99–103 · *The diary of Bulstrode Whitelocke, 1605–1675*, ed. R. Spalding, British Academy, Records of Social and Economic History, new ser., 13 (1990), 150–53, 155, 162, 185, 191, 503, 509, 551 · J. R. Woodhead, *The rulers of London, 1660–1689* (1965), 39–40 · *DNB* · K. Lindley, *Popular politics and religion in civil war London* (1997), 145, 191, 193, 214 · P. Thomas, ed., *Oxford royalist newsbooks*, 4 vols. (1971), 1.426–7; 3.10, 221, 228, 257–8, 285 · G. W. E. Marshall, 'Sir Richard Browne', *The Genealogist*, 3 (1879), 377–9 · G. W. E. Marshall, note, *The Genealogist*, 4 (1880), 128–9 · *The journal of Thomas Juxon*, ed. K. Lindley and D. Scott, CS, 5th ser., 13 (1999), 55–6, 78–9, 113, 165 · *The visitation of London, anno Domini 1633, 1634, and 1635, made by Sir Henry St George*, 1, ed. J. J. Howard and J. L. Chester, Harleian Society, 15 (1880), 115 · R. Ashton, *Counter-revolution: the second civil war and its origins, 1646–8* (1994), 397 · lists of common councilmen, CLRO, 98, 100 · *The obituary of Richard Smyth … being a catalogue of all such persons as he knew in their life*, ed. H. Ellis, CS, 44 (1849), 83 · administration, PRO, PROB 6/46, fol. 11v · 'Boyd's Inhabitants of London', Society of Genealogists, London, 9166

Likenesses oils, 1648, NPG · engraving, repro. in Vicars, *England's worthies*, 99 · engraving, repro. in *A perfect list of all the victories obtained … by the parliament's forces … to August 1646* (1646) [Thomason Tracts, 669 fol. 10/79] · line engraving, BM, NPG; repro. in J. Ricraft, *Survey of England's champions* (1649) · silver medal, BM · wash drawing, AM Oxf.

Wealth at death Debden Hall, Essex, and manor of Debden: GEC, *Baronetage*, 3.92; administration, PRO, PROB 6/46, fol. 11v

Browne, Sir Richard, baronet (1605–1683), diplomat, was born on 6 May 1605, the only son of Christopher Browne (d. 1645) of Saye's Court, Deptford, and Thomasine (b. 1563), daughter of Benjamin *Gonson (c.1525–1577) [see under Gonson, William], treasurer of the navy. Browne's grandfather had served with the earl of Leicester in the Low Countries and was a courtier under both Elizabeth I and James I, and his godfathers, Sir Robert Bannister and William Lancaster, were both prominent at court in the early seventeenth century. Browne matriculated on 26 June 1623 from Christ Church, Oxford, but it was from St Alban Hall that he graduated BA the same day. He was

briefly from 1624 a fellow of Merton College and proceeded MA on 28 June 1628, but had already, on 23 February 1627, been admitted to Gray's Inn, where he commenced a legal education. It was probably during the late 1620s that Browne married Elizabeth (c.1610–1652), daughter of Sir John Pretyman of Dryfield in Gloucestershire; they had one son and one daughter. Only the latter, Mary (d. 1709), who married the diarist John Evelyn, survived him.

Some time before 1631 Browne was appointed secretary to Isaac Wake, English ambassador in Venice, and between 1631 and 1633 Browne also served him while he was resident in Paris. Between 1636 and 1640 Browne was in Paris again as secretary to another English ambassador, John, Viscount Scudamore, during which time he made a number of visits to England on official business. Amid rumours of his impending appointment as secretary to Sir Henry Vane sen., Browne was sworn clerk-in-ordinary of the privy council on 27 January 1641. In the following month he was sent on his first diplomatic mission as ambassador, to the queen of Bohemia and the elector palatine, who were then in the Low Countries, and in the following July he was dispatched as resident to Paris. He was to remain there until 1660, acting as ambassador to Charles I during the civil wars and to Charles II in exile during the Commonwealth. During this period his chapel became a focal point for those royalists who were attached to the liturgy of the Church of England, and he is reported to have protected clerics who argued against Catholicism. As his son-in-law noted, this was 'no small honour, and in a time when it was so low as many thought utterly lost' (*Diary of John Evelyn*, ed. Wheatley, 3.247). However, Browne himself suffered severe financial difficulties during this period as a result of the king's financial straits. Browne and his father had alienated much of the family estate in order to finance the embassy, and Browne's penurious condition was the subject of frequent comment. In March 1649 Browne himself reflected on having 'consumed my whole estate', but added that he was 'ambitious of nothing more than to spend the last drop of my blood in service of so good a master' (BL, Add. MS 37047, fol. 1).

In spite of such poverty, Browne resisted the attempt by agents of the new regime in London to win him over to the republic, and Charles II on 1 September 1649 rewarded him with the baronetcy which had been intended for him since 1644. In spite of his loyalty, however, and his efforts to secure the publication of a French translation of the *Eikon basilike*, Browne's position appears to have been less secure after 1649, and he may have fallen foul of divisions among the exiles. Catholic courtiers evidently sought to undermine someone whom they perceived to be overly hostile to the Romish faith and overly attached to the policies of the 'Louvre' group, who favoured an alliance with the Scots in order to revive royalist fortunes. In the autumn of 1651 Browne was accused by Christopher, Lord Hatton, of having worked secretly to advance the presbyterian cause. Browne dismissed such allegations as 'uncharitable calumnies' emanating from 'backbiting lips', and protested against 'arrant lies suggested by a diabolical, malicious, whispering spirit' (BL, Egerton MS 2534, fols. 110–11). Although Browne was friendly with controversial pro-Scottish royalists such as Robert Long, he was probably someone who sought to remain aloof from factional squabbles. This is indicated by the fact that he received support from prominent 'old royalists' such as Sir Edward Nicholas and Sir Edward Hyde (later earl of Clarendon), who were no friends of the Louvre party. It was they who became Browne's most important friends and allies in ensuing years. Nevertheless, the affair may have proved damaging. Having briefly suffered imprisonment in late 1652, for reasons unknown, Browne was dispatched to Brittany in order to oversee the attempt to raise funds from captured English ships, in what may have been a deliberate attempt to cast him into the political wilderness. By the time he returned to Paris in 1656, the embassy faced a serious threat, in the form of a treaty between the Cromwellian protectorate and the French government and the arrival of a new ambassador, Sir William Lockhart. Browne's credentials were eventually revoked in May 1657, although he remained in Paris, from where he continued to relay news to other royalists, and from where he noted in 1659 how he wished those in power in England 'disorder, disunion, and ruin' (BL, Egerton MS 2536, fol. 363). He also expressed his confidence, however, that a restoration of the Stuart dynasty was imminent, since 'the rebels' disorders in England seem more and more to thicken into a dark chaos of confusion, out of which we may speedily see some auspicious beam of light by a blessed feat from above' (BL, Add. MS 15857, fol. 148).

Browne returned to England in June 1660, was finally called to the bar, and resumed his position as clerk of the privy council, in addition to which he was made muster master-general. It was during this period that Samuel Pepys recorded his impression of Browne as being 'a dull, but it seems upon action a hot man' (Pepys, 4.430). The crown sought to find ways to relieve Browne's financial position and to repay their debt to someone who had been a loyal servant for many years. Nevertheless, Browne, who claimed to have been owed £12,000, struggled financially until the end of his life. In 1661 he was nominated as a prospective warden of Merton College, but failed to secure unanimous support when a single fellow objected. The choice then fell to Archbishop Juxon, who selected Sir Thomas Clayton, a decision which led to some acrimony. Browne resigned his clerkship of the privy council in 1672, after which he served as master of Trinity House in 1673. Thereafter Browne may have lived in retirement until his death, at Saye's Court, on 12 February 1683. He was buried in the churchyard of St Nicholas's, Deptford, on 19 February. His voluminous official and personal papers form an extensive part of the Evelyn papers in the British Library.

J. T. PEACEY

Sources *Diary of John Evelyn*, ed. W. Bray, new edn, ed. H. B. Wheatley, 4 vols. (1906) · Evelyn, *Diary* · R. Bell, ed., *Memorials of the civil war … forming the concluding volumes of the Fairfax correspondence*, 2 vols. (1849) · *Calendar of the Clarendon state papers preserved in the Bodleian Library*, ed. O. Ogle and others, 5 vols. (1869–1970) · *The Nicholas papers*, ed. G. F. Warner, 4 vols., CS, new ser., 40, 50, 57, 3rd ser., 31 (1886–1920) · *CSP dom.*, 1631–76 · GEC, *Baronetage* · G. M. Bell, *A handlist of British diplomatic representatives, 1509–1688*, Royal Historical Society Guides and Handbooks, 16 (1990) · Pepys, *Diary* · BL, Evelyn–Browne MSS · *Report on the manuscripts of Lord De L'Isle and Dudley*, 6, HMC, 77 (1966) · E. Corp, 'An inventory of the archives of the Stuart court at Saint-Germain-en-Laye, 1689–1718', *Archives*, 23 (1998), 118–46 · Foster, *Alum. Oxon.* · J. Foster, *The register of admissions to Gray's Inn, 1521–1889, together with the register of marriages in Gray's Inn chapel, 1695–1754* (privately printed, London, 1889), 180

Archives BL, Browne–Evelyn papers, corresp., Add. MSS 12184–12186, 15856–15858, 15865, 15948, 34702, JE A1, JE A8/1 | BL, letters to R. Long, Add. MS 37047 · BL, letters to Sir Edward Nicholas, Egerton MSS 2534, 2536, 2547 · Christ Church Oxf., corresp. with first earl of Clarendon · PRO, state papers, SP 78/88, fols. 90, 93, 104–7, 111–14

Likenesses P. Audinet, line engraving, 1818 (after R. Nanteuil), BM, NPG; repro. in Bray and Wheatley, eds., *Diary of John Evelyn*, vol. 1, p. 295

Browne, Richard (1647/8–1693/4?), physician, the son of Thomas Browne of Barton, Westmorland, matriculated at Queen's College, Oxford, on 29 March 1667, aged nineteen. Although he apparently did not take a degree, he may have begun practising medicine a few years later, since he wrote *Medicina musica, or, A mechanical essay on the effects of singing, musick and dancing on human bodies* (1674; republished 1729). On 20 September 1675 he matriculated in the medical faculty at Leiden University; again there is no evidence of his having completed a degree. Browne was in London by mid-August 1676, when he began the three-part examination of the College of Physicians; on 30 September he was formally awarded the licentiate of that body, allowing him to practise in the metropolis. He published another book in the spring of 1678, *Peri archōn liber in quo recepta veteribus rerum principia funditus evertuntur et nova*, which showed his medical learning.

Browne also began to translate Latin works. The first published was *The Cure of Old Age* (1683), which contained translations of two medieval works on the preservation of health, by Roger Bacon and by Edward Madeira Arrais. This was shortly followed by *Of Natural Affection towards One's Offspring* (1684), from Plutarch. A year later Browne published *Prosodia pharmacopaeorum, or, The Apothecary's Prosody* (1685), translated with additions from the work of Olaus Borrichius: an etymological dictionary, which could also serve apothecaries as a pronunciation guide. Browne showed himself sympathetic to the surgeons, too: on 7 December 1685 he registered with the Stationers' Company a new edition of the works of Alexander Read, which appeared anonymously, late in 1687, as *Chirurgorum comes*. It was a learned and compendious volume, using Read's organizational framework, but adding more recent works (some translated from Latin), and Browne's own observations. In its preface, Browne complained that since the time of Erasistratus medicine had become divided into three parts, which he wished to reunite.

About March 1687 Browne and Christopher Crell (a Polish Socinian with an MD from Leiden) took out a five-year lease, at £32 per year, on a property in King's Street,

London, known as the Golden Angel and Crown, and containing several rooms. On 12 August 1687 they drew up a document bringing three other college licentiates into the practice. The group collected a stock of drugs (the 'repository'), saw patients by turns, and held a weekly meeting to divide the profits. At the same time, each continued his private practice. They advertised by distributing handbills and by printing the jointly authored *Oracle for the Sick* (1687), which contained a series of medical questions with answers, which the patient could fill out and send in for a diagnosis and medicines in the return post. Browne also circulated private handbills advertising his 'London Pills', which prevented and cured 'all Diseases, wherein Purging is proper', such as scurvy, venereal disease, gout, dropsy, coma, lethargy, and so on. The pills were sold at many places, including his house, to the left of the arch in Great Winchester Street.

In the autumn of 1687 the censors of the College of Physicians attacked Browne for advertising his pills, accusing him of acting like an empiric and so bringing the faculty of physicians into disrepute. In December, members of the college also brought charges against Browne for frequently disobeying the new statute that required members not to consult with unlicensed practitioners; for this Browne was fined 10s. Browne legally gave up all claims on the *Oracle* practice on 23 December 1687. Following the revolution of 1688, Browne joined with a group of fellows and licentiates in petitioning the House of Lords on 12 June 1689 against restoring the college charter obtained from James II, and in the following years he opposed plans for the college's dispensary. Nevertheless, Browne attacked quackery in the advertisements for his pills, and in the *Oracle*. His interest in language continued to manifest itself with the publication of his *English Examiner* (1692).

In the spring of 1693, when the Admiralty sought physicians for the Red squadron, Browne obtained one of the posts. Since he was still listed as a licentiate of the college in the printed catalogue of members in 1693, but not in the catalogue of 15 June 1694, he would appear to have lost his life in service. A final book, the *General History of Earthquakes* (1694), and two translations from Plutarch, *Natural Questions* (1694) and *Platonick Questions* (1694), probably appeared posthumously. HAROLD J. COOK

Sources Arber, *Regs. Stationers* · E. Arber, ed., *The term catalogues, 1668–1709*, 3 vols. (privately printed, London, 1903–6) · Foster, *Alum. Oxon.* · R. W. Innes Smith, *English-speaking students of medicine at the University of Leyden* (1932) · H. J. Cook, *Trials of an ordinary doctor: Joannes Groenevelt in 17th-century London* (1994) · J. J. Keevil and others, *Medicine and the navy, 1200–1900*, 4 vols. (1957–63)

Browne, Richard (1700–1756). *See under* Brown, Richard (1736–1816).

Browne, Robert (1550?–1633), religious separatist, was probably born at Tolethorpe Hall, Rutland, the third of seven children of Anthony Browne (c.1515–c.1590) and his wife, Dorothy (d. 1602), daughter of Sir Philip Butler (or Boteler) of Watton-at-Stone, Hertfordshire, and his wife, Elizabeth, daughter of Sir Robert Drury of Hawstead, Suffolk. The Browne family was well established in the ranks

of influential county gentry. Indeed, Browne was distantly related to William Cecil, Lord Burghley, whose later intercessions on his behalf helped to insulate him from the full rigour of the law.

Browne attended Corpus Christi College, Cambridge, where he graduated BA in 1572, probably aged twenty-two. While there he associated with a group of 'forward' protestant students and 'carefull and zelous' local reformers (*Writings of Harrison and Browne*, 397). Following his graduation he became a schoolteacher, although where he taught remains unclear. While teaching he grew concerned about his students, and he meditated on the sad state of the world in which they had to live. Ultimately he came to believe that the cause of all the trouble was 'the wofull and lamentable state of the church' (ibid.). Browne's opinions brought him into conflict with the local minister, however, and he had to give up his post. In late 1578 or 1579 he lived with the puritan minister Richard Greenham at Dry Drayton, not far from Cambridge. He even seems to have preached in Greenham's church without an episcopal licence.

Shortly afterwards, when he was asked to preach at his old college of Corpus, Browne experienced a crisis of conscience. He had come to believe that the bishops had usurped authority in God's kingdom and that the real power to call and depose ministers belonged to individual congregations. He had also concluded that the whole ecclesiastical system was unscriptural, and therefore unacceptable to God. By early 1580 Browne was becoming disillusioned with reforming the ecclesiastical establishment from within. Instead, he considered beginning the kingdom of God with 'the worthiest, were thei never so fewe' (*Writings of Harrison and Browne*, 404). As a result, he resigned his Cambridge position, preaching in St Benet's, next door to Corpus, and started holding conventicles. Forbidden to preach, he denied the bishops' authority, and shortly afterwards persuaded his friend Robert Harrison to espouse similar views.

Browne soon moved to Norwich where he stayed with Harrison. About this time both men signed a petition titled 'A supplication of Norwich men to the queen's majesty', urging her to institute an eldership in her church and remove non-preaching ministers. Additionally, some time before the spring of 1581, Browne appears to have written a document that became a portion of 'A view of Antichrist', which was subsequently printed in *A Parte of a Register* (1593?). In this writing Browne took a presbyterian position, arguing that the church should be composed of ministers and elders chosen by the congregation to watch over it.

By April 1581 Browne was attracting attention around Bury St Edmunds, Suffolk. Bishop Freake of Norwich reported to Burghley that Browne had been arrested for holding conventicles in private homes there. Burghley replied that he should be treated charitably and sent to him in London if he remained obstinate. These measures left Browne unfazed, and with Harrison and their followers he soon separated from the Church of England. Instead, they agreed to 'joine them selves to the Lord, in one covenant and followeshipp together, and to keep and seek agrement under his lawes and government'. They also promised to avoid 'disorders and wickednes', obey those whom they chose to instruct them, and abide by procedures for teaching, warning, and rebuking each other (*Writings of Harrison and Browne*, 422). Their goal was to make one another 'obedient to Christ' and judge 'all thinges by the worde of God' (ibid., 277). These ideas reflected Browne's desire to create a church grounded upon the scriptural model, where the gospel could be truly preached, the sacraments truly dispensed, and discipline rightly administered by the whole congregation guided by its officers. The new church chose Browne as its pastor and Harrison as its teacher.

Persecutions and imprisonments by ecclesiastical officials and assize judges caused the congregation to emigrate to Middelburg in the Netherlands some time between May and August 1582. After its arrival Browne published three treatises, which were distributed as one volume. In the best-known of these works, *A Treatise of Reformation without Tarrying for Anie*, he pressed for immediate reformation of the church and condemned those who evaded this responsibility by pleading dependence on the secular state. *A Book which Sheweth the Life and Manners of All True Christians* provided a kind of catechism for the spiritually uninstructed and a guide for daily religious life, while *A Treatise upon 23. of Matthewe* denounced the empty self-serving preaching of many contemporary clergymen. On 30 June 1583 a royal proclamation was issued in England against these writings and their author.

Meanwhile, Browne's church was disintegrating as internal dissensions wracked the congregation. He narrated these troubles in *A True and Short Declaration* (1583?). Late in 1583, therefore, he left Middelburg for Scotland, where he sought admission to the Edinburgh kirk. The Edinburgh session refused him because of his unorthodox views and arrogant manner. He then denounced the entire Scottish system of church discipline and asserted that he would appeal to the secular authorities. He was gaoled, but subsequently freed on the authority of King James, who was incensed with the kirk over the Ruthven raid.

Disillusioned, Browne returned to England in 1584, travelled abroad in early 1585, and returned to England later that year. During this period he received a copy of a letter from Thomas Cartwright to Harrison, expressing the hope that Harrison would reunite with the established church. Browne replied to Cartwright, denying that the Church of England was a true church of God. This rejoinder was subsequently published under the title of *An Answere to Master Cartwright* (1585?).

Following his return Browne was arrested and charged with publishing *An Answere*. He admitted authorship but denied having the work printed. Burghley asked Archbishop Whitgift for leniency, and Browne, whose religious disappointments, family responsibilities, and legal problems were increasing, accepted an accommodation. On 7 October 1585 he signed a 'submission'. In this document he acknowledged Archbishop Whitgift's authority over him, accepted the Church of England as the church of God, promised to receive the sacraments, and pledged to keep the peace of the church.

In November 1586 Browne was elected master of St Olave's School, Southwark, on condition that he sign articles of good behaviour. His conformity stirred debate. For the next two years he found himself embattled on two fronts. First, the puritan Stephen Bredwell charged him with hypocrisy in *The Rasing of the Foundations of Brownisme* (1588). Second, Browne became engaged in a controversy with the separatists Henry Barrow and John Greenwood. Champlin Burrage claimed to have found Browne's manuscript answer to them, which he published under the title of *The 'Retractation' of Robert Browne* (1907). None the less some historians have questioned Browne's authorship of this work, while others have rejected it, arguing that it is radically at variance with Browne's earlier writings, both in tone and substance, and citing evidence for Thomas Cartwright's authorship; perhaps Browne copied this treatise with the intention of replying to it. It may also be significant that, while Browne was supposedly writing *The 'Retractation'*, Bredwell was denouncing him for converting a woman to separatism.

By late 1588 Browne had left St Olave's and written a letter to a Mr Flower, published in 1904 under the title *A New Years Guift*, in which he now seems to reveal himself as an 'Erastian congregationalist', denouncing both Scottish presbyterianism and lordly bishops, while defending the magistrates' power in ecclesiastical affairs. Other writings from this period survive only in fragments.

In 1591 Browne accepted the rectorship of Little Casterton from his brother Francis and was instituted on 30 June. That summer he moved to the parish of Thorpe Achurch, Northamptonshire, where he was presented on 24 August, instituted on 2 September, and ordained deacon and priest on 30 September. There, with his wife Alice—whom he had married before moving to Middelburg—and their eight or nine children, he lived quietly for the next twenty years. Alice was buried on 9 July 1610 and Browne subsequently married Elizabeth Warrener of Stamford St Martin's, Northamptonshire, on 14 February 1613. This marriage produced domestic strife that divided not only the new couple but the parish as well. By late 1615 Browne had moved out of the parsonage and probably separated from his wife. He may have settled at Thorpe Waterville. Elizabeth apparently continued to live in the parsonage, and on 29 October 1623 sued Browne for restitution of conjugal rights.

Perhaps because of this irregular situation, Browne's nonconformist tendencies reappeared. Church court records, the only reliable source for this period, indicate that he was apparently suspended in 1617 and ceased to conduct services at Achurch. Then on Palm Sunday 1626 he suddenly returned and resumed his pastoral duties. On 8 November 1627, however, he was presented for nonconformity, and responded by bringing suit against several parishioners. The court cases continued until his excommunication in late 1631 and the sequestration of his living, evidently in September 1632. This was not the end of Browne's troubles. In late August 1633, Robert Greene, his godson and parish constable, rudely requested that he pay a rate. Browne refused and struck Greene, who complained to the local JP. When Browne proved obstinate, the magistrate sent him to gaol in Northampton, where he died. He was buried on 8 October 1633 at St Giles's Church, Northampton. Four years later, in a dispute over his will, Elizabeth Browne was said to have goods of her late husband's worth £240 in her possession.

Browne was intelligent, strong-willed, and strong-minded, with a harsh individualistic spirit that prevented him from co-operating well with others. However, these traits gave him the strength to withstand great hardships and to become the first English separatist to demand publicly the formation of a true church composed of sincere Christians in gathered congregations. He supported this demand with trenchant arguments based on the scriptures. His subsequent defection deeply distressed other separatist leaders. They rejected the opprobrious label of 'Brownists' and alleged that they drew their inspiration directly from God and his scriptures. Nevertheless Stephen Offwood reported in 1632 that the great Elizabethan separatist Henry Barrow had read Browne's works and found them persuasive. Browne's views on ecclesiology, church polity, and church discipline eventually merged with those of other separatist, semi-separatist, and puritan thinkers to influence the development of congregationalism in England, the Netherlands, and America.   MICHAEL E. MOODY

Sources A. Peel and L. Carlson, eds., *Cartwrightiana*, Elizabethan Nonconformist Texts Series, 1 (1951), 197–201 · *The writings of Robert Harrison and Robert Browne*, ed. A. Peel and L. Carlson, Elizabethan Nonconformist Texts Series, 2 (1953) · *The writings of Henry Barrow, 1587–1590*, ed. L. H. Carlson (1962), 49–50 · B. R. White, 'A puritan work by Robert Browne', *Baptist Quarterly*, 18 (1959), 109–17 · D. C. Smith, 'Robert Browne, Independent', *Church History*, 6 (1937), 289–349 · B. R. White, *The English separatist tradition from the Marian martyrs to the pilgrim fathers* (1971), 44–66 · M. Moody, 'A critical edition of George Johnson's *Discourse* (1603)', PhD diss., Claremont Graduate School, 1979 · A. Peel, *The Brownists in Norwich and Norfolk* (1920) · T. Fuller, *The church history of Britain*, ed. J. S. Brewer, new edn, 6 vols. (1845), vol. 5, pp. 62–70 · S. Bredwell, *The rasing of the foundations of Brownisme* (1588) · *The 'retractation' of Robert Browne, father of congregationalism*, ed. C. Burrage (1907) · R. Browne, *A new years guift* (1904) · R. Clutterbuck, ed., *The history and antiquities of the county of Hertford*, 2 (1821), 476 · *A parte of a register* [1593] · R. Serjeantson, *The history of the church of St Giles, Northampton* (1911), 188–202 · F. Ives Cater, 'Robert Browne's ancestors and descendants', *Transactions of the Congregational Historical Society*, 2 (1905–6), 151–9 · F. Ives Cater, 'The later years of Robert Browne', *Transactions of the Congregational Historical Society*, 3 (1907–8), 303–16 · C. Burrage, *Early English dissenters in the light of recent research*, 2 vols. (1912), 1.94–117 · HoP, *Commons, 1509–58*, 1.555–6 · S. Ofwod [S. Offwood], *An advertisement to Jhon Delecluse and Henry May the elder* [1632], 40
Wealth at death at least £240: *Writings*, ed. Peel and Carlson, 540–44

Browne [Brown], **Robert** (*bap.* 1672, *d.* 1753), history painter, the son of John and Diana Browne, was baptized in the parish church of Ottery St Mary, Devon, on 19 May 1672. By 1712 he was a student at Kneller's academy in Great Queen Street, London; there, under the tuition of Sir James Thornhill, he began to specialize in decorative painting in churches. Vertue, writing in 1720, includes 'Mr. Brown', with Thornhill himself, among the 'present History painters' working in the manner of Louis Laguerre (Vertue, 2.126). During 1715–21, when Thornhill was painting scenes from St Paul's life in grisaille around the interior of the dome and lantern of St Paul's Cathedral, Browne was his chief assistant, and is generally credited with having, through sheer presence of mind, saved Thornhill's life upon one occasion. Working on scaffolding high up under the dome, Thornhill stepped backwards to assess his work on one of the apostles, and might have fallen to his death had not Browne diverted him by dashing a brushful of colour across the apostle's face. 'Sir James ran hastily forward, crying out "Bless my soul, what have you done?" "I have saved your life!" replied his friend' (letter from Joseph Highmore to Sir Edward Walpole, 3 March 1764, in *GM*, 302).

Browne worked independently from about 1721, receiving commissions for work in several London churches, including St Botolph, Aldgate; St Andrew's, Holborn; and the chapel of St John, Bedford Row. The only surviving examples of such work are the monochrome spandrels in the nave of St Andrew Undershaft, now much obliterated. Browne designed the lower row of 7 foot high figures in the west window in the nave of Westminster Abbey, executed in stained glass by the younger William Price; unveiled in 1736, these survive. Horace Walpole noted that Browne was 'admired for his skill in painting crimson curtains, apostles, and stories out of the New Testament' (Walpole, 4.39). Browne is remembered now chiefly as the master of his nephew Francis Hayman (son of his elder sister, Jane), whom he accepted as an apprentice in 1718, for a fee of £84; the articles of apprenticeship describe Browne as 'citizen and history painter' (Index of apprentices), the 'citizen' status presumably relating to his membership of the Painter–Stainers' Company.

Several of Browne's works were engraved in mezzotint, including *The Annunciation* (by Valentine Green), *Salvator mundi* and *Precursor Domini* (by James McArdell), and a variant *Salvator mundi* (by John Faber). According to Walpole, Browne painted two signs for City of London taverns ('the Paul's head in Cateaton Street, and The Baptist's Head at the corner of Aldermanbury') that were 'much admired' (4.40). By the 1740s, his commissions for original work appear to have declined. In 1748–9 he repainted (for a fee of £42) Alexandre Souville's figures of the *Virtues* in the Paper Buildings, Inner Temple. In 1749 he was an unsuccessful applicant for the post of drawing master at Christ's Hospital (given to Alexander Cozens). Browne died on 26 December 1753, the *Gentleman's Magazine* recording his death as that of 'Mr. Robert Brown, history painter' (590).   JUDY EGERTON

Sources E. Croft-Murray, *Decorative painting in England, 1537–1837*, 1 (1962), 73–4, 263–4 · E. Croft-Murray, *Decorative painting in England, 1537–1837*, 2 (1970), 259 · Vertue, *Note books*, 2.126 · H. Walpole, *Anecdotes of painting in England: with some account of the principal artists*, ed. J. Dallaway, [rev. and enl. edn], 4 (1827), 39–40 · B. Allen, *Francis*

Hayman (1987), 2, 48–9 · H. Tapley-Soper, ed., *The register of baptisms, marriages and burials of the parish of Ottery St Mary, Devon, 1601–1837*, 2 vols., 1, Devon and Cornwall RS, 3 (1908–29), 1.38, 345, 351 · index of apprentices, 1710–62, GL, vol. 45, 7/13 · I. Bignamini, 'George Vertue, art historian, and art institutions in London, 1689–1768', *Walpole Society*, 54 (1988), 1–148, esp. 74, list 3/15 · *Daily Advertiser* [London] (8 March 1736) · GM, 1st ser., 86/1 (1816), 302 · mezzotint engravings after Browne, BM, department of prints and drawings · GM, 1st ser., 23 (1753), 590

Browne, Samuel (1574/5–1632), Church of England clergyman, was born in or near Shrewsbury, Shropshire, where his father was a burgess, perhaps the Thomas Browne (*d.* 1606?), draper, who used evangelical language in a letter to Queen Elizabeth; Samuel's baptismal name implies a firmly protestant family. He was educated first at Shrewsbury School, and later at St Paul's School, London, from where the Mercers' Company gave him an exhibition for part of his degree. He entered All Souls College, Oxford, as a servitor in 1594, aged nineteen, and matriculated on 28 November 1595, graduating BA in 1601 and proceeding MA in 1605, when he was also ordained by the bishop of Oxford. At an unknown date he married Martha (probably *née* Fluellin), with whom he had at least eight children.

On 2 April 1619 Browne was chosen as minister of the peculiar of St Mary's, Shrewsbury, by the bailiffs of the council. They were influenced by his predecessor, William Bright, who on his deathbed advised them to avoid choosing a nonconforming minister who would divide the town. Browne's theological interests were wide, embracing Thomas Aquinas as well as books by the Calvinists Francis Bunny and bishops Babington, Carleton, and Morton, and his stance was moderate. Although strongly Calvinistic in matters of faith, as is evident from his catechism on the Lord's prayer, *The Summe of the Christian Religion* (1630), he did not use his independent ecclesiastical jurisdiction to set up a presbyterian system of discipline. However, when Bishop Morton of Lichfield visited him as subject to his authority, Browne argued that he held a royal free chapel. When the bishop was reduced to quoting a decree of Pope Innocent in favour of episcopal jurisdiction, Browne diplomatically but firmly referred him to the bailiffs of the town, who silenced him by quoting Edward IV's pronouncement that such a claim was 'to the contempt, prejudice, and disinheritance of the Crowne of England' (Owen and Blakeway, 365). Browne changed ceremonial practice from taking down the communion rails for the eucharist and replacing them afterwards; rather, he had the chancel evenly paved and the communion table permanently railed there in 1621. His surplice was washed more frequently than his predecessor's, but both men were equally diligent in repairing church fabric, and ensuring the bells could be rung.

As public preacher of the town, Browne was remembered long afterwards 'by precise people' for his edifying and frequent preaching, and planned to publish some sermons (Wood, *Ath. Oxon.*, 2.531). Despite his diligence and good character he was opposed by nonconforming puritans in Shrewsbury, who, according to the Laudian polemicist Peter Studley, 'showed an insolent contempt of his talents and pains' (Studley, 180), and had set up a more radical lecture at St Alkmund's. Browne died in 1632, possibly from the plague sweeping the town at the time, and was buried on 6 May at St Mary's. He was survived by his wife and six of their children.   ELIZABETH ALLEN

Sources H. Owen and J. B. Blakeway, *A history of Shrewsbury*, 1 (1825), 365–6, 413 · PRO, PROB 11/161, fol. 23v [Browne's will] · Shrops. RRC, P257/B/3/1, fols. 231, 236–7, 243v, 278–279v · Foster, *Alum. Oxon.* · Shropshire Parish Register Society, 12 (1911), 59, 61, 65, 67–8, 76, 79, 81, 85 · Shropshire Parish Register Society, 15 (1913), 46 · P. Lake, 'Puritanism, Arminianism, and a Shropshire axe-murder', *Midland History*, 15 (1990), 37–64, esp. 46–7 · P. Studley, *The lookingglasse of schisme*, 2nd edn (1635), 180 · Wood, *Ath. Oxon.*, new edn, 2.531 · Oxf. dioc. MSS, Oxfordshire Archives, c264, fols. 12–14v · *Reg. Oxf.*, 2/2, 211 · E. Calvert, ed., *Shrewsbury School regestum scholarium, 1562–1635: admittances and readmittances* [1892], preface, 103 · M. McDonnell, ed., *The registers of St Paul's School, 1509–1748* (privately printed, London, 1977), 96–7 · Shrops. RRC, 3365/2590 (K2) · K. Fincham, *Prelate as pastor: the episcopate of James I* (1990), 233 · Shrops. RRC, 3365/68, fol. 41v · *Some account of the ancient and present state of Shrewsbury* (1808), 222

Browne, Sir Samuel (*b.* in or before **1598**, *d.* **1668**), politician and judge, was the son of Nicholas Browne, vicar of Polebrook, Northamptonshire and prebendary of Peterborough, and Frances, daughter of Thomas St John, third son of Oliver, Lord St John. He was admitted pensioner of Queens' College, Cambridge, on 24 February 1614 and entered Lincoln's Inn on 28 October 1616; he was called to the bar on 16 October 1623 and eventually elected reader in Michaelmas term 1642. About May 1629 he married Elizabeth, daughter of John Meade of Nortofts, Finchingfield, Essex.

Browne's renown derives less from his work as a jurist than from his astute performance as a parliamentary manager during the critical years of the English civil war. He was first elected to parliament in October 1641, representing part of Devon, and almost immediately assumed a leading role in close association with his cousin, Oliver St John, the future justice of common pleas during the interregnum. Though frequently associated with parliamentary radicals and their ideas, Browne, St John, and their associates were in fact political and religious moderates, committed to the preservation of England's constitutional monarchy, subject to the special limitations imposed in 1641, and to a tolerant, albeit Erastian, church settlement. They have been appropriately described as 'Royal Independents', because of their willingness vigorously to pursue military victory over Charles I in order to achieve these ends.

Browne's success as a parliamentary manager derived from his reputation as a man of genuine integrity. He was widely admired by moderates and radicals alike for his intelligence, his learning, and his consummate professionalism. It was doubtless that reputation (together with the influence of his patrons) which led to his appointment as a commissioner of the great seal in November 1643, a position he held until 1646. He was appointed to the committee to manage the impeachment of Archbishop Laud in March 1644 and took the lead in arguing successfully for Laud's attainder before the House of Lords the following January. In July 1645 he was appointed to chair the Commons committee investigating the so-called 'Savile affair', an accusation of high treason placed against leading moderates Denzil Holles and Bulstrode Whitelocke for their part in the Uxbridge negotiations. Browne pursued the accusation with considerable zeal in the face of substantial evidence that the charges were in fact insupportable. He appears to have acted largely as St John's agent, and in the pursuit of a personal vendetta against Denzil Holles, and his own reputation for fairness was to some extent compromised as a result.

None the less, in November 1647 Browne was chosen to draft articles and preconditions for further negotiations with the king and the following September was nominated by the lower house to treat with the king at Newport, Isle of Wight. The proposed settlement in 1648 included a wholesale reconstruction of the judiciary which envisaged Browne's appointment as chief baron of the exchequer. That plan had to be amended for political reasons, and he was eventually made serjeant-at-law and instead appointed justice of king's bench.

In matters of religion Browne was an Erastian presbyterian. He played a key role in fashioning the settlement of 1645–6, working successfully to reconcile the conflicting demands of presbyterians, Independents, and his own middle group colleagues. It was Browne who suggested the establishment of a standing committee of Lords and Commons to act as arbiters of religious offences, in place of lay county commissioners, and he himself was elected a parliamentary trier in October 1645.

The failure of the Newport negotiations and the resulting trial and execution of the king led Browne to resign his seat on the bench and withdraw from public life altogether during the interregnum. He was eventually elected MP for Bedford in 1659, and for Bedfordshire in 1660. He was knighted by Charles II and rewarded for his loyalty during the interregnum with reinstatement as serjeant-at-law in Trinity term 1660 and with elevation to the bench of common pleas in the Michaelmas term following. He served as justice in common pleas until his death in London on 11 April 1668. He was buried at Arlesey in Bedfordshire, where he lived.   JAMES S. HART JR

Sources DNB · Foss, *Judges*, vol. 7 · B. Whitelocke, *Memorials of English affairs*, new edn, 4 vols. (1853), vol. 1, pp. 457–81; vol. 2, p. 459 · diary of Sir Simonds D'Ewes, BL, Harleian MS 145, fol. 224v · *The journal of Sir Simonds D'Ewes from the first recess of the Long Parliament to the withdrawal of King Charles from London*, ed. W. H. Coates (1942) · *Mercurius Pragmaticus*, 17 (4–11 Jan 1648) · JHC, 4 (1644–6), 506, 511, 518 · JHC, 5 (1646–8), 248, 330, 370 · JHL, 10 (1647–8), 566, 570 · *The manuscripts of his grace the duke of Portland*, 10 vols., HMC, 29 (1891–1931), vol. 1, p. 593 · V. Pearl, 'The Royal Independents in the English civil wars', TRHS, 5th ser., 18 (1968), 69–96 · V. Pearl, 'Oliver St John and the "middle group" in the Long Parliament, August 1643 – May 1644', EngHR, 81 (1966), 490–519 · D. Underdown, *Pride's Purge: politics in the puritan revolution* (1971), 68, 72–3, 87, 104, 113, 203 · P. Crawford, 'The Savile affair', EngHR, 90 (1975), 76–93 · W. Palmer, *The political career of Oliver St John, 1637–1649* (1993), 64, 83, 93–4, 96–7 · B. Worden, *The Rump Parliament, 1648–1653* (1974), 179, 278 · M. W. Helms and L. Naylor, 'Browne, Samuel I', HoP, *Commons, 1660–90*
Likenesses J. M. Wright, oils, Lincoln's Inn, London
Wealth at death considerable wealth: Helms and Naylor, 'Browne, Samuel I'

Browne [Broun], **Samuel** (*bap.* **1611**, *d.* **1665**), printer, was baptized on 16 November 1611 in St Dunstan-in-the-West, Middlesex, the youngest son of John Browne (*d.* 1622), bookseller, and his wife, Alice. Apprenticed to the London bookseller Humphrey Robinson on 1 August 1627, he was sworn in as a freeman of the Stationers' Company on 3 June 1633, and elected to the company's livery on 1 June 1640. Entries in Frankfurt book fair catalogues suggest he was already dealing in books on the continent by 1631, possibly as an apprentice to William Fitzer, publisher of Harvey's *Circulation of the Blood* (Frankfurt, 1628). In 1636 William Laud sent Browne to Leiden to buy oriental type for the Oxford University Press, for which 2300 guilders were paid.

On 15 April 1639 Browne married Jeanne Hall (*b.* 1616), daughter of Nathaniel Hall. In the same year he opened a bookshop in St Paul's Churchyard, first under the sign of the Fountain and then at the White Lion and Ball, and started publishing books: his first endeavour, a reissue of an edition of Herodian's *Historiae*, originally published by Fitzer in 1627 and 1630, is evidence of his continental contacts and interests. Subsequent publications included the first English edition of Jean Ogier de Gombauld's *Endimion* (1639); the second part of the *Cid* in Joseph Rutter's translation, commissioned by Charles I (1640); the collected sermons of royal chaplain Isaac Ambrose, illustrated by Wenceslaus Hollar (1640); and sermons by Thomas Morton, bishop of Durham (1642).

Browne's career came to a temporary halt during the first civil war, in which he may have fought on the king's side. His goods were sequestrated by parliament in 1643, after which 'ever avoyding any compliance with any power in England since the Surrender of Oxford', he found himself 'necessitated to reside in fforaigne parts' (PRO, SP 29/2/94, fols. 25–6). In 1646, he escaped to the Netherlands, together with his wife, their daughter Alice, and his brother Thomas; he set up shop in The Hague, where in January 1647 he signed a lease on a house adjacent to the English church. In 1648 he moved to another property, where he opened his English Printing-House, and from 1651 onwards he occupied a stall in the Great Hall on the Binnenhof.

Working as a printer now as well as continuing as a publisher, Browne soon established himself as the most important distributor of royalist news and propaganda within the exile community on the continent, producing in 1649 alone more than thirty pamphlets and newspapers discussing political events in the British Isles. He took up the printing of the *Eikon basilike* as soon as the book was banned in England, having secured the exclusive rights in the Netherlands for all Latin, French, Dutch, and English editions. These activities must have been well known to his London colleagues, for they used his name or initials in their false imprints of the *Eikon*, suggesting their books were printed in The Hague and then smuggled into England. Between 1649 and 1652 Browne dominated the Dutch market for English news, selling newspapers—both his own publications and those imported from London—to the Dutch authorities on a regular basis. He translated English royalist pamphlets into Dutch, and his outspoken prefaces show how hard he tried to influence public opinion in favour of the royalist party.

In January 1651, in line with their neutrality politics, the Dutch states general issued a general ban on publications discussing foreign states or governments. Two months later Browne was summoned to the court of Holland on account of a controversial pamphlet which he had published anonymously, and in which he rhetorically questioned the legitimacy of the 'murderous mock-parliament' (*Vrage ofte Meer behouden*, 1651, fol. 1). Although he was sentenced to a heavy fine and banishment from the province of Holland, he remained in The Hague, occasionally even employed by the states general as a translator.

Through his brother Thomas, personal chaplain to princess royal Mary Stuart, Browne was closely connected to English court circles in The Hague. He supplied the exiled king with books, and he printed sermons preached by Anglican divines for Mary and Charles II in The Hague and Breda. Between 1649 and 1654 he published several books written by eminent churchmen in exile such as John Bramhall, Richard Watson, and Isaac Basire, as well as royalist plays, for instance William Cavendish's *The Country Captaine* (1649), which was performed at Mary's court. In 1651 he produced Nathaniel Highmore's handsomely illustrated *Corporis humani disquisitio*, dedicated to Highmore's friend and mentor William Harvey—the first book to incorporate Harvey's ideas and discoveries. Browne's shop, where, according to a parliamentary spy in 1651, 'daily a little Exchange [is] held, of Romance news', and where many would gather to catch up on the latest news from England—often commented upon by the 'bold Bookseller, sometime a Captain under the late King'—was well known within the royalist exile community (*Mercurius Politicus*, 637). It was often used as a postal address for letters and money sent to and from England.

In November 1655 Browne moved to Heidelberg where, as printer to the recently reopened university, he specialized in academic publications for the next five years. His brother looked after business in The Hague until 1659, when Browne signed a partnership with his son-in-law Joannes de L'Escluse. After the Restoration, Browne returned to England, where he asked Charles II in May 1660 for a compensation for his sufferings, and applied for a loan from the Stationers' Company to bring over his printing materials from the Netherlands. Imprints between 1660 and 1663 alternately show a Hague, Heidelberg, and London address, the last at the sign of Queen's Arms in St Paul's Churchyard. In August 1665 'Mr. Brown, once a bookseller at the Hague … died at the Pest house' (Ellis, 66). He was buried on 21 September 1665 'at the Upper end of the North Isle' in the church of St Christopher-le-Stocks (parish register). On 2 October the administration of his estate was granted to Anna Sawtell alias Browne.　　　　　　　　　MARIKA KEBLUSEK

Sources M. Keblusek, 'Boekverkoper in ballingschap: Samuel Browne, boekverkoper/drukker te Londen, 's-Gravenhage en Heidelberg 1633–1665', MA diss., University of Leiden, 1989 • E. Weil, 'Samuel Browne, printer to the University of Heidelberg, 1655–1662', *The Library*, 5th ser., 5 (1950–51), 14–26 • papers, Stationers' Company, Stationers' Hall, London • STC, 1475–1640 • Wing, STC • parish register, Middlesex, St Dunstan-in-the-West, 16 Nov 1611 [baptism] • parish register, London, St Bartholomew-the-Less, 15 April 1639 [marriage] • parish register, Middlesex, St Christopher-le-Stocks, 21 Sept 1665 [burial] • Municipal Archives, The Hague, Notarial papers • National Archives, The Hague, Court of Holland Archives • PRO, State papers domestic (1660–61), SP 29 • University Archives, Heidelberg • Bodl. Oxf., Clarendon MSS • F. F. Madan, *A new bibliography of the Eikon basilike of King Charles the First* (1950) • *Mercurius Politicus* (27 Feb–6 March 1651) • *The obituary of Richard Smyth … being a catalogue of all such persons as he knew in their life*, ed. H. Ellis, CS, 44 (1849), 66 • administration, PRO, PROB 6/40, fol. 121r
Wealth at death see administration, PRO, PROB 6/40, fol. 121r

Browne, Samuel (*d.* 1698), botanist, was a surgeon employed by the East India Company and stationed at Fort St George, Madras. He sent a series of collections of dried plants, collected near Madras by himself and by agents further afield, along with their Indian names and uses, to England. There they were described by James Petiver, and published in the *Philosophical Transactions* in a series of papers in vols. 20 (1698) and 23 (1703). Browne also collected plants on his journey to India and was sent material from China and Ceylon. Petiver's plants passed into the hands of Sir Hans Sloane, and were subsequently incorporated into the herbarium of the Natural History Museum. Petiver praised Browne's indefatigable industry and from the notes on his herbarium specimens it is clear that he was a keen observer and well versed in the literature of his time. Browne died at Fort St George on 22 September 1698.　　　　　　B. D. JACKSON, rev. P. E. KELL

Sources R. Pulteney, *Historical and biographical sketches of the progress of botany in England*, 2 (1790), 38–9, 62 • J. Britten and J. E. Dandy, eds., *The Sloane herbarium* (1958), 99–102 • Desmond, *Botanists*, rev. edn
Archives BL, Sloane MSS, accounts of his sixth book of East Indian plants; letter to G. J. Camellus, 1699; letters to James Petiver, 1698

Browne, Sir Samuel James (1824–1901), army officer, was born on 3 October 1824 in India, a son of John Browne of the East India Company's medical service and his wife, Charlotte Isabella, daughter of Captain S. Swinton RN. After education in England he returned to India in 1840, joining the 46th Bengal native infantry as an ensign. During the Second Anglo-Sikh War, Browne was present at the cavalry action at Ramnagar on 22 November 1848, at the passage of the River Chenab on 1 December by Sir Joseph Thackwell, and at the battle of Sadulapur (a few miles north of the River Chenab) on 3 December. He later took part in the battles at Chilianwala on 13 January 1849 and at Gujrat on 21 February, receiving the medal and clasp for his services. After the campaign he was selected

Sir Samuel James Browne (1824–1901), by unknown photographer, 1860

by Sir Henry Lawrence for the newly raised Punjab frontier force. He raised the 2nd Punjab irregular cavalry which became, in 1927, Sam Browne's cavalry (12th frontier force). Browne was promoted captain on 10 February 1855, and from 1851 to 1863 he was adjutant and later commanding officer of the 2nd Punjab cavalry. He served mainly on the Punjab north-west frontier, and was engaged in numerous operations against the Pathans.

During the Indian mutiny Browne commanded the 2nd Punjab cavalry at the siege of Lucknow in 1858, and after the capture of the city formed part of the movable column, under Sir James Hope Grant, which defeated the rebels on numerous occasions in 1858. With 230 sabres of his regiment and 350 native infantry Browne made a surprise attack on the rebels at Sirpur in the Adilabad district of Hyderabad at daybreak on 31 August 1858. Attacking from the enemy's rear, he charged them almost single-handed and prevented their gunners from reloading and firing on the advancing infantry. In this hand-to-hand fight his left arm was severed; he was also twice wounded in the knee. For this act of gallantry he was awarded the Victoria Cross in 1861.

As a result of the loss of his left arm Browne invented a belt to balance the carrying of his sword; it was later called the Sam Browne belt and was widely used. The original belt is displayed in the Indian Army Room at Sandhurst. Browne, who was thrice mentioned in dispatches, received the thanks of the commander-in-chief and the government of India. He had already been given the brevet rank of major on 20 July 1858, and on 26 April 1859 he was promoted lieutenant-colonel. In 1860 he married

Lucy, daughter of R. C. Sherwood MD of the East India Company's medical service. On 17 November 1864 Browne attained the rank of colonel, and was given command of the Guides. On 6 February 1870 he was promoted major-general, and in 1875 was chosen to represent the Indian army during the Indian tour of the prince of Wales. In 1876 he was made KCSI, and became lieutenant-general on 1 October 1877.

From 9 August to 5 November 1878 Browne was military member of the governor-general's council, and as such was concerned with the preparations for the Afghan war in 1878–9. He knew from experience the character of the Afghans, and he told the viceroy, Lord Lytton, of the immense difficulties that a British invasion of Afghanistan involved. His advice, however, was disregarded, and it was only reluctantly that the viceroy acceded to the insistent demands of Browne and Sir Frederick Haines, the commander-in-chief, for reinforcements for the Kandahar field force. Browne himself was given command of the 1st division of the Peshawar field force, with orders to force the Khyber Pass, which was strongly held by the Afghans. His progress was much hampered by the inefficiency of the commissariat, transport, and hospital arrangements, but on 21 November 1878, by a skilful turning movement, he captured with little loss the fortress of Ali Masjid, together with thirty-two guns. Little opposition was offered to his subsequent advance, and Jalalabad was occupied on 20 December. Browne however had much difficulty in keeping his communications open, and had to send for further reinforcements.

The magnitude of Browne's task was increased by his ignorance of Lord Lytton's policy; nor was he allowed to exercise the political power with which he had been invested. Further advance was hindered by the threatening attitude of the Khyber people. After consultation with Sir Frederick Haines, Browne was ordered to prepare a scheme for an advance on Kabul. This report, which was sent to the viceroy in April 1879, amounted to a demonstration of the impossibility of the undertaking, but did not shake Lord Lytton's determination to bring the war to an end by the capture of Kabul. Meanwhile the victory of General Sir Charles Gough at Fatehabad on 2 April 1879 enabled Browne to occupy Gandamak. On the withdrawal of British troops from Afghanistan, Lord Lytton, despite the protests of Sir Frederick Haines, blamed Browne for the failure of his transport service, although that was mainly due to inadequate preparations by the government. Browne was not reappointed military member of the council, and was relegated to the command of the Lahore district. Nevertheless he was made a KCB in 1879, and received the thanks of the government of India and both houses of parliament. He retired from active service shortly afterwards.

Browne was promoted general on 1 December 1888 and made a GCB in 1891. After his retirement he resided at The Wood, Ryde, Isle of Wight, where he died on 14 March 1901, survived by his wife. After cremation his remains were buried at Ryde. [ANON.], *rev.* JAMES LUNT

Sources W. Blackwood, *The journal of Sir Sam Browne* (1937) · *The Times* (15 March 1901) · *The Times* (19 March 1901) · *Army and Navy Gazette* (16 March 1901) · W. H. Paget, *A record of the expeditions against the north-west frontier tribes, since the annexation of the Punjab*, rev. A. H. Mason (1884) · J. W. Kaye and G. B. Malleson, *Kaye's and Malleson's History of the Indian mutiny of 1857–8*, new edn, 6 vols. (1897–8) · Lord Roberts [F. S. Roberts], *Forty-one years in India*, 30th edn (1898) · W. H. Russell, *The prince of Wales's tour* (1877) · G. J. Younghusband, *The story of the Guides* (1908) · H. B. Hanna, *The Second Afghan War*, 3 vols. (1899–1910) · B. Robson, *The road to Kabul: the Second Afghan War, 1878–1881* (1986) · R. S. Rait, *The life of Field-Marshal Sir Frederick Paul Haines* (1911) · *CGPLA Eng. & Wales* (1901)
Archives NAM, diary · NAM, family papers and letters | NL Wales, letter to Johnes family
Likenesses photograph, 1860, BL OIOC [*see illus.*] · C. K. Robertson, portrait, 1904 · J. Hughes, photograph, NAM · C. Vivian, portrait, East India Club, 16 St James's Square, London · portrait, repro. in Roberts, *Forty-one years in India*, vol. 1, p. 409 · wood-engravings, repro. in *ILN* (1876–9)
Wealth at death £564 8s. 3d.: probate, 25 April 1901, *CGPLA Eng. & Wales*

Browne, Dame **Sidney Jane** (1850–1941), nurse, was born on 5 January 1850 in Bexley, Kent, one of the four children of Benjamin Stocks Browne and his wife, Jane Sidney, formerly Deane. Sidney grew up in a medical family: her father was a surgeon and her two brothers were doctors. She was educated at home, and when she was twenty-eight started nursing at the Guest Hospital, Dudley, before transferring in 1879 to the West Bromwich District Hospital to undertake a formal three-year training. As a qualified nurse she worked briefly at St Bartholomew's Hospital, London, before joining the army nursing service in 1883. While at St Bartholomew's she was influenced by the matron, Ethel Manson (later Mrs Bedford Fenwick), who believed that nursing was a profession and should command professional education and status.

As an army sister Browne was posted to the Royal Victoria Hospital, Netley. At this time the army nursing service consisted of about twenty sisters, and their role was ill-defined. In peacetime they were responsible for the nursing in the large military hospitals, but their small number meant that the nursing work was done by orderlies with the sisters acting as superintendents. Between 1885 and 1899 Browne held a series of increasingly responsible positions in the army nursing service, which included active service in the Sudan wars, for which she was awarded the khedive's star and the Egyptian medal and bar. She served at the military hospitals at Woolwich, Malta, and Curragh Camp, Ireland, and at the Herbert Hospital, Woolwich. With the outbreak of the Second South African War in October 1899 she was ordered to South Africa and served for three years as superintending sister at three different base hospitals. Following severe criticism of the War Office's handling of the medical services during the war, fundamental reforms were introduced. One of these was the establishment of a proper army nursing service, to be known as Queen Alexandra's Imperial Military Nursing Service. Browne was recalled to England to take up the position of matron-in-chief of the new service. For her service in South Africa she was awarded the Royal Red Cross.

Dame Sidney Jane Browne (1850–1941), by Langfier

By the standards of the War Office, Browne had advanced ideas about the status of nurses. As matron-in-chief she worked for the establishment of the new service on professional lines and argued successfully for members of the service to hold officer rank. Against strong disapproval from the traditional Royal Army Medical Corps, she introduced a new system for the training of the nursing orderlies, transferring their training from the medical staff to the nursing sisters. When she retired in 1906, at the age of fifty-five in accordance with army regulations, the number of nurses in the service stood at 400. Two years later she was closely involved in another army reform, the establishment of the Territorial Force Nursing Service. With her good friend Elisabeth Haldane, sister of R. B. Haldane, secretary of state for war, she worked with the War Office to establish this reserve of trained civilian nurses who would serve in military hospitals at home in the event of war. The success of the service relied on the recruitment of civilian nurses; helped by the mood of the time, nurses responded to the opportunity to take an active part in the defence of their country. When the First World War started in 1914, Browne was responsible for the mobilization of the service and also for its rapid expansion from 3000 members to over 7000 strong, with approximately 25 per cent of its members serving at the war front. As matron-in-chief she travelled all around the country and abroad, under wartime conditions, inspecting the living and working conditions of the nurses.

Throughout the war there was a shortage of trained

nurses, and the issue of how to control the use of untrained volunteer nurses in the military hospitals was of great concern to trained nurses. Browne played a key role in mediating between the establishment and the profession. She had been a supporter of the campaign for state registration for trained nurses since qualifying and was an active member of the various associations set up to promote the cause. As a result of the war, the balance of opinion among trained nurses shifted in favour of registration and the College of Nursing was founded to provide a uniform standard of training and examination. Browne became a member of the college, and her administrative experience and financial abilities were of great value to the new organization. She became the first president and the first nurse honorary treasurer of the college.

Browne's contribution to the great channelling of women's energy during the war was recognized at the Exhibition of Women's War Work, organized by the Imperial War Museum in 1918, where her portrait hung beside those of Dr Garrett Anderson and Dr Flora Murray. She received many tributes for her war work, including a bar to her Royal Red Cross and her appointment as DBE; the University of Leeds awarded her an honorary nursing diploma, the League of Red Cross Societies awarded her the international Florence Nightingale medal, and she was the first woman to receive the freedom of the city of West Bromwich.

After the war Browne retired from many of the offices she held, including the position of matron-in-chief and that of British representative of Lady Minto's Indian Nursing Association. She continued to play an active role in the College of Nursing until she left London in 1927. The rest of her life was spent in Cheltenham with her longstanding friend Hilda Hoole. When she died, at 11 Tivoli Road, Cheltenham, on 13 August 1941, at the age of ninety-one, she was described as the 'modern Florence Nightingale'. The funeral, which was held on 16 August at St Stephen's Church, Cheltenham, where she was buried, was of a semi-military character. A Red Cross flag, which had flown over the army sisters' quarters at Springfontein, covered her coffin.   SUSAN McGANN

Sources Royal College of Nursing Archives, Edinburgh, Sidney Browne MSS · military nursing establishment, nursing sisters nominal rolls, 1861–91, PRO, WO 25/3955 · QARANC Museum, Aldershot, Sidney Browne MSS · QAIMNS register, 1903–26, PRO, WO 25/3956 · reorganization of the royal army medical corps and nursing services, corresp. and papers, 1901, PRO, WO 30/114 · advisory board for army medical services, reports on military hospitals in Great Britain, 1902–4, PRO, WO 30/133 · S. Browne, 'Army nursing', *The science and art of nursing* (1910), vol. 1, pp. 149–67 · S. Browne, 'Women's work in the war, I', *The Times history of the war* (1918), vol. 4, pp. 241–80 · S. Browne, 'Women's work, III: war services', *The Times history of the war* (1918), vol. 17, pp. 433–64 · *Nursing Times* (23 Aug 1941) · S. McGann, 'The battle of the nurses', *Sidney Browne: a great matron-in-chief* (1992), 80–101 · b. cert. · d. cert.
Archives Queen Alexandra's Royal Army Nursing Corps Museum, Aldershot, MSS · Royal College of Nursing, Edinburgh, archives, MSS | NL Scot., letters to Lord Haldane
Likenesses three photographs, 1901–22, Royal College of Nursing, archives · Langfier, photograph, NPG [*see illus.*] · photographs,

Queen Alexandra's Royal Army Nursing Corps Museum, Aldershot
Wealth at death £1234 2s. 9d.: probate, 1941

Browne, Simon (*c.*1680–1732), dissenting minister and religious controversialist, was born of unknown parents in Shepton Mallet, Somerset, where his education began under John Cumming, the pastor of the local congregation. He completed it at the academy of John Moore, dissenting minister, in Bridgwater, and started to preach before he was twenty. He was minister first in Portsmouth and then to the Old Jewry congregation in London, where he moved in 1716. After publishing some of his sermons separately, he collected others in a volume printed in 1722. Two essays as well as his *Hymns and Spiritual Songs* had already appeared. He was involved in the Salters' Hall controversy (1719) between advocates of subscription to the doctrine of the Trinity and the majority who, like Browne himself, objected to such a constraint even though they held the Trinitarian doctrine. The controversy incited further polemic between him and Thomas Reynolds, a leading defender of subscription, in 1723.

For reasons that remain uncertain, a sudden depression drove Browne to abandon the ministry later that year. In a funeral sermon Anthony Atkey cited 'a complicated domestic affliction', which other sources specify as the death of Browne's wife and only son. Unless the circumstances of this loss inspired guilt, however, it would not explain his conviction that his creator had begun to destroy the 'thinking substance' in him (Hawkesworth, 2.93). Another cause may have been Browne's supposed encounter with a highwayman near Shepton Mallet. When challenged by the highwayman, the minister threw him down on the ground, only to discover that he had killed him. The shame of violating the fifth commandment might have unbalanced him but no evidence other than oral tradition confirms the incident.

Browne's congregation regretted his departure so greatly that they waited two years before appointing another pastor to replace him. He struggled to convince his friends that he had really lost his mind as his attempts to prove his loss of rationality actually demonstrated the contrary. He attributed their doubts that he was speaking the truth to God's anger with him. In his writings he insisted that the loss of his mind had deprived him of the very means to worship God. Eventually, however, his distraction changed to melancholy and he withdrew his opposition to his friends' praying for him, provided they acknowledged his loss of reason. Urged to say grace before a dinner, he refused several times, but finally did say one imploring God's mercy for himself. When confronted with a contradiction between his obsession and a principle in which he believed, he would react with silent perplexity.

Browne's friends claimed that his intellectual powers had actually increased after his bout of depression. After returning to Shepton Mallet he wrote books for children, a grammar and spelling manual, translated Latin and Greek poetry, collected fables, and compiled an abstract of the Bible and a dictionary of classical themes. None of these works is extant. Later, he defended Christian orthodoxy in three works published in 1732. *A Fit Rebuke to a Ludicrous Infidel* answers the *Fifth Discourse*, on the question of resurrection, by the freethinker, Thomas Woolston (although in his preface Browne deplored the civil prosecution of Woolston for blasphemy). In *A Defence of the Religion of Nature and the Christian Revelation* Browne refuted Matthew Tindal's separation of nature and revelation in *Christianity as Old as Creation*. Browne's friends persuaded him to withdraw from publication a dedication to Queen Caroline in which he describes his degradation and implores her prayers on his behalf. His *Sober … Disquisition Concerning … the Trinity* relies on traditional apologetic arguments.

Browne's monomania continued for the last nine years of his life, during which time he refused to take physical exercise, and suffered mortification of his leg, from which he died in 1732 at Shepton Mallet. He was buried in the meeting-house at Shepton Mallet and was survived by several of his daughters. WILLIAM H. TRAPNELL

Sources A. Atkey, *The rectitude of providence under the severest dispensations: a funeral sermon on the late Revd Simon Browne … (1733)* · *Protestant Dissenter's Magazine*, 4–5 (1797–8) · W. Wilson, *The history and antiquities of the dissenting churches and meeting houses in London, Westminster and Southwark*, 4 vols. (1808–14), vols. 1–2 · *Town and Country Magazine*, 2 (1770), 689–93 · J. Hawkesworth and others, *The adventurer*, rev. edn, 2 vols. (1771) · A. Kippis and others, eds., *Biographia Britannica, or, The lives of the most eminent persons who have flourished in Great Britain and Ireland*, 2nd edn, 3–4 (1784–9) · *GM*, 1st ser., 32 (1762), 453–5 · *DNB*

Archives BL, corresp. and papers, Add. MS 4367

Browne, Stanley George (1907–1986), leprologist and medical missionary, was born on 8 December 1907 at 77 Bousefield Road, New Cross, London, the second of the five children of Arthur Browne (1874–1967), Post Office clerk, and his wife, Edith Lillywhite (1887–1927). His formal instruction started when, after much pleading, he entered Waller Road elementary school, New Cross, at the age of three. In 1919 Browne left to continue his education at Brockley central school, but, because of the prolonged illness of his father, he left here in 1923 and obtained the post of junior clerk in the town clerk's department at Deptford town hall. He studied at night school and passed matriculation in the first division in June 1926. Browne was awarded one of the first London county council (LCC) non-vocational scholarships in 1927 and entered King's College, London, the following autumn. His two-year scholarship was extended to three, which enabled him to follow a medical course, and he obtained a further LCC scholarship which enabled him to complete his medical studies, qualifying MB, BS, at London University in 1933. Browne won many prizes during his medical education and also took the theology course available to students who were not studying divinity; he passed as an associate of King's College with first-class honours. He became a member of the Royal College of Physicians in 1934 and a fellow of the Royal College of Surgeons in 1935.

Browne spoke fluent French and, in 1936, after obtaining the diploma in tropical medicine from the Institut de Médecine Tropicale Prince Léopold, Antwerp, he joined

Stanley George Browne (1907–1986), by Elliott & Fry, 1956

the staff of the Baptist Missionary Society hospital at Yakusu in the Belgian Congo. As well as his duties in the hospital he undertook the training of the African *infirmiers*, or medical auxiliaries, and carried out disease surveys in outlying areas, where he discovered that the incidence of leprosy was extremely high. He also undertook missionary duties. Browne returned to Britain on leave in 1939 and, just before his return to Africa in 1940, he met his future wife, Ethel Marion Williamson (b. 1912), known to her family as Mali, a teacher, and the daughter of the general foreign secretary of the Baptist Missionary Society. Browne returned to Yakusu in April 1940 where he was joined by Ethel; they married on 15 November 1940 and their three sons were all born in Africa.

When he was in England on furlough Browne continued preaching in chapels all over the country. Soon after his return to Yakusu a leprosarium was opened nearby at Yalisombo. Because of the painful and unreliable treatment with chaulmoogra oil, along with food shortages in the settlement, the leprosarium had an uncertain beginning; but the American Mission to Lepers sent out a new drug, diasone, for Browne to try, which proved more effective. In 1954 he also worked on the increasing rate of onchocerciasis, or river blindness, and the control of its vector, the blackfly *Simulium damnosum*, whose larval stage he discovered. The leprosarium at Yalisombo became internationally known and Browne was urged to concentrate on leprosy by the distinguished leprologist Robert Cochrane, a suggestion which was opposed by some who interpreted medical and missionary policy differently, and by others out of professional jealousy.

After his return on leave to England in 1958 Browne resigned from the Baptist Missionary Society and the following year he was invited by the Nigerian government to become senior leprologist at the Leprosy Research Unit, Uzuakoli in eastern Nigeria. There he continued his work with trials of new drugs, in particular B663 (subsequently called clofazimine), and maintained his lecturing and preaching. During 1963 sponsorship by the World Health

Organization enabled him to visit leprosy research centres throughout the world. He was invited to be chairman of the working group on the treatment of leprosy at the International Congress on Leprosy at Rio de Janeiro in 1963, and was asked to advise on the establishment of the All Africa Leprosy Training and Rehabilitation Centre. He recommended its placement at Addis Ababa.

During these years Browne published extensively in both English and French on leprosy, onchocerciasis, and other tropical diseases, as well as on medical ethics. At the beginning of 1966, in succession to Robert Cochrane, he took up the appointment of director of the Leprosy Study Centre, London, and remained in the post until the centre's closure in 1980. Browne campaigned against the stigma attached to the disease, and it was in part as a result of his efforts that the Mission to Lepers changed its name to the Leprosy Mission. He was awarded many international prizes and honours both for his work on leprosy and for his missionary activities, and was visiting lecturer on leprosy to hospitals throughout the world. He was appointed OBE in 1965 and the CMG in 1976, as well as receiving Belgian honours. He was president of the Royal Society of Tropical Medicine and Hygiene from 1977 to 1979, and president of the Baptist Union from 1980 to 1981. Browne's manner demonstrated great warmth and friendliness to all and he had the gift of making others feel that what they did was of great value.

Browne made a visit to China soon after receiving treatment for cancer of the larynx. He died suddenly at his home, 16 Bridgefield Road, Sutton, Surrey, on 29 January 1986, from a ruptured aorta; his funeral took place at Sutton Baptist Church on 11 February 1986, and he was cremated. He was survived by his wife.   MARY E. GIBSON

Sources P. Thompson, *Mister Leprosy* (1980) • *WWW* • Munk, *Roll* • S. Duncan and P. Duncan, *Bonganga: experiences of a missionary doctor* (1958) • *Transactions of the Royal Society of Tropical Medicine and Hygiene*, 80 (1986), 496 • *BMJ* (15 Feb 1986), 491 • memorial and resolution of the Baptist Missionary Society, 18/3/1986 • private information (2004)
Archives London School of Hygiene and Tropical Medicine, lecture notes and papers relating to leprosy • priv. coll. • Wellcome L., papers
Likenesses Elliott & Fry, photograph, 1956, NPG [*see illus.*] • group portrait, coloured photograph (with family), repro. in N. Martin, *Battle against leprosy: story of Stanley Browne* (1985) • photograph, repro. in *Record of presidents of the Royal Society of Tropical Medicine and Hygiene* • photograph, repro. in *Transactions of the Royal Society* • photograph, repro. in *BMJ* • photographs, repro. in N. Martin, *Battle against leprosy: story of Stanley Browne* (1985)
Wealth at death £59,246: probate, 9 May 1986, *CGPLA Eng. & Wales*

Browne, (Frances Worsley) Stella (1880–1955), feminist and abortion law reformer, was born at Halifax, Nova Scotia, Canada, on 9 May 1880, elder daughter of Daniel Marshall Browne RN (1843–1883) and his second wife, Anna Dulcibella Mary Dodwell (1848–1919). Her father drowned on duty with the Canadian marine when she was three.

Related, through her mother's sister's marriage to Sir Alexander Siemens, to the Anglo-German engineering dynasty, Stella Browne was educated partly in Germany, and at St Felix School, Southwold. She attended Somerville College, Oxford, from 1899 to 1902, achieving second-class honours in modern history. A teaching career ended when her health broke down from strain and privation. From 1907 to 1912 she was librarian at Morley College in south London. From 1912 she seems to have supported herself (rather precariously) by reviewing, journalism, translating, and lecturing, eked out by occasional clerical jobs.

Stella Browne participated in the famous *Freewoman* debate of 1912 on chastity and sexual desire in women, and corresponded with Havelock Ellis from 1914 until his death in 1938. She was active in the British Society for the Study of Sex Psychology. The papers she gave to the society, entitled 'The sexual variety and variability among women and their bearing upon social reconstruction' (1915; published, 1917) and 'Studies in female inversion' (1918; published, 1923), emphasized the need for women to speak about their own experiences. In both principle and practice Stella was a convinced believer in free love, known to have had various lovers, certainly some male, and possibly some female, though these cannot be reliably identified. She translated and annotated significant works of continental sexology including Van de Velde's *Ideal Marriage* (1928) and *Fertility and Sterility in Marriage* (1931), F. Muller-Lyer's *Marriage* (1931), and Max Hodann's *History of Modern Morals* (1937). She also translated German poetry, including that of Otto Braun (published in an English translation of Braun's *Autobiography*, 1924).

Stella Browne's vigorous support for birth control (well predating the First World War) and abortion (her earliest published statement dates from 1915), largely conducted through the auspices of the Malthusian League, was part of a wide-ranging agenda of feminist and socialist reform. She desired to place in women's own hands the means to control their fertility, while also working to relieve the stigma on illegitimacy. In evidence to the interdepartmental (Birkett) committee on abortion in 1937, she courageously revealed that if abortion 'was necessarily fatal or injurious, I should not be here before you' (B. Brookes, *Abortion in England, 1900–1967*, 1988, 122).

Stella Browne was also involved with other organizations, including the Women's Social and Political Union, the Divorce Law Reform Union, the No-Conscription Fellowship, the Humanitarian League, and the Federation of Progressive Societies and Individuals. She was an early member of the British Communist Party and was also active in the Chelsea branch of the Labour Party and the Fabian Society. Though often alleged to have been a eugenicist she repeatedly criticized the criteria of 'fitness' propounded by the Eugenics Society. However, she did join the society for a short period (1938–42), probably to represent the interests of the Abortion Law Reform Association of which she was a founder (1936).

In her later years, with sight deteriorating and other health problems, Stella Browne lived with her younger sister (Alice) Sylvia Lemira Browne in Liverpool, far from comrades in the struggle. Stella none the less remained actively in touch and constantly wrote to the press to keep alive the issue of legalizing abortion. Her associates regularly described her as 'indomitable'.

Stella Browne died from heart disease during the night of 8 May 1955 at her home, 39 Hawarden Avenue, Sefton Park, Liverpool. She was cremated and her ashes scattered on 11 May at Landican cemetery, Birkenhead, where a memorial plaque to her was later erected. The campaigns she fought for seemed at the time to be in eclipse; twelve years later, however, the Abortion Law Reform Association was instrumental in aiding the passage of David Steel's act of 1967, which did not, however, go as far as Stella Browne would have wished in leaving the decision entirely to the woman concerned. Her writings remain of considerable pertinence to feminist debates.

LESLEY A. HALL

Sources S. Rowbotham, *A new world for women: Stella Browne, socialist feminist* (1977) · private information (2004) · BL, Havelock Ellis MSS · Wellcome L. · Public Archives of Nova Scotia · d. cert. **Archives** BL, letters to Havelock Ellis, Add. MS 70539 · L. Cong., Margaret Sanger MSS · Ransom HRC, British Society for the Study of Sex Psychology MSS · Smith College, Massachusetts, Sophia Smith collection · Wellcome L., Abortion Law Reform Association **Likenesses** group photograph, *c.*1923 (with Bertrand Russell and Dora Russell), International Institute for Social History, Amsterdam, Dora Russell MSS · photograph (aged *c.*fifty-eight), repro. in Rowbotham, *New world for women*

Browne, Sir Stewart Gore- (1883–1967), settler and politician in Northern Rhodesia, was born in London on 3 May 1883, the elder son of the barrister Sir Francis Gore-Browne (1860–1922), and his wife, Helenor (*b.* 1858), elder daughter of John Archibald Shaw-Stewart. His grandfather Sir Thomas Gore *Browne had been governor of New Zealand and Tasmania. After attending Wixenford preparatory school, Wokingham (1892–7), he was educated at Harrow School for three years, and passed into the Royal Military Academy at Woolwich in 1900. He was commissioned into the Royal Field Artillery, and in 1902–4 did survey work in Natal. Back in England, he took up motor-racing at Brooklands, on the track laid out by his uncle, Hugh Locke King. In 1911 he went to Northern Rhodesia on an Anglo-Belgian boundary commission. Here, he decided, he could fulfil his boyhood ambition to own an estate, and perpetuate the sort of patrician regime which seemed threatened in Britain. On his way home in April 1914 he found the site he sought, beside a lake called Shiwa Ngandu, among the Bemba people in the north-east of the country.

During the First World War, Gore-Browne served on the western front, reaching the rank of lieutenant-colonel. He proved a highly effective staff officer; during the battle of the Somme his skill in liaison with regimental officers was especially valued. He was awarded the DSO and twice mentioned in dispatches. In 1920 he retired from the army and returned to Northern Rhodesia, settling at Shiwa Ngandu where, with hundreds of resident African workers, he sought to produce essential oils for making perfume from geraniums, limes, and oranges. In 1931–3 he built a mansion, of Italian aspect, in bricks and tiles made locally; its avowed exemplar was John Buchan's *Lodge in the Wilderness* (1906). However, Gore-Browne's manorial

economy owed less to the trade in feminine allure than to that in male bravado: it was heavily subsidized by the Locke Kings' fortune from Brooklands. Shiwa Ngandu failed to make a profit until the Second World War closed off supplies of essential oils from the rivieras of France and Bulgaria.

In 1927 Gore-Browne married Lorna Grace Bosworth (1908–2001), daughter of the microbiologist Professor Edwin Goldmann. They had two daughters, but from 1934 they spent much time apart, and were divorced in 1950. Gore-Browne's deepest and most lasting attachment was to his aunt Dame Ethel Locke *King (1864–1956), with whom he corresponded from childhood until her death.

Gore-Browne's political career began in 1935, when he was elected to represent one of seven constituencies of white voters in the Northern Rhodesia legislative council. He immediately raised the tone of public debate, at a time when large-scale copper mining had just got under way. He castigated British colonial 'trusteeship', and looked instead to a future of 'partnership', seeking for settlers a larger share in government, but arguing the interdependence of white and black prosperity. Unlike other white politicians, such as his friend Roy Welensky, a trade union leader, Gore-Browne felt no threat from African social and educational advance. From 1938 to 1951 he sat in the legislative council as a member nominated to represent African interests, for which services he was knighted in 1945. He also served on the executive council from 1939 to 1951. When African mineworkers struck in 1940 Gore-Browne played a key role in limiting the use of force. He sought out African opinion, both rural and urban, denounced the various forms of colour bar, welcomed the growth of African welfare societies and trade unions, and got the government to set up African representative councils. In Britain his diverse contacts included Dr Hastings Banda (the future president of Malawi), and his faith in African abilities was strengthened in 1946–7 by visits to Uganda and west Africa.

By 1946 Welensky was campaigning for amalgamation with Southern Rhodesia, where settlers enjoyed self-government. Gore-Browne opposed amalgamation, and therefore resigned as leader of the elected members. Instead, he devised a scheme for 'responsible government', intended to appeal to both white and black people, but he so mishandled its presentation in 1948 as to alienate his African supporters. By 1950 he felt he no longer had a role in politics, and resigned from the legislative council early in 1951.

Gore-Browne's later years were mostly spent at Shiwa Ngandu, where citrus crops were replaced by cattle. But he remained actively interested in politics. Federation—imposed on the Rhodesias and Nyasaland in 1953—had for him discredited the idea of 'partnership'. By 1960 he was committed to African majority rule, and was friendly with Kenneth Kaunda, leader of the United National Independence Party. In 1962 Gore-Browne stood for that party in the general election, though he failed to win enough white votes to qualify. In 1964 he attended Zambia's independence ceremonies in Lusaka as an honoured guest. He died from pneumonia at Kasama Hospital, Zambia, on 4 August 1967; his burial at Shiwa Ngandu two days later was a state occasion.

Gore-Browne was of medium height, military in bearing, and monocled. He drove himself hard. His anger could be frightening; and the Bemba called him Chipembere ('the Rhinoceros'). But he was respected for his courtesy, his good humour, and his patent belief that *noblesse oblige*. He amassed a library that included the works of J. B. Bossuet and Voltaire, and he loved serious music. He was a forbearing, generous, and ceremonious host. One custom at Shiwa Ngandu was the issue of a glass of port after dinner to the senior house staff, who drank it standing behind their master. To a guest who asked him if they liked port, Gore-Browne replied, 'D'you know, I never asked them' (personal knowledge).

A. D. ROBERTS

Sources R. I. Rotberg, *Black heart: Gore-Browne and the politics of multi-racial Zambia* (1978) · personal knowledge (2004) · private information (2004) [Lady Gore-Browne] · *DNB* · *CGPLA Eng. & Wales* (1968)
Archives Bodl. RH, corresp. | Bodl. RH, corresp. with Sir R. Welensky and papers · National Archives of Zambia
Likenesses R. I. Rotberg, photographs, 1962–7, repro. in Rotberg, *Black heart*, frontispiece · I. Mackinson, pastels, Shiwa Ngandu, Zambia
Wealth at death £3802 effects in England: probate, 18 Sept 1968, *CGPLA Eng. & Wales*

Browne, Theophilus (*bap.* 1762, *d.* 1835), Unitarian minister, was born in Derby and baptized at there All Saints Church on 26 August 1762. He was the son of Theophilus Browne and his wife, Margaret, who died, widowed, on 21 February 1795, aged seventy-six. The younger Theophilus Browne was admitted to Christ's College, Cambridge, on 23 June 1780, migrating to Peterhouse on 27 May 1783. He graduated BA in 1784 and MA in 1787, was ordained deacon on 19 December 1784 and priest on 24 December 1786, and on 15 July 1785 was made a fellow of Peterhouse.

In December 1793 Browne was presented to the college living of Cherry Hinton, Cambridgeshire. On 15 July 1794, at the parish church in Harston, Cambridgeshire, he married Ann Hurrell. While vicar of Cherry Hinton he adopted the theological opinions of the Priestley school of Unitarians and resigned his living. In 1800 he became minister of the Presbyterian congregation at Warminster, Wiltshire, leaving in 1807 to become classical and mathematical tutor at Manchester College, York, an unsatisfactory appointment for all concerned. In January 1809 he preached as a candidate at the Octagon Chapel, Norwich, to the annoyance of the college authorities, whom he had not notified of his intention. He left York for Norwich at midsummer for a short and unhappy tenure. His new congregation had not enquired beyond his academic attainments and his act of conscience in leaving the church, but they soon found that, as Taylor, the historian of the congregation, put it, he retained establishment notions of the priestly office, publicly and privately rebuking those who differed from him and insisting, when the congregation fell away, that he was secure in the endowment and would preach to bare walls. On 25 December 1810 he was asked to

resign, with a promised payment of £200 (raised in January to £300) if he would leave by midsummer 1811. He remained in Norwich for a time, advertising his availability in a letter to the *Monthly Repository* on 10 March 1812.

After serving as minister at Congleton, Cheshire, from 1812 to 1814 and briefly as supply at Chester, Browne settled at Barton Street Chapel, Gloucester, in 1815. There in November 1818 he established a fellowship fund, and shortly after created some consternation by proposing that Unitarian fellowship funds—the main purpose of which was to aid other, struggling, congregations—should be invested in state lotteries, with a view to gaining windfalls for denominational purposes. As at Norwich, his tenure in Gloucester ended in recrimination. He complained to his friend J. H. Bransby (1783–1847) that because his congregation rejected his efforts to secure their 'eternal good', he was forced to tell their leaders that he would choose to incur their displeasure rather than the Creator's. Wondering how ministers raised in dissent could ever keep on terms with their people, he determined never again to be a pastor (Browne to Bransby, 7 Jan 1823, JRL, Bransby MSS). Accordingly, at the end of 1823 he retired to Bath, preaching only occasionally.

He took great interest in education and was president of the Bath Mechanics' Institution. His friend George Browne Brock (1805–1886) speaks of him as 'conscientious almost to a fault' and very generous to the poor. Browne's wife, Ann, three years his senior, died on Christmas day 1834, and he died at Bath, after a short illness, on 19 or 20 May 1835. He was buried on 26 May at the burial-ground belonging to the Trim Street Chapel, Bath, in nearby Lyncombe Vale. His only daughter, following a brief, unhappy marriage, drowned herself in the River Avon at Bath on 17 February 1836.

Browne edited collections of sermons (1818) by Joshua Toulmin and of devotional addresses and hymns (1818) by William Russell of Birmingham and published a collection of forms for public worship (1803) and a selection from the Bible intended as a lectionary (1805). An anonymous appeal in a Gloucester newspaper that the community refuse to support the Unitarian Sunday school resulted in 1819 in a grandiloquently titled pamphlet, *Religious Liberty and the Rights of Conscience and Private Judgment Grossly Violated*. He dedicated it to Thomas Belsham, 'to whom, if to any … may be justly applied the title HEAD OF THE UNITARIAN CHURCH', a phrase that gave great offence to his co-religionists.

R. K. WEBB

Sources *DNB* · G. B. B. [G. B. Brock], 'Memoir of Rev. Theophilus Browne', *Christian Reformer, or, Unitarian Magazine and Review*, 2 (1835), 507–8 · Venn, *Alum. Cant.* · J. Taylor and E. Taylor, *History of the Octagon Chapel* (1848), 55–6 · *Christian Reformer, or, Unitarian Magazine and Review*, 2 (1835), 805–6 · *GM*, 1st ser., 65 (1795), 349 · G. E. Evans, *Vestiges of protestant dissent* (1897) · vestry book of the Octagon Chapel, Norfolk RO, FC/13/1/2 · *Monthly Repository*, 7 (1812), 64, 272 · *Monthly Repository*, 13 (1818), 750–51 · *Monthly Repository*, 14 (1819), 18–19, 300–02 · *Monthly Repository*, 15 (1820), 392–3 · JRL, Bransby MSS · *IGI* · parish register, Trim Street, Bath, 26 May 1835 [burial] · parish register, All Saints' Church, Derby, 26 Aug 1762 [baptism] · T. P. R. Layng, *Extracts from marriage registers for Harston*

(1972) • J. Hunter, 'Biographical notices of some of my contemporaries who have gained some celebrity', BL, Add. MS 36527, fols. 55–6

Wealth at death under £6000: estate duty registers, PC 3/611

Browne, Thomas (*c.*1535–1585), Church of England clergyman and headmaster, was born in London. He was a king's scholar at Westminster School from about 1546 to 1550, whence on 13 August 1550 he was admitted as a scholar of King's College, Cambridge; he matriculated in 1550 and took his BA in 1554/5, coming first in his year. Further academic honours followed. A fellow of King's from 1553 until 1564, Browne graduated MA in 1558 and BTh in 1569. He was ordained deacon in the diocese of London on 18 October 1561 and was appointed university preacher in the following year. Browne acquired many ecclesiastical positions, including the rectory of Dunton Waylett, Essex (on the presentation of King's College, Cambridge), between 1564 and 1585. On the presentation of the dean and chapter he was admitted on 11 July 1567 to the rectory of St Leonard, Foster Lane, London. On 7 June 1574, at about the time of his resignation from St Leonard, and on the presentation of Anna, duchess of Somerset, and her brother Francis Newdigate, he was admitted to the rectory of Chelsea. On 20 April 1566 he was presented by the queen to the first prebend of Westminster Abbey and was also appointed as a subdean of the diocese. Browne held this canonry, and the rectory of Chelsea, until his death.

Browne was headmaster of Westminster School between 1564 and 1570. Little is known of his mastership, and the school was not then as prestigious as it became under his successors Edward Grant and William Camden. To Grant's Greek primer, *Spicilegium Graecae linguae* (1575), Browne contributed a prefatory poem. He and Grant both provided a verse for each of two works of historical geography, *Historiae Brytannicae defensio* (1573) by Sir John Price, and the translation by Thomas Twyne, issued in the same year, of *The Breviary of Britain* by Humphrey Llwyd. Browne seems, in fact, to have been an open-minded and cultured individual, who saw even in tavern music 'a sensible fit of that harmony which sounds in the ears of God' (Porter, 395–6). It is very probable that he was the Thomas Browne who on 6 April 1574 signed from Westminster the epistle to the reader in *A Sermon Preached before the Queen* by Richard Curteys, bishop of Chichester.

In September 1584 Archbishop Whitgift proposed changes in the episcopate, in which William Day was to become bishop of London, and Browne would fill Day's place as provost of Eton, but the scheme did not come to fruition. Thomas Browne died on 2 May 1585, and was buried the next day in Westminster Abbey.

STEPHEN WRIGHT

Sources *Old Westminsters*, vols. 1–2 • Venn, *Alum. Cant.* • Cooper, *Ath. Cantab.* • *Fasti Angl., 1541–1857*, [Ely] • H. C. Porter, *Reformation and reaction in Tudor Cambridge* (1958) • R. Newcourt, *Repertorium ecclesiasticum parochiale Londinense*, 1 (1708) • J. C. C. Smith, *Some additions to Newcourt's Repertorium, vol. II* (1899) • J. Strype, *The life and acts of John Whitgift*, new edn, 3 vols. (1822), vol. 1

Browne [Broun], **Thomas** (*bap.* **1604**, *d.* **1673**), Church of England clergyman, was baptized on 24 October 1604 at St Dunstan-in-the-West, London, the eldest son of John Browne (*d.* 1622), bookseller, and his wife, Alice (possibly *née* Medley). In October 1621 he matriculated as student of Christ Church, Oxford, graduating BA in 1624 and proceeding MA in 1627. As a student Browne wrote panegyric poetry and in 1629 published a translation of the second part of Camden's *Annals*. He contributed an elegy to the 1633 edition of John Donne's poetry. In April 1636 he was chosen senior proctor of the university and in August he preached for Charles I in Oxford, castigating those who would have 'no altars or images, no kings or bishops'—a sermon thought 'excellent' by William Laud, who made him one of his domestic chaplains (*Works of … William Laud*, 5.150). Browne proceeded BD in 1637, and the following year became rector of St Mary Aldermary, London. In 1639 he was appointed canon of Windsor, and in 1640 rector of Oddington, Oxfordshire.

In 1642 Browne was forced by the 'impetuous Presbyterians' (Wood, *Ath. Oxon.*, 524) to leave his London parish. He returned to Oxford as chaplain to Charles I, and received his DD by letters patent in February 1643. Two years later he published anonymously a defence of the king and queen, *A Key to the King's Cabinet* (1645), the autograph of which is in the Bodleian Library (MS West 29186). He was officially discharged from St Mary Aldermary on 21 April 1646 and, with his brother Samuel, a bookseller, he fled to the Netherlands, where he became personal chaplain, 'confessor and Closet-clerk' (*Mercurius Politicus*, 39, 1651, 637) to Charles's daughter Mary Stuart, princess of Orange. He preached for Charles II whenever the exiled king was in The Hague, and in Breda, where he would replace the minister of the local English church, acting as the king's chaplain and assisting him in the touching of the sick. In 1651 Browne was summoned by the Hague classis to subscribe to the Dutch Reformed church, but he refused, stating that he had already subscribed to the Thirty-Nine Articles. The classis accused him of denouncing the Dutch Reformed church as schismatic, stating that he sometimes used controversial, and possibly misunderstood, quotations from the church fathers, which he denied. In 1658–9 the classis questioned Browne on his Socinian preaching, but he refused to respond to the allegations. His strict manners were commented upon by his contemporaries, and it was remembered that he once treated Princess Mary 'to a dinner consisting of 30 dishes without either flesh nor fish' ('Diary of Dr Edward Lake', 13) in his country house near The Hague, which he had bought in 1657 from Charles II's mistress, Lucy Walter.

During his time in the Netherlands, Browne kept in close touch with other royalist exiles. He financed his brother's publishing enterprises and occasionally lent money to Charles II. In 1658 he tried to get William Sancroft a post as chaplain to Mary. He was a close friend of exiled Anglicans such as Michael Honywood—from whose Utrecht library he borrowed several books and manuscripts—and John Bramhall, who inscribed presentation copies of his books to 'Dr Browne'. He also moved in Dutch intellectual circles, befriending the lawyer and linguist Janus Vlitius, to whom he gave an incunable edition of Frisian laws (Bodl. Oxf., MS Marshall 60), and the scholar Isaac Vossius, with whom he corresponded and who later, in 1672, dedicated a book to him. He wrote a defence of Hugo Grotius, published in 1646 under the pseudonym Justus Pacius.

After the Restoration, Browne recovered his benefices. In 1661 Charles II recommended him for the provostship of Eton, but revoked his request when Browne was accused of 'certain crimes of schisme & heresis' (PRO, SP 29/446, no. 45). As a member of the Windsor chapter he acted alternately as steward, auditor, lecturer, and treasurer, compiling in 1667 an inventory of the chapel's possessions, which mentions a pair of silver candlesticks and a silver basin that were presented to the chapel as a gift from Mary in 1660 on Browne's instigation. His keen interest in the history of Windsor is evident from a letter to Elias Ashmole in 1667.

In May 1673 Browne's old friend Isaac Vossius was also made canon of Windsor. Soon afterwards they agreed that if Browne should die first he would leave Vossius his manor of Southley, but were Vossius the first to die he would leave Browne his magnificent library. On 3 December 1673 Browne fell ill of a cold and 'being impatient to aid himself of it … took a vomit which cast him into a fever', of which he died three days later in Windsor (PRO, SP 29/338, 56). He was buried in St George's Chapel. His will caused a scandal, for he had named as his executor Lady Mary Heveningham, wife of the regicide William Heveningham, 'to whom he was no way related, and to whose family he was a stranger' (*Diary of Dr Edward Lake*, 13). The major part of his belongings, consisting of his estate, as well as his books and papers, Browne duly left to Vossius, expressing the hope that he might find in the notebooks something 'which may make me live by his pen after my departure'. Browne's manuscripts and books were deposited in Leiden University Library, while his papers went to the University Library of Amsterdam. They show his wide-ranging interests in chronology, etymology, antiquity, and patristics. In 1687 his 'Dissertatio de therapeutis Philonis' was posthumously published in Patrick Young's edition of Pope Clement's *Epistolae duae ad Corinthios*. Vossius characterized Browne in the inscription over his monument as a 'man of learning and erudition, a penetrating critic, a fluent orator and a skilled antiquarian and historian' (S. M. Bond, ed., *The Monuments of St George's Chapel*, 1958, no. 50).   MARIKA KEBLUSEK

Sources Foster, *Alum. Oxon.* · Wood, *Ath. Oxon.*, 2nd edn · F. Madan, *Oxford books: a bibliography of printed works*, 3 vols. (1895–1931); repr. (1964), vols. 2, 3 · *The works of the most reverend father in God, William Laud*, 5, ed. J. Bliss (1853), 123, 149–50 · papers in the library of the Remonstrant church, University Library, Amsterdam · Hague classis, National Archives, The Hague · notarial archives, Municipal Archives, The Hague, inv. 456–7, fol. 9 (1658), fol. 4r–4v (1659) · BL, Sancroft papers, Harley MS 3783, fols. 202–3 · Clarendon state papers, Bodl. Oxf., MSS Clarendon · Chapel Acts, St George's Chapel, Windsor · 'Diary of Dr Edward Lake … in the years 1677–8', ed. G. P. Elliott, *Camden miscellany, I*, CS, 39 (1847), 13 · will, PRO, PROB 11/344, sig. 2; PROB 11/346, sig. 137 · parish register, London, St Dunstan-in-the-West, 24 Oct 1604, GL [baptism] · PRO, SP 29/338, SP 29/446

Archives BL, Sancroft papers, Harley MS 3783 · Bodl. Oxf., Clarendon state papers · Municipal Archives, The Hague, notarial archives · National Archives, The Hague, Hague classis · University of Amsterdam, library of the Remonstrant church
Wealth at death estate with lands; endowments; £640; plate, 400 shillings: will, 1673, PRO, PROB 11/344, sig. 2; PRO, PROB 11/346, sig. 137

Browne, Sir Thomas (1605–1682), physician and author, was born (he told John Aubrey in a postscript of 24 August 1672) on 19 November 1605 (fixed as between 5.05 and 6.23 a.m. by the astrological details given in *Religio medici*, II.11) in the parish of St Michael-le-Querne, Cheapside (burnt down in 1666), London, the son of Thomas Browne, liveryman of the Mercers' Company of London, and Anne Garraway, his wife. Of his father, who died in October or November 1613 Browne remembered, according to his daughter Elizabeth Lyttelton, that he 'used to open his breast when he was asleep, and kiss it in prayers over him … that the Holy Ghost would take possession there' (E. Lyttelton, 'Sir Thomas Browne', in *Works*, ed. Wilkin, 1, 1835). By 5 July 1614, however, Browne's mother had married courtier and Low Country captain Sir Thomas Dutton (1575–1634), to whom she had already lent money out of the yet unsettled but already part 'wasted & consumed' estate. Though favoured by Robert Cecil, by James I (who made him a gentleman of the privy chamber, scoutmaster-general in Ireland for life in 1610, and recommended in 1612 that he be given dead men's pay), and later by Charles I and the duke of Buckingham, Dutton was a habitual debtor and borrower, and notorious for killing his colonel, Sir Hatton Cheke, after the siege of Juliers in a duel on the sands at Calais in 1610 (vividly recorded by Arthur Wilson in *The History of Great Britain*, 1653, 50), which perhaps prompted Browne's verses on 'the cruell & heedlesse villainy of duell' (*Works*, ed. Keynes, 3.236). Dutton's extravagance and the illiteracy of his letters to his 'write Honrabell' patrons about his 'trubulls' place him among that 'rabble even amongst the gentry … ignorant *doradoes*' denounced in *Religio medici* (II.1). From a blow received 'amongst some Low-Country Friends' in London on St George's Day 1634 he died on 16 May and was buried three days later at Isleworth, Middlesex. Lady Dutton lived on in Ireland until at least the Irish rising in 1642, when she and the youngest of Browne's four sisters, Ellen or Elinor, lost their possessions and nearly their lives. Another sister, Jane, married Thomas *Price (1599–1685), later archbishop of Cashel.

Early years and education Browne's mother and stepfather having 'wasted & consumed' part of the inheritance, the court of aldermen intervened to stop 'very great losse … to the five orphans', and induced her to relinquish executorship. Responsible administration of the estate by his uncle Edward Browne enabled Thomas Browne in 1616, having 'scarcely ever Simpled further than Cheap-side' (*Religio medici*, II.8), to enter Winchester College as a scholar under Hugh Robinson. Failing to win a scholarship at New College, he matriculated on 5 December 1623 as a commoner at Broadgates Hall, Oxford, where his tutor was the witty, eloquent, and popular preacher

Sir Thomas Browne (1605–1682), by Robert White, pubd 1686

Thomas Lushington, Neoplatonist and amateur mathematician. The energetic principal was Thomas Clayton, regius professor of physic and first Tomlins lecturer in anatomy, who taught concern for the patient's soul as well as body, and jointly inaugurated the physic garden at Oxford in 1622. Ten Latin couplets to William Camden, a former Broadgates man ('as old Dr Clayton told mee'), in Oxford's memorial volume, *Camdeni insignia* (1624, sig. C3v), constituted Browne's first published writing; he was then chosen to deliver the undergraduate oration when the hall was incorporated as Pembroke College in August 1624. From his Oxford years he later recalled Henry Briggs, Savilian professor of astronomy, and 'with some content' his 'old freind' Robert Hues, the geographer, with whom he had often discussed Ptolemy, Euclid, and Aristotle. Browne was admitted BA on 31 January 1627 and proceeded MA on 11 June 1629.

Ireland It was probably in the late summer of 1629 (since Dutton died soon after Browne's graduation at Leiden) that, according to his daughter Elizabeth Lyttelton's memoir, Browne's stepfather 'shewed him all Ireland in some visitation of the forts and castles', of which Dutton, as scoutmaster-general based in Dublin, commanded ten

or more in Ulster and Connaught, also holding estates in Longford and Leitrim. There are scant memories of Ireland in Browne's writings—of spiders in *Pseudodoxia epidemica* (1646, VII.15), and of burnt trees in a letter to William Dugdale (16 November 1659)—but the Irish Sea brought forth twenty-eight lines of verse, preserved by Elizabeth, 'writt by my Father at the Crowe Inne in Chester at his coming from Ireland' (*Works*, ed. Keynes, 3.236–7). In a letter to her of 15 September 1681 he still recalled how 'I came once from Dublin to Chester at Michaelmas and was so tossed, that nothing but milk and Possets would goe down with me 2 or 3 days after'.

Montpellier After Ireland (and signing an acknowledgement on his twenty-fourth birthday, 19 November 1629, that he had received all his inheritance), Browne proceeded abroad, where he 'spent some yeares' (letter to Aubrey) and 'the greatest part of his Patrimony' (J. Whitefoot, 'Some minutes for the life', in Browne, *Posthumous Works*, xxxvi) at medical schools. The first was at Huguenot Montpellier, which, though recently reconquered and ravaged by his Catholic majesty Louis XIII and the plague, was still hospitable to students from protestant countries. Intellectually independent, Montpellier was a centre of herbal medicine under Lazare Rivière, who also promoted the chemical medicines of Paracelsus and William Harvey's doctrine of the circulation of the blood, of which the first trumpet-blast in 1628 set murmuring all the schools of Europe, according to Browne in a 1680 draft of a projected Harveian lecture (*Works*, ed. Keynes, 3.190), to be delivered by his son Edward *Browne (1644–1708). In *Pseudodoxia* (IV.1) Browne recalls the insect 'by Zoographers called *mantis*, and by the Common people of Province, *Prega Dio*, the Prophet and praying Locust', and in *A Letter to a Friend* (XI), 'that Endemial Distemper of little Children in *Languedock*, called the *Morgellons*, wherein they critically break out with harsh Hairs on their Backs'; in his tract 'Of languages' he gives a specimen paragraph of Provençal, in one manuscript draft mentioning that he had been 'often delighted with their songs and poems in that speech' (*Works*, ed. Keynes, 3.81). In France he shared without surprise or disgust 'their dishes of frogges, snailes, and toadstooles' (*Religio medici*, II.1). Experiences such as becoming:

> familiarly acquainted in France, [with] a Divine and man of singular parts, that on [the immortality of the soul] was so plunged and gravelled with three lines of *Seneca*, that all our Antidotes, drawne from both Scripture and Philosophy, could not expell the poyson of his errour   (*Religio medici*, I.21)

may have heightened the tensions between his classical, Christian, and medical educations which produced *Religio medici*.

Padua Browne went next to Padua, which was under the protection of Venice, similarly independent of Roman domination, and so open to protestant students. This university of medical pioneers such as Vesalius, Fallopius, and Fabricius in anatomy, and Sanctorius in iatrophysics (works by all of whom, including the 1631 edition of Sanctorius's work on errors in medicine, Browne owned), with its renowned anatomy theatre and herb garden, was still pre-eminent as in Harvey's day in its tradition of empirical study, and Browne retained a lifelong belief in dissection as the ground of medicine. But the imprints were not only professional: as well as 'an old Italian long ago' asserting that most people died 'when the moon was descending from the meridian' (*Letter to a Friend*, manuscript draft) he also remembered 'a Doctor in Physick of Italy, who could not perfectly believe the immortality of the soule, because *Galen* seemed to make a doubt thereof' (*Religio medici*, I.21). It was presumably there that he ate locusts and grasshoppers with Jews (ibid., II.1), and by experience of their synagogues and commerce, their houses and conversation, disproved the superstition he later refuted, in *Pseudodoxia* (IV.10), 'That Jews stink'.

Leiden Finally, on 3 December 1633, Browne matriculated at Leiden, and graduated MD only eighteen days later. However, he probably spent longer in Leiden than these dates suggest, merely deferring matriculation until it was required. Here also the professors of medicine augmented Hippocrates and Galen by dissecting cadavers; displayed more than a thousand plants (many exotic) in the school's botanical garden, and hundreds more on field-trips; and added the bedside study of patients. Leiden was also the university of the rationalist Arminian Hugo Grotius, author of 'an excellent Tract of the verity of Christian Religion' (*Pseudodoxia*, I.7), and of the anti-Calvinist and anti-Socinian moderate Joannes Polyander, whom, after his death in 1646, Browne praised in verse as plain, just, wise, and formidable, yet cheerful and meek, but morally brave, a living example of his lessons, often giving peace to the wounded mind (*Works*, ed. Keynes, 3.237–8). He mentions the elegant building, learned lecturers, and international audience of Leiden's anatomy theatre in a letter to his son Edward (11 November 1680) suggesting ideas for a Harveian lecture. Browne's medical education is reflected in a 1646 letter of advice to Henry Power, the son of his friend John Power of Halifax, stressing anatomy as basis and autopsy as faithful guide, and in a long list of books adding to the classics the best books available in the early 1630s, including 'Dr. Harvey's piece *De Circul. Sang.* which discovery I prefer to that of Columbus' (*Works*, ed. Keynes, 4.255, corrected from A. Kippis, *Biographia Britannica*, 2, 1780, 633).

Religio medici Back in England, Browne served a medical apprenticeship in Oxfordshire, according to Anthony Wood (Wood, *Ath. Oxon.*, 2.713), or in Halifax, according to Samuel Midgley (Midgley, 88–9). It was perhaps then (or on an unrecorded visit to Ireland in connection with his mother after his stepfather's death), 'in such a place … that … I had not the assistance of any good book' (1643 preface), that he wrote the first version of *Religio medici* in 1635–6; he is not yet thirty in I.41, but his life 'is a miracle of thirty yeares' in II.11, and in the 1643 preface he says 'about seven yeares past'. A non-autograph manuscript of an early version, shorter than other texts, but also containing passages not included in them, is in Pembroke College, Oxford.

Having returned home after finding out that 'I am no Plant that will not prosper out of a Garden. All places, all ayres, make unto me one Country; I am in *England*, every where' (II.1), Browne nevertheless seeks to clarify his Englishness in religion. In this 'private exercise … rather a memoriall unto me than an example or rule unto any other' ('To the reader') he evaluates his religious position after seeing the Roman Catholicism of Ireland (and his stepfather's fierce hostility to it), France, and Italy, and the Calvinism of the Netherlands, neither of which he wholly condemns or accepts, preferring a middle way guided by scripture above all, by the Anglican church, and in default of them, by his own powers of reason. His orthodoxy is blended with Christianized versions of classical schools, such as the stoic, Neoplatonist, and sceptic, and interlaced with idiosyncratic perceptions and ingenious queries, expressed in a style which combines biblical sonorities with fresh and lively expression, and the symmetries of traditional rhetoric with a syntax which accommodates the unforeseen excursions of his mind.

The two parts treat broadly of faith and of charity: Browne's relationships to his God and fellow creatures. In the first, confronting the proverbial assumption that two doctors out of three were atheists, he proclaims himself a convinced Christian (though inclined rather to pity than to hate Turks, infidels, and Jews), and protestant—'but cannot laugh at the fruitlesse journeys of Pilgrims', declining the 'popular scurrilities and opprobrious scoffes' of extremists (I.1, 3, 5). In divinity he prefers 'to keepe the road, and … follow the great wheele of the Church' of England, forsaking some heresies of 'my greener studies' such as mortalism, the remission of eternal punishment, and prayer for the souls of the dead (I.6–7). It seems to him that 'there be not impossibilities enough in Religion for an active faith … I love to lose myself in a mystery, to pursue my reason to an *oh altitudo*'. With regard to 'those involved aenigma's and riddles of the Trinity … Incarnation and Resurrection … I can answer all the objections of Satan, and my rebellious reason, with that odde resolution I learned of *Tertullian*, *certum est quia impossibile est*' (I.9). But submission to authority in religion does not entail total withdrawal: 'The world was made to be inhabited by beasts, but studied and contemplated by man: 'tis the debt of our reason wee owe unto God' (I.13). Above all he studies 'the Cosmography of my selfe … a *compendium*' of that natural world which is a second book 'whence I collect my Divinity'. He learns from 'the Heathens' of Greece and Rome to 'suck Divinity from the flowers of nature', holding there to be 'a generall beauty in the works of God … I cannot tell by what Logick we call a Toad, a Beare, or an Elephant, ugly … nature is the Art of God' (I.16). He admits that his scientific knowledge prompts doubts about the literal truth of scripture—'whilst I labour'd to raise the structure of my reason, [the Devil] striv'd to undermine the edifice of my faith' (I.20, added in 1643)—but accommodates any intellectual difficulty with the analogy of man as 'that great and true *Amphibium*, whose nature is disposed to live … in divided and distinguished worlds; … the one visible, the other invisible' (I.34). Among other Christian concerns, he asserts a belief in witches to be inseparable from belief in spirits (I.30), and explains his equable attitude to death, although he has not become 'insensible of the dread and horrour thereof … by raking into the bowells of the deceased' (I.38). Though disturbed by extreme Calvinists, 'Insolent zeales that doe decry good workes and rely onely upon faith' (I.60), Browne seems comfortable in God's world, sure of a special personal providence and his own salvation.

In the second part, the 'mercifull disposition, and humane inclination I borrowed from my Parents' inclines Browne to 'honour, love, and embrace' not just his own class or nation, but all human beings, whether poor, ignorant, or foreign, though, as in his religion, there are limits to his tolerance and desire to avoid dispute: though 'at the sight of a Toad, or Viper, I finde in me no desire to take up a stone to destroy them', he scorns and laughs at 'the multitude' in which the 'reason, vertue and religion' of individuals become submerged. He stresses that there is a 'rabble even amongst the Gentry … men in the same Levell with Mechanickes, though their fortunes doe somewhat guild their infirmities, and their purses compound for their follies' (II.1). He affirms his own duty, 'as calling my selfe a Scholler', to be generous with his learning, and charitable to ignorance (II.3). While obliged as a Christian to honour 'the nearest of my blood', it is for his friend (possibly the original addressee of *Religio medici*) that he feels passionate love, delivering a paean to 'the wonders in true affection' (II.5–6) which struck a responsive chord in late-nineteenth-century readers such as Walter Pater and Charles Sayle. Browne is in conflict only with his own vices, but minimizes them; in claiming not to be proud of knowing 'besides the *Jargon* and *Patios* of severall Provinces … no lesse then six Languages', the climates, provinces, cities, 'Lawes, Customes and Policies' of several countries, 'all the constellations in my Horizon', and 'most of the Plants of my Country and of those about mee', he seems to show some self-satisfaction (II.8, added in 1643).

Perhaps thinking of his mother, Browne is 'resolved never to be married twice'. However, it is his temper 'to affect all harmony', which includes beauty, and shows in his care for the shape and the sound of his prose. His pain at religious discord around him intrudes in 'Whatsoever is harmonically composed, delights in harmony; which makes me much distrust the symmetry of those heads which declaime against all Church musicke' (II.9), words written after its century of excellence in England and published in the year when the organ in Norwich Cathedral was wrecked (famously deplored by Browne's 'honord freind' and patient, whose works he praises in 'Repertorium', the ejected bishop, Joseph Hall). In a letter of 22 April 1661 to his son Tom, Browne notes 'a sweet Organ' has replaced it. Browne was temperamentally thoughtful (even at times desiring death, as in *Religio medici*, I.38):

> At my Nativity, my ascendant was the watery signe of *Scorpius*, I was borne in the Planetary houre of *Saturne*, and I think I have a peece of that Leaden Planet in me. I am no way facetious, nor disposed for the mirth and galliardize of

company, yet in one dreame I can compose a whole Comedy … and laugh my selfe awake … were my memory as faithfull as my reason is then fruitfull, I would never study but in my dreames. (*Religio medici*, II.11)

Norwich and marriage On 10 July 1637 Browne was incorporated as DM (Oxon), and at the prompting of his former tutor Thomas Lushington, Justinian Lewin, who took his DCL from Pembroke in the same year, and others, moved to Norwich, where he practised for the rest of his life. Despite his wish 'that there were any way to perpetuate the world without this triviall and vulgar way of coition' (*Religio medici*, II.9), characterized as 'unmanly' by James Howell in *Epistolae Ho-Elianae* (1645), reproached by Sir Kenelm Digby, and rebutted by Alexander Ross, in 1641 he married Dorothy Mileham (1621–1685), 'a Lady of such a Symetrical Proportion to her Worthy Husband,' wrote John Whitefoot, 'both in the Graces of her Body and Mind, that they seemed to come together by a kind of Natural Magnetism' ('Some minutes for the life of Sir Thomas Browne', in Browne, *Posthumous Works*, xxxii). She was the fourth daughter of Edward Mileham of Burlingham St Peter, Norfolk, and his wife, Dorothy Hobart, daughter of John Hobart of Salle. Browne thus augmented his existing acquaintance in Norfolk with connections among other local gentry families, such as Knyvett, Townshend, Astley, Pettus, Paston, Tenison, and Le Gros. The marriage appears to have been contented (Browne chose to hang in his parlour 'a draught' of Rubens's *Baucis and Philemon*); Dorothy bore eleven children, of whom six survived to adulthood, and four outlived her. She expresses her care and concern for them in letters from 1660 to 1682.

Fame In 1642 Browne was surprised by the unauthorized printing of *Religio medici*, 'which being communicated unto one [possibly John Power] it became common unto many, and was by transcription successively corrupted, until it arrived in a most depraved copy at the press', where it was twice 'most imperfectly and surreptitiously published' without attribution, by Andrew Crooke. Hereupon Browne prepared what, in a letter to Digby (see below), he termed 'the true and intended original'. In fact the authorized edition of 1643, though altered and expanded, was set from an incompletely corrected copy of the first 1642 edition. The revisions noticeably moderate some statements, while emphasizing his Anglican orthodoxy, and he cuts out some vulnerable points, such as having made friends with a Jesuit whose sermon he had attended, and lacking hate for the Devil, while adding, for instance, a substantial dismissal of the healing efficacy of relics such as the alleged 'ashes of John the Baptist' (I.28) in Genoa. Wary of dogmatic arguments, he draws back from some possible clashes between the religion and natural philosophy he is attempting to reconcile, though risking others in additional passages on the location of Hell (I.51) and on the inclusion of Africa and Asia in Christendom (I.56). Revising in time of civil war (when especially 'wee are beholding unto every one wee meete hee doth not kill us', I.44), Browne the royalist deletes some material susceptible to political interpretation—a hint of multiple authority in the kingdom, a comparison of himself to 'a king without a crown', and lack of sympathy with 'raving against the times'—but strengthens his anti-sectarian arguments, as 'particular Churches and Sects usurpe the gates of heaven, and turne the key against each other, and thus we goe to heaven against each others wills, conceits and opinions' (I.56). He cuts potentially embarrassing admissions (disregard of 'physic', experience of taverns); and, perhaps sensitive about his passages on male friendship, disclaims 'the constitution of *Nero* in his Spintrian recreations' (II.7). Despite the state of his widowed, now destitute mother, he expands his personal resolve to commendation of all 'who never marry twice' (II.9).

In a letter of 3 March 1643 (printed with *Religio medici*, 1643) to Sir Kenelm Digby, Browne vainly attempted to stay publication of the latter's *Observations upon 'Religio medici'* (1643; reprinted, 1644). Digby's *Observations* on the unrevised edition criticized Browne's metaphysics from a Roman Catholic point of view, and reproved the prominent authorial presence, more engaging to later readers, that 'true Anatomy of my selfe' (II.1), the happy egotism of 'The world I regard is my selfe, it is the Microcosme of mine owne frame, that I cast mine eye on; for the other, I use it but like my Globe, and turne it round sometimes for my recreation'. This was intensified in the 1643 revision: 'whilst I study to finde how I am a Microcosme, or little world, I finde my selfe something more than the great' (II.11). A Norwich Quaker, Samuel Duncon (*d*. 1679), wrote privately praising certain 'sound assertions' and suggesting 'personall conferrance … concerning the principalls of our religion' (*Works*, ed. Wilkin, 1.352). In contrast to such a peaceable approach and to Digby's repeatedly expressed admiration, Alexander Ross, dogmatic Aristotelian and militant anti-Catholic, abused Browne's work unsparingly in *Medicus medicatus, or, The Physicians Religion Cured, by a Lenitive or Gentle Potion* (1645). Between them Digby and Ross may have prompted the hopeful prefatory claim for *Pseudodoxia epidemica*: 'We cannot expect the frowne of *Theologie* herein' ('To the reader'). Ross's book was not reprinted, but Browne's went through a further eight English editions in his lifetime (from 1656 with annotations by Thomas Keck). Revisions in the author's hand in a copy of the 1672 quarto edition of *Pseudodoxia epidemica* and *Religio medici* in Norwich Central Library corroborate some of the changes and additions to the text of 1643 in the 1678 edition of *Religio medici*, showing that late in Browne's life, perhaps when he was working on *Christian Morals*, he returned to the tract that had made him famous, of whose title there had already appeared seven imitations (of an eventual eighty or more), beginning in 1645 with *Religio laici*, by Edward Herbert, first Baron Herbert of Cherbury.

A Latin version of *Religio medici* in 1644 met likewise with a mixed reception in the Netherlands, France, and Germany. According to a letter of 1 October 1649 from the translator, John Merryweather, of Magdalene College, Cambridge, 'it found some demurr in the first impression at Leyden': the first bookseller he approached was

deterred by Salmasius's opinion 'that there were indeed in it many things well said, but that it contained many exorbitant conceptions in religion, and would probably find but frowning entertainment, especially amongst the ministers', and two printers subsequently refused it (*Works*, ed. Wilkin, 1.366–8), though Hackius found response enthusiastic enough to justify reprints in 1644 and 1650. The warning was borne out for the first Dutch translation (1665; enlarged with more notes from Keck, and Digby's *Observations*, 1683) by Dr Abraham van Berckel, as he wrote to Browne in a letter of 27 March 1666 (*Works*, ed. Keynes, 4.333). Merryweather's Latin version was immediately pirated in France (1644; repr. Zürich, 1743) with a preface claiming Browne as almost a Roman Catholic—an Anglican only through accident of birth and since then through fear of the English inquisition—and piously hoping he might renounce his errors and receive divine enlightenment. From Paris, Gui Patin, dean of the faculty of medicine, reported that people were making much of *Religio medici*, and he himself repeatedly mentioned and praised it in letters (1644–57) to Charles Spon. On the contrary part, an imputation of 'atheism' (commonly a broad term for any deviation from one's own beliefs) was raised in Germany. Rome placed it on the *Index expurgatorius* in 1645, which did not prevent printings at Strasbourg with notes by L. N. von Moltke in 1652, 1665, and 1677 (reissued Frankfurt, 1692). From van Berckel's Dutch it was translated into French (1668), into Dutch a second time (from the 1686 *Works*) by a Quaker, William Séwel, for *Alle de werken van Thomas Brown* (1688), and into German 'aus dem Original' (1746). Edward Browne reported that in Vienna in 1669 the emperor Leopold's librarian, Petrus Lambecius:

> recommended a Translation of *Religio medici* unto him, wherewith the Emperour was exceedingly pleased, and spake very much of it … and desired me to send him [Lambecius] that Book in the Original *English*, which he would put into the Emperours Library. (Browne, *Account of Several Travels*, 85)

The copy of the 1669 edition sent by Edward (illustrated in its original fine English binding by A. Hobson, *Great Libraries*, 1970, 148) is still in Vienna in the Österreichische Nationalbibliothek. Wilkin reprints the prefaces to the Merryweather, Paris (1644), Moltke, and 1665 French editions (*Works*, ed. Wilkin, 2.153–8). There are twentieth-century translations into Italian (1931), French (1947), Swedish (1948), Italian again (1958), and Japanese (1963).

Pseudodoxia epidemica Despite Browne's working 'by snatches of time, as medical vacations and the fruitless importunities of uroscopy would permit', and starting a family (his eldest child, Edward, was born in 1644), a decade of reading, observation, and experiment bore fruit in *Pseudodoxia epidemica, or, Enquiries into very many received tenents and commonly presumed truths* (1646; revised and enlarged, 1650, 1658, 1672; reprinted, 1658, 1669, and in *Works*, 1685–6). It is addressed not to 'the people (whom Bookes doe not redresse …) but unto the knowing and leading part of Learning', among whom, *Religio medici* having made him famous for piety and wit, *Pseudodoxia* now earned his reputation as scholar and naturalist. In this, his most substantial work, almost an encyclopaedia of seventeenth-century misconceptions and new knowledge, Browne took up numerous false beliefs particularized in the *Apology* of George Hakewill; and, with a larger number of his own finding (some already mentioned in *Religio medici*), he put them in the framework suggested by Francis Bacon in his *Advancement of Learning* (as translated by Gilbert Watts, 1640) of 'a calendar of falsehoods and of popular errors now passing unargued in natural history and in opinions, that sciences be no longer distempered and embased by them'. Browne still had religious motives: to 'repaire our primarie ruins' (I.5), the loss of Adam's universal knowledge of the natural world by the fall, and 'to enforce the wonder of its Maker' (II.3), and theology as well as philosophy figure in the first book's systematic survey of the causes of error, from the fall of man, through logical and verbal misunderstanding, laziness, deference to antiquity and authority, to the wiles of the Devil. In the following six books, he subjects to 'the three determinators of truth, Authority, Sense and Reason' (III.5)—in a 1658 tribute to William Harvey reduced to 'the two great pillars of truth, experience and solid reason' (III.28)—a host of misbeliefs concerning the natural world, human physiology, pictorial representation, geography, history, biblical interpretation, and classical antiquity. While he records about a hundred personal experiments on subjects animal, vegetable, and mineral (ranging from amber, ants, and bitterns to toads, turkeys, and yew berries), he cites twelve times as many authors: in *Certain Physiological Essays* (1661) Robert Boyle accordingly respects him as both 'the learned Dr *Brown*' and 'so faithful and candid a Naturalist'. The science and learning are sharpened with witty irony as Browne disposes of the 'misapprehension, fallacy or false deduction, credulity, supinity, adherence unto Antiquity, Tradition and Authority' of two millennia, which have conceived a world of shrieking mandrakes, lopsided badgers, griffins, phoenixes, mermaids, ominous owls, the wandering Jew, Pope Joan, and Aeschylus brained by a tortoise, through to the last chapter, in which he points out a bright side to the all too believable account of necrophiliac embalmers in Egypt: 'Surely, if such depravities there be yet alive, deformity need not despaire; nor will the eldest hopes be ever superannuated, since death hath spurres, and carcasses have beene courted' (VII.19).

The first printed response was again from Alexander Ross, who in *Arcana microcosmi* (1651), after a confident account 'of one that lived some years without a Brain', challenged the enterprises of Bacon, Harvey, and Browne as 'new conceits and whimzies … like the apples of *Sodom*', for which 'they reject *Aristotles* pure Fountains' and 'go a whoring (as the Scripture speaketh) after their own inventions'. Approval of *Pseudodoxia* in its century came mostly from medical men: Walter Charleton in 1650 and Noah Biggs in 1651; two Norwich doctors, John Bulwer in 1653 and John Robinson (a contemporary at Leiden), who in *A Calm Ventilation of 'Pseudo-doxia epidemica'*, subjoined to his *Endoxa* (Latin 1656; English, enlarged, 1658),

examines 'what we have in private, without infringing the limits of Amity, more loosely discussed'; Browne's disciple the microscopist Henry Power in his *Experimental Philosophy* (1664; used by Browne without acknowledgement in his 1672 edition); Robert Plot and John Webster (1611–1682), both in 1677; and Edward Tyson in 1699 (Keynes, 178–204). A patient, Sir Hamon L'Estrange of Hunstanton (*d.* 1654), father of Sir Hamon L'Estrange (1605–1660), in response to a postscript enquiry of 11 June 1653 sent Browne substantial 'Observations' (BL, MS Sloane 1839), also used without acknowledgement in Browne's chapter on the sperm whale. Extensive annotations by Christopher Wren, dean of Windsor (1591–1658), in his copy of the first edition (Bodl. Oxf.) were partly printed by Wilkin in *Sir Thomas Browne's Works* (1836) and almost completely by Robbins in 1981. Versions of *Pseudodoxia* in Dutch (1668), German (1680, expanded), French (1733, bowdlerized), and thence Italian (1737), enhanced the continental reputation secured by *Religio medici*, though Isaac Gruter, editor of three of Browne's authorities, William Gilbert, Grotius, and Francis Bacon, never accomplished the Latin version he projected in 1649, and a 1652 translation into Danish remained in manuscript (Kongelige Bibliotek, Copenhagen). A publisher attempted to profit from Browne's reputation by publishing under his name in 1657 a curious work on natural history and physiology, *Nature's Cabinet Unlock'd*, loftily disclaimed in a notice, 'From the stationer to the reader', added to the 1658 editions of Browne's next published works.

Hydriotaphia, The Garden of Cyrus, and A Letter to a Friend Despite Browne's county-wide medical practice and the urge to revise and enlarge *Pseudodoxia*, he found time for the thought and reading that produced shorter tracts for his friends. *Hydriotaphia, Urn-Burial, or, A Discourse of the Sepulchral Urns Lately Found in Norfolk* for Thomas Le Gros of Crostwick or Crostwight, and *The garden of Cyrus, or, The quincuncial, lozenge, or network plantations of the ancients, artificially, naturally, mystically considered*, for Nicholas Bacon of Gillingham, were published together in 1658. Some dozen surviving copies corrected in Browne's hand were evidently for presentation. Although professedly works of invention, and therefore displaying *Religio medici*'s wide and witty imagination, *Hydriotaphia* and *The Garden of Cyrus* had serious ends in view. They were written, like *Pseudodoxia*, out of books as well as experience, extracting and reweaving much erudite information on the funerary and horticultural practices of the ancients to provide a large context for personal observations. *Hydriotaphia* may be one of the first archaeological monographs in English, but the pictured and comparatively briefly described urns, now in the British Museum, are Saxon rather than (as Browne tentatively guessed) Roman, and the work's sole contribution to knowledge was Browne's discovery 'in an Hydropicall body ten years buried in a Church-yard' of 'a fat concretion' (later termed 'adipocere'). The tract has been enjoyed less for factual content than for its wit and solemn music, from the first chapter's reflection that the shallow burial of the deceased has 'left unto our view some parts, which they never beheld themselves' to the concluding declamation on the futility of all monuments compared to 'the extasie of being ever'. The addressee lost his father, Browne's patient, Sir Charles Le Gros, in 1656, which suggests that the much admired peroration on the triumph of Christian immortality over time, death, and oblivion was always the ultimate goal of the piece.

The Garden of Cyrus, after expounding ancient patterns of planting, including much modern botanical information, and gathering together examples of quintuplicity in human artefacts, the natural world, and pagan and Christian numerology, likewise concludes in religious mood, invoking 'the mystical Mathematicks of the City of Heaven' which will ordain 'that time, when … all shall awake again'. Nicholas Bacon, too, had recently been bereaved, in his case of successive heads of the family, his uncles Sir Edmund Bacon (Browne's 'true and noble friend') and Sir Robert Bacon, premier baronets, in 1649 and 1655. The dedication justifies coupling the tracts 'since the delightful world comes after death, and paradise succeeds the grave; since the verdant state of things is the symbol of the Resurrection, and to flourish in the state of glory, we must first be sown in corruption'. Both tracts, therefore, may have been conceived as works of consolation, exercises in the genre of Seneca's *Moral Essays*.

A third such piece, *A Letter to a Friend upon Occasion of the Death of his Intimate Friend* (probably not the author's title), survives in two versions: an untitled manuscript draft (BL, MS Sloane 1862; Browne, ed. Martin), perhaps an expansion of the original letter; and a version three times as long, following the manuscript's final readings, published posthumously in 1690 (by Edward Browne, according to the *Posthumous Works*, 1712). The *Letter* claims to be written 'not very many days' (I) after the death in early May (IV; year unspecified) about midnight (VII, not in manuscript) 'fifteen days after' his nativity (VIII), of a patient who in the manuscript thinks he has lived too long in seeing 'one Lustre more than his Saviour' (that is, to thirty-eight); but in the printed version (perhaps an imaginative idealization), 'had scarce out-lived the second Life of *Lazarus* [thirty years], esteeming it enough to approach the Years of his Saviour [thirty-three]' and so aged thirty-one or thirty-two (XXV). Browne describes the patient in the last stages of consumption, digresses into medical and literary reflections prompted by his appearance and circumstances, meditates on mortality, and praises his wisdom, prudence, chastity, and temperance, concluding with exhortations to virtue, religious, civil, and personal. Greatly extended in the 1690 version, these exhortations overlap with and were expanded for *Christian Morals*.

The subject of the *Letter* was identified by F. L. Huntley as a probable patient of Browne, Robert Loveday, who died of consumption in 1656, aged thirty-five. Less plausibly, Huntley has claimed the original addressee to be Loveday's patron and neighbour Sir John Pettus (1613–1690) of Chediston, Suffolk (to be distinguished from two contemporary namesakes, one his elder half-brother, the other the third baronet, of Rackheath, Norfolk, referred

to in Browne's letters), whose age (forty-three), and standing as a favoured state servant, make him an unlikely target for Browne's injunctions to be sober, temperate (though 'not to preserve your body in a sufficiency for wanton ends'), liberal, and pious. R. F. Hall suggests that the addressee might be the 'R. W.', of Loveday's *Letters Domestick and Forrein* (1659), who went abroad to the Low Countries, France, and Italy: perhaps one Robert Waller, a contemporary at Cambridge (MD, Leiden, 1650), of whose father's death Loveday himself had to send news (received through his brother Anthony) from R. W.'s married sister in Norfolk.

Later works Thirteen more epistolary essays on natural history, ancient customs, holy scripture, classical and modern verse, languages, oracles, facetious prophecy, and mock antiquarianism constitute *Certain Miscellany Tracts*, first selected and ordered by Dame Dorothy's relative Thomas Tenison, former incumbent of St Peter Mancroft, Browne's parish from 1649, and published in 1683, the year after Browne's death. Browne mentioned to Aubrey (14 March 1673) 'some miscellaneous tracts which may bee published', and Tenison notes that he 'had procured *Transcripts*', probably 'for publick use' (T. Tenison, preface to 'Certain miscellany tracts', in *Works*, ed. Wilkin, 4, 1836). Browne's wide-ranging mind produced learned, ingenious, and sometimes whimsical discourses for friends and serious authors in search of information. At the suggestion of their friend Robert Paston, later earl of Yarmouth, he sent 'discourses, and the Acoustic Diagramme, &c.' on 21 January 1660 to John Evelyn, who noted in his copy of *Certain Miscellany Tracts* (now at Norwich) that most of them were written (like *The Garden of Cyrus*) to Nicholas Bacon, but that 'Of garlands' was called forth by his own letter to Browne of 28 January 1660 seeking material for his projected (but never completed) *Elysium Britannicum*. Browne followed it with a catalogue of plants possibly suitable for grafting. His description in a letter of 1663 of a great lime tree at Deopham, Norfolk (though not his accompanying recall of a giant yew near Winchester) was used by Evelyn in *Sylva* (1664), a copy of which he presented to Browne, as he had of his *Sculptura* in 1662 (*Works*, ed. Keynes, 3.374–8; 4.273–81; Keynes, 141). In his diary for 17 October 1671 Evelyn recorded a visit to Browne:

> his whole house and Garden being a Paradise and Cabinet of Rarities … especialy Medails, books, Plants, natural things … a collection of Eggs of all the foule and birds he could procure … as Cranes, Storkes, Eagles etc: and variety of Water-foule.

Another recipient was William Dugdale, for whose *History of Imbanking and Draining* (1662) there survive some of Browne's draft notes, and their correspondence from 1658 to 1662, including the actual text of 1658 on burial mounds which became 'Of artificial hills, mounts or burrows' (*Works*, ed. Keynes, 3.84–7, 255–6; 4.301–27, omitting a letter from Browne of 11 Sept 1661, now in Pembroke College, Oxford, acknowledging the gift of volume 2 of *Monasticon Anglicanum*). Browne himself received a steady flow of information, as in Thomas Lawrence's letter on 'Subterraneal cockle, muscle, and oyster shels' found at

Shotesham, Norfolk, which was published in 1664 as *Mercurius centralis*.

Tenison's preface to *Certain Miscellany Tracts* mentions 'other brief Discourses', including 'a brief Account of all the Monuments of the *Cathedral* of *Norwich*', which 'may come forth … at such due distance from these Tracts, that They may follow rather than stifle them'. The *Posthumous Works* published by Edmund Curll in 1712 opens with an anonymous brief life, perhaps at least partly by Elizabeth Lyttelton, but less valuable than the appended 'Minutes for the life of Sir Thomas Browne' (also referred to by Tenison), by his 'learned and faythfull old freind Mr. John Whitefoot, Rector of Heigham'. 'Repertorium, or, The antiquities of the cathedral church of Norwich' is a response to the depredations described in the prefixed 'Account of the sacrilege and prophanation of this church, in the time of the civil wars', inaccurately reprinted from Joseph Hall's 'Hard measure'. In a letter to Aubrey of 24 August 1672 Browne explains that:

a clark of the church [in 'Repertorium' called 'John Wright … above 80 yeares old'] told mee that in the late times above an hundred brasse inscriptions were stolne out of the church, and therefore to prevent all oblivion of the rest I tooke the best account I could of them at the Kings returne from an understanding singing-man of 91 yeares old [in 'Repertorium' mentioned as 'Mr John Sandlin … who lived 89 yeares and … told mee that hee was a chorister in the reigne of Queen Elizabeth'].

As sole repository of otherwise lost information, 'Repertorium' did not entirely deserve the contempt of Thomas Hearne (Keynes, 109). 'An account of some urnes, &c. found at Brampton in Norfolk, anno 1667' is a short description, factual rather than learned, literary, or meditative, of the relics and artefacts, including late third-century Roman coins, excavated from an ancient cemetery 'not much more then a furlong from Oxned park', where similar objects were found by 'my noble & honor'd freind, Sr. Robert Paston'. The rest of the 1712 volume comprises letters between Dugdale and Browne, *A Letter to a Friend*, and a couple of lesser pieces from manuscript.

Christian Morals was termed by Elizabeth Lyttelton in her dedication to David Erskine, ninth earl of Buchan (husband of Frances, sixth daughter of Sir Thomas's daughter Anne Fairfax), 'the Last Work of our Honoured and Learned Father' (Browne, ed. Martin, 201). White Kennett recorded her report that when she fetched back from Tenison the box of their father's manuscripts which Edward Browne had lent him 'in the reign of James II' (presumably for the selection and preparation of the 'other brief discourses' promised in Tenison's preface to *Certain Miscellany Tracts*) her brother 'complained that he misst the choicest papers, which were a continuation of his Religio Medici, drawn up in his elder years, and which his son Dr. Brown had now intended to publish'. According to the 1716 preface by the editor, John Jeffery, incumbent of St Peter Mancroft in Browne's last years, 'Search was lately made in the Presence of the Lord Arch-Bishop of Canterbury [as Tenison now was], of which his Grace, by Letter, informed Mrs LITTLETON, when he sent the MS to Her … the Original MS of the Author' (Browne, ed. Martin, 202).

As Jeffery, who had 'read the MS. of the Author immediately after his Death' acknowledges, a reader of *Religio medici* might 'Doubt, whether the same Person was the Author of them both', such is the contrast between the imperative precepts in *Christian Morals* for living and dying and the thirty-year-old Browne's 'soft and flexible sense' 'rather a memoriall unto me then an example or rule unto any other'. With its prescriptive aphorisms in the style of Epictetus and Marcus Aurelius, but Christianizing their secular stoicism into a bidding 'to sit quiet in the soft showers of Providence' (III.5), *Christian Morals* thus seems rather a counterpart than a continuation, though, opening and closing with words from *A Letter to a Friend* and *Hydriotaphia*, it shares the inventive thought and rich allusion of Browne's earlier writings. Its greater formality (to Lytton Strachey it seemed 'like an elaborate and magnificent parody of the Book of Proverbs') shows it was written for a general public readership.

Commonplace books Browne's manuscripts were extensively quarried by Simon Wilkin and Geoffrey Keynes for their editions of the works. They contain, apart from drafts of parts of most of Browne's publications, pieces of verse, notes from reading on his usual wide range of topics—'not trite or vulgar' (*Works*, ed. Keynes, 3.285), he writes in a paragraph perhaps drafted for an epistolary tract—anatomical observations, presumably for Edward's lectures, extensive notes, observations and trials in natural history, with particularly rich records for Norfolk, and records of numerous experiments on boiling, bubbles, coagulation, and freezing. Covering the last thirty years of Browne's life, they typify, though lacking in system and quantification, the interests of an intelligent natural philosopher of that time.

Correspondence The bulk of Browne's correspondence surviving in author's copy or original is with his sons Edward and Tom: dating from 1660 to 1668, these are informal letters of moral and practical advice. The younger, 'Honest Tom' (1647–1667?), dispatched at the age of fourteen for an educational tour in France from 1660 to 1662, was enjoined by his father to 'Learn the languadge and … singing painting or danceing … painting will be most usefull if you Learn to draw Landskips or buildings … Cast of[f] *Pudor Rusticus* and take up a Comendable boldness', but to be careful in La Rochelle, 'a very drinking town, as I observed when I was there'. Tom's dutiful journal of his sightseeing in France, and his lively, good-humoured account of a trip to Derbyshire with Edward, were preserved among Browne's manuscripts (*Works*, ed. Wilkin, 1.17–42). Later there followed solicitous advice and congratulations on Tom's brave and intelligent conduct in various naval actions from 1665 to 1667, and on his keeping up serious reading:

I must not fayle to tell you how well I like it, that you are not only *Marti* but *Mercurio*, and very much pleased to find how good a student you have been at sea, and particularly with what successe you have read divers bookes there, especially Homer and Juvenal, … you are like to prove not only a noble navigator butt a great schollar, which will bee much more to your honour and my satisfaction and content.   (*Works*, ed. Keynes, 4.24)

Browne's interest in education persisted: in 1672 he formally certified the proficiency of the six-year-old William Wotton in reading Latin, Greek, and Hebrew aloud; later he contributed to a new building at his old school, Winchester, to the new library at his son Edward's old college, Trinity College, Cambridge (designed by the latter's friend Christopher Wren), and to repairs to Christ Church, Oxford.

Over a hundred of Browne's surviving letters are addressed to Edward. They concern Edward's travels in France and Italy in 1664–5, and in the Austro-Hungarian and Ottoman empires in 1668–9 and 1673, and his resulting books and papers; the father's and son's respective medical practices (with evocative detail); draft lectures to the College of Physicians; dissections of humans and animals (including Edward's ostrich); other exotica seen (such as ginseng); Edward's non-medical reading; and family, national events, and other topics, including the father's growing infirmities and the expense of his family. Letters to both sons contain Norfolk and family news, with occasional maternal additions by Dorothy Browne. The assiduous but duller Edward's intellectual dependence on his father is manifested in his travel books, where there are occasional paragraphs in Sir Thomas's richer style, with ingenious reflections encompassing his characteristic spread of ancient and modern learning; these presumably evolved during the consolidation and polishing revealed by the letters. The sons' halves of the correspondence and journals of their travels are printed by Wilkin but not by Keynes. There are four letters to his daughter Elizabeth in Guernsey in 1681 after her marriage, one consoling her after seeing a ship wrecked with loss of life.

Outside his family Browne corresponded with some of the intellectual leaders of Charles II's reign, including fellows of the Royal Society, such as Dugdale and Evelyn. Writing to Browne on 28 January 1660 the latter desiderated 'a society of learned and ingenuous men, such as Dr Browne, by whome we might hope to redeem the tyme that has bin lost, in pursuing vulgar errours' (*Works*, ed. Keynes, 4.275); but, though known or esteemed for his work by a couple of dozen fellows (some close to him, such as Paston, Power, and his son Edward), Browne never became a member. Presumably, financial need to maintain his practice as Norfolk's leading physician, and the two or three days it still took to reach London—for Edward, enviably, 'Miles about London are short and 4 horses go farre in a summers daye' (letter of 11 June 1679)—made the obligatory attendance at meetings impracticable and the expense of subscriptions pointless. However, he received the *Transactions*; on 27 February 1668 he sent curiosities, including a large fossil bone from a cliff near Winterton, Norfolk (draft of letter in *Works*, ed. Keynes, 3.350–51), and with four letters from 31 May to 25 October 1669 he sent the secretary, Henry Oldenburg, Edward's observations of mines in central Europe, to be read to the society.

Browne's letters to three other fellows cover his usual range from superstition to science. To Elias Ashmole he sent information concerning the alchemical and astrological interests, books, and manuscripts of John Dee, obtained from the latter's son Arthur, Browne's 'familiar freind' and 'old acquaintance'; and to Aubrey (who in his *Brief Lives* hailed *Religio medici* as the book 'which first opened my understanding'), biographical and autobiographical particulars of Lushington, himself, and others. He favoured Christopher Merrett with materials (of which numerous sections exist in various manuscript drafts as well as the letters) for his proposed enlarged edition of *Pinax rerum naturalium Britannicarum*, which was never accomplished. The materials were passed on to another Browne acquaintance, John Ray, who also borrowed drawings for Francis Willughby's *Ornithologia*, 1676. While Browne's own volumes were never decorated with the laudatory poems written to him by George Daniel of Beswick, John Collop of Flitwick, James Duport of Cambridge, and Joshua Barnes, he contributed commendatory letters 'To his Endeared Friend, Mr Daniel King', engraver, in *The Vale-Royall of England, or, The County Palatine of Chester Illustrated* (1656), by William Smith, William Webb, and others; and 'To the Author', in both *A Compleat Treatise of Preternatural Tumours* (1678) and *A Compleat Discourse of Wounds* (1678) by John Browne (1642–1702/3), whom Thomas Browne, however, in a letter to Edward of 10 May 1679, deemed over-ambitious and conceited. Wilkin prints some of the letters from correspondents to whom Browne's letters have disappeared. Two wrote with information used in the third edition of *Pseudodoxia* (1658): the botanist William Howe or How wrote on 20 September 1655 concerning sundew and catmint (*Pseudodoxia*, II.vii), and an Icelandic clergyman, Theodore Jonas (Jónssen) of Hitterdal, wrote on '2 Idus Julias' (that is, 14 July) 1651, concerning 'the *Aetites* or *Aegle-stone*' (ibid., II.v.9). This and two more (1656, 1664) of what appear to have been regular July letters from Jonas (perhaps after returning from trips to Yarmouth on trading vessels) on the natural history of the island occur in Wilkin; and Browne submitted two others, with an abstract by himself (*Posthumous Works*; *Works*, ed. Keynes, 3.355–6), to the Royal Society on 15 January (or 24 March) 1664, followed by a sample of black rock in 1672. He also received letters from a Norwich minister named L'Escaillot (presumably Huguenot) at Surat in India. His friend Paston writes to Browne, presenting ancient medals and discussing alchemy, on 19 September 1662, 5 April 1669 and 10 September 1674 (*Works*, ed. Wilkin, 1.417–19, 256–70, 424–42, 409–13).

Later life   Little trace remains of Browne's life, during the civil war and the interregnum, other than as author and family man. His post-Restoration letters to his sons show awareness of public events and strong opinions about the killing of Charles I, but the only political act during the civil war and the interregnum of which evidence survives is his refusal in 1643 (along with 431 other members of the gentry and professions) to subscribe money to parliament for the recapture of royalist-held Newcastle. After 1660, however, he played a more open role in the establishment. In *Religio medici* (I.30) he had declared: 'I have ever beleeved, and doe now know, that there are Witches' (a belief shared by Bacon, Harvey, and Boyle). The anonymous account of *A tryal of witches, at the assizes held at Bury St. Edmonds for the county of Suffolk; on the tenth day of March, 1664* (1682, 41–2), 'in the sixteenth year of … Charles II', reports that Browne was:

> clearly of Opinion, that [the seven alleged child-victims] were Bewitched; … he conceived, that these swouning Fits were Natural, and nothing else but that they call the Mother, but only heightned to a great excess by the subtilty of the Devil, co-operating with the Malice of these which we term Witches, at whose Instance he doth these Villanies.

Compared to the vehement and vivid stories of a dozen prosecution witnesses, mostly superstitious or vindictive parents in collusion with their histrionic offspring (experimentally but fruitlessly exposed as frauds during the trial), Browne's opinion, while not helping the defendants at all, may not have borne much weight. He did nothing to identify those in the dock as blameworthy; the judge, Sir Matthew Hale, directed the jury that this decision finally lay with them (having reminded them that scripture and the law affirmed the existence of witchcraft). The jury found against the defendants, who were hanged. In a commonplace book probably filled in the 1660s, Browne noted that:

> We are no way doubtfull that there are wiches, butt have not been alwayes satisfied in the application of their wichcrafts or whether the parties accused or suffering have been guiltie of that abomination, or persons under such affliction suffered from such hands. (MS Sloane 1869; *Works*, ed. Keynes, 3.293)

Had such been the tenor of his recorded testimony at the trial, he might have avoided the anachronistic obloquy he suffered in succeeding centuries. His belief was still too widely shared to inhibit the College of Physicians from electing him to an honorary fellowship in December 1664 (diploma awarded 6 July 1665), or Charles II from knighting him in 1671. Three weeks later John Evelyn made the visit to Norwich recorded above, and toured the city with Browne.

Soon after, Browne requited the king by sending to Newmarket 'collars' of a dissected dolphin, of which Dame Dorothy had 'an art to dresse & cooke the flesh so as to make an excellent savory dish'. Such glimpses of domestic life are frequent in the letters to Edward, with their mentions of his sisters: Frances, who married John Boswell at St Benet Paul's Wharf, on 19 November 1687; Elizabeth, who married George Lyttelton (*d.* Windsor, 1717) in St Peter Mancroft, on 19 December 1680 ('Hee is of a very good Humor and Temprat as can be', wrote her mother two days before); Anne, who married, probably in 1669, Henry Fairfax of Hurst, Berkshire ('one who must have drinck and company', his father-in-law warns Edward on 10 May 1679); and Mary (*d.* 1676); Browne also writes of Edward's first child, Thomas, lovingly looked after in

infancy by his grandparents and mentioned in their letters from 1677 to 1681; and of family friends and acquaintances.

Appearance and habits Apart from portraits and his writings (*Religio medici* in its entirety is a self-portrait), Browne's personal appearance and manner are chiefly preserved in the 'Minutes' of John Whitefoot (the 'old Mr Whitefoote' of Browne's letters of 1679–80), who had known him since he was about thirty-two, that is, when he moved to Norwich:

> His Complexion and Hair was answerable to his Name, his Stature was moderate, and Habit of Body neither fat nor lean … he had an Aversion to all Finery, and affected Plainness, both in the Fashion and Ornaments. He ever wore a Cloak, or Boots, when few others did. He kept himself always very warm, and thought it most safe so to do … His Memory … was Capacious and Tenacious, insomuch as he … not only knew all Persons again that he had ever seen at any distance of Time, but remembered the Circumstances of their Bodies, and their particular Discourses and Speeches … he was Excellent Company when he was at leisure, and express'd more Light than Heat in the Temper of his Brain … He was never seen to be transported with Mirth, or dejected with Sadness; always Chearful, but rarely Merry, at any sensible Rate, seldom heard to break a Jest; and when he did, he would be apt to blush at the Levity of it: … They that knew no more of him than by the Briskness of his Writings, found themselves deceived in their Expectation, when they came in his Company, noting the Gravity and Sobriety of his Aspect and Conversation; so free from Loquacity … that he was something difficult to be engaged in any Discourse; though when he was so, it was always Singular, and never Trite or Vulgar [Browne's own phrase in a commonplace book, above]. Parsimonious in nothing but his Time, whereof he made as much Improvement, with as little Loss as any Man in it; when he had any to spare from his drudging Practice, he was scarce patient of any Diversion from his Study; so impatient of Sloth and Idleness, that he would say, he could not do nothing. (J. Whitefoot, 'Some minutes for the life of Sir Thomas Browne', in Browne, *Posthumous Works*, xxvii–xxxi)

Last days Whitefoot also provides an account of Browne's end:

> In his last Sickness, wherein he continued about a Weeks time, enduring great Pain of the Cholick, besides a continual Fever, with as much Patience as hath been seen in any Man … I visited him near his End, when he had not Strength to Hear or Speak much; the last words which I heard from him, were, beside some Expressions of Dearness, that he did freely submit to the Will of God, being without Fear: He had oft triumphed over the King of Terrors in others, and given many Repulses in the Defence of Patients; but when his own Turn came, he submitted with a Meek, Rational, and Religious Courage. (Whitefoot, 'Minutes', xxxiv–xxxv)

Browne died at his house in the Haymarket, Norwich, on 19 October 1682, a month short of his seventy-seventh birthday, and was buried in the chancel of St Peter Mancroft, where a tablet erected by Dame Dorothy, who survived him by over two years, commemorates his piety, honesty, and learning.

To his widow Browne left a substantial property in the Haymarket, Norwich (mostly demolished in 1842, the rest in 1961). The personal collection of books out of which he compiled much of his work passed mostly to his son

Edward, and thence to the latter's only son Thomas. After Thomas's fatal fall while riding home to Northfleet, Kent, from a night's drinking at Gravesend, extinguishing the male line, the books were sold at auction in January 1711. Most of Browne's surviving thirty-five autograph manuscripts and those he possessed of the works of others were acquired at about the same time by Hans Sloane and Richard Rawlinson, and are now in the British and Bodleian libraries respectively, while the urns of *Hydriotaphia* remain in the British Museum, and his herbarium has passed to the Natural History Museum, London.

'To be gnaw'd out of our graves', Browne had observed in *Hydriotaphia*, 'to have our sculs made drinking-bowls, and our bones turned into Pipes, to delight and sport our Enemies, are Tragicall abominations, escaped in burning Burials': though his own skull was spared such ensuing indignities, it was removed from the family vault in 1840. Before reinterment in 1922 under the supervision of Sir William Osler it was subjected to laboratory measurement which authenticated as likenesses: the double portrait of Browne (with 1640s-style collar) and his wife, Dorothy, attributed to their friend Joan Carlile (1606?–1679), once belonging to the family of Browne's friend Sir Hamon L'Estrange (NPG); the Buccleuch miniature (with 1650s-style collar); and the inferior or crudely retouched painting in St Peter Mancroft, given about 1739 by Dr Edward Howman, son of Dr Roger Howman, Sir Thomas's co-subscriber (29 May 1682) for a work by Nehemiah Grew (presumably his *Anatomy of Plants*, 1682), who occupied Browne's house after Dame Dorothy's death. The collar in the St Peter Mancroft painting and hair-line in the Buccleuch miniature suggest derivation from the double portrait, the most finely modelled of the three. All other paintings and engravings appear to be derived from one of these, or to be inauthentic.

Posthumous reputation For Samuel Johnson 'there is no science, in which he does not discover some skill; and scarce any kind of knowledge, profane or sacred, abstruse or elegant, which he does not appear to have cultivated with success'. His style Johnson found complicated by 'exuberance of knowledge, and plenitude of ideas … but the spirit and vigour of his persuit always gives delight' though its virtues had matching vices: vigorous but rugged, learned but pedantic, deep but obscure, striking but not pleasing, commanding but not alluring; 'his tropes are harsh, and his combinations uncouth'. None the less, Johnson's own prose, like that of lesser writers such as Walter Charleton in *A Ternary of Paradoxes, Written Originally by J. B. Van Helmont* (1650), Noah Biggs in *The Vanity of the Craft of Physic* (1651), and Agricola Carpenter in *Pseuchographia anthropomagica* (1652), showed the influence of Browne's diction and syntax, as did that of Charles Lamb in 'Witches, and Other Night-Fears' (1821), Herman Melville, and Walter Pater.

Browne himself acknowledged the difficulty readers of *Pseudodoxia* might find with his neologisms, explaining that 'the quality of the Subject will sometimes carry us into expressions beyond meere English apprehensions'. A fruitful source for Thomas Blount in his *Glossographia, or, A*

Dictionary, Interpreting … Hard Words (1656), Browne is the first recorded user of over a hundred word-forms in the *Oxford English Dictionary*, such as analogous, compensate, computer, cylindrical, electricity, exhaustion, generator, gymnastics, hallucination, inconsistent, indigenous, indoctrination, invigorate, jocularity, literary, locomotion, medical, polarity, precocious, pubescent, recurrence, and vitreous. Many of them are merely extensions of already naturalized words, but about half of them are entirely new to English. Most of these may be traced to his continental Latin sources; a couple of dozen, at least, such as antediluvian, approximate, aquiline, bisect, carnivorous, coexistence, coma, cryptography, disruption, follicle, herbaceous, insecurity, mucous, precarious, prostate, protuberant, suicide, ulterior, ultimate, and variegation, not only illustrate Browne's wide range of interests but are still commonly used, while more specialist coinages, particularly in zoology, became standard terms of classification.

In the first half of the nineteenth century appreciation of Browne's style and imagination reached its highest pitch since the seventeenth among readers and writers such as Lamb, Coleridge ('a brain with a twist'), Leigh Hunt, Hazlitt, De Quincey, Southey, and Carlyle, some praising quaint whimsy and fanciful humours, others finding depth of thought. Later in the century a wider readership found Browne reflecting its concern with the relationship of science to religion: after Wilkin's *Works* in 1836, *Religio medici*, with or without other pieces, had been reprinted fifteen times when W. A. Greenhill's scholarly edition of *Religio medici, Letter to a Friend, and Christian Morals* appeared in 1881; it was itself reprinted eleven times by 1923, during which period there were a couple of dozen other printings. Browne's religious attitudes appealed to Christians up to the twentieth century; later, his royalism and anti-populism alienated some readers, while others have been less interested in Pater's stylist, John Addington Symonds's 'mental aristocrat' akin to Walt Whitman, or Sir William Osler's ideal Christian physician, than in Browne as creator of a persona, epistemologist, Baconian discoverer, and popularizer of the new learning.   R. H. ROBBINS

Sources J. S. Finch, *Sir Thomas Browne: a doctor's life of science and faith* (1950) [fullest biography] · *Sir Thomas Browne's works, including his life and correspondence*, ed. S. Wilkin, 4 vols. (1835–6) [incl. much material not in edn by Keynes] · *The works of Sir Thomas Browne*, new edn, ed. G. Keynes, 4 vols. (1964) · T. Browne, *Religio medici and other works*, ed. L. C. Martin (1964) [incl. *Hydriotaphia, The garden of Cyrus, A letter to a friend, Christian morals*, MS version of *A letter to a friend*] · T. Browne, *Pseudodoxia epidemica*, ed. R. H. Robbins (1981) · T. Browne, *Posthumous works* (1712) · C. W. Schoneveld, 'Sir Thomas Browne and Leiden University in 1633', *English Language Notes*, 19 (1981–2), 335–59 · F. L. Huntley, *Sir Thomas Browne: a biographical and critical study* (1962) [possible subject of *A letter to a friend*] · R. F. Hall, 'Studies in Sir Thomas Browne's *Letter to a friend*', MLitt diss., U. Oxf., 1972 · N. J. Endicott, 'Sir Thomas Browne as "Orphan", with some account of his stepfather, Sir Thomas Dutton', *University of Toronto Quarterly*, 30 (1960–61), 180–210 · N. J. Endicott, 'Browne's *Letter to a friend*', *TLS* (15 Sept 1966), 868 · N. J. Endicott, 'Sir Thomas Browne's *Letter to a friend*', *University of Toronto Quarterly*, 36 (1966–7), 68–86 · K. J. Höltgen, 'Browne's *Letter to a friend*', *TLS* (20 Oct 1966), 966 · D. Tyler, 'A review of the interpretation of Sir Thomas

Browne's part in a witch trial in 1664', *Anglia*, 54 (1930), 179–95 [quotes orig. account] • A. B. Shaw, *Sir Thomas Browne of Norwich* (1982) [local information, reproduces portraits] • E. Browne, *An account of several travels through a great part of Germany* (1677) • M. L. Tildesley, 'Sir Thomas Browne: his skull, portraits and ancestry', *Biometrika*, 15 (1923), 1–76; pubd separately (1923) [authoritative evidence, genealogy] • S. Wilkin and C. Williams, 'The pedigree of Sir Thomas Browne', *Norfolk Archaeology*, 15 (1902–4), 109–13 [basis for Tildesley]; pubd separately (*c.*1903) • M. Toynbee, 'Some friends of Sir Thomas Browne', *Norfolk Archaeology*, 31 (1955–7), 377–94 • G. C. R. Morris, 'Sir Thomas Browne's daughters, "Cosen Barker", and the Cottrells', *N&Q*, 231 (1986), 472–9 [later family relationships] • G. C. R. Morris, 'Sir Thomas Browne's nativity', *N&Q*, 228 (1983), 420–21 • A. Hobson, *Great libraries* (1970), 148 [illustrates presentation copy of *Religio medici* in the Österreichische Nationalbibliothek, Vienna] • F. Stubbings, 'A Latin verse epistle of Joshua Barnes to Sir Thomas Browne', *Transactions of the Cambridge Bibliographical Society*, 10 (1991–5), 86–91 [poem not listed in Keynes's *Bibliography*] • G. L. Keynes, *A bibliography of Sir Thomas Browne* (1968) [full information on all known edns, biography and criticism, and imitators] • D. G. Donovan, M. G. H. Herman, and A. E. Imbrie, *Sir Thomas Browne and Robert Burton: a reference guide* (1981) [updates Keynes] • P. Beal, *Index of English literary manuscripts*, ed. P. J. Croft and others, 1/1 (1980) • J. S. Finch, *A catalogue of the libraries of Sir Thomas Browne and Dr Edward Browne, his son* (1986) [listing most of Browne's bks, with introduction and notes] • A. Wilson, *The history of Great Britain: being the life and reign of King James the First* (1653) • Wood, *Ath. Oxon.*, 2nd edn • S. Midgley, *Halifax and its gibbet-law* (1708) • BL, MS Sloane 1839, 1869
Archives BL, corresp. and papers, Sloane MSS • Bodl. Oxf., letters and papers • NHM • Pembroke College, Oxford, early version of *Religio medici*, with annotations possibly in his hand | Norfolk RO, Wilkin MSS
Likenesses attrib. J. Carlile, double portrait, oils, *c.*1641–1650 (with his wife), NPG • F. H. Van Hove, line print, BM; repro. in Browne, *Pseudodoxia epidemica* (1672), frontispiece • P. Vanderbank, line print, BM, NPG; repro. in T. Browne, *Certain miscellany tracts*, ed. T. Tenison (1683) • R. White, line print, BM, NPG; repro. in T. Browne, *Works* (1686) [*see illus.*] • miniature (after R. White), NPG • oils, St Peter Mancroft, Norwich • oils (after J. Carlile), RCP Lond.
Wealth at death left substantial house in Norwich to widow; also books and MSS: will, *Works*, ed. Keynes (1964), vol. 4

Browne, Thomas (*bap.* 1673, *d.* 1710), physician, the son of Edward *Browne (1644–1708), physician, and Henrietta Susan Terne (*d.* 1712), daughter of Christopher Terne, physician, was born in London, and baptized at St Andrew Undershaft on 21 January 1673. His childhood was spent with his grandfather Sir Thomas *Browne at Norwich, as is known from the numerous references to 'Tomey' in Sir Thomas's correspondence with his son. He entered Trinity College, Cambridge, in 1690, after attending St Paul's School, and graduated MB in 1695, MD in 1700. He was admitted a candidate of the Royal College of Physicians on 30 September 1704, and a fellow on 30 September 1707. He was made a fellow of the Royal Society in 1699. In 1698 he married his cousin Alethea (*d.* 1704), daughter of Henry Fairfax, but had no children. He inherited his father's estate at Northfleet, Kent, in 1708, and is said to have led a dissolute life.

Browne died in 1710, as a result of falling drunk from his horse on a journey between Gravesend and Southfleet. He was interred in the church at Northfleet. He was not eminent as a physician, and is remembered chiefly because of his family connections. He wrote, however, an account of

an antiquarian tour through England in company with Robert Plot, which is printed in *Sir Thomas Browne's Works* (1836), edited by Simon Wilkin.

J. F. PAYNE, *rev.* MICHAEL BEVAN

Sources *Sir Thomas Browne's works, including his life and correspondence*, ed. S. Wilkin, 4 vols. (1835–6) • Munk, *Roll* • Venn, *Alum. Cant.*

Browne, Thomas (1702–1780), herald and land surveyor, was born in Derby, the second son of John Browne of Ashbourne, Derbyshire. He was first employed as surveyor to John Warburton, Somerset herald, and then to the dukes of Beaufort. He entered the College of Arms in 1728 as Blanch Lyon pursuivant. He progressed to Black Lyon pursuivant in 1730 and became Bluemantle pursuivant in 1741, Lancaster herald in 1743, Norroy king of arms in 1761, Clarenceux in 1773, and Garter in 1774. He produced maps of estates mainly in Yorkshire and southern England and was well regarded as a land surveyor; he was called Sense Browne, to distinguish him from his contemporary Lancelot Brown, who was known as Capability Brown. He lived at Little Wimley, near Stevenage, Hertfordshire, which came to him through his marriage with Martha (*d.* in or before 1778), youngest daughter of George Needham of Wymondley Priory in Hertfordshire. They had two sons and four daughters. Browne and his family later moved to Camville Place, Essendon, Hertfordshire. He died at his town house in St James's Street, Bedford Row, London, on 22 February 1780 and was buried in Essendon churchyard.

THOMPSON COOPER, *rev.* J. A. MARCHAND

Sources F. W. Steer and others, *Dictionary of land surveyors and local map-makers of Great Britain and Ireland, 1530–1850*, ed. P. Eden, 2nd edn, 2, ed. S. Bendall (1997), 69 • *GM*, 1st ser., 50 (1780), 103 • M. Noble, *A history of the College of Arms* (1804)
Likenesses W. Dickinson, engraving (after portrait by N. Dance)
Wealth at death £5000 to each daughter; fourth share of his interest in the Eddystone Lighthouse left to daughter, Elizabeth Wightwick; estate at Camville Place incl. 75 acres, plus estates at Driffield and Skirne in East Yorkshire left to son: will, 1772

Browne, Thomas Alexander [*pseud.* Rolf Boldrewood] (1826–1915), novelist, was born in London on 6 August 1826, the eldest child of Sylvester John Brown, merchant and shipowner, and his wife, Elizabeth Angell, *née* Alexander. He lived in Australia from the age of five, when his father settled in Sydney after delivering a cargo of convicts to Hobart Town in his own barque, the *Proteus*. The family moved to the new settlement at Port Phillip (Melbourne) in 1839, but Thomas stayed in Sydney as a boarder at Sydney College until 1841. After joining his family in Melbourne he was tutored by the Revd David Boyd, his former classics master at Sydney College. In 1844 he took up a cattle run called The Swamp near Port Fairy in Victoria, in partnership with his brother-in-law William Walker. He named it Squattlesea Mere, after the seat of Sir Roger Wildrake in Sir Walter Scott's novel *Woodstock*; in his own novel *The Squatter's Dream* (1890) it is called Marshmead. It remained his home until 1858, when he bought a larger run, Murrabit, on the Murray River, but began to spend most of his time in Melbourne, where his family returned to Hartlands, the house his father had built at Heidelberg in 1839–40.

Brown visited England and Ireland in 1860 and the following year, on 1 August, married Margaret Maria Riley at St Thomas's Church in Mulgoa, near Sydney, officially changing the spelling of his surname to Browne soon after. His wife belonged to the colonial aristocracy, her father and grandfather having been among the first importers of Saxon merino sheep into Australia. Browne and his wife had four sons and five daughters. Immediately after his marriage he suffered a financial collapse that brought his career as a landed proprietor to an end. From 1864 to 1869 he subsequently managed another sheep station, Bundidgeree, near Narrandera, New South Wales, owned by two of his wife's brothers. In April 1871, thanks to family influence, he began a new career as a public servant, being appointed police magistrate and, soon after, gold commissioner at Gulgong, then the centre of the richest goldfield in New South Wales. After ten years there he served successively as magistrate and mining warden at Dubbo, Armidale, and Albury, before retiring to Melbourne in 1895. He died at his home, Iona, Kensington Road, South Yarra, Victoria, on 11 March 1915 and was buried in Brighton cemetery, Melbourne.

Browne wrote sixteen novels, all under the pseudonym Rolf Boldrewood, borrowed from Scott's *Marmion*. Eleven of them were serialized in Australian magazines in the 1870s and early 1880s, but it was not until *Robbery under Arms*, his classic tale of bushranging, cattle stealing, and goldmining, was published in London in 1888 that he became well known. Like his other novels, of which the best is *The Miner's Right* (1890), it exactly suited the prevailing British taste for exotic adventure stories. In Australia, Browne's exaggerated respect for rank and his predilection for gentlemanly English heroes were mocked by his younger, more nationalistic contemporaries, but for all their romantic absurdities his best novels were deservedly praised for the authenticity of their scenes of life in the bush, their convincing rendition of Australian speech and character, and their lively evocation of recent historical events. P. D. EDWARDS

Sources A. Brissenden, *Rolf Boldrewood* (1972) · P. de Serville, *Rolf Boldrewood: a life* (2000) · T. I. Moore, 'Boldrewood, Rolf', *AusDB*, vol. 3 · K. Banke, *Thomas Alexander Browne (Rolf Boldrewood): an annotated bibliography, checklist, and chronology* (1956) · *CGPLA Eng. & Wales* (1915)
Archives BM · Mitchell L., NSW · State Library of Victoria, Melbourne, La Trobe manuscript collection
Wealth at death £247 15s. 5d.: Australian probate sealed in London, 14 Dec 1915, *CGPLA Eng. & Wales*

Browne, Thomas Arthur (1870–1910), illustrator and painter, was born at Nottingham on 8 December 1870, the son of Francis and Maria Browne. He left St Mary's national school, Nottingham, at the age of eleven to become an errand boy, first at a milliner's and later at a lace market, and when he was fourteen he was apprenticed to a firm of lithographic printers. His career as a black and white artist and humorous draughtsman began

Thomas Arthur Browne (1870–1910), by Kay Robertson, 1906

at the age of seventeen when he discovered that he could draw and make comic illustrations of his friends. One of them persuaded him to send some of his drawings to the comic paper *Scraps*, issued by the London publisher James Henderson. Browne was paid 30s., equivalent to three months' wages. Henderson printed his first published work in *Scraps* on 27 April 1889, entitled, prophetically, 'He knew how to do it'. After finishing his apprenticeship Browne immediately went to a local art school for three months; it was the only formal art training he had, and he later described it as 'dull'.

Browne soon moved to London, and for the next few years he contributed work on a freelance basis to periodicals issued by Henderson, Alfred Harmsworth (later Lord Northcliffe), and others. His breakthrough to success and subsequent public recognition came when he was asked to contribute to the front page of *Illustrated Chips*, a tabloid comic weekly published by Harmsworth, who financed his future newspaper empire on the profits of his comics. For the issue dated 16 May 1896 Browne drew a picture strip entitled *Innocents on the River* and in the process created a pair of tramps—Weary Waddles and Tired Timmy—who were later renamed Weary Willie and Tired Tim. The pair were modelled on Don Quixote and Sancho Panza, Browne's favourite characters. The strip was an important creation, one of the earliest in Britain to feature regularly appearing comic characters. Weary Willie and Tired Tim became two of the longest-running comic characters in the world, spawning scores of tramp-character imitations and ending their run only when *Chips* itself ceased publication on 12 September 1953. Browne drew the pair until 1900. Among the many who declared an influence was Charlie Chaplin, a keen fan in his youth who, when talking about his own tramp character, admitted: 'I started the little tramp simply to make people laugh and because those other old tramps, Weary Willie and Tired Tim, had always made me laugh' (P. Haining, *Charlie Chaplin*, 1989, 30).

Browne also found a ready market for his work in magazines such as *Black and White, Captain, Cassell's, Cycle, Cycling, Eureka, The Graphic, Illustrated Sporting and Dramatic News, Lady's Realm, London, Moonshine, Odd Volume, Pearson's, Pick-Me-Up, Printer's Pie, Punch, Royal, The Sketch, The Tatler, To-Day,* and *Wheel.* His other endeavours were successful too. He was signed up by the picture postcard publishers Davidson Brothers, and in the next few years he drew nearly 1000 pictures for the firm's cards. His work also appeared on the greetings cards of Tuck, Valentine, Collins, Hartmann, and others. In 1897 he was a founder of the lithographic colour-printing firm of Tom Browne & Co. of Nottingham. Browne designed advertisements for Fry's, Beecham's, Sunlight Soap, and Raleigh Bicycles (he was a great cycling enthusiast) and created the famous striding Regency gent for Johnnie Walker whisky. He had his own comic annual (published 1899–1905), *Tom Browne's Comic Annual* (later *Tom Browne's Christmas Annual*), and books he illustrated included *Tom Browne's Cycle Sketch Book* (1897), *The Khaki Alphabet Book* (1901), *Letters to Dolly* (1902), *The one before* (1902), *The Night Side of London* (1902), *The Man who Lost his Past* (1903), *Larks and Levities* (1903), and *The World that Never Was* (1908). In 1904 he travelled to the USA where he was well received and drew *Boston Types* for the *Commercial Tribune.* He returned two years later and for four months worked for the *Chicago Tribune.* As special artist for *The Graphic* he travelled through Egypt, China, and Japan.

Browne later turned his talents to painting, and his watercolours and oils drew considerable acclaim. In 1898 he was elected a member of the Royal Society of British Artists and in 1901 he became a member of the Royal Institute of Painters in Water Colours; from 1897 to 1901 he exhibited each year at the Royal Academy, sending seven pictures in all. He joined the Langham Sketch Club in the 1890s, and later he founded, with his friend Dudley Hardy (and others), the London Sketch Club; he was appointed president in 1907. He was also a long-time member of the Savage Club and belonged to the Yorick Club. An active freemason, he was a past master of the Pen and Brush lodge. He was married with one son, Noel, and two daughters. Tragically Browne died of throat cancer on 16 March 1910, aged only thirty-nine. As he had been a lance-corporal in the City of London rough riders and later held a commission in the Woolwich company of Army Service Corps, he was entitled to be buried with full military honours at Shooters Hill cemetery.

Browne was, with Phil May, one of the most popular and respected pen-and-ink artists of the late Victorian and Edwardian era. The happy geniality which distinguished his life, as well as his pictures, won him hosts of friends; he also inspired generations of black and white comic artists. It is odd that, despite all the many thousands of drawings he completed before and after establishing his studio at Blackheath, relatively few pen-and-ink originals appear to survive.   ALAN CLARK

Sources A. E. Johnson, *Tom Browne RI* (1909) · J. A. Hammerton, *Humorists of the pencil* (1905) · M. Bryant and S. Heneage, eds., *Dictionary of British cartoonists and caricaturists, 1730–1980* (1994) · M. Bryant, *Dictionary of twentieth-century British cartoonists and caricaturists* (2000) · DNB · d. cert.
Likenesses K. Robertson, portrait, 1906, priv. coll. [*see illus.*]

Browne, Sir Thomas Gore (1807–1887), army officer and colonial governor, was born on 3 July 1807 at Aylesbury, Buckinghamshire, the son of Robert Browne of Morton House, near Buckingham, a colonel of the Buckinghamshire militia, and his wife, Sarah Dorothea, the second daughter of Gabriel Steward MP, of Nottington and Melcombe, Dorset. His youngest brother, Edward Harold *Browne, became bishop of Winchester.

Browne joined the army at the age of sixteen, when he was commissioned as ensign in the 44th foot (14 January 1824). He exchanged to the 28th foot on 28 April 1824, became lieutenant on 11 July 1826, and was promoted captain on 11 June 1829. He had his first experience of civil administration when he served as aide-de-camp to Lord Nugent, the high commissioner of the Ionian Islands, from 1832 to 1835. He obtained a majority in the 28th on 19 December 1834, and exchanged to the 41st on 25 March 1836. When the 41st regiment took part in the First Anglo-Afghan War, Browne had the opportunity, in the absence of senior officers, briefly to command the regiment. When, on its way to join Major-General Nott at Kandahar, the British army was repulsed at Hykulzie (28 March 1842), Browne covered its retirement and repulsed the enemy. He was involved in the fighting at Kandahar on 29 May, in the march on Kabul, and in the storming of Istalif. As the armies returned through the Khyber Pass to India he was with the frequently engaged rearguard; he was made brevet lieutenant-colonel on 23 December 1842, and CB on 27 September 1843.

Browne returned to England with the 41st in 1843, and became its lieutenant-colonel on 22 July 1845. He exchanged to the 21st on 2 March 1849, and, having been appointed governor and military commander of St Helena on 20 May, went on half pay on 27 June 1851. On 22 August he was given the local rank of colonel; while governor he improved the water supply at St Helena.

On 6 November 1854 Browne was appointed governor of New Zealand. That same year, *en route* to take up his new post, he married Harriet Louisa, the daughter of James Campbell of Craigie, Ayrshire. They had several children, including Harold, the eldest son, who commanded the 1st battalion King's Royal Rifle Corps in the Second South African War of 1899–1900, and was at the defence of Ladysmith.

Browne landed at Auckland on 6 September 1855. As governor, he was to be best remembered for his involvement in Maori affairs. Having presumed that his only task would be to implement the letter of the 1852 constitution and to introduce responsible government, he was ill-prepared to manage the relations between Maori and settlers, which were already strained. In a climate in which the Maori population was steadily shrinking and the claims of settlers to their lands apparently insatiable, matters came to a head when, early in 1859, he chose to persist in the purchase of some land at Waitara in northern Taranaki against the wishes of the chief of the tribe, Wiremu-kingi Te Rangitake. When Browne ordered a survey to be made of the land for further investigation, Wiremukingi, supported by Taranaki, Ngati Ruanvi, and Waikato followers of the Maori king, refused to co-operate, and Browne sent troops to enforce his orders. On 17 March 1860 a guerrilla war broke out which was to last for a year, leaving the land devastated and no clear victory on either side.

Browne's actions in Taranaki had some legal justification and the full support of his ministers, but nevertheless represented a serious error of judgement. They were much criticized in England by opponents of the Stafford ministry and by leading Anglican clergymen, including Archdeacon Octavius Hadfield and Bishop G. A. Selwyn. It would be misleading, however, to see the Taranaki affair as typical of Browne's governorship, and he soon used his influence to begin to repair the damage caused by the war. In July 1860 he summoned a large gathering of chiefs to Auckland to calm fears about the fighting, and it was during this month-long Kohimarama conference that the necessary trust for future consultative government began to be established. In August of the same year the Colonial Office asked him to write a full report on the right of a tribal chief to forbid the sale of land by one of his members, which he finished on 4 December. Browne's report, with its insistence that plunder taken from Taranaki be returned and that land sales and road building be allowed to proceed, met with opposition from the Maori leadership, but there were already signs that opinion, both in England and in New Zealand, was beginning to turn. When the newly elected house of representatives met on 3 June, Browne was promised unanimous support in the event of a second war, and even the clergy who had taken the Maori side in 1859 put pressure on Waikato Maori to accept the governor's terms. Combined military and moral pressure on the Maori, in conjunction with Browne's recommendations for a comprehensive Maori policy, which included a training school for Pakeha and Maori entering the native service, local self-government, and a Maori land tribunal, made imminent capitulation of the Maori leadership likely.

On 25 May 1861 Sir George Grey was appointed as Browne's successor in the hope that he would be able to prevent hostilities from breaking out again. But Browne had actually smoothed the way for a reconciliation, which it was easy for Grey to seem to have managed single-handedly. The secretary of state nevertheless complimented Browne on the 'sound and impartial judgement, the integrity, intelligence, and anxiety for the public good' which had characterized his government of the colony for nearly six years. The Maori afterwards made plain

their preference: 'Browne was like a hawk, he swooped down upon us; Grey was like a rat, he undermined us.'

On 5 March 1862 Browne was appointed governor of Tasmania, where he remained until the end of 1868. He continued to follow the affairs of New Zealand, though he refused to be drawn into the renewed dispute over the Waitara land after its surrender by Grey in 1863; he was, however, the only governor to respond to an appeal by Grey in sending troops. He was made KCMG on 23 June 1869. His last appointment was as temporary governor of Bermuda, from 11 July 1870 to 8 April 1871. He died at his home, 7 Kensington Square, London, on 17 April 1887.

E. M. LLOYD, rev. LYNN MILNE

Sources *The Times* (19 April 1887) · D. A. N. Lomax, *A history of the services of the 41st—the Welch—regiment* (1899) · W. Gisborne, *New Zealand rulers and statesmen, 1840–1885* (1886) · B. J. Dalton, 'Browne, Thomas Robert Gore', *DNZB*, vol. 1 · *CGPLA Eng. & Wales* (1887) · H. A. Amos, 'Browne, Sir Thomas Gore', *AusDB*, vol. 3
Archives Archives New Zealand, Wellington, corresp., letter-books, and papers · Bucks. RLSS, papers relating to Corfu · NRA, priv. coll., diaries
Wealth at death £18,978 8s. 10d.: probate, 6 May 1887, *CGPLA Eng. & Wales*

Browne, Sir Thomas Henry (1787–1855), army officer, was born on 8 September 1787 in Liverpool, the eldest of the seven children of George Browne, of Irish descent, merchant, banker, and imperial and Tuscan consul at Liverpool, and his wife, Felicity Dorothea (1766–1827), daughter of Benedict-Park Wagner, of North Hall near Wigan, of Italian descent, wine merchant, and imperial and Tuscan consul-general at Liverpool. His sister was the poet Felicia *Hemans (1793–1835); and his brothers were Lieutenant-Colonel George Baxter Browne, who served in the Peninsula and became chief commissioner of police in Ireland, and Claude Scott Browne (*d.* 1821), deputy assistant commissary-general in Upper Canada. As a result of financial problems, about 1800 the family moved from Liverpool to north Wales, initially settling at Gwrych, near Abergele, Denbighshire. In 1809 they moved to Bronwylfa, near St Asaph, Flintshire, an area with which Browne maintained close links for much of his life.

Browne entered the army on 28 October 1805, as a non-purchase ensign in the 2nd battalion 23rd foot (Royal Welch Fusiliers). On 18 September 1806 he was promoted first lieutenant. He was present at the bombardment and siege of Copenhagen in July 1807, receiving £97 as a subaltern's share of the prize money for the capture of the Danish fleet. In January 1808, as a result of the war scare which followed the Chesapeake incident, he was posted with the 2nd battalion to Nova Scotia, where he remained until November 1808. The battalion then took part in the Martinique expedition, on which he was in several actions. During the siege of Fort Desaix he was seriously wounded in the arm.

From March 1809 to November 1810 Browne was again stationed in Nova Scotia. From Halifax the 23rd moved to Portugal, arriving in November 1810. Following the withdrawal of French forces under Marshal Masséna, the regiment participated in Wellington's advance from the lines of the Torres Vedras. Browne was not present at the siege of the fortress of Badajoz or the battle of Albuera, having been assigned temporary duties in Lisbon with the adjutant-general's department. During 1812 he was appointed deputy assistant adjutant-general on the staff of the adjutant-general, before his promotion to captain in 1813.

As a staff officer Browne participated in every significant battle in Spain and France, from Salamanca (22 July 1812) to the British army's last major engagement of the Peninsular War, at Toulouse (10 April 1814). At Vitoria (21 June 1813) he received a sabre wound to his head and was subsequently captured by French troops, then rescued by the 15th hussars.

After Napoleon's exile to Elba the 2nd battalion of the 23rd was disbanded and its officers placed on half pay. In August 1814 Browne was ordered to join the British forces in North America, as deputy assistant quartermaster-general, but the order was soon cancelled and he returned to England on leave. Wellington had requested that he again be appointed to his staff during the Waterloo campaign. This, however, was rejected by the administrative authorities at the Horse Guards, to the duke's displeasure. Browne, therefore, was not present at the battle of Waterloo, serving instead as aide-de-camp to Lieutenant-General Sir Charles Stewart at the Vienna headquarters of the Austrian, Prussian, and Russian armies. He was described by the whig MP H. G. Bennet as 'a creature of Lord Stewart's' (*Letters of George IV*, 2.301). Following the defeat of Napoleon he was attached under Stewart to the allied forces occupying Paris, before returning as a private secretary at the British embassy in Vienna. With the reduction of the British army he was placed on half pay, as regimental captain, on 25 December 1815.

With the end of the Napoleonic wars Browne returned to Bronwylfa. His promotion thereafter was slow, though he received several distinctions. In June 1817 he was appointed brevet major. In 1818 he was made KH; and in January 1819 he was promoted brevet lieutenant-colonel. His appointment as KCH in 1821 entitled him to the half pay of a lieutenant-colonel.

Recommended by Lord Stewart and able to speak Italian, Browne in 1818 had been appointed a member of the three-man 'Milan commission'. Appointed by Sir John Leach, the vice-chancellor, for the prince regent, who wanted divorce with ministerial consent, the commission went to Italy to investigate the scandalous conduct of Caroline, princess of Wales. Browne was keen but imprudent, and caused 'a little breeze' (*Letters of George IV*, 2.301) with the Austrian government. In November 1818 he had 'no doubt of everything being completely proved' and that there was 'sufficient evidence to warrant a public enquiry' (Hibbert, 137). In Milan in January 1821 two men apparently tried to murder Browne, and instead wounded him; allegedly they were partisans of Caroline. In 1823 Browne requested a household place in recompense for his Milan commission services. The king considered his conduct 'altogether wrong-headed' (*Letters of George IV*, 3.23) and refused.

Browne became sheriff of Flintshire in 1824 and a knight bachelor in 1826. He was not, however, promoted colonel until January 1837. In June 1854 he was promoted lieutenant-general and in August became colonel of the 80th regiment.

Browne was married three times. His first wife, Louisa Anne Gray, daughter of Robert Gray, lord bishop of Bristol, died in childbirth in July 1823. His second wife, Elizabeth Anne, daughter of Rowland Burdon of Castle Eden, co. Durham, also died in childbirth, in February 1826. In March 1828 he married Elizabeth, eldest daughter of the Revd Henry Brandling of Gosforth House, near Newcastle upon Tyne. The couple had two sons: Henry Ralph, the elder, joined the army and became a general, and Ralph Charles became a clergyman. Browne and his third wife had separated, however, by the time of his death from pneumonic complications on 11 March 1855, aged sixty-seven, at his London home, 19 Camden Terrace, Camden New Town. He was buried in the cathedral in St Asaph, north Wales, where his son erected a memorial tablet in his honour.   STEWART M. FRASER

Sources *The Napoleonic war journal of Captain Thomas Henry Browne, 1807–1816*, ed. R. N. Buckley (1987) • Boase, *Mod. Eng. biog.* • Burke, *Gen. GB* (1871) • *The Times* (15 March 1855) • C. Hibbert, *George IV*, 2: *Regent and king* (1973) • L. Melville, *The first gentleman of Europe*, 2 (1906) • *The letters of King George IV, 1812–1830*, ed. A. Aspinall, 2–3 (1938), vols. 2, 3 • P. W. Trinder, *Mrs Hemans* (1984) • H. F. Chorley, *Memorials of Mrs Hemans*, 1 (1836) • *GM*, 2nd ser., 43 (1855), 451
Archives priv. coll.
Likenesses miniatures, repro. in Buckley, *Napoleonic war journal*

Browne, Valentine (*c*.1594–1672), Franciscan friar, was born in Galway. The Brownes were one of the prominent families known as the Tribes of Galway. He was related to the Burke and Blake families, perhaps given the name Valentine from the association with the latter. He studied at home and at the Irish College at Douai in the Spanish Netherlands, whence he entered the Franciscan order at St Anthony's College, Louvain, on 20 August 1617. It is unlikely, as is sometimes suggested, that he was 'a distinguished lawyer' beforehand (Jennings, 'Abbey', 112). He became a lecturer in theology and taught Franciscan students in Galway. The friars had a house there in 1629, when he was elected minister provincial on 15 August. A proclamation from Dublin Castle of 1 April 1629 ordered the closing of religious houses, yet he visited all Franciscan dwellings in Ireland twice before September 1632. During this time he corresponded with Luke Wadding in Rome on the state of the Franciscans—they were living with relatives or friends, engaged in trying to send students abroad. From June to September 1631 he put up a spirited defence against the questionable propositions allegedly preached by the religious in Ireland which Patrick Cahill publicized in Paris.

On 5 May 1632 Browne, who was interested in acquiring books on Franciscan history, gave his official blessing to the work of the Franciscan historian Michel Ó Cléirigh. During his provincialate, which lasted until 1633, he received Peter Walsh into the order. The chapter bill for 1639 shows him continuing as guardian in Galway, and that county was his base from then on. In 1642 he welcomed to Galway a group of Poor Clares, among them the future abbess Mary Bonaventure Browne, possibly a relative, who later wrote her recollections in Spain. In 1643, with the confederate Catholics in control of Galway, he preached the sermon at the first solemn mass for nearly 100 years celebrated in the old friary, which the friars occupied from 1641 to 1652. In 1644 he was chosen prechapter visitator of the Irish Franciscans.

Described as 'inveterately Anglo-Irish' (Jennings, *Michael O Cleirigh*, 83) Browne supported James Butler, marquess of Ormond within the city. In 1648 he preached against the excommunication issued by the nuncio, Rinuccini, of supporters of the truce with the commander Murrough O'Brien, Lord Inchiquin, and was suspended from public ministry on 12 July 1648. He apologized, but then relapsed. With other friars he rejected the authority of the minister provincial and accepted that of the controversial visitator Redmond Caron. Caron's supporters were excommunicated by the Franciscan order on 22 June 1649 and had to retract at the chapter of 1650. Browne remained an Ormondist, and in 1652 was one of the few who favoured the surrender of Galway to English forces. In that year he was described as 'the man that gave seven several opinions, one contrary to the other, since the coming of the Lord Nuncio' (Gilbert, *Contemporary history*, 3.73).

In 1658 Browne was appointed titular guardian of Galway and nominated for visitator. He was a known Valesian, or supporter of Peter Walsh (Valesius) and of his one-sided statement of Catholic loyalty to the king. On 31 March 1662 he signed a very florid approval of the remonstrance drawn up by Walsh, but later revoked this. He was a Franciscan commissary and visitator in August 1664, when at least seventy years old. In June 1665 he was present at a meeting of the friars at Killeigh to show fidelity to Charles II. On this occasion the wording of Walsh's 'loyal formulary' was changed, though it still proved unacceptable to Ormond, now again lord lieutenant. Browne's nephew Mark Browne OFM was visitator for the chapter of 1666 and allowed his uncle, a former provincial, to vote. Mark Browne's behaviour was challenged at home and abroad and the chapter aborted. He had been in Spain for years and was known to the Spanish minister-general, Salizanes, a relationship which may have helped his uncle. Valentine Browne attended the chapters at Meelick in 1669 and Athlone in 1670, and died two years later at the friary of Baile an Chláir, or Bally Clare, now Claregalway, co. Galway. Peter Walsh described him as 'a man esteemed both of sound learning, and great holiness' (Walsh, 556), but an opponent thought him pompous, calling him 'a little lump of a dwarfish quiditative, participating both of human and assnical subsistence … assumed to a transcendent degree of dignity' (Gilbert, *Contemporary history*, 3.74).   IGNATIUS FENNESSY

Sources MSS, Franciscan Library, Killiney, co. Dublin · C. Giblin, ed., *Liber Lovaniensis: a collection of Irish Franciscan documents, 1629–1717* (1956) · B. Jennings and C. Giblin, eds., *Louvain papers, 1606–1827*, IMC (1968) · B. Jennings, ed., *Wadding papers, 1614–38*, IMC (1953) · P. Walsh, *The history and vindication of the loyal formulary, or Irish remonstrance* (1674) · J. T. Gilbert, ed., *A contemporary history of affairs in Ireland from 1641 to 1652*, 3 vols. (1879–80) · B. O'Ferrall and D. O'Connell, *Commentarius Rinuccinianus de sedis apostolicae legatione ad foederatos Hiberniae Catholicos per annos 1645–1649*, ed. J. Kavanagh, 6 vols., IMC (1932–49) · [R. L. Browne], 'A history of the Franciscan order in Ireland by Donagh Mooney', *Franciscan tertiary* (1897), 353 · B. Jennings, *Michael O Cleirigh, chief of the four masters, and his associates* (1936) · B. Jennings, 'The abbey of St Francis, Galway', *Journal of the Galway Archaeological and Historical Society*, 22 (1946–7), 101–19 · *Relatio veridica & sincera status provinciae Hiberniae … sub regimine F. Petri Marchant* (1651) · C. O'Brien, ed., *Recollections of an Irish Poor Clare in the seventeenth century* (1993) · M. J. Hynes, *The mission of Rinuccini in Ireland: nuncio extraordinary to Ireland, 1645–1649* (Dublin, 1932)
Archives Franciscan Library, Killiney, co. Dublin · St Isidore's College, Rome, archives

Browne, William (1590/91–1645?), poet, was the son of Thomas Browne and Joane Healen of Tavistock, Devon. According to Wood, he attended Tavistock grammar school and was sent to Exeter College, Oxford, about 1603, but left without taking a degree (Wood, *Ath. Oxon.*, 2.364–5). There is no record of his attendance at this time and there may be some confusion with his later stay at Oxford in 1624–5. His ancestry can be traced to Sir Thomas Browne of Betchworth Castle near Dorking in Surrey, whose grandson, John, moved to Tavistock, Devon (BL, Harley MS, 6164, fol. 37).

The inns of court and literary friendships, 1612–1616 Browne was admitted to the Inner Temple on 1 March 1612 after transferring from Clifford's Inn. He seems to have been the quasi-official poet for the Inner Temple from about 1613 to 1616. The majority of the verses before the first book of his *Britannia's Pastorals* (1613) were from inner templars, including John Selden, Edward Heyward, and Thomas Gardiner, who stood as one of Browne's sureties on admission to the Inner Temple. His volume of pastoral eclogues, *The Shepheards Pipe* (1614), included an elegy for a fellow inner templar, Thomas Manwood, and he provided the masque for the 1614–15 Christmas festivities which was performed on 13 January 1615 to an audience which crowded the Inner Temple hall. After the event, part of the cloisters had to be repaired, having been 'broken down by such as climbed up at the windows of the hall to see the mask' (Inderwick, 2.95, xliii).

Browne's first known work was the elegy for Prince Henry that was published alongside an elegy from Christopher Brooke from Lincoln's Inn in the volume *Two Elegies, Consecrated to the Memorie of Henry Prince of Wales* (1613). It was expensively produced with Henry's crest printed on a black-inked page and an inserted engraving of the prince lying in state by William Hole. Browne may have sought the patronage of Prince Henry as his accounts record a payment to a 'Mr Browne for a booke given to his highnes' on 8 October 1608 (Parsons, 503), possibly an early draft of *Britannia's Pastorals*. In the first song he speaks of being 'not twice ten suns' and he would have been seventeen or eighteen when this book was presented to Henry. Its eventual dedicatee was Lord Edward Zouche, a member of the privy council and fiercely anti-Spanish. Browne celebrates his Hampshire estate, Bramshill, in his dedicatory verse to Zouche before *The Shepheards Pipe*.

With his first major work, *Britannia's Pastorals*, Browne set himself the ambitious task of composing a pastoral epic on a national theme. The poem's title recalls William Camden's *Britannia* (1586) and announces its affinities with the antiquarian impulse to map the land. Browne's pastoral epic found a companion in this enterprise in Michael Drayton's long chorographical poem, *Poly-Olbion* (1612). Like *Poly-Olbion*, *Britannia's Pastorals* is an experimental poem that mixes literary genres in the effort to find a form to represent the nation. Browne followed the first book with a second published in 1616. These two books are very different in form and tone. The first combines Italianate pastoral tragicomedy with Spenserian allegory to give the poem an English flavour. The fifth song includes Browne's previously published elegy for Prince Henry sung by Idya (England) in the Vale of Woe, who also laments the fate of that other protestant martyr-hero, Robert, earl of Essex, and of Sir Walter Ralegh, and Arabella Stuart, imprisoned under James I. The prince's loss is redeemed by the marriage of Princess Elizabeth and Frederick, elector palatine, figured in the story of the union of Alethia (Protestant Truth) and Amintas, and the first book ends with the poet looking towards a future when his muse will:

> make the Courtly Swaines
> Enamour'd on the *Musicke* of the Plaines.
> (p. 109)

The second book, published three years later, is much darker in tone and satire and elegy dominate. The poem criticizes James I's husbandry of the nation through the allegory of Famine, and laments the decay of the navy and, by association, the decline of the English empire that had triumphed under Elizabeth. For inspiration the poet turns to his fellow 'English Shepheards' and to the land of his birth, Devon, and its rivers. The elegiac and incomplete third book, which remained unpublished during his lifetime, is dominated by the theme of exile. The speaker has now left 'My *Tavy's* flowry shore' (*Poems of William Browne*, 2.28) for a foreign land and finds a sympathetic companion in the unnamed shepherd of the first song who has found refuge in the 'Den of Oblivion'. *Britannia's Pastorals* has been criticized for its disorienting formlessness. This feature of the poem perhaps should be seen less as a fault than as a function of the poem's decentralizing vision of the national landscape.

The Shepheards Pipe (1614) was published together with 'Other Eclogues: by Mr. Brooke, Mr. Wither, and Mr. Davies'. Browne was already acquainted with Brooke and probably knew George Wither through the inns of court. Wither was in prison for his satire *Abuses Stript, and Whipt* (1613) during this time. Browne may have come into contact with John Davies of Hereford through their mutual friend Drayton, who was known to Browne by 1613 when he placed a commendatory poem before *Britannia's Pastorals*. Drayton is often identified with this community of poets influenced by Spenser although he does not make an appearance in this volume. Brooke and Wither had also

contributed verses to *Britannia's Pastorals* and Wither, in his eclogue appended to *The Shepheards Pipe*, claimed to have met Browne and Brooke at a gathering of inns of court men to hear Browne read from *Britannia's Pastorals* at the Devil and St Dunstan tavern in Fleet Street. Browne, Brooke, and Wither appear throughout the eclogues under the pastoral pseudonyms of Willy, Cuddy, and Roget. This literary community was renewed in Wither's *The Shepherd's Hunting* (1615), which has Roget (Wither) visited in the Marshalsea prison by Cuddy (Brooke) and Willy (Browne), who are joined by Alexis (William Ferrar). Ferrar was Browne's fellow inner templar and had placed a poem before *Britannia's Pastorals*. Richard Brathwaite honoured 'bonny Browne', 'lovely Wither', 'solid *Seldon*', and 'their *Cuddy*' in his *A Strappado for the Divell* (1615, C4r). Browne and Brooke were the only new poets in the second edition of the Elizabethan pastoral anthology *Englands Helicon* (1614). Since the editor, Richard More, had published the *Two Elegies* it is possible that they had some type of working relationship. In 1616 Browne and Brooke contributed companion verses to *Sir Thomas Overburie his Wife with New Elegies upon his (now Knowne) Untimely Death*.

The commendatory verses to the second book of *Britannia's Pastorals* (1616) were again dominated by inner templars; Davies and Wither also contributed verses, as did Jonson, who had previously placed a poem before Brooke's *The Ghost of Richard the Third* (1614). The first song of this second book opens with an elegy for a friend, 'Alexis', drowned at sea. In the second song he praises Chapman, Drayton, Jonson, and Daniel alongside Brooke, Wither, and Davies. The third song closes with the poet moving off to greet Roget who is accompanied by:

> the lovely herdess of the dell
> That to an oaten quill can sing so well,
> (*Poems of William Browne*, 2.3.84)

perhaps an allusion to Wither's *Fidelia* (1615), which was answered in manuscript by Browne's 'Fido: an Epistle to Fidelia'.

Browne seems to have become involved in antiquarian circles through the inns of court. He began acquiring medieval manuscripts in his youth, including volumes from the libraries of John Stow and Sir Thomas North. Hoccleve held a special interest for Browne and he published a modernized version of one of his *Gesta* tales in *The Shepheards Pipe*. These interests appear to have drawn him to John Selden and the two shared books and information.

The 1620s The names of Browne and Drayton were frequently coupled in this period. Abraham Holland celebrated his recent friendship with Browne in the verse addressed 'To my honest father, Mr Michael Drayton, and my new, yet loved friend, Mr Will[iam] Browne', which appears to have been written soon after the 1616 publication of *Britannia's Pastorals* (Bodl. Oxf., MS Ashmole 36). Browne, together with Wither, placed verses before the second part of Drayton's *Poly-Olbion* (1622). Samuel Austin in his *Urania* (1629) urged Browne and Drayton to join him and turn their talents to divine poetry rather than secular amatory and pastoral verse. Drayton addressed an epistle

'To my Noble Friend Master William Browne, of the Evill Time' in his *The Battle of Agincourt* (1627) which is thought to date from the early 1620s. He seems to sympathize with Browne's decision to leave the third book of *Britannia's Pastorals* unpublished in these 'arsey varsey' (p. 191) times and:

> sit out of the way
> Of this ignoble age.
> (p. 193)

Browne's ode to Drayton, 'Awake, fair muse', appears to respond to this epistle; while it allows that some may now seek 'Honour by the victorious steel' (*Poems of William Browne*, 2.211), the times make the poet:

> affect (where men no traffic have)
> The holy horror of a savage cave.
> (ibid., 2.212)

Browne probably composed the first two songs of the third book of *Britannia's Pastorals* between 1624 and 1625 (J. Holmer, 'Internal evidence for dating William Browne's *Britannia's pastorals*, book III', *Papers of the Bibliographical Society of America*, 70, 1976, 347–64, see 362–4). The second song includes a witty satiric fairy poem that may have influenced Drayton's *Nimphidia, the Court of Fayrie* (1627), and a refutation of Sir William Monson's attack on Sir Richard Grenville in his *Naval Tracts*, written about 1624. This book remained unfinished. Browne supported a war in defence of Elizabeth and Frederick of Bohemia and produced 'An epitaph on Sir John Prowde, lieutenant-colonel to Sir Charles Morgan, slain at the siege of Groll, and buried at Zutphen, 1627'. In 1625 he wrote an elegy for the merchant Richard Fishbourne, a patron of Thomas Middleton.

The Herbert family, Oxford, and France The second book of *Britannia's Pastorals* was dedicated to William Herbert, third earl of Pembroke, and initiated a successful patronage relationship with the Herbert family that lasted until Browne's death. On 18 April 1615 a William Browne was granted the office of pursuivant of the court of wards and liveries. Hazlitt identified this Browne as the poet and suggested that he was preferred to the post by Pembroke, although, as he points out, there were two William Brownes in the Inner Temple at this time (*Whole Works*, 1.xv–xvi).

In the 1620s and 1630s Browne acted as 'the official poet of the Herbert family' (Brennan, 190), producing elegies for Mary Herbert, the dowager countess of Pembroke, Susan Vere, countess of Montgomery, her son, Charles, Lord Herbert of Cardiff and Shurland, and Pembroke's chaplain, John Smyth. He may have been the author of an elegy on Anne Prideaux, the daughter of John Prideaux, a client of Pembroke. The elegies for the members of the Herbert family appear to have had a very limited circulation, and may have been confined to the family itself. The exception is the well known and highly regarded epitaph 'On the Countess Dowager of Pembroke' ('Underneath this sable hearse / Lies the subject of all verse'), which seems to have been the official memorial put out by the Herbert family; it was included in a letter from Chamberlain to Carleton on 13 October 1621, circulated widely in manuscript, and appeared in print. Of equal interest is 'An Elegy on the Countess Dowager of Pembroke', attributed to Browne in BL, Lansdowne MS 777. These two poems are the only recorded verse commemorations for Mary Herbert.

Between 1623 and 1625 Browne acted as tutor to Robert Dormer (later earl of Carnarvon), the ward of Philip Herbert, earl of Montgomery, at Eton and Exeter College, Oxford. They matriculated on the same day, 30 April 1624 (Browne's age was given as thirty-three), and Browne was created MA on 16 November 1624. Both Browne and Dormer contributed a Latin poem on the marriage of Charles and Henrietta Maria to *Epithalamia Oxoniensia* (1625). Jack Markham, a 'late gentleman-usher to the queen', told Aubrey that the tutelage of Dormer 'was worth to [Browne] 5 or 6000 li., i.e. he bought 300 li. per annum land' (*Brief Lives*, 1.312; 2.43).

Browne attracted a group of younger writers at Exeter College. William Kidley wrote his long heroic poem, 'Kidley's Hawkins', modelled on *Britannia's Pastorals*, at Exeter in 1625 under the guidance of Browne. Nathanael Carpenter, a fellow of the college, praised his 'worthy friend *Mr. W. Browne*' in his *Geographie* (1625), dedicated to Pembroke. Browne produced a number of elegies for his Oxford associates, such as John Deane of New College (*d.* 1626/1627), and Francis Vaux of Broadgates Hall. In the mid-1630s current and past members of the college produced a series of verses encouraging him to continue the third book of *Britannia's Pastorals* that were inserted in a 1625 edition of the poem which may have been presented to the college by Browne (Beloe, 58). These verses may have coincided with a visit by Browne to his college. In his elegy on Richard Turner of St Mary's Hall, who died in 1637, he claimed to have met Turner in Oxford eight days before his death.

Browne would have accompanied Dormer on his grand tour after his marriage to Montgomery's daughter, Anna Sophia, in February 1625; the tour may have been organized in conjunction with Montgomery's journey to the French court in May 1625 to escort Henrietta Maria to England for her marriage (Brown and Piva, 401). A passage in song 3 of the third book of *Britannia's Pastorals* records a journey from the Seine to the Loire (Saumur) to Thoué (Thouars) that may have been undertaken in 1625. Browne maintained his ties with the Herberts and Dormer into the 1640s. He ended a letter to Sir Benjamin Rudyerd, dated November 1640, written from his home in Dorking, with prayers 'for my honord Lord the Lord Chamberlayne' (Philip Herbert, fourth earl of Pembroke) and 'my good Lord and Master the Earle of Caernarvon' (Bodl. Oxf., MS Ashmole 830, fol. 288). Herbert sponsored Browne's *The History of Polexander*, a translation of a romance by Gomberville, and took responsibility for its posthumous publication in 1647. According to Bullen a copy of the French original is in the library at Wilton (*Poems of William Browne*, xxxiii).

Sussex and Surrey, 1628–1645 On 24 December 1628 at Horsham, Browne married Timothy Eversfield (*bap.* 1600, *d. c.*1662), the daughter of Sir Thomas Eversfield from

Denne, outside Horsham, in Sussex. Her father's will allowed her a dowry equivalent to 1000 marks. There may have been some conflict over the dowry. Lady Eversfield in her will, dated November 1640, stated that she owed 'my son Browne not one farthing of my daughter's portion for use nor yet principal' (*Poems of William Browne*, xx–xxi). Timothy may have been the 'Caelia' to whom Browne addressed many of his sonnets and lyrics. This identification was first suggested by Bullen, who also suggested that he had had a previous wife who died in 1614 (ibid., ix–xx). Moorman and Briggs argue that the mistress of his lyrics was possibly a Browne of Betchworth who died in the mid-1620s, as she is associated with Betchworth Castle (Moorman, 12–13; Briggs, 147–56).

Browne appears to have lived with the Eversfields at Horsham. The list of gentry from the Herald's College visitation of Sussex in 1634 includes 'William Browne, of the Inner Temple, (son of Thomas Browne, of Tavistock)' (*Sussex Archaeological Collections*, 39.110). His sons were born in Horsham: Robert was baptized on 27 September 1629 and died on 22 October; a second son, also called Robert, was baptized on 20 March 1631 and was buried two days later; a third son, Ambrose, was baptized on 13 November 1635. He may have been named after Sir Ambrose Browne of Betchworth Castle (Briggs, 177–8).

Between 1634 and 1640 Browne moved to Dorking in Surrey, near the seat of the Browne family of Betchworth. His wife's family were parliamentarians during the civil war. On 6 November 1645 the administration of his estate was granted in the prerogative court of Canterbury to his widow, Timothy. The date of his death is not given and he is described as 'late of Dorking, in the county of Surrey, Esquire' (Briggs, 6–7, 183). It is therefore highly unlikely that he returned to his birthplace to die, as is often thought.

Reputation Browne's verses circulated widely in manuscript among a contemporary inns of court and university audience. Milton imitated Browne in his early poetry as did Vaughan in his 'To the River Isca'. In his lifetime he gained a name as a Devonshire poet: Nathanael Carpenter in his *Geographie* (1625) said that he would leave the writing of Devon's literary heritage to Browne who could draw 'out the line of his *Poeticke* Auncestors, beginning in *Iosephus Iscarus*, and ending in *himselfe*' (Rr2v–4v). His reputation, however, soon faded. Aubrey was unable to find anyone in the household of the second earl of Carnarvon that had heard of Browne. Winstanley speaks favourably of Browne in his *Lives of the most Famous English Poets* (1687), but attributes a passage to *Britannia's Pastorals* that is not his, strongly suggesting that he had not read Browne's poems. John Prince reprinted this passage in his *Worthies of Devon* (1701), so its seems that he too was not familiar with Browne's poetry. Thomas Davies in the preface to his 1772 edition of Browne's works lamented that 'the public scarce know that such a man ever existed' (p. ii) and attributed this to the scarcity of copies of his poems.

Further editions appeared throughout the nineteenth century. In 1815 Sir Samuel Egerton Brydges edited the poems in BL, Lansdowne MS 777, preferring 'the natural and uncalled chain of ideas' to the rigidity of Augustan poetry (p. 3). Browne was admired by the Romantic poets. Coleridge claimed Browne, his fellow countryman, as a distant relative; he and Southey attributed epitaphs in the church at Ottery St Mary to Browne. Clare read the extracts from Browne in Southey's *Selected Works of the British Poets* (1831) with great enthusiasm, saying that 'there is a freshness & beauty about them that surprised [*sic*] me' (*Letters*, 548). Keats adopted lines from *Britannia's Pastorals* for the motto to his *Poems* (1817), as did Elizabeth Barrett Browning in her 'A Vision of the Poets'. Hazlitt published *The Whole Works of William Browne* (1868–9) with a detailed biography that depicted Browne primarily as a love poet.

In the mid-twentieth century Browne, along with other Spenserians, was neglected in surveys and anthologies of seventeenth-century poetry—disparaged as a throwback to the Elizabethan age. There has been a slow revival of interest in Browne. *Britannia's Pastorals*, in particular, has drawn the attention of critics interested in early modern nationhood. Browne's verses in manuscript and print, such as *The Shepheards Pipe*, can tell us much about the processes of intellectual and textual exchange in a range of communities, from the inns of court and universities to the Herbert circle. MICHELLE O'CALLAGHAN

Sources E. S. Briggs, 'Browne of Tavistock: a biographical and critical study', PhD diss., Harvard U., 1956 · *The whole works of William Browne of Tavistock, and of the Inner Temple*, ed. W. C. Hazlitt, 2 vols. (1868–9) · *The poems of William Browne of Tavistock*, ed. G. Godwin, 2 vols. (1894) [incl. introduction by A.H. Bullen] · F. W. Moorman, *William Browne: his Britannia's pastorals and the pastoral poetry of the Elizabethan age* (1897) · M. O'Callaghan, *The 'shepheards nation': Jacobean Spenserians and early Stuart cultural politics* (2000) · Wood, *Ath. Oxon.*, new edn, 2.364–6 · *Brief lives, chiefly of contemporaries, set down by John Aubrey, between the years 1669 and 1696*, ed. A. Clark, 2 vols. (1898), vol. 1, pp. 130, 312; vol. 2, p. 43 · P. Beal and others, *Index of English literary manuscripts*, ed. P. J. Croft and others, [4 vols. in 11 pts] (1980–), vol. 2 · C. Brown and M. Piva, 'William Browne, Marino, France and the third book of Britannia's pastorals', *Review of English Studies*, new ser., 29 (1978), 385–404 · J. Prince, *Danmonii orientales illustres, or, The worthies of Devon* (1701) · W. Beloe, *Anecdotes of literature and scarce books*, 6 vols. (1807–12), vol. 6 · M. Brennan, 'The literary patronage of the Herbert family, earls of Pembroke, 1550–1640', DPhil diss., U.Oxf., 1982 · L. Parsons, 'Prince Henry (1594–1612) as a patron of literature', *Modern Language Review*, 47 (1952), 503 · F. A. Inderwick and R. A. Roberts, eds., *A calendar of the Inner Temple records*, 2 (1898) · J. Comber, *Sussex genealogies*, 3 vols. (1931–3), vol. 1 · N. Carpenter, *Geographie delineated forth in two bookes*, 2nd edn (1635) · T. Westcote, *A view of Devonshire in MDCXXX, with a pedigree of most of its gentry*, ed. G. Oliver and P. Jones (1845) · *The letters of John Clare*, ed. M. Storey (1985) · *The notebooks of Samuel Taylor Coleridge*, ed. K. Coburn, 4 vols. (1957–90), vols. 2, 3 · W. Pattison, *The poetical works of William Pattison* (1728)

Archives BL, Add. MSS 23147, 34360, 35298 · BL, Stowe MSS 68, 952 · Bodl. Oxf., MSS Ashmole 40, 45, 46, 59 · Bodl. Oxf., pair of emblem books, second in Browne's hand, MS Ashmole 767 · U. Durham, MS Cosin V III.9 | Bodl. Oxf., letter to Sir Benjamin Rudyerd, MS Ashmole 830, fol. 288 [copy]

Browne, William (1629/30–1678), botanist, was born at Oxford, the son of either William Brown, a mercer of that city, or—according to another account (Wood, *Ath. Oxon.*)—John Browne, one of its bailiffs. Admitted to the university in 1644 while Oxford was under siege in the civil war, he had a distinguished career at Magdalen College, where he graduated BA in 1647 and was elected fellow in 1657, praelector of moral philosophy the next year, and dean of divinity the year after that, gained a BD in 1665, and finally became vice-president for 1669–70. By his student years he had developed a keenness for field botany, ranging widely over the Oxford region and as far afield as Northamptonshire and Sussex in search of plants. Many records by him, including the first of the military and monkey orchids in Britain, feature in William How's own annotated copy of his *Phytologia* (1650), some of which were published in Merrett's *Pinax* (1666). William Coles acknowledged his help in his *Adam in Eden* (1657), as did Robert Plot in his *Natural History of Oxfordshire* (1677). According to Anthony Wood, who rated him one of the best botanists of the time, he was also the principal of the three authors credited with the revised catalogue of the Oxford Physic Garden of 1658. He died suddenly of apoplexy on 25 March 1678 and was buried in the antechapel of his college, where a marble tablet commemorates him.   B. D. JACKSON, *rev.* D. E. ALLEN

Sources R. T. Gunther, *Early British botanists and their gardens* (1922), 298–302 · G. C. Druce, *The flora of Oxfordshire*, 2nd edn (1927), 69–73 · G. C. Druce, *The flora of Berkshire* (1897), 106–7 · Wood, *Ath. Oxon.: Fasti* (1820), 104, 282 · A. Wood, *The history and antiquities of the colleges and halls in the University of Oxford*, ed. J. Gutch, appx (1790), 344 · J. R. Bloxam, *A register of the presidents, fellows … of Saint Mary Magdalen College*, 8 vols. (1853–85)

Browne, Sir William (1692–1774), physician, was born in co. Durham, the son of a physician. After attending school in Durham he entered Peterhouse, Cambridge, in 1707; he graduated BA in 1711 and MA in 1714. In 1716, having received a licence from the university, he began to practise medicine at Lynn, Norfolk, where he lived for over thirty years. He was considered to be eccentric, but he succeeded in making a fortune, and in 1749 he moved to London, where he lived for the rest of his life in Queen Square, Bloomsbury. In 1721 he took his MD degree at Cambridge. In 1725 he was admitted a candidate at the Royal College of Physicians, and in the next year a fellow. On 1 March 1739 he was admitted a fellow of the Royal Society, and in 1748 he was knighted through the influence of the duke of Montagu.

After settling in London, Browne held various offices of the College of Physicians, and in 1765 and 1766 he was president. At this time there was a violent dispute between the college and the licentiates. Browne was a defender of the privileges of the universities, and had offended the licentiates by his pamphlet in the college's dispute with Isaac Schomberg (*Vindication of the Royal College of Physicians*, 1753). Samuel Foote caricatured him on the stage in his farce *The Devil on Two Sticks*. Browne sent Foote a card complimenting him on his accuracy, but sending his own muff to complete the likeness. He found it difficult to maintain his dignity at the college, and on one occasion, when he was holding the *comitia*, the licentiates forced their way tumultuously into the room. Resolving to avoid such an affront in future, Browne decided to resign his office instead of holding it for the usual term of

five years. On resigning the chair he delivered a humorous address, which was published in Latin and English. In this he declared that he had found fortune in the country and honour in the college, and that he now proposed to find pleasure at the medicinal springs. He accordingly went to Bath, where he called upon William Warburton at Prior Park. Warburton gives a ludicrous description of the old gentleman, with his muff, his Horace, and his spyglass, showing all the alacrity of a boy both in body and mind.

Browne returned to London, where, on St Luke's day 1771, he appeared at Batson's coffee house in a laced coat and fringed gloves to show himself to the lord mayor. He explained his healthy appearance by saying that he had neither wife nor debts. His wife had died on 25 July 1763, in her sixty-fourth year; they had one daughter. Browne died on 10 March 1774. He was buried at Hillington, Norfolk, under a Latin epitaph written by himself. He left a will profusely interlarded with Greek and Latin, and directed that his Elzevir Horace should be placed on his coffin. He left three gold medals worth 5 guineas each to be given to undergraduates at Cambridge for Greek and Latin odes and epigrams. He also founded a scholarship of 20 guineas a year, at Peterhouse.

Browne wrote a number of works on a wide range of subjects, his best-known production probably being the Cambridge answer to the much better Oxford epigram upon George I's present of Bishop Moore's library to the University of Cambridge:

The king to Oxford sent a troop of horse,
For tories own no argument but force;
With equal care to Cambridge books he sent,
For whigs allow no force but argument.

LESLIE STEPHEN, *rev.*

Sources Munk, *Roll* · Venn, *Alum. Cant.* · [W. Warburton], *Letters from a late eminent prelate to one of his friends*, ed. R. Hurd [1808] · Nichols, *Lit. anecdotes*, 3.315–30
Archives RCP Lond., commonplace book
Likenesses T. Hudson, oils, 1767, RCP Lond. · T. O., etching, 1771, Wellcome L. · caricature, etching, 1771, NPG · J. Dixon, mezzotint (after T. Hudson), BM, NPG, Wellcome L.
Wealth at death had succeeded in earning a fortune

Browne, William (1737–1802), public official and colonial governor, was born in Salem, Massachusetts, on 27 February 1737 to Samuel Browne, a merchant, and Catherine Winthrop (*b. c.*1716). He graduated AB from Harvard College as valedictorian of the class of 1755, ranked third behind Henry Appleton, the son of a member of the Harvard Corporation—an understandable departure from Harvard's tradition of ranking graduates according to the prestige of their family lineage. His MA oration in 1757 defended the proposition that not all warfare violates Christian charity.

Browne read law under Edmund Trowbridge, but instead of seeking admission to the bar he devoted himself to the management of his inheritance of £5000 and more than 100,000 acres in Connecticut and other settled parts of New England. He could have avoided public service, but in 1761, at the age of twenty-four, he accepted appointment as justice of the peace in Salem, and in 1764 agreed to assume the office of collector of customs for Salem and Marblehead when his predecessor was caught flagrantly taking bribes from importers of wine and fruit and allegedly sharing the booty with the governor, Francis Bernard. In 1762 the voters of Salem elected him to the Massachusetts house of representatives where he supported Chief Justice Thomas Hutchinson while at the same time serving as a trusted adviser to Hutchinson's rival, James Otis. In 1768 Browne became a marked man when he voted to rescind the Massachusetts circular letter which had condemned the controversial Townshend duties (British direct taxes on internal American trade).

With family connections going back to the Winthrops and Dudleys, Browne did not need affiliation with the dominant Hutchinson–Oliver faction as a prop to his social pre-eminence, and accordingly the Sons of Liberty treated him gingerly. After the younger James Otis received a serious blow to the head in a fracas with a customs agent in a Boston tavern in 1769, a sheriff arrested Browne as an accessory. A crowd of more than 2000 followed Browne and the sheriff to Fanueil Hall, where he was questioned by two Boston justices of the peace and then released. A year later a writer in the *Essex Gazette* attacked Browne for cancelling his subscription in protest against the newspaper's radical politics. In 1770 he failed to gain re-election to the house. Governor Hutchinson retaliated by appointing Browne to a seat on the Essex court of common pleas and to the rank of colonel in the colony's militia. Although condemned as a lackey of the Hutchinson faction, by this time Browne had, in fact, earned his militia command by years of service in the ranks. But the gulf between Browne and his whig neighbours had grown too large to be closed by the old civilities. In April 1774 he paraded the Essex militia for Governor Hutchinson and then compounded the offence by serving the governor tea purchased from the Tea Act consignee, Richard Clarke, in violation of the Boston patriots' boycott of East India Company tea.

His record of support for British authority earned Browne an unsought appointment to the mandamus council under the Coercive Acts, which were designed to punish the Bostonians for the tea party, and, in consequence, condemnation by a mass meeting of Essex county freeholders in September 1774. He wrote to his Essex county neighbours that they had no grounds to question his 'fidelity' to the public good nor his 'due regard to their true interest'—a careful statement of Massachusetts orthodoxy on the role and duty of an office-holder. Stung by this language the Essex county whigs demanded that Browne explain how 'you, Sir' could 'draw your sword and sheathe it into the bowels of your countrymen and fellow citizens' (Shipton, 554).

On 26 March 1776 Browne and his son, William, left Boston for London carrying with them General William Howe's dispatches to the North ministry. His wife, Ruth, *née* Wanton, about whom little is known, joined him in exile in the spring of 1778. With only his judicial salary of £200 to live on, the family rented a small house in Cowbridge, Glamorgan. His close friend Richard Saltonstall, also descended from early puritan stock, took a room at a Cowbridge tavern so that he could enjoy Browne's company. At Browne's behest other Massachusetts exiles— John Murray, William Apthorp, Henry Caner, Samuel Mather, Daniel Oliver, and Thomas Flucker—settled in Cowbridge or in nearby Cardiff. Browne was the lynchpin of this exile community, and after his departure the group scattered.

In May 1781 Browne was appointed governor of Bermuda. When he arrived there he found the governor's residence 'in ruins' despite assurances that a garden capable of supplying his table would be restored in preparation for his arrival. Browne told the assembly that his long experience in colonial New England equipped him to understand 'their real wants and reasonable expectations', another example of his ability to articulate the assumptions of British official orthodoxy. As he later reported to Lord North, he got along well with the planter class by adhering to 'the principle of being well with every one and familiar with no one' (Shipton, 559). When the ministry privately asked Browne's advice about abolishing the slave trade, Browne reported that importation of Africans in Bermuda did not exceed ten a year and that the planters regarded the sale of slaves as morally reprehensible.

Browne secretly visited the United States in 1784 in hopes of recovering his property under the terms of the peace settlement. But he was too late. His Salem mansion was already listed for auction by the committee on the sale of confiscated estates—it was the only loyalist property in Salem not recovered by the original owners. Browne returned to Bermuda, and prepared a claim for compensation from the British government for his Salem property and more than 10,000 acres of land in Connecticut (estimated value, £33,256) which he personally presented before the claims commissioners in Halifax, Nova Scotia, in the summer of 1786. There is no record of his claim's being paid, and his £200 compensation for service on the mandamus council and £750 salary as governor of Bermuda were in line with the minimal compensation that successful loyalist supplicants received.

These distractions compounded Browne's inability to suppress illegal trade between Bermuda and the United States and probably contributed to his recall in 1788. He took up lodging in the city of Westminster, and continued to receive a partial salary until 27 February 1790. His daughter married John Harvey Tucker, a Yale graduate (class of 1796), but his emotionally troubled son, William, for whom Browne had secured a commission in the 58th regiment of the British army, committed suicide in 1786. During the last decade of his life Browne devoted himself unsuccessfully to recovering unpaid salary and fees from the crown and a loan from the Winthrop family to Joseph Wanton which Browne had co-signed years earlier. He died in Westminster on 13 February 1802 following twelve days of a painful abdominal illness.

ROBERT M. CALHOON

Sources C. K. Shipton, *Sibley's Harvard graduates: biographical sketches of those who attended Harvard College*, 13 (1965), 551–60 • *The journal of Samuel Curwen, loyalist*, ed. A. Oliver (1972) • M. B. Norton, *The British Americans: the loyalist exiles in England, 1774–1789* (Boston, 1972)
Archives Mass. Hist. Soc., letter-book • PRO, corresp., PRO 30/55 | Government Archives, Hamilton, Bermuda archives, corresp. and papers [copies]

Browne, William. *See* Brown, William (1748–1825).

Browne, William Alexander Francis (1805–1885), alienist, was born on 24 June 1805 in Stirling, the son of William Browne (c.1785–1806), a lieutenant in the Cameronians, who drowned in the wreck of a troopship on the Goodwin Sands, and his wife, Jessie (d. 1861). Brought up in the home of his paternal grandparents, The Enclosure, Stirling, by his mother and her two unmarried sisters, Browne was a member of the Scottish Episcopal church. He was educated at the local high school, studied medicine at the University of Edinburgh, and qualified as a licenciate of the Royal College of Surgeons of Edinburgh in 1826. Elected a fellow of the Royal Medical Society on 25 November 1825, he became its president on 8 December 1826 and its senior president for 1827–8. Like many ambitious but ill-connected young professionals in the 1820s, Browne was strongly attracted to the phrenological doctrines of F. J. Gall (1757–1828) and J. G. Spurzheim (1776–1832), and he became a close friend and disciple of the leading Scottish phrenologists, the brothers George and Andrew Combe. Vice-president of the Edinburgh Phrenological Society between 1830 and 1832, Browne was for a time one of the more popular phrenological lecturers in the city.

In 1828 Browne left Edinburgh for the continent, entrusted with the care of a well-to-do lunatic being treated through travel and changes of scene. For two years, as they travelled through Belgium, France, and Italy, Browne made a practice of visiting local asylums, forming a close attachment in Paris to the French alienist J. E. D. Esquirol (1772–1840), with whom he returned to study for several months in 1832. Subsequently he sought to establish himself as a general practitioner in his home town of Stirling. In 1834, however, with the support of the Combes, he secured the vacant superintendency of the Royal Lunatic Asylum at Montrose. That same year he married Magdalene Howden Balfour, daughter of Andrew Balfour, physician and publisher of the *Edinburgh Encyclopaedia*. They had eight children, three of whom died in infancy; two others—James Crichton-*Browne (1840–1938) and John Hutton Balfour Browne (1845–1921)—achieved eminence in medicine and law respectively.

A talented administrator, Browne began his tenure at Montrose by introducing the new system of moral treatment pioneered by William Tuke at the York Retreat, and by Philippe Pinel and Esquirol in Paris. He enjoyed considerable success with this new system, which minimized the use of physical coercion and sought to employ carefully designed techniques and a controlled environment to induce patients to collaborate in their own recovery. A course of public lectures delivered at the asylum in the autumn of 1836 and published in May 1837, *What asylums were, are, and ought to be*, brought him national and international attention. Its harrowing, if over-simplified, descriptions of the worst horrors of the traditional madhouse were drawn directly from evidence presented to a series of early nineteenth-century parliamentary inquiries, and its powerful propaganda on behalf of the new therapeutic regime significantly advanced the cause of reform in the treatment of lunatics.

The book also secured for Browne the superintendency of the new and handsomely endowed Crichton Royal Asylum, then being constructed in Dumfries, and he arrived in time to play a major role in designing, equipping, and staffing the asylum. Browne obtained his MD from Heidelberg in January 1839 and then sought over the next eighteen years to turn the Crichton Royal into an actual example of his utopian vision of the perfect asylum. Within an institution carefully designed to preserve existing class distinctions, patients were encouraged to engage in work or other physical activity, to learn languages or musical instruments, to participate as audience or actors in plays, and to submit themselves to a minutely organized and rigidly structured routine. Browne also insisted on the importance of making use of drugs as an additional aid in the treatment of mental disorder, and he experimented aggressively with a variety of possible pharmacological remedies. Yet despite his extraordinary energies and talents, and the virtual absence of the material constraints that hampered other Victorian asylum superintendents, Browne's annual reports at the Crichton Royal revealed that his experience essentially paralleled theirs: declining cure rates; the accumulation of chronic patients; and on his part a growing pessimism about the prospects and even the desirability of curing mental illness.

Browne shared with his fellow Scots an abhorrence of the English poor law. He was proud of the fact that Scotland's asylums were charitable enterprises, and when in the mid-1850s the American reformer Dorothea Dix (1802–1887) sought to extend the English model of centrally supervised, tax-funded pauper asylums north of the border, he fought publicly to block her plans. When the legislation was passed anyway, he manoeuvred behind the scenes to secure his appointment as one of the two Scottish lunacy commissioners, a position he assumed in 1857.

Browne spent much of the next fifteen years on the official circuit. The task seems to have suited him less well than the day-to-day challenges of running an asylum, but his official post added to his visibility within the profession. In 1865 his stature was recognized by his election as president of the Medico-Psychological Association of Great Britain and Ireland for 1865–6. By this time he had published *Endemic Degeneration* (1862), *Epileptics* (1865), and *Sisterhoods in Asylums* (1866). In 1870, on a tour of inspection in East Lothian, Browne was thrown from his carriage, and suffered severe head injuries that left him blind.

Forced into an unwanted retirement, he spent the last fifteen years of his life at the home he had established in 1857, Crindan, Dumfries, cared for by his two unmarried daughters, Madeline and Margaret. He died suddenly of a heart attack at Crindan on 2 March 1885.

ANDREW SCULL

Sources A. Scull, ed., *The asylum as Utopia: W. A. F. Browne and the mid-nineteenth-century consolidation of psychiatry* (1991) • A. Scull, C. MacKenzie, and N. Hervey, *Masters of Bedlam: the transformation of the mad-doctoring trade* (1996) • C. Cromhall Easterbrook, *The chronicle of Crichton Royal, 1833–1936* (1940) • *BMJ* (14 March 1885), 568–9 • *The Lancet* (14 March 1885) • R. Cooter, *Phrenology in the British Isles: an annotated historical biobibliography and index* (1989)
Archives Harvard U., Houghton L., Dorothea Dix MSS • NL Scot., corresp. with George Combe
Likenesses photograph, repro. in Easterbrook, *Chronicle of Crichton Royal*

Browne, William Charles Denis (1888–1915), composer and music critic, was born on 3 November 1888 at Lynnwood, 111 Lillington Avenue, Leamington Spa, the youngest of the five children of William Denis Browne (1836–1916), retired land agent and juror at the 1883 Phoenix Park murder trials, and his wife, Louisa Hackett (1843–1926). Both parents were Irish. His mother's family hailed from Moor Park and Riverstown, Birr, King's county. His paternal grandfather, the Very Revd Denis Browne, was dean of Emly, and his great-grandfather, the Rt Hon. Denis Browne, was MP for Mayo and younger brother of the first marquess of Sligo. Relatives called him Billy, while friends favoured Denis—the first half of his composite surname. All remarked on a charming personality, inspiring yet unassuming. Portraits also project a serene gaze.

Denis Browne won classics scholarships to Rugby School (1903) and Clare College, Cambridge (1907). Rupert Brooke, his contemporary and lifelong friend, wrote for him 'An Easter-day Song in Praise of Cremation' (1906) and 'The Dance' (1915), but no musical settings survive. Both men were active in student productions by the Marlowe Dramatic Society. For Milton's *Comus* in 1908, Denis Browne helped E. J. Dent to combine Henry Lawes's songs with tunes from 'Elizabeth Rogers hir virginall booke' (BL, Add. MS 10337). One anonymous 'Allmayne' (fol. 32) pervaded *To Gratiana Dancing and Singing* (1913). *Diaphenia* and *Epitaph on Salathiel Pavy* (1912) were also intended as 'Two Elizabethan Songs'. The influence of transcription on his creativity foreshadowed the work of Peter Warlock, as did his championship of ultra-modern music. But whereas Warlock was always a reluctant executant, Denis Browne excelled as pianist, accompanist, organist, and conductor. Dent rated him 'by far the cleverest of the musicians' (Dent, 86) at Cambridge, comparing him with Arthur Bliss, Armstrong Gibbs, Clive Carey, and Steuart Wilson.

Denis Browne was intended for the civil service until a poor degree and pleas from family and friends convinced his father to countenance a career change. As Clare's organ scholar from 1910 to 1912, he studied composition with Charles Wood, the organ with Alan Gray, the piano with a former pupil of Ferruccio Busoni, Ursula Newton, and history with Dent. His Magnificat and Nunc dimittis

(1911) and *Two Dances* (1912) were premièred by Clare College choir and orchestra. Six songs (1908–1910?) are unremarkable, though two Tennyson settings, 'Move Eastward, Happy Earth' and 'The Snowdrop', were published in 1909. A seventh song, 'Dream-tryst' (1909), anticipated the experimental *Arabia* (1914).

Denis Browne sang in the chorus of Ralph Vaughan Williams's *The Wasps*, and played *On Wenlock Edge* and *Hugh the Drover* while they were still work in progress. Vaughan Williams's assertion in a reference that Denis Browne had 'a most musical nature and his artistic judgement and perception are remarkable' (1911, priv. coll.) helped to secure his appointment at Repton in April 1912. He dedicated the motet 'God is our strength and song' (1912) to the school and passed his MusB with distinction in May.

After Denis Browne visited Busoni in Berlin, overzealous piano practice caused neuritis and threatened paralysis. He resigned from Repton and succeeded Carey as organist of Guy's Hospital in December 1912. He supplemented his income by deputizing for Gustav Holst at Morley College, conducting choral societies in London and Surrey, and writing for John Middleton Murry and Katherine Mansfield's *Blue Review*. He also contributed eight columns to *The Times* (1913–14) and seven to the *New Statesman* (1914), including shrewd critiques of Stravinsky and Skryabin. Denis Browne became the favourite of Edward Marsh's Georgian circle when Brooke was abroad between 1913 and 1914. He attended breakfast and supper parties, first nights, and private views with Mark Gertler and Wilfrid Wilson Gibson, and the latter commemorated him in *Friends* (1916, 14).

Denis Browne's eight-part Nunc dimittis was performed at Westminster Cathedral on Palm Sunday 1914. He gave the London première of Anton Berg's sonata op. 1 on 11 May, and a lecture entitled 'Modern musical tendencies' before the Musical Association on 19 May. On 15 July he accompanied Wilson in a recital at 10 Downing Street. 'The Comic Spirit', a ballet-pantomime intended for Bristol's Theatre Royal, was unfinished when war began.

Marsh engineered commissions for Denis Browne and Brooke in the Royal Naval division and, after the abortive Antwerp expedition, they sailed for the Dardanelles. Denis Browne passed the journey playing duets with F. S. Kelly and directing the Hood battalion band. He chose Brooke's Skyros grave, and his evocative account of the burial is widely cited. Shot through the neck on 8 May 1915, he recuperated in Egypt and insisted on returning to the front before he was fully fit. His prescient last message came from a trench at Kerever Dere on 4 June, the same day on which he was killed in action: 'I've gone now, too; not too badly, I hope. I'm luckier than Rupert, because I've fought. But there's no one to bury me as I buried him, so perhaps he's better off in the long run' (W. Denis Browne to Edward Marsh, 4 June 1915, priv. coll.). His body was never retrieved, and his achievement cannot be fully assessed. Dent feared another hysterical response to Gallipoli's 'second great loss to art' (Forbes, 1.264) and destroyed many manuscripts.

RHIAN DAVIES

Sources R. Davies, 'Composers of the Great War', MA diss., U. Wales, Aberystwyth, 1985 • private information (2004) [family] • W. C. Denis Browne, letters, 1908–15, priv. coll. • W. C. Denis Browne, letters, 1908–15, King's Cam. • H. Taylor, 'The life and work of W. Denis Browne' (photocopy), Barclay Squire essay, U. Cam., 1973 [author's collection] • T. Hold, *Parry to Finzi: twenty English song-composers* (2002) • [M. D. Forbes], ed., *Clare College, 1326–1926*, 2 vols. (1928–30) • *Duet for two voices: an informal biography of Edward Dent compiled from his letters to Clive Carey*, ed. H. Carey (1979) • E. J. Dent, *Selected essays*, ed. H. Taylor (1979) • R. Vaughan Williams, testimonial, 1911, priv. coll. • *CGPLA Eng. & Wales* (1916) • L. Denis Browne, letter to E. J. Dent, 22 Sept 1915, CUL, Add. MS 7973 • Commonwealth War Graves Commission, Maidenhead

Archives Clare College, Cambridge, compositions • priv. coll., letters to his parents and sisters • priv. coll., scrapbook | CUL, W. Denis Browne, MS Dd.2.11, fols. 1–23 [transcription] • King's Cam., letters to E. J. Dent • priv. coll., letters to Rupert Brooke • priv. coll., letters to Edward Marsh

Likenesses L. Caswell Smith, photograph, 1914?, priv. coll. • facsimile, NPG

Wealth at death £79 16s. 3d.: probate, 1916, *CGPLA Eng. & Wales*

Browne, William George (1768–1813), traveller, was born on Great Tower Hill, London, on 25 July 1768, son of George Browne, wine merchant, and descended from a Cumberland family. He was educated privately until entering Oriel College, Oxford, where, receiving 'no encouragement and little assistance in his academical studies', he strove to educate himself. After leaving Oxford (BA 1789) he for a time studied law in the Temple until he inherited money on his father's death. He was deeply stirred by the French Revolution and had reprinted several political tracts of the period and seemed inclined to a public career, when, after reading James Bruce's travels in Abyssinia and the first report of the African Association, he decided to devote himself to the exploration of Africa. Among his qualifications he enumerated 'a good constitution, though by no means robust, steadiness of purpose, much indifference to personal accommodations and enjoyments, together with a degree of patience which could endure reverses and disappointments without murmuring'. He also knew the classics, modern languages, and some chemistry, botany, and mineralogy.

Browne left England in 1791, arriving at Alexandria in January 1792, and after two months' residence proceeded westwards along the coast to visit the ruins at Siwa, which he pronounced not to be the remains of the temple of Jupiter Ammon. In May 1792 he arrived at Cairo, where he spent two months studying Arabic and investigating the geography and antiquities of the country, then little known to Europeans. Being prevented by war from entering Nubia, he visited the vast Roman quarries at Quseir on the Red Sea, which he explored in oriental disguise, and then decided to accompany the great Sudan caravan to Darfur, a country west of Abyssinia and north of the White Nile not previously described by any European, from which he hoped to penetrate into Abyssinia and then the interior of Africa. After encountering great hardships he reached Darfur in July 1793, only to contract dysentery, to be robbed of most of his property, and to be detained, although not ill-treated, for nearly three years by the sultan. He spent his time examining the character and products of the uninviting country, solacing his ennui by the

education of two young lions. At length the sultan released him to prevent reprisals on Darfurian merchants in Egypt, and Browne returned to Cairo with the caravan of 1796 having gained some information, especially on the course of the Nile, which later proved correct. Having journeyed through Asia Minor to Constantinople, he arrived in England in September 1798. His *Travels* (1799) were rather poorly received in Britain, not least for their odd style, but were translated into French (1800) and German (1801) and went to a second English edition. They aroused some controversy because of their considerable sympathy towards, and admiration of, the East.

From 1800 to 1802 Browne travelled again in Turkey and the Levant, and collected much valuable information, partially published after his death in Walpole's *Travels in Various Countries of the East* (1820). He spent the next ten years in England, 'leading the life of a scholar and recluse', but intimate with several men of similar tastes, before in 1812 he again left England hoping to reach Tartary via Persia. Travelling through Asia Minor and visiting Armenia, he reached Tabriz, which he left for Tehran towards the end of the summer of 1813, accompanied by two servants. A few days later, about 120 miles from Tabriz, he was murdered, though whether for his money or because he had caused offence by his Turkish dress, the Persians being deeply suspicious of the Turks, and whether the Persian government was involved, was never fully resolved. His body could not be recovered, having been eaten by birds of prey, but his effects, except his money, were restored to the English ambassador, and after some time bones allegedly his were brought to Tabriz and interred.

Browne's apparent reserve disguised considerable warmth, generosity, and kindness. In politics he was a republican, in religion a freethinker. His intellectual endowments were rather solid than shining; exactness and veracity made his travel narratives informative, if not attractively written.

RICHARD GARNETT, rev. ELIZABETH BAIGENT

Sources R. Walpole, *Travels in various countries of the East* (1820) • W. R. Dawson and E. P. Uphill, *Who was who in Egyptology*, 3rd edn, rev. M. L. Bierbrier (1995) • R. Porter, *Travels in Georgia, Persia, Armenia* (1821) • H. J. Rose, *A new general biographical dictionary*, ed. H. J. Rose and T. Wright, 12 vols. (1853) • C. Knight, ed., *The English cyclopaedia: biography*, 1 (1856) • Allibone, *Dict.* • R. Wharton, *Observations on the authenticity of Bruce's travels in Abyssinia in reply to some passages in Brown's travels* (1800) • W. Beloe, *The sexagenarian, or, The recollections of a literary life*, ed. [T. Rennell], 2nd edn, 2 vols. (1818)

Archives BL, journal, Add. MS 6132 • Shrewsbury School Library, travel diaries and papers • University of Western Ontario, London, Ontario, memoirs and papers

Brownell [*married names* Blair, Pitt-Rivers], **Sonia Mary** [*known as* Sonia Orwell] (1918–1980), literary editor, writer, and friend of artists and intellectuals, was born Sonia Mary Brownell on 25 August 1918 at Mesra Thaua, Ranchi, Bihar, India, the younger daughter of Charles Neville Brownell (1882–1918), a freight broker in Calcutta, and Beatrice Edith Binning (1890–1959). On 5 January 1920 Beatrice married Edgar Geoffrey Dixon (1880–1953), a successful chartered accountant, whose alcoholism wrecked

Sonia Mary Brownell [Sonia Orwell] (1918–1980), by unknown photographer, 1949 [left, at the offices of *Horizon*]

1950; subsequently she mostly used the surname Orwell. On 12 August 1958 she married Michael Augustus Lane Fox Pitt-Rivers (1917–1999), a wealthy farmer, but the marriage ended in divorce in 1965.

From 1951 to 1956 Sonia worked as a reader and editor for Weidenfeld and Nicolson and persuaded them to publish Saul Bellow, Nigel Dennis, Elizabeth Hardwick, Dan Jacobson, and Mary McCarthy. She helped to organize the successful Writers' Conference at the 1962 Edinburgh Festival and from 1964 to 1965 in Paris she was a co-editor of the international review *Art and Literature*. She translated many articles from French and in 1966 translated *Days in the Trees*, by her friend Marguerite Duras, for the Royal Shakespeare Company.

Sonia took her duties as Orwell's literary executor seriously and was resolute that his work should not be misrepresented or commercialized. She gave all his papers to the Orwell Archive, as a founder trustee, when it was set up in 1961 at University College, London, to create a centre for Orwell studies. She was responsible for the publication in 1968 of the four-volume *Collected Essays, Journalism and Letters of George Orwell*, edited by herself and Ian Angus, which further enhanced Orwell's reputation. When Mary McCarthy disparaged Orwell and alleged bias in the editing of the *Collected Essays*, Sonia wrote a trenchant and witty rebuttal (*Nova*, June–July 1969), which makes it a matter for regret that she so undervalued her own literary ability that she wrote less than a score of articles and reviews. Orwell's injunction in his will that no biography of him be written resulted in her upsetting several people and caused her anguish up to her death. She was also tormented while she was dying by an impending lawsuit about the Orwell estate that she had initiated but was forced reluctantly to settle out of court because of her physical condition.

Sonia could be bossy, high-handed, presumptuous, noisy, and anti-male, which set many against her, particularly when her behaviour, at certain periods, was fuelled by too much drink or accompanied by strong language, but, in Stephen Spender's words, she 'still remained underneath the warm-hearted, generous, spontaneous person she was all her life' (Spender, 435). She had a devoted circle of friends, which included J. R. Ackerley, W. H. Auden, Francis Bacon, Ivy Compton-Burnett, Michel Leiris, and Angus Wilson. Prompted by her passionate love of literature and her admiration of imagination and intelligence, Sonia was enthusiastic in her encouragement of writers she befriended and frequently helped them materially. She was lavish in her hospitality and responded instantly and tirelessly to the emotional, physical, and financial needs of her friends who were in distress, as when, for instance, she financially supported Jean Rhys and in 1975 organized an appeal, after Cyril Connolly died in debt, which raised over £40,000 for his widow and children. Sonia was rewarded by being cared for affectionately by her friends when she was dying of cancer. She died in St Stephen's Hospital, Chelsea, London, on 11 December 1980, and was buried on 18 December in the

his career in Calcutta and broke up his marriage after the family returned to England in 1927. Sonia had a sister, Bay, and a younger half-brother, Michael, and from 1931 Beatrice brought up her children unaided. Raised a Roman Catholic, Sonia was educated at the Convent of the Sacred Heart, Roehampton, London, from 1927 to 1935 and perfected her French at Neuchâtel, Switzerland, but in the summer of 1936 had to be brought back to London, distraught, the sole survivor of a boating tragedy.

In 1938 Sonia worked for Professor Eugene Vinaver on his edition of Malory's *Morte d'Arthur*. By this time she had firmly renounced her Roman Catholicism. Also in 1938 she began sitting for portraits at the Euston Road School of Drawing and Painting, who named her the Euston Road Venus on account of her radiant blond beauty. She was drawn by Rodrigo Moynihan and painted by Claude Rogers and William *Coldstream. Coldstream and she were lovers from 1939 to 1941 and through him she met Stephen Spender and Cyril Connolly, co-editors of *Horizon*, and its financial backer, Peter Watson, who were to remain her lifelong friends. After working as John Lehmann's secretary on *New Writing* in 1941 and doing war work at the Ministry of War Transport, in 1945 she joined *Horizon* as editorial secretary and became, in effect, Cyril Connolly's working partner when Connolly (then sole editor) and Peter Watson were absent. In late 1945 she had a very brief affair with the recently widowed George Orwell (pseudonym of Eric Arthur *Blair) and later an unhappy affair with the French philosopher Maurice Merleau-Ponty (1908–1961). On 13 October 1949 she married Orwell, seriously ill with tuberculosis, who died on 21 January

Putney Vale cemetery. She left everything she derived from Orwell, which was the bulk of her estate, to his adopted son, Richard Blair.   IAN ANGUS

Sources *The Times* (12 Dec 1980) · *The Times* (16 Dec 1980) · M. Shelden, *Friends of promise: Cyril Connolly and the world of 'Horizon'* (1989) · G. Orwell [E. A. Blair], *Our job is to make life worth living*, ed. P. Davison, I. Angus, and S. Davison (1998), vol. 20 of *The complete works of George Orwell*, ed. P. Davison (1986–98), 169–71, 306–9 · H. Spurling, *The girl from the fiction department: a portrait of Sonia Orwell* (2002) · S. Spender, *Journals, 1939–1983*, ed. J. Goldsmith (1985) · private information (2004) · personal knowledge (2004) · *WWW* · b. cert. · m. certs. · d. cert.
Archives U. Sussex, Gorer MSS · UCL, Orwell archive · University of Tulsa, Oklahoma, McFarlin Library, Cyril Connolly MSS
Likenesses C. Rogers, oils, 1938, Laing Art Gallery, Newcastle upon Tyne · W. Coldstream, oils, 1939, priv. coll. · photograph, 1949, UCL, Orwell archive [*see illus.*]
Wealth at death £289,109: probate, 5 May 1981, *CGPLA Eng. & Wales*

Brownhill, Rowland William (1834–1895), engineer and local politician, was born in Tipton, Staffordshire, the second of seven sons in a family of ten; his parents, William Brownhill (*b.* 1789), iron founder, and his wife, Elizabeth, were nonconformists. Brownhill's education and early training are obscure, but he married on 30 October 1860 and with his wife, Emily (*b.* 1832/3), from Bilston, the daughter of Samuel Foley, a boiler maker, raised a son and four daughters. During the late 1870s Brownhill was living at Walsall, where William Brownhill & Sons were in business at Green Lane Foundry; another Brownhill operated a brickworks.

In 1873 Brownhill filed his first patent for machines to weigh trucks and other heavy goods; another seventeen patents followed over the years, one for brickmaking and several others for weighing machines. Brownhill was prominent in civic life. Elected to the town council in 1867 and made alderman a few years later, he was mayor from 1872 to 1874; he retired from the corporation in 1880. His brothers William and Theophilus Paul also served as mayor. For much of his period of office Brownhill was chairman of the corporation's gas committee. In 1877 Walsall erected a new gasworks and the borough authorities purchased the whole of the gas undertaking of the Birmingham gas works within Walsall. For more than twenty years the town enjoyed the distinction of supplying itself with gas at a cheaper rate than any other in Britain; the profits abated the borough rate, to the extent that in 1883–4 no rate was levied on the residents.

By this time Brownhill had moved to Victoria House, Trinity Road, Birmingham, where he practised as an engineering valuer. The most enduring of his inventions was described in his patent no. 7012, of 1887, a coin-operated gas meter delivering a measured supply of gas. Tested in a group of small dwellings in Birmingham, it soon came into general use, with Brownhill continuing to patent various improvements. Coin-operated machines were no novelty; the first English patent had been filed in 1857 for a machine delivering cigarettes and other small items in exchange for a coin, and Brownhill himself had patented a coin-operated weighing machine earlier in 1887. He arranged for the meters to be manufactured by W. Parkinson & Co. The pre-payment meter allowed gas to be supplied to many homes which would not have otherwise been considered creditworthy, bringing to their occupants the benefits of gas lighting and gas water-heaters.

On 4 February 1895 Brownhill assigned his gas-meter patents and his licence rights to the new Pre-Payment Gas Meter Company for £50,000, of which £5000 was to be in cash. It seems, however, that neither he nor his immediate family derived any benefit from this arrangement. Brownhill died unexpectedly at 30 Birchfield Road, Aston Manor, Aston, on 11 August 1895, survived by his wife, leaving an estate valued at only £40. His obituarist wrote, 'Being of great amiability of disposition, conciliatory, resourceful, and generous, deceased made many friends, who will deeply regret his removal from among them' (*Journal of Gas Lighting*, 66, 1895). By December 1904 the *Journal of Gas Lighting* could state that Brownhill's pre-payment gas meter had brought 'the spread of light and comfort to almost every home in the land', and it attributed to him 'the creation of what is practically a new industry'.   NORRIS McWHIRTER

Sources *Gas Industry Genealogical Index* · census returns for Bloxwich, Walsall, 1851 · register of deaths, St Catherine's House, London · *Staffordshire Chronicle* (17 Aug 1895) · private information (1997) · *Journal of Gas Lighting* (1895) · *Journal of Gas Lighting* (Dec 1904) · *CGPLA Eng. & Wales* (1895) · m. cert. · d. cert.
Likenesses portrait, Walsall town hall
Wealth at death £40: probate, 10 Sept 1895, *CGPLA Eng. & Wales*

Browning [*married name* Dugdale], **Amy Katherine** (1881–1978), painter, was born on 31 March 1881 at Great Bramingham Hall Farm, near Luton, Bedfordshire, the second daughter of eight children of James Day Browning (1858–1933), bailiff and later tenant farmer, and his wife, Katherine Lucy Saunderson (1857–1946). Amy was educated at a small private school in Luton, and because of her early aptitude for drawing she attended weekly drawing lessons. In 1897 the family moved to a remote farm several miles away. Having witnessed the drudgery of housekeeping and childbearing that her mother had to endure, Amy resolved to escape and train to be a professional artist. In September 1899, with her parents' support, Amy, nicknamed Brownie by her contemporaries, entered the Royal College of Art to study painting and gain a diploma in the teaching of art.

In 1901 Browning had to leave college when her mother, at the age of forty-four, was pregnant again after a lapse of eight years. As her older sister was married it was considered Amy's duty to return to run the household. A year later, desperate to return to the college, and realizing that her father could not afford to pay her fees, she applied to the London county council and won two outside scholarships. On her return to the college she met and became friends with Sylvia Pankhurst, and later assisted her in the mounting of the Women's Exhibition of 1909 held at the Prince's Club skating rink in Knightsbridge. Later, during the First World War, she worked alongside Pankhurst to raise money and provide work for women in the East End of London. At the college Browning was the star pupil of the head of painting, Gerald Moira, who sent her up to the men's studio to show them how to paint. She left in 1906 with glowing recommendations from Moira and the same year had a picture accepted for the Royal Academy Summer Exhibition. She continued to exhibit there annually for the next sixty-two years apart from a three-year period during the First World War. She always signed her paintings A. K. Browning so that her sex would remain unknown and she could be judged fairly alongside the men.

In the following years Browning supported herself by teaching, only returning to Bedfordshire for the vacations, when she compelled members of the family to be her models. She was extremely productive, painting large pictures more suitable for public galleries than domestic interiors, family groups, portraits, as well as flower paintings, still lifes, and landscapes. At the 1913 Paris Salon Browning won the silver medal for *Chequered Shade* which, with *The Red Shawl* (1914), was bought by the French government. The latter is to be seen at the Musée Baron Gerard, Bayeux. When the Paris Salon resumed after the war she won the gold medal for *Lime Tree Shade* (Ipswich Museum) in 1922 and continued to exhibit there *hors concours* all through the 1920s and 1930s and in other major exhibitions all over the world. She also exhibited widely in Britain and was made a member of the Royal Institute of Oil-Painters, the New English Art Club, the Royal Society of Portrait Painters, and the Society of Women Artists. Browning's style was 'British Impressionist': there is a wonderfully subtle feeling of light in all her work. Her paintings tend to be low in tone, but the result is never muddy. Although her brushstrokes appear to be very free, as if applied quickly and spontaneously, she was (apart from her very quick sketches) a slow worker. Towards the end of her life, when working on commissions, she felt that the tastes of her clients dictated a smoother application of paint, but, when painting for her own pleasure, she retained her old vivacity.

While at the Royal College Browning had met Thomas Cantrell Dugdale (1880–1952), later a highly regarded portrait painter and Royal Academician. So that she could continue teaching they did not marry until 15 June 1916. (It was only after the outbreak of the First World War that married women were allowed to teach.) Their marriage was a happy one; they had no children. He spent most weekdays in London at their studio flat while she painted and gardened at their home in Suffolk. This way of life lasted for over twenty-five years. She had always kept some small dog for companionship and in almost every photograph of Browning she is to be seen clutching a terrier, long-haired and snappy, both of them peering out from under their respective fringes.

In 1952 Tommy Dugdale died, leaving Amy virtually penniless. She gave up their rented house in Suffolk and spent the next twenty-three years in their rented Chelsea studio flat. Thereafter she painted mainly family groups and portraits, including one of Lady Churchill with whom she did not get on. In 1975 she had a stroke and went to live with her youngest sister in Hertfordshire. She died at St Catherine's Nursing Home, Letchworth, on 27 January 1978 at the age of ninety-six and was cremated on 11 February at Golders Green. Further examples of her work are held in Luton Museum and Art Gallery; Wolverhampton Museum and Art Gallery; Ipswich Museum and Art Gallery; Kelvingrove Museum, Glasgow; and the Royal Academy collection, London.   JOANNA DUNHAM

Sources J. Dunham, *Amy K. Browning: an impressionist in the women's movement* (1995) • A. Bury, 'The art of A. K. Browning', *Bedfordshire Magazine*, 4 (1953–4), 255–60 • a list of paintings by Amy Katherine Browning exhibited over her lifetime, RA • P. Dunford, *A biographical dictionary of women artists in Europe and America since 1850* (1990) • *CGPLA Eng. & Wales* (1978) • b. cert. • m. cert. • private information (2004) • d. cert.
Wealth at death £20,027: probate, 3 April 1978, *CGPLA Eng. & Wales*

Browning [*née* Moulton Barrett], **Elizabeth Barrett** (1806–1861), poet and writer, was born on 6 March 1806 at Coxhoe Hall, co. Durham, the first of the twelve children of Edward Barrett Moulton Barrett (1785–1857), plantation owner, and his wife, Mary, *née* Graham (1781–1828).

Family origins Elizabeth Barrett Browning's family origins are documented in Jeannette Marks's *The Family of the Barrett*, in R. A. Barrett's *The Barretts of Jamaica*, and in *The Brownings' Correspondence*. Her mother's parents were John and Arabella Graham (after 1786, Graham-Clarke) of Newcastle upon Tyne. John Graham-Clarke owned Jamaican sugar plantations, ships trading between Newcastle and Jamaica, a brewery, flax spinning mills, and glassworks. Her father's parents were Charles and Elizabeth Moulton (1763–1830), who had married in Jamaica on 28 August 1781. Edward Barrett Moulton Barrett's fortune came not from his father, who soon separated from his wife, but from his maternal grandfather, Edward Barrett (1734–1798), owner of Cinnamon Hill, Cornwall, Cambridge, and Oxford estates on Jamaica's north side: more than 10,000 acres in total (Barrett, 128). Edward Barrett's income was 'fifty thousand a year', his great-granddaughter told fellow poet Robert *Browning (1812–1889), during the courtship recorded in their famous love letters (*Correspondence*, 13.24).

The desire to hand down the family's patronymic together with its wealth explains the doubled Barrett in the poet's maiden name. By 1798 all three of Edward Barrett's sons had predeceased him, making his two grandsons by Elizabeth Moulton, Edward and Samuel Barrett Moulton (1787–1837), his principal male heirs. A clause in the will of his son George Goodin Barrett (1761–1795) had made legacies for the Moulton sons conditional on their adding and bearing 'the Surname of Barrett' on turning twenty-one. In 1798 they successfully obtained a royal licence to do so. Their grandfather then added a clause to his own will stipulating that all heirs to his Jamaican estates 'use the surname of Barrett'. The poet's father customarily shortened his name to Edward Moulton Barrett, without hyphenation; his descendants adopted the hyphenated form after his death in 1857 (Barrett, 37, 44, x).

Elizabeth Barrett Browning (1806–1861), by Field Talfourd, 1859

The poet herself customarily retained the forename Barrett and dropped the surname Moulton, using Elizabeth Barrett Moulton Barrett only for legal documents like her marriage certificate. When she did not refer to herself as Ba, the pet name family members and close friends called her by throughout her life, she signed her letters and poems during her maiden years with varying forms of Elizabeth Barrett Barrett, often simply using 'EBB'. She used 'Elizabeth B. Barrett' for *The Seraphim, and other Poems* (1838), her third published collection and the first to bear her name. In the two-volume *Poems* (1844) that established her international fame and prompted Browning to write to her on 10 January 1845, she identified herself, more resoundingly, as 'Elizabeth Barrett Barrett'. As the courtship progressed, Browning happily noted that, in marrying him, she would remain 'EBB' (*Correspondence*, 11.248–9).

After their marriage on 12 September 1846, Elizabeth Barrett Browning maintained her characteristic use of her signature initials. A charming instance appears in a fair copy of the anti-slavery poem 'The Runaway Slave at Pilgrim's Point', dating from autumn 1846. Here the signature 'EBB' in her hand is enclosed in brackets added in Browning's hand and preceded by his underlined word '*my*' (Armstrong Browning Library, D802). Her signature practices have been ignored by biographers and critics, who usually identify her as 'Elizabeth Barrett', as 'Mrs Browning', or, since the 1970s feminist revival of interest in her works, as 'Barrett Browning'. Yet the poet rarely

identified herself by the first two names, while the third is an anachronistic formation. Given her own practice and the continuity between her maiden and married identities conveyed by her initials, this article henceforth refers to her as EBB.

EBB's explanation of her complicated name to Browning in 1845 has provoked some speculation about her ancestry:

> My true initials are *EBMB*—my long name, as opposed to my short one, being … Elizabeth Barrett Moulton Barrett!—… Christian name—Elizabeth Barrett:—surname, Moulton Barrett … to make it portable, I fell into the habit of doubling it up & packing it closely,—& of forgetting that I was a *Moulton*, altogether. … Yet our family-name is *Moulton Barrett*, & my brothers reproach me sometimes for sacrificing the governorship of an old town in Norfolk with a little honorable verdigris from the Heralds' Office—As if I cared for the *Retrospective Review*! Nevertheless it is true that I would give ten towns in Norfolk (if I had them) to own some purer lineage than that of the blood of the slave!—Cursed we are from generation to generation!—I seem to hear the 'Commination service'. (*Correspondence*, 11.252)

Citing this passage, Julia Markus concluded in 1995 that the poet 'believed that she had African blood through her grandfather Charles Moulton' (Markus, 106).

Although Markus was not the first to contend that EBB had African blood, evidence does not support the speculation. There *were* racially mixed branches of the Barrett family: for example, the children of the poet's great-uncle George with Elissa Peters, a slave. He freed these children and directed in his will that they be educated in England and take up residence in countries where 'distinctions respecting colour' were 'not maintained'; the oldest of these, Thomas Peters, visited Coxhoe Hall in January 1808 (Barrett, 36, 58). However, genealogical research has uncovered no indication of African blood in EBB's lineage (Marks, 313; Barrett, 64). What the poet herself may have believed is another matter. Yet there is no mention of possible mixed ancestry in the hundreds of letters written by EBB and the Barrett family published in part or whole. Moreover, the poet's remarks imply that the 'curse' she speaks of does not stem, as Markus infers, from the Moulton side (in Norfolk where Moultons date back to the sixteenth century), but from the Barrett side.

Given her reference to the 'Commination service' for sinners, and her anti-slavery sentiments, it is more likely that EBB was alluding to the Barrett family's complicity in the 'curse' of profiting from the blood of slaves, as she shared her family history with Browning. His father also had Jamaican ancestors (on the maternal side), although Robert Browning sen. (1782–1866) had rejected the potential profits of the slavery system, remaining in England instead and living on a bank clerk's salary. In 1833, when the Emancipation Act abolishing slavery in British colonies was passed, EBB declared that she was 'glad' that 'the negroes' were 'virtually—free!' even though her father thought that the West Indies would be 'irreparably ruined' (*Correspondence*, 3.81, 86). During the courtship she also ironically discussed with Browning the 'infinite traditions' of her 'great great grandfather' Samuel Barrett (1689–1760) who had 'flogged his slaves like a divinity' (ibid., 13.24)—traditions passed on by 'Treppy' or Mary Trepsack, a planter's orphaned daughter who became the lifelong companion of the poet's beloved grandmother Moulton. Treppy believed in 'the beatitude of the slaves', but EBB presents a very different picture in 'The Runaway Slave at Pilgrim's Point', portraying a slave woman who has been whipped, raped, and impregnated cursing her oppressors. As she said to John Ruskin in 1855, 'I belong to a family of West Indian slaveholders, and if I believed in curses, I should be afraid' (*Letters*, 2.220). The humane attitude that EBB's father and uncle adopted towards their slaves spared them from the worst effects of the Jamaican slave uprising of 1831–2 (Barrett, 84). Yet a kind of curse did seem to shape the Barrett family's history, manifested in thirty-eight years of chancery litigation among Edward Barrett's various descendants over slaves, cattle, and land beginning in 1801, aggravating the financial reverses experienced by his heirs as sugar prices dropped. Still, EBB's family was far from poverty-stricken; while Browning's father earned under £300 a year, her father's annual income was more than £4000 in 1807 (ibid., 47, 55).

Childhood and early education In her early years EBB was relatively untroubled by her family's Jamaican roots. She passed her childhood and youth at Hope End, an idyllic estate in Herefordshire near Ledbury, where her father had a Turkish-style mansion built to accommodate his growing family. Elizabeth or 'Ba' was soon followed by Edward or 'Bro', the closest companion of her childhood, Henrietta, Mary (who died at age three), Samuel, Arabella, and six more sons: Charles, George, Henry, Alfred, Septimus, and Octavius. By virtue of her age, force of character, and precocity, Ba reigned over her siblings in the nursery. Educated in early childhood by her mother, who acted as 'publisher' for some of her compositions by transcribing collections of 'Poems by Elizabeth B. Barrett', she soon displayed the striking abilities that led her father, whom she affectionately called 'Puppy', to designate her as the 'Poet Laureate of Hope End'. The result of her irrepressible literary activity is one of the largest bodies of juvenilia produced by any English writer.

'At four I first mounted Pegasus but at six I thought myself priviledged [*sic*] to show off feats of horsemanship', EBB recalls in 'Glimpses into my own life and literary character', written principally when she was fourteen (*Correspondence*, 1.348–56). She breathlessly records how, at six, she began reading novels; at eight she was enraptured by Pope's translations of Homer; at ten she began to study Greek with Bro's tutor Daniel McSwiney; at eleven she began writing her own Homeric epic *The Battle of Marathon*; and on her fourteenth birthday in 1820 she exulted to see her epic privately printed in fifty copies (a gift from her father). She 'was familiar with Shakespeare Milton Homer and Virgil Locke Hooker Pope', reading Homer and Virgil 'in the original with delight inexpressible' (ibid., 1.352). By 1821 she had also read Mary Wollstonecraft's *Vindication of the Rights of Woman* (1792), responding with such enthusiasm that her mother teased her about founding hopes for female happiness 'on yours & Mrs. Wolstonecrafts system' (ibid., 1.132).

EBB's 'Glimpses' closes with contracting possibilities on the verge of her fifteenth year, as the girl who had aspired to mount Pegasus mourns the departure of Bro for Charterhouse and the formal education denied to his gifted sister. During this period her life was also transformed by an illness that struck all three Barrett daughters, but left lasting marks on only the eldest, who passed almost a year in a Gloucester spa. Her symptoms, as detailed by Dr William Coker [*sic* for Cother], included head and back pains, loss of mobility and appetite, debility, and regular 'paroxysms' accompanied by convulsive twitching of the diaphragm. Dr Cother offered the tentative diagnosis of spine disease, acknowledging 'positive proofs' were wanting (*Correspondence*, 1.325–7). Evidence indicates that EBB did have a serious illness; she did not bring her suffering on herself, as the story recorded in the *Dictionary of National Biography* suggests, by falling and injuring her spine while impatiently trying to saddle her pony Moses alone. The symptoms of her adolescent illness also differed substantially from the chronic lung disease that later afflicted her in 1837. The treatments she received—opiates, cupping, the use of setons (passing thread or tape on a needle through folds of skin), and suspension in a spine crib—may also have increased her debility (Forster, 24–5). She was to become dependent on opiates, a standard medical treatment, throughout much of her life. As Alethea Hayter notes, the effect of opium on 'an integrated personality with a brilliant imagination' may have contributed to the sensory vividness and metaphoric originality of her poetry (Hayter, 62).

In her mid-thirties EBB recalled the exuberant aspirations predating her adolescent illness in a wryly whimsical sketch of a girl named Beth (*Correspondence*, 1.360–62). Ten-year-old Beth is a 'warrior' and a 'poet', who plans to become Lord Byron's lover, wear men's clothes, 'live on a Greek island', and become the 'feminine of Homer. Many persons w^d. be obliged to say that she was a little taller than Homer', in fact. But Beth 'had one great misfortune. She was born a woman.' Despising 'nearly all the women in the world' except Madame de Staël for their 'littlenesses called delicacies, their pretty headaches, & soft mincing voices', Beth 'thanked her gods that she was not & never w^d. be feminine. Beth could run rapidly & leap high.' After her adolescent illness, EBB would never again 'leap high'. Undeterred by her physical weakness, however, she directed her spirit of conquest to learning and poetry instead.

Apprenticeship years: 1821–1840 EBB's long apprenticeship reflects the lack of opportunity she experienced as a woman in an isolated setting, with no access to higher education. She made her début in the world of letters with two poems on Greece in the *New Monthly Magazine* in 1821. Other poems followed, including 'Stanzas on the Death of Lord Byron' in 1824. From 1824 to 1826 she engaged in an intensive programme of self-education, recording analytical comments on works by Locke, Hume, Hobbes, Berkeley, Byron, Southey, Mary Shelley, Felicia Hemans, Maria Edgeworth, Letitia E. Landon (L.E.L.), and other writers. Some of this reading is reflected in the title-poem of *An*

Essay on Mind, with other Poems (1826), combining her passion for Byron and Greek politics with an exploration of the human mind's powers. The poem never directly considers how gender influences genius and the prospects for fame. But clearly this is an underlying concern, as it is in 'The Development of Genius', a long Byronic poem that she worked on in 1826-7, only to have it condemned by her father as 'insufferable' in its hero's 'egotism', 'most *wretched*', and '*beyond [her] grasp*' after he had read less than half of it (*Correspondence*, 1.359). The days were past when Puppy was uniformly delighted with the achievements of the Poet Laureate of Hope End. Autumn 1828 brought a more serious loss with the death of her mother, her first 'publisher', on 7 October—although, immersed in childbearing and dominated by her husband, the intelligent, artistic Mary Moulton Barrett could not provide a role model for her daughter. 'Scarcely I was a woman when I lost *my* mother', EBB later wrote to Browning—'[a] sweet, gentle nature, which the thunder a little turned from its sweetness', she added, alluding to the effect of her father on his wife (ibid., 13.305-6). Her mother's unmarried sister Arabella Sarah Graham-Clarke (1785-1869), called 'Bummy', helped to mother the Barrett children, but the strong-willed eldest Barrett child clashed with her aunt on more than one occasion.

EBB encountered a more sympathetic, learned response to 'The Development of Genius' from two classical scholars near Hope End—Uvedale Price and Hugh Stuart Boyd—led to correspond with her by *An Essay on Mind*. EBB's correspondence with Price on classical Greek pronunciation was cut short by his death in 1829, but her friendship and correspondence with Boyd lasted from 1827 until his death in 1848. Boyd was blind, but the two studied Greek together, Boyd drawing on his wide knowledge of classical poetry and EBB working as his amanuensis. Bored with country-house life and knowing no young men who interested her, she embraced this opportunity for intellectual partnership as zealously as Dorothea in George Eliot's *Middlemarch* embraces the pedantic Casaubon. And Boyd responded, presenting her with a splendid edition of Homer, inscribed in Greek, 'For the nearest and dearest', words which she inscribed in turn in a diary she kept from June 1831 to April 1832 (*Diary*, 57). The diary reflects her reading of Keats, Shelley, and other writers, as well as her complicated feelings for Boyd and the tensions these created with Mrs Boyd, whom EBB quietly scorned as '[e]mpty minded' (ibid., 48).

In the same period EBB emphatically expressed her family's whig sympathies to Boyd in letters about the first Reform Bill, describing Bro's speaking for the reform cause and exulting, when the bill was passed, that the English were 'a freer people' (*Correspondence*, 3.23, 25). Her keen interest in politics had been stimulated by her close relationship with her uncle Samuel, member of parliament for Richmond in Yorkshire from 10 March 1820 to February 1828, until he left England to oversee the family's Jamaican estates. On his death in December 1837 he left EBB a legacy of several thousand pounds plus shares in the ship *David Lyon*. Her uncle's legacy, combined with £4000 she received on her grandmother Moulton's death in 1830, gave EBB £8000 for investment (Barrett, 81, 100; *Correspondence*, 13.229).

The year 1832 was a time of dramatic change for the Barrett family as well as for the nation. Financial difficulties intensified by Edward Moulton Barrett's legal disputes forced the sale of Hope End. With characteristic secrecy about his affairs, he did not discuss the sale or plans for their new residence with his children, leaving EBB 'haunted' by the fear the family might move to Jamaica (*Correspondence*, 2.307). On 23 August the Barretts left for rented accommodation in Sidmouth, where they lived from August 1832 to December 1835. 1833 brought the Emancipation Act, compounding her father's financial reverses. In Sidmouth EBB maintained her friendship with Boyd, but outgrew her intellectual dependence with the publication of *Prometheus Bound, Translated from the Greek of Aeschylus, and Miscellaneous Poems* (1833). She later condemned her translation as a 'Prometheus *twice* bound' (ibid., 5.26); to make amends, she undertook a second translation in 1845, published in her 1850 *Poems*. Yet the production of an accurate translation of Aeschylus by a young woman with no university training remains an extraordinary feat. 'Aeschylus presents difficulties to the manliest Greek scholar', a reviewer observed; 'think of these rugged obstacles to a woman's mind!' (ibid., 4.390).

EBB's distinctive voice begins to emerge in the ballads she published in periodicals and annuals during the 1830s, including 'The Poet's Vow' and 'The Romaunt of the Page'. She was encouraged in the writing of these by the older, successful woman writer Mary Russell Mitford, whom she met in May 1836, after her family moved to 74 Gloucester Place, London. Mitford, who came to act as a literary mother to EBB and became her most regular correspondent, was introduced to her by John Kenyon (1784-1856), a wealthy distant cousin of her father's who shared her literary interests and the Barretts' Jamaican connections. The day after her meeting with Mitford, EBB met William Wordsworth and Walter Savage Landor at Kenyon's house. It was a propitious time for her. The move to London, which became permanent when the Barretts settled into 50 Wimpole Street in April 1838, promised to open up a stimulating world. In June *The Seraphim, and other Poems* appeared, including her ballads and numerous other works. Like the title-poem, portraying the crucifixion from the perspective of the angels, many of these reflect EBB's Congregationalist religious faith, derived from a dissenting background but modified by her increasingly unorthodox mistrust of established religions (Lewis, 11). 'The Seraphim' was criticized as an ambitious failure, but the collection led Wordsworth to praise the author's 'Genius and attainments' (*Correspondence*, 4.347).

Between 1822 and 1837 improvements in EBB's health had permitted her to lead a relatively normal life. In 1837-8 she was stricken with a second prolonged illness which continued over four years, in which she suffered from 'blood spitting, irregular heart action, loss of voice', elevated body temperature, fainting, and insomnia, symptoms associated today with either bronchiectasis or 'tuberculous ulceration of the lungs' (Hayter, 59). On 25 August 1838 she left the polluted air of mid-Victorian London for Torquay; she was not to return to Wimpole Street until 11 September 1841. During this period two tragedies struck in quick succession. On 17 February 1840 her brother Samuel died of fever in Jamaica; on 11 July Bro, the brother dearest to her, drowned in a sailing accident in Babbacombe Bay. Bro's death was a near-mortal blow, intensified by the guilt she experienced because her father had agreed, against his wishes, to allow Bro to stay with her in Torquay. 'That was a very near escape from madness, absolute hopeless madness', she later told Mitford (*Correspondence*, 5.82). Out of this tribulation, however, came some of her finest poems, including 'De profundis' and the sonnet 'Grief'.

The middle years, 1840–1850: fame, courtship, marriage, and Italy In both academic and popular versions of EBB's life story, Browning is credited with miraculously curing 'Miss Barrett' and awakening her poetic creativity when he rescued her from her dragon of a father, the legendary Mr Barrett of Wimpole Street. In fact, however, EBB experienced a return to moderately better health, as well as a flowering of her poetic powers, at least two years before first meeting Browning in May 1845, although she remained confined to her Wimpole Street room after returning to London in 1841. Her growing vitality is evident in her correspondence of the early 1840s with writers and artists on both sides of the Atlantic. She corresponded with the painter Benjamin Robert Haydon concerning Keats, Napoleon, and the nature of genius, supplying him with a vivid verbal portrait of herself, but refusing to meet him in person:

> I am 'little & black' like Sappho, en attendant the immortality … five feet one high, … eyes of various colours as the sun shines … [n]ot much nose … but to make up for it, a mouth suitable to a larger personality—oh, and a very little voice. (*Correspondence*, 8.128)

She also corresponded at length with the poet, critic, and dramatist Richard Hengist Horne, collaborating with him on a lyrical drama, 'Psyche apocalypté', that never advanced beyond various manuscript fragments; contributing to *The Poems of Chaucer, Modernized* (1841); and collaborating with him on *A New Spirit of the Age* (1844). In fact, she wrote entire sections of the essays on Carlyle and Tennyson for this critical collection, although she chose not to make her role public (ibid., 8.353–67). Her richest literary correspondence during this period, however, is with Mitford, who sent letters and gifts of flowers to revive EBB's interest in life after Bro's death and gave her additional reason to live with the gift of the spaniel Flush in January 1841. Their letters teem with discussions of English, American, and European authors, particularly women writers such as Mary Wollstonecraft and Jane Austen, and writers of the day such as Tennyson and George Sand (*Letters … to Mary Russell Mitford*).

Between 1841 and 1844 EBB also prolifically produced new poetical works, translations, and two substantial critical essays for 1842 issues of *The Athenaeum*: 'Some account of the Greek Christian poets' and 'The book of the poets', a comprehensive 'Survey of the English poets' under the pretence of a review (*Correspondence*, 5.349). Her physicians had warned her that writing might endanger her health, but she literally wrote herself back to life. In 1839, at work on her 'wild and wicked ballad' about a cursing nun, 'The Lay of the Brown Rosary', despite a medical prohibition against writing, she described herself discovered with 'a pen guilty of ink' by her side and Dr Barry exclaiming 'In the very act, Miss Barrett!' (ibid., 4.169, 174). Following her brush with death in 1840–41, the guilty pen was again in action producing, among much else, sonnets to George Sand; 'A Vision of Poets', an allegorical representation of the quest for poetic immortality; 'The Lost Bower', a Wordsworthian depiction of nature's regenerative power; and 'A Drama of Exile', in which she takes up Milton's story where it ends in *Paradise Lost*, boldly justifying her focus on Eve's story after the fall because it is 'more expressible by a woman than a man' (*Complete Works*, 2.144). Inspired as well by Horne's work in 1841–2 with the royal commission for the investigation of the employment of children in mines and factories, she wrote 'The Cry of the Children'. First published in *Blackwood's* in 1843, it was credited with rousing support for Lord Shaftesbury's Ten Hours Bill (1844). The result of this prolific creativity was *Poems* (1844), establishing her as Tennyson's rival and a candidate for poet laureate in 1850. In America, where this collection appeared as *A Drama of Exile: and other Poems*, the reception was particularly favourable, leading Edgar Allen Poe to dedicate *The Raven and other Poems* (1845) to her as the 'noblest of her sex'. EBB observed to her cousin Kenyon 'What is to be said, I wonder, when a man calls you the ["]noblest of your sex" … "Sir, you are the most discerning of yours"!' (*Correspondence*, 12.165).

The new ballads in the *Poems* of 1844 became EBB's most popular works. 'Rhyme of the Duchess May', with its star-crossed lovers plunging to their deaths on a stallion from a tower, had such a sensational effect that one lady reportedly fell 'into hysterics' (*Correspondence*, 10.140). 'Lady Geraldine's Courtship', subtitled 'a romance of the age', was the most celebrated, with its story of a love match between an earl's daughter and a peasant poet. It was EBB's answer to Tennyson's 'Locksley Hall', although it is best known today for its salute to Robert Browning for poems likened to pomegranates, with 'a heart within blood-tinctured, of a veined humanity' (suggested by Browning's *Bells and Pomegranates* series, in which 'dramatic lyrics' such as 'My Last Duchess' had appeared). EBB had long admired Browning as an 'indubitable genius' and one of the 'demigods': a 'master in clenched passion … burning through the metallic fissures of language' (ibid., 7.14, 55, 6.325). She had particularly praised *Paracelsus*, *Pippa Passes*, and Browning's dramatic 'impersonations'. She also sympathized with the charges of obscurity levelled against his poetry, given similar criticisms of her own. Browning for his part had long admired her works. In 1842, after reading the 'Greek Christian poets', he expressed his interest to Kenyon (a mutual friend) of being introduced at her 'sofa-side' (ibid., 5.290); in 1843, seeing 'The Dead Pan' in manuscript, he called it '[m]ost noble!' (ibid., 7.137).

The sensuous compliment to Browning for poems revealing a 'heart' like 'blood-tinctured' pomegranates led to his first letter of 10 January 1845, beginning 'I love your verses with all my heart, dear Miss Barrett' and proceeding to his praise of their 'fresh strange music, the affluent language, the exquisite pathos and true new brave thought' (*Correspondence*, 10.17). Her reply, 'I thank you, dear Mr. Browning, from the bottom of my heart', echoed, as his letter had done, the imagery of the heart she had used to salute him in print, initiating a pattern of returning quotation for quotation pervading their correspondence. Their shared artistic aspirations, dissenting backgrounds, family situations (both were still living at home, he at thirty-two, she at thirty-eight), passion for Greek literature, and circles of literary friends led to an immediate intellectual intimacy, then to a deepening spiritual and emotional bond. EBB boldly indicated her desire to write a 'novel-poem' as 'completely modern' as 'Lady Geraldine's Courtship', 'meeting face to face & without mask the Humanity of the age', obliquely spoke of how '[a]nguish' had 'instructed' her 'in joy', and confessed her fear that her seclusion and intense 'inner life' were a 'disadvantage' to her art, making her like a *blind poet*'. Browning, frustrated by the critical misunderstandings of his writings, described his sense that his works were the imperfect 'escapes' of an 'inner power' leaping out like the 'light' in 'crazy Mediterrean phares' he had watched at sea (ibid., 10.102–3, 112, 133, 70). As spring approached, he hinted more directly his wish to meet EBB in person, spoke of his desire to write something 'in concert' with her, and promised one day to describe to her a 'country' seen in his 'soul only, fruits, flowers, birds and all' (ibid., 10.201, 166). She demurred about a meeting; after telling him that she was '*essentially better*' and had been 'for several winters', she postponed the idea of his calling on her, then finally agreed, writing to warn him that her poetry was 'the flower' of her: 'the rest of me is nothing but a root, fit for the ground & the dark' (ibid., 10.111, 216).

They finally met in person on 20 May 1845 in EBB's room. The event was rapidly followed by Browning's impulsive declaration of love (in a letter that he subsequently reclaimed from her and destroyed), precipitating her withdrawal in alarm, given her invalidism, age, and feelings of inadequacy. Then began the rocky restoration of a relationship restricted to friendship. The conflicts Browning's love aroused in EBB are eloquently expressed in the *Sonnets from the Portuguese*, but a more unguarded response appears in two unpublished fragments in a 'Poems and Sonnets' note book at Yale, 'We are not equal …' and 'I dared to love …' (leaf 23*v*). After this turbulent beginning, the two poets settled into a growing intimacy, and Robert began to record the date and duration of each meeting. In total, he called on EBB ninety-one times between 20 May 1845 and their marriage in September 1846 (*Correspondence*, 10.226). Initially, they refracted their growing love through literature, as Browning requested

EBB's help in revising the *Dramatic Romances and Lyrics* published in November 1845; she provided pages of detailed commentary (ibid., 11.375–401). August and September brought a turning point, however, as EBB received medical advice urging her to travel to Italy to avoid another London winter, but found her father firmly opposed to the idea. Unsuccessful appeals to him left her distraught and embittered. Browning, after a summer of holding his love in check, condemned the 'veriest slavery' her father subjected her to and declared on 25 September 'I would marry you now', saying that he would be 'no more than' a brother to her if her health necessitated it. His visit the next day led her to affirm in return 'I am yours for everything but to do you harm', promising that she would be to him what he chose if God freed her from her 'trailing chain' of ill health (ibid., 11.98, 100).

Once EBB had chosen '"Not Death, but Love"', as she later wrote in the *Sonnets from the Portuguese*, she did everything in her power to live. Although Italy was not an immediate possibility, winter 1845–6 was unusually mild. One warm day, 17 January 1846, she astonished her brothers and sisters when she 'put on a cloak & walked down stairs into the drawing room' (*Correspondence*, 12.4). By that point her sisters, Henrietta and Arabella, knew of her relationship with Browning, although they maintained strict secrecy about it, convinced that their father would be opposed to any of them marrying. Henrietta, in particular, sympathized, given her long courtship with her cousin William Surtees Cook. As 1846 progressed, the two poets moved towards more definite plans of marriage, discussing finances, including the costs of EBB's opiate prescription. Fortunately, her £8000 invested in the funds and shares in the ship *David Lyon* gave them the financial means to consider a marriage in which both might remain dedicated to their art even if she were disinherited by her father (as she was). The story of this courtship and their private marriage at St Marylebone parish church on 12 September 1846, followed by their flight to Italy with EBB's maid, Wilson, and Flush, has often been told. Markus emphasizes the tyranny of Mr Barrett and EBB's recollection of Henrietta's knees 'ring[ing] upon the floor' before him for the very suspicion of a romantic relationship (Markus, 33–5). Margaret Forster offers more sympathetic insight into Edward Moulton Barrett, while Dorothy Mermin and Daniel Karlin analyse the subtle intellectual and emotional exchange between two deeply intelligent, forceful personalities.

The romantic flight to Italy and EBB's subsequent 'vivid' life on the continent are most fully described in her intimate letters to Arabella (*Letters … Arabella*, 1.434). During their honeymoon stop in Paris, where EBB described herself as 'living as in a dream', in a 'new life' that seemed like 'riding an enchanted horse', the Brownings encountered their mutual friend, author and art critic Anna Jameson, with 'eyes open as wide as Flush' exclaiming, '"Can it be possible? … You dear abominable poets! Why what a ménage you will make!"' (ibid., 1.2–3). They subsequently stopped at Avignon to visit Vaucluse, made immortal by the love of Petrarch and Laura, where Ba startled her husband by making her way 'over the boiling water to a still rock in the middle of it'—a scene A. S. Byatt draws on in her 1990 novel *Possession* (ibid., 1.16). The only jarring element came in the news from home. EBB had expected her father's outrage. She did not expect the indignation of her brothers, and their long refusal to have any contact with Browning, whom they saw as a lower-class upstart eager to exploit their sister's income. This family opinion was still evident in 1930, when EBB's nephew Edward Alfred Moulton-Barrett exclaimed that his Aunt Ba had married a man whose grandfather 'kept a public house on Hampstead Heath' (Marks, 6).

In Italy the Brownings lived from 18 October 1846 until 20 April 1847 in Pisa, where on 21 March EBB experienced a miscarriage in the fifth month, after denying the possibility that she could be pregnant (*Letters … Arabella*, 1.67). A second miscarriage followed in spring 1848, a third in autumn 1849, and a fourth on 28 July 1850, with serious haemorrhaging (ibid., 1.163, 297, 331, 337). Between her second and third miscarriages, however, on 9 March 1849, EBB gave birth to a healthy son, Robert Wiedeman Barrett Browning, or Penini (shortened to Pen). '*E un miraculo quello bambino e venuto da quel corpo*', the Italian nurse declared ('it's a miracle that baby came from that body'; Markus, 130). Sadly, the happy event was rapidly followed by Browning's mother's death on 18 March.

Pen was born in the Casa Guidi apartments that the Brownings furnished and settled into during May 1848, after moving to Florence in April 1847 and living in various temporary quarters. Thereafter, although they made extended journeys to France and England in 1851–2 and 1855–6, Casa Guidi became their principal home. During the hot summer months they retreated to Bagni di Lucca in Tuscany, or to Siena. 1858 brought a change in this pattern as EBB's health declined. From July to September 1858 they stayed in Paris and Le Havre. In 1853–4 and from 1858 to 1861 they passed the winters in Rome.

1846–8 was not a period of great poetic activity for EBB; she was too immersed in the poetry of life. Soon, however, the passion of the struggle for Italian liberation, together with Pen's birth, generated a new kind of poetry. Late in 1847 she began work on *Casa Guidi Windows* (1851), a lyrical epic about the birth of a nation interwoven with personal reflections on motherhood. But she worked on this intermittently. In summer 1849 she finally revealed to Robert the sonnets she had written during their courtship, including them at his insistence in the expanded two-volume *Poems* of 1850 (a third edition appeared in 1853, and a fourth in 1856). The title *Sonnets from the Portuguese*, meant to serve as a mask for the personal content, was suggested by the association of 'Catarina to Camoens', one of Browning's favourite poems, with the Portuguese poet Luis de Camões (*Letters … Arabella*, 1.368). Poignantly, EBB's 1850 *Poems* retained the dedication to her father from her 1844 edition. But the gesture and her many letters to him had no discernible effect. He refused to communicate with her up until his death in 1857, and died '[w]ithout a word, without a sign—It's like slamming a door on me as he went out', EBB said to Arabella (ibid., 2.298).

Married life, mature works, and final illness: 1851–1861 After her marriage EBB developed friendships with many writers, artists, intellectuals, and activists. In 1849 she met Margaret Fuller and was saddened by her death by shipwreck in 1850. On 15 February 1852 she also met George Sand, whose genius she had long admired; she disapproved of her bohemian companions, yet noted with approval that Sand seemed respected as '*the man* in that company' (*Letters*, 2.56). The Brownings' journey back to England in 1851 led to social exchanges with Tennyson in Paris, and John Forster, Samuel Rogers, and the Carlyles in London. Later, EBB also met Charles Kingsley and became friends with John Ruskin. In Italy, the Brownings' circle of friends and acquaintances included Fanny and Adelaide Kemble; the American artists William Page and his wife, and William Wetmore Story and his wife; William Makepeace Thackeray and his daughters (Anne Thackeray Ritchie later wrote the 1886 *Dictionary of National Biography* entry on EBB); Frederick Tennyson, brother of the poet laureate; Robert Lytton, son of Sir Edward Bulwer-Lytton; Walter Savage Landor, befriended by the Brownings in his stormy old age; Isa Blagden, one of their closest friends; the sculptor Harriet Hosmer, who lived the life of a 'perfectly "emancipated female"' (ibid., 2.166); and, in 1857 and 1860, Harriet Beecher Stowe, who shared EBB's keen interest in spiritualism.

Conflicting views of the table-moving and spirit-rapping sessions generated by the public fascination with spiritualism in 1852–3, combined with earlier conflicts over Louis Napoleon's *coup d'état* in France during their Paris winter of 1851–2, led to the first serious differences in the Brownings' otherwise happy marriage. The years from 1851 to 1855 were generally very productive for both poets, however. By 1853 EBB had commenced serious work on *Aurora Leigh* (published in November 1856, but dated 1857), developing the idea for the novel-poem she had first mentioned in 1844. Meanwhile, Browning was writing the dramatic monologues published in *Men and Women* (1855). From July to October 1855 they were in England, as Browning attended to the proofs of his new book. In London they saw many other writers, including Ruskin, Carlyle, and Adelaide Proctor. One memorable evening during this stay the Brownings were visited by Tennyson, Dante Gabriel Rossetti, and his brother William Michael Rossetti.

D. G. Rossetti did a sketch of the poet laureate as he read 'Maud' 'to E. B. B.' and the others (*Letters … Arabella*, 2.175–6). *Casa Guidi Windows*, with its focus on Italian politics and its searing critique of the English imperialism embodied in the 1851 Great Exhibition, had not added greatly to EBB's reputation in England. By contrast, *Aurora Leigh*, which she described in its dedication (to John Kenyon) as the 'most mature' of her works, expressing her 'highest convictions upon Life and Art', was an immediate success. As Margaret Reynolds's scholarly edition of *Aurora Leigh*

(1992) reveals, EBB's aim was not only to portray a representative woman artist, but also to take her subject matter 'from the times, "hot and hot"' (Reynolds, 85), confronting the 'social question' of the gulf between the classes, as well as the 'woman question' much debated in mid-Victorian periodicals. Addressing the issues of women's rights to education and work, battered wives, and systemic prostitution, *Aurora Leigh* simultaneously represents the threat of class conflict and the reforms it precipitated. It is also much concerned with questions about art, as the heroine, Aurora, and her high-born cousin Romney, a socialist reformer, debate the relative worth of artistic creation and pragmatic political action. Aurora gives no quarter in this debate, defiantly rejecting both Romney's patronizing dismissal of female artistic aspiration and his attempt to conscript her as helpmate (and wife) in his socialist mission. Years later she finally marries Romney, but she is now a successful author. He is blind (like Rochester in *Jane Eyre*), and has learned to appreciate her mission in life as well as his own.

Some reviewers were shocked by 'brazen-faced Aurora', and by the elliptical depiction of the rape and ensuing pregnancy experienced by Aurora's working-class friend, Marian, saying the 'book should be a closed volume' to the author's own sex. Others called *Aurora Leigh* the work of a 'master mind', a 'modern epic', saying, 'It sings of our actual life, embodying the schemes and struggles, the opinions and social contrasts of our day' (Stone, 141–5). Dorothy Mermin's balanced summary (Mermin, 223–4) indicates that critical responses were as diverse as the conflicting agendas of its readers. *Aurora Leigh* had no shortage of admirers, however. Terming it 'a unique work of audaciously feminine' genius, Swinburne said in 1898 'The advent of *Aurora Leigh* can never be forgotten by any lover of poetry who was old enough at the time to read it.' Ruskin called it 'the greatest poem' of the century; George Eliot read it three times because no other book gave her 'a deeper sense of communion with a large as well as a beautiful mind'; Elizabeth Gaskell turned to it for the epigraph of *The Life of Charlotte Brontë* (1857); and Susan B. Anthony carried it with her as she criss-crossed America, lecturing on women's rights, inscribing her copy with the wish that women might be 'more & more like Aurora Leigh' (Stone, 32; Kelley and Coley, 573).

The success of *Aurora Leigh* was attended by three personal sorrows for EBB: the death of her benevolent cousin John Kenyon on 3 December 1856 and the death of her father on 17 April 1857, following rapidly on Treppy's death on 9 March 1857. In his will Kenyon left £4500 for EBB and £6500 for Browning (*Correspondence*, 3.317). Her father excluded EBB entirely from his will, along with Henrietta and Alfred (like EBB, both had married against his wishes), giving his Jamaica properties to his eldest living son and dividing his English estate, worth more than £63,000, among his remaining children (ibid., 1.288). After 1857 EBB's health grew frailer and she wrote relatively little for a period. Her father's death was followed by Henrietta's on 23 November 1860. In these years she was

drawn to the consolations Swedenborgianism and spiritualism seemed to offer, forming a particularly close relationship with the wealthy American amateur medium Sophia Eckley, until she recognized Sophia's deceptions.

In 1859 EBB was intensely absorbed in Italian politics again, as Louis Napoleon, now self-crowned as Emperor Napoleon III, intervened in Italy and the liberation longed for by so many seemed imminent—until the treaty of Villafranca. These events are the subject of *Poems before Congress* (1860)—in America, entitled *Napoleon III in Italy*—a collection that provoked an outcry in England because reviewers assumed the thundering concluding poem, 'A Curse for a Nation', was the poet's curse on her own country (in fact, it was an anti-slavery poem first published in the 1856 issue of the abolitionist annual *The Liberty Bell*, as a curse on America). A storm of abuse descended on EBB from conservative quarterlies like *Blackwood's* and the *Saturday Review*. Denounced as a fanatic, she was told that woman's function was to bless, not to curse. Among Italians, however, *Poems before Congress* was more favourably received.

At the beginning of June 1861 the Brownings returned from a winter in Rome, where EBB had been seriously ill, to her final spring in Florence. Her condition did not improve, despite her husband's tender care and the use of morphine to relieve her pain. On 29 June, as dawn approached, she died in her husband's arms, after what Browning described to her brother George as 'the most perfect expression of her love to me within my whole knowledge of her'; she died 'smilingly, happily, and with a face like a girl's. … Her last word was—… "*Beautiful*"' (Mermin, 247). On 1 July she was buried in the protestant cemetery in Florence. A memorial tablet erected by 'Grateful Florence' at Casa Guidi paid tribute to the poet and the scholar 'whose poems forged a golden ring / Between Italy and England'.

Changing critical assessments EBB's *Last Poems* (1862), edited by her husband, included works on Italian politics, accomplished dramatic monologues, and the powerful lyric 'A Musical Instrument'—exploring the beauty cruelly extracted by the gods of poetry from the artist's pain. The reviews of *Last Poems*, together with the obituaries, reflect the conflicting critical assessments typical of the next few decades. On the one hand EBB was called 'one of the foremost poets' of the age (*British Quarterly Review*, 34, October 1861), or one of the 'chief poets of the century', more welcomed in America 'than any English poet since the time of Byron' (*Harper's New Monthly Magazine*, 23, September 1861). At the very least, she was ranked as the 'greatest woman poet of whom we have any record' (*North British Review*, 36, May 1862), showing that 'Genius has no sex' (*The Athenaeum*, 6 July 1861). On the other hand she was criticized for eccentricity, obscurity, and faulty rhymes by reviewers who deplored her meddling with political questions viewed as beyond women's scope. The *Edinburgh Review* of October 1861 concluded that her career was 'some proof of the impossibility that women can ever attain to the first rank in any imaginative composition'. The *Saturday Review* more bluntly observed, 'no woman can hope to achieve what Mrs. Browning failed to accomplish' (*Saturday Review*, 12, 13 July 1861). *Aurora Leigh* is recognized as her major work in the obituaries, but preference is expressed for more conventionally feminine works, including the *Sonnets from the Portuguese*. Focus on the *Sonnets* permitted reviewers to assert that, if Mrs Browning 'exceeded her sex in strength and aspiration, it was only to foreshow what a woman may gain in her proper sphere' (*North American Review*, 94, April 1862).

A better index of EBB's historical significance appears in her widespread influence on other writers, intellectuals, and activists for women's rights in Britain, America, and Europe. In his youth Dante Gabriel Rossetti knew many of her poems of 1844 by heart, while Christina Rossetti's works reflect her complex response to the writer she acknowledged as her greatest female precursor. In America *A Drama of Exile: and other Poems* circulated in circles that included Margaret Fuller, James Russell Lowell, and the Hawthornes, as well as Poe. EBB's anti-slavery poems led Frederick Douglass, the great American orator and abolitionist, to pause by her grave in Florence in tribute during his travels in Italy. Certain works, such as the *Sonnets from the Portuguese*, were later translated into French, German, and Italian; in the case of 'The Cry of the Children' the interest extended to Russia.

EBB had a particularly powerful effect on women writers and reformers. Barbara Leigh-Smith (later Bodichon) wove quotations from *Aurora Leigh* into her pamphlet *Women and Work* (1857); Bessie Rayner Parkes, who helped establish the *English Woman's Journal* in 1858, paid tribute to her in 'To Elizabeth Barrett Browning'; Dora Greenwell mourned her death in 'To Elizabeth Barrett Browning, in 1861'; and Frances Power Cobbe used her achievement as an example of women's powers in art in 'What shall we do with our old maids?' (1862). George Eliot's *Armgart* (1874) clearly owes a debt to *Aurora Leigh*, like Katherine Bradley's *Arran Leigh* (1875), published before she began to collaborate with Edith Cooper as Michael Field; Louisa Sara Bevington also published her first volume of poems in 1876 under the pseudonym Arbor Leigh. By 1900 over twenty editions of *Aurora Leigh* had appeared, and in America a new edition 'could sell ten thousand copies' (Reynolds, 149). 'There may be greater poems in our language than "Aurora Leigh", but it was many years before it was possible for me to suppose it', the American author Elizabeth Stuart Phelps observed, recalling that she 'could have repeated a large portion of it' from memory after she read it at sixteen in 1860 (Stone, 191). Emily Dickinson also wrote three poems to EBB, among them 'I think I was enchanted', and listed her among the authors she most treasured.

While many late Victorian critics continued to approach EBB as one of the century's major poets, those hostile to the implications of her achievement increasingly carried the day—like Edward Fitzgerald, who expressed 'relief' over her death: 'no more Aurora Leighs, thank God! A Woman of real Genius, I know; but what is the upshot of it all? She and her Sex had better mind the Kitchen and their Children; and perhaps the Poor'

(Mermin, 248). The comment infuriated Browning when it was published in 1889, shortly before his own death. By the early twentieth century, hostility to the author of *Aurora Leigh* had subsided, but at the cost of reducing EBB to an appendage of her husband. Literary histories began to relegate consideration of 'Mrs. Browning' to supplementary sections of chapters on Browning, focusing on the story of her courtship and singling out *Sonnets from the Portuguese* as her best work. The *Sonnets* appeared in edition after edition from 1900 to 1970, while *Aurora Leigh* lapsed into virtual oblivion, and its author, whose reputation had eclipsed Browning's in her lifetime, was cast as the handmaid of her husband's genius. In 1908 John W. Cunliffe argued that she was more important for her influence on Browning than for her own poetry. 'Her best work is to be found not in her own writings, but in his.' By 1931 her reputation had sunk so low that Virginia Woolf sardonically described her as relegated to the 'servants' quarters' in the 'mansion of literature' (Stone, 209–12). In the same period, numerous popularized accounts of her life—most notably Rudolph Besier's 1930 play, *The Barretts of Wimpole Street*, made into Hollywood motion pictures in 1934 and 1959—established her as the pining Miss Barrett rescued by the dashing Robert Browning (Taplin, 419–20). Woolf and G. K. Chesterton both offered serious critical assessments of EBB's poetry at this time, but theirs were voices crying in the wilderness, like Alethea Hayter's thirty years later (1962). Gardner Taplin's 1957 scholarly biography did little to question the prevailingly dismissive attitudes towards her artistic achievement.

The women's movement of the 1970s, together with changing critical perspectives, generated a dramatic recovery of EBB's reputation, manifested in Cora Kaplan's 'Introduction' to the 1978 Women's Press edition of *Aurora Leigh*. In the 1980s new readings of the poetry of 'Barrett Browning' multiplied in books by Angela Leighton (1986), Helen Cooper (1988), Dorothy Mermin (1989), and Glennis Stephenson (1989), and in hundreds of entries listed in Sandra Donaldson's annotated bibliography (1993). *Aurora Leigh* has been the principal focus of these reinterpretations, but attention has also been directed to EBB's ballads and her 1844 *Poems* (Stone) and to her religious poetry (Lewis). Reassessment has been hampered by the lack of a scholarly complete edition of her writings, including criticism published under Richard Hengist Horne's name and poems such as 'Aeschylus' Soliloquy', mistakenly attributed to Browning for decades and occasioning repeated exchanges in the pages of the *Times Literary Supplement*. The lively letters that make her correspondence such a window on her age are comprehensively appearing, however, in the *Correspondence* edited by Philip Kelley, Ronald Hudson, and Scott Lewis.

While EBB has earned unanimous praise for her letters, the poetry that was her primary achievement has provoked more controversy. This controversy was as vigorous in the late twentieth century as it was in the 1850s and 1860s, and intertwined as it was then with debates concerning the nature of women, political issues, and aesthetic preferences. Few can deny, however, that Elizabeth

Barrett Browning was one of the most influential poets of her time. Aptly termed the 'wellhead of a new female tradition' (Mermin, 3), she was also an author whose daring experiments with poetic conventions and subject matter extended the possibilities for all writers who succeeded her, male as well as female. Popular stereotypes still cast her as the passive heroine of Wimpole Street. But her husband and fellow poet knew better. In *The Ring and the Book*, a novel in verse that owes much to the precedent of *Aurora Leigh*, Browning links his work to the golden ring of Elizabeth Barrett Browning's achievement, paying high tribute to her as '[b]oldest of hearts that ever braved the sun'.

MARJORIE STONE

Sources *The Brownings' correspondence*, ed. P. Kelley, R. Hudson, and S. Lewis, [14 vols.] (1984–) · *The letters of Elizabeth Barrett Browning to her sister Arabella*, ed. S. Lewis, 2 vols. (2002) · *The letters of Elizabeth Barrett Browning*, ed. F. G. Kenyon, 2 vols. (1897) · *The letters of Elizabeth Barrett Browning to Mary Russell Mitford*, ed. M. B. Raymond and M. R. Sullivan, 3 vols. (1983) · *The complete works of Elizabeth Barrett Browning*, ed. C. Porter and H. A. Clarke, 6 vols. (1900); repr. (1973) · *Diary by E.B.B.: the unpublished diary of Elizabeth Barrett Barrett, 1831–32*, ed. P. Kelley and R. Hudson (1969) · R. A. Barrett, *The Barretts of Jamaica: the family of Elizabeth Barrett Browning* (2000) · D. Mermin, *Elizabeth Barrett Browning: the origins of a new poetry* (1989) · J. Marks, *The family of the Barrett: a colonial romance* (1938) · J. Markus, *Dared and done: the marriage of Elizabeth Barrett and Robert Browning* (1995) · M. Stone, *Elizabeth Barrett Browning* (1995) · M. Forster, *Elizabeth Barrett Browning: a biography* (1988) · L. M. Lewis, *Elizabeth Barrett Browning's spiritual progress: face to face with God* (1998) · C. Kaplan, 'Introduction', in E. B. Browning, *Aurora Leigh* (1978) · G. Taplin, *The life of Elizabeth Barrett Browning* (1957) · D. Karlin, *The courtship of Robert Browning and Elizabeth Barrett* (1985) · M. Reynolds, notes and introduction, in E. B. Browning, *Aurora Leigh* (1992) · E. B. Browning, *Hitherto unpublished poems and stories*, ed. H. Buxton Forman, 2 vols. (1914) · A. Hayter, *Mrs Browning: a poet's work and its setting* (1962) · G. Stephenson, *Elizabeth Barrett Browning and the poetry of love* (1989) · P. Kelley and B. Coley, *The Browning collections: a reconstruction with other memorabilia* (1984) · S. Donaldson, *Elizabeth Barrett Browning: an annotated bibliography of commentary and criticism, 1826–1990* (1993) · W. Barnes, *A bibliography of Elizabeth Barrett Browning* (1967) · *The Athenaeum* (6 July 1861) · *British Quarterly Review*, 34 (Oct 1861) · *EdinR*, 114 (Oct 1861) · *Harper's New Monthly Magazine*, 23 (Sept 1861) · *North American Review*, 94 (April 1862) · *North British Review*, 36 (May 1862) · *Saturday Review*, 12 (13 July 1861) · M. H. Shackford, 'The authorship of "Aeschylus' soliloquy"', *The Times*, literary suppl. (21 March 1842) · G. D. Hobson, '"Aeschylus's soliloquy"', *The Times*, literary suppl. (11 April 1842) · I. Jack, 'Browning translations', *TLS* (31 July 1987) · private information (2004) [P. Kelley] · Baylor University, Waco, Texas, Armstrong Browning Library, D 802 · 'Poems and sonnets' note book, Yale U., Beinecke L.

Archives Baylor University, Waco, Texas, Armstrong Browning Library · BL, address book, Ashley 5718 · BL, letters and literary MSS, Add. MSS 42227–42231, 43487, 60391, 60574–60575 · Boston PL, corresp., literary MSS, and papers · Eton, Barrett Browning collection · FM Cam., personal and family corresp. · Hunt. L., letters and literary MSS · Morgan L., letters and literary MSS · NRA, priv. coll., corresp. · Ransom HRC, letters and literary MSS · Wellesley College, Massachusetts, corresp., literary MSS, and papers · Yale U., Beinecke L., papers | BL, letters to Robert Browning and others, Ashley 2522 · BL, letters to Richard Henry Horne, MS Facs Suppl X · BL, letters to John Kenyon, RP2087 · BL, letters to Mary Eliza Minto, Add. MS 41323 · BL, letters to Thomas Westwood, Add. MS 40689 · Herts. ALS, corresp. with Lord Lytton · Morgan L., letters to George Moulton Barrett; letters to Richard Hengist Horne · NYPL, Henry W. and Albert A. Berg Collection of English and American Literature, letters and literary MSS · University of Chicago Library, corresp. with Bryan Procter and Anne Procter

Likenesses crayon drawing, c.1820, Wellesley College, Massachusetts · M. Moulton-Barrett, slightly tinted pencil drawing, 1821, repro. in Kelley and Coley, eds., *Browning collections*, 1, facing p. 132 · W. M. Thackeray, drawing, 1845, Hunt. L. · T. B. Read, oils, 1853, Hist. Soc. Penn. · M. Gordigiani, oils, 1858, NPG; repro. in Forster, *Elizabeth Barrett Browning*, cover · R. Lehmann, pencil drawing, 1859, BM · F. Talfourd, chalk drawing, 1859, NPG [*see illus.*] · Alessandri, photograph, 1861, Baylor University, Waco, Texas, Armstrong Browning Library; repro. in Markus, *Dared and done*, 329 · Alessandri, photograph, 1861, Wellesley College, Massachusetts; repro. in Markus, *Dared and done*, 327 · W. W. Story, posthumous bust, 1861, Keats and Shelley Memorial Museum, Rome · T. O. Barlow, line and stipple (after photograph by Macaire of Le Havre, 1858), BM · J. Brown, stipple (as a child; after Mayou), BM · G. Cook, line and stipple (aged nine; after C. Hayter), BM · photograph, U. Texas, Gernsheim collection · stipple prints, repro. in E. B. Browning, *Poetical works* (1889–90), vols. 1, 2, 3

Browning [*née* Chadwick], **Ethel** (1891–1969), toxicologist and factory inspector, was born on 16 March 1891 at 36 Audlam Street, Bury, Lancashire, the daughter of James William Chadwick, cotton spinner, later a gentleman (1916), and sometime managing director of a soap factory, and his wife, Elizabeth Ann (*née* Morris). She was educated at Hough Green high school, Widnes, Lancashire, and, between 1909 and 1914, the University of Liverpool, where she studied medicine. She was an accomplished musician and at one time hoped to become a concert pianist, but was unable to fulfil this ambition either because a shoulder injury prevented her from completing her training or because her hands were too small. As a medical student she won several awards, including the Kanthack medal in pathology, the Holt medal in physiology, and the university prize in medicine. For two years she was the Lyon Jones scholar. In July 1914 she graduated MB BCh with first-class honours; she achieved distinctions in medicine, surgery, and obstetrics. Following graduation she was briefly house surgeon at Liverpool Stanley Hospital. There she contracted a serious infection of the hand which led to septicaemia and pericarditis. For several years, including two in which she was confined to bed, illness prevented her from pursuing a medical career. During brief periods of remission she worked as assistant school medical officer in Liverpool and medical officer to the infant welfare centre at Garston. Otherwise, she read history and wrote medical and other articles for the popular press. For about two years she worked as a journalist on a literary magazine.

It was probably at Liverpool that Ethel met her first husband, Basil Browning (*b.* 1891/2), a medical graduate of the University of Manchester, who was a house surgeon in the same institution. He was the son of a clergyman, Henry Browning. The marriage, which took place on 12 July 1916, produced no children. About 1919 the couple moved for a short while to St Just in Cornwall, where Basil became a partner in a general practice. A few years later they moved to Twickenham in Middlesex. In 1924 Ethel published her first article in the medical press: 'Case of diabetes treated with decreasing dosage of insulin'. She was briefly lecturer in nursing at St John's Hospital in Twickenham, but was increasingly occupied in medical research and writing, including for her MD thesis. In 1927 she submitted a thesis entitled 'B-vitamin deficiency as a cause of intestinal stasis', the research for which had been carried out at the Knightsbridge laboratories in Sloane Street, London. Her external examiner considered the thesis to be of 'excellent merit' and, initially, suggested that no oral examination was required (Report of R. H. A. Plimmer, 19 Nov 1927, in Liverpool University Archives). Her internal examiner, on the other hand, regarded the work as 'seriously defective' and insisted on a viva (Report of W. Ramsden, 25 Nov 1927, in Liverpool University Archives). The degree of MD was awarded in 1927. Ethel and Basil divorced in 1928; Ethel was the petitioner and no co-respondent was identified. On 14 March 1931 Ethel married the pathologist Ernest Thomas Ruston (b. 1902/3). He was the son of a retired schoolmaster, Albert Ernest Ruston. This marriage was also childless. In 1928, the year in which she became assistant pathologist at the Pickett Thomson Research Laboratory at St Paul's Hospital in London, Ethel published her first two books of many: *Heritage of Ills: some Common Diseases and their Prevention* and *The Machine of Life*. *The Graphic* reviewed the former as a 'thoroughly modern' guide to the 'true foundations of good health'. Over the next forty years she published a number of papers in medical journals and a further ten books on specialist and popular areas of medicine and science. She was also general editor of a series of Elsevier monographs on industrial toxic agents.

Browning became known as a specialist in dietetics and publication of her book *The Vitamins* (1931) led in 1935 to her appointment as medical officer to Energen Foods. At about this time the Medical Research Council's industrial health board, in an inspired move, invited her to compile for publication information on the health effects of solvents used in industry. Notwithstanding her lack of experience of industrial medicine she produced 'the first useful textbook on the subject' (*The Lancet*, 17 Jan 1970). Entitled *Toxicity of Industrial Organic Solvents* (1937), it soon became the standard reference work. In constant demand, a revised edition was issued in 1953. Related titles continued to appear until the year of her death. These included *Harmful Effects of Ionising Radiations* (1959). With an encyclopaedic knowledge of the field based on factory floor experience, exhaustive library study, and formidable knowledge of chemistry rather than experimental work, 'Ethyl' Browning, as she was once dubbed, became the leading authority on industrial toxicology, and enjoyed an international reputation. In 1940, following reports of high mortality among women using radioactive paint in New Jersey, the senior medical inspector of factories, Dr John Bridge, requested her to make a six-month study of luminizers. She not only accepted the commission but joined the medical inspectorate of factories, remaining in post until her retirement in 1958.

Browning was a tiny, frail woman, whose weight probably never exceeded 6 stones. Although she had a delicate constitution and suffered repeated bouts of serious illness, she possessed great energy, enthusiasm for life, and

strength of character. She was also a magnificent cook, outstanding musician, and talented linguist, with at least four languages at her command. Professionally busy until well into her seventies, including a post as adviser on toxicology to Courtaulds, she died on 18 December 1969 at her home, Overdale, 30 Oakfield Road, Birkby, Huddersfield. Her second husband survived her.   P. W. J. BARTRIP

Sources *BMJ* (17 Jan 1970), 177 · *The Lancet* (17 Jan 1970), 150 · *Transactions of the Society of Occupational Medicine*, 20/2 (April 1970), 74 · *The Times* (12 Jan 1970) · *Medical Directory* (1914–69) · student dossier, U. Lpool L., special collections and archives · M. Kipling, *A brief history of HM medical inspectorate* (1979) · b. cert. · m. certs. · decree absolute, 11 June 1928, no. folio 161/1928 · d. cert. · *The lady's who's who: who's who for British women … 1938–9* (1939) · private information (2004)

Wealth at death £90,361: new grant, 19 May 1971, *CGPLA Eng. & Wales* · £90,361: administration, 18 March 1970, *CGPLA Eng. & Wales* [revoked]

Browning, **Sir Frederick Arthur Montague** (1896–1965), army officer and courtier, often known as Boy Browning, or as Tommy to intimates, was born on 20 December 1896, at 31 Hans Road, Brompton, London, the second child and only son of Frederick Henry Browning and his wife, Anne (*née* Alt). His father was a London merchant who was made an honorary colonel and appointed CBE for his work as a censor of overseas mail in the First World War; he later moved with his family to Flaxley Abbey in Gloucestershire.

Browning was educated at Eton College from 1910 to 1914. On the outbreak of the First World War he entered the Royal Military College, Sandhurst, and in June 1915 he was commissioned into the Grenadier Guards; he received promotion to lieutenant next month. He joined the 2nd battalion, Grenadier Guards, on the western front in October 1915, and was made acting battalion adjutant and an acting captain in 1917. Browning served with the battalion throughout the war, distinguishing himself during the German counter-attack at Cambrai in December 1917, for which he received the DSO and the Croix de Guerre. He also gained a reputation for his love of military display, which throughout his life he held to be indivisible from fighting ability. He continued after the war as adjutant of his battalion, and was promoted captain in 1920. He was appointed adjutant at Sandhurst in 1924, and introduced the famous tradition in which the ceremonial passing out parade ended with the adjutant on his white horse following the cadets up the steps and through the doors of Old Building. This was his only military experience outside his battalion, which he rejoined as a major in 1928, and he did not attend the Staff College.

Although his handsome appearance and physical prowess won him admirers, contemporaries saw Browning as an emotional and theatrical character. Utterly confident of his own innate superiority, and of his place in society, he was inclined to sulk if thwarted (one family nickname was 'Moper') and became prone to displays of bad temper and in later life a tendency to fantasize. Accounts of his athletic prowess seem to have grown with the telling. Although he spent much time away from his battalion on sports and social events, and was throughout his life a

Sir Frederick Arthur Montague Browning (1896–1965), by Sir
Gerald Kelly, 1923

keen sailor, he also emerged from the First World War
with unspecified 'tummy trouble' which may have contributed to later illnesses (he was also slightly colour
blind). In the 1924 winter Olympics he was reserve for one
of the two British four-man bobsleigh teams. But repeated
stories that he was national champion at the high hurdles
and represented his country in the Olympic games at that
sport, are quite untrue.

On 19 July 1932 Browning married Daphne *Du Maurier
(1907–1989), novelist and second daughter of Sir Gerald
*Du Maurier, at the church of Lanteglos by Fowey, in
Cornwall; they settled in the nearby house of Menabilly.
She idealized Browning, and he was probably the inspir-
ation for Sir Richard Grenvile in her novel The King's
General (1946). They had three children, Tessa (b. 1933), Fla-
via (b. 1937), and Christian (b. 1940).

In 1936 Browning was promoted lieutenant-colonel
commanding his battalion, with which he served in Egypt
in 1936–8, and on ceremonial duties at Windsor in 1938–9.
At the start of the Second World War he was promoted to
brigadier, and given a series of training appointments in
Britain as commandant of the small arms school at
Netheravon (1939–40), commanding the 128th infantry
brigade (1940), and commanding the 24th guards brigade
(1940–41). In October 1941 he was promoted major-general
in command of the airborne forces (paratroops and glider
troops), and next month he was given the additional post
of commanding the newly formed 1st airborne division.

Although he did not found the airborne forces, Browning ensured their institutional survival and expansion
from a handful of small units to a full Airborne Corps of
two divisions (and an attached Special Air Service brigade)
by January 1944, with himself as the lieutenant-general
commanding. Fellow senior airborne officers saw his
institutional and social connections as important in overcoming resistance to the airborne forces by the RAF in particular, although both Browning and his staff were also
criticized as more concerned with institutional politics
than military planning. His handsome charm also
appealed to many senior British figures, including Winston Churchill, General Sir Alan Brooke as chief of the
Imperial General Staff, and Lord Louis Mountbatten as
chief of combined operations. In addition, Browning was
responsible for creating an airborne identity, particularly
within the Parachute regiment, by means of distinctive
dress and insignia, including the famous 'red beret'.

From the north African campaign of 1942–3 onwards,
British airborne forces operations were increasingly
mounted in conjunction with American forces, and
became virtually dependent on American military aircraft. Unfortunately to many Americans Browning
appeared almost as a caricature of an English fop.
Although his airborne forces were used successfully in the
Sicilian and Italian campaigns of 1943, and again on D-day
in Normandy in June 1944, Browning played no direct role
in the planning or conduct of these battles.

Browning's only operational command in the Second
World War involved him in what turned out to be a failure
surrounded by controversy and mutual recrimination. In
August 1944 he received the further appointment of deputy commander, first allied airborne army, which combined British, American, and other allied airborne troops
under the American airman Lieutenant-General Lewis
Brereton. In early September Field Marshal Sir Bernard
Montgomery, commanding Twenty-First Army group,
devised Operation 'Market-Garden', an ambitious plan for
supporting an armoured drive by the British Second Army
into the Netherlands with an airborne assault by two
American and one British airborne divisions, which
would capture critical bridges for the advance. Browning
was placed in charge of the airborne operation, and on 17
September he and his Airborne Corps headquarters
landed with the first wave. The attack failed to achieve its
objectives, German resistance being much stronger than
had been expected. British 1st airborne division, landing
furthest away at Arnhem, was virtually wiped out, the survivors being withdrawn to safety on 26 September. The
story circulated that Browning had warned Montgomery,
'we might be going a bridge too far'; but senior officers
who used this phrase in Browning's lifetime have since
confirmed that they did not hear it at the time. In the 1977
film that took its title from Browning's supposed words,
the fictionalized Browning character was played by Dirk
Bogarde.

In November 1944 Browning was sent to the Far East as
chief of staff to Mountbatten, where he became closely
associated with Mountbatten's set, including the young

Prince Philip (later the duke of Edinburgh), and where his courtier's political skills were used to the greatest advantage. After the war he was appointed military secretary in 1946, and left the army in 1948 to become comptroller of the household for the newly married Princess Elizabeth and Prince Philip. In 1952, following the royal succession, he became treasurer and comptroller for the duke of Edinburgh. He retired from this post through ill health in 1959 to Menabilly House, and was made deputy lord lieutenant for Cornwall in 1960. In 1964 his left leg was amputated below the knee owing to circulatory problems, and on 14 March 1965 he died at home of a blood clot to the heart.

STEPHEN BADSEY

Sources V. Dover, *The sky generals* (1981) · T. B. H. Otway, ed., *Airborne forces, or, The Second World War 1939–1945 army* (1951?); repr. (1990) · J. Cook, *Daphne* (1991) · C. Ryan, *A bridge too far* (1974) · N. Hamilton, *Monty*, [3]: *The Field Marshal, 1944–1976* (1986) · F. Ponsonby, *The grenadier guards in the Great War*, 3 vols. (1920) · R. E. Urquhart, *Arnhem* (1958) · F. G. L. Fairlie, ed., *Official report of the VIIIth Olympiad, Paris, 1924* (1925) · *The Times* (15 March 1965) · *DNB* · *WWW* · *Army List* · *CGPLA Eng. & Wales* (1965) · b. cert. · d. cert.
Archives IWM, private MSS | Airborne Forces Museum, Aldershot, Airborne forces MSS | FILM BFI NFTVA, 'Japs take surrender orders', *British News*, 17 Sept 1945 · BFI NFTVA, news footage · IWM FVA, actuality footage
Likenesses G. Kelly, oils, 1923, priv. coll. [*see illus.*] · W. Stoneman, photograph, 1944, NPG · A. C. Davidson-Houston, oils, 1950, NPG · D. Fildes, oils, 1950–59, Airborne Forces Museum, Aldershot · W. Stoneman, photograph, 1955, NPG
Wealth at death £26,478: probate, 28 April 1965, *CGPLA Eng. & Wales*

Browning, John (d. 1612?), Church of England clergyman and theological disputant, is of obscure origins; nothing is known of his life before his arrival at Cambridge University. It cannot have involved great wealth, however, for he matriculated sizar at Trinity College on 14 November 1558. He was awarded a scholarship in 1560, became a fellow of Trinity in 1563, and graduated BA in 1562/3 and MA in 1566. Ordained as a deacon in the diocese of Ely on 2 June 1570, he was appointed a university preacher in the same year.

Browning quickly ran into trouble, however, on account of his sympathies with the radical reformers. The authorities were informed that in a Christmas sermon given in 1572 in St Mary's, Cambridge, he advocated perfectionist doctrines associated with the third century schismatic Novatius. Called before John Whitgift, then deputy chancellor, and the college heads, he was forbidden to preach. When Browning defied the ban, he was committed to the Tolbooth in Cambridge on 27 January 1573. His release in February was secured only on payment of a bond of £200 on his own account and of £40 each by two of his college fellows. Strype states that these very large sums were demanded as surety for his appearance to answer charges 'touching of great matters (matters of state I suppose)' (Strype, *Parker*, 2.195–7). Strype was ill-disposed towards Browning, whom he considered a 'turbulent, hot spirit', associated with 'a great faction' in Trinity 'disaffected to the present ecclesiastical settlement' (ibid., 2.195; Strype, *Whitgift*, 1.93), and this suggests that the political misdemeanours in question may have involved sympathy towards presbyterian church discipline. Chancellor

Burghley does not seem to have considered them very grave: he interviewed Browning, who signed a confession recanting his doctrinal errors. Burghley sent this to the vice-chancellor and heads together with a letter urging them to be sure that the miscreant would 'continue in that conformity and submission that he pretended', but recommending that if this should prove to be so, they should 'do well to receive him and cherish him with all good countenance and usage' (Strype, *Reformation*, 2/1.280–81).

Having survived this dangerous episode, Browning was awarded his BTh in 1577. He was then employed as a chaplain by Francis, earl of Bedford. He graduated DTh at Oxford on 8 July 1580. But when Browning returned to Cambridge and sought incorporation in this degree, he met with official opposition. Dr Still, the master of Trinity, objected that Browning had failed to perform the required exercises or to secure an exemption from them. Browning won his case, and Still was persuaded to sign the grace for his incorporation in the degree of doctor of theology at Cambridge on 8 December 1581.

Despite this success, Browning seems to have become convinced that the master had been impelled by personal and religious animus, and had invoked the university statutes to conceal the fact beneath a cloak of legalism. In 1584, having been appointed as vice-master of Trinity College, Browning seized the opportunity for revenge. On 7 September he suspended the authority of Dr Still 'for his marriage contrary to his oath, and divers and sundry other breaches of statute, both in the government and not husbanding the goods of Trinity college'. Enraged, Still ordered him ejected from the fellowship:

> but Dr Browning, however, would not depart, keeping his chamber door shut till some were sent to pull him out; a decree being passed from the vice chancellor and the heads, to have the proctors enter with force: and Dr Still made a decree, the next day by eight o'clock his doors should be broke open. And this was acordingly done, and they carried him out by strong hand. (Cooper, *Ath. Cantab.*, 2.239)

But Browning continued his tenacious resistance in the sphere of politics. In October he petitioned the queen, sought with some success to enlist the sympathy of Archbishop Whitgift, and persuaded the earl of Bedford to write on his behalf to Burghley. For a second time Burghley wrote to the heads of colleges in his favour, recalling much 'good experience of his sufficiency in the sound preaching of the truth, and of his godly conversation in my own family' (Cooper, *Ath. Cantab.*, 2.239). But it seems that even such powerful support was insufficient to secure Browning's readmission. Nothing further is known of him with certainty. However, one John Browning, a bachelor of theology, is listed as rector of South Stoke, in the diocese of Chichester, from 1589 until his successor's institution in 1612. It seems probable that the contentious fellow of Trinity spent his last years in the obscurity of the Sussex countryside.

John Browning of Trinity should not be confused with another **John Browning** (d. 1648), who was born in Worcester; his mother was named in his will as Katherine

Austyn of London, widow. This man attended Cambridge University, matriculating as a pensioner at Peterhouse in 1610 and graduating BA in 1613/14. A fellow of Jesus College from 1616 to 1626, he graduated MA there in 1617, and was incorporated at Oxford on 15 July 1617. Browning graduated BD in 1624 and was ordained priest in the diocese of Peterborough on 23 May. His will mentions a wife, Elizabeth, and lands held by copyhold at Much Hadham and Ware, in Hertfordshire. Browning was instituted to three Essex rectories—Raworth in 1625, Little Easton from 1634 to 1639, and Great Easton from 1639. In 1636 appeared his only published work, *Concerning Publike Prayer and the Fasts of the Church*. He is reported to have acted as a chaplain to Bishop Williams. On 1 February 1642 the Commons ordered that he be 'sent for as a delinquent … for speaking words of dangerous consequence against this House', though it allowed him bail on 14 February (*JHC*, 2.408). But Browning became a committed royalist. He was ejected by commissioners sitting at Maldon, and acted as chaplain to Prince Rupert from 1643. He signed his will on 19 May 1647, died on 22 September 1648, and was buried at St Peter-le-Poer, London, on the 26th. The funeral sermon was preached by Stephen Hall, also a sequestered minister and a former fellow of Jesus College, Cambridge.   STEPHEN WRIGHT

Sources Venn, *Alum. Cant.* · Cooper, *Ath. Cantab.* · H. C. Porter, *Reformation and reaction in Tudor Cambridge* (1958) · J. Strype, *The life and acts of Matthew Parker*, new edn, 3 vols. (1821), vol. 2 · J. Strype, *The life and acts of John Whitgift*, new edn, 3 vols. (1822), vol. 1 · J. Strype, *Annals of the Reformation and establishment of religion … during Queen Elizabeth's happy reign*, new edn, 2/1 (1824) · G. L. Hennessy, *Chichester diocese clergy lists* (1900) · C. H. Cooper, *Annals of Cambridge*, 2 (1843) · Walker rev. · P. Benton, *History of Rochford hundred* (1867) · H. I. Longden, *Northamptonshire and Rutland clergy from 1500*, ed. P. I. King and others, 16 vols. in 6, Northamptonshire RS (1938–52) · *JHC*, 2 (1640–42)

Browning, John (d. 1648). *See under* Browning, John (d. 1612?).

Browning, John (1830/31–1925), scientific instrument maker, was born in Kent, the son of William Browning (d. 1862) and his wife, Susan. William Browning conducted an instrument-making business at 111 Minories, London, which his son later claimed had been established as early as 1765. It has been suggested that this was the shop Charles Dickens had in mind in describing that of Solomon Gills in *Dombey and Son*. According to his Royal Astronomical Society obituarist, John Browning was intended for the medical profession and entered Guy's Hospital after passing the necessary examination. A breakdown in health, however, led him to abandon this career, and about the age of fifteen he joined his father's business as an apprentice. In the academic year 1848/9 he was working in the shop every other day while attending classes at the recently founded Royal College of Chemistry under Professor A. W. Hoffmann.

In 1856 Browning took over his father's business. He was already expert in the design and manufacture of precision scientific instruments; between 1856 and 1872 he obtained various provisional patents, for stereoscopes, telescopes, cameras, barometers, and photometers, but did not seek to obtain full protection. He improved electric lamps and the condensers used with induction coils, and in 1862 he received a prize medal at the International Exhibition in London for his temperature-compensated aneroid barometers. He was a keen observer of Mars and Jupiter, and his preferred researches led him to construct and market affordable reflecting telescopes, and to undertake numerous experiments with telephones and phonographs.

Browning was a member of several learned societies: on 11 November 1863 he was elected to the Microscopical Society of London, in 1865 he was elected fellow of the Meteorological Society (he resigned in 1874), and from 6 May 1871 he was a member of the Royal Institution (he resigned on 3 April 1882). He was elected to the Royal Astronomical Society (RAS) on 10 March 1865, and published regularly in its *Monthly Notices*. He was also a member of its council from 1870 to 1873.

As a member of the joint council of the Royal Society and RAS set up to carry out the solar eclipse expedition in 1871, Browning was put in charge of the instrumentation, but, to avoid possible allegations of a vested interest, he did not take up this task. In 1863 John Phillips (1800–1874) had constructed and exhibited the first Mars globe, which enabled different observations to be compared. Browning improved this globe, which he presented at the RAS meeting in spring 1868, and from which pictures were taken for Proctor's *Stereograms*. Browning was held in high esteem in the scientific community because for many years he was the leading English designer and manufacturer of spectroscopes, both for laboratories and especially for those attached to telescopes: William Huggins and J. Norman Lockyer depended on his skills to enable them to pursue their early research in astronomical physics. General Sabine, in an address to the Royal Society, spoke at length on Browning's technical improvements to optical instruments. His instruments were favourably mentioned in works on spectroscopy by scientists such as Roscoe, Lockyer, Suffolk, Schellen, and Gassiot, who commissioned from Browning a six-prism spectroscope, a masterpiece at the time; it was presented to the new observatory of the University of Oxford in 1875 but was since lost. About 1870 Browning undertook the reconstruction of all the self-registering meteorological instruments at the Royal Observatory, Greenwich, then under the direction of Sir George Airy, and also turned his attention to improvements in the microscope, making a special one for Professor Hermann von Helmholtz.

In 1872 Browning's business, which employed some seventy men besides 'bunting girls', or flagmakers, was transferred to 63 Strand. When the factory at 6 Vine Street became inadequate, new premises were acquired in Southampton Street and Exeter Street, both close to the Strand, and after 1904 other premises in the Strand were acquired for the shop. At the time of the 1871 census Browning was a widower, living at 4 Greville Road, Richmond, Surrey, with three younger sisters. Nothing is known of his first wife, but he was described as a widower at his marriage, on 18 February 1874, to a widow, Charlotte Hotten, daughter of William Stringer, carver and designer.

Browning's medical training and skill with lenses enabled him to develop the ophthalmic side of his business: in 1876 he was prescribing and making astigmatic lenses, and he improved Lindsay Johnson's ophthalmoscope. He took great interest in the subject, voicing his opinion in public when, in 1894, the surgeons sought to get an act of parliament to prevent opticians using the ophthalmoscope; he was also a founder member of the British Optical Association and its first president, from 1895 to 1900. He published various popularizing books, including *How to Use our Eyes* (1883), which reached its fifteenth edition in 1894, having sold 22,000 copies. Later editions contained many testimonials by satisfied users of his spectacles. In 1898 he was admitted to the Spectaclemakers' Company. He wrote *A Plea for Reflectors* (1867), with descriptions of various telescopes and instructions for their use, and *How to Work with the Spectroscope* (1878), about the instrument of which he was for many years the leading maker, and provided an introduction to H. Renlow's *The Human Eye and its Auxiliary Organs* (1896). One of his favourite research topics was the importance of the rain band in the solar spectrum, for which he devised special spectroscopes.

The scope of Browning's personal interests was as broad as that of his work: from 1870 to 1880 he was a member of the Royal Aeronautical Society and its council; in his obituary in *Dioptric Review* he was credited with installing the first complete sets of telephonic apparatus at Buckingham Palace and Windsor Castle for Queen Victoria's personal use. He was a passionate cyclist in his leisure time and a member of various cycling clubs, having built himself his first tricycle at the age of seventeen. He wrote a series of papers influencing the reduction of the diameter of cycle wheels, and devised a new form of brake to act simultaneously on both wheels.

Browning was a scrupulous craftsman; perhaps because of his reluctance to part with a less than perfect instrument, Norman Lockyer was denied being the first to observe a prominence on the uneclipsed sun, and Browning always regarded himself as largely responsible for the delay. He was also a conscientious employer, encouraging his workmen to sing during the long working day. Among them in the early 1870s was Adam Hilger, who was employed by Browning on arriving from Paris with his brother at the outbreak of the Franco-Prussian war in 1870, and became his foreman. Hilger later became a notable maker of spectroscopes and optical instruments in his own right.

Browning's second wife predeceased him, and on 24 July 1890 he married Annie, daughter of Josiah Woolley, a licensed victualler. She was a spinster aged twenty-five from Monmouth, with a child, Minna Woolley. In later years Browning's business declined, and about 1905 he retired and went to live first at Kelsey, Gloucestershire, then at Cheltenham, where he died, at his home, Strathcona, Albion Street, on 14 December 1925. He was survived by his wife and by Minna Woolley, librarian at the Bradford Library and Literary Society. The firm continued to operate under his name until 1945.   ILARIA MELICONI

Sources 'The British Optical Association: its founders and formation', *Dioptric Review and British Journal of Physiological Optics*, new ser., 5/1 (1945), 1–5 · *Monthly Notices of the Royal Astronomical Society*, 90 (1929–30), 359–62 · 'John Browning', *Dioptric and Ophthalmometric Review* (1897), 122–6 · *British Optical Association Yearbook* (1914) · G. Clifton, *Directory of British scientific instrument makers, 1550–1851*, ed. G. L'E. Turner (1995) · census returns, 1841, 1851, 1871, 1881, 1891 · CUL, G. B. Airy MSS, RGO 6 · RAS, 31.9; 31.10; Add. MS 90 · patents, 1856–72 · H. Roscoe, *Spectrum analysis: six lectures delivered in 1868, before the Society of Apothecaries of London* (1869) · 'Minna Woolley Browning', *Bradford Library Association Record* (Aug 1966), 313 [NF] · R. Routledge, *Discoveries and inventions of the nineteenth century* (1900), 422–36 · GL, Grocers' Company MSS, 11595/2, 11587/1 · private information (2004) · d. cert. · m. certs.
Likenesses two photographs, 1860–1869?, repro. in *British Optical Association Yearbook*, 144 · photograph, repro. in 'The British Optical Association' · photograph, RAS

Browning, Louisa (1807–1887), school proprietor, was born in London, the sixth child and fourth daughter of Robert Browning (1749–1833), principal clerk of the bankstock division at the Bank of England, and his second wife, Jane Smith (1771–1848), whom he married in 1794. Robert's eldest son by his first marriage to Margaret Tittle (1754–1789), also Robert, was the father of Robert Browning, the poet; thus Louisa was half-aunt to the poet, with whom she maintained cordial but not close relations.

Equipped by her father with an initial capital of £200 Louisa set up a boarding-school for ladies at 4 Dartmouth Row, in Blackheath. She was assisted by her sister Sarah, and another sister, Jemima, also appears to have helped out before her marriage in 1845. Among the pupils were Sophie and Annie Crow, daughters of an alkali manufacturer from Gateshead, and five of the six daughters of Newson Garrett, corn and coal merchant of Aldeburgh, including the future Dr Elizabeth Garrett Anderson and Dame Millicent Garrett Fawcett. Elizabeth met Emily Davies for the first time when staying with the Crows in the school holidays.

The Browning establishment seems to have had more pretension and less rigour than some other successful schools of this period. Elizabeth Garrett recalled 'the stupidity of the teachers … with shudders' and Miss Browning's insistence that French was the language of all school transactions meant that she became fluent in the language 'as spoken in Blackheath' (Anderson, 33). At least the experience did not destroy her appetite for learning. Millicent Garrett, on the other hand, recalled Louisa Browning as 'a born teacher', writing approvingly of her thoroughness and method. She noted also her refusal to be overawed by institutionalized religion and her distinct unconventionality in refusing to have needlework taught in her school. This, Louisa thought, should be taught at home, and if she saw a girl with a needle in her hand, 'would call out in her most commanding tones, "A guinea a stitch, my dear, a guinea a stitch!"' (Fawcett, 38). Both Elizabeth and Millicent agreed on Louisa's ample size, powerful presence, her passion for bright colours in dress, and her enthusiasm for fresh air. By the time Millicent left in 1862 the school had changed hands, and Louisa and her sister Sarah retired to live at 1 Maitland Park Crescent on Haverstock Hill in north London. Louisa died there on 6 September 1887.   GILLIAN SUTHERLAND

Sources J. Maynard, *Browning's youth* (1977) • M. G. Fawcett, *What I remember* (1924) • L. G. Anderson, *Elizabeth Garrett Anderson, 1836–1917* (1939) • J. Manton, *Elizabeth Garrett Anderson* (1965) • d. cert.
Wealth at death £5088 17s. 4d.: probate, 24 Oct 1887, *CGPLA Eng. & Wales*

Browning, Sir Montague Edward (1863–1947), naval officer, was born on 18 January 1863 at Fornham St Martin, Suffolk, the eldest child of Captain Montague Charles Browning, who subsequently became a justice of the peace for Suffolk when living at Manningtree, and his wife, Fanny Allen, daughter of the Revd Edward Hogg, rector of Fornham St Martin.

Browning entered the Royal Naval College, Dartmouth, as a naval cadet in July 1876 and after two years was appointed midshipman in the *Invincible*, Mediterranean station. In September 1880 he was transferred to the corvette *Carysfort* on special service and served in her as acting-lieutenant during the Egyptian campaign of 1882, being awarded the war medal and the Khedive's bronze star. Promoted sub-lieutenant in July 1882 he returned home to the *Excellent* gunnery school at Portsmouth for examinations and obtained first-class certificates in all subjects. He remained in the *Excellent* until November 1884. While doing a year's sea service, he was promoted lieutenant in June 1885, and, except for three years as gunnery lieutenant in the battleship *Dreadnought*, he was employed almost continuously in the *Excellent* until promoted commander in January 1897, and then was specially employed on the preparation of a handbook for quick-firing guns. He served as commander in the *Prince George*, channel squadron, from January 1898, and then in September 1900 he was chosen to be secretary of the committee which had been appointed by G. J. Goschen to report on the controversy regarding the respective merits of the cylindrical and water-tube types of boiler and on those of the Belleville and other types of water-tube boilers. In 1890 he married Ruth, daughter of Lieutenant-General George Neeld Boldero. They had one daughter.

After promotion to captain in January 1902, Browning remained for six months with the committee until the presentation of its first report, and then joined Sir Archibald Douglas, commander-in-chief, North America and West Indies station, as flag captain in the *Ariadne*. In 1905 he became flag captain to Sir Lewis Beaumont at Devonport. In May 1907 he commissioned the battleship *Commonwealth* in the Channel Fleet and a year later was transferred to the *King Edward VII* as chief of staff to Charles Beresford. In July 1909 he took command of the *Britannia*, and at the end of the next year was given the appointment of inspector of target practice, in recognition of his reputation as a gunnery expert. He continued in this duty after promotion to flag rank (September 1911) until August 1913. While in this role he was criticized for opposing the more accurate system of centralized 'director firing' of guns. Browning and others wanted to continue the practice of

Sir Montague Edward Browning (1863–1947), by Walter Stoneman, 1919

independent gunlaying, a decision the developer of director firing attributed to 'simply professional jealousy' (cited Marder, 1.415). The new system was ultimately introduced, but the delays meant the navy did not have its benefits in the early part of the war.

Browning then hoisted his flag in the *Hibernia* as rear-admiral in the 3rd battle squadron of the Grand Fleet. In July 1915 he was appointed to the command of the 3rd cruiser squadron, with his flag in the *Antrim*, which with the 3rd battle squadron had been stationed at Rosyth since the war began. In April 1916 both squadrons were detached from the Grand Fleet and moved to the Swin (Thames estuary), then returned north after the battle of Jutland.

In August 1916 Browning was appointed commander-in-chief of the North America and West Indies station with the acting rank of vice-admiral with his flag in the *Leviathan*. In that capacity he represented his country in discussions with the United States naval authorities on joint action in the conduct of the war at sea. He was promoted vice-admiral in April 1917, and in February 1918 returned to the Grand Fleet to take command of the 4th battle squadron with his flag in the *Hercules*. After the armistice of November 1918 he was appointed president of the allied naval armistice commission, and paid visits in the *Hercules* to the German naval ports to see that the settled terms were duly carried out. His approach to this role was described by J. M. Keynes as having 'no idea in his head but the extirpation and further humiliation of a despised and defeated enemy' (Keynes, 13). Browning joined the Board of Admiralty as second sea lord in March 1919 and was promoted admiral on 1 November. He had no previous experience of administrative work in Whitehall and was more happily placed at Devonport where he became commander-in-chief for three years in September 1920. He was appointed first and principal naval aide-de-camp to the king in May 1925 and placed on the retired list in October 1926. He returned to court duty in March 1929 as rear-admiral of the United Kingdom, became vice-admiral of the United Kingdom in February 1939, and finally retired in June 1945.

Browning was appointed MVO (1908), CB (1916), KCB (1917), GCMG (1919), GCB (1924), and GCVO (1933). He held a number of foreign decorations. In 1889 he had the misfortune to lose his left hand through an accident while visiting the *Inflexible*. Thereafter he wore an iron hook. After retirement he lived near Winchester and became a JP and deputy lieutenant for Hampshire. He died at his home, Sleepers Hill House, Winchester, Hampshire, on 4 November 1947 and was buried at Magdalen Hill cemetery, Winchester, on 7 November.

Regarded as a fine type of sea officer, Browning had great natural ability, good brains, and a thorough knowledge of the navy. A stern disciplinarian with a determined character, he was never unfair, and was liked and trusted by his subordinates, in spite of his somewhat grim manner.   V. W. BADDELEY, rev. MARC BRODIE

Sources *The Times* (6 Nov 1947) · A. J. Marder, *From the Dreadnought to Scapa Flow: the Royal Navy in the Fisher era, 1904–1919*, 5 vols. (1961–70) · J. M. Keynes, *Two memoirs* (1949) · S. W. Roskill, *Naval policy between the wars*, 2 vols. (1968–76) · *CGPLA Eng. & Wales* (1948) · private information (1959) · personal knowledge (1959)
Archives IWM, papers
Likenesses W. Stoneman, photograph, 1919, NPG [*see illus.*] · A. S. Cope, group portrait, oils, 1921 (*Naval officers of World War I, 1914–18*), NPG
Wealth at death £22,007 18s. 2d.: probate, 9 March 1948, *CGPLA Eng. & Wales*

Browning, Oscar (1837–1923), teacher and historian, was born on 17 January 1837 at 8 Cumberland Terrace, Regent's Park, London, third son of William Shipton Browning (d. 1853), distiller, of Smithfield, and his wife, Mariana Margaret (1799–1889), daughter of Thomas Bridge (1772–1858), captain in the Royal Navy, of Southwark. He was a tiny, premature baby and a nervous, ardent, delicate child, who grew steadily in hardihood to become a formidably tough old man. Convinced that he was reserved for great work by his survival (his elder twin died at birth) and by the ambition of his mother (who lost a little daughter in the month before his birth), his yearning for fame was always marred by a sensitivity to affronts verging on paranoia. After attending Dr Robertson's boarding-school at Upton Park in the late 1840s, Browning was tutored for two years (1848–50) by his brother, a curate at Everdon, Northamptonshire. In 1851 he was sent to Eton College, where he was unpopular and ill-treated in the house of William Johnson Cory, which he found coarse, brutal, dirty, and unloving. The food was so meagre that he nearly starved. When later he was a housemaster he ensured that the

Oscar Browning (1837–1923), by Ignacio Zuloaga y Zabaleta, 1900

atmosphere of his house was high-minded, affectionate, and urbane. At Eton he became infatuated with a fellow pupil called Dunmore: 'I have found that he is a lord, but I loved him before' (Wortham, 33). Snobbery and homosexuality were entrenched for life.

In 1856 Browning was elected to a scholarship at King's College, Cambridge. He graduated BA in 1860, being placed fourth in the classical tripos. He proceeded MA in 1863, and was elected in 1859 to a fellowship at King's, which, as he never married, by prevailing college regulations he retained until his death. Ostracized by his fellow Etonians at King's for speaking at the union, of which he became president (1859), he befriended men at Trinity, where he found an intellectual set in which strong affections were sublimated into high educational ideals.

An Eton master In 1860 Browning accepted an assistant mastership at Eton, where he ran a boarding-house from 1862. His house had a controversially Pre-Raphaelite tone; the food was nourishing and plentiful, the curtains were by William Morris, and James FitzJames Stephen complained that a boy at Browning's had been lent a novel by Gautier with Walter Pater's approval. There was much jolliness and ragging led by the man–boy at the centre, but the bronzes and marbles in his corridors discouraged rough-housing. Though he participated in many sports, and was elected to the Alpine Club (1864), OB—as he became universally known—detested the cult of athleticism. His history lessons were highly successful, but shocked the headmaster, James Hornby, who thought that both Queen Anne and the French Revolution were dangerous subjects for study. OB passionately desired to reform Eton so that it could educate an effective governing class for a democratic age; these new rulers, in his ideal, would rest their power on the Platonic virtues of wisdom and goodness as well as hereditary privilege. To foster this élite, he urged reform of the curriculum to emphasize modern history and foreign languages and to minimize science and mathematics; he also advocated more school prizes for intellectual achievements and fewer rewards for athletic success. True education, he thought, was possible only by personal contact and must never be confused with mere coaching.

Browning's proposed reforms would have ensured for him luxurious living and unbounded intimacy with favourite boys, but were resisted by the forces of staid inanition; Edmond Warre was his most formidable opponent. Many of his colleagues were pompous, small-minded, and vindictive, and he showed them much rancour. Meanwhile he cultivated intelligent boys (such as Cecil Spring-Rice), to whom he lent books and whom he teased with Socratic provocations. He went abroad every school vacation, travelling in princely style with a courier, usually to Italy and often accompanied by an Eton boy: he took, for example, Gerald Balfour to Sicily in 1869. Though his favouritism was often beneficial, he could be cruel and tyrannical in abruptly repudiating his idols during puberty. He encouraged sexual confidences, and despite his own erotic fantasies, took a strong purifying line against masturbation and spooning. His activities as a moral busybody were unabated by the conviction in 1873 of his friend Simeon Solomon on a charge of gross indecency. His intimate, indiscreet friendship with a boy in another boarding-house, G. N. Curzon—later the politician and viceroy—provoked a crisis with Hornby (1874). OB was incapable of corrupting anyone (he had the saving vice of pride, which saved him from many meaner sins), but his openness was hated by more repressed men. Amid national controversy he was dismissed in 1875 on the pretext of administrative inefficiency but actually because his influence was thought to be sexually contagious.

At King's College, Cambridge Hornby's innuendoes left a residual odium, and some senior members of King's were dismayed by OB's return as a resident fellow. Nevertheless, he helped to expand the college and was for a time a useful colleague. He did good work in promoting King's to higher intellectual standards: the nascent historical tripos received his eager support, and he was an innovative tutor, requiring a weekly essay from his history pupils. He hoped to remodel King's to emulate Balliol or the École Normale in Paris. In a memorandum of 1877 he proposed a college of 150 honours students

> provided with the best teaching which the University can afford, which should be given them to a great extent at the expense of the College, enjoying the stimulus of a very cultivated and energetic society, protected from the temptations of a larger college, and directed with a careful

and sympathetic attention from the older men. (Wilkinson, 14)

OB obtained a college lectureship at King's in 1880 and a university lectureship in 1884. As part of his professional rehabilitation he became a fellow of the Royal Historical Society (1884) and chairman of its council (1885). It had hitherto been an amateurish, undistinguished body, but OB thereafter coaxed or cajoled many professional historians into membership. He was in 1885 the first professional historian to contribute to its *Transactions*, with papers on the triple alliance of 1788 and the Anglo-French commercial treaty of 1786. For the society's Camden Series he transcribed and annotated *The Political Memoranda of Francis, Fifth Duke of Leeds, 1774–1796* (1884) and two volumes of the third duke of Dorset's diplomatic dispatches from Paris from 1784 to 1790 (1909–10). His edition for the Camden Series of *Earl Gower's Despatches* (1885) was also competent. The focus of his historical interests on high politics and foreign affairs indicated that, despite his role in the professionalization of history teaching, he regarded history as a tool in training statesmen, and himself as a professional educator rather than a professional historian.

Browning produced one notable book, in 1887, an affectionate account of Mary Ann Evans (George Eliot), who was the only important woman in his life apart from his mother. The solitude of research, however, did not suit him. He was a dangerously self-confident writer, who once prepared an article on Florentine art for a guidebook while sitting in a hotel lounge in Lucerne without consulting a single source. His carelessness is evident in *Wars of the Nineteenth Century* (1899), his *History of Europe, 1814–1843* (1901), and his *History of the Modern World, 1815–1910* (1912). His lectures, like his scholarship, were superficial, inaccurate, and diffuse. In college his arbitrariness, obstinacy, boasting, disparagement of colleagues, captious indiscretion, and grievance-mongering ruined his standing. He became detested by dons, if not undergraduates, as a bore 'all coated and scaled with egotism, and covered with prickles' (*Diary of … Benson*, 120).

OB wrote many articles on education and books, including *History of Educational Theories* (1881; translated into Hungarian and Serb) and *Aspects of Education* (1888). With unglamorous worthiness OB also strove to improve elementary education as secretary of the teachers' training syndicate (1879–1909) and as an autocratic principal from its inception of the Cambridge University Day Training College (1891–1909). His genius as an educator was inspired by his love of boys and young men, but he had no scholarly gifts.

As an admirer of symposial culture, Browning pioneered the use of seminars in English university education by founding the Political Society, of which he was president (1876–1908). This influential and exclusive society was conceived as a training ground for national leaders at which undergraduate historians read papers intended to encourage discussion. Browning was founding treasurer of Cambridge University Liberal Club, and contested the constituencies of Norwood (1886), East Worcestershire

(1892), and the West Derby division of Liverpool (1895). Although he enjoyed rowdy meetings, his oratory was closer to political lectures than to electioneering speeches. His early support of Irish home rule increased his unpopularity in the university. His improvidence as treasurer of the Cambridge Union Society (1881–1902) was also notorious. As president of Footlights (1887–95) he brought that dramatical society to the brink of bankruptcy and failed in his efforts to obtain reduced rates for its members at the Turkish baths in Emmanuel Street.

Character, later years, and death Life for Browning was 'long stretches of dullness interspersed with moments of rapture' (Browning, *Sixty Years*, 94). In London and overseas he pursued monarchs, noblemen, cabinet ministers, poets, and other exalted personages. He was the luckiest of snobs: when two strangers took refuge from the rain under his holiday balcony, it was typical fortune that they were Alfred Tennyson and Benjamin Jowett. He travelled constantly, even when old, and maintained an extensive correspondence with a polished horde of celebrities. He had an attractive mixture of the high-spirited and self-important. He was the only man to have sung with the future Queen Mary 'The Man who Broke the Bank at Monte Carlo', accompanied by a barrel organ. He also declared that, when faced with a hard decision, he asked himself what Napoleon would have done in his place. He passionately desired to be the Cambridge tutor of the heir presumptive to the throne, the duke of Clarence and Avondale, and imagined himself becoming an intellectual king-maker like Thomas Hobbes.

Undergraduates are the most inflammable of gossips: OB made himself the centre of a set where his smallest gestures were magnified into significance and he became a tremendous Cambridge personality. His eccentricities enabled his protégés to share emotional intimacy without impermissible sexual contact. Sir Desmond MacCarthy has depicted one of OB's 'at homes', on a Sunday evening, as a convivial gathering of undergraduates, metaphysicians, and peers at which no one thought it strange that there was 'a Tommy in scarlet uniform' playing the clarinet or that when OB finished 'trolling out *Voi che sapete* with immense gusto' on the piano 'the clarinet-player gave him a spanking' (MacCarthy, 37–8). His friendships were never intense or soulful but cheerful affairs with young sailors, artisans, and stable-lads to whom he was kind and hospitable. He was generous and romantic with perpetual hope of finding a mute, inglorious Milton: a shopboy in Hastings who impressed him as a genius was one of many grateful youths whom he employed as a secretary. He preferred to sleep at night with a muscular companion lest he was seized by sudden illness.

In appearance Browning was pug-like—squat, with a great head, noble features, hefty trunk, absurdly short legs, and rolling gait. At table his manners were indelicate. He was a hearty trencherman who ate lobster for breakfast and recommended hock and oysters at bedtime as a cure for indigestion. His conversation was ample, and for many years witty, but with increasing age his anecdotage

became offensively self-centred. He had prodigious vitality and magnificent *élan*. His admirers found him affectionate, generous, lavish of money, self-mocking, Rabelaisian, and impulsive; but A. C. Benson in 1905 judged him 'greedy, vain, foul-minded, grasping, ugly, sensual' (Anstruther, 174), and deplored his visage: 'loosely moulded out of dough, smeared with train oil; a climbing, upturned face' (Gere and Sparrow, 46). He had, though, prodigious gifts: Polish was his fortieth language; others were Yiddish and Esperanto. OB always adored music, notably Mozart, and attended the first Bayreuth performance of Wagner's *Ring* cycle (1876). He joined the Society for Psychical Research, dallied with positivism in the 1860s, and became a freemason. In 1906 he was converted to Christian Science by the mayor of Bexhill while travelling to that town.

Browning's years at King's from 1905 were especially acrimonious as his enforced retirement became imminent. In 1909 he was forcibly superannuated from his lectureship. Caught in Italy by the outbreak of war in 1914, he remained at Rome until his death, of heart failure, on 6 October 1923, at his home, Palazzo Simonetti, via Pietro Cavallini 12, Rome. His ashes were deposited in a vault at the west end of King's College chapel, Cambridge, on 27 October.   RICHARD DAVENPORT-HINES

Sources *The Times* (8 Oct 1923) · O. Browning, *Memories of sixty years at Eton, Cambridge and elsewhere*, 2nd edn (1910) · O. Browning, *Memories of later years* (1923) · H. Wortham, *Oscar Browning: Victorian Eton and Cambridge* (1927) · I. Anstruther, *Oscar Browning* (1983) · R. Croft-Cooke, *Feasting with panthers: a new consideration of some late Victorian writers* (1967) · D. MacCarthy, *Portraits* (1931), 34–8 · L. P. Wilkinson, *A century of King's* (1980) · *The diary of Arthur Christopher Benson*, ed. P. Lubbock (1926), 119–21 · R. J. A. Skidelsky, *Hopes betrayed, 1883–1920* (1983), vol. 1 of *John Maynard Keynes* (1983–2000) · J. A. Gere and J. Sparrow, *Geoffrey Madan's notebooks* (1981) · K. Rose, *Superior person* (1969) · D. Gilmour, *Curzon* (1994)

Archives CUL · Eton · King's Cam., corresp. and papers · Yale U. | BL, letters to W. E. Gladstone, Add. MSS 44412–44513, *passim* · BL OIOC, corresp. with Lord Curzon, MSS Eur. F 111–112 · CUL, letters to Lord Acton · CUL, letters to C. R. Fay · HLRO, corresp. with Herbert Samuel · King's Cam., letters to Henry Bradshaw, etc. · King's Cam., letters to John Maynard Keynes · King's Cam., letters to Sir John T. Sheppard · King's Cam., letters to Charles Webster · King's Cam., letters to Nathaniel Wedd · NRA Scotland, Balfour MSS · priv. coll., Footlights archives · Staffs. RO, letters to John Maynard Keynes · U. Texas, corresp. with John Lane · UCL, letters to Karl Pearson

Likenesses S. Solomon, pen-and-ink drawing, 1865, repro. in Browning, *Memories of sixty years*, frontispiece · photograph, 1872, repro. in K. Rose, *Superior person*, facing p. 65 · photograph, 1872, repro. in Browning, *Memories of sixty years* · G. H. Teague, oils, 1887?, Eton · M. Beerbohm, caricature, chalk and watercolour drawing, *c*.1892, King's Lond. · J. Palmer Clarke, photograph, 1900, repro. in O. Browning, *Memories of sixty years*, 100 · I. Zuloaga y Zabaleta, oils, 1900, King's Cam. [*see illus.*] · J. Tenniel, cartoon, 1902, repro. in Browning, *Memories of sixty years*, 252 · L. Dickinson, portrait, 1903, Cambridge Union Society · M. Beerbohm, caricature, chalk and watercolour drawing, 1908, repro. in Anstruther, *Oscar Browning*, facing p. 118 · C. Gill, portrait, 1914, King's Cam. · H. Lerche, bronze head, *c*.1920, U. Cam., faculty of education · N. Los, bronze bust, 1921, King's Cam. · E. Gliecenstein, portrait, 1923, priv. coll. · photographs, priv. coll.

Wealth at death £294 2s. 1d.: probate, 25 Jan 1924, CGPLA Eng. & Wales

Browning, Robert (1812–1889), poet, was born on 7 May 1812 in Camberwell, London, the first of the two children of Robert Browning (1782–1866) and his wife, Sarah Anna, *née* Wiedemann (1772–1849).

Ancestry, childhood, and adolescence Robert Browning's grandfather, also called Robert Browning (1749–1833), was of Dorset yeoman stock, and moved to London at the age of twenty. He eventually rose to a prominent position in the Bank of England, and married Margaret Tittle (1754–1789) who came from a family of some wealth emanating from the West Indies. The couple had a son, Robert, the father of the poet. After the death of his first wife, Browning's grandfather married a younger woman, with whom he had nine children. There was soon conflict between his first son and his new wife, and Browning's father was sent to the West Indies to work on a sugar plantation. Revolted by the slavery there, he soon returned to England and found employment as a clerk in the Bank of England, where he remained until 1852.

In 1811 Browning's father married Sarah Anna Wiedemann. She was ten years his senior, and came from a middle-class family originally from Dundee, which had settled in Camberwell, where the pair took a cottage. It was there that Robert Browning was born, and his birth was followed by that of his sister, Sarianna Browning (1814–1903).

By all testimony Robert Browning was a precocious child who insisted on showing off. He learned to read at an early age and from his largely self-taught cultivated parents he gained a love of music and classical literature. He seems to have attended a local dame school at the age of five but, owing to his superior knowledge, was sent home to avoid embarrassing the older boys. At seven he began at the Misses Readys' weekly boarding-school in nearby Peckham, where he was both lonely and bored; and then at about ten he moved to the tutelage of the Misses Readys' brother, the Revd Thomas Martin Ready, master of Peckham School, where again he believed that he was taught nothing. It was at home during weekends that his real education took place. His father helped him with Latin declensions by turning them into rhymes, encouraging him in Greek literature, and teaching him to draw and appreciate pictures at the nearby Dulwich Picture Gallery. His mother instructed him in the names of flowers, taught him to play the piano (at which she was quite talented), and encouraged him in the love of music. At home the four Brownings proved an extraordinarily close-knit family. Robert Browning left Peckham School at fourteen, and for the next two years, from 1826 to 1828, was tutored at home, primarily with the aim of making him a gentleman. It was, however, mostly from his eclectic reading in his father's library that Browning gained the wide-ranging erudition later manifested in his poetry.

As for verse, Browning had begun making rhymes as soon as he could talk. Although he was familiar with Shakespeare from earliest childhood, some of his earliest lines were in imitation of Macpherson's Ossian, whence he moved on to the English Romantics. His earliest poems, however, he destroyed. His parents were impressed by a

Robert Browning (1812–1889), by Field Talfourd, 1859

collection of verse of somewhat later date and modestly entitled 'Incondita', and they unsuccessfully looked for a publisher. Only two poems, dating from his fourteenth year, survive: 'The Dance of Death', modelled on a poem of republican sympathies by Coleridge, and 'The First-Born of Egypt', demonstrating the influence of Byron, whose rebellious attitudes and dandiacal attitudes the young Browning found worthy of imitation in life as well as in verse.

After the imitative pieces of 'Incondita' Browning seems to have ceased writing poetry for five or six years, music becoming his chief means for finding expression, although he continued to regard the poet's calling as pre-eminent. Byron's influence on him began to wane at this time, and was replaced by that of Shelley, whom Browning found far less egotistic and cynical. Late in 1826 or in 1827 Browning's maternal cousin James Silverthorne gave him a copy of Shelley's *Miscellaneous Poems* (1826), in which he found set forth his own dreams and aspirations with a startlingly fresh beauty. Wanting to have more of the poet's work, he persuaded his pious mother to purchase for him the works of an evangelizing atheist. Reading them voraciously, Browning soon became an atheist and a vegetarian, and for the next few years 'Shelley was his God' (Domett, 141).

Fired with Shelley's beliefs and Byron's dandyism, the young Browning acted in such ways as to distress his parents, whom he felt did not appreciate him. Seeking to widen his acquaintance, he began calling regularly on the artistic, older Flower sisters. Eliza, a talented musician, may have given Robert music lessons, and, idolizing her, he composed a stream of verses and letters to her. Sarah was a poet also interested in the theatre. Together they probably exerted the greatest influence on Browning's adolescence, serving as models of artistic activity and providing him with a sentimental education. The young man, however, also had an influence on them, especially on Sarah, who wrote in November 1827 to her spiritual confessor that Robert had unsettled her religious beliefs.

To help in finding a publisher for Browning's 'Incondita', Eliza showed the poems to William Johnson Fox, a famed Unitarian minister and journalist of compelling personality. Liking them, but recognizing their derivative nature, Fox praised them in person to the young poet but advised against their publication, probably because of their extensive debt to Byron, and it may have been through Fox that the young poet disavowed Byron's great influence over himself and destroyed all copies of 'Incondita'. In any case, Browning acknowledged Fox as his 'literary father' (Orr, *Life*, 43).

Following his two years of tutoring at home, Browning entered the newly founded University of London. His father had earlier subscribed £100 towards its foundation and this allowed him, as one of the 'proprietors', the right to free tuition for his nominee. In April 1828 the elder Browning applied for admission for his son, who was accepted. Robert, settled into a rooming-house in or near Bedford Square, began his classes in German, Greek, and Latin in late October. He was disappointed from the beginning, finding student life drab and the lectures for the most part perfunctory. He soon withdrew from his student lodging and went home to live while continuing his classes. At the end of the academic year he withdrew from the university.

The question then arose as to how the boy of seventeen was to make a living. His father had hoped that by attending the university he might qualify for the bar, but Browning expressed contempt for the legal profession. His father then suggested the medical profession, but although he visited Guy's Hospital, Browning's interest in medicine was merely that of the detached observer. What he undertook then was study with no goal in view, following an unsystematic course of reading in his father's library. As he was later to say, '[B]y the indulgence of my father and mother, I was allowed to live my own life and choose my own course in it' (Orr, *Life*, 378).

The years from 1829 to 1833 are the least-known period in Browning's life. What is known is that he continued his self-education. He read widely in European culture in his father's library, the diverse subject matter that he hoped to master proving unending. The result was that Browning became, with the possible exception of Milton, the most learned of the great English poets. But more important than his gain of general knowledge during this period was his discovery of a philosophy far different from that of Shelley, which he had hitherto followed so devotedly.

What Browning perceived was that there is no stable centre of selfhood accessible to the thinking subject. The subject, he learned, is accessible only obliquely, not in the continuity of its self-consciousness but in the discontinuity of its shifting forms. And following this perception, he saw that truth and meaning are not fixed but, instead, are always becoming. Further, he saw that the questions posed determine to no small degree the answers reached, and that the angle of view limits visions of the whole. This apprehension caused Browning to conclude that not enough questions or enough points of view can ever be asked to gain a complete, encompassing overview of any matter. At best, one gains approximations of the truth which are always subject to better formulations. Absolute truth, then, is never present in the phenomenal world, although informing it. It was with such newly gained belief that he recoiled from Shelley's mythopoeic, visionary expressions about a world that can be redeemed by poets who are the unacknowledged legislators of mankind.

Early published poetry Yet it was not easy to break with Shelley. Browning's first act of exorcism occurred in *Pauline; a Fragment of a Confession*, composed late in 1832 and published anonymously by the firm of Saunders and Otley in March 1833, with the subsidy of £30 offered by a maternal aunt. In a kind of poetic autobiography, the speaker looks back over his past life in which he had deserted Pauline (who may have been inspired by Eliza Flower) and had foregone his inherited religious faith under the influence of the Sun-treader (Shelley). At the end, expressing a willingness to submit to the world of limitations and not seek hereafter for a world in which he will know all, he embraces God, Pauline, and the Sun-treader. Yet in the final verse paragraph it becomes clear that the poet's betrayal of Shelley the Sun-treader is a greater source of remorse than his forswearing of his traditional religious faith. Reviews of *Pauline* were mixed, W. J. Fox praising it and others despising it as unintelligible.

In February 1834 Browning took his first trip abroad: to St Petersburg at the invitation of the Russian consul-general to accompany him there. Browning was so fascinated by court life on this occasion that for a brief period he considered a diplomatic career. On his return to London he met in summer 1834 a young Frenchman, Count Amédée de Ripert-Monclar (1807–1871), an aristocrat who loved art and literature and was in close touch with the cultural life of France. They became close friends, and their friendship lasted until the 1840s, when they seem to have drifted apart. Monclar was an important influence on Browning in many ways, and he even seems to have influenced Browning's poetic development, in that he was to suggest Paracelsus as the subject for an extended piece of verse (Orr, *Life*, 72).

Browning began this poem early in October 1834, and completed it in mid-March 1835. His father bore the expense of publication, and *Paracelsus* was published anonymously on 15 August 1835. Although its format is that of a play—it was divided into five scenes and contained four characters—the author claims in the preface that it is not a drama nor a dramatic poem, but that each scene presents Paracelsus at a critical moment of his inner life in which he is brought by an articulation of his 'mood' to new insights. In effect, the five scenes are five monologues, in the first of which Paracelsus begins as a

Shelleyan visionary whose role is to encounter the divine and reveal the results to mankind. At the close he comprehends how his pursuit was misconceived, for he learns that the noumenal, even if partially touched by means of language, cannot be communicated to others through the phenomenal, which is language. The reviews of the poem were largely favourable, although the work did not gain the author a great deal of money. For a number of years thereafter the title-pages of Browning's new works bore the legend 'By the Author of *Paracelsus*'.

In the mid-1830s Browning was introduced to a number of literary figures through the agency of W. J. Fox. Although some of them (like Thomas Carlyle) found his dandyism in dress and manner off-putting, they soon discerned beneath the foppish surface a serious though ironic personality. In May 1836 Browning attended a supper at which he was toasted by Francis Talfourd, the host, Walter Savage Landor, and Wordsworth. Of most immediate importance, however, was the fact that William Charles Macready, the actor and producer of plays, asked the young poet to write a play for him.

Browning's *Strafford* was produced at Covent Garden on 1 May 1837, after some conflict with Macready and John Forster over its nature as a play. In the end, it ran for only five performances. It was not well received—apparently because, as the author said in the preface to the published play, his aim was 'Action in Character rather than Character in Action'. Following his disappointment with the reception of *Strafford*, Browning visited Paris and in spring 1838 made a three-month tour of Europe. For the previous four or five years he had been working on a long poem devoted to the Italian troubadour Sordello, but he was so taken with Italy that he was unable to finish the poem among the scenes described in it. *Sordello* was not published until March 1840, again at the expense of his father.

Browning's conception of the poem had changed several times and his intractable materials could not be fused into a harmonious union. But to the poet this was no drawback, for, in his opinion, conventional formal unity and logical coherence were attributes merely of poetry of the past. His aim was to be one of the

> setters-forth of unexampled themes,
> Makers of quite new men.
> (*Sordello*, 1.26–7)

This is why his speaker bids Shelley depart early on so that his poem, finally of approximately 5800 lines of rhymed couplets, can get down to business. Speaking in his own voice, the poet admits to a new kind of narrative presentation and to a new kind of genre (which mixed many genres). One of the chief characteristics of the poem that gives it its distinctive voice is parabasis: that is, the presence of digressions in which the author addresses the audience on personal or topical matters. After devoting six books often relating in a roundabout way to Sordello, in the end the narrator suggests that the real subject was not Sordello but rather the poet himself and his efforts to write the poem. Carefully ordered but appearing unstructured, purportedly historical but in fact deeply personal, generically indeterminate and stylistically complex, *Sordello* is unique in literary history.

Bells and Pomegranates   Browning believed that *Sordello* would make his reputation, but for the next two decades it had the opposite effect, as its critical reception was almost universally condemnatory. The poem 'became notorious for its obscurity', partly because Browning unreasonably assumed that his readers would be familiar with the thirteenth-century Italian history that was key to its narrative structure. Even Elizabeth Barrett, who was soon publicly to praise the young poet's work, had difficulty with *Sordello*, and the confusion prevailed well into the modern era, with only Ezra Pound finding the poem 'a model of lucidity', and consequently being 'probably the only person who has ever seriously claimed to have understood *Sordello*' (*Poems*, 1.1040). Certainly in his own time, the work damaged the young poet's standing, and his publisher, Edward Moxon, attempted to redeem Browning's reputation (as well as his own), with the suggestion that his next poetry be printed in a series of inexpensive paperbound pamphlets, the cost to be borne by Browning's ever supportive father. Browning agreed and chose the general title *Bells and Pomegranates* hoping by this title to 'indicate an endeavour towards something like an alternation, or mixture, of music with discoursing, sound with sense, poetry with thought; which looks too ambitious, thus expressed, so the symbol was preferred' (ibid., 1.1069). The eight pamphlets were to contain seven plays and two collections of poems and were published between April 1841 and April 1846.

Pippa Passes (April 1841), the first number, contests Romantic notions of poetry as lyric effusion, a view summed up and advocated by J. S. Mill in two essays in 1833 in which he maintained that the greatest poetry is by nature soliloquy, not heard but overheard. In *Pippa Passes*, Browning presents a heroine whose key mode of utterance is lyric poetry overheard by others. The innocence and religiosity of Pippa's song which is inadvertently overheard by the various characters is crucial. As she sings famously at the beginning of the poem:

> God's in his heaven—
> All's right with the world!

But all is emphatically not right in the world of *Pippa Passes*, and the overheard lyric acts as a commentary on the auditors' situations, and acts on the characters to great effect, causing significant changes in their viewpoints and actions. In working out the implications of this mode of poetic utterance Browning showed that the poet has a dialogic relationship with the audience and a responsibility from which he or she cannot escape. In effect, in the four scenes Browning shows how poetry is theatre, or performance, before an interactive audience.

The next pamphlet and four more of them were plays, which Browning designed for stage production. The only one produced, by Macready against his better judgement, was *A Blot in the 'Scutcheon*. Presented in February 1843, it was withdrawn after three performances, at which point Browning's break with Macready was complete and so, effectively, were his hopes for the stage. The plays offer little plot and almost no action, their interest (as in *Strafford*) centring on action in character rather than character in action. The root conception of Browning's plays lies in the conflict between love and duty, or love and power, which is for the most part worked out within a political situation. However interesting to Browning, this was far from being the primary focus that theatregoers expected.

Pamphlets three and seven—*Dramatic Lyrics* (1842) and *Dramatic Romances and Lyrics* (1845)—contain some of Browning's best-known poems, such as 'My Last Duchess', 'Porphyria's Lover', and 'The Bishop Orders his Tomb at St Praxed's Church'. These are dramatic monologues (called by the poet dramatic lyrics or dramatic romances), which take the form of narratives told in the first person by a carefully characterized narrator who, so distanced, is understood to be distinct from the poet. Browning's achievement in grounding these narrators in their historical milieu was memorably praised in *Modern Painters* by Ruskin, who commented that in 'The Bishop Orders his Tomb at St Praxed's Church', Browning had put 'nearly all that I said of the central Renaissance in thirty pages of the *Stones of Venice* into as many lines' (*Poems*, 1.1093). The narrator in one of Browning's dramatic monologues usually speaks to an auditor within the poem, and inadvertently reveals his true nature to the reader through his words. The monologues internalize plot and deal with an interior conflict of which the speaker is frequently not consciously aware. As Browning said in the preface to *Dramatic Lyrics*, the poems in this genre are 'for the most part Lyric in expression, always Dramatic in principle, and so many utterances of so many imaginary persons, not mine'. In other words, the utterance by the fictitious speaker is lyric to the degree that it is expressive of self, and dramatic to the degree that it is suggestive of conflicting motives and tendencies. The dramatic monologue became the chief genre that Browning employed and experimented with for the remainder of his career, and in large part because of his skilful manipulation of its peculiar characteristics, it became one of the dominant genres employed by poets over the following century. Recognizing his young friend's amazing achievement, Walter Savage Landor published a poem in November 1845 attesting to Browning's majority, as having become a name to be listed, along with those of Chaucer and Shakespeare, among the greatest English writers.

Marriage and early life in Italy Another poet, whom Browning had recently come to know, was equally enthusiastic. Elizabeth Barrett [*see* Browning, Elizabeth Barrett (1806–1861)], among the most famous poets of the day, had praised Browning's poetry in a journal article in 1842 and in one of her poems published in 1844. Browning was full of gratitude, and posted a letter to her on 10 January 1845 telling her that 'I love your verse with all my heart … and I love you too' (*Brownings' Correspondence*, 10.17). She replied the next day thanking him for his letter and proclaiming herself 'a devout admirer & student' of his works (ibid., 10.19). Thereafter they began to exchange letters every few days.

Elizabeth Barrett fended off Browning's requests to visit her for some time, as she feared his reaction on seeing an ageing invalid some six years his senior confined to a sofa. But he persisted, and she finally allowed him to come to 50 Wimpole Street on 20 May 1845. He fell in love with her almost at first sight, as he told her in his letters. For her part, she could not believe that someone could love a seemingly incurable invalid and was also terrified that her tyrannical father, who had forbidden his children to marry, would learn about her admirer. But after many letters and visits, she was ready to declare her love for him in forthright terms in November 1845, although she told none of her friends or family. When, however, her father became suspicious of Robert's visits, she came to recognize her father as a despotic egoist and agreed to discuss the possibility of marriage.

One obstacle to marriage was money. Browning was completely dependent financially on his parents, but Elizabeth had inherited a fortune that yielded about £350 annually. Browning would not hear of taking any money from her and for a time considered several careers that he might take up. At last the money question was settled when he agreed that they would live on her income in Italy, where they proposed to go in part because of southern benefits for her health. He was adamant, however, that she must write a will bequeathing her property to her brothers and sisters.

The couple were married in St Marylebone Church on 12 September 1846 in the presence of two witnesses, Browning's cousin James Silverthorne and Elizabeth's maid, Wilson. Elizabeth returned home alone, with Robert not visiting her for the next few days. On 19 September the pair, joined by Wilson and Elizabeth's dog, Flush, fled to Paris, where they rested for several days; thence to Avignon and Marseilles; thence by ship to Leghorn; and finally by train to Pisa, where they arrived on 14 October.

In Pisa the Brownings found an apartment and settled in for winter 1846–7. Elizabeth's health immediately improved, but in March she suffered a miscarriage, which caused them both much grief. In mid-April they set out on a tour of northern Italy, and although they had intended to return to Pisa, they were so smitten by Florence that they decided to move there. They found an unfurnished apartment in Casa Guidi, opposite the Pitti Palace and a short walk from the Ponte Vecchio, and for the next thirteen years this was their home. They were so happy with their active life in Florence that for the next two years Browning devoted little time to writing. Their main interest during 1848–9 was the revolutionary fervour being manifested all over the continent. They had both espoused the Italian nationalist cause while in England, and now in Italy they became enthusiastic partisans of Italian liberty. They remained united in espousing the cause even after it began to fail in spring 1849. This is more than can be said for their views on Louis Napoleon's later *coup d'état*—Elizabeth saw it as an unfortunate necessity, but Browning detested the action. Admirably suited though they were in so many other ways, their differences on this particular political issue continued for the rest of their married life.

Amid all the military activity Elizabeth was pregnant, and gave birth to a son, Robert Wiedeman Barrett Browning (soon called Pen), on 9 March 1849. Browning was delighted, yet his joy was diminished a few days later by letters from his sister announcing their mother's illness and then her death. To escape from his continuing sadness, the Brownings went to Bagni di Lucca. Yet Browning's despondency persisted, aggravated by his having nothing to do. Elizabeth showed him for the first time her *Sonnets from the Portuguese*, to be published in 1850, poems that she had written to him during their courtship. He was greatly appreciative, yet ashamed that he himself had written almost nothing. He had, however, published in two volumes with his new publishers, Chapman and Hall (Moxon being judged too slow), the first collection of his works, excluding the unfavourably received *Pauline*, *Strafford*, and *Sordello*.

Late in 1849 Browning began a new work, which he published as *Christmas-Eve and Easter-Day* the following spring. 'Christmas-Eve' is the dramatic narrative of a speaker in London on Christmas eve 1849 who enters a dissenting chapel to escape the rain. Therein he falls asleep and envisions several kinds of religious observance on that date, ending up with the belief that what he had regarded as absolute religious truth was truth only to him and that other modes of worship, other than his own dissenting one, have their own validity. While 'Christmas-Eve' is a monologue, 'Easter-Day' is the first of Browning's 'parleyings', a dialogue in which the poet divides himself up into two voices to express, through relation of a visionary experience in the past that may or may not be valid, how belief in the supremacy of the infinite resides in the perception of the infinite through the finite. The volume was respectfully but not widely reviewed, and after 200 copies had been sold within a fortnight of publication, the rest were remaindered, and were still being sold in the 1860s. On the other hand, Elizabeth, who was proposed by several journals to succeed Wordsworth as poet laureate on his death on 23 April 1850, had a new edition of her *Poems* in two volumes published in the autumn that received many reviews and enjoyed good sales.

Travels outside Italy, 1851–1852 In July 1850 Elizabeth suffered her fourth miscarriage, in the course of which she lost a large amount of blood. At her doctor's suggestion the Brownings rented a villa above Siena until November. By 1850 they had established an interesting circle of friends among the foreigners in Italy, mainly Englishmen and Americans. Yet by 1851, for all the liveliness of Florence, there remained the attraction of England and the friends and relatives whom they had not seen in almost five years. And so they returned for a visit, landing in London on 22 July 1851. They rented a house on Devonshire Street, within walking distance of the Barretts' home. Elizabeth and the baby called on her sisters and brothers when their father was out, while Browning spent long hours with his father and sister at New Cross, another suburb south of the Thames where the Brownings had lived

since 1840. They also saw many old friends, and called on the Carlyles. John Kenyon, Elizabeth's relation who had supplemented her income by the gift of £100 annually after Pen was born, visited them frequently during their stay. Because of the Great Exhibition everything about London seemed lively, and they hated leaving.

But late in September, accompanied by Carlyle, the Brownings travelled to Paris, where they found lodgings on the Champs Elysées. They met a number of French literary figures, including George Sand, by whom Browning was appalled. More importantly, they met Joseph Milsand, a native of Dijon who had recently published a perceptive and laudatory article on Browning's poetry. Browning soon came to rely on Milsand's judgement, eventually even sending him proof sheets of his work for final revision before publication.

While in Paris, Browning was commissioned by Edward Moxon to write a preface to some letters by Shelley that he had purchased and proposed to publish. The 'Essay on Shelley', as it has come to be known, is Browning's major critical document. He had published another piece anonymously, on Thomas Chatterton, in 1842 in John Forster's *Foreign Quarterly Review*, but the essay on Shelley is far more important. In it Browning contrasts the 'objective' and 'subjective' poets. The objective poet is the 'fashioner', with the work so fashioned 'substantive, projected from himself and distinct'. The subjective poet, by contrast, is the 'seer', with the work produced an 'effluence' that 'cannot be easily considered in abstraction from his personality' (Browning, 'Essay on Shelley', in *Poems*, 1.1001–2). Browning demonstrates that in cyclically alternating periods one or the other type of poet is dominant, and places Shelley firmly in the 'subjective' camp. The essay in part attempts to deal with the overwhelming legacy of the Romantics, and to articulate a useful role for the nineteenth-century poet. In support of this, Browning accords the objective poet at least equal status to the subjective by naming Shakespeare as its chief example. Ultimately, however, he maintains that there is no reason why the two modes of poetic faculty might not be combined into 'the whole poet' who fully displays the objective and subjective modes. Evidently, this was the kind of poet that Browning conceived himself to be. The collection of letters was published early in 1852, but the letters were soon discovered to be spurious and the book was suppressed.

The Brownings spent summer 1852 in London. Robert went there first because of a breach of promise and defamation of character suit that had been brought against his father by a widow to whom he had offered and then withdrawn a proposal of marriage. She won the suit, the court's judgment awarding her £800 in damages. Browning found his father and sister in deep depression, and to help them escape paying the damages he accompanied them to Paris in mid-July and saw them settled in an apartment. Later in July he and Elizabeth went to London, where they again saw old friends, met new ones, and cemented their friendship with the Tennysons, whom they had met in Paris the previous summer. They departed for Paris in October and by mid-November 1852 were home in Florence.

Life in Italy, 1853–1855, and *Men and Women* (1855) Winter 1852–3 passed pleasantly. In summer 1853 the Brownings were again in Bagni di Lucca, where they re-encountered William Wetmore Story, an American sculptor, and his family, whom they had first met in 1848. The Storys, who by and large alternated between Rome and Florence, were highly cultivated and interesting people and were among the closest friends the Brownings made in Italy. In October, after many mutual visits in Bagni, both families returned to Florence and the next month went on to Rome, where the Storys arranged lodgings for the Brownings, and introduced then to interesting foreign circles. But Rome proved expensive, and tragically the Storys' son died. Their daughter also fell ill, and Pen was struck by the same disease; by late spring the Brownings gave up on Rome.

By early June 1854 the Brownings were back in Florence, where, settled into a more orderly routine, both set diligently to work. Robert had a certain stock of poems on hand to which he intended to add. Elizabeth continued to suffer from chest pains, however, and Browning was often in attendance on her as a result. In spite of this, he had managed to compose some 8000 lines of verse by June 1855. Rumours of cholera in a nearby neighbourhood meant that they left Florence soon after their return.

On 24 June the Brownings took an apartment in Paris in the same building where Robert's father and sister lived. On 12 July they were back in London, settled into an apartment not far from Wimpole Street. In Paris they had made possible the marriage of the maid, Wilson, who was pregnant, to their manservant, Ferdinando Romagnoli; and while in London they sent Wilson north to her family for her confinement, leaving Ferdinando responsible for household chores and (warily) for Pen. They again visited many friends and relatives. Dante Gabriel Rossetti, long an admirer, drew Browning's portrait, and hosted a soirée during which Browning and Tennyson each read one of their poems to the guests. Browning and Elizabeth also attended a séance held by the famous American spiritualist Daniel Dunglas Hume, at which she was thrilled and he disgusted, and not reluctant to show his feelings.

Browning took the manuscript of his fifty poems to Chapman and Hall soon after he arrived, and it was decided that it should be published in two volumes. In September he added another poem, 'One Word More', and before the end of the month he was reading proofs. In October he and Elizabeth retired to Paris to await publication on 10 November.

The title of *Men and Women* probably derived from the twenty-sixth poem in *Sonnets from the Portuguese* (1850), which states:

I lived with visions for my company
Instead of men and women, years ago.

The subject matter of the volume centres on love, art, and religion, and contains some of Browning's best-known poems, such as 'Fra Lippo Lippi', 'Andrea del Sarto', 'An

Epistle … of Karshish', 'Childe Roland to the Dark Tower Came', and 'Cleon'. It contains quite a few important dramatic monologues in Browning's best style, and he maintains that throughout he has gathered men and women 'Live or dead or fashioned by my fancy' so as to:

Enter each and all, and use their service,
Speak from each mouth.
('One Word More', ll. 130–32)

There are several instances, however, where he departs from the securities of the dramatized narrator, such as in the coda to 'The Statue and the Bust', and in the monologue 'Old Pictures in Florence', where the speaker's voice and situation are hardly to be differentiated from the poet's. And yet Browning concludes with 'One Word More', in which, while he purports to 'speak this once in person' (l. 137), he speaks ironically, as in this final poem of *Men and Women* his aim is essentially the same as in the preceding fifty poems: to question the familiar by placing it within a new artistic network of relationships. Browning concludes with a refusal to articulate meaning, saying that he sees novel sights

undreamed of,
Where I hush and bless myself with silence.
(ll. 196–7)

Although *Men and Women* has become arguably the most highly regarded of all Browning's works, it was not well received at the time of its publication. Both the Brownings had believed that it would prove popular, but as they read the reviews, many charging obscurity and unable to understand that the poet was working in unconventional modes, they were bitterly disappointed. Critical opinion continued to depress Browning for the rest of his life in Italy. As Elizabeth wrote to his sister in 1861, 'his treatment in England affects him' for 'nobody there, except a small knot of pre-Raffaellite men, pretend to do him justice. Mr. Forster has done the best,—in the press …—and for the rest, you should see Chapman's returns [from sales]!' (Orr, *Life*, 233–4). By spring 1856 the Brownings had left Paris and had gone to London, where Elizabeth submitted her verse novel *Aurora Leigh* to her publisher, while Browning devoted himself to her work.

Last years in Italy The Brownings left for Florence in mid-November 1856, and later in the month *Aurora Leigh* was published, immediately attaining critical and popular success. As Browning, more than Elizabeth, basked in the praise and the couple were considering how royalties from its sales would lighten their financial situation, they learned that John Kenyon had died and had left them £11,000, which meant that they would never again have to worry about money.

Winter 1856–7 was uneventful, but April 1857 saw the death of Elizabeth's father, which caused her great grief. The Brownings went to Bagni di Lucca late in July and returned to Florence at the end of the summer. Early in summer 1858 they went to France, stopping in Dijon to visit Milsand, and in Paris to find Browning's father and sister in good health. After two months in Normandy they returned to Florence for six weeks and then in November travelled to Rome, in search of warmer weather for Elizabeth. Excited by the war declared on Piedmont by Austria and by France's declaration of war on Austria, the Brownings returned in May 1859 to Florence to find French troops encamped. When in June Napoleon III made peace with Austria, Elizabeth, who had been almost delirious over the exploits of the French emperor and the Piedmontese king, suffered a physical collapse, all her hopes for a united Italy erased.

For a change of scene the Brownings travelled to Siena, where they were joined by the Storys and the octogenarian W. S. Landor. Landor's characteristic irascibility had been exacerbated by old age and mental decline, and he had become estranged from his family as a result. Through the agency of John Forster, Browning agreed to act as guardian for Landor, and to administer the £200 annuity granted to the old man. They settled Landor into the house of Elizabeth's former maid, who had left their service after the birth of her second child and was living with her husband in Florence. The Brownings then returned to Rome for winter 1859–60, for the sake of Elizabeth's health, but it had continued to worsen, and she was becoming increasingly dependent on morphine, which she had been taking for years. The Storys feared that she would not survive the winter.

In June 1860 the Brownings were briefly back in Florence, and then spent the summer in Siena, with the Storys having a villa close by. In Rome again for the next winter, they learned that one of Elizabeth's sisters had died, and Elizabeth never entirely recovered from the shock. Browning wrote no poetry at this point; all his time was spent in nursing Elizabeth and in overseeing Pen's education. They returned to Florence late in spring 1861. There Elizabeth caught a cold in June, which inflamed her lungs. As she grew worse Robert sat by her day and night, and in the early morning of 29 June 1861 she died in his arms.

Elizabeth's funeral took place on 1 July, and was attended by fewer people than the Storys expected, although they also found Browning in better control of himself than they had anticipated. Out of respect, the shops in the neighbourhood were closed, and a crowd followed the coffin to burial in the protestant cemetery. After the funeral Browning immediately made plans to reorder his life. He had Pen's long curls cut and the boy's dress, which Browning had always contended with Elizabeth was too elaborate, was simplified. As he wrote to correspondents, he wanted his future life to resemble his past fifteen years of exile as little as possible. He packed belongings at Casa Guidi during the day, and he and Pen spent the night at the home of Isa Blagden, the Brownings' devoted friend for most of their years in Florence. Browning and his son left Florence on 1 August, accompanied by Isa Blagden. She left Paris after a few days while Browning and Pen stayed on with his father and Sarianna in Paris and Brittany until October, when they went on to London. Browning never again returned to Florence.

In London Browning and Pen took temporary lodging before settling into the rented house at 19 Warwick Crescent that was their home for the next twenty-five years.

Browning found a suitable tutor for Pen and met Elizabeth's sole surviving sister, Arabella, and old friends like Carlyle and Forster; otherwise he occupied himself mainly in solitary walks. But he was too sociable not to seek company, so by spring 1862 he took to dining out. He was elected to the Athenaeum Club in February, and in March was offered the editorship of the *Cornhill Magazine* on the retirement of Thackeray. He refused it, but was gratified by the offer, which he took as a sign of increasing appreciation of his work. Before turning to his own work, he guided Elizabeth's *Last Poems* (1862) through the press and prepared a group of her essays for publication in 1863. He then began preparation for a collected edition of all his poems (save for *Pauline*). Published in three volumes in 1863, the poems of 1842, 1845, and 1855 were broken up and regrouped, and *Sordello* was radically revised and enlarged by 181 lines. The edition was dedicated to Forster, with *Sordello* inscribed to Milsand. A volume of *Selections* (1863) was put together by Forster and B. W. Procter (Barry Cornwall), an old friend to whom number 6 of *Bells and Pomegranates* had been dedicated. Both the collected edition and the selections sold so well and were so respectfully reviewed that a new volume of Browning's completed poetry was not published until the following year.

Life in the mid-1860s and *The Ring and the Book* The monologues of *Dramatis Personae* (1864) are more deeply concerned with matters of contemporary importance than Browning's earlier work in the genre. Spiritualism, biological evolution, higher criticism of the Bible, current social conditions, modern love—these are but some of the topics dealt with in these poems. By and large, the verse demonstrates a working-out, in generally new and more complex ways, of the poet's long held ideas. Among them are 'James Lee's Wife', 'Mr Sludge', 'The Medium', 'A Death in the Desert', 'Caliban upon Setebos', and 'Abt Vogler'. *Dramatis Personae* was such a critical and popular success that a second edition was soon called for. Within the space of a year Browning's reputation had dramatically changed.

Although now a celebrity, regularly dining at the great houses and meeting foreign and domestic dignitaries, Browning never neglected his son. What he wanted more than anything was the admission of Pen to Balliol College, Oxford, where Benjamin Jowett, the regius professor of Greek, was a tutor. Browning greatly admired Jowett for his liberal views on theology, and hoped that Pen would come under his influence. Browning, therefore, diligently oversaw his son's education—but it became increasingly evident that Pen's academic qualifications were not high. Jowett helped the boy in every way he could and Pen took almost a year of academic preparation at Oxford, but he failed the matriculation examination in 1868 and returned home to his disappointed father. During Pen's scholarly preparations, however, Browning was awarded an Oxford master of arts degree by convocation in June 1867, and this was followed by his election to an honorary fellowship at Balliol.

While overseeing Pen's studies Browning made regular visits to Paris to see his father and sister. In June 1866 his father died in Browning's presence, and soon Sarianna came to live at 19 Warwick Crescent. She became the companion, confidante, and housekeeper of her brother for the rest of his life. In June 1868 Arabella Barrett, Elizabeth's surviving sister who had been so concerned with Robert and Pen when they came to live in London, died in Browning's arms.

As partial relief from the sadness caused by deaths of loved ones, Browning turned more and more to writing a long poem. In June 1860 he had purchased in Florence what he later called 'the Old Yellow Book', containing pamphlets, legal documents, and manuscript letters concerning a 1698 murder trial in Rome. The accused was Count Guido Franchesini, an impoverished nobleman from Arezzo, who was ultimately found guilty of multiple murders, including that of his wife, Pompilia, whom he had believed guilty of adultery with a young priest. He had also killed Pompilia's parents. Browning was intrigued by the case, mainly because, as the Latin lettering on the volume related, the trial 'disputed whether and when a Husband may kill his Adulterous Wife without incurring the ordinary penalty'. Reading through the matter, written in Latin and Italian, Browning began to ask himself whether the wife was adulterous and, if so, why. He made enquiries about the case in Rome and Arezzo, and in 1862 Isa Blagden obtained a supplementary manuscript account for him. He began writing about the case in autumn 1864 and, working on it for three hours every morning, completed the poem's 21,000 lines, divided into twelve books, in spring 1868.

Browning chose a new publisher for his poem: Smith, Elder & Co., whose senior partner, George Murray Smith, the poet had known since 1843. Initially contemplating serial publication in magazines, the poet and his new publisher finally decided on the appearance of the poem in four volumes. Named *The Ring and the Book*, perhaps because this suggested the poet's own initials, the volumes were published in monthly instalments in the last two months of 1868 and the first two of 1869.

In the first book, Browning, barely disguised as the narrator, offers three versions of the murder case and instructs his audience to choose the true account. In the following ten books Browning presents the accounts and interpretations of various figures, including 'Half-Rome'; 'The Other Half-Rome'; Count Guido; the priest accused of adultery; and Pompilia herself, whose account is ostensibly related on her deathbed. Even the pope is given a book of the poem in which to state his views on the murder. In book 12 the narrator again offers several versions of the story, and the audience for whom this piece of Roman history has been resuscitated is presented not with the poet's claim of truth, but with a kind of documental drama from which they must decide for themselves. At the end of this work, Browning asks the reader to take away:

This lesson, that our human speech is naught,
Our human testimony false, our fame
And human estimation words and wind.
Why take the artistic way to prove so much?

Because, it is the glory and good of Art,
That Art remains the one way possible
Of speaking truth, to mouths like mine, at least.
(*The Ring and the Book*, XII.834-40)

In Browning's view, a right interpretation of the case, like that of the Bible, is almost provisional: an approximation for the time being. But, ultimately, this does not devalue the attempt to seek out that truth.

The 'British public, ye who like me not' (I.405, 1371) were wooed and won, as Browning's wish that it 'may like me yet, / (Marry and amen!)' (XII.831) was finally fulfilled. Sales were high, and reviews were adulatory, *The Athenaeum* of 20 March 1869 calling *The Ring and the Book* 'the *opus magnum* of our generation … the most precious and profound spiritual treasure that England has produced since the days of Shakspeare'. Even the queen was impressed by the poet's new reputation, inviting him to an audience in March along with Carlyle and two other eminent men. About the same time Browning also received and declined an invitation to become lord rector of St Andrews University. But the pleasure in public acclaim was lessened when he seems to have learned of his son's sexual activities in Brittany the previous summer. And at about this time he became seriously ill and for several months remained housebound.

The Lady Ashburton episode During summer 1869, with Browning unable to enjoy his usual holiday in Brittany, he, Sarianna, and Pen joined the Storys in Scotland, where he had never been before. Plagued by the bad weather and uncomfortable lodgings, they received an invitation to the 'lodge' at Loch Luichart to visit Louisa, the widowed Lady Ashburton, whom Browning had known since before her marriage to the wealthy second Baron Ashburton. Although he had earlier refused such an invitation, Browning, along with the others, felt compelled by her insistence to accept the invitation. Some days after they arrived, Lady Ashburton apparently suggested that since both he and she were widowed and struggling to bring up a child, their marriage might be felicitous. Browning was politely evasive, and seems to have defused the situation, for when he and his party left, everyone was cheerful.

Browning and the Storys went on to visit their friends George and Rosalind Howard (later earl and countess of Carlisle) at their castle in Cumberland. There the Storys' 25-year-old unmarried daughter, Edith (Edy or Edie), confided to her hostess that Lady Ashburton had declared her love for the poet, that Browning had asked Edie's advice, and that she had advised him that it was not right to marry a woman simply for her position and his son's sake. Edie further reported that a letter had come from Lady Ashburton wishing to settle the matter and that Browning had replied saying no. Edie also claimed that Browning was in love with her and was forcing his attentions on her, but Rosalind Howard did not believe her on this point, and assumed that the passion she ascribed to the poet was probably Edie's own for him.

Browning returned to London in September and for the next seven or eight months was often away from Warwick

Crescent, visiting the country houses of the great and famous, and visiting Pen at Christ Church, Oxford, where he had arranged for his admission, believing it to be easier than Balliol. In June 1870 Pen failed his examinations and was forced to leave Christ Church. Browning became disconsolate and angry with his son not only for his academic failures but also for his spendthrift nature and idleness.

In summer 1871 Browning and Pen set off for another holiday in Scotland. Pen had visited Lady Ashburton and her daughter earlier in the year at their home in the south, and perhaps because of this, they again visited Loch Luichart. Lady Ashburton raised the issue of marriage once more, and Browning told her that his heart lay buried in Florence and any attractiveness of marriage lay in its advantage to Pen. Browning left the next day, realizing that her vanity was wounded. She nevertheless wrote to him in derogatory language, he reported to a friend, and she also told others that he had ill-treated her. Thereafter he met her only on large social occasions and viewed her as contemptible and unworthy of conversation.

Long poems of the 1870s In spring 1871 Browning began composing a poem published in August of the same year: *Balaustion's Adventure: Including a Transcript from Euripides*. The greater part of the poem is the young Balaustion's account of the performance of the first extant drama by Euripides, the *Alcestis* of 438 BC. Elizabeth Barrett Browning had admired Euripides, and the motto of the poem comes from her *Wine of Cyprus* (1844). The poem is a modern adaptation, rather than a strict translation, forming what Browning called a 'transcript'—scenes are shortened and deleted, the Chorus's role is reduced, and the descriptions and actions of the main characters are altered. The general movement of the play differs from that of the original, with Balaustion's interpretation shoring up her main concern of salvation through love and art. Her account interweaves her commentary on the characters with Euripides dramatic colloquies, so that Admetus learns the meaning of love and loss, while Heracles is Christianized into a god-man devoted to relieving the sufferings of others. What Balaustion in effect presents is a 'higher criticism' of the play that looks beyond the actual text in an attempt to grasp Euripides essential meaning. Some critics feel that the poem has autobiographical elements, with the portraits of Alcestis and Admetus 'affected by points of resemblance to Mrs Browning and the poet himself' (*Poems*, 1.1170). Admetus, for instance, is insistent that he will not remarry, and this emphasis may well have derived from Browning's recent experience with Lady Ashburton. In the epilogue Balaustion is revealed as the mask of the poet, who, quoting from his late wife and still smarting from earlier critical neglect, nevertheless asserts his self-confidence by asking in the final line 'Why crown whom Zeus has crowned in soul before?' It was well received at the time, with the 2500 copies of the first edition quickly selling out.

While in Scotland, Browning began to write a poem conceived of in rough draft in Rome in 1860. *Prince Hohenstiel-Schwangau, Saviour of Society* (December 1871) was based on the career of Napoleon III, who had been defeated (to

Browning's delight) by the Germans the previous year, and had taken refuge in England. Although he had never shared his wife's enthusiasm for the emperor, Browning had on occasion seen some good in him. In the poem, a long monologue, he addresses the problem of why people with good intentions fail to pursue them, in the end showing that this person who claims to be a man of action is merely an indecisive *homme sensuel*. The poem sold well initially, 1400 copies in five days, but sales soon tailed off. Reviewers were also baffled by a work which asks the reader to be both sympathetic and judgemental of the monologuist, and although Browning himself thought it to be 'a sample of my very best work' (*Poems*, 1.1177) it is now among the least read of his poems.

Soon after its publication Browning began another poem dealing with the same issue: good intentions unfulfilled. *Fifine at the Fair* (1872) is composed of 2355 rhymed alexandrines, with a prologue and epilogue of 108 lines. Dealing with conjugal inconstancy, *Fifine at the Fair* may touch on Browning's qualms concerning disloyalty to his dead wife for even briefly considering Lady Ashburton's proposal of marriage, and on his father's disloyalty to his mother in proposing to marry another woman. The main part of the poem is an almost cinematic monologue of shifting perspectives in time and space, but its narrative hardly matters. What is significant is the internal action, structured on the Browning-esque interplay between the wish for constancy and law, on the one hand, and the desire for change and lawlessness, on the other.

Browning expected that most readers would find the poem difficult to understand—in April 1872 he said that the poem was 'the most metaphysical and boldest he had written since *Sordello*', and that he 'was very doubtful to its reception' (*Poems*, 2.975). Readers did indeed have difficulty with it. As the *Westminster Review* put it on 1 October 1872: 'for the ordinary reader it might just as well have been written in Sanscrit'. One of the saddest events resulting from its publication was the rupture of friendship with Dante Gabriel Rossetti that it caused. Browning had sent him a copy, and the poem enraged Rossetti for what he saw as its satire of him and his poetry. At stake specifically was Rossetti's poem *Jenny*, which had been roundly criticized by Robert Buchanan in *The Fleshly School of Poetry* (1871). It is likely that Browning had used the poem as a source, and Rossetti saw him as part of the conspiracy that he felt was being ranged against the pre-Raphaelites at this time. Their friendship never recovered.

Browning's next work was based on a story he had heard concerning the suicide of a man in Calvados and involving love, sex, religion, and social roles. As with 'the Old Yellow Book', the poet threw himself imaginatively into the situation, so fascinated that he asked for legal documents and collected accounts of people in the neighbourhood to try to come up with its truth. Published in May 1873, *Red Cotton Night-Cap Country* is a first-person narrative in four parts and 4247 lines of blank verse. Its internal auditor was Anne Thackeray, daughter of the novelist, who had been staying at Lion, about 5 miles from the scene of the suicide. As the poem states, she referred to the region as

'White Cotton Night-Cap Country', and Browning changed the 'white' to 'red' in part to point up the bloody nature of his tale. Anne Thackeray was not entirely happy with her association with the poem, particularly when hostile reviews of it appeared. Readers had problems with the sordid nature of the story, and with 'its grotesque blend of savage humour, whimsical humour and intense seriousness' (*Poems*, 2.986). It was generally disliked, but Browning seems to have borne up well to the criticism, and probably as a diversion he made another translation of Euripides, this time of *Heracles*.

Laying aside his translation, Browning turned to Aristophanes, who had denigrated Euripides. In the 1870s there was general hostility to Euripides, stimulated by German criticism claiming that the playwright had destroyed classical Greek poetry. Browning wanted to prove otherwise, and during his annual summer holiday in France during 1873 he was deeply involved in a study of Greek books, especially the works of Aristophanes. Over the next year he read widely about Greek dramatists, including arcane scholarship. In mid-August 1874 he began composing the material surrounding *Heracles* and completed it the following November. *Aristophanes' Apology* (1875), composed of 5705 lines, is the third longest of Browning's works. It acts as a kind of sequel to *Balaustion's Adventure*, and is formally complex. It progresses by statement and counterstatement, and is divided into three different modes—the apology of Aristophanes, Balaustion's admonishment of him, and a translation of *Heracles*—with a prologue and a conclusion. The poem is Browning's boldest experiment with the dramatic monologue, and it concludes that all individual points of view are in some way or other deficient, and that tensions of opposites should be recognized and accepted, a paradox joyfully expressed by Balaustion at the close of her monologue when she sings:

> There are no gods, no gods!
> Glory to God—who saves Euripides.

When published on 15 April 1875, *Aristophanes' Apology* proved again a bewildering work to most of the reviewers. Copies of the first edition were still being sold after the poet's death.

Browning's next work is formally entirely different from anything he had previously published. It is like *Sordello* in being a dramatic poem in which the narrator sets the scene and ends the action. It is also like *The Ring and the Book*, in that the point of departure is a text; but here the text is not one interpreted by the narrator or the actors, but is a text written by the characters themselves and inscribed into an album. *The Inn Album* was published in autumn 1875. Although 1100 copies of the 2000-copy print run were sold within three weeks of publication, no second edition was called for. Reviews, including that by Henry James in *The Nation* (20 January 1876), were generally negative, although Swinburne praised the poem. Browning was irate with the criticisms, as they yet again featured the old charge of obscurity.

Poems of the later 1870s and 1880 Browning's next work, *Pacchiarotto and how he Worked in Distemper* (1876), embodies the poet's discontent with the reviewers and offers a stern warning to all who tried to delve into his private life. In the prologue the speaker lives in a 'house, no eye can probe'. In 'Of Pacchiarotto' the critics come to the house under the pretence of helping with housekeeping, but bring in filth and are told to stay away. Whether they like him or his house is to Pacchiarotto a matter of supreme indifference, as his only concern is to please the 'Landlord' to whom he pays rent for the 'freehold'. The nineteen poems of *Pacchiarotto*, unsurprisingly, were not cordially received, and Browning claimed that he had written them only to amuse himself at the expense of his critics. Over the previous six years he had written six highly experimental but largely unappreciated long poems totalling about 20,000 lines. He was at this time willing to relax, and published a volume that was largely a *jeu d'esprit*.

Browning went on to accept Carlyle's suggestion that he translate the Greek tragedians. He undertook the translation of the *Agamemnon* of Aeschylus, who in the nineteenth century was generally regarded as an obscure writer, just as Browning himself had come to be. *The Agamemnon of Aeschylus Transcribed by Robert Browning*, more a transcription than a translation and reading like Greek English, was published in October 1877.

Browning's next poem was an elegy, *La Saisiaz*, in memory of Anne Egerton Smith, a close friend who had died in the Jura mountains when she was staying in a chalet there with Browning and Sarianna. As the speaker works his way through 'facts' and 'fancies' about the soul and an afterlife, he expresses belief in his own being, 'soul', and a power outside and independent of himself—'God'. That these 'facts' surpass his ability to prove them, in fact:

> proves them such:
> Fact it is I know I know not something which is fact as much.
> (ll. 223–4)

The poem was published in May 1878 along with its sequel, *The Two Poets of Croisic*, in a volume taking its title from the names of the two individual poems. In *The Two Poets of Croisic*, the first poet is one who, after writing a poem prophesying an event that comes true, feels himself divinely inspired, gives up poetry, and retires to a secluded life. The other poet is one who becomes famous when his sister claims authorship of his worthless verse, but who loses fame when he reveals himself to be its writer. From these stories of the two poets, the speaker concludes that fame is dependent on externals, and cannot be a criterion for true value. In his estimation, the great poet is one who will 'Yoke Hatred, Crime, Remorse, / Despair: but ever 'mid the whirling fear' and 'tumult' will let 'break the poet's face / Radiant' (*The Two Poets of Croisic*, CLIX.1269–72). In other words, the great poet will be one like Robert Browning.

Late in summer 1878, still suffering from Anne Egerton Smith's death and upset over the sexual peccadillos of Pen, who had decided to undertake formal training as a painter, Browning, with Sarianna, spent a month in Switzerland before going on to Italy and delighting in Asolo and

Venice. They both liked Venice, with its large English and American community, so much that they returned there in seven autumns over the next eleven years. While on this vacation, Browning wrote several poems that he joined with others to publish as *Dramatic Idyls* in April 1879. The title inevitably forced comparisons with Tennyson's 'idylls', and Browning defined what he meant by the term in this way in 1889:

> a succinct little story complete in itself; not necessarily concerning pastoral matters, by any means, though from the prevalency of such topics in the idyls of Theocritus, such is the general notion. These of mine are called 'Dramatic' because the story is told by some actor in it, not the poet himself. (*Poems*, 2.1067)

The poems are in rhymed verse, and the metres approximate those of Greek idylls. '[B]esides the measure of formal unity in the volume, there is also some kind of thematic unity in the stress on conscience and remorse' (ibid.). Browning was so pleased that the book was well received (for the first time since *Balaustion's Adventure* a second edition was called for), that he wrote another series of poems, and published them as *Dramatic Idyls, Second Series* (June 1880). The second series, however, was not as popular as the first, and a second edition was not required.

Growing fame, and poems of the early 1880s By 1880 Browning had become recognized, along with Tennyson, as one of the greatest poets of the period. He was awarded an LLD degree by Cambridge in 1879, and in summer and autumn 1881 a group of his admirers founded the Browning Society. The poet was amazed and elated by this outpouring of support, and he was further delighted and surprised when Browning societies began to spread around the world—there were twenty-two of them within the next three years. In 1882 he was given an honorary DCL at Oxford. In America his reputation spread so that in Chicago, for example, some of his works were printed on railway timetables, and bookstores could not keep up with the demand for copies of his works. In addition, foreign visitors in London sought glimpses of him as well as autographs. Browning was delighted and, resting on his laurels for the next three years, published nothing. He and Sarianna continued to spend their summers abroad. During the rest of the year he became a strenuous diner-out and attender at all sorts of social functions, dressed so dapperly that he was, according to the weekly *World* of 7 December 1881, 'as far a dandy as a sensible man can be'.

Browning ended his period of printed silence with *Jocoseria* (March 1883). Containing ten poems in the mode of the dramatic idylls, all treating the theme of desire, the volume is largely undistinguished, 'Ixion' being the only poem now recognized as worthy of mention. At the time, however, *Jocoseria* was well received. A second edition was needed almost immediately, and a third edition was published in 1885. Browning himself was not very pleased with this collection, remarking that it had 'had the usual luck of the little-deserving' (*Poems*, 2.1084). He was increasingly aware that he was now proclaimed a sage by the Browning societies, and he felt that he must therefore address philosophical and religious issues in a higher way.

He began trying to improve his German, and it may be that in Goethe's *Westöstlicher Divan*, a collection of poems with a Persian backdrop divided into twelve books, he found a suitable setting and persona for a religiophilosophical poem. *Ferishtah's Fancies*, published in November 1884, contains twelve 'fancies', analogies and parables of the great theological problems, plus a prologue and epilogue. Each of Ferishtah's theological speculations is followed by a love lyric, thereby indicating that the 'fancies' of the intellect are authenticated by the 'facts' of love. The poem 'is important as a fairly direct statement of the poet's mature religious beliefs ... Browning did not pretend that Ferishtah was more than a transparent disguise for himself' (ibid., 2.1096). The poem sold well—two further editions were needed in 1885.

Last long poem Browning apparently began his next poem when he was seventy-three. He worked on it for several years and wanted it to be the summation of his career, so he found the writing difficult. Aiming at a kind of intellectual autobiography told in a conversational style, he designed it to be of epic, encyclopaedic scope. *Parleyings with Certain People in their Day* (1887) was modelled both on *Faust* and *The Divine Comedy*, and consists of seven parts with prologue and coda. Each 'parleying' deals with the appearance of a ghost from the past and its stimulation of a current thought or attitude to be argued with. This means that there are three points of view to be considered: those of the speaker, the figure from the past, and a contemporary. Further, each parleying poses two basic questions: is life good or bad? and what makes it tolerable? Among the contemporaries treated are Carlyle, Lady Ashburton, Rossetti, William Morris, Swinburne, Disraeli, critics of Pen Browning's art, and contemporary poets (like Tennyson, Arnold, Swinburne, Morris, and possibly Shelley) who adopt Greek models and attempt to write in a Greek style. Both in its philosophical complexity and daring design, the *Parleyings*, dedicated to the memory of Joseph Milsand, who had died in September 1886, is the boldest work of Browning's later career. Ranging from classical Greece through the middle ages and the Enlightenment to the later nineteenth century, it deals with the evolution of man's art, thought, morals, and religion. Most reviewers found the *Parleyings* bewildering and seemed to share the reviewer's opinion in *The Spectator* of 5 February 1887 that 'Mr. Browning does not condescend more generously to the minds of his readers in age than he did in youth'. No second edition was called for.

Final years In April 1887, owing to defects in the rented Warwick Crescent property, Browning bought a grander house at 29 De Vere Gardens, Kensington; he and Sarianna moved there in June. On 4 October Pen, who had become a somewhat popular artist because of his father's many busy efforts to promote him, married the heiress Fannie Coddington, an American by parentage but English in upbringing and a great admirer of Browning's poetry. Browning could now reduce the amount of money he had been giving Pen and, after a conversation with the bride-to-be, he told Pen that he could provide the couple with £300 annually.

Browning's main business during 1887 and 1888 was to prepare his collected works, issued in sixteen volumes monthly between April 1888 and July 1889. He and Sarianna spent three months in Venice in late summer and autumn 1888, where they followed the negotiations that Pen (with his wife's financial backing) was making to buy and refurbish the baroque Palazzo Rezzonico. Back at De Vere Gardens, Browning continued during winter 1888–9, as when in Venice, to correct proofs of his collected edition. In July he read in a recently published edition of the deceased Edward FitzGerald's letters a letter derogatory of Elizabeth Barrett Browning. Greatly angered, Robert wrote a vituperative sonnet, which was published in *The Athenaeum* on 13 July. The poem caused an uproar, and Browning felt that he had humiliated both himself and his dead wife.

Although Browning's health had appeared good, during the winter both he and his acquaintances thought him lacking in his usual energy. The FitzGerald incident worsened matters, and he fell ill. But he revived sufficiently to attend some prominent social events, and by September he and Sarianna were on their way to Italy. They stopped first in Asolo, which stimulated in him a burst of creative energy, and the preparation of a new volume of poems incorporating verse written there. In mid-October he sent off the poems to his publisher and then he and Sarianna went on to Venice to stay with Pen and Fannie in the splendidly restored Palazzo Rezzonico. Late in October Robert became ill with what he thought was a cold, but which was diagnosed as bronchitis and a weakened heart. As he became worse, friends were notified of his critical condition, which soon became known to the press and aroused the world's curiosity.

On 12 December 1889, soon after hearing Pen read to him a telegram from his publisher that the book, published that day, had received highly favourable reviews and was almost sold out, Browning slipped in and out of consciousness and then, about ten o'clock that evening, he died. Pen had hoped to bury his father alongside his mother in Florence, but was told that the cemetery was closed. A message then came from the dean of Westminster offering burial in the abbey, and it was accepted. A preliminary funeral service was held in Venice in the great hall of the Palazzo Rezzonico, followed by a cortège of funeral gondolas down the Grand Canal out to the island of San Michele. Soon thereafter the body was returned to London by train. The splendid funeral in Westminster Abbey on 31 December 1889 ended with burial in Poets' Corner.

After the funeral, Pen and Fannie remained in London until spring 1890 to settle the poet's affairs. Browning's will, executed in 1864 in the presence of Tennyson and Francis Palgrave, was proved on 19 February 1890. The administration of his effects was granted to Pen, the residuary legatee, and the estate valued at £16,744. Sarianna, who became seriously ill soon after the funeral, stayed on at De Vere Gardens for another year and then went to Venice to live with Pen and Fannie, where Pen's old nurse, Wilson, and her husband also came. In April 1891 sixty-six cases of household effects were shipped to Venice. Pen had a memorial plaque to his father installed on the Palazzo Rezzonico and contributed to a window commemorating him in the English church in Venice.

In time Pen and Fannie, who had no children, drifted apart, although they never divorced. Thereafter he and Sarianna more or less settled in Asolo, where Pen had purchased some property that his father had wished to buy, and thereon built Pippa's Tower in his father's honour. Sarianna lived with him until 1903. Pen himself, who had grown obese, sickly, and almost blind, died of a heart attack in 1912 and received a splendid funeral and burial in Asolo. Ten years later Fannie had his body moved to Florence. She died in 1935.

On six days in May 1913 Pen's effects—which included his parents' manuscripts, pictures, books, and furniture—were auctioned at Sothebys in London. There were 1417 lots, described in a 170-page catalogue. After Pen's enormous debts were paid, one-third of the residue of the sale went to Fannie and two-thirds to sixteen Barrett cousins.

Posthumous reputation By the time of his death Browning was one of the most famous people in the English-speaking world, although never as popular as Tennyson—the sales of his works being a fraction of the poet laureate's. Chiefly admired as a philosopher and thinker, Browning became less well regarded in the 1890s, when moral instruction as the end of art (something Browning had always denied) was regarded as deplorable. The last public meetings of the London Browning Society were held in the season of 1891–2, although meetings continued in members' homes for several years and other Browning societies continued in America. Several critical works over the next ten or so years attacked Browning's approach to serious thought, the most important being George Santayana's 'The poetry of barbarism' (1900). Nevertheless, there were centennial celebrations in 1912, producing a large number of books and two editions (the centenary and the pocket version of the Florentine) of the poet's works that were more or less standard for at least fifty years. But in the 1920s, when there was a reaction to almost everything Victorian, Browning's reputation suffered almost total collapse, kept alive by only a few poets (notably Hardy, Yeats, Pound, and Frost) and lovers of Victorian verse. In the 1950s scholarly interest in his work began to revive, and in the early twenty-first century Browning's centrality in the history of English poetry is largely taken for granted. There are Browning societies in both Britain and America; there is a Browning Institute in New York; there is the Browning apartment preserved at the Casa Guidi and open to the public; and there is the Browning shrine and great repository of his printed works and autographs, the Armstrong Browning Library at Baylor University in Texas. There are the journals *Browning Society Notes*, *Browning Institute Studies* (now renamed *Victorian Literature and Culture*), and *Studies in Browning and His*

Circle. Numerous books and essays have appeared in increasing number since 1965, in addition to John Pettigrew's 1981 scholarly edition of his works.

CLYDE DE L. RYALS

Sources The Brownings' correspondence, ed. P. Kelley, R. Hudson, and S. Lewis, [14 vols.] (1984–) · J. Maynard, Browning's youth (1977) · W. Hall Griffin and H. C. Griffin, The life of Robert Browning, 3rd edn (1938) · C. de L. Ryals, The life of Robert Browning (1993) · W. Irvine and P. Honan, The book, the ring, and the poet (1974) · W. C. DeVane, A Browning handbook, 2nd edn (1975) · A. L. Orr, Life and letters of Robert Browning, new edn (1908) · A. L. Orr, A handbook to the worlds of Robert Browning, 6th edn (1927) · Robert Browning: the poems, ed. J. Pettigrew, 2 vols. (1981) · The diary of Alfred Domett (1953) · V. Surtees, The Ludovisi goddess: the life of Louisa Ashburton (1984) · M. Ward, The tragicomedy of Pen Browning (1849–1912) (1972) · W. S. Peterson, Interrogating the oracle: a history of the Browning Society (1969) · F. G. Kenyon, ed., Robert Browning and Alfred Domett (1906) · Robert Browning and Julia Wedgwood: a broken friendship as revealed in their letters, ed. R. Curle (1937) · Dearest Isa: Robert Browning's letters to Isabella Blagden, ed. E. C. McAleer (1951) · New letters of Robert Browning, ed. W. C. DeVane and K. L. Knickerbocker (1951) · G. R. Hudson, ed., Browning to his American friends: letters between the Brownings, the Storys, and James Russell Lowell (1965) · The Brownings to the Tennysons: letters from Robert Browning and Elizabeth Barrett Browning to Alfred, Emily, and Hallam Tennyson, 1852–1889, ed. T. J. Collins (1971) · Browning's trumpeter: the correspondence of Robert Browning and Frederick J. Furnivall, 1872–1889, ed. W. S. Peterson (1979) · More than friend: the letters of Robert Browning to Katharine de Kay Bronson, ed. M. Meredith (1985)
Archives Balliol Oxf., corresp. and poems · Baylor University, Waco, Texas, corresp. and papers · BL, address book, Ashley 5718 · BL, biographical papers, Add. MSS 45558–45564 · Boston PL, letters, literary MSS, and papers · L. Cong., papers · Morgan L., literary MSS and papers · NRA, corresp. · Ransom HRC, corresp., literary MSS, and papers · Yale U., Beinecke L., papers | BL, corresp. with Lord and Lady Carnarvon, Add. MS 60865 · BL, letters to Alfred Domett, Add. MS 45876 · BL, corresp. with Michael Field, Add. MS 46866 · BL, letters to Edmund Gosse, Ashley B.238, B.252–253, etc.; 5739 · BL, letters to Norman MacColl, Ashley 276, A.2549 · FM Cam., misc. letters · Herts. ALS, corresp. with Earl of Lytton · Herts. ALS, letters to Lord Lytton · Hunt. L., letters, documents, literary MSS · JRL, corresp. with John Leicester Warren · Lincoln Central Library, letters to Alfred Lord Tennyson · Morgan L., letters to George Marlton Barrett · Morgan L., letters to Frederic Chapman · Morgan L., letters to William Angus Knight · Somerville College, Oxford, letters to Amelia Edwards · Syracuse University, New York, corresp. with Sir John Simeon · TCD, letters to Mrs Lecky · U. Leeds, Brotherton L., letters to Sir Edmund Gosse · University of Chicago Library, corresp. with Bryan Procter and Anne Procter · University of Sheffield, letters to Maria Theresa Mundella and Anthony John Mundella · Wellesley College, Massachusetts, letters to Elizabeth Browning and papers · Yale U., Beinecke L., letters to Sophy Landor
Likenesses A. Ripert-Monclar, drawing, 1837, Armstrong Browning Library, Waco, Texas · H. Hosmer, bronze cast, 1853, NPG · W. Fisher, oils, 1854, Wellesley College, Massachusetts · W. Page, oils, 1854, Baylor University, Texas · D. G. Rossetti, watercolour, 1855, FM Cam. · D. G. Rossetti, watercolour drawing, 1855, FM Cam. · T. Woolner, bronze medallion, 1856, Birmingham Museums and Art Gallery · M. Gordigiani, oils, 1858, NPG · R. Lehmann, crayon drawing, 1859, BM · F. Talfourd, chalk drawing, 1859, NPG [see illus.] · London Stereoscopic Co., carte-de-visite, 1860–69, NPG · W. W. Story, bust, 1861, Keats and Shelley Memorial Museum, Rome · J. M. Cameron, carte-de-visite, 1865, NPG · S. Laurence, oils, 1866, Baylor University, Texas · G. F. Watts, oils, 1866, Armstrong Browning Library, Waco, Texas · G. F. Watts, oils, 1866, NPG · W. W. Story, two drawings, 1869, Morgan L. · photograph, c.1869, Armstrong Browning Library, Waco, Texas · J. M. Cameron, photograph, 1870, Hult. Arch. · R. B. Browning, oils, 1874, St Andrews School, Tennessee · R. Lehmann, oils, 1875, Baylor University, Texas; version, 1884, NPG · W. Fisher, oils, 1877, Baylor University, Texas · A. Legros, oils, 1879, V&A · R. B. Browning, oils, 1882, Balliol Oxf. · F. Moscheles, oils, 1884, Wesleyan University, Ohio · R. B. Browning, bust, 1886, Browning Hall, Walworth, Connecticut · R. B. Browning, oils, 1889, Baylor University, Texas · G. D. Giles, drawing, 1889, Baylor University, Texas · H. S. Montalba, bust, 1889, probably University of Oxford · E. Myers, photographs, 1889, NPG · R. Bryden, print, 1898, V&A · Ape [C. Pellegrini], chromolithograph, NPG; repro. in VF (20 Nov 1875) · M. Beerbohm, cartoon, AM Oxf. · E. Edwards, carte-de-visite, NPG · G. D. Giles, drawing (Last life-picture, Venice, 14 November 1889), Armstrong Browning Library, Waco, Texas · photograph (death bed portrait), Poetry Society, London · photographic prints, NPG
Wealth at death £16,744 19s. 4d.: administration, 19 Feb 1890, CGPLA Eng. & Wales

Browning, Robert (1914–1997), Byzantinist, was born at 64 Airlie Street, Glasgow, on 15 January 1914, the oldest of the three sons of Alexander Martin Browning, cardboard box manufacturer, and his wife, Jeanie Murray, *née* Miller, primary school teacher. After attending Kelvinside Academy, where for a time under parental pressure he had studied science, he entered Glasgow University with a scholarship of about £40 per annum in 1931. He graduated in 1935, having won the Snell exhibition, which took him to Balliol College, Oxford, where he achieved a double first in classics, winning various prizes, including the Ireland scholarship in 1937, and taking finals in 1939.

While still a student Browning had travelled in eastern Europe, arriving in Vienna at the time of the *Anschluss*. When the Second World War broke out he joined the Royal Artillery as a second lieutenant. On 7 December 1940 he married Mary Doughty (*b.* 1915/16), actress and daughter of William Horn, property owner. Browning was sent to Cairo to do intelligence work. On the long and roundabout voyage he used his spare time to acquire Georgian; as a student he had begun to dabble in Slavonic languages, in which he later became very adept. From Cairo he went in 1944 to Italy, then to Sofia and Belgrade, where he was assistant to the military attaché in 1945–6. His first marriage having ended, he married, in 1946, Galina Chichekova, a Bulgarian. They had two daughters, one of whom died as a young adult.

Browning returned to Oxford as a Harmsworth senior scholar at Merton College in 1946, but in 1947 took up an appointment as a lecturer in classics at University College, London. He had an enviably wide range of interests in the classics—he published on topics as far apart as Linear B and Petronius—and it was some years before Byzantine studies became the dominant element in his output. He became a reader in 1955 and in 1965 (the year he was appointed to the editorial board of *Past and Present*) was elected to the chair of classics and ancient history at Birkbeck College, which he held until he retired in 1981. Several books and articles appeared during this period. Some of the books might be described as works of *haute vulgarisation*; the most important and influential was his manual *Medieval and Modern Greek* (1969, rev. 1983), which admirably traced the evolution of the language. His articles, in several of which he published important texts for the first time, included pioneering studies of the history of scholarship and education in Byzantium, probably his greatest contribution to learning. Recognition of their excellence came, a little later than it should have, with his election to a fellowship of the British Academy in 1978. The Academy of Athens made him a member in 1981 and he received many other honours from Greece, where he was known for his support of the campaign for the return of the Elgin marbles to Athens. His second marriage having ended in divorce, he married, on 1 July 1972, Ruth Gresh, translator and daughter of Bernard Papert, doctor of medicine. Browning had first met her in Cairo during the war. There were no children of this third marriage.

Browning was noted for his unfailing courtesy and helpfulness to colleagues and students. Though a fluent speaker, he had also a kind of reticence, as a result of which he often managed to conceal from pupils another facet of his life. His political sympathies were with the Communist Party; this allegiance, which probably went back to his time at Oxford, survived the shock of 1956. For many years he contributed to left-wing papers. He also maintained links with numerous academics in the Soviet bloc, including both party members and dissidents. His sympathy for eastern Europe sometimes led him to take a more favourable view of its scholarly output than seemed justified in the opinion of Western colleagues. On the other hand, in his own works he never allowed his political bias to distort the picture.

In retirement Browning remained as vigorous as ever and became a regular visitor at Harvard University's centre for Byzantine studies at Dumbarton Oaks, Washington, DC, where he had a chance to continue his didactic activity. He also served as an adviser when the University of Cyprus was being set up. His last major publication, undertaken in collaboration with C. N. Constantinides, was a corpus of dated manuscripts probably written in Cyprus between the tenth century and 1570. He received two Festschriften, *Maistor* (1984) and *Philhellene* (1996). He died on 11 March 1997 at the Royal Free Hospital, Camden, of bronchopneumonia and pulmonary embolic disease. He was survived by his wife, Ruth, and his daughter Tamara. He was a freeman of the city of Athens, and the expenses of his secular cremation were met by the Greek state.   N. G. WILSON

Sources A. M. Cameron, 'Robert Browning', *PBA*, 105 (2000), 289–306 · *The Guardian* (13 March 1997) · *The Independent* (14 March 1997) · *The Times* (18 March 1997) · *Daily Telegraph* (26 March 1997) · *WWW* · personal knowledge (2004) · b. cert. · m. certs. · d. cert.
Likenesses photograph, repro. in *The Guardian* · photograph, repro. in *The Independent*
Wealth at death £297,386: probate, 18 July 1997, CGPLA Eng. & Wales

Brownlie, James Thomas (1865–1938), trade unionist, was born on 23 June 1865 at Port Glasgow, Renfrewshire, the son of Thomas Brownlie, marine engineer, and his wife, Jessie Robertson. Educated at Wason's academy, Paisley, he served an engineering apprenticeship and worked for many years at Woolwich arsenal. He was a member of the management committee of the Royal Arsenal Co-operative Society between 1900 and 1910. He married Ellen Anderson and they had two sons and three daughters.

In 1910 Brownlie stood unsuccessfully as a Labour parliamentary candidate at Govan. He later stood at Crewe in 1918 and Sunderland in 1931, but his subsequent career was principally within the Amalgamated Society of Engineers (ASE). The union was then struggling to cope with the integration of its extensive welfare benefits into the national insurance system and with the defeat of its long tradition of an exclusive, craft-based unionism in the 1897–8 engineering lock-out.

In September 1910 Brownlie attacked the ASE's executive committee as the most unpopular body within the union and proposed constitutional reforms. The 1912 delegate meeting, the union's 'parliament', changed many rules and created a new paid post of independent chairman, elected by the entire membership. The existing executive committee made several unsuccessful attempts to challenge the meeting, by appealing directly to the membership, by refusing to leave the union's offices until physically ejected, and through legal action.

Brownlie had led the assault on the old executive committee and was personally attacked in their manifesto to the membership. In reply he noted that he had never stood for election to the executive, but in June 1913 he became the first independent chairman of the ASE. The union had traditionally been led by its general secretary but a contested election in 1913, ending in a libel suit, greatly damaged the post's status and it became an essentially administrative position. Brownlie was consequently the pre-eminent leader of the engineers until his retirement in 1930.

In 1915 Brownlie joined the new national advisory committee on war output and was centrally involved in discussions of 'dilution', the use of labourers and women to expand military output and free men for the front. Union leaders agreed to suspend craft practices but met resistance from the membership, especially on Clydeside, and Brownlie visited Paisley to justify dilution, with partial success. He served on several wartime government committees and was made CBE in 1917.

In 1920 the ASE became the Amalgamated Engineering Union (AEU) with Brownlie as president. However, the upheavals of 1912–13 reflected the union's diminishing status within the union movement: in 1910 the ASE was third in size after the Miners' Federation of Great Britain and the Lancashire Weavers, and arguably the largest genuinely national union; by 1933 the AEU came fifth and overall leadership had shifted to the miners and to newer unions of the unskilled, Ernest Bevin's Transport and General Workers Union and the General and Municipal Workers Union.

In the 1920s Brownlie was a typical moderate unionist. In 1919 and 1920 he supported a campaign for higher productivity as the only basis for higher wages. In 1920 he was attacked for having secretly accepted additional employment as the labour adviser to the Hulton newspaper group. In 1924 he was accused by Will Thorne of collaboration with the employers. He had close relations with Allan Smith of the Engineering Employers' Federation, lunching at his club. However, his views were broadly representative of the AEU's executive committee, whose policies changed little on his retirement, and of much of the membership, supporting the old ideals of craft unionism.

Brownlie died at sea from a heart attack on 13 October 1938 while returning from Canada on the *Duchess of Richmond*. In its *Monthly Journal* for November 1938, his union recalled his outstanding ability as a negotiator and power as an orator, but also his brusque and dominating personality, commenting 'a curious amalgam, his nimble mind was often unable to tolerate many of his own qualities when used by those in opposition.'

HUMPHREY SOUTHALL

Sources WWW · J. B. Jefferys, *The story of the engineers, 1800–1945* [1946]; repr. (1970) · H. A. Clegg, A. Fox, and A. F. Thompson, *A history of British trade unions since 1889*, 2 (1985) · *Monthly Journal of the Amalgamated Society of Engineers, later the Amalgamated Engineering Union* (Nov 1938), 433 · E. Wigham, *The power to manage: a history of the Engineering Employers' Federation* (1973) · B. Weekes, 'The Amalgamated Society of Engineers, 1880–1914: a study of trade union government, politics and industrial policy', PhD diss., University of Warwick, 1970 · E. A. Chapman and W. C. Rust, *The case against J. T. Brownlie* (1920) · b. cert. · d. cert., General Register Office for Scotland, Edinburgh [Marine Register Book] · *CGPLA Eng. & Wales* (1938)
Archives U. Warwick Mod. RC, Amalgamated Society of Engineers/Amalgamated Engineering Union collection
Wealth at death £2215 10s. 2d.: probate, 10 Dec 1938, *CGPLA Eng. & Wales*

Brownlow [*formerly* Chamberlain], **Arthur** (1645–1711), landowner, was born on 20 March 1645 at Ardee, co. Louth, the eldest son of Patrick Chamberlain of Nizelrath, co. Louth, and his wife, Lettice (d. 1699), eldest daughter of Sir William Brownlow of Brownlows Derry and Elinor O'Doherty, who came from an Irish family of Innishown, co. Donegal. His maternal great-grandfather John Brownlow and his maternal grandfather, Sir William Brownlow, arrived in Ireland in 1610 from Epworth in Lincolnshire and together obtained grants totalling 3500 acres in Doughcorn in Oneilland barony, co. Armagh, later known as Brownlows Derry and later still as Lurgan. Sir William had no surviving sons and his estates passed to Arthur Chamberlain as eldest son of his eldest daughter, Lettice. Under his grandfather's will he was required to assume the name of Brownlow. Lettice Brownlow survived four husbands, acquiring property, mainly in co. Louth, from each of them, while retaining a life interest in her father's estate. The Chamberlains were an Old English family which had been in Ireland from at least the beginning of the fourteenth century, while the Brownlows were a plantation family, and the O'Dohertys Gaelic Irish. Thus Arthur Brownlow grew up in a background which not only gave him a claim in all sections of the community, but also indicated that divisions were sometimes more blurred than is commonly believed. He was educated first at Mr Jones's school, and then entered Trinity College,

Dublin, on 20 September 1660, aged fifteen. He graduated BA in 1664.

Brownlow was an Irish scholar and collector of manuscripts, his prize possession being the Book of Armagh, now displayed with the Book of Kells in the library of Trinity College, Dublin. In addition to being a transcriber and translator of Gaelic manuscripts, including an elegy on Owen Roe O'Neill, he carried out experiments on fossilized wood from Lough Neagh, close to his estate, with a view to finding out whether it was a vegetable or a mineral. As a politician he trod a careful middle way and appears to have done so very successfully. His real concern was with his role as a country gentleman and a landlord in co. Armagh. During the reign of Charles II he acted as an agent for disarming Catholic Irish when there were fears of an uprising in 1673 and 1678. Nevertheless, he was tolerant in matters of religion, as, although of the established church, he allowed the Presbyterians to establish a church in Lurgan and his tenants included Quakers to whom he also gave the right to build a meeting-house in Lurgan. He appears to have preferred reliable tenants regardless of their religion. His lease book for 1667–1711 is still extant. He also had lands in counties Monaghan and Louth. He developed the town of Lurgan, encouraging the linen trade and founding the Lurgan linen market.

Brownlow was high sheriff for co. Louth in 1667 and for co. Armagh in 1679 and 1686. In March 1686 he was described to the lord lieutenant, the earl of Clarendon, as 'a loyal honest gentleman' and to this recommendation Clarendon responded: 'this needs no answer'. He was one of the few sheriffs appointed by Clarendon allowed to retain their posts by his successor Tyrconnell (Singer, 1.287). As the reign of James II progressed and civil war appeared imminent many protestants fled to England or Scotland. Brownlow did not, and on 12 April 1689 he wrote to his neighbour William Waring:

> I am sorry you left this kingdom yourself, your tenants and some of your neighbours have suffered by it. I believe you might have stayed as well as any man, for I know none of your station in Ulster that behaved themselves more innocently and inoffensively to all.

Brownlow sat in the parliament of James II, though he 'withdrew before the end of the session' (Gillespie, 12); apparently having offended a Catholic MP he escaped dressed as a Quaker. But, most interestingly, he was one of the half dozen MPs who sat in the 1692 parliament of William III. He also sat in the 1695 parliament and in the first parliament of Queen Anne.

The 1692 parliament was short-lived, but in 1695 Brownlow supported Lord Chancellor Porter against the unsuccessful accusations of Jacobite sympathies and favouritism to Roman Catholics brought against him by some MPs. In 1696 he signed the Association for the protection of William III in the country. During Queen Anne's reign he was a supporter of the administration. He was listed for three committees in 1692, for twenty-eight in the 1695–9 parliament, and for twenty-four between 1703 and 1709 in the first parliament of Queen Anne.

About 1677 Brownlow had married Jane, daughter of Sir

Standish Hartstonge, bt. They had six surviving children, including four sons, William, Standish, John, and Philemon. His eldest son, William (1683–1739), succeeded his father as MP for co. Armagh and sat for the county until his death; his grandson the Rt Hon. William Brownlow (1726–1794), also MP for co. Armagh, was one of the most highly respected MPs in the Irish House of Commons. Both of his daughters, Anne and Lettice, married MPs. Brownlow died at Lurgan in March 1711 and was buried in the Brownlow vault at Shankill, co. Armagh.   E. M. JOHNSTON-LIIK

Sources E. M. Johnston-Liik, *History of the Irish parliament, 1692–1800*, 6 vols. (2002) · T. G. Paterson, 'The Chamberlains of Nizelrath: the Brownlows', *County Louth Archaeological Journal*, 11 (1945–8), 282–5 · W. S. Brownlow, 'The Brownlows', *Upper Ards Historical Society Journal*, 11 (1987), 8–9 · B. Ó Buachalla, 'Arthur Brownlow', *Ulster Local Studies*, 2 (1982), 24–8 · J. G. Simms, *Jacobite Ireland* (1969), 75 · PRO NIre., T 581, vol. 3, 234–5, Society of Genealogists, London · Burke, *Peerage* (1903) · Burke, *Peerage* (1906) · J. L. J. Hughes, ed., *Patentee officers in Ireland, 1173–1826, including high sheriffs, 1661–1684 and 1761–1816*, IMC (1960) · Burtchaell & Sadleir, *Alum. Dubl.* · R. G. Gillespie, ed., *Settlement and survival on an Ulster estate: the Brownlow lease book, 1667–1711* (1988), xi–xiii · J. G. Simms, *War and politics in Ireland, 1694–1730*, ed. D. W. Hayton and G. O'Brien (1986), 68 · *The correspondence of Henry Hyde, earl of Clarendon, and of his brother, Laurence Hyde, earl of Rochester*, ed. S. W. Singer, 1 (1828), 287 · *Dublin Intelligence* (27 March 1711)

Archives PRO NIre., MSS

Brownlow [*née* Morgan], **Jane Macnaughton Egerton** (1854/5–1928), educationist and suffragist, was born in Paisley, the daughter of Captain George Bernard Morgan. Her father was town major at Gibraltar when she married Captain Edward Francis Brownlow (1839–1875), of the 71st highland light infantry, at King's Chapel, Gibraltar, on 20 August 1872. Her husband was a distant connection of the family of Baron Lurgan; after his early death she returned to Britain, and in 1881 was living in Grantchester, near Cambridge, as a student. She subsequently moved from Cambridge to London, where she brought a feminist perspective to the issues of state schooling and the position of women in the labour market. She was also an uncompromising supporter of women's suffrage and it seems likely that she joined a suffrage society.

A member of the Fabian Society, the Humanitarian League, the Pioneer Club for Women, the Teachers' Guild, and the Women's Progressive Society, Mrs Brownlow could draw on almost twenty years' experience in the educational world by the time she became manager of an elementary school in Finsbury (1891). Within two years she was criticizing the domestic curriculum for working-class girls in a Pioneer Club debate covered in the feminist journal *Shafts*. In 1896 she condemned the uneven provisions of the Technical Education Act, commenting in a letter to *Shafts* that: 'framed by men in the interests of men, they make it impossible for instruction to be given in any trade to persons not already working at that trade' (*Shafts*, 1896, 84).

In the autumn of 1894 Jane Brownlow put herself forward as a candidate for the London school board. Campaigning as a Progressive in Finsbury, she was a strong supporter of higher elementary schools and argued that a great injustice had been done to the really intelligent children. At the same time she did not endorse socialist proposals to provide maintenance for school children out of public funds. As a Liberal she advocated a charitable solution to the problem of school feeding. Speaking at a campaign meeting in Horsleydown, Mrs Brownlow acknowledged the work of her predecessor, Helen Taylor, who represented Southwark between 1876 and 1885: having heard much praise of Taylor's involvement with the local schools she vowed to 'strive to follow in her footsteps' (*Southwark Recorder*, 10 Nov 1894). With the support of the London Nonconformist Council she polled 7121 votes, finishing fifth in the contest for four divisional seats on the board.

An active member of the Women's Liberal Federation, in 1896 Jane Brownlow supported an attempt to withdraw female support for anti-suffrage parliamentary candidates. She seconded a resolution to this effect moved by Mrs W. Grove of Southport, in the absence of Mrs Eva McLaren, at the annual council meeting in June (*Woman's Signal*, 18 June 1896, 189–90). In the end the proposal was defeated, after a turbulent debate that raised the spectre of more party secessions. Six months later she reiterated her position during a public debate at Trinity Hall, London: 'I will not', said Mrs Brownlow, 'lift a finger to help any man who will not help my sisters' (*Woman's Signal*, 3 Dec 1896, 357).

Jane Brownlow was an outspoken critic of protective legislation which restricted or prohibited women's work in certain fields or limited their duties or hours of work. In her view the link between lack of political rights and potential economic disenfranchisement was clear, since the new Factory Acts applied only in areas worked also by men. As she put it in 1896: 'No legislator has yet attempted to make laws which shall prevent women from taking night work when nursing, or acting, or dancing' (Brownlow, *Women and Factory Legislation*, 4). However, she also took up the issue of child labour, working with Margaret Macdonald and Ruth Homan on the committee on wage-earning children, which was formed by the Women's Trade Union League to increase the efficiency and promote the reform of the existing legislation.

Quite apart from her political commitments, Mrs Brownlow was an accomplished author and linguist, whose works included a translation entitled *The English Woman: Studies in her Psychic Evolution* from the French work by David Staars (1909). The book starts by providing a general introduction to the idea of character, moving on to look at the English mind, English women during the Renaissance, and the position of English women in the eighteenth century. Final sections describe the advent of organized feminist campaigns in the nineteenth century. At the start of the twentieth century she turned naturally to the Women's Local Government Society as a political organization; she made a significant contribution to its agitation against the Education Act of 1902, which restricted the opportunities for women in local educational administration. A decade later, fresh legislation meant her handbook for women seeking elected office

(1911) was used to promote women's work in local government. Jane Brownlow died on 14 November 1928 at her home, 59 Seymour House, Compton Street, London.

JANE MARTIN

Sources J. M. E. Brownlow, *Women and factory legislation* (1896) · D. Staars, *The English woman: studies in her psychic evolution*, trans. J. M. E. Brownlow (1909) · J. M. E. Brownlow, *Women's work in local government* (1911) · J. Edwards, ed., 'The directory of lecturers and reformers', *Labour Annual* (1897), 241–6 · *School Board Chronicle* (11 Nov 1894), 583 · *Shafts*, 3 (1894), 366–7 · *Shafts*, 4 (1895), 22 · *Southwark Recorder* (3 Nov 1894) · *Woman's Signal* (18 June 1896), 189–90 · *Woman's Signal* (3 Dec 1896), 357 · 205/59 committee on wage earning children, 9th and 10th Annual Reports, 1909–10, London Metropolitan University, Gertrude Tuckwell MSS, Women's Trade Union League · m. cert. · d. cert. · E. Lodge, *The peerage of the British empire* (1881) · census returns, 1881, 1901

Archives LMA, school board for London · LMA, Women's Local Government Society | London Metropolitan University, TUC Collection, Gertrude Tuckwell MSS, Women's Trade Union League

Wealth at death £3633 6s. 1d.: probate, 25 Jan 1929, *CGPLA Eng. & Wales*

Brownlow, Margaret Eileen (1916–1968). *See under* Grieve, Sophia Emma Magdalene (*b.* 1858, *d.* after 1933).

Brownlow, Richard (1553–1638), legal official, was born on 2 April 1553 and baptized on 12 April at St Andrew's, Holborn, Middlesex. He was the son of John Brownlow of High Holborn and his wife, a daughter of Sir John Zouche of Stoughton Grange in Leicestershire. While little is known of Brownlow's early education, he probably trained as a clerk within the offices of the court of common pleas. He entered the Middle Temple in 1583, but though he became a bencher in 1591, and served as treasurer in 1606, he made his career within the judicial bureaucracy rather than at the bar. By 1589 he had secured the office of exigenter in common pleas, which he ran from chambers in Clement's Inn. On 9 October 1590 he became chief protonotary of the court of common pleas, one of the most important and lucrative clerical offices in a period when court business was growing at an unprecedented pace. Holding the post until his death, he estimated in the late 1620s that it was worth £3000 a year. He owned a house in Holborn, where a street still bears his name, and in the 1590s began to accumulate property in Middlesex and Lincolnshire, crowning his estate in the 1610s with the purchase for £4100 of the reversion to Belton, Lincolnshire. In 1613 his legal action challenging the newly erected *supersedeas* office, which cut into his fee income, gave rise to the famous arguments over the writ *non procedendo rege inconsulto*. Like other court officials, he was regularly questioned during the early Stuart period by royal commissions appointed to investigate the tenure of office-holders and increases in their fees, but his position brought him into close contact with the common pleas advocates, the serjeants-at-law, and he was sometimes consulted by the judges, with whom he remained on good terms.

Thanks to his long tenure and careful record keeping, Brownlow also gained a notable posthumous reputation as an expert on matters related to his office. In 1651 the legal booksellers Matthew Walbancke and Henry Twyford

Richard Brownlow (1553–1638), by Thomas Cross, pubd 1653

published a collection of judicial 'observations' by the common pleas judges, which was attributed to Brownlow and another protonotary, John Goldsborough, along with a collection of *Reports* that had evidently been gathered by Brownlow alone. *Writs Judiciall … Collected out of the Learned and Accurate Presidents of Richard Brownlow* (1653), which was also published by Twyford, is probably less authentic, but *Declarations, Counts and Pleadings* (1654), a translation into English of Brownlow's Latin precedents for plea roll entries, is a lengthy and detailed work that gives specific references to the court records, most of which date from *c*.1600–1615. Clearly timed to coincide with the short-lived decision by parliament to make English rather than Latin the legal language of record, the latter work was published several times in the 1650s, and then reappeared after 1660 in various editions in which the English was translated back into Latin. The *Reports* had three editions up to 1675.

Brownlow married Katherine, the daughter of John Page of Wembley, Middlesex, one of the first governors of Harrow School; they had three sons and three daughters. He died at Enfield on 21 July 1638, but was buried at Belton, Lincolnshire, on 1 August; there is a monument of him in his protonotary's gown in Belton church. Among other legacies, he left £200 to the parish of St Andrew's, Holborn, to be lent yearly to four poor tradesmen, and £52 3s. p.a. for six almsmen and one almswoman of the parish of

Kirkby Underwood in Lincolnshire, an allowance designed to enable them to 'spend their aged yeares in praying and serving of God nowe they are unable to worke for thier lyvinge' (PRO, PROB 11/177, fols. 317–19).

CHRISTOPHER W. BROOKS

Sources C. W. Brooks, *Pettyfoggers and vipers of the commonwealth: the 'lower branch' of the legal profession in early modern England* (1986) · E. Cust, *Records of the Cust family*, 3 vols. (1909), 1 · *DNB* · will, PRO, PROB 11/177, fols. 317–19 · Baker, *Serjeants* · Holdsworth, *Eng. law*, vol. 5 · *The works of Francis Bacon*, ed. J. Spedding, R. L. Ellis, and D. D. Heath, 14 vols. (1857–74), vol. 7, pp. 683ff. · monument, Belton church, Lincolnshire

Archives Lincs. Arch., account books and papers

Likenesses J. Marshall, bust on funeral monument, 1638, Belton church, Lincolnshire · T. Cross, line engraving, pubd 1653 (after a portrait), BM, NPG, V&A [*see illus.*] · oils, Belton House, Lincolnshire

Wealth at death houses and land in Holborn, Middlesex, and Lincolnshire; office valued at £3000 p.a.: will, PRO, PROB 11/177, fols. 317–19; Cust, *Records of the Cust family*; Brooks, *Pettyfoggers and vipers*

Brownrigg, Elizabeth (c.1720–1767), murderer, of whose parentage and early life nothing is known, is first heard of in the late 1740s working as a servant for a family residing in Prescot Street, Goodman's Fields, London. According to the *Gentleman's Magazine* she was then about twenty-seven years old, at which age she married James Brownrigg, a house painter, with whom she moved to Greenwich. The marriage produced sixteen children, of whom only three sons outlived their mother. About 1763 the family moved to Fleur de Luce Court, Fetter Lane, London, where Brownrigg practised midwifery, being appointed as midwife to the poor in the parish of St Dunstan-in-the-West in 1765. At this time she was said to have displayed 'great skill and humanity' in this role as well as being 'a faithful wife' and 'affectionate parent' (*GM*, 433).

The family income was supplemented by Elizabeth Brownrigg's taking in girl apprentices from the parish workhouse for a sum of £5 per child. It was as part of this scheme that two fourteen-year-olds, Mary Mitchell and Mary Jones, were sent to Fetter Lane in the early part of 1765. Here they were subjected to a punishing regime of work and a catalogue of beatings, near drownings, humiliation, and imprisonment. Attention was drawn to the house following Jones's escape to the Foundling Hospital in July 1765, but no action appears to have been taken against the family and indeed a third child, Mary Clifford, was sent there in February 1766. Brownrigg, along with her husband and son, continued to torture the children, intensifying her attacks on Clifford in particular, who was regularly stripped and beaten, strangled with a chain, and hanged from a hook in the kitchen. A particularly vicious beating in August 1767 attracted the attention of Brownrigg's neighbours, and after several searches of the house by the parish overseers both girls were removed. Clifford, whom a surgeon described as 'all one wound from her head to her toes' (*GM*, 433), died of her injuries on 9 August. Elizabeth Brownrigg was charged with wilful murder and after a three-day search was discovered in hiding with her son in Wandsworth. All three family members were tried on 12 September. James and his son were

acquitted but Elizabeth was found guilty and was hanged at Tyburn on 14 September, after which her body was displayed in the surgeon's hall at the Old Bailey. The terrible nature of Brownrigg's crimes provoked various reactions from the ghoulish to the sober social analysis found in *Gentleman's Magazine*, which questioned how children could suffer 'in such a *metropolis* as London' (*GM*, 437). Similar themes were raised in several contemporary pamphlets, including *An Appeal to Humanity* (1767), as well as in later publications such as *The Cries of the Afflicted* (1795), *Brownrigg the Second, or, A Cruel Stepmother* (1812), and *The Atrocious Life and Horrid Cruelties of Elizabeth Brownrigg* (1830), which reveal her enduring infamy in the popular imagination.

PHILIP CARTER

Sources *GM*, 1st ser., 37 (1767), 433–7 · *DNB* · H. Wilson, *Wonderful characters*, 3 vols. (1821) · G. H. Burrow, *Celebrated trials and remarkable cases* (1875)

Likenesses N. Dance, etching, pubd 1767, BM · R. Cooper, engraving, 1825, repro. in Wilson, *Wonderful characters* · line engraving, BM · prints, NPG

Brownrigg, Ralph (1592–1659), bishop of Exeter, was the son of a merchant of Ipswich, who died during his infancy. He was educated at Ipswich grammar school and in 1606 went to Pembroke College, Cambridge, as a scholar of the college. In 1611 he graduated BA and was elected a fellow, sooner than the college statutes allowed. He proceeded MA in 1614. Conversations four years later in the privacy of his college rooms nearly brought him punishment when he was informed on by David Owen, an upholder of the divine right of kings, for discussing whether kings might be deposed for breaking fundamental laws. In the event his career continued smoothly. He proceeded BD in 1621 and DD in 1627. He combined his college duties with holding various livings, all within 12 miles of Cambridge: he became vicar of Madingley in 1615, of Barton in 1619, and of Stretham in 1621. He was from 1621 rector of Barley, Hertfordshire, where he adjusted his preaching and catechizing to his congregation, 'fitting his net to the fish he was to catch' (Gauden, 158). He was appointed a prebendary of Ely by the love and favour of Bishop Felton in 1621 and received three more offices—the prebend of Lichfield in 1629, the archdeaconry of Coventry in 1631, and the prebend of Durham in 1641 through his friendship with Thomas Morton, bishop of Lichfield and later of Durham, to whom he had been a chaplain.

Brownrigg was a noted Calvinist and gained a reputation as an opponent of Arminianism early in his career at Cambridge, yet his words to Simonds D'Ewes on his election as master of St Catharine's College in 1635 show his readiness to be conciliatory. He said that 'as I account it my duty to promote conformity to the orders of our church so I shall undertake that service in the spirit of love and levity, being assured that I am amongst those whose dispositions are tractable' (Cliffe, 102). As master he drew more students to the college, raised the standard of scholarship, and improved the buildings and revenues. With regard to university affairs he was one of a group of nine heads of college who tried to prevent sermons in favour of Laudian views. He was vice-chancellor from 1637 to 1639, when he reformed the standard of behaviour at the university, and he served again as vice-chancellor from 1643 to 1645. His stance on discipline and conformity perhaps provides the explanation for his appointment as a chaplain-extraordinary to the king on 4 March 1638.

When parliament met in 1640 Brownrigg was drawn towards the centre of affairs, partly through his relationship to John Pym; at an unknown date he had married Pym's niece (she died about 1632). His credentials as an impeccable Calvinist were confirmed by an invitation to preach at the communion service for the Short Parliament on 3 May. As an archdeacon he sat in the lower house of convocation and was active in opposition to the canons of 1640. When the Long Parliament met Brownrigg became one of the ecclesiastical advisers to a group, led by the earl of Bedford and including Pym, which was planning a broader settlement of government. In January 1641 Brownrigg was one of those deputed to wait upon the king with the group's views on the episcopacy. In March he became a chaplain-in-ordinary to the king and in the same month was appointed to a subcommittee under the bishop of Lincoln to prepare material for the committee of lords and bishops created to settle the affairs of the church. He was an assiduous member of this subcommittee and was one of the seven signatories to its report, which condemned innovations of both doctrine and discipline. In September the secretary of state, Sir Edward Nicholas, recommended the king to counter the antipopery of his subjects by filling the vacant bishoprics with men free from any suspicion of favouring popish parties. The king followed Nicholas's advice and filled five bishoprics, Brownrigg being appointed to the see of Exeter.

Brownrigg was consecrated in Henry VII's chapel at Westminster on 3 May 1642, when the sermon was preached by his constant friend and long associate, Dr Edward Young. Brownrigg never visited his diocese, being enthroned in the person of his proctors, Timothy Shute and Dean Peterson, on 1 June. He created a commission dated 27 November 1643 for the institution of clerks, with Dr George Parry (the diocesan chancellor) and Dean Peterson as the most active commissioners. He also made some appointments such as that of Young to the archdeaconry of Exeter. In his absence an ordination was conducted in the cathedral by the bishop of Bristol on 26 October 1645.

Brownrigg remained at Cambridge when he became bishop of Exeter. He was the Cambridge representative to the Westminster assembly in 1643 but was excused from attendance on the grounds of being vice-chancellor. His active career ended in 1645 when he was arrested for the sermon he preached before the university as vice-chancellor on the anniversary of the king's coronation (2 February). Ironically, in view of the incident thirty years earlier, he was reported to have 'denied any capacity in Christian Subjects to resist their Sovereign Princes, for which they had neither Christs precept nor any good Christian practice'; they had 'only the choice to obey actively or passively, to do or to suffer; and rather to suffer than to sin by doing or resisting in any unlawful way'. In

response 'he was immediately proscribed and outed of his place in the University, and deprived of his liberty' (Gauden, 182). John Gauden learnt of this sermon when he visited Brownrigg in prison. The committee of both kingdoms had ordered his arrest on 2 April, and on 5 April committed him to prison at Winchester House, moving him to Mr Dillingham's house three days later, when a subcommittee was named to examine his sermons. On 26 June 1645 Brownrigg petitioned that, after ten weeks under restraint, he should be either bailed or discharged. On 1 August he was allowed bail of £5000 with leave to go to Cambridge for twenty days and give up his accounts.

Brownrigg, now deprived of his college and university positions, was soon to lose the benefits of his episcopal office. In 1646 ordinances were passed establishing a presbyterian form of church government and on 9 October the episcopal constitution of the church was abolished and the property of bishoprics confiscated to the state. Brownrigg's sole income was now money left him by his wife; they had no children and he moved between the homes of various friends accompanied by one servant and always paying for his entertainment. He was most often at the houses of Mr Thomas Rich at Sonning, Berkshire, and at Wimbledon.

Although Brownrigg had been deposed from his episcopal office, he continued to discharge its spiritual functions as far as possible. He carried out some ordinations in accordance with the rites of the Church of England, most notably that of Edward Stillingfleet, later bishop of Worcester. Seth Ward, later dean and bishop of Exeter, acted as his chaplain and Brownrigg appointed him honorary precentor of Exeter Cathedral about 1650. In the last year of his life the Honourable Society of both Temples invited Brownrigg 'to bless them with his residence', and when his health would permit, 'with his fatherly instruction and prayers' (Gauden, 221). The society allowed him an annual grant and provided him with handsomely furnished lodgings. He preached seven or eight times during the Easter term to crowded congregations and in spite of suffering from the stone preached his last sermon there on 5 November 1659, when he reiterated the views that had caused his arrest in 1645. He died in London at Temple Lodgings on 7 December and was buried in the Temple Church ten days later.

Although Brownrigg was prevented from being an active bishop he achieved a posthumous reputation from Gauden's *Memorials of the Life* (1660), and from his *Fourty Sermons* published by William Martyn the following year so that 'the World may know that pious, practical Preaching and Prelatical Dignity are not inconsistent'. The sermons are not dated, but most of them were delivered either on the four main festivals of the church or on the two occasions for thanksgiving for the Stuart monarchs—5 November and the anniversary of the coronation of Charles I. In one of these he showed his admiration of the king's faith:

> Did England ever know a Prince more frequent, more
> constant, more attentive and devout in the worship of God.
> We commend it in private persons; and 'tis justly

commendable; how much more in a king? To keep his constant times for prayer, to bring his children daily to the worship of God; to teach them betimes to know the God of their Father.   (R. Brownrigg, *Fourty Sermons*, 1661, 45)

The *Memorials*, largely delivered after the funeral sermon, revealed Brownrigg as a bishop who upheld episcopal government but was without 'secular pomp and vain ambition', who esteemed the liturgy of the church but was not a stickler for matters of ceremony, regarding them as the shadows not the substance of religion, and who was 'against those unquiet and pragmatick spirits which affect endless controversies, vanities and novelties in Religion'. Gauden described him as 'a Primitive Prelate … here was the learned industry and humble piety of ancient Christian Bishops' (Gauden).   MARY WOLFFE

Sources J. Gauden, *Sermon preached at funeral of Ralph Brownrig DD late lord bishop of Excester in Temple Chappel: the memorials of the life and death of the Right Reverend Father in God Dr Brownrig late lord bishop of Excester* (1660) · C. Russell, *The fall of the British monarchies, 1637–1642* (1991) · Devon RO, Chanter 23, 50, 57 · E. E. Rich, ed., *St Catharine's College, Cambridge, 1473–1973: a volume of essays to commemorate the quincentenary of the foundation of the college* (1973) · *Walker rev.* · Venn, *Alum. Cant.* · Fuller, *Worthies* (1811), vol. 2 · *The diary of John Evelyn*, ed. W. Bray, 2 vols. (1907); rev. edn (1952); repr. (1966) · *CSP dom.*, 1641–5; 1660–61 · Sixth report, HMC, 5 (1877–8) · N. Tyacke, *Anti-Calvinists: the rise of English Arminianism, c.1590–1640* (1987) · will, PRO, PROB 11/299, fol. 159 · Foster, *Alum. Oxon.* · G. Oliver, *Lives of the bishops of Exeter, and a history of the cathedral* (1861) · J. F. Chanter, *The bishop's palace, Exeter, and its story* (1932) · J. B. Pearson, 'Edward Young, dean of Exeter', *Report and Transactions of the Devonshire Association*, 39 (1907), 194–7 · J. T. Cliffe, *The puritan gentry: the great puritan families of early Stuart England* (1984) · D. Hoyle, 'A Commons investigation of Arminianism and popery in Cambridge on the eve of the civil war', *HJ*, 29 (1986), 419–25 · J. P. Somerville, *Politics and ideology in England, 1603–1640* (1986) · J. Walker, *An attempt towards recovering an account of the numbers and sufferings of the clergy of the Church of England*, 2 pts in 1 (1714)

Likenesses W. Faithorne, line engraving, BM, NPG; repro. in *Sermons* (1661) · oils, Pembroke Cam.

Wealth at death £100 to nephew; other bequests from £1 to £30: will, PRO PROB 11/299, fol. 159

Brownrigg, Sir Robert, first baronet (1759–1833), army officer and colonial governor, was born at Rockingham, co. Wicklow, Ireland, the second of the four sons of Henry Brownrigg (*d.* 1793) and his wife, Mary Alcock (*d.* 1819). Gazetted as ensign in 1775, his progress in the army was at first slow, his family lacking both wealth and influence. However, on 8 April 1789 Brownrigg married Elizabeth Catharine (*d.* 1804), daughter of William Lewis of Jamaica. They had six sons and a daughter, and it seems likely that it was wealth acquired by this marriage that enabled Brownrigg's career to progress. After service in varied regiments, in 1793 Brownrigg joined the staff of Frederick, duke of York, as a lieutenant-colonel in his first disastrous Netherlands campaign against the French revolutionary armies. As the protégé and personal friend of the 'grand old duke of York', his career thereafter prospered. Appointed the duke's military secretary when the duke became commander-in-chief at the Horse Guards, Brownrigg later filled the same position in the further unsuccessful expedition to The Helder in 1799. He became quartermaster-general at the Horse Guards in 1803 with

Sir Robert Brownrigg, first baronet (1759–1833), by Sir Thomas Lawrence, *c.*1809

the rank of major-general. Raised to lieutenant-general in 1808, the following year he was with the fruitless and fever-wracked expedition to Walcheren, before returning again to Whitehall. Failure though the duke of York had been in the field, his reforms at the Horse Guards did much to rebuild the army that helped defeat Napoleon. As one of the duke's main assistants, Brownrigg received much credit for the part he played.

In 1811 Brownrigg sailed for Ceylon as governor and commander-in-chief, having married on 24 June 1810 Sophia (*d.* 1834), the attractive daughter of the Revd Dr John Bissett of the Isle of Wight. Sophia was to accompany him to Ceylon. At that time the British controlled only the maritime provinces of Ceylon, the interior being ruled by Sri Wikrama, the king of Kandy. In 1803 the British made an attempt to seize the mountainous and jungle-clad interior and were severely repulsed by the Kandyans, as had been their Portuguese and Dutch colonial predecessors.

With Napoleon threatening Europe, unnecessary and distracting overseas military adventures were to be discouraged. Consequently, Brownrigg's instructions from his government were that no further attempt was to be made to conquer Kandy. Nevertheless, he reached Ceylon determined to bring the whole island under British control. He awaited the right moment.

At last, in October 1814, ten traders, natives of Colombo, were robbed as they entered Kandyan territory, denounced as spies, killed, and mutilated. With his plans for the conquest of the interior already in hand, it was the excuse Brownrigg awaited. Six battalions of infantry were at his disposal, two British and four of the Ceylon regiment, the latter manned by Malays, Indians, Javanese, and Africans. Dividing his force into self-contained columns marching on Kandy by five routes, Brownrigg's meticulous preparations were an indication of his professional ability.

Although by then heavily built and suffering from gout, the 55-year-old governor accompanied his leading column. The campaign was little more than a triumphal procession: not a single member of the invading force was killed, and deaths from disease were few. A brutal reign of terror only recently imposed had cost the king the support of both his chieftains and his people. An emotional man, Brownrigg burst into tears at dinner when the news of the king's capture reached him. In early March 1815 a convention was signed with the Kandyan chiefs whereby they retained their powers but were answerable not to a king but to a resident, the governor's representative. In 1816 Brownrigg's economical and speedy victory was rewarded with a baronetcy. In January 1815 he had been gazetted GCB.

The peace was short-lived. Happy though they were to get rid of Sri Wikrama, the Kandyans did not welcome exchanging his tyranny for a foreign bureaucracy. The result was that an almost spontaneous and unexpected major rebellion erupted in October 1817. The rising occurred when Brownrigg was on an extended tour of his recently acquired provinces; it was his custom to travel widely, and he was accompanied by his wife, escorted by only a few mounted troopers. On hearing the news, he rode straight away to Kandy to take personal command of the counter-measures. Quelling the rebellion was to prove a harder task than the initial conquest of Kandy. With only two British and two local battalions at first available, it took more than a year. Brownrigg remained up-country throughout, conducting the campaign from his sickbed, crippled by both the gout and a vicious skin disease. Against guerrilla warfare, the only effective counter-measure was to devastate the countryside. When resistance at last collapsed in the autumn of 1818, more than 1000 troops had died, most from disease. Kandyan losses were never calculated.

During his time as governor Brownrigg introduced into Ceylon many much needed judicial and administrative reforms, including substantial steps towards the abolition of slavery. Promoted general in August 1819, he returned to England the following year. Handsome though he had been when he left for Ceylon, he now looked an old man. From 1823 he was governor of Landguard Fort until his death at his home, Helston House, near Monmouth, on 27 May 1833.   GEOFFREY S. POWELL

Sources G. Powell, *The Kandyan wars: the British army in Ceylon, 1803–1818* (1973) · J. Davy, *An account of the interior of Ceylon and of its inhabitants* (1821) · H. Marshall, *Ceylon: a general description of the island and its inhabitants, with an historical sketch of the conquest of the colony by the English* (1846) · T. Vimalananda, *The great rebellion of 1818* (1970) · C. R. De Silva, *Ceylon under British occupation, 1795–1833*, 1 (1969) · E. F. C. Ludowyk, *The story of Ceylon* (1962) · L. A. Mills, *Ceylon under British rule, 1795–1932* (1933) · *Debrett's Peerage* (1819) · *Debrett's Peerage* (1840) · *Army List* · will, PRO, PROB 11/1819, sig. 488 · Burke, *Peerage* (1939)

Archives NAM, papers as quartermaster-general · PRO, Colonial Office MSS, 54, 55 · PRO, letterbooks and papers, WO 133 | BL, corresp. with earl of Chichester, Add. MSS 33101–33105, *passim* · BL, corresp. with Sir Ambrose Hardinge Giffard, etc., Add. MS 56367 · BL, corresp. with Sir J. W. Gordon, Add. MSS 49505, 49517 K–M, *passim* · BL, letters to Lord Hardwicke, Add. MSS 35642–35733, *passim* · BL, corresp. with William Huskisson, Add. MSS 38736–38742, *passim* · Bucks. RLSS, corresp. with Richard Vyse · Morgan L., letters to Sir James Murray-Pulteney · Mount Stuart Trust, Isle of Bute, letters to Lord Hastings · NA Scot., corresp. with lords Melville · NAM, corresp. with Sir George Nugent · NL Scot., corresp. with earl of Minto · NRA Scotland priv. coll., letters to Sir John Hope · U. Durham L., corresp. with first Earl Grey
Likenesses T. Lawrence, oils, *c.*1809, NAM [*see illus.*] · J. Jackson, mezzotint, 1820, NAM · J. Jackson, stipple, 1824, NAM · J. Thompson, engraving (after J. Jackson, 1824) · W. Ward, mezzotint (after J. Jackson, 1820), BM, NPG
Wealth at death approx. £28,000: will, PRO, PROB 11/1819, sig. 488

Brownrigg, Thomas Marcus (1902–1967), naval officer and television company executive, was born on 8 July 1902 at Homeleigh, Shooters Hill, Plumstead, London, the son of Major, later Colonel, Henry John Watt Brownrigg (1859–1908) and his wife, Evelyn Mary, daughter of the Revd Hugh Huleatt, vicar of Shalford in Surrey. Thomas Brownrigg was educated at the Royal Naval College at Osborne and Dartmouth. He was gazetted midshipman in 1919, first seeing service on board the battleship *Warspite*. After attending a lieutenant's course at the Royal Naval College, Greenwich, he became sub-lieutenant from 15 August 1923. He was posted to the Yangtze (Yangzi) River in China on the gunboat *Scarab* as first lieutenant, but he took over command aged only twenty-one on the captain's illness. Later regarded as a fine navigator, Brownrigg attended a special navigation course in 1926, after which he was promoted lieutenant and served as navigation officer on several naval vessels. He married Joyce Chiesman (1902–1995), daughter of Sidney Chiesman, at St Peter's, Eaton Square, Belgravia, in London, on 27 November 1926; they had one son and one daughter.

Brownrigg was promoted to lieutenant-commander on 30 August 1931 and he attained the rank of commander on 31 December 1936. He went out to Singapore as commander of the dockyard and as king's harbour master at the Changi naval base from 1937 until 1939. At the outbreak of the Second World War, Brownrigg was appointed to the old naval post of master of the fleet and to the post of staff officer (operations), serving again on the battleship *Warspite*. He was on the personal staff of the commander-in-chief, Mediterranean, Andrew Cunningham, who was to have a considerable influence on Brownrigg's life and naval career. Brownrigg was present, as fleet navigator, in July 1940 when *Warspite* caused considerable damage to the leading Italian battleship *Cesare*; he was also in a major victory in March 1941 at the battle of Cape Matapan.

In 1942 Brownrigg went to Washington, DC, to join Admiral Cunningham, then head of the British Admiralty delegation, for discussions of the combined chiefs of staff on the plans for the allied invasion of French north Africa, code-named operation Torch. On returning to London he joined a small team at Norfolk House in St James's Square for the colossal task of translating those plans into detailed operational orders for Torch. The simultaneous landings of over 65,000 allied troops at the three Vichy government-controlled bases of Casablanca, Oran, and Algiers on 8 November 1942 were a success, with little resistance and no effective interference from axis forces. He was promoted to captain from 31 December 1942. Cunningham, in his memoirs, *A Sailor's Odyssey* (1951), commended Brownrigg as an officer of great operational experience and exceptional attainments, and he mentioned in particular Brownrigg's contribution to the planning of the allied landings in north Africa. From January 1943 Brownrigg served as staff officer (plans), again under Admiral Cunningham, who had resumed his former post as commander-in-chief, Mediterranean. Brownrigg was concerned with day-to-day operations and planning. The most pressing tasks for the Royal Navy following the surrender of axis forces in Tunisia were clearing the minefields, so that allied shipping might pass safely through the Mediterranean to the Middle East, and planning for the invasion of Sicily. On 10 September 1943 Brownrigg accepted the surrender of the Italian fleet on behalf of Admiral Cunningham, an honour of which he was extremely proud. He boarded the *Eugenio di Savoia*, the flagship of the Italian line, which he then navigated from off the north African coast to the British naval base at Malta.

Returning to Britain for Overlord, the allied invasion of Normandy, Captain Brownrigg took command of the cruiser *Scylla* on 4 November 1943, ready for the operation Neptune assault phase landings the following year. The eastern naval task force, of which *Scylla* was the flagship of the inshore squadron of Sir Philip Vian, was responsible for landing the British Second Army on the beaches codenamed Sword (Ouistreham), Juno (Courseulles), and Gold (Asnelles-Arromanches). Though it was damaged by mines Brownrigg succeeded in getting *Scylla* back to port. Neptune saw nearly 7000 ships and landing craft in action, landing over 850,000 men, between D-day, 6 June, and the

end of the month. Brownrigg was appointed DSO on 15 November 1944 'for gallantry, skill, determination and undaunted devotion to duty during the landing of Allied Forces on the coast of Normandy'. He was made OBE in 1942 (for his part in the battle of Cape Matapan) and promoted CBE in 1943. After the war Brownrigg commanded first the *Merganser* and then the aircraft-carrier *Theseus* before going to the Imperial Defence College in 1947 and then to the Admiralty as director of plans in January 1948. In April 1950 he became chief of staff, Mediterranean (as commodore, first class), based at Malta, under Admiral Sir John Edelsten, as commander-in-chief, Mediterranean station. He was appointed naval aide-de-camp to the queen in 1952. On retirement from the navy in 1952 Brownrigg took up the post of general manager of Bracknell new town development corporation, where he became a driving force in the creation of this post-war new town.

In 1954 Brownrigg entered the very different world of the new commercial television industry, in which he would use his leadership and organizational abilities to make a pioneering contribution. On 24 November 1954 he was appointed general manager of Associated-Rediffusion, later renamed Rediffusion Television. The company, formed by Associated Newspapers, proprietors of the *Daily Mail*, and Broadcast Relay Service (Rediffusion), a part of British Electric Traction, had been awarded the contract by the Independent Television Authority to provide the London weekday programme service for Independent Television. Despite having had practically no previous knowledge of television or advertising, he took on the job and built up the television station into a successful operation. He gave the company the motto 'Never baffled', which he certainly lived up to himself. Brownrigg had a philosophy of management that was clearly based on his naval experience, as outlined in the Rediffusion house magazine *Fusion*: 'no one is a successful general manager unless he serves. In our case he has to serve the viewers, the staff and the shareholders. Also, of course, he has to manage' (*Fusion*, 33, 1963, 3). Brownrigg took over Adastral

Thomas Marcus Brownrigg (1902–1967), by unknown photographer, 1960s [with his wife, Joyce Brownrigg]

House in London, the former Air Ministry building, ironically for a naval man, where he rapidly established a large headquarters, incorporating television studios, and recruited over 1000 staff in ten frantic months.

Associated-Rediffusion went on air on Thursday 22 September 1955 with a gala opening for ITV, presented jointly with the Associated Broadcasting Company (later renamed Associated Television), the weekend programme contractor for London. The following day Rediffusion became the first ITV station to begin regular broadcasting. Brownrigg was justifiably proud of Associated-Rediffusion programmes, especially of starting the first regular schools programmes in the United Kingdom in 1957 and of broadcasting a generally high standard of popular drama and light entertainment. ITV's early acquired reputation for good quality news and current affairs, including such series as *This Week*, was due in part to Brownrigg's personal interest in current affairs and his belief that Rediffusion should have a Fleet Street style and ethos. He was influential in the running of the ITV network through his position on all inter-company liaison committees, including his chairmanship of Independent Television News. He commanded Rediffusion as if it were a battleship, referring to the executive offices as the 'bridge' and the studios as the 'engine room'. Though perhaps he never quite understood the artistic temperament of television, and he certainly was not all things to all men, he was a colourful and respected figure in the company and the industry. He retired from Rediffusion Television in 1964. The decision of the Independent Television Authority in 1967 not to reappoint Rediffusion Television to the London ITV contract, but instead to enforce a merger with rival company ABC Television (to form Thames Television), saddened him considerably. In a letter to *The Times* (17 June 1967) he questioned the decision, loyally defending the record of the company and staff. 'It is sad and I am baffled', he concluded. Brownrigg died of heart failure at his home, Vann House, Finchampstead, Berkshire, on 9 October 1967. He was buried at St James's Church, Finchampstead. Attendance at his memorial service at St Martin-in-the-Fields, Trafalgar Square, London, reflected his varied life. The lesson was read by Admiral Sir David Luce, and an address by a colleague who had served under Brownrigg in the Royal Navy and at Rediffusion paid tribute to his qualities as a brilliant navigator of the Mediterranean Fleet during the Second World War and his achievements in the television industry, describing him as 'a very remarkable man'. BARRIE MACDONALD

Sources WWW · *The Times* (10 Oct 1967) · A. Cunningham [first Viscount Cunningham], *A sailor's odyssey: the autobiography of admiral of the fleet, Viscount Cunningham of Hyndhope* (1951) · O. Warner, *Cunningham of Hyndhope: admiral of the fleet* (1967) · Navy List (1919–52) · citations for distinguished service order awards, *The Times* (15 Nov 1944) · T. M. Brownrigg, 'Balance', *Fusion*, 2 (1958), 8–9 [magazine of Rediffusion Television] · T. M. Brownrigg, 'We want better quality programmes', *Fusion*, 8 (1959), 22–3 · T. M. Brownrigg, 'The general manager's farewell', *Fusion*, 33 (1963), 3–4 · R. Everett, 'A very remarkable man', *Fusion*, 48–9 (1967), 7–8 · P. Hunt, 'A third man's view', *Fusion*, 48–9 (1967), 8–9 · B. Sendall,

Origin and foundation, 1946–62 (1982), vol. 1 of *Independent television in Britain* (1982–90) · b. cert. · m. cert. · d. cert.
Archives priv. coll., unpublished draft of his memoirs | FILM IWM FVA, HMS *Scylla* at the Normandy landings, 7 June 1944, Film ref: ADM 1256
Likenesses A. John, pencil sketch, c.1927–1929, priv. coll. · photograph, 1960–67, priv. coll. [see illus.] · C. Dobson, oils (commissioned by Associated Rediffusion), priv. coll.
Wealth at death £64,624: probate, 1 March 1968, CGPLA Eng. & Wales · English probate resealed in Hong Kong, 22 July 1968, CGPLA Eng. & Wales

Brownrigg, William (1711–1800), physician and chemist, was born at High Close Hall, Cumberland, on 24 March 1711, the eldest of seven children of George Brownrigg (d. c.1760). After being apprenticed to a local physician and then studying medicine in London, 1733–5, he completed his education at the University of Leiden under Hermann Boerhaave, graduating MD in 1736. His thesis, *De praxi medica ineundi* (1737), was a manual for physicians about to enter the profession.

In early 1737 Brownrigg settled in Whitehaven, Cumberland, a port town noted for its coal trade. His practice grew and soon he was drawing patients from as far away as 40 miles. On 3 August 1741 he married Mary (1721–1794), the charming and vivacious daughter of John Spedding of Whitehaven, steward for the Lowther family estates. The Brownriggs had no children.

Explosions, fires, and bad air which killed, maimed, and debilitated miners, led Brownrigg to explore the nature of mine gases. This work, the first of its type, resulted in four papers which were read before the Royal Society during 1741–2 but which, except for one abstract, were not published. On the strength of this work, Brownrigg was elected fellow of the Royal Society on 20 May 1742. The following year Sir James Lowther, owner of the Whitehaven coalmines and Brownrigg's sponsor in the Royal Society, paid half the costs of building a laboratory for him, the furnaces of which were heated by fire-damp (methane) piped from the mines. Brownrigg learned to predict mine explosions by reductions in barometric pressure, helped perfect a flint-on-steel continuous sparking device for mine lighting, and outlined, but did not publish, a history of coalmines.

In addition to his work on mine gases, Brownrigg engaged in a range of scientific enquiries with practical import. His illustrated 295-page book, *The Art of Making Common Salt* (1748), covers both processes and economics and calls on government to build and manage salt works and to regulate salt quality. An abridgement was published in the *Philosophical Transactions of the Royal Society* and an edition came out in the American colonies in 1776. He also issued the first scientific report on the properties of platinum, which he based on experiments made by the assayer Charles Wood, using samples which Wood brought from the West Indies in 1741. Finally, in 1756, he showed that the efficiency of steam engines could be increased by agitating the water in the boiler and by superheating the steam in pipes passed either through the boiler's firebox or up its flue, technology which was not adopted for another century.

Besides his medical and scientific pursuits, Brownrigg invested both time and money in a rope factory, iron mining, timber production, turnpike construction, farms, and farm improvements. He also promoted tourism in the area, acted as political agent for Sir James Lowther, and held sinecures of patent searcher and receiver general of taxes.

In 1766 the Royal Society awarded Brownrigg its highest honour, the Copley medal, for his work on the 'mineral elastic spirit or air' contained in water from the German resort town of Spa (*PTRS*, 55, 1765, 218–35). This award placed him among the most eminent scientists of the time and encouraged him into further research. According to J. Dixon, his first biographer, Brownrigg pioneered the use of the pneumatic trough for collecting 'airs', but it seems that John Mayow (1641–1679) used a similar apparatus much earlier. However Brownrigg was the first person to recognize that there were different gases, not just different forms of air, and to show that the fixed air emitted by mineral water was exactly the same as that emitted in fermentation. He was also the first to recognize the acid nature of fixed air, and to show its toxic effects on animal life and that water solutions of it dissolve calcium and iron oxides. He was interested in both botany and mineralogy and his last published article described twenty specimens of various mine salts. His paper on woollen cloth manufacture and a book on the history of Cumberland were never published.

From the start of his medical career, Brownrigg kept detailed case histories on his patients. He came to believe that disease was spread by direct contact, and was a strong advocate of quarantine. Following the outbreak of the plague in Europe in 1771, he published a forty-page book on the causes and prevention of contagion. He was one of the founders of the Whitehaven Dispensary in 1783 and served as vice-president until his death in 1800. He studied the classics, knew French, Greek, and Latin, was an excellent mathematician, and an astute agriculturist. Contemporaries described him as kind, amiable, polite, modest, and benevolent. Although a devout Christian, he was accused of 'infidelity and irreligion' (Dixon, 89).

About 1770 Brownrigg went to live in semi-retirement at Ormathwaite, his villa near Keswick, where he built a fine laboratory, mineral museum, art collection, and library. In 1772 Benjamin Franklin, while a house guest there, experimented during a storm with stilling the waves on Derwentwater by pouring oil on the turbulent surface. When poor management led Brownrigg into financial difficulty, he was saved from ruin by a young relative. After his wife died in 1794 his mind began to fail, and he came to need supervised care. He died on 6 January 1800 at the age of eighty-eight, and was buried on 12 January at Crosthwaite church. A plaque honouring him and his wife was placed in the chancel there. HERBERT T. PRATT

Sources J. Russell-Wood, 'A biographical note on William Brownrigg', *Annals of Science*, 6 (1948–50), 186–96 · J. Russell-Wood, 'The scientific work of William Brownrigg [pt 1]', *Annals of Science*, 6 (1948–50), 436–47 · J. Russell-Wood, 'The scientific work of William Brownrigg [pts 2–3]', *Annals of Science*, 7 (1951), 77–94, 199– 206 · J. E. Ward and J. Yell, eds. and trans., *The medical casebook of William Brownrigg* (1993) · J. V. Beckett, 'Dr William Brownrigg, FRS: physician, chemist and country gentleman', *Notes and Records of the Royal Society*, 31 (1976–7), 255–71 · J. R. Partington, *A history of chemistry*, 3 (1962), 123–7 · J. Dixon, *The literary life of William Brownrigg, MD, FRS* (1801) · *GM*, 1st ser., 70 (1800), 386–8 · D. McDonald, *A history of platinum: from the earliest times to the eighteen-eighties* (1960), 23–5 · D. I. Duveen, *Bibliotheca alchemica et chemica* (1986), 104 · *A scientific autobiography of Joseph Priestley*, ed. R. E. Schofield (1966), 130

Archives Cumbria AS, Carlisle, accounts and papers · RS · Tullie House Library, Carlisle, casebook | American Philosophical Society, Philadelphia, Franklin MSS · BL OIOC, corresp. with Sir John Benn Walsh, MS Eur. D 546 · Cumbria AS, Carlisle, Lonsdale MSS · Cumbria AS, Carlisle, Lord Ormathwaite MSS · Linn. Soc., Ellis MSS

Likenesses oils, *c.*1790–1795, West Cumberland Hospital, Whitehaven

Wealth at death had £8000 of debts by 1781; paid off by relative in exchange for estate after death: Beckett, 'Dr William Brownrigg'

Brownswerd, John (*d.* 1589), poet and schoolmaster, was probably born in Cheshire in or near Witton, where he attended the grammar school. There he was taught by John Bracegirdle, a zealous reformer 'putting to flight the shadows of loathsome error' (Fripp, 768), to whom he paid tribute in several Latin poems. Wood in his *Athenae Oxonienses*, on which most later accounts of Brownswerd's life are based, claims that he attended both Oxford and Cambridge, but no trace of him has been found except in records which are based on Wood. His first post was probably as a teacher of grammar at the school in Wilmslow; in a poem addressed to Bracegirdle he complained of scanty leisure, poverty, and tiresome rivals. He had a connection with Manchester grammar school as he dedicated poems to two high masters and a trustee, Sir Edmund Trafford. Thomas Brownswerd, almost certainly a relative of John, received the remainder of a messuage and 40 acres in Stretford, Lancashire, from Trafford's son in 1569.

Brownswerd seems to have conformed outwardly during Mary's reign, as he kept his employment and one of his poems is a hymn to the virgin. He also wrote a poem deploring the discord in Manchester church in 1560, but his cautious language and the absence of firm evidence make it unclear what he was referring to. In January 1561 he was appointed to the free grammar school at Macclesfield as headmaster, with a salary of £13 6s. 8d. Perhaps it was to be near his mentor, Bracegirdle, that he moved to the school at Old Burgess Hall, Warwick, in September 1564; he taught there until March 1565. Brownswerd then transferred to Stratford upon Avon, where Bracegirdle was the minister; the latter had removed Romish ornaments from the church and supervised repairs, including the refurbishment of the headmaster's house by John Shakespeare (father of William). Brownswerd had a wife by this time, as she is mentioned in his contract with the Stratford bailiff and burgesses. He agreed to 'serve in their Free School, as a good and diligent schoolmaster ought to do, for the term of two years … in consideration of the sum of £20 yearly and his dwelling house' (Fripp, 773). Bracegirdle died in June of the same year leaving two books by near contemporaries to Brownswerd in his will,

Musculus upon Mathew (Wolfgang Musculus, a Calvinist teacher and preacher from Lorraine) and *Homilia Nauseae* (Frederick Nausea, bishop of Vienna, the author of several *Homilies*).

There were draconian penalties should Brownswerd break his contract and he worked out his two years at Stratford. He then returned to Macclesfield and resumed his post as headmaster (his former pupil, Thomas Newton, had taught there during his absence) which he retained until the year before his death, in Macclesfield, in 1589. He was buried in the church and there is a memorial tablet to him on the south wall of the chancel. Brinsley's *Grammar Schoole* (1612) bears witness to Brownswerd's fame as a schoolmaster, praising his method of teaching Latin, and he is cited by Simon (1966) for maintaining good educational standards. His Latin poems survive in a 56-page volume, *Joannis Brunsuerdi, Maclesfeldensis gymnasiarchae progymnasmata quaedam poetica* (1590), through the piety of Thomas Newton who published them. Newton is better known than his teacher as he translated Latin works into English and is occasionally mentioned in modern studies; the most recent literary reference to Brownswerd which has been found is in Warton (1778)—his elegant classicism was not admired by vernacular writers. MARGARET LUCILLE KEKEWICH

Sources *Joannis Brunsuerdi, Maclesfeldensis gymnasiarchae progymnasmata quaedam poetica*, ed. T. Newton (1590) · Wood, *Ath. Oxon.*, 1st edn, 1.194 · J. Simon, *Education and society in Tudor England* (1966), 362 · E. I. Fripp, 'The minister who baptised Shakespeare', *Hibbert Journal*, 18 (1919–20), 767–75 · *VCH Warwickshire*, vol. 2 · *VCH Lancashire*, vol. 4 · *VCH Cheshire*, vol. 3 · D. Wilmot, *A short history of the grammar school, Macclesfield, 1503 to 1910* (1910) · T. Warton, *The history of English poetry*, 4 vols. (1774–81), vol. 3, p. 878 · J. Brinsley, *Ludus literarius, or, The grammar schoole* (1612), 84 · G. Ormerod, *The history of the county palatine and city of Chester*, 3 (1819), 287, 366
Archives BL, Add. MS 5864, fol. 19r

Broxbourne. For this title name *see* Smith, Derek Colclough Walker-, Baron Broxbourne (1910–1992).

Broxholme, Noel (1686–1748), physician, the son of Robert Broxholme, was probably born at Stamford, Lincolnshire. He was admitted on the foundation at Westminster School in 1700, and in 1704 was elected to Trinity College, Cambridge. He proceeded, however, to Christ Church, Oxford, where he was nominated student on 23 July 1705, and graduated BA on 20 May 1709 and MA on 18 April 1711. In 1709 he began his medical studies under Richard Mead at St Thomas's Hospital, London, and in 1715 was elected to one of the first of the Radcliffe travelling fellowships. On his return he moved to University College, Oxford, as a member of which he took his degrees in physic by accumulation, proceeding MD on 8 July 1723. Broxholme then began practice in London, was admitted a candidate of the Royal College of Physicians on 23 December 1723, and became a fellow on 22 March 1725. He was censor in 1726, and delivered the Harveian oration in 1731.

Broxholme was one of the six physicians appointed to St George's Hospital at the first general board held on 19 October 1733, and in the following year was made first physician to the prince of Wales, 'with salary annexed', an

office which he resigned in 1739. He resigned from his post at St George's Hospital in 1735. At Lord Hervey's suggestion Broxholme was the first physician summoned to assist George Tessier in Queen Caroline's last illness. In 1729 he published *A Letter from a Lady to her Husband Abroad*. Broxholme married on 7 May 1730, at Knightsbridge Chapel, Amy, widow of William Dowdeswell of Pull Court, Worcestershire, daughter of Anthony *Hammond (1668–1738), the wit and poet, and sister of James Hammond (1710–1742). In 1746 Broxholme was the recipient of a *Letter to Dr Sangrado* [i.e. Broxholme], *in answer to Thomsonus redivivus*. Broxholme died at Hampton Court, Middlesex, by his own hand, on 8 July 1748, and was buried on 13 July at Hampton. In his will he bequeathed the sum of £500 for the benefit of the king's scholars at Westminster 'in such manner as the two upper masters of the said school shall think fit', and a like sum to Christ Church 'to be applied towards finishing the library'. Mrs Broxholme survived her husband by six years, dying in 1754.

William Stukeley, a fellow student at St Thomas's Hospital, said that Broxholme

> was a man of wit and gayety, lov'd poetry, was a good classic … got much money in the Misisipi project in France. At length he came over and practised, but never had a great liking to it, tho' he had good encouragement. (*Family Memoirs*, 96)

'He was always nervous and vapoured' wrote Horace Walpole, 'and so good-natured that he left off his practice from not being able to bear seeing so many melancholy objects. I remember him with as much wit as ever I knew' (*Letters*, 120). In 1754 there appeared *A collection of receipts in physic, being the practice of the late eminent Dr. Bloxam* [sic]: *containing a complete body of prescriptions answering to every disease, with some in surgery*. He was an accomplished Latin poet, part of the literary circle that included the physicians John Freind and John Wigan, and the poet Anthony Alsop (whom he assisted to return from exile).

GORDON GOODWIN, rev. KAYE BAGSHAW

Sources Munk, *Roll* · Foster, *Alum. Oxon.* · Venn, *Alum. Cant.* · *N&Q*, 12 (1855), 303, 353, 390 · *N&Q*, 2nd ser., 2 (1856), 249–50 · *GM*, 1st ser., 4 (1734), 628 · *GM*, 1st ser., 7 (1737), 699 · *GM*, 1st ser., 9 (1739), 328 · *GM*, 1st ser., 18 (1748), 333 · *The letters of Horace Walpole, earl of Orford*, ed. P. Cunningham, 2 (1857), 20, 120 · J. Hervey, *Memoirs of the reign of George the Second*, ed. J. W. Croker, 2 vols. (1848), vol. 2, p. 493 · *The family memoirs of the Rev. William Stukeley*, ed. W. C. Lukis, 1, SurtS, 73 (1882), 46, 81, 96 · L. Bradner, *Musae Anglicanae: a history of Anglo-Latin poetry, 1500–1925* (1940) · D. K. Money, *The English Horace: Anthony Alsop and the tradition of British Latin verse* (1998)
Wealth at death left £500 to Westminster School and £500 to Christ Church, Oxford

Bruarne [Bruerne], **Richard** (1519–1565), Hebrew scholar, was born on 10 March 1519, according to a note by him in Hebrew and Latin in his copy of Giralmo Cardona's *Libelli quinti* (1546) in the British Library. He studied at Lincoln College, Oxford, taking his BA on 8 February 1537 and his MA on 2 May 1539. He was appointed a fellow of the college in 1538. In March 1546 he was appointed to the living of Mapledurham, Oxfordshire, but he resigned it a few months later. In 1548 he received a BD degree, was elected a fellow of Eton College, and appointed regius professor of

Hebrew at Oxford. In 1550 he was appointed to Mapledurham again.

Richard Bruarne was Catholic in his religious allegiance. He gave evidence for Bishop Stephen Gardiner at his trial in 1551. On Mary I's accession in 1553, Peter Martyr was dispossessed as a canon of Christ Church and his stall was given to Bruarne. The next year he was one of twelve theologians of Oxford and Cambridge who witnessed a disputation in Oxford with Archbishop Thomas Cranmer, Hugh Latimer, and Bishop Nicholas Ridley on three articles concerning the mass, and judged them guilty of heresy. This action caused him to be detested by the reformers. Mary I rewarded him with a canonry at St George's Chapel, Windsor, and in 1557 Cardinal Pole appointed him to the living of St Dunstan's-in-the-East, London, which he held until his death.

In 1559, soon after the accession of Elizabeth, Bruarne was obliged to resign his Oxford chair and the living at Mapledurham after being detected in a homosexual relationship with an undergraduate, Roger *Marbeck. On 25 July 1561 the fellows of Eton College elected him as their provost without seeking the queen's permission. Edmund Grindal, bishop of London, wrote to Sir William Cecil:

> It is a shame that such a sort of hedge priests should presume so far upon an obsolete statute, knowing the Queen's Majesty's prerogative so long exercised without interruption, and that they should do it *impune* or that it should stand in force. (*CSP dom.*, 1547–80, 183)

The queen appointed Matthew Parker, archbishop of Canterbury, Robert Horne, bishop of Winchester, and Sir Anthony Cook as visitors to Eton to investigate and correct the matter. They took evidence there and at St George's Chapel in September 1561. Bruarne's enemies came forward with copious denunciations. He was accused of popery, adultery, conjuring with the aid of a familiar spirit, and Judaizing (by eating a paschal lamb at Easter). The visitors deprived several of the Eton fellows, accepted Bruarne's resignation, and ordered the college to pay him £10 in compensation. When in 1562 he supplicated for a DD at Oxford it was refused, no doubt because of his role in the trial of Cranmer, Latimer, and Ridley.

In 1563 the library at Christ Church, Oxford, was founded. Bruarne, who was receiver of the college, gave it a fine English medieval Hebrew manuscript Pentateuch, recording the donation on the flyleaf in ungrammatical Hebrew, marred by an incorrect use of the construct case (MS1, Westminster Abbey Library). Bruarne also owned a nine-volume folio Talmud (now in the Valmadonna Library, London), and a copy of Isaac Arama's *Akedat Yitzhak* (now at Westminster Abbey), both printed by Daniel Bomberg, bound in Oxford, and stamped with his initials. After Bruarne's death in 1565, Thomas Sampson, dean of Christ Church, complained to Archbishop Parker that a large sum due from him to the college was unaccounted for. At the time of his death, Bruarne had been vicar of Sherborne in Dorset, and also possessed the advowson of Kiddermorton, Leicestershire. He left his residuary estate to Raphael and Robert Bruarne, sons of William Bruarne of Bury, Lancashire, who were probably his nephews. He

was buried in St George's Chapel, Windsor. Richard Bruarne was a pioneer in the revival of Hebrew in England. The inscription in his manuscript Pentateuch shows that his Hebrew was rudimentary, but there was then little competition among English students of the scriptural tongues and he was reputed an expert.

EDGAR SAMUEL

Sources R. Bruarne, MS notes in G. Cardona, *Libelli quinti* (1546), BL · R. Bruarne, flyleaf inscription, Westminster Abbey Library, MS 1 · Foster, *Alum. Oxon.* · H. C. Maxwell Lyte, *A history of Eton College, 1440–1910*, 4th edn (1911) · *Report on manuscripts in various collections*, 8 vols., HMC, 55 (1901–14), vol. 7, p. 35, document XV.19 [St George's Chapel, Windsor] · E. Samuel, 'The provenance of the Westminster Talmud', *Transactions of the Jewish Historical Society of England*, 27 (1978–80), 148–50 · J. Strype, *Memorials of the most reverend father in God Thomas Cranmer*, new edn, 2 vols. (1840), vol. 2, p. 1090 · *Correspondence of Matthew Parker*, ed. J. Bruce and T. T. Perowne, Parker Society, 42 (1853), 150 · J. Fines, '"Judaising" in the period of the English Reformation—the case of Richard Bruern', *Transactions of the Jewish Historical Society of England*, 21 (1962–7), 323–6 · *The acts and monuments of John Foxe*, ed. S. R. Cattley, 8 vols. (1837–41), vol. 6, pp. 213, 500 · D. Goldstein, 'Hebrew printed books in the library of Westminster Abbey', *Transactions of the Jewish Historical Society of England*, 27 (1978–80), 151–4 · *The works of John Jewel*, ed. J. Ayre, 4 vols., Parker Society, 24 (1845–50), vol. 4, pp. 1199, 1201 · *Fasti Angl.* (Hardy), 2.54 · *CSP dom.*, 1547–80 · Tanner, *Bibl. Brit.-Hib.* · H. Robinson, ed. and trans., *The Zurich letters, comprising the correspondence of several English bishops and others with some of the Helvetian reformers, during the early part of the reign of Queen Elizabeth*, 1, Parker Society, 7 (1842), 12, 66 · *DNB* · PRO, PROB 11/48, sig. 13

Archives BL, MS inscription in Giralmo Cardona, *Libelli quinti* · Valmadonna Trust, Babylonian Talmud, specimens of Hebrew handwriting · Westminster Abbey Library, flyleaf inscription, MS 1

Wealth at death possessed living at Sherborne, Dorset and advowson at Kiddermorton, Leicestershire: will, PRO, PROB 11/48 sig. 13

Bruce, Alexander, earl of Carrick (d. 1333). *See under Bruce, Edward, earl of Carrick (c.1280–1318).*

Bruce, Alexander, second earl of Kincardine (c.1629–1680), landowner and politician, was the second son of Sir George Bruce (d. 1643) and his wife, Mary, daughter of Sir John Preston of Valleyfield. In 1645 Bruce matriculated at St Leonard's College, St Andrews. Probably on account of his involvement in the royalist cause, Bruce left Scotland in 1657, initially settling at the White Swan inn at Bremen, from where he started a remarkable correspondence with Sir Robert Moray which lasted until Moray's death in 1673. Over 100 of Moray's letters to Bruce survive, encompassing discussions of chemistry, physics, mathematics, mining, horticulture, divinity, heraldry, and moral philosophy. When Bruce became ill with the ague in 1658, Moray entertained his friend with 'letters of 5 or 6 houres long', not expecting Bruce to reciprocate likewise, but acknowledging his desire 'to set every line I get from you in diamonds' (NL Scot., MS 5049, fols. 113, 111). Following his recovery Bruce moved to Hamburg where he collaborated with Hugen de Zulinchem and Christiaan Huygens in attempts to devise a pendulum clock that could be used at sea to determine longitude. By a contract dated 19 June 1659 Bruce married Veronica (c.1633–1701), daughter of Cornelius van Arsen, Baron Somelsdyk, with whom he

Alexander Bruce, second earl of Kincardine (*c*.1629–1680), by Adriaen Hanneman, *c*.1660

had five sons, three of whom died in infancy, and four daughters.

Following Charles II's restoration Bruce returned to his Scottish family estate at Culross where extensive stone and marble quarries, coalmines, and salt works had been established by his grandfather, Sir George *Bruce (*c*.1550–1625). Having attended the foundation meeting of the Royal Society on 28 November 1660, Bruce was duly encouraged by Moray to 'behave your self lyke a true member of the Royall Society' (NL Scot., MS 5049, fol. 104) by communicating detailed accounts of subterranean mining experiments conducted at Culross and he duly became a fellow on 20 May 1663. In 1662 Bruce succeeded as second earl of Kincardine following the death of his elder brother, Edward (who had gained the title in 1647), and thereafter assumed responsibility for managing the family's commercial enterprises. Visiting Greenwich with Charles II in 1664 Moray informed Kincardine that he had seen masons 'laying some of your stone' and that the king had 'lyked your stone well' (ibid., fol. 138). Charles evidently also contemplated using Portland stone from Culross at Whitehall and in the interior of St Paul's Cathedral but was dissuaded by the punitive import duties levied upon Scottish stone. At this time Kincardine also became involved in a protracted dispute with Huygens over patenting rights for their earlier chronometric experiments. Regarding a specific mechanism, Bruce protested that he was 'sure it was my inventione', confident that 'any rationall man will judge that no other person should pretend the advantages of this inventione' (NL Scot., MS

5050, fol. 122). A relevant patent was granted in the Royal Society's name in 1665.

According to the testimony of his friend Gilbert Burnet, however, Kincardine took 'a wrong turn' in sacrificing the financial welfare of his Culross estates to civic duty (*Burnet's History*, 1.189). Since Moray remarked in August 1665 that it was 'easy for me to judge you are in straights', public employment provided lucrative potential (NL Scot., MS 5050, fol. 145). Kincardine's initial attempts to secure public office were, however, frustrated by Archbishop James Sharp of St Andrews, who allegedly informed Charles II that Kincardine had attended an unauthorized presbyterian service in his home parish of Tollialoun. Incensed, Kincardine decided to 'expostulat with a freedom beyond ordinar', informing Sharp that he considered 'a well ordered Episcopacy the best of Governments' and judged himself 'bound in conscience to defend Episcopacie with my lyfe & fortune, so long as his Matie & the laws are for it' (BL, Add. MS 23123, fols. 220, 223).

During the Pentland rising of 1666 Kincardine commanded a troop of horse and was made an extraordinary lord of session the following year on 10 July 1667. After the Scottish Treasury was put into commission, he became a Treasury commissioner on 3 September 1668. As policy towards religious nonconformity fluctuated between coercion and conciliation, Kincardine acknowledged to John Maitland, earl of Lauderdale, that he supported 'a qualified toleration, but I wold have it given & not taken' (Airy, *Lauderdale Papers*, 3.125). Participating in an episcopalian evangelizing tour of south-west Scotland in April 1670 he remained wary of the inflammatory potential of unlicensed extempore preaching, wishing that 'the people may have the Scriptures read to them without their glosses', so that 'the perspicuity of the Scriptures may be asserted in their practice' (NL Scot., MS 7004, fols. 48, 33).

As a Treasury commissioner Kincardine attended the inconclusive negotiations held to consider increased commercial and parliamentary union between Scotland and England during 1669–70. Endorsing the benefits of union, he declared himself 'glad w^t all my heart [that] they beginne to talk seriously of the union wch is the only remedi I can thing of' for the 'great many evills that are upon us' (NL Scot., MS 7003, fol. 172). Keen to remove economic prejudices against Scottish traders, he also attempted to interest Moray and Lauderdale in founding a Scottish East India Company in 1671, believing that the establishment of Scottish plantations would render the future commercial enterprises of both Scottish colonists and banished convicts of economic benefit to Scotland, not England. At home, however, Kincardine benefited personally from prevalent attachment to economic protectionism when a new salt monopoly was created and responsibility for collecting the relevant customs and excise duties was granted to him for an annual rent of £2000 Scots. Since all salt imports were banned, unless for use by the fishing industry, 'complaints throng'd in daily' as salt prices allegedly quadrupled (Mackenzie, 243). As opposition escalated, Kincardine 'most handsomely offered to lay down' the five-year monopoly in November 1673, receiving compensation of £2000 (Airy, *Lauderdale Papers*, 3.244).

When attempts were made to impeach the duke of Lauderdale for misgovernment in Scotland by the English House of Commons in January 1674, Kincardine refused to testify, protesting that the Commons 'could pretend no jurisdiction over Scotland' (Airy, *Lauderdale Papers*, 3.32). In mid-1674, however, he withdrew his support from Lauderdale and was 'reputed by all worthy to succeed him in his office as Secretary' of Scotland. According to his cousin Sir George Mackenzie of Rosehaugh, however, Kincardine's failure to secure promotion was engineered by the duchess of Lauderdale. Inferring that Kincardine's presence in London was connected with the Commons' impeachment, she observed him 'in frequent conversations' with his 'strict friend', Burnet, who had already testified against Lauderdale. Mutual suspicion between Kincardine and Lauderdale thereafter grew 'soon into an open rupture' as both politicians 'most foolishly embark'd in a war, wherein neither could expect honour or success' (Mackenzie, 314–16). According to a contemporary anecdote circulating in May 1675, when Lauderdale noticed Kincardine and Charles II conversing in St James's Park he immediately hurried over, placing himself between so as to 'put his face to the King's face ... and his breech to E. Kincardin's bellie', forcing Kincardine to retire (letter, J. Turner to earl of Arran, 3 June 1675, NA Scot., GD 406/1/2881).

When Kincardine later challenged the legality by which the covenanter James Kirkton was prosecuted, the Scottish privy council requested Charles II to adopt 'some speedie cours to prevent these obstructions in the future' (Airy, *Lauderdale Papers*, 3.84). Implicated as disloyal, Kincardine was removed from the council on 12 July 1676. Having defected from Lauderdale's faction, Kincardine did not immediately join the duke of Hamilton's opposition, preferring instead 'to stand upon his oune legs at court' (ibid., 3.78). The duchess of Lauderdale was likewise informed that Kincardine's heart was 'full of resentment' (ibid., 3.82) as he allegedly endeavoured 'to give a bad character' of Lauderdale and his wife 'unto persons he judges inclinable to receive a bad impression' (BL, Add. MS. 23138, fol. 3).

Kincardine's heir, Charles, died on 12 January 1680 and Kincardine himself died on 9 July, survived by his wife, who died on 28 April 1701; he was succeeded as third earl by his second son, Alexander (*bap.* 1666, *d.* 1705). Kincardine was buried in the Bruce family chapel at Culross. Described by Sir George Mackenzie as being 'naturally stiff' (Mackenzie, 316), according to Burnet, Kincardine was 'both the wisest and the worthiest man that belonged to his country'. As Burnet recalled, Kincardine's 'thoughts were slow, and his words came much slower: but a deep judgement appeared in every thing he said or did' (*Burnet's History*, 1.189).   CLARE JACKSON

Sources O. Airy, 'Correspondence of Sir Robert Moray with Alexander Bruce, 2nd earl of Kincardine', *Scottish Review*, 5 (1885), 22–43 · A. J. Youngson, 'Alexander Bruce F.R.S., 2nd earl of Kincardine (1629–1681)', *The Royal Society*, ed. H. Hartley (1960), 251–8 · R. Moray, letters to the earl of Kincardine (transcripts), 2 vols., 1657–74, NL Scot., MSS 5049–5050 · C. Dobell, 'The Kincardine papers', *Notes and Records of the Royal Society*, 4 (1946), 174–8 · O. Airy, ed., *The Lauderdale papers*, 3 vols. (1884–5) · *Burnet's History of my own time*, ed. O. Airy, new edn, 2 vols. (1897–1900) · G. Mackenzie, *Memoirs of the affairs of Scotland from the restoration of King Charles II* (1822) · acta rectorum, U. St Andr. L., MS VI/503/3 · earl of Kincardine to earl of Tweeddale, 3 Nov 1668, NL Scot., MS 7003, fol. 172 · NL Scot., MS 7004, fols. 33, 48 · NL Scot., Tweeddale MSS · James Turner to earl of Arran, 3 June 1675, NA Scot., GD 406/1/2881 · earl of Kincardine to Archbishop James Sharp, BL, Add. MS 23123, fols. 220, 223 · Lauderdale papers, BL, Add. MS 23138, fol. 3 · *Scots peerage* · monument, Bruce family chapel, Culross, Fife

Archives NL Scot., corresp. and papers · NL Scot., lecture notes | BL, letters to Lauderdale, Charles II, etc., Add. MSS 23114–23137 · Buckminster Park, Grantham, Lincolnshire, corresp. with duke of Lauderdale · NL Scot., letters to marquess of Tweeddale

Likenesses A. Hanneman, portrait, *c.*1660, priv. coll. [*see illus.*]

Wealth at death obtained dowry from wife's family of 80,000 guilders (1659): *Scots peerage*; Youngson, 'Alexander Bruce'

Bruce, Alexander (*d.* 1729), lawyer, was the second son of Andrew Bruce (*d.* 1696) of Earlshall, Fife, and his cousin and second wife, Anna, daughter of Robert Bruce, minister of Ballingry, Fife, and Anna, daughter of George Seaton. He may have been the Alexander Bruce who matriculated at Leiden in 1694, but the name is not uncommon. He was admitted advocate on 5 December 1702.

Bruce was the author of a number of legal works, including *Disputatio juridica de re militari* (1702), *Principia juris feudalis* (1713), *Tutor's guide, or, Principles of civil and municipal laws and customs relating to pupils and minors and their tutors or curators* (1714), and *An Institute of Military Law, Ancient and Modern* (1717). Of these the *Principia juris feudalis* is noted by Professor John Girvan as perhaps 'entitled to a passing reference in respect of the freshness with which he handles from the time to time the subject' (McKechnie, 204), while D. M. Walker notes that the *Institute of Military Law* 'shows considerable learning and acquaintance with continental jurists' (Walker, 304). Indeed, in all these works Bruce treated Scots law within a framework of the learned *jus commune* of Europe.

In 1713 Bruce was appointed collector of decisions for the Faculty of Advocates in succession to William Forbes. He planned to compile a dictionary of decisions from the institution of the college of justice, but this grand scheme made little progress. He produced *Decisions* for 1714/15, published in 1720 and also bound with Lord Kames's *Remarkable Decisions* (1728). His *Decisions* for 1716/17 were printed in 1772 as a supplement to the third volume of *Faculty Collections*. The Faculty of Advocates' minute book discloses Bruce's steady decline into illness, poverty, and debt, and his many appeals to the faculty for financial assistance. He was dismissed from his post as collector in 1723. He continued until 1725 as clerk of the Faculty of Advocates, much of this work, however, being done by Thomas Ruddiman, the clerk depute. James Boswell refers to him as 'poor Bruce' (*Applause of the Jury*, 18). Bruce married, on 24 April 1698, Janet, daughter of William Home, a merchant in Edinburgh; they had at least six children. She predeceased him in 1726. Alexander Bruce died on 6

August 1729. His son, Andrew (d. 1745), who was disabled, became a faculty pensioner. Two of his daughters, Anne and Barbara, were still drawing a faculty pension as late as 1778. W. D. H. SELLAR

Sources F. J. Grant, ed., *The Faculty of Advocates in Scotland, 1532–1943*, Scottish RS, 145 (1944) • M. D. Young, ed., *The parliaments of Scotland: burgh and shire commissioners*, 2 vols. (1992–3) • J. M. Pinkerton, ed., *The minute book of the Faculty of Advocates*, 1: *1661–1712*, Stair Society, 29 (1976) • J. M. Pinkerton, ed., *The minute book of the Faculty of Advocates*, 2: *1713–1750*, Stair Society, 32 (1980) • A. Stewart, ed., *The minute book of the Faculty of Advocates*, 3: *1751–1783*, Stair Society, 46 (1999) • H. McKechnie, ed., *An introductory survey of the sources and literature of Scots law*, Stair Society, 1 (1936) • D. M. Walker, *The Scottish jurists* (1985) • *Boswell: the applause of the jury, 1782–1785*, ed. I. S. Lustig and F. A. Pottle (1982), vol. 12 of *The Yale editions of the private papers of James Boswell*, trade edn (1950–89) • I. S. Ross, *Lord Kames and the Scotland of his day* (1972) • R. Douglas and others, *The baronage of Scotland* (1798) • G. du Rieu, ed., *Album studiosorum academiae Lugduno Batavae, MDLXXV–MDCCCLXXV: accedunt nomina curatorum et professorum per eadem secula* (The Hague, 1875)

Bruce, Alexander Balmain (1831–1899), Free Church of Scotland minister and theologian, was born at West Lodge, Dupplin, in the Perthshire parish of Aberdalgie on 13 January 1831, the son of David Bruce, a farmer and joiner, and his wife, Margaret Robertson. Bruce received his early education at Auchterarder parish school. At about the time of the Disruption, which occurred in May 1843 and resulted in the creation of the Free Church of Scotland under the moderatorship of Thomas Chalmers, the Bruce family moved to Edinburgh, where Bruce continued his studies, entering first Edinburgh University in 1845, then the Divinity Hall of the Free Church of Scotland in 1849. His studies precipitated a profound crisis of faith which, however painful it may have been for the young scholar, seems to have contributed to the richness of the critical insights characteristic of his mature scholarship.

Upon completion of his studies in Edinburgh, Bruce entered the ministry of the Free Church, and served as assistant minister at Ancrum, in Roxburghshire, and Lochwinnoch, in Renfrewshire, until in 1859 he became minister in Cardross, Dunbartonshire, where he remained for nine years. While serving as minister in Cardross he delivered to the congregation a series of lectures on the gospels, which would be published in 1871 under the title *The Training of the Twelve* (2nd edn, 1877). Bruce, in 1868, accepted a call to become minister of the east Free Church at Broughty Ferry, Forfarshire. In 1874 he presented the Cunningham lectures in Edinburgh. His lectures provided a meticulous survey of the doctrine of Christology from the primitive church to those theologians contemporary with the author; it was published as *The Humiliation of Christ* (1876; 2nd edn, 1881). Bruce continued as minister in Broughty Ferry until 1875, when he was appointed to the chair of apologetics and New Testament exegesis in the Free Church Hall at Glasgow, following the death of Patrick Fairbairn (1805–1874). As an apologist Bruce refused to accept as a final position 'either the agnosticism of modern culture, or blind adherence to traditional dogmatism' (A. B. Bruce, *The Chief End of Revelation*, 1881). His work as a biblical scholar (as seen in *The Kingdom of God, or, Christ's Teaching According to the Synoptical*

Gospels, 1889; 2nd and 3rd edn, 1890) was marked by an appreciation for the emerging field of biblical criticism, leavened with modesty and Christian piety. As a teacher, during his twenty-four years in Glasgow, he has been characterized as exercising a strong influence over his students, 'both from his wide knowledge and on account of the magnetism of his mind' (*DNB*).

Bruce's appreciation for biblical criticism evoked both censure and respect: 'He and William Robertson Smith were the first Scottish scholars whose authority was regarded with respect among German biblical critics' (*DNB*). But Bruce, Smith, and Marcus Dods all faced considerable criticism in their ecclesiastical context because of their treatment of biblical texts. Bruce's statement of defence for Smith in 1881, when Smith was removed from his professorship in the Free Church college at Aberdeen, argued that the church should embrace a future 'in which she shall appear orthodox yet not illiberal, evangelical yet not Pharisaical, believing yet not afraid in inquiry' (Black and Chrystal, 439). Nearly a decade later, in 1890, Bruce and Dods were themselves called before the general assembly of the Free Church to answer for their own writings, following the publication of Bruce's *The Kingdom of God* (1889); but the assembly pronounced their writings consistent with the standards of that church. The moderate tone of Bruce's critical studies is demonstrated especially well in his 1886 Ely lectures at Union Theological Seminary, New York (published as *The Miraculous Element in the Gospels*, 1886), and in the essay 'Ferdinand Christian Baur and his theory of the origins of Christianity and of the New Testament writings' (published in *Present Day Tracts on the Higher Criticism*, 1888).

In addition to his contributions to biblical studies, Bruce also invested significant effort in Christian apologetics, writing *Apologetics, or, Christianity Defensively Stated* (1892), and serving as Gifford lecturer in Glasgow University for 1896–7. The lectures were published under the titles *The Providential Order of the World* (1897) and *The Moral Order of the World in Ancient and Modern Thought* (1899). Bruce described his task as an apologist to be 'a preparer of the way of faith, an aid to faith against doubts whencesoever arising, especially such as are engendered by philosophy and science' (A. B. Bruce, *Apologetics*, 1892, 37). His biblical and apologetical studies coincided in his 1899 publication *The Epistle to the Hebrews: the First Apology for Christianity* (1899), which Bruce understood as a companion to *The Kingdom of God* and *St Paul's Conception of Christianity* (1894). Other major works by Bruce included *The Parabolic Teaching of Christ* (1882), *The Galilean Gospel* (1884), *The Life of William Denny* (1888), *With Open Face, or, Jesus Mirrored in Matthew, Mark, and Luke* (1896), and the synoptic gospels in the Expositor's Greek Testament (ed. W. R. Nicoll, 1897).

Bruce was active in the life of the Free Church, serving as convenor of hymnal committees that published in 1882 the *Free Church Hymn Book* and in 1888 the *Church Hymnary* for use in all Scottish presbyterian churches. Beginning in 1894 he also assisted T. K. Cheyne in editing the Theological Translation Library. On 1 May 1860 Bruce married Jane Hunter Walker (b. 1832/3), the daughter of James

Walker of Fodderslee, Roxburghshire, and his wife, Janet Gladstone. He died on 7 August 1899 at 32 Hamilton Park Terrace, Glasgow, and was buried on 10 August at Broughty Ferry. He was survived by his wife, a son, David, and a daughter.   MICHAEL JINKINS

Sources *Glasgow Herald* (8 Aug 1899) · *The Scotsman* (8 Aug 1899) · J. S. Black and G. Chrystal, *The life of William Robertson Smith* (1912) · A. L. Drummond and J. Bulloch, *The church in late Victorian Scotland* (1978) · *DNB* · parish register (baptism), Aberdalgie, Perth, 20/2/1831 · m. cert.
Wealth at death £5316 12s. 2d.: confirmation, 30 Oct 1899, *CCI*

Bruce, Alexander Hugh, sixth Lord Balfour of Burleigh (1849–1921), politician, was born at Kennet, Alloa, on 13 January 1849, the only son of Robert Bruce of Kennet (1795–1864), MP for Clackmannanshire, and his second wife, Jane Dalrymple Hamilton, daughter of Sir James Fergusson of Kilkerran, fourth baronet. His ancestor Robert *Balfour, fifth Lord Balfour of Burleigh, was attainted in 1716, and the title was restored in 1869. He was educated at Loretto School, Musselburgh, and at Eton College, and graduated in 1871 at Oriel College, Oxford, with a second class in law and modern history. On 21 November 1876 he married Lady Katherine Eliza (1852–1931), youngest daughter of George John James Hamilton-Gordon, fifth earl of Aberdeen (1816–1864), and his wife, Mary, *née* Baillie (d. 1900). They had two sons and three daughters, of whom the youngest was Victoria *Bruce, governor of Aylesbury girls' borstal. After leaving Oxford, Balfour of Burleigh began a strenuous public career. Unusual among the Scottish peers of the late nineteenth century in being an able Conservative, Balfour of Burleigh became in 1876 a representative peer for Scotland, and sat in the Lords in that capacity until his death. His Conservatism was largely a product of his establishmentarianism. His shrewdness, business ability, and sound knowledge of local government were early recognized; and his biography is largely a record of his work on royal and other commissions, the reports of which became authoritative documents, noted especially for their thorough accumulation of evidence rather than for any startling line of recommendation. He was chairman of the royal commission on Sunday closing in Wales (1881–90), the educational endowments commission (1882–9), the metropolitan water supply commission (1893–4), the rating commission (1896), the royal commission on local taxation (1899–1902), the cable communications inter-departmental committee (1902), the royal commission on food supply in time of war (1903), the Lords' select committee on overseas life insurance (1906), the royal commission on closer trade relations between Canada and the West Indies (1909), and the committee on commercial and industrial policy after the war (1916–17). In 1888–9 he was lord-in-waiting to Queen Victoria, and from 1889 to 1892 parliamentary secretary to the Board of Trade. Entering the third Salisbury cabinet in 1895 as secretary for Scotland, an office which he held for eight years, he showed himself a very able administrator. His unwearied efforts to further the welfare of Scotland by wise and beneficent legislation were universally recognized. During his term of office the Scottish Parish Councils Act

became operative, while his legislative achievements included the codification and amendment of the Public Health Acts (Scotland) 1897; the establishment of the congested districts board (1898); and an act (1899) simplifying and cheapening the promotion of private Scottish bills by municipalities and other corporate bodies. Balfour of Burleigh worked well with Liberals as well as Conservatives and though in the cabinet was seen as a rather non-political figure. He was, however, an uncompromising free-trader. This led to his dismissal by A. J. Balfour, the prime minister, at the cabinet of 14 September 1903, along with C. T. Ritchie; the duke of Devonshire wrote on 15 September: 'I never heard anything more summary and decisive than the dismissal of the two Ministers' (Gollin, 132). Balfour of Burleigh was subsequently an active Unionist free-trader. In 1904 he was appointed lord warden of the stannaries, in virtue of which he presided over the council of the duchy of Cornwall during the minority of the prince of Wales.

In his later years Balfour of Burleigh was perhaps the most outstanding figure in the public life of Scotland. In 1896 he became lord rector of Edinburgh University; in 1900 chancellor of St Andrews University; and in 1917 chairman of the Carnegie trust for the universities of Scotland. In the affairs of the Church of Scotland he took a leading part. He organized the fund for aged and infirm ministers, and was at all times a stout defender of the church establishment. Balfour of Burleigh drew a sharp distinction between the defence of the establishment and the accommodation of the Free Church. He was uncompromising on the former, becoming in 1882 convener of the church interests committee of the general assembly, which at the 1885 general election organized a highly effective petition against disestablishment, which forced Gladstone onto the back foot and had the effect of making the Scottish Liberals demote the question, so that in the 1892–5 Liberal government it was Welsh disestablishment which took first place. Balfour of Burleigh combined this sustained campaign with movement towards union with the Free Church, which he supported both for itself and as a means of removing a chief cause of the pressure for disestablishment. He moved sometimes strongly opposed motions in the general assembly to that end. From the 1890s he was prominent in the talks which led eventually, and after his death, to the union of the Church of Scotland and the United Free Church. He was the author of *An Historical Account of the Rise and Development of Presbyterianism in Scotland* (1911).

Balfour of Burleigh became a privy councillor in 1892, a knight of the Thistle in 1901, GCMG in 1911, and GCVO in 1917. He was DCL of the University of Oxford (1904) and an honorary LLD of the four Scottish universities. He died on 6 July 1921 at his London residence, 47 Cadogan Square. His main residence was Kennet House, near Alloa, Scotland. In 1891 he sold the estate of Blairgowrie, Perthshire, but retained significant property in the southern highlands. Balfour of Burleigh had a commanding presence and much charm of manner. Without brilliance, he yet represented the best type of public servant—conscientious, purposeful, and with a gift for mastering complicated details and presenting them lucidly and cogently.

W. F. GRAY, *rev.* H. C. G. MATTHEW

Sources *The Scotsman* (7 July 1921) · *British Monthly* (Dec 1904) · F. Balfour, *A memoir of Lord Balfour of Burleigh* (1925) · A. Gollin, *Balfour's burden* (1965) · A. Sykes, *Tariff reform in British politics, 1903–1913* (1979) · A. L. Drummond and J. Bulloch, *The church in late Victorian Scotland* (1978) · F. Balfour, *Ne obliviscaris: dinna forget*, 2 vols. [1930] · GEC, *Peerage*
Archives NRA Scotland, priv. coll., corresp. and papers · U. Edin., New Coll. L., corresp. and papers relating to church union | BL, corresp. with Arthur James Balfour, Add. MS 49800, *passim* · BL, letters to Sir Charles Dilke, Add. MSS 43915–43917 · Bodl. Oxf., letters to Herbert Asquith · Bodl. Oxf., corresp. with Lord Selborne · HLRO, corresp. with John St Loe Strachey · NA Scot., corresp. with A. J. Balfour · U. Birm. L., corresp. with Joseph Chamberlain · University of Sheffield, corresp. with W. A. S. Hewins
Likenesses Russell & Sons, woodburytype, *c.*1891, NPG · C. M. Hardie, oils, 1899, Scot. NPG · W. Stoneman, photograph, 1917, NPG · Melhuish & Gate, photograph, NPG; repro. in *Our conservative and union statesmen* [1898], vol. 2 · G. Reid, pencil drawing, Oriel College, Oxford · Spy [L. Ward], chromolithograph caricature, repro. in *VF* (14 Aug 1902) · oils, U. St Andr. · print (after G. Reid), NPG
Wealth at death £49,308 11*s.* 2*d.*: confirmation, 13 Sept 1921, *CCI*

Bruce, Alice Moore (1867–1951), educationist, was born in London on 29 April 1867, the youngest of six daughters and two sons of Henry Austin *Bruce, first Baron Aberdare (1815–1895), and his second wife, Nora Creina Blanche (*d.* 1897), daughter of General Sir William *Napier. Among her brothers was the army officer and mountaineer Charles Granville *Bruce; there were also two daughters and one son surviving from Lord Aberdare's first marriage. Her father's chairmanship of the departmental committee on intermediate and higher education in Wales (1880–81) generated the blueprint for educational reform in Wales. Her mother was one of the leading protagonists in the establishment of the Aberdare Hall for women students at Cardiff in 1883, and was president of the hall from 1883 to 1895. Educated at home and at Bedford College, London, Alice entered Somerville Hall, Oxford, in 1887, where she gained a second in modern history in 1890.

After four years at home Alice Bruce returned to Somerville in 1894 as secretary to the new principal, Agnes Maitland. From 1898 until her retirement in 1929 she was vice-principal. She was elected an official fellow in 1922 and honorary fellow in 1929. She consecrated years of devoted administrative and tutorial work in English and French to her alma mater, claiming to have held every office in the college except for the tutorships in science and classics. An accomplished tennis player, she encouraged sports in the college. Elsewhere, she gave devoted service on many committees at Oxford, and as council member and vice-president of the Girls' Public Day School Trust. She represented the privy council on the council of the University College of South Wales and Monmouthshire.

From 1929 to 1936 Alice Bruce served as president of Aberdare Hall, Cardiff, where she consolidated her mother's efforts on behalf of women's higher education in Wales. The virtues of residence in a university hall were highlighted, a personal library of modern language books donated in 1935, and a £500 bequest given in her will. In character and temperament she was warm-hearted and impulsive, but also critical and discriminating. Generations of students, including Vera Brittain, recalled her 'gentle, diffident shyness' (V. Brittain, *The Women at Oxford*, 1960, 121), generous and deeply affectionate nature, love of music, and lively interest in public affairs. She was an effective participant in committees, where her knowledge of educational matters and wise judgement proved invaluable. In 1951 a former fellow of Somerville recalled her 'wise and tolerant view in college affairs' and her quest for 'the constitutional basis of any questions' (*The Times*, 20 Nov 1951). Alice Bruce died at her home, Whitegables, Headington Hill, Oxford, on 4 November 1951, and was buried at St Andrew's, Old Headington, Oxford, on 8 November.

W. GARETH EVANS

Sources *The Times* (9 Nov 1951) · *The Times* (17 Nov 1951) · P. Adams, *Somerville for women: an Oxford college, 1879–1993* (1996) · S. B. Chrimes, ed., *The University College of South Wales and Monmouthshire: a centenary history, 1883–1983* (1983) · Aberdare Hall: minutes of the Ladies' Hall committee, 1885–1936, U. Wales, Cardiff, archives · *Daily Telegraph* (6 Nov 1951) · CGPLA Eng. & Wales (1951)
Likenesses photograph, 1929, repro. in Adams, *Somerville for women*, pl. 34
Wealth at death £18,988 16*s.* 9*d.*: probate, 29 Dec 1951, *CGPLA Eng. & Wales*

Bruce, Archibald (*bap.* 1748, *d.* 1816), minister of the Secession church and author, was born at Broomhall, near Denny, Stirlingshire, the son of John Bruce and Isobel, *née* Tayler. Both his parents were early adherents of Ebenezer Erskine's Secession church, and he himself was baptized at the St John Street Associate Secession church in Stirling on 12 November 1748. He was educated privately and, until 1761, at the University of Glasgow. He then studied theology at the Anti-Burgher theological hall at Alloa, under William Moncrieff, and was ordained in the Associate (Anti-Burgher) congregation in Whitburn, Linlithgowshire, on 24 August 1768. This was to be his only charge. In 1786 he was appointed professor of divinity for the General Associate Synod, despite the initial objections of his fellow Anti-Burgher, Adam Gib.

Between 1786 and 1806 Bruce taught about 150 students. Through his writing as well as his teaching he gained a reputation as a man of great erudition and piety. 'Living in a sequestered part of the country, his flock small and his privacy subject to few interruptions, he gave his days and nights to study' (Scott, 520). His list of publications is long (M'Kerrow, 897–9), with a particular focus on the relation between civil government and religion; his model was the Reformed Church of Scotland in its purest times. He strenuously defended religious and political liberty, though he paradoxically justified legal restraints against Roman Catholics in his *Free Thoughts on the Toleration of Popery*, published in 1780, afraid that Catholicism would threaten his prized civil and religious freedoms; his knowledge of the 'Romish controversy' was said to be unrivalled. He was a whig in politics, and in the nervous times of the French Revolution he published *Reflections on* the *Freedom of Writing* (1794), to oppose a government proclamation against seditious publications. His *Right and Duty of Private Judgement and Due Freedom of Enquiry* appeared posthumously in 1817. So difficult did Bruce find it to get his books published at some periods that he imported to Whitburn a printing press bought in Edinburgh and hired a printer to assist in the production process. The output of this private press was of poor printing quality but was redeemed by the excellence of the writing. Bruce's 'serious and amusing' poetry included *The Kirkiad* (1774), a satire on the 'moderate' party in the Church of Scotland, and *A Penitential Epistle* (1797), which lampooned the superstitions of Roman Catholicism.

Bruce's influence was spread further by the successes of those of his pupils who went on to serve in many areas of the church in Scotland and Ireland, or as missionaries in America. The elder and younger Thomas McCrie; Robert Shaw, Bruce's successor at Whitburn; and John Duncan—later famous as 'Rabbi' Duncan—professor of oriental languages at New College, Edinburgh, served as prominent ministers. James Watt became a leading Baptist in Glasgow, and Thomas Campbell proceeded to America by way of his native Ireland, becoming one of the founders of the Disciples of Christ. In 1856 Duncan described Bruce as one of the last ministers to wear a full-bottomed wig and silver-buckled knee-breeches, while others, like the younger McCrie, spoke of his dignity, neat appearance, sedateness, and 'polite bearing' (Scott, 519). He spoke in the muffled tones of the 'Dead march' in *Saul*, but uttered a depth of wisdom worthy of being listened to by a whole conclave of bishops. His stipend at Whitburn was £50 per annum, reduced from a slightly higher figure 'because of a vote he gave on a political question' (ibid., 439). In 1804 Bruce and a few other ministers protested against the 'New Narrative and Testimony' of his church, by which the synod altered its teaching regarding the relation of civil magistrates and the church. On 7 October 1806 he was deposed by his former colleagues, having in the previous August, along with four other ministers, formed the Constitutional Presbytery. He continued to teach in the much smaller theological hall of that branch of the Secession until he died, unmarried, on 18 February 1816 at Whitburn, where he was buried.   DEREK B. MURRAY

Sources *DNB* · D. Scott, *Annals and statistics of the original Secession church* (1886) · W. Mackelvie, *Annals and statistics of the United Presbyterian church*, ed. W. Blair and D. Young (1873) · J. M'Kerrow, *History of the Secession church*, rev. edn (1854) · *DSCHT* · *Scots Magazine and Edinburgh Literary Miscellany*, 78 (1816), 318–19 · R. Small, *History of the congregations of the United Presbyterian church from 1733 to 1900*, 2 vols. (1904) · *IGI* · Viewfield Associate Secession church, Stirling, records, NA Scot. · gravestone, parish church, Whitburn, Linlithgowshire

Bruce, Lady **Augusta Elizabeth Frederica**. *See* Stanley, Lady Augusta Elizabeth Frederica (1822–1876).

Bruce, Brenda Margaret (1919–1996), actress, was born on 7 July 1919 at 44 Richmond Avenue, Prestwich, Lancashire, the daughter of George Alexander Findlay Bruce, tobacco sales manager, and his wife, Ellen Isabella Dwerryhouse Vowles. Bruce was educated at the convent of the Holy Family of Nazareth and studied ballet dancing with Margaret Saul and, later, the Ballet Rambert. By the age of three she had informed her mother that she was going to become a fairy, and spent much of her childhood tottering up and down corridors in high-heeled shoes imagining she was Marlene Dietrich. By the time she had become a backbone member of the Royal Shakespeare Company in its formative years, she had acquired wide experience in revue, repertory theatre, and in the West End.

Bruce's first stage appearance was in 1934 at the Theatre Royal, Exeter, in a ballet of *The Babes in the Wood*. She made her London début in the following year as a chorus girl in *1066 and All That*. 'Irresistibly sweet and charming' (*The Guardian*, 22 Feb 1996), according to a contemporary, she was petite, bright-eyed, button-nosed, with a distinctive mop of shiny red hair that she kept in good order all her life. She joined Sir Barry Jackson's Birmingham repertory theatre for three years in 1936, playing such roles as Lydia Languish in Sheridan's *The Rivals* and Anne in *The Brontës of Haworth Parsonage*. She toured in revue with the Entertainments National Service Association during the Second World War and in 1943 played one of her favourite roles, Vivie Warren, in Shaw's *Mrs Warren's Profession*. She had additional success with Shaw as Eliza Doolittle in *Pygmalion* at the Lyric, Hammersmith, in 1947.

Bruce married her first husband, Roy Rich (1911–1970), on 18 January 1946. He later directed her in a season of one-act Shaw plays at the Aldwych. She was soon well-established in the West End, playing a series of leading roles at the Arts Theatre. Her range was exceptional, as she proved throughout the 1950s in plays by authors as diverse as Somerset Maugham, Jean Anouilh, and Sir John Mortimer—and she played Peter Pan at the Scala in 1952. With Roy Rich, who was a television executive, she presented a television chat show, *Rich and Rich*, filmed in a studio replica of their Bloomsbury flat. In 1962 she was nominated television actress of the year after a series of starring performances. At the end of 1962 she played in the British première of Samuel Beckett's *Happy Days* at the Royal Court, replacing Joan Plowright at short notice. As Beckett's heroine, Winnie, defying mortality while buried up to her waist, then her neck, in the scorched earth of some post-nuclear disaster area, she won critical acclaim for a performance of 'dogged valour' and 'hypnotic power' (*Daily Telegraph*, 22 Feb 1996).

This proved a turning point in her career. Having cut back on stage work to bring up her adopted twin daughters, she began a period of intense activity with the Royal Shakespeare Company in 1964, moving to Wellesbourne, near Stratford upon Avon, where she and Rich ran the King's Head, an eleven-bedroom hostelry. She played Mistress Page in *The Merry Wives of Windsor* on three different occasions for the Royal Shakespeare Company and excelled, too, as the Nurse in *Romeo and Juliet* and as an unutterably moving Paulina in Trevor Nunn's all-white *The Winter's Tale* in 1969.

Roy Rich died of cancer in 1970; later that year, on 24

December, she married fellow Royal Shakespeare Company actor Clement Schuyler McCallin (1913–1977), who died of leukaemia in 1977. Her adopted son, Sam, died of asthma aged fourteen in 1975. She worked tirelessly and unostentatiously for both Asthma Research and Amnesty International.

Brenda Bruce was as intense as she was reliable as an actress, combining qualities of rough-edged humanity and emotional sparkle, and she was blessed with a voice of great sensuality, crackle, and bite. She always evinced a spirit of enthusiasm and joy rooted, no doubt, in her vast experience as well as in her ability to overcome tragedy in her personal life. She died as she lived, quickly and without fuss, on 19 February 1996, suffering heart failure after entering the Middlesex Hospital, Westminster, London, for tests. Cancer had been diagnosed one month before, though she never stopped working, filming D. H. Lawrence's *The Widowing of Mrs Holroyd* for the BBC in her final weeks.   MICHAEL COVENEY

Sources *The Guardian* (22 Feb 1996) · *The Times* (22 Feb 1996) · *The Independent* (22 Feb 1996) · *Daily Telegraph* (22 Feb 1996) · I. Herbert, ed., *Who's who in the theatre*, 16th edn (1977) · S. Beckett, *Happy days*, ed. J. Knowlson (1978) · b. cert. · m. cert. · d. cert. [Roy Rich] · d. cert. [Clement McCallin] · *CGPLA Eng. & Wales* (1996)
Likenesses photograph, repro. in *The Guardian* · photograph, repro. in *The Times* · photograph, repro. in *Daily Telegraph* · photograph, repro. in *The Independent*
Wealth at death £255,657: probate, 1996

Bruce, Charles Granville (1866–1939), army officer and mountaineer, was born in London on 7 April 1866, the youngest son of Henry Austin *Bruce, first Baron Aberdare (1815–1895), politician, and his second wife, Nora Creina Blanche (d. 1897), youngest daughter of Lieutenant-General Sir William Napier. He was the second youngest in a large family in which three brothers, from both Lord Aberdare's marriages, and eight sisters (including Alice Moore *Bruce) reached adulthood. They lived at Dyffryn, an estate in Glamorgan, and at Queen's Gate, London. Charlie Bruce was educated at Harrow School (1879–80) and Repton School (1881–4), and spent two years in the militia in York, where he was a noted wrestler and runner. He was commissioned in the Oxfordshire and Buckinghamshire light infantry in 1887; and he served briefly with an Indian regiment in Madras and Burma before moving in 1889 to the 5th Gurkha rifles, the regiment with which he served for most of his career. Stationed at Abbottabad, he saw much service on the northwest frontier of India: in Black Mountain (Hazara), 1891; Miranzai, 1891; Chitral, 1893; Waziristan, 1894–5; and Tirah, 1897–8. In all he received six clasps to his two frontier medals, three mentions in dispatches, and a brevet majority in 1898. During the Tirah campaign Bruce cut the Gurkhas' tight-fitting breeches off above the knee, an improvisation that was once said to have introduced shorts into the Indian and British armies. In 1891 Bruce studied the equipment of Italian mountain troops in Turin, and he ran a training course for frontier scouts from 1891 to 1913. He taught staff college instructors in his training methods on the slopes of Snowdonia in 1910.

Charles Granville Bruce (1866–1939), by George Percy Jacomb-Hood, 1913

Bruce travelled widely in the Himalayas and organized porters for several important mountaineering expeditions. In 1892 William Martin Conway chose Bruce to join an expedition to the Karakoram since his father had been president of the Royal Geographical Society. Bruce made several ascents including that of Pioneer Peak (22,600 feet/6890 metres) on Baltoro Kangri, but he injured his back and leg in a crevasse on the return from the Karakoram. In 1895 he joined A. F. Mummery's expedition to Nanga Parbat. A severe attack of mumps forced Bruce to leave before Mummery and two Gurkhas were killed. In 1907 Bruce accompanied T. G. Longstaff and A. L. Mumm's expedition to Garhwal. A knee injury prevented him from reaching the summit of Trisul (23,360 feet/7120 metres) with them and Karbir Burathoki, one of the many Gurkhas whom he introduced to climbing. In 1907 and 1910 Bruce developed serious proposals for the ascent of Mount Everest that were abandoned for political reasons. On 12 September 1894 he had married Finetta Madeline Julia (1866/7–1932), third daughter of Colonel Sir Edward Fitzgerald Campbell, second baronet; their only child, a son, died in infancy in the Himalayas, an occurrence Bruce considered the greatest blow in his life. He described his travels in *Twenty Years in the Himalaya* (1910), and *Kulu and Lahoul* (1914), both of which included chapters by Mrs Bruce, who often accompanied him and was the author of *Kashmir* (1911).

After being adjutant and second-in-command of the 5th

Gurkha rifles he was promoted lieutenant-colonel in May 1913, and in May 1914 he was appointed to command the 6th Gurkha rifles. He went with them to Egypt for the defence of the Suez Canal on the outbreak of war in 1914. In Gallipoli he commanded the depleted battalions of the 29th Indian brigade, including the 5th and 6th Gurkhas at Gurkha bluff, for which he was thrice mentioned in dispatches and promoted brevet colonel in November 1915. Severely wounded in the leg, he was evacuated before the withdrawal, and on discharge from hospital was appointed general officer commanding the independent frontier brigade at Bannu, a position he held from 1916 to 1919. He commanded the North Waziristan field force in 1917, and served in the Third Anglo-Afghan War (May 1919). In these operations he was mentioned twice in dispatches. His health deteriorated in the heat, and he was invalided out of the service with the honorary rank of brigadier-general in 1920. He then became secretary to the Glamorganshire Territorial Association in Cardiff.

When Tibet unexpectedly granted permission for a Mount Everest expedition, Bruce could not obtain leave to join the first reconnaissance in 1921, but he was appointed leader of the next expedition in 1922. He was too old to take part in the climbing, but his knowledge of Himalayan languages and military organization, his cheerfulness and joviality, and the Gurkhas he brought to organize the porters all contributed to the expedition's success. Captain John Geoffrey Bruce (1896–1972), a Gurkha officer and Bruce's cousin, and George Ingle Finch, a chemist, supported by Lance-Naik Tejbir Bura, a Gurkha NCO, reached a record elevation of 27,300 feet (8310 metres) using oxygen. Afterwards Bruce resigned his Territorial Association appointment, moved to Kensington Crescent, London, and with other climbers wrote *The Assault on Mount Everest, 1922* (1923). In 1924 Bruce was again appointed Everest leader, but contracted malaria on a tiger hunt immediately before the expedition. On the march to Everest he became seriously ill and turned the leadership over to Colonel E. F. Norton. Bruce became the model for later Everest leaders. When Colonel John Hunt was chosen to lead the successful 1953 Everest expedition, the organizers were looking for 'another General Bruce' (Goodfellow to Hunt, 10 July 1952, RGS, EE 68).

During his lifetime Bruce was respected as an authority on the Himalayas and its peoples, though his ability to understand the 'native mind' was more ambiguous than his contemporary reputation suggested. For example, Bruce and Zatul Rinpoche, the head lama at the Rongbuk monastery at the foot of Everest, each left very different accounts of their encounter in 1922. According to Bruce, he told the lama that 'we regarded the whole Expedition, and especially our attempt to reach the summit of Everest as a pilgrimage'. According to Rinpoche the general told him that 'As this snow peak is the biggest in the world, if we arrive on the summit we will get from the British government a recompense and high rank' (Hansen, 721). Their meeting is recorded in John Noel's silent film, *Climbing Mount Everest* (1922). Undoubtedly Bruce's boisterous conviviality, exuberant horseplay, and combination of

geniality and dignity, endeared him to many people in both the Himalayas and Britain.

Bruce was rotund as well as jocund. His strength, endurance, and appetite enjoyed a phenomenal reputation, but his burly frame eventually suffered from his strenuous exertions. Early photographs depict the youthful, muscular officer with moustache; by the 1920s he was overweight, wore a pince-nez, and had been advised by his doctors to avoid exercise. Bruce was appointed MVO in 1903, and CB in 1918. The Royal Geographical Society awarded him the Gill medal in 1915, and the founder's medal in 1925. On behalf of the Everest expedition he received a special Olympic medal in 1924. He was president of the Alpine Club from 1923 to 1925, an honorary member of European climbing clubs, and an enthusiastic founder member of the Himalayan Club. He received the honorary degrees of DSc from Oxford and Wales, DCL from Edinburgh, and LLD from St Andrews. From 1931 to 1936 he served as colonel of the 5th Gurkha rifles. After his wife's death in 1932 he wrote an autobiography, *Himalayan Wanderer* (1934), and moved to 27 St Mary Abbot's Terrace, London, where he died on 12 July 1939. A funeral service was held on 17 July at St Martin-in-the-Fields, and he was buried at Thames Ditton churchyard.

KENNETH MASON, *rev.* PETER H. HANSEN

Sources *The Times* (13 July 1939) · *The Times* (15 July 1939) · *The Times* (18 July 1939) · *The Times* (16 Sept 1939) · *Alpine Journal*, 52 (1940), 101–7 · *Himalayan Journal*, 13 (1946) · B. E. M. Gurdon, *GJ*, 96 (1940), 301–3 · C. G. Bruce, *Himalayan wanderer* (1934) · *Debrett's Peerage* · *WW* · RGS, Everest expedition archives · P. H. Hansen, 'The dancing lamas of Everest: cinema, orientalism and Anglo-Tibetan relations in the 1920s', *American Historical Review*, 101 (1996), 712–47 · A. Macdonald, 'The lama and the general', *Kailash*, 1 (1973), 225–33 · M. G. Dauglish and P. K. Stephenson, eds., *The Harrow School register, 1800–1911*, 3rd edn (1911) · *Repton School Register, 1557–1910* (1910) · m. cert. · *CGPLA Eng. & Wales* (1939)

Archives Alpine Club, London | RGS, Mount Everest expedition MSS | FILM BFI NFTVA, British Pathé Newsreels, *Climbing Mount Everest, 1922*, London, G1078–1924

Likenesses photograph, 1895, repro. in Bruce, *Himalayan wanderer*, 129 · photograph, *c.*1910, repro. in C. G. Bruce, *Twenty years in the Himalaya* (1910), frontispiece · photograph, 1912, repro. in C. G. Bruce, *Kulu and Lahoul* (1914), 136 · G. P. Jacomb-Hood, portrait, 1913, repro. in Bruce, *Himalayan wanderer*, frontispiece [*see illus.*] · J. Noel, photograph, 1922, repro. in Bruce, *Himalayan wanderer*, 280 · photograph, 1924, repro. in Bruce, *Himalayan wanderer*, 288 · photographs, RGS

Wealth at death £2466 18s. 11d.: probate, 13 Sept 1939, *CGPLA Eng. & Wales*

Bruce, Christian (d. 1356), noblewoman, was one of the many daughters of Robert (VI) de *Brus, earl of Carrick (1243–1304), and his wife, Marjorie; *Robert I was her brother. She is supposed to have married Gartnait, earl of Mar, in the 1290s, but a number of objections have been raised against this. In the first place, she is never described as countess of Mar, nor even just 'of Mar'. Second, there is no evidence of any communication between her and Donald, earl of Mar, who should have been her son, when both were imprisoned in England after 1306. Abbot Walter Bower (d. 1449) explicitly states that Gartnait married the eldest Bruce daughter, a description never applied to

Christian, and made unlikely by the date of her death. Her later holding of Kildrummy Castle, the centre of the earldom of Mar, could point to a connection, but if there was one its nature remains incapable of definition.

Before 1305 Christian undoubtedly married Sir Christopher *Seton (c.1278–1306), a knight with lands in Annandale and northern England. He was captured at Loch Doon Castle and executed by Edward I in 1306; she kept sacred his sacrifice in her brother's cause as late as 1324, when she founded a chapel in Dumfries to his memory. In 1306 she herself was captured by Edward, along with her sister Mary, her niece Marjorie, Bruce's queen, Elizabeth, and the countess of Buchan, at Tain in Ross-shire, possibly *en route* for Norway, where another sister, Isabel, was queen. Christian's punishment was captivity in the Gilbertine nunnery of Sixhills in Lincolnshire; her freedom was secured only in 1314 with the exchange of prisoners following the battle of Bannockburn. At some point after her release she was granted the lands of the Garioch, Aberdeenshire, which had come to the Bruces as part of their inheritance from David, earl of Huntingdon (d. 1219).

Although it is possible that she was the sister of King Robert whom English sources rumoured was intended for the hand of Andrew Harclay, earl of Carlisle, when he made an unsuccessful attempt to negotiate a peace treaty with Scotland early in 1323, Christian did not remarry until 1326. Perhaps the memory of the fate of her first husband was sufficient to deter her from a speedy second marriage, or perhaps her brother, now king, was keen to prevent the arrival of another nephew to complicate the succession so long as he himself remained without an heir. Her second husband was Sir Andrew *Murray (1298–1338), son of the joint victor of the battle of Stirling Bridge, a man most certainly many years her junior. Being a member of the royal family, Christian took part in the coronation of her nephew *David II in 1331 and shared a room in the palace at Scone with her nieces, the new king's sisters. When war broke out again shortly afterwards, Murray played a prominent role, as guardian of Scotland, in repulsing the attempts at conquest of Edward Balliol and Edward III of England. To this end he entrusted Christian with the keeping of Kildrummy Castle, and in 1335 she defended it against the earl of Atholl, Balliol's commander in the north. One of two vital defences of castles by women in this period (the other was that of Dunbar by Agnes Dunbar in 1338), her resistance enabled her husband to confront Atholl at Culblean and defeat him. Christian remained in custody of Kildrummy even after the death of Murray in 1338, entertaining her nephew's wife, Queen Joan, there in 1342. King David permitted her to draw an income from a number of sources, including the customs of Aberdeen. The final reference to her in the exchequer rolls suggests that she died, surely at least in her seventies, in 1356.　　　FIONA WATSON

Sources G. W. S. Barrow and others, eds., *Regesta regum Scottorum*, 5, ed. A. A. M. Duncan (1988) · *Scots peerage*, vol. 2 · G. Burnett and others, eds., *The exchequer rolls of Scotland*, 1 (1878) · W. Bower, *Scotichronicon*, ed. D. E. R. Watt and others, new edn, 9 vols. (1987–98), vol. 6 · G. W. S. Barrow, *Robert Bruce and the community of the realm of Scotland*, 3rd edn (1988)

Bruce, Clarence Napier, third Baron Aberdare (1885–1957), athlete, was born in London on 2 August 1885. He was the second son of Henry Campbell Bruce, second Baron Aberdare (1851–1929), and grandson of Henry Austin *Bruce, first Baron Aberdare and home secretary. His mother, Constance Mary Beckett (d. 1932), was a granddaughter of J. S. Copley, Baron Lyndhurst. Bruce was educated at Winchester College, where he was in the cricket eleven and was captain of rackets in 1903 and 1904, and at New College, Oxford. At Oxford he represented the university at cricket in 1907 and 1908 (when he scored 46 for the winning side) and also at golf, rackets, and real tennis, at which he won the silver racket in 1907. He gained third-class honours in modern history in 1908. In 1911 he was called to the bar by the Inner Temple, and on 12 December the following year married Margaret Bethune (d. 1950), only daughter of Adam Black. With her he had two sons and two daughters. Between 1914 and 1919 he served with the Glamorgan yeomanry, with the 2nd Life Guards, on the staff of the 61st division, and with the guards machine-gun regiment. He retired with the rank of captain; the death in action of his elder brother in 1914 left him heir to the title.

From 1919 Bruce began to play cricket for Middlesex, which he had represented twice in 1908. One of his best years was 1925, when he scored 527 runs in nineteen appearances. On 23 June, at Nottingham, his county were set 502 runs to win in the fourth innings, and achieved that total. Hendren and Bruce added 154 together in 95 minutes, and Bruce finished with 103 to his name; *Wisden* justly describes this as one of the great matches in the history of Middlesex cricket. His last game for the county was in 1929.

Bruce was a good golfer and competent at all ball games, but he excelled at the two great indoor court games, rackets and real tennis. At rackets he was the amateur champion in 1922 and 1931 and was ten times winner of the doubles with different partners. His finest achievement was to become open champion of the British Isles in 1932 by defeating J. C. F. Simpson. Although the loser was the best receiver of service playing, Aberdare's service was devastating and his court craft superb. He was the singles champion of Canada in 1928 and 1930 and won the doubles in Canada and the United States (with H. W. Leatham) in the latter year. He was real tennis champion of the United States in 1930, and of England in 1932 and 1938; he also won the MCC gold or silver prize every year from 1930 to 1937. Here too his superb fitness assisted him and he was a master tactician. In 1938 he defeated L. Lees, champion for five years and a younger man, in the semi-final 3–2, after being two sets down. His service was always accurate (although he eschewed the American variety) and his attack on the dedans deadly. In the final he won easily, finishing with a spectacular winning gallery shot. In France he won the Coupe de Paris six times. At doubles he had a happy knack of bringing out the best in his partners. With E. B. Noel, he was the author of an admirable work on *First Steps to Rackets* (1926) and he edited the Lonsdale Library volume *Rackets, Squash Rackets, Tennis, Fives and Badminton* (1933).

After his succession to the barony on 20 February 1929 Aberdare played an increasing part in public life. From 1931 to 1946 he was a member of the Miners' Welfare Committee, an appointment that reflected the long connection between his family and the south Wales coal field. He took a great interest in youth welfare and was treasurer of the National Association of Boys' Clubs in 1935 and chairman from 1943 until his death. Another lifelong interest was the Queen's Institute of District Nursing, of which he became chairman in 1944. In February 1937 Oliver Stanley announced the creation of a new National Advisory Council for Physical Training and Recreation of which Aberdare was chairman until 1939. Aberdare was an admirable choice; he was good in the chair, unruffled, and modest, while his reputation brought in money and support. In a speech in 1938 he declared that his great ideal was to give everyone 'a chance of making the human body a fit instrument for the human soul'. In that year he himself was amateur tennis champion, and in 1939, at the age of fifty-three and partnered by his son, he attained the final of the doubles at rackets.

In Wales, Aberdare continued the family interest in the university (of which his grandfather was the first chancellor) as president of the Welsh National School of Medicine; he received an honorary LLD in 1953. In 1948 he became prior of the Welsh priory of St John of Jerusalem, and was a knight of the order which he had long aided. He spoke in the House of Lords on the subjects dear to his heart; in 1944 he twice voiced the claims of youth in the debates on the Education Bill, and at the end of the same year urged that youth club leaders should not be forgotten in the demobilization programme. During the Second World War he served in the Home Guard; he was honorary colonel of the 77th (later renumbered 282nd) (Welsh) heavy anti-aircraft brigade. He was appointed CBE in 1949 and promoted GBE in 1954.

In 1931 Aberdare had joined the executive committee of the international Olympics. He attended the games at Los Angeles in 1932, Berlin in 1936, and after the war in London (1948), Helsinki (1952), and Melbourne (1956). On 12 September 1957 he married as his second wife Grizelda Harriet Violet Finetta Georgiana, daughter of Dudley Francis Amelius Hervey; while returning with her from an Olympic meeting in Sofia, he was killed in a car accident at Morinj, near Koton, in Yugoslavia, on 4 October 1957. He was succeeded by his elder son, Morys George Lyndhurst (*b*. 1919). MICHAEL MACLAGAN, *rev.*

Sources *The Times* (5 Oct 1957) · *The Times* (10 Oct 1957) · *The Times* (11 Oct 1957) · *The Times* (14 Oct 1957) · private information (2004) · Burke, *Peerage* (1967) · *CGPLA Eng. & Wales* (1957)
Archives Glamorgan RO, Cardiff, diaries and scrapbooks
Likenesses F. Lion, oils, 1947, NMG Wales
Wealth at death £70,264 15s. 3d.: administration, 18 Dec 1957, *CGPLA Eng. & Wales*

Bruce, David. *See* David II (1324–1371).

Bruce, David (*fl. c.*1650–1686), physician, was the son of Andrew Bruce DD (youngest of the ten sons of the laird of Fingask), who held the post of principal of St Leonard's College, St Andrews, from 1630 to 1647. After graduating MA at the University of St Andrews, Bruce travelled to France, where he studied physic at Paris and Montpellier. As was the custom in the period, he intended to proceed to another university in order to take his MD, and had chosen Padua, but an outbreak of plague in Italy prevented him from doing so. He therefore remained in France, and following a period of study in Lyons, finally graduated MD at Valence in Dauphiny on 7 May 1657. He returned to England and was incorporated as doctor of physic at Oxford on 27 March 1660. He then joined his great-uncle, Sir John Wedderburne, in the service of the duke and duchess of York. After spending a number of years assisting Wedderburne as physician to the duke and duchess, Bruce gave up this office, 'being wearied by the court toil' (Wood, 2.805), and burdened by Wedderburne's advancing infirmity, which resulted in an increased workload, particularly following the latter's retirement from royal service. After a further period of travel abroad, he settled in Edinburgh, and in the early 1690s was still apparently 'in good repute for his practice' (ibid.). Bruce was admitted as a candidate of the College of Physicians, London, on 24 December 1660, and became a fellow of the Royal Society on 20 May 1663, having been proposed by Alexander Bruce, second earl of Kincardine, and Sir Robert Murray, lord of exchequer and high commissioner of Scotland. However, he paid no subscriptions to the society, took no part in its affairs, and was expelled in 1675, along with nine others, because of inactivity and arrears of subscriptions. He married Mrs Rachel Hamilton, a widow, in Edinburgh on 2 September 1686.

SIDNEY LEE, *rev.* HELEN M. DINGWALL

Sources Wood, *Ath. Oxon.* · M. Hunter, *The Royal Society and its fellows, 1660–1700: the morphology of an early scientific institution*, 2nd edn (1994) · Munk, *Roll* · H. Paton, ed., *The register of marriages for the parish of Edinburgh, 1595–1700*, Scottish RS, old ser., 27 (1905) · *Fasti Scot.*, new edn

Bruce, Sir David (1855–1931), bacteriologist and parasitologist, was born in Melbourne, Australia, on 29 May 1855, the only son of David Bruce, of Edinburgh, and his wife, Jane, daughter of Alexander Hamilton, of Stirling. His father was presumably an engineer, who went to Australia to install a crushing plant in a goldfield near Sandhurst, about 100 miles from Melbourne. When Bruce was five years old the family returned to Stirling in Scotland, and he attended Stirling high school until he was fourteen. He then worked for three years in business in Manchester. From his early interest in natural history he turned to the pursuit of athletics and boxing, until a severe attack of pneumonia intervened.

In 1876, at the age of twenty-one, Bruce entered the University of Edinburgh to read zoology. However, he was advised by a fellow student to study medicine, and he graduated MB CM in 1881. After qualifying Bruce's first position was as assistant to Dr Herbert Stanley Stone, at Reigate in Surrey. It was here that Bruce met his future

Sir David Bruce (1855–1931), by unknown photographer, 1894–6

wife, Mary Elizabeth Sisson (1849–1931), daughter of John Sisson Steele MRCS, Stone's predecessor in the practice. They were married in 1883, and began a lifelong partnership in science and travel; there were no children.

Shortly after their wedding Bruce was commissioned a surgeon in the Army Medical Service, and passed first from the Army Medical School at Netley, on Southampton Water, on 4 August 1883. In 1884 Bruce received his first overseas commission to Malta, and accompanied by his wife he joined the Mediterranean commission in Valletta. At this time the naval and military hospitals at Malta contained large numbers of cases of an obscure continued fever with a high mortality rate; even in milder cases it was associated with prolonged ill health and disability. So seriously was the incidence of this disease regarded that the naval and military medical officers were already collecting information on the clinical nature and epidemiology of the disease. Bruce worked on its pathological and bacteriological aspects. Bacteriology was then in its infancy and the introduction by Robert Koch in 1880 of solid media and other technical methods of isolating organisms, and the recent identification of the organisms of typhoid fever, respiratory tuberculosis, and cholera, directed Bruce to investigate the aetiology of Malta fever using the new laboratory methods. Within two years he had found in the spleens of fatal cases an organism which he named *Micrococcus melitensis*, later known as *Brucella melitensis*. His research proved conclusively that this was the cause of Malta fever.

In 1888 Bruce left Malta on leave and worked with his wife in Koch's laboratory in Berlin. On his return to England he was appointed assistant professor of pathology at the Army Medical School at Netley. In his five years here from 1889 to 1894, he introduced courses in bacteriology and improved the teaching of pathology. He was disappointed not to be made full professor when, in 1892, a civilian, Almroth Wright, was brought in to fill the vacant post.

In 1894 Bruce was posted overseas again, this time to Pietermaritzburg in Natal, South Africa. In Zululand at this time a fatal disease, known as nagana or tsetse-fly disease,

was devastating the domestic animals of the native population and settlers. The governor of the colony, Sir Walter Hely-Hutchinson, who had been lieutenant-governor of Malta at the time of Bruce's successful work on Malta fever, had Bruce seconded to investigate the disease. Within two months Bruce reported the discovery of a single-celled parasite, later named *Trypanosoma brucei*, in the blood of infected animals, and that this was the cause of both tsetse-fly disease and nagana, then thought to be two distinct diseases. In December 1896 he was seconded for a further period. He and his wife spent two years in an isolated camp in the bush at Ubombo in Zululand. They lived and worked in wattle and daub huts and ate wild game which they themselves shot. By the end of this period they had established the main facts regarding trypanosomiasis in domestic and wild animals and its transmission by the tsetse-fly. This confirmed Bruce's reputation as a scientist of remarkable capacity, and while still absent in South Africa he was elected a fellow of the Royal Society (1899). In the Second South African War in 1899 the Bruces were caught in the siege of Ladysmith. Bruce had charge of a large military hospital and acted as an operating surgeon, while his wife assisted him as sister in charge of the operating theatre. Following the relief of Ladysmith (in March 1900) Bruce was made a member of the committee investigating typhoid and dysentery in the field, as these diseases were decimating the troops.

In 1901 Bruce returned to England and was appointed to the advisory board of the Army Medical Services department at the War Office. In February 1903 he was seconded to supervise the Royal Society's sleeping sickness commission in Uganda. Sleeping sickness had reached epidemic levels among the lake-shore population, and the commission had been dispatched to find its cause and mode of transmission. As often happens, the actual discovery of the cause of sleeping sickness was not wholly attributable to any one individual, though it was Bruce's systematic research that first established the nature and cause of this fatal infection. Trypanosomiasis in animals caused by *T. brucei* does not affect man; however, J. E. Dutton, working in the Gambia, had seen parasites in the blood of a case of fever which he recognized as a trypanosome and which in 1902 he named *T. gambiense*. In 1903, shortly before Bruce's arrival, Aldo Castellani, an existing member of the commission, had found trypanosomes in the cerebrospinal fluid of five out of fifteen cases of sleeping sickness. He had disregarded this in favour of a bacterium he had also isolated. Castellani told Bruce of his work and in the three weeks before he left for England found these organisms in twenty out of twenty-nine further cases. Bruce recognized the implications of Castellani's observations and related this to his own experience with nagana. He collected information about the distribution of the disease and of tsetse-flies and set up fly-feeding experiments using the Zululand research as a model. By August 1903, when the Bruces returned to England, he had established that sleeping sickness was also a trypanosome disease carried by the tsetse-fly and that it could be transmitted from sick to healthy individuals by the bite of this insect.

Bruce's career now followed the path of a roving researcher, heading a series of successful investigations, until the outbreak of war in 1914. Thus in 1904 he revisited Malta, in charge of the Royal Society's Malta fever commission. It identified the source of infection in Malta fever as the goat, transmission occurring when contaminated milk was consumed. In 1908 Bruce visited Uganda as director of the third sleeping sickness commission, and in 1911 he led a further commission to Nyasaland to investigate human trypanosomiasis. With the outbreak of war in 1914 Bruce was appointed commandant of the Royal Army Medical College, Millbank. He had held the rank of surgeon-general since 1912 after a special promotion in recognition of his scientific work. He chaired the War Office pathological committee, and supervised those investigating tetanus and trench fever. He retired in 1919 on completion of the written reports. Following his retirement he served as chair of the governing body of the Lister Institute. For reasons of health he spent the winters in Madeira, though he continued to keep in touch with research at home and to give to workers the benefit of his experience and advice.

In all his work Bruce was assisted by his wife, who accompanied him throughout his foreign service, working in the laboratory and taking charge of camp arrangements. Immediately before his own death, four days after his wife's, Bruce expressed the wish that her role in his scientific work should be recognized. She had been honoured with the Royal Red Cross for her work with the wounded in the siege of Ladysmith, and was appointed OBE for her work for the committees on trench fever and tetanus during the First World War.

Among Bruce's many honours were a royal medal from the Royal Society in 1904 and its Buchanan medal in 1922. In 1923 Bruce was presented with the Albert medal of the Royal Society of Arts. From his peers in the field of tropical medicine he received the Mary Kingsley medal from the Liverpool School of Tropical Medicine in 1905, the Leeuwenhoek medal of the Dutch Academy of Sciences in 1915, and the Manson medal of the Royal Society of Tropical Medicine and Hygiene (of which he was president from 1917 to 1919). He was also awarded four honorary degrees and the membership of several foreign academies and societies. He was Croonian lecturer of the Royal College of Physicians in 1915 and president of the British Association in 1924. He was appointed CB in 1905, and, having been knighted in 1908, KCB in 1918.

Bruce was a man of strong physique and forceful mind. His research into the aetiology and transmission of animal and human trypanosomiasis helped to establish tropical medicine as a postgraduate speciality in Britain. His approach to research problems was simple, logical, vigorous, and direct, and he had an intuitive perception of the essential point for attack. He contributed more than 172 scientific papers, of which thirty were co-authored by his wife. Bruce had a reputation for being reserved and self-contained, and Lady Bruce often smoothed the way for him. Among his contemporaries he was renowned for his loyalty, and his integrity of mind and purpose. At the time of his death he was living at Artillery Mansions Hotel, Victoria Street, London. He died on 27 November 1931, at Christchurch, Westminster, during the funeral of Lady Bruce, following a long period of ill health. He was cremated at Golders Green crematorium on 1 December.

S. R. CHRISTOPHERS, rev. HELEN J. POWER

Sources B. J. S. Grogono, 'Sir David and Lady Bruce', *Journal of Medical Biography*, 3 (1995), 79–83, 125–32 · E. E. Vella, 'Major General Sir David Bruce, KCB', *Journal of the Royal Army Medical Corps*, 119 (1973), 131–44 · A. E. Hamerton, 'Major-General Sir David Bruce', *Transactions of the Royal Society of Tropical Medicine and Hygiene*, 25 (1931), 305–12 · J. R. B., *Obits. FRS*, 1 (1932–5), 79–85 · J. J. Joubert, 'Ubombo and the site of David Bruce's discovery of *Trypanosoma brucei*', *Transactions of the Royal Society of Tropical Medicine and Hygiene*, 87 (1993), 494–5 · *BMJ* (5 Dec 1931), 1067–9 · *The Lancet* (5 Dec 1931), 1270–71 · *The Times* (28 Nov 1931)

Archives RCP Lond., letters relating to Croonian lectures · Stirling central regional council archives, career records · Wellcome L., diary and reports on tsetse-fly in Zululand · Wellcome L., papers especially relating to sleeping sickness and incl. papers of Mary Bruce · Wellcome L., paper on Malta fever | Wellcome L., Royal Society of Tropical Medicine and royal army medical corps MSS

Likenesses photograph, 1894–6, Wellcome L. [*see illus.*] · W. Stoneman, photograph, 1918, NPG · Elliott & Fry, photograph, Wellcome L. · photograph, repro. in *Obits. FRS* · photograph, repro. in *BMJ* · photomechanical print, Wellcome L.

Wealth at death £16,106 6s. 1d.: probate, 16 Jan 1932, *CGPLA Eng. & Wales*

Bruce, Dorothy Morris Fairlie [Dorita Fairlie] (1885–1970), children's writer, was born in Palos, Spain, on 20 May 1885. Her father, Alexander Fairlie Bruce (1857–1944), a Scottish engineer, was working in Spain at the time, and to this she owed her Spanish nickname. Her mother was Katherine Elizabeth (*c*.1861–1931), daughter of William Freebairn of Drummilling, West Kilbride, Ayrshire. Bruce's early childhood was spent in Scotland, first at Blanefield, Strathblane, Stirlingshire, and then at Blairgowrie, Perthshire, where her brother was born in 1894, but in 1895 her father was commissioned to build the Staines Reservoir and the family moved south to Ealing in west London. Bruce was educated at Clarence House, Roehampton (originally a branch of the Royal School for the Daughters of Military Officers), an experience which she evidently enjoyed. From the age of seven she had determined on a writing career and on leaving school was able to live at home and pursue it. Later, her mother's ill health and death imposed housekeeping duties on her, but otherwise she was free to write.

Bruce's love for her Scottish homeland had to be content with holidays, in her teenage and early adult years with her maternal grandparents. She disliked their strictness, but it was Ayrshire and the Firth of Clyde which she came to use as the background of the bulk of her books with Scottish settings.

From 1905 Bruce was publishing poems and short stories for girls and children, but in 1920 came her first full-length book, *The Senior Prefect* (later reissued as *Dimsie Goes to School*); over the next thirty-five years she produced thirty-eight books and numerous short stories. All were aimed at middle-class teenage girls, and the majority were school stories, a genre then at its height and which Bruce helped to shape. Some later books dealt with slightly older girls, grappling with life and careers, and she wrote four historical novels with Scottish settings.

The interest of Bruce's school stories depends chiefly not on romantic settings or exciting incidents (although both occur) but on the interplay of characters and the resolution of personal dilemmas within the limits of a small, clearly defined community. Her plots are tightly constructed and her school backgrounds very real; her popular Dimsie series is recognizably set in her own old school. She was the first major writer to produce a school series, a form she liked as giving more scope for development, but she was careful not to overextend it. Compared with the mammoth series of her compeers Elsie J. Oxenham (an Ealing older contemporary) and Elinor M. Brent-Dyer (thirty-six and fifty-nine books respectively) Bruce's series of nine volumes or less appear modest, though their overall quality is higher. Besides the Dimsie books (which were very popular in Britain and, in Swedish translations, in Scandinavia), her best work is to be found in her Nancy and Springdale series.

In appearance Bruce was tall and well-set, with a fresh complexion, loosely knotted hair and blue-grey eyes. She enjoyed gardening, needlework, and animals, and was a private person who avoided publicity and was content with her family and close friends.

Bruce was a devout member of the Church of Scotland, sustained and impelled by a deep faith. From her twenties until the Second World War she was much involved with the Girls' Guildry, an organization similar to the Girl Guides but largely church-connected. Its motto, Wise unto that which is good, was certainly the ideal which her heroines followed, and might very well serve as her own epitaph.

Not until 1949, after the deaths of her parents, did Bruce return to Scotland to live. Her last twenty-one years were spent in Upper Skelmorlie, Ayrshire, on Wemyss Bay, where, in her own house, Triffeny, she died on 21 September 1970.   HILARY CLARE

Sources E. M. Löfgren, *"Schoolmates of the long-ago": motifs and archetypes in Dorita Fairlie Bruce's boarding school stories* (1993) · Oxford University Press, archives · M. Cadogan and P. Craig, *You're a brick, Angela!* (1976) · M. Cadogan, *Chin up, chest out, Jemima!* (1989) · S. Sims and H. Clare, *The encyclopaedia of girls' school stories* (2000), vol. 1 of *The encyclopaedia of school stories*, ed. R. Auchmuty and J. Wotton · b. cert. · Burke, *Peerage* · directories, Ealing
Archives Oxford University Press, archives, contracts, and letters · priv. coll., MSS and family papers
Likenesses photograph, repro. in D. F. Bruce, *Nancy at St Bride's*, new edn (1965), cover · photographs, priv. coll.
Wealth at death £20,918 18s.: confirmation, 5 Nov 1970, *CCI*

Bruce, Edward, earl of Carrick (*c*.1280–1318), soldier and claimant to the Irish throne, was the third, or possibly fourth, son of Robert VI de Brus (*d*. 1304), son of the claimant for the Scottish throne, and Marjory, countess of Carrick. He had two older brothers, *Robert (King Robert I), and Neil, and was probably older than Alexander and Thomas; he also had four sisters, the oldest, Isabel, married to Erik II, king of Norway.

Nothing is known of Bruce's childhood save a hint that

for a time he was fostered with an Irish family; in 1304, not yet knighted, he was in the household of Edward, prince of Wales, in Scotland. With the murder of John Comyn in February 1306 and seizure of the Scottish throne by his brother, Robert, he was drawn into the desperate war for the family's right. In the early phase he is depicted by Barbour as being with Robert, but also sent as messenger to Comyn, a task which other sources ascribe to his brothers Thomas and Alexander, never mentioned by Barbour. They, not Edward, were sent to Ireland to bring help, and died on the gibbet for it; his brother Neil, taken at Kildrummy, met the same end. Thus by February 1307 Edward was the sole surviving brother of the king, apparently sticking fairly closely to him during the fraught summer of 1307. A month after the Bruce victory of Inverurie, Edward Bruce led an invasion of Galloway on 21 June 1308 by forces from the western seaboard, suggesting that he had been there since autumn 1307. The campaign was outstandingly successful, with victories at the Cree (against overwhelming odds, according to Barbour) and the Dee; English forces and hostile Galloway kindreds were driven from the west and Buittle became the westernmost English stronghold from 1308 to 1312. As Edward retired north he took Rutherglen.

Bruce appears at the St Andrews parliament of March 1309 as lord of Galloway, but is not prominent in the following years. Strikingly it was Thomas Randolph, not Bruce, whom the king appointed as royal lieutenant, and in 1312 Randolph became earl of Moray before Bruce was given the much smaller earldom of Carrick (1313) with no trace of the regalian powers conferred on Moray. Barbour ascribes to him the taking of Dundee, in early April 1312, but it was surrendered to the king in terms of a prior agreement during a siege, and Bruce's role was probably subordinate.

In 1314, however, Carrick seems to have seized an initiative. The northern English counties had bought a truce to last until 29 September, but Edward II had promised to be in Scotland by 24 June. The king gave Moray the task of taking Edinburgh Castle, but during that siege, on 27 or 28 February 1314, Douglas took Roxburgh Castle by surprise; on receipt of the news the king sent Carrick across country to render its defences ineffective. Then, on 14 March, Edinburgh fell, and, according to the Lanercost chronicle, the Scots marched to set siege to Stirling, a siege which the life of Edward II ascribes to King Robert. Carrick cannot have been with them, for on 16 April with an army he invaded Cumberland, burning towns, killing people, and rustling cattle, all because the blackmail due had fallen into arrears. Barbour is emphatic, however, that the agreement for the surrender of Stirling if not relieved by 24 June, was made by Carrick and forcefully deprecated by the king. Barbour is wildly wrong in ascribing this agreement to the absurd date of Lent 1313; record evidence reveals that it was made about mid-May 1314, which would fit with Carrick's taking over the siege after his Cumbrian campaign. And it looks as though during all these months the king was in uncertain health.

That illness, probably recurrent, had receded when

Edward II approached Stirling. The king had placed Carrick in command of one of the three Scottish divisions, and when the battle of Bannockburn opened, it was by an assault of the English van upon Carrick's force. Evidently they held steady and wreaked carnage among the English cavalry, but no individual role is ascribed to Carrick then or in the aftermath, until, about 1 August, he led a large force which devastated Northumberland, took blackmail from Durham, and returned by the west, ravaging sometimes, taking money at others.

Carrick had shown his want of judgement at Stirling, but the return of the king's daughter and her proposed marriage now raised the critical issue of the succession; at an assembly at Ayr on 27 April 1315, it was agreed that Carrick, as 'a vigorous man, most highly skilled in warfare for the defence of the freedom of the kingdom, and his heirs male' should succeed the king unless he had a son, but if he did and died, the regent for the child was to be not Carrick but Moray (Dickinson, Donaldson, and Milne, 1.149–50). In fact Carrick was already in communication with the kings and chiefs of Ulster, with whom it was later said he had been brought up, and the Ayr assembly must have agreed to back his decision to cross, and to drive the English from Ireland, with the aid of Ulster chiefs and recognition of him as king of Ireland.

King Robert and Carrick had always been conscious of the Gaedhealtachd off Britain's western seaboard, seeking allies and troops there in difficult times. Now they committed themselves, with men and supplies from lowland and Gaelic Scotland, to establishing a permanent Bruce kingdom in Ireland, to reconciling the native Irish rulers sufficiently to replace their rivalries with a royal authority strong enough to conquer Dublin and other urban centres of English power. Neither Carrick nor Robert showed the slightest acquaintance with a strategy which might have achieved those ends.

Carrick landed near Carrickfergus on 26 May 1315, with a force which included Moray. In early June (and not, as is often said, in May 1316) he was recognized as king of Ireland, and, after a foolish delay of about a month, he crossed into Airgialla. Outside Ulster he ravaged and burned, pressing south into Louth, then retreating to Coleraine and Connor, where he had an encouraging success in battle against the earl of Ulster and government forces. At the end of that year he again marched south, picking up Moray and reinforcements at Dundalk. Avoiding Dublin he marched through Wicklow, almost into Carlow, and defeated an incompetently led government force at Arscoll (or Skerries) before returning to Ulster in February 1316. About the end of August 1316 he at least secured the surrender of Carrickfergus Castle, probably with King Robert's help, and they both returned to an assembly at Cupar, Fife, on 16 September 1316, where Edward and the Scottish magnates put their seals to an unusual royal charter confirming Moray's possessions; relations between Moray and Carrick seem to have been fraught.

Late in 1316 Edward was back in Ireland, and, confident of the control of the Irish Sea by his privateers, sent a letter which almost defies belief to 'all those [in Wales] desiring freedom'. The Welsh and the Scots, 'who proceed from one root of origin or kinship and country in the beginning', have suffered from the oppression of the English. If it is the will of the Welsh, he will carry forward their joint struggle if they will commit to him the prosecution of their cause and the chief lordship which their prince formerly exercised (*Regesta regum Scottorum*, 5, no. 571). About the same time the native Irish of Ulster were preparing their Remonstrance against English misdeeds to Pope John XXII, a document where Edward is invoked as king only at the very end and because he will protect the liberties of the Irish church; he had little support in his 'kingdom' and none in Wales.

None the less, in January 1317 King Robert and Moray, committed to the whole enterprise, crossed to Ireland, and with Edward launched an assault on the south. Dublin was in a panic as they approached, but perhaps because the Scots lacked supplies in what were lean years, they made no attempt to seize or besiege it, and the force went on to ravage south and west as far as Limerick and Tipperary, returning north without achieving anything decisive. From the return of Robert and Moray to Scotland in May 1317 a silence falls on Carrick's activities until, in October 1318, probably buoyed by the promise of reinforcements from Scotland, he marched again. Outside Dundalk, at Faughart, a government force under John Bermingham blocked his way. Urged to await reinforcements under King Robert which had just arrived at Carrickfergus, he refused, and without support from the native Irish, most of whom were heartily sick of him, attacked the stronger enemy on 14 October 1318. He was killed, his body decapitated, and the head taken to Edward II by Bermingham. King Robert went home to sort out the succession yet again. There is much colourful detail about the Irish war, but a confusion of the first two campaigns, in Barbour's poem; it is possible that behind this there lies a minstrel's account of Edward Bruce, written in the last year of his life.

The explanation of Barbour for the sorry tale of his end was that Edward found Scotland too small for himself and his brother; Fordun is blunter, claiming that Edward asked Robert for half the Scottish kingdom, and when refused determined to win Ireland. Other sources make much the same comment, bearing out Barbour's judgement that Edward was brave but completely lacking in 'mesur', that moderation which we would call common sense. Even his marital life was a mess. He seems to have been affianced to Isabel, daughter of John, earl of Atholl (executed 1306), probably to mark the earl's commitment to the Bruces in the early summer of 1306; they had a son, Alexander, and they may even have married, as Barbour's confused account claims. If so, the marriage was annulled, for he married another Isabel, daughter of William, earl of Ross. In 1306 William had handed over to the English Elizabeth, queen of Robert I, and may have been responsible for their taking the earl of Atholl. According to the papal dispensation of 1317, the marriage of Edward was arranged to end Ross's feud with the Bruces, and therefore can be dated to the earl's submission to King Robert in October 1308. There were no surviving children. The Atholls bore a lasting grudge against Edward, wherefore Isabel's brother, Earl David, deserted the Bruce cause at a critical moment, the battle of Bannockburn.

Robert I conferred the earldom of Carrick on his own son and heir, David, a practice which the Stewarts later revived, and which continues today. In 1326 or 1327 Isabel of Atholl and her son, **Alexander Bruce**, earl of Carrick (*d.* 1333), received grant of lands in Dumfriesshire and later the king gave Alexander, his 'nephew', land in Angus and Wigtownshire. His role, if any, at the end of Robert's reign is obscure, and he is not named as participating in the Weardale campaign of 1327, nor is he a witness to royal charters. On the outbreak of war in 1332, Alexander Bruce seems to have avoided serving in the Guardian's army at Dupplin, but when the newly crowned king, Edward (Balliol), came south to spend Christmas at Annan, Bruce joined him. The party was interrupted by a patriotic assault which killed Henry Balliol, and from which Bruce escaped only because he was recognized by the earl of Moray. By the time Edward III invaded and set siege to Berwick in the summer of 1333, Bruce had been bribed back to loyalty to David II by the conferment of the earldom of Carrick; he was in the Scottish army which, seeking to relieve the town, was thoroughly defeated at Halidon Hill on 19 July 1333. Carrick was one of five earls killed. He had married Eleanor, daughter of Sir Archibald *Douglas ('Tyneman') and sister of William, first earl of Douglas, but they had no surviving children. She remarried several times and died after 1376.

A. A. M. DUNCAN

Sources J. Barbour, *The Bruce*, ed. A. A. M. Duncan (1997) · J. Stevenson, ed., *Chronicon de Lanercost, 1201–1346*, Bannatyne Club, 65 (1839) · W. Bower, *Scotichronicon*, ed. D. E. R. Watt and others, new edn, 9 vols. (1987–98), vols. 6–7 · T. W. Moody and others, eds., *A new history of Ireland*, 2: *Medieval Ireland, 1169–1534* (1987); repr. with corrections (1993) · G. W. S. Barrow, *Robert Bruce and the community of the realm of Scotland*, 3rd edn (1988) · G. W. S. Barrow and others, eds., *Regesta regum Scottorum*, 5, ed. A. A. M. Duncan (1988) · *Scots peerage*, 2.435–7 · G. Burnett and others, eds., *The exchequer rolls of Scotland*, 1 (1878) · S. Duffy, 'The Bruce brothers and the Irish Sea world, 1306–29', *Cambridge Medieval Celtic Studies*, 21 (1991), 55–86 · J. M. Thomson and others, eds., *Registrum magni sigilli regum Scotorum / The register of the great seal of Scotland*, 2nd edn, 1, ed. T. Thomson (1912) · W. C. Dickinson, G. Donaldson, and I. A. Milne, eds., *A source book of Scottish history*, 2nd edn, 1 (1958), 149–50

Bruce, Edward, first Lord Kinloss and first Baron Bruce of Kinloss (1548/9–1611), lawyer and administrator, was the second son of Sir Edward Bruce of Blairhall, Clackmannanshire (1505–1565), and his wife, Alison, daughter of William Reid of Aitkenhead, Clackmannanshire; he was thus a nephew of Robert Reid, bishop of Orkney, and elder brother of Sir George *Bruce, mining industrialist and landowner. Educated at St Andrews University, he matriculated in 1568 and graduated MA in 1571. In the following decade Bruce apparently developed a legal career and is infrequently referred to in public records, mostly as a lawyer. By 1583 he had acquired some prominence and

had attracted the notice of the government, and in that year he was appointed a judge of the commissary court of Edinburgh, and one of the deputies of the lord justice-general. Also in 1583 he received a grant of the abbey of Kinloss in Moray, to be held for life *in commendam*, subject to an annuity payable to the abbot and a rent of 500 merks to the crown. Some time before 1586 Bruce married Magdalen, daughter of Sir Alexander Clark of Balbirnie, Fife.

Although English observers consistently labelled Bruce a protestant, his conduct suggests that he was considerably more moderate in his views than other government officials. It would appear that he followed the lead of James VI in such matters, and was more concerned with the political implications of the king's attempts to secure religious harmony than with the fine details of devotional form and practice. His legal experience and social position enabled Bruce to play an important part in shaping the government's approach to religious affairs. In 1587 the government exploited his legal skills to thwart the political initiatives of an increasingly radical Scottish church. The general assembly petitioned James to bar from parliament the bishops and other spiritual lords (by this time consisting mostly of the holders of secularized monastic commendatorships) in favour of church representatives nominated by the assembly. Addressing parliament as a member of the spiritual estate, Bruce set out the government's position, one opposed to such a change in the parliamentary constitution, and the king refused the petition. After 1587 James increasingly confided legal matters of a particularly sensitive nature to Bruce, who typified the professional legal administrators increasingly cultivated by the king in his government of Scotland.

In the 1590s affairs of state which were of personal importance to the king were also entrusted to Bruce. He was the lawyer and junior political member on three embassies to England, in 1594, 1598, and 1601. The first of these, led by James Colville of Easter Wemyss, bore a complaint to Queen Elizabeth that the earl of Bothwell was being harboured in England and sought a subsidy to crush the earl's conspiracy. Bruce also complained that the English ambassador to Scotland, Edward, Lord Zouche, had attempted to conduct secret negotiations with Bothwell. A modest subsidy was secured, ostensibly to suppress religiously motivated conspiracy in Scotland. In 1597 Bruce was appointed a commissioner to levy an aid granted by parliament, and on 2 December that year he was made a judge in the court of session, the kingdom's highest civil court. In March 1598 he was again sent to the English court, to make King James's apologies for offences complained of by Elizabeth, and to discuss other matters of state concerning the two realms and their borders. Probably he was also secretly instructed to sound out the queen and her council about James's position with regard to the English succession, but if so his mission appears to have been fruitless in that respect.

Early in 1601, on the eve of the eruption of the Essex plot, King James, who had for some time been in secret correspondence with the conspirators, determined to send Bruce and the earl of Mar to London on a mission which was ostensibly of no special importance but which was really intended to ascertain the precise state of affairs in England and the prospects for the plot, with a view to co-operating with it. However, the envoys did not start until February, and therefore did not arrive until after Essex's execution. In view of the changed circumstances, James instructed his ambassadors to seek a formal declaration from the queen and her council that he was guiltless of involvement in any of the intrigues against her, particularly in the late conspiracy, and the assurance of his succession to the English throne after her death. They obtained an early audience with Sir Robert Cecil, who exacted from them a pledge that James would abandon all his efforts to obtain formal recognition of his title as the condition of continued communications, and that all such communications should be kept secret. The result was a celebrated correspondence between James and Cecil. Following his return to Scotland, on 2 February 1602, Bruce was made Lord Kinloss.

Bruce accompanied King James to England in 1603, was naturalized as an English subject by act of parliament, and worked for the crown from London until his death. He was made a member of the privy council in both realms. On 18 May 1603 he was made master of the rolls and given lands in Yorkshire, and on 8 July 1604 he was created Baron Bruce of Kinloss, a further Scottish peerage, probably because there were legal doubts over the 1602 creation. On 30 August 1605 Oxford University conferred the degree of MA upon him. Although his career in England tended towards legal administration, and was less noteworthy than his very active service in Scotland, Bruce remained closely involved in government and high in James's favour. When his daughter Christiana [see Cavendish, Christian] married William Cavendish, later second earl of Devonshire, on 10 April 1609, the king gave the bride away and made her wedding portion up to £10,000. Bruce died suddenly on 14 January 1611, aged sixty-two, and was buried in the Rolls Chapel in Chancery Lane, London; a splendid monument marks the tomb.

The Bruces had three sons, Robert, Edward, and Thomas, and two daughters, Christiana and Janet. Robert predeceased his father, who was therefore succeeded in his lands and title by Edward, who, however, was killed in a duel by Sir Edward Sackville at Bergen op Zoom in August 1613. Thomas succeeded his brother and in 1633 was created earl of Elgin during Charles I's visit to Scotland. Janet (who is recorded as illegitimate in Crawford's *Scottish Peerage*) married Thomas Dalziel of the Binns, Linlithgowshire, an Edinburgh lawyer. Lady Bruce remarried, to Sir James Fullerton, and died about the end of 1630.

R. R. ZULAGER

Sources G. Brunton and D. Haig, *An historical account of the senators of the college of justice, from its institution in MDXXXII* (1832) • *Scots peerage*, 3.474–7 • GEC, *Peerage*, 2.350–51 • *CSP Scot. ser.*, 1589–1603 • DNB • G. Crawfurd, *The peerage of Scotland: containing an historical and genealogical account of the nobility of that kingdom* (privately printed, Edinburgh, 1716) • *Correspondence of King James VI of Scotland with Sir Robert Cecil and others in England during the reign of Elizabeth*, ed. J. Bruce, CS, old ser., 78 (1861) • D. Dalrymple, *The secret correspondence of Sir Robert Cecil with James VI* (1766)
Likenesses Barrett, line engraving (after tomb effigy), NPG • G. P. Harding, drawing (after portrait, 1604), NPG • funeral monument, Rolls Chapel, Chancery Lane, London • tomb effigy, Public Record Office Museum, London

Bruce, (Josephine) Esther (1912–1994), seamstress, was born on 29 November 1912 at 15 Dieppe Street, Fulham, London, the only surviving daughter of Joseph Adolphus Bruce (1880–1941), builder's labourer and coach painter, originally from British Guiana, and his Scottish wife, Edith (d. 1918), daughter of James Brooks, journeyman printer. A younger sister died in infancy. Her father (who brought Esther up on his own after the death of his wife) had settled in Edwardian London at a time when very few people of African descent were living in the capital. A proud man, he always made a defiant stand against racism. In the early 1920s he was responsible for the sacking of a teacher who instructed his daughter and her (white) classmates at North End Road School, Fulham, 'not to talk to coloured people' (Bourne and Bruce, 4). A few years later Esther (who left school at fourteen to work as a seamstress) was sacked by a new manager from her job at Barker's, a department store in Kensington High Street, for, she said, 'being coloured'. She later recalled,

> Dad was very angry and went to Barker's the next day. He raised the roof. He said: 'You can't do this to my child.' He even wrote a letter to our MP at the House of Commons, but that's as far as it went.   (Bourne and Bruce, 7)

Joseph Bruce married second, in 1928, Jennie Edwards, a children's nurse, also from British Guiana; she died of tuberculosis in 1933, at the age of forty.

For many years Joseph and Esther Bruce were the only black members of their tight-knit working-class community. Esther fondly recalled the community spirit that existed before and during the Second World War. 'In the old days the people of Fulham used to be one big happy family and we helped each other. … We were poor but people cared about each other. People were friendly and that meant a lot' (Bourne and Bruce, 14). In the 1930s she befriended two famous black people living in London: the Jamaican nationalist leader Marcus Garvey (who also lived in Fulham) and the American singer Elisabeth Welch (for whom she made dresses). She said, 'Marcus Garvey was a nice chap. He told me the English are no good but I said there are *some* good people in this world' (ibid., 7).

During the Second World War Bruce worked as a ward cleaner and fire-watcher in Brompton Hospital. After the death of her father in 1941 she was 'adopted' by her neighbour Hannah Johnson (1877–1952). Johnson was the matriarch of Dieppe Street, affectionately known in their community as Granny Johnson. Said Bruce, 'Granny Johnson was like a mother to me. She was an angel' (Bourne and Bruce, 10). After the war Bruce continued working in Brompton Hospital as a seamstress in the linen room. She stayed there until 1956, when she left to work for a curtain manufacturer in Fulham. She retired in 1972, but boredom brought her out of retirement and she continued

(Josephine) **Esther Bruce** (1912–1994), by Sandra Knight

working as a seamstress until poor eyesight forced her to retire finally at the age of seventy-four.

A friendly, outgoing woman, Bruce integrated easily into the new, multi-cultural society of post-war Britain which began with the arrival of Caribbean settlers on the *Empire Windrush* at Tilbury docks in 1948. But from time to time racism still reared its ugly head. She recalled in particular the aftermath of the Notting Hill riots in 1958: 'It was a terrible time for black people. I didn't think anything like that would ever happen in this country. Afterwards I noticed a change in some white people' (Bourne and Bruce, 13). She believed that 'if they'd stopped Enoch Powell and the National Front right at the beginning they wouldn't have got a hold' (ibid., 14).

In 1991 Hammersmith and Fulham's Ethnic Communities Oral History Project published *Aunt Esther's Story*, Bruce's autobiography, co-authored with her nephew Stephen Bourne, for which the project, Bruce, and Bourne received the Arts Council of Great Britain's Raymond Williams prize for community publishing. Simon Reade described Bruce's story as

A personal yet archetypal chapter in the history of working-class London, one which is usually overlooked in the grand catalogue of great men. It should inspire young people to explore the thoughts and observations of an older generation of family and friends, thus discovering shared experiences throughout our multi-racial, culturally diverse metropolis. (*City Limits*, 23–30 Jan 1992)

For two years an exhibition of photographs from the book—including several contemporary portraits by Val Wilmer—toured various venues in London. In 1994 the Museum of London featured the exhibition in a historical

event called the Peopling of London. A revised and updated edition of the book was published in 1996. David Mathews commented, 'Inspirational and enlightening, focussing on everyday realism, the book gets to the heart of the matter: black people are, and have been, an integral part of British history for centuries' (*Caribbean Times*, 10 Oct 1996).

Bruce, who never married, died at the Chelsea and Westminster Hospital, Chelsea, on 17 July 1994 of heart failure. Following her cremation at Mortlake crematorium on 27 July 1994 her ashes were scattered on her parents' unmarked grave in Fulham cemetery.

STEPHEN BOURNE

Sources S. Bourne and E. Bruce, *Aunt Esther's story*, 2nd edn (1996) · S. Bourne, 'Point of departure: my Aunt Esther', *History Today*, 50/2 (2000) · S. Bourne, *The Independent* (29 Aug 1994) · J. P. Green, *Black Edwardians: black people in Britain, 1901–1914* (1998) · S. Okokon, *Black Londoners, 1880–1990* (1998) · b. cert. · d. cert. · cremation cert. · personal knowledge (2004) · private information (2004)
Archives priv. coll., MSS
Likenesses S. Knight, photograph, 1992, repro. in *The Independent* · S. Knight, photograph, priv. coll. [*see illus.*] · photographs, priv. coll. · photographs, repro. in Bourne and Bruce, *Aunt Esther's story* · photographs, repro. in Bourne, 'Point of departure: my Aunt Esther'

Bruce, Frederick Fyvie (1910–1990), biblical scholar, was born on 12 October 1910 in Elgin, the eldest of the seven children of Peter Fyvie Bruce (1874–1955), an evangelist among the Christian Brethren, and his wife, Mary Maclennan (1883–1965). From Elgin Academy (1921–8) he proceeded to study classics at Aberdeen (MA, 1932) and Cambridge (BA, 1934), followed by a year in Vienna as holder of the Sandys scholarship. The possibility of further doctoral study in philology was overtaken by appointment to a junior teaching post in Greek in Edinburgh (1935–8) and then to a lectureship in classics in Leeds (1938–47). During this period he developed his scholarly interest in biblical studies and in the New Testament in particular; he won the Crombie scholarship in biblical criticism in 1939 and took a diploma in Hebrew in 1943. Although he had no degree in biblical or theological subjects and was never ordained he was appointed to the headship of the newly created department of biblical studies in Sheffield in 1947, and worked to such good effect that he was appointed to a chair in 1955 and was awarded an Aberdeen honorary DD in 1957. In 1959 he was appointed to the Rylands chair of biblical criticism and exegesis in Manchester (in the distinguished succession of A. S. Peake, C. H. Dodd, and T. W. Manson) where he remained until retirement in 1978.

Bruce had an international reputation as a biblical scholar. He travelled and lectured in institutions throughout the world. He shared with only one other scholar the honour of being president of both the (British) Society for Old Testament Study (1965) and the (international) Studiorum Novi Testamenti Societas (1975); he was elected a fellow of the British Academy (1973) and was awarded its Burkitt medal (1979). He was awarded a DLitt from Leeds University in 1988. He received three Festschriften by colleagues and former students.

Bruce was a prolific writer with some fifty books and hundreds of articles to his credit. His scholarly career began with a major commentary on the Acts of the Apostles (1951) in which he dealt with the Greek text linguistically and historically from the vantage point of a classical scholar; simultaneously he was also at work on a more theologically orientated volume, *The Book of the Acts* (1953). From Acts he moved naturally into the Pauline literature and wrote commentaries of varying scale on most of the letters; those on Galatians (1982) and 1 and 2 Thessalonians (1982) are the most substantial. A host of public lectures and essays formed the basis for his major study, *Paul: Apostle of the Free Spirit* (1977). He also wrote a fine commentary on Hebrews (1964). He was among the first scholars to discuss the impact of the discovery of the Dead Sea scrolls on biblical studies (*Second Thoughts on the Dead Sea Scrolls*, 1956; *Biblical Exegesis in the Qumran Texts*, 1959). He wrote standard textbooks on early Jewish history (*Israel and the Nations*, 1963) and the history of the early church (*The Spreading Flame*, 1953; *New Testament History*, 1969).

Bruce's scholarship was marked by the way in which he brought his classical training to the study of the biblical texts. This tended to liberate him from the theological bias and even prejudice that can interfere with objective biblical study. He was able to harvest the results of archaeological study for the illumination of the written texts of the Bible. Writing initially at a time when so-called 'higher criticism' often disparaged the historical value of the biblical writings, he came to a much more positive evaluation of their historical worth. Admittedly this conclusion was congenial to his own theological position. He was nurtured in a conservative, evangelical tradition in the Christian Brethren and never wavered from it, but his scholarly conclusions were not preformed but relied on sober study of the evidence, and he was certainly not afraid to differ from his more conservative colleagues when he was convinced that the evidence required him to do so. At the same time he was respected by scholars who took a more radical view of the evidence than he did, precisely because he respected them and their work.

Bruce played an important part in stimulating the development of biblical and theological scholarship in his own evangelical Christian constituency. He was a founder member and sometime chairman of the Tyndale Fellowship for Biblical Research, and he was honorary president of the Inter-Varsity Fellowship in 1955. Particularly in Manchester he guided the studies of a remarkable number of doctoral students.

Bruce was an outstanding example of the genus *Scholar* rather than *Researcher*. He had an encyclopaedic and exact knowledge in many fields, and the ability to express himself in a lucid and attractive manner. His scholarship was entirely free from eccentricity and weakly based hypotheses.

Bruce was an active member of the church and much in demand as a lay preacher and speaker. His spoken style could be somewhat dry, but he shone in panel discussions and informal occasions when his capacity for relating anecdotes and his pawky Scottish humour came to the fore. He wrote an autobiographical account, *In Retrospect: Remembrance of Things Past* (1980), which is a delightful description of the academic and Christian scene, especially during his earlier years in the north-east of Scotland. He married Annie Bertha Davidson, known as Betty (1910–1994), daughter of A. B. Davidson, a Scottish farmer, on 19 August 1936, and they had two children, Iain and Sheila. He was an essentially humble and ordinary person with no side, able to fit in with whatever company he was in. He never drove a car nor acquired a computer; he corrected the proofs of the English translation of the *Theologisches Wörterbuch zum Neuen Testament* on his daily train journeys. Bruce died at his home, The Crossways, 2 Temple Road, Buxton, on 11 September 1990 and was buried at Buxton cemetery a week later.

I. HOWARD MARSHALL

Sources F. F. Bruce, *In retrospect: remembrance of things past* (1980); rev. edn (1993) · I. H. Marshall, 'Frederick Fyvie Bruce, 1910–1990', *PBA*, 80 (1993), 245–60 · I. H. Marshall and others, 'The contribution of Frederick Fyvie Bruce', *Journal of the Christian Brethren Research Fellowship*, 22 (1971), 4–47 · L. Gasque and W. Gasque, 'Frederick Fyvie Bruce: an appreciation', *Aware*, 69/11 (Nov 1990), 1–4 · A. R. Millard, 'Frederick Fyvie Bruce, 1910–1990', *Journal of Semitic Studies*, 36 (1991), 1–6 · *CGPLA Eng. & Wales* (1993) · d. cert. · private information (2004) [family; A. Millard]
Wealth at death £236,419: probate, 23 Sept 1993, *CGPLA Eng. & Wales*

Bruce, Sir Frederick William Adolphus Wright- (1814–1867), diplomatist, was the youngest son of Thomas *Bruce, seventh earl of Elgin (1766–1841), and his second wife, Elizabeth (1790–1860), youngest daughter of James Townshend Oswald of Dunnikier, Fife. He was born at Broomhall, Fife, on 14 April 1814. After a short legal career, on 9 February 1842 he was attached to Lord Ashburton's mission to Washington and returned to Britain in September of that year. On 9 February 1844 he was appointed colonial secretary at Hong Kong, a position he held until 1846, when on 27 June he became lieutenant-governor of Newfoundland. His next posting was to Sucre, where he was appointed consul-general in the republic of Bolivia on 23 July 1847; on 14 April 1848 he was accredited as chargé d'affaires. On 29 August 1851 he was named chargé d'affaires to the Oriental Republic of the Uruguay, and on 3 August 1853 he became agent and consul-general in Egypt, replacing the Hon. C. A. Murray.

In April 1857 Bruce went to China as principal secretary, accompanying his brother James *Bruce, the eighth earl of Elgin, who had been appointed ambassador-extraordinary there. Having played a minor but not unimportant part in its negotiation, he brought home (18 September 1857) the treaty with China signed at Tientsin (Tianjin) on 26 June 1858, and was made a CB on 28 September. On 2 December 1858 he was appointed envoy-extraordinary and minister-plenipotentiary to the Chinese emperor (and from 1 March 1859 he was chief superintendent of British trade there). His mission was to proceed to Peking (Beijing) with his French counterpart, to exchange the ratified treaty. At Shanghai, however, he found the mouth of the Peiho (Beihe) River barred. Acting on Bruce's orders, Admiral Sir James Hope attempted to force entry to the river but failed ignominiously. Palmerston in effect replaced Bruce by sending back his brother, Lord Elgin, as ambassador to China, accompanied by a punitive expedition. Bruce followed his brother to Peking in November 1860, after the treaty had been ratified (24 October 1860); he finally met Prince Gong, China's foreign minister, on 2 April 1861.

Bruce's career took some time to recover from this episode, but he was not wholly out of favour. He was made a KCB of the civil division on 12 December 1862, and received the grand cross of the order on 17 March 1865. He was appointed umpire by the commission named under the convention of 1864, concluded between the United States of America and the United States of Colombia, for the adjustment of claims of American citizens against the Colombian government. He was appointed, from 1 March 1865, to succeed Lord Lyons as British envoy in Washington. There he found himself at the centre of the storm over the American claims against the British government for damages caused by the warship *Alabama* (sold to the South by a British firm during the civil war). Bruce 'played the moderator to perfection' and helped pave the way for the Gladstone government's later arbitration (Cook, 72).

Bruce died unmarried at Tremont House, Tremont Street, Boston, USA, on 19 September 1867; his remains were embalmed and, after being conveyed to Scotland, were interred at Dunfermline Abbey on 8 October. The American press spoke in eulogistic terms of his amiable personal qualities and of the able manner in which he exercised his ministerial functions. When a young lawyer, he handled the affairs of a widow, Mrs Wright, who on her death left him her fortune. He added Wright to his surname, but he was always known simply as Bruce. He was regarded in his family as a confirmed bachelor, very susceptible to blushing, which in later life he mostly concealed by sporting thick whiskers, the blush being observable only at the top of his bald head.

G. C. BOASE, *rev.* H. C. G. MATTHEW

Sources *GM*, 4th ser., 4 (1867), 677–8 · *FO List* (1868) · E. Holt, *The opium wars in China* (1964) · A. Cook, *The Alabama claims: American politics and Anglo-American relations, 1865–1872* (1975) · *CGPLA Eng. & Wales* (1868) · private information (2004)
Archives priv. coll. · University of Rochester, New York, Rush Rhees Library, letter-book | BL, corresp. with C. G. Gordon, Add. MSS 52386–52387, *passim* · Lpool RO, corresp. with fifteenth earl of Derby · priv. coll., letters to Lord Monck · Wilts. & Swindon RO, corresp. with Sidney Herbert
Wealth at death under £70,000: probate, 9 Jan 1868, *CGPLA Eng. & Wales*

Bruce, Sir George (*c.*1550–1625), mining industrialist and landowner, was probably born about 1550, the youngest of the three sons of Sir Edward Bruce (1505–1565) of Blairhall near Culross, in Perthshire, and Alison Reid of Aitkenhead, a sister of the bishop of Orkney. Sometimes described in documents as a 'merchant' or 'burgess of Culross', Bruce came from an established and well-connected landed family. His brother Edward *Bruce was a senior figure in the Scottish legal and political establishment, ennobled as Lord Kinloss for his part in securing the throne of England for James VI in 1603. Both brothers

were privy councillors. George himself filled a number of important offices, including member of the Scottish parliament for Culross from 1593. He married Margaret, daughter of Archibald Primrose, of Burnbrae, and Margaret Blaw, and they had three sons and five daughters.

In 1575 Bruce was allowed to become the lessee of the former monastic coalworks at Culross on the shore of the Firth of Forth, west of Dunfermline, 'for his great knowledge and skill in machinery such like as no other man has in these days; and for his being the likeliest person to re-establish again the Colliery of Culross' (Cunningham, 53). Bruce used innovative mechanical drainage, ventilation, and haulage techniques—notably an 'Egyptian wheel'—to solve the problems of exploiting deep and under-sea coalmines. In addition he ran saltworks which burned coal to evaporate sea water. In their day, Bruce's mines and saltworks were a tourist attraction, probably the largest and certainly the most technically advanced such enterprise in Scotland. John Taylor, 'the water poet', penned an epic poem about their operation in 1618. James VI knighted Bruce, probably in 1610, and visited his house and industrial businesses in 1617. Bruce's house or 'great lodging', and several other buildings in the picturesque burgh of Culross, were subsequently acquired by the National Trust for Scotland and opened to the public.

While no commercial records survive, Bruce's business was clearly profitable, to judge from his sprawling, attractive mansion (built in stages between 1597 and 1611) and from the impressive tomb in the Culross Abbey church: testaments to the benefits enjoyed by a successful industrialist even in an age when most wealth came from agriculture. George Bruce was also a shipowner and merchant, as well as a substantial landowner or 'laird'. His principal lands, purchased in 1602, were at nearby Carnock. With Bruce's help Culross became an important trading community and was elevated to the status of a royal burgh in 1588. Shortly before his death there in 1625 Bruce's showpiece enterprise was largely destroyed by a great storm, but Culross enjoyed commercial and industrial significance for a further century before the baton of economic development passed elsewhere in Scotland.

R. A. HOUSTON

Sources D. Beveridge, *Culross and Tulliallan, or, Perthshire on Forth*, 2 vols. (1885) · J. Hatcher, *Before 1700: towards the age of coal* (1993), vol. 1 of *The history of the British coal industry* (1984–93) · *Scots peerage* · A. S. Cunningham, *Culross: past and present* (1910), 53
Likenesses effigy, after 1625 (with family), Culross Abbey church

Bruce, Sir George Barclay (1821–1908), civil engineer, was born at Newcastle upon Tyne on 1 October 1821, the younger son of John Bruce (1775–1834), founder of the Percy Street Academy there, and Mary Jack. John Collingwood *Bruce was his eldest brother. Robert Stephenson was among his father's pupils, and Bruce, who was educated in his father's school, served five years' apprenticeship (1836–41) in the locomotive works of Robert Stephenson & Co. He worked for two years on the construction of the Newcastle and Darlington Railway and spent a year as resident engineer on the Northampton and Peterborough line, before being appointed, at the age of twenty-four, resident engineer of the Royal Border Bridge between Tweedmouth and Berwick, by Robert Stephenson and Thomas Elliot Harrison, the engineers-in-chief. The bridge was opened by Queen Victoria in August 1850, and in 1851 Bruce presented an account of it to the Institution of Civil Engineers, for which he was awarded a Telford medal. Bruce married in 1849 Helen Norah, daughter of Alexander H. Simpson, solicitor, of Paisley; they had one son and four daughters.

While working on the construction of the Haltwhistle and Alston Moor branch of the Newcastle and Carlisle Railway, Bruce was called to India, and for the remainder of his life was mostly concerned with Indian railways. After working on the Calcutta section of the East Indian Railway until 1853, he served as chief engineer of the Madras Railway, laying out and constructing some 500 miles of line before ill health compelled his return home in 1856.

Upon his return to Britain Bruce established himself as a consulting engineer in Westminster, from 1888 in partnership with Robert White. He was consulting engineer for fifty years to the 1 metre gauge South Indian Railway, and from 1894 to the Great Indian Peninsula and Indian Midland railways of 5 ft 6 in. gauge—the broader gauge which Bruce preferred.

Bruce's work included the Kettering, Thrapston and Huntingdon, the Peterborough, Wisbech and Sutton, the Whitehaven, Cleator and Egremont, and the Stonehouse and Nailsworth railway lines. Abroad he constructed the Tilsit–Intersburg, East Prussian, and Berlin–Gorlitz lines. During 1873-6 he constructed works for the shipment of ore from the Rio Tinto copper mines at Huelva in Spain, including a railway and a large pier of innovative construction. He also did engineering work for the East Argentine Railway, the Buenos Aires Grand National tramway, and the Beira Railway in southern Africa.

Bruce was elected a member of the Institution of Civil Engineers in 1850, became a member of council in 1871, and was president in the jubilee year, 1887. He served a second term as president in 1888, when he was knighted. In 1883, while vice-president, he represented the institution in Canada at the opening of the Northern Pacific Railway. In 1889 he was created a chevalier of the French Légion d'honneur for his contribution to the engineering displays at the Paris Exhibition of that year. He became a member of the Institution of Mechanical Engineers in 1874, and served on the royal commissions on the water supply of London of 1892 and 1897.

Outside his professional work Bruce was deeply interested in the Presbyterian church in England and in public education, and gave time and money liberally to the extension of the Presbyterian church at home and abroad. He was an elder of his local Presbyterian congregation in St John's Wood for thirty years, and served as convenor of both the church extension committee and the home mission committee from 1879 until his death. He actively promoted the union of Presbyterians in England, which was effected in 1876. At Wark he built a church and manse. He

was a member of the school board for London, representing Marylebone from 1882 to 1885. He died at his home, 64 Boundary Road, St John's Wood, on 25 August 1908.

W. F. SPEAR, *rev.* RALPH HARRINGTON

Sources *The Times* (26 Aug 1908) · PICE, 174 (1907-8), 369-72 · *The Engineer* (28 Aug 1908) · J. Marshall, *A biographical dictionary of railway engineers* (1978) · d. cert.
Likenesses W. M. Palin, oils, 1888, Inst. CE · O. Edis, photograph, c.1902, NPG
Wealth at death £57,579 19s. 6d.: probate, 20 Oct 1908, CGPLA Eng. & Wales

Bruce, George Wyndham Hamilton Knight- (1852–1896), bishop of Mashonaland, was born on 23 March 1852 at Keston, Kent, the eldest son of Lewis Bruce Knight-Bruce (*b.* 1820), of Roehampton Priory, Surrey, and his wife, Caroline Margaret Eliza, the only daughter of Thomas Newte of Tiverton, Devon. Sir James Lewis Knight-Bruce was his grandfather. George was educated at Eton College, and studied at Merton College, Oxford, from 13 April 1872. He graduated BA in 1876 and MA in 1881, and was created DD on 23 February 1886. He was ordained deacon in 1876, by the bishop of Gloucester and Bristol, and priest in 1877, as curate of Bibury in Gloucestershire. Knight-Bruce married Louisa, daughter of John Torr of Carlett Park in Cheshire, on 21 August 1878. They had one daughter. From 1878 to 1882 Knight-Bruce was curate of St Michael-at-Wendron, near Helston in Cornwall, and from 1882 to 1883 he was vicar of St George, Everton, Liverpool. In 1883 he offered his services as curate in the East End of London, and from 1884 to 1886 was curate in charge of St Andrew's, Bethnal Green, during the period in which the Oxford House Settlement was established.

On 25 March 1886, in St Mary's Church, Whitechapel, Knight-Bruce was consecrated third bishop of Bloemfontein. Reserved by nature, he was not entirely successful in his new country; however, his work in reorganizing and restoring order to the bishopric was admirable. He recognized Kimberley as a mission field which drew miners from every nearby country, and he was a keen explorer who, before the charter of the South African Company, made a preliminary expedition northwards, and reached as far as the Zambezi. He visited Lobengula, the chief of the Matabele (Ndebele), and, supported by the Society for the Promotion of the Gospel, obtained permission from the principal Mashona chiefs to accept missionaries into their lands.

After the charter of the British South Africa Company was granted in October 1889, Knight-Bruce followed the pioneer force into the country, and in 1891 he accepted the post of first bishop of Mashonaland in Southern Rhodesia. With the help of his wife, who shared his love for the native inhabitants, he ministered to local people as well as to English immigrants. While acknowledging the assistance of Cecil Rhodes and the company, he remained independent in his views. He repudiated the 'moral right' of Lobengula to rule over Mashonaland, but entirely disapproved of the Matabele campaign. In 1893 he joined the expeditionary force, but declined the post of chaplain, because he insisted that the Matabele were as much under

George Wyndham Hamilton Knight-Bruce (1852–1896), by unknown engraver, pubd 1896 (after Ball)

his diocesan care as the company's troops. From the same principles, he cared for the sick and wounded of both sides, even on the battleground when necessary.

Ill health forced Knight-Bruce to retire from the bishopric in 1894. He returned to England, and went immediately to Devon, where he worked for a time with the bishop of Exeter. In 1895 he was nominated to the crown living of Bovey Tracey, and shortly afterwards he became assistant bishop to Dr E. H. Bickersteth, then bishop of Exeter. He died at the vicarage of Bovey Tracey on 16 December 1896, survived by his wife.

Knight-Bruce left autobiographical accounts in his *Journals of the Mashonaland Mission* (1892, 2nd edn 1893) and *Memories of Mashonaland* (1895). An alabaster tablet to his memory was unveiled in Exeter Cathedral about 1900.

E. I. Carlyle, *rev.* Lynn Milne

Sources G. W. H. Knight-Bruce, *Journals of the Mashonaland mission, 1888 to 1892*, ed. L. K. B. [L. K. Bruce], 2nd edn (1893) · G. W. H. Knight-Bruce, *Memories of Mashonaland* (1895) · *The Times* (17 Dec 1896) · *Mission Field*, 42 (1897), 46–54 · *The Guardian* (23 Dec 1896), 2079–80 · *ILN* (26 Dec 1896), 880 · Boase, *Mod. Eng. biog.* · L. Baillie and P. Sieveking, eds., *British biographical archive* (1984) [microfiche]
Likenesses engraving (after photograph by Ball), NPG; repro. in *ILN* [*see illus.*] · photograph, NPG · portrait, repro. in *ILN*, 850
Wealth at death £2066 15*s.* 2*d.*: 20 March 1897, *CGPLA Eng. & Wales*

Bruce, Henry Austin, first Baron Aberdare (1815–1895), politician, was the second son of John Bruce (later Bruce Pryce; 1784–1872), and his first wife, Sarah, daughter of Hugh Williams Austin, rector of St Peter's, Barbados. Bruce was born at Dyffryn Aberdâr in Glamorgan on 16 April 1815, but spent his life from the age of six to twelve at St Omer in France. At this point the family returned to Wales, and Bruce was sent to Swansea grammar school. Instead of proceeding to Oxford or Cambridge, he left school for the chambers of his uncle, James Lewis (afterwards Lord Justice) Knight-Bruce; among his fellow pupils was the future Lord Cranbrook, his immediate predecessor as home secretary. He was called to the bar from Lincoln's Inn in 1837 at the age of twenty-two, but though he studied law fitfully for a few years, he had little zeal for the work, and, as a consequence, only a small practice. Furthermore he was plagued by indifferent health. He retired

from the bar in 1843 and spent the next two years on the continent recuperating.

First marriage, and the Dyffryn estate On returning to England in 1845, Bruce married Annabella, daughter of Sir Richard Beadon. Together they moved back to Wales to live at Dyffryn Aberdâr. This estate, long the Bruce family's residence, had by then passed formally into the hands of his father who inherited it in 1837 from his cousin Thomas Pryce. Bruce senior, who added Pryce to his surname on his inheritance, subsequently moved, however, leaving Dyffryn vacant and thus allowing his son to return. The move marked a watershed in Bruce's life. Up to this point, as he had complained to a friend in 1843, his life had been aimless and he felt himself to be 'a useless member of society' (W. N. Bruce, 220). On his return, however, he became involved in both the direction of the estate and in the administrative life of the burgeoning south Wales industrial belt.

Bruce's later prominence owed much to the events of this period. In the first place, it was in these years that the Bruce family fortune was made. Mineral royalties from the Dyffryn Aberdâr estate had risen steadily to reach about £1800 per annum by 1852, but subsequent expansion in the market for steam coal, a resource in which the estate was particularly rich, sent income soaring. By 1860 mineral royalties from Dyffryn Aberdâr were worth nearly £12,000. Bruce's consequence grew with the fortunes of the estate.

Magistrate and MP for Merthyr Tudful It was not to his wealthy background alone, however, that Bruce owed his prominence. He also established a reputation in these years as a sound man of business. In 1846 he was appointed a justice of the peace and a deputy lieutenant of Glamorgan, but the principal focus of his endeavours was Merthyr Tudful, for which he became a stipendiary magistrate in 1847. The work attached to the post was not arduous (the business of Merthyr required his presence for approximately three hours a day on three days of the week; Aberdâr, which he also visited, a further two hours on one day each week), but Bruce considered that he discharged his responsibilities with considerably more attention than either of his predecessors had. The great attraction of the post, however, was the income of £600 it provided, which allowed Bruce to become financially independent of his father for the first time. Altogether, Bruce estimated that his annual income at this period amounted to about £850.

The years of Bruce's magistracy saw the beginning of his interest in the education question. He recognized the explosive nature of society in frontier towns such as Merthyr, where the population increased sixfold in the first half of the nineteenth century to stand at 46,378 in 1851. He considered that the provision of both educational and 'rational' recreational facilities was essential to their civilization. In 1850–51 he delivered two lectures on this theme, remarking that there were no fifth-rate towns in France and Germany so backward in these respects as was the supposedly first-rate borough of Merthyr. His proposed solution contained the seeds of later policy: he was church rates (26 May 1853). He pursued his interest in questions relating to education, serving on the select committee on endowed schools in 1859.

The undramatic start to Bruce's parliamentary career may be explained by a combination of domestic circumstances and the demands of business in his native county. In 1852 his first wife died, and in 1854 he married again. His second wife was Nora Creina Blanche (d. 1897), younger daughter of Sir William Napier, the historian of the Peninsular War, of whom Bruce edited a *Life* in 1864. Soon after his marriage he contracted a bad case of scarlet fever, which also took its toll. Nevertheless the reputation that Bruce had gained from his years as the Merthyr magistrate was now translated into the vice-chairmanship of the county quarter sessions, a place on the board of directors of the Vale of Neath Railway Company, and a place as a trustee of the Dowlais ironworks. This last appointment, in 1856, represented a particularly important accretion of local political influence for the Merthyr MP. Again, Bruce proved himself a good choice. In tandem with his co-trustee, G. T. Clark, he reorganized the management structure of the works and immediately took out a licence to produce steel using the Bessemer process.

Henry Austin Bruce, first Baron Aberdare (1815–1895), by Lock & Whitfield, pubd 1882

among those urging the involvement of the state in making education compulsory if voluntary effort failed to fill the gap.

Bruce resigned the Merthyr magistracy in the autumn of 1852, and was elected as the town's MP in December on the death of Sir John Guest. Although the Dyffryn Aberdâr family had traditionally been tory supporters, Bruce sat as a Liberal. The foundation of his political philosophy seems to have been his confidence in the people. He was impressed by the self-control that was manifested in Merthyr during the Chartist revival of 1848. He mixed freely with the crowds at Chartist meetings, and later told a friend that he 'never got an uncivil word or look' (Aberdare, 88). As a consequence he was prepared to countenance a further extension of the franchise, declaring in 1851: 'My idea of the British constitution is that it is sufficiently elastic to admit to a share of political power all those whom education and good conduct have qualified for the trust' (W. N. Bruce, 227).

An active back-bencher Once in parliament, as his *Times* obituary writer suggested, Bruce made his way 'steadily, though not rapidly' (*The Times*, 26 Feb 1895). He gave general support to Lord Palmerston's government, and as a constituency MP was sedulous in the promotion of local interests. His maiden speech (16 February 1854) was in support of a bill to amend the Truck Act, and he also sat on several select committees set up to deal with both the Truck Act and various aspects of mining. Furthermore, though he was himself a stout Anglican, he reflected the wishes of his dissenting constituents by seconding the motion of Robert Phillimore to amend the system of

At the Home Office: under-secretary and secretary It was in the 1860s that Bruce began his rise to national prominence. His now well-recognized administrative skills earned him the offer of the governorship of Madras in September 1860, which he declined. In November 1862, however, he accepted an under-secretaryship at the Home Office, where he remained until 1864. His chief was Sir George Grey, a man for whom he expressed great admiration, and someone who held Bruce's own talents in equally high esteem, often quoting his subordinate's opinions in the cabinet. His most important work during his tenure of the position was to oversee the extension of the Factory Acts to the potteries. In April 1864 he became vice-president of the committee of Council on Education in succession to Robert Lowe, and was sworn a member of the privy council. He held these offices, together with that of second church estates commissioner, until the fall of Lord John Russell's government in the summer of 1866.

Although Bruce continued to take considerable interest in mining affairs (he served on the 1862 royal commission on the condition of mines), it was matters relating to education that preoccupied him during this period. Not only was he prepared to countenance state intervention, but he acknowledged that any compulsory measure must respect the denominational scruples of nonconformists. His background in Wales undoubtedly played a role in convincing him of this. Speaking during the debate on the education estimates in 1861, he observed that as a trustee of the Dowlais works he had found school places for 2300 children. The schools in the area were run by the National Society and yet not 10 per cent of the children had been Anglicans. As a consequence, Bruce had disaffiliated the schools and handed over control of them to the British and Foreign School Society. In 1866 he published a speech to the Social Science Association on national education, and in 1867 with W. E. Forster sponsored an Education of the Poor Bill. This permissive measure, which could be adopted by a majority of ratepayers in any area, would have allowed a popularly elected committee of management to raise a rate for the erection and running of a new school, which might give whatever religious instruction it thought fit. The bill was withdrawn, but Bruce introduced a revised measure in 1868 which contained provisions aimed at compelling local authorities to ensure that there was an adequate supply of schools in any given area. This too was withdrawn. A substantially similar measure was introduced during Gladstone's first government, and became the famous Elementary Education Act of 1870; although Bruce's name appeared on the bill, it was piloted through parliament by W. E. Forster.

Bruce became home secretary in December 1868 in Gladstone's first government but he sat for Renfrewshire, having suffered the humiliation of defeat at Merthyr in the 1868 general election. The 1867 Reform Act had increased the electorate in Merthyr elevenfold, and the traditional influence of the mine and factory owners was supplanted by the interests of organized nonconformity on the one hand and radical working-class politics on the other. Bruce's parliamentary record on behalf of the nonconformists was one of which he was justifiably proud, though he did not agree with the policy of disestablishment for Wales which some of his constituents espoused. On working-class issues, however, he was perceived to be much weaker. He had become obnoxious to former Chartists for his refusal to back universal suffrage and vote by ballot, but his defeat in 1868 appears to have derived almost entirely from differences of opinion on the general question of safety in mines, and, in particular, his apparent support for the introduction of a double-shift system into the Welsh coalfield. Bruce was 'vexed & mortified' to be beaten at Merthyr (Bruce to A. H. Layard, BL, Add. MS 38995, fol. 375), and the Welsh Liberal press likewise lamented his defeat. Within a week of the defeat, he had apparently been offered the chance to fight any one among three county seats, but he declined, and eventually came in for Renfrewshire (25 January 1869) where the sitting member had died. His letters during the campaign pointedly drew attention to the intelligence of the Scottish working men compared with those of other areas.

Bruce remained home secretary until 9 August 1873. Although Gladstone congratulated himself on having found a 'heaven-born Home Secretary' (DNB), Bruce's tenure of the post is best remembered for his abortive Licensing Bill of 1871. The reform of the law relating to the sale of alcohol had been an important issue during the 1868 election. Bruce's bill, introduced before the Easter recess, proposed that all existing licence holders remain in possession for a further ten years, but that there be no increase in the overall number of licences granted. Any 'vacancies' in the existing pool of licence holders were to be filled by granting the licence to the highest bidder, the money

raised to be applied to a worthy local object. These proposals drew opposition not only from the brewing interest, but also from the temperance lobby within Bruce's own party. During the recess, many protest meetings were held and, when parliament reconvened, the bill was defeated. A much milder measure, regulating the hours of opening, was introduced into the House of Lords the following session by Lord Kimberley, and passed. Bruce's most considerable achievements as home secretary were the Trades Union Act of 1871, which gave unions statutory protection but included controversially worded clauses outlawing the intimidation of members, and the Mines Regulation Act of 1872, which aimed to increase safety and further curtail the employment of boys in coal pits. He also played an important role during 1870 in helping Gladstone to choose a Welsh-speaking bishop of St Asaph.

Peerage: a variety of interests In the summer of 1873, Gladstone's need to move Robert Lowe, his unpopular chancellor of the exchequer, led him to ask Bruce to make way at the Home Office. In return, Bruce was offered a choice of three appointments: the lord lieutenancy of Ireland, the viceroyalty of Canada, or the lord presidentship of the council. Bruce chose the last and was raised to the peerage (22 August 1873) with the title of Baron Aberdare. He held the position only until February 1874, when the Liberal Party was turned out of office following a heavy defeat at the general election. The scale of the defeat was, in some quarters, blamed on the opposition roused by Bruce's Licensing Bill.

Although Bruce (now Lord Aberdare) attended the House of Lords regularly during his remaining twenty-one years, 1874 marked the end of his official political life. When Gladstone came to form another cabinet in 1880, he was overlooked. He did not withdraw from public life, however, and his abilities as a chairman were constantly in demand. On the nomination of successive governments, he chaired royal commissions on noxious vapours (1876), reformatory and industrial schools (1881), and the aged poor (1893), the last under great pressure from Gladstone himself. He was also involved with many learned societies. In 1875, as president of the Social Science Congress, he delivered an important address on crime and punishment, and on 20 January 1876 he was elected FRS. From 1878 to 1892 he was president of the Royal Historical Society, and in 1881 became the president of the Royal Geographical Society. He was also involved with the Royal Horticultural Society and the Royal Society for the Prevention of Cruelty to Animals. In 1882, meanwhile, he became chairman of the National African Company (later the Royal Niger Company), actively presiding over its operations in tandem with its founder Sir George Taubman Goldie. He was made a GCB on 7 January 1885.

Welsh education Despite this varied array of interests, Lord Aberdare's chief commitment during the last fifteen years of his life was to the cause of intermediary and higher education in Wales. Although he himself always averred that the greatest credit for the attainment of these objects should be given to Sir Hugh Owen, there is no doubt that Aberdare's connections benefited the movement for Welsh educational reform. The first principal of Cardiff College in 1883 described him as 'Commander-in-Chief of the Welsh Educational Army' (W. N. Bruce, 247).

Although education was one of the chief themes running throughout Bruce's parliamentary career, his practical involvement with the specifically Welsh aspects of the question only began in 1875, when he became president of the new college at Aberystwyth. In 1880–81 he headed the departmental committee appointed to inquire into higher education in Wales and Monmouth. Under his chairmanship, the committee proved a model of speed and efficiency. Issued on 25 August 1880, its final report was signed on 18 August 1881. Furthermore, it had eschewed the use of assistant commissioners, preferring to travel around Wales (fourteen places were visited) and collect evidence directly. The report, in addressing the problem of intermediate education, recommended that existing grammar schools be extended and that new schools, funded by the government, be established where there was still a deficiency. The Intermediate Education Act (Wales) of 1889, based on the new structures put in place by the County Councils Act of the previous year, was the fruit of this proposal. With regard to higher education, the report recommended the establishment of two further university colleges in Wales, one each in the north and south, and that a grant of £4000 be given to both. After much wrangling, these new colleges, established at Cardiff (1883) and Bangor (1884), were joined with Aberystwyth to form the University of Wales in 1893. Aberdare was unanimously elected to be the first chancellor of the new institution. He wrote to one of his children: 'I feel Wales could bestow on me no greater honour' (W. N. Bruce, 48).

Death and reputation Aberdare died of influenza at his London home, 39 Princes Gardens, on 25 February 1895. He was buried at Mountain Ash, near Aberdâr. He had four children with his first wife, of whom three survived him—one son, Henry Campbell Bruce, his successor in the peerage, and two daughters. From his second marriage he left two sons, including Charles Granville *Bruce, army officer and mountaineer, and six daughters, including Alice Moore *Bruce, educationist. A statue of Lord Aberdare was erected shortly after his death in Cardiff.

Aberdare's death robbed public life of one of its most active, yet unassuming, notables. Popular in society, of 'fine appearance', and with a deep fund of interesting conversation reflecting his many interests, he yet freely admitted, with typical self-deprecation that, 'of original ideas I have had none. I put my shoulder to the wheel when others have set it going' (W. N. Bruce, 250). This remark undoubtedly contained an element of truth: even the conclusions of his famous report in 1881 had been substantially prefigured by those of the school enquiry commission of 1864–7. Its veracity might also be reflected in the limited amount of published work Bruce bequeathed to posterity: a few published speeches aside, this amounted to his life of Sir William Napier (1864) and an

introductory notice to the *Early Adventures* of his lifelong friend Sir Austin Henry Layard in 1894. What Bruce's self-assessment underestimates, however, is the contribution he made as an administrator. He was among the most active MPs of his generation in undertaking select committee work in the House of Commons, and, as the demand for his services after he had left office indicated, a fine chairman. He exemplified an ideal in which the country's social élite took upon themselves a large share of the unpaid work of the state, at both national and local level, discharging their duties with the utmost probity. It was men like Bruce who, as one contemporary remarked, did 'so much to keep public life wholesome and to make it bear good fruit' (ibid.).

As a statesman he cannot be considered a major figure. In politics, his first loyalty always lay with Gladstone. Even after he had been overlooked for the 1880 cabinet, he supported Gladstone's policy on Ireland, and bowed to his wish that he head the royal commission on the aged poor in 1893 despite a conviction that the issue was not ripe for discussion, and that the team he had been given to conduct the investigation was ill-chosen. To Sir Algernon West, Gladstone's secretary, the events of 1880 summed up the qualities of Henry Austin Bruce better than anything. He recalled:

> Bruce's character was in some respects one of the finest with which I have ever been acquainted in public life. I could see no self-seeking in him anywhere. He was not without ambition and he liked office; but he accepted his exclusion, when it came, without a murmur, and without a disloyal thought towards the party of the chief who set him aside. I know of no greater test of character than this. (A. West, *Recollections*, 1, 1899, 352)

MATTHEW CRAGOE

Sources Lord Aberdare, *Life and letters*, 2 vols. (1902) · H. A. Bruce, *Lectures and addresses* [1895] · W. N. Bruce, 'Henry Austin Bruce', *Welsh political and educational leaders in the Victorian era*, ed. J. V. Morgan (1908) · *The Times* (26 Feb 1895) · H. Thomas, 'Duffryn Aberdare', *Morgannwg*, 21 (1977), 9–41 · I. G. Jones, 'The election of 1868 in Merthyr Tydfil', *Explorations and explanations: essays in the social history of Victorian Wales* (1981), 193–214 · 'Welsh MPs and select committees, 1852–65', M. Cragoe, *Parliaments, estates, and representations* (1994) · Gladstone, *Diaries · CGPLA Eng. & Wales* (1895)
Archives Bodl. Oxf., family corresp. · Glamorgan RO, Cardiff, corresp. and diary · Hunt. L., corresp. · TCD, corresp. relating to Irish universities | BL, Gladstone MSS, Add. MSS 44086–44087 · BL, corresp. with Sir A. H. Layard, Add. MSS 38995–39119, 58159, *passim* · BL, corresp. with Lord Ripon, Add. MSS 43534–43535 · Bodl. Oxf., letters to Lord Clarendon · Bodl. Oxf., corresp. with Lord Kimberley · Cardiff Central Library, letters to Sir Hugh Owen · King's AC Cam., letters to Oscar Browning · LPL, corresp. with A. C. Tait · NL Ire., letters to W. Monsell · NL Wales, letters to T. C. Edwards · NL Wales, letters to Lord Rendel · NL Wales, letters to Thomas Thomas · NL Wales, letters to H. H. Vivian · PRO, corresp. with Lord Granville, PRO 30/29
Likenesses oils, c.1850, Gov. Art Coll. · J. Watkins, carte photograph, c.1860, NPG · Lock & Whitfield, photograph, pubd 1882, NPG [see illus.] · J. M. Griffith, marble bust, exh. RA 1889, University College, Cardiff · Ape [C. Pellegrini], chromolithograph caricature, NPG; repro. in *VF* (21 Aug 1869), 1, 29 · H. Hampton, plaster bust, NMG Wales · H. Hampton, statue, Cardiff · C. Holl, stipple (after H. T. Wells), BM, NPG · W. Holl, stipple (after H. T. Wells), BM, NPG · plaster bust, RGS · portrait, repro. in *ILN*, 106 (1895), 25 ·

print (after an unknown artist), NPG · woodcut, repro. in *Harper's Weekly*, 13 (1869), 36

Wealth at death £74,408 0s. 8d.: resworn probate, Feb 1896, *CGPLA Eng. & Wales* (1895)

Bruce, Sir Henry Harvey (1862–1948), naval officer, was born at Stoke Damerel, Devonport, on 8 May 1862, the only son of Commander Sir Thomas Cuppage Bruce, who became superintendent of packets, Dover, and his first wife, Elizabeth, daughter of Henry Wise Harvey, of Middle Dealhouse, Kent. Bruce entered the *Britannia* in 1875, and next served in the *Black Prince*, one of the first two iron-clads in the Royal Navy, and then went to the Mediterranean in the screw frigate *Raleigh*. In November 1879 he transferred to the iron turret-ship *Monarch*, and in her took part in the bombardment of Alexandria in July 1882, being awarded the Egyptian medal and khedive's bronze star. He returned home in August 1882 following his promotion to sub-lieutenant in June and spent some months at the Royal Naval College, Greenwich, before joining the gunboat *Swinger* on the Australia station. He was promoted lieutenant in December 1884 and went to the cruiser *Porpoise* on the China station in February 1888 and to the sloop *Beagle* on the south-east coast of America in August 1891. Although not a gunnery specialist, he was appointed for gunnery duties to the cruiser *Marathon* in the East Indies in January 1894, and after a short gunnery course in the *Excellent* in 1897 joined, as gunnery lieutenant, the cruiser *Sirius*, which was employed carrying relief crews out to the Mediterranean.

In July 1898 Bruce took over his first command, the torpedo gunboat *Jason* which, like the *Sirius*, was employed on special duties. After his promotion to commander in June 1901 he commanded successively the store-ship *Tyne* in the Mediterranean and the cruiser *Medea* in home waters. In 1905 he was naval officer in charge and king's harbour master at Bermuda, where he gained the firsthand experience of dockyard administration which was destined to prove so useful to him during the First World War. Promoted captain at the end of 1905 he commanded the reserve cruiser *Blenheim* which during his term of command was converted into a destroyer depot and repair ship at Chatham. After attending a senior officers' war course at Portsmouth in 1908, he took over command of the cruiser *Arrogant*, and later the battleship *Prince George*, both in the Home Fleet.

For two years Bruce commanded the *Defence*, one of the four cruisers to escort the liner *Medina* carrying George V and Queen Mary to and from India for their coronation durbar in December 1911. For this service Bruce was appointed MVO. In 1913 he married Nina Catherine Marian Broome (d. 1915), daughter of Frederick Edward Nicholson, solicitor, of Ashfield Balby, and Leicester House, Doncaster; they had one son. Bruce was again attending a war course in April 1913 but in June became captain of the battleship *Hercules* which he commanded in the Grand Fleet during the opening months of the war. In June 1915 he became the first commodore superintendent of the new Rosyth Dockyard and remained there for five vital

Sir Henry Harvey Bruce (1862–1948), by Francis Dodd, 1919

years, being promoted rear-admiral and admiral superintendent in April 1917. Rosyth developed into the most up to date of the fleet bases, and the efficiency of its organization under Bruce was invaluable to the fleet, by reason of its geographical position. He was appointed CB in 1917 and KCB in 1920. He retired with the rank of vice-admiral in 1922 and was promoted admiral in 1926.

Bruce was a thickset bearded man of fine physique and medium height, a man of great physical energy and strength of character. Although outwardly brusque, beneath the surface he possessed a kindly and considerate personality and was ever solicitous for the welfare of the officers and men under his command. He maintained a lively interest in service charities and at his death was patron of the metropolitan branch of the British Legion. He was knocked down by a motor car in London on 18 August 1948 and died from his injuries on 14 September at his home, 67 Elizabeth Street, Eaton Square.

J. H. LHOYD-OWEN, *rev.*

Sources *The Times* (16 Sept 1948) · *WWW* · private information (1959) · personal knowledge (1959) · *CGPLA Eng. & Wales* (1948)
Archives Hydrographic Office, Taunton, Admiralty Library, Rosyth diaries | FILM IWM FVA, actuality footage
Likenesses F. Dodd, charcoal and watercolour drawing, 1917, IWM · F. Dodd, engraving, 1919; Sothebys, 22 Oct 1970, lot 4 [*see illus.*]
Wealth at death £1225 1s. 4d.: probate, 12 Oct 1948, *CGPLA Eng. & Wales*

Bruce, James (1660/61–1730), minister of the Presbyterian General Synod of Ulster, was the eldest son of the Revd Michael *Bruce (1635–1693), minister of Killinchy, co. Down, and his wife, Jean (fl. 1659–1683); he was born at the time that his father was ejected for nonconformity by Bishop Jeremy Taylor. Having been educated at Edinburgh University (MA 1678) he was ordained by Down presbytery at Killyleagh some time between 1684 and 1687. On 25 September 1685 he married Margaret (*d.* 1706), daughter of Lieutenant-Colonel James Traill of Tollychin, Killyleagh, a former parliamentary army officer; her mother, Mary Hamilton, was a niece of the first Viscount Claneboye. In the spring of 1689, when the Jacobite forces swept northwards, defeating the protestants at Dromore and Killyleagh, Bruce sought refuge in Scotland but returned after the Williamite victory in 1691. Killyleagh was a centre of Presbyterian influence; in 1696 Bruce secured from its proprietors, Gawn Hamilton, William Hamilton, and Hans Stevenson, endowments for the three Presbyterian ministers on the estate, consisting of a lease of lands at a nominal rent. In 1697 he persuaded the proprietors to sponsor the setting up of a 'philosophical school' at Killyleagh, which he proposed for the training of Presbyterian ministers in their native land. Despite strong opposition from Episcopalian clergy it continued for seventeen years; it closed on the departure of its preceptor, James McAlpin. Its most celebrated pupil was the philosopher Francis Hutcheson.

Bruce was one of the most influential and efficient members of the synod of Ulster and served on numerous committees. In 1699 he was appointed one of the trustees for the management of the *regium donum*, an office which he held until his death; in 1703 he was elected moderator of synod. During his ministry at Killyleagh a new and larger church was erected to accommodate the congregation. In the nonsubscription controversy (1720–26) Bruce sided with the subscribers, and in 1721 signed the Westminster confession, but he was unwilling to ban the nonsubscribers from fellowship. In 1725 synod divided Down presbytery into two new presbyteries, Bangor and Killyleagh; Bruce and those well disposed to the nonsubscribers were placed in the latter. He died in Killyleagh on 17 February 1730. In his will (dated February 1725) he directed that his mortal remains be interred at Killyleagh; tradition states that his grave (now unmarked) is in the grounds of the Episcopal church. Of his ten children three sons and three daughters survived him. Michael *Bruce was minister at Holywood; Patrick was minister successively of Drumbo, Kilellan (Renfrewshire), and Killyleagh, and the ancestor of the Hervey Bruces who were created baronets in 1804; and William *Bruce was a publisher in Dublin. Of his daughters Mary married the Revd James Fleming of Lurgan, and Eleanor and Magdalen died unmarried.   ALEXANDER GORDON, *rev.* W. D. BAILIE

Sources A. M'Creery, *The Presbyterian ministers of Killyleagh* (1875) • C. Porter, *The seven Bruces: Presbyterian ministers in Ireland in six successive generations* (1885) • *Records of the General Synod of Ulster, from 1691 to 1820*, 3 vols. (1890–98) • J. McConnell and others, eds., *Fasti of the Irish Presbyterian church, 1613–1840*, rev. S. G. McConnell, 2 vols. in 12 pts (1935–51) • W. B. Armstrong, *The Bruces of Airth and their cadets* (1892) • Burke, *Gen. Ire.* (1958) • [J. Kirkpatrick], *An historical essay upon the loyalty of Presbyterians in Great Britain and Ireland from the Reformation to the present year* (1713)

Wealth at death see will, Armstrong, *Bruces of Airth*

Bruce, James, of Kinnaird (1730–1794), traveller in Africa, was born at Kinnaird House, Kinnaird, Stirlingshire, on 14 December 1730, son of David Bruce (*d.* 1758), laird of Kinnaird, and Marion (*d.* 1733), daughter of Judge James Graham, dean of faculty at Edinburgh University. Bruce was educated in the family of Councillor William Hamilton in London, and in 1742, a scholarly but sickly boy, he went to Harrow School. Although inclined to become an Anglican clergyman on leaving school in 1746, he complied with his father's wishes and in May 1747 enrolled in the law faculty at Edinburgh University.

Entry into business and marriage Bruce showed little enthusiasm for his legal studies, however, and, still dogged by bad health, spent his time reading Ariosto and Petrarch before dropping out of university. He then spent several years at Kinnaird, recovering his health in the leisurely pursuit of field sports. In 1753 he set off for London, intending to embark as a 'free trader' with the East India Company. In London, however, he fell in love with Adriana Allan (1734–1754), daughter of a deceased Scottish wine merchant, and the couple were married on 3 February 1754, Bruce taking a share in the Allan family wine business. In September of the same year, the pregnant Adriana set off for France (to be joined by her husband) in the hope of curing her galloping consumption. Tragically, she died shortly after arrival in Paris and, to Bruce's indignation, as a protestant she was denied burial in consecrated ground.

Bruce returned, grief-stricken, to London, and set about studying languages, drawing, and architecture in preparation for a European tour. In July 1757 he embarked for Spain and Portugal (under pretence of studying the vintage), landing at Corunna and carrying out some amateur espionage at the port of Ferrol. He travelled through France, the German states, and the Netherlands, and purchased Job Ludolf's *History of Ethiopia* (1681), a work which whetted his appetite to know more about the ancient Christian kingdom of Abyssinia, a region virtually unknown to Europeans in the eighteenth century. In Brussels in 1758 he received the news that his father had died, and returned to Scotland to assume his responsibilities as laird of Kinnaird. He signed a contract on 4 November 1760 to supply the Carron ironworks with coal from his mines at Kinnaird. The contract provided him with the capital and the leisure to travel the world.

Algiers and Tunis Bruce submitted a plan to capture the Spanish fort of Ferrol, first to William Pitt, and then (after war broke out with Spain) to George Grenville, and lords Egremont and Halifax. Although his plan came to nothing, Halifax was impressed by Bruce and offered him the post of consul-general at Algiers with a commission to examine and draw the classical ruins of Algiers and Tunis for the king's collection. According to Bruce the offer was accompanied by the hint of a reward of a baronetcy and pension, although these were never forthcoming. Despite the fact that he had recently fallen in love with a sixteen-year-old Stirlingshire neighbour, Margaret Murray, Bruce prepared for his departure, planning to spend some time

James Bruce of Kinnaird (1730–1794), by John Smart, 1776

in Italy (under the pretext of a diplomatic mission to Malta), in order to develop his artistic skills before proceeding to Algiers. He departed in April 1762, equipped with a formidable array of books and scientific instruments. In Italy, Bruce prepared treatises on the architecture of ancient and modern Rome and the ruins of Paestum, conversed with the exiled Scots Jacobite antiquary Andrew Lumisden, had his portrait painted by Pompeo Battoni, and studied drawing at Florence.

In February 1763 Bruce departed for his diplomatic posting, with the brief of maintaining Britain's 1682 treaty with the bey of Algiers. The system of safe passes to preserve British ships from attack by Barbary corsairs had collapsed, and it appeared to Bruce that the bey was taking unwarrantable liberties. His recommendations that the Foreign Office employ the eighteenth-century equivalent of gunboat diplomacy to overawe the bey went unheeded, and he quickly alienated his superiors in London. A replacement consul was dispatched in June 1765, much to his fury, though his irascible temper and overbearing manner evidently made Bruce quite unsuitable for a diplomatic career. While in Algiers, Bruce secured the services of a young Bolognese artist called Luigi Balugani to act as his 'secretary' and draughtsman. Balugani was an invaluable and loyal servant, although he is hardly mentioned in Bruce's account of their journey (*Travels to Discover the Source of the Nile in the Years 1768–73*, 1790), in which Bruce predated Balugani's death to before the expedition to discover the source of the Nile, probably in order to claim sole credit for the discovery. Bruce and Balugani set off to draw the Roman ruins of Algiers and Tunis. They filled three bound volumes with architectural and antiquarian drawings, presented to George III upon Bruce's return,

which he claimed as his own work. In August 1766 Bruce proceeded from Tunis to Tripoli and Benghazi where he visited the principal sites of the ancient Pentapolis. Shipwrecked on the Libyan coast *en route* for Crete in November, Bruce was robbed of much of his equipment.

Arrival in Abyssinia His plans frustrated and his health in ruins, Bruce arrived at the Syrian port of Aleppo, where an English doctor, Patrick Russel, cured him of fever and instructed him in the treatment of tropical diseases. Bruce next set off across the desert to visit Palmyra and Baalbek, already explored and described by his friend Robert Wood. His connections in Europe, including naturalist and fellow mason Buffon, meanwhile replaced his lost scientific instruments on the understanding that Bruce would undertake an expedition to Abyssinia in order to discover the source of the Nile. Equipped with firmans from the Ottoman Porte and letters of credit from his bankers in London, he arrived at Alexandria on 20 June 1768, assuming the disguise of a wandering fakir. In Cairo Bruce cured Ali Bey (the city's mameluke ruler) of a stomach upset and procured further firmans to enable him to travel to Abyssinia. Sailing up the Nile to Aswan, he visited the ruins of Thebes, where he reported a painting of a harpist in the tomb of Rameses III, subsequently publishing an article on the subject in Charles Burney's *History of Music*. Visiting Karnak and Luxor, Bruce began making detailed terrestrial observations and charting the course of the Nile.

Having chosen to approach Abyssinia from the Red Sea town of Massawa, Bruce retraced his steps back from the first Nile cataract in order to make the desert crossing to Quseir on the Red Sea. Arriving at Jiddah in early May 1769 after an eventful sea-crossing, he stayed for three months in the company of the British East India Company captains who frequented the port, employing the time to survey and chart the Red Sea. Bruce also persuaded the powerful Metical Aga, swordbearer to the reigning pasha of Jiddah and a former Ethiopian slave, to write letters of safe conduct to the much-feared naybe of Massawa. The naybe, on whose island (situated on what is now the Eritrean coast) he landed on 19 September 1769, controlled the gateway to Abyssinia. It was just over seven years since Bruce's departure from England.

Bruce stayed two months in Massawa awaiting permission from Ras Michael Sehul of Tigré, effective ruler of Abyssinia, to proceed into the mountainous hinterland. Bruce—posing as 'El hakim Yagoube', a skilful Syrian physician—had been recommended to Ras Michael by his ally Metical Aga at Jiddah. Eventually managing to outwit the manipulative naybe of Massawa, Bruce's caravan began the laborious ascent into the mountains of central Abyssinia, bound for the then capital, Gondar. Enduring physical hardships and surmounting technical difficulties in carrying delicate surveying instruments over the rough mountain terrain, Bruce first witnessed the Abyssinian custom of eating raw beef cut from living beasts, his account of which met with great scepticism upon his return to England. After stopping to visit the ruins of Aksum, capital of Abyssinia from the fifth century AD, he arrived at Gondar on 14 February 1770, after an arduous journey through territory which bore all the signs of Ras Michael's bloody policy.

Bruce was only the second European to visit the isolated mountain kingdom of Abyssinia since the 1630s. He arrived at the start of a long period of chaos in which the powerless emperors of the ancient Solomonic dynasty were at the mercy of powerful regional warlords. In 1769 the machiavellian Ras Michael Sehul had crowned the fifteen-year-old Tekle Haimanout II as puppet emperor, and was currently waging war with the rebellious Fasil of Damot and his Galla army. Bruce's first task was to establish good relations with Ras Michael, although the fact that the springs of the Little Abbai (considered the major tributary of the Nile) at Gish lay within Fasil's territory made it imperative for Bruce to conciliate him as well.

Bruce's knowledge of the Tigrinya and Amaharic languages, the favour his medical knowledge won him with the royal ladies, and his insistence, having dropped his Syrian disguise, that he was no hated Roman Catholic but a protestant Christian, were instrumental to his success at court in Gondar, and the emperor made him governor of the province of Ras-el-Fil, on the Sudanese border. In the spring of 1770 he accompanied Michael's army on an expedition against Fasil which enabled him to explore Lake Tana and visit the falls of Tissisat: but Michael's army was forced to retreat and Bruce had to abandon his first quest to reach the springs of the Nile at Gish.

The source of the Nile   On 28 October 1770 Bruce and his party once again left Gondar bound for Gish, which the emperor had granted him as a fiefdom. The main obstacle to his reaching the source of the Nile was the presence of Fasil and his army, but after Bruce had impressed the warlord by taming a wild horse and by his marksmanship, Fasil sped him on his way with a bodyguard. On 4 November 1770 the party crossed the Little Abbai, by this point a tiny stream, arriving at the swampy 'Nile source' at Gish. Bruce triumphantly toasted George III, Catherine the Great, and the mysterious 'Maria' (possibly Bruce's fiancée), and gave vent to the 'sublime of discovery':

> it is easier to guess than describe the situation of my mind at that moment—standing in that spot which had baffled the genius, industry, and inquiry, of both ancients and moderns, for the course of nearly three thousand years.   (Bruce, 3.597)

The depression which followed may have been prompted by Bruce's realization that Gish had already been visited by the Jesuit Pedro Paez in 1618 (although Bruce went to great lengths to deny this fact) and also that the springs of Gish, flowing into Lake Tana, represent only one of several tributaries of the Blue Nile. More damagingly, the source of the larger White Nile, whose confluence with the Blue Nile at Halfaya (Khartoum) Bruce would see on his return journey, was over 500 miles away at Lake Victoria, to be discovered nearly a century later by John Hanning Speke.

The journey home   When Bruce returned to Gondar on 19 November, he discovered the capital in turmoil, in the midst of which Balugani died (apparently of natural causes). Michael and the emperor granted Bruce permission to leave Abyssinia as soon as the rebel warlords were

defeated. At the end of March 1771 Michael marched out of the city to confront his enemies. Bruce, in chain mail and a plumed helmet, astride a Sudanese charger 17 hands high, commanded the emperor's black horse, and must have looked an imposing sight. The stout, 6 foot 4 inch, red-headed Bruce was later described by Fanny Burney: 'His Figure is almost Gigantic! He is the Tallest man I ever saw [in another version, Burney inserted the word "gratis"] & exceeding well made, neither too fat or lean in proportion to his amazing height' (*Early Journals and Letters*, 44–5). But after a series of inconclusive battles at Serbraxos, Michael was deposed and exiled. Bruce, having escaped with only light wounds, anxiously sought to leave amid the ensuing turmoil. Not until 28 December 1771, however, was he able to set off for home. He was laden with botanical, zoological, and archaeological specimens, journals, maps and measurements, a history of medieval Ethiopia copied from a manuscript in the monastery of Debra Libanos, and, perhaps most important of all, an Ethiopic text of the apocryphal book of Enoch, which he later presented to the Bodleian Library.

Desert ordeal   Bruce's 1200 mile return journey to Egypt via the Sudanese desert was the most dangerous stage of his whole expedition, and it remains a mystery why he did not retrace his steps via Massawa and the Red Sea. Giving the slip to the importunate Sheikh Fidele of Teawa, he was hospitably received by the Nuba people, and in the spring of 1772 arrived in the Fung kingdom of Sennar, posing as an itinerant dervish. Delayed by the schemes of King Ismain of Sennar, on 6 September he finally managed to escape, following the Blue Nile to its confluence at Halfaya, and thence to Chendi. Striking out across the great Nubian Desert, rather than following the much longer Nile loop, Bruce's caravan soon ran out of food and water. At Saffeiliyyah the small party slaughtered and ate their last camel, struggling on to Aswan on foot, having abandoned all specimens and journals. They arrived at the Egyptian frontier city on 29 November 1772, after a twenty-day desert ordeal; as soon as he had recovered his strength Bruce plunged back into the desert to retrieve his jettisoned baggage. Suffering from severely swollen feet, guinea worm in his leg, and malaria, he hastened to Cairo, where he negotiated a customs treaty for East India Company shipping at Suez with Ali Bey. Proceeding to Alexandria, he took ship for Marseilles, where he arrived on 23 March 1773. French savants flocked to meet the man whom most Europeans had long presumed to have vanished in the interior of Africa.

Back in Europe   After having enjoyed the hospitality of the court of Louis XV the invalided Bruce travelled to Italy. At Florence he was portrayed standing in front of the Medici Venus in Zoffany's famous painting, the *Tribuna degli Uffizi*. By chance he encountered his former fiancée, Margaret Murray, now married to the Marchese Accoramboni; Bruce challenged the terrified Italian to a duel, but was eventually pacified by an apologetic letter. After having been presented to Pope Clement XIV, Bruce turned for home, and finally arrived in England in June 1774. For a time he was, according to Fanny Burney, 'the Lyon of the Times' (*Early Journals and Letters*, 44), stealing the show from Captain Cook and Joseph Banks, the recently returned Pacific explorers. Horace Walpole wrote: 'There is just returned a Mr Bruce who has lived for three years in the court of Abyssinia, and breakfasted every morning with the maids of honour on live oxen. Otaheite and Mr Banks are quite forgotten' (Walpole, *Corr.*, 24.21, letter to Sir Horace Mann, 10 July 1774). Although he was presented at court and elected FRS, Bruce's baronetcy was not forthcoming, and the king did not pay him the £6000 due for his paintings and consulship until 1780. Moreover, the British public's initial euphoria was soon replaced by scepticism concerning the truth of Bruce's claims, not least because Dr Johnson, translator of Jerome Lobo's *Travels in Abyssinia*, author of *Rasselas*, and self-appointed Abyssinian 'expert', took a critical view of his vaunted achievements.

Travels to Discover the Source of the Nile   Bruce returned to Kinnaird to nurse his resentment, oversee his collieries (amid endless litigations with the Carron Company), and, in May 1776, to marry Mary (1754–1785), the daughter of his neighbour Sir Thomas Dundas, with whom he had three children. Unwisely, he postponed the composition of his *Travels* for sixteen years (although a brief account by his distant relative James Boswell had been published in the *London Magazine* for August and September 1774), finally putting pen to paper to console himself after Mary's early death in 1785. He hired William Logan and later Benjamin Latrobe to edit his chaotic notes and journals. Anxious to emulate the form of James Cook's *Voyage to the Pacific Ocean* (one of the best-selling travel books of the century), Bruce published his 3000-page *Travels to Discover the Source of the Nile* in five quarto volumes in 1790. In conformity with eighteenth-century conventions of travel writing, it is an 'immethodical miscellany', ranging from striking adventure stories, reported dialogues, and Shandean asides boasting of his success with African women, through a pedantic history of ancient Ethiopia (which occupies most of the first two volumes), to vivid sketches of contemporary Abyssinian life, politics, and natural history. It was immensely successful, most of the original edition being sold to retail booksellers within thirty-two hours, and was rapidly translated into French and German. Despite favourable reviews in the *Analytical Review*, the *Critical Review*, the *London Chronicle*, and the *Journal des Scavans*, however, Bruce's credit was widely impugned; a sequel to Baron Münchhausen's travels was dedicated to him, the popular satirist John Wolcot (Peter Pindar) mocked him in his *Complimentary Epistle to James Bruce, Esq.* (1790), and, more damagingly, Lord Valentia and Henry Salt, the first British travellers to visit Abyssinia after Bruce, would cast serious doubts on his veracity.

Death and reputation   Bruce did not live to fulminate long at his critics; on 26 April 1794 the now corpulent traveller fell down stairs at Kinnaird House, and died of his injuries, an ignominious end for one who had braved the perils of the Sennar Desert. He was buried on 1 May 1794 in Larbert

old churchyard beside his wife, where an inscription on his cast-iron obelisk (manufactured at Carron works) proclaims: 'By the unanimous voice of mankind, his name is enrolled with those who were conspicuous for genius, for valour, and for virtue'. His *Travels* went into a second (1804–5) and a third (1813) edition, both edited by the oriental scholar Revd Alexander Murray, whose painstaking examination of Bruce's papers established a more reliable text of his travels and whose biography of Bruce (1808) is an important contemporary source. Although subsequent travellers did much to restore Bruce's credit, his reputation never fully recovered and he was canonized (perhaps unjustly) as a travel liar. His long and energetic narrative nevertheless remains one of the great travel accounts of the eighteenth century. Charles Lamb, one of the Romantic generation who greatly admired Bruce's work, captures something of its charm in an effusive letter of 1806:

> We just read thro' Bruce's Travels, with infinite delight where all is alive & novel & about kings & Queens & fabulous Heads of Rivers Abyssinian wars & the line of Solomon & he's a fine dashing fellow & intrigues with Empresses & gets into Harems of Black Women & was himself descended from Kings of Scotland: rot farmers & mechanics & industry.
> (*Letters of Charles and Mary Lamb*, ed. E. Marr, 1975–8, 2.199)

NIGEL LEASK

Sources   J. Bruce, *Travels to discover the source of the Nile in the years 1768–73* (1790) • A. Murray, *Account of the life and writings of James Bruce of Kinnaird* (1808) • *The early journals and letters of Fanny Burney*, ed. L. E. Troide, 3 vols. (1988–94) • F. B. Head, *The life of Bruce, the African traveller*, 2nd edn (1836) • *DNB* • J. M. Reid, *Traveller extraordinary: the life of James Bruce of Kinnaird* (1968) • M. Bredin, *The pale Abyssinian: a life of James Bruce, African explorer and adventurer* (2000) • Madame D'Arblay [F. Burney], *Memoirs of Doctor Burney*, 3 vols. (1832) • H. Marcus, *A history of Ethiopia* (1994) • G. Annesley [Viscount Valentia], *Voyages and travels to India, Ceylon, the Red Sea, Abyssinia, and Egypt*, 3 vols. (1809) • Peter Pindar [J. Wolcot], *Complimentary epistle to James Bruce, esq.* (1790)

Archives   Bodl. Oxf., MSS • NL Scot., papers and corresp. • priv. coll. • Yale U. CBA, Paul Mellon collection • Yale U. CBA, corresp. and papers | NL Scot., corresp. with Mackenzies of Delvine

Likenesses   P. Batoni, oils, 1762, Scot. NPG • J. Zoffany, group portrait, oils, 1772–8 (*Tribuna degli Uffizi*), Royal Collection • E. Topham, caricature, etching, pubd 1775, NPG • J. Smart, miniature, 1776, NPG [*see illus.*] • R. Stainier, stipple, 1790, BM, NPG; repro. in *European Magazine* (1790) • I. Cruikshank, caricature, 1791 • J. Kay, double portrait, caricature, etching, pubd 1791 (with Peter Williamson), BM • P. Batoni, oils, NG Scot. • attrib. J. Bogle, watercolour on ivory, Scot. NPG • J. Heath, stipple (after D. Martin), BM, NPG; repro. in Bruce, *Travels* • D. Martin, portrait, NG Scot. • miniature, Scot. NPG • oils, NPG • wash drawing (after D. Martin), Scot. NPG

Bruce, James (*c*.1765–1806), journalist and priest, was born in the county of Forfar. In 1777 he began studying at the University of St Andrews, and in 1785 he matriculated from Emmanuel College, Cambridge. He graduated BA in 1789, and took orders in the English church. About 1800 he was again in Scotland, where for a short time he officiated as a clergyman in the Scottish Episcopal church. Towards the end of this period was published his only separate literary work, *The Regard which is Due to the Memory of Good Men* (1803), a sermon preached at Dundee on the death of George Teaman.

In 1803 Bruce went to London to devote himself to literature, and was soon a prolific contributor to the *British Critic* and *The Anti-Jacobin Magazine and Review*, the latter a weekly journal started almost contemporaneously with, and conducted on the same principles as, its more famous namesake *The Anti-Jacobin* (associated with George Canning). A large proportion of the articles published in this review from 1803 to 1806 are from Bruce's pen; written with considerable ability, they are chiefly on theological and literary subjects. The former are characterized by a keen spirit of partisanship, and are aimed especially against the Calvinistic and evangelical parties in the church. His contempt for the whole tendency of the thought of revolutionary France informed the character of the *Anti-Jacobin Magazine*.

Bruce's life in London was obscure and probably unfortunate. He was found dead in the passage of the house in which he lodged in Fetter Lane, on 24 March 1806.

AGNES MACDONELL, *rev.* H. C. G. MATTHEW

Sources Anderson, *Scot. nat.* · Irving, *Scots.* · Venn, *Alum. Cant.*

Bruce, James (1808–1861), journalist and author, was born at Aberdeen. Educated in his native city, he remained there after leaving college to take up a career in journalism, contributing articles to the *Aberdeen Observer*, *Aberdeen Journal*, *The Constitutional*, and others. In 1840 he published *The Black Kalendar of Aberdeen*, an account of the more remarkable cases tried before the criminal courts between 1745 and 1830. This was followed in 1841 by *Lives of Eminent Men of Aberdeen*, a collection of biographies which included those of John Barbour, Bishop Elphinstone, chancellor of Scotland under James III, the artist Jamieson, and the poet Beattie. He published in 1844 *The Aberdeen Pulpit and Universities*, a series of sketches of the Aberdeen clergy and professors. He was also a contributor to the *Caledonian Mercury* and *The Scotsman*, and editor of the *Fifeshire Journal* in the early 1840s.

In 1845 Bruce published a collection of short papers on miscellaneous subjects under the title *Table Talk*. A descriptive *Guide to the Edinburgh and Northern Railway* followed in 1847. This same year he was appointed by *The Scotsman* to inquire into highland destitution during the great famine. He toured the highlands for three months, his observations appearing in *The Scotsman* from January to March 1847. These were later published in a pamphlet entitled *Letters on the Present Condition of the Highlands and Islands of Scotland*, in which he advocated a compulsory poor law, education, mass emigration, and the integration of potato patches into small farms as a means to ameliorate economic conditions in the highlands. He attributed the cause of destitution to the neglect and selfishness of the proprietors, and to the indolence and lethargy of the highlanders. He later undertook another commission for *The Scotsman*, reporting on the moral and sanitary condition of Edinburgh.

Bruce's attempt to launch a literary journal in Edinburgh called *The Lyceum* proved unsuccessful. He spent several years in India, where he learned several dialects of the local language, while continuing his career, as editor of the *Madras Athenaeum*. He edited the *Newcastle Chronicle* and, prior to his death, the Belfast *Northern Whig*. He also contributed occasional articles to *The Athenaeum*, and at the time of his death was engaged on a series of papers for the *Cornhill Magazine*. His most widely known books are *Classic and Historic Portraits* (1853) and *Scenes and Sights in the East* (1856). The former is a series of sketches describing the personal appearance, private habits, and tastes of over thirty ancient historical figures, interspersed with criticism on their moral and intellectual character. The latter work is a collection of observations on life and landscape in southern India and Egypt.

Bruce was an accomplished scholar with a remarkable knowledge of classical and modern languages. He mastered at least five European languages and was widely read in literature of every kind. His enquiring mind led him away from the popular and familiar into a variety of unexplored corners. His original and forcible style and strength of expression made his work more than eloquent. He wrote on topics and in a manner entirely for his own satisfaction. In failing to realize contemporary tastes and needs he may not have attained the recognition and public acclaim his work deserved. A number of his contemporaries considered his career in journalism to have been a waste of his talents. However, there were few who could rival him as a reviewer and a critic.

Retiring and unobtrusive in character, Bruce was of a kind and amiable disposition. He disliked dullness and quarrelled only with hypocrisy and persecution. Contemporaries admired him for his intellect and humour, and for his complete lack of hatred and cunning. He was regarded with both affection and esteem. Having suffered from heart disease for some time James Bruce died at his home, 6 Mount Charles, Botanic Road, Belfast, on 19 August 1861, aged fifty-three. CHRISTINE LODGE

Sources *The Scotsman* (22 Aug 1861) · *Aberdeen Herald and General Advertiser* (24 Aug 1861) · *Aberdeen Free Press* (23 Aug 1861) · *Aberdeen Journal* (28 Aug 1861) · *Belfast News-Letter* (20 Aug 1861) · *Northern Whig* (20 Aug 1861) · *The Athenaeum* (24 Aug 1861) · BL cat. · DNB

Bruce, James, eighth earl of Elgin and twelfth earl of Kincardine (1811–1863), governor-in-chief of British North America and viceroy of India, was born on 20 July 1811 at Park Lane, London, the first of the eight children of Thomas *Bruce, seventh earl of Elgin and eleventh earl of Kincardine (1766–1841), and his second wife, Elizabeth (1790–1860), daughter of James Oswald of Dunnikier House, Kirkcaldy, Fife. His father's first marriage, to Mary Hamilton Nisbet (1778–1855), had ended in a bitter and notorious divorce which had been dragged through the courts in both London and Edinburgh; the son of this marriage, George Charles Constantine Bruce, was heir to the titles and estates until his premature death in 1840. Only then did James Bruce become the heir.

Education and early career With his seven brothers and sisters and his four half-sisters and one half-brother, James Bruce was brought up in Paris in straitened circumstances. Their father had impoverished himself by the purchase of the Elgin marbles, for although the British government had bought the marbles from Elgin, the price

James Bruce, eighth earl of Elgin and twelfth earl of
Kincardine (1811–1863), by Disderi & Cie

failed to recompense him for his heavy expenditure. This
background of family poverty determined the life and career of James Bruce, who had no option but to seek an
income from government service. He was educated at
Eton College and at Christ Church, Oxford, from which
university he graduated with a first in classics in 1832, and
where he was a friend of William Ewart Gladstone: both
young men were distinguished by their serious attitude to
life, an inheritance in both cases effected by maternal
evangelical earnestness.

After leaving Oxford, Bruce retired to Scotland, where
he managed the family estates at Broomhall, Fife. It was a
frustrating period: land was farmed, coalmines were
sunk, small local railways were built, but the profits
which accrued were never enough to counterbalance the
inevitably heavy capital outlay. In 1837 he stood, unsuccessfully, for the Fife parliamentary seat in the Conservative interest. In 1841, with his election expenses paid by Sir
Robert Preston, an old friend of his father, he was elected
as a Conservative with liberal tendencies for Southampton. On 24 August that year he seconded an amendment to
the address, his only speech in the House of Commons. A
petition raised by his opponent at Southampton became
irrelevant when, on the death of his father on 14 November 1841, James Bruce succeeded as eighth earl of Elgin

and twelfth earl of Kincardine. Although the position of
Scottish earls with regard to parliament was legally
unclear, the succession effectively prevented Elgin from
sitting in the House of Commons; nor was he entitled to
sit in the House of Lords, unless he was elected as one of
the twelve representative Scottish peers. The family
estates remained heavily encumbered, and were a continual source of worry to the earl.

In April 1842 Elgin was appointed governor of Jamaica.
Thereafter, until his own death, he was continually to
serve his country overseas, in Jamaica, Canada, China,
Japan, and India. Outwardly, he epitomized the high-
ranking British imperialist; inwardly, his letters and diaries were full of anxiety about Britain's aggressive expansion. Jamaica proved a difficult posting for Elgin, both personally and politically. On 22 April 1841 he had married
Elizabeth Mary (Elma; 1821–1843), only child of Charles
Lennox Cumming Bruce of Dunphail and Roseisle, Ross-
shire. In 1842 she bore a daughter, but Jamaica did not suit
her and she faded and died there on 7 June 1843. Following
a long and bitter campaign slavery had been abolished in
the British empire in 1833, but until 1840 the former slaves
had been required to continue to work for their former
owners as 'apprentices'. The problems of Jamaica were, in
the short run, incapable of solution: the planters, who
wanted to keep their former apprentices working in their
fields, were full of resentment, for the former slaves
themselves, finally freed, preferred to cultivate their own
plots of land. Elgin continued to struggle with the apparently intractable problems of Jamaica, but found it unre-
warding work, given the intransigence of the planters and
the volatility of the former slaves. In the spring of 1846 he
retired from his post, regarding himself as a failure.

Governor-in-chief of British North America On his return to
Scotland, a sorrowing, lonely widower, he met Lady Mary
Louisa Lambton (1819?–1898), daughter of John George
*Lambton, first earl of Durham. Her family was connected
with that of Lord Grey, then secretary of state for the colonies, and was wealthier and more influential than the
Bruces. They were married on 7 November 1846, and produced five children during the seventeen years of their
marriage. Elgin's service in Jamaica, and perhaps his marriage, encouraged the new whig government to offer him,
in the summer of 1846, the position of governor-in-chief
of British North America. There had been rebellions in
both Upper and Lower Canada in 1837 and 1838, and, as a
result, Lord Durham had been sent to Canada to report. He
had made two recommendations: that Upper and Lower
Canada be united into a single polity, and that Canadians
might aim for responsible government, from which independence might eventually emerge. The Canada Act of
1840, in theory, brought the two parts of Canada together.
Elgin's primary task as governor-in-chief was to reconcile
and conciliate the disparate elements of the Canadian
population. Lower Canada was at this time controlled by
the Anglo-Scots, who, despite being a minority in the capital, Montreal, dominated the French-Canadian majority.
There was intense hostility between the two groups, both
of which focused exclusively on their own immediate

interests. Upper Canada, centred on Toronto, had its own parties eager for power, but they made less impact in Montreal.

When Elgin opened the Canadian parliament in February 1848, speaking in both French and English, he announced that both tongues would be official languages in Canada, to the outrage of the Anglo-Scots. At the subsequent election, in which for the first time the governor-in-chief did not intervene, the tories were ousted, and Elgin sent for the reform leaders, Louis LaFontaine and Robert Baldwin, to head the government. There was much anger and alarm among the tories, who saw their political and economic certainties shattered, but it remained unfocused until the Rebellion Losses Bill was introduced into parliament. It sought to allow compensation to be paid to those in Lower Canada whose property had been damaged in the riots of 1837–8. The bill gave the tories a cause, and they argued that it would compensate those who had previously been rebels. Elgin was caught in a dilemma: if he did anything other than sign the bill when it was passed by parliament he would be retreating from the responsible government so recently established. He signed the bill on 25 April 1849. Within hours the parliament building was razed to the ground, and Sir Allan MacNab, one of the tory leaders, rushed from the building bearing aloft the portrait of the young Queen Victoria. Elgin himself retreated from the mob violence on the streets to Monklands, the governor-in-chief's residence outside the city, and when he returned on 30 April to receive an address his carriage was pelted with stones, forcing his return to Monklands, amid fears of continuing public disorder. A restrained policy on the part of the government eventually re-established calm, although many tories responded by signing the annexation manifesto of 1849, calling for union between Canada and the United States. Elgin resumed his policy of attempting to conciliate as many groups as he could. He travelled widely in Upper and Lower Canada; although he met with some opposition in Upper Canada, notably from the Anglican bishop John Strachan, in general Toronto supported the governor-in-chief, sensing that it might benefit from the demotion of Montreal as capital.

Elgin's final significant action in Canada was the negotiation in 1854 of the reciprocity treaty with the United States. Persuaded that only economic prosperity would prevent Canadians from preferring union with the United States to independence within the British empire, Elgin successfully persuaded Washington (where southern senators opposed union on grounds of upsetting the balance between slave and free states) that a reciprocity treaty would serve to prevent, rather than promote, annexation. Elgin resigned following the adjournment of parliament on 18 December 1854 and returned to Britain.

Two sons had been born in Canada: in 1849, Victor Alexander *Bruce, later ninth earl, for whom Queen Victoria stood sponsor as an expression of her approval of Elgin's actions, and in 1851, Robert, who was born in Quebec, which since the Montreal riots had alternated with Toronto as the capital of Canada. Back in Britain, Elgin

declined the invitation to serve as chancellor of the duchy of Lancaster under Lord Palmerston, and also turned down the governorship of Madras. In the spring of 1857 he was appointed high commissioner and plenipotentiary in China and the Far East to assist in the process of opening up China and Japan to Western trade. His remit developed from the *Arrow* affair, in which a British vessel had been boarded and its Chinese crew taken prisoner. The British had retaliated with some ineffectual military action against Canton (Guangzhou), and much indignation was felt both in Britain and the Far East. Palmerston was determined to punish the Chinese, and saw Elgin, whom he placed in overall command of a large military and naval force, as his instrument of vengeance. Elgin accepted the commission, but privately was deeply troubled by Britain's aggressive policy. In April he left for the East, but on arriving in Singapore he received an urgent message from Lord Canning, the governor-general of India, about the serious mutiny which had recently broken out. Elgin was urged to send the troops which had been allocated for his use in China to India to help suppress the rebellion; he ordered all his transports to proceed to India, and in this way helped to preserve British rule in India.

Canton and Japan It was not until the end of 1857 that Elgin and his forces were ready to make their move against Canton. Anxious as ever to mediate, but having failed to wring any concessions from Governor Ye of Canton, Elgin finally gave the order to attack. For twenty-seven hours, on 28 and 29 December, Canton was bombarded by the British, and then occupied. Ye was among the prisoners. 'I never felt so ashamed of myself in my life,' Elgin wrote to his wife. After Canton, he moved on to Shanghai, from where he proposed to negotiate with the Chinese government in Peking (Beijing). There followed months of tedious negotiation, during which the Chinese deployed their only real weapons, prevarication and promises, with great skill. Elgin himself, much to his own distaste, played the part of the 'uncontrollably fierce barbarian'. Eventually the treaty of Tientsin (Tianjin) was signed on 26 June 1858.

After the months of inactivity Elgin resolved to move on to Japan, where the Americans had been at work following the visit of Commander Perry in 1854. Japan proved more to his liking, because there, not knowing of the underlying power struggles, he succeeded in making a treaty (which in fact followed that of the United States) in rather less than four weeks. The British treaty with Japan was signed on 26 August 1858. He thereafter returned to Shanghai and Canton, arranging, among other things, the legalization of the opium trade. He finally reported back to the Foreign Office in London on 19 May 1859.

Elgin returned to Britain a hero. Whereas the sterling service he had performed in Canada drew only criticism, his exploits in 'saving' India, and taming China and then Japan, fuelled the nation's pride. He was praised in the House of Lords and fêted throughout the country. He had been made GCB in 1858, subsequently served briefly as postmaster-general (1859–60), and was elected lord rector of the University of Glasgow (1859–62). Unfortunately, events in China were not encouraging. There had been a sorry defeat at the Taku (Dagu) forts in June 1859, where Elgin's brother, Frederick *Bruce (1814–1867), newly appointed minister in China, had attempted to make his way up the Peiho (Beihe) River towards Peking. The country, and Palmerston, were outraged. A mere eleven months after returning from 'this abominable East' Elgin was invited to return there. This time he was to be provided with an army of 30,000 men, and the French were to provide 10,000, for a mission aimed directly at Peking. He accepted the mission, although he was inwardly wearied, and had thoroughly appreciated his brief period of family life.

The journey to China was long and hazardous, and Elgin and the French ambassador were shipwrecked off Ceylon. Elgin reached Hong Kong in June 1860, and met up with his brother Frederick in Shanghai on 28 June. The large assembly of troops moved northwards and, after further delay, attacked the Taku forts, forcing their way through to Tientsin. The British and French received various groups of Chinese emissaries as power struggles raged in Peking. An advance party, including Harry Parkes, was captured by one group of the Chinese. They were brutally treated, and only Parkes, James Loch, and five soldiers out of a party of some thirty men survived. This incident hardened Elgin's resolve. The allies had fought their way to the outskirts of Peking, and the French had stormed and looted the emperor's summer palace outside Peking. Elgin had agreed not to enter Peking immediately, and argued that to destroy the summer palace would strike at the emperor and not his people; on 18 October 1860 the palace was put to the torch, and a great pall of smoke hung over Peking as the palace complex burned. Six days later Elgin and his army entered Peking, and Frederick Bruce was presented to the Chinese as the queen's representative in China. Leaving a considerable army behind him, Elgin left China for the last time.

Viceroy of India Elgin arrived back in England in April 1861, and was again received with public acclaim. Almost immediately he was charged with another duty, this time the post of viceroy of India, in succession to Lord Canning. On 12 March 1862 he was inducted into office in Calcutta. But the Indian climate caused him difficulties, and Elgin, who had updated his will in London shortly before his departure, was reminded of his gloomy prognostications: he had told his Fife neighbours that 'the prospect of our again meeting is more remote and uncertain' (inaugural address to the Dunfermline Young Men's Literary Society, 22 Nov 1861, priv. coll.). Although Lady Elgin and their youngest daughter had arrived safely in India on 8 January 1863 Elgin remained anxious. He studied the multitude of problems with which India was wracked and considered the conflicting demands of the various interest groups. He decided to travel, holding a series of durbars at which he would meet the rulers of the different parts of the country. En route for Simla, where they would spend five comfortable months in the mountains, they met Indians of various faiths and beliefs. From Simla, in the autumn of 1863, the viceroy set out for Peshawar, travelling at high altitudes. They journeyed at 13,000 feet over the Rotung

Pass and then came to the gorge across the Chandra River, which was to be crossed by a worn and broken twig bridge. Elgin managed to struggle across, but his heart was severely strained. On 22 October he suffered another attack and was carried, with great difficulty, to Dharmsala, a military station, where he and his party arrived on 4 November. He rallied from time to time, but died there on 20 November 1863. He was buried there the following day, having been viceroy for only eighteen months.

Elgin was a man of courage and ability who, in the strong tradition of aristocratic tribute, served the British empire well for over twenty years. He was a successful proconsul, in that he did what was required of him with skill and sensitivity, but in so doing he was at least in part at war with himself. In the Far East, especially, he was ambivalent about the British imperial policy of forcing trade on the peoples in China and Japan. He deplored what he called the 'commercial ruffianism' which effectively determined British policy responses. Though his behaviour in China epitomized the triumph of imperial might, some contemporaries regarded him as overly sympathetic to the interests of indigenous peoples. His major triumph, which was only dimly perceived during his lifetime, was to encourage the Canadian people to accept the responsibilities which representative government imposed on them; this led quite quickly to the establishment of the dominion of Canada in 1867, the precedent for so much imperial constitutional development. In this sense, Elgin was one of the great whigs.

OLIVE CHECKLAND

Sources S. Checkland, *The Elgins, 1766–1917: a tale of aristocrats, proconsuls and their wives* (1988) • J. L. Morison, *The eighth earl of Elgin: a chapter in nineteenth-century imperial history* (1928) • L. Oliphant, *Narrative of the earl of Elgin's mission to China and Japan in the years 1857, 1858 and 1859*, 2 vols. (1860) • T. Walrond, *Letters and journals of James, eighth earl of Elgin* (1872) • M. Bence-Jones, *The viceroys of India* (1982) • S. Osborn, *A cruise in Japanese waters* (1859) • G. J. J. Tulchinsky, *The river barons, Montreal businessmen and the growth of industry and transportation* (1977) • J. M. Ward, *Colonial self-government: the British experience, 1759–1856* (1976) • GEC, *Peerage* • W. L. Morton, 'Bruce, James', DCB, vol. 9

Archives BL OIOC, corresp. and papers relating to India, MS Eur. F 83 • NRA, priv. coll., corresp. and papers | BL, corresp. with W. E. Gladstone, Add. MSS 44352–44397, *passim* • Bodl. Oxf., corresp. with Sir John Fiennes Crampton • Hants. RO, corresp. with Lord Malmesbury • Lpool RO, letters to Lord Stanley • NA Canada, corresp. with third Earl Grey • PRO, corresp. with Lord John Russell, PRO 30/22 • U. Durham L., corresp. with third Earl Grey • U. Edin., New Coll. L., letters to Thomas Chalmers • U. Nott. L., corresp. with fifth duke of Newcastle • Wilts. & Swindon RO, corresp. with Sidney Herbert

Likenesses Swinton, portrait, 1844 • Doan of Nova Scotia, daguerreotype photograph, c.1849, repro. in Checkland, *Elgins*, 135 • G. Richmond, portrait, c.1856 • F. Beato, photograph, 1860, repro. in Checkland, *Elgins*, 135 • F. Grant, portrait, c.1860, Cupar council offices, Fife • W. Behnes, marble bust, 1861, federal government of Canada; on loan to Lord Elgin Hotel, Ottawa, Canada • F. Grant, oils, exh. RA 1862, Dunfermline town hall • J. B. Philip, medallion on monument, 1868, Calcutta Cathedral • H. H. Crealock?, colour portrait, repro. in Checkland, *Elgins*, facing p. 178 • Disderi & Cie, carte-de-visite, NPG [*see illus.*] • T. Fairland, tinted lithograph (after J. R. Swinton), BM • W. Holl, stipple (after G. Richmond), BM, NPG • C. Mayer, line print, BM; repro. in *Almanach de Gotha* (1861) • D. J. Pound, stipple and line print (after photograph by J. Watkins), NPG; repro. in *Illustrated News of the World* • J. Sartain, process engraving (after photograph by Fariss), NPG • miniature (as a young man), repro. in Checkland, *Elgins*, facing p. 90 • portraits, priv. coll. • wood-engraving (after medallion by J. B. Philip, 1868), NPG; repro. in *ILN* (4 Dec 1869)

Wealth at death £105,889 17s. 5½d.: inventory of estate in Scotland and England, 11 Oct 1864; £12,599 6s. 6d.; £3875 6s. 8d.; £727 4s.; £20,000; £7300; £225,576 15s. 8d.; £13,515 6s. 4d.: personal estate in India; £1169 5s. 8½d.: estate in sundry places; £612 10s.; £3000: shares and bonds: NA Scot., SC 20/50/36, pp. 1136–93

Bruce, Sir James Lewis Knight- (1791–1866), judge, was born at Barnstaple on 15 February 1791, the youngest son of John Knight of Fairlinch, Devon, and his wife, Margaret, the daughter and afterwards heir of William Bruce of Llanblethian, Glamorgan.

Knight was educated at King Edward's Grammar School, Bath, and the King's School, Sherborne. He left Sherborne in 1805, and, after two years with a mathematical tutor, was articled to a solicitor in Lincoln's Inn Fields. When his articles expired, on 21 July 1812 he was admitted as a student of Lincoln's Inn. On 20 August 1812 he married Eliza, the daughter of Thomas Newte of Duvale, Devon; they had several children.

On 21 November 1817 Knight was called to the bar, and for a short time was on the Welsh circuit. The increase of his chancery practice soon caused him to abandon the common-law bar, and he confined himself to practising in the equity courts. In the autumn of 1829 he was appointed a king's counsel, and on 6 November in the same year was elected a bencher of Lincoln's Inn. On becoming king's counsel he chose the vice-chancellor's court, where Sir Edward Sugden, afterwards Lord St Leonards, was the leader. Knight had daily contests with him until Sugden's appointment as lord chancellor of Ireland in 1834.

Knight was politically conservative, and in April 1831 he became member of parliament for Bishop's Castle, a pocket borough belonging to the earl of Powis. His parliamentary career was short-lived, however, since the borough was disfranchised by the 1832 Reform Act. In 1834 Knight received the honorary degree of DCL from the University of Oxford. In 1835 he was one of the counsel heard at the bar of the House of Lords on behalf of the municipal corporations against the Municipal Reform Bill, and in 1851 on behalf of the deans and chapters against the Ecclesiastical Duties and Revenues Bill. In 1835, and again in 1837, he unsuccessfully contested the borough of Cambridge.

In September 1838 Knight changed his surname by royal licence to Knight-Bruce. When the court of exchequer in equity was abolished and its jurisdiction transferred to the court of chancery, on 28 October 1841 Sir Robert Peel appointed him one of the two additional vice-chancellors. He was soon knighted, and on 15 January 1842 was sworn in as a member of the privy council. In the autumn (Michaelmas term) of 1842 he took on the further duties of chief judge in bankruptcy, and seven years later the jurisdiction of the old court of review. In 1842–3 he held the yearly office of treasurer of Lincoln's Inn, and laid the foundation-stone of the new hall and library of the inn on 20 April 1843. On the creation of the Court of Appeal in

Chancery, Lord John Russell appointed Knight-Bruce and Lord Cranworth the first lords justices (8 October 1851). Knight-Bruce sat in this court for fifteen years.

At the bar, Knight-Bruce was noted for his quick grasp of the salient facts of a case and for his excellent memory; he had a particular aptitude for business law. As a judge he was determined to shorten procedures and save time in the discussion of legal technicalities. While his briskness was admired, several of his decisions were afterwards overruled. Yet some of his short cuts anticipated later reforms of the legal system. Knight-Bruce frequently sat on the judicial committee of the privy council, where he was able to display his familiarity with the civil law and foreign systems of jurisprudence.

Knight-Bruce retired as a judge in October 1866, with failing eyesight and still grieving for his wife, who had died the previous year. He died within a fortnight, on 7 November 1866 at his home, The Priory, Roehampton, Surrey, and was buried in Cheriton churchyard, near Folkestone, on 14 November.

G. F. R. BARKER, *rev.* HUGH MOONEY

Sources *Law Magazine*, 4th ser., 22 (1896–7), 278–93 • *Law Journal* (19 Oct 1866), 564–5, 607–8 • *Solicitors' Journal*, 11 (1866–7), 25, 53–4, 79 • *Law Times* (10 Nov 1866), 21; (17 Nov 1866), 48, 57; (16 Feb 1866), 303 • *GM*, 4th ser., 2 (1866), 681, 818, 833–5 • *Annual Register* (1866), 218–19

Archives BL, letters to Sir Robert Peel and others • Bodl. Oxf., corresp. with Sir Thomas Phillipps

Likenesses W. Walker, mezzotint, pubd 1850 (after T. Woolnoth), BM • J. Evans, marble bust, Royal Courts of Justice, London • pencil drawing, NPG • portrait, repro. in *Green Bug*, 13 (1901), 445 • stipple, NPG

Wealth at death under £14,000: probate, 29 Nov 1866, *CGPLA Eng. & Wales*

Bruce, John (1744–1826), historian, was the elder son of Andrew Bruce (1710–1761) of Grangemyre or Grangehill, shipmaster at Kinghorn, Fife, and Jean (*b.* after 1719), daughter of the Revd John Squyre of Forres, Elgin. He was baptized at Forres on 8 November 1744. In 1776 he was admitted heir male of the family of Bruce of Earlshall, ancient cadet of the royal house of Bruce, of which the main line had failed at the death of Helen, Lady Earlshall, in 1774. Her lands, however, passed to Sir Robert Henderson of Fordell, nephew of her late husband. Bruce never married. He had a brother, Robert (*d.* in or before 1797), lieutenant-colonel in the Bengal artillery, and a sister, Margaret, who died unmarried.

With a small patrimony, Bruce was reliant on patronage but adept at getting it. He entered the University of Edinburgh in 1764. He was immediately a founding member of the Speculative Society, established for student debate with the encouragement of principal William Robertson to help in livening the place up. In 1774 Bruce won appointment as joint or assistant professor of logic with the aged John Stevenson. Some months later he became the temporary occupant of the full chair of moral philosophy, held by Adam Ferguson, who wanted to go off for a year as tutor to the earl of Chesterfield on a grand tour. Members of the corporation of Edinburgh, supposed to have patronage of the post, objected to this irregular substitution as a job, but they were foiled by Robertson. Bruce became full professor of logic in 1778, when he also took his MA. He published his lectures as *First Principles of Philosophy* (1780) and *Elements of the Science of Ethics* (1786). He held the chair until 1792, and became a fellow of the royal societies of Edinburgh, London, and Göttingen.

Robertson's influence waned, but Bruce smoothly transferred his allegiance to Henry Dundas, the political manager of Scotland. It was a coup to be asked to go as tutor with Dundas's son Robert on a continental journey in 1786–7. They arrived in Paris armed with an introduction to the Abbé Morellet from Adam Smith, who called Bruce his 'particular friend' (*Correspondence of Adam Smith*, 295). They proceeded to Göttingen, where the young man attended the university. 'I have too anxious a temper', Bruce conceded in a report back (NL Scot., Melville MSS, GD 235/9/7/6), and his faintly neurotic intellectual force-feeding may have given his pupil a carapace of amiable complaisance never quite lost. He was rewarded with reversion of the patent of king's printer for Scotland. It did not come to him until 1809, but made his fortune with its accompanying monopoly to print and publish the Bible north of the border, where holy writ remained the most popular reading.

Dundas continued to employ Bruce to lend academic weight to his pragmatic policies, noting that the professor's sole joy was to be 'buried in old records' (*Fortescue MSS*, 2.306). The duties were formalized in an official position as historiographer to the East India Company in 1793. It had been clinched by Bruce's *Historical View of Plans for the Government of British India* (1793), fruit of three years' research exploring options for the imminent renewal of the company's charter. Despite its pernickety style, it sufficiently softened up public opinion for a plan which Dundas wished to air without taking personal responsibility, the creation for himself of a post of president of the Board of Control for India, served by a permanent staff. In 1796 Bruce produced a historical review of the balance of power in Europe. In 1798 his report on defence guided measures to meet the French threat. Bruce was to write a similar report on the requirements of the circumstances created by the uneasy peace of Amiens in 1801. A report published in 1799 dealt with the Anglo-Scottish union, as a precedent for the projected Irish union. By then Dundas thought Bruce's tireless hackwork deserved some interim reward, and made him Latin secretary to the privy council and keeper for life of the state papers. Into these, according to Charles Abbot, speaker of the House of Commons, he introduced confusion. In 1810 appeared his *Annals of the East India Company from 1600 to 1707–8*, a fully documented narrative history in three volumes.

At last in receipt of the reversion, Bruce began a short parliamentary career when, in 1809, he was brought in for Mitchell by Sir Christopher Hawkins, the Cornish borough-monger, in return for patronage from Dundas, now Viscount Melville. Bruce always supported the government. In 1812 he served as secretary to the Board of Control under his former pupil, the second Viscount Melville. In 1813 he was a member of the East India committee of the House of Commons, preparing a further renewal of the company's charter. To no avail, he sought to uphold its trading monopoly, in support of which he had written another report in 1811; he also published his speech in committee vindicating its privileges on historical grounds. He retired from the House of Commons in 1814.

Afterwards Bruce gave his energies to his biblical publishing business in Edinburgh and 'applied himself to being a country gentleman as he had in other pursuits' (*GM*, 87). In 1820 he bought Falkland, Fife, with the remains of the royal palace, which he began restoring. He acquired further estates nearby and 'must have been one of the largest landowners in the county'. He died at one of them, Nuthill, on 16 April 1826, 'in his 82nd year' and was buried in St Cuthbert's churchyard, Edinburgh. Beside £2000 to Melville, he left his estate to his brother's daughter 'by a native lady in India' (Armstrong, 48–9) Margaret Stuart Bruce (*d.* 1869). Since the county could, or would, provide no match for her, she married in 1828 a lawyer from Bristol, Onesiphorus Tyndall (*d.* 1855), who took the name Tyndall-Bruce. Bruce's money was put to good use, for with it the couple completed restoration of Falkland Palace and built the House of Falkland to the design of William Burn.   MICHAEL FRY

Sources W. B. Armstrong, *The Bruces of Airth and their cadets* (1892) · HoP, *Commons, 1790–1820* · M. Fry, *The Dundas despotism* (1992) · *The correspondence of Adam Ferguson*, ed. V. Merolle, 1 (1995) · *The correspondence of Adam Smith*, ed. E. C. Mossner and I. S. Ross (1977), vol. 6 of *The Glasgow edition of the works and correspondence of Adam Smith* · *GM*, 1st ser., 96/2 (1826), 87 · *The manuscripts of J. B. Fortescue*, 10 vols., HMC, 30 (1892–1927) · bap. reg. Scot. · *Fasti Scot.* · private information (2004) [Revd John Jarvie] · NL Scot., Melville MSS, GD 235/9/7/6

Archives BL, papers relating to diplomatic history, Add. MSS 38779–38780 · BL OIOC, Home misc. series, corresp. and papers relating to East India Company · NA Scot., letters · NA Scot., corresp., family papers, and literary MSS · NL Scot., letter-books · University of the Witwatersrand Library, Johannesburg, history of Cape of Good Hope [copy] | NA Scot., corresp. with Henry Dundas · NL Scot., Melville MSS

Likenesses H. Raeburn, oils, *c.*1794, Scot. NPG

Bruce, John (1802–1869), antiquary, a native of London, although of a Scottish family, was educated partly at private schools in England, and partly at the grammar school of Aberdeen. He trained as a lawyer, but did not practise after 1840, and from that time devoted himself entirely to historical and antiquarian pursuits, in which he was already interested. He took a prominent part in the foundation of the Camden Society on 15 March 1838, held office in it as treasurer and director, and contributed various historical works to its publications: *The Historie of the Arrivall of Edward IV* (1838), the first volume of the society's works; *Annals of the First Four Years of Queen Elizabeth* (1840); *Correspondence of Robert Dudley, Earl of Leycester* (1844); *Verney Papers* (1845); *Letters of Queen Elizabeth and James VI* (1849); and various prefaces and other writings. His last few publications were *Accounts and Papers Relating to Mary Queen of Scots* (1867), published conjointly with A. J. Crosby, *Journal of a Voyage … by Sir Kenelm Digby* (1868), and *Notes of the*

Treaty of Ripon (1869). He was for some time treasurer and vice-president of the Society of Antiquaries, and contributed many papers to the *Archaeologia*, among which his 'Inquiry into the authenticity of the Paston letters' is of particular interest. He wrote occasionally in the *Edinburgh Review* and other periodicals, and was for some years the editor of the *Gentleman's Magazine*. For the Berkshire Ashmolean Society he edited a volume of *Original Letters Relating to Archbishop Laud's Benefactions* (1841), and for the Parker Society the *Works of R. Hutchinson* (1842), and conjointly with the Revd T. Perowne the *Correspondence of Archbishop Parker* (1853). In 1857 he contributed an edition of Cowper's poems to the Aldine edition of poets. He edited twelve volumes of the calendars of state papers (domestic series, Charles I, 1625–39) published under the direction of the master of the rolls from 1858 to 1871, the last volume being completed by W. D. Hamilton; and in 1867 he printed privately papers relating to William, first earl of Gowrie. In 1861 he was appointed by the Society of Antiquaries as a trustee of Sir John Soane's Museum. He had been a widower for some years before his sudden death in Montagu Square, London, on 28 October 1869. His library was sold at Sothebys from 27 April to 2 May 1870.

WILLIAM HUNT, rev. NILANJANA BANERJI

Sources T. Cooper, *A new biographical dictionary*, new edn (1883) [with suppl.] • *Men of the time* (1862) • *The Times* (3 Nov 1869) • J. G. Nichols, *A descriptive catalogue of the first series of the works of the Camden Society*, 2nd edn, CS (1872) • *N&Q*, 4th ser., 4 (1869), 443–4 • Boase, *Mod. Eng. biog.*
Archives BL, corresp. and papers, Add. MSS 28197–28202, 29716, 31998–32000 • Bodl. Oxf., historical collections | Shakespeare Birthplace Trust RO, Stratford upon Avon, letters to J. G. Nichols • U. Edin. L., letters to James Halliwell-Phillipps
Wealth at death under £3000: probate, 17 Dec 1869, *CGPLA Eng. & Wales*

Bruce, John Collingwood (1805–1892), antiquary, was born at Albion Place, Newcastle upon Tyne, on 15 September 1805, the eldest son of John Bruce (1775–1834) of Newcastle and his wife, Mary Jack. He was educated at the Percy Street Academy, a well-known school in Newcastle run by his father, and afterwards (1819–21) at Mill Hill School, Middlesex. He entered Glasgow University in 1821, graduated MA in 1826, and became an honorary LLD in 1853. In early life he studied for the Presbyterian ministry, but never sought a 'call' from any congregation. In 1831 he began to assist in the management of his father's school, of which he became sole proprietor in 1834, when his father died. He retired from the school, after a successful career, in 1863.

Bruce was an enthusiastic antiquary, who recognized the importance of the central section of Hadrian's Wall, and who synthesized the findings of others as to its chronology. In 1851 he published *The Roman Wall*, followed in 1861 by *The Wallet Book of the Roman Wall*, which appeared in later editions as *The Handbook of the Roman Wall*. Revised periodically, this had reached its thirteenth edition by the end of the twentieth century. He acted as editor, from 1870 to 1875, of the *Lapidarium Septentrionale*, issued by the Newcastle Society of Antiquaries. For forty years Bruce visited

various parts of the wall annually, and organized 'pilgrimages' there in 1851 and 1886. These have continued at approximately decennial intervals.

Aided in his researches by his friend John Clayton FSA, Bruce was a secretary and vice-president of the Newcastle Society of Antiquaries; fellow of the Society of Antiquaries of London; and corresponding member of the Royal Archaeological Institute of Rome. He revived public interest in the folk music of Northumberland, and edited with John Stokoe *Northumbrian Minstrelsy* (1882). Bruce was a frequent contributor to *Archaeologia Aeliana* and to similar periodicals. Apart from his books on Hadrian's Wall he also wrote *The Handbook of English History* (1848) and *The Bayeux Tapestry Elucidated* (1856). He was also chairman of the Royal Infirmary, Newcastle, and a founder of the Newcastle YMCA.

Bruce married in 1833 Charlotte, daughter of T. Gainsford of Gerrards Cross, Buckinghamshire; they had two sons and two daughters. Their eldest son, Sir Gainsford Bruce (1834–1912), was a High Court judge. Bruce died, after a short illness, at his home, 2 Framlington Place, Newcastle, on 5 April 1892, and was buried on 8 April in the old cemetery, Jesmond. Some of his maps and drawings were presented by his son in 1893 to the Newcastle Society of Antiquaries.

W. W. WROTH, rev. C. M. FRASER

Sources T. Hodgkin, 'Obituary notice of the Rev. J. C. Bruce', *Archaeologia Aeliana*, new ser., 15 (1892), 364–70 • 'Biographies of contributors to the society's literature', *Archaeologia Aeliana*, 3rd ser., 10 (1913), 212–17 • R. Welford, *Men of mark 'twixt Tyne and Tweed*, 1 (1895), 415–22 • *Slater's directory*
Archives Arberia Roman Fort and Museum, South Shields, library and papers relating to Hadrian's Wall • Society of Antiquaries of Newcastle upon Tyne | U. Newcastle, Robinson L., letters to Sir Walter Trevelyan
Likenesses P. Graham, photograph, repro. in Hodgkin, 'Obituary notice', 364–5 • R. Lehmann, portrait • Swan Electric Engraving Co. (after R. Lehmann), repro. in *Archaeologia Aeliana* (1913), 212–13
Wealth at death £16,992 19s. 10d.: resworn probate, Oct 1892, *CGPLA Eng. & Wales*

Bruce, Sir John Hope, of Kinross [*formerly* John Hope], **seventh baronet** (1684?–1766), soldier and politician, was the third son of Sir Thomas Hope, sixth baronet, of Craighall, Fife, and his wife, Anne, the sole heir of Sir William Bruce of Kinross, first baronet. On the death of his elder brothers without heirs, he succeeded to the estates on 5 April 1729, taking the additional name of Bruce.

Bruce's first wife was Catherine, daughter of Sir Charles Halket, whose sister, Elizabeth, Lady Wardlaw, is the real author of 'Hardyknute', once attributed to Bruce. They had three sons who all predeceased Bruce. With his second wife, Marianne, daughter of the Revd William Denune, whom he married in 1706, he had a daughter.

Bruce had gone into the army as a younger son, but sold his commission in 1718. He was recommended by a kinsman to Lord Carteret, British ambassador in Sweden, and travelled there in 1719. When Carteret became secretary of state in 1721, Bruce was made governor of the Bermudas. He was parliamentary representative for Kinrossshire from 1727 to 1734, and again from 1741 to 1747.

How the imitation ballad—an account of a thirteenth-century battle between the Scots and Northmen, with stylistic and structural similarities to such canonical favourites as 'Sir Patrick Spense'—came to be associated with Bruce's name is convoluted. Although the text was not published until 1719, it was clearly talked about in some circles before then. Sir John Hope Bruce, knowing undoubtedly the identity of the ballad imitator, sent an account of its presumed discovery in an old vault in Dunfermline together with a supposed transcript of the text to Lord Binning. Authorship was often withheld in hopes that an imitation would pass as authentic, and one widely used proof of antiquity was the evidence of the 'found manuscript'. This latter trope seldom fooled anyone and John Pinkerton, himself a notorious forger and author of 'Hardyknute Part II', on receipt of a copy of the Bruce–Binning correspondence, assumed that this was a recognized subterfuge to hide Bruce's own authorship. Thus Pinkerton named Bruce as author.

Thomas Percy, in the second edition of *Reliques of Ancient English Poetry* (1767), named Lady Wardlaw as author on intelligence sent him by David Dalrymple, Lord Hailes, who had transmitted the text together with the jewels of the Scottish ballad canon to him originally. Since that date, most analysts have accepted Lady Wardlaw and not her brother-in-law as the writer of 'Hardyknute'. Bruce died on 5 June 1766; the baronetcy passed to his cousin Thomas *Hope (c.1681–1771). MARY ELLEN BROWN

Sources DNB · R. Chambers, *The romantic Scottish ballads: their epoch and authorship* (1849) · T. Percy, ed., *Reliques of ancient English poetry*, rev. H. B. Wheatley, 3 vols. (1886); facs. edn (1966) · J. Pinkerton, *Ancient Scottish poems*, 2 vols. (1786), vol. 1 · Burke, *Peerage* (1879) · HoP, *Commons, 1715–54*
Archives NA Scot., commissions; corresp.; letters regarding birth, death, and funeral; service papers | NA Scot., letters to duke of Montrose

Bruce, Marjorie (c.1296–1316). *See under* Stewart family (*per.* c.1110–c.1350).

Bruce, Michael (1635–1693), Church of Scotland minister, was born at Newtown, Stirlingshire, the third and youngest son of Patrick Bruce and his wife, Janet, daughter of John Jackson, an Edinburgh merchant. After receiving his MA degree from Edinburgh University in 1654 Bruce began to preach about 1656. In a letter dated 3 July 1657 the presbyterian minister John Livingston recommended Bruce to his former congregation at Killinchy, co. Down, where Bruce was ordained in October. On the recommendation of John Drysdale and Robert Cunningham, Bruce and four other presbyterian clergymen were approved for state stipends in June 1658. On 30 May 1659 he married his cousin Jean Bruce (*fl.* 1659–1683), daughter of Robert Bruce of Kinnaird; they had four children, Robert, Michael, Anne, and James *Bruce (1660/61–1730), the future minister at Killyleagh, co. Down. In 1660 Bruce declined an invitation to become the minister at Bothkennar, Stirlingshire.

The following year Jeremy Taylor, bishop of Down and Connor, ejected Bruce from the living at Killinchy for refusing to conform. For a time Bruce remained in Ireland, preaching in barns and forests, sometimes at night. Although his fellow minister Patrick Adair praised him for his gifts, zeal, and peaceful temperament, he deemed Bruce and other young clergy reckless for endangering all presbyterian ministers by defying the magistrates. When the government began arresting presbyterian clergy in June 1663 following the discovery of the Dublin plot, Bruce fled to Scotland. With Henry Hunter and James Campbell he returned to Ireland in January, apparently hoping for *de facto* toleration; they asked their followers to petition Ormond on their behalf, seeking his agreement to have them tried by an assize judge rather than an ecclesiastical court should they be charged with any offence. By June, Bruce may have returned to Scotland, for on the twenty-third its privy council, having been informed of 'the seditious and factious doctrine and practises' of Bruce and John Crookshanks, both of whom it described as fugitives from Scotland, ordered them to appear before it by 27 July. The council also commanded government troops to apprehend the two ministers (*Reg. PCS, 1661–4*, 551). When Bruce and Crookshanks had not appeared by 9 August, the council outlawed them. Irish magistrates were equally unsuccessful in apprehending them in late 1664 despite intelligence reports that Bruce was in the Ards peninsula in co. Down.

Bruce's whereabouts for the next two years are unknown, though he may have been in Scotland with Crookshanks, for the latter and unnamed ejected clergy were preaching to large conventicles in autumn 1666. Bruce almost certainly did not participate in the Galloway rising in November, but in its aftermath he continued to preach to Scottish conventicles. In a sermon on Mark 9: 43 preached at this time he called on covenanters to remain steadfast, giving up houses, lands, spouses, and children if necessary: 'The man that ventures most for God now shall be the least ashamed man in Scotland' (Howie and Kerr, 331). It was probably about this time that he preached on Psalm 119: 133 at West Calder, Edinburghshire, boldly depicting conforming clergy as Baal's ministers and urging his audience not to become 'mongrel professors' (ibid., 315) by listening to their sermons. Beseeching his listeners to travel as much as 12 miles to hear covenanting ministers, he castigated those who placed their families' welfare above the gospel. In another sermon, on Genesis 42: 25, perhaps preached about the same time, he lashed out at those who charged the godly with treason and rebellion because they faithfully kept their covenant obligations.

Early in 1668 Bruce and Crookshanks were successfully persuading people in the Irish baronies of Dunluce, Kilconway, Glenarm, and Cary to subscribe the covenant. Bruce was back in Scotland by May, holding a conventicle at Anstruther, Fife, which prompted the archbishop of St Andrews to complain to Lauderdale. Early in June 1668 the governor of Stirling Castle arrested Bruce after a struggle in which Bruce and one of his captors sustained injuries. On 4 June the privy council ordered that he be detained in the castle, with access only by physicians or surgeons. A plan by a group of Edinburgh women to rescue Bruce when he was transported to the capital on the eighteenth came to naught, and he was confined in the Tolbooth. After finding him guilty of sedition, faction, disturbing the peace, and contravening the acts of parliament and council, the latter sentenced him on 2 July to banishment from the three kingdoms and to execution should he return. Bruce signed a bond agreeing to obey and preached a farewell sermon in the Tolbooth on Psalm 140: 12–13. Subsequently published, its title-page indicates that he expected to be sent to Virginia. Instead, on 9 July, the council received instructions to convey him to London by sea at its earliest convenience. Taken from Edinburgh on 13 September, Bruce was carried to London and incarcerated in the gatehouse at Westminster. Although the government decreed his exile to Tangier, his preaching at the Tolbooth impressed the countess of Castlemaine, who helped his wife petition the king. Charles relented, allowing Bruce to name the site of his exile. He promptly selected Killinchy, to which he returned in April 1670. By this point, his relative, Robert Bruce, earl of Elgin, had obtained a writ suppressing his prior sentences.

In the summer of 1670 Bruce's congregants built a meeting-house for their use. He again found himself in trouble after Robert Leslie, bishop of Raphoe, urged Roger Boyle, bishop of Down and Connor, to repress nonconformists in his diocese. Boyle summoned Bruce and eleven other presbyterian ministers to his court in order to excommunicate them, and when none appeared, Boyle declared them contumacious and issued another summons. The twelve sent two of their number, Drysdale and Alexander Hutcheson, to entreat Boyle to act moderately, but it was Archbishop James Margetson's intervention that made Boyle back off. Bruce visited Scotland in the spring of 1672, on which occasion he preached on a May night in the churchyard at Carluke, Lanarkshire, taking as his text Ezekiel 37: 7–8. Published the same year, as *The Rattling of the Dry Bones*, it reflects Bruce's oratorical power. Depicting himself as a prophet, much as John Knox had done, he decried the Church of Scotland as dead, focused on the twin themes of individual and national sin, and exhorted his audience to look within themselves for evidence of the Spirit shaking their dry bones. Without substantive reform, he averred, such a spiritual experience was impossible.

Although Bruce was among the most visible covenanters who held conventicles in Scotland and Ireland, the magistrates could not suppress him. A report on such activity in July 1674 depicted Bruce as 'a fierce & pernicious Zealott' who was assisted by Hutcheson and Alexander Ferguson (BL, Stowe MS 214, fol. 232r). All three men were among the fifteen signatories of a petition to Ormond disavowing knowledge of the Bothwell Bridge rising, submitted on 25 June 1679, only three days after the battle. In February and May 1683 the United Societies, a radical splinter group in the covenanting movement, invited Bruce to preach and administer the sacraments to them, but he declined. When civil war erupted in 1689 Bruce fled to Scotland, where he accepted a call from the church at Anwoth, Kirkcudbrightshire. He was also offered the pastorate at Jedburgh in September 1689, but he refused. In 1690 he was a member of the general assembly of the Church of Scotland, and the following year he returned to Ireland to attend the synod of Ulster. Bruce died at Anwoth in 1693 and was interred in the parish church there. A number of his sermons, including *Soul Confirmation* (1709), were published posthumously. One of the most powerful and popular preachers at field-conventicles, Bruce stopped short of supporting physical rebellion against the government.

RICHARD L. GREAVES

Sources *Reg. PCS*, 3rd ser., vols. 1–2, 6, 14 • P. Adair, *A true narrative of the rise and progress of the Presbyterian church in Ireland (1623–1670)*, ed. W. D. Killen (1866) • J. Howie and J. Kerr, eds., *Sermons delivered in times of persecution in Scotland, by sufferers for the royal prerogatives of Jesus Christ* (1880) • *DNB* • *Fasti Scot.*, new edn, 2.386 • R. L. Greaves, *God's other children: protestant nonconformists and the emergence of denominational churches in Ireland* (1997) • Bodl. Oxf., MSS Carte 32, 45 • St J. D. Seymour, *The puritans in Ireland, 1647–1661* (1912) • Hunt. L., MS 14398 • U. Edin. L., MS 2512, fol. 116 • M. Shields, *Faithful contendings displayed* (1780) • *CSP Ire.*, 1663–5 • BL, Stowe MS 214, fol. 232r

Archives U. Aberdeen L., fragments of lectures and speeches, notes made for use in his sermons • U. Edin. L., MS 2512 | Bodl. Oxf., MS Carte 32, 45 • Hunt. L., MS 14398

Bruce, Michael (1686–1735), non-subscribing Presbyterian minister, was born on 27 July 1686, the eldest son in the family of ten children of James *Bruce (1660/61–1730), minister of Killyleagh, co. Down, and Margaret Traill (d. 1706). The bookseller William *Bruce was a younger brother. Having been educated at Edinburgh University he was licensed by the Down presbytery at Downpatrick on 27 October 1708 after subscribing to the Westminster confession and promising not to 'follow any divisive courses all the days of my life'. He was ordained minister of Holywood, co. Down, on 10 October 1711, and acquired the reputation of a quiet, solid preacher. In 1716 he married Mary Ker; they had four children, one of whom, Samuel (1722–1767), became minister of the Wood Street Presbyterian congregation in Dublin.

Bruce was a member of the ministerial club founded in 1705 and subsequently known as the Belfast Society. This club, headed by John Abernethy, exerted a powerful influence in challenging the theological orthodoxy of Ulster Presbyterianism. When in 1720 the non-subscription controversy broke out Bruce joined Abernethy in refusing to subscribe to the Westminster confession; his father, by contrast, became a subscriber. In 1724 he protested against the exclusion of his fellow non-subscriber Thomas Nevin of Downpatrick for alleged heresy. On 5 January 1725 he preached before the sub-synod of Belfast what was intended to be a healing sermon, 'The duty of Christians to live together in religious communion', the only sermon of his to be published. Later that year he and the other non-subscribers were placed in a separate presbytery of Antrim. Bruce acted as clerk for the Antrim presbytery, which formally broke with the general synod in 1726. A subscribing congregation was soon formed at Holywood under William Smith, and most of Bruce's congregation deserted him, leaving him with a handful of families who could provide him only with a stipend of barely £4. To supplement his income a fortnightly evening lecture was established in the First Belfast Congregation and Bruce appointed lecturer at £20 a year. He resigned in 1731.

Though Bruce was highly regarded as a minister he wrote so little that it is hard to judge his significance. He was responsible, however, for most of the non-subscribers' historical statement that was published as *A Narrative of the Proceedings of Seven General Synods of the Northern Presbyterians in Ireland* (1727). He died on 1 December 1735, and was buried on 7 December at Holywood, where Samuel Haliday preached his funeral sermon, on Psalm 37: 37.   ALEXANDER GORDON, *rev.* S. J. SKEDD

Sources S. Haliday, *A sermon occasioned by the death of the Revd. Michael Bruce* (1735) · J. Duchal, 'Brief memoirs of the life and character of the Revd. Samuel Haliday', *A sermon on occasion of the much lamented death of the late Revd. Samuel Haliday* (1741) · J. S. Reid and W. D. Killen, *History of the Presbyterian church in Ireland*, new edn, 3 (1867), 290n, 389n · 'Death of the Rev. William Bruce, D.D.', *Bible Christian*, 3rd ser., 3 (1841), 109–30 · T. Witherow, *Historical and literary memorials of presbyterianism in Ireland, 1623–1731* (1879), 295–8 · C. Porter, *The seven Bruces: Presbyterian ministers in Ireland in six successive generations* (1885) · J. McConnell and others, eds., *Fasti of the Irish Presbyterian church, 1613–1840*, rev. S. G. McConnell, 2 vols. in 12 pts (1935–51), 91

Bruce, Michael (1746–1767), poet, was born on 27 March 1746 at Kinnesswood in Portmoak, Kinross-shire, the fifth of eight children of Alexander Bruce (*d.* 1772), weaver, and Ann, *née* Bruce (1710/11–1798). Bruce's father was a significant local figure, notably as an elder of the seceding church of Thomas Mair of Orwell. Michael followed the family tradition of godliness, quickness of sensibility and wit, and delicacy of health. A precocious child, Bruce could write his name and read from the Bible before he started at the village school, at which he formed significant friendships with long-time correspondent David Pearson, and William Arnot, the son of David Arnot, laird of Portmoak. The death of William while still at school had a profound effect on Bruce's sensibility (he wrote the elegy 'Daphnis' in his memory in May 1765) and had the effect of drawing him into a close friendship with Arnot of Portmoak, from whom Bruce acquired his knowledge of English literature and with whom he held a lifelong correspondence (often in Latin).

In 1762 Bruce's father inherited a sum of money that allowed Michael to enrol in the Greek class at Edinburgh University, where he proved to be something of a polymath even though poetry remained his primary interest. He completed three sessions at Edinburgh, before re-establishing the school at Gairney Bridge in Cleish, about 2 miles south of Kinross. Although Bruce apparently had neither the qualifications, vocation, nor temperament for teaching, his time at Gairney Bridge (on the opposite bank of Loch Leven from Kinnesswood) seems to have been happy, and while boarding with Grieve of Classlochie he fell in love with the daughter of his host

and one of his pupils, Magdaline. Magdaline has been identified with the Eumelia and Peggy celebrated in various of Bruce's poems, although it is possible that one Margaret White of Kinnesswood should be more properly identified with Peggy (Mackenzie). In any case, Bruce never declared his affections and Magdaline was to marry someone else.

Bruce had long held the desire to enter the ministry, and, having been turned down by the Anti-Burgher synod on account of his connections with Mair, he enrolled in the Associated Synod College at Kinross. With the closure of the college, the autumn of 1766 saw him taking the school at Forrest Mill in Clackmannanshire. The cold damp climate of Forrest Mill did not suit Bruce's delicate constitution, and it was during the miserable autumn of this year, with his health entering its terminal decline, that he composed 'Lochleven', his great evocation of life on the banks of the loch where he spent so much of his short life. That winter he gave up the school and returned home to Kinnesswood. The following spring, with his consumption entering its final stages, he wrote his final poem, the touching 'Ode to Spring', an elegy for himself. He was found dead in bed on 5 July 1767 and was buried in the kirkyard at Portmoak.

Although he contemplated a volume of verse while at Gairney Bridge, Bruce formally published no poems during his lifetime. In 1767 a sometime schoolfriend, John Logan, gathered Bruce's writings (both poetry and correspondence) and in 1770 published *Poems on Several Occasions, by Michael Bruce*. The highly selective contents of this seventeen-poem volume proved controversial (it was notably short of Bruce's religious works), but attempts by Alexander Bruce to recover his son's papers were only partly successful (the most regrettable loss being the quarto volume Bruce had copied his work into in the last months of his life). To add insult to injury, Bruce's 'Ode to the Cuckoo' subsequently appeared in print twice under different names, most notably under Logan's own in his 1781 *Poems*, a volume in which Bruce's erstwhile editor also appropriated a number of Bruce's hymns.

A slight pale man, Bruce's learning, piety, and refinement of feeling earned him the admiration and affection of all who encountered him. Many of his hymns were adopted by the Scottish kirk in its 1781 *Paraphrases* from whence they have appeared in many hymnbooks. His verse is broadly bucolic, tinged with a gentle melancholy, and while the style and convention of the poems are overtly classical they generally avoid rigidity or self-consciousness. Equally the tragically blighted life of the (by cosmopolitan standards at least) all-but self taught 'natural genius', sometime shepherd-boy, and archetypal 'man of feeling' appealed to the sentimental tastes of the 1770s and 1780s and ensured some posthumous recognition. While Bruce's published verse did not fulfil the expectations of friends who predicted that he would join the pantheon of great poets writing in English, his verse and memory inspired a set of devoted followers into the twentieth century.   D. R. MOORE

Sources J. G. Barnet, *The life and complete works of Michael Bruce, poet of Lochleven* (1926) • W. Mackelvie, *Life of Bruce* (1837) • J. Mackenzie, *Life and complete works of Michael Bruce* (1914) • *DNB*

Bruce [*née* Petre], **Mildred Mary** (1895–1990), motorist and aviator, was born on 10 November 1895 at Margaretting, Ingatestone, Essex, the daughter of Lawrence Joseph Petre (1864–1944), landowner, of Coptfold Hall, Essex, and his wife, Jennie Maginness, *née* Williams (*d.* 1943), an actress. She was educated at the convent of Sion.

Growing up among five brothers, Mildred Bruce learned early in life how to sail, ride, motorcycle, and drive a car. Her love of motoring was encouraged by her marriage, on 16 February 1926, to the Hon. Victor Austin Bruce (1897–1978), youngest son of Hugh Campbell Bruce, second Baron Aberdare. Victor Bruce, winner of the Monte Carlo rally in 1926, introduced her to long-distance motor touring and to racetracks, and in 1927 Mildred won the *coupe des dames* at the Monte Carlo rally, covering 1700 miles in seventy-two hours. In December 1927 husband and wife shared the driving at Montlhéry to set an endurance record of 15,000 miles in nine days, averaging around 68 m.p.h. They also undertook a mammoth car journey, beginning at John o' Groats and ending in London, during which they circled the western Mediterranean through France, Italy, Sicily, north Africa, and Spain. The Hon. Mrs Victor Bruce, as she was now known, speedily wrote a book on the tour entitled *Nine Thousand Miles in Eight Weeks* (1927); the lively narrative, noted *The Times*, travelled 'as competently as the motor-car which endured the long test' (*The Times*, 8 July 1927). In the following year she produced *The Woman Owner–Driver* (1928), a response to 'the growing tendency for women to drive and look after their own cars' (Bruce, *The Woman Owner–Driver*, inside cover).

Bruce returned to Montlhéry in June 1929 to claim a speed record for a single-handed twenty-four-hour drive, travelling 2164 miles at an average of 89.57 m.p.h. In between her record-breaking motor drives she established, in September 1928, the fastest time for a Dover–Calais channel crossing by motor boat. Her feats mirrored those of her own fictional creation Penelope, the heroine of a series of humorous short stories that appeared in *Sketch*. They were later collected in a book, *The Peregrinations of Penelope* (1930), accurately described as 'Wodehouse *manqué*' (Cadogan, 77). As well as conquering land and water, Penelope took to the air, and in the summer of 1930 Mildred Bruce, passing a car showroom off Bond Street, saw a Blackburn Bluebird light aircraft for sale at £550. It bore the sign 'Ready To Go Anywhere': on enquiring if the plane would travel round the world she was assured by the salesman, 'Of course … easily!' (Bruce, *The Bluebird's Flight*, 2). Before long she had decided to buy it and was planning to visit her mother's birthplace in New Albany, Indiana, via Japan. She learned to fly in a matter of weeks at Brooklands School of Flying and in the early hours of 25 September 1930 set off from Heston aerodrome, armed with route maps provided by the Automobile Association and forty hours of flying in her logbook. *Bluebird* bore the identifier G-ABDS and when one of its engineers was asked by an onlooker what this stood for he replied 'A B—y Daft Stunt' (ibid., 9). Such scepticism was general and few expected her even to manage to leave England.

The following day Bruce surprised her husband by telephoning him not from Kent but from Munich, and in the next five months she proved herself a serious aviator, covering 20,000 miles by air and averaging over 400 miles a day in forty-seven days of flying. She arrived in Rangoon on 30 October 1930, Shanghai on 15 November, and Tokyo on 24 November. From Japan she took *Bluebird* across the Pacific by ship and resumed flying at Vancouver, then travelled across the United States from Seattle and reached New York on 5 February. Pilot and plane then sailed the Atlantic on the *Île de France* and Bruce was honoured with a dinner in Paris by the Aero Club de France. On the final leg of her journey, from Lympne to Croydon on 20 February 1931, she was joined by five Bluebirds, one piloted by Winifred Spooner, and a lone Puss Moth belonging to Amy Johnson, whose flight to Australia in May of the previous year had inspired Mildred Bruce's own adventure. A sizeable crowd gathered to greet her and the under-secretary of state for air welcomed her home on behalf of the Air Council. Her flight, he said, 'testified to the nation's technical development', while her 'unpretentious efficiency' would do much to convince the public of the progress being made in air travel (*The Times*, 21 Feb 1931).

A series of celebratory dinners followed, including one given by the Women's Automobile and Sports Association. *Flight* judged Bruce's venture 'one of the most meritorious that has been made by a woman' (*Flight*, 182), and *Aeroplane* particularly praised her passage over the Annam Mountains, and the 600 mile stage along the Yellow Sea to Osaka, 'severe enough tests of navigation and nerve' (*Aeroplane*, 40/8, 25 Feb 1931, 337). In her own account of the voyage, *The Bluebird's Flight* (1931), she made light of the difficulties she had faced, prompting one reviewer to observe that readers might well underrate the courage she had shown: 'Her journey was a series of narrowest escapes' (*The Times*, 13 Nov 1931).

Bruce's attempt on the world endurance record in August 1932 met with less acclaim. Piloting a Saro Windhover flying boat, with an accompanying aircrew, she remained airborne for 55 hours. It was well short of the world record, but was nevertheless hailed as a British record, a point vigorously disputed in an editorial in *Aeroplane*. The journal considered the exercise to be of dubious technical value, and not comparable to the non-stop flight of two RAF pilots from Cranwell to Karachi in April 1929, a journey of almost 51 hours. Its tone betrayed a clear reaction against the sensational way that aviation was presented to the public:

> It all comes under the generic heading of humbugging the press and the people, like putting on bogus Heroes of the Air at movie palaces, and knocking down pylons which were not hit, and claiming records for women when male pilots did the flying, and so on. (*Aeroplane*, 43/7, 17 Aug 1932, 332)

It was a process in which Bruce had become unwittingly caught up. In November 1934 she embarked upon an ambitious flight to the Cape in an autogiro, intending to be 'home by Christmas'. She planned to cross the Sahara, and to fly by night as well as by day. These were hazardous courses even with a back-up plane and the venture was abandoned when the autogiro was damaged in strong winds approaching Nîmes.

Three years later, in 1937, Bruce founded Air Dispatch Ltd, a small Croydon-based company carrying freight and passengers. It claimed the quickest air service to France and regularly delivered London newspapers to Paris breakfast tables. During the war the company moved to Cardiff and concentrated on aircraft repair. In 1941 Bruce divorced her husband of fifteen years; they had one son. She announced her intention to stand for parliament at Stroud as an independent in 1945, but withdrew before the election. She died at her home, Croftway House, 298 Finchley Road, Hampstead, London, on 21 May 1990.

Mildred Bruce was one of the few women of her day to pursue a successful career in aviation. Her epic journey around the world confirmed to the public the stamina of women pilots, while the very casualness of her approach made travel by light aircraft seem less exceptional. It helped in the portrayal of the light plane as the 'aerial motor car'. Both as a motorist and as an aviator she won the respect of the male establishment and after her failed endurance record bid in 1932 *Aeroplane* saluted her: 'she has always proved herself to be full of real courage and energy … and whenever she has been beaten she has proved herself to be a thorough sportsman' (*Aeroplane*, 43/7, 17 Aug 1932, 332).   MARK POTTLE

Sources Mrs V. Bruce [M. M. Bruce], *Nine lives plus: record-breaking on land, sea, and in the air: an autobiographical account* (1977) · V. Moolman, *Women aloft* (1981) · M. Cadogan, *Women with wings: female flyers in fact and fiction* (1992) · *The Times* (8 July 1927) · *The Times* (10 Sept 1928) · *The Times* (8 June 1929) · *The Times* (8 July 1929) · *The Times* (18 Sept 1930) · *The Times* (21 Feb 1931) · *The Times* (28 Feb 1931) · *The Times* (13 Nov 1931) · *The Times* (12 Aug 1932) · *The Times* (26 Nov 1934) · *The Times* (28 Nov 1934) · *The Times* (1 Dec 1934) · *The Times* (2 June 1945) · *The Times* (25 May 1990) · Mrs V. Bruce [M. M. Bruce], *Nine thousand miles in eight weeks: being an account of an epic journey by motor-car through eleven countries and two continents* (1927) · Mrs V. A. Bruce [M. M. Bruce], *The Bluebird's flight* (1931) · WWW · Burke, *Peerage* (1999) [Aberdare; Petre] · b. cert. · d. cert. · W. Boase, *The sky's the limit: women pioneers in aviation* (1979) · 'Mrs Victor Bruce's return', *Flight* (27 Feb 1931) · *The Aeroplane* (25 Feb 1931), 337 · *The Aeroplane* (17 Aug 1932), 330–32

Archives Wilts. & Swindon RO, corresp. and papers
Likenesses photographs, repro. in Bruce, *Nine lives plus*
Wealth at death £168,394: probate, 21 Sept 1990, CGPLA Eng. & Wales

Bruce, (William) Nigel Ernle (1895–1953), actor, was born on 4 February 1895 in Ensenada, Mexico, the second son of Sir William Waller Bruce, tenth baronet (1856–1912), who was holidaying there while negotiating a land deal in southern California, and his wife, Angelica Mary (*d.* 1917), daughter of General George Selby, officer in the Royal Artillery. After being educated at The Grange, Stevenage, and Abingdon School, he was training as a stockbroker when the First World War broke out and he enlisted in the Honourable Artillery Company. He was wounded within weeks of arriving in France and spent many months in convalescence. He was eventually gazetted as a captain in

the Somerset light infantry's home battalion, but the legacy of his injuries caused him to be invalided out of the service.

After returning to London, Bruce began acting, with parts in *Why Marry?* and *The Creaking Chair*, a mystery play by Allene Tupper Wilkes (both 1920), at the Comedy Theatre, before serving as stage manager on H. V. Esmond's and Eva Moore's 1920 Canadian tour. On 19 May 1921 he married the actress Violet Mary Pauline Shelton (stage name Campbell; 1891–1970), daughter of Colonel Willington Augustus David Shelton, army officer, of Bruree House, co. Limerick; they had two daughters, Pauline and Jennifer. Making his mark as Ensign Blades in J. M. Barrie's *Quality Street* at the Haymarket in 1921, Bruce developed into a versatile performer over the next decade, attracting attention in both Edgar Wallace mysteries and Noël Coward revues. He was particularly impressive as Philip Downes in *Lean Harvest* (1931) at the St Martin's Theatre, a role he re-created on Broadway, where he also scored a considerable triumph in *Springtime for Henry* (1931). He reprised the latter performance on film in 1934, some five years after making his screen début in the British silent film *Red Aces* (1929).

Resident in the United States from 1934, Bruce opted to concentrate on cinema, having proved an effective foil to Shirley Temple in *Stand up and Cheer* (1934). In company with his old friend C. Aubrey Smith, he pursued his hobbies of golf, cricket, and shooting, and quickly became a key member of Hollywood's English colony, though he retained membership of the Garrick and Bucks clubs in London. Despite a shambling manner that seemed to invite his being cast as amiable buffoons and cuckolded dullards, he soon carved himself a niche in literary adaptations, playing the prince of Wales in *The Scarlet Pimpernel*, Squire Trelawney in *Treasure Island* (both 1934), Professor Holly in *She*, and Joseph Sedley in *Becky Sharp* (both 1935), RKO's reworking of *Vanity Fair* which is now primarily remembered as the first feature to be filmed in three-strip Technicolor.

Bruce was equally in demand for historical melodramas, including *The Charge of the Light Brigade* (1936), *Suez* (1937), and *A Dispatch from Reuter's* (1940). Alfred Hitchcock took a liking to him, teaming him twice with Joan Fontaine, in *Rebecca* (1940) and *Suspicion* (1941). But he was only rarely allowed to demonstrate his versatility, most notably as Ronald Colman's butler in *The Man who Broke the Bank at Monte Carlo* (1935) and as a construction engineer in the frontier western *The Trail of the Lonesome Pine* (1936). He will, however, always be remembered for his partnership with Basil Rathbone in a series of fourteen Sherlock Holmes films. Although Bruce in no way resembled the Dr Watson of Conan Doyle's stories, his avuncular presence provided the perfect counterbalance to Rathbone's briskly omniscient sleuth. Financed by Twentieth Century Fox, *The Hound of the Baskervilles* (1939) was widely considered the best Holmes film to date. It prompted the *Motion Picture Herald* to declare that the advertising campaign for it should be addressed to 'the millions who have read the book, and such other millions who have not got round to reading it, but have meant to for some time, and now under the circumstances needn't' (Davies, 64). It was rapidly followed by *The Adventures of Sherlock Holmes* (1939), in which George Zucco played the part of Professor Moriarty. As in the earlier film, Watson was given plenty to do, though as the series wore on his almost accidental discoveries were essentially used as comic relief to Holmes's uncanny powers of deduction.

Fox dropped the duo in 1940, though by this time they had already assumed the roles on radio, making over 200 broadcasts between 1938 and 1945. In 1942 the pairing was signed by Universal Studios, which reinvented the residents of 221B Baker Street as contemporary figures. This eliminated the need for period trappings, while also enabling them to boost morale by confounding the Nazis in such cases as *Sherlock Holmes and the Voice of Terror*, *Sherlock Holmes and the Secret Weapon*, and *Sherlock Holmes in Washington* (all 1942).

Unfortunately, the standard of the films tailed off after *Spider Woman* and *The Scarlet Claw* (both 1944). It was perhaps ironic that the final one, *Dressed to Kill* (1946), should contain a scene in which Holmes berates Watson for the sensationalism of his *Strand* magazine articles: 'If you must record my exploits, I do wish you would put less emphasis on the melodramatic and more on the intellectual issues involved' (Davies, 95).

In the last decade of his life Bruce struggled to emerge from Watson's shadow, falling back on period pieces such as *Frenchman's Creek* (1944) and *Dragonwyck* (1946). He played a cameo role in Charlie Chaplin's *Limelight* (1952) before rounding off his career with the 3-D jungle adventure *Bwana Devil* (1952) and the posthumously released *World for Ransom* (1954). He was considering a stage reunion with Rathbone when he died from heart failure in St John's Hospital, Santa Monica, California, on 8 October 1953. He was cremated at the Chapel of the Pines crematory, Los Angeles, and was survived by his wife and daughters.   DAVID PARKINSON

Sources J. Vinson, ed., *The international dictionary of films and filmmakers: actors and actresses* (1986) · D. S. Davies, *Holmes of the movies* (1976) · *The Times* (9 Oct 1953) · *Daily Mail* (9 Oct 1953) · *News Chronicle* (9 Oct 1953) · *Variety* (14 Oct 1953) · *Motion Picture Herald* (17 Oct 1953) · *Picturegoer* (1 Aug 1936) · *Leader Magazine* (19 June 1948) · D. Parkinson, ed., *Mornings in the dark: the Graham Greene film reader* (1993) · *The Spectator* (8 March 1940) · m. cert. · Burke, *Peerage*
Likenesses photographs, 1928–45, Hult. Arch. · photographs, Ronald Grant Archive · photographs, Kobal collection · photographs, Huntley Archive

Bruce, Peter Henry (1692–1757), military engineer, the son of James Bruce (d. after 1705), army officer in the Brandenburg service, and Elizabeth Catherina Detring (d. after 1724), was born at his mother's family home, Detring Castle in Westphalia. Bruce recorded that his father was the son of a Scottish emigrant who had joined the elector of Brandenburg's forces to escape Cromwell's rule. His father also joined a Scots regiment in the service of Brandenburg, under the command of David Melville, third earl

of Leven. Leven was also acting as the agent of William of Orange in Berlin and James Bruce appears to have joined a regiment of Scottish exiles formed privately by Leven, which accompanied William's expedition to Torbay in 1688 and garrisoned Portsmouth briefly. Bruce's father served with Leven in Scotland, his regiment—later the 25th regiment of foot, and then the King's Own Scottish Borderers—distinguishing itself at Killiecrankie in 1689. The regiment subsequently served in Ireland and Flanders, where in 1692 the infant Bruce and his mother joined his father. The family moved with the regiment to Fort William in 1698.

Bruce spent three years at school in Cupar, Fife, where his great-uncle lived, and after three more years in Fort William joined his mother's family in Germany. There, he was sent to a military academy in Berlin, and in 1706 he entered the Prussian army where he studied fortification. Bruce's first active campaign was that of 1707 and during 1708 he was present at the battle of Oudenarde and worked with the pioneer corps at the siege of Lille. For his conduct in taking temporary command after the death of the engineer he was promoted to ensign. In 1709 at the siege of Tournai he was employed for the first time as an engineer and was directly involved in the attack upon the French entrenchments at the battle of Malplaquet, where he was shot through the leg. During the campaign of 1710 he was again employed as a military engineer in several sieges, including that of Douai.

In the winter of 1711 Bruce left the Prussian service with the rank of captain and, upon the invitation of a distant relative, James Daniel Bruce (1669–1735), a general and master of the ordnance under Peter the Great, entered the Russian service as a military engineer with a commission as captain of a company of artillery. He was immediately employed in the expedition against the Turks which led to the battle of Pruth, and was sent to Constantinople with diplomatic dispatches. He remained there for several months and described the city, its people and customs, in his memoirs. He returned to St Petersburg in October 1711, where he lived when he was not on missions for Peter the Great. Upon Bruce's arrival in Berlin in May 1718 in command of a party of ceremonial grenadiers—a gift from Peter the Great to the king of Prussia—his family attempted to secure his release from the Russian service but he was ordered to join Field Marshal Count Sheremetev at Copenhagen as an aide-de-camp and later served in the same capacity with General Weyde at Mecklenburg. His release was again refused in 1717 and in 1719 he was directed by the tsar to strengthen the fortifications at Revel. In 1720, by way of compensation, he was transferred to the tsar's own division as captain of a company of the Astrakhan regiment, following a further refusal of release. In 1721 he took part in the expedition against Sweden and was ordered to destroy the fort at Helsinki.

In late October of that year Bruce received news that he had inherited his late uncle's estate at Cupar in Fife, which secured from the tsar a promise of leave, deferred until after a new expedition to the Persian frontier to punish the local tribes for their depredations against Russian merchants. Thus in 1722 Bruce sailed with the tsar's force down the Volga River from Nizhniy Novgorod to Astrakhan and along the western shore of the Caspian Sea to Derbent, passing through the lands of several tribes, of whose manners and customs he gives a good account. Bruce's main task was to design and oversee the construction of fortifications on the River Sulak and in 1723 he was ordered to carry out a survey of the shores of the Caspian Sea, the circumnavigation of which he completed by September, and described as 'the most pleasant jaunt I ever had in my whole life' (Memoirs, 386). Upon his return to Astrakhan, in October, he took command of a small expedition against the Kalmyk Tartars, repulsing a pre-emptive attack. He returned to Moscow in January 1724 to present the report of his survey to the tsar. Fearing a return to the Caspian to build more fortifications he resolved 'to get out of this state of slavery … from which it was impossible for anyone that was serviceable to extricate himself with honour' (ibid., 412). After numerous petitions he was at last granted a year's leave to settle his affairs in Scotland and, as an inducement to return, his back pay as an engineer (1200 roubles) and his property in St Petersburg were withheld. But Bruce was determined not to return and he lost his Russian estate.

Bruce left St Petersburg in late May 1724 and after an eventful journey—the vessel in which he took passage from Riga for Montrose struck rocks off the island of Bornholm—he arrived at Cupar on 20 August, where he joined his mother, brother, and sister, after an absence of twenty years. Bruce settled down, married, had several children, and for the next sixteen years farmed the small estate at Cupar. Then, with the onset of war with Spain in 1739, which led to an increase in demand for military engineers, Bruce was recommended by the duke of Argyll to the master-general of the ordnance, the duke of Montagu, and in 1740 was employed by the Board of Ordnance as a chief engineer with the rank of captain and the salary of 20s. per day. As he recounts, Bruce 'once more launched into a new world for the sake of my family, which were by this time becoming pretty numerous' (Memoirs, 442). His orders were to proceed to the Bahamas to strengthen the defences at Nassau, the capital on the island of Providence. He sailed out with John Tinker, the new governor, on HMS Rose with a small convoy, arriving via Charles Town in April 1741. The old fort at Nassau was dilapidated and Bruce quickly brought the artillery up to strength with supplies from England. His first construction was a new fort, Fort Montagu, sited on the shore of the eastern approach to Nassau harbour, the likeliest place for a hostile landing. This, together with a new battery, Bladen's battery, was completed by July 1742. Bruce declined a place on the governor's council, but took a seat in the local assembly, where he used his position to secure civilian aid and materials for the rapid completion of the new fort, to thwart a much rumoured Spanish descent upon the town.

Awaiting further money and supplies from England to start work on the old fort, Bruce's frustration led to a greater involvement in local politics and a growing antagonism with the governor and his coterie. When Bruce quarrelled with Lieutenant Stewart of the local independent company, the governor placed him under house arrest for two weeks. Bruce threatened to sail for Charles Town, where there was a great demand for his skills, and money was then found from local funds for work to commence on the old fort. This was completed by December 1744. The sections of Bruce's memoirs which deal with this episode, which were separately published in 1949, provide a fascinating, if one-sided, account of the history of the colony in the mid-eighteenth century, and an important source for later historians of the Bahamas.

In January 1745 Bruce left Providence for Charles Town where, at the governor's request, he drew up plans to strengthen the defences, receiving a fee of 50 guineas. In the absence of instructions from the board he declined the offer of further employment to complete the works and took passage for England on 1 June, arriving at London on 25 July. He was immediately sent north to inspect the fortifications at Hull, following the news of the rising in Scotland, but finding matters well in hand journeyed on to Doncaster where General Wade's army was mustering. There followed a series of marches tracking the Young Pretender's army, in which Bruce took part; he was also employed in strengthening Berwick Castle. But his health was badly affected by the sudden transition from a warm to a cold and wet climate, and made worse by the rigours of campaigning, and he retired from military service to his estate at Cupar, where he died in 1757, in his sixty-fifth year.

Bruce's memoirs, which break off in 1745, were originally written in the form of a private journal in his native German. These he translated into a clear and unfussy English in 1755, but they remained unpublished at his death. In 1782 they were published in London 'for his widow' (about whom little is known) and a second edition came out in Dublin the following year. A German edition was issued in 1784 and a modern imprint was published in 1970. The book was favourably reviewed by the Monthly Review and the Gentleman's Magazine in 1782. Bruce's anecdotes of the Russian court were the main point of interest for contemporary reviewers, but they remain an interesting and well-written account of an eventful life—the life of a Scottish military man abroad.   JONATHAN SPAIN

Sources Memoirs of Peter Henry Bruce (1783) · Bahamian interlude: being an account of life at Nassau … from The memoirs of Peter Henry Bruce, ed. R. Kent (1949) · Monthly Review, 67 (1782), 410–19 · GM, 1st ser., 52 (1782) · C. Dalton, ed., English army lists and commission registers, 1661–1714, 6 vols. (1892–1904) · M. Craton, A history of the Bahamas (1962) · R. T. Higgins, The records of the king's own (Scottish) borderers (1873) · J. Grant, The Scottish soldiers of fortune (1889) · R. Woollcombe, All the blue bonnets: the history of the king's own Scottish borderers (1980) · D. G. Fedosov, 'The 1st Russian Bruces', The Scottish soldier abroad, 1247–1967, ed. G. G. Simpson (1992), 55–64 · A. Stewart, Scottish influences in Russian history (1913), 95–106 · DNB

Bruce, Robert de. See Brus, Robert de (supp. d. 1094).

Bruce, Robert (I) de. *See* Brus, Robert (I) de, lord of Annandale (*d.* 1142).

Bruce, Robert (II) de. *See* Brus, Robert (II) de, lord of Annandale (*d.* 1194?).

Bruce, Robert (V) de. *See* Brus, Robert (V) de, lord of Annandale (*c.*1220–1295).

Bruce, Robert (VI) de. *See* Brus, Robert (VI) de, earl of Carrick and lord of Annandale (1243–1304).

Bruce, Robert. *See* Robert I (1274–1329).

Bruce, Sir Robert, lord of Liddesdale (*c.*1293–1332), royal bastard, was the eldest son, albeit illegitimate, of Robert Bruce, earl of Carrick (1274–1329), later *Robert I. The identity of his mother is unknown, though she perhaps resided on or near the Bruces' Scottish estates, given that all her son's activities took place in Scotland. A French chronicler asserted that a royal bastard, surely this Robert, was one of those knighted by the king before Bannockburn; since the minimum age for knighthood was supposedly twenty-one, this suggests that he was born about 1293, when his father was a very young man. On the other hand, his sudden appearance in government records in 1321 may indicate that he reached his majority in that year, having been born *c.*1300. But the latter point is entirely hypothetical, and in any case does not preclude his having fought at Bannockburn.

In 1321 Bruce was granted Sprouston in Roxburghshire, forfeited by the English heirs of the Vescy family. In that or the following year he received the important border lordship of Liddesdale, recently forfeited by William Soulis for his part in the conspiracy of 1320 against King Robert. Liddesdale had as its caput the impressive castle of Hermitage, which dominated the western border between England and Scotland, and was thus a grant of some responsibility. Bruce was also given lands in Angus. He played a part in royal government, albeit sporadically, witnessing eight of his father's acts between 1323 and 1328, where he was usually acknowledged by the king as 'our son'. In 1328 Robert I bestowed on him a gift of 500 merks. Most importantly, the younger Robert was involved in the rebuilding of the church of St Fillan; having successfully invoked the help of that saint before Bannockburn, the king had intended to found a daughter house of Inchaffray Abbey (to which St Fillan's Church and sanctuary were now attached) in Glendochart, Perthshire. Responsibility for the task passed to his son after his death.

On 6 August 1332 Bruce was one of the leaders of the force which unsuccessfully resisted English troops landing at Kinghorn in support of Edward Balliol's claim to the throne. On 11 August his career was cut short at the battle of Dupplin Moor, Perthshire. At the outset of the battle Bruce engaged in a violent quarrel with the guardian of Scotland, Donald, earl of Mar, whom he accused of pro-Balliol and pro-English sympathies. The result was a furious competition as to who could most clearly demonstrate his patriotism by reaching the enemy lines first, which had the effect of disrupting the Scottish attack and did much to ensure the loss of the battle. Both men were killed. Bruce does not appear to have married, and the lands of Liddesdale were later taken over by Sir Archibald Douglas.   FIONA WATSON

Sources G. W. S. Barrow, *Robert Bruce and the community of the realm of Scotland*, 3rd edn (1988), 262, 318, 367, n.42 · G. W. S. Barrow and others, eds., *Regesta regum Scottorum*, 5, ed. A. A. M. Duncan (1988), no. 172 · J. M. Thomson and others, eds., *Registrum magni sigilli regum Scotorum / The register of the great seal of Scotland*, 2nd edn, 1, ed. T. Thomson (1912) · G. Burnett and others, eds., *The exchequer rolls of Scotland*, 1 (1878) · R. Nicholson, *Edward III and the Scots: the formative years of a military career, 1327–1335* (1965), 85–93

Bruce, Robert (*d.* 1602), political agent and spy, was 'the son of a poor gentleman and a merchant's daughter' (*CSP Scot.*, 1597–1603, 609), and a brother of the laird of Bynnie. He acted for some time as secretary to James Beaton, archbishop of Glasgow and envoy from Mary, queen of Scots, to the French court. The termination of the earl of Morton's regency in 1578 encouraged a revival among the Marian and Francophile party in Scotland. Robert Bruce had a distinct if obscure role in the chain of contacts linking that country with the Guise party in France and with Spain. He acted for many years as a courier between Beaton, the Guise family, the duke of Parma, and Philip II. In February 1579 he was summoned to appear before the Scottish privy council to answer unspecified charges. When he failed to appear he was outlawed, and George, Lord Seton, was ordered to bring him to justice. Seton was a committed Marian who had been imprisoned for his pro-French sympathies by Regent Morton. Seton admitted that Bruce had been in his company not long before but was unable or unwilling to produce him.

On his return to France, Bruce left Beaton's service and entered the newly founded Scottish seminary at Pont-à-Mousson in Lorraine, where he studied philosophy and theology and may have been ordained priest. At the seminary he became familiar with the Scottish Jesuits who administered it, including Father Edmund Hay with whom he was to be associated in later years. In 1585 Bruce wrote to Queen Mary telling her that he had left Beaton's household; he offered to be of service to her, asked for a pension, and told her that he was employed by the duc de Guise on various missions. In August 1585 Bruce and four Jesuits, including Edmund Hay, landed in the north of Scotland with the connivance of the sixth earl of Huntly, leader of the conservative, Francophile, and anti-English party among the nobility. Huntly's contacts with the Guises and Spain were to be useful in providing a constant stream of foreign subsidies which bolstered his domestic position and increased the influence of his party. Bruce and the Jesuits were to try to meet the king and interest him in the Catholic cause. They brought with them 6000 crowns to encourage support. The comparative freedom of movement enjoyed by Bruce and his Jesuit companions encouraged Walsingham in London to believe that James VI had assented to their arrival.

Bruce now assumed an important role as a middleman between the Guise family and the Catholic league in France, the exiled Scottish Marians, and Philip II. Having resolved on an invasion of England in order to secure his position in the Low Countries, Philip allied with the Guises in order to destabilize France and prevent any interference in his schemes elsewhere. In May 1586, as the Spanish Armada was being prepared, Bruce carried blank signed letters from the Scottish Catholic nobles to the duc de Guise, who in turn drew up proposals encouraging Philip II to support the Catholic party in their efforts to secure custody of James VI and convert him to Catholicism. Bruce carried the letters to Madrid where he persuaded the king to add a Scottish dimension to his grand strategy. He then returned first to Guise and then to Parma, the Spanish commander in the Netherlands. Initially Parma opposed intervention in Scotland, but the execution of Queen Mary on 8 February 1587 prompted hopes that James would wish to avenge her death. Philip II offered a subsidy of 150,000 crowns to the Scottish lords if they rose in rebellion and gained custody of James VI. Parma was to embark a substantial force from the Netherlands for Scotland to aid the conservative lords. Bruce now found himself a key player in this strategy and set about an ultimately unsuccessful attempt to provide Scottish ships which would convey the foreign troops to Scotland. Meanwhile, James seemed to be offering encouragement to the conservative party at home and abroad. He made Archbishop Beaton in Paris his ambassador to France, and took the Catholic bishops of Ross and Dunblane under his protection since they acted as useful channels of communication with Rome.

In May 1587 Bruce arrived in Scotland, having sailed from Brittany with the money for Parma's ships sewn into his doublet. He met the king at Hamilton and at Blantyre and was also invited to see him at Falkland; at one of these meetings he was able to deliver a letter from Philip II. James expressed pleasure at receiving the letter, giving the appearance of distancing himself from England just in case Spain should defeat England and turn her eyes to an invasion of Scotland, while in reality remaining loyal to his league with England. Consequently Bruce at first provided optimistic reports to Spain and the Guises about the potential for a Catholic coup in Scotland, but by August 1588 had become convinced of James's unreliability. He advised Philip II to work through the Catholic lords in opposing the king and that Huntly, among others, was willing to submit to Spanish sovereignty. In February 1589 the English ambassador in Scotland presented James VI with copies of letters to Parma from the earls of Huntly, Erroll, and Crawford and other conservative nobles, regretting that Spain had not used Scotland in its attack on England. In the ensuing reaction Bruce, who had been part of Huntly's entourage, was pursued until he eventually fled the country towards the end of the year.

Bruce's patron, Parma, was seriously wounded in the French campaign of spring 1592 and died on 3 December. In August Bruce wrote from Calais to Robert Bowes, the English ambassador in Scotland, and also to James VI and Chancellor Maitland, offering to disclose the names of the Spanish agents in Scotland. The price for this was to be his free return to Scotland. In November James granted Bruce a pardon for treason. When Bowes complained James said that he had been tricked into signing it without reading it. Nevertheless, in November 1593 Bruce was reported to be back in Scotland from Flanders with further Spanish subsidies, directed towards the king himself, his guard, and other significant figures at court.

In May 1594, already an agent of the Scottish government, Bruce offered once more to work for the English. He had now also fallen out with his Jesuit associates. In 1595 the Jesuit John Myreton was arrested in Scotland with letters containing accusations by Bruce against James Gordon and William Crichton, leading Scottish members of the order. They had eliminated Bruce as a distribution channel for foreign subsidies, and he was increasingly isolated and distrusted. In 1596 he was described as being in great straits and in danger of death, while in 1598 he made overtures to Cecil and was alleged to be writing a book against the Jesuits. In 1600 he was charged by the exiled Scots in Flanders with treachery, misappropriation of Spanish subsidies, and with attempting to make himself the sole channel of communication between Scotland, France, and Spain. He was imprisoned for fourteen months, but a year later is found at Brie in France reporting to James VI on the movements of the bishop of Dunblane and Father William Crichton. Visiting Scotland in 1601 under the alias of Peter Nene, he was accused of attempted murder by two English travellers whom he had met in the borders. During his examination he spoke of his dealing with Catholics and boasted of his connection with Robert Cecil. He was sentenced to death but did not suffer execution, being released to return to Paris where he died of plague in 1602.

At his death Bruce left a manuscript attack on the Jesuits which he had intended for publication, presumably the one he was reported as writing four years earlier. His heir—unidentified, but said to be a man of little fortune—was offered 1000 écus for it by the Huguenots, but as he was a Catholic was prepared to sell it to the papal nuncio in France, Innocenzo del Bufalo, for only 400. However, the general of the Jesuits refused to pay, on the grounds that to buy up every attack on his order would be a process without end, and a brief correspondence ended with Cardinal Aldobrandini advising the nuncio to try to get the manuscript for less, or, better still, to persuade its owner of the evil effects for the Catholic church, not to mention his own soul, if he permitted the Huguenots to have it. No book appeared, so one or other of these arguments must have been effective.   ALLAN WHITE

Sources Reg. PCS, 1st ser., vols. 3–4 · CSP Scot., 1574–1603 · J. Bain, ed., The Hamilton papers: letters and papers illustrating the political relations of England and Scotland in the XVIth century, 2, Scottish RO, 12 (1892), 673, 685 · CSP Rome, 1558–78 · CSP Spain, 1580–1603 · A collection of state papers ... left by William Cecill, Lord Burghley, ed. W. Murdin, 2 (1759) · J. B. A. T. Teulet, ed., Papiers d'état, pièces et documents inédits ou peu connus relatifs à l'histoire de l'Écosse au XVIème siècle, 3 vols., Bannatyne Club, 107 (Paris, 1852–60) · Calendar of the manuscripts of the most hon. the marquis of Salisbury, 4, HMC, 9 (1892) · J. Goodan and M. Lynch, eds., The reign of James VI (2000) · B. Barbiche, ed., Correspondance du nonce en France Innocenzo del Bufalo, évêque de Camerino (1601–1604) (Rome, 1964) · DNB

Bruce, Robert (1554–1631), Church of Scotland minister, was the second son of Sir Alexander Bruce of Airth and Janet, daughter of Alexander, fifth Lord Livingston. Educated at St Andrews University, where he graduated MA, he was sent by his father, who served as an elder in Airth parish church, first to France and then to the University of Louvain to study law. On returning home he acted as a procurator 'for his father's effeares and his frinds' in the court of session in Edinburgh (*Autobiography and Diary of … Melvill*, 147), but abandoned law in favour of divinity in the hope of entering the ministry. For ten years he wrestled with his conscience until on 31 August 1581, as he lay in his room at Airth Castle, he experienced an inward call to the ministry. Accordingly he cast aside his 'vain and glorious apparel, sent my horse to the fair and emptied my hands of all impediments' and 'resolved to go to St Andrews to Mr Andrew Melville', principal of St Mary's College, to study theology. Initially, he found himself 'so bashful, and oppressed with shame and blushing' that he had to be coaxed to open his mouth in class; but on gaining confidence he took his turn to preach, 'with great confluence and motion' (Bruce, 8–9).

After completing his studies and attending the 'exercise' for theology students, Bruce was called to the ministry of Edinburgh on the recommendation of Andrew Melville in 1587. He also received a call to become minister of St Andrews, which had the support of 'the whole university and all the gentlemen round about', and although he 'liked better to go to St Andrews, for I had no will of the Court, for I knew very well that the Court and we could never agree', he bowed to the entreaties of the provost and council in Edinburgh to become their minister (Bruce, 8–9). Melville also introduced him to the general assembly in June 1587, where he was urged to accept the call to Edinburgh, but he asked for more time before announcing his decision. In February 1588 he found himself elected moderator of the general assembly, an office which he again held in February 1589 and in May 1592. On 22 August 1590 Bruce married Martha Douglas (*d.* 1620), second daughter of Sir George Douglas of Pittendreich.

It was at this time that Bruce acted as a kind of extraordinary privy councillor, for which he was warmly thanked by the king—James had been absent in 1589–90 to escort his royal bride home. Bruce anointed Queen Anne at her coronation in 1590. In 1592, however, he required the king 'to humble himself upon his knees and to confess his negligence before God' in failing to take effective action against Roman Catholics but James, 'farre from humbling himself on his knees', accused him of treason for harbouring Francis Stewart, earl of Bothwell, a charge which Bruce denied (Calderwood, 5.168, 187). It was to Bruce that Bothwell had made his repentance in 1589, 'for all his bypast sinnes' and in 1594 Bruce declared in a sermon that, by siding with the presbyterians in objecting to James's leniency towards the northern Catholic earls, Bothwell 'had taikin the protection of the good caus, at least, the pretence therof, to the king's shame' (*Autobiography and Diary of … Melvill*, 277; Calderwood, 5.295).

In December 1596, when the king ordered Bruce and the

ministers of Edinburgh to leave the burgh after a riot which he blamed on the ministers, Bruce, in a sermon underlining the doctrine of the two kingdoms, showed the need to resist 'the manifest usurpation that is made upon the spirituall kingdome and this encroaching upon our spirituall liberteis' (Calderwood, 5.517). After the riot in Edinburgh, Bruce and his colleague Walter Balcanquhall left for Yorkshire where they set to work on an apologia vindicating their innocence. By July 1597 the ministers of Edinburgh were permitted to preach once more and in the following year the king declared himself reconciled with Bruce and his colleagues. Bruce himself in 1597 had made his peace by promising James:

> to serve you, and to studie by all meanes to your preservatioun, so that I sall not [be] privie to the tuiche of the lap of your mantle, lett be of your person; for I know your calling is high, and person is great, and therefore craveth due reverence of all your subjects. (Calderwood, 5.653)

With the division of Edinburgh into several parishes in 1598 Bruce, as one of the ministers who lacked the imposition of hands, was required on the king's personal intervention to receive the ceremony before he could be readmitted as minister. He declined to accept the ceremony as other than a confirmation of his ministry. To do otherwise, and to accept it as ordination, seemed to him to call into question the validity of his earlier ministry. When James pressed him 'to take a new ordination', the Edinburgh presbytery was ready to acknowledge the following of Bruce:

> [He] was and is yit a lauchfull pastor of the kirk of Edinburgh having ane lauchfull calling of the generall assemblie thairto and as to this impositioun of handis, the use is not as a ceremonie of ordinatioun to the ministrie, bot as a ceremonie of ordinatioun to his particular flock. (Kirk, *Second Book of Discipline*, 72)

Bruce was firmly opposed to the idea of ecclesiastical representation in parliament and proved an outspoken opponent of episcopacy, 'for which caus he was never suffered to returne to Edinburgh again' (Calderwood, 6.59). For declining to accept the king's version of the Gowrie conspiracy in 1600, he was warded and then ordered to leave the country. After several months in France he returned to England and was finally given permission to return to Scotland. Still unrepentant he remained reluctant to profess himself thoroughly resolved with the king's account of the Gowrie plot. In 1605 he was forbidden to preach and was warded in Inverness until 1609, despite a plea in 1606 from the nobility for his liberation, at the general assembly's request. In 1621 he was again warded, first in Edinburgh Castle and then in Inverness, for breaking the bounds of his confinement.

With James's death and the accession of Charles I, Bruce was allowed to return to his estate at Kinnaird near Falkirk, where he died on 27 July 1631. He left net assets amounting to a mere £300—not wholly surprising, for he had been deprived of his stipend. His wife had died in November 1620, with debts in excess of her assets. Renowned for his eloquent preaching, Bruce produced

Sermons Preached in the Kirk of Edinburgh, printed by Robert Waldegrave in Edinburgh in 1591, and *The Way to True Peace and Rest*, published in London in 1617. JAMES KIRK

Sources D. Calderwood, *The history of the Kirk of Scotland*, ed. T. Thomson and D. Laing, 8 vols., Wodrow Society, 7 (1842–9) · *The autobiography and diary of Mr James Melvill*, ed. R. Pitcairn, Wodrow Society (1842) · J. Spottiswoode, *History of the Church of Scotland*, ed. M. Napier and M. Russell, 3 vols., Spottiswoode Society, 6 (1847–51) · J. Row, *The history of the Kirk of Scotland, from the year 1558 to August 1637*, ed. D. Laing, Wodrow Society, 4 (1842) · W. K. Tweedie, ed., *Select biographies*, 2 vols., Wodrow Society, 7 (1845–7) · T. Thomson, ed., *Acts and proceedings of the general assemblies of the Kirk of Scotland*, 3 pts, Bannatyne Club, 81 (1839–45) · R. Bruce, *Sermons*, ed. W. Cunningham, Wodrow Society, 6 (1843) · A. I. Cameron, ed., *The Warrinder papers*, Scottish History Society, 3rd ser., 19 (1932), vol. 2 · J. Kirk, *Visitation of the diocese of Dunblane*, Scottish RS, new ser., 11 (1984) · J. Kirk, *The Second Book of Discipline* (1980) · *Reg. PCS*, 1st ser. · W. B. Armstrong, *The Bruces of Airth and their cadets* (1892) · J. Kirk, *Patterns of reform: continuity and change in the Reformation kirk* (1989) · register of Stirling testaments, 30 Nov 1631, NA Scot.
Wealth at death £300: NA Scot., register of Stirling testaments, 30 Nov 1631

Bruce, Robert, second earl of Elgin and first earl of Ailesbury (*bap.* 1626, *d.* 1685), nobleman, was born in the parish of St Bartholomew-the-Less, London, and baptized there on 19 March 1626, the only son of Thomas Bruce, first earl of Elgin (1599–1663), and his wife, Anne (*c.*1605–1627), daughter of Sir Robert Chichester KB. Although known in later years for his intellectual curiosity—he amassed a collection of antiquities and historical manuscripts and was a fellow of the Royal Society—his formal education seems to have been minimal. He toured Europe from 1642 to 1646; in 1645 he met John Evelyn in Venice. He was once again in London on 16 February 1646, when he married Lady Diana Grey (*d.* 1689), daughter of Henry *Grey, first earl of Stamford (*c.*1599–1673). Their marriage was a fruitful one, producing seventeen children.

Although Bruce's father was a moderate parliamentarian, serving on the Bedfordshire county committee in 1644–7, Bruce himself was by 1659 an active royalist conspirator. In May 1659 he brokered a donation to Charles II from a woman who was probably his aunt Christian *Cavendish, dowager countess of Devonshire. He gave £1000 himself in June and in July he was deeply involved in plans for a royalist uprising. Bruce was to raise Bedfordshire, though in the end the plan came to nothing and he was arrested on 15 August. He revealed nothing under questioning, and was subsequently granted bail.

After the Restoration, Bruce's royalist credentials stood him in good stead. In 1660 he was named to the Bedfordshire bench, given the command of a regiment of militia horse, and, more importantly, appointed joint lord lieutenant of Bedfordshire (along with the earl of Cleveland). He began, at the same time, an active career in the House of Commons. First elected to the convention for Bedfordshire, he returned to the house, where he sat on many committees and played an important part in the campaign to reward old cavaliers. His father's death on 21 December 1663 elevated him to the Scottish peerage but on 18 March 1664 he was translated to the English House of Lords as earl of Ailesbury.

As an English peer Ailesbury continued to play an active political role. He became sole lieutenant of Bedfordshire after Cleveland's death in 1667. A friend of the earl of Danby and the court, he also actively championed the anti-exclusionist cause in Bedfordshire, where he enjoyed only mixed success against the formidable interest of his neighbours the Russells. He told the duke of Ormond in April 1680 that 'I have had no little share of the calumnies that have been laid of late on those who endeavour to keep things in the old frame both as to Church and State' (*Ormonde MSS*, new ser., 5.313). But his efforts earned him the confidence of both Charles and James II. He was appointed lord lieutenant of Huntingdonshire in 1681, and Cambridgeshire in 1685. He bore St Edward's staff at James's coronation, and was appointed lord chamberlain of the household on 30 July 1685. He did not enjoy his court office long, however, and died on 20 October 1685 at his home, Houghton Park, Ampthill, Bedfordshire. He was buried on 26 October at Maulden, near Ampthill. His son Thomas *Bruce (1656–1741) succeeded him. His wife died on 8 April 1689. T. F. HENDERSON, *rev.* VICTOR STATER

Sources M. W. Helms and L. Naylor, 'Bruce, Robert', HoP, *Commons, 1660–90*, 1.737–9 · GEC, *Peerage* · *Memoirs of Thomas, earl of Ailesbury*, ed. W. E. Buckley, 2 vols., Roxburghe Club, 122 (1890) · *The manuscripts of the duke of Somerset, the marquis of Ailesbury, and the Rev. Sir T. H. G. Puleston, bart.*, HMC, 43 (1898) · N. Luttrell, *A brief historical relation of state affairs from September 1678 to April 1714*, 6 vols. (1857) · *Calendar of the manuscripts of the marquess of Ormonde*, new ser., 8 vols., HMC, 36 (1902–20), vol. 5, p. 313 · J. Godber, *History of Bedfordshire* (1969) · D. Underdown, *Royalist conspiracy in England, 1649–1660* (1960), 259, 266, 300
Archives Beds. & Luton ARS, Brudenell-Bruce MSS, household accounts · Wilts. & Swindon RO, Brudenell-Bruce MSS, estate papers, Ampthill, Bedfordshire | NA Scot., corresp. with Sir William Bruce of Balcaskie, GD 29
Likenesses R. Dunkarton, mezzotint, pubd 1814 (after P. Lely), BM, NPG · W. Faithorne, line engraving, BM · attrib. P. Lely, oils, Deene Park, Northamptonshire · R. White, line engraving (after P. Lely), BM, NPG · mezzotint (after P. Lely), BM, NPG

Bruce, Stanley Melbourne, Viscount Bruce of Melbourne (1883–1967), prime minister of Australia, was born on 15 April 1883 at Grey Street, St Kilda, Melbourne, Australia, the youngest of five children of John Munro Bruce (1840–1901) and his wife, Mary Ann Henderson (1848–1908), both Irish-born of Scottish descent. His father, a partner in Paterson, Laing, and Bruce, soft goods importers, bought out his partners in 1897 to form a limited proprietary company of which he became chairman of directors. Stanley was educated at Melbourne Church of England grammar school, where he captained football, cricket, athletics, and rowing, and was lieutenant of cadets and school captain in 1900–01.

After a year in the warehouse, Bruce entered Trinity Hall, Cambridge. He rowed in the winning Cambridge crew of 1904 and graduated BA in 1905. He went to Ashurst, Morris, and Crisp, a leading firm in commercial law in London, and read for the bar at the Middle Temple. Admitted in 1907 he practised in the equity jurisdiction, specializing in company law. Appointed chairman of

Paterson, Laing, and Bruce, he attended regularly its London office. He travelled to Mexico in 1908 and to Colombia in 1912 on legal commissions, and to Melbourne in 1910 and 1914 to relieve his brother Ernest as general manager of the family firm, which prospered under the brothers' direction.

On 12 July 1913 at Sonning, Berkshire, Bruce married Ethel Dunlop (1879–1967), Australian-born daughter of the late Andrew George Anderson, pastoralist, and his wife, Elizabeth Mary Synnot Manifold. It was a happy marriage. They shared an enthusiasm for theatre, and enjoyed golf, motoring, and bridge. Bruce said his political career became Ethel's hobby.

Bruce joined the Inns of Court Officers' Training Corps and was commissioned on 21 January 1915 in the Worcester regiment. Seconded to the Royal Fusiliers, he fought with the 29th division in the Gallipoli campaign. He was wounded, promoted temporary captain, severely wounded on 25 September and invalided to London. He won a Military Cross and Croix de Guerre *avec palme*. Bruce was back at Paterson, Laing, and Bruce while convalescent, and in 1917 returned to Melbourne as general manager. He took his military discharge on medical grounds in June 1917.

Political career Bruce was elected to the federal parliament in 1918 as a Nationalist. He stressed the need to apply business methods to government and took a sympathetic interest in former servicemen's problems. He travelled on family business in 1919 and again in 1921, when he represented Australia at the League of Nations. On his return he became treasurer. Prime Minister W. M. Hughes, under threat from the Country Party, had tried to negotiate a coalition but failed. Hughes needed to shore up support among his own supporters. Bruce was thought to be

marked as a future leader by National Union power-brokers. Fortunate in coming to the treasury at the turning point of the recession, he reduced taxes, gave the states money for roads, and balanced the budget. He borrowed to expand post and telephone services, explaining that the financing of reproductive works by loans was internationally approved.

The 1922 federal election gave the Country Party the balance of power. Earle Page's refusal to serve under Hughes forced the prime minister to recommend Bruce. During the campaign Bruce had said he would do anything for good relations with the Country Party. However, he was not prepared to form a minority government. He insisted the Country Party share responsibility and form a joint ministry (9 February 1923 to 22 October 1929). Bruce ceded the treasury and five of eleven portfolios, a more generous allocation of ministries than Country Party numbers called for. It was the basis of a formidable urban–rural alliance which dominated Australian politics for decades. In 1924, to forestall moves to 'go it alone', Bruce negotiated the first of a series of electoral pacts.

Page later claimed credit for much of the Bruce–Page programme, though the achievement was more truly Bruce's. Bruce was systematic. He sought advice, he listened, when he had reached a decision he stood by it. Page came to respect his judgement. He would discuss an idea with Bruce before publicly committing himself, and continued to do so after Bruce left politics. Bruce brought an orderliness to administration notably lacking under Hughes.

Bruce wanted improved communications with Britain and co-ordinated development of empire resources. He knew the importance of developing radio and aviation, which linked centre to periphery. He promoted both. He

Stanley Melbourne Bruce,
Viscount Bruce of Melbourne
(**1883–1967**), by Howard
Coster, 1939

preached the mutual benefits of empire. Through a redistribution of population Britain could solve its unemployment problem and expand the market for its manufactures. Australia needed a larger population. With efficient use of natural resources it could support more people at existing living standards. Bruce spoke of a national duty to develop natural resources. The capital needed would come from Britain. He expected the benefits to flow on, creating additional investment opportunities. Crucial to the whole undertaking was the securing of markets for Australian produce. And for that he looked to Britain. Bruce would be remembered as the 'Men, Money and Markets' prime minister.

At Bruce's request an Imperial Economic Conference was called in 1923 alongside an Imperial Conference. Bruce argued persuasively the case for imperial preference, but the promised tariffs became an election issue and were lost. Australian tariff schedules already included preference for British manufactures. A tariff board had been established to advise on the cost of protection. An additional appointment representing rural interests had a moderating influence on Country Party criticism. The promise held out to its supporters was of protection all round. A mix of export control boards, subsidies, and home price support schemes went some way towards overcoming farmers' marketing difficulties.

Bruce's strategy was to enlarge the scale of existing migration and settlement agreements and to make development scientific. A £34 million agreement was signed in 1925 with terms broadened to include public works associated with closer settlement. A development and migration commission was created with wide-ranging investigatory powers, and specific responsibility for the approval of projects under the agreement. The Imperial Economic Conference had adopted Bruce's proposal for an Imperial Economic Committee; through an Empire Marketing Board funded by the British government, it financed research, and promoted empire produce. Bruce funded generously a Commonwealth Institute of Scientific Research, which tapped Empire Marketing Board funds.

When Bruce took office the federal public service was small and largely recruited from school-leavers. He looked elsewhere for expert advice, borrowing British civil servants and consulting academics. His penchant for appointing royal commissions before initiating reforms was criticized as a device for postponing action, but is more rightly seen in the context of increasing public use of professional expertise. Warned by the tariff board of spiralling costs of tariff and wages, Bruce commissioned an investigation by economists. He arranged an official tour of Australia by leading British businessmen, ostensibly to reassure the City of London of Australia's capacity to service debt, but also to showcase investment opportunities. The economists warned against further tariff increase but concluded, more positively, that without protection it would not have been possible to support the same population at existing living standards. The British economic mission, also reporting in 1929, bluntly stated Australia was living beyond its means.

At the 1923 Imperial Conference Bruce helped draft the resolution on defence. His government would accept responsibility for Australia's defence as far as finance permitted, a subjective criterion and inevitably so. He approved the addition of two cruisers, two submarines, and a seaplane carrier to the Australian navy. The advice on submarines was ill-founded. He deferred a decision on coastal defence, while the merits of fixed as against aerial defence were disputed.

With an overriding concern to strengthen the empire, Bruce resisted moves to formalize dominion status. He resented, as did other prime ministers, a British summons to dispatch troops—in the Chanak crisis—when the policy productive of the crisis was pursued without consultation. Bruce wished to know in time to put the Australian point of view. The solution he found was to place a 'liaison officer' (his friend R. G. Casey) in the British cabinet secretariat with privileged access to confidential papers. What influence he commanded he used to dissuade Britain from any action to which another dominion objected. Bruce valued the diplomatic unity of empire. At the 1926 Imperial Conference he contributed to the ambiguity of the Balfour declaration of dominion autonomy by securing omission of the word 'independence'. When the seat of government moved to Canberra in 1927, Bruce arranged for a royal duke to perform the ceremony. After 1926 only the crown held the empire together constitutionally.

The most important unresolved federal issue concerned state revenue. There was general agreement that fiscal independence was desirable, but various schemes for reserving specified taxes for the states were rejected. Under threat of terminating per capita payments Bruce secured the states' consent to a financial agreement (adopted as a constitutional amendment in 1928) which established a loan council, with authority to determine the amount and allocation of government loans, and replaced per capita payments with an arrangement slightly more favourable to the states in which the commonwealth helped fund state debts. An earlier voluntary loan council had operated satisfactorily but without New South Wales participation. The statutory loan council proved a more powerful weapon against recalcitrant states than Bruce envisaged.

The fall in world prices late in the 1920s had immediate impact on export industries and cumulative consequences for other industry. Unemployment rose. Industrial relations deteriorated. In 1919 after travel abroad, Bruce noted Australia's industrial troubles were small compared with those of the United Kingdom. In his first term in office he adroitly played militants against others, and in 1925 ran a law and order campaign to win additional seats. He took a complex constitutional amendment to the electorate in 1926 seeking extensive powers to intervene in industrial disputes, and lost. The introduction of a licensing system on the waterfront intended to break a militant union, new restrictions and penalties for striking unions, and a requirement that the arbitration court consider the likely effects on the economy and on the industry concerned when making an award, precipitated the worst industrial conflict for a decade. The government lost seats in the 1928 election. Bruce made overlapping state and federal jurisdictions the reason for withdrawing the commonwealth altogether from industrial regulation, except for shipping. Hughes led a revolt which brought down the government. It lost the October 1929 election. Bruce himself was defeated. However, the dissolution of the lower house only ensured that control of the senate remained with the National and Country parties.

Bruce was re-elected in 1931. Dissident Labor members had joined Nationalists to form a United Australia Party under J. A. Lyons's leadership. Bruce became honorary minister assisting the treasurer. He led the Australian delegation to the Ottawa conference in 1932, where a series of intra-imperial trade agreements was negotiated. He went then to London to oversee loan transactions. Bruce was patient and persuasive in his wrangles with the chancellor of the exchequer; and then in the terms he negotiated with the underwriters. Bruce finely judged the market for a series of conversion loans which substantially reduced interest payments.

High commissioner After a year as resident minister in London, Bruce resigned from cabinet and parliament. He served as Australian high commissioner in London from 1933 to 1945. He kept a watchful eye on the trade concessions gained at Ottawa, alerting his government to any threat to Australia's position from other nations. He negotiated bulk purchase of Australia's major exports during the war. He represented Australia at world conferences and at the League of Nations. Later he boasted Australia was better informed on international affairs and had more influence on British policy than all the rest of the empire together, but he was modest about his own considerable influence on Australian policy. With foreknowledge gained from the liaison officer's reading of confidential papers and his own important contacts he would alert his government to a likely eventuality and draft an appropriate response. Senior ministers trusted Bruce's judgement and usually responded as he suggested.

Bruce's expectations for the league were always tempered by realistic assessment of its limited peacekeeping power without United States membership. He opposed any measure thought likely to bar future United States membership. When Italy invaded Abyssinia he acknowledged a league obligation to apply sanctions but warned of ineffectiveness. He pushed Britain hard for firm commitments regarding Singapore and Pacific security. It was Bruce's insistence in 1933, Sir Maurice Hankey recalled, which brought the first effective steps in rearmament. Bruce was no naïve believer in empire invincibility and tried, through personal contact with American presidents, to elicit a promise of support. The danger lay in a German–Italian–Japanese alliance and against that he pressed for economic appeasement. As an industrializing nation Japan needed markets. Bruce envisaged credit arrangements whereby China opened its market to Japan's cheap manufactures, reserving capital goods for American and British industry. Bruce believed the freeing-

up of trade would moderate international tension. He proposed a new mandate arrangement for non-self-governing colonies and territories, to which Germany could be admitted. It would give Germany access to tropical raw materials and markets.

Colonial development meshed neatly with another Bruce project linking nutrition and agriculture. Rather than restrict production to raise price levels, as was proposed at the 1933 world economic conference, Bruce proposed a scheme to use surplus produce to raise nutritional standards and, by restoring purchasing power to agricultural countries, give a stimulus to international trade. From 1935 Bruce was spokesman at the League of Nations for this movement. In 1936 he presided at the London meeting of the council during the Rhineland crisis. He chaired the Montreux conference which approved a revision of the Straits convention acceptable to Turkey. He was judged among the ablest of league chairmen. The special committee on league reform, which he also chaired, became known as the Bruce committee. Its recommendations shifted the emphasis in league functions from peacekeeping to social and economic reform.

Bruce was worried by the pace of British rearmament. His scheme for large-scale aircraft manufacture in Australia was undermined by British military and commercial interests. He returned to Australia in 1939 for consultation and after Lyons's death declined an invitation to re-enter politics. He resisted R. G. Menzies's request to go to Washington as Australia's first ambassador. After the conquest of Poland, Bruce anticipated German 'peace feelers' and was distressed by the British failure to address the issue. He believed neutral opinion could be influenced by positive plans for a post-war settlement, in which restoring Poland had priority. His detailed suggestions incorporated the social and economic reforms earlier pursued through the league. He failed to persuade Winston Churchill and pushed the issue beyond tolerance. Their relationship was further strained by Churchill's decisions on strategy and use of Australian troops, and his discounting the likelihood of a Japanese invasion of Australia. At the gravest point in the Pacific war Churchill conceded membership of the war cabinet to Bruce, but when he did not want Bruce present, Bruce was not told cabinet was meeting. Bruce became resigned to Churchill's dominating ways. His influence on post-war planning came through President Roosevelt. Bruce and F. L. McDougall, the Australian government's economic adviser, planned to make the marriage of health and agriculture the first programme to give real meaning to the Atlantic charter promise of freedom from want. The Hot Springs conference in 1943 agreed the United Nations would establish a Food and Agriculture Organization.

Bruce was minister to the Netherlands government in exile from 1941 to 1945 and in close contact with important neutral powers. He used his exceptional prestige with the Turks, from Atatürk onwards, to strengthen Turkish neutrality, and kept himself briefed on Spain through friendship with Sir Samuel Hoare. He cultivated relations with the Russians. When his term as high commissioner ended he was offered a peerage but declined. In Australia he found his old party 'too reactionary' and the Labor government offered nothing. His name was among those discussed for secretary-general of the United Nations Organization, but the decision was for someone younger. Bruce accepted several directorships in London and agreed to chair a preliminary committee for a world food board. As initially envisaged by J. B. Orr and Bruce, the board would establish buffer stocks to control price fluctuations. This was too radical for Americans. Bruce guided the committee to a compromise recommendation, a world food council as the executive of the Food and Agriculture Organization. He was appointed its chairman but resigned in 1951 finding it powerless.

Bruce accepted a viscountcy in 1947. It gave him a platform to promote ideas on nutrition and colonial development. From 1947 to 1957 he chaired the Finance Corporation for Industry which had been established to finance the re-equipment and modernization of British industry. He was the first chancellor of theAustralian National University (1951–61), travelling occasionally to Canberra to preside at meetings.

The three things which pleased him most, Bruce said, were his Cambridge blue, his captaincy of the Royal and Ancient Golf Club of St Andrews, and his fellowship of the Royal Society (1944). Throughout a long career he looked to science for solutions for environmental, industrial, and political problems. The tragedy of the depression overshadowed his later years in office and his name is still linked in popular memory with bitter industrial conflict. His international standing was not widely known in Australia though is now better appreciated. W. J. Hudson places Bruce along with F. L. McDougall among the most innovative contributors to international life in the interwar period.

Bruce died in his London flat, no. 16, 7 Prince's Gate, on 25 August 1967. His wife, to whom he was devoted, had died in March 1967. They were childless. Bruce was no longer wealthy. He left several bequests to learned institutions and directed that his ashes be scattered over Canberra. HEATHER RADI

Sources I. M. Cumpston, *Lord Bruce of Melbourne* (1989) · A. Stirling, *Lord Bruce: the London years* (1974) · C. Edwards, *Bruce of Melbourne* (1965) · W. J. Hudson, *Australia and the League of Nations* (1980) · G. Sawer, *Australian federal politics and law, 1901–1929* (1956) · *Documents on Australian foreign policy, 1937–49*, 1–8 (1975–89) [vols. 1 and 2 ed. R. G. Neale; vol. 3 ed. H. Kenway, H. J. W. Stokes and P. G. Edwards; vols. 4–8 ed. W. J. Hudson] · *Letters from a 'secret service agent': F. L. McDougall to S. M. Bruce, 1924–1929*, ed. W. J. Hudson and W. Way (1986) · *My dear P.M.: R. G. Casey's letters to S. M. Bruce, 1924–1929*, ed. W. J. Hudson and J. North (1980) · W. J. Hudson, *Casey* (1986) · G. T. Powell, 'The role of the commonwealth government in industrial relations, 1923–1929', MA diss., Australian National University, 1974 · J. McCarthy, *Australia and imperial defence, 1918–39* (1976) · G. Sawer, *Australian federal politics and law, 1929–1949* (1963) · E. Page, *Truant surgeon* (1963) · *DNB* · *AusDB*, vols. 3, 7 · W. H. Richmond, 'S. M. Bruce and Australian economic policy, 1923–1929', *Australian Economic History Review*, 23 (1983), 238–57 · W. K. Hancock, *Problems of economic policy, 1918–39* (1942), vol. 2 of *Survey of British Commonwealth affairs* · R. S. Gilbert, *The Australian loan council in federal fiscal adjustments, 1890–1965* (1973) · J. B. Orr and D. Lubbock, *The white man's dilemma: food and the future* (1953) · R. Ovendale, 'Appeasement' and the English speaking world (1975) · A. W. Martin and P. Hardy, *Robert Menzies: a life*, 2 vols. (1993–9) · B. D. Graham, *The formation of the Australian country parties* (1966) · *The diaries of Sir Alexander Cadogan*, ed. D. Dilks (1971) · E. Lyons, *Among the carrion crows* (1972) · *CGPLA Eng. & Wales* (1968)

Archives Australian National University, Canberra, records · National Archives of Australia, Canberra, papers, CRS A1420–21, M100–14, A1486–96 Accession CP 362/4–5 | NL Aus., Brookes papers; Edwards MSS; Latham papers; officer papers; Page papers; Pearce papers; corresp. with first Viscount Stonehaven | FILM BFI NFTVA, documentary footage; news footage

Likenesses H. Coster, photograph, 1939, NPG [see illus.] · W. B. McInnes, portrait, Parliament House, Canberra · photographs, repro. in Edwards, *Bruce of Melbourne* · photographs, repro. in Stirling, *Lord Bruce* · portraits, NL Aus.

Wealth at death £35,479: probate, 1968, *CGPLA Eng. & Wales*

Bruce, Thomas, second earl of Ailesbury (1656–1741), nobleman and memoirist, was born on 26 September 1656, probably at Ampthill, Bedfordshire, the fifth but first surviving son of Robert *Bruce, first earl of Ailesbury (*bap.* 1626, *d.* 1685), and his wife, Diana (*d.* 1689), daughter of Henry *Grey, first earl of Stamford (*c.*1599–1673). He was educated privately. His first marriage, on 30 October 1676, to Elizabeth Seymour (1656–1697), daughter of Henry Seymour, Lord Beauchamp, and sister and coheir of William Seymour, third duke of Somerset (*d.* 1671), brought Lord Bruce, as he was then styled, an interest in three Wiltshire boroughs, though he hoped to make his political début as knight of the shire for Bedfordshire. Even though his father was lord lieutenant of the county, in the first Exclusion Parliament Bedfordshire's electors preferred supporters of the Russell interest. Bruce represented Marlborough in the last two Exclusion parliaments, where he supported the court. In the country he was a busy proponent of loyal addresses aimed at whigs and dissenters.

Appointed a gentleman of the bedchamber by Charles II only a month before the king died (at a cost of £5000), Bruce retained the post after James II's accession. He served as a page of honour at the coronation, and was elected to James's first parliament as knight of the shire for Wiltshire. He succeeded his father in October 1685, replacing him as the king's main supporter in Bedfordshire, where he was now lord lieutenant. The king added the lieutenancy of Huntingdonshire to his offices, and Ailesbury also served as recorder of Bedford and high steward of Huntingdon, where he strove, at times against his own better judgement, to advance the king's policies. Although he advised the king against it, following the royal instruction of 25 October 1687, he dutifully asked his deputy lieutenants the infamous three questions, namely, would they support the repeal of the penal and test acts if elected as MPs, would they endorse the candidature of others who did, and would they acquiesce in practice in a declaration of indulgence. When most were sacked for their negative answers Ailesbury sent commissions to new, more pliable gentlemen—along with a letter requesting that they stay away from his house, as he had no desire to meet them. Despite his misgivings about James's actions, Ailesbury remained loyal. When William of Orange landed at Torbay, he stayed at the king's side. He accompanied James back to London after his capture at Faversham in December 1688, and urged him to remain in the country. After the king's departure Ailesbury remained behind, fighting a rear-guard action in his behalf. He acted as teller for the 'not contents' when the Lords voted to declare James's abdication in February 1689, and soon he was deeply involved in Jacobite plotting.

In 1695 Ailesbury travelled to France, where he solicited Louis XIV's aid in a plot to overthrow William III. He later hosted conspiratorial meetings at his London house, according to informers, and was finally imprisoned in the Tower in February 1696. The authorities intercepted his mail and refused to allow his wife to accompany him. While he was still in gaol, she died on 12 January 1697 in childbed, a tragedy for which Ailesbury blamed the government. Although perhaps not as culpable as Sir John Fenwick, executed for his part in the plot, Ailesbury was much more than a minor figure. His health weakened by his long imprisonment, he was finally bailed in February 1697, and in 1698 he left the country after the king refused him further leave to stay.

Ailesbury settled in Brussels, where he continued to keep in touch with political developments at home and remained in contact with the Jacobite court. In 1711 he wrote to Lord Oxford asking for the appointment of his son Charles, Lord Bruce, to the lieutenancy of Bedfordshire, and after the Hanoverian succession he corresponded with the new court, even as he was promising James Stuart (the Pretender) his assistance. His commitment to either side seems to have been fairly weak by this time, however, for he put down deep roots in Brussels. On 27 April 1700 he married a Flemish heiress, Charlotte Jacqueline D'Argenteau, countess of Esneux (1679–1710), and thus came to control considerable property in and around the city. His daughter with Charlotte, Marie Thérèse, married the prince van Hornes, and was the grandmother of Charles Edward Stuart's wife. Ailesbury also seems to have converted to Catholicism. As he put it in his memoirs, 'I live in a sort of retreat … I hear all things, but say nothing, nor meddle in any business but the care of my house' (*Memoirs of … Ailesbury*, 1.189). Along with his gardens, he had one other important pastime while in exile: his memoirs. Begun about Christmas 1728, they were an important first-hand account of English politics from the exclusion crisis to the revolution. Ailesbury died in Brussels on 16 September 1741, and was buried there at the Brigittine church, beside his second wife, who had died on 13 July 1710. His heart was carried to Maulden, Bedfordshire, where it was interred with his first wife. His son, Charles Bruce (1682–1747), succeeded to the earldom.   VICTOR STATER

Sources *Memoirs of Thomas, earl of Ailesbury*, ed. W. E. Buckley, 2 vols., Roxburghe Club, 122 (1890) · GEC, *Peerage* · J. P. Ferris, 'Bruce, Thomas', HoP, *Commons, 1660–90*, 1.739–40 · *The manuscripts of the duke of Somerset, the marquis of Ailesbury, and the Rev. Sir T. H. G. Puleston, bart.*, HMC, 43 (1898) · *CSP dom.*, *1696*; *1698* · *Report on the manuscripts of the marquis of Downshire*, 6 vols. in 7, HMC, 75 (1924–95), vol. 1, pp. 276, 280, 644; vol. 5, pp. 725–6, 652–3 · *Calendar of the Stuart papers belonging to his majesty the king, preserved at Windsor Castle*, 7 vols., HMC, 56 (1902–23), vol. 2, pp. 319, 443; vol. 7, p. 421 · *The manuscripts of the House of Lords*, 4 vols., HMC, 17 (1887–94), vol. 2, p. 18 · V. L. Stater, *Noble government: the Stuart lord lieutenancy and the transformation of English politics* (1994)
Archives Wilts. & Swindon RO, corresp. and papers | NA Scot., corresp. with Sir William Bruce of Balcaskie, GD 29
Likenesses F. Harrewijn, line engraving (after his earlier work), BM, NPG

Bruce, Thomas, seventh earl of Elgin and eleventh earl of Kincardine (1766–1841), diplomatist and army officer, was born at the family home, Broomhall, Fife, Scotland, on 20 July 1766, the son of Charles Bruce, fifth earl of Elgin and ninth earl of Kincardine (1732–1771), and his wife, Martha (d. 21 June 1810 in her seventy-first year), only child of Thomas White, banker, of London. He succeeded to the titles and estates on the death of his brother, William Robert Bruce, sixth earl (1764–1771), on 15 July 1771. He entered Cormick's School, Wandsworth, before attending (from 1775) Harrow School and (from 1778) Westminster School. Elgin then attended the University of St Andrews (1782–6), and later he studied public and civil law in Paris. He also spent a year in Dresden, mainly in order to learn German, and made visits to several other German cities. The Elgin family was closely allied politically to the party of William Pitt and Henry Dundas, under whose patronage Elgin made his political and diplomatic career.

In 1785 Elgin joined the army as an ensign in the 3rd (Scots) guards; he was responsible, after war began in 1793, for raising a regiment of Elgin fencibles of which he was appointed colonel. Later, despite not having seen active service, he progressed through the upper ranks before being appointed general in 1837. In 1790 Elgin, a tory, was elected a representative peer for Scotland, a position he retained until 1807. In 1808 he was sent, at short notice, as envoy-extraordinary to the court of Vienna, Sir Robert Keith, the previous British representative, having been taken ill. His mission, seen as vital as the nations of Europe prepared for war against revolutionary France, was to persuade the emperor Leopold into an alliance. When Keith recovered and returned to his post Elgin was sent to Brussels, capital of the Austrian Netherlands; much of his time there was spent with the Austrian army. During the years 1794 and 1795 he spent part of his time in London and part in Scotland, until in 1795 he was appointed minister-plenipotentiary at the court of Prussia in Berlin. He returned to London, following the accidental drowning of another of his brothers in 1798. In 1799 he was appointed ambassador to Constantinople.

Much of Elgin's energy when he was at home was devoted to the opening up of lime quarries and coal mines in Fife. With his new wealth Elgin rebuilt Broomhall on the Firth of Forth in the Grecian style. It was at the suggestion of Thomas Harrison, the architect, that he decided to use his mission to Constantinople, as he was often to say, 'to improve the arts in Great Britain'. The plan was to make, and then publish, accurate architectural drawings of the classical Greek buildings surviving in Athens,

Thomas Bruce, seventh earl of Elgin and eleventh earl of
Kincardine (1766–1841), by Anton Graff, 1787

which was at that time a small town in the European territories of the Ottoman empire, and to make full-scale plaster casts of the chief architectural and sculptural features. By providing British artists with reliable examples of what was considered the best art, he hoped he would help to raise the standards of British art and design.

Although the government declined to assist him financially Elgin decided to go ahead at his own expense. When it emerged that British artists, including J. M. W. Turner, were unwilling to go on the terms offered, Elgin's private secretary recruited a party of artists and moulders in Italy. The government did, however, agree that Joseph Dacre Carlyle, a Cambridge professor, should be attached to the mission in the hope of finding and obtaining manuscripts of unknown ancient texts from the libraries of Constantinople, Athos, and elsewhere, a hope which was not to be fulfilled.

On 11 March 1799, shortly before setting off for Constantinople, Elgin married Mary Nisbet (1778–1855), only child of William Hamilton Nisbet, of Dirleton; she was from a Scottish landowning family who lived not far away, and heir to a large fortune. They had two sons and three daughters. After divorcing her for adultery by legal actions in 1807 and 1808 in the English and Scottish courts—and by act of parliament—which caused much public scandal, Elgin on 21 September 1810 married Elizabeth (1790–1860), youngest daughter of James Townsend

Oswald of Dunnikier; they had five sons, including James *Bruce (1811–1863), governor-in-chief of British North America and viceroy of India, and Sir Frederick Wright-*Bruce, diplomatist, and three daughters. The first countess later married Robert Ferguson of Raith (1777–1846) who had been cited in the divorce.

During Elgin's first years as ambassador to Turkey his credibility with the Ottoman government was constantly undermined by Sir Sidney Smith and his brother Spencer Smith who also held official positions in the eastern Mediterranean area. Napoleon blamed Elgin personally for the fiasco of the convention of al-ʿArish. However, when, in 1801, British forces expelled the French invading forces from Egypt, Elgin, as the representative of Turkey's best ally, suddenly found himself the recipient of many official favours.

It was in these circumstances that, in May 1801, he obtained a firman, an official letter from the Ottoman government to the governor and chief justice of Athens requesting them to grant extensive facilities to the artists who were then in Athens. Elgin's chaplain and private secretary, Philip Hunt, who had recently visited Athens, had been appalled to see the severe damage that was being inflicted on the monuments, both by members of the Turkish garrison and by the officers and tourists from western Europe who, from the middle of the eighteenth century, were visiting Greece in large numbers. Although the firman did not give explicit authority to allow the removal of antiquities from the buildings, Hunt, using a mixture of bribes and threats, persuaded the authorities at Athens to permit Elgin's agents to take down, and later export, many of the surviving sculptures of the Parthenon and other buildings. His agents also arranged excavations on the Acropolis and elsewhere, amassing a large collection of ancient inscriptions, vases, jewellery, and other antiquities besides sculptures.

The work of removal continued, with interruptions, with the full co-operation of the authorities in Athens for several years. When, some years later, the French ambassador and others raised doubts with the Ottoman government about the legality of what had been done under the terms of the firman, Elgin and his successors at Constantinople obtained further firmans which gave legitimation under Ottoman law to the removals of the antiquities and their subsequent export.

As Elgin was returning from Constantinople in 1803 he and his family were arrested by the French government. He was kept, mostly under close arrest, at various locations in France, during which time the French authorities unsuccessfully attempted to incriminate him by drawing him into secret intrigues. Elgin also rejected suggestions deriving from Napoleon that he could obtain his freedom by selling his collection of antiquities to the Louvre which, at that time, was being filled with works of art taken from museums all over Europe. In 1806 Elgin was allowed to leave France, under a parole which required him to return to France whenever the French government asked him to do so. Since, until the fall of Napoleon in 1815, no British government could employ him under such conditions, the giving of the parole effectively ended his public career.

Deep in debt as a result of his expenditure in Athens, Elgin began a long campaign to sell his collection to the nation. As soon as the sculptures of the Parthenon were seen in London, the artists of the day, almost without exception, declared that they were the most perfect works of art they had ever seen. Modern appreciation of ancient art was immediately changed. Although most of Elgin's contemporaries regarded the removals from Athens as an act of rescue, in 1812, with the publication of *Childe Harold's Pilgrimage*, Lord Byron changed the terms of the debate, portraying Elgin as a plunderer. Some of the attacks which followed were highly personal. For example, from an early age Elgin had suffered from an ailment which was described as rheumatism but which was almost certainly syphilis. The disease, which ate into his nose, made him, and his family, who included an epileptic son, the targets of many cruel jokes.

In 1816, following an inquiry by a select committee of the House of Commons which vindicated Elgin from the charge of having misused his powers, the Elgin marbles, as the collection of antiquities was officially called, were bought on behalf of the British nation, and entrusted to the British Museum. Thereafter Elgin retired into private life. He died in Paris on 4 November 1841. It was mainly because the estates were still heavily encumbered with debt that his third son, James Bruce, the eighth earl, spent most of his life abroad.

The sculptures of the Parthenon in the British Museum at once became the classic site for the artistic and cultural concerns of each succeeding age. To the Romantic imagination, for example, as given expression by Benjamin Robert Haydon, Henry Fuseli, John Keats, and many others, the Elgin marbles were the supreme example of great art as creation, the nearest to the divine to which human beings could aspire, unsurpassed and unsurpassable, exempt from the contingencies of time, of place, and of history. Later they exemplified the imperial claims of London to be the inheritor of the ancient tradition as well as the political and financial metropolis of the modern world. The history of the sculptures illustrates vividly the changing meanings conferred on ancient works of art, the place of asserted pedigrees in the constructions of national identity, the difference between history and heritage, the discourses of legality, rescue, duties of stewardship, and post-colonial restitution, and many other questions and issues relating to the evolving notions of cultural property. The 1998 and 1999 revelations that the surfaces of many of the sculptures were whitened with abrasives in 1937 and 1938 at the instigation of Lord Duveen, and that the British Museum authorities withheld the facts about the episode from the public, have added new dimensions to the debate. The Greek government has asked for the return of the marbles on many occasions.   WILLIAM ST CLAIR

Sources W. St Clair, *Lord Elgin and the marbles*, 3rd edn (1998) • W. St Clair, 'The Elgin marbles: questions of stewardship and accountability', *International Journal of Cultural Property*, 8 (1999),

391–521 • A. H. Smith, 'Lord Elgin and his collection', *Journal of Hellenic Studies* (1916) • S. Checkland, *The Elgins, 1766–1917: a tale of aristocrats, proconsuls and their wives* (1988) • GEC, *Peerage* • GM, 2nd ser., 17 (1842), 95–6

Archives BL, corresp. and papers relating to Turkey, RP 1016, 1542 [copies] • BL OIOC, corresp. relating to Turkey, Home misc. series • NA Scot., letters • NA Scot., estate, business, and legal corresp., and papers, GD 241 • priv. coll., corresp. and MSS • priv. coll., diplomatic and personal MSS • PRO, Foreign Office Archives, esp. FO 78 (Turkey) • PRO, letter-books and corresp., FO 353 • Yale U., Beinecke L., corresp. and papers relating to Prussia, MS c206 | Balliol Oxf., letters to James Mallet du Pan • BL, corresp. with Lord Grenville, Add. MSS 59006–59008 • BL, corresp. with duke of Leeds, etc., Add. MSS 34430–34450, *passim* • BL, corresp. with earls of Liverpool, Add. MSS 38237–38380, 38570–38571, *passim* • BL, corresp. with Sir Robert Peel, Add. MSS 40350–40428, *passim* • BL, corresp. with Lord Wellesley, Add. MSS 13788–13792 • CKS, letters to William Pitt • Herefs. RO, corresp. with Sir Harford Jones • Hunt. L., letters to Grenville family • NA Scot., corresp. with Lord Melville • NL Scot., letters to earl of Minto • NL Scot., letters to Patrick Tytler • NMM, letters to Lord Keith • priv. coll., corresp. with Oswald family • priv. coll., corresp. with Spencer Perceval • Suffolk RO, Ipswich, corresp. with Alexander Straton and Lord Grenville • U. Edin., New Coll. L., letters to Thomas Chalmers • U. Southampton L., letters to first duke of Wellington

Likenesses A. Graff, portrait, 1787, priv. coll. [*see illus.*] • G. P. Harding, engraving (after A. Graff, *c.*1795) • G. P. Harding, wash over pencil drawing (after A. Graff), BM

Wealth at death deep in debt

Bruce, Victor Alexander, ninth earl of Elgin and thirteenth earl of Kincardine (1849–1917), politician and viceroy of India, was the eldest son of James *Bruce, eighth earl of Elgin (1811–1863), and his second wife, Lady Mary Louisa Lambton (1819–1898), daughter of the first earl of Durham. He was born on 16 May 1849 at Monklands (Government House), near Montreal, his father then being governor-in-chief of British North America. He had three brothers and a sister, and a half-sister. He was educated at Trinity College, Glenalmond—an English-type public school in Perthshire—and afterwards, from the age of twelve, at Eton College; and then at Balliol College, Oxford, where he graduated in 1873 with a second-class degree in *literae humaniores*. For the next twenty years he lived chiefly at his family seat at Broomhall, near Dunfermline, Fife (to which he had succeeded on the death of his father while viceroy of India in 1863), running the estate and taking an active part in county and Scottish affairs, including the promotion of higher education. He became a director of the North British Railway and of the Royal Bank of Scotland. By 1899 he had an annual income of about £14,000. In 1881 he accepted the chairmanship of the Scottish Liberal Association, and, as a loyal supporter of Gladstone on home rule, found himself in 1886 in the Liberal government as treasurer of the household and subsequently as first commissioner of works. Meanwhile, on 9 November 1876 he married Lady Constance Carnegie (1853–1909), daughter of James Carnegie, sixth earl of Southesk. They had eleven children, six boys and five girls; but the end result was to turn the countess into a semi-permanent invalid who died in 1909. Four years later he married again: Gertrude Lilian Ogilvy, *née* Sherbrooke

Victor Alexander Bruce, ninth earl of Elgin and thirteenth earl of Kincardine (1849–1917), by Elliott & Fry, 1886

(d. 1971), was a widow who eventually gave birth to his posthumous son, Bernard.

Elgin inherited a snub nose and modest stature (5 feet 7 inches), but he had a noble head, enhanced quite early in adult life by a generous dark beard, which turned grey. He was not an intellectual, but neither was he an archetypal Victorian aristocrat, since he disliked riding and hunting, and disdained equally smartness (whether social or sartorial), conspicuous consumption, and Edwardian ebullience. He was not even a freemason, which was a highly unusual omission in his family. He was notoriously silent; he did not smoke; he hated the telephone. He enjoyed nothing more than a day spent alone cutting down trees, though occasionally he took an interest in cricket or curling.

Considerable pressure had to be put upon him (by his friend and admirer Lord Rosebery) to accept the viceroyalty of India, and in the event he did not make a reputation as a particularly good viceroy; he held the office from January 1894 to January 1899. The Indian Councils Act of 1892 had only just come into operation, so his political masters in a weak Liberal government had no further initiatives to suggest. Not called on to make a political advance, and preoccupied by a series of difficult administrative problems, his historical reputation has also suffered from his being succeeded by the flamboyant Lord Curzon, who, while privately appreciative of Elgin's handling of Indian affairs, found it necessary publicly to point up his own superiority by comparisons decidedly invidious. It may be conceded that unfortunately Elgin did not tackle the first major issue before him with sufficient decisiveness, and he was unable to resolve the conflicting interests involved. Tariff duties were imposed on Indian imports in a way which was criticized for acting protectively on Lancashire cotton goods, despite a reduction to 3½ per cent. Nevertheless, in other respects his viceroyalty does not deserve the harsh assessment made of it by Sir Frank Herbert Brown in the *Dictionary of National Biography*. The official papers subsequently made available reveal an effective, intelligent, and sensible hand at the helm on all sorts of questions, from venereal disease among British soldiers to relations with the Waziri tribesmen. Although he was not unsympathetic to the aspirations of the Indian National Congress, he was not persuaded of the readiness of Indians as yet for self-rule. His best assets—administrative skills and liberal optimism—showed to advantage in the stimulus he gave to railway building. About 3000 miles of track were completed, and a further 3000 miles were sanctioned: a notable achievement. His army policy was also sound, and helpful to the military, emphasizing as it did the need for better logistics and transport. Moreover, he reversed the planned withdrawal from Chitral (a strategic outpost on the extreme north-west frontier). This was an important decision which had a good effect on frontier stability for many years to come. Interestingly, it brought him into unpleasant conflict with his Liberal colleagues at home, but was upheld by the incoming Conservative and Unionist government of 1895. A catastrophic famine hit India in 1896. It proved to be one of the worst of the century. Elgin's organization of relief measures was equal to the occasion. Indeed, his predecessor, Lord Dufferin, regarded it as one of the most remarkable achievements of the British raj.

After his return from India in 1899 Elgin was invited by the Conservative government to undertake three public inquiries. The first was to investigate the damage being done to British salmon rivers by pollution. This was one of the first environmental surveys ever undertaken. The second was to chair a major royal commission to examine deficiencies in the military preparations for the Second South African War and various logistical matters relating to its conduct. Its unanimous report of July 1903 led eventually to the formation of the Territorial Army. The third inquiry (also a royal commission, of 1905) concerned an arcane, bitter, and protracted ecclesiastical dispute between the Presbyterian churches of Scotland and the division of their property. In all three cases Elgin's chairmanship was conspicuously successful.

When Sir Henry Campbell-Bannerman formed his Liberal government in December 1905, Elgin's appointment to the Colonial Office was favourably received across a wide spectrum of opinion, partly because it was relatively non-political. He was well equipped to deal with most of its problems as secretary of state (11 December 1905–8 April 1908). The biggest challenge, perhaps, was to work with his exuberant and ambitious parliamentary undersecretary, Winston Churchill, who was determined to make his mark in his first ministerial post. Churchill's private secretary, Edward Marsh, described Elgin as 'a rugged old thane of antique virtue', and believed that 'their qualified esteem was mutual' (*A Number of People: a Book of Reminiscences*, 1939, 150). Certainly each found much to admire in the other's complementary qualities. Elgin, however, found it tiresome that his subordinate—'a curious and impulsive creature' (letter to Lady Elgin, 16 June 1907, Elgin MSS)—was so adept at stealing the limelight. The famous story of a sharp exchange on the minute sheets (Churchill, 'These are my views'; Elgin, 'But not mine') is probably apocryphal, though well within the spirit of their frequent disagreements.

The main task of Elgin's colonial secretaryship was to calm down the post-war tensions in South Africa and find a way forward. Lord Milner's controversial experiment with Chinese labour in the Witwatersrand goldmines was terminated with all possible speed. Elgin masterminded the introduction of responsible self-government for the Transvaal (1906) and Orange River Colony (1907). The appalling mess of overlapping land concessions in Swaziland was sorted out, and attempts by Boer politicians to incorporate it were strongly resisted. A Zulu rebellion in Natal focused attention on an intransigent local settler regime which Churchill denounced as 'the hooligan of the British empire' (PRO, CO 179/243, no. 2605, 27 June 1907). This episode only made progress towards unification in South Africa seem more desirable, and Elgin did much to prepare for it. The permanent under-secretary at the Colonial Office, Sir Francis Hopwood, paid Elgin the tribute of recognizing that 'in contradistinction to the acts of any of your predecessors, you have applied a healing salve to the wounds and sorrows of South Africa' (letter to Elgin, 11 April 1908, Elgin MSS).

Elgin was much concerned with the problems of 'native policy' in Africa, even proposing a comprehensive and exhaustive survey of the whole subject. Although in Kenya 'the Elgin pledge' (1908) reserved the 'white highlands' to European farmers, he was far from convinced that Kenya could or should develop as 'a white man's country'. A modest start was made with development policies, especially cotton-growing in Uganda and Nigeria, and with railway extension. In Nigeria, Lord Lugard's militaristic tendencies were put on a tighter rein. Outside Africa the principal issues ranged from the cod disputes of Newfoundland to the pearl fisheries of Ceylon, from incipient enosis (union with Greece) in Cyprus to land questions in Fiji, from the establishment of the Anglo-French condominium in the New Hebrides to withdrawal of the West Indies from the international sugar convention of 1902. At the colonial conference of April–May 1907 the pretensions of the 'imperial federationists' were successfully held off in favour of a more loosely structured 'commonwealth', a term just beginning to emerge.

Almost all the Colonial Office staff approved of Elgin, and he enjoyed the work. He was indeed closer in temperament to civil servants than to his political colleagues. He was fundamentally an administrator rather than a politician. He resented having to make speeches in the House of Lords in support of government bills he did not care about. In cabinet he scarcely opened his mouth on

subjects outside his department. It was for these reasons that H. H. Asquith as incoming prime minister in April 1908 dropped him from his team, thus forcing Elgin into retirement at the age of fifty-nine, the latter grumbling (with considerable justification) that 'even a housemaid gets a better warning' (letter to Lord Tweedmouth, 20 April 1908, Elgin MSS).

Elgin died at home on 18 January 1917 and was buried in the tiny village graveyard at Limekilns, close to Broomhall. Curzon, to his credit, managed to pronounce a fairminded eulogy: Elgin, he said, maintained 'the highest ideals of duty in public life', and was 'one of those wellendowed but unassuming men whose abilities and services are not less useful because they are to some extent concealed by instinctive modesty from the public gaze' (*Hansard 5L*, 24, 1917, cols. 19–20).

Never an autocrat, always cautious, sometimes pedestrian and unimaginative, Elgin was never weak or slavishly dependent on his officials. He was a man of sound judgement, with a sure instinct for the essentials of a case. He was an excellent administrator who was a better viceroy of India than his reputation suggests and who ran the Colonial Office with considerable command of its wideranging business during one of its more significant periods of achievement.   R. HYAM

Sources S. Checkland, *The Elgins, 1766–1917: a tale of aristocrats, proconsuls and their wives* (1988), chaps. 17–21 · R. Hyam, *Elgin and Churchill at the colonial office, 1905–1908* (1968) · P. L. Malhotra, *Administration of Lord Elgin in India, 1894–99* (1979) · H. L. Singh, *Problems and policies of the British in India, 1885–1898* (1963) · G. J. Alder, *British India's northern frontier, 1865–1895* (1963) · *The Times* (19 Jan 1917) · 'India under Lord Elgin', *QR*, 189 (1899), 313–36 [review] · private information (2004) · Broomhall, Dunfermline, Fife, Elgin MSS · d. cert. · 27 June 1907, PRO, CO 179/243, no.2605 · *Hansard 5L* (1917), 24.19–20 · Burke, *Peerage* (1999)
Archives BL OIOC, corresp. and papers as viceroy of India, MS Eur. F 84 · priv. coll., corresp. and papers · PRO, Colonial Office files | BL, corresp. with Sir Henry Campbell-Bannerman, Add. MSS 41214, 52515–52516 · BL, corresp. with Lord Ripon, Add. MS 43552 · BL OIOC, letters to Lord Curzon, no. 291 · BL OIOC, corresp. with Arthur Godley, MS Eur. F 102 · BL OIOC, corresp. with Lord George Hamilton, MSS Eur. C 125–126, D 508–510, F 123 · BL OIOC, corresp. with Lord Wenlock, MS Eur. D 592 · Bodl. Oxf., letters to Herbert Henry Asquith · Bodl. Oxf., corresp. with earl of Kimberley · Bodl. Oxf., corresp. with Lord Selborne · CAC Cam., Winston Churchill MSS · NL Aus., corresp. with Alfred Deakin · NL Scot., corresp. mainly with Lord Rosebery · PRO, letters to Lord Northcote, PRO 30/56 · Trinity Cam., corresp. with Sir Henry Babington Smith and Lady Babington Smith · UCL, Galton MSS
Likenesses Elliott & Fry, photograph, 1886, NPG [*see illus.*] · C. M. Hardie, group portrait, oils, 1899 (*Curling at Carsebreck*), Scot. NPG · C. M. Hardie, oils, 1899, Scot. NPG · F. Sargent, etching, NPG · Spy [L. Ward], chromolithograph caricature, NPG; repro. in *VF* (27 April 1905) · cartoons, repro. in *Punch* · miniature, priv. coll. · photographs, priv. coll.; repro. in Checkland, *The Elgins* · portrait, Scot. NPG
Wealth at death £212,494 10s. 11d.: confirmation, 20 Sept 1917, *CCI*

Bruce, Victoria Alexandrina Katherine (1898–1951), prison governor, was born on 13 September 1898 at Kennet House, Clackmannan, the youngest by fifteen years in the family of two sons and three daughters of Alexander Hugh *Bruce, sixth Lord Balfour of Burleigh

(1849–1921), secretary for Scotland in Lord Salisbury's cabinet from 1895 to 1903, and his wife, Lady Katherine Eliza Hamilton-Gordon (d. 1931), youngest daughter of George John James Hamilton-Gordon, fifth earl of Aberdeen. She was probably educated at home, then became interested in social work, and after working from 1928 to 1931 as voluntary librarian of the boys' prison in Wandsworth, a special wing of Wandsworth prison for boys who had been removed from their borstals for bad behaviour or who had been recalled from parole, she was appointed a probation officer in the juvenile courts in London.

In 1937 Victoria Bruce was offered the job of deputy governor of the Aylesbury Borstal Institutions, where Lilian Barker had been governor from 1923 to 1935, transforming the Aylesbury borstal, the only girls' borstal in the country, which had opened in 1912 in the former state inebriate reformatory in the wing of the women's prison. Borstal training, so called because the first experiment had been in the wing of a prison in Borstal, near Rochester, had been established as part of the penal system in 1908, as a result of the efforts of Sir Evelyn Ruggles-Brise, who held the view that up to a certain age every criminal was potentially a good citizen, and that a prison sentence was inappropriate for young offenders. Alexander Paterson had developed a system of institutional training followed by a closely supervised period of parole.

Victoria Bruce spent three years at Aylesbury borstal before moving to Manchester in 1940 as deputy governor of the prison. In 1943 she returned to Aylesbury as governor of the borstal institution for girls, which now housed 250 girls. She introduced the house system, modelled on the English public school, and continued the work of preparing the girls for domestic and farm work, but Aylesbury borstal, which shared the prison block with the long-term women's prison, was still too large and prison-like to be suitable for young girls. She remained there until 1946, when she was appointed governor of HM prison, Duke Street, Glasgow, a women's prison.

Victoria Bruce died on 25 November 1951 at 6 Cathedral Square, Glasgow, after a short illness, and was buried on 28 November at Clackmannan church, Clackmannan, Scotland. She was unmarried.   ANNE PIMLOTT BAKER

Sources E. Gore, *The better fight: the story of Dame Lilian Barker* (1965) · L. Fox, *The English prison and borstal systems* (1952) · S. Leslie, *Sir Evelyn Ruggles-Brise* (1938) · *The Times* (26 Nov 1951) · *The Times* (27 Nov 1951) · *WWW* · Burke, *Peerage* · *CGPLA Eng. & Wales* (1952) · b. cert. · *WW* · d. cert.
Wealth at death £33,355 14s. 4d.: probate, 26 April 1952, *CGPLA Eng. & Wales*

Bruce, Sir William, first baronet (c.1625–1710), architect and politician, was born into minor Perthshire gentry, the second son of Robert Bruce, Lord Bruce of Blairhall, and Catherine (or Jean), daughter of Sir John Preston of Valleyfield. His early life is obscure but if he is identified with the William Bruce who matriculated at St Salvator's College, University of St Andrews, in 1637, he must have been born in the 1620s.

1660: political patronage Bruce is not recorded again, however, until 1660, when, according to Douglas, he played an important role in the Restoration, both in bringing General Monck round to the royalist cause and as an intermediary between Monck and the exiled Stuart court (Douglas, 245). Royalist sympathies were a defining factor in Bruce's subsequent career and Charles II rewarded him with a knighthood c.1660 and a baronetcy in 1668. With the favour of the king and the patronage of John Maitland, duke of Lauderdale, Bruce obtained a series of political appointments between 1660 and 1685, the most lucrative of which allowed him to buy the estate of Balcaskie, near Anstruther, Fife, in 1665 and the larger one of Kinross ten years later. These were to become not only expressions of his architectural prowess but also, particularly in the case of Kinross, the vehicles for his dynastic and political ambitions.

Many of the offices held by Bruce were also connected with his rights and status as a landowner; thus he represented first Fife (1669–74) and then Kinross-shire (1681–2 and 1685–6) in the Scottish parliament. A number of his appointments were connected with the Restoration: as clerk of the bills and receiver of fines, he was responsible for collecting the indemnity imposed on supporters of the Commonwealth and other fines imposed by the new regime against those, such as the covenanters, who did not submit to the new settlement. Others may be seen as extensions, sometimes lucrative, and often prestigious, of his more local responsibilities. Thus, in the realm of taxation, he was not only a commissioner for the valuation of Fife (1682 and 1684), but also collector-general of a cess imposed on the whole of Scotland to finance the army there in 1667. Most important of all in this area was his success in winning the farm of the Scottish customs in 1671, which allowed him to collect customs dues for an agreed fee, with everything beyond that representing his profit. Similarly, Bruce was active both in the administration of justice at the local level, as justice of the peace in Fife (from 1673) and sheriff of Kinross (from 1682), and at the national level, with his appointment to the privy council in 1685. This represented the peak of his political career but it was short-lived. With the king's death in the same year the viscountcy that he reportedly coveted (Dunbar, 1) never materialized and, despite lobbying in London over the autumn and winter of 1685–6, his political advancement ceased. He was removed from the privy council in May 1686.

If James VII and II was unsympathetic to Bruce, the post-revolution regime after 1690 was actively hostile. Bruce was suspected, on very good grounds, of being a Jacobite sympathizer, and as a result from 1694 onwards spent periods under house arrest or in prison. In 1702 he was declared a rebel and, at a time of national paranoia about Jacobite plots and French invasion, he was arrested in both 1707 and 1708, and only the intercession of David, second earl of Melville, protected him from being shipped south to the Tower of London as a traitor.

Family life As Bruce's political career declined, its disappointments were mirrored in his family life. He married Mary (d. 1699), daughter of James Halket of Pitfirrane, Fife. They had two children: Anne, who married Sir Thomas

Hope of Craighall, and John. William Bruce's ultimate ambition was to found an aristocratic dynasty, with Kinross as its principal seat and power base. John was carefully educated, including a grand tour to France and the Low Countries in 1681–3, and in 1687 married Christian Leslie, daughter of John Leslie, seventh earl of Rothes, and widow of James Graham, third marquess of Montrose. In the same year Sir William made over the Kinross estates to his son, partly as a protection against possible confiscation but also signifying the transition of the family fortunes from one generation to the next.

The estates were, however, something of a poisoned chalice by this time. Kinross House was still under construction and a project that had ultimately depended on the largesse of the regime of Charles II became a struggle and a major source of friction between father and son. They fought not only over the furniture and furnishings of the house but also over the upkeep of the beautiful but expensive formal gardens designed by Sir William. There were also other, related sources of friction between them. John's failure to produce an heir was an even greater threat to his father's family ambitions than the precarious state of the family finances, and with the death of Bruce's wife, Mary, in 1699 relations between the two grew even worse. Added to the financial problems were the issues of Bruce's decision to live in Edinburgh rather than in the bosom of his grieving family in Kinross and his decision to marry, within a year of his wife's death, Magdalene Clerk, *née* Scott, daughter of David Scott, brother of the laird of Galashiels and widow of George Clerk, merchant burgess of Edinburgh; this decision raised unfounded fears among the younger generation about the safety of their inheritance.

Architectural career However, even as these misfortunes befell him, Bruce was increasingly acknowledged as the foremost architect in Scotland, credited with introducing a sophisticated brand of European classicism that helped form the basis for Scottish classical architecture in the following century. As a politician and gentleman his architectural interests were those of the erudite amateur rather than the professional, but as his career developed, his architectural interests became increasingly important and his knowledge was clearly far beyond that of a mere dilettante. Most of his early work involved giving advice to kinsmen or contacts among the Scottish nobility. Thus he assisted the earl of Rothes at Leslie House, Fife, in 1667–72, as well as advising both John Hay, second earl of Tweeddale (1670), and John Kennedy, seventh earl of Cassillis (1673–4). This aspect of his architectural career remained a constant and even in 1709, shortly before his death, he was writing to the countess of Atholl offering advice on the House of Nairne.

Bruce's first major commission was of great importance. In 1671 he was appointed surveyor-general of the royal works in Scotland, a position he held until 1676. There his main undertaking was the modernization of the palace of Holyroodhouse in Edinburgh. The remodelling of the old palace involved the demolition of Cromwellian additions, the modernization of the old building, and, to

some extent, the completion of a sixteenth-century design begun by James V of Scotland c.1530. The new palace symbolized the restoration of the monarchy and the continuity (and therefore the legitimacy) of the Stuarts; it also symbolized the presence of the monarch himself in his Scottish capital. Bruce, ably assisted by Robert Mylne, master mason to the Scottish crown, produced a building that underscored but updated the French influence that was evident in the work of James V. In layout and planning the key sources for Bruce were the modern, baroque palaces and hotels of contemporary France. In stylistic terms, Holyrood was also important to the architectural history of Scotland as it represents the first use of modern, European classicism there, including the first use of the classical orders ascending in their correct hierarchy on the three storeys of the building and the first use of the hipped roof, which became so important in country house design over the following fifty or sixty years. It was also an excellent model of how an older building could be modernized and made regular in tune with modern tastes. Bruce had put some of these ideas into practice in his own country house at Balcaskie in Fife and, alongside the Holyroodhouse project, he remodelled houses at Lethington, Brunstane, and, most importantly, Thirlestane, for the duke of Lauderdale, using many of the same craftsmen who were working at Holyrood and demonstrating a knowledgeable familiarity with mainly French sources, including both le Muet and du Cerceau.

In 1679 Bruce was given the opportunity to build two rather similar new houses, both in Perthshire. The results, at Dunkeld and Moncreiffe, are two astylar and rather austere classical houses. His greatest achievement in this period, however, was his own house on his new estate at Kinross, built c.1679–93. Here Bruce took an increasingly familiar pattern from contemporary English country houses of a double-pile plan and two main storeys and an attic over a semi-basement. To this, however, he added his increasingly sophisticated understanding of European classical architecture. The house is built in precisely cut and fitted ashlar and adorned with a giant Corinthian order of pilasters clasping the corners. The attic, which he developed from those at Moncreiffe and Dunkeld, does not break through the slates, but sits squeezed in between the entablature and the eaves. Owing to his fall from grace, the interior, strongly influenced by Dutch architecture, was never finished, but the plan was a clever combination of the very formal and the comfortable and domestic, which, along with the work of his contemporary James Smith, proved a powerful model for the next generation of Scottish architects.

The advanced classicism employed by Bruce at Kinross was developed elsewhere, most notably at Hopetoun House in Linlithgowshire, which he designed between 1698 and 1710. The result was a house that developed a number of trends evident in his earlier work, including the deep, almost square, plans of Moncreiffe, Dunkeld, Melville House, Fife (1697), and Craigiehall, Linlithgowshire (1698), which at Hopetoun becomes a top-lit, Greek-cross-in-square plan showing the influence of Palladio.

Other influences included Le Vau in France and Dutch seventeenth-century classicism. A further Palladian influence is evident in the use of quadrant links from the main body of the house to the service wings, picking up on a theme that can be traced through a number of buildings right back to Balcaskie in Bruce's work and locating Hopetoun among those proto-Palladian houses built in the period immediately before the great upsurge in neo-Palladianism in Britain, in the early eighteenth century.

Bruce's importance to country-house architecture also extended to garden design. It was Bruce who was mainly responsible for the introduction of the baroque formal garden to Scotland in the late seventeenth century, with a whole series of great designs in which the house was integrated into a formal layout, controlled in every case by a strong, single axis that terminated on some feature in the distant landscape. At Balcaskie House, Fife, he employed the Bass Rock in the Firth of Forth for this purpose, at Kinross, the rather closer Loch Leven Castle, and at Hopetoun, North Berwick Law, some 25 miles distant, was aligned with the main avenue.

Bruce's architectural interests also extended beyond the country house. He is credited with the design of Stirling toll-booth, 1703–5, and was involved in a whole series of proposals for Edinburgh, from the mundane but very practical concern with water supply to the design of a new merchants' exchange in the city (built 1676–82). By the mid-1680s he was even involved in the proposals of James VII and II to extend the city to the site of the present New Town, a proposal that was brought to an end by James's fall in 1688.

Death and posthumous reputation Bruce died on 1 January 1710 and was buried at Kinross old parish kirk. His son and daughter-in-law survived him by only a few months and his dynastic and aristocratic ambitions died with them. However, his success as an architect is unquestionable, as the foremost figure in the first generation of Scottish classicism. JOHN LOWREY

Sources J. Dunbar, *Sir William Bruce, 1630–1710* (1970) [exhibition catalogue, Scottish Arts Council, Edinburgh] · Colvin, *Archs.* · H. Fenwick, *Architect royal: the life and works of Sir William Bruce, 1630–1710* (1970) · NA Scot., Bruce of Kinross MSS, GD 29 · NA Scot., Bruce of Arnot MSS, GD 242 · *Acts of the privy council of Scotland*, 3rd ser., vols. 1–13 · R. S. Mylne, *The master masons to the crown of Scotland* (1893) · Holyrood contracts and drawings, BL, Egerton MSS 2870–2871 · R. Miller, *The municipal buildings of Edinburgh* (1895) · H. F. Kerr, 'Sir William Bruce', *Quarterly of the Royal Incorporation of Architects of Scotland* (1924) · NRA Scotland, Hopetoun House MSS, 888 · M. Wood, ed., *Extracts from the records of the burgh of Edinburgh, 1665–1680*, [11] (1950) · R. Douglas and others, *The baronage of Scotland* (1798)

Archives NA Scot., corresp. and papers, GD 29, GD 242 | Buckminster Park, Grantham, Lincolnshire, corresp. with duke of Lauderdale · NA Scot., Annandale MSS, Craigiehall material · NA Scot., Hamilton MSS, GD 406 · U. Edin., Laing MSS

Likenesses J. M. Wright, oils, 1665, Scot. NPG; copy, Kinross House · J. B. Medina, oils, *c*.1705, Scot. NPG · wash drawing (after J. B. Medina), Scot. NPG

Bruce, William (1702–1755), bookseller, was born on 6 September 1702 at Killyleagh, co. Down, the youngest son

in the ten children of James *Bruce (1660/61–1730), Presbyterian minister of Killyleagh, and his wife, Margaret Traill (*d*. 1706). His two elder brothers, Michael *Bruce and Patrick, became ministers. Bruce matriculated at Glasgow University on 10 March 1718.

By July 1725 Bruce had become a partner in the Dublin bookselling and publishing business established in 1722 by John Smith and William Smith. John Smith had attended Glasgow University between 1716 and 1722 but had been expelled. The Smith partnership published the first book by Bruce's cousin, on his mother's side, the philosopher Francis Hutcheson, *An Inquiry into the Original of our Ideas of Beauty and Virtue*, in 1725. About 1726 William Smith left the business to work in Amsterdam; John Smith and William Bruce remained in partnership until the end of 1737 trading at the Philosopher's Head, Blind Quay, and thirty-eight publications are recorded with their imprint, trading alone or in conjunction with other businesses. In Dublin, Bruce associated with the Wood Street Presbyterian congregation and was active with John Abernethy in agitating for the repeal of the Test Acts in 1733; he was the co-author of *Reasons for the Repeal of the Sacramental Test* published in Dublin in 1733. He was a close friend of Hutcheson, who in November 1737 sent him a manuscript of his *System of Moral Philosophy* 'chiefly for his and Mr. Abernethy's approval'. Hutcheson, who died in 1746, bequeathed Bruce £100 in his will.

Bruce retired from bookselling in 1738 but remained on friendly terms with Smith. He became tutor to Joseph Henry, son of Hugh Henry, a Dublin banker and MP for Antrim 1715–27, travelling with him to Cambridge, Oxford, and possibly also Glasgow. T. D. Hincks, his nineteenth-century biographer, who had access to Bruce's family papers, believed him to have settled permanently in Dublin by 1745, where he became an elder in the Wood Street congregation. In 1750 he was instrumental in promoting a pension fund for ministers' widows and was among those asked to draw up an appropriate scheme. In 1751 the General Synod of Ulster voted him the thanks of the house 'for his care and zeal in projecting and carrying on the scheme' (*Records*, 2.363).

Bruce is also credited with the authorship of *Some Facts and Observations Relative to the Fall of the Late Linen Bill* (Dublin, 1753) and *Remarks on a Pamphlet Entitled 'Considerations on the Late Bill for Paying the National Debt'* (Dublin, 1754), both of which defend the privileges of the Dublin legislature.

Bruce died, unmarried, on 11 July 1755 at his lodgings on Blind Quay and was buried on 13 July in the same tomb as Hutcheson in St Mary's graveyard, Mary Street, Dublin. He left his property to Alexander Stewart of Newtownards, co. Down, father of the first marquess of Londonderry, for distribution to his relatives. His death prompted a highly laudatory *Essay on the Character of the Late Mr. W. Bruce in a Letter to a Friend* (Dublin, 1755) by Gabriel Cornwall and *A Monody to the Memory of Mr. Bruce* by Alexander Halliday.

C. J. BENSON

Sources NL Ire., Bruce papers, MS 20869 · NL Scot., Dunlop MS 9252 · certified copy of will, NL Ire., D 27112 · T. D. Hincks, 'Notices of William Bruce, and of his contemporaries and friends', *Christian Teacher*, new ser., 5/19 (1843), 72–92 • W. B. Armstrong, *The Bruces of Airth and their cadets* (1892) • W. R. Scott, *Francis Hutcheson* (1900) • C. Innes, ed., *Munimenta alme Universitatis Glasguensis / Records of the University of Glasgow from its foundation till 1727*, 4 vols., Maitland Club, 72 (1854) • [G. Cornwall], *An essay on the character of the late Mr. William Bruce in a letter to a friend* (1755) • *Records of the General Synod of Ulster, from 1691 to 1820*, 3 vols. (1890–98) • M. Pollard, *A dictionary of members of the Dublin book trade 1550–1800* (2000) • M. Pollard, *Dublin's trade in books, 1550–1800* (1989) • A. McCreery, *Presbyterian ministers of Killileagh* (1875) • parish register, Dublin, St Mary, 13 July 1755 [burial] • *Pue's Occurrences* (12 July 1755)

Archives NL Ire., papers, MS 20869 • NL Scot., Dunlop papers, MS 9252

Bruce, William (1757–1841), non-subscribing Presbyterian minister, was born in Dublin on 30 July 1757, the son of Samuel Bruce (1722–1767), minister of the Wood Street (later Strand Street) Presbyterian congregation in the city, and of Rose Rainey of Magherafelt, co. Londonderry. His family had supplied Presbyterian clergymen in both Dublin and Ulster over four generations. His grandfather the Revd Michael *Bruce of Holywood (1686–1735) had played a prominent role in the subscription controversy which divided Irish Presbyterians in the 1720s, and from that time the family was associated with the non-subscribing, or New Light, camp. His great-uncle was the Dublin bookseller and patriotic pamphleteer William *Bruce (1702–1755), who had founded the Presbyterian Widows' Fund.

Although technically barred as a dissenter Bruce entered Trinity College, Dublin, in 1771. Four years later he obtained a scholarship and graduated BA, having supported himself by private tuition. In 1776 he went to Glasgow University for a session, where he delivered a paper to the college society opposing capital punishment, and in 1777 he went to Warrington Academy, where for two years he studied divinity under John Aikin. He received a DD from Glasgow in 1786. He married, on 25 January 1788, Susanna Hutton (1753–1819); they had twelve children, of whom four died in infancy.

On 8 August 1779 Bruce was called to the congregation of Lisburn, and on 4 November he was ordained by the presbytery of Bangor, one of the most strongly New Light presbyteries in the General Synod of Ulster. His involvement in public affairs also began at this time, with his decision to join the Lisburn True Blues, the local volunteer company. On 24 March 1782 he received a call from his father's old congregation of Strand Street, Dublin, as colleague to John Moody DD (1742–1813), where he ministered for the next eight years. He sat in the national convention of volunteers that met on 10 November 1783, as a representative of Carrickfergus. Regarded as one of the more advanced reformers at that meeting, he brought forward a proposal for vote by secret ballot. He was also a delegate at the national congress which met in Dublin in the winter of 1784–5.

It is with Belfast, however, that Bruce's name is associated. In October 1789 he was called to the First Congregation, the wealthiest in Ulster, as colleague to the Revd James Crombie DD (1730–1790), founder of the Belfast Academy (1786). This call he declined; but on being again

William Bruce (1757–1841), by Thomas Hodgetts, pubd 1819 (after Thomas Clement Thompson)

invited (11 March 1790), following Crombie's death, and at the same time elected principal of Belfast Academy, he accepted both posts. The congregation was affiliated to the independent, non-subscribing presbytery of Antrim, in which Bruce became the dominant figure, devoting much of his time to managerial business and the examination of candidates for the ministry. At the academy meanwhile he acted as schoolmaster, and from 1802 lectured on history, *belles lettres*, and moral philosophy; he also suppressed a violent barring-out in April 1792. In 1794, following the publication of Thomas Paine's *Age of Reason*, he delivered a series of lectures entitled 'Christian evidences', but like most New Light ministers he steered clear of doctrinal controversy.

The same cannot be said for Bruce's role in politics. Following the outbreak of the French Revolution and the publication of Paine's *Rights of Man* (1791) he opposed the radical programme of the new Society of United Irishmen. Visiting Belfast late in 1791 Wolfe Tone witnessed a 'furious battle' over the Catholic question, during which Bruce defended the penal code on the conventional grounds that the Catholics would use political power to establish their church and recover the estates forfeited by their ancestors (Bartlett, 126). At the Belfast town meeting of 28 January 1792, convened to draw up a petition for Catholic emancipation, he led a minority of moderates who favoured 'progressive' (that is, piecemeal) rather than immediate abolition of the penal laws. In 1794 he collaborated with his kinsman Henry Joy (1754–1835), editor of the *Belfast News-Letter*, on a volume of addresses, reports, and resolutions entitled *Belfast Politics*, in an unsuccessful attempt to stem the tide of radical opinion in the north. Further clashes with the radicals followed with the raising of yeomanry units under government control. Recruitment in Belfast began in January 1797, opposed not only by the United Irishmen but by moderate reformers who regarded enrolment as a betrayal of the old independent volunteers. Concerned to set an example, Bruce enrolled that month and served with the Belfast Merchants' infantry during the rising of 1798. With the radicals in disarray following the defeat of the rebels he went on to become a powerful advocate of the Act of Union in 1799–1800, using his influence with Viscount Castlereagh to secure legal and financial advantages for Irish Presbyterians within the new United Kingdom of Great Britain and Ireland.

During the last quarter of the eighteenth century a spirit of compromise on the issue of subscription to the Westminster confession of faith had allowed the General Synod of Ulster to contain a range of doctrinal opinions. By the 1820s, however, the rise of evangelicalism, combined with a series of controversies among heterodox dissenters in England, put pressure on New Light Presbyterians to define their position on the doctrine of the Trinity. In *Sermons on the Study of the Bible and the Doctrines of Christianity* (1824) Bruce announced his adherence to Arianism, which he claimed was making progress in both his own presbytery of Antrim and the General Synod of Ulster. He thus helped to spark off the second subscription controversy, which eventually led to the expulsion of the Arians from the synod and the emergence of Unitarianism as a distinct denominational identity. Although he resigned from the Belfast Academy in November 1822 he continued to minister at First Belfast with the assistance of his son William *Bruce (1790–1868), who had been appointed co-pastor in 1812. In addition to his *Treatise on the Being and Attributes of God* (1818) and his *Sermons* (1824) he compiled a twenty-three part history of non-subscription in Ireland for John Scott Porter's periodical, the *Christian Moderator*. He supported the Hibernian Bible Society in letters to the *Newry Telegraph* (reprinted in the *Belfast News-Letter*, 16 November 1821) and assisted in the formation of the Unitarian Society for the Diffusion of Christian Knowledge (9 April 1831).

Bruce dominated the wider cultural life of Belfast too. He served on the committee of the Belfast Society for Promoting Knowledge, better known as the Linen Hall Library, and was one of the founders of the Belfast Literary Society (1801), contributing papers on the advantages of classical education and on meteorological observations. His *State of Society in the Age of Homer* (1827) was originally read to the society about 1805, as were his *Literary Essays* (1811); other essays read to the society were published in the *Newry Magazine*. He was also a member of the Royal Irish Academy and in 1828 contributed to their transactions his 'Memoir of James VI'.

On 21 January 1834, with his sight deteriorating, Bruce retired from the ministry, and in November 1836 he moved back to Dublin with his daughter Maria. He died there on 27 February 1841 and was buried in St George's burying-ground. He was survived by six of his children: Samuel, William, Haliday, Emily, Maria, and Henry. 'His mind', as his son Samuel recorded, 'was softened down to universal tolleration [*sic*], & disregard of sectarian distinctions' (Samuel Bruce to John H. Houston, 1841, PRO NIre., Bruce MS, T/3041/1/E123). Though blind during his last years he had continued his studies with the aid of an amanuensis, and a commentary on a passage of scripture that he had dictated appeared in the *Christian Reformer* several days after his death. Contemporaries commented on his powerful oratory, his erect bearing, and his aristocratic countenance, something of which is evident in the several extant portraits of him. I. R. MᶜBRIDE

Sources PRO NIre., Drennan–Bruce MSS, D 553 · PRO NIre., Drennan MSS, D 591 · PRO NIre., Bruce MSS, D 2673, T 3041 · minutes of the presbytery of Antrim, PRO NIre., T 1053 · Linen Hall Library, Belfast, Joy papers · NL Ire., MSS 27116, 20881, 20894 · *The history of the proceedings and debates of the volunteer delegates of Ireland, on the subject of parliamentary reform* (1784) · *Memoirs and correspondence of Viscount Castlereagh, second marquess of Londonderry*, ed. C. Vane, marquess of Londonderry, 12 vols. (1848–53) · W. T. W. Tone, *Life of Theobald Wolfe Tone*, ed. T. Bartlett (1998) · J. Anderson, *History of the Belfast Library and Society for Promoting Knowledge, commonly known as the Linen Hall Library* (1888) · J. Armstrong, *History of the Presbyterian churches in the city of Dublin* (1829) · *The Drennan–McTier letters*, ed. J. Agnew, 3 vols. (1998–9) · G. Benn, *A history of the town of Belfast from earliest times to the close of the eighteenth century* (1877) · P. Brooke, 'Controversies in Ulster presbyterianism, 1790–1836', PhD diss., U. Cam., 1980 · A. Gordon and G. K. Smith, *Historic memorials of the First Presbyterian Church of Belfast* (1887) · A. Gordon, 'William Bruce, D.D.', *Belfast Literary Society, 1801–1901: historical sketches with memoirs of some distinguished members* (1902), 29–34 · I. R. McBride, *Scripture politics: Ulster Presbyterians and Irish radicalism in the late eighteenth century* (1998) · J. W. Nelson, 'The Belfast Presbyterians, 1670–1830: an analysis of their political and social interests', PhD diss., Queen's University of Belfast, 1985 · C. Porter, *The seven Bruces: Presbyterian ministers in Ireland in six successive generations* (1885) · J. S. Porter, *The Christian's hope in death: a discourse delivered in the meeting-house of the First Presbyterian Congregation, Belfast, on Sunday, March 7, 1841; on occasion of the death of the Rev. William Bruce, D.D. senior pastor of the congregation: and published at the request of the committee* (1841) · [J. S. Porter (?)], 'Death of the Rev. William Bruce, D.D.', *Bible Christian*, 3rd ser., 3 (1841), 109–30 · J. S. Reid and W. D. Killen, *History of the Presbyterian church in Ireland*, new edn, 3 vols. (1867) · A. T. Q. Stewart, *A deeper silence: the hidden roots of the United Irish movement* (1993); repr. as *A deeper silence: the hidden origins of the United Irishmen* (1998) · *DNB*

Archives NL Ire., corresp., sermons, lectures, and papers · PRO NIre., papers, D 2673; T 3041

Likenesses T. Hodgetts, mezzotint, pubd 1819 (after T. C. Thompson), BM, NPG, NG Ire. [*see illus.*] · G. Adcock, stipple (after miniature by Hawksett), NPG · Adcock, engraving, repro. in *Christian Moderator* (1827) · Thompson?, oils, Linen Hall Library, Belfast · J. Wilson, portrait, Ulster Museum, Belfast

Wealth at death two farms left to two sons; £500 to other two sons; sums of £100, £50, £30, £25, and £10 to various relatives, friends, and servants: will, 1839, NL Ire., Bruce MS 20881

Bruce, William (1790–1868), non-subscribing Presbyterian minister, was born at Belfast on 16 November 1790. He was the second son of William *Bruce (1757–1841), Presbyterian minister, and his wife, Susanna Hutton (1753–1819), of Dublin. He was initially educated at Belfast Academy under his father, and then entered Trinity College, Dublin, in July 1804, where he obtained a scholarship and graduated BA on 20 July 1809. He pursued his theological studies under the direction of Antrim presbytery by attending two sessions at Edinburgh University between 1809 and 1811. His subjects included moral philosophy and church history under Dugald Stewart, Hugh Meiklejohn, and others. He was licensed by the presbytery on 25 June 1811. On 19 January 1812 he was called to First Belfast Presbyterian Church as colleague to his father, and ordained on 3 March. He was not as gifted as his father but nevertheless developed a good relationship with his congregation, who came to hold him in high esteem. Theologically he closely followed his father's line of thought. It is believed that he edited the Belfast edition (published in 1819) of *Sermons on the Christian Doctrine*, by Richard Price (originally published in 1787), which contain a mild assertion of a modified Arianism, as a middle way between Calvinism and Socinianism.

In 1821 Bruce came forward as a candidate for the vacant classical and Hebrew chair in the Belfast Academical Institution. Two-thirds of the Arian vote went against him, in consequence of the hostility previously shown to the institution by his family; but Sir Robert Bateson, the episcopalian leader, and Edward Reid of Ramelton, moderator of the General Synod of Ulster, openly supported Bruce, and he was elected on 27 October by a large majority. The appointment conciliated those who had stood aloof from the institution on the ground that it had sympathized with unconstitutional principles. However, Bruce's successful candidature was also controversial. It figured prominently in Dr Henry Cooke's intensified campaign to expose the heresy of Arianism. Bruce, still keeping his congregation, remained aloof from the polemics and held the chair until the establishment of Queen's College in 1849 reduced the Academical Institution to the rank of a high school. The Hebrew chair was separated from that of classics in the 1820s, when Thomas Dix Hincks, another Arian, was appointed to fill it, an event which further increased the debate on orthodoxy within the Presbyterian church.

In later life Bruce headed the conservative minority in the Antrim presbytery, maintaining that non-subscribing principles not only allowed but required a presbytery to satisfy itself as to the Christian faith of candidates for the ministry. The discussion was conducted with much acrimony (not on Bruce's part), and ended in the withdrawal of five congregations, later recognized by the government as a distinct ecclesiastical body, the Northern Presbytery of Antrim, of which, at its first meeting, on 4 April 1862, Bruce was elected moderator. In the same year the jubilee of his ordination was marked by the placing of stained-glass windows in his meeting-house in Rosemary Street, Belfast. He retired from active duty on 21 April 1867. From 1832 he had as colleague John Scott Porter, who remained sole pastor.

On 20 May 1823 Bruce married Jane Elizabeth (1798/9–1878), only child of William Smith of Barbados and his wife, Catherine Wentworth. They had four sons and six daughters. Bruce continued his services to many of the charities and public bodies of the town, such as the Belfast Literary Society and the Chemico-Agricultural Society for

Ulster. Although he was a regular contributor to Unitarian periodicals, he published only a few works during his life, most of which were sermons. His last sermon was at a communion in Larne on 28 April 1867. He died at his home, The Farm, Belfast, on 25 October 1868, and was buried at Holywood, co. Down, on 28 October; his wife survived him. A memorial tablet was erected in First Belfast in 1881. Bruce was a faithful, non-controversial minister of his congregation and denomination and was one of Belfast's leading citizens.

ALEXANDER GORDON, rev. DAVID HUDDLESTON

Sources C. Porter, 'Seven Bruces', *Northern Whig* (25 May 1885) • J. S. Porter, *The new heavens and new earth: a sermon preached … on … 1st of November 1868, on occasion of the death of the Rev. William Bruce* (1868) • G. Benn, *A history of the town of Belfast from the earliest times to the close of the eighteenth century*, 2 (1880), 195 • J. S. Reid and W. D. Killen, *History of the Presbyterian church in Ireland*, new edn, 3 (1867), 445 • J. L. Porter, *The life and times of Henry Cooke, D.D.* (1871), 62–4 • P. Brooke, *Ulster Presbyterianism* (1987), 147–9 • *Christian Unitarian*, 1 (1862), 112–18 • *Christian Unitarian*, 1 (1862), 133 • *Christian Unitarian*, 1 (1862), 375 • R. F. Holmes, *Our Irish Presbyterian heritage* (1985), 100–01 • *Christian Life* (7 Dec 1878), 595 • J. Jamieson, *The history of the Royal Belfast Academical Institution, 1810–1960* (1959, [1960]) • A. Gordon and G. K. Smith, *Historic memorials of the First Presbyterian Church of Belfast* (1887) • *CGPLA Ire.* (1868)

Likenesses engraving (after portrait), repro. in Gordon and Smith, *Historic memorials*

Wealth at death under £20,000: probate, 21 Dec 1868, *CGPLA Ire.*

Bruce, William Speirs (1867–1921), polar scientist and explorer, was born at 43 Kensington Gardens Square, Paddington, London, on 1 August 1867. He was the fourth child of a family of eight children and had one younger brother and six sisters. His father, Samuel Noble Bruce MRCS, was a successful general practitioner in this fashionable part of London and came originally from Edinburgh. His maternal grandmother, Charity Isbister, was born in Orkney, and his paternal grandfather, the Revd William Bruce, from Edinburgh, was minister of the Swedenborgian church, Hatton Garden, London. His mother, Mary, daughter of L. Wild Lloyd, an architect, was of Welsh origin. Although born in London, Bruce yearned for the lands of his forefathers, and eventually made Scotland his permanent residence as well as his spiritual home. While at university in Edinburgh he became a member of the St Andrew's Society and a fervent advocate of Scottish nationalism. He married in 1901 Jessie (d. 1942), daughter of Alexander Mackenzie, a merchant, of Tain, Easter Ross, and they had a son, Eillium (b. 1902), and daughter, Sheila (b. 1909).

Until he was eleven Bruce was educated privately at home, and subsequently he entered the independent Norfolk county school, North Elmham. In 1887 he attended a summer school at Granton, near Edinburgh, and came under the influence of the polymath Sir Patrick Geddes and other teachers from the University of Edinburgh, where Bruce then enrolled to study medicine. Thereafter Scotland became his workplace and his passion as well as his permanent home; he turned exclusively to Scottish patrimony to support his later polar exploration and increasingly became estranged from his family and antipathetic to English institutions.

William Speirs Bruce (1867–1921), by unknown photographer

As a student Bruce specialized in natural science. Adopting a holistic approach to environmental problems, he obtained valuable expertise in zoology, geology, botany, and oceanography in the *Challenger* laboratories, where he worked on the expedition records as a volunteer at weekends. In 1892–3 he sailed in the whaler *Balaena* as surgeon and naturalist as part of the Dundee whaling expedition to the Weddell Sea. He had a disappointing scientific survey but came back enthusiastic: 'I am burning to be off again anywhere, but particularly to the far south where I believe there is a vast sphere for research' (Bruce MSS). An account of the expedition is given in a book written by his artist friend and companion W. G. Burn Murdoch, *From Edinburgh to the Antarctic* (1894).

Bruce now abandoned his medical studies and devoted himself to polar science. He was given the opportunity in 1895–6, as first assistant, to help direct the high-level meteorological observatory on Ben Nevis. From there he was invited to join the Jackson–Harmsworth expedition as naturalist in its second year in Franz Josef Land (Zeml'a Franca-Iosifa). Here he collected numerous biological specimens and met the Norwegian Fridjof Nansen, who was returning from the *Fram* expedition. In 1898 he accompanied, as scientist, Major Andrew Coats in the *Blencathra* to Kolguyev, Novaya Zemlya, and the Barents Sea, and was then invited to sail with the prince of Monaco in the *Princesse Alice*, the finest of all oceanographic survey ships at that time, to Hope Island, Bear Island, and Spitsbergen. He returned with the prince to Spitsbergen in 1899 to survey Red Bay in the north of the archipelago.

Bruce in 1900 was among the best-equipped and most experienced of all polar scientists in Britain. He had amassed a large collection of rocks and biological specimens, and was an experienced land and marine surveyor and a competent meteorologist. He offered his services in 1899 to Clements Markham, president of the Royal Geographical Society, who was organizing an Antarctic expedition to be led by Robert Falcon Scott (the *Discovery* expedition, 1901–4). Bruce proposed himself as a member of the scientific staff, as either leader or deputy, but Markham delayed long in his reply and offered only a junior post. Bruce had already firm plans for his own expedition. Markham saw him as a rival to Scott: 'I do not understand why this mischievous rivalry should have been started, but I trust that you will not connect yourself with it' (Bruce MSS).

With the blessing of the Scottish Geographical Society, Bruce raised funds for the Scottish national Antarctic expedition in the well-equipped *Scotia* (1902–4). The entire crew and scientists were virtually all Scottish, and the funds came from Scottish subscribers, notably James and Andrew Coats of Paisley. Two summers were spent in biological and oceanographical work in the Weddell Sea and the south Atlantic. New coastline was discovered and named Coats Land, and the intervening winter was spent in Scotia Bay and on Laurie Island, South Orkneys, where an observatory, Omond House, was built, which remains as the oldest of all scientific observatories in Antarctica.

This highly successful expedition returned to Scotland with large scientific collections which formed the basis of the Scottish Oceanographical Institute, founded by Bruce in Edinburgh in 1907. Seven volumes of scientific reports from the *Scotia* expedition were published between 1907 and 1919.

Bruce returned to Spitsbergen in 1906 and 1907, and was instrumental in founding a mineral exploration company, the Scottish Spitsbergen Syndicate, in 1909. He was again in Spitsbergen in 1912, 1914, 1919, and 1920, and made a vain effort to raise a second expedition to Antarctica in 1910–11. The Oceanographical Institute closed in 1919 through lack of funds, but by this time Bruce's health was failing, and he died on 28 October 1921 in Liberton Hospital, Morningside, Edinburgh. He was cremated in Glasgow and his ashes scattered, according to his wishes, off South Georgia in the south Atlantic on 2 April 1923.

Bruce was awarded the honorary degree of LLD by Aberdeen University (1906), the gold medal of the Royal Scottish Geographical Society (1904), the patron's medal of the Royal Geographical Society (1910), the Neill prize and medal of the Royal Society of Edinburgh (1913), and the Livingstone medal of the Hispanic Society of America (1920). He never, however, achieved the fame of other contemporary polar explorers of the heroic age of polar exploration, nor did he court public acclaim.

PETER SPEAK

Sources R. N. Rudmose Brown, *A naturalist at the poles: the life, works and voyages of Dr W. S. Bruce, the polar explorer* (1923) · W. S. Bruce, *The log of the 'Scotia' expedition*, ed. P. Speak (1992) · P. Speak, *William S. Bruce: Scottish polar explorer and nationalist* [forthcoming] ·

P. Speak, 'William Speirs Bruce: Scottish nationalist and polar explorer', *Polar Record*, 28 (1992), 285–92 • R. N. Rudmose Brown, *Scottish Geographical Magazine*, 38 (1922), 46–8 • *Scottish Geographical Magazine*, 39 (1923), 92 • *The Scotsman* (31 Oct 1921) • W. G. Burn Murdoch, *From Edinburgh to the Antarctic* (1894) • Scott Polar RI, Bruce MSS • b. cert. • private information (2004) [S. M. Willman, daughter; G. Swinney, National Museums of Scotland, Chambers Street, Edinburgh]

Archives Hunterian Museum and Art Gallery, Glasgow, artefacts and MSS • National Museums of Scotland Library, artefacts • National Museums of Scotland Library, corresp. and papers • NL Scot., MSS • Scott Polar RI, corresp. and journals | NL Scot., corresp. with W. L. McKinlay • Scott Polar RI, letters to R. N. R. Brown • Scott Polar RI, letters to J. G. Ferrier • Scott Polar RI, corresp. with Sir Clements Markham • Scott Polar RI, letters to H. R. Mill

Likenesses photographs, 1900–21, Scott Polar RI • photograph, Scott Polar RI [*see illus.*]

Wealth at death £6714 8s. 1d.: confirmation, 16 Feb 1922, *CCI*

Bruce-Gardyne. For this title name *see* Gardyne, John Bruce-, Baron Bruce-Gardyne (1930–1990).

Brück, Hermann Alexander (1905–2000), astronomer, was born on 15 August 1905 in Berlin, the only child of Hermann Heinrich Brück, an officer of the Prussian army, killed in 1914 at the battle of Łódź, and his wife, Margaret Anne, *née* Weylandt, (*d. c.*1945). He attended the Kaiserin Augusta Gymnasium in Charlottenburg. His mother would have preferred him to become a lawyer, but his uncle, a distinguished bacteriologist, urged that science could also be a respectable profession.

Brück started his university career in Kiel; but he found no inspiration there, and moved on after one semester. He was far more fortunate in Munich, where he completed his first degree. He was taught by the legendary, charismatic physicist Arnold Sommerfeld, in the exciting years when quantum mechanics was being formulated—indeed, he attended the colloquium where Heisenberg first presented the famous 'uncertainty principle'. He obtained his doctorate in 1928 for work on the physics of crystals. Sommerfeld then encouraged him to read the recently published book *The Internal Constitution of the Stars* by the eminent British astrophysicist Arthur Eddington; Brück thereafter focused his interest on astronomy. He moved to a post at the Potsdam observatory, and within a few years became a lecturer at the University of Berlin, where luminaries such as Max von Laue, Erwin Schrödinger, and Albert Einstein were on the faculty.

The pre-Nazi years in Berlin, about which Brück wrote a detailed memoir, were among the happiest and most productive of his life. But he left Germany abruptly in 1936. This was the start of a lengthy cosmopolitan career during which he contributed greatly to astronomy—especially to the modernization of observatories and the improvement of observational techniques. His first post after leaving Berlin was at the Vatican observatory in Castel Gandolfo, where he worked on stellar classification. Although he stayed only one year, this was a formative period spiritually as well as scientifically. Brück, previously a Lutheran, was received into the Roman Catholic church by Romano Guardini and Johannes Pinsk, two of the most distinguished theologians of the age. His intense commitment to the church continued throughout his long life, and of all the organizations to which he later belonged, none gave him greater satisfaction than his membership of the Pontifical Academy of Sciences. (He was especially proud to have been elected to that body when its president was the eminent cosmologist Georges Lemaître, whom he came to know well.)

Brück's next move, in 1937, was to the Cambridge observatories in England, where Arthur Eddington was the director. After war broke out he was interned as an enemy alien, but within six months his release was secured and he returned to Cambridge, becoming acting director after Eddington's death. In 1947 he received a personal invitation from Eamon de Valera, then prime minister of the Irish republic, to become director of the Dunsink observatory and professor of astronomy at the new Dublin Institute for Advanced Studies, where he joined his friend Erwin Schrödinger who had been invited to be professor of theoretical physics.

After a decade in Ireland, where he was particularly successful in promoting scientific collaboration between north and south, Brück moved again. On the personal initiative of Sir Edward Appleton, then vice-chancellor of Edinburgh University, he was invited to take up the posts where he made his most substantial and enduring contributions: director of the Royal Observatory in Edinburgh, and astronomer royal for Scotland. Brück's personal scientific interests were in the physics of the interstellar medium, questions of stellar evolution, and the formation of stars from diffuse interstellar material. But his impact was wider through his influence on others—his courteous dignity and traditional style (his everyday dress was a formal suit and bow tie) overlay an original intellect and a far-sighted innovator.

Brück's tenure at Edinburgh lasted from 1957 until his retirement in 1975, and during that time the observatory staff numbers expanded from eight to more than one hundred. He fostered the work of P. Fellgett on automatic plate scanning machines and that of V. C. Reddish (his successor at Edinburgh) on new telescopes. He thereby prepared the way for instruments which greatly boosted the UK's international standing in astronomy—especially the 40-inch UK Schmidt telescope in Australia, which produced a photographic survey of the southern sky, and the pioneering Cosmos machine which could automatically scan the resulting photographic plates at high speed. He also laid the groundwork for the UK infra-red telescope and the James Clerk Maxwell radio telescope in Hawaii. He championed the establishment of observing stations in climates better than that of Great Britain and was a prime advocate of a United Kingdom northern hemisphere observatory in the Canary Islands.

Brück's first wife was Irma Waitzfelder (1905–1950), whom he married on 8 September 1936 and with whom he had one son and one daughter. On 21 November 1951 he married Mary Teresa Conway (*b.* 1925), herself an astronomer; they had one son and two daughters. Throughout his long and active retirement he and Mary lived in Penicuik, near Edinburgh. They co-authored *The Story of Astronomy in Edinburgh* (1983) which traced the subject's emergence back to the Scottish Enlightenment, and also *The Peripatetic Astronomer* (1988) a highly readable biography of an eccentric nineteenth-century astronomer Charles Piazzi Smyth, one of Brück's predecessors in Edinburgh, who pioneered stereoscopic photography, but gained embarrassing notoriety through his obsession with the numerology of the Great Pyramid.

Brück was elected to the Royal Irish Academy in 1948, to the Royal Society of Edinburgh in 1958, and appointed CBE in 1966. He was elected in 1955 to the Pontifical Academy; he served on its council for twenty years, and gained special satisfaction from a study week he organized in 1981 on its behalf, the proceedings of which appeared as a book entitled *Astrophysical Cosmology*. On his ninetieth birthday Pope John Paul appointed him knight grand cross of the order of St Gregory the Great. He died in the Royal Infirmary, Edinburgh, from pulmonary embolism, on 4 March 2000, and was buried on 11 March at Mortonhall cemetery, Edinburgh. He was survived by his wife.

MARTIN J. REES

Sources T. Dalyell, *The Independent* (8 March 2000) • A. Steven, *The Scotsman* (10 March 2000) • *The Times* (17 March 2000) • P. Brand, *Astronomy and Astrophysics*, 41/6 (2000), 35 • personal knowledge (2004) • private information (2004) [family]
Archives Royal Observatory, Edinburgh, papers | Bodl. Oxf., Society for Protection of Science and Learning and Home Office files
Wealth at death £47,081.66: confirmation, Scotland, 2000

Bruckner, John (1726–1804), Lutheran minister and author, was born on 31 December 1726 at Cadzand in Zeeland, a few kilometres north-west of Bruges and not far from the present-day Belgian frontier. French influence was strong in this little town that had been colonized by the French in the late seventeenth century, and Bruckner grew up bilingual in Dutch and French. As he was intended for the protestant ministry from an early age, he also learned Latin, Greek, and Hebrew. He pursued his studies in Franeker at the academy founded in 1585 to teach Calvinist doctrine. In the mid-eighteenth century its leading lights were the Hellenist Valckenaer, Schultens the elder, and Hermannus Venema, a professor tolerant in religious matters who stressed the importance of philology in scriptural exegesis.

Bruckner's first ecclesiastical appointment was as assistant to Monsieur de Loche, the minister in Leiden. The Walloon community in Norwich was at that time looking for a new minister, and while Paul Colombine, one of the elders of the church, was in the Netherlands for business, he offered Bruckner the appointment. The stipend was £40 a year, with £10 for removal expenses. The Norwich consistory signified approval on 27 January, and, on taking the oath, Bruckner was received as pastor on 27 October 1751.

Bruckner was, however, unable to maintain, let alone expand, the Walloon congregation in Norwich; Dr Van Sarn's Dutch congregation in Blackfriars in London was

dwindling too. Not surprisingly, since Bruckner was capable of preaching in Dutch as well as in French, Latin, and English, the precedent set the previous century was followed: about 1766 he became minister to the Dutch church as well as to the French. He exercised the plurality with a certain willingness to tolerate flexibility in the form and order of religious observances.

Bruckner's duties even in his dual capacity were not arduous, so he found suitable and congenial employment and the means of augmenting his income by teaching French, for Norwich grammar school provided such classical tuition as was required, and Dutch was not in demand. As the literature of the classical period and the Enlightenment was highly esteemed, and as some familiarity with French was reckoned a genteel accomplishment for young ladies, Bruckner had little difficulty in finding pupils. As well as conducting classes in private schools, he called regularly at the houses of well-to-do members of his congregation, particularly in the Colegate area favoured by the Huguenot community, to give private lessons. His most famous pupils were William Taylor (1765–1836) and Amelia Opie. Gazing at the picture of Bruckner painted in 1800 by her husband, John Opie, Amelia left an affectionate impression of his benignity in the third 'Portrait' in her *Lays for the Dead*.

Translations into English by Thomas Cogan in 1768, and thence into German by C. Garvé in 1769, testify to considerable contemporary interest in Bruckner's *Théorie du système animal* (1767); allusions to classical literature and to a body of contemporary scientific writing underpin an argument that nature is ordered despite apparently random wastefulness. In *Thoughts on Public Worship* (1792), of which only the first part was published, Bruckner uses scripture and history to rebut Gilbert Wakefield's eccentric views. The ascription of *Criticisms on the Diversions of Purley by John Cassander* (1790) to Bruckner is doubtful. As well as being scholarly and sincerely religious, Bruckner was a proficient musician and a gifted draughtsman; he also enjoyed country sports. The cultural life of Georgian Norwich, which owed much to Huguenot influence generally, appreciated, as Taylor wrote, his 'learning and good sense'.

Bruckner married in 1782 one of his former pupils, Mary Cooper from Guist, near Foulsham, Norfolk. As he grew older, depression set in; on 12 May 1804, at Norwich, he hanged himself. He was buried beside his wife, who had predeceased him, at Guist.

CHRISTOPHER SMITH

Sources W. J. C. Moens, *The Walloons and their church at Norwich: their history and registers, 1565–1832*, Huguenot Society of London, 1 (1887–8) • *Norfolk tour*, 2 (1829), 1074 • J. Menzies-Wilson and H. Lloyd, *Amelia* (1937–40) • W. Habasch, *Sir William Hale und John Bruckner: mit einer Geschichte der vormalthuschen Bevölkerungstheorie* • *DNB* • will, PRO, PROB 11/1409, fols. 348r–359r
Likenesses J. Opie, oils, 1800; photograph, Courtauld Inst.

Brude mac Bile [Bridei son of Beli] (d. **693**), king of Picts, was overking of the Picts from 672 until his death. Irish annals call him 'king of Fortriu' (Anderson, *Early Sources*, 1.193) and his mother presumably belonged to the royal matrilineage of that Pictish province (roughly the southern half of modern Perthshire). Ecgfrith (d. 685), king of Northumbria, was said to have been his cousin (*fratruelis*), and it seems that Ecgfrith's uncle, King Eanfrith, may have been the maternal grandfather of Brude's mother; not, as is sometimes supposed, her father [see Picts, kings of the]. Brude's father is stated to have been a king of Ail Cluathe ('Rock of Clyde', present-day Dumbarton). There are two kings called Beli in the Strathclyde royal genealogy (Bile seems to have been the Pictish form of the British Beli, adopted into Irish); to identify either Beli as Brude's father is possible, but strains the chronological evidence to its limits.

Brude succeeded in the Pictish kingship to Drust, Donuel's son, who had been expelled in 672 after an abortive revolt against Ecgfrith (the Picts had been subject to Northumbria since the 650s) ended in the slaughter of the Pictish army. In 682 Brude is said to have 'destroyed' the Orkney Islands and between 680 and 683 the annals record several 'sieges' within what might well have been Brude's sphere of interest, though he is not named in connection with any of them.

In 685 King Ecgfrith, apparently without provocation, invaded the country of the Picts. A Pictish force, by a series of deceptive withdrawals, led the Northumbrians on beyond the rivers Earn and Tay, and on Saturday 20 May inflicted a heavy defeat upon them in swampy ground at Nechtansmere, or Dunnichen Moss, near Forfar. Ecgfrith himself died. An Irish verse says that Brude was fighting for 'the heritage of his grandfather' (Anderson, *Early Sources*, 1.194). It has been suggested that his maternal grandfather may have been the king of, or a nobleman in, the province of Círchenn (modern Angus and Mearns). A further possibility is that the grandfather was Donuel, the father of Gartnait and Drust, Brude's immediate predecessors. Brude could thus provide an example of a nephew succeeding to his maternal uncle(s) in a matrilineal society; however, other explanations of his ancestry have been put forward. As a result of the Pictish victory (or perhaps, rather, of Ecgfrith's death), the Picts were free thenceforward from Anglian dominion and occupation.

Brude died in 693 and was believed to have been buried in Iona. He was remembered partly for having freed his kingdom from Northumbria, and partly for having been a friend of Adomnán, the ninth abbot of Iona, who died in 704. A story in an Irish homiletic life of St Adomnán tells of his distress when Brude's body was brought to the island for burial. MARJORIE O. ANDERSON

Sources *Ann. Ulster* · M. O. Anderson, *Kings and kingship in early Scotland*, rev. edn (1980), 248, 262, 266, 272, 280 · A. O. Anderson, ed. and trans., *Early sources of Scottish history, AD 500 to 1286*, 1 (1922); repr. with corrections (1990), xvii, 194 · A. O. Anderson, ed., *Scottish annals from English chroniclers, AD 500 to 1286* (1908); repr. (1991), 36, 42 · Bede, *Hist. eccl.*, 53, 295 · M. Herbert and P. Ó Riain, eds. and trans., *Betha Adamnáin: the Irish life of Adamnán*, ITS, 54 (1988), 58, 82 · K. Grabowski and D. Dumville, *Chronicles and annals of mediaeval Ireland and Wales: the Clonmacnoise-group texts* (1984), 124 · F. T. Wainwright, 'Nechtansmere', *Antiquity*, 22 (1948), 82–97

Brude [Bridei] **mac Maelchon** (d. *c.*586), king of Picts, was the earliest of seven 'historical' bearers of the name Brude in the Pictish king-lists [see Picts, kings of the]. That name, not certainly of Celtic origin, was Brude or Bruide in Irish. Its principal Pictish forms, perhaps later than the Irish, were Bridei (known to Bede *c.*731) and Bredei. Maelchon is sometimes used by modern writers as a nominative, because the true nominative of Brude's father's name is in doubt. Chronologically, he could have been Maelgwyn, king of Gwynedd in north Wales, who died in 547 or 549.

There is no contemporary record of Brude. He was remembered, it seems, for having checked an eastward expansion of Scots into Pictish territory, about 558 [see Dál Riata, kings of]. The event is noted laconically—'Flight before Maelchon's son' (Anderson, *Early Sources*, 1.21)—in the annals of Ulster, and more explicitly in later versions.

Adomnán of Iona, writing his life of Columba about 700, believed that Columba had travelled at least once to the country of the Picts, by way of the Great Glen and Loch Ness, to visit their king Brude in a fortified residence near the River Ness (the site of the medieval castle of Inverness has been suggested). These chapters of the life are far more concerned with Broichan, a malign magician and the foster father of Brude, than with the king himself. However, one chapter represents Brude as exercising lordship over a king of Orkney, which surely implies considerable sea power. Adomnán says nothing of Brude's relations with southern Picts; but Bede (about 731), after drawing a distinction between northern and southern Picts, seems to imply that Brude, 'a very powerful king' (Bede, *Hist. eccl.*, 222), had been sovereign over both.

Brude may have been the first king of a Pictish province to claim sovereignty over all the Picts. Certainly he is the first Pictish king to be mentioned by the annalists, but perhaps only because the monastery of Iona, ultimate source of much annal information, had been founded in his reign. Bede believed that it was 'the Picts' who had granted the island to Columba. Adomnán has nothing to say on that matter. He relates that Brude was initially hostile to the saint, but for the rest of his own life treated him with the greatest honour. He does not suggest that Brude was converted by Columba, or even that he was ever a Christian.

Brude's death is dated by the annals of Ulster to 583, perhaps intended for 586 or 587. The lists say that he reigned for thirty years. The dating of his death, and those of several of his successors, may have been calculated from a regnal list and, if so, cannot claim to have independent authority. MARJORIE O. ANDERSON

Sources *Ann. Ulster*, s.a. 557, 583 · M. O. Anderson, *Kings and kingship in early Scotland*, rev. edn (1980), 248, 262, 266, 272, 280 · *Adomnán's Life of Columba*, ed. and trans. A. O. Anderson and M. O. Anderson, rev. edn, rev. M. O. Anderson, OMT (1991) · Bede, *Hist. eccl.* · K. H. Jackson, 'The Pictish language', *The problem of the Picts*, ed. F. T. Wainwright (1955), 129–66 · T. F. O'Rahilly, *Early Irish history and mythology* (1946), 360, 535 · I. Henderson, 'Inverness, a Pictish capital', *The hub of the highlands* (1975), 91–108 · A. O. Anderson, ed. and trans., *Early sources of Scottish history, AD 500 to 1286*, 2 vols. (1922); repr. with corrections (1990)

Brudenell, Adeline Louisa Maria, countess of Cardigan. *See* Lancastre Saldanha, Adeline Louisa Maria de, Countess de Lancastre (1824–1915).

Brudenell, James Thomas, seventh earl of Cardigan (1797–1868), army officer, only surviving son of Robert, sixth earl of Cardigan (d. 1837), and his wife, Penelope Ann Cooke (d. 1826), was born at the Manor House, Hambleden, Buckinghamshire, on 16 October 1797; he had seven sisters. He grew tall and slender, with long golden hair and whiskers, pale blue eyes, and an aristocratic nose. From 1811 until 1813 he attended Harrow School, and then lived at the family home of Deene Park, Northamptonshire, before studying at Christ Church, Oxford (1815–17). Subsequently, he undertook the grand tour, and became an accomplished shot, swordsman, and horseman. In 1823 Captain Frederick Johnstone obtained £1000 damages from Brudenell for holding 'criminal conversation' with his wife, but declined further satisfaction with duelling pistols. A life of adultery and bravado had truly begun. Following her divorce, Brudenell married Elizabeth Johnstone (née Tollemache) (1797–1858) on 26 June 1826 in the chapel at Ham House, Richmond, Surrey.

Brudenell sat in parliament for the corporation borough of Marlborough, controlled by his cousin Charles, second earl of Ailesbury, from 1818 until 1829, when his tenure was terminated for opposing the Catholic Relief Bill. He represented another rotten borough, Fowey in Cornwall (1830–32), until its abolition by the Reform Act. He was then elected MP for the northern division of Northamptonshire in December 1832 and re-elected three years later, but left the Commons in 1837 after succeeding to a peerage.

Never devoted to politics, Brudenell instead yearned to join the army. In November 1819 he raised a troop of yeomanry from the tenants at Deene Park, and on 6 May 1824 purchased a regular commission as cornet in the 8th hussars. Gazetted lieutenant on 13 January 1825, after three months on half pay he secured a vacancy in the 8th hussars, advancing (again by purchase) to captain on 9 June 1826 and major on 3 August 1830. Four months later, on 3 December 1830, Brudenell went on half pay as a lieutenant-colonel until 16 March 1832, when he reputedly paid over £35,000 for command of the 15th hussars. His overbearing manner and violent temper brought frequent clashes with regimental officers. He twice put Captain Augustus Wathen under arrest and, when a court-martial vindicated Wathen, he was removed from command, returning to the half-pay list on 21 March 1834. Thoroughly incensed, Brudenell lobbied furiously for another regiment. Through his sister Harriet, married to Queen Adelaide's chamberlain, Lord Howe, he sought royal support; and he subjected senior politicians and influential officers to personal pressure. The military secretary at the Horse Guards, Lord Fitzroy Somerset (later Lord Raglan), after one of many confrontations, remarked: 'Lord Brudenell favoured me with another of his disagreeable visits yesterday' (Sweetman, 94). Brudenell's offensive paid off: on 30 March 1836 he obtained command of the 11th hussars for some £40,000, joining his new regiment in India shortly before it returned to England.

James Thomas Brudenell, seventh earl of Cardigan (1797–1868), by George Zobel, pubd 1856 (after Henry Wyndham Phillips)

Brudenell's father died on 14 August 1837 (his mother had died in 1826), and he succeeded as seventh earl of Cardigan. He inherited an estimated annual income of £40,000 with Deene Park and other properties in Northamptonshire, Leicestershire, Yorkshire, and London, where one house (17 Carlton House Terrace) was later leased to the French exile Louis Napoleon (afterwards Emperor Napoleon III). Cardigan rode with the Quorn, Pytchley, and Cottesmore hunts, frequented London clubs (the Travellers', White's, Boodle's, and the short-lived Military and Country Service Club), gambled excessively, bought the steam yacht *Dryad* for £10,000, and entertained lavishly at Deene Park. His marriage, however, had by then failed, though the Cardigans would never divorce. The seventh earl found solace elsewhere, reputedly siring several illegitimate offspring, and being publicly accused by Lord William Paget of conducting an affair with his wife.

Cardigan petitioned in vain to become lord lieutenant of Northamptonshire and to be awarded the Garter. Professionally, his eccentric and authoritarian behaviour brought no better relations with officers of the 11th hussars than with those of the 15th, though a letter in the *United Service Gazette* (12 October 1850) would praise his concern for the welfare of his soldiers. He had Captain John Reynolds arrested for supposedly drinking porter at a mess dinner in the notorious 'Black Bottle' incident, court-martialled Captain Richard Reynolds, placed Lieutenant William Forrest under arrest for a minor offence, causing that officer to complain to the commander-in-chief, and verbally harassed and bullied others. On 12 September 1840, Cardigan fought a duel with a former officer, Harvey Tuckett, and was arrested; but in April 1841 the House of Lords, before whom he had opted to be tried, acquitted him on a legal technicality. Attacked in the press, hissed and booed at in theatres, Cardigan was further reviled for the 'atrocity' of ordering a flogging after divine service on Easter Sunday 1841. In exasperation the commander-in-chief, Lord Hill, exclaimed: 'I am thoroughly sick of the 11th! And all that belongs to it!' (Sweetman, 96). The United Service Club repeatedly blackballed him.

Promoted colonel on 9 November 1846, Cardigan still eschewed popularity, concentrating on rigorous discipline and creating a sartorially elegant regiment, towards which he contributed a considerable amount of his own money. When the Crimean War broke out he was appointed brigadier-general in command of the light brigade of the cavalry division. With no experience of active service and aged fifty-six, Cardigan suffered from piles, constipation, chronic bronchitis, and urinary discomfort. Nevertheless, he set out enthusiastically from London on 8 May 1854, reaching Scutari sixteen days later. On 20 June 1854 he became a major-general, which did not prevent confrontation with his brother-in-law and tetchy superior officer, the earl of Lucan. When the light brigade moved to Bulgaria, Lucan remained at Scutari; Cardigan therefore believed himself to be independent of the divisional commander, which Lucan hotly disputed. Raglan's appeal to them as 'both gentlemen of high honour, and of elevated position in the country, independently of their military rank' (Sweetman, 235) failed to quell the acrimony. Raglan unwittingly exacerbated the situation by praising Cardigan for his conduct during a lengthy reconnaissance with his brigade along the Danube in June and July, and at the first skirmish in the Crimea on the Bulganek River on 19 September, where 'it was impossible for any troops to exhibit more steadiness' (Sweetman, 220).

When the allied invaders laid siege to Sevastopol from uplands to the south, the cavalry division camped on the plain below ready to protect the British supply port of Balaklava. Owing to his medical condition, Cardigan dined and slept on the *Dryad* in Balaklava harbour. Thus he was not with the brigade shortly after dawn on 25 October, as Russian troops overran a line of redoubts along a ridge north of Balaklava and an enemy cavalry squadron was turned back near the village of Kadikoi by the 'thin red line'. He had assumed command when another, stronger cavalry force swept over the captured ridge, to be checked by the heavy brigade as the light brigade remained immobile on its left flank. Criticized for lethargy, Cardigan replied that Lucan had ordered him to move only if attacked by the Russians. Lucan maintained that he had required Cardigan 'to attack anything and everything that shall come within reach of you' (Sweetman, 247).

The main action (the 'charge of the light brigade') took place shortly after 11 a.m. Seeing the Russians about to withdraw captured British guns from the redoubts, Raglan sent Captain L. E. Nolan with a written order to Lucan for 'the cavalry to advance rapidly to the front, and try to prevent the enemy taking away the guns' (Sweetman, 249). Instead of advancing towards the ridge, Cardigan led his brigade down the valley against enemy cannon drawn up ahead: they advanced 'to the front', certainly, but the guns were not being taken away. Of the 673 men and horses that started out, 113 men and 475 horses were killed, 247 men and 42 horses badly injured. Rebuked by Raglan, Cardigan pointed to a direct order from Lucan. Lucan in turn blamed Nolan, who had died in the action, for imprecise clarification of the order; but Raglan officially censured Lucan. Whoever was at fault, Cardigan's personal bravery was acknowledged by a survivor, Captain William Morris: 'He led like a gentleman' (Thomas, 253).

Before the close of the year Cardigan had been invalided home. In England he was lauded in the press, dined with the queen, attended banquets in his honour, and was greeted in Northampton by the strains of 'See the conquering hero comes'. The United Service Club even made him an honorary member. He was also created KCB (7 July 1855), commander of the Légion d'honneur, and knight second class of the Mejidiye. Cardigan's querulous nature, though, had not been calmed. Learning that A. W. Kinglake was writing an account of the charge, Cardigan subjected him to lengthy and tedious correspondence. He reacted vigorously to the assertion by one of Raglan's aides-de-camp, the Hon. S. J. G. Calthorpe, in his book *Letters from Headquarters*, that he had returned down the valley at Balaklava without waiting to rally survivors: he started legal proceedings and challenged Lucan to a duel for supporting Calthorpe. Farce then ensued when Lucan arrived in Paris after his would-be opponent had recrossed the channel. Cardigan's legal action also failed, having been initiated five years after the alleged libel.

In 1859 Cardigan became colonel of the 5th dragoon guards, relinquishing that post the following year for a similar one with the 11th hussars, at whose annual dinner in 1865 he and 'Black Bottle' Reynolds, now both white-haired but erect, made their peace. In May 1866 Cardigan reviewed his old regiment on its departure for India. Appointed inspector-general of cavalry in 1855, after the normal period in post he retired in 1860, and he was promoted lieutenant-general on 9 March 1861.

At the age of sixty-five Cardigan fell badly while hunting and thereafter suffered occasional seizures. His taste for flirtation hardly diminished, however: he seduced Sir William Leeson's young wife, and in 1857 took as his mistress Adeline De Horsey [*see* Lancastre Saldanha, Adeline Louisa Maria de (1824–1915)]. Elizabeth, Cardigan's estranged wife, died on 12 July 1858, and on 28 September Cardigan married Adeline in the garrison chapel, Gibraltar, though his new bride was never fully accepted by his social circle. Cardigan still frequented race meetings, owned an expensive yacht, and remained a member of the Royal Yacht Squadron and commodore of the Royal Southern Yacht Club. His extravagance, however, led to his mortgaging part of the estate in 1864, and when he died on 28 March 1868, two days after again falling from his horse, Adeline faced estimated debts of £365,000 with assets of £60,000. After lying in state at Deene Park, Cardigan's body was entombed in the Brudenell chapel of St Peter's Church. The earldom devolved on Cardigan's second cousin, the marquess of Ailesbury.

Undoubtedly bad tempered, intolerant, and ultra-conservative, Cardigan was nevertheless motivated by a perverse sense of duty, which caused him bravely to advance at the head of the light brigade, be solicitous towards old soldiers, and encourage others formally to adhere to the Anglican faith, as he did himself. Belying the mischievous contention that a childhood riding accident had left him empty-headed, Cardigan published two books, *Eight Months on Active Service* (1855), and *Cavalry Brigade Movements* (1861); and three pamphlets, *Trial of James Thomas, earl of Cardigan, before the Right Honourable House of Peers, for felony* (1841), *The Earl of Cardigan v Lieutenant-Colonel Calthorpe, Proceedings in the Queen's Bench* (1863), and *Statement and Remarks upon the Affidavits Filed by Lieutenant-Colonel Calthorpe* (1863). JOHN SWEETMAN

Sources Army List · D. Thomas, *Charge! hurrah! hurrah! A life of Cardigan of Balaclava* (1974) · J. Sweetman, *Raglan: from the Peninsula to the Crimea* (1993) · C. Woodham-Smith, *The reason why* (1958) · C. Hibbert, *The destruction of Lord Raglan* [1961] · A. W. Kinglake, *The invasion of the Crimea*, 4 (1868) · P. Compton, *Cardigan of Balaclava* (1972) · J. Wake, *The Brudenells of Deene* [1953] · S. David, *The homicidal earl: the life of Lord Cardigan* (1997)
Archives Northants. RO, corresp., military notebook, and papers | BL, corresp. with Sir Robert Peel, Add. MSS 40419–40560, *passim* · BL, letters to marquess of Tweeddale · CUL, letters to A. W. Kinglake regarding the battle of Balaklava · Lpool RO, letters to fourteenth earl of Derby · NAM, corresp. with Lord Raglan · NL Scot., corresp. with Sir George Brown · Northants. RO, letters to the rector of Deene
Likenesses J. E. Ferneley, group portrait, oils, 1850, Deene Park, Northamptonshire · J. Sant, oils, 1855, Deene Park, Northamptonshire · attrib. H. W. Phillips, oils, 1856, Deene Park, Northamptonshire · G. Zobel, mezzotint, pubd 1856 (after H. W. Phillips), NPG [*see illus.*] · G. H. Laporte, oils, 1868, Deene Park, Northamptonshire · A. F. de Prades, oils, 1868, Deene Park, Northamptonshire · J. E. Boehm, figure on monument, St Peter's Church, Deene, Northamptonshire · R. Buckner, oils, Deene Park, Northamptonshire · G. Hayter, group portrait, oils (*The House of Commons, 1833*), NPG · L. MacDonald, marble bust, Grawsworth Hall, Cheshire · A. F. de Prades, oils, NAM · bust; formerly, United Service Club, London · pencil and watercolour drawing, NPG · portraits, repro. in Wake, *Brudenells of Deene*
Wealth at death under £60,000: probate, 23 June 1868, *CGPLA Eng. & Wales*

Brudenell, Sir Robert (1461–1531), judge, was a younger son of Edmund Brudenell (*d.* 1469) of Amersham, Buckinghamshire, and his second wife, Philippa, daughter of Philip Englefield of Englefield. He is said, rather doubtfully, to have spent some time at King's College, Cambridge. It is a more certain fact that he entered the Inner Temple about 1480 and delivered his first reading about ten years later on the statute *De donis*. His second reading, in Lent 1500, was on the statute *De mercatoribus*. He was a governor of the inn by 1496, and at some time before 1503 served as treasurer. Meanwhile he had started practising at the bar, and is first mentioned in the year-books in 1490 as counsel in a king's bench case. Among his regular clients in the time of Henry VII were Peterborough Abbey

Sir Robert Brudenell (1461–1531), by unknown sculptor, *c.*1531 [with his wives, Margaret Entwistle and Philippa Power]

and Edward, Lord Hastings. A year after taking the coif in 1503 he was made one of the king's serjeants, and held the office until 1507 when he became a puisne justice of the king's bench. At an unknown date he was knighted. On 23 April 1520 he was translated to the common pleas as chief justice, and remained in that office until 22 November 1530 when his successor was appointed.

Until his first marriage Brudenell lived in his paternal county of Buckinghamshire, where his father had given him lands in Burnham and Stoke Mandeville, and he was appointed to the commission of the peace for that county in 1489. In 1495 he married Margaret (*d.* 1502), sister and coheir of Thomas Entwistle, widow of William Wyville of Stonton Wyville, Leicestershire, and settled at the manor of Stonton. Her husband's directions for a memorial brass indicate that Margaret died in 1502, though her arms were impaled with his in the windows of Serjeants' Inn, Fleet Street. They had four sons and a daughter. In 1505 Robert married as his second wife Philippa Rufford, *née* Power (*d.* 1531), widow of Thomas Rufford of Beachampton, Buckinghamshire, who survived him by only a few months; they had no children. During his years as a serjeant he purchased lands in Leicestershire, Rutland, Buckinghamshire, Lincolnshire, and Northamptonshire; and in 1514 he purchased the manor of Deene, Northamptonshire, which became the Brudenell seat. Brudenell died on 30 January 1531, and was buried in Deene church, Northamptonshire, where, as directed in his will, there is an effigy in robes and collar of SS lying with his two wives. His eldest son, Sir Thomas (*d.* 1549), a barrister of the Inner Temple, has a brass at Deene. The chief justice left him 'all my bookes of the law or concerning the lawe with all other bookes whatsoever they be except masse bookes, porteses and prymers for my wifes chapleyns'; several of the law books survive. Thomas was appointed by his father as clerk of the essoins in 1521, and as a filazer of the common pleas in 1523, an office that he relinquished on his father's death. His grandson was created earl of Cardigan; and from the same line were descended the dukes of Montagu (1766–1845). The third son, Robert, was also a member of the Inner Temple and was given the clerkship of assize on the Oxford circuit by his father in 1511, although it was taken over by Thomas in 1527. The second son, Anthony, inherited the Stonton estates besides other land in Northamptonshire.   J. H. BAKER

Sources M. E. Finch, *The wealth of five Northamptonshire families, 1540–1640*, Northamptonshire RS, 19 (1956), 135–7 · J. Wake, *The Brudenells of Deene* [1953] · Baker, *Serjeants* · Cooper, *Ath. Cantab.*, 1.43 · E. W. Ives, *The common lawyers of pre-Reformation England* (1983) · Foss, *Judges*, 5.140–42 · *The reports of Sir John Spelman*, ed. J. H. Baker, 2, SeldS, 94 (1978), 2.358, 372, 387 · *Coat of Arms*, 6.328, 12.2–11 · *The notebook of Sir John Port*, ed. J. H. Baker, SeldS, 102 (1986), xxxv, xxxvii, 176–80 · will, PRO, PROB 11/24, sig. 2 · will, PRO, PROB 11/24, sig. 16 [widow's will]
Likenesses oils, 1527 (after monument), Deene church, Northamptonshire; repro. in Wake, *Brudenells of Deene*, facing p. 16 · alabaster effigy on monument, *c*.1531, Deene church, Northamptonshire [*see illus.*]

Bruen, John (1560–1625), iconoclast, the eldest son of John Bruen (1510–1587) and his wife, Dorothy Holford, was born at Bruen Stapleford, Cheshire, in 1560 (some time before 18 January) into a gentry family that had dominated that village since the thirteenth century. He was baptized the same year. Much of what is known of Bruen's career derives from the hagiographic biography by William Hinde (1568/9–1629), who served as curate of the nearby parish of Bunbury from about 1603. Initially educated under the tutorship of the schoolmaster James Roe in the household of his uncle at Dutton between about 1565 and 1570, Bruen and his younger brother Thomas were sent to St Alban Hall, Oxford, in 1577, where they remained for two years. Despite a youthful reputation for revelry, and especially for dancing and hunting, Bruen's marriage in 1580 to Elizabeth Cowper (1552–1595/6), the widow of a Chester alderman, connected him to the influential puritan network of Elizabeth's father, Henry Hardware, the reformist mayor of Chester responsible for suppressing the city's mystery plays.

According to Hinde, it was the death of Bruen's father in 1587 that prompted a radical transformation in Bruen's lifestyle. Whether because of a spiritual crisis or because of the financial constraints imposed by his new responsibilities towards eleven siblings, including his sister Katherine Bruen [*see* Bretterall, Katherine] (to become famous in 1601 because of her putative deathbed loss of faith), Bruen imposed a strict code of piety on the household. He began by disparking the estate and suppressing hunting and gaming, and subsequently enforced a culture of discipline on family, servants, and tenants alike. This not only involved prayers seven times daily but also attendance at both morning and evening sermons on Sundays, usually without departing from the church in between. The knowledge of scripture among even his illiterate household servants became legendary: Hinde drew particular attention to 'Old Robert', **Robert Pashfield** (*fl. c.*1600), servant, whose familiarity with the Bible was such that he could cite chapter and verse of almost any scriptural text, despite his inability to read. Bruen also suppressed the drinking, dancing, and sport associated with the annual festivities of the St Andrew's day wakes that he (and Hinde) regarded as popish and profane. Following

the death of Elizabeth, who was buried on 18 January 1596, Bruen moved to Rhodes, near Manchester, and it was at a prayer meeting in Manchester that he met Ann (*d. c.*1616), the daughter of the martyrologist John Foxe, whom he married before a return to Bruen Stapleford in 1601. The Bruen household rapidly earned a reputation for both religiosity and hospitality, and as many as twenty-one boarders (including the children of the prominent Cheshire families of Done, Dutton, Egerton, Grosvenor, and Wilbraham) regularly stayed there. This pattern of religious economy was disrupted only after Ann's death, about 1616, when Bruen temporarily broke up the household and lived in Chester for about four years. He had nine children by Ann, and a further two by his third wife, Margaret.

Bruen's claim (made in a letter to a fellow member of the household of faith, Robert Harley of Brampton Bryan, Herefordshire) to the title 'Bishop' Bruen, intending a visitation to suppress immorality and profanity without tarrying for the magistrate, is vindicated not only by Hinde's euphemistic references to the 'removal' of stained glass in Tarvin church, but also by two sets of judicial records which confirm that Bruen and members of his household were twice prosecuted for iconoclasm (BL, Add. MS 70001, fol. 1). On May day 1603 his servants allegedly smashed the stained glass, especially an image of St George and the dragon, in the windows of the local Tarvin church, an act of spontaneous iconoclasm that earned them a summons before a privy sessions held before Bishop Vaughan of Chester at Tarvin. Some ten years later, it was alleged that other members of Bruen's household, including several who had been prosecuted for the first offence, had engaged in the systematic destruction of 'popish' crosses in the churchyards and highways of several Cheshire parishes. Bruen himself was on this occasion prosecuted along with his ally John Ratcliffe, alderman of Chester, but the tribunal involved was now Star Chamber and the prosecution was initiated by Attorney-General Sir Francis Bacon, an indication of just how seriously the offence was regarded. Six members of Bruen's household were convicted and fined £550 between them. Bruen none the less continued to campaign for the suppression of popish and immoral behaviour, writing to the secretary of state, Conway, only months before his death about the dangers of failing to protect godly magistrates who were forced to run a gauntlet of mockery and assault as they attempted to stamp out drunkenness, swearing, and gaming.

Bruen died on 18 January 1625 at the age of sixty-five of an unspecified illness, and was buried at Bruen Stapleford in the same month. By this time his local reputation as a godly activist was already assured. His fame spread as a consequence of Hinde's biography, which was completed and published by Hinde's son in 1641.   STEVE HINDLE

Sources W. Hinde, *A faithful remonstrance of the holy life and happy death of John Bruen of Bruen Stapleford* (1641) · W. Harrison and W. Leigh, *Death's advantage little regarded, and the soules solace against sorrow … at the buriall of Mistress Katherin Bretterall*, 1st–5th edns (1602–17) [later edn known as *The Christian life and death of Mistris*

Katherin Brettergh] • G. Ormerod, *The history of the county palatine and city of Chester*, 2nd edn, ed. T. Helsby, 2 (1882), 320–22 • R. C. Richardson, *Puritanism in north-west England: a regional study of the diocese of Chester to 1642* (1972) • PRO, STAC 8/21/6 • Ches. & Chester ALSS, QJF 32/1/78–84 • S. Hindle, *The state and social change in early modern England, c.1550–1640* (2000), 66–7 • S. Hindle, 'Aspects of the relationship of the state and local society in early modern England with special reference to Cheshire, c.1590–1630', PhD diss., U. Cam., 1993, 99–103 • M. Aston, 'Puritans and iconoclasm, 1560–1660', *The culture of English puritanism, 1560–1700*, ed. C. Durston and J. Eales (1996), 92–121 • Foster, *Alum. Oxon., 1500–1714*, 1.200

Archives BL, commonplace book of 'Bruen's cards', Harley MS 6607 • PRO, household MSS, PRO STAC 8/21/6 | BL, corresp. with R. Harley, Add. MS 70001, vol. 1 • Ches. & Chester ALSS, proceedings at privy sessions before Bishop Vaughan at Tarvin, QJF 32/1/78–84

Likenesses line engraving, NPG • portrait, repro. in S. Clarke, *The marrow of ecclesiastical history*, 3rd edn, 2 (1675); copy, Ches. & Chester ALSS, D/39777

Wealth at death manor of Bruen Stapleford valued at £15 17s. 3d.

Bruerne, Richard. *See* Bruarne, Richard (1519–1565).

Bruges, William (*c*.1375–1450), herald, was the son of Richard Bruges, Lancaster king of arms, and Katherine, whose maiden name may have been Hawley. He was appointed Chester herald on 7 June 1398 by letters patent under the seal of the new principality of Chester. He was later attached to the household of Henry of Monmouth (the future Henry V), then prince of Wales, earl of Chester, and duke of Aquitaine, though from 1407 to 1410 Henry IV employed him on various royal missions.

Bruges may well have been promoted to Guyenne king of arms on the accession of Henry V. He was very probably the Guyenne who was present at the coronation in 1413 and was sent to France in early 1414. As Guyenne he accompanied the king on his Agincourt campaign when, in September 1415, he was sent on a mission to the dauphin. In February 1416 as Aquitaine king of arms Bruges was entrusted with letters for the emperor-elect, Sigismund, and magnates of the empire; the titles Aquitaine and Guyenne were interchangeable at this time. Soon after, he entertained the emperor-elect at his own home in Kentish Town. He was still Guyenne on 22 May 1417.

A copy of his father's will, dated July 1415, refers to Bruges as both Guyenne and Garter king of arms. However, the latter title may have been a gloss on the original will, the copy not appearing in the registers until 1420, some years after Bruges's promotion to that position. He was certainly Garter by 13 September 1417 and probably promoted before the king's departure for France in late July. It was the first time a king of arms had been specifically appointed for the service of an order of chivalry and by virtue of his title held permanent authority over the provincial kings. No letters patent were issued and the new office was not at first endowed, though Bruges did later receive *ad hoc* payments.

Bruges's appointment as the first Garter king of arms coincided with a series of moves to regulate heraldic matters, some of which he may well have initiated himself. In June 1417 the king clamped down on the unauthorized wearing of coat armour. In September the duke of Clar-

William Bruges (*c*.1375–1450), manuscript illumination, *c*.1430 [kneeling, right]

ence ruled on matters of precedence between the heralds and the serjeants-at-arms, and later that month he laid down orders for the fees for heralds on the display of banners. Some time before 1420 Bruges petitioned Henry to establish certain rights and privileges for his new office and for the office of arms in general. In January 1421 the English heralds held their first chapter and directed that a common seal for that office be made. Resolutions were to govern the office of arms and its members, with chapters summoned by Garter. Bruges must have given much thought to the organization and management of the office. In the same year, as part of Henry's revival of the Order of the Garter, some statutes of the order were revised and at about the same time many heraldic stall plates of former companions were set up in St George's Chapel, Windsor. Both tasks would have involved Bruges, and it is very probable that his research for the latter was included in his 'Garter book', produced about 1430—the earliest known armorial of the order.

In 1421 Bruges took part in the coronation of Queen Catherine, and in the following year he officiated at Henry V's funeral. Under Henry VI there was scarcely a year in which he was not sent on at least one mission, sometimes staying abroad for many months. He was usually concerned with France, but he also visited Normandy and Brittany, Flanders, Hainault and Holland, Scotland, Spain, Portugal, and Italy. Sometimes he was the senior or sole member of the mission.

Bruges lived from at least 1416 until his death on 9 March 1450 in sizeable property in Kentish Town. He was buried in St George's Church, Stamford. He had married, before 1415, Agnes (possibly Haddon). They had three daughters, one of whom, Katherine, married John Smert, Bruges's successor as Garter.   ADRIAN AILES

Sources H. Stanford London, *The life of William Bruges, the first Garter king of arms*, ed. A. Wagner, 2 vols. in 1, Harleian Society, 111–12 (1970) · W. H. Godfrey, A. Wagner, and H. Stanford London, *The College of Arms, Queen Victoria Street* (1963) · A. Wagner, *Heralds of England: a history of the office and College of Arms* (1967) · J. Anstis, ed., *The register of the most noble order of the Garter*, 2 vols. (1724) · A. R. Wagner, *A catalogue of English mediaeval rolls of arms*, Harleian Society, 100 (1950) · F. Taylor and J. S. Roskell, eds. and trans., *Gesta Henrici quinti / The deeds of Henry the Fifth*, OMT (1975) · N. H. Nicolas, ed., *Proceedings and ordinances of the privy council of England*, 7 vols., RC, 26 (1834–7), vol. 2 · J. Ferguson, *English diplomacy, 1422–1461* (1972) · C. E. Wright, *English heraldic manuscripts in the British Museum* (1973) · R. Marks and A. Payne, eds., *British heraldry from its origins to c.1800* (1978) · *Chancery records* · Coll. Arms, MSS SML 64, 246 · P. J. Begent, 'The creation of the office of Garter king of arms', *Coat of Arms*, new ser., 11/172 (1995), 134–40 · A. Ailes, 'The creation of the office of Garter king of arms: a postscript', *Coat of Arms*, new ser., 11/182 (1998), 239–40
Archives BL, Stowe MS 594 · Coll. Arms, MSS SML 64, 246 | Drapers' Company, London, grant of arms to the Drapers' Company
Likenesses manuscript illumination, *c.*1430, BL, Bruges's Garter book, Stowe MS 594, fol. 5*v* [*see illus.*] · manuscript illumination, before 1450, Bodl. Oxf., Ashmole MS 764, fol. 1
Wealth at death £120 p.a.; owned sizeable property in Kentish Town, generous benefactions to St George's Church, Stamford: London, *Life of William Bruges*

Brugha, Cathal [*formerly* Charles William St John Burgess] (1874–1922), president of Dáil Éireann, was born on 18 July 1874 at 13 Richmond Avenue, Dublin, one of fourteen children born to Thomas Burgess (1827–1899), an importer of works of art, and his wife, Marianne, *née* Flynn. He was educated at Colmcille School and at Belvedere College (1888–90). In 1909 he became a partner in the Lalor brothers' company, which provided altar candles for churches. Influenced by the Irish-Ireland movement, he changed his name to Cathal Brugha.

Brugha joined the Keating branch of the Gaelic League in 1906. The branch was often in conflict with Patrick Pearse and the Gaelic League executive, culminating in an extraordinary Ard Fheis (National Convention) on 9 June 1908. Brugha became president of the branch on 30 October 1909. The separatist attitude of the branch became more pronounced as Brugha was also a member of the Irish Republican Brotherhood (IRB), and the Easter rising was planned from its headquarters at 46 Parnell Square, Dublin.

Brugha joined the Irish Volunteers on their foundation in 1913, and was in charge of the advance party of volunteers at Howth on 26 July 1914, which received rifles from the yacht *Asgard*. When the Easter rising broke out on 24 April 1916 Brugha acted as vice-commandant of the 4th battalion of the Dublin brigade at the South Dublin Union. Having fought bravely and suffered many wounds, he was treated in several hospitals. He was discharged

soon after hearing that the internment order on him had been revoked on 23 August.

Brugha was resolved to fight on for the Irish republic, and he encouraged the first moves to revive the volunteers at the end of 1916. He was opposed to the restoration of the IRB. He also played a central role in the reshaping of nationalist politics after 1916, aligning himself with Count Plunkett and his stand for the ideals of the Easter rising.

After a nationalist convention at the Mansion House on 19 April 1917 Brugha served on various committees which prepared the way for the Sinn Féin convention on 25–26 October 1917. He was largely responsible for article 2 of the constitution, which stated that 'Sinn Fein aims at securing the International recognition of Ireland as an independent Irish Republic'. Eamon de Valera was elected president, and Brugha was elected to the executive with 688 votes, a number exceeded only by Eoin MacNeill.

At the volunteer convention on 27 October de Valera was appointed president of the national executive, and Brugha was elected as chairman of the resident executive. He presided over the meeting which elected Richard Mulcahy as chief of staff in 1918, and he himself made plans to assassinate members of the British cabinet during the conscription crisis. In the election of December 1918 Brugha was elected as the Sinn Féin member for Waterford.

Brugha was elected speaker of Dáil Éireann at its first meeting on 21 January 1919, and he read out the Declaration of Independence in Irish, which ratified 'the establishment of the Irish Republic'. On the following day, 22 January, he was appointed president of the ministry *pro tempore*. He retained this position until 1 April 1919, when de Valera took his place.

In de Valera's ministry Brugha was appointed minister of defence. He brought the army under the control of the Dáil by successfully proposing, on 20 August 1919, that the volunteers should take an oath of allegiance to Dáil Éireann. This was an important step in making the volunteers the Irish Republican Army.

Brugha co-operated with Mulcahy, chief of staff, during the War of Independence, but both before and after the treaty negotiations, which began on 11 October 1921, serious differences appeared. The influence of the IRB in the army was central to this antipathy. Matters came to a head at a cabinet meeting on 25 November 1921, when Brugha reconfirmed the general headquarters staff in their positions, but secured the resolution that 'the supreme body directing the Army is the Cabinet'.

Throughout the peace negotiations Brugha participated regularly in the cabinet meetings. When faced by the British articles of agreement on 3 December 1921, he agreed with de Valera that the terms should be rejected and that the policy of 'external association' should be reaffirmed. After the signing of the articles by Griffith and Collins on 6 December Brugha spoke and voted against the treaty but was among the minority of three to four in cabinet on 8 December, and of fifty-seven to sixty-four in Dáil Éireann on 7 January 1922. In the new ministry of

Griffith, he was replaced as minister of defence by Mulcahy on 9 January 1922.

Acute differences appeared between Brugha and Michael Collins during the treaty debates. The origin of these difficulties lay in the decision of Collins to sustain the IRB as a parallel organization to Dáil Éireann, with inevitable conflicts over the lawful chain of military command and of allegiance to the Dáil. However, Brugha's bitter speech on 7 January 1922 against Collins was provoked particularly by an editorial in the *Freeman's Journal* of 5 January. This editorial recommended a vote for the treaty and for Collins, the man who had won the war and who had £10,000 on his head. Brugha denied both the primacy of Collins in the conduct of the war, and the £10,000 reward on his head (on both counts he was proved correct). The severity of Brugha's attack was inspired, in large part, by his belief that British influences were using the popularity of Collins to undermine the anti-treaty position in the days before the vote on the treaty. On this matter he was again proved correct. It is now known that Andy Cope, an official at Dublin Castle, was in close contact with Martin Fitzgerald, editor of the *Freeman's Journal*.

Brugha campaigned strongly against the treaty, once it had been passed, but attempted to preserve unity, even in the army, by securing a republican dimension in the Free State constitution. With this intention he supported the pact on 20 May between de Valera and Collins, but its rejection by Collins, after pressure from Lloyd George, led to a divisive election on 16 June 1922.

Although Brugha was re-elected for his constituency, redrawn as Waterford and Tipperary East since 1921, the anti-treaty side had a minority of seats, thirty-six to fifty-eight. Brugha still worked for unity, and it was only after the Free State forces had attacked the Four Courts, on 28 June, that he reported back for active duty in the army. He was wounded in an action at the Granville Hotel, near O'Connell Street, Dublin, and died in the Mater Hospital on 7 July 1922. He was buried in Glasnevin cemetery two days later.

Brugha had married Cathleen Kingston (1879–1959) on 8 February 1912, and she was left to care for six young children on his death. She succeeded him as Sinn Féin representative for Waterford in 1923 and 1927, and continued to embody his ideals. These ideals were described, in a legal judgment on Sinn Féin in 1948, as 'transcendental', a fitting description of the timeless qualities that are part of the republican legacy of Cathal Brugha.

BRIAN P. MURPHY

Sources *Minutes of the proceedings of the first parliament of the Republic of Ireland, 1919–1921*, Dáil Éireann (1921) · *Official report for the period 16–26 August 1921, and 28 February to 8 June 1922*, Dáil Éireann (1922) · *Debate on the treaty between Great Britain and Ireland signed in London on 6 December 1921*, Dáil Éireann (1922) · J. J. O'Kelly [Sceilg], *A trinity of martyrs* (Dublin, [1947]) · F. O'Donoghue, *Cathal Brugha: Anniversary brochure, 1922–1972* (1966) · B. P. Murphy, *Patrick Pearse and the lost republican ideal* (1991) · S. Ua Ceallaigh, *Cathal Brugha* (1942) · T. Ó Dochartaigh, *Cathal Brugha a shaol is a thréithe* (1969) · ministerial career (DE 2/369) and 1916 internees (14698/16), NA Ire. · personal file, PRO, WO 35/206 · University College, Dublin, Mulcahy MSS · M. Valiulis, *Portrait of a revolutionary: General Richard Mulcahy and the founding of the Irish Free State* (1992) · private information (2004) · b. cert. · m. cert.
Archives NA Ire., ministerial career and 1916 internees, DE 2/369; 14698/16 · PRO, personal file, WO 35/206 | NL Ire., McGarrity MSS · NL Ire., William O'Brien MSS · NL Ire., Stack MSS · University College, Dublin, Mulcahy MSS | FILM BFI NFTVA, news footage
Likenesses O. Sheppard, bronze bust, 1939, NG Ire. · D. Hone, portrait, Cathal Brugha Barracks, Dublin, Ireland, Officers' mess · J. Kelly, portrait, Dáil Éireann, Dublin, Ireland · A. Power, death mask, National Museum of Ireland, Dublin

Brugis, Thomas (*b.* in or before **1620**, *d.* in or after **1651**), surgeon, was probably born no later than 1620, since he practised for seven years as a surgeon during the civil war. He does not record on which side he served, though his *Vade mecum, or, A Companion for a Chyrurgion* (1651) is dedicated to William Cavendish, third earl of Devonshire, who had been a prominent royalist. Brugis's medical qualifications are obscure. He styles himself 'doctor in physick' on the title page of the *Vade mecum*, which is written from Rickmansworth, Hertfordshire, where he both lived and practised. On a later page he acknowledges his 'ever honoured master Dr Riolan', Galenist and anatomist, who taught at the University of Paris (Brugis, *Vade mecum*, 406). This, and passing respectful references to James Primrose (1600–1659), suggest that Brugis may have been a younger contemporary of Primrose, both of them students of Riolan at Paris. Both Riolan and Primrose were critics of William Harvey.

Brugis is probably the author of a satirical 36-page work: *The discovery of a projector, shewing the beginning, progress, and end of the projector and his projects* (1641). Many projects became the consumer industries of the seventeenth and eighteenth centuries, such as those which involved leather working, textile weaving, or wood and madder growing for dyes. Other ventures failed. Brugis took a traditionalist view of the grander schemes formulated by projectors drawn from among lawyers, merchants, mongers, craftsmen, and foreigners, who were half-dreamers, half-technocrats, 'begotten on a fair faggot pile between the man in the Moone and Tom Lancaster's Laundresse'. 'Their curse was to try and apply their theories in practice prematurely and thus bring themselves and others to disaster' (Wilson, 7). Brugis's attitude to medicine is similarly conservative: 'thou mayest cure any wound … without any new devices which many use' (Brugis, *Vade mecum*, preface).

Brugis's first medical book, *The Marrow of Physicke* (1640), is a handbook in Galenic tradition; it was reprinted in 1669. The *Vade mecum* proved more popular. It ran to seven editions, though neither book contains anything original, as the author admits. Of minor note in the *Vade mecum* is a small contribution to forensic medicine in the shape of rules for the reports which a surgeon might have to make before a coroner's inquest. It is, with due acknowledgement, a précis of part of Ambroise Paré's 'Rapports et du moyen d'embaumer les corps morts', translated into English by Thomas Johnson as part of Paré's *Works* in 1634.

This section of the *Vade mecum* had disappeared by its seventh edition in 1689, which was amended and augmented by Ellis Prat. There is nothing to indicate whether Brugis was still alive at that date.   JENNY WARD

Sources T. Brugis, *Vade mecum, or, A companion for a chyrurgion*, 2nd edn (1653) • T. Brugis, *The marrow of physicke* (1640) • *DNB* • 'Cavendish, William, third earl of Devonshire', *DNB* • C. Wilson, *England's apprenticeship, 1603–1763* (1965) • J. Thirsk, *Economic policy and projects: the development of a consumer society in early modern England*, another edn (1988)
Likenesses T. Cross, line engraving, 1652, Wellcome L. • T. Cross, group portrait, line engraving, BM, NPG, V&A; repro. in T. Brugis, *Vade mecum or, A companion for a chirurgion*, 3rd edn (1657) • engraving, repro. in T. Brugis, *Vade mecum or, A companion for a chirurgion*, 7th edn (1689), frontispiece

Brühl, John Maurice [Hans Moritz], **Count von Brühl** (1736–1809), diplomatist and patron of science, was born on 20 December 1736 at Wiederau, north-west of Dresden, the son of Friedrich Wilhelm, Count von Brühl (1699–1760), of Martinskirche, in Saxony. His younger brother Heinrich was the well-known Brühl of Carlyle's *Frederick the Great*, whose vanity Carlyle so despised. Hans Moritz matriculated on 1 June 1750 from Leipzig University and studied under Christian Fürchtegott Gellert, with whom he corresponded for many years thereafter. He spent two years at Paris before embarking on a diplomatic career, being dispatched to Warsaw in 1759–60, and possibly returning to Paris before arriving in London in 1764 as minister-plenipotentiary from the elector of Saxony. Already addressed as Count von Brühl from before the time of his father's death in 1760, he was proposed as a fellow of the Royal Society by four eminent members of the Académie des Sciences plus Ferdinand Berthoud, chronometer maker, and with further English support was elected. He seldom visited Saxony thereafter, probably because Prussian troops burnt Martinskirche during the Seven Years' War and ransacked the family's Dresden house. Brühl's only non-scientific publication, *Recherches sur divers objets de l'économie politique*, published in Dresden in 1781, treated matters of commerce in a fairly impersonal style without criticizing the laws in his native or adopted countries. From 1788 he was on the Saxon privy council, and in February 1792 he was involved in the proposed commercial treaty between Great Britain and Saxony. On 9 May 1783 the Polish king Stanisław II August created him knight of the order of the White Eagle. In 1793 he was named associate of the Imperial Academy of Sciences of St Petersburg.

On 6 July 1767 Brühl married Alicia Maria, countess of Egremont (d. 1794), daughter of George, second Baron Carpenter of Killaghy, co. Kilkenny, and widow of Charles *Wyndham, second earl of Egremont, at whose death in 1763 she was left with a large family, a London house at 94 Piccadilly, and an estate at Petworth, in Sussex. In 1778 she was at Windsor as a lady-in-waiting to Queen Charlotte. For a short time Brühl had a country house at Blackheath; he subsequently acquired Harefield House, in the village of Harefield, Middlesex, and when Alicia died in May 1794 she was buried at Harefield. Their eldest son, George (1768–1856), lived a quiet life in England; there was also a

daughter, Harriet (b. 1772), who married Hugh Scott of Harden, later Lord Polwarth, and possibly another son, Ernest, who died young.

Soon after his arrival in England Brühl became acquainted with Thomas Mudge (1715/16–1794), a noted horologist and one of several people then working on the problems of constructing a precision sea-going watch, hoping for a substantial reward from the board of longitude. Brühl became a patron of Mudge. About 1770 he commissioned Nathaniel Dance to portray Mudge in oils, and when declining health obliged Mudge to retire to Plymouth, where his brother, a physician, was living, Brühl was able to get him appointed in 1776 watchmaker to the king, a post which carried a small pension. Franz Xaver von Zach (1754–1832), an Austrian who went to London in 1783 and became tutor to George Brühl, overreached himself by claiming in 1786 that Mudge's watches were so accurate that he, Zach, had discovered errors in the *Nautical Almanac*. He sent these allegations direct to the Revd Thomas Hornsby at Oxford, who was so impressed that he obtained an honorary doctor's degree for Zach. But when the tables were recalculated, the *Almanac* computers were vindicated, and when Hornsby proposed Zach as a fellow of the Royal Society he was blackballed. Meanwhile, in 1784 the Brühls spent the summer on the Egremont estate at Petworth, in Sussex. The Egremonts traced their ancestry from Henry Percy, ninth earl of Northumberland, who had been a patron of the mathematician Thomas Harriot, and at Petworth Brühl found the long-lost manuscripts of Harriot, untouched since 1632. He drew them to Zach's attention; Zach began immediately to publicize this discovery and in 1786 proposed to the delegates of Oxford University Press that he should write a life of Harriot and edit the manuscripts. He was allowed to take away some of the documents, but nothing was ever published and the manuscripts, hitherto preserved as a whole, were thereafter dispersed, causing untold despair to generations of Harriot enthusiasts. Zach took Mudge's chronometer on the continent, perhaps when he accompanied Brühl and his son in 1785–6 as they made a circuit of Brussels, Frankfurt, Dresden, and Paris to ascertain latitudes and longitudes; Zach also took the chronometer on a sea voyage from Hyères to Genoa, after which it was returned to Brühl, who took up Mudge's cause with vigour in his disputes with the board in general and with Maskelyne in particular. In 1786 Brühl recommended Zach to his friend Duke Ernst of Saxe-Gotha-Altenburg, who needed an astronomer for his new observatory at Seeberg, and after organizing the provision of apparatus, he departed from Brühl's employ in 1788.

In his support of Mudge, Brühl made full use of his contacts inside and outside parliament, and in 1793 a select committee of the House of Commons awarded Mudge a further £3000. Brühl owned several fine watches by Mudge and Emery, and, by reference to his own astronomical observations, kept accurate records of their going. His published records (*Three Registers of a Pocket Chronometer*, 1785; *Latitudes and Longitudes of Several Places Ascertained*, 1786; *A Register of Mr Mudge's Timekeepers*, 1794; and various translations) helped to support Mudge's claims. The letters from Mudge to Brühl written between the years 1772 and 1787 were published by Mudge's lawyer son, also Thomas Mudge, in *A Description … of the Time-Keeper Invented by the Late Mr Thomas Mudge* (1799). Brühl also owned two orreries, probably also made by Mudge.

Brühl's interest in astronomy was part and parcel of his concern for accurate timekeeping. About 1787 he constructed a small observatory, probably on the flat roof of Harefield House. He was conveniently situated within easy reach of several other passionate amateur astronomers, notably Alexander Aubert in Highbury and William Herschel at Slough. He was also a familiar visitor to the important observatories of Greenwich and Blenheim. Among his own notable instruments was the 2 foot astronomical circle which he purchased from Edward Troughton, who erected it at Harefield in July 1793. Brühl commented that it bore the stamp of originality and exquisite workmanship, and although he made but few observations with it, they exceeded in accuracy any that had been made hitherto.

When Brühl had been in Brussels in 1786, he had met the Italian astronomer Barnaba Oriani, *en route* from his observatory at Milan to England where he proposed to buy various instruments. When Oriani arrived in England, he was regularly invited to dine with Brühl, and was escorted, with Ernst, duke of Saxe-Gotha-Altenburg, who was also on a buying visit for his Seeberg observatory, to Aubert's and Herschel's observatories and those at Greenwich, Oxford, and Mount Edgecumbe. Brühl's wife made drawings of clockwork which Oriani took back for his own mechanic to make up. The Hungarian Baron Vay de Vaja was also escorted round the observatory circuit; in May 1787 Sir Henry Englefield, Aubert, and Brühl visited Herschel to see the great reflecting telescopes that were so much admired throughout Europe. Brühl, on the other hand, was unimpressed by Herschel's claims to have seen volcanoes on the moon and sought to query this identification, without giving offence. In 1793 Brühl received one of the five Herschel 10 foot reflecting telescopes ordered by George III as gifts for his friends. (It was later sent to Dresden, where it was destroyed during the Second World War.) He acted as agent for several continental astronomers wishing to purchase apparatus from the London workshops of Troughton and Jesse Ramsden, and his tussles with the notoriously slow Ramsden are vividly recounted in his correspondence with Duke Ernst now in the National Archives of Scotland.

A second marriage on 24 November 1796 to Maria (d. 1835), daughter of Thomas Chowne of Alfriston, Sussex, may have coincided with Brühl's move from his London house at 34 Dover Street to 20 Cumberland Place or with his move in the same year to 33 Old Burlington Street, Westminster. In the autumn of 1789 he injured his leg and was lame for some weeks; in the summer of 1799 he was 'banished' to Rottingdean—'a very bleak spot'—for his health, but on 15 July was on his way home 'without having acomplished the purpose of my banishment' (Herschel MSS B154 and B158). This may not have been his only

ailment, as a letter to Herschel on 3 October 1800 refers to 'this awful scrawl of an almost blind writer' (Herschel MS B160). In 1802 Zach, who by this time had moved to the Seeberg observatory, commented in a letter to Sir Joseph Banks that communication with Brühl had ceased since his illness. Brühl's collection of instruments, including the Troughton circle and a Troughton barometer and sextant, was given to the Leipzig observatory, where it arrived on 9 July 1803. Another circle, made by Cary, went to the Seeberg observatory. Brühl died on 22 January 1809 and was buried at Harefield church. ANITA McCONNELL

Sources M. T. Baillie, *What I have been told concerning my great-grandmother and my great-grandfather* (1900) · B. Oriani, 'Del cronometrio ossia oriuolo di S. E. il sig. conte di Bruhl', *Opuscoli scelti sulle scienze e sulle arte*, 11 (1788) · A. Mandrino, G. Tagliaferri, and P. Tucci, eds., *Un viaggio in Europa nel 1786* (1994) · correspondence with William Herschel, RAS, Herschel MSS, W1/B137–161 · Brühl corresp. and papers, NA Scot., GD 157, 3284–3471 · *GM*, 1st ser., 42 (1772), 434; 66 (1796), 966; 79 (1809), 186 · *The scientific papers of Sir William Herschel*, ed. J. L. E. Dreyer, 1 (1912), l–li · Farington, *Diary*, 2.335–7, 532; 3.776 · D. Penney, 'Thomas Mudge and the longitude: a reason to excel', *The quest for longitude*, ed. W. A. H. Andrewes (1996), 294–310 · *C. F. Gellert's Briefwechsel*, ed. J. F. Reynolds, 4 vols. (1983–96), vols. 1–3 · J. G. Meusel, *Das gelehrte Teutschland*, ed. G. C. Hamburger, 5th edn, 17 vols. (1796), 1.457 · D. Lysons, *Middlesex parishes* (1800), 124 · DNB
Archives NA Scot., corresp. and papers, GD 157, 3284–3471 | RAS, letters to William Herschel, W1/B137–161
Likenesses J. Northcote, oils, Petworth House, West Sussex

Brummell, George Bryan [*known as* Beau Brummell] (**1778–1840**), dandy and socialite, was born on 7 June 1778 in Downing Street, Westminster, the last of three children of William Brummell (d. 1794), private secretary to the prime minister, Lord North, and his wife, Miss Richardson (d. 1793), daughter of the keeper of the lottery office. George, known in adult life as Beau Brummell, was baptized on 2 July 1778 at St Margaret's, Westminster, and spent his childhood at the family home, The Grove, Donnington, Berkshire, which had been bought by his father in 1782. The purchase of The Grove signified the upward mobility of the Brummell family during the third quarter of the eighteenth century. This improvement in fortunes owed much to the lucrative offices bestowed on William Brummell while he was serving as North's secretary. William's desire to provide for his family also extended to his sons' schooling. In 1786 George was sent to Eton College and, though he later eschewed learning, he was initially a talented student, proving particularly accomplished in the writing of Latin verse. He was also popular among fellow students for his wit, refinement, and a fascination with matters of dress and poise which defined his adult life and, as a schoolboy, earned him the sobriquet Buck Brummell. In his early life there also appears to have been a degree of compassion to others; finding himself among a group of boys intent on throwing a boatman into the Thames, for example, he is reported to have requested that the man be spared since it was 'a certainty that he will catch cold'. Such sensitivities were later abandoned in the competition of fashionable London society. George left

George Bryan Brummell [Beau Brummell] (**1778–1840**), by R. Dighton, 1805

Eton in 1793 and entered Oriel College, Oxford, in May of the following year. His university career was brief: Brummell left after one term having received about £20,000 from his father's estate following William's death in March 1794. His principal achievement while at Oxford was to perfect the 'cut', the English art of ignoring people though conscious of their presence; Brummell's favoured targets were former schoolfriends whom he considered students at inferior colleges.

While at Eton, Brummell had become a regular guest at society balls organized by members of the whig élite centred on Carlton House. It was through his attendance at these functions that, aged sixteen, he met George, prince of Wales, who in May 1794 offered him a cornetcy in his personal regiment, the 10th hussars. Brummell's duties required him to accompany the prince at numerous social engagements which dominated the life of the regiment. In April 1795 he attended the prince at his marriage to Caroline of Brunswick, and in the following year he was promoted captain, a rank which he held until leaving the army in 1798. Brummell, in truth, was never destined to be a soldier, nor indeed anything that required effort or the subordination of an inflated personality dedicated to the pursuit of elegance. His departure from the regiment is said to have been precipitated by an order to garrison in Manchester, a location which the beau considered beneath his dignity.

Brummell's retirement from the army also coincided

with his coming of age and his acceptance of an inheritance of about £30,000. With his new wealth he established himself as a leading member of London society. He moved to 4 Chesterfield Street, Mayfair, where he entertained the friends—including the prince of Wales, the duke and duchess of York, and Lord Alvaney—he had made while at Eton and in the army. The years between Brummell's move to Chesterfield Street and his departure from England in 1816 witnessed the apogee of the fashion for dandyism of which Brummell was the leading exponent. The culture was characterized by its reaction against the excessive dress and manners of eighteenth-century men of fashion whose gentility had been defined by the magnificence and luxury of clothing and the fineness or delicacy of conversation. Dandyism, by contrast, drew on earlier English qualities—independence, self-command, capriciousness, and a hint of puritanism—to offer a rival style based on meticulous but simple tailoring and imperious, and therefore often impolite, displays of mannered etiquette.

Brummell's dress set the standard for his acolytes who included members of the aristocracy and the prince of Wales. Day wear included plain Hessian boots, the new pantaloons, a blue coat, and a buff waistcoat then favoured by supporters of whig politics (in which Brummell showed token interest); for evening engagements he favoured a blue coat, white waistcoat, trim black pantaloons buttoned to the ankle, and striped silk stockings. Not surprisingly, Brummell's appearance gave rise to some wonderful, but unproven, anecdotes concerning his efforts to achieve such a nonchalant air: some, for example, said that the fingers of his gloves were made by different, specialist glovers; others that his boots were washed in champagne. The epitome of the Brummell style was the highly, though never excessively, starched cravat which was precisely tied to obscure the throat and raise the head, the desired effect being superiority, simple elegance, and rigorous self-possession. Such qualities were also evident in Brummell's manners which, centred on the dos and don'ts of fashionable society, were invariably snobbish, competitive, and for public entertainment. His place among the dandies was sufficiently secure for him to criticize not just his social inferiors and equals but also titled acquaintances including the duke of Bedford ('Bedford, do you call this thing a coat?') or his own brother William who, during a visit, was kept from view until his new wardrobe arrived. Famed at the time for his wit, the majority of his sayings are today remarkable only for a sourness and dullness characteristic of dated camp.

Brummell's not inconsiderable self-confidence, bolstered by his celebrity, now brought him into conflict with his patron, the prince of Wales. George had himself aped dandy fashions, though it was evident that his predilection was always for self-indulgence and excess rather than for Brummell's strictly defined and regulated concept of elegance. As the prince grew ever more corpulent, and thus increasingly at odds with the trimness of dandyism, he became a target for Brummell's wit, being dubbed Big Ben after an overly large porter then working at Carlton

House. The prince's mistress Mrs Fitzherbert became Benina, an affront which led to a final quarrel and the breaking off of relations in 1811. For Brummell, for whom style was the key to life, the prince's place in the social order counted for nothing: I made him and therefore shall break him, he was reported to have said at the end of their friendship. There followed several bitter exchanges which culminated in an immaculate and justly celebrated put-down. Promenading with Lord Moira in St James Street, Brummell had encountered the prince who greeted Moira but ignored his companion. 'Pray who is your fat friend?' asked Brummell in a sufficiently loud voice on resuming their walk.

As he predicted, Brummell's split with George, now prince regent, failed to undermine his reputation as a socialite. In 1812 he moved to 13 Chapel Street (later Aldford Street), where he established a new locus of fashionable society centred on the duke and duchess of York, and from where he organized a celebrated fête at the Argyll Rooms in July of the following year. Such entertainments demanded an income exceeding his inheritance and, opposed to employment, he turned to the gaming tables which formed a central part of London's club society. Brummell had mixed fortunes as a gambler. He was said in 1813 to have won £26,000 at one card game, and a further £30,000 from betting on horse races. But in the following year he lost 'an unfortunate £10,000'—his last—and was effectively ruined and later denounced by fellow members of White's Club. It was most likely his desperate financial situation which prompted him to leave England on 16 May 1816 when, after attending the opera and dining as usual, he departed London for Dover and from there sailed to Calais.

Brummell remained in France for the rest of his life, staying until 1830 in Calais, where he rented rooms at the rue Royale. During this period he is known to have returned to England on at least one occasion in July 1822 to negotiate (unsuccessfully) the publication of his *History of Male and Female Costume from Ancient Greece to Modern Times* (it eventually appeared in 1932). During the 1820s Brummell's lifestyle followed a similar, if somewhat reduced, pattern to that in London, for which he was dubbed the King of Calais. Visitors in this period included Lord Alvaney, though a visit to the town by the prince regent, now George IV, did not produce a reconciliation. Increasingly, however, Brummell was losing touch with the high London society in which he had fashioned his reputation and which had once sought his favour. Without money and standing he was now cast less as the innovative arbiter of elegance than a dated upstart from an era preoccupied with the trivialities of fashion.

The late 1820s saw Brummell involved in further financial difficulties. It was a result of this situation that he finally resorted to work, accepting the office of consul for the department of Calvados. He entered his new position, which was located at Caen, in September 1830, where he took up residency at the Hôtel d'Angleterre. But, as at Oxford, his term as consul was short. Never committed to his new lifestyle he was dismissed in March 1832 having complained about the insignificance of the post. Unemployment exacerbated the problems he had in repaying existing debts. In April 1835 he was arrested and gaoled for failing to repay an outstanding sum of 15,000 francs. During his four-month imprisonment he continued to display the fastidiousness and snobbery which had made him famous. In reality Brummell, who by 1835 had suffered three strokes, was no longer able to maintain his once meticulous appearance and conduct. Reduced to living on handouts from the shopkeepers of Caen, he was moved in May 1839 to the local Bon Sauveur asylum, where he died, aged sixty-two, on 30 March 1840. He was buried in the town's protestant cemetery.

To his early biographers Brummell was a figure from a lost age, though opinion differed as to the lessons to be drawn from his rise and fall. Captain William Jesse's *The Life of Beau Brummell* (1844) cast its subject as the epitome of a hedonistic and irresponsible society and equated Brummell's decline as an eloquent warning on the dangers of imitation. By contrast, in *Du dandyism et de George Brummell* (1845) Jules Barbey d'Aurevilly passed over Brummell's ruin (despite having met his subject during the final years at Caen) in favour of a celebration of the essentially English dandy culture he inspired. To Barbey, Brummell was 'Dandyism incarnate' being possessed of a 'God given elegance' (pp. 77, 82). Praised in his lifetime by the likes of Lord Byron (who claimed he would rather be a Brummell than a Bonaparte), he was later celebrated by Baudelaire and Oscar Wilde. Subsequent popular memoirs have, like Barbey's, looked sympathetically on a man who combined snobbery with nonconformity in an elegant world, extravagantly portrayed in the 1954 film *Beau Brummell* with Stewart Granger in the title role. More recent academic studies (Moers, 1960), while acknowledging Brummell's success as intimately linked with Regency manners, have located him within a longer nineteenth- and early twentieth-century history of European dandyism and male aestheticism. For Walden (2002) the capriciousness and popularity of Brummell has found new life as the studied 'cool' of an albeit democratic celebrity culture. Among older generations Brummell's legacy is also evident in the ever-useful 'cut' and in the now classic equation of elegant male dress with a precision and control epitomized by the dinner jacket.   PHILIP CARTER

Sources H. Cole, *Beau Brummell* (1977) · K. Campbell, *Beau Brummell* (1948) · W. Jesse, *Life of Beau Brummell*, 2 vols. (1844) · *GM*, 1st ser., 64 (1794), 285 · W. Connely, *Beau Brummell* (1940) · E. Moers, *The dandy: Brummell to Beerbohm* (1960) · A. Ribeiro, *The art of dress* (1995) · *Blackwood* (June 1844) · J. Barbey d'Aurevilly, *On dandyism and Beau Brummell*, trans. G. Walden (2002) · G. Walden, *Who's a dandy?* (2002) · *DNB*
Likenesses J. Reynolds, oils, 1781–2, Kenwood House, London · R. Dighton, pencil and watercolour, 1800, repro. in Ribeiro, *The art of dress* · R. Dighton, engraving, 1805; Christies, 21 March 1989, lot 79 [*see illus.*] · pencil, 1835?, repro. in Cole, *Beau Brummell* · J. Cook, line engraving, pubd 1844 (after miniature), BM, NPG; repro. in Jesse, *Life* · I. Sedlecka, statue, 2002, Piccadilly Arcade, Jermyn Street, London · R. H. Cole, etching, NPG · J. Cook, miniature, BM
Wealth at death imprisoned for debt; died in poverty

Brundish, John Jelland (1750/51–1786), poet and school-master, the elder son of the Revd John Brundish, clerk of Bury St Edmunds, Suffolk, was born at Northwold, Norfolk. He was educated at Bury St Edmunds, and at seventeen entered Gonville and Caius College, Cambridge, as a sizar on 4 July 1768. He matriculated in the Michaelmas term 1769, by which time his father had become rector of Great Cressingham, Norfolk. His brother, Benjamin, was admitted to Caius in the following year. Brundish developed into an accomplished scholar. He was senior wrangler, senior classical medallist, and first Smith's prizeman in 1773, the year he graduated BA. He obtained a curacy in his father's parish in 1774, and was ordained deacon in Norwich on 12 June. He proceeded MA and was elected to a fellowship at Caius in 1776, becoming chaplain in the same year, and subsequently holding various other college appointments. He was taxor, and moderator to the university in 1777. Benjamin also was elected to a fellowship of Caius in 1777, and he died in college on 21 June 1779. Brundish was ordained priest in Peterborough on 17 December 1780, and he was appointed master of the Perse School in Cambridge, by trustees resident in Caius, between 1781 and 1782. His tenure coincided with a sharp decline in the school's fortunes, and in 1785 the school had no pupils at all.

Brundish's sole printed contribution to literature, *An Elegy on a Family-Tomb*, was first published anonymously in Cambridge in 1782 and subsequently republished in 1783 with an accompanying Italian metrical translation by his friend J. B. Seale of Christ's College, Cambridge. The *Elegy* mourns the deaths, in quick succession, of a parent, his sister Mary, or Maria, and his brother, Benjamin. The loss of these near relatives, within a short space, is said to have marked his personality with a melancholy cast. The *Elegy*'s concluding allusion to 'Arria', a female name associated with the virtues of constancy and magnanimity by Pliny and Martial, might imply that Brundish had also suffered a frustrated romantic attachment. The inscription of 'Miss Wale' in a contemporary, or near-contemporary, hand in the margin of a copy of the *Elegy* preserved in the British Library (11632.e.27) perhaps identifies the object of Brundish's affections. In any event, he remained unmarried at his death, which, as in the case of his brother, occurred in college, on 28 February 1786. In the month preceding his death, the *Elegy* was reprinted in the *European Magazine and London Review*. There is a family memorial inscription in the parish church of St Michael's, Didlington, Norfolk.   JAMES WILLIAM KELLY

Sources BL, Add. MS 19166, fol. 205 • J. J. B. [J. J. Brundish], *An elegy on a family-tomb* (1782) [signed copy, Gon. & Caius Cam., C.13.16] • [J. J. Brundish and J. B. Seale], *An elegy on a family-tomb, translated into Italian verse by a friend of the author* (1783) • D. Jones, *A vision realised: a history of the Perse and its move from Gonville Place to Hills Road forty years ago* (2001) • *Cantabrigiensis graduati; sive catalogus, exhibens nomina eorum, quos, ab anno 1659, usque ad annum 1787* (1787), 59 • Venn, *Alum. Cant.* • J. Venn, *The register of baptisms, marriages, and burials in St Michael's parish, Cambridge, 1538–1837* (1891) • *European Magazine and London Review*, 9 (Jan 1786), 49–50

Brundrett, Sir Frederick (1894–1974), government scientist, was born on 25 November 1894 at Sunny Bank, Ebbw Vale, Monmouthshire, the eldest in the family of seven sons and three daughters of Walter Brundrett, of Hinxhill, Kent, general secretary and accountant with the Ebbw Vale Steel, Iron, and Coal Company, and his wife, Ada, daughter of James Richardson, of Chorlton-cum-Hardy. He was educated at Rossall School, Fleetwood, Lancashire, and at Sidney Sussex College, Cambridge. He obtained a first class in part one of the mathematical tripos (1914) and was a wrangler in part two (1916). He then served in the Royal Naval Volunteer Reserve, joining the wireless branch in 1916. After demobilization in 1919 he joined the scientific staff of the Admiralty and was appointed to the Royal Naval Signal School. In 1920 Brundrett married Enid, daughter of George Richard James, schoolmaster, of Chesterton, Cambridgeshire. Their only child, a son, was killed in Italy in 1944. He remained at the signal school until 1937, when he was transferred to the headquarters of the Royal Naval Scientific Service in London and promoted to principal scientific officer. He became a superintending scientist in 1939, assistant director of scientific research in 1940, deputy director in 1942, and in 1946 succeeded Sir Charles Wright as chief of the Royal Naval Scientific Service. In 1950 he was appointed deputy scientific adviser to the minister of defence, serving first under Sir Henry Tizard and then under Sir John Cockcroft, whom he succeeded in 1954 as scientific adviser and chairman of the defence research policy committee.

During his service in the Royal Naval Volunteer Reserve Brundrett became engaged in research work on underwater communications with submarines. At the signal school he played a leading part in the development of short-wave radio. He would not, however, have claimed to have made a great contribution to fundamental scientific knowledge, and he once described himself as the worst circuit engineer who ever joined the Royal Naval Scientific Service. His great strength lay in his ability to apply scientific principles to the practical development of new types of equipment. He also showed a great talent for administrative work in the field of science and it was this that enabled him to play such an effective role, first as chief of the Royal Naval Scientific Service and later during his time at the Ministry of Defence. Before he became scientific adviser himself, he had taken an increasing share of the workload, especially after Tizard's retirement, when Cockcroft combined the position of scientific adviser with that of head of the Atomic Energy Research Establishment. He was thus well prepared and established when he himself succeeded in 1954.

In those days, before the absorption of the separate service departments and the Ministry of Supply into the Ministry of Defence, the scientific adviser's function lay in the co-ordination of policy towards scientific research and the development of new equipment for the armed forces. Brundrett fulfilled this with great skill. He won the confidence not only of successive ministers, but also of successive members of the chiefs of staff committee, who came to rely more and more upon his practical approach and valued his advice on problems ranging well beyond the strictly scientific. Much of the co-ordinating work was done in the defence research policy committee or in specially appointed working groups. Brundrett, being a shrewd judge of people, proved a masterly chairman.

In 1954 Brundrett became an honorary fellow of Sidney Sussex College. He was appointed CB in 1946, KBE in 1950, and KCB in 1956. He received an honorary DSc from Manchester in 1956. After his retirement from the Ministry of Defence in 1959, Brundrett undertook many other tasks in the public service. He was a civil service commissioner for seven years (1960–67), chairman of the Air Traffic Control Board, and chairman of the naval aircraft research committee of the Aeronautical Research Council (1960–66).

In appearance Brundrett was small and spare, with bright blue eyes and the air of an inquisitive bird. His approach was direct, his personality warm and outgoing, his interests wide, and, despite the controversies in which he inevitably became involved, he made no enemies. Throughout his life he was keenly interested in agriculture, and he was himself a very successful farmer. He was chairman of the council of the Red and White Friesian Cattle Society, and an authority on the management of contagious abortion in cattle. He became president of the Agricultural Co-operative Association and devoted much energy to the development of co-operative marketing for poultry and eggs. He was an enthusiastic and skilful player of ball games, excelling particularly in hockey, where he was captain of the Hampshire county and civil service teams. He also played cricket for the civil service, and was an eminent stamp collector. He lived latterly at Fieldside, Prinsted, Southbourne, Sussex. Brundrett died at Fieldside on 1 August 1974.   RICHARD POWELL, *rev.*

Sources *The Times* (6 Aug 1974) · *The Times* (12 Aug 1974) · personal knowledge (1986) · b. cert. · d. cert.
Archives CAC Cam., papers | CAC Cam., corresp. with Sir Edward Bullard
Likenesses W. Stoneman, photograph, 1954, NPG · W. Bird, photograph, 1965, NPG
Wealth at death £117,760: probate, 14 Feb 1975, *CGPLA Eng. & Wales*

Brunel, Sir (Marc) Isambard (1769–1849), civil engineer, was born on 25 April 1769 at Hacqueville on the direct road from Paris to Rouen in Normandy, where his family had farmed for more than three hundred years. He was the second son of Jean Charles Brunel and the second of his four wives, Marie Victoire Lefèvre. Brunel's parents intended him for the church and he was sent at the age of eight to school in Gisors to begin the appropriate studies. However, he showed aptitude in other areas—in drawing, model making, and a general interest in mechanical devices. At the age of eleven he was sent to the seminary of St Nicaise at Rouen whose principal, accepting that Brunel's talents lay elsewhere, helped his transfer to pupillage with the American consul in Rouen, François Carpentier, a retired sea captain, for training in hydrography and draughtsmanship in preparation for service in the French navy. In 1786 he was commissioned as *volontaire d'honneur* and sailed for the West Indies aboard the corvette *Le Maréchal de Castries* for six years' service,

Sir (Marc) Isambard Brunel (1769–1849), by James Northcote, 1812–13

throughout which he used an ebony quadrant he had made himself. The revolutionary terror was in full swing when he returned to Paris in 1792, and he left for Rouen, a sensible move in view of his royalist sympathies. There he met his future wife, Sophia, orphan daughter of William Kingdom, contracting agent for the navy and the army, who, despite the troubled times, had been sent to France to improve her knowledge of the language. From Rouen Brunel managed to obtain a passport for America, and sailed for New York on 7 July 1793.

Brunel's first venture in America, with two fellow French refugees, was to undertake a large land survey near Lake Ontario. Through a meeting with an American, Thurman, he was next commissioned to survey the line of a canal to link the Hudson River with Lake Champlain, and at this point he decided to become an engineer in preference to rejoining the French navy. His first major success was the winning design for a new congress building in Washington, which was, however, never built on grounds of cost. In a modified form and resembling the *Halle aux grains* in Paris it was built as the Park Theatre in New York, which was destroyed by fire in 1821. At the age of twenty-seven he was appointed chief engineer of New York, in which capacity his major achievements included a design for a new cannon factory and advice on the defences for the navigation channel between Long Island and Staten Island. Brunel's interest in Britain was kindled through Major-General Hamilton, then serving as a British diplomat in Washington, who gave him an introduction to Earl Spencer of Althorp, first lord of the Admiralty: he sailed from New York on 20 January 1799. Having arrived in Britain he married Sophia Kingdom on 1 November 1799. They had two daughters, Sophia and Emma, followed on 9 April 1806 by a son, Isambard Kingdom *Brunel. His wife supported him in all his work and in all his privations. He was never a rich man, suffered many misfortunes, and, towards the end of his life, depended on his son for financial support.

Once in Britain, Brunel used his connection with Earl Spencer to develop his interests in the design of ships' block-making machinery for the Royal Navy, making use of the remarkable skills of Henry Maudslay to manufacture the machines. After initial rebuffs, the designs attracted the attention of Sir Samuel Bentham, inspector-general of naval works and an accomplished engineer, who was already planning improvements in block making. The government adopted his proposals in 1803. By 1806, forty-three machines for executing different processes in making blocks were in use at Portsmouth Dockyard, with the claim that six men could thereby do the previous work of sixty, allowing annual savings in cost estimated at £24,000. He also worked on a pantograph for copying drawings and on a machine for winding cotton thread, but he omitted to secure a patent for this successful device, an omission he made more than once. Between 1805 and 1812 Brunel was increasingly engaged in designing wood-working machinery for government mills at Woolwich and elsewhere, subsequently investing in his own sawmills at Battersea. On observing the wretched state of the soldiers returning from Corunna, he persuaded the government to commission him to supply boots stitched by machine. Sales were not guaranteed, however, and peace in 1815 led to large unwanted stocks at his expense. His Battersea sawmills were largely destroyed by fire in 1814, an event which exposed the fact that his partner in the enterprise had failed to keep control of the finances. These circumstances contributed to his increasing financial problems, culminating in arrest for debt in 1821 and confinement in the king's bench prison (with the company of Sophia) until rescued by his patrons and friends who had secured an honorarium of £5000 from the government in recognition of the value of his past unrewarded services.

Brunel also designed a wide variety of machines for textile, printing, and several other industries. In 1812 he undertook experiments in steam navigation on the Thames, utilizing double-acting piston engines with paddle-driven propulsion. He demonstrated this capability to the navy, which in 1814 accepted his proposals for steam-driven tugs. In 1816, however, the Navy Board reneged, describing his scheme as 'too chimerical to be seriously entertained', and he was left to bear the costs of experiments. He returned to civil engineering by designing bridges and docks, including in due course Liverpool's first floating landing stage in 1826. In 1812, a scheme devised by him was undertaken at Chatham Dockyard, comprising a sawmill connected to a timber pond (the South Mast pond) by a short canal tunnel, with transport at the surface achieved by wide-gauge rail track. In 1820 he had prepared designs for a bridge over the Seine at Rouen

and for a timber bridge of 880 feet span across the Neva at St Petersburg, but neither project proceeded. His design for a 122 feet span bridge to withstand hurricanes for the French island of Bourbon was, however, manufactured, pre-erected, and tested in Britain, then shipped and built in the early 1820s.

While working at Chatham in 1816 Brunel observed the means whereby the mollusc *Teredo navalis* advanced itself by muscular action as it bored through ships' timbers. From this observation developed his initial ideas for a tunnelling shield. The first application was for an unadopted scheme for a carriage tunnel under the Neva at St Petersburg in 1818, and in the same year he applied for a patent in which he called one such a device a 'teredo or auger'. He understood that, to overcome problems being experienced at that time by unsuccessful efforts to tunnel beneath the Thames, it was necessary in such ground to provide continuous support to the working face and to the periphery of the tunnel ahead of any permanent lining by the use of a self-propelling device, not yet known as a tunnelling shield.

Proposals were being considered in the early 1820s for a tunnel beneath the Thames between Rotherhithe and Wapping, principally to connect the docks under construction to reduce theft from ships moored in the river. The project had attracted the patronage of the duke of Wellington, who also saw the consequential strategic benefits of a river crossing below London. Brunel proposed the use of his shield and was appointed as chief engineer. For this purpose he modified his original ideas for circular shields to a large rectangular form, comprising twelve frames each containing three cells set one above the other, the overall height related to the dimensions of the miner who had to occupy each cell. One important advantage of such an arrangement lay in the standardization of the many castings and machined components. He returned to Maudslay to supply the parts for this the first tunnelling shield. Each frame supported poling boards at the face by means of adjustable screws and was advanced separately, but always no more than a few inches ahead of its neighbour, by thrusting against the brickwork whose progress followed the shield. Overhead and to each side, the ground was supported by 'staves' attached by sliders to the frames and advanced independently. A bill for the tunnel received royal assent on 24 June 1824, with the proviso that all funding should be privately raised. Brunel started in 1823 to prepare plans, to explore the availability of land and to make models. The first brick was laid on the cast-iron kerb of the Rotherhithe shaft on 2 March 1825 and the shield launched through the shaft wall in December.

The project encountered extraordinary difficulties, largely on account of the unexpected nature of the geology which comprised water-bearing sands and gravels where Brunel had expected clay. Moreover there was no experience of the complexities of successful operation of such a machine. Progress was in consequence slow. The river broke into the tunnel on several occasions, calling for considerable ingenuity and much courage in filling cavities in the river bed by clay and other materials, while restoring damage sustained to the shield. A major irruption on 12 January 1828 led to suspension of the work for more than seven years, the tunnel only half completed and the budget exhausted. The restart had to await arrangements for a government loan, and removal of the original damaged shield and its replacement by a shield of improved design, more robust but generally similar in concept, in a skilfully designed chamber in the disturbed ground under the river. During the first half of the work, his son Isambard, as resident engineer, made major contributions to the solution of problems encountered, to the development of novel techniques, and to maintaining the morale of the men which, in view of the appalling conditions, remained for the most part remarkably high. Throughout their careers, father and son constantly consulted each other and each worked on several projects attributed to the other. The tunnel was completed between the two working shafts in December 1841 and opened as a pedestrian tunnel in March 1843. The vehicular access shafts were never built but in 1869 the tunnel was first used for a railway and was subsequently absorbed into London's underground railway system.

Brunel was well known to the leading scientists of his day and was elected a fellow of the Royal Society in 1814. He discussed with Humphrey Davy and Michael Faraday many common interests including the design of a gas engine. In 1833 he witnessed operation of the (improved) calculator (difference engine) of Charles Babbage and was one of the leaders in the attempt to obtain government support for its further development. He was knighted in 1841, shortly before the completion of the tunnel. In 1829 he received the French Légion d'honneur. He was also elected a member of the Royal Academy of Science in Stockholm. A member of the Institution of Civil Engineers from 1823, he took an active part in meetings, being presented with the Telford silver medal in 1839 for his account of the shield employed in the construction of the Thames tunnel.

Brunel suffered a stroke in 1842 and another in 1845. He died at 1 Park Prospect, St James's Park, London, on 12 December 1849 and was buried in a vault at Kensal Green cemetery, where he had collaborated with A. W. N. Pugin to design a modern necropolis. His wife lived for another five years.　　　ALAN MUIR WOOD

Sources R. Beamish, *Memoir of the life of Sir Marc Isambard Brunel* (1862) • C. Gladwyn, 'The Isambard Brunels', *PICE*, new ser., 50 (1971), 1–14 • A. M. M. Wood, 'The Thames tunnel, 1825–43: where shield tunnelling began', *PICE*, new ser., 102 (1994), 130–39 • L. T. C. Rolt, *Isambard Kingdom Brunel* (1957); repr. (1970) • *DNB* • I. Brunel, *The life of Isambard Kingdom Brunel, civil engineer* (1870) • C. B. J. Noble, *The Brunels, father and son* (1938) • P. Clements, *Marc Isambard Brunel* (1970) • d. cert.
Archives Inst. CE, diaries and letters relating to Thames tunnel • NMM, letter-book • Notts. Arch., draft report on John Heathcote's lace-making machine • Sci. Mus., papers relating to Thames tunnel • University of Bristol Library, corresp., diaries, and papers, mainly relating to Thames tunnel | BL, letters to Charles Babbage, Add. MSS 37183–37192 • BL, letters to Earl Spencer • Lancs. RO, corresp. with George Harrison, mayor of Chester, concerning the construction of New Dee Bridge • NA Scot., letters to Lord Dundonald • Sci. Mus., letters to Henry Maudslay and Joshua Field • U. Southampton L., letters to duke of Wellington
Likenesses J. Northcote, oils, 1812–13, NPG [*see illus.*] • C. Turner, mezzotint, 1815 (after J. Northcote), NPG • E. V. Rippingille, oils, *c.*1820, Bristol City Art Gallery • W. Brockedon, chalk drawing, *c.*1834, NPG • C. C. Vogel, drawing, 1834, Staatliche Kunstsammlungen, Dresden • A. Bry, lithograph (after A. Farcy), NPG • J. Carter, mezzotint (in old age; after S. Drummond), NPG • S. Drummond, oils, NPG • J. C. Horsley, portrait (after J. Northcote), Inst. CE • engraving (after C. Turner), Inst. CE • engraving (after J. Carter), Inst. CE • plaster bust, Sci. Mus.

Brunel, Isambard Kingdom (1806–1859), civil engineer, was born at Portsea, Portsmouth, on 9 April 1806, the third child and first son of Sir Marc Isambard *Brunel (1769–1849), civil engineer, and his wife, Sophia Kingdom (*d.* 1854). As a child Brunel soon demonstrated that he had inherited his father's mechanical and artistic aptitudes, and under careful parental instruction he quickly added skills in draughtsmanship and the use of tools. He was educated at the Revd Weeden Butler's school in Chelsea from 1814 and later attended Dr Morrell's school, Hove. In 1820 his father arranged for him to attend schools in France and to spend some time in the workshop of Louis Bréguet, the leading French clockmaker of the time. At the age of sixteen, however, he returned to England to complete his apprenticeship with his father, who was then becoming heavily involved in plans to construct the first tunnel under the River Thames in London, from Rotherhithe to Wapping, using his ingenious tunnelling shield. Young Isambard soon became his father's chief assistant engineer on this ambitious project, to which both father and son devoted intense effort for several years, struggling to push the shield forward through the clay under the Thames and repelling repeated incursions of the river into the tunnel. In the most serious of these, in January 1828, the younger Brunel almost lost his life and sustained internal injuries which made necessary a lengthy convalescence. It also led to a cessation of work on the tunnel and effectively marked the end of his active commitment to the project because by the time it could be resumed he had become preoccupied with other large projects of his own.

Bristol and the Great Western Railway The first of these new projects derived directly from Brunel's convalescence, part of which he spent in Clifton, the affluent residential suburb of Bristol. While there he became interested in the scheme to build a bridge across the Clifton Gorge, through which the River Avon flows from Bristol to the sea. He submitted several designs for the competition to provide this bridge, but these and other entries were all turned down by Thomas Telford, the doyen of British engineering in the 1820s and the adjudicator for the competition. However, the promoters of the competition, the Bristol Society of Merchant Venturers, did not like Telford's alternative proposal and held a second competition, and this time Brunel won with one of his modified plans. Thus he came to design the elegant suspension bridge which still provides one of the finest sights in Bristol. But he did not build it, because even though construction began with high hopes in 1836 the funds ran out when only the two

Isambard Kingdom Brunel (1806–1859), by Robert Howlett, 1857

towers had been completed; the project was abandoned during the remainder of Brunel's lifetime and was revived only after his death as a memorial to him, and completed in 1864.

The Clifton Bridge introduced Brunel to a circle of Bristol merchants and entrepreneurs who were of inestimable importance to him in determining the direction of his career. They secured for him a commission to advise the Bristol Docks Company on improvements to the condition of the Bristol City docks, which he carried out with considerable success, establishing a steady flow of water through the enclosed docks which prevented the formation of shoals threatening to impede navigation. They also made sure that he was considered for the important post of engineer to the new railway company which was proposing to construct a main line from London to Bristol, so that in March 1833, when still not quite twenty-seven, Brunel was appointed engineer to the Great Western Railway (GWR). For the next fifteen years he devoted much of his phenomenal energy and talent to the construction of what he intended to be 'the Finest Work in England' (Rolt, 171). The line from Paddington Station in London to Temple Meads in Bristol, a masterpiece of skilful surveying and careful grading, became the first thread in a network which covered much of south-west England and provided an unprecedented service of high-speed passenger transport. Its many splendid engineering structures included the viaducts at Hanwell and Chippenham, the Maidenhead and other masonry bridges, the Box Tunnel, and the iron structures of the Chepstow and Saltash bridges on the Great Western line and its extensions. All these exhibited boldness of conception, taste in design, and great skill in the use of materials.

To achieve this Brunel recognized at the outset that he needed to design a complete system, combining a well-engineered permanent way with superlative locomotives and services which catered for the safety and comfort of passengers. He decided that the stability of trains at the speeds which he envisaged required a broader gauge than that adopted by previous railways, so that the GWR was built on a 'broad gauge' of 7 feet instead of the conventional 'narrow' gauge of 4 feet 8½ inches. Stability was further ensured by laying the rails on longitudinal sleepers rather than on independent stone blocks or—as became general practice subsequently—evenly spaced cross-sleepers. It seems clear in retrospect that, even though the broad gauge gave the GWR an initial advantage over its rivals, the narrow gauge was capable of improvements which quickly made it fully competitive as well as considerably cheaper to construct, so that the broad gauge soon became a costly liability. During Brunel's lifetime, however, the GWR remained committed to the broad gauge, and it was in this form that the system was extended on from Bristol to Exeter, Plymouth, and Penzance, and as the South Wales Railway, to Cardiff, Swansea, and Milford Haven. Other branches linked with Gloucester, Oxford, and beyond to Birmingham, Wolverhampton, and even to the Mersey, although it must be admitted that on these north-westerly extensions the problems of linkages with narrow gauge railways obliged the GWR to allow some narrow gauge working in its own system. As an engineering system, the GWR was distinctive and comprehensive, with a high standard of performance which reflected in virtually every detail of its operation the inspiration of its designer.

The *Great Western* and the *Great Britain* Within a few months of work beginning on the GWR, Brunel surprised his directors by suggesting that the line should be extended to New York by way of a steamship operating out of Bristol. The result of this suggestion was the creation of a subsidiary company, the Great Western Steamship Company, with Brunel as its engineer, commissioned with the task of designing and building the largest steamship of its day, the SS *Great Western*. This was a paddle-wheeled, wooden-hulled ship of 2300 tons displacement. It was designed by Brunel and built in Bristol in defiance of the conventional wisdom of the time which believed that no viable service could be operated by a steamship on a transatlantic route because it would be obliged to use all its space to carry fuel. Although he had no previous experience as a shipbuilder, Brunel had calculated that while the power to drive a ship increases as the square of its dimensions (depending on its cross-sectional resistance) the carrying capacity increases as the cube of those dimensions, so that it could more than keep pace with the increasing requirement for fuel. These calculations were amply vindicated in 1838 when the *Great Western* made her successful maiden voyage, arriving in New York with fuel to spare.

Having made his point and established the feasibility of transatlantic steam navigation, Brunel needed to provide a sister-ship for the *Great Western* to allow the company to secure the lucrative mail contract and exploit the tremendous potential of this traffic. However, even though the company lost little time in making a decision, the mail contract went to Cunard, operating a fleet of reliable steamships out of Liverpool, and when the Bristol company began to build a second ship Brunel could not settle for a mere sister-ship of the *Great Western*. Instead, he built the *Great Britain*, which was substantially larger than its predecessor with a displacement of 3018 tons, and which incorporated two striking innovations: it was the first large iron ship, having a strong hull of riveted wrought-iron plates, and it was the first large screw-propelled ship. Brunel had initially designed it as another paddle-ship but, on observing the efficiency of a small screw-ship, he made a radical change of plans which involved not only providing for propulsion by a single screw but also designing the unusually large steam engine required to drive it. The new ship was built in Bristol City docks and was launched on 19 July 1843, but she was unable to leave until December 1844 because the entrance locks were too small to accommodate her. Only the combination of an exceptionally high tide with the dismantling of some of the lock masonry allowed her to pass into the River Avon, and once through she did not return to Bristol until her rusting hull was brought home in triumph from the Falkland Islands in 1970.

The SS *Great Britain* had a long and successful operating career, but she worked mainly out of Liverpool. A serious accident in 1846, when she was stranded on the coast of northern Ireland, caused the Great Western Steamship Company to go into liquidation and other owners took over the operation of the vessel. Apart from the early transatlantic runs and a period as a troopship in the Crimean War, she spent most of her working life on the run to Australia.

The *Great Eastern* Brunel, meanwhile, went on to design his third and mightiest ship, the SS *Great Eastern*. The conception of this vessel derived from the potential demand for a ship large enough to make the journey to India and the Far East under steam, and without relying on replenishments of fuel *en route*. Brunel undertook a huge scaling-up of his previous ships to design an iron vessel with two sets of engines, one to drive a pair of paddle wheels, and the other to drive a screw. The hull was like an enormous wrought-iron beam, largely double-skinned and sectionalized to give lateral as well as longitudinal strength. Even though he took an active part in the capital-raising and company-promotion aspects of the enterprise, Brunel recognized that he did not possess the facilities to build this leviathan himself, so he took into partnership the eminent shipbuilder John Scott Russell to be responsible for the construction work at his London shipyard on the Isle of Dogs. Unfortunately, the terms of the partnership do not appear to have been uniformly interpreted, and discord quickly grew to intense antipathy between Brunel and Russell over methods of construction, the supply of

material, the organization of the labour force, and personal styles of leadership.

Despite all these problems and acute financial difficulties, work on the ship gradually progressed between 1854, when the first contracts were let, and her launch in January 1858. An earlier attempt to launch her, in the previous November, was abandoned after trouble with the unorthodox sideways launch specially designed by Brunel because he considered that the width of the River Thames at this point would make a more conventional longitudinal launch unsafe. It was found, however, that the great weight of the ship caused some distortion in the slipway so that she stuck fast and required the installation of a battery of hydraulic presses to push her into the river. Once afloat, the problems of the *Great Eastern* were not over, but after a hectic period of fitting-out she was ready to depart on her maiden voyage in September 1859. By this time Brunel (who suffered from kidney disease) was mortally sick, and he had his last seizure on the deck of the ship shortly before her projected departure. He lingered for a few days, just long enough to receive the devastating news of the explosion in the boiler room of the *Great Eastern* as she steamed down the English Channel, an explosion which would have destroyed any lesser ship. The SS *Great Eastern* survived; at 32,000 tons displacement she was by far the largest ship of her time and remained such until she was scrapped in 1888. Never a commercial success, she did, all the same, demonstrate the technical feasibility of the systems incorporated in her design, and proved herself well equipped for one distinctive task—that of laying the transoceanic telegraph cables. However, her engines soon became obsolete, and the time had not yet arrived for a vessel of such a large capacity.

Engineering achievements and London life By 1859 Brunel had established the main lines of the Great Western Railway; he had designed three pioneering steamships which had transformed the pattern of transoceanic navigation; and he had completed many other exemplary works of civil engineering including dock improvements at Bristol and Sunderland, and railways in Italy. His Clifton Bridge, it is true, was still unfinished, but his two innovatory wrought-iron truss bridges at Chepstow and Saltash had been completed as part of the railway network: the Royal Albert Bridge, which crossed the Tamar at Saltash, was opened to traffic shortly before his death in 1859. It had two spans of 455 feet each, and a central pier built on the rock 80 feet below high-water mark. He had also built a suspension bridge across the Thames at Hungerford in 1841–5, but this was demolished in 1862 and the chains were reused in the construction of the Clifton suspension bridge.

Not all Brunel's works were successes: the GWR continued to struggle with the 'break of gauge' and other problems associated with his controversial broad gauge; and his early experiments in locomotive engineering for the GWR were conspicuous failures, though his reputation in this respect was saved by the excellent engines which Daniel Gooch produced for the railway. Brunel adopted too hastily the 'atmospheric railway' system for the South Devon Railway in the belief that it would meet the difficulties of a heavily graded line, only to have to abandon it a year later, to the considerable loss of the shareholders. In addition, the *Great Eastern*, for all its technical excellence, was a major financial disaster. Even his disasters tended to assume epic proportions, however, and none of them did serious damage to his reputation as one of the greatest civil engineers of the nineteenth century.

Throughout his professional career, Brunel was based in London. He acquired a house at 18 Duke Street in Westminster, convenient for parliament and Whitehall, and established his home there above his office. On 5 July 1836, at Kensington church, he married Mary Elizabeth (*b.* 1813), the eldest daughter of William *Horsley (1774–1858), organist and composer, who came from an accomplished musical and artistic family. She outlived him. They lived in some style and had two sons and a daughter: Isambard, the elder son, became a lawyer and the younger, Henry Marc, followed in his father's footsteps to become an engineer, and entered into partnership with Sir John Wolfe-Barry, designer of the Tower Bridge. Brunel's daughter, Florence Mary, married an Eton schoolmaster. When Brunel began to think about a country estate he found one which suited him very well at Watcombe, on the edge of Torquay, where he laid out an extensive garden and began to build a mansion which was never finished.

From his office in Duke Street, Brunel was able to control his wide range of projects. At the height of his career, in the 1840s, he had a large team of approaching thirty, including assistant engineers, a secretary and clerks, and several pupils serving apprenticeships with him. Brunel obtained a high reputation for his evidence given before the parliamentary committees on schemes of which he was engineer. He spent much of his time away from the office, travelling to the sites of his projects, visiting firms from whom he had commissioned work, and performing 'consultancies'—although he did not care for the term, as he always expected to be made totally responsible for any project on which he was engaged. He was a keen supporter of the Institution of Civil Engineers, of which he became an associate in 1829, and a member from 1837. Although he never found time to deliver a paper, he was made a member of the council of the institution in 1845, and at the time of his death was a vice-president, expecting to serve a term as president. He was elected a fellow of the Royal Society in June 1830, and, when they were held in a convenient place, he attended meetings of the British Association for the Advancement of Science. He was an active member of the buildings committee of the commission for the Great Exhibition of 1851, and supported Paxton's design for the Crystal Palace. He applied himself to military improvements in the Crimean War, and designed the prefabricated hospital constructed at Renkioi in Turkey for the reception of wounded soldiers. Brunel had few close friends, though he did share confidences with his brother-in-law, the artist John Horsley (who painted two excellent portraits of Brunel), and he always enjoyed the company of Robert Stephenson, even though the two men were frequently professional rivals. Assistants and contractors found him distant and autocratic, but many of them developed a deep attachment for him. In 1857 he was awarded an honorary degree of DCL from the University of Oxford.

Reputation and death Brunel was one of the great engineers of the 'heroic age' of British engineering. He had the good fortune to be alive in a time of national expansion for which his talents were peculiarly appropriate, and he was able to exploit his advantage to the full. In many ways, he was a man of his times—a believer in free enterprise untrammelled by state regulations, a man who showed some reservation about religious commitment, and a firm supporter of British national and imperial pretensions. When he died at his home, 18 Duke Street, Westminster, London, on 15 September 1859, he was only fifty-three, but his reputation was already securely established, even though the wealth which had accompanied his prime years had been severely depleted by the losses incurred with the *Great Eastern*. He was buried on 20 September 1859 in the family vault in Kensal Green cemetery, in which his father had collaborated with A. W. N. Pugin to design a modern necropolis. Colleagues in the Institution of Civil Engineers promoted the completion of the Clifton suspension bridge in his memory in 1864 and commissioned the Marochetti statue on the Embankment in London. A memorial window in the south aisle of Westminster Abbey was erected by family and friends, but most significantly many of his great engineering works survive as a monument to his extraordinary vision and enterprise.   R. ANGUS BUCHANAN

Sources I. Brunel, *The life of Isambard Kingdom Brunel, civil engineer* (1870) · C. B. J. Noble, *The Brunels, father and son* (1938) · L. T. C. Rolt, *Isambard Kingdom Brunel* (1957) · G. S. Emmerson, *John Scott Russell: a great Victorian engineer and naval architect* (1977) · R. Beamish, *Memoir of the life of Sir Marc Isambard Brunel* (1862) · P. Clements, *Marc Isambard Brunel* (1970) · E. Corlett, *The iron ship: the history and significance of Brunel's 'Great Britain'* (1975) · A. M. M. Wood, 'The Thames tunnel, 1825–43: where shield tunnelling began', *PICE*, new ser., 102 (1994), 130–39 · C. Gladwyn, 'The Isambard Brunels', *PICE*, new ser., 50 (1971), 1–14 · *CGPLA Eng. & Wales* (1858)

Archives Bodl. Oxf., corresp. · Hammersmith and Fulham Archives and Local History Centre, letters relating to London–Birmingham, Great Western Railway, etc. · Hunt. L., memorandum and letter-books · Institution of Mechanical Engineers, London, MSS and papers · NRA, priv. coll., journal · U. Newcastle, Robinson L. · UCL, letters to the Society for the Diffusion of Useful Knowledge · University of Bristol Library, corresp. and papers; further papers incl. bank books, diaries, and notebooks | BL, letters to Charles Babbage, Add. MSS 37184–37200 · Cornwall RO, corresp. relating to Cornwall Railway · Devon RO, corresp. and plans relating to Great Western Railway · Inst. CE, M. I. Brunel MSS · PRO, corresp. and papers relating to Great Western Railway, Rail 1008/70–75, 79, 1148–1149

Likenesses J. C. Horsley, portrait, *c.*1836 · J. C. Horsley, portrait, *c.*1844, Bristol Art Gallery · J. C. Horsley, oils, 1848, Museum of British Transport, York · J. Lucas, group portrait, oils, *c.*1853 (*Conference of engineers at Britannia Bridge*), Inst. CE · J. C. Horsley, oils, 1857, NPG · R. Howlett, photographs, 1857, NPG [*see illus.*] · photographs, 1857–9, Brunel University, London · R. Howlett, photographs, 1858, Library of Institution of Mechanical Engineers, London · J. J. E. Mayall, engraving, pubd 1859 (after photograph by D. J.

Pound), BM, NPG · E. W. Wyon, marble bust, c.1862, Great Western Railway Museum, Swindon · C. Marochetti, bronze statue on monument, 1877, Victoria Embankment, London · R. Howlett, engraving (after photograph by H. Harval), NPG; repro. in *ILN* (16 Jan 1858) · D. J. Pound, line print (after photograph by Mayall, c.1858), NPG; repro. in *Illustrated News of the World* · C. Vogel, drawing, Staatliche Kunstsammlungen, Dresden · group portrait, photograph (with Lord Alfred Paget, Mr Yates, and the harbour master), NPG

Wealth at death under £90,000: probate, 10 Oct 1859, *CGPLA Eng. & Wales*

Bruning, Anthony (1716–1776), Jesuit, was born on 7 December 1716, the eldest son of George Bruning of East Meon and Foxfield, Hampshire, and his first wife, Mary, daughter of Christopher Bryon of Sussex. The Jesuit priest George *Bruning (1738–1802) was his half-brother. Educated at the English College at St Omer (1726–33), Anthony then studied at Liège, and was ordained priest about 1741. He entered the Society of Jesus in 1733, and became fully professed in 1751. He was sent on the English mission and was afterwards appointed professor of philosophy at Liège, where he died on 8 August 1776. He wrote manuscript treatises entitled 'De gratia', 'De Deo', and 'De trinitate'. THOMPSON COOPER, rev. ROBERT BROWN

Sources G. Oliver, *Collections towards illustrating the biography of the Scotch, English and Irish members, SJ* (1838) · H. Foley, ed., *Records of the English province of the Society of Jesus*, 7 vols. in 8 (1875–83) · G. Holt, *The English Jesuits, 1650–1829: a biographical dictionary*, Catholic RS, 70 (1984) · A. de Backer and A. de Backer, *Bibliothèque des écrivains de la Compagnie de Jésus*, ed. C. Sommervogel, new edn, 3 vols. (Liège and Paris, 1869–76) · Gillow, *Lit. biog. hist.*

Bruning, George (1738–1802), Jesuit, was born on 19 September 1738 in Hampshire, the youngest son of George Bruning of East Meon and Foxfield, Hampshire, and his second wife, Anne, daughter of Thomas May of Ramsdale in the same county. He was educated at the English College at St Omer, and then studied for the priesthood at Watten and Liège. He was ordained priest about 1763. His elder half-brother, Anthony *Bruning (1716–1776), was also a Jesuit priest. George entered the Society of Jesus in 1756 and served the mission of Southend, Soberton, Hampshire, for some years, living afterwards at Britwell, Oxfordshire, and at East Hendred, Berkshire, the seat of Thomas John Eyston, who had married his half-sister, Mary Bruning. He retired to Isleworth, and died there on 3 or 5 June 1802. Bruning published *The Divine Oeconomy of Christ* in London in 1791 and *Remarks on the Rev. Joseph Berington's examination of events termed miraculous, as reported in letters from Italy, addressed to the public* in 1796. THOMPSON COOPER, rev. ROBERT BROWN

Sources G. Oliver, *Collections towards illustrating the biography of the Scotch, English and Irish members of the Society of Jesus* (1835) · Gillow, *Lit. biog. hist.* · H. Foley, ed., *Records of the English province of the Society of Jesus*, 7 vols. in 8 (1875–83) · G. Holt, *The English Jesuits, 1650–1829: a biographical dictionary*, Catholic RS, 70 (1984) · A. de Backer and A. de Backer, *Bibliothèque des écrivains de la Compagnie de Jésus*, ed. C. Sommervogel, new edn, 3 vols. (Liège and Paris, 1869–76)

Brunlees, Sir James (1816–1892), civil engineer, was born on 5 January 1816 at Kelso, Scotland, the son of John Brunlees and his wife, Margaret, daughter of John Rutherford of Kelso. His father was gardener and steward to a Mr Innes, the duke of Roxburghe's agent. Brunlees was educated at the parish school and afterwards at the local private school. At the age of twelve he began in gardening and farm work with a view to becoming a landscape gardener; but he had a natural taste for engineering work. Through Innes, Brunlees met the civil engineer Alexander J. Adie, then carrying out work on the Roxburghe estates, picked up a considerable knowledge of surveying, and was eventually employed to make a survey of the estates. During this time he saved money to pay for classes at Edinburgh University, where he studied for several sessions.

In 1838 Adie took him on as his pupil and assistant on the Bolton and Preston Railway line. He subsequently carried out surveys for Joseph Locke and John Edward Errington on the Caledonian line to Glasgow and Edinburgh, before becoming an assistant to John Hawkshaw on the Lancashire and Yorkshire Railway for about five years. At this time he met his wife, Elizabeth, daughter of John Kirkman of Bolton-le-Moors, Lancashire, a laundry master; they married in 1845. They had two sons and one daughter; the elder son, John, subsequently became his father's partner.

In 1850 Brunlees set up his own practice, becoming engineer to the Londonderry and Coleraine Railway in Ireland. This involved the construction of embankments under difficult conditions across Rosse's Bay in the River Foyle. Brunlees's success here helped him obtain the appointment as engineer to the Ulverston and Lancaster Railway. This scheme was promoted by the Brogden family of contractors and ironmasters, as were several of Brunlees's later works. It involved embankments across Morecambe Bay, and iron viaducts on screw-pile foundations across the Leven and Kent estuaries. Brunlees freely acknowledged the help of Harry Brogden in developing a method of sinking piles using water jetting. These works were described by Brunlees in papers to the Institution of Civil Engineers (*Minutes of Proceedings of the Institution of Civil Engineers*, 14, 1854–5, 239–45; and 17, 1857–8, 442–7), which helped consolidate his reputation.

At this time Brunlees was based in Manchester, but in 1856 he was appointed engineer to the São Paulo Railway in Brazil, and shortly afterwards he moved to London where he remained for the rest of his career. The São Paulo Railway crossed the steep slopes of the Serra do Mar, and he had to adopt a system of inclined planes and stationary engines. This was fully described in a paper by the resident engineer, D. M. Fox (*Minutes of Proceedings of the Institution of Civil Engineers*, 30, 1869–70, 29–77). Other lines in Brazil designed by Brunlees were the Porto Allegre and New Hamburg, and Minas and Rio. In 1873 he was appointed to the order of the Rose of Brazil for his railway work. Other work in South America included the Central Uruguay and Hyugentas Railway, the Bolivar mineral line in Venezuela, and a 400 ft long iron pier in the River Plate.

The design of iron structures for tidal waters was a continuing theme throughout Brunlees's career. Although Eugenius Birch is more commonly associated with the design of seaside piers, Brunlees was responsible for impressive examples, at Llandudno, New Brighton, Southport, and Southend, the longest built. As engineer to the Solway Junction Railway he designed an iron viaduct across the firth 1¼ miles long.

Several of Brunlees's later railway projects were associated with the dock and harbour works for which he was engineer, at King's Lynn, Whitehaven, and Bristol. The most important dock scheme was that at Avonmouth (1868–75) for the city of Bristol, the trade of the city having suffered severely from the difficulties of approach through the narrow and tortuous course of the River Avon. He was engineer for several railway lines in Lancashire and Cheshire, of which the most important was the Mersey Railway, with the tunnel under the river between Birkenhead and Liverpool. He was joint engineer with Charles Douglas Fox, and on the completion of the work in May 1886 they were both knighted. He was also, with Hawkshaw, engineer to the original Channel Tunnel Company.

On the continent Brunlees was engineer for the Mont Cenis Railway, a mountain line linking Savoy to Italy prior to the completion of the Mont Cenis Tunnel. This was built according to the Fell system, which made use of horizontal wheels beneath the locomotive, pressed against a central rail, to gain extra adhesion on severe gradients. He also designed the Alcoy and Gandia Railway and harbour in Spain.

There are several distinct specialist strands in Brunlees's work—the design of iron piers and viaducts, mountain railways, and tunnels. The variety of these reflect his belief that no specialist knowledge could be useless, even if its immediate professional application was by no means obvious. These views were impressed upon his pupils and colleagues, and were reflected in his own career when he drew on his agricultural background in the solution of engineering problems. His reputation led to his frequently acting as arbitrator, and his involvement in the Tay Bridge inquiry in 1880.

Brunlees became a member of the Institution of Civil Engineers in 1852, and was president during 1882–3. He was also a member of the Institution of Mechanical Engineers from 1870, and a fellow of the Royal Society of Edinburgh. He died at his home, Argyle Lodge, Wimbledon, on 2 June 1892 at the age of seventy-six. His wife died in 1888.   MIKE CHRIMES

Sources *PICE*, 111 (1892–3), 367–71 • *The Times* (4 June 1892) • *Institution of Mechanical Engineers: Proceedings* (1892), 223–4 • *Engineering* (10 June 1892), 729–30 • *The Engineer* (10 June 1892), 503 • L. Blake, 'Railroad to ruin', *Estates Gazette* (18 Oct 1997), 167 • Burke, *Peerage* • m. cert. • d. cert. • *CGPLA Eng. & Wales* (1888) [Elizabeth Brunlees]
Archives Inst. CE, membership records • PRO, railway records
Likenesses Moira & Haigh, carte-de-visite, *c.*1860, Inst. CE • Papworth, bust; formerly at Inst. CE; Phillips, 1973
Wealth at death £31,699 3s. 9d.: resworn probate, July 1893, *CGPLA Eng. & Wales* (1892)

Brunner, Sir John Tomlinson, first baronet (1842–1919),

chemical manufacturer and politician, was born on 8 February 1842 in Everton, Liverpool, the second of the three sons and the fourth of the five children of John Brunner, a Swiss protestant minister, who migrated to Lancashire in

Sir John Tomlinson Brunner, first baronet (1842–1919), by Augustus John, exh. New English Art Club 1906

1832 and became a Unitarian and a schoolmaster, and his wife, Margaret Curphey, from the Isle of Man. Brunner's mother died in 1847 and in 1851 his father married Nancy Inman, who had run a successful school near Birkenhead. He was educated at his father's school, St George's House, Everton, until, at the age of fifteen, of his own volition, he decided to pursue a commercial career. The young Brunner had been greatly influenced by both his father's liberal Unitarian teaching and his affectionate stepmother's businesslike principles of household management.

Brunner spent four years at a Liverpool shipping house and then in 1861 obtained a clerical post at Hutchinson's alkali works in Widnes. During the next twelve years he rose to the position of general manager, in charge of finance and personnel, and during this time established a reputation in the business community for ability and honest dealing. Here, about 1862, he first met and befriended Ludwig *Mond [see under Mond family (per. 1867–1973)], born at Kassel in 1839, a chemist educated at Heidelberg.

In 1864 Brunner married Salome, daughter of James Davies, a Liverpool merchant. She died in 1874 leaving a family of three sons and three daughters. In 1875 he married his children's governess, Jane (d. 1910), daughter of William Sanderson Wyman, a Kettering physician. They had three daughters.

The bond struck between Brunner and Mond, both ambitious men, was to endure. In 1873 they formed a partnership, born of mutual respect and trust, to manufacture soda ash at Winnington in Cheshire. Having little money they required financial backing and Brunner's high business reputation, no less than Mond's scientific eminence, was crucial for their success. After two years of grinding work they produced a small profit, which was to herald the creation of wealth unsurpassed in the British chemical industry of the nineteenth century. A managing partner from the start, Brunner was chairman of Brunner, Mond & Co. from 1891 until 1918. When the company became a founder member of ICI in 1926 the enterprise, which had been launched in 1873 with less than £20,000, had a capitalization of more than £18 million.

In 1885 Brunner became Liberal MP for Northwich and held the seat, with one short break, until he resigned in 1909. His eldest son, John Fowler Leece Brunner, sat with him in the House of Commons from 1906. In the management of their chemical business Brunner and Mond were ahead of their times in introducing such socially enlightened measures as sickness and injury insurance, apprentice education, shorter working hours, and holidays with pay. As an MP Brunner could now promote his philanthropic principles through parliament. A supporter of home rule, trade unions, and free trade, he was an influential back-bencher and a prominent Liberal advocate, whose wide business experience informed his sometimes humorous but always cogent participations in debate. Before 1914 he earned himself obloquy in some quarters by urging a less provocative British stance towards Germany. He was created baronet in 1895 and sworn of the privy council in 1906. He declined several offers of a peerage.

Brunner was a generous benefactor. In Cheshire alone he provided schools, guildhalls, and social clubs, and he gave Northwich a free library. He endowed three chairs at Liverpool University and funded many scholarships. His benefactions included gifts to the Landesmuseum in Zürich and a hospital, now the Spital Bülach, for the town of his father's birth in canton Zürich. In the political field he supplied munificent financial support to the Liberal Party and its numerous causes. Dubbed by The Times a 'chemical Croesus', he rejoiced in using his wealth for philanthropic ends. Brunner died on 1 July 1919 at his home, Silverlands, Chertsey, Surrey.   FRANCIS DICK, rev.

Sources S. E. Koss, Sir John Brunner: radical plutocrat, 1842–1919 (1970) · W. F. L. Dick, A hundred years of alkali in Cheshire (1973) · Brunner, Mond archives, Ches. & Chester ALSS · m. certs. · d. cert. · private information (2004) [Hugo Brunner, great-grandson]
Archives Ches. & Chester ALSS, Brunner Mond & Co. Ltd, Winnington · U. Lpool L., corresp. and papers | BL, letters to Lord Gladstone, Add. MSS 46057–46066 · Ches. & Chester ALSS, corresp. with Ludwig Mond, etc.
Likenesses A. John, portrait, exh. New English Art Club 1906, U. Lpool, art collections [see illus.] · A. Hacker, portrait, Harris Man. Oxf.
Wealth at death £899,112 11s. 0d.: probate, 13 Jan 1920, CGPLA Eng. & Wales

Brunning, Benjamin (bap. 1623, d. 1680), clergyman and ejected minister, was the eldest son of John Brunning (1597–1663), for forty years rector of Semer in Suffolk, who baptized him there on 8 October 1623. His mother, Anna Brand (d. 1676), was daughter of John Brand, lord of the manor of nearby Edwardstone; she married John in 1620

and they had three more sons and two daughters. John Bruning, ship carpenter of Ipswich and a donor to its town library about 1613, may have been Benjamin's grandfather.

Brunning matriculated as a pensioner at St Catharine's College, Cambridge, at Michaelmas 1644, proceeding BA the following spring, when he was elected a fellow at Jesus College and took his MA there three years later. Calamy wrote of his 'great usefulness' and of his

> general reputation in the university for his wit and learning. He was a man of large and deep thoughts, and his province required it; he having the most judicious persons in the town and country, both ministers and people, for his audience. (Calamy, 2.645)

After ordination he became rector of Great Waldingfield and, about 1654, married Elizabeth Fuller (1629–1699), the daughter of John Fuller, incumbent at St Peter's, Ipswich, from 1647 to 1651. They had a son, Benjamin (b. 1655), and two daughters, Dorcas and Anna. In August 1656 he was persuaded, not without difficulty, to accept the town preachership of Ipswich. Stephen Marshall had died in the post of town preacher in November 1655, and over the following months the corporation had tried and failed to lure Matthew Newcomen from Dedham, so made sure of Brunning by offering him also the incumbency of St Mary-le-Tower, the principal church, and the removal of his possessions to the house appointed in Lower Brook Street, later adding an extra 'lettle room … next the staircase into the orchard' at his request (Ipswich corporation assembly book, 31 Jan 1659). The Best Wisdome, the sermon he preached at the election of knights of the shire for the county in April 1660 on the eirenic text of James 3: 17, was dedicated to the successful candidates; Edmund Calamy was the publisher.

In June 1662 Brunning told the corporation that he could not 'preache the Lecture of this towne in regard he is not at present justified to conforme to the late Act of Parliament' and asked for time to consider 'whether he can conforme or noe' (Suffolk RO, Ipswich corporation assembly book, 9 June 1662). In September they had reluctantly to accept his resignation and the following summer he moved from the house provided to another in St Clement's parish. There he may have continued as a minister of the gospel to those who would hear him, but he is not listed as a pastor of a conventicle in the 1669 episcopal returns, nor did he take out a licence in 1672. St Clement's was the parish where Brunning's conforming friend Samuel Golty became incumbent in succession to John Ward (brother of Ipswich's celebrated puritan town preacher Samuel Ward) who, by dying in April 1662, had escaped Brunning's dilemma.

Brunning wrote, but apparently never published, a further work, 'against Impositions and Conformity, from the Second Commandment' (Calamy, 2.645). He died at his home in St Clement's on 20 November 1680 and was buried in St Clement's Church two days later under a black ledger stone, where his wife joined him three days after she died on 9 May 1699. Samuel Golty oversaw Brunning's burial and will. Brunning left all his books to his son, Benjamin, who was admitted a sizar at Christ's College, Cambridge, in 1673 and ordained the year after his father died. He resigned all his livings in Nottinghamshire and Lincolnshire within a month of James II's coming to the throne. The elder Benjamin's younger brother Samuel, also a minister, held the living of St Mary-le-Tower for three years until his death in 1677, the year after that of their widowed mother, Anna: both Samuel and Anna were buried at Semer. Of father, brothers, and son, only Benjamin Brunning chose the path of exclusion from the Restoration Church of England.   J. M. BLATCHLY

Sources Calamy rev. · Semer, Great Waldingfield, and St Clement's, Ipswich, parish registers and monumental inscriptions · Ipswich corporation assembly books, 1655–63, Suffolk RO, Ipswich · will, 1680, Suffolk RO, Ipswich, IC/AA1/110/130 · E. Calamy, ed., An abridgement of Mr. Baxter's history of his life and times, with an account of the ministers, &c., who were ejected after the Restauration of King Charles II, 2nd edn, 2 vols. (1713), vol. 2, p. 645 · G. L. Turner, ed., Original records of early nonconformity under persecution and indulgence, 3 vols. (1911–14)

Brunt, Sir David (1886–1965), meteorologist, was born on 17 June 1886 at Staylittle, near Llanidloes, a small village in a remote Welsh-speaking part of Montgomeryshire, the youngest of five sons and four daughters of John Brunt, then a lead miner, and his wife, Mary Jones. In 1896 the family moved to Llanhilleth in Monmouthshire where his father obtained work as a collier. So, when he was ten, the young Brunt's education changed from the ambience of a small village school, with instruction in Welsh, to one of large classes and instruction in English. Despite these difficulties he was successful in gaining scholarships, first from his local school to Abertillery intermediate school, and from there to the University College of Wales, Aberystwyth. There he graduated in 1907 with first-class honours in mathematics, and was awarded a sizarship (later converted to a scholarship) at Trinity College, Cambridge, where he obtained first classes in parts one (1909) and two (1910) of the mathematical tripos. He was awarded the Isaac Newton studentship in 1911 and remained at Cambridge for research in astronomy under H. F. Newall. In 1913 he took a lectureship in the University of Birmingham and from 1914 to 1916 he was lecturer in mathematics at the teachers' training college at Caerleon.

Brunt had little opportunity to exercise his talents at Caerleon, but during his time there, on 10 August 1915, he married Claudia Mary Elizabeth, daughter of William Roberts, schoolmaster, of Nant-y-glo, Monmouthshire. She had been a fellow pupil at Abertillery and Aberystwyth, where she studied French with distinction. The formative point of his scientific career came in 1916, when he joined the meteorological section of the Royal Engineers in France. He was commissioned and in due course became meteorologist at the independent air force headquarters. The RE section had been formed around a nucleus of staff recruited from the civilian Meteorological Office and, when he was demobilized in 1919, Captain Brunt, as he had become, accepted a permanent post in the office as superintendent of the army services division.

In 1921 the Meteorological Office was absorbed into the Air Ministry. At that time the expanding needs of aviation dominated meteorological services which in peacetime were in limited demand from the army. Brunt found time for research and also to fill the role of visiting lecturer in the new meteorological department at Imperial College under Napier Shaw. He had had early success with a textbook on mathematical statistics, *Combination of Observations* (1917), and went on to publish several original contributions to theory. Belief in meteorological periodicities was dimmed by his periodogram analyses, while he excelled at selecting those aspects of a problem that were of physical significance. He was also writing his renowned textbook *Physical and Dynamical Meteorology*, a pioneer work first published in 1934, which became a standard text.

Brunt's duties in the Meteorological Office also included one feature of far-reaching importance. Experience of wartime usage of poisonous gases had shown the need for comprehensive research and in 1921 the Chemical Warfare Experimental Station was set up at Porton. Brunt became chairman of the meteorological subcommittee of the chemical warfare (later defence) committee, an office he held for the following twenty-one years. He created at Porton a team to study the problems of diffusion and turbulence, and it contributed much to the evolution of micrometeorology as a quantitative scientific study. Arising in a context of chemical warfare the work was veiled in secrecy, but the problems were fundamental to meteorology and the advances made founded the scientific reputations of two future heads of the Meteorological Office—Nelson K. Johnson and (Oliver) Graham Sutton—and put other workers on their paths to fellowships of the Royal Society. No comparable effort in meteorological research was initiated until the great expansion after the Second World War and Brunt's enterprise in seizing a unique opportunity cannot be overestimated.

The Meteorological Office of that time, preoccupied with weather services and with no research programme, was not the ideal environment for a theoretician of Brunt's calibre, and his appointment in 1934, in succession to Sir Gilbert T. Walker, to the chair of meteorology at Imperial College, was wholly advantageous. Brunt's department, which expanded both before and after the Second World War, mostly for postgraduate work, earned great repute; his former students were later to be found in responsible positions all over the world.

Brunt was elected a fellow of the Royal Society in 1939, served on its council in 1942–3, and was physical secretary in 1948–57, and vice-president in 1949–57. He performed these duties with distinction and was active in organizing the UK contribution to the International Geophysical Year (1957–8); much of the success of the Royal Society expedition to Halley Bay, Antarctica, was due to his planning. The ice shelf upon which the expedition's base stood was named after him.

Brunt was knighted in 1949 and appointed KBE ten years later. He was president of the Royal Meteorological Society in 1942–4 and of the Physical Society in 1945–7, and chairman of council of the British Gliding Association in

1935–46. He became ScD of Cambridge in 1940 and received honorary doctorates from Wales (1951) and London (1960). He was awarded a royal medal of the Royal Society (1944), and the Buchan prize (1933) and Symons gold medal (1947) of the Royal Meteorological Society. From 1952, when he retired from his chair at Imperial College, he became chairman of the Electricity Supply Research Council of the Central Electricity Authority.

Smart in appearance and alert in manner, Brunt had an admitted liking for influence, not to say intrigue, a ready wit in ordinary conversation, but a direct and unequivocal approach to scientific discussion. Occasionally he seemed to form dislikes for little reason and to be less than fair in his judgements, but with his students and those who worked smoothly with him he was open and friendly and widely regarded with warm affection. His later years were saddened by his wife's illness and the sudden death of their only child, Geoffrey, who was unmarried. Brunt died at the Hunters Moon Nursing Home, Ottways Lane, Ashtead, Surrey, on 5 February 1965.

REGINALD C. SUTCLIFFE, rev. JIM BURTON

Sources O. G. Sutton, *Memoirs FRS*, 11 (1965), 41–52 · *WWW* · P. A. Sheppard, *Quarterly Journal Royal Meteorological Society*, 91 (1965), 403–1 · O. G. Sutton, 'Scholar, teacher, administrator', *Meteorological Magazine*, 85 (1956), 161–4 [tribute upon Brunt's retirement] · S. Petterssen, *Bulletin of the American Meteorological Society*, 46 (1965), 362 · personal knowledge (1981) · private information (2004) · b. cert. · m. cert. · d. cert.

Likenesses Lafayette Ltd, photograph, repro. in *Memoirs FRS*, 11 (1965), facing p. 41

Wealth at death £74,654: probate, 5 April 1965, *CGPLA Eng. & Wales*

Brunt, John Thomas (1782–1820). *See under* Cato Street conspirators (*act.* 1820).

Brunton, Alexander (1772–1854). *See under* Brunton, Mary (1778–1818).

Brunton, Elizabeth. *See* Yates, Elizabeth (1799–1860).

Brunton, George (1799–1836), lawyer and journalist, was born on 31 January 1799 in St Cuthberts, Midlothian, the son of George Brunton and his wife, Agnes Baxter, and was educated at the Canongate high school, Edinburgh. He was admitted a solicitor in 1831, and in the following year, with David Haig, brought out *An Historical Account of the Senators of the College of Justice* (1832). This volume, which was at first undertaken as a republication of the *Catalogue of the Lords of Session* prepared by Lord Hailes in 1767, with a continuation to the time of its issue, became a collection of short biographies. Brunton was a frequent contributor to various magazines and journals and a committed Liberal. He established in 1834 a weekly Saturday newspaper called *The Patriot*, which was dropped upon his death. Brunton died on 2 June 1836, in Paris, where he had gone for health reasons.

ARTHUR H. GRANT, rev. ERIC METCALFE

Sources Irving, *Scots.* · *Caledonian Mercury* (11 June 1836) · *Edinburgh Almanack* (1831–7) · *GM*, 2nd ser., 6 (1836), 111 · *Tait's Edinburgh Magazine*, new ser., 3 (1836) · b. cert.

Wealth at death £458 11s. 2d.: inventory, 27 Dec 1836, NA Scot., SC 70/1/54, p. 735

Brunton, John (1741–1822), actor and theatre manager, was born in Norwich on 10 November 1741, the son of John Brunton, a soap maker, said to have come from a Scottish family tracing its descent from James II of Scotland. Young John Brunton went to Norwich grammar school before serving his apprenticeship to a wholesale grocer in the city. He then married Elizabeth Friend (1744–1826), daughter of a Norwich merchant, and with her settled and started a family in London, where he engaged in business as a grocer and tea dealer in Drury Lane.

However, according to *The Secret History of the Green Rooms* 'the Drama had long floated in his imagination' (2.176) and he conceived the idea of converting his propensity for 'what he had hitherto considered an amusement' (ibid.) into a livelihood. His chance came in 1774, when, at the suggestion of his friend Joseph Younger, actor and prompter at Covent Garden, he appeared first at Younger's own benefit on 11 April, in the title role of John Hoole's tragedy *Cyrus*, then at the benefit of Mr and Mrs Kniveton on 3 May, in the role of Hamlet. A year later—at the age of thirty-three and neither tall nor very handsome, but with an intelligent eye and resonant voice—he was playing leading parts at the Theatre Royal, Norwich.

He opened in late March 1775 with three consecutive performances as Hamlet, and in the following weeks he proceeded to build up a repertory of parts as diverse as Romeo and Richard III, Achmet in John Brown's *Barbarossa*, and Belville in Hugh Kelly's *The School for Wives*. The public, no doubt predisposed to applaud a fellow citizen, gave him a great reception, esteeming him, according to *The Thespian Dictionary* (1805), 'the best actor that had ever appeared on that stage'. John Bernard, who had been in the company with Brunton, described him as 'our leading tragedian and one of the best Shylocks … I ever saw' (Bernard, 121). In accomplishing so much so quickly, in spite of his inexperience, Brunton quite possibly had help from the manager, Richard Griffiths, who had a gift for coaching young actors, as Bernard recalled in acknowledging his own debt to him. 'Mr Griffiths', he wrote, 'exerted himself in that peculiar element in which he had ability, the opening to me a knowledge of the mechanism of my performance, as the means of my attaining a good style' (ibid.). That the actors themselves do not seem to have resented the sudden incursion of Brunton into their midst may have been at least partly a tribute to his genial temperament and generosity of disposition.

After five years on the Norwich circuit (which varied, but typically included Colchester, Ipswich, Bury St Edmunds, Yarmouth, and King's Lynn) Brunton tried his fortune again in London, in a single performance of *Richard III* on 1 July 1780. The audience was cordial enough but the press was grudging, conceding his natural attributes but finding him lacking in technique. He spent the rest of the summer at Bristol before joining the Bath company in September, at the beginning of their 1780–81 season. Characteristically he took his family with him and during the next five years, while himself acting both at Bath and in Bristol, chiefly in supporting roles, he also began to introduce his older offspring to the stage. Elizabeth, John, and Harriet, now ten, seven, and five years old, all took their first bow in 1782 but it was on his eldest daughter, Anne, born in London in 1769, that Brunton's hopes were centred. With his instruction and encouragement she made a brilliant début in April 1785 as Euphrasia in Arthur Murphy's *The Grecian Daughter*, Brunton playing her father, Evander. In October they were offered a brief engagement together at Covent Garden, where Anne had a promising reception, her father a cool one. They returned to Norwich, where Anne played for a while before spreading her wings in the theatrical firmament.

Brunton resumed his place as leading actor in what had become one of the most important theatres in the provinces. Things had changed in his absence. Griffiths had retired because of ill health in 1780 and the new manager, Giles Linnett Barrett, was also lessee. On 24 May 1788 the *Norwich Mercury* announced:

> Mr Barrett, with the consent of the Proprietors, has disposed of the remaining five years of his lease, as Manager of our Theatre, to Mr Brunton, father of the celebrated actress of that name … From the well-known abilities of Mr Brunton, the public may naturally expect to be highly gratified in their theatrical amusements, under his direction.

Brunton was an excellent manager, shrewd and reliable in business, popular with the public, considerate to his actors, and liberal in support of the Norwich Theatrical Fund for Retired Actors; generous, in fact, to anyone in need, from a rival manager in dire straits to a small school threatened with closure. He was also good company and at home in Norwich society. Under him the theatre had the most distinguished and prosperous decade in its history. However, towards the end of his third term as lessee it became clear that maintenance of the theatre buildings was not a high priority with him, and in January 1799 the proprietors decided, by sixteen votes to eleven, to grant the patent, not to him but to William Wilkins, architect, who had submitted detailed proposals for a complete structural overhaul of the Norwich house. Still immensely popular, Brunton retired gracefully from the scene at the end of May 1800.

Meanwhile two more of Brunton's children had sought the limelight. Elizabeth (1771–1799) had had an affecting début in 1790 at her now famous sister Anne's benefit at Covent Garden. Later she acted at Norwich but she died in 1799, a year after her marriage there to Peter Columbine. John (though intended for the law) had made the theatre his career and in 1792 he had married an actress, Anna Ross (b. 1773); both acted at Norwich under Brunton. Harriet (1778–1859) had not taken to the stage but had married Francis Noverre (1773–1840), son of Augustin Noverre and nephew of the famous Chevalier Jean Georges Noverre. It was now the turn of Louisa *Brunton (1782x5–1860) to follow her sisters to Covent Garden, as she did on 5 October 1803, charming the audience with her beauty.

In 1804 Brunton became manager of the Brighton (Duke Street) Theatre, the fortunes of which he improved, securing for it the active patronage of the prince of Wales (later George IV) and the title of Theatre Royal. When, in 1805 and 1806, Louisa came from Covent Garden to play for her father, the prince of Wales attended her benefits in both seasons. Among other noble patrons was William, first earl of Craven (1770–1825), and on 12 December 1807 at his house in Charles Street, Berkeley Square, he took Louisa from her father's hand in marriage. By April of that year the Duke Street theatre had been demolished and replaced by a new one in New Road, with Brunton as first lessee, this time with his son John, who also played Laertes to Charles Kemble's Hamlet at the opening on 6 June. Two more young Bruntons acted at Brighton, Kitty and Thomas, but the youngest of the family, Richard (1789–1859), was to take a different path, serving in the army through the Peninsular War, at Waterloo, and in India, and becoming lieutenant-colonel of the 13th light dragoons.

Brunton continued at Brighton until 1811, at some time after which he and his wife moved to Hamstead Marshall, in Berkshire, close to the Craven family seat at Hamstead Park. There he died, after an illness of only three days, on 18 December 1822. In its report the *Norwich Mercury* (28 Dec 1822) described him as 'alike distinguished by his own talents and those of his family'. As manager he had had 'a degree of success no former patentee had obtained'. As actor, it said:

> [he] was of the school of Garrick. He was natural, easy and graceful; and his manner in certain parts was powerful and affecting. His *Iago*, *Shylock* and *Old Dornton* are still remembered by many in the district, as perhaps the most perfect representations they have ever seen of these difficult characters. In the walks of private life few men were so amiable. His conversation was particularly animated, and informed by sense, vivacity and anecdote.

His wife, Elizabeth, lived on until 14 May 1826. She had been married to Brunton for over fifty years and borne fourteen children but had not followed his example in taking to the stage.   MOIRA FIELD

Sources records of the Norwich theatre and circuit, Norfolk RO · D. H. Eshleman, ed., *The committee books of the Theatre Royal, Norwich, 1768–1825* (1970) · [J. Haslewood], *The secret history of the green rooms: containing authentic and entertaining memoirs of the actors and actresses in the three theatres royal*, 2 vols. (1790) · *The thespian dictionary, or, Dramatic biography of the eighteenth century* (1802) · *Norwich Mercury* (1775–1826) · playbills for Norwich, Bristol, Bath, and Brighton theatres, 1775–1811, various collections · C. Mackie, *Norfolk annals: a chronological record of remarkable events in the nineteenth century*, 1: 1801–1850 (1901) · H. B. Baker, *The London stage: its history and traditions from 1576 to 1888*, 2 vols. (1889) · H. Bryant, A. Hare, and K. Barker, eds., *Theatre Royal, Bath: a calendar of performances at the Orchard Street Theatre, 1750–1805* (1977) · B. S. Penley, *The Bath stage: a history of dramatic representations in Bath* (1892) · K. Barker, *The Theatre Royal, Bristol, 1766–1966* (1974) · A. Dale, *The Theatre Royal, Brighton* (1950) · *Strictures, in verse, on the performances at the Theatre-Royal, Norwich towards the close of the season of 1799* [1799] · J. Bernard, *Retrospections of the stage*, ed. W. B. Bernard, 2 vols. (1830) · C. E. Noverre, *Some notes of the Norfolk Noverres and Bruntons* (1916) · Highfill, Burnim & Langhans, *BDA* · E. Grice, *Rogues and vagabonds, or, The actor's road to respectability* (1977)

Archives Bath Central Library, local collections · BL, playbills · Norfolk RO, collection of records and press cuttings relating to Norwich circuit theatres and actors · Norwich Central Library, playbills · Suffolk RO, Bury St Edmunds, Bury St Edmunds theatre collections · Suffolk RO, Bury St Edmunds, H. R. Eyre collection ·

University of East Anglia, Williams collection · Bristol, local collections
Likenesses school of Reynolds, portrait, c.1780, repro. in Grice, *Rogues and vagabonds*; formerly in Theatre Royal, Norwich

Brunton, Louisa [*married name* Louisa Craven, countess of Craven] (**1782×5–1860**), actress, was born in Norwich, the daughter of John *Brunton (1741–1822), actor and theatre manager, and his wife, Elizabeth Friend (1744–1826). She had six sisters, two of whom, Anne and Elizabeth, had some success as actresses. Louisa, who was considered a great beauty, made her first appearance at Covent Garden on 5 October 1803 as Lady Townly in *The Provoked Husband*, opposite John Philip Kemble. This performance, and a later one as Beatrice in *Much Ado about Nothing*, received favourable comment in the *Theatrical Inquisitor* (November 1803): Brunton was described as 'extremely handsome and striking', and her features as 'expressive of archness [and] vivacity'. She went on to play a series of secondary parts, principally in comedy. Her last recorded appearance was as Clara Sedley in Reynolds's comedy *The Rage* on 21 October 1807.

On 12 December 1807 Louisa Brunton married William Craven, first earl of Craven (1770–1825), and left the stage. They had three sons and a daughter. Craven, who was the son of the playwright Elizabeth Craven [*see* Elizabeth, margravine of Brandenburg-Ansbach-Bayreuth], had previously been among the early patrons of the courtesan Harriette Wilson; his wife, though accepted in society, was viewed somewhat askance by the aristocracy. She outlived her husband by thirty-five years, and died on 27 August 1860 at Hamstead Lodge, Hamstead Marshall, Berkshire. She was buried at Binley, near Coventry. Were it not for her socially elevated marriage, it is unlikely that Louisa Brunton's career would have been noticed.

K. D. REYNOLDS

Sources DNB · GEC, *Peerage* · Boase, *Mod. Eng. biog.* · *GM*, 1st ser., 77 (1807), 1172 · Mrs C. Baron-Wilson, *Our actresses*, 2 vols. (1844) · *CGPLA Eng. & Wales* (1860) · L. Melville, *Regency ladies* (1926) · *The girlhood of Queen Victoria: a selection from her majesty's diaries between the years 1832 and 1840*, ed. Viscount Esher [R. B. Brett], 2 vols. (1912) · Highfill, Burnim & Langhans, *BDA* [John Brunton]
Likenesses prints, BM, NPG
Wealth at death under £8000: probate, 17 Dec 1860, *CGPLA Eng. & Wales*

Brunton [*née* Balfour], **Mary** (**1778–1818**), novelist, was born on 1 November 1778 on Burray, one of the Orkney Islands, the daughter of Colonel Thomas Balfour (1752–1799) of Elwick and his wife, Frances Ligonier, who was the daughter of Colonel Francis Ligonier of the 13th dragoons. She had little formal education, but her mother taught her music, French, and Italian. On 4 December 1798 she eloped with and married the Revd Alexander Brunton (1772–1854) [*see below*] and settled in the manse of Bolton, near Haddington. With her husband's guidance she developed an interest in the philosophy of mind, especially that of Thomas Reid; in history she particularly enjoyed the works of William Robertson. In a letter of 1818 to Mrs Mary Balfour, her sister-in-law, she said that she was in favour of women's studying ancient languages

and mathematics, 'such accomplishments as are absolutely incapable of being converted into matter of exhibition' (Brunton, xcvi). In 1803 Mary and Alexander Brunton went to live in Edinburgh. In 1809 they travelled to Harrogate to take the waters, for the sake of Mary Brunton's health, and visited the Lake District with Mrs Izett, Mary Brunton's English friend.

Mary Brunton's first novel, *Self-Control*, was published in 1811; it was dedicated to Joanna Baillie, to whom she wrote that she 'merely intended to shew the power of the religious principle in bestowing self-command; and to bear testimony against a maxim as immoral as indelicate, that a reformed rake makes the best husband' (Brunton, xlii). Jane Austen made the comment in a letter that the book was an 'excellently-meant, elegantly-written work, without anything of Nature or Probability in it' (*Jane Austen's Letters*, 234). In pitching self-control against sensibility, however, Brunton was also trying to redefine femininity. *Self-Control* went into a third edition in 1812. A second novel, *Discipline*, came out in December 1814; it was also well received (going into three editions within two years), especially for its highland scenes, which had been conceived independently of Walter Scott's in *Waverley* (1814), but were influenced by Maria Edgeworth's Irish tales. In 1815 the Bruntons took advantage of repair work on the Tron Church to spend some time in London and the southwest of England. This was the year in which Mary Brunton began to study Gaelic. She now planned a series of domestic tales and made considerable progress in the writing of one of them, *Emmeline*. While stressing that for her a moral, 'a *lofty* moral' (Brunton, xxxii), was a necessary part of a work of fiction, she chose the then improper subject of a divorced woman whose second marriage is ruined by her guilty feelings and social ostracism. In this unfinished story she avoids the implausibilities of romantic plotting and the rhetoric of sensibility.

After giving birth to a stillborn son, her only child, on 7 December 1818 Mary Brunton succumbed to a fever and died on 19 December. She was buried in her father's tomb in Canongate churchyard, Edinburgh, on 24 December. A seven-volume edition, *The Works of Mary Brunton*, came out in 1820. *Self-Control* and *Discipline* were republished in Colburn and Bentley's Standard Novels in 1832, and in cheap editions in 1837 and 1852, an index to their lasting success. A French translation of *Self-Control* appeared in Paris in 1829. The portrait by W. I. Thomson printed in the 1819 volume shows Mary Brunton to have been an attractive, placid-looking woman with short, dark hair and an upturned nose. Her novels are significant because they show the aporias of the ethical-psychological model of sensibility prevalent in the late eighteenth century. Their proclaimed religious purpose is often at odds with their narrative logic. Mary Brunton also contributed to introducing in fiction a greater geographical specificity and a more dynamic image of the human psyche.

Mary Brunton's husband and biographer, **Alexander Brunton** (**1772–1854**), Church of Scotland minister and scholar of oriental languages, was born in Edinburgh, and baptized in Peebles on 4 October 1772, the son of James

Brunton, cordner (shoemaker), and his wife, Christian, *née* Cranston. He became minister of Bolton in 1797, of the New Greyfriars Church, Edinburgh, in 1803, and of the Tron Church in the same city in November 1809, remaining in the latter parish until his death. He was professor of oriental languages in the University of Edinburgh from May 1813; in December of the same year he became a doctor of divinity. In 1818 Brunton published *Sermons and Lectures*, and after his wife's death he compiled a volume in 1819 which included a memoir of Mary Brunton and selections from her travel diary for 1812 and 1815, as well as aids to devotion and her unfinished novel *Emmeline*. In 1822 his *Outlines of Persian Grammar* appeared, and he was made moderator of the general assembly of the Church of Scotland in May 1823. He was also convenor of the Indian mission committee from 1834 to 1847, and published *Forms of Public Worship in the Church of Scotland* in 1848. Alexander Brunton died on 9 February 1854 at Jordonstone House, Coupar Angus, Perthshire. ISABELLE BOUR

Sources A. Brunton, 'Memoir', in M. Brunton, *'Emmeline', with some other pieces* (1819) · R. P. Fereday, 'Mrs Mary Brunton—a moralising novelist', *The Orcadian* (23 July 1987) · *Jane Austen's letters*, ed. D. Le Faye, new edn (1997) · *Fasti Scot.*, 1.737 · Boase, *Mod. Eng. biog.* · bap. reg. Scot. [baptism of Alexander Brunton, 4 Oct 1772] · m. reg. Scot. · bur. reg. Scot.

Archives Orkney Archives, Balfour MSS, D2

Likenesses J. Thomson, stipple, pubd 1820 (after G. Clint), BM · H. Meyer, sculpture, repro. in M. Brunton, *'Emmeline', with some other pieces* · W. I. Thomson, drawing, repro. in M. Brunton, *'Emmeline', with some other pieces* · stipple, BM

Brunton, Sir Thomas Lauder, first baronet (1844–1916), physician and pharmacologist, the third son of James Brunton (1781–1863), and his second wife, Agnes (1805/6–1848), daughter of John Stenhouse of White Lee, was born at Hiltonshill, Roxburghshire, on 14 March 1844. Educated privately, he entered the University of Edinburgh, where he had a distinguished academic career, graduating MB CM with honours in 1866. For a year after graduation he acted as house physician in Edinburgh Infirmary. During this time he undertook research involving experiments on himself. The results were published in his thesis on the action of digitalis for which he was awarded MD with gold medal in 1868. As a Baxter natural sciences scholar Brunton travelled abroad to study pharmacology in Vienna and Berlin. He went on to Amsterdam, where he studied physiological chemistry with Willy Kuhne, and to Leipzig to work in the laboratory of the physiologist Carl Ludwig.

After returning to Britain in 1870 Brunton was appointed lecturer in materia medica and pharmacology at the Middlesex Hospital, and in the following year to the same position at St Bartholomew's, both in London. Regarding this as a responsibility that involved more than the mere delivery of lectures, and in emulation of the pharmacological laboratories that were just beginning to be established in Germany, he secured as his first laboratory the only place available, a hospital scullery, measuring 12 feet by 6 feet. He remained on the active staff of St Bartholomew's as casualty physician for four years, as assistant physician for twenty years, and as physician for nine. During this time he gradually became an acknowledged leader of the medical profession, with a more than European reputation. His fruitful researches and his wide knowledge of scientific and medical literature, his friendships with British and foreign workers, his personal charm and integrity, added to his fame as the most widely known consulting physician in London. Brunton married, in 1879, Louisa Jane, daughter of the Ven. Edward Adderley Stopford, archdeacon of Meath. They had three sons and three daughters. Brunton's researches on the physiology and therapy of the cardiovascular and digestive systems contributed to the development of experimental pharmacology. In 1867, while still a house physician in Edinburgh, he observed in a patient suffering from angina pectoris that the nightly attacks of pain were accompanied by a rise in the blood pressure. Unpublished experiments by Arthur Gamgee had shown that nitrite of amyl lessened arterial tension in man and animals. Using this knowledge Brunton administered the substance by inhalation to his patient as an alternative to bleeding which was the only other treatment known to have any effect in relieving the pain. He analysed the action of the drug in Ludwig's laboratory and found the reduction in blood pressure to be due to a dilatation of the blood vessels. He regarded the success of amyl nitrite, the first known vasodilator, as an example of rational therapeutics based on pharmacological data.

Brunton made numerous original contributions to medicine and pharmacology, including studies on the action of digitalis, the diuretic effect of mercury, the physiology of digestion, and the action of enzymes. He was elected a fellow of the Royal Society in 1874. It was said of him that 'his aim was to leave therapeutics, if possible, as a science instead of merely an art, as he found it'.

Brunton was regarded as a great teacher and organizer of medical knowledge. His lectures at St Bartholomew's were described by one who attended them as 'the most interesting and instructive of all the lectures given there at that time'. His published works were influential in connecting the practice of medicine with the sciences upon which it came to be based. His most important work was his *Textbook of Pharmacology, Therapeutics and Materia medica* (1885). In this work, which was translated into several languages, Brunton abandoned the classical materia medica and emphasized the physiological actions of pure drugs. In the Goulstonian lecture of 1877 he discussed the relation of pharmacology to therapeutics. The disorders of digestion were the subject of his Lettsomian lectures in 1886 and in the Croonian lectures in 1889 he discussed the relation between chemical structure and physiological activity.

Brunton had imperial as well as academic interests. He was one of the founders of the National League for Physical Education, and was a steadfast and active advocate of schemes in favour of national health, school hygiene, and military training. In a letter to Brunton in 1915 Sir Douglas Haig wrote, 'You and I have often talked about the certainty of this war, and have done, each of us, our best to prepare in our own spheres for it.' Brunton was knighted in 1900 and given a baronetcy in 1908. The death of his devoted wife in 1909, the symptoms of heart disease, and the death of his second son, killed in action in 1915, clouded the last years of his life. Of somewhat frail build, he was impressive only when he spoke. His learning, originality, and practical skill entitle him to rank as one of the founders of modern pharmacology. This, combined with his enthusiasm, his capacity for friendship, and unfailing kindness of heart made him an outstanding and cosmopolitan figure for over a quarter of a century. He died at his home, De Walden Court, New Cavendish Street, London, on 16 September 1916 and was buried at Highgate.   J. A. GUNN, rev. M. P. EARLES

Sources *The Lancet* (23 Sept 1916), 572–5 · *BMJ* (23 Sept 1916), 440–42 · C. A., *PRS*, 89B (1915–17), xliv–xlviii · *DSB*, 2.547–8 · *The medical who's who* (1915) · Munk, *Roll* · L. Holmstedt and G. Liljestrand, *Readings in pharmacology* (1963), 99–102 · Burke, *Peerage* (1931)

Archives NL Scot., corresp · Wellcome L., corresp. and papers | NL Ire., letters to A. S. Green · RCP Lond., letters to Sir Thomas Barlow · Wellcome L., corresp. with Sir Leonard Rogers

Likenesses G. Jerrard, photograph, 1881, Wellcome L. · photogravure, 1890 (after chalk drawing by L. D. C.), Wellcome L. · H. von Herkomer, oils, 1913, St Bartholomew's Hospital, London · C. d'O. P. Jackson, bronze medal, 1923, Scot. NPG · H. Solomon, oils, 1925, Wellcome L. · photograph, repro. in *BMJ*, facing p. 440 · photograph, repro. in *The Lancet*, 573 · photomechanical print, Wellcome L.

Wealth at death £28,151: unsettled estate; £26,457: net personalty: *BMJ*

Brunton, William (1777–1851), engineer, was the eldest of three sons of Robert Brunton, a watch- and clockmaker at Dalkeith, Edinburghshire, Scotland, where he was born on 26 May 1777. He studied mechanics in his father's shop and engineering under his grandfather, who was a local colliery viewer. In 1790 he commenced work in the fitting shops of the New Lanark cotton mills, and stayed there until he obtained employment in 1796 at the famous Soho works of Boulton and Watt, where he eventually became foreman and superintendent of the engine factory.

Brunton left Soho in 1808 and joined William Jessop's Butterley works in Derbyshire, which specialized in the production of castings, and in the course of his work made the acquaintance of John Rennie, Thomas Telford, and other eminent engineers. He married on 30 October 1810 Anne Elizabeth Button, adopted daughter of John and Rebecca Dickinson of Summer Hill, Birmingham. They had three daughters and three sons, two of whom became well-known engineers.

In 1815 Brunton became a partner and engineering manager in the firm of Francis, Smith, Dearman, and Brunton (the Eagle Foundry) of Broad Street, Birmingham. This company manufactured various metal products, including Brunton's own ingeniously designed mechanical stokers and revolving fire grates (1819, patent 4387; 1820, patent 4449; 1822, patent 4685). While working at the foundry he lived at first in Regent Street but later took up residence at 3 Camden Street, Birmingham.

About 1825 Brunton moved to London, where he practised as a civil engineer and bought a house in Canonbury Square, Islington. His brother Robert and son John were employed in his drawing office at East India Chambers, Leadenhall Street, and assisted with his work, which included railway construction. For this he designed a machine (1833, patent 6500) for excavating the ground and forming embankments, and in 1836 issued a publication on the subject.

On leaving London in 1835 Brunton took a share in the Cwmafon tin works, Glamorgan, where he designed and erected copper smelting furnaces and rolling mills at the foot of the Foel Mountain. A feature of the development was a massive chimney built on the mountain to remove noxious gases from the works. He then became connected with the Maesteg ironworks and also with the Vale of Neath brewery in 1838; but by 1847 the latter had failed and his life savings were lost.

An early member of the Institution of Civil Engineers, Brunton developed a number of original methods of reducing ore and manufacturing metals (1841, patent 9135; 1842, patent 9351) and the machinery for the processes. He played an important part in the introduction of steam navigation by making some of the original engines for craft on the Humber and Trent, and some of the earliest on the Mersey, including those for the vessel which first plied on the Liverpool ferries in 1814. He fitted out the *Sir Francis Drake* at Plymouth in 1824, the first steamer to take a man-of-war in tow. His calciner (1828, patent 5621) was used at many tin mines in Cornwall, as well as at silver ore works in Mexico; and his fan regulator was also a most useful invention. At Butterley he introduced the principle of rapidly rotating moulds for casting iron pipes and here designed one of the most ingenious of his inventions. This was the walking machine called the 'mechanical traveller' or 'steam horse' (patent 3700), which he built in 1813, and which worked at the Newbottle colliery, co. Durham. On 31 July 1815, after receiving a new boiler, this machine exploded because of the driver's carelessness, and unfortunately several people were killed and many injured.

William Brunton was a clever, energetic, and totally dedicated engineer, but one who derived little remuneration from his inventions. Latterly he turned his attention to the subject of improved ventilation for collieries, and sent models of his inventions to the Great Exhibition in Hyde Park. His publication *On the Ventilation of Coal Mines* appeared in 1849. Brunton's wife died at Eaglebush House, Neath, Glamorgan, in 1845; and after moving to Cornwall about 1848, Brunton himself died at the residence of his son William Brunton, at Camborne Cross, Camborne, on 5 October 1851.

G. C. BOASE, rev. CHRISTOPHER F. LINDSEY

Sources *PICE*, 11 (1851–2), 95–9 · J. Brunton, *John Brunton's book: being the memories of John Brunton, engineer, from a manuscript in his own hand written for his grandchildren and now first printed* (1939) · L. St L. Pendred, 'A note on Brunton's steam horse, 1813', *Transactions* [Newcomen Society], 2 (1921–2), 118–20 · 'Newbottle colliery accident', *Durham Advertiser* (5 Aug 1815) · J. Morris, 'Evan Evans and the Vale of Neath brewery', *Morgannwg*, 9 (1965), 38–60 · D. Brownlie, 'John George Bodmer, his life and work, particularly in relation to the evolution of mechanical stoking', *Transactions* [Newcomen Society], 6 (1925–6), 94–6 · J. W. Hall, 'Joshua Field's diary of a tour in 1821 through the midlands, with introduction and notes', *Transactions* [Newcomen Society], 6 (1925–6), 1–41, esp. 3–6, 32–3 · P. Riden, *The Butterley Company, 1790–1830*, 2nd edn, Derbyshire RS

(1990) · G. T. Eaton, 'Cwmavon and some early notabilities', *Transactions of the Port Talbot Historical Society* (1965), 48–9 · L. G. Charlton, 'William Brunton', in L. G. Charlton, *The first locomotive engineers: their work in the north-east of England* (1974), 43–5 · d. cert. · private information · census returns for Camborne, Cornwall, 1851, PRO, HO 107/1916, fol. 114 · *DNB* · *IGI*

Archives Birm. CL, Boulton and Watt collection, letters and MSS · Birm. CL, draft deeds, Solicitor's collection-Lee Crowder/118, Eagle Foundry circular Z 370 · LUL, Goldsmiths' Library of Economic Literature, Basing to Bath railway plan

Wealth at death £200: PRO, death duty register, IR 26/1922, fol. 378

Brunyard, William (*supp. fl.* **1349–1350**), supposed Dominican friar and theologian, is recorded by the late fourteenth-century bibliographer Henry Kirkestede as an English Dominican who flourished in 1349 and wrote a good *summa* and a collection of *distinctiones*. Kirkestede's account is followed by Bale, who, however, gives his *floruit* as 1350, and adds a set of *determinationes*. Brunyard occurs in similar terms in the writings of Pits and Tanner. There is, however, no good reason for supposing that William Brunyard ever existed, and it seems clear that he originated in an error by Kirkestede, who accidentally created a fiction and endowed him with the writings of the famous Dominican theologian and preacher John *Bromyard, whose *Summa praedicantium* was one of the best-known collections of pulpit *exempla* of the later middle ages.

HENRY SUMMERSON

Sources Tanner, *Bibl. Brit.-Hib.*, 132 [Kirkestede's catalogue] · Bale, *Cat.*, 429–30 · J. Pits, *Relationum historicarum de rebus Anglicis*, ed. [W. Bishop] (Paris, 1619), 479 · R. Sharpe, *A handlist of the Latin writers of Great Britain and Ireland before 1540* (1997), 756

Bruodin [MacBrody, Mac Bruaideadha], **Anthony** (*d.* **1680**), Franciscan friar, was born at Ballyhogan, co. Clare, the son of Miler Bruodin, a landowner, and Margaret O'Mollony, a relative of two bishops of Killaloe, Malachy and John O'Mollony. The MacBrody or Mac Bruaideadha were a bardic family [*see* Mac Bruaideadha family (*per.* 1558–1636)]. After early education in Ireland Bruodin entered the Franciscan order at the age of twenty, and left Ireland in 1643. He pursued ecclesiastical studies at St Isidore's College, Rome, completing them in 1650, and asked to join his relative Bernardine Clanchy at the Irish College of the Immaculate Conception, Prague. Luke Wadding recommended Bruodin to the general as a 'good student' but opposed his appointment as lector at the Irish College in Prague, where Bruodin would teach philosophy and theology in the archiepiscopal seminary. Possibly due to overcrowding in the Irish College there, at the end of 1651 Bruodin was transferred from the Irish Franciscan province to the Bohemian province of St Wenceslas and was appointed prefect of studies in the philosophical school attached to the friary at Olmutz. On 8 September 1659 he was elected a definitor at the provincial chapter held at Neuhaus and from 1662 to 1663 was guardian of the convent of Olmutz. As lector jubilate he presided over the disputation at the 1664 general chapter of the order held in Aracoeli, the headquarters of the Franciscan order in Rome, when Father Anthony William Brauczek defended a thesis under the auspices of Emperor Leopold I, the first

Bohemian friar to do so. In 1667 he was again invited to preside over a discussion at the general chapter when another Bohemian Franciscan defended. From 1668 to 1670 he was guardian of the friary of Our Lady of the Snows, Prague, the mother house of the Bohemian province, and in 1672 became guardian of Neuhaus. He was one of the leaders of the province's efforts to retain its independence from the Austrian province of the order.

Bruodin published a manual of theology entitled *Oecodomia minoriticae scholae Salomonis* in Prague in 1663, the first volume of a *summa* for students, of which he published the second volume, *Corolla oecodomiae minoriticae scholae*, in 1664. This second volume was prohibited, pending correction, by the Congregation of the Index on 29 November 1667. Among his other works, *Propugnaculum catholicae veritatis*, published in 1669, narrated about 200 Irish Catholic martyrdoms, with an index of 164 persons arranged by Christian name as in martyrologies. In the chapter headed 'De Carve seu Carrani erroribus et impostoribus' of its fifth book he attacked the controversial Irish secular priest Thomas Carew's *Lyra*, prompting a fiery polemic with Carew (or Carve). Carew replied in a small work entitled *Enchiridion apologeticum* (1670), published in Nuremberg, to which Bruodin responded in *Anatomicum examen* (1671), published under the pseudonym Cornelius O'Mollony, which contained accounts of Irish Franciscan martyrs. Carew replied again in 1672 with his *Responsio veridica*, which questioned Bruodin's veracity as a writer of the lives of the Irish martyrs.

In 1675 Bruodin transferred back to the Irish province but remained in Prague, attached to the community of the College of the Immaculate Conception. He died there during the plague of 1680. In 1721 his *Descriptio regni Hiberniae sanctorum insulae, et de prima origine miseriarum & motuum in Anglia, Scotia, & Hibernia regnante Carolo primo rege* was published at Rome. Bruodin has been considered 'a somewhat troublesome man … celebrated for his lack of tact' and a 'facile, imaginative writer, given at times to exaggeration' (Millett, *The Irish Franciscans*, 151, 247). His works are among the 'few sources of knowledge of the fate of Irish catholic victims of religious persecution, but are not always reliable' (Millett, 'Irish literature', 580).

STEFANO VILLANI

Sources G. Cleary, *Father Luke Wadding and St Isidore's College, Rome* (1925), 136–8 · K. McGrath, 'The Bruodins in Bohemia', *Irish Ecclesiastical Record*, 5th ser., 77 (1952), 333–43 · T. Wall, 'Bards and Bruodins', *Father Luke Wadding: commemorative volume*, ed. Franciscan Fathers dún Mhuire, Killiney (1957), 438–62 · B. Millett, 'Some lists of Irish Franciscans in Prague, 1656–1791', *Collectanea Hibernica*, 36–7 (1994–5), 59–84 · C. McGrath, 'Materials for a history of clann Bhruaideadha', *Éigse*, 4 (1943–4), 48–66 · B. Millett, *The Irish Franciscans, 1651–1665* (1964) · S. Sousedík, *Jan Duns Scotus* (Prague, 1989) · B. Jennings, 'The Irish Franciscans in Prague', *Studies: an Irish Quarterly Review*, 28 (1939), 210–22 · C. McNeill, 'Irish confessors and martyrs', *Catholic encyclopaedia* (1913) · P. Minges, 'Scotism and Scotists', *Catholic encyclopaedia* (1913) · *Index librorum prohibitorum* (1940), 67 · S. Villani, 'Uomini, idee, notizie tra Inghilterra della Rivoluzione e Italia della Controriforma', diss., Scuola Normale Superiore di Pisa, 1998–9 · B. Millett, 'Irish literature in Latin, 1550–1700', *A new history of Ireland*, ed. T. W. Moody and others, 3: *Early modern Ireland, 1534–1691* (1976), 561–86

Brus [Bruce], **Robert de** (*supp. d.* 1094), supposed noble-man, was once thought to have been the ancestor of the Brus (later Bruce) family. The search for the origins of the family led nineteenth-century historians, including Aeneas Mackay writing in the *Dictionary of National Biography*, to accept late medieval lists of those who fought at Hastings, such as that cited by John Leland (*d.* 1552) in his *Collectanea*, as evidence for Brus's existence at that time. These lists are, however, wholly unreliable. The real founder of the family's fortunes in Britain was Robert (I) de *Brus (*d.* 1142). It was this Robert who had extensive holdings in northern England, the first of which were granted by Henry I, perhaps soon after 1106, and were added to the Yorkshire section of Domesday Book between 1114 and 1119.   EMMA COWNIE

Sources A. Farley, ed., *Domesday Book*, 2 vols. (1783) • *DNB* • *Joannis Lelandi antiquarii de rebus Britannicis collectanea*, ed. T. Hearne, [2nd edn], 6 vols. (1770), vol. 1, p. 202 • W. Farrer and others, eds., *Early Yorkshire charters*, 12 vols. (1914–65), vols. 1–3, see also index

Brus [Bruce], **Robert (I) de**, **lord of Annandale** (*d.* 1142), baron and soldier, has been said without authority to be the son of a Robert (sometimes Adam) de *Brus, who was alleged to have fought at Hastings. The subject of this memoir came from Brix, south of Cherbourg, where he was an ally of Henry I, whose conquest of Normandy he presumably supported. Perhaps soon after the battle of Tinchebrai (September 1106) Henry gave him some eighty Yorkshire manors, chiefly in Claro wapentake, then a fur-ther thirteen manors around Skelton, formerly of the count of Mortain, and *c*.1119 Hart and Hartness in co. Dur-ham. Brus's importance is shown by the addition, between 1114 and 1119, of the first of these holdings to the Yorkshire Domesday, while the second, the lordship of Skelton, formed one of a series of castellanies whereby Norman control of northern England was consolidated. He attested several charters of Henry I, especially after 1106, and was with him at Lyons la Forêt in 1129, and at Woodstock (with David I also) at Easter 1130. But he undoubtedly spent much time in the north, where, for example, he was at a gathering of magnates at Durham in 1121, when the monks of Durham and St Albans fell out over Tynemouth. He founded the Augustinian priory of Guisborough in the North Riding of Yorkshire, probably in 1119, endowing it richly with some thirty carrucates of land; the first prior was his brother, William. David I, king of Scots, knew Brus well, perhaps starting in Normandy, where Brus gave the church of Querqueville to St Mary's York for the souls of Earl David (as he then was) and his parents. Their absences from Henry's court seem to coin-cide, and they may have campaigned together, for instance after 1107, in compelling Alexander I to hand over to David the southern Scottish appanage left him by King Edgar.

After David succeeded as king in 1124 he gave Annandale with its castle to Brus, possibly at his inauguration in that year, since the charter is dated at Scone. The castle has been alleged to imply an earlier grant—only 'Normans' could build castles. He was a frequent witness of those charters of David I whose witnesses are known, whether

issued in England or Scotland; he was usually named first among the Anglo-French barons, and his friendship with David I was surely close. But after the death of Henry I, Brus, who may be presumed to have taken the oath in favour of Matilda's rights, none the less supported King Stephen, and was present with him at the siege of Exeter in 1136, and later at York. In 1138, therefore, he was one of the leaders of the northern English army which opposed David I's invasion at Cowton Moor, and was sent to per-suade him to withdraw, for which occasion Ailred of Rie-vaulx puts in his mouth a memorably eloquent speech about David's previous dependence on English and Nor-mans. David was moved, but William fitz Duncan, accus-ing Brus of treason, persuaded the king to fight. Brus for-mally broke his fealty and homage to the king, no mere gesture, for it greatly impressed contemporaries. The Eng-lish army, said to have included Brus's older son, Adam, crushingly defeated King David, whose former relation-ship with Brus was never re-established. Robert died on 11 May, in 1141 according to a fourteenth-century family chronicle, which has many unreliable dates; John of Hexham, who places the death about Easter (19 April), 1142, is to be preferred: he died on 11 May 1142.

Robert (I) de Brus married an Agnes, probably daughter of Geoffrey Bainard (sheriff of York before 1100), with whom he had two sons, Adam, and Robert (II) de *Brus (*d.* 1194?). A Peter de Brus was not, as has sometimes been claimed, a middle son, though he may have been Robert's brother. The male descendants of Adam (who died in 1143) continued to hold the Yorkshire lands as lords of Skelton for a further four generations, until the death of Peter de Brus in 1272, when they passed to his sisters and coheirs.

A. A. M. DUNCAN

Sources W. Farrer and others, eds., *Early Yorkshire charters*, 12 vols. (1914–65), vol. 2, pp. 11–19 • P. Dalton, *Conquest, anarchy, and lordship: Yorkshire, 1066–1154*, Cambridge Studies in Medieval Life and Thought, 4th ser., 27 (1994), 90–94 • A. C. Lawrie, ed., *Early Scottish charters prior to AD 1153* (1905), nos. 52, 54; pp. 27, 42, 51, 52, 55, 70, 71, 73, 78, 82, 87, 89, 99 • Dugdale, *Monasticon*, new edn, 6.267 • A. O. Anderson, ed., *Scottish annals from English chroniclers, AD 500 to 1286* (1908), 192–5 • A. A. M. Duncan, 'The Bruces of Annandale, 1100–1304', *Transactions of the Dumfriesshire and Galloway Natural History and Antiquarian Society*, 3rd ser., 69 (1994), 89–102

Brus, Robert (III) de (*d.* before 1191). *See under* Brus, Rob-ert (II) de, lord of Annandale (*d.* 1194?).

Brus [Bruce], **Robert (II) de**, **lord of Annandale** (*d.* 1194?), baron, was the son of Robert (I) de *Brus (*d.* 1142) and his wife, Agnes. Described as *iuvenis* ('a youngster') on his seal and in one of his father's charters, he was probably born after *c*.1120. A late family chronicle claims that the younger Robert had already been given Annandale by his father when he was in David I's army at Northallerton in 1138, that he was taken prisoner by his father at the battle of the Standard, and handed over to King Stephen, who courteously gave him to his mother. Staying in his father's house, he complained that wheaten bread was unobtain-able in Annandale, so his father gave him Hart and Hart-ness (co. Durham) for wheat growing. This pleasant fable is unreliable in every respect, and Robert may not have been at Northallerton and may have received his lands after the battle; Hartness he and his heirs held of the senior (Skelton) line of the family, but Annandale of the Scottish king. He was also assessed as having five knights' fees in Yorkshire, but these have not been identified. Edenhall in Cumbria, given by Henry II, was later held by him of Bruce of Skelton.

Robert (II) de Brus was one of those who sought unsuccessfully on behalf of David I and the empress to cajole the monks of Durham into electing William Cumin as bishop of Durham in 1141, but thereafter he is hard to trace in politics, Scottish or English. He was a frequent witness to charters of David I (r. 1124–53) and Malcolm IV (r. 1153–65), but was distant from William the Lion (r. 1165–1214), witnessing only three of his charters; perhaps he had failed to support William's claims to the earldom of Northumberland in 1157. Before 1173 the Scottish king gave a charter at Lochmaben confirming the lordship of Annandale as held by Robert's father, but with exceptions which trimmed their extensive franchises; it was to be held for the service of ten knights, a figure not disclosed in earlier charters and high for Scotland. In 1173–4 Brus supported Henry II against the young king and William the Lion.

In the 1140s Brus had welcomed Malachy at Annan, and granted the future saint's wish that a thief be pardoned; the following morning Malachy saw the thief on the gibbet and put a curse on Annan, where the river obligingly washed away part of the motte. Robert probably built the extensive motte and bailey at the new *caput* of Annandale, Lochmaben, whose cost may help to explain his borrowing of over £237 from Aaron the Jew. He settled a long-running dispute with Ingram and Jocelyn, bishops of Glasgow, over the churches of Annandale, which had been given to Guisborough Priory, of which he was a careful patron (and where he was probably buried).

Robert (II) de Brus married Euphemia, niece of William, earl of Albemarle, who bore three sons, Robert, William, and Bernard, and a daughter, Agatha, who married Ralph, son of Ribald of Middleham. He was alive at the time of the pipe roll of 1193; but in that of 1194 both he and his heir occur, so he probably died in that year, on either 17 February or 26 August. His first son, **Robert (III) de Brus** (d. before 1191), married an illegitimate daughter of King *William the Lion in 1183, and had died without surviving children by 1191, so that on his father's death Annandale and Hartness passed to the second son, **William de Brus**, lord of Annandale (d. 1211/12), of whom almost nothing is known. The pipe rolls show him reluctant to pay King John's scutages, but making a part payment of £25 in 1209, and he died on 16 July in 1211 or 1212, having witnessed one charter of King William and bought for Hartlepool a market and fair at a cost of 20 marks in 1201. He had married a Christina, who bore two sons; the younger, who was a hostage in King John's hands in 1213, was possibly called William de Brus, and the elder was **Robert (IV) de Brus**, lord of Annandale (c.1195–1226x33). He was of age in 1215, when King John made him minor conciliatory grants on the eve of, and soon after, conceding Magna Carta. Unlike his distant cousin Peter de Brus, lord of Skelton, he played

no known part in the civil and Anglo-Scottish wars of 1215–17, though Alexander II would surely have demanded his knight-service. He attested the marriage settlement of that king at York in 1221 and owed scutage until 1226, but is not recorded thereafter. His marriage to Isabel, second daughter of *David, earl of Huntingdon, which annals once attributed to John Fordun placed before Earl David's death in 1219, was probably not long before, and there is no authority for the often repeated claim that his son was born in 1210. This marriage would have given him some lands in the south which perhaps kept him in England. Robert (IV)'s death has been placed wrongly in 1245: his fief of Hart was in his kinsman's wardship when Richard Poor was bishop of Durham (1228–37), and the bishop's grant of privileges to the borough of Hartlepool in September 1230 may place the wardship that early; indeed there is no evidence that he was alive after 1226, and he was certainly dead by March 1234. He died on 21 April or 26 August, between 1226 and 1233, and was buried at Guisborough Priory. Isabel died in 1251 and was buried at Sawtry Abbey in Huntingdonshire. They had one son, Robert (V) de *Brus. The Beatrice who married Hugh de Neville was a daughter of Robert de Briwes, a justice who was confused with Brus by nineteenth-century editors. A. A. M. DUNCAN

Sources G. W. S. Barrow, ed., *Regesta regum Scottorum*, 1–2 (1960–71) · A. C. Lawrie, ed., *Early Scottish charters prior to AD 1153* (1905) · Dugdale, *Monasticon*, new edn, 6.267 · A. A. M. Duncan, 'The Bruces of Annandale, 1100—1304', *Transactions of the Dumfriesshire and Galloway Natural History and Antiquarian Society*, 3rd ser., 69 (1994), 89–102 · Pipe rolls · T. D. Hardy, ed., *Rotuli litterarum clausarum*, 2 vols., RC (1833–4) · *CDS*, vol. 1, nos. 621, 624, 700, 707, 808 · A. O. Anderson, ed., *Scottish annals from English chroniclers, AD 500 to 1286* (1908) · P. Dalton, *Conquest, anarchy, and lordship: Yorkshire, 1066–1154*, Cambridge Studies in Medieval Life and Thought, 4th ser., 27 (1994), 90–94 · F. H. M. Parker, ed., *The pipe rolls of Cumberland and Westmorland, 1222–1260*, Cumberland and Westmorland Antiquarian and Archaeological Society, extra ser., 12 (1905), 5, 9, 15 · W. Brown, ed., *Cartularium prioratus de Gyseburne*, 2, SurtS, 89 (1894), 342 · W. Brown, 'The Brus cenotaph at Guisbrough', *Yorkshire Archaeological Journal*, 13 (1894–5), 226–61, esp. 249–50
Archives PRO, duchy of Lancaster, cartae miscellaneae, DL 36

Brus, Robert (IV) de, lord of Annandale (c.1195–1226x33). *See under* Brus, Robert (II) de, lord of Annandale (d. 1194?).

Brus [Bruce], **Robert (V) de** [called Robert the Noble], **lord of Annandale** (c.1220–1295), magnate and claimant to the Scottish throne, was a minor at the death of his father, Robert (IV) de *Brus (c.1195–1226x33) [see under Brus, Robert (II) de], when Peter de Brus of Skelton had wardship of his English lands. He was first named among the Scottish barons promising in 1237 that they would compel observance of the treaty of York, but was probably not then of age, though he had come of age by June 1242. In 1252 he succeeded to the extensive estates of his mother, Isabel (d. 1251), second daughter of *David, earl of Huntingdon, in Essex and Garioch (Aberdeenshire). At this time he played little part in Scottish politics, though he was named as an acceptable councillor by Alexander III and approved by Henry III on the exclusion of the Comyns and their supporters in 1255. Henry III sent him to Scotland in 1257, an association which may explain why he was not in the compromise Scottish council of 1258.

Henry III's excursion into Scottish politics in September 1255 clearly influenced him to appoint Brus as sheriff of Cumberland on 22 August, a post from which he was sacked, after Henry had got his way in Scotland, on 28 October. There is no evidence that he was active in the English baronial reform movement though he was cited as a 'friend' by his brother-in-law, the earl of Gloucester, on 14 March 1259. He probably stayed in Scotland until 1262 when, with John Comyn, he joined Henry III's *mesnie*, witnessing royal charters in October and December 1263. Thereafter he must have retreated to Hartness or Scotland, returning in the northern force raised for Henry III and the Lord Edward in April–May 1264; despite their defeat and the capture of Henry, Edward, and Brus at Lewes, where many Scots were killed, the action was probably critical for Robert's future, in establishing a close link with Edward. Brus was ransomed by his son, Robert (VI) de *Brus, and after Evesham joined in the royalist exploitation of the unfortunate rebels, profiting from the lands of Walter de Fauconberg and John de Melsa. Constable of Carlisle Castle in 1267–8, he was sent to Scotland by Henry III to forward the king's business there in 1269, and was apparently with Alexander III at Scone for an assembly in March 1270, in which a dispute over their rights in the churches of Annandale was settled; the royal letter recording this is unique in that it is in French, perhaps because that was Brus's first language. Later in 1270 his sons intended to join the crusade of the Lord Edward, but are not known to have gone; this failure (and it is clear that his heir stayed at home) may explain why in 1271 Robert himself, aged about fifty, sailed with the second expedition, under the Lord Edmund, and served with Edward in Palestine. On his way home he visited the tomb of St Malachy at Clairvaux, to undo the saint's curse laid upon Robert (II) de Brus. In 1278 his son accompanied Alexander III to Tewkesbury, possibly a sign of Robert's advancing years, though he was sheriff of Cumberland in 1283–5.

In 1284 Brus was among the Scottish magnates who swore to accept Margaret, the Maid of Norway, as heir presumptive to Alexander III. The king's death, and the soon-discovered pregnancy of his widow, in 1286 raised many uncertainties. In September 1286 a gathering of Brus's distinguished supporters at his son's castle of Turnberry undertook to help two Irish magnates, a bond which has always been seen as preparation for the rising of Brus after the queen miscarried in November. Presumably he now sought the Scottish throne by virtue of his descent from Earl David. A number of royal and Balliol castles in the south-west were taken, but support was quite inadequate and the guardians restored peace by the spring of 1287. For two years Robert's influence must have languished—he and his supporters had charge of no royal castles in this period—and in 1288 he was at Hart. But in 1289, when negotiations with England and Norway began, the Scottish envoys were three guardians and Brus in place of the fourth, James Stewart, an uncertain supporter of his.

He was party to the treaties which were intended to bring the Maid to Scotland and marry her to Edward I's heir.

As soon as rumours of the Maid's death reached the Scots assembled at Scone to greet her in October 1290, Robert moved to settle the issue by force, in alliance with the earl of Atholl. Again he was contained, and the Scots agreed to involve Edward I in identifying the rightful heir to the throne, an uneasy period in which, about Christmas 1290, Brus complained to Edward about the supporters of John de Balliol, and invoked the claims of seven earls who should make the king—an ambiguous assertion about an unidentifiable cohort. That memorandum contains the earliest version of the story which gave Florence, count of Holland, a claim to the Scottish throne. Robert also urged Edward to come north to assert the overlordship which Richard I had wrongfully sold in 1189, and then to do right to Brus's claim to the kingdom. It can scarcely be coincidence that Edward I arrived at Norham in May 1291, with Florence in his train, to demand that the Scots acknowledge his lordship, a demand with which Florence, Brus, and John Hastings hastened to comply.

The history of the Great Cause, in which Brus and Balliol were the only serious contenders (for they appointed forty members of the court each), is complex and needs careful reassessment. Brus's claim made appeal to a 'law by which kings reign' (Barrow, 45), which was different from the ordinary law by which lands of inferior tenures descended by primogeniture (Balliol's claim). Brus put forward two propositions: he was the nearest surviving descendant of Earl David in degree, and nearness in degree was the principle which precedent justified for kingdoms. And secondly, as between male (Brus) and female (Dervorguilla de Balliol) of the same degree, the male is to be preferred, even if of the junior line; therefore Dervorguilla had no right to transmit to her son. The pleadings survive only in fragmentary form, but they fudge the distinction between these propositions, contain other internal contradictions, and show a remarkable willingness to invent and distort, most notably in the tale, occurring in three different forms, that Alexander II, when childless, had recognized Robert as his heir (this would have to be about 1238), a recognition supposedly accepted by the barons, written down, and mysteriously lost.

A similar tale of lost documents recording even more absurd events was put forward by Count Florence in a form which shows its inspiration in the Brus camp, and Brus actually did a deal with Florence on 14 June 1292, whereby if one gained the throne he would grant substantial lands to the other. Since the court was dealing with the question of whether Balliol or Brus had the better right and had not yet looked at the other claims, it is unclear how this agreement would have worked, though it was surely intended to block the way for Balliol. So too was the belated claim of King Eric of Norway, behind which the hand of Brus can also be seen. The consultations with Paris lawyers, ordered by the court in June–July 1292, show that Brus was already considering his fall-back position, that if Balliol became king the kingdom should be partitioned like a barony between the three coheirs of Earl David: Balliol, Brus, and Hastings.

On 6 November 1292 judgment was given for Balliol against Brus and the court turned to other claims; Brus and Hastings were now permitted to submit a new claim alleging partibility, but after seven days of argument all were swept aside and Edward I gave judgment for Balliol on 17 November. Brus later executed a document ante-dated to 7 November 1292 resigning his claim to the throne to his son, but this was a device to enable him to hold Annandale of King John without prejudicing the claim. There can be no doubt that Robert (V) de Brus was convinced of his lineage's right to the kingship, but in such varying circumstances (before and after the death of the Maid, before and after Edward I's lordship) as to suggest that ambition and opportunity had more to do with his conviction than a knowledge of law, custom, and the European kingdoms to which he rightly appealed. Like Balliol he had good lawyers; his forty nominees to the court were less impressive socially than Balliol's, but it may be doubted if, in the end, that mattered much. He expected a favourable verdict from Edward I in return for supporting overlordship, and there are hints, no more, that Edward I was at first tempted in that direction. If so, the temptation was resisted.

Robert (V) de Brus played no active role after the inauguration of King John. In May 1240 he had married Isabel (d. in or after 1264), daughter of Gilbert de Clare, earl of Hertford and Gloucester, who despite her lineage brought him only a single manor as marriage portion. They had two sons, Richard, who died in 1285 or 1286, and Robert (VI) de *Brus (1243–1304), the father of Robert I, king of Scots. Robert (V) remarried, between 1270 and May 1275; his new wife was called Christina (d. 1305), daughter and heir of a Cumberland knight, Sir William of Ireby, who bore him no children. Robert died at Lochmaben, where the remains of a great stone castle beside the loch may be attributed to his efforts, on 31 March 1295 and was buried on 17 April beside his father at Guisborough Priory.

A. A. M. DUNCAN

Sources A. A. M. Duncan, 'The Bruces of Annandale, 1100—1304', *Transactions of the Dumfriesshire and Galloway Natural History and Antiquarian Society*, 3rd ser., 69 (1994), 89–102 · G. W. S. Barrow, *Robert Bruce and the community of the realm of Scotland*, 3rd edn (1988) · GEC, *Peerage*, new edn, 2.358–60 · E. L. G. Stones and G. G. Simpson, eds., *Edward I and the throne of Scotland, 1290–1296*, 2 (1978) · *The chronicle of Walter of Guisborough*, ed. H. Rothwell, CS, 3rd ser., 89 (1957)
Archives PRO, duchy of Lancaster, cartae miscellaneae, DL36
Likenesses seals, BM, casts 15646–15660, 15651, 15653, 15654–15656

Brus [Bruce], **Robert (VI) de**, **earl of Carrick and lord of Annandale** (1243–1304), magnate, was the elder son of Robert (V) de *Brus (d. 1295) and Isabel de Clare (d. in or after 1264), and was probably born at his father's manor of Writtle in Essex in 1243. He ransomed his father in 1264 and evidently shared in his father's speculations in the lands of English rebels by 1268. In 1270 he belatedly offered to join the Lord Edward's crusade, but was in England in 1271, so he clearly did not go. He had hitherto remained unmarried but, possibly during his father's

absence, he married the widowed Marjory, countess of Carrick. John Fordun has a pleasant tale that he met her while hunting, and that she took him back to Turnberry, where after fifteen days' pressure he married her, much to the fury of Alexander III (r. 1249–86), who briefly seized her lands; the lack of royal consent is likely enough. Of their fruitful marriage there survived five sons: *Robert I, king of Scots; Neil; Edward [see Bruce, Edward, earl of Carrick]; Alexander, dean of Glasgow; and Thomas. There were also five surviving daughters: one who married Gartney, earl of Mar; Isabel, queen of Eric II of Norway; Mary, wife of Sir Neil Campbell and Sir Alexander Fraser; Christian *Bruce, wife of Sir Christopher Seton and Sir Andrew Moray; and Matilda, wife of Hugh, earl of Ross. In addition Robert had a daughter Margaret, who was probably illegitimate. Countess Marjory died before 1293 and Robert married a second wife, Eleanor, of unknown lineage.

Earl Robert attended the Westminster parliament of 1278, where he swore fealty to Edward I on behalf of Alexander III, an occasion on which some attempt was made to extract homage for Scotland. In 1281 he was one of a Scottish delegation of sixteen to Guy, count of Flanders, to arrange the marriage of the Lord Alexander (d. 1284) to Guy's daughter, a delegation which bravely defined the custom of succession to the throne of Scotland. In 1284 he acknowledged Margaret, the Maid of Norway, as heir presumptive, but in 1286 joined in the Turnberry band and helped his father in their revolt of 1286–7; then, retreating from opposition to the Maid's succession, he was among those Scottish nobles who confirmed the treaty of Birgham in 1290. He swore fealty to Edward I as overlord of Scotland on 13 June 1291 and witnessed his father's deal with Florence, count of Holland, on 14 June 1292. He would also be party to the deal with King Eric of Norway, who undertook to marry Robert's daughter, and he had leave to sail with her to Norway on 28 September 1292, though he may not have gone until the following spring. After the Great Cause went against his father, the latter resigned to him the family claim to the throne; at the same time Carrick resigned his earldom to his own eldest son, the future king, leaving himself with English lands, the claim, and no need to do homage to John, king of Scots. These transactions were antedated to 7–9 November 1292.

With the death of his father in 1295, Brus inherited Annandale, but probably refused homage to King John for it. In the winter of 1295–6 he also refused to answer a summons to the Scottish host, and Annandale was given by King John to John Comyn though Brus was certainly in possession again from 1297. In England he had been made constable of Carlisle Castle on 6 October 1295, and when Edward I enforced his overlordship of Scotland in the spring of 1296 Robert and his son, the new earl of Carrick, were in his army. After the victory of Dunbar, at which Brus fought, 'Fordun's' annals claim that Robert asked Edward to fulfil his promise and give him the kingdom, to which Edward replied 'Have we nothing else to do but win kingdoms for you?' (*Chronica gentis Scottorum*, 1.326). This answer caused Brus to withdraw to England, never to return to Scotland. The same source claims that 'Robert de Brus who became king' (ibid., 1.330) fought for Edward I at Falkirk in 1298, and turned the Scottish flank, hence ensuring an English victory. It is possible that Robert (V) de Brus was there, for his son, who would have been called Carrick, was certainly not. But Brus did not serve Edward in France and seems to have lived quietly at Writtle. In February 1304 the Scottish leaders submitted to Edward; Robert set out forthwith for Annandale, but died on the way very soon after Easter (29 March) and before 4 April 1304. He was buried at Holmcultram Abbey, in Cumberland. His eldest son at last inherited his claim to the Scottish throne.   A. A. M. DUNCAN

Sources A. A. M. Duncan, 'The Bruces of Annandale, 1100—1304', *Transactions of the Dumfriesshire and Galloway Natural History and Antiquarian Society*, 3rd ser., 69 (1994), 89–102 • G. W. S. Barrow, *Robert Bruce and the community of the realm of Scotland*, 3rd edn (1988) • GEC, *Peerage*, new edn, 3.55–6 • *Johannis de Fordun Chronica gentis Scotorum / John of Fordun's Chronicle of the Scottish nation*, ed. W. F. Skene, trans. F. J. H. Skene, 1 (1871), 326, 330

Likenesses casts of seals, BM, 15652, 15865–15866, 15868–15869

Brus, William de, lord of Annandale (*d.* 1211/12). *See under* Brus, Robert (II) de, lord of Annandale (*d.* 1194?).

Brushfield, Thomas Nadauld (1828–1910), lunacy specialist and antiquary, the son of Thomas Brushfield of Derbyshire, JP and deputy lieutenant of the Tower of London, and his wife, Susanna Shipley, was born on 10 December 1828 and was baptized at Christ Church, Stepney, London, on 31 December. Brushfield's grandmother Ann Nadauld was a descendant of the Huguenot Henri Nadauld who settled in England after the revocation of the edict of Nantes, became a sculptor, and in 1698 created statuary and friezes to decorate Chatsworth House. Brushfield was educated at a private boarding-school at Buckhurst Hill, Essex. In 1845 he entered the London Hospital where he studied medicine and surgery and won numerous honours including gold medals for chemistry in 1847 and for medicine and physiology in 1849. He matriculated with honours at London University in 1848. Two years later he became MRCS and in 1862 graduated MD at St Andrews. After serving as house surgeon at the London Hospital he moved to the Bethnal House Asylum where he joined Dr Millar and first experienced working with lunacy. In 1852 he was appointed house surgeon at Cheshire County Lunatic Asylum, where he subsequently became the first resident medical superintendent. Brushfield married, on 5 August 1852, Hannah, daughter of John Davis of London; they had three sons and three daughters.

In 1865 Brushfield was appointed medical superintendent of the proposed Surrey County Asylum at Brookwood; he assisted in planning the buildings there, and also subsequently helped to design the cottage hospital. He pioneered the non-restraint treatment of lunatics and attempted to brighten the life of asylum patients by making the wards cheerful and by organizing entertainments. He wrote articles on lunacy, including 'Medical certificates of insanity' (*The Lancet*, 1880) and 'Practical hints on the symptoms, treatment, and medico-legal aspects of

insanity', which was read before the Chester Medical Society in 1890.

Brushfield retired from professional work in 1882 and settled at Budleigh Salterton on the south Devon coast near Hayes Barton, the birthplace of Walter Ralegh. He became a member of the Devonshire Association in 1883, and was elected president in 1893–4. He was elected FSA in 1899, and in 1904 was a founder member of the Devon and Cornwall Record Society. He made the career of Ralegh the major subject of his research, producing a series of papers called 'Raleghana' which was published in the *Transactions* of the Devonshire Association between 1896 and 1907, followed in 1909–10 by the first two parts of 'Ralegh miscellanea'. He contributed many other papers on similar themes to other journals. His bibliography of Ralegh appeared serially in volume 5 of the *Western Antiquary* in 1885 and 1886. He was a reader for the *New English Dictionary*, contributing more than 72,000 slips.

Brushfield died on 28 November 1910 at his home, The Cliff, Cliff Road, Budleigh Salterton, and was buried in the town. He was survived by his wife and children. Most of his library of about 10,000 volumes and manuscripts was dispersed after his death but the more important Ralegh items were placed in the Exeter Public Library together with the lantern slides which he used to illustrate his very popular lectures. About thirty early editions of Ralegh's works, and the slides, were later deposited in the Devon County Local Studies Library in Exeter.

HARRY TAPLEY-SOPER, *rev.* CHRISTINE NORTH

Sources *Devon and Cornwall Notes and Queries*, 6 (1910–11), 161 • private information (2004) [Devon County Library] • *Kelly's directory of Devon and Cornwall* (1910) • private information (1912) • personal knowledge (1912) • IGI

Archives Devon RO, commonplace books and notes • Wellcome L., lecture notes and papers | Ches. & Chester ALSS, letters to Thomas Hughes • U. Birm., special collections department, corresp. with Edward Arber

Wealth at death £16,161 5*s.* 9*d.*: resworn probate, 17 Jan 1911, CGPLA Eng. & Wales

Brutton, Nicholas (1780–1843), army officer, descended from the old Devonshire family of Brutton or Bruteton, entered the army as ensign in the 75th foot in 1795. He was posted to India, served at the battle of Seedaseer in 1799, was aide-de-camp to Colonel Hart throughout the Mysore campaign, and led one of the storming parties at Seringapatam on 4 May 1799, when he was severely wounded. He served through the campaign in Kanara, at the siege and assault of Jamalabad, and under Lord Lake through the campaigns of 1804–5. At Bharatpur he led a storming party, and was again very badly wounded.

Brutton exchanged into the 8th hussars, serving in the Sikh country in 1809 under General St Leger, and as brigade-major to General Wood during the Pindari campaign of 1812. At the outbreak of the Anglo-Nepal War in 1814 he commanded three troops of the 8th hussars, and led the assault on the fort of Kalunga at the head of 100 dismounted troopers, where he was again severely wounded. He served as brigade-major at the siege and capture of Hathras, and in the Pindari campaign of 1817 was promoted to major in the 8th hussars; on the regiment's return to Europe in 1821 he exchanged into the 11th hussars, with whom he served at the siege and capture of Bharatpur. In 1830 he was promoted lieutenant-colonel and commanded the 11th hussars until 1837, when he sold out, and was succeeded by James Thomas Brudenell, seventh earl of Cardigan.

Brutton, who had been present at the siege and capture of the six strongest fortresses in India, received a wound pension of £100 a year. He died in retirement at Bordeaux on 26 March 1843.

F. B. GARNETT, *rev.* STEWART M. FRASER

Sources PRO, War Office Records · *Colburn's United Service Magazine*, 2 (1843), 1174 · P. Moon, *The British conquest and dominion of India* (1989)

Bruyn, Theodore de (1730–1804), landscape painter, was born in Amsterdam. He studied at Antwerp under Nicholaes van den Bergh, and moved to England to carry out decorative work for the duke of Norfolk in 1768. He entered the Royal Academy Schools in October 1773, aged forty-three, as a sculptor, but proceeded to exhibit landscape paintings at the Royal Academy, the Society of Artists, and the Free Society of Artists over the next twenty years. He contributed elegant, well-designed works to the genre of country house views. His *View of Painshill*, exhibited in 1790, was sold at Christies in 1950; others included *Luxborough House, Essex, Sudley House*, and *Lulworth Manor*. He also exhibited rustic landscapes with cattle and figures. His grisaille paintings of sculpture bas-relief were well regarded. The chapel at Greenwich Hospital and Carlton Towers, Yorkshire, contain grisaille decorations by de Bruyn. He died in London in 1804. His two sons, John, born on 9 September 1764, and Henry (*b.* 1772), both entered the Royal Academy Schools as painters in 1782 and 1792 respectively, and subsequently exhibited at the Royal Academy.

ERNEST RADFORD, *rev.* R. J. LAMBERT

Sources Waterhouse, *18c painters* · Bryan, *Painters* · M. H. Grant, *A dictionary of British landscape painters, from the 16th century to the early 20th century* (1952) · S. C. Hutchison, 'The Royal Academy Schools, 1768–1830', *Walpole Society*, 38 (1960–62), 123–91, esp. 139, 147, 154 **Archives** Courtauld Inst., Witt Library, UK folder

Bruyne, Norman Adrian de (1904–1997), aeronautical engineer, was born on 8 November 1904 at Punta Arenas, Magallanes, Chile, the fourth and youngest son of Dr Pieter Adriaan de Bruyne, a sheep farmer originally from the Netherlands, and his wife, Maude, *née* Mattocks, of English descent. His father had left Holland for South America in 1887. He prospered in Chile, became Netherlands consul and a director of the Bank of Punta Arenas, started a whaling company, and owned, and operated, the first refrigerated ship to bring mutton to Europe. In 1906 the de Bruyne family settled in England, first in Redhill in Surrey, and, from 1910, at Littlehampton in Sussex. De Bruyne went to Wellesley House preparatory school and then from September 1918, Lancing College, which he did not enjoy because of its excessive preoccupation with divinity and games. Eventually he blossomed as head of house, and in the sixth form, under a new headmaster, he won the school essay prize. In his final report de Bruyne's headmaster wrote, 'he has great literary gifts as well as an

intense enthusiasm for his ideas … [If] he is properly directed and does not let his humour or his originality run away with him, he will show a first-class intellect' (de Bruyne, 35).

In 1923, with a higher certificate in physics and maths and a distinction in chemistry, de Bruyne passed into Trinity College, Cambridge, spending the final summer months before going to university on research into high-vacuum electrical equipment at the Wembley offices of the British General Electric Company (GEC). Having gained first-class honours in the natural sciences tripos he went on to three years of research for his PhD at the Cavendish Laboratory under Lord Rutherford, while—to augment his work at the GEC—he put in for a prize fellowship at Trinity on the field emission of electrodes. That fellowship achieved, he received for four years 'free rooms, free dinner, and £400 a year'. He wrote, 'I felt that I had joined the best club in the World—and was being paid for it too' (de Bruyne, 65).

By 1930, now with his MA and PhD, de Bruyne was invited to become Trinity's junior bursar, a member of the college council, and secretary of its committees, and responsible for all its buildings. It added up to no more than a total of three hours' work each morning and evening. So, with time to spare and some private funds, de Bruyne made his first flight in a de Havilland Moth belonging to Trinity College's wealthy and eccentric the Revd Canon F. A. (Simbo) Simpson. 'It gave me a feeling of intense exhilaration', de Bruyne wrote (de Bruyne, 68). He determined to become involved with aircraft and their construction. To implement this he spent the rest of the summer of 1931 at the De Havilland technical school at Stag Lane, studying aircraft design. He qualified there as an aircraft ground engineer and welder, and learned to fly as Arthur Marshall's first pupil at Fen Ditton aerodrome. He then bought a de Havilland Gipsy Moth and, in those days of the universal biplane, became convinced that there was scope for original work.

In a lifelong quest 'to do things differently and better', de Bruyne undertook—in a shed at Marshall's aerodrome—first to design, and then to build, a four-seat enclosed cabin cantilever monoplane. It turned out to be a four-year task, based on first principles and achieving, when complete, a lighter structure than any before in a comparable size of aircraft. De Bruyne's design was submitted to the airworthiness department of the Royal Aircraft Establishment (RAE) at Farnborough. Despite check stressing by Harold Roxbee Cox, later Lord Kings Norton, of the RAE itself, de Bruyne's design was summarily rejected by the RAE experts. That impasse was, however, resolved by K. T. Spencer, director of research and development at the Ministry of Supply, who contrived that duplicate components of the projected aircraft should be tested to destruction. In the event they passed triumphantly. The new aircraft, named *The Snark*, was first flown by de Bruyne himself on 16 December 1934. It received its certificate of airworthiness and, with his brother and his wife on board, was flown by de Bruyne to Berlin and back in April 1936. To his intense satisfaction he then sold it to the

Air Ministry for research into the characteristics of cantilever wings by the already renowned Sir Bennett Melville Jones.

Having thus confirmed his calculations on a wooden aircraft assembled with traditional casein glues, de Bruyne, always pioneering, turned his thoughts to the use of the wholly new epoxy resins for the ultimate bonding of wood to wood, wood to metal, and eventually metal to metal, in the form of immensely strong laminated honeycomb forms of aircraft construction. De Bruyne's epoxy resins were first used in the wartime building of the de Havilland Mosquito fighter-bomber for the RAF and in the production of large numbers of Airspeed Horsa military gliders. During the next four years Aero Research Ltd—a £100 company founded by de Bruyne himself in April 1934—became the leading producer and supplier to the British aircraft industry (led by the de Havilland Aircraft Company) of a range of new epoxy resin adhesives which became increasingly used in place of riveted assemblies. These successes—with the production and sales from Duxford of what were termed successively Aerolite, Araldite, and Redux epoxy resin adhesives, used for aircraft and powerboat construction—led, in 1948, to a merger between Aero Research Ltd at Duxford and the Society of Chemical Industry, Basel (CIBA), and to de Bruyne's decision to become managing director of his own pioneering company, Techne Ltd. In 1950 he started another successful enterprise, Techne Inc., based in Princeton, New Jersey, to build and market scientific instruments. Meanwhile, on 26 June 1940 de Bruyne married Elma Lilian Marsh (b. 1906/7), musician, and daughter of Francis Marsh, farmer and miller. They had one son and one daughter.

De Bruyne was, for almost twenty-two years—from October 1936 to June 1958—managing director of Aero Research Ltd, and for a further nine years—from June 1958 to February 1967—managing director of CIBA (ARL) Ltd at Duxford. Nevertheless D. B., as he was widely known, looked for pastures new. He found these initially in an invitation from Anthony Wedgwood Benn, minister of power, to become a non-executive director of the Eastern Electricity Board under its chairman, Sir Ronald Edwards. It was, he wrote, 'a most interesting experience' (de Bruyne, 126). He resigned his directorship when he left with his wife for the United States as a protest against the Labour government's nationalization of so much of British industry. In Princeton, Techne Inc. prospered.

After twenty-one years as Techne Inc.'s president in December 1993, de Bruyne, at the age of eighty-nine, returned to England on a visit. By then his acute deafness was being, more or less successfully, relieved by his final invention of a bone-conducted hearing aid. He died at Pyne's House, 8 Chapel Street, Duxford, Cambridgeshire, on 7 March 1997, of heart failure. He was survived by his wife, son, and daughter.   PETER G. MASEFIELD

Sources WWW · *The Times* (31 March 1997) · *Daily Telegraph* (15 March 1997) · N. de Bruyne, *My life* (1996) · m. cert. · d. cert.
Likenesses photograph, repro. in *The Times* · photograph, repro. in *Daily Telegraph*

Brwmffild, Mathau [Mathew] (*fl. c.*1525–*c.*1545), poet, is an obscure figure of unknown origins. Although his name suggests an affinity with the lordship of Bromfield in north-east Wales, the few pieces of extant poetry, about twenty in all, picture an itinerant poet—on one occasion he would bemoan 'Rhoed ym boen … rhodio o bell 'r hyd y byd' ('Mine is a wretched lot … traversing far to all corners of the land'; Brogyntyn MS 2, fol. 541)—whose panegyric duties took him to distant Carmarthenshire (he was buried in Carmarthen), Cardiganshire, and Anglesey, where he visited the homes of some of the most important public figures of his day, nearly all renowned for their poetic patronage. However, he was forced to seek reconciliation with two of his patrons—Elis Prys (Price) of Plasiolyn, and Rowland Gruffudd of Plas Newydd, Porthaml, Anglesey—a possible indication of the itinerant poet's inevitable involvement in the ever-present power struggle between feuding factions.   A. CYNFAEL LAKE

Sources DWB · J. T. Jones, *Geiriadur bywgraffyddol o enwogion Cymru*, 2 vols. (1867–70) · I. Foulkes, *Geirlyfr bywgraffiadol o enwogion Cymru* (1870) · R. Williams, *Enwogion Cymru: a biographical dictionary of eminent Welshmen* (1852) · J. Davies, *Dictionarium duplex* (1632) · BL, Add. MS 31055 · NL Wales, Brogyntyn papers

Brwynllys, Bedo. *See* Bedo Brwynllys (*fl.* 1469).

Bry, Theodore de [Dirk de Brij] (1528–1598), engraver, was born at Liège, at that time an independent state controlled by prince-bishops. He came from a family of engravers active in the Low Countries and Germany. By 1570 he had left the city as a protestant refugee and in 1589 was living at Frankfurt am Main. De Bry engraved plates for a number of notable works, including the first four volumes of Boissard's *Roman Antiquities* (1597–1602), those for the fifth and sixth volumes being engraved by J. T. and J. I. De Bry.

De Bry travelled to London in 1586/7, where he engraved a depiction of the elaborate funeral procession and obsequies of Sir Philip Sidney, as staged by Thomas Lant, Portcullis pursuivant, on 16 February 1587. He also illustrated Hakluyt's English translation of Thomas Hariot's *Briefe and True Report of the New Found Land of Virginia* (1590). De Bry died at Frankfurt on 27 March 1598.

ERNEST RADFORD, *rev.* HELEN PIERCE

Sources A. M. Hind, *Engraving in England in the sixteenth and seventeenth centuries*, 1 (1952) · W. V. Seidlitz, 'Bry, Theodor', Thieme & Becker, *Allgemeines Lexikon*, 5.162–3 · H. Walpole, *Anecdotes of painting in England … collected by the late George Vertue, and now digested and published*, 2 (1762) · Redgrave, *Artists* · Bryan, *Painters* (1849) · V. Hanschke, 'Bry, niederland-dt Kupferstecher und Verleger Familie', *Allgemeines Künstlerlexikon: die bildenden Künstler aller Zeiten und Völker*, ed. G. Meissner, [new edn, 27 vols.] (Munich, 1992–), vol. 14, pp. 620–21
Likenesses T. De Bry, self-portrait, engraving, 1597, repro. in Hind, *Engraving*

Bryan, Augustine (d. 1726), classical scholar and Church of England clergyman, was the son of Augustine Bryan of London. He was educated at St Paul's School, London, and was admitted to Trinity College, Cambridge, on 30 March 1708. He became a scholar in the following year and graduated BA (1712) and MA (1716). He was ordained a deacon at Ely on 13 March 1715 and became rector of Piddlehinton,

Dorset, on 16 January 1722. Bryan's will records his marriage to Anne, and that the couple had two children, George and Penelope.

In 1718 Bryan published a sermon on the election of the lord mayor. Just before his death (which occurred on 6 April 1726) he finished the printing of a well-respected edition of Plutarch's *Lives*, which was completed by Moses du Soul, and published in five volumes under the title of *Plutarchi Chaeronensis vitae parallelae, cum singulis aliquot, Graece et Latine, adduntur variantes lectiones ex MSS. codd. veteres et novae, doctorum virorum notae et emendationes, et indices accuratissimi* (1723–9). The Greek text is printed from the Paris edition of 1624, with a few corrections; the Latin translation is also chiefly adopted from that edition.

THOMPSON COOPER, *rev.* PHILIP CARTER

Sources Venn, *Alum. Cant.* · Nichols, *Lit. anecdotes*, 4.286 · Nichols, *Illustrations*, 4.375 · W. T. Lowndes, *The bibliographer's manual of English literature*, ed. H. G. Bohn, [new edn], 6 vols. (1890) · A. Boyer, *The political state of Great Britain*, 31 (1725), 344 · J. Hutchins, *The history and antiquities of the county of Dorset*, 2nd edn, ed. R. Gough and J. B. Nichols, 2 (1803), 352–3 · A. Bryan, will, PRO, PROB 11/609, fols. 202r–203v

Bryan, Benjamin [*nicknamed* Big Ben] (**1753–1794**), prizefighter, sometimes named Benjamin Brian or Brain, was born in Bristol; nothing is known about his parents or upbringing. It is unclear whether he had any formal education; however, letters (apparently from Bryan) which appeared in the press towards the end of his life suggest that he was literate. During his early years Bryan worked as a collier in Kingswood, Bristol, during which time he defeated two noted fighters, Clayton and Harris. In 1774 he moved to London, working for several years as a coal porter at a wharf in the Strand. 'Good looking, clean and respectable' (Miles, 65), Bryan had a mild and sociable demeanour, stood 5 feet 10 inches tall, and weighed less than 14 stone.

Bryan's prize-fighting career began on 31 October 1786 when he defeated the 'Fighting Grenadier' at Bloomsbury. Bryan owed this victory to the intervention of a physician who, taking advantage of a disruption to the bout, lanced a swelling on Bryan's eye, enabling the badly bruised fighter to continue the contest. On 31 December 1788, in a bout that took place in atrocious weather, Bryan defeated Corbally at Navestock, Essex. In the following year he was due to fight the legendary pugilist Tom Johnson for £500, but had to pay £100 default because his health was too poor to take part in the bout. By 23 October 1789 he had recovered sufficiently for him to defeat Jacombs at Banbury in a 'most dreadful battle of one hour and twenty six minutes' (Miles, 66–7). On 30 August 1790 Bryan tried to fight the 'Tinman' Bill Hooper at Newbury for 100 guineas, but after receiving one blow Hooper became so frightened that instead of fighting he:

> fell every time Ben's hand reached him, and even before; ran all over the stage, filled his mouth with water and spirted it in Ben's face, accompanied by provoking and blackguard epithets to irritate Ben and throw him off his guard. (ibid., 67)

Hooper fell 133 times and after three and a half hours, and

with night having set in, the bout was declared drawn (*Sporting Magazine*, 4, 1794, 77).

Despite the farcical nature of this contest Bryan's patron, the duke of Hamilton, was sufficiently impressed to back him for 500 guineas for a rematch with Tom Johnson at Wrotham, Kent. On 17 January 1791 Bryan and Johnson fought, the latter being 7–4 on favourite. However, Bryan won a very fierce battle in twenty-one minutes, partly through luck since Johnson 'broke the metacarpal bone of his middle finger by striking the rail of the stage', but also due to his ability, especially 'his straight and severe right hand deliveries' (Miles, 69, 65). Despite the severity of the bout, a few days later Bryan displayed great agility in sparring matches at the Grecian Theatre in London's Strand, as noted in the *Daily Advertiser* (22 January 1790). Such regular displays, coupled with his role as a second to other fighters, provided Ben with a living between 1790 and 1794. However, on 24 February 1794 he came out of retirement and agreed to fight William Wood. Unfortunately, the battle did not take place because Bryan fell ill, dying at his house in Gray's Inn Road on 8 April 1794. Many 'supposed at the time that his death happened in consequence of some inward bruise which he got in one of the many desperate battles' (*Sporting Magazine*, 4, 1794, 45). As it was, when Bryan's body was opened they discovered that he was suffering from a 'scirrhous liver' (Miles, 69). On 11 April he was buried at St Sepulchre's churchyard in Snow Hill, London. Among his mourners were Johnson, Wood, and two other prize-fighters, Bill Warr and John Symonds. These pugilists composed the following epistle that appeared on his tombstone:

> Farewell, the honours of my brow
> Victorious wreaths, farewell!
> one blow from death has laid me low,
> By whom such brave ones fall
> Yet bravely I'll dispute the prize,
> Nor yield, though out of breath,
> Tis not the fall—I yet shall rise,
> And conquer even death.
> (Miles, 70)

ADRIAN N. HARVEY

Sources H. D. Miles, *Pugilistica: the history of British boxing*, 1 (1906) · *Sporting Magazine*, 1 (1792–3), 290 · *Sporting Magazine*, 4 (1794), 44–5, 77–8 · P. Egan, *Boxiana, or, Sketches of ancient and modern pugilism*, 5 vols. (1812–29) · T. Gee, *Up to scratch: bareknuckle fighting and heroes of the prize-ring* (1998)

Bryan, Sir Francis [*called* the Vicar of Hell] (*d.* 1550), courtier and writer, was the first surviving son of Sir Thomas Bryan (*d.* 1518), courtier, of Ashridge in Hertfordshire and his wife, **Margaret Bryan** [*née* Bourchier], *suo jure* Baroness Bryan (*d.* 1552), daughter of Sir Humphrey Bourchier and his wife, Elizabeth, and sister of John *Bourchier, second Baron Berners (*c*.1467–1533). His grandfather was the chief justice of the common pleas, Sir Thomas *Bryan (*d.* 1500). In his boyhood Bryan may have been brought up in the Northamptonshire household of Sir Thomas Parr of Kendal, Westmorland, for he later called him his special patron.

Like her son, Lady Bryan was best known as a courtier. Her father was a Yorkist and was killed at the battle of

Barnet on 14 April 1471. Her mother was the daughter and heir of Frederick Tilney of Boston, Lincolnshire, and his wife, Elizabeth, and married Thomas *Howard, second duke of Norfolk (1443–1524), as his first wife on 20 April 1472. She died on 4 April 1497. Sir Thomas Bryan was a knight of the body to Henry VII and Henry VIII and vice-chamberlain to Katherine of Aragon. On the birth of Princess Mary on 18 February 1516 his wife was appointed lady mistress and a baroness. She was governess to the royal children thereafter. Bryan had died by 31 January 1518 and his widow married again. Her second husband, David Soche (Zouche), had died by 1536, at which time she was governess to Princess Elizabeth and, uncertain of the child's status or of her own after the execution of Anne Boleyn on 19 May, she wrote to Thomas Cromwell for reassurance. She sought his support in the ordering of the princesses' household at Hunsdon, Hertfordshire, and for her way of bringing them up. In her letters delight at the childish amusements of the royal children is juxtaposed with the terrors of court life. In 1539, as lady mistress to Edward, prince of Wales, as well as the princesses, she wrote again to Cromwell, fearful for the future of her daughter, Elizabeth, shortly after the execution of Elizabeth's husband, Nicholas *Carew, and for herself should she lose her. Lady Bryan retained her position of lady mistress when Edward VI succeeded his father in 1547 but mainly lived at Leighs in Essex during her last years, on an impressive annuity of £70 per annum. She made her will on 20 August 1551, stipulating that her debts and servants' wages be paid and petitioning to receive the remainder of her annuity 'for my poor service done as well unto his majesty in his tender age, as also unto his dearly beloved sisters' (*Literary Remains*, 1.xxxii). Her will was proved on 21 June 1552.

Early career, 1513–1531 Francis Bryan's first command was in April 1513 as captain of the *Margaret Bonaventure* during the admiralty of his kinsman Sir Edward *Howard (1476/7–1513). He soon won the favour of Henry VIII by his prowess at jousting. In April 1514 the king lent horses and armour to Bryan and to Nicholas Carew, who became Bryan's brother-in-law that year. Bryan played a leading part in the court entertainments at Richmond Palace in April 1515, at Eltham Palace at Christmas 1515, and at Greenwich Palace in July 1517. In 1516 he was appointed the king's cupbearer. Bryan's passion for hunting gave him proximity to Henry in his favourite pastime and in 1518 he became, and remained throughout the reign, master of the toils.

In September 1518 Henry appointed Bryan to the newly created post of gentleman of the privy chamber. Bryan accompanied Henry to the court of François I of France, and there they disported themselves in disguise in the streets of Paris. Bryan and the king's other young favourites, the 'minions', returned 'all French, in eating, drinking and apparel, yea, and in French vices and brags', 'high in love with the French court' (Hall, fols. 67v, 68v). In May 1519 the royal council, alarmed by the familiarity with which the king's minions treated him, to his dishonour,

banished Bryan and Carew, but they were receiving breakfast in the royal household again by October. Bryan returned to France in 1520, in attendance upon Henry at the Field of Cloth of Gold, and in July 1522 served in Brittany under Howard, now earl of Surrey, where, after the capture of Morlaix on the 2nd, he was knighted for his noble courage. By March 1522 Bryan was married to Philippa (d. 1542), daughter and heir of Humphrey Spice of Black Notley in Essex and widow of John Fortescue of Ponsbourne in Hertfordshire. They had no children. In October 1523 Surrey summoned young gentlemen of the court to join the Scottish campaign, urging their duty of military service to the king before that of dancing and dicing. Bryan went north against the Scots, but he had already gained a reputation for gambling and court vice which he would never lose. He began to hold local office in the early 1520s—collecting the subsidy in Essex in 1524 and joining the commissions of the peace in Buckinghamshire and Bedfordshire from 1525—but was still favourite at the court. At the Christmas festivities in 1524 Bryan defended Castle Loyal with Sir Thomas Wyatt the elder, with whom his life would be closely linked. By 1526 he was chief cupbearer, and master of the henchmen, Henry's pages, with whom he lodged when at court.

In July 1527, in the aftermath of the sack of Rome, Bryan attended Cardinal Thomas Wolsey to his meeting with François. By the following June, if not before, he was restored to the post of gentleman of the privy chamber, and in August was sent to accompany Cardinal Lorenzo Campeggi on his long-awaited journey to England to decide the legality of Henry's first marriage. Bryan had an audience with the French king on the way. Throughout the time when Henry was preoccupied with his Great Matter, Bryan was his trusted emissary to those with most power to bring about the king's remarriage: Clement VII and François. Bryan's self-interest lay with advancing the cause of his cousin, *Anne Boleyn (c.1500–1536) (their mothers were half-sisters). On 26 November 1528 he was sent as special ambassador to the court of Rome to persuade Clement to dispense so that Henry could contract a second marriage. There he conducted a separate correspondence with Anne, and took her part in her opposition to Wolsey. In December he passed on to Henry François's warning that there were some among his advisers who were opposed to his divorce. As the mission failed the English ambassadors despaired, and Bryan told the king in April 1529 that the pope would do nothing to help him and that whoever had promised him otherwise—by implication, Wolsey—had misled him.

Bryan became known for his unusual willingness to tell the king the truth, but also for his employment of dubious means to gain diplomatic ends. Early in May 1529 he told Henry that he had revealed all to the pope 'first by fair means, and afterwards by foul means, but neither fair nor foul will serve here' (*State Papers, Henry VIII*, 7.169). Later it was alleged that in order to gain intelligence Bryan slept with a courtesan at the papal court. Returning to England on 22 June 1529, he was promptly dispatched to France as resident ambassador with a diet of £1 6s. 8d. per day, on 14

July at the time of the negotiations for the peace of Cambrai. He was recalled in October, but sent on special missions to France in 1530 and appointed resident ambassador at the French court on 13 October, charged to promote the king's matrimonial cause. In November 1531 Bryan followed François to Hainault, ostensibly to hunt, but more importantly to discover whether the reported meeting between Charles V and the French king, which Henry dreaded, would take place, and to foment trouble between them.

Courtier and diplomat, 1532–1539 In Calais in March 1532 Bryan's uncle Lord Berners completed his translation of *The Golden Book of Marcus Aurelius*, made at the behest of his nephew. This work of ethical counsel and stoic consolation had an appeal for one who understood political mutability. Through 1532 Bryan served in the privy chamber for six weeks in every twelve, spending the other six weeks in the country. At court he gambled with the king for high stakes at dice, primero, bowls, and 'Pope Julius' game'. Bryan's replacement by Carew in the retinue which accompanied Henry and Anne Boleyn to Calais in October was taken as the sign of some rupture. However, his testimony in April 1533 of Katherine's reaction to her summons before the archiepiscopal court was crucial in the declaration of her as contumacious. Late in May Bryan accompanied Thomas *Howard, third duke of Norfolk (1473–1554), in embassy to France, to attend upon François as he went south to meet the pope and to try to dissuade him from the meeting. In August it was Bryan who took the news of Henry's excommunication to the French king. He waited in Marseilles for the pope's arrival, and left in mid-November. Returning to court, Bryan used his access to Henry to pursue patronage for his friends and clients and for himself. In Buckinghamshire, he was *custos rotulorum* from 1528, sheriff, served as JP in the county assizes for Bedfordshire, Buckinghamshire, and Hertfordshire, and was zealous in hunting heresy in the Chilterns. He entered the House of Commons by the time of the penultimate session of the Reformation Parliament (November–December 1534) as knight of the shire for Buckinghamshire, and was named on a list of members with a particular connection with the Treasons Bill.

As the king became alienated from his second queen, Bryan distanced himself from the Boleyns, quarrelling with George Boleyn, Viscount Rochford (d. 1536), at the end of 1534. He spent from November 1535 until January 1536 in embassy to France, and was expected to return there. In April 1536 he went to court after a long absence, but soon left for his Buckinghamshire estate. As his fellow members of the privy chamber were charged with treason in May 1536 Bryan was sent for in haste upon his allegiance, and was only admitted to the royal presence after an interview with Thomas Cromwell. His early distancing of himself from the Boleyns saved him and he may have reached an accommodation with Cromwell. By 13 May he had become chief gentleman of the privy chamber and was granted £100 of the revenues of the bishopric of Winchester, to the fury of Stephen Gardiner, but was denied the groomship of the stool. Cromwell now referred to Bryan as the Vicar of Hell. On 17 May Bryan took the news of Anne Boleyn's condemnation to Jane Seymour (1508/9–1537), the second of his cousins to become queen. Soon afterwards Bryan, with Carew, was accused of working to restore Princess Mary to the succession.

Bryan, still under suspicion, was sent to prove his loyalty by leading forces against the Pilgrimage of Grace in autumn 1536. At the end of November he was emissary between the king and his commanders in the north, reporting Norfolk's stratagem to offer pardon and to temporize rather than fight an overwhelming rebel army. Bryan's own sympathies lay with the traditional religion which the rebels were defending. He insisted that he would have no one in his household who was an adherent of the 'new learning'. His friends and clients within monastic houses looked to him for favour and patronage. For all his libertinism and his anticlerical jokes, Bryan's faith was genuine. His motto was *Je tens grace* ('I look for salvation'). The figure of Bryan who appeared in the satire Wyatt addressed to his friend had one aspiration: 'next godly things, to have an honest name' (*Complete Poems*, 151.83). Bryan knew the Bible well enough for Wyatt to send him a coded warning which depended upon his knowledge of Ecclesiasticus 27. He owned a copy of the Matthew Bible of 1537, and was intrigued by the humanist enterprise of scriptural translation and exegesis. Although he could not translate scripture himself, he was the patron of scholars of Greek who could, and his own household was a kind of academy. As master of the henchmen he arranged the education of the royal wards. Leading figures of the coming political generation were brought up in his household, some with religious convictions quite different to their master's.

In April 1537 Bryan was in Paris. His official mission was to prevent the French king from receiving the papal legation of Cardinal Reginald Pole, sent to stir the Catholic powers to crusade against England; his undercover mission was to arrange for the kidnap or even assassination of Pole. Pole escaped because he was forewarned, and there were suspicions that the warning came via Bryan himself. Bryan left France at the end of May and played a prominent part at Edward's baptism in October. In January 1538, as Henry's amity with François faltered, Bryan was sent to France, and returned there again as special ambassador in April. In May, during his absence, investigations at Woburn Abbey in Bedfordshire, where Bryan was steward, revealed his close friendship with the abbot, Robert Hobbes, to whose treasonable utterances Bryan had listened and with whose opposition to evangelical preaching Bryan had concurred. Bryan had warned his old friend Arthur Plantagenet, Viscount Lisle, another conservative, of the need for secrecy, but had been unguarded himself.

In May 1538, as the French king and the emperor prepared to declare a truce which would threaten England, Bryan, ambassador to François, and Wyatt, ambassador to Charles, were in Nice, charged to act in concert in the most delicate diplomacy. Unusually Bryan was denied audience with François. During the stalemate he gambled recklessly and was ransomed from debt by Wyatt. English diplomacy was in disarray and Henry blamed his ambassadors. Bryan, in disgrace for his drunkenness, his undiplomatic exchanges with François, and his intemperate dispatches, was recalled in July to face the royal fury. Ominously, the king asked to see the book of all Bryan's offices and fees, which were very many. In 1537 he had become chief butler of England. An inquisition began, conducted by the agents of Cromwell, who had long resented Bryan's influence, into his embassy, and into his part in an alleged scheme for reconciliation with Rome. Bryan fell so ill that his life was in danger. He recovered, but was eclipsed in the king's favour and replaced in the office of chief gentleman by the end of 1538 by his own former servant Anthony Denny. In proof of his loyalty Bryan sat on the jury which found his brother-in-law and court companion, Carew, guilty of treason on 14 February 1539.

Final years, 1539–1550 Bryan's worth as ambassador had rested not in his skills as bureaucrat or scholar—his embassy in 1531 was afforced because he lacked Latin—but as courtier and orator, and in the trust which kings reposed in him. He was received as Henry's close servant, and François had granted him frequent access and confided in him. Bryan had not attended any university and was not formally trained in rhetoric, but he was naturally skilled in the arts of eloquence, and his letters are full of rhetorical balance, alliteration, and antithesis. He was a torrential talker, and often complained that it would take him a week to write what he could say in an hour. He preferred the directness of proverbs to golden diction, and spoke proverbially not only to his friends but to an emperor and a queen. However, after 1538 Bryan lost the trust of the French king and his own. He never returned to the French court as ambassador, and was not on embassy again until sent to the emperor in October 1543.

In the last years of Henry's reign Bryan remained gentleman of the privy chamber and continued to serve at court, but with diminished influence. His closeness to the king had brought him many lands, pensions, and offices, which he continued to hold, and he made handsome gains of dissolved monastic lands, especially in Bedfordshire and Buckinghamshire. By 1545/6 his estates were worth at least £888 per annum. By 1539 he was knight of the shire for Buckinghamshire again and in 1542 he was the senior knight of the shire in parliament and provided 200 demilances for the war against Scotland. In January 1543 he was appointed vice-admiral and ordered to sail to the Firth of Forth and to intercept the ship carrying Claude de Lorraine Guise, first duc de Guise, to Scotland. At sea, beset by storms, he acted independently, contravening the instructions of the lord admiral, John Dudley, Viscount Lisle. His command was revoked at the end of February. In October he was sent as ambassador to Charles to cement the Anglo-imperial alliance, and to make plans for their common war against France. On 24 October he had audience with the emperor outside Landrecy. In the following year he served in the rearguard of the army in France, and was among the commanders at the siege of Montreuil in September; his embassy ended on 28 December 1544. In July 1545 he reviewed the defence of the

south-west coast with his old friend, Sir John Russell, who suggested Bryan as the best man to deputize for him. He attended the reception of the admiral of France in 1546.

In the last crisis of Henry's reign Bryan made a politic transfer of allegiance from his Howard cousins, with whom he had been closely associated, to the Seymours. The conferment of the freedom of the City of London in October 1546 recognized his part in the new political order, and after the execution of Henry Howard, earl of Surrey (1516/17–1547), Bryan inherited his gown of gold. For his part as commander of the horse in the expedition against Scotland in September 1547 led by Edward Seymour, duke of Somerset and lord protector, Bryan was made knight banneret. His last service, and his last rewards, lay in Ireland. His first wife died some time after May 1542, whereupon he followed Wyatt's satirical advice to marry a wealthy widow. Accordingly in 1548, in order to achieve political security, Bryan married the most powerful widow in Ireland, Joan Butler, dowager countess of Ormond, daughter of James fitz Maurice Fitzgerald, tenth earl of Desmond, and his wife, Amy; her husband had died in October 1546. Through his marriage Bryan wielded Ormond authority in south Leinster, controlling the estates of Thomas *Butler, tenth earl of Ormond (1531–1614), in his minority and a private army of gallowglasses in co. Kilkenny. However, his wife resisted his control; her loyalty lay with her Desmond relatives, and she was allegedly in collusion with Irish rebels. Through the office of lord marshal, to which he was appointed in January 1549, he commanded royal forces in Ireland. Although the lord deputy, Sir Edward Bellingham, protested at the appointment of a courtier and gambler who had seized lands, fees, and the royal treasure, and Sir John Alen claimed that Bryan's command would have cost Edward VI £40,000, Bryan's subsequent reputation in the pale was for probity. Bryan insisted that he 'would not borrow of the law as my lord of Ormond did' (*CSP Ire.*, 1509–73, 102). On 27 December 1549 Bryan was appointed lord justice, but having made a journey into Tipperary to check the incursions of the O'Carrolls, he died suddenly at Clonmel on 2 February 1550. The news at the English court was that Bryan's last words were 'I pray you, let me be buried amongst the good fellows of Waterford (which were good drinkers)' ('The letters of Richard Scudamore to Sir Philip Hoby', *Camden Miscellany*, 30, CS, 4th ser., 39, 1990, 121–2).

No portrait remains of Bryan, but he may be imagined as Wyatt described him—restless, fine-drawn, highly-strung:

> To thee, therefore, that trots still up and down
> And never rests, but running day and night
> From realm to realm, from city, street, and town,
> Why dost thou wear thy body to the bones?
> (*Complete Poems*, 151.11–14)

He had lost an eye while jousting in 1526 and could joke about it, for he wrote of the one-eyed Robert Aske 'I know him not, nor he me … yet we have but two eyes' (*LP Henry VIII*, 11.1103). As befitted so grand a courtier he dressed in rich apparel of the latest fashion, and the magnificence of his embassies was noted, and resented, by his contemporaries. Roger Ascham remembered Bryan as being perennially youthful, even in age.

Bryan retained a dual reputation in Europe as fearless teller of truth to princes and as Henry's Vicar of Hell. This view of him, disseminated by Nicholas Sander in *De origine ac progressu schismatis anglicani* (1585), was drawn upon but changed by Nicolaus Vernulaeus for his Neo-Latin drama *Henricus octavus* (1624). There the character Brianus appears as an archetypal flatterer, which Bryan had not been in life. In *Areopagitica* (1644) John Milton remembered that Henry had had a 'Vicar of Hell'. Bryan's other sixteenth-century reputation was as a poet. Francis Meres named him as 'the most passionate among us to bewail and bemoan the perplexities of love' (*Palladis tamia*, 1598, fol. 284), and Michael Drayton included Bryan, together with Wyatt and Surrey, as a contributor to the courtly anthology known as *Tottel's Miscellany*. But of Bryan's love poetry none can be identified. His only extant poem is a collection of moral precepts and ethical counsels, which he drew, with more earnestness than elegance, into ottava rima—'The proverbes of Salmon do playnly declare'. In 1548 his translation of a French version of Antonio de Guevara's *A Dispraise of the Life of a Courtier* was published. This work, with its themes of the mendacity and mutability of life at court, was close to the real experience of Bryan, whom Wyatt had saluted as one:

> who knows how great a grace
> In writing is to counsel man the right.
> (*Complete Poems*, 151.9–10)

SUSAN BRIGDEN

Sources *LP Henry VIII* · *State papers published under … Henry VIII*, 11 vols. (1830–52) · *CSP Spain, 1509–52* · [E. Hall], *The union of the two noble and illustre famelies of Lancastre and Yorke*, ed. [R. Grafton] (1548) · *Sir Thomas Wyatt: the complete poems*, ed. R. A. Rebholz (1978) · *CSP Ire., 1509–73* · D. Starkey, 'The court: Castiglione's ideal and Tudor reality', *Journal of the Warburg and Courtauld Institutes*, 45 (1982), 232–9 · R. S. Kinsman, '"The proverbes of Salmon do playnly declare": a sententious poem on wisdom and governance, ascribed to Sir Francis Bryan', *Huntington Library Quarterly*, 42 (1979) · HoP, *Commons, 1509–58*, 527–9 · S. Brigden, '"The shadow that you know": Sir Thomas Wyatt and Sir Francis Bryan at court and in embassy', *HJ*, 39 (1996), 1–31 · R. Bagwell, *Ireland under the Stuarts*, 1 (1909) · D. Starkey, *The reign of Henry VIII: personalities and politics* (1985) · *Literary remains of King Edward the Sixth*, ed. J. G. Nichols, 2 vols., Roxburghe Club, 75 (1857) · *Calendar of the manuscripts of the most hon. the marquis of Salisbury*, 24 vols., HMC, 9 (1883–1976)
Archives BL, Add. MSS; Cotton MSS; Harley MSS · PRO, SP 1, SP 3
Wealth at death landed wealth assessed for subsidy at £888 p.a.: HoP, *Commons*, 527–9

Bryan, George (1731–1791), merchant and revolutionary politician in America, was born on 11 August 1731 in Dublin, the fourth of eight children, and eldest son, of Samuel Bryan, merchant, and his wife, Sarah Dennis. His parents were Irish Presbyterians. In 1752 his father thought him sufficiently schooled in trade and sent him to Philadelphia to be a partner to the merchant James Wallace. After two years Bryan established his own mercantile business. He married Elizabeth (1733–1799), daughter of Philadelphia merchant Samuel Smith, on 22 April 1757. They had ten children. His firm flourished until 1771, when Bryan, probably because of defalcations of merchants in other ports, went bankrupt.

In 1755 Bryan became an ally of Benjamin Franklin's effort to overcome Quaker pacifism and provide for colonial defence, while asserting Pennsylvanians' rights against the Penn proprietors. Bryan and two other exuberant 24-year-olds, William Franklin and Joseph Galloway, concocted a vicious screed against the proprietary governor. By 1758 Bryan, unhappy with continuing Quaker opposition to defensive war, drew away from Benjamin Franklin's coalition. In the heated 1764 political campaign over Franklin's efforts to bring royal government to Pennsylvania, Bryan defeated Franklin in the Philadelphia burgess election. As a reward, Governor John Penn commissioned Bryan a judge. He remained a judge throughout his life, and his judicial income supported him after 1771. A revitalized anti-proprietary party ousted Bryan and his cohorts in 1765, and he held no other elective office until 1777.

As a leading proprietary assemblyman, Bryan was a delegate to the Stamp Act Congress of 1765. In 1768 he published a denunciation of British Admiralty jurisdiction over the colonies. However, he never served on any of the committees that were formed during this period to resist British impositions. Business reverses and bad health in the early 1770s may explain this in part, but his rigid and uncompromising mindset also may have alienated important Philadelphians.

In February 1777, after the promulgation of Pennsylvania's controversial state constitution, with its unicameral legislature and plural executive, Bryan reappeared as a supporter of the constitution and a candidate for the supreme executive council from Philadelphia. He won election because many anti-constitutionalists boycotted the voting, and other potential constitutionalist candidates were away with the army. Because he had legislative experience and represented Philadelphia, the assembly and council elected him council vice-president. When the president died in May 1778 he assumed that post, but reverted to the vice-presidency on election of a new president in 1779. His major achievements were to rally the state against British invasion and occupation of Philadelphia, and enforce harsh laws against suspected loyalists.

Bryan's tenure was successful enough for Philadelphia to elect him, at the end of his council term in 1779, to the legislature. Here he achieved his most important goal: passage of the first gradual slave emancipation act in the United States. His motives and arguments were both religious and based on whig views of liberty. He had advocated emancipation since 1778, but only when he entered the legislature was he able to push passage of a very moderate bill that was yet a major start toward abolition. Bryan's elevation to the supreme court in 1780 ended his productive legislative career. His election to the council of censors in January 1784 was politically insignificant, and after this he held no more elective posts.

Bryan's final political efforts were to oppose the federal constitution of 1787 and to oppose any new constitution for Pennsylvania. He organized a state convention in September 1788 to propose amendments to the recently ratified federal constitution, but this body mainly made unwelcome proposals for a return of power to the states. In March 1789, when the Pennsylvania assembly voted to hold an election for a constitutional convention, Bryan's opposition was completely ineffectual, and in 1790 a new state constitution with checks and balances replaced that of 1776. Bryan remained on the supreme court, but, having been ill since 1789, died from influenza on 5 January 1791, in Philadelphia. He was buried there in the Second Presbyterian churchyard.　　　BENJAMIN H. NEWCOMB

Sources J. S. Foster, *In pursuit of equal liberty: George Bryan and the revolution in Pennsylvania* (1994) · L. Gragg, 'Bryan, George', *ANB* · R. L. Brunhouse, *The counter-revolution in Pennsylvania, 1776–1790* (1942) · J. T. Main, *The antifederalists: critics of the constitution* (1961) · *Minutes of the supreme executive council of Pennsylvania* (1851–3) · B. H. Newcomb, *Franklin and Galloway: a political partnership* (1972) · B. H. Newcomb, *Political parties in the American middle colonies, 1700–1776* (1995) · R. A. Ryerson, *The revolution is now begun: the radical committees of Philadelphia* (1978)

Archives Hist. Soc. Penn., MSS · L. Cong., diary | New York Historical Society, Joseph Reed MSS

Likenesses oils, Hist. Soc. Penn.

Wealth at death very poor: Foster, *In pursuit of equal liberty*

Bryan, George Hartley (1864–1928), applied mathematician, was born on 1 March 1864 at 12 Trumpington Street, Cambridge, the only child of Robert Purdie Bryan, fellow-commoner of Clare College, and his wife, Fanny, daughter of George Martell, a surgeon. His father died in 1865 at the age of twenty-five while a student of law and Bryan's subsequent upbringing and education were undertaken by his mother and grandparents.

An only child and in delicate health, Bryan had an indulgent childhood, the family spending much of its time abroad in France, Italy, and Germany, especially the warmer climes of the Italian and French rivieras. This unusual upbringing gave him an excellent knowledge of languages and a lifelong fascination with the natural world, particularly of the rivieras, but it also led to a rather noticeable personal eccentricity. He was never allowed to go to school, and even when he became an undergraduate at Peterhouse, Cambridge, in 1883 he still lived at home. Having graduated as fifth wrangler in the mathematical tripos of 1886, in the next year Bryan was placed in the first division of the first class in part two of the tripos and in due course was second Smith's prizeman. He was elected a fellow of Peterhouse in 1889, his fellowship terminating automatically in 1895. In 1896 he was appointed professor of pure and applied mathematics at the University College of North Wales, Bangor, a position he held, with a special period of leave for research in 1917–20, until his retirement in 1926. His eccentric and absent-minded behaviour gave rise to numerous anecdotes among the Bangor students of the time. Bryan was elected

a fellow of the Royal Society in 1895 and honorary fellow of Peterhouse in 1915. On 17 July 1906 he married Mabel Williams (1870–1958), headmistress of the Bangor kindergarten school. Their only daughter, Margaret, was born in 1909.

Bryan's unique and lasting contribution to mathematics was the formulation of the theory of aircraft stability. As early as 1896 he recognized the importance of stability and control when addressing the Royal Artillery Institution on progress in manned flight. In June 1903, even before the first powered flight by the Wright brothers, he and his former student W. E. Williams communicated an epoch-making paper to the Royal Society on the longitudinal stability of gliders. Once certain characteristic quantities related to an aircraft were known, it became possible to study mathematically its stability—though only (at this stage) in the direction of its flight. Early aviators constructed their machines empirically and Bryan's work had little impact. However, persevering in his efforts, he published *Stability in Aviation* in 1911, completing the mathematical treatment of aircraft stability in all dimensions. Soon, using wind tunnels, the necessary characteristics of an aircraft could be experimentally evaluated and Bryan's theory became an integral part of all aircraft design. In 1914 his work was recognized by the award of the gold medal of the Royal Aeronautical Society. He was also elected president of the Institution of Aeronautical Engineers.

Stability was a recurring theme in Bryan's work. His first papers in 1888 were on the stability of elastic systems and the stability of a rotating cylinder of liquid, but he spread his very considerable and highly productive talents in applied mathematics widely. In 1891 and 1894 he produced important reports for the British Association on thermodynamics (the study of the general laws governing heat and energy), becoming a world authority on the subject. The article on thermodynamics published in the *Encyklopädie der mathematischen Wissenschaften* (1898–1934) is his. His 1900 paper on the mathematical theory of the action of bilge keels in extinguishing the oscillations of a ship led, in 1901, to the award of the gold medal of the Institution of Naval Architects.

Bryan was committed to raising the standards and status of mathematical education in Britain, and produced, mainly with W. Briggs, over a dozen student textbooks, such as the *Elementary Text Book of Mechanics* of 1894. In 1907, while president of the Mathematical Association, he introduced local branches by setting up the first in north Wales.

Bryan was an accomplished naturalist, contributing many articles on botany, entomology, and microscopy to such journals as *Science-Gossip* and the *International Journal of Microscopy and Natural Science*. He served as president of the Cambridge Entomological Society and the Postal Microscopical Society. A man with very wide interests, his great love of music led him to experiments with pneumatic piano-players on which he published a paper in the *Proceedings of the Royal Institution* (21, 1915, 397–406). On retirement in 1926 Bryan moved to his beloved Italian riviera. He died, after a short illness, at his villa, Le Lucciole, in Bordighera on 13 October 1928.   D. J. WRIGHT

Sources S. Brodetsky, *Nature*, 122 (1928), 849–50 · A. E. H. Love, *Journal of the London Mathematical Society*, 4 (1929), 238–40 · F. Hacker, *Flight stability and control* (1970) · b. cert. · m. cert. · d. cert. · *CGPLA Eng. & Wales* (1928)
Archives U. Wales, Bangor, archives
Wealth at death £8238 10*s.*: probate, 13 Dec 1928, *CGPLA Eng. & Wales*

Bryan, John (*b.* 1492/3, *d.* after 1521), logician, was a native of London. His family connections are unknown, but he was acquainted with Pietro Carmeliano, Latin secretary to Henry VII, and may have been his protégé. In 1505 he was sent to Eton College; from there he proceeded to King's College, Cambridge, where he was admitted on 17 August 1510, aged seventeen. He became a fellow in 1513, commenced BA in 1515, and incepted as MA in 1518. During Bryan's years as an undergraduate Erasmus spent his longest period of continuous residence in Cambridge, and Bryan was one of a select group of Cambridge scholars, including Henry Bullock and John Watson, who enjoyed the great humanist's particular favour. Bryan seems to have learned Greek at least partly as a result of attending Erasmus's Cambridge lectures, since Greek was not taught at Eton in his time. While he was in Cambridge Erasmus occasionally employed Bryan as scribe and messenger for his correspondence. In November 1513 he reported to Andrea Ammonio that Bryan had completed a history of France. This has not survived. After his inception as MA Bryan taught logic for two years. His lectures are said to have been based not on the thorny disputes of the realists and nominalists, but on the original sources.

John Bryan is last attested as a member of Cambridge University in 1521. Two years later a man of the same name was instituted as rector of the parish of Shellow Bowells in Essex. He died before 30 October 1545. It is not entirely certain that the Cambridge graduate and the parish priest were one and the same person, since the rector of Shellow Bowells is not described as master of arts. It is as a humanist and a disciple and friend of Erasmus that Bryan is remembered.   S. F. RYLE

Sources Venn, *Alum. Cant.*, 1/1.243 · *Opus epistolarum Des. Erasmi Roterodami*, ed. P. S. Allen, 1–3 (1906–13) · S. Knight, *Life of Erasmus* (1726), 146–7 · R. Newcourt, *Repertorium ecclesiasticum parochiale Londinense*, 2 (1710), 522 · BL, Add. MS 5814, fol. 156 · *DNB* · P. G. Bietenholz and T. B. Deutscher, eds., *Contemporaries of Erasmus: a biographical register*, 1 (1985), 208–9 · D. R. Leader, *A history of the University of Cambridge*, 1: *The university to 1546*, ed. C. N. L. Brooke and others (1988), 296–7, 310 · D. F. S. Thomson and H. C. Porter, *Erasmus and Cambridge* (1963), 218 · A. Tilley, 'Greek studies in England in the early sixteenth century [pt 1]', *EngHR*, 53 (1938), 221–39

Bryan, John (*d.* 1676), clergyman and ejected minister, was the son of Susanna Bryan, later Hopkins (*d.* 1673), and elder brother of another ejected minister, Jarvis (or Gervase) Bryan, twenty years his junior. John Bryan matriculated from Emmanuel College, Cambridge, in 1620, graduated BA in 1627, and proceeded MA in 1632. He was created BD in 1645 and DD in 1651. He was ordained deacon in September, and priest in December, 1623. In June 1632 he was presented by Serjeant Rowley Ward to the living of Barford, Warwickshire. The name of his first wife, like that of his father, is unknown, though it is known that three sons (and probably a fourth) were born between 1628 and 1635—John, Noah, Samuel, and probably Nathaniel—who were to follow their father to Cambridge. In the 1630s Bryan belonged to a moderate puritan group which was associated with a ministerial lecture at Warwick and which regularly met at the dining-table in Warwick Castle of the puritan Lord Brooke, who was Bryan's patron in that decade. The activities of this group are recorded in the diary of Bryan's close friend Thomas Dugard.

In the civil war John Bryan was treasurer to the parliamentary garrison at Warwick (receiving proposition money), and also its preacher and chaplain, until 1644. In May 1643 he preached a conciliatory sermon the day after new recruits had accidentally fired on their own side; two months later he was one of those ministers who petitioned parliament about the plight of soldiers wounded at Edgehill who had been sent to Warwick. In May 1644 he became vicar of Holy Trinity, Coventry, at a salary of £80 per annum (he had received £140 at Barford), with the promise that the city would add £20 to this. It was in Coventry that he became acquainted with certain godly orthodox divines who would remain his friends. They included Obadiah Grew, Richard Vines, and Richard Baxter. Coventry was then a bastion of puritan orthodoxy, but the radical sects did have some following there. In December 1646 Bryan and Grew, vicar of St Michael's, held a successful public disputation with the Baptists Hanserd Knollys and William Kiffin.

On 23 December 1646 Bryan preached at a day of public humiliation in the city, called because of the recent unseasonable rains and floods. He argued that they had been caused by divine anger at the people's 'discontentment with our present government', their discontent with taxes, and with the abolition of 'Popish holy days', especially the imminent feast of Christmas. His sermon *A Discovery of the Probable Sin Causing this Great Judgement of Rain and Waters* was printed in 1647 (Hughes, *Godly Reformation*, 1–2).

In 1647 the Holy Trinity vestry agreed to augment Bryan's stipend. However, he and Grew were becoming increasingly discouraged by their lack of maintenance. In January 1652 Bryan received an approach from the town of Shrewsbury, and promised to move there. There was great alarm in Coventry at this prospect, and in May 1652 a meeting took place in Stourbridge at which, it seems, Baxter and other Worcestershire ministers were asked to arbitrate between the competing claims of Shrewsbury and Coventry. Eventually Baxter, realizing that Dr Bryan was now regretting his promise, persuaded the people of Shrewsbury that Bryan would stay in Coventry. Bryan and Grew remained unhappy about their remuneration, particularly from the city (they were both city lecturers); after representations from William Purefoy and others the situation somewhat improved. Bryan built houses and laid out gardens in the city.

Probably in December 1654 Bryan and other ministers set up the Kenilworth classis, the 'Associated Presbytery within the County of Warwick and the City and County of Coventry'. Bryan, who had exercised 'presbyteriall government' in his parish for several years, preached a series of lectures on 'gospel order' (parochial elderships), which provoked a public challenge from the General Baptist John Onley. An account of the disputation between Bryan and Onley at Kenilworth was published in 1655 under the direction of Onley, and in 1658 John Ley, a member of the classis, complained that 'Mr. Onley so enervateth the vigour of [Bryan's] discourse as if he had suffered a failing of his faculties' (Ley, 78). It would appear that Bryan was the key figure in the classis, which had over twenty ministerial members. On 14 October 1658 Bryan was married again, to Susanna Bathars, in Holy Trinity Church, Coventry.

Bryan was ejected in 1662, and, though he would not conform as a minister, he chose thenceforth to attend the services of the established church as a layman. From that time until his death in 1676 he lived at Coleshill and at Coventry, and he ministered to nonconformist congregations in both places. In 1670 he published *Dwelling with God … in Eight Sermons*. In a letter of 28 February 1670 Sir Joseph Williamson was told that the book 'is making a great noise; the sixth sermon offends his people as defending the liturgy' of the established church (*Calamy rev.*, 83). In 1672 he was licensed a presbyterian minister at Coventry.

The friendship with Baxter begun in Coventry continued to Bryan's death. In 1651 Bryan took a copy of Baxter's *Saints Everlasting Rest* (the second edition) to the mayor and corporation of Coventry, and in 1657 Bryan wrote to thank Baxter for the gift of two of his works. In 1660, when refusing a bishopric, Baxter named Bryan as one of sixteen possible substitutes. He later called him 'an ancient Learned Divine, very humble, faithful and of a godly, upright life' (*Reliquiae Baxterianae*, 3.93). In 1670 he contributed a preface to Bryan's controversial *Dwelling with God*.

John Bryan died at Coventry on 4 March 1676 (he was buried in Holy Trinity on the 7th), and his funeral sermon was preached by Nathaniel Wanley, who had replaced him as vicar of Holy Trinity in 1662. He left two sons, John, a nonconformist minister in Shrewsbury, and Samuel, also a minister, besides his widow, Susanna, who died in 1680. In his will, dated 16 February 1676, he appointed as his sole executor the strongly puritan Major Robert Beake, a former mayor and MP for Coventry. His inventory, taken on 30 July 1676, totalled £263 2s. 11d., including 'Bookes' valued at £60.

John Bryan was a man of holy life and an exemplary pastor. It would seem that he was more interested in preaching and catechizing than in making for himself a literary reputation. He was also, as Baxter noted, an inspired trainer of young ministers, or aspirants to the ministry. He worked for a purified national, comprehensive church. He was a man who also worked quietly, and despite all discouragements, for the full reformation of the church he knew. In the 1658 words of his friend John Ley, he was:

as painful, powerful and profitable a minister … as any … this day in England … for besides his preaching which is very frequent both on the Sabbath and on the week day, he catechizeth daily from house to house every person in every family within his parish, and yet doth much good service in other places as just occasion requireth and opportunity serveth both as a learned man and as a godly minister. (Ley, 95–6, 104)

C. D. GILBERT

Sources A. Hughes, *Politics, society and civil war in Warwickshire, 1620–1660* (1987) · A. Hughes, *Godly reformation and its opponents in Warwickshire, 1640–1662*, Dugdale Society, 35 (1993) · *Reliquiae Baxterianae, or, Mr Richard Baxter's narrative of the most memorable passages of his life and times*, ed. M. Sylvester, 1 vol. in 3 pts (1696) [1 vol. in several pts] · A. Hughes, 'Coventry and the English revolution', *Town and countryside in the English revolution*, ed. R. C. Richardson (1992), 69–99 · T. John, *Coventry's civil war, 1642–1660*, Coventry and County Heritage Booklet, 20 (1994) · A. Hughes, 'Thomas Dugard and his circle in the 1630s—a "parliamentary–puritan" connexion?', *HJ*, 29 (1986), 771–93 · *Calendar of the correspondence of Richard Baxter*, ed. N. H. Keeble and G. F. Nuttall, 2 vols. (1991) · J. Ley, *A discourse of disputations* (1658) · A. Laurence, *Parliamentary army chaplains, 1642–1651*, Royal Historical Society Studies in History, 59 (1990) · *Calamy rev.* · will and inventory of John Bryan, Lichfield RO · F. B. Burbidge, *Old Coventry and Lady Godiva* (1952) · E. Calamy, *A continuation of the account of the ministers … who were ejected and silenced after the Restoration in 1660*, 2 vols. (1727) · Venn, *Alum. Cant.* · H. I. Longden, *Northamptonshire and Rutland clergy from 1500*, ed. P. I. King and others, 16 vols. in 6, Northamptonshire RS (1938–52), 2.269

Wealth at death £263 2s. 11d.: inventory, 30 July 1676, Lichfield RO

Bryan, Margaret, *suo jure* Baroness Bryan (d. 1552). *See under* Bryan, Sir Francis (d. 1550).

Bryan, Margaret (*fl.* 1795–1816), educator and writer on natural philosophy, was a noted early example of a woman teaching natural science to other women. Little is known about her life; such information as is available comes from her own writings. She was married to a Mr Bryan, and had two daughters. She ran a boarding-school for girls at Blackheath from 1795 to 1806, opened a school in London in 1815, and moved to Margate in 1816, where she also ran a school. The curriculum in her schools differed from that of most peer institutions by including mathematics and science as suitable subjects for girls.

In 1797 Margaret Bryan published her early lecture notes as *A Compendious System of Astronomy*. In the preface to this book she denied demonstrating any originality, proclaiming that the subject had already been extensively considered 'by the ablest mathematicians and by philosophers of the most penetrating genius' (Bryan, 1799, vii). She explained that her goal was to make obscure subjects clear and, continuing in an apologetic tone, stated that if she had failed 'through the imbecility of my judgment, I hope the motive may be my apology' (ibid.). Her tone reveals her awareness that she was doing something very unusual, and she noted that her lectures were not written for publication but for her students. Explaining that she had published these notes at the insistence of friends, she expected censure from those with 'false and vulgar' prejudices but expected fair treatment by those who acknowledged 'truth, although enfeebled by female attire' (ibid.).

Margaret Bryan (*fl.* 1795–1816), by William Nutter, pubd 1797 (after Samuel Shelley, 1797) [with her daughters]

first book, feeling the need to explain why she might appear to be overstepping the line of propriety and venturing into what might be considered the public sphere, she reasoned that to do so was to engage in responsible motherhood. Although this approach probably did not represent a deliberate strategy, it nevertheless served as a means to open scientific education to girls. Her works emphasized her femininity; on the frontispieces of her books were portraits of herself and her two daughters. This encouraged the *Dictionary of National Biography* biographer to describe her as 'beautiful and talented'. It is not known when Margaret Bryan died; her move to Margate in 1816 was her last recorded action.

MARILYN BAILEY OGILVIE

Sources M. Bryan, *A compendious system of astronomy*, 2nd edn (1799) · M. Bryan, *Lectures on natural philosophy: the result of many years' practical experience of the facts elucidated* (1806) · M. Benjamin, 'Elbow room: women writers on science, 1790–1840', *Science and sensibility: gender and scientific enquiry, 1780–1945*, ed. M. Benjamin (1991), 27–59 · E. C. Krupp, 'Astronomical musings', *Griffith Observer*, 39 (1975), 8–18 · N. A. Hans, *New trends in education in the eighteenth century* (1951) · Watt, *Bibl. Brit.* · DNB

Likenesses J. Heath, stipple (after T. Kearsley), BM, NPG; repro. in Bryan, *Lectures on natural philosophy* · T. Kearsley, portrait, repro. in Bryan, *Lectures on natural philosophy*, frontispiece · W. Nutter, group portrait, stipple (after S. Shelley, 1797), BM, NPG; repro. in Bryan, *Compendious system of astronomy* (1797) [*see illus.*] · S. Shelley, group portrait, repro. in Bryan, *Compendious system of astronomy*, frontispiece

Margaret Bryan succeeded in obtaining the endorsement of Charles Hutton, acknowledged leader of the London based philomaths, who noted his pleasure in finding 'that even the learned and more difficult sciences are … beginning to be successfully cultivated by the extraordinary and elegant talents of the female writers of the present day' (Bryan, 1799, xiii). Hutton stated that he was honoured to support Bryan's work, and this praise encouraged her to publish her *Lectures on Natural Philosophy* (1806), a work consisting of thirteen lectures on hydrostatics, optics, pneumatics, and acoustics. In this work, she was anxious to impress upon her students the mutual relationship between religion and science as expressed by William Paley in his *Natural Theology*. Since her first book had received such good reviews, she was more confident and less apologetic in this work. In 1815 she published *An Astronomical and Geographical Class Book for Schools*. Her work was often confused with that of Jane Marcet, who sometimes published anonymously. In the eighth London edition of the anonymous *Conversations on Chemistry*, the 'Advertisement' credits Bryan as author of the book later acknowledged to be by Marcet. Similar misattributions are found in Robert Watt's *Bibliotheca Britannica* and in the *Biographical Dictionary of Living Authors* (1916).

Though her work was a very public intrusion into a male sphere, Bryan sought rhetorically to accommodate her scientific work to her domestic role. In her *Lectures on Natural Philosophy*, she wrote that she was pleased with her domestic responsibilities and saw her teaching as an extension of her role as 'Parent and Preceptress' ('Address to my pupils', *Lectures on Natural Philosophy*). Earlier in her

Bryan, Matthew (1645/6–1699), nonjuring Church of England clergyman, was born at Limington in Somerset, the son of Robert Bryan, a clergyman. He matriculated on 23 October 1665, aged nineteen, as a semi-commoner at Magdalen Hall, Oxford, where his tutor was Robert Plot, the first keeper of the Ashmolean Museum. Bryan left the university without graduating. His precipitate departure was explained by John Lloyd, principal of Jesus College, Oxford, and vice-chancellor of the university in a letter twenty years later, dated 11 June 1685, in which he told his correspondent how Bryan 'was called away by extraordinary business and detained by deaths of some of his relations, and [now] desires to accumulate degree of bachelor and doctor of laws' (*Ormonde MSS*, 7.344). This desire was satisfied when, on 10 July 1685, Bryan proceeded bachelor and doctor of laws.

After holding a benefice in the diocese of Bath and Wells (possibly Limington, where his son was born in 1670 or 1671) for about ten years Bryan was presented to the living, which had been held by his father, of St Mary, Newington Butts, Surrey. He was also appointed afternoon lecturer at St Michael, Crooked Lane, in the City of London. A sermon preached by Bryan in 1684 in both these churches on a text from St Paul's second epistle to the Corinthians led to an accusation being laid against him before the dean of arches alleging the sermon to be treasonable and seditious in that it ascribed a lack of even-handedness to the king's courts. To vindicate himself Bryan published the sermon in 1685 under the title *The Certainty of the Future Judgment Asserted and Proved*. Notwithstanding the passages that stated 'even in the Courts of Judicature 'tis impossible that Justice should be universally and equally administred' and 'not to speak of the corruption of the Judge's heart, and the blinding of his eyes by Bribes' (p. 16) William Sancroft, archbishop of Canterbury, quashed the charge of sedition, judging it to be baseless. Apart from any potentially seditious passages the sermon is remarkable for its inventive metaphors, especially where the preacher describes himself and his fellow Christian ministers as 'Physicians in Ordinary to the King of Kings, and the World [as] his great Hospital, where do lye abundance of impotent Folk … who are in our Care' (p. 7).

A sermon published in 1686 under the title *A Perswasive to the Stricter Observation of the Lords Day* marks Bryan's contribution to a literature enjoining frequent church attendance. This appears to have been a distinct literary genre, popular in the 1680s, and exemplified by *A letter of advice to all the members of the Church of England to come to the divine service morning and evening every day* (1688) and a pamphlet, attributed to Thomas Comber, published under the title *The Christians best exercise: being an earnest invitation to the frequenting of the common prayer* (1689).

Bryan refused the oaths of allegiance to William and Mary and in 1689 was suspended from his church duties from 1 August 1689 until 1 February 1690. He did not take the oaths during the period of suspension and as a consequence was deprived of his preferments in 1690, and became minister of a nonjuring congregation. This ministry often brought him into trouble with the government. On 26 March 1692 a meeting of one hundred people was discovered in Mitre Court, Fleet Street, where 'Dr. Bryan, a nonjuror, read prayers and preacht, praying for the late royall family by name' (Luttrell, 2.398). Later, on 3 January 1693, a meeting of about one hundred presided over by Bryan in Johnson's Court, Fleet Street, was raided and the names of those present were taken (Luttrell, 3.1). It was perhaps as a result of this discovery that on 10 January 1693 a warrant, addressed to the keeper, or his deputy, of the Gatehouse prison in Westminster ordered that Bryan should be taken into custody for writing treasonable and seditious pamphlets and holding unlawful assemblies. Earlier, on 29 October 1689, Bryan had appeared before the court of king's bench which admitted him to bail.

In the highly charged political atmosphere of the 1690s those who were known to favour the exiled Stuarts were regarded with suspicion and were liable to arrest. Bryan was in this camp and gave expression to his Jacobite and nonjuring principles in *A copy of a letter sent to the Reverend Dr Beveridge, upon occasion of the second edition of the paper of remarks upon his sermon about restitution*, published anonymously, together, on the verso, with a poem entitled 'An eucharisticon occasion'd by his seasonable and excellent sermon about restitution', in 1691. 'An eucharisticon' vilifies those who had deposed James II and scoffs at any who would describe the deposition as an abdication by saying 't'Abdicate by Force, seems, by the By,/ A Monstrous Riddle, and Unlearned Lye:' adding in a note: 'To abdicate an Office, supposes a voluntary Act, and the consent of him who quits it' (Bryan, 'Eucharisticon'). The occasion of this polemic was the selection in 1691 of William Beveridge,

archdeacon of Colchester, to fill the see of Bath and Wells vacated by the deprivation of Thomas Ken and in it Bryan asks whether 'To enter upon the *Right* and *Possession* of another, Is it, I pray, agreeable to the *Golden Rule*, which, you observ'd, our *Saviour* recommended—*Whatsoever ye would that Men should do to you, even so do ye to them-?*' (Bryan, *Copy of a Letter*). Beveridge yielded to the pressure exerted by Bryan and other Jacobites and, even though he had at first accepted the preferment, finally declined it.

A polemical purpose also lies behind Bryan's identifying himself with St Paul as the prisoner of the Lord in a sermon, published in 1692, which had as its text Ephesians 4: 1 ('I therefore, the prisoner of the Lord, beseech you that ye walk worthy of the vocation wherewith ye are called'):

> How unlikely is this Lecture, this Epistle to prevail with the Auditors, which is deliver'd, which is sent by *Paul the Prisoner*, who talks of Riches and Honour, and Power and Liberty for his Disciples, when himself is poor, and despised, and weak and in bonds? (Bryan, *St. Paul's Triumph*, 3)

That this sermon is polemic aimed at those who had taken the oaths of allegiance to William and Mary is clear from a passage in which Bryan stigmatizes him who

> to avoid the loss of a little trival Profit, or to secure his Estate, when he is threatened with the loss of it … will *lye*, and *swear*, or *forswear*, and act against his Conscience, and the word of God, and his own words too … He refuses to *fight under the Banner of Christ*, notwithstanding his Vow; but is a perfidious, base Deserter, and runs over to the Enemies Camp. (ibid., 10)

It may be that Matthew Bryan was the Mr Bryenne described as having 'returned and fallen ill of the gout' (*CSP dom.*, 1698, 401). If this man was indeed Bryan his condition pointed to a more serious underlying disease. Bryan died on 10 March 1699 and was buried in St Dunstan-in-the-West, Fleet Street. Nothing is known of his family life save that he had a son, Robert, and therefore a marriage is presumed.   ROGER TURNER

Sources Foster, *Alum. Oxon.*, 1500–1714, 1.201 · Wood, *Ath. Oxon.*, new edn, 4.779–80 · Wood, *Ath. Oxon.: Fasti* (1820), 396–7 · *Calendar of the manuscripts of the marquess of Ormonde*, new ser., 8 vols., HMC, 36 (1902–20), vol. 7, p. 344 · N. Luttrell, *A brief historical relation of state affairs from September 1678 to April 1714*, 6 vols. (1857), vol. 2, p. 398; vol. 3, p. 1 · *CSP dom.*, 1689–90, 308; 1693, 8; 1698, 301 · *DNB* · J. H. Overton, *The nonjurors: their lives, principles, and writings* (1902), 474 · M. Bryan, *The certainty of the future judgment asserted and proved* (1685) · [M. Bryan], *St Paul's triumph in his sufferings for Christ, with some directions how a Christian ought to behave himself under, and may reap advantage by his sufferings* (1692) · [M. Bryan], *A copy of a letter sent to the Reverend Dr Beveridge, upon occasion of the second edition of the paper of remarks upon his sermon about restitution* (1691) · [M. Bryan], 'An eucharisticon occasion'd by his seasonable and excellent sermon about restitution, on St Luke 19.8 preach'd at St Laurence's London, Tuesday, March 12. 1690', *A copy of a letter sent to the Reverend Dr Beveridge, upon occasion of the second edition of the paper of remarks upon his sermon about restitution* (1691), verso

Bryan, Michael (1757–1821), art historian and dealer, was born in Newcastle upon Tyne on 9 April 1757 and baptized on 23 May 1757 at St Nicholas's Church; he was the son of Michael and Elizabeth Bryan. He was educated at the Newcastle Free School and appears to have remained in Northumberland in the years immediately after leaving school, taking up a number of short-lived employments, first as a schoolmaster and then as an actor among 'country performers' (Farington, *Diary*, 6.2433). Towards the end of the 1770s he moved to London where he took up work as a 'rider to some mercantile House' (Farington, *Diary*, 2.500), and it was under their auspices that he moved to Bruges in 1781. Some accounts record his travelling to Flanders in the company of his brother—who was later described as a 'Clothier in Yorkshire in great business' (Farington, *Diary*, 6.2433)—and it is possible that Bryan also began his career in the cloth trade.

Although he had shown some interest in art while still in London, this nine-year period in Flanders was the time in which Bryan's taste, knowledge, and collection of art was much enhanced. On a personal level, too, this stay proved fundamental to the later, successful development of his business as a fine art dealer: his marriage, on 7 June 1784, to the 'very plain and very proud' (Farington, *Diary*, 6.2433) Juliana Talbot, sister of the earl of Shrewsbury—whom Bryan is supposed to have met on a return crossing to London—benefited Bryan enormously; once he was joined to this aristocratic family, his social prestige and connections in the world of patrons and purchasers were assured.

On his final return to London, in 1790, Bryan quickly established himself as an authority on, and a dealer in, fine art. From his gallery on Savile Row he dispensed opinions, and exhibited and sold the many expertly selected works that he imported from the Netherlands and Flanders and, as a consequence, cultivated friendships among Royal Academicians and the growing number of aristocratic collectors of fine art. Indeed, Joseph Farington's diaries reveal how 'Bryant's [*sic*] Gallery' became a fashionable centre where artists and their patrons regularly met to view and discuss the paintings on display, which included important works by Dutch, Flemish, and Italian masters. His great learning and fair prices earned Bryan a reputation as 'a very honest man' (Farington, *Diary*, 6.2217); his obituarist similarly remembered him as a 'worthy man, and an enlightened member of the most intellectual circles' (*Literary Gazette*, 187).

Throughout the 1790s the standard of the works on offer in Bryan's gallery was maintained owing to his constant buying trips to the continent; but these journeys were not without hazard during such a politically tense period. In 1797, after purchasing 150 pictures in the Netherlands, he was thrown into prison for three weeks, unable to procure a passport for his return at a time when the French government were expelling all English residents. It was of course a result of these upheavals in Europe that some of the finest French aristocratic collections were dispersed and, through his various continental connections, Bryan was able to secure the rights to sell paintings from the Calonne collection in 1795, as well as the Italian masters from the cabinet of the duc d'Orléans in 1797. Before the foundation of the National Gallery few master works of such quality had ever been on open display and so, once the paintings from these collections arrived in London, Bryan mounted a six-month display, for the benefit of artists and exhibition goers, before

delivering the various canvases to purchasers who included the duke of Bridgewater, the marquess of Stafford, the earl of Carlisle, and John Julius Angerstein. Naturally Bryan raised impressive sums from the sale of such masterpieces, and while no business records appear to survive, Farington talks of total figures in the region of thousands of pounds. The exhibitions of the two collections bore other than financial fruits: the display of the Orléans collection, which included works by Raphael, Titian, Guido Reni, and the Carracci, fired William Hazlitt's fascination with art. In his essay 'On the pleasure of painting', Hazlitt recalled that 'A new sense came upon me, a new heaven and earth stood before me … From that time on I lived in a world of pictures' (*The Complete Works of William Hazlitt*, ed. P. P. Howe, 8, 1931, 14).

In the early 1810s Bryan retired from business and began to write his *Biographical and Critical Dictionary of Painters and Engravers*. Published in parts between 1813 and 1816, this two-volume work, with its lively and authoritative artists' biographies, was widely acclaimed and quickly took its place as an outstanding reference text for the history of art: although undergoing numerous revisions and enlargements, it retained its prominence until the early twentieth century, and still features in bibliographical citations. Bryan died of a stroke at his house in Portman Square on 21 March 1821.　　　LUCY PELTZ

Sources W. Buchanan, *Memoirs of painting: with a chronological history of the importation of pictures by the great masters into England*, 2 vols. (1824) • Farington, *Diary* • *GM*, 1st ser., 91/1 (1821), 379 • *Literary Gazette* (24 March 1821), 187 • G. Meissner, ed., *Allgemeines Künstlerlexikon: die bildenden Künstler aller Zeiten und Völker*, [new edn, 34 vols.] (Leipzig and Munich, 1983–) • J. Turner, ed., *The dictionary of art*, 34 vols. (1996) • W. T. Whitley, *Artists and their friends in England, 1700–1799*, 2 vols. (1928) • IGI

Likenesses W. Haines, stipple, pubd 1813 (after miniature by A. Pope), repro. in Bryan, *Painters* (1816–49)

Bryan, Stephen (*c*.1685–1748). *See under* Berrow, Harvey (*bap.* 1719, *d.* 1776).

Bryan, Sir Thomas (*d.* 1500), judge, was born in obscure circumstances, though he assumed arms containing three piles in allusion to those of Sir Guy Bryan (*d.* 1390) whose barony became extinct in 1456. His early career suggests that he was the son of a Londoner, and the most probable lineage is that of John Bryan (*d.* 1395), citizen and fishmonger, whose son John (*d.* 1418) owned property in various parts of London, Buckinghamshire, Middlesex, and Essex. Sir Thomas likewise had property in London and Buckinghamshire.

Thomas Bryan may have attended university before turning to legal study in the 1440s. An incident in the year-books for 1496, when he dismayed Sir Roger Townshend by referring to universal and particular negatives, the figure, and a sophister's verse, certainly suggests a more advanced scholastic background than was usual for a common lawyer. By 1456, when he acted as a feoffee of Gray's Inn, he was doubtless already a bencher, and in the same year he made his first appearance in the year-books. At this period he was acting as counsel to several London companies, and by 1459 he was steward of St Bartholomew's Hospital. In 1460 he was elected common serjeant of London, an office which he held until his creation as a serjeant-at-law in 1463. By April 1470 he had become one of the king's serjeants.

On the accession of Edward IV in 1471 Bryan was appointed chief justice of the common pleas, and in 1475 was created a knight of the Bath. In 1472 he received a remarkable patent of reappointment 'during good behaviour', the usual form of judicial appointment being 'during the king's pleasure'. The plea roll for Hilary term 1477 contains a badly defaced drawing which shows Bryan, in robes, receiving an amended version of this patent from the king. His tenure of the chief justiceship, which lasted for a little over twenty-nine years until his death, was the longest ever, though his lasting influence was staid rather than innovative. He always maintained that the common law should be guided by equity and justice, and he was not unaware of social changes: for instance, he favoured the new-found protection of the copyholder against his lord by an action of trespass. Nevertheless, in a period when the king's bench, under Hussey and Fyneux, was developing new remedies and becoming a rival court for court of common pleas, Bryan's judicial conservatism set the court of common pleas on a course which by the end of the sixteenth century would seem distinctly reactionary.

Bryan did not favour the current movement to find a means of barring entails. Although the doubts which he expressed in *Taltarum's case* (1472) failed to prevent the common recovery from becoming established in the early years of his presidency, he was scrupulous to protect the interests of leaseholders and remaindermen. Such considerations seem to have weighed less with his fellow judges, but the legacy of his cautious approach was the elaborate scheme of double and triple vouchers developed in the following century. In *Hulcote's case* (1493) he stopped counsel from disputing the 'common learning' that a landowner's freedom to dispose of the fee simple could not be restrained by condition, while in the same case approving a condition against barring an entail: this distinction encouraged a spate of 'perpetuity clauses', to counter the common recovery, which were not finally declared ineffective until 1613. Bryan was also opposed to the circumvention of wager of law by means of actions on the case, the issue later to provide the main source of contention between the two benches.

Bryan married Isabel (*d.* 1467), widow of Thomas Blount, treasurer of Calais, whose jointure lands lay in Lincolnshire. The couple settled, however, at Ashridge in Hertfordshire, where Bryan desired to be buried if he died within 20 miles. Bryan also owned London houses in the parishes of St Andrew, Holborn, and St Sepulchre; he had some connection with St George's Inn and in 1475 purchased the freehold of Thavies Inn, both in the latter parish. He died on 14 August 1500.

Bryan's only son, Sir Thomas (*d.* 1518), was admitted to Gray's Inn, but became a knight of the body, and vice-chamberlain to Katherine of Aragon. The younger Sir Thomas Bryan had a son, Sir Francis *Bryan (*d.* 1550), who was a courtier, diplomat, and man of letters, and had two daughters, Elizabeth Dilcock and Joan Clement.

J. H. BAKER

Sources E. W. Ives, *The common lawyers of pre-Reformation England* (1983) · Baker, *Serjeants*, 164, 263 · *The reports of Sir John Spelman*, ed. J. H. Baker, 2, SeldS, 94 (1978) · J. H. Baker and S. F. C. Milsom, eds., *Sources of English legal history: private law to 1750* (1986) · N. L. Ramsay, 'The English legal profession, c.1340–1450', PhD diss., U. Cam., 1985 · N. Doe, *Fundamental authority in late medieval English law* (1990) · will of John Bryan, 1418, PRO, PROB 11/2B, sig. 42 · plea rolls of the common pleas, PRO, CP 40 · P. E. Jones, ed., *Calendar of plea and memoranda rolls preserved among the archives of the corporation of the City of London at the Guildhall*, 5: 1437–1457 (1954), 145, 177, 180, 182 · E. Williams, *Early Holborn and the legal quarter of London*, 2 vols. (1927) · arms in Gray's Inn Hall, BL, Harley MS 1042, fol. 11v · will, PRO, PROB 11/12, sig. 13

Likenesses pen drawing, PRO

Bryant, Sir Arthur Wynne Morgan (1899–1985), historian, was born on 18 February 1899 at Dersingham on the royal Sandringham estate in Norfolk, the elder son of Francis Morgan Bryant (1859–1938), chief clerk to the prince of Wales, and his wife, May, elder daughter of H. W. Edmunds of Edgbaston. Two years later, on the accession of Edward VII, Bryant's father joined the royal secretariat, becoming registrar of the Royal Victorian Order in 1916, and being knighted in 1920. Bryant's childhood was spent in a house in Lower Grosvenor Place, London, close to the Royal Mews. He attended two fashionable day schools in London before going to Pelham House, Sandgate, followed by Harrow School. In 1916 he gained a history exhibition to Pembroke College, Cambridge, but instead joined the Royal Flying Corps in 1917, becoming a pilot officer. In January 1919 he returned to England, and entered the Queen's College, Oxford, where in 1920 he gained a distinction in the former servicemen's shortened modern history honours course.

Bryant started his career as a teacher in a London council school in Holloway. He was called to the bar by the Inner Temple but in 1923 was appointed principal of the Cambridge School of Arts, Crafts, and Technology. On 16 July 1924 he married Sylvia Mary Shakerley (1900/01–1950), daughter of Sir Walter Geoffrey Shakerley, third baronet, of Somerford Park, Cheshire. Within a year, on his appointment as lecturer in history for the University of Oxford department of extra mural studies, they moved from Cambridge to White House, East Claydon, north Buckinghamshire, where he was to live for the next twenty years.

In 1929 Bryant became educational adviser to the Bonar Law College at Ashridge, Hertfordshire, and produced his first book, *The Spirit of Conservatism*, imbued with nostalgic Baldwinite traditionalism. Soon he was editing the *Ashridge Journal*. His nostalgia for an ideal English past had been further expressed in the successful historical pageants he had organized in the vicinity of Cambridge, and then Oxford, which were to lead to his role as co-ordinator of the Greenwich pageants in London in the 1930s.

Bryant's first book of history was *King Charles II* (1931), a biography favourable to that monarch as a protector of traditional English interests, which was dramatic in its impact, and also readable; so much so, that it became a best-seller, and the Book Society's monthly choice. A modern reader of it will note the detailed research involved, but also at times the rather sentimental, mannered tone, which was to be a constant in his output. Both aspects were to the fore in his highly successful life of Samuel Pepys, in three volumes (1933, 1935, and 1938), the making of his reputation as a historian.

Bryant was asked, in 1936, to succeed G. K. Chesterton as writer of 'Our note book' in the *Illustrated London News* (which he was to write regularly for the rest of his life). In the same year he left his post with the University of Oxford department of extra mural studies, and was from now on to be a freelance writer. In 1937 he became general editor of the National Book Association, a tory counterblast to the Left Book Club.

Bryant's politics, like those of many people on the right, were affected from 1933 onwards by a naïve pro-Nazism. In 1934 he had published a collection of essays entitled *The Man and the Hour: Studies of Six Great Men of our Time*, in which his 'Summary' described Hitler as a 'mystic' who had enabled Germany to 'find her soul' (pp. 143–4). In the late thirties he was still publicly railing against the calumnies with regard to Germany that he believed 'warmongers' to be spreading.

All this would seem comparatively innocuous, and typical of the attitudes of many at the time; but, even after war broke out, when so many others had recanted, Bryant continued in the same vein, publishing in January 1940 a book (based in part on earlier work), entitled *Unfinished Victory*; this, while purporting to be an explanation of Germany's attitudes, attempted among other things to justify Germany's actions against the Jews: 'The native Germans … were confronted with a problem—that of rescuing their indigenous culture from an alien hand and restoring it to their own race' (p. 141). The book ended with a triumphant evocation of the victory of the German revolution. Bryant, in his continual use and reuse of everything he had written, had failed to notice that times had changed. The public reactions to his book soon showed him that they had.

Bryant swiftly embarked, in responsive reaction, upon his well-known career as a writer of patriotic history, starting with *English Saga* (1940), and continuing with *The Years of Endurance, 1793–1802* (1942), and *The Years of Victory, 1802–1812* (1944). Clear parallels were drawn between Napoleon and Hitler, and England's heroic role in the Napoleonic Wars was given a contemporary gloss. These books lacked the detailed research that had marked his writing of the thirties, but were strongly popular in their appeal. They were widely read, and did much to raise public morale.

In 1939 Bryant's first marriage had been dissolved, and on 29 January 1941 he married Anne Elaine Primula, daughter of Bertram Willes Dayrell Brooke, a retired captain in the Royal Artillery and heir to the last raja of Sarawak (they were to be divorced in 1976). There were no children of either marriage.

Bryant had always been a very prolific writer. In the post-war period his output was prodigious, with, apart from his journalism, more than twenty books, and many shorter works. Many of these were in the nature of potboilers, but his two-volume edition of the diaries of Lord Alanbrooke, *The Turn of the Tide* (1957) and *Triumph in the West* (1959), showed that he was still capable of research. The volumes caused something of a furore, because of the criticisms of Churchill contained in them and because they exposed the extent of Anglo-American rivalry over the European campaign in 1944–5. Much of his other output could be best described as 'generalist' history. He had, however, become something of a national institution, and as Britain's leading writer of patriotic history was showered with honours, becoming CBE (1949), a knight (1954), and CH (1967). His one venture into politics, in this period, was his opposition to Britain's entry to the European Common Market.

Bryant died at New Hall Hospital, Bodenham, Salisbury, Wiltshire, on 22 January 1985. The reputation he left as a historian is a mixed one. Academics have tended to disdain his particular form of popular history. There is a good story about the reactions of A. J. P. Taylor when Bryant was introduced to him as 'our greatest living historian'; yet, to many people, he was just that. His writings have performed a very important function, because by making history a 'good read' he encouraged countless people, who would not otherwise have thought of doing so, to take a real interest in the events of the past.

RICHARD GRIFFITHS

Sources King's Lond., Liddell Hart C., Bryant MSS · P. Street, *Arthur Bryant: portrait of a historian* (1979) · A. Roberts, *Eminent Churchillians* (1994) · R. Griffiths, *Patriotism perverted: Captain Ramsay, the Right Club and British anti-Semitism* (1998) · *The Times* (24 Jan 1985) · *DNB* · J. Kenyon, *The Observer* (18 Feb 1979) · m. certs. · d. cert. · *WWW, 1929–40*

Archives Bucks. RLSS, MSS relating to Crafton Farm · IWM, MSS and military corresp. · King's Lond., Liddell Hart C., corresp., diaries, MSS, and memoranda | Bodl. Oxf., corresp. with Lord Woolton · CUL, corresp. with Sir Samuel Hoare · HLRO, corresp. with Lord Beaverbrook · HLRO, corresp. with Viscount Davidson · King's Lond., Liddell Hart C., corresp. with Sir B. H. Liddell Hart | FILM BFI NFTVA, news footage | SOUND BL NSA, Bow dialogues, 11 Sept 1973, C812/36 C1 · BL NSA, performance recordings

Likenesses photographs, 1930–72, Hult. Arch. · P. Tanqueray, photograph, 1931, NPG · H. Coster, photographs, *c.*1934, NPG · double portrait, photograph (with his first wife), repro. in Roberts, *Eminent Churchillians*, facing p. 181 · double portrait, photograph (with Admiral Sir Barry Domville), repro. in Griffiths, *Patriotism perverted*, following p. 116 · portrait, repro. in Kenyon, *The Observer*

Wealth at death £779,352: probate, 29 May 1985, *CGPLA Eng. & Wales*

Bryant, Benjamin [Ben] (1905–1994), naval officer, was born in India on 16 September 1905, the third and youngest child of John Forbes Bryant of the Indian Civil Service and his wife, Mary Ada, *née* Genge. Having been to Oundle School, Ben (as he was invariably known) was a cadet at

Benjamin Bryant (1905–1994), by Walter Stoneman, 1956

the Royal Naval College at Osborne and Dartmouth (1919–23), and first went to sea as a midshipman in the battleship *Ramillies* in 1923. He volunteered for submarines in 1927, his first boat being *L52* at Devonport. In 1929 he was appointed first lieutenant of *R4*, known as The Slug for her appearance and speed, acting as a target off Portland. He returned to general service in 1930 for a year in the battleship *Royal Oak*. After service in the submarines *Osiris* and *Perseus* on the China station, he then passed the submarine commanding officer's qualifying course (the 'Perisher') in 1933. His first command was *H49*, a boat of First World War vintage, in the training flotilla at Portland. In 1936 he was seconded to the Royal Australian Navy and served for two years in the cruiser *Australia* in the Mediterranean.

In 1939 Bryant was appointed to the submarine *Sealion*, which he commanded for the next three years in home waters, off Norway, and in the Mediterranean. He was awarded the DSC in May 1940 for successful submarine operations against the enemy, and was mentioned in dispatches for *Sealion's* clandestine missions off the coast of Brittany. His sailors relied on him utterly, and he in turn drew strength from them. Off Norway in 1940 the clear water, sudden freshwater rips, almost continuous daylight, and constant air surveillance made submarine operations extremely difficult and hazardous. Off Stavanger in July 1940 Bryant had what he called his 'worst patrol', during which *Sealion* was depth-charged several times and attacked by aircraft whenever she surfaced to try and recharge her main batteries. Once, after *Sealion* was forced

to remain dived for nearly twenty-four hours, her air quality was so poor that when she finally surfaced the diesel engines would not start until the boat had been ventilated. It was one of the few times when Bryant was downcast. The war was going badly, and two submarines commanded by friends of his had just been lost. But when he went up to the fore ends, where the sailors lived, his mood changed:

> Suddenly the atmosphere of unworried serenity passed from them to me. I realised that they would go into action on the morrow without backward thoughts, that with crews such as I was privileged to command we could not be beaten; the depression left me. (Bryant, 104–5)

Bryant never took any exercise, because he had noticed that men who did so on their return from patrol often fell sick. He stayed fit throughout the war. Even when most of *Sealion's* officers and men were prostrated by influenza, Bryant remained immune, dispensing aspirins and Dover tablets to the afflicted until the epidemic was over.

Appointed to command *P211* (later renamed *Safari*) in the Mediterranean in late 1941, Bryant made ten war patrols between May 1942 and April 1943, sinking some 30,000 tons of enemy shipping and winning a DSO and two bars. In the Mediterranean in 1942 submarine losses were so high that at one time a boat's chances of survival were no better than fifty–fifty. But Bryant never lost the attacking spirit. He often said he 'loved to hunt and chase the enemy and beat him up on his own doorstep' (*The Independent*, 3 Dec 1994). Tracking and sinking the enemy was to him 'the finest sport in the world' (*The Times*, 25 Nov 1994). His first DSO was awarded in March 1943, for sinking nine enemy ships in the Mediterranean between July and October 1942. His first bar, awarded in May 1943, was for sinking enemy ships in the eastern Mediterranean in November and December 1942, when *Safari* took part in the 'Torch' landings in north Africa. His second bar, awarded in July 1943, was for his last six war patrols. Bryant excelled at surface gun actions, using *Safari* as a submersible gunboat to disrupt coastal traffic, and several times even shelling coastal railway lines and rolling stock. In his tenth and last patrol, described by the commander-in-chief Mediterranean as 'one which will rank among the classic exploits of the submarine service' (*Daily Telegraph*, 25 Nov 1994), *Safari* sank an armed liner, a tanker, a tramp steamer, a minesweeper, an anti-submarine brigantine, and a trading schooner. Bryant reproached himself for only severely damaging a store ship: 'We should have sunk that ship', he said (Bryant, 235). By the time he left *Safari* Ben Bryant was a full commander and one of the most experienced submarine commanding officers in the navy, but he never allowed himself to become overconfident.

Promoted captain in June 1944 Bryant was appointed in command of the depot ship *Cyclops* and the 7th submarine flotilla at Rothesay, and then the depot ship *Forth* and the 2nd flotilla in Holy Loch. In 1945 he went to Fremantle in Australia to command the depot ship *Adamant* and the 4th flotilla in the British Pacific Fleet. In 1947 he went to HMS

Dolphin, Fort Blockhouse, Gosport, in command of the 5th flotilla and the submarine school. He was commodore of Devonport barracks from 1951 to 1953 and then commanded the cruiser *Glasgow* as flag captain to the commander-in-chief Mediterranean until 1954, when he was promoted rear-admiral. Bryant's final appointment before he retired in 1957 was as deputy chief of naval personnel (training and manning). He was appointed CB in 1956. In retirement, he took a course in business management and was staff personnel manager of Rolls-Royce's Scottish factories from 1957 to 1968. He published *One Man Band*, his wartime memoirs, in 1958 (reissued as *Submarine Command* in 1975).

Bryant actually looked the part. Edward Young, one of *Sealion*'s officers, who later became a submarine commanding officer himself, wrote of him:

> With his erect height, his sea-dog beard and arrogant eye, he was a typical submarine captain of the public imagination. He had a fine command of the English language, which he used to good effect in recounting yarns in the wardroom, inventing ballads or expressing his opinion of some ineptitude on the part of one of his officers or men. He had the rare gift of being able to switch without loss of dignity from CO to entertaining messmate.   (Young, 62)

Bryant was married twice. On 6 April 1929 he married Marjorie Dagmar Mynors Symonds (*b.* 1906/7), daughter of Reginald Wynne Symonds, gentleman, of New Milton, Hampshire; they had a son and a daughter. She died in 1965, and on 7 April of the following year Bryant married Heather Elizabeth Williams (*b.* 1917/18), a widow, and daughter of Julian Henry Reginald Hance, merchant. His second wife died in 1989. Bryant himself died in a nursing home in Worthing, Sussex, on 23 November 1994. He was survived by his son and daughter.   JOHN WINTON

Sources B. Bryant, *One man band* (1958) · *Daily Telegraph* (25 Nov 1994) · *The Times* (25 Nov 1994) · *The Independent* (3 Dec 1994) · E. Young, *One of our submarines* (1952) · *Navy List* · records, Royal Navy Submarine Museum, Gosport, Hampshire · private information (2004) · personal knowledge (2004) · *WWW* [forthcoming] · *CGPLA Eng. & Wales* (1995) · m. certs.
Likenesses W. Stoneman, photograph, 1956, NPG [*see illus.*] · photograph, repro. in *The Times* · photograph, repro. in *The Independent* · photograph, repro. in Young, *One of our submarines*, facing p. 65 · photographs, repro. in Bryant, *One man band*
Wealth at death £593,287: probate, 24 April 1995, *CGPLA Eng. & Wales*

Bryant, Henry (*bap.* 1722, *d.* 1799), botanist, was baptized at St Peter's, Norwich, on 22 May 1722, one of at least three sons of John Bryant, a weaver, of Norwich, and his wife, Ann, *née* Harper. Admitted to St John's College, Cambridge, in 1746, he graduated BA in 1749 and proceeded MA in 1753. Bryant entered the church, and took up botany about 1764, after the death of his wife, whose name is unknown. He is said to have been a man of great acuteness and attainments in mathematics. From Norwich he was presented to the vicarage of Langham in 1758, removing afterwards to Heydon, and thence to the rectory of Colby. His brother Charles Bryant, also a botanist, died shortly before him. Bryant was the author of *A Particular Enquiry*

into the Cause of that Disease in Wheat Commonly called Brand (1784), and contributed to J. Sowerby and J. E. Smith's *English Botany*. He died at Colby on 4 June 1799.

B. D. JACKSON, *rev.* ANITA MCCONNELL

Sources Venn, *Alum. Cant.* · *GM*, 1st ser., 69 (1799), 532 · J. E. Smith, 'Biographical memoirs of several Norwich botanists, in a letter to Alexander MacLeay', *Transactions of the Linnean Society of London*, 7 (1804), 295–301, esp. 297–300 · *IGI*

Bryant, Jacob (*bap.* 1717, *d.* 1804), antiquary and classical scholar, was born in Plymouth, where his father, Anthony Bryant, was a customs officer, and where he was baptized on 19 August 1717. The family later moved to Chatham, Kent. He attended school at Luddesdon, near Rochester, and from 1730, Eton College. Elected to King's College, Cambridge, in 1736, he graduated BA in 1741, proceeded MA in 1744, and became a fellow of the college. He was then employed as a private tutor, first to Sir Thomas Stapylton and afterward to George Spencer, marquess of Blandford, and his brother, Lord Charles Spencer. In 1756 Bryant was appointed secretary to his charges' father, Charles Spencer, third duke of Marlborough, a master-general of the ordnance, and accompanied him to Germany in 1758, where the duke died suddenly at Munster. On Bryant's return to England, the Marlborough family generously provided him with a sizeable income, living quarters at Blenheim, and use of their famous library.

Having attained financial independence, Bryant devoted the rest of his long life to arcane researches, book collecting, and authorship. Though once actually elected, he twice refused the mastership of the Charterhouse School in London. In his first book, *Observations and Enquiries Relating to Various Parts of Ancient History* (1767), Bryant attacked selected opinions in the works of such celebrated antiquarian scholars as Theodore Beza (1519–1605), Hugo Grotius (1583–1645), Samuel Bochart (1599–1667), and Richard Bentley (1662–1742). His work was favourably received. Suitably encouraged, he next published the book for which he is most often remembered, *A New System, or, An Analysis of Ancient Mythology*, with plates (3 vols., 1774–6). This work, according to its subtitle, was 'an attempt … to divest tradition of fable, and to reduce the truth to its original purity', a goal in which he always believed, but the actual result was simply a fantastic hodgepodge of spurious etymology (in the manner of Bochart) and riotous imagination.

Bryant took as his subject matter the whole of ancient history from the deluge of Noah to the dispersion of peoples occasioned by the subsequent wanderings of Noah's three sons. He argued that many of the old stories, such as the expedition of Jason to Colchis, were entirely fabulous, but that the Mosaic account to be found in Genesis was true in all respects, and many other myths, like those of the Greek god Poseidon, were simply distorted recollections of Noah. The deluge, he argued, was the grand epocha of every ancient kingdom, including those of Egypt, Babylon, Chaldea, Ethiopia, and others. Of the three sons of Noah—or Noachidae, as he called them—Bryant was most interested in Ham, whom he believed to be the father of a great 'Amonian' family who were the disseminators of culture worldwide. Though indebted for much of his deluge material to a French work by Nicolas-Antoine Boulanger (1766), Bryant rarely acknowledged his extensive use of sources.

While speculative mythology was a genre of some importance in the learned literature of the eighteenth century, it has been entirely superseded since. A field of study that began by explaining the myths of the ancient world as distortions of facts recorded in the Bible ended by questioning whether biblical events like the flood were not merely myths themselves. Unlike Bryant, later generations of scholars have had at their disposal a more reliable understanding of word origins, a more critical approach to history, a strikingly revised view of scripture, and a developed science of archaeology, all of which have shown what Bryant (and others) wrote to be nonsense.

Ironically, Bryant's importance to modern readers lies in the influence he had upon the poet and artist William Blake, who in his own time was generally considered mad. The many plates appearing in Bryant's *Mythology* were prepared and signed by James Basire, a well-known London engraver, to whom Blake was apprenticed from 1771 to 1778. It is possible that several of the plates in Bryant's *Mythology* were Blake's work, and the final, unsigned one (on the last page of volume three) almost certainly is. In his prose *Descriptive Catalogue* (1809), written to accompany an exhibition of his art, Blake affirmed that all myths 'are the same thing, as Jacob Bryant and all antiquaries have proved'. In his long self-illustrated poem *Jerusalem* (1804–20), Blake also followed Bryant in placing the Erythrean (Red) Sea not surrounding Sinai but in the Indian Ocean. In illustrating the same poem, he depicted the Ark as a crescent moon, just as he had done on the last page of Bryant's *Mythology*. Blake scholars therefore find Bryant still of some interest.

Bryant's views in the *Mythology* did not escape censure in his own time. For example, his account of the Apamean medal was disputed by an anonymous writer in the *Gentleman's Magazine* and he published a 28-page 'Vindication' in his defence (1775). More seriously, John Richardson (1741–1811?), assisted by Sir William Jones, opposed some of Bryant's more outlandish antiquarian fantasies in the dissertation on languages affixed to his *Dictionary of Persian, Arabic, and English* (1777). When Bryant replied in an anonymous pamphlet *Apology*, Richardson revised his former preface and added a second part comprising *Further Remarks on the 'New Analysis of Ancient Mythology'* in 1778. Bryant again replied, this time with a 100-page *Farther Illustration of the 'Analysis'* the same year. Criticism from the Dutch scholar Wyttenbach also required a response.

The otherwise favourable public reception of his weighty *Mythology* encouraged Bryant to speak out freely (if sometimes imprudently) on controversial issues for the rest of his life. In 1775, four years after the death of his friend Robert Wood, he revised and published Wood's *Essay on the Original Genius and Writings of Homer*, the original of which had been privately printed (seven copies only) in 1769. In 1777 Bryant's *Vindiciae Flavianae* endorsed

the authenticity of Josephus's testimony regarding Jesus Christ which, it was said, even convinced Dr Joseph Priestley. Bryant then boldly published *An Address to Dr. Priestley … on Philosophical Necessity* (1780) to which Priestley replied the same year. Priestley would publish his well-known *History of the Corruptions of Christianity* in 1782 and his *History of Early Opinions Concerning Jesus Christ* in 1786. When, in a further controversy, Thomas Tyrwhitt exposed the presumed Rowley poems of Thomas Chatterton as forgeries, Bryant—together with Dr Robert Glynn of King's College, Cambridge—replied with two volumes of *Observations on the poems of Thomas Rowley, in which the authenticity of those poems is ascertained* (1781). His views did not prevail.

In 1783 Bryant's former pupil, George Spencer, fourth duke of Marlborough, underwrote the publication of *Gemmarum antiquarum delectus*, a privately printed and luxurious two-volume folio in which the antique gem collection of the Marlboroughs was described and depicted, with plates by Francesco Bartolozzi. The first volume was written in Latin by Bryant and translated into French by Paul Henry Maty. The second volume was written by William Cole and translated by Louis Dutens. In 1785 Bryant read to the Royal Society a paper, 'On the Zingara or Gypsey language', subsequently published in *Archaeologia*. His disquisition, 'On the land of Goshen', written about 1767, was published the same year in William Bowyer's *Miscellaneous Tracts*. After several years of comparative silence, Bryant undertook an anonymous *Treatise on the Authenticity of the Scriptures* (1791) at the behest of the dowager countess of Pembroke, daughter of his patron. Signed editions followed in 1793 and 1810 with all profits going to charity. There followed *Observations on a Controverted Passage in Justin Martyr, also upon the Worship of Angels* (1793); and the 440-page *Observations upon the Plagues Inflicted upon the Egyptians* (1794), a work probably influenced by the concurrent reign of terror in France.

In 1794 Andrew Dalzel published his own translation from the French of Chevalier's *Tableau de la plaine de Troye* (1791) as *Description of the Plain of Troy*. In his bizarre responses, *Observations upon a Treatise … [on] the Plain of Troy* (1795) and *A Dissertation Concerning the War of Troy* (1796?; 2nd edn., 1799), Bryant denied not only that there had ever been a Trojan War but that Troy had even existed. He won no converts to his views and was roundly attacked by such critics as William Vincent, Gilbert Wakefield, and J. B. S. Morritt. Shaken by the number and ability of his opponents, Bryant replied intemperately to a criticism of his views appearing in the *British Critic* and misidentified its author as Wakefield rather than Vincent.

Unable to retire gracefully, Bryant next appeared before the public with a fanciful treatise, *The Sentiments of Philo-Judaeus Concerning the Logos or Word of God* (1797). His final literary labour, *Observations upon some Passages in Scripture* (1803), dealt with Balaam, Joshua, Samson, and Jonah. Short, slight, and unmarried, in his later years Bryant lived at Cypenham in Farnham Royal, near Windsor, keeping dogs with him for company. George III often visited him there for the sake of his conversation, which was said to be pleasing, instructive, and slyly humorous. In his eighty-ninth year Bryant injured a leg while reaching for a book in his library, developed an unstoppable infection, and died of gangrene on 14 November 1804. He was buried in his parish church, with a nearby monument erected to his memory. The classical part of his library was donated to King's College, Cambridge. During his lifetime he had donated many valuable books to George III. He also left money to charities.

In the ironic assessment of Edward Hungerford:

Jacob Bryant was an astonishing person. Financially well off, a protégé of the Marlboroughs and a friend of the king, he devoted a very long life to scholarship, during the nine decades of which he came to not a single correct conclusion. His erudition was equaled only by his capacity to misuse it. He proved that Chatterton did not forge the Rowley poems, that there had never been a Troy, and he set up a system of mythology which dazzles the imagination. At last, as if Learning could no longer endure the outrage, a book fell on him while he was at work in his study, and he died from the injury. (Hungerford, 20)

But perhaps we should think better of him than that.

DENNIS R. DEAN

Sources *DNB* · Venn, *Alum. Cant.* · E. B. Hungerford, *Shores of darkness* (1963) · S. Foster Damon, *A Blake dictionary* (1965) · F. E. Manuel, *The eighteenth century confronts the gods* (1959) · M. L. Clarke, *Greek studies in England, 1700–1830* (1945)
Archives Boston PL, letters and papers · King's Cam., corresp. as librarian to duke of Marlborough
Likenesses H. R. Cook, stipple (after J. Bearblock), BM; repro. in *Analysis of ancient mythology* (1807); related etching, pubd 1801, NPG
Wealth at death left thousands of pounds in legacies; did not own large real estate: *DNB*

Bryant [*née* Broad], **Mary** (*b.* 1764), convict, was born in April 1764 in the town of Fowey, Cornwall, the second of the four children of William Broad, a master mariner, and his wife, Grace. In 1785, for reasons that remain unclear, although it is on record that times were particularly hard, she became a highwaywoman, and in January 1786 she was captured after holding up a woman from whom she stole jewellery worth 11 guineas. Committed for trial to Exeter assizes, on 20 March 1786 she was sentenced to death, but the sentence was commuted a week later to transportation.

While in the prison hulks at Plymouth Dock (Devonport) Mary Broad became pregnant, the most likely father being one of the officers in charge of the prisoners, since male and female prisoners were segregated. On 13 May 1787 she sailed to Australia with the first fleet, and halfway through the voyage gave birth to a daughter, Charlotte, named after the transport ship. Following her arrival in January 1788, on 10 February she married William Bryant (1762–1791), a Cornish fisherman sentenced for smuggling, with whom she had a son, Emmanuel, born in April 1790. To some extent Mary was in a privileged position, since Bryant's skills were in great demand as food was so short; they even had a hut to themselves. Also, most unusually, they seem to have been trusted by the Aborigines, particularly a man called Bennelong and his family. However, after three years of privation, during the winter

of 1790–91 Mary determined to escape, a decision reached after Bryant had been condemned to a hundred lashes for bartering fish for vegetables—a criminal offence.

After the arrival of the Second Fleet, bringing with it convicts who had suffered the most appalling privations on the voyage, Mary deliberately made friends with Captain Detmer Smith, the sympathetic Dutch captain of a cargo ship, from whom she acquired compass, quadrant, a barrel for fresh water, two old muskets, and a chart. On 28 March 1791 the Bryants with their infants and seven other convicts, James Martin, James Cox, Sam Bird, William Allen, Nathaniel Lilly, William Moreton, and Samuel Broom, succeeded in stealing the governor's own boat and escaped under cover of darkness. Their ensuing voyage of 3254 miles to Kupang in East Timor was later described by Captain Bligh as one of the most remarkable journeys ever made in an open boat. Afterwards the convicts praised Mary for her seamanship—James Martin in his account of the voyage noting how she had urged them to fight for their lives and continue bailing out the boat when they would otherwise have given up. In Kupang they claimed to be victims of shipwreck, but Bryant, careless in drink, bragged too openly of the escape.

This proved fatal, as the group came to the attention of Captain Edward Edwards, who had been dispatched to the Pacific to search out and arrest *Bounty* mutineers. Notorious for his inhumanity, he had wrecked his own vessel after refusing to take advice on the position of dangerous reefs. Having learned of the escape, he realized who the convicts were and arrested them, after which he chartered a ship and set sail for England. Both the handful of *Bounty* mutineers who had survived the wreck and the convicts were kept in conditions of great cruelty, shackled in open cages on the deck. Before the ship left the East Indies Mary had lost both husband and baby, and three more convicts died on the voyage to Cape Town. Once there, however, they were transferred to a naval ship bringing back officers sent to guard the original penal colony who were now being recalled for the war with the French. Shortly after leaving Cape Town, Mary's daughter, Charlotte, also died. One of the naval officers, Watkin Tench, captain of marines, to whom we owe a great deal of our knowledge of the early years of the penal colony, wrote in his diary: 'I confess that I have never looked at these people without pity and astonishment. They had miscarried in a heroic struggle for liberty; after having combated every hardship and conquered every difficulty' (Cook, 190). Mary, he said, was distinguished for her courage and behaviour.

The convicts arrived in England to become the centre of attention—Mary being described in the press of the day as 'The Girl from Botany Bay'. She was quoted as saying, 'I would rather suffer death than return to the Fatal Shore' (*London Chronicle*, 3 July 1792). She was sent to Newgate gaol, once again under threat of death, the standard penalty for returning from transportation. Her demeanour when finally brought before a judge and the frankness with which she answered questions greatly impressed the crowd that packed the court: her story fired the imagination of James Boswell, lawyer and biographer of Dr Johnson, who visited her in prison, offering to represent her to ensure she would not hang. Mary told him she would rather die than suffer further imprisonment. Boswell therefore determined she should have a free pardon and devoted himself to that end, which he finally achieved on 2 May 1793.

Mary remained in London for six months and possibly became Boswell's mistress. Certainly during this period Boswell not only visited her regularly but also sought out her sister, whom he discovered to be in service in London. When she finally told him she wanted to return home he was greatly saddened. On 12 October she left London for Fowey, Boswell taking her to Southwark to see her embark on the ship. 'I had settled on her an Annuity of £10 yearly … and that, therefore, being independent, she might quit her relations whenever she pleased!' (*Journal of Boswell*, xxx). She gave him her only souvenir of her sojourn in Australia, dried sarsaparilla leaves pulled from the bush by her cabin on the night of her escape.

Mary drew the annuity until Boswell's death in 1795 (when his family stopped it), after which she disappears from Fowey parish records completely; there is no record of her burial either there or in any of the surrounding parishes. However, it is possible she was the Mary Bryant who in 1807 married a Richard Thomas in the parish of Breage, some 40 miles away, since, unlike all other entries in the parish register, 'Mary Bryant' is described as neither 'widow' nor 'spinster' and Bryant had said openly that he did not consider the shipboard marriage to be binding. If it was, then that year she gave birth to a daughter, Mary Anne.   JUDITH COOK

Sources J. Cook, *To brave every danger* (1993) · W. Tench, *A narrative of the expedition to Botany Bay, with an account of New South Wales* (1789) · *The journal of James Boswell, 1789–1794*, ed. G. Scott and F. A. Pottle (New York, 1934), vol. 18 of *Private papers of James Boswell from Malahide Castle* (1928–34) · gaol book, PRO, Assizes 5/144, western circuit 23/8 · W. Bligh, journals, Mitchell L., NSW · UCL, Bentham MSS, box clxix, fols. 179–204 · *A complete account of the settlement at Port Jackson* (1793) · parish registers, Fowey, Cornwall RO · convict archive, Mitchell L., NSW · F. A. Pottle, *Boswell and the girl from Botany Bay* (1938)
Archives PRO, gaol books; transportation orders, etc., Assizes 5/44, 23/8 | Mitchell L., NSW, W. Bligh, journals · Mitchell L., NSW, Macarthur MSS · Nationaal Archief, The Hague, Dutch colonial archives · UCL, Bentham MSS

Bryant [*née* Willock], **Sophie** (1850–1922), educationist and suffragist, was born in Sandymount, near Dublin, on 15 February 1850, the third of the six children of the Revd William Alexander Willock, fellow of Trinity College, Dublin, mathematician, and his wife, daughter of J. P. Morris of Skreen Castle. As a child she was mainly taught by her father, but in 1866, three years after the family moved to England, she won a scholarship to Bedford College, London. The Cambridge local examinations had only just been opened to girls, and her performance in mathematics placed her alone in the first class. She married in 1869, but her husband, Dr William Hicks Bryant, died the next year. In 1875 she was appointed to teach mathematics

Sophie Bryant (1850–1922), by W. & D. Downey, pubd 1894

by Frances Buss of the North London Collegiate School. The conventional view that this was not a subject for girls was challenged by Sophie Bryant's success, notably in sending a succession of North Londoners to study mathematics at Girton. She worked at the same time for her own degree and in 1881 took a BSc (London), gaining a first in mental and moral science and a second in mathematics. Three years later she became the first woman to be awarded a DSc.

George Bernard Shaw, a friend of her youth, remembered Sophie as having a sunny and engaging personality; and this personal warmth, combined with intellect, moral purpose, culture, and commitment to making girls think, launched her as an outstanding teacher, Frances Buss's right hand and natural successor. By the time she herself became headmistress of the North London in 1895 she was well known in wider circles, as a member of the London county council's technical education board and of the Bryce commission on secondary education, and as the author of *Educational Ends* (1887) and of many articles in journals of education and philosophy. She was an apostle of teacher training, and as the first woman to be elected to the senate of London University promoted the foundation of the London Day Training College and the accompanying chair in education.

'Ireland was in the heart of her heart', said Sir Michael E. Sadler, and Sophie Bryant always felt a touch of the exile's longing. A Gladstonian Liberal, she backed home rule, pressing that cause among English people. In Ireland she heartened the embryonic movement for the higher education of women by personally securing the involvement in it of the Roman Catholic convent-school nuns. Three of her ten books were about Ireland, and she was awarded in 1904 an honorary DLitt from Dublin University.

Bryant's feeling for freedom as 'the condition of all development' infused her teaching, her patriotism, and her support for women's suffrage. In Hampstead she was president of the local committee of the National Union of Women's Suffrage Societies. She took great delight in physical freedom, was one of the first women to cycle, loved to row, and climbed the Matterhorn twice. She retired in 1918. On holiday in 1922 she disappeared, climbing alone near Chamonix. Her death is recorded as having taken place on 14 August 1922. After a search her body was found on 28 August 1922.   SHEILA FLETCHER, *rev.*

Sources S. Burstall and others, *Sophie Bryant D.Sc, Litt.D, 1850–1922* (privately printed, 1922) · E. Doorly, 'Mrs Bryant', *The North London Collegiate School, 1850–1950*, ed. R. M. Scrimgeour (1950)
Likenesses W. & D. Downey, photograph, pubd 1894, NPG [*see illus.*]
Wealth at death £11,676 19s. 8d.: probate, 10 Nov 1922, *CGPLA Eng. & Wales*

Bryant, Wilberforce (1837–1906), match manufacturer, was born in Plymouth on 25 January 1837, the eldest of four sons (there was also a daughter) of William Bryant (1804–1874) and his wife, Elizabeth Carkeet. William Bryant, who had become a Quaker on his marriage, ran a malodorous business making tallow, candles, blacking, sugar, and locomotive lubricants. In 1844 he teamed up with a fellow Quaker, Francis *May, as general merchants in the City of London. Eleven years later they bought from a Swedish firm the patent rights for the newly invented safety matches; in 1861 they began match manufacture in Bow, east London, and the following year they were awarded a gold medal at the 1862 International Exhibition.

After education at a Quaker school, Wilberforce Bryant in the mid-1850s joined the Plymouth business, and then became manager of the match factory in 1861, later with the assistance of his three brothers. Father and sons were already contriving to ease out May, who refused to go quietly; he did not finally depart until 1875, shortly after William Bryant's death. A year later Wilberforce made a good marriage, to Margaret, second daughter of William Lowson, deputy lieutenant of Perth. She presented him with an estate in Gloucestershire, a son who died in infancy, and three daughters.

As senior partner Bryant strove hard to make his firm the leading match manufacturer in Britain. He introduced mechanization and promoted new specialities, such as wax vestas and decorated metal containers. Overseas, in the 1880s the firm began to build up its export markets, especially in the British empire and the Far East. High

Wilberforce Bryant (1837–1906), by Augusto Stoppoloni

American tariffs thwarted an attempt to enter that market via an agreement with the Diamond Match Company there.

In 1884 Bryant and the one brother remaining in the firm, Frederick Carkeet Bryant, registered Bryant and May Ltd, with a large capital. The financial press was soon condemning the firm for its annual reports—'the most cynically meagre and imperfect documents published by any board in the country'—and for its insider dealings to rig the share prices for its own ends (*Financial News*). This widespread mistrust of the company was fanned by the celebrated matchgirls' strike of 1888, when the implacable Bryants crossed swords with the equally tenacious Annie *Besant. The matchgirls had their main grievance—concerning arbitrary fines and deductions—remedied, and secured the right to a trade union which proved short-lived, collapsing after a wildcat strike in 1903. They were also given a women's club with subsidized canteen, recreation rooms, and a library.

By the 1890s Bryant was losing his touch, letting slip the opportunity to acquire the rights to Diamond Match's latest match-making technology. Instead, he spent much time as a magistrate and high sheriff of Buckinghamshire in 1892, as a keen gardener and amateur photographer, and in hosting at his Stoke Poges home local agricultural and horticultural shows. Diamond Match lost no time in erecting a very modern works in Liverpool, which so eroded its rival's sales that in 1901 Bryant and May was forced to join Diamond Match as a minority partner. The considerable autonomy granted to the British directors

(Bryant by then being no more than a titular chairman) allowed them to expand overseas sales further and to open up branches in parts of the empire.

Bryant lacked entrepreneurial flair, sacrificing the goodwill of the outside world to short-term advantage and driving the matchgirls into a strike which irredeemably tarnished the name of Bryant and May. He embodied too much of Quakerism's darker side—a narrow-minded exclusiveness and a dogged refusal to let go—yet was in some ways generous to the workforce, as no doubt to his local community. While remaining nominally a Quaker, he became a staunch Anglican and patron of the Church of England Temperance Society. He was a conservative in politics, fond of driving, and an excellent whip. He died at home at Stoke Park, Stoke Poges, on 3 February 1906, and was buried in the parish churchyard at Stoke Poges on 7 February.   T. A. B. CORLEY

Sources T. A. B. Corley, 'Bryant, Wilberforce', *DBB* · *Royal album of arts and industries of Great Britain* (1887) · *Slough Observer* (10 Feb 1906) · *Annual Monitor* (1907) · T. A. B. Corley, 'Huntley Boorne & Stevens and tin box manufacturing in Berkshire, 1832–1985', *Berkshire Archaeological Journal*, 72 (1983–5), 59–67 · H. Lindgren, *Corporate control: the Swedish match industry in its global setting* (1979) · N. C. Soloen, *Women in British trade unions, 1874–1976* (1978) · A. Stafford, *A match to fire the Thames* (1961) · *The Link* (1888) · *Financial News* (7 Feb 1887) · Quaker birth records, RS Friends, Lond. · *The Times* (5 Feb 1906) · d. cert. · Burke, *Gen. GB*
Archives Hackney Archives, London, Bryant and May archives
Likenesses photograph, *c.*1890, repro. in *Royal album of arts* · A. Stoppoloni, drawing; Christies, 3 Oct 2001, lot 371 [*see illus.*]
Wealth at death £118,155 9s. 2d.: probate, 13 March 1906, CGPLA Eng. & Wales

Bryce, Alexander (*bap.* 1713, *d.* 1786), applied mathematician and Church of Scotland minister, was baptized on 12 April 1713 in Boarland, Kincardine-on-Forth, Perthshire, the son of John Bryce and Janet Campbell. He attended Kilmadock School in Doune, Perthshire, and the University of Edinburgh, where he distinguished himself in the study of mathematics and astronomy under Professor Colin Maclaurin and graduated MA in May 1735. Five years later he went to Caithness under Maclaurin's patronage to be the tutor of a gentleman's son and to devise a map of the treacherous northern coast of Scotland. After three difficult years, during which he had to travel armed because some of the local inhabitants feared that his cartographic activities would reduce their plundering and smuggling from shipwrecks, he produced 'A map of the north coast of Britain, from Raw Stoir of Assynt, to Wick, in Caithness; by a geometrical survey, with the harbours, rocks, and an account of the tides in the Pentland Firth', which was published by the Edinburgh Philosophical Society in 1744, and dedicated to his first patron, James, earl of Morton. Upon returning to Edinburgh in 1743 Bryce verified and revised the actuarial calculations of Alexander Webster for the clergy's Widows Fund. Later he conducted a geographical survey of Edinburgh at the request of the Philosophical Society (of which he was a member by the 1750s), using 'a very fine astronomical instrument' to determine the meridian, longitude, and

latitude with precision. For this achievement he was proclaimed 'an excellent mathematician' by Richard Gough (Gough, 2.578).

Bryce had continued his divinity studies at the University of Edinburgh, and on 12 June 1744 was licensed to preach by the presbytery of Dunblane. He was presented by the earl of Morton to the parish of Kirknewton, a few miles south-west of Edinburgh, and was ordained there on 22 August 1745. During the Jacobite rising of 1745–6 he supplied the duke of Cumberland's army with information regarding the geography and roads of northern Scotland. At the same time he was teaching the mathematics classes at the University of Edinburgh at the request of the dying Maclaurin, whom he subsequently eulogized in verse. Despite the support of the earl of Morton, however, his candidacy for the mathematics chair was unsuccessful after Maclaurin died in June 1746. On 23 October 1750 Bryce married a daughter of the provost of Stirling, Janet Gillespie (*d.* 1807), with whom he had nine children, including Sir Alexander *Bryce (1766–1832), army officer, and William Bryce (*b.* 1770), minister of Aberdour. Seven months before his marriage Bryce was presented to the adjacent parish of East Calder by the duke of Buccleuch, and Kirknewton and East Calder were then joined into a united parish, with a new church. In a legal confrontation with some of his parishioners Bryce defended himself in February 1756 in *Answers for Mr. Alexander Bryce minister of the united parishes of Kirknewton and East Calder, to the petition of Helen, Isobel and Elizabeth Hodges, and others.*

Among Bryce's greatest accomplishments were the discovery and mathematical analysis of the Stirling jug, which the Scottish parliament had established in 1618 as the legal standard for measuring the value of a Scotch pint. After a two-year search, in 1752 he found what he believed to be the authentic Stirling jug among the discarded belongings of a dispossessed Jacobite coppersmith called Urquhart. He took the jug to Edinburgh and calculated the number of cubic inches it contained, from which it then became possible to establish mathematically precise standards for all liquid and dry measures in Scotland, as well as for all weights. Bryce himself adjusted the weights and measures in the possession of the dean of guild in Edinburgh, and in January 1754 was made a burgess and guild brother for his trouble.

Bryce had wide-ranging interests in mathematics, natural science, and engineering. In 1766 he sent two letters to the earl of Morton, then president of the Royal Society of London, that were published in its *Philosophical Transactions*, one containing his observation of a comet (read 17 April; 56.66–7) and the other on 'a new manner of measuring the velocity of the wind, and an experiment to ascertain to what quantity of water a fall of snow is equal' (read 19 June; 56.224–9). As a surveyor and engineer he was consulted about the Forth and Clyde Canal in May 1767, obtained the freedom of the town of Stirling in gratitude for his services in planning a water supply system in the spring of 1774, and served as sole arbiter in disputes concerning the boundaries of fields. As a practical astronomer he made observations on the transits of Venus on 6

June 1761 and 3 June 1769, designed an astronomical observatory at Belmont Castle for James Stuart Mackenzie, and in 1776 calculated a large-scale epitome of the solar system that was later erected by the earl of Buchan at Kirkhill. He is said to have published numerous meteorological and scientific observations in Ruddiman's *Weekly Magazine*, and in 1772 wrote a paper on the use of barometers in measuring altitudes which he sent to Mackenzie the following year. While pursuing his scientific activities he remained a conscientious pastor and was said to be particularly distinguished for his pulpit lectures, which were spoken from notes. In 1770 James Stuart Mackenzie arranged his appointment as one of George III's chaplains-in-ordinary.

As a young man Bryce gained acclaim for composing lyrics that he set to Scottish airs, including popular stanzas in 'The Birks of Invermay'. During the last three years of his life he wrote pious poetry intended for private circulation among friends. Bryce died at the age of seventy-two on 1 January 1786 and was buried in the church at Kirknewton, where he had served for more than forty years. A plaque placed along the east wall of the church commemorated him as 'a man of true piety, of great benevolence, and of general science' (*New Statistical Account of Scotland*, 1.440).   RICHARD B. SHER

Sources Anderson, *Scot. nat.*, 447–8 · Chambers, *Scots.* (1835) · R. L. Emerson, 'The Philosophical Society of Edinburgh, 1748–1768', *British Journal for the History of Science*, 14 (1981), 133–76 · R. L. Emerson, 'The Philosophical Society of Edinburgh, 1768–1783', *British Journal for the History of Science*, 18 (1985), 255–303 · R. G. [R. Gough], *British topography*, [new edn], 2 vols. (1780) · *The new statistical account of Scotland*, 1 (1845), 440 · 'Scots origins', www.scotsorigins.com · *Fasti Scot.*, new edn, 1.151 · E. G. R. Taylor, *The mathematical practitioners of Hanoverian England, 1714–1840* (1966)

Bryce, Sir Alexander (1766–1832), army officer, was born on 23 January 1766, the son of Alexander *Bryce (*bap.* 1713, *d.* 1786), applied mathematician and Church of Scotland minister, and his wife, Janet, *née* Gillespie (*d.* 1807). He had a twin brother, James (1766–1826), who became a fellow of the Royal Society of Edinburgh. Bryce entered the Royal Military Academy, Woolwich, on 7 October 1782, and passed out as second lieutenant, Royal Artillery, on 25 August 1787. In autumn 1787 he was employed with Captain W. Mudge in carrying out General Roy's system of triangulation for connecting the meridians of Greenwich and Paris, and in the measurement of a 'base of verification' in Romney Marsh.

Bryce was transferred from the Royal Artillery to the Royal Engineers in March 1789, and became a captain in 1794. After serving for some years in North America and the Mediterranean he became senior engineer officer with the army sent to Egypt under Sir Ralph Abercromby, and he was present at the landing, in the battles before Alexandria, and at the surrender of Cairo. He directed the siege operations at Abu Qir, Fort Marabout, and Alexandria. He received the brevet rank of major and was awarded the Ottoman order of the Crescent. Later, as colonel, he served some years in Sicily. In the descent on Calabria he commanded the detachment of Sir John

Stuart's army that captured Damienti; and he was commanding engineer in the expedition to the Bay of Naples in 1809 and in the defence of Sicily against Murat. He was awarded the order of St Ferdinand and Merit by the king of the Two Sicilies.

In 1814 Bryce received the rank of brigadier-general, and was appointed president of a commission to report on the restoration of the fortresses in the Netherlands. He was made CB and knighted (KCH). He became a major-general in 1825, colonel commandant of the Royal Engineers in 1829, and in 1830 inspector-general of fortifications. Much esteemed in private life as well as professionally, he died, after a few hours' illness, at his home in Hanover Terrace, Regent's Park, London, on 4 October 1832.

                   H. M. CHICHESTER, *rev.* DAVID GATES

Sources *Army List* · H. Bunbury, *Narratives of some passages in the great war with France, from 1799 to 1810* (1854) · *GM*, 1st ser., 102/2 (1832), 474 · J. Kane, *List of officers of the royal regiment of artillery* (1815) · R. T. Wilson, *History of the British expedition to Egypt*, 2nd edn, 2 vols. (1803) · P. Mackesy, *The war in the Mediterranean, 1803–1810* (1957) · *Fasti Scot.*

Bryce, (John) Annan (1843–1923), merchant and politician, was born in Belfast on 12 August 1843, the son of the mathematician and geologist James *Bryce the younger (1806–1877) and his wife, Margaret, *née* Young (1813–1903). His elder brother was James *Bryce, Viscount Bryce (1838–1922). Educated at Glasgow high school, he studied from 1858 at the University of Glasgow, graduating MA in 1866, and at the University of Edinburgh. He went on to Balliol College as Brackenbury history scholar, graduating BA in 1872, after serving as first the secretary, then treasurer, and in 1871 the president of the Oxford Union Society. He married Violet (*d.* 1939), daughter of Captain Champagné L'Estrange RA. They had two daughters and a son.

In 1875 Bryce joined Wallace Brothers, East India merchants, and was sent to work as an assistant for the Bombay-based arm of the company, Wallace & Co. The firm held leases of extensive teak forests in British and Upper Burma through its subsidiary, the Bombay Burma Trading Corporation, and in 1878 Bryce moved to Rangoon to assist in extending its activities. In 1880 he and a colleague, H. Maxwell, visited King Thibaw in Mandalay, and after prolonged negotiations they were able to confirm existing leases, and obtain new ones, to teak forests in Upper Burma. The following year Bryce travelled extensively in the Chindwin forests, identifying areas suitable for further expansion. In 1884 he visited upper Siam to explore opportunities for working the teak forests of that country, and his report was instrumental in Wallace Brothers' decision to open an office in Bangkok in 1886.

Bryce took an active part in the business life of Rangoon, serving as a chairman of the Rangoon chamber of commerce, and on the legislative council of Burma. In 1881 he was made a resident partner in the head office of Wallace & Co. in Bombay, and in August 1884 he returned to London, on becoming a partner in the parent company, Wallace Brothers. Bryce's knowledge of Burmese and Siamese affairs proved invaluable to the London partners, and his analysis of the political situations at the royal courts in

Mandalay and Bangkok was sent to British government officials in 1884, when the company lobbied for action to counter French moves to extend their commercial interests in the region.

It seems that Bryce was sent abroad only rarely after 1888, when he visited the Caucasus to investigate the state of the oil industry there, prior to Wallace Brothers' negotiation of contracts for the supply of refined kerosene. Maintaining his interest in travel and exploration, however, Bryce was a member of the council of the Royal Geographical Society, 1886–9, and frequently contributed to discussions at their meetings in the 1880s and 1890s. He also served as a member of the council of the London chamber of commerce, 1891–1902.

Bryce retired from Wallace Brothers in 1906, on his election as the Liberal MP for the Inverness burghs. He represented the constituency until 1918, when he declined to seek re-election. Although his political career effectively ended, he remained active in business, and was a director of London, County, and Westminster Bank; the Bombay, Baroda, and Burma railway companies; the English, Scottish, and Australian Bank; and the Atlas Assurance Company. He was also chairman of British Westinghouse Company.

Possessing a strong interest in Irish affairs, Bryce served on the royal commission on congestion in Ireland, 1906–8, and he spoke frequently in favour of home rule. In October 1920 he wrote to *The Times* from Glengariff, co. Cork, complaining of reprisals carried out against the local population by soldiers seeking revenge for republican attacks on troops and loyalists. Later that month, his wife, Violet, was arrested at Holyhead, *en route* for Tonypandy, where she had been invited to speak about reprisals. Violet Bryce was detained under the Restoration of Order in Ireland Act, on the grounds that she was in possession of documents (the notes for her speech and a copy of a cartoon from an English newspaper) which libelled the Royal Irish Constabulary. She was deported to Dublin and held in the bridewell for several hours, before being released without charge—a situation Bryce deplored in a series of letters to *The Times*. The issues raised by his wife's arrest, and Bryce's denunciations of the increasing authoritarianism of British rule in some areas of Ireland, fuelled controversy in the press and in the House of Commons over the government's policy in Ireland.

Bryce died at his home, 35 Bryanston Square, London, on 25 June 1923, and was cremated at Golders Green, Middlesex. He had been an enthusiastic collector of art throughout his adult life, and his collection of oriental *objets d'art* was so highly regarded as to merit exhibition at the Imperial Institute in 1892. In November 1923 the contents of his home, consisting of 2200 lots, which included Italian masters, English furniture, and Persian rugs, were sold at auction.

To his contemporaries in the world of business, Bryce was probably best known for his services in opening up and protecting British interests in the teak forests of Burma and Siam. However, his support for Irish home rule and his outspoken criticism of British policy in Ireland after the First World War brought him a degree of wider fame, or notoriety, late in life.   IAIN F. RUSSELL

Sources *The Times* (1 Feb 1923) · *The Times* (26 June 1923) · A. C. Pointon, *Wallace Brothers* (1974) · *The Times* (1 Oct 1920) · *The Times* (1 Nov 1920) · *The Times* (2 April 1920) · *The Times* (2 Nov 1920) · *The Times* (9 Nov 1920) · *The Times* (10 Nov 1920) · *The Times* (12 Nov 1920) · J. A. Bryce, 'Burma, the country and people', *Proceedings* [Royal Geographical Society], new ser., 8 (1886), 481–501 · *WWW* · *CGPLA Eng. & Wales* (1923) · Bodl. Oxf., MSS Bryce
Archives Bodl. Oxf., corresp. and papers
Wealth at death £30,870 16s. 3d.: probate, 8 Oct 1923, *CGPLA Eng. & Wales*

Bryce, David (1803–1876), architect, was born on 3 April 1803 in Buccleuch Place, Edinburgh, the second of four children of William Bryce, builder. John Bryce (1805–1851), architect, was his younger brother. After attending the Royal High School, Edinburgh, built by his father, where he displayed a talent for drawing, he entered his father's office. Supplementing his income in these early years, Bryce established at what was 15 South James's Street a school which he called the Architectural Academy, a name that confirmed the young architect's ambitious nature. The death on 5 September 1823 of his brother William, then a clerk in the office of one of Scotland's leading architects, William Burn, provided a crucial opening in the office for David, and in 1825 he joined Burn, his mentor and future partner.

Burn, recognizing the young man's talent, quickly elevated Bryce to the post of head clerk and, in 1841, partner. From the 1830s Burn's ever-increasing focus on the field of country house design enabled Bryce to gain invaluable first-hand experience from one of the masters of country house architecture of his day, a skill he developed later in his own practice. In addition, Burn's interests allowed Bryce to develop his wider interests in commercial and ecclesiastical work. In 1844, when Burn decided to move his practice to London, Bryce moved into the firm's house and office at 131 George Street, in place of Burn, and began to play the leading role in the Scottish practice. With his master's departure Bryce could also learn about the practical matters of running a large firm. Though the partnership was not formally dissolved until 1850, from even before Burn's departure to London Bryce was already beginning to reveal an individual and creative hand in the practice. Bryce's wide-ranging interests and eclectic tastes, in perfect sympathy with mid-nineteenth-century Scotland, found a stimulating outlet as partner in Burn's successful practice, with the opportunity to experiment as well as to learn. It should be remembered, too, that Burn's office also saw a number of other architects of significant calibre, including George Meikle Kemp and J. T. Rochead, and it is a tribute to Bryce's talent that he should have been singled out for advancement by the senior figure.

In the field of country houses Bryce naturally remained hugely indebted to Burn, and followed his master's efficient and practical laying out at the same time as he evolved his own style from the more classically disposed

David Bryce (1803–1876), attrib. John Zephaniah Bell

manner of Burn. If Burn may be credited with the introduction of Scottish baronial detail in the practice, Bryce, from 1839 and with his further extensions at Kilconquhar, Fife, displayed his ability to sympathize with informal compositional arrangements, thereby giving his work not only more energy but also more historical integrity. Enriching the picturesque variety of Burn's work by introducing freely composed features such as canted bays below corbelled corners, as at Kilconquhar House (1839), Bryce enlivened the elevation and details, and revealed a looser hand and a free interpretation of a wider range of sources. He focused also on the more popular features of Burn's more experimental designs, such as the elevation of rooms over a basement behind a cantilevered terrace as at Langton House, Berwickshire (1862; dem.), or the creation of a coherent series of rooms, essentially classical in the disposition given the source in Burn's work, as at Kimmerghame House, Berwickshire (1851). Indeed his success in re-creating an essentially Victorian variant of Burn's late Georgian planning, distinguished not least by a greater differentiation between the different functional parts of the house—for example at Castlemilk, Dumfriesshire (1862–3)—ensured that the vast majority of Scottish practice remained with Bryce after Burn's departure for London. In itself, this was also an impressive feat of diplomatic engineering.

Undoubtedly, too, Bryce's familiarity with and sympathy for the development of R. W. Billings's *Baronial and Ecclesiastical Antiquities of Scotland*, published between 1845 and 1852, supported originally in part by Burn, provided Bryce with a more contemporary vocabulary from which

to develop his own distinctive manner. Yet Bryce's inherently pluralistic aesthetic, revealing a genius for eclectic manners within a consistently impressive drama, may be seen to be perfectly adapted to succeed in Scotland within the Victorian period. This is all illustrated by the contrast between his two most prominent secular commissions in Edinburgh. The baroque Italianate extension and encasing of the Bank of Scotland on Bank Street (from 1864), the classical language of which reflects only in part the pre-existing fabric, looks down on Princes Street with almost baronial gusto. The contemporary Fettes College, a French Gothic château-style building adapted to house a boys' boarding-school endowed by Sir William Fettes (1750–1836), has only slightly more dramatic a silhouette, even given its central five-storey plus attic and spire tower rising above the already busy skyline.

Ecclesiastical architecture was one of Bryce's least prolific building types but here, too, he exercised significant influence, at least in elevational matters, and advanced the type far beyond Burn's limited repertory. From as early as his St Mark's Unitarian Church on Castle Terrace (1834–5) Bryce realized the potential for adapting freely revised continental baroque to enrich street elevations. The St George's Free Church (1866–9; now St George's West) is more Anglo-Italianate, and though the tower intended by Bryce was not built, it remains a key work.

Bryce's scholarly and professional procedure is consistent, too, whether looking to Italian, French, or Scottish sources. His appreciation of architectural quality over matters of style ensured that his response to older buildings was unusually sympathetic for his day. His remodelling of the hall of Thomas Hamilton's neo-classical College of Physicians was masterly in its sensitivity to artistic character and requisite improvements, as it reformed the axis of the room to accord better with the building as a whole. No less sympathetic, if more typical, was the remodelling and extension of Blair Atholl, Perthshire, which though much changed after its mainly post-1400 construction, became in Bryce's hands one of the most striking examples of Scottish baronial architecture.

Bryce was a determined, astute businessman with a precise but patient mind of solid determination, all exemplified by his adopted motto 'Do well, doubt not'. In 1841 his application for membership of the ill-fated Institute of Architects in Scotland was blackballed because of his position of clerk inside Burn's office. He continued to enhance his position, however, through his alliance with professional associations. He became a fellow of the Royal Institute of British Architects in 1845 and of the Society of Antiquaries of Scotland in 1849, an associate of the Royal Scottish Academy in 1855 and a fellow in 1856, and was serving as a trustee of the academy at his death. As grand architect to the masonic grand lodge of Scotland from 1850 onwards, he refitted their George Street premises. He was also a member of the exclusive New Club of Edinburgh, whose premises he enlarged in 1859.

Bryce's office became one of the most important sources for the masters of later Victorian architecture in Scotland, including Charles Kinnear, John Starforth, and

James M. Wardrop, James McLaren of Dundee, Andrew Heiton of Perth, John Milne of St Andrews, and J. B. Pirie of Aberdeen, and J. J. Stevenson, whose own office in turn spurred on another generation of Scottish architects, while about 1873 he was briefly in partnership with Robert Rowand Anderson. Following his death on 7 May 1876, after a prolonged attack of bronchitis, in his office and home at 131 George Street, Bryce was interred in the New Calton cemetery, Edinburgh, where a monument was erected to him. He was unmarried and left a son, David, for whom he provided in his will, while his office was continued by his nephew John before it passed to his nephew John Brechin, who finally closed it in 1928. Bryce's large collection of European pattern books was acquired by the art and architecture library of George Washington University, St Louis, Missouri, in 1932. An exhibition to mark the centenary of Scotland's great Victorian architect was held at the University of Edinburgh and travelled to Dundee, Aberdeen, Inverness, Glasgow, and London in 1976–7.

SEÁN O'REILLY

Sources *The Builder*, 34 (1876), 507–8 · *The Scotsman* (12 May 1876) · Irving, *Scots.* · D. M. Lyon, *History of the lodge of Edinburgh* (1873), 30, 341 · *Proceedings of the Royal Society of Edinburgh*, 9 (1875–8), 216–18 · A. K. Placzek, ed., *Macmillan encyclopedia of architects*, 1 (1982), 316–17 · *Royal Scottish Academy Report* (1876), 10 · V. Fiddes and A. J. Rowan, *David Bryce, 1803–1876: an exhibition to mark the centenary of Scotland's great Victorian architect* (1976) [exhibition catalogue, U. Edin., Talbot Rice Gallery, 2 Nov – 11 Dec 1976] · E. Berry, ed., *Catalogue of books in architecture and allied subjects, which belonged to the eminent Scottish architect, David Bryce* (1928) · CCI (1877) · *Sessional Papers of the Royal Institute of British Architects* (1876–7), 4

Archives NRA, priv. coll., corresp. and estimates relating to Meikleour House

Likenesses attrib. J. Z. Bell, drawing, Scot. NPG [*see illus.*] · line engraving, repro. in Lyon, *History of the lodge of Edinburgh*, 30

Wealth at death £37,973 3s. 6d.: confirmation, 6 Nov 1876, CCI

Bryce, Dame Isabel Graham [*née* Isabella Lorrain Smith] (1902–1997), public servant, was born on 30 April 1902 at Westbourne, Windsor Avenue, Belfast, the fourth of five children of James Lorrain Smith (1862–1931), a professor of pathology, and his wife, Isabella, *née* Meek-Edmond (*b.* 1864). Her father moved to Manchester in 1904, then in 1912 to Edinburgh, where his medical career had begun; from 1919 until his death he was dean of the university's medical faculty. He was also chairman of the English Association, so his children enjoyed a rich cultural life, while his four daughters were encouraged to follow their mother's enthusiasm for public service.

Isabel was tutored at home, then attended St Leonard's School at St Andrews before going to Edinburgh University, where she graduated with a general MA. Influenced by her father's researches into the effects of humidity and ventilation in cotton weaving sheds, she became in 1926 an investigator for the Industrial Fatigue Research Board, looking at the effects of humidity in shoe factories in Leicester. She undertook a year of psychological research in Cambridge and in 1928 successfully competed for a post as HM inspector of factories, an unusual job for a woman at that time. The work took her to London and Manchester, where during her six years in the post she took a special interest in the cotton industry, and gained valuable experience of working conditions and of how workers sought to adapt to difficult situations. She later remarked on the lip-reading skills acquired by staff in noisy factories.

On 25 January 1934 Isabel married Alexander Graham Bryce (1890–1968), a surgeon and consultant to several Manchester hospitals. After raising their two sons, Isabel joined the boards of Princess Christian College (which trained nannies) and of the Manchester Babies' Hospital. In 1938, as the nation prepared for war, she joined the Women's Voluntary Service (WVS) and, as centre organizer for the Manchester area, arranged the escorts to accompany child evacuees. In 1940 Isabel and her sons were themselves evacuated to Toronto, where she was involved with the WVS in Canada, and then in the USA. At Harvard she undertook research into pilot fatigue. She returned to England in one of the first repatriation convoys.

Back in Manchester, Isabel resumed her voluntary work, helping the Princess Christian College to develop a new curriculum for training nursery nurses and, at the Children's Hospital, participating in a study of nurses' work. She also joined two organizations which remained of great interest to her for the rest of her life: the National Council of Women (she became chairman of the Manchester branch), and the Federation of University Women.

In 1948, with the introduction of the National Health Service (NHS), the previous hospital boards became hospital management committees (HMCs). Isabel sat on the HMC for the Manchester Children's Hospital, and when a national association of committees was established she became the Manchester representative. Her longstanding concern for staff welfare led to her appointment to the General Nursing Council, which set standards for recruitment, training, and the quality of nurses. She also sat as a magistrate in both adult and juvenile courts.

Alexander Graham Bryce retired in 1955, and the couple moved to East Grinstead, Sussex. Isabel joined the HMC of Queen Victoria Hospital, where Sir Archibald MacIndoe had his famous burns unit. She also joined the board of the Eastman dental clinic and helped to establish a programme for dental auxiliaries. From 1962 to 1968 Isabel was a non-executive director of British Transport Hotels, where she was concerned with staff working conditions. To her surprise, she was also invited to join the Independent Television Authority for five years, which she enjoyed so much that she readily accepted a non-executive directorship with the Associated Television Company, then the contractors for the midlands region.

After her next move, to Upper Basildon, Berkshire, Isabel was invited onto the Oxford Regional Hospital Board, which covered parts of the adjacent counties and, with the new city of Milton Keynes, held a rapidly increasing population. In 1963 she was appointed chairman in succession to Sir George Schuster, under whom the board had established a reputation for innovation. Her appointment as the first woman to hold a regional chairmanship reflected the respect in which she was held. She spent nine years in the post; and under her leadership the region continued to enhance its reputation and privileged position, securing new hospital buildings and new medical specialities. Her award of the DBE in 1968 was widely recognized as well deserved, but it was soon followed by her husband's death on 24 October that year.

In 1967 Isabel was asked to chair the new national nursing staff committee, and two years later she chaired the national staff committee for administrative and clerical staff. This was a time of considerable upheaval, ahead of the first major reorganization of the NHS in 1974, which reformed the management structure. Isabel stepped down in 1975 when the new structure was up and running. She held no more official positions after 1978, confining herself to voluntary work.

Dame Isabel's natural gifts as a chairman combined well with her considerable experience of boards and committees and her concerns for staff welfare, and she saw her chairmanships as the high point of her career. She was tall, with a stately presence, and impressed those who met her. She received great loyalty from those who sat with her, because of the confidence she inspired and her charismatic leadership. She remained, however, approachable and essentially kind and considerate. She died in the John Radcliffe Hospital, Oxford, on 29 April 1997.

ALEX GATHERER

Sources *The Independent* (19 June 1997) · b. cert. · m. cert. · d. cert. · C. Webster, *The health services since the war*, 2 vols. (1988–96) · R. Klein, *The politics of the NHS*, 2nd edn (1989) · *Diary of a regional health authority, 1947–1994: a year-by-year history of Oxford Regional Hospital Board and Oxford Regional Health Authority* (1996) · private information (2004) [Dame Rosemary Rue, Alastair Graham Bryce]

Bryce, James (1767–1857), founder of the Associate Presbytery of Ireland, was born at Airdrie in Lanarkshire on 5 December 1767. He was the son of John Bryce and Robina Allan (d. 1796). They were both descendants of landowners in Lanarkshire who had subsequently lost most of their property during the seventeenth century, as they had espoused the covenanting cause.

Bryce attended the parish school of New Monkland before entering Glasgow University in 1782, which he later left without graduating. He spent some time at the Divinity Hall of the Anti-Burghers and was licensed to preach on 29 October 1792. He was ordained minister of the Anti-Burgher Secession church at Wick, Caithness, on 20 September 1795. He married Catherine Annan of Auchtermuchty, Fife, on 25 April 1796. Their family rose to eminence—Reuben was principal of Belfast Academy, Archibald was principal of the high school, Edinburgh, while James *Bryce, the younger, was principal of the high school, Glasgow, and father of the politician James Bryce, Viscount Bryce.

In 1797 Bryce was accused of latitudinarianism before the General Associate Synod, because he had minimized the difference between his own and other denominations of Christians, had condemned the extreme assumption of power by the clergy, and had argued that the dogmatic creeds of the church received too much respect as compared with the scriptures. He was suspended for two

years, and although restored to his functions, he accepted an invitation to visit Ireland, where he ultimately settled in 1805 as minister of the Anti-Burgher congregation at Killaig in co. Londonderry.

At this time the ministers of the Anti-Burgher and Burgher bodies in Ulster had been offered a share in the *regium donum*, an annual endowment paid by the lord lieutenant to the Presbyterian ministers. (It was abolished in 1869.) This had been distributed as a free gift without conditions; it was now for political reasons proposed greatly to increase its amount, but to require the recipient first to take the oath of allegiance, and to give the lord lieutenant an absolute veto on its bestowal. The ministers of Bryce's denomination vehemently denounced these terms, but eventually accepted them, and the stipend. Bryce alone stood firm, holding that the requirements were dishonouring to Christ as the supreme head of the church, and tended to enslave a minister of religion and to degrade his office. Although this position separated him from his fellow ministers, and he was unsupported by the parent church in Scotland, he maintained his principles, and thus, as others gradually gathered round him, became the founder of a branch of the Presbyterian church which took the name of the Associate Presbytery of Ireland (established formally in 1816). This body was ultimately united with the Scottish United Presbyterian church, which had by that time come to adopt similar views of spiritual independence. Bryce died at Killaig, at the age of eighty-nine, on 24 April 1857, having preached twice on the Sunday preceding his death.

[ANON.], rev. DAVID HUDDLESTON

Sources 'The Rev. James Bryce of Killaig', *United Presbyterian Magazine*, new ser., 2 (1858), 17–21, 64–76, 116–21, 164–70 · *A history of congregations in the Presbyterian Church in Ireland, 1610–1982*, Presbyterian Church in Ireland (1982), 549 · D. Stewart, *The seceders in Ireland* (1950) · J. S. Reid and W. D. Killen, *History of the Presbyterian church in Ireland*, new edn, 3 (1867), 420–21 · *Evangelical Witness* (1 June 1864), 152–6 · W. T. Latimer, *A history of the Irish Presbyterians*, 2nd edn (1902)

Bryce, James (1806–1877), schoolteacher and geologist, was born on 22 October 1806 at Killaig, near Coleraine, Ireland, the third son of the family of four sons and at least one daughter of James *Bryce (1767–1857), Scottish Presbyterian minister, and his wife, Catherine Annan of Auchtermuchty, Fife. He was educated first by his father and eldest brother, the Revd Reuben John Bryce (1797–1888), and at fourteen entered the University of Glasgow, where he graduated MA in 1828, having won the Blackstone prize for classics. His desire to study for the bar was frustrated by the expense and he turned instead to teaching, becoming mathematics master at Belfast Academy where his eldest brother was then principal, and another brother, Thomas Annan Bryce (d. 1875), also taught. His *Treatise on Algebra* (1837) went through several editions. In 1836 Bryce married Margaret (1813–1903), daughter of James Young of Abbeyville, co. Antrim. Their eldest son was James *Bryce, later Viscount Bryce (1838–1922), politician and diplomat; a younger son, (John) Annan *Bryce

(1843–1923), became an East India merchant and politician.

In 1846 Bryce was appointed to the high school at Glasgow, where he remained until 1874. He was a brilliant and successful teacher of mathematics and geography, but his special interest lay in the study of natural history which, as it was not part of the curriculum, he taught voluntarily. He was an enthusiastic geologist, exploring first in the north of Ireland, where his researches on the fossils of the Lias, greensand, and chalk beds of Antrim were published in the *Philosophical Magazine* from 1831. On the basis of this and other articles he was elected a fellow of the geological societies of London (1834) and Dublin. He afterwards worked in Scotland and its western islands, leading to his outstanding paper 'On the Jurassic rocks of the islands of Skye and Raasay', read to the Geological Society of London in 1873 (published in the society's *Quarterly Journal*, 29, 1873, 317–39). His major papers, including his investigations and descriptions of the structure of the Giant's Causeway, appeared in the *Transactions* of the London society, others in the *Proceedings* of the Belfast Natural History Society and of the Philosophical Society of Glasgow, of which he was president in 1868–71. The geological survey of the region which he provided for the British Association for the Advancement of Science (BAAS) meeting of 1855 held in Glasgow, *Arran and the other Clyde Islands* (1855), was long relied on as a local guide. From its formation in 1869 he was on the BAAS committee on earthquakes in Scotland.

Bryce was a pioneer in urging reform of the constitution of the Scottish universities, for which he received the honorary degree of LLD from Glasgow in 1858, and in campaigning to make the Scottish educational system independent of London. Among other minor reforms he favoured the introduction of a decimal system of currency and weights and measures. After resigning his post at Glasgow he settled in Edinburgh; he was elected fellow of the Royal Society of Edinburgh in 1875 and published his later researches in its *Transactions*. Always a keen and accurate observer, he remained physically fit and continued his fieldwork in the highlands with unflagging zeal to the end of his life. He died on 11 July 1877; it was presumed that, while examining a mass of granite in the Inverfarigaig Pass, on the shores of Loch Ness, he disturbed some loose stones, precipitating a rock fall which killed him instantly. His lifeless body was found a few hours later.   [ANON.], rev. ANITA MCCONNELL

Sources P. Macnair and F. Mort, eds., *History of the Geological Society of Glasgow, 1858–1908* (1908), 195–6 · A. Boyle and F. Bennet, eds., *The Royal Society of Edinburgh: scientific and engineering fellows elected, 1784–1876* (1984), vol. 5 of *Scotland's cultural heritage* (1981–4) · *Proceedings of the Royal Society of Edinburgh*, 9 (1875–8), 514–18 · *Weekly Scotsman* (14 July 1877) [repr. *Geological Magazine*, new ser., decade 2/4 (1877), 383–4] · P. M. Duncan, *Quarterly Journal of the Geological Society*, 34 (1878), 35 · *Nature*, 16 (1877), 236 · *CCI* (1923) · d. cert.
Archives Bodl. Oxf., corresp. and papers · NL Scot. · U. Edin. · U. St Andr. L.
Wealth at death £2456 0s. 2d.: confirmation, 5 Nov 1877, *CCI*

Bryce, James, Viscount Bryce (1838–1922), jurist, historian, and politician, was born in Arthur Street, Belfast, on

James Bryce, Viscount Bryce (1838–1922), by George Charles Beresford, 1902

10 May 1838, the eldest son of James *Bryce (1806–1877), schoolteacher and geologist.

Family and education The Bryce family had been bonnet lairds (landowning farmers) in Dechmont in the north of Lanarkshire, near Coatbridge. Bryce's grandfather James *Bryce the elder (1767–1857) became a leader of the more liberal element in the Scottish Anti-Burgher Secession church, taking charges both in the far north of the country, at Wick, in Caithness, and after 1805 in Killaig, in the Glens of Antrim; his son married Margaret (1813–1903), the daughter of James Young, a Belfast merchant. As Ulster Scots the Bryces—a talented family of eleven children (including (John) Annan *Bryce)—were part of that Presbyterian enlightenment which had its issue in the United Irishmen and in the political ideas of such as William Drennan and Henry Joy MacCracken: a political community which was, ironically until the union of 1800, virtually indivisible from the covenanting radicalism of south-west Scotland, which had such a profound impact on the ideology of the American revolutionaries. While Presbyterianism was forced into line, the Bryces continued radical, refusing the state's offer of subvention through the *regium donum*, thus preserving the republicanism of the Cameronians and the Queensferry manifesto. Even in his obituary, *The Times* observed that James Bryce's 'language and views undoubtedly encouraged hostility to British monarchical and aristocratic institutions' (*The Times*, 23 Jan 1922).

Bryce spent his first eight years in Ulster, but in 1846 followed his father, who was appointed rector, to the high school of Glasgow, and then for a year went to study under his uncle Dr Reuben John Bryce in Belfast, before entering the University of Glasgow in 1854, at a time when the deductive traditions of the Scottish Enlightenment were still alive, though his personal development also owed much to the sort of close, and alternately didactic and libertarian, family life characteristic of the Scottish professional classes, particularly on long summer holidays in the highlands or on the Antrim coast. He inherited a family fascination with natural history and at the age of twenty-one he contributed to a *Flora of the Island of Arran*, published by his father in 1859. Bryce acquired a delight in walking, swimming, fishing, and climbing, and shared his Irish relatives' absorption in their own Celtic traditions. He attended Glasgow University while it still occupied its Renaissance buildings in the High Street, torn down a decade later: 'There was no better way', he wrote at the end of his life, 'of understanding the Scotch spirit as it has been ever since the middle of the sixteenth century' (Fisher, *James Bryce*, 1.16). His professor of logic, Robert Buchanan, was a disciple of the great Thomas Reid. Reid's 'commonsense' philosophy, with its assumption of an immanent core of 'consciousness' linking and moderating sense perception, remained the basis of Bryce's non-dogmatic Christianity (H. A. L. Fisher found him 'curiously exempt from metaphysical misgivings and scruples'), as well as of the catholicity of his social and political interests. But the university was also beginning to change with the immigration of English academics, notably Edmund Law Lushington, Tennyson's brother-in-law. It seems to have been Lushington's influence that sent Bryce south in 1857, after his Glasgow degree, on a scholarship to Trinity College, Oxford. Curiously, Bryce did not compete for a Snell exhibition to Balliol, the usual route for Glasgow graduates; but his seceder convictions would be against giving any aid to the Scottish Episcopal church: the ground for Snell's benefaction.

Despite an attempt to make him subscribe to the Thirty-Nine Articles by the tory president, Dr John Wilson (one suspects that Wilson was immobilized by the complexity of Scottish sectarian legalism), Bryce had a very successful career at Trinity from 1857 to 1862, following the *literae humaniores* (Greats) curriculum which also contrived to have much deliberate reference to contemporary politics. He took a first class in moderations in 1859, the best first of the year in Greats in 1861, and graduated BA in 1862, although, as a nonconformist, he never proceeded to the MA. This was a particularly exciting period in the history of the university, when the reforms of the Oxford University Act of 1854 were beginning to take effect, and the insistence on open competition for fellowships meant that many colleges were being colonized, notably from next-door Balliol under the sway of Benjamin Jowett. Bryce's relation with Jowett was one of guarded friendliness, but he encountered as a private tutor one Balliol graduate who became his lifelong friend and collaborator, Albert Venn Dicey. Most of Bryce's friends, not surprisingly, were from this milieu: enlightened, radical, and in origins to a great extent Scottish or northern English. Although active in the union (then important for its library) as librarian, secretary, and in 1863 president, Bryce joined most of his intellectual contemporaries in such groups as the Oxford Essay Society, founded by the somewhat older generation of Matthew Arnold, George Joachim Goschen, and Arthur Hugh Clough, and the smaller Old Mortality Society, which included Algernon Charles Swinburne, Thomas Hill Green, Courtenay Ilbert, Aeneas Mackay, and Thomas Edward Holland. The latter group adopted advanced democratic radicalism, secularism, and university extension, and warmed in particular to the project of Italian unity, represented in Oxford by the Taylorian teacher of Italian, Aurelio Saffi, one-time triumvir of the Roman Republic (1848–9) along with Giuseppe Mazzini.

A radical of the 1860s Bryce's enthusiasm for Italy almost led him to volunteer to join Garibaldi in the latter's Sicilian campaign of 1860, but he chose to finish his degree, stay in Oxford, and compete for a fellowship at Oriel, to which he was elected in 1862, retaining it until his marriage in 1889. Within this Oxford milieu he was noted less for originality of mind or the secular saintliness of T. H. Green as for his endless good humour and organizational ability: 'He does not seem to possess extraordinary, so much as admirably balanced, talents', wrote Dicey during a visit to Heidelberg in 1863. 'He stirs us all up, rushes around like a shepherd's dog, collects his friends, makes us meet, leads us into plans and adventures and keeps everything going' (Fisher, *James Bryce*, 1.59). Both in the university and during reading-party tours to the continent (he studied law under Karl Adolf von Vangerow at Heidelberg University in 1863) he established many enduring links with continental jurists and historians. As with many of his contemporaries, Bryce used the expansion of the European railway and steamer system to extend his range as a walker and mountaineer. Besides the almost obligatory ascents in Switzerland, he climbed in Iceland in 1872, the Pyrenees in 1873, Mauna Loa in Hawaii in 1883, the Rockies, Mount Etna in 1903, and even (at the age of seventy-five) Mount Myogi-San in Japan in 1913. Mount Bryce, in the Rockies, was named after him. Before his death he had in fact visited practically every part of the globe except the polar regions and present-day Indonesia. In 1876 he was the first European to climb Mount Ararat, after travelling with his friend Aeneas Mackay, largely by river-steamer, from St Petersburg via Moscow to the Caucasus. An ascent of the Tatras in Carpathia followed in 1878. Not surprisingly he was elected to the Alpine Club in 1879, and was its president in 1899–1901.

As was common with young graduates of the period Bryce moved to London and studied for the bar, at Sir John Holker's chambers in Lincoln's Inn, being called in 1867 and joining the northern circuit. With Frederic Harrison, he also acted as a lecturer and examiner in law for the inns of court. At the same time he contributed to liberal literary and political periodicals, notably the *Contemporary Review* and the *Fortnightly Review*, writing in particular on European politics, history, and academic reform. Educational improvement became of immediate concern between 1865 and 1866, when under Frederick Temple and with two other college fellows, T. H. Green and Joshua Girling Fitch, he served as an assistant commissioner on the Taunton commission into endowed schools, something which developed his interest in secondary education and, because he was given the north-west to report on, led to a close acquaintance with Manchester. In 1868 he became part-time lecturer in law, and later professor at the city's Owens College, founded in 1850, drafting its act of incorporation in 1871. This connection, which lasted until 1874, forged enduring links with Manchester's radical and nonconformist élite, the Darbishires, Taylors, and Ashtons, and the city's liberal bishop, James Fraser. But Bryce's real influence in Manchester was exerted in favour of the reform and extension of Oxford University, in support of which he organized a substantial demonstration on 8 April 1866 in the Free Trade Hall. He also involved himself in the agitation for women's legal equality and higher education. He was a founding member of Girton College, Cambridge, and later, as an MP, he carried the Guardianship of Infants Bill in 1886, which gave women equal rights in custody cases. But (perhaps influenced by Frederic Harrison and his positivist friends) at no time did he support women's suffrage.

Bryce took an active part in the life of literary London, frequenting the social circles of Arthur Stanley (Dean Stanley) and Marian Evans (George Eliot), and becoming a founder member of the Century Club, the forerunner of the National Liberal Club, along with Leslie Stephen, Henry Sidgwick, Frederic Harrison, and other Liberals and radicals (Harrison, 376). In the 1860s he accepted the general political leadership of Goldwin Smith, regius professor of history at Oxford since 1858, who was the confidant of Richard Cobden and John Bright. This link led to an energetic commitment to the cause of the North in the American Civil War, an issue which sharply divided English literary and leisured society. The support which the upper classes showed for the Confederacy, on anti-democratic grounds, propelled the academics to the left, and led in great measure to the strength of the democratic views shown by the symposia *Essays on Reform* and *Questions for a Reformed Parliament*, which Bryce had a substantial hand in editing, along with Albert Osliff Rutson, in 1867. Their contributors included Goldwin Smith, Leslie Stephen, Frederic Harrison, Lord Houghton, and A. V. Dicey; Alexander Macmillan was the enthusiastic publisher, and Bryce remained with the firm for the rest of his life. He contributed an essay entitled 'The historical aspect of democracy', in which he attacked critiques of Greek and Roman political history which were not founded in accurate knowledge of the politics and society of the city states and the republic. His lucid and informative *Studies in Contemporary Biography* (1903), though largely made up of obituary notices, provides a fine picture of the high-minded milieu in which he moved in those years.

Historian, jurist, and academic reformer *Essays on Reform* was published by Macmillan only three years after it had produced the first of many editions of Bryce's *The Holy Roman Empire*, which had its origins in an Arnold prize essay of 1863. The result was both a popular success—it had run through sixty-five editions on both sides of the Atlantic by 1958—and of intellectual importance in introducing to British historical studies the historical and anthropological jurisprudence associated with Karl von Savigny (1779–1861). The work was also steeped in the pro-Germanism which characterized most of British academic life after the impact of the 'liberal Anglicans' and

Carlyle, but it went beyond this in its exploration of the conditions for the exercise of supranational authority (Kleinknecht, 108–14). The success of this work further strengthened Bryce's contacts with British historians, notably the volatile high-church liberal Edward Augustus Freeman. But his 'Anglo-Saxonism' was limited, and his closest link was with the radical John Richard Green and the dissenting Anglo-German Catholic Sir John Emerich Edward Dalberg Acton. Later Bryce played an important role, in the organizational sense that Dicey had highlighted, in the foundation of the *English Historical Review* in 1885, following a meeting of Acton, Dean Church, Mandell Creighton, Richard Garnett, Sir Adolphus Ward, and Robertson Smith which was convened at Bryce's house in Bryanston Square. With his Oxford colleagues he was also instrumental in organizing the *Law Quarterly Review*, founded in 1883.

A visit with Dicey to the eastern seaboard states of America in 1870, besides sustaining an enthusiasm for American politics and society which was to last the rest of his life (with seven visits before 1921), acquainted Bryce with Edwin Lawrence Godkin (1831–1902), another radical Irish Presbyterian and alumnus of the Academical Institution, who had emigrated to New York in 1856 and founded *The Nation* in 1865 (Tulloch, 82). Godkin, the original 'mugwump' (or principled republican reformer), gave him a commission to write a regular report on British politics for the weekly, which Bryce regarded as 'the best ... not only in America but in the whole world'. He was to contribute more than 300 articles to it in the next half-century, a useful source of income for an undemonstrative performer who was never likely to make a fortune at the bar, although he stuck it until 1882, and whose sole purely legal publication was *The Trade Marks Registration Act, with Introduction and Notes on Trade Mark Law*, in 1877.

Bryce's position as a college fellow who was not (as the law insisted) an Anglican was paradoxical and even uncomfortable. Along with most of his Oxford friends, however, he was insistent on pressing the issue of further university reform, opening all fellowships, professorships, and college emoluments to men of all faiths and none, on a not wholly enthusiastic Gladstone. This campaign, organized jointly between Liberals at the two universities, who to this end founded the Ad Eundem dining club in 1864, had its fulcrum among the 'non-resident' graduates in London, headed by Bryce's friend Charles Saville Roundell, fellow of Merton, on the Oxford side and Professor Henry Fawcett, representing Cambridge. A representative selection of 121 of these 'lights of liberalism' turned out at a rally in the Freemasons' Tavern, London, on 10 June 1864 to support a tests repeal measure moved by J. G. Dodson MP. These included, besides Bryce, Leslie Stephen, T. H. Green, T. H. Huxley, Thomas Hughes MP, John Bright MP, and Dean Stanley (Harvie, *Lights of Liberalism*, 246–56). The political connections which were then built up, particularly with politicians and organized nonconformity, bore fruit, after a ten-year campaign, in the abolition of university tests in 1871.

In the previous year Gladstone, now reconciled to

reform, had appointed Bryce regius professor of civil law, a position he held until 1893. This position was more of political than of educational significance, since both civil law and professorships were marginal to Oxford studies; but it did give Bryce the high profile of presenting the candidates for higher degrees at the annual encaenia, and with his usual application he made the best of it by involving himself with the movement for the endowment of research.

Mark Pattison's plea, in *Suggestions on Academical Organisation* (1868), for Oxford and Cambridge as centres of research rather than teaching had no more enthusiastic supporter: it was 'the best thing that any of us have produced'. Bryce was more consistently the ally of research than the mercurial Pattison, particularly in the field of comparative constitutional studies. The outcome of this was a series of lectures and papers on constitutional issues which were to have a considerable subsequent impact, although not quite in the way in which Bryce intended. Although he had sympathized with European nationalist movements, *The Holy Roman Empire* had still postulated the importance of an overarching authority from which subordinate legislatures derived their legitimacy; it was, for a Scots Presbyterian, a rather Catholic conception of mixed sovereignty, but not foreign to the Scottish tradition of 'civic humanism', with its conception of the fundamental importance of law rather than force in political life. This became apparent in a lecture, 'Flexible and rigid constitutions', delivered in the 1870s but not published until 1901, in which he contrasted the hard and fast codes of continental and American models with the ability of British politicians to agree on types of convention better fitted to the efficient and equitable dispatch of business. Nevertheless, by that time Bryce was less persuaded that the British paradigm offered checks against populistic interventions in the market and the jingoism which he and other Liberals had encountered during the Eastern question agitation.

Radical politician and home rule The Eastern question agitation of 1876–8 proved an early peak in a developing political career. A limited income delayed Bryce's start (between £1000 and £3000 was necessary to contest a promising seat in 1868). After a defeat as a radical Liberal, standing against the 'moderate Liberal' telegraph magnate Sir John Pender in the Wick burghs in 1874, when the Liberals lost power, in his view, because of lack of policy—a radical view at the time—he played a leading part in the Bulgarian agitations in 1876. He and A. O. Rutson had both travelled in the area in 1876, and his friend Freeman had strong sympathies with the Orthodox church. With the trade unionists Henry Broadhurst and George Howell, and the artist and designer William Morris (*en route* to a much more radical position), Bryce went on to organize the National Liberal League in 1878, trying to unite working- and middle-class radicals behind an 'advanced policy'. Probably as a result of this, and other causes such as his chairmanship of the Commons Preservation Society, he was selected by Liberal activists to fight the Tower Hamlets constituency in 1880. Bryce's 1876 visit also brought

him into contact with the Armenian subjects of the Turkish empire, whose repression he combated through the founding of the Anglo-Armenian Society in 1879.

As a rather fastidious academic, however, Bryce was almost overwhelmed by having to cope with the problems of a packed slum constituency during the depression. Although most of his Commons activity concerned working-class issues, and he played a notable part in the process of involving Oxford University in the social problems of the East End by helping create Toynbee Hall in 1883 with Canon Samuel Barnett, as a memorial to the young Oxford historian Arnold Toynbee and to his close friend T. H. Green, his constituency experience did not make him confident about the future of democracy in an increasingly urban population. When the chance came to move to loyal and undemanding South Aberdeen in 1885, he took it. Subsequently he would visit his constituency for two weeks every year, putting aside one day to discuss problems with constituents. Nevertheless he reacted aggressively to what he encountered in the House of Commons in 1880: 'The thorough-going selfishness of the plutocracy and especially of the landlords makes me more disposed to sweeping measures unfavourable to what they think their privileges than I should have otherwise been' (letter to R. J. Bryce, 1880, Bryce MSS). But his major concerns were subsequently to lie with foreign and educational issues rather esoteric to the electorate as a whole. He was also prepared theoretically to move towards a more 'rigid' type of constitution, for two reasons. One was his involvement with Godkin and Sir John Seeley in the Imperial Federation League of 1884, in which he saw not only the possibility of constitutional co-operation among the self-governing colonies but the possible reconciliation with Britain of the United States. He wrote to a sceptical Freeman in December 1886 that his object was

> to maintain our English citizenship and nationality over the whole world … I wish we could bring in the U.S.A. too: we ought never to have let them go out; nor do I despair of some sort of permanent arrangement with them in the future. (Harvie, 'Ideology and home rule', 313)

The other reason was the looming confrontation in Ireland.

'Personally I think that no two men unless it be Morley and Hartington have gained so much by this crisis as you and myself', Bryce wrote to Dicey in July 1886, at the height of the controversy over Gladstone's first Home Rule Bill (Harvie, 'Ideology and home rule', 298). In the Liberal administration of 1886 Bryce occupied the non-cabinet position of under-secretary for foreign affairs, junior to the earl of Rosebery. A loyal middle-of-the-road Liberal as well as a close academic friend of Gladstone, Bryce was a qualified home-ruler out of conviction. He had tried to create a Liberal protestant pressure group, the committee on Irish Affairs, to mediate between the Parnellites and the government after 1881, directing its propaganda mainly at Ulster Liberals, but he had started by mid-1884 to think in terms of a subordinate legislature in the pamphlet *England and Ireland*. Although Gladstone in the autumn of 1885 decided on a much more drastic measure Bryce quickly reconciled himself to it, much to the chagrin of many of his Ulster Liberal relatives, and academic friends, who became Unionists, Dicey and Goldwin Smith notable among them. The neurasthenic Smith and Bryce did not correspond for more than a decade, but relations with Dicey (whose physical infirmities made it necessary for Bryce to act as his unofficial literary agent) became even closer. Ironically, Dicey's conviction of the absolute sovereignty of the Westminster parliament, which he elevated into a timely dogma in 1886 with the publication of his *Introduction to the Study of the Law of the Constitution*, was in its essentials a development of Bryce's 'Flexible and rigid constitutions' argument. But Dicey, as 'the prophet of the obvious', got through to most MPs, who found themselves lost in Bryce's subtler and more referential arguments.

Bryce attempted to mediate between the radical Unionists and the Gladstonians in 1886, without success. Joseph Chamberlain denounced him as 'a snivelling professor' (Hurst, 381). But his suggested modification to the Government of Ireland Bill, the retention of a reduced number of Irish MPs at Westminster, brought some rebels back into the fold and was the basis of Gladstone's revived bill in 1893. Paid by the secret service fund, he set about organizing *Essays on Reform*-type symposia to further the cause of Irish home rule: *Five Centuries of Irish History* and *The Handbook of Home Rule*, with R. Barry O'Brien, came out in 1887, including two contributions by Godkin. At the same time he was, rather apprehensively, trying to warn Gladstone off Scottish home rule. In fact, he participated little in issues which engaged the Scots electorate, such as land reform and the disestablishment of the kirk, although he merits a mention in the history of Scottish recreation by his attempts in the 1880s and 1890s to secure walkers statutory public access to the Scottish mountains.

The American Commonwealth Out of office Bryce, in his contemporaries' judgement a better performer in the House of Commons library than on the floor of the house, devoted himself to writing his greatest work, *The American Commonwealth*. Initially his ambition had been to write a life of Justinian (482–565), Eastern emperor and codifier of Roman law, and his discovery of an unknown manuscript life was published in the *English Historical Review* in 1887, but this biography was continually deferred by contemporary concerns. Following two trips to America, in 1881 and 1883, on both occasions travelling to the west and in 1883 as far as Hawaii, he decided to concentrate on a book which would revise Alexis de Toqueville's famous critique of 1838, *Democracy in America*. He was urged in this direction by Gladstone who, following the settlement of the *Alabama* arbitration in Geneva in 1871, wanted to build up a transatlantic co-operation which would repair the hostility of the 1860s (Tulloch, 70–73).

This was a particularly demanding assignment in view of the westward expansion of the Union, the incorporation of the post-bellum South, and a population which, at 50 million in 1880, had more than doubled since 1840.

Bryce became an adept collector and analyst of 'state constitutions, published government commissions, statistical compilations, party slip tickets, campaign literature, newspapers, advertisements, political memoirs such as Blaine's *Twenty Years in Congress*, reformist tracts, satirical descriptions of city politics such as *Solid for Mulhooly*' (Tulloch, 80). He had often to codify and rationalize information that was difficult to obtain and to create his own statistical series. In this he was aided by a huge academic and political network, the members of which eagerly responded to requests for opinions and material: something that made his work, ultimately, more significant for America than for his own country.

Bryce's trips in the 1880s subsequently involved countless conversations with politicians and citizens at all social levels; when resident in Britain this was supplemented by a vast correspondence and involvement in daily and periodical journalism. It was Bryce's philosophy never to rely wholly on the printed word, and his recordings of dialogues and interviews, and observations of scenery, organizations, and customs, gave the book an enduring value as a comprehensive study of civil society which did much to counter the pessimism with which he had viewed American political life from the Grant presidencies of 1868–77 to the 'gilded age' of the 1880s.

However, Bryce's sources were on the whole derived from 'high politics'. Hugh Tulloch comments of his treatment of stump and machine politicians that

> his upbringing, his Presbyterian conscience and the American circles in which he moved, all combined to restrict his empathy … essentially he surveyed this class from the elevated heights of a Henry Adams rather than from below in Graziano's Shoeshine Parlor, where George Washington Plunkitt held daily court. (Tulloch, 90)

In the struggle between two of his closest associates, the mugwump Godkin and the practical reformer in the 'muddy whirlpool', Theodore Roosevelt, he carefully refused to take sides, to the latter's chagrin (Tulloch, 95–9).

With successive revisions after its publication in 1888, *The American Commonwealth* went through three comprehensive new editions, in 1889, 1893–5, and 1910, and remained in print long after his death. The National Union Catalog lists 101 editions by 1950, about a third of these being abridgements for American school use. Bryce took the line that the American constitution was essentially conservative, but that, in the flexibility of its civil society, something that it derived from the British tradition, America would be likely to avoid class conflict. 'America marks the highest level, not only of material well-being but of intelligence and happiness, which the race has attained'; the optimism of his final conclusion was not shared by his friend Acton: 'Where you speak like Macaulay speaking of 1688, I speak like Michelet speaking of 1789' (Acton to Bryce, 1888, Bryce MSS).

Marriage and society On 23 July 1889, now fifty-one, Bryce married Elizabeth Marion Ashton (*d.* 1939), the partly American daughter of a Manchester mill owner, a charming and intelligent woman twenty years his junior. Miss

Ashton brought a substantial income, which enabled the Bryces to live well, with a town flat at 3 Buckingham Gate, London—friends noted ugly maids and glaring electric light—and Hindleap, a country house in an arts and crafts style near Forest Row in Sussex, built in 1898 and surrounded with an extensive garden stocked with the booty of Bryce's foreign trips. From the couple's letters the relationship seems to have been more partnership than passion; it saved Bryce from the fate of becoming a walking encyclopaedia or of falling down crevasses on solo jaunts, but there were no children. Aspects of the man were, however, less orthodox than those of most of his academic contemporaries. Bryce dressed in the somewhat bohemian manner of the Pre-Raphaelites: reefer jackets, loosely knotted bright blue ties, and fold-down collars; he was a pipe smoker throughout his long life and also rolled his own cigarettes. This radicalism could have odd moments of revival. In October 1892, on Tennyson's death, he suggested his old friend William Morris to Gladstone as poet laureate, albeit with a caveat about the acceptability of Morris's republicanism and revolutionary socialism; his second choice was the even more implausible Swinburne, then, rather despairingly, Coventry Patmore—'at least he is a poet'. Lord Salisbury later appointed the unforgettably awful Alfred Austin, who at least was a tory.

Liberal governments When Gladstone regained power in 1892 Bryce entered the cabinet as chancellor of the duchy of Lancaster. In this capacity he appointed the first working-class JPs in the duchy and accompanied Queen Victoria to Florence as minister in attendance. She liked 'Mr Bryce, who knows so much and is so modest'. Lord Rosebery advanced him to the presidency of the Board of Trade in 1894. His achievements were not great, something partly to be accounted for by the short and troubled Liberal period in office (though Arthur Acland made an impressive success of the Board of Education in the same period). It was in fact Acland who suggested Bryce's most constructive work in this decade, as chairman of the royal commission on secondary education (1894–6). The commission also considered girls' schools, and Bryce insisted on the appointment of the first (three) women members of a royal commission, one of whom was Eleanor Mildred Sidgwick, wife of his Cambridge friend Henry Sidgwick and sister of the Conservative leader of the Commons, Arthur Balfour. The commission envisaged a ministry of education, taking over a range of existing authorities. Its findings were to figure in the Balfour Education Act of 1902, setting up the county councils as education authorities for England and Wales and funding secondary education out of the rates; but some younger Liberals, notably Richard Burdon Haldane, regarded Bryce as fixed in a humanistic Oxford mould and slow to move on the development of provincial university colleges and technical education. Shortly afterwards he played a major part, along with his friends Sidgwick and Donald Mackay, Lord Reay, in establishing the British Academy in 1900 in a belated attempt to secure prestige, if not endowment, for

research in the humanities. He was president of the Academy from 1913 to 1917, a foreign member of the Institut de France in 1904, and a member of the academies of Brussels (1896), Turin (1896), Naples (1903), and Stockholm, and the Imperial Academy of St Petersburg. The 1890s also saw Bryce's strongest 'chivalric' commitment, to the cause of the Armenians in the Ottoman empire (Dicey was similarly active on behalf of the Jews, and their friend John Westlake on behalf of the Finns). Bryce played a part in mobilizing the now retired Gladstone on his last crusade, in 1895–6, on the Armenians' behalf. In 1902, together with H. N. Brailsford and the Buxton brothers, he went on to found the Balkan Committee.

By this time Bryce's red hair had gone pure white, and with his jutting eyebrows and full moustache and beard he looked alarmingly like an energetic West Highland terrier. He had a vast range of information, few enemies, but a somewhat fact-bound cast of mind, which was scholarly rather than political, something which among party colleagues occasionally caused hilarity rather than conviction: 'He knew every place, how to get there, how long it took you to get to the railhead, and how long it took you to cross the desert by camel, and all the rest of it' (Harvie, *Lights of Liberalism*, 238).

Bryce's zest for travel also intervened. Like Anthony Trollope, whom he knew from the 1860s, he took advantage of the expansion of railways and steamer routes and wrote serious-mindedly about this. *Transcaucasia and Ararat* came out in 1877 and *Impressions of South Africa* in 1897. In the latter case he was over-influenced by the persuasiveness of Cecil Rhodes into an unwontedly imperialist attitude, but forecast the mounting tensions which were to erupt in the Second South African War. In this conflict he moderated his position and took the same critical but not explicitly pro-Boer stance as his Glasgow contemporary and friend the new Liberal leader, Sir Henry Campbell-Bannerman, with whose old-fashioned radicalism he thoroughly agreed, backing him on free trade and bringing his own American expertise to bear on the 'trustification' of industry. By this time he was somewhat of a back number in the house. Arthur Balfour, in a letter to Edmund Gosse, was scathing about his performances:

> I assure you his appearances in the House of Commons are those of a gabbling, foolish, muddled old man. Nobody could be older in mind, less elastic than Bryce … Bryce is a standing instance of the uselessness of the higher education.
> (Harvie, 'Ideology and home rule', 13)

When the Liberals took power in 1905 Campbell-Bannerman did not offer Bryce the Foreign Office, which he had thought himself fitted for, but the much more arduous and less rewarding portfolio of the Irish chief secretaryship. His tenure of this was brief and unsuccessful. He hoped to be able to carry an Irish council bill, as a partial step towards home rule, but saw this dismissed out of hand by John Redmond and the nationalists. The Irish, having experienced in Gerald Balfour and George Wyndham two Unionists running far ahead of their party in sympathy for Irish causes, regarded the cautious Ulster Presbyterian as something of a backslider. An attempt at an Irish university bill failed, but nevertheless the royal commission on Irish university education, which he convened in 1907, did much to settle the awkward problem of relationships between the Catholic church and the movement for higher educational reform, which had plagued governments since Gladstone's abortive bill of 1873.

Ambassador to Washington, 1907–1913 Moreover Bryce, whose economic views were broadly those of Cobden and Bright, was out of sympathy with the radical tenor of the Liberal government's policies—being suspicious of the trade unions, of redistributive taxation, and, above all, of Lloyd George. Campbell-Bannerman's solution was the elegant one of sending Bryce to Washington as ambassador in 1907, the permanent under-secretary at the Foreign Office, Sir Charles Hardinge, remarking cynically:

> I realised he would be greatly appreciated in America as knowing more of the history and constitution of America than most Americans. He had also the quality of liking to make long and rather dull speeches on commonplace subjects which I knew to be a trait that would be possible with the American masses. He had also a charming and agreeable wife. (Harvie, *Lights of Liberalism*, 238)

Refusing a peerage in 1907 and 1910, but being awarded the Order of Merit in 1907, Bryce stayed in Washington until 1913. He made two lengthy excursions, one to South America and the other to Australia, respectively in 1909 and 1912, from which stemmed *South America: Observations and Impressions* (1913) and part of the book *Modern Democracies* that he had first planned in 1904. His mission greatly enhanced the friendly co-operation between the two powers, less through close relationships with presidents Theodore Roosevelt and William Howard Taft than through his popularity with the American public. Roosevelt was devoted to the same sort of strenuous exercise that Bryce enjoyed, while Bryce's sympathies had generally lain with the republicans since the days of Abraham Lincoln, yet despite earlier co-operation on *The American Commonwealth* Roosevelt was privately dismissive, sharing his wife's opinion that Bryce was a 'worthy and dull old person' (Perkins, 277). Nor were relations with Roosevelt's successor, Taft, particularly close. With Taft's opponent, Woodrow Wilson, he shared an affinity as a political scientist of south-west Scottish Presbyterian origins, but Wilson took office only in the last year of Bryce's embassy.

Bryce's diplomatic achievements were qualified. He carried through a limited arbitration treaty between Britain and the USA, finalized on 4 April 1908. He also paid studious attention to Canadian interests after a visit to Ottawa in April 1907, noting that the dominion was beginning to chafe against British suzerainty. The co-operation which he negotiated over fishery, financial, and boundary issues was to have valuable results when war broke out. Attempts at the conclusion of more extensive free trade and a permanent arbitration commission, however, foundered on opposition in congress. The dispute between Britain and the USA about the privileges granted to American shipping using the new Panama Canal remained unresolved (though it was settled in 1914). But more influential than anything else was Bryce's sympathy with and absorption in American intellectual and social life, from the standpoint of a rather circumspect American progressive. Booker T. Washington was entertained at the embassy, and another Ulster Presbyterian, Sir Roger Casement, introduced to Roosevelt to publicize his inquiry into the maltreatment of Brazilian rubber workers in Putumayo. In the course of his embassy 'Old Man Bryce' visited every state, revelling in a life which he was convinced had improved while that of Europe had deteriorated.

Liberal peer On his return from America (via Japan, China, and India) Bryce was ennobled (on 28 January 1914) as Viscount Bryce of Dechmont in the county of Lanark, and took an active role in the upper house, which he found more congenial than life as an MP. But within months war had broken out, and Bryce had enrolled as a reluctant partisan. His reputation had been that of a pro-American and a thorn in the flesh of successive British governments in the cause of civil rights, so the choice of him by the British Foreign Office in September 1914 as the chairman of a six-man committee to investigate German conduct in occupied Belgium was an inspired act. The work of the Bryce committee, which reported in May 1915, remains controversial, and many of the stories of atrocities which it publicized were shown up as false (Knightley, 84). Evidence was taken by lawyers in England, without corroboration, and all the proceedings of the inquiry were subsequently destroyed, although Bryce himself learned about the distortions only after the war. His report was blamed for creating 'atrocity fatigue' during the Second World War, when the British public simply refused to believe the far worse (and true) stories of Nazi genocide. Bryce was temperamentally, and as a historian, pro-German, so this reversal of expectations, however provoked, had a violent effect on his outlook: 'Better anything than the destruction of morality which has come in Germany!' Yet the tribulations of the Belgians were to be as nothing compared to the genocide practised by the Turks on Bryce's Armenian friends. Much of this pessimism was conveyed in his private correspondence with British and American academics and politicians, notably Dicey, President Eliot of Princeton, and Governor Charles Evans Hughes, and in the tone of his last lengthy work, *Modern Democracies*, undertaken during the war.

These two volumes made up a very uneven survey which covered the white dominions, America, and Europe (but not Britain), and was published in 1921. Although Bryce's confidence in America was undimmed, his diagnosis of the other liberal nationalisms was gloomy, at a time when the Versailles treaty had invested so much in their example. The Fabian Graham Wallas had attacked Bryce's 'rationalist fallacy' in *Human Nature in Politics* (1908):

> What does Mr Bryce mean by 'ideal democracy'? If it means anything, it means the best form of democracy which is consistent with the facts of human nature. But one feels … that Mr Bryce means by these words the kind of democracy which might be possible if human nature were as he himself would like it to be, and as he was taught at Oxford to think that it was. (Wallas, 126)

The war, and the power of élites in 'welfarist' politics, seemed to bear out Wallas's post-Freudian stress on political 'behaviourism', though recent interest in the constitution of 'principled societies' may have swung the argument back in Bryce's favour.

However, other wartime work was more fruitful; Bryce was a member of the allied inter-parliamentary conference and the chair of a joint conference of both houses into the future of the House of Lords which recommended in 1917 a 326-member second chamber. Some 246 members were to be elected by groups of MPs arranged by region and voting by single transferable vote, and 80 were to be elected for twelve years by a joint committee of both houses of parliament. Differences between the two houses would be settled by joint consultation. Nothing, however, came of these proposals. From 1914 Bryce also helped set up various informal bodies which pressed for the creation of a League of Nations. He joined figures from the Union of Democratic Control, such as Goldsworthy Lowes Dickinson, Graham Wallas, and J. A. Hobson, in drafting 'Proposals for the prevention of future wars' (1915)—'by far the most influential of the preliminary schemes for a League of Nations', and pressed for the creation of a permanent council for the league (Brennan, 146). The Bryce memorandum to the British government on 8 August 1917, outlining a structure for the league and insisting on the participation of the United States, was a key document in the Versailles negotiations, although its hopes were to be betrayed by American non-ratification. Despite his suspicion of socialism and abhorrence of Bolshevism, Bryce co-operated with many younger Liberals and progressives in this cause, and that of other minorities, such as the Jews and the Macedonians. Although siding with Asquith after the split in the Liberal Party, he remained in contact with the Lloyd Georgeites through his friend, and later executor and biographer, the Oxford don H. A. L. Fisher, education minister in 1916–22.

Death and assessment Bryce continued active in the House of Lords, moving in December 1921, with another former Irish chief secretary, John Morley, the resolution which greeted the signing of the treaty between Britain and the forces which would constitute the Irish Free State. Still commanding all his powers, he died, quite unexpectedly, of heart failure in his sleep while on holiday at the Victoria Hotel, Sidmouth, Devon, on 22 January 1922: 'It was euthanasia', commented a colleague. After cremation at Golders Green and an Anglican memorial service in Westminster Abbey (and Greek and Armenian services in their own London churches) his ashes were buried next to those of his parents in the Grange cemetery in Edinburgh. Lady Bryce lived on until 27 December 1939.

One of Bryce's volumes of essays was called *The Hindrances to Good Citizenship* (1909). This characterized the heavily ethical content of his liberalism, which subsequent behaviourist analysis tended to dismiss as wilfully fastidious. However, his essentially 'civic republican' doctrine, and his sense of the need for a moral bond between civil society and a decentralized state, can be seen as fitting him into the 'civic humanism' of the tradition explored by John Pocock in *The Machiavellian Moment* (1975), and his essay 'Flexible and rigid constitutions' has been praised by Judge David Edward of the European Court of Justice as a precedent for the constitution of the European Union, in both its federal and regional aspects.

CHRISTOPHER HARVIE

Sources *The Times* (23 Jan 1922) · *The Times* (24 Jan 1922) · *The Times* (31 Jan 1922) · H. A. L. Fisher, *James Bryce*, 2 vols. (1927) · H. A. L. Fisher, 'Viscount Bryce of Dechmont, O. M., 1838–1922', *PBA*, 12 (1926), 297–305 · Bodl. Oxf., MSS Bryce · E. S. Ions, *James Bryce and American democracy, 1870–1922* (1968) · T. Kleinknecht, *Imperiale und internationale Ordnung: eine Untersuchung zum anglo-amerikanischen Gelehrtenliberalismus am Beispiel von James Bryce, 1838–1922* (1985) · C. Harvie, *The lights of liberalism: university liberals and the challenge of democracy, 1860–86* (1976) · C. Harvie, 'Ideology and home rule: James Bryce, A. V. Dicey and Ireland, 1880–1887', *EngHR*, 91 (1976), 298–314 · P. Neary, 'Grey, Bryce, and the settlement of Canadian-American differences, 1905–1911', *Canadian Historical Review*, 49 (1968), 357–80 · T. Wilson, 'Lord Bryce's investigation into alleged German atrocities in Belgium', *Journal of Contemporary History*, 14 (1979), 369–83 · A. C. Hepburn, 'The Irish Councils Bill and the fall of Sir Anthony Macdonnell, 1906–7', *Irish Historical Studies*, 17 (1970–71), 470–98 · F. Harrison, *Realities and ideals* (1908) · P. Knightley, *The first casualty: the war correspondent as hero, propagandist and myth maker from the Crimea to Vietnam* (1975) · H. Pelling, *America and the British left* (1956) · B. Perkins, *The great rapprochement: England and the United States, 1895–1914* (1969) · H. Tulloch, *James Bryce's 'American Commonwealth': the Anglo-American background* (1988) · Gladstone, *Diaries* · G. Wallas, *Human nature in politics* (1908) · M. Hurst, *Joseph Chamberlain and liberal reunion* (1967) · D. Edward, *Federalism and democracy* [forthcoming] · J. W. Brennan, 'Bryce, James, first Viscount', *BDMBR*, vol. 3, pt 1

Archives Bodl. Oxf., corresp. and papers · Boston PL, letters · NL Ire., corresp. and papers relating to Ireland · NL Scot., Add. MSS 1011–1015 · PRO, corresp. relating to Hungary, FO 800/331–335 | BL, letters to William Archer, Add. MS 45290 · BL, corresp. with Sir Henry Campbell-Bannerman, Add. MS 41211 · BL, corresp. with Lord Carnarvon, Add. MS 60775 · BL, letters to T. H. S. Escott, Add. MS 58776 · BL, letters to Lord Gladstone, Add. MSS 46019, 46064 · BL, corresp. with W. E. Gladstone, Add. MSS 44463–44789, *passim* · BL, corresp. with Macmillans, Add. MSS 55086–55088 · BL, corresp. with Lord Ripon, Add. MS 43542 · BL, corresp. with C. P. Scott, Add. MS 50909, *passim* · BL, letters to J. A. Spender, Add. MSS 46391–46392 · Bodl. Oxf., corresp. with H. H. Asquith · Bodl. Oxf., letters to H. A. L. Fisher · Bodl. Oxf., corresp. with Sir William Harcourt and Lewis Harcourt · Bodl. Oxf., corresp. with Lord Kimberley · Bodl. Oxf., letters to Gilbert Murray · Bodl. Oxf., letters to C. H. Pearson · Bodl. Oxf., letters to Lord Ponsonby · Bodl. Oxf., corresp. with Lord Selborne · CAC Cam., corresp. with Sir Cecil Spring-Rice · CAC Cam., letters to W. T. Stead · Christ's College, Cambridge, Stead MSS · CUL, letters to Lord Acton · CUL, corresp. with Lord Hardinge · Cumbria AS, Carlisle, letters to Lord Howard of Penrith · DWL, letters to Henry Allon · HLRO, letters to David Lloyd George · HLRO, corresp. with Herbert Samuel · HLRO, corresp. with John St Loe Strachey · JRL, letters to C. P. Scott · King's Cam., letters to Oscar Browning · NA Canada, corresp. with Earl Grey · NA Canada, corresp. with Sir George Parkin · NA Scot., corresp. with G. W. Balfour · NA Scot., corresp. with Philip Kerr · NL Aus., letters to Alfred Deakin · NL Ire., letters to A. S. Green · NL Ire., corresp. with Sir John Redmond · NL Scot., corresp., mainly with Lord Rosebery and Sir Patrick Geddes · Plunkett Foundation, Long Hanborough, Oxfordshire, corresp. with Sir Horace Plunkett · Society of Psychical Research, London, corresp. with Sir Oliver Lodge · TCD, corresp. with John Dillon · U. Birm. L., corresp. with W. H. Dawson · U. Newcastle, Robinson L., letters to R. S. Watson and E. S. Watson · U. St Andr. L., letters to Wilfred Ward · UCL, letters to James Sully · University of Toronto Library, corresp. with James Manor · Wellcome L., letters to Sir Thomas Barlow · Yale U.,

Sterling Memorial Library, corresp. with Edward House | FILM BFI NFTVA, propaganda film footage (Hepworth Manufacturing Company)

Likenesses A. Cope, oils, 1880–81, priv. coll. · W. & D. Downey, woodburytype photograph, pubd 1893, NPG · A. Delecluse, oils, 1895–9, priv. coll. · B. Stone, photograph, 1898, NPG · J. Wilson Forster, oils, c.1899, Trinity College, Oxford · G. C. Beresford, photographs, 1902, NPG [see illus.] · G. Reid, oils, 1905, Oriel College, Oxford · E. Moore, oils, 1907, NPG · S. Thomas, oils, c.1912, National Liberal Club, London · B. Robinson, pen-and-ink drawing, 1913, NPG · W. Stoneman, photograph, before 1917, NPG · H. Furniss, drawings, NPG · S. P. Hall, pencil drawing, NPG · W. Orpen, oils, Aberdeen Art Gallery · W. Rothenstein, chalk drawing, Scot. NPG · J. Russell & Sons, photograph, NPG · Spy [L. Ward], cartoon, repro. in *VF* (25 Feb 1893) · Wright, chromolithograph, NPG; repro. in *VF* (25 Feb 1893) · bust; presented to Lady Bryce in 1923 · drawings, NPG

Wealth at death £36,205 14s. 0d.: probate, 15 July 1922, *CGPLA Eng. & Wales*

Bryce, John (*bap.* 1717, *d.* 1787), printer and bookseller, was baptized in Glasgow on 10 March 1717, the younger son of Patrick Bryce, hammerman, and Janet Watson. Nothing more is known of his background or early life. His name first appears in a Glasgow imprint in 1742, when an edition of James Fisher's *Review of the Preface to a Narrative of the Extraordinary Work at Kilsyth* was 'printed for John Bryce and sold by him at the Gallowgate Printing house, and by Patrick Bryce at his shop above the Cross'. Patrick, a bookseller, was John's elder brother, and kept the shop referred to until 1757. In 1744 John and Patrick collaborated on another religious publication, a sermon by John Bisset.

Bryce's name did not appear in another work until he began printing in partnership with David Paterson in 1752. The address of their printing house, according to the imprint of John Lawson's *Speech Concerning the Settling of Parishes* (1752), was 'second close above the Saltmercatwell'. In the *Glasgow Journal* for 16 May–2 June 1755 the partners advertised a change of address, together with a description of the work they were prepared to undertake:

John Bryce and David Paterson, printers in Glasgow, have removed their printing office from the 4th story of Gibson's land to the second story of that land in New-street opposite to the new bank, which was lately occupied by a stocking factory, where they continue to do all kinds of printing work.

On 8 February 1757 Bryce became a Glasgow burgess and member of the guild of hammermen by right of his father. The following year Bryce and Paterson moved again, this time to premises in the Bridgegate, near the old bank, but the partnership ended in 1759, with Bryce retaining the Bridgegate printing house. Between 1760 and 1762 he printed a number of books there in partnership with Archibald McLean junior. After that he ran the Bridgegate printing house alone until 1775, though his work as a printer was undistinguished. He also sold books from various addresses in the Saltmarket and published many titles.

Bryce's output consisted almost entirely of religious works. Throughout the 1760s, 1770s, and early 1780s he was the foremost publisher of evangelical books in Glasgow, and perhaps in all of Scotland. His publications included reprints of Reformation classics by Samuel Rutherford, as well as modern works by the historian and biographer John Howie and by Presbyterian seceders such as Ralph and Ebenezer Erskine. A number of his titles were published by subscription, with support coming largely from pious weavers and tradesmen in the Glasgow vicinity. His connections with seceders probably account for the fact that for many years he printed the acts of the Associate Presbytery.

Bryce's first wife, Margaret Glen, died of consumption aged fifty-two, and was buried on 14 April 1760. On 12 October of that year Bryce married Janet Inglis, widow of John Smith, weaver in the Baronie. She died in June 1786 at the age of fifty, and on 19 December 1787 Bryce himself died in Glasgow, soon after leaving his shop at the end of the day. He was buried in Glasgow on 1 January 1788; the burial register gives the cause of death as 'stomach cramps'. His heir was his son John, a Glasgow workman who in 1792 advertised for sale two tenements which had belonged to his father. There is some evidence to suggest that he continued his father's business for a time, but he is not listed in the Glasgow directories of the period.

R. A. GILLESPIE

Sources parish registers, Glasgow · H. R. Plomer and others, *A dictionary of the printers and booksellers who were at work in England, Scotland, and Ireland from 1726 to 1775* (1932) · *Decennial indexes to the services of heirs in Scotland*, 4 vols. (1863–89) · *Glasgow Mercury* (26 Dec 1787) · *Glasgow Mercury* (2 Jan 1788) · J. Morris, 'Scottish book trade index', www.nls.uk/catalogues/resources/sbti/ · R. B. Sher and A. Hook, 'Introduction: Glasgow and the Enlightenment', *The Glasgow Enlightenment*, ed. R. B. Sher and A. Hook (1995)

Brychan Brycheiniog (*fl. c.*500), king of Brycheiniog, was allegedly son of the Irish king Anlach, son of Coronac, and of Marchell ferch Dewdrig of south Wales. He was the legendary dynastic founder and eponym of the early medieval kingdom of Brycheiniog (Brecknockshire) in south Wales. Nothing historically reliable is known about his life or rule, though later hagiographical and genealogical accounts would suggest that he flourished in the late fifth or early sixth century. According to the dynastic origin-legend, Brychan was son of one Marchell, a daughter of a local petty king called Tewdrig. Marchell was sent to Ireland to marry the king, Anlach son of Coronac (perhaps Cormac), on the understanding that if a son issued from the union he should return to Wales to reclaim his rightful kingdom. Thus, when Brychan was born, the couple returned thither with the child. As a youth he is said to have been sent as 'hostage' to the kingdom of Powys where he violated Banhadlwedd ferch Banadl, the daughter of the king, who subsequently gave birth to Cynog, afterwards St Cynog. Brychan is most famous for his allegedly large progeny by three wives—Eurbrawst, Rhybrawst, and Proestri—numbering twelve sons and twenty-four daughters according to the earliest lists, and both figures increase in later accounts. His daughters are linked to a number of figures of saintly and secular importance, most notably with St David and Cadog and the kings Urien Rheged and Maelgwn Gwynedd. There are also some entirely different accounts of Brychan's saintly descendants located in Cornwall and Ireland. Brychan is said to have been buried at 'Ynys Brychan', near 'Mannia' or 'Manar', but the location has not been identified.

Although much of this account is probably hagiography and origin-legend, and therefore difficult to credit historically, Brychan's alleged connection with Ireland is important. His name probably derives from the Irish personal name Broccán, and the region of Brecknockshire contains a large number of ogham inscriptions suggesting significant Irish settlement in the region, perhaps in the fifth century. Also Brycheiniog houses the only known example of a crannog, or lake settlement, outside Ireland and Scotland, at Ynys Bwlc at Llan-gors, again implying an Irish connection. This was probably the 'Brecenanmere' destroyed by Æthelflæd, 'lady of the Mercians', in 916. However, the settlement probably dates no earlier than the ninth century. This would be too late for Brychan of c.500, but it is worth noting that his father's name has also been identified as the Irish name Amlaíb (from Olaf), suggesting a ninth- or tenth-century origin. Whether this affects understanding of Brychan himself is not clear.

DAVID E. THORNTON

Sources A. W. Wade-Evans, 'The Brychan documents', *Y Cymmrodor*, 19 (1906), 18–50 • P. C. Bartrum, ed., *Early Welsh genealogical tracts* (1966) • P. Ó Riain, ed., *Corpus genealogiarum sanctorum Hiberniae* (Dublin, 1985) • *ASC*, s.a. 916 [text C] • N. Edwards and A. Lane, eds., *Early medieval settlements in Wales, AD 400–1100: a critical reassessment and gazetteer of the archaeological evidence for secular settlements in Wales* (1988)

Brydall, John (*b. c.*1635, *d.* in or after **1705**?), lawyer, was the son of John Brydall, of Chatsworth, Derbyshire, who may have been the John Bridell who matriculated from Jesus College, Cambridge, in 1636. John Brydall the younger matriculated as a commoner in Queen's College, Oxford, on 15 July 1652, graduating BA on 28 June 1655. Four months earlier, on 22 February, he had enrolled as an inner barrister at Lincoln's Inn, being listed in the admission register there as the 'heir app[arent]' of his father (Lincoln's Inn, 270). He was called to the bar in 1662. Thirty years later Anthony Wood noted that Brydall, who was 'afterwards a common lawyer … hath published several things of his profession' (Wood, *Ath. Oxon.*, 2.786). Some sources state that he served as a secretary to Sir Harbottle Grimston, Charles II's master of the rolls. The details of his career are vague, however, and he may have been confused sometimes with his father. He could not have written the first of the sixteen works for which 'Brydall (John)' is listed as the author in the British Museum's *Catalogue of Printed Books* (1965); it was published in 1641. It also seems unlikely that he was the 'J. B.' who edited *The Rights of the People Concerning Impositions, Stated in a Learned Argument, etc.*, in 1658. But he may well have written *Jus sigilli, or, The Law of England Touching his Majesties Four Principal Seales*, published in 1673, and certainly the secretary to the master of the rolls might be expected to be an expert on that subject.

Generally, the works ascribed to him reflect a very wide range of jurisprudential expertise, covering such topics as the laws and customs of London, the rights and privileges of the nobility and gentry, conveyancing, bastardy, and lunacy. They also indicate a strongly conservative and pro-monarchical frame of mind. The latest publication date, 1705, suggests that he lived into the middle years of Queen Anne's reign.

MICHAEL DE L. LANDON

Sources Wood, *Ath. Oxon.*, 1st edn, 2.786 • W. P. Baildon, ed., *The records of the Honorable Society of Lincoln's Inn: admissions*, 1 (1896), 270 • *British Museum general catalogue of printed books … to 1955*, BM, 263 vols. (1959–66), vol. 28, pp. 936–7 • Foster, *Alum. Oxon.*, 1500–1714, 1.202 • A. Chalmers, ed., *The general biographical dictionary*, new edn, 2 (1813), 211–12
Archives Bodl. Oxf., letters and legal papers

Bryden, Beryl Audrey (1920–1998), jazz singer and washboard player, was born on 11 May 1920 at 17 Rowington Road, Norwich, Norfolk, the only child of Amos Wilfred Bertram Bryden, a commercial traveller, and his wife, Elsie Maud Tyler Reeves Jones. She was educated at Norwich high school, and while still a teenager started collecting records. At seventeen she joined the local branch of the national Rhythm Club movement. These were social forums where jazz records were played and analysed and 'live' music sessions held, and she was the Norwich club's secretary by 1941, when members travelled to London to attend the first English public jam session. On this visit, she also heard black musicians playing at the raffish Jigs Club in Soho, an experience that changed her life.

In 1942 Bryden moved to Cambridge, where she ran that city's Rhythm Club and began singing Billie Holiday's songs. She settled in London when the war ended, determined to become part of the jazz world. She did secretarial work for the Entertainments National Service Association, and visited nightclubs where she got to know the small community of black musicians as well as members of the burgeoning 'revivalist' movement which was seeking to rekindle interest in early New Orleans jazz. Among these was Humphrey Lyttelton, whom she met as an employee at Selmer's instrument shop in Charing Cross Road when he came to purchase his first cornet; subsequently she sang with his band. She also worked at 'Doc' Hunt's percussion centre, where she encountered the leading drummers, and thus formed a relationship with the Jamaican percussionist Clinton Maxwell. As interest grew in the revival of traditional jazz, Bryden sang with its leading exponents in a semi-professional capacity. She worked as a record company secretary and appeared with the pianist George Webb, the clarinettist Cy Laurie, and the cornettist John Haim's Jelly Roll Kings, before making her recording début in 1948 with the trumpeter Freddy Randall (whose business affairs she conducted). At Rudy Evans's Caribbean Club she admired the French guitarist Django Reinhardt and the American singer Lena Horne, but it was typical of Bryden that, while gaining musical inspiration from so eclectic a range of models, she herself performed material from a jazz repertory that was simple

Beryl Audrey Bryden (1920–1998), by David Redfern, 1990

and basic. She sang early songs by the likes of Bessie Smith and accompanied herself by strumming with thimble-tipped fingers on a metal washboard, a rhythm instrument with a history predating jazz that Smith herself, even in the 1920s, would probably have scorned.

In May 1949 Bryden formed Beryl's Back-Room Boys, with whom she broadcast before joining the trumpeter Mike Daniels as commère and singer at his Delta Jazz Club in Soho. It was there, in 1952, that she met the French clarinettist Maxime Saury; he engaged her to sing with his band at the Vieux Colombier in Paris, her first professional engagement. That city became a second home, and there she formed friendships with notable American expatriates, among them the trumpeter Bill Coleman, the singer Billie Holiday, and the pianist Mary Lou Williams, with whom she recorded. These associations inspired her and gave her the impetus to sit in at 'jam' sessions with such distinguished jazz artists as the saxophonist Sidney Bechet. As European re-creations of pre-war traditional jazz grew in popularity in the 1950s, Bryden sang and recorded with the trombonist Chris Barber and played the washboard with his guitarist Lonnie Donegan; their record of *Rock Island Line* (1956) sold 2 million copies and entered the British and United States hit parades. She continued to travel in Europe, where she worked with the Dutch Swing College Band and then, as the 'trad boom' became big business in Britain, was heard with the genre's more sophisticated representatives such as the trumpeter Alex Welsh.

Away from the jazz scene, Bryden filled lengthy residencies at the elegant Blue Angel nightclub in Mayfair, where she appeared opposite the Grenada-born entertainer Leslie Hutchinson. To outsiders she remained indelibly identified with the raucous milieu of white 'trad' and its music-hall trappings, yet she enjoyed contact with a sophisticated artist such as 'Hutch', for he had once played the piano in Harlem and was connected to the source of the black music she loved. She maintained her early links with Caribbean settlers, and when the American vibraphonist Lionel Hampton arrived in London in 1957 she took him to the Sunset Club to 'jam' with the newly arrived musicians. In later years she became a confidante of the singer Adelaide Hall, who had settled in London before the war.

Although her talent was modest, Bryden became a fixture of the British jazz scene. It was impossible to overlook her, a larger-than-life figure who dressed in dramatic zebra-striped gowns, wore sculptured blonde wigs, and strummed on a star-spangled washboard. She seldom deviated from a repertory of songs taken from the lighter side of jazz, and sang these with little variation or rhythmic finesse, yet she earned respect for her sincerity in a male-dominated world that routinely showed hostility to women. She fashioned a carefree, unpoliticized image for herself, but her fascination with authenticity never abated. She continued to travel widely and to practise her hobbies of photography and deep-sea diving, and lived for many years at 166 Gloucester Terrace, Paddington, London, where her walls were covered with jazz memorabilia and her bathroom filled with shells, coral, and other souvenirs brought back directly from the depths of the sea. She was unmarried. Bryden died from cancer on 14 July 1998 at St Mary's Hospital, Paddington, London.

VAL WILMER

Sources P. Vacher, 'A life and soul in British jazz', *The Guardian* (16 July 1998) · V. Wilmer, 'A Norwich fan', *The Guardian* (17 July 1998) · S. Voce, *The Independent* (16 July 1998) · *Daily Telegraph* (16 July 1998) · *The Times* (16 July 1998) · J. Chilton, *Who's who of British jazz* (1997) · B. Kernfeld, ed., *The new Grove dictionary of jazz*, 2 vols. (1988) · B. Bryden, 'Beryl Bryden '54', *Music Mirror* (Jan 1955), 32 · personal knowledge (2004) · b. cert. · d. cert.
Archives SOUND BL NSA, oral history [recorded Feb, March 1989; ref. 6248, 6249]
Likenesses V. Wilmer, photographs, 1965, priv. coll. · D. Redfern, photograph, 1990, Redferns Music Picture Library [*see illus.*] · D. Redfern, photographs, Redferns Music Picture Library

Bryden, James Lumsdaine (1833–1880), surgeon and medical statistician, was born in Edinburgh; little is known of his parents or his early life. He attended Edinburgh high school and then Edinburgh University, where he obtained the licentiateship of the Royal College of Surgeons of Edinburgh and graduated MD in 1855, winning the gold medal for his thesis. Bryden joined the Bengal medical service in 1856 and arrived in India later that year. He was engaged initially in the military wing of the service, and saw action during the mutiny of 1857 at the siege of Delhi and the relief of Lucknow. Soon afterwards Bryden was appointed civil surgeon of Buxar, a post which he held until his transfer to statistical duties in Calcutta. In 1866 he became the statistical officer to the newly formed sanitary commission, and later to J. M. Cuningham, the first sanitary commissioner of the government of India.

Bryden is best known for his *Vital Statistics of the Bengal Presidency* (1866–79) and his numerous reports on cholera, including *Epidemic Cholera in Bengal* (1869) and *The Cholera History of 1875 and 1876* (1878). Having observed cholera in Bengal, where the disease was endemic, Bryden was well placed to record its seasonal fluctuations and was struck by its apparent conformity to unknown laws. Soon after being appointed statistical officer, he was called upon to investigate the epidemic form of the disease, which had appeared in India in 1817, and which had spread through Asia to Africa and Europe. He concluded that cholera became 'epidemic' only under certain conditions, and that these related closely to the onset of the monsoon. According to Bryden, the cholera germ flourished in a humid atmosphere and was transported beyond its endemic area by monsoonal air currents. It was his firm belief that India was epidemiologically unique and that cholera on the subcontinent differed fundamentally from that in Europe, in that the disease was never transmitted by water or human contact. Bryden's opinion of medical statistics was so high that he believed that epidemics of cholera could be predicted; as he put it in his *Reports bringing up the Statistical History of the European Army in India … to 1876*, 'Statistics are the Sibylline Books of modern times … an unerring guide to the future' (Bryden, *Reports*, 313).

However, medical opinion in Britain tended increasingly to attribute the spread of cholera either to contaminated water or to close human contact, and Bryden's airborne theory and his predictive claims were widely ridiculed during the 1860s. In India, however, Bryden was not without support and his views underpinned the government's approach to the prevention of cholera until 1870. If not actually formative of government policy, his airborne theory provided a medical rationale for opposition to the quarantines imposed against Indian shipping from 1866. Nevertheless, when the government realized that its position had become untenable, it began to distance itself from Bryden and to solicit advice from other doctors in India and elsewhere. This may explain why Bryden became depressed towards the end of his career. He also suffered from Bright's disease, a kidney complaint which caused his retirement from the medical service and his return to England in August 1880. He died in Upper Norwood, London, from kidney failure on 18 November of that year, leaving a wife, Grace Edith Bryden, and three young children. He was buried in Norwood cemetery on 22 November.

Bryden was said to have been a sensitive and retiring man, and he was greatly esteemed for his selfless devotion to duty and breadth of knowledge. Although discredited towards the end of his career, he was considered by many of his Indian colleagues to have been a statistician and medical thinker of the first rank.   MARK HARRISON

Sources *The Lancet* (4 Dec 1880), 915–16 · D. G. Crawford, ed., *Roll of the Indian Medical Service, 1615–1930* (1930) · M. Harrison, *Public health in British India: Anglo-Indian preventive medicine, 1859–1914* (1994) · J. L.

Bryden, *Reports bringing up the statistical history of the European army in India … to 1876* (1878), 313 · J. L. Bryden, *The cholera history of 1875 and 1876* (1878) · CGPLA Eng. & Wales (1881)

Wealth at death under £3000: probate, 22 Feb 1881, CGPLA Eng. & Wales

Brydges [née Stanley], **Anne**, Lady Chandos [*other married name* Anne Touchet, countess of Castlehaven] (**1580–1647**), noblewoman, was born in May 1580, the first of three daughters of Ferdinando *Stanley, Lord Strange, later fifth earl of Derby (1559?–1594), and his wife, Alice (1559–1637), daughter of Sir John Spencer of Althorpe and Katherine Kytson. Six years after the untimely death of her father, her mother married Thomas *Egerton (1540–1617), lord keeper to Elizabeth I and later lord chancellor to James I, who also created him Baron Ellesmere and Viscount Brackley. On behalf of Anne's family, Ellesmere waged a lengthy lawsuit against the sixth earl of Derby, Ferdinando's brother William, over property, particularly the Isle of Man, which after a protracted battle passed in 1609 to Earl William and his wife, Elizabeth de Vere. As the eldest daughter, Anne Stanley received £8000 and property in settlement.

Through her mother and sisters Anne was connected to some of the most powerful families in England. Her sister Frances married John Egerton, later first earl of Bridgewater, son of their stepfather Lord Ellesmere, and her sister Elizabeth married Henry Hastings, later fifth earl of Huntingdon. Despite rumours as early as 1603 that Anne had married Grey Brydges, fifth Baron Chandos (c.1579–1621), a man said to be as profligate as she was, the generally accepted date for the union is 28 February 1608. The marriage produced six children: Robert, who died in infancy; George (1620–1652), who succeeded as sixth baron; William (1621–1676), who succeeded as seventh baron on his brother's death; Elizabeth (1614/15–1679), later countess of Castlehaven; Frances, who married Edward Fortescue; and Anne, whose married name may have been Torteson.

In 1621 Chandos died in Germany, and on 22 July 1624, at her mother's estate at Harefield in Middlesex, Anne made a disastrous marriage with Mervin *Touchet, second earl of Castlehaven (1593–1631). The year before this marriage Touchet's niece Lucy, daughter to his sister Lady Eleanor Davies (afterwards Douglas) and her husband Sir John Davies, had been married at age eleven to Ferdinando Hastings, nephew to Anne. These marriages were followed by the marriage of Anne's daughter Elizabeth Brydges, then aged thirteen, to Castlehaven's son and ostensible heir, James Touchet, who in 1631 charged his father before Charles I with depravity involving Anne and her daughter, his wife. Both women gave deposition at the subsequent trials of Castlehaven and two of his servants, Lawrence (or Florence) FitzPatrick and Giles Brodway; all three defendants were executed for sodomy and for the rape and sexual abuse of Anne and her daughter Elizabeth.

Although Castlehaven and one of his servants alleged that the countess and her daughter were complicitous, it is unclear why the two women required pardons from the king; however, Alice, countess dowager of Derby, took custody of the remaining Brydges children but delayed reconciliation with Anne and Elizabeth until the pardons were granted. Anne was also publicly labelled Jezebel and 'A Lye Satan' in an anagram by Lady Eleanor, Castlehaven's sister, who blamed the scandal on Anne and all the Derby women.

After the execution of her husband Anne resumed the title of Lady Chandos and lived quietly either at her younger son's estate at Heydons in Middlesex or at her mother's estate at Harefield, which she inherited in 1637. She died at Ruislip in October 1647, and was buried at the Harefield estate later in the month.

MARY ANN O'DONNELL

Sources C. B. Herrup, *A house in gross disorder: sex, law, and the 2nd earl of Castlehaven* (1999) · CSP dom., 1631–3 · miscellaneous documents, incl. brief summary of the Castlehaven trial, 1631, Hunt. L., Huntington MS, EL 7979 · brief account of the beginning of the Castlehaven trial and a list of the Lords hearing the case, 25 April 1631, Hunt. L., Huntington MS, HA legal box 5 (2) · *The arraignment and conviction of Mervin, Lord Audley, earl of Castlehaven, (who was by 26 peers of the realm found guilty of committing rapine and sodomy) at Westminster, on Monday, April 25, 1631 (1642/3) · The trial of the Lord Audley, earl of Castlehaven, for inhumanely causing his own wife to be ravished, and for buggery (1679) · The second and last part of impotency &c. debated, vol II, containing: the trial of Mervin, Lord Audley, earl of Castlehaven, for sodomy and a rape, Anno 1631 (1715) · State trials, 3.401–26 · E. Davies, *Woe to the house* (Amsterdam, 1633) · DNB, 'Stanley, Ferdinando', 'Egerton, Thomas', 'Touchet, James', 'Brydges, Grey', 'Spencer, Robert', 'Kytson, Sir Thomas' · GEC, *Peerage*, new edn, vols. 1, 14 · Burke, *Peerage* (1999) · J. P. Collier, ed., *The Egerton papers*, CS, 12 (1840) · W. Ffarington, *The Derby household books*, ed. F. R. Raines, Chetham Society, 31 (1853)
Archives BL, Egerton papers, papers relating to the trial · Hunt. L., Ellesmere papers; Hastings papers
Likenesses W. P. Sherlock, engraving (after tomb by M. Colt), NPG · portrait, Church of St Mary, Harefield, Middlesex

Brydges, Cassandra, duchess of Chandos. *See* Willoughby, Cassandra (1670–1735).

Brydges, Edmund, second Baron Chandos (*d.* 1573), soldier, was the eldest son of John *Brydges, first Baron Chandos (1492–1557), and Elizabeth (*d.* 1559), daughter of Edmund Grey, ninth Baron Grey of Wilton. Well established by the beginning of the fifteenth century, the Brydges family held the majority of its land in Gloucestershire, centred about the castle and manor of Sudeley. Edmund was one of the army that besieged Boulogne in 1544, and a participant in Protector Somerset's victory over the Scots at the battle of Pinkie in September 1547, when he was created a knight-banneret. However, his main services to the crown were performed as a leading member of the Gloucestershire nobility. Before inheriting his father's title in April 1557 he sat as an MP, first for Wootton Basset in 1545 and latterly in 1553 as one of the knights for the county of Gloucestershire. From 1547 until his death he served as justice of the peace for both Gloucestershire and Wiltshire, and in 1559 he was appointed lord lieutenant of Gloucestershire. In January 1572 he sat on the jury that tried the fourth duke of Norfolk for treason and five months later received the Order of the Garter.

Brydges married, before 1548, Dorothy (1529/30–1605),

fifth daughter and coheir of Edmund, first Baron Bray, with whom he had at least two sons and two daughters. At his death on 11 or 12 March 1573 he bequeathed the bulk of his much expanded estate, including lands in Wiltshire and Worcestershire, to his eldest son, Giles. As third Baron Chandos, **Giles Brydges** (1548–1594) continued the role of his father as a central figure in the administration of Gloucestershire. MP for Cricklade in 1571 and then for Gloucestershire in 1572, Giles participated in a variety of commissions concerned with recusancy, ecclesiastical abuses, and local disorder. He was appointed lord lieutenant of Gloucestershire in 1586 and sat on the council in the marches of Wales from 1590. The queen visited him at Sudeley in 1576 and 1592. Brydges married Frances (*d.* 1623), fifth daughter of Edward Clinton, first earl of Lincoln, but he had no heirs with her and it was his younger brother William who succeeded to the title upon his death on 21 February 1594. Like his father, he was buried at Sudeley.

LUKE MACMAHON

Sources LP Henry VIII · HoP, *Commons, 1509–58*, 1.531 · HoP, *Commons, 1558–1603*, 1.508 · GEC, *Peerage*, 3.126–7 · CSP dom., 1547–80
Likenesses H. Custodis, oils (Giles Brydges), Woburn Abbey, Bedfordshire

Brydges, Sir (Samuel) Egerton, first baronet, styled thirteenth Baron Chandos (1762–1837), writer and genealogist, was born at Wootton Court, Wootton, between Canterbury and Dover, on 30 November 1762, the eighth child of Edward Bridges (or Brydges; 1712–1780) and his wife, Jemima (1728–1809), daughter of William Egerton, prebendary of Canterbury and chancellor of Hereford. Sir John William Head Brydges (1764–1839), MP for Coleraine, was his younger brother. He was educated at Maidstone School (1771–5), King's School, Canterbury (1775–80), and Queens' College, Cambridge (October 1780–Christmas 1782). He left without taking a degree, preferring the study of poetry in seclusion from his contemporaries. He entered the Middle Temple, London, in 1782 and was called to the bar in 1787, but never practised. On 24 January 1786 he married Elizabeth Byrche (1766/7–1796), the only surviving daughter and heir of the Revd William Dejovas Byrche of Canterbury, 'much too early', according to his autobiography (Brydges, 1.15) which otherwise ignores his wives. The couple had two sons and three daughters: Thomas Barrett (1789–1834), colonel in the Grenadier Guards; John William Egerton (1791–1858), of the dragoons; Elizabeth Jemima; Jemima Anne Deborah (1793–1822), who later married the poet Edward *Quillinan (1791–1851); and Charlotte Catherine (*b.* 1796). Brydges and his wife moved to Hampshire to be near his sister, Ann Lefroy, Jane Austen's favourite mentor; the Austens were distant relatives.

An interest in topography and antiquities resulted in *The Topographer*, edited by Brydges and Stebbing Shaw between 1789 and 1791, and his own *Topographical Miscellanies* (1792). He was elected a fellow of the Society of Antiquaries in 1795. After living briefly in London he bought and restored at great expense Denton Court, near his birthplace, to which he retired in 1792 to devote himself to literature and genealogy. Following the death of his wife on 30 July 1796, he married, on 15 September, Mary, daughter of the Revd William Robinson, rector of Burfield, Berkshire. They had five sons and five daughters: Grey Matthew (1797–1812), midshipman; Edward William George (1800–1816); Egerton Anthony (1802–1849); Anthony Rokeby (*b.* 1803); Ferdinand Stanley Head (1804–1863); Anne Mary (*b.* 1799); Mary Jane (*b.* 1805); Ellen (*b.* 1808); Frances Isabella (*b.* 1810); and Jane Grey.

Through his mother, a descendant of lord chancellors Hardwicke and Egerton, Brydges was related to many noble houses and liked to claim he had a better right to the throne of England than the current incumbent. In October 1789 he persuaded his elder brother the Revd Edward Tymewell Brydges (1749–1807) to claim the recently extinct barony of Chandos. The case began before the committee of privileges of the House of Lords on 1 June 1790 and lasted until June 1803, when the lords resolved that the claim to the title had not been proven. The barony of Chandos had been created in 1554 and, after descending through the male lines of the two eldest sons, had become extinct in 1789. Edward Tymewell Brydges claimed to be the descendant of the third son, Anthony, of the first baron through an Edward Bridges of Maidstone (*bap.* 25 March 1603), allegedly Anthony's grandson. There were grounds, however, for believing that Egerton Brydges and his brother were really descended from an obscure family of yeomen and grocers who had lived at Harbledown, near Canterbury, quite unconnected with the Chandos family. There were also suspicions that crucial entries in parish registers—reproduced by R. H. Goodsall in *Archaeologia Cantiana* (77, 1962, 1–26)—were insertions, though no direct accusations were ever made. The Chandos case was thoroughly investigated in 1834 by George Beltz, Lancaster herald, who concurred that the claim was not well founded.

Brydges was publicly humiliated but never ceased to maintain the justness of the claim, though he never appealed to the law courts. After the death of his brother, who left no male heir, Egerton Brydges styled himself '*Per legem terrae*, Baron Chandos' and even bought the ruined Sudeley Castle in Gloucestershire. In 1808 he accepted with considerable delight the knighthood of the Swedish order of St Joachim, a bogus distinction. He henceforth wrote the letters K. J. after his name and improperly styled himself Sir; he was created an English baronet in 1814 after intense pressure. His genealogical investigations led him to commence in 1806 an augmented edition of Collins's *Peerage of England*, published in 1812 in nine volumes. In 1825 he published *Stemmata illustria*, charting his presumed descent from Charlemagne, and in 1831 wrote *Lex terrae: a Discussion of the Law of England Regarding Claims of Inheritable Rights of Peerage* to prove that he was not bound by the peers' decision.

But literature was Brydges' first love. His *Sonnets and other Poems* was published in 1785 to a lukewarm reception, causing six years of depression; an enlarged fourth edition appeared as *Poems* in 1807 (repr., 1978). Throughout his life he suffered from 'morbid sensitiveness' (Brydges, 1.ix) due to the utter neglect his poetry received. Convinced of his own talents, he poured out a stream of books and articles in praise of his literary heroes, such as Milton and Gray, and attacking his own critics. His novels, *Mary De-Clifford* (1792) and *Arthur Fitz-Albini* (1798), fared better. The latter was semi-autobiographical and deeply upset his country neighbours, those 'book-hating squires' (ibid., 1.87), who recognized themselves. His unpopularity, however, was probably more connected to his inability to manage his estates; he was permanently in debt, despite inheriting vast properties from both parents and his wives.

Brydges was enormously productive in republishing long-forgotten works of literature, particularly of the Tudor period. He disparaged these achievements, but his real talent rested in that field. He produced an enlarged edition of Edward Phillips's *Theatrum poetarum anglicanorum* (1800); '*Censura literaria*', containing titles, abstracts, and opinions of old English books, with original disquisitions, articles of biography, and other literary antiquities (10 vols., 1805–9); *British Bibliographer*, with Joseph Haslewood (4 vols., 1810–14); '*Restituta*', or, *Titles, Extracts, and Characters of Old Books in English Literature Revived* (4 vols., 1814–16); and *Excerpta Tudoriana* (2 vols., 1814–18).

Brydges, who possessed a fine library, became a founder member of that exclusive bibliographical society, the Roxburghe Club, in 1812. In October 1810 he had moved to Lee Priory, Ickham, near Canterbury, the residence of his eldest son, where in 1813 he established a private printing press with a compositor and pressman from the firm of Bensleys. Brydges provided 'copy', while the printers made what profits they could. Print-runs were purposely small, and copies were sold at high prices; their quality compares favourably with the products of the Strawberry Hill press. Brydges rendered an important service to English literature by reprinting over thirty rare works, chiefly poetical, including poems of Nicholas Breton, William Browne, Raleigh, Margaret, duchess of Newcastle, and Robert Greene. He also reprinted Lord Brook's *Life of Sir Philip Sydney* and the duchess of Newcastle's *Autobiography*, and himself contributed *The Sylvan Wanderer* (3 vols., 1813–21) and a poem, *Bertram* (1814). Considerable expense was incurred, and the press was given up in 1823.

In 1812 Brydges was elected MP for Maidstone after defeating a whig; unsuccessful attempts elsewhere are related in his novel *Arthur Fitz-Albini*. He seldom spoke, though he assisted with the Poor Law Act of 1817 and helped amend the Copyright Bill to extend authors' rights. Failing to gain re-election in 1818 and in serious financial embarrassment, he moved to Europe. He travelled to Paris and Switzerland and toured Italy between 1819 and 1821 before settling permanently near Geneva. His literary urges continued unabated with *Res literariæ* (3 vols., 1821–2), *The Anti-Critic* (1822), *Polyanthea librorum vetustiorum* (1822), *Cimelia* (1823), *An Impartial Portrait of Lord Byron* (1824), *The Anglo-Genevan Critical Journal for 1831*, *The Lake of Geneva: a Poem* (1832), and countless tracts on the peerage. His last years were peaceful and perhaps happier than before, but he never shook off his melancholia nor a sense of injustice. His *Recollections of Foreign Travel* (2 vols., 1825) contain many personal opinions, while the self-serving but entertaining *Autobiography, Times, Opinions, and Contemporaries of Sir Egerton Brydges* (2 vols., 1834) is an appropriate summit to his career.

Brydges' only return to England was from June 1826 to October 1828 in a vain attempt to sort out his affairs. He was swindled many times over his estates but refused to take personal care of them, and Denton Court became dilapidated and was demolished in 1822. His sons and former son-in-law Edward Quillinan devised a fraudulent scheme to rescue their father's fortune, and upon its discovery the family was disgraced. Thomas, his eldest son, fled to France and died in poverty; Egerton Anthony, now rector of Denton, was thrown into the Fleet for debt and only released as a lunatic; Quillinan, who later married Wordsworth's daughter, was gravely compromised. Brydges' own responsibility is unclear.

Egerton Brydges died at Campagne Gros Jean, near Geneva, on 8 September 1837 and was buried in Geneva. None of Brydges' sons married; the baronetcy passed to John William Egerton, then to Ferdinand Stanley Head, becoming extinct on his death in 1863. K. A. MANLEY

Sources E. Brydges, *The autobiography, times, opinions, and contemporaries of Sir Egerton Brydges*, 2 vols. (1834) · *Collins peerage of England: genealogical, biographical and historical*, ed. E. Brydges, 9 vols. (1812), vol. 6, pp. 704–40 · M. K. Woodworth, *The literary career of Sir Samuel Egerton Brydges* (1935) · J. B. Nichol, *GM*, 2nd ser., 8 (1837), 534–9 · G. F. Beltz, *A review of the Chandos peerage case* (1834) · R. H. Goodsall, 'Lee Priory and the Brydges circle', *Archaeologia Cantiana*, 77 (1962), 1–26 · W. P. Jones, 'New light on Sir Samuel Egerton Brydges', *Harvard Library Bulletin*, 11 (1957), 102–16 · B. Murphy and R. G. Thorne, 'Brydges, Samuel Egerton (1762–1837)', HoP, *Commons, 1790–1820* [draft] · *GM*, 1st ser., 66 (1796), 705
Archives Bodl. Oxf., corresp.; letterbook; notebook · Boston PL, corresp. and papers · Harvard U., Houghton L., corresp. and papers · Hunt. L., letters; literary MSS · London Library, corresp. and papers · NL Scot., papers relating to a baronetage in Scotland · NRA, priv. coll., corresp. · U. Birm. L., special collections department, sonnets and writings · Yale U., Beinecke L., corresp.; journal; memoranda book; literary MSS | Hants. RO, Bolton MSS · NL Scot., letters to J. G. Lockhart · V&A NAL, letters to Alexander Dyce and Pickering · Yale U., Beinecke L., papers relating to poor laws, incl. corresp. with Montagu Pennington · Yale U., Beinecke L., letters to John Warwick
Likenesses B. Burnell, chalk drawing, 1817, NPG · Carloni, portrait, 1819, repro. in Brydges, *Autobiography*, frontispiece · G. B. Nocchi, line engraving, 1820 (after P. Carloni), BM, NPG · F. Danby, etching, 1834, NPG; repro. in Brydges, *Autobiography*, frontispiece · F. Danby, drawing, V&A · D. Maclise, lithograph, NPG; repro. in *Fraser's Magazine* (1834)

Brydges, George, sixth Baron Chandos (1620–1655), royalist nobleman, was born on 9 August 1620, presumably at Sudeley Castle, the eldest son of Grey *Brydges, fifth Baron Chandos (1578/9–1621), and his wife, Anne *Brydges (1580–1647), daughter of Ferdinando Stanley, fifth earl of Derby. His childhood was hardly stable; his father died in 1621 and his mother married Mervin *Touchet, the notorious second earl of Castlehaven. Whether the young Chandos was ever exposed to the depravities of their

household, as his sister Elizabeth was, is unknown. On 14 December 1637 he married Susan Montagu (1621?–1652), daughter of Henry *Montagu, first earl of Manchester, with whom he had three daughters. He thereby added estates in Middlesex to his vast Gloucestershire and Wiltshire patrimony.

Because Chandos was the only resident peer in Gloucestershire, his allegiance was hotly sought in the slide to civil war. Chandos supported some measures of the Long Parliament in the Lords, including giving the Commons control of the militia, and on 10 February 1642 he was named lord lieutenant of Gloucestershire. By July, however, he was in the king's camp. On 15 August he tried to execute the commission of array at Cirencester but badly misjudged the local mood. Over a thousand men blockaded the streets against horsemen and, after he was let in with a few followers, harried him into swearing to uphold the privileges of parliament. Next day his Cotswold allies smuggled him away, fearing for his life. This ended any possibility of a unified command under local leadership in Gloucestershire.

In late 1642 Chandos raised a horse regiment, which he commanded for eighteen months. He became notorious for putting his men to hard service and narrowly cheated death several times. After three horses had been shot under him charging parliamentarian lines at the first battle of Newbury on 21 September 1643, the king offered him an earldom but he 'modestly declined till it might please God to restore his Majesty to the peaceable enjoyment of his rights' (Dugdale, 3.396). Chandos was the archetypal cavalier: brave and dashing, but reckless, unstable, quarrelsome, and politically naïve. He lost out to Sir William Vavasour in the choice of a county commander-in-chief in early 1644; instead he garrisoned Sudeley. Vavasour's command soon collapsed, but, despite much local and court support, Chandos was again passed over as local deputy in Prince Rupert's presidency of south Wales in favour of Nicholas Mynne, like Vavasour an experienced outsider. Deeply disillusioned, he slipped away from Oxford and surrendered to black rod on 6 June—although he may have secured a pass as early as 1 April.

Chandos spent the next seven years trying to minimize his losses. Sudeley, which had been ransacked by local parliamentarians in January 1643, was sacked by Waller in June 1644; it was garrisoned again in 1648, before finally being slighted, at Chandos's expense, by March 1650. Between 1644 and 1651 Chandos fought this and the composition process through the parliamentary committees, finally compounding for £3976. Despite his increased wariness of committing himself, royalist hopes for Gloucestershire soon focused on him again and he was briefly imprisoned in April 1651 when the plot in which he had become involved was betrayed to the government.

On 13 May 1652, a month after his wife's burial, Chandos killed Colonel Henry Compton in a duel on Putney Heath. He briefly fled to France but, to save his estates, returned to stand trial. He and his second, Lord Arundel of Wardour, were convicted of manslaughter on 17 May 1653 in upper bench, pleaded benefit of clergy, and were burned in the hand. They were the only peers ever to suffer this indignity. In the interim, on 17 January 1653, Chandos had married Jane Savage (d. 1676), daughter of John Savage, Earl Rivers, and they had at least two daughters. His will settled most of his lands on Jane and left his dull and pious parliamentarian brother and heir, William, little more than the title. Perhaps appropriately his sudden death near Covent Garden in London, from smallpox, in February 1655, effectively prevented any Gloucestershire participation in Penruddock's rising.

ANDREW WARMINGTON

Sources GEC, *Peerage*, new edn, vol. 3 · W. Dugdale, *The baronage of England*, 2 vols. (1675–6) · *CSP dom.*, 1641–3; 1649–51; 1655 · M. A. E. Green, ed., *Calendar of the proceedings of the committee for compounding … 1643–1660*, 5 vols., PRO (1889–92) · A letter sent to a worthy member … concerning the Lord Shandois coming to Cisseter, 1642, BL, E 113 (6) · J. Corbet, 'An historicall relation of the military government of Gloucester', *Bibliotheca Gloucestrensis*, ed. [J. Washbourne], 1 (privately printed, Gloucester, 1823), 1–152 · Clarendon, *Hist. rebellion* · G. A. Harrison, 'Royalist organisation in Gloucestershire and Bristol, 1642–1646', MA diss., University of Manchester, 1961 · *JHL*, 5–6 (1642–4) · *DNB* · E. Dent, *Annals of Winchcombe and Sudeley* (1877) · the arraignment of Mervyn, Lord Audley, earl of Castlehaven … (1643), BL, E 84 (2) · R. Atkyns, *The vindication of Richard Atkyns*, ed. P. Young (1967)
Likenesses C. Jansen, oils, c.1642, priv. coll.; repro. in E. Delt, *Annals of Winchcombe and Sudeley* (1872)
Wealth at death estate £3120 p. a. in 1642, but less at time of death; most estates to widow; little more than title to brother and heir

Brydges, Giles, third Baron Chandos (1548–1594). *See under* Brydges, Edmund, second Baron Chandos (d. 1573).

Brydges, Grey, fifth Baron Chandos (1578/9–1621), courtier and landowner, was the son of William Brydges, fourth Baron Chandos (d. 1602), and his wife, Mary Hopton (d. 1624), daughter of Owen *Hopton. He was presumably born at the family seat at Sudeley, Gloucestershire. He matriculated from Exeter College, Oxford, on 1 December 1592, aged thirteen.

Brydges served as MP for Cricklade, Wiltshire, in the parliament of 1597–8. In February 1601 he was briefly imprisoned in the Fleet prison with Henry Cuffe and five others for suspected complicity in the Essex rebellion. His father had, like Grey, been at Essex House on the morning of the rebellion but was not imprisoned and was even appointed to the commission that tried Essex. Grey Brydges succeeded to the barony on his father's death on 18 November 1602. He inherited a large estate in the Cotswolds and his father's feuds, notably that against Grey's cousin Elizabeth Brydges, daughter and heir of Giles *Brydges, third Baron Chandos [see under Brydges, Edmund], over parts of the inheritance. In June 1602 Grey had assaulted her at a conference called to resolve matters. A proposal to settle matters by their marrying fell through when he inherited the title. The quarrel was apparently composed by December but the new Lord Chandos vented his wrath on Elizabeth again after she married Sir John Kennedy, a Scottish favourite of James I, in 1603. He declined to help her after her marriage ended violently in 1609, and she ultimately died in poverty.

Chandos was among the lords of the council who wrote to inform the commissioners at Breame on 28 March 1603 of King James's accession. Four months later he was one of four who were 'proposed to be brought in' to the privy council over the Bye plot to put Arabella Stuart on the throne. The charge seems to have been groundless, though it gave Henry Berkeley, Lord Berkeley, another great Gloucestershire magnate, the opportunity to step in and acquire the lord lieutenancy to the county that Chandos had been expecting in succession to his father. By a compromise, they were made joint lord lieutenants; Chandos continued as sole lieutenant after Berkeley's death in 1613. None the less, King James was fond of Chandos and bestowed other honours on him. He was named a knight of the Bath in January 1605 when Prince Charles was created duke of York and was among the courtiers created MA by the University of Oxford upon the king's visit on 30 August 1605. He had been admitted an honorary member of the Middle Temple a year before. On 2 July 1609 Chandos was granted the keepership of Ditton Park in Buckinghamshire for life, a place he sold on to Secretary Winwood in 1614.

Chandos's life was not simply that of a courtier. It is recorded that:

> having an ample fortune, [he] was a noble house keeper. By a winning behaviour, he contracted so great an interest in Gloucestershire (where he kept open house three days every week) and had such numerous attendants when he came to Court, that he was commonly called the King of Cotswold. (Nichols, 1.477)

Between 1605 and 1608 he was at odds with Sir Thomas Lowe, alderman of London, over a manor in Wiltshire which Chandos unscrupulously seized when Lowe was lord mayor and unable to leave London. On 28 February 1608 Chandos married Lady Anne Stanley [see Brydges, Anne (1580–1647)], daughter and coheir of Ferdinando *Stanley, fifth earl of Derby. They had two or three daughters, Elizabeth, Frances, and possibly Anne, and two sons who in turn succeeded Chandos: George *Brydges, the sixth baron (1620–1655), and William, the seventh baron (d. 1676). Another son, named after his friend Robert Cecil, earl of Salisbury, died in infancy in 1611. Like his father, Chandos was the patron of a company of players, who appeared in Norwich in 1604 and 1609 and in Somerton in 1605 and 1606, and were last recorded in 1610. He also appeared in tournaments and masques at court, including Ben Jonson's *Challenge at Tilt at a Marriage* in March 1614. From 1610 Chandos spent increasing amounts of time abroad. In that year he went with Edward, Lord Herbert of Cherbury, to join the English reinforcements to the Dutch army besieging Juliers, though he is not known to have taken part in the fighting. In June 1611 he was at Orléans and on 23 July 1612 it was reported that he had gone to 'the Spa' to take the waters—presumably Spa in the Spanish Netherlands. On 9 September 1613 court gossip was that he was to fight a duel with Lord Hay, one of the king's Scottish minions. There was also talk on 14 June 1616 of his being granted the presidency of the council in the marches of Wales, but in the event he lost out to Lord Gerard. On 8 November 1617 he was appointed to receive the Muscovite ambassadors at court. Next year, still in poor health, he tried the waters at Newenham Mills, Warwickshire. His last known appearance at court was at Queen Anne's funeral on 13 May 1619.

Some authorities ascribe to Chandos the authorship of *Horae subsecivae*, a work published in 1620 and apparently written about 1615, though others attribute it to Gilbert or William Cavendish, sons of the duke of Devonshire. The bulk of *Horae subsecivae* is a well written, if rather conventional, series of observations on such characteristics as ambition, affectation, and self-will and issues like relations between masters and servants and the country life. The author—whose identity was also unknown to the publisher—was undoubtedly from the upper landed gentry and his eulogy of traditional hospitality makes Chandos a possible candidate, as do the seventeenth-century hands that identify him as the author on some copies. Against his candidature are his failing health in these years, that the author visited Rome, which Chandos is not known to have done, and the fact that his own behaviour over the years had shown precious few of the virtues on which the author discoursed so eloquently.

Chandos died on 10 August 1621; according to Lucy, countess of Bedford, this was 'hastened by drinking Spa water' (*CSP dom.*, 1619–23, 286). While reports differ as to whether he died at Spa itself, in his coach on his way home, or at Sudeley, the firmest account, confirmed by the report of Sir William Trumbull, the agent at Brussels, is that he did indeed die at Spa. His body was taken back to England, and although he is recorded as having been buried at Winchcombe he was in fact buried at Sudeley in the family chapel.

Chandos was succeeded by his elder son, George, aged one year and one day at his father's death, who was brought up by his maternal grandmother, Alice, dowager countess of Derby. The high living of Chandos and his wife left the latter with the relatively modest income for a woman of her status of £800 per annum. Three years later she married Mervin *Touchet, second earl of Castlehaven, a superficially advantageous match bringing together her high status and his wealth, followed by the marriage of her elder daughter, Elizabeth, at the age of thirteen to Castlehaven's heir, James *Touchet, Lord Audley (later third earl of Castlehaven). However, the accusations and counter-accusations of sexual and social disorder within the Castlehaven household were to bring social disgrace to the women, both branded as adulteresses, and death to the earl, convicted of sodomy and acting as an accessory in the rape of his wife.   ANDREW WARMINGTON

Sources *CSP dom.*, 1598–1601; 1603–23; addenda, 1580–1625 • GEC, *Peerage* • J. Nichols, *The progresses, processions, and magnificent festivities of King James I, his royal consort, family and court*, 4 vols. (1828) • *Horae subsecivae* (1620) • Foster, *Alum. Oxon.* • R. C. Gabriel, 'Bridges, Gray', HoP, *Commons, 1558–1603* • W. J. Jones, 'Brydges, William', HoP, *Commons, 1558–1603* • C. Williams, *The history of Sudeley Castle* (1791) • *An autobiography of Edward, Lord Herbert of Cherbury*, ed. S. Lee (1906) • A. Douglas and P. Greenfield, eds., *Records of early English drama: Cumberland, Westmorland and Gloucestershire* (1986) • D. Galloway, ed., *Records of early English drama: Norwich, 1540–1642* (1984) • J. Stokes and R. J. Alexander, eds., *Records of early English drama: Somerset*, 2 vols. (1996) • E. Lodge, ed., *Illustrations of British history*, 2nd edn, 3 vols. (1969) • private information (2004) [Sudeley archivist] • PRO, State Papers Flanders, 1620–21, SP 77/14 • C. B. Herrup, *A house in gross disorder: sex, law and the 2nd earl of Castlehaven* (1999) • administration, PRO, PROB 6/10, fol. 169r

Wealth at death see administration, PRO, PROB 6/10, fol. 169r

Brydges, Sir Harford Jones, first baronet (1764–1847), diplomatist and author, was the son of Harford Jones of Presteigne and his wife, Winifred, daughter of Richard Hooper of the Whittern, Herefordshire. He was born on 12 January 1764. On 16 February 1796 he married Sarah, eldest daughter of Sir Henry Gott of Newland Park, Buckinghamshire, and widow of Robert Whitcomb, of the Whittern; they had one son and two daughters. In commemoration of his descent, through his maternal grandmother, from the family of Brydges of Old Colwall, Herefordshire, he assumed, by royal signature, dated 4 May 1826, the additional name of Brydges.

Early in life Jones entered the service of the East India Company, working as assistant and factor at Basrah, 1783–94, and its president in Baghdad, 1798–1806. He acquired great proficiency in oriental languages, and with the assistance of Robert Dundas's patronage he was appointed envoy-extraordinary and minister-plenipotentiary to the court of Persia, where he remained from 1807 to 1811. In 1807 he was created a baronet in recognition of the importance of the mission (Yapp, 47). His main achievement was the Preliminary treaty of 1809 which effectively barred France from the route to India. He began the involvement of British military instructors in the Persian army and he prevented peace between Persia and Russia. On his return from Persia, seeing no immediate prospect of promotion in the service of the East India Company, he severed his connection with it. Throughout life he cherished a warm interest in the welfare both of Persians and Indians. In 1833 he published *The Dynasty of the Kajars, Translated from the Original Persian Manuscript*, in the following year *An account of his majesty's mission to the court of Persia in the years 1807–11, to which is added a brief history of the Wahanby*, and in 1838 a *Letter on the Present State of British Interests and Affairs in Persia*. He pleaded the cause of the emirs of Sind in a letter of 1843 to the court of directors of the East India Company, denouncing the policy of annexation and conquest.

Jones Brydges was 'a man who was underrated both at the time and subsequently' (Yapp, 59). His years in Baghdad changed the direction of British policy in the Middle East and on his Persian mission he proved resourceful and effective. In politics a decided whig, he took an active interest in the election contests of Radnorshire, where he founded a political association known as the Grey Coat Club. On 15 June 1831 he received the honorary degree of DCL from the University of Oxford. In 1832 he was sworn of the privy council, and in 1841 was appointed deputy lieutenant of the county of Hereford. He died at his seat at Boultibrook, near Presteigne, on 17 March 1847.

T. F. HENDERSON, *rev.* H. C. G. MATTHEW

Sir Harford Jones Brydges, first baronet (1764–1847), by Sir Thomas Lawrence, completed 1829

Sources *GM*, 2nd ser., 28 (1847), 86 · *Annual Register* (1847), 219 · M. E. Yapp, *Strategies of British India: Britain, Iran and Afghanistan, 1798–1850* (1980)

Archives BL OIOC, Home misc. series, corresp. relating to India · Herefs. RO, corresp. and papers · NL Wales, letter-books and papers | Balliol Oxf., letters to David Morier · Duke U., Perkins L., letters to James Willis · Leics. RO, letters to Lord Minto [microfilm] · NL Scot., letters to first earl of Minto · priv. coll., corresp. with Lord Elgin · PRO, letters to Stratford Canning, FO 352 · PRO NIre., corresp. with Lord Castlereagh · W. Sussex RO, letters to duke of Richmond

Likenesses T. Lawrence, oils, completed 1829, Kentchurch Court, Herefordshire [*see illus.*]

Brydges, James, first duke of Chandos (1674–1744), politician and patron of music, was born at Dewsall, Herefordshire, on 6 January 1674, the eldest son of James Brydges, eighth Baron Chandos (1642–1714), who held estates in Herefordshire and Radnorshire, and Elizabeth Barnard (1643–1719), who came from a successful merchant family. Having inherited the attributes of both the landed gentry and of merchant bankers, the young James made use of them to achieve a status and a lifestyle that earned him the description 'princely'. He grew up at Dewsall and in London and was educated at Westminster School (1686–90) and New College, Oxford, which he left in 1692 without a degree but having learned to take pleasure in books and music. His gift of £100 to the college helped to pay for its garden quadrangle and ornamental gates. He then went to Wolfenbüttel Academy in northern Germany. Wolfenbüttel was one of the principal towns of the duchy of Brunswick-Wolfenbüttel, adjacent to the electorate of Hanover. There he combined study with making influential acquaintances at the electoral court and engaging in

indiscreet love affairs that led to his recall to England at the end of two years. On 27 February 1696 he married Mary Lake (*bap.* 1668, *d.* 1712), of Cannons, Middlesex, and in 1698, thanks to family influence in the city, he was elected member of parliament for Hereford. His opponent, Sir Thomas Southwell, shrewdly forecast his future as 'a great courtier … who would certainly be a pensioner if once chose Parliament man' (Baker, 19).

Between 1697 and 1702, according to entries in his journal, Brydges tirelessly pursued useful contacts among politicians, businessmen, and courtiers, frequenting the clubs, coffee houses, and theatres in London where these might be found. Meanwhile, he regularly attended as a member meetings of the Royal Society and of the Society of Gentlemen Performers of Music, started to collect paintings, and to invest in promising commercial ventures. In 1703, through connections at court, he secured an appointment as a commissioner to the Admiralty, a post for which he had neither experience nor liking. In 1705, under the patronage of the Marlboroughs, he was made paymaster of the queen's forces, from which he had profited by £600,000 when he resigned in 1713. This was an outstanding amount even at a time when public office was regarded as a legitimate source of profit, though a subsequent scrutiny of his accounts revealed no evidence of wrongdoing.

In 1712 his first wife died, leaving two surviving sons and claims to an estate at Cannons which Brydges promptly bought with his acquired fortune. His ambitions for this were capably supported by his second wife, Cassandra *Willoughby (1670–1735), daughter of his aunt Emma Barnard, whom he married on 4 August 1713, and who, though childless, proved a good stepmother to his sons and an intelligent, equable companion for Brydges himself. Links forged earlier with the electoral court further advanced Brydges' fortunes when George I succeeded to the English throne in 1714. Intending for the moment to remain in the Commons, Brydges obtained an earldom, of Carnarvon, for his father, who died on 16 October 1714 before the patent had passed the great seal; on 19 October the new Lord Chandos was thus created earl of Carnarvon instead. In 1719 he was promoted as duke of Chandos in recognition of his services to the state.

After acquiring Cannons, Chandos determined to emulate other men of importance who were establishing themselves in the public eye by their building projects and affluent lifestyle. At the centre of the estate he established what came to be regarded as the finest house in England. Leading architects including Talman, Gibbs, and Vanbrugh were involved in its design and the finest materials and craftsmen employed to furnish and decorate it. Lord Burlington, foremost arbiter of style at the time, gave Cannons his approval. Among its most striking features were a magnificent marble staircase, a well-stocked library, a picture gallery, and a chapel decorated in baroque style where a choir and orchestra under the direction of Dr Pepusch performed music which included anthems specially composed for the duke by Handel. Household arrangements were elaborate and protocol all-important,

James Brydges, first duke of Chandos (1674–1744), by Michael Dahl

yet ducal hospitality was liberal and Cannons was rarely without guests who enjoyed the modern amenities in the house, meals accompanied by music, and the attractions of well laid out and meticulously maintained grounds guarded by Chelsea pensioners. The poet Pope was one of the few people who remained unimpressed, condemning 'Timon's Villa' as the epitome of tastelessness and misspent wealth, though Chandos chose to regard this criticism as unintentional (Pope).

As well as Cannons, Chandos rebuilt the parish church of St Lawrence, at Little Stanmore, Middlesex, where he and his household worshipped regularly and where he had erected for himself and his two wives a marble tomb designed and carved by Grinling Gibbons. After first renting town houses Chandos bought Ormond House in St James's Square, gave it his own name and refurbished it to suit his needs. When the fashionable world moved west he acquired land in Cavendish Square and had two houses built there for himself and his son. In 1726 he bought Shaw Hall near Newbury to use as a country retreat and a stopping place when he journeyed to Bath and the west. Chandos's third wife, Lydia, found Shaw more homely

than their London dwellings and chose to spend her last years there after her husband's death. Finally, Chandos employed James Wood to rebuild and modernize four houses at Bath with the idea of providing superior lodgings for himself and others visiting the spa.

Chandos had by now settled into a life typical of his class, busying himself with the care of his family and his estates but also concerned with public duties as lord lieutenant of Herefordshire and Radnor, governor of the Charterhouse and of the Foundling Hospital, chancellor of St Andrews University, ranger of Enfield Chace, and clerk of the hanaper office. At the same time he was following the fashion for dabbling in any business that held the slightest promise of gain. The Sun Life Assurance Company, the York Buildings Water Supply Company, and shares in the Mississippi and Africa companies were sound prospects in view of contemporary residential developments in London and commercial expansion overseas, but his plans to turn Bridgwater into a rival port to Bristol, to develop land in New York state and Nova Scotia, and to found an oyster fishery off the Essex coast came to nought and he got little return for money he put into mining projects and experiments with various ores. The duke was clearly more naïve than most in his trust of fellow businessmen, and according to Onslow's epitaph 'was a bubble to every project and a dupe to men that nobody else almost would keep company with' (Baker, 337). He lost money when the South Sea Company collapsed in 1720 and thereafter was always anxious about his finances, especially as his second son (his elder son died in 1717) and heir, Henry, marquess of Carnarvon, was an irresponsible spendthrift.

The death of Duchess Cassandra in 1735 saddened Chandos deeply and that he remarried in 1736 was an indication of his constant need for companionship and reassurance. His bride was Lydia Catharina (*bap.* 1693, *d.* 1750), widow of Sir Thomas Davall (*d.* 1714) and daughter of John Vanhatten, from a London mercantile background; she was an established member of the Chandos circle. During his remaining years, while continuing to supervise his estates, entertain at Cannons, and visit members of his family in the west country, he became a prey to fears about his health and the victim of dubious remedies advocated by his doctors and friends.

Chandos died at Cannons on 9 August 1744 after a short illness and was buried on 23 August at the church of St Lawrence, Little Stanmore, in the tomb where his first two wives already rested. His epitaph on the monument and contemporary reports of his death commended his benevolence and humanity; in the 'register', a record of the Brydges family begun by Lady Chandos and continued by the duchesses Cassandra and Lydia, the last named wrote of the generosity, compassion, and unfailing civility of her husband. It is indeed unlikely that the duke ever aroused lasting resentment, for if shaken out of his habitual goodwill he was always quick to make amends. On the unique occasion when anger over an insult to his father drove him to fight a duel, he disarmed his opponent then offered his apologies and an invitation to dine that evening. He exploited patronage to further his career, but he became a generous patron in his turn and readily gave financial support to his family and dependants and secured appointments for them. He was called 'princely' but behind his apparent stateliness there was no inclination to dominate but rather an anxiety to please and to serve, and a modesty that was reflected in his wish for a simple and unceremonious funeral. Cannons was sold and pulled down in 1747–8 and his other building projects have decayed or been changed, but his voluminous correspondence remains as evidence of his conscientiousness, his enthusiasms, and his capacity for inspiring and sustaining lasting affection and friendships.

JOAN JOHNSON

Sources Hunt. L., Stowe papers • C. H. C. Baker and M. I. Baker, *The life and circumstances of James Brydges, first duke of Chandos, patron of the liberal arts* (1949) • J. Johnson, *Excellent Cassandra: the life and times of the duchess of Chandos* (1982) • J. Johnson, *Princely Chandos: the life of James Brydges, 1st duke of Chandos* (1984) • J. M. Beattie, *The English court in the reign of George I* (1967) • C. Gildon, *The vision* (1718) • S. Humphreys, *Cannons* (1728) • A. Pope, *Epistle to Lord Burlington: on the use of riches* (1731) • G. Beard, *Craftsmen and interior decoration in England, 1660–1820* (1981) • M. Girouard, *Social life in the English country house* (1981) • J. Lees-Milne, *English country houses, 1638–1715* (1970) • B. S. Allen, *Tides in English taste, 1619–1800* (1969) • J. Summerson, *Georgian London*, rev. edn (1962) • IGI

Archives Herefs. RO • Hunt. L., papers, incl. commonplace books, corresp., letter-books, etc. • Northants. RO, papers, incl. letter-book | BL, letters to Lord Hardwicke, Add. MSS 35584–35604, *passim* • CUL, letters to Sir Robert Walpole • Glos. RO, Chamberlayne MSS • NA Scot., letters to John Drummond • NA Scot., letters to Sir A. Grant • North London Collegiate School, Stanmore, Cassandra Willoughby letter-book • Shakespeare Birthplace Trust RO, Stratford upon Avon, Stoneleigh MSS

Likenesses G. Kneller, group portrait, oils, 1713 (with family), National Gallery of Canada, Ottawa • G. Gibbons, marble statue on monument, 1717, church of St Lawrence, Little Stanmore, Middlesex • H. van der Myn, oils, after 1719, NPG • J. Wootton, group portrait, oils, 1737, Royal Collection • B. Reading, line engraving, pubd 1820 (after M. Dahl), BM • M. Dahl, oils, Denver Art Museum, Colorado [*see illus.*] • C. F. Zincke, enamel miniature, Buccleuch estates, Selkirk

Wealth at death wealthy: will, Baker and Baker, *Life and circumstances*, 465–8

Brydges, John, first Baron Chandos (1492–1557), landowner and soldier, was born on 9 March 1492 at Coberley, Gloucestershire, the eldest of three sons and three daughters of Sir Giles Brydges (d. 1511), landowner, and his wife, Isabel (fl. c.1475–1511), daughter of Thomas Baynham of Clearwell, Gloucestershire. His younger brother was Thomas *Brydges (d. 1559). Nothing is known about John's education, but presumably this was provided by Sir Edward Darrell, when he became his ward after his father's death.

Soon Brydges received possession of Coberley and the three manors at Blunsdon, Wiltshire. His father's position as knight of the body to Henry VIII proved advantageous to Brydges by providing an entrée at court. In 1513 he served at Thérouanne and Tournai and was knighted about October for his good service. He had married Elizabeth (d. 1559), daughter of Edmund Grey, ninth Baron Grey of Wilton, and his wife, Florence, by 1520. They had

seven sons, including Edmund *Brydges, second Baron Chandos (d. 1573), and three daughters. In 1528 Katherine of Aragon appointed Brydges steward of Beesley, Gloucestershire. He was MP for Gloucestershire in 1529 and JP for Gloucestershire and Wiltshire from 1529. He was of the quorum for Gloucestershire from 1547. He accompanied the king to Calais in October 1532, was appointed knight of the body by 1533, and in 1536 was named, with his brother Thomas Brydges, keeper of Cornbury and Langley parks, near Oxford. By 1539 he was groom of the privy chamber and attended many ceremonial state functions.

Brydges was sheriff of Wiltshire in 1537–8 and of Gloucestershire in 1549–50. He was constable of Sudeley Castle, Gloucestershire, from 1538 to 1542. This, and the stewardship of Winchcombe and the hundreds of Greatstone, Holford, and Kiftsgate in Gloucestershire, was held with his son Edmund Brydges from 1542. In 1536 he was summoned to attend the king with two hundred men against the rebels during the Pilgrimage of Grace. He participated in the 1544 war against France and afterwards became lieutenant of the castle at Boulogne. In 1546 he was promoted to high marshal of Boulogne, though Edward Seymour, earl of Hertford, suggested that Brydges be advised by a more experienced soldier. He became deputy governor and lieutenant of Boulogne in September 1547 and was relied on by his brother-in-law, William *Grey, thirteenth Baron Grey of Wilton. In 1547 he was given Brimsfield and Norton, Wiltshire, for his services and in 1548 he purchased Coberley chantry, Gloucestershire.

Brydges had an intense personality. Sir Thomas Palmer wrote to the duke of Somerset (Hertford) that Brydges was too demanding and even Grey of Wilton complained of his insubordination and disrespect. Brydges, himself, wrote to Somerset from Boulogne in 1548, describing how he had been addicted to the king's service since the cradle. He successfully participated in the defence of Boulogne in 1549 against the French siege, personally led by Henry II.

During the succession crisis after the death of Edward VI, Lady Jane Grey wrote to Brydges and Sir Nicholas Poyntz on 18 July 1553. She asked them to support her against Princess Mary by raising their clienteles, as well as the royal retinue on the crown estates they administered, and to march to Buckinghamshire, 'because we doubt not but this our most laufull possession of the Crowne … is both playnley knowen, and accepted of you, as our most loving subiects' (BL, Harley MS 416, fol. 30r). The lateness of this letter suggests it was an act of desperation. It was unsuccessful. Like his cousin, Richard Brydges [see below], Sir John Brydges was a noted Catholic. With his brother Thomas Brydges he rallied in support of Mary and accompanied her on her triumphal entry into London. He was among Princess Elizabeth's retinue when she entered London to congratulate her sister on 29 July. Lady Brydges attended Mary at her coronation. For his loyalty he was appointed lieutenant of the Tower of London from August 1553 to June 1554 and granted Sudeley Castle.

During Wyatt's rebellion, Brydges threatened to fire on the rebel forces (possibly defying royal orders). This caused Sir Thomas Wyatt to abandon hope of entering London by way of London Bridge and forced him to march via Kingston instead. It had a decisive effect on the collapse of the rebellion. When Wyatt was brought to the Tower, Brydges shouted at him: 'Ohe! thou villayn and unhappie traytour!', and shook him rigorously (Nichols, *Chronicle*, 51–2). Brydges was so moved by the charms of Lady Jane Grey (distantly related to Lady Brydges) while she was in the Tower, that he begged her for a written memento. She gave him her English prayer book, on which she wrote a homily encouraging him to 'live to die' (Froude, 6.185–6). When Elizabeth was in the Tower in early 1554 he was accused of treating her too leniently— she was allowed to walk in the garden and a little boy of four even took flowers to her—and Sir Henry Bedingfield was given her custody in March. This courtesy and gentleness contrasts with his tetchy relations with military colleagues.

Brydges was created first Baron Chandos of Sudeley on 8 April 1554 at the reception of Philip II and was granted the reversion of the monastery of Winchcombe and lands in Sudeley. This elevation was in preparation for Philip's war with France but Chandos did not take part in this. He died at Sudeley Castle on 13 April 1557 and was buried on 3 May at the local church.

Sir Richard Brydges (*c*.1500–1558), landowner and administrator, was born about 1500, the only son of Sir Henry Brydges (*c*.1470–1538/9), landowner and administrator, of Newbury, Berkshire, and his wife, Margery Bedford, a widow, of Newbury. He had a sister. Brydges was admitted to the Middle Temple on 2 November 1518. He frequently sat as MP for Ludgershall and Berkshire between about 1523 and 1558. By 1525 he had married Anne, daughter of Richard Norris of West Shefford, Berkshire; they had no known children. In 1537 he became steward of the lands in Berkshire formerly belonging to Jane Seymour, was JP for Berkshire from 1538 to 1558 and of Wiltshire from 1543 to 1558, and was sheriff of Berkshire and Oxfordshire in 1539–40 and 1554–5. He was keeper of Ludgershall, Wiltshire, from 1539 to 1558 and groom of the privy chamber from about 1539. His first wife having died, Brydges married Jane (*d*. 1593), daughter of Sir William Spencer of Althorp, Northamptonshire, by 1543. They had two sons, Anthony (*b*. 1542/3) and Edmund Brydges, and two daughters. He was in the army that supported Charles V in the Low Countries in 1543 and served during the Boulogne campaign the following year. He was knighted on 19 October 1553, for supporting Mary I. He died on 1 August 1558 and was buried on 9 September in Ludgershall church.   M. M. NORRIS

Sources *LP Henry VIII* · J. A. Froude, *History of England*, 2nd edn, 12 vols. (1858–66), vol. 6 · J. G. Nichols, ed., *The chronicle of Queen Jane, and of two years of Queen Mary*, CS, old ser., 48 (1850) · HoP, *Commons, 1509–58* · GEC, *Peerage* · J. Nichols, *The progresses and public processions of Queen Elizabeth*, new edn, 3 vols. (1823), vols. 1, 3 · *The diary of Henry Machyn, citizen and merchant-tailor of London, from AD 1550 to AD 1563*, ed. J. G. Nichols, CS, 42 (1848) · will, PRO, PROB 11/17, sig. 21 · will, PRO, PROB 11/39, sig. 16 · D. Loades, *The reign of Mary Tudor: politics, government and religion in England, 1553–58*, 2nd edn (1991) · W. A. Shaw, *The knights of England*, 2 (1906), 68

Archives PRO, letters and other state papers
Wealth at death properties

Brydges, Sir Richard (*c*.1500–1558). *See under* Brydges, John, first Baron Chandos (1492–1557).

Brydges, Thomas (*d*. 1559), landowner and administrator, was the second son of Sir Giles Brydges (*d*. 1511) of Coberley, Gloucestershire, and his wife, Isabel Baynham. His elder brother was John *Brydges, first Baron Chandos. He married first Jane, daughter and coheir of John Sydenham of Orchard, Somerset. His second wife, mentioned in his will, was named Anne. His brother's influence at court was crucial to his career: one of Thomas's earlier appointments, as a keeper of the wardrobe, was made when John was clerk. The building up of a large estate began with the stewardships (held jointly with his brother) of several royal manors and parks in Oxfordshire. It progressed with the leases of the monastic estates of Bruern and Langley in the same county—all this under Henry VIII—and culminated between 1550 and 1553 with the grant of the episcopal borough and manor of Chudleigh, Devon, and the purchase of 1200 acres at Bruern and the estates of the abbey of Keynsham, Somerset.

Brydges' public life, local then national, mirrored his amassing of wealth. He was an active official for Oxfordshire, and mustered troops there for the campaign of 1544; he was later posted to Boulogne as surveyor. As a substantial landowner, he sat on commissions that confiscated church property; as a justice of the peace, he attended the burning of Thomas Cranmer at Oxford in 1556. Two years before, as deputy lieutenant of the Tower under his brother, he was at the execution of Lady Jane Grey. He sat as an MP for Oxfordshire in Elizabeth's first parliament in January 1559, and died on 14 November the same year. He was buried at Chadlington, Oxfordshire. His son Thomas was drowned off London Bridge in 1553.

ROGER ASHLEY

Sources *LP Henry VIII* · *CPR, 1548–9; 1550–53; 1553* and appx · will, PRO, PROB 11/43, fols. 99r–101r · *CSP dom., 1547–58* · HoP, *Commons, 1558–1603* · 'Brydges, Sir John, first Baron Chandos', *DNB*
Wealth at death see will, PRO, PROB 11/43, fols. 99r–101r

Brydon, John McKean (1840–1901), architect, was born at Dunfermline, the son of John Brydon, tailor and draper, and his wife, whose maiden surname was McKean. He was educated at the Commercial Academy in Dunfermline. Articled to the Liverpool architects William and James Hay from 1856 to 1859, he then worked for David Bryce in Edinburgh (1860–63) and J. J. Stevenson and Campbell Douglass in Glasgow (1863–6) before moving to London to the office of Richard Norman Shaw and W. Eden Nesfield (1866–71). In 1869 he joined a group of Scottish expatriates as a partner in Cottier & Co., a decorating firm inspired by William Morris's attempts to link architecture and the decorative arts. Although he set up in independent practice in 1871, he is recorded to have spent much of his time designing furniture.

Two of Brydon's architectural pupils at a time when women were unusual in the profession were Agnes *Garrett and her cousin Rhoda *Garrett [*see under* Garrett,

Agnes], who established themselves as London's first women interior decorators in the early 1870s. Agnes was the sister of Elizabeth Garrett Anderson (1836–1917), the first woman in England to qualify in medicine, and through them Brydon got the commissions for the New Hospital for Women, Euston Road (1889–90; now the Elizabeth Garrett Anderson Hospital), and the London School of Medicine for Women, Hunter Street (1897–1900), which Anderson founded.

Brydon is remembered mainly for his public buildings, although he designed a number of private houses that early in his career showed the influence of Shaw and Nesfield. Later domestic work included the remodelling and extension of the Château de Buillon, near Besançon, France (1895), for the painter James Tissot. Success came with his competition entries for the Chelsea vestry hall (1885–7; now the town hall), Chelsea Library (1889), and South Western Polytechnic (1891), and also much work in Bath between 1891 and 1898 in a free classic style, again won in competition: the municipal buildings, technical schools, Victoria Art Gallery and Library, Pump Room extensions, and remodelling of the old Roman baths. This led to his appointment as architect for the new government offices on Great George Street, London (1898–1912), but he died suddenly of a throat infection just after the foundations had been put in, and the superstructure was completed by Sir Henry Tanner of the office of works.

Through his works and lectures Brydon encouraged a 'Wrenaissance'—a revival of interest in seventeenth-century English architects such as Inigo Jones and Christopher Wren. Their buildings, he thought, were in a classical style of quiet dignity ideally suited to contemporary imperial needs, which also permitted the integration of painting and sculpture according to arts and crafts ideals. Brydon was popular with his contemporaries, who found him forthright but fair, a safe but conscientious designer who 'would never have done anything which he might live to regret in the way of triviality or experimentalism' (*British Architect*, 55, 1901, 377). He died on 25 May 1901 at his home, 31 Steele's Road, Haverstock Hill, London, and was buried on 29 May in Highgate cemetery. He was survived by his widow, Edith Mary Brydon.

PAUL WATERHOUSE, rev. IAN DUNGAVELL

Sources J. S. Gibson, 'The late John McKean Brydon', *RIBA Journal*, 8 (1900–01), 400–05 · *The Builder*, 80 (1901), 540–41 · *British Architect*, 55 (1901), 377, 395–6 · W. J. Loftie, 'Brydon at Bath', *ArchR*, 18 (1905), 3–9, 51–9, 147–54 · M. D. Conway, *Travels in South Kensington, with notes on decorative art and architecture in England* (1882) · CGPLA Eng. & Wales (1901) · A. S. Gray, *Edwardian architecture: a biographical dictionary* (1985)

Likenesses studio of Bassano?, photograph, *c.*1890, repro. in *Building News*, 58 (1890), 202

Wealth at death £11,931 16s. 9d.: probate, 20 Sept 1901, CGPLA Eng. & Wales

Brydon, William (*c.*1811–1873), army surgeon, born in London, was descended from a Scottish border family, one member of which had distinguished himself as provost of Dumfries during a siege of that town; another, who farmed his own land, had horsed a troop of cavalry for the Young Pretender. Brydon received his education from Dr

William Brydon (*c.*1811–1873), by R. & E. Taylor, pubd 1873 (after John Stuart)

Robert Booth Rawse, at Bromley in Kent, before going on to study medicine at University College, London, and at the University of Edinburgh.

In October 1835 Brydon entered the service of the East India Company as an assistant surgeon. He spent three years' service in the North-Western Provinces of India, with various regiments, both British and native. He was then sent on escort duty, first with the commander-in-chief, Sir Henry Fane, and later with the governor-general, Lord Auckland, to the court of Ranjít Singh at Lahore.

In 1839, at the outbreak of war with Afghanistan, Brydon was posted to the 5th native infantry. When the main body of the army returned to India, he remained behind with the occupation force in Kabul. Brydon is renowned for being one of the few survivors of the ill-fated retreat from Kabul in January 1842. The retreating garrison was massacred by Afghan fighters on their journey to Jalalabad through narrow passes and gorges, their progress hampered by snow. Brydon and five other British officers managed to escape as far as Fatehabad, 4 miles short of Jalalabad. Here his companions were slain. Brydon continued on to Jalalabad, almost the only one left of a garrison which had totalled over 16,000 people. He received wounds to the knee and to the left hand, and had received a near-fatal blow to the head from an Afghan knife, being saved from death by a copy of *Blackwood's Magazine* stored under his forage cap. To Europeans in India he was known by the sobriquet 'last man', and his arrival at Jalalabad is immortalized in *The Remnants of an Army*, a painting by Lady Butler. Brydon served in the subsequent defence of Jalalabad as part of Sir Robert Sale's 'illustrious garrison'.

Brydon returned to India and in 1849 he was promoted to surgeon and posted with the 40th native infantry, with which he served in Burma. In 1853 he returned home on sick leave for three years. He then returned to India once more, and at the time of the mutiny of the Bengal army was stationed at Lucknow. During the siege of that garrison, in July 1857, he was severely wounded when a rifle bullet passed through his loins, injuring his lower spine.

Brydon was awarded medals for his service in Jalalabad, Kabul, Burma, and Lucknow, and in 1858 was appointed a companion of the Bath. In the following year he retired from the Indian service. He settled in the highlands of Scotland, and in 1862 became honorary surgeon to the Highland rifle militia. He died at his home, Westfield House, Nigg, Ross-shire, on 20 March 1873, and was buried in the same month at the Rosemarkie burial-ground. His wife, Colina Maxwell Brydon, survived him.

CLAIRE E. J. HERRICK

Sources *BMJ* (26 April 1873), 480 · J. P. J. Entract, 'The remnants of an army', *Journal of the Royal Army Medical Corps*, 106 (1960), 137–40 · D. G. Crawford, *A history of the Indian medical service, 1600–1913*, 2 (1914), 206, 261, 263, 265 · *Medical Press and Circular* (2 April 1873), 304 · N. Cantlie, *A history of the army medical department*, 1 (1974), 475, 493 · N. Cantlie, *A history of the army medical department*, 2 (1974), 238–40 · D. G. Crawford, *A history of the Indian medical service, 1600–1913*, 1 (1914), 184 · *The Lancet* (29 March 1873), 465 · *Calcutta Gazette* (8 Dec 1857) · J. W. Kaye, *History of the war in Afghanistan*, 3rd edn, 1 (1874), 389 · *The Times* · *CGPLA Eng. & Wales* (1873)
Likenesses E. Butler, painting, exh. RA 1880 (*The remnants of an army*); formerly at Somerset County Museum · R. & E. Taylor, wood-engraving (after photograph by J. Stuart), NPG; repro. in *ILN* (19 April 1873) [*see illus.*]
Wealth at death under £200: probate, 28 May 1873, *CGPLA Eng. & Wales*

Brydone, Patrick (1736–1818), traveller and author, was born on 5 January 1736, probably in Coldingham, Berwickshire, Scotland, one of the seven children of Robert Brydone (1686?–1761), minister of Coldingham, and Elizabeth, daughter of the previous minister, John Dysart, or Dysert, who were married on 30 June 1727 at Coldingham. Brydone is listed in the matriculation roll at St Andrews University for the year 1750/51 in the class of Walter Wilson, professor of Greek. At some point after completing his education he must have served in the army, since he is occasionally referred to as Captain (for example in 1778 by James Boswell in his *Life*, 3.356). As a young man, inspired by Benjamin Franklin's work, Brydone developed his enduring interest in electricity. During the 1760s he travelled in Switzerland, where he conducted electrical experiments, and in 1768 he travelled as tutor to the young William Beckford of Suffolk, who later wrote an account of Jamaica. He may also have travelled to Spain and Portugal since he refers knowledgeably to these countries in his 1773 travelogue. During the summer of 1770 he travelled from Naples to Sicily and Malta in the company of the seventeen-year-old William Fullarton (later colonel and commissioner of Trinidad), a friend named Glover, and several servants. At this time Sicily was virtually unknown to British travellers. Brydone's record of the journey was published in 1773 as *A tour through Sicily and Malta: in a series of letters to William Beckford, esq. of Somerly in Suffolk* (2 vols.). The work met with critical acclaim and the vulcanological and electrical observations it contained earned Brydone election to the Royal Society in either 1772 or 1773. He was also elected fellow of the Royal Society of Edinburgh and a fellow of the Society of Antiquaries. In 1780 Horace Walpole spent an evening at Mrs Keene's in Richmond where the company included Lord and Lady North and 'Brydone, the Sicilian traveller, who having wriggled himself into Bushy, will I suppose soon be an envoy, like so many other Scots' (Walpole, *Corr.*, 43.98). In 1781 Brydone was appointed for life to the comptrollership of the stamp office, which brought him about £600 a year. Thereafter little is known about his life: indeed, his obituary writer for the *Annual Biography* in 1820 observes that 'It is greatly to be lamented, that the materials for a life of this ingenious gentleman are scanty and incomplete' (p. 85). He must have married: his eldest daughter was Mary (1786–1853) who in 1806 married Gilbert Elliot Murray Kynynmound, second earl of Minto (1782–1859). Brydone died on 19 June 1818 at Lennel House in Berwickshire, having spent the latter part of his life in 'retirement, and almost in obscurity' (ibid., 109).

Brydone contributed letters on electrical phenomena and the therapeutic effects of electricity to the *Philosophical Transactions* of the Royal Society, but was chiefly celebrated in his day for the *Tour*, which went into at least nine editions in his own lifetime and was translated into French by Demeunier in 1776 and into German in 1777. Samuel Johnson praised the *Tour* in 1775, but Brydone's speculations on the age of the earth prompted Johnson to observe, in a conversation with Fullarton in 1778, that 'If Brydone were more attentive to his Bible, he would be a good traveller' (Boswell, *Life*, 3.356).

In the offending passage in the *Tour* Brydone reports and enlarges upon the work of a Signor Recupero, a Sicilian priest who wrote upon the natural history of Etna. Brydone notes that there are 'several strata of lavas' (Brydone, 1.131) around Etna, the most recent of which were recorded by Diodorus Siculus as having occurred 'in the time of the second Punic war' (ibid., 114), over 2000 years previously. This leads Brydone to the following thoughts:

> if it requires two thousand years or upwards, to form but a scanty soil on the surface of a lava, there must have been more than that space of time betwixt each of the eruptions that has formed these strata. But what shall we say of a pit they sunk near to Jaci, of a great depth. They pierced through seven distinct lavas one over the other, the surfaces of which were parallel, and most of them covered with a thick bed of fine rich earth. Now, says he [Recupero], the eruption that formed the lowest of these lavas, if we may be allowed to reason from analogy, must have flowed from the mountain at least 14,000 years ago.
>
> Recupero tells me he is exceedingly embarrassed, by these discoveries, in writing the history of the mountain.—That Moses hangs like a dead weight upon him, and blunts all his zeal for inquiry; for that really he has not the conscience to make his mountain so young, as the prophet makes the world. (ibid., 131–2)

Ralph Griffiths in the *Monthly Review* notes that Brydone's observation 'strongly tends to subvert all our common received notions of chronology, and the age of the world' (49, 1773, 28), but the radical implications of Brydone's vulcanology were not developed either by himself or by his contemporaries: it was only with Charles Lyell's *Principles of Geology* (1830–33) that James Ussher's (1654) dating of creation to 4004 BC began to be seriously questioned. The *Annual Biography* takes pains to diminish the significance of Brydone's philosophical speculations, reporting that 'his insinuations against the Mosaic account of the creation have been answered by several eminent divines, to which, we believe, he on his part never took the trouble to reply' (p. 111).

In the less controversial sections of the *Tour* Brydone makes shrewd observations on classical remains and natural history and on the manners and customs of modern Sicily. His style is conversational, yet elegant, and his professed aim is to 'make ourselves masters of the reader's imagination, to carry it along with us through every scene' (Brydone, 1.100). Especially striking is his use of the sublime when describing the wonders of Etna: stupendous effects of light, shade, and perspective are vividly evoked, and although Brydone is careful always to provide a scientific explanation, a sense of awe persists: 'All appears enchantment; and it is with difficulty we can believe we are still on earth' (ibid., 89). Similarly, as a sensible Scot he analyses the causes of his sentimental responses to distressed females (especially nuns), without entirely debunking the then highly fashionable interest in such emotions. The *Tour* consciously promotes an ideal of rational and manly Britishness and in sum may be considered one of the most accomplished eighteenth-century travel books. KATHERINE TURNER

Sources GM, 1st ser., 88/1 (1818), 643 · *Annual Biography and Obituary*, 4 (1820), 85–111 · [Clarke], *The Georgian era: memoirs of the most eminent persons*, 3 (1834), 464 · P. Brydone, *A tour through Sicily and Malta: in a series of letters to William Beckford, esq. of Somerly in Suffolk*, 2 vols. (1773) · *Fasti Scot.*, 1/2. 431 · J. Foster, *The peerage, baronetage, and knightage of the British Empire for 1883*, 1 [1883], 492 · J. M. Anderson, ed., *The matriculation roll of the University of St Andrews, 1747–1897* (1905), 3 · *Court and City Register* (1779–1813) · IGI · Boswell, *Life*, 2.345–6, 467–8 · Walpole, *Corr.*
Archives NL Scot., letters to Lord and Lady Minto · NRA Scotland, priv. coll., corresp. and papers, incl. military and scientific papers and journals during travels
Likenesses W. Ward, mezzotint (after A. Geddes), BM

Brydson, Thomas (1804–1855), clergyman and poet, was born in Glasgow on 12 October 1804, the son of William Brydson, merchant, and his wife, Margaret, *née* MacGeorge. After completing courses of study at the universities of Glasgow and Edinburgh he became a licentiate of the established church of Scotland. He officiated as assistant successively at the Middle Church in Greenock, in Oban, and in Kilmalcolm, and in 1839 was ordained minister of Levern Chapel, near Paisley. In 1842 he was presented to the parish of Kilmalcolm, where he remained until his death. Brydson wrote two volumes of verse, *Poems* (1829), and *Pictures of the Past* (1832). He also contributed to the *Edinburgh Literary Journal*, the *Glasgow Republic of Letters*, and several London annuals. He died suddenly, after some years of ill health, at the manse, Kilmalcolm, on 28 January 1855. T. F. HENDERSON, *rev.* SARAH COUPER

Sources C. Rogers, *The modern Scottish minstrel, or, The songs of Scotland of the past half-century*, 4 (1857), 172 · Boase, *Mod. Eng. biog.*, 1.456–7 · J. G. Wilson, ed., *The poets and poetry of Scotland*, 2 (1877), 286 · *Greenock Advertiser* (30 Jan 1855) · *Fasti Scot.* · bap. reg. Scot. · d. cert.

Bryer, Henry (*d.* in or before **1782**), engraver and printseller, was apprenticed to the engraver and stationer Edward Ryland, for the premium of £50, in 1758. Apart from the Society of Arts' premium, for etching and engraving, which Bryer won in 1762, 1763, and 1764, little is known of the early stages of his career. We can assume that he completed his training about 1765 as it was in that year that he went into business with his master's son, William Wynne Ryland. From their shop on Cornhill, London, the publishing partnership of Ryland and Bryer became 'The most prolific publisher of modern art' (Clayton, 195). Their reputation was built on the work of the most fashionable artists and their willingness to adopt innovative methods of print publishing. For example, in 1765 they published a collection of picturesque landscape views by Paul Sandby and in 1769 they commissioned the painting *Ceyx and Alcyone* from Richard Wilson, expressly so that they could publish the engraving. Theirs was evidently a winning formula and their print shop is thought to have made about £800 per annum.

Not satisfied with their success in the domestic market, in 1770 Ryland and Bryer decided to export prints in the belief that they could make money out of the British community in India. Entering into two separate business deals with Captain Charles Mears of the East India Company ship *Egmont* and James Haddock, purser of the *Morse*, they borrowed huge amounts of money and hoped to earn 500 per cent profit on the stock being shipped to India. When the two ships returned, 'the venture was reported a fiasco: the cost price of the prints had not even been covered' (Hayward and Kirkham, 6). So great was the loss that Ryland and Bryer were declared bankrupt in December 1771.

Shortly after this débâcle Bryer turned back to engraving. From a new London address in Rathbone Place he sent mezzotints to the Society of Artists' exhibitions of 1773 and 1774. He also published the occasional mezzotint, and was ever open to seemingly lucrative possibilities. This entrepreneurial streak can be seen in his strategy for stipple engravings, in which he continued to favour the same group of artists as he had when in partnership with Ryland. Indeed, after Ryland, Bryer is described as the most prominent publisher of the work of Angelica Kauffman, and a number of his independent publications were after this sentimental artist.

Nothing is known of the circumstances of Henry Bryer's early death but he died in or before 1782, when Robert Dossie listed him as deceased. Moving to Poland Street, his widow, Ann, continued 'to publish prints from the pictures of Angelica Kauffman &c.' (Strutt). LUCY PELTZ

Sources J. Strutt, *A biographical dictionary, containing an historical account of all the engravers, from the earliest period of the art of engraving to the present time*, 2 vols. (1785–6) · H. Hayward and P. Kirkham, *William and John Linnell* (1980) · T. Clayton, *The English print, 1688–1802* (1997) · M. Postle, *Reynolds: the subject pictures* (1995) · Redgrave, *Artists* · W. W. Roworth, ed., *Angelica Kauffman: a continental artist in Georgian England* (1992) · C. Lennox-Boyd and others, *Theatre: the age of Garrick. English mezzotints from the collection of the Hon. Christopher Lennox-Boyd* (1994) [exhibition catalogue, Courtauld Inst., 1994] · Graves, *Soc. Artists* · I. Maxted, ed., *The British book trades, 1710–1777: an index of the masters and their apprentices* (1983) · H. T. Wood, *A history of the Royal Society of Arts* (1913) · R. Dossie, *Memoirs of agriculture, and other oeconomical arts*, 3 vols. (1782)

Brygandyne [Brickenden], **Robert** (*c*.1465–*c*.1525), naval administrator, was born into a substantial yeoman family at Smallhithe near Cranbrook in Kent. Nothing is known about his parents, but the name (usually spelt Brickenden) was common in the region at that time. Exactly how or when he entered the king's service is not known, but he was sufficiently well regarded by 1490 to be granted an annuity of £10 for life, and to be allowed to purchase (for £20 3s. 4d.) a seven-year lease of the subsidies on cloth sold in Kent. Five years later, in May 1495, as a yeoman of the crown, he succeeded William Commersall as clerk of the king's ships. Brygandyne was both literate and numerate, and although nothing is known about his education, it would seem to have been typical of that given to the sons of substantial merchants. As clerk of the ships he was paid 12d. a day for himself, and 6d. for a clerk. This was not a full-time job, and he would have continued to be rewarded for whatever general service he provided in the king's chamber. Two sets of Brygandyne's accounts survive from Henry VII's reign, which show him to have been responsible for between four and seven ships when they were not in service. Henry seems to have regarded him as a naval expert, and consulted him directly over matters relating to the ships.

Brygandyne's patent was renewed on 23 July 1509 by Henry VIII, and reveals that his fee and expenses were paid out of the customs of Exeter and Dartmouth. Although the clerk was not responsible for operational expenses, Henry's build-up of the navy during the war of 1512–14 inevitably meant far more work, and in 1512 a second official was appointed when John Hopton, a gentleman usher of the chamber, became clerk comptroller. Hopton was superior to Brygandyne in status, although Brygandyne was not directly responsible to him. The clerk was relocated to Portsmouth, the main base in wartime, and continued to account independently. Brygandyne's experience was still regarded as important, but he was no longer consulted as he had been by Henry VII. He was granted a release of debts, as clerk of the ships 'and purveyor of stuffs and timber for the same' on 22 March 1523, and seems to have retired at that point. He was succeeded by Thomas Jermyn, and a reference to him as clerk in October 1525 would appear to have been a mistake. By 1523 the king had built up a standing navy of over thirty ships, and Brygandyne's long period of service covered one of the most formative periods in the history of the English navy.

Brygandyne was married, and his wife may have been called Alice, but nothing is known certainly about his domestic affairs. His son John was old enough to be 'overseer and ruler' of two of the king's great ships, the *Regent* and the *Sovereign*, in March 1512, when he may have been acting as assistant to his father. At about the same time John was also granted for life three tenements in Portsmouth, which would suggest that the family had already moved there. A William Brygandyne, who was probably a kinsman, was supplying timber to Calais at the same date. Robert probably died about 1525; no will appears to have survived. One Robert Brickenden of Smallhithe left 20d. to Smallhithe Chapel in a will dated 22 November 1517, and another man of the same name and place, described as 'a

wealthy clothier', gave £100 for the refurbishment of Cranbrook church in 1520. It seems unlikely that either of these was the clerk of the ships, especially as the clothier is specifically described as resident in Smallhithe, when the clerk was certainly in Portsmouth. The family may have returned to Kent after Brygandyne's retirement, but there is no conclusive evidence. Apart from having provided long and trustworthy service at a crucial time, Brygandyne is also important for having led an early example of what would later be called a 'navy board' family. The Gonsons and the Hawkins are similar and better-known families from the next two generations.

DAVID LOADES

Sources M. Oppenheim, ed., *Naval accounts and inventories of the reign of Henry VII, 1485–8 and 1495–7*, Navy RS, 8 (1896) • *LP Henry VIII*, 1/1, nos. 132, 632; 1/2, no. 3608; 3/2, nos. 1744, 2992 • *Archaeologia Cantiana*, 55 (1943), 27 • W. K. Jordan, 'Social institutions in Kent, 1480–1660: a study of the changing patterns of social aspirations', *Archaeologia Cantiana*, 75 (1961) [whole issue], esp. 120 • W. Tarbutt, *The annals of Cranbrook church*, 3 pts (1870–75) • PRO, E101 • D. M. Loades, *The Tudor navy* (1992)

Bryhtwell [Bryghtwell], **Thomas** (d. 1390), ecclesiastic and suspected heretic, was born in the diocese of Salisbury, possibly at either Brightwell or Britwell, both in Berkshire, the son of John Welle. First recorded in 1364, as a fellow of Exeter College, Oxford, he was a fellow of Merton College by 1368. By 1382 he had the degree of DTh. On 24 February in that year John of Gaunt, duke of Lancaster, presented him to the deanery of the collegiate church of St Mary in the Newarke, Leicester. He may not in fact have been admitted to this benefice, but he did become a prebendary in St Mary's on 5 March following. Gaunt was still at this time a patron of John Wyclif and his followers, several of whom had connections with the Leicester area. Among these were William Swinderby (who preached in St Mary's in the Newarke) and Philip Repyndon. The latter, who was a canon of Leicester Priory, and as such must have been well known to Bryhtwell, was also, like Bryhtwell, an Oxford academic. Consequently it seems highly likely that Bryhtwell was a member of the Oxford congregation who enthusiastically applauded the sermon preached by Repyndon on 5 June 1382, upholding Wycliffite doctrines that had only just been condemned by Archbishop Courtenay and his Blackfriars Council.

On 12 June 1382 Bryhtwell was therefore summoned to appear before the Blackfriars Council in London, along with Robert Rygge, the chancellor of the university. Rygge immediately submitted, but Bryhtwell 'at first and for a time hesitated a little', undergoing 'a diligent examination by the archbishop' before agreeing to condemn Wyclif's opinions (Wilkins, 3.159). His hesitation implies a genuine sympathy for Wycliffism, rather than mere resentment of archiepiscopal interference with university privileges. But henceforward Bryhtwell apparently abandoned his heretical leanings. He accumulated benefices which included prebends in St Paul's, London, and Lincoln Cathedral, and on 25 May 1388 was elected chancellor of Oxford University; by then he was indisputably dean of St Mary's in the Newarke. As dean he headed the royal commission (dated 23 May 1388) charged with arresting Lollards and seizing their books in Leicester, and in November 1389 he supervised the public penance of local heretics in his decanal church. More ironically still, his death in 1390 (between 10 February, when he made his will, and 25 November, when his successor was appointed) most probably occurred during a mission to that Roman papal curia so loudly condemned by John Wyclif.

CHARLES KIGHTLY

Sources Emden, *Oxf.* · [T. Netter], *Fasciculi zizaniorum magistri Johannis Wyclif cum tritico*, ed. W. W. Shirley, Rolls Series, 5 (1858), 297–308 · D. Wilkins, ed., *Concilia Magnae Britanniae et Hiberniae*, 3 (1737), 157–9 · will, Lincs. Arch., episcopal register XI [in register of Bishop John Buckingham], vol. 2, fol. 373 [orig. pagination] · *John of Gaunt's register, 1379–1383*, ed. E. C. Lodge and R. Somerville, 1, CS, 3rd ser., 56 (1937), 5–6 · A. H. Thompson, *History of the new college of St Mary in the Newarke, Leicester* (1937), 104–5, 231–2, 253 · *Knighton's chronicle, 1337–1396*, ed. and trans. G. H. Martin, OMT (1995), 306–15, 430–31, 438–43 [Lat. orig., *Chronica de eventibus Angliae a tempore regis Edgari usque mortem regis Ricardi Secundi*, with parallel Eng. text] · Chancery records · K. B. McFarlane, *John Wycliffe* (1966), 109

Wealth at death see will, register of Bishop John Buckingham, Lincs. Arch., episcopal register XI, vol. 2, fol. 373

Brynach [St Brynach, Bernachius, Bernacius] (*fl.* **6th cent.**), founder of the church of Nevern, Pembrokeshire, was not of Welsh descent. His pedigree is in neither of the two main collections of saints' genealogies, *Bonedd y saint* and *Achau'r saint*, and his life, twelfth-century in its present form, fails to give the names of his parents, though it does say, probably as a mere hagiographical formula, that he was of noble descent. Much of the substance of the life is a collection of traditional narrative motifs, some purely hagiographical (such as voyaging upon a rock), others more general; it is, however, a well-constructed text written in good and vigorous Latin. There are two main sections: first, the saint's wanderings, and, second, his dealings with Maelgwn Gwynedd.

The life portrays Brynach as a pilgrim–saint (*peregrinus*), who moved from one place to another as soon as his reputation for holiness endangered his monastic seclusion. First, he travelled from his homeland (not named) to Rome, where he freed the citizens from the attentions of 'a pestiferous monster' ('Vita sancti Bernacii', chap. 2). His fame then caused him to journey to Brittany, where, again, his reputation made it impossible for him to stay. He took ship, on a rock, and came to Milford Haven, where he temporarily settled. Here, however, it was the amorous attentions of a nobleman's daughter that made it impossible to remain: once rejected her love turned to hatred, and she arranged an attack in which Brynach was wounded. He then moved to Pontfaen, and from there to a nearby site on the River Nyfer. Here, with his companions, he prepared a permanent settlement, but each night their day's work vanished. Brynach decided that they should await illumination. This came in the form, traditional in Irish hagiography, of an angelic message declaring that their present site was not Brynach's 'place of resurrection' ('Vita sancti Bernacii', chap. 7). He was directed to follow a white sow with white piglets which would lead them to their dwelling place. Once established at Nevern, Brynach

made friends with a local ruler, Clechre, who had prophesied Brynach's arrival, and whose twenty sons were instructed in the monastic life and became 'coheirs' with the saint. The descendants of Clechre were, in the language of the Irish laws, 'the kindred of the land', while Brynach was the patron saint; since he had no descendants (as a *peregrinus* and an ascetic), they became the hereditary kindred of Nevern. The theme of the first half of the life, the *peregrinatio* of the patron saint, thus led naturally to a preordained conclusion, the alliance between saint and kindred, joint heirs of Nevern.

The second part of the life had an equally clear purpose and achieved it with similarly entertaining narrative detail. The link between the two halves was an account of the character of the saint's life—so holy that, not only did he enjoy converse with angels, but the very wild beasts were tame at his bidding. In particular, the one cow of the community was guarded by a wolf, the friend and servant of the saint. The protagonists in the second part of the life were the saint, Brynach, and the king, Maelgwn Gwynedd. Maelgwn arrived and demanded a night's hospitality (*gwest*). This was refused and the king sent men to take the one cow. The wolf complained to Brynach, who put his case before Heaven. Maelgwn Gwynedd and his men, now afflicted by extreme hunger, were distressed to find that, however high they stoked the fire, the water in their stewing-pot remained stubbornly cold. By this miracle they were compelled to acknowledge the authority of the saint. Brynach then changed tactics—having revived the cow—and invited Maelgwn and his men for dinner and a night's rest. Given the exemplary ascetic poverty of the community, such entertainment required miracles: loaves were found growing on trees; the water of the local stream turned into wine; Maelgwn and his men were royally entertained. The king, duly impressed, granted to Brynach a perpetual immunity from royal exactions for the monastery and all its possessions; it was at Nevern that he was to die, on 7 April in an unspecified year, and where he was buried, outside the east wall of the church.

The king chosen to grant this privilege was a king of Gwynedd, not a king of Dyfed. Otherwise, Brynach's career in Wales was confined to Dyfed: it was where he landed and all his settlements, up to and including Nevern, were within the one kingdom. There may be two reasons: first, Maelgwn had already appeared in a similar role in the life of St Cadog, likewise a southern saint. More interestingly, however, it was prudent to obtain such a grant from an over-king and to get it not just for Nevern but for all the possessions of Brynach. Although the life does not mention it, Llanfrynach, 2 miles to the south-east of Brecon, was another important church of the saint. A mere local privilege, from the king of Dyfed, would not have helped a church situated in Brycheiniog.

The main evidence for the early importance of Nevern is the surviving sculpture. This falls into three groups. First, there are two fifth- or sixth-century inscriptions, both bilingual (Irish and Latin). If they attest an early cemetery of the period when Irish settlers ruled Dyfed, this need not yet have been ecclesiastical and they do not, therefore, provide good evidence for a church. Second, there are three stones, of the seventh to the ninth centuries, at a farm some 3 miles to the south, Tre-bwlch. Third, two stones of the tenth and eleventh centuries are on the site of the church. One of them is highly ornate, in the same style as the Carew stone commemorating a king of Dyfed, Maredudd ab Edwin (d. 1035). Only this third group confirms the importance of the church in the pre-Norman period. T. M. CHARLES-EDWARDS

Sources 'Vita sancti Bernacii', *Vitae sanctorum Britanniae et genealogiae*, ed. and trans. A. W. Wade-Evans (1944), 2–15 · P. C. Bartrum, ed., *Early Welsh genealogical tracts* (1966) · V. E. Nash-Williams, *The early Christian monuments of Wales* (1950), nos. 353–60 · *Gir. Camb. opera*, 6.3–152 · S. Baring-Gould and J. Fisher, *The lives of the British saints*, 4 vols., Honourable Society of Cymmrodorion, Cymmrodorion Record Series (1907–13) · E. R. Henken, *Traditions of the Welsh saints* (1987), no. 45 · E. R. Henken, *The Welsh saints: a study in patterned lives* (1991) · M. Richards, *Welsh administrative and territorial units* (1969)

Bryne, Albertus (c.1621–1668), organist and composer, was possibly born in the Spanish Netherlands, the son of an English father and a mother he named in his will as Myldmann Buggs. He was a pupil of John Tomkins, whom he succeeded as organist of St Paul's Cathedral in 1638, when he was, on his own account, about seventeen. During the Commonwealth he taught harpsichord and organ. At the Restoration he returned to St Paul's. He made a petition to Charles II to be organist in the king's chapel at Whitehall, claiming that his skills had been very considerably advanced through practice since Charles I had chosen him for St Paul's, but this was unsuccessful. After the fire of London in 1666 he moved to Westminster Abbey.

Bryne was apparently well known among contemporaries as a gifted organist, but he also composed harpsichord and sacred vocal music, and indeed was the most outstanding keyboard composer of his day after Matthew Locke. His seven harpsichord suites show considerable imagination and complexity and were influential on the next generation of composers. Three of these are among the earliest examples of English four-movement suites for the instrument. On the other hand, his anthems suggest a pre-Restoration style with absence of declamatory elements in verse writing, and were copied into partbooks in Durham and Lichfield. His service with verses was copied into the Chapel Royal partbooks in the year 1680–81, and texts to his anthems appear in Clifford's *Divine Services and Anthems Usually Sung in his Majesties Chappell*.

Bryne had three children with his wife, whose name is unknown—Albertus (d. 1713), organist of All Hallows Barking by the Tower and Dulwich College, Elizabeth, and Mary. Bryne died, presumably in Westminster, on 2 December 1668. His place of burial is unknown, and no evidence can be found for claims that he was buried at Westminster Abbey.

W. B. SQUIRE, rev. DAVID S. KNIGHT

Sources D. Dawe, *Organists of the City of London, 1666–1850* (1983) · I. Spink, ed., *The seventeenth century* (1992) · I. Spink, *Restoration cathedral music, 1660–1714* (1995) · H. W. Shaw, *The succession of organists of the Chapel Royal and the cathedrals of England and Wales from c.1538* (1991)

Bryskett, Lodowick [Lewis] (c.1546–1609×12), administrator and writer, probably born in Hackney, was the fifth of the eight children of Antonio Bruschetto (d. 1574), merchant, and his wife, Elizabeth (d. 1579), an Italian whose lineage remains unknown. Antonio was a native of Genoa who had taken up residence in England by 1523 and was granted letters of denization on 4 December 1536. Lodowick began school at Tonbridge before the age of five, but was soon forced to withdraw owing to the onset of 'a quartaine ague' (Bryskett, 98). He matriculated at Trinity College, Cambridge, on 27 May 1559, but left the university without taking a degree.

Bryskett was intended by his father for a career in medicine, but 'providence had otherwise determined … and made me of a scholer to become a servant' (Bryskett, 17). He paid his first visit to Ireland in 1565 in the service of the lord deputy, Sir Henry Sidney, and acted as temporary clerk to the council in Ireland for a brief period in 1571. Chosen to accompany Sir Philip Sidney on his grand tour (1572–4), he witnessed the St Bartholomew's day massacre in Paris and visited Strasbourg, Frankfurt, Vienna, Venice, and Genoa (Bryskett, 160–61). From 1575 to 1582 he served as clerk to the council in Ireland and in 1577 he was also appointed clerk in chancery for the faculties, an office in which he was succeeded in 1581 by his close friend Edmund Spenser.

Bryskett was granted the lucrative post of general controller of the customs on wines in Ireland in 1579; he appears to have married about the same time, although nothing is known of his wife's identity beyond her given name, Ellen. The birth of a son is recorded on 28 April 1580 and the baptism of a daughter on 9 May 1600. In 1581 Bryskett petitioned for the post of secretary of state for Ireland on the death of Sir John Challoner, but was rejected in favour of Geoffrey Fenton. In 1583, however, he succeeded in securing appointment as clerk to the Council of Munster, an office in which he employed Spenser as his deputy. As a reward for his services to the crown he was granted a small estate in Wexford in 1593 and he served for a time as sheriff for the county. In 1594 he became clerk of the casualties. The following year he contributed two poems (adapted from Tasso) to Spenser's *Astrophel* in memory of their common patron, Sir Philip Sidney. He also appeared under the persona of Thestylis in *Colin Clouts Come Home Againe* and was addressed in the thirty-third sonnet of the *Amoretti*.

In 1600, having fled Ireland on account of the worsening situation during the Nine Years' War, Bryskett surrendered the office of clerk to the Council of Munster to Richard Boyle, later first earl of Cork, and in 1604 he was deprived of the office of clerk of the casualties on the grounds of non-residence. During this period he repeatedly petitioned Sir Robert Cecil for financial assistance in order to defray debts which 'the common calamity of Ireland hath brought upon me' (Plomer and Cross, 66). While on an official mission to the continent in 1601 he was taken captive in Flanders on the orders of Count Mansfelt, but was released in 1603 in exchange for some Catholic prisoners held in England, including the Jesuit Ferdinand Cardin.

In 1606 Bryskett published *A Discourse of Civill Life*, translated and heavily adapted from Giambattista Giraldi Cinthio's *Tre dialoghi della vita civile*, being the second part of *De gli hecatommithi* (1565). Although the work is dedicated to the earl of Salisbury, internal evidence indicates that it was written in the mid-1580s and originally intended for Lord Arthur Grey of Wilton, former lord deputy of Ireland (1580–82). It contains one of the earliest descriptions of *The Faerie Queene* (placed in the mouth of Spenser himself), supplies much autobiographical information, and reflects upon the Irish colonial situation. The date and place of Bryskett's death are uncertain, but he was again active in Ireland in 1609 and must have died before the end of 1612, since his widow was involved in a suit in the Irish court of chancery in January 1613.

RICHARD A. MCCABE

Sources H. R. Plomer and T. P. Cross, *The life and correspondence of Lodowick Bryskett* (1927) · D. Jones, 'Lodowick Bryskett and his family', *Thomas Lodge and other Elizabethans*, ed. C. J. Sissons (1933) · Venn, *Alum. Cant.* · L. Bryskett, *A discourse of civill life: containing the ethike part of morall philosophie* (1606)

Bryson, Alexander (1802–1869), naval surgeon, began his professional studies at Edinburgh and continued them at Glasgow, where he qualified in 1827 and was admitted to the Royal Faculty of Physicians and Surgeons. In the same year he entered the navy as assistant surgeon; he was promoted surgeon in 1836, deputy inspector-general in 1854, and inspector-general in 1855. In January 1864, on the retirement of Sir John Liddell, he was appointed director-general of the medical department of the navy.

Bryson was also appointed honorary physician to the queen, in 1859, and subsequently he was made a companion of the Order of the Bath. He became a fellow of the Royal College of Physicians in London in 1860, and he was also a fellow of the Royal Society. He compiled the *Statistical Reports on the Health of the Navy* and published accounts of his experience of disease in Africa.

Bryson was neither an efficient nor a popular director-general. Blunt in manner and somewhat cold and dry, he was interested more in statistics than in the problems of naval medical officers. He also lacked any substantial hospital experience. He was suddenly dismissed from his post in 1869, failed to receive the customary knighthood, and spent his last months haggling over his pension.

Bryson had for some time suffered from severe headache, vertigo, and loss of memory. He collapsed after walking in the garden of his home at The Hermitage, Barnes, Surrey, and died without regaining consciousness on 12 December 1869.

JAMES MILLS

Sources *The Lancet* (18 Dec 1869), 860–61 · *BMJ* (18 Dec 1869), 670 · Munk, *Roll*

Wealth at death under £6000: administration with will, 2 Feb 1870, CGPLA Eng. & Wales

Bryson, James (c.1730–1796), minister of the Presbyterian General Synod of Ulster, the son of John Bryson (1685–1788), was probably born in Holywood, co. Down. He was licensed by the Armagh presbytery on 1 June 1762 and, after preaching at Banbridge in 1763–4, he was ordained minister of Lisburn by Bangor presbytery on 7 June 1764, giving a modified form of subscription. A new meeting-house was opened in Lisburn on 18 May 1766, Bryson's congregation using the Anglican church while the building was under way. In 1774 he accepted a call to Belfast's (non-subscribing) Second Congregation, on condition that he did not have to sever his connection with the general synod, indicating the rapprochement that then existed between the synod and the presbytery of Antrim. In June 1778 he was elected moderator of the synod meeting at Lurgan.

Bryson rapidly gained a reputation as an able preacher, although Martha McTier said that his sermons contained 'many good things and pretty expressions—but … that is all' (Agnew, 101). A number of his sermons were published, including *The Objections of Infidels* (1769) and *Obtaining the Divine Approbation* (1772; 2nd edn, 1773). His most important publication was *Sermons on Several Important Subjects* (1778), a collection of thirteen sermons dedicated to his cousin William Bryson (1730–1815). As a freemason Bryson preached frequently before lodges in dissenting meeting-houses and occasionally in the established church; his *Duties of Masonry*, preached before the Orange lodge of Belfast, number 257 (a masonic precursor of the Orange order), were published in 1782. He was also an enthusiastic supporter of the volunteer movement and on a number of occasions preached to companies of volunteers. In Belfast the Second Congregation built a new meeting-house for him in 1790, but his ministry was not to last much longer.

Bryson married twice. His first wife, with whom he had at least two children, died on 19 January 1790. Shortly afterwards he remarried but became embroiled in a scandal which alienated a large proportion of his congregation. With his supporters he left the Second Congregation in 1791 to form a new congregation, worshipping in the parish church until the new meeting-house was opened on 18 May 1794. The venture was not immediately successful, Bryson recording on the flyleaf of his sermon that the sacrament was celebrated on 23 April 1796, when 'few indeed' were present (Bryson MSS, sermons, vol. 12). He died in Belfast on 3 October 1796, and was survived by his wife.

ALEXANDER GORDON, rev. A. D. G. STEERS

Sources J. Bryson, MS sermons, 13 vols. (vol. 9 missing), Queen's University Belfast, Antrim Presbytery Library, special collections, B.3.XI · S. S. Millin, *History of the second congregation of Protestant dissenters in Belfast … 1708–1896* (1900), 32–6, 119 · T. Witherow, *Historical and literary memorials of presbyterianism in Ireland, 1731–1800* (1880), 141–4 · J. McConnell and others, eds., *Fasti of the Irish Presbyterian church, 1613–1840*, rev. S. G. McConnell, 2 vols. in 12 pts (1935–51) · *Belfast News-Letter* (22 Jan 1790) · *Belfast News-Letter* (3 Oct 1796) · *Records of the General Synod of Ulster, from 1691 to 1820*, 3 (1898) · *The Drennan–McTier letters*, ed. J. Agnew, 3 vols. (1998–9) · A. Gordon, 'Belfast: list of ministers, second congregation', *The Disciple*, 3 (1883), 114–15 · S. S. Millin, *Additional sidelights on Belfast history* (1938), 68–70

Archives Queen's University, Belfast, Antrim Presbytery Library, sermons, B.3.XI

Likenesses oils, All Souls' Non-Subscribing Presbyterian Church, Elmwood Avenue, Belfast; repro. in Millin, *History of the second congregation of protestant dissenters*

Bryson, William (1729/30–1815), non-subscribing Presbyterian minister, was born in co. Down, the second son of Patrick Bryson; the Presbyterian minister James Bryson was a cousin. He matriculated at Glasgow University in 1756 but appears not to have taken a degree. In August 1764 he was ordained by the presbytery of Antrim to be the minister of the non-subscribing Presbyterian congregation of Antrim, his one and only charge. While at Antrim he married; his wife was said to be a daughter of Alexander Maclaine, minister at Antrim from 1742 to 1759, and a granddaughter of John Abernethy, minister at Antrim from 1703 to 1730. Together they had six children.

Bryson soon adopted very radical theological views. Alexander Gordon, who had sight of Bryson's (now lost) manuscript sermons, described them as 'thoughtful and unconventional, direct and practical in their tone, and … distinct in their presentation of a robust Unitarian theology' (Gordon, 'Our old burying ground', 15). His Christology was strongly Arian and he rejected the doctrines of original sin and imputed righteousness. Nevertheless, although a member of the presbytery of Antrim, he enjoyed close relations with the orthodox General Synod of Ulster, frequently serving on committees of the synod and preaching in its churches. His published work amounts to just two (or possibly three) sermons, copies of which are now very rare. His first publication was *The Practice of Righteousness* (1782), the funeral sermon for Thomas Crawford, minister at Crumlin; the second was *The Duty of Searching the Scriptures* (1786), preached at the ordination at Ballyclare of Futt Marshall. A funeral sermon for Robert Sinclair of Larne (*d.* 1795) may have been published.

In politics Bryson remained staunchly loyalist during the troubles of the 1790s, in sharp contrast to many in his congregation. Before the United Irishman and member of the Antrim congregation William Orr was hanged in 1797, at Orr's request it was not Bryson who attended on him in Carrickfergus gaol but other ministers who shared his political views. In November 1810 Bryson resigned his charge, due to increasing infirmity, and John Carley was ordained as assistant and successor on 3 April 1811. Bryson died at Antrim on 6 May 1815 in his eighty-sixth year, his wife having predeceased him; William Bruce preached his funeral sermon on 18 June. Bryson is said to have been buried at Antrim, in the graveyard of his meeting-house; a tombstone there marks the burial place of five of his children.

A. D. G. STEERS

Sources T. Witherow, *Historical and literary memorials of presbyterianism in Ireland, 1731–1800* (1880), 256–9 · A. Gordon, 'Our old burying ground', *The Disciple*, 1 (1881), 12–15 · A. Gordon, 'Antrim old Presbyterian congregation', *The Disciple*, 3 (1883), 38–9 · presbytery of Antrim minute book, First Presbyterian Church, Belfast · *Belfast News-Letter* (12 May 1815) · *Records of the General Synod of Ulster, from 1691 to 1820*, 3 (1898) · W. I. Addison, ed., *The matriculation albums of the University of Glasgow from 1728 to 1858* (1913), 56 · F. J. Bigger, *The northern leaders of '98, No. 1: 'remember Orr'* (1906), 15–16 · Bryson family tombstone, former old Presbyterian meeting-house, Antrim, graveyard

Likenesses C. Pike, silhouette, 1893 (after P. Bryson), Old Presbyterian Church, Templepatrick, co. Antrim · P. Bryson, silhouette, First Presbyterian Church, Rosemary Street, Belfast

Bryt [Brytte], **Walter** (*fl.* 14th cent.), astronomer, was of Welsh origins. His only authentic surviving work is a *Theorica planetarum*, a textbook on planetary theory known in thirteen manuscripts, seven of which are in Oxford and the rest in London, Cambridge, Gloucester, Norwich, and Lincoln. In four manuscripts the author is called *dominus* (not *magister*) Walterus Bryt, to which in Bodl. Oxf., MS Digby 15, fol. 96*v*, is added 'quondam socius collegii de Merton' ('formerly fellow of Merton College'). The incipit of the text is 'Circulus eccentricus, circulus egresse cuspidis et circulus egredientis centri idem sunt'. This is very similar to the 'Circulus eccentricus, vel egresse cuspidis vel egredientis centri dicitur qui non habet centrum suum cum centro mundi' with which the anonymous and widely used *Theorica planetarum* from the thirteenth century begins. This confused the two texts until in 1905 A. A. Bjørnbo showed them to be different. Bryt has also been credited with works now known to be by John Sacrobosco and others.

Walter Bryt's *Theorica* is clearly inspired by the earlier treatise, but is by no means an unoriginal rehash of the old text. On the contrary, a closer study reveals several important innovations. The first *Theorica*'s very disorderly and confused chapter on motions in latitude and other topics is omitted, and the relevant theories are described in the various chapters on motion in longitude; also, the final astrological chapter is left out. Moreover, the purely geometrical models of the earlier treatise are now embedded in a cosmological machinery of celestial 'spheres', in agreement with the 'physical' cosmology of the late middle ages. Also of interest are the numerical parameters, quoted in much greater abundance than in the previous *Theorica* and now taken from the Alfonsine tables which became known in Britain in the first quarter of the fourteenth century.

Of even greater interest are the kinematical ideas introduced by Bryt. The traditional terms of 'equal' and 'unequal' motion are replaced by *uniformis* and *difformis*, which were key words in the new kinematics developed in the fourteenth century by a number of scholars, many of them connected with Merton College, Oxford. According to Bryt, physicists speak of uniform motion when a point passes through equal spaces in equal times, whereas astronomers mean that a point 'in equal times describes equal angles around some fixed centre, or when in equal times it cuts equal arcs from the circumference of some circle' (Bodl. Oxf., MS Digby 15, fol. 60*r*). This leads to the proposition that all points on a line rotating uniformly around a centre at rest will move uniformly around the centre. So even if the term 'angular velocity' is not used, it is clear that the author is familiar with the concept, and may have been the first to use it in theoretical astronomy.

All that is known about Bryt is that he was Welsh, that at one time he taught astronomy at university level and tried to modernize the curriculum, and that he may have been connected with Merton College, although his name seems to be absent from the college register. That he is called *dominus* instead of *magister* seems also to indicate that his academic career was not complete. However, in 1674 Anthony Wood tried to identify Bryt with a certain Gualterius Bryte who was denounced as a Lollard in 1390 and tried before Bishop John Trefnant of Hereford (*d.* 1404). The ensuing process was reported in great detail by John Foxe, and the original documents were published in 1916 by W. W. Capes. Although Bryte described himself as a 'layman and sinner', his long defence in fluent Latin shows that he was also a scholar. In 1393 he recanted his errors and nothing more is heard of him. Such an identification would explain the obscurity of Bryt's university life, and would also date the *Theorica* to before 1390. But against it can be set the fact that the astronomical treatise is completely free of astrology, while the suspected heretic uses astrological arguments concerning a great conjunction of Saturn and Jupiter (perhaps in 1385), which is taken as a portent of the second coming of Christ. Thus the question remains open.   OLAF PEDERSEN

Sources O. Pedersen, 'The problem of Walter Brytte and Merton astronomy', *Archives Internationales d'Histoire des Sciences*, 36 (1986), 227–48 · A. A. Bjørnbo, 'Walter Bryte's *Theorica planetarum*', *Bibliotheca Mathematica*, 6 (1905), 112 ff. · R. T. Gunther, *Early science in Oxford*, 2: *Astronomy*, OHS, 78 (1923), 65–6 · J. L. E. Dreyer, *Nature*, 113 (1924), 38–40 · G. C. Brodrick, *Memorials of Merton College*, OHS, 4 (1885), 324 · Emden, *Oxf.*, 1.270 · J. Foxe, *The first volume of the ecclesiasticall history, contayning the actes and monumentes*, 3rd edn (1576), 457–84 · W. W. Capes, ed., *Registrum Johannis Trefnant*, CYS, 20 (1916), 231–411 · A. Wood, *Historia et antiquitates universitatis Oxoniensis*, trans. R. Peers and R. Reeve, 2 vols. (1674), vol. 2, p. 87 · L. Thorndike and P. Kibre, *A catalogue of incipits of mediaeval scientific writings in Latin*, rev. edn (1963) · L. Thorndike, *A history of magic and experimental science*, 8 vols. (1923–58), vol. 3, p. 523 · G. Sarton, *Introduction to the history of science*, 3 (1947), 1500 f. · C. H. Talbot, 'Simon Bredon (*c.*1300–1372): physician, mathematician, and astronomer', *British Journal for the History of Science*, 1 (1962–3), 19–30 · Bodl. Oxf., MS Digby 15, fols. 60*r*, 96*v*

Archives BL, Egerton MS 847 · Bodl. Oxf., MSS Digby 15, 98

Brzeska, Henri Alphonse Séraphin Marie Gaudier- (1891–1915), sculptor and draughtsman, was born on 4 October 1891 at Vomimbert, St Jean-de-Braye, on the outskirts of Orléans, France, the only son and eldest of the three children of Germain Gaudier (1864–1934) and Marie-Alexandrine, *née* Bourgoin (1865–1954). Both parents came from French artisan families, his father being a carpenter–joiner and his maternal grandfather a wheelwright. In 1907 Gaudier's academic and linguistic ability won him a two-year state scholarship for study abroad, which he spent at the Merchant Venturers' Technical College in Bristol, and working for a coal exporter, Fifoot, Ching & Co., in Cardiff, before travelling to Germany, where he stayed in Nuremberg and Munich. During this period he determined, though entirely self-taught, on an artistic career aiming at magazine illustration, though his efforts in this direction under the name Gérald proved unsuccessful.

On his return to France in September 1909, Gaudier worked briefly in Paris for a publisher, a lens manufacturer, and a textile firm while studying voraciously in the libraries and museums. He drew people, animals, and the

Henri Alphonse Séraphin Marie Gaudier-Brzeska (1891–1915), self-portrait, 1912

urban scene, laying the basis of his rapid and immensely versatile draughtsmanship. In May 1910 he met Sophie Suzanne Brzeska (1871–1925), a Polish woman who became his lifelong companion in a volatile but probably platonic relationship. They moved to London in January 1911, adopting the surname Gaudier-Brzeska and the identity of a Franco-Polish brother and sister to lend respectability to their cohabitation.

While employed from March 1911 to July 1913 as a foreign-language clerk with Wulfsberg & Co., a timber importer in the City, Gaudier-Brzeska spent all his spare time studying in libraries, museums, and galleries and making work from clay, cut plaster, and bought, begged, or stolen offcuts of stone. Despite his job and Sophie's sporadic employment as a governess, they were scarcely able to make ends meet and led a penurious existence in a series of rented rooms in Chelsea and Fulham. During protracted separations they exchanged letters; this correspondence, of which only his side survives, and Sophie Brzeska's autobiographical writings (now at the Musée des Beaux-Arts, Orléans, Cambridge University Library, and Essex University Library), provide vivid insights into their lives and thoughts.

During 1912 Gaudier-Brzeska began to establish himself as a sculptor, first in clay and then, probably from mid-1912, in stone, assimilating the influence of Rodin, fauvism, cubism, Brancusi, and examples of non-

European art from China, Africa, and Oceania, in rapid succession; a fluidly modelled bronze, *Dancer* (1913, Tate collection), for which the painter Nina Hamnett modelled, preceded by only weeks an aggressively primitivistic carving in Mansfield stone, *Redstone Dancer* (1913, Tate collection). Stylistically eclectic but formally inventive and often savagely humorous, he had 'an amazing faculty for synthesis' (Pound, 7). His sculptures during 1912–13 were primarily Rodinesque figure studies, including theatre, ballet, and wrestling subjects, and modelled portraits of friends, including the writer Enid Bagnold (1912, priv. coll.), the journalist Frank Harris (1913), and fellow artists Alfred Wolmark (1913) and Horace Brodzky (1913). Meeting Jacob Epstein in June 1912 confirmed his interest in direct carving which increasingly took over but never entirely superseded modelling in his working practice. Animal and bird studies remained a favourite theme evolving from quick zoo sketches to the semi-geometric primitivism of *Stags* (alabaster, 1914, Art Institute of Chicago) and *Bird Swallowing a Fish* (plaster, 1914, Kettle's Yard, Cambridge) and the intuitive cubism of *Birds Erect* (limestone, 1914, Museum of Modern Art, New York). However, despite his self-conscious modernism, he could still draw inspiration from the classical tradition, as seen in his small marble *Torso* (1913, Tate collection), *Maternity* (1913), and *Seated Woman* (1914, both Musée National d'Art Moderne, Paris).

During 1913–14, working from a comfortless studio, first at 454A Fulham Road (January to September 1913) and then Arch 25, Winthrop Road, Putney, Gaudier-Brzeska became an increasingly prominent figure within the London avant-garde, especially after beginning to exhibit his sculpture at the London Salon in July 1913. There he met the American poet Ezra Pound, to whom his slight, sinewy figure appeared 'like a well-made young wolf or some soft-moving, bright-eyed wild thing' (Pound, 45). His friendly relationships with a wide range of artists within otherwise mutually antipathetic groups—Roger Fry's Grafton Group and Omega workshop artists, Camden Town artists such as Harold Gilman and Robert Bevan, as well as Wyndham Lewis and his circle—were indicative both of his eclecticism and of the respect which his talent and sharply critical intelligence commanded. He was elected to the London Group in February 1914 and was chosen as chairman of the artists' committee for the 1914 London Salon. However, he sold few sculptures and received only a handful of small private commissions.

Through his friendship with Pound, Gaudier-Brzeska became increasingly identified with the nascent vorticist group during 1914 [see Vorticists]. His sculptures, whether large like the so-called *Hieratic Head of Ezra Pound* (1914, R. Nasher Collection, USA), commissioned by the poet himself, or very small like the carved metal *Torpedo Fish* (1914, Art Gallery of Ontario, Toronto) and *Doorknocker* (1914, Kettle's Yard, Cambridge), take on increasingly sharp-edged, geometric, and abstract forms in keeping with the vorticists' virile, machine age aesthetic. He was one of the signatories of the vorticist manifesto and contributed two seminal articles, 'Vortex—Gaudier-Brzeska',

to the 1914 and 1915 issues of *Blast*. In these he revealed literary gifts and an impressive grasp of the history of sculpture. His opening statement,

> Sculptural energy is the mountain.
> Sculptural feeling is the appreciation of masses in relation.
> Sculptural ability is the defining of these masses by planes.
> (Gaudier-Brzeska, 1.155)

became a rallying call for modern British sculpture, influencing Henry Moore and Frank Dobson among others.

In September 1914 Gaudier-Brzeska returned to France and enlisted as a private in the 129th regiment of the French army, serving in the Craonne sector near Rheims. Twice promoted—to corporal and sergeant—he was due for officer training when he was killed by a single bullet through the head on 5 June 1915 at Neuville-St Vaast in Artois and was buried in the military cemetery there.

Sophie Brzeska inherited his work by an *inter vivos* gift; on her death, insane and intestate, in 1925, it was valued at £545. The enthusiasm of artists and the publication of Pound's *Gaudier-Brzeska: a Memoir* (1916) and H. S. Ede's *Savage Messiah* (1931) led to a growing appreciation of his catalytic role in the birth of modernist sculpture in Britain but he remained until the late 1950s virtually unknown in his native country. His life with Sophie Brzeska, as told by Ede, acquired mythic status, notably in Ken Russell's film *Savage Messiah* (1971), but as early as 1934 their relationship was the acknowledged inspiration for the artist and writer protagonists in *The Laughing Woman*, a play by Elizabeth Mackintosh writing under the name of Gordon Daviot.

EVELYN SILBER

Sources E. Pound, *Gaudier-Brzeska: a memoir* (1916) · H. S. Ede, *A life of Gaudier-Brzeska* (1930) · H. S. Ede, *Savage Messiah*, 2nd edn (1971) · R. Cole, *Gaudier-Brzeska: artist and myth* (1995) · E. Silber, *Gaudier-Brzeska: life and art* (1996) · H. Brodzky, *Henri Gaudier-Brzeska* (1932) · R. Secrétain, *Un sculpteur 'maudit': Gaudier-Brzeska, 1891–1915* (1979) · H. Gaudier-Brzeska, 'Vortex—Gaudier-Brzeska', *Blast*, 1, 2 (1914–15) · R. Cole, *Burning to speak: the life and art of Henri Gaudier-Brzeska* (1978) · University of Essex Library, Colchester, Gaudier-Brzeska MSS · Musée des Beaux-Arts, Orléans, Brzeska MSS · d. certs. [Germain Gaudier and Marie-Alexandrine Gaudier]

Archives Kettle's Yard, Cambridge, sketchbooks and papers · University of Essex Library, Colchester, corresp. and papers, incl. diaries and literary MSS of Sophie Brzeska · V&A NAL, corresp. | Tate collection, corresp. with Kitty Smith · U. Hull, corresp. with E. Marsh · University of Essex Library, Colchester, corresp. with S. Brzeska · V&A NAL, corresp. with H. MacFall · Yale U., corresp. with E. Pound | SOUND BL NSA, 'Vortex-Gaudier-Brzeska', 19 May 1965, NP6943WR

Likenesses H. Gaudier-Brzeska, self-portrait, chalk drawing, 1912, NPG [*see illus.*] · H. Brodzky, oils, 1913, Musée des Beaux-Arts, Orléans, France · A. Wolmark, oils, *c.*1913, Musée des Beaux-Arts, Orléans, France · W. Benington, photographs, Leeds City Art Gallery · W. Benington, photographs (copies), Tate collection · H. Gaudier-Brzeska, self-portrait, pastel drawing, Southampton City Art Gallery · H. Gaudier-Brzeska, self-portrait, pen drawing, Leeds City Art Gallery · H. Gaudier-Brzeska, self-portrait, pencil drawing, NPG · H. Gaudier-Brzeska, self-portraits, pen-and-ink, pencil, and crayon drawings, Kettle's Yard, Cambridge

Buachalla, Domhnall Ua. See Buckley, Daniel Richard (1866–1963).

Bubwith, Nicholas (*c.*1355–1424), administrator and bishop of Bath and Wells, was born at Menthorpe in the

East Riding of Yorkshire, and brought up in nearby Bubwith. T. S. Holmes speculated that he was the son of Thomas and Isabel Bubwith and had two brothers, Henry and Thomas. His protégé and servant, Thomas Bubwith (son of William), was almost certainly a kinsman. If he was ever at Oxford University, he left no mark. His family evidently had existing contacts with royal administration, and he may well have been a chancery clerk as early as June 1379, enjoying church preferment regularly thereafter, although only on 7 February 1387 was he first called 'king's clerk'.

Bubwith's career in chancery remained solid if unspectacular throughout the 1390s. During Richard II's two Irish expeditions (in 1394–5 and 1399), he served as attorney in England for many leading participants. Early in 1399 he was promoted master in chancery. The revolution of 1399 affected him not at all. Briefly, in 1402, he became Henry IV's secretary, proof of that king's continuing difficulty in running an effective government rather than of special intimacy. He returned to his chancery career as keeper of the rolls from 24 September 1402.

In these years Bubwith was frequently a proctor for prelates and religious institutions in parliament. In March 1404 he was nominated to serve on the king's council, again as proof to sceptics of the king's intentions to provide competent government. None the less, he did not attend until his appointment as keeper of the privy seal on 2 March 1405, a post he held until his promotion to the episcopate. In faction-ridden and difficult times for governments Bubwith's value had been his simple ability to keep the machinery of state in motion, and for that he was well rewarded. In March 1403 his numerous benefices were reckoned to be worth over £800 a year.

Since July 1400 Bubwith had been archdeacon of Dorset, absentee but perhaps not without interest. In 1401–2 he briefly also held the powerful northern archdeaconry of Richmond. On 26 September 1406 he was consecrated at Mortlake after his promotion to the see of London. In a period of fraught domestic politics and Anglo-papal aggravations Bubwith was twice translated in reshuffles in 1407, first to Salisbury (which he never visited as bishop) and then, on 7 October, to Bath and Wells, not unwillingly. The temporalities were restored on 2 December. Still a councillor, he was persuaded on 15 April 1407 to assume the office of treasurer of the realm, and he rode out yet another financial crisis before retiring on 14 July 1408. Even thereafter, when factional purges were regular, Bubwith was always named to the council. In fact he rarely came out of Bath and Wells, where he was proving a conscientious diocesan, predictably of a brisk, administrative turn of mind.

Such congenial rustication was unexpectedly disturbed by Bubwith's appointment as a principal envoy of Henry V to the Council of Constance on 20 October 1414. While his colleague Robert Hallum of Salisbury was chosen to provide the intellectual lustre, Bubwith was selected for his reliability. Only in spring 1418 could Bubwith return to England and his diocese. His vigour left him in September 1422. His deathbed will of 10 October 1424 reflected him

fairly: considerable wealth, portioned out in particular for the completion of ambitious rebuildings of Bubwith church (£300) and Wells Cathedral (£667), roadworks in Somerset (£667), and prayers for his soul, especially by poor priests in Oxford and friars in London and his diocese (£667). It was in character that he referred to detailed oral instructions about all this. He died on 27 October 1424 and was buried in Wells Cathedral, in the chantry chapel which, of course, he had already constructed.

R. G. DAVIES, *rev.*

Sources Emden, *Oxf.*, 1.294–6 · J. Otway-Ruthven, *The king's secretary and the signet office in the XV century* (1939) · E. F. Jacob, ed., *The register of Henry Chichele, archbishop of Canterbury, 1414–1443*, 2, CYS, 42 (1937), 298–302 · T. S. Holmes, ed., *The register of Nicholas Bubwith, bishop of Bath and Wells, 1407–1424*, 2 vols., Somerset RS, 29–30 (1914) · GL, MS 9531/4, fols. 21–36v · register of Richard Mitford and Nicholas Bubwith, Wilts. & Swindon RO
Archives Wilts. & Swindon RO, register
Wealth at death £2300 monetary wealth: will, Jacob, ed., *Register*

Buc, Sir George. See Buck, Sir George (*bap.* 1560, *d.* 1622).

Buccleuch. For this title name *see* Scott, James, duke of Monmouth and first duke of Buccleuch (1649–1685); Scott, Anna, duchess of Monmouth and *suo jure* duchess of Buccleuch (1651–1732); Scott, Henry, third duke of Buccleuch and fifth duke of Queensberry (1746–1812); Scott, Walter Francis Montagu-Douglas-, fifth duke of Buccleuch and seventh duke of Queensberry (1806–1884); Scott, Charlotte Anne Montagu-Douglas-, duchess of Buccleuch and Queensberry (1811–1895) [*see under* Scott, Walter Francis Montagu-Douglas-, fifth duke of Buccleuch and seventh duke of Queensberry (1806–1884)].

Bucer, Martin (1491–1551), theologian, was born on 11 November 1491 in Schlettstadt (Sélestat) in Alsace. Little is known of his parents: his father, Claus Butzer (*d.* 1540), was a cooper by trade, while his mother, Eva (*d.* 1538), is thought to have been a midwife. Nothing is known of any siblings.

Early years, 1491–1523 Early in Bucer's life his parents moved to Strasbourg (where they later became citizens), leaving him in the care of his paternal grandfather. It is likely (though not proven) that Bucer received his early education at the famous Latin school of Schlettstadt. To continue his education he chose to enter the Dominican order at the convent in Schlettstadt in 1507, and took his vows in 1508. In 1515 he was sent to study for the priesthood, first at Heidelberg and then in 1516 at Mainz, and was probably ordained in 1516 when he reached the canonical age of twenty-five. He matriculated at the university in Heidelberg on 31 January 1517, where in due course he took the degrees of MA and BTh. While at Heidelberg he was present at Luther's disputation on 18 April 1518, which proved to be one of the most formative events of Bucer's career. Whereas earlier he was much under the influence of Erasmus of Rotterdam, Bucer now came under the spell of Luther. His advocacy of Luther led to persecution by his superiors, and Bucer was able finally to secure release from his monastic vows on 29 April 1521; he then became a secular priest.

Martin Bucer (1491–1551), by unknown engraver

For the next few years Bucer held a number of positions, first as chaplain to the count palatine, Friedrich, and then from May 1522 as pastor of Landstuhl (in the gift of Franz von Sickingen). It was there that he married the former nun Elisabeth Palass or, more commonly, Silbereisen (*d.* 1541), thus becoming among the first of the soon-to-be reformers to take a wife. They had several children. Later in that same year he left Landstuhl with the permission of Sickingen, who offered to provide support to Bucer in order to undertake study with Luther. On his way to Wittenberg, Bucer passed through the town of Weissenburg (Wissembourg), where the preacher Heinrich Motherer persuaded him to remain and assist in the work of Reformation. Here he laboured through the winter, with the final result that he was (with Motherer) excommunicated and the two were forced to flee to Strasbourg in April 1523.

The beginning of reform in Strasbourg, 1523–1529 Bucer was able to secure protection from the city on the grounds that his father was a citizen, and he subsequently attained citizenship in his own right on 22 September 1524. Almost immediately upon his arrival Bucer began lecturing on the Bible at the request of a number of citizens. Though initially restrained from further public preaching by order of the town council (in view of his excommunicate status), by the end of 1523 Bucer was appointed by the council as a salaried lecturer on the New Testament. Bucer joined Matthäus Zell (priest to the Strasbourg Cathedral parish), Wolfgang Capito (dean of the collegiate chapter of the church of St Thomas), and Caspar Hedio (the principal

cathedral preacher) in agitating for reform in Strasbourg. They were supported in this by the councilman Jacob Sturm, with whom Bucer formed a close working relationship. Bucer produced in 1523 his first major treatise, *Das ym selbs Niemant, sonder Anderen leben soll* ('That no one should live for himself but for others'), in which Bucer emphasized the church as a community of believers living a life of mutual service and love. These two themes—the church as a community and the Christian life as one of service to others—marked much of Bucer's subsequent writing and work, and gave it a strongly ethical character. In April 1524 the parishioners of St Aurelien chose him as their minister, as a result of which the town council was able to assume authority for subsequent pastoral appointments. Bucer thus began what would be a long career of parish ministry in Strasbourg. In 1531 he became pastor of St Thomas, and subsequently dean of its collegiate chapter in succession to Capito.

Bucer's work for the establishment of reform (in which he soon took the lead among the Strasbourg theologians) proceeded along two fronts, principally in the face of opposition from the Catholic bishop of Strasbourg, but also against the Anabaptists. He was largely responsible for the *Grund und Ursach* ('Ground and basis'), written in 1524, which set forth the programme of reform for Strasbourg. While he remained on good terms with Luther (and translated a number of Lutheran works from Latin into German), Bucer began to be drawn towards Ulrich Zwingli, in part because of their common struggle against Anabaptists but especially on the question of the eucharist or the Lord's supper. For a number of years Bucer worked closely with Zwingli and other Swiss reformers (including Johannes Oecolampadius of Basel), and participated with them in the disputation of Bern (1528). In addition to his struggles against the Catholic hierarchy and the Anabaptists (during which he produced several treatises against each), Bucer also published a number of highly regarded commentaries on books of the Bible, beginning in 1527 with a harmony of the synoptic gospels and a commentary on Ephesians, and then in 1528 commentaries on the gospel of John and the prophecy of Zephaniah, and then his massive commentary on the Psalms in 1529. His works on John, Psalms, and the gospels went through a number of later editions; the last of his major commentaries published during his lifetime was that on Romans (1536).

Ecclesiastical organizer and mediator among protestants, 1529–1536 Led by Bucer, reform in Strasbourg proceeded at a measured pace during these years, and reached a culmination in the synod of 1533 and the institution of a church order and catechism in 1534. In addition to completing the break with the Catholic hierarchy (the mass had already been abolished in 1529), the Strasbourg theologians successfully concluded a long struggle against the Anabaptists at this time. Bucer's reputation as an ecclesiastical organizer led to his invitation to take part in the reform of other towns and territories in Germany—Ulm (1531), Augsburg (1534–7), and then later Hesse (1538–9) and Cologne (1543). He also began to emerge as the leading protestant theologian in southern Germany. During the Diet of Augsburg (1530) it was Bucer who (with Capito) was responsible for drafting the Tetrapolitan confession (1530), to which Strasbourg, Konstanz (Constance), Memmingen, and Lindau subscribed when they were unable to accept the Lutheran Augsburg confession.

However, his most significant labours during these years were his efforts to achieve concord between the Swiss protestants and the Lutherans on the issue of the eucharist. The often bitter dispute not only divided protestantism theologically, but also prevented the formation of a united political front in opposition to the emperor. As noted above, Bucer gravitated towards the position of Zwingli on this issue. Following the Zürich reformer, he adopted a symbolic and memorialistic understanding of the Lord's supper, holding that Christ is spiritually present by faith and thus only to believers. In contrast the Lutherans insisted that there is a real, substantial presence of Christ in the sacrament, explaining it as a presence 'with, in and under' the elements rather than replacing them (thus in distinction from the Roman Catholic doctrine of transubstantiation), and they maintained that Christ is present in the sacrament to believers and unbelievers alike. Bucer became convinced towards the end of the 1520s that Luther and Zwingli held to the same position regarding the presence of Christ even though they expressed themselves differently. The key was his understanding of Christ's 'sacramental' presence, a phrase he found in Luther's writings at this time. Since Bucer believed that the difference was one of words, the solution would be found in a properly formulated statement of doctrine to which the major parties could subscribe.

This conviction became a cause for Bucer, who spent the years after the colloquy of Marburg (1529) travelling throughout Germany and Switzerland in search of an agreement. In the process of this undertaking he drew closer to the Lutherans (whom earlier he had alienated during his own Zwinglian phase) and as a consequence antagonized the Swiss protestants. An agreement was sealed in the Wittenberg concord between the Lutherans and the protestants of southern Germany in 1536. Unfortunately for Bucer's efforts the Swiss-German protestants refused to subscribe, in part because of their zealous protection of Zwingli's memory and continued suspicion of Luther, but also because they held fast to their belief that Christ was present in the supper only to those who believed. Bucer, for his part, continued to maintain that belief was central to the question of Christ's presence, and made a distinction between unworthy believers (to whom Christ was present) and rank unbelievers (to whom he was not). In spite of the Swiss-German rejection of the agreement, it was nevertheless (politically speaking) partially successful, for it did provide the theological basis for the Schmalkaldic League of the German protestant states.

Emergence as an ecclesiastical statesman, 1536–1543 In the 1530s both Catholic and protestant theologians within Germany began to suggest that a compromise might be arrived at by means of a national church council, thus preventing an irrevocable schism. Bucer was among the first to promote this idea, producing in 1533 his *Furbereytung zum Concilio* ('Groundwork for a council') and in 1534 *Defensio adversus axioma Catholicum* ('Defence against the Catholic principle'). In the latter, among his proposals was a suggestion that where scripture was not explicit the church of the first five centuries be used as a standard against which reform could be measured in non-doctrinal matters, specifically ceremonies and practice. The possibility of a national council of the German estates to reform the church, mooted for a number of years, began to look more promising as a result of a number of colloquies held in the late 1530s in which Bucer took part. He emerged alongside—in some ways even overtook—Philip Melanchthon as the leading protestant collocutor and advocate of a general council, turning out numerous tracts (some anonymously) in support of the idea. He was supported in his efforts by Landgrave Philip of Hesse, a leader in the Schmalkaldic League (whose bigamous marriage Bucer reluctantly supported).

In these years Bucer made the transition from being a leading protestant churchman in southern Germany to being perhaps the leading protestant churchman in the empire, and he attended colloquies with Catholics at Leipzig (1539), Hagenau (1540), and Worms (1540). At Worms he worked in secret with Johann Gropper (theological adviser to Hermann von Wied, archbishop of Cologne) to produce a text upon which discussions were to proceed, while Melanchthon and Johann Eck publicly negotiated the issues. This work, known as the Worms-Regensburg Book, became the centrepiece of the Regensburg colloquy of 1541, where Bucer joined Melanchthon and Johann Pistorius for the protestant side, faced on the Catholic side by Gropper, Eck, and Julius Pflug. Though the collocutors were able to reach agreement on the doctrine of sin, and even on that of justification, the process of reconciliation came to grief when the discussion turned to the eucharist, and the colloquy failed to achieve its goal.

Yet Bucer forged ahead, producing in the aftermath of Regensburg further treatises on the matter of reform in the empire, as well as an account of the ill-fated colloquy. Whereas his reputation with many fellow protestants had suffered as a result of his apparent willingness to compromise with the Catholics to the threshold of betrayal, his more definitively protestant stance at this time began to restore his reputation. In late 1542 he was invited by the archbishop of Cologne (who was also an elector of the empire) to join with Gropper in the reform of the diocese of Cologne. This was probably the greatest commission of Bucer's career. He believed that, if successful, he could establish a measured approach to reform that could function as a standard for the entire empire. The commission had not only ecclesiastical implications, but also far-reaching political implications, for if the electoral territory of Cologne became protestant the balance of power among electors within the empire would shift in favour of the protestant movement. Bucer laboured through 1543, joined by Melanchthon and then Pistorius. Though he had the full support of the archbishop, Gropper and the cathedral chapter were implacably opposed to him. With Melanchthon he produced in 1543 a plan for reform, the *Einfaltiges Bedencken* ('A simple consultation'), later translated into Latin as *Simplex ac pia deliberatio* (1545). Bucer was responsible for the latter half of the work, which dealt with ecclesiastical practices and the liturgy, and it displays his measured approach to reform. But despite high expectations, political circumstances caused the failure of the effort. The attempt at Cologne proved to be the last major effort on Bucer's part at a measured, comprehensive reform within the German empire, and marked the high point of his career as an ecclesiastical statesman.

The final years in Strasbourg, 1536–1549 Though the synod of 1533 and the catechism of 1534 marked the triumph of the Strasbourg theologians over both the Catholics and the Anabaptists, Bucer was dissatisfied with what he had achieved thus far, and pushed ahead with plans for a more complete reformation. It was his aim to establish a church order independent from, but working in co-operation with, the municipal authorities, and to this end he laboured for the remaining years of his career in Strasbourg in the face of increasing resistance from the city council. His concern for an institution of Christian discipline became more pronounced, and in his major work of pastoral theology, *Von der Waren Seelsorge* ('Concerning true pastoral care', 1538), he identified discipline as one of the marks of the true church. In this (as in some other areas) he influenced John Calvin, recently expelled from Geneva, who spent several formative years in Strasbourg (1538–41). In 1539 Bucer presided at a second Strasbourg synod, through which he hoped to further his plans of reform, but the city council was increasingly reluctant to be guided by their leading theologian in the paths he sought to lead them. In 1541 his wife, Elisabeth, died of the plague, as did some of his children and his close friend Wolfgang Capito. In 1542 Bucer married the widow of Capito, Wibrandis, *née* Rosenblatt (1504–1564), who had also been the wife of Oecolampadius, and before him of Ludwig Keller.

Bucer was elected to the collegiate chapter of St Thomas in 1541, and to the post of dean in 1544. His election in the latter year as the head of the newly established Kirchen Konvent ('college of preachers') marked the apex of his authority in Strasbourg, but he was soon to find that authority slipping away from him. Beginning in the winter of 1546–7 and against the backdrop of the Schmalkaldic war, *christlichen Gemeinschaften* ('Christian fellowships') were formed in a number of the Strasbourg parishes with the intention to put into practice the kind of piety Bucer had been advocating for the past decade. These fellowships were envisaged as voluntary societies of committed believers within the several parishes. Participants were to pledge themselves to live in mutual love and service according to the pattern first described by Bucer in *Das ym selbs* (1523) and to be subject to the kind of Christian discipline that Bucer had sought to institute since the early 1530s. The hope was that the fellowships would become the nucleus for a further reformation of Strasbourg, leading the wider church community by example. Bucer wrote in support of these fellowships, and was joined in his advocacy by Paul Fagius (minister of New St Peter), but several other pastors opposed him and most importantly the city council came to oppose the practice. His already strained relationship with the magistrates and especially with Jacob Sturm reached its nadir when Bucer returned from the Augsburg diet of August 1548, held in the aftermath of the decisive defeat of the Schmalkaldic League and at which the emperor, Charles V, imposed the settlement known as the Interim. Whereas he had initially subscribed to the Interim (though under some duress), upon his return to Strasbourg Bucer vigorously opposed it. In fact Strasbourg at first resisted becoming a signatory to the agreement, but was compelled to submit in 1549. As the most visible opponent of the Interim, Bucer was forced to go into exile (along with Fagius), and he left Strasbourg on 6 April 1549. Of the many invitations that lay before him the one he chose to accept was that of the archbishop of Canterbury, Thomas Cranmer.

Arrival in England, 1549 Bucer's direct relations with England long antedated his arrival in 1549, beginning formally in 1531 when he was among the continental theologians consulted in the matter of Henry VIII's divorce from Katherine of Aragon. After this initial contact he retained a keen interest in England. Bucer approved of Stephen Gardiner's *De vera obedientia* (1535) and even wrote a positive preface to it. However, after the Act of Six Articles in 1539 Bucer judged that Gardiner was the principal obstacle to further reform in England. Following their meeting at the Regensburg colloquy they engaged in a polemical exchange on the doctrine of justification, which led to Bucer's *Gratulatio ad ecclesiam Anglicanam* ('Congratulation to the English church', 1548). Though ostensibly written for the purpose its title suggests, it was largely a bitter attack on Gardiner. But it was Bucer's relationship with Thomas Cranmer that proved to be the most important, and it probably began in connection with the consultation regarding Henry's divorce. Bucer demonstrated his regard for Cranmer in dedicating to him his 1536 commentary on Romans, warmly approving of the proposal for an alliance of all protestant churches, more specifically between England and the Schmalkaldic League. The two subsequently exchanged letters, and in time Bucer came to be a significant influence upon Cranmer's eucharistic thinking. This was especially the case in November 1547, when Cranmer received a letter from Bucer on this doctrinal issue that moved him decisively away from a Lutheran position. Cranmer had also followed closely the events of the attempted reform of Cologne (and with them Bucer's efforts). The treatises produced during that time were of great interest to him, especially Bucer's *Bestendige Antworten* ('Steadfast response') of which Cranmer had a manuscript Latin translation (*Constans defensio*), as well as Bucer's proposed reform for Cologne, the *Einfaltiges Bedencken* (also in the possession of Cranmer in its Latin version). This last work, in addition to providing a model of the kind of measured reform for which Cranmer strove, is generally regarded—in view of its lengthy treatment of the reform of liturgy and its own character as a synthesis of other liturgical texts and thus a model for liturgical reform—as a significant source for the composition of the 1549 Book of Common Prayer. This was particularly the case with respect to the order for the communion service, where a number of the texts, as well as the exhortation and the prayers of confession, humble access, and the absolution were drawn from Bucer's work. Further, another treatise of Bucer's, *De ordinatione legitima* ('On restoring lawful ordination', 1549?), was a source for the ordinal appended to the prayer book. It is not surprising that Cranmer should have been keen to recruit Bucer for the Reformation in England, and had been writing to him for this purpose since December 1547.

Bucer and Fagius arrived in England on 23 April 1549 and spent several months in the company of Cranmer, moving between Lambeth and Croydon. They were presented to the king on 5 May. During these months Bucer and Fagius were given the task of translating the Bible into Latin and of providing a commentary on the text. The purpose of the project (in which Cranmer himself joined) was to provide a critical Latin text from which a fresh English translation would be made. Bucer's proximity to and close relationship with Cranmer at this time were a cause of much concern to the Zwinglian party among the English, who were striving to increase the influence of Zürich and particularly of Heinrich Bullinger over the English church and saw Bucer as a principal obstacle to that goal.

Professor at Cambridge, 1549–1551 In the first week of July 1549 Bucer arrived at Cambridge, where he was intended to take up a teaching post as regius professor of divinity (Fagius was to become the regius professor of Hebrew), and where—apart from a few trips—he spent the remainder of his English sojourn. It was in Cambridge that Bucer exerted his greatest personal influence in these final two years of his life. Though not confirmed in his post until late in the year (the letters patent were not signed until December, a point of much embarrassment to Cranmer), once he began to exercise the duties of his office his impact was profound. He was the greatest foreign divine to come to England since Erasmus (also a one-time resident at Cambridge). The extent of his personal influence cannot be measured with any precision, but it was none the less wide and deep. For several decades afterwards his words were cited with great reverence by those who were up at university during these years—including those on opposite sides of an argument, such as John Whitgift and Thomas Cartwright, who quoted Bucer against each other in the admonition controversy some twenty years after his death.

Bucer finally took up his duties as regius professor in January 1550, lecturing on Paul's letter to the Ephesians before large numbers of students and senior members of university. He also began presiding at disputations, and is reported to have begun a series of sermons in Latin (he did not speak English) on John 6. These elicited the wrath not only of the Zwinglians (whose opposition Bucer felt keenly) but also of the Catholic party, which was still strong at Cambridge, especially in Trinity College. Upon his installation Bucer became a member of Trinity (to which college his professorship, itself a royal foundation, was attached). He lived in a house owned by the college, the foundations of which are now under the present Great Court, and in which his friend Nicholas Carr subsequently lived. Though on the whole his time in Cambridge was beneficial for him it was not without sorrow, trials, and disappointment. He was deprived by death of his close friend Fagius on 13 November 1549, a blow that compounded his depression arising from homesickness and the fact that his appointment was delayed. After his assumption of duties he was forced on several occasions to suspend his lectures due to his own poor health, and he never seems to have adjusted to the Cambridge climate or the English diet. Compounding these problems were Bucer's sense of isolation from the court and his belief that he was insufficiently employed in the service of English reform, as he pointed out more than once in correspondence with the continental reformers John Calvin and Johannes Brenz. A progressively more critical view of the course of the Reformation in England also becomes manifest in his letters during these months and eventually in some of his writings. He came to note with some sharpness how far courtiers were using the Reformation to enrich themselves, and above all he lamented the establishment's failure adequately to promote the preaching ministry of the church, which he thought essential to the promotion of reform.

Theological debate Bucer's trials were not all of a personal nature, and his time in Cambridge was not without controversy or opposition. His relations with members of Trinity (apart from the master, John Redman) do not appear to have been good, and may have given rise to the often negative views he expressed in his correspondence about aspects of university life, especially about the resistance to evangelical reform. In June 1550 a disputation was held before royal visitors between three Catholic fellows (Thomas Sedgwick and John Young of Trinity College, and Andrew Perne of Peterhouse) and Bucer on the subjects of justification by faith, the sufficiency of scripture, and whether the church could err. The next month Bucer went to Oxford, accompanied by John Bradford, in order to visit Pietro Martire Vermigli. While Bucer was away Young began a series of lectures on 1 Timothy in which he attacked Bucer personally, taking aim in particular at his teaching on justification. When Bucer returned he protested at Young's actions and then submitted a written account of the earlier dispute to Young and Sedgwick asking for a response in writing from them. The strife went on into August, and Bucer's anxiety is seen in the letter he wrote to Edmund Grindal (the vice-master of Pembroke College) regarding the affair, asking him to convey the details to the bishop of London, Nicholas Ridley (also master of Pembroke) that he might intervene. In the end, the matter seems to have exhausted itself without decisive resolution.

In addition to controversy with Catholics, Bucer also faced opposition from the Zwinglian or Zürich party within the English church. Following their mentors in Zürich, members of this party regarded Bucer with deep suspicion—if not, indeed, as a traitor—on account of his rapprochement in 1536 with the Lutherans on the issue of the Lord's supper, and they were deeply concerned that he would lead Cranmer (whom they hoped to enlist for the Zürich camp) to adopt his own understanding of it. In September 1550 Bucer was visited by the Polish reformer John à Lasco (a leading Zwinglian) who desired to discuss matters of doctrine, principally the Lord's supper and the question of the real presence, with the aim of either persuading Bucer to change his views or at least of neutralizing his influence. The interview ended amicably but inconclusively. Shortly afterwards Bucer sent a statement of his position to à Lasco, which the latter annotated in order to refute him and which he then in turn forwarded to Cranmer in an effort to influence him away from Bucer. Bucer began to compose anew a fuller statement of his position, which was incomplete upon his death.

Involvement in English reform All was not strife and disappointment, and whatever he may have thought in his darker moments Bucer was far from being ignored. At some point in the latter months of 1550 he was consulted on the matter of the demolition of altars. In November 1550 he became involved in a controversy over vestments at the centre of which stood the bishop-elect of Gloucester, John Hooper, and in which he generally supported Cranmer and Ridley against Hooper. Most important, he was commissioned to review the 1549 Book of Common Prayer, a task he completed on 5 January 1551 and conveyed to Bishop Thomas Goodrich of Ely, who in turn would have sent it on to Cranmer. It was through this work, the so-called *Censura*—a careful analysis of the 1549 prayer book with suggestions for improvements—that Bucer exercised what was probably his greatest direct influence on the English church, as well as his most lasting influence. Though the extent of its impact upon the 1552 prayer book is difficult to determine with any precision, it does seem that a number of changes reflect his critique—for instance his calls for the reduction in vestments used, the abolition of private communion, the elimination of prayers for the faithful departed, and his suggestion that services no longer be celebrated in the choir but in the presence of the people, all changes found in the revised prayer book.

While death prevented Bucer's taking part in the framing of the forty-two articles (1553) and the work of canon law revision, one can only assume that had he been alive his living voice would have made a contribution here as well. In his magnum opus, *De regno Christi* (a presentation copy of which was sent to Edward VI by way of John Cheke on 21 October 1550), one can sense the ways in which his continued active influence might have been felt, especially in regard to the reform of canon law. The work, written at the suggestion of friends and in grateful response to Edward's gift of money for two German heating stoves to enable Bucer better to endure the bitter Cambridge winter, was a blueprint for the thorough reformation of English society. It consisted of two parts: in the first Bucer set

forth his understanding of the kingdom of Christ, and then articulated the rationale for his programme; in the second part he proposed fourteen laws by which the reform of English society was to be achieved. This work not only displayed to the full the ethical character of Bucer's theology, but also demonstrated a remarkable knowledge of the social and economic situation of England. Though it was never translated in its entirety, portions of *De regno Christi* relating to poor relief were published in English in the reign of Elizabeth I (*A Treatise, How by the Worde of God, Christian Mens Almose Ought to be Distributed*, no date), while the lengthy section on divorce was translated by John Milton (*The Judgement of Martin Bucer, Concerning Divorce, Writt'n to Edward the Sixt, in his Second Book of the Kingdom of Christ. And now Englisht*, London, 1644).

Death and influence Bucer's health, never good in these years, finally turned for the worst, and he died (probably of tuberculosis) while at Cambridge some time in the night of 28 February/1 March 1551. His funeral was attended by some 3000 people, both town and gown, and he was buried on 3 March in Great St Mary's Church. Walter Haddon gave the Latin eulogy and Matthew Parker preached the English sermon. On the following day John Redman presided at a memorial communion service. Haddon and Parker were the executors of his will. His property, consisting of household goods and his library, was valued at £380. The library was divided in three. The king was to receive the manuscripts, and the books were divided between Catherine Brandon, duchess of Suffolk (a close friend to Bucer), and Cranmer. In fact the manuscripts and at least some of the books ended up in the possession of Parker. Bucer's story in Cambridge does not end with his death, for during the reign of Mary I his remains and those of Fagius were disinterred and burnt on Market Hill, on 6 February 1557, a heresy trial having been held previously. The condemnation was reversed in July 1560, when a ceremony was held to restore to full honour the names of both reformers.

The full measure of Bucer's importance for the Reformation has yet to be taken. Work on various aspects of his theology has begun to pick up pace with the production of a critical edition of his works, but he remains less understood than many of his fellow reformers. No doubt the extreme illegibility of his handwriting has much to do with this (Grindal once said it required a conjuror to make sense of it), but the difficult style and verbosity of his writing has proved an obstacle as well. Calvin said Bucer could not lift his pen from the paper, and Luther termed him a *klappermaul* ('blabbermouth'). Yet there is no gainsaying his importance as the leading theological mediator of his day, or his stature as an ecclesiastical statesman and organizer. His personality, especially his generosity of spirit, was such that he was on good terms even with many of those who were at odds with him, and this remained true throughout his entire career. His standing as a theologian must be assessed with respect to his constant involvement in negotiation, but in any case he was more a pastoral theologian than a systematic one. Perhaps he would have left a more substantial imprint on the theology of the period had he remained in his study in Strasbourg and written more, but such was not to be his calling.

With respect to his impact upon the course of the Reformation during the reign of Edward VI and beyond, its measure must be taken through Cambridge, for it was here that he made his closest English friends—many of whom were significant participants in both Edward VI's regime and that of Elizabeth I. During his eighteen months in Cambridge he came to know not only Parker, Haddon, Cheke, Carr, and Bradford, but also Roger Ascham, Grindal, and Edwin Sandys. Yet care must be taken not to confine his sphere of influence for these years to Cambridge alone, for he continued to be a significant part of the wider Reformation as it was played out in the England of Edward VI as well as that of Elizabeth I. This final phase of Bucer's career was short, but its importance in relation both to England and to his career as a whole proved to be significant. Indeed, as one commentator has observed, 'in view of all that subsequently transpired in Strasbourg, it could be argued that it was in England that the echo of Bucer's voice resounded longest' (Collinson, 25).   N. SCOTT AMOS

Sources M. Greschat, *Martin Bucer: ein Reformator und seine Zeit* (Munich, 1990) · H. Eells, *Martin Bucer* (1931) · H. Vogt, 'Martin Bucer und die Kirche von England', diss., University of Münster, 1968 · C. Hopf, *Martin Bucer and the English Reformation* (1946) · A. E. Harvey, 'Martin Bucer in England', PhD diss., University of Marburg, 1906 · D. MacCulloch, *Thomas Cranmer: a life* (1996) · R. Stupperich, 'Bucer, Martin (1491–1551)', *Theologische Realenzyklopädie*, ed. G. Krause, G. Müller, and S. Schwertner, 7 (Berlin, 1981), 258–70 · D. F. Wright, ed., *Martin Bucer: reforming church and community* (1994) · A. N. Burnett, *The yoke of Christ: Martin Bucer and Christian discipline* (1994) · M. U. Chrisman, *Strasbourg and the reform: a study in the process of religious change* (New Haven, Connecticut, 1967) · G. C. Gorham, *Gleanings of a few scattered ears, during the period of the Reformation in England* (1857) · H. Robinson, ed. and trans., *Original letters relative to the English Reformation*, 1 vol. in 2, Parker Society, [26] (1846–7) · D. F. Wright, *Commonplaces of Martin Bucer* (1972) · M. Köhn, *Martin Bucers Entwurf einer Reformation des Erzstiftes Köln* (Witten, 1966) · T. Brady, *Protestant politics: Jacob Sturm (1489–1553) and the German Reformation* (Atlantic Highlands, New Jersey, 1995) · C. Krieger and M. Lienhard, eds., *Martin Bucer and sixteenth-century Europe: actes du colloque* [Strasbourg 1991], 2 vols. (1993) · R. Bornert, *La Réforme protestante du culte à Strasbourg au XVIe siècle* (Leiden, 1981) · J. Rott, 'Le sort des papiers et de la bibliothèque de Bucer en Angleterre', *Revue d'histoire et de philosophe religieuses*, 46 (1966), 346–67 · P. Collinson, *Godly people: essays on English protestantism and puritanism* (1983)

Archives CCC Cam., Parker collection, letters and papers | Archives (Départementales et Régionales) du Bas-Rhin, Strasbourg · Archives Municipales de Strasbourg, Archives du chapitre Saint-Thomas · Archives Municipales de Strasbourg · Bibliothèque Nationale et Universitaire de Strasbourg, Thesaurus Baumianus, papers, MSS 660–709

Likenesses F. Hagenauer, medal, 1543, Staatliche Münzesammlung, Munich · R. Boyvin, engraving, 1561–2, Bibliothèque Nationale et Universitaire de Strasbourg · woodcut, 1581, BM, NPG; repro. in T. Beza, *Icones*, new edn (1581) · monogrammiste SD [DS], print, 1586, Bibliothèque Nationale et Universitaire de Strasbourg · J. Faber senior/R. Houston, mezzotint (after unknown artist), BM, NPG · line engraving, NPG [see *illus.*] · print, BL; repro.

in J. J. Boissard and others, *Icones quinquaginta virorum*, 4 vols. (Frankfurt, 1597–9)

Wealth at death £380—property in England: 12 May 1551, letter of Matthew Parker and Walter Haddon to the guardians of Bucer's children, Cambridge, Robinson, ed. and trans., *Original letters*, 2.361–2

Buchan. For this title name *see* individual entries under Buchan; *see also* Comyn, Alexander, sixth earl of Buchan (d. 1289); Comyn, John, seventh earl of Buchan (c.1250–1308); Stewart, Alexander, earl of Buchan (c.1345–1405); Stewart, John, tenth earl of Buchan (c.1380–1424); Stewart, James, earl of Buchan (1441/2?–1499/1500); Erskine, James, sixth earl of Buchan (d. 1640); Erskine, David Steuart, eleventh earl of Buchan (1742–1829).

Buchan, Alastair Francis (1918–1976), writer on strategic and international affairs, was born at 76 Portland Place, London, on 9 September 1918, the third son and the fourth and youngest child of John *Buchan, first Baron Tweedsmuir (1875–1940), and his wife, Susan Charlotte (1882–1977), daughter of Captain Norman de l'Aigle Grosvenor, third son of the first Baron Ebury. He was educated at Eton College and at Christ Church, Oxford, where he took second-class honours in modern history in 1939. After spending a short while at the University of Virginia, he was commissioned in the Canadian army in 1939 (his father being at that time governor-general of the dominion) and saw active service at Dieppe in 1942 and, as a major, in north-west Europe in 1944–5. On 11 April 1942 he married Hope Gordon (d. 1997), daughter of David Gordon Gilmour, of Ottawa, Canada, lumberman. They had two sons and a daughter.

After demobilization Buchan turned to journalism. He served as assistant editor of *The Economist* from 1948 until 1951, when he went to Washington as correspondent for *The Observer*. There he remained until 1955, observing at close quarters the political turmoil resulting from the Korean War and the witch-hunts initiated by Senator McCarthy. It was then that he laid the foundations of his expertise in the major problems of defence and nuclear armament that were of increasing concern to decision makers at this period in Washington and elsewhere; and his writing on this topic gained him the respect of senior officials and political figures, as well as his fellow journalists, in both the United States and Europe.

In 1955 Buchan returned to London and continued to work for *The Observer* as its diplomatic and defence correspondent. He was there able to pursue a private interest in the life and work of the founder of *The Economist*, Walter Bagehot, which led to the publication in 1959 of an excellent brief study, *The Spare Chancellor*. But his main interest lay in the increasingly complex and controversial field of defence and nuclear deterrence, and he accepted with alacrity the invitation to become the first director of the newly formed Institute for Strategic Studies in 1958.

The object which the founders of the institute had in mind was to make generally available information on defence questions, in order to educate public opinion in a debate that was at that time engendering more heat than light. An essential element in this programme was to persuade responsible officials to release more information and share their concerns with a wider public. A difficult path had therefore to be trodden in order to retain the confidence both of Whitehall and of Fleet Street, and in this Buchan succeeded brilliantly. Further, his contacts in the United States enabled him to enlist the interest of such seminal strategic thinkers in that country as Bernard Brodie, Albert Wohlstetter, Thomas Schelling, and Henry Kissinger. European thinkers such as Raymond Aron in France and Helmut Schmidt in Germany were also drawn in. As a result the International Institute for Strategic Studies (as it later became) developed from a simple information centre into the principal forum of strategic debate in the Western world, where officials, journalists, academics, and military men met and freely exchanged ideas. To these ideas Buchan himself made a continuing contribution with his books and articles; but his real talents were entrepreneurial, the capacity to draw ideas out of others. The increasing intelligence and moderation with which such questions as nuclear deterrence, nuclear proliferation, and arms control were publicly discussed in the 1960s in all Western countries owed a very great deal to Buchan's influence.

Buchan retired from the directorship of the institute in 1969 to take up an appointment as commandant of the Imperial Defence College: the first non-official civilian ever to hold the post. Under his leadership the syllabus was broadened and the membership extended, its changed role being expressed in a new title: the Royal College of Defence Studies. In 1972, at the conclusion of his tour of duty, he became Montague Burton professor of international relations at Oxford, and began to develop a serious graduate school of international politics in that university. He had time barely to lay the foundations, however, when he died suddenly in his sleep on 4 February 1976, in his home, Waterloo House, Brill, near Oxford. His funeral was held in Brill on 10 February. A readership in international relations was established in his memory by Oxford University in 1980.

Although Eton and Christ Church had equipped Buchan with the agreeable worldliness of an upper-class Englishman, he was fundamentally a Scot, with formidable powers of work and a granite-hard integrity which impressed people even more than did his intellectual ability and the literary fluency he inherited from his father. He was appointed MBE in 1944 and CBE in 1968. In 1973 he gave the Reith lectures, with the theme 'Change without war'.

MICHAEL HOWARD, rev.

Sources *The Times* (5–6 Feb 1976) · R. D. Edwards, *The pursuit of reason: The Economist, 1843–1993* (1993) · *WWW* · personal knowledge (1986) · Burke, *Peerage* (2000)
Archives Arundel House, Temple Place, London, archives of the International Institute for Strategic Studies · Bodl. Oxf., corresp. with William Clark · NL Scot., letters to his brother, Lord Tweedsmuir | SOUND BBC, Reith lectures, 1973
Likenesses D. Poole, portrait, International Institute for Strategic Studies, London
Wealth at death £66,227: probate, 11 May 1976, *CGPLA Eng. & Wales*

Buchan, Alexander (1829–1907), meteorologist, was born on 12 April 1829 in Kinnesswood, Kinross-shire, the youngest of the four children of Alexander Buchan (*bap.* 1779), weaver, and his wife, Janet Hill (1791–1869). He was educated locally and at the Free Church Normal School in Edinburgh. He qualified as a teacher and between 1848 and 1860 was schoolmaster of the Free Church schools in Banchory, Blackford, and Dunblane. Initially his favourite science was botany and in 1858 he took part in an expedition to the Alps led by Professor Balfour of Edinburgh University.

Because of a weakness of the throat, Buchan could not continue with his teaching career and late in 1860 he was looking for another profession. Simultaneously the council of the Scottish Meteorological Society, which had been founded in 1855, decided not to renew the appointment of the current secretary, A. H. Burgess, and on 21 December 1860, following interviews with members of the council, Buchan was appointed as meteorological secretary. The primary object of the society was to investigate Scottish meteorology and this required a network of reliable climatological stations across Scotland. James Stark, the first secretary (and also superintendent of statistics for the Scottish registrar-general), initiated the network in 1855 and it expanded further under Buchan. The stations were manned by unpaid, voluntary observers, who had to follow strict regulations concerning the methods of observation and the completion of monthly returns. Regular inspection visits were made by the secretary to the stations. The secondary objects included the investigation of the general laws regulating atmospheric changes, the discovery of which might lead to a knowledge of the coming weather, and Buchan, though never directly involved in weather forecasting, played a major role in advancing this object.

From 1861 to 1863 Buchan attended classes at the University of Edinburgh and graduated MA in 1864. On 19 July 1864 he married Sarah Ritchie (1829–1900); their only son, Alexander Hill Buchan, who later studied medicine and became a general practitioner, was born in 1868. Also in 1868 **Jessie Hill** [*formerly* Janet Hill] **Buchan** (1848–1905), daughter of Buchan's elder brother Thomas Hill Buchan (1823–1895), a church officer, and his wife, Margaret Russell (*d.* 1895), became Buchan's assistant. She was born at Kinnesswood on 23 July 1848 and was often dux at school. She worked for the society until her sudden death from a heart attack on 7 December 1905 at 2 Dean Terrace, Edinburgh. She never married. As an expert calculator she was an invaluable assistant and special tributes to her work were paid in Buchan's memorial notices.

From 1856 *Quarterly Reports* of the proceedings of the society were published but 1864 saw the first publication of the *Journal of the Scottish Meteorological Society*. As well as being editor Buchan was the principal contributor to the journal, for which he wrote or co-wrote about sixty papers. He also published papers in the *Transactions* and *Proceedings* of the Royal Society of Edinburgh, of which he was elected a fellow in 1869; he was curator of its library from 1878 to 1906. In 1898 he became a fellow of the Royal Society of London.

Buchan published many papers relating to the weather and climate of Scotland and was particularly interested in how variations in temperature, rainfall, and wind were related to interactions between large scale weather systems and the geography of the country. He attributed the apparent interruptions which he found in the smooth annual progression of temperature (often called 'Buchan's spells') to a tendency for certain types of changes in pressure pattern to occur around certain dates. He published the first monthly and annual maps of mean sea level pressure and temperature for the British Isles in the *Journal of the Scottish Meteorological Society* (vol. 6, 1883). Maps of monthly and annual rainfall averages for Scotland for the period 1866–90 were published in the *Journal of the Scottish Meteorological Society* (vol. 10, 1894), based on data from 324 stations. Averages for stations with incomplete records were corrected by reference to full period stations.

In 1883 the Scottish Meteorological Society launched a public appeal to establish a meteorological observatory at the summit of Ben Nevis (1344 m), the highest mountain in Scotland. It operated from November 1883 to September 1904, when insufficient financial support from government sources forced its closure. Under Buchan's editorship the hourly observations from the mountain observatory and the low level one at Fort William (from 1890) were published in the *Transactions of the Royal Society of Edinburgh*, providing a comprehensive resource of mountain weather data.

Meteorology requires observations on a global scale and Buchan, through his contacts with meteorologists in many countries and his ability to handle large quantities of data, played a major role in determining the salient features of mid-latitude storms. Buchan's published analyses, using surface synoptic charts, of storms which could be traced from the United States across the Atlantic into Europe and other analyses in his *Handy Book of Meteorology* (2nd edn, 1868) demonstrated clearly the general application of the relationship (later known as Buys Ballot's law) between surface isobars and the wind field.

Buchan's greatest achievement was probably the publication of the first maps of mean atmospheric surface pressure and prevailing winds over the globe for individual months and the year (*Transactions of the Royal Society of Edinburgh*, 25, 1869). During the next thirty years, as more data became available, notably during the period of the *Challenger* expedition in 1872–4, he published refinements of these maps and added others for mean temperature.

Buchan's contribution to meteorology was widely acknowledged. He was one of the two British representatives to the international congresses in Leipzig (1872) and Vienna (1873), which standardized methods of making and reporting weather observations. From 1887 to 1904 he served on the council (set up by the Royal Society of London) which supervised the administration of the parliamentary grant for meteorology. In 1887 he was awarded the honorary degree of LLD by the University of Glasgow

and in 1902 he was the first recipient of the Symons' memorial medal of the Royal Meteorological Society.

Buchan was a tall man, whose long, silky beard concealed his mouth, but the laughter lines around the eyes, clearly apparent in his photographs, corroborate the description by his contemporaries of a friendly and congenial personality. His interests were by no means confined to science, and he and his wife were part of the vibrant intellectual social life which flourished in Edinburgh at that time. He had a profound knowledge and appreciation of literature and quickly recognized the talents of Robert Louis Stevenson, son of the lighthouse engineer Thomas Stevenson, who was honorary secretary of the Scottish Meteorological Society from 1872 to 1887. Throughout his life he retained his pedagogic abilities and H. R. Mill, in his memorial notice, described 'the kindly care with which he instructed me in the art of meteorological observing' (Mill, 104). Religion played an important part in Buchan's life and he was an elder in St George's United Free Church in Edinburgh.

Buchan's marriage and family life were extremely happy, but on 19 May 1900 his wife died at their home at 42 Heriot Row and he and his son moved to 2 Dean Terrace. He continued as secretary of the Scottish Meteorological Society until his death at his home from pneumonia on 13 May 1907. He was buried beside his wife in Warriston cemetery in Edinburgh.   MARJORY G. ROY

Sources A. Mitchell and others, 'Contributions towards a memorial notice of Alexander Buchan, M.A., L.L.D., F.R.S.', *Journal of the Scottish Meteorological Society*, 3rd ser., 14 (1908), 101–18 [includes bibliography of his publications] • H. R. Mill, *Quarterly Journal of the Royal Meteorological Society*, 34 (1908), 131–5 • minute books of the Scottish Meteorological Society, 1859–81, Scottish Weather Observations Centre, Edinburgh, Scottish Climatological Archives • Reports of the council to the general meetings of the Scottish Meteorological Society, *Proceedings of the Scottish Meteorological Society* (1856–63) • Reports of the council to the general meetings of the Scottish Meteorological Society, *Journal of the Scottish Meteorological Society*, 1–14 (1864–1908) • Scottish Weather Observations Centre, Edinburgh, Scottish Climatological Archives, Buchan MSS • *The Scotsman* (14 May 1907) • A. Buchan, *Handy book of meteorology*, 2nd edn (1868) • *Edinburgh University Calendar* (1860–64) • H. H. Hildebrandsson and L. Teisserenc de Bort, *Les bases de la météorologie dynamique: historique—états de nos connaissances* (1898) • b. cert. [Alexander Buchan] • b. cert. [Jessie Buchan] • m. cert. [Alexander Buchan] • d. cert. [Alexander Buchan] • d. cert. [Jessie Buchan] • d. cert. [Sarah Buchan] • private information (2004) • parish register (birth, baptism), Portmoak, Kinross-shire • records of Warriston cemetery, Edinburgh • parish register (mother's birth), Orwell

Archives Meteorological Office, Bracknell, Berkshire, National Meteorological Library and Archive, meteorological journals and observations • NRA, priv. coll., notebook; papers, mainly articles and offprints • Scottish Weather Observations Centre, Edinburgh, Scottish Climatological Archives, papers and MSS

Likenesses photograph, Scottish Weather Observations Centre, Edinburgh, Scottish Climatological Archives • photograph, repro. in Mitchell and others, 'Contributions towards a memorial notice …'

Wealth at death £2373 18s. 9d.: confirmation, 19 June 1907, CCI

Buchan, Alexander Peter (*bap.* **1764**, *d.* **1824**), physician, was the son of William *Buchan (1728/9–1805), physician and author of *Domestic Medicine*, and his wife, Elizabeth, *née* Peter. He was baptized on 17 May 1764 at Nether Chapel (Independent) in Sheffield. He was educated at Edinburgh high school and Edinburgh University, studied anatomy and medicine in London under John and William Hunter and George Fordyce, and proceeded to Leiden, where he graduated MD on 11 July 1793. Buchan then settled in London, and he became physician to the Westminster Hospital in 1813. He resigned that office in 1818 but was re-elected in 1820.

Buchan's works include *Enchiridion syphiliticum* (1797); *Treatise on Sea Bathing, with Remarks on the Use of the Warm Bath* (1801); *Bionomia, or, Opinions Concerning Life and Health* (1811); *Symptomatology* (1824); a translation of M. Daubenton's work on indigestion, in 1807; and an edition of George Armstrong's *Diseases Incident to Children*, in 1808. He also edited and made additions to several of his father's works.

Buchan died at his house in Percy Street, Rathbone Place, London, on 5 December 1824 and was buried in the west cloister of Westminster Abbey.

G. T. BETTANY, *rev.* KAYE BAGSHAW

Sources Munk, *Roll* · *IGI*

Buchan [Rathven], **Andrew of** (*d.* in or before 1304), bishop of Caithness, is first recorded in 1284, as abbot of the Cistercian house of Coupar Angus. A late transcript calls him 'of Rathven', probably the Banffshire Rathven. As abbot he witnessed charters of the earl of Buchan and Mar, and he also acted as a royal envoy in 1284 and as an exchequer auditor in 1289. He is recorded as paying homage to Edward I at Perth on 24 July 1291, and at Berwick-on-Tweed on 28 August 1296. In the latter year he became bishop of Caithness. The death of Bishop Alan in 1291 had been followed by a prolonged vacancy. The election of the archdeacon of Caithness was quashed in April 1296 by Boniface VIII, who provided Adam, precentor of Ross; but Adam, having been consecrated at the curia, died at Siena before the end of the year. On 17 December, therefore, Boniface provided Andrew of Buchan to the see, and must have summoned him to Rome for consecration. However, circumstances made it impossible for him to attend, for on 1 August 1297 a mandate to the bishops of Aberdeen, Glasgow, and Ross directed them to consecrate Andrew, who was unable to travel to Rome 'on account of the wars that are imminent in those parts and the dangers of the way, which is long and perilous' (Theiner, no. 360). Buchan held the bishopric until his death, some time before 16 June 1304, when his successor-elect received a safe conduct to visit the curia for confirmation. The earl of Ross was keeper of the see in 1304/5, and handed over issues amounting to £40.

BARBARA E. CRAWFORD

Sources D. E. R. Watt, ed., *Fasti ecclesiae Scoticanae medii aevi ad annum 1638*, [2nd edn], Scottish RS, new ser., 1 (1969) · D. E. Easson, ed., *Charters of the abbey of Coupar-Angus*, 2, Scottish History Society, 3rd ser., 41 (1947), 269–70 · J. Anderson, introduction, *The Orkneyinga saga*, ed. J. Anderson, trans. J. A. Hjaltalin and G. Goudie (1873), lxxxv–lxxxvi · *CDS*, 2.438, 1752 · A. Theiner, *Vetera monumenta Hibernorum et Scotorum historiam illustrantia* (Rome, 1864), no. 360

Buchan, Anna Masterton [*pseud.* O. Douglas] (1877–1948), author, was born in Fife, at Inglewood, Smeaton Road, Pathhead, Kirkcaldy, on 24 March 1877, the elder of two daughters and second of six children of John Buchan (1847–1911), minister of the Free Church of Scotland, and his wife, Helen Jane (1857–1937), daughter of John Masterton, farmer, of Broughton Green, Peeblesshire. Anna's father, the son of a distinguished Peeblesshire lawyer, served congregations at Broughton, Perth, and Kirkcaldy, and John Knox Church in the Gorbals district of Glasgow. Her mother exercised great influence on the Buchan children, one of whom was the novelist John *Buchan (1875–1940). Anna's sister died, aged five, in 1893.

When Anna was eleven the family moved to Florence Villa, 34 Queen Mary Avenue, Crosshill, Glasgow. Anna went to Queen's Park Academy and then to Hutcheson's Girls' Grammar School. She found Hutcheson's somewhat overwhelming, and completed her secondary education privately in Edinburgh, where she lived with a colleague of her father's. While her brothers embarked on careers in the professions Anna went to Queen Margaret College, Glasgow, which was founded in 1884 for the higher education of women in Scotland. In Edinburgh she acquired a certain independence and also a love of Shakespeare. She wanted to be an actress, but as a daughter of the manse devoted herself to charitable work in her father's parish, including readings—from authors such as J. M. Barrie—that displayed her talent for mimicry and accurate characterization. Of average height, with an imposing presence, and (with a prominent Buchan nose) handsome rather than pretty, she possessed many social aptitudes and was much liked. Her recreations included acting, theatre-going, and climbing. She had an urban upbringing, but the Buchans were mainly of borders stock, and this tightly knit family delighted in the country, returning frequently to visit the Mastertons at Broughton Green (and later to stay at Gala Lodge, Broughton, which Helen Buchan inherited in 1918). After the death of her uncle in 1906 Anna and her unmarried brother J. Walter Buchan (1882–1953)—head of the Commercial Bank and town clerk—moved to Bank House, Peebles (which still bears a plaque commemorating them).

Anna Buchan's first novel, *Olivia in India: the Adventures of a Chota Miss Sahib* (1913), was based on a visit in 1907 to her brother William, who had become a distinguished Indian civil servant, in Calcutta. It consists of letters home from the heroine, Olivia Douglas; 'G' is Gladys Helder, whom Anna met on board ship and with whom she maintained a lifelong friendship. She wrote under an assumed name because her brother John had already established the literary reputation of the Buchans (but it probably pleased her when a Canadian enthusiast later dubbed John Buchan 'the brother of O. Douglas' and her mother admitted to preferring Anna's novels to his). Before the book was published William Buchan died, aged thirty, in 1912.

Further family misfortune followed when during the First World War Anna's youngest brother was killed. Her second novel, *The Setons*, was published in 1917; it describes life in a Glasgow manse immediately before the war. It has uncritical sentimental qualities that have caused some critics to place Anna Buchan firmly in the 'kailyard' school of writers, which included Barrie. Moira Burgess, however, detects a significant detachment in her writing, and Beth Dickson, in *A History of Scottish Women's Writing* (1997), considers that 'she avoids Barrie's sentimentality and [Annie S.] Swan's woodenness' (p. 341). Anna Buchan's best-known novel, *Penny Plain*, appeared in 1920; it is set in Peebles and mentions Neidpath Castle, which once belonged to the notorious duke of Queensberry—Wordsworth's 'degenerate Douglas'—who may have given Anna her pen name. The heroine, Jean Jardine, is well loved and the author displays considerable skill in drawing a variety of amusing minor characters. *Ann and her Mother* (1922) is a fictionalized life of Helen Buchan. *Pink Sugar* (1924) was written at Broughton; *Eliza for Common* (1928) is another novel about a Glasgow manse.

During the 1920s and early 1930s Anna Buchan enjoyed considerable success. *Priorsford* (1932), *The Home that is our Own* (1940), and several other novels are set in the borders. *The Proper Place* (1926) and *The Day of Small Things* (1930) are both partly about Fife. Peebles, where Anna spent most of her life, is Priorsford in several of her novels. A distinguished speaker, she came to occupy a position of importance in the town, serving for example as justice of the peace and, despite her unmarried status, as president of the Peeblesshire League of Wives and Mothers. In retirement her father also lived in Peebles. Some believe that the Buchans 'got above' themselves (Scott). Her talented older brother, John Buchan, later Lord Tweedsmuir, governor-general of Canada, his wife, Susan, and their children, to whom Anna was a benign aunt, were regular visitors to Peebles and Broughton. Anna visited them at Elsfield, in Oxfordshire, where she began more than one of her novels, and she visited Canada, with their mother, in 1936 and in 1939; she also extended hospitality in Peebles to many Canadians.

When both her parents were seriously ill Anna Buchan undertook many family duties; indeed in one of her novels the heroine declines a proposal of marriage to look after her brothers, and it may be that a sense of duty explained why Anna herself did not marry. At the end of her life she wrote a reflective family biography, *Unforgettable, Unforgotten* (1945), a significant source of information about John Buchan. She died, of cancer, at Bank House, Peebles, on 24 November 1948. Following cremation her remains were scattered in Peebles cemetery, where there is a monument to her in the Buchan family plot. *Farewell to Priorsford* (1950), compiled as a tribute, appeared in 1950.   LOUIS STOTT

Sources S. Scott, *O. Douglas* (1993) • O. Douglas [A. Buchan], *Ann and her mother* (1922) • O. Douglas [A. Buchan], *Unforgettable, unforgotten* (1945) • S. Tweedsmuir, *John Buchan, by his wife and friends* (1947) • W. Forrester, *Anna Buchan and O. Douglas* (1995) • D. Gifford and D. McMillan, eds., *A history of Scottish women's writing* (1997) • T. Royle, *The Macmillan companion to Scottish literature* (1983) • M. Green, *Biography of John Buchan and his sister Anna* (1990) • J. M. Speedy, 'Remembering O. Douglas', *Borders Life*, 2/11 (1967) • *DNB* • M. Burgess, *Imagine a city* (1998) • b. cert. • d. cert.

Archives NL Scot., literary MSS, notebooks, lectures, etc. • NL Scot., further papers, Acc 11627 | Biggar Museum Trust, Lanarkshire
Likenesses portrait, Biggar Museum Trust, Lanarkshire

Buchan, Charles Murray (1891–1960), footballer and journalist, was born at 151 Reidhaven Road, Plumstead, London, on 22 September 1891, the son of William Buchan and his wife, Jane Murray. His father had been born in Aberdeen and was a colour sergeant in a Highland regiment before moving to London and a job as a blacksmith in the Woolwich arsenal. Charles played football on Plumstead Common with his three brothers, two of whom would also become professionals, and at his elementary school, High Street, Plumstead, and at the Bloomfield Road higher grade school, to which he went at the age of eleven. From there it was Woolwich Polytechnic, with the aim of becoming a schoolteacher but by the time he left the 'Poly' at the age of seventeen his football powers had become the talk of the south-east London football *cognoscenti*.

Buchan described in his autobiography, *A Lifetime in Football* (1955), how he alternately ran and walked the 2 miles from his home to the polytechnic because he could not afford the tram fare, often kicking a small ball against the kerb and controlling the rebound as he went. He played for numerous local teams not only on Saturday afternoons but also on Sunday mornings, at a time when the Football Association opposed organized football on the sabbath. It was while he was at the polytechnic that Woolwich Arsenal Football Club, who then played at Plumstead, asked him to play for their reserves. He played four times for them as an amateur in 1909–10 but left after their secretary–manager refused to pay him the 11s. expenses which he claimed; the cost of travel for training and away games. It would cost the club a much larger sum to get him back.

For the remainder of that season Buchan played as an amateur for Northfleet in the Kent senior league. With both the championship and the Kent senior cup won, the club's players were attracting the attention of the professionals. Buchan turned down offers from Bury and Fulham, the latter because he thought the wage offered not enough, but eventually signed for Leyton in the southern league in May 1910. This was the first step in a professional career which was to last for eighteen years. Fifteen of those years were spent with Sunderland, for whom he signed in March 1911 for a then record fee of £1250 and a £10 signing-on fee for himself, which he used partly to buy a new, lined overcoat as he had been told it could get cold in the north.

Buchan was a tall and willowy inside right, 6 feet ¾ inch tall, who looked awkward as he walked onto the field, but he had exemplary control of the ball. His passes were 'gentle, deft and accurate, his dribbling close and he was unsurpassed when the ball was in the air' (Joy, 35). He was quick to appreciate an opening and this helped him to score over 200 goals for Sunderland, for whom he was a key member of the team which won the championship in 1912–13 and narrowly lost to Aston Villa in the cup final.

Charles Murray Buchan (1891–1960), by unknown photographer, 1925

He was a thoughtful player, a chess master rather than a master athlete, and it was this aspect of his game, as well as his ability to score goals, which made him one of the earliest signings made by Herbert Chapman when he was building the new Arsenal team in 1925. Buchan probably contributed as much to the innovation of the defensive centre half as Chapman himself.

It was a peculiar transfer. Buchan was nearly thirty-four and Sir Henry Norris, the Arsenal chairman, thought the fee that Sunderland were demanding was too high. The Sunderland manager, Bob Kyle, pointed to Buchan's goal-scoring and said he would score twenty in his first Arsenal season. Norris asked if he was prepared to back that opinion; Kyle agreed, so a fee of £2000 was fixed, plus £100 for every goal in 1925–6. Buchan scored nineteen in the league and two in the cup, Arsenal finished in their highest ever league position—second—and Sunderland were £2000 richer.

It was surprising that Buchan played only six times for England, matches in which he scored four goals. It was said he was sometimes too subtle for his colleagues. Another factor may have been his intelligence and independence. He was aware of his worth as a man and as a footballer. He was on the committee of the players' union between 1922 and 1925. He was also argumentative and often complained to referees of what he thought were the unfair things opponents were doing to him. It may be that none of this went down too well with the international selectors during Frederick Wall's long secretaryship of the Football Association.

Buchan was a prime example of a working-class man trying to improve the standard of living of himself and his family and, having done it, to maintain it and enjoy a modest social mobility. He qualified as a teacher and both taught at Cowan Terrace School in Sunderland and played for the club in 1919–20. In the latter year he opened a sports shop in Blandford Street with Amos Lowings, a professional cricketer. He married Ellen (b. 1892/3), daughter of John Robson, a ship's outfitter of Bishopwearmouth,

on 2 February 1914. They had a son, Angus, and a daughter. He volunteered for the army, at the end of the football season in 1915, and joined the Grenadier Guards. He saw action as a sergeant at the Somme, Cambrai, and Passchendaele and was awarded the Military Medal. He was recommended for a commission and completed the officer training course at Catterick just before the war ended in 1918.

Buchan retired from football in 1928, his last game for Arsenal being the one in which Dixie Dean scored his record sixtieth goal of the season. He then built up a second successful career as a football journalist. He had contributed regularly to newspapers in Sunderland and Newcastle before the war. Now he was offered a job on the *Daily News*, and he was its football correspondent through its transformation into the *News Chronicle* until his second retirement in 1956. He became a regular broadcaster on BBC radio, his contributions to *Sports Report* and his summaries of the Saturday results on the Home Service making him a national figure.

In September 1951 Buchan launched *Charles Buchan's Football Monthly*, which has some claim to be the first modern football magazine. It was aimed mainly at boys and young men, and its mixture of club and player profiles, feature and historical articles, gossip, and photographs, brightened the lives of many football-struck teenagers. Its circulation had reached 350,000 by the late 1950s, and it continued until 1973 and was later revived. It was generally uncontroversial, reflecting the man himself by the 1950s, but at least Buchan did not claim that footballers were better in his day and he was generous to the contemporary player during a period when he came in for a lot of criticism. Charlie Buchan died suddenly of a heart attack while on holiday with his wife in Monte Carlo on 25 June 1960. He was cremated in Marseilles and the ashes brought back for burial in Scotland. It does not seem too much of an exaggeration to say, as a *News Chronicle* colleague did, that 'if football had a father figure, it was him' (MacAdam). His career as writer and broadcaster brought his views and south London voice to an even greater public than his long and impressive playing career with the old giants Sunderland and the modern Arsenal.

TONY MASON

Sources C. Buchan, *A lifetime in football* (1955) • B. Joy, *Forward Arsenal!* (1952) • J. Harding, *For the good of the game* (1991) • M. Farror and D. Lamming, *A century of English international football, 1872–1972* (1972) • *Daily Telegraph* (27 June 1960) • J. MacAdam, *News Chronicle* (27 June 1960) • *The Times* (27 June 1960) • *Charles Buchan's Football Monthly* (Sept 1960) • b. cert. • m. cert. • *CGPLA Eng. & Wales* (1960)
Archives FILM BFI NFTVA, news footage • BFI NFTVA, sports footage
Likenesses photograph, 1925, Hult. Arch. [*see illus.*] • photograph, NPG
Wealth at death £17,818 11s. 11d.: probate, 1 Sept 1960, *CGPLA Eng. & Wales*

Buchan, David Duncan (1939–1994), folklorist, was born in Aberdeen on 7 January 1939, the only son of Joseph Duncan Buchan (1905–1979), marine scientist, and his wife, Elsie Anne (*née* Robb; 1906–1991), legal secretary. He was educated in the fishing village of Findochty, Banffshire, and in Aberdeen, where he received his secondary education at Robert Gordon's College. This unique institution, established by a cadet of the great Gordon family who had amassed a fortune in the Baltic, had an excellent teaching staff who inspired him to study English at Aberdeen University and gave him a lifetime interest in the theatre. He was active in student dramatic societies, writing a number of plays. He graduated in 1960.

Awarded a postgraduate research fellowship (with spells in the middle and end as an instructor of English at the University of Victoria), Buchan was encouraged to work on ballads; this was surprising, for such ethnological studies were looked down upon by the British academic community. But the folk music revival was under way, and the School of Scottish Studies, Edinburgh, was demonstrating that balladry had great research potential. He came across two impressive collections of folksong in the Aberdeen University archives. These were carefully preserved and guarded, and initially he had difficulty in persuading the librarian, Dr Douglas Simpson, to allow them to be handled by a mere student. The Glenbuchat MSS consisted of four volumes of some sixty ballads purportedly collected by a local parish minister in the early nineteenth century. The librarian was impressed by Buchan's work on these, and persuaded the library committee to allow him to edit and publish the manuscripts. He was unable fully to complete the project before he died. Also on the library shelves was the Greig–Duncan folksong collection, one of the largest and most comprehensive ever made, consisting of some 3500 texts and 3100 tunes. Only the great ballads (as categorized by Francis Child)—some 13 per cent of the whole—had been published posthumously in a 1925 volume edited by Alexander Keith, entitled *Last Leaves of Traditional Ballads and Ballad Airs Collected in Aberdeenshire by the Late Gavin Greig*. Although the now aged Keith was hardly encouraging—'I wouldna bother. It's aa been deen' (Olson, 'Foreword', xiv)—Buchan sustained a doctoral thesis in 1965 using Greig and Duncan's manuscripts.

On 2 September 1965 Buchan married Moyra Jean Nisbet (*b.* 1941), a social worker. They had a daughter and a son. Following the award of his PhD, Buchan taught in North America, at the universities of Victoria, British Columbia, and Massachusetts, before returning in 1968 to the new University of Stirling as lecturer and then senior lecturer in English studies, and convenor and sole lecturer for the folklife studies component of the English studies with folklife studies degree programme. During this period he expanded his thesis into *The Ballad and the Folk* (1972). In 1979 he was appointed professor of folklore and head of department at the Memorial University of Newfoundland, where he remained—apart from visiting professorships at Binghampton, Guelph, Aberdeen, and Sheffield universities—for the rest of his life. In early 1994 he was appointed to the newly created chair of Scottish ethnology at the University of Aberdeen (only the second such chair to be established in the United Kingdom), despite making clear to the committee that he had cancer. He had hoped for sufficient time to firmly establish the chair

and its research institute, but fell gravely ill and died within the year.

Buchan's lectures and publications were extremely wide-ranging, from sixteenth-century Scottish ballads to Glasgow prison humour, from urban legends to medical folklore, from the didactic *Scottish Tradition* (1984) to the final *Folk Tradition and Folk Medicine in Scotland* (1994), but the work that initially made him famous was his *tour de force* of 1972. Taking up the cudgels of the oral-formulaic approach to balladry initiated by the publication of Albert Lord's *The Singer of Tales* in 1960, Buchan claimed that the great classical ballads could be understood only in relation both to the re-creative nature of their performance (and performers) and to the society—including its history, geography, and sociology—which sustained them. *The Ballad and the Folk* remains the most widely quoted (and contested) work of its kind.

A well-built, handsome, and cheerful man (with a dismaying penchant for appalling puns), Buchan was an enthusiastic sportsman and hill-walker. Throughout a distinguished and productive career, which brought him an international reputation, he was noted for the thoroughness of his work, imaginative handling of complex and difficult problems, and generosity and kindness to colleagues and students alike. His first marriage having ended in divorce in 1985, on 27 August 1994 he married his fellow folklorist Diane Ellen Goldstein (*b.* 1956). He died of a recurrence of bowel cancer at his home, 6 Catherine Street, St John's, Newfoundland, on 22 October 1994, and was cremated following a service in St Andrew's Presbyterian Church, St John's, on 26 October. His ashes were scattered in Aberdeen and Pennan. He was survived by both wives and by the two children of his first marriage.

IAN A. OLSON

Sources G. Bennett, 'David Buchan: a folklore bibliography', *Folklore*, 106 (1995), 101–2 · I. A. Olson, foreword, in D. Buchan, *The ballad and the folk* (1997), ix–xv · I. A. Olson, 'Editing the Glenbuchat ballads: David Buchan's legacy', *Aberdeen University Review*, 57 (1997–8), 29–45 · W. F. H. Nicolaisen, 'The ballad and the folklorist', *Aberdeen University Review*, 57 (1997–8), 327–33 · I. A. Olson, *Aberdeen University Review*, 56 (1995–6), 119–20 · *The Scotsman* (26 Oct 1994) · *The Independent* (4 Nov 1994) · *The Times* (22 Nov 1994) · personal knowledge (2004) · private information (2004) [family] · University roll, U. Aberdeen
Archives Memorial University, Newfoundland · U. Aberdeen
Likenesses photograph, repro. in *Folk Music Journal*, 7 (1995), 121 · photograph, repro. in *The Scotsman*

Buchan [*née* Simpson], **Elspeth** (*c.*1738–1791), founder of the Buchanites, was born in Banffshire, the daughter of John Simpson and Margaret Gordon (*d. c.*1741), who kept an inn at Fitmy-Can, halfway between Banff and Portsoy, Banffshire. Her mother died when she was three years old, after which her father remarried and sent her into service. She was later employed by a distant female relative who taught her to read and write, but they separated in Greenock when her employer left for the West Indies. Travelling to Ayr she became acquainted with a potter, Robert Buchan, and followed him to Glasgow, where she secured a servant's position in his employer's household. The couple married and moved to Banff, where they had a number of children, of whom only two girls and one boy survived. They later separated; her husband returned to Glasgow while she opened a dame-school in Banff to support her family. She temporarily rejoined her husband in Glasgow in 1781.

Buchan believed she received a special commission from God in 1774, but it was not until she encountered Hugh White, a minister in the Relief church, at a communion service in Glasgow in 1782 that she found the support which enabled her ministry to flourish. In 1783, after an exchange of correspondence, White invited Buchan to speak to his congregation. Initially welcomed by the Irvine Relief Church, her unorthodox beliefs attracted criticism and she was forced to leave. White continued to support her visionary insights and was subsequently deposed from office. A Society of Buchanites was formed in Irvine in 1783, where their meetings attracted interest as well as hostility. Buchan, a tall, plump woman with long, dark hair, was a gifted speaker with a kind and gentle manner. Among her followers she became known as Friend Mother in the Lord, but outsiders often referred to her as Luckie Buchan, the witch-wife. Robert Burns shared the general view that Buchanite beliefs were a 'strange jumble of enthusiastic jargon; among others she pretends to give them the Holy Ghost by breathing on them' (R. Burns to J. Burness, Aug 1784, *Letters*, 1.22).

Opposition swelled against Buchan, and on May Fair day 1784 she was expelled from Irvine, taking White and some forty-six followers with her. They left, according to a young John Galt, singing as they passed through the crowded streets. The Buchanites moved to New Cample, Dumfriesshire, and established a celibate community of some sixty people. According to a merchant who visited them in 1783 they paid great attention to the Bible and declared the 'last day to be at hand' while waiting expectantly for Christ's return (*Scots Magazine*, vol. 46). In 1785 White published, with Buchan's endorsement, *The Divine Dictionary* on behalf of the society. The dictionary identified Buchan as the woman of Revelation 12: 1, while she identified White as the male child of Revelation 12: 5. In 1786 the Buchanites embarked on a forty-day fast to prepare for the moment of their translation, the failure of which left many members disillusioned. In 1787 they relocated to a farm in Auchengibbert, Dumfriesshire, where Buchan died on 29 March 1791. On her deathbed she announced she would return after either six days or ten or fifty years, depending on the purity of her followers' faith. Her body was kept in a barn for six days and then temporarily buried in Kirkgunzeon churchyard.

After Buchan's death the sect dispersed, with about half moving to the United States with White. The Scottish remnant established a prosperous livelihood in Crocketford, Dumfriesshire. The longest surviving member, Andrew Innes, kept Buchan's body with him awaiting her return. He died in 1846 and her coffin was placed underneath that of his own in his grave so that he would wake when she arose. The Buchanites, including Buchan, were buried in the garden of their final dwelling, Newhouse, in Crocketford.　　　　　JILL SÖDERSTRÖM

Sources J. Train, *The Buchanites from first to last* (1846) • *Scots Magazine*, 46 (1784) • *Scots Magazine*, 48 (1786), 589–90 • *Castle Douglas Miscellany*, 3 (Feb 1826), 249–59 • *Christian Journal*, 3 (1835), 7–12 • J. Cameron, *History of the Buchanite delusion, 1783–1846* (1904) • H. White, *The divine dictionary, or, A treatise indicted by holy inspiration*, rev. E. Simpson (1785) • H. White and E. Buchan, *Eight letters between the people called Buchanites*, ed. J. Purves (1785) • H. MacDiarmid [C. M. Grieve] and A. Riach, *Scottish eccentrics*, [new edn] (1993) • W. Robertson, *Old Ayrshire days* (1905) • G. Struthers, *The history of the rise, progress, and principles of the Relief church* (1843) • A. Chalmers, 'The Buchanites & Crocketford', *Dumfriesshire & Galloway Natural History & Antiquarian Society …*, 3rd ser., 1 (1912–13), 285–303 • *The letters of Robert Burns*, ed. J. de Lancey Ferguson, 2nd edn, ed. G. Ross Roy, 2 vols. (1985) • J. Galt, *The autobiography of John Galt*, 2 vols. (1833)
Archives NL Scot., Train MSS

Buchan [*née* Macduff], **Isabel**, **countess of Buchan** (*b. c.*1270, *d.* after 1313), noblewoman, was the daughter of Earl Colban of Fife and Countess Anna, who was perhaps a daughter of Alan Durward (*d.* 1275) [*see under* Macduff family, earls of Fife]. She was probably born about 1270 and in due time married John *Comyn, earl of Buchan (*d.* 1308). She is first recorded in October 1297, when she was said to be managing her husband's estates in England. Buchan, captured after the Scottish defeat at Dunbar in 1296, had recently been set free and had returned to Scotland. Isabel's life then continued unremarkably until 1306, when she achieved fame (or infamy) by placing the coronet on Bruce's head at his enthronement on 25 March. The earls of Fife had long performed this important function, which some said was essential for the validity of the ceremony; the current earl, Isabel's nephew Duncan, was a teenager who adhered completely to Edward I and therefore had no inclination to attend. Although one chronicler asserts that the countess left her husband dishonestly, it seems more likely that he was in England and Isabel, who could have stayed at her own house at Balmullo in Fife before the ceremony, might thus have been able to travel to Scone with comparative ease. None the less, she never saw her husband again: his close relationship to John Comyn of Badenoch, whom the new king had murdered as recently as 10 February, rendered her actions unforgivable. Rumours that she was or wanted to be Bruce's mistress were almost *de rigueur* in the circumstances.

The countess remained with the new royal family during the following difficult months, staying initially at Kildrummy Castle in Mar and then moving north with the queen and other royal women when that proved unsafe. However, they were captured at St Duthac's shrine at Tain in Ross-shire by William, earl of Ross, in September 1306. Isabel's role at Robert I's enthronement ensured her harsh treatment: she and Mary Bruce were incarcerated in wooden cages within the walls of the castles of Berwick and Roxburgh respectively. Although the women were provided with a privy, the degradation and humiliation of this punishment, which may have been Italian in inspiration, testified to both the seriousness of their offences and the frustration felt by King Edward at this new rebellion. Sir Robert Keith and Sir John Mowbray made an attempt to secure the countess's release in the next few years through the offices of Duncan of Fife, but this came to nothing. Isabel was finally removed from her cage in

June 1310 to the comparative luxury of the Carmelite friary in Berwick. Three years later she was handed over to the safe keeping of Sir Henry de Beaumont (*d.* 1340), husband of Buchan's niece and coheir, Alice, and lived the rest of her life in obscurity. It is not known when she died.   FIONA WATSON

Sources *Scots peerage*, 2.258 • G. W. S. Barrow, *Robert Bruce and the community of the realm of Scotland*, 3rd edn (1988), 151, 162 • *CDS*, vols. 2, 5 • Marquess of Bute, 'Notice of a manuscript of the latter part of the fourteenth century', *Proceedings of the Society of Antiquaries of Scotland*, 19 (1884), 166–92 • *The chronicle of Walter of Guisborough*, ed. H. Rothwell, CS, 3rd ser., 89 (1957), 367 • H. R. Luard, ed., *Flores historiarum*, 3 vols., Rolls Series, 95 (1890), vol. 3, p. 324 • *Scalacronica, by Sir Thomas Gray of Heton, knight: a chronical of England and Scotland from AD MLXVI to AD MCCCLXII*, ed. J. Stevenson, Maitland Club, 40 (1836), 130

Buchan, Jessie Hill (1848–1905). *See under* Buchan, Alexander (1829–1907).

Buchan, John, first Baron Tweedsmuir (1875–1940), author, publisher, and governor-general of Canada, was born at Perth on 26 August 1875, the eldest child in the family of four sons and one surviving daughter of John Buchan (1847–1911), Free Church of Scotland minister, and his wife, Helen Jane (1857–1937), daughter of John Masterton, farmer, of Broughton Green, near Peebles. His sister, Anna *Buchan, was the novelist O. Douglas. The father was a lively character, an enthusiast for border ballads and other Scots songs which he recited or sang to the family or played on a penny whistle, and he was indulgent when a Free Church minister might have been expected to be strict. The mother made up for this. She epitomized Free Church virtues: she was hard, spare, and respectable, hated Rome, and distrusted established churches generally. Between them the parents gave young John two Scottish points of reference on which much of his fiction rested. Their different attitudes to respectability likewise provided a fertile tension, for there developed in Buchan a very sharp awareness both of the need to be respectable and of the sense that it is the eccentrics that get things done.

Youth and education In 1876 the family moved to the small mining town of Pathhead, Fife, when Buchan's father became Free Church minister there. Aged five John fractured his skull in a carriage accident, leaving him with a permanent scar on the left forehead of his otherwise chiselled, classical features. Buchan was expelled from a dame-school for upsetting a broth pot. He attended Parkhead board school and then the burgh school in nearby Kirkcaldy and Kirkcaldy high school. Aged eleven he published a hymn for the new year of 1887 (in Buchan, *Poems*, 8). Buchan played on the shore of the Forth, and relished his holidays on his relatives' farm at Broughton in the borders where he first engaged with the border rivers, hills, and shallow glens and their people, which were the staple of so much of his best writing.

In 1888 the Revd John Buchan was called to the John Knox Church in the Gorbals in Glasgow, thus presenting to his children an almost Manichaean contrast between

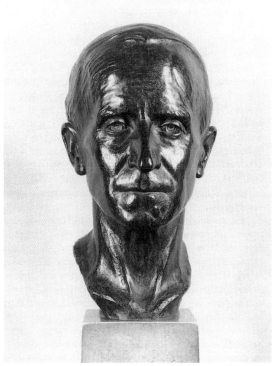

John Buchan, first Baron Tweedsmuir (1875–1940), by Thomas John Clapperton, 1935

their city and country life. John Buchan attended Hutcheson's Boys' Grammar School until 1892. School was for him, he recalled, 'only a minor episode. The atmosphere I lived in was always that of my home' (*Memory Hold-the-Door*, 29). That atmosphere was one of moderate Calvinism (Buchan's father was not normally a protagonist in the theological disputes over biblical criticism in the Free Church, though he intervened on the conservative side in 1902), but John and his siblings found the social life of the manse somewhat stifling. In 1890 he went onto the classical side at Hutcheson's and, taught by James Cadell, found the classics a liberation. In 1892 he won a John Clark bursary to Glasgow University, where he chiefly studied classics, being taught and influenced by the young Gilbert Murray (more perhaps than he realized) and the philosopher Henry Jones. Buchan had by this time that formidable range of reading and reference which, with his accurate memory, enabled him to write so authoritatively and swiftly. Though a diffident youth, he was from a very early stage authorially ambitious. As a Glasgow student he published in the *Glasgow University Magazine* and developed his considerable ability as a poet. He also edited Bacon's *Essays and Apothegms* with an introduction (1894). Buchan was a natural Edinburghian (it was to be his chief place of work for many years but never his home) and although his Glasgow years supplied much fodder for later novels, he was keen to move on. He wrote about this time:

And often I dream that yonder,
Beyond the red sea haze,

Is that wonderful El Dorado
Men sung of in former days.
(*Poems*, 15)

He did not, however, see Edinburgh as his El Dorado, but rather Oxford.

In 1895 Buchan won a junior Hulme scholarship to Brasenose College, Oxford (attracted thither by interest in two of the dons, Walter Pater and Richard Lodge), and before he matriculated in October 1895, wrote and published his first novel, *Sir Quixote of the Moors*, and began work on *John Burnet of Barns* (1898). It was during his time at Brasenose that Buchan met the public-school set whose ethos and patois his best-known novels were to record. His friends included Raymond Asquith, Auberon and Aubrey Herbert, Harold Baker, F. E. Smith, Stair Gillon (who wrote his *Dictionary of National Biography* memoir), and Thomas *Nelson [see under Nelson family], his future employer and publishing partner. He won the Stanhope prize for history (1897) and was librarian of the Oxford Union (1898) and its president (1899). While an undergraduate he entered *Who's Who* in 1898 (listing five publications) and was invited by his college to write its history. He was placed in the second class in honours moderations, and in the first class for *literae humaniores* in 1899, but failed, perhaps fortunately for him, in the All Souls prize fellowship examination. In that year he published *Grey Weather*, a collection of short stories mostly set in the Scottish borders; it contains some of his best scenic writing.

Oxford gave Buchan easy access to London society, and he chose to establish himself there rather than return to Scotland. He read for the bar at the Middle Temple, paying his way by journalism, especially, like H. H. Asquith before him, for *The Spectator*, then a Liberal Unionist periodical, and for the tory *Blackwood's Edinburgh Magazine* (his short stories for it form the bulk of *The Watcher by the Threshold*, 1902). He was called to the bar in June 1901 and joined the northern circuit.

Buchan had an impatience with the Liberal Party and especially with what he saw as woolly-headed radicals. He was seen at Oxford as 'a Tory-Democrat Jacobite' (*Isis*, 28 Jan 1899, cited in Adam Smith, *John Buchan*, 71) but he also had an insistence on the practical and the rational and, despite himself, his values throughout his life were those of a free-trade Liberal Unionist rather than of a tory. At the end of his life, he felt he was 'becoming a Gladstonian Liberal' (to G. M. Trevelyan, cited in Parry, 234). While his novels recognized the importance of the irrational and of sudden and direct action (and in that sense recognize the importance in society of tendencies which fascists were later to see as desirable values), Buchan's own life was in a physical sense non-adventurous. Even in his mountaineering—in which, like many of his contemporaries, he found an outlet for excitement bonded with some of the extremes of nature—there was an absence of the sense of danger, for Buchan had 'the opposite of vertigo, for I found a physical comfort in looking down from great heights' (*Memory Hold-the-Door*, 140; however, on one occasion he experienced real panic when in the hills, an episode on which he drew in several novels). Buchan always drove himself hard, as his upbringing had taught him to do, but the danger which many of his heroes underwent physically was in his own case the danger of social and literary failure.

The metropolitan political and legal society in which Buchan had chosen to move was grappling with the problem of Britain's over-extension in world affairs, a weakness clearly exposed by the Second South African War, which began in October 1899. Buchan was attracted by the romance of imperial deeds of daring, but he was too canny to be wholly seduced by them. *The Half-Hearted* (1900), his first novel in a contemporary setting, is in two parts, the first describing country-house life in the borders (with the chief character loosely moulded from Raymond Asquith, to whom, among others, the novel is dedicated), the second a heroic 'great game' adventure in Kashmir and Bardur, the hero dying while saving India from invasion. The novel is broken-backed, but it staked out much of Buchan's future stamping ground, and it showed his remarkable capacity for depicting a landscape which he had not visited. 'What is remarkable about these adventure stories is the completeness of the world they describe' noted Graham Greene, and this quality is apparent in this early attempt (Greene, 104).

South Africa and its aftermath Buchan proved a good but not outstanding barrister; he was becoming established as a writer of ability. Neither calling fully satisfied him and he was unwilling to yield fully to either the demands of public life or the loneliness of full-time creative writing. He had persuaded himself with some anxiety that 'it was not my duty to volunteer for active service' when the Second South African War began in 1899 (*Memory Hold-the-Door*, 91), but he felt some malaise as a result. When Leo Amery suggested Buchan to Alfred Milner, Milner, then high commissioner in South Africa, invited Buchan in August 1901 to assist in the reconstruction of the Transvaal and the Orange Free State, the Afrikaners' defeat by then being a matter of time. Milner used Buchan, who arrived in October 1901, as 'a sort of political Private Secretary' (letter of 7 Oct 1901, cited in Lownie, 73) and he also became legal adviser to Johannesburg town council with the large salary of £2000 per annum. In South Africa he believed he 'ceased to be an individualist and became a citizen' (*Memory Hold-the-Door*, 92). He had some responsibility for reducing the mortality rate in the concentration camps in which Afrikaners were confined, and for the land settlement department, which he ran until March 1903. He travelled extensively in the South African hinterland, described in *The African Colony* (1903), his only imperial travelling before the 1930s. Though he toured the Mediterranean and Europe he never made the grand imperial tour common for young men at that time. Buchan returned to London and the bar in October 1903. The Milner group was politically discredited and the Unionist Party was split over tariff reform: a long Liberal government was in the offing. Buchan had many Liberal friends, such as R. B. Haldane, who wrote an introduction to Buchan's *The Law Relating to the Taxation of Foreign Income*

(1905); but in terms of political advancement he was harnessed to the wrong horse. Nothing came of expectations of a post in Egypt. He was approached by the South Edinburgh Unionist Association but could not afford to become an MP, supposing that he could win the seat (Lownie, 88). He became part-time assistant editor of *The Spectator* in 1908. In that year he published *A Lodge in the Wilderness*, a didactic fictional discussion of imperial values and objectives which remains one of the clearest and fairest analyses of British imperial endeavours, and shows Buchan resisting the strong protectionist imperialism followed by most of the Milnerites in the 1900s. He shared their suspicion of but not their contempt for party politics, and he remained a free-trader.

Marriage, publishing, and writing One aspect of Buchan's lack of direction was resolved when on 15 July 1907 at St George's, Hanover Square, London, in a great society wedding, he married Susan Charlotte Grosvenor (1882–1977), daughter of Norman de l'Aigle Grosvenor (1845–1898), son of Lord Robert *Grosvenor (1801–1893), and his wife, Caroline Susan Theodora, *née* Stuart-Wortley (d. 1940). Susan Grosvenor was very well connected but not rich; she mirrored, perhaps reinforced, Buchan's ambivalent relationship to English society, though her lineage and Anglicanism greatly upset Buchan's mother (Lownie, 96). Before marriage she had worked as a volunteer for the Charity Organization Society. She had a distaste for aristocratic life. The Buchans lived initially in London at 40 Hyde Park Square, then at 13 Bryanston Street, and from 1912 at 76 Portland Place (a neighbourhood used in several of Buchan's novels). Their first child, Alice, was born in 1908, followed by John Norman Stuart in 1911.

To finance his marriage Buchan worked for Nelsons, the Edinburgh publishers owned by the family of his friend Thomas Nelson, visiting Edinburgh at least monthly, and sometimes for longer spells. Buchan brought flair to cheap, quality publishing, compiling an excellent list which included Conrad, H. G. Wells, and George Douglas Brown. His reassociation with Scotland prompted Buchan to try to turn the *Scottish Review and Christian Leader* into a Scottish *Spectator*. He achieved this in terms of its contributors—a distinguished group representing the Scottish, imperial, and metropolitan strands of his life—and through his own columns; but the periodical failed financially, folding in 1908.

Buchan balanced this apparent move towards the literary side of his life by attempting to find a parliamentary seat, eventually succeeding in March 1911 in being adopted by the Unionists for the predominantly Liberal seat of Peeblesshire and Selkirk, the area of his youthful holidays within which several of his relatives were prominent and where both Buchan's father and his brother William died in 1911. No general election was likely before 1915, but Buchan began nursing the seat, his experience of public meetings providing a memorable episode in *The Thirty-Nine Steps*. Since *The Half-Hearted*, Buchan had not essayed a narrative novel, though he had written striking short stories, collected in *The Moon Endureth* (1912), which included the remarkable 'The Grove of Ashtaroth'. In 1910

he published, initially serially, *Prester John* (*The Great Diamond Pipe* in the USA), his first significant money-maker; the novel is often regarded as the crudest of his imperial pieces, but it shows perception of the different social and political forces in southern Africa. He accompanied this with biographies of Sir Walter Ralegh (1911) and the marquess of Montrose (1913), and a memoir of his friend Andrew Jameson, Lord Ardwall (1913). Also in 1913, *The Power House* was serialized in *Blackwood's*, though not published in book form until 1916. In the summer of 1914 Buchan was overworked and exhausted by a variety of family problems. Even so, as something of a relaxation, he wrote a novel, described in its introductory note as 'that elementary type of tale which Americans call the "dime novel," and which we know as the "shocker"', provisionally entitled *The Black Stone* but published as *The Thirty-Nine Steps* in September 1915 after serialization in *Blackwood's* in 1914 under the pseudonym H de V (Adam Smith, *John Buchan*, 197). Its hero, Richard Hannay, was loosely based on Edmund Ironside and others of Buchan's contemporaries in South Africa. Hannay initially represented the values of the outsider, equal to but not part of the British ruling élite.

Buchan and the First World War Buchan was too ill for active service in 1914 or subsequently; this was a psychological blow from which he perhaps never fully recovered. His response was to write, with assistance, *Nelson's History of the War* (24 vols.), published regularly from February 1915 to July 1919 in instalments of 50,000 words. The series had by far the largest circulation of any war commentary (Grieves, 'Early responses', 30). The enterprise, together with his growing reputation as a writer and his support for the war, gave prominence to his role as correspondent for *The Times* and the *Daily News*. By 1916 he was working for Haig drafting communiqués for the War and Foreign offices, with permission also to continue the war series. In 1916 he became second lieutenant in the intelligence corps. He published a series of books on the battles of Jutland, the Somme, and Picardy in 1915–16. His volume for Nelson on the Somme emphasized individual courage within a general strategic analysis which rather took for granted the reader's awareness of the scale of the slaughter, and its conclusion, much valued by contemporaries, is a lyrical evocation of the validity of war sacrifice. His intelligence work in part inspired *Greenmantle* (1916), set in the Middle East, its chief character, Sandy Arbuthnot, drawn from Aubrey *Herbert (see M. Fitzherbert, *The Man who was Greenmantle*, 1983) with a dash of T. E. Lawrence (whom Buchan did not then know personally). Buchan in *Greenmantle* found some romance in the war, as he also did in *Mr Standfast* (1919), though he was careful about the political implications of the plot.

Work for C. F. G. Masterman's propaganda department at Wellington House gave Buchan experience in this new field, for which his talents naturally equipped him. When Lloyd George's coalition was formed in December 1916 Buchan was asked to prepare for the new war cabinet a memorandum on propaganda policy, which he delivered in January 1917. On the urging of Milner, a member of the war cabinet, Buchan was appointed on 9 February 1917 director of a new department of information (created by a cabinet minute of that day), with direct responsibility to the prime minister and a salary of £1000 p.a. (Adam Smith, *John Buchan*, 200; Messinger, 89). The same month Buchan, whose health had been under strain for some time, underwent an only partially successful operation for a duodenal ulcer (Lownie, 127); for the rest of his life he was often in pain and was never wholly fit.

In principle independent, Buchan's department was in practice an annexe of the Foreign Office, reflecting the degree to which wartime propaganda was seen as directed at allies and neutral countries rather than at the home population, though Buchan personally recognized the importance of the latter. Buchan divided the department into four sections: art and literature (under Masterman at Wellington House); press and cinema; intelligence; administration (located in the Foreign Office). The reporting structure did not work well. By July 1917 Lloyd George had decided that Buchan 'was not the right man for the job' (Sanders and Taylor, 71). He and the department were viciously attacked by the Northcliffe press and ministers made little effort to defend him. Though Buchan himself had in May 1917 raised the question of home propaganda with the cabinet, the latter's solution was in August 1917 to establish the national war aims committee, independent of Buchan and responsible to Sir Edward Carson. In December 1917 a committee chaired by Robert Donald recommended reorganization; the response by Buchan was 'swift, detailed, and resentful' (Sanders and Taylor, 74) and that month Sir Edward Carson, another member of the war cabinet, was given a supervisory role over the department, Buchan remaining executive head. This also caused difficulties and on 4 March 1918 the department became a ministry, with Lord Beaverbrook as minister and Colonel Buchan as director of intelligence. At the end of the war, ironically, Buchan was appointed liquidator of the Ministry of Information, which he closed down on 31 December 1918.

Buchan handled war propaganda liberally, continuing for the most part the tradition of Masterman, who continued at Wellington House and worked well with Buchan. Both men staunchly resisted the gaucheries of Northcliffe's *Times*. Buchan was a moderate innovator. He increased the scale of government propaganda considerably and, with his assistant, T. Lennox Gilmour, greatly extended the use of film in British propaganda, as a means of both educating the home population and informing allies and neutrals of the allied case. The two large-scale films made were D. W. Griffith's *Hearts of the World* (1917) and Herbert Brenon's *The Invasion of Britain* (not completed until the end of the war and never shown). Many information films were made, including the popular 'tags', which were added onto newsreels. Buchan began active propaganda in enemy states, though in Germany he stopped short of encouraging social revolution (the most effective

means of ending the war). Behind the façade of the gentlemanly amateur which he so sedulously cultivated, Buchan was a tough and professional propagandist. However, considering the scale and slaughter of the war his propaganda was attempting to win in 1917–18, his methods remained for the most part within the canons of democratic behaviour. It was a paradox that in practice Buchan played by the rules of the political system of representative government which his novels and sometimes his non-fiction so often seemed to deride.

After the war Buchan did not stand for election in the 'coupon' election of December 1918 and turned down offers of Peeblesshire (1920) and Glasgow Central (1922; Adam Smith, *John Buchan*, 299). He bought the Manor House, Elsfield, 4 miles north-east of Oxford, and established a new routine for himself and his family (the Buchans' third child was William de l'Aigle (*b.* 1916), and their fourth Alastair Francis *Buchan (1918–1976), who became director of the Institute of Strategic Studies). Though he continued to play a part in Nelsons in Edinburgh, his main post-war focus shifted southwards, and chiefly to writing, though he was from 1919 on the board of Reuters and was also a curator of the chest at Oxford University. As a trustee of the Pilgrim Trust he was able to benefit Oxford and other institutions. He visited Canada and the USA in 1924. At Elsfield, Buchan to an extent played the academic squire. The Manor became something of a social centre for the large Buchan circle, eclectic but essentially liberal-tory, rather as Garsington Manor, similarly close to Oxford, did contemporaneously for the liberal-socialist Morrells. T. E. Lawrence was quite a regular visitor.

Buchan at Elsfield first concentrated on further military writings, rather hastily revising his history of the war for republication in four volumes (1921–2), an edition less well received than the original, and writing *The Battle-Honours of Scotland, 1914–1918* (1918), and the history of the South African forces in France (1920) and of the Royal Scots Fusiliers (1925), in part a tribute to his youngest brother, Alastair, killed in action in 1917. He declined a request to write the life of Haig, though in his *Nelson's History* he had praised Haig's military ability (Grieves, 'Early responses', 34). He also wrote *These for Remembrance* (1919), memoirs of some of his friends killed in action, and a memoir of Francis and Riversdale Grenfell (1920); these were important contributions to the literature of the 'missing generation'.

Photographs of Buchan in the country show him dressed with exaggerated precision and wearing country clothes like a uniform. Indeed, all his photographs suggest a very carefully presented public persona. But he was by no means fully Anglicized, in either religion or culture. His *Poems, Scots and English* (1917) showed how in moments of stress he turned to writing Scots vernacular verse. In Scotland he was seen not as the chronicler of clubland but as an important if not wholly engaged literary figure, part of the inter-war Scottish literary renaissance. An LLD from Glasgow University was the chief recognition of his war work, when the London establishment declined him the desired KCMG. His poems were included in two of C. M. Grieve's *Northern Numbers* (1920–21); Grieve (Hugh MacDiarmid) dedicated his *Annals of the Five Senses* to Buchan in 1923, and Buchan wrote an introduction to Grieve's *Sangshaw* (1925). In 1924 Buchan edited *The Northern Muse: an Anthology of Scots Vernacular Poetry*, one of the renaissance's better selling volumes, which MacDiarmid, who disliked Buchan's novels, thought 'by far the best anthology of Scottish poetry available at the time' (MacDiarmid, 257). Buchan was, however, rightly one of MacDiarmid's 'Strange Bedfellows' and it was an improbable long-term involvement. Buchan soon became chiefly a commentator on vernacular Scottish literature rather than a participant.

Fiction and biography between the wars Buchan also began, with *The Three Hostages* (1924), a remarkable series of novels: every year until 1937 he published at least one popular novel, many of which remain in print. These fell into three chief categories: historical novels, Scottish novels, and what may be called imperial novels. Several of Buchan's best historical novels, notably *Midwinter* (1923) and *The Blanket of the Dark* (1931), were set in the Cotswolds and showed a natural affinity with English rural life and the interplay between paganism and Christianity, and between the countryside and the town. *The Path of the King* (1921) traced the concept of kingship through several centuries. *Witch Wood* (1927)—Buchan's personal favourite—and *The Free Fishers* (1934) were historical novels with Scottish settings and preoccupations. *Witch Wood* poignantly combined many of Buchan's interests, in landscape, Calvinism in the seventeenth century, the fate of Scotland. The theme of town and country was developed in a series of novels depicting Dickson McCunn, a Glaswegian trader, in a variety of contemporary adventures: *Huntingtower* (1922), *Castle Gay* (1930), *The House of the Four Winds* (1935). Buchan's best work is to be seen in *Witch Wood* and *The Blanket of the Dark*, but it is for his stream of 'shockers' that he is chiefly remembered as a creative writer. In the inter-war years, the chief of these were *The Three Hostages* (1922), *The Dancing Floor* (1926), *The Gap in the Curtain* (1932), *A Prince of the Captivity* (1933), and *The Island of Sheep* (1936, reusing with quite different content the title of a book 'by Cadmus and Harmonia' he had written with his wife and published privately in 1919). Richard Hannay became a Cotswold squire, the guardian rather than the observer of British values. These novels, together with the earlier 'shockers', are among Britain's most striking political fiction. Their chief themes—the individual accidentally caught up in great affairs of state, the vulnerability of nations to evil conspiracies with worldwide connections, the excitement and detail of the chase, the dislocation between the city and the country, the psychology of disguise—were articulated in a distinctive authorial voice epitomized in the opening chapter of *The Thirty-Nine Steps*:

> I got the first hint in an inn on the Achensee in Tyrol. That set me inquiring, and I collected any other clues in a fur-shop in the Galician quarter of Buda, in a Strangers' Club in Vienna,

and in a little bookshop off the Rachnitzstrasse in Leipsig. I completed my evidence ten days ago in Paris.

Buchan caught the tone of Edwardian and inter-war English public life, the anxiety which accompanied complacency, its instinctive antisemitism, its male, public-school culture. His imperial novels are a pastiche of that culture and of the fiction it encouraged; their force in part derives from the fact that they are written against the grain of Buchan's inherent liberalism. Buchan was much blamed subsequently for élitism and antisemitism: the charge derives from these novels and fails to recognize their intention of pastiche, even of parody (and latterly self-parody). As the preface to *The Thirty-Nine Steps* makes clear, Buchan adopted a conscious pose when writing his shockers. His other work is written in a quite different voice.

In addition to this substantial corpus of fiction Buchan was an excellent essayist—as is shown by *A Book of Escapes and Hurried Journeys* (1922) and *The Last Secrets*, on exploration and mountaineering (1923)—and he was a notable biographer. He never completed his life of Lord Mansfield on which he worked for many years, but a steady stream of lives flowed from his pen, notably *Lord Minto* (1924); *Montrose* (1928, an improvement on his under-researched book of 1913); two on classical figures, *Julius Caesar* (1932) and *Augustus* (1937); *Oliver Cromwell* (1934); and—prepared for via *Some Notes on Sir Walter Scott* (1924) and *The Man and the Book* (1925)—*Sir Walter Scott* (1932), 'a book which I was bound one day or other to write' (p. 7). These were not works of primary historical research, but in the British genre of generalist biography they stand as perceptive, humane accounts, successfully appealing to the general reader without cheating the specialist. His concluding chapter on Scott as 'the greatest, because the most representative, of Scotsmen … [Scotland's] great liberator and reconciler' (*Scott*, 372) stated a notable credo, as much perhaps Buchan's as Scott's. In the face of Lytton Strachey's *Eminent Victorians* (1918) and Buchan's own shockers, their tone was respectful and balanced. His literary eminence was recognized by the award of the Companionship of Honour in 1932.

Buchan's inter-war literary output was remarkable. He wrote fluently and with little correction. His secretary, who typed out his spidery handwriting, recorded that he 'always worked to a time-table … and as a rule this time-table was not only adhered to, but was completed a little beforehand' (*Buchan by his Wife and Friends*, 279). With this literary punctiliousness went an obsession with punctuality and tidiness. He wrote chiefly in the morning, from 9.30 until 1 (and never in the evening) in the library he built for himself at the top of the house. He relaxed at Elsfield especially by walking, on several occasions walking the perimeter of the hills surrounding Oxford in a day. He did not, as it was sometimes said, write his novels on the train, but he often travelled third-class so as to meet characters and situations useful for his fiction. His punctilious appearance masked an easy and friendly manner, and he often surprised young people by the relaxed and unconventional way he spoke to them, Catherine *Carswell, for example, being much taken by him (*Buchan by his Wife and Friends*).

Politics and political life 'Publishing is my business, writing my amusement and politics my duty', Buchan was wont to remark (Lownie, 206). In 1927 he accepted the Unionist candidacy at a by-election for one of the three Scottish university seats, winning easily. He held the seat until 1937. It was a convenient seat, for university members were conventionally allowed a good deal of latitude by the Unionist whips. He supported, for example, the MacDonald government's Education Bill in 1930 and its decision to recognize the Soviet Union. He was instrumental in establishing what became the tory Education Institute at Ashridge. He campaigned for a school leaving age of fifteen. He was chairman of the parliamentary pro-Palestine committee in 1932 and spoke in Shoreditch in 1934 at a mass demonstration by the Jewish National Fund. His bill for the protection of birds was enacted in 1933. Always cautious about commitment, Buchan was as friendly with Labour MPs as with those of his own party: Ramsay MacDonald (depicted in *A Prince of the Captivity*), with whom he shared attendance in Lady Londonderry's circle, and several of the Clydeside group of socialists, particularly James Maxton and Tom Johnston (Adam Smith, *John Buchan*, 317 ff.). In the latter days of MacDonald's premiership, Buchan used to bolster the flagging prime minister with walks round St James's Park, just as he had earlier formed a friendship with the aged and largely forgotten Lord Rosebery, whose *Miscellanies* Buchan edited (without credit on the title-page) in two volumes in 1921. Despite these inter-party contacts, Buchan was not one of those Scottish tories who in the 1930s supported devolution or independence. He romanticized the extent to which, as he saw it, the First World War had broken down class barriers and killed 'a shoddy gentility', and his jubilee celebration of the reign of George V, *The King's Grace, 1910–1935* (1935)—an interesting essay on wartime and inter-war Britain—expressed the belief that 'the young man of the educated classes today is at home, as his father could never have been, in a Hull trawler, or working the soil with unemployed miners' (*The King's Grace*, 313). Buchan expected but received no political office when the tories returned to office in the National Government of 1931. This was unsurprising, for in politics Buchan was a novelist, just as in literary circles he presented himself as a man of affairs. Only in publishing was he a professional, and even there not a wholly committed one.

The branch of the Free Church of Scotland to which Buchan belonged became part of the Church of Scotland in 1929. Buchan was an active elder of the Church of Scotland in London (St Columba's Church) and in Oxford. With George Adam Smith he wrote *The Kirk in Scotland* (1930) to mark the union of the Church of Scotland and the United Free Churches in 1929. In 1933–4 he was lord high commissioner to the general assembly, investing that slightly Ruritanian office with great significance. The appointment greatly pleased his still active mother and himself. As high commissioner he visited the tiny assembly of the remnant of the Free Church.

Governing Canada In 1933 Buchan was sounded out by Baldwin with respect to the governorship of Burma; nothing came of this, for the necessary reforms to create the governorship were delayed. In 1935 Buchan, on MacDonald's nomination, accepted a much more suitable appointment, as governor-general of Canada, an office whose significance increased considerably as war became probable, for dominion support was both important and by no means initially certain. Though the governor-general was responsible only to Canada, Buchan knew his imperial duty. He was created Baron Tweedsmuir of Elsfield in 1935 and sworn of the privy council. It was rare for a governor-general to be well known in another capacity, and having a famous person in the office carried some risks. Tweedsmuir saw these clearly and avoided them. The appointment came at a propitious moment for him, for he was disillusioned with British politics and saw its leaders in the 1930s as mediocre. Canada gave him a new public role and a fresh sheet of paper on which to write. Tweedsmuir was a high-profile and generally popular governor-general, whose speaking (in French as well as English) and writing abilities were employed to the full. He travelled extensively and exceptionally within Canada. His intention was to develop a Canadian as well as a provincial loyalty. He set a pace and range of activity which his successors were unable to match.

In 1937 Tweedsmuir was elected chancellor of Edinburgh University (easily defeating Lord Lothian), though his Canadian commitments circumscribed his activities as such; his contesting of the election occasioned some official criticism. Later that year he toured the Arctic area of Canada, believing that 'I may be able to do some good work in awakening Canada to the real meaning of its possessions in the northern wilds' (Adam Smith, *John Buchan*, 408). One fruit of this expedition was Buchan's last novel, *Sick Heart River*, published posthumously (1941), in which the pastiche tone of the shockers is dropped and the best qualities of his historical novel writing are brought to bear on contemporary themes, the plights of an introspective imperial soul facing death and of a starving Canadian Indian tribe. His treatment in that novel of what were then called French Canadians was exceptional and anticipated the more subtle subsequent approach to the Québecois which more recent English language authors have attempted.

Tweedsmuir was active in encouraging association with the United States, with a view to ensuring American support in the event of war. His contacts with Roosevelt were significant and he arranged, in 1936, the first official visit to Canada by an American president. In 1937 Tweedsmuir in turn visited the USA, had talks with Roosevelt in Washington, shared a press conference with him, addressed congress (the first Briton to do so), and in 1938 he received honorary doctorates at Harvard and Yale. On dominion day 1937 Roosevelt broadcast to Canada and Tweedsmuir reciprocated. He encouraged the calling of a diplomatic conference in Washington, but received little support from Neville Chamberlain, the British prime minister. Even so Tweedsmuir strongly supported, on pragmatic grounds, Chamberlain's Munich agreement. In 1939 Tweedsmuir superintended the royal tour of Canada, for which he had worked since becoming governor; it was the first by a reigning monarch in a dominion and an important consolidation of the Commonwealth on the eve of war. Following a decision by the Canadian parliament he declared Canada at war with Germany on 10 September 1939 (the week subsequent to the British declaration, giving valuable time for Canadian requisitioning in the USA). Between 1938 and 1940 he wrote what he called a 'journal of certain experiences'—in effect a partial autobiography—intended for publication at the end of his governorship in September 1940 (he was offered but declined a further five years). It was posthumously published, with two excellent essays on fly-fishing, as *Memory Hold-the-Door* (1940), a remarkably candid work for so eminent a figure and influential on the genre of autobiography. It was quoted by George VI in his Christmas broadcast in 1943 and was one of President Kennedy's favourite books.

Death and reputation The royal tour of Canada was deemed a great success, but it left Tweedsmuir exhausted. On 6 February 1940 he had a cerebral thrombosis while shaving; he died on 11 February in the Neurological Institute, Montreal. His body lay in state in Ottawa. Following a funeral service in St Andrew's Church, Ottawa, he was cremated in Montreal. His ashes were returned by destroyer to Britain, where they were buried in Elsfield churchyard, under a fine gravestone designed by Sir Herbert Baker. His chauffeur and friend of twenty years, Amos Webb, who suffered a stroke soon after, was buried next to him. Tweedsmuir's wife, Susan, who suffered from depression during the years in Canada, herself wrote several historical novels and other books after her husband's death; she died in 1977. Tweedsmuir was succeeded in the title by his first son, John Norman Stuart Buchan (1911–1996), whose country enthusiasms had figured in several of his father's novels. Buchan's library and artefacts form the basis of the John Buchan Collection in Queen's University, Kingston, Ontario; and the Free Church in Broughton, of which his father was briefly the minister, is now the John Buchan Centre.

Buchan retained his readership throughout the twentieth century through the subtle universalism of his tales which underlay the localism of the scenery and the period charm of the plots and the characters. He reached a wider public through film, television, and radio adaptations of his novels, the first to be filmed being *Huntingtower* in 1925, starring Harry Lauder. He showed considerable interest in film and was active in the foundation of the British Film Institute. The most striking adaptation—almost a recreation—was Alfred Hitchcock's 1935 version of *The Thirty-Nine Steps* starring Robert Donat as Richard Hannay, and one of Hitchcock's best films, anticipating many of Hitchcock's later action films and introducing the cinematic audience to the grammar of the twentieth-century spy movie; later versions in 1959 and 1978 were more faithful to Buchan's narrative but of little cinematic significance. This popularity was not reflected in literary critical interest, except of a hostile sort. Buchan's body of

writing was too miscellaneous and too patchy for him to appear in English literature courses, and he suffered from the same anti-imperial reaction as Rudyard Kipling; to some of a later generation, the tone of Buchan's shockers shocked. Interest in him revived with Janet Adam Smith's fine biography (1965) and other studies, and at the end of the century much of his Scottish writing was rediscovered. Literary criticism began to show an interest. Buchan's large body of work was mostly of good quality but was too voluminous to achieve consistent excellence. It drew its strength from the unusually wide range of his cultural and public experience, and from his sense of individual evil in mass society. He was perhaps too fair-minded to match Kipling and Conrad, though he covered the same ground; but in his shockers he anticipated and shaped much of the non-sexual popular fiction of the latter part of the century. H. C. G. MATTHEW

Sources DNB · J. Buchan, *Memory hold-the-door*, [another edn] (1941) · R. G. Blanchard, *The first editions of John Buchan: a collector's bibliography* (1981) · J. Adam Smith, *John Buchan* (1965) · J. Adam Smith, *John Buchan and his world* (1979) · A. Lownie, *John Buchan* (1995) · A. Buchan, *Unforgettable, unforgotten* (1945) · S. Buchan, ed., *John Buchan by his wife and friends* (1947) · Lady Tweedsmuir [S. C. Buchan], *The lilac and the rose* (1952) · *John Buchan's collected poems*, ed. A. Lownie and W. Milne (1996) · W. Buchan, *John Buchan* (1982) · M. Green, *A biography of John Buchan and his sister Anna* (1990) · H. MacDiarmid [C. M. Grieve], *The company I've kept* (1966) · G. Greene, *The lost childhood and other essays* (1951) · D. Daniell, *The interpreter's house: a critical assessment of John Buchan* (1975) · R. Usborne, *Clubland heroes*, 2nd edn (1974) · G. Himmelfarb, 'John Buchan: an untimely appreciation', *Encounter*, 15/3 (1960), 46–53 · J. P. Parry, 'From the Thirty-Nine Articles to *The thirty-nine steps*: reflections on the thought of John Buchan', *Public and private doctrine: essays in British history presented to Maurice Cowling*, ed. M. Bentley (1993), 209–35 · G. S. Messinger, *British propaganda and the state in the First World War* (1992) · M. L. Sanders and P. M. Taylor, *British propaganda during the First World War, 1914–18* (1982) · C. Harvie, *The centre of things: political fiction in Britain from Disraeli to the present day* (1991) · C. Harvie, 'Second thoughts of a Scotsman on the make', *SHR*, 70 (1991), 31–54 · C. Harvie, '"For Gods are Kittle Cattle": J. G. Frazer and John Buchan', *John Buchan Journal*, 9 (winter 1989), 14–26 · J. Kruse, *John Buchan (1875–1940) and the idea of empire* (1989) · A. Kirk-Greene, 'Buchan and Burma', *John Buchan Journal*, 1 (spring 1983), 3–7 · *The Roosevelt letters: being the personal correspondence of F. D. Roosevelt*, ed. E. Roosevelt, 3 vols. (1949–52) · E. B. Nixon, ed., *Franklin D. Roosevelt and foreign affairs*, 3 vols. (1969) · W. L. Morton, *The kingdom of Canada*, 2nd edn (1969) · K. Grieves, '"Nelson's history of the war": John Buchan as a contemporary military historian, 1915–22', *Journal of Contemporary History*, 28 (1993), 533–55 · K. Grieves, 'Early responses to the Great War: Fortescue, Conan Doyle and Buchan', *The First World War and British military history*, ed. B. Bond (1991), 15–39 · R. Low, *The history of the British film, 1914–1918* (1950) · C. J. Walker, 'Greenmantle's absent Armenians', *Armenian Review*, 45 (1992), 1–38 · J. Marshall-Cornwall, *Wars and rumours of wars* (1984) · D. Trotter, 'The politics of adventure in the early British spy novel', *Intelligence and National Security*, 5 (Oct 1990), 80–91 · D. Stafford, *The silent game: the real world of imaginary spies* (1988)

Archives NL Scot., corresp. and papers; final copies and drafts of letters as governor-general of Canada · NL Scot., letters · NRA, corresp. and literary papers · Queen's University, Kingston, Ontario, corresp., literary MSS, notebooks, papers, speeches · Royal Arch. | BL, corresp. with Macmillans, Add. MS 54971 · BL, corresp. with Albert Mansbridge, Add. MS 65253 · BL, corresp. with Lord Northcliffe, Add. MS 62161 · BL OIOC, letters to Sir Malcolm Seton, MS Eur. E 267 · Bodl. Oxf., corresp. with Lord Lovelace and

Lady Lovelace · Bodl. Oxf., corresp. with Gilbert Murray · Bodl. Oxf., corresp. with Lord Simon · Brown University, Providence, Rhode Island, John Hay Library, letters to W. M. Colles · Brown University, Providence, Rhode Island, John Hay Library, letters to Sir Henry Newbolt · CUL, letters to Stanley Baldwin · Cumbria AS, Carlisle, letters to Lord Howard of Penrith · Dartmouth College, Hanover, New Hampshire, letters to James Pinker · HLRO, corresp. with Lord Beaverbrook · HLRO, corresp. with John St Loe Strachey · King's Lond., Liddell Hart C., corresp. with Basil Liddell Hart · NA Scot., corresp. with Lord Lothian · NL Scot., letters to Frederick Britten Austin · NL Scot., letters to Lord Beaverbrook · NL Scot., corresp. with Blackwoods · NL Scot., letters to Donald and Catherine Carswell · NL Scot., letters to Donald Macleod · NL Scot., corresp. with H. P. Macmillan · NL Scot., letters to fifth earl of Rosebery · PRO NIre., letters to Lady Londonderry · Ransom HRC, corresp. with John Lane, incl. reader's reports · Royal Society of Literature, London, letters to Royal Society of Literature · U. Aberdeen L., letters to Alexander Keith · U. Edin., corresp. as director of Nelson & Sons | FILM BFI NFTVA, documentary footage; news footage

Likenesses G. C. Beresford, photograph, 1906, NPG · H. Coster, photograph, 1931, NPG · T. J. Clapperton, bronze head, 1935, Scot. NPG [*see illus.*] · W. Stoneman, photograph, 1935, NPG · T. J. Clapperton, cast, NPG · portraits, repro. in Adam Smith, *John Buchan and his world*

Wealth at death £24,513 5*s.* 5*d.*: confirmation, 2 July 1940, *CCI*

Buchan, Peter (1790–1854), folk-song collector, historian, and publisher, was born on 4 August 1790 at Peterhead, Aberdeenshire, the only son of Peter Buchan, a ships' pilot from Peterhead, and his wife, Janet Buchan of St Fergus, Aberdeenshire. On 20 June 1813 he married Margaret Matthew, a dressmaker in Peterhead; they had seven sons and three daughters. Buchan had a varied literary career, but his chief claim to fame is as one of the most important early collectors of folk-songs and folk-tales in Scotland.

Buchan was restless and ambitious, determined to make a mark for himself in the literature of his country. After ten days' training at a chapbook house, the Randall Press, in Stirling, he set up the first printing shop in Peterhead, where on 24 March 1816 he commenced as jobbing printer, publisher, and general man of letters. 'I was obliged', he wrote, 'to be author, caseman, pressman, &c. and many … pages never were in manuscript, being actually composed while printing them' (Taylor, 2). A stream of publications poured from his small press, most of them written by Buchan himself. He had published his first volume of poems and songs, *The Recreation of Leisure Hours: Being Original Songs and Verses, Chiefly in the Scottish Dialect*, in 1814, which he followed with two works of local history, *Annals of Peterhead* (1819) and *An Historical and Authentic Account of the Ancient and Noble Family of Keith* (1820). His popular miscellany, *The Selector*, ran from June to November 1817, and contained short articles, literary essays, and serial fiction, much of it probably written by himself. *The Selector* was one of the earliest products of the Useful Knowledge movement in Scotland, anticipating *Chambers's Edinburgh Journal* by several years. Buchan's literary output was diverse, including collections of ballads and songs, popular theology, political tracts, poems and stories, and even a play, a melodrama called *The Peterhead Smugglers* (1834), which introduced the local warlock, Adam Donald, the prophet of Bethelnie. In 1831 Buchan

wound up his business and settled in Aberdeen for the education of his children, moving in 1838 to live with some of his sons in Glasgow. In 1845 he bought a small estate in Stirlingshire which he named Buchanstown; financial difficulties eventually forced him to retire to the home of his eldest son in Ireland.

As a young man in Peterhead, Buchan made frequent walking tours throughout the north-east of Scotland, during which he collected songs and ballads so assiduously that, by 1827, he had amassed two substantial manuscript volumes. A foretaste of the collection was published in 1825 as *Gleanings of Scotch, English, and Irish, Scarce Old Ballads*. Its success gained him admission to the circle of Sir Walter Scott who, with fine condescension, referred to him as 'the hirsute poet of Peterhead'. From Buchan's original manuscript collection two volumes were edited by Scott's associates David Laing and Charles Kirkpatrick Sharpe. While they were carefully southernizing Buchan's northern idiom, with 'meen' being changed to 'moon', 'abeen' to 'aboon', and 'fa' to 'wha', for example (Walker, 160–61), the collector was travelling the country recruiting subscribers. The two volumes of *Ancient Ballads and Songs of the North of Scotland* were published in 1828. Only a fraction of the material gathered during Buchan's later extensive fieldwork, comprising traditional songs and tales (notably his famous collection of bawdy songs, *Secret Songs of Silence*), was published during his lifetime.

Scott's coolness may have derived from the fact that Buchan sought to establish the north-east rather than the borders as the *locus classicus* of 'tradition' in Scotland, a task which was to occupy several later generations of northern intellectuals, and include such figures as Walter Gregor and Gavin Greig. Buchan was a plebeian, largely self-taught, a classic 'outsider', a man incapable of giving his ballad texts the sumptuous literary patina of a Percy or a Scott. It was upon him, therefore, that the brunt of the attack fell in the nationalistic ballad wars that followed his death, during which Scottish and English scholars struggled to establish their own as the dominant tradition. Since Buchan's texts were closest to what the people actually sang, he was the key to the whole Scottish position, and it was essential therefore to discredit him. He was castigated by J. W. Ebsworth as 'fraudulence personified' and 'wholly unreliable', but later collectors were able to confirm that his work was essentially trustworthy. One-third of the prestigious 'A' texts in Francis James Child's magisterial *English and Scottish Popular Ballads* (1882–98) were collected in Aberdeenshire, of which thirty-seven came from Buchan.

Although Buchan's status as a relatively faithful collector and editor was eventually vindicated by William Walker, the full extent of his contribution to folk-song studies has yet to receive the attention it deserves. He died of cholera in London on 19 September 1854, and was buried in Norwood cemetery two days later.

WILLIAM DONALDSON

Sources W. Walker, *Peter Buchan and other papers* (1915) · J. A. Fairley, *Peter Buchan, printer and ballad collector, with a bibliography* (1903) ·

BUCHAN, STEVENSON

D. M. Bertie, *Literary families: an exhibition to commemorate the bicentenary of the birth of Peter Buchan* (1990) [exhibition catalogue, North East of Scotland Museums Service, 1990] · W. L. Taylor, *Bibliography of Peterhead periodical literature* (privately printed, Aberdeen, 1889) · D. Buchan, *The ballad and the folk* (1972), 205–22 · W. Donaldson, 'Popular literature: the press, the people, and the vernacular revival', *The history of Scottish literature*, ed. C. Craig, 3: *Nineteenth century*, ed. D. Gifford (1988), 203–15 · W. Donaldson, introduction, in G. Greig, *Logie O'Buchan: an Aberdeenshire pastoral* (1985) · U. Aberdeen, Peter Buchan MSS 230311–230319
Archives BL, 'Collection of ancient Scottish and English ballads', Add. MSS 29408–29409 · Harvard U., Child Memorial Library · NL Scot., letters · U. Aberdeen, collection of MSS, corresp., notes, and family papers | NL Scot., letters to Robert Anderson · U. Edin. L., letters to David Laing · U. Glas. L., corresp. with William Motherwell [copies]
Likenesses J. Forbes, oils, Arbuthnot Museum, Peterhead, Aberdeenshire Heritage Collection

Buchan [*née* Thomson], **Priscilla Jean Fortescue**, **Lady Tweedsmuir and Baroness Tweedsmuir of Belhelvie** (1915–1978), politician, was born at 13 Rosary Gardens, Kensington, London, on 25 January 1915, the younger daughter of Major Alan Fortescue Thomson (1880–1957) of the Royal Artillery and his wife, Edythe Mary Unwin. She was educated in England, Germany, and France. On 14 May 1934 she married Sir Arthur Lindsay Grant, eleventh baronet (1911–1944), of Monymusk, Aberdeenshire. They had two daughters. Her husband, who served as a major in the Grenadier Guards, was killed in action in Normandy on 18 July 1944.

Lady Grant began her political career in the general election of 1945, when she stood as the Conservative candidate in Aberdeen North. She was defeated, but in November 1946 she was elected to parliament at a by-election in Aberdeen South. When she entered the House of Commons in 1946 she was a pretty war widow with fair hair and blue eyes, and the mother of two small children. She was also, at the age of thirty-one, the youngest woman in the House of Commons at the time and one of only two Conservative women. Not surprisingly, she quickly attracted the attention of the press, who dubbed her the 'glamour girl'. She held the Aberdeen South seat for twenty years.

On 27 July 1948 Lady Grant married John Norman Stuart Buchan, second Baron Tweedsmuir (1911–1996), of Elsfield Manor, Oxfordshire, son of the author John *Buchan. They had one daughter. Lady Tweedsmuir was a delegate to the consultative assembly of the Council of Europe from 1950 to 1953, and was a member of the Commonwealth parliamentary delegation to the West Indies in 1955. In November 1957 she became the second woman to move the address in reply to the queen's speech at the opening of parliament. She was elected a member of the executive of the 1922 committee of the Conservative Party, only the second woman to have reached this position. During 1960–61 she served as one of the British delegates to the United Nations general assembly. She was joint parliamentary under-secretary of state at the Scottish Office from 1962 until the Labour victory of 1964.

Lady Tweedsmuir lost her Aberdeen seat in the general election of 1966. Her political career seemed at an end, and she established business connections, becoming, notably, a member of the management team at Cunard from 1966 to 1970. However, in 1970 she was elevated to the House of Lords in her own right, with a life peerage, as Baroness Tweedsmuir of Belhelvie. At this point her career entered a new and even more distinguished phase. She served as minister of state at the Scottish Office from 1970 to 1972. As the Scottish minister in the Lords, she was expected to reside in Scotland and undertake local responsibilities there, while the secretary of state stayed in London. Her success in this position was rewarded in 1972 by a promotion to minister of state at the Foreign and Commonwealth Office, the first woman to be appointed to ministerial office in that department. As a Scottish MP she had learned a great deal about the fishing industry, and was well qualified to be chief negotiator during the first so-called 'cod war' with Iceland. In 1974 she was sworn of the privy council, and became a deputy speaker of the Lords.

Lady Tweedsmuir's greatest achievement, however, was her role as chair, from 1974, of the European Communities select committee of the House of Lords. Although a committed European, she was quite ready to examine the community's actions with a critical eye. She recruited about eighty lords of different backgrounds—trade unionists, judges, and former diplomats, among others—to examine in detail all proposed legislation of the European Community. They did so with a thoroughness that put to shame the equivalent House of Commons committee. It was said of the committee: 'Time and again the Lords select committee produced reports based on weeks of close examination and careful analysis that provided cogent evidence of the malfunctioning of the Brussels bureaucracy which gave other European parliamentarians cause to marvel' (*The Times*, 13 March 1978). Her achievement was also constitutionally significant, for she managed to establish a politically effective body within the House of Lords. Lady Tweedsmuir resigned from this position in 1977 because of ill health, and died on 11 March 1978.

G. E. MAGUIRE

Sources *The Times* (13 March 1978) · *WWW* · *Hansard 5C* · Burke, *Peerage* (1939) [Grant of Monymusk] · Burke, *Peerage* (1999) [Tweedsmuir] · b. cert. · P. Brookes, *Women at Westminster: an account of women in the British parliament, 1918–1966* (1967) · G. E. Maguire, *Conservative women* (1998) · S. McGowan, *Widening horizons: women and the conservative party* (1975) · Bodl. Oxf., conservative party archive
Archives NL Scot., business, personal, and political corresp. and MSS · NL Scot., corresp. and papers
Wealth at death £169,358: probate, 15 Aug 1978, *CGPLA Eng. & Wales*

Buchan, Stevenson (1907–1996), geologist, was born on 4 March 1907 at 32 Queen Street, Peterhead, the only child of James Buchan (1864–1943), fish trader, and his second wife, Christian Ewen (1870–1933), daughter of James Stevenson and his wife, Eliza Simpson. He had a half-brother, James, the child of his father's first wife. His education began at the Central School, Peterhead, and continued at the Peterhead Academy before he entered Aberdeen University in 1925. Active in university life, Steve, as he was known, earned a full athletics blue and became president of both the scientific and geological societies. A prizeman and medallist, he graduated in 1929 with first-class honours in geology. During 1930 he undertook research into the granites and dykes around Peterhead while demonstrating in the geology department.

In 1931 Buchan joined the (then) Geological Survey of Great Britain (GSGB) centred in Jermyn Street, London, and from 1934 in South Kensington at the Geological Museum. He served the GSGB and its successor, the Institute of Geological Sciences (IGS), in three roles over a period of forty years—as a field geologist, a hydrogeologist, and an administrator. In his fieldwork he surveyed Cretaceous strata around Sevenoaks, Jurassic in the Bridport district, and Eocene on the Isle of Sheppey. The summers of 1933 and 1934 also saw him mapping Dalradian metamorphic rocks and the Old Red Sandstone on Foula and Devonian lavas on Papa Stour in the Shetland Isles. He published three papers on these studies as well as contributions to the several maps and memoirs. In 1933 he was awarded a PhD for his research around Peterhead.

From 1934 Buchan prepared for publication many of the 1:10,000 scale geological maps of the capital. This necessitated formally documenting the several hundred records of wells and boreholes drawing water supplies from the Tertiary strata and the underlying Chalk of the London basin, which led to the publication in 1938 of a classic memoir *The Water Supply of the County of London from Underground Sources*. On 29 December 1937 he married Barbara Hadfield (*b.* 1914); they settled in Banstead, Surrey, and had a daughter Anne, and a son Stuart, a petroleum geologist. The wartime search for strategic minerals and the resolution of many groundwater problems in all parts of the country occupied Buchan between 1939 and 1945. An early task was the identification of a network of wells in London suitable for emergency water supplies; subsequently he was involved in locating sites for boreholes for the supply of many military camps, airfields, and wartime industries. These varied researches were recognized by the Geological Society through the award of the Lyell fund in 1944.

Buchan played an influential part in the drafting of those sections of the Water Acts of 1945 and 1946 relating to the management of groundwater as a national resource. Appointed head of the water department in 1945, he recognized the need for a comprehensive review of the thousands of well records already in the collections and the increasing importance of quantitative analysis of hydrogeological problems. The obligations placed on the GSGB by the new Water Acts provided the mechanism. All new well records had to be notified to the GSGB, but in addition a licensing system for both new and existing wells was introduced leading to the ongoing creation of a national database. To ensure the accuracy of the well records a bevy of young women geologists—the 'water babies'—visited the sites and checked the details; summaries were subsequently published in a Well Catalogue

Series. These basic data enabled colleagues to compile for the first time a series of regional resource studies of the principal aquifers and to introduce new methods of quantifying groundwater assessments. Their reports formed the basis of advice to government, local authorities, and industry. Buchan's own research at that time related to artificial recharge of the overdeveloped aquifers beneath north-east London and to an early study of groundwater pollution in Europe.

In 1960 Buchan toured North America as a visiting international scientist under the auspices of the American Geological Institute. The same year he was promoted to assistant director, responsible for a broad spectrum of GSGB's activities, and from 1968 as deputy director, for all work in the UK. He was heavily involved in the merger in 1965–6 of the GSGB and the Overseas Geological Surveys to form the IGS. International activities occupied Buchan throughout his career. Within the International Association of Hydrology he was president of the International Groundwater Commission; chaired the standing committee on hydrogeological maps; and was British delegate to the co-ordinating council of UNESCO for the hydrological decade. A founder member of the International Association of Hydrogeologists, he served as president in 1972–7. He was elected a fellow of the Royal Society of Edinburgh in 1962 and chaired the hydrology subcommittee of the Royal Society, as well as Section C of the British Association in 1968.

Appointed CBE in 1971, Buchan retired to Rockland St Mary, Norfolk, where he perfected his technique of producing a range of powerful liqueurs. A man of energy and resource with a deep sense of responsibility, he devoted himself wholeheartedly to the task of introducing rational management systems for the nation's groundwater resources. Buchan's encouragement and ability to delegate led his colleagues to develop many research techniques with which to tackle this task. He published fifty papers and articles in a wide range of scientific and engineering journals, thereby encouraging the integration of the role of groundwater in the two professions, which he recognized as necessary for the successful investigation and development of groundwater resources. He died at All Hallows Hospital, Ditchingham, on 24 July 1996 and was cremated at Earlham, Norwich, on 30 July. He was survived by his wife, daughter, and son.   DAVID A. GRAY

Sources WW (1984), 308 · *Summary of progress of the geological survey of Great Britain and the Museum of Practical Geology* (1931–8) · staff files, BGS · *Daily Telegraph* (29 Aug 1996) · *Annual Report* [Geological Society of London] (1996), 18–19 · D. A. Gray, *Year Book of the Royal Society of Edinburgh* (1996–7), 113–15 · personal knowledge (2004) · private information (2004)
Archives BGS
Likenesses photograph, 1971, Institute of Geological Sciences; repro. in *Yearbook of the Geological Society* (1971), frontispiece
Wealth at death £417,967: probate, 12 Nov 1996, CGPLA Eng. & Wales

Buchan, Thomas (*c.*1641–1724), Jacobite army officer, was the third of four sons, of the eight children of James Buchan of Auchmacoy (*d. c.*1659) and Margaret, daughter of Alexander Seton of Pitmedden. He was descended of a family who had been proprietors of Auchmacoy, in Logie-Buchan parish, Aberdeenshire, since at least 1445, and cherished an imaginary descent from the old Comyn earls of Buchan. The family, royalist and in debt, had a crypto-Catholic strain—Thomas's eldest nephew, Alexander, heir to Auchmacoy, became a Jesuit—which allowed Thomas to convert to Catholicism, furthering his career.

Buchan entered French military service about 1668. On 15 May 1671 Louis XIV, who was quadrupling the size of Douglas's infantry regiment (the Royal Scots, then in French pay), commissioned Buchan a captain to raise a new company in Scotland. In Louis's Dutch War (1672–8) he served mainly with the regiment on the German front. About 1678 he entered the Dutch service's Scots brigade (by the duke of York's order, he later stated) and by 1680 was lieutenant-colonel under Colonel Hugh Mackay, later the general opposing him. His younger brother, John Buchan (c.1650–c.1724), also entered the brigade in 1678, as a captain.

On 7 December 1682 Charles II's government appointed Thomas lieutenant-colonel of the earl of Mar's regiment (the Royal Scots Fusiliers) and ordered him home to Scotland. The regiment was quartered mainly in the south-west as hostilities with the covenanters escalated into the 1684–6 'killing time'. Buchan took a leading part, at first under John Graham of Claverhouse, for which he received the privy council's thanks on several occasions. Presbyterian chroniclers show him enforcing harsh laws, but not, like several colleagues, wantonly exceeding them. On 29 July 1686 he became colonel of the regiment on Mar's dismissal. Appointed brigadier-general of foot on 12 November 1688, he served in the campaign against William's invasion. Having followed James II to Ireland, Thomas was on 19 April 1689 promoted major-general for Scotland. He was intended to cross with three crack Irish regiments to reinforce Viscount Dundee, but he and they were diverted to the siege of Londonderry. He commanded there at the second battle of Windmill Hill on 4 June, a defeat blamed largely on his over-optimism, and served throughout the siege. That winter, he was commander in Drogheda and its vicinity.

On 24 January 1690 Buchan sailed from Dublin to Mull to take command of the Jacobite highland army. Although he repeated James II's promise that the duke of Berwick would follow shortly with reinforcements, the clan chiefs were disheartened. However, at a council of war in mid-February they determined to fight on, and Buchan organized a regiment of his own. His brother John (now lieutenant-colonel), who had fought for William at Killiecrankie, at this point took over Thomas's personal assets, 27,600 Scottish merks in bonds from individuals, to avert government confiscation. Despite this, though the brothers served in Scotland on opposite sides throughout 1690–91, neither apparently was suspected (unlike some aristocratic families) of any treacherous collusion. John in January 1691 received his own regiment, which he commanded under William in Flanders during 1692–7.

On 1 April 1690 Buchan assembled detachments from several Jacobite clans with which to raid along the 'highland line' in the north-east, harassing the enemy, seizing provisions for the intended main summer campaign, and, perhaps, inspiring the disaffected local episcopalians to rebel. By 30 April, the force marching down the River Spey had grown to 1200–1500. Ignoring prudent highland custom and specific warnings, Buchan had his men camp on flat riverside ground at Cromdale, opposite a Williamite chief's castle. However, his attempt to encourage local sympathizers resulted only in his forces suffering a serious defeat by the Williamite Sir Thomas Livingstone, who routed the encamped and unprepared highlanders with his cavalry early on May 1, killing an estimated 300–400 and capturing 100, including Buchan's nephew. Buchan himself, without coat, hat, or sword, fled east. The catastrophe is the subject of the humorous Scottish ballad 'The Haughs o' Cromdale'. Buchan's responsibility for it permanently alienated the clans, and the highland army never reassembled.

In August 1690 Buchan advanced eastwards through Aberdeenshire with some cavalry and 600 Braemar highlanders, and bluffed the local commander, the master of Forbes, into fleeing to Aberdeen. The Aberdeenshire and Kincardineshire lowland episcopalian gentry briefly rose and joined Buchan, swelling his force to perhaps 1800. But it lacked a solid core of highland foot, and he was soon after forced to retreat under the challenge of his former commander, Major-General Mackay. Buchan hurried to the Inverness area to join Kenneth Mackenzie, fourth earl of Seaforth, who had just raised his clan; but Mackay, pursuing, drove Buchan away and browbeat Seaforth into surrender. After some futile raiding, Buchan disbanded his tiny remaining force in September.

The exhausted Jacobite clans could not rise in 1691. Buchan, persuaded by Sir George Barclay, and several chiefs therefore met John Campbell, first earl of Breadalbane, to discuss peace terms. However, other chiefs opposed these moves, and the easily influenced Buchan feared general Jacobite condemnation if he conceded too much while French assistance remained possible. The Achallader agreement of 30 June 1691 established a conditional three-month truce, during which Buchan could obtain James's authorization to submit. He later sent Barclay to solicit for this; but, not having obtained it, and with the chiefs turning against the agreement, he was unable to conclude a pacification with Breadalbane that autumn. The failure led to the massacre of Glencoe in February 1692. In March, Buchan and his officers were allowed to travel by ship to France. On arrival Buchan, though in disgrace for Achallader, was ordered, seconding the French invasion attempt of May 1692, to sail from Dunkirk with 100 Scottish officers to north-east Scotland to start a new rising. The naval defeat of La Hogue in late May prevented this.

Thereafter Buchan and other field officers remained on small pensions at the Jacobite court. After James II's death in 1701, Buchan unsuccessfully sought the colonelcy of a run-down Scottish regiment in the army of the French-controlled Spanish Netherlands. He returned home under the amnesty proclaimed by Anne's Scottish privy council in 1703. They at first allowed him only a short stay to settle his private affairs; yet he risked a clandestine farewell visit to the court at St Germain that December. By summer 1704 he had married Elizabeth (*fl.* 1660–1710), only daughter of Patrick Urquhart of Meldrum and Lady Margaret Ogilvy, a royalist heroine and daughter of the first earl of Airlie. Her family also had crypto-Catholic traditions, and she was widow of the overt Catholic Sir George Gordon, ninth laird of Gight. Her late brother Adam Urquhart of Meldrum had been Buchan's fellow soldier and persecutor of covenanters. Buchan's assets remained with his brother John and nephew James (laird of Auchmacoy), secured by bond, leaving him the freer for Jacobite plotting. He was a main channel for St Germain's communications with the Errol family, the most active north-eastern Jacobites, partly via his nephew George Buchan, now a French officer. The main French agent, Nathaniel Hooke, still blamed Thomas for the failure of the highland rising, but employed him in June 1707 to report on the state of the citadels at Fort William and Inverness for the proposed 1708 invasion and rising, in which he intended to serve as a volunteer under the earl of Moray. He was arrested and taken to London with the other Jacobite suspects.

As the rising of 1715 began, Alexander, marquess of Huntly, wrote on 22 September commending Buchan's 'frankness to go with me, in our King and cuntrays caws' (HMC, *Fourth Report*, 1.529). After participating, Buchan escaped by sea to Bordeaux in August 1716, and spent some months at the court of the Pretender (James Stuart) at Avignon and Rome. About November 1717 he returned home from Paris after government troops left north-eastern Scotland, and again he became a Jacobite intermediary for the Errol family. He died in May 1724 at Ardlogie, in Fyvie, his wife's property, and was buried at Logie-Buchan.

The episcopalian author of the 1732 *View of the Diocese of Aberdeen* called Buchan 'a man eminent for courage and antient honesty' (Keith, 361). His obvious fault as a general was over-confidence, exacerbated in 1690 by ignorance of highland warfare. Yet, persevering after Cromdale, he almost succeeded in spreading the highland rising to his native north-eastern lowlands.   PAUL HOPKINS

Sources P. A. Hopkins, *Glencoe and the end of the highland war* (1986) • [James, sixteenth earl of Caithness], 'The Buchans of Auchmacoy', Auchmacoy, Aberdeenshire [family history, composed 1880s; photocopy in NRA Scotland, West Register House, Edinburgh] • *Correspondence of Colonel N. Hooke*, ed. W. D. Macray, 2 vols., Roxburghe Club, 92, 95 (1870–71) • *Memoirs of the Lord Viscount Dundee, the highland clans, and the massacre of Glencoe … by an officer of the army* (1714) • H. Mackay, *Memoirs of the war carried on in Scotland and Ireland*, ed. J. M. Hog and others, Bannatyne Club, 45 (1833) • J. Macpherson, ed., *Original papers; containing the secret history of Great Britain …*, 2 vols. (1775) • *Fourth report*, HMC, 3 (1874), 528–9 • *Calendar of the Stuart papers belonging to his majesty the king, preserved at Windsor Castle*, 7 vols., HMC, 56 (1902–23), vols. 1–5 • J. Buchan, *The history of the royal Scots fusiliers, 1678–1918* (1925) • testamentary inventories, NA Scot.: James Buchan, 13 Dec 1726, CC1/6/7; John Buchan, 20 June 1726, CC1/6/9; Thomas Buchan, 2 Sept 1728, CC1/6/9, 25 June 1741, CC1/6/22 • R. Wodrow, *The history of the sufferings of the Church of Scotland from the Restoration to the revolution*, ed. R. Burns, 4 vols. (1828–30), vols. 3–4 • J. Ferguson, ed., *Papers illustrating the history of the Scots brigade in the service of the United Netherlands, 1572–1782*, 3 vols., Scottish History Society, 32, 35, 38 (1899–1901) • [A. Keith], 'A view of the diocese of Aberdeen', *Collections for a history of the shires of Aberdeen and Banff*, ed. J. Robinson (1843), 69–632 [1732] • D. Nairne, journal, NL Scot., MS 14266, fols. 175, 185v–187v, 191, 198v • register of the privy council of Scotland, 1703–7, NA Scot., PC 1/53

Archives priv. coll., Buchan of Auchmacoy MSS, commissions, and official letters, bundle 57 | NA Scot., archive of the 'Highland Army', Leven & Melville MSS GD 26/8 • Scottish Catholic Archives, Edinburgh, 'An acct of the affaires of Scotland from ye 1st of May to ye 27th May 1690', SM 2/1/14 • West Highland Museum, Fort William, letters to Macpherson of Cluny

Likenesses oils, repro. in Buchan, *History*; priv. coll.

Wealth at death only surviving information from 1721 will in official records concerns a bond for £5700 Scots from brother, to whom he bequeathed 6000 merks Scots of it: inventory, NA Scot., CC1/6/9, Col. John Buchan, 20 June 1726; Major-General Thomas Buchan, 2 Sept 1728

Buchan, William (1728/9–1805), physician and author, was born at Ancrum in Roxburghshire, where his father had a small estate and also rented a farm. He was educated at Jedburgh grammar school and then went to the University of Edinburgh, intending to enter the ministry. He seems to have spent about nine years at the university, devoting much time to botany, astronomy, and mathematics. It is said that he supported himself to some extent by acting as a private tutor in mathematics. He also studied medicine. He most probably left Edinburgh in 1758. He practised first in rural Yorkshire and in 1759 was appointed medical officer to a branch of the Foundling Hospital at Ackworth, Yorkshire. There he wrote his MD thesis, 'De infantum vita conservanda', which was published in Edinburgh in 1761. In 1760 he married Elizabeth Peter, daughter of a Mr Peter, whose wife was related to the family of Lord Dundas. They had a daughter and two sons, one of whom, Alexander Peter *Buchan, became a physician.

In 1762 after government support for foundling hospitals was withdrawn Buchan began to practise in Sheffield. He returned to Edinburgh about 1766. In 1769 he published *Domestic Medicine, or, The Family Physician*. It cost 6s. and the 5000 copies which were printed rapidly sold out. It was dedicated to Sir John Pringle, a distant relative by marriage and at that time president of the Royal Society. That Buchan was the sole author of this work was disputed by Robert Kerr in his *Memoirs* (1811) of the Edinburgh printer and polymath William Smellie. Citing Smellie's son, Kerr claimed that the printer had entirely rewritten Buchan's original draft of the book. This judgement seems plausible. Smellie, a self-educated man, was certainly equipped for the task. There is, however, no corroborative evidence, except that only the first edition bore Smellie's imprint. The second edition was extensively revised. Before the twentieth century, no single health guide enjoyed as much popularity as *Domestic Medicine*. Between 1769 and the last edition, which appeared in Philadelphia in 1871, there were at least 142 separate

William Buchan (1728/9–1805), by John Flaxman, 1783

English-language editions. It was particularly popular in the United States, an American reprint first appearing in 1772. Later editions were edited by other hands, some of whom added their names to the title page. There were also French, Spanish, Portuguese, Italian, German, Russian, and Swedish translations. The empress of Russia sent Buchan a gold medal and a commendatory letter. It was said that Buchan sold the copyright for £700, and that the booksellers made that profit annually by its sale.

Domestic Medicine was a novel work with only one obvious predecessor, S. A. Tissot's *Avis au peuple sur sa santé* of 1761. *Domestic Medicine* combined two older genres. It was a volume to be read as a guide to preserving health, and a book to use to identify and prescribe for diseases. Approximately the first third was devoted to explicating rules of healthy living, and the remainder to describing diseases and their cures. The 1772 revision provided a separate index of remedies and a separate dispensatory was added to its third edition. The book was also informed by the common-sense philosophical views of the Edinburgh medical professor John Gregory, cousin of Thomas Reid, whom Buchan and Smellie knew well. In Gregory's view medical knowledge should be easily accessible to the public. Other members of the Edinburgh medical faculty, notably William Cullen, were not of this opinion.

In 1772 Buchan became a fellow of the Royal College of Physicians of Edinburgh, and when John Gregory died in 1773 Buchan was a candidate for the vacant chair of the Institutes of Medicine. He failed to achieve this, however, since the appointment was apparently awaiting the graduation of James Gregory, John Gregory's son, who succeeded to the chair in 1778. In the same year in Edinburgh, Buchan briefly gave public lectures on experimental philosophy, using apparatus bequeathed by his friend the astronomer James Ferguson. In his will Ferguson had given Buchan first option of disposal of the instruments.

In 1778 Buchan moved to London where Ferguson's entire collection was acquired from Buchan, probably shortly after his arrival, by the physician John Coakley Lettsom. Buchan practised regularly at the Chapter Coffee House, near St Paul's, which he is said to have visited daily. It was the resort of literary men. While in London he published several minor works, of which *On the Offices and Duties of a Mother* (1800) and *Advice to mothers on the subject of their own health, and on the means of promoting the health, strength and beauty of their offspring* (1803) were probably the most popular. He was said to be of an athletic frame, convivial, full of anecdotes, and compassionate. He became ill about a year before his death, which occurred at his son's house in Percy Street, Rathbone Place, London, on 25 February 1805. He was buried in the west side of the cloisters of Westminster Abbey on 5 March.

CHRISTOPHER LAWRENCE

Sources *GM*, 1st ser., 75 (1805), 286–8, 378–80 · *European Magazine and London Review*, 47 (1805), 167–9 · C. J. Lawrence, 'William Buchan: medicine laid open', *Medical History*, 19 (1975), 20–35 · R. Kerr, *Memoirs of the life, writings and correspondence of William Smellie*, 2 vols. (1811) · C. Rosenberg, 'Medical text and social context: explaining William Buchan's *Domestic medicine*', *Bulletin of the History of Medicine*, 57 (1983), 22–42 · J. R. Millburn, *Wheelwright of the heavens: the life and work of James Ferguson* (1988) · IGI
Archives Royal College of Physicians of Edinburgh, papers | BL, letters to G. Cumberland, Add. MSS 36494–36497, *passim*
Likenesses J. Flaxman, Wedgwood medallion, 1783, BM [*see illus.*] · line engraving, 1815, Wellcome L. · J. Mills, line print (after A. Mills), NPG; repro. in *European Magazine* (1805) · R. Page, stipple, Wellcome L. · W. Ridley, stipple (after painting by J. Wales), Wellcome L. · Sellier, line engraving, Wellcome L. · J. Thomson, stipple (after painting by J. Wales), Wellcome L. · engravings, Wellcome L. · line engraving, Wellcome L. · medallion, Westminster Abbey, London · pen and wash drawing, RCS Eng. · stipple, Wellcome L. · Wedgwood medallion, Scot. NPG

Buchanan, Andrew (1690–1759), merchant and lord provost of Glasgow, was born on 29 January 1690 in Glasgow, the second of four sons of George Buchanan, maltster, and Mary Maxwell.

In 1716 Buchanan was admitted a burgess of Glasgow by right of his father, and quickly revealed himself to be an energetic businessman. During the 1720s he and his younger brothers Neil and Archibald became involved in the city's growing trade in tobacco with the American colonies, and by 1730 Andrew Buchanan, Bros. & Co. was Glasgow's largest tobacco importer, shipping over 500,000 lbs per annum. The company, and successor firms Andrew and Archibald Buchanan & Co. and Andrew Buchanan, Son & Co. re-exported the bulk of their tobacco from Scotland to France.

In 1750 Andrew Buchanan was one of six prominent merchants who founded the Ship Bank, Glasgow's first bank. He also held shares in a sugar house in the city's King Street, a Glasgow linen works, a Pollokshaws printfield, and a ropeworks and sailcloth factory in Greenock. With his brothers George, Neil, and Archibald, Buchanan formed in 1725 the Buchanan Society, a charitable institution for the benefit of people of that surname, providing apprenticeships for poor boys, and financial assistance to the widows of subscribers.

Buchanan served as Glasgow's dean of guild in 1728–9, and was elected lord provost in 1740 and 1741. He was one of the six commissioners appointed in September 1745 to negotiate with John Hay, the quartermaster in Charles Edward Stuart's army, and persuaded the Jacobites to reduce the loan they demanded from the city from £15,000 to £5500. When the Jacobites occupied Glasgow in December, Buchanan was told that his house would be plundered if he did not pay a levy of £500. He refused, but the threat was not carried out.

In 1735 Buchanan purchased the estate of Drumpellier in Lanarkshire, where he built a mansion, Drumpellier House. Between 1719 and 1740 he acquired strips of land on the city's western boundary, and in 1753 he began to lay out a new street there, which he called Virginia Street.

On 30 January 1723 Buchanan married Marion Montgomery (1711–1743). After her death, on 1 July 1744 he married Elizabeth Binning. When he died on 20 December 1759, he was survived by his second wife, and two sons and four daughters from his first marriage. Both of his surviving sons became prominent in Glasgow business and politics. The elder, James Buchanan of Drumpellier (1724–1786), was lord provost of Glasgow from 1768 to 1770 and from 1774 to 1776. He was a partner with his cousin Andrew Buchanan in the tobacco firm Buchanan Hastie & Co., which failed in 1777 during the American War of Independence, forcing James to sell his house in King Street and the Drumpellier estate. The younger George Buchanan of Mount Vernon (1728–1762) made his fortune in the tobacco trade, and built one of Glasgow's finest houses, Virginia Mansion, in Virginia Street.

Although little known today, Andrew Buchanan was an important figure in the development of Glasgow's mercantile economy during the early eighteenth century, and one of the first of the city's famous 'tobacco lords'.

IAIN F. RUSSELL

Sources J. R. Anderson, ed., *The provosts of Glasgow from 1609 to 1832* (1942) · G. Stewart, *Curiosities of citizenship in old Glasgow* (1881) · T. Annan, J. O. Mitchell, and others, *The old country houses of the old Glasgow gentry*, 2nd edn (1878) · J. O. Mitchell, *Old Glasgow essays* (1905) · J. M. Price, 'Buchanan and Simson, 1759–1763: a different kind of Glasgow firm trading to the Chesapeake', *William and Mary Quarterly*, 40 (1983), 3–41

Buchanan, Sir Andrew (1807–1882), diplomatist, the only son of James Buchanan of Blairvadoch, Ardinconnal, Dunbartonshire, and Janet, eldest daughter of James Sinclair, twelfth earl of Caithness, was born on 7 May 1807. He entered the diplomatic service on 10 October 1825, and was attached to the embassy at Constantinople. On 13 November 1830 he was named paid attaché at Rio de Janeiro, but he did not remain long in South America, as he served temporarily with Sir Stratford Canning's special embassy to Constantinople from 31 October 1831 until 18 September 1832, after which he became paid attaché at Washington on 9 November. He was with Sir Charles Vaughan's special mission to Constantinople from March 1837 to September 1838, and he then proceeded to St Petersburg as paid attaché from 6 October of the same year. He went through a greater number of changes than most in the diplomatic service; he was secretary of legation at Florence from 24 August 1841, and chargé d'affaires from July 1842 to October 1843, and from March to May 1844. At St Petersburg he was appointed secretary of legation in 1844, and between that time and 1851 acted several times as chargé d'affaires. He was then rewarded for his various services by his appointment, on 12 February 1852, as minister-plenipotentiary to the Swiss confederation. In the following year, on 9 February, he was named envoy-extraordinary to the king of Denmark, and he acted as the British representative at the conference at Copenhagen in November 1855 for the definite settlement of the long-standing dispute about the payment of due by ships passing through the sound between Zealand and Sweden. He was transferred to Madrid on 31 March 1858, and then to The Hague on 11 December 1860. He became ambassador-extraordinary and plenipotentiary to the king of Prussia on 28 October 1862. His pro-Danish sympathies during the Schleswig-Holstein crisis in 1864 led to Queen Victoria's intervention to have him moved from Berlin. He became ambassador-extraordinary to Russia on 15 September 1864, and served as ambassador to Austria from 16 October 1871 to 16 February 1878. He then retired on a pension, Disraeli having found him 'a hopeless mediocrity', 'a perfectly useless' ambassador (Seton-Watson, 45, 201). In fact, he was one of the shire-horses of the Victorian diplomatic corps. He received the usual honours: he was made CB on 23 May 1857, KCB on 25 February 1860, and GCB on 6 July 1866, and he was sworn of the privy council on 3 February 1863.

Buchanan married first, on 4 April 1839, Frances Katharine, daughter of Edward Mellish, dean of Hereford (she died on 4 December 1854); and second, on 27 May 1857, the Hon. Georgiana Eliza, third daughter of Robert Walter Stuart, eleventh Lord Blantyre. Among the children from his first marriage was George William *Buchanan, diplomatist. He was created a baronet on 14 December 1878, and died at Craigend Castle, Milngavie, near Glasgow, on 12 November 1882.

G. C. BOASE, rev. H. C. G. MATTHEW

Sources *The Times* (15 Nov 1882) · *FO List* (1882) · R. W. Seton-Watson, *Disraeli, Gladstone and the eastern question: a study in diplomacy and party politics* (1935) · *Dearest mama: letters between Queen Victoria and the crown princess of Prussia, 1861–1864*, ed. R. Fulford (1968) **Archives** priv. coll. · U. Nott. L., corresp. and papers | BL, corresp. with Sir Austen Layard, Add. MSS 39012–39030, *passim* · Bodl. Oxf., corresp. with Lord Kimberley · CUL, corresp. with Lord Mayo · Hants. RO, corresp. with Lord Malmesbury · LPL, letters to A. C. Tait relating to continental chaplaincies · Lpool RO, corresp. with fifteenth earl of Derby · NL Scot., letters to Sir Henry Elliot · Notts. Arch., letters to John Saville · PRO, corresp. with Lord John Russell, PRO 30/22 · PRO, letters to Odo Russell, FO 918 **Likenesses** G. F. Watts, pencil drawing, Scot. NPG **Wealth at death** £12,572 11*s*. 6*d*.: probate, 1883, *CCI*

Buchanan, Claudius (1766–1815), East India Company chaplain, was born on 12 March 1766 at Cambuslang, a village near Glasgow, the second son of Alexander Buchanan (*d.* 1788), schoolmaster at Inveraray, Argyll, and his wife, the daughter of Claudius Somers. He commenced his education at Inveraray, and at the age of fourteen became tutor in a gentleman's family. In 1782 he entered the University of Glasgow, where he spent the two following years; he left prematurely to engage in private tuition but returned to obtain his degree in 1786.

It was hoped by his pious parents that Buchanan would enter the ministry in the Church of Scotland but he was to disappoint them bitterly. At the age of twenty-one he formed a wild scheme to travel through Europe on foot, supporting himself by playing on the violin. He carefully withheld the true nature of his plans from his parents, telling them that he had been engaged by a gentleman to travel on the continent with his son. However, Buchanan did not venture further than London, where, undergoing great hardship for some months, he eventually obtained poorly paid employment in a solicitor's office. For the next four years he continued to conceal his whereabouts from his parents. Leading a fairly dissolute life he often had to pledge his clothes in order to find the money to eat. Even his father's death in 1788 did not induce Buchanan to put an end to the sham.

In 1790 Buchanan started to reform his life. He introduced himself to John Newton (1725–1807), then rector of St Mary Woolnoth in the City, under whose influence a complete change in his character took place. This led to his decision to become ordained in the Church of England. The bishop, however, refused to ordain him unless he went to an English university. Henry Thornton, who had met Buchanan through Newton, stepped into the breach and provided the necessary funds (repaid in 1802) to enable him to go to Cambridge. He entered Queens' College in 1791. Although he had not previously studied mathematics he took the college prize and also came first in Latin. In 1794 Newton suggested that Buchanan should go to India. This idea gradually took root, reinforced by his friendship with Charles Simeon, the Cambridge evangelical. Buchanan took his degree in 1795, and in the same year was ordained deacon and commenced his clerical life as Newton's curate. In the following year he was appointed to a chaplaincy in Bengal, the first of a band of evangelical chaplains brought to India through the influence of Simeon. Isaac Milner, president of Queens' College, wrote his recommendation for the post, saying of Buchanan that 'much may be expected from his ability and industry and discretion ... His uncommon zeal is tempered and directed by sound and well-informed understanding' (Pearson, 130).

On his arrival at Calcutta early in 1797 Buchanan lodged for a few months with David Brown (1763–1812), then presidency chaplain. Buchanan was sent to Barrackpore, where he remained for two years. This was an unhappy time for him. There was no church and no British regiment quartered there, and the climate was debilitating. Buchanan passed his time studying the scriptures in the

Claudius Buchanan (1766–1815), by Frederick Christian Lewis senior, pubd 1815 (after J. Slater, 1814)

original tongues, and in Persian and Hindustani. On 3 April 1799 he married Mary Whish, third daughter of Richard Whish, rector of Northwold, Norfolk. In December he was transferred to Calcutta, where he quickly impressed Lord Wellesley, who directed that Buchanan's sermon at the thanksgiving service for the successes achieved in the recent war in Mysore should be circulated throughout India.

Wellesley next appointed Buchanan vice-provost of his new college for East India Company servants at Fort William. Buchanan stated that much of the impetus for the college had come from himself and David Brown, who was appointed provost. 'The whole direction of the College lies with me. Every paper is drawn up by me and everything that is printed is revised by me' (*Memoir*, 15). His duties as vice-provost were to act as 'censor-morum and arbiter of official and personal proprieties' in the college. In addition he gave lectures on Greek, Latin, and English classics (Pearson, 205). He had high hopes for the college, believing that it had been founded to 'enlighten the oriental world, to give science, religion, and pure morals to Asia, and to confirm in it the British power and dominion' (Pearson, 368). He became the chief apologist, defender, and promoter of the college, doing all he could to help Wellesley fight the battle to keep it open. Buchanan also edited *Primitae Orientales* (Calcutta, 1802–4) and *The College of Fort William* (1805) in an attempt to publicize the college's work in England. His influence could clearly be seen in the topics chosen for the college's public disputations and essays: some concerned the advantages of an academic institution in the East and the benefits to the Indian people of British rule, and others were directed towards the benefits and best methods of propagating Christianity in India. Buchanan hoped the college would prove the means of evangelizing Asia.

Although as a company chaplain Buchanan could not engage directly in missionary operations, he laboured zealously for the promotion of Christianity and education among the people of India. He raised money and gained support for translations of the scriptures, working closely with the Baptists at Serampore. Out of his own pocket he offered liberal prizes to several universities and public schools for essays and poetical compositions in Greek, Latin, and English on the restoration of learning in the East; on the best means of civilizing the subjects of the British empire in India, and of diffusing the light of the Christian religion throughout the Eastern world; and on other similar topics. He paid the salary of Lassar, an Armenian Christian born in China, to translate the scriptures into Chinese. He made two tours of south India in 1806 and 1807, which were undertaken almost entirely at his own expense, and the information he gleaned and the way in which he publicized it was to do much to further the cause of Christianity in India. He established good relations with the Syrian Christians in Malabar, which resulted in the publication of the New Testament into Malayalam.

However, Buchanan alienated the Jews in Cochin by taking valuable manuscripts by force, and although accounts of his travels were published in literary and religious periodicals and aroused great interest his zeal occasionally overran his discretion. His disputations on religious themes aroused opposition from his Indian colleagues, who regarded them as infringements of the religious toleration accorded them by the East India Company. In 1804 the governor-general, Lord Wellesley, prohibited one of his disputations. Buchanan also tended to treat the Baptist missionaries at Serampore as subordinates, and he attempted to gain control of their translations with his proposal for the formation of an institution to be called 'British propaganda', to be based at Serampore; this led to friction and distrust with the missionaries.

Buchanan's wife died on 18 June 1805, leaving two daughters, and in March 1808 Buchanan returned to England. He became curate of Ouseburn, Yorkshire, in 1810. In February of that year he married Mary Thompson (d. 1813), daughter of Henry Thompson of Kirkby Hall, Scarborough: she had two sons, dying in childbirth on 23 March 1813.

Back in Britain Buchanan campaigned in earnest to force the East India Company to do more to further Christianity in India. The creation of an episcopate for India, at the renewal of the East India Company's charter in 1813, was largely due to his efforts. Buchanan had started his campaign in 1805 by writing his *Memoir of the Expediency of an Ecclesiastical Establishment for British India*. He had lobbied the leading bishops and, using the same argument as he had employed to enlist support for Fort William College, pointed out that his proposal would tend to confirm Britain's dominion of India. In 1813 he published *Colonial ecclesiastical establishment, being a brief view of the state of the colonies of Great Britain and of her Asiatic empire in respect to religious instruction*. There was even talk of his becoming the first bishop in India, but he had no wish for such an honour.

Buchanan was as much concerned to promote missionary work in general as to promote the Church of England. He was a key publicist against the company's censorship of Christian works, and later, at the renewal of the company's charter, he supported the campaign to force the company to grant missionaries unrestricted access to India. In 1811 he wrote *Christian Researches in Asia*, which went through nine editions in two years. Another important work was his *Apology for Promoting Christianity in India* (1813). Central to his argument was his depiction of a degraded Hindu society which could only be reformed through the introduction of Christianity. His dramatic descriptions of juggernaut, suttee, and hook-swinging contributed powerfully to change both British opinion towards India and the role that the propagation of Christianity was to play. By 1813 the image of India prevalent in Britain was not the glorious India of the past depicted by men like Sir William Jones, but the degraded India of the present portrayed by Buchanan and other evangelicals. Buchanan's writings were considered authoritative in America and helped to stimulate the American missionary movement and to shape American attitudes towards non-Christians.

Buchanan was awarded the degree of DD by the universities of Glasgow, Aberdeen, St Andrews, Dublin, and Cambridge. In 1811 he had two strokes, and he died of a third on 9 February 1815 at Broxbourne, Hertfordshire, where he was engaged in revising a Syriac translation of the New Testament. His remains were returned home to Yorkshire, and buried at Ouseburn. He was survived by Charlotte and Augusta, daughters of his first marriage.

PENELOPE CARSON

Sources *Memoir and Christian researches of the Rev. Claudius Buchanan, DD* (1841) • H. N. Pearson, *Memoirs of the life and writings of the Rev. Claudius Buchanan, DD*, 2 vols. (1817) • A. K. Davidson, *Evangelical attitudes to India: missionary publications of Claudius Buchanan with a text of Buchanan's Memoir of the expediency...* (1990) • M. E. Gibbs, *The Anglican church in India, 1600–1970* (1972) • S. Neill, *A history of Christianity in India, 1707–1858* (1985) • H. Cnattingius, *Bishops and societies: a study of Anglican colonial and missionary expansion, 1698–1850* (1952) • M. A. Sherring, *History of protestant missions in India from their commencement in 1706 to 1881*, ed. E. Storrow, new edn (1884)
Archives BL OIOC, letters • CUL | BL, letters to Thomas Yeates, Add. MS 21557 • U. Birm. L., Church Missionary Society archives
Likenesses F. C. Lewis senior, stipple, pubd 1815 (after J. Slater, 1814), BM, NPG [see illus.] • R. Page, stipple, BM • I. Whessell, engraving, repro. in Pearson, *Memoirs of the life and writings*, frontispiece

Buchanan, David (c.1595–1652), author, was the second son of William Buchanan of Arnprior and thus related to George *Buchanan (1506–1582), the great Scottish humanist. He entered St Leonard's College, St Andrews, as a student in 1609, and matriculated in January 1610. He graduated MA on 26 July 1613 and was placed among the best students of his year. He may then have moved to St Mary's College, the theological college of the university: his writings presuppose a good education in classical and biblical languages. Buchanan's activity during the next twenty years or so of his life is somewhat uncertain. He probably pursued his studies on the continent, and, since he is known to have acquired a good knowledge of French, almost certainly in France, where he might have been a professor in one of the protestant colleges. According to James Gordon of Rothiemay, he was tutor to James Stuart, fourth duke of Lennox, and he may have accompanied the young man in his travels to France, Spain, and Italy from 1624 to 1633 (Gordon, 18, 62).

In 1636 Buchanan's *Historia animae humanae* was published, almost certainly in Paris. In a letter of dedication to William Craven dated 24 March 1636, he stated that he had spent the previous years in France but was now in England. The book itself runs to upwards of 600 pages, much of which is concerned with ethics, and was based on extensive studies. The following year Melchior Mondiere republished the work in Paris at Buchanan's expense. In 1638 Buchanan's *L'histoire de la conscience* was almost certainly also published there. Thereafter much of Buchanan's time was devoted to preparing his edition of John Knox's *Historie of the Reformation in Scotland*. First published in London in 1644, it was republished in extended form in the same year in Edinburgh, 'in all probability under his own inspection' (*Works of John Knox*, 1.xlii). The 1644 edition contained five books and some other writings and a sermon by Knox. It was subsequently republished several times in the eighteenth century and in the early decades of the nineteenth. Buchanan's entire work has earned a well-merited condemnation from David Laing, the nineteenth century's leading authority on Knox's writings, who wrote that so many unwarranted liberties had been taken by Buchanan in altering and adding passages 'as for a length of time to throw discredit on the whole work' (1.xlii) that 'it might have been well had this publication been actually prohibited' (1.xlii). As well as frequent instances of 'palpable blunders' (2.584ff.) he had added various allusions to his own times and omitted passages or modified expressions, which might have proceeded from the 'Licencer of the Press in London rather than from Buchanan himself' (2.584ff.). However, Buchanan deserves some credit for having preserved and published the fifth book, covering September 1564 to August 1567, the work of an unknown continuator but derived from Knox's papers.

According to James Gordon, Buchanan 'looked upon Episcopacye and all the English ceremonies [which Charles I was introducing to Scotland] with an evil eye', and Gordon attributes the fact that the fourth duke of Lennox, despite his well-known loyalty to the monarch, 'was inclyned to the Covenant of his owne accorde' to his having had Buchanan at some time as his tutor (Gordon, 18, 62). In the early 1640s Buchanan was in London and between 1643 and 1652 became involved on the periphery of the Westminster assembly on behalf of Scottish commissioners, whose views on episcopacy and independency he shared. Anxious to obtain help from leading continental Reformed scholars and churches, Robert Baillie, one of the leading commissioners, requested Buchanan, with his known continental links, to write to 'some of the ministers of Paris, Geneva and Berne' informing them that 'a mighty faction' was pressing for 'liberty of conscience for all sects', whereas most of the Scots, the

assembly, and parliament favoured a form of presbyterianism (*Letters and Journals of Robert Baillie*, 2.179ff.). When Buchanan's efforts were less successful than expected, Baillie encouraged him to elucidate further the issues dividing the presbyterians from the Independents, and to underline the urgency of securing a Reformed declaration against the Independents. In fact Baillie wanted to use Buchanan to uphold the reputation of the Scots presbyterian covenanters against adverse reports circulated abroad by both their episcopal and Independent opponents.

Drawing, according to Baillie, on copies of papers presented by the Scottish commissioners to the Westminster assembly, Buchanan published *Truth its manifest, or, A short and true relation of divers main passages of things in some whereof the Scots are particularly concerned* (1645) and *Some papers of the commissioners of Scotland, given in lately to the Houses of Parliament, concerning propositions of peace* (1646), 'hazard[ing] to print them with a Preface of his owne, and an introduction, both very harmless' (*Letters and Journals of Robert Baillie*, 2.367). When, again according to Baillie, 3000–4000 copies of these works were sold in two days, the enraged Independents secured from both houses of parliament their condemnation, which included burning by the common hangman. Only Buchanan's preface and introduction, of which he admitted authorship, were finally judged offensive. Ordered to appear at the bar of the House of Commons, he failed to attend. On 28 July 1646 it was reported to the House of Commons that he was in Newcastle. It was decreed that he be 'forthwith sent for as a Delinquent' (*JHC*, 4, 1646, 505–17, 628) but on 24 April 1646, more than a month earlier, Baillie had written to a correspondent that 'Mr Buchanan is gone to a place safe enough' and hinted that this might be abroad (*Letters and Journals of Robert Baillie*, 2.367). How long Buchanan remained in his place of safety is not known. Thereafter he discreetly discontinued any activity in the interests of the Scottish presbyterians in London.

Buchanan's interest for the remaining years of his life centred on Scottish history and topography. Much of his work, however, remained unprinted while he lived, or if printed did not signify his authorship. As a friend of Robert Gordon of Straloch and his son, James Gordon, parson of Rothiemay, Buchanan took over from the former some of his work on the preparation of Bleau's *Theatrum Scoticae*. Writing to him on 31 March 1650 from Edinburgh, Buchanan mentioned that he had provided descriptions of some of 'our western regions' and that he would shortly give them and several more to John Scot of Scotstarvet. In a postscript he added that he was working on a history of 'our people' in the vernacular (Stuart, 1.43–4). Buchanan was almost certainly the author of 'Provinciae Edinburgenae descriptio' (Mitchell, 2.614, 622) and 'Edinburgi descriptio' (ibid., 2.623, 628), 'commonly regarded as having been composed to accompany the well-known 1647 *Bird's-Eye View of Edinburgh* prepared for the Magistrates of the City by James Gordon, Parson of Rothiemay … and … known to have been "in print"' (ibid., 2.xlviiff.). It is quite possible that Buchanan himself produced and saw to the printing of a French translation.

William Buchanan stated that David Buchanan 'wrote a large Natural History which was not completed at the author's death, and therefore never printed, to the great loss of the learned and curious' (Buchanan, *Historical ... Essay*, 154), and that he had written 'a large Etymologion of all the Shires, Cities, Rivers, and Mountains in Scotland, which was printed, tho' not in many Hands' (ibid.). Robert Sibbald stated that in writing his *Historia literaria* he had derived the greatest assistance from the manuscript of Buchanan's *De scriptoribus Scotis*, a collection of brief and rather derivative biographies of some 115 persons, not all of whom can be classified as Scottish and some of whose writings are totally unknown. From a historical point of view they are now of little or no value. Buchanan made his will on 19 August 1652, and died in Edinburgh shortly thereafter. The cause of death is not recorded. The testament, confirmed on 19 January 1653, made his 'loving brother Mr. William Buchanan' his only executor, and confirms that he had independent means, and had not married.

Seventeenth-century writers thought highly of Buchanan: Robert Baillie wrote of him as 'a most honest and worthy man' (*Letters and Journals of Robert Baillie*, 2.367), and Sir Robert Sibbald in the preface to *Historical Inquiries Concerning the Roman Monuments and Antiquities in Scotland* included, next to Timothy Pont, David Buchanan and Robert Gordon of Straloch as those to whom he had been most indebted. At the beginning of the eighteenth century he was described by William Buchanan as a 'gentleman of great learning' (Buchanan, *Historical ... Essay*, 154) and in the nineteenth century David Laing, despite his critical appraisal of Buchanan's edition of Knox's *History*, could refer to him as 'a person of literary distinction' (*History of the Reformation*, 2.465). In the twentieth century, however, Buchanan's work received little attention. As regards his scholarship, Buchanan might today justifiably be judged guilty of some eccentricities, as for example in his search for the derivation of the name Edinburgh, as he was by William Nicolson, who wrote that the manuscripts of Buchanan, such as he had seen, 'discover their author's skill in the Hebrew and Celtic languages to have been more considerable than his acquaintance with the Greek and Roman writers, who are never to be made friends with some of his opinions and etymologies' (Nicolson, 33).

JAMES K. CAMERON

Sources *The works of John Knox*, ed. D. Laing, 6 vols., Wodrow Society, 12 (1846–64) • *The letters and journals of Robert Baillie*, ed. D. Laing, 3 vols. (1841–2), vols. 2–3 • W. Buchanan, *Historical and genealogical essay upon the family and surname of Buchanan* (1723), 61 • W. Buchanan, *An enquiry into the genealogy and present state of ancient Scottish names* (1819), 206 • matriculation register; graduation register, St Andrew's University, MS UY 305.3, fol. 143; MS UY 305.3, fol. 321 • J. Gordon, *History of Scots affairs from 1637–1641*, ed. J. Robertson and G. Grub, 3 vols., Spalding Club, 1, 3, 5 (1841) • Venn, *Alum. Cant.* • 'Stuart, James, fourth duke of Lennox', *DNB* • 'Craven, William (1606–1697)', *DNB* • J. Knox, *The history of the Reformation of the Church of Scotland*, sel. edns (1644–1812) • *John Knox's History of the Reformation in Scotland*, ed. W. C. Dickinson, 2 vols. (1949) • W. Nicolson, *Scottish history library*, new edn (1776) • J. Stuart, ed., *The miscellany of the Spalding Club*, 1, Spalding Club, 3 (1841) • D. Laing, ed., *The* *Bannatyne miscellany*, 2, Bannatyne Club, 19a (1836) • *Geographical collections relating to Scotland made by Walter MacFarlane*, ed. A. Mitchell, 2, Scottish History Society, 52 (1907) • *Remains of Sir Robert Sibbald* (1837) • D. Buchanan, *De scriptoribus Scotis libri duo*, ed. D. Irving, Bannatyne Club, 55 (1837) • *Thomae Dempsteri Historia ecclesiastica gentis Scotorum, sive, De scriptoribus Scotis*, ed. D. Irving, rev. edn, 2 vols., Bannatyne Club, 21 (1829) • I. D. McFarlane, *Buchanan* (1981) **Archives** NL Scot., Sir Robert Sibbald's MS, Adv. MSS 33 7 17 –18 **Wealth at death** see will repr. in Buchanan, *De scriptoribus Scotis*, 136–8

Buchanan, David (1745–1812), printer and publisher, was born at Montrose. A descendant of the ancient family of Buchanan of Buchanan, nothing is known of his parents or his early life. He studied at the University of Aberdeen, where he graduated MA. He began the business of printing in his native town at a time when it was conducted in few of the provincial towns of Scotland, and his enterprise as a publisher was shown by the issue of good editions of the dictionaries of Johnson, Boyer, and Ainsworth. He abridged Johnson's dictionary for the earliest pocket edition. Among his other publications special mention may be made of his miniature series of English classics. He died in 1812, survived by a number of children, including William *Buchanan, lawyer, David *Buchanan, editor, and George *Buchanan, civil engineer.

T. F. HENDERSON, rev. DOUGLAS BROWN

Sources Anderson, *Scot. nat.*

Buchanan, David (1779–1848), newspaper editor and author, son of David *Buchanan (1745–1812), printer and publisher, was born at Montrose. William *Buchanan, lawyer, and George *Buchanan, civil engineer, were his brothers. He learned the business of his father and, like him, possessed intellectual tastes and sympathies. Early in his career he contributed to William Cobbett's *Political Register*, and possibly to the *Edinburgh Review* in April 1807 (the article on Lord Henry Petty's financial plan may be by Buchanan). In 1808 he accepted an invitation to start in Edinburgh a liberal newspaper, the *Weekly Register*. The paper lasted less than a year; when it folded Buchanan edited the *Caledonian Mercury*. He held this post until 1827, when he accepted the editorship of the *Edinburgh Courant*, editing it until his death. Buchanan also wrote on political economy, editing Adam Smith's works, with notes and additional matter, in 1814, and publishing an *Inquiry into the Taxation and Commercial Policy of Great Britain* in 1844 (a work supporting free trade but opposing income tax and David Ricardo's theory of rent). He also brought out an edition of the *Edinburgh Gazetteer*, in six volumes, contributed numerous geographical and statistical articles to the seventh edition of the *Encyclopaedia Britannica*, and supplied a large portion of the letterpress for the *Edinburgh Geographical Atlas* (1835). He died in Glasgow on 13 August 1848.

T. F. HENDERSON, rev. H. C. G. MATTHEW

Sources Anderson, *Scot. nat.* • *Montrose Standard* (18 Aug 1848)

Buchanan, Dugald [Dughall Bochanan] (1716–1768), Gaelic poet, was born on the farm of Ardoch, Strathyre, in the parish of Balquhidder, western Perthshire, the son of John Buchanan, a quiet, God-fearing man who rented a farm and owned a small meal mill, and Janet Ferguson. His mother was a great influence during Buchanan's early years and imbued him with a lifelong sense of the importance of spirituality. She died, however, on 6 December 1722 when Buchanan was six. He attended a local school established by the Society for Promoting Christian Knowledge (SPCK), and at the early age of twelve served as a household tutor to children whose mother was a devout Christian. However, the irreligious behaviour of the children caused Buchanan mental distress, and he left after a short time.

In 1730 Buchanan went to Stirling to further his education. After two years he continued the process with a six-month stay in Edinburgh, where he was led astray by his involvement with wild companions. Having been ordered home at the age of eighteen he was apprenticed to a carpenter, first of all at Kippen and then at Dumbarton, and travelled around as the work demanded. During these years he survived a serious attack of fever, was twice rescued from drowning, and was nearly bayoneted by a drunken soldier. There is evidence that he attended divinity college in Glasgow in the early 1740s. He frequented many parish churches and took part in moorland communions. During George Whitefield's second visit to Scotland in the summer of 1742, Buchanan was deeply impressed by the evangelism of that great preacher. His early religious instincts deepened and, conscious of his sins, he became an earnest searcher for spiritual truth, a process that he recorded in a diary written in English.

This diary, kept by Buchanan between 1741 and 1750, was written in the mode of an autobiographical sequence of confessions, and was based on John Bunyan's spiritual autobiography, *Grace Abounding*. In it Buchanan reveals his early profanity, recklessness, and irreligion, and analyses in vivid detail his fits of remorse, violent mental agony, and fear of the judgment of God. It is this struggle, from which he emerged intellectually and spiritually, that provides the key to his *laoidhibh spioradail* ('spiritual hymns'), only eight in number, which have been reprinted many times.

In 1749 Buchanan married Margaret Brisbane (*d.* 1824), daughter of a land steward of the earl of Louden, and settled on his father's farm at Ardoch. The life of a farmer did not suit him and he soon took to itinerant teaching. In 1753 he was appointed by the SPCK as a teacher, and subsequently as catechist, at a school at Kinloch Rannoch in the estate of Duncan Robertson of Strowan. There he played an important role in bringing education, stability, and religion to the inhabitants.

Because of his proficiency in Gaelic, Buchanan was chosen, together with the Revd James Stewart of Killin, to assist with the translation and publication of the first edition of the Gaelic New Testament. While performing this task in Edinburgh he attended classes in natural philosophy, astronomy, and anatomy at the university, and in 1767 he published the first edition of his own poems. He also met many of the city's literary celebrities, including David Hume. Hume challenged him to quote anything as sublime as a passage from *The Tempest*; Buchanan met the challenge by reciting from memory verses from the Revelation of St John.

The tone of Buchanan's poems is the result of his deeply personal experience of religious conversion. Although his subject matter is not new, he compensates for this with his skilful poetic technique. The striking accuracy of his imagery tends to reflect the daily life and environment of a Perthshire countryman. His poem *Là a' bhreitheanais* translates crisply into Scots. His particular debt to the poetry of Isaac Watts is highlighted by Donald Meek in a two-part article in *Gairm* (nos. 147 and 148, summer and autumn 1989). The 'graveyard' influence of the poetry of Edward Young and Robert Blair can also be detected. Buchanan conveys to his readers a vivid sense of Christ's suffering and God's splendour. Spiritual values and responses are more important than the physical achievements of the heroes of some traditional Gaelic poets. Death will come all too soon and with it judgment for each individual's earthly sins. Afterlife punishment can only be avoided by early repentance.

In 'Morachd Dhe' ('The greatness of God') Buchanan meditates on the nature of God; 'Fulangas Chrisiod' ('The sufferings of Christ') is an account of the passion of Christ; *Là a' bhreitheanais*, his longest and widely regarded as his greatest poem, portrays dramatically the universal and moral upheaval of the day of judgment; 'Am bruadar' ('The Dream') contrasts religious contentment with the futility of avarice and ambition; 'An gaisgeach' ('The Hero') declares that true courage is the result of spiritual and moral strength rather than physical strength; 'An claigeann' ('The Skull') pours bitter criticism upon a variety of social types; 'An geamhradh' ('Winter') uses the metaphor of a highland winter to provide a parable of death; and 'Urnuigh' ('A Prayer'), written shortly before the poet's death, is his Nunc dimittis that presents the doctrine of atonement by means of a devout, penitential prayer of adoration.

In 1768 Buchanan was called home to tend his fever-stricken family. He caught the infection and died at Ardoch in his fifty-second year. He was survived by two sons and two daughters, and by his widow, who continued to live at the family farm until her death in 1824.

RICHARD D. JACKSON

Sources D. Buchanan, *Laoidhe spioradail* (1767) · *Laoidh spioradail le Dughall Bochannan* (1773) · *Comh-chruineacha do laidhibh spioradail le Doughal Buchannain* (1784) · *The diary of Dugald Buchanan, author of 'Laoidhean spiordaeil', with a memoir of his life* (1836) · *Laoidhean spioradail le Dughall Bochannan* (1837) [spiritual hymns by Dugald Buchanan with life of the author in English] · *Reminiscences of the life and labours of Dugald Buchanan, family teacher and evangelist at Rannoch, Perthshire with his 'Spiritual songs' and an English version of them by the Rev. A. Sinclair*, 21st edn (1875), viii, 194 · *Beatha agus iompachadh Dhùghaill Bochannain* (1875) · *Dugald Buchanan's spiritual songs, translated into English verse*, trans. L. Macbean (1884) · *The spiritual songs of Dugald Buchanan*, ed. D. Maclean, new edn (1913) · *Dain spioradail le Dughall Bochannan*, [new edn] (1946) · D. S. Thomson, 'Gaelic poetry of the 18th century: Dughall Bochanan', *An Gaidheal* [The Gael], 53/9 (1958), 87–9 · D. Meek, 'Ath-sgrudadh: Dughall Bochanan (I and II)' ('A study of Dugald Buchanan'), *Gairm*, 147 (summer 1989), 267–80; *Gairm*, 148 (autumn 1989), 319–31 · *Là a' bhreitheanais (The* *day of judgment*) *le Dughall Bochanan*, translated into Scots by James Robertson (1999) • J. MacInnes, *The evangelical movement in the highlands of Scotland, 1688–1800* (1951), esp. 280–83 • D. E. Meek, *DSCHT*, 106 • D. S. Thomson, *Gaelic poetry in the eighteenth century* (1993), 139–43

Buchanan, Francis Hamilton. *See* Hamilton, Francis, of Buchanan (1762–1829).

Buchanan, George (1506–1582), poet, historian, and administrator, was born about 1 February 1506 at a farm called The Moss in Killearn parish, Stirlingshire, the fifth of eight children of Thomas Buchanan (*d. c.*1512) and Agnes Heriot, traditionally said to be of the Heriots of Trabroun, Haddingtonshire. His father and grandfather, Robert Buchanan of Drumikill, died while he was a child and he was brought up by his mother, who was given a lease of lands near Cardross, Menteith, in 1513. He probably spoke Gaelic. One of his five brothers, Patrick, became known as a humanist. A nephew Thomas succeeded him as keeper of the privy seal, and Thomas's wife Janet was Buchanan's executor.

Early studies and writings A few details of Buchanan's early life are given in his autobiographical *Vita*, first published in 1598. Its authenticity is generally accepted, though Peter Young, assistant tutor to James VI, has been suggested as a possible author. At the instigation of his uncle James Heriot he left local schooling at the age of fourteen to go to Paris. His uncle's death caused him to return to Scotland within two years. During 1523 he undertook military service with French troops led by the duke of Albany in a campaign of retaliation against English invasion, and was present at the siege of Wark in October. After a winter's illness he went to St Andrews to study under John Mair or Major. He took his BA degree at St Andrews on 3 October 1525 and though in a later epigram he described his teacher as 'Major in name alone' (Buchanan, *Opera*, 2.373), he followed him to Paris where he was admitted BA on 10 October 1527. He began to teach in the Collège de Sainte-Barbe, noted for its Greek studies, and became procurator of the German nation in 1529. For the next five years he was tutor to Gilbert Kennedy (later third earl of Cassillis) to whom he dedicated his first published work, a translation from English into Latin of Linacre's *Rudimenta grammatices* (1533), and whom he later commemorated in an elegy.

Buchanan had returned to Scotland with Kennedy by 1536 and was appointed tutor to Lord James Stewart, an illegitimate son of James V who died in 1557. He wrote a satirical poem describing a dream in which St Francis asked the author to join the Franciscan order. He replied that there was more honesty found outside the church. He developed the themes of the *Somnium* at more length in the *Palinodiae*, intended as a middle way between offending the Franciscans and being too mild for the king, and in the more pointed *Franciscanus*. These poems, not published until later, showed Buchanan's familiarity with classical models. They also involved him in religious controversy: he had eaten meat in Lent and taken an interest in Lutheran questions. Condemned as a heretic he was thrown into prison, but he escaped and fled to London,

George Buchanan (1506–1582), after Arnold Bronckorst, 1581

where he stayed about six months and was assisted by Sir Thomas Rainsforde. After a month in Paris he left for Bordeaux in September 1539.

Teacher and playwright While Buchanan was at the Collège de Guyenne in Bordeaux (he had been invited by the principal, André Gouvea, nephew of the principal of Sainte-Barbe) he continued his acquaintance with scholars including the elder Scaliger, as he did during a year or so at the Collège du Cardinal Lemoine in Paris. He visited Toulouse in 1544 and then returned to Bordeaux where Montaigne was among his pupils. At this time he did not appear to be in danger on account of his religious views.

During these years Buchanan worked on his plays: *Baptistes*, written and produced in 1542, *Medea* which was produced in 1543 but may have been drafted earlier, and *Jephthes* and *Alcestis* which were not produced at that time. *Medea* and *Alcestis* were translations of Euripides; the two original plays, on biblical themes, were directed against tyranny and religious hypocrisy, *Baptistes* being of more interest for the author's political views but *Jephthes* being more mature in structure. Various suggestions have been made for the target of *Baptistes*, and James V of Scotland, François I of France, and Henry VIII of England have all been identified with King Herod.

Inquisition and poet In 1547 André Gouvea was invited by King João III of Portugal to become principal of the college at Coimbra, and Buchanan was among those who accompanied him there to teach the classical authors and the rudiments of Aristotelian philosophy. Gouvea died the following year, however, and under his successor Diogo Gouvea, probably a brother, the administration of the college deteriorated and the inquisitor-general decided to make enquiries about some of the college staff. Buchanan was taken into confinement and put on trial for heresy between August 1550 and January 1551. He feared that the *Franciscanus* would be held against him and suspected the involvement of Cardinal Beaton, but a variety of theological matters were discussed, including the sacrament, justification, and confession. Buchanan was directed to make public abjuration on 29 July 1551 and to be sent to the monastery of San Bento for further instruction. He was released from there in February 1552. Buchanan's own account of the inquisition episode was not wholly accurate. The reasons behind the proceedings probably included personal jealousies at Coimbra involving Diogo Gouvea; neither Beaton nor the Jesuits were likely to have had much influence, and Buchanan's response was neither ignominious nor heroic. He left Portugal and reached Paris later in the year after a few months in England.

Buchanan wrote several poems relating to Belchior Beleago who taught at Coimbra. The satirical tone was continued in poems about the meretricious Leonora; other poems conveyed a tone of sincere respect. There were also a few poems commenting unfavourably on Portuguese politics, for instance the colonization of Brazil by undesirable characters. The best-known work associated with his period of detention was his Latin version of the Psalms which he may have planned earlier as it was a genre which attracted contemporary French writers. Dedicated to Mary, queen of Scots, when published, it is the work which does most to justify Henri Estienne's description of Buchanan as easily the leading poet of his time. His principal characteristics as a poet may be described as mastery of the Latin language and variety of subject matter. He uses several metrical forms and follows different literary traditions, such as pastoral and the epigrams of the Greek anthology, as well as echoing the major Latin authors. His allusions may be to classical mythology or to contemporary events, and his tone ranges from sharply satirical to devotional. His personal epigrams convey admiration, as for the earl of Moray, hostility, as for John Hamilton, archbishop of St Andrews, or respect, as for John Calvin.

In Paris Buchanan continued his literary and scholarly links and also his contacts with members of aristocratic society. He was appointed tutor to Timoléon de Cosse, son of the maréchal de Brissac, in 1554 or 1555, and spent the next five years in northern Italy and Paris, probably also making a visit to Lyons which apprised him of the death of Florence Wilson and led to a poem in tribute. According to Estienne, Buchanan was invited to join the maréchal's council of war. In 1560 Brissac was replaced as commander in northern Italy by the duc de Guise, and Buchanan returned to Scotland about that time. In 1558 he obtained the prebend of Mulleville in Coutances Cathedral, a gift which demonstrates the gratitude of the Brissac family but does not imply that he was in holy orders. In these years his court poetry developed and the unfinished *De*

sphaera, five books on the old Ptolemaic system of cosmology, was dedicated to Timoléon. Buchanan probably first thought of this work in the 1540s—when the Copernican theory revived ancient controversy over whether the earth moved—began it in the 1550s, and continued it until the 1570s (book 5 refutes the emphasis on astrology in Tycho Brahe's *De nova stella*, published in 1572). He was well-informed rather than expert on astronomy and besides using classical sources such as Pliny's *Natural History* and Aristotle's *De caelo* he presented a synthesis of contemporary thinking on astronomy and features of the earth, including such topics as the relationship of the intellect to heaven. The subject matter was traditional, and the work original perhaps only in its literary improvement and moralizing, for instance on the futility of strife and the insanity of avarice.

Involvement in politics On his return to Scotland Buchanan quickly gained the favour of the crown. He is mentioned in a letter from Randolph to Cecil dated 7 April 1562 as reading Livy with the queen. In the treasurer's accounts, payments of £125 to Buchanan were recorded for the terms of Martinmas 1561, Whitsunday 1562, and Martinmas 1562. He was named by the privy council on 6 February 1562 'to interpreit the writtis product in proces, writtin in Spanis langage, furth of the samin in Franche, Latyne or Inglis, that the Quenis Grace and Counsale mycht thaireftir understand the samin' (*Reg. PCS*, 1545–69, 234), and in 1563 parliament included Buchanan among commissioners to investigate the University of St Andrews. In 1564 he was granted the temporalities of Crossraguel Abbey, and in an entry under 16 October the privy council, following a complaint by Buchanan that the earl of Cassillis had refused to hand the abbey over following the death of the last abbot, ordered the earl to do so within six days. The queen, Randolph noted that month, would have made Buchanan abbot: but 'with spiritualities he wyll not meddle, bejcawse he cane not preache' (*CSP Scot.*, 1563–9, 88). About 1566 Buchanan was in France again, possibly on government business. Over the next few years he was closely associated with James Stewart, earl of Moray (c.1531–1570). He became principal of St Leonard's College in St Andrews in 1566, an appointment in the hands of Moray as commendator of St Andrews Priory.

In 1567, following Darnley's murder, Mary's marriage to Bothwell, and her forced abdication and imprisonment at Lochleven, Buchanan attached himself to the party opposed to her. His exact motives are still not entirely clear. Some have argued that he owed a duty of loyalty to Mary. Form of religion does not seem to have been a dominant factor (he had conformed to protestantism from his return to Scotland), nor opposition to women rulers. Nor is the theory that the educated and well-travelled Buchanan had a particular ancestral attachment to Darnley wholly convincing. In fact there is no simple explanation of the issues dividing the queen's party and king's party. Loyalties fluctuated. For instance the earl of Moray, whom Buchanan admired, had been opposed to Mary's marriage to Darnley. In the early 1560s Buchanan may have established personal links with men like the lawyer

James MacGill, who remained loyal to the queen when Moray rebelled in 1565, though he later turned against her. Buchanan may have done the same.

In September 1568 Buchanan went to York as secretary to the commission attending the conference summoned by Queen Elizabeth which was subsequently transferred to Westminster. Buchanan declared that the casket letters, passed to Moray by the earl of Morton, were genuine, and he probably took part in formulating the book of articles containing the charges against Mary. His *Detection*, first printed in a Latin edition in 1571, may also have been written under political instructions. At any rate it contains allegations, for instance Mary's impulsive ride from Jedburgh to visit Bothwell in October 1566, which are clearly false. Another pamphlet against Mary, the *Actio contra Mariam Scotorum reginam*, has been attributed to Buchanan but was probably not written by him. In 1570 he wrote his two vernacular works, the *Admonition*, directed against the Hamiltons, and *Chamaeleon*, against William Maitland of Lethington.

Public servant During Moray's regency and after—he was reported to have been much distressed by the regent's murder on 23 January 1570—Buchanan continued to play a significant part in public affairs. He had been moderator of the general assembly of the kirk in 1567. The treasurer's accounts record letters sent to Buchanan in St Andrews in May and June 1568 and allocations of black velvet and money in August and November 1570 by the regent's command. For a short time in 1570 Buchanan was director of chancery, and he was keeper of the privy seal from that year until 1578 when he was succeeded by his nephew. He attended the privy council at intervals until 1579, being made temporary secretary by parliament sitting at Stirling in 1578. He served on commissions for digest of the laws, reform of the universities, and compilation of a Latin grammar.

One of the best-known of Buchanan's duties in those years was his tutorship, along with that of Peter Young, to King James, an appointment which was renewed in 1572 and 1578. James Melville in his memoirs wrote that Buchanan held the king in great awe, unlike another of the four principal masters who carried himself warily 'as a man who had a mind to his own weal, by keeping of his majesty's favour'. Melville wrote:

> Mr George was a Stoick philosopher, who looked not far before him. A man of notable endowments for his learning and knowledge of Latin poesie. Much honoured in other countries, pleasant in conversation, rehearsing on all occasions moralities short and instructive, whereof he had abundance, inventing where he wanted. He was also of good religion for a poet; but he was easily abused, and so facill that he was led with any company that he haunted for the tym, quhilk maid him factious in his old dayis; for he spoke and writ as they that were about him for the tym informed him; for he was become sliperie and careless, and followed in many things the vulgar opinions; for he was naturally populair and extreme vengeable against any man that had offendit him, quhilk was his gratest fault. (*Memoirs of His Own Life*, 262)

Although the king trembled at the approach of an official

who reminded him of his pedagogue and later denounced Buchanan's *History*, he was not wholly averse to his former tutor:

> Buchanan I reckon and rank among poets, not among divines, classical or common. If the man hath burst out here and there into some traces of excess or speech of bad temper, that must be imputed to the violence of his humour and heat of his spirit, not in any wise to the rules of treu religion rightly by him conceived before. (Willson, 21)

In a speech at Stirling he praised his master's Latin learning: 'I follow his pronuncation, both of his Latin and Greek, and am sorry that my people of England do not the like; for certainly their pronunciation utterly fails the grace of these two learned languages' (Grant, 1.174).

Political theorist and historian Not until 1579 did Buchanan publish his *De jure regni*, a dialogue between the author and Thomas Maitland which defended a kind of constitutional monarchy in which bad kings could be legitimately deposed. Earlier writers such as John of Salisbury and John Mair had proposed the punishment of kings for misdemeanours, depriving Buchanan's doctrine of some of its originality, and in any case the latter did not expound the actual working of the constitution, giving the *De jure* something of the character of a literary exercise after the manner of Plato. Nevertheless, it provoked contemporary opposition from Adam Blackwood, Ninian Winzet, and William Barclay, and in 1584 it was condemned by act of parliament, though it still had considerable influence on political thought in the seventeenth century.

Buchanan's most substantial work, *Rerum Scoticarum historia*, was published in the year of his death. The preface to James, suggesting that it could be a substitute for the tuition which ill health prevented him giving, and the reference to Bothwell's death, which took place in 1578, confirm that Buchanan was working on the *History* late in his life. A few of his letters have survived, as have letters to him from Theodore Beza, Elias Vinet, Hubert Languet, and Tycho Brahe, and this correspondence shows his friends' anxiety to see his *History* completed, notwithstanding the increasing illness of its author during the 1570s. A letter from Ferrerius to Robert Reid in 1555, on the other hand, implies that Buchanan may have written some historical work much earlier.

In his letters Buchanan reveals something of his approach to his work: 'I am besy with our story of Scotland to purge it of sum Inglis lyis and Scottis vanite,' he writes (Brown, 377), and later adds, 'I am occupiit in writyng of our historie, being assurit to content few, and to displease mony thar throw' (Buchanan, *Opera*, 1, fol. 2v). His wish to eradicate the vanity of fables is also emphasized in the text. Another aim, expressed in the preface, is to provide exemplars for King James to follow. Although he does not explicitly write much about the practice or philosophy of history there are indications of weighing up evidence and consciously arranging material. It is perhaps surprising, given his tenure of senior administrative posts, that he showed no interest in consulting official records, perhaps because of infirmity or because he was writing about the recent past from his own recollection.

The first two books of the *History* comprise a philological discussion of the nomenclature of the British Isles, a geographical description of Scotland, and an account of the origins of the peoples of Britain. Some have thought that this was one of the latest portions to be written, others that it was written, or at least drafted, first. There have been equally diverse opinions about the value of this section: on the one hand that it shows Buchanan's academic expertise, and on the other that his dispute with Humphrey Llwyd, who had attacked the historical writings of Hector Boece, was trivial and old-fashioned. On the Scottish-origin legend and the mythical forty kings from Fergus I to Fergus II in book 4, Buchanan, though still in error, was more sceptical than his predecessor Boece and the earlier chroniclers. The doctrine that underlay Buchanan's political theory was also fundamental to his historical writings. He stated that the source of power was the people, that the king must accept limitations upon the authority committed to him, and that it was lawful to resist and punish tyrants. For him this was not simply an abstraction, but was borne out by the fortunes of Scotland's early kings. His critics later claimed that he had composed his account in order to support his own views, but similar opinions were probably widely held in late sixteenth-century Scotland, and are ascribed to a figure as eminent as the Regent Morton. However, the accusation by Thomas Innes in the early eighteenth century that Buchanan knew the falsity of his own account but retained it for political purposes goes too far.

The third book consists of passages from ancient authors on Britain. The historical narrative proper begins in book 5, with a disproportionate number of the twenty books on the recent past. Although the author had already penned an account of Mary's deposition, the treatment in the *History* is in some respects different and the narrative continues up to 1572 when it comes to an unpolemical conclusion. Commentators have likened his style to various authors but in outlook he perhaps reflects a growing Renaissance interest in Tacitus.

Death In September 1581, when Buchanan's work was in the press, Andrew and James Melville, who had been his pupils at St Andrews, and his cousin Thomas Buchanan, came to see him in Edinburgh. They found him teaching his servant to read, and after they had spoken of his industry he showed them his epistle of dedication to the king. Andrew Melville pointed out some defects in it. 'Sayes he,' James Melville wrote in his diary:

> 'I may do na mair for thinking on another mater.' 'What is that?' sayes Mr. Andro. 'To die,' quoth he, 'but I leave that and many ma things for you to helpe.' We went from him to the printars' wark hous, whom we fand at the end of the 17 Buik of his Cornicle, at a place quhilk we thought verie hard for the tyme, quhilk might be an occasion of steying the haill werk onent the buriall of Davie. Therefor steying the printer from proceiding, we cam to Mr. George again and fund him bedfast by his custome, and asking him how he did, 'Even going the way of weilfaire,' says he. Mr. Thomas his cusing schawes him of the hardness of that part of his Storie, that the king wald be offendit with it, and it might stey all the wark. 'Tell me man,' sayes he, 'giff I have tauld the treuthe?' 'Yes,' sayes Mr. Thomas, 'sir, I think sa.' 'I will byd his fead

and all his kins then,' quoth he. 'Pray to God for me, and let him direct all.' Sa be the printing of his Cornicle was endit that maist lerned, wyse, and godlie man endit this mortall lyff. (*Autobiography and Diary of ... Melvill*, 120)

Memorials Buchanan died on 28 September 1582 and was buried the following day in Greyfriars churchyard, Edinburgh. The exact place is not known, but a monument was erected in 1878 and a memorial window was inserted in the church. A monument was also erected in Killearn. Perhaps surprisingly Buchanan died poor, his only resources being £100 due from his allowance from Crossraguel. Several portraits exist, but their authenticity is not certain. His skull, held by Edinburgh University's anatomy museum, was used in 1996 for a forensic reconstruction to establish which was the best representation.

Although his reputation has fluctuated Buchanan has never ceased to be a figure of considerable stature. The first reasonably complete edition of his poems and the first to be published in Scotland was Andro Hart's in 1615; the verse had been gathered into a somewhat artificial arrangement, partly by metre. In the constitutional struggles of the seventeenth century Buchanan's works were a powerful influence on political thinking. The edition of *Opera omnia* (1715) by Thomas Ruddiman, later principal keeper of the Advocates' Library, was a great achievement but did not meet with universal approval. Particularly in editing the *History*, Ruddiman was criticized for his treatment of earlier editions and for the intrusion of his own political views. The outcome was a series of controversies which kept Buchanan at the centre of attention. When William Lauder expressed a preference for Arthur Johnston's version of the Psalms over Buchanan's, John Love supported Buchanan. When William Benson repeated Lauder's opinion Ruddiman came to Buchanan's defence, but with the passing years he became less sympathetic to his author, not least because of controversy over the crown in Scotland touching such questions as the succession of the early kings, the relative merits of Bruce and Balliol, and the marriages of Robert II. Thus when Love published *A Vindication of George Buchanan* in 1749 Ruddiman replied bitterly with *Animadversions*. In 1753 James Man published *A censure and examination of Mr Thomas Ruddiman's philological notes on the works of the great Buchanan*, with contributions from Love. Although this and Ruddiman's two responses, *Anticrisis* and *Audi alteram partem* (which also contained notes on Burman's 1725 edition), included some trivial disputes, mainly concerning the text of the *History*, a good deal of learning was in evidence and Buchanan was never again subject to such detailed study. The *History* was not reprinted after Man's edition of 1762, though James Aikman's translation in 1827 has been much consulted.

To Sir Walter Scott (in a note in his novel *Ivanhoe*) Buchanan was 'the celebrated George Buchanan'. The sympathetic biography by Peter Hume Brown (1890), which views the *History* as an 'honest attempt to produce a narrative such as he believed would be finally accepted as just and true', long remained the standard account. It was soon followed by publications in 1906 and 1907 respectively by the universities of Glasgow and St Andrews, marking the quatercentenary of Buchanan's birth, and by a study in 1939 of the inquisition records concerning him. I. D. McFarlane's *Buchanan* (1981) is outstanding on Buchanan's continental connections and on the complex background to the publication of his poetry. The *Miscellaneorum liber* (a collection of Latin verses) was published in 1983 in Philip J. Ford's *George Buchanan, Prince of Poets*. However, the development of Scottish historical studies in the later twentieth century in some ways did not benefit Buchanan, not least because the study of other sources showed how much his *History* had been superseded. A further problem was that knowledge of Latin and Greek from the schools upwards was in decline and even those with a reasonable knowledge could find it difficult to assess Buchanan's writings competently, ranging as they do from composition in lyric metres to sixteenth-century politics. Moreover, although a great deal is known about Buchanan, there are still points at which lack of information makes interpretation difficult. A further obstacle to study has been the lack of easily available basic texts. It was planned that this should be remedied by a programme of publications to commemorate the quatercentenary of his death in 1982, but the programme was not completed.   D. M. ABBOTT

Sources I. D. McFarlane, *Buchanan* (1981) · P. Hume Brown, *George Buchanan and his times* (1890) · J. Durkan, *Bibliography of George Buchanan* (1995) · G. Buchanan, *Opera omnia*, ed. T. Ruddiman (1715) · G. Buchanan, *Tragedies*, ed. P. Sharratt and P. G. Walsh (1983) · J. R. Naiden, *The sphera of George Buchanan* (1952) · P. J. Ford, *George Buchanan, prince of poets* (1983) · I. B. Cowan and D. Shaw, eds., *The Renaissance and Reformation in Scotland: essays in honour of Gordon Donaldson* (1983) · *The autobiography and diary of Mr James Melvill*, ed. R. Pitcairn, Wodrow Society (1842) · *Memoirs of his own life by Sir James Melville of Halhill*, ed. T. Thomson, Bannatyne Club, 18 (1827) · A. Grant, *The story of the University of Edinburgh during its first three hundred years*, 2 vols. (1884) · *Reg. PCS*, 1st ser., vols. 1–3 · *CSP Scot.*, 1563–9 · C. T. McInnes, *Compota thesaurariorum regum Scotorum / Accounts of the lord high treasurer of Scotland*, ed. J. B. Paul, 11–13 (1916–78) · T. Innes, *A critical essay on the ancient inhabitants of the northern parts of Britain, or Scotland*, 2 vols. (1729) · W. Scott, *Ivanhoe* (1820), note V · J. M. Aitken, *The trial of George Buchanan* (1939) · D. H. Willson, *King James VI and I* (1956)
Archives NL Scot., corresp. · U. Edin. L., papers
Likenesses oils (after A. Bronckorst, 1581), NPG [*see illus.*] · oils, other versions (after A. Bronckorst, 1581), Scot. NPG, U. St Andr. · portraits, Scot. NPG
Wealth at death £100: *DNB*

Buchanan, George (*c.*1790–1852), civil engineer, the third son of David *Buchanan (1745–1812), a printer and publisher at Montrose, was born in Edinburgh. His father was a Glasite and an accomplished classical scholar, who published numerous editions of the Latin classics, which were highly regarded for their accuracy. David *Buchanan (1779–1848) and William *Buchanan (1781–1863) were his elder brothers. Buchanan was educated at Edinburgh University, where he was a favourite pupil of Sir John Leslie. About 1812 he began business as a land surveyor, but his strong scientific bent soon led him to devote himself to the profession of a civil engineer. In this capacity he was engaged upon several important public works in connection with the construction of harbours and bridges, and made a considerable local reputation. In 1822 he was invited by the directors of the Edinburgh School of Arts to deliver a highly successful course of lectures on mechanical philosophy in the Freemasons' Hall. He later gave occasional courses of lectures on natural philosophy, but his increasing business as an engineer interfered with any further educational work.

In 1827 Buchanan drew up a report on the South Esk estuary at Montrose in connection with a local salmon-fishing dispute. This report attracted the attention and the marked approval of lord justice clerk Hope, then solicitor-general, who subsequently employed Buchanan on many occasions as a technical adviser in cases involving scientific evidence. When the tunnel of the Edinburgh and Granton Railway was being constructed under the new town in 1845–6, and the adjacent buildings were considered in imminent danger, Buchanan was commissioned by the sheriff of Edinburgh to supervise the works on behalf of the city. He was also responsible for the erection in 1848 of a huge chimney, nearly 400 feet in height, at the Edinburgh gasworks, and he carried out an exhaustive series of experiments to assure its stability.

Buchanan produced many writings on technical and engineering subjects, and contributed a large number of papers to the *Transactions of the Royal Scottish Society of Arts*. He was a fellow of the Royal Society of Edinburgh, and was elected president of the Royal Scottish Society of Arts for the session 1847–8. He died of lung disease on 30 October 1852.   ROBERT HARRISON, *rev.* RALPH HARRINGTON

Sources *The Scotsman* (7 Nov 1852) · *The Courant* (19 June 1851) · *Transactions of the Royal Scottish Society of Arts*

Buchanan, George (1827–1906), surgeon, born at Glasgow on 29 March 1827, was the son of Moses Steven Buchanan (1796–1860) and his wife, Agnes Leechman. Moses Buchanan was surgeon to the Glasgow Royal Infirmary and lecturer on anatomy in the Portland Street medical school from 1836 to 1841, when he was appointed professor of anatomy in the Andersonian University. George Buchanan was educated at the University of Glasgow, where he graduated MA in 1846. After studying under his father and others at the Andersonian University, in 1849 he became MD at St Andrews and LRCS (Edin.), and in 1852 he was made a fellow of the Faculty of Physicians and Surgeons of Glasgow. He married Jessie Shaw Blair, daughter of Patrick Blair of Irvine.

In early life Buchanan volunteered to have chloroform anaesthesia demonstrated on himself, when his father performed a minor operation on him. He began to practise in Glasgow, but in 1856 he went to the Crimea as a civil surgeon. He returned to Glasgow at the end of the war, and was one of the first to practise there purely as a consulting surgeon. In 1860, when he succeeded his father as professor of anatomy in the Andersonian University, he was also appointed surgeon to the Glasgow Royal Infirmary. He soon became known as a bold and skilful operator, and as a good teacher. He was the first to point out (in 1865 and 1867) the possibility and safety of removing half the tongue in cases of cancer, and he was among the first surgeons to remove the upper jaw (in 1864 and 1869). He gave reasons for preferring lithotrity to lithotomy in operating for stone in the adult male, in 1868, and he was the first to perform ovariotomy successfully in the west of Scotland, in 1863. Until 1869 Buchanan had as a colleague Joseph Lister, who in 1867 described in *The Lancet* his antiseptic method of wound treatment. In 1871 Buchanan published *Camp Life as Seen by a Civilian*. In 1873 his re-edited and largely rewritten ninth edition of Erasmus Wilson's *The Anatomist's Vade Mecum* appeared.

Buchanan moved to the Western Infirmary when it opened in 1874 and held the post of professor of clinical surgery from 1874 until 1900; he then retired, with the title of emeritus professor of clinical surgery in the University of Glasgow, and settled at Balanton, Stirling. He died there on 19 April 1906, and was survived by his wife and one son, Dr George Burnside Buchanan, assistant surgeon to the Western Infirmary, Glasgow.

D'A. POWER, rev. CHRISTOPHER LAWRENCE

Sources *Glasgow Medical Journal*, new ser., 65 (1906), 354 · *BMJ* (5 May 1906), 1078 · private information (1912) · *CGPLA Eng. & Wales* (1906)
Archives Royal College of Physicians and Surgeons of Glasgow, journals of travel in Europe, Turkey, and the Crimea
Likenesses G. Jerrard, photograph, 1881, Wellcome L. · photograph, Wellcome L.

Buchanan, Sir George (1831–1895), epidemiologist and civil servant, was born on 5 November 1831 at Myddleton Square, Islington, London, the elder son of George Adam Buchanan, general practitioner, and his wife, Sarah Mary, daughter of Thomas Harrison. He was educated in London at University College School, where he revealed marked literary and mathematical abilities, and gained a BA degree at London University in 1851 before studying medicine at University College. He qualified MB in 1854 and MD with distinction in the following year. Buchanan married twice. His first wife, Mary Murphy, was the sister of Shirley Murphy, later first medical officer of health to London county council; his second wife, Alice Mary Asmar Seaton, whom he married in 1865, was the daughter of Edward Cator *Seaton (1815–1880), Buchanan's predecessor as medical officer at the Local Government Board. Sir George Seaton *Buchanan (1869–1936) was their son. There were five other children from the two marriages.

In the first decade of his professional life Buchanan acquired a variety of appointments, as was then necessary to secure an adequate income. He continued to live in London, and established a private practice in Gower Street, acted as a resident medical officer at the London Fever Hospital, where he afterwards served as physician (1861–8) and consulting physician, and was an assistant physician at the children's Hospital, Great Ormond Street, between 1855 and 1860. In 1856 he was made first medical officer of health to the parish of St Giles-in-the-Fields, an appointment which was to determine the direction of his life. St Giles was then notorious for its insanitary slums, criminal population, and mortality rates of 20 per cent

above the London average. From the first, Buchanan's reports displayed a deep interest in the disease ecology of the parish and a comprehensive grasp of current epidemiological concepts and techniques, notably on the statistical side. It was in St Giles that he first began to study issues in public health and epidemiology which were to recur throughout his life and work. These included infant mortality, tuberculosis, overcrowding, and the health of animals intended for human consumption. Beyond the immediate problems of his district, however, he was beginning to formulate general epidemiological concepts, and to articulate them in his reports. In 1860, for example, he set out the law of disease distribution in an epidemic year:

> Given, a number of localities habitually affected to different degrees by diseases of a certain class. Let these diseases occur with exceptional prevalence, either in the way of increase or subsidence. Then it is those localities which habitually suffer *most* from such diseases that are chiefly affected by their *exceptional* incidences in whichever direction the exception may be. (G. Buchanan, *Medical Officer's Annual Report*, London, St Giles's Vestry, 1860, 12)

This was a prescription which enabled public health officers to target their efforts at specific areas in times of epidemic outbreaks. Regarded as important at the time, there is little evidence that it was put to practical use by contemporaries, nor has it survived into modern epidemiological lore.

The quality of Buchanan's annual reports, both literary and epidemiological, attracted the attention of John Simon, then medical officer to the privy council, and in 1861 Simon began using Buchanan as an occasional investigator for the medical department. Between 1861 and 1869, when he joined the department on a permanent basis, Buchanan undertook several investigations that became public health classics. The first of these, undertaken with Edward Seaton, was a systematic inquiry into the working of the vaccination laws and the incidence of smallpox in London; published in 1863, the inquiry led in 1867 to the amendment of the existing legislation on compulsory infant vaccination. When typhus broke out in Lancashire with the cotton famine of 1862, Buchanan was dispatched to make a thorough inquiry into the health of the cotton operatives. He thereafter became something of an authority on the epidemiology of typhus, undertaking further investigations into the disease in Liverpool and Warrington in the later 1860s. The conclusions which he reached with regard to typhus causation—as hinging on domestic overcrowding and squalor—provided the justification for more active public health measures and were considered by contemporaries to have played a significant part in the virtual elimination of typhus from English cities after 1870.

The work which had the greatest impact on nineteenth-century epidemiological thought sprang, however, from an originally more prosaic undertaking. In 1865 Buchanan was assigned to investigate the effects of structural sanitary works (such as drainage systems and the improvement of water supplies) on the mortality and morbidity in twenty-five towns, selected on the grounds that their sanitary works were the oldest and were thought to offer the best opportunity for judging their impact on death rates. In the course of this inquiry Buchanan noted that where drainage improvements had resulted in the drying out of town subsoils, death rates from respiratory tuberculosis had invariably fallen. Further research on the incidence of the disease in south-east England led him to conclude that its prevalence was directly associated with dampness of soil. The methodology employed in the investigation was very highly statistical, and it was rapidly accepted by contemporaries as conclusive; this judgement, in England at least, survived the discovery of the tuberculosis bacillus and the subsequent elucidation of the infectiousness of the disease.

In 1869 Buchanan became a permanent member of the privy council medical department, and when the department was transferred to the Local Government Board in 1872 he was made an assistant medical officer. Between 1869 and 1879, he was occupied in the routine of departmental inquiries: for example, he investigated the incidence of infectious diseases in Aston and Birmingham in 1874, and an outbreak of scarlet fever among middle-class families in South Kensington, London. Such activities served to extend Buchanan's epidemiological experience and expertise, and when, in the autumn of 1879, the health of Edward Cator Seaton, Simon's successor as medical officer and Buchanan's father-in-law, began to fail, Buchanan was appointed to succeed him. He took up the medical officership on 31 December 1879.

In his capacity as medical officer Buchanan showed himself also to be a capable administrator, with a decided flair for applied epidemiology; he was concerned that all advice coming from his department should have a definite scientific basis, and he had a dogged determination to promote and maintain the causes of public health and medicine with his official superiors, notably the successive presidents of the Local Government Board, the Liberals John George Dodson, Sir Charles Dilke, Charles Ritchie, and, in the early 1890s, the conservative John Burns. Although his preoccupations after 1880 were largely administrative, Buchanan's annual reports testify to the breadth of his perspectives on public health and his abilities as a meticulous and exact expositor of the work done by his department. At a time when the English medical community was beginning to come to terms with the germ theory of disease, Buchanan steered a judicious path between the old disease theories and the new, while encouraging his scientific staff to investigate problems associated with newly discovered micro-organisms of disease. In retirement, and on the death of Lord Basing, Buchanan was appointed chairman of the royal commission on tuberculosis.

Throughout his life Buchanan retained an active interest in University College, London, of which he was elected a fellow in 1864, and in the University of London itself. In 1858 he helped to obtain the representation of graduates on the governing body by means of convocation, and in 1882 he was one of the first graduates to be elected by convocation to the senate. He was active in securing the admission of women both as students at University College and to the degrees of London University. He had a long-standing involvement in the Society of Apothecaries, of which he was a member and later one of the court of assistants.

Buchanan was elected a fellow of the Royal College of Physicians in 1866, served as censor there in 1892–4, and was Lettsomian lecturer in 1867. He was president of the Epidemiological Society in 1881 and was elected a fellow of the Royal Society in 1882. He was knighted in 1892 and in 1893 he was made an honorary LLD of Edinburgh University.

Buchanan died suddenly of heart failure at Fitzroy House, Fitzroy Square, London, while recovering from an apparently successful operation, on 5 May 1895. He was buried at Brookwood cemetery, Woking, Surrey. His wife survived him. Buchanan had received a subscription at his retirement from the Local Government Board in 1892, and was able to endow, in 1894, a gold medal to be awarded triennially by the Royal Society for services to sanitary science. ANNE HARDY

Sources *BMJ* (11 May 1895), 1066–7 · *Transactions of the Epidemiological Society*, new ser., 14 (1894–5), 113–17 · *Public Health*, 7 (1894–5), 311, 315, 320–22 · Munk, *Roll* · *PRS*, 59 (1895–6), xli–xliii · *The Lancet* (11 May 1895), 1224–5 · *The Times* (7 May 1895) · *CGPLA Eng. & Wales* (1895) · *DNB* · Burke, *Peerage* (1894)
Archives NL Scot., corresp. and family papers · Wellcome L., report on cotton operatives
Likenesses G. Jerrard, photograph, 1881, Wellcome L. · photograph, repro. in *Transactions of the Epidemiological Society* · photograph, Wellcome L. · wood-engraving (after photograph by Fradelle & Young), NPG; repro. in *ILN* (18 May 1895)
Wealth at death £7739 6s.: probate, 11 June 1895, *CGPLA Eng. & Wales*

Buchanan, George (1890–1955), politician, was born in Glasgow on 30 November 1890 in Naburn Street, Gorbals, the constituency he would later represent as MP. His father, George Buchanan, a joiner, came from Kilberry in Argyll and his mother, Ann Mackay, was born in Creich, Sutherland, in a poor croft where her family had been forced to settle following the highland clearances.

Buchanan's family were respectable working class; his father was a craftsman and both parents were supporters of the Independent Labour Party (ILP). While one son and daughter were put through university there was not enough money for George, whose education was limited to the local Camden Street School in the Gorbals and later evening classes. His first jobs were as a messenger and copy-boy in a newspaper office before entering an apprenticeship as an engineer's patternmaker. As a youth and, indeed, when older, he enjoyed an active social life: in the Boys' Brigade, in the Rechabites, and as a junior footballer, billiards player, and keen dancer. At the same time he was attracted to politics, when in his teens joining both his trade union, the United Patternmakers, and the ILP, in which his brother Willie, also a skilled engineer, was a member.

Buchanan became a prominent local propagandist for

George Buchanan (1890–1955), by Walter Stoneman, 1946

the ILP before 1914 but really began to make his mark during the war. Alongside John Wheatley and John S. Taylor, both city councillors, he was one of the leading anti-war ILP members in Glasgow and suffered at least one serious assault when attacked for intervening during a pro-war meeting addressed by the dockers' leader Havelock Wilson. A shop steward and delegate to the trades council, Buchanan was active in the famous forty-hour strike of January 1919, supporting the demand for a thirty-hour week, and became a member of his union's executive.

Between 1918 and 1923 Buchanan sat as one of the councillors for the Hutchesontown ward (he was the youngest councillor ever elected) and in 1922 was returned as MP for Gorbals, within which constituency his ward was located. He continued to live there after his marriage, on 19 July 1924, to Annie Masterton McNee (b. 1885/6), the daughter of William McNee, a wood turner, and his wife, Catherine. The early post-war years saw him concentrate much of his political activity in representing constituents at tribunals dealing with pension and welfare benefits, and this became a constant preoccupation with him for the rest of his political career. In particular he became expert in the intricacies of the numerous pieces of legislation dealing with the unemployed. While the wider labour movement tended to protest over the means test and levels of benefit, Buchanan and some of his Clydeside colleagues consistently argued against the iniquities of the 'genuinely seeking work' clause. The background to this was the very

high levels of unemployment on Clydeside in the early 1920s and the use of the offending clause in Glasgow labour exchanges to deny claimants benefit and thereby encourage skilled men, of which there was now deemed a surplus, to move south.

Whether it be Conservative, Labour, or National governments Buchanan was a constant and often violent voice of protest. His notoriety was established early in his parliamentary career in 1923 when he joined James Maxton and John Wheatley in calling a tory MP who supported cuts in health grants a 'murderer' and was subsequently suspended from the House of Commons. This was to be the first of many suspensions resulting from the willingness of Buchanan and his ILP colleagues to deliberately create 'scenes' at Westminster. While this infuriated Ramsay MacDonald it was regarded as a necessary tactic by those who saw themselves as representing the poor and the unemployed. Relations with MacDonald had not been helped by the leader's failure to provide additional parliamentary time for the Government of Scotland Bill in 1924. As a result this effort at home rule, in preparation by the Labour Party in Scotland since 1920 and introduced to the house by Buchanan, was talked out by hostile Conservatives.

Buchanan was one of the large intake of Labour MPs returned for Glasgow and neighbouring industrial areas in 1922. Though often referred to as the Clydesiders, there was no real unity among them apart from the smaller group comprising Buchanan, Wheatley, Maxton, and Campbell Stephen. This was the real 'rebel' group, with Wheatley being replaced after his death in 1930 by John McGovern. Maxton, Campbell Stephen, and Buchanan were particularly close friends, sharing bachelor digs in London for many years. This group was to play a critical role in the growing estrangement between the Labour Party and the ILP and the eventual disaffiliation of the latter from the parent party in 1932. Although Buchanan has sometimes been presented as unhappy over this decision, at the time he was an even more vociferous supporter of the break than Maxton. At the Scottish ILP conference in late 1931, Maxton argued against immediate disaffiliation while Buchanan spoke in its favour.

Prior to the general election in 1931 George Lansbury had offered Maxton and Buchanan front-bench positions which they refused. Along with McGovern and Maxton, Buchanan resisted the National Government tide and held his seat. Indeed, even with the intervention of the communist Harry McShane he enjoyed a majority of over 8000 votes, a remarkable achievement in the circumstances. In spite of the loss of Campbell Stephen, the ILP now had three of the four remaining Labour seats in Glasgow and they operated as an independent opposition in parliament, often outshining a Labour Party which had been shell-shocked by the rout at the polls.

In 1935 Buchanan held Gorbals with a massive majority of over 17,000 despite facing an official Labour Party candidate. His growing disagreements over ILP policy on matters such as Abyssinia and unity with the communists, and the difficulty of his position as president (1932–48) of the

United Patternmakers' Union, which was affiliated to the Labour Party, ultimately led him to rejoin the Labour Party in 1939. After the war Attlee offered him the post of minister of national insurance and was surprised when he preferred to take the much more junior position of undersecretary at the Scottish Office. Buchanan's motivation was that he wanted to make a contribution to solving Scotland's dreadful housing conditions, but it was not the first time he had refused an attractive offer: in 1934 he had turned down a post on the statutory unemployment committee and the very handsome salary of £2000 per annum. In 1947 he became minister of pensions and the following year was sworn of the privy council. A few months after this his parliamentary career came to an end when he was appointed chairman of the newly created National Assistance Board, resigning the Gorbals seat which he had held for twenty-six years.

Under Buchanan's chairmanship the National Assistance Board established a reputation for enlightened treatment of claimants and this cemented the already high affection in which he was held. After his term as chairman expired in 1953 he continued as a board member almost until his death. Buchanan, the last of the four original 'Clyde Brigade', died in Glasgow on 28 June 1955, where he was cremated. He was survived by his wife; they had no children.

Buchanan was described in the 1930s as 'the physical embodiment of … the poor but honest workman of the Gorbals' (Paton, 225). With his sandy hair, normally in some disorder, broad physique, large face, booming voice, and pugnacious manner, it was a role he was perfectly suited to. In spite of his later achievements in office, it is the earlier Buchanan, the resolute and irreconcilable member for the Gorbals, who will be chiefly remembered.   JAMES J. SMYTH

Sources W. Knox, ed., *Scottish labour leaders, 1918–39: a biographical dictionary* (1984) · DNB · R. K. Middlemas, *The Clydesiders: a left-wing struggle for parliamentary power* (1965) · J. Paton, *Left turn: the autobiography of John Paton* (1936) · A. Deacon, 'Concession and coercion: the politics of unemployment insurance in the 1920s', *Essays in labour history, 1918–1939*, ed. A. Briggs and J. Saville (1977), 9–35 · R. E. Dowse, *Left in the centre: the independent labour party, 1893–1940* (1966) · F. Brockway, *Socialism over sixty years: the life of Jowett of Bradford* (1946) · R. Skidelsky, *Politicians and the slump: the labour government of 1929–1931* (1967) · D. Marquand, *Ramsay MacDonald* (1977) · M. Keating and D. Bleiman, *Labour and Scottish nationalism* (1979) · J. Brand, *The national movement in Scotland* (1978) · W. Gallacher, *Revolt on the Clyde: an autobiography* (1936) · *Glasgow Herald* (29 June 1955) · *The Times* (29 June 1955) · *Forward* (2 July 1955) · *Forward* (9 July 1955) · m. cert.

Archives FILM BFI NFTVA, documentary footage | SOUND BL NSA, current affairs recording

Likenesses W. Stoneman, photograph, 1946, NPG [*see illus.*] · photograph, repro. in Middlemas, *The Clydesiders*, 129

Wealth at death £11,836 4s. 7d.: confirmation, 7 Sept 1955, CCI

Buchanan, Sir George Cunningham (1865–1940), civil engineer, was born at Islington on 20 April 1865, the eldest son of George Buchanan, of Westminster, also a civil engineer, and his wife, Emily, youngest daughter of Thomas Boosey, of London. As a trainee engineer he worked on civil engineering projects along the Tyne from 1882 until 1886, first under J. Watt Sandeman and then under P. J. Messent, chief engineer to the Tyne improvement commission. From 1886 he was associated for ten years with railway and other works in Venezuela, Nova Scotia, Argentina, Spain, and Jamaica. On his return to England in 1895 he became resident engineer for the construction of a graving dock at Blyth, and in the following year he was appointed chief engineer to the Dundee harbour trust.

In 1901 Buchanan left Dundee to become chairman and chief engineer of the Rangoon port trust, and during the fourteen years for which he held that position designed new port works and carried out extensive improvements on the river (for which he received the Watt gold medal from the Institution of Civil Engineers in 1916). At the end of 1915 he went to Basrah as adviser to Sir John Nixon, the commander-in-chief of the Mesopotamian campaign, on all matters connected with the port, including its administration, engineering works, and river conservancy, and in 1917 he attained the rank of brigadier-general. For his work at Basrah, which he described in his book *The Tragedy of Mesopotamia* (1938), he was twice mentioned in dispatches, and his services and powers of organization were acknowledged by the government of India to have 'sensibly promoted' the ultimate success of British arms in Mesopotamia. His war services also included membership of the Indian munitions board (1917–19).

After the war Buchanan entered into partnership with C. S. Meik and was appointed consulting engineer for the Back Bay reclamation scheme at Bombay, which provided for the reclamation of more than 1100 acres of land by the construction of a sea wall 4 miles long, the area within it being filled with silt dredged from the sea bed outside. In this undertaking he had less than his usual success, for his estimates proved faulty and his plans miscarried.

In 1922 Buchanan visited South Africa at the request of the union government to report on the transport problems of the country, particularly in connection with ports and harbours. In 1925 he undertook a similar mission in Australia for the commonwealth government, and prepared a report on the development and administration of northern Australia.

Buchanan was appointed CIE in 1911, and after having been knighted in 1915, KCIE in 1917. He was twice married, first in 1894 to Elizabeth Isabelle (d. 1926), younger daughter of William Mead, of Plymouth; they had a son and a daughter. His second marriage, in 1930, was to Joan, second daughter of Lieutenant John George Haggard RN, later consul at Malaga, who survived him. He died at his home, Nunnery Farm, Ditchingham, Norfolk, on 14 April 1940.   H. M. ROSS, *rev.* RALPH HARRINGTON

Sources *The Times* (15 April 1940) · *The Engineer* (19 April 1940) · *Engineering* (19 April 1940)

Buchanan, Sir George Seaton (1869–1936), expert in public health, was born in London on 19 February 1869, the elder son of Sir George *Buchanan (1831–1895), and his second wife, Alice Mary Asmar, daughter of Edward Cator

*Seaton (1815–1880). He was educated in London at University College School and then University College, and at St Bartholomew's Hospital. He graduated MB, with a gold medal, in 1891, and MD in 1893. He married Rhoda Agnes (d. 1959), fifth daughter of Thomas Atkinson, of Plumgarths, Westmorland, in 1896; their son died as the result of an accident in 1927, and their daughter married the Eton College housemaster Hubert Hartley.

After early hospital appointments Buchanan joined the medical department of the Local Government Board as an inspector, in 1895. Apart from service with the army sanitary committee during the First World War (he was appointed CB in 1918), Buchanan's entire career was spent at the medical department, where he was promoted to chief assistant medical officer in 1911, and its successor (from 1919) the Ministry of Health, where he was the senior medical officer, responsible for the medical intelligence section. He retired in February 1934. Within this institutional framework, his career had three distinct phases. As an inspector between 1895 and 1906 he conducted a variety of local investigations, notably into outbreaks of typhoid fever, in which he proved himself an able epidemiologist; his inquiry into housing conditions in the Northumberland town of Alnwick in 1898 was considered a classic contribution on slum clearance, both for the clarity with which Buchanan stated the case for slum demolition and for the way in which he proposed it should be carried out. Secondly, from 1900 to 1904, Buchanan was involved in inquiries into arsenical poisoning from beer. This was one of a series of disclosures about dangerous food-handling practices which led the medical department to set up a sub-department of food inspection and control in 1905. Initially intended to supervise all national food supplies, the sub-department's activities were restricted by statute in 1907 to cover only imported and canned foods.

Shortly before the outbreak of war in 1914 Buchanan embarked on the third phase of his career, when he was sent to Paris as the official British delegate to the permanent committee of the Office International d'Hygiène Publique (he was elected its president in 1932). After the war he resumed his connection with this institution, and he became a foundation member of the health organization of the League of Nations. Buchanan became Britain's principal representative on the inter-war international public health scene. The rest of his career was largely devoted to international public health work, and in particular to the design and drafting of the International Sanitary Convention of 1926. It was, for example, Buchanan who initiated a measure to provide for the free treatment of sexually transmitted diseases for merchant seamen of all nationalities at ports throughout the world; he was also among the first to recognize the epidemiological hazards of international air travel, and instigated measures to prevent the transmission of yellow fever along air routes. Indeed, Buchanan's later career illustrates the trend towards growing medical internationalism which, though apparent before 1914, accelerated in

the inter-war period partly as a result of the experience of war but also because of concern over the consequences of international trade, in which the new nautical and aeronautical technologies enabled people to travel from one side of the world to the other within the incubation time of the major infectious diseases.

Buchanan was tall, fair, and blue-eyed, a man of great charm with a pleasant sense of humour, which made him a popular figure both abroad and with his colleagues. Although his general scientific culture was superficial and he was not a good public speaker, he was a highly effective manager of committees. He was also an indefatigable worker, who had few interests beyond his official preoccupations. None the less, when in London he lunched daily at the Athenaeum, and when in Paris he preferred to lunch alone at a special corner at Prunier's.

Buchanan was knighted in 1922, elected FRCP in 1925, and was master of the Society of Apothecaries in 1934–5. He was vice-president of the international health organization of the League of Nations, president of the league's cancer commission, and in 1929 member of a commission for the reorganization of public health services in Greece. In 1934 he gave the Milroy lectures, entitled 'International co-operation in public health', which were published under the same title in the same year.

Buchanan's health began to fail shortly after his retirement, and he died at 12 Exmoor Street, Kensington, London, after a long illness, on 11 October 1936. He was survived by his wife. ANNE HARDY

Sources The Times (12 Oct 1936) · Public Health, 50 (1936–7), 36 · Munk, Roll · Nature, 138 (1936), 832 · The Lancet (17 Oct 1936), 947–9 · BMJ (17 Oct 1936), 788–9 · BMJ (10 Feb 1934), 247 · d. cert. · CGPLA Eng. & Wales (1936) · DNB
Archives NL Scot., letters and papers · PRO, sanitary reports, MH 113 | CUL, corresp. with Lord Kelvin
Likenesses Topical Press Agency, photograph, repro. in BMJ, 788
Wealth at death £6760 10s. 3d.: probate, 25 Nov 1936, CGPLA Eng. & Wales

Buchanan, Sir George William (1854–1924), diplomatist, was born at Copenhagen on 25 November 1854, the fifth son of Sir Andrew *Buchanan (1807–1882), of Dunburgh, and his wife, Frances Katharine (d. 1854), daughter of Edward Mellish, dean of Hereford. He was educated at Wellington College and entered the diplomatic service in 1876. After serving first as attaché under his father, who was then ambassador at Vienna, and subsequently in the Foreign Office, he transferred successively to Rome (1878) and Tokyo (1879), to which he travelled through the United States, before returning to Vienna in 1882. On 25 February 1885 he married Lady Georgina Meriel Bathurst (1863–1922), daughter of Allen Alexander, sixth Earl Bathurst (1832–1892), and Meriel Leicester (d. 1872).

After periods at the Foreign Office and at Bern, in 1893 Buchanan became chargé d'affaires at Darmstadt, an important listening post as members of the Russian, German, and British royal families were frequent visitors there to the grand duke of Hesse and by Rhine; in this capacity he was brought into contact with Queen Victoria,

Sir George William Buchanan (1854–1924), by Walter
Stoneman, 1918

The Balkan wars of 1912–13 brought new dangers to the Anglo-Russian entente and sharp disputes over Russian policy towards Turkey, though Grey was unwilling to move too far away from St Petersburg. The maintenance of the entente therefore required the closest co-operation on the one hand between Buchanan and Sazanov, the foreign minister in St Petersburg, and on the other between Sir Edward Grey, Sir Arthur Nicolson, and Count Benckendorff, the Russian ambassador in London. Buchanan's task was made no easier by the existence of a strong pro-German party at the court in St Petersburg and by the inability of Sazanov to control his subordinates in the face of court and bureaucratic influences. Buchanan, however, remained totally convinced of the crucial importance of the entente for Britain's imperial and European security: his dispatches were full of warnings about the consequences of its disruption and the possibility of a Russo-German settlement. Like Sir Arthur Nicolson, the permanent under-secretary at the Foreign Office, Buchanan pressed Grey to turn the entente into an alliance, though he recognized that public opinion in Britain made this politically impractical. The ambassador observed the growth of internal discontent in Russia and feared that any European war would be followed by revolution. If Germany was faced with the knowledge that Russia and France could count on British support, Buchanan believed, she would never risk launching such a war.

When the crisis of 1914 occurred, Buchanan was just going on leave. His health was indifferent and he had considered a transfer to Vienna but was persuaded to stay in Russia. His main efforts after the outbreak of war were directed to obtaining the maximum effort from the Russians, and later, to combating pro-German influences and demands for a separate peace. He became exceedingly close to Tsar Nicholas II but, though he tried to steer the tsar towards some form of constitutional reform, his advice was not taken and his warnings of impending catastrophe were dismissed. Buchanan liked the emperor whom he considered a lovable, if weak, man and a loyal ally, and he acquitted the empress of any desire to assist Germany, though he believed her reactionary influence over the tsar was instrumental in causing the final tragedy. Owing to his bluntness and willingness to speak his mind, Buchanan made enemies and (paradoxically) was bitterly attacked later by some Russian émigrés for promoting the revolution because of the recommendations he made to avert it.

Buchanan attained a position of great personal influence in Russia and in 1916 was granted the freedom of the city of Moscow, an honour conferred previously only on one foreigner and eight Russians. He was helpless, however, in the face of the military defeats of 1915, the weakness of the emperor, and the utter incompetence of the administration. In February 1917 he predicted that the internal political and economic situation was so disastrous that disagreeable surprises might be at hand. After the March revolution and the abdication of the tsar he was instructed to recognize the provisional government, but

owing to her close relationship with the Darmstadt court. In 1898 he served as the British agent on the Venezuela boundary arbitration tribunal at Paris and afterwards was secretary of the embassy at Rome (1900) and Berlin (1901). In 1903, with the rank of minister, he became agent and consul-general at Sofia, where he made his diplomatic reputation during the Near East crisis which followed the Turkish revolution, the annexation of Bosnia and Herzogovina, the proclamation of Bulgarian independence, and the recognition in 1908 of Prince Ferdinand as king. The agency became a legation and Buchanan, who enjoyed excellent relations with Ferdinand, was made envoy-extraordinary. He was awarded the Hague legation in 1908 and after little more than a year's residence in the Netherlands was made ambassador to Russia in 1910.

This appointment was a critical one as, though Anglo-Russian relations were cordial after the conclusion of the conventions of 1907, misunderstandings, particularly over Persia, were frequent; these were the subject of debates in the House of Commons, where there was considerable criticism of Sir Edward Grey's pro-Russian policies, particularly among the radical members of his own party. The harsh methods adopted by Russian agents and consuls and their forward tactics at Tehran violated the spirit if not the letter of the Anglo-Russian agreement and caused Grey considerable discomfort. It seemed clear that the Russians were not only prepared to treat northern Persia as part of the Russian empire but were trying to move into the neutral zone as well. There were continuing conflicts, too, in Tibet, Afghanistan, Mongolia, and Turkestan.

he was exceedingly pessimistic about its future. He foretold a period of revolution and counter-revolution for he did not think Russia ripe for democratic government. During these difficult months, his main effort was concentrated on preventing a separate peace, but his already eroded position was further undermined when Lloyd George sent Arthur Henderson to St Petersburg in the spring of 1917 to contact the revolutionary leaders and if necessary to replace Buchanan. Henderson decided against the latter course of action and returned to Britain. On 7 January 1918, however, two months after the Bolsheviks took power, Buchanan, his health broken by the strain, left Russia to make his way home by a circuitous route through the north of Sweden.

In London, Buchanan was without an assignment, though his advice was sought on Russian questions. He was among those advocating armed intervention in Russia to avoid the German seizure of its resources and to prevent the spread of communism throughout Asia and Europe. His appointment in 1919 as ambassador to Rome was a great relief, but his position was complicated by the effective existence in London of two foreign offices that did not pull together—one run by Lord Balfour, the foreign secretary, but the other located at 10 Downing Street, where Lloyd George directed his own foreign policy. Buchanan retired from the service in the autumn of 1921. His wife, a woman of extraordinary energy and remarkable individuality, died a few months later. Lady Georgina was responsible for the organization of the hospital for the Russian wounded created by the British colony in St Petersburg. When one of the provisional government's women's battalions (created in 1917 to shame the men into continuing the war) was seized by the Bolsheviks after participating in the defence of the Winter Palace in October 1917, it was largely owing to her firmness and courage that the safety of the women was assured. After returning to England, Lady Georgina was tireless in organizing relief for Russian refugees.

Buchanan was tall and handsome, a good shot and horseman, and an excellent linguist (though without Russian); he was widely read in French, German, and Italian, as well as English literature, and translated parts of Goethe's *Faust* and selections from Dante into English. He also published *My Mission to Russia, and other Diplomatic Memories* in 1923. He was the model for Sir Herbert Witherspoon, Somerset Maugham's fictional ambassador in the short story 'His Excellency', and Maugham endowed his hero with some of Buchanan's idiosyncrasies, including his notorious absent-mindedness as a card player. Contemporaries sometimes referred to Buchanan's 'baffling simplicity', but his dispatches were clear and to the point and he had a very wide knowledge of foreign countries and foreign affairs. He was urbane and courteous, but outspoken and firm in dealings with foreigners, and honest and clear-minded with his superiors.

Buchanan was created KCMG in 1909, GCMG in 1913, and GCB in 1915, and also received several foreign decorations. He was sworn of the privy council in 1910. He died at his home, 15 Lennox Gardens, London, on 20 December 1924, two years after his wife. He left one daughter, Meriel, who herself wrote on her experiences in Russia in a number of books, including *Ambassador's Daughter* (1958).

ZARA STEINER

Sources G. Buchanan, *My mission to Russia, and other diplomatic memories*, 2 vols. (1923) · M. Buchanan, *Ambassador's daughter* (1958) · *The Times* (22 Dec 1924) · W. Somerset Maugham, 'His excellency', *Sixty-five short stories* (1976), 479–99 · Z. S. Steiner, *The foreign office and foreign policy, 1898–1914* (1969) · K. Neilson, *Britain and the last tsar: British policy and Russia, 1894–1917* (1995) · R. H. Bruce-Lockhart, *Memoirs of a British agent* (1932) · H. J. Bruce, *Silken dalliance* (1946) · *CGPLA Eng. & Wales* (1925)
Archives CUL, corresp., mainly with Lord Hardinge · HLRO, Lloyd George MSS, letters to David Lloyd George · Hove Central Library, Sussex, letters to Lord Wolseley · PRO, letters to Sir William White · U. Leeds, Brotherton L., letters to Sir Edmund Gosse · U. Newcastle, Robinson L., corresp. with Walter Runciman · U. Nott. L., letters to Sir Andrew Buchanan
Likenesses W. Stoneman, photograph, 1918, NPG [*see illus.*] · Adèle, cabinet photograph, NPG · K. Scott, bronze bust, Gov. Art Coll. · E. Walker, photograph, repro. in Buchanan, *My mission to Russia*, vol. 1, frontispiece
Wealth at death £14,869 2*s.* 7*d.*: probate, 4 Feb 1925, *CGPLA Eng. & Wales*

Buchanan, James (1696–1758), merchant, was born and baptized on 31 May 1696, the second of four sons of Archibald Buchanan of Drumhead in the parish of Cardross, Dunbartonshire, a minor Scottish laird, and his wife, Jannet Anderson. It was common for the younger sons of lairds thereabouts to be put into trade, and, like his eldest and youngest brothers, Buchanan's initial career was as a merchant in Glasgow. He may have spent some time in America at the beginning but, if so, he soon returned to Glasgow. In 1725, when he was twenty-nine, he was one of the original members of the Buchanan Society of Glasgow, which was founded to provide for poor members of the clan Buchanan, and is described in their records as a merchant of Glasgow. Scottish firms in Virginia needed London correspondents for commercial and banking services and by 1727 Buchanan had settled in the capital, where he acted at first for the Glasgow firm of John Luke & Co., major tobacco importers. He was soon a respected figure in the London Virginia trade, if never himself a tobacco importer of the first rank. In his later years he was the London financial agent of Lieutenant-Governor Robert Dinwiddie of Virginia and a member of the policy committee of the London association of merchants trading to the Chesapeake. In the latter capacity he participated in negotiations with the secretary of state, William Pitt, and other ministers on matters relating to their trade and navigation.

While his Glasgow kin engaged in a direct trade to the Chesapeake through stores maintained there, Buchanan in London was a merchant factor, acting on commission for principals in Virginia who consigned him tobacco for sale, and drew bills of exchange on him for the proceeds or authorized him to make purchases for them of return goods. Only half his correspondents were planters, the remainder being mostly country merchants. His planter correspondents were a select group, including many with names prominent in Virginia, while at least three-fifths were justices of the peace or higher officials. However, his dealings with country traders were more substantial. After his death, more than 70 per cent of the sums owing to his firm in Virginia was from merchants. Buchanan's activity in this cargo trade with American merchants placed his among the more progressive houses in the London Chesapeake trade. In addition to his Virginia business, Buchanan developed some West Indies trade in his last years. In 1756 he was also one of the bondsmen or guarantors for the army forage contract of Richard Oswald, a fellow Glaswegian migrant to London. Such sureties usually had a financial interest in the contract guaranteed.

Buchanan at various times had places of business in Mincing Lane, Mark Lane, and Crutched Friars in the south-east corner of the City. In addition he possessed a country residence in Highgate. He married Jane Crichton on 17 October 1733 in Dunstable; they raised a son, Archibald, and two daughters, Jane and Rebecca. Finding himself in ill health and his only son still a minor, in December 1757 Buchanan reorganized his business as James Buchanan & Co., a partnership involving himself (with a half share), John Hyndman (a third), and Richard Lancaster (a sixth). Lancaster had been his chief clerk, while Hyndman, a Scot, had been in business at Smithfield in southern Virginia, corresponding with Buchanan and some of the Glasgow Buchanans. Less than a year after this reorganization, Buchanan died at his country residence at Highgate on 24 August 1758. By his will, a third of his estate went to his widow, a third to his son, and a sixth to each of his two daughters. Since his daughter Jane's portion was £10,000 when she married in 1762, it seems likely that Buchanan's total estate was in the vicinity of £60,000, of which only a tenth was invested in the capital of his new firm. Hyndman capably managed the affairs of that concern (in which Buchanan's estate retained its half interest) and expanded both its general turnover and its activity in the West Indies. The old partnership was wound up after 1768, though Hyndman and Lancaster continued a similar business in partnership with Thomas Main (Hyndman's nephew) and Robert Bunn. The firm lasted under Main until about 1810.   JACOB M. PRICE

Sources J. M. Price, 'The last phase of the Virginia–London consignment trade: James Buchanan & Co., 1758–1768', *William and Mary Quarterly*, 43 (1986), 64–98 · R. M. Buchanan, *Notes on the members of the Buchanan Society, numbers 1 to 366, 1725–1829* (1931) · J. Guthrie Smith, *Strathendrick and its inhabitants* (1896) · PRO, T 11/371/41 · G. Eyre-Todd, *History of Glasgow*, 3 (1934), 201–2 · *The Buchanan Society* (1927) · IGI · will, PRO, PROB 11/840, sig. 257
Archives Northumbd RO, Riddell MSS
Wealth at death approx. £60,000: Northumbd RO, Morpeth, Riddell MSS

Buchanan, James (1784–1857), headmaster, was born in Edinburgh on 10 March 1784. Nothing is known of his ancestry or early life. He married twice. With his first wife, whose name is not known, he had a son, William. He married his second wife, Isabella Anderson, in Edinburgh and was living at Haddington in 1812 when his son Ebenezer was born. A weaver by trade and a Primitive Methodist lay preacher, he served in the militia in Scotland during the

Napoleonic war, moving to New Lanark in June 1814 to obtain employment in the recently opened mills.

Buchanan's association with Robert Owen began in January 1816 when the Institution for the Formation of Character was opened and he became the first master in a 'rational infant school'. This day school for children aged between two and six was an integral part of the system, which included evening classes for older children and adults. Kindness was all-important, corporal punishment was forbidden, and competition had no place. Buchanan received specific instructions from Owen on many aspects of child education and evolved his own approach with emphasis on music, marching, movement, gymnastics, and concern for moral welfare. In 1819 Buchanan was recruited by Henry Brougham to open the first infant day school in England (the Westminster Free Day Infant Asylum), 'according to Mr. Owen's Plan', at 23 Brewers Green, later moving to Carey Street, Vincent Square, Westminster. The original school was administered by a committee representing mainly whig, radical, and nonconformist interests, charging no fees and relying solely on private philanthropy; but by 1824 a weekly fee of 1d. was charged, substantially less than the fees then current in dame-schools and child-minding establishments.

Buchanan's methods, predominantly personal, reflected the view that moral education was as important as basic subjects in the curriculum for working-class children. An excellent storyteller, he encouraged children's self-expression during simple object lessons when they did most of the talking, learning to observe and describe. Such interaction between teacher and child differed from the usual monitorial school relationships and impressed numerous influential visitors to Westminster, which served as a model for other infant schools. Contemporaries recalled that he never grew up, was simple-hearted and natural with a child's power to imagine and dramatize. Mystical, eccentric, completely unpractical, he was unable to cope with everyday school activities without the assistance of his wife, who was responsible for maintaining basic standards of behaviour and cleanliness.

Buchanan was an active member of the New Jerusalem Church based on Emanuel Swedenborg's doctrines which endorsed the innocence of infancy and believed knowledge was derived from the senses. Samuel Wilderspin, who opened Spitalfields infant school in 1820, and David Goyder, master of Bristol Meadow Street infant school in 1821, both Swedenborgians, frequently visited Buchanan's school and acknowledged his influence on infant school methodology which they subsequently developed and publicized. Thomas Bilby, another protégé, who taught at Vincent Square, opened infant schools in Chelsea and the West Indies and published *The Infant Teacher's Assistant* in 1831.

Buchanan conducted the London infant school, with the assistance of his wife and daughter Anne, for almost twenty years, with only a year's absence in 1826 when he established an infant school at Crich in Derbyshire. In 1839 he accepted an invitation from the New Zealand Land

Company to promote infant schools but on reaching Cape Town, where his eldest son was living, he was persuaded to stay and was joined by his wife and daughter. Buchanan continued to support infant school development, moved to Natal in 1856 to join his sons, and died in Pietermaritzburg on 14 January 1857. G. Jeffrey Machin

Sources G. J. Machin, 'The Westminster Free Day Infant Asylum', *Journal of Educational Administration and History*, 20 (1988), 43–6 · B. I. Buchanan, *Buchanan family records: James Buchanan and his descendants* (privately printed, Capetown, 1923) · D. Salmon and W. Hinshaw, *Infant schools: their history and theory* (1904) · R. Owen, *The life of Robert Owen written by himself*, 2 vols. (1857–8)
Likenesses W. Brodie, bronze bust, Dean cemetery, Edinburgh · photograph, repro. in R. R. Rusk, *A history of infant education* (1933), 135

Buchanan, James (1804–1870), Free Church of Scotland minister and theologian, was born in Paisley in Scotland on 14 April 1804, son of James Buchanan, a wine merchant, and his wife, Annabella Orr. He studied at the University of Glasgow before pursuing a theology course at Edinburgh. In 1827 he was ordained as a minister of the Church of Scotland at Roslin, near Edinburgh; in 1828 he received and accepted a call to the parish in North Leith, where he remained until 1840. On 10 February 1829 he married Elizabeth, daughter of John Cochrane, a Glasgow merchant; they had a son and a daughter before her early death in May 1832. On 12 December 1836 he married Mary, daughter of John Morison; they had a daughter.

While serving at North Leith, Buchanan was said to have 'attained great fame as a preacher, being remarkable for a clear, vigorous, and flowing style, a graceful manner, a vein of thrilling tenderness, broken from time to time by passionate appeals, all in the most pronounced evangelical strain' (*DNB*). During his ministry there he also wrote *Comfort in Affliction* (1837), *Improvement of Affliction* (1840), and *The Office and Work of the Holy Spirit*, which went through six editions between 1842 and 1849. The last work was remarkable both for the clarity of its style and its faithfulness to the task of biblical exposition.

In 1840 Buchanan accepted a call to St Giles's Church, Edinburgh, but he remained there only three years, leaving at the Disruption to join the new Free Church of Scotland. He became the first minister of St Stephen's Free Church, Edinburgh, where he ministered until 1845. In this year he was appointed professor of apologetics in the New College, the divinity hall of the Free Church in Edinburgh; in 1847, upon the death of Thomas Chalmers, he took the chair of systematic theology, which he held until his retirement in 1868.

Although Buchanan was more widely respected for his lucid style than for the originality of his thought, he produced several well-received books, including two topical volumes, *On the Tracts for the Times* (1843)—a response to the Tracts for the Times published by leaders of the Oxford Movement—and *The 'Essays and Reviews' Examined* (1861)—a reply to the notorious volume of essays published in 1860 in which the necessity of free enquiry in religious matters was advocated. He also published studies in apologetics,

Faith in God and atheism compared in their essential nature, theoretical grounds and practical influence (1855) and *Analogy Considered as a Guide to Truth and Applied as an Aid to Faith* (1864). In 1866 Buchanan delivered the second series of the Cunningham lectures, which were published in 1867 under the title *The doctrine of justification: an outline of its history in the church and its exposition from scripture*. Here Buchanan revisited Reformation theology, instructing his contemporaries to hold firm to the doctrine of justification by faith alone as the only effective antidote to rationalism and ritualism, which he regarded as the great tendencies of the age. Although principally remarkable for his avoidance of constructive and original thought, this work proved to be the most durable of Buchanan's works and was reprinted as recently as 1985. With James Bannerman, Buchanan edited the works of William Cunningham (1805–1861).

Buchanan received an honorary DD from Princeton College, New Jersey, in 1844, and a LLD from the University of Glasgow in 1851. He died on 19 April 1870 at 51 Lauriston Place, Edinburgh, survived by his wife. Unlike his younger contemporaries William Robertson Smith, Alexander Balmain Bruce, and Marcus Dods, Buchanan's relationship with the Free Church was without controversy and conflict, in part because his 'delicate health and a retiring disposition' (*DNB*) kept him out of ecclesiastical politics after the Disruption, but perhaps also because his unoriginal conservative theology did not threaten the accepted views of his denomination. Michael Jinkins

Sources *DNB* · J. A. Wylie, *Disruption worthies: a memorial of 1843*, ed. J. B. Gillies, new edn (1881) · *Fasti Scot.* · parish register (birth), Renfrewshire, Paisley High, 14 April 1804 · d. cert. · H. Watt, *New College, Edinburgh: a centenary history* (1946)
Archives U. Edin., New Coll. L., letters to Thomas Chalmers
Likenesses W. Walker, stipple, pubd 1838 (after S. Mackenzie), BM, NPG
Wealth at death £25,765 5s. 3d.: inventory, 5 Oct 1870, NA Scot., SC 70/1/150/22

Buchanan, James, Baron Woolavington (1849–1935), Scotch whisky blender and philanthropist, was born on 16 August 1849 at Brockville, Ontario, Canada, the third and youngest son of Alexander Buchanan, the son of a farmer from Bankhill, Stirlingshire, and his wife, Catherine, daughter of William McLean. His parents were Scottish emigrants but returned to Scotland when James was still an infant and he was brought up in Larne, where his father was a quarry manager for Charles Tennant & Co., chemical manufacturers. Because of ill health James was educated privately. His first job, at the age of fourteen or fifteen, was as an office boy with William Sloan & Co. of Glasgow, shipping agents. He was hired for three years on a salary which rose from £10 a year to £30. He was promoted to the post of custom house and clearing clerk but at the age of nineteen decided to join his brother, William, a grain merchant in Glasgow. After nearly ten years in the grain trade, including a period when he tried unsuccessfully to work on his own, he moved to London in November 1879 as agent for Charles Mackinlay & Co. of Leith, Scotch whisky blenders. Not satisfied to continue as an agent, Buchanan decided in 1884 to start his own business.

According to Buchanan's memoirs, 'The extraordinary thing is that the possibility of failure never once occurred to me. I had it always before me in my mind that sooner or later I was bound to make a success' (*DCL Gazette*, January 1931, 6). Success is almost an inappropriate word for Buchanan's achievement and it came sooner rather than later. By 1903, when his firm was incorporated as a private limited liability company, he had built a business worth over £0.75 million. By 1909 Buchanan's sales were larger than those of his longer established competitors, John Dewar & Sons and John Walker & Sons. Buchanan's growth was remarkable because it was achieved with minimal investment in production facilities. What he created, through necessity rather than choice, was a marketing company. Lacking capital Buchanan turned to his old friend William Lowrie, the chairman of W. P. Lowrie & Co., a Glasgow blending company. Lowries were large stockholders, suppliers of bulk blended whiskies to the trade, and provided Buchanan with whisky on credit. Rather than use one of Lowrie's established blends, Buchanan developed his own, a decision based on his assessment of the London market:

> The wants of the Licensed Trade in London were pretty well met by Messrs. Greenlees whose Lorne Whisky practically held the monopoly of the supply. I found many of the licensed houses were users of 'self whiskies'—heavy Highland malts and Lowland malts—with the public inclination certainly inclining towards the use of Scotch whisky. What I made up my mind to do was to find a blend sufficiently light and old to please the palate of the user. (ibid.)

Buchanan's blend

> was first put on the market in a black bottle with a plain white label. These characteristic colours prompted the public to refer to it—when they were unable to recall the name 'Buchanan' as 'that black and white whisky'. This apt title, by which the licensed victualler knew instantly to what blend they were referring, grew rapidly, until it was decided to embody it in the label. ('History of the house of Buchanan', 68)

On 5 December 1891 Buchanan married a nurse thirteen years his junior, a widow with a son and daughter, Mrs Annie Eliza Bardolph (1860/61–1918), daughter of Thomas Pounder, upholsterer. They had a daughter, Catherine, and a son who died in infancy. During the First World War Buchanan's wife nursed the wounded in London hospitals. She died suddenly in October 1918.

Buchanan derived enormous satisfaction from business, attributing his success to 'continuous and unremitting hard work' and 'taking pains, and giving attention to small matters' ('Lord Woolavington tells of his early experiences', 7). He realized the importance of obtaining orders from the owners of multiple retail outlets and, in an age when social emulation mattered, sought prestigious clients, particularly royalty and great institutions. A particularly noteworthy client was the House of Commons, with whose refreshment department Buchanan first secured a supply contract in 1885. He subsequently included the words 'As specially selected for the House of Commons' on the label of his bottles, as well as the text of the letter of appointment. In 1898 Buchanan was granted royal warrants to supply his whisky to the prince of Wales, the duke of York, and Queen Victoria. Buchanan's success was also the product of his effective use of publicity, whether in matters of personal appearance, such as driving a black pony and red-wheeled buggy with a smartly liveried boy on the back, or in using two Highland terriers, one black and one white, with the title 'REAL SCOTCH' on his label.

Buchanan developed his sales from his metropolitan base, the opposite approach to most blenders, and visited overseas markets to promote sales (and for health reasons). The first overseas branch office opened in Paris in 1902, shortly followed by one in New York. By then branches had been established in major cities outside London. Buchanan also moved into malt distilling at Glentauchers distillery on Speyside, which began production in 1898. By 1906, two more malt distilleries had been acquired.

In 1906 the one-time debtor became owner when Buchanan acquired W. P. Lowrie & Co. Lowrie had been hit by the slump in mature whisky prices and the prospect of financial failure highlighted Buchanan's dependence on his supplier. Control was followed by a programme of expansion in mechanized production facilities in Glasgow in order to meet growing sales of bottled whisky. Backward integration to control malt distilling and bottling was common to most large blending firms but Buchanan was the first to move into bottle manufacturing in 1907, when he acquired an interest in the North British Bottle Manufacturing Company to gain access to the Owens automatic bottle-making machine. This machine lowered the price of bottles and produced a more uniform bottle better suited to mechanical filling. Buchanans also acquired its own case-making facilities in 1907 by purchasing the Acme Tea Chest Company of Glasgow. Again, the works were extended and modern machinery was installed.

These investments created the capacity to handle sales which were still growing in the first decade of the twentieth century when Scotch whisky consumption was declining. James Buchanan's increasing market share did not blind him to the cost of achieving it. To him, as to his competitors, Dewars and Walkers, or 'the big three' as they called themselves, amalgamation seemed a solution and in April 1909 the three firms invited the accountant, Edwin Waterhouse, to prepare a scheme. When the principals—James Buchanan, Sir Thomas Dewar, and George Walker—met on 19 October 1910 Buchanan emphasized 'the manifest advantages that would accrue to all three companies by the cessation of costly and aggressive competition, and the further advantages to be derived from a united policy of action in home and foreign markets' (John Dewar & Sons Ltd, Cameron papers, 19 Oct 1910, United Distillers archive). He urged that in valuing their firms they should 'take the lean years with the fat' and offered to sell his firm for £20,000 to £30,000 less than it was worth if this would secure an amalgamation (ibid.).

Buchanan had personal reasons for backing an amalgamation. He was the oldest of the proprietors, had never enjoyed good health, and had no one in his family to take over the business, or at least no one equipped according to contemporary social values: 'Mr Buchanan has an only daughter, who cannot be expected to aid in the management' (John Dewar & Sons Ltd, memorandum on amalgamation, 29 July 1914, United Distillers archive). Unfortunately Buchanan's magnanimity failed to convince Walkers. In May 1914 he again approached Dewars and in April 1915 the firms formed a holding company, Scotch Whisky Brands Ltd. This was renamed Buchanan Dewar Ltd in 1919 by which time it was the thirty-third largest British manufacturing company and three times larger than the Distillers Company. It looked ideal for resolving what had become known as 'the big question', the merger between the Distillers Company and 'the big three'. When that amalgamation occurred in 1925 it was under the aegis of the Distillers Company. Buchanan joined DCL's board, one of its 'five noble lords' whose salesmanship had made Scotch whisky into a national and international drink (DCL board minute book 18, 12 Sept 1935, United Distillers archive). Aged seventy-six and in failing health he played little part in the group, attending only one board meeting between 1925 and 1935, though he did secure the election of his son-in-law Captain Reginald Macdonald-Buchanan MC to the board in 1930.

James Buchanan had many interests outside the whisky trade. He supported Joseph Chamberlain's tariff reform campaign and was a vice-president of the Tariff Reform League. In 1903 he bought Lavington Park, Petworth, Sussex, an estate of 3000 acres, where he created a stud farm. He was a successful racehorse owner. His first classic victory was in the St Leger of 1916 with Hurry On, who sired his Derby winners of 1922 and 1926, Captain Cuttle and Coronach. He was elected to the Jockey Club in 1927. Buchanan owned properties in British East Africa and Argentina, and was part owner, with Lord Aberdeen, of a 20,000 acre fruit farming estate in British Columbia. His hobbies included hunting, shooting, breeding pedigree cattle, sheep, and thoroughbred horses, and salmon fishing at Torridon, the family's summer home. He was appointed high sheriff of Sussex in 1910, created a baronet in 1920, raised to the peerage as Baron Woolavington of Lavington, Sussex, in 1922, and appointed GCVO in 1931.

Much of Buchanan's wealth was devoted to philanthropy. He bought the logbook of the Victory and presented it to the British Museum, provided the funds to fit out the Implacable as a training ship, and gave £10,000 to Edinburgh University for its animal breeding research department in 1926 (the university subsequently conferred an honorary doctorate in law on him). In 1928 he donated £125,000 to the Middlesex Hospital in memory of his wife to provide an equipped wing for middle-class paying patients; other gifts included £50,000 for the restoration of the nave of St George's Chapel, Windsor, £10,000 to the London Hospital for a ward for paying patients of moderate means, £5000 to the West of Scotland Agricultural College, and £2500 each to the Licensed Victuallers' School and Licensed Victuallers' Benevolent Institution.

Buchanan died within a week of his eighty-sixth birthday, on 9 August 1935, at Lavington Park, Petworth, Sussex, leaving personal estate with a gross value of over £7m. He was buried at Graffham churchyard, Sussex.

RONALD B. WEIR

Sources R. B. Weir, 'The distilling industry in Scotland in the nineteenth and early twentieth centuries', PhD diss., 2 vols., Edinburgh, 1974, 2.552–60 • B. Spiller, The chameleon's eye: James Buchanan & Company Limited, 1884–1984 (1984) • R. B. Weir, The history of the Distillers Company, 1877–1939 (1995) • 'Lord Woolavington tells of his early experiences', DCL Gazette (Jan 1931), 6–12 • B. Spiller, 'Buchanan, James, Lord Woolavington', DSBB • CGPLA Eng. & Wales (1935) • m. cert. • United Distillers Archive, John Dewar & Sons Ltd, Cameron MSS, 19 Oct 1910 • United Distillers Archive, John Dewar & Sons Ltd, memorandum on amalgamation, 29 July 1914 • DCL board minute book 18, 12 Sept 1935, United Distillers Archive • 'History of the house of Buchanan', DCL Gazette (April 1931), 7
Archives United Distillers archive, Brands Publicity Scotland, Barbour Building, Banbeath, Leven, Fife, records of James Buchanan & Co. Ltd | FILM BFI NFTVA, sports footage
Likenesses J. J. Shannon, portrait, 1918, RA • W. Stoneman, photograph, 1925, NPG • A. P. F. Ritchie, cigarette card, NPG • Spy [L. Ward], caricature, Hentschel-colourtype, NPG; repro. in VF (20 Nov 1907) • portrait, repro. in Spiller, Chameleon's eye, inside cover
Wealth at death £7,150,000: probate, 26 Sept 1935, CGPLA Eng. & Wales

Buchanan, John Lanne (fl. 1780–1816), author, was born in Menteith, Perthshire, a descendant of the Leny, Lenoch, or Lane family of that district. Nothing is known of his immediate family. He was educated at the grammar school in Callander and at the University of Glasgow. For some years he was assistant to Robert Menzies, minister of Comrie, and, on Menzies' death in 1780, he went as a missionary of the Church of Scotland to the Western Isles. His knowledge of Gaelic and his religious zeal fitted him for this work and his later writings show him to have been a keen advocate of the rights of the poor. Afterwards he lived in London. He was the author of Travels in the Western Hebrides (1793), which was published in German in 1795, and A Defence of the Scots Highlanders (1794). The miscellaneous writer William Thomson (1746–1817) edited Buchanan's Travels in the Western Hebrides from a huge mass of material and, without Buchanan's knowledge, inserted some severe criticisms of the Scottish clergy and others which Buchanan in his General View of the Fishery of Great Britain (1794) indignantly disclaimed. The quarrel between the two men was aired in public and Buchanan seems to have come off worse. There is no record of Buchanan after 1816. He was a sincere but unskilled writer whose works achieved modest circulation in his lifetime. They have some interest as records of areas of Britain remote from London, and his work on fisheries was republished in 1976 (on microfilm).

T. F. HENDERSON, rev. ELIZABETH BAIGENT

Sources A new catalogue of living English authors: with complete lists of their publications, and biographical and critical memoirs (1799) • [J. Watkins and F. Shoberl], A biographical dictionary of the living authors of Great Britain and Ireland (1816)

Buchanan, Sir John Scoular (1883–1966), aeronautical engineer, was born at Cambuslang, Lanarkshire, on 23 November 1883, the son of Joseph Buchanan, a steel smelter, and his wife, Janet M. Scoular Hogg. They also had another son and a daughter who emigrated to Canada. Buchanan was educated at Allan Glen's School, Glasgow, and served a marine engineering apprenticeship at G. and J. Weir of Glasgow before going on to the Royal Technical College, Glasgow, after winning a Whitworth exhibition in 1906. In 1908 he became an inspector of factories in the Newcastle district; in 1914 he joined the Royal Naval Volunteer Reserve as a technical officer attached to the Royal Naval Air Service (RNAS). In 1910 in Cathcart he had married Helen, daughter of Walter Parker, a cotton operative. They had one son, Ian Scoular Buchanan MD MRCP.

The merger of the Royal Flying Corps and Royal Naval Air Service as the Royal Air Force on 1 April 1918 brought military and naval personnel together. Buchanan was posted to the Royal Aircraft Establishment at Farnborough which had been set up by the War Office in 1909 for aeronautical research, and which had inspired the design of most of the early war aircraft until the nascent British industry began to take over.

Following the armistice all aircraft contracts were terminated, and the number of RAF squadrons declined from ninety-six to twenty-three, of which only ten were fully serviceable owing to drastic demobilization. Winston Churchill, then war and air minister, informed the air staff that no war planning was necessary for ten years (an instruction which was extended for the same period in 1925, and cancelled only in 1929) and that the RAF budget would be kept down to £15 million.

At the end of the war Buchanan joined the Air Ministry research and development department, but in the early 1920s little money was left for new government contracts, and the meagre funds were devoted to research, the building of the new RAF College at Cranwell, and mechanics' schools. Although the Royal Aircraft Establishment continued its fundamental research and testing, analysing in the greatest detail all established aspects of flying, aviation had perforce to be left to private enthusiasm, and sporting contests had to be stimulated by the Royal Aero Club.

In 1923 and 1924 Buchanan was an official observer at the light aeroplane trials at Lympne, for aircraft fitted in 1923 with motor cycle engines not exceeding 750 cc (followed in 1924 with 1100 cc engines). His report (*Journal of the Royal Aeronautical Society*, 28, 1924, 676–85) showed that there was nothing structurally new in any of the planes, although they exceeded the expected performance in stunt flying. In July 1926 Buchanan presented a similar paper on the Schneider trophy seaplane race in Baltimore, USA, at which he was the Air Ministry observer (*Journal of the Royal Aeronautical Society*, 30, 1926, 434–52). Buchanan proved convincingly that although the British had bad luck, America had slipped ahead in high-speed flying in what had been a sporting event but which had become a fiercely nationalistic contest with political implications. He pinpointed the need for an RAF team to be formed for

Sir John Scoular Buchanan (1883–1966), by Walter Stoneman, 1944

high-speed flight, and concluded that the American planes had been structurally and aerodynamically improved. The outcome was that an RAF high-speed flight was set up; increasing government money was devoted to the development of the design of the seaplanes, and a Rolls Royce engine was specially developed. The subsequent contests at Venice in 1927, Cowes in 1929, and again at Cowes in 1931 were won by Britain and the trophy was finally secured for British possession.

In 1935, as deputy of technical development, Buchanan, with his director, Air Commodore Verney, and Ralph Sorley, the director of operational requirements, persuaded the air staff to accept the experimental aircraft which developed into the Spitfire.

Throughout the 1930s Buchanan was held in the highest regard for his integrity and impartiality. He was short, with a charming Scots accent, and a face like that of an ancient Greek philosopher. Essentially conservative in disposition, when faced with a new suggestion he would first ponder on its possible disadvantages rather than its potential benefits. He would often say reflectively, 'No I don't think I would do that. No I wouldn't agree with that', and so won a reputation for immense sagacity.

The entire technical staff of the Air Ministry was transferred to the new Ministry of Aircraft Production on 10 May 1940, and the fruits of their labours over five years were gathered by the minister, Lord Beaverbrook.

Buchanan, though now ranking as deputy director-general of production, was overshadowed. However, his inherent knowledge and wisdom were not lost by the industry which perhaps surreptitiously sought him out. It was not until 1942, when Sir R. Stafford Cripps had become minister, that Buchanan emerged from eclipse as assistant chief executive, and gave great personal service in introducing Cripps to the industry and the understanding of its aeronautical intricacies. For his services Buchanan was knighted in 1944, having been appointed CBE in 1934.

After serving some years on the council of the Royal Aeronautical Society, Buchanan became president in 1949–50 and led the society's deputation to the USA to meet its opposite number, the Institute of Aeronautical Sciences, for the first of what became a biennial gathering alternately held in Britain and America, with valuable results.

From 1945, after retirement, Buchanan was appointed until 1948 a technical director of Short Bros. and Harland, flying boat builders. From 1949 until 1960 he was chairman of the London and south-eastern regional board for industry, a government appointment. Buchanan died on 5 April 1966 in Dudley Road Hospital, Birmingham. He was survived by his wife.

G. P. BULMAN, rev. ANITA McCONNELL

Sources M. M. Postan, D. Hay, and J. D. Scott, *Design and development of weapons* (1964) · A. Cairncross, *Planning in wartime aircraft production in Britain, Germany and the USA* (1991) · *The Times* (9 April 1966), 10f · *WWW* · personal knowledge (1981) · d. cert., 1981 · *CGPLA Eng. & Wales* (1966)
Likenesses W. Stoneman, photograph, 1944, NPG [*see illus.*] · photograph, repro. in *The Times*
Wealth at death £4658: probate, 27 July 1966, *CGPLA Eng. & Wales*

Buchanan, John Young (1844–1925), chemist and oceanographer, was born at Dowanhill, Glasgow, on 20 February 1844, the son of John Buchanan of Dowanhill (1807–1876), a merchant, and his wife, Jane (d. 1899), the daughter of John Young of Rowmore, Dunbartonshire. Both his parents came from prosperous Glasgow merchant families. Buchanan was the second of four sons, of whom the eldest died young and the third, Thomas Ryburn *Buchanan (1846–1911), became a member of parliament. There were also four daughters. Buchanan was educated at Glasgow high school and the University of Glasgow. He graduated MA in 1863 and then spent several years abroad, studying chemistry at Marburg, Leipzig, and Bonn and at the École de Médecine in Paris (1867), before becoming assistant to Alexander Crum Brown, professor of chemistry at Edinburgh. His investigation into the hydrolysis of chloroacetic acid to glycolic acid (1871) was subsequently exploited by J. H. van't Hoff in his establishment of the laws of chemical kinetics.

In 1872 Buchanan was selected to join the scientific team sailing round the world in HMS *Challenger* (1872–6) in the first major scientific study of the sea. His work both during the voyage and subsequently was pivotal to the development of oceanography. He studied the chemistry of the sea in its broadest sense, contributing to all the main divisions of marine science. Observations on the chemical and physical properties of sea water, on sea ice, and on marine deposits begun in the *Challenger* formed the basis for much of his later research. However, his best known observation during the voyage was the discovery that T. H. Huxley's *Bathybius*, thought by many to be a primitive life form inhabiting the ocean floor, was in fact an inorganic residue created when sediment samples were stored in alcohol. He further showed that the black 'rocks' the *Challenger* dredged from the sea-bed were in fact concretions of manganese and other metals.

After the expedition's return Buchanan continued working on problems in oceanography and related sciences for the rest of his career. However, apart from a brief spell as lecturer in geography at Cambridge (1889–93) he held no official position. He had a substantial private income and lived in the family home in Edinburgh until his mother died in 1899, subsequently moving to London. Both houses were equipped with a private laboratory but for twenty years Buchanan also occupied rooms in Christ's College, Cambridge. He appreciated the social side of college life and freedom to work unhindered by formal society obligations or, latterly, by teaching commitments. Some people found him 'cold and distant' (Mill, *Autobiography*, 50) but in Cambridge he was welcomed as a gifted conversationalist. Although reserved and sensitive in disposition, he was a man of strong family feeling, and generous in case of need. He inspired great affection among a small circle of close friends and colleagues, some in the upper echelons of European society. Chief among these was Prince Albert I of Monaco, who also devoted a substantial part of his life and fortune to the study of oceanography.

Buchanan listed travel as his recreation in *Who's Who*. During the 1880s and 1890s he made a number of scientific voyages in cable ships and in Prince Albert's yachts. He was often in South America, looking after family property in Argentina, and in 1885 journeyed on up the Pacific coast. In Europe he visited friends and, increasingly, spas, but whatever the reason for the journey he employed his habit of observation, on his special fields of scientific interest if appropriate, if not, on other topics. A trip to Switzerland in 1893, for example, intended as a rest-cure, led to a long-term study of glaciers.

Buchanan's scientific researches ultimately covered oceanography, chemistry, limnology, and meteorology. While many arose out of his work in the *Challenger*, he also identified important new areas of interest. He was an outstanding experimentalist; during the *Challenger's* voyage he had devoted much attention to methods of measuring the temperature and specific gravity of sea water, devising a stopcock water bottle (named after him) and piezometers for measuring pressure and temperature in the ocean depths. His observational work was admired by contemporaries for its painstaking accuracy, but it was felt that his preoccupation with detail prevented him from publishing his results fully. A colleague wrote: 'I never knew a man who did so much work and wrote so little about it' (Mill, *Autobiography*, 50). Nevertheless, Buchanan still published over a hundred scientific papers. Late in life he collected the most important in three volumes, published by Cambridge University Press: *Scientific Papers, vol. 1* (1913), *Comptes rendus of Observations and Reasoning* (1917), and the best known, *Accounts Rendered of Work done and Things Seen* (1919).

Buchanan helped write the narrative of the *Challenger* but because of a dispute with the Treasury only part of the expedition's chemical results—'Specific gravity of samples of ocean water'—appeared under his name in the official report. This contribution included the first global chart of the surface salinity of the oceans. He continued to work extensively on the chemistry of marine deposits and on the formation and distribution of oceanic and littoral manganese concretions, his interest in this topic being augmented by his discovery in 1878 of manganese nodules in Loch Fyne, while dredging off the west coast of Scotland in his specially built steam yacht, *Mallard*. He also investigated the seasonal variation of temperature in the sea and in lakes, together with their freezing and the nature of ice and brines. His findings, in both fresh and salt water, contributed to the concept of thermocline formation, and influenced later development of ideas on the thermohaline circulation of the ocean. He was also probably the first person to draw attention to the oxygen minimum layer in the ocean.

Observing cold water off the west coast of South America in 1885 Buchanan concluded that this could not be due to a surface current from the south polar regions, as had been previously supposed, but was due to upwelling of cold deep water off a windward shore, and further that this occurred in similar sites elsewhere. Another feature he recognized to be of great significance in ocean circulation was the equatorial undercurrent, discovered off the African coast when he was in the cable ship *Buccaneer* in 1886. The same voyage revealed the existence of huge submarine canyons in continental shelves. On an earlier trip, in the *Dacia*, Buchanan had drawn scientific attention to the existence of isolated seamounts rising from the deep-sea floor. Lack of resources meant that it was not until the second half of the twentieth century that these phenomena were more widely investigated and their full significance understood.

As Buchanan was meticulous to a fault and lacked the ability to relinquish old projects as he added new ones, the internal pressures on him grew. From the 1890s onwards he increasingly complained of ill health which appears to have been at least partly stress-related, and in 1912 he suffered a nervous breakdown. The outbreak of war in 1914 exacerbated his depression and he sold his London house and went to North America, only returning after hostilities were over. His final years were spent as a recluse, the enthusiasm of his youthful personality transformed into profound pessimism about the destructive power of modern civilization, both towards itself and on indigenous peoples and habitats.

Buchanan became a fellow of the Royal Society of Edinburgh in 1870 and was awarded its Keith prize in 1887, in which year he was also elected fellow of the Royal Society of London. He was an active member of other scientific societies and the Royal Scottish Geographical Society, which he had helped found, awarded him its gold medal in 1911. He held honorary memberships of the Berlin Gesellschaft für Erdkunde (Geographical Society) and of the Société Helvétique des Sciences (Swiss Natural Sciences Society). Prince Albert made him a vice-president of the Comité de Perfectionnement of the Institut Océanographique in Paris and conferred on him the order of St Charles of Monaco. Buchanan never married. He died suddenly in London on 16 October 1925.   MARGARET DEACON

Sources A. E. S. [A. E. Shipley], *PRS*, 110A (1926), xii–xiii • H. R. Mill, *Proceedings of the Royal Society of Edinburgh*, 45 (1924–5), 364–7 • *Nature*, 116 (1925), 719–21 • G. Kutzbach, 'Buchanan, John Young', *DSB* • D. Stoddart, 'The *Challenger* expedition: Buchanan—the forgotten apostle', *Geographical Magazine*, 44 (1971–2), 858–62 • A. W. Patrick-Buchanan, *The Buchanan book* (1911) • M. J. McPhaden, 'The equatorial undercurrent: one hundred years of exploration', *Eos* (7 Oct 1986), 762–5 • *Glasgow Herald* (19 Oct 1925) • *The Times* (17 Oct 1925) • R. Damien, *Albert 1er, prince souverain de Monaco* (1964) • H. R. Mill, *An autobiography* [1951] • J. Peile, *Biographical register of Christ's College, 1505–1905, and of the earlier foundation, God's House, 1448–1505*, ed. [J. A. Venn], 2 (1913) • J. W. Goodison, *Catalogue of the portraits in Christ's, Clare and Sidney Sussex colleges, Cambridge* (1985)
Archives RGS, paper on Antarctic expedition | NRA Scotland, priv. coll., letters to his parents • Scott Polar RI, letters to W. S. Bruce
Likenesses J. P. L. Tinayre, oils, 1909, Christ's College, Cambridge • photograph, repro. in Shipley, 'John Young Buchanan, 1844–1925' • photograph, repro. in J. Y. Buchanan, *Papers*, 1 (1913), frontispiece • photograph, NHM, Earth Sciences Library, Murray collection • photograph, RS • photographs, repro. in *Scottish Geographical Magazine*, 28 (1912), facing pp. 169, 184
Wealth at death £166,854 17s. 3d.: confirmation, 13 Jan 1926, *CCI*

Buchanan, Robert (1786–1873), university professor and playwright, was a cadet of the clan Buchanan. He was born on 16 February 1786 at Trean, Callander, the son of John Buchanan, a farmer. He graduated MA from the University of Glasgow in 1808, where he specially distinguished himself in the philosophy classes. He was for a period tutor in the family of Francis, sixth earl of Wemyss and fourth earl of March. After completing his divinity course, he was in 1812 licensed as a preacher of the Church of Scotland by the presbytery of Haddington, and in 1813 was presented to the parish of Peebles. In 1824 he was appointed assistant and successor to George Jardine in the chair of logic at Glasgow University and, becoming sole professor in 1827, he held the office until 1864; the university conferred on him the degree of LLD in 1869. He retired to Ardfillayne, Dunoon, where he died, unmarried, on 2 March 1873.

Buchanan was the author of *Fragments of the Table Round* (1860); *Vow of Glentreuil, and other Poems* (1862); *Wallace: a Tragedy* (1856); and *Tragic Dramas from Scottish History* (1868). He also published anonymously, in 1868, *Canute's Birthday in Ireland, a Drama in Five Acts*. His tragedy *Wallace* was performed twice for a charitable object at the Prince's Theatre, Glasgow, in March 1862, the principal characters being played by students of the divinity and art classes.

Though averse to independent and original speculations, Buchanan had a thorough mastery of Scottish philosophy, and his highly cultivated taste was manifested not only in his verse, but in the correct and chaste style of his lectures. In commemoration of his services as occupant of the logic chair for forty years (during which tenure he became familiarly known as 'Logic Bob') the Buchanan prizes were instituted in 1866 for students of the logic, moral philosophy, and English literature classes. By his will he bequeathed £10,000 for the founding of Buchanan bursaries in connection with the arts classes of the university.   T. F. HENDERSON, *rev.* M. C. CURTHOYS

Sources *Fasti Scot.* · *Glasgow Herald* (3 March 1873) · R. Inglis, *The dramatic writers of Scotland* (1868) · W. I. Addison, *A roll of graduates of the University of Glasgow from 31st December 1727 to 31st December 1897* (1898)
Archives U. Glas. L., lecture notes
Wealth at death £15,051 16s. 6d.: confirmation, 25 March 1873, NA Scot., SC 51/32/18/385

Buchanan, Robert (1802–1875), Free Church of Scotland minister, was born on 15 August 1802 in the village of St Ninians, near Stirling, the sixth son of Alexander Buchanan, brewer and farmer. Educated at the universities of Glasgow (1817–20) and Edinburgh (1820–25), Robert was licensed as a preacher in the Church of Scotland by the presbytery of Dunblane in 1825. After serving briefly as a tutor to the Drummond family of Blair-Drummond, he was presented through their influence as minister of the parish of Gargunnock, near Stirling, in late 1826. He was translated to the parish of Saltoun, in East Lothian, in 1829 and then to the prestigious Tron parish in Glasgow in 1833. It was at the Tron that Thomas Chalmers had begun his Glasgow ministry in 1815, initiating many innovative programmes for the urban parish ministry. Buchanan shared Chalmers's evangelical convictions and intended to carry on his work in the Tron, but his energies were soon diverted to ecclesiastical controversies at the national level.

In 1834 the evangelical party, under Chalmers's leadership, gained control of the general assembly of the Church of Scotland and initiated reforms designed to make the established church more popular and effective. They reformed patronage with the Veto Act, giving the majority of male communicants in a parish the right to veto an unacceptable patron's candidate for the ministry of that parish. They also began a church extension campaign, intended to build hundreds of new parish churches and schools in response to Scotland's growing population. Buchanan emerged to national prominence as an eloquent evangelical promoter of the extension of the established church. In 1835 he was appointed to a deputation charged with negotiating for a parliamentary grant to support Scottish church extension. However, although his dignified bearing and refinement made a favourable impression at Westminster, parliament declined to provide a grant for church extension, and relations between church and state in Scotland grew strained.

The tensions erupted into open conflict in 1838, when the civil courts declared the church's Veto Act to be illegal and demanded the reimposition of the old system of church patronage. The established church, the civil courts insisted, had no authority to interfere with the civil right of patrons. Buchanan stood firmly with the evangelical party in supporting the congregational veto. In the general assembly of 1838 he moved the celebrated 'independence resolution', which insisted that the appointment of ministers was a spiritual function and that the church could not allow the civil courts authority over such appointments without sacrificing its 'spiritual independence'. As the controversy between church and state grew more heated, Buchanan served on church deputations sent to London to negotiate a parliamentary settlement. Efforts to resolve the conflict, however, failed, and at the Disruption of 1843 Buchanan joined Chalmers and over a third of the clergy and lay members in leaving the Church of Scotland.

Those going out formed the Free Church of Scotland, and Buchanan took a prominent role in building and consolidating the new denomination. Invited to write the history of the struggle that culminated in the Disruption, he produced a scholarly and balanced account, *The Ten Years' Conflict* (1849), which went far to justify to the educated public the actions of those who went out. In 1847 he became convener of the Sustentation Fund, which had been devised by Chalmers to provide for the Free Church's financial needs by ensuring that wealthier congregations helped support poorer congregations. Buchanan presided over the Sustentation Fund for nearly thirty years, giving the Free Church a firm financial foundation. In the late 1840s he returned to his early interests in urban home mission, initiating a movement based on Chalmers's ideas in the deprived Wynds district of Glasgow. This led to the creation of several new churches in the Wynds, and encouraged a national movement for territorial home missions across Scotland.

Buchanan was also a leading figure in the movement that emerged out of the revival of 1859 to reunite the several presbyterian denominations in Scotland. He presided over the Free Church union committee during its lengthy but ultimately unsuccessful union negotiations with the United Presbyterian church between 1863 and 1873. By the early 1870s he became convinced that the presbyterian churches of Scotland could be united only on the basis of independence from the state. This led him to support the campaign to disestablish the Church of Scotland after 1872.

Buchanan was a tall and handsome man, who had been a fine athlete in his youth and had the bearing of a statesman—though some found him aloof and too much the ecclesiastical politician. He married Anne Handyside on 5 March 1828; she died in 1841, and on 31 October 1843 he married Elizabeth Stoddart (d. 1898). There were children from both marriages, seven of whom survived him. He served as moderator of the Free Church general assembly in 1860, and was to be appointed principal of the Glasgow Free Church College in 1875. However, before that appointment could be confirmed he died while on holiday, at the Palazzo Torlonia, via Angelo Custode 25, Rome, on 31 March 1875 after a brief illness. The body was returned to Glasgow and honoured with a great public funeral on 18 May, before burial in the Glasgow necropolis. STEWART J. BROWN

Sources N. L. Walker, *Robert Buchanan, D.D.: an ecclesiastical biography* (1877) · *Fasti Scot.* · R. Rainy, 'Robert Buchanan', *Disruption worthies: a memorial of 1843* (1876), 325–34 · R. Buchanan, *The ten years' conflict*, 2 vols. (1849)
Archives BL, letters to Lord Aberdeen, Add. MS 43237 · BL, corresp. with Sir Robert Peel, Add. MS 40508 · NL Scot., letters to George Combe · U. Edin., New Coll. L., letters to Thomas Chalmers
Likenesses A. H. Ritchie, marble bust (after model by S. Joseph), U. Edin., New College · chalk drawing, Scot. NPG · engraving, repro. in Walker, *Robert Buchanan*
Wealth at death £9231 5s. 10d.: confirmation, 13 May 1875, NA Scot., SC 36/48/76/604–8

Buchanan, Robert (1813–1866), socialist, was born at Ayr. After working as a tailor, he joined the Huddersfield Owenites in 1837 and between 1838 and 1842 was a peripatetic socialist lecturer and missionary. Despite his socialism, Buchanan was also a contributor to the Chartist *Northern Star*, though not as a supporter of physical force.

In 1840 Buchanan engaged in a bitter confrontation with the Christian polemicist the Revd Joseph Barker, and his refutation of the latter's *The Abominations of Socialism Exposed* was one of a number of works attacking the practices and doctrines of the established church that Buchanan published while at Manchester between 1839 and 1841. The same year he became embroiled in a legal conflict with the religious authorities. His *Socialism Vindicated* (1840) was a reply to the attack upon the Owenites by the Revd W. J. Kidd, rector of Didsbury, who successfully prosecuted them for illegally charging for admission to Sunday lectures at their 'Hall of Science'. As the Owenites claimed to be an organization of protestant dissenters, Kidd and T. P. Bunting, the son of Wesleyan minister Jabez Bunting, induced the stipendiary magistrate to tender to Buchanan the oaths required of a dissenting minister. Buchanan vacillated but eventually took the oath—earning himself the sobriquet of the 'Rev.-swear-at-last' from G. J. Holyoake (J. McCabe, *Life and Letters of Holyoake*, 1908, 1.58). Bunting then managed to elicit from him a declaration that he did not believe in the orthodox doctrines of damnation and Buchanan was fined 50s. for refusing to take the oaths of supremacy.

Buchanan married Margaret Williams (d. 1894), daughter of a local solicitor favourable to socialism, in the autumn of 1840, at a civil service in Stoke-on-Trent, attended by Robert Owen. In May 1841 he moved to Glasgow and, while he was on a lecture tour, his son Robert Williams *Buchanan, later a distinguished poet and dramatist, was born in Caverswall, Staffordshire, on 18 August 1841. A serious physical assault on Buchanan at a Methodist chapel in Whitehaven, Cumberland, in January 1842 brought his missionary career to a close. He moved to Norwood, Surrey, and sent his wife and young son to the Ham Common community in Surrey while he earned a living as a reporter for *The Sun* newspaper. Still an Owenite, he joined the League of Social Progress as a member of its

Robert Buchanan (1813–1866), by unknown engraver

inaugural central committee in December 1848. The league campaigned for home colonization and co-operation, and Buchanan contributed to Holyoake's *Spirit of the Age* on these topics in 1849.

In 1850–51 Buchanan returned to Glasgow to edit and later own the freethinking *Glasgow Sentinel*, through which he fomented much local hatred for his attacks upon religion and capitalism. Buchanan built up a printing and publishing business but his acquisition of the *Glasgow Times* and the *Penny Post* led to his bankruptcy in 1856 and complete ruin by 1860.

Buchanan died at his son's house at Bexhill, Sussex, on 4 March 1866. He was survived by his wife, who died in 1894. MATTHEW LEE

Sources H. Jay, *Robert Buchanan* (1903) · J. A. Cassidy, *Robert W. Buchanan* (1973) · E. Royle, *Victorian infidels: the origins of the British secularist movement, 1791–1866* (1974) · C. W. Sutton, *A list of Lancashire authors* (1876) · G. J. Holyoake, *Sixty years of an agitator's life*, 2 vols. (1875–9) · *New Moral World* (1838–42) · *DNB*
Likenesses engraving, NPG [*see illus.*] · portrait, repro. in Jay, *Robert Buchanan*, facing p. 8
Wealth at death ruined by 1860; lived modestly at Glasgow 1859–c.1864 and then at Kentish Town

Buchanan, Robertson (1769–1816), mechanical and civil engineer, was born in Glasgow, the sixth son of George Buchanan and his first wife, Jane Gorvie. The Buchanans were immensely wealthy merchants with interests in North America and the West Indies. It is not known where or how Robertson learned his trade as a millwright, civil engineer, and surveyor, but it seems likely that he learned something of the craft working in the textile mills owned by the family in Glasgow. By 1791 he was working at David Dale's Rothesay cotton mills and was soon appointed overseer, or acting partner, of the works and elected to the burgh council and nominated as a commissioner of supply for Argyll. While in Rothesay he developed an interest in milling machinery, methods of heating mills, and in manual marine and fire engine pumps, patenting his own invention in 1796. He considered opening a works in London to manufacture these during 1800, but abandoned the idea when the Navy Board's response was lukewarm. At about this time he seems, also, to have become a consulting engineer, installing heating apparatus in mills owned by the Houldsworth family in the west of Scotland and Manchester, the mills of James Finlay & Sons (in which his father was a partner), and in other mills throughout central Scotland. By 1804 he was back in Glasgow describing himself as a cotton spinner in a transaction to purchase land to build a footbridge over the Clyde at the foot of the Saltmarket to be called Hucheson's Bridge. He seems to have been working at Finlay's Adelphi Mills in Huchesontown.

Buchanan published his first treatise in 1807, *On the Warming of Mills and other Buildings*, which included the results of the experiments he had carried out at the Adelphi Mills and readings from other mills where he had worked. The following year he published a much larger volume, *Practical and Descriptive Essays on Mill Works and other Machinery* (1808), which contained seven individual essays—some of which were printed separately. This volume was regularly reprinted over the next thirty years with editions by Thomas Tredgold (1823) and George Rennie (1842). During 1808 Buchanan was employed in building the Cranstonhill waterworks in Glasgow on land belonging to Henry Houldsworth. This was a large undertaking, costing £60,000, which drew water from a tunnel running parallel with the Clyde and pumped it into the city using two large steam engines. With his experience of both steam powered and water driven mills Buchanan was well qualified to supervise the work. He continued to act as consulting engineer to the water company at least until 1811 when he reported on the stoppage of water in Cowcaddens, one of the city's suburbs.

In 1809 Buchanan set up in business at the York Street Foundry, Port Dundas (the harbour of the Forth and Clyde Canal in Glasgow), building on his extensive business in supplying equipment for heating mills. During 1809 he surveyed and replaced the bridges over the White and Black Cart in the parish of Inchinnan, Renfrewshire. Two years later he surveyed the estate of North Barr, the property of his brother James, also in Inchinnan, and constructed wharves at the mouth of the Cart. Buchanan was admitted a burgess of Glasgow in 1810. In the following year he was commissioned to prepare a 'report relative to the proposed Rail-Way from Dumfries to Sanquhar', which was designed to give the isolated Sanquhar coalfield access to a wider market. This was one of the first railway proposals in Scotland to forecast the development of

passenger services and to suggest that the line's very existence would stimulate the local economy and generate new demands. The York Street Foundry also supplied stoves for heating public buildings. In 1815 he fitted two of his stoves in the Northwest church 'rendering the congregation now in cold weather very comfortable' (Renwick, 327); but unfortunately the congregation had to appeal to the town council for help in meeting the bill of £124. Also in 1815 he patented a wholly impractical invention for making the paddles on a steamboat enter the water perpendicularly. This was, perhaps, not the best qualification for his publication in 1816 of *A Practical Treatise on Propelling Vessels by Steam*, which was translated into German the following year. He died at the home of his step-grandfather (the father of his father's third wife), Dr Alexander Innes of Creech St Michael, near Taunton, on 22 July 1816.

MICHAEL S. MOSS

Sources *The Post Office directory of Glasgow* (1809–16) · surveys of bridges at Inchinnan, 1809, at North Barr Estate for James Buchanan, 1911, Mitchell L., Glas., Glasgow City Archives · R. Renwick, *Extracts from the records of the burgh of Glasgow, AD 1809–1822*, 10 (1915), 327–8 · R. Buchanan, report on the stoppage of water in Cowcaddens Port done at the request of James Hill, 18 Jan 1811, NL Scot., MS 5327 no. 186 · notes by David Murray on copy of R. Buchanan, *Practical essays on millwork* (1841), U. Glas. L., Murray collection, special collection
Wealth at death £83 8s.: confirmation, 1818

Buchanan, Robert Williams (1841–1901), poet and novelist, was born at Caverswall, Staffordshire, on 18 August 1841, the only surviving child of Robert *Buchanan (1813–1866) and his wife, Margaret Williams (*d.* 1894), daughter of a socialist lawyer from Stoke-on-Trent. His father, originally a tailor in Ayr, had by the time of his son's birth become an itinerant lecturer in support of Robert Owen's socialist and anti-religious theories. The family eventually settled in Norwood, Surrey, where Buchanan's father worked as a journalist on radical newspapers. Buchanan attended schools at Hampton Wick and Merton during his early years, but much of his education seems to have taken place at his parents' home in Norwood; visitors included the French socialist exiles Louis Blanc and Marc Caussidière, and the Chartist champion of the co-operative movement, (Patrick) Lloyd Jones. Buchanan was brought up to share his parents' socialist, humanitarian, and anti-religious beliefs and these beliefs played an important though by no means unquestioned role throughout his subsequent intellectual career.

About 1850 the family went to Glasgow, where Buchanan's father had moved to edit the *Glasgow Sentinel*, a socialist newspaper which he was eventually to own. After attending a small day school, Buchanan was sent to a school at Rothesay, on the island of Bute, from which he was expelled for his 'mutinous spirit' (Jay, 25). He returned to Glasgow and continued his education at Glasgow Academy and Glasgow high school, and enrolled in Greek and Latin classes at Glasgow University in 1856. During his student years he became an ardent devotee of the theatre, and especially of Shakespeare; in his reminiscences he describes how one particular production of *King Lear* 'focused [his] feelings into humanitarianism, and gave to

Robert Williams Buchanan (1841–1901), by Barraud, pubd 1893

[his] mind no little of the human sympathy which … it possesses' (ibid., 34). He also made the acquaintance of various actors, among them the young Henry Irving. A fellow student at the university, David Gray, became a close friend, and together they developed a passionate enthusiasm for poetry.

Following the collapse of his father's newspaper business Buchanan went to London in 1860 with Gray to seek literary fame and fortune. Their early experiences of hardship and the circumstances leading up to Gray's death in December 1861 are vividly delineated by Buchanan in *David Gray and other Essays* (1868). He had already made some contributions to Glasgow newspapers, and in London he managed to obtain employment on *The Athenaeum* and other periodicals. He also enjoyed some success writing for the stage, collaborating with Charles Gibbon on *The Rathboys* (1862) and having a verse-play entitled *The Witch-Finder* produced at Sadler's Wells two years later. His circle of literary acquaintances expanded to include G. H. Lewes, George Eliot, Robert Browning, and Charles Dickens, the last of whom accepted some contributions to *All the Year Round*. The influence of another friend, Thomas Love Peacock, can be detected in *Undertones* (1863), Buchanan's first volume of 'pseudo-classic poems' (Jay, 103). Both this and his second volume, *Idyls and Legends of Inverburn* (1865), were warmly received by reviewers; he was awarded a medal by the Society of Fine Arts for the former, while the latter strongly appealed to the publisher Alexander Strahan and to Roden Noel, both of

whom became valued friends. In *London Poems* (1866), a volume which confirmed his growing reputation as a poet, he returned to his socialist roots to produce a powerful series of portraits of the poor and outcast in London.

On 2 September 1861 Buchanan married Mary Jay (*d.* 1881), whose younger sister Harriet eventually became his biographer; and a few years later his parents joined them in London. After his father's death in 1866, however, he decided to return to Scotland, settling near Oban from 1866 to 1874, living as a country gentleman, and writing steadily, both verse—chiefly narrative—and prose sketches and criticisms. It was during this period that he became involved in the acrimonious and protracted controversy for which he is chiefly remembered. On 4 August 1866 he reviewed Algernon Charles Swinburne's *Poems and Ballads* in *The Athenaeum*, describing Swinburne as 'unclean for the mere sake of uncleanness' and making thinly veiled allusions to his homosexuality. He followed this up in *The Spectator* on 15 September 1866, publishing under the pseudonym Caliban a poem called 'The Session of the Poets' in which he ridiculed Swinburne's drunken antics at a literary party given by the publisher Edward Moxon. Swinburne's friend William Michael Rossetti retorted on his behalf in a pamphlet on *Poems and Ballads* issued in 1867 by calling Buchanan 'a poor and pretentious … poetaster'. Buchanan later claimed that it had been Swinburne's derogatory reference to David Gray's 'poor little book' in a review of Matthew Arnold's *New Poems* (*Fortnightly Review*, new ser., 1, Oct 1867, 414–45) which led him to vow 'to avenge it if ever I had the opportunity' (Jay, 161). The offending words, however, were not in fact added to Swinburne's review until it was reprinted in his *Essays and Studies* (1875), by which time the dispute had intensified considerably. In October 1871 Buchanan, under the pseudonym Thomas Maitland, contributed to the *Contemporary Review* an article entitled 'The fleshly school of poetry: D. G. Rossetti', in which he severely criticized Rossetti's *Poems* (1870) and ridiculed the friendly reviewers (including Swinburne) who had praised the volume. Rossetti protested in *The Athenaeum* against 'the stealthy school of criticism' (16 Dec 1871), while Swinburne, with biting causticity, denounced Buchanan in *Under the Microscope* (1872). Having revised and amplified his attack, Buchanan then issued it as a pamphlet under his name, entitled *The Fleshly School of Poetry and other Phenomena of the Day* (1872). The warfare was long continued. Swinburne, under the mocking signature of Thomas Maitland St Kilda, renewed his attack on Buchanan in a letter entitled 'The Devil's due', published in *The Examiner* on 28 December 1875, in which he called Buchanan 'a polypseudonymous libeller'. Buchanan brought an action for libel against the proprietor of the newspaper, Peter Taylor, and after three days' trial (29 June–1 July 1876) won £150 damages. Buchanan subsequently acknowledged the excessive nature of his assault and sought to make amends by dedicating his novel *God and the Man* (1881) to an 'old enemy', later explicitly identified as Rossetti, and by declaring in *The Academy* on 1 July 1882 that 'Mr Rossetti … never was a Fleshly Poet at all'.

During this period Buchanan's health and his financial situation both deteriorated. In 1869 he tried to better his finances with a reading tour in London, but poor health soon forced him to abandon the enterprise. In 1870 Gladstone granted him a civil-list pension of £100, but by 1874 his circumstances were so serious that he left Oban and settled in Rossport, co. Mayo, in an attempt to reduce his expenses. A collection of his poems in three volumes appeared that year and met with some public acclaim; but his next poetic production, an epic entitled *Balder the Beautiful: a Song of Divine Death* (1877), was received with indifference. Buchanan was, meanwhile, diversifying his literary output in an attempt to restore his fortunes. He returned to writing for the stage with an adaptation of Walter Scott's novel *Woodstock* called *A Madcap Prince* (1874); and in 1876 his first novel, *The Shadow of the Sword*, was published. His subsequent output in these two genres was prolific. He went on to write or collaborate in no fewer than forty-seven additional plays during the remaining twenty-seven years of his life—seven in 1890 alone—and to publish a further twenty-four novels. His plays include adaptations of his own novels *The Shadow of the Sword* and *God and the Man*, and a version of Dostoyevsky's *Crime and Punishment* called *The Sixth Commandment* (1890). His plays and novels proved more popular than his poetry and the upturn in his fortunes enabled him to move back to London in 1877.

In November 1881 Buchanan's wife died, and he dedicated his *Selected Poems* (1882) to her memory 'in sure and certain hope of a heavenly resurrection', language scarcely consistent with the Owenite and anti-religious beliefs with which he had been brought up. From this point onward his family consisted of his mother and his wife's younger sister Harriet. Harriet became an author in her own right, writing novels and co-authoring some plays with Buchanan; and in 1884 she accompanied him to the United States to oversee the production in Philadelphia of one of their joint efforts, *Alone in London*. During this visit he took the opportunity to make the acquaintance of Walt Whitman. He had long been one of Whitman's most enthusiastic and vociferous British supporters, having championed the American writer's work as early as 1868, and having urged British readers to send the impecunious American poet financial assistance.

Although his literary and dramatic profits were substantial, Buchanan, who was generous in his gifts to less successful writers, was always improvident. He took up gambling, and was eventually bankrupted by an unwise speculation on the production of his own play, *A Social Butterfly*, in 1894. Just a few months later, in November 1894, his mother died, casting a further shadow over the remaining years of his life. Buchanan suffered a stroke in October 1900 and died in comparative poverty at Streatham, London, on 10 June 1901. He was buried at Southend-on-Sea, Essex, according to the rites of the Church of England.

Buchanan's voluminous literary output was little read after the nineteenth century. His chief claim to the modern reader's interest appears increasingly to reside in his critical and journalistic work. The 'fleshly' controversy is a central but in many ways misleading episode in his life. It appears, at first sight, to cast him as a stereotypical Victorian prude disgusted by the 'loose' morals of Swinburne, Rossetti, and their followers, but other elements of his work indicate a continuing allegiance to the radical socialist heritage of his parents. He was, for instance, outspoken in his condemnation of British imperialism during the last decade of his life; and one of his last articles was an attack on Rudyard Kipling's 'Barrack-Room Ballads' entitled 'The voice of the hooligan' (*Contemporary Review*, Dec 1899).   J. P. PHELAN

Sources H. Jay, *Robert Buchanan* (1903) · J. A. Cassidy, *Robert W. Buchanan* (1973) · *The Swinburne letters*, ed. C. Y. Lang, 6 vols. (1959–62) · *Letters of Dante Gabriel Rossetti*, ed. O. Doughty and J. R. Wahl, 4 vols. (1965–7)
Archives BL, corresp. and papers, MSS, Add. MS 52480 | NL NZ, Turnbull L., letters to Robert Browning · NL Scot., letters to J. S. Blackie
Likenesses Barraud, photograph, pubd 1893, NPG [*see illus.*] · W. Roffe, stipple and line print (after photograph by Elliott & Fry), NPG · R. Taylor & Co., wood-engravings, BM, NPG; repro. in *ILN* (15 Oct 1892) · bust, St John's Church, Southend-on-Sea, Essex · photographs, repro. in Jay, *Robert Buchanan*, frontispiece and facing p. 308

Buchanan, Thomas Ryburn (1846–1911), politician, was born at Partick, Lanarkshire, on 2 April 1846, the third son of John Buchanan (1807–1876), of Dowanhill, Glasgow, a merchant and founder of the Dowanhill prizes in Glasgow University, and Jane (d. 1899), daughter of John Young. According to the account of his funeral in *The Times* he had two surviving brothers and four sisters. His elder brother, John Young *Buchanan FRS (1844–1925), achieved distinction as a scientist. The family name had been made in the last quarter of the eighteenth century by Buchanan's grandfather, James, who founded the trading firm of Buchanan, Steven & Co. Buchanan was educated at Glasgow high school, Sherborne School, and Balliol College, Oxford. He graduated BA in 1870, after a highly successful undergraduate career, gaining a double first in classics and mathematics, and the Stanhope prize in 1868; he graduated MA in 1872. Buchanan was elected a fellow of All Souls College, Oxford, in 1871 and in 1873 was called to the bar at the Inner Temple. As a fellow of All Souls he was in charge of the Codrington Library, building up something of a reputation as a bibliophile. His connection with the college ended with his marriage in 1888 to Emily, daughter of T. S. Bolitho of Trengwainton, Cornwall. The marriage appears to have been childless.

In his political career Buchanan was affected more than most by the vicissitudes the Liberal Party experienced at this time. At the general election of 1880 he stood in East Lothian against Lord Elcho, later the earl of Wemyss, but lost by forty-four votes. Compensation came the following year when he was elected unopposed for Edinburgh City at a by-election. In July 1886 he was returned as a Liberal Unionist for Edinburgh West and was therefore in parliament at the time of the political crisis over Irish home rule. It is recorded that he was:

a sensitive man, perhaps too sensitive for the rough works of politics, and his position at this crisis was far from comfortable. He found the arguments against Mr. Gladstone's policy unanswerable, but it cost him a painful effort to vote against his leader and his party. (*The Times*, 8 April 1911)

Within two years the pain had proved too much and he returned to his Gladstonian allegiance, resigning his seat and narrowly winning the by-election consequently held in February 1888. At the general election of 1892, however, he was heavily defeated. Buchanan re-entered parliament at a by-election held in Aberdeenshire East in December 1892 and continued to represent that constituency until he was again defeated in 1900. At this time and later in Perthshire East, which he represented between February 1903 and his retirement in January 1910, he appears in his efforts to win the support of his constituents to have struggled with his own manner and peculiar accent, which was said to have suggested Oxford rather than agricultural Scotland. His voting record shows him, despite his lapse in 1886–7, to have been on the whole a faithful Gladstonian. He was for restraint in public expenditure, especially on the armed forces, and for disestablishment of the Scottish and Welsh churches.

Buchanan's ministerial career began late in life, a function of his party's being out of office for so long at the turn of the century. He was nearly sixty when he was appointed financial secretary to the War Office in December 1905. He had no opportunity to shine in this department under Viscount Haldane, but he did make a valuable contribution to the reorganization of the army and territorials that was undertaken at this time. The peak of Buchanan's career was his period as parliamentary under-secretary for India, an office he held from April 1908 until June 1909 when illness forced him to resign. Lord Morley, the India secretary, was in the Lords, which left Buchanan as the government's front man in the Commons. As such he was responsible for responding to criticisms, especially by radicals, of its reform of Indian government. Buchanan died at Fontmel Priory in Bournemouth, on 7 April 1911, the victim of the chronic Bright's disease that had forced his resignation nearly two years before. His funeral was held in Arborfield near Reading. His wife survived him.

GORDON F. MILLAR

Sources *The Scotsman* (8 April 1911) · *Glasgow Herald* (8 April 1911) · *The Times* (8 April 1911) · *The Times* (12 April 1911) · *Dod's Parliamentary Companion* (1909) · G. Stronach, *25 years of politics, or, The political record of Mr T. R. Buchanan* (1906) · Foster, *Alum. Oxon.* · d. cert.
Archives BL, diary, Add. MS 52520 [fragment] · Bodl. Oxf., MSS collection · priv. coll. | All Souls Oxf., letters to Sir William Anson · BL, letters to Sir Henry Campbell-Bannerman, Add. MSS 41232–41242
Wealth at death £144,767 2s. 6d.: resworn probate, 22 May 1911, CGPLA Eng. & Wales

Buchanan, Walter John [Jack] (1890–1957), actor and theatre manager, was born on 2 April 1890 at Helensburgh, near Glasgow, the son of Walter John Buchanan (d. 1902), auctioneer, and his wife, Patricia Purves McWatt (d. 1936). When his father died leaving little provision, the family, including Jack's elder sister, Jessie, moved to Glasgow where his mother took in boarders. Educated at Glasgow Academy, Buchanan tried his father's old profession, but

Walter John Buchanan (1890–1957), by unknown photographer, 1929

his failure encouraged dreams of a theatrical career. He had a hard professional apprenticeship in the rough world of the northern music-hall as Chump Buchanan, patter comedian, adopting his schoolboy nickname; the rowdy hostility of the audiences remained engraved on his memory. But he persisted, finally making his West End début, in September 1912, as a dancing master in Lausi Wylie's comic opera, *The Grass Widow*.

Buchanan was declared unfit for military service, his health damaged by years of malnutrition. He began to attract notice for his immaculate attire and languid elegance, and emerged as a possible successor to George Grossmith when he appeared in Fred Thompson's *Tonight's the Night* at the Gaiety Theatre in April 1915. Stardom came in André Charlot's revues, beginning with *Bubbly* in 1917. Buchanan starred opposite Gertrude Lawrence in Charlot's most successful revue, *A to Z* (1921), where he first performed what became his signature song, 'And her mother came too'. Transferred to Broadway as *André Charlot's Revue of 1924*, the show successfully introduced the American public to the distinctive charms of the intimate revue as opposed to the Ziegfeld spectaculars.

On his return to Britain Buchanan established himself as London's pre-eminent actor–manager of musical comedy. From the Ruritanian antics of Douglas Furber and Harry Graham's *Toni* (1924) through to Furber and L. Arthur Rose's *It's Time to Dance* (1943), his shows followed a set pattern, designed to demonstrate his versatility as a comedian, singer, and dancer. He performed with several glamorous *ingénues*, including Binnie Hale, but his long-term partner was Elsie Randolph, starting with Furber's *That's a Good Girl* in 1928. His throwaway nonchalance was complemented superbly by her spirited vivacity. Theirs was a world of light-hearted facetiousness played out in glamorous modern settings created by leading designers such as Ernest Stern. Buchanan rarely strayed from this milieu. When he played the romantic lead in *The King's Rhapsody* after the sudden death of Ivor Novello in 1951, it was from duty not choice.

Buchanan starred in two early Hollywood talkies, *Paris* (1929), and *Monte Carlo* (1930) directed by Ernst Lubitsch. However, he was supplanted by the Gallic charms of Maurice Chevalier and reverted to British films, which were usually straightforward adaptations of his stage successes, including *That's a Good Girl* (1933) and *This'll Make you Whistle* (1936) for Herbert Wilcox's British and Dominion. His romantic lead in Wilcox's *Goodnight Vienna* (1932) opposite Anna Neagle was an exception. *Brewster's Millions* and *Come out of the Pantry* (both 1935) were better tailored to his image as the affable playboy. He made a late return to Hollywood in MGM's *The Band Wagon* (1953). His duet with Fred Astaire showed the profound differences between American pep and English aristocratic nonchalance.

Buchanan's popularity was augmented by sales of sheet music, records, and his frequent performances on radio especially during the Second World War, including *The Jack Buchanan Programme*. The eight-part series *Man about Town* (1955) was a huge success, recreating many of his most famous sketches and numbers. He also compèred many variety shows on radio and subsequently television and made guest appearances on both sides of the Atlantic.

Buchanan had extensive business interests. In various partnerships he built and owned the Leicester Square Theatre and the Imperial in Brighton and also controlled the Garrick and the King's Theatre in Hammersmith. In partnership with J. Arthur Rank and Charles Woolf, in 1937 he formed Jack Buchanan Productions which owned Riverside Studios in Hammersmith. He jointly owned, with his schoolfriend John Logie Baird, Television Limited, an innovative manufacturing and rental company. His ambitious plans were often beset with financial difficulties, but among his fellow professionals Buchanan was known for his probity, generosity, and loyalty.

Buchanan's reputation as the 'eternal bachelor' was maintained by guarding the secret of his marriage, on 25 November 1915, to Saffo Arnau (*b.* 1893), a singer known professionally as Drageva; it was annulled in 1920 and the *Daily Mail*, at the time of Buchanan's death, suggested that it had been a marriage of convenience to allow Saffo Arnau British citizenship. In 1947 he met the American Susan Bassett, twenty-five years his junior. They were married on 14 January 1949 and lived with Theo, the daughter from her previous marriage. Buchanan also kept secret that he was suffering from cancer and he continued performing on stage, films, radio, and television right to the end. His last professional appearance was at the opening of Scottish ITV at the Theatre Royal, Glasgow, in August

1957. His final film, *The Diaries of Major Thompson*, writer–director Preston Sturges's satire of the English gentleman, was released posthumously. Jack Buchanan died in the Middlesex Hospital, London, on 20 October 1957. His property ventures had depleted his estate, which was relatively modest. A private memorial service was held on board the *Queen Mary*, his ashes scattered on Southampton Water. An official service followed, at St Columba's, the foremost Scottish church in London.

Buchanan's achievement was to become an international male icon. He incarnated the urbane, fashionably elegant man about town, Mr Mayfair, able to overcome any obstacle in an easy-going manner. As his generation's Beau Brummell, in 1924 he introduced the prince of Wales to the American-style double-breasted dinner jacket, which rapidly became the modern norm. On stage or screen his tall, slim figure was always immaculately clothed, most often in midnight-blue tails, white tie, and silk top hat, with a black malacca cane. His limber dancing, apparently casual and spontaneous, was complemented by a slightly husky light tenor voice considered both pleasant and alluring. His whole style was especially notable for a relaxed, affable grace and charm which gave him tremendous sex appeal, but he was also admired by men who envied and hoped to emulate his insouciant *savoir faire*. It was a particularly British form of male display: understated, apparently effortless, the quintessence of 'good form' that refused to take itself too seriously.

ANDREW H. SPICER

Sources M. Marshall, *Top hat and tails: the story of Jack Buchanan* (1978) · K. Gänzl, *The British musical theatre*, 2 (1986) · W. Macqueen-Pope, *The footlights flickered* (1959) · S. Wilson, 'Jack, Bobby and Ivor', *The rise and fall of the matinée idol*, ed. A. Curtis (1974), 75–84 · *The Times* (21 Oct 1957) · *Manchester Guardian* (21 Oct 1957) · *Daily Telegraph* (21 Oct 1957) · *Daily Mirror* (21 Oct 1957) · *Daily Mail* (21–2 Oct 1957) · DNB · R. Low, *The history of the British film*, 7: *1929–1939: film making in 1930s Britain* (1985) · R. Mander and J. Mitchenson, *Musical comedy* (1969) · R. Mander and J. Mitchenson, *Revue* (1971) · S. Morley, *Spread a little happiness: the first hundred years of the British musical* (1987) · H. Wilcox, *Twenty-five thousand sunsets* (1967) · A. Nicoll, *English drama, 1900–1930* (1973) · J. Richards, *The age of the dream palace: cinema and society in Britain, 1930–1939* (1984) · A. Spicer, 'Jack Buchanan: the "Man about Town" of British musical-comedies in the 1930s', *Musical moments: film and the performance of song and dance*, ed. I. Conrich and E. Tinknell [forthcoming]

Archives V&A NAL, miscellaneous material | FILM BFI NFTVA, performance footage · 'Tribute to Jack Buchanan', ITV (21 Oct 1957) [no copy exists] | SOUND BBC NSA, 'The Jack Buchanan story', 13 May 1958, LP38486

Likenesses A. Bassano, photographs, 1919, NPG · photograph, 1929, Kobal Collection, London [*see illus.*] · Baron, photograph, 1940–1949?, Garrick Theatre; repro. in Marshall, *Top hat and tails* · F. Coudrill, drawing, priv. coll. · J. H. Dowd, drawing, repro. in *Punch* (1 June 1938) · W. K. Haselden, drawing, repro. in *Punch* (21 May 1924) · J. Nash, drawing, priv. coll. · G. L. Stampa, drawing, repro. in *Punch* (24 Oct 1945) · R. P. Staples, drawing, priv. coll. · film and publicity stills, BFI, London · photographs, Hult. Arch. · photographs, repro. in Marshall, *Top hat and tails* · stills, Theatre Museum, London

Wealth at death £24,489 12s. 9d.: probate, 22 Jan 1958, CGPLA Eng. & Wales

Buchanan, William (1781–1863), lawyer, was born in Montrose, the son of David *Buchanan (1745–1812), printer and publisher; his brothers were David *Buchanan (1779–1848), editor of the *Edinburgh Courant*, and George *Buchanan (c.1790–1852), civil engineer. William Buchanan was educated at Edinburgh University; he studied law and was called to the bar in 1806. He married Elizabeth, daughter of James Gregory, minister of the parish of Banchory, Aberdeenshire; they had several children.

At the outset of his career Buchanan showed a strong leaning to whig principles, but he never made politics a profession and devoted himself to the bar. In 1813 he published *Reports of certain remarkable cases in the court of session and trials in the high court of justiciary*. These reports are marked by their purity of expression and their methodical arrangement. In 1856 he was appointed queen's advocate and solicitor of teinds, or tithes, on the death of Sir William Hamilton. He was now the oldest member of the Scottish bar, and peculiarly fitted for his office by his antiquarian bent. He published in November 1862 *A Treatise on the Law of Scotland on the Subject of Teinds*, which instantly became the standard authority on the subject. Towards the end of his career he largely withdrew from active work because of illness.

For the last forty years of his life Buchanan was one of the elders of the Glasite church. In the autumn of 1863 his health began to give way, and he died after a lingering illness on 18 December.

B. C. SKOTTOWE, *rev.* ERIC METCALFE

Sources *GM*, 3rd ser., 16 (1864), 392

Buchler, Adolph (1867–1939), college head, was born into a poor family of rabbinic stock on 18 October 1867 in the Slovakian village of Priekopa, then in Hungary. His father died in Adolph's infancy. He and his sister were brought up by their mother, whose brother was Adolph Neubauer (1831–1907), bibliographer and professor in biblical Hebrew at Oxford. Between 1887 and 1892 Buchler studied at the Budapest Jewish Seminary (where in 1892 he was ordained rabbi), Budapest University (philosophy), Leipzig University (where in 1890 he gained his doctorate on his—later published—dissertation on the Hebrew accents), and at the Breslau Jewish Seminary.

After some months in 1892 as assistant rabbi in Budapest, Buchler spent a year in Oxford as assistant to his uncle in identifying the Hebrew manuscripts at the Bodleian. In 1893 he was appointed to teach at the Vienna Jewish Seminary in Jewish studies. Buchler married Hermione Lowenthal (d. 1956) in 1895. They had six children. In 1906 his fame as pedagogue and original scholar led to his appointment as chief assistant to the ailing principal of Jews' College, London, Michael Friedlander, whose retirement was followed by Buchler's succession on 1 August 1907. The college was the Orthodox seminary intended principally for the training of rabbis and ministers for the congregations of the United Synagogue in London and the many synagogues beyond which followed its pattern.

The new principal was a classicist, modern linguist, grammarian, and master of the substance and methods of the latest Jewish scholarship. According to his pupil and

successor, Isidore Epstein, there was hardly a highway or byway of Jewish learning that did not attract Buchler's attention. His special field was Jewish life in Palestine in the generations both before and after 70 CE. His pioneering use of Talmudic sources, in addition to classical, was esteemed by Christian and Jewish scholars alike. Among the best-known of his numerous works were *The Political and Social Leaders (of the Jews) in Sepphoris in the Second and Third Centuries* (1909) and *Studies in Sin and Atonement in the Rabbinic Literature of the First Century* (1928).

Buchler was slightly built, with an angular face and quizzical expression. He was firmly Orthodox, with a deep sense of duty in all things. He readily shared his vast knowledge and remarkable memory with fellow scholars. His famously meticulous preparation of his lectures was matched by his interest in the welfare and progress of his students, who revered him as instructor and friend. When the chief rabbi, J. H. Hertz, described him in 1927 as 'a scholar's scholar', it was intended as a compliment. But the quality was not unreservedly welcomed by the doubters of the practical utility of higher levels of rabbinic study in the training of the Jewish 'clergy'. They declared their preference for 'a wide secular education and considerable general culture', and also for the transfer of Jews' College to Oxford or Cambridge. Buchler led the opposition, and the plan was not proceeded with.

Buchler's modest bearing belied his readiness to fight for his point of view. The contrasting opinions and consequent tensions remained throughout his tenure. On 24 March 1931 he used the celebration of the college's seventy-fifth anniversary (1930) to deliver a tirade against his community's lay leaders, many of whom were present, for their limited concern for—and neglect of—Jewish higher studies generally. While his immense contribution to Jewish scholarship was acknowledged, his ambitions for the college were unfulfilled. He saw the inadequate provision of resources as a reflection of communal priorities which were not his.

Buchler died suddenly on 19 February 1939 at his home, 261 Goldhurst Terrace, Hampstead, and was buried on 21 February at the Willesden Jewish cemetery in London. Among the mourners was the chief rabbi of Palestine, Isaac Herzog. ISRAEL FINESTEIN

Sources B. Marmorstein, 'Adolph Buchler', *Jewish Historical Studies*, 30 (1987–8), 219–26 [extended bibliography, pp. 227–34] · A. M. Hyamson, *Jews' College, London, 1855–1955* (1955) · A. Buchler, *Studies in Jewish history*, ed. I. Brodie and J. Rabbinowitz (1956), xxiii–xxx [with biographical memoir by then principal of the college, Rabbi Dr Isidore Epstein, and bibliography] · J. H. Hertz, 'Memoir', *Jews' College Annual Report* (1939) [including parts of Hertz's tribute to Buchler in 1927] · *Jewish Chronicle* (24 Feb 1939) · *Jews' College jubilee volume* (1906) [with history of the college by Isidore Harris (pp. 175–6 on Buchler)] · private information (2004) [family] · *CGPLA Eng. & Wales* (1939)
Archives Hebrew University, Jerusalem, papers
Likenesses photograph, c.1906, repro. in *Jews' College jubilee volume* · photograph (in later years), repro. in Hyamson, *Jews' College*
Wealth at death £14,340 19s. 1d.: probate, 18 April 1939, *CGPLA Eng. & Wales*

Buchman, Frank Nathan Daniel (1878–1961), evangelist, was born on 4 June 1878 in Pennsburg, Pennsylvania, the

Frank Nathan Daniel Buchman (1878–1961), by Howard Coster, 1938

second of two children of Franklin Buchman (1840–1921), merchant and hotelier, and his wife, Sarah Anna Greenwalt (d. 1925). Both parents were of Swiss German extraction, their ancestors having emigrated to America in the middle of the eighteenth century. His parents and the culture of Pennsylvania Dutch society (Buchman's father was more at home speaking Pennsylvanian Dutch than English) had a profound influence on him. According to Buchman, he learned from his father how to understand people, while he inherited from his mother his personal reserve, a sense of order, and an understanding of the line which divides right from wrong (Lean, 9). The Buchmans were orthodox Lutherans, and it was Mrs Buchman's cherished desire that her son should become a minister, a wish with which Buchman readily complied, especially after realizing the transformative power of religion at the tender age of five, when one Sunday he observed a well-known drunk of Pennsburg signalling his decision to reform by taking the penitent's stool in church.

At the age of eight Buchman attended Perkiomen Seminary at Pennsburg, run by the Schwenkfelders, a liberal German sect which advocated a personal and spiritual religion and believed—similarly to the Quakers—that 'the inner light' came through the direct inspiration and rule of the Holy Spirit. In 1894 Buchman went to Allentown high school and then to Muhlenberg College, a liberal arts institution owned and run by the Lutheran Ministerium. He graduated in 1899 at the age of twenty-one, with honourable mention and the Butler analogy prize. After three years at the Lutheran seminary at Mount Airy in Philadelphia (1899–1902) he was ordained a minister of the Lutheran church. While Buchman was at Mount Airy he became acquainted with the church's increasing emphasis on its mission to the poor and he began to see his future in that area. An evangelical conference in 1901 convinced him that winning people for Christ should be his main objective in life. After graduation Buchman started a new church, the Church of the Good Shepherd, in Overbrook, one of Philadelphia's growing suburbs. In 1904, inspired by the Christian hospices and the work of Friedrich von Bodelschwingh in Germany (with which he became acquainted during a holiday in 1903), Buchman opened a hospice himself and later, copying the work of Canon Barnett in the East End of London in the 1880s, he opened Settlement House in 1906, a place for children from the streets. After initial support by the Lutheran Church's home missions board, relations became strained over finances and Buchman resigned in October 1907.

A second visit to Europe led Buchman to attend the Keswick convention in Cumberland, an annual gathering of evangelical Christians, where he experienced his 'poignant vision of the Crucified' and realized 'I was as wrong as anybody else. I was most in need of change' (Howard, *Buchman's Secret*, 21). In January 1909 he accepted the post of YMCA secretary at Pennsylvania State College, the 'most godless university in the country' (Lean, 33), which became his laboratory to test the principles on which to work for change. His approach affected the lives of the most unlikely people and had a wider impact in the college. Buchman's practice of keeping a 'quiet time' every morning to receive 'guidance' started there, as did the emphasis on personal interviews and on encouraging individuals to testify to their decision of giving their lives unreservedly to Christ. Buchman's meetings spread and his methods were applied at other colleges. Despite his successes, Buchman was accused of self-advertisement and name-dropping by some critics.

After travels to India and China in 1915 and 1916, Buchman took a part-time job, extension lecturer in personal evangelism, at Hartford Theological Seminary, a small, non-sectarian college in New England with an evangelical tradition. In April 1919 he became convinced that a radical reawakening of faith was the long-term answer to the 'breakdown of civilisation' in the post-war period and that the young people in the universities needed to be won for this reawakening. Buchman started with conferences at Hartford and other colleges and in July 1920 he set the 'peripatetic fellowship' on the move with another visit to Europe. In May 1921, while at Cambridge, England, he had the sense that God was calling him to a wider task—'You will be used to remake the world' (Lean, 93)—which filled him with the sense of a specific mission. At

Oxford he was invited to join the Beef and Beer Club after which the first 'house party' took place in August 1921. It became a characteristic feature of Buchman's work—hence 'drawing-room conversion' (Eister)—as a way of bringing together an assortment of people for several days in a friendly, relaxed atmosphere where they might be able to take fundamental decisions for their lives. It had the flavour of the contemporary social house party but the essential purpose of a religious retreat, the main difference being the kind of people invited. In February 1922 Buchman resigned from Hartford and never held any paid position again.

Thus Buchman began a life and a career of a different kind, which had neither institutional affiliation nor salaried income. Throughout his life he relied entirely on voluntary donations to finance his activities and those working full-time for the movement. When he died, he owned no more than his family home in Allentown and a few thousand dollars given to him on his recent birthday. Although centred on Buchman, the movement underwent change as it expanded worldwide and as Buchman's outlook and emphasis shifted in the light of political events. The initial house parties increased in number and scale, although the core teachings remained the four 'absolutes' (absolute honesty, absolute purity, absolute unselfishness, absolute love), complemented by the practice of sharing—the confession of sins—and guidance. The name 'A First Century Christian Fellowship' was chosen in late 1922 to secure support and define aims. According to Buchman, it was to be 'a voice of protest against the organised, committeeised and lifeless Christian work' and an 'attempt to get back to the beliefs and methods of the Apostles' (Lean, 97).

The movement gained the designation the Oxford Group after a trip of Oxford students to South Africa, and in 1937 it was registered as a legal body under that name. In 1938 Moral Re-Armament was launched in east London, with Buchman proclaiming that 'The next great move in the world will be a movement of moral re-armament for all nations' (Lean, 262). The term Buchmanism was subsequently coined by an opponent and critics referred to Buchmanites. Buchman's personal approach and his conviction that nations and their leaders needed to be directed 'Godwards' and put under 'God control' brought him in contact with key people, political, religious, and trade union leaders across the world, who were open to his message. However, his attempts to take his methods to Germany during the Nazi regime—Buchman had contact with Heinrich Himmler and tried to meet Hitler—roused controversy and raised suspicion, especially in the light of an interview in 1936 in which he was quoted as having stated 'I thank heaven for a man like Adolf Hitler, who built a frontline of defense against the anti-Christ of Communism' (Lean, 239). After the Second World War, Buchman focused on reconciliation between nations, notably France and Germany, on trade relations, on the emerging countries in Africa, on east Asia, and on the cold war. In the early 1940s the former Palace Hotel (Mountain House)

at Caux-sur-Montreux in Switzerland was turned into the European meeting-place for Moral Re-Armament assemblies, while in America, Mackinac Island in the Great Lakes was used as the training centre for Moral Re-Armament.

Apart from Buchman's alleged attitude towards Hitler, there had also been fierce debates over whether the group should be allowed to use Oxford for its registered name (in 1937), and whether Moral Re-Armament's lay evangelists should qualify for exemption from conscription (in the late 1930s). In the movement's earlier phase, concerns were voiced about public confessions at meetings. Buchman was criticized for 'hobnobbing with the nabobs', for disdaining the efforts of other Christians, for paying uncritical deference to people of birth and social position, and for being prone to exaggerations. (Buchman hated understatement.) In the cold war period, Moral Re-Armament was suspected of being an instrument for anti-communist propaganda in America. Princeton University, a working party of the Church of England's social and industrial council, and the secretariat of the international confederation of free trades unions all commissioned inquiries, and the Roman Catholic church distanced itself sharply from the movement with a warning to Catholics.

Buchman's evangelist mission is not easy to categorize, as it evolved over time and was stamped by his personality. He was not particularly original in his teachings, using Robert E. Speer's summary of Christ's moral teachings as his main tenets and deriving his practices, such as the 'quiet time' and personal interviews, from advice given by F. B. Meyer. The idea for a spiritual and moral re-armament came from the Swedish socialist author Harry Blomberg. Nor was Buchman a prolific writer; there is a collection of speeches (*Remaking the World*), together with some widely circulated statements towards the end of his life. However, Buchman used—probably intuitively—the powerful sway of the narrative, both in house parties and assemblies, when individuals told their conversion stories, and in numerous plays and musicals, such as *The Forgotten Factor* (1940), *The Vanishing Island* (1955), *The Road to Tomorrow* (1955), *The Crowning Experience* (1958), and *Hoffnung* (1960), which toured the world and some of which were made into films. They were written by close collaborators, such as Peter Howard and Alan Thornhill, or by participants at meetings.

Buchman seems to have been neither particularly charismatic nor attractive, yet he had a way of drawing people towards him. Sir Arthur Lunn commented:

> He has no charisma that I can see. He isn't good-looking, he
> is no orator, he has never written a book and he seldom even
> leads a meeting. Yet statesmen and great intellectuals come
> from all over the world to consult him, and a lot of
> intelligent people have stuck with him, full time without
> salary, for forty years, when they could have been making
> careers for themselves. Why? (Lean, 2)

His appearance was that of a tall, stoutish, quietly dressed man with 'a long pointed nose in a round face' (Lean, 228), with rimless glasses and a pleasant voice. He was obviously American, 'with that mien of scrupulous shampooed, and almost medical cleanness or freshness' (ibid., 134, 106).

Buchman remained unmarried throughout his life, feeling that a single man could do better work than a married man, although he was not opposed to marriage and liked children. In 1942 he suffered a severe stroke, which impaired his speech and paralysed his right side. He recovered, but his right leg and hand remained affected. Combined with a long-term heart condition and from 1956 failing eyesight, Buchman's health forced him to slow down and rely on his entourage for organization and communication. By 1959 his strength was strictly limited and he was generally moved about in a wheelchair. In 1961 Buchman went to Freudenstadt, Black Forest, Germany, to rest and regain strength. He died there on 8 August 1961, at the age of eighty-three. On 18 August 1961 Buchman was buried in Allentown in the family plot, after a funeral service at St John's Lutheran Church, Allentown, where he had been ordained.   ELISABETH ARWECK

Sources H. W. Austin, *Frank Buchman as I knew him* (1975) • D. C. Belden, 'The origins and development of the Oxford group (Moral Rearmament)', DPhil diss., U. Oxf., 1975 • F. Buchman, *Remaking the world: speeches on Moral Rearmament* (1958) [translated into German as *Für eine neue Welt: Gesammelte Reden von Frank N. D. Buchman* (1961)] • *Moral Re-Armament* (1955) [Church Information Board and Social and Industrial Council of the National Assembly of the Church of England (Church Assembly)] • R. Dilly, *Discovering Moral Re-Armament* (1995) • T. Driberg, *The mystery of Moral Re-Armament: a study of Frank Buchman and his movement* (1964) • A. W. Eister, *Drawing-room conversion* (1950) • N. G. Ekman, *Experiment with God: Frank Buchman reconsidered* (1972) • P. Howard, *Innocent men* (1941) • P. Howard, *The world rebuilt: the true story of Frank Buchman and the men and women of Moral Rearmament* (1951) • P. Howard, *Frank Buchman's secret* (1961) • G. Lean, *Frank Buchman: a life* (1985) • G. Marcel, *Fresh hope for the world: Moral Rearmament in action* (1960) • G. Williamson, *Inside Buchmanism: an independent inquiry into the Oxford group movement and Moral Rearmament* (1954)

Likenesses H. Coster, photograph, 1938, NPG [*see illus.*]

Buck, Adam (1759–1833), miniature and portrait painter, was born in Castle Street, Cork, the elder son of Jonathan Buck, a silversmith, of Castle Street, and brother of Frederick Buck [*see below*]. His artistic training remains obscure but an anonymously published article in volume 26 of the *Journal of the Cork Historical and Archaeological Society* (1920) records that he studied under a little-known artist called Minasi. However, Anthony Pasquin states that he was self-taught (Pasquin, 41).

By the 1780s Buck was well established in Ireland as a miniature portrait painter working in watercolour on ivory. He lived in Cork and later moved to Dublin but travelled about the country for commissions. He specialized in painting small, whole-length portraits in watercolour on card, a type of portrait he popularized. He also did portraits on card with a special wax crayon which he invented. His early portraits, such as his group portrait in watercolour on paper of the Edgeworth family (1787, priv. coll.; exh. Dublin, Belfast, and London 1969–70) and the miniatures of the Ellis family (National Gallery of Ireland, Dublin), show that he had evolved his own decorative neo-

Adam Buck (1759–1833), self-portrait, 1813 [*The Artist and his Family*]

classical style early in his career. This was commented on by Pasquin, who may have known Buck when he was in Ireland. In an account of Buck's life, written along with a note on beauty, Pasquin stated: 'He [Buck] appears to study the antique more rigorously than any of our emerging artists and by that means he will imbibe a chastity of thinking, which may eventually lead him to the personification of apparent beauty' (Pasquin, 41).

In 1795 Buck moved permanently to London, where he lived at 174 Piccadilly (1795–8), Frith Street, Soho (1799–1802), and Bentinck Street (1813–20). He had a fashionable clientele which included George IV, the duke of York, the duke's mistress Mary Anne Clarke, the opera singer Angelica Catalani, the politician Sir Francis Burdett, the art collector Thomas Hope (all National Portrait Gallery, London), the seventh earl and the countess of Cavan, Lady Chatterton, and the actor J. P. Kemble. He also taught drawing and portrait painting. From 1795 to 1833 he exhibited over 170 miniatures and small, full-length portraits at the Royal Academy. He also exhibited at the British Institution and the Society of British Artists in Suffolk Street. He only exhibited once in Ireland, in 1802, when he sent a portrait to the Society of Artists in Ireland exhibition at the parliament house, Dublin.

Buck influenced Regency taste through his work, which was engraved and widely published. He did fashion plates, produced decorative engravings, and did illustrations (1801) for Sterne's *Sentimental Journey*. The decorative pieces were fanciful genre pictures of mothers and children, personifications of Faith, Hope, and Charity, and classical subjects such as Cupid and Psyche. Sentimental figurative pieces were used to decorate furniture and were adapted as designs for the decoration of china, embroidery, and fans.

Buck was greatly influenced by the Greek Revival and he

included Greek vases and sculpture, as well as Greek-inspired furniture, in his portraits. His sitters wear high-waisted muslin dresses and have curly hair-styles *à la grecque*. He was a collector of Greek vases and was familiar with private collections which he used as devices in his work, as in his *Self-Portrait with his Family* (Yale U. CBA).

Buck published a prospectus for a book on Greek vase painting: *Proposals for publishing by subscription 100 engravings from paintings on Greek vases which have never been published, drawn and etched by Adam Buck from private collections now in England, dedicated to the earl of Carlisle* (1811). This publication was intended as a continuation of Sir William Hamilton's *Collection of Engravings from Ancient Vases ...* (1791–7) and the prints were to be issued in fascicles of ten, over a period of one year. Public interest must have been slight, as only one instalment of ten etched outlines seems to have been issued (on 31 March 1812), and contrary to almost all accounts of Buck's life the book *Paintings on Greek Vases* was never published. The only recorded copy of the prospectus is in the British Museum. The drawings and aquatint engravings for the unpublished book are in the Library of Trinity College, University of Dublin.

Adam Buck died in 1833 at his home, 15 Upper Seymour Street, London. He was survived by his wife, Margaret, and two sons, Alfred (b. c.1813) and Sidney (b. c.1813), the latter of whom also became a miniature painter. A miniature self-portrait by Buck is in the Victoria and Albert Museum, London; other work is in the collections of the National Gallery of Ireland, Dublin; the British Museum, National Portrait Gallery, and Kenwood House (the Draper gift), London; the Yale Center for British Art, New Haven, Connecticut; the Metropolitan Museum of Art, New York; and the Art Institute of Chicago.

Adam Buck's brother **Frederick Buck** (1771–c.1839/40) was also a miniature painter. He was admitted as a pupil to the Dublin Society's drawing school in 1782. He practised over a long period as a miniature painter in Cork, where he executed many portraits of officers prior to their embarkation on ships bound for the Peninsular War. His work is inferior to that of his brother, the features often badly drawn and modelled; this is probably the result of their being imposed on partly painted ivories to which he hastily added faces and regimental facings. He also engraved some book-plates. Successful in his work, Buck retired some years before his death about 1839 or 1840. Examples of his miniatures are in the Victoria and Albert Museum, London, and the National Gallery of Ireland, Dublin. PAUL CAFFREY

Sources W. G. Strickland, *A dictionary of Irish artists*, 1 (1913), 117–23 · B. S. Long, *British miniaturists* (1923), 52–3 · D. Foskett, *Miniatures: dictionary and guide* (1987) · I. Jenkins, 'Adam Buck and the vogue for Greek vases', *Burlington Magazine*, 130 (1988), 448–57 · P. Caffrey, 'Irish portrait miniatures, c.1700–1830', PhD diss., Southampton Institute, 1995 · P. G. Lee, *Journal of the Cork Historical and Archaeological Society*, 2nd ser., 26 (1920), 40–41 · A. Pasquin [J. Williams], *An authentic history of the professors of painting, sculpture, and architecture who have practiced in Ireland ... to which are added, Memoirs of the royal academicians* [1796], 41 · P. J. Noon, *English portrait drawings and miniatures* (New Haven, CT, 1979) [exhibition catalogue, Yale U. CBA, 5 Dec 1979 – 17 Feb 1980] · A. M. Stewart, ed., *Irish art loan exhibitions, 1765–1927*, 1 (1990), 89 · A. Crookshank and the Knight of Glin [D. Fitzgerald], *The watercolours of Ireland: works on paper in pencil, pastel and paint, c.1600–1914* (1994) · A. Crookshank and the Knight of Glin [D. Fitzgerald], eds., *Irish portraits, 1660–1860* (1969) [exhibition catalogue, Dublin, London, and Belfast, 14 Aug 1969 – 9 March 1970] · A. Le Harivel, ed., *National Gallery of Ireland: illustrated summary catalogue of drawings, watercolours and miniatures* (1983) · *Proceedings of the Dublin Society*, 19 (1782–3), 42 · DNB · IGI
Likenesses A. Buck, self-portrait, miniature watercolour on ivory, 1804, V&A · A. Buck, self-portrait, watercolour on card, 1813 (with members of his family), Yale U. CBA, Paul Mellon collection [see illus.]

Buck, Charles (1771–1815), theological writer and Independent minister, was born at Hillsley, near Wotton under Edge, Gloucestershire, and began preaching at the age of seventeen in a room in Black Horse Court, Fleet Street, London. He was pastor of an Independent congregation in Sheerness until 1797, when he moved to Princes Street, Moorfields, where he remained five years before moving to Wilson Street. After seven years he made his final move, to the City Chapel, Grub Street (later Milton Street). He also served as secretary to Hoxton Academy.

Buck was the author of a well-known work, of which many editions appeared both in England and America, entitled *A theological dictionary, containing definitions of all theological and ecclesiastical terms; an impartial account of the several denominations that have subsisted in the religious world; remarkable transactions and events in ecclesiastical history, and a biographical sketch of writers in theological science*. The first edition appeared in London in two volumes in 1802; a new, enlarged edition was published by Ebenezer Henderson in 1833, and again in 1841. Buck was also author of a *Collection of Anecdotes* (1799), which went through many editions, and of several lesser religious works. He died on 11 August 1815 and was buried in Bunhill Fields.

W. G. BLAIKIE, rev. K. D. REYNOLDS

Sources *A religious encyclopaedia, or, Dictionary of biblical, historical, doctrinal and practical theology: based on the real encyklopadie* (sic) *of Herzog et. al.*, ed. P. Schaff, 2 vols. (1883) · J. A. Jones, ed., *Bunhill memorials* (1849)
Archives DWL, corresp. and papers as secretary of Hoxton Academy
Likenesses I. W. Ridley, stipple (after Robinson), BM, NPG; repro. in *Evangelical Magazine* (1803)

Buck, Frederick (1771–c.1839/40). *See under* Buck, Adam (1759–1833).

Buck, Sir George (*bap.* 1560, *d.* 1622), master of the revels and historian, was baptized in Holy Trinity, Ely, Cambridgeshire, on 1 October 1560, the eldest son and probably second of the four children of Robert Buck (*d.* 1580), church official, and Elizabeth Nunn, *née* Petterill, of Brandon Ferry, Suffolk. He studied under Henry Blaxton first at Higham Ferrers, Northamptonshire, then probably at Chichester Cathedral school, and proceeded to Cambridge, possibly to Trinity Hall. By 1580 he was in London, where he became a probationer at Thavies Inn, and in 1585 he entered the Middle Temple from New Inn. He was envoy to France in 1587 and in 1588 served against the Spanish Armada under his patron, Lord Admiral Charles Howard. Howard recommended him to Queen Elizabeth, who was favourably impressed by him, and procured for him the parliamentary seat of Gatton, Surrey, in 1593 and 1597. Buck served on the Cadiz expedition in 1596 and was envoy from the commanders to the queen. His account of the expedition appears anonymously in John Stow's *Annales*. He was appointed esquire of the body in 1588. On James I's accession he became a gentleman of the privy chamber and was knighted. He served on diplomatic missions to Flanders in 1601 and Spain in 1605.

In 1603 King James granted Buck the reversion of the mastership of revels, which Queen Elizabeth may have promised him. In 1606 Buck obtained the authority to license plays for publication, a function independent of the revels office. Though this has led to the assumption that he assisted his predecessor, Edmund Tilney, in the revels office, there is no evidence that he did so; he succeeded Tilney as master in 1610. His main responsibilities, during this most flourishing period of English dramatic activity, were censoring plays for stage performance and selecting and arranging for entertainments at court during the revels season from the end of October to the end of February and also at special events—feasts such as Easter and Whitsun, visits of foreign dignitaries, and annual triumphs celebrating the king's accession. His duties, which took him to Whitehall, Somerset House, the palace at Greenwich, and other royal residences, included arrangement of bear-baitings, dancing, and tilts. They required, he claimed, expertise in grammar, rhetoric, logic, philosophy, history, music, mathematics, and other arts (Buck, 'Third Universitie', sig. Oooo 3v). As censor he seems to have been conscientious but not severe; his comments and markings for deletion, revealed in manuscripts of the anonymous *Second Maiden's Tragedy* (BL, MS Lansdowne, 807, fols. 29–56) and of Fletcher and Massinger's *Sir John Van Olden Barnevelt* (BL, MS Add. 18653), show him learned and gentlemanly. He implemented strictures against profanity, blasphemy, religious controversy, presentation of royalty on the stage and politically sensitive issues, and showed a concern—as in his scholarly works—for historical accuracy. Shakespeare's later plays all passed through his hands, and he was responsible for court performances by the King's Men of *The Tempest*, *The Winter's Tale*, *Much Ado about Nothing*, *Othello*, *1* and *2 Henry IV*, *Pericles*, and *Twelfth Night*, as well as plays by Massinger, Fletcher, Marston, Dekker, and Middleton, and masques by Samuel Daniel and Ben Jonson.

In addition to his court career, Sir George was a scholar and author. Highly regarded by William Camden and other leading scholars of his day, with whom he regularly exchanged books and information, he was probably a member of the original Society of Antiquaries; in 1620 the duke of Buckingham listed him as one of the scholars best qualified to compose an English Academy. Like his fellow scholars, he was interested in research into original records and in classifying and critically assessing historical sources. His main interests were genealogy and history, particularly in areas where recoverable fact conflicted with tradition. His first published work (1605, written 1602) was *Daphnis Polystephanos: an Eclog Treating of*

Crownes, and of Garlandes, a poem honouring James I's coronation and celebrating the king's ancestors. It contains the first hint of Buck's championship of Richard III and is as learned and heavily documented as his historical treatises. His 'Third Universitie of England' (1612), published as an appendix to the 1615 edition of John Stow's *Annales*, details the subjects—law, divinity, medicine, and various arts and sciences—that can be effectively studied in the capital, with the histories of the foundations that profess them. He wrote a treatise on the art of revels which does not survive, but we have his assessment of the theatre of his day: 'The first and most ancient kind of Poesy, the Dramatik, is so lively expressed and represented upon the publicke stages of this citty, as *Rome* in the *Auge* of her pompe & glorie, never saw it better performed' (Buck, 'Third Universitie', sig. Oooo lv). His huge work on the history of English titles and offices, *The Baron*, is not extant but some of the material he collected for it survives (Bodl. Oxf., MS Arch. Selden. B. 66). His only extant genealogical work is a manuscript 'Commentary upon … Liber domus Dei' (Bodl. Oxf., MS Eng. misc. b.106), tracing the history of the families who came in with the Conqueror. He wrote short poems in English, French, and Latin, translated part of *Orlando Furioso*, and devised dumb shows for the anonymous play *Locrine*.

The work for which Buck is known is *The History of King Richard the Third*, which, though he began a fair copy in 1619, he left in manuscript in a state of incomplete revision (BL, Cotton Tiberius E. X). His interest in the subject sprang from the fact that his great-grandfather John Buck supported Richard III at Bosworth and was executed and attainted after the battle. This pioneering revisionist study of the king is in five books: the first two detail the events of Richard's life and reign, the third examines and refutes the accusations against him, the fourth expounds the legality of his title, and the fifth surveys his achievements. Buck's method is that of a lawyer, pointing out that in law suspicion is not proof. Even though his style is tautological and his sympathy for Richard is evident, he lays down and generally adheres to high standards of historical writing: impartiality, critical appraisal of sources, and careful documentation. He considers the conditions under which the Tudor historians were obliged to write and exposes their bias, refuting it by reference to original documents. The public records had recently become available for consultation, enabling him to discover the 'Titulus regius', the document ratified by parliament which sets forth Richard's right to the throne. He also discovered the 'Second continuation' of the 'Chronicle of Croyland Abbey', a significant contemporary source, and used other manuscripts and oral reports.

From 1613 Sir George suffered difficulties with the exchequer over wages, and in 1618 a marriage mooted between him and Elizabeth Meutis of West Ham came to nothing. Becoming incompetent, he was succeeded as master of the revels by Sir John Astley on 29 March 1622, and declared a lunatic on 12 April. Taken in by his sister Susan and her husband, Francis Heydon, vicar of Broadwater, Sussex, he died there on 31 October that year, and was buried there on 15 November. His considerable estate was apparently left to his brother Robert (1570–1648), a Jesuit, but his nephew Stephen Buck presented a will, either forged or made after Sir George became insane, designating himself and his son George the heirs; they had already embezzled many of his effects during his madness, including many manuscript works.

Although in the next century William Maitland cited Buck as a major early historian and although all subsequent Ricardian apologists, including Horace Walpole, Sir Clements Markham, and Paul Murray Kendall, followed his structure and methods, Buck's scholarly reputation suffered eclipse for centuries because his great-nephew George Buck revised and passed off the work as his own, first making manuscript copies dedicated to various potential patrons, then publishing a drastically shortened version in 1646. He deleted personal and contemporary references, including firsthand information from reliable authorities, omitted much of the documentation, changed emphasis to make a reasoned defence read more like a harangue, made many careless errors, and rewrote passages in a florid and obscure style. Since the original manuscript, already difficult to read due to the author's revisions, suffered damage in the Cotton Library fire of 1731, most readers relied on the great-nephew's published edition, mistakenly assuming it to be the author's revised version, and thus concluded that Buck was a careless scholar. It was not until a modern edition of Sir George's original manuscript was published in 1979 that assessment could be made of his scholarly methods and competence. ARTHUR KINCAID

Sources M. Eccles, 'Sir George Buc, master of the revels', *Thomas Lodge and other Elizabethans*, ed. C. J. Sisson (1933), 408–507 · G. Buck, *The history of King Richard the Third*, ed. A. N. Kincaid (1979); repr. with corrections (1982) · R. Dutton, *Mastering the revels: the regulation and censorship of English Renaissance drama* (1991) · W. H. Challen, 'Sir George Buck, kt., master of the revels', *N&Q*, 202 (1957), 290–93, 324–7 · W. R. Streitberger, ed., *Jacobean and Caroline revels accounts, 1603–1642* (1986) · G. E. Bentley, *The Jacobean and Caroline stage*, 7 vols. (1941–68) · G. Buck, 'Commentary upon the new roulle of Winchester, comonly called Liber domus Dei', Bodl. Oxf., MS Eng. misc. b. 106 · G. Buck, 'The third universitie of England', in J. Stow, *The annales, or, Generall chronicle of England … unto the ende of this present yeere, 1614*, ed. E. Howes (1615), 958–88 · E. K. Chambers, *The Elizabethan stage*, 4 vols. (1923) · T. H. Howard-Hill, 'Buc and the censorship of *Sir John van Olden Barnavelt* in 1619', *Review of English Studies*, new ser., 39 (1988), 39–63 · T. M. McCoog, *English and Welsh Jesuits, 1555–1650*, 1, Catholic RS, 74 (1994), 130 · *CSP dom.*, 1619–23, 511 · J. Nichols, *The progresses, processions, and magnificent festivities of King James I, his royal consort, family and court*, 1 (1828), 215

Archives Bodl. Oxf., collections, draft chapters, and notes for *The Baron, or, The magazine of Honor* | BL, Add. MSS · BL, Cotton MSS · BL, Egerton MSS · BL, Lansdowne MSS · PRO

Wealth at death lands in Lincolnshire valued at £125 p.a.; house in St Peter's Hill, London; clothing, jewellery, plate, furniture, pictures, and books valued at approx. £3000; estate value suggested elsewhere £1400–£1500: *CSP dom.*, 511; Eccles, 483–96

Buck, John William (1780/81–1821), barrister, was the only son of John Buck of Town Hill, near Bradford, Yorkshire. He matriculated at Lincoln College, Oxford, on 27 April 1797 at the age of sixteen, and was admitted to the Middle Temple on 10 December 1805. He was called to the bar on 8 February 1811 and was admitted to Lincoln's Inn on 6 July 1813 as a barrister. He recorded the first forty-four pages of a volume of English reports of cases in bankruptcy decided by Lord Eldon, Sir Thomas Plumer, and Sir John Leach, from Michaelmas term 1816 to Michaelmas term 1820. The volume—the only one to appear—was published as *Cases in Bankruptcy* in Buck's name in 1820. Buck died on 23 August 1821 at his home, 31 Montagu Place, Russell Square, London.

ROBERT HARRISON, *rev.* BETH F. WOOD

Sources *GM*, 1st ser., 91/2 (1821), 284 · W. P. Baildon, ed., *The records of the Honorable Society of Lincoln's Inn* [incl. *Admissions*, 2 vols. (1896), and *Black books*, 6 vols. (1897–2001)] · Allibone, *Dict.* · Foster, *Alum. Oxon.* · H. A. C. Sturgess, ed., *Register of admissions to the Honourable Society of the Middle Temple, from the fifteenth century to the year 1944*, 2 (1949), 423

Buck, Nathaniel (*fl.* 1724–1759). *See under* Buck, Samuel (1696–1779).

Buck, Sir Percy Carter (1871–1947), musician, was born Percy Hartshorn Buck on 25 March 1871 in West Ham Lane, West Ham, Essex, the son of William Richard Buck, clerk in the War Office, and his wife, Alice Emmeline Wilson. He was educated at Merchant Taylors' School, and in 1891, after studying the organ with Walter Parratt at the Royal College of Music, he won an organ scholarship to Worcester College, Oxford, where he was awarded a BMus in 1892. Although he had completed the work for a DMus by 1893, the degree was not conferred until 1897. After leaving Oxford in 1894 he taught for a short time at Rugby School, taking up the post of organist at Wells Cathedral in 1896. In 1896 he married Lucy (d. 1940), eldest daughter of Thomas Bond FRCS, a surgeon at Westminster Hospital: they had three sons (one of whom was killed in the First World War) and two daughters. In 1899 he was appointed organist of Bristol Cathedral.

Buck became director of music at Harrow School in 1901, where he took the line that as very few of his piano pupils were likely to become concert performers, it was more important to turn them into useful musicians: accordingly he taught them to accompany, to transpose, and to extemporize. He also wrote three school songs: 'You?', 'Avete', and 'The Silver Arrow', and several hymn tunes for the Harrow School hymnbook. While at Harrow, Buck began a secret affair with the writer (Nora) Sylvia Townsend *Warner (1893–1978) which lasted for some seventeen years. Although Buck remained at Harrow until 1927, he took on several part-time positions as well: from 1910 to 1920 he was non-resident professor of music at Trinity College, Dublin, and he joined the staff of the Royal College of Music in 1919, appointed by the new director, Hugh Allen, to teach theory. In 1925 he was appointed King Edward professor of music at the University of London, a chair he held until 1937. Buck was particularly concerned with the training of music teachers, and at the Royal College of Music he helped to set up the teachers' training course, for which he lectured on psychology. In *The Scope of Music* (1924), based on his Cramb lectures at the University of Glasgow in 1923, he stressed the importance of the study of psychology for music teachers, and his topics included memory, habit, interest and attention, how to practise, and the art of explaining, with many practical examples and much useful advice. *Psychology for Musicians* (1944) remained in print for thirty years. He was also responsible for framing the syllabus of the graduate of the Royal Schools of Music (GRSM) diploma, designed to give school music teachers the same status (and pay) as university graduates. His influence on music education was not confined to the training of music teachers. From 1925 to 1937 he was musical adviser to the education committee of the London county council, and as well as revising the music curriculum in the elementary and secondary schools he selected talented children for music lessons at the Royal College of Music and the Royal Academy of Music. He was also professor of music at the University of Sheffield from 1927 to 1928.

Buck's other books included *The Organ: a Complete Method for the Study of Technique and Style* (1909), *Unfigured Harmony* (1911), and *Acoustics for Musicians* (1918). He edited the introductory volume (1929) to the *Oxford History of Music*, and revised the first two volumes, *The Polyphonic Period* (1929 and 1932) of the second edition, originally written by H. E. Woolridge in 1901. He edited the *Oxford Song Book*, volume one (1929) and the *Oxford Nursery Song Book* (1934), and was co-editor of *The English Psalter* (1925). The only organist on the editorial committee of the ten-volume *Tudor Church Music* (1922–9), published for the Carnegie Trust, he used his skill as a contrapuntist to supply missing parts. Buck was also a composer, and his published works include three organ sonatas (1896, 1902, and 1904), piano pieces, anthems, and songs. Fourteen of his hymn tunes were used in the 1916 edition of *Hymns Ancient and Modern*. In addition he wrote chamber music, including a string quintet, a piano quartet, and a violin sonata, and an overture, *Cœur de lion*: these were unpublished. His books and the manuscripts of many of his early unpublished works were destroyed in an air raid during the Second World War, a loss he felt deeply.

Buck was knighted in 1936. He died on 3 October 1947 in Stoneycrest Nursing Home, Hindhead, Surrey, after a short illness. ANNE PIMLOTT BAKER

Sources W. S. Lloyd-Webber, 'Sir Percy Carter Buck', *Music in Education*, 11 (1947–8), 167–9 • H. W. Shaw, *The succession of organists of the Chapel Royal and the cathedrals of England and Wales from c.1538* (1991), 41, 291–2 • 'Buck, Sir Percy Carter', *New Grove*, 2nd edn • *The Times* (7 Oct 1947) • *The Harrovian* (15 Oct 1947) • *WW* • b. cert. • d. cert. • *CGPLA Eng. & Wales* (1947) • C. Harman, *Sylvia Townsend Warner* (1989)

Likenesses photograph, repro. in Lloyd-Webber, 'Sir Percy', 167 • photograph, repro. in *The Harrovian*, 41/1 (25 Feb 1928)

Wealth at death £28,879 1s. 3d.: probate, 17 Nov 1947, *CGPLA Eng. & Wales*

Buck, Sir Peter Henry [*called* Te Rangi Hiroa] (1877?–1951), anthropologist and physician, was born in Urenui, Taranaki province, New Zealand. There is uncertainty over his birth date since it was not registered. Buck believed that he was born in 1880, but October 1877, the date recorded in his primary school register, is probably more accurate. His father, William Henry Buck (*d.* 1920), was born in co. Galway and migrated to New Zealand in 1862. He served in the armed constabulary, and settled at Urenui, Taranaki, where he married Ngarongo-ki-tua of the Ngati Mutunga people. However, she did not conceive, so a relative, Rina, was brought in to give William Buck a child. Rina died soon after Peter's birth.

Peter Buck regarded both sides of his ancestry as equally important. Binominal and bilingual, he believed that his mother's blood gave him a unique appreciation of the psychology and culture of Polynesian peoples, while his father's language enabled him to interpret them to the world. He was educated at the Urenui state primary school and Te Aute College, an Anglican secondary school for Maori boys in Hawkes Bay. Here he learned Latin and Greek in preparation for a professional career. After three years, Buck matriculated, was dux of the school, and passed his medical preliminary exam for Otago University's medical school.

At Otago, Buck was equally successful. He captained the athletics and rugby teams and graduated MB ChB in 1904. While serving as a house surgeon in Dunedin Hospital, Buck married, on 4 October 1905, Margaret Wilson, who had been born in northern Ireland. Though he could have become a conventional medical practitioner, Buck decided to work in Maori health. In November 1905 he became a medical officer to the Maori, and deputy to another Maori medical graduate, Maui Pomare. They campaigned vigorously to improve Maori health and clean up squalid living conditions—helping to facilitate the first increase in Maori population since European colonization began.

In 1909 Buck's career took an unexpected new turn. Under the patronage of the native minister, James Carroll, Buck entered parliament as member for Northern Maori. Here he joined the brilliant young lawyer Apirana Ngata, also a Te Aute graduate, who had been elected for Eastern Maori in 1905. In 1911 they were joined by Pomare. The trio formed a Young Maori Party. Each of them held cabinet office, though Buck did so for only a few months in 1912. His heart was not in politics and he did not seek re-election for Northern Maori in 1914.

Buck was becoming more interested in anthropology. In 1910 he completed an MD thesis, 'Medicine amongst the Maoris in ancient and modern times'. He extended his interest to the Pacific. During parliamentary recesses in 1910 and 1912–13 he served as medical officer to the Cook Islands and Niue, carried out anthropological fieldwork, and published his findings in Dominion Museum bulletins and the *Journal of the Polynesian Society* (*JPS*).

Buck's horizons were further extended during the First World War. In February 1915 he became medical officer to the Maori volunteer contingent that fought in the disastrous Gallipoli campaign. Buck was twice mentioned in dispatches and appointed DSO. After Gallipoli the Maori force was sent to France. Buck transferred to combat duty, was promoted to major, and became second in command of the battalion. In 1918 he was posted to the New Zealand General Hospital in Codford. Buck met several British anthropologists who provided him with instruments to measure the physique of the Maori troops on their way home from the war. The results were published as 'Maori somatology' in the *JPS* in 1922–3.

In 1919 Buck became director of the Maori hygiene division in the department of health. But medicine soon gave way to anthropology. He continued to publish in the *JPS*, and also a memoir, *The Evolution of Maori Clothing*. Buck was becoming a celebrated lecturer. His 'Coming of the Maori', delivered at the Cawthron Institute at Nelson in 1922 and the Melbourne Pacific Science Congress in 1923, was repeated many times afterwards. It was published in 1925, reprinted in 1929 and republished in a much expanded form in 1949. That edition has been reprinted numerous times.

Buck was also attracting international attention. At the Melbourne congress he met Herbert E. Gregory, director of the Bernice P. Bishop Museum in Hawaii. The museum funded Buck's field trip to the Cook Islands in 1926. He published the results as *The Material Culture of the Cook Islands* (Aitutaki) in 1927.

In that year Buck's career took an important new direction. Gregory offered him a five-year research fellowship at the Bishop Museum. Buck was now fifty and could have contemplated a more sedate life but, on the advice of his old friend Apirana Ngata, Buck decided to go. It was the beginning of Buck's lifelong expatriation from New Zealand, graphically recorded in his lengthy correspondence with Ngata.

From the Bishop Museum, Buck worked his way around the Polynesian island groups, starting in Samoa. He published his findings in a succession of museum bulletins on Samoa, Tongareva, Mangaia, Mangareva, the Cook Islands, Kapingamarangi, and Hawaii. These works, profusely illustrated with fine line drawings, established Buck as the world authority on Polynesian material culture. They also provided material for his most popular work, *Vikings of the Sunrise*, published in 1938.

Buck wanted to end his career in New Zealand, but there was no academic post for him. Though he visited his homeland briefly in 1930, 1935, and 1949, he gradually realized that he would end his career abroad. When his fellowship at the Bishop Museum ended in 1932, Buck went to Yale as visiting professor in anthropology for two years. In June 1933 he was named as Gregory's successor as director of the Bishop Museum. Gregory did not retire for three more years so Buck carried out more fieldwork in the Pacific.

When he became director, Buck was not content to be a desk-bound administrator. He continued fieldwork, published extensively, and was forever in demand as a public lecturer and after-dinner raconteur. His term at the Bishop was regularly renewed. He even became chairman of the museum's board of trustees. He received numerous academic awards, including the Hector Memorial prize, and the Rivers Memorial, S. Percy Smith, and Huxley medals. He received honorary degrees from the universities of New Zealand, Rochester, Hawaii, and Yale. But the honour that Buck most coveted, a New Zealand knighthood, was long denied him because it was wrongly assumed that he had become an American citizen. When

the error was finally discovered in 1946, Buck was nominated a KCMG.

Stricken with terminal cancer, Buck made a final pilgrimage to New Zealand in 1949, where he attended the Pacific Science Congress, received his knighthood from the governor-general, Sir Bernard Freyberg, kept company with his old and ailing friend, Sir Apirana Ngata, and revisited the Maori *marae* (meeting grounds) of his youth. Buck died in harness as director of the Bishop Museum at Honolulu on 1 December 1951. His ashes were returned to New Zealand in 1953 and entombed on 8 August 1954 at Okoki in an impressive monument, with a canoe prow pointing to Hawaiki, near Urenui. His wife Margaret briefly survived him and her ashes were interred with his. But there were no children to carry on the legacy of a man who, in his bicultural origins and impressive scholarship, had himself become a viking of the Pacific.

M. P. K. SORRENSON

Sources M. P. K. Sorrenson, ed., *Na to hoa aroha* (*From your dear friend*): *the correspondence between Sir Apirana Ngata and Sir Peter Buck, 1925–50*, 3 vols. (1986–8) • M. P. K. Sorrenson, 'Buck, Peter Henry', *DNZB*, vol. 3 • J. B. Condliffe, *Te Rangi Hiroa: the life of Sir Peter Buck* (1971) • E. Ramsden, *A memoir … Te Rangihiroa* (1954) • K. Luomala, 'Necrology: Peter Henry Buck (Te Rangi Hiroa)', *Bernice P. Bishop Museum Bulletin*, 208 (1951), 36–44 • M. P. K. Sorrenson, 'Polynesian corpuscles and Pacific anthropology: the home-made anthropology of Sir Apirana Ngata and Sir Peter Buck', *Journal of the Polynesian Society*, 91 (1982), 7–27
Archives NL NZ, Turnbull L., MSS | NL NZ, Turnbull L., Maori Purposes Fund Board MSS • NL NZ, Turnbull L., Ngata MSS • NL NZ, Turnbull L., Polynesian Society MSS • NL NZ, Turnbull L., Ramsden MSS | SOUND BL NSA, recorded talk • Radio New Zealand, Wellington, recordings of speeches
Likenesses E. Beckman, drawing, 1931, Bishop Museum, Honolulu, Hawaii • M. Tennant, portrait, Bishop Museum, Honolulu, Hawaii

Buck, Samuel (1696–1779), topographical draughtsman, engraver, and print publisher, is usually said to have been born in Richmond, Yorkshire, though firm evidence of his birth place is lacking. Hauxwell, 4½ miles south of Richmond, has also been suggested. His father was living near Elvil Bridge, Durham, in 1722, but no other information about his parents is known. Although Buck's familiarity with shorthand could suggest an original intention to enter the legal profession, by 1719 he was known to the Leeds antiquary Ralph Thoresby as an amateur, though useful, artist. Thoresby introduced him to John Warburton, an antiquary then engaged in writing a county topography for Yorkshire. Sketches made by Samuel Buck in 1719 and 1720 for plates intended for this later abandoned topography can be found in the British Library.

In 1720 Buck published proposals for two large engraved prospects of Leeds and Wakefield. These two prints proved to be the first in a series of town prospects. Eventually there were ten in the first series (1720–25), the others being of York, Newcastle upon Tyne, Durham, Stockton-on-Tees, Maidstone (two), Sunderland, and Lincoln. Measuring on average about 410 mm x 1000 mm, each was printed on two sheets, and no more were printed off than were subscribed for. Today they are extremely rare.

By this time Buck had moved to London. The first

address he gave for subscribers was the White Swan, Brownlow Street, off High Holborn. Later he operated from his brother's address at the Golden Buck, Warwick Street, near Golden Square, Soho, and also at the Golden Buck, Great Russell Street, Bloomsbury, and at 1 Garden Court, Middle Temple. The Green Canister, next to the Crown and Anchor in the Strand, seems to have been his residence. From his arrival in London he worked closely with the fellows of the Society of Antiquaries, attending their meetings at The Mitre tavern in the Strand and showing them specimens of his town prospects. In 1724 and 1725 he accompanied the society's secretary, William Stukeley, on two of his antiquarian peregrinations. The resulting drawings are in the Bodleian Library, Oxford. A view of the gatehouse of Thornton College, Lincoln, carries a Stukeley inscription: 'Mr. Saml. Buck now with me whom I engaged to begin his drawings of Antiquitys' (Gough Top. 17512, fol. 56, Bodleian Library, Oxford).

In January 1724 Buck issued proposals for publishing a collection of twenty-four perspective views ('antiquities') in the county of York. These views were published in 1726. A number of the prints were based on sketches he had made when with Warburton. Thanks largely to the fellows of the Society of Antiquities, who had encouraged its publication, it was a success. In proposals issued in May 1726 Buck announced that he was working on a second set of twenty-four antiquities, representing 'remarkable ruins' in Lincolnshire and Nottinghamshire, places drawn when he accompanied William Stukeley. These were published in 1727, the same year he married Catherine Faussett, on 20 April. By this date Buck had developed a more ambitious plan. In November 1726 he announced his intention of systematically recording ruins throughout England. The castles, religious foundations, and other remains of antiquity throughout the kingdom, he argued, were in a lamentable condition. He would 'rescue the mangled remains' of 'these aged & venerable edifices from the inexorable jaws of time' (S. Buck, 'Proposals for the publication of ... twenty-four views of castles ... in the counties of Lincoln and Nottingham', 1 Nov 1726, copy in priv. coll.), by visiting and recording them.

Samuel's brother, **Nathaniel Buck** (*fl.* 1724–1759), was associated with this project from the start, taking in subscriptions at the Golden Buck, Warwick Street, Soho. It is assumed that he was born in or near Richmond, Yorkshire, though the earliest mention of him is not until 1724. In the summer of 1727 Nathaniel accompanied Samuel on a peregrination of Lancashire, Cheshire, and Derbyshire. The third antiquities collection thus consists of ruins in those counties, and the views are signed either 'S. B. delin. N. B. sculp.' or vice versa. In 1728 the brothers announced their plan to undertake the remaining counties of northern England, but they discovered enough recordable ruins in Durham and Northumberland for the following year's set of twenty-four, and Cumberland and Westmorland had to wait. In 1729–31 they took their sketch-boards to the midlands, between 1732 and 1736 they covered the counties in the south of England and also in Monmouthshire, in 1737 they covered the counties of East Anglia, and in 1738 they completed England by dealing with Cumberland and Westmorland. Finally they produced sets for Wales, apparently touring the counties of Wales in 1739–41. With the publication in 1742 of Anglesey, Caernarvonshire, Denbighshire, Flintshire, Merioneth, Montgomeryshire, and Radnor, the antiquities project was completed.

This project constituted only half of the Buck brothers' enterprise. From 1728 they had worked on a parallel project: producing and publishing a series of long prospects of English and Welsh 'Cities, Sea-ports, and Capital Towns'. In this second, 'principal' series of townscapes each prospect consisted of an image on a single sheet measuring 305 mm x 775 mm. They are taken in most cases from the nearby countryside, 1 or 2 miles from the town, and from an elevated spot where possible. In the cases of London and of Greenwich and Deptford (two views that abut to form one) they are taken from several

Samuel Buck (1696–1779), by Richard Houston, pubd 1774 (after Joseph Highmore) [left, with his brother, Nathaniel Buck]

viewpoints. All the town prospects carry a numbered key and most are accompanied by a diligently compiled panegyric. The Bucks' usual practice was to market the town prospects in sets of six.

The drawings for the town prospects were usually made on the same peregrinations as those for the antiquities. After the completion of the antiquities, however, Cambridgeshire, Lincolnshire, Nottinghamshire, and Leicestershire were revisited and their principal towns recorded. Because several towns in the north had been dealt with in the first series, the Bucks left that area of England until last. They then turned their attention to Wales in 1748, publishing prospects of the six principal Welsh towns. The set, which was supposed to conclude the project, consisting of London in five sheets plus a sheet for Portsmouth, appeared on 11 September 1749. However, on the same day the brothers issued the finest of all their town prospects—two long views of Richmond, Yorkshire, the town with which they had been so closely associated. These were surely intended as the grand finale. Nevertheless, in 1752 they published second views of Birmingham and Oxford. Nathaniel died some time between 1759 and 14 May 1774, when Garden Court, Middle Temple, was to be disposed of on behalf of his executrix, Mrs Rebecca Buck.

Samuel Buck continued to advertise and sell his antiquities and town prospects. He advertised that he would instruct young ladies and gentlemen in their own houses in the art of drawing and painting in oils and watercolours; he made flower drawings; he sold drawings specially designed for young beginners to copy and improve their skills; he offered to clean and mend pictures; and he exhibited at the Royal Academy, the Free Society, and the Society of Artists. Two years before he died he issued proposals for a set of four perspective views in Yorkshire from drawings made on the spot by himself.

In their proposals for the Glamorgan, Brecknockshire, and Cardiganshire antiquities the Bucks firmly stated that they 'do design and draw the Views on the spot and engrave their own Copper-Plates' (copy inserted in collections for a third edition of Gough's *British Topography*, vol. 4, 161, in the Bodleian Library). These claims must be treated with caution. The Bucks were not the only people involved. Other artists were employed to strengthen their drawings, to draw the staffage, and generally to bring their awkward drawings to life. These artists included Thomas Rosse, Hubert-François Gravelot, Jean-Baptiste Claude Chatelain, Peter Monamy, and probably Samuel Scott. The style of engraving changes markedly from time to time. Engravers employed for the first series of town prospects included John Harris and Gerard Vandergucht. Chatelain may have been the engraver of the various towns that concluded the principal series.

In his proposals for the prospects of Durham and Stockton in the first series Buck announced: 'Any Gentleman may have his Seat drawn and engraved by the same Hand at a reasonable Rate' (*Newcastle Weekly Courant*, 15 Sept 1722). He made drawings of Bolton in Yorkshire, and prints of Chilham Castle in Kent, Powderham Castle in Devon, Melton Constable in Norfolk, Aston in Warwickshire, and Worksop Manor in Nottinghamshire. In Cornwall the Bucks produced four views of St Michael's Mount.

Samuel Buck's final years were spent in poverty. Richard Gough supported him out of his own pocket and encouraged his friends to follow suit, publishing an appeal in the *Gentleman's Magazine* and elsewhere, and attempting to present it in the chamber of the Society of Antiquaries. It provoked a generous response, and in his last six months Buck was free from financial anxiety. He died at eighty-three on 17 August 1779, and was buried in the churchyard of St Clement Danes three days later.

The copper plates for printing the antiquities and the principal series of town prospects were acquired by the Fleet Street printmaker Robert Sayer. Sayer reissued the prints in 1774, making them available in single sheets, or bound into three volumes with the comprehensive title *Buck's Antiquities*. The Sayer impressions have the original imprints but can be distinguished from the impressions made by Buck by the plate numbers Sayer added at the top right corner. They are listed in print catalogues as late as 1813, by which date some of the prints had been on the market for eighty-seven years. Only the London prospect was updated, though not thoroughly.

Large numbers of preparatory drawings for Buck's antiquities and town prospects survive in libraries, art galleries, museums, and record offices, drawn by the Bucks themselves or by the artists they employed. Some are inscribed with shorthand notes. Though the Buck brothers were not the only ones producing views of antiquities and town prospects in the eighteenth century they were much the most prolific. They published 428 engravings of monasteries, abbeys, castles, and other ruins, three unsigned engravings of Fountains Abbey, two town plans, an engraving of Bristol high cross, and eighty-seven long prospects of English and Welsh towns. Collectively their engravings constitute a national survey of ruins of the period, and provide us with an indispensable record of what English and Welsh towns looked like before the industrial revolution. RALPH HYDE

Sources R. Hyde, *A prospect of Britain: the town panoramas of Samuel and Nathaniel Buck* (1994) · E. Croft-Murray and S. O'Connell, MS catalogue of eighteenth-century British drawings in the British Museum, BM · *Diary of Ralph Thoresby* (1850) · *Samuel Buck's Yorkshire sketchbook* (1979) · W. B. Crump, 'The "Warburton" sketchbook (Lansdowne MS 914, British Museum)', *Yorkshire Archaeological Journal*, 35 (1940–43), 61–4 · *GM*, 1st ser., 49 (1779), 67–8, 424 · D. Moore and M. Moore, 'Buck's engravings of Glamorgan antiquities', *Stewart Williams's Glamorgan Historian*, 5 (1968), 133–51 · D. B. Brown, *Catalogue of the collection of drawings in the Ashmolean Museum*, 4 (1982), 206–10

Archives BL, Lansdowne MSS 895, 899, 914 · Bodl. Oxf., Gough Top. 17512, 17553, Linc. 15 · S. Antiquaries, Lond., Society of Antiquaries minute books, vol. 1, and treasurer's book

Likenesses R. Houston, double portrait, mezzotint (with his brother, Nathaniel Buck; after J. Highmore), BM, NPG; repro. in S. Buck, *Buck's antiquities*, 3 vols. (1774) [see illus.]

Buck, Zechariah (1798–1879), organist, was born on 9 September 1798 in the parish of St Peter-per-Mountergate, Norwich, of poor parents. He was recruited into the choir of Norwich Cathedral as a boy by the organist, Thomas Garland, who apparently heard him singing while playing in the streets. A chorister from 10 September 1807, he was trained for a short while by Garland and by his successor, John Christmas Beckwith, but principally by Beckwith's son John Charles Beckwith, to whom he became an apprentice. He was assistant organist of St Peter Mancroft from 1818 to 1821, and in October 1819 he succeeded the younger Beckwith as cathedral organist.

The Norwich musical tradition at this date was of a considerably higher standard than that of many other cathedrals, and Buck was able to build on solid traditions. Very early in his career he made a tour of other cathedrals to learn how their musical establishments were run, and while still only in his twenties he built up a considerable reputation as a trainer of boys' voices. Although he was an able piano teacher, he was not particularly renowned as an organist, and he played very little in the cathedral after the 1840s. Perhaps for that reason he established a succession of articled pupils who undertook the main duties of organ playing in his stead, not only in the cathedral, but also supplying music for many of the numerous Norwich churches. This left Buck able to concentrate on supervising the boys in the choir stalls, in an age when there was little direct influence of a cathedral organist upon his choir during divine service.

Buck's training methods included such unconventional practices as using custom-made wooden spacers to accustom the boys to opening their mouths properly, yet the theories behind his rigorous attention to the physical requirements for a basic vocal technique were sound, and the accounts of his achievements are thereby the more credible. In the 1840s, when cathedral music had not begun to be revitalized, there were newspaper articles by musical correspondents from London testifying to the expertise of Buck's choir. He was also fanatical about the amount of rehearsal he would give the boys, especially if important solos were to be sung. This was often to the detriment of the very rudimentary general education which the choristers received, although Norwich's lack in this area was no different from that of many other cathedrals at the time. While Buck was a hard taskmaster, he could also show great generosity towards his organist pupils. This is typified in his taking many of them to London, at his own expense, shortly before they were to be discharged from their apprenticeships, so that they might experience the wider range of music-making in vogue there.

Among Buck's seventy-two pupils were the cathedral organists Robert Janes (Ely, 1830–66), Frederick Atkinson (Norwich, 1881–5), Arthur Mann (King's College, Cambridge, 1876–1929), and George Gaffe (St Albans, 1880–1907), while a further thirty or so went on to be organists of major parish churches, or to gain other prominence as professional musicians. Buck thus had a wide influence on more than a generation of church musicians at precisely the time that music in the Anglican church was receiving a new impetus as a result of ecclesiastical reform. The

degree of MusDoc was conferred on him by the archbishop of Canterbury in 1847. His compositions are not remarkable. They include an evening service in A, six anthems, five hymn tunes, and twenty-three chants.

Buck married, in 1819, the eldest daughter of the Revd Peter Hansell. Although the couple had eight children, only two survived into adulthood; his wife herself died in the early 1830s. In 1832 Buck married Lucy Holloway, a daughter of John Holloway, by whom he had four sons and a daughter. He retired from Norwich Cathedral in 1877 and died at the home of his eldest son by his second marriage, Henry, in Newport, Essex, on 5 August 1879.

ANDREW PARKER

Sources F. G. Kitton, *Zechariah Buck: a centenary memoir* (1899) • H. W. Shaw, *The succession of organists of the Chapel Royal and the cathedrals of England and Wales from c.1538* (1991) • *Norfolk Chronicle* (1848–65), *passim* • Norfolk RO, archives of the dean and chapter of Norwich
Likenesses R. J. Lane, lithograph (after S. Gambardella), NPG
Wealth at death under £4000: probate, 9 Sept 1879, *CGPLA Eng. & Wales*

Bucke, Charles (1781–1846), playwright and writer, was born at Worlington in Suffolk on 16 April 1781. For over thirty years he worked in poverty, until he found a generous benefactor in Thomas Grenville, from whom he regularly received £5 a month. He also obtained several grants from the Royal Literary Fund. His poetic sensibility, encyclopaedic reading, and considerable gifts as a popular moralist are shown in his earlier works. They include *Amusements in retirement, or, The influence of science, literature, and the liberal arts, on the manners and happiness of private life* (1816), and *On the beauties, harmonies, and sublimities of nature, with occasional remarks on the laws, customs, manners, and opinions of various nations* (4 vols., 1821; 3 vols., 1837). The latter was originally published anonymously in 1813, under the title *The Philosophy of Nature*; it was reprinted in New York in 1843. Bucke left an enlarged version in twenty manuscript volumes at his death.

Bucke is primarily known, however, for the controversy surrounding his five-act verse drama *The Italians, or, The Fatal Accusation: a Tragedy*. Its preface 'containing the correspondence of the author with the committee of Drury Lane Theatre, P. Moore, Esq., M.P., and Mr. Kean' was sensational enough to see the publication through seven editions in 1819, and an eighth in 1820. The affair concerned the playwright's clash with Edmund Kean, then at the height of his acting career, and Bucke's account of the events is illuminating for its depiction of the uneasy relations between authors and the theatrical establishment of the time. *The Italians* had been accepted by the Drury Lane committee in November 1817, but its presentation was delayed by the theatre's three-week closure on the death of Princess Charlotte. Shortly after its reopening Edmund Kean became interested in Bucke's play, but William Dimond's *Bride of Abydos* had priority. Other complications followed, including a production of Christopher Marlowe's *The Jew of Malta* for which the committee asked a prologue of Bucke. This was too much for the sensitive moralist:

I felt ashamed in being accessory to the cruelty of offering such an undeserved, as well as unprovoked, insult to the great body of the Jews:—all of whom took so much offence at the representation—particularly as it occurred during Passover. (Bucke, 'Preface', *The Italians*, viii–ix)

As preparations to present Bucke's tragedy went ahead, Kean began to raise objections. He complained that certain subsidiary characters 'would excite too much interest' and detract from his central role as Albanio, 'that no one should write a tragedy for that House, without making the entire interest centre in the character HE should perform' (ibid., ix). Bucke was further disgusted by Kean's deliberately careless acting in the presentation of Jane Porter's tragedy *Switzerland* and withdrew consent for the presentation of *The Italians*, which he then printed. Nevertheless, on 3 April, the tragedy was 'performed at Drury Lane Theatre against the author's consent, and withdrawn on the second night of performance in consequence of a violent party having been made against it by the partisans of Mr. Kean' (Bucke, 'Dedication', *The Fall of the Leaf*). *The Italians* was performed on 15 June 1819 at Nottingham. Bucke reveals that at this period the effect of broken promises left himself, his 'excellent' wife, and his children in want, and refers to 'a series of afflictions' (Bucke, 'Preface' to 3rd edn, xxx–xxxi, 24 March 1819).

The prefatory memoir to *Julio Romano, or, The Force of the Passions, an Epic Drama* (1830) further illustrates the problematic relations between authors and the theatre at this time. Bucke realized that his piece was not adapted to theatrical presentation and sought the help of 'a celebrated dramatic reader', who explained that its lengthy dramatic readings would not hold an audience. Bucke therefore decided to publish the work, but before doing so sought some assurance from Drury Lane and Covent Garden that they would not pirate the work:

since proprietors of theatres profess to enjoy the right of appropriating all published dramas to their own use; entailing all the personal hazard, and all the disgrace, in case of failure, on the author; and retaining for themselves all the pecuniary benefit, in the event of success.

The responses were far from reassuring and Bucke proceeded to seek protection for dramatic works by an act of parliament. His petition was presented in the house on 4 June 1829 by Sir James Mackintosh. It referred to the more favourable treatment of authors in France and Russia and sought protection during the author's life, or fourteen years from the first publication. It met with only partial success, primarily in making the issue public.

Bucke's later works included *A Classical Grammar of the English Language* (1829), *The Life of John, Duke of Marlborough* (1839), and *Ruins of Ancient Cities* (1840). He died at 10 Pulteney Terrace, Islington, London, on 31 July 1846, leaving 'a widow with two sons (the elder imbecile from his birth) and two daughters' (*GM*). JOHN D. HAIGH

Sources *GM*, 2nd ser., 27 (1847), 558 · *N&Q*, 2nd ser., 10 (1860), 307 · *N&Q*, 4th ser., 1 (1868), 267 · *N&Q*, 4th ser., 1 (1868), 419–20 · *N&Q*, 4th ser., 1 (1868), 520 · C. Bucke, 'Preface', *The Italians, or, The fatal accusation*, 1st and 3rd edns (1819) · C. Bucke, preface, *Julio Romano, or, The*

force of the passions, an epic drama (1830), v–xxv · C. Bucke, 'Dedication', *The fall of the leaf: and other poems* (1819) · d. cert.

Archives BL, letters relating to application to the Royal Literary Fund, loan no. 96

Buckenham, Robert (*fl. c.*1523–1539), Catholic polemicist and prior of Cambridge, took at Cambridge the degrees of BTh about 1523 and DTh in 1530–31. He is also said to have studied in Bologna in 1526, being sent back to England the following year. Early in January 1530, after Hugh Latimer had preached his 'Sermon on the Cards' in Cambridge, advocating *inter alia* the reading of the English Bible, Buckenham answered with a sermon on 'Christenmasse dice', suggesting a throw of *quater* to represent the four doctors of the church, and a *cinque* to list five texts of scripture, which, if available in the vernacular, could mislead lay readers into neglecting their vocations. Latimer responded later that day, and, according to Foxe, Buckenham 'was so dashed, that never after hee durst peepe out of the pulpit agaynst M. Latymer' (Foxe, 1735). In fact Buckenham seems to have continued the controversy, as he is probably the 'Mr. Proctor of the blak frears' who was commanded with others on 29 January 1530 to cease attacking Latimer from the pulpit (taking 'proctor' to be a misreading of 'prior' (Lamb, 16)).

An advocate of the papal supremacy, Buckenham faced threatening prospects under Henry VIII, and he therefore left England for Edinburgh before 7 June 1534; by Easter 1535 (28 March) he had arrived in Louvain, where he and a fellow exile stayed in the Dominican house, supported by Henry Phillips. Buckenham was not privy to Phillips's initial plot against William Tyndale, but once the latter had been imprisoned, Buckenham was probably one of the two translators of his works into Latin for the trial, and it is also likely that he was among the English divines from Louvain who examined Tyndale at Vilvorde. In exile Buckenham wrote a number of letters (no longer extant) to his contacts in England, and Tanner records that a work of his, *De reconciliatione locorum s. scripturae*, rested in the English College at Rome, though it is no longer traceable. On 28 April 1539 Buckenham was one of a number of persons named in a parliamentary attainder, accused of advocating papal supremacy, indicating that he was then believed to be still living. The date of his death is unknown.

Buckenham has been confused with William Bokenham, master of Gonville Hall from 1514 to 1536, and has also mistakenly been identified as chancellor of Cambridge University and archdeacon of Lewes, though he held neither post. Foxe refers to him as 'Priour of our Lady fryars' in the first English edition of the *Actes and Monuments* (1563), but this is corrected in subsequent editions. Foxe also mentions a nickname, Domine Labia, though without explanation; in a marginal note he calls him 'D. Dewsace' (deuce-ace), a jibe aimed at his dice sermon.

MARTIN HOLT DOTTERWEICH

Sources *LP Henry VIII*, 7, no. 805; 8, no. 1151; 9, nos. 182 (and 493n.), 1097; 14/1, no. 867 · J. Foxe, *The seconde volume of the ecclesiastical historie, conteining the acts and monuments of martyrs*, 4th edn (1583), 1734–5 · J. Lamb, ed., *A collection of letters, statutes and other documents ... illustrative of the history of the University of Cambridge during the Reformation* (1838), 15–18 · *The whole workes of W. Tyndall, John Frith,* *and Doct. Barnes*, ed. J. Fox (1572–3), vol. 1, fol. B2v · J. F. Mozley, *William Tyndale* (1937), 304, 327, 333 · Venn, *Alum. Cant.*, 1/1.427 · *Fasti Angl., 1300–1541*, [Chichester], 14, n. 3 · A. G. Chester, *Hugh Latimer: apostle to the English* (1954), 38–48 · C. F. R. Palmer, 'The Friar-Preachers, or Blackfriars, of Cambridge', *The Reliquary*, 25 (1884), 141 · Tanner, *Bibl. Brit.-Hib.*, 137 · D. R. Leader, *A history of the University of Cambridge, 1: The university to 1546*, ed. C. N. L. Brooke and others (1988)

Bucker, George [*alias* Adam Damplip] (*d.* **1543**), religious radical, is first recorded in 1536 when he was in Padua with Reginald Pole and Alvise Priuli. He then tried to attach himself to Cosmo Gheri, bishop of Fano. He claimed to have been John Fisher's mass priest, and told Priuli many of Fisher's sayings. Bucker had begun by expressing 'certain depraved and heretical opinions especially against the unity of the church and the authority of the Roman pontiff' as well as condemning the reason Fisher had died, but when he saw that Pole and Priuli disapproved, he changed his opinion and gave them a 'discourse on both sides [*in utramque partem*] on papal authority' (Bodl. Oxf., Bodl. MS Ital. C. 25, fol. 147r) that Pole thought he must have heard from Fisher. Gheri regarded Bucker's arrival in Fano as providential, since Pole had just asked Gheri to write Fisher's life. Bucker set down Fisher's opinions *De oratione* ('On prayer'), *De predestinatione et libero arbitrio* ('On predestination and free will'), and *De potestate pontificis* ('On papal power'), the last only in a copy which Bucker had hidden in his house in England. Only the first of these is known, but many of Fisher's works were destroyed by his enemies. Along with discussions of the late bishop, Bucker spoke on the Pauline epistles. He told Gheri that after Fisher's imprisonment he adhered to Henry VIII but repented after the bishop's death, inspired by a vision of Fisher asking him about his desertion. He undertook a pilgrimage to Rome, where he attached himself to an Englishman, one of whose servants he killed. Gheri offered to secure absolution for him, and Bucker tried to enlist Ludevico Beccadelli's assistance.

Bucker next appeared in Calais about the end of April 1538, looking for passage to England and calling himself Adam Damplip or perhaps just Adams. He was persuaded to stay and preach. Damplip alleged that he could have had a good living from Pole had he stayed in Rome—Pole wished him to read there three times a week and sent money after him to get him back. This gift would become the fatal French crown that according to John Foxe led to Damplip's execution for treason. Foxe is one of the most important sources for the rest of Damplip's story, but his tale changed between the first edition of 1563 and that of 1570. Despite the alterations, Foxe's main story agrees well enough with Ellis Gruffudd's contemporary chronicle and other sources to make it possible to reconstruct Damplip's actions in Calais with fair confidence.

Lord Lisle, the deputy of Calais, gave Damplip money and strong support, subsequently denying only that he had known that Damplip came from Pole. Lisle pronounced Damplip's sermon on the epistle to the Romans the best he had heard, and he recommended Damplip to Archbishop Thomas Cranmer. The Carmelite prior John

Dove by contrast attacked Damplip for saying that each Christian should understand the significance of the mass. On Whitsunday (9 June), Damplip preached at the destroyed site called Resurrection where a supposedly miraculous host had been exposed by royal commissioners. The council of Calais warned Cranmer's commissary John Butler on 19 June 1538 that Damplip should preach nothing on Corpus Christi (20 June) contrary to royal ordinances, and shortly thereafter he was summoned to England. He allegedly responded that he had a licence (from Butler) 'to tarry there as long as he would and to depart when he would' (*Lisle Letters*, 5.186). A month later Thomas Cromwell ordered an investigation.

No sooner had Damplip sent in a written opinion than he was taken to England by a member of Lisle's household, with a letter of recommendation from Butler to Cranmer. As soon as he arrived, Cranmer sent him first to Cromwell with a letter asking that he be allowed to return to Calais, and then to a committee of bishops. Warned by Cranmer that he was in danger of imprisonment, Damplip submitted a written statement of his opinions and escaped (according to Foxe), but nothing more happened until 1539. In the interval, Damplip may have taken service with Nicholas Shaxton, bishop of Salisbury, while Foxe asserts that he kept a school in the west country for one or two years. Then on 27 May 1539 Cromwell told the council of Calais that the allegations against Damplip did not amount to much. The council rejoined to Cranmer that Damplip 'preached here directly against the sacraments of the altar and baptism' (*Lisle Letters*, 5.516), and a few days later Cromwell himself wrote that, if true, the articles against Damplip were 'very pestilent' and 'most detestable and cankered heresy' (ibid., 5.523). On 27 June Lisle and the council informed bishops Clerk, Sampson, and Rugg that Damplip had caused recent disturbances in Calais. They were especially concerned to discover whether anyone had heard him preach that 'the very body of God was not really and substantially contained in the sacrament … And the priest with his mumming cannot make a god' (ibid., 5.567).

Almost another year passed, and then a royal commission was dispatched to Calais. It took sixty depositions and reported on 5 April 1540 that Damplip had engendered division. Lisle asked William, Lord Sandys, who was hearing depositions along with Sampson, to have Dove brought over to London to testify, and Sandys agreed. On 22 July Damplip was attainted of treason for his contacts with Pole. Most of the dénouement comes from the 1570 edition of Foxe, drawing on the letters of John Marbeck who had been imprisoned in the Marshalsea with Damplip for about a month (Foxe says a year). Foxe's chronology is out by a year overall and by about a week in its essential details, but much of his narrative seems plausible. After Damplip had been in prison for about two years, at Easter (25 March) 1543 he decided Stephen Gardiner had forgotten him and wrote offering his submission. Gardiner replied by having him sent back to Calais. When the news arrived, Damplip discerned that it meant his death. Nevertheless he ate a hearty dinner, asking the keeper 'Do you think I have been God's prisoner so long in the Marshalsea and have not yet learned to die?' (Foxe, *Actes and Monuments*, 1583 edn, 1229). On 2 May he was taken to Calais, following orders from the privy council on 22 and 29 April about the manner of his execution. On 5 May he was hanged, drawn, and quartered. The parson of Notre Dame preached as directed, and Sir Ralph Ellerker prevented Damplip from speaking in his own defence.

Volatile in his opinions in a way far from untypical of this period, Damplip illustrates the pervasiveness of Pauline Christianity in the early Reformation, as well as the degree to which it turned on questions of ecclesiology. His arguments in his interrogation of 1538 also had a significant impact on Cranmer's eucharistic theology.

T. F. MAYER

Sources G. B. Morandi, ed., *Monumenti di varia letteratura*, 2 vols. (Bologna, Istituto per le scienze, 1797–1804), 1/2. 286, 293, 296, 300, 306–7, 319–22 · Bodl. Oxf., MS Ital. C. 25, fols. 147r–v, 151v · *LP Henry VIII*, 13/1, nos. 1219, 1436, 1446; 13/2, no. 97; 15, no. 728, no. 498c.60 · M. St C. Byrne, ed., *The Lisle letters*, 6 vols. (1981), vol. 5, nos. 1189–90, 1196, 1429, 1437, 1443, 1447, 1464, 1470a; vol. 6, nos. 1664, 1674 · J. Foxe, *Actes and monuments* (1563), 656–7, 665–6 · J. Foxe, *The first volume of the ecclesiasticall history contayning the actes and monumentes of thynges passed*, new edn (1570), 1400–01, 1406–7 · J. Foxe, *Actes and monuments*, 4th edn, 2 vols. (1583), 1223–4, 1228–9 · *APC*, 1542–7, 117, 123 · S. E. Lehmberg, *The later parliaments of Henry VIII, 1536–1547* (1977), 110–12 · F. van Ortroy, ed., 'Vie du bienheureux martyr Jean Fisher', *Analecta Bollandiana*, 12 (1893), 97–287, 211–14

Buckeridge, John (*d.* 1631), bishop of Ely, was born, according to Anthony Wood and Thomas Fuller, in the parish of Draycot Foliat, Wiltshire, the son of William Buckeridge and Elizabeth Keblewhite or Kibblewhite (*d.* in or after 1631?); his father's name is sometimes given as Thomas Buckeridge. Elizabeth Keblewhite was first cousin (not niece, as Wood and other sources suggest) of Sir Thomas White, founder of St John's College, Oxford, and co-founder of Merchant Taylors' School, London. Although Wood states that Buckeridge attended the school, there is no record of him in the registers, unlike seventeenth-century entrants from the family. However, in 1578 he was elected to one of six fellowships at St John's for founder's kin. He graduated BA in July 1582, and proceeded MA in April 1586. The tradition that he was presented to a canonry at Rochester in 1587 is erroneous. His appointment in 1589 as college tutor to William Laud, later archbishop of Canterbury, was of lasting significance: since the seventeenth century the latter's biographers have credited Buckeridge with instilling or confirming in Laud his reverence for patristic learning, liturgical ceremonialism, anti-Calvinist views on grace, and a hatred of puritanism. Buckeridge's later career was marked indelibly by his association with his former student, but he rose to some prominence in his own right as a preacher, controversialist, and court bishop.

Having proceeded BD in November 1592 and supplicated for a licence to preach on 9 December, by 1595 Buckeridge was chaplain to the earl of Essex, who actively but unsuccessfully sought from Lord Keeper Sir John Puckering his preferment to several livings. By 1596 he had probably transferred his service as chaplain to Archbishop

John Buckeridge (*d.* 1631), by Thomas Murray, 1697 [inscribed with the donor's name]

John Whitgift, thereby joining a cadre of other anti-puritan chaplains that included Lancelot Andrewes. In that year he was appointed by the queen to the rectory of North Fambridge, Essex, which he resigned in 1599 upon royal appointment to Kilworth, Leicestershire; that year he proceeded DD. In this period Buckeridge was granted repeated leaves of absence from St John's to carry out his parochial and chaplain's duties. When resigning his fellowship in 1600 upon accepting Kilworth, he noted that he had not been regularly resident in Oxford for five years. From 1597 Whitgift appointed him one of the Lent preachers at court, in which series Buckeridge then appeared every year until his death. Important early evidence of his avant-garde conformity is found in notes of a sermon by him at the Temple Church in June 1602, where he wryly observed that 'in tymes past men were afeared to commit synn, but ready to make confession; nowe the world is changed, for nowe every one dares comitt anie synne, but is ashamed to make confession' (*Diary of John Manningham*, 73). This oblique criticism of puritan presumption, coupled with a nostalgic commendation of the lapsed Catholic practice of auricular confession, matches Andrewes's controversial promulgation of the same views at court and at St Giles Cripplegate in the late 1590s.

Contrary to previous assumptions, Buckeridge never served as chaplain to Queen Elizabeth; his name does not appear in Whitgift's list of her chaplains at her death in 1603. Whitgift did, however, list him as one of those who were not royal chaplains but 'fitt to preach' to the new king (Westminster Abbey, muniment book 15, fol. 6). Like many others in Whitgift's circle, Buckeridge's anti-puritanism and skill in the pulpit swiftly won him preferment from King James. In July 1603 he was granted the next vacant canonry at Windsor. In March 1604 he was appointed archdeacon of Northampton and prebendary of Colewall at Hereford; in the following year he succeeded Andrewes as vicar of St Giles by the king's appointment. On 18 January 1606 Buckeridge was elected president of his Oxford college, and in April he received his promised canon's stall at Windsor. In September, James appointed him one of four select preachers chosen to propound the scriptural validity of episcopacy, and the royal supremacy over the church, to Andrew Melville and other Scottish Presbyterians at Hampton Court. William Barlow, bishop of Rochester, and John King, dean of Christ Church, asserted the clerical hierarchy, and Buckeridge and Andrewes offered uncompromising defences of the supremacy. Buckeridge deployed James's favourite trope of stigmatizing presbyterians as 'many Popes' who, like the bishop of Rome, 'doeth extoll himselfe above the Emperor' (*A Sermon Preached at Hampton Court* 1606, sig. B4r). Andrewes was reported to be irked with Buckeridge, however, for 'comming immediately before him', Buckeridge 'preoccupated much of his matter' (*The Letters of John Chamberlain*, ed. N. E. McClure, 2 vols., 1939, 1.233). In 1610 Buckeridge was presented to the rectory of Southfleet, Kent, by his associate Richard Neile, bishop of Rochester. In the same year his standing with the king among Whitgift's former clients found further testament in James's command to Archbishop George Abbot that Andrewes and Buckeridge alone had the 'perusal of such writings' left in the locked study of Whitgift's successor, Richard Bancroft, recently deceased (PRO, SP 14/58/46).

In the following spring, after Neile's translation to Coventry and Lichfield, the king appointed Buckeridge to the see of Rochester; he was consecrated at Lambeth on 9 June by Abbot, assisted by Andrewes and other bishops. He thereupon resigned Kilworth, Southfleet, his Hereford canonry, and his college headship, nominating Laud as his successor, but he retained the vicarage of St Giles and Windsor canonry. He remained close to Neile and his circle: both he and Neile were part of a group gathered at Bromley in October 1611 (according to a letter from the latter's half-brother Robert Newell to Laud), and when Neile left for Lichfield in November, Buckeridge, Laud, and others accompanied him. With Neile and Andrewes he sat on the high commission; he was also prominent in the court of delegates, where, as an honorary member of Doctors' Commons, he seems to have deployed considerable expertise. In September 1613 Buckeridge joined bishops Andrewes, Thomas Bilson, and Neile in their controversially slim majority decision in favour of the divorce of the earl of Essex, which pitted them and the king against the less morally dubious views of Abbot and others on the jury. Buckeridge, like Andrewes, also entered the lists in the print controversy sparked by James's promulgation and defence of the oath of allegiance. In 1614 appeared his largest original work, *De potestate papae*, a response to Cardinal Bellarmine's

Tractatus de potestate summi pontificis, in which Buckeridge refuted papal claims to temporal authority, especially the endorsement of regicide. Like Andrewes, and anticipating later Laudian anti-Roman controversial writing, Buckeridge not only avoided any denial of the pope's spiritual power, but even allowed some historical primacy to the see of St Peter.

James's renewed attempts later in the decade to achieve Scottish conformity with the English church, and the pressures on the church of his pro-Spanish foreign policy, allowed Buckeridge and other Arminian ceremonialists greater confidence in their campaign against conformist Calvinism [*see also* Durham House group]. In Lent 1618 Buckeridge preached before the king on the text 'O come, let us worship, and fall downe, and kneele … before the Lord our Maker' (Psalm 95: 6). The sermon, published by the king's printer with an appended 200 page dissertation on kneeling at communion, was a landmark in the Jacobean turn toward what would become Laudianism. In it Buckeridge not only argued for ceremonial conformity in both kingdoms out of duty to the king, but insisted, radically for the time, that ritual bodily worship was also a duty to God that could not 'be ommitted as an indifferent thing' (*A Sermon Preached before his Majestie*, 1618, 18). In such statements Buckeridge was even bolder than Andrewes, whose indictments of sermon-centred piety he also intensified. The tract on kneeling at communion privileged the eucharist in a way foreign to mainstream Calvinism by maintaining that, above all the other sacraments, and certainly over preaching, the communion (celebrated on an altar, not a table) offered the believer the most real and efficacious participation with God's grace.

In summer 1625 Buckeridge joined Andrewes, Laud, and other Arminians who vouched for the orthodoxy of Dr Richard Montague's pamphlets on Roman error and royal power, which were simultaneously condemned by parliament for crypto-popery. In February 1626 he took a leading part in the York House Conference convened by the duke of Buckingham to debate the issues raised by Montague's books. Buckeridge, the Episcopal spokesman for the Arminian side, re-articulated his party's views on universal grace and on the sacraments as efficacious in their own right without the prerequisite of predestination. On 11 November 1626 Buckeridge preached the sermon at Andrewes's funeral in St Saviour's, Southwark. Perhaps sensitive to accusations against their circle for straying too far from reformed orthodoxy during the Montagu controversy, Buckeridge used the occasion to preach an extremely careful exposition of the anti-Calvinists' theological position on sacrifice. In it he denied a literal repetition of Christ's sacrifice in the eucharist, but maintained that 'the Action of CHRIST'S sacrifice, which is long since past, should continue as long as the Eucharist shall endure'. He then extolled the 'sacrifices' of proper liturgical worship and works of charity. From his text's affirmation that in these 'GOD is well pleased' (Hebrews 13: 16), Buckeridge preached a narrow middle-ground between claiming the inherent efficacy of works or a Calvinist view of solely imputed grace: with works, '*God* may be both pacified and pleased, and yet no *merit in us*, but *acceptation in God*' (*A Sermon Preached at the Funerall*, 1–2, 14). The sermon, which concluded with an invaluable biographical sketch of Andrewes, was appended to Andrewes's *XCVI Sermons* (1629). At this time Buckeridge was already collaborating with his former pupil Laud on their edition of Andrewes's works under a royal warrant. The edition, one folio volume of English sermons and a quarto volume of Latin works, appeared with a dedication to King Charles in 1629.

In March 1628 Laud's influence with Charles had secured his former tutor's translation to the diocese of Ely, whereupon Buckeridge relinquished St Giles and his Windsor stall. Few diocesan records and no visitation articles for either of Buckeridge's episcopates survive. Almost no testimonials of Buckeridge's personal character survive. One exception is that of the St John's College steward and MP Sir James Whitelock, who recorded loaning 'my ancient frend Mr. Docter Buckridge, against his consecration to … Rochester … 400*l*', which Whitelock 'set downe to shew my love unto him, and how far from covetousnes he had lived' (*Liber famelicus*, 26). In October 1630 Abbot wrote that Buckeridge was 'very sick of the dropsey' and had retired to London 'for help of the phisitians' (PRO, SP 16/174/96). He died at Bromley in Kent on 23 May 1631, and was buried in St Peter's Church on 31 May, 'but had no memorial whatever put over him' (Hasted, 1.567). His will provides some further insight into his character and associations. Buckeridge's preamble is striking for the personal intensity with which it articulates an Arminian piety, convinced of his 'most miserable sinfull soule', not trusting in any hint of assurance through predestination, but only hoping 'that I maie obtaine mercie and grace when I shall appeare before his Throne … washe[d] throughlie in the blood of thy sonne' (will, fols. 16*v*–17*v*). Buckeridge left legacies to his mother, four brothers—Arthur, George, Thomas, and Nicholas—a sister, Katherine Phillipps, and their children. To St John's College he left the fine silver communion service from his episcopal chapel modelled on that used by Andrewes, twenty books for the college library (the communion service and books remain in the college's possession), and £500 for investment to support undergraduate fellows. Special intimacy is suggested in bequests of domestic furniture to Dorothy and Paul Neile, wife and son of Bishop Richard Neile, and to Sir William Paddy, king's physician and benefactor of St John's. Laud, Neile, and Sir Thomas Eden DCL were appointed overseers. Buckeridge's brothers had become prosperous London merchants or landowners; Nicholas was notable for his involvement in the East India Company and his narrative accounts of trading expeditions to Persia. P. E. McCULLOUGH

Sources P. Lake, 'Lancelot Andrewes, John Buckeridge, and avant-garde conformity', *The mental world of the Jacobean court*, ed. L. Peck (1991) • W. H. Stevenson and H. E. Salter, *The early history of St John's College, Oxford*, OHS, new ser., 1 (1939) • Foster, *Alum. Oxon.* • *CSP dom.*, 1603–31 • Fuller, *Worthies* (1811), 2.444 • Wood, *Ath. Oxon.*, new edn, 2.506–10 • will, PRO, PROB 11/160, sig. 70 • LPL, MS 943, fol. 59 • DWL, Morice MS J sub 1631, fol. 10 • P. Heylyn, *Cyprianus Anglicus* (1668) • A. Milton, *Catholic and Reformed: the Roman and protestant churches in English protestant thought, 1600–1640* (1995) • K. Fincham, *Prelate as pastor: the episcopate of James I* (1990) • K. Fincham, ed., *Visitation articles and injunctions of the early Stuart church*, 2 vols. (1994–8) • N. Tyacke, *Anti-Calvinists: the rise of English Arminianism, c.1590–1640* (1987) • *The diary of John Manningham of the Middle Temple, 1602–1603*, ed. R. P. Sorlien (Hanover, NH, 1976), 72–3 • *Liber famelicus of Sir James Whitelocke, a judge of the court of king's bench in the reigns of James I and Charles I*, ed. J. Bruce, CS, old ser., 70 (1858) • muniment book 15, Westminster Abbey Archive • P. E. McCullough, *Sermons at court: politics and religion in Elizabethan and Jacobean preaching* (1998) [incl. CD-ROM] • PRO, SP 14/58/46 and SP 16/174/96 • E. Hasted, *The history and topographical survey of the county of Kent*

Archives St John's College, Oxford, MSS • St John's College, Oxford, notes and draft of anti-papal tract, MS I. 4

Likenesses oils, 1600–40, St John's College, Oxford • T. Murray, oils, 1697, St John's College, Oxford [*see illus.*]

Wealth at death cash bequests of approx. £1000; plus leaseholds in Middlesex and Bromley, Kent: will, PRO, PROB, 11/160, sig. 70

Buckhurst. For this title name *see* Sackville, Thomas, first Baron Buckhurst and first earl of Dorset (*c*.1536–1608).

Buckingham. For this title name *see* Stafford, Humphrey, first duke of Buckingham (1402–1460); Stafford, Henry, second duke of Buckingham (1455–1483); Stafford, Edward, third duke of Buckingham (1478–1521); Villiers, George, first duke of Buckingham (1592–1628); MacDonnell, Katherine, duchess of Buckingham and marchioness of Antrim (1603?–1649); Villiers, George, second duke of Buckingham (1628–1687); Villiers, John, styled third earl of Buckingham (*c*.1677–1723); Grenville, George Nugent-Temple-, first marquess of Buckingham (1753–1813).

Buckingham, James Silk (1786–1855), author and traveller, was the youngest child of Christopher and Thomazine Buckingham, born at Flushing, near Falmouth, on 25 August 1786. He was drawn to a seafaring life from an early age, having only a limited education at various local schools. While on his third voyage, in 1797, he was taken prisoner by the French and was confined for several months at Corunna as a prisoner of war. In February 1806 he married Elizabeth Jennings (1786–1865), daughter of a farmer near Penryn. They had several children, the youngest being Leicester Silk *Buckingham.

Buckingham spent much of his early life as a sailor in the Atlantic and the Mediterranean, and between 1813 and 1818 travelled extensively in Egypt, Palestine, and Persia. In October 1818 he established at Calcutta a newspaper called the *Calcutta Journal*. His forthright criticisms of the East India Company and the Bengal government led to his expulsion from India and the suppression of the paper by the acting governor-general, John Adam, in April 1823. Buckingham campaigned for financial compensation for many years and redress was recommended by a select committee of the House of Commons in August 1834; but it was not until long afterwards that the East India Company conceded the injustice of the suppression by granting him a pension of £200 a year.

Having returned to London, Buckingham published accounts of the lands which he visited on his way to and

James Silk Buckingham (1786–1855), by Henry William Pickersgill, exh. RA 1825 [with his wife, Elizabeth Jennings]

from India, notably *Travels in Assyria, Media and Persia* (1829). He devoted considerable energy to the establishment of several journals, including the monthly *Oriental Herald and Colonial Review* (1824–9), which continued his campaign against the East India Company and promoted colonial self-government; *The Sphynx* (1827–9), a weekly journal of politics, literature, and news; and *The Athenaeum*, the first number of which came out on 2 January 1828. Buckingham was editor of this last journal for only a few weeks, parting with his interest in it to John Sterling. In this year he also founded a London evening paper called *The Argus*, but it lasted only four weeks. In July 1830, he published a prospectus for a government-sponsored voyage around the world, but this scheme was later abandoned.

From December 1832 to July 1837 Buckingham represented the new borough of Sheffield in the first reformed parliament. In the House of Commons he took special interest in social reforms, advocating an end to flogging in the army and navy, the abolition of press-gangs, the improvement of safety at sea, the repeal of the corn laws, and the provision of parks, museums, and libraries in cities. He also took an active part in promoting the temperance movement, presiding over a select committee of the House of Commons on drunkenness.

After retiring from parliament, in October 1837 Buckingham undertook an extensive tour through North America, lasting nearly four years. In 1844 he was instrumental in the foundation of the British and Foreign Institute in Hanover Square. This literary and social club, of which he was appointed resident director, drew the ridicule of *Punch*, which persisted in calling it the 'Literary and Foreign Destitute'. The institute was closed in 1846. In 1847 and 1848 Buckingham travelled through various parts of western Europe, writing extensive accounts of his tours. In 1849 he published *National Evils and Practical Remedies*, which proposed a quasi-socialist plan for a model town, in some respects anticipating the works of Ebenezer Howard. In 1851 he became the president of the newly formed London Temperance League, and on 1 September was granted a pension of £200 a year from the civil list, 'in consideration of his literary works and useful travels in various countries'. For some few years before his death he took little active part in public life, and he died after a long illness at Stanhope Lodge, Upper Avenue Road, St John's Wood, London, on 30 June 1855, in his sixty-ninth year.

Buckingham was a voluminous writer. He published numerous books on his foreign travels—which are especially notable for the information they provide about social conditions in the many countries he visited—and wrote a large number of pamphlets on social and political subjects. He was probably best known, however, as a lecturer, undertaking speaking tours in both Britain and North America. His enthusiasm for campaigns of reform was unrestrained; in his own words, he could 'never find anything in a defective state without feeling an instinctive desire to *improve* it'. The sheer variety of his undertakings was not perhaps well calculated to ensure him immediate success in any one of them individually; indeed, his many critics judged him capricious and shallow. His seemingly eclectic political creed has puzzled historians as much as it infuriated his opponents. In sum, the remarkable range of his travels, the diversity of his interests, and the extent of his writings testify to a life of energy if not of achievement.   G. F. R. BARKER, *rev.* FELIX DRIVER

Sources J. S. Buckingham, *Autobiography of James Silk Buckingham*, 2 vols. (1855) · R. Turner, *James Silk Buckingham, 1786–1855* (1934) · *GM*, 2nd ser., 44 (1855), 322–3 · *Annual Register* (1855), 289 · H. Mackay, 'Buckingham, James Silk', *BDMBR*, vol. 2 · J. Rockey, 'Victorian ideal cities', *Town Planning Review*, 54 (1983) · S. Arnot, *A sketch of the history of the Indian press* (1829)

Archives BL, journals relating to Nubia, Add. MS 26602 · BL OIOC, letters relating to India, MSS Eur. C 249 · NA Canada, corresp. | BL, corresp. with J. C. Hobhouse, Add. MSS 36460–36466, *passim* · BL, corresp. with Sir R. Peel, Add. MSS 40485–40595, *passim* · Lambton Park, Lambton estate office, Chester-le-Street, Durham, letters to earl of Durham · PRO, corresp. with Lord Ellenborough, PRO 30/12 · U. Newcastle, Robinson L., letters to Sir Walter Trevelyan and Lady Trevelyan · W. Sussex RO, letters to duke of Richmond

Likenesses J. Reynolds, group portrait, 1780–82 (with his father and family), NG Ire. · W. Beechey, oils, 1802, Stowe School, Buckinghamshire · H. W. Pickersgill, double portrait, exh. RA 1825 (with his wife), RGS [*see illus.*] · W. Theed, bust, 1845, Cutler's Hall, Sheffield · G. T. Doo?, portrait, *c.*1855, repro. in Buckingham, *Autobiography* · W. H. Brooke and R. Havell, etching with aquatint, repro. in J. S. Buckingham, *Travels in Assyria, Media and Persia* (1829) · R. Cooper, stipple (after miniature by G. L. Saunders), BM, NPG · G. Hayter, group portrait, oils (*The trial of Queen Caroline*, 1820), NPG

Buckingham, John (*c.*1320–1399), administrator and bishop of Lincoln, was born on 23 June about 1320; his family was of much less than gentry rank. Earliest references link him to Thomas Beauchamp, earl of Warwick (d. 1369). Buckingham's arms, gules a cross bottonny or, were closely based on the Beauchamp arms, and he was instituted to both Compton Murdack prebend in St Mary's College, Warwick, in 1344, and to Sutton Coldfield rectory in 1346 at Warwick's presentation. In April 1347 Warwick, the hereditary chamberlain, appointed him deputy chamberlain of the king's exchequer of receipt, and thereafter Buckingham's rise in royal service was steady; on 14 February 1350 he was appointed keeper of the great wardrobe, on 5 January 1353 controller of the wardrobe, and keeper of the wardrobe from 23 February 1353 to 26 February 1357; on 4 April 1357 he became an exchequer baron. With Robert Herle, another Beauchamp adherent, Buckingham was co-lieutenant of Brittany for a year from 29 September 1358, the only clerk to be appointed lieutenant of a duchy during the Hundred Years' War. When Edward III led an expedition to France in the autumn of 1359 Buckingham became keeper of the privy seal of the regent, Thomas of Woodstock (d. 1397), his duties running from 28 October for 204 days. On 1 July 1360 he was promoted keeper of the king's privy seal and continued in this position until 9 June 1363. Buckingham thus held a senior government position during the negotiations leading to the treaty of Brétigny, and was present at Calais on 24 October 1360 to witness ratification of the treaty.

Meanwhile, Buckingham's ecclesiastical career was prospering. An acolyte by 1344, he was ordained priest by the bishop of Worcester in 1346, by virtue of a letter dimissory from the bishop of Lichfield. In 1348 he was presented to Olney church, Buckinghamshire, by Warwick's son-in-law Ralph Basset, and by Edward III to a prebend in St Stephen's College, Westminster. In 1349 he was briefly archdeacon of Nottingham but resigned in November, preparatory to promotion to the deanship of Lichfield in early 1350, in which post he proved energetic and conscientious. In 1351, following a dispute over prebends in Lincoln Cathedral, he obtained that of Gretton. His election as bishop of Ely during the autumn of 1361 was set aside by the provision of Simon Langham (d. 1376) on 10 January following; Buckingham, apparently consoled at first by promotion to several lucrative prebends, was subsequently elected bishop of the major see of Lincoln, by 4 October 1362, in succession to John Gynewell. However, Urban V (r. 1362–70) was unwilling to confirm the election until Buckingham had been examined to prove his educational fitness for the position; this examination, along with the support of both Edward III and the captive Jean, king of France, was successful in persuading the pope of Buckingham's suitability. He was provided on 5 April 1363 and consecrated at Wargrave, Berkshire, on 25 June, two days after receiving his temporalities from the king.

After becoming bishop of Lincoln, Buckingham ceased at once to hold any formal position in government or to undertake diplomatic missions. He was replaced as keeper of the privy seal on 10 June 1363. His itinerary shows that he was a resident, working diocesan whose favourite residence was Lyddington, Rutland; most journeys outside the diocese can be accounted for by attendance at parliament or convocation. Nevertheless, Edward III appointed him an executor on 7 October 1376. Granted life exemption from attending parliament on account of age and infirmity in 1384, he attended two later parliaments in 1390 and 1394. From autumn 1390 he became much less active, staying almost entirely at his three Lincolnshire manors, and he remained continuously at Stow Park, Lincolnshire, for six months during the winter of 1395–6.

Buckingham was a strong supporter of the Carthusian order. He founded a cell in both the London and the Coventry charterhouses, and was a visitor to (in August 1386), and benefactor of, the Hull charterhouse. At Lincoln he left his mark on two works undertaken in his episcopate, the cathedral choir stalls and the entrance range of the vicars' court, both decorated with his arms. He is, however, best known as the bishop in whose diocese John Wyclif (d. 1384) lived and wrote, and in which Lollardy first took root. As a man without university education, and the bishop who in 1367 had seen episcopal authority over Oxford finally quashed by the papacy, Buckingham was in no position to discipline members of the university, but he took action against a number of other heretics, notably William Swinderby of Leicester, John Corringham, vicar of Diddington, Huntingdonshire, Thomas Compworth of Thrupp, Oxfordshire, Sir Thomas Latimer, lord of Braybrooke, Northamptonshire, and the Lollards of Northampton, especially the anchoress Anna Palmer. He attended the Blackfriars Council in May 1382, where the issue of heresy was taken firmly in hand. Beset on one side by heresy, Buckingham battled on the other against superstition, especially in Lincolnshire; the veneration of trees and the apparent substitution of bacon and eggs for the elements at Easter mass were among his concerns.

Walsingham's assertion that Buckingham was a political ally of John of Gaunt, duke of Lancaster, is unsubstantiated; the two had extensive contacts but only of a formal nature. Both were executors of Edward III's will and trustees of that property which eventually came to three religious houses, notably the abbey of St Mary Graces, London. Buckingham, the last surviving trustee, on 1 March 1399 released to St Mary Graces his rights in seven Kentish and two Surrey manors.

By then Buckingham had only a short time to live. He was not permitted to end his days at Lincoln, for on 27 February 1398 he was translated to the see of Coventry and Lichfield to make way for the promotion of Henry Beaufort (d. 1447) to Lincoln. Walsingham regarded the move as the responsibility of Beaufort's father, John of Gaunt. But Buckingham refused to move to Lichfield, and continued to rule Lincoln diocese until 12 July 1398. His movements then are obscure until around 25 August, by when he had arrived at Canterbury, where he spent the last few months of his life in Meister Omers, a house (still standing) which was part of the infirmary of Christ Church Priory. He died on 10 March 1399. His will, dated 9 February 1399, directed his burial in Canterbury Cathedral where his damaged memorial brass was seen by William Somner before 1640. Buckingham died a wealthy man. Precise bequests totalled upwards of £530, and his executors gave Canterbury Cathedral a further £1200 to found a chantry for his soul. Though he evidently had a large collection of vestments (but only declared two books, both psalters), Buckingham nevertheless directed that his funeral was to be conducted without worldly pomp.　A. K. McHARDY

Sources Lincs. Arch., Registers of Bishop Buckingham, 10, 11, 12, 12B [institutions I, institutions II, memoranda, royal writs] · A. K. McHardy, 'The crown and the diocese of Lincoln during the episcopate of John Buckingham, 1363–98', DPhil diss., U. Oxf., 1972 · A. K. McHardy, 'John Buckingham and Thomas Beauchamp, earl of Warwick', *Nottingham Medieval Studies*, 19 (1975), 127–35 · A. K. McHardy, 'The early ecclesiastical career of John Buckingham', *Lincolnshire History and Archaeology*, 8 (1973), 3–11 · A. K. McHardy, 'Bishop Buckingham and the Lollards of Lincoln diocese', *Schism, heresy and religious protest*, ed. D. Baker, SCH, 9 (1972), 131–46 · A. K. McHardy, 'The promotion of John Buckingham to the see of Lincoln', *Journal of Ecclesiastical History*, 26 (1975), 127–35 · C. E. Woodruff, ed., *Sede vacante wills*, Kent Archaeological Society Records Branch, 3 (1914) · *Chancery records* · Tout, *Admin. hist.* · Rymer, *Foedera*, new edn, vol. 3, pt 1 · BL, MS Arundel 68 · Lichfield Cathedral chapter act book, 1321–85, Bodl. Oxf., MS Ashmole 794 · *John of Gaunt's register*, ed. S. Armitage-Smith, 2 vols., CS, 3rd ser., 20–21 (1911) · *John of Gaunt's register, 1379–1383*, ed. E. C. Lodge and R. Somerville, 2 vols., CS, 3rd ser., 56–7 (1937) · *Thomae Walsingham, quondam monachi S. Albani, historia Anglicana*, ed. H. T. Riley, 2 vols., pt 1 of *Chronica monasterii S. Albani*, Rolls Series, 28 (1863–4) · W. Somner, *The antiquities of Canterbury*, ed. N. Battely, rev. edn (1703) · G. L. Harriss, *Cardinal Beaufort: a study of Lancastrian ascendancy and decline* (1988)

Archives Bodl. Oxf., MS Ashmole 794 · Lincs. Arch., registers | PRO, E101, E403

Wealth at death approx. £2000: Woodruff, ed., *Sede vacante wills*

Buckingham, Leicester Silk

Buckingham, Leicester Silk (1825–1867), playwright, the youngest son of James Silk *Buckingham (1786–1855), oriental traveller, and Elizabeth Jennings (1786–1865), was born at 11 Cornwall Terrace, Regent's Park, London, on 29 June 1825. Under the name of L. S. F. Y. Buckingham he married, at the age of eighteen, on 5 April 1844 at Gretna Green, Caroline Sarah, the fourth daughter of Captain Frederic White of her majesty's packet service, Weymouth; she later became a well-known and much respected actress under the stage name of Mrs Buckingham White.

In early life Buckingham accompanied his father on visits to the United States, France, and the East and acquired experiences that he later put to good use when he was a lecturer. When the Panopticon (afterwards the Alhambra in Leicester Square) was established in 1854 as a scientific institution, he was selected to write and deliver the explanatory description of the views of various countries. Later he was the lecturer engaged at the Egyptian Hall to illustrate Hamilton's 'Tour of Europe'. In his early years he associated himself with the stage and produced several light pieces at the Strand Theatre under J. Payne's direction in 1856–7, and for a short time undertook the responsibilities of management. Among the most successful comedies he afterwards wrote were *The Merry Widow* (1863), *Silken Fetters* (1863), *The Silver Lining* (1864), and *Faces in the Fire* (1865). As a dramatist he was largely indebted to the French stage, and the majority of his pieces were founded on the works of Parisian writers. His talents, however, were equal to much more than the work of a skilful adapter. From 1857 to 1867 he was dramatic and musical critic of the *Morning Star*. A singularly fluent and graceful writer, he was even more remarkable as a speaker.

Buckingham began writing at the age of nineteen, when he compiled the *Memoir of Mary Stuart, Queen of Scotland* (1844). This was followed by *Life and times of Louis Philippe, by the Rev. G. N. Wright. Continued to the Revolution of 1848 by L. F. A. Buckingham* (1850). *Belgium, the Rhine, Italy, Greece, and the Mediterranean, by the Rev. G. N. Wright and L. F. A. Buckingham* appeared in 1851, and in 1853 he published *The Bible in the middle age, with remarks on the libraries, schools, and religious aspects of mediaeval Europe*. He was also the author of more than thirty-five burlesques, comedies, and farces, of which many were written in conjunction with various members of the Savage Club, namely J. R. Planché, Frank Talfourd, H. J. Byron, Andrew Halliday, Frederick Lawrence, E. Falconer, and William Brough. During his comparatively short life he was known probably by a greater variety of first names than were almost any of his contemporaries. On various occasions he used Leicester, Leicester Ambrose, Leicester Silk (his birth-name), Leicester Forbes Ambrose, Leicester Stanhope, Leicester Stanhope Forbes, Leicester Stanhope Forbes Young, and Leicester Stanhope Forbes Young Ambrose. He also made use of the pseudonym Matthews & Co. when producing his first drama, *Aggravating Sam*, at the Lyceum in 1854. He died at Margate, Kent, on 15 July 1867, having converted to the Roman Catholic faith. His copyrights passed to the theatrical publisher Thomas Hailes Lacy, who in September 1873 bequeathed them to the Royal General Theatrical Fund.

G. C. BOASE, *rev.* NILANJANA BANERJI

Sources *N&Q*, 5th ser., 11 (1879), 244, 295 · Boase & Courtney, *Bibl. Corn.*, 1.48–9, 3.1099 · *The Era* (21 July 1867), 10 · *GM*, 4th ser., 4 (1867), 264

Buckingham, Thomas

Buckingham, Thomas (d. 1349), schoolman, probably came from Buckinghamshire. He is first recorded in 1324 as a fellow of Merton College, Oxford, a college which emphasized theology, and where he completed his studies for a master's degree c.1330, after which he began work on a doctorate. By 1338 he was commenting on the *Sentences* of Peter Lombard and he remained a full-time student until 1340, when he vacated his fellowship to become rector of the parish of Deene, Northamptonshire. The move brought little real change in his life, as he was given leave to continue his studies for two further years shortly thereafter. By 1346 he had both achieved his doctorate in theology and taken on ecclesiastical responsibilities. Bishop John Grandison of Exeter (d. 1369), who had studied at Paris and wished to encourage learning in his diocese, in that year appointed Buckingham to be chancellor of his cathedral church. It was during his few years in this position as chancellor that Buckingham discussed the fate of souls preceding the coming of Christ and composed the work for which he is remembered as a minor thinker of the period, the *Quaestiones theologicae*. Buckingham's career was cut short in 1349, most probably by the black death.

Buckingham's main intellectual interests were the relationship of free will and predestination, the nature of future contingents, and in what way the conclusions about these subjects influence our view of God and man. In his *Quaestiones super Sententias* (written *c*.1339, printed in 1505) he shows some predilection for untraditional notions, particularly on the topic of grace and sin. He argues for a neutral zone between the two wherein the absence of one does not imply the existence of the other. The existence of this middle ground (*medius status*) is necessary in order to ensure God's complete freedom. A lack of sin should not force God to supply grace. The middle ground is possible because of God's total or absolute power (*potentia absoluta*) and Buckingham's emphasis thereon is driven by his desire to portray God as infinitely free and completely omnipotent.

Similar tendencies and concerns permeate Buckingham's major work, his *Quaestiones theologicae*. It was written in direct response to Thomas Bradwardine's *De causa Dei*, composed in 1344, and deals primarily with questions about merit, demerit, free will, and action. Buckingham (who is reported to have engaged in a disputation with Bradwardine in Paris in 1343) is initially intent on claiming that he is not a Pelagian, one who believes that man is himself the prime mover towards his spiritual salvation. He was reacting against Bradwardine's virtual elimination of creaturely action in favour of God's immediate role in all decisions of rational creatures. Buckingham desired to rebut the accusation of Pelagianism which Bradwardine often levelled against those with whom he disagreed. This is not to say that Buckingham was particularly original in either his arguments against Bradwardine or his doctrines. He was indebted to both Duns Scotus (*d.* 1308) and William Ockham (*d.* 1349) and has been characterized by one authority as a follower of Scotus. Thomas Aquinas had argued that a distinction between proximate and ultimate causes, coupled with another distinction between absolute and suppositional necessity, was sufficient to maintain free will and the total immutability of God. Buckingham rejected this traditional Thomistic explanation of the seeming contradiction between an omniscient and omnipotent God and the doctrine of free will. To Buckingham this was insufficient and he, therefore, argued against Bradwardine's idea of God's 'necessitating' certain acts of 'free will'. He rightly pointed out that 'necessary acts of free will' were very much contradictory.

In one of his important arguments Buckingham is indebted to both Scotus and Ockham for some central concepts. He wants to maintain God's immutability while preserving the contingency of God's decisions. He argues that God can decide on a thing (eternally) and then decide something different. The trick is that the second decision wipes out the first. In this way the first is erased backwards for all eternity. To Buckingham (and in this portion of his argument he appears to be original) this does not suggest

mutability in God because change requires some transition from one term relative to another. Since God is eternal and beyond time, there is not in divine reality a 'before' or an 'after'. So any God-determined change proceeds backwards throughout eternity (God's timelessness) to erase the said 'change'. Such an argument gives one an inkling of the lengths to which Buckingham and many other theologians would go to preserve contingency and immutability in God. He is a disciple of Ockham in giving preponderance to God's omnipotence. Any human understanding of God as some entity with consistent attributes disappears. The construction of a God that remains immutable by changing as the future approaches the present is part of the fourteenth century's tendency to create a God more remote from man. In this sense Buckingham was very much a part of his age's movement towards the destruction of the ideal of a union between reason and faith. Whereas Bradwardine retreated to the Thomistic certainties of the previous generation, Buckingham joined the forces of nominalism and indeterminacy which ultimately led to the destruction of that edifice called the scholastic synthesis. PETER K. BENBOW

Sources B. R. de la Torre, *Thomas Buckingham and the contingency of futures* (1987) · G. Leff, *Bradwardine and the Pelagians* (1957), 227–41 · J. A. Robson, *Wyclif and the Oxford schools* (1961), 32–69 · A. R. Lee, 'Thomas Buckingham: a critical edition with commentary of the first question of the *Questiones super Sententias*', BLitt diss., U. Oxf., 1975 · M. D. Chenu, 'Le "Questiones" de Thomas de Buckingham', *Studia medievalia in honorem admodum reverendi patris Raymundi Josephi Martin*, ed. [B. L. van Helmond] (Bruges, 1948), 229–41 · W. A. Pantin, *The English church in the fourteenth century* (1955), 113–15 · Emden, *Oxf.* · A. Maier, *Die Vorlaufer Galileis im 14. Jahrhundert: Studien zur Näturphilosophie der Spätscholastik* (1949), 96 · P. S. Allen and H. W. Garrod, eds., *Merton muniments*, OHS, 86 (1928) · F. C. Higeston-Randolph, ed., *The register of John D. Grandisson, bishop of Exeter, 1331–1360* (1897), pt 2 of *The register of John D. Grandisson, bishop of Exeter, AD 1327–1369*
Archives Merton Oxf., MS 143 · New College, Oxford, MS 134

Buckingham and Chandos. For this title name *see* Grenville, Richard Temple-Nugent-Brydges-Chandos-, first duke of Buckingham and Chandos (1776–1839); Grenville, Richard Plantagenet Temple-Nugent-Brydges-Chandos-, second duke of Buckingham and Chandos (1797–1861); Grenville, Richard Plantagenet Campbell Temple-Nugent-Brydges-Chandos-, third duke of Buckingham and Chandos (1823–1889).

Buckingham and Normanby. For this title name *see* Sheffield, John, first duke of Buckingham and Normanby (1647–1721).

Buckinghamshire. For this title name *see* Hobart, John, first earl of Buckinghamshire (1693–1756); Hobart, John, second earl of Buckinghamshire (1723–1793); Hobart, George, third earl of Buckinghamshire (1731–1804); Hobart, Albinia, countess of Buckinghamshire (1737/8–1816) [*see under* Hobart, George, third earl of Buckinghamshire (1731–1804)]; Hobart, Robert, fourth earl of Buckinghamshire (1760–1816).

Buckland. For this title name *see* Berry, (Henry) Seymour, Baron Buckland (1877–1928).

Buckland, Francis Trevelyan (1826–1880), pisciculturist and naturalist, was born at Christ Church, Oxford, on 17 December 1826, the son of William *Buckland (1784–1856), canon of Christ Church, and his wife, Mary *Buckland (1797–1857), daughter of Benjamin Morland of Abingdon, Berkshire. He was baptized on 28 June 1827, in the college.

From his boyhood Buckland, who was always known as Frank, was an ardent lover of exotic pets. Among other animals, he kept at Christ Church a monkey, an eagle, a marmot, and a bear (which was at one time introduced to Charles Lyell), all of which, it seems, were allowed to roam about the college fairly freely. He was educated at Cotterstock, Northamptonshire (1835–7), at Laleham (1837–9) under his uncle, John Buckland, at Winchester College (1839–44), and at Christ Church, Oxford, where he proceeded BA on 18 May 1848. During the vacation of 1845 and subsequently, Buckland travelled to Giessen in Germany, to study chemistry with Liebig. After graduating he turned to medicine, going to St George's Hospital, London, first as a student from 1848 to 1851, and then as house surgeon from 1852 to 1853.

On 14 August 1854 Buckland became assistant surgeon in the 2nd Life Guards, with whom he remained until 1863. During this time he lived mainly in London, and eagerly embraced every opportunity of examining curious specimens of natural history, and abnormal growths, describing his observations in his *Curiosities of Natural History*, begun in 1858. The following year, among other eccentric activities, he engaged himself in the task of finding the remains of the great surgeon and anatomist John Hunter (1728–1793), for whom he held a deep reverence. Hunter's body had been interred in the vaults of St Martin-in-the-Fields, which were, at the time, being cleared. After weeks of searching Buckland found the coffin bearing Hunter's name, and his remains were duly transferred to Westminster Abbey, where Buckland's father had been dean since 1845. In 1860 Buckland applied for promotion to the position of senior surgeon with the Life Guards. His application was unsuccessful and he resigned his commission to pursue his literary and scientific career, with which he was having growing success. Buckland married on 11 August 1863, Hanna, née Papes (1829–1920), with whom he had previously had a son, Francis John (1851–1856).

In 1856 Buckland had joined the staff of the *Field* newspaper. He wrote largely for that paper until 1865 when he started a weekly journal of his own—*Land and Water*—in which most of his later writings appeared. *Land and Water* was described as an 'independent channel for diffusing knowledge of practical natural history, and fish and oyster culture'. It was about the time of its establishment that Buckland began to turn his attentions almost exclusively to matters concerning fish and fishing. He applied himself to the many economic questions affecting the artificial supply of salmon, the length of the close season, the condition of different salmon rivers, and similar investigations, gradually becoming the highest authority on pisciculture. In February 1867, following the resignation of Frederick Eden, one of the first of the two inspectors to be created by the Salmon Fisheries Act of 1861, he was appointed inspector of salmon fisheries. No more congenial post could have been offered to him, and from then on he devoted all his energies not merely to the duties of his office, but to the study of every point connected with the history of the salmon, and endeavoured in every way to improve the condition of British fisheries and those employed in them. This involved frequent visits to the rivers and coasts of the country, when he was always a welcome guest among people of all classes.

In May 1865 Buckland was appointed scientific referee to the South Kensington Museum. This required him to give a course of lectures and demonstrations, and in order to illustrate them he established a large collection of hatching apparatus, models of fish passes, casts of fish, implements of fishing, and so on at the museum. The collection, to which Buckland was constantly adding, expanded to form the basis of the International Fisheries Exhibition of 1883 and remained an important part of the Science Museum, as it was later known, in the late twentieth century. In the years that followed Buckland undertook a multitude of fisheries work. His last report was presented on 31 March 1880, by which time his health was breaking. During the following months he prepared new specimens for his museum, which he determined to leave to the nation. In June he underwent an operation for dropsy but died at his home, 37 Albany Street, Regent's Park, London, on 19 December 1880. Five days later he was buried at Brompton cemetery.

In his lifetime Buckland was regarded as one of the most whimsical of naturalists and, with all its stories of his doings and escapades, his biography was published in popular fiction as a 'good romance'. Besides numerous papers published in the *Field* and *Land and Water*, Buckland, in his capacity of inspector of salmon fisheries, reported annually on the salmon fisheries. He also wrote reports on the Scottish salmon fisheries, the Norfolk fisheries, and the crab and lobster, Scottish herring, and sea fisheries. He was the author of several books, of which his best known was *Curiosities of Natural History*.

M. G. WATKINS, rev. GILES HUDSON

Sources G. C. Bompas, *Life of Frank Buckland* (1885) • G. H. Burgess, *The curious world of Frank Buckland* (1967) • W. E. Snell, 'Frank Buckland—medical naturalist', *Proceedings of the Royal Society of Medicine*, 60 (1967), 291–6 • J. Dobson, 'Frank Buckland and rare Ben Jonson', *Proceedings of the Royal Society of Medicine*, 60 (1967), 296–8 • CGPLA Eng. & Wales (1881)
Archives Devon RO, corresp. and papers • Sci. Mus., collection of fishes | NHM, corresp. with William Clift and Richard Owen, letters • U. Newcastle, Robinson L., letters to Sir Walter Trevelyan
Likenesses photograph, June 1870, RCS Eng. • S. A. Walker, photograph, repro. in S. A. Walker, *Notes and jottings from animal life* (1882) • wood-engraving, NPG; repro. in *ILN* (1 Jan 1881)
Wealth at death under £10,000: probate, 2 April 1881, CGPLA Eng. & Wales

Buckland [Bocland], **Geoffrey of** (d. 1225), justice and administrator, was, like many contemporary government officials, a close associate of Hubert Walter. He witnessed several of Hubert's deeds and they appeared together in final concords, for example at Oxford in November 1195, St Benet of Hulme in April 1197, and Shrewsbury in January 1198. Final concords likewise record his activities as a justice, for example at Dunwich in July 1201, at the Tower of London in August 1202, and at Westminster in August 1204. He was also an itinerant justice in the east of England in 1194, and in the south under Geoffrey fitz Peter in 1202. However, and again like many Angevin administrators, Buckland did not exercise his talents in any one field. He devoted considerable time to the exchequer. When Robert de Bernières had his farm for Ormesby in Norfolk reduced in 1199 it was through Buckland that the justiciar passed this information to the exchequer barons. The pipe roll of 1203 mentions a roll of fines which Geoffrey of Buckland entered into the treasury, and he may at times have acted as the justiciar's deputy at the exchequer. An account of a lengthy dispute between the monasteries of Crowland and Spalding also reveals his prominence, reporting that when judgment was given in 1202 he was one of many 'nobles' who were at court for the business of the realm.

Buckland's importance at this time clearly stemmed in part from his close relationship with the justiciar, Geoffrey fitz Peter, whose sister-in-law had married William of Buckland, probably Geoffrey's elder brother. Indeed on one occasion after the justiciar's death a chancery clerk mistakenly described the two Geoffreys as brothers, when ordering Geoffrey of Buckland to sell to the king the corn and stock of Geoffrey fitz Peter's estate at Berkhamsted. Buckland witnessed several of the justiciar's writs, including the earliest surviving returned writ of novel disseisin, and various of Geoffrey fitz Peter's charters recording gifts to the church, for example the foundation of Shouldham Priory in Norfolk, which Buckland attended together with Hubert Walter.

Buckland's ecclesiastical career had begun by 24 September 1198 when he was archdeacon of Norwich, a post he may have held until about 1203. He received the churches of Teynham and Pagham in 1205 and 1206 respectively, and by 1210 he had been made dean of St Martin's-le-Grand. A dispute of the early 1220s shows him in conflict with the canons of St Martin's-le-Grand over the vicarage of Witham, while in 1224 a claim was made against him by the archdeacon of Colchester for Newport, an important portion of the deanery, and he obtained a writ of prohibition against the archdeacon. Buckland appears to have been less prominent in royal administration after c.1203–4, but late in John's reign the king entrusted him with the custody of Aylesbury. However, he became involved in the baronial revolt, and although he received letters of safe conduct to appear before the king, in 1216 his manor of Datchworth in Hertfordshire was forfeited and granted to Nicholas of Yealand. He returned to favour with the accession of Henry III and was still serving the king in 1224. He appears to have become a baron of the exchequer, and was an itinerant justice in eastern England 1218–21. He died between 31 August and 14 September 1225.

JOHN HUDSON

Sources D. M. Stenton, ed., *Pleas before the king or his justices*, 4 vols., SeldS, 67–8, 83–4 (1952–67) · *Chancery records* · *Pipe rolls* · *Curia regis rolls preserved in the Public Record Office* (1922–) · *Fasti Angl., 1066–1300*, [Monastic cathedrals] · S. Painter, 'Norwich's three Geoffreys', *Speculum*, 28 (1953), 808–13 · D. A. Carpenter, *The minority of Henry III* (1990) · D. Crook, *Records of the general eyre*, Public Record Office Handbooks, 20 (1982) · D. M. P. Stenton, *English justice between the Norman conquest and the Great Charter, 1066–1215* (1965) · C. R. Cheney, *Hubert Walter* (1967) · F. J. West, *The justiciarship in England, 1066–1232* (1966) · *CPR*

Buckland [Bocland], **Hugh of** (*d.* 1116x19), administrator, was sheriff of Berkshire and several other counties. He took his name from the manor of Buckland, near Faringdon, of which he was tenant under the monastery of Abingdon. Before the death of William Rufus he was already sheriff of Berkshire, Hertfordshire, and also possibly Bedfordshire. He is stated in the Abingdon history to have been one of the people who profited by the unjust transactions of Modbert, whom the king had appointed to administer the affairs of the monastery in the interest of the royal revenues, during the period when the office of abbot was vacant. A grant of 3 hides at Hanney was made to Buckland because he was sheriff of Berkshire and a royal justice. He was ordered by Henry I to restore to the abbey the possessions that he had in this manner wrongfully obtained. Notwithstanding this, the Abingdon historian gives him a high character for uprightness and wisdom. The same authority states that he was held in great esteem by Henry I, and that in 1110 he was sheriff of eight counties. The evidence of charters enables us to identify six of these, namely, Berkshire, Hertfordshire, Bedfordshire, Buckinghamshire, Essex, and London and Middlesex. Buckland was an addressee of the copy of Henry I's coronation charter that was sent to Hertfordshire. He held 10 hides at Buckland from the abbey of Abingdon for one knight's service, 1 hide from Richard of Winchester, perhaps at Missenden, and land at Ludgate from Roger of Salisbury. In 1102 Henry I granted him warren in his land of Kensworth, Hertfordshire. He may have been a canon of St Paul's, holding the prebend of Harlesden.

The date of Buckland's death is uncertain; he witnessed a royal charter on 28 December 1115, but a charter of the queen in 1116 or 1117 refers to him as if he had died shortly before. The Abingdon history says that William de Bochelande, presumably a son of Hugh, was sheriff of Berkshire in 1119, so it can be inferred that Hugh of Buckland was certainly dead by then.

Another Hugh of Buckland, who may have been a grandson of the subject of this article, was sheriff of Berkshire from 1170 to 1176, and was one of the itinerant justices in 1173 and 1174. In 1166 he held one knight's fee in chief, another from Abingdon, and Faringdon at farm.

HENRY BRADLEY, *rev.* JOHN HUDSON

Sources J. Stevenson, ed., *Chronicon monasterii de Abingdon*, 2 vols., Rolls Series, 2 (1858) · *Reg. RAN* · *Pipe rolls* · J. A. Green, *The government of England under Henry I* (1986) · J. A. Green, *English sheriffs to 1154* (1990) · C. N. L. Brooke, 'The composition of the chapter of St Paul's, 1086–1163', *Cambridge Historical Journal*, 10 (1950–52), 111–32 · E. J. Kealey, *Roger of Salisbury, viceroy of England* (1972) · Foss, *Judges*, vol. 1

Buckland [*née* Morland], **Mary** (1797–1857), geological art- ist and curator, was born on 20 November 1797 in St Hel- en's parish, Abingdon, Berkshire, the eldest daughter of Benjamin Morland (1768–1833), solicitor (and a member of the West Ilsley brewing family), and his wife, Harriet Baster (1777–1799). Benjamin Morland was much involved in local politics and had made money during the Napo- leonic wars. He was also involved in both canal promo- tions and Forest of Dean coalmines.

Mary Morland's mother died just over a year after her birth and it was her father who first aroused in her an interest in geology. She was educated in Southampton but also developed a close relationship with the childless regius professor of anatomy at Oxford, Sir Christopher *Pegge (1764/5–1822), and spent some of her childhood with him and his wife in Oxford. Pegge had been an early advocate of the importance of teaching geology at Oxford, and had given a number of private lectures in mineralogy. His admiration of Mary Morland culminated in his bequest to her in 1822 of 'his mineral cabinets and all the minerals and fossils contained in them at the time of my decease and all my books of natural history and compara- tive anatomy as a mark of my esteem and regard for her' (will of Christopher Pegge).

On 31 December 1825, at Marcham, Berkshire, Mary Morland married William *Buckland (1784–1856), profes- sor of geology and mineralogy at Oxford University, who was thirteen years her senior. She clearly brought her own geological interests to this marriage, so the famous 1839 anecdote of their introduction—in a Dorset coach dis- covering a mutual admiration for Georges Cuvier—may have had some truth to it. Mary was certainly involved in independent geological investigations by 1819, when Buckland first mentions his extensive obligations to her and had been sending Georges Cuvier drawings of *Megalo- saurus* (later published by William Buckland) from 1822.

Mary Buckland played a vital, if now forgotten, role in her husband's meteoric rise as geologist and founder of the Oxford school of geology. She accompanied him on a year-long wedding tour of the continent, and on their return she created a home for him in which the 'dust and rubbish [were] held sacred to geology' (Fox, 1.83). She cor- rected Buckland's fine prose and wrote much of it at his dictation. Her skill as an artist was also put to use in Buck- land's wonderfully illustrated *Reliquiae diluvianae* (1823) and his *Bridgewater Treatise* (1836). She was 'neat and clever in mending fossils' with specially developed cements, in making models of them, and in assisting Buckland's experiments to reproduce fossil tracks—all vital evidence for Buckland's science. She was Buckland's curator, and 'hardly a fossil or bone in the Oxford Museum … [had] not her handwriting upon it' (Kölbl-Ebert, 33).

Mary Buckland also played a vital role in the education of the five of her nine children who survived childhood; the eldest, Francis (Frank) *Buckland (1826–1880), became a renowned naturalist. Worn out with caring for her hus- band, who had slipped into mental decline from about 1842 and had been placed in John Bush's Mental Asylum at

Clapham in London in 1850, Mary Buckland died on 30 November 1857 at St Leonards, Sussex. She was buried at Islip, Oxfordshire.   H. S. TORRENS

Sources E. O. Gordon, *The life and correspondence of William Buck- land* (1894) • M. Kölbl-Ebert, 'Mary Buckland, *née* Morland 1797– 1857', *Earth Sciences History*, 16 (1997), 33–8 • F. T. Buckland, 'Memoir of Very Rev William Buckland', in W. Buckland, *Geology and miner- alogy* (1858), xxxv–xxxvii • C. Fox, *Memories of old friends*, ed. H. N. Pym (1882), 1.83–4 • G. C. Bompas, *Life of Frank Buckland* (1885) • P. Taquet, 'Cuvier–Buckland–Mantell et les dinosaures', *Actes du symposium paléontologique G. Cuvier*, ed. E. Buffetaut, J. M. Mazin, and E. Salmon (1983), 475–94 • census returns for Abingdon and Clapham, London, 1851 • Burke, *Gen. GB* (1937) [under Morland] • F. T. Buckland, *Curiosities of natural history*, 2nd ser. (1900), 54–64 • will of Christopher Pegge, PRO

Archives MHS Oxf., William Buckland MSS • RCS Eng., letters to Frank Buckland • Trinity Cam., letters to Whewell

Likenesses photograph (in old age), repro. in G. H. O. Burgess, *The curious world of Frank Buckland* (1967) • silhouette, repro. in Gordon, *Life and correspondence*, 103

Buckland, Ralph (1564–1611), Roman Catholic priest, was the son of Edmund Buckland and was descended from an ancient family at West Harptree, Somerset. After studying at the Merchant Taylors' School from June 1571 he became a commoner of Magdalen College, Oxford, in the Michael- mas term 1579. Before taking a degree he went up to Lon- don to study law at the inns of court. There 'he spent a great deal of time in reading books of controversy, which filled him with scruples concerning the religion of his country, and at last ended in his conversion to the Cath- olic faith' (Dodd, 2.385) and his departure for the English College at Rheims. From Rheims he was sent to the other English College at Rome in February 1586; he was ordained priest at the Lateran on 7 August 1588. After returning to Rheims he was sent to the English mission in December 1588. He lived in England for several years, dur- ing which time he worked on his translations of Surius's *Saints Lives* and Victor's *Vandal Persecution*.

With the accession of James I, Buckland was prompted to write his major work, *Seven Sparkes of the Enkindled Soule*, along with 'four lamentations composed in the hard times of Q. Elizabeth'. The work evidently belongs to the years 1603–5, considering its pious aspirations for the rec- onciliation of Britain with Rome such as occupied the minds of English Catholics on James's accession. This book acquired subsequent notoriety from a sermon preached by the primate of Ireland, James Ussher, at St Mary's Church, Oxford, on 5 November 1640. From it Ussher cited passages to show that English Catholics were aware of the Gunpowder Plot beforehand and prayed for its success. One such passage was from Psalms 2, 'But the memory of novelties shall perish with a crack: as a ruin- ous house falling to the ground'. The accusation is, how- ever, rejected as fanciful by Wood.

Another book of Buckland's, *An Embassage from Heaven*, has its setting in the aftermath of the Gunpowder Plot, when many Catholics were hastening, with the encour- agement of certain priests, to prove their loyalty to the king not only by taking the new oath of allegiance but also by attending services and sermons in the Anglican church. To his title, therefore, the author adds: 'Christ giveth to understand his iust indignation against al such as being catholikely minded, doe yeelde their presence to the rites and praier of the malignant church'. To the end of his book he appends a metrical epilogue which shows some signs of poetical talent. About this time Buckland was arrested and banished, and he arrived at Douai on 24 July 1606. Yet soon afterwards he risked a return to England, where he laboured as a missioner until his death in 1611. He is said to have left behind him the character of 'a most pious and seraphical person, who went beyond all of his time for fervent devotion' (Wood, 2.107).

PETER MILWARD

Sources C. Dodd [H. Tootell], *The church history of England, from the year 1500, to the year 1688*, 2 (1739), 385–6 · Wood, *Ath. Oxon.*, new edn, 2.105–7 · Gillow, *Lit. biog. hist.*, 1.332–3 · G. Anstruther, *The seminary priests*, 1 (1969), 57 · P. Milward, *Religious controversies of the Jacobean age* (1978), 159 · DNB

Buckland, Richard (d. 1436), merchant and administrator, was a member of the Fishmongers' Company in the city of London and treasurer of Calais. The names of his parents are unknown, although he had a brother, Christopher. The bequest in his will to the collegiate church of St Mary Ottery in Devon may indicate that he came originally from the west country.

Buckland was a man of drive, energy, and enterprise who served both Henry V and the duke of Bedford when he was regent of France and conducted his own business as a merchant and shipowner. He made an advantageous marriage, his wife, Joan, being the daughter of Richard Gifford, also a member of the Fishmongers' Company. Buckland probably married Joan some time before 1407, since their only child, Agnes, was married by 1420 to Robert *Whittingham. Joan herself was a minor when her father died in 1399 leaving property in the city, mostly in Distaff Lane near St Paul's, and £35 for gifts to the poor and for obits. His widow, Agnes (d. 1427), originally from Essex, looked after the interests of her young family energetically. Joan, however, benefited from the fact that one brother and one sister entered monastic orders, and the remaining brother, Thomas, died in 1435. She, therefore, came to control the bulk of her late father's property. This may not have been as great a help to her husband as the connection with the Fishmongers' Company; he was elected in 1409 with the help of John Hill, his father-in-law's executor, who at the time was the tenant of Joan's inherited tenement in Distaff Lane.

Buckland now began to prosper. By 1415 he was collector of tunnage and poundage in the port of London and made the first of many loans to the crown to support the Agincourt campaign. Two of his own ships assisted in the siege of Harfleur; for this he was rewarded with a grant of The Peacock inn in the captured town. Later he had a half share in the *Antony of London* (280 tuns) and obtained the *Grand Marie* (126 tuns) in 1423 from William Soper, the clerk of the king's ships, to whom he occasionally supplied naval stores. Like many of his colleagues he trod a delicate line between legitimate trade, for example supplying goods for the royal wardrobe, and employing sharp practice—in 1419, for instance, his mariners, with doubtful legality, took a rich and varied cargo of luxury foods and wines from a Genoese carrack off Plymouth.

The main area of Buckland's activities from 1417 was Calais, where he was first victualler and from 1421 to 1436 also treasurer. Through these offices he had close contact with the duke of Bedford, whose councils in both England and France he joined by 1426, later becoming one of his executors. He must have journeyed frequently between London and Calais on business, since he was also involved in more mundane royal commissions to take musters, to hear admiralty cases, and the like. He even found time to sit as an MP for Northamptonshire in the parliaments of 1425 and 1431. None of these jobs was a sinecure: at Calais he not only had to deal with day-to-day administration but also to concern himself with such matters as the apparent loss on the way from Lombardy of armour for the king himself. He may have been guilty of sharp practice here too, since he was accused with his son-in-law and successor, Whittingham, of diverting timber and bricks from the Calais works for repairs to his own properties in Edgcote and London.

Throughout his life Buckland had invested in property in the city (valued at £100 in 1436), in Northampton, and elsewhere. His main London house, bought in 1417, was in the parish of All Hallows-the-Great, near the Steelyard. His country house was at Edgcote, near Banbury, held with nearby farmland at Sewell; in 1428 he also bought further lands in the midlands from his fellow MP Thomas Chambre and his wife and, in 1434, a manor in Essex, Copthall. He died in All Hallows-the-Great on 10 August 1436, a very wealthy man; his widow, however, was faced with the need to fight appeals in two maritime cases and great difficulties in settling his accounts as treasurer and in concluding his responsibilities regarding the Bedford executorship. The crown owed Buckland at his death over £3433, of which £1100 was still outstanding in 1445. A magnificent jewelled cross pledged by Bedford to Buckland in 1433 was finally obtained by Joan in 1456 in part settlement of debts of over £1000. In his will, made five days before his death, he left over £350 for masses and charitable gifts, and £100 and an unusual columbine-shaped silver cup to his daughter, Agnes. Joan, his widow, was also well provided for: her will (dating from 1450, though she survived until 1462), lovingly lists bequests of her plate, linens, and elegant gowns furred with miniver and marten, as well as legacies for charity and to the local clergy. The inheritance of Buckland's real property was complicated by the facts that Agnes died before her mother in 1456 and her own eldest son was attainted as a Lancastrian in 1461. Provision was made for his younger brother, Richard, to inherit, but the properties came into the hands of Richard Clarell, apparently once Buckland's apprentice, who in his late fifties married Richard's daughter Margaret. Buckland asked for his marble gravestone in the Pardon churchyard at St Paul's to be carved with his coat of arms and the words, 'Mercy and Grace', a modest epitaph to his active life.

SUSAN ROSE

Sources J. Stratford, 'Joan Buckland (*d.* 1462)', *Medieval London widows, 1300–1500*, ed. C. M. Barron and A. F. Sutton (1994), 113–28 · S. Rose, ed., *The navy of the Lancastrian kings*, Navy Records Society (1982), 232 and *passim* · J. Stratford, *The Bedford inventories: the worldly goods of John, duke of Bedford, regent of France, 1389–1435* (1993), 211–12, 402–3, 408 · PRO · *Letters of Queen Margaret of Anjou and Bishop Beckington and others written in the reigns of Henry V and Henry VI*, ed. C. Monro, CS, 86 (1863), 18–24, 34–45 · F. J. Furnivall, ed., *The fifty earliest English wills in the court of probate, London, AD 1387–1439*, EETS, original ser., 78 (1882), 104–8 · A. Clark, ed., *Lincoln diocese documents, 1450–1544*, EETS, 149 (1914), 37–44 · J. Bridges, *The history and antiquities of Northamptonshire*, ed. P. Whalley, 2 vols. (1791), vol. 1, pp. 118–20, 201, 239–6; vol. 2, p. 34 [genealogy is erroneous] · R. Brown, H. M. Colvin, and A. J. Taylor, eds., *The history of the king's works*, 1–2 (1963) · G. Baker, *The history and antiquities of the county of Northampton*, 1 (1822–30), 492–6 · P. H. Reaney and M. Fitch, eds., *Feet of fines for Essex*, Essex Archaeological Society, 4: 1423–1447 (1964), 20–21 · L. Drucker, ed., *Warwickshire feet of fines*, 3, Dugdale Society, 18 (1943), 146

Wealth at death very wealthy; left charitable donations of over £350; also £100 to daughter, and £20 to any child of hers for their marriage; £20 to brother and £10 to nephew; also left varying sums of money to servants, friends, and executors totalling £88 13*s.* 4*d.*; further bequest gave every married couple in Edgecote 2*s.* and every single man and child 1*s.*: Furnivall, ed., *The fifty earliest English wills*, 104–8

Buckland, William (1784–1856), geologist and dean of Westminster, was born on 12 March 1784 at Axminster, Devon, the eldest son of Charles Buckland (1750–1828/9), rector of Templeton and Trusham, and his first wife, Elizabeth (1756–1812), daughter of John Oke, of Combpyne near Axminster. His interest in natural history and geology was aroused when he was a boy exploring the quarries and woods of his native Devon, often with his father. He was educated at home by his father until he entered Blundell's School, Tiverton, for a year in 1797, before continuing to Winchester College, where he extended his fossil collecting to sponges and others from the chalk of the nearby downs. Partly through the interest of his uncle, John Buckland, fellow of Corpus Christi College, Oxford, he obtained a scholarship to that college in 1801, gaining his BA in classics and theology three years later; he was elected a fellow of his college in 1808, when he was ordained priest. Buckland's meagre salary from the college, eked out by fees from undergraduates whom he tutored in classics, enabled him to pursue his growing interest in natural history, particularly in minerals and geology in general. He attended the lectures of John Kidd, reader in mineralogy, and of Sir Christopher Pegge on anatomy. At the same time he engaged in field investigations around Oxford and beyond, often with his younger friend W. J. Broderip of Oriel College, and from 1808 to 1812 he rode on horseback over extensive areas of southwest and midland England, collecting rocks and fossils that would in time form the nucleus of the University Museum collection.

Lecturer in geology On Dr Kidd's resignation in 1813 Buckland was appointed reader in mineralogy, and to the new readership in geology in 1818. The following year he delivered his inaugural lecture, *Vindiciae geologicae*, in which he

William Buckland (1784–1856), by Thomas Phillips, 1836

reassured his audience that the facts of geology are consonant with the record of the Bible. In particular, the distribution of older gravels ('diluvium') capping isolated hills around Oxford could not be explained by the action of present-day rivers, and seemed to Buckland convincing evidence for 'an universal deluge' which he equated with Noah's flood. Much of the *Vindiciae* was derived from material supplied by his friend and mentor William D. Conybeare of Christ Church (Edmonds, '*Vindiciae geologicae*').

Buckland's lectures on geology and mineralogy, given in the old Ashmolean Museum, were for many years the most popular in the university. They were attended mainly by senior members of the university including heads of colleges, future bishops and archbishops, and such luminaries as Arnold, Hampden, Keble, Newman, Pusey, Whately, Wilberforce, and, notably, Charles Lyell, later the leading geologist of the mid-nineteenth century and Darwin's geological mentor. By all accounts Buckland's lectures were anything but dull: they were enlivened by his benevolent good humour, by jokes, and even by impersonations of the gait of extinct animals. They were copiously illustrated by maps, drawings, and spectacular fossils and mineral specimens. Parts of his courses were given in quarries and on hills around Oxford and further afield, sometimes from horseback.

Buckland's fame spread as a result of his investigations

of fossil cave faunas. These started in Germany during a visit in 1816, and led to his excavations in 1821 of Kirkdale Cavern, Yorkshire (brought to his attention by one of his 'pupils', Edward Legge, bishop of Oxford and warden of All Souls). There he discovered and identified numerous bones of hyenas, with those of elephant, hippopotamus, rhinoceros, ox, deer, bear, fox, water rats, and birds. Bones of exotic animals found in Britain had previously been dismissed as remnants of Roman importations or as jumbled collections swept in from tropical countries by Noah's flood: Buckland's brilliant interpretation of the cave as an 'ante-diluvial' den of hyenas which had dragged in carrion or prey caused a sensation. He backed up his hypothesis (in the face of much scepticism) by comparing rounded fossil objects from the cave with modern hyena faeces; and by feeding ox bones to captive hyenas he obtained splintered bones identical to fossil bones from Kirkdale. The results were published in his *Reliquiae diluvianae* of 1823, and have been used to claim that he can be regarded as the first palaeoecologist (Brook; P. J. Boylan, 'Foundations of taphonomy').

Life at Christ Church By 1825 Buckland, then aged forty, was still existing on £200 per annum from his two readerships, with a few guineas from his students, and was considering leaving Oxford for a position, such as vicar, elsewhere. However, with the help of influential friends (including Sir Robert Peel) he succeeded in obtaining a glittering prize in the form of a canonry of Christ Church. Charles Lyell commented in some astonishment and envy in a letter to Gideon Mantell (20 July 1825): 'Buckland, as you know, is made by Lord Liverpool a canon of Christ Church, a good house, 1000l. per annum, and no residence or duty required. Surely such places ought to be made also for lay geologists' (*Life, Letters, and Journals*, 1.1611). Buckland lost no time in marrying, on 31 December 1825; his wife, Mary *Buckland, *née* Morland (1797–1857), was a talented naturalist and scientific illustrator who had worked for him in tracing the distinctive quartzite pebbles in the Oxford 'diluvium' to the Lickey Hills near Birmingham. Five of their nine children reached adulthood; the eldest, Francis Trevelyan *Buckland (1826–1880) became a renowned naturalist.

The next two decades were the heyday of Buckland's fame and achievement. He and his wife presided over an extensive set of rooms at Christ Church, overflowing with geological specimens and a great variety of exotic pets, where Buckland delighted in entertaining guests to such delicacies as toasted field mice, crocodile steaks, hedgehog, puppy, ostrich, and snail. His avowed ambition was to eat his way through the animal kingdom, and he lost no opportunity in sampling a new member. This was not altogether a frivolous purpose, however, for one of the declared aims of the 1825 prospectus of the Zoological Society of London (of which Buckland was a founder member) was the introduction of new and useful animals with a view to improving the inadequate diet of most of the population.

Contemporary portraits show Buckland as of medium height and good looking. He affected a somewhat eccentric dress, and always wore his academic gown in the field. He was seldom seen without a large blue bag, from which he delighted to draw out (in senior common rooms and at dinner parties) his latest treasures, such as fossil bones of all kinds, mammoth teeth and skin, hyena skulls, and fossil faeces of giant marine reptiles. These last Buckland had first obtained and identified from Lyme Regis (where he worked with the famous fossil collector Mary Anning) and named coprolites, a term he bequeathed to the English tongue. From their contents he deduced the diet of these extinct monsters whose discovery was astonishing the scientific world. While most of his audiences were charmed, amused, and instructed, some of his peers were critical of his pre-Victorian, sometimes scatological, sense of humour and lack of the *gravitas* deemed appropriate for a scientific savant of the time. These included Darwin, who was definitely not amused by Buckland's showmanship and buffoonery. The affection in which Buckland was held by his contemporaries, however, is attested in numerous humorous satirical poems and cartoons by his friends such as De la Beche and Sopwith.

Later years and reputation Buckland published some forty papers and books, and the major work of his later years, his lavishly illustrated Bridgewater Treatise (1836), in which he abandoned his former belief in the universal effects of the Noachian deluge, was highly influential. The spectacular coloured representation of the history of the earth contained in the Treatise, showing the reconstructed fauna and flora of each geological period, strikingly illustrates the idea of a progressive history of life on earth, which Lyell at the time was denying. Buckland's research into and understanding of the adaptive hydrostatic function of the shell of ammonites, long ignored, has been recognized as correct and ahead of its time (Jacobs). He was the first to describe and name what became a fossil dinosaur, *Megalosaurus*, and from the same Jurassic deposit the sensational fossil 'Stonesfield opossums'—the first pre-Tertiary mammalian fossils known. He excavated and described the bones of the so-called Red Lady from Paviland, a cave in south Wales, though his interpretation of this as probably a camp follower of the Roman army was far from the mark. This important relic is now established as the skeleton of a man of the Gravettian period (palaeolithic), and claimed to be the first fossil human remains recovered. From the outset Buckland, although ever a sincere Anglican, was never a biblical literalist. He recognized that vast periods of geological time, possibly even 'millions of millions' of years had existed before the creation of Adam. After a visit in 1838 to Switzerland, where his friend Agassiz convinced him that glaciation had been far more extensive in the past, he reinterpreted his vast collection of observations for a catastrophic flood over Britain as evidence for the new and revolutionary glacial theory, which he and Agassiz introduced to an initially sceptical British geological establishment.

Wherever possible, Buckland employed experimental methods. One night, puzzling over some newly discovered and problematic fossil footprints, he roused his sleeping wife and asked her to prepare a slab of dough in her kitchen at Christ Church. Then he caused his pet tortoise to walk across it, the results convincing him that the fossil footprints had been made by a long extinct relative. This demonstration was repeated at a party in Roderick Murchison's house for a group of 'geologists and savants'; before a proper consistency was attained, the dough had to be kneaded afresh and it was 'a glorious scene to behold all the philosophers, flour-besmeared, working away with tucked up sleeves' (Murray IV, 8). Buckland's 'geopolitical' achievements were considerable: he was a leading light of the Geological Society, of which he was twice president, fellow of the Royal Society, president of the British Association for the Advancement of Science in 1832, and an active member of many other scientific societies. Buckland's reputation in the field of archaeology is attested by the invitation in 1842 to perform the unrolling of a mummy in Shrewsbury (he declined). His support of Henry De la Beche in the foundation of the fledgeling Geological Survey of Great Britain was probably crucial.

By 1845 Buckland was becoming dissatisfied with the academic scene in Oxford, which he perceived as hostile to science, and accepted appointment (procured largely through his patron, Robert Peel) as dean of Westminster; this was coupled with the rectorship of Islip, near Oxford. Initially he continued to travel to Oxford to deliver his courses on geology. He began to introduce reforms and improvements to the fabric of the abbey and the nearby Westminster School, including clearing the cesspits of centuries' worth of ordure, and constructing a system of lined sewers. In 1849 in his sermon on the occasion of thanksgiving for the abatement of a cholera epidemic he took the text 'Wash and be clean', urging good sanitation and hygiene and castigating avaricious slum landlords who neglected the dwellings of the poor. These views caused quite a sensation, and possibly some resentment among the establishment members of his London congregation. In 1850 (and probably for several years before) signs of a severe mental breakdown (possibly resulting from a fall from a coach) became apparent, and prevented Buckland from performing his duties as dean or professor. He retired to Islip, but later was placed in The Retreat, John Bush's mental asylum at Clapham, where he died on 14 August 1856. He was buried at Islip church.

For a century after his death Buckland's reputation suffered a decline: he was largely remembered as an eccentric figure who tried unsuccessfully to reconcile geology with Old Testament accounts, and as a champion of 'diluvialism' and an outmoded catastrophism which was destroyed and superseded by the 'uniformitarianism' of Lyell. However, recent reappraisals, in particular those by Rupke (1983) and Boylan (1997), have shown that, on the contrary, Buckland was one of the leading figures in the golden age of geology. It could be argued that more than anyone else he was responsible for making geology, and in particular the concept of 'deep time', acceptable to the Anglican establishment centred on Oxford, and so for paving the way for the Darwinian revolution.

NEVILLE HAILE

Sources Mrs. Gordon, *Life and correspondence of William Buckland, D.D., F.R.S.* (1894) · N. A. Rupke, *The great chain of history: William Buckland and the English school of geology, 1814–1849* (1983) · F. T. Buckland, 'Memoir of the Very Rev. William Buckland', in W. Buckland, *Geology and mineralogy considered with reference to natural theology*, [3rd edn], ed. F. T. Buckland, 2 vols. (1858), xvii–lxx · H. S. Torrens, 'Geology and the natural sciences: some contributions to archaeology in Britain, 1780–1850', *The study of the past in the Victorian age* (1998) · *A catalogue of the valuable scientific library of the William Buckland* (1857) [sale catalogue, 1857] · P. J. Boylan, 'William Buckland (1784–1856) and the foundations of taphonomy and palaeoecology', *Archives of Natural History*, 24 (1997), 361–72 · A. J. Brook, 'The Rev. William Buckland, the first palaeoecologist', *Biology*, 40/4 (1993), 149–52 · G. L. Davies, *The earth in decay: a history of British geomorphology, 1578 to 1878* [1969] · J. M. Edmonds, 'Patronage and privilege in education: a Devon boy goes to school, 1798', *Report and Transactions of the Devonshire Association*, 110 (1978), 95–111 · J. M. Edmonds, 'Founding of the Oxford readership in geology', *Notes and Records of the Royal Society*, 34 (1979–80), 33–51 · J. M. Edmonds, 'Vindiciae geologicae, published 1820; the inaugural lecture of William Buckland', *Archives of Natural History*, 18 (1991), 255–68 · J. M. Edmonds and Douglas, 'William Buckland, FRS (1784–1856), and an Oxford geological lecture, 1823', *Notes and Records of the Royal Society*, 30 (1975–6), 141–67 · D. K. Jacobs, 'The support of hydrostatic load in cephalopod shells', *Evolutionary Biology*, 26 (1992) · G. V. Cox, *Recollections of Oxford* (1868), 350 · P. J. Boylan, 'Dean William Buckland, 1784–1856: a pioneer in cave science', *Studies in Speleology*, 1/5 (1967), 237–55 · P. J. Boylan, 'An unpublished portrait of Dean William Buckland, 1784–1856', *Journal of the Society of the Bibliography of Natural History*, 5 (1968–71), 350–54 · D. R. Dean, *Gideon Mantell and the discovery of dinosaurs* (1999) · *Life, letters, and journals of Sir Charles Lyell*, ed. Mrs Lyell, 1 (1881), 161 · d. cert. · private information (2004) · J. Murray IV, *John Murray III, 1808–1892: a brief memoir* (1919) · S. Aldhouse-Green, ed., *Paviland Cave and the 'Red Lady'* (2000)

Archives BGS, drawings and lecture notes · BL, corresp., Add. MS 38091 · Bodl. Oxf., Radcliffe Science Library · Christ Church Oxf. · Devon RO, corresp. and papers · FM Cam. · Linn. Soc., letters to Linnean Society · Linn. Soc. · NL Wales, corresp. · NMG Wales · Oxf. U. Mus. NH, lecture notes and corresp. · Philpott Museum, Lyme Regis · RS · University of Bristol Library, corresp. | BL, letters to Charles Babbage, Add. MSS 37183–37200, *passim* · BL, letters to Philip Bliss, Add. MSS 34569–34581, *passim* · BL, letters to Lord Grenville, Add. MS 58995 · BL, corresp. with Sir Robert Peel, Add. MSS 40355–40600, *passim* · Castle Ashby, Northampton, letters to the marquess of Northampton · FM Cam., corresp. with William Baker and Thomas Webster, notes, and papers · ICL, corresp. with Lord Playfair, Sir Robert Peel, and others · MHS Oxf., letters to Andrew Bloxam · NA Scot., corresp. with Sir Charles Murray · NHM, letters on the fossil Edentata of South America to J. B. Pentland and W. Parish · NHM, letters to members of the Sowerby family · NL NZ, Turnbull L., letters to Gideon Algernon Mantell · NMG Wales, letters to Sir Henry de la Beche · RBG Kew, letters to Sir William Hooker · RCS Eng., letters to Sir Richard Owen · Trinity Cam., letters to Sir William Whewell · U. Newcastle, Trevelyan MSS · U. St Andr. L., corresp. with James Forbes · University of Bristol Library, Eyles MSS

Likenesses A. Edouart, silhouette, 1828, Woodwardian Museum, Cambridge · S. Howell, oils, exh. RA 1829, CCC Oxf. · T. Phillips, oils, 1832, Westminster Abbey, London, deanery · T. Phillips, portrait, 1836; photograph, U. Oxf., department of geology and mineralogy [*see illus.*] · W. Brockedon, black-and-red chalk drawing, 1838, NPG · W. Brockedon, chalk drawing, 1838, NPG · H. Weekes, marble bust, 1856, Westminster Abbey, London · H. Weekes, marble bust, exh. RA 1858, Oxf. U. Mus. NH · H. Weekes, bust, 1860, Geological Museum, London · A. Hooker, oils, 1894 (after T. C. Thompson), Oxf. U. Mus. NH · A. Claudet, engraving (after daguerreotype), NPG · C. Hullmandel, lithograph (after G. Rowe), NPG · T. H. Maguire, lithograph (after daguerreotype by Claudet), NPG; repro. in T. H. Maguire, *Portraits of honorary members of the Ipswich Museum* (1852) · T. Phillips, oils, NPG · G. Rowe, lithograph (after C. Hullmandel), NPG · H. Weekes, bronze bust, NPG · mezzotint (after engraving), NPG

Buckland, William Warwick (1859–1946), jurist, was born on 11 June 1859 at Moor Park, Aller, near Newton Abbot, Devon, the fifth son of Francis Buckland, furniture dealer, and his wife, Sarah Segar (or Mortimer). Buckland, whose twin brother did not survive, was one of ten children. His mother died when he was very young and his father married again, and moved to Edmonton where he practised as a surveyor. Buckland was educated at Guînes, near Calais, at St John's College, Hurstpierpoint, at the Crystal Palace School of Engineering, and at Gonville and Caius College, Cambridge. He was placed first in the first class of the law tripos in 1884 and was awarded the chancellor's medal for legal studies in 1885. He became a scholar of his college in 1884, and a fellow in 1889, the year in which he was called to the bar by the Inner Temple, London. In 1890 Buckland married Eva Taylor, with whom he was said to have enjoyed 'a perfect married life' until her death in 1934 (McNair and Duff, 283). They had one daughter.

Buckland became a college lecturer at Cambridge in 1895, but in 1900 he suffered an attack of tuberculosis. There followed a long period of precarious health, during which he underwent two operations and spent many months in South Africa and the Canary Islands, accompanied by his wife and daughter. Eventually he made a good recovery and, though he was always small and thin, and in his later years suffered from hearing loss, he was active and alert in body and mind to the end of his life.

In 1903 Buckland became a tutor of Caius College and from 1912 he was senior tutor, until his appointment in 1914 as regius professor of civil law. During the First World War he served for a time in the Ministry of Munitions. In 1923 he was elected president (vice-master) of his college, in which capacity he was particularly adept in his relations with the younger fellows. He lectured at the Harvard law school in 1925. During his visit to America he also delivered the Storrs lectures at the Yale law school. He retired from the professorship in September 1945, but lectured for one more term.

Buckland taught all branches of English law before he became regius professor. He was an excellent lecturer, provided his audience was able and willing to follow the speed of his thought and speech. However, he evidently was at his 'very best' in 'a small class of advanced students where he could provoke discussion' (McNair and Duff, 285). Perhaps he might have become a historian of English law had his close friendship with and great admiration for F. W. Maitland started sooner. Instead, Buckland's enduring monument is what he wrote about Roman law. His

William Warwick Buckland (1859–1946), by Sir James Gunn, 1936

first book was *The Roman Law of Slavery* (1908), a thorough and masterly survey of 'the most characteristic part of the most characteristic intellectual product of Rome' (p. v.). *Equity in Roman Law* (1911) and *Elementary Principles of the Roman Private Law* (1912) were shorter works, difficult, but stimulating. His masterpiece was *A Text-Book of Roman Law from Augustus to Justinian* (1921; 2nd edn, 1932; 3rd edn, 1963; revised by Peter Stein). At the close of the twentieth century, Buckland's treatise remains possibly the most important work on Roman law ever published in English. Its broad principles are plainly expounded, but closer study reveals an endless wealth of detail and countless independent and acute judgments on disputed issues. *A Text-Book* fully reflects Buckland's most impressive scholarly assets—a razor-sharp analytical mind, 'massive erudition' (Hoeflich, 121), and 'extraordinary mastery of the texts' (Nicholas, 271). Moreover, despite its formidable length—744 pages—it may be 'the easiest to read of all Buckland's books' (McNair and Duff, 289). In 1922 it received the Ames prize of the Harvard law school, awarded for the best law book or legal essay written in English, and published between one and five years before the award.

Buckland also wrote a number of other works on Roman law. *A Manual of Roman Private Law* (1925; 2nd edn, 1939) covers the whole subject briefly for beginners, while *The Main Institutions of Roman Private Law* (1931) is an advanced discussion of selected topics. In addition, Buckland collaborated with his former pupil A. D. McNair (later president of the International Court of Justice) in *Roman Law and Common Law* (1936; 2nd edn by Professor F. H.

Lawson, 1952); and he produced with Hermann Kantorowicz *Studies in the Glossators of the Roman Law* (1938). Moreover, Buckland published many articles in English, French, and American legal periodicals. Here he gave freer rein to his pen than he thought appropriate in his books and showed himself not only a redoubtable, but also a witty, controversialist. A good example is his 'Interpolations in the Digest' in volume 33 of the *Yale Law Journal* (February 1924, pp. 343–64).

Although Buckland tended to focus on Roman law, he also wrote about jurisprudence. His best-known work on this subject is *Some Reflections on Jurisprudence* (1945), a short, lively book full of common sense and realism. To an extent, it reiterates ideas that he had expressed fifty-five years earlier in his very first article ('Difficulties of abstract jurisprudence', 1890), which is in essence a critique of the underlying assumptions of the prevailing English philosophy of law. Buckland particularly objected to the supposition of universal legal principles or truths.

Buckland was an exceptional scholar who was arguably 'the greatest master of Roman law that the English-speaking world has ever produced' (Duff, 2). He received honorary degrees from the universities of Oxford, Edinburgh, Harvard, Lyons, Louvain, and Paris. He was elected a fellow of the British Academy in 1920 and president of the Society of Public Teachers of Law in 1925. Finally, he 'never seemed to grow old, either mentally or physically. At the age of eighty-five he still ran up and down stairs like a young man' (Goodhart, 138). He continued to work until four days prior to his death in Cambridge on 16 January 1946.   P. W. DUFF, rev. WILFRID E. RUMBLE

Sources A. D. McNair and P. W. Duff, 'William Warwick Buckland', *PBA*, 33 (1947), 283–91 • B. Nicholas, *An introduction to Roman law* (1975) • W. W. Buckland, 'Difficulties of abstract jurisprudence', *Law Quarterly Review*, 6 (1890), 436–45 • A. L. Goodhart, 'William Warwick Buckland, 1859–1946', *Law Quarterly Review*, 62 (1946), 137–8 • M. H. Hoeflich, *Roman and civil law and the development of Anglo-American jurisprudence in the nineteenth century* (1997) • P. W. Duff, 'Roman law today', *Tulane Law Review*, 22 (Oct 1947), 2–12 • *The Times* (17 Jan 1946) • W. W. Buckland, 'F. W. Maitland', *Cambridge Law Journal*, 1 (1921–3), 279–301 • J. H. Beale, 'William Warwick Buckland', *Cambridge legal essays written in honour of and presented to Doctor Bond, Professor Buckland and Professor Kenny*, ed. P. H. Winfield and A. D. McNair (1926), 9–13 • personal knowledge (1959)
Likenesses photograph, 1932, NPG • J. Gunn, portrait, 1936, Gon. & Caius Cam. [*see illus.*]
Wealth at death £19,855 16s. 11d.: probate, 20 June 1946, *CGPLA Eng. & Wales*

Buckle, Sir Claude Henry Mason (1803–1894), naval officer, grandson of Admiral Matthew Buckle (1716–1784) and second son of Admiral Matthew Buckle (1770–1855) and his wife Henrietta, daughter of Henry Reveley of Clifford Street, London, and Blackheath, Kent, commissioner of excise, was born at Blackheath on 13 December 1803. He entered the Royal Naval College, Portsmouth, in August 1817. In March 1819 he passed out, and after serving a few months in the channel was appointed to the *Leander*, going out to the East Indies. In her and in her boats he served in the First Anglo-Burmese War and at the capture of Rangoon in May 1824.

Buckle returned to England in January 1826 and was appointed in April to the *Ganges* (84 guns), going out to the South American station as flagship of Sir Robert Waller Otway, and in her was promoted lieutenant on 17 April 1827. He afterwards (1829–33) served in the *North Star* and the *Tweed*, on the West Indian station; from 1833 to 1836 was flag-lieutenant to Sir William Hargood at Plymouth; and on 4 May 1836 was promoted to the rank of commander. From December 1841 to October 1845 he commanded the steam sloop *Growler*, on the coast of Brazil and afterwards on the west coast of Africa, and in February 1845 led the boats of the squadron under the command of Commodore William Jones at the destruction of several barracoons up the Gallinas River. On returning to England he was advanced to post rank on 6 November 1845, and married in 1847 Harriet Margaret, daughter of Thomas Deane Shute of Bramshaw, Hampshire; they had one son.

In January 1849 Buckle was appointed to the *Centaur* as flag-captain to Commodore Arthur Fanshawe, going out as commander-in-chief on the west coast of Africa, where, in December 1849, being detached in command of the boats of the squadron, together with the steamer *Teazer* and the French steamer *Rubis*, he 'administered condign punishment' to a horde of pirates who had established themselves in the River Geba and had captured some small trading vessels.

Towards the end of 1850 Buckle was compelled by failing health to return to England; and in December 1852 he was appointed to the steam frigate *Valorous*, attached during 1853 to the channel squadron, and in 1854 to the fleet up the Baltic under Sir Charles Napier, and more particularly to the flying squadron under Rear-Admiral James Hanway Plumridge in the operations in the Gulf of Bothnia. At the end of 1854 the *Valorous* was sent out to the Black Sea, where she carried the flag of Houston Stewart at the capture of Kinburn.

On 5 July 1855 Buckle was nominated a CB. From 1857 to 1863 he was superintendent of Deptford Dockyard, and on 14 November 1863 was promoted rear-admiral. In November 1867 he was appointed commander-in-chief at Queenstown, where he remained until he retired, under Childers's scheme, in 1870. He was made a vice-admiral on 1 April 1870, KCB on 29 May 1875, admiral on 22 January 1877, and was granted a good-service pension on 30 October 1885. He died at his home, 59 Rutland Gate, London, on 10 March 1894.   J. K. LAUGHTON, rev. ROGER MORRISS

Sources *The Times* (12 March 1894) • *Navy List* • O'Byrne, *Naval biog. dict.* • Boase, *Mod. Eng. biog.* • *CGPLA Eng. & Wales* (1894)
Archives W. Sussex RO, corresp., diaries, and naval papers
Wealth at death £20,388 16s. 3d.: resworn probate, Sept 1894, *CGPLA Eng. & Wales*

Buckle, (James) Desmond (1910–1964), political activist, was born on 29 March 1910 in Accra, capital of the British colony of the Gold Coast, in west Africa. He was the second of five children born to Vidal James Buckle, a prominent and wealthy lawyer, and his wife, Ellen Konadu Buckle, a member of the equally prominent Bannerman family.

The Buckle family originated from Sierra Leone and Desmond Buckle's forebears were of African-American and Caribbean origin. Desmond first came to Britain as a child at the age of ten, shortly after the death of his father, and was educated at Truro College in Cornwall, and in 1928 began medical studies at University College, London. He failed to complete his medical studies and in the early 1930s became increasingly active in several student and black political organizations, including the League of Coloured Peoples, the Gold Coast Students' Association, of which he was secretary from 1936 to 1937 and president from 1937 to 1938, and the communist-led Negro Welfare Association.

During the late 1930s Buckle became the first west African and almost certainly the first African to join the Communist Party of Great Britain, and by 1943 was a member of the party's colonial committee. He subsequently worked in the party's international affairs and Africa committees, and from 1950 to 1954 was editor of the latter committee's *Africa Newsletter*. He was a regular contributor to such publications as *World News and Views*, the *Daily Worker*, and *Labour Monthly*. It was Desmond Buckle who presented the report on Africa and the West Indies to the conference of communist parties of the British empire in London in 1947.

Buckle was also involved with the work of the National Council for Civil Liberties and spoke at several of the organization's conferences both on the anti-colonial struggles in Africa and on the problem of racism and the colour bar in Britain. In 1945 he drafted *Manifesto on Africa in the Post-War World*, which British-based African and pan-African organizations sent to the newly formed United Nations and which among other things called for 'full self government within a definite time limit' for all the African colonies.

After 1945 Buckle was active in the international peace and trade union movements. He represented the Transvaal Council of Non-European Trade Unions at the founding of the World Federation of Trade Unions in Paris in 1945. He was subsequently a member of the general council of the federation, and he played a leading role in the work of the preparatory committee of the All-African Trade Union Congress which met in Dakar, Senegal, in 1951. He was also a member of the permanent committee of the World Peace Congress, and was elected to the presidium of the Second World Peace Congress, held in Warsaw in 1950.

During the post-war period Buckle was employed as a journalist by TASS, the Soviet news agency, reporting mainly on sport and African affairs. He also wrote for several European papers including the German publications *Tägliche Rundschau*, *Neue Berliner Illustrierte*, and *Zeit im Bild*. A committed internationalist, he even acted as Paul Robeson's secretary during his four-month stay in Britain in 1949. Desmond Buckle was a regular speaker at meetings and conferences throughout Europe and one of the founders of the British-Hungarian Friendship Society. He died of stomach cancer at St George's Hospital in London on Sunday 25 October 1964, and his ashes were interred at Highgate cemetery, Middlesex, on 31 October.

HAKIM ADI

Sources private information (2004) · *Daily Worker* (26 Oct 1964), 1 · *Daily Worker* (31 Oct 1964), 5 · UCL, records office
Likenesses portrait, repro. in *Daily Worker* (26 Oct 1964)
Wealth at death £3213: administration, 4 Jan 1965, *CGPLA Eng. & Wales*

Buckle, Francis [Frank] (*c.*1770–1832), jockey, was born at Newmarket, where his father was a saddler, and was apprenticed to Lord Grosvenor's horse-racing establishment, one of the most lavish at the sport's headquarters. Among his earliest major successes was victory in the 1792 Derby on a Scottish horse paradoxically named John Bull. In all he was to win twenty-seven classic races, including some notable doubles. His dual successes on Champion in the Epsom Derby and the Doncaster St Leger in 1800 did much to give the latter race national status. He twice more won the Derby and the Oaks in the same year, in 1802 and 1823. Buckle also rode in several famous two-horse matches, including wins on Champion over Hambletonian for a £3000 stake in 1799 and on Orlando over Gaoler in 1803, both at Newmarket. Even his notable failures were readily explicable. He lost on Allegro to Alicia *Thornton, the horsewoman who had caused such a sensation at York races in 1804, but he was giving her a weight advantage of 4 pounds; and riding Colonel Henry Mellish's Sancho (on which he won the St Leger and which the owner now backed to win £20,000) against Lord Darlington's Pavilion, his horse went lame when in the lead.

Both Buckle's skills as a jockey and his honesty won him high regard. He was an excellent judge of a horse and of a race. He could urge on his mount without any great show of force but was equally adept at 'gammoning'—seeming to drive a horse vigorously when not in fact doing so, thereby making it difficult for rivals to know what pace they have to contend with. As to his integrity, it is perhaps best exemplified by an incident at Lewes when, expecting to be a spectator, he had bet heavily on one of the runners but then was himself engaged to take a late ride on another horse—and won.

It was said that Buckle never had to 'reduce himself' and rode always at 7 stone 11 lb. Known as the 'Pocket Hercules', he was obviously very short in stature and, while he was said to look completely at home on a horse, he was bow-legged and ungainly otherwise. In a period when professional sport rarely provided long-term security, Buckle became a wealthy man, a landowner and farmer. He enjoyed his generally old-fashioned pleasures: breeding greyhounds, bulldogs, and fighting cocks, and at one stage became a master of foxhounds. However, his enthusiasms also extended to the theatre and he would from time to time commission plays to be performed in country towns where he was racing.

Buckle married twice. The first marriage was childless but there were several children from the second, though he expressed a wish that none of his sons would themselves become jockeys. He lived to a good old age and was, in the words of Pierce Egan's obituary, highly respected and 'always considered an ornament to the Turf' (Egan, 187). His last race was at the Houghton meeting in 1831, and his death was reported early in 1832.

DENNIS BRAILSFORD

Sources P. Egan, *Book of sports* (1832) · J. Tyrrel, *Racecourses on the flat* (1989) · *Sporting Magazine* (1792–1825) · *Racing Calendar* (1790–1810) · GM, 1st ser., 102/1 (1832), 286
Likenesses R. Dighton, hand-coloured etching, pubd 1806 (after his portrait), BM, NPG · B. Marshall, group portrait, oils (Mr Wastell with his jockey Frank Buckle, his trainer and stable lad), repro. in S. Deuchar, *Sporting art in eighteenth-century England: a social and political history* (1988), 162

Buckle, George Earle (1854–1935), newspaper editor and historian, was born at Twerton, near Bath, on 10 June 1854, the eldest of the four sons of George Buckle, successively fellow of Oriel College, Oxford, vicar of Twerton, rector of Weston-super-Mare, and canon and precentor of Wells Cathedral, and his wife, Mary Hamlyn Earle, sister of the philologist John Earle. He was educated at Honiton grammar school, whence he gained a scholarship to Winchester College. In 1873 he became a scholar at New College, Oxford. There he read classical and mathematical moderations, won the Newdigate prize for 'David Livingstone' (1875), and was awarded a first class in *literae humaniores* (1876), and in modern history (1877). From 1877 to 1885 he was a fellow of All Souls. At Lincoln's Inn he read in the chambers of John Rigby. Almost at once, however, journalism furnished him an alternative opportunity, for he was offered the post of assistant editor at the *Manchester Guardian*. Although he declined, he accepted another newspaper post five months before being called to the bar in November 1880. The proprietor of *The Times*, John Walter, appointed him assistant to the editor, Thomas Chenery, on whose death on 11 February 1884, Buckle, at twenty-nine, became editor.

The editorial tradition of *The Times* was to support the existing government, and Buckle, whose interest always remained home politics, continued the policy, causing Gladstone's private secretary, Edward Hamilton, to record in his diary in August 1892 that his opinion of Buckle's 'wholly disinterested motives' had 'gone up enormously'. Under Buckle *The Times* did not shift much in either direction from the political centre. 'Thundering out' was already unfashionable when he accepted the post. Despite contending, in his last years with *The Times*, that it was 'madness … to try to confine the Editor to political directions', he intruded very little into the work of sub-editors, though he regularly read the proofs to ensure consistency of style and language. He and his staff recognized *The Times* as a national institution almost beyond personal convictions and private profit. Not, thus, a dominating force as editor, he made few political mistakes of his own, and weathered the complications of factional loyalties over Irish home rule that split the Liberals early in his tenure. Eager for a scoop, however, *The Times* blundered into publication of the forged Charles Stuart Parnell letters in 1888, allegedly linking him to Irish political murders. Although responsibility lay with the proprietor, Buckle

George Earle Buckle (1854–1935), by unknown photographer

stood by the genuineness of the letters even after rumours questioning them surfaced. Once Richard Pigott, their perpetrator, was about to confess early in 1889, *The Times* publicly apologized and Buckle offered to resign, a sacrifice not accepted. Yet he realized that, in reading the paper's proofs, he should have recognized language and even spelling uncharacteristic of Parnell. Humiliated, *The Times* would pay a substantial libel settlement.

Soon after, Buckle saw his day-to-day control weakened by unrelated administrative alignments necessary to maintain the paper's health in an era of harsh competition. Walter's death in 1894 led to increasing decline. Ownership became divided among several heirs, impairing overall management. Decentralization cost Buckle the supervision of the expanding foreign department and gradually reduced his functions as editor to the writing of leading articles and the determining of political orientation. Resisting modernization, Buckle refused a personal office telephone and would not use a typewriter, but the essential new technology was installed elsewhere at Printing House Square. An editor along the unhurried old lines, Buckle found his position awkward, but he hung on despite the erosion of his authority, which was accelerated when, in 1908, Alfred Harmsworth, later Lord Northcliffe, purchased a controlling interest in the paper and continued, even more impatiently, the process of change. He saw Buckle as an anachronism in the aggressive new age of journalism and the staid *Times* under Buckle as alien to his view of the intrusive role of proprietorship. The sudden death of C. F. Moberly Bell, the managing director, in 1911, removed the last restraint upon Harmsworth, who forced his editor's retirement. Buckle's letter of resignation was dated 31 July 1911. He had despised the 'penny press' as opposed to his vision of newspaper responsibility, but Harmsworth dramatized his own personal style by lowering the price of *The Times* from 3*d.* to a penny, and watched both circulation and advertising rise.

Buckle was not at leisure long. After the death of William F. Monypenny, the Beaconsfield trustees on 26 February 1912 commissioned Buckle to continue the *Life of Benjamin Disraeli*. His labours of the next eight years were devoted to the last four of its six volumes (published 1914–20). Even with censorship imposed upon him about aspects of Disraeli's private life, and a biographical structure already established, Buckle 'reconstructed for those who never knew Lord Beaconsfield', Viscount Esher wrote, 'that strange figure of a Jew of Aragon, which Disraeli loved to think he was, clothed in the robes of the most ancient order of Christian chivalry'. Wary as a biographer after his embarrassment as editor over the Parnell letters, Buckle refused to accept the contention that Sir Robert Peel, in the famous debate of 15 May 1846, had Disraeli's obsequious job-soliciting letter of 1841 in his dispatch case but had spurned the opportunity to read it on the floor of the house. Since Disraeli's political future hung in the balance, Buckle's handling of the incident exemplified his innate caution. Goldwin Smith in his *Reminiscences* (1910) had claimed to have the revelation first-hand from Lord Lincoln, who had accompanied Peel to the house and recalled seeing the letter, but Buckle apparently weighed the story against logic—that people seldom carry five-year-old letters with them—and against Smith's outspoken antisemitism and hatred of Disraeli. Buckle's picture of the public man always in the plans of the young Disraeli was engrossing. Years later, Lord Morley, who had written an even more guarded biography of Gladstone, wrote to Buckle: 'We have each of us done his best to keep public life and public opinion on a wholesome and self-respecting level: and we have done our best to make the two great political rivals immortal'.

After the final volume of the Disraeli life had appeared on 12 June 1920, Buckle was approached about continuing the editing of *The Letters of Queen Victoria*, which had been carried to 1861, and the death of Prince Albert, by A. C. Benson and Lord Esher in 1907. Since the reputations of august persons still living were involved, and the mass of documentation was frank and intimidating, Buckle was hesitant about accepting the commission. Ironically, he had, even as editor of *The Times*, made a practice of destroying his own correspondence. Only on 28 January 1922 did he accept the offer of George V. Two series, 1862–85 and 1886–1901, each of three substantial volumes, appeared between 1926 and 1932. In June 1932, on the release of the final volumes, the king praised Buckle's work and gave him a signed portrait. The encomium was valid. Perhaps the greatest impact of the letters was in dispelling legends and misunderstandings that had grown up during the years of the queen's post-Albert seclusion, and in tracing the gradual recovery of public trust, culminating in the jubilees of 1887 and 1897. Yet Buckle did not conceal the queen's limitations—her lack of confidence without Albert, her arrogance and selfishness, her vindictiveness, and her acerbity. In balance he brought out dramatically her shrewd political sense, her restored devotion to duty, her broad sympathies, and her burgeoning rapport with her subjects. With the royal family to consider as well as the needs of state, Buckle's challenges were daunting, but the result was a model of clarity and elucidation. His editing and selection through the six substantial volumes triumphantly combined boldness and discretion and created an enduring self-portrait of Victoria.

Buckle was seventy-eight, his tasks accomplished, when he conceived a *History of The Times*. Despite his years he worked energetically with another former editor, Geoffrey Dawson, as well as with Theodore Morison, Dermot Morrah, and R. M. Barrington-Ward, his collaborators often dependent upon Buckle's intimate knowledge of nineteenth-century newspaper and political history. The first volume was published just before he died, after a brief illness, on 13 March 1935 at 62 Oakley Street, Chelsea.

Despite widespread recognition of his public work, the full-bearded Buckle remained a very private person. The demands of a morning newspaper limited social life; his evenings, into the early morning hours, were spent at his office. He lived simply when with *The Times*, first in Queen Square, then in Ashley Gardens, and finally in Warwick Square. In retirement he moved to Oakley Street, Chelsea, and, as a literary man, made his club, the Athenaeum, a place for daily recourse. Early in the new century he declined a baronetcy offered by A. J. Balfour, but he accepted honorary degrees from the universities of St Andrews (1899) and Oxford (1932). Uninterested in foreign travel but for a post-retirement voyage in 1912 to visit a brother in South Africa, he spent his holidays on country walks, and developed a passion for golf. He was twice married: first in 1885, to Alicia Isobel (d. 1898), third daughter of the novelist James Payn; then, in 1905, to his first cousin, Beatrice Anne (d. 1938), second daughter of John Earle. A son and daughter were born of the first marriage.

While not in the pantheon of great newspaper editors despite nearly three decades with *The Times*, Buckle did furnish it with a judicious continuity that substantiated its reputation as the paper of record. Buckle remains more memorable for his role in two publishing monuments of the Victorian age.

STANLEY WEINTRAUB

Sources DNB · [S. Morison and others], *The history of The Times*, 3 (1947) · S. E. Koss, *The rise and fall of the political press in Britain*, 1 (1981) · S. E. Koss, *The rise and fall of the political press in Britain*, 2 (1984) · *The diary of Sir Edward Walter Hamilton, 1885–1906*, ed. D. W. R. Bahlman (1993) · *The Times* (13 March 1935) · Viscount Esher [R. B. B. Esher], *Cloud-capp'd towers* (1927) · R. Blake, *Disraeli* (1966) · R. Kee, *The laurel and the ivy: the story of Charles Stewart Parnell and Irish nationalism* (1993)

Archives News Int. RO, papers | All Souls Oxf., letters to William Anson · BL, corresp. with Arthur James Balfour, Add. MS 49797, *passim* · BL, corresp. Lord Northcliffe, Add. MSS 62242–62243 · Bodl. Oxf., corresp. with Sir Henry Burdett · CAC Cam., corresp. with Lord Randolph Churchill · NL Scot., corresp. mainly with Lord Rosebery

Likenesses F. Pegram, pencil sketch, c.1888–1889, V&A · photograph, c.1930, Times Picture Library, London · Dawson & Fries, photograph, repro. in Dawson, *History of The Times*, vol. 3, facing p. 688 · Dawson and Fries, charcoal drawing (in youth), repro. in Dawson, *History of The Times*, vol. 3, facing p. 4 · photograph, NPG [*see illus.*]

Wealth at death £3516 3s. 1d.: probate, 12 April 1935, *CGPLA Eng. & Wales*

Buckle, Henry Thomas (1821–1862), historian, was born on 24 November 1821 at Lee in Kent, the son of Thomas Henry Buckle (1779–1840), partner in a London shipping firm, and his wife, Jane Middleton (*d.* 1859) of Yorkshire. He had two sisters. Originally from Westmorland, the Buckle family had lived in London for more than two centuries. An ancestor, Sir Cuthbert Buckle, was lord mayor of London in 1593. Henry Thomas was born while his parents were visiting his father's brother, but the family's home was in Mecklenburg Square, where he grew up.

Education and early travels As a boy, Buckle was frail and not suited for the usual schooling or games of a middle-class youth. He was educated at home by his mother, to whom he was devoted until her death in 1859. She taught him to read the Bible, the *Arabian Nights*, *Pilgrim's Progress*, and Shakespeare. His father read theology and literature and occasionally recited Shakespeare to the family in the evenings. At the age of fourteen Buckle was sent to Gordon House School, but his spell of formal education proved to be brief. In his first year he won a prize in mathematics, and when his delighted father asked him what reward he would like, Buckle answered, 'To be taken away from school'. His father agreed, and thereafter Buckle was self-taught, which he regarded as a blessing: 'I was never much tormented with what is called education, but allowed to pursue my own way undisturbed … Whatever I may now be supposed to know I taught myself' (St Aubyn, 2).

Buckle's father insisted that Henry enter the family shipping business when he was seventeen. In his three months in this office he found the routine dreary and confining. But his father, suffering from consumption and the shock of breaking an arm, died in 1840. Henry experienced fainting fits for some weeks after his father's death, but he inherited £20,000, which allowed him to leave the shipping business for the pleasures of reading and travel. In July 1840 Buckle, his mother, and his sister Mary embarked on a tour of Europe that lasted almost a year, with extended stays in Germany, Italy, and France. Buckle studied the language, literature, and history of each place they visited, as he was to do on subsequent visits to the continent. His aptitude for languages was prodigious: by 1850 he could read eighteen foreign languages and could speak six of them—albeit with an atrocious accent.

Private life Buckle spent most of the rest of his life in a rigid routine of study and writing, living first in lodgings in Norfolk Street, London, and later with his mother at 59 Oxford Terrace (now 115 Sussex Gardens), London. A methodical person, constantly concerned about his

Henry Thomas Buckle (1821–1862), by Mayall & Co., 1850s

health, Buckle rose, worked, walked, dined, and retired with remarkable regularity. He kept a careful account of what he read. He was likewise careful in his expenditure of money, for while his inheritance enabled him to live comfortably, he felt it necessary to harbour his resources. His only extravagances were fine cigars, of which he smoked three a day, and books, of which he collected a splendid library of 22,000 volumes. Despite his solitary scholarship, Buckle was not a recluse: he and his mother enjoyed giving dinners for small numbers of friends, and they also dined out frequently. Buckle was thought by most acquaintances to be a good conversationalist. He had an excellent memory, deep knowledge of a wide range of subjects, and an eagerness to pursue interesting topics exhaustively. Some people found him tedious or egotistical, for he tended to dominate conversations and did not suffer the ignorant gladly. He became an excellent chess player, capable of defeating international masters even though he spent no time in serious study of the game.

In appearance Buckle looked older than he was, for he was prematurely bald and rather stooped in posture. He never married, though when he was seventeen he proposed to Annie Jane Holloway, who was the daughter of his headmaster and five years older than Buckle; but she was not attracted to him. In later life he enjoyed female companionship and in 1854 became close friends with Emily Shirreff (1814–1897) and Maria Grey (1816–1906), two intellectual sisters interested in women's education.

Intellectual views During the year of travel following his father's death, Buckle became a radical in politics and a freethinker in religion. He seems to have been repelled by foreign despotisms and attracted by German higher criticism. Thus, although his father had been a strong Anglican and tory and his mother a Calvinist, Buckle became a deist and a devotee of rationalism and natural science. He regarded John Stuart Mill as the greatest living thinker, but he also learned much from Enlightenment philosophers such as Voltaire, Montesquieu, Adam Smith, and Kant. He was influenced by the work of Auguste Comte, but even more by that of the statistician Adolphe Quételet. From these various thinkers Buckle concluded that all human behaviour is subject to law, and therefore that there can be a science of human society. Many critics in his own day and later thought of Buckle as the English disciple of Comte, but, as Mill declared, Buckle agreed with the founder of positivism on little other than the basic notions of the regularity of human behaviour and the historical progress of civilization from superstition to science. Buckle explicitly rejected Comte's political ideas as 'monstrously and obviously impracticable' (St Aubyn, 163).

History of Civilization in England Buckle's fame rests entirely on one book, his *History of Civilization in England*, which was published in two volumes in 1857 and 1861. These thick volumes amounted to only a fragment of what Buckle originally intended. He initially wanted to write a history of medieval civilization, and then hoped to write a general history of world civilizations, on the model of eighteenth-century 'philosophical history'. The magnitude of that task led him to restrict his scope to the history of English civilization, in comparison with those of France, Spain, Scotland, Germany, and the United States. He planned in his introductory volumes to discover the fundamental laws of human progress, and then in the main body of the work, which would have comprised many volumes, to apply these laws to English history. Despite prodigious labours, however, he was able to produce of this scheme only a portion of his introduction, including five chapters of historical theory, one on Spain, seven on France, four on Scotland, and only one on England.

In his introductory chapters on historical theory, Buckle had an agenda of several items. First, he contended that it was time for history to be brought up to the level of accomplishment reached by other departments of knowledge, such as physics and astronomy; he would do for history what Kepler and Newton had done for their subjects. Second, he argued that grand generalization, necessarily based on very wide reading rather than specialized research, is the true function of the historian. Third, he insisted that human society over time changes in conformity to laws like those of the natural sciences. And finally, he claimed that all history is the record of the mutually determining interactions of human minds and external nature. In particular, he believed that in Europe progress had been determined by the growing power of mind over nature—that is, by developments in the various national intellects. Paradoxically, therefore, Buckle's

belief in the regularity of human behaviour led him to focus on intellectual history.

Buckle thought that the new science of statistics proved that there can be a science of history. Statistics of the rates of murder, suicide, and marriage in any society show that the actions of people 'are the result of large and general causes' (*History of Civilization*, 1.21). He did not deny free will altogether but set the doctrine aside, explaining that when we do any action, we do it because of some set of motives. Since all motives are caused by 'antecedents', all behaviour 'must have a character of uniformity' (ibid., 18). This uniformity can be revealed by a comprehensive analysis of the antecedents to any act, plus a knowledge of 'all the laws of their movements'. Buckle then reasoned that all antecedents—that is, causes of motives—are either internal or external to the mind, and therefore that all history is the result of the interaction of human minds and external nature.

Buckle believed that national civilizations differ in the relative weight of influence exercised by mind and nature. Nature, he said, works its influence through four agents: climate, food, soil, and the 'General Aspect of Nature' (ibid., 36). Outside Europe, these physical agents increased the authority of the imagination, while in Europe they strengthened that of the understanding. In Europe, in contrast to the rest of the world, there has been a steady increase in the dominion of the mind over 'the agencies of the external world'. Buckle concluded that in Europe progress has been due more to mental than to physical laws.

According to Buckle, mental laws fall into two categories—moral and intellectual. Since moral capacities change very little, the obvious progress of European civilization has been due to the intellectual development of Europeans. Thus, for example, both religious persecution and the warlike temper have declined in Europe as both knowledge and the influence of the 'intellectual classes' have grown.

In his only chapter on English history, Buckle gave an optimistic account of English progress that he contrasted with the records of France, Spain, and Scotland. He claimed that the 'English intellect' from the sixteenth century to the end of the eighteenth was shaped by the growth of scepticism, toleration, and liberty. His argument was that of a philosophic radical, a believer in the 'march of mind', and was a tribute to English exceptionalism. He compared the English story to that of a healthy person, while that of France was 'diseased'. In France progress had been impeded by the continuing power of the 'protective spirit' (by which he meant a stultifying belief in social hierarchy and paternalism) of the clergy, aristocracy, and monarchy. He treated the French Revolution as a reaction, partly stimulated by the English example, against the protective spirit. Spain likewise suffered from the protective spirit of the state and church, encouraged as it was by the irrational loyalty of the Spanish people.

In his chapters on Scotland, Buckle told a story of slow progress that resulted from the continual conflict between religious superstition on the one hand and political rebelliousness on the other. For Buckle, the great paradox of Scottish history is the Scots' love of liberty in matters of government and their subordination to the clergy in religion. His explanation of the paradox is that for more than a century after the establishment of protestantism in Scotland, the monarchy either ignored or persecuted the church. This drove the clergy into an alliance with the people. Consequently, the eighteenth century witnessed a revolutionary development of the Scottish intellect, but Scottish intellectuals nevertheless held to a deductive style of reasoning that conformed to the religious way of thinking. The deductive mode limited the benefits of an otherwise progressive Scottish Enlightenment. In England, Buckle argued, the Baconian (inductive) style of thought had eroded the power of the clergy and largely accounted for English progress.

Reception of the History Buckle's *History of Civilization in England* made a huge splash with the general public but met with strong criticism from both Christian thinkers and academic historians. His first volume made him a London literary lion overnight in 1857 and won him introductions to W. M. Thackeray, Herbert Spencer, T. H. Huxley, Charles Darwin, and Charles Greville. He was elected to the Athenaeum and the Political Economy Club in 1858. Although John Stuart Mill felt that Buckle erred in regarding human moral quality as fixed, he admired the work and said that Buckle was serving 'a most valuable function in popularizing many important ideas, and stimulating the desire to apply general principles to the explanation and prediction of social facts' (St Aubyn, 31). Darwin spoke for many in the general reading public when he described the book as 'wonderfully clever and original, and written with astonishing knowledge' (F. Darwin, ed., *Life and Letters of Charles Darwin*, 1887, 2.315). The book likewise made a great impact in Europe and America; it was translated into German, French, and Russian, and it was especially influential with young Russian intellectuals.

But if Buckle was taken up by secularists, radicals, and liberals, and by middle-class readers who liked his combination of bold interpretations, vigorous prose, and belief in progress and the superiority of England, he was fiercely condemned by more conservative religious and academic writers. Scottish Presbyterians were, perhaps understandably, hostile to the work; and so were other Christian writers, who deprecated the book's anti-clerical message. Lord Acton, for instance, treated Buckle as simply a positivist historian, and, like all positivists, only half-educated; furthermore, he argued, Buckle ignored the influence of classical antiquity and the Christian religion and rejected the obviously true doctrine of free will. Mark Pattison felt that Buckle did not give enough credit to passion in human affairs, and at the same time accused Buckle of not practising the historical science that he preached, for Buckle gave too much credit to the influence of individuals. Historians such as Macaulay thought that Buckle did not know enough about any aspect of his subject, and others felt that Buckle's intention of establishing a science of history was invalid. Bishop William Stubbs

declared, 'I do not believe in the Philosophy of History, and so do not believe in Buckle' (W. H. Hutton, ed., *Letters of William Stubbs*, 1904, 42). Even Leslie Stephen, who belonged to the same sceptical and rationalist school as Buckle, was very critical. Buckle, he wrote, lacked both specialist knowledge and sympathy with past epochs, and he wrote too early to take into account evolutionary views. By the time of the *Dictionary of National Biography*, Stephen could say (in his 1886 entry on Buckle) that the immense reputation of the *History of Civilization in England* had already faded. Despite vigorous defences by John Mackinnon Robertson in 1895 and G. A. Wells in 1956, a favourable modern biography by Giles St Aubyn in 1958, and a laudatory exposition by H. J. Hanham in 1970, the book remains today largely unread by both the general public and academic historians. It shared with whig histories of the day a commitment to a progressive view of the past, but Buckle did not share the whig historians' devotion to research in primary documents, which came to be a touchstone of the emerging professional academic history. Buckle's book today is regarded by professional historians as evidence of the Victorian fascination with science and progress.

Other works Buckle devoted himself almost exclusively to his book and published only three other pieces in his lifetime. The first, an article in *Fraser's Magazine* of April 1858, derived from a public lecture he delivered to the Royal Institution on 'The influence of women on the progress of knowledge'. In it Buckle argued that women could make important contributions to knowledge because of their special facility in deductive reasoning, a mental quality that he associated with female traits: emotion, enthusiasm, imagination, and intuition. A second publication was a long and laudatory review of Mill's *On Liberty* in *Fraser's Magazine* for May 1859. Here Buckle praised Mill for his unique combination of profound speculative philosophy and sound practical sense. The third was a substantial pamphlet on the case of Thomas Pooley, the Cornish well-digger who was tried and convicted in 1857 for writing some offensive phrases against Christianity on a fence gate. Buckle first wrote about the case in his review of *On Liberty*, where Mill had mentioned it in his defence of individual liberty. Buckle expressed dismay that an English judge would sentence to imprisonment a man who had never caused his community any harm and who was obviously not in full possession of his wits. Buckle accused the judge in the case, Sir John Taylor Coleridge, nephew of the poet, of intolerance and cruelty. Many of Buckle's friends, as well as leading members of the legal profession, rushed to Judge Coleridge's defence. When the judge's son John Duke Coleridge published a vigorous letter to *Fraser's Magazine*, Buckle answered with a pamphlet defending his earlier charges and insisting that the case was a battle in an old and crucial 'warfare between liberty and repression', and that it was his duty as a literary man to uphold 'the weak against the strong' (H. Taylor, ed., *The Miscellaneous and Posthumous Works of Henry Thomas Buckle*, 1885, 1.240). This pamphlet was not widely read, and meanwhile

Coleridge had pardoned Pooley when he learned of Pooley's mental condition.

Later travels and death The Pooley controversy coincided for Buckle with a period of grief following the death of his mother, who had begun to decline not long after publication of the first volume of the *History of Civilization in England*. Buckle was further exhausted by work on the second volume, and later in the year of its publication (1861) he decided to go to Egypt for a change of scenery that might revive him. Much to his friends' surprise, Buckle invited one Elizabeth Faunch, the widow of a carpenter, to join him. This seemed especially scandalous because Buckle had taken responsibility during the trip for two impressionable sons of his friends Mr and Mrs Henry Huth. Mrs Faunch refused his invitation, but there is some evidence that the two had been engaged in a liaison for some time. This situation did not stop one of the Huth sons, Alfred, from writing a biography of Buckle some years later: *Life and Writings of Henry Thomas Buckle* (1880). Buckle and the Huths' two sons arrived in Alexandria in October 1861, travelled to Cairo, and then went up the Nile to Thebes and Aswan. Buckle was feeling better and, having returned to Cairo, decided to journey through Sinai to Palestine and Syria. His party reached Jerusalem in March 1862 and in the next month visited Jericho, Nazareth, and Bethlehem. Late in April he contracted typhoid fever but, not realizing the danger, he pushed on to Beirut and Damascus. Although treated by French and American doctors, Buckle died in Damascus on 29 May 1862. He was buried in the protestant cemetery there the same day. His sole surviving sister, Mary Allatt, provided a gravestone in 1866. The epitaph she specified was 'I know that he shall rise again'; but the sister of the British consul in Damascus added, in Arabic, more appropriate lines:

> The written word remains long after the writer;
> The writer is resting under the earth, but his works
> endure.

THOMAS WILLIAM HEYCK

Sources G. St Aubyn, *A Victorian eminence: the life and works of Henry Thomas Buckle* (1958) · *DNB* · A. H. Huth, *Life and writings of Henry Thomas Buckle*, 2 vols. (1880) · H. J. Hanham, introduction, in H. T. Buckle, *On Scotland and the Scottish intellect*, ed. H. J. Hanham (1970) · G. A. Wells, 'The critics of Buckle', *Past and Present*, 9 (1956), 75–89 · J. M. Robertson, *Buckle and his critics* (1895) · J. S. S. Glennie, *Pilgrim memories* (1880) · A. W. Benn, *The history of English rationalism in the nineteenth century*, 2 vols. (1906)
Archives BLPES, catalogue of library; notes on Germany and America · University of Illinois, Urbana-Champaign, corresp.; literary MSS and papers
Likenesses Mayall & Co., photograph, 1850–59, NPG [*see illus.*] · two portraits, repro. in Huth, *Life and writings*
Wealth at death under £20,000: administration, 19 Sept 1862, *CGPLA Eng. & Wales*

Buckler, Benjamin (1716/17–1780), antiquary, was born at Warminster, Wiltshire, the son of Thomas Buckler, gentleman, of Warminster. He matriculated on 15 February 1733 aged sixteen as a member of Oriel College, Oxford, whence he graduated BA in 1736 and proceeded

Benjamin Buckler (1716/17–1780), by unknown artist

MA in 1739, when he was elected a fellow of All Souls College. He obtained the degree of BD in 1755 and DD in 1759. In 1755 he was appointed to the vicarage of Cumnor, near Oxford, by Willoughby Bertie, later fourth earl of Abingdon, and he also obtained the small rectory of Frilham in Berkshire. He wrote a short history of Cumnor for John Nichols's *Bibliotheca Topographica Britannica* (8 vols., 1780–90, vol. 4, no. 16, 12–25).

Buckler became the close, and flamboyant, friend of Sir William Blackstone, who joined him as a fellow of All Souls in 1743. He succeeded Blackstone as a bursar of the college in 1752 and received from him the *Dissertation on the Accounts of All Souls College, Oxford* which was published by the Roxburghe Club in 1898. Quite early during his fellowship Buckler became involved in a controversy concerning Oxford's strangest ritual, the college's mallard ceremonies. There are many legends about its origin, but the most popular tradition asserts that when the foundations of the college were laid in 1438 an unusually large mallard, or wild duck, was discovered in an ancient drain, and since the seventeenth century this has been celebrated by a song at a gaudy on St Hilary's day (14 January), the first day of the Hilary term. In 1749 John Pointer in his *Oxoniensis academia* declared, to the indignation of the college's fellows, that this illustrious bird was merely a common goose. Buckler brought out anonymously *A Complete Vindication of the Mallard of All Souls College*, which was published in 1750 and republished in 1751. This provoked in 1752 an ironical prospectus, usually attributed to Edward Rowe Mores, announced as *Preparing for the Press … a Complete History of the Mallardians … in Three Parts*, and in the same year there was printed *The swopping-song of the mallardians, an ode as it is to be performed on Tuesday the 14th. of January*, the original of which is among the Tanner manuscripts in the Bodleian Library.

In the contest between whigs and tories in the university, called the 'new interest' and 'old interest', Blackstone and Buckler became the leaders of the tory phalanx at All Souls, and did much to secure the election of Sir Roger Newdigate as a burgess in parliament for the university in 1750 and the election of John Fane, seventh earl of Westmorland, as chancellor of the university in 1759. In that year, at St Mary the Virgin, the university church, Buckler preached a sermon, 'The alliance of religion and learning considered', stating that such a union, which upheld the church and constitution, was dependent on the continuation of the university as sustained by Westmorland. This sermon was his sole publication as a divine. He readily supported the tory cause, however, with his pen. In a satirical tract entitled *A Proper Explanation of Oxford Almanack for the Present Year* (1755) he alluded to the general election of the previous year, which produced what was among the most notorious of the county elections under the unreformed parliament, when the second duke of Marlborough contested tory dominance of Oxfordshire, long known for its opposition to whiggism. Although the university had no official concern in the election, the almanac supported the high-church, tory cause, and Buckler described its opponents as representing 'Folly, Stupidity and Debauchery' (Ward, 203). He certainly contributed greatly to the electoral debate, and wrote many pungent articles for the local newspaper *Jackson's Oxford Journal*.

Buckler was credited in the *Dictionary of National Biography* with involvement in a 1756 dispute concerning the right of the Oxford proctors to appoint a delegate of the university press without consulting the vice-chancellor, then George Huddesford, president of Trinity College and a tory. Huddesford issued a pamphlet, *Observations relating to delegates of the press with an account of their succession from their original appointment*, which was rapidly answered in *A Reply to Dr. Huddesford's 'Observations relating to delegates of the press'*. However, as Buckler was proctor in the year 1756–7, and the dispute concerned 1755–6, it is more probable that the pamphlet was written by the proctors for the earlier year, John Tracy and C. Mortimer, perhaps in collaboration with William Blackstone.

By the middle of the eighteenth century, since the fellowships at All Souls had become financially more attractive, graduates claiming kinship with the founder, Archbishop Chichele, sought entry. As these candidates often had little else to recommend them, Blackstone sought in 1750 to check this practice by argument in his *Essay on Collateral Consanguinity*, in which he was assisted by Buckler. In 1765 Buckler published anonymously his *Stemmata Chicheleana*, which contained the genealogies of the families entitled to college fellowships through descent from the founder. When the college acquired some manuscripts of John Anstis, the Garter king of arms, on the sale of his library, Buckler compiled a supplement to this work in 1775.

Buckler was elected keeper of the archives of the university in 1777, his duty being to take charge of and arrange all the muniments and papers concerning either the estates, possessions, rights, and privileges of the university or the endowments of professorships, and all the records and registers of the university. He was among the candidates for the task of completing John Bridges' history of Northamptonshire, but he withdrew and Peter Whalley was appointed instead.

Buckler died at Cumnor on 24 December 1780, and was buried in the parish church. He was able and possessed much wit and miscellaneous learning, but he lacked personal ambition. In his epitaph on Buckler, Blackstone declared that he possessed:

> talents, which in all probability would have advanced him to high station had they been less under the influence of those honest principles, which, although they greatly dignify a character, are not ways of use on the way to preferment. (*GM*, 1792)

LEONARD W. COWIE

Sources M. Burrows, *Worthies of All Souls* (1874), appx · R. G. [R. Gough], *British topography*, [new edn], 2 vols. (1780) · Nichols, *Lit. anecdotes* · Nichols, *Illustrations* · Foster, *Alum. Oxon.* · *GM*, 1st ser., 61 (1791), 1128–9 · *GM*, 1st ser., 62 (1792), 224–5 · W. R. Ward, *Georgian Oxford: university politics in the eighteenth century* (1958) · *Hist. U. Oxf.* 5: *18th-cent. Oxf.* · C. Grant Robertson, *All Souls College* (1899) · W. Blackstone, *Dissertation on the accounts of All Souls College, Oxford* (1898) · *DNB* · private information (2004) [M. St John Parker, S. Wearne] **Archives** Bodl. Oxf., Rawlinson MSS · Bodl. Oxf., Tanner MSS **Likenesses** oils, All Souls Oxf. [*see illus.*] **Wealth at death** various bequests: will, PRO, PROB 11/1073, sig. 4

Buckler, John (1770–1851), artist and architect, was born on 30 November 1770 at Calbourne, Isle of Wight, and baptized there at All Saints' Church on 27 December, the eldest son of Edward Buckler (1741–1792) and his wife, Hannah (1745–1809), daughter of William Jacob. He developed an early interest in drawing through an association with George Fisher, younger son of the rector of Calbourne, and in 1785 he became clerk to Fisher's elder brother, R. B. Fisher, steward of Magdalen College, Oxford. He thus began a lifelong involvement in managing the college's estate in London, and soon afterwards he was articled for seven years to the surveyor and builder Charles Thomas Cracklow of Southwark, for whom he drew plans and elevations for a speculative development on college property on the site of the present London Bridge railway station in 1792. On 21 August 1791 he married Ann (1769–1847), daughter of John Chessell of Brading, Isle of Wight, and John Chessell Buckler [*see below*], the first of their eleven children, was born two years later.

In or soon after 1801 Buckler was given the title of bailiff and collector of rents for Magdalen College in Freeman's Court (near the Bank of England) and Southwark, and he retained this post until his retirement in 1849, when he was granted a pension for life by the college. He was living 'near the Jamaica House, Bermondsey' in 1798, but had moved by 1801 to Spa Road in the same parish. He later moved to 15 Rockingham Row, New Kent Road, Newington, and it was there that he died on 6 December 1851. He was buried at St Mary Newington, London.

Buckler is chiefly remembered for his skill and industry as a topographical artist, a calling which he pursued in the seemingly generous spare time allowed him by Magdalen College. His first recorded drawings were of Wolvercote church, north of Oxford; one of his drawings was exhibited at the Royal Academy in 1798, and he exhibited there every year until 1849. In 1797, with the encouragement of Martin Routh, president of Magdalen, whom he later described as his 'early and constant friend' (Buckler, 50), he published two aquatint engravings of the college, and two years later, in 1799, again with Routh's support, he made an engraving of Lincoln Cathedral, the first of a series of engraved views which by 1814 had grown to include all the English cathedrals and many of the major collegiate and parish churches. Soon after 1800 he was commissioned by the antiquary and historian Richard Colt Hoare of Stourhead, Wiltshire, to produce ten volumes of drawings of churches and other old buildings in Wiltshire (now in Devizes Museum, Wiltshire), and this commission, in the words of his grandson, 'decided his brains for antiquarian pursuits' (ibid., 51); he himself wrote in 1849:

> to build, repair, or survey warehouses and sash-windowed dwellings, however profitable, was so much less to my taste than perspective drawing with such subjects before me as cathedrals, abbeys and ancient parish churches, that I never made any effort to increase the number of my employments as an architect. (*The Builder*, 10, 3 Jan 1852, 7)

Commissions from other antiquaries, among them William Salt of Stafford, and from several noblemen, gentlemen, and clergymen, followed rapidly, and by the end of his life Buckler could claim authorship of 13,000 drawings of buildings throughout England and Wales, with Somerset, Yorkshire, Oxfordshire, Buckinghamshire, Hertfordshire, Staffordshire, and Wiltshire especially strongly represented. (Taunton Museum, Somerset, holds a collection of Buckler's drawings, as does the Bodleian Library, Oxford.) These meticulous works of art, in pencil or pen and wash, supplied an invaluable body of information about medieval and later buildings, many of them previously unrecorded, and many subsequently demolished or drastically altered. In 1810, after some opposition, he was elected a fellow of the Society of Antiquaries. In later life he ascribed his artistic productivity to his 'uniformly temperate and regular method of living' (Buckler, 51). Forty-two volumes of his sketches are in the British Library.

From about 1810 John Buckler was assisted in his vast output of drawings by his eldest son, **John Chessell Buckler** (1793–1894), artist and architect, who was born on 8 December 1793, possibly at Bermondsey. He received an artistic training from the watercolour painter Francis Nicholson. On 12 May 1818 he married Esther Fair. John Buckler's youngest son, George Buckler (1811–1886), later became involved in the enterprise, and subsequently wrote that the three 'worked together in perfect harmony and without any confusion of labour' (Bodl. Oxf., MS Eng.

lett. a. 1, c. 335, fol. 52). John Chessell Buckler was responsible for the text of *Views of the Cathedral Churches of England and Wales* (1822), incorporating his father's engravings, and in the following year he published a pamphlet, *Observations on the Original Architecture of St Mary Magdalen College, Oxford*, in which he criticized recent alterations to the college's fifteenth-century quadrangle. He subsequently brought out *Sixty Views of Endowed Grammar Schools* (1827); *A Historical and Descriptive Account of the Royal Palace at Eltham* (1828); *Remarks on Wayside Chapels* (1843); and *A History of the Architecture of the Abbey Church of St Alban* (1847). The last two of these were produced in partnership with his son Charles Alban Buckler (1824–1905). These publications made an important contribution to the growing body of scholarship of English medieval architecture.

Three successive generations of the Buckler family practised as architects, starting with John, whose works include Halkyn Castle, Flintshire (1824–7), Pool Park, Denbighshire (c.1828), and the tower of Theale church, Berkshire (1827–8), a Magdalen College living. He also restored the monument to William Waynflete, founder of Magdalen College, in Winchester Cathedral, and he was responsible in 1828 for re-erecting the tomb of Waynflete's father, formerly in Wainfleet church, Lincolnshire, in Magdalen chapel. About 1830 he made over his practice to his eldest son, who worked until 1842 in partnership with his younger brother George. John Chessell Buckler's first important building was the Tudor-Gothic Costessey Hall, Norfolk (1826). He carried out a sensitive restoration of the fifteenth-century chancel at Adderbury church, Oxfordshire, in 1831–4, and was second prizewinner in the competition for the new houses of parliament in 1836. Later works include Butleigh Court, Somerset (1845), and Dunston Hall, Norfolk (begun 1859); and restoration work at Lincoln Cathedral, Oxburgh Hall, Norfolk, and Hengrave Hall, Suffolk. He completed the superb series of 145 drawings of Oxford begun in 1811 by his father (now in the Bodleian Library); he also carried out restorations at several Oxford colleges and at the university church of St Mary the Virgin, and designed new premises for Magdalen College School (1849–51; now the college library) and the front of Jesus College to Turl Street (1854–6). He did little architectural work after 1860, retiring to Melbury House, Cowley, Oxford, where he died at the age of 100 on 10 January 1894. His son Charles Alban Buckler, a convert to Roman Catholicism, was also an architect, designing several impressive Catholic churches, including Our Lady and St Dominic, Haverstock Hill, London (1874–83), and carrying out the spectacular restoration and remodelling of Arundel Castle, Sussex, for the fifteenth duke of Norfolk in 1890–1903, one of the last great achievements of the Gothic revival in English secular architecture.

GEOFFREY TYACK

Sources C. A. Buckler, *Bucleriana: notices of the family of Buckler* (1886) · *Oxford Herald* (20 Dec 1851) · *The Builder*, 10 (1852), 7 · letters, Magd. Oxf., MS 460 · Colvin, *Archs.* · *Catalogue of the drawings collection of the Royal Institute of British Architects: B* (1972) · letters, Bodl. Oxf., MSS Eng. lett. a. 1, c. 335 · C. L. Eastlake, *A history of the Gothic revival* (1872) · *Drawings of Oxford by J. C. Buckler, 1811–27*, Bodleian Library, Oxford (1951)

Archives Bodl. Oxf., letters, sketches, drawings, and family papers · Lewisham Library, London, Lewisham Local Studies Centre, letters · Magd. Oxf., letters

Likenesses J. Outrim, line engraving, pubd 1850 (after portrait by W. J. Newton, 1847), NPG

Wealth at death wrote on retirement (18 July 1849) that he was almost deprived of income 'at all times slender and now reduced within very narrow limits': Magd. Oxf. MS 460, fol. 33

Buckler, John Chessell (1793–1894). *See under* Buckler, John (1770–1851).

Buckler, William (1814–1884), artist and entomologist, was born on 13 September 1814 at Newport, Isle of Wight, the son of William Buckler. The topographical artist John Buckler (1770–1851) was his uncle. He was educated at Newport, and then through the influence of Captain Ffarrington of Woodvale, he entered the studio of Mr Sass of Soho, London, where he showed much taste for drawing. He became a student of the Royal Academy Schools. Although initially an oil painter, he became more interested in watercolours, a medium in which he gained some reputation as a portrait painter; between 1836 and 1856 he exhibited sixty-two pictures at the Royal Academy.

About 1848 Buckler moved from Portman Square, London, to Emsworth, Hampshire. There he became interested in entomology, exchanging drawings for specimens with his friend the Revd John Hellins. Buckler's first entomological article, 'Captures of Lepidoptera', was published in the *Entomologist's Weekly Intelligencer* in 1856. In 1857, in response to a request in that journal for a portrait painter, he became engaged to contribute drawings of the Tineina larvae and their food-plants. In the course of the next three years he contributed about 120 figures, but eventually found the work too time-consuming, and in 1860 he requested to be released from the undertaking. However, he did contribute additional descriptions of larvae to the *Weekly Entomologist* (1862) and to the *Entomologist's Monthly Magazine*.

By 1873 Buckler estimated that he had produced at least 5000 larvae drawings, figuring more than 850 species in various stages of growth. This was despite his being afflicted by attacks of scrivener's palsy, from which he sought relief in carpentry and making cabinets. Furthermore his sight was so poor it prevented him from becoming a successful collector in his own right, and meant all his work had to be done at home with a magnifying lens. During the winter of 1882–3 Buckler began learning German in order to be able to correspond with foreign entomologists. However, on 9 January 1884 he died (presumably unmarried), at Lumley, Westbourne, Sussex, as a result of bronchopneumonia. At his death his work on the Macrolepidoptera of Britain remained unfinished. His *Larvae of the British Butterflies and Moths* (considered his most important work) was edited by Henry T. Stainton and E. T. Porrst and published in six volumes between 1886 and 1901.   YOLANDA FOOTE

Sources *Entomologist's Monthly Magazine*, 20 (1884), 229–36 · Boase, *Mod. Eng. biog.* · Mallalieu, *Watercolour artists*

Archives NHM, collection of fly-fishing; corresp.; notebook relating to Lepidoptera

Wealth at death £172 12s. 6d.: probate, 31 Jan 1884, *CGPLA Eng. & Wales*

Buckley [*married name* Fisher], **Arabella Burton** (1840–1929), popularizer of science and writer, was born on 24 October 1840 in Brighton, the daughter of John Wall Buckley, vicar of St Mary's, Paddington Green, and his wife, Elizabeth (d. 1889), daughter of Thomas Burton; Henry Burton *Buckley, first Baron Wrenbury (1845–1935), was her brother. Little is known of her education and early life. An authoritative popularizer of science, and from 1864 to 1875 secretary to Sir Charles Lyell (for whose entry in the *Encyclopaedia Britannica* she wrote the expert's addendum), she was personally familiar with the leading scientists and scientific theories of her day. She lectured on natural science from 1876 until 1888, was editor of Mary Somerville's *Connexion of the Physical Sciences* (1877) and Heinrich Leutemann's *Animals from Life* (1887), and produced a set of botanical tables for the use of junior students (1876). In her own first book, *A Short History of Natural Science* (1876), she recalled that she 'often felt very forcibly how many important facts and generalizations of science, which are of great value … in giving a true estimate of life and its conditions, [were] totally unknown to the majority of otherwise well-educated persons' (pp. vii–viii). Her *Short History* was intended 'to supply that modest amount of scientific information which everyone ought to possess, while, at the same time … form a useful groundwork for those who wish afterwards to study any special branch of science' (p. viii) and as such was praised by Charles Darwin. On 6 March 1884 she married Thomas Fisher MD (1819/20–1895), a widower twenty years her senior.

Although Arabella Buckley also wrote a *History of England for Beginners* (1887), traditional history never gave full scope to her distinctive penchant for narrative, which was better exercised in her books retelling the story of evolution. Grounded in evolutionary theory and in all aspects of the new geology, she re-created this knowledge in two popular books whose narratives are highly imaginative, *Life and her Children* (1881) and *Winners in Life's Race* (1883). In them Buckley presented seven divisions of life: *Life and her Children* covers the first six, from the amoebas to the insects, and *Winners in Life's Race* is entirely devoted to the seventh, the 'great backboned family'.

Buckley was one of a small number of nineteenth-century Darwinians who realized the deficiencies in Darwin's thinking with regard to the development of moral qualities in the animal kingdom, set out in his discussion of 'social instincts' in *The Descent of Man* (1871). Darwin had observed the competitive advantage species can gain from a well-developed social instinct but had difficulty in explaining its evolution, particularly with respect to parental affections for their offspring. Far from being daunted by this aspect of evolution, Buckley made parents' care for their offspring central to her books on evolution and continued Darwin's observations with far greater emphasis on mutuality. For her the *raison d'être* for evolution was not just the preservation of life, but the development of altruism as well.

Buckley's work is concurrent with Karl Kessler's 'On the

law of mutual aid' (1880), the lecture which stimulated Peter Kropotkin to re-examine Darwin. Kessler died in 1881, the year that saw the publication of Buckley's *Life and her Children*; it then took Kropotkin ten years to challenge Thomas Henry Huxley over the importance of mutual aid in the pages of *Nineteenth Century*, and another ten to formulate his classic *Mutual Aid: a Factor in Evolution* (1902). Meanwhile, Buckley's last book, *Moral Teachings of Science* (1891), was devoted to this idea and written to unite science and philosophy—to study morality from 'within outward' and 'without inward' (p. 4). For Buckley, 'these [were] not really two, but only different methods of arriving at one result, namely, the knowledge of laws by which we and all the rest of nature are governed' (p. 5).

Buckley was deeply aware of the nature of science writing and realized that science, though based in fact or experiment, was transmitted as a literary construction. Two other books, *The Fairy-Land of Science* (1879, reissued in a number of late nineteenth-century editions) and its sequel, *Through Magic Glasses* (1890), demonstrate her skill at telling the stories of science. In *Fairy-Land* Buckley generated interest in her scientific subjects by borrowing the language of fairy stories and wizardry to reinforce her ultimate belief that the wonders of science not only paralleled but surpassed the wonders of fairyland. In its sequel, *Through Magic Glasses*, she focused more closely on what childlike eyes can see, calling on the help of the telescope, stereoscope, photographic camera, and microscope, and a fictional guide, a magician into whose chamber the reader immediately enters and through whose eyes the world is viewed. Her last work showed the same concern with vision and the visible and was written for Cassell's series *Eyes and No Eyes* (1901–24). Buckley died of influenza at her home, 3 Boburg Terrace, Sidmouth, Devon, on 9 February 1929. BARBARA T. GATES

Sources *WWW*, 1929–40 • C. Darwin, *The descent of man, and selection in relation to sex*, 2 vols. (1871) • P. Kropotkin, *Mutual aid: a factor in evolution* (1902) • m. cert. • d. cert.
Wealth at death £16,998 4*s.*: resworn probate, 1929, *CGPLA Eng. & Wales*

Buckley, Cecil William (1828–1872), naval officer, entered the navy in 1845. He served in the frigate *Miranda*, one of the squadron which, on the outbreak of the war with Russia, was sent to the White Sea.

In the following winter the *Miranda* was sent to the Black Sea, and on 29 May 1855 Buckley, with Lieutenant Burgoyne and Mr Roberts, a gunner, volunteered to land and burn stores at Genichersk. They did so, narrowly escaping Cossacks, who almost cut them off from their boat. A few days later Buckley, accompanied by Mr Cooper, the boatswain, again landed at Taganrog, and burned the stores and government buildings. In acknowledgement of these services, Buckley was promoted commander on 27 February 1856, and was awarded the Victoria Cross on the occasion of its institution.

Buckley as commander served on the Cape station, and for some time in the *Forte*. He was promoted captain on 16 April 1862, and from 1868 to 1870 commanded the *Pylades* on the Pacific station. In December 1871 he was appointed to command the *Valiant*, coastguard ship in the Shannon, from which failing health obliged him to retire in the following October, to Catcott in Somerset. He died in Madeira on 7 December 1872. He had married Catharine Senhouse, who survived him, and they had a son and a daughter. J. K. LAUGHTON, *rev.* ROGER MORRISS

Sources R. W. O'Byrne, *The Victoria cross* (1880), 44 • private information (1886) • Boase, *Mod. Eng. biog.* • *CGPLA Eng. & Wales* (1873)
Wealth at death under £450: administration with will, 28 Oct 1873, *CGPLA Eng. & Wales* • under £50: further action, 13 Jan 1876, *CGPLA Eng. & Wales*

Buckley, Daniel Richard [Domhnall Ua Buachalla] (1866–1963), Irish nationalist and last governor-general of the Irish Free State, was born on 3 February 1866 at Maynooth, co. Kildare, the fourth of the six children of Cornelius Buckley, merchant, and his wife, Sarah (1838–1918), daughter of Joshua Jacob of Dublin and his wife, Sarah. Educated at Belvedere College and at Catholic University School, Dublin, he subsequently inherited his father's business. An early member of the Gaelic League, he began to refer to himself as Domhnall Ua Buachalla but was also known as Dan or Donal Buckley or Donal O Buachalla. His marriage on 3 June 1897 to Jane Walsh (*c.*1870–1918) of Dublin produced seven children; after her death on 4 July 1918 he remained a widower.

Upright, determined, and self-effacing, not dissimilar in appearance to George V, Buckley was a devout and lifelong Roman Catholic. A member of the Irish Republican Brotherhood and of the Irish Volunteers, he fought valiantly during the 1916 Easter rising and, after some time in Knutsford gaol and Fron-goch, was released the following Christmas. Standing as a Sinn Féiner in the 1918 general election, he was returned for North Kildare. He attended the first meeting of Dáil Éireann, voted against the treaty/articles of agreement in January 1922, and failed to secure re-election in June. Joining the anti-treaty forces upon the outbreak of hostilities, he was arrested and escaped from Dundalk gaol. After his electoral success as a member of Fianna Fáil in June 1927, he entered Dáil Éireann on 12 August with his party colleagues. Retaining his seat in the September 1927 election, he lost it in February 1932.

Asked by President de Valera to accept the governor-generalship, Buckley agreed in order to help prepare the way for an Irish republic. He was appointed on 25 November 1932 and sworn in the following day. As governor-general (seanascal), he resided not in the vice-regal lodge but in private accommodation, first at Booterstown and then at Dún Laoghaire, received a considerably reduced salary, and led no official social life. After the abolition of the governor-generalship in December 1936 he lived quietly in Dublin at Stillorgan Park and later at Eglinton Road, Donnybrook. He died of renal failure at the Pembroke Nursing Home, Dublin, on 30 October 1963 and was buried with full military honours on 2 November at Laraghbryan, Maynooth. BRENDAN SEXTON

Sources B. Sexton, *Ireland and the crown, 1922–1936: the governor-generalship of the Irish Free State* (1989)
Likenesses photograph, 1932, repro. in *Irish Times* [Dublin] • photograph, Áras an Uachtaráin, Phoenix Park, Dublin

Wealth at death £8539: probate, 16 Dec 1963, *CGPLA Éire*

Buckley, Henry Burton, first Baron Wrenbury (1845–1935), judge and legal writer, was born in London on 15 September 1845, the fourth of six sons of John Wall Buckley (1809–1883), vicar of St Mary's Church, Paddington Green, and his wife, Elizabeth (*d.* 1889), daughter of Thomas Burton; Arabella Burton *Buckley (1840–1929) was his sister. From Merchant Taylors' School, London, he entered Christ's College, Cambridge, as a scholar (1864). He was ninth wrangler in the mathematical tripos of 1868. During his undergraduate career he was stroke of the college boat and obtained in 1866 the Tancred law studentship at Lincoln's Inn. On 18 April 1868 he was elected fellow of Christ's (the same day as John Fletcher Moulton, also destined for a distinguished judicial career), an emolument he retained until resignation in 1882. In 1901 he was elected an honorary fellow of the college. He was called to the bar by Lincoln's Inn (7 June 1869), and became a master of the bench in 1891, having taken silk in 1886 and having served on the bar committee and bar council. On 12 April 1887 he married Bertha Margaretta (*d.* 1960), third daughter of Charles Edward Jones of South Kensington; they had four sons and four daughters.

In 1900 Buckley was appointed a judge of the Chancery Division of the High Court and was knighted (3 May 1900). In October 1906 he was promoted to the Court of Appeal and made a privy councillor. In recommending the promotion to the prime minister (Campbell-Bannerman) the lord chancellor (Loreburn) had written that:

> Mr Justice Buckley is the man whose appointment would be most approved in the legal profession and with justice I think. He is a first rate man and has proved a very fine judge of the Chancery Court in all ways. (Heuston, 147)

On his retirement from the bench in 1915 he received a peerage (12 April 1915) as Baron Wrenbury, of Old Castle, Sussex, but he did not retire from judicial work, for over the next two decades he sat frequently in both the judicial committee of the privy council and the House of Lords.

Buckley first established his professional reputation as a legal author in the field of company law. The first edition of *The law and practice under the Companies Act 1862, 1867, 1870, the Life Assurance Companies Act 1870, 1871, 1872 and other acts relating to joint stock companies* appeared in 1873, being a commentary on the texts of the relevant statutes, and the work reached its eleventh edition in the author's lifetime, when he was eighty-five years old. The book continues in later editions as an authoritative work of reference in its field.

Apart from his special knowledge and experience in the field of company law, Buckley was a general equity lawyer of the highest calibre, and as an appellate judge he displayed considerable talent in other areas of law and the common law at large. Over a span of thirty-five years his contributions to case law through the law reports were numerous and weighty. A good example of his style is the reasoning in his judgment in *Hurst* v. *Picture Theatres Ltd* (1915), a highly controversial decision on the revocability of contractual licences, and the appropriate remedies for the breach of such contracts, in which he displayed a high degree of faith in the sanctity of contract, an attitude which he shared with his judicial contemporary Fletcher Moulton. Another decision of great jurisprudential consequence was *Sinclair* v. *Brougham* (1912–14) on the distribution of loss as a consequence of *ultra vires* banking loans, a case in which Buckley was unable to aid depositors as against the bank's shareholders, though the House of Lords ultimately held otherwise by means of a tracing order.

Generally Buckley's judicial career covered the years in which the effects of the fusion of law and equity after the Judicature Acts were being worked out, and the more fluid equity of earlier times was being rapidly refined by rules of greater precision and of a more specific character. This legal climate was congenial to Buckley's temperament as a lawyer, his mind being both subtle and cautious. Later, in the House of Lords, he developed a more independent approach and, though loth to dissent, he was not afraid to do so. Thus in *Bourne* v. *Keane* (1919) he dissented from all his colleagues in their re-interpretation of a sixteenth-century enactment against superstitious uses and their decision that a bequest for masses for souls of the dead was legally valid. Wrenbury was not prepared to overrule earlier cases binding on the house, remarking that 'certainty in the law is a thing greatly to be desired'. To change the law, he felt, was for the legislature.

Buckley had interests in many directions other than the law. He founded in 1904 a scholarship in political economy tenable at Cambridge University, and the consolidation of income tax law in 1918 owed much to his participation in the work of the parliamentary committee on the subject; later he contributed letters and articles to *The Times* newspaper on a variety of topics connected with political economy. Towards the end of his life he published, in 1930, a collection of essays, *Of Immortality and other Thoughts*, seventeen short disquisitions, apparently written over a period of years, in which he reflected on the mysteries of human individuality and the nature of human experience. Since his early days in Cambridge he retained a strong taste for scholarship; from 1916 to 1918 he served as vice-president of the Selden Society. He died at his London home, 7 Melbury Road, Kensington, on 27 October 1935, and was cremated at Golders Green. His fourth son, Sir Denys Burton Buckley (*b.* 1906), who assisted editorially with later editions of his textbook on company law, had a distinguished legal career, serving as a lord justice of appeal from 1970 to 1981. His fourth daughter, Ruth Burton Buckley (1898–1986), was called to the bar by Lincoln's Inn in 1926 as one of the first generation of women barristers, served as chairman of East Sussex county council (1952–5), and was appointed DBE in 1959.

D. E. C. YALE

Sources W. R. C. [W. R. Cornish], 'Buckley, Henry', *Biographical dictionary of the common law*, ed. A. W. B. Simpson (1984) · *The Times* (28 Oct 1935) · Venn, *Alum. Cant.*, 2/1 · J. Peile, *Biographical register of Christ's College, 1505–1905, and of the earlier foundation, God's House, 1448–1505*, ed. [J. A. Venn], 2 (1913), 581 · *Christ's College Magazine*, 33 (1923), 237–40 · Sainty, *Judges*, 191 · *Law reports* · Burke, *Peerage* (1969) · GEC, *Peerage* · R. F. V. Heuston, *Lives of the lord chancellors, 1940–1970* (1987)

Archives UCL, letters to Sir Francis Galton
Likenesses J. Collier, portrait, 1897, priv. coll. · J. Collier, portrait, 1907, priv. coll. · W. Stoneman, two photographs, 1917–28, NPG · Spy [L. Ward], chromolithograph caricature, NPG; repro. in *VF* (5 April 1900)
Wealth at death £14,654 15s. 9d.: resworn probate, 30 March 1936, *CGPLA Eng. & Wales*

Buckley, Olivia Francisca (1799–1847). *See under* Dussek, Sophia Justina (1775–1847).

Buckley, Robert [*name in religion* Sigebert] (1516/17–1610), Benedictine monk, was almost certainly one of the postulants admitted to Westminster Abbey on 21 November 1556, the day after that house's refoundation by Queen Mary. He took minor orders on 17 December 1557 and became a priest on 4 June 1558. As a very old man Buckley, known as Sigebert, would recall that the manner of life in the abbey was 'much like to that which he saw observed in cathedral churches as for the divine office' and that it followed 'the laws and customs of colleges and Inns of Court' (McCann and Cary-Elwes, 69). Like the rest of the community, Buckley left Westminster at its second dissolution in May 1559; he retained his Catholic allegiance and consequently spent long periods in prison, in the Marshalsea (1582–6) and at Wisbech (1588–99) and Framlingham (1599–1603).

It is his longevity which has given Buckley his importance for posterity. By the beginning of the seventeenth century English monks in Spanish and Italian monasteries were coming together to revive the monastic tradition in England and establish a Benedictine mission to recusants there. Late in 1603 a small group of monks of the Cassinese congregation landed in Norfolk; they knew that Buckley still lived, and since he had just been released from prison on the orders of James I they were able to meet him at the house of Francis Woodhouse at Caston, Norfolk. On that occasion Buckley renewed his monastic vows in their presence. Four years later, on 21 November 1607, after he had moved to Clerkenwell, he aggregated Robert Sadler and Edward Maihew into the old English congregation and on 15 December 1609, though by now blind, he solemnly confirmed his action before witnesses. He died on 22 February 1610 at the house of Thomas Lovedon, near West Meon, Hampshire, aged ninety-three and was buried in the chapel of Ponshall near by.

Although the aggregation was soon ratified by Pope Paul V (*Cum sicut accepimus*, 1609) and approved in full in a papal brief of 1612, the enactments being later incorporated into the bull *Plantata* of 1633, none the less there is a note of caution in all these instruments, probably arising from uncertainty about how far Buckley was legally capable of transmitting the rights and privileges once enjoyed by the medieval English Benedictines. The latter had never formed a body with a discrete juridical identity of the sort envisaged for monastic congregations following the Council of Trent, and it must therefore be doubted whether Buckley could hand on any rights other than those of Westminster Abbey in the days of its restoration. In the last resort the significance of Buckley's actions lies primarily in their symbolic character, in the link they represented between the embattled Catholicism of the early seventeenth century and its Marian and medieval past.

ANTHONY MARETT-CROSBY

Sources J. McCann and C. Cary-Elwes, *Ampleforth and its origins* (1952) · D. Knowles [M. C. Knowles], *The religious orders in England*, another edn, 3 (1979) · J. Bossy, *The English Catholic community, 1570–1850* (1975) · D. Lunn, *The English Benedictines, 1540–1688* (1980)

Buckley, Theodore William Alois (1825–1856), classical scholar, was born on 27 July 1825 at Paddington, Middlesex, the eldest son of William Richard Buckley and his wife, Olivia Francisca *Buckley, *née* Dussek (1799–1847) [*see under* Dussek, Sophia Justina], daughter of the composer J. L. Dussek. His mother was a gifted musician, and he acquired considerable proficiency as a pianist. He was a protégé of the well-known Greek scholar George Burges. He regularly attended the British Museum Library, where he was described as 'a fresh-coloured youth, with flaxen and slightly curling hair, poring over works of which some of the best scholars knew little more than the name'. One of the earliest projects on which he worked there was an edition of *Apuleius de Deo Socratis*, for which he collected material with a view to publication. For this he had no means; he was very poor, and from the age of twelve he was self-taught. His library, which when transferred to Oxford weighed a ton and a half, was picked up at old bookstalls at the cheapest prices. In this manner he collected a very nearly complete set of the quarto Dutch Latin classics. He was fortunate in his purchases. He is said, for instance, to have procured an Aldine Aristophanes for 4s., the title-page of which was supposed missing, but was afterwards discovered by him merely to have been misplaced. The expense of printing his *Apuleius de Deo Socratis* was defrayed by the book collector Thomas Grenville, to whom it was dedicated, in 1844.

Some friends had the idea of sending Buckley to study at Oxford and approached the classical scholar Thomas Gaisford, the dean of Christ Church, who secured for him a servitorship at Christ Church in 1845. Buckley's Latin prose was acknowledged by the dean the purest he had ever met, but his lowly status as a servitor barred his way to promotion. His experience as a menial student in an aristocratic college inspired a work of social observation, *The Natural History of Tufthunters and Toadies* (1848). After graduating BA in 1849 and proceeding MA in 1853, he returned to London where he wrote for booksellers. Besides contributions to many periodicals, including Charles Dickens's *Household Words*, *Eliza Cook's Journal*, *Sharpe's Magazine*, *Freemason's Journal*, *Parker's Miscellany*, and *The Press*, he undertook many translations between 1849 and 1853 for H. G. Bohn's series of classical authors. He also edited many works for Routledge. His output during these years was prodigious, and included, according to Edward Bradley, a novel, *The Adventures of Mr Sydenham Greenfinch* (1854). His poetic power found expression in an ode to Florence Nightingale, published in *Punch* and reprinted in *The Times*. In 1852 Gaisford appointed him to a minor chaplaincy at Christ Church but he went into decline as illness caused him to resort to opium and subsequently to alcohol. He died of fever on 30 January 1856, and was buried in Brookwood cemetery, Woking.

JAMES MEW, *rev.* M. C. CURTHOYS

Sources GM, 3rd ser., 1 (1856), 314–16 • N&Q, 4th ser., 7 (1871), 534 • N&Q, 4th ser., 8 (1871), 255 • Foster, *Alum. Oxon.*

Buckley, William (1518/19–1571), mathematician, born at Lilleshall, Shropshire, was educated at Eton College from about 1532, proceeding on a king's scholarship to King's College, Cambridge, in 1537. He graduated BA in 1542 and MA in 1545, held a fellowship from 1540 to 1550, and briefly in 1549 was a prebendary of Lichfield.

Described by Robert Mulcaster as 'very well studied in the mathematicalls' (Taylor, 169), Buckley was mathematics tutor to Edward VI from 1545 to 1548. While at court, at her request, he made a ring dial for Princess Elizabeth, which he presented in 1546, with a tract explaining its use. He was probably also the maker of an astronomical quadrant, designed for the king by Sir John Cheke, royal tutor, and signed 'W. B.'. In 1548, when Cheke was provost of King's College, he sent for Buckley to teach arithmetic and geometry to the students. Buckley also served as schoolmaster to the royal pages from 1550 to 1552. In algebra Buckley was able to extract square roots in the manner of Cardan and John of Seville, and his *Arithmetica memorativa* (1550?), consisting of the rules of arithmetic set out in Latin verse, for easy memorizing, was the first treatise published in England to develop a theory of combination. Buckley died in 1571.

THOMPSON COOPER, *rev.* ANITA MCCONNELL

Sources Cooper, *Ath. Cantab.*, 1.292 • W. Sterry, ed., *The Eton College register, 1441–1698* (1943), 54 • W. W. R. Ball, *A history of the study of mathematics at Cambridge* (1889), 22 • E. G. R. Taylor, *The mathematical practitioners of Tudor and Stuart England* (1954); repr. (1970), 169

Buckley, William (1780–1856), convict and settler in Australia, was born at Marton, near Macclesfield, Cheshire, the son of small farmers. He learned to read at evening school before being apprenticed as a bricklayer. At nineteen he enlisted in the local militia, then the 4th regiment of foot and served in Holland. Upon his return he was convicted at the Sussex assizes on 2 August 1802 for receiving a roll of stolen cloth and was transported to Port Phillip. On Christmas day 1803 he absconded from the infant settlement. While near death after months of privation in the bush, he was claimed by the Wathaurung people of Geelong as a transmogrified dead relative. Murrangurk, as he was known, was incorporated into the group, 'retaught' their language, customs, and hunting practices, and claimed to have been protected by them. His great height (6 ft 6 in.), large frame, and the stories he told of England and Europe, marked him as a unique (but it seems not powerful) individual among them. Buckley's account of his thirty-two years among the Wathaurung, as told to John Morgan in 1852 (seventeen years after Buckley's return to white society), is a mixture of unmatched ethnographic material and exaggerated and ethnocentric claims of Aboriginal violence and savagery: in short, the fascinating but telescoped memories of an illiterate

seventy-year-old retold by a journalist for 'our mutual benefit'.

In June 1835 an advance party from Van Diemen's Land, illegally attempting to settle the uninhabited south-eastern coast of Australia, camped at Indented Head, near Geelong. Buckley, bearded and clad in possum skin, entered the camp on 6 July. Through signs, and the tattoo 'W. B.' on his arm, he made himself known and warned of an imminent Aboriginal attack. After ten days his English language returned sufficiently for him to be useful as an interpreter. Once the party's leaders, John Batman and John Wedge, arrived, a pardon was arranged from Hobart and he was placed on Batman's payroll as an interpreter. In March 1836 he toured with the governor, Sir Richard Bourke, visiting his former residence, a cave on the Barwon River. He was made a government interpreter and special constable in September 1836.

Buckley was vulnerable, caught between the Europeans of his birthright who saw him as a savage and an ex-convict, and the Wathaurung who shared his years in the wilderness only to be rejected upon the arrival of white settlers. Worse still, he lived in Melbourne, amid the Woiworung, the enemies of his former Wathaurung kin. These many tensions surfaced in April 1837 when he was to search for Gellibrand and Hesse, settlers believed murdered by Aborigines. Buckley's horse was mysteriously hamstrung, putting him out of the search (horses then being rare commodities). Buckley resigned in October 1837 and petitioned Governor Bourke for help, claiming he could not earn his livelihood in white society after being separated from 'civilized life' for thirty-two years, and could not rejoin the Wathaurung as he had displeased them. Sir Richard Bourke lobbied for a £100 pension, but the British government refused to pay this former escapee. Buckley emigrated to Hobart in December 1837 and, in May of the next year, secured a government job as assistant storekeeper and then a gatekeeper, first at the Female Factory Hospital and then at the nursery at Dymnyrne. He married Julia Egar, a widow with one daughter, on 27 January 1840. He was pensioned off by the government of Van Diemen's Land in 1852 at £12 a year, to which sum the Victorian government added £40 a year. He was fatally injured when he fell from a carriage in December 1855, dying at home in Hobart on 30 January 1856.

His contemporaries saw Buckley as the archetypal 'wild man'—curious, dangerous, and of obvious 'low intelligence' having lived so long with 'cannibals'. Later observers have been fascinated by his exotic, courageous, and elusive life, told in four books and numerous press articles. RICHARD BROOME

Sources J. Morgan, *The life and adventures of William Buckley: thirty-two years a wanderer amongst the Aborigines of the unexplored country round Port Phillip* (1852) • P. Jones, ed., *Beginnings of permanent government* (1981), vol. 1 of *Historical records of Victoria*, ed. M. Cannon • *The Aborigines of Port Phillip, 1835–1839* (1982), vol. 2A of *Historical records of Victoria*, ed. M. Cannon • *Aborigines and protectors, 1838–1839* (1983), vol. 2B of *Historical records of Victoria*, ed. M. Cannon • *The early development of Melbourne* (1984), vol. 3 of *Historical records of Victoria*, ed. M. Cannon • P. L. Brown, ed., *The Todd Journal 1835* (1989) [Geelong Historical Society] • M. Tipping, *Convicts unbound: the story of the Calcutta convicts and their settlement in Australia* (1988) • T. F. Bride, ed., *Letters from Victorian pioneers* (1898) • J. H. Wedge, 'Narrative of an excursion amongst the natives of Port Phillip, on the south coast of New Holland', State Library of Victoria, Melbourne, La Trobe manuscript collection, MF 63 • *Hobart Town Courier* (31 Jan 1856) • *Tasmanian Daily Register* (28 Dec 1855)

Likenesses C. H. T. Constantini, portrait, State Library of New South Wales, Dixson Wing; repro. in *Cornwall Chronicle* (Sept 1837) • F. Gross, wood-engraving (after N. Chevalier), State Library of Victoria, Melbourne, La Trobe picture collection; repro. in *Newsletter of Australasia* (Aug 1857) • W. McLeod, portrait, repro. in A. Garran, ed., *The picturesque atlas of Australasia* (1888), vol. 1, p. 103 • oils, State Library of Victoria, Melbourne, La Trobe picture collection, LT 787 • sketch, State Library of Victoria, Melbourne, La Trobe picture collection, J. H. Wedge's Field Book, 1835, MS 9302

Buckman, James (1814–1884), naturalist and agriculturist, was born on 20 November 1814 in Cheltenham, a son of John Buckman (1767–1851), shoemaker and cordwainer, and his wife, Mary Bishop (*b.* 1777). He was first articled to Stephen H. Murley, a Cheltenham surgeon-apothecary, who inculcated in him an interest in science. From about 1835 Buckman studied medicine in London, but his first publication (listing plants found at Battersea in 1835–6) demonstrated his growing interest in natural history. About 1837 he abandoned medical studies and established himself as an analytical and dispensing chemist in Cheltenham, but his interest in botany remained and he joined the Botanical Society of London. He soon developed a reputation as a Cotswold naturalist, especially in the fields of botany and geology, and by 1842 he was honorary secretary and lecturer to the Cheltenham Literary and Philosophical Institution (CLPI). In the latter year he was elected fellow of the Geological Society and published *Our Triangle. A Geological Chart of the Cotswolds* followed in 1843 and *Botanical Guide to Cheltenham* in 1844. He also published, together with Hugh Strickland, an important revision of R. I. Murchison's *Geology of Cheltenham*.

In 1844 Buckman's brother Edwin, a Cheltenham ironmonger, went bankrupt; from about this time Buckman began to seek a new career in science, away from both pharmaceutical chemistry and Cheltenham. He resigned from the CLPI in 1845 and early in 1846 was appointed as professional secretary, curator, and resident lecturer to the Birmingham Philosophical Institution. The institution failed financially, and in 1848 Buckman became professor of geology, botany, and zoology at the Royal Agricultural College, Cirencester. There he found new interests in archaeology amid the nearby Roman remains and helped form the Corinium Museum. He was an early member of the Cotswold Club from 1846 and the Worcestershire Naturalists' Club from 1847, and was elected a fellow of the Linnean Society in 1850. In 1852 he married Louisa Elizabeth Dunn (*b.* 1826); she died in childbirth within a short time. Buckman visited the United States of America as a mineral consultant in 1854, and in 1858 married Julia (1834–1865), daughter of pharmacist John Savory (1800–1871). They had five children, including Sydney Savory *Buckman (1860–1929).

On his arrival at the Royal Agricultural College, Buckman had started botanical experiments to solve the problem of the identity of species. Papers were read to the British Association for the Advancement of Science from 1856, and funded by the association from 1857. Buckman's experiments involved both wild and cultivated plants, yielded a new 'Student parsnip of delicious flavour' in 1860, and were praised in Charles Darwin's *Origin of Species* in 1859. Buckman was in turn a supporter of Darwin; in his report of 1860 to the infamous meeting of the British Association for the Advancement of Science at Oxford he backed Darwin's theories of evolution. The Anglican principal of the Royal Agricultural College (the Revd John Constable, 1825–1892) found this distasteful and by 1863 had forced Buckman's resignation from the college. Buckman had published more books, including *Stone Steps* (1852 and 1855) and *British Grasses* (1858), while at the college, but his botanical garden had been ploughed up in the summer of 1862, on the principal's orders.

In October 1863 Buckman moved to farm 'on scientific principles' at Bradford Abbas, Dorset, one of the most richly fossiliferous areas in the world. In 1865 his second wife, Julia, died in childbirth, leaving Buckman with five children. By now a recognized agricultural authority, Buckman became active as a teacher of private agricultural students, founded the Dorset Natural History and Antiquarian Field Club, and wrote an immense number of articles, both popular and learned. He died at The Villa, Bradford Abbas, on 23 November 1884 after an extraordinarily productive career, and was buried in the churchyard there on 27 November. The *Royal Society Catalogue* lists a total of sixty-five periodical articles, but the full list is many times longer (he made nearly 300 contributions on agriculture alone).

H. S. TORRENS

Sources H. S. Torrens, 'What price the advancement of science? James Buckman as a professional scientist, 1846–63', paper presented to the 150th British Association for the Advancement of Science meeting, 1988, Royal Agricultural College, Cheltenham • J. Buckman, *An address on resigning his professorship* (1863) • *Cheltenham Looker-On* (29 Nov 1884) • *Sherborne Journal* (1 Dec 1884) • *Gloucester Journal* (29 Nov 1884) • J. C. Mansel-Pleydell, 'In memoriam—Professor James Buckman', *Proceedings of the Dorset Natural History and Antiquarian Field Club*, 7 (1886), 1–4 • W. D. Lang, 'The Buckmans: father and son', *Proceedings of the Dorset Natural History and Archaeological Society*, 82 (1960), 73–6 • T. G. Bonney, *Quarterly Journal of the Geological Society*, 41 (1885), 43 • H. J. Riddlesdell and others, eds., *Flora of Gloucestershire* (privately printed, Cheltenham, 1948) • R. Sayce, *The History of the Royal Agricultural College, Cirencester* (1992) • H. S. Torrens and M. A. Taylor, 'Geological collectors and museums in Cheltenham, 1810–1988', *Geological Curator*, 5 (1988–94), 173–213 • E. Garrett, *Bradford Abbas: the history of a Dorset village* (1989) • Bishop's transcript, Glos. RO • S. S. Buckman, *Type ammonites*, 4 (1922–3), 29–36 • *CGPLA Eng. & Wales* (1885)

Archives BGS, botanical and geological notebooks, and letters • BGS, corresp., notebook, and papers | BGS, letters to F. L. Kitchin

Likenesses P. N. Marshall, portrait, *c.*1844, repro. in S. S. Buckman, *Type Ammonites 3* (1920), 23 • K. Witchell, portrait, 1883, repro. in Buckman, *Type Ammonites 4* • photograph, 1886, repro. in Mansel-Pleydell, 'In memoriam'

Wealth at death £2259 15s. 8d.: probate, 13 Feb 1885, *CGPLA Eng. & Wales*

Buckman, Sydney Savory (1860–1929), geologist and palaeontologist, was born on 3 April 1860 at Dollar Street, Cirencester, the eldest son of James *Buckman (1814–1884), naturalist, and his wife, Julia, *née* Savory (1834–

1865). After his father lost his job as professor of botany and geology at the Royal Agricultural College, Cirencester, in 1863, the family moved to Bradford Abbas, Dorset, one of the most richly fossiliferous districts in the world. His mother died two years later; thus Buckman's main influences were his naturalist father and Dorset's palaeontological riches.

Between 1871 and 1879 Buckman attended Sherborne School. In 1877, while still at Sherborne, he read a paper on fossil *Astarte* (*Bivalvia*) to the Dorset Field Club. The paper was awarded the club's prize, and was published in 1878. First intentions were that Buckman should enter the church, but with the encouragement of his grandfather John Savory (1800–1871), a London pharmaceutical chemist, Buckman set off in 1879 to study at the Chemischen Laboratoriums, run by the Fresenius family in Wiesbaden, Germany. However, the following year Buckman returned to England, where he spent the next two years studying to become a land agent under one of his father's former students, Robert Holland (1829–1893), estate agent of Norton Hill and Mobberley, Cheshire. The two years were also spent courting Holland's daughter, Maude Mary (1860–1946), whom Buckman married on 14 June 1882.

In 1881 Buckman published his first paper in the *Quarterly Journal of the Geological Society*. In it he disagreed with his father's views about the age of sands at Yeovil and the value of fossil 'zones' in dating such rocks. The following year he was elected fellow of the Geological Society. It was also in 1882 that Buckman began farming at Upper Hampden, Gloucestershire, a profession he abandoned in March 1886 after being defeated by the great agricultural depression. He now started a new, but precarious, career as a novelist, commercial writer, and dealer in fossils, in order to support his scientific work on Jurassic rocks.

Buckman started work on a Palaeontographical Society monograph on the ammonites of the Inferior Oolite in 1887. In 1889 the first of his critically important papers was published, demonstrating that southern English sands of Toarcian to Aalenian age were diachronous. It remains the classic demonstration of this phenomenon, where identical strata distinguished by their fossil assemblages differ in age from place to place. In 1893 his paper on the subdivision and detailed dating of the Inferior Oolite of Dorset followed. This broke new ground in showing how precisely such condensed and eroded rocks could be subdivided, and how necessary it was to separate the stratal record from the chronological. Buckman was the first to show how precisely time could be revealed from fossils. The first of his pioneering studies of homeomorphy in brachiopods followed in 1901.

In 1904 Buckman suffered a breakdown in health, caused by over-exertion as a cycling geologist. He moved to Thame, Oxfordshire, in order to be closer to scientists based in London and Oxford. However, the move brought a loss of contact with the fieldwork which had been so critical to the quality of his work earlier. This, and the ever-increasing multiplicity of names he was giving to ammonites, caused the council of the Palaeontographical Society

to abandon his monograph in 1907. In 1909 he commenced publication of *Type Ammonites*, initially those from Yorkshire, as a private venture without interference from referees. The work reached seven volumes by the time of his death.

Buckman's scientific work before 1904 was of a quality quite unequalled for its time, but its worth has only recently become clear. His later work, as an early and 'consultant palaeontologist' largely outside government or academic circles, was done in too much isolation from other professional scientists. Buckman was a man of extraordinary breadth, a good linguist, and much interested in political and social reform, having been an advocate of 'rational dress' for women cyclists. In 1910 he published his minor, if forgotten, classic, *Marriage, Mating and the Status of Women*.

Buckman's work polarized geological opinion, but he was awarded the Lyell medal of the London Geological Society in 1913. In 1914, now busy as a consultant, he was offered a post with the Geological Survey of Canada, but the First World War prevented his appointment. Buckman died at his home, Southfield, Long Crendon, Buckinghamshire, on 26 February 1929. He left only £1474 and asked to be cremated, with no religious service of any kind. In 1930 his widow was awarded a civil-list pension for his services to geology. In 1933 his ashes were spread over Thorncombe Beacon, Dorset.   H. S. TORRENS

Sources 'Autobiography', 1860–82, priv. coll. [incomplete] • A. M. Davies, 'The geological life work of Sydney Savory Buckman', *Proceedings of the Geologists' Association*, 41/3 (1930), 221–40 • W. D. Lang, 'The Buckmans, father and son', *Proceedings of the Dorset Natural History and Archaeological Society*, 82 (1960), 73–6 • J. H. Callomon, 'Time from fossils: S. S. Buckman and Jurassic high-resolution geochronology', in M. J. Le Bas, *Milestones in geology* (1995), 127–50 • H. S. Torrens, 'The Sherborne School museum', *Proceedings of the Dorset Natural History and Archaeological Society*, 98 (1978), 32–42 • J. W. Tutcher, 'S. S. Buckman', *Naturalist* (1929), 187–8 • R. Austin, 'S. S. Buckman', *Proceedings of the Cotteswold Naturalists' Field Club*, 23 (1930), 287–8 • C. H. Crickmay, 'S. S. Buckman', *Science*, 70 (1929), 87–8 • A. M. Davies, 'S. S. Buckman', *Quarterly Journal of the Geological Society of London*, 86 (1930), lxiii–lxvi • D. T. Donovan, 'History of the classification of mesozoic ammonites', *Journal of the Geological Society of London*, 151 (1994), 1035–40 • O. Buckman, *Life is a mountain* (1987) • *CGPLA Eng. & Wales* (1929)

Archives BGS • NHM • priv. coll. | Bristol City Museum and Art Gallery, Tutcher MSS

Likenesses photograph, 1906, repro. in S. S. Buckman, *Type ammonites*, 3 (1921), 25 • P. Buckman, portrait, 1907, repro. in Buckman, *Life is a mountain*, 21, fig. 4

Wealth at death £1474 3s. 9d.: probate, 4 June 1929, *CGPLA Eng. & Wales*

Buckmaster, Maurice James (1902–1992), intelligence officer and businessman, was born on 11 January 1902 at Ravenhill, Brereton, Staffordshire, the son of Henry James Buckmaster (c.1857–1943), brewer, and his wife, Eva Matilda, *née* Nason (b. c.1868). He was educated at Eton College from 1915 to 1920 and secured a classics exhibition to Magdalen College, Oxford, but lack of money stopped him from continuing his academic studies. Instead, he taught French to schoolchildren, worked briefly for *France Soir*,

Maurice James Buckmaster (1902–1992), by unknown
photographer

and spent six years at J. Henry Schroeder & Co., merchant
bankers, in London. On 2 July 1927 he married May Dorothy Steed (b. 1904/5), daughter of Frederick Othnill Steed,
silk merchant; they had a son and two daughters. In 1929
Buckmaster began his long association with Ford Motors.
He was personal assistant to the chairman of the English
branch for three years, from 1932 to 1936 managed Ford
SA France, and then spent three years as head of the European department at Dagenham.

Buckmaster was commissioned into the intelligence
corps in October 1939, and after a war intelligence course
at Minley Manor and a course on photographic interpretation at Farnborough was posted as an intelligence officer
to 50 division in the British expeditionary force in France.
He was mentioned in dispatches for services in that role
during the retreat to Dunkirk, from which he was evacuated on 2 June 1940. He served as a liaison officer at Weymouth during the battle of Britain, and then joined the
Dakar expedition as a GSO3 (intelligence). After it failed,
he rejoined 50 division, and was briefly an instructor on
the intelligence course at Bridgwater.

In the spring of 1941, on the invitation of Gerald Templer, Buckmaster joined the Special Operations Executive
(SOE) with the rank of major, and spent the summer on
courses. He then, after a brief spell in the Belgian section,
became head of the independent French (F) section in
November 1941. On 18 December the same year, his first
marriage having ended in divorce, he married Anna Cecilia Frances Stevenson (1903/4–1988), daughter of Michael
Reinstein, of independent means, and divorced wife of
Aubrey Melford Steed Stevenson. She was thereafter his
constant companion at home, but could know nothing of
his secret work. This consisted in finding, training, and
dispatching to France—usually by parachute—men and
women who could pass for French, who would prepare
tasks of sabotage and subversion that would assist an
eventual British armed re-entry into France. They came, as

Buckmaster came, under the orders of the chiefs of staff,
passed down through SOE's command channels (Buckmaster, often wrongly described as SOE's head, stood four
steps down its staff ladder). He had fluent French (spoken
with an English accent) and friendly manners, but no direct experience of Nazi occupation methods, and too little
detailed information from 'the field' about what life in
France was currently like.

Buckmaster's section sent nearly 500 agents into
France, over 100 of whom died, either in action or in concentration camps. Eighteen of them were dropped, unper-
ceived by Buckmaster, directly into Gestapo hands.
General de Gaulle strongly disapproved of their presence,
but they inflicted substantial damage on the enemy and
on French collaborators, imposing for example substantial delays on reinforcements for the Normandy front in
June 1944. After the liberation of France in September
1944, Buckmaster, by now promoted full colonel, made a
progress round that country, thanking those who had supported his leading agents, and he made sure that his men
and women secured plenty of decorations, including
three George crosses (all for women) and over a score of
appointments to the DSO. He was himself made a civil
OBE in 1943, and a chevalier of the Légion d'honneur in
1945 (promoted officier in 1978).

Buckmaster was released from the army late in 1945 and
returned to Ford, for whom he worked in England for
another fifteen years, first as head of the European department, then, from 1950, as director of public relations.
From 1960 he was a freelance publicity consultant, specializing in champagne imports, and was much in
demand in France at reunions of those who had worked
with him. The 'réseaux Buck' (Buck networks) are now
established as part of French resistance history, and several towns have streets named after him. He published
two books, Specially Employed (1952) and They Fought Alone
(1958), crammed with anecdotes, most of them true,
though few of them applied to the correct places and
agents. His health began to fail when he was in his eighties
and he retired from London to Forest Row in Sussex. He
died at his home there, the Walhatch Country Hotel, of
heart failure, on 17 April 1992. He was survived by the
three children of his first marriage. A memorial service
was held at Holy Trinity, Brompton, on 2 July 1992.

M. R. D. FOOT

Sources M. R. D. Foot, *SOE in France: an account of the work of the
British Special Operations Executive in France, 1940–1944*, 2nd edn
(1968) · *The Independent* (25 April 1992) · *The Times* (20 April 1992) ·
The Times (22 April 1992) · *The Times* (25 April 1992) · *The Times* (3 July
1992) · *The Guardian* (21–2 April 1992) · personal knowledge (2004) ·
private information (2004) · *WWW, 1991–5* · b. cert. · m. certs. · d.
cert.
Archives PRO, SOE files
Likenesses photograph, c.1943, repro. in Foot, *SOE in France* ·
photograph, c.1943, Special Forces Club, London · photograph,
repro. in *The Times* (20 April 1992) · photograph, repro. in *The Independent* · photograph, News International Syndication, London
[see illus.]
Wealth at death £145,373: probate, 3 June 1992, *CGPLA Eng. &
Wales*

Buckmaster, Stanley Owen, first Viscount Buckmaster (1861–1934), lord chancellor, was born on 9 January 1861 at 2 New Road, off St John's Hill, Wandsworth, London, the third of four sons of John Charles Buckmaster (d. 1908), professor of chemistry, and his wife, Emily Anne (d. 1890), eldest daughter of George Goodliffe, of Trumpington, near Cambridge. John Buckmaster was a remarkable man who, beginning as an agricultural labourer at the age of ten in the village of Slapton in Buckinghamshire, became successively a joiner, a platform speaker in the campaign against the corn laws, and, after attending a teacher training college, a teacher of chemistry first at the college where he had trained and then at the Imperial College of Science and Technology.

Stanley Buckmaster was sent to Aldenham grammar school (now Aldenham School). The school was then in low water and the boys suffered hardships which Buckmaster never forgot. However, thanks to the encouragement of one outstanding teacher, Buckmaster won a junior studentship in mathematics at Christ Church, Oxford, in 1879. He led an active and sociable life at Oxford, but was disappointed by obtaining a second class in both mathematical moderations (1881) and the final honours school (1882) rather than the first class for which he had hoped and which his two elder brothers had obtained.

Buckmaster was called to the bar by the Inner Temple in 1884. His first few years were a struggle, but from 1887 onwards he began to acquire a general practice on the midland circuit, and became a familiar figure in the county courts and magistrates' courts. However he also acquired a Chancery practice which eventually became the dominant part of his work.

On 29 December 1889 Buckmaster married Edith Augusta (d. 1935), fourth daughter of Spencer Robert Lewin of Widford, Hertfordshire. They had one son and two daughters. The elder daughter, Margaret, was a woman of outstanding ability who devoted her life to social reform and predeceased her father. Buckmaster's marriage was not, at least in later years, happy. In a letter to a friend in the last year of his life, he described himself as having had 'a broken home' (letter to Sir Lancelot Sanderson, June 1934, Heuston, 307).

Chancery silk and Liberal politician Buckmaster's practice as a senior barrister became very successful, and he took silk in 1902. At that time Chancery silks normally practised in the court of a particular judge, and Buckmaster attached himself to the court of Mr Justice Buckley, later Lord Wrenbury. In the same year he joined Lincoln's Inn; he became a bencher of the inn in 1910 and became its treasurer in 1934, the last year of his life.

After taking silk, Buckmaster, who had always been an enthusiastic Liberal, turned his attention to politics and sought election as a member of parliament. In 1903 he was adopted as the Liberal candidate for Cambridge, and he won the seat in the Liberal landslide in January 1906. Unusually, he chose to make a controversial maiden speech (on 6 July 1906), defending Mr Justice Grantham against allegations of pro-Conservative bias in the hearing of two election petitions. Buckmaster opposed his party

Stanley Owen Buckmaster, first Viscount Buckmaster (1861–1934), by Walter Stoneman, 1915

by objecting to the Criminal Appeal Act 1907, which introduced the court of criminal appeal. In the following years, he rarely spoke in the House of Commons and was frequently absent.

In spite of this, Buckmaster was highly regarded by the Liberal leadership, and after he lost his seat at Cambridge in the general election of January 1910 and failed to regain it in December 1910, a place was found for him as candidate in a by-election for the Keighley division of Yorkshire, which he won in October 1911. Thereafter he became very active both professionally and politically. He appeared regularly not only in the Chancery Division of the High Court but also in the King's Bench and the judicial committee of the privy council. He told his family that he was earning the then enormous sum of £40,000 a year. From 1910 to 1913 he was standing counsel to Oxford University.

In the House of Commons in 1912 Buckmaster made a powerful speech in defence of the ministers involved in the Marconi scandal, in particular the then attorney-general, Sir Rufus Isaacs. Buckmaster's reputation for personal integrity gave his speech great weight in the house, and was instrumental in persuading the house to accept the explanations given by the ministers. In October 1913 Isaacs was appointed lord chief justice and the solicitor-general, Sir John Simon, was promoted to replace him as attorney-general. Buckmaster was appointed to replace Simon and was knighted. In the consequent by-election (resulting from the rule then in force that newly appointed ministers had to resign and stand for re-election) Buckmaster was again returned for Keighley. His work as solicitor-general was widely praised and enhanced his reputation.

On the outbreak of war in 1914 Buckmaster (while remaining solicitor-general) was appointed director of the press bureau, the department responsible for control of the press. This was not a successful appointment. Buckmaster was not fitted for the office by background or personality. Relations between the press and the armed forces (particularly the Admiralty) were bad and the newspaper proprietors were powerful figures who resisted control. Buckmaster's statement in the House of Commons on 12 November 1914 that he was prepared to block criticism which 'might destroy public confidence in the government which at this time is charged with conduct of the war, or might in any way weaken the confidence of the people in the administration of affairs' (*Hansard 5C*, 58.129) suggested an authoritarian attitude excessive even in time of war.

Lord chancellor In May 1915 the prime minister, Herbert Asquith, was forced to form a coalition government. One of the terms on which the Conservatives insisted was the removal from office of the then lord chancellor, Lord Haldane. Simon was offered the post but refused it. Buckmaster was Asquith's next choice. He received the great seal on 27 May and was sworn of the privy council on the same day. He was elevated to the peerage as Baron Buckmaster of Cheddington in the county of Buckingham on 14 June.

Buckmaster held office as lord chancellor for only eighteen months. Asquith was forced to resign on 6 December 1916, and Buckmaster as a member of his government resigned on the same day. When David Lloyd George formed the new government, Buckmaster was replaced by a Conservative, Sir Robert Finlay.

His short period of office and the government's concentration on the war effort deprived Buckmaster of the chance to make a significant impact as lord chancellor. He was responsible for only two appointments to the High Court, those of A. F. Peterson and H. A. McCardie. He made no appointments to the office of king's counsel, taking the view that to do so would be unfair to juniors absent on war service. However, a war cabinet had not yet been created and Buckmaster, as a member of the cabinet, was involved in decisions affecting war strategy. He was strongly opposed to the decision, following the withdrawal from the Dardanelles, to send an expeditionary force to Salonika. He was also closely involved in the decision not to grant a reprieve to Sir Roger Casement from the death sentence which had been imposed on him for treason.

Law lord In October 1917 Buckmaster was appointed one of the members of the inter-allied council to co-ordinate the purchase of war material from the USA. In December 1917 he publicly supported the 'Lansdowne letter', the letter written to the *Daily Telegraph* by the fifth marquess of Lansdowne calling for a negotiated peace.

After the war Buckmaster strongly attacked the atrocities committed in Ireland by the 'Black and Tans', the auxiliary police force recruited by the British government. He became recognized as one of the leading orators of his day, speaking on a wide variety of subjects both in the House of Lords and on public platforms. He never wrote out his speeches in advance, but relied on scribbled notes. Subjects on which he spoke ranged from the treatment of Germany after the war to the protection of lapwings (for which purpose he secured the passage of the Protection of Lapwings Act 1928). He supported improved housing for the poor, birth control, the abolition of capital punishment, and women's suffrage.

Unlike most people, Buckmaster became more radical, particularly on social issues, as he grew older. He was particularly active in the field of divorce reform, where he sought to provide for divorce on grounds other than adultery, which at that time was the only ground recognized by the law. In November 1918 he introduced a bill adding desertion as a ground for divorce, which was defeated. In March 1920 he moved the second reading in the House of Lords of a bill which would have provided five additional grounds for divorce. This bill was narrowly passed by the House of Lords but it failed because the government never introduced it in the House of Commons. Similar bills were introduced in the House of Lords in 1921 and 1924 but failed to get enough support to be enacted. Buckmaster's only success was to pilot through the House of Lords the Matrimonial Causes Act 1923 which made a limited extension to divorce law by allowing women to obtain a divorce on the ground of their husband's adultery alone; previously women (but not men) had had to prove cruelty as well as adultery.

Buckmaster's personal loyalty to Asquith and the decline of the Liberal Party after 1918 ruled out any return to office. However, as a former lord chancellor he regarded it as his duty to sit regularly as a member of the House of Lords in its judicial capacity and the judicial committee of the privy council. Two of the best-known cases in which he took part come from the beginning and the end of his judicial career. In *Bowman* v. *Secular Society* (1917) he held, together with a majority of his colleagues, that the purposes of a society formed to challenge Christian doctrine were not illegal. In *Donoghue* v. *Stevenson* (1932)—a case familiar to every first-year law student—Buckmaster found himself in a minority in objecting to the extension of a manufacturer's liability in negligence to include liability to the ultimate purchaser of the manufactured goods (in the case in question, a bottle of ginger beer alleged to have contained a decomposed snail). Buckmaster was not a creative or reforming judge—he stuck firmly to the maxim that hard cases make bad law—but he was highly regarded by other leading judges of his day. Lord Birkenhead described him as 'a consummate judge' (Heuston, 301). Lord Dunedin was asked, 'Whom do you regard as the greatest colleague you have had?' and replied:

> You will be surprised when I tell you—Buckmaster; I have not and I never have had any sympathy with Buckmaster's political ideas and performances and I think him to be a sentimentalist—until he is sitting on his arse on the bench; there he is one of the most learned, one of the most acute, and the fairest judge I ever sat with.   (*DNB*)

In 1925 Buckmaster abandoned his judicial work for a time to go into the City, giving up his judicial pension during this period although he was under no obligation to do so. His purpose was to right what he believed to be wrongs suffered by the shareholders of an oil company at the hands of their directors. However, the City was not to his taste and he soon returned to his judicial work. In 1929 Buckmaster was appointed chairman of the political honours scrutiny committee, which had been set up in 1924 in order to stop the abuses of the honours system which had occurred during Lloyd George's premiership. He was reappointed in 1931. He also served, for three years before he became solicitor-general and again from 1925 until his death, as the umpire for deciding disputes about wages and conditions in the boot and shoe industry. In 1923 he was proud to become chairman of the governing body of Imperial College, where his father had taught.

Buckmaster was awarded honorary degrees by the universities of Toronto (1925), Oxford, and Edinburgh (both 1933). In 1930 he was awarded the GCVO. In 1933 he was belatedly raised to the rank of viscount.

An observer described Buckmaster in 1925 as:

> a man of medium height; and lean. He has a lean face; high cheek bones, hollow cheeks, an aquiline nose, deep set blue eyes, and an earnestness of manner that reaches the quality of solemnity … He speaks with an admirable, clear and easily heard voice, which never falters, which speaks admirable, choicely arranged, finely inflected language. (Heuston, 298)

Buckmaster was a popular member of the Garrick Club, to which he was elected in 1909.

Buckmaster's short tenure of office, during a period when life was dominated by the First World War, means that he is one of the lesser lord chancellors of the twentieth century. His importance rests perhaps more on his roles as social reformer and judge after his retirement from office as lord chancellor. There is a notable dichotomy here—he was a judicial conservative but a liberal on social issues. He was a man of outstanding integrity and great powers as an orator, who might well have returned to office had it not been for the collapse of his party.

At the end of 1933 Buckmaster's health failed. After a year's illness he died at his home, 1 Porchester Terrace, Hyde Park, on 5 December 1934. He was cremated at Golders Green and his ashes were interred in the graveyard of the parish church at Widford in Hertfordshire, the village from which his wife had come and where he owned a country house. He was succeeded by his only son, Owen Stanley Buckmaster. His wife, who had long been an invalid, died the following year.

WILLIAM GOODHART

Sources R. F. V. Heuston, *Lives of the lord chancellors, 1885–1940* (1964) · *DNB* · *Law reports* [for Buckmaster's judgments] · J. Johnston, *An orator of justice: a speech biography of Lord Buckmaster* (1932) · GEC, *Peerage*
Archives ICL, corresp. and papers relating to Imperial College · priv. coll., MSS | BL OIOC, letters to Lord Reading, MSS Eur. E 238, F 118 · Bodl. Oxf., corresp. with Herbert Asquith · Bodl. Oxf., corresp. with Lewis Harcourt · Bodl. Oxf., corresp. relating to Society for the Protection of Science and Learning · NL Ire., letters to John Redmond
Likenesses J. Russell & Sons, photograph, 1915, NPG · W. Stoneman, photograph, 1915, NPG [*see illus.*] · G. F. Watt, oils, *c.*1920, Lincoln's Inn, London · E. Kapp, drawing, 1929, Barber Institute of Fine Arts, Birmingham · T. Cottrell, cigarette card, NPG · R. Eves, oils (posthumous), Christ Church Oxf. · H. Furniss, ink caricature, NPG · T. McKegger, portrait, priv. coll. · Owl, mechanically reproduced caricature, NPG; repro. in *VF* (19 Nov 1913)
Wealth at death £93,309 14*s*. 1*d.*: probate, 21 Feb 1935, *CGPLA Eng. & Wales* · £92,838 15*s*. 5*d.*: probate, further grant, 13 May 1935, *CGPLA Eng. & Wales*

Buckmaster, Thomas. *See* Buckminster, Thomas (1531/2–1599).

Buckmaster, William (*d.* 1546), scholar, graduated BA in 1513–14 as a student of Peterhouse, Cambridge, where he was admitted a fellow in 1517. He was admitted MA the same year, and was ordained deacon in the diocese of Lincoln on 18 September 1518 and priest on 18 December. He was admitted BTh in 1525 and DTh in 1528, the year of his appointment as Lady Margaret preacher. Elected vice-chancellor of Cambridge University in 1529, he found himself caught up in the problem of the king's divorce from Katherine of Aragon.

Early in 1530 Henry VIII wrote to the universities of Oxford and Cambridge, asking them for a determination as to the canon law status of his marriage to the widow of his deceased brother, Arthur. The king had already sought and found persuasive supporters at Cambridge, including Robert Wakefield and Edward Foxe. But the attitude of the university authorities was crucial in obtaining a favourable answer, and Buckmaster did not disappoint. At a preliminary meeting in February 1530 Stephen Gardiner and Foxe found him anxious to serve the king in the matter. When the congregation of the university convened, Buckmaster read out the king's letter, with its request for a determination of the law, stressing the university's responsibility to provide one. He began the process of asking each doctor in turn for his opinion, hoping to conclude with a formal vote which would find that the marriage was illegal. But it quickly became clear that many among the congregation dissented, and Buckmaster found it necessary to abandon the consultation process. A commission was proposed, but this provoked opposition, since those nominated had already expressed themselves against the marriage.

Probably on 21 February 1530, a more tractable commission of twenty-nine men was created, which expressed itself favourably. On 9 March Buckmaster was able to present its findings at a congregation of the university, which endorsed them. The determination thus made was then entrusted to the keeping of Buckmaster, who journeyed to Windsor and on 13 March presented it to the king.

Henry, however, was not pleased, since the scholars had ruled the marriage illegal only in the case that Arthur and his wife had consummated their marriage, devoutly to be denied by Queen Katherine. And they had neither been asked for, nor considered, the question of whether the pope could dispense from the law in such matters.

Henry thus found it necessary to ask his vice-chancellor to arrange further deliberations, and Buckmaster is known to have been active in this. If he is to be believed, Henry was not slow to offer bribes to get his way: the king 'talked with me a good while. He much lauded our wisdoms and good conveyance in the matter with the great quietness in the same. He shewed me also what he had in his hands for our University'; the following day 'twenty nobles' were conveyed to him (Burnet, 6.33). Buckmaster seems to have been thoroughly unnerved by the whole experience. The next morning, as he records, he departed 'glad to be out of the court', 'thinking more than I did say'. To his friend John Edmonds, master of Peterhouse, he confirmed the strength of opposition aroused at Cambridge by the decision in the king's Great Matter. Buckmaster's arrest of 'Parson Dakers', an opponent of the divorce, led to a rowdy protest with 'such boying and crying out against our college that all Cambridge might perceive it was in spite of me' (ibid., 34). As a result of the decision, Buckmaster complained, he had lost a benefice which the patron Mr Throckmorton 'hath faithfully promised unto me many a time, but now his mind is turned and alienate from me' (ibid.). It seems likely, however, that this was the rectory of Barcheston, Warwickshire, to which he was presented in April 1530.

Buckmaster was certainly no hot reformer, if his opinion whether confirmation was a sacrament may be taken as a guide. Although warrant for such a claim might:

> be not expressly had in scripture, yet ought we reverently and obediently to accept and receive the same: for as much as the Church, that is to say, the whole multitude of Christen people, hath so allowed and received them hitherto. (Strype, vol. 3, pt 2, 359–62)

Nevertheless, Buckmaster was a signatory of the 1536 articles of faith, and of a declaration the following year concerning the functions of bishops and priests.

Little else is known of Buckmaster's life, though his loyalty did not go unrewarded. Between 1532 and 1544 he was a fellow of the new foundation of King's Hall, Cambridge. In 1534 he became rector of St Mary Woolwich. He served again as vice-chancellor of Cambridge in 1538 and 1539. He also became rector of Stanwick, Northamptonshire, and succeeded Ralph Pole (whose will is dated 12 March 1539) in the prebendal stall of East Withington in the cathedral of Hereford. On 9 April 1541 he was collated to the prebend of Holborn in the diocese of St Paul's, retaining the living until his death, which occurred in 1546.

STEPHEN WRIGHT

Sources T. A. Walker, A biographical register of Peterhouse men, 1 (1927) · G. Burnet, The history of the Reformation of the Church of England, rev. N. Pocock, new edn, 7 vols. (1865) · G. B. Skelly, 'Henry VIII consults the universities of Oxford and Cambridge', Le 'divorce' du roi Henry VIII, ed. G. Bedouelle and P. Le Gal (1987), 59–72 · J. Strype, Ecclesiastical memorials, 3/2 (1822) · Fasti Angl., 1541–1857, [St Paul's, London] · will, PRO, PROB 11/31/23
Wealth at death see will, PRO, PROB 11/31, fols. 184v–185r

Buckminster [Buckmaster], **Thomas** (1531/2–1599), Church of England clergyman and almanac writer, was vicar of Twickenham from 1562 to 1563, then rector at All Hallows-the-Great, London, 1564–72, and rector at St Mary Woolnoth from 1572 until his death. He is sometimes supposed to have been a relative of William Buckmaster, vice-chancellor of the University of Cambridge under Henry VIII. Between 1566 and 1599 he produced annual almanacs—usually entitled A New Almanack and Prognostication and calculated for the meridian of London—for the printers Watkins and Roberts. A number of his almanacs are extant and a facsimile edition of his almanac for 1598 was published by the Shakespeare Association in 1935. The content of his almanacs is unremarkable, conventional, and middle-of-the-road; they are made up of the usual calendrical and astronomical information, advice on the most propitious times for planting and harvesting, bleeding of patients, and other mundane matters. They are notably patriotic, deferential, and religious in tone, and the monthly pages are headed with moral exhortations in indifferent verse, usually promoting the virtues of honesty and charity. Buckminster died in 1599.

JOSEPH GROSS

Sources B. S. Capp, Astrology and the popular press: English almanacs, 1500–1800 (1979) · STC, 1475–1640, vol. 1

Bucknill, Sir John Charles (1817–1897), psychiatrist, was born in Market Bosworth, Leicestershire, on 25 December 1817, one of the five children of a local surgeon, John Bucknill. He was educated at Rugby School and Market Bosworth grammar school, working as an assistant to his father before beginning his formal medical education in Dublin in 1837. In 1838 Bucknill transferred to University College, London, and graduated MB in 1840; he obtained his LSA and membership of the College of Surgeons in the same year. Appointed as surgeon's dresser to Robert Liston at University College Hospital, Bucknill was passed over in 1841 when he applied for the post of its apothecary, and left to enter private practice in Chelsea. In 1842 he married Maryanne Townsend (d. 1889), only child of Thomas Townsend of Hillmorton Hall, near Rugby. They had three sons, Lieutenant-Colonel John Townsend Bucknill MP, Sir Thomas Townsend Bucknill (1845–1915), a High Court judge and MP, and Charles Bucknill (1846–1895).

A tall (6 ft 1½ in.) and taciturn man, whom even his children found reserved, uncommunicative, and difficult, Bucknill had little success in establishing himself as a metropolitan practitioner, and by 1843 unspecified health problems forced him to move to Devon. The following year he successfully applied for the vacant post of superintendent at the new Devon County Asylum in Exminster, where he remained for the next eighteen years. From this point forward, his career was centrally involved with the treatment of mental illness and the administration of the lunacy laws.

Bucknill believed that mental disease was rooted in

abnormal states of the brain and was convinced of the value of medicine's standard therapeutics in the treatment of insanity. An early convert to the merits of treating patients without recourse to mechanical restraint—strait-jackets and the like—his abilities as an asylum administrator quickly won him the approbation of the lunacy commissioners, the national inspectorate set up in 1845. As Bucknill acquired confidence in his new role, he gradually sought a wider and more substantial professional reputation as a member of the Association of Medical Officers of Asylums and Hospitals for the Insane (AMOAHI), subsequently the Medico-Psychological Association, and as spokesman for the emerging profession in his role as editor and co-founder of the *Asylum Journal*. Appearing every six weeks between 1853 and 1855, the journal became a quarterly and changed its name to the *Journal of Mental Science* from 1856. Bucknill remained its editor until 1862. In a profession riven with divisions between the heads of the new publicly funded pauper asylums and the profit making private sector, he sought to serve as a unifying figure, emerging as a major spokesman for what he insisted were their shared interests. In 1858, together with Daniel Hack Tuke, great-grandson of the founder of the York Retreat, he published the first comprehensive British textbook on insanity, *A Manual of Psychological Medicine*, writing the key sections on diagnosis, pathology, and treatment. The book was an international success, appearing in a fourth edition in 1879. In 1860–61 Bucknill's central role in the profession was recognized by his election as president of the AMOAHI.

Bucknill had received his MD from University College, London, in 1852; he became LRCP in 1853, and FRCP in 1859. During the 1850s, he wrote extensively on insanity and its legal relations, and on Shakespeare's knowledge of insanity. He also lobbied the War Office, and in 1852 secured permission to create a corps of citizen soldiers, officially styled the 1st Exeter and Devonshire Rifle Volunteers. In 1862, tiring of the demands of administering a large and increasingly overcrowded asylum, Bucknill secured an appointment as lord chancellor's visitor in lunacy, supervising the care and treatment of mostly well-to-do chancery lunatics.

In his last years at Devon, Bucknill had begun to break with professional orthodoxy, experimenting with boarding patients out in the community and supplementing the large centralized asylum with smaller, cottage-like accommodation in the grounds. Subsequently, however, he was to become even more of a professional maverick, expressing growing doubts, often using intemperate language, about the value of asylum treatment, and worries about the civil liberties of the insane, eventually calling for the complete abolition of private, profit-making asylums, and their replacement by state run institutions. His similarly controversial pronouncements on the treatment of inebriety and harsh criticisms of American alienists for continuing to employ mechanical restraint in managing their patients (which followed a visit to North America in 1875) further distanced him from his erstwhile colleagues.

Having resigned his official position, from 1876 Bucknill worked from consulting rooms in Wimpole Street as a lunacy specialist, helping to establish a style of private practice based upon office consultancy rather than institutional care. A member of the Garrick and Athenaeum clubs, Bucknill's metropolitan prominence and social connections brought him election as FRS in 1866. He became increasingly influential in the affairs of the Royal College of Physicians; he was elected Lumleian lecturer in 1877, was censor in 1879–81, and subsequently served as a member of council. Together with James Crichton-Browne, David Ferrier, and John Hughlings Jackson, in 1878 he founded the new journal, *Brain*, which fostered a neuropsychiatric approach to understanding the physical pathology of insanity. His accession to his wife's family's country estate in Warwickshire, his appointment as a Warwickshire justice of the peace, and his enthusiasm for, and spirited participation in, fox-hunting, fishing, and shooting completed his transformation into an eminent Victorian physician and country gentleman. Following the death of his wife in 1889, Bucknill moved to Bournemouth, Hampshire. He was knighted in 1894 for his role in founding the Devon Volunteers as much as for his prominence in medicine. He died on 19 July 1897 at his home, East Cliff House, Bournemouth, of septic inflammation brought on by kidney disease, and was buried at Clifton-on-Dunsmore, near Rugby, three days later.

ANDREW SCULL

Sources A. Scull, C. MacKenzie, and N. Hervey, *Masters of Bedlam: the transformation of the mad-doctoring trade* (1996) · DNB · *Journal of Mental Science*, 43 (1897), 885–9 · *The Lancet* (24 July 1897) · *BMJ* (24 July 1897), 255 · *CGPLA Eng. & Wales* (1897)
Likenesses engraving (after photograph by Debenham & Gould), NPG; repro. in *ILN* (2 June 1894) · engraving (after photograph by Elliott & Fry), NPG; repro. in *ILN* (31 July 1897)
Wealth at death £48,274 16s. 9d.: probate, 6 Oct 1897, *CGPLA Eng. & Wales*

Buckshorn [Boxhorn], **Joseph** (*fl.* 1670), painter, was a native of the Netherlands. Of his parents nothing is known. He settled in London about 1670 where he worked for Sir Peter Lely, whose pupil he had been. He was much praised by Vertue for his copies after Lely: 'whose manner he came so near, that several Heads of his have been mistaken, by good Judges, for that Grate Masters' (Vertue, *Note books*, 2.134). Compared with that of his master, his style was 'rather stronger, not so broad but [of] great force & Softness' (ibid., 80). Thomas Bardwell also wrote well of him: 'Buckshorn was one of the last good copiers we have in England; the rest that followed him and his master Lely soon dwindled to half-artists' (Bardwell, 21). Pictures by him, however, are scarce. Vertue mentions a portrait of Davenant, the son of Sir William, and another of his wife, and all sources mention a copy in the possession of Lord Rockingham at Wentworth Woodhouse made by Buckshorn after Van Dyck's *Earl of Strafford*. A portrait by him of Mary Isham in Lamport Hall, Northamptonshire, is documented in a letter from David Loggan to Sir Thomas Isham of 29 December 1675, saying that 'Mr Boxhorn' had promised it would be done in about three weeks, and adding that it 'is very well painted, but I could wisch that it was more Leick' (Isham, 87). Buckshorn died at about the age of thirty-six and was buried in St Martin's churchyard, London. GORDON GOODWIN, rev. SARAH HERRING

Sources E. K. Waterhouse, *The dictionary of British 16th and 17th century painters* (1988), 38–9 · G. Meissner, ed., *Allgemeines Künstlerlexikon: die bildenden Künstler aller Zeiten und Völker*, [new edn, 34 vols.] (Leipzig and Munich, 1983–) · Vertue, *Note books*, 1.82, 106; 2.5, 80, 94, 134 · G. Isham, *A catalogue of the pictures at Lamport Hall, Northamptonshire* (1933), 11–12 · [B. Buckeridge], 'An essay towards an English school of painters', in R. de Piles, *The art of painting, with the lives and characters of above 300 of the most eminent painters*, 2nd edn (1744), 354–430, esp. 359–60 · Redgrave, *Artists* · A. von Wurzbach, *Niederländisches Künstler-Lexikon*, 1 (Vienna and Leipzig, 1906), 221 · C. Kramm, *Geschiedenis van der beeldende kunsten in der Nederlanden*, 1–2 (Amsterdam, 1664), 186 · T. Bardwell, *The practice of painting and perspective made easy* (1756), 21 · H. Walpole, *Anecdotes of painting in England: with some account of the principal artists*, ed. R. N. Wornum, new edn, 3 vols. (1888), vol. 2, p. 102 · G. Isham, 'The correspondence of David Loggan with Sir Thomas Isham: 2', *The Connoisseur*, 154 (1963), 84–91

Buckstone, John Baldwin (1802–1879), actor, playwright, and theatre manager, was born at Hoxton, London, on 14 September 1802, the son of John Buckstone, a retired shopkeeper. After brief service as a ship's boy on a man-of-war at the age of eleven, he returned to his studies at Walworth grammar school and was subsequently articled in a solicitor's office. Soon, however, he developed an interest in acting, and made his first appearance at a fit-up theatre in a barn at Peckham, as Captain Aubri in a benefit performance of *The Dog of Montargis*, an adaptation of Guilbert de Pixérécourt's melodrama. When he was nineteen he left home to join a troupe of strolling players, with whom he appeared at Wokingham, Berkshire, as Gabriel in Thomas Morton's *The Children in the Wood*. He then spent three years with a theatrical circuit company serving towns in south-east England, during which time he became acquainted with Edmund Kean, who seems to have been impressed by his comic talent and to have encouraged him to persevere in his chosen profession. Possibly through Kean's recommendation, he made his London début at the Surrey Theatre on 30 January 1823, as Ramsay the watchmaker in *The Fortunes of Nigel*, based on Scott's novel. In October 1824 he became a member of the resident company at the Coburg, where he remained until 1827; he then moved to the Adelphi under Daniel Terry's management, and first appeared there on 1 October as Bobby Trot in his own domestic melodrama *Luke the Labourer*, which had been premièred anonymously on the same stage a year earlier.

While at the Adelphi, Buckstone was introduced by Terry to Sir Walter Scott, a meeting which apparently inspired him to devote himself to writing, and it was at this theatre, then the home of spectacular melodrama, that some of his most popular plays were later to be presented. He was the original Gnatbrain in Douglas Jerrold's *Black-Eyed Susan*, produced at the Surrey on 8 June 1829. In 1833 his drama *Ellen Wareham*, with Elizabeth Yates as the heroine, was staged at the Haymarket, where between April of that year and 1839 he also performed in several farces of his own, one of them, *Uncle John* (October 1833),

including in its cast such eminent artists as William Farren the younger, Benjamin Webster, and Julia Glover, as well as Buckstone himself. But initially his engagement at the Haymarket was for the summer months only and he would return each winter to the Adelphi.

After an indifferently received visit to the United States in 1840–42 Buckstone rejoined the Haymarket company as its principal low comedian. At the same time he fulfilled short engagements with Alfred Bunn at Drury Lane and Madame Vestris at the Lyceum, where in 1847 he created the role of Box in J. M. Morton's farce *Box and Cox*. In the following year, when he was ill-advisedly cast as First Witch opposite Charles Kean's Macbeth at the Haymarket, the familiar voice of the comedian, issuing from the grim figure of the witch, had the effect of reducing the house to helpless laughter. In March 1853 he took over from Benjamin Webster as manager of this theatre, a position he retained until three years before his death. Under his easy-going but resourceful management the Haymarket prospered for some years, achieving a prominence and a consistent drawing power it had not previously enjoyed and becoming identified with English comedy at its best. This was due in large measure to the distinguished body of seasoned players with whom he surrounded himself, including at one time or another Henry Compton, Amy Sedgwick, Mr and Mrs Chippendale, Mr and Mrs Charles Mathews, Henry Howe, A. E. Sothern, J. S. Clarke, William Farren junior (the third actor of that name), Mr and Mrs Kendal, and Ada Cavendish, though his short-sighted reliance on a largely unchanging company progressively impaired its appeal. He did, however, produce much new work, by J. R. Planché, Tom Taylor, A. W. Dubourg, Westland Marston, Edmund Falconer, T. W. Robertson, H. J. Byron, John Oxenford, F. C. Burnand, W. S. Gilbert, Stirling Coyne, Leicester Buckingham, Maria Lovell, and Catherine Crowe, in most of which he also appeared.

If, as an actor, Buckstone's powers were restricted to broad comedy, within that range he reigned supreme, being quick, inventive, and unselfish towards his fellow performers, and possessing, despite the handicap of severe deafness, the rare gift of communicating to audiences an infectious sense of fun. To a singular and intensely mobile face he added a twinkle in the eye and a chuckle in his drawling voice, the mere sound of which would send a ripple of laughter through the house even before he appeared on stage. While he remained substantially himself in every part he played, his evident enjoyment of the absurdities he was called upon to enact served only to enrich that of the spectators. At times he also had a way of pausing before delivering a joke and, having wound up the audience to a pitch of expectancy, of discharging it with a rapidity and an exuberance that were irresistible. Buckstone excelled in such established comic parts as Sir Andrew Aguecheek, Launcelot Gobbo, Touchstone, Grumio, Speed, Tony Lumpkin, Maw-Worm, Scrub, Marplot, Sir Benjamin Backbite, and Bob Acres, but he was equally acclaimed for performances in his own plays and those of his contemporaries. The 160 or so pieces he wrote, ranging from melodrama to farce, burletta, and pantomime, exhibit a sure grasp of stage effect, a good deal of broad humour, and a proclivity for strong characterization and edifying pathos. Many of them were highly successful in his day, notably *The Wreck Ashore* (1830), *Victorine* (1831), *The Dream at Sea* (1835), *The Green Bushes* (1845), and *The Flowers of the Forest* (1847) at the Adelphi; *Second Thoughts* (1832), *Nicholas Flam* (1833), *Married Life* and *Rural Felicity* (both 1834), *The Irish Lion* (1838), *Single Life* (1839), and *Leap Year, or, The Ladies' Privilege* (1850) at the Haymarket; and *Popping the Question* (1830) and *Our Mary Anne* (1838) at Drury Lane, but none has held the stage.

As a man Buckstone possessed the abundant geniality which he threw into his acting, and was never more at home than at the weekly club which he founded at the Haymarket. He was also a very amusing speaker. His addresses at the dinners of the General Theatrical Fund and on his own benefit nights were always well received. At one time he contributed a few articles to periodicals, and a sketch in the *New Monthly Magazine* which, describing the career of an optimist corrupted into a misanthrope by his experience of life, reveals in its cynicism of tone and seriousness of intent qualities very different from those which he displayed as an actor. In 1859 he wrote a preface to the Revd Henry Bellows's *An Address upon the Claims of the Drama*.

Buckstone was apparently married twice, although there is no evidence that his reputed first marriage, to the actress Fanny Elizabeth *Fitzwilliam (*née* Copeland), shortly before her death in 1854, actually took place. No record of the marriage has been traced, but Buckstone described himself as 'widower' at his marriage to Mrs Fitzwilliam's cousin Isabella Copeland, on 20 August 1857. Ultimately, financial difficulties brought about by his own improvidence, coupled with failing health, undermined his fortunes as a manager and, in 1877, forced him to retire from the stage altogether, after which he went into a steady decline. In March 1878 he was declared bankrupt, and he died at his home, Bell Green Lodge, Lower Sydenham, on 31 October 1879, the cause of death being given as paralysis. One daughter, Lucy Isabella, and two sons, John Copeland and Rowland, became professional actors.

DONALD ROY

Sources *The Times* (1 Nov 1879) · *Daily Telegraph* (1 Nov 1879) · *Daily News* (1 Nov 1879) · *The Era* (7 Nov 1879) · T. Taylor, 'Impressions of John Baldwin Buckstone', *The Theatre*, new ser., 3 (1879), 26–7 · *Annual Register* (1879) · C. E. Pascoe, ed., *The dramatic list*, 2nd edn (1880) · Boase, *Mod. Eng. biog.* · J. E. Mayall, *Mayall's celebrities of the London stage* (1867–8) · W. Bates, *The Maclise portrait-gallery of 'illustrious literary characters'* (1883) · *Encyclopaedia Britannica*, 11th edn (1910–11), vol. 4 · M. Banham, ed., *The Cambridge guide to world theatre* (1988) · P. Hartnoll, ed., *The Oxford companion to the theatre*, 3rd edn (1967) · A. Nicoll, *Late nineteenth century drama, 1850–1900*, 2nd edn (1959), vol. 5 of *A history of English drama, 1660–1900* (1952–9)

Archives BL, Lord Chamberlain's collection · Hunt. L., letters, document, literary MS · Theatre Museum, London, letters | BL, letters as sponsor to the Royal Literary Fund, loan no. 96 · BL, letters to W. S. Gilbert, Add. MSS 49330–49331, *passim*

Likenesses D. Maclise, oils, *c*.1836, NPG · G. Little, photograph, 1856, Theatre Museum, London · J. P. Knight, oils, 1859, Garr. Club · D. J. Pound, stipple and line print, pubd 1860 (after photograph by Mayall), NPG · caricature, 1863, Theatre Museum, London · A. Bryan, caricature, watercolour drawing, NPG · D. Maclise, lithograph, NPG; repro. in *Fraser's Magazine* (1836) · H. Watkins, pencil drawing, NPG · cartes-de-visite, NPG · photographs, Theatre Museum, London · portrait, repro. in *ILN*, 1 (1842), 384 · portrait, repro. in *ILN*, 75 (1879), 457 · portrait, repro. in F. Waddy, *Cartoon portraits and biographical sketches of men of the day* (1873), 116–17 · portrait, repro. in Bates, ed., *Maclise portrait gallery* · prints, BM, Harvard TC, NPG

Buckton [*née* Williams], **Catherine Mary** (1826/7–1904), promoter of household science teaching, was born in London, the daughter of John Morgan Williams, a surgeon, later of Llandaff, Glamorgan. On 22 March 1849 she married Joseph Buckton, a Leeds cloth merchant, with whom she had a son and a daughter. She was a founder member of the Leeds Ladies' Educational Association (1869), which promoted women's higher education and organized the Cambridge local examinations in the city. She was also active on the Yorkshire Ladies' Council of Education, a voluntary body which in 1871 began evening classes for working girls employed in factories, shops, and as domestic servants. Members of the Ladies' Council, drawn mainly from influential professional and business families, were supporters of sanitary reform, and they were concerned by the evidence which these classes brought to light of a widespread ignorance of the laws of health and domestic economy. Statistics gathered by a Leeds medical practitioner, James Braithwaite, exposed the comparatively high mortality rate in the city. During the winter of 1871–2 Catherine Buckton gave a course of lectures to working women and mothers at Holbeck Mechanics' Institute on 'domestic physiology and the laws of health', parallel courses being given by Emily Kitson and Mary Anne Baily. These culminated in a conference at Leeds town hall in November 1872 on the teaching of hygiene.

In 1873, standing as a Liberal, Catherine Buckton was elected the first woman member of the Leeds school board, the second largest school board in the country after London. Industrious and intellectually able, she was an effective school board member, gaining re-election in 1876 and 1879 at the top of the poll. Her experience of evening classes convinced her that only by systematic teaching of hygiene in board schools could the health of future generations be improved. From 1874 she gave annual physiology and health lectures to the oldest board school girls, of whom sixty were subsequently chosen each year to attend the Yorkshire School of Cookery, founded in 1874 by the Ladies' Council, to gain practical instruction. In due course, health, hygiene and cookery instruction became an essential part of the Leeds school board curriculum. Catherine Buckton personally determined the syllabus, rebutting criticisms from some teachers that it was overloaded, and she was generally welcomed by head teachers into their schools to give practical cookery demonstrations. Few schools adopted her advice to establish specialist cookery rooms, but as most working-class homes did not have separate kitchens she acknowledged the need to teach girls to manage efficiently in a small space.

From 1875 Catherine Buckton began to publish her health, hygiene, and basic cookery advice. *Health in the*

House (1875) and *Food and Home Cookery* (1879) were also popular with school boards outside Leeds and continued to be reprinted into the 1880s. Her love of nature, combined with her desire to improve the children's home environment, led to hundreds of children growing and exhibiting their own plants. Her subsequent *Town and Window Gardening*, based on her lectures, was published in 1879. In due course all her works became required reading in the cookery training schools, giving her a national, as well as a local, reputation.

A strong Unitarian, Catherine Buckton's educational interests extended beyond developing the quantity and quality of girls' schooling. Despite persistent and vociferous opposition from supporters of denominational schools on the Leeds board, including some of her fellow Liberals, she vigorously campaigned for free secular education. After visiting schools on the continent, she became convinced that the first stage of schooling was the most important. She persuaded the board to experiment with the new Froebel kindergarten method and to introduce the phonic system of spelling into all Leeds board schools. Sensitive towards children's needs, she managed to convince board members in 1876 of the need for a half-time day industrial school which could provide work, schooling, and daytime meals for difficult children. She subsequently monitored progress at the industrial school, condemning excessive punishments and objecting in 1882 to the appointment of a former prison gaoler as the school's superintendent.

In 1882, overworked and worn down by the continual denominational battles over elementary education, Catherine Buckton retired from the board and moved to London, where she continued to write on health and hygiene issues. Before she left Leeds she produced an influential *Address* on education in the city, which the Liberals used in their successful 1882 school board election campaign. Her concern for women's rights made her a keen advocate of equal pay and women's suffrage. Her last publication was *Comfort and Cleanliness: the Servant and Mistress Question* (1894).

Catherine Buckton has secured an important place in the history of the British domestic science education movement. With her contemporaries Fanny Calder, in Liverpool, and Edith Clarke, in London, she was responsible for the introduction of cookery and hygiene onto the school curriculum. In contrast to Miss Calder, who chose teachers with a good general education and then taught them about cookery, Mrs Buckton believed domestic science teachers should first and foremost be expert cooks. This approach tended to exclude some women who would otherwise have made good instructors. She died, a widow, at her London home, 27 Ladbroke Square, Kensington, on 20 May 1904. An obituary in the *Yorkshire Post* praised her as a pioneer of 'much that is now esteemed as most useful and practical in the education of girls'.

JANET SHEPHERD

Sources *Yorkshire Post* (23 May 1904) • I. Jenkins, 'The Yorkshire Ladies' Council of Education, 1871–91', *The Thoresby Miscellany*, 17 (1979), 27–71 • m. cert. • d. cert. • *Souvenir of the Leeds school board, 1870–1903* (1903) • Leeds school board, Education committee minutes, 1873–6, W. Yorks. AS, Leeds • Yorkshire School of Cookery records, W. Yorks. AS, Leeds, 149–50 • Leeds school board triennial reports, 1879–82, W. Yorks. AS, Leeds • *Women's Suffrage Journal* (1 June 1885), 98 • *Leeds Mercury* (1876–9) • *School Board Chronicle* (1874–82) • M. A. Travis, 'The work of the Leeds school board', *Research and Studies* (1953) • H. Sillitoe, *A history of the teaching of domestic subjects* (1933) • P. Hollis, *Ladies elect: women in English local government, 1865–1914* (1987) • *CGPLA Eng. & Wales* (1904) • census returns, 1881 **Archives** W. Yorks. AS, Leeds, Leeds school board records • W. Yorks. AS, Leeds, Yorkshire School of Cookery records **Wealth at death** £19,901 16s. 2d.: resworn probate, 25 June 1904, *CGPLA Eng. & Wales*

Buckton, George Bowdler (1818–1905), entomologist, was born at Hornsey on 24 May 1818, the eldest son of George Buckton, a proctor of the prerogative court of Canterbury, of Doctors' Commons and Oakfield, Hornsey, and his wife, Eliza, daughter of Richard Merricks of Runcton House, Mundham, Sussex. He was privately tutored, having been deprived of a public school education by a childhood accident which left him partially paralysed.

An early friendship with the zoologist Thomas Bell (1792–1880) gave Buckton a taste for natural history, and led to his introduction to the Linnean Society in 1845. Following the death of his father, Buckton moved to London and became a student at the Royal College of Chemistry in 1848. He remained there for seven years, serving part of the time as research assistant to Professor August Hofmann. Buckton published several papers on chemical topics from 1845 to 1865; his studies included the cyanide compounds and insecticides. He was elected FRS in 1857, and contributed fourteen papers to scientific periodicals, two of them in conjunction with Professor Hofmann, and one with Dr Odling.

In 1865 Buckton married Mary Ann, daughter of George Odling of Croydon and sister of Professor William Odling of Oxford. They settled at Weycombe, Haslemere, and later that year Buckton abandoned the study of chemistry in favour of his earlier interest in entomology. His first important research in natural history was a study of parthenogenesis in aphids. This led to his *Monograph of British Aphides* (1876–83), which he dedicated to Thomas Bell. This was followed, in turn, by a *Monograph of British Cicadae or Tettigiidae* (2 vols., 1890–91), the *Natural History of Eristalis tenax or the Drone Fly* (1895), and a *Monograph of the Membracidae of the World* (1901–03).

Buckton was also interested in astronomy. His house at Haslemere, which he designed himself, included an observatory. In 1882, however, while trying to reach the long focus of a Newtonian telescope, he fell, fracturing his leg in two places, and his astronomical studies were brought to a close. He died at his home, Weycombe, Haslemere, Surrey, on 25 September 1905, following a short illness, and his ashes were interred in Haslemere churchyard on 30 September. He was survived by his wife, son, and five daughters.

ROBERT STEELE, rev. YOLANDA FOOTE

Sources W. F. Kirby, *PRS*, 79B (1907), xlv–xlviii • *Nature*, 72 (1905), 587–8 • J. Spiller, *JCS*, 91 (1907), 663–5 • *Allingham's Diary* (1910) • *Men and women of the time* (1899)

Archives NHM, drawings · Oxf. U. Mus. NH, Hope Library, corresp. and drawings
Likenesses R. Hope-Pinker, bust, exh. RA 1904
Wealth at death £5760 6s. 4d.: probate, 7 Nov 1905, CGPLA Eng. & Wales

Buckton, Raymond William [Ray] (1922–1995), trade unionist, was born on 20 October 1922 in Rillington, near Malton, Yorkshire, the eldest of seven children of William Ernest Buckton, farm labourer, and his wife, Hannah Young. Although his father was a farm worker, Buckton was born into a railway family, and after attending Appleton Roebuck elementary school he followed his uncles onto the footplate and became an engine cleaner at York depot at the age of sixteen. While still employed as a 'third man' he helped to fire the *Flying Scotsman*. At nineteen he became the youngest branch secretary in the Amalgamated Society of Locomotive Engineers and Firemen (ASLEF). He also became active in local politics, becoming chairman of the constituency Labour Party and the youngest alderman on the city council. On 20 March 1954 he married Barbara Gerry (b. 1928/9), a chef, daughter of Robert Langfield, a locomotive driver. They enjoyed what appeared to be a perfect marriage, and had two sons.

Buckton became a full-time employee of ASLEF as the society's Irish officer, based in Dublin, in 1962. Nevertheless, the following year he became assistant general secretary, and in 1970 general secretary, serving until his retirement in 1987. As general secretary during a prolonged period of industrial strife on the railways, he was one of Britain's most widely hated trade union leaders, whose notoriety derived from his perceived position as the militant head of a small but 'irresponsible' craft union. He arrived at his union's splendid offices in Arkwright Road, Hampstead (the birthplace of Sir Thomas Beecham), just in time for three crucial battles with the British Railways board, one and a half of which he won.

The first reached its climax in 1974 and concerned the fourteen-year erosion of the so-called Guillebaud formula. This sought to link railway pay to rates for similar work in the private sector. After sporadic industrial action all three railway unions agreed to submit their claims to the railway's own arbitration machinery—a commendable, if rare, example of inter-union solidarity. The result was a substantial rise in real pay for all railway grades, in exchange for promises of improved performance.

The second battle peaked in the early 1980s and centred on the board's determination to introduce single manning of footplates and a differential payment for driving high-speed trains. ASLEF fought this struggle alone, with its traditional mixture of obduracy and perseverance. Eventually Buckton was forced to accept the first objective, but persuaded the board to postpone the second, at least for the foreseeable future.

The third struggle was by far the most bitter and protracted. It concerned the terms demanded for what was called 'flexible rostering', that is, the freedom of management to rearrange shifts so that drivers spent more time at the controls. In 1983 Buckton demonstrated, before

Raymond William Buckton (1922–1995), by Frank Barratt, 1977 [left, with Bill Ronksley, president of ASLEF]

another hearing of the industry's own tribunal, that the board had little idea of the actual savings involved. They had also worked out few answers to his many practical objections. His difficulty was that once again he had no support among the other unions. In the end he was forced to sign an agreement of sorts, though it was by no means clear that management extracted many worthwhile concessions.

Buckton served on the general council of the TUC from 1973 to 1986, and was its president in 1984–5. He was a conscientious committee man, representing the TUC on a number of public bodies. He tirelessly supported the policies of the left on council, and it was a much noted irony on the right that he found himself president during the disastrous year of the miners' strike. He did his best to mobilize support for the miners' cause, on the impossible terms demanded by their leaders. This time he failed completely, and regarded the result as the biggest disappointment of his life.

At the rostrum Buckton was voluble, sonorous, and sometimes over the top. In negotiation he was perspicacious, astute, and capable of sudden concessions. Off duty he was gregarious, genial, and relaxed. He sang to his own accordion and played the mouth organ well. He always claimed that he never bothered about the things irate commuters stuck through his letter box; he said he did not mind about the death threats and abusive phone calls. He laughed off the tin of paint thrown at his windscreen while he was waiting at a red light. What the public did not know, or care about, was that his was a union run by its full-time lay executive. Buckton had no vote and few levers of influence. His job was to convince the executive to go out and persuade the members to accept the inevitable, for the best price he could squeeze out of the board. It was a strategy that defied public explanation or excuse.

On his retirement Buckton and his wife opened a Mexican bistro in Bushey, Hertfordshire, but they sold it after a year to buy a villa in Albufeira, Portugal. There he kept busy organizing the expatriate vote for Labour, with the help of his friend Clive Dunn (Corporal Jones from the television comedy *Dad's Army*). Ray Buckton died of stomach cancer in Albufeira on 7 May 1995; he was survived by his wife and two sons. WILLIAM MCCARTHY

Sources *The Times* (9 May 1995) · *The Independent* (9 May 1995) · *WWW*, 1991–5 · personal knowledge (2004) · private information (2004)
Likenesses F. Barratt, photograph, 1977, Hult. Arch. [*see illus.*] · D. Rose, photograph, 1987, repro. in *The Independent* · photograph, repro. in *The Times*
Wealth at death £16,995: probate, 29 June 1995, *CGPLA Eng. & Wales*

Budai, István. *See* Parmenius, Stephen (d. 1583).

Budd, George (*fl.* 1745–1756), painter, is thought to have been born in London, where for some time he kept a hosier's shop. Eventually he abandoned the hosiery business and devoted himself wholly to art. He painted a wide variety of subjects, including historical scenes, portraiture, landscape, and still life, mostly executed in oil. He also taught drawing, and for several years gave lessons at Dr Newcome's academy at Hackney, Middlesex. A portrait by him of Timothy Bennett, 'the patriotic shoemaker', of Hampton Wick, who successfully maintained an action against Princess Amelia, when she was ranger, for attempting to close the public road through Bushey Park, was mezzotinted by W. McArdell in 1756. Another painting by Budd representing the execution of lords Balmerino and Kilmarnock in 1746 is also engraved. The Tower and surrounding buildings form the background, while the whole picture is crowded by a dense mass of small figures. Budd is known to have produced a series of landscape paintings, though these are now lost.

GORDON GOODWIN, *rev.* ASIA HAUT

Sources Redgrave, *Artists* · E. Edwards, *Anecdotes of painters* (1808); facs. edn (1970), 8–9 · J. Gould, *Biographical dictionary of painters, sculptors, engravers and architects*, new edn, 2 vols. (1839) · M. H. Grant, *A dictionary of British landscape painters, from the 16th century to the early 20th century* (1952) · Mallalieu, *Watercolour artists*

Budd, George (1808–1882), physician, was born at North Tawton, Devon, in February 1808, the third son of Catherine Wreford (1778/9–1869) and her husband, Samuel Budd (1772–1841), a surgeon, who practised there, and seven of whose nine sons, including William *Budd, practised medicine. Five of them, who all became wranglers, went to Cambridge. Owing to poor health George Budd was educated at home. He then entered St John's College, Cambridge, in 1827, but he subsequently transferred to Gonville and Caius and became a fellow of his college after taking his degree in 1831. He was elected a fellow of the Royal Society in 1836.

Budd pursued his medical studies in Paris and at the Middlesex Hospital, London, and graduated MD at Cambridge in 1840. He attracted notice by writing an important article on the stethoscope as an acoustic instrument, which was published in the *Medical Gazette* in 1837. In the same year, while still a bachelor of medicine, he was appointed physician to the *Dreadnought* seamen's hospital ship at Greenwich. Here, with George Busk, he did extensive research on cholera and scurvy, and acquired considerable knowledge about diseases of the stomach and liver.

In 1840 Budd was elected professor of medicine at King's College, London, and in 1841 he became a fellow of the Royal College of Physicians, where he served as censor between 1845 and 1847. On 15 November 1859 he married Louisa-Matilda, daughter of Thomas Russell MD, of Toulouse.

In 1863 Budd retired from his chair at King's College, of which he was then made an honorary fellow, and in 1867, owing to ill health, he gave up his large practice in London. After travelling on the continent he retired to Barnstaple, Devon, in 1869. In 1880 he was made an honorary fellow of Caius College, Cambridge, having given up his former fellowship on his marriage. Budd died on 14 March 1882 at Ashleigh House, Barnstaple, Devon.

Budd was a very able physician and medical teacher and made many valuable contributions to medical literature on the gastroenterological tract. He published numerous brief papers and lectures in medical journals, especially the *Medico-Chirurgical Transactions* (London) and the *Medical Gazette*, where his Goulstonian lectures (1843) and Croonian lectures (1847) at the College of Physicians may be found. Budd was an original thinker, he was lucid in writing and speaking, and he drew his information from a large fund of close personal observation.

S. J. A. SALTER, *rev.* MARY E. GIBSON

Sources J. Marshall, 'Address', *Medico-Chirurgical Transactions*, 66 (1883), 8–10 · J. P. [J. Paget], *PRS*, 34 (1882–3), i–iii · *GM*, 2nd ser., 42 (1854), 503 · R. E. Hughes, 'George Budd, 1808–1882, and nutritional deficiency diseases', *Medical History*, 17 (1973), 127–35 · personal knowledge (1886) · *CGPLA Eng. & Wales* (1882)
Archives Wellcome L., lecture notes · Wellcome L., corresp. and papers
Likenesses photograph, 1836, RS
Wealth at death £49,127 6s. 7d.: resworn probate, June 1883, *CGPLA Eng. & Wales* (1882)

Budd, Henry (1774–1853), Church of England clergyman, born at Newbury, Berkshire, on 25 September 1774, was the son of Richard *Budd (1746–1821) and his wife, Mary, *née* Stabler (d. 1837). Emma Hamilton (Nelson's mistress) was a maid in the household in his youth. Budd attended Winchester College and then St John's College, Cambridge, from October 1793 to June 1797, and graduated BA in 1798 and MA in 1801. He was admitted at Lincoln's Inn in 1793, but chose a clerical career. After his ordination on 31 December 1797 he became curate of Aldermaston, Berkshire, and was appointed chaplain of Bridewell Hospital, London, in 1801, which he resigned in 1831. He was instituted to the rectory of White Roothing, Essex, on 18 March 1808. Budd married on 22 February 1803 Eliza Henrietta Lewin, who died after a year's illness on 12 June 1806, having borne one child. On 25 May 1814 he married Jane, eleventh daughter of General Hale of the Plantation, near Guisborough. She was, like Budd, a fervent evangelical. They had at least two children before her death in August 1821.

Budd, an active worker in all church matters, was one of the founders of the Prayer Book and Homily Society, on 21 May 1812, and for some time acted as its secretary; he was connected with the Newfoundland Society for the Education of the Poor, the African Missions, and the Church Missionary Society. He was a chief instigator of the Widow's Friend and Benevolent Society, which was an important stimulus to the system of lay district visitors in London. He was also one of those instrumental in introducing daily church services in London. For over fifty years Budd wrote regularly to C. J. Bird, rector of Mordiford, Herefordshire; the correspondence is an interesting record of London evangelicalism and is published in the *Memoir of the Rev. Henry Budd* (1855). Budd's chief publications were *Infant Baptism, the Means of National Regeneration* (1827; 3rd edn, 1841), *The Present Controversy in the Bible Society Briefly Considered* (1832), and *Helps for the young, or, Baptismal regeneration according to the services of the established church* (2 vols., 1832–9). Unusually among evangelicals, Budd used the political crisis of 1832 to call for 'a complete reform' of the church, its discipline and liturgy, adumbrated in his *Petition … to the Three Estates of the Legislature* (1833). Budd died at White Roothing on 27 June 1853 and was buried in the churchyard there.   H. C. G. MATTHEW

Sources *A memoir of the Rev. Henry Budd … comprising an autobiography, letters, papers, and remains* (1855) • Venn, *Alum. Cant.* • *Christian Observer* (1856), 194–211 • DNB

Likenesses R. Woodman, stipple and line print, pubd 1855, NPG • engraving, repro. in *Memoir of the Rev. Henry Budd*

Budd, Richard (1746–1821), physician, was born in Newbury, Berkshire, where his father, Richard Budd, was a banker. He matriculated at Balliol College, Oxford, in 1764, and afterwards at Jesus College, Cambridge; he graduated MB in 1770 and MD in 1775. After practising for some years in Newbury he moved to London, in 1780, and in the same year he was appointed physician to St Bartholomew's Hospital, an office which he held until his retirement in 1801. In 1771 Budd was elected a fellow of the College of Physicians, in which he attained considerable official status; he was censor six times between 1780 and 1798, Goulstonian lecturer and Harveian orator in 1781, treasurer from March 1799 to April 1814, and elect from December 1797 to July 1818. For a while, Budd was physician to Christ's Hospital, where under his influence potatoes were introduced as part of the boys' diet. He lived at Chatham Place, Blackfriars, where two maids in his service became famous: Emma Hamilton was a nursemaid for a time, and the celebrated actress Mrs Powell had been employed as a housemaid.

Budd did not exert himself greatly in private practice, having married Mary Stabler (d. 1837), the daughter of a wealthy merchant. One of their sons, the Revd Henry *Budd, became well known as the chaplain of Bridewell and a leading evangelical clergyman. The chaplaincy was secured by his father's indefatigable canvassing. Budd is described as a man of strong will, impetuosity, and of great social influence. He died at Battersea Rise, Clapham, on 2 September 1821, and was buried at Speen, near Newbury.   G. T. BETTANY, *rev.* CAROLINE OVERY

Sources Munk, *Roll* • Venn, *Alum. Cant.* • Foster, *Alum. Oxon.* • *A memoir of the Rev. Henry Budd: comprising an autobiography, letters, papers, and remains* (1855)

Likenesses W. Daniell, etching, pubd 1812 (after G. Dance, 1798), BM, NPG, Wellcome L.

Budd, William (1811–1880), physician and epidemiologist, was born on 14 September 1811 at Melhuishes in the village of North Tawton, Devon, where his father, Samuel (1772–1841), practised as a surgeon until his death. Previous generations had been educated at Oxford, but Samuel appears to have studied medicine via apprenticeship and service in the navy. William's mother, Catherine Wreford, of a Devon family, was a woman of forceful character who died aged ninety in 1869. William was the fifth son and sixth child in a family of ten children, eight of whom were university educated and six of whom graduated in medicine. Of William's brothers the best-known is George *Budd (1808–1882); William was closest to Richard, FRCP 1863, who settled at Barnstaple.

After an early education at home William gained a thorough grounding in medicine, studying from 1828 to 1837 in Paris, London, and Edinburgh. He seems to have taught himself French, German, and Italian, as well as draughtsmanship and photography, all of which are evident in his later research. Letters preserved by Richard Budd record William's responses to his teachers and his estimates about how best to establish his career. During the three separate periods he spent in Paris, Budd was influenced, but not dominated, by the localist pathology vigorously advocated by François Broussais, and by the clinician Pierre Charles Alexandre Louis. He also suffered from an attack of typhoid (enteric or continued fever), the disease on which he was to write his major work. After a winter at the Middlesex Hospital in London he moved to Edinburgh, graduating MD in August 1838. During periods at home he assisted his father and made observations on local epidemics. He worked on the seamen's hospital ship *Dreadnought* at Greenwich and at King's College Hospital under his brother George's aegis, but plans to establish himself in London seem to have been given up after another major bout of illness which Budd himself attributed to typhoid. After recuperation at North Tawton he finally settled in Bristol in 1841, putting up his plate as a surgeon in Park Street. Later he moved to Clifton, first to 15 Lansdown Place, and then to the Manor House.

Budd quickly gained a foothold in Bristol, being appointed physician to St Peter's, a poor-law hospital, in 1842, and progressing in 1847 to become physician to the Bristol Royal Infirmary. For ten years from 1845 he was lecturer in medicine at the Bristol medical school, claimed to be the first school in England and Wales outside London. He was active in local medical societies, particularly the Provincial Medical and Surgical Association (PMSA, later the British Medical Association), being president of his local branch in 1855–6. On 7 April 1847 he married Caroline Mary Hilton (d. c.1887), and they had three sons and six daughters. Their third son, George Turnavine Budd, became, as a medical practitioner in Plymouth, well known for his eccentric abilities, and provided material for the stories of Conan Doyle.

Budd's Edinburgh dissertation, for which he was awarded a gold medal, was on rheumatism, and he wrote another on the spinal cord. His earliest intentions were to make the nervous system 'the work of my life. It is the finest subject in nature' (corresp., William Budd to Richard Budd, 1841). However he was also attracted to chemical pathology, not least because he deplored the experimental use of vivisection by French physiologists. He was struck by the 'simplicity and sublimity' of the new organic chemistry of Justus Liebig, whom he met in 1842. His first major project, on what he saw as the law of symmetry in disease, involved consideration of 'blood medicines' working by elective affinity. His focus of attention then shifted, but he retained a deep concern for the practical outcomes of medical ideas, as well as reflecting contemporary interest in humoral pathology. A paper on cancer given in 1842 and based on microscopical observations shows the early maturity of his characteristic theories of epidemic disease; Richard Budd later revived the claims of this paper to suggest that cancer was contagious. Of his English teachers Budd was probably most influenced by the clinician Thomas Watson, who provided valuable support throughout his career. Like Budd, Watson took smallpox, as a contagious disease originating in an 'animal poison' affecting the blood, as providing the definitive type of epidemic disease. Budd developed a confident, single-factor approach which depended upon assimilating less well-defined diseases, like typhoid, into the smallpox model. He was planning a book on fever as early as 1842; in 1839 he had entered for the Thackeray prize, awarded for the best essay on the 'common continued fevers' of Britain by the PMSA. The manuscript of his entry (which did not win) was identified and edited by Smith in the 1980s.

Budd's lifelong concern for the prevention of epidemic disease first became linked to the wider movement for sanitary reform when he gave evidence to the health of towns commission soon after his arrival in Bristol, then regarded as the third most unhealthy city in the country. Many of Budd's later interventions were designed to influence official opinion, but, possibly because of his extensive practice, he never took on any official public health responsibilities. He did however later develop a close relationship with Bristol's first medical officer of health, David Davies, and in the 1840s he also sat on the first board of directors of the Bristol Waterworks Company, an involvement which may have caused the severe financial losses he suffered at this time. He became more widely known from 1849, when, during the second cholera epidemic to strike Britain, he joined other Bristol medical men in asserting that the disease was caused by a fungus, identifiable in discharges from the body and in contaminated water and air. Perhaps as a result of the ensuing controversy Budd was never afterwards specific about the nature of the causative agents entailed by his explanations of epidemic disease, beyond the properties of independent life and self-propagation. The features he continued to emphasize were those suggested by the smallpox model: specificity, contagiousness, and the production of morbid matter in a manner characteristic of the disease. In terms of prevention he placed great

stress on disinfection. Unlike his contemporary John Snow he was not unduly concerned about the medium by which the causative agent travelled from one body to another. Again unlike Snow he felt that the nature of a disease was best established, once and for all, by observations made in closed institutions or small localities. Budd's epidemiology was not in the least quantitative; he was unusual among public health reformers in making almost no use of statistics. He was even more distinctive in the attention he gave to epidemic diseases of animals, such as anthrax ('malignant pustule'), variola ovina ('sheep's smallpox'), 'pig typhoid', and cattle plague, which broke out in 1865. He linked animal and human diseases, which he saw as analogous, in a classic set of experimental principles to be applied to the investigation of epidemic disease.

Budd was most active between 1852 and 1864. Many of his papers, written with vigour and strong feeling, were drafted during this period, well before they were actually published. His views on tuberculosis, released in 1867, had been held back for a decade. His major work on typhoid, *Typhoid Fever, its Nature, Mode of Spreading and Prevention*, appeared in 1873, but was mainly a reworking of papers published some years earlier. These were written in opposition to the consensual 'pythogenic' theory of Charles Murchison (which saw typhoid as caused by a putrefactive process) and gained the partial acceptance of John Simon, medical officer of health to the privy council. In 1871, somewhat belatedly, Budd was elected fellow of the Royal Society. Of robust physique and 'brave presence', Budd suffered a mental and physical decline in later life which his contemporaries attributed to overwork and his unusual sensitivity to suffering. In 1873 he was incapacitated by a stroke, which left him hemiplegic. He died on 9 January 1880 at Castle Villa, Walton in Gordano, Clevedon, Somerset, and was buried on 14 January in Arnos Vale cemetery in Bristol.   MARGARET PELLING

Sources E. W. Goodall, *William Budd, MD Edin, FRS: the Bristol physician and epidemiologist* (1936) · M. Pelling, *Cholera, fever and English medicine, 1825–1865* (1978) · *'On the causes of fevers' (1839) by William Budd*, ed. D. C. Smith (1984) · IGI · correspondence, London School of Hygiene and Tropical Medicine · University of Bristol, medical library, William Budd box · d. cert.
Archives London School of Hygiene and Tropical Medicine, corresp. · priv. coll., family papers · University of Bristol, medical library, William Budd box · Wellcome L., autograph letter collection | Bristol Central Library, Estlin collection
Likenesses photograph, University of Bristol, medical library; repro. in Goodall, *William Budd*, frontispiece · photographs, University of Bristol, medical library
Wealth at death under £12,000: probate, 4 March 1880, *CGPLA Eng. & Wales*

Budden, John (1566–1620), civil lawyer, was born at Canford, Dorset, the son of John Budden. He matriculated from Merton College, Oxford, on 14 December 1582, aged sixteen, was admitted a scholar of Trinity College, Oxford, on 30 May 1583, and graduated BA on 29 October 1586. At the request of Thomas Allen, the mathematician, about 1587 he migrated to Gloucester Hall, where he proceeded MA on 27 June 1589 and began the study of civil law. He also studied philosophy and was selected as reader in metaphysics for the visit of Queen Elizabeth to Oxford in 1592. On 8 July 1602 he received the degrees of BCL and DCL. Budden was admitted as an advocate in the court of the arches on 26 February 1605, but he did not practise in the ecclesiastical or admiralty courts, choosing instead to pursue an academic career. When in 1605, Alberico Gentili, the regius professor of civil law at Oxford, began his service as advocate for the Spanish embassy in the high court of admiralty, Budden assumed the duties of reader in civil law, and in 1611 he was appointed regius professor.

Anthony Wood observed that Budden was a man 'of great eloquence, an excellent rhetorician, philosopher, and a most noted civilian' (Wood, *Ath. Oxon.*, 1.382). Unlike Gentili, Budden did not publish any legal works. He wrote Latin lives of Bishop Waynfleet and Archbishop Morton and translated Sir Thomas Smith's *De republica Anglorum* into Latin. In 1614 he translated a work by the French civilian Pierre Ayrault into English as *A Discourse for Parents Honour and Authority over their Children*. In his dedication of this work to Archbishop Tobie Matthew (whose own son Tobie had converted to Catholicism) Budden claimed that Ayrault's son, by joining the Jesuits' order without his father's permission, had committed a heinous injury to his parents. Budden served as principal of New Inn Hall from 1609 until 1616, and in 1619 he was elected principal of Broadgates Hall (later Pembroke College). He died there on 11 June 1620 and was buried in the neighbouring church of St Aldate.　　　　　BRIAN P. LEVACK

Sources Wood, *Ath. Oxon.*, new edn, 1.382–3 · *Reg. Oxf.*, 2/1; 2/3 · B. P. Levack, *The civil lawyers in England, 1603–1641* (1973) · B. P. Levack, 'Law', *Hist. U. Oxf.* 4: *17th-cent. Oxf.*, 558–68 · *CSP dom.*, 1603–10, 489 · LPL, Bancroft Register, I, fol. 129*v* · Oxf. UA, vice-chancellor's court, administrations A–B, and inventories BR–C · Venn, *Alum. Cant.*
Archives Bodl. Oxf., letter, MS Bodley 1.699 (Arch. F.C.O. fol. 107)
Wealth at death £110 9*s.*: 1620, Oxf. UA, vice-chancellor's court, inventories BR–C

Buddicom, William Barber (1816–1887), mechanical and civil engineer, was born in Everton on 1 July 1816, the second son of the Revd Robert Peddie Buddicom of St George's in Everton, later principal of St Bees College. He was educated at home and in 1831 was apprenticed to Mather, Dixon & Co. of Liverpool.

In 1836 Buddicom was appointed resident engineer of the Liverpool–Newton Bridge section of the Liverpool and Manchester Railway, with responsibility for its maintenance including the winding engines for the steeply graded tunnel sections at Edge Hill, as well as for the replacement of the original rails which were far too light to carry heavy traffic. At this time he came to the attention of Joseph Locke, who was to play an important part in developing his career. In 1838 Locke invited him to become resident engineer on the Glasgow–Paisley railway. In 1840, on Locke's recommendation, he became locomotive superintendent of the Grand Junction Railway where he introduced to locomotive drivers a system of premiums for economies in fuel and oil, which enabled working

expenses to be reduced considerably. He was involved with Alexander Allan, the works manager at Liverpool, in rebuilding existing inside-cylinder locomotives, the crank axles of which frequently fractured, with outside-cylinder drive. This was the origin of the Crewe locomotive type, which was built on a large scale after the transfer of the Grand Junction Railway works to Crewe, in the planning of which Buddicom was deeply involved.

In 1841 Locke invited Buddicom to France to work on the Paris–Rouen railway, which opened in 1843 and was subsequently extended to Le Havre. There he became manager with William Allcard of the Allcard Buddicom works near Rouen. These works were founded by Buddicom in association with the contractors William Mackenzie and Thomas Brassey, and capitalists involved in the line, to supply locomotives and rolling stock for the railway, and to manage its operation. In 1845 he married Marie Jeanne (d. 1892), daughter of Joseph Robert Howman RN, who had been involved from 1832 in the management of the Martin Cie ironworks at Sotteville. They had three daughters and at least three sons.

During the revolutionary period in France which followed the fall of Louis Philippe in 1848, Buddicom struggled valiantly to keep the railway in operation despite considerable financial problems and physical danger to himself and to his family. In addition to work for the Paris–Rouen–Le Havre lines, Buddicom supplied locomotives and equipment for the Orléans–Tours and Amiens–Boulogne railways. In 1849 a second works was built at Bordeaux-La Bastide to meet the locomotive and rolling-stock requirements of the Midi (Southern) Railway. The Buddicom company was wound up in 1861, after the works had been bought by the Chemin de Fer de l'Ouest on the expiration of existing contracts.

In 1854 a contractors' consortium, in which the Belgian contractors Parent and Schaecken joined Thomas Brassey and Buddicom, undertook to build the Bellegarde tunnel, 2½ miles long, for the Lyon–Geneva railway, and in 1860 Buddicom and Brassey undertook the conversion of the Rouen to Dieppe railway from single to double track. In 1863 Parent, Brassey, and Buddicom undertook to build part of the southern railway of Italy and Buddicom joined Brassey and Charles Jones in the construction and supply of motive power and rolling stock for the Maremma Railway in that country. With the deaths of Parent and Brassey in 1870 Buddicom wound up the partnership.

Buddicom purchased an estate near Mold in 1853 and became a JP and high sheriff of Flintshire (1864). In 1847 he was made a member of the Légion d'honneur by Louis Philippe for his services to France. He was a member of the institutions of civil and mechanical engineers and of the Société des Ingénieurs Civils de France. Buddicom died at his home, Penbedw, Nannerch, Holywell, Flintshire, on 4 August 1887, and was buried at St Mary's, Nannerch.

　　　　　GEORGE W. CARPENTER, *rev.* MIKE CHRIMES

Sources PICE, 91 (1887–8), 412–21 · *Engineering*, 44 (1887), 170 · *La vie du rail*, Paris (24 Sept 1967) · M. M. Chrimes, M. K. Murphy, and G. Ribeill, *Mackenzie: giant of the railways* (1994) · d. cert.

Buddle, Adam (*bap.* 1662, *d.* 1715), botanist, was baptized on 17 April 1662 at Deeping St James, Lincolnshire, the son of Richard Buddle. He was educated at St Catharine's College, Cambridge, graduating BA in 1681 and MA in 1685. He was a fellow of the college from 1681 to 1691, when he was ejected as a non-juror, having refused to pledge his oath to the new king, William III; he subsequently complied and was ordained into the Church of England in 1702.

Buddle married, at Freston, Suffolk, on 13 February 1695, Elizabeth Eveare, with whom he had several children. In 1696–8, while he was living at Henley, Suffolk, he corresponded with Doody and Petiver, to whom he lent his collection of grasses and mosses, then the best in the kingdom; these were afterwards lent to Tournefort, Bobart, and others. This collection revealed Buddle's great skill in identifying mosses. Dillenius eventually used the material in revising the third edition of Ray's *Synopsis* (1724). William Vernon at this time called Buddle 'the top of all the moss-croppers' (Turner, 73). In 1699 Buddle paid a visit to the elderly John Ray. In 1703 he was presented to the living of North Fambridge, Essex, and he was also reader at Gray's Inn, under the patronage of an appropriately named Cambridge friend, Robert Moss.

By 1708 Buddle had compiled specimens for a complete English flora with accompanying text. He bequeathed these to Sloane, who valued them highly. The flora was never printed although Petiver and others made good use of the information that it contained. Dawson Turner's note (Turner, 151), that 'justice was not done him by those of his immediate successors who more particularly benefited by his labours', seems fully justified. His flora is preserved among the Sloane manuscripts, and his herbarium with that of Sloane, with further specimens in the Oxford Herbarium. Buddle died at Gray's Inn and was buried at St Andrew's, Holborn, on 15 April 1715. It is popularly supposed that Linnaeus later named the flowering shrub buddleia after Buddle, although the attribution is uncertain.

JAMES BRITTEN, *rev.* JANET BROWNE

Sources *Extracts from the literary and scientific correspondence of Richard Richardson*, ed. D. Turner (1835) · D. H. Kent, *The historical flora of Middlesex*, Ray Society, 150 (1975), 14–15 · C. E. Raven, *John Ray, naturalist: his life and works* (1942), 393 · S. O. Linberg, 'The mosses of Buddle's *Hortus siccus*', *Journal of Botany, British and Foreign*, 12 (1874), 36–47 · parish register, Holborn, St Andrew, 15 April 1715 [burial] · parish register, Holborn, St Andrew, 17 April 1662 [baptism]
Archives NHM, specimens · U. Oxf., department of plant sciences, specimens | BL, botanical memoranda, etc., Sloane MSS, MSS 2201, 2305–2306, 2970–2980

Buddle, John (1773–1843), mining engineer, was born at Kyo, near Lanchester, Durham, on 15 September 1773, the fourth of six children and the only son of John Buddle (1743–1806) and Anne Reay, a farmer's daughter. His father is said to have been a schoolmaster (though he was never licensed), but by 1777 was described as a coal viewer (or mining engineer), and it is clear that he was taking an interest in local mining matters from the 1760s. By 1792 the father's reputation was such that he was appointed viewer to Wallsend colliery, on the Tyne, as well as viewer to the bishop of Durham, and subsequently also to the dean and chapter. John Buddle himself recorded that he was 'initiated into the mysteries of pit work when not quite six years old' (Buddle to Londonderry, 14 June 1842, Durham RO, NCB1/JB/2556). He seems to have had little formal schooling, but to have been educated by his father, as well as receiving from him his mining training. Having served as his father's assistant at Wallsend, by 1801 Buddle was receiving salaries and fees for colliery viewing independent of his father, and on the latter's death in 1806 he was already established as a distinguished viewer in his own right. Within a few years he himself was described as having a good many apprentices. Throughout his life he remained a practical colliery worker, and told a House of Commons committee in 1836 that he knew his native county 'better underground than above', and as late as his sixty-sixth year he spent, on one occasion, eight hours underground. He prided himself on being 'a good pitman' (Buddle to Londonderry, 27 June 1832, Durham RO, D/LO/C142) and expressed regret when managerial functions increasingly drew him away from his underground work. Those he appointed to subsidiary positions had first to meet the criterion of being sound in pit work, and he consistently preferred those with long experience underground to college-trained engineers, whom he despised.

As a viewer Buddle was employed by numerous collieries on the rivers Tyne and Wear, and by 1808 was commanding £1200 in salaries for this work. Later in his career he added collieries in the newly developed south Durham coalfield to his viewing brief, and in 1837 he was appointed to the post once held by his father, as viewer to the bishop of Durham. In addition he was in demand as check-viewer at many north-east collieries, including the powerful Hetton and Lambton enterprises, which rivalled those of his long-term employer, the third marquess of Londonderry. Buddle was also employed further afield, as check-viewer to Lord Elgin in Scotland, as well as to Sir Josiah Guest in Wales, and his opinions on mining matters were sought from as far away as Portugal, South America, Russia, and Nova Scotia.

More than any other, perhaps, Buddle was responsible for converting the old style colliery viewer into the more modern mining engineer; when it was put to him by a House of Commons committee that he was not an engineer, he firmly replied, 'I believe I am', citing his membership of the Institution of Civil Engineers (1832) as a proof of his claim. His engineering work was wide-ranging. He advised on railway working, for instance on the Stanhope and Tyne Railway; and in 1832 he surveyed the route for the proposed Durham Junction Railway, commenting that the work 'was the sort of thing which I have at my fingers' ends' (Buddle to Londonderry, 23 Sept 1832, Durham RO, D/LO/C142). One of the earliest steam locomotives in British North America was named the *John Buddle*, in recognition of the advice he had provided to railway builders in Nova Scotia. In 1808 he advised the Thames Archway Company on their (unsuccessful) attempt to construct a tunnel from Limehouse to Rotherhithe. He investigated the mineral wells at Harrogate, and devised a central heating scheme for the new theatre in Newcastle in 1836. As well as his most famous engineering project, the planning and construction of Seaham harbour for Lord Londonderry, he was also consulted by Sir Matthew White Ridley over improvements to Blyth harbour, and by the Exchequer Bill Loan Commissioners on improvements to Warkworth.

Buddle's chief engineering contributions, however, naturally focused on underground mine working. In 1810 he devised a system of underground ventilation, known as double or compound ventilation, which improved on James Spedding's system of 'coursing the air'. Buddle's system produced fresher air underground and reduced the hazards from ventilating furnaces; it was first employed at Wallsend, and then extended to other collieries under his control, such as Percy Main, Hebburn, and Heaton. Within a few years it was in general use throughout the north-east. Another innovation, also pioneered at Wallsend's A pit, was the panel system of underground working, where solid barriers of coal were left in order to divide the workings into districts, within which the pillars of coal could be worked, thus considerably increasing productivity. Although this 'pillar and stall' system was later replaced by the 'longwall' method of working a seam along its length, for many years Buddle's method of operation remained the preferred working method in the coalfields of Northumberland and Durham. As well as devising new working methods himself, he was ready and willing to adapt the innovations of others: he helped to test and disseminate John Curr's flat ropes and shaft conductors; T. Y. Hall's tub-and-slide system for raising coals in the shaft; Chapman's locomotive; and perhaps most notably the Davy lamp, the necessity for which he had advocated in a paper to a Sunderland society for the prevention of accidents in mines, following a disastrous explosion at Felling in 1813. Another disaster, the fatal inundation of Heaton colliery, for which Buddle was viewer, led him to call for a permanent deposit of mining records.

As well as his viewing work, Buddle was both a coal owner, and a manager of collieries. As owner, he had investments in Benwell, Heaton, Sheriff Hill, Backworth, and Elswick collieries, among others, and he held a quarter share in the Stella Coal Company. On the whole his partners looked to him for his technical expertise, while he claimed that he made little profit in the fluctuating fortunes of the early nineteenth-century coal trade. Nevertheless, with these and other investments in land, shipping, railways, and banking, he was said to have left £150,000 at his death (Flinn, 63–4). He managed Wallsend colliery for the Russells of Brancepeth (for whom he also acted as consultant at Washington and North Hetton), and

was in charge of Tanfield Moor colliery for William Morton Pitt, a Dorset landowner. But his chief managerial function, and one that absorbed the whole of his later career, was as general manager and agent to the third marquess of Londonderry, a post to which he was appointed in 1819 (when the future marquess inherited the Vane-Tempest colliery empire on marriage), and which he retained until his death. Buddle not only supervised for Londonderry both his extensive mining interests and the construction of the town and port of Seaham (devised to avoid the costs of shipping at Sunderland), but he also represented the Londonderry collieries on the powerful committee of the north-east coal owners who sought to regulate the quantity and price of coal on the London market.

As in all his dealings, Buddle sought a fair and honest regulation of the coal trade, designed to provide a steady income through stable prices. He was usually critical of his own employer and others who aimed for short-term gains through a 'fighting' trade of unrestricted competition. However, by the end of his life, with the expansion of the coalfields and the coming of the railways, Buddle recognized that the days of a regulated trade were numbered, and it survived him by only a year. Buddle also managed the estate property, and spent much energy on Londonderry's difficult financial concerns. The two men had a sometimes tempestuous relationship, with Buddle's frank expostulations at his employer's lack of fiscal prudence provoking quarrels and suspicion. Nevertheless, Buddle was strictly loyal to his employer and his concerns, to the extent of foregoing his salary in times of financial difficulty; indeed he even lent Londonderry over £5000, telling him, 'I have always been ready to assist a friend' (Buddle to Londonderry, 27 June 1832, Durham RO, D/LO/C142), and he paid for the *Lord Seaham*, the first collier trading out of the new port of Seaham. After Londonderry had secured Buddle's appointment as a magistrate in 1842 (following long delays because of a disinclination to appoint colliery agents to the bench), the marquess described his employee as a man of 'high intellectual endowments, high character, and complete independence' (Londonderry to Rowland Burdon, 1 Nov 1842, Durham RO, D/LO/C142).

As a coal owner and manager Buddle had mixed relationships with his colliers. During the strike of 1831 he reported that plans existed to murder him, and his effigy was burnt by the strikers outside his own house. On another occasion, however, his workmen chaired him, and he was 'obliged to abscond to avoid the honour of being drawn in grand procession from Wallsend to Newcastle'; as he wryly commented at the time, 'so much for popular odium, or popular favour' (Buddle to Londonderry, 23 June 1831, Durham RO, D/LO/C142). He knew many pitmen personally, and while throughout his life he totally opposed trade union activity among them (retaining a network of spies within the collieries when strikes threatened) he nevertheless exercised a largely paternal attitude and was willing to listen to individual grievances. Though generally a believer in the practical training of pitmen, rather than in schooling—'the labour of the *pen* is already more plentiful than that of the *pick*' (Durham RO, NCB1/JB/1788)—he was unfairly blamed for disrupting the proposal to exclude children under thirteen from pit work; in fact his role was that of go-between for the northern coal owners and Lord Ashley, while the latter thought he was a negotiator.

By religious affiliation Buddle was a Unitarian, and in politics he described himself as a reforming tory, being naturally conservative in disposition yet seeing the inevitable nature (and indeed desirability) of the first Reform Act. He never married, but was cared for by his unmarried sister, Ann. He lived frugally; a visitor reported that 'a man of his great reputation and wealth slept in a room carpetless and nearly bare of furniture, and showed that whatever fortunes he was instrumental in making for others, he cared little for luxury himself' (Hiskey, 44). As well as a wide circle of engineering and scientific friends, including Thomas Sopwith (1803–1879) and William Buckland (1784–1856), Buddle had a large social acquaintance, including many of the north-east aristocracy, as well as the writer Harriet Martineau. He was a keen musician and concert-goer, an accomplished cellist, and leader of a chamber group in Newcastle from 1825.

Although by the end of Buddle's life a deep rift had opened between him and Londonderry, it was as a result of the two men's riding over 'our collieries' (Londonderry to Nathaniel Hindhaugh, 11 Oct 1843, Durham RO, D/LO/C326) in bad weather that Buddle became ill; he died at his home, Wallsend House, Wallsend, on 10 October 1843. He was buried at St James's Church, Benwell, Newcastle; the building had been erected on land he himself had given to the church, and a bust and memorial plaque were erected there in his honour.   A. J. HEESOM

Sources C. E. Hiskey, 'John Buddle (1773–1843): agent and entrepreneur in the north-east coal trade', MLitt diss., U. Durham, 1978 • W. Fordyce, *The history and antiquities of the county palatine of Durham*, 2 vols. (1857) • R. Welford, *Men of mark 'twixt Tyne and Tweed*, 3 vols. (1895) • M. W. Flinn and D. S. Stoker, *The industrial revolution: 1700–1830* (1984), vol. 2 of *The history of the British coal industry* (1984–93) • R. Church, A. Hall, and J. Kanefsky, *Victorian pre-eminence: 1830–1913* (1986), vol. 3 of *The history of the British coal industry* (1984–93) • Durham RO, National Coal Board MSS • Durham RO, Londonderry MSS • 'Select committee on the South Durham Railway Bill', *Parl. papers* (1836), 27 • M. Dunn, 'History of the viewers', *c*.1811, Northumbd RO • parish register, Lanchester, co. Durham
Archives Durham RO, corresp. relating to Lord Londonderry's mines • Durham RO, corresp., diaries, and papers • Lambton estate office, Lambton Park, Chester le Street, co. Durham, reports and corresp. relating to the earl of Durham's estate • Northumbd RO, memoranda and reports • Tyne and Wear Archives Service, Newcastle upon Tyne, reports on collieries • U. Durham L., reports on Blenkinsopp colliery | Durham RO, Londonderry MSS • Northumbd RO, coal trade MSS
Likenesses bust, St James's Church, Newcastle upon Tyne • portrait, Literary and Philosophical Society, Newcastle upon Tyne
Wealth at death under £1500: will, 1844 • left £150,000: Flinn and Stoker, *Industrial revolution*, 63–4

Budge, Edward (1799/1800–1865), theological writer and geologist, was the son of John Budge, and was a native of Devon. He was educated at Saffron Walden, Essex, and was admitted at Christ's College, Cambridge, on 14 March 1820, when twenty years old. In 1824 he took the degree of BA, and in the same year was ordained deacon by the bishop of Exeter. After holding several curacies in the west of England, he was instituted in 1839 to the small living of Manaccan, Cornwall, and remained there until 1846, when he was appointed by the bishop of Exeter to the more valuable rectory of Bratton Clovelly, north Devon. He died at his rectory on 3 August 1865, his wife, Ann, surviving him. At his death his family was left with little provision for their support. In the hope of raising money for their necessities, the Revd R. B. Kinsman, the vicar of Tintagel, published in 1866 a collection entitled *Posthumous Gleanings*, drawn from Budge's works and from essays which he had contributed to the *Saturday Review*.

Budge was a learned theologian and a skilled geologist. For E. B. Pusey's *Library of Fathers of the Holy Catholic Church* he translated the homilies of St John Chrysostom on the statues, and his scientific views were reflected in the numerous articles which he supplied to the Geological Society, and to the Royal Institution (of Cornwall), on the geology of the Lizard district. For the Revd H. A. Simcoe's periodical, *Light from the West*, he wrote a series of articles republished as the *Christian Naturalist* (1838). His *Lives of Men of Great Aeras* was issued in 1851. He published many visitation and other sermons.

W. P. COURTNEY, *rev.* H. C. G. MATTHEW

Sources *GM*, 3rd ser., 19 (1865), 391 • Venn, *Alum. Cant.* • *Posthumous gleanings*, ed. R. B. Kinsman (1866) • Boase & Courtney, *Bibl. Corn.* • *CGPLA Eng. & Wales* (1866)
Wealth at death under £1500: probate, 7 April 1866, *CGPLA Eng. & Wales*

Budge, Sir Ernest Alfred Thompson Wallis (1857–1934), orientalist, was born on 27 July 1857 in Turf Street, Bodmin, Cornwall, the son of Mary Ann Budge. The identity of his father is unknown. He became interested in Hebrew, Syriac, and Akkadian at an early age, and studied these languages in his spare time while employed by W. H. Smith & Son (1870–78). During the same period he was encouraged by Samuel Birch, keeper of oriental antiquities in the British Museum, who taught him ancient Egyptian and gave him access to the library in the museum's oriental department.

Budge went up to Cambridge as a non-collegiate student in 1878 to read for the recently established Semitic languages tripos. He was able to do so thanks to the support of W. E. Gladstone and other prominent individuals who took a personal interest in his education. In 1879 he won the Otway exhibition at Christ's College for Hebrew and Assyrian. He became a scholar of the college in 1881. The following year, after taking his degree, he was awarded the Tyrwhitt university scholarship for Hebrew.

On 24 March 1883 Budge married Dora Helen Emerson (*d*. 1926), daughter of Titus Emerson, rector of Allendale, Northumberland. They had no children. In the same year, upon leaving the university, he was appointed as an assistant in the British Museum's department of oriental antiquities. He remained there for the rest of his career. In January 1892 he became acting assistant keeper of the department, now renamed Egyptian and Assyrian antiquities. In February 1894 he was promoted to keeper, a post which he held until his retirement in 1924.

As an official of the British Museum, Budge devoted himself whole-heartedly to its service. He worked zealously to expand the museum's collections of Egyptian and western Asiatic antiquities, display them for the benefit of the general public, and make the more significant texts and objects available to scholars in the form of printed editions and catalogues.

Between the years 1886 and 1913 Budge made numerous journeys to the Near East in order to acquire antiquities. For the first six years of this period his work abroad was concentrated upon Mesopotamia. In all he carried out three missions to that region for the trustees of the British Museum, each one lasting several months. After his promotion in 1892, however, with its attendant increase in administrative responsibilities, Budge was no longer in a position to spend such protracted periods away from London. Accordingly the focus of his missions shifted to Egypt, which he now visited virtually on an annual basis for short periods of no more than a month or two. He also travelled to the Sudan on five occasions, the first time accompanying the Anglo-Egyptian forces under Kitchener which had been sent out to crush the Mahdist uprising.

Budge was responsible for a limited amount of excavation and clearance work at various sites, for example, Aswan in Egypt and Deir in Mesopotamia. However, most of the antiquities which he brought back from his missions were obtained not as a result of digging but through purchase, either from local dealers or from other inhabitants of the places that he visited. He made effective use of agents, who would write to inform him whenever an interesting find of antiquities had been made.

Budge enjoyed great success as a collector of papyri, statues, stelae, inscribed clay tablets, and other artefacts for the trustees of the British Museum. The total number of items with which he enriched the museum's collections runs to several thousand, many of them of major importance. His knowledge was sufficiently wide to enable him to recognize significant objects when he encountered them and assess them at their true worth, even when they fell outside his immediate field of expertise. His critical faculties were sufficiently developed to permit him to distinguish the best from what was merely good. His personal manner was such that he was able to gain the trust and co-operation of those with whom he dealt in the course of his travels. It was his expressly declared aim to make the collections under his charge as comprehensive as possible, an aim which he undeniably achieved.

There was, however, a negative side to Budge's collecting activities. For one thing he was careless, even in official reports, about giving precise information as to where and when objects were acquired. Such details as he did provide, when later subjected to careful scrutiny, have often proved to be contradictory or inaccurate. More seriously, in purchasing antiquities and dispatching them to the British Museum from their countries of origin, Budge sometimes deliberately ignored the laws governing the export of such objects. It is clear, for instance, that a number of his more important Egyptian acquisitions were removed from that country without ever having passed through customs. Under the laws then in force, their shipment abroad would have been prohibited.

Budge made no attempt to conceal this, but rather justified his conduct by reference to what he saw as the inequity of the laws regulating the antiquities trade in Egypt and elsewhere, and the arbitrary way in which such legislation was applied. Although he had his detractors, both at home and abroad, there is no evidence that his superiors in the British Museum ever expressed any disapproval of his activities, and theirs was the only authority which he was disposed to regard seriously.

Budge published his first book in 1878, before he went up to Cambridge as an undergraduate. His last book appeared in the year of his death, one of five from his pen to do so. In all he published well over 100 monographs, some of them multi-volume works, together with numerous articles in periodicals. He wrote prolifically on many subjects, producing editions of cuneiform, ancient Egyptian, Coptic, Syriac, and Ethiopic texts, accounts of Egyptian history, literature, and religion, guidebooks, catalogues of antiquities, dictionaries, and elementary grammars.

Budge's books were written very quickly, and not always with due care. Consequently his published works contain numerous errors and inaccuracies, which might have been eliminated had he taken greater pains over their preparation. He was, moreover, resistant to change and innovation, refusing, for instance, to accept many of the advances in the understanding of the ancient Egyptian language that were made during his lifetime. Despite this, a number of his Egyptological works can still be consulted with profit. Chief among these are perhaps his publications of various 'Book of the dead' papyri. Some of his editions of Coptic and Syriac manuscripts remain serviceable as well. His other writings, however, particularly those on cuneiform subjects, which he produced near the beginning of his career, are now largely outdated. Nevertheless it is thanks to him that a number of texts of fundamental importance were first made available to scholarship.

Budge was the recipient of honorary degrees from the universities of Oxford (DLitt), Cambridge (LittD), and Durham (DLitt). He was knighted in 1920. After his wife's death in 1926, he established two memorial foundations in her name for the encouragement of Egyptology: one at his old college, Christ's, in Cambridge; the other at University College, Oxford, where he had been incorporated as a member in 1898. Over the years these foundations have provided support for the research of numerous Egyptologists from Britain and abroad. Budge died at 16 Fitzroy Square, London, on 23 November 1934, and was buried at Nunhead cemetery.   M. SMITH

Sources E. A. W. Budge, *By Nile and Tigris* (1920) • E. A. W. Budge, *The Egyptian Sudan*, 1 (1907), 64–504 • W. R. Dawson and E. P. Uphill, *Who was who in Egyptology*, 3rd edn, rev. M. L. Bierbrier (1995), 71–2 •

Journal of Egyptian Archaeology, 21 (1935), 68–70 · *Bulletin of the John Rylands University Library*, 19 (1935), 5–8 · A. W. Shorter, 'Ernest A. Wallis Budge', *Journal of the Royal Asiatic Society of Great Britain and Ireland* (1935), 436–8 · *WWW* · private information (2004) · b. cert. · m. cert. · *CGPLA Eng. & Wales* (1935)

Archives BM, department of Egyptian antiquities | BL, letters to Mrs Robert Crawshay, Add. MS 58211 · BL, letters to W. E. Gladstone, Add. MSS 44456–44520 · Castle Howard, letters to Lord Carlisle · CKS, letters to Lady Stanhope · U. Durham L., corresp. with Sir Reginald Wingate · U. Oxf., Griffith Institute, corresp. with Sir A. H. Gardiner · W. H. Smith Archive, corresp. with W. H. Smith

Likenesses B. Stone, photograph, 1906, Birmingham Reference Library · photograph, repro. in *Journal of Egyptian Archaeology*, plate VII, facing p. 68 · photograph, repro. in Bierbrier, *Who was who in Egyptology*, 71

Wealth at death £43,523 15*s*. 6*d*.: resworn probate, 7 Jan 1935, *CGPLA Eng. & Wales*

Budgell, Eustace (1686–1737), writer, was born at Symondsbury, Dorset, on 19 August 1686, the eldest son of Gilbert Budgell DD (*c*.1650–1710), rector of Symondsbury, and Anne Gulston (*bap.* 1667). His maternal grandfather was Bishop William Gulston of Bristol, whose sister was Joseph Addison's mother. Budgell matriculated at Trinity College, Oxford, on 31 March 1705, moving to the Inner Temple on 3 December 1705. But his connection with Addison led initially to a career in writing and politics, much against his father's will. Addison took him as a clerk in his office when he was secretary to Lord Wharton, lord lieutenant of Ireland. During the last years of Queen Anne, Budgell contributed to *The Spectator* the papers signed with an 'x', and perhaps others, totalling some twenty-nine to the original series and about ten in the continuation. He also contributed to *The Guardian*, *The Lover*, and other papers, wrote a popular epilogue to Ambrose Philips's *The Distressed Mother* (1712), and published a translation, the *Moral Characters of Theophrastus* (1714). In all these endeavours it was said (by Pope and Johnson, for example) that Addison was the real author.

Addison was re-appointed secretary to the lord lieutenant of Ireland (now Lord Sunderland) on the accession of George I and made Budgell his under-secretary; Budgell was also clerk of the council and secretary of the lords justices in Ireland. He was MP for Mullingar in the Irish parliament from 1715 to 1727. In these offices he served with some distinction. When Addison left Ireland, he procured for Budgell the post of accountant-general of the revenue, worth some £400 per year; Budgell held the appointment from 10 August 1717 to 11 December 1718, when he quarrelled with Edward Webster, the secretary of the new lord lieutenant, the duke of Bolton. Budgell wrote two offensive vindications of himself on his return to England, the first of many such pamphlets (*A Letter to the Lord ****, 1718, and *A Letter from a West-Country Freeholder to the Right Hon. Mr Secretary Web-r*, 1719). Addison died in 1719, depriving Budgell of a political future. He travelled on the continent, and in the following year lost (by his own, perhaps inflated, account) £20,000 in the South Sea Bubble. Aided by the duke of Portland, who had also lost heavily, Budgell published numerous protests against the company (*The Speech Made by Eustace Budgell, Esq; at a General Court of the South-Sea Company* and *The Second Speech* both

appeared in 1720). He also made efforts to have his literary works republished.

The rest of Budgell's life was defined by legal troubles and increasing persecution mania. His father had died in 1710, leaving him an estate of about £950 per year, encumbered with debt; an eleven-year legal wrangle ensued, ending with defeat for Budgell's attempt to deprive his sisters of their legacies. He was also involved in a long-running dispute over estates in Essex, Devon, and Oxfordshire, which led to chancery cases, a trial at Chelmsford in 1727, and a suit in king's bench, all of which he lost. Having been finally called to the bar on 25 June 1726, he took the case by writ of error to the House of Lords, acting as his own lawyer, but lost again. He is supposed to have spent £5000 of his own money in an unsuccessful attempt to get into parliament; in 1727 he gained verbal but not financial support from the duchess of Marlborough for another attempt, and tried to enlist Swift's influence in 1731. He was convicted of libel in 1728, and in May 1730 he was in the Fleet prison for debt. In 1732 he successfully sued a bailiff for false arrest, winning damages of £5 (he claimed privilege through Lord Orrery, whose secretary he was, and whose biography he wrote in 1732).

Budgell developed the view that all his troubles could be blamed on the king's minister Sir Robert Walpole who was, he claimed, attempting to have him murdered. After the accession of George II he attempted to offer the new king lunch as he passed close to one of Budgell's properties, celebrated the event (*A Poem upon his Majesty's Late Journey to Cambridge and Newmarket*, 1728), and petitioned him (and the queen) directly for Walpole's removal (*A Letter to The Craftsman from Eustace Budgell*, 1730). He expressed the same views to Walpole himself in a private letter (CUL, MS Chol. 1585). All this was laid bare in his own writings with an abject and voluminous sensationalism: *A Letter to Cleomenes, King of Sparta* (1731) and *A Letter to his Excellency Mr. Ulrick d'Ypres* (1731) put the political case, while the two-part *Liberty and Property* (1732) gave a detailed narrative of his litigation grievances and his supposed persecution by government spies. *Verres and his Scribblers* (1732), an account of Walpole's propaganda machine, is also ascribed to him. The Scriblerian satirists had already identified Budgell as a soft whig target, and Pope in particular mocked his dependence on Addison, manic self-obsession, and litigious failures (in *The Dunciad*, *Epistle to Dr Arbuthnot*, *Sober Advice from Horace*, and other poems). Budgell was also attacked, more viciously, by the pro-government press (*A Letter to Eustace Budgell, Esq*, 1730; *A Proper Reply, to a Scurrilous Pamphlet*, 1732). Both of these forms of attack derived further fuel from the events of the last four years of his life.

In February 1733 Budgell became a freemason (Bodl. Oxf., MS Rawl. J. 4° 5, fol. 175). Later that year he became involved with the deist Matthew Tindal, who left his rooms in All Souls College, Oxford, to take up residence in Cold Bath Fields, where he was much courted by Budgell and Lucy Price, widow of the judge Robert Price. He died there on 16 August, and Lucy Price invited his nephew Nicholas Tindal to discuss the terms of the will, which gave £2100 and some other property to Budgell 'that his great Talents may serve his Country'. Nicholas Tindal, who had been expecting to inherit his uncle's estate, but was merely named residuary legatee, discovered that virtually all his uncle's assets (some £1900 stock) had already been loaned to Budgell, and refused to administer the will. A bond for £1000 was missing; the will itself was written out by Lucy Price and showed other suspicious signs, and after obtaining such property as remained Nicholas Tindal published what amounted to an accusation of forgery in *A Copy of the Will of Dr. Matthew Tindal* (October 1733). The *Grub-Street Journal* persistently ridiculed Budgell's own frenzied attempts (in his own periodical, *The Bee*) to explain the circumstances of his friendship with Tindal and the details of the will; Budgell blamed this literary agitation against him on Pope.

On 4 September Lucy Price sent a letter to Walpole, supposedly written by Tindal but again in her hand, asking for an instalment of a government pension to be transferred to Budgell; Nicholas Tindal also claimed the money. Walpole's ministry was keeping an interested eye on the case, and the bookseller Edmund Curll, who also published a copy of Tindal's will, supplied them with further information, some of it gleaned from Budgell himself. This lends some credence to Budgell's claim that he was being targeted. Behind the controversial exchanges between *The Bee* and the *Grub-Street Journal* was an actual lawsuit contesting the will in the name of Anne Pare (Nicholas Tindal's sister), which seems to have petered out early in 1734. Budgell wrote to Philip Yorke (later the earl of Hardwicke) on 18 and 19 March 1737 to complain about frauds in chancery, where another case of his was being pursued; but on 4 May 1737 he filled his pockets with stones, took a boat from Dorset steps, and jumped out near London Bridge. His body, with £161 in gold and notes on it, was found a week later. He left a note justifying the suicide on the basis of Addison's *Cato* (1713) and leaving what remained of his estate to Ann Eustace, his natural daughter (possibly the daughter of his housemaid, Mary Harris), aged about twelve. (She later became an actress at Drury Lane; her guardian, Paul Wells, was executed for forgery at Oxford in 1749.) The coroner's jury recorded a verdict of lunacy; evidence was presented that Budgell was expecting an execution in his house and was especially anxious about other forthcoming legal cases. It was widely assumed that his suicide was the result of difficulties ensuing from the Tindal scandal. It was also said that he had sold the manuscript of the second part of Tindal's controversial *Christianity as Old as the Creation* to Bishop Gibson, who destroyed it.   PAUL BAINES

Sources L. G. Morrison, 'Eustace Budgell and his family background', *N&Q*, 217 (1972), 178–83, 209–16 · L. G. Morrison, 'The Bee, or, Universal Weekly Pamphlet, 1733-1735', PhD diss., U. Texas, 1953 · P. Baines, 'Authenticity and forgery in 18th-century Britain', PhD diss., University of Bristol, 1988, chap. 2, appx 3 · R. Shiels, *The lives of the poets of Great Britain and Ireland*, ed. T. Cibber, 5 (1753), 1–16 · L. G. Morrison, 'Eustace Budgell and the duchess of Marlborough', *N&Q*, 218 (1973), 212–13 · P. Smithers, *The life of Joseph Addison* (1954) · L. G. Morrison, 'Eustace Budgell's proposals', *N&Q*, 218 (1973), 8–9 · J. Eggart and C. Rosales, 'A bibliography of holdings of the works of Eustace Budgell in the Bodleian Library', typescript, University of Oklahoma, 1985, Bodl. Oxf. · D. Berman and S. Lawlor, 'The suppression of *Christianity as old as the creation*, volume II', *N&Q*, 229 (1984), 3–6 · correspondence, CUL, Cholmondley MSS · Bodl. Oxf., MS Rawl. J, 4°5, fol. 175 · F. A. Inderwick and R. A. Roberts, eds., *A calendar of the Inner Temple records*, 4 (1933), 146 · *IGI* · *GM*, 1st ser., 7 (1737), 315

Archives BL, Hardwicke papers · BL, letters to the duchess of Marlborough, Add. MS 61476 · BL, letters to Lord Sunderland, Add. MS 61636 · CUL, Cholmondley papers

Likenesses J. Faber, mezzotint (after D. Firmin, 1720), BM

Wealth at death approx. £161; goods and chattels to daughter: *GM*; will, PRO, PROB 11/684, sig. 175

Budgen, Nicholas William (1937–1998), barrister and politician, was born on 3 November 1937 at 50 Palace Road, Streatham, London, the son of George Nicholas Budgen (*d.* 1942), businessman, and his wife, Mary Helen, *née* Bather. He was baptized into the Church of England by the grandfather of Enoch Powell, a politician who much later significantly influenced his life. His father, a captain in the army, was killed at Tobruk. Budgen was educated at St Edward's School, Oxford, where he gained a reputation as a talented but difficult child, always ready to argue niceties with authority.

Unlike many young men of his time, Budgen—perhaps influenced by romantic memories of his father—looked forward to his national service. When he was called up he joined the North Staffordshire regiment (the prince of Wales's). He was commissioned in April 1957 and posted to Germany. He became devoted to his regiment and seriously considered a military career. When he took up, instead, a political career he demonstrated constant vigilance in the interests of the army, and the regimental march of the North Staffs—'The days we went a'gypsyin'—was played at his memorial service. In the army, too, he discovered what became a lifelong passion for horses. He became an enthusiastic, if not notably successful, steeplechaser, and helped to set up and run the regimental saddle cup.

Appropriately, in view of his disputatious nature, Budgen went on to read law at Corpus Christi College, Cambridge. In 1962 he was called to the bar by Gray's Inn. He joined chambers in Birmingham and specialized in criminal practice on the Oxford and midland circuit. He was always busy, if never particularly outstanding. He had inherited a 200 acre farm in Staffordshire, and so was a farmer as well as a barrister. On 4 April 1964 he married Madeleine Elizabeth (*b.* 1941/2), solicitor, daughter of Raymond Montague Cecil Kittoe, schoolmaster. They had a son and a daughter.

Outside his professional life Budgen became interested in politics and joined the Birmingham Bow Group, subsequently becoming its chairman. During these years he formed a close alliance with a fellow member of the bar, a young man of similar political enthusiasm, Kenneth Clarke. In 1966 the two wrote a pamphlet on immigration and race relations, *Immigration, Race Relations and Politics*, which aroused controversy because of its tough, and even minatory, attitude. In later years, when Clarke was chancellor of the exchequer in John Major's governments of

Nicholas William Budgen (1937–1998), by Robin Mayes

1990–97, he was the butt of many sallies, sometimes funny, but often bitter, from Budgen. Their personal relations, none the less, remained amicable.

Budgen was anxious to get into parliament, and was envious when Clarke gained Rushcliffe in 1970. Three times he tried and failed to gain the nomination in safe Conservative seats. Then, in 1974, a thunderbolt struck party and national politics alike. Enoch Powell, who had been dismissed from the shadow cabinet by Edward Heath because of a speech on immigration in 1968, announced that, because of Heath's European policy, he could not stand as a tory candidate in his constituency of Wolverhampton South-West. His constituents were shocked. Many supported Powell's views, and sought a candidate who shared them. Budgen stepped forward. As John Biffen wrote later: 'A great many [tories] partially supported Powell or were glad to have his views aired. These were the à la carte Powellites; Budgen wanted the full menu' (The Guardian, 27 Oct 1998). On the doctrine of a balanced budget, on immigration—where he believed that the Heath government had grown lax—and above all on Britain's relations with Europe, Budgen was at one with Powell. He was duly returned for Wolverhampton in February 1974.

Given Budgen's views it was impossible to imagine Heath appointing him to shadow office after the general election defeat of February 1974. Budgen amused himself by pursuing his favourite causes from the back benches and excited media interest, partly because he was 'the successor to Enoch' and partly because of his perceived eccentricities. He was notably parsimonious, and bought most of his clothes from charity shops. One colleague observed that they were invariably ill-fitting; Budgen explained that he had to save money for his horses.

Margaret Thatcher's succession to Heath as Conservative leader in 1975 did not bring preferment to Budgen. Thatcher was too preoccupied with silencing the big guns of the Heath years, while bringing forward senior figures of her own persuasion, to concern herself with minor gadflies such as Budgen. In September 1981, however, her chief whip, Michael Jopling, who believed in the old adage that it is better to have members of the awkward squad inside, rather than outside, the political tent, invited Budgen to join him as an assistant whip. Budgen took the job, but was unhappy. Office did not suit him because it silenced him on so many subjects on which he was determined to dilate. In 1982 the government proposed to create a general assembly of all parties in Northern Ireland. Budgen saw this as a betrayal of Ulster Unionism and in May resigned his office.

Budgen continued in his amiably independent way throughout the Thatcher years, serving for a time as a member of the Treasury select committee. But, though well disposed to the prime minister and to the general direction of her policy, he never compromised his own principles, and these came into serious play when John Major succeeded her in 1990. The following years saw continuous conflict over the Maastricht treaty and the entry of Britain into the European exchange rate mechanism. Major's bold decision, in November 1994, to withdraw the Conservative whip from Budgen and seven other tory MPs who constantly challenged his authority was widely regarded as headstrong. Following a conciliatory article by Budgen in The Times the whip was restored. None the less, the rift in the party thus opened was extremely damaging to the government. Major attributed a large share of the blame for the ending of his political career at the general election defeat of 1997 to the eight rebels, among whom he singled out Budgen. In the circumstances his portrait of Budgen was not unfair. Budgen was, he wrote, 'a dry, short and cheerfully miserly, holes-in-his-socks barrister, a specialist in mischief. You never quite knew where you were with him. He adopted Wolverhampton right-wingery as a sort of Powellite intellectual challenge'. This adoption, Major caustically observed, 'failed to save his seat' (Major, 356).

From then on it was downhill. Budgen tried and failed to gain a seat in the European parliament. In 1998 cancer was diagnosed. 'With characteristic matter-of-factness', wrote Charles Moore, 'he set about making the necessary arrangements … selling his horses, and organising his funeral' (Daily Telegraph, 27 Oct 1998). To the end Budgen was the same brave, independent stoic he had always been. He died on 26 October 1998 at Staffordshire General Hospital, Stafford. He was survived by his wife and their two children. PATRICK COSGRAVE

Sources *The Guardian* (27 Oct 1998) · *The Independent* (27 Oct 1998) · *Daily Telegraph* (27 Oct 1998) · *The Times* (27 Oct 1998) · S. Heffer, *Like the Roman: the life of Enoch Powell* (1998) · J. Major, *The autobiography* (1999) · *WWW* [forthcoming] · private information (2004) · personal knowledge (2004) · b. cert. · m. cert. · d. cert. · *CGPLA Eng. & Wales* (1999)
Likenesses photograph, 1974, repro. in *Daily Telegraph* · photograph, 1992, repro. in *The Times* · photograph, 1996, repro. in *The Independent* · R. Mayes, photograph, News International Syndication, London [*see illus.*] · photograph, repro. in *The Guardian*
Wealth at death £261,503—gross; £55,352—net: probate, 31 March 1999, *CGPLA Eng. & Wales*

Budgett, Samuel (1794–1851), merchant and philanthropist, was born on 27 July 1794 at Wrington, Somerset, the seventh of the twelve children of James Budgett (1747–1823), shopkeeper, and his second wife and cousin, Elizabeth Budgett (d. 1831). In 1801, after residing in Backwell and Nailsea, his father obtained a grocer's shop in Kingswood, a notoriously lawless coalmining community located outside the civic boundaries of Bristol. Two years later the family moved to Coleford, on the southern edge of the Somerset coalfield, but the Kingswood grocery business was retained and successfully developed by Budgett's elder half-brother, Henry Hill Budgett (1778–1849), a leading member of the local Wesleyan Methodist community and the Kingswood Benevolent Society.

Budgett was educated at local dame-schools in Kingswood and Kilmersdon and was then a weekly boarder at Midsomer Norton. In 1809 he was apprenticed to his brother and returned to Kingswood, though not without presenting his parents with a tangible demonstration of his commercial aptitude in the form of £30 accumulated by trade on his own behalf in the neighbourhood and at the markets of Shepton Mallet and Bath. Surprisingly, however, in 1812, with the apprenticeship half served, Samuel was given a month's notice to quit, for want of ability, but before this period expired obtained employment with a grocer in Bristol. About six months later, his brother Henry, combining a promise of financial reward and a call to duty, persuaded him to return to Kingswood where he completed his apprenticeship.

With the business under Samuel's capable supervision, H. H. Budgett engaged in a campaign, which echoed the earlier efforts of John Wesley and George Whitefield, to civilize Kingswood through the provision of a school and chapel, to which Samuel contributed as an enthusiastic Sunday school teacher. After holding a salaried position for three years, during which time his reputation grew as an honest purveyor of quality products, Samuel Budgett accepted the offer of a partnership in the business which subsequently prospered as H. H. and S. Budgett. In 1822 he married Ann Smith (1791–1866) of Midsomer Norton; they had four sons and three daughters.

Determined to expand the business, Budgett introduced a delivery service to neighbouring villages which was soon extended to cater for smaller shops in the vicinity. He built his reputation and business on clear principles: he

insisted on prompt cash payment, rather than credit, and guaranteed regular deliveries to his customers at competitive prices. He developed a business system which enforced the operation of specified procedures within an organizational structure that integrated several departments and eventually employed 300 workers. This required the imposition of strict labour discipline which rewarded good timekeepers and fined those who were not; however, Budgett also demonstrated a keen paternalistic interest in the welfare of individual employees. With the intention of raising efficiency and increasing motivation among his employees, he significantly shortened the working day, supervised training, introduced a sickness benefit scheme, and financed an annual fête. His personal savings also contributed to the survival of the business when his brother's banking enterprise, Jones, Brain, and Budgett, collapsed.

Shortly after Budgett took sole control of the business, in 1842, the Kingswood premises were largely destroyed by a fire, though the financial losses were mitigated by insurance policies which recouped over £8000. Budgett's immediate response was to move his headquarters to an established depot at Nelson Street, Bristol, which quickly demonstrated its advantageous location. Further expansion saw the development of a wholesale business which eventually delivered to customers throughout the south west of England and south Wales and the establishment of a London branch under the management of his eldest son, James Smith Budgett.

Budgett campaigned nationally to raise funds for the Wesleyan chapel at Kingswood, engaged in many nonsectarian charitable acts, and encouraged communal religious devotions at work. He died on 29 April 1851, probably from a stroke, at The Park, Tabernacle Road, his Kingswood home, and was buried on 7 May 1851 in the churchyard of the Wesleyan chapel, Kingswood Hill, Somerset. Posthumously he achieved international significance as the subject of the Revd William Arthur's extraordinarily popular biography, *The Successful Merchant* (1852), which portrayed him as a paragon who had combined devoutly held Christian ethics with a natural talent for business. PETER WARDLEY

Sources W. Arthur, *The successful merchant: sketches of the life of Mr Samuel Budgett, late of Kingswood Hill* (1852) · D. P. Lindegaard, *The Budgetts of Kingswood Hill and their Bristol family* (1988) · *Bristol Times and Mercury* (10 May 1851) · *Western Daily Press* (20 Oct 1900) · d. cert.
Likenesses stipple and line print, c.1840, Bristol City Museum and Art Gallery

Budworth, William (1699/1700–1745), schoolmaster, was born in Marston Montgomery, Derbyshire, one of at least nine children of Luke Budworth, vicar of Cubley (1695–1700) and Longford (1700–22), in Derbyshire, and his wife, Elizabeth. His father later became rector of the parishes of Tittleshall and Wellingham, in Norfolk. William was educated at Derby grammar school under Anthony Blackwall. Aged seventeen he was admitted sizar of Christ's College, Cambridge, on 26 February 1717, and graduated BA (1721) and MA (1726). Having been ordained deacon in June 1723 and priest in September 1724, he became master of Rugeley grammar school, in Staffordshire. He married Lucy Lane at Rugeley on 23 July 1728; they had eleven children, of whom ten were stillborn and the last did not live long enough to be baptized.

Budworth was appointed headmaster of the free grammar school at Brewood, Staffordshire, on the death of the previous head, Dr Hillman. He was presented to Brewood vicarage by the dean of Lichfield and to the nearby donative chapel of Shareshill by Sir Edward Littleton, whose nephew was educated at the school. Budworth did not take up residence for two years, while the dilapidated schoolhouse was being repaired, but he proved to be a skilful teacher and the school grew in size and reputation under him. In 1736 he considered engaging the young Samuel Johnson as usher but rejected him apparently on the grounds that his paralytic affliction might be ridiculed by the boys.

Following the death of his wife Budworth became embroiled in a protracted chancery case with her relatives. Though he mourned her death he made a concerted effort to find another wife, but without success. He risked his livelihood when he invited a widow, Mrs Vaughan, and her daughter to live with him and keep house, for the presence of a young unmarried woman in the house prevented him from boarding some of his pupils, which was an important source of income. His hopes of marrying Mrs Vaughan were dashed by her death.

One of Budworth's most eminent pupils was Richard Hurd, later bishop of Worcester, who wrote that he 'possessed every talent of a perfect institutor of youth in a degree which I believe has been rarely found in any of that profession since the days of Quinctilian' (Nichols, *Lit. anecdotes*, 3.383). This admiration for Budworth was not shared by his parishioners, who thought him aloof and arrogant and dreaded meeting him in the street. A shy and reserved man, he drove his congregation away by delivering dry and abstruse sermons. He took to employing some of the worst preachers in the area to demonstrate his own merit, but eventually gave up preaching in favour of his curate. He was a fine singer and especially fond of music. Though a high-churchman he was not a Jacobite, as demonstrated in his published sermon on the rising of 1745. Budworth died of an apoplectic fit while talking to an acquaintance in his school garden in September 1745. He was succeeded as headmaster by his former usher, Mr Bromley, who, by contrast, was very popular in the village.

THOMPSON COOPER, *rev.* S. J. SKEDD

Sources Nichols, *Lit. anecdotes*, 3.332–55, 383, 759; 6.469–70 • Venn, *Alum. Cant.* • N. Carlisle, *A concise account of the endowed grammar schools of England and Wales*, 2 vols. (1818), vol. 2, p. 476 • J. Boswell, *Life of Johnson*, ed. R. W. Chapman, rev. J. D. Fleeman, new edn (1970); repr. with introduction by P. Rogers (1980), 1385 • F. Kilvert, *Memoirs of the life and writings of the Right Rev. Richard Hurd* (1860) • IGI

Bufton [*married name* Swanborough], **Eleanor** (1842–1893), actress, was born in Llanbister, Radnorshire, Wales, on 2 June 1842, the daughter of Mary Bufton, an unmarried and illiterate woman. She made her first professional

Eleanor Bufton (1842–1893), by unknown photographer

appearance at an early age in Edinburgh, as the chambermaid in *The Clandestine Marriage*. In 1854 she played at the St James's Theatre, London, and by 1856 had progressed from there to a round of Shakespearian roles with the Princess's company under Charles Kean, the first of which was on 15 October 1856, as Hermia in *A Midsummer Night's Dream*. The most notable of her performances was as Ferdinand in *The Tempest*, a curious experiment, said to have been the first time the role had been played by a woman, and the propriety of this casting was disputed. On 21 February 1860 she married Arthur (d. 1895), the son of Henry Valentine Swanborough (formerly Smith), whose wife, Ada, was the manager of the Strand Theatre. Their daughter-in-law played various burlesque parts, some original, at the Strand, and then moved back to the St James's, where she performed with Henry Irving in Thomas Morton's *The School of Reform* in November 1867. She remained there until 1870, when she returned to the Strand, as Cicily Homespun in Colman's *The Heir-at-Law*. On the opening of the Court on 25 January 1871 she was the first Miss Flamboys in W. S. Gilbert's *Randall's Thumb* and on 29 May the first Estella in the same author's adaptation of *Great Expectations*.

Eleanor Bufton was the victim of a railway accident in 1871 which was said to have affected her memory. She obtained damages of £1600 and for some years appeared on the stage only sporadically. On her recovery in December 1872 a complimentary benefit was given her at Drury Lane, when she played Constance in Sheridan Knowles's *The Love Chase*. She was engaged by Irving to play in *Book the Third, Chapter the First* at the Lyceum in 1879. After this she was reduced mainly to supporting roles, the last being on 16 April 1892 in *The Tin Box* at the Globe. Bufton was tall and good-looking, and was more successful in burlesque than in comedy. She died of influenza at her home, 169 Strand, London, on 9 April 1893, and was buried in Brompton cemetery. She was survived by her husband and at least one daughter.   JOSEPH KNIGHT, *rev.* J. GILLILAND

Sources Adams, *Drama* · Boase, *Mod. Eng. biog.* · F. Hays, *Women of the day: a biographical dictionary of notable contemporaries* (1885) · C. E. Pascoe, ed., *The dramatic list* (1879) · E. Reid and H. Compton, eds., *The dramatic peerage* [1891]; rev. edn [1892] · Hall, *Dramatic ports.*, vol. 1 · S. D'Amico, ed., *Enciclopedia dello spettacolo*, 11 vols. (Rome, 1954–68) · *The Era* (15 April 1893) · *The life and reminiscences of E. L. Blanchard, with notes from the diary of Wm. Blanchard*, ed. C. W. Scott and C. Howard, 2 vols. (1891) · H. B. Baker, *The London stage: its history and traditions from 1576 to 1888*, 2 vols. (1889) · E. Kilmurray, *Dictionary of British portraiture*, 3 (1981), 29 · C. Scott, *The drama of yesterday and today*, 2 vols. (1899) · b. cert. · d. cert. · D. Bank and others, eds., *British biographical archive* (1984–98) [microfiche; with index, 2nd edn, 1998]

Archives Theatre Museum, London, letters

Likenesses cartes-de-visite, NPG · photograph, NPG [*see illus.*] · photographs, Harvard TC

Wealth at death £372 4*s.* 8*d.*: administration, 4 Aug 1893, *CGPLA Eng. & Wales*

Bufton, Sydney Osborne (1908–1993), air force officer, was born on 12 January 1908 at Teviot, Temple Avenue, Llandrindod Wells, Radnorshire, the second son in the family of four sons and one daughter of James Osborne Bufton, a tobacconist, and later an estate agent, alderman, and JP, and his wife, Florence, *née* Peters. Educated at Llandrindod Wells community school (1920–22) and Dean Close School, Cheltenham (1922–6), he showed an early aptitude for radio, constructing one of the first crystal sets in Wales. In 1926–7 he was an engineering pupil at Vickers; he attended evening classes at Erith Technical College and in June 1927 gained an intermediate BSc.

Bufton then successfully applied for RAF pilot training, reporting to Uxbridge on 16 December 1927 for an initial drill and discipline course, and was posted to 4 flying training school, Abu Sueir, Egypt. Instructed on Avro 504Ks, he gained his wings on 22 October 1928; then, as a pilot officer, he was posted in December to 100 squadron, which had Horsley day bombers. After seventeen months there he was sent to the Central Flying School, and in August 1930 he was posted to 5 flying training school as an instructor. But in order to gain a specialist qualification and a permanent career in the RAF he applied for an aeronautical engineering course at the home aircraft depot in Henlow. In September 1932 he was awarded a permanent commission, and in July 1933 he completed his course.

In October 1933 Bufton was posted as engineering officer to the aircraft depot in Hinaidi, Iraq. Having bought a Rolls-Royce Silver Ghost for £8, he had it shipped out to Basrah, then drove it to Baghdad. It proved to be an invaluable unit transport. In June 1934 he passed a colloquial Arabic exam; and while on UK leave in August that year he was cabled by Lady Hoare, the wife of the British minister in Tehran, asking if he would fly out a DH Gipsy Major Moth. He agreed and made the flight with Flying Officer Jack Larking of 55 squadron, based at Hinaidi. Then in June 1935 he was asked by the Iraq Petroleum Company if he would fly a DH Dragon back to the UK, which he did in July after applying for twenty-eight days' annual leave. When in July 1936 his overseas tour ended he was posted to the department of training in the Air Ministry, where his work involved overseeing the practical implications of the RAF expansion schemes.

In January 1939 Bufton was sent on the Staff College course at Andover and completed it just before the outbreak of war, when he was posted to France with no. 2 mission. He then served at the British air forces headquarters until they were ordered to move to Nantes; he left there as the Panzers rolled in and was flown back to the UK on 17 June 1940. Bufton was posted to nos 19 and 20 operational training units to fly Whitleys before being sent to command 10 squadron, with which he undertook nineteen operations. In November 1940 he was awarded the DFC. On the night of 24–5 October his youngest brother, John, flying with 49 squadron, had been lost when his Hampden came down in the sea near Skegness.

On 12 April 1941 Bufton was posted to Linton on Ouse to form 76 squadron with Halifaxes. He converted to the new type but was then promoted group captain and ordered to open up Pocklington, which he commanded to the end of October. With effect from 1 November he was deputy director, bomber operations, at the Air Ministry. In this appointment, and as director from March 1943 to June 1945, he deployed his considerable writing skill to bring about operational improvements in Bomber Command—the provision of three emergency airfields, radar navigation, and target-finding aids, and the establishment of a Pathfinder force (which he proposed, despite opposition from the commander-in-chief, Sir Arthur Harris, and in which his younger brother Hal served with great distinction). In 1944 he advocated attacks on precision targets such as oil supplies and the ball-bearing industry rather than area bombing of German cities. Arguing cogently and with clarity, he was 'beating Bert [Harris] at his own game', as the chief of the air staff, Sir Charles Portal, put it.

On 1 January 1943 'the little Air Commodore' (as Churchill called him) married (Maureen Anthony Osra) Susan Browne (*b.* 1921), who served in the WRNS and modelled for recruiting photographs; she was the daughter of Colonel Edgar Browne, army officer. They had two daughters, Carol and Marilyn. In the 1945 new year honours he was made a CB; he was also made a commander of the Legion of Merit by the president of the USA in October 1945, and a commander (with swords) of the order of Orange Nassau by the queen of the Netherlands in November 1947.

Bufton held a succession of important post-war appointments: air officer commanding Egypt (1945–6); officer commanding tactics wing, central bomber establishment

(1946–8); assistant chief of air staff (operation/plans), air forces, Western Europe (1948–51); director of weapons, Air Ministry (1951–2); air officer administration, Bomber Command (1952–3); air officer commanding British forces, Aden (as an air vice-marshal) (1953–5); senior air staff officer, Bomber Command (1955–8); and finally assistant chief of air staff (intelligence) (1958–61). He retired in October 1961.

Bufton then returned to one of his youthful interests, radio, and founded Radionic Products, which after eight years' successful trading was bought out by Philips. He was often called upon to comment upon books and programmes about the bombing offensive in the Second World War, telling a BBC researcher that 'without Bomber Command the war would have been lost' (private information). In 1967 he was appointed high sheriff of Radnorshire, and three years later he was elected a fellow of the Royal Aeronautical Society, sponsored by Dr Barnes Wallis and Sir Frank Whittle.

Buf Bufton was a keen sportsman, playing hockey for Wales, the combined services, and the RAF, and excelling at other sports; he was also an amateur artist and poet. He died at Epsom General Hospital on 29 March 1993 following a stroke, shortly after he and his wife had celebrated their golden wedding; he was survived by his wife and their two daughters. At a service of thanksgiving for his life in St Mark's Church, Reigate, on 6 April his poem 'Flight', extolling the airman's freedom in his element— 'Gods now, not men. No longer bound to earth'—was read by his grandson Alex Hieatt.   HUMPHREY WYNN

Sources *The Times* (3 April 1993) · *Daily Telegraph* (3 April 1993) · Royal Air Force record of service · R. Cording, unpublished biography, priv. coll. · *WWW* · D. Saward, *'Bomber' Harris: the authorised biography* (1984) · C. Messenger, *'Bomber' Harris and the strategic bombing offensive, 1939–1945* (1984) · H. Probert, *Bomber Harris, his life and times: the biography of Marshal of the Royal Air Force Sir Arthur Harris, wartime chief of bomber command* (2001) · D. Richards, *The hardest victory: RAF bomber command in the Second World War* (1994) · J. Maynard, *Bennett and the Pathfinders* (1996) · private information (2004) [Mrs Carol Downer, daughter] · personal knowledge (2004) · b. cert. · m. cert. · d. cert.

Archives CAC Cam., papers and photographs, mainly on service with bomber command · priv. coll., Royal Air Force and autobiographical papers

Likenesses photograph, repro. in *The Times* · photographs, priv. coll.

Wealth at death under £125,000: probate, 10 May 1993, *CGPLA Eng. & Wales*

Bugg, Francis (1640–1727), Quaker apostate, was born at Mildenhall, Suffolk, on 10 March 1640 and baptized on 14 March. His father was Robert (d. c.1667), the second son of Francis and Margaret Bugg; his mother, Joan, the daughter of Thomas and Mary Holman. Bugg noted that his parents were 'of good yeomen-family' of 'good repute', and brought him up according to the Church of England (Bugg, *Pilgrim's Progress*, 1). They lived on a large farm at Undley-Hall, in the parish of Lakenheath, Suffolk, which brought the family £200 per annum, with a further £100 a year from a fen farm (ibid., 2). Bugg received an education until about fifteen, and apparently excelled for he wrote: 'I was capable to write, and read English very well; as also

Francis Bugg (1640–1727), by Frederick Hendrick van Hove, 1700

to cast account, few lads went beyond me' (ibid.). It appears, however, that the family fell on bad times for Bugg recorded how his father had need for his assistance during the summer months which resulted in Francis being 'prevented, of attaining to that degree they once designed' (ibid.). He afterwards became an apprentice and lamented the loss of much of his previous learning.

The Quaker, 1657–c.1675 In his early years Bugg had 'a love to religion' (Bugg, *Pilgrim's Progress*, 2), though enjoyed company, dancing, and music. His first experience of the Quakers came in 1657 when Thomas Symonds of Norwich visited Lakenheath to appoint meetings and Bugg wrote that 'tho' I went to church in the forenoon, yet I had itching ears to hear the Quakers' (ibid., 3). He was impressed by the patience they displayed in their sufferings, their plainness of living and sincerity, and 'their so much insisting on the dictates of our consciences, which prompts to good, and checks for some evils' (ibid.). He believed that he fell in with the Quakers because of 'the scandalous practice of our minister' (ibid.), though refrains from providing further detail on the matter, except to suggest that he did not lead an exemplary life. Bugg notes that over a period of a few years he became 'very zealous that way' and began to attend the silent meetings of the Quakers (ibid., 4).

In *A modest defence of my book, entitled, 'Quakerism expos'd'* (1700), Bugg outlines his early relations with the Quakers, noting that he was 'of good repute and esteem amongst them', he 'entertained their teachers with no little charge … put clothes on the backs of some, and money in the purses of others'. He was also register to the monthly and quarterly meeting for around sixteen to eighteen years and contributed £20 towards the building of a meeting-house, meetings before having been held at his home (Bugg, *Modest Defence*, dedication). Bugg mentions elsewhere that he also served as deputy of the yearly meeting and six weeks' meeting in London, all at his own expense (Bugg, *Quakerism a Grand Imposture, or, The Picture of Quakerism Continued*, 1716, pt 4, 144).

His aunt Ann *Docwra, a Quaker minister who turned against him for his later opposition to Friends, noted that he was initially quite poor, but increased his wealth following his father's death when he was left £30 a year. He bought an estate at Mildenhall 'with a fair brick house upon it, built by a knight baronet' (Docwra, *Apostate*, 5). According to his aunt he was a 'wool-man' and owned a shop and an 'Adventure at sea, in a coal ship at Ipswich', which he eventually disposed of (ibid., 6). She confirms in *The Second Part of an Apostate-Conscience Exposed* (1700) that he was married, though does not give the name of his wife; a son Francis is mentioned, and a further source confirms that there was another son, Robert, who was elected churchwarden for Mildenhall from 1690 to 1693.

At some point in the late 1650s Bugg may have moved to Ely, for he attended several meetings there. He suffered three years and four months' imprisonment for the Quaker cause. On 16 February 1663 he, Thomas Richardson, and John Ives were removed from a meeting by constables and taken to Ely gaol, where they were kept until the assizes five months later. There they were tendered the oath of allegiance, which they refused, and were sent back to prison. They lived in terrible conditions which led to the death after two and a half years of Richardson, while Bugg and Ives remained there for another six months. At Ely in 1670 Bugg had goods distrained worth £42 18s. 4d. for attendance at several meetings, and in 1673 he also suffered distraints for a meeting at Mildenhall.

Falling out, 1675–1680 About 1675 some trouble arose between Bugg and another Quaker, Samuel Cater, over a fine for attending a meeting which Bugg appears to have paid. It was alleged that Bugg, for financial gain, had told informers of the meeting and later had a third of the fine returned, but continued to hold Cater, the preacher of Lakenheath, responsible for payment. Bugg stated that he had suffered the fine himself because Cater had refused to tell the informers his name to avoid prosecution. The matter was disputed for a long time and Bugg relates that he pursued the matter through his monthly, quarterly, and yearly meetings for three years. In 1677 Bugg is noted as attending the yearly meeting where he complained to William Penn that county Friends had refused him justice. Two arbitrations, the latter during 1679–80, held that

Cater was not liable, leaving Bugg dissatisfied, with the result that a George Smith offered to pay half the sum. It is alleged that Bugg, as proof of good faith, asked for the money, which Smith, not possessing, borrowed with the condition that Bugg would not keep it, only to find that he did so. Bugg's refusal to return the money apparently led to the Quaker meeting deciding in favour of Smith, which, according to Friends, was the reason for Bugg's departure from the society. Bugg had a different account of the incident; he stated that Smith gave him the money and that the episode was not the reason for his disaffection with the Quakers, for he had written a letter to Cater in May 1675 relating his dislike of 'Friends forcing their apprentices to stand bare-headed before them' (Bugg, *Quakerism a Grand Imposture*, 142).

Bugg seems to have left the Quakers in 1680 when he began writing against them but his exact reasons for doing so are uncertain. His aunt believed that he feared that the statute of £20 a month would be executed against him unless he conformed. However there do seem to have been other reasons for his disenchantment for even Docwra noted in 1682 that while at her home in Cambridge he 'made great complaint of George Fox, that he had brought in innovations into the church about marriages' (Docwra, *Apostate*, 6). Bugg was perhaps referring to the idea that intentions for marriage should be submitted before the women's as well as the men's meetings.

Anti-Quaker polemicist, 1680–1727 According to Ann Docwra, Bugg conformed to the Church of England in 1684. From 1680 his anti-Quaker output was considerable, the last work being published in 1724. *De Christiana libertate* (1682), one of his major works, contains some of his favourite themes: Quakerism as tantamount to Catholicism, the repressive nature of Quaker central organization, and George Fox's 'laws'. He exclaims in the second part of this:

> it is a popish principle, to believe as the Church believes, barely because she so believes: to take all for granted our leaders say, without any further examination, to read no books, but what are licensed and approved on by this general council, or that Second-Day's Meeting, to pin my faith on their sleeves, to see with their eyes instead of my own. (Bugg, *De Christiana libertate*, 2nd pt, 215)

These ideas are echoed in *The Quakers Detected* (1686), in which he bemoans the pre-eminence of George Fox, who, he believed, 'began to set task-masters over us' with the establishment of the local meeting system, and 'several outward orders, laws and canons ecclesiastical' (p. 4). In *A Letter to the Quakers* (1690) Bugg accuses Friends of inconstancy and hypocrisy, for espousing 'the good old cause and the cause of your dear friend O. C. and R. C. Protectors' [Oliver and Richard Cromwell] and then owning the king at the Restoration (p. 1). Likewise, in a tract of 1693 entitled *New Rome Arraigned* Bugg pointed to the radicalism of some early Quakers and then stated, ''tis now common for the Quakers to call and be called master and mistress, sir, and to drink wine, eat dainty dishes, wear silk and velvet, and perriwigs' and to have 'rich houses as any body' (p. 65). Bugg's many works were answered by leading Quakers such as William Penn and George Whitehead, the latter interestingly observing that Bugg left the Quakers because 'he deemed us guilty of apostasy from our first principle and profession' (Whitehead, epistle dedicatory).

In 1698 Bugg had urged the Norfolk clergy to appoint a debate with Quakers which took place in West Dereham church on 8 December; it was attended by both local Friends and five from London. Quaker sources state that Bugg 'stood at the Priests Elbows and was their Agent to look out places, quotations, &c.'. Along with the clergy he was accused of rudeness and of 'hooteing and hallooing and laughing', though according to the source the Quakers seem to have won the debate, much to Bugg's dissatisfaction (letter from John Tomkins to Sir John Rodes, 3 Jan 1699, Lampson, 151–2). In 1701 Bugg was at another debate at Sleaford, Lincolnshire, with Henry Pickworth, which he describes in his *A Narrative of the Conference at Sleeford* (1702).

In 1702 Bugg challenged Mr Richard Vivers of Banbury to a debate in the town on 21 September to defend the society from Bugg's charges of heresy and blasphemy. He discussed these in *Quakerism Drooping and its Cause Sinking* (1703); among the charges mentioned were: a lack of respect for the scriptures and Christ, denial of the Trinity, and contempt of church ordinances. The work also contains an interesting drawing entitled 'Quakerism drooping', showing a Quaker on crutches, each one labelled 'sinless perfection' and 'infallibility' (between pages 72 and 75 and replicated between 179 and 181). Bugg also returns in this work to his familiar allegation of Quaker hypocrisy and inconstancy, writing that, 'Formally, they pretended to infallibility of judgement, and a sinless perfection, but now, 'tis the Spirit of God only that is infallible' (Bugg, *Quakerism Drooping*, 181). Much to Bugg's disdain Vivers failed to appear at the meeting and Bugg's supporter, Benjamin Loveling, vicar of Banbury, believed this to be because 'the Quakers have discovered one of the chief causes of their indignation against Mr. B. He comes about … with several of his books, and thereby exposes the mystery of their iniquity to the view and abhorrence of all good Christians' (ibid., 13).

Bugg's plethora of anti-Quaker writings apparently left him in some financial distress for he wrote in 1700 that he had been reduced by his 'constancy of writing for more than twenty years together, and by the charge of printing' (Bugg, *Modest Defence*, dedication). He acknowledged the help of the gentry, justices of the peace, clergy, and some protestant dissenters who had provided him with support. His aunt wrote that he had 'scribbled away his estate' and was hundreds of pounds in debt 'and now goes about a begging, with a certificate from the Bishop of Norwich' (Docwra, *Apostate*, 6). In 1703 Bugg felt compelled to defend his name and reputation, issuing a certificate which was signed by his friends and his son Francis.

Despite his difficulties Bugg continued to write profusely against the Quakers into the third decade of the eighteenth century. In 1712 he wrote *A Finishing Stroke*, in which he attacked George Fox, accusing him of bewitching the people. In relation to the book Daniel Defoe wrote 'I am told it is very difficult for him to write anything he has not printed before, and that has not been often answered' (*Journal of George Fox*, ed. N. Penney, 2 vols., 1911, 2.500).

Little is known of the remainder of Bugg's life except that he was imprisoned for some unknown cause at Ely, and appears to have spent the remainder of his days at Mildenhall. He died in 1727, presumably at Mildenhall for the register of burials in Woollen, Mildenhall, records a Francis Bugg senior, aged eighty-six (though he would in fact have been eighty-seven), with the date 1 October 1727. It is hard to capture a clear picture of his character and exact activities, entangled as it is in the polemical writings of himself and his Quaker opponents. He seems, initially, to have been genuinely attracted to the Friends, and although his works have been castigated for their repetitive nature they often point to grievances, particularly in terms of Quaker organization, which are reflected, in part, in the works of Quaker separatists from around the 1670s onwards. An interesting engraving of Bugg in his fifty-eighth year can be seen in his *Pilgrim's Progress* (1698), together with a plate entitled 'The Quakers' synod'.

CAROLINE L. LEACHMAN

Sources F. Bugg, *The pilgrim's progress from Quakerism to Christianity, &c.* (1698) · F. Bugg, *A modest defence of my book, entitled, 'Quakerism expos'd'* (1700) · A. Docwra, *An apostate-conscience exposed* (1699) · J. Besse, *A collection of the sufferings of the people called Quakers*, 1 (1753) · J. Smith, ed., *A descriptive catalogue of Friends' books*, 1 (1867) · A. Docwra, *The second part of an apostate-conscience exposed* (1700) · *Journal of the Friends' Historical Society*, 13 (1916), 166–7 · M. Storey, 'The defence of religious orthodoxy in Mildenhall in the 1690s: the "Quaker–protestant" debate', *Religious dissent in East Anglia* [Norwich 1996], ed. D. Chadd (1996), 168–86 · G. W. [G. Whitehead], *A rambling pilgrim, or, Profane apostate, exposed* (1700) · Mrs G. L. Lampson, ed., *A Quaker post-bag* (1910) · W. C. Braithwaite, *The second period of Quakerism*, ed. H. J. Cadbury, 2nd edn (1961) · *DNB* · F. Bugg, *De Christiana libertate* (1682) · F. Bugg, *The Quakers set in their true light* (1698) · G. W. Marshall, ed., *The Genealogist*, 3 (1879), 239–40 · will, PRO, PROB 11/269, sig. 44

Archives Sion College, MS | RS Friends, Lond., A. R. Barclay MSS, 221, 226, 234, 241, 323–324

Likenesses F. H. van Hove, engraving, 1700, NPG [*see illus.*] · F. H. Van Hove, line engraving (aged fifty-eight), BM, NPG; repro. in F. Bugg, *The pilgrim's progress from Quakerism to Christianity* (1698) · engraving, repro. in F. Bugg, *A seasonable caveat against the prevalency of Quakerism* (1701), frontispiece · photograph, RS Friends, Lond.

Bugga (*fl.* late 7th–early 8th cent.), abbess, was the daughter of King *Centwine of Wessex (*r.* 676–85). She is known chiefly from a poem written by Aldhelm to celebrate a church she had built dedicated to the Virgin Mary; her nunnery is the earliest recorded in the kingdom of the West Saxons. The poem gives some interesting information on the operation of the mixed community of monks and nuns over which Bugga presided. It reveals, for instance, that the monks and nuns formed separate choirs, that male and female lectors read the lessons, and that the chanting of the psalms was accompanied by a psaltery and a lyre. There are also references to a cross of gold and silver with jewels, a golden chalice with jewels, and gold-embroidered cloths. Unfortunately the location of her foundation is not known. Various attempts have been made to identify Bugga with other religious women known by that name or having names ending in '-burh' or '-burg' from which it is likely to have been derived, but none carry conviction. In particular it should be noted that there are no grounds for equating her either with Boniface's correspondent Bugga (Hæaburh) of Kent or with Abbess Bugga of Withington (Gloucestershire). A Latin verse epitaph survives for her, which reveals that she was abbess for thirty-four years.   BARBARA YORKE

Sources *Aldhelm: the poetic works*, trans. M. Lapidge and J. Rosier (1985), 40–41, 47–9 · M. Lapidge, 'Some remnants of Bede's lost *Liber epigrammatum*', *EngHR*, 90 (1975), 798–820, esp. 815–17 · B. Yorke, 'The Bonifacian mission and female religious in Wessex', *Early Medieval Europe*, 7 (1998), 145–72

Bugga [Hæaburh] (*d.* 759×65), abbess, had the full name Hæaburh and was related to the Kentish royal house. She is first known from a letter she sent to Boniface, early in his career in Germany, with her mother, Eangyth, who was abbess of a Kentish monastery, to which Bugga subsequently succeeded. Their letter contains some interesting insights into the problems of running a double monastery, including rebellious monks and excessive demands from the king and his officials. Hostility from the king (Wihtred), presumably because they belonged to a rival branch of the royal house, had forced other members of their family to go abroad, including a cousin of Bugga's called Denewald (who later joined Boniface's mission), and Eangyth and Bugga sought Boniface's advice about also going overseas on a pilgrimage. One subsequent letter from Bugga to Boniface survives and two from him to her which testify to the mutual support they provided to one another throughout their lives. Although Boniface had been discouraging about the advisability of a pilgrimage, Bugga did eventually travel to Rome, probably in 738–9, where she met Boniface and asked him to pray for her kinsman King Æthelbert II of Kent, as the king subsequently recalled in a letter to the missionary. In old age she gave up her position as abbess to follow a more contemplative life. Archbishop Bregowine, writing between 759 and 765, reported to Lull that her *depositio* was celebrated on 28 December, but the exact year of her death is not known.   BARBARA YORKE

Sources M. Tangl, ed., *Die Briefe des heiligen Bonifatius und Lullus*, MGH Epistolae Selectae, 1 (Berlin, 1916), nos. 4, 14, 27, 94, 105, 117 · B. Yorke, 'The Bonifacian mission and female religious in Wessex', *Early Medieval Europe*, 7 (1998), 145–72

Bugge, Agnes (*fl.* 1417–1430). *See under* Women traders and artisans in London (*act. c.*1200–*c.*1500).

Buhler, Robert (1916–1989), artist, was born on 23 November 1916 at the French Hospital, Shaftesbury Avenue, London, the only son and elder child of Robert Buhler, a Swiss aircraft designer with Handley Page, who later became a journalist, and his wife, Lucy Kronig, who came from the village of Täsch in the Valais. He held Swiss– British nationality all his life. He attended Westbourne Park grammar school in 1926–9, and was then further educated in Switzerland for a short time, before leaving school in

Robert Buhler (1916–1989), self-portrait, 1948 [*Portrait of the Artist*]

his early teens to study commercial art at the *Kunstgewerbeschule* in Zürich, and then at the *Kunstgewerbeschule* in Basel. In 1933 he returned to London, where he spent two terms at Bolt Court School of Photo-Engraving and Lithography. There he met (J.) Keith Vaughan, who encouraged him to take up fine art. In 1934 he became a painting student at St Martin's School of Art, where he was taught by (R.) Vivian Pitchforth, (G. C.) Leon Underwood, and Harry Morley. In 1935 he won a senior county scholarship to the Royal College of Art (RCA). He responded to the teaching of Barnett Freedman and John Nash, but only stayed there for six weeks.

Having inherited a little money, Buhler relinquished his scholarship, and rented a studio in Camden Town. He made an income from teaching at Wimbledon School of Art, and from illustrating for various newspapers. He was also commissioned by Jack Beddington of Shell to design a very successful poster depicting Hawker Hurricane fighter aircraft. He began to exhibit in 1936, and showed at the first British Artists' Congress (1937), organized by the Artists' International Association. His work attracted the attention of the collector and patron Sir Edward Marsh, and his *Portrait of Dickie Green* was illustrated in Herbert Read's review of the exhibition in *The Listener*.

Buhler's mother, by then separated from his father, ran a bookshop and café in Charlotte Street, frequented by staff and students of the nearby Euston Road School; from 1937 Buhler became acquainted with them, but did not attend the school himself. He was, however, influenced by their approach to painting, using restrained colour and close tones for the composition of soberly executed portraits, still lifes, landscapes, and urban scenes. The Contemporary Art Society bought his portrait of Stephen Spender, then a student at the Euston Road School, in 1938. Buhler shared exhibitions with Vivian Pitchforth and also with Lawrence Gowing in the early 1940s, while serving in the Auxiliary Fire Service during the Second World War. In 1945 he began teaching at the Central School of Arts and Crafts in London, and also at the Chelsea School of Art. He exhibited at the Royal Academy (RA) in 1945, at the New English Art Club (becoming a member in 1946), and at the Royal Society of British Artists. In 1947 he was elected ARA, and the following year joined the London Group. He was invited in 1948 by Robert (Robin) Darwin to teach at the RCA. He was an intelligent and sensitive teacher, who encouraged students of very varied talents. His first one-man show was at the Leicester Galleries in 1950, and in 1956 he was made an RA, one of the youngest until then to achieve that distinction.

In 1975 Buhler became a trustee of the RA. In that year he resigned from the staff of the RCA, and travelled very widely in Europe and the United States over the next few years. In 1982 he won the Wollaston award for the most distinguished exhibit at the RA, *Water-Meadow Dusk*, and in 1984 he won the Hunting Group prize for *Vineyards, Neufchâtel*. His work is in the permanent collections of national and provincial galleries all over the world. In addition to his many commissioned portraits, Buhler painted a number of portraits of his friends and fellow artists for his own satisfaction. In his later work he tended to seek an underlying geometry or pattern in nature. His oil paintings were matt in texture, brush strokes were almost suppressed, and detail was all but eliminated in favour of muted but luminous blocks of colour.

(H. G.) Rodrigo Moynihan's group portrait, *The Painting School Teaching Staff of the RCA* (1949–52), depicts Buhler, of average height, dark-haired, and handsome, with dark eyebrows and a markedly cleft chin, wearing a dark suit, standing at the centre of the composition with his hand on the back of a chair. A sophisticated man of cosmopolitan background, he was a sociable and witty person. On 12 February 1938 he married Eveline Mary (b. 1915/16), daughter of William Gadsby Rowell, joiner. They were divorced in 1951. They had one son, and Buhler was also the father of a daughter, the mother of whom he did not marry. On 5 April 1962 he married Prudence Mary Brochocka (b. 1929/30), whose previous marriage was dissolved, daughter of Hubert William Hastings Beaumont, solicitor. They had two sons, and were divorced in 1971. Buhler died at his home, Flat 5, 38 Onslow Square, Chelsea, London, on 20 June 1989.   ALAN WINDSOR, *rev.*

Sources C. Hayes, *Robert Buhler* (1986) · R. Buhler, conversation with Mervyn Levy, 1984, BL NSA · *CGPLA Eng. & Wales* (1989) · m. certs.
Archives SOUND BL NSA, Robert Buhler in conversation with Mervyn Levy, 9/1984
Likenesses R. Buhler, self-portrait, oils, 1948, unknown collection; copyprint, NPG [*see illus.*] · L. H. Rosoman, acrylic, 1979–84, NPG · H. G. R. Moynihan, portrait, repro. in H. G. R. Moynihan, *The painting school teaching staff of the RCA* (1949–52)

Wealth at death £174,090: probate, 11 Oct 1989, *CGPLA Eng. & Wales*

Buissière [Bussière], **Paul** (d. 1739), surgeon and anatomist, was a native of France, and a protestant who had left his country on account of his religion. Before leaving France he had practised with distinction in the principality of Orange. He settled in the first instance at Copenhagen, then, after moving to Britain, was naturalized on 10 October 1688. He afterwards based himself in Suffolk Street, Pall Mall, London, where he rapidly attained the highest reputation and success. He was the surgeon who attended Robert Harley when he was stabbed at the privy council table by the marquis de Guiscard, in March 1711; he also attended the attacker after his committal to Newgate, and was called in to the consultation on the last illness of Queen Caroline. Lord Hervey, in writing of the last event in November 1737, states that 'although fourscore years old the king and queen had a great opinion of [Buissière], and preferred [him] to every other man of his profession'.

Buissière was one of the first to introduce a course of lectures on anatomy and physiology into England. He had been approved as a fellow of the Royal Society on 22 March 1699, and was transferred from the 'Persons of other nations' category to the main list in 1713. To the *Philosophical Transactions* he contributed six papers on anatomical topics. Other papers are to be found in the *Mémoires* of the Academy of Sciences, Paris, of which he became a corresponding member in March 1699, and in the *Acta Eruditorum*. He also maintained a scientific correspondence with Sir Hans Sloane, which was preserved in the archives of the Royal Society. Buissière died at his house in

Paul Buissière (d. 1739), by unknown artist

Suffolk Street in January 1739. His will, dated 19 July 1737, was proved on 22 January 1739. By it he bequeathed the sum of £200 to the French hospital in London, of which he had been elected governor in 1729.

GORDON GOODWIN, *rev.* MICHAEL BEVAN

Sources D. C. A. Agnew, *Protestant exiles from France in the reign of Louis XIV, or, The Huguenot refugees and their descendants in Great Britain and Ireland*, 2nd edn, 3 vols. (1871–4) • E. Haag and E. Haag, *La France protestante*, 10 vols. (Paris, 1846–59) • Nichols, *Lit. anecdotes* • J. Hervey, *Memoirs of the reign of George the Second*, ed. J. W. Croker, 2 vols. (1848) • will, PRO, PROB 11/694, sig. 3 • *GM*, 1st ser., 7 (1737), 699 • J. S. Burn, *The history of the French, Walloon, Dutch and other foreign protestant refugees settled in England …* (1846) • M. Hunter, *The Royal Society and its fellows, 1660–1700: the morphology of an early scientific institution*, 2nd edn (1994)
Likenesses portrait, RS [*see illus.*]
Wealth at death £200 to the French hospital, London: will, PRO, PROB 11/694, sig. 3

Buist, George (1804–1860), newspaper editor and scientist, was born at Tannadice, Forfarshire, on 17 November 1804, the second of the nine children of the Revd John Buist (1752/3–1845) and his wife, Margaret Jafferson. After being taught at home by his father until 1817 he was educated at St Salvador's and St Mary's colleges, St Andrews University. (He was awarded an honorary doctorate by St Andrews University in the early 1840s.) In 1824 he enrolled as an occasional student of theology and church history at the University of Edinburgh, and in 1826 he qualified as a minister. He preached irregularly for six years, while pursuing skilful amateur studies in geology, topography, and natural history. In 1832 he became editor of the *Dundee Courier* (subsequently *The Constitutional*), and used the paper to oppose what he saw as the excessive liberalism of his times. In 1834, having quarrelled with his partners, he established a rival journal, the *Dundee Guardian*, and also the *Scottish Agricultural Magazine*, both short-lived ventures. In 1835 he accepted the editorship of the *Perth Constitutional*, followed in November 1837 by that of the tory *Fifeshire Journal*. In November 1839 he sought and won the editorship of the *Bombay Times*.

Buist soon dominated Bombay's literary and scientific circles. From 1842 until 1845 he held the honorary position of inspector of the Colaba observatory, superintending the recording of over 300,000 observations and the production of numerous meteorological reports. He was also secretary to the Geographical Society of Bombay and the Agri-Horticultural Society of Western India, and experimented, at his own cost, with the reclamation of local salt flats for vegetable cultivation. In 1850, under Lord Elphinstone's patronage, he founded the Bombay Reformatory School of Industry. He formed the geological collection for the museum of Elphinstone College, Bombay. He published papers in the transactions of most of Bombay's scientific societies.

Buist's personal life in India was marred by the death in May 1845 of his first wife, Jessie Hadow (*b.* 1817/18), daughter of Dr Hunter, professor of logic at St Andrews. They had married on 4 December 1843 after a long courtship. After Jessie's death Buist returned to Britain for a few months and while there prepared for publication the compendious *Bombay Observatory Report for 1844*. He also obtained funding from the Admiralty to establish, on his return journey to Bombay, twelve observatories from Cape Comorin to the Red Sea for meteorological and tidal research.

In 1846 Buist was appointed to the honorary position of sheriff of Bombay. On 12 November of that year, in Bombay, he married Anna-Maria, daughter of Joseph Dillon. She was to survive him, along with a daughter, Katherine Anna, born in 1847. A son, George Alexander, died in infancy.

Buist was initially considered a competent editor. He opposed the policy of retaliation after the Kabul massacres of 1842 and relentlessly criticized the invasion of Sind. In 1852 he backed the attempts of prominent Indians in Bombay to found a pressure group along the lines of Calcutta's British Indian Association, and in 1853, on leave in Britain, he appeared before the select committee on Indian government in defence of the Anglo-Indian press. In time, however, his strident, combative tone was seen to compromise the paper's independence. Deteriorating relations with the paper's Parsi proprietors came to a head during the rebellion of 1857. Buist was in Britain when fighting broke out, having left the paper in the hands of Roger Knight who, alone of all the Anglo-Indian editors, supported Canning's policy of conciliation. Having hurried back to Bombay, Buist reversed Knight's editorial line and poured forth leaders vilifying Indians. On 23 December 1857, offended at his indiscriminate hatred, Buist's Parsi employers sacked him, whereupon local Scots came to his aid with capital to start a rival daily, the *Bombay Standard*. This lasted barely a year before being absorbed into the *Bombay Times* as the *Bombay Times and Standard*.

The affair was an unhappy end to Buist's long association with Bombay's public-spirited community of educated Indians and Europeans. In 1859 he accepted the post of superintendent of the government press at Allahabad, but before he could settle into the job he succumbed to dysentery, at Calcutta, on 1 October 1860. He was buried the following day at St Andrew's Church, Calcutta.

KATHERINE PRIOR

Sources G. Buist, *Memoir with testimonials, etc of George Buist, LLD* (1846) • S. C. Sanial, 'History of the press in India—Bombay', *Calcutta Review*, 130 (1910), 80–118 • ecclesiastical records, BL OIOC • D. E. Wacha, *Shells from the sands of Bombay* (1920) • *Bombay Times and Standard* (4 Oct 1860) • *GM*, 3rd ser., 9 (1860), 680 • *DNB*
Archives BL | U. Edin., New Coll. L., letters to Thomas Chalmers
Likenesses D. O. Hill and R. Adamson, print, 1845, NPG

Buíte mac Brónaig (*d.* 519/20). *See under* Meath, saints of (*act. c.*400–*c.*900).

Bülbring, Edith (1903–1990), pharmacologist and physiologist, was born on 27 December 1903 in Bonn, Germany, the youngest of four children and third daughter of Karl Daniel Bülbring, professor of English at Bonn University, and his wife, Hortense Leonore Kann, a Dutch woman, daughter of a Jewish banker's family in The Hague. Edith's father died prematurely in 1917, and his eldest child, a son,

Edith Bülbring (1903–1990), by Walter Bird

law to declare their ancestry, the fact that she was half Jewish caused her dismissal. She returned home to Bonn in late 1933.

Intending to go to Holland to practise medicine, Edith Bülbring first joined a sister and a friend on a holiday in England. While there, she visited her old chief at the Virchow Krankenhaus, Ulrich Friedemann, from Berlin, a refugee working in Sir Henry Dale's laboratory in Hampstead. Dale assumed she also was looking for a job, and contacted J. H. Burn, who was setting up a biological standardization laboratory for the Pharmaceutical Society in Bloomsbury Square, London; he offered her a post. Thus began her scientific career. When Burn was appointed to the Oxford chair of pharmacology in 1937, she moved to Oxford, where she became successively a departmental demonstrator (1937), university demonstrator and lecturer (1946), *ad hominem* reader (1960), and finally, in 1967, *ad hominem* professor. She was elected to a professorial fellowship at Lady Margaret Hall in 1960. She had been naturalized in 1948. Initially Edith Bülbring worked in collaboration with Burn on the autonomic nervous system, and the effects of catecholamines and acetylcholine and their interactions. She acted as Burn's research assistant for some fifteen years, but in her early forties began more independent research. She decided to concentrate on trying to unravel the physiology of smooth muscle, a tissue that had previously always irritated her by its unpredictability. It was here that she made the greatest impact, and she will be remembered as one of the world's most influential scientists in this field. Under her influence, the study of smooth muscles became first respectable, and then increasingly important. She published *Smooth Muscle* in 1970. The techniques developed in her laboratory led to increasing knowledge of the physiology of smooth muscle, and the activities of the many scientists who spent time working with her spread her interest and enthusiasm for these tissues throughout the world. She was elected a fellow of the Royal Society in 1958, received honorary degrees from Groningen, Louvain, and Homburg (Saar), was awarded the Schmiedebert-Plakette of the Deutsche Pharmakologische Gesellschaft in 1974 and won the Wellcome gold medal in pharmacology in 1985.

Edith Bülbring never married, but in Oxford lived first with her younger sister, Maud, in Cumnor, and then finally built a house at 15 Northmoor Road, where after Maud's death she lived with her elder sister, Lucy. In appearance Edith was not distinguished, being of medium height and build. In early photographs she looked decidedly plain, and one would have guessed that she was quiet and unassuming, but she was remembered as vivacious. Later in life she became progressively more attractive and feminine in appearance. Her health was good and she continued active work well after her official retirement. Eventually atherosclerosis led to amputation of one leg below the knee when she was in her seventies. She did not allow this to handicap her, but she had progressive loss of circulation in her other leg, and could not tolerate the thought of a second amputation. Instead, she

was killed in action in 1918. Edith was educated at the Klostermann Lyzeum, Bonn. Her father's death and the hyper-inflation of the post-war years caused a financial strain, but her mother's brothers set up accounts for the three girls, giving each a modest income for life. After a period of private tuition she entered Bonn Gymnasium in 1922 to study chemistry, physics, and mathematics for the municipal examinations, which she passed at Easter 1923, entitling her to enter Bonn University, where she started preclinical studies for medicine.

Bülbring's decision to read medicine at university was a surprise and perhaps a disappointment to her mother, since she had early shown exceptional talent as a pianist; an accomplishment that gave her and her friends considerable pleasure in later life (she had two grand pianos in Oxford). Her clinical training was undertaken in Munich, Freiburg, and Bonn, and she qualified in May 1928. She then moved to Berlin, where she spent a year as house physician and two years as research assistant to Paul Trendelenburg, an eminent professor of pharmacology and an old family friend, who thought she was wasting her talents as a physician. Unfortunately, he died of tuberculosis before Edith had become sufficiently confident to decide on a research career, and she returned to medicine in 1931, as a paediatrician for a year in Jena (Germany). This seems to have been her first paid position. She then returned to Berlin, to the infectious disease unit of the Virchow Krankenhaus. This was during the rise of Adolf Hitler and national socialism, and, when citizens were required by spent much of her last two years trying different treatments, culminating in her final operation, an attempt at a venous graft which she knew would be highly risky. The graft was probably a success, but there were multiple emboli which affected her heart and probably caused her minor strokes. She died three days later on 5 July 1990 in the John Radcliffe Hospital, Oxford.

A. F. BRADING, rev.

Sources T. B. Bolton and A. F. Brading, *Memoirs FRS*, 38 (1992), 67–95 · *The Times* (10 Sept 1993) · **Archives** Bodl. Oxf., corresp. with the Society for the Protection of Science and Learning · Wellcome L., corresp.; notebooks · **Likenesses** W. Bird, photograph, RS [*see illus.*] · photographs, repro. in Marren, *The new naturalists* · **Wealth at death** £690,136: *The Times*

Bulfin, Sir Edward Stanislaus (1862–1939), army officer, was born in Dublin on 6 November 1862, the second son of Patrick Bulfin JP, of Woodtown Park, Rathfarnham, co. Dublin, and his wife, Teresa Clare (*née* Carroll). He was educated at Stonyhurst College (1873–6), Kensington Catholic Public School, and Trinity College, Dublin, but did not take his degree. He was commissioned into the Princess of Wales's Own (Yorkshire) regiment (Green Howards) on 12 November 1884 at the age of twenty-two after militia service with the 3rd battalion Royal Irish Fusiliers. His early career was mundane. The turning point, as for many of his generation, came with the Second South African War.

Bulfin had been in South Africa since November 1898 in the congenial appointment of assistant military secretary and aide-de-camp to his fellow Irishman and fellow Roman Catholic, Lieutenant-General Sir William Butler. All careers need a slice of luck. Bulfin's came in the summer of 1899 when he escaped the fate of his chief, who was recalled after tendering unwelcome advice to the British government. By November 1899 he found himself brigade major, 1st (guards) brigade, under Lord Methuen. He saw action at Belmont, Enslin, Modder River, and Magersfontein. His performance not only won him a staff promotion to deputy assistant adjutant-general (DAAG) but also the command of a mobile column with the opportunity to establish a reputation as a field commander. Bulfin had married Frances Mary Lonergan (*d.* 1947) on 11 January 1898. They had a son and a daughter.

After the Second South African War, Bulfin's career took the staff path. From 1902 until 1904 he was DAAG with 1st corps; from 1906 until 1910 assistant adjutant and quartermaster-general (AAQMG), Cape Colony. On his return he was given command of the Essex infantry brigade, Territorial Force. It was unusual to reach this level without having commanded a battalion. In June 1913 he was promoted to the prestigious command of the 2nd infantry brigade. He took this unit to war in August 1914 with the original British expeditionary force (BEF) and commanded it throughout the epic fighting of 1914.

During 1914 Bulfin established a reputation among his peers as an outstanding fighting soldier. The desperate days round Ypres at the end of October 1914 displayed Bulfin's courage, steadfastness, and powers of leadership at their best. On 31 October, at the critical moment of the first battle of Ypres, with Gheluvelt lost and reserves exhausted, he organized a scratch force of six weak battalions known as 'Bulfin's force' and led a counter-attack which drove back the German line half a mile. He was wounded on the following day.

In December 1914 he returned to command the newly raised 28th division, a regular unit. He commanded this in heavy fighting during the German gas attack at Ypres in April 1915 and again towards the end of the battle of Loos in October. On 11 October 1915 he returned to England sick and thus avoided being sent to Salonika with his division. He returned to the western front in June 1916 in command of the 60th (2nd / 2nd London) division, a territorial unit; 60th division was sent to Salonika in the following December, but Bulfin spent only six months in that malarial backwater. In June 1917 60th division was transferred to the Egyptian expeditionary force under the new and invigorating command of General Sir Edmund Allenby. Bulfin soon caught Allenby's eye. On 2 August 1917 he was promoted temporary lieutenant-general and given command of 21st corps.

As a corps commander Bulfin displayed those same qualities of steadfastness and dependability which had brought him to notice. Allenby knew his man. He saw Bulfin as a bludgeon, his other corps commander (and fellow cavalryman), Sir Philip Chetwode (general officer commanding, 20th corps), as a rapier. This was a cause of some resentment to Bulfin, but there was much work for the bludgeon in the harsh hills of Judaea. At the decisive battle of Megiddo (September 1918) a reinforced 21st corps was given the key role, smashing through the Turkish defences and paving the way for the cavalry to inflict an overwhelming defeat. Bulfin was appointed KCB in 1918.

Bulfin was a man of moral as well as physical courage, never afraid to tell his superiors uncomfortable truths. His penetrating grey eyes could instil fear as well as respect in his subordinates, but he never lost the regimental officer's concern for the welfare of his men and he could bestow praise as well as blame, a characteristic not always common in regular officers of his generation but an important consideration in a man whose corps command included many citizen soldiers.

General Sir Edward Bulfin retired from the army on 1 January 1926. He died on 20 August 1939 at his home, 5 Woodland Avenue, Boscombe, Bournemouth, Hampshire, and was buried in Bournemouth cemetery on 23 August. His son, Captain James Joseph Bulfin MC, died in Palestine in 1929 while serving with the 2nd battalion Green Howards.

J. M. BOURNE

Sources G. MacMunn and C. Falls, *Military operations: Egypt and Palestine*, 3 vols., History of the Great War (1928–30) · C. Falls, *Armageddon, 1918* (1964) · Marquess of Anglesey [G. C. H. V. Paget], *A history of the British cavalry, 1816 to 1919*, 5 (1994) · L. James, *Imperial warrior. The life and times of Field-Marshal Viscount Allenby, 1861–1936* (1993) · G. de S. Barrow, *The fire of life* (1942) [autobiography] · *Stonyhurst Magazine*, 341 (July 1940), 391–3 · *The Times* (22 Aug 1939) · *The Times* (24 Aug 1939) · *DNB* · Burke, *Peerage* · *WWW* · **Archives** FILM IWM FVA, actuality footage · IWM FVA, news footage

Likenesses J. McEvoy, portrait, 1918, IWM · W. Stoneman, photograph, 1920, NPG · F. Irwin, photograph, Stonyhurst College; repro. in F. Irwin and C. Chichester-Constable, *Stonyhurst war record* (1927), xii · St. H. Lauder, portrait, regimental depot, Green Howards, Richmond, Yorkshire · photograph, repro. in *The Times* (22 Aug 1939) · photograph, repro. in *The Times history of the war*, 3 (1915), 456

Bulger, James Patrick (1990–1993), murder victim, was born in Liverpool on 16 March 1990, the first child of Ralph S. Bulger (*b*. 1964) and his wife, Denise Matthews (*b*. 1965). A younger brother was born after his death, and his parents separated in 1994. The family lived in Kirkby, Lancashire. James Bulger was an attractive, soft-featured child with fair skin, blue eyes, and light-brown tousled hair; he was 2 feet 6 inches tall when he died.

On 12 February 1993 James accompanied his mother to the Strand shopping centre in Bootle, whence he was abducted by Robert Thompson and Jon Venables, both aged ten, who were playing truant from school. They walked with him for 2½ miles, meeting *en route* many adults who did nothing to intervene, despite his obvious distress. The boys took him to a railway line near Walton Lane police station and Anfield cemetery. There, shortly before dusk, they subjected him to cruel indignities before battering him to death using bricks and an iron bar. His body (subsequently further damaged by a passing train) was found on 14 February. The police had meanwhile released poignant, grainy photographs taken from a security surveillance video camera of two unknown boys leading the child away from the shopping centre. This led to the identification of Thompson and Venables, who on 20 February were charged with James's abduction and murder, and with the attempted abduction of another child on the same day.

James's murder precipitated an anguished national debate on the moral state of Britain, especially about the nature of evil, the possibly innate depravity of some children, the vulnerability of children, urban deprivation, the 'sickness' in society, and the failure of adults collectively to take responsibility for children's welfare. In a speech at Wellingborough on 19 February, the shadow home secretary, Tony Blair, summarized reactions.

> The news bulletins of the last week have been like hammer blows struck against the sleeping conscience of the country, urging us to wake up and look unflinchingly at what we see. We hear of crimes so horrific they provoke anger and disbelief in equal proportions … These are the ugly manifestations of a society that is becoming unworthy of that name. (Rentoul, 200)

His call for communities as well as individuals to recover their moral identity struck a responsive chord in public opinion. James's murder led the prime minister, John Major, to declare a national crusade against crime, insisting that 'society needs to condemn a little more, and understand a little less' (Smith, 2; *The Times*, 22 Feb 1993, 1; *Oxford Dictionary of Twentieth-Century Quotations*, 204). A mistaken belief that James's murder was linked to 'video nasties', cheap horror films with titles such as *Child's Play 3*, was one factor behind the stricter censorship rules introduced in 1994.

The trial of Thompson and Venables opened on 1 November 1993 at Preston crown court and ended with their conviction on 24 November. They were the youngest people to be convicted of murder in British criminal history. The trial judge, Sir Michael Morland, recommended that they serve a minimum of eight years. Subsequently Lord Chief Justice Taylor of Gosforth raised their minimum sentence to ten years. After James's parents had collected 207,000 signatures for a petition that the murderers be imprisoned for their lifetimes, the home secretary, Michael Howard, in 1994, imposed a minimum tariff of fifteen years. This was characterized by Lord Donaldson of Lymington as 'institutionalised vengeance' by 'a politician playing to the gallery' (*The Times*, 10 Oct 1995, 2). The European Court of Human Rights in 1999 rejected Thompson's and Venables's claim that their trial had amounted to inhuman or degrading treatment, but found that they had been denied a fair hearing by being exposed to a public trial in an adult court. This judgment aroused widespread public distaste. In the same court in 1999 lawyers representing James's parents argued in vain that victims of crime should have a right to help determine criminals' sentences. Following a further judgment by Lord Chief Justice Woolf in 2000, and despite considerable media disquiet, Thompson and Venables were released on parole in 2001, with new identities and with the media restrained by law from seeking them out and reporting on their whereabouts.

A memorial garden was established in James's memory in Sacred Heart primary school, Westhead Avenue, Northwood, Kirkby, the school James would have attended had he lived. RICHARD DAVENPORT-HINES

Sources D. J. Smith, *The sleep of reason* (1994) · B. Morrison, *As if* (1997) · *The Times* (14–15 Feb 1993) · *The Times* (18 Feb 1993) · *The Times* (21–2 Feb 1993) · *The Times* (24 Feb 1993) · *The Times* (2–25 Nov 1993) · *The Times* (5–6 Nov 1994) · J. Sopel, *Tony Blair* (1995), 156–7 · J. Rentoul, *Tony Blair* (2001), 200–1 · *Oxford dictionary of twentieth-century quotations* (1998) · b. cert.
Archives FILM security video footage from the Strand shopping centre, Bootle, 12 February 1993
Likenesses photographs, 1993?

Bulkeley, Arthur (*c*.1495–1553), bishop of Bangor, was the son of Richard Bulkeley, a merchant of Beaumaris, Anglesey. His claim to kinship with the first Sir Richard Bulkeley, courtier and agent of Thomas Cromwell, was acknowledged by Sir Richard, whose influence was instrumental in his progress. On 2 May 1524 he supplicated to the University of Oxford, as a BCL with twelve years' study and practice in civil and canon law, to proceed to BCnL and DCnL and was accordingly admitted in 1525. He had been rector of St Peter-le-Bailey, Oxford, since 1 June 1523. Subsequent livings indicate links with London and north Wales, including prebends of Bangor and St Asaph cathedrals, but his occupancy of livings in north Wales was challenged in disputes after 1537 in which Thomas Cromwell supported his opponents. From 15 July 1531 he was also rector of St James Garlickhythe, London, probably incidental to his career as an ecclesiastical lawyer. Recorded as proctor in the Oxford chancellor's court in

1520, he was admitted on 16 April 1526 to the College of Advocates and by 1537 was a master in chancery. From *c*.1530 he was chaplain to Charles Brandon, duke of Suffolk, through whom he had contact with the royal court and was involved in the debate over religious change, affirming his support for the six articles in 1539. This may reflect political support of Henry VIII against the more radical Cromwell, with whom Bulkeley was then out of favour, rather than theological conservatism.

Bulkeley seems to have served Cromwell until the spring of 1537, and had direct knowledge of Cromwell's disparaging view of religious and social conditions in a diocese as remote from London as Bangor. Cromwell, he reported, was 'offended at the incestuous and abominable living both of priests and laymen therein' (*LP Henry VIII*, 12/2, no. 255). He recommended himself about June 1537 as a commissary who, with previous experience as proctor of Bangor, would restore discipline among its clergy, but was refused. He was clearly out of favour by November 1537, and Sir Richard Bulkeley's recommendation that he should become Cromwell's chaplain in October 1537 was rejected. As signatory to the declaration of the convocations of Canterbury and York on 9 July 1540 annulling the Cleves marriage he was clearly opposed to Cromwell, whose fall in July 1540 improved his fortune.

Operating as intermediary between centre and locality, in 1529 Bulkeley represented the deans of both Bangor and St Asaph at convocation and was proctor for the Bangor clergy; in 1537 he was described as a proctor who had served the king well in that diocese. On 8 June 1536 he attended the chapter at St Asaph that elected the conservative Robert Wharton as bishop. His appointment as bishop of Bangor late in 1541 to succeed John Bird must be seen against this background of legal expertise, intimacy with the court and central administration, unfailing support of the crown, and an awareness of local conditions. Elected on 18 November, he was consecrated in St Paul's on 19 February 1542 by John Bird, having already been licensed on 23 October 1541 to hold *in commendam* for three years four rectories and two prebends to supplement Bangor's meagre income; he resigned all rectories by October 1544.

Acclaimed as the first resident bishop of Bangor and the first born in north Wales for over a century, Bulkeley continued to spend periods in London during Henry's reign, being present at court on 27 May 1543, attending parliament in January 1547, and taking part in Henry VIII's funeral ceremony in February 1547, but was less active there during Edward VI's reign and was absent from parliament during the religious debates of 1549–52. This has been interpreted as evidence of private unease with radical protestant doctrine. Nevertheless, at Bangor itself, he actively promoted the crown's religious policy. His injunctions of 1542 aimed to improve spiritual conditions by ordering priests to instruct in the vernacular, recognizing Welsh rather than English as the vernacular of his diocese—he was the first modern prelate known to have acknowledged the desirability of using Welsh. His views parallel those of Sir John Price, whose translations of the

creed, the Pater noster, and the ten commandments were included in the first Welsh printed book, *Yny lhyvyr hwnn …* (1546). They may well have met in the course of ecclesiastical administration; both were commissioners to inquire into the chantries in Wales in 1546. This insistence on using the vernacular, and his charge that schoolmasters and heads of families should join clerics in instruction, suggest concern for reform; Bulkeley's visitation articles of 1551, based on those of Ridley for London, indicate further accommodation with protestantism before his death. He bequeathed to the cathedral two English bibles, and his private library included humanist works approved by reformers, such as Erasmus's *Paraphrase upon the Epistles* in English. Though unmarried himself, he certainly tolerated clerical marriage after it was sanctioned in February 1549; over 16 per cent of the Bangor clergy were ejected during the Marian campaign against married clergy after December 1553, including his dean, Robert Evans.

Bulkeley drew on his legal skills to assert diocesan interests, with mixed results. Prolonged litigation to secure rights of presentation in a dispute with the Catholic apologist John Gwynneth failed, culminating in Bulkeley's attainder on 17 June 1544 for contravening the Statute of Provisors and for maintaining papal authority, although his actions as bishop contradict this accusation. He was granted a pardon on 21 July 1544. He had greater success in securing clerical discipline by depriving George Woolflete, the non-resident rector of Tywyn, Merioneth, in 1546 for not paying clerical taxes. Such action earned him a reputation as protector of the diocese and a good canonist. His well-ordered register commencing in 1542, a record of ordinations from 1544, and early eighteenth-century transcripts of other documents indicate sound administration and a mind well versed in legal processes. He also took care of the fabric of the cathedral, and his bequest of books to the dean and chapter expressly to establish a library at Bangor suggests humanist endeavour. A tradition recorded by Francis Godwin in 1616 that he was struck blind as divine punishment for selling five cathedral bells had no currency in Bangor, but Bulkeley's will of 1553 noted money raised from the sale of cathedral goods and used by the advice of the chapter to repair the church. He was also accused of impoverishing the see by making long leases and alienating advowsons, sometimes granting church property and key benefices to the Bulkeley family, but the *acta* of Bangor do not reveal alienation on a scale larger than during any other episcopate. He died on 14 March 1553 in the bishop's residence at Bangor. His will instructed that he be buried in the choir of the cathedral; the grave is unmarked.   NIA M. W. POWELL

Sources *LP Henry VIII*, vols. 4–5, 11–12, 14–19, 21 · PRO, SC1/16/377; SC2/3/56–8; SC2/16/376–8; SC/2/33/71; C3/28/27; C3/16/7; C2Eliz/ B11/19; SP1/111/89; SP1/112/260; SP1/116/117v–118r; SP1/117/10v–11r; SP1/120/4; SP1/126/35 · NL Wales, B/BR/1 (ii), fol. 16; B/BR/2; ECE/ SA/145 [1832 return]; B/MISC/227–228; B/MISC/27; B/DL/138, 141, 142, 400, 437, 439 · B. Willis, *A survey of the cathedral church of Bangor* (1721), 101–4, 247–62, 331–6, 342 · *Fasti Angl., 1300–1541*, [Welsh dioceses], 5, 16, 48 · Wood, *Ath. Oxon.*, new edn, 1.247; 2.764–8 · Emden, *Oxf.*, 4.81–2 · D. C. Jones, 'The Bulkeleys of Baron Hill,

1440–1621', MA diss., U. Wales, Bangor, 1958, 73–92, 336–57, 384–404, pedigree 7 · G. Williams, *Wales and the Reformation* (1997), 65–7, 120–22, 145, 171–2, 181, 185–6, 196–7 · U. Wales, Bangor, Baron Hill MSS 570, 1425, 1428, 1676, 1731 · Anglesey plea roll, 1509–17, U. Wales, Bangor, Porth yr Aur Additional MSS, memb. 3, 27, 29, 32–3 · U. Wales, Bangor, Henblas MS 4, 255–7 · *CSP dom.*, 1547–53, nos. 16, 431 · A. I. Pryce, *The diocese of Bangor in the sixteenth century* (1923), 6, 8, 9–14, 48–9, 85 · LPL, Cranmer register, fols. 160, 171v, 178, 277v · Bodl. Oxf., MS Jesus College 115, fols. 379–86 · Bodl. Oxf., MSS Willis 41, fols. 333–71; 50; 66, fols. 195–218; 72, fols. 167–72 · W. H. Frere and W. P. M. Kennedy, eds., *Visitation articles and injunctions of the period of the Reformation*, 2, Alcuin Club, Collections, 15 (1910), 262–6 · *Reg. Oxf.*, 1.99 · R. R. Hughes, *Biographical epitomes of the bishops and clergy of the diocese of Bangor from the Reformation to the reconstitution*, pt 9 (Bishops) (1932) · F. Godwin, *De praesulibus Angliae commentarius* (1616), 650 · Foster, *Alum. Oxon.*, 1500–1714, 1.207 · T. Richards, *Baron Hill MSS*, 1 (1938) · E. G. Jones and J. R. V. Johnston, *Catalogue of the Bangor Cathedral Library* (1961)

Archives Bodl. Oxf., Ashmole MSS; Jesus College MSS; Willis MSS; Wood MSS · NL Wales, Bangor diocesan records

Wealth at death personal estate, incl. furnishings and books: will

Bulkeley, Launcelot (1568/9–1650), Church of Ireland archbishop of Dublin, was probably born in Beaumaris, Anglesey, one of the six surviving children of Sir Richard Bulkeley (*c*.1523/4–1572) of Beaumaris and of Cheadle in Cheshire, MP for Anglesey, and his second wife, Agnes (*d*. 1623), daughter of Thomas Needham of Stanton, Shropshire. Agnes Bulkeley was accused of poisoning her husband, but on 7 July 1575 she reached legal settlement with Bulkeley's half-brother Sir Richard *Bulkeley (*c*.1540–1621). Launcelot Bulkeley had ten half-siblings from his father's first marriage to Margaret, daughter of John Savage of Clifton, Cheshire, and further half-siblings from his mother's second marriage, to Lawrence Cranage.

Bulkeley entered Brasenose College, Oxford, as a commoner in 1587. He graduated BA on 10 February 1591 and then moved to St Edmund Hall, Oxford, from where he proceeded MA on 28 June 1593. On 13 November 1593 he was ordained deacon by Hugh Bellot, bishop of Bangor, and ordained priest the following year. He became rector of Llanddyfnan and later acquired the livings of Llandegfan and Beaumaris, all in Anglesey. His wife, Alice (*d*. 1652), daughter of Roland Bulkeley, came from Conwy. They had three children, William, Grissell, and Mary. In 1613 he became archdeacon of Dublin, and was promoted to archbishop in 1619. In 1623 he revived the controversy over the primacy of the Irish church, but in 1634 Thomas Wentworth, lord deputy, settled the case in favour of the archbishops of Armagh. He was awarded the degree of doctor of divinity by the University of Dublin. The pamphlet *Proposals for Sending Back the Nobility, and Gentry of Ireland* was attributed to him by John D'Alton, but this was probably written by his son William (*d*. 1671), archdeacon of Dublin from 1636. Bulkeley was a member of the Irish privy council and from 1634 was treasurer of Cashel. He accrued land in Dublin, Wicklow, and Kildare. He vigorously pursued Catholic recusants through regular visitations of his diocese (returns for 1630 survive as Trinity College, Dublin, MS 843/13) and through prosecution for non-payment of recusancy fines. On St Stephen's day 1629 he raided a Catholic mass in a Carmelite friary and was

stoned in the street. In 1638 he signed the black oath, repudiating the Scottish national covenant. After 1641 he seems to have only irregularly signed council letters reporting on the Irish rising. In 1646 he signed the peace forged between the marquess of Ormond and the confederate Catholics. With Dublin in the hands of the English Commonwealth he was stripped of his lands and honours on 8 March 1649 and was imprisoned for using the Book of Common Prayer, prohibited by the English parliament in 1647. He died at Tallaght, co. Dublin, on 8 September 1650, aged eighty-one, and was buried in St Patrick's Cathedral, reputedly under the communion table.

T. F. HENDERSON, *rev.* AMANDA L. CAPERN

Sources E. G. Jones, ed., 'History of the Bulkeley family (National Library of Wales, MS 9080E)', *Transactions of the Anglesey Antiquarian Society and Field Club* (1948), 1–99 · Wood, *Ath. Oxon.*, new edn, 4.806–7 · [C. B. Heberden], ed., *Brasenose College register, 1509–1909*, 1, OHS, 55 (1909), 71 · J. D'Alton, *The memoirs of the archbishops of Dublin* (1838), 258–75 · H. Cotton, *Fasti ecclesiae Hibernicae*, 1–5 (1845–60) · *The whole works of Sir James Ware concerning Ireland*, ed. and trans. W. Harris, rev. edn, 1 (1764), 355–6 · Fuller, *Worthies* · O. T. Bulkeley, *Pedigree of the ancient family of Bulkeley* (1902) · 'Archbishop Bulkeley's visitation of Dublin, 1630', ed. M. V. Ronan, *Archivium Hibernicum*, 8 (1941), 56–98 · G. Ormerod, *The history of the county palatine and city of Chester*, 3 (1819), 137, 320 · J. P. Earwaker, *East Cheshire: past and present, or, A history of the hundred of Macclesfield*, 1 (1877), 171–81 · J. E. Griffith, *Pedigrees of Anglesey and Carnarvonshire families* (privately printed, Horncastle, 1914) · R. Bagwell, *Ireland under the Stuarts*, 1 (1909); repr. (1963), 186–7, 206–7, 239, 274 · W. A. Phillips, ed., *History of the Church of Ireland*, 3 (1933), 6–7 · *Calendar of the manuscripts of the marquess of Ormonde*, new ser., 8 vols., HMC, 36 (1902–20), vol. 2 · T. W. Moody and others, eds., *A new history of Ireland*, 3: *Early modern Ireland, 1534–1691* (1976), 241–2; repr. with corrections (1991) · Beecham's genealogical abstracts, PRO

Archives TCD, record of visitation, MS 843/13

Bulkeley, Peter (1583–1659), minister in America, was born on 31 January 1583 in Odell, Bedfordshire, to Dr Edward Bulkeley, rector of Odell (*d*. 1621), and his wife, Olive (Olyff) Irby. He studied at St John's College, Cambridge, where, in 1605, he graduated BA and became a fellow; he proceeded MA in 1608. Ordained at Ely, he became a prebendary of Lichfield Cathedral in 1609; the following year he was named university preacher at Cambridge and succeeded his father as rector of Odell; in the same year he was incorporated at Oxford. He inherited substantial property—a gentleman's estate, says Cotton Mather, whose *Magnalia Christi Americana* is the main source for Bulkeley's life and character. With two wives, Jane Allen (*c*.1588–1626) and Grace Chetwode (*c*.1602–1669), he had thirteen children; sons Edward, John, and Gershom followed him into the ministry.

A discreet nonconforming clergyman, Bulkeley enjoyed the protection of John Williams, bishop of Lincoln, until 1635, when he was silenced by Archbishop William Laud. Later that year he sold his property and took his family and servants to New England, where he settled for a time at Newtown (later Cambridge) in the Massachusetts Bay Colony. In 1636, with other proprietors, he founded the town of Concord at Musketaquid, some 20 miles inland from Boston, on lands purchased from Native Americans.

There he acquired large holdings of land as well as interests in a gristmill and an ironworks.

In July 1636 Bulkeley led Concord's settlers in forming the Bay Colony's twelfth church; in April 1637 he and John Jones were installed as the new congregation's teacher and pastor respectively. After Jones migrated to Connecticut in 1644, accompanied by a good many of Concord's people, Bulkeley filled both offices. Prominent members of the Boston church, such as the governor, Henry Vane, and John Cotton, boycotted his ordination service at Newtown for doctrinal reasons. Bulkeley had already sparred with Cotton on the subject of the union of believers with Christ, a central issue in the so-called antinomian controversy, which was then developing.

Bulkeley appears in Mather's pages as a learned, diligent preacher, an earnest catechizer, a strict sabbath keeper, and a stickler for plain garb and short hair—the image of a puritan's puritan. His relations with his flock were marked by tensions arising from the 'great exactness of his piety' (Mather, 1.402). But although he took a relatively high view of clerical prerogatives, and his congregation sometimes chafed against his autocratic temper, Mather says he held their affection by 'a sort of winning and yet prudent familiarity' and commanded their respect by force of moral character (ibid., 1.401–2). He seems to have led the colony's churches in the practice of publicly catechizing on the sabbath. He pursued a liberal policy on baptism of church members' children, anticipating the half-way covenant of 1662. Laypeople's narratives of religious experience, such as those of John Fiske or Thomas Shepard, attest to his pastoral power.

Concord's remoteness and Bulkeley's physical infirmities kept him from participating very actively in the colony's public affairs, but he served, with Thomas Hooker, as moderator of the synod of 1637 that condemned theological positions held by, or attributed to, Anne Hutchinson and her associates, and he joined in harrying Hutchinson out of the Boston church in 1638. In the years that followed, Bulkeley and Cotton conducted an amiable correspondence on theological matters.

Bulkeley's work *The Gospel-Covenant, or, The Covenant of Grace Opened* originated as sermons preached in response to the antinomian challenge. Published in quarto in London in 1646, with a revised edition in 1651 (reissued 1674), these sermons defined a salient element of New England's emergent orthodoxy; their effects can be traced in British religious thought, particularly in the development of covenant or federal theology. Fervidly millennial and committed to New England's puritan mission, Bulkeley followed John Winthrop in promoting New England as a 'Citie upon an hill … a Beacon on the top of a mountaine' (Bulkeley, *Gospel-Covenant*, 1646, 15).

Bulkeley's exposition of covenant theology sweeps a broad field of doctrinal topics and experiential concerns. Focal among the issues he addressed are the means of grace, the role and place of faith in the process of redemption, the relations of justification and sanctification, union with Christ, and assurance of salvation. Current scholarship views him as a leading exponent of 'preparationist' principles. His book has been seen as formally sustaining divine preveniency while tilting the scale towards human agency both substantively, by stressing conditions attached to the covenant of grace, and rhetorically, by encouraging efforts to perform those conditions. He is believed to have translated one or two psalms for the *Bay Psalm Book* of 1640. Mather reproduces some of his Latin verses. An elegy in English to Thomas Hooker, by P. B., appears in Nathaniel Morton's *New-Englands Memoriall* (1669).

Little is known about Bulkeley's later life. He died in Concord on 9 March 1659, aged seventy-six. His will left his house and outbuildings, some 1600 acres, a mill, cash, and books to his wife, five surviving children, and the widow of a sixth, with the proviso that these latter legatees not 'prove disobedient to their mother, or otherwise vitious & wicked' ('Will of Peter Bulkely', 168). He had earlier given a portion of his library to Harvard College.

MICHAEL McGIFFERT

Sources C. Mather, *Magnalia Christi Americana*, 3rd edn, 7 bks in 2 vols. (1853–5) · *DNB* · D. L. Jacobus, *The Bulkeley genealogy* (1933) · R. C. Anderson, G. F. Sanborn, and M. L. Sanborn, eds., *The great migration: immigrants to New England, 1634–1635*, 1 (Boston, MA, 1999), 459–65 · M. McGiffert, 'The problem of the covenant in puritan thought: Peter Bulkeley's *Gospel-covenant*', *New England Historical and Genealogical Register*, 130 (1976), 107–29 · 'Will of Peter Bulkely', *New England Historical and Genealogical Register*, 10 (1856), 167–70 · B. Brook, *The lives of the puritans*, 3 vols. (1813) · *The correspondence of John Cotton*, ed. S. Bush (2001) · D. D. Hall, ed., *The antinomian controversy, 1636–1638: a documentary history*, 2nd edn (Durham, NC, 1990) · E. B. Holifield, *The covenant sealed* (1974) · E. Johnson, *Johnson's wonder-working providence*, ed. J. F. Jameson (1910) · J. Knight, *Orthodoxies in Massachusetts* (1994) · 'Letter from certain ministers and others of New England to Cromwell' (1650), *Collections of the Massachusetts Historical Society*, 4th ser., 2 (1854), 115–18 · P. Bulkeley, letter to Governor Endicott and Deputy Governor Bellingham, *Collections of the Massachusetts Historical Society*, 3rd ser., 1 (1825), 48–9 · S. E. Morison, *The tercentennial history of Harvard College and University, 1636–1936*, 1: *The founding of Harvard College* (1935) · N. Morton, *New-Englands memoriall* (1669) · D. Neal, *The history of the puritans or protestant nonconformists*, ed. J. Toulmin, new edn, 2 (1822), 239 · N. Pettit, *The heart prepared* (1966) · R. G. Pope, ed., *The notebook of the Rev. John Fiske, 1644–1675* (1974) · J. M. Poteet, 'A homecoming: the Bulkeley family in New England', *New England Quarterly*, 47 (1974), 30–50 · *Thomas Shepard's Confessions*, ed. G. Selement and B. C. Woolley (1981) · L. Shattuck, *A history of the town of Concord* (1835) · W. K. B. Stoever, *'A faire and easie way to heaven': covenant theology and antinomianism in early Massachusetts* (Middletown, Connecticut, 1978) · J. von Rohr, *The covenant of grace in puritan thought* (1986) · *The journal of John Winthrop, 1630–1649*, ed. R. S. Dunn, J. Savage, and L. Yeandle (1996)

Likenesses oils, Odell church, Bedfordshire · portrait, repro. in P. M. Jones and N. R. Jones, eds., *Salvation in New England* (1977), 25

Wealth at death house, outbuildings, 1600 acres of land, mill, etc.: 'Will of Peter Bulkely'

Bulkeley, Sir Richard (c.1540–1621), landowner and courtier, was the eldest of six sons and the heir of Sir Richard Bulkeley (c.1523/4–1572), landowner, of Hen Blas, Beaumaris, Anglesey, and Cheadle, Cheshire, and his first wife, Margaret, daughter of Sir John Savage of Clifton and Rocksavage, Cheshire, and his wife, Elizabeth. The MP Thomas Bulkeley (d. 1593) was a younger brother, and their kinsman was Arthur *Bulkeley (c.1495–1553), bishop of

Bangor. The Cheshire Bulkeleys had held a prominent position in north Wales since the late fourteenth century through involvement in trade, the church, and administration. Sir Richard Bulkeley (d. 1547) was also involved in central administration, serving Cardinal Thomas Wolsey and Thomas Cromwell, and both he and his son Sir Richard Bulkeley (d. 1572) were courtiers.

After tuition under Edmund Bonner, bishop of London, the third Sir Richard Bulkeley was admitted to Lincoln's Inn on 22 January 1558. He applied this training directly in litigation throughout his life and was also a member of the council in the marches of Wales from 1602, if not earlier. His early career, however, reflected aristocratic and court connections. His father, in the service of John Dudley, earl of Warwick, later duke of Northumberland, since before 1547, survived the plot of 1553 to place Lady Jane Grey on the throne, and Richard Bulkeley himself was present at Mary I's coronation on 1 October 1553, but the Dudley connection was maintained. About 23 April 1560 he married Katherine (d. 1573), daughter of Sir William Davenport of Bramhall, Cheshire. The couple had nine children, but only a son and a daughter survived infancy. During the 1560s Bulkeley served Robert Dudley, earl of Leicester, and this was an instrumental factor in his introduction to court, where he became a particular favourite of Elizabeth I. Noted as an expert horseman and tilter, on 16 February 1568 he was admitted gentleman pensioner; he retained this position until 1581/2. Bulkeley's wife died on 21 October 1573. He was knighted by Elizabeth on 16 February 1577, the day before his marriage at court to his second wife, one of the queen's maids of honour, Mary (d. 1640), daughter of William Burgh, fourth Baron Burgh, and his wife, Frances. The couple had seven surviving children, two sons, Sir Richard Bulkeley and Thomas Bulkeley (d. 1659), and five daughters. Later in 1577 Bulkeley entertained Elizabeth at Lewisham in Kent, and again in May 1602.

During the 1560s Bulkeley divided his time between London and Cheadle rectory, Cheshire, his main country residence until the late 1580s. The Bulkeleys' Cheshire estates were under his supervision before he inherited them after his father's death on 8 September 1572, and included the moiety of the manor of Cheadle, the advowson of its church, and landed interests in Occleston, Newton, Churchulme, Sutton, Middlewich, Whatcroft, and Timperley, producing by 1580 an estimated income of £516. His prominence was reflected in membership of the Cheshire commission of the peace from about 1587 to 1620, but the Cheshire estates were reduced during the 1580s. All his lands in Churchulme were sold in July 1580 to Edward Cotton; in April 1587 the crown lease of the rectory of Middlewich expired and the greater part of other Bulkeley property there was sold to Sir Thomas Venables for £1500. This coincided with the restoration and extension of Hen Blas and the enclosure of a deer park at Red Hill there. Hen Blas thus replaced Cheadle as Bulkeley's main residence, and by 1622 the rents of the Cheshire estates had declined by 29 per cent to £367.

By contrast Bulkeley's involvement in north Wales increased. On 28 May 1561 he was granted the reversion of his father's office of constable of Beaumaris Castle for life, and he was returned as knight of the shire for Anglesey in 1563. He was returned to parliament again for the shire in 1604 and 1614, sitting on more than fifty committees. His influence at court was instrumental in securing in June 1562 a charter of incorporation for Beaumaris which ensured family domination of borough governance and control over its parliamentary representation. He was from 1573 to 1621 of the quorum for Anglesey, the only *custos rotulorum* noted during the period, and was also JP for Caernarvonshire from 1584 to 1621, but played a less prominent part in its governance. As vice-admiral of north Wales from 1572 to 1585, he controlled maritime trade, but he lost the position through complicity in piracy. Bulkeley was, nevertheless, appointed deputy lieutenant for Anglesey in December 1587. Court connections enabled him to profit from grants of land on favourable terms and to consolidate and expand landed interests in Anglesey and Caernarvonshire. The total income from his Anglesey estates was £726 in 1580, the town of Beaumaris contributing £124; by 1622 this had increased by 76 per cent to about £1275. His Caernarvonshire interests were mainly concentrated in Conwy and the north-east, where he most actively purchased land after 1584. A total income of £229 in 1580, excluding the town of Caernarfon and rents in kind, increased to £551 by the 1620s. Shrewd commercial activity accumulated further wealth and business interests associated with the port of Beaumaris may explain the increasing frequency of Bulkeley's residence there at the expense of Cheadle. Ships owned by him imported Spanish and French wines; fish caught off Greenland were used as barter in Spain. Trading privileges brought further profits, including the farm of sea coal in Chester from 1582 and the prisage of wines from 1593; as constable of Beaumaris he also collected prisage of wine landed there. Wider commercial interests attracted him to become a shareholder of the Virginia Company in January 1621. Association with Lancashire and north Wales pirates, including his brothers and kinsmen, and with smuggling, provided further lucrative illicit profits and compromised his position as vice-admiral; his London residence was used to sell contraband sugar.

A combination of landed and commercial profits gained by exploiting all opportunities made Bulkeley the wealthiest gentleman in north Wales. His annual income was estimated at over £4000 at the end of his life. Wealth at home and influence abroad made him a formidable figure who entertained lavishly in London and Beaumaris, where he welcomed travellers to Ireland. Baron Hill, a new mansion near Beaumaris, was constructed about 1618 expressly to welcome Henry, prince of Wales. Bulkeley travelled with an armed retinue of twenty to twenty-four men, and his dominating personality and promotion of personal interests generated conflict within and without his family, leading to legal actions in which he took little heed of any authority. Concern to protect Bulkeley interests in Anglesey brought him after 1580 into conflict with his patron, Leicester. The earl aroused antagonism in Caernarvonshire over his efforts from 1574 to inquire into encroachments onto crown lands in the forest of Snowdon. The dispute extended into Anglesey, over which there was a question of whether it was in the forest. Leicester took it to be so, and this directly affected Bulkeley interests, especially after the earl was granted concealed lands there in March 1575. Bulkeley was acclaimed by a later history for securing a royal proclamation on 15 December 1579 which was a general suspension of all concealed land grants. Although he answered before the council in the marches in September 1580 that he had acted in Leicester's interest throughout the 1570s, the event marked the beginning of a rift between them, the earl later claiming, according to a later history, that his former client had caused him a loss of over £10,000. This culminated in an alleged attempt, according to the same source, to murder Bulkeley in London during the late 1580s, with only the queen's personal intercession securing a cool reconciliation between them until Leicester's death in September 1588. The proclamation of 1579 concluded that all suits already in the courts over concealed land were not suspended but that compounding was to be arranged. Bulkeley was summoned to the council in the marches in 1580 because of his attempts to persuade freeholders of Anglesey in general to compound when most of the land in question belonged to him. This appears to be confirmed by the book of concealed Snowdon lands (BL, Lansdowne MS 27, fols. 187r–206r). Almost all the lands in Anglesey were Bulkeley's.

Involvement in factional disputes in north Wales was the product of local conflicts rather than a reflection of court divisions. Opposition from Anglesey gentlemen developed over land transactions and the exercise of authority. This was led by Lewis ab Owen Meyrick of Bodeon, who had risen to prominence during Bulkeley's absence from Anglesey at court before the 1580s, and his nephew Owen Wood. Challenged by Bulkeley's increasingly direct involvement in Anglesey, but emboldened by the rift between Leicester and him, they attacked him with complaints to the privy council and in Star Chamber between 1588 and 1589. These quickly escalated from charges of maladministration as deputy lieutenant to more serious charges of treason (alleging involvement with Thomas Salisbury), lack of religious conformity, indifference to the Spanish threat, and complicity in piracy. There may have been truth in some charges, particularly those relating to piracy, but Bulkeley's intimacy with London circles enabled him to escape with a mere rebuke. Further charges by Wood in Star Chamber in 1589 included the imperious oppression and rapaciousness of Bulkeley during the 1580s; abuse of his position as JP and deputy lieutenant; browbeating other JPs and subverting justice; harbouring pirates; misappropriating borough lands; and falsely accusing his stepmother, Agnes Bulkeley (d. 1623), of poisoning his father in 1572. The outcome was to detain Bulkeley in London during the winter of 1590–91, but he was released by order of the privy council

in May 1591 to return to Anglesey to organize its defences. Wood's continuing outspoken opposition and insubordination led to a counter-complaint by Bulkeley to the privy council which resulted in the former's permanent removal as JP in 1592. This finally secured Bulkeley's unquestioned supremacy in Anglesey until his own death in 1621.

In Caernarvonshire, although identified during the 1580s with gentry who opposed Leicester, Bulkeley also remained on intimate terms with his Gwydir kinsmen, foremost supporters of the earl in the forest of Snowdon dispute. Relations remained cordial until Bulkeley's increasing interest in the eastern Caernarvonshire land market threatened Wynn interests there about 1607 and turned rivalry into hostility. This led to Bulkeley's successful attempt to secure a greater balance of power in Caernarvonshire by supporting gentlemen who challenged Gwydir's domination, led by John Griffith of Cefnamwlch. Griffith's defeat of Richard Wynn of Gwydir in his election as MP for Caernarvonshire in 1620 could not have been achieved without Bulkeley's support.

Relations within Bulkeley's immediate family were often turbulent. In 1572, in an attempt to deprive her of her jointure, he accused Agnes Bulkeley of adultery and poisoning his father in March 1572. She was acquitted in July 1573 and was granted lands in Newton, Cheshire, following arbitration in 1575. Relations were equally strained with his first wife, Katherine Bulkeley. In 1618 he declared that he had married her against his will when under-age in 1560 and had contemplated divorcing her in 1573. Their children, Elizabeth and Richard Bulkeley (1573–1619), were brought up by the Davenports at Bramhall; they were disinherited by a settlement in 1577, and Sir Richard Bulkeley later denied his son. Relations became increasingly acrimonious over an allowance granted to Richard Bulkeley of Bramhall in 1593, especially after he married against his father's wishes in 1604. The problem was resolved only after the death of father and son. In 1632 Bulkeley lands in north-west England were settled on Richard Bulkeley, eldest son of Richard Bulkeley of Bramhall. The north Wales lands were settled on the issue of Sir Richard Bulkeley's second wife, with whom his relations were more cordial. Owing to the fecklessness of his heir, the fourth Sir Richard Bulkeley, the son of his second wife, he settled his property by will on 4 April 1614 on his grandson, yet another Richard Bulkeley (d. 1645). Shortly before his death at Hen Blas on 28 June 1621, another dispute erupted over the guardianship of this grandson between his wife and her second son, Thomas Bulkeley, on one part, and the child's parents, the fourth Sir Richard Bulkeley and Anne, on the other. The latter retained control of the estate on behalf of their son. Sir Richard Bulkeley was buried privately in his own tomb at Beaumaris church in July 1621 in the absence in London of his widow. A public funeral was held in her presence at Beaumaris in October 1621, the funeral sermon delivered by Gruffyth Williams, later bishop of Ossory.

NIA M. W. POWELL

Sources W. Williams, 'A history of the Bulkeley family', 1673/4, transcribed and ed. E. G. Jones, *Transactions of the Anglesey Antiquarian Society* (1948), 7–99 • U. Wales, Bangor, Bangor MS 1921, 1–34 • U. Wales, Bangor, Baron Hill MSS • Anglesey plea roll, 1509–17, U. Wales, Bangor, Porth yr Aur Additional MSS, memb. 3, 27, 29, 32–3 • U. Wales, Bangor, Penrhos MS 2 • *APC, 1581–88, 1591–2, 1595–6* • NL Wales, MSS 1531D, 4710, 9051–6E, 9080E, 9081D; Add. MSS 464E, 465E, 466E; Mostyn MS 145, 490–95 • BL, Lansdowne MS 45, fols. 190r–192r • BL, Lansdowne MS 167, fol. 192r • BL, Lansdowne MS 737, fol. 162r • R. Flenley, ed., *A calendar of the register of the queen's majesty's council in the dominion … and principality of Wales and the marches of the same, 1569–1591, transcribed from Bodley 904* (1916), 32, 119–20, 127–34, 194, 213, 218–21 • P. Williams, *The council in the marches of Wales under Elizabeth I* (1958), 87, 218–19, 237–40, 246–8, 253, 266–9, 274, 309–10, 314, 344–5 • J. G. Jones, *The Welsh gentry, 1536–1640: images of status, honour and authority* (1998), 9, 18–19, 41, 47, 57, 62, 91, 120–25, 151, 215 • BL, Cotton MS Claudius C.iii, fols. 171r, 217r • BL, Harley MS 1535, fols. 3r, 36r • BL, Harley MS 2180, fol. 296r • BL, Harley MS 7004, fol. 236r • BL, Egerton MS 2882, fol. 20r • HoP, *Commons, 1558–1603*, 1.513–14 • G. Williams, *Recovery, reorientation and reformation: Wales, c.1415–1642* (1987), 86, 97, 102–3, 301, 348, 363–6, 378–9, 389, 392, 440 • D. C. Jones, 'The Bulkeleys of Baron Hill, 1440–1621', MA diss., U. Wales, Bangor, 1958, 149–299, 363, 366–83, 414–36, pedigrees V, VI • W. O. Williams, 'The Anglesey gentry as businessmen in Tudor and Stuart times', *Transactions of the Anglesey Antiquarian Society* (1948), 100–14
Archives U. Wales, Bangor, Baron Hill MSS | NL Wales, Panton papers • NL Wales, Wynn of Gwydir papers
Wealth at death income assessed at £4000 p.a. in 1632 and 1638: PRO, C2ChasI/B43/12; Hunt. L., MS 7155 • widow's est. £4300 p.a.: Williams, 'History of the Bulkeley family', 32 • will, 4 April 1614, U. Wales, Bangor, Baron Hill MS 35 • inquisition post mortem covering lands, 22 Feb 1622, PRO, C142/393/168

Bulkeley, Richard (1626/7–1650), royalist army officer, was born at Llanfairfechan, Caernarvonshire, the second of five sons (there were also four daughters) of Thomas Bulkeley (*bap.* 1585, *d.* 1659), landowner (created Viscount Bulkeley of Cashel, co. Tipperary, in the Irish peerage in January 1644), and his first wife, Blanche Coytmore (*d.* 1664), daughter of Robert Coytmore, of Coetmor, Caernarvonshire.

There is some doubt whether Bulkeley attended Westminster School, but he was certainly admitted, aged fifteen, as a fellow-commoner to St John's College, Cambridge on 28 January 1642. About 1641 he married Katherine Mostyn, daughter of Sir Roger Mostyn, of Mostyn, Flintshire; she had died without issue by 1644. Bulkeley was described by William Williams, compiler of a family history about 1673, as 'a handsome person, of very affable and courteous deportment' (Jones, 75). Early in the civil war he gained military experience in the campaign to defend Chester, but he was back home by mid-1643. Anglesey's importance in overall royalist strategy grew as the coastline controlled from Beaumaris became a vital landing area, given the increased royal dependence on men and supplies from the marquess of Ormond in Ireland.

After the royalist surrender of Chester (3 February 1646) Lord Byron, royalist commander-in-chief in north Wales, appointed Bulkeley, aged only twenty, governor of Beaumaris. Although he was, in his own estimation, a seasoned campaigner, it is difficult to know why Byron put him in charge of such an important fortress, especially as he was later to call Bulkeley an 'ignorant and wilful young man'

(Clarendon, *State Papers*, 1767, 2.418). Byron may have hoped that Bulkeley would be the man to override the localism of the Anglesey gentry, who had forced him a few months earlier to accept one of their number, David Lloyd, as governor, and from whom Bulkeley seized the castle in May 1646. By that time Thomas Mytton, the plain-dealing parliamentarian commander in north Wales, was besieging Caernarfon, and he sent commissioners to Beaumaris for formal discussions about surrender. The country gentry, led by Lord Bulkeley, and fearful for their estates, were in favour; but Richard Bulkeley, young enough to be impatient of his elders' timid compromises and puffed up by his colonelcy, resented the opening of negotiations and protested at the stationing of two parliamentary men-of-war in the Menai Strait to prevent waterborne supplies reaching Beaumaris. However, the capitulation of Caernarfon and the vote of a general county meeting for surrender led to terms being signed on 14 June 1646. Bulkeley seems not to have suffered for his actions as governor and went off to help in the defence of Harlech.

In the second civil war (1648) Bulkeley and his father were both present at the royalist defeat by Mytton at Y Dalar Hir, on the Caernarvonshire coast (5 June), but, at the instigation of Lord Byron, they signed the flamboyant declaration of the Anglesey gentry for the king (July). To Byron's annoyance they chose as their commander the over-confident and inexperienced Bulkeley rather than himself, and he left them to their fate. Mytton's troops were checked at the straits for lack of shipping, but Bulkeley made little use of the respite to strengthen the Beaumaris defences, and failed to prevent his family's enemy, Richard Cheadle, providing fifty ships and guiding Mytton's forces across to Anglesey. The Bulkeley rivalry with the Cheadle family, originally the Bulkeleys' agents and rent-collectors, had been ongoing since the mid-1620s, and in 1644 Lord Bulkeley had wounded Cheadle in a scuffle. A sharp cavalry skirmish on the shore was followed by an affray on Red Hill outside Beaumaris and the royalists were driven into the castle, which, in no condition to sustain a siege, was soon surrendered (2 October 1648). Bulkeley was imprisoned in Hen Blas, the family home, until ransomed, and then went abroad, travelling in France, Flanders, and the Netherlands. Making his peace with the Long Parliament, he returned to Anglesey in 1649, but on 19 February 1650, after visiting a Dutch squadron sheltering in the Menai Strait, an altercation with Richard Cheadle on Lavan Sands led to his heart being pierced by a rapier. He was buried (21 or 22 February 1650) in the family vault in the chancel of Beaumaris parish church. Cheadle was hanged at Conwy for the murder.

BASIL MORGAN

Sources N. Tucker, 'The military activity of Colonel Richard Bulkeley', *Transactions of the Anglesey Antiquarian Society and Field Club* (1965), 7–24 • A. H. Dodd, 'Anglesey in the civil war', *Transactions of the Anglesey Antiquarian Society and Field Club* (1952), 1–33 • [J. Ballinger], ed., *Calendar of Wynn (of Gwydir) papers, 1515–1690, in the National Library of Wales* (1926) • B. D. Roberts, 'Cheadles against Bulkeleys', *Transactions of the Anglesey Antiquarian Society and Field Club* (1945), 25–37 • E. G. Jones, ed., 'History of the Bulkeley family

(National Library of Wales, MS 9080E)', *Transactions of the Anglesey Antiquarian Society and Field Club* (1948), 1–99 • G. Roberts, ed., 'The parliamentary history of Beaumaris, 1555–1832', *Transactions of the Anglesey Antiquarian Society and Field Club* (1933), 97–109 • GEC, *Peerage*, new edn • *Old Westminsters*, vols. 1–2 • Venn, *Alum. Cant.* • E. Parry, *Royal visits and progresses to Wales* (1851) • B. D. Roberts, *Mitre and musket: John Williams, 1582–1650* (1938) • J. Lodge, *The peerage of Ireland*, rev. M. Archdall, rev. edn, 5 (1789) • J. P. Earwaker, *East Cheshire: past and present, or, A history of the hundred of Macclesfield*, 1 (1877), 183 • A. I. Price, 'Westminster School and its connection with north Wales prior to the Victorian era', *Transactions of the Anglesey Antiquarian Society and Field Club* (1932), 91–104 • J. F. Rees, *Studies in Welsh history* (1947) • R. Hutton, *The royalist war effort, 1642–1646* (1982)

Archives NL Wales, Baron Hill MSS

Likenesses portrait, *c.*1649–1650, repro. in Tucker, 'The military activity of Colonel Richard Bulkeley', 6; priv. coll.

Bulkeley, Sir Richard, second baronet (1660–1710), scientist and author, was born on 17 August 1660 in Dublin, the first son of Sir Richard Bulkeley, first baronet (1634–1685), and his first wife, Catherine, *née* Bysse (*d.* 1662). He entered Trinity College, Dublin, in September 1676, graduating BA in 1680, and MA in 1682. Bulkeley was incorporated BA at Christ Church, Oxford, in May 1680, made a fellow of Trinity College, Oxford, in 1682, and was a member of the Royal Society. He served as a member of the Irish parliament for Fethard, co. Wexford, in 1692–3, 1695–9, and 1703–10. Bulkeley succeeded to the baronetcy on his father's death on 17 March 1685, inheriting Old Bawn, the family estate near Dublin. Bulkeley also owned a manor at Ewell in Surrey. He married Lucy Downing (1665–1710) at Westminster Abbey on 16 February 1686. The couple had no children.

Involved in new scientific developments, Bulkeley was an enthusiastic inventor and experimenter. He developed plans for an engine to power mechanical devices, and he designed an air pump for ships. Included in the *Transactions of the Royal Society* for 1685 is Bulkeley's description of his experiments with a carriage constructed to resist overturning. Bulkeley was also an avid horticulturist, and on his lands in Ireland and Surrey he cultivated many different types of plants. Again in the Royal Society's *Transactions* (1693) are Bulkeley's descriptions of his experiments with the planting of maize as a more productive substitute for peas, and of a successful method for propagating elm trees from seed. He was also interested in the growing of other kinds of trees, and in raising wheat and potatoes.

Bulkeley was hunchbacked and endured a number of physical ailments. He described his suffering from terrible headaches, recurring fevers, kidney stones, and a hernia, as well as rheumatism. It was in the context of these afflictions that in later life Bulkeley became involved with an enthusiastic sect among French Huguenots in London.

Holding millenarian beliefs, the central figures of the French prophets, as the group came to be known, were three men who had fled a revolt in the Cévennes region of France and arrived in England in 1706. Durand Fage, Elie Marion, and Jean Chevalier, believed to be inspired by prophetic visions, first attracted followers among French exiles, but soon gathered English supporters as well. Bulkeley became involved with the group late in 1706, and in *An Answer to Several Treatises Lately Publish'd on the Subject of the Prophets* (1708) he defended the prophets' claims through scriptural argument and based on his personal experiences. He described how his physical maladies had ceased after being blessed by the prophets, thus proving their spiritual powers. Bulkeley also published 'An impartial account of the prophets of the Cevennes' as a preface to a work entitled *Prophetical Extracts* (1708). In publicly defending the three prophets after they were pilloried in December 1707 Bulkeley proclaimed that 'Though there is at present not above two or three hundred of the Inspired, yet before a Twelve-Month comes about, there will be more than ten-thousand of them' (Schwartz, 112). Bulkeley later broke from the main group in support of Abraham Whitrow, a new English prophet from among the French prophets' followers. Bulkeley and Whitrow implemented policies of charity, giving money to the poor in both England and Ireland.

Owing to his financial support of the French prophets, and later of Whitrow's cause, Bulkeley went heavily into debt. He died at Ewell on 7 April 1710, and his house there was sold in order to meet the financial obligations he had left. Bulkeley was buried in the church at Ewell, with an inscription including his coat of arms. His widow, Lucy, married her stepfather several months after Bulkeley's death, but she died six months after her former husband and was interred beside him at Ewell.

WARREN JOHNSTON

Sources GEC, *Baronetage*, 4.207 • Foster, *Alum. Oxon.* • Burtchaell & Sadleir, *Alum. Dubl.*, 110 • H. Schwartz, *The French prophets: the history of a millenarian group in eighteenth-century England* (1980) • J. Aubrey, *The natural history and antiquities of the county of Surrey*, 2 (1718), 220–21 • A. Kippis and others, eds., *Biographia Britannica, or, The lives of the most eminent persons who have flourished in Great Britain and Ireland*, 2nd edn, 3 (1784), 144

Archives Bodl. Oxf., letters to Martin Lister • TCD, corresp. with William King

Bulkeley [*née* Stuart], **Lady Sophia** (*fl.* 1660–1718), Jacobite sympathizer, was the younger daughter of Walter Stuart or Stewart (*d.* in or before 1657), a physician and MP for Monmouth, and his wife, Sophia (*d.* 1702/3), a dresser to Queen Henrietta Maria; her father was the third son of Walter Stuart or *Stewart, first Lord Blantyre (*d.* 1617), and her elder sister was the celebrated court beauty Frances Teresa *Stuart or Stewart (1647–1702), 'Mrs Stewart', afterwards married to Charles, fifth duke of Richmond. The Stuarts were royalists and went into exile in France during the interregnum, returning to England after the Restoration. In 1668, on Sunday 30 August, shortly after her sister's marriage, Sophia Stuart was seen by Pepys walking in St James's Park with her sister when she was pronounced 'very handsome' (Pepys, *Diary*, 9.294). Sophia was appointed a maid of honour to Queen Catherine in 1671 and about November 1673 she married (with a portion of £5000 provided by the crown), Henry Bulkeley (*c.*1641–

1698), fifth but third surviving son of Thomas, first Viscount Bulkeley of Cashel near Beaumaris; he was master of the household to Charles II and James II, MP for Anglesey and Beaumaris, and brother of royalist officer Richard Bulkeley (d. 1650). About 1680 it was rumoured that Sidney Godolphin was enamoured of her, a report referred to in a line of a satire written in that year, 'Bulkeley's Godolphin's only care' (Lord and others, 2.342). In 1684 she was granted the place and precedence of the daughter of an English earl, perhaps in anticipation of her appointment in 1685 as a lady of the bedchamber to Queen Mary. She attended Mary at the birth of the prince of Wales in 1688, being one of the deponents who swore as to the truth of the birth in October that year, and in December she and her children followed Mary to France. She had six children, of whom James became a resident in France, and left a family there; Charlotte married Charles O'Brien, styled fifth Viscount Clare; and Ann married James, duke of Berwick, the natural son of James II. Sophia remained faithful to the Jacobite cause, although a report of the early 1690s that she 'was very curious in prying into all that passed at St. Germains' and was under arrest for corresponding with Godolphin suggests that she may not have been entrusted thereafter with Jacobite intrigues (Sir J. Dalrymple, Memoirs, 1771, 2, pt. 2, 189). Sophia made a visit to England in 1702 in an attempt to claim a legacy left to her by her sister but, having returned without leave, was ordered to depart immediately. Later requests to be allowed to return to England, in 1713 and in 1718, were rebuffed and Lady Sophia presumably died in exile.

JENNETT HUMPHREYS, rev. S. M. WYNNE

Sources C. H. Hartmann, La belle Stuart: memoirs of court and society in the times of Frances Teresa Stuart, duchess of Richmond and Lennox (1924) • Calendar of the Stuart papers belonging to his majesty the king, preserved at Windsor Castle, 7 vols., HMC, 56 (1902–23), vols. 6–7 • HoP, Commons, 1660–90, 1 (1983) • Report on the manuscripts of Allan George Finch, 5 vols., HMC, 71 (1913–2003), vol. 3 • G. de F. Lord and others, eds., Poems on affairs of state: Augustan satirical verse, 1660–1714, 7 vols. (1963–75), vols. 1–2, 4 • W. A. Shaw, ed., Calendar of treasury books, 1–7, PRO (1904–16) • CSP dom., 1663–4, 1683–4, 1687–9, 1691–2 • Foster, Alum. Oxon. • entrybook of the queen's lord chamberlain, 1665–83, NL Scot., Adv. MS 31.1.22, fol. 152 • wills of Henry Bulkeley, 1698; Frances Teresa Stuart, duchess dowager of Richmond and Lennox, 1702; Sophia Stuart, 1703, PRO, Prob. 11/448, sig. 245, 11/468, sig. 14, 11/468, sig. 166 • J. Y. Akerman, ed., Moneys received and paid for secret services of Charles II and James II from 30th March 1679 to 25th December 1688, CS, 52 (1851) • E. Chamberlayne, Angliae notitia, or, The present state of England, new edn (1687) • W. D. Christie, ed., Letters addressed from London to Sir Joseph Williamson, 2, CS, new ser., 9 (1874)
Likenesses R. Dunkarton, mezzotint, pubd 1814 (after H. Gascar), NPG • H. Gascar, mezzotint, BM

Bulkeley, William (1691–1760), diarist, was born on 4 November 1691 at Brynddu in the parish of Llanfechell, Anglesey, the second son of William Bulkeley (d. 1699) and Lettice (d. 1750), daughter of Captain Henry Jones of Llangoed in Anglesey. His father died when he was a mere boy and his mother married a second and third husband.

William Bulkeley received a sound education and may have attended the grammar school at Beaumaris. On 22 March 1710 he married Jane (1693–1714), the daughter of Ambrose Lewis, rector of Llanrhuddlad, a neighbouring parish. After bearing three children, Catherine, Mary, and William, Jane died in January 1714 on the day her son was baptized; William Bulkeley did not remarry. On coming of age he had inherited his father's estate which consisted of Brynddu and some scattered farms in nearby parishes.

Bulkeley lived a fairly uneventful life, but he recorded the latter part of that life in two volumes of a personal diary, the first covering the period from 30 March 1734 until 8 June 1743, the second 1 August 1747 to 28 September 1760. These diaries, along with other complementary sources, provide a valuable insight into the daily life of a fairly typical Anglesey landowner: Bulkeley's running of his estate, cattle-dealing in the local fairs, his duties as justice of the peace, his extended visit to Dublin and its playhouses, his references to Anglesey politics, and his religious convictions. The diaries also disclose that he was burdened with a heavy debt, that he opposed the unfortunate marriage in 1738 of his daughter Mary to Fortunatus *Wright, the famous privateer from Liverpool, and that he accepted resolutely the waywardness and death of his only son and heir in 1751.

Although references to William Bulkeley's adherence to Welsh culture in the diaries are brief, for example his patronizing of Welsh harpists, other sources confirm his interest in Welsh poetry, music, and antiquities. He was distantly related to Lewis Morris, and it was probably due to the latter's influence, which had begun in 1725, that he undertook the task of copying into one volume (NL Wales, MS 832) a variety of Welsh poems, a substantial number of which are seventeenth-century works in free metre. He was an active member of Lewis Morris's group of friends in Anglesey until 1742, but his fairly strict religious attitude would have prevented him sharing in Morris's experiments with ribald poetry and prose.

When Bulkeley was fifty-one years old nonconformity took a hold in central Anglesey. The Anglican clergy actively resisted the nonconformists, who were persecuted in their homes, in their public worship, in the civil and especially the ecclesiastical courts, and through the printed word. True to his character Bulkeley was incensed by the opposition of the clergy to the nonconformists and made his views on the subject public. His stand reached a climax in 1747, when the Revd Thomas Ellis of Holyhead published the first edition of a Welsh tract, Byrr Grynhôad, attacking the nonconformists, to which Bulkeley responded with a handwritten tract which was circulated, but of which no copy has survived. In a second edition of Ellis's tract there are hurried additions which are a direct response to Bulkeley's tract, and include an invitation to him to set a farm to the chief nonconformist. Needless to say Bulkeley set one of his farms to William Prichard, the leader of the Anglesey nonconformists. There are several other references which confirm Bulkeley's sympathetic attitude to the beleaguered nonconformists in Anglesey.

William Morris, brother of Lewis Morris and himself a staunch churchman, wrote in 1754 that Bulkeley was an unhypocritical and honest person, a view which he restated when he heard of Bulkeley's death in October 1760 at Bryndu. Bulkeley was buried on 28 October 1760 at the parish church of Llanfechell.

DAFYDD WYN WILIAM

Sources William Bulkeley, diaries, U. Wales, Bangor, Henblas MSS 18–19 · D. W. Wiliam, *Wiliam Prichard, Cnwchdernog, neu, Hanes ymneilltuaeth* (1992) · J. H. Davies, ed., *The Morris letters* (1909), vols. 1–2
Archives U. Wales, Bangor

Bulkley, Charles (1719–1797), General Baptist minister, was born in London on 18 October 1719, the fourth son of Thomas Bulkley, silk merchant in Ludgate Street, London, and his wife, Esther Henry (*b.* 1694), the daughter of Matthew *Henry, the biblical commentator, and his second wife, Mary Warburton. His early education was under Lancaster, a clergyman at Chester, and his ministerial training was undertaken at Philip Doddridge's academy in Northampton, where he was a student from 1736 to 1740.

In the summer of 1740 Bulkley became minister to the Presbyterian congregation at Welford, Northamptonshire, but he soon moved to Colchester, where he became pastor of the chapel in St Helen's Lane. While at Colchester he abandoned orthodox Calvinism to embrace the Arminian views of the General Baptists, a conversion which owed much to John Ashworth, brother of Caleb Ashworth. In 1743 Bulkley succeeded John Ashworth as minister at White's Alley, Little Moorfields, and in 1745 succeeded Dr James Foster at the Barbican, taking with him his congregation from White's Alley. In 1749 he married Ann Fiske (*d.* 1783) of Colchester; they had no children. Some years later, when Foster retired in January 1752 from the Sunday evening lectureship at the Old Jewry, Bulkley again succeeded him. By the late 1770s the General Baptist cause in London was declining, and in 1780 Bulkley's congregation amalgamated with three others to form a new congregation in Worship Street, Finsbury. Here, despite growing infirmities, he remained as minister until his death.

Bulkley enjoyed great popularity as a minister and for some years preached to a crowded audience at the Old Jewry, even though he was no great orator. Like his friend Foster, he adopted anti-Trinitarian views, while his views on communion became too liberal for many 'closed communionists' within the General Baptists and brought him into conflict with Grantham Killingworth, a leading General Baptist layman of Norwich. He was considered to be a great thinker and a prolific writer, being the author of numerous religious, moral, and philosophical treatises, most of which were 'written in a true spirit of piety in a clear and animated style' (Allibone, *Dict.*, 1.279). Although most of his publications appeared before 1770, the work for which he is perhaps best remembered, *Notes on the Bible*, was published posthumously in 1802, with a preface by Joshua Toulmin.

Bulkley, whose wife died in August 1783, remained active in the ministry until his death, though a stroke in 1795 shattered his health and affected his speech. He died on 15 April 1797 at his home in Ironmonger Row, Old Street, London, and was buried on 25 April in the graveyard behind the meeting-house in Worship Street.

ALEXANDER GORDON, *rev.* M. J. MERCER

Sources C. Surman, index, DWL · A. Chalmers, ed., *The general biographical dictionary*, new edn, 32 vols. (1812–17) · Allibone, *Dict.* · W. Wilson, *The history and antiquities of the dissenting churches and meeting houses in London, Westminster and Southwark*, 4 vols. (1808–14) · R. Brown, *The English Baptists of the eighteenth century* (1986) · *GM*, 1st ser., 67 (1797), 439 · G. E. Evans, *Vestiges of protestant dissent* (1897) · J. Toulmin, 'Preface', in C. Bulkley, *Notes on the Bible*, 3 vols. (1802) · J. Evans, *A sermon preached at Worship Street … April 30 1797, on the decease of the … Reverend Charles Bulkley* [1797] · IGI

Bulkley [*née* Wilford; *other married name* Barrisford], **Mary** (1747/8?–1792), dancer and actress, was the daughter of Edward Wilford (*d.* 1789), a minor official at Covent Garden. Wilford's sister Priscilla Steevens had in 1744 married John Rich, the proprietor of Covent Garden Theatre, as her second husband. Mary was brought up in some comfort at the centre of the theatrical establishment and moved naturally into a career on the stage.

Mary first appeared at Covent Garden in 1758 as a dancer, and in 1761 she became a member of the company. She remained with them until 1780, first as a dancer (until 1765) and thereafter as an actress specializing chiefly in comedy. Her acting début was as Miranda in Susanna Centlivre's *The Busy Body*. She later played all the main female roles in Shakespearian comedy, as well as Cordelia and Portia, and innumerable parts in contemporary plays. She was the first Miss Richland in Oliver Goldsmith's *The Good-Natur'd Man* (1768), the first Kate Hardcastle in his *She Stoops to Conquer* (1773), and the first Julia in Richard Brinsley Sheridan's *The Rivals* (1775). Her beauty helped to ensure her initial success. Hugh Kelly praised her thus:

> Blest with a person wholly without fault;
> Tho' polish'd, gay, and natural, though taught,
> See where that Wilford elegantly moves,
> Leads up the graces, and commands the loves.
> (*Thespis* II, 1767)

He noted, however, that her voice was not strong, and in his life of Johnson James Boswell records an occasion in 1773 when Goldsmith commented that she could not sing.

In her personal life Mary was exuberant and profligate. Her marriage to George Bulkley (*d.* 1784), of the Covent Garden orchestra, on 9 August 1767 produced a daughter, of whom nothing is known after her baptism at St Paul's, Covent Garden, on 9 November 1768. Bulkley had 'a grateful heart and useful virtues' (*Theatrical Biography*, vol. 2) but she found him dull. In the summer of 1768, during the annual closure of the London theatres, when metropolitan actors customarily worked in the provinces, the Bulkleys were engaged at the King Street Theatre, Bristol. Also in the company were James William *Dodd (*c.*1740–1796) and his wife, Martha, both of Drury Lane. Mary Bulkley's indiscretions with Dodd gave rise to scandal and Martha refused to accompany her husband again to Bristol in the following year. She died shortly afterwards and public sympathy moved against the lovers. The relationship persisted, however. In London they worked in separate theatres and were on the whole successful; in the vacations they worked together with mixed fortunes. In the summer of 1774 they had a disastrous season in Dublin:'Some recent transactions had excited strong prejudices against them' (Hitchcock, 2.259). Dodd was left penniless and was bailed out by Garrick, and Bulkley returned temporarily to her husband. In contrast their season for Tate Wilkinson in York in 1779 was highly successful. They had by this time set up house together, an arrangement which lasted until another scandal erupted, this time with Dodd as the wronged party. Mary's lovers were reputed to include John Banks, a notable Harlequin, and John Brown Williamson, a minor actor.

Mary Bulkley ceased to appear regularly at Covent Garden after the 1779–80 season and her career was clearly in decline. From 1781 until 1788 she worked in the summers at the Haymarket Theatre. She was engaged by Drury Lane for one season only, in 1783–4, and she made one last, single appearance at Covent Garden in 1789–90. In the winter months, with neither of the patent theatres employing her, she was probably hard-pressed for money. She reached the bottom of her career as a member of a company of strolling actors in Shrewsbury in 1784. Edward Cape Everard, another Covent Garden child dancer whose own downward spiral had set in early, relates in his *Memoirs of an Unfortunate Son of Thespis* (1818) the arrival of John Jackson, proprietor of the Edinburgh theatre, who recruited four of the Shrewsbury troupe for his own company. Jackson remembered Mary Bulkley as a girl, with admiration and affection, and was clearly rescuing her.

Sadly public disapproval followed Mary to Scotland and her first benefit was a failure, but she overcame the hostility when she played Hamlet successfully on 23 March 1784. On 22 July 1788 she married Captain Ebenezer Barrisford and used his name henceforward. She remained with the Edinburgh company until 1791, by which time she was drinking heavily. She died in poverty on 19 December 1792 in Dumfries, survived by her husband; the *Newcastle Courant* of 29 December 1792 gave her age as forty-four. She was buried in Dumfries churchyard. JOHN LEVITT

Sources G. W. Stone, ed., *The London stage, 1660–1800*, pt 4: 1747–1776 (1962) · C. B. Hogan, ed., *The London stage, 1660–1800*, pt 5: 1776–1800 (1968) · Highfill, Burnim & Langhans, *BDA* · *The letters of David Garrick*, ed. D. M. Little and G. M. Kahrl, 3 vols. (1963) · [J. Haslewood], *The secret history of the green rooms: containing authentic and entertaining memoirs of the actors and actresses in the three theatres royal*, 2 vols. (1790) · *Theatrical biography, or, Memoirs of the principal performers of the three Theatre Royals*, 2 vols. (1772) · T. Wilkinson, *Memoirs of his own life*, 4 vols. (1790) · T. Wilkinson, *The wandering patentee, or, A history of the Yorkshire theatres from 1770 to the present time*, 4 vols. (1795) · R. Jenkins, *Memoirs of the Bristol stage* (1826) · J. Jackson, *The history of the Scottish stage* (1793) · R. Hitchcock, *An historical view of the Irish stage from the earliest period down to the close of the season 1788*, 2 vols. (1788–94) · E. C. Everard, *Memoirs of an unfortunate son of Thespis* (1818)

Archives BL, letters to Oliver Goldsmith, Add. MS 42515

Likenesses J. H. Ramberg, oils, 1785, BM · I. Roberts, engraving (as Lady Dainty), BM · I. Roberts, engraving, NPG · I. Roberts, engraving, repro. in J. Bell, *Bell's British Theatre* (April 1778)

Bulkley, Peter. *See* Bulkeley, Peter (1583–1659).

Bull [*née* Hicks], **Amy Maud** (1877–1953), suffragist, was born at Great Holland Hall, Essex, on 16 July 1877, the daughter of a farmer, Charles Thompson Hicks (1838–1892), and his wife, Lilian Martha, *née* Smith (1853–1924). The family included another daughter, Beatrice, and a son, Charles, who died in the First World War. Amy Hicks was educated privately and at North London Collegiate School, before going up to Girton College, Cambridge, in 1895 to read classics. She graduated in 1899 with a first-class degree, having been awarded the college's Agnata Butler prize in 1897 and 1898 and the Thérèse Montefiore memorial prize in 1899. She was a visiting lecturer at Westfield College in 1900–01, class mistress at Belvedere High School, Liverpool, from 1901 to 1904, and a fellow of Bryn Mawr College, Pennsylvania in 1904–5.

Amy Hicks's mother, brought up by a father who 'was a great believer in woman's capability, and trained both his daughters to manage their own affairs and depend on their own judgment just as carefully and thoroughly as he trained his sons' (*The Vote*, 2 April 1910), had worked for many years with the Charity Organization Society and as a school manager, both in East Anglia and then in north St Pancras, and for the suffrage cause from the early 1880s. By 1902 both mother and daughter were members of the Central Society for Women's Suffrage. In December 1906 they joined the Women's Social and Political Union (WSPU) on the occasion of the banquet given by the constitutional suffrage society at the Savoy to celebrate the release from prison of the first militant suffragettes, but left that organization in October 1907 to join the newly founded Women's Freedom League (WFL). Amy Hicks had become the WFL's literary secretary by 1909. In July of that year she was imprisoned for three weeks on a charge of obstruction. In 1910 she both gave support to the New Constitutional Society for Women's Suffrage and rejoined the WSPU. In 1910 Amy Hicks was a member of the committee of the Tax Resistance League and in November of that year was arrested, with her mother, during the struggles with the police in Parliament Square on 'black Friday'. In March 1912 she was imprisoned for four months after taking part in the WSPU's window-smashing campaign in the West End of London. She spent time both in Holloway and Aylesbury, for a period in solitary confinement, went on hunger strike, and was forcibly fed. She was considered by the Home Office to be one of the ringleaders of the hunger strike at Aylesbury. On 27 May 1913 Amy Hicks was, with Sylvia Pankhurst, a founder of the East London Federation of the WSPU. With her mother she later became a member of the United Suffragists. During the First World War Amy Hicks joined the Women's Volunteer Reserve (Green Corps), which had been founded by Evelina Haverfield, a fellow suffragette.

On 4 August 1927 at St Peter's Church, Belsize Park, Amy Hicks married a widower, John Major Bull (1858/9–1944), who had been a clerical officer in the War Office, and was the son of Archibald Bull, accountant. There were no children of the marriage. Amy Bull served as a rural district councillor in Chelmsford from 1927 to 1930, and lectured to Women's Institutes on the production and preservation of home-grown food. She was made an MBE some time before 1948. She died of pneumonia at her home, General's Orchard, Little Baddow, near Chelmsford, on 11 February 1953. In her will she left £1000 each to Girton College and to the National Trust.

ELIZABETH CRAWFORD

Sources E. Crawford, *The women's suffrage movement: a reference guide, 1866–1928* (1999) · *The Vote* (2 April 1910) · K. T. Butler and H. I. McMorran, eds., *Girton College register, 1869–1946* (1948) · b. cert. · m. cert. · d. cert. · will [Amy Bull]
Likenesses photograph, repro. in *The Vote* (16 April 1910)
Wealth at death £24,988: probate, 19 May 1953, *CGPLA Eng. & Wales*

Bull, Daniel (*bap.* 1633?, *d.* 1697/8), clergyman and ejected minister, was probably the Daniel, son of Christopher Bull, curate of the parish of Sturminster Marshall in Dorset, who was baptized there on 1 December 1633, although nothing certain is known of his origins or early life. It is possible that Bull attended Cambridge University: a sizar of his name matriculated from Emmanuel College in September 1647, graduated BA in 1650 and MA in 1652 from Christ's College, was incorporated at Oxford in 1654, and was fellow of Christ's 1650–54, but this man might be another Daniel Bull, ordained priest at Lincoln on 1 September 1662. The future nonconformist is first definitely encountered in August 1655 as rector of Wyke Regis, Dorset.

Perhaps it was while Bull was still in the west country that he met and married Elizabeth (*d.* 1671), daughter of Sir George Vaughan of Tiverton, in Devon, but their eldest son, Nathaniel, was baptized on 3 May 1659 at Stoke Newington, Middlesex, where Bull had been chosen as minister by the vestry on 27 September 1657, Cromwell confirming the appointment on 25 November. At the Restoration in 1660 the former rector, William Heath, was reinstated but Bull continued to preach in the parish, perhaps as curate, until August 1662. Though he was reported in 1664 as preaching in Smithfield and the Minories, it is clear that Bull stayed at Newington and he was probably the founder of the presbyterian congregation there. He also renewed his connection with Dorset, preaching in 1669 with Edward Buckler, ejected minister and former rector of Wyke Regis, at several places including the house of Michael Hervey JP at Yetminster, before sixty or seventy people. In April 1672 he was granted a licence to preach at his house at Stoke Newington.

Bull later became assistant to John Howe, ejected minister of Great Torrington, Devon, and pastor of the presbyterian congregation at Haberdashers' Hall from 1676. In 1681, however, Bull was discovered in an adulterous relationship. This was highly embarrassing for it gave credence to traditional charges of hypocrisy, and in vain did Edmund Calamy protest that Bull's behaviour was unique among the ejected clergy of 1662. He was dismissed from his position. Howe preached before the congregation a sermon, *Of Charity in Reference to Other Men's Sins* (1681)

which stressed the evil of taking pleasure in their exposure, but it was effectively the end of his colleague's career. In February 1691 Bull travelled to Carlisle, hoping 'to reside there among a poor inconsiderable number of people' (Gordon, 24), but it appears they were unable to provide for him and, probably before the appointment as minister there of Daniel Jackson in 1692, Bull returned to London. He was living at St Giles Cripplegate at the time of his death, which occurred before 4 February 1698 when the administration of his estate was awarded to his son Nathaniel. Samuel Stancliff, formerly minister at Rotherhithe, witnessed Bull's 'last hours and dying prayers and tears', and thought him 'a penitent sinner and a returning backslider. He gave up the ghost in his closet, craving any place where Christ was, though it was but eternally to lie at his footstool' (Calamy, *Abridgement*, 2.472).

STEPHEN WRIGHT

Sources *Calamy rev.* · G. L. Turner, ed., *Original records of early nonconformity under persecution and indulgence*, 1 (1911) · A. Gordon, ed., *Freedom after ejection: a review (1690–1692) of presbyterian and congregational nonconformity in England and Wales* (1917) · E. Hobday, 'The registers of Sturminster Marshall', *Dorset Records*, 7 (1901) · administration, PRO, PROB 6/74, fol. 31r · E. Calamy, ed., *An abridgement of Mr. Baxter's history of his life and times, with an account of the ministers, &c., who were ejected after the Restoration of King Charles II*, 2nd edn, 2 vols. (1713) · W. Robinson, *The history and antiquities of the parish of Stoke Newington* (1820) · IGI
Wealth at death see administration, PRO, PROB 6/74, fol. 31r

Bull, George (1634–1710), bishop of St David's, was born on 25 March 1634 in the parish of St Cuthbert, Wells, Somerset, the son of George Bull (*d.* 1638/9), merchant and twice mayor of Wells, and his wife, Elizabeth Perkins (*d.* 1634?). His mother died soon after his birth and his father died when George was aged four, after which Bull went to live with a sister.

Education and early career Before his entrance at Oxford University Bull studied at the grammar school at Wells and then the free school at Tiverton, Devon. His master at Tiverton, Samuel Butler, was an excellent grammarian, who provided him with a good foundation in the classics. At the age of fourteen, on 10 July 1648, Bull matriculated as a sojourner of Exeter College, Oxford. He left Oxford in January 1650, after refusing the oaths of allegiance to the Commonwealth, and followed his tutor Baldwin Ackland to North Cadbury, Somerset, staying with him there until his nineteenth birthday.

Choosing to pursue ordination to the ministry, Bull studied with the eminent puritan divine William Thomas (1593–1667), rector of Ubley, Somerset. Bull found this period of study frustrating, as Thomas directed his studies to reading reformed systems of divinity, but Samuel Thomas (1627–1693), the son of Bull's teacher, introduced Bull to episcopalian divines including Richard Hooker, Henry Hammond, and Jeremy Taylor, and convinced the future bishop of St David's of his need for episcopal orders. He subsequently applied to Robert Skinner, the ejected bishop of Oxford, for ordination in 1655, and Skinner ordained the 21-year-old Bull as deacon and priest the same day, after which Bull was given the small benefice of St George, Bristol, worth £30 per year. There he read from

George Bull (1634–1710), by Michael Vandergucht, pubd 1721

the Book of Common Prayer and preached twice every Sunday, gaining renown for his preaching.

Marriage and ministry at Siddington While at St George, Bull spent two months annually at Oxford using the libraries, stopping during his journeys at the home of Sir William Masters of Cirencester, Gloucestershire. It was there that he met the minister of Cirencester, Alexander Gregory, and his daughter Bridget (1637–1712), to whom he was married on 20 May 1658 according to the Book of Common Prayer. Their marriage endured for fifty-two years, Bridget being described as 'fruitful, as well as a provident and obedient wife, agreeably to the prayer of her wedding ring' (Kippis, 2.698). The couple had eleven children, of whom only two survived them.

In 1658 Bull was presented to the rectory of St Mary, Siddington, near Cirencester. The young cleric would also preach occasionally in his father-in-law's parish at Cirencester. During this period Bull was privy to plans for the restoration of Charles II, serving as host to a meeting of conspirators. After the restoration of the monarchy the earl of Clarendon, at the recommendation of Dr William Nicholson, bishop of Gloucester, presented Bull to the vicarage of St Peter, Siddington (1662). These two benefices provided him with an annual income of £100. While at Siddington, Bull continued to preach twice on Sundays,

basing his preaching on scripture, but making the message understandable for everyone. As parish minister Bull applied himself diligently to the tasks of catechizing, performing baptisms, and celebrating the eucharist at least seven times a year. He also made it his custom to take a collection for the poor.

Well trained in both the classical and biblical languages, Bull not only devoted himself to his parish duties, but also engaged himself in his studies, which his biographer Robert Nelson says was his 'chief delight'. His study was the

> scene of his most exquisite pleasure; and he would freely own, with great assurance, that he tasted the most refined satisfaction in the pursuit of knowledge, that the present state of human nature was capable of; and that when his thoughts were lively and lucky in his compositions, he found no reason to envy the enjoyment of the most voluptuous epicure. (*Works*, 8.76)

He devoted the greater part of each evening to his studies, working on little sleep, a practice that later compromised his health. Yet this 27-year period was his most productive. At Siddington he wrote most of his works including the *Harmonia apostolica* (1670) and the *Defensio fidei Nicenae* (1685).

Later career Bull had gained esteem (if also some notoriety) for his theological publications (discussed below) and for his diligence as a pastor. On the recommendation of John Tillotson, then dean of St Paul's, Bull was appointed to a prebend of Gloucester Cathedral in 1678 by the lord chancellor, Daniel Finch, earl of Nottingham. He was installed on 9 October 1678. After serving at Siddington for nearly three decades, he was presented to the rectory of Avening, Gloucestershire, in 1685, a benefice valued at £200 per annum. Avening had the reputation of a dissolute and immoral parish, and Bull overcame significant resistance to bring it under his control through his 'prudent conduct and diligent discharge of duty' (Kippis, 2.702–3). Shortly thereafter Archbishop William Sancroft appointed him archdeacon of Llandaff, Wales (1686), after which Bishop John Fell of Oxford nominated him to Oxford University for the doctor of divinity to honour the publication of the *Defensio fidei Nicenae*. This honour came despite his never having taken an academic degree. Diligent study and hard work more than compensated for his lack of academic credentials. As Anthony Wood recounted, 'the excellency of his riper and more pregnant parts, seconded by sever industry, and unwearied diligence that compensated in some measure that loss which he sustain'd, thro' his removal hence so soon' (Wood, *Ath. Oxon.*, 2nd edn, 1721, 2.954). Strongly anti-Catholic, he began to preach against the errors of Rome at Avening and elsewhere soon after the accession of James II. After the revolution in 1689 he was appointed to the commission of peace. In this position he attempted to use the agency of the state to enforce his understanding of Christian holiness. He hoped to fight immorality and profanity in the kingdom in this way, so that 'those whom he could not convince by his arguments, nor persuade by his affectionate way of enforcing them, might be terrified into better manners by the sword of justice which was put into his hands' (*Works*, 8.312).

A diligent and loyal priest, Bull served the church with his prodigious learning, but he was not promoted to the episcopacy until late in life. On 29 April 1705 the 71-year-old Bull was consecrated at Lambeth Palace as bishop of St David's, Wales. He had initially rejected Queen Anne's offer, but reluctantly took the position upon the encouragement of friends and family. His son, George, succeeded him as archdeacon of Llandaff, but died two years later on 11 May 1707. His son's premature death grieved Bull tremendously, especially as he had hoped his son would assist him in his episcopal duties. As bishop of St David's, Bull sat in the House of Lords, voting for the union of the two kingdoms of Scotland and England.

In spite of his age and infirmities Bull resided in his diocese, taking up residence at Brecon in July 1705 because the episcopal palace at Abermarlais was in disrepair. That summer he delivered a charge to his clergy, which was later published as *A companion for the candidates of holy orders, or, The great importance and principle duties of the priestly office* (1714). This charge gives evidence of the great esteem with which he held the pastoral calling. Prevented by illness from conducting a diocesan visitation that year, Bull commissioned several clergy to conduct it for him. In 1708 illness again impeded his conduct of a triennial diocesan visitation, but his son-in-law Joseph Stevens, husband of his daughter Anne (1662–1703) and archdeacon of Brecon, with William Powell, prebend of Brecon, conducted the visitation. He also offered services of confirmation at Brecon, and at neighbouring parishes, and every September he held services of ordination there. He used his episcopal revenues to provide for charitable work, though this diminished his estate for his family. His charitable work included the provision of a meal each Sunday for sixty indigent people and he provided funds to help widows, orphans, prisoners, and impoverished clergy and their widows.

Bull died in 1710 after a series of severe illnesses that began in September 1709 and entered their final stages in February 1710. Knowing that the end was near, he made his final confession to his son-in-law, Archdeacon Stevens, and two other clergy. He then met with his wife and children and prayed with them. Death came a little after nine in the morning on 17 February 1710 at Abermarlais. He was buried a week later at Brecon between two of his predecessors. The inscription on his tomb described him as 'excellently learned, pious and charitable' (Kippis, 2.706). His widow, Bridget, followed him in death on 16 November 1712 and was buried beside her husband. Of their eleven children only their son Robert, rector of Tortworth, Gloucestershire, and prebendary of Gloucester, and their daughter Bridget survived the death of their parents.

Published works Bull's rise to prominence in English church circles can be attributed in large part to his renown as a writer. Most of his theological works were written in Latin, being directed to a learned and educated community, with his first publication being the most controversial. Begun when he was twenty-six, his *Harmonia apostolica* was published in London in 1670, after an earlier attempt at Oxford between 1664 and 1666 had been blocked when the vice-chancellor refused to grant the book a licence. Dedicated to Bull's friend William Nicholson, bishop of Gloucester, the *Harmonia* addressed the doctrine of justification of faith by attacking the solafideism he found in the protestant theology of the day. He sought to reconcile the biblical writers Paul and James, by interpreting Paul in the light of James, insisting that the epistle of James responded to misinterpretations of Paul's doctrine of justification. According to Bull, James clarified Paul's doctrine by teaching that good works proceed from faith and are required by God for justification. The *Harmonia* engendered significant opposition, beginning with presbyterian Charles Gataker's anonymous response (1671), to which Bull replied in 1675 with his *Examen censurae*. George Morley, bishop of Winchester, issued a pastoral charge forbidding his clergy to read or preach on the book. Thomas Barlow, Lady Margaret professor of divinity at Oxford, denounced Bull's book in his lectures as an act of 'parricide' against the Church of England and socinian in the role it assigned to works, while Thomas Tully, principal of St Edmund's Hall, wrote in support of Barlow's response, declaring Bull's views heretical. Bull responded to Barlow and Tully in 1674 with the *Justificatio Paulina sine operibus, ex mente ecclesiae Anglicanae*. Despite the opposition engendered by his *Harmonia* and *Examen censurae*, these books helped advance Bull to the prebend of Gloucester.

In 1680 Bull wrote the *Defensio fidei Nicenae* to defend himself against the charge of Socinianism. Though three publishers refused to publish the work, William Jane, regius professor of divinity at Oxford, convinced Bishop Fell to intervene and have it published in 1685. Despite the delay in publication, it received the endorsement of Jacques-Benigne Bossuet, the Gallican bishop of Meaux, and the acclamation of his English colleagues, making the work the standard defence of Nicene orthodoxy. In 1694 Bull supplemented and defended the *Defensio* with his *Judicum ecclesiae catholicae*, reaffirming there the Nicene anathema against the denial of Christ's divine sonship. Bull's friend and biographer, Robert Nelson, sent the *Judicum* to Bossuet, who in turn passed it to his French episcopal colleagues, who praised the book for its forthright defence of Catholic doctrine.

In 1703 John Ernest Grabe edited Bull's Latin works, publishing them in a one-folio volume. Included in this volume was Bull's final work, *The primitive and apostolical tradition of the doctrine received in the Catholic church, concerning the divinity of our Saviour Jesus Christ*, which responded to Prussian unitarian Daniel Zwicker, arguing that Justin Martyr's logos Christology did not distort primitive Christian orthodoxy.

After Bull's death Robert Nelson published a three-volume edition of Bull's English works under the title *Some important points of primitive Christianity maintained and defended, in several sermons and other discourses* (1713).

Attached to this set was Nelson's biography of Bull. The twenty sermons and five discourses (one being in Latin) in this set appeared in print for the first time. In 1714 Bull's charge to the clergy of St David's was published under the title *A companion for the candidates of holy orders, or, The great importance and principle duties of the priestly office.*

Though Bull wrote most of his theological works in Latin, an English translation of the *Harmonia* appeared in 1801, followed by an English translation of the *Judicum ecclesiae catholicae* in 1825. As a testament to the esteem in which he was held by later high-church Anglicans, the *Harmonia*, *Examen censurae*, *Defensio*, and *Judicum* all appeared in English translation in the Tractarian-sponsored Library of Anglo-Catholic Theology (1842-55).

Bull's influence Bull's influence came largely through his published works, which set him up as a leading theological interpreter of Anglican orthodoxy at the end of the seventeenth century. His episcopal colleague, Gilbert Burnet, wrote of the *Defensio* that it was 'the most learned treatise that this age has produced of the doctrine of the primitive church concerning the Trinity' (*Burnet's History*, 767).

As a writer Bull represented a new theological movement that John Spurr suggests obscured 'the theological distinction between justification and sanctification' (Spurr, 312). Bull did in an academic context what parish clergy always did, and that was to recognize the difficulty of distinguishing between faith and works. Although Bull was assuredly more Arminian than Calvinist, Spurr emphasizes that these terms 'tell only half the story'.

Bull's concern for proper Christian living, which elicited his theological publications, was also expressed in his diligence as a parish priest and in his preaching, for which he became well known. It is odd, therefore, that his advancement to the episcopate came so late in life when age and infirmity prevented him from becoming the exemplary bishop suggested by his parish work. The biographer Mark Noble wrote that 'the only particular to be lamented in Dr. Bull's life, is, that he was not sooner a bishop, that he might have done more service to a church, of which he was a principal ornament' (Noble, 2.93).

ROBERT D. CORNWALL

Sources The works of George Bull … to which is prefixed the life of Bishop Bull by Robert Nelson, ed. E. Burton, 7 vols. in 8 (1827) • A. Kippis and others, eds., Biographia Britannica, or, The lives of the most eminent persons who have flourished in Great Britain and Ireland, 2nd edn, 5 vols. (1778-93), vol. 2, pp. 698-707 • Wood, Ath. Oxon., 2nd edn, vol. 2 • Nichols, Lit. anecdotes • A biographical history of England, from the revolution to the end of George I's reign: being a continuation of the Rev. J. Granger's work, ed. M. Noble, 3 vols. (1806) • Fasti Angl. (Hardy) • Bishop Burnet's History of his own time, new edn (1850) • J. Spurr, The Restoration Church of England, 1646-1689 (1991) • A. McGrath, 'The emergence of the Anglican tradition on justification, 1600-1700', Churchman, 98 (1984), 28-43 • C. J. Abbey, The English church and its bishops, 1700-1800, 2 vols. (1887) • N. Sykes, From Sheldon to Secker: aspects of English church history, 1660-1768 (1959) • R. Cornwall, 'Education for ministry in the Augustan age: Gilbert Burnet, George Bull, and the modern church', Anglican Theological Review, 78 (1996), 241-57 • W. H. Hutton, 'Divines of the Church of England', The Cambridge history of English literature, 8, ed. A. W. Ward and A. R. Waller (1912), 294-308 • N. Tyacke, 'Religious controversy', Hist. U. Oxf. 4: 17th-cent. Oxf., 569-620, esp. 591, 606-9
Likenesses oils, 1700, Exeter College, Oxford • M. Vandergucht, line engraving, pubd 1721, BM, NPG [see illus.]

Bull, George Stringer (1799-1865), Church of England clergyman and social reformer, was born on 12 July 1799 at Stanway, Essex, the sixth child and sixth son of eight sons and two daughters of the Revd John Bull (1767-1834), curate of Stanway, and his wife, Margaret Towndrow (1766-1833). He joined the Royal Navy at the age of eleven and served in the Napoleonic wars. In 1816 he left the navy and went to live with his father, by now rector of Tattingstone, near Ipswich. In 1818 he sailed to Sierra Leone to work as a missionary and teacher under the auspices of the Church Missionary Society, but sickness forced him to return to England in 1820. Three years later he was ordained and became curate of Hessle, near Hull, where he met Mary Frances Coulson (1796-1878), the daughter of a Hull merchant, whom he married on 5 December 1825 and with whom he had six children.

After moving to the West Riding of Yorkshire in 1825 Bull was initially curate of Hanging Heaton, near Dewsbury, and then, from 1826 until 1839, of Byerley (Bierley), near Bradford, where he became known as 'Parson Bull of Byerley'. He campaigned for slave emancipation abroad and temperance at home, and from 1831, having become increasingly aware of the often appalling conditions in many Yorkshire factories, he allied himself with Michael Sadler, Richard Oastler, and John Wood in the Ten Hours Movement, which long pressed for a reduction in the working hours of children and young people. Bull laboured tirelessly in this cause, thereby earning the nickname 'the Ten Hours Parson'. He organized and spoke at rallies and demonstrations, wrote numerous pamphlets, and was co-editor of the *British Labourer's Protector, and Factory Child's Friend* (1832-3). It was he who in 1833 was largely responsible for persuading Lord Ashley, later the seventh earl of Shaftesbury, to lead the agitation for a Ten Hours Act in parliament. Though a firm churchman he advocated the reform of abuses in the Church of England, notably in his pamphlet *The Church her Own Enemy* (1834). He was sympathetic towards the emerging trade unions and opposed the Poor Law Amendment Act of 1834, which he regarded as a retrograde measure. However, during his later years at Byerley he drew back somewhat from public campaigning because of the growth of militant Chartism, of which he disapproved. In 1840 Bull went to Birmingham. He became perpetual curate of the newly formed district of St Matthew, Duddeston, and from 1847 rector of St Thomas's, near the Bull Ring, a parish of 30,000 people. By 1864 he was in poor health and accepted the benefice of Almeley, Herefordshire, where he died on 20 August 1865. He was buried in St Thomas's churchyard, Birmingham, on 26 August.

Throughout his ministry Bull, small in stature but stockily built, was an energetic and highly effective pastor, establishing numerous schools and other parochial institutions and attracting large congregations. His outspoken advocacy of social reform ensured that he was a very popular and respected figure among the working classes in industrial areas, but his uncompromising tory churchmanship and his prominence within the Ten Hours Movement led to periodic clashes with both dissenters and Liberals. In the novel *Michael Armstrong* (1840), Frances Trollope, mother of Anthony, depicts factory life in Derbyshire and introduces Bull, thinly disguised as 'George Bell of Fairly'.   STEPHEN GREGORY

Sources J. C. Gill, *Parson Bull of Byerley* (1963) · J. C. Gill, *The ten hours parson: Christian social action in the eighteen-thirties* (1959) · J. T. Ward, *The factory movement, 1830–1855* (1962) · D. M. Lewis, ed., *The Blackwell dictionary of evangelical biography, 1730–1860*, 2 vols. (1995) · *Birmingham Daily Post* (22 Aug 1865) · *Birmingham Daily Post* (28 Aug 1865) · *Birmingham Daily Gazette* (22 Aug 1865) · E. Hodder, *The life and work of the seventh earl of Shaftesbury*, 1 (1886), 147–51 · E. Stock, *The history of the Church Missionary Society: its environment, its men and its work*, 1 (1899), 111 · *Clergy List* (1846) · *Clergy List* (1864)
Archives LUL, Goldsmith's Library of Economic Literature
Likenesses photograph, *c*.1850–1859, repro. in Gill, *Ten hours parson*, frontispiece · photograph, *c*.1860–1865, repro. in Gill, *Parson Bull of Byerley*; priv. coll., *c*.1863
Wealth at death under £2000: probate, 30 Sept 1865, *CGPLA Eng. & Wales*

Bull, Sir Graham MacGregor (1918–1987), physician, was born on 30 January 1918 at Nyaunghla, Upper Burma, the eldest in the family of two sons and one daughter of Arthur Barclay Bull, medical practitioner to an oil company and later in practice in Simonstown, and his wife, Margaret Petrie MacGregor. He was educated at Diocesan College, Rondebosch, Cape Province, South Africa, and at the University of Cape Town, where he obtained his MB, ChB with distinction in 1939. He worked in the department of medicine at the University of Cape Town at Groote Schuur Hospital from 1940 to 1946, gaining an MD degree in 1947 on the subject of postural proteinuria. As a result of this work he was awarded a fellowship by the South African Council for Scientific and Industrial Research to continue his research at the postgraduate medical school in Hammersmith, London, the post-war mecca of most Commonwealth medical academics. Under the direction of John McMichael, the postgraduate medical school provided an exciting environment in which bright young people were encouraged to think critically and pursue novel, and intellectually challenging, research. Bull thrived in this environment, and in 1947 was appointed to a lectureship in the school. His research concerned the management of acute kidney failure, for which he devised a treatment that became internationally known as the 'Bull regime'. The basis of the regime was simplicity itself. Bull argued from the analogy of a blocked lavatory. One's natural reaction was to pull the chain, so that more water flowed into the basin, which then overflowed; it would be better to leave things as they were until the blockage was relieved. For patients who were unable to pass urine, Bull recommended replacement only of the fluid and electrolytes they lost. In this way they were not overloaded and were kept in balance until kidney function returned spontaneously. The Bull regime saved countless lives by preventing over-enthusiastic

attempts to 'flush out' the kidneys, but was eventually superseded by dialysis techniques, through which a similar balance could be maintained. The recognition of Bull's work soon led to his appointment in 1952 to a chair of medicine at Queen's University, Belfast, where he gained an immense reputation as an all-round clinician and teacher. A paper he published from Belfast examined marking systems applied to essay questions in medical examinations and he was able to demonstrate that individual variability led to highly discrepant and irreproducible outcomes. More than anyone else Bull was responsible for the switch from essays to multiple-choice questions, which later became the basis of most written examinations in medicine. He became FRCP (London) in 1954. Following the untimely death of the director designate, John Squire, Bull was asked in 1966 to become the director of the new Medical Research Council clinical research centre at Northwick Park, Harrow. Squire's was a difficult place to fill, but Bull did so superbly, displaying the tact, wisdom, and concern for high standards that eased the centre into its role as a world-class clinical and investigative institution, despite many difficulties that stood in its path. His novel idea was to integrate a clinical research centre and a general district hospital, and, by the time he retired in 1978, he was in charge of an 800-bed hospital (Northwick Park Hospital) and a clinical research centre, designed as a single unit. His own research activity had, not unexpectedly, diminished over the years, but he remained abreast of the latest scientific advances and encouraged the excellent medical and scientific personnel at the centre to tackle big and exciting research problems—much in the same way as John McMichael had lent support to his young people some twenty to thirty years earlier.

Bull was a member of the Medical Research Council from 1962 to 1966, and for many years chairman of its tropical medicine research board. From 1970 to 1983 he was a member of the executive committee of the CIBA Foundation, serving as its chairman from 1977 to 1983. He was also vice-president of the Royal College of Physicians of London in 1978–9, and in 1988 the Sir Graham Bull memorial prize was founded there, to be awarded annually for meritorious research carried out by a scientist under the age of forty-five in the broad field of clinical research, in which Bull personally had excelled and guided so many young doctors. He had been knighted in 1976.

Bull was a kind and humane man, greatly respected and liked by patients, students, and colleagues. He was an excellent institutional head, always willing to listen sympathetically to people's ideas or problems and to offer sensible and helpful advice. He had many outside interests—travel, cooking, wine making—and he and his wife were exceptional and popular hosts. A little above average height, he was of solid build and tended to put on weight latterly. His brown hair fell over his forehead; in later years it silvered and thinned and, with his rather aquiline nose, this gave him a distinguished, almost patrician appearance. His eyes were strikingly direct and penetrating. In 1947 he married Megan Patricia, daughter of Thomas Jones, doctor of medicine, of South Africa. She had been a fellow medical student of his at Cape Town and became governor of Holloway prison in 1973, having previously served as its medical officer. The Bulls had three sons and a daughter, whose occupations—doctor, accountant, biologist, and musician—reflected the wide interests of their parents. Bull died suddenly on 14 November 1987 after surgery, at the National Heart Hospital, London. RAYMOND HOFFENBERG, *rev.*

Sources The Times (18 Nov 1987) · The Independent (4 Dec 1987) · The Lancet (5 Dec 1987) · MRC News, 38 (March 1988) · Munk, Roll · personal knowledge (2004) · CGPLA Eng. & Wales (1988)
Wealth at death under £70,000: probate, 25 Nov 1988, CGPLA Eng. & Wales

Bull, Hedley Norman (1932–1985), university teacher, was born on 10 June 1932 in Englewood Hospital, Burwood, Sydney, New South Wales, the third and youngest child of (Joseph) Norman Bull (1891–1972), insurance broker, and his wife, Doris Annie, *née* Hordern (1893–1967), whose family had developed a chain of department stores in Australia. He had a stable childhood in Sydney, attending Burwood primary school (*c.*1937–43) and Fort Street high school, Petersham (*c.*1944–8), one of the most prominent in the New South Wales state system.

At Sydney University (1949–52) Bull read history and philosophy, took an active part in student journalism and societies, and had a busy social life. Exceptionally, he completed both honours courses in four calendar years, gaining a first in philosophy and a second in history. The most important influence on his thinking was John Anderson, Challis professor of philosophy: his iconoclasm, tough realism, devotion to teaching, and love of grappling with statements of a contrary position in their strongest form, all left their mark on him. Bull later wrote: 'My greatest intellectual debt is to John Anderson … the impact of his mind and his example have been the deepest factors in shaping the outlook of many of us whom he taught' (*The Anarchical Society: a Study of Order in World Politics*, 1977, x). While at Sydney, he became engaged to a fellow history student, Frances Mary Lawes (*b.* 1930). On 13 March 1954 they married at Oxford. Mary Bull developed an expertise in Commonwealth history, becoming a research assistant to Margery Perham. They had three adopted children.

Bull arrived at University College, Oxford, in 1953 with the help of a Woolley travelling fellowship. He had intended to do the BPhil in philosophy, but was discouraged by the emphasis on linguistic analysis. Instead he did the BPhil in politics under a galaxy of teachers, including Herbert Hart, Isaiah Berlin, Kenneth Wheare, John Plamenatz, and Norman Chester. He showed no interest in the academic field of international relations, not well developed at Oxford at the time. After Oxford he intended to teach in Britain for some years before returning to Australia. About to take up a post in political philosophy at Aberdeen, he was unexpectedly offered an assistant lectureship in international relations at the London School of Economics and Political Science (LSE) by Charles Manning, Montague Burton professor of international relations there since 1930. The future shape of Bull's career and intellectual interests was settled.

At the LSE, learning his trade while practising it, Bull was particularly influenced by his colleague Martin Wight, whose lectures on international theory he attended. As Bull wrote in 1976: 'Ever since that time I have felt in the shadow of Martin Wight's thought—humbled by it, a constant borrower from it, always hoping to transcend it but never able to escape from it' ('Martin Wight and the theory of international relations', *British Journal of International Studies*, 2/2, July 1976, 101). He was impressed by Wight's exposition of three distinctive traditions of thought (labelled realist, rationalist, and revolutionist) in terms of which debates about international relations in any era could be understood.

Bull's first published academic work was on disarmament, on which he was critical but also constructive. In 1957–8 he was reinforced in this approach when, with the help of a grant from the Rockefeller Foundation, he visited the main centres in the USA of new thinking about arms control. In 1959–60 he acted as rapporteur for a study group on arms control of the newly formed Institute for Strategic Studies in London. The resulting book, *The Control of the Arms Race* (1961), quickly gained worldwide recognition as a rigorous exposition of the view that selective measures of arms limitation had a better chance of contributing to international order than did the utopian pursuit of general and complete disarmament.

Much of Bull's subsequent writing was on the nature of international society and the appropriate means of studying it. In a celebrated article in *World Politics* in April 1966, under the deceptively mild title 'International theory: the case for a classical approach', he attacked certain aspirants to the 'scientific' study of international relations with characteristic gusto. Although his controversialism could occasionally hurt, it was never vicious or mean-spirited, but rather reflected a love of intellectual combat. Tall, well built, and self-assured, he assaulted political cant and academic folly with a twinkle in the eye, a smile, and a real appreciation of outlandish viewpoints.

The remarkable course of his sadly brief career reflected the quality of Bull's published work. After being promoted to a readership at LSE in 1963, in 1965–7 he was appointed the first director of the newly formed arms control and disarmament unit at the Foreign Office in London. In May 1965 he took up UK citizenship.

In 1967 Bull was tempted back to Australia, to the professorship of international relations at the Australian National University, Canberra. It was there, helped by study visits to India, the USA, and Oxford, that he wrote his major work, *The Anarchical Society: a Study of Order in World Politics* (1977). This is a magisterially clear statement of the view that the system of sovereign states, although lacking a strong central authority, constitutes a society with common norms and institutions. Force, law, revolutionary and conservative perspectives all have a part to play. The book displayed an understanding of 'third-world' criticisms of Western dominance that was to be the theme of later studies, including *The Expansion of International Society*, which he edited with Adam Watson (1984).

In 1977 Bull returned to Oxford, taking up the Montague Burton professorship of international relations and a fellowship at Balliol College. In both Canberra and Oxford he played a key part in building up departments of international relations: his evident intellectual distinction helped make the subject academically respectable, he gained a formidable reputation as a supervisor of graduate students, and he managed to continue with his own research and writing. In 1984 he was elected a fellow of the British Academy. He died at his home at 5 Warnborough Road, Oxford, on 18 May 1985 after a long fight against cancer, and was cremated four days later at Oxford crematorium. His wife survived him.

ADAM ROBERTS

Sources J. D. B. Miller, 'Hedley Bull, 1932–1985', *Order and violence: Hedley Bull and international relations*, ed. J. D. B. Miller and R. J. Vincent (1990), 1–12 [incl. bibliography of Bull's pubns] · M. Howard, 'Hedley Norman Bull, 1932–1985', *PBA*, 72 (1986), 395–408 · A. Roberts, 'Hedley Norman Bull, 1932–1985', *Balliol College Annual Record* (1985), 24–8 · R. O'Neill and D. N. Schwartz, eds., *Hedley Bull on arms control* (1987) · K. Alderson and A. Hurrell, eds., *Hedley Bull on international society* (2000) · private information (2004)
Archives Bodl. Oxf., letters, MSS
Likenesses Ramsey & Muspratt, photograph, c.1977, Balliol Oxf. · photographs, priv. coll.

Bull, Henry (*d.* 1577), theological writer and physician, was born in Warwickshire. In 1537 he entered Magdalen College, Oxford, where he was admitted BA in June 1539 and became a fellow the following year. His colleagues included John Foxe, Robert Crowley, and Thomas Cooper, and their mutual interest in reform provided an air of dissidence at chapel and high table. Eventually Foxe and several of the others resigned their fellowships, under some pressure, in the mid-1540s, but Bull, who became MA in 1543, managed to keep his place, and was vice-president of the college in 1549–50. On 23 March 1553 he was admitted rector of Courtenhall, Northamptonshire, but soon after Mary came to the throne he was expelled from Magdalen, as a result of a protest he made with Thomas Bentham (the future bishop of Lichfield) at the restoration of the mass, when they snatched the censer out of the hand of the officiating priest to forestall what they believed was the idolatrous offering of incense. Courtenhall was recorded as vacant in November 1553.

The manner in which Bull passed the dangerous years that followed remains obscure. Already by 1550 he had developed friendships with continental reformers, and he might have turned to them for aid. But although Wood reports that Bull fled to the continent, his name does not appear among the lists of exiles. In an Elizabethan letter to Foxe, William Wyntropp acknowledged Bull as among those who 'have not bowed theyr knees to baall' (BL, Harley MS 416, fol. 106*r*), which may indicate that even if Bull

did not escape abroad, he managed to avoid mass, as well as the authorities, during Mary's reign. He had supplicated the university for leave to practise medicine in Michaelmas term 1552, and it is possible that he earned his living as a physician during these years. Bull may have been one of the linchpins of a covert London congregation that helped to ensure the ultimate survival of protestantism in England.

After Elizabeth's accession, from 1560 onward Bull joined Foxe in the challenging undertaking of finding and editing the documents that were left behind by the Marian martyrs, as a legacy 'in behalfe of the churche of God' (Hooper, *Apologye*, preface). He was a frequent visitor at the house of Foxe's collaborator and printer John Day. Much of Bull's work was performed in symbiosis with Foxe's larger and more far-reaching effort to edit and re-edit the *Actes and Monuments*, the comprehensive history of the Christian Church in which the martyrdom of those who had suffered persecution (particularly under Henry VIII and Mary Tudor) was central. Before the first English version of Foxe's *Actes and Monuments* was printed in 1563, Bull called publicly for the recovery of documents by the Marian martyrs. The collection of manuscripts that he helped to amass has been preserved by Emmanuel College, Cambridge, from its earliest days (MSS 260, 261, and 262). They include letters by John Hooper, John Bradford, and John Philpot.

Bull issued the writings of the martyrs in individual editions, as collections of letters or brief pamphlets, very much in the form that they were originally conceived by their authors. In this sense Bull provided an associated literature which must be understood as an important adjunct to Foxe's great book of martyrs, which also mined the letters Bull discovered. Bull's first book was an edition of a tract with letters that Hooper, the Edwardine bishop of Gloucester and Worcester (burnt 1555) had written in prison, *An Apologye … againste the Untrue and Sclaunderous Report* that he had encouraged those who had treasonably cursed Queen Mary in January 1555. It appeared in 1562, with the approval of Bishop Edmund Grindal of London (who, with Foxe in exile, originally conceived of the plan to bring the martyrs' writings to the press).

Bull's most important contribution to the shared effort to print the written 'monuments' of those who had died, was to serve as the actual editor of the collection *Certain Most Godly, Fruitful, and Comfortable Letters of … True Saintes and Holy Martyrs of God*, which was issued under Miles Coverdale's name and printed by Day in 1564. Close inspection of the surviving holograph letters of the martyrs, preserved at Emmanuel College, shows that the numerous editorial markings are in Bull's handwriting. His subtle editing tended to heighten the timeless quality of the letters by emphasizing the writers' intense biblicism, building upon the martyrs' desire to send comforting epistles to their followers in the style of St Paul. Bull chose to delete any material from the letters that he deemed 'superfluous' (Emmanuel College, MS 260, fol. 33*r*), removing many personal allusions to the martyrs' friends and supporters. Some of these letters Foxe too incorporated into the next edition of the *Actes and Monuments* in 1570, and frequently with Bull's changes.

Bull's most popular book was a collection of *Christian Prayers and Meditations*, which went through six editions by 1590, and continued to be reprinted in the seventeenth century.

In the last years of his life, Bull lived in London, serving as a physician. By the early 1560s he had married Margaret Litler and settled in the parish of St Dunstan-in-the-West. He died in London between 13 March and 4 July 1577. Two books were issued posthumously. His translation *Commentarie upon the Fiftene Psalmes*, from the work by Luther, includes a moving preface by Foxe, describing how Bull had received from this dying labour the greatest 'spirituall consolation' of his life. In 1580 a collection of Hooper's *Certeine Comfortable Expositions ... upon the XXIII. LXII. LXXXIII. and LXXVII. Psalmes*, of which Bull was joint editor, was printed (perhaps under the guidance of Foxe's wife, Agnes).

In the first edition of the *Actes and Monuments*, Foxe explained that he was impelled to bring the writings of the martyrs 'of our time' into wider currency, for the sake of 'the encrease of the gospel'. Otherwise, their writings would lie buried 'in the pit of oblivion' (sigs. B6r–B6v). Henry Bull was among those who worked with Foxe to preserve their words for future generations.

SUSAN WABUDA

Sources J. Foxe, *Actes and monuments* (1563), 1475–640 • J. Foxe, *The first volume of the ecclesiasticall history contaynyng the actes and monumentes of thynges passed*, new edn (1570) • M. Coverdale, ed., *Certain most godly, fruitful, and comfortable letters* (1564) • BL, Harley MSS 416–426, 590; Add. MS 19400 [Foxe MSS] • H. B[ull], ed., *Christian praiers and holy meditations* (1570) • J. Hooper, *An apologye ... againste the untrue and sclaunderous report*, ed. H. Bull (1562) • M. Luther, *A commentarie upon the fiftene Psalmes*, trans. H. Bull (1577) • J. Hooper, *Certeine comfortable expositions ... upon the XXIII. LXII. LXXIII. and LXXVII. psalmes*, ed. [H. Bull] (1580) • S. Wabuda, 'Henry Bull, Miles Coverdale, and the making of Foxe's Book of martyrs', *Martyrs and martyrologies*, ed. D. Wood, SCH, 30 (1993), 245–58 • Wood, *Ath. Oxon.*, new edn, 1.424–5 • Emmanuel College, Cambridge, MSS 260–262 • Emden, *Oxf.*, 4.82 • will, PRO, PROB 11/59, fols. 218v–220r • B. Usher, 'Backing protestantism: the London godly, the exchequer, and the Foxe circle', *John Foxe: an historical perspective* [Oxford 1997], ed. D. Loades (1999), 105–34
Archives Emmanuel College, Cambridge, MSS assembled by him, 260, 261, 262
Wealth at death no value given: will, PRO, PROB 11/59, fols. 218v–220r

Bull, Herbert Arthur (1854–1928), headmaster, was born at Harrow on 21 May 1854, the son of William John Bull (*d.* 1890), an assistant master at Harrow School, and his wife, Augusta Jane (*née* Marshall). Educated at Rugby School from 1867 to 1873, Bull entered Trinity College, Cambridge, in 1873, graduating with a pass degree in 1877. He represented Cambridge against Oxford at rugby football, tennis, and racquets. His first teaching post was as an assistant master at Wellington College, where he taught modern languages from 1880 to 1886. He left Wellington to set up, in partnership with his brother, Reginald Alfred Bull (*b.* 1857), a private preparatory school at Westgate-on-

Sea, which they named Wellington House. They started with only one boy, but by 1896 there were over fifty; many proceeded with scholarships to Wellington College, with which Bull maintained close ties. Reginald Bull set up a preparatory school (St Andrew's, Southborough, Kent) on his own account in 1890, leaving Herbert as sole headmaster at Wellington House until his retirement in 1920. Bull ran the school with the help of his wife, Elinor, daughter of Alfred Willett, a surgeon, whom he married in 1889. Wellington House closed in 1970.

Ordained in 1884, Bull was deeply religious, and built a chapel for the school. Simple and honest in his approach to the education of boys, he could also be a frequent user of the cane. A lifelong enthusiast for sport, he was one of the original members of the Hockey Association.

Bull was a leading light in the formation of the Association of Preparatory Schools (APS) in 1892, seeing the importance of having a public body to bring the heads of public and preparatory schools together. He was twice elected chairman (1899 and 1910). Holding high ideals about the teaching of the young, he saw the APS members as a band of brothers dedicated to the early teaching of the leaders of the nation. He could, however, be impatient with those who did not share his views. His last appearance at the APS conference was in 1917, when he defended the retention of the scripture paper in the common entrance examination.

After his retirement Bull was active in local government and became chairman of Westgate-on-Sea urban district council. He was appointed rural dean of Westbere, Thanet, in 1917. He died at his home, Idene Place, Benenden, Kent, on 10 August 1928.

DONALD P. LEINSTER-MACKAY

Sources *The Times* (28 Aug 1928) • *Preparatory School Review* (Dec 1928) • C. W. Trevelyan, 'Memories of Herbert Bull', 1970 • Venn, *Alum. Cant.* • D. P. Leinster-Mackay, *The rise of the English prep school* (1984) • b. cert.
Wealth at death £46,322 3s. 4d.: probate, 8 Nov 1928, *CGPLA Eng. & Wales*

Bull, Joan (*supp. fl.* 1928–1946), fictitious epitomist of enfranchised women, the analogue of John *Bull, was created by the cartoonist David *Low (1891–1963) to symbolize the women aged between twenty-one and thirty who obtained the vote in 1928 despite opposition from the 'diehard dimwits'—clear precursors of Low's Colonel Blimp. Championing flapper fashions against the old fogies, speaking up for birth control and against restrictive clothing, Low showed a radical enthusiasm for the healthy political influence that newly enfranchised women might exert. His cloche-hatted, short-skirted, and high-heeled 'Miss 1929' featured in the *Star* on 11 June 1927 is the prototype for the Joan Bull who first appeared in the *Evening Standard* on 23 January 1928. Low had earlier portrayed a Mrs J. Bull in the *Star* on 10 November 1922 as a buxom middle-aged housewife. His Mrs Bull of 24 April 1924 was middle-aged and double-chinned and wore a Britannia helmet—echoing an earlier embodiment of patriotic domesticity popularized during the French Revolutionary Wars. Joan Bull, by contrast, sported a top hat, a Union

Joan Bull (*supp. fl.* 1928–1946),
by David Low, 1928

Jack dress, and boots. When confronted by the claims and aspirations of politicians she appeared innocent, incredulous, and puzzled, though her questions—as later with the wife of Strube's John Citizen—issued from a shrewd and somewhat pert intelligence guaranteed to infuriate the male. Wide-eyed, open-minded, sceptical, and slightly humourless, she patronizingly gave party leaders a hearing as they competed for her vote.

Joan Bull stopped appearing regularly in Low's cartoons after the early 1930s and never rivalled his Colonel Blimp as a well-known stereotype. Low had less use for her once the general elections of 1929 and 1931 had exposed earlier exaggerations of the distinctive electoral influence that could be expected from women. Besides, in the 1930s there were more important issues for cartoonists and others to think about. Joan Bull made a brief return (in slacks, sandals, and a Union Jack brassière) with Low's other pre-war symbols—his dog, Blimp, and the TUC cart-horse—in his cartoon *The Models Return*, published in the *Evening Standard* on 6 August 1946. Thereafter Low made no further use of her, and when in need of a national symbol in 1951 he reverted to the traditional and less contentious female archetype of *Britannia.

BRIAN HARRISON

Sources P. Mellini and R. T. Matthews, 'John Bull's family arises', *History Today*, 37/5 (1987), 17–23 · R. T. Matthews and P. Mellini, 'From Britannia to Maggie: the fall and rise of John Bull's descendants', *History Today*, 38/9 (1988), 17–23
Likenesses D. Low, caricature, University of Kent at Canterbury, Centre for the Study of Cartoons and Caricatures; repro. in *Evening Standard* (23 Jan 1928) [*see illus.*] · D. Low, caricature (*The models return*), repro. in *Evening Standard* (6 Aug 1946)

Bull, John (1559×63–1628), composer, was born either in 1562 or 1563 (according to a 1589 portrait) or, less plausibly, in 1559 or 1560 (according to his marriage licence of December 1607), probably in Hereford or the surrounding area but possibly in Radnorshire; nothing is known of his parents. On 31 August 1573 he was admitted as a choirboy of Hereford Cathedral and about 1574 he was enlisted for the Chapel Royal choir, the master of the children at that time being William Hunnis. At some stage Bull was also a student of John Blitheman. In January 1578, presumably after his voice had broken, he was apprenticed to the Merchant Taylors' Company; his sponsor was Thomas Radcliffe, third earl of Sussex. On the recommendation of the earl's brother-in-law, Sir Henry Sidney, president of the council of Wales and the marches, the dean and chapter of Hereford Cathedral appointed Bull as organist there on 24 December 1582—at first jointly with John Hodges, who had held the post since 1538.

On 21 January 1583 Bull was also appointed master of the choristers, in place of Thomas Mason who had been negligent in his duties. His own relationship with the dean and chapter did not always run smooth: he was temporarily dismissed from his two posts on 1 February 1585 because he had taken longer leave than had been granted, and on 5 June the same year he was suspended because he had been absent when required to play the organ and had been disrespectful to the precentor. Nevertheless, following his admission in January 1586 as a gentleman of the Chapel Royal, Bull maintained his association with Hereford for some years. He was granted new rooms there on 16 September 1587, and again (at the request of the archbishop of Canterbury) on 18 January 1591. Meanwhile, on 9 July 1586 he graduated BMus at Oxford, having 'practised the fac[ulty] of Musick for 14 years' (Wood, *Ath. Oxon.*: *Fasti*, 1.756), and on 7 July 1592 he proceeded DMus by incorporation, having almost certainly taken the Cambridge MusD degree in the meantime; a minute in the journal book of the common council of the City of London (23 March 1597) reveals an affiliation to King's College, Cambridge.

John Bull (1559x63–1628), by unknown artist, 1589

At the court of Elizabeth I The gentlemen of the Chapel Royal were appointed primarily as singers, and in May 1592 Bull was apparently the first organist to receive any special remuneration for his services in that capacity. When on Easter day 1593 the queen went to communion, 'Dr Bull was at the organ playinge the Offertorye' (Rimbault, 150). Gentlemen of the chapel were well placed to receive supplementary income through royal patronage. For example, in November 1593 Bull was granted a twenty-one-year lease in reversion 'for 5 tenements … in consideration of his service', together with the parsonage of Middleton, Norfolk, and land in Yorkshire and Warwickshire, with a rental amounting to £14 10s. per annum (Ashbee, 6.61). On the queen's recommendation he was also appointed on 30 November 1596 by the mayor and aldermen of the City of London the first reader in music at the newly founded Gresham College, at a salary of £50 per annum. According to the ordinances of 16 January 1597 the twice-weekly music lecture was to consist of 'the theorique part for one half hour or thereabouts, and the practique by concent of voice or of instruments for the rest of the hour' (Ward, viii); it could be 'altogether in English' (rather than Latin and English). Bull's inaugural lecture, given on 6 October 1597, was later printed by Thomas East. Only the title-page and an offset of the first page of the lecture have survived; the latter includes the phrases 'a quick sighted bird' (undoubtedly a reference to Byrd) and 'My Master [Byrd] liveth … and I his scholar not worthy … in his presence to speak of this Art and Science' (A. H. King, 'Fragments of early printed music in the Bagford collection', *Music and Letters*, 40, 1959, 269–73, 270–71). Some insight into Bull's own studies is given by two books

surviving from his library. One (Fitzwilliam Museum, Cambridge, Mus MS 782) contains music manuscript paper printed by 'T. E.' (Thomas East); several hands have written in it, but none of them appears to be that of Bull. The other, slightly smaller, volume (CUL, Rel.c.56.4) contains three printed books, Sebastiani's *Bellum musicale* (1563), Arbeau's *Orchésographie* (1596 edn), and Holborne's *Cittharn Schoole* (1597).

It is possible that Bull was involved in the production of instruments at this period. On 7 January 1599 a privy council warrant refers to a certain Thomas Boultele or Boultelt, employed by Bull in the making of musical instruments for the queen. There is evidence (Jeans and Neighbour, 585–6) that Bull himself was later involved in an organ building project.

Although clear confirmation is lacking, it is also possible that in 1601 and/or 1602 Bull travelled in Europe. A chequebook entry for 3 April 1601, recording the appointment of Arthur Cocke 'to supplye the wantes of organistes which may be throughe sicknes or other urgent causes' (Rimbault, 37), has been taken to imply his absence, or planned absence; furthermore, on 22 June 1601 Bull requested on grounds of sickness leave of absence from his Gresham readership, eventually granted on 5 February 1602. According to Wood, Bull 'took occasion to go incognito in France and Germany' (he does not say when), and, to the amazement of a famous musician at the cathedral of St Omer, added forty more parts to an existing song of forty parts. However, on 29 April 1602 Bull received a payment as a member of the chapel; he was certainly present at the funeral of Queen Elizabeth on 28 April 1603, and in June of that year he resumed his readership at Gresham College.

At the court of James I In the early years of James's reign Bull's career was on an 'upward curve'. In the Chapel Royal chequebook he heads the list of gentlemen present at the coronation, on 5 December 1604 his annual salary (like that of his colleagues) was increased from £30 to £40, and on 13 April 1605 he was awarded an additional payment of £40 per annum for life, apparently for his organ playing duties. In 1606 the king gave Bull as a new year gift a chain of gold weighing almost 1 lb. On 15 December 1606 Bull was admitted a freeman of the Merchant Taylors' Company. A few months later, on 16 July 1607, the company gave a feast in honour of King James and Prince Henry, at which Bull 'in a cittizens gowne, cappe, and hood, played most excellent melodie upon a small payre of organes placed there for that purpose onely' (Stow and Howes, 891). The following day he and Nathaniel Giles, master of the children at the Chapel Royal, were admitted to the livery of the company, without fee.

On 20 December 1607 Bull resigned his Gresham readership, since he was about to marry Elizabeth Walter. According to the marriage licence, issued on 22 December, she was about twenty-four years old and had been in the service of the marchioness of Winchester. Evidence that Bull had a child appears in a rather puzzling letter which he addressed on 26 April 1613 to Sir Michael Hicks, secretary to the earl of Salisbury, asking that his name in some letters patent, producing £40 per annum, be replaced by that of his child.

By June 1611 Bull was at the head of Prince Henry's musical establishment, formed a year earlier; his annual salary was again £40. On 5 May 1612 he was paid £35 for having provided 'sondry sortes of musick bookes' for the prince's use (Ashbee, 4.212), and when the prince died that November, Bull received mourning livery for the funeral. In the winter of 1612–13 he taught Princess Elizabeth the virginals, and on 14 February 1613, when she married Frederick, the elector palatine, at Whitehall, he composed a setting of the benediction 'God the father, God the son' (now lost). Also in celebration of the marriage was the publication, some time between the engagement on 27 December and the wedding ceremony, of *Parthenia*, a volume of keyboard music by Byrd, Bull, and Orlando Gibbons, printed from engraved copper plates, to which Bull contributed seven pieces.

Netherlands, 1613–1628 Later that year, however, Bull's court career came to an abrupt end. According to Archbishop George Abbot of Canterbury, writing on 15 December to William Trumbull, the English ambassador in Brussels, Bull fled across the seas as a result of having been charged in the high commission court with adultery and other grave offences, although the composer himself later explained his flight as occasioned by 'information [being] laid against him that he was of the Catholic faith' (Dart, 'An unknown letter', 177). Bull secured a position as one of the organists in the chapel of the Archduke Albert in Brussels, being appointed on 24 September 1613 and paid regularly at the rate of 750 florins per annum until the end of August 1614, but he did not keep it long. When Trumbull informed the archduke of Bull's misdemeanours and James I's displeasure the archduke dismissed Bull—apparently unwillingly, for he continued to make occasional payments to him up to 23 April 1618, and possibly thereafter. Meanwhile, as the composer sought alternative employment, writing in November 1614 to the mayor of Antwerp, seeking the post of organist-pensioner, more of his work appeared in print in England in Sir William Leighton's *The Teares or Lamentacions of a Sorrowful Soule* (1614).

From September 1615 Bull was assistant organist to Raymond Waelrant at Antwerp Cathedral, and on Waelrant's death (15 September 1617) he was appointed probationary organist; the position was confirmed on 29 December 1617. His salary, of 80 florins plus a supplement of 20 florins, was later increased to 160 florins. As in England there were supplementary sources of income, such as playing and maintaining an organ in the cathedral acquired in 1617 by the Guild of Our Lady, advising in December 1617 on a new organ to be installed in the cathedral at 's-Hertogenbosch, and acting as city organist. In 1620 Bull moved into a house by the south door of the cathedral, and later he occupied rooms in the Papenhof (vicars' close). On 15 July 1625 Elisabeth Boll—perhaps Bull's wife—died in Antwerp. In 1626 and 1627 deputy organists were appointed by the cathedral chapter to cover for Bull's illness. He died at Antwerp on 12 or 13 March 1628 and was buried on 15 March in the Groenplats cemetery to the south of the cathedral. No will survives, but the chapter received his bequest of 24 florins on 26 October 1628.

Reputation According to Wood, Bull had 'a most prodigious hand on the Organ' (Wood, *Ath. Oxon.: Fasti*), and it is mainly on his keyboard music, notably in the celebrated Fitzwilliam virginal book but also surviving in Paris (Bibliothèque Nationale, Rés. 1185), that his reputation rests. The forms he used were those developed by his predecessors (and teachers) Blitheman and Byrd: plainsong settings, fantasias, grounds and variations, and dances such as pavans and galliards. Much of the music is technically demanding and brilliant in effect, though, oddly enough, the piece entitled *Doctor Bulls my Self* (Musica Britannica, 19, rev. edn 1970, no. 138), with its haunting melody, is more restrained. It was probably his friend Guilielmus Messaus, choirmaster of the Antwerp church of St Walburga, who preserved the chief collection of Bull's compositions in the Netherlands (BL, Add. MS 23623). Bull composed a large number of canons for unspecified instruments; of the 120 surviving in Vienna (Österreichische Nationalbibliothek, MS 17771) all but four are on the plainsong *Miserere*. A few other works for viol consort are ascribed to him. Finally, a modest number of English anthems survive: four full and three verse anthems (others are incompletely preserved). Unusually for a British composer of his generation, Bull wrote no madrigals. With his liking for contrapuntal device and highly patterned figuration, and his frequent use of plainsong cantus firmi, Bull, in the apt words of William Barclay Squire, 'approaches more nearly the Flemish school than the Italian' (*DNB*). ALAN BROWN

Sources T. Dart, 'Calendar of the life of John Bull', *John Bull: keyboard music*, ed. J. Steele and F. Cameron, 2nd edn, pt 1, Musica Britannica, 14 (1967), xxi–xxvi · S. Jeans and O. W. Neighbour, 'Bull, John', *New Grove*, 2nd edn · A. Ashbee, ed., *Records of English court music*, 4 (1991); 6 (1992); 8 (1995) · E. F. Rimbault, ed., *The old cheque-book, or book of remembrance, of the Chapel Royal, from 1561 to 1744*, CS, new ser., 3 (1872) · J. Ward, *The lives of the professors of Gresham College* (1740) · Wood, *Ath. Oxon.: Fasti*, 1st edn, 756 · J. Stow and E. Howes, *The annales, or, Generall chronicle of England ... unto the ende of the present yeere, 1614* (1615) · H. R. Hoppe, 'John Bull in the archduke's service', *Music and Letters*, 35 (1954), 114–15 · T. Dart, 'An unknown letter from Dr John Bull', *Acta Musicologica*, 32 (1960), 175–7 · R. Rasch, 'The Messaus-Bull codex: London, British Library, additional manuscript 23,623', *Revue Belge de Musicologie*, 50 (1996), 93–127 · W. Cunningham, *The keyboard music of John Bull* (1984) · P. Chappell, *A portrait of John Bull, c.1563–1628* (1970)

Archives Österreichische Nationalbibliothek, Vienna, MS 17771 · Bibliothèque Nationale, Paris, Rés. 1185 · BL, Add. MS 23623 · CUL, Rel. c. 56.4 · FM Cam., Mus MS 782 | FM Cam., Fitzwilliam Virginal Book, Mus MS 168

Likenesses oils, 1589, U. Oxf., library of the faculty of music [*see illus.*]

Wealth at death 24 florins to Antwerp Cathedral: cathedral chapter records

Bull, John (d. 1642), self-proclaimed prophet, is an obscure figure. Nothing is yet known of his early life. Shortly after his death an anonymous pamphlet appeared relating the 'true story' of 'two Weavers (late of Colchester) *viz. Richard Farnham* and *John Bull*; who affirmed themselves the two great Prophets which should come in the end of the world' (Revelation 11: 3; *False Prophets Discovered*, title-page). It is possible that Bull came from the Colchester area—he was known to two people living in the town in the 1630s. Perhaps he learned his trade there. Equally, he may have been apprenticed in London, though no one by that name was admitted as a freeman of the Weavers' Company between the years 1600 and 1646. By the spring of 1636 Bull appears to have been living in St Botolph, Aldgate.

On 20 February 1636 the king's commissioners for causes ecclesiastical issued a warrant to John Wragg, messenger of the chamber. They had been informed that in London, its suburbs, and many other places 'there are at this present … sundrie sorts of Separatists and sectaries, as namely Brownists, Anabaptists, Arrians, Thraskists, Famalists, Sensualists, Antinomians, and some other sorts'. Wragg was required to root out such 'sectaries or schismatiques' in 'anie house or place' suspected of hosting private 'Conventicles' and to search for 'all unlawfull and unlicenced' books, writings, and papers (PRO, SP 16/314, no. 34, fols. 78v–79r). Bull and Richard *Farnham seem at this time to have attended a conventicle, for a Rose Thurgood records that 'I reasoned with my brothers Richard Farnam & John Bull concerning prayer' (Thurgood, MS 875, fol. 203v). Though the pastor of this congregation is unknown, it is suggestive that Colchester was the seat of 'an old Church of the Separation' (C. Burrage, *The Early English Dissenters*, 2 vols., 1912, 2.299). Bull and Farnham were taken by warrant (Farnham was apprehended in Long Lane near 'Whittington's cat') and examined on 16 April 1636. A pamphlet by Thomas Heywood appeared that same year relating their 'Opinions' (Heywood, title-page). Farnham was said to affirm:

that hee hath the very spirit of God, which revealeth unto him all secrets whatsoever … He likewise affirmeth, that he must first be slaine, and after that rise againe, and after that be made King of that very *Jerusalem* in which King *David* and King *Salomon* once reigned. He saith also that he himselfe is one of the two witnesses spoken of in the *Revelation* … and that his brother *Bull* is another also; and shall be a Priest at the same time when he is made a King. (ibid., 9)

Bull was said to be 'besotted with the like Lunacy', affirming that 'hee shall also be slaine at *Hierusalem* where *Christ* suffered, and shall rise againe; and after that his resurrection, he shall reigne there as a Priest' (ibid., 10–11). The writer added that the two believed that 'when they shall come to *Hierusalem*, they shall be inspired with the *Holy Tongue*, the very same in which the Patriarchs and Prophets spake, and prophesied' (ibid., 12). He noted without elaboration that these doctrines seemed 'to smell of the Sect of the *Thraskites* and *Sabbatarians*' (ibid., 13). The first of these labels was a reference to John Traske, who had been an early victim of Wragg's sweep against sectaries, had emphasized the applicability of Old Testament laws to Christians in his teaching, and kept the dietary laws of the Jews and—the meaning of the second label—observed the sabbath on Saturday.

On 4 May 1636 Bull was sent to Bridewell by warrant from the court of high commission. There he remained, ordered to work and with company kept from him. After enduring months in 'the laborious' task of 'beating hempe: to the sore afflickting of his weake bodie' he petitioned Archbishop Laud, requesting that he be brought to trial (PRO, SP 16/375, no. 95). Farnham, who was imprisoned first in Newgate and then in Bethlem Hospital (Bedlam), wrote similar entreaties, successively petitioning Laud, the privy council, the governors of Bridewell and Bethlem hospitals, and Charles I. At some point Farnham 'sickned', while Bull was said to have 'gone abroad at his pleasure'. In December 1641 Bull was reportedly 'shut upp in an house visited with the sicknes' (*False Prophets Discovered*, sig. A3). Doubtless this was at one Richard 'Curtains house in Rosemary lane', where Curtain, Farnham, and Bull all 'dyed' (ibid.). Curtain died first, apparently of 'the plague' (ibid., sig. A3v). He was followed to the grave by Farnham, who was buried on 4 January 1642. Three days after Farnham's demise Bull and three female followers (all married) allegedly claimed that they had witnessed his resurrection. John Bull was buried on 14 January 1642 in the parish of St Mary, Whitechapel. It is possible that a few days before his death he was baptized by a member of a branch of the semi-separatist church which had been founded by Henry Jacob and continued by John Lathorp.

In December 1648 one Anne Curtyn was committed to the New Prison at Clerkenwell by warrant for denying 'Jesus Christ to be a p[ro]fit & his p[ro]pheticall office, for being a p[ro]fessed Jew & causing children to be circumcised' (Middlesex Sessions, Jan 1649, fol. 10). She may have been Richard Curtain's wife, at whose house Farnham and Bull died.

ARIEL HESSAYON

Sources *False prophets discovered* (1642) · T. H. [Thomas Heywood], *A true discourse of the two infamous upstart prophets* (1636) · R. Thurgood, 'A lecture of repentance', JRL, MS 875, fols. 201–74 · petition of John Bull, 1637?, PRO, SP 16/375, no. 95 · court minute book of governors of Bridewell and Bethlem hospitals, GL, MS 33011/8, fols. 87r, 90r, 363r · parish registers, St Mary Whitechapel, 1558–1643, LMA, P 93/MRY/1 · Middlesex sessions, Jan 1649, LMA, MJ/SBB/82 · D. Featley, *Katabaptistai kataptystoi, the dippers dipt*. (1645)

Likenesses supposed portrait, repro. in T. H., *True discourse*, title-page

Bull, Mrs John (supp. *fl.* 1712–*c*.1930). *See under* Bull, John (supp. *fl.* 1712–2000).

Bull, John (supp. *fl.* 1712–2000), fictitious epitomist of Englishness and British imperialism, first appeared in print in *The History of John Bull*, a political allegory—sometimes wrongly attributed to Jonathan Swift, but now accepted as the work of John *Arbuthnot, Queen Anne's physician. The *History* appeared in five parts between March and July 1712 at the time of the War of the Spanish Succession. In this satire John Bull was a small cloth merchant, embroiled in a law suit with his European neighbours, Nicholas Frog (the Dutch), Lewis Baboon (Louis Bourbon of France), Philip Baboon (the king of Spain), Esquire South (the Austrian archduke), Sister Peg (Scotland), and various others. Arbuthnot's work was a thinly veiled attack on whig foreign policy and on the financiers who were benefiting from English intervention in Europe. Arbuthnot's

THE BRITISH ATLAS, or John Bull supporting the Peace Establishment.

John Bull (*supp. fl.* **1712–2000**), by Charles Williams, *c.*1816

John Bull—'an honest plain-dealing Fellow, Cholerick, Bold, and of very unconstant Temper' (Arbuthnot, 9)—had prospered from trade, but had been duped by his lawyers into a suit which they had promised would be settled in a year or two, but had now dragged on for over a decade, causing him much financial misery. The *History* was not the first portrayal of the archetypal Englishman as blunt, irritable, and prone to take to the bottle, nor the first association of Englishness with bovine characteristics: the bull, the ox, and beef had often symbolized the English nation. Nor was Arbuthnot's *History* the first tory allegory on the whig junta which had effectively controlled the country's fortunes since the revolutionary settlement of 1688–9. But Arbuthnot's *History of John Bull* was the first to combine all these ingredients in the persona of John Bull, and as such it remained a remarkably influential work, reprinted in 1727 and 1751, and still inspiring parodies such as *Sister Peg* in 1761, once thought the work of David Hume but now identified as that of the historian and philosopher Adam Ferguson.

From the 1760s onwards John Bull began his long history in the visual media as the embodiment not so much of England, but of the English people. The explosion of political propaganda which accompanied the accession of George III and the ministry of the third earl of Bute saw John Bull being drawn by the caricaturists for the first time, initially sometimes as a bull, but increasingly by the 1780s as a shopkeeper or farmer, depending on the artist.

Whatever the preferred depiction of the various cartoonists and print-sellers, the characteristics associated with John Bull remained quite close to the genre established by Arbuthnot. He was a reluctant nationalist—reluctant because he knew going to war with other countries meant higher taxes. The focus of his nationalism might change—Bute and the Scots in the 1760s, the Jacobin constitution in the 1790s, Napoleon's nation in arms after 1802—but his reputation as a down-to-earth, liberty-loving, beer-drinking, and pugnacious admirer of all things English remained intact. And as in Arbuthnot's original incarnation, the John Bull of the late eighteenth-century print was gullible, lacked much foresight, and was easily led by scheming politicians of all parties (but especially the whigs). But if the proclivities and preoccupations of John Bull remained constant over time, the late eighteenth century did see a concerted attack on his status as the authentic 'everyman' of public opinion. Alarmed at the seizure of power by the demos of Paris, the sansculottes, some caricaturists in 1789—particularly James Gillray and Charles Williams—produced versions of John Bull which made him appear as a sort of Frankenstein's monster of democracy: coarse, plebeian, physically disfigured, and grotesque. Other propagandists—for example William Jones in his anti-Jacobin Bull family letters—lauded his loyalism, peasant-like stoicism, and deference, and this stereotype became common during the invasion scares of 1802–3.

One consequence of Jones's focus on Bull's family was the growing prominence of **Mrs John Bull** (*supp. fl.* 1712–*c.*1930) in accounts designed to show the effects of radicalism and war on British domestic as well as political life. Thus, in Jones's letters Mrs Bull and her sister-in-law anxiously discuss the impact of a now godless France on national attitudes to marriage. James Gillray's contemporary cartoon *John Bull's Progress* offered a similarly bleak picture: with her once 'happy' home destroyed by war, Mrs Bull is forced to pawn her possessions and now sits in rags awaiting John's return from the army. By contrast, the original Mrs Bull, dating from 1712, had offered little loyalty, being a 'luxurious Jade' who 'lov'd splendid Equipages'. Arbuthnot's decision to kill off the first Mrs Bull left John free to remarry a more suitable 'sober Countywoman … the reverse of the other in her Temper' (Arbuthnot, 13, 15) who, practical, sensible, and respectful, willingly lent her support during the later political crisis.

As the Napoleonic wars drew to a close and war in Europe gave way to civil instability at home, radical publishers and prints associated with William Benbow, George Cruikshank, and William Hone appropriated the tax-hating, free-born Englishman that was John Bull for their own purposes, making him the figurehead of their attacks on 'old Corruption', or, as in an 1816 print, the bearer of the establishment's excessive fiscal burden. In this struggle John was once more assisted by Mrs Bull, who over the course of the war emerged as a somewhat more forceful and independent figure: for example, marching beside her husband at Taunton's peace parade in June 1814 or helping him driving away a 'swarm of tax gatherers' in Charles Williams's cartoon *Blessing of Britain* (1817). Tory writers responded in kind. At the time of the Queen Caroline affair, for example, the *John Bull* newspaper, established under tory colours and edited by Theodore Hook, took the new king's side in the acrimonious attempt to impose a divorce on the estranged queen. Thus by the early nineteenth century there was as little agreement about who John Bull was as there was consensus about the nation's affairs in general.

A more stable version of John Bull began to emerge in the middle decades of the nineteenth century. As taxes fell and Britain retreated from military involvement on the European continent, the burdens of John Bull lightened. And as the threat posed by republican democracy eased off, the disputes over John Bull's social origins subsided. By the time of the Reform Act of 1832 the rotund, usually rural, shabby farmer or even squire was beginning to become the dominant depiction of John Bull. In this guise he featured as the bemused but complacent 'everyman' of H. B.'s [John Doyle's] prints in the late 1820s and 1830s, and then in *Punch* from 1842 onwards. John Leech's and John Tenniel's drawings for *Punch* provide what remains the best-known and most easily recognizable version of John Bull: a portly, ruddy-cheeked and side-whiskered farmer, with boots and a shabby hat, and an aggressive mastiff at his side. The mid-nineteenth century John Bull was in party terms essentially neutral—his rural appearance did not indicate a preference for, for instance, a protectionist agenda. And during the heyday of Gladstone and Disraeli the party prints, for example the Liberal *Punch* and the tory *Judy* (mainly drawn by William Boucher) and *Fun* (where he was depicted by J. Gordon Thomson), enlisted John Bull with equal credibility. It was left to foreign commentators to produce more pejorative versions. In 1819 Washington Irving produced a modern rendition of Arbuthnot's original, attributing England's propensity to meddle in the affairs of other countries to being 'a little fond of playing the magnifico abroad' (Irving, 250). Max O'Rell's *John Bull and his Island* (1883) extended the criticism, dubbing John Bull an aggressive imperialist—'a large land-owner, with muscular arms, long, broad, flat, and heavy feet, and an iron jaw that holds fast whatever it seizes upon' (O'Rell, 1). These caricatures began to stick, and overseas representations of John Bull carried in the illustrated press in the last decades of the nineteenth century invariably represented John Bull as a land-grabbing capitalist, annexing more and more of the non-European world.

In the Edwardian years John Bull shed much of his political and social neutrality. As the notion of the English 'public' expanded, especially after the extension of household suffrage to the counties in 1884, the representation of the typical Englishman as a squire or small landowner became more problematic. Repudiating jingoism in the Second South African War, Canon Scott Holland pronounced the John Bull stereotype 'ludicrously obsolete'— fat in an age when 'the fat man's day is past and gone' and

when the 'long lean Australian' had become a more accurate image for empire. Scott Holland went on to complain that John Bull 'has no brains. He embodies, in his fatuous good-humour, in his farmer's suit, in his obvious provincialism, the British horror of ideas' (S. Paget, ed., *Henry Scott Holland*, 2nd edn, 1921, 217). The cartoonists of the labour movement—for example, Will Dyson—likewise tended to avoid 'John Bull' if they wished to invoke 'everyman'. And some radical cartoonists of the late nineteenth century depicted exploitative employers or inhumane agricultural landlords in caricatures remarkably similar to the stock John Bull. With the massive acceleration of usage of political posters by the two main parties in elections after 1885 (peaking in the three elections of 1906 and 1910), John Bull's image became traded around with the same degree of competition and contestation that had occurred in the 1790s. Perhaps the most famous version of the Edwardian John Bull came in Horatio Bottomley's eponymous newspaper, which he edited from 1906 until 1921. Bottomley's John Bull, now with a union jack waistcoat, and dressed out in a top hat, riding gear, and crop, rather than in the unkempt farming garb of old, was a persistent critic of the state interventionism of Asquith's Liberal government, and in particular of its fiscal policies. Bottomley's John Bull also savaged the venality and corruption of the Liberal Party's relations with big business. The figure featured heavily too in the 'free trade versus protection' election campaigning which dominated the Edwardian years, with the illustrators of both parties using John Bull to support their calls for either greater indirect or greater direct taxation.

The constitutional crisis over the 'people's budget', which ran from 1909 to 1911, was the climax of the party-political career of John Bull. Thereafter, he still featured in political caricature—increasingly, but not always on the conservative end of the spectrum—but more frequently after the First World War as a symbol of imperial nostalgia. John Bull was, for example, a prominent element in the advertising strategy of the Empire Marketing Board in the 1920s and 1930s and was again supported by a middle-aged matronly wife who, in David Low's *Star* cartoon (24 April 1924), donned Britannia's helmet; both were joined later by Low's youthful Joan *Bull, who epitomized the recently enfranchised woman. John Bull ended his active political life very much as he had begun it—a repository of various meanings and associations, a composite and far from univocal national character. MILES TAYLOR

Sources M. Taylor, 'John Bull and the iconography of public opinion, *c.*1712–1929', *Past and Present*, 134 (1992), 93–128 · D. Donald, *The age of caricature: satirical prints in the reign of George III* (New Haven, 1996) · J. Brewer, ed., *The common people and politics, 1750–1790s* (1986) · H. T. Dickinson, ed., *Caricatures and the constitution, 1760–1832* (1986) · M. Duffy, ed., *The Englishman and the foreigner* (1986) · M. D. George, *English political caricature: a study of opinion and propaganda*, 2 vols. (1959) · J. Surel, 'La première image de John Bull, bourgeois radical, Anglais loyaliste (1779–1815)', *Mouvement Social* (1979) · J. Surel, 'John Bull', *Patriotism: the making and unmaking of British national identity*, ed. R. Samuel, 3 vols. (1989), 3.3–25 · M. Jouve, 'La formation de l'image de John Bull dans la caricature anglaise au XVIIIe siècle', *Linguistique, civilisation, litterature—actes* *du Congrès de la Société des anglicistes de l'Enseignement supérieur de Tours, 1977* (Paris, 1980) • J. Arbuthnot, *The history of John Bull*, ed. A. W. Bower and R. A. Erickson (1976) [edn of 5 pamphlets pubd 1712] • W. Irving, 'John Bull', *The sketch book of Geoffrey Crayon, gent.* [1819]; ed. H. Springer as vol. 8 of *The complete works of Washington Irving* (1978) • M. O'Rell, *John Bull and his island* (1883) • P. Mellini and R. T. Matthews, 'John Bull's family arises', *History Today*, 37/5 (1987), 17–23 • R. T. Matthews and P. Mellini, 'From Britannia to Maggie: the fall and rise of John Bull's descendants', *History Today*, 38/9 (1988), 17–23

Likenesses C. Williams, caricature, engraving (coloured impression), *c.*1816, BM [*see illus.*] • portraits, before 1832, repro. in Brewer, ed., *Common people* • portraits, before 1832, repro. in Dickinson, ed., *Caricatures* • portraits, before 1832, repro. in Duffy, ed., *Englishmen and the foreigner*

Bull, Phil (1910–1989), racehorse owner and punter, was born on 9 April 1910 at 3 Cemetery Road, Hemsworth, West Riding of Yorkshire, the only son and eldest of the three children of William Osborne Bull (*c.*1870–1954), a coalminer who later became a sanitary inspector, and his wife, Lizzie Jessop (Dolly) Watson (1884–1972), schoolteacher. He was educated at Hemsworth church school and then, by way of scholarships, at Hemsworth grammar school (1921–8) and Leeds University (1928–31), where he took a degree in mathematics. He worked first as a schoolteacher in London but left that profession to devote himself to racing. He specialized in betting and selling advice to other punters, either directly or via his own racing publications, initially under the *non de plume* William K. Temple. His meticulous accounts show that when he gave up serious betting about 1974 he had taken the equivalent (in early twenty-first-century terms) of over £5 million from the bookmakers. He was not a gambler but a rational placer of bets who gained intellectual stimulus from the challenge of the new set of horses that appeared each year.

The basis of Bull's betting was past racing performance, but not merely the relative finishing positions used by most students of form. He maintained that a moderate horse could never become a great one but that any horse which ran a fast time was capable of replicating the feat when conditions were propitious. From this idea came his development of *Timeform*, which he introduced to the racing public in 1948. In this detailed publication every racehorse in Britain was rated according to achieved speed. This major original contribution to racing became internationally recognized, and was eventually mirrored by the Jockey Club in its handicapping system.

Although Bull always maintained that for the public racing was about betting, not breeding, he was himself interested in the latter aspect of the sport. He founded the Hollins Stud in 1947, though this was not a tangible entity but a corporate name for his breeding operations. He was unusual for an owner–breeder in that every year he offered all his stock for sale. Perhaps this contributed to his never winning a classic, although his fillies Arietta and Aureoletta were third respectively in the One Thousand Guineas and the Oaks.

A socialist by upbringing—his uncle Gabriel Price (1879–1934) was Labour MP for Hemsworth—and an egalitarian

by conviction, Bull had little time for the racing establishment, especially for those members of the Jockey Club who had been public-school educated. Many of his writings were trenchant criticisms of the club's conservatism and of its failure to act in the interests of punters, who, as Bull often pointed out, made a major contribution to racing via the betting levy. Well before they were adopted he advocated electronic timing, Sunday racing, and prominently displayed betting odds boards. He was never invited to join the Jockey Club; in 1980, however, he was appointed to the chair of the horseracing advisory committee. He lasted just over four months before he resigned from what he termed a 'cosmetic charade' (Wright, 223), a body not treated seriously by either the Jockey Club or the Horserace Betting Levy Board, which were the key players in running and financing racing. In any event Bull was not by nature a compromiser and he found it difficult to curb his individualism to the needs of committee work. Although he felt that kindness was a virtue he had no such regard for tolerance, believing that one should speak out against people and policies with which one disagrees.

Bull married three times. His first marriage, on 15 June 1935, was to a fellow teacher, Doris Astley, who was five months pregnant at the time with his son David. They soon separated and were divorced in June 1944. By then Bull had been living for almost four years with another teacher, Eleanor (Nell) Oxley, with whom he had two children, Anne and Raymond. On 4 November 1949 he married Wendy Carter, and on 2 September 1963 Patricia Scott Finlay. Patricia had replaced Wendy as his personal assistant at *Timeform*, and both eventually left Bull for younger men.

Instantly recognizable with his ginger beard (first retained as a protest after a headmaster demanded he shave it off), heavy glasses, and ubiquitous cigar, Bull cultivated his image of bluntness and liked to play the showman. Away from the racetrack and the study where he spent hours working on his betting plans he indulged his passion for classical music, chess, and snooker. He was a humanist who maintained that all religions were superstitious nonsense and that the Christian faith in particular had brought immeasurable unhappiness to the world. He died at his home, The Hollins, Warley, Halifax, Yorkshire, on 11 June 1989.   WRAY VAMPLEW

Sources H. Wright, *Bull: the biography* (1995) • R. Mortimer, R. Onslow, and P. Willett, *Biographical encyclopedia of British flat racing* (1978) • b. cert. • d. cert.

Archives Halifax, *Timeform* records

Likenesses photographs, repro. in Wright, *Bull: the biography*

Wealth at death £1,288,491: probate, 28 March 1991, *CGPLA Eng. & Wales*

Bull, William (*bap.* 1738, *d.* 1814), Independent minister and college head, one of five children of John Bull, was born at Irthlingborough, Northamptonshire, and baptized there on 17 December 1738. Concern for the upbringing of the children, together with their father's growing financial difficulties, led to them being brought up by their grandfather, Francis Bull, at Newport Pagnell. As a child, Bull showed a capacity for learning, teaching himself Hebrew and the rudiments of mathematics. His great ambition was to enter the nonconformist ministry. Accordingly he gave up his secular employment in 1758 and went to live with his elder brother John at Bedford. There, as a preliminary to his course of ministerial training, he studied Latin under Revd Samuel Saunderson and Greek under Revd James Belsham (d. 1770), the minister at Newport Pagnell who resided at Bedford. In 1759 he was admitted to the dissenting academy at Daventry, then under the direction of Caleb Ashworth. Unlike many students who emerged from the academy holding heterodox views, Bull remained an orthodox Calvinist. On completing his course of studies he was ordained on 11 October 1764 as minister of the Independent chapel at Newport Pagnell in succession to James Belsham, a position he retained for the rest of his life.

To supplement his slender income of £37 10s. per annum Bull started a school for boys, some of whom later attained important positions—one, John Leach, became master of the rolls. On 7 June 1768 he married at St Mary's, Bedford, Hannah (1737–1804), daughter of Thomas Palmer, deacon of the Old Meeting-House in Bedford. They had several children but only one, Thomas, survived infancy. At Newport Pagnell, Bull proved a popular and enthusiastic preacher who 'maintained a strong hold on the affections of his people' (Hillyard, 134). His preaching, which was described as 'eloquent', became more attractive as he grew older, and his sermons were said to be 'characterised by a remarkable depth and earnestness of feeling' (J. Bull, 363). By the time of his death his congregation of 115 was seven times larger than at the time of his ordination, and the place of worship had been repeatedly enlarged. From 1780 he also preached to congregations at the neighbouring villages of Astwood, North Crawley, Bradwell, Sherrington, and Stoke Goldington, while for many years he was on the rota of preachers at the Tabernacle, Tottenham Court Road, and Surrey Chapel. His services were attended by persons of all religious denominations. He was also president of the Bedford Union of Christians from its foundation in 1797 until his death.

Early in 1770 Bull got to know John Newton, the Anglican curate of Olney, and William Cowper, the poet and co-author with Newton of the 'Olney hymns'. The three remained close friends, regularly corresponding with each other for the remainder of their lives. Through Newton, Bull came to know many of the leading members of the evangelical party and of the Clapham Sect, including John Thornton, John Clayton, Henry Venn, Zachary Macauly, Thomas Babington, and Mrs Wilberforce, aunt of William Wilberforce and sister of John Thornton. It was Newton who in 1782 first mooted the idea for an academy to train evangelical ministers along non-denominational lines. Encouraged by prominent members of the Clapham Sect, he drew up *A Plan of Academic Preparation for the Ministry*, which formed the basis on which the new academy was founded. It was designed to produce gospel preachers rather than profound scholars; Bull, who since 1772 had privately trained on an intermittent basis young men for

the ministry, was seen as the obvious choice to superintend the institution and Newport Pagnell as its ideal location. Bull was appointed principal of the Newport Pagnell Evangelical Institution in January 1783, and the first two students were admitted in June. Throughout Bull's principalship the 'great object of its foundation was to secure pious and suitable candidates for the ministry, without regard to their particular views as to the forms of church government' (*Account*, 21). Consequently the academy attracted both dissenters and members of the established church. John Thornton was so impressed with the scheme that in January 1786 he generously offered to undertake the entire cost of maintaining the academy. In his will, dated 2 April 1790, he bequeathed to Bull, for the period of his natural life, an annuity of £200 for this purpose. This financial security enabled the trustees to appoint as assistant tutor Samuel Greatheed, who was succeeded in 1789 by Bull's son, Thomas.

While Bull never deviated from orthodox Calvinism, 'he had in his soul an element of mysticism' ('Bull, Cowper and Newton', 817) and admired the poetry of Madame Guyon. He persuaded his friend Cowper to translate her hymns which he, with Cowper's consent, later published in 1801, adding a preface of his own. His knowledge of Hebrew enabled him to make a new translation with notes of the Psalms of David. The work does not appear to have been published, but a manuscript version is in Dr Williams's Library. He also contributed four papers to John Thornton's new edition of Bogatzky's *Golden Treasury*, published in 1775, and was co-author with his son, Thomas, of *A Brief Narrative of the Rise and Progress of the Independent Church of Newport* (1811). While on a visit to Ireland in 1785 he wrote a tract entitled *The Seasonable Hint*, hundreds of copies of which were distributed on this preaching tour.

Bull had never enjoyed robust health. Since childhood he had suffered from severe headaches and depression and from the 1770s he began to suffer from nephritis, a condition which eventually caused his death at Newport Pagnell on 23 July 1814. His funeral service was preached by his former student Revd Samuel Hillyard of Bedford. He was succeeded in his offices of minister and academy principal by his son. M. J. MERCER

Sources J. Bull, *Memorials of the Rev. William Bull*, 2nd edn (1865) · F. W. Bull, 'The Newport Pagnell Academy', *Transactions of the Congregational Historical Society*, 4 (1909–10), 305–22 · F. W. Bull, 'History of the Independent church, Newport Pagnell', *Transactions of the Congregational Historical Society*, 4 (1909–10), 266–8 · S. Hillyard, 'Memoir of the late Rev. William Bull', *Evangelical Magazine and Missionary Chronicle*, 23 (1815), 133–8 · 'Bull, Cowper and Newton', *Evangelical Magazine and Missionary Chronicle*, [3rd ser.], 6 (1864), 814–19 · H. McLachlan, *English education under the Test Acts: being the history of the nonconformist academies, 1662–1820* (1931), 241–4 · *An account of the origins and history of the Newport Pagnell Evangelical Institution* (1831) · *GM*, 1st ser., 85/1 (1815), 650 · J. Watson, *A discourse on the studies of Newport Pagnell College, delivered on 26 Oct 1842* (1843) · R. G. Martin, *The story of the Congregational church, Newport Pagnell* (1960), 7–8 · C. Surman, index, DWL · *IGI* · *DNB*

Archives DWL, essays and translations of the Psalms, New College archives L12/3 · LPL, corresp. and MSS · LPL, further corresp.

and papers · LPL, MS 2935 | NRA, priv. coll., letters to S. Whitbread
Likenesses R. M. Meadows, stipple, pubd 1801 (after J. Robinson), NPG · print (after engraving by W. Harvey), repro. in Bull, *Memorials*

Bullaker, Thomas [*name in religion* John Baptist] (*bap.* **1598**, *d.* **1642**), Franciscan friar, was baptized on 2 November 1598 at St Andrew's, Chichester. He was the son of Dr John Bullaker, or *Bullokar (*bap.* 1574, *d.* 1627), physician and lexicographer, and his wife, Ellinor (*d.* in or after 1631). His grandfather was William *Bullokar, grammarian and phonetician. As both his father and grandfather were schoolteachers he received a good education in comfortable surroundings in the family home in West Street, Chichester. In 1621, after a retreat with the Jesuit fathers at St Omer, he was admitted to the English College at Valladolid. In 1622 he entered the convent of the Franciscan Recollects at Abrojo. He was professed in 1624, ordained in 1628, and petitioned to go on the mission to the West Indies.

Instead Bullaker was sent on the English mission. He travelled overland to Bordeaux and from there took ship to Plymouth. On arrival he was arrested and imprisoned on the information of the captain of the vessel. He was transferred to Exeter, where he was confined until the spring assizes of 1630. He was then released and, for the next twelve years, lived the secret life of a missionary priest. For a few years he acted as secretary to Francis Davenport, the Franciscan provincial. In 1640 he was appointed titular guardian of Oxford and, for a short time, was titular guardian of Chichester. In 1641 he took up residence in London. He was arrested on 11 September 1642 while saying mass in the house of Margaret Powell, being seized by the pursuivant Wadsworth. He was interrogated before the sheriff of London and committed to Newgate prison. He was indicted, tried, and sentenced to death for treason for being a seminary priest and was hanged, drawn, and quartered at Tyburn on 12 October 1642. Thomas Bullaker was one of the eighty-five martyrs who were beatified by Pope John Paul II on 22 November 1987.

TIMOTHY J. McCANN

Sources Angelus à Sancto Francisco [R. Mason], *Certamen seraphicum provinciae Angliae pro sancta Dei ecclesia* (1649) · F. de Marsys, *Histoire de la persecution présente des Catholiques en Angleterre*, 3 pts (1646) · *An exact relation of the apprehension, examination, execution and confession of Thomas Bullaker* (1642) · R. Challoner, *Memoirs of missionary priests*, ed. J. H. Pollen, rev. edn (1924), 428–35 · J. M. Stone, *Faithful unto death* (1892), 132–52 · A. Hope, *Franciscan martyrs in England* (1878), 130–55 · T. J. McCann, 'Some unpublished accounts of the martyrdom of Blessed Thomas Bullaker OSF of Chichester in 1642', *Recusant History*, 19 (1988–9), 171–82 · T. J. McCann, 'The Catholic recusancy of Dr. John Bullaker of Chichester, 1574–1627', *Recusant History*, 11 (1971–2), 75–86 · Franciscus à Sancta Clara [C. Davenport], *Manuale missionariorum regularium*, 2nd edn (1661) · E. Henson, ed., *The registers of the English College at Valladolid, 1589–1862*, Catholic RS, 30 (1930) · R. Trappes-Lomax, ed., *The English Franciscan nuns, 1619–1821, and the Friars Minor of the same province, 1618–1761*, Catholic RS, 24 (1922) · parish records, W. Sussex RO, Par. 37/1/1/1, fol. 12 · LMA, MJ/SR 916/97 · Stonyhurst, Grene MSS, collectanea M, fols. 44, 45 · Franciscan Library, Killiney, Ireland, MS D4. 452r · English College of Friars Minor, Forest Gate, London, archives · Convent of the Institute of Mary, Nymphenburg, Bavaria
Likenesses line engraving, BM; repro. in Angelus, *Certamen seraphicum* · portrait, Carmelite convent, Lanherne, Cornwall · portrait, St Alban's College, Valladolid, Spain

Bullar, John (1778–1864), schoolmaster and campaigner for liberal causes, was born on 27 January 1778 in the parish of Holy Rood, Southampton, probably at 95/96 High Street, the son of John Bullar (1744–1836), peruke maker and hairdresser of Southampton High Street, and his wife, Penelope Rowsell (1755–1799), the sister of a neighbouring wheelwright. John Bullar was the eldest of their eleven children, of whom only three survived childhood. He was educated at King Edward VI Grammar School in Southampton under the Revd Dr Mant, but in early adulthood he left the Church of England to join the dissenting chapel at Above Bar, to which he belonged for sixty-seven years, forty-three of them as an elected deacon. On 28 June 1806 he married Susannah Sarah Whatman Lobb (1778–1835), daughter of a Southampton linen draper and silk merchant; they brought up a family of four sons and two daughters.

Through his energy and commitment John Bullar became intimately associated with the development of nineteenth-century Southampton. For nearly forty years he was well known as a schoolmaster, teaching in his schools at Bugle Street, Moira Place, and Prospect Place many boys who later became civic leaders. A regular speaker at mechanics' and literary institutes, he was a life-long friend of Henry Robinson Hartley, despite the latter's atheism, and was instrumental in determining how Hartley's bequest should be used for the benefit of the town. The Hartley Institute, later to develop into the University of Southampton, may be supposed to have satisfied in part Bullar's ambitions for the town—that it should have 'a copious public library, an imposing museum, and well-frequented lecture rooms' and that 'energetic alliances with science and literature' sought by commerce elsewhere should be replicated in his birthplace (J. Bullar, *Hints to Assist the Enquiries of Visitors*, 1846, 14).

In his youth Bullar was a prominent campaigner against slavery, and as such attracted the enmity of several wealthy and influential Southampton families. Following retirement in 1840 he supported his two sons doctors Joseph and William Bullar in establishing an infirmary which rapidly developed into the Royal South Hampshire Hospital. In 1846, during the meeting in Southampton of the British Association attended by the prince consort, the family was host to Sir John Herschel in Prospect Place. Bullar himself addressed the meeting on the need for a rational science incorporating Christian belief. *Hints to Assist the Enquiries of Visitors* (1846), his guide to Southampton and the Isle of Wight, was produced for delegates.

Though enfeebled by age John Bullar remained active in worthwhile causes until shortly before his death. This life-long dedication grew out of his deep affection for Southampton and his absolute commitment to his faith. He was a founder and secretary of the Southampton branch of the British and Foreign Bible Society, established in 1814,

John Bullar (1778–1864), by Richard Cockle Lucas, 1854

and faith underpinned his diverse writings which ranged from a series of locally based historical and geographical tourist guides, to a collection of edifying poetry with which he sought to counter the anti-religious tide of popular culture epitomized by the poetry of Lord Byron. Although he was classically educated, interest in contemporary science is a consistent theme in his writing. His other published writings include biographies and lectures as well as sermons and pamphlets in support of Christian and dissenting causes. By his own efforts he became a leading citizen of early nineteenth-century Southampton and he was a significant force in shaping the modern city's major institutions.

John Bullar died on 13 May 1864 at his home in Basset Wood, having finally succumbed to 'the gradual decay of those natural powers which have carried him far beyond the allotted span of human existence' (*Southampton Times*, 7 May 1864, 2). He was buried at St Nicholas's Church, North Stoneham, on 20 May amid widespread mourning. His estate was valued at less than £800 but his obituary in the *Southampton Times* (14 May 1864, 2) valued his contribution to the history of the town thus: 'The life of Mr. Bullar is in fact the life of Southampton during the past fifty years.'   BARBARA SPENDER

Sources *Southampton Times* (14 May 1864) • T. Adkins, *A voice from the dead: a sermon preached on the occasion of the death of Mr Bullar* (1864) • Above Bar Congregational Chapel, church book, Southampton City Archive • parish register, Southampton, Holy Rood Church, Hants. RO, vol. 1 • W. J. C. Moens, ed., *Hampshire allegations for marriage licences granted by the bishop of Winchester, 1689 to 1837*, 1, Harleian Society, 35 (1893) • Genealogical Society, Monumental Inscriptions, Churchyard of St Mary's, Southampton, Hampshire Records Office • A. Anderson, *Hartleyana—Henry Robinson Hartley* (1987) • alphabetical list of voters, Southampton, 1790–1830, Southampton Reference Library • *CGPLA Eng. & Wales* (1864) • S. Stainer, *History of the Above Bar Congregational Church* (1909) • Roe family scrapbook, Southampton City Archive • 'Southampton local news', *Southampton Times* (7 May 1864) • 'Funeral of the Lte Mr John Bullar', *Southampton Times* (21 May 1864) • parish register, Southampton, Holy Rood Church, Hants. RO, vol. 3 • parish register, Southampton, St Mary's, Hants. RO, vol. 1 • J. Rowsell, will, 1816, Hants. RO, MS 17.1817A/58 • *Southampton Directory, 1811*, 1811, Southampton City Archive • *Hampshire Trades Directory, 1784*, Hants. RO • *Royal South Hampshire Infirmary Yearbook, 1855*, Southampton City Archive • H. Dayman, *Beloved physician: a memoir of the late Dr Joseph Bullar* (1869) • *Pigot's Southampton Directory, 1823–4*, 1823, Southampton Reference Library • *Fletcher's Directory of Southampton, 1836*, 1836, Southampton Reference Library • R. I. Murchison, *Address to the British Association* (1846)

Likenesses R. C. Lucas, wax, 1854; Sothebys, 24 Jan 1974, lot 42; 26 July 1976, lot 11 [*see illus.*] • engraving, repro. in R. Morrison, *A grammar of the Chinese language* (1815)

Wealth at death under £800: probate, 25 Aug 1864, *CGPLA Eng. & Wales*

Bullard, Sir Edward Crisp (1907–1980), marine geophysicist, was born on 21 September 1907 at 1 Heigham Grove, Earlham Road, Heigham, Norwich, the only son and eldest of four children, of whom the last were twins, of Edward John Bullard (1875–1950), a Norwich brewer, and his wife, Eleanor Howes (1877–1962), daughter of Sir Frank *Crisp, first baronet (1843–1919), solicitor and vice-president of the Linnean Society, and his wife, Catherine (*née* Howes). Bullard's first schooling was in the mixed primary classes at Norwich High School for Girls, which took both girls and boys in the lower class, and in 1916 he went on to Norwich grammar school, where he was extremely unhappy; things improved when he was sent to Aldeburgh Lodge (now Orwell Park School), Suffolk, in 1919, and his lifelong interest in physics was kindled while at Repton School, Derbyshire (1921–6). He entered Clare College, Cambridge, in 1926 and obtained first-class honours in both parts of the natural sciences tripos, taking physics, chemistry, mathematics, and mineralogy in part one (1928) and specializing in physics in part two (1929).

On graduation Bullard began research for his PhD at the Cavendish Laboratory under Patrick Blackett and Lord Rutherford. He initially worked with Harrie Massey (1908–1983) on a study of electron scattering in gases and, later, with Philip Moon building an analogue device to solve Schrödinger's equation (which describes the wave-like behaviour of electrons in the atom). At the height of the economic depression in 1931 he took Rutherford's advice to 'take any job you can get' (Munk, v) and accordingly accepted an invitation from Sir Gerald Lenox-Conyngham to join his fledgeling department of geodesy and geophysics as a demonstrator. On the strength of this post Bullard married Margaret Ellen (*b.* 1907), daughter of Frederick Bevan Thomas, a civil engineer with the Indian railways, and his wife, Annie Whitmarsh (*née* Phelps), on 25 July 1931. Described as 'an immensely talented [but] restless romanticist' (Revelle, 4), Margaret assisted Bullard with much of his early experimental work, 'keeping many of the notebooks and making the thermal conductivity measurements' (McKenzie, 76). In the 1950s she published three novels based on their lives in Cambridge, Toronto, and La Jolla.

On joining Lenox-Conyngham, Bullard developed techniques greatly to improve the accuracy of the department's large invariable pendulum, used to measure the strength of the earth's gravity field. As a result, he became a consultant to the Anglo-Iranian Oil Co. and gained his

PhD (in physics and atomic physics) in 1932, and his application of this geophysical method to investigate the geological structure of the east African rift valley in 1933–4 established his reputation. He was awarded a Smithsonian research fellowship of the Royal Society (1936–43) and Cambridge's Sedgwick prize in March 1937. By 1936 he had recognized the potential for academic research of the secret seismic survey techniques used by oil companies. Aided by Leslie Flavill, an instrument designer and mechanic of genius, C. Kerr-Grant, Thomas Gaskell, and the geologist Brian Harland, Bullard built equipment and by refraction survey during 1937–8, combined with evidence from boreholes, successfully elucidated the sub-surface structure of much of eastern England.

In contrast the geology of the ocean floor was at this time still largely unknown. In the autumn of 1936 Bullard met the American geologist Richard Field (1885–1961), who described measurements of the thicknesses of sediments on the continental shelf off the Virginia coastline made by Maurice Ewing (1906–1974) the previous year. Field recommended similar work on the opposite side of the Atlantic, and invited Bullard to accompany Ewing on a cruise to observe the seismic techniques used. Consequently in July 1938 and June 1939, Bullard, Gaskell, and Flavill improved on Ewing's refraction survey technique with sea-floor geophones by using hydrophones floating close to the sea surface (thereby paving the way for modern marine seismic surveys), and measured sediment thicknesses on a transect south-west of Land's End, Cornwall. This showed that, as Ewing had found, the basement sloped down towards the continental edge and confirmed the existence of a major Atlantic sedimentary basin.

Although many measurements of the increase of the earth's temperature with depth had been made in the nineteenth century using mines and boreholes, lack of knowledge of the thermal conductivity of the rocks through which they passed made it impossible to know whether observed variations in thermal gradient were caused by changes in heat-flow or conductivity. At the instigation of Harold Jeffreys (1891–1989), reader in geophysics in Lenox-Conyngham's department, in 1935 the British Association for the Advancement of Science established a committee to remedy this situation. Bullard developed improved techniques for measurement of thermal conductivity, setting definitive standards which 'have remained largely unchanged' (McKenzie, 75) since. Unexpectedly low temperature gradients had recently been reported from very deep boreholes in South Africa. In 1938–9 Bullard's measurements showed that the anomalous results were accounted for by high thermal conductivities of the local rocks through which the boreholes passed. This enabled him to obtain the first reliable estimate of heat-flux through the continents.

In November 1939 Bullard joined HMS *Vernon*, the Royal Naval Mine and Torpedo School, Portsmouth. Ships naturally acquire a magnetic field during their construction and this made them an easy prey to German magnetic mines. Bullard was placed in charge of finding ways to protect ships from magnetic and acoustic mines. Demonstrating when necessary an utter disregard for the formalities of normal civil service rules his group, which included Flavill and Gaskell, successfully developed methods for sweeping mines and neutralizing ship magnetic fields. Within eighteen months shipping losses from mines had been reduced to such an extent that, in 1941, Bullard could move to London to join Blackett's naval operational research group in the Admiralty. He first worked on strategies for conducting marine warfare; on analysis of data which Reginald Jones's (1911–1997) scientific intelligence unit at the air ministry was obtaining regarding the German rocket and flying-bomb programme; and then on strategies for attacking firing sites in northern France. In 1944 Bullard was appointed assistant director of operational research. In later years he 'thought of these wartime accomplishments when he was so young as the most important things he had ever done' (Revelle, 2). He remained an adviser to the Admiralty until his retirement from Cambridge in 1974.

Bullard returned to Cambridge as reader in experimental geophysics in 1945, then head of department in 1947. He tried to continue with seismic and heat-flow research and, as a result of his wartime duties, began work on problems of the earth's magnetic field, but he became increasingly frustrated by lack of equipment, financial support, and ship time. In the spring of 1948 (the year he gained his ScD in geophysics from Cambridge) he became chairman of the physics department at the University of Toronto. There he continued work on heat-flow, and began theoretical studies to show how movement of fluid material in the core of the earth could act as a self-sustaining dynamo, and hence as the source of the geomagnetic field. He encouraged departmental research in geochemistry and methods for the dating of rocks using natural radioactive decay. Despite this, both he and his family were unhappy in Canada, and he accepted directorship of the National Physical Laboratory, Teddington. In June–July 1949 at the Scripps Institution of Oceanography, La Jolla, California, he designed and, with graduate student Arthur Maxwell (b. 1925), built a prototype of the first deep-sea probe capable of accurately measuring the thermal gradient in the sediments of the ocean floor.

Although he could be forgetful, Bullard was a skilled and sometimes buccaneering manager and an excellent academic supervisor: 'Running things needs confidence … I learned a lot from Rutherford. A thing you must do is spend time with people who are in trouble, either emotional, financial or scientific … you have to remain calm, sympathetic and reasonable' (McKenzie, 80–81). So, despite his 'disconcerting and invigorating habit of dropping into a laboratory or office, hearing what the occupant was doing, and almost always telling him how to do it better' (Cook, 16), he was an effective and well-liked director of the National Physical Laboratory and was created knight bachelor in 1953 in recognition of this service and his wartime work. While at the laboratory he pursued development of the heat-probe—'I had superb facilities and no question as to who was going to use them. … If I said do something, they did it' (Shor, 74). The first successful measurements were made in the deep ocean basin southwest of Ireland, in July 1952. Bullard was now able to complete calculations underpinning his dynamo model, one of the first non-military applications of computational fluid-mechanics, using the ACE computer at the National Physical Laboratory.

In 1955 Bullard returned to Cambridge (at a third of his Teddington salary) as Bye fellow of Gonville and Caius College; he became assistant director of research in the department of geology and geophysics (1956), reader in geophysics (1960), and the first professor of geophysics (1964–74). He was a fellow of Churchill College from 1960 and a visiting professor at the La Jolla laboratories of the Institute of Geophysics and Planetary Physics, University of California (1963–74). He was by now a firm champion of the idea that the ocean floor was essentially different in nature from the continents, while his own principal fields of research continued to be geomagnetics and heat-flow, and his department became a major centre for palaeomagnetic and marine research. By 1954 analysis of heat-flow data obtained in collaboration with Roger Revelle (1909–1991) and Maxwell of the Scripps Institution, from the Pacific and Atlantic, had shown results hotter than anticipated, and by 1956 Bullard had located a zone of high heat-flow associated with the mid-oceanic ridge. This supported his 1954 hypothesis that excess heat-flow could be explained by upwards transportation of heat from the inner earth by convection. In 1959, although Alfred Wegener's (1880–1930) theory of continental drift was still regarded as complete heresy by the majority of geologists, Bullard, although recognizing that there could be counter-arguments, suggested that recent palaeomagnetic evidence of polar-wandering paths (obtained by his former student Keith Runcorn (1922–1995) and others), also indicated that drift could be a reality, and that the mid-Atlantic ridge might mark the place at which the ocean was widening. Evidence from palaeomagnetism and magnetic and gravity surveys of the sea floor continued to accumulate and Bullard and his colleague Maurice Hill (1916–1966) were among the first to introduce computer processing methods to marine geophysical data reduction. However, interpretation of what such results implied remained controversial. In 1963, in a lecture to the Geological Society, London, Bullard 'at last came out in favour of continental drift without reservations' (Bullard, 16), concluding that the consensus of evidence supporting drift was now convincing and that thermal convection currents, driving sea-floor spreading, provided a plausible mechanism. Inspired by Jeffrey's disbelief in previous attempts to demonstrate the closeness-of-fit of the margins of the continental shelves across the Atlantic, Bullard now recalled Euler's (1776) theorem, that any motion of a sphere over itself can be regarded as a single rotation about a given axis. Working with Alec Smith and J. E. Everett he used the theorem to compute a very convincing match, which they presented at a symposium on drift organized by Blackett, Runcorn, and Bullard in 1964. With growing understanding of the nature of spreading at mid-

oceanic ridges and Tuzo Wilson's (1908–1993) recognition of the presence of major transform-faults, Bullard's computational method underpinned the eventual acceptance, in 1966–7, of the concept of plate tectonics. Thereafter, his research was mainly concerned with the origin of the earth's magnetic field.

In quite different roles Bullard participated in the 1958 conference of experts held in Geneva to establish the technical criteria necessary to monitor a nuclear test-ban treaty; as joint chairman of the Anglo-American ballistic missile committee; and in the Pugwash conferences in the 1960s. As a result he maintained an interest in the detection of underground nuclear explosions. He also served on a number of committees in the Ministry of Defence; as a director of the family firm, Bullard & Sons (1950–55), and of IBM UK (1964–75); and as a consultant to the US president's office of science and technology policy, the California energy commission, and the jet propulsion laboratory of the California Institute of Technology on high-level radioactive waste disposal (1975–8). He was elected to the Royal Society in 1941 and received many honours, including its Hughes and royal medals (1953, 1975); the Chree medal (Physical Society, 1956); Day medal (Geological Society of America, 1959); gold medal of the Royal Astronomical Society (1965); Agassiz medal (US National Academy of Science, 1965); Wollaston medal (Geological Society, London, 1967); the Bowie and Ewing medals (American Geophysical Union, 1975, 1978); the Vetlesen prize (often regarded as the geological equivalent of the Nobel prize, 1968); and honorary ScD degrees from the Memorial University of Newfoundland (1970) and the University of East Anglia (1976). His favourite was reputed to be the stuffed albatross awarded to him in 1976 by the American Miscellaneous Society for 'the most incomprehensible paper of the decade in geophysics' (Revelle, 6)—a reference to his work on the dynamo theory.

There were four daughters from Bullard's first marriage (Belinda, Emily, Henrietta, and Polly), the middle two of whom were twins. The marriage was dissolved in January 1974 and on 11 June he married Mrs Ursula Margery Curnow (1924–1989), daughter of Ernest James Cooke, medical practitioner, of Christchurch, New Zealand. Although his health was beginning to fail, Bullard and his new wife emigrated to California in September 1974, where he resumed his (previously visiting) position as a professor at the Scripps Institution. With the 'calm and steady' painter and sculptor, Ursula, Lady Bullard, he was able to 'find peace and … genuine happiness' (Revelle, 4). After a courageous fight against prostate cancer Bullard died in his sleep on 3 April 1980, at his home, 2491 Horizon Way, La Jolla, California, a few hours after the completion of the manuscript (with S. R. C. Malin) of his 196th scientific article, a historical review of the direction of the earth's magnetic field at London since the sixteenth century. His ashes were scattered at sea off the La Jolla coast. Memorial services were held at the Scripps Institution on 16 April, and in Cambridge on 24 May, 1980.

RICHARD J. HOWARTH

Sources D. P. McKenzie, *Memoirs FRS*, 33 (1987), 67–98 · R. R. Revelle, 'The search for Teddy Bullard', 1980, U. Cal., San Diego, Scripps Institution of Oceanography, biographical information files, Box 2 Bj-Croc · E. N. Shor, 'E. C. Bullard's first heat probe', *Eos*, 65 (1984), 73–4 · [D. Matthews], 'Sir Edward Bullard: an outstanding scientist of his time', *The Times* (5 April 1980), 16 · C. C. Bates, T. F. Gaskell, and R. B. Rice, *Geophysics in the affairs of man* (1982) · E. C. Bullard, 'The emergence of plate tectonics: a personal view', *Annual Review of Earth and Planetary Sciences*, 3 (1975), 1–30 · E. C. Bullard, T. F. Gaskell, W. B. Harland, and C. Kerr-Grant, 'Seismic investigations on the Palaeozoic floor of east England', *PTRS*, 239A (1940), 29–94 · A. H. Cook, 'Sir Edward Bullard', *The Times* (15 April 1980), 16 [letter] · J. P., 'Sir Edward (Crisp) Bullard', *Annual Obituary*, 1 (1981), 215–17 [St Martin's, New York] · H. E. LeGrand, *Drifting continents and shifting theories* (1988) · H. S. W. Massey, 'Sir Edward Bullard', *Physics Today* (Aug 1980), 67–8 · R. M. Wood, *The dark side of the earth* (1985) · W. H. Munk, 'Dedication', *Topics in nonlinear dynamics: a tribute for Sir Edward Bullard*, ed. S. Jorna, American Institute of Physics Conference Proceedings, 46 (1978), v–viii [ghosted by Bullard] · E. N. Shor, 'Edward C. Bullard, 1907–80', *Eos*, 65 (1984), 74–5 · private information (2004) [Dr B. Bullard; W. Munk]

Archives CAC Cam., corresp. and papers | Norfolk RO, Norwich, corresp. and papers relating to Bullard & Sons, brewers · RS, corresp. with Lord Blackett · U. Cal., San Diego, Scripps Institution of Oceanography | FILM BFI NFTVA, *Seismic experiments at sea 1938 & 1939*. Great Britain c.1938, colour and black/white, 16mm, 20mins. | SOUND CAC Cam., tape recordings of lectures by Bullard · CAC Cam., interviews with family and colleagues recorded while preparing McKenzie (1987) · U. Cal., San Diego, Scripps Institution of Oceanography Archives, audio cassette recording (60 min) and typed transcript of oral history interview with Bullard conducted by Elizabeth Noble Shor and George Shor on August 5, 1973 specifically on the history of the heat-flow probe (published in Shor, 1984) · U. Cal., San Diego, Scripps Institution of Oceanography Archives, audio tape recordings of the First International Oceanographic Congress (1959) at which Bullard gave a paper · U. Cal., San Diego, Scripps Institution of Oceanography Archives, audio recording (reel to reel) of memorial service for Bullard held on 16 April 1980

Likenesses photographs, 1953–60, repro. in *Scienziati e Tecnologi Contemporanei*, 1, 196 [Milan, 1974] · B. Dunstan, portrait, c.1955, National Physical Laboratory, Queens Road, Teddington, Middlesex · photograph, 1967, repro. in Shor, 'Edward C. Bullard', 74 · portrait, c.1975, repro. in Bullard, 'The emergence', facing p. 1 · photograph (middle-aged), repro. in McKenzie, *Memoirs FRS*, facing p. 67, frontispiece · photograph (as young man), repro. in J. P., *Annual Obituary*, 215 · portrait, repro. in Massey, 'Sir Edward Bullard', 67 · portrait (in old age; after photograph?), repro. in *McGraw-Hill modern men of science*, 1 (1966), 77

Bullard, Sir Giles Lionel (1926–1992). *See under* Bullard, Sir Reader William (1885–1976).

Bullard, Sir Reader William (1885–1976), diplomatist, was born in Walthamstow, London, on 5 December 1885, the younger child and only son of Charles Bullard (1850–1912), dock labourer, and his wife, Mary, née Westlake. The unpropitious opening to this life was conveyed in the first paragraph of Bullard's autobiography *The Camels must Go* (1961):

> Very early one morning in December 1885 a man of thirty-five walked from a small house in Walthamstow to the London docks, a distance of some eight miles, in the hope of being taken on for a day's work, helping to load or unload some vessel. Having failed to catch the foreman's eye, and holding that it was the willingness of casual labour to hang about all day that encouraged employers to depend on casual labour, he walked home again, and having earned no money he bought no food. On his return home he found that besides

Sir Reader William Bullard (1885–1976), by Walter Stoneman, 1950

a daughter of five years old he now had a son, and he decided to give him the odd christian name his father had—Reader. It happened to be the man's own birthday, and at the moment it seemed unlikely that any returns of the day there might be would be very happy for either of them.   (Bullard, 17)

After a short spell in Canada in 1886–7 (which was not a success) the family returned to various homes in and near London, and a few years later Bullard's father obtained regular employment as a foreman on the British and Foreign Wharf, near Tower Bridge, at 42s. a week. At the age of eleven Bullard won an Essex county scholarship worth £16 a year for two years, which took him to Bancroft's School at Woodford. He trained as a schoolmaster and spent one year as a pupil teacher, and at the age of eighteen he briefly became an assistant master at a poor school in Walthamstow. All this time he had been following an intensive course of self-education. He 'read everything', showed an early aptitude for languages, enjoyed excellent health, and so emerged successfully from the 'curious [educational] steeplechase' (ibid., 44) in which he had been engaged.

Bullard's future was determined after he had seen a crammer's prospectus which gave particulars of, among other careers, the Levant consular service, the examination for which required an English essay, arithmetic, good handwriting, and six languages, including compulsory Latin and French. He added Greek, German, Spanish, and Italian, and in 1906 successfully came third out of twenty-five candidates. There followed two years at

Queens' College, Cambridge, studying Arabic, Turkish, and Persian under Professor E. G. Browne.

Bullard's first posting was to Constantinople, first in the consulate-general and then in the embassy as a student interpreter (third dragoman), where he was in time to see the last few weeks of the rule of Abdul Hamid. After two spells as acting consul in Trebizond and Erzurum, in the summer of 1914 he was asked to go to Basrah to take the place of the consul there, who was due to go on leave. This meant a complicated journey—a fortnight's ride to Diyarbakır, then by *kelek* (a raft of inflated goatskins) down the Tigris to Baghdad, and finally by steamer to Basrah. He expected to stay in Mesopotamia for six months, but was to be there for six years.

After Turkey entered the war in October 1914 and an Indian expeditionary force was landed in Basrah, Bullard was naturally attached to it as political officer, helping to erect the rudiments of a civil administration. His chief was Sir Percy Cox, whom he accompanied on two missions to Tehran. After a brief period of leave in England in 1919 (he had survived the war without serious illness except malaria and without any leave) he returned to Iraq in May 1920 as military governor of Baghdad, with the rank of major.

There followed two years back in London as a member of the new Middle East department of the Colonial Office, set up by the colonial secretary, Winston Churchill, who was 'trying to clear up the confusion in the Middle East' (Bullard, 117). Bullard's colleagues there included Herbert Young and T. E. Lawrence, but his responsibility was confined to Iraq. He attended the Lausanne conference in December 1922, where he was concerned with drawing the frontier between Turkey and the Mosul province of the new Iraqi state.

In June 1923 Bullard took up his post as consul in Jiddah, where the consulate was 'dilapidated though airy and picturesque' (Bullard, 124) (there was no electricity, so no air-conditioning or refrigerator) and the haunt of a lot of noisy owls. Hejaz was at that time ruled by the Hashemite King Hussein, father of Feisal and Abdullah, now installed in Iraq and Transjordan. Hussein suffered from a keen sense of betrayal, as he saw it, at the hands of the allies, and had become a cantankerous old man who often sorely tried Bullard's exemplary patience. The main income of Hejaz was from pilgrims, and the main task of the consul was to prevent them from being cheated by guides or monarch and to look after the welfare of those, mainly from India, who were British subjects. It was from this time that he acquired the name by which he was always known, Haji. By the time he left in July 1925, the man who was to turn Arabia into a unitary state, ʿAbd al-ʿAziz ibn Saʿud, was battering on the gates of Jiddah, which he finally entered in December 1921, by which time Hussein was an exile in Cyprus.

Bullard's next two postings, Athens from 1923 to 1928 and Addis Ababa from 1928 to 1930, were comparatively uneventful, but after the resumption of diplomatic relations with the Soviet Union he asked for a posting there,

curious to see at first hand the much vaunted 'new civilization'. In November 1930 he became consul-general in Moscow, transferring the following June to Leningrad. His four years in the Soviet Union saw the end of the first five-year plan and the beginning of the second. He left Leningrad just before the murder of Kirov, which provided Stalin with the excuse to stage-manage the series of great show trials, but Bullard had seen enough of the iron grip of the secret police and the adulation of Stalin to appreciate how wide was the gulf between the picture painted by unremitting Soviet propaganda and the reality. There was not a great deal of activity in the consulates but, as Bullard said, if there was little bread there were plenty of circuses, and he enjoyed the theatre, opera, and ballet, as well as reading widely and perfecting his Russian.

Bullard was next offered the post of consul-general in Strasbourg, which he would have liked, but turned down in favour of a colleague from the Levant consular service whose health problems he felt gave him priority. Instead, two years in Morocco proved an equally pleasant contrast. That legacy of the old Ottoman empire, capitulations, was still alive there and involved Bullard in a good deal of legal business. Rather to his surprise, in 1936 he was transferred from the Levant consular service to the foreign service proper and was sent back to Jiddah as minister. He was appointed KCMG at the same time.

Ibn Saʿud was a much more rewarding monarch to deal with than King Hussein. Pilgrims were still a major source of revenue (oil was not in commercial production until late in 1939) but they were now much better looked after. One agreeable duty which fell to Bullard was to escort Princess Alice, granddaughter of Queen Victoria, and her husband, the earl of Athlone, brother of Queen Mary, who had been invited by Ibn Saʿud to be his guests in a crossing of Arabia from Jiddah to Bahrain via Taʿif and Riyadh. The visit was a great success, Ibn Saʿud for the first time entertaining a European lady to a meal.

In December 1939 Bullard was appointed, now that the country was at war, to one of the key posts in the diplomatic service, Tehran, first as minister but from 1943 as ambassador. The sympathies of Reza Shah, the autocrat who had ruled Persia since 1921, were with the axis, and there were a great many Germans in the country posing as specialists or businessmen. Pressure to secure their removal increased after the German invasion of Russia in June 1941, and in August British and Russian troops entered the country. The next month Reza Shah, under the mistaken impression that Russian troops were approaching the capital, abdicated in favour of his son Mohamed Reza, and was taken in a British ship to South Africa, where he died.

Britain and Russia were now allies, and the north–south railway which Reza Shah had built became one of the main routes for the supply to Russia of arms and other essentials. But the interests of the allies were not always easily reconciled. Ensuring adequate food supplies for the local population became one of Bullard's constant headaches, the Russians holding the main grain-growing areas in the north and being reluctant to release supplies to areas where they were most needed.

Many important visitors passed through Tehran on their way to or from Russia, and at the end of 1943 it became the venue for the first time of conferences of the 'big three'. Much organizational work fell on Bullard and his staff, and an inscription on a wall in the embassy drafted by Bullard commemorated the dinner there on 30 November, at which Churchill sat between Roosevelt and Stalin and, opposite them, Bullard sat between Marshal Voroshilov and Molotov. For his services during the Tehran conference, Bullard was appointed KCB.

At the end of the war, though invited to accept another post, Bullard preferred to retire. His retirement was as busy as his diplomatic career. He was from 1951 to 1956 director of the Institute of Commonwealth Studies, Oxford; he wrote for Hutchinson's University Library *Britain and the Middle East* (1951), a model of brevity; he edited the third volume of the Chatham House *Middle Eastern Survey* (1958); and he chaired both the Libyan currency commission and the abortive attempt to adjudicate on the rival claims of Saudi Arabia, Muscat, and Abu Dhabi, to the Buraimi oasis. He also took some part in local government affairs and did much lecturing in Britain and America. In 1961 he published his autobiography, *The Camels must Go*.

But it was for his personality that Bullard was chiefly remembered. He was a humble man. Short and stocky, with a craggy face and deep set eyes, he gave an immediate impression of rock-like solidity. A tireless worker, deeply conscious of his country's past and of the highest standards she had the right to demand from her servants, he was no less conscientious in his attention to detail, for example always arranging (and paying for) Christmas presents for the ever expanding embassy staff.

In spite of his multifarious duties in Tehran Bullard found time to give two talks to the British Council, on Dr Johnson and Dickens, and another on a subject particularly dear to his heart, 'Changes in the English language in my lifetime'. His love of the literature of many languages was unconfined. He thought he must be slipping when it took him a whole morning to read a book of the *Aeneid* (in a Jiddah summer); at the other end of the spectrum, when in bed 'with a really bad cold—the first for years', he read, among much else, Dorothy Sayers's *Gaudy Night* for the sixth time. 'If I ever fall into the water', he wrote, 'and appear to be drowned, bring in a new book and see if the smell of printer's ink doesn't bring me round' (*Letters from Tehran*, 132).

Bullard was an honorary fellow of Queens' College, Cambridge, Lincoln College, Oxford, and the School of Oriental and African Studies, London. He married on 18 August 1921 at Bamburgh, Northumberland, Miriam Catherine (Biddy; 1888–1973), daughter of Arthur Lionel *Smith (1850–1924), master of Balliol College, Oxford. She stayed with him briefly in Jiddah and Leningrad and for a longer time in Addis Ababa, but they realized that if their children were to be properly educated a house of their own in Oxford was a necessity. The choice was vindicated. They had a daughter and four sons, two of whom followed

him into the foreign service, Giles [*see below*] and Julian (*b.* 1928), a fellow of All Souls and ambassador in Bonn. Bullard survived his wife by three years, dying in his son Giles's house in West Hendred, near Wantage, on 24 May 1976. Asked for a recipe for longevity he suggested that 'while I do not make a fetish of exercise, I think that a brisk walk—say about every other Easter—does nobody any harm' (Bullard, 283).

Sir Giles Lionel Bullard (1926–1992), diplomatist, was born in Oxford on 24 August 1926, the second of four sons and the third of five children of Sir Reader Bullard and his wife, Miriam Catherine (Biddy), *née* Smith. He was educated at the Dragon School, Oxford, and at Blundell's School, Tiverton, where he was head of the school. He won a scholarship to Balliol, which he attended from 1944 to 1945, before three years of national service, including a year with the West African Rifles, which he much enjoyed. In 1948 he returned to Balliol, where he was president of the junior common room, and played cricket and rugby for the college, and rugby for the university in 1950 and 1951, in the latter year as captain of the side that beat Cambridge 13–0, he himself contributing most of the Oxford score. In 1952 he captained an Oxford team which made an unbeaten tour of Japan. He graduated with a second in modern history in 1951. On 20 December 1952 he married Hilary Chadwick (*d.* 1978), daughter of J. C. Brooks, of London; they had two sons and two daughters.

After three years with a shipping firm, mostly in Norway, Bullard joined the foreign service in 1955, serving in Bucharest, Panama, Bangkok, and Islamabad. He had two home postings, in the mid-1960s to the personnel department of the Foreign Office, and in the mid-1970s as a senior inspector, both posts requiring great tact, a quality with which Bullard was notably endowed.

Bullard spent a year at the Centre for South-East Asia Studies in Cambridge, and from 1977 to 1980 was consul-general in Boston, where he met his second wife, Linda Rannells, *née* Lewis (*d.* 1992), whom he married in 1982. She brought Bullard four step-children in addition to his own children. His next post was as ambassador in Sofia, where for three years in those Warsaw pact days he was only allowed to meet officials. He did, however, manage to visit the Museum of Humour, where he bought volumes of Bulgarian jokes which he declared to be worth their weight in lead.

A more congenial posting was as high commissioner to the West Indies, based in Bridgetown, Barbados. Only two months after his arrival came the American invasion of Grenada, to topple a left-wing regime and a suspected pro-Cuban plot. This armed intervention in a Commonwealth country was greeted in London with official outrage, but Bullard, who knew the strong feelings about the Grenada regime in other West Indian countries, advised co-operation with the Americans, or at any rate doing nothing to hamper them. The fact that his advice was ignored was something he never referred to, though he was sorely tempted to do so in the face of American criticism. He was appointed CMG in 1981 and KCVO in 1985.

After his retirement in 1986 Bullard lived at the Manor

House, West Hendred, near Wantage, where he was able to engage in many country pursuits and local interests. Like his father, Bullard was quietly spoken, a rock of integrity, and a man of wide reading and subtle humour. He died at his home on 11 November 1992.

E. C. HODGKIN

Sources R. Bullard, *The camels must go: an autobiography* (1961) · E. C. Hodgkin, ed., *Letters from Tehran: a British ambassador in World War II Persia* (1991) · *Two kings in Arabia: Sir Reader Bullard's letters from Jedda*, ed. E. C. Hodgkin (1993) · M. Weir, memorial address for G. L. Bullard, 23 Jan 1993, Balliol Oxf. · personal knowledge (2004) · *The Times* (27 May 1976) · *The Times* (17 Nov 1992) · *The Independent* (16 Nov 1992) · *DNB* · *CGPLA Eng. & Wales* (1976)
Archives St Ant. Oxf., Middle East Centre | St Ant. Oxf., Middle East Centre, Cecil Edmonds MSS; H. St J. Philby MSS | FILM BFI NFTVA, news footage
Likenesses W. Stoneman, photograph, 1950, NPG [*see illus.*] · photograph, repro. in *The Times* (17 Nov 1992) · photograph, repro. in *The Times* (24 Nov 1992) · photograph, repro. in *The Independent*
Wealth at death £27,805: probate, 24 Aug 1976, *CGPLA Eng. & Wales*

Bulleid, Oliver Vaughan Snell (1882–1970), mechanical engineer, was born on 19 September 1882 in Invercargill, New Zealand, the eldest in the family of two sons and a daughter of William Bulleid, a businessman from North Tawton, Devon, and his wife, Marian (daughter of Oliver Vaughan Pugh), from Llanfyllin, Montgomeryshire, to which she returned with her children in 1889 on the death of her husband. Bulleid was educated at Spa College, Bridge of Allan, Scotland, and at Accrington Technical School. In 1901 he began a four-year premium apprenticeship for the Great Northern Railway at their Doncaster works, under Henry Alfred Ivatt, locomotive carriage and wagon superintendent, with academic studies at Sheffield and Leeds universities. In 1908 Bulleid married Ivatt's youngest daughter, Marjorie Campbell (1888–1985). They had three sons (one of whom died in 1938 at the age of fifteen) and one daughter.

In the same year Bulleid became assistant works manager and chief draughtsman at the French Westinghouse Company's brake and signal works in Paris, where he had his first contacts with French railway engineers. In 1910 and 1911 he was mechanical engineer for the Board of Trade at the British pavilions at the Brussels and Turin exhibitions.

In 1911 Bulleid returned to railway service as personal assistant to H. Nigel Gresley who had just taken over from Ivatt on the Great Northern Railway. This was the beginning of a close association and collaboration lasting for twenty-six years, interrupted only by Bulleid's war service from 1915 to 1919, when he was involved mainly in the operation of military railways serving ammunition dumps near the front in France. He attained the rank of lieutenant-colonel in the Royal Engineers. Shortly after his return Gresley appointed him assistant carriage and wagon superintendent, and they introduced numerous innovations including modernized train interiors; twin articulated sleeping cars; a completely articulated five-coach train set carried on only six bogies, in whose kitchen electric cooking was pioneered.

In 1923 Gresley became chief mechanical engineer of the London and North Eastern, the second largest group railway, formed from six individual companies, with Bulleid as his personal assistant. Bulleid's innovative outlook on design matters and study of overseas engineering practice complemented Gresley's, and they were both closely involved in the technical work of the International Railway Congress Association. Bulleid was an active participant in developing Gresley's locomotives and rolling-stock and was a pioneer in the application of welding, including its use for boilers.

In 1937 Bulleid succeeded Richard Maunsell, chief mechanical engineer of the Southern Railway, which had concentrated its capital expenditure on widespread electrification and relatively little on improvement of its steam-operated services. Bulleid strongly advocated the need for more modern and powerful steam locomotives and obtained authority for these. His first heavy main-line passenger and fast freight locomotive, of the 4–6–2 type, was built in 1941. It was of striking 'air-smoothed' outline and embodied many innovations, including welded steel fire-box and totally enclosed internal driving mechanism housed in an oil-bath. It rapidly demonstrated its power and haulage capacity, despite teething troubles, and 140 of these and a slightly smaller variant transformed train operation over most of the steam-worked Southern lines. From 1942 a class of more powerful 0–6–0 freight locomotives also gave excellent results. Bulleid introduced new and more comfortable main-line and electric suburban trains, the latter including a double-deck prototype train for the crowded Kent suburban lines and a revolutionary prototype general-purpose steam locomotive carried on two steam-driven power bogies.

On retirement in 1949, after the formation of the nationalized British Railways system, Bulleid was invited to join Coras Iompair Eirann, the Irish state transport system, as consulting mechanical engineer and later chief mechanical engineer. He was responsible for introducing modern carriage and wagon designs embodying welded construction, workshop modernization, and, encouraged by the high cost of imported coal, diesel locomotives and railcars. He also produced a prototype steam locomotive burning indigenous peat, which embodied features of the prototype Southern locomotive. He retired again in 1958.

Bulleid was president of the Institution of Mechanical Engineers in 1956–7, of the Institution of Locomotive Engineers in 1939–45, and of the Institute of Welding in 1949. He was also an honorary member of the American Society of Mechanical Engineers. He was appointed CBE in 1949 and received an honorary DSc from Bath University (1967). He combined great innovative ability and enthusiasm with charm, humour, and kindness to his staff, many of whom were devoted to him. He was a devout Roman Catholic. Bulleid died on 25 April 1970 in Malta.

GEORGE W. CARPENTER, rev.

Sources H. A. V. Bulleid, *Master builders of steam* (1963) · S. Day-Lewis, *Bulleid, last giant of steam* (1964) · H. A. V. Bulleid, *Bulleid of the Southern* (1977) · private information (1993) · private information (2004) [H. A. V. Bulleid, son]

Archives National Railway Museum Library and Archives, York, corresp. with John Click and others, incl. interview

Wealth at death £19,642 in England: probate, 23 Dec 1970, *CGPLA Eng. & Wales*

Bullein, Richard (d. 1563). *See under* Bullein, William (c.1515–1576).

Bullein, William (c.1515–1576), physician, was probably born about 1515 in the Isle of Ely, the eldest of the three sons of William Bullen and his wife, Alice Tryvet. His family may have been distantly related to that of Anne Boleyn. He was clearly educated, and it has been asserted that he studied at both Cambridge and Oxford, but there are no records of his presence at either university.

On 9 June 1550 Bullein was instituted to the rectory of Blaxhall in Suffolk, a town in which he was related to one of the principal families. His fervent protestantism led to his resignation by 5 November 1554, at the beginning of Queen Mary's reign. His timing was fortunate, as the new bishop of Norwich, John Hopton, proved to be a particularly rigorous suppressor of protestants in the area. Although he left the region Bullein did not lose the contacts he had made among a group of influential protestant gentry in Suffolk, among them Sir Robert Wingfelde and Henry Carey, Lord Hunsdon, to whom he later dedicated medical works.

After resigning his rectorship Bullein turned his attention to medicine, which he may have studied for a time in Germany, though it does not appear that he took an MD. He then began to practise in Northumberland and Durham, where he acquired the patronage of Sir Thomas Hilton, baron of Hilton. Hilton had been a leading participant in the pilgrimage of grace, for which he had been pardoned, and had been made captain of Tynemouth Castle by Queen Mary.

The first of Bullein's medical books, *A Newe Booke Entituled the Gouernement of Healthe* (1559), was written in Hilton's home and dedicated to him. This work maintained a traditional emphasis on the importance of regimen and diet to health, criticizing gluttony and intemperance. Structured as a dialogue between John, an epicure, and Humfrey, a learned physician, it includes a number of rhymes to aid the learning of medical knowledge, and a lengthy exposition of the nature and use of a range of herbs and simples. Hilton died soon after this book was published, and his widow, Agnes (or Anne), married Bullein. He moved to London about this time, renting a house in June 1560 in Grub Street, in the parish of St Giles Cripplegate, where his brother Richard [*see below*] was rector.

Bullein was now, however, accused of 'no lesse crime than of [the] moste cruell murder' of Sir Thomas by his brother, William Hilton, who had him arraigned before the duke of Norfolk. Bullein denied the charge, claiming that Sir Thomas had died of a fever 'sent onely by God' (Bullein, *Bulwarke*, fol. 84). The case was apparently dismissed, possibly through the influence of Bullein's Suffolk patrons, who were neighbours and clients of the duke. Interestingly, the dedication to Hilton in the

VV. B.

William Bullein (c.1515–1576), by unknown engraver, pubd 1805 [original, 1559]

Gouernement of Healthe was a lengthy attack on those who slander physicians as poisoners, and called for patients to have faith in their skills, suggesting that Bullein had not been free from suspicion while Hilton was alive. Although frustrated in the murder charge, William Hilton continued to pursue Bullein and his wife, and some time in 1559 or 1560 prosecuted them for debt, demanding 350 marks that he claimed he had been owed by Sir Thomas. William Hilton won the case at the York assizes, although Bullein later asserted that this was thanks to a corrupt jury and threats against his life which prevented him from attending, and he therefore sought to overturn the verdict in chancery in 1560 (Whelpy, 5).

While Bullein and his wife were imprisoned for debt Bullein wrote his next work, *Bulleins Bulwarke of Defence Againste All Sicknes, Sornes, and Woundes*, which he finished in March 1562 and published that year with a dedication to Henry Carey, Lord Hunsdon. This book replaced a manuscript lost when the boat transporting his possessions to London was shipwrecked. Openly inspired by Sir Thomas Elyot's *Castle of Health* (1539), the text was again framed as a dialogue, but was much more extensive in plan, covering surgery, compound medicines, and the responsibilities of physicians, surgeons, and apothecaries, as well as a much more extensive treatment of the simples which had been the main subject of his earlier work. Although substantially Galenist in approach, the book contains some of the earliest printed references to Paracelsus and chemical medicines in English medical writing, together with a discussion of a number of mineral and chemical substances and methods of distillation. This text is also the main source for William Hilton's prosecution, suggesting that Bullein's reputation had been damaged by what he claimed were 'sondrie malicious and devilish invencions' (Bullein, *Bulwarke*, 'To the reader'). He also mentioned trouble he had faced from another former patient, a gentleman named Bellises of Jarrow in Durham, who, although Bullein had cured him of the 'palsie', had later sought 'divers ways to haue murthered me', employing ruffians to assist him in his 'bloody purpose' (ibid., fol. 39).

In 1562 Bullein obtained release from prison. He published his third book, *A Comfortable Regiment … Against the … Pleurisi*, in December that year, dedicating it to Sir Robert Wingfelde of Lethryngam. After a brief survey of plagues and other divine judgements throughout history, it contains a discussion of the causes and treatment of pleurisy, which was apparently the cause of a great number of deaths that winter. Although the work seems to have been written in response to this crisis, Bullein suggests that it would also be the first of a series of books in which he was going to address a further thirty diseases.

Bullein published his last and most popular work, *A Dialogue … Against the Fever Pestilence*, in 1564. The book was dedicated to Master Edward Barrette of Belhouse in Essex, in whose house Bullein seems to have written some of it. This work saw him move away from the overwhelmingly medical concerns of his previous writing, and extend his use of dialogue beyond the didactic to a more lively style in which he mixed medicine, morality, and entertainment. Like the authors of many plague tracts, Bullein takes the epidemic as his starting point for a broad criticism of the sins of society, attacking engrossing and enclosure in the countryside and the sudden charity of the afflicted, and parodying hypocritical and atheistic physicians and apothecaries, and the desperation of usurious merchants when faced by death. The need for spiritual reform is clear: among the sections is a Utopian passage in which one of the characters describes a reformed and godly city named 'Nodnol' (London) or 'Ecnatneper' (Repentance), in a land, supposedly beyond the Americas, 'Taerg Natrib' (Great Britain). Although plague was primarily understood as an act of God, like most of his contemporaries Bullein sees it as operating through natural means, particularly bad air, and therefore interspersed throughout the text are useful treatments, preventatives, and remedies against the plague.

Bullein seems to have found growing success as a physician over his next few years in London. He never became a fellow of the College of Physicians, but escaped their censure. His first wife, Agnes, died early in the 1560s, and on 30 October 1566 he married Anne Doffield, with whom he had a daughter, Margaret, who was baptized on 12 October 1567. He seems to have written little after the *Dialogue*, his last known publication being some commendatory verses prefacing John Sadler's *The Four Bookes of Flavius Vegetius Ranatus* (1572) translated from the Latin.

Little evidence of Bullein's practice survives, although

some indication of a continued involvement in controversy is suggested in further editions of the *Dialogue*, published in 1573 and 1578. Among the changes in 1573 is the name of the deceiving and atheistic physician he criticizes, named Antonius Capistranus in 1564, which now became 'Doctor Tocrub' (Burcot spelt backwards). This referred to Burchard Kranich (*d.* 1578), a German immigrant miner, metallurgist, and physician. Kranich, possibly a Catholic escaping the upheavals of the Reformation, had arrived during the reign of Queen Mary, who gave him a patent to mine and refine metals, mainly in Devon and Cornwall. This enterprise seems to have failed, and he moved to London in the mid-1560s, where he established a successful practice as a physician under the name of Burcot. His metallurgical skills were not forgotten, however, and he was consulted by the royal mint about Frobisher's gold in 1577. The origin of Bullein's animosity toward him is unclear, but it may have stemmed from rivalry for the patronage of Lord Hunsdon, whom both knew, or from the debtors' prison, where Kranich may have been incarcerated at the same time as Bullein.

Bullein died on 7 January 1576 in the parish of St Giles Cripplegate. He was buried two days later in the church of St Giles Cripplegate, in the same grave as his brother Richard. A few years later John Foxe, the martyrologist, was also interred there. A monument in Latin commemorating the three of them was placed over the tomb, in which it is said of Bullein that 'medicamina semper habebat, aeque pauperibus danda, ac locupletibus aeque' ('he always had medicines, which he gave to rich and poor alike'; Strype, 3.209, Appendix).

Bullein is mainly known from his writing. Apparently popular among contemporaries, his continued reputation as a writer is suggested by Thomas Nashe's claim that he framed *Have with You to Saffron Walden* (1596) 'in the nature of a Dialogue, much like Bullen' ('Address'), and as a physician by reprints of his books in the 1580s and 1590s. Bullein's work was distinguished by his clear and entertaining prose and fine use of dialogue. The medical content was not generally novel, although his works do number among the first vernacular herbals, and include some of the earliest published references to Paracelsus, and mineral and chemical medicines in English. The works rely on a combination of sources, principally a range of classical and more recent medical authors, including Fuchs and Gesner. They are marked with a strong scriptural vein, and are unsurprisingly fervent in their anti-Catholicism.

Richard Bullein (*d.* 1563) was a younger brother of William Bullein, and, like his brother, appears to have combined a vocation as a priest, as rector of St Giles Cripplegate, London, with an interest in physic. He was described by his brother as 'a Zealous lover in Physicke, more for the consolacion and help of thafflicted sicke people beyng poore, than for the lucre and gaine of the money of the welthie and riche' (Bullein, *Bulwarke*, pt. 2, fol. xlviii). He was presumably the author of some commendatory verses printed at the start of *The Governement of Healthe*

(1559) signed R. B., and according to his brother wrote an unpublished treatise on the stone.

Richard Bullein died on 16 October 1563 and was buried in the church of St Giles Cripplegate in the grave where his brother and John Foxe were later interred.

PATRICK WALLIS

Sources W. H. Whelpy, 'An unanswered question on Bullein and Hilton', *N&Q*, 202 (1957), 3–6 · C. C. Manbretti, 'William Bullein and the "lively fashions" in Tudor medical literature', *Clio Medica*, 9 (1974), 285–97 · M. B. Donald, 'Burchard Kranich (*c.*1515–78), miner and queen's physician', *Annals of Science*, 6 (1948–50), 308–22 · A. Kippis and others, eds., *Biographia Britannica, or, The lives of the most eminent persons who have flourished in Great Britain and Ireland*, 2nd edn, 5 vols. (1778–93) · D. MacCulloch, *Suffolk and the Tudors: politics and religion in an English county, 1500–1600* (1986) · W. S. Mitchell, 'William Bullein, Elizabethan physician and author', *Medical History*, 3 (1959), 188–200 · J. Strype, *Annals of the Reformation and establishment of religion … during Queen Elizabeth's happy reign*, 3rd edn, 4 vols. (1731–5) · R. Surtees, *The history and antiquities of the county palatine of Durham*, 4 vols. (1816–40) · *DNB* · W. Bullein, *Bulleins bulwarke of defence againste all sicknes, sornes, and woundes, that dooe daily assaulte mankinde* (1562) · W. Bullein, *A newe booke entituled the gouernement of healthe* (1559)

Likenesses woodcut, 1579, Wellcome L. · W. Stukeley, pen drawing, 1722, Wellcome L. · engraving, pubd 1805 (original, 1559), NPG [*see illus.*] · line engraving, 1805, Wellcome L. · line engraving, pubd 1805 (after woodcut, 1559), BM, NPG · heliograph, Wellcome L.

Bullen, Arthur Henry (1857–1920), literary editor and publisher, was born in London on 9 February 1857, the second son of George *Bullen (1816x18–1894), and his first wife, Eliza Mary Martin (*d.* 1887). He was educated at the City of London School, where the headmaster, Dr Edwin Abbott, encouraged the reading of Elizabethan literature and where Bullen was noted for his knowledge of both Elizabethan and contemporary writers. He matriculated at Worcester College, Oxford, in 1875, with an open classical scholarship, and took a first in classical moderations in 1877. His prospects were set back, however, when he graduated with only a third class in *literae humaniores* in 1879. On 2 August of the same year he married Edith (*b.* 1858/9), daughter of William John Goodwin, head of the map department of the ecclesiastical commissioners; they had two sons and three daughters. They lived first in Margate, where Bullen worked as a classics tutor. He soon moved back to London, however, and embarked on a remarkable programme of scholarly publication which began with *The Works of John Day* (1881). His English Dramatists series comprised complete editions of the plays of Marlowe (1885), Middleton (1886), Marston (1887), and Peele (1888) and his seven-volume *A Collection of Old English Plays* (1882–90) included a number of plays never published before. He also published a number of collections of lyric poems, including *Selections from the Poems of Michael Drayton* (1883), *Lyrics from the Song-Books of the Elizabethan Age* (1886), and *The Works of Dr Thomas Campion* (1889).

During the same period Bullen wrote over 150 articles for the early volumes of the *Dictionary of National Biography*, chiefly on English authors of the sixteenth and seventeenth centuries. He did some teaching at Toynbee Hall in London, and in February and March 1889 he delivered a series of lectures in Oxford, organized by the university

Arthur Henry Bullen (1857–1920), by unknown photographer

extension office, on Elizabethan dramatists (these were eventually published in 1924, with some additional essays, under the title *Elizabethans*). Bullen must have hoped that these activities and his many publications would help him to obtain a university post. He was unsuccessful, however, in his application for the chair of English language and literature at University College, London, in 1889 (the successful candidate was W. P. Ker) and this disappointment seems to have precipitated a change of direction in his career.

In 1891, in partnership with H. W. Lawrence, Bullen set up the publishing house of Lawrence and Bullen. The firm quickly acquired a reputation for fine books and sympathetic treatment of its authors, who included George Gissing and W. B. Yeats. It folded in 1900, but Bullen continued to publish under the imprint 'A. H. Bullen', and found a new partner in Frank Sidgwick, nephew of Henry Sidgwick. In 1904 they set up the Shakespeare Head Press at Stratford upon Avon, in a house once lived in by Shakespeare's contemporary Julius Shaw, with the intention of publishing the first complete edition of Shakespeare's works to be published in the town of his birth (Bullen characteristically claimed that the idea for this project had come to him in a dream). The Stratford Town Shakespeare, which remains of bibliographical if not academic interest, was published in ten volumes between 1904 and 1907. Under the imprint of the Shakespeare Head Press Bullen also published a collected edition of the works of W. B. Yeats (1908).

As publisher or editor Bullen assisted in many works of

scholarship, such as R. B. McKerrow's edition of Nashe, W. W. Greg's edition of Henslowe's *Diary*, and G. C. Moore Smith's edition of Gabriel Harvey's *Marginalia*. For a short period, in 1906, he also edited the *Gentleman's Magazine* for Lord Northcliffe. He was awarded a civil-list pension in 1912, but was unable to raise public support for the Shakespeare Head Press, which struggled as a business until it was bought by Basil Blackwell and his associates after Bullen's death.

A colourful and energetic character, Bullen was admired by his contemporaries for his scholarship and great enthusiasm for Elizabethan literature. As an editor he modernized his texts, so they did not remain standard scholarly editions, but some of his individual insights survive: he was the first editor of Marlowe's *Doctor Faustus*, for example, to realize that the mysterious word 'Oncaymaeon', in Faustus's important opening speech, was a transliteration of the Greek philosophical phrase *on kai mē on* ('being and not being'). His greatest achievement, both as publisher and editor, was to make the literature he loved more widely known and available. His anthologies, in particular, were acknowledged by Sir Arthur Quiller-Couch as an important source for the *Oxford Book of English Verse* (1900). He died at Stratford upon Avon at 26 Evesham Place on 29 February 1920, and was buried at Luddington. A small volume of his poems, *Weeping-Cross*, was published shortly after his death. RICHARD STORER

Sources *Application of A. H. Bullen for the English chair at University College, London* (1889) · K. Tynan, 'A. H. Bullen', *The Bookman*, 58 (1920), 10 · A. H. Bullen, *Weeping-cross and other rimes* (1921) · 'H. F. B. Brett-Smith's foreword to Shakespeare's sonnets', *Frank Sidgwick's diary and other material relating to A. H. Bullen and the Shakespeare Head Press at Stratford-upon-Avon* (1975) · P. Morgan, 'Arthur Henry Bullen (1857–1920) and the Shakespeare Head Press', *Frank Sidgwick's diary and other material relating to A. H. Bullen and the Shakespeare Head Press at Stratford-upon-Avon* (1975) · H. Jones, 'Arthur Henry Bullen and the Stratford Town Shakespeare', *Antiquarian Book Monthly Review*, 12 (1985), 128–33 · A. L. P. Norrington, *Blackwell's 1879–1979: the history of a family firm* (1983) · I. Rogerson, 'Shakespeare Head Press', *British literary publishing houses, 1881–1965*, ed. J. Rose and P. J. Anderson, DLitB, 112 (1991)

Archives Birm. CA, corresp. and papers · Bodl. Oxf., corresp. · Hunt. L., letters | Bodl. Oxf., letters to Bertram Dobell · Bodl. Oxf., letters to Frank Sidgwick relating to Shakespeare Head Press · Bodl. Oxf., legal and financial papers and corresp. with Sidgwick and Jackson · Bodl. Oxf., notes on Aurelian Townsend · Shakespeare Birthplace Trust RO, Stratford upon Avon, corresp. and papers relating to Shakespeare Head Press; personal papers · U. Edin. L., letters to James Halliwell-Phillipps · U. Warwick Mod. RC, letters to Clara Collet · University of Bristol, letters to J. A. Symmonds

Likenesses E. Walker, photograph, repro. in Bullen, *Weeping-cross* · photograph, repro. in *Frank Sidgwick's diary* · photograph, NPG [*see illus.*]

Wealth at death £2980 5s. 10d.: probate, 1 July 1920, CGPLA Eng. & Wales

Bullen, Sir Charles (1769–1853), naval officer, was born on 10 September 1769 at Newcastle upon Tyne, the son of John Bullen (surgeon-general on the coast of North America, 1779–81) and his wife, Ruth, daughter of Charles Liddell and cousin of Lord High Chancellor Eldon. He entered the navy in February 1779 on board the *Europe*, the flagship of Vice-Admiral Arbuthnot, on the North American station. During the peace after the treaty of Versailles (1783) he was mostly in the Mediterranean, and was promoted lieutenant on 9 August 1791. In the same year he married a distant relative, Miss Wood (*d.* 10 July 1842); they had children. In 1794 he was a lieutenant of the *Ramillies*, one of the fleet with Lord Howe in the battle of the 'Glorious First of June'. In 1797 he was first lieutenant of the *Monmouth*, one of the ships implicated in the Nore mutiny; she was afterwards at Camperdown, on 11 October, when Bullen, having been sent to take possession of the Dutch ship *Delft*, found her in a sinking state and remained trying to save the wounded until she went down. Bullen was rescued and, in recognition of his exertions, was promoted commander on 2 January 1798.

In 1801 Bullen commanded the sloop *Wasp* on the west coast of Africa; he was promoted captain on 29 April 1802. In 1804 he was appointed flag-captain to Lord Northesk in the *Britannia*, which he commanded at Trafalgar. The *Britannia* was the fourth ship in the weather line led by Nelson himself, and was thus early in action, continuing closely engaged until the end, with a loss of ten killed and forty-two wounded.

During the years 1807–11 Bullen commanded successively the frigates *Volontaire* and *Cambrian* in the Mediterranean, off Toulon, and on the coast of Spain; from 1814 to 1817 he commanded the *Akbar* (50 guns) on the North American station; and from 1824 to 1827 he was commodore on the west coast of Africa, on the *Maidstone*. In July 1830 Bullen was appointed superintendent of Pembroke dockyard, and also captain of the yacht *Royal Sovereign*, both of which offices he held until he became rear-admiral on 10 January 1837. He had no further employment afloat, but was advanced by seniority to the rank of vice-admiral on 9 November 1846 and that of admiral on 30 July 1852. He was created CB on 4 June 1815; KCH on 13 January 1835; KCB on 18 April 1839; and GCB on 7 April 1852. He also received the gold medal for Trafalgar, and a £300 good-service pension (1843). He died at Shirley, near Southampton, on 2 July 1853.

J. K. LAUGHTON, *rev.* ROGER MORRISS

Sources O'Byrne, *Naval biog. dict.* · *GM*, 2nd ser., 40 (1853), 309 · Boase, *Mod. Eng. biog.*

Likenesses oils, 1843–6, NMM · A. Grant, oils, 1849, NMM · portrait, Greenwich, painted hall

Bullen, Edward (1813–1868), legal writer, was born at Taunton, on 3 April 1813, the son of Robert Uttermare Bullen, an attorney. He was educated at the Benedictine College of Douai, and was admitted to Lincoln's Inn in 1833. (He should not be confused with a Gray's Inn barrister of the same name, called in 1852.) As a Roman Catholic he was unable to subscribe to the oaths required for call to the bar, and therefore followed the course set by others in the same plight—notably Charles Butler (*d.* 1832), also of Douai and Lincoln's Inn—by practising 'below the bar'. Such practitioners had no rights of audience in court, but were permitted to engage in chambers practice either as conveyancers or special pleaders. Bullen chose pleading, and became one of the most celebrated pleaders of the century. He is first mentioned in the *Law List* for 1838, when he was practising at 2 Elm Court. The privilege of reading as a pupil in his chambers was highly prized.

Bullen wrote *A Practical Treatise on the Law of Distress for Rent and of Things Damage Feasant* in 1842, a work which achieved a second edition in 1899 but which was destined to be overtaken by more detailed treatises on the same subject. A pamphlet which he published in 1853 on the changing relationship between landlord and tenant indicates his continuing interest in that branch of the law. His lasting renown, however, was due to his classic *Precedents of Pleadings in Common Law*, compiled in collaboration with a former pupil, Stephen Martin Leake, and which first appeared in 1860. The object was to produce a collection of simple modern precedents in conformity with the new pleading system introduced by the Common Law Procedure Act 1852, and the rules made under it, which put an end to the fictions and prolix formalities which had characterized special pleading during the first twenty years of Bullen's professional life. The book was an enormous success and became the *vade mecum* of every common-law barrister; an extended second edition appeared in 1863, and by the time of the fourth edition (1882) the work's original length had been doubled. Despite the many further reforms introduced throughout the next century, which necessitated heavy revision by successive editors, the work of Bullen and Leake was still in use (as Bullen, Leake, and Jacob) in the thirteenth edition of 1990.

Bullen died at his London home, 82 Belsize Park Gardens, on 19 July 1868, after reading the proofs of the third edition of *Precedents of Pleadings*. He was survived by his wife, Louise. Three of his sons were barristers who had served as pupils in his chambers. His eldest son, Edward Uttermare, born about 1838, was admitted to the Middle Temple in 1856, called to the bar in 1860, and joined the western circuit. The second son, Charles Louis, became a member of the same inn in 1857 but does not appear to have been called or to have practised. Another son, Thomas Joseph, born in 1845, joined the Inner Temple in 1864, and practised as a special pleader until 1883, when he was called to the bar. He assisted Leake in the completion of the third edition of *Precedents of Pleadings*, was co-editor of the 1882 edition, and also helped to prepare the 1899 edition of Bullen's *Distress*.　　J. H. BAKER

Sources *Law Times* (25 July 1868), 235 · *Law Journal* (31 July 1868), 508 · Boase, *Mod. Eng. biog.* · *CGPLA Eng. & Wales* (1868)

Likenesses H. W. Pickersgill, portrait, exh. RA 1860 · photograph, c.1865, Middle Temple Library, London

Wealth at death under £14,000: administration, 16 Oct 1868, *CGPLA Eng. & Wales*

Bullen, Frank Thomas (1857–1915), merchant seaman and writer, was born at 40 Alfred Road, Paddington, London, on 5 April 1857, the son of Frank Robert Bullen, journeyman stonemason of Crewkerne, Dorset, and his wife, Margaret, *née* Brown. When he was eighteen months old the family broke up, his upbringing passing to a maiden aunt. An elder sister disappeared, and he saw his mother only once again, though he re-established contact with his father later in life. Existence depended on his aunt's ability at home sewing, yet two foundations of his later development were laid down: an awareness of literature and familiarity with religion. A natural pre-school reader, he attended dame- and junior schools and a Sunday school chapel in Paddington, but was otherwise cloistered until, in 1866, aged nine, he was thrown out on the streets following his aunt's death. Thereafter he was self-educated.

In and out of errand-boy jobs, Bullen now lodged for the cost of his keep or, between jobs, slept rough and lived on scraps. Thus he learned a 'street wisdom' which helped him through similar periods between passages at sea. In January 1869, when not yet twelve, he persuaded an uncle, a ship's master, to take him as cabin-boy. So began the most influential phase of his life, largely in the lower strata of British merchant shipping. By the age of thirteen he had twice been shipwrecked and had survived two epidemics of yellow fever, a hurricane, and two serious illnesses. Most of his sea service was in sail. He served in over twenty-five ships, rising to able seaman and, after passing the examinations for second mate and first mate, in those capacities when such employment offered.

On 1 September 1879 Bullen married Amelia (*d*. 1945), daughter of Voltaire Lucifer Grimwood, shoemaker. They had two sons, both of whom died young, and three daughters. The couple separated about 1905. In 1882 he became a clerk in the Meteorological Office, augmenting his income by running simultaneously a picture-framing business and haberdashery shop in London. This led to a collapse from overwork and, in the mid-1890s, to voluntary bankruptcy. Although he disliked clerical employment, his writing ability and theoretical understanding of marine science were developing. Following a conversion at sea he became an evangelical Christian, and through spare-time preaching he developed an ability at public speaking.

The acceptance of Bullen's first article about 1894 led to regular contributions to popular journals, including *The Spectator* and the *Cornhill Magazine*, with syndication in American journals. Appointed columnist on the *Morning Leader*, and financially stable, he left the Meteorological Office in 1899 and also began accepting engagements as a paid circuit lecturer. His illustrated lectures commanded large audiences. Later he undertook lecture tours in Australia, New Zealand, and North America. His first of thirty-six books, and most widely acclaimed, *The Cruise of the 'Cachalot'* (1898), established his international reputation.

All Bullen's writing and lectures derived from his sea experience, keen observation, and a good memory, and were concerned mainly with marine science and sea life. His easy, natural style made his non-fictional writing compulsive reading and he did much to explain the maritime world to the public ashore. Maritime historians rate his revelations of seafaring conditions in the 1870s highly, though his fictional work was not of the same calibre. Born the same year as Joseph Conrad, his reputation became established earlier, though his work did not retain the same general literary esteem.

Bullen was awarded a civil-list pension in 1912. He died

on 26 February 1915 at Reid's Palace Hotel in Funchal during a visit to Madeira and was buried there on the 27th in the English cemetery. He was survived by his wife.

ALSTON KENNERLEY

Sources F. T. Bullen, *The log of a sea waif: being recollections of the first four years of my sea life* (1899) · F. T. Bullen, *With Christ at sea: a religious autobiography* (1900) · F. T. Bullen, *Confessions of a tradesman* (1908) · F. T. Bullen, *Recollections: the reminiscences of the busy life of one who has played the varied parts of sailor, author and lecturer* (1915), frontispiece · NMM, Board of Trade records · Board of Trade records, PRO · Memorial University, St John's, Newfoundland, Maritime History Archive · F. T. Bullen, *Cruise of the 'Cachalot' round the world after sperm whales* (1898) · A. Kennerley, 'Frank Thomas Bullen, 1857–1915: whaling and nonfiction maritime writing', *American Neptune*, 56 (1996), 353–70 · A. Kennerley, 'Frank Thomas Bullen: Christian maritime author', *Maritime Mission Studies*, 4 (1995), 49–55 · *The Times* (2 March 1915) · *The Times* (31 May 1915), 9c · private information (2004) [D. Peters] · census returns for London, 1861 · b. cert. · *CGPLA Eng. & Wales* (1915) · *London Directory* (1892–4) · *London Directory* (1896–1902) · parish register, Paddington, Holy Trinity, 28 June 1863 [baptism] · parish register, Paddington, St Marylebone, 1 Sept 1879 [marriage] · parish register, Funchal, Madeira, English cemetery [burial]

Archives University of North Carolina Library, Chapel Hill, A. P. Watt archive

Likenesses S. van Abbé, engraving?, c.1900, repro. in F. T. Bullen, *Cruise of the 'Cachalot' and The log of a sea waif* (1953) · Vandyk, photograph, c.1914, repro. in Bullen, *Recollections*, frontispiece · photographs, repro. in F. T. Bullen, *With Christ in Sailortown* (1901), frontispiece · portrait, repro. in *Bookman*, 37 (Oct 1909), 59 · portrait, repro. in *Reader Magazine*, 5 (Dec 1904), 118

Wealth at death £551 7s. 11d.: probate, 26 May 1915, *CGPLA Eng. & Wales*

Bullen, George (1816x18–1894), librarian, was born in Ireland, probably at Clonakilty, co. Cork. He is said to have been born on 17 or 27 November 1816 or 1817, but his tombstone records that he was seventy-six when he died in October 1894. He was educated at St Saviour's Grammar School, Southwark, London, and spent some time as a private tutor of the classics. In January 1838 he became a supernumerary assistant in the department of printed books in the British Museum, and thus inaugurated a connection with the museum which lasted for more than half a century. At the date of his appointment the institution was undergoing several changes. Antonio Panizzi had just been made keeper of printed books, the demolition of the old Montagu House was about to begin, and part of the buildings in Bloomsbury which had been erected on the site of its garden were ready for the reception of the library. Bullen's earliest work was to assist in the arrangement of the books on the shelves in the new premises. In the following year he took part in the preparation of the catalogue of the library which the trustees had resolved to prepare. Only one volume of this edition was printed; it was published in 1841 and covered the letter A. To this folio volume Bullen contributed the article on Aristotle, which filled fifty-six columns. Although Panizzi prevented any more volumes being printed, because he insisted that the whole catalogue must be revised before it was sent to the press, work on the new version continued. Forty years later the enterprise of printing the museum catalogue was resumed, and was then carried through successfully.

In 1849 Bullen was made a permanent assistant in the library. In 1866 he was promoted, in succession to Thomas Watts, to one of the two posts of assistant keeper in the department; he also became superintendent of the reading-room. Bullen's genial temper gained him popularity in this role. In 1875 he succeeded W. B. Rye in the higher office of keeper of printed books, and thus became chief of the department which he had first entered thirty-seven years earlier. During his fifteen years as keeper the great task of printing the museum catalogue was begun, in 1881; but this was despite his opposition, and because of pressure from Edward Bond, the principal librarian, and Richard Garnett, one of the assistant keepers of printed books. Bullen was much more interested in the *Catalogue of the English Books in the Library Printed before 1640* (3 vols.), which was compiled under his supervision and published in 1884. An index of the printers and publishers whose productions were noticed in the text is a valuable feature of the work. Bullen retired from the keepership of printed books in 1890, and was succeeded by Richard Garnett.

Although no scholar of a formal type, Bullen was much interested in literary research, and throughout his life he devoted much time to literary work. He was a frequent contributor to *The Athenaeum*; he wrote articles in 1841 for the *Biographical Dictionary* of the Society for the Diffusion of Useful Knowledge; and he compiled in 1872 a *Catalogue of the Library of the Royal Military Academy at Woolwich*. His bibliographical skill was probably displayed to best advantage in his *Catalogue of the Library of the British and Foreign Bible Society*, which appeared in 1857. In 1877 he helped to organize the Caxton celebration at South Kensington, and edited the catalogue of books exhibited there.

In 1883 Bullen arranged in the Grenville Library at the British Museum an exhibition of printed books, manuscripts, portraits, and medals illustrating the life of Martin Luther, and prepared a catalogue with a biographical sketch. In 1881 he prefixed a somewhat unsatisfactory introduction to a reproduction by the Holbein Society of the first printed edition of the *Ars moriendi* (c.1465) in the British Museum; and in 1892 he edited a facsimile reprint (in an issue limited to 350) of the copy, then recently acquired by the museum, of the *Sex quam elegantissimae epistolae* edited by Peter Carmelianus, and printed by Caxton in 1483.

Bullen was a vice-president of the Library Association, and took a prominent part in many of its annual congresses. He was elected a fellow of the Society of Antiquaries on 11 January 1877; the University of Glasgow conferred on him the honorary degree of LLD in 1889; and he was created CB in 1890. Bullen was twice married: his first wife was Eliza Mary Martin, who died in 1887; his second wife's name is unknown. With his first wife he had at least two sons, one of whom, Arthur Henry *Bullen (1857–1920), edited Elizabethan works. He died at his house, 62 Abingdon Road, Kensington, on 10 October 1894, and was buried in Highgate cemetery on 15 October.

SIDNEY LEE, *rev.* P. R. HARRIS

Sources *The Times* (13 Oct 1894) · *The Athenaeum* (13 Oct 1894) · *The Library*, 6 (1894), 367 · personal knowledge (1901) · d. cert.

Archives BL · BM · Holborn Library, Camden, London, corresp. | U. Edin. L., letters to J. Halliwell-Phillips · UCL, letters to Society for the Diffusion of Useful Knowledge
Likenesses photograph, BL · wood-engraving (after photograph by Barraud), NPG; repro. in *ILN* (20 Oct 1894)
Wealth at death £3772 18s. 9d.: probate, 29 Oct 1894, *CGPLA Eng. & Wales*

Buller, Arthur Henry Reginald (1874–1944), botanist and mycologist, was born on 19 August 1874 at Moseley, Birmingham, the son of Alban Gardner Buller JP, solicitor, and his wife, Mary Jane Huggins. He was educated at a preparatory school at Moseley, then at Queen's College, Taunton. At the age of eighteen he entered Mason College, Birmingham, to study science, including botany. He obtained the BSc (London) in 1896, having been awarded the Heslop memorial gold medal in 1895.

In 1897 Buller went to Leipzig to research under the plant physiologist Wilhelm Pfeffer. While there he won an 1851 Exhibition scholarship. In 1900 he moved to Munich, where, working under Robert Hartig, he acquired a lifelong interest in fungi. He returned to Birmingham in 1901 as assistant lecturer in botany and was awarded the DSc degree of the newly established university in 1903. In 1904 he was appointed the first professor of botany at the University of Manitoba, where he was influential in shaping university policy. He soon built up a successful botanical department in Winnipeg and continued active researches on fungi. He returned to England every summer to work at Birmingham University or at the Royal Botanic Gardens, Kew.

The results of Buller's investigations chiefly appeared in seven volumes entitled *Researches on Fungi*. Six were issued during his lifetime: in 1909, 1922, 1924, 1931, 1933, and 1934; the last was published posthumously, for the Royal Society of Canada, in 1950. *Researches on Fungi* made an important contribution to knowledge of their general biology and sexuality, especially in the higher groups. Buller showed the adaptation of common fungi to their environment and the intimate relation of the structure of their parts to function. The volumes contain abundant illustrations and are written with an enthusiasm that shows Buller to have been an observant field naturalist as well as a skilful experimentalist.

Buller was an inspiring teacher of botany and was in great demand as a lecturer on fungi in both academic and popular circles; he had a remarkable talent for communicating his enthusiasm to his audience. He was also much interested in the history of mycology, and his presidential address to the British Mycological Society in 1914 was entitled 'The fungus lore of the Greeks and Romans'. He was instrumental in arranging for an English translation, published in 1931, of the mycological classic *Selecta fungorum carpologia*, written by the brothers Tulasne in Latin. During his early residence at Winnipeg he witnessed the great expansion of wheat cultivation in western Canada, which he described in his 1919 book *Essays on Wheat*.

Buller took an active part in the general scientific life of Canada, especially in connection with its Royal Society

and National Research Council. The former elected him president for 1927–8 and in 1929 conferred on him the Flavelle medal for distinction in scientific attainment. He was elected FRS in 1929 and received a Royal medal in 1937. He was honorary LLD of the universities of Manitoba (1924), Saskatchewan (1928), and Calcutta (1937), and honorary DSc of the University of Pennsylvania (1933). He was interested in all aspects of country life and was a great bird-watcher; having musical talent he could repeat the songs of birds. He also wrote humorous verse on all sorts of topics, including fungi. He composed limericks, of which one on relativity, published in *Punch* on 18 December 1923, became famous.

Buller retired from the chair of botany at Winnipeg in 1936. He returned to England and lived chiefly at Kew, where he regularly worked in the herbarium. Early in 1939 he went for the last time to Winnipeg, where he continued his researches until he fell ill. He died there unmarried on 3 July 1944.   F. T. BROOKS, *rev.* V. M. QUIRKE

Sources F. T. Brooks, *Obits. FRS*, 5 (1945–8), 51–9 · *Nature*, 154 (1944), 173 · personal knowledge (1959) · *WWW*, 1941–50
Archives RBG Kew, botanical notebooks and papers

Buller, Sir Arthur William (1808–1869). *See under* Buller, Charles (1806–1848).

Buller, Charles (1806–1848), politician and wit, was born in Calcutta on 6 August 1806, the son of Charles Buller (1774–1848), civil servant in India and politician, and his wife, Barbara Isabella Kirkpatrick (d. 1849), daughter of Major-General William Kirkpatrick of the East India Company service. Renowned as a great beauty in Calcutta, Buller's mother was part Irish; his paternal family were from east Cornwall, where they controlled the parliamentary borough of West Looe, which his father represented, nominally as a whig, from 1812 to 1816 and from 1826 to 1830.

Early life: the Cornish Voltaire and first spell in parliament At eleven Buller was brought to England by his aunt and uncle; he suffered a fall during a stopover at St Helena that left him with a flattened nose (a feature he shared with a later friend, William Thackeray) and a limp. He was sent to Harrow School, where his greatest preoccupation was the literature of pugilism. From 1822 to 1823 he took classes in Latin and Greek at Edinburgh University and was tutored by Thomas Carlyle. The itinerant urges of Buller's mother took the family thereafter to Kinnaird House, Perthshire, and from thence to Kew Green and Shooters Hill in the London environs, followed by an increasingly irascible Carlyle, who early saw Charles's potential but worried about his lack of serious application. In 1824 Buller proceeded to Trinity College, Cambridge, where he was admitted to the Conversazione Society, the 'Apostles', then a serious and exclusive debating group, and acquired the nickname of the Cornish Voltaire. He was president of the union in 1827. At this time he first embraced Benthamite utilitarianism; this disappointed Carlyle, who none the less became a lifelong

Charles Buller (1806–1848), by Edward Scriven, pubd 1840 (after Bryan Edward Duppa)

friend. He was welcomed into the London Debating Society in 1826 by John Stuart Mill, to whom he remained ideologically close. In 1828 he joined another such forum started by George Grote, a future colleague in the parliamentary grouping which became known as the philosophic radicals. An early foray into journalism came in June 1829, when he contributed an anonymous satirical article to *Blackwood's Magazine*, which charted the mental contortions of an Anglican clergyman over Catholic emancipation. The piece displays early evidence of the irreverent, occasionally flippant humour which, depending on the viewpoint of the commentator, either distinguished or disfigured his political career.

Buller replaced his father as the MP for West Looe in February 1830. His maiden speech featured a provocative attack on William Cobbett, and his early months in parliament gave little hint of his later radicalism. He first showed his cards as a parliamentary reformer in a pamphlet, published in February 1831, entitled *On the Necessity of a Radical Reform*. It proposed equal electoral districts, a franchise based on eligibility for jury service, and vote by ballot. He privately dismissed most of the Grey ministry as place-hunters—'a heartless, spiritless, canaille', he told his Cornish neighbour Sir William Molesworth (M. G. Fawcett, *Life of Sir William Molesworth*, 1901, 40)—but he was impressed by the boldness of their reform proposals, which he supported by speech and vote. On other issues, such as his opposition to newspaper stamp duty, he remained at odds with the government. He was, as a cousin later recalled, 'not allowed' to come in again for West Looe at the general election in March 1831 (*Cornhill*

Magazine, new ser., 3, 1897, 396); it is likely that the patron, his uncle John Buller, preferred to return a member—another of his uncles, Sir Anthony Buller—who would vote for its preservation. In the form that it passed, the Reform Act duly cast West Looe into electoral oblivion.

Lawyer, journalist, and radical back-bencher Belonging to a cadet branch of a minor gentry family, Buller needed to work for a living, a consideration which influenced his career as well as, perhaps, his beliefs. In June 1831 he was called to the bar of Lincoln's Inn (to which he had first been admitted in 1824) and practised law on the western circuit. Convinced that its rejection would lead to 'a most horrible convulsion' (Sweetman, 105–6), he also busied himself speaking in support of the Reform Bill in Cornwall. He secured his own election for Liskeard, close to his family home, in the first election under the new franchise in December 1832, and held the seat for the rest of his life (ironically furnishing a case in point of the ineffectiveness of the first Reform Act—which Buller himself decried—in ending the influence of local landed proprietors in small boroughs).

Journalism was an important sideline for Buller. He wrote for the *Westminster Review*, the *London Review* (and the subsequent amalgamation of the two), *The Globe*, and *The Constitutional*, a short-lived radical daily begun in 1836. His subject matter ranged from national and international politics to literary reviews. With Henry Cole, a civil servant at the record commission with whom Buller co-operated in seeking to reform that body, he started the *Weekly Chronicle* (1837); it lost money, and they sold out to Henry George Ward, then a radical MP. Buller also co-edited with Cole, again in 1837, the *Guide to Knowledge*. One article, in the *Foreign Quarterly Review* in May 1832, on a widely criticized book on English society by Prince Plückler-Maskau, captures the essence of his radical credo at the time:

> The dullness of English intercourse, and the arrogance which renders the English disagreeable to foreigners, spring from the same source as some of the worst features of our morality—from the reverence and rivalry of wealth—the utter contempt of social merit as a claim to distinction in society, and the vicious systems of *caste*, which are the only checks on the predominating influence of money.
> (Haury, 65)

Yet despite such manifest dissatisfaction with the existing order, social stability was for Buller, as for all the philosophic radicals, an all-pervading concern. It was, he believed, being undermined by a loss of confidence in aristocracy, which was compounded by the 'decorous lifelessness of the Church of England' (ibid., 66). Opposition to the established church as constituted was a constant thread in his politics; he opposed obliging nonconformists to pay for it through tithes, wanted bishops removed from the House of Lords, thought compulsory sabbath observance the epitome of aristocratic double standards, and went as far as to describe the Church of Ireland as an 'abominable institution' (22 July 1834, *Hansard* 3, 24.358). Little is known of his own religious and spiritual beliefs beyond that he later dabbled in mesmerism.

Surveying the radical parliamentary contingent in March 1833, John Stuart Mill judged that Buller possessed the 'finest understanding … but wants strength of will' (*Early Correspondence*, 1.145). Buller shared his colleagues' view of the 1832 Reform Act as a partial measure, and kept up the pressure for a widening of the franchise and the abolition of the property qualification for MPs. The introduction of voting by secret ballot he regarded as of paramount importance; his speech in support of this on 2 June 1835 was an early instance of his—or anyone's—public use of the term 'liberal' as a self-description, and in something approaching the political sense it would acquire a generation later (*Hansard 3*, 28.429). Buller was among those, too, who recalled that the desire for reduced taxation had been behind much of the previous agitation for parliamentary reform. An opponent of the corn laws, he was from 1835 a member of the Political Economy Club. In 1836 he initiated and chaired an inquiry into the state of the public records, held in the wake of the destruction of much of the Palace of Westminster by fire two years before. His proposal that they should be stored in 'commodious and suitable apartments, in accessible situations, and under a perfect system of arrangement' resulted in an act of 1838, and the eventual establishment of the Public Record Office (Brookfield, 115). In 1837 he chaired another inquiry, into the reform of Commons committees to settle disputed elections, the decisions of which frequently reflected nothing more than their political composition. Some of its recommendations were later adopted, though not the far-sighted suggestion that trained lawyers should oversee the deliberations of such tribunals.

Buller's growing prominence in the Commons owed much to his attention to presentation; he took lessons from the actor William Charles Macready, which slowed his delivery and added cadence to his monotone. (It is not known whether he acted on his mother's suggestion that he might take opium as an aid to oratory.) The conversational tone he adopted anticipated the technique of later generations, and his deadpan, often self-deprecating wit became legendary: 'All the speaking in the house of commons is extempore and on the spur of the moment, except the impromptus, which are, of course, very carefully prepared' was one of the epigrams attributed to him that was much borrowed and adapted later (Wrong, 17). His humour and affability were all the more marked by their contrast with the stiffness of radical colleagues like Grote and John Roebuck. Buller had a fondness, too, for elaborate practical jokes, often hatched with his friend (and political opponent) Richard Monckton Milnes. In May 1842 they caused a fictitious account to be published in the *Morning Chronicle* of a furious reaction in the French chamber of deputies to the news that Queen Victoria and Prince Albert would be attending a costume ball dressed as Edward III and Queen Phillippa. It was solemnly reported that the French ambassador would, in response, go along dressed as Joan of Arc; a diplomatic incident was averted because Peel, the prime minister, was in on the ruse. Four years earlier, Peel had lost patience with Buller

during a debate, accusing him of buffoonery. Buller felt the force of the rebuke, and endeavoured to temper his ebullience, but the unfortunate perception that as a wit he could not also be a serious politician remained widespread until shortly before his untimely death.

Canada: the Durham report; other colonial interests Buller was an early enthusiast for Edward Gibbon Wakefield's scheme of 'systematic colonization' as a means of dealing with home surpluses of capital and labour, and was a member of Wakefield's National Colonization Society. In January 1838 he accepted, after initial reluctance, the post of chief secretary to Lord Durham, the nominal leader of the radical party, who had been appointed as governor of the British North American colonies in the wake of the French Canadian rising of the previous year. Buller was more sympathetic than his chief to the grievances of the colonists though, from his own account, his attitude hardened in the light of experience. (The Anglicization and assimilation of the French-speaking population was in any case a working assumption of all concerned.) Buller was appointed to the executive and special councils of Lower Canada in June 1838. He was given responsibility for several subcommissions of inquiry, and accompanied Durham on part of his tour of the territories. He was also responsible for advising the governor on the fate of the insurgent prisoners; most were granted amnesty, but eight ringleaders were marked for banishment to Bermuda. This, and other aspects of the mission, prompted a critical barrage in Britain; the hostility of some of Buller's radical colleagues, such as Roebuck, was a large factor in the final demise of the philosophic radicals as a distinct parliamentary grouping. The government refused to sanction the deportation ordinance, and Durham resigned in September.

The achievement of the mission lay in Durham's *Report on the Affairs of British North America* (1839), the main recommendation of which—the unification of Upper and Lower Canada—was implemented by his successor, Charles Poulett Thomson. Once lauded as the blueprint for the development of the British empire for much of the following century, the significance of the report has been called into question by more recent historians. Many contemporaries gave Buller the credit for being its real author; the story may have originated with Lord Brougham, Durham's rival, and Buller denied it. Given the size of the undertaking, it is likely, however, that the report was a collaborative effort, and Durham's reliance on Buller's advice on Canada was widely attested. No such doubt exists about the authorship of *Responsible Government for Colonies* (1840), although it was published anonymously, initially as a series of articles for the *Colonial Gazette*. Written by Buller after his return to England in December 1838, the pamphlet proposed devolved colonial government with a representative component; control over foreign policy, trade, and grants of crown land was to be reserved to Westminster. Aware that indifference to the subject was widespread both inside parliament and out, he set out his arguments with typical verve and directness, setting up an Aunt Sally in 'Mr Mothercountry', a meddlesome Colonial Office mandarin, almost certainly modelled on James Stephen, the under-secretary at the time. *Responsible Government* was widely read, and many of its key proposals were put into practice in Canada by Poulett Thomson. Another literary legacy of Buller's Canadian sojourn was Harriet Martineau's *History of England during the Thirty Years' Peace* (1849–50), the Canadian section of which was based on Buller's journals.

On the Canadian mission Buller had taken with him his brother **Sir Arthur William Buller** (1808–1869), then 'a very junior barrister' (Thomas, 387). Arthur, like Charles, had been born in Calcutta (5 September 1808) and gone on to Trinity College, Cambridge, before being called to the bar at Lincoln's Inn in 1834. In Canada he was appointed commissioner in charge of inquiry into education. His report of November 1838 was in several respects anticipatory, not least in its recommendation of a compulsory school tax. Like his brother, however, he took French-Canadian assimilation for granted and antagonized the churches with his proposal for a unified, school-based system of religious education. Later he went on to be queen's advocate in Ceylon (1840–48), a post apparently obtained through Charles's influence, and afterwards a judge in Calcutta (1848–58). He was knighted in 1848. After returning to England, he sat in the House of Commons for Devonport from 1859 to 1865 and for Charles's old constituency at Liskeard from 1865 until his death. A Liberal, he was, like his brother, in favour of the ballot and colonial self-government. He had married, in 1842, Anne Henrietta Maria (*d.* 28 January 1907), daughter of Francis James Templer; they had a son and two daughters. He died at 6 Half Moon Street, Piccadilly, on 30 April 1869.

Charles Buller was also a director of the South Australian Association (1834), and served as a (paid) legal agent for the Australian Patriotic Association (1837–40); he was uncomfortable with the latter body's defence of transportation, which he regarded as inimical to the establishment of a successful, autonomous colony. On their behalf he drafted a constitution for New South Wales in 1838, which contained as large an element of popular participation in government as he believed the Westminster parliament would countenance. The eventual act, passed four years later, was based on this scheme. Buller joined the short-lived New Zealand Association in 1837; later he drafted the charter of the New Zealand Company and acted as their agent and representative in the difficult negotiations with the Colonial Office after 1840. In one vigorous parliamentary defence of the company he found another outlet for his anti-clericalism, accusing missionaries in New Zealand of land grabbing. A river and gorge were named after him in the South Island, and his memory was also perpetuated in Australia at Mount Buller in Victoria.

Move to the political centre; early death The radicals suffered losses both at the general election of 1837 and from defections; Buller, with a mixture of reductionism and levity, ascribed the latter to the talent of the cook employed by the whig speaker, Charles Shaw Lefevre. The end of the radical dreams of a political realignment in

their favour led many to give up politics, and Buller considered seeking an appointment as an Indian judge. He was already emerging, however, as a bridge-builder with the whig leadership, having generally recommended a line of constructive support for the Melbourne administration in earlier debates about tactics. Having refused the same office in August 1839, he accepted the post of secretary to the Board of Control in June 1841. His admission to the political mainstream was rubber-stamped by his conscription, by the agency of Macaulay, to write for the *Edinburgh Review*. When prompted, Buller assured its editor, Macvey Napier, that he 'need not have specified "moderation" and "hesitation", for if there are two qualities in the world that I excel in, these are the very two' (Hamburger, 268). By 1844 he was ready to admit that 'he had grown out of being a utilitarian' (ibid., 269).

Buller's taste of government was brief, as the ministry fell in August 1841. He took up law again, practising before the judicial committee of the privy council in cases dealing with colonial and Indian appeals, and took silk in 1842. In parliament he continued to press for a government-regulated programme of colonization as a means of solving both short- and long-term social and economic problems at home; his speech of 6 April 1843—a *tour de force* that was subsequently reprinted, along with *Responsible Government*, in Wakefield's *A View of the Art of Colonisation*—sought to exploit his hearers' fear of chartist-led popular unrest. He was notably unconvinced, however, that emigration was the answer for Ireland; his death deprived Lord John Russell, then premier, of a valuable supporter of measures of inward investment there to reclaim wastelands. Throughout the 1840s Buller had pressed for government action on Irish distress, and endeavoured to edge the whigs into co-operation with O'Connell (on the premise, always, of the indissolubility of the union). Another cause to attract his support was the campaign for a ten-hour day for factory workers; he also spoke on education, church rates, and income tax.

In July 1846, following the whigs' return to office, Buller took the sinecure office of judge advocate-general. Unusually, he was not made a privy councillor, which would have made him, by custom, unable to practise as a lawyer in a lower court than the House of Lords. In December 1847 he accepted the post of chief poor-law commissioner, 'with the hope of doing good' (Wrong, 58). The remit, which dovetailed with his abiding interest in colonization, suited him, but before he could do more than begin a series of reforms, he died of typhus on 29 November 1848 at his London home, 2 Chester Place, Chester Square. The illness was apparently preceded by erysipelas, which was blamed on a botched operation. Though physically imposing—Carlyle called him 'a great tower of a fellow, six feet three in height, a yard in breadth' (J. A. Froude, *Thomas Carlyle: a History of the First Forty Years*, 1908, 1.218)—he had always suffered from poor health, notably asthma. His death was the subject of a leader in *The Times*, and tributes were paid to his wit and integrity from across the political spectrum (he had generally managed to conduct arguments without rancour, and made few enemies).

The grief of his friends was heartfelt; Bulwer Lytton was inspired to poetry:

> Farewell fine humorist, finer reasoner still
> Lively as Luttrell, logical as Mill.
> (St Stephens, 1860)

His mother, who doted on him and had acted as his political hostess, had been widowed only six months previously; she died, heartbroken, on 13 March 1849. Buller was buried at Kensal Green cemetery. A bust commemorates him in Westminster Abbey.

Buller's will, apart from playfully leaving the works of Adam Smith and J. S. Mill to Carlyle, left clues about his private life. One legatee of his meagre personal estate was Harriet Baring, Lady Ashburton, the supposed object of his unrequited love; another, one Theresa Reviss, has been identified as his illegitimate daughter conceived with an actress, also named Theresa (W. G. Elliot, *In my Anecdotage*, 1925, 27–8). Her paternity was also ascribed to his brother Arthur (J. Pope-Hennessey, *Monckton Milnes*, 1949–51, 156–7); at all events, she was adopted by the Bullers' parents, who indulged her. She made two advantageous marriages into foreign aristocracy, became a well-known society figure in Calcutta, and was the putative model for Becky Sharp, the *femme fatale* of Thackeray's *Vanity Fair*. Clearly she disregarded Buller's testamentary instruction 'to be a good girl'.

Historians have found Buller as attractive a figure as did his contemporaries. The early twentieth-century editor of *Responsible Government* discovered 'much to admire and nothing to dislike' in his personality; as a result, his appended biographical sketch was 'longer than I intended' (Wrong, preface). In some quarters the suspicion that he was a lightweight has persisted: one historian has postulated that Buller's acceptance of Wakefield's theories on colonization and their economic base was without a real awareness of their novelty or implications (Semmel, 86). This is difficult to assess; what is certain is that his 'cheerful and pragmatic outlook' (Thomas, 417) made him an exceptionally able proselytizer of these ideas and a most effective politician, whose record of achievement compares favourably with many of his better known (and longer-lived) radical colleagues. The most recent biographical study of Buller charts his influence on Liberal Imperialism in the later nineteenth century; if its author occasionally overstates his case, it is because his subject's contribution to the development and direction of the British empire has so often been undervalued.

H. J. SPENCER

Sources D. A. Haury, *The origins of the liberal party and liberal imperialism: the career of Charles Buller, 1806–1848* (1987) · E. M. Wrong, *Charles Buller and responsible government* (1926) · H. J. Spencer, 'Buller, Charles', HoP, *Commons, 1820–32* [draft] · L. P. Audet, 'Buller, Arthur William', *DCB* · H. Lysons-Balcon, 'Buller, Charles', *DCB* · E. A. Sweetman, 'Life and times of Charles Buller', PhD diss., U. Lond., 1952 · W. Thomas, *The philosophic radicals: nine studies in theory and practice, 1817–1841* (1979) · J. Hamburger, *Intellectuals in politics: John Stuart Mill and the philosophical radicals* (1965) · P. Burroughs, *The colonial reformers and Canada, 1830–1849* (1969) · F. M. Brookfield, *The Cambridge Apostles* (1906) · B. Semmel, 'The philosophic radicals and colonialism', in A. G. L. Shaw, *Great Britain and the colonies, 1815–1865* (1970) · M. R. G. Grylls, 'Charles Buller and radical imperialism', *Contemporary Review*, 174 (1948), 365–8 · P. Gray, '"Shovelling out your paupers": the British state and Irish famine migration, 1846–50', *Patterns of Prejudice*, 33/4 (1999), 47–65 · G. Martin, *The Durham report and British policy: a critical essay* (1972) · *The early correspondence of John Stuart Mill*, ed. Mineka, 2 vols. (1963) · *DNB* · will, PRO, PROB 11/2086/9 · *WWBMP* [Arthur Buller] · Burke, *Gen. GB* (1937) · *The letters and private papers of William Makepeace Thackeray*, ed. G. N. Ray, 4 vols. (1945–6)
Archives CUL, corresp. and papers · NA Canada, corresp. and papers relating to Canada | BL, letters to Macvey Napier, Add. MSS 34620–34626, *passim* · BL, corresp. with Sir Robert Peel, Add. MSS 40488–40569, *passim* · Bodl. Oxf., letters to Sir William Napier · Lpool RO, letters to Lord Stanley · NA Canada, corresp. with Lord Durham and Lady Durham · U. Durham L., letters to third Earl Grey · UCL, corresp. with Edwin Chadwick
Likenesses H. Weekes, marble bust on monument, 1848, Westminster Abbey · B. E. Duppa, portrait · E. Scriven, stipple (after B. E. Duppa), BM, NPG; repro. in I. Saunders, *Portraits and memoirs of eminent political reformers* (1840) [*see illus.*] · bust, Liskeard library · bust, Reform Club, London
Wealth at death under £2000: PRO, death duty register, IR 26/1835/35 · will, PRO, PROB 11/2086/9

Buller, Sir Francis, first baronet (1746–1800), judge, was born at Downes, near Crediton, Devon, on 17 March 1746, the third son of James Buller and his second wife, Lady Jane Bathurst, second daughter of Allen, first Earl Bathurst. He demonstrated that 'Notwithstanding the incredulity of country-gentlemen, some lawyers have pedigrees' (Townsend, 1.2). He was born into a venerable and respected Cornish family from Morval, with a history of service in politics, the church, and the law. He attended Ottery St Mary grammar school, where he lived in the house of the Revd John Coleridge, father of Samuel Taylor Coleridge. Precocious throughout his life, he entered the Inner Temple at the age of seventeen to study special pleading under the pupillage of William Ashurst, later a puisne justice with Buller on the court of king's bench. The same year, 1763, he married Susanna (d. 1812), daughter and heir of Francis Yarde of Churston Court, Devon. He began practice as a special pleader in 1765 and met with immediate success. His uncle, Henry Bathurst, was at the time an experienced judge on the court of common pleas, and in 1767 had published an anonymous work (shown as 'by a learned judge') with which Buller would later be associated, *An Introduction to the Law Relative to Trials at Nisi prius*. Buller edited the work, and indeed may have been responsible for much of the arrangement and content of the 1767 version, publishing the first edition under his name in 1772. The book went through seven editions and was widely used as a guide for conducting jury trials, and as a circuit companion.

Buller was called to the bar in Easter term 1772 and rapidly acquired an extensive practice. An examination of cases argued at king's bench between 1774 and 1778 shows Buller as counsel in most cases of consequence. On 24 November 1777 he was made king's counsel, and three days later was made the second judge of the county palatine of Chester. He early came to the notice of Lord Mansfield, who recommended him for appointment to fill a vacancy when Richard Aston died in 1778. On 6 May 1778,

Sir Francis Buller, first baronet (1746–1800), by Mather Brown, 1792

at the age of thirty-two, Buller joined Lord Mansfield and fellow puisne judges William Ashurst and Edward Willes on the court of king's bench. His energetic work habits, quickness of intellect, and congeniality instantly overcame any prejudice there might have been about his youth. While Buller was yet serving on king's bench, a biographer wrote: 'Nature designed him for a lawyer … for very early in life he seems to have *entered into a recognizance*, to talk and think of nothing but law; his knowledge of *practice and cases*, left him without a competitor' (Rede, 62). However, Buller was constantly subjected to malicious hostility, no doubt because of his early elevation to the bench; and some critical views were recorded by a retired barrister in his notebook (Espinasse).

The expansiveness of Buller's capacity for the law and the extent of his collaboration with Lord Mansfield can be readily seen in the 'Buller paper books' held by Lincoln's Inn Library. Part of the Dampier manuscripts, the collection includes extensive research notes and draft opinions in Buller's autograph that show remarkable assiduity and learning. The papers show that some opinions of the court delivered by Lord Mansfield, especially in Mansfield's last few active years on the bench, were actually written by Buller. They also show that Buller occasionally discarded his own tentative opinions in order to follow his chief. He regarded Mansfield as having been a 'second Father', indeed he was a named beneficiary in Mansfield's will. Nevertheless, Buller carefully prepared and presented his own opinions, and although, especially by the mid-1780s, he was prepared to differ from Mansfield, there was rarely a need to do so since the two judges held compatible views

on most issues. One point of departure was over the dividing line between what should be decided by the judge and what by the jury. *Tindal v. Brown* (1786) was the last in a series of cases that came before the court turning upon what constituted reasonable notice to bankers or merchants in commercial transactions. Mansfield hesitated to take the issue away from the jury, but Buller, being strongly of the view that the issue was the judge's responsibility, declared:

> The numerous cases on this subject reflect great discredit on the courts of *Westminster*. They do infinite mischief in the mercantile world; and this evil can only be remedied by … considering the reasonableness of time as a question of law and not of fact. (C. Durnford and E. H. East, *Term Reports in the Court of King's Bench*, new edn, 8 vols., 1817, vol. 1, p. 169)

Palpable self-confidence and keen abilities usually left Buller in full control of his courtroom during the conduct of trials, but he met his match in the flamboyant brilliance of Thomas Erskine. Erskine, who had once been pupil to Buller in chambers, was counsel to the dean of St Asaph during the dean's trial for seditious libel before Buller in 1783. The jury attempted to return a verdict of 'guilty of publishing *only*', and Buller, in keeping with the law as it then stood, pressed them to return a general verdict of guilty or not guilty. Erskine insisted that the word 'only' be recorded. Buller scolded: 'Mr Erskine, sit down, or I shall be obliged to interpose in some way', but Erskine refused, Buller did nothing, and recorded a verdict of 'guilty of publishing, but whether a libel or not the jury do not find' (*State trials*, 21.950–55). This led to a motion for a new trial based on misdirection of the jury, and left Buller in a momentary state of professional embarrassment.

Buller was regarded as sometimes arrogant and impetuous, leaping to conclusions too quickly. Foss declared that 'notwithstanding his urbanity, he was not a popular judge' (Foss, *Judges*, 8.254), but this claim is too broad. Buller may have been occasionally precipitate or harsh in criminal trials, yet he was universally respected in civil cases, particularly those involving commercial affairs. As was true of Mansfield, however, Buller tended on occasion to blend law and equity. John Scott, first earl of Eldon, remembered in a letter to John Singleton Copley, Baron Lyndhurst, that Buller sat frequently under a commission permitting puisne judges to assist in chancery, and that Buller 'in some measure in Chancery made a Mixture of Law with Equity, which spoiled both—as in the King's Bench he made a Mixture of Equity with Law, which likewise spoiled both' (letter, not dated [1830], Glamorgan RO, Lyndhurst MSS, D/D Ly 19/79). Buller suffered as a result of an unfortunate remark attributed to him, that a husband could punish his wife with impunity provided that the rod or stick he used was no thicker than his thumb. Foss claimed that, despite a searching investigation, 'no substantial evidence has been found that he ever expressed so ungallant an opinion' (Foss, *Judges*, 8.252); none the less, James Gillray published a caricature on 27 November 1783 of Buller as 'Judge Thumb', carrying two bundles of 'thumbsticks'—'for family correction: warranted lawful!'

During the ten years he shared on king's bench with

Lord Mansfield, Buller was effectively the second in command, despite being junior to his fellow puisne judges. Mansfield wished to have Buller succeed him as chief justice, as Mansfield declared in a letter to Lord Chancellor Thurlow on 27 November 1786 suggesting that it was time to resign. There was resistance to Buller in the administration, chiefly from Pitt, and Mansfield's resignation waited another two years, when Sir Lloyd Kenyon was appointed chief justice. During those two years Mansfield was incapacitated, and Buller conducted most of the trials and ran the business of the court. He stayed on king's bench after Kenyon's appointment and on 13 January 1790 received the consolation of being made baronet. He remained vigorous in his judicial duties, as was attested to by James Scarlett, later Lord Abinger, who attended the northern circuit in the spring of 1792 when Buller was the sole judge. Scarlett wrote in his memoirs:

> There were eighty-six causes to be tried at York, one of which was a boundary cause that lasted sixteen hours, thirty-six at Lancaster, and forty to fifty prisoners at each place; but Mr. Justice Buller concluded the whole Circuit in three weeks. (Scarlett, 49)

In Easter term 1794 Buller transferred to common pleas, where he served until his death on 5 June 1800, at the age of fifty-four, in Bedford Square, London. The last major trial over which he presided was that at Maidstone in 1798 of state prisoners Arthur O'Connor and others for treason. In his last years he suffered frequent attacks of gout and a mild stroke, and he had arranged to resign a few days before he died. He was buried quietly near the remains of his first-born son, Edward, at St Andrew's, Holborn, London, on 11 June.

Short of stature, but with handsome, commanding features and a piercing gaze, Buller lived his professional life to the fullest, with almost a preternatural intensity. He was generous as a mentor to young men starting out in the profession, including Thomas Erskine, Charles Fearne, Vicary Gibbs, and Francis Hargrave. His only known recreations outside the law were a notorious love of card-playing, especially whist, and, in later years, his estate at Princetown, on Dartmoor. He owned 600 acres and experimented with rotation of crops and improving agricultural methods, communicating about these matters with Arthur Young. He was survived by a son, who succeeded him, and his grandson was made Baron Thurston.

James Oldham

Sources W. C. Townsend, *The lives of twelve eminent judges*, 2 vols. (1846) · H. Bathurst, *Introduction to the law relative to trials at nisi prius* (1767) · J. Oldham, *The Mansfield manuscripts and the growth of English law in the eighteenth century*, 2 vols. (1992) · *Strictures on the lives and characters of the most eminent lawyers of the present day* (1790) · Lincoln's Inn, London, Dampier MSS, Francis Buller MSS · *State trials* · Foss, *Judges* · *The works of James Gillray from the original plates*, 3 vols. (1847–51) · P. C. Scarlett, *A memoir of the right honourable James, first Lord Abinger* (1877) · A. Young, ed., *Annals of agriculture and other useful arts*, 46 vols. (1784–1815) · John, Lord Campbell, *The lives of the chief justices of England*, 3 vols. (1849–57) · D. Duman, *Judges of England, 1730–1875* (1979) · [I. Espinasse], 'My contemporaries: from the notebooks of a retired barrister', *Fraser's Magazine*, 6 (1832), 224–8 · *IGI* · *GM*, 1st ser., 70 (1800)

Archives Lincoln's Inn, London, legal papers

Likenesses M. Brown, chalk drawing, *c*.1792, Scot. NPG · M. Brown, oils, 1792, NPG [*see illus.*]

Buller, Sir George (1802–1884), army officer, was the third son of General Frederick William Buller of Pelynt and Lanreath in Cornwall, who had himself served with distinction in the 57th foot in the Low Countries and the West Indies. George Buller was gazetted a second lieutenant in the rifle brigade on 2 March 1820. For the first twenty-five years he saw no active service, but climbed the military ladder steadily: he was promoted captain (19 August 1828), major (31 December 1839), lieutenant-colonel (27 August 1841), and colonel (November 1841). He commanded the 1st battalion the rifle brigade from 1841 to 1854. Buller joined his battalion in February 1847 at the Cape, where the Cape Frontier War with the Xhosa tribes, or 'war of the axe', had just broken out. Buller was at once given command of a brigade and eventually of the 2nd division. In September 1847 he was appointed second in command to General Berkeley, the commander-in-chief, and the tempo was greatly increased by the employment of mobile patrols to strike at cattle and corn. Sandile was the most powerful chief and Buller's battalion chased him so hard that he surrendered to Buller on 19 October 1847 and was confined in Grahamstown. Buller was made CB in December 1847.

A new governor arrived in the same month: Major-General Sir Harry Smith, a rifleman like Buller. On 3 March 1848 Smith proclaimed the queen's sovereignty over the territory between the Orange and Vaal rivers, resulting in conflict with the Boers living there, led by Andries Pretorius. At the battle of Boomplaats on 29 August 1848 Buller was severely wounded and had his horse killed under him. The Boers were, however, defeated and on 2 September Smith entered Bloemfontein and proclaimed the queen's sovereignty. Soon afterwards Buller and his battalion returned home.

A new Cape Frontier War broke out in 1850. Buller returned to the Cape with the rifle brigade and commanded a brigade in General Somerset's division. He burnt kraals in the Waterkloof and was at the battle of Berea which concluded the campaign against the Sotho. By then, however, Smith had been recalled, having lost the confidence of the colonial secretary, Lord Glenelg. He was replaced by Lieutenant-General Sir George Cathcart who publicly thanked Buller for his services. Buller succeeded Somerset in command of his division in August 1852. In October 1853 his battalion was ordered home, and Buller insisted on accompanying it, despite Cathcart's entreaties to remain, and the promise that he would remain a brigadier were he to do so.

War was declared on Russia on 28 March 1854, and an expeditionary force was formed to go to the aid of Turkey. Buller commanded a brigade in the light division under Lieutenant-General Sir George Brown. Buller's brigade landed in the Crimea on 18 September 1854. It consisted of the 19th, 77th, and 88th foot, and the 2nd battalion rifle brigade. In the advance to Sevastopol the army found its way barred by the River Alma, with the Russians deployed on the heights beyond. When the battle began the light division was on the British left, or exposed, flank. Sir George Brown ordered Buller to 'Advance in line, and do not stop until you have crossed the river.' Buller crossed the river but in doing so lost contact with the 19th foot which became absorbed into the adjoining brigade. After the crossing, Buller, in default of any further orders, formed up to defend the left flank of the army against possible cavalry attack. Indeed he ordered the 88th foot to form square to repel cavalry, though no such attack materialized and some of his troops went forward with Codrington's brigade. Buller was later criticized for not playing a more active part in the battle.

The next battle was Inkerman on 5 November 1854. It was fought initially in a fog, and has been described by Fortescue as 'a series of detached combats' (Fortescue, *Brit. army*, 13.118). Buller took four companies of the 77th foot into the fog and could not at first believe that the figures looming out of the obscurity towards him were Russians. It was his aide-de-camp, Captain the Hon. Henry Clifford of the rifle brigade, who told him, 'In God's name fix bayonets and charge!' (Clifford, 88). They did so and held their ground but Buller was badly wounded in the left arm. He also had two horses shot under him. His brigade stopped the Russians outflanking the 2nd division down the Wellway, the 77th and 88th foot holding the western end of the Home Ridge. They also saved the 47th foot from being overrun. Much of the fighting was with the bayonet; overnight rain and damp had made the rifles so wet that the charges would not explode. None the less the Russian plan to roll up the British and French besieging Sevastopol was foiled. In December 1854 Buller was promoted major-general but his wound compelled him to return home in March 1855. He was made KCB in July 1855. In the same year Buller married Henrietta, daughter of General Sir John Macdonald, adjutant-general, who may have helped his rapid promotion. They had one son and four daughters.

Buller saw no further active service. He commanded the division in the Ionian Islands from 1856 to 1862, in which year he was promoted lieutenant-general on 9 November. He had been made colonel-commandant of the rifle brigade in 1860. He commanded the troops in the southern division at Portsmouth from 1865 to 1870, was made GCB in 1869, and was promoted general on 25 October 1871. He was a commander of the Légion d'honneur and a knight of the second class of the order of the Mejidiye. He died at his house, 23 Bruton Street, Berkeley Square, London, on 12 April 1884.   H. M. STEPHENS, rev. JAMES LUNT

Sources W. Cope, *The history of the rifle brigade* (1877) · W. R. King, *Campaigning in Kaffirland*, 2nd edn (1855) · A. W. Kinglake, *The invasion of the Crimea*, [new edn], 5 (1877) · Fortescue, *Brit. army*, vol. 11–13 · J. H. Lehmann, *Remember you are an Englishman: a biography of Sir Harry Smith* (1977) · C. Hibbert, *The destruction of Lord Raglan* (1961) · *Hart's Army List* · Marquess of Anglesey [G. C. H. V. Paget], *A history of the British cavalry, 1816 to 1919*, 2 (1975) · L. James, *1854–56 Crimea: the war with Russia from contemporary photographs* (1981) · H. Clifford, *Letters and sketches from the Crimea* (1956)
Archives NL Scot., letters to Sir George Brown
Wealth at death £86,196 13s. 9d.: resworn probate, July 1884, CGPLA Eng. & Wales

Buller, Dame (**Audrey Charlotte**) **Georgiana** (1883–1953), worker for the disabled, was born on 4 August 1883 at Downes, Crediton, Devon, the only child of Sir Redvers Henry *Buller (1839–1908), landowner and army officer, and his wife, Lady Audrey Jane Charlotte (1844–1926), youngest daughter of the fourth Marquess Townshend and widow of the Hon. Greville Howard. She was considerably influenced by her father, who was highly respected locally both as a landowner and for his leadership in the army. During the Second South African War he was responsible for organizing the relief of Ladysmith, in 1900, and he was regarded as a hero both locally and nationwide. Georgiana was educated at home and at the Phonetic Institute, Bath, where she gained a Pitman's shorthand certificate in 1907. She was actively involved with charitable organizations, especially the Voluntary Aid Organization (British Red Cross Society), and by 1914 she was deputy county director for Devon. She was very keen on hunting but injured her spine in a fall. In early 1914 it was thought that war was likely, and the Voluntary Aid Organization was asked to prepare hospital accommodation in Exeter. Georgiana Buller was asked to supervise this; she ended her convalescence and set to work.

It was originally estimated that 160 beds would be needed, but by August 1915 more than 1400 beds were in use. The Red Cross Voluntary Aided Hospital in Exeter, which Buller organized, was taken over by the War Office in 1915 as the Central Military Hospital with Georgiana Buller as administrator, the only woman to hold such a post. She was also responsible for forty-four affiliated auxiliary hospitals. During the war more than 35,000 patients passed through the hospital, staying on average twenty-five days. Georgiana Buller and her voluntary staff worked very hard. She had extremely high standards, and some found her demands unreasonable. On being demobbed in 1920 she was exhausted and went into a physical and mental decline. She was awarded the Royal Red Star (first class) by the British Red Cross Society in 1920 and was made a DBE on 24 December 1920.

Dame Georgiana Buller was next informed by two medical friends of the great need in Devon for an orthopaedic hospital for children. When she began to plan ways of raising money she quickly realized how acute the need was, as she discovered that many children were suffering at home from orthopaedic conditions simply because there was no hospital nearby. In 1927 the Princess Elizabeth Orthopaedic Hospital was opened in Exeter. Dame Georgiana also worked with the Central Council for the Care of Cripples and was chairman of the Devon Association for Cripples Aid. She then became aware of another problem in relation to disability: the lack of training facilities for those permanently disabled. From 1935 onwards she concentrated her energies on establishing two training colleges, the St Loyes Training Centre for Cripples in Exeter, and Queen Elizabeth College in Leatherhead. Dame Georgiana's aim was for each person with disabilities to become independent through learning a marketable skill. She met with opposition when insisting that disabled people deserved training, but then enlisted the support of the minister of labour Ernest Bevin. Bevin had gone to school in Crediton and had often stolen apples from her father's orchards which were next to the village school.

Dame Georgiana also established the British Council for Rehabilitation and believed that the resources of the state and the voluntary spirit could be combined for the benefit of the disabled. Funds were always needed for the training centres and she harnessed volunteers to run events as diverse as a flower ball in the Savoy Hotel in November 1947 and a 'Play-time work' exhibition in Exeter. Portland College, near Nottingham, was founded on the same lines as the St Loyes centre, as were other centres throughout Britain.

Dame Georgiana was chairman at St Loyes for many years. She supported the Girl Guides, the Boy Scouts, and the St John Ambulance Brigade. She was a JP for twenty years. In 1947 she initiated preparatory training for those facing long stays in hospital and who could enjoy academic work. On 11 March 1953 she was interviewed on the BBC radio programme *Woman's Hour* about her life and her work for the disabled. She died from carcinoma on 22 June 1953 at her home, Bellair House, Topsham Road, Exeter, and was buried on 26 June at Holy Cross Church, Crediton, Devon.   CATHARINE M. C. HAINES

Sources Devon RO, Buller papers, 2065 M add. F 357; 2065 M add. 7; 2065 M add. 11 [personal notebook]; 2065 M add. 2/SS, 12–84 · *The Times* (23 June 1953) · Lord Clinton and S. A. S. Malkin, tributes, *The Times* (27 June 1953) · N. C., 'In memoriam, Dame Georgiana Buller, RRC, DBE, 1884–1953', *Journal of Bone and Joint Surgery*, 35B (Nov 1953), 673–5 · *The house and the man— 2. Sir Redvers Buller at Downes*, BBC Radio, 26–7 April 1939 · 'Guest of the week', *Woman's Hour*, BBC Radio, 11 March 1953 · *WWW, 1897–1915* · *WWW, 1951–60* · W. Fothergill Robinson, ed., *Voluntary aid in Devon* (1915) · 'The Red Cross and voluntary aid in Devonshire, 1914–1917'; 'The Red Cross and voluntary aid in Devonshire, 1917–1918'; 'Annual reports of the war organisation of the British Red Cross Society and the order of St John of Jerusalem', British Red Cross Society Archives, London · L. Childs, *Ladysmith: Colenso / Spion Kop / Hlangwane / Tugela* (1998) · b. cert. · d. cert.
Archives Devon RO, address to the British and Foreign Bible Society, 2065 M add. 2/SS, 64–66/69–84 · Devon RO, note about play written by G. Buller, 2065 M add. F 357 · Devon RO, notebook containing selected verses and quotations from the Bible, 2065 M add. 11 | SOUND British Broadcasting Society sound archives, Caversham, Reading, *The house and the man—2. Sir Redvers Buller at Downes*, talk by Dame Georgiana Buller [broadcast on Western Programme, 26 April 1939, 8–8.15 pm, and on Regional Programme, 27 April 1939, 1–1.15 pm] · British Broadcasting Society sound archives, Caversham, Reading, *Woman's Hour*, 'Guest of the week': Dame Georgiana Buller [broadcast on Light Programme, 11 March 1953, 2–3 pm]
Likenesses group photograph, 1915, Devon RO, 2065 M add. F357 · photograph, 1953, repro. in *Journal of Bone and Joint Surgery* · photograph, Devon RO, 2065 M add. F 357; repro. in *Western Evening Herald* (3 Nov 1939) · photograph, Devon RO, 2065 M add. F 357; repro. in *Western Morning News* (14 July 1950)
Wealth at death £64,244 9s. 8d.: probate, 30 July 1953, CGPLA Eng. & Wales

Buller, Sir Redvers Henry (1839–1908), army officer, was born at the family seat of Downes, Crediton, Devon, on 7 December 1839, the second son of James Wentworth Buller, whig MP for Exeter (1830–35) and North Devon (1857–65), and Charlotte Juliana Jane Howard-Molyneux-

Sir Redvers Henry Buller (1839–1908), by Charles Knight, c.1900

Howard, niece of the twelfth duke of Norfolk. Buller's mother, to whom he was devoted, died in December 1855 and his father in March 1865. The family estates, over 5000 acres in Devon and Cornwall, passed to Buller on the death of his elder brother in October 1874. In many respects he was the archetypal squire, returning as frequently as his career permitted to Downes, and popular in the locality as a model landlord. Independently minded and of Liberal sympathies, he was asked to stand for North Devon as a Liberal in 1879 and was again offered seats in 1906, by which time he had come to regard himself more as a Liberal Unionist. Excelling at country sports, he was a man of courage and of great physical strength and endurance. Only in his later years did good living and long hours at a War Office desk sap his physique: even then he was still capable of fourteen hours in the saddle at Colenso in December 1899.

Education and early career Buller was educated primarily at Eton College, having briefly attended Harrow after preparatory schooling. As a younger son the army was a natural choice, and Buller was commissioned ensign by purchase in the 60th rifles (the King's Royal Rifle Corps) on 23 May 1858. He joined the 2nd battalion at Benares and embarked with it for the Second Opium War in February 1860. He saw little action, though a kick in the mouth from a horse left him with a minor speech impediment. Purchasing his lieutenancy on 9 December 1862 he was next posted to the 4th battalion in Canada, where he was greatly influenced by the commanding officer, Colonel Robert Hawley. When Buller was considering giving up regimental duty, Hawley offered him the adjutantcy and inculcated something of his own professionalism. Buller returned to England with the battalion in 1869 but, having purchased a captaincy on 28 May 1870, was posted to the next vacancy in the 1st battalion, serving back in Canada. The battalion had been detailed for Colonel Garnet Wolseley's Red River expedition to overthrow a rebel provisional government at Fort Garry, 600 miles beyond Lake Superior in the far north-west. Buller's sheer strength in manhandling boats and supplies over the unnavigable portages—it was said that he was the only man in the expedition capable of carrying a 100 lb barrel of pork over a portage on his back—soon came to the notice of Wolseley. Thus, although the rebels had fled by the time Wolseley reached Fort Garry in August 1870, Buller's future was assured as one of the emerging *Wolseley ring.

African campaigns Wolseley failed to secure a brevet majority for Buller, but encouraged him to enter the Staff College, Camberley, at the end of 1871. However, in August 1873, before Buller had completed the course, Wolseley offered him the post of deputy assistant adjutant and quartermaster-general, with responsibility for intelligence, on his Asante expedition. There Buller gained much useful information and led a company of native scouts in Wolseley's advance on Kumasi, receiving a slight wound at Ordahsu and succumbing to a serious bout of fever in February 1874. For his services he received a brevet majority and the CB on 1 April 1874, and from 1874 to 1878 he was deputy assistant adjutant-general in the War Office. On 30 January 1878 he was appointed a special service officer with Major-General the Hon. Frederic Thesiger for the Cape Frontier War in South Africa.

On 22 April 1878 Buller received command of the frontier light horse, a locally raised corps of undisciplined irregulars. Fearless, indefatigable, and outspoken, Buller won their respect and moulded them into a fine fighting unit before the campaign against the Ngqika ended in June. Mentioned in dispatches, Buller received a brevet lieutenant-colonelcy on 11 November 1878. That same month an ultimatum was presented to the Zulu king, Cetshwayo, with the intention of removing the threat posed to South African federation by his independent kingdom. Buller's corps was attached to no. 4 column at Utrecht, commanded by his old friend and fellow Wolseley protégé Brevet Colonel Evelyn Wood, and it was intended to form the northern arm of Chelmsford's advance into Zululand.

However, when the main Zulu army overwhelmed the camp of no. 2 column at Isandlwana on 22 January 1879, Wood was compelled to entrench at Khambula. In the words of W. H. Russell, Wood and Buller became 'relentless cattle lifters' (H. F. Ponsonby to his wife, 14 Sept 1879, Royal Archives, Ponsonby MS Add. A36), harassing the local Zulu to draw attention from Chelmsford's attempt to relieve no. 1 column, which had similarly entrenched itself at Eshowe in the south. Wood resolved in March to raid the Zulu stronghold at Hlobane Mountain, discounting rumours that Cetshwayo had decided to send his own army to eradicate the British at Khambula. On 28 March

Buller, with some 400 colonial horse and 300 native auxiliaries, ascended the eastern face of Hlobane while Wood supported a smaller diversion to the west. Unknown to Wood and Buller, the main Zulu army was rapidly advancing from the south-east and Buller had to make a hasty retreat from the mountain down the almost sheer Devil's Pass. Fifteen officers and seventy-nine men were killed, an error by Buller in the confusion sending his close friend Captain Robert Barton, together with thirty men of the frontier light horse, into the path of the main Zulu body. Buller himself heroically rescued three men on the descent, for which he was awarded the Victoria Cross on 17 June 1879, one of five given for the action. None the less, the reputation of Wood and himself would have been seriously damaged if the Zulu had not pressed a frontal assault on Khambula the following day. They were driven off by British firepower with perhaps 2000 dead: Khambula effectively shattered Zulu offensive power. Lionized by the press he despised as the Bayard of South Africa, Buller served with Wood's flying column for the second invasion of Zululand in late May, and he was present at the battle of Ulundi on 4 July 1879.

Wolseley had been sent out to supersede Chelmsford, but arrived too late to do more than preside over the pursuit of Cetshwayo. He wanted Wood and Buller to remain but both were exhausted; Buller had such painful sores on his hands that they were permanently affected. He and Wood went home to an enthusiastic reception in August, Buller receiving the appointment of aide-de-camp to the queen and promotion to colonel on 27 September. He was also created CMG on 19 December 1879, and both he and Wood were summoned to Balmoral to be interviewed personally by the queen, who noted Buller as being 'reserved & shy, with rather a dry, gruff manner' (Royal Archives, R8/82).

Following leave Buller was due to return to his regiment, in which he still ranked only as a captain, although he received a half-pay majority on 13 March 1880. However, in April he was appointed assistant adjutant and quartermaster-general in Scotland and was transferred to Aldershot in July. In February 1881 he was sent back to South Africa as chief of staff to Wood, who had succeeded to the command in Natal on the death of another Wolseley protégé, George Colley, at Majuba. Buller received the local rank of major-general on 29 March. Wood had been instructed to negotiate, and a peace agreement restoring self-government to the Transvaal was concluded.

Marriage Buller therefore returned to England in December. On 10 August 1882 he married Lady Audrey Jane Charlotte Howard (1844–1926), daughter of the fourth Marquess Townshend and widow of his own cousin, the Hon. Greville Howard. Lady Audrey already had four small children, to whom Buller proved a considerate stepfather, and the couple had one daughter, (Audrey Charlotte) Georgiana *Buller, born in 1883.

Egypt and the Sudan Wolseley had expressed the hope that marriage would not prevent Buller campaigning, and he now offered employment in his forthcoming expedition to Egypt. Buller returned at once from honeymoon on 21 August 1882 and joined Wolseley at Alexandria on 1 September as head of intelligence. Buller reconnoitred the Egyptian position at Tell al-Kebir four days later and was present at the subsequent battle. Again mentioned in dispatches, he was made KCMG on 24 November 1882, having returned to England in October. In July 1883 Buller became assistant adjutant-general at the War Office, but returned to Egypt in February 1884 to command the 1st infantry brigade of the force sent to Suakin under Sir Gerald Graham against the Mahdist threat of Osman Digna. Wolseley had heavily influenced the choice of commanders and Buller was effectively second in command. He distinguished himself at al-Teb on 29 February and at Tamai on 13 March, his command saving the 2nd brigade from being overrun at the latter. For his services Buller was promoted major-general on 21 May 1884.

Buller enjoyed only a short leave before he was again summoned by Wolseley, and appointed chief of staff to the Gordon relief expedition on 26 August 1884. Wolseley's highly personalized command system was being weakened by the increasing seniority of his subordinates and their often considerable military reputations. Wolseley increasingly complained that Buller was belittling others, particularly Herbert Stewart, commanding the desert column. Tension also developed between Buller and both William Butler and Henry Brackenbury.

Moreover, Wolseley's capacity to control affairs personally decreased as the scale of operations grew, the Nile campaign being conducted over almost 1700 miles, the distance between Cairo and Khartoum. While Wolseley claimed to give Buller a free hand, in reality he demanded that Buller keep him constantly informed of all he was doing. Buller, too, interpreted his duties in a limited way, as being primarily to move the field force forward to Dongola and bring up sufficient supplies to enable it to operate beyond there. So in December 1884 Buller was at Wadi Halfa while Wolseley was 360 miles further on at Korti, Buller complaining that he had seen Wolseley personally for only eight hours in the previous two months. Their relationship deteriorated, and Wolseley concluded that, in any future campaign, Brackenbury rather than Buller would be the chief of staff. Nevertheless, Wolseley recognized Buller as the best available fighting general when Stewart was fatally wounded at Methemmeh and sent him forward at once to command the desert column. By the time Buller reached Gubat on 11 February Khartoum had fallen, and he withdrew the column to Gakdul before rejoining Wolseley at Korti. Once more Buller had cause to complain as, while Wolseley returned to Cairo, he was left at Dongola uninformed of Wolseley's plans.

At the War Office Having overseen the withdrawal from the Sudan, Buller remained in Egypt until October 1885, receiving the KCB for his services. On 1 November he became deputy adjutant-general to Wolseley at the War Office, but on 16 August 1886 the new Conservative government appointed him special commissioner for the Irish counties of Kerry and Clare, with the task of restoring law and order. Having earned the trust of the police,

Buller reduced crime, and in November was made under-secretary for Ireland and an Irish privy councillor. However, his sympathy for the Irish peasantry and criticism of their landlords aroused controversy, and it was with relief that Buller took up the post of quartermaster-general on 15 October 1887, remaining so until succeeding Wolseley as adjutant-general, a post he held from 1 October 1890 until 30 September 1897. He thus spent ten years at the War Office. He was promoted lieutenant-general on 1 April 1891 and general on 24 June 1896, receiving the GCB on 26 May 1894. He also became colonel-commandant of the King's Royal Rifle Corps on 13 July 1895 and honorary colonel of the 1st volunteer battalion, Devonshire regiment, on 4 May 1892.

Buller's period at the War Office was one of frequent change in organization and in the responsibilities of individuals. While the authority of the commander-in-chief was extended over such matters as transport and supply, financial control remained firmly with the civilians. Nor had the reorganization resolved the problem of the proper provision of military advice to the secretary of state when the commander-in-chief was overburdened with additional responsibilities. A continental-style chief of the general staff was recommended by the Hartington commission in 1891, but the opposition to a general staff shared by Liberal politicians, the queen, the commander-in-chief (the duke of Cambridge), and Wolseley (who hoped to succeed the duke with untrammelled powers) resulted only in a War Office council. A still more unhappy compromise by an order in council of 1895 made the commander-in-chief responsible to the secretary of state for all decisions on military matters while allowing the heads of military departments access to the civilian head and increased responsibility. The situation was exacerbated by the duke's and Wolseley's resentment of perceived political interference and by their own mutual hostility.

In spite of the difficulties involved in War Office administration Buller won the confidence of the duke and of successive secretaries of state, so that by the time he became adjutant-general he had considerable influence. He took a leading role in the changes to improve the conditions for ordinary soldiers following the Wantage commission in 1892, contributed to the production of the new drill book in 1896, and, above all, sponsored the establishment of the Army Service Corps in December 1888. Buller's position on administrative reform was to advocate a dual responsibility of the heads of civil and military departments within the War Office to both secretary of state and commander-in-chief through a chief of staff, and in 1895 he was prepared to accept a certain diminution of the powers of the commander-in-chief as suggested by Campbell-Bannerman, who again became secretary of state in 1892.

Almost commander-in-chief Campbell-Bannerman held Buller in high regard and offered him the chief command in India, but Buller had no wish to serve there and declined the offer in November 1892. Three years later he was Campbell-Bannerman's choice to succeed the duke as commander-in-chief; unable to secure the appointment of her son, the duke of Connaught, the queen approved that of Buller on 16 June. Buller was reluctant to accept, as the obvious choice was Wolseley, and Campbell-Bannerman failed to secure Buller's immediate appointment. The government fell on 21 June and the incoming prime minister, Salisbury, distrusted Buller, presumably for his perceived liberalism. In addition, the new secretary of state, Lansdowne, was an Irish landlord, and wanted Lord Roberts to be commander-in-chief. However, it was Wolseley who finally secured the prize, and succeeded the duke on 1 November 1895.

Wolseley believed that he had been betrayed by Buller over the appointment, and subsequently virtually ignored him 'except when he wanted to get something said disagreeable to the S of S [Lansdowne] when he asked AG to do it' (Buller to A. J. Bigge, 12 Dec 1897, Royal Archives, W13/164). None the less, Buller served Wolseley loyally, particularly as Wolseley's mental powers rapidly failed with declining health. However, Buller disliked Lansdowne almost as much as did Wolseley, and rarely agreed with the War Office permanent under-secretary, A. L. Haliburton—these not being circumstances conducive to harmony.

The Second South African War: commander-in-chief in South Africa At the end of his tenure as adjutant-general Buller was on half pay for twelve months, but on 9 October 1898 he succeeded Connaught in the Aldershot command. Buller did not distinguish himself in the revived autumn manoeuvres; he had had no experience in handling so large a force as a corps and had never exercised independent command in the field. He plainly stated as much when he was summoned by Lansdowne in June 1899 to discuss the increasing possibility of war against the Boers. Buller had little enthusiasm for the command, judging Wolseley or Wood more suitable, and he was hardly assisted by the government's continuing refusal to undertake the military preparations necessary for such a war. Buller eventually felt obliged to approach Salisbury without consulting Lansdowne to press for active preparations and, as a result of his memorandum on 8 September, the cabinet finally authorized a limited reinforcement of Natal under Sir George White.

Buller favoured holding Natal, Kimberley, and vulnerable points in Cape Colony with some 20,000 men while advancing through the Orange Free State to Bloemfontein with a field force of a further 30,000 men, but it was not until 23 September that he was formally requested to present a plan of campaign, and the full army corps required for the offensive could not then reach South Africa before December. Mobilization was not ordered until 7 October, with Buller himself appointed as commander-in-chief only two days later, embarking on 14 October. By the time he reached South Africa on 30 October, White had already retreated into Ladysmith, and Kimberley and Mafeking were also besieged. Buller had little option but to recast his plan and abandon the offensive towards Bloemfontein in order to relieve Ladysmith and Kimberley.

Having managed to assemble 20,000 men in southern Natal, Buller moved to Colenso and made a frontal assault on the strong Boer positions along the Tugela on 15 December 1899. He had intended to try and turn the position, but the defeats suffered by Lord Methuen attempting to relieve Kimberley at Magersfontein on 11 December and by General Gatacre at Stormberg in Cape Colony on the previous day compelled him to reconsider exposing his communications to an enemy elated by success. The decision was doomed by the lack of detailed topographical knowledge and serious errors by Buller's subordinates, with the result that the attack broke down in the face of concentrated Boer firepower which caused over 1100 casualties and led to the loss of ten guns. Buller himself was hit in the side by a spent shell fragment while trying to direct the rescue of the guns. The effects of this, together with the thirty-six hours he had gone without rest and his frustration at Lansdowne's apparent interference in operations in ordering that Sir Charles Warren's newly arrived 5th division should be sent to Kimberley rather than Natal, appear to have contributed to Buller's ill-considered message that evening to Lansdowne suggesting that Ladysmith be 'let go' and to White the next day counselling that he surrender on the best terms available. Buller later maintained that the first was intended only to imply the suspension of active operations for the time being and the second to stir White from his torpor. Upon receipt of the message in London, however, Lansdowne engineered the appointment of Roberts to supersede Buller, without consulting the queen or Wolseley: Buller would be confined to operations in Natal.

Commanding in Natal Roberts had been pressing to go to South Africa even before Colenso, and Buller's reputation had also suffered from criticism by a partisan of Roberts, the young Leo Amery, head of *The Times* war correspondents in South Africa and later editor of the influential *Times History of the War in South Africa*. As Roberts arrived in South Africa in January 1900, Buller was making a further attempt to reach Ladysmith by a wide sweep westward. However, this failed disastrously at Spion Kop on 24 January, a result of divided responsibility between Buller and Warren, in whom Buller had little confidence but whose status as his designated second in command, appointed by Lansdowne, appears to have convinced him that he could not be removed. Recrimination followed and Buller was invited to rewrite the dispatch in which he gave full vent to his criticism of Warren; he declined to do so, and the papers were initially published in an edited and sanitized form, though including Roberts's own criticism of Buller. A third attempt to force a way through to Ladysmith by way of Vaal Krantz also failed in early February, but by mid-month Buller began to gain possession of the Hlangwane heights to the east of Colenso and finally relieved Ladysmith on 28 February 1900.

Roberts, advancing through the Orange Free State, declined to authorize Buller to do more than occupy the Boers' attention on the Biggarsberg. Buller, who had learned the lessons of the early phase of the war, pushed on to Laing's Nek and reached Standerton on 23 June, linking with Roberts on 4 July. Subsequently Buller advanced on Middelburg, defeating a Boer force at Bergendal on 27 August, and then proceeded to Lydenburg, as the conventional part of the war came to an end and his army was broken up for garrison duties.

Return from South Africa, dismissal, death Buller asked Roberts to release him and returned to England on 9 November to a rapturous reception, receiving the GCMG. He resumed command at Aldershot in January 1901, and when this was merged in a new First Army corps took command of that on 1 October. Roberts was now commander-in-chief and St John Brodrick, son of another Irish landlord, was secretary of state. Press criticism orchestrated by Amery arose when it was announced that the new corps would be commanded in peace by those who led it in war, and Buller was provoked into an impromptu and flustered public defence of his Ladysmith 'surrender telegram' at a luncheon at Queen's Hall, Westminster, on 10 October 1901. It was interpreted as a breach of king's regulations and Buller was dismissed his command by Brodrick on 21 October. Never again holding command, although retained on the active list for a further five years, he presented a case before the royal commission on the war in South Africa in February 1903, but this did not prevail. There is certainly a sense in which he was a convenient scapegoat for much that was wrong with the army.

Buller retired to Devon, where he remained popular, as shown by the unveiling of the statue of him at Exeter in September 1905. He died of carcinoma of the gall bladder and liver at Downes on 2 June 1908 and was buried at Crediton three days later. Though Buller was popular with the ranks he commanded, and in the west country, his reputation as a commander was for many years low, partly because of the *Times History*, which dominated British historiography of the Second South African War for more than fifty years. However, since the 1970s, revisionist historians, notably Thomas Pakenham with *The Boer War* (1979) and Geoffrey Powell with *Buller: a Scapegoat?* (1994), have been more critical of Roberts and more favourable in their assessment of Buller.   IAN F. W. BECKETT

Sources C. H. Melville, *The life of General the Rt Hon. Sir Redvers Buller*, 2 vols. (1923) · G. Powell, *Buller: a scapegoat?* (1994) · T. Pakenham, *The Boer War* (1979) · J. Symons, *Buller's campaign* (1963) · E. M. Spiers, *The late Victorian army, 1868–1902* (1992) · *In relief of Gordon: Lord Wolseley's campaign journal of the Khartoum relief expedition, 1884–1885*, ed. A. Preston (1967) · E. Muenger, *The British military dilemma in Ireland: occupation politics, 1886–1914* (1991) · *The Frontier War journal of Major John Crealock, 1878*, ed. C. Hummel (1989) · J. H. Lehmann, *All Sir Garnet: a biography of Field-Marshal Lord Wolseley* (1964) · P. Gon, *The road to Isandlwana* (1979) · I. Knight, *Brave men's blood: the epic of the Zulu War, 1879* (1990) · J. P. C. Laband, ed., *Lord Chelmsford's Zululand campaign, 1878–1879* (1994) · P. Warwick and S. B. Spies, eds., *The South African War: the Anglo-Boer War, 1899–1902* (1980) · Viscount Wolseley [G. Wolseley], *The story of a soldier's life*, 2 vols. (1903) · 'Report of the commissioners appointed to inquire into the military preparations ... connected with the war in South Africa: minutes of evidence', *Parl. papers* (1904), 41.169–85, 617–30, Cd 1791 · E. Wood, *From midshipman to field marshal*, 2 vols. (1906) · E. Gosse, 'Sir Redvers Buller: a character study', *North American Review* (Jan 1900), 108–20 · J. Symons, *England's pride: the story of the Gordon relief expedition* (1965) · B. Robson, *Fuzzy-wuzzy: the campaigns in the eastern Sudan, 1884–85* (1993) · W. S. Hamer, *The British army: civil–military relations, 1885–1905* (1970) · R. Lock, *Blood on the Painted Mountain: Zulu victory and defeat, Hlobane and Khambula, 1879* (1995)

Archives Devon RO, corresp. and papers · priv. coll. (NRA), corresp. and papers, WO 132 · Royal Arch., esp. E39, 40, 41; P2, 3, 4; W12, 13 · Royal Arch., Ponsonby MSS. Add. A36 | BL, corresp. with Arthur James Balfour, Add. MS 49807 · BL, corresp. with Henry Campbell-Bannerman, Add. MS 41212 · BL, corresp. with E. T. H. Hutton, Add MS 50086, *passim* · Bodl. Oxf., corresp. with Sir Edmund du Cane · Bodl. Oxf., corresp. with Lord Milner · Bodl. RH, corresp. with Sir Godfrey Lagden · CKS, letters to Edward Stanhope · Glos. RO, corresp. with Sir Michael Hicks Beach · Hove Central Library, Sussex, letters to Viscount Wolseley etc. · NA Scot., corresp. with earl of Airlie · NAM, letters to Earl Roberts · Natal Archive Depot, corresp. with Sir Evelyn Wood · PRO, corresp. with Sir J. C. Ardagh, PRO 30/40 · University of Natal, Durban, Killie Campbell Africana Library, Wood MSS

Likenesses H. T. Wells, portrait, 1889 · C. Knight, photograph, *c*.1900, NPG [*see illus.*] · A. Jones, statue, 1905, Queen's Street, Exeter · B. Mackennal, marble bust on monument, *c*.1911, Winchester Cathedral · Spy [L. Ward], chromolithograph caricature, NPG; repro. in *VF* (18 Jan 1900) · photographs, repro. in *Navy and Army Illustrated* · photographs, repro. in H. W. Wilson, *With the flag to Pretoria* (1900–02) · portrait, repro. in Powell, *Buller*, cover; priv. coll.

Wealth at death £34,992 13*s*. 2*d*.: probate, 30 July 1908, *CGPLA Eng. & Wales*

Buller, Reginald Edward Manningham-, first Viscount Dilhorne (1905–1980), lawyer and politician, was born at Latimer House, Amersham, Buckinghamshire, on 1 August 1905, the eldest of five children and the only son of Sir Mervyn Manningham-Buller, third baronet (1876–1956), a soldier and later MP, and his wife, Lilah Constance Cavendish (*d*. 1944), daughter of the third Lord Chesham. He was a direct descendant of Sir Edward Coke, who held high legal and political offices in the reigns of Elizabeth I and James I.

Manningham-Buller was educated at Eton College and Magdalen College, Oxford, where he secured a third in law in 1926. Heavily built and suffering from poor eyesight, he was not obviously athletic, but he proved a more than competent oarsman and his strong constitution proved an asset in the long hours and hard work his legal and political careers required. In later years his ample figure was described as overlapping both sides of the lord chancellor's woolsack.

After being called to the bar at the Inner Temple on 29 June 1927, Manningham-Buller soon established himself at the chambers of F. Beney of Brick Court, where he remained until he became a government law officer in 1951, and he built up a small practice on the midland circuit. On 18 December 1930 he married Lady Mary Lilian Lindsay, fourth daughter of David Alexander Edward *Lindsay, the twenty-seventh earl of Crawford. The marriage produced one son, John Mervyn, and three daughters.

By the outbreak of the Second World War, Manningham-Buller was already thirty-four, though his eyesight would also have been a barrier to military service. Instead he worked in the judge advocate general's department and also embarked upon a political career when, under the terms of the wartime party truce, he was returned unopposed to the House of Commons as MP for Daventry in 1943. The constituency was redesignated as

Reginald Edward Manningham-Buller, first Viscount
Dilhorne (1905–1980), by Elliott & Fry, 1962

South Northamptonshire in 1950 and Manningham-
Buller continued to represent it until July 1962.

Law officer He briefly held office as parliamentary secretary to the minister of works in Churchill's caretaker government (May–July 1945) but it was in opposition between
1945 and 1951 that he established himself as a hard-
working and valuable MP, becoming chairman of the
party's legal committee. His career at the bar also prospered and he took silk in August 1946. Nevertheless, there
was some surprise when Churchill appointed him
solicitor-general at the formation of the Conservative government in November 1951. Doubts were soon stilled, as
Manningham-Buller proved an efficient and successful
minister, his achievements stemming more from sheer
hard work than from an outstanding intellect. He was a
tough and effective debater, though his abrasive style
never really endeared him to the House of Commons,
even on his own side of the chamber. To many he was best
summed up by the nickname of Sir Reginald Bullying-
Manner. The Labour MP Tony Benn recalled an appearance before the Commons privileges committee at which
Manningham-Buller 'bullied and hacked at me as if I was a
man who had been caught red-handed in the act of rape
and was then pleading mistaken identity. He really
behaved in a most unpleasant and hostile way' (R. Win-
stone, ed., *Tony Benn, Years of Hope*, 1994, 368).

In government, on the other hand, Manningham-
Buller's work was appreciated and in Churchill's reshuffle

of October 1954 he was promoted to attorney-general.
There he was prominent in the tribunal of enquiry set up
in November 1957 into alleged leaks of information about
an increase in the bank rate. Earlier that year he led for the
prosecution at the trial of Dr John Bodkin Adams who was
accused of murdering an elderly woman patient. After
retiring for less than three-quarters of an hour the jury
returned a verdict of not guilty—an outcome which damaged Manningham-Buller's standing in parliament and
further afield. It may also have played a part in blocking
his elevation, upon the retirement of Lord Goddard in
September 1958, to the lord chief justiceship, an appointment to which an incumbent attorney-general had hitherto been thought to have first claim. A leading article in
The Times on 29 May 1958, which declared that appointment to the chief justiceship should not be regarded as
'some political plum', was widely believed to have been
directed at Manningham-Buller's claims. For all that, government colleagues saw him as the very model of a law
officer. Harold Macmillan particularly appreciated his
handling in parliament in 1959 of the Devlin report into
the deaths while under detention of Mau Mau guerrillas
in Nyasaland.

Lord chancellor and law lord It was some indication of his
competence that Manningham-Buller served for ten years
and nine months under three different prime ministers
before finally succeeding Kilmuir as lord chancellor after
Macmillan's radical reshaping of his cabinet in July 1962,
the celebrated 'night of the long knives'. Having succeeded his father as fourth baronet in 1956, Manningham-
Buller now took the title of Baron Dilhorne of Towcester
in the county of Northampton and received the great seal
on 16 July. Though it is doubtful whether his appointment
helped Macmillan to realize his declared intention of reju-
venating the image of his government—Dilhorne was a
less politically prominent figure than his predecessor had
been—the new lord chancellor's two years in office were
dominated by his political rather than by his legal responsibilities.

At the end of May 1963 the prime minister asked Dilhorne to conduct an investigation into allegations concerning the relationship between John Profumo, secretary of state for war, and Christine Keeler, a society prostitute. After little over a fortnight the lord chancellor told
the cabinet that from the security point of view no further
enquiry was necessary. But it was his role in the emergence of Macmillan's successor as prime minister that
probably represents the most controversial moment of
his career. The premier was taken ill shortly before the
Conservative Party conference opened in Blackpool in
October 1963, and decided to resign. Dilhorne was charged by Macmillan with sounding out the views of cabinet
ministers about the succession, a task he performed,
according to R. A. Butler, 'like a large Clumber spaniel
sniffing the bottom of the hedgerows' (*DNB*). The lord
chancellor began his enquiries at Blackpool and continued them in London the following week. Ministers
were summoned to meet him in his small bedroom at the
Imperial Hotel. As one recalled,

there was a touch of incongruous farce about sitting on the Lord Chancellor's unmade bed, while he, his massive frame poised in a creaking wooden chair, made a note of the view of a Cabinet Minister as to who should be Prime Minister of England. (Boyd-Carpenter, 175–6)

Yet in carrying out his task Dilhorne may have found it difficult to separate the roles of committed partisan and impartial recorder of others' opinions. He himself began by favouring the claims of Lord Hailsham but was alienated by the latter's over-exuberant conference performance and, like Macmillan, transferred his allegiance to the foreign secretary, Lord Home. In the event Dilhorne reported that at least half the cabinet favoured Home, a figure which seems inherently improbable, given the known preferences of several of those polled. A charitable interpretation is that Dilhorne reached the questionable conclusion of preponderant positive support for Home on the basis of an absence of outright hostility towards him on the part of most members of Macmillan's cabinet. If true, this was a curious error for a trained lawyer to make; rumours persisted, which the lord chancellor did little to contradict, that he had deliberately misled the prime minister about the preferences of his cabinet colleagues. Such an interpretation was strengthened by Dilhorne's refusal of requests from senior ministers to convene a cabinet meeting to discuss the whole question of the leadership.

Dilhorne remained in office under Sir Alec Douglas-Home, as Lord Home now became, but his occupancy of the woolsack came to an end when the Conservative government lost the general election of 1964. He was made a viscount in the dissolution honours list. He now became deputy leader of the opposition in the House of Lords, and retained this post when Edward Heath succeeded Douglas-Home as Conservative leader in August 1965, but he left the shadow cabinet without acrimony after the general election of the following year. Though he sat on a Conservative constitutional committee to consider Scottish devolution, which reported early in 1970 with a recommendation for a directly elected Scottish assembly, Dilhorne's time was now devoted largely to the law, and in 1969 he gratefully accepted an offer from Harold Wilson's Labour government to become a lord of appeal in ordinary. In this position he proved by common consent a considerable success and he worked diligently until his retirement at the age of seventy-five in 1980. As a law lord he sat in no fewer than 205 appeals. He was also treasurer of the Inner Temple in 1975.

Dilhorne was not in the highest flight of English lawyers and his tenure of the woolsack was not a period of conspicuous reform. He was out of sympathy with much of the changing mood of the 1960s, opposing the abolition of the death penalty and the legalization of homosexuality. By contrast, he was in favour of majority verdicts and the abolition of the practice of cautioning suspected offenders. He believed that courts should retain their discretion over the question of sentencing but was concerned by the variations in sentences handed down by magistrates' courts and tried to ensure that newly appointed JPs should be subjected to a course of compulsory

training. His reputation was badly tarnished by the unusual decision of Lord Devlin, the presiding judge, to publish an account of the Bodkin Adams trial in 1985. From this he emerged as a heavy-handed and unimaginative lawyer who scarcely merited the high offices he had attained. According to Devlin, 'what was almost unique about him and makes his career so fascinating is that what the ordinary careerist achieves by making himself agreeable, falsely or otherwise, Reggie achieved by making himself disagreeable' (Devlin, 39). Such attacks provoked statements of support for Dilhorne from distinguished jurists, including lords Scarman and Bridge. In his public life Dilhorne evoked more respect than affection, but those who knew him more intimately recognized a kindly man, devoted to his family.

Dilhorne died suddenly at Knoydart, Inverness-shire, on 7 September 1980, only a month after his retirement as a law lord. He was buried at the parish church of Deene in Northamptonshire.   D. J. DUTTON

Sources R. F. V. Heuston, *Lives of the lord chancellors, 1940–1970* (1987) · *The Times* (29 May 1958) · *The Times* (10 Sept 1980) · *DNB* · P. Devlin, *Easing the passing* (1985) · R. Lamb, *The Macmillan years* (1995) · J. Ramsden, *The winds of change: Macmillan to Heath, 1957–1975* (1996) · J. Boyd-Carpenter, *Way of life* (1980) · D. R. Thorpe, *Selwyn Lloyd* (1989) · D. R. Thorpe, *Alec Douglas-Home* (1996) · A. Seldon, *Churchill's Indian summer* (1981) · A. Horne, *Macmillan*, 2: 1957–1986 (1989) · S. Heffer, *Like the Roman: the life of Enoch Powell* (1998)

Likenesses Elliott & Fry, photograph, 1962, NPG [*see illus.*] · A. M. Burton, portrait, Inner Temple, London

Wealth at death £120,060: probate, 20 March 1981, *CGPLA Eng. & Wales*

Buller, Sir Walter Lawry (1838–1906), ornithologist, was born on 9 October 1838 at Newark Wesleyan mission station in Pakanae, Hokianga region, New Zealand, the second of the ten children of James Buller (1812–1884), Wesleyan missionary, and his wife, Jane Tonkin Martin (1808–1884), both of Helston, Cornwall. He grew up on mission stations and then completed his education at the missionaries' Wesleyan college in Auckland. His knowledge of Maori gained him a position as an official interpreter, and by 1862 he was appointed resident magistrate—effectively government agent—among the Maori of the Manawatu district in Wellington province. On 24 April that year he married Charlotte Mair (1838–1891), daughter of the pioneer settler Gilbert Mair; they had four children. After their marriage Buller joined the Church of England.

Alongside his official career Buller developed a childhood interest in natural history into a scientific avocation. With a confidence unusual in colonial scientists he set out to describe and name new species of birds himself rather than submitting them to the metropolitan authorities. His *Essay on the Ornithology of New Zealand*, written for the Dunedin Exhibition in 1865, established him as a local authority on the subject, and, after he sent copies to influential scientists in Britain and Europe, also brought him to wider attention. In 1871 he used the *Essay* to obtain the degree of doctor of natural history from the University of Tübingen. By this time he had assembled the materials for

Sir Walter Lawry Buller (1838–1906), by Ethel Mortlock, *c*.1901

a comprehensive work, and obtained leave to go to London to publish it. *A History of the Birds of New Zealand* (1872–3), illustrated by the ornithological artist J. G. Keulemans, was a fine bird book in the best style.

While in London, Buller also took the opportunity to read law at the Inner Temple, and on his return to New Zealand began a lucrative practice as a barrister. Again taking advantage of his knowledge of Maori, he specialized in native land court business. At the same time he energetically pursued his ornithological collecting and writing, and in 1879, with the help of friends in London, he was elected a fellow of the Royal Society.

By 1886 Buller was able to retire from his law practice a wealthy man. He returned to London for the Colonial and Indian Exhibition held that year and, after pledging £5000 for the prince of Wales's struggling project to turn the exhibition into a permanent 'imperial institute', was made KCMG. He went on to publish an enlarged and more sumptuous edition of his *History* (1887–8). This became a New Zealand classic, and Keulemans's illustrations the definitive images of its native birds.

In his scientific writing Buller articulated the colonists' view that all the natives—plants, birds, and Maori people—would inevitably be displaced by more vigorous European immigrants. On the Maori, he quoted I. E. Featherston's maxim that the colonists could only 'smooth down their dying pillow'. Buller described the native birds, too, as doomed—indeed this gave them, and

Buller's books, much of their interest to collectors and scientists—and he rejected as hopeless early proposals to conserve or protect them. Even so, in 1891, after returning to New Zealand to try to rescue several mining companies in which he had taken London directorships, Buller allied himself with the governor, Lord Onslow, in his plea for statutory protection of some species of native birds and for the creation of sanctuaries. (Despite now advocating these moves Buller remained, however, equivocal about their value and privately continued to take specimens of the protected species for his own and other collections.)

Lady Buller died on 1 November 1891. The following year Buller established a country home at Lake Papaitonga, Horowhenua, on land leased and purchased from a Maori friend and client, Keepa Te Rangihiwinui. However, in 1895, after Buller had criticized government actions in purchasing another section of Keepa's tribal land at Horowhenua for a state farm, the minister of lands, John McKenzie, turned on Buller and accused him in parliament of obtaining Papaitonga by fraud. McKenzie carried his feud against Buller through a succession of inquiries and court actions, but in the legal arena he was no match for Buller; much evidence emerged of dubious dealings, but none of the charges against Buller was sustained. Eventually, in 1899, having gained clear title to Papaitonga, he was able to return to London.

Buller had gained his fame and fortune by exploiting the opportunities of his colonial position, while striving to throw off the imputation of inferiority from his colonial origins. In the end, although expressing nostalgia for the bush and birds of New Zealand in a final *Supplement to the 'Birds of New Zealand'* (1905), he was more at home in England. Sir Walter Buller died at his daughter's home, Pondtail Lodge, Fleet, Hampshire, on 19 July 1906. He was buried at Fleet. R. A. GALBREATH

Sources R. A. Galbreath, *Walter Buller: the reluctant conservationist* (1989) · J. Buller, 'Journal', NL NZ, Turnbull L., MS 1838–1844 · J. Buller, NL NZ, Turnbull L., J. Buller MSS, MS papers 180 · m. cert. · d. cert.

Archives American Museum of Natural History, New York · Canterbury Museum, Christchurch, New Zealand · Carnegie Institute and Museum, Pittsburgh · National Museum of New Zealand, Wellington · NL Aus. · NL NZ, Turnbull L., corresp. and papers | Auckland Institute and Museum, Thomas Cheeseman MSS · Auckland Public Library, letters to Sir George Grey · McGill University, Montreal, Richard Bowdler Sharpe MSS · NHM, letters to A. Gunther and R. W. T. Gunther · NHM, Sir Richard Owen MSS · NHM, L. Walter Rothschild MSS · NL NZ, Turnbull L., John Ballance MSS · NL NZ, Turnbull L., W. B. D. Mantell MSS · NL NZ, Turnbull L., Donald McLean MSS · RBG Kew, Hooker MSS · U. Cam., department of zoology, Alfred Newton MSS

Likenesses photographs, 1860–1906, repro. in Galbreath, *Walter Buller* · E. Mortlock, oils, *c*.1901, National Museum of New Zealand, Wellington [*see illus.*] · photograph, 1901, Auckland Institute and Museum, New Zealand · engraving (after photograph), repro. in W. L. Buller, *Supplement to the 'Birds of New Zealand'* (1905), frontispiece

Wealth at death £15,842 0s. 11d.: resworn probate, 16 Aug 1906, *CGPLA Eng. & Wales*

Buller, William (1735–1796), bishop of Exeter, was born at Morval, Cornwall, on 9 August 1735, the fourth son of John

Francis Buller (*bap.* 1695, *d.* 1751) of Morval and Shillingham, and his wife, Rebecca (*d.* 1743), third daughter and coheir of Sir Jonathan *Trelawny, bishop of Winchester. William matriculated from Oriel College, Oxford, on 10 April 1753, aged seventeen, but soon moved to Christ Church. He graduated BA in 1757 and MA in 1759; he subsequently took the degrees of BD and DD in 1781.

Buller's career in the church owed a great deal to an astute marriage, on 19 April 1762, to Anne (*d.* 1800), daughter and coheir of John *Thomas (1696–1781), bishop of Winchester and, from 1763, clerk of the closet to George III. Buller's father-in-law had previously granted him the lucrative rectory of Brightwell in Berkshire, which he held until 1766, and named him canon of the twelfth prebend in Winchester Cathedral. Buller subsequently received the rectories of Wonston and Houghton in Hampshire, followed by the rectories of Alresford and Overton in 1776. A mandamus was issued for Buller's preferment as a canon of Windsor on 22 December 1773.

Buller resigned this last stall when he was elected dean of Exeter on 25 March 1784. The high point of his office was entertaining George III, Queen Charlotte, and members of their family at the deanery during the royal visit to Exeter in August 1789. Buller, who was 'very civil and in high glee' (*Diary and Letters*, 1.310), followed a service in the cathedral with a private tour for the party and made sure it was he rather than the city authorities who entertained the king and queen. A grateful monarch took a special interest in enabling Buller, in 1790, to exchange one deanery for another, namely Canterbury, on George Horne's promotion to the episcopate. Buller was not slow to follow Horne to the House of Lords, returning to Exeter as bishop in 1792 in a career move that was unusual for the Hanoverian church but popular locally because of Buller's west-country background. As with Horne, Buller was past his best by the time of his last promotion, suffering from continuous ill health and domestic loss. He was a dutiful, orthodox cleric whose family associations and connections held the key to his advancement. As a bishop his major undertaking was to hold a primary visitation for the Exeter diocese in 1793–4, and was one of the supporters of the 1796 act to improve the income of poor curates. Indeed, the number of ordinands in the diocese ran at its highest level for the century during Buller's episcopate. He was made a freeman of Exeter in August 1793.

Buller enjoyed episcopal rank for only four years before dying of dropsy in the chest on 12 December 1796 at Downes, near Crediton in Devon, the seat of his son-in-law. He was buried in the south choir aisle of Exeter Cathedral on 17 December. His wife, Anne, died on 28 August 1800 and was buried on 3 September 1800. One son, Richard, survived him as did two daughters, Anne and Susannah Catherine. He published only sermons, including one preached before the House of Lords on 9 March 1796 for the general fast.   NIGEL ASTON

Sources *GM*, 1st ser., 66 (1796), 1061 · *GM*, 1st ser., 67 (1797), 78 · Burke, *Gen. GB* (1858) · J. L. Vivian, ed., *The visitations of Cornwall, comprising the herald's visitations of 1530, 1573, and 1620* (1887), 58–9 · B. H. Williams, *Ancient westcountry families and their armorial bearings*, 1

(1916), 39–40 · J. Polsue, *A complete parochial history of the county of Cornwall*, 3 (1867–72); repr. (1974), 379 · Boase & Courtney, *Bibl. Corn.*, 1.82 · Foster, *Alum. Oxon.* · *Fasti Angl.* (Hardy), 1.383, 389; 3.410 · *Fasti Angl.*, 1541–1857, [Canterbury], 14, 106 · A. J. Robertson, *A history of Alresford* (1969), 46, 52 · J. N. Dolben, ed., *The manuscripts of St George's Chapel, Windsor Castle* (1957), 79 · A. Warne, *Church and society in eighteenth century Devon* (1969) · G. Oliver, *Lives of the bishops of Exeter, and a history of the cathedral* (1861), 164–5 · R. J. E. Boggis, *A history of the diocese of Exeter* (1922), 468 · J. F. Chanter, *The bishop's palace, Exeter, and its story* (1932) · J. Gidley, *Notices of Exeter: comprising a history of royal visits to the ancient and loyal city* (1863) · J. M. Cowper, *The lives of the deans of Canterbury* (1900), 201 · C. J. Abbey, *The English church and its bishops, 1700–1800*, 2 (1887), 270 · *Diary and letters of Madame D'Arblay (1778–1840)*, ed. C. Barrett and A. Dobson, 1 (1904), 310 · M. Spurrell, ed., *The Brightwell parish diaries*, Oxfordshire RS, 62 (1998), 87

Archives Cornwall RO, Buller of Morval, BU/349, 355–356, 602 · Devon RO, Ac. 56/10, box 34; 53/6, box 36; Z16/3/13–14 · Devon RO, Buller of Crediton, Buller pedigree, 2065M/F5/5

Likenesses portrait, 1796, bishop's palace, Exeter · portrait, 1796, Canterbury deanery; repro. in Cowper, *Lives of the deans of Canterbury*, 201

Bullett, Gerald William (1893–1958), writer and broadcaster, was born on 30 December 1893 at 107 Brockley Rise, Forest Hill, London, the third of the three sons of Robert Bullett (1851–1914), a schoolmaster, later a coal agent, and Ellen, *née* Pegg (1848–1904), a farmer's daughter from Ullesthorpe, Leicestershire. In 1895 the family moved to Muswell Hill in north London, where Gerald was educated at a small private day school. His mother died when he was ten, and at sixteen he became a bank clerk. He wrote his first novel (unpublished and later destroyed) at eighteen. His second, *The Progress of Kay*, a study of suburban adolescence, was immediately accepted by Constable, and published in 1916, when he was serving with the Royal Flying Corps in France.

On demobilization Bullett applied for entry to Cambridge as an ex-serviceman, and sent some poems and a copy of *The Progress of Kay* to Sir Arthur Quiller-Couch, who persuaded Jesus College to accept him. He read English, graduated with first-class honours in 1921, and married Edith Marion (Rosalind) Barker, *née* Gould (1887–1982) on 5 December the same year. Their marriage proved fulfilling and purposeful, Rosalind acting as housekeeper, hostess, and secretary. Since both preferred country life, they lived frugally in a succession of rented houses in the home counties, finally settling in an Elizabethan farmhouse at East Harting in Sussex. They had one daughter.

After Cambridge Bullett began reviewing for the *Times Literary Supplement* and other journals, and then embarked on a career as an assiduous short story writer and poet, small-time publisher, and editor and author of some forty published books.

In 1923 Bullett published a critical study of G. K. Chesterton. In April 1926 he was the first author to broadcast his own short story, 'The Baker's Cart', from the BBC's 2LO station, and thereafter he frequently adapted and performed his own work for radio. From 1926 to 1934 he acted as reader for the publishing firm of Gerald Howe, and served on the selection committee of the Book Society. He published a number of novels during this period including *The History of Egg Pandervil* (1928) and *Nicky, Son of Egg* (1929), which chronicle the impact of the First World War on a rural family. In the 1930s he brought out *Helen's Lovers* (1932), a collection of short stories, *I'll Tell you Everything* (1932), a detective novel written jointly with J. B. Priestley, *The English Galaxy* (1933), an anthology of short poems, *The Bubble* (1934), one of a few selections of his own poetry, *The Happy Mariners* (1935), a story for children, and *The Jury* (1935), which has a neat plot, delicate character drawing, and an engaging style. *The Snare of the Fowler* (1936), a retelling of the Oedipus legend in a contemporary setting, created a stir among his regular readers and prompted some reviews which made him apprehensive for his future as a writer. Although Alfred Knopf enthused over its fine qualities, publishing it in the USA in the same year, and Quiller-Couch and E. M. W. Tillyard, to whom Bullett turned for reassurance, did their best to rebuild his confidence by pointing out the book's many merits, he never again attempted such a problematic or ambitious theme. The regular annual appearance of Bullett's novels was interrupted only by the Second World War. From 1940 to 1943 he was employed by the BBC Overseas Service as a talks producer. He broadcast a series of talks entitled *Life at Home*, describing everyday activities, and the unassuming heroism of the civilian population. After 1945 he chaired literary discussions and reviewed novels and poetry, giving succinct assessments of Elizabeth Gaskell and George Eliot (he published a biography of her in 1947). In 1946, in collaboration with Tsui Chi Lai, he made a 'rendering' of a sequence of poems by Fan Cheng-ta written in 1186. Although attacked by serious English scholars of Chinese poetry, it reads well (it was reprinted in Hong Kong, with the original Chinese text interleaved, in 1980). Of his post-war novels *The Elderbrook Brothers* (1945), *The Alderman's Son* (1954), *The Daughters of Mrs Peacock* (1957), and *The Peacock Brides* (1958) are among the most interesting. He also wrote two detective novels, *One Man's Poison* (1956) and *Odd Woman Out* (1958) under the pen name Sebastian Fox.

Bullett's fiction is pervaded by feeling for his maternal midland roots, and memories of his Edwardian childhood in Muswell Hill among the 'middle middle-class' (Kunitz and Colby). The contentment of his thirty productive years in Sussex, from where he was lured to London only by agents or publishers, never quite obliterated his 'terror of being at the world's mercy'. He disliked intrusions into his private life from any quarter, saying:

> On the rare occasions when I pick up a book of my own and glance through it, the intimacy of the revelation almost makes me blush. There I am, written down. What more can the most inquisitive reader demand?

He remained, in Storm Jameson's words, 'one of God's honest stubborn … eternally youthful English'.

Storm Jameson, who knew Bullett as a young man, said that his 'clumsy head and body housed a poet of extreme elegance'. His novels pay a measured tribute to the decency, obstinacy, and compassion with which ordinary English men and women attempted to order their lives during the first troubled decades of the twentieth century.

Bullett died on 3 January 1958 in the Royal West Sussex Hospital, Chichester, and was cremated on 8 January in Brighton. His posthumous *Collected Poems* was published in 1959, and contains many attractive lyrics.

FELICITY EHRLICH

Sources WWW, 1951–60 · S. J. Kunitz and V. Colby, eds., *Twentieth-century authors: a biographical dictionary of modern literature, first supplement* (1955) · S. Jameson, *Journey from the north*, 1 (1969), 205–6 · *Hants and Sussex News* (8 Jan 1958) · *The Times* (6 Jan 1958); (8 Jan 1958); (22 Jan 1958) · private information (2004) · b. cert. · d. cert.
Archives BBC WAC, contributor files relating to Bullett and scripts on microfilm · Bodl. Oxf., corresp. and literary papers, MSS Eng. misc. c. 354, d. 495, e. 457–458 | BL, corresp. with League of Dramatists, Add. MS 63366 · BL, corresp. with Society of Authors, Add. MS 56678 · U. Reading L., letters to the Bodley Head Ltd | SOUND BL NSA, appreciation of W. J. Turner, tape, 16 Dec 1946, by Gerald Bullett, T11388
Likenesses photograph, c.1942, repro. in Kunitz and Colby, eds., *Twentieth-century authors* (1942); priv. coll.
Wealth at death £8182 13s. 5d.: probate, 25 Feb 1958, *CGPLA Eng. & Wales*

Bulley [*married name* Brooke], (**Agnes**) **Amy** (1852–1939), promoter of women's education and women's trade unionism, was born on 20 April 1852 at Liscard, New Brighton, Cheshire, one of several sons and daughters of Samuel Marshall Bulley, cotton broker, and Mary Rachel Bulley, *née* Raffles. The Bulleys held progressive views on women's education and, influenced by Anne Jemima Clough, the first warden of Newnham College and a family friend, sent three of their daughters, Ella, Amy, and Caroline, to Cambridge. After studying at Laleham School, Clapham, Amy became a student at Emily Davies's college in 1871, residing first at Hitchin and then at Girton. In 1873 she moved to Newnham in order to take a fourth year of study, thus joining her two sisters. She and Mary Paley became the first women to sit for the moral science tripos in 1874; both were successful, with Amy Bulley placed in the second class, although of course she received no degree.

In 1876 Amy Bulley joined the staff of Manchester High School for Girls as an assistant mistress, and thus began ten years of active involvement with the fledgeling movement to advance academic education for girls and young women. When negotiations between Owens College and the Manchester Association for the Higher Education of Women resulted in the setting up of the independent Manchester and Salford College for Women in Brunswick Street in 1877, Amy Bulley became its secretary, a post she held until 1883 in conjunction with her teaching duties at the high school. The aim was to prepare students for a certificate, and thus to prove their academic ability. The lecturers included Amy Bulley's elder sister, Mrs Ella *Armitage, the wife of a Congregational minister and subsequently herself a distinguished historian. After strong pressure from campaigners, in 1883 the college was replaced by a women's department, which was constituted as a formal part of Owens, thus enabling its students to sit for degrees.

After leaving the high school in 1885 Amy Bulley developed an interest in women's employment, which marked the beginning of a lifelong attachment to the labour movement. An award-winning essay entitled *Middle Class Education in England*, which had been published in 1881, was the start of a distinguished career in journalism, during which time she contributed to the *Manchester Guardian* and wrote for a number of quarterly periodicals and women's journals. She was a fine writer and produced well-informed and astute articles on progressive political and labour issues, including 'Domestic service: a social study' in the *Westminster Review* (1891) and a 'Report on the employment of women' (*Fortnightly Review*, Jan 1894). In the latter year she also published *Women's Work* with Margaret Whitley, a full-length and comprehensive study of the new white-blouse professions and industrial trades. When the Women's Liberal Federation held its second annual conference in Manchester in December 1889, she delivered a paper entitled 'The political evolution of women', which was subsequently published in the *Westminster Review* (July 1890): she expressed support for women's suffrage, but warned against the moralizing tendency within the women's movement, and the presumption of moral superiority which underpinned the desire for political and social reform.

The founding of the Manchester, Salford and District Women's Trades Union Council in 1895, which sought to organize women in local trades, factories, and workshops, was part of the new spirit of the age in which progressive Liberals and feminist reformers forged an alliance with Christian socialists and the embryonic labour movement. Amy Bulley served as chair of the council from 1897 to 1906, and directed its investigation subcommittee, which carried out research into local conditions of employment, particularly in the homework and clothing trades where sweating was rife. In 1906 she and the council joined with the Women's Co-operative Guild to present Manchester's version of the much-publicized Sweated Industries Exhibition in the Co-operative Hall. She worked alongside organizers Sarah Dickenson and Eva Gore-Booth, and welcomed visits from many of the leading women trade unionists of the day, including Lady Dilke, Gertrude Tuckwell, and Isabella Ford. Her wider network of colleagues and acquaintances included C. P. Scott, Margaret Ashton, and members of Manchester's liberal and academic intelligentsia.

On 26 October 1907, at the age of fifty-five, Amy Bulley married a cotton merchant named Joseph Brooke (1836–1912), the recently widowed husband of her sister Mary, and withdrew from public work until his death in 1912. The following year she moved to Bushey in Hertfordshire. In the 1920s, tremendously vigorous still in mind and body, she helped to build the labour movement in Watford, and, although unsuccessful, stood for three consecutive years as the Labour candidate for Bushey urban district council (1926–8). She lectured on behalf of the League of Nations Union, and as a Labour nominee was among the first women to be appointed JPs after the Sex Disqualification Removal Act of 1919. She sat on the Watford bench from 1920 to 1937.

Born into a highly musical family, Amy Bulley wrote songs, including 'The Peace Song of Ireland' (1911), and

served on the council of the Watford School of Music. Her intellectual interests were wide-ranging and included a published essay on Edwin Waugh, the Lancashire poet (*Temple Bar*, October 1890), and an anthropological study, *The Eucharist*, in 1910. She died of cerebral thrombosis, aged eighty-seven, on 16 November 1939 at her home, 14 Nightingale Road, Bushey, and was cremated at Golders Green crematorium on 20 November. Both a Victorian and a 'modern', she embraced the twin causes of women and workers with absolute conviction. LINDA WALKER

Sources K. T. Butler and H. I. McMorran, eds., *Girton College register, 1869–1946* (1948) · [A. B. White and others], eds., *Newnham College register, 1871–1971*, 2nd edn, 1 (1979) · M. P. Marshall, 'Mrs E. Armitage (Ella Sophie Bulley)', *Newnham College Roll Letter* (1932), 37–40 · *Watford Observer* (17 Nov 1939) · Manchester, Salford and District Women's Trades Union Council: annual reports (1895–1919) · JRL, Manchester University archive collections, material relating to the education of women, UA/4/1–24 · JRL, Manchester Guardian Archive, correspondence of C. P. Scott · Manchester High School for Girls: annual reports (1877–86) · M. Tylecote, *The education of women at Manchester University, 1883–1933* (1941) · B. A. Clough, *A memoir of Anne Jemima Clough*, new edn (1903) · M. P. Marshall, *What I remember* (1947) · S. A. Burstall, *The story of the Manchester High School for Girls, 1871–1911* (1911) · *Manchester Guardian* (3–6 Dec 1889) · *Manchester Guardian* (17 Nov 1939) · b. cert. · m. cert. · d. cert. · *Englishwoman's Yearbook and Directory* (1904–7)

Archives JRL, Manchester Guardian Archive, corresp. of C. P. Scott · JRL, Manchester University archive collections, material relating to the education of women

Likenesses group portraits, photographs, 1872–4 (with student group), Newnham College, Cambridge · oils, Newnham College, Cambridge

Wealth at death £164 3s. 7d.: probate, 8 Jan 1940, CGPLA Eng. & Wales

Bullingham, John (*d.* 1598), bishop of Gloucester, was probably born in Gloucestershire. He was educated at Oxford and had graduated BA by 1550, when he was elected a probationer fellow of Magdalen College. He left England to live in exile in Rouen, France, shortly thereafter, as a result of the increasingly radical direction being taken by English protestantism during the later years of Edward VI's reign. The accession of Mary and the restoration of Catholicism prompted his return, and he resumed his position and studies at Magdalen. He proceeded MA and was ordained to the priesthood in 1554. That same year he became rector of Boxwell in the diocese of Gloucester on the presentation of the queen, and three years later he was granted the vicarage of Creche in the diocese of Bath and Wells.

By 1562, three years after Elizabeth had succeeded Mary as queen and England had returned to protestantism, Bullingham had apparently reconciled himself to the new religion (or at least wanted the martyrologist John Foxe to think so). In that year he wrote a letter to Foxe lamenting his earlier Catholic allegiance and his rejection of the Marian martyr Julins Palmer (a former Magdalen man like both Foxe and Bullingham himself). Bullingham told Foxe how he had met with Palmer in St Paul's after returning to England early in Mary's reign, and how after arguing with him about the cathedral's recently erected rood, he told Palmer, 'I will never have to do with you again'. Clearly he now wanted Foxe to believe that he regretted his words, adding that by Palmer's words and deeds 'it appeareth that God had elected him' (*Acts and Monuments*, 8.204–5).

Bullingham seems to have completed the rehabilitation of his ecclesiastical career by the mid-1560s—in 1565 he was collated to the prebend of Wenlocksbarn in St Paul's, London. He also continued his association with Magdalen and received the degrees of BTh and DTh in 1566 and 1567 respectively. In the latter year he was appointed archdeacon of Huntingdon by Nicholas Bullingham, bishop of Lincoln, who may have been a kinsman. In any event, John Bullingham benefited from Nicholas's patronage on several subsequent occasions. He became a canon of Lincoln with the prebend of Louth in 1568, rector of Brington and Bithorne in the diocese of Lincoln in 1569, and a canon of Worcester in 1570, all through the patronage of the bishop of Lincoln. Then in 1571, after Bishop Bullingham was translated to Worcester, he presented John to the living of Withington in the diocese of Gloucester. John was subsequently incorporated DTh of Cambridge in 1575, and the following year was a commissioner to conduct the metropolitical visitation of the diocese of Hereford for Archbishop Grindal. He seems to have held his accumulated positions until 1581, only relinquishing them when he was named bishop of Gloucester and, like his predecessor Richard Cheyney, granted Bristol *in commendam*. The see of Gloucester was poorly endowed, its annual income being calculated at just over £330 at this time. Bristol's equally slender revenues nevertheless allowed Bullingham to maintain the dignity of a bishop, but it must be doubted whether the archbishop of Canterbury's officials allowed him effective control over Bristol's diocesan affairs, regarding it rather as a vacant see and administering it accordingly. When Richard Fletcher was consecrated bishop of Bristol in 1589 Bullingham complained to Lord Burghley that his lost income from the see had been 'the onely stay of my living' and petitioned for a benefice *in commendam* to make up for it (BL, Lansdowne MS 61, fol. 9r). He received the rectory of Kilmington in the diocese of Bath and Wells, holding it until his death. John Aylmer, bishop of London, who had originally opposed Bullingham's elevation, was by 1592 sufficiently sympathetic to his plight to propose that he be allowed to hold the see of Oxford *in commendam* following the death of John Underhill.

By the time he was elevated to Gloucester, Bullingham seems to have reconciled himself fully to the new religion. In 1583 he was one of a number of bishops who presented a set of articles to the queen for the government of the church, urging her to execute the laws against recusants, and to promote preaching, reading the Bible, admission to orders, and clerical marriage. He seems to have been active against nonconformity, but most of his energies were devoted to attempts to control the behaviour of his chancellor, William Blackleech, whom he accused of corruption in the execution of his office. Blackleech followed another corrupt diocesan chancellor, Thomas Powell, and, like his predecessor, Cheyney, Bullingham had little success in either reforming or removing the offending official. Like Cheyney, Bullingham was supported more than once by the privy council, obtaining letters and commissions to help him in asserting his episcopal authority, although the effect of such actions was probably negligible. Early in 1589 Bullingham selected Gilbert Bourne to replace Blackleech. Bourne was sworn in and took the oath of supremacy on 13 March 1589; but Blackleech refused to acquiesce in his own removal and presided over the diocesan consistory court on 7 April, having forced Bourne to give way, allegedly at sword-point. Two days later Bullingham issued a decree, declaring that in the interest of maintaining the reputation of the court he would henceforth preside in person.

Bourne disappears from the records at this point but the episcopal decree was no more of a deterrent to Blackleech than Bullingham's previous attempts to gain control of his consistory court. The chancellor continued to preside over the court through the summer of 1590. When on 6 October 1590 the bishop attempted to preside himself, his recalcitrant chancellor challenged his authority by disrupting the proceedings. Blackleech tried to prorogue the session, announcing that it would be reconvened that afternoon in a nearby parish church, and then:

> departed out of the corte with dyvers clients apparitors and others following them. And walked up and downe in the Cathedral Churche of Gloucester. And the sayd Lord Bushoppe continued his judiciall sitting … and [later] the same forenoone the same Mr Blackleeche came againe into the consistory place and standing bare headed without the Inner Bar …

interrupted the proceedings to announce that he would reconvene the court immediately in the neighbouring parish (rather than waiting until afternoon). The bishop responded by telling those present 'that they should stay there before his Lordship and appear'. The records show that some stayed and others followed the chancellor to his session (Gloucester diocesan records, vol. 63, 6 Oct 1590).

The battle of wills continued until 11 April 1592, with both Bullingham and Blackleech presiding over simultaneous sessions held in different places within the cathedral. Then a compromise of sorts was reached that left Blackleech as chancellor presiding over the court. Soon afterwards, however, Bullingham accused Blackleech of ignoring injunctions emanating from higher courts (including the court of requests), though apparently to no avail. Once again Blackleech appears to have acted with flagrant disregard for higher authority, and once again the bishop was unable to do anything about it.

Bullingham's ineffectiveness was consistent with other aspects of his performance, first as a priest and then as a bishop. In 1568 Matthew Parker, archbishop of Canterbury, had chosen Bullingham to preach on Good Friday at Paul's Cross in place of the bishop of Winchester, who was ill. Subsequently Parker heard Bullingham preach and concluded that he lacked the rhetorical style and temperament appropriate for a court preacher. He vowed that he would not select him to preach before the queen again, because 'he would that her Highness had the best' (*Correspondence*, 378). Following his elevation to Gloucester, Bullingham was viewed by some as a weak member of the

Elizabethan bench. He was one of the bishops selected for particular mention and pointed ridicule in the Marprelate tracts, where he was characterized as 'unlerned' and an 'olde stealecounter masse priest' (Marprelate, *Epistle to the Terrible Priests*, 3; *Hay any worke for Cooper*, 6). He died on 20 May 1598 at Kensington and was buried in Gloucester Cathedral.   CAROLINE LITZENBERGER

Sources APC, 1542–98 · CPR, 1553–82 · CSP dom., 1547–1603, with addenda, 1580–1625 · DNB · M. Marprelate, *An epistle to the terrible priests* [1588]; repr. in *The Marprelate tracts (1588–1589)* (1967) · M. Marprelate, *Hay any worke for Cooper* [1559]; repr. in *The Marprelate tracts (1588–1589)* (1967) · Hockaday Abstracts, Chronological, 1554–8, Gloucester City Library · diocesan records, Gloucester, Glos. RO, vols. 2a, 27a · K. Fincham, *Prelate as pastor: the episcopate of James I* (1990) · Foster, *Alum. Oxon., 1500–1714*, 1.208 · *The acts and monuments of John Foxe*, new edn, ed. G. Townsend, 8 vols. (1843–9) · *Fasti Angl.*, 1541–1857, [St Paul's, London] · *Fasti Angl.*, 1541–1857, [Ely] · *Fasti Angl.*, 1541–1857, [Bristol] · *Fasti Angl.*, 1541–1857, [Lincoln] · *Correspondence of Matthew Parker*, ed. J. Bruce and T. T. Perowne, Parker Society, 42 (1853) · F. D. Price, 'Bishop Bullingham and chancellor Blackleech: a diocese divided', *Transactions of the Bristol and Gloucestershire Archaeological Society*, 91 (1973), 175–98 · *STC, 1475–1640* · D. M. Smith, *Guide to bishops' registers of England and Wales: a survey from the middle ages to the abolition of the episcopacy in 1646*, Royal Historical Society Guides and Handbooks, 11 (1981) · J. Strype, *Annals of the Reformation and establishment of religion ... during Queen Elizabeth's happy reign*, new edn, 4 vols. (1824) · J. Strype, *The life and acts of Archbishop Whitgift* (1821) · J. Strype, *The history of the life and acts of the most reverend father in God Edmund Grindal*, new edn (1821) · J. Strype, *Historical collections of the life and acts of ... John Aylmer*, new edn (1821) · J. Strype, *The life and acts of Matthew Parker*, new edn, 3 vols. (1821) · Wood, *Ath. Oxon.*, new edn, 2.842–3
Archives Glos. RO

Bullingham, Nicholas (1511?–1576), bishop of Lincoln and of Worcester, was the son of Thomas Bullingham (*d.* in or before 1549) of Worcester, bailiff in 1528 and 1530, and his wife, Susan (*d.* 1562), whose maiden name may have been Archbold. His brother Richard was a clothier who followed their father in the city élite, becoming bailiff (1561, 1563) and MP in 1563.

Education and early career Bullingham emerges from obscurity in 1536, when as a student of law he became a fellow of All Souls, Oxford. He was dean of the faculty there in 1543 and bursar in 1544–5, having supplicated for the degree of BCL in 1539. He was not admitted until 1541. He supplicated unsuccessfully for the degree of DCL in 1546, thereafter resigning his fellowship and apparently abandoning Oxford.

It is possible that protestant sympathies were proving an obstacle to Bullingham's further advancement at Oxford and that he looked elsewhere for promotion. He was certainly appointed chaplain to Thomas Cranmer, archbishop of Canterbury, and in December 1547 was collated by Bishop Henry Holbeach to the prebend of Welton Westhall in Lincoln Cathedral. This he exchanged for the more valuable Empingham (£25 6s. 5d. p.a. rather than £9 10s.) the following August. He had already appeared as a proctor of the Lincoln lower clergy in convocation in November 1547. On 22 September 1549 he was installed as archdeacon of Lincoln and also became the bishop's vicar-general, uniting two sometimes divisive arms of ecclesiastical jurisdiction. He protested major residence at Lincoln

a year later, thereby gaining £83 11s. p.a. from the common fund to add to £180 from his archdeaconry. His brother Richard meanwhile started to acquire rights of next presentation in Lincoln chapter. Bullingham was named to the commission of 1550 against Anabaptists and heretics, though not of the quorum, and then to the commission of 1551 to enforce the Edwardian prayer book. In 1552 Matthew Parker became dean of Lincoln, Bullingham acting as proxy at his installation—he was later to act in effect as Bullingham's patron.

In 1553 Bullingham was presented to the rectory of Thimbleby, Lincolnshire, worth £13 11s. p.a. The accession of Mary meant that he did not enjoy it long enough to pay first fruits; the exchequer wrote these off in view of his deprivation on 23 May 1554 as a married clerk—not, as has been suggested, as one with insufficient orders. He had been replaced as archdeacon on 5 May. His wife was Margaret (*d.* 1566), daughter of Hamond Sutton of Washingborough, Lincolnshire. They had two sons, Francis (1553–*c.*1636) and Nicholas (1566–1639), and two short-lived daughters both named Susan (*b.* and *d.* 1561, and *b.* 1563, *d.* 1564). In an Elizabethan sermon Bullingham pointedly reproved married priests who in Mary's time 'forsooke unnaturalye ther wives and marryede bennefycis. God graunte them to repent with Abrah[a]m', who abandoned Sarah for temporal benefit (LPL, MS 739, fol. 5r).

After a period of concealment Bullingham made his way to Emden. He was enrolled there as a citizen on 5 November 1555, presumably after a year's residence. Possibly he helped edit the Latin edition of Cranmer's *Defence of the True and Catholick Doctrine of the Sacrament*, published there in 1556. He is supposed to have added theological studies to his legal ones. His Lincolnshire interests were not wholly neglected, for although he had to abandon his house in the cathedral close on deprivation, somebody negotiated a lease for him on another one in 1556.

Bishop of Lincoln The month after Elizabeth I's accession a prominent Lincolnshire gentleman, Sir Francis Ayscough, successfully pressed Sir William Cecil for Bullingham's restoration as archdeacon, his deprivation tending 'to his utter undoing' (PRO, SP 12/1/46). In 1559 he proceeded DCL at Cambridge. Archbishop-elect Parker made him a chaplain. On 9 December 1559 he appeared as proxy for Parker at the latter's confirmation as archbishop, and together with Edmund Guest (both vested, whatever their own views, in silken copes) assisted at his consecration; he also shared Parker's commission to confirm Edmund Grindal as bishop of London on the 20th. Moreover he provided legal opinions on the nomination of new bishops, favouring the *supplentes* clause, affirming the capacity of royal authority to supply any defects.

Parker was said to have intended to make Bullingham an ecclesiastical judge, but to have been prevented by his nomination in November 1559 to the see of Lincoln. Bullingham had been absent from the various lists of possible episcopal nominees drawn up at Elizabeth's accession, and was not employed in the royal visitation of 1559. His apparently well-established Lincolnshire connections must eventually have been a factor, especially since a vast diocese and a reduced income would make the see a difficult one for an outsider. Along with his brother Richard, eleven Lincolnshire gentlemen (including Ayscough) gave security for the first fruits on his official income of £894 18s. 1½d. p.a. Bullingham was consecrated at Lambeth on 21 January 1560 and assisted with further consecrations over the next two months; the temporalities were restored on 18 April. However, the uncertain financial position of the see was acknowledged by a licence to retain the archdeaconry *in commendam* for three years; in the event he held it until April 1562.

Bullingham's nomination was surprising—his legal background made him a unique figure among Elizabethan English, as distinct from Welsh, bishops. It also lent a degree of plausibility to a curious allegation. Before Pope Pius V issued the bull *Regnans in excelsis* deposing Elizabeth in February 1570, evidence was taken at Rome on her episcopal appointments, among other subjects. Bullingham was a star example, as it was alleged by William Alott of Lincolnshire that 'I was a friend of his and familiarly acquainted, and I know him *not to be a priest*, but a heretic' (Dixon, 6.256). This has been taken to be a denial of any form of valid ordination, but it is more probably a reference to the fact that he was not ordained until after the introduction of the Edwardian ordinal: Ayscough's damaged petition of 1558 seems to refer to Bullingham's being 'made minister according to the booke' (PRO, SP 12/1/46). From the Catholic point of view the same charge of 'heresy' could have been levelled at several of his episcopal colleagues, and it may be that Bullingham was singled out merely because Alott happened to be acquainted with him personally.

Bullingham has been characterized as one of Parker's most constant supporters in his drive for ritual conformity during the 1560s, but, like most Marian exiles, he had little time for church ceremonial. He denounced popular nostalgia, now that 'the glisteringe of Antichriste's churche is gonne … coppes, cross, challis are gonne'; there should be 'no reliques' of it (LPL, MS 739, fols. 21v, 31v). At Lincoln, like Jewel at Salisbury, Bullingham restricted his oath to observe the cathedral statutes to those not contrary to the laws of God and the realm. His reply to the queries to bishops of 1564 on the religious stance of JPs took advantage of the request for comments in the manner of Robert Horne and Thomas Bentham rather than of the more conservative Richard Cox, with particular stress on the need for commissions extending 'to places exempt … for reformacion of disorders in religion' and indeed of 'papisticall orders and usages in cathedrall and collegiat churches' (Bateson, 32–3). He also wanted archdeacons added to peace commissions and suggested that they preach at quarter sessions.

In 1565 Bullingham struck at the conservative leaders of Lincoln's chapter, dismissing from residence Roger Bromhall, the subdean, Roger Dalyson, the precentor, and probably also John Salisbury, the chancellor, on the pretext of financial irregularities. Death or resignation removed them altogether within a few years. His diocese also saw the systematic defacement of 'superstitious' monuments,

primarily at the instigation of John Aylmer, archdeacon of Lincoln from 1562. Bullingham also showed himself sympathetic to protestants displaced by troubles on the continent, announcing a collection for them from his diocese in February 1568.

Episcopal activities Perhaps because of his legal background Bullingham became one of the most active bishops in the House of Lords, being appointed to no fewer than twenty-six committees during the parliaments of 1563, 1566, 1571, and 1572—a tally which outstrips (and that within a period of only ten years) all Elizabethan bishops and archbishops except Thomas Cooper and Thomas Bilson. Despite the concurrent distractions of convocation, he recorded a parliamentary attendance of nearly 90 per cent in 1563, a figure he maintained consistently and even exceeded as late as 1572. This made him a natural choice as proxy for other prelates including Parker, Grindal, and Richard Cox of Ely.

Following Bullingham's consecration Parker used him as his deputy at Lambeth ordinations: at over 170, he was by far the most prolific ordainer of 1560. His own Lincoln register records at least 150 ordinations in 1562, 85 in 1563, some 80 in 1564, 90 in 1565, and 75 in 1566. Bullingham's successor at Lincoln, Thomas Cooper, found only 55 per cent of his predecessor's ordinands to be well versed in scripture, but Bullingham was not alone in finding choice limited in the provinces at the beginning of Elizabeth's reign.

In the convocation of 1563 Bullingham was one of the deputies nominated to act for Parker on 5 February (in the event Edmund Grindal did so), and he and Edwin Sandys of Worcester led the session dealing with the clerical subsidy on 15 February. Moreover he was among those with whom Parker discussed Alexander Nowell's *Catechism*. Bullingham was also appointed, with Grindal, Robert Horne of Winchester, and John Scory of Hereford, to a committee to consider questions of discipline, without any agreed result.

Bullingham and Horne joined Parker, Grindal, and Cox, all episcopal members of the ecclesiastical commission, in drawing up the 'advertisements' on ritual in 1565. Thereby Bullingham and other bishops eschewed the full implications of their own initial broadsides against inherited Catholic traditions. That Bullingham's sympathies had not fundamentally changed, however, appeared in the case of Edward Brocklesby. The brother of one of Bullingham's group of first fruits sureties, Brocklesby was collated by the bishop to the vicarage of Hemel Hempstead, Hertfordshire, in 1564; when the ecclesiastical commission decided to deprive Brocklesby the following year for rejection of the surplice, Bullingham was in no hurry to replace him, and either he or Cooper, his successor at Lincoln, gave Brocklesby the prebend of Sexaginta Solidorum there in 1571. In the latter year, however, Bullingham was one of the bishops who received the submission of the radical puritan Christopher Goodman.

Roman Catholicism did not divide Bullingham's sympathies in the same way as protestant nonconformity, but demands to act against it could still have practical inconveniences. The deprived bishop of Bath and Wells, Gilbert Bourne, was committed to the custody of Bullingham in Lincolnshire, but he claimed that he lacked the space to accommodate Bourne in London when attending the parliament of 1566. In 1560 Bullingham had needed a pardon for the escape of prisoners in his custody; whether religious or secular suspects is unclear.

In 1565 Bullingham visited King's College, Cambridge, in response to complaints about the popish tendencies of the provost, Philip Baker. He contented himself with 'admonitions and certain injunctions', such as the removal of Catholic ornaments, and also 'earnestly requested' Baker to give the fellows an account of college property (Cooper, *Annals*, 2.225, 247). This was ineffective, and the fellows next resorted to Grindal at London rather than to their visitor. A commission under Cox, the diocesan, finally displaced Baker in 1570.

Parker named Bullingham in 1568 as one of the translators of the Bishops' Bible, with responsibility for the non-Pauline epistles and the Apocalypse. However, these books were eventually published with the initials H. L.: Hugh Jones, bishop of Llandaff, presumably took over, possibly because Bullingham's Greek was insufficient for such an undertaking.

Bullingham's is one of the instances suggesting that anecdotes about Elizabeth I's hostility to bishops' marriages, and even more to second marriages, may have been taken too seriously. At the end of 1569 or beginning of 1570 he married Elizabeth (*b.* 1535, *d.* in or after 1581), widow of a London mercer, Richard Hill, and daughter of Sir William *Lok, alderman. With her he had a third son, John (*bap.* 1570), but also acquired thirteen stepchildren, at least some of whom came to live with him at Worcester. There is no indication that this second marriage created any problem either over his translation to Worcester or over his reception of the queen there.

Bishop of Worcester On Edwin Sandys's translation to London, Bullingham succeeded him as bishop of Worcester, apparently after James Calfhill had been nominated but removed by death. A *congé d'élire* was issued for Bullingham on 27 November 1570; he received the royal assent on 17 January 1571 and the temporalities on 14 February. The translation was allegedly to ease the ageing prelate, Worcester being a richer diocese, with a nominal income of £1049 17s. 3d., and also smaller and more manageable. Bullingham was detained at first in London by convocation business, subscribing the forty articles and the canons of 1571. He was named in the high commission patent of June 1572, before taking up residence at Worcester later that month.

Bullingham remained on close terms with Parker, who in 1575 bequeathed him a horse called Packington. In August that year the queen visited his country palace of Hartlebury Castle before making a ceremonial progress through the city of Worcester itself. By then Bullingham may have already entered his last illness. In February 1576

he received licence to be absent from parliament and he performed his last institution on 14 April. He died intestate, probably at Hartlebury Castle, four days later. The queen was sent a petition on his family's behalf for financial relief, reckoning his debts at £1224 6s. 8d. and his assets at only £1052 11s. 6d., including plate worth £300 and 'goods and cattell' valued at £486 (PRO, SP 12/108/45–6). Although he should have paid his first fruits within three years of his translation in 1571, the sum of £205 was still outstanding.

Bullingham's apparent poverty might be attributed to many different causes. Sandys's stewardship of the estates during the 1560s is a possible factor, but the petition particularly stresses the burden of debt that had resulted from Bullingham's failure to obtain compensation for dilapidations at Lincoln after 1560. His own 'great howse keeping' (Pearce, 114), particularly in view of Elizabeth's recent visit, was also stressed. He had, moreover, undertaken repairs at the old palace in Worcester, at Hartlebury, and at Grimley, the last a residence unused by his immediate predecessors. Nor, perhaps, had he survived long enough either to capitalize on Worcester's remaining assets or to deploy them judiciously. His successor, John Whitgift, claimed that Bullingham had leased out the grain at his manor of Hallow, near Grimley, for only one quarter of its potential value.

Bullingham and the Elizabethan church Bullingham's burial was registered at Hartlebury on 16 May 1576, but he now lies in the north aisle of Worcester Cathedral, with a monument in which his effigy is curiously cut in two, the middle disappearing behind a slab inscribed:

> Here born, here bishop, buried here,
> A Bullyngham by name and stock,
> A man twise maried in Gode's feare,
> Chief pastor late of Lycolne flock,
> Whom Oxford trained up in youthe,
> Whom Cambridge doctor did create,
> A painful preacher of the truthe,
> He changed this life for happie state.
> (Moore Ede, 106)

His effigy's partial disappearance perhaps encapsulates Bullingham's career: he was a highly competent lawyer who proved a sound, rather than a distinguished, bishop. As a specialist in matters pertaining to canon law he was something of a Janus figure, who attempted loyally to set the fractured bones of what was left of the ancient canon law as it had survived under Henry VIII and Edward VI to meet the requirements of the Elizabethan settlement. For Parker he seems to have fulfilled a utilitarian role while showing signs of religious proclivities more radical than the archbishop's own. He published no theological work, and all that survives of his sermons is a large body of notes by a listener, now preserved in Lambeth Palace Library as MS 739, taken from sermons preached in London probably mainly in 1560 and 1562–3. It appears that he was quite a popular choice for livery companies' feasts (sixteen of them) and burials.

Bullingham's financial position at death may exculpate

him from any suspicion of stripping the bishopric of Worcester for his family's benefit, but betrays hints of extravagance and probably administrative ineptitude. Helped perhaps by the strong Lincoln connections that he seems to have cultivated during the Edwardian period, he had rather established his family in the legal oligarchy of that diocese. He himself had employed his cousin, formerly his mother's ward, Edward Archbold, who married one of his stepdaughters, Elizabeth Hill. His eldest son, Francis, became registrar of Lincoln after his father's death, and was MP for Lincoln (1601) and Boston (1604–11). John Bullingham, the future bishop of Gloucester, whom Nicholas helped to prebends successively at Lincoln and Worcester, may also have been a cousin.

Besides the episcopal finances, the Worcester church courts remained something of a reproach to a legal specialist like Bullingham. If a principal reason for regarding Richard Cheyney as 'one of the least efficient of Elizabethan bishops' (Price, 104) is his failure to check the corrupt practices of his chancellor Thomas Powell, the same criticism applies to Bullingham, who had the doubtful benefit of Powell's services as archdeacon of Worcester, a position from which he was ejected only in 1579.

JULIAN LOCK

Sources Emden, *Oxf.*, 4.83 • J. Strype, *The life and acts of Matthew Parker*, new edn, 3 vols. (1821) • J. Strype, *The history of the life and acts of the most reverend father in God Edmund Grindal*, new edn (1821) • J. Strype, *Annals of the Reformation and establishment of religion … during Queen Elizabeth's happy reign*, new edn, 4 vols. (1824) • *Correspondence of Matthew Parker*, ed. J. Bruce and T. T. Perowne, Parker Society, 42 (1853) • V. J. K. Brook, *A life of Archbishop Parker* (1962) • W. P. Haugaard, *Elizabeth and the English Reformation* (1968) • B. Usher, 'Edward Brocklesby: "the first put out of his living for the surplice"', *From Cranmer to Davidson: a Church of England miscellany*, ed. S. Taylor (1999), 47–68 • Cooper, *Ath. Cantab.*, 1.350–51, 563; 3.74 • C. H. Cooper, *Annals of Cambridge*, 2 (1843) • A. J. Carlson, 'The bishops and the queen: a study of "puritan" episcopal activity in early Elizabethan England, 1558–1566', PhD diss., Princeton University, 1962, 90–95, 102–4, 154, 158–61, 196–7, 234, 256–7, 300 • J. A. Berlatsky, 'The social structure of the Elizabethan episcopate', PhD diss., Northwestern University, 1970 • *JHL*, 1 (1509–77) • E. H. Pearce, *Hartlebury Castle* (1926) • W. R. Buchanan-Dunlop, 'Old Worcester families: Archbold', *Transactions of the Worcestershire Archaeological Society*, new ser., 31 (1954), 8–19 • HoP, *Commons, 1558–1603*, 1.515 • *The autobiography of Sir John Bramston*, ed. [Lord Braybrooke], CS, 32 (1845), 11–12 • M. Bateson, ed., 'A collection of original letters from the bishops to the privy council, 1564', *Camden miscellany, IX*, CS, new ser., 53 (1893) • state papers domestic, Elizabeth I, PRO, SP 12/1/46, 12/46/37, 12/108/45–46 • *CPR, 1549–51; 1558–66; 1569–72* • R. W. Dixon, *History of the Church of England*, 6 (1902) • *Fasti Angl., 1541–1857*, [Lincoln] • *Fasti Angl., 1541–1857*, [Ely] • exchequer, first fruits office, composition books, PRO, E334/3, 4, 7, 8 • exchequer, first fruits office, plea rolls, PRO, E337/1, m. 202 • episcopal registers, Lincs. Arch., Lincoln diocesan archives, Reg. XXVIII–XXVIIIA • Worcester episcopal register, Worcs. RO, BA 2648/10(i) • parish register, Hartlebury, Worcs. RO, 16 May 1576 [burial] • J. B. Wilson, ed., *The parish book of St Helens in Worcester*, 2 vols. (1900), vol. 2, p. 87 • J. Nichols, *The progresses and public processions of Queen Elizabeth*, 2nd edn, 3 vols. (1823), vol. 1, pp. 533–51 • D. MacCulloch and P. Hughes, eds., 'A bailiff's list and chronicle from Worcester', *Antiquaries' Journal*, 75 (1995), 235–53 • C. H. Foster, ed., *Parish registers of St Margaret in the Close of Lincoln, 1538–1837*, Lincoln RS, 2 (1915), 5 • C. W. Foster, ed., *Lincoln episcopal records*, Lincoln RS, 2 (1912) • R. E. G. Cole, ed., *Chapter acts of the cathedral church of St Mary of Lincoln*, 3, Lincoln RS, 15 (1920) • R. B. Walker, 'Lincoln Cathedral in the reign of Queen Elizabeth I', *Journal of Ecclesiastical History*, 11 (1960), 186–201 • C. H. Garrett, *The Marian exiles: a study in the origins of Elizabethan puritanism* (1938) • A. Pettegree, *Marian protestantism: six studies* (1996), 70 • J. Harington, *A briefe view of the state of the Church of England* (1653), 81 • F. O. White, *Lives of the Elizabethan bishops of the Anglican church* (1898) • F. Heal, *Of prelates and princes: a study of the economic and social position of the Tudor episcopate* (1980) • M. Prior, 'Reviled and crucified marriages: the position of Tudor bishops' wives', *Women in English society, 1500–1800*, ed. M. Prior (1985), 118–48 • E. D. Price, 'The administration of the diocese of Gloucester, 1547–1579', BLitt diss., U. Oxf., 1939 • B. F. Westcott, *General view of the history of the English Bible*, rev. W. A. Wright, 3rd edn (1905) • A. W. Pollard, *Records of the English Bible* (1911) • W. M. Ede, *The cathedral church of Christ and the Blessed Virgin Mary of Worcester: its monuments and their stories* [1925], 106–10 • LPL, MS 739

Archives Lincs. Arch., Lincoln diocesan archives, episcopal registers, Reg. XXVIII–XXVIIIA • Worcs. RO, Worcester episcopal register, BA 2648/10(i)

Likenesses funerary monument, Worcester Cathedral; repro. in S. E. Lehmberg, *The reformation of cathedrals* (1988), 291

Wealth at death assets £1052 11s. 6d.; debts £1224 6s. 8d.: PRO, SP 12/108/45

Bulloch, Archibald Stobo (1730–1777), planter and revolutionary politician in America, was born in Charles Town, South Carolina, the son of James Bulloch (1701–1780) clergyman and planter, and Jean Stobo. Archibald studied law and was admitted to the bar before 1758, when he moved to Georgia with his parents. He soon acquired a rice plantation on the Georgia side of the Savannah River across from Purysburg, South Carolina. On 9 October 1764 he married Mary de Veaux; the marriage produced four children: James, Archibald, Jane, and William Ballinger. Bulloch entered the public arena in 1768 when he was elected to the Georgia Commons house of assembly as a delegate from Savannah. Politically and socially he was closely associated with Noble Wimberly Jones (Jones's sister Mary became Bulloch's father's fourth wife in 1779), and he succeeded Jones as speaker in 1771.

With Jones, George Walton, and John Houstoun, Bulloch signed a notice printed in the *Georgia Gazette* on 14 July 1774 inviting Georgians to attend an American patriotic rally at Tondee's Tavern in Savannah, but only a few persons attended. By 15 January 1775 dissatisfaction with parliamentary measures had increased and a Georgia provincial congress that met on that date elected Bulloch, Jones, and John Houstoun to the continental congress. Because not all the Georgia parishes were represented, the delegates declined to attend the congress in Philadelphia, apologizing to congress for Georgia's backwardness in the revolutionary movement.

The Georgia second provincial congress, meeting in July, elected Bulloch president and also named him a delegate to the continental congress. Bulloch took his seat in Philadelphia in September and on 5 November 1775 signed a preliminary draft of a declaration of independence. Bulloch returned to Georgia at a critical time when British warships threatened Savannah. The provincial congress named Bulloch president of the council of safety and left him to deal with the crisis. On 15 February 1776 Bulloch wrote a confidential letter to the South Carolina council of safety appealing for help; he could rely on the loyalty of his own people but needed support from the neighbouring colony. The Carolina council ordered Colonel Stephen Bull to muster the militia in the Beaufort district and march to Savannah. Before the Carolina troops arrived, British warships sailed into the Savannah River and took away fifteen merchant vessels loaded with rice. The incident is referred to as 'the Battle of the Rice-Boats'. On learning that fugitive slaves had gathered on Tybee Island in the expectation of finding freedom with the British, Bull devised a plan of employing friendly American Indians in an attack on the slaves, thus causing animosity between Georgia's American Indians and blacks. Bulloch led the attack on 25 March with a company of Cussita Indians and white men disguised as American Indians. However, the two hundred or so slaves had already gone aboard British vessels. On 31 March the British fleet and the Georgia refugees sailed north with the captured rice.

On 15 April 1776 the Georgia provincial congress adopted a temporary constitution and elected Bulloch president. At the opening of the June session of the new assembly Bulloch appealed for unanimity. When news of the Declaration of Independence reached Georgia on 8 August, Bulloch read the document to an enthusiastic crowd in Savannah.

An attempted invasion of British-controlled Florida was launched on 19 August 1776 during Bulloch's presidency, but failed even to reach Florida. A constitutional convention produced a new Georgia constitution on 5 February 1777. Before elections could be held for a governor, Bulloch died in Savannah, on 22 February 1777, and was buried there at the colonial cemetery. His most important asset was his ability to lead both the radical and conservative factions in the revolutionary movement. 'Georgians!' proclaims the inscription to his monument, 'let the memory of Archibald Bulloch live in your breasts, tell your children of him and let them tell another generation.'

Bulloch was the great-great-grandfather of Theodore Roosevelt and the great-great-great-grandfather of Eleanor Roosevelt.   EDWARD J. CASHIN

Sources Georgia Historical Society, Savannah, Archibald S. Bulloch papers, coll. 3 · E. A. Ford, 'The Bullochs of Georgia', *Georgia Review*, 6 (1952), 319–31 · G. A. Rogers and R. F. Saunders, 'Bulloch, Archibald', *Dictionary of Georgia biography*, 2 vols. (Athens, Georgia, 1983), 1.134–6 · J. F. Cook, *Governors of Georgia* (Huntsville, Alabama, 1979), 24–6 · A. D. Candler, *The revolutionary records of the state of Georgia*, 3 vols. (1908) · R. F. Saunders, 'Bulloch, Archibald', *ANB*
Archives Georgia Historical Society, Savannah, papers
Likenesses attrib. H. Benbridge, group portrait, oils, *c*.1774 (*The Bulloch family*), Georgia Historical Society, Savannah

Bulloch, James Dunwoody (1823–1901), naval officer and merchant, was born near Savannah, Georgia, USA, on 25 June 1823, the son of Major James Stephens Bulloch, a member of the company which owned the pioneer steamship *Savannah*, and his wife, Hester Amarintha. His half-sister Martha married Theodore Roosevelt sen.

James Bulloch joined the US navy as midshipman in 1839 and served in several ships, including the battleship *Delaware*, before attending the Navy School at Philadelphia from 1844 to 1845. The navy provided a few lieutenants to serve in the east coast–California mail steamers

as a means of expanding the pool of steam expertise, and Bulloch was given command of the *Georgia*. In 1853 he retired from the navy and went into the merchant service, first in the California mails, later sailing between New York and the southern ports. On 19 November 1851 he married Elizabeth Euphemia Caskie (*d*. 23 Jan 1854) and in January 1857 he married Mrs Harriott Cross Foster (*d*. 1900), daughter of Brigadier-General Osborne Cross of Maryland. He had five children.

When the American Civil War broke out in 1861 Bulloch resigned, and was commissioned into the Confederate navy and dispatched to England as chief agent. His task was to procure warships, to supplement the hopelessly inadequate fleet—and building capacity—of the South. He naturally based himself in Liverpool, where there were shipyards, good communications with major weapons manufacturers, banking facilities provided by Charles Prioleau, and many Confederate sympathizers in the local business community. By far his most spectacular success was the purchase of the commerce raider *Alabama* (commissioned 1862), which at one stage he had expected to command, but his superiors rightly placed a higher priority on his procurement activities. Under the command of Captain Raphael Semmes *Alabama* was so successful as to affect the overall pattern of the war, and was the focus of American outrage, leading to an arbitration arranged by Gladstone's government of 1868–74.

Bulloch negotiated the construction or purchase of eleven further warships in Britain and France, though Union agents succeeded in having seven of these seized by the British and French governments as breaches of neutrality. Three were ironclad ram steamers with turret guns, of such speed and power that they could conceivably have changed the outcome of the war.

Bulloch did not fall within the terms of the amnesty proclamations, which is perhaps unsurprising as he had probably done more harm to the Union war effort than any other one man. Bulloch was unable to return to the USA but his Liverpool friends remained loyal to him, and he set up in business trading as Bulloch and Robertson, commission merchants, reputedly specializing in cotton. He continued to mix in the upper echelons of local society, and lived in the (then) prestigious Upper Parliament Street. In retirement he moved to a smaller house, at the edge of Sefton Park. His daughter Jessie married Maxwell Hyslop-Maxwell jun., a member of a long-established and highly respected family of North American merchants.

In 1883 Bulloch published a remarkable book entitled *The Secret Service of the Confederate States in Europe*, which extends to over 900 pages, and describes in minute detail the complex technical, financial, legal, and moral issues involved, along with the espionage, and counter-espionage practised by both sides.

Little is known of Bulloch's personal life or qualities. In Liverpool he remained reticent about his past and was said to have 'a distinguished personality, magnetic courtly manners, and was courteous and kind' (*DAB*, 3.258). Theodore Roosevelt jun. visited him three times in Liverpool, and left some descriptions of 'Uncle Jimmy', including the statement that he was 'utterly unable to "get on" in the worldly sense of that phrase' (Roosevelt, 15).

Bulloch died at Maxwell Hyslop-Maxwell's home, 76 Canning Street, Liverpool, on 7 January 1901. He was buried in Smithdown Road cemetery, Liverpool, where his grave is still occasionally visited by historians of the Confederacy.   ADRIAN JARVIS

Sources P. Van Doren Stern, 'Introduction', in J. D. Bulloch, *The secret service of the Confederate states in Europe* (1959) • R. I. Lester, *Confederate finance and purchasing in Great Britain* (1975) • *DAB*, 3.257–8 • P. E. Coletta, 'A selectively annotated bibliography of naval power in the American Civil War', *Civil War History*, 42/1 (March 1996), 32–63 • *Liverpool Daily Post* (8 Jan 1901) • T. Roosevelt, *Theodore Roosevelt: an autobiography* (1913), 15 • *CGPLA Eng. & Wales* (1901) • A. Cook, *The Alabama claims: American politics and Anglo-American relations, 1865–1872* (1975)
Archives Merseyside Maritime Museum, Liverpool, Fraser, Trenholm papers
Likenesses engraving, repro. in Bulloch, *Secret service of the Confederate states in Europe*, frontispiece
Wealth at death £200 2s. 3d.: administration, 31 Jan 1901, *CGPLA Eng. & Wales*

Bulloch, John (1805–1882), brass-finisher and literary scholar, was a native of Aberdeen. For most of his life he worked as a brass-finisher, and lived in very humble circumstances, but he devoted much of his leisure to literary pursuits. He contributed to *The Athenaeum* several articles on decimal coinage, and in 1859 delivered a lecture entitled 'Reminiscences of the past half century', which was later published. The works of Shakespeare were, however, the chief subject of his study; and when W. G. Clark became editor of the Cambridge Shakespeare in 1863, Bulloch suggested a number of textual emendations, which were introduced into the notes of that edition. In 1878 he published by subscription *Studies of the Text of Shakespeare*, in which he displayed a very shrewd capacity for textual criticism. He died in December 1882 in Aberdeen, and was survived by a son, also John, who was the father of the pathologist and bacteriologist William *Bulloch.

                              SIDNEY LEE, *rev.* NILANJANA BANERJI

Sources *The Times* (3 Jan 1883) • *The Athenaeum* (30 Dec 1882), 899 • *The works of William Shakespeare*, another edn, ed. W. G. Clark, W. A. Wright, and others, 9 vols. (1863–6) [preface]

Bulloch, William (1868–1941), bacteriologist and pathologist, was born at Aberdeen on 19 August 1868, the younger son of John Bulloch and his wife, Mary, daughter of Andrew Malcolm, schoolmaster, of Leochel-Cushnie. John Malcolm Bulloch (1867–1938), journalist and genealogist of the house of Gordon, was his elder brother. His father, an engraver and later a businessman, edited *Scottish Notes and Queries* in his spare time and was the son of another John *Bulloch, the author of *Studies of the Text of Shakespeare* (1878).

After early education at Aberdeen grammar school, Bulloch entered Aberdeen University. In 1884 he joined the faculty of arts, but in 1886 he transferred to medicine. He graduated MB CM with highest honours in 1890, winning the Murray medal, and in 1894 he graduated MD with equal distinction and was awarded the Struther gold medal in anatomy. After qualification Bulloch studied pathology for nine months under D. J. Hamilton at Aberdeen and worked as an assistant in private practice. Not liking this latter pursuit, he went to Europe to study in Leipzig, Vienna, Paris, and Copenhagen, where he formed lifelong friendships with the famous pathologists and bacteriologists of his day. Birch-Hirschfeld, Roux, and Salomonsen were his teachers, and he counted among his friends Ehrlich, Koch, Mechnikov, Madsen, and Lord Lister.

On his return to Britain, Bulloch was appointed assistant to Victor Horsley, professor of pathology at University College, London. In July 1895 he was appointed assistant bacteriologist, and later bacteriologist, to the antitoxin laboratories of the British (later Lister) Institute of Preventive Medicine. He became bacteriologist to the London Hospital in 1897, and in 1919 he was elected first Goldsmiths' Company professor of bacteriology. On retirement in 1934, he was appointed consultant bacteriologist to the London Hospital and emeritus professor of London University. In 1913 he was elected FRS, and received an honorary degree from Aberdeen in 1920. Bulloch also held a number of administrative posts. He was an original member of the Medical Research Committee (later Council), served actively on other government committees, and was chairman of the governors of the Lister Institute from 1932 until his death.

Bulloch was a prolific writer and did much in the way of research and teaching. His publications—alone and in collaboration—number well over a hundred. In addition to these he contributed hundreds of anonymous reviews and abstracts to medical periodicals and assisted in the works both of pupils and colleagues, and of the committees on which he served. His research concentrated on serology and immunology. He was the inventor of the Bulloch jar, used for cultivating anaerobic bacteria (1900). He also had an enduring interest in haemophilia, on which he contributed (with Paul Fildes) an important monograph to The Treasury of Human Inheritance (1912), edited by Karl Pearson. His manuscript record of the incidence of this complaint in the royal family was deposited after his death with the Royal Society of Medicine, of which he was an early fellow and honorary librarian. In addition he was an authority on the preparation of catgut for surgical use.

Bulloch also wrote a number of works on medical history and biography, and his Heath Clark lectures on this subject were published as *The History of Bacteriology*, in 1938. It was a work based on a profound study of the sources and personal knowledge of many pioneer bacteriologists. Like all his writings it is characterized by clarity in thought, accuracy in data, simplicity in expression, and the exactitude of its references. Two other historical works were left incomplete and unpublished—a detailed inquiry into the life and works of Spallanzani, and, most importantly, a biographical *Roll of the Fellows of the Royal Society* from its foundation. The manuscript of the latter was acquired by the society after his death.

In 1923 Bulloch married Irene Adelaide, daughter of Alexander Peyman, and widow of Alfred Augustus Baker, a stockbroker. They had no children. In the last years of his life Bulloch was hampered by gradually progressing Parkinson's disease, and he died after an emergency operation in the London Hospital on 11 February 1941. His wife survived him.

In appearance Bulloch was short, thickset, clean-shaven, with dark hair and light-brown eyes. Despite long residence in the capital he never lost his native Doric accent. An informal and helpful man, he had friends in many walks of life all over the world. Lively, humorous, and energetic, yet he took no exercise and played no games; his only hobby was historical research.

CLIFFORD DOBELL, *rev.* CLAIRE E. J. HERRICK

Sources J. C. G. Ledingham and C. Dobell, *Obits. FRS*, 3 (1939–41), 819–52, incl. bibliography · *Journal of Pathology and Bacteriology*, 53 (1941), 297–308 · *BMJ* (1 March 1941), 341–2 · *The Lancet* (22 Feb 1941), 263 · *BMJ* (15 March 1941), 422 · S. Duncan and L. Hill, 'William Bulloch', *Aberdeen University Review*, 28 (1940–41), 119–22 · private information (1959) · personal knowledge (1959)

Archives UCL, letters to Karl Pearson and W. P. Elderton

Likenesses P. Fildes, photograph, *c*.1911 · L. Fildes, oils, 1913, U. Aberdeen · W. Stoneman, photograph, 1917, NPG · photograph, repro. in Ledingham and Dobell, *Obits. FRS*

Wealth at death £13,423 8s. 1d.: resworn probate, 29 April 1941, *CGPLA Eng. & Wales*

Bullock, Christopher (*bap.* 1691?, *d.* 1722), actor and playwright, was the son of the successful actor William *Bullock (*d.* 1742); he may have been the Christopher Bullock, son of William Bullock and his wife, Dennis, who was baptized at St Giles Cripplegate, London, on 5 February 1691, although by that date his father may have been married to his better-documented wife, Margaret. The first recorded mention of him appears on 31 December 1707, when he performed in George Farquhar's *The Recruiting Officer* at the Queen's Theatre, thus beginning what was to be a distinguished but highly abbreviated career. He is also named in a lord chamberlain's listing of performers sworn as members of the royal household on 15 January 1708.

As a performer Bullock attained success in more than three dozen plays across fourteen years. Mainly a comic actor, he performed a variety of roles, from the servant Scrub in Farquhar's *Beaux' Stratagem* to the ostentatious fop Sir Novelty Fashion in Colley Cibber's *Love's Last Shift*, the latter accomplishment leading Giles Jacob to remark in the *Theatrical Register* that Bullock was Cibber's only rival. Perhaps his greatest achievement, however, was his creation of the lively Colonel Fainwell in Susanna Centlivre's *A Bold Stroke for a Wife* (3 February 1718), the memory of which endured for decades.

As a dramatist Bullock created, between February 1715 and October 1718, at least seven verified plays, of which at least two had continuing appeal later in the century. *The Slip*, his first effort, is a farce derived from Thomas Middleton's *A Mad World my Masters*. First performed on 3 February 1715 at the recently reopened Lincoln's Inn Fields Theatre, the play exemplifies Bullock's early and ongoing interest in adaptation. On 24 October of the same year was staged *A Woman's Revenge*, his highly successful conflation of Aphra Behn's *The Revenge* and John Marston's *The Dutch Courtezan*, which John Philip Kemble later drew upon as the basis for his *Trick upon Trick* (1789). On 24 January 1716 appeared *The Cobler of Preston*, derived from Shakespeare's *The Taming of the Shrew*, which was no doubt quickly hurried into production to upstage Charles Johnson's play of the same title that was presented at Drury Lane barely a week later. Not two months had passed when Bullock presented his next effort, and his first play of entirely original design, *The Adventures of Half an Hour* (19 March 1716, Lincoln's Inn Fields), and on 4 December 1716, to conclude his *annus mirabilis*, followed *A Woman is a Riddle*, which owes something to Pedro Calderón de la Barca's *La dama duende*. Bullock's most successful dramatic enterprise, this play was performed from time to time for sixty years, was abridged as an afterpiece in 1776, and served as the foundation of at least two adaptations by 1788.

After *A Woman is a Riddle* Bullock's pace slowed and he wrote only two more known plays. *The Per-Juror* (12 December 1717) attempted to profit from the recent popularity of Colley Cibber's *The Non-Juror*, which had appeared only a week earlier. While Bullock's comedy did not thrive on the stage it warranted at least four published editions in the first month, indicating lively topical appeal. His last known play is based on both James Shirley's and Antony Rivers's tragedies entitled *The Traytor* (11 October 1718). With this final adaptation Bullock apparently exhausted his creative energies, thus concluding a remarkable four-year burst, though in 1720 he was still considered a viable target by the anonymous author of *The Stage Pretenders, or, The Actor Turn'd Poet*, a lively satire of Bullock, Cibber, and several other playwrights.

Bullock also ventured into management for several years. Along with Theophilus Keen he rented from John and Christopher Rich, on 18 September 1717, the sagging Lincoln Inn Fields enterprise. Their efforts were futile and the company struggled to survive, Bullock being unable to pay his taxes on the theatre during 1717; nevertheless on 23 May of that year he married the actress Jane Rogers (*d.* 1739), daughter of Robert Wilks and an actress also named Jane Rogers. The management agreement, originally intended to run for four years, until late 1721, was terminated early in May 1720, due to a falling out between the Riches and Bullock and his wife, thus ending Bullock's brief foray into theatrical administration.

Apparently the victim of consumption Bullock struggled with health problems off and on for about two years before his demise. Reports of his illness first appear in late 1720, and by January 1721 a newspaper notice suggests that he is dangerously ill. The end came on 5 April 1722, 'of a Fistula and a Consumption' (Highfill, Burnim & Langhans, *BDA*); he was buried three days later at Hampstead, thus ending a short but noteworthy career. The Bullocks had at least three children, although nothing is known of their lives. It is said that a portrait in the Garrick Club, once thought to be of Christopher Bullock, is now known to be of his father, William (ibid.); another portrait, purportedly bearing his likeness, is located at the Huntington Library.   WILLIAM J. BURLING

Sources C. A. Prettiman, 'Caldéron, Richard Savage, and Christopher Bullock's *Woman is a riddle*', *Philological Quarterly*, 68 (1989), 25–36 · [G. Jacob], *The poetical register, or, The lives and characters of the English dramatick poets*, 2 vols. (1719–20) · W. J. Burling, *A checklist of new plays and entertainments on the London stage, 1700–1737* (1993) · Highfill, Burnim & Langhans, *BDA* · *The stage pretenders, or, The actor turn'd poet* (1720) · lord chamberlain's papers, 15 Jan 1708, PRO, LC 5/166/211 · chancery documents, 18 Sept 1717, PRO, C 11/1006/22 · chancery documents, 19 Jan 1719, PRO, C 11/1411/37 · affidavit relating to 18 July 1720, PRO, C 107/171 · exhibit in a lawsuit from 1728, PRO, C 11/2661/17 · IGI
Likenesses portrait (of Bullock?), Hunt. L.

Bullock, Sir Christopher Llewellyn (1891–1972), public servant and businessman, was born on 10 November 1891 at Whiston, Northamptonshire, the second child and second son in the family of seven children (one of whom died at birth) of the Revd Llewellyn Christopher Watson Bullock (1866–1936), later rector of Great and Little Wigborough, Essex, and his wife, Cecil Augusta Margaret Isabella, daughter of Edmund Robert Spearman CMG, British consul in Chantilly and formerly secretary of the Public Works Loan Board, and granddaughter of the fifth earl of Orkney. He was educated at Rugby School, where his father was a master, becoming captain of the running eight and gaining a classical scholarship to Trinity College, Cambridge, where he had a remarkable career. He won not only the Abbott and Porson university scholarships in classics, the members' Latin essay prize, and the Browne medals for Latin ode (twice) and Greek epigram, but also the Charles Oldham Shakespeare scholarship and the Whewell scholarship in international law. He was placed in the first division of the first class of the classical tripos in 1913 and was offered a fellowship at Trinity.

It was, however, to the public service that Bullock turned. After taking first place in the open competition for the home and Indian Civil Services in 1914 he chose India. But the First World War intervened before he took up his appointment and he volunteered for service with the rifle brigade. He was seriously wounded at Ypres in 1915 and was mentioned in dispatches; later, seconded to the Royal Flying Corps, he gained his wings first as an observer and then as a pilot. Becoming unfit for flying in 1917, he was appointed to the air staff and, in 1919, became principal private secretary to Winston Churchill, the secretary of state for air. From 1923 to 1930 he served successive secretaries of state in the same capacity and in 1931, at the exceptionally early age of thirty-nine, he was promoted directly to permanent secretary of the Air Ministry and member of the Air Council.

It was at the Air Ministry that Bullock's best work was done. In 1919 the government had decided to establish a permanent independent Royal Air Force and Sir Hugh Trenchard was given the task of creating and building up the new service. Bullock became his right-hand man on the civilian side and Trenchard, when he retired in 1929, recorded his gratitude for Bullock's great contribution during what he called 'the hardest years that I think any

Department could pass through'. For there were forces in Whitehall, particularly in the other service departments and in the Treasury, that were hostile to the young Royal Air Force and its very survival as a separate service was at times in doubt. Bullock fought with partisan ferocity for the interests of his ministry and it was in this testing atmosphere that his administrative temperament was forged.

Later the rising menace of Nazism made the expansion of the RAF a concern of first importance, and Bullock's part was again crucial. Against the pacific temper and financial stringency of the times he strove to awaken public and parliament to the need for strengthening the RAF to meet the dangers ahead. His powerful intellect and superb administrative skills were harnessed unstintingly to the task and he drafted nearly all of the important air staff papers for the cabinet himself. It was during these critical years that decisions were taken in the Air Ministry that were vital to Britain's air defence capability when war finally came. Bullock also made a major contribution during the 1920s and 1930s to developing civil aviation, in particular to the pioneering empire air mail scheme.

Bullock had a strong personality, and once embarked upon a course in which he believed was not easily turned aside. Viscount Templewood thought him 'combative by nature' and elsewhere he was described as 'a fluent talker and not always a patient listener' (Templewood, 51; Stephen Roskill, *The Times*, 30 May 1972). In the bitter interdepartmental battles of the day he conveyed 'a high degree of arrogance' and undoubtedly made enemies (Dean, 89). This told heavily against him when, in 1936, he became the subject of a board of inquiry, appointed by the prime minister, following allegations that he had misused his official position by writing to the chairman of Imperial Airways about the possibility of joining the board of the company should he retire prematurely from the civil service. The approach was made when the Air Ministry was still negotiating with the company about the empire air mail scheme, and a *Times* leader was strongly critical of Bullock. As a result of the inquiry the prime minister approved summary dismissal, though Stanley Baldwin later wrote that, had he known the whole story, he would never have done so. And Bullock's chief, Lord Hankey, wrote in November 1937: 'the more I think of it the more I feel that the punishment did not fit the crime' (Roskill, *Hankey*, 3.360). The injustice done to Bullock was implicitly recognized during the Second World War, when Bullock was invited to resume a permanent secretary's appointment in the civil service, an offer that he declined because of existing commitments in industries connected with vital war work. Public acknowledgement that his dismissal had been mistaken was belatedly made at his memorial service. It was attended by a representative of the prime minister, members of the air force board, and the permanent under-secretary of the Ministry of Defence.

After 1936 Bullock showed great fortitude in developing a range of business interests, becoming a director of a number of well-known companies; he remained active in business until his late seventies. He married, on 18 April 1917, Barbara May, daughter of Henry Lupton, a stuff merchant in Leeds, and they had two sons, both of whom enjoyed successful careers in the public service.

Bullock was appointed OBE in 1919, CBE in 1926, CB in 1929, and KCB in 1932. He died in London on 16 May 1972.

GEOFFREY-LLOYD, rev. MARK POTTLE

Sources personal knowledge (1986) · private information (1986) · *The Times* (19–20 May 1972) · S. W. Roskill, *The Times* (30 May 1972) · *The Times* (16 June 1972) · S. W. Roskill, *Hankey, man of secrets*, 2 (1972) · S. W. Roskill, *Hankey, man of secrets*, 3 (1974) · M. Dean, *The Royal Air Force and two world wars* (1979) · Viscount Templewood, *Empire of the air: the advent of the air age, 1922–1929* (1957) · *CGPLA Eng. & Wales* (1972)
Archives IWM, papers | Bodl. Oxf., corresp. with Lord Monckton · CUL, corresp. with Sir Samuel Hoare · King's Lond., Liddell Hart C., corresp. with Sir B. H. Liddell Hart · NL Wales, corresp. with Thomas Jones
Wealth at death £138,765: probate, 27 June 1972, *CGPLA Eng. & Wales*

Bullock, Sir Ernest (1890–1979), organist and music teacher, was born in Wigan, Lancashire, on 15 September 1890, the youngest child of Thomas Bullock and his wife, Eliza Stout. He had one sister, the eldest of the family, and four brothers, and both his parents died while he was still at school. As a small boy he joined the choir at Wigan parish church, an event that proved decisive by bringing him into the care of E. C. Bairstow, then organist at Wigan. Bairstow recognized the boy's talent and his difficult circumstances, and took him as an articled pupil, providing general education at Wigan grammar school. When Bairstow moved to Leeds parish church in 1906 he took the pupil with him into his own home, and assumed responsibility for his musical education. Bullock received his BMus (Durham) in 1908 and passed the FRCO examination in 1909. Appointed in 1912 to be assistant to S. H. Nicholson at Manchester Cathedral, Bullock soon became known as a promising composer of church music, chamber music, and songs. In 1914 he obtained his DMus (Durham) but it was not until 1919, after four years of distinguished service in France as a captain and adjutant in the King's Own Yorkshire light infantry, that he was able to return to music. A few months as organist at St Michael's College, Tenbury, Worcestershire, prepared him for an important spell from October 1919 to January 1928 as organist at Exeter Cathedral, where, with determination that was considered at times ruthless, he put new life into the music of the cathedral, the diocese, and the region. In 1919 he married Margery, daughter of George Hope Newborn, solicitor, of Epworth, Lincolnshire. They had two sons and a daughter.

When Bullock moved to Westminster Abbey in 1928 he brought similar reforming energy into a reorganization of the daily choral offices and many special occasions, the most spectacular of which was the coronation of George VI on 12 May 1937, for which Bullock composed fanfares and acted as joint musical director. After the bombing in 1940, in which his house (with all his property and papers) was destroyed, the abbey's musical establishment had to be dispersed, and Bullock's career seemed to be in ruins.

In 1941, however, he was appointed to be principal of the Royal Scottish Academy of Music and Drama, a post at that time involving also the Gardiner professorship of music in the University of Glasgow. In his eleven years in Glasgow Bullock made a significant contribution to Scottish music, and he chaired the music committee of the Scottish Arts Council from 1943 to 1950. He was also a member of the music panel of the Arts Council of Great Britain (1945–7).

Bullock returned to London in January 1953 to succeed Sir George Dyson as director of the Royal College of Music, where his skill in dealing with temperamental students and even more temperamental professors was much admired. His own musical influence, moreover, was more far-reaching than was immediately recognized, his classes in improvisation, in particular, being considered as among the finest experiences that the curriculum offered. From 1952 until 1960 he was joint chair of the associated board of the Royal Schools of Music.

Although circumstances did not allow him to devote a major part of his time to composition, Bullock produced throughout his career a steady stream of music, principally for church use. His published output included three evening services, two Te Deums, and a Jubilate, twenty anthems and motets, and a small quantity of organ music and secular songs. His style, derived from Sir C. H. H. Parry and Sir C. V. Stanford, is today regarded as highly conservative, but his music remains effective in the liturgical context for which much of it was intended. In his music, as in his life, Bullock was disciplined, fastidious, and somewhat austere. His friends could rely on absolute loyalty and generosity but realized that there was no welcome for anything frivolous, pretentious, or effusive.

Bullock was appointed CVO in 1937 and was knighted in 1951. In 1955 he was given an honorary LLD at Glasgow University. He was also honorary RAM and president of the Incorporated Society of Musicians (1947) and of the Royal College of Organists (1951–2). After retirement from the Royal College of Music in 1960 he settled at Welby Cottage in Long Crendon, Buckinghamshire, where he died on 23 May 1979. His wife, a devoted companion for sixty years, survived him by only a few months.

THOMAS ARMSTRONG, rev. MERVYN COOKE

Sources M. Turner, 'Bullock, Ernest', *New Grove* · L. Duck, 'Bullock, Ernest', *Die Musik in Geschichte und Gegenwart*, ed. F. Blume, 17 vols., suppl. (1973), 1189 · H. C. Colles and J. Cruft, *The Royal College of Music: a centenary record, 1883–1983* (1982) · *Debrett's Peerage* (1961) · H. Foss, 'Salute to Ernest Bullock', *Music Teacher*, 30 (1951), 346 · G. Baker, 'Sir Ernest Bullock', *Music Teacher*, 36 (1957), 37 · *The Times* (16 Nov 1979)
Archives Royal College of Music, London | SOUND BL NSA, performance recordings
Likenesses J. Ward, portrait, 1960, Royal College of Music, London
Wealth at death £18,841: probate, 11 July 1979, *CGPLA Eng. & Wales*

Bullock, George (1520/21–1572), theologian, was probably born at Newcastle upon Tyne. He studied at Cambridge

(BA, 1538; MA, 1541; BTh, 1554; DTh, 1557) and became a fellow of St John's College by 1538. (There is no clear evidence to support earlier conjecture that he had been educated at Eton College.) As a fellow he inclined to the conservative side in religion, and in 1542 was one of the 'appellants' who challenged the governance of the master, John Taylor, in a *cause célèbre* which was in effect a power struggle between evangelicals and conservatives for the control and future of the college. The conservatives did not win the day, and from that time more and more of them left the college. But Bullock, like Alban Langdale, stayed on. He is mentioned once in the correspondence of Roger Ascham (another fellow of St John's, of evangelical beliefs), but with no particular marks of affection or esteem. He served as proctor in the academic year 1549–50, and appeared as a witness at the trial of Bishop Stephen Gardiner early in 1551, when he was recorded as thirty years old. Shortly after this he found he could no longer assent to the ever more radical changes in religion, and fled the country, taking refuge for two years at the abbey of Ninove in the southern Netherlands, and then making his way to Louvain, where he matriculated in the university in December 1552.

Bullock returned home after the accession of Mary Tudor, and enjoyed a considerable degree of royal favour throughout her reign. Almost at once she presented him to the rectory of Great Mongeham in Kent (18 November 1553) and soon afterwards to a canonry at Durham (1 May 1554). His ambitions seem to have been scholarly, for he returned to Cambridge, where he took the degree of BTh in 1554, and, on 12 May was elected master of St John's, apparently by a unanimous vote (by this time most of the evangelicals would have fled) but probably also at the instigation of the queen. During Bullock's mastership the college set aside the statutes promulgated for it by Henry VIII in the 1540s, reverting to the final recension of the statutes sanctioned by Bishop John Fisher, dating from 1530. On 20 December 1554 the queen presented him to the vicarage of St Sepulchre in London. In 1556 he resigned this post as the queen had presented him to the rectory of Much Munden, Hertfordshire, on 9 September. He signed the Roman Catholic articles of religion which were promulgated for members of Cambridge University in 1555. During the visitation of the university by Cardinal Pole's delegates, he was one of those examined to substantiate the posthumous charges of heresy against Bucer and Fagius, in proceedings that culminated in the exhumation and burning of their remains on 6 February 1557. Later that year he was given a grace to proceed DTh, although in June 1558 and again in January 1559 he was granted leave to defer his doctoral disputation on grounds of illness. This did not prevent him from taking office as Lady Margaret professor of divinity at Michaelmas 1558.

Bullock's fortunes were reversed upon the accession of Queen Elizabeth and the consequent return to a protestant religious settlement. Although he was still master of St John's on 28 March 1559, he was on borrowed time. He refused to take the oath to the royal supremacy during the visitations of that year, and was as a result deprived of all his ecclesiastical and academic preferments. He was at Durham for the visitation in September 1559, when he refused the royal supremacy with the defiant assertion that 'the bishop of Rome hath and ought to have the jurisdiction ecclesiasticall within this realme' and that 'the sea of that bishope was the sea Apostolicke' (Kitching, 25). In proceedings on 25–6 September he was deprived of his canonry there in favour of John Rudd, whom he had himself displaced back in 1554. He left England for the second time, and, in his own words 'at sea, while fleeing the pestilent infection of heresy and heretics, was taken prisoner and despoiled by pirates' (Bullock, sig. +3r). Bullock landed in France and proceeded to Paris, whence he was invited once more by his old friend the abbot, Jean de Avene, to take refuge in the monastery at Ninove in the Netherlands.

Bullock stayed there about eight years before moving to Antwerp in the Netherlands, probably for the sake of seeing his life's work, the *Oeconomia methodica concordantiarum scripturae sacrae*, a massive biblical concordance, through the press. He registered once more at the University of Louvain on 9 September 1568. In his dedication of the work to Pope Gregory XIII he speaks of it as a project of many years' standing, and twice interrupted by exile. The famous printer Christopher Plantin took this immense, and immensely expensive, task as a prestige project to rival the achievements of the Estienne press of Paris or the printers of Basel. Bullock speaks of having experienced further but unspecified troubles at the hands of heretics in both France and the Netherlands, which may go some way to explain the gap between the licensing of his book in 1567 and its eventual appearance at Antwerp in 1572. In the meantime his patron, the abbot of Ninove, died, so that the second dedication of the work was to his successor, Michael Malenus. Bullock migrated to the monastery of St Michael in Antwerp, serving as the divinity lecturer. He died in October or November 1572, a few months after the publication of his book, and was buried at the monastery of St Michael. Plantin covered Bullock's debt in a complex financial arrangement with Bullock's heirs and the abbey of Ninove.   RICHARD REX

Sources W. G. Searle, ed., *Grace book Γ* (1908) • J. Venn, ed., *Grace book Δ* (1910) • *CPR, 1553–7* • G. Bullock, *Oeconomia methodica concordantiarum scripturae sacrae* (Antwerp, 1572) • J. Foxe, *Acts and monuments*, ed. G. H. Townsend, 8 vols. (1843–9), vol. 6, pp. 225–6 • C. J. Kitching, ed., *The royal visitation of 1559: act book for the northern province*, SurtS, 187 (1975) • *Matricule de l'Université de Louvain*, 4, pp. 463, 744 • BL, Cole MS 42 • BL, Add. MS 5863 • T. F. Knox and others, eds., *The first and second diaries of the English College, Douay* (1878) • *Rogeri Ascham epistolarum, libri quatuor*, ed. W. Elstob (1703) • Cooper, *Ath. Cantab.*, 1.429 • L. Voet, ed., *The Plantin Press (1555–1589): a bibliography of the works printed and published by Christopher Plantin at Antwerp and Leiden*, 6 vols. (Amsterdam, 1980–83)

Bullock, George (1782/3–1818), sculptor and cabinet-maker, was one of at least two sons of William Bullock and Elizabeth, *née* Smallwood, the owners of a travelling waxworks. His brother, William *Bullock, became an artist, naturalist, explorer, and museum proprietor. Nothing is known of Bullock's early life, but by March 1797 'Mrs Bullock and Son' were conducting modelling and drawing lessons at their 'Modelling and Statuary Warehouse' at 29 Bull Street, Birmingham.

On 16 September 1799 Bullock advertised as a 'modeller in rice paste' at 12 Ann Street, Birmingham. He remained in Birmingham until 1801. His brother William, who had started a 'cabinet of curiosities' in Birmingham in 1800, moved to Liverpool in 1801 and opened a museum. George moved to Liverpool and produced his first documented work, a wax portrait relief of Henry Blundell of Ince, the connoisseur and sculpture collector. This is signed 'G. Bullock 1801'. Bullock worked as a sculptor, showing six busts at the Royal Academy in London in 1804. In 1804–5 he was in partnership with William Stoakes as general furnishers and marble workers and in 1809–10 with the architect J. M. Gandy as 'architects, modellers, sculptors, marble masons, cabinet-makers and upholsterers' (Wainwright, *George Bullock*, 144).

By 1806 Bullock had purchased 'some marble quarries containing two beds of rocks, the one resembling, in colour and effect, the Oriental porphyry, and the other the *verd antique*'. This was on the Isle of Anglesey and Bullock, using the ancient Welsh name as a clever marketing ploy, began to sell his 'Mona marble'. At this time of war continental marbles were hard to obtain and his chimney pieces and marble tops for furniture sold very well. Capitalizing on this patriotic British theme he soon manufactured furniture made of native woods and decorated with elaborate brass inlay based upon native plants, depicting hops, for instance, instead of grapes. He provided the furniture and marble fittings for a number of houses, including Cholmondeley Castle in Cheshire, Storrs Hall in Westmorland, and Hafod in Wales.

In 1809 William Bullock moved to London and in 1812 George sold up and joined him at the Egyptian Hall in Piccadilly. In 1813 he formed a partnership with Charles Fraser, a colonel in the East India Company's service, as 'upholder, cabinet-maker and marble mason' (Levy, 146). This probably brought the injection of capital needed to establish extensive cabinet-making and marble-working workshops. They leased a grand house at 4 Tenterden Street, just off Hanover Square, the garden of which ran north and contained the workshops which fronted on to Oxford Street.

The furniture which Bullock manufactured (and unusually for a cabinet-maker also largely designed) was stylistically in advance of any then being made. His firm expanded, supplying Sir Walter Scott, Sir Geoffrey Webster, the dukes of Atholl and Buccleuch, and the marquess of Abercorn. His most famous commission was to supply all the furniture and furnishings for the house constructed for Napoleon on St Helena.

Strikingly handsome with an artistic and very engaging personality, Bullock entertained fashionable London at Tenterden Street. He was perhaps married twice, for on 29 March 1799 a George Bullock was married to Elizabeth Mansell, a pawnbroker's widow in Birmingham. At his death he had been married for at least nine years to a wife called Margaret. He died at home in Tenterden Street on 1 May 1818, and was buried at St George's, Hanover Square, where the burial register notes that he was aged thirty-five.   CLIVE WAINWRIGHT, *rev.*

Sources C. Wainwright, *George Bullock: cabinet maker* (1988) [exhibition catalogue, London, 24 Feb–19 March and Liverpool 21 Feb–26 March, 1988] · M. Levy, 'George Bullock's partnership with Charles Fraser, 1813–18, and the stock-in-trade sale, 1819', *Furniture History*, 25 (1989), 145–213 · G. Beard and C. Gilbert, eds., *Dictionary of English furniture makers, 1660–1840* (1986) · A. Chuplin, *A St. Helena who's who* (1919)

Bullock, Henry (*d.* 1526), humanist scholar, entered the University of Cambridge about the year 1500. His family background is unknown. Fuller believed that he was 'most probably' born in Berkshire, 'where his ancient name appears in a worshipful estate' (Fuller, 95). The archives of Queens' College, Cambridge, however, describe him as originating from the diocese of Coventry and Lichfield. He graduated BA in 1504, was admitted a fellow of Queens' in 1506, and incepted MA the following year. Between 1510 and 1513 he held the university lectureship in mathematics. Having resigned his fellowship in 1513, perhaps in order to pursue further study abroad, he was re-elected two years later. In 1514–15 he was chosen to be one of the university preachers. He was admitted a bachelor of theology in 1516–17, and during that session delivered lectures on St Matthew's gospel. He received the doctorate in theology in 1519–20. Finally in 1524–5 he was vice-chancellor of the university.

Bullock, whose name was Latinized by his fellow humanists as Bovillus, became one of the closest English friends of Desiderius Erasmus. The two men may have met for the first time in 1506, when Erasmus is said to have lodged at Queens', probably on the occasion of a visit to Cambridge by Henry VII. In 1511 Erasmus was persuaded to take up the offer of a lectureship in Greek at Cambridge, and Bullock took charge of the arrangements for his arrival. Through his attendance at Erasmus's lectures Bullock made rapid progress in Greek studies: in a letter of May 1512 Erasmus states that Bullock 'is learning Greek assiduously' ('Bovillus gnaviter Graecatur'; *Opus epistolarum*, ep. 262, line 9). When Erasmus issued his edition of the New Testament in 1516 Bullock wrote to him expressing his welcome for the publication. Erasmus, aware that many theologians were opposed to his project, used his reply to mount an elaborate defence of the critical approach to biblical scholarship. At the same time he took the example of the changes in the teaching curriculum of Cambridge during the previous thirty years, including the introduction of Greek studies, as a paradigm of the advances in learning that humanism had brought about. The following year Bullock informed Erasmus that he had made copious use of the latter's annotations when lecturing on St Matthew. The last known contacts between the two men occurred during 1518, when Erasmus wrote three letters, of successively decreasing length, to his Cambridge friend. Thereafter no further correspondence between them is extant.

Bullock was instrumental in establishing the short-lived printing press run by John Siberch at Cambridge during the early 1520s. He was one of the four guarantors of a loan of £20 made to Siberch by the university. The first two works printed by Siberch were a Latin oration by Bullock, delivered on the occasion of a visit to Cambridge by Cardinal Wolsey in October 1520, and Bullock's Latin version of the work by Lucian on snakes whose bite induces raging thirst (*Peri dipsadōn*).

Bullock appears to have been an opponent of Luther. He is said to have written a work against Luther's *De captivitate Babylonica* (having been compelled to do so by Wolsey, according to Bale), and he was one of the commissioners who supervised the burning of Luther's books in front of St Paul's Cathedral in London on 12 May 1521. He became one of Wolsey's chaplains, and in April 1523 was appointed rector of St Martin Ludgate. His health may never have been robust: he fell gravely ill during the spring of 1517, and mentioned in a letter to Erasmus the virtual loss of the sight of one eye. He made his will on 24 May 1526, and died before 4 July. After his death twenty-four of his books were purchased by Queens' College.   S. F. RYLE

Sources Emden, *Cam.*, 105 · *Opus epistolarum Des. Erasmi Roterodami*, ed. P. S. Allen, 1–3 (1906–13) · P. G. Bietenholz and T. B. Deutscher, eds., *Contemporaries of Erasmus: a biographical register*, 1 (1985), 220 · *DNB* · Bale, *Cat.*, 1.707 · Fuller, *Worthies* (1662), 1.95 · D. R. Leader, *A history of the University of Cambridge*, 1: *The university to 1546*, ed. C. N. L. Brooke and others (1988), 295–7 · E. P. Goldschmidt, *The first Cambridge press in its European setting* (1955), 2–4, 69–71 · D. F. S. Thomson and H. C. Porter, *Erasmus and Cambridge* (1963), 218 · P. L. Rose, 'Erasmians and mathematicians at Cambridge in the early sixteenth century', *Sixteenth Century Journal*, 8 (1977), 47–59 · A. Tilley, 'Greek studies in England in the early sixteenth century [pt 1]', *EngHR*, 53 (1938), 221–39 · G. Hennessy, *Novum repertorium ecclesiasticum parochiale Londinense, or, London diocesan clergy succession from the earliest time to the year 1898* (1898)
Wealth at death no value given: will, 1526

Bullock, Shan Fadh [*formerly* John William Bullock] (1865–1935), novelist, was born on 17 May 1865 on the island of Inisherk on Lough Erne, part of the Crom Castle demesne, near Newtownbutler, in south-eastern co. Fermanagh, the son of Thomas Bullock (1840–1917) and Mary Wheery. He was the eldest of eleven children; eight survived to adulthood. Bullock experienced a strict evangelical protestant upbringing, which despised fiction as lies. His father was steward to the earl of Erne and a tenant farmer with 200 acres at Killynick, on the shore of Lough Erne; as a JP and auctioneer he was a man of some status locally. Bullock's tense relationship with his father shaped his life; he admired the old man's strength and determination and used his memories of local events, but resented his harsh authority over wife and children (including severe corporal punishment into his son's late teens). Most of Bullock's siblings emigrated (in some cases as a result of quarrels with their father); two brothers emigrated to America and another to South Africa, while a sister became a journalist in Australia.

Bullock was educated at the local Church of Ireland national school and at Farra College, Westmeath, a small protestant school originally founded as an agricultural college. His experiences there were fictionalized in *The Cubs* (1906). He failed a Trinity College, Dublin, scholarship

examination, and after a year caretaking on his father's farm went to London in 1883 as a civil service clerk in Somerset House. His father openly expressed contempt for this decision, calling townsmen weaklings and wage slaves; at some level Bullock agreed. At a later stage he transferred to the office of the public trustee, where he remained until his retirement.

In London Bullock went through a period of rebellion. He adopted the Gaelic Shan Fadh ('Long John'—Bullock was extremely tall and thin) instead of his baptismal names, John William; his father refused to acknowledge the change. Bullock went through an excruciating period of religious doubt, and was saved from despair by his marriage on 14 March 1889 to Emma (1858/9–1922), daughter of Henry Mitchell, clerk, and by the writings of Matthew Arnold, which led him back to broad-church Anglicanism. He remained active in the church for the rest of his life; in retirement he served as a churchwarden and edited a parish magazine, but his final religious position was mildly pantheistic, possibly influenced by the poet A. E. (George Russell).

The Bullocks had two children, Norah and Sydney. Bullock supplemented his salary with journalism, and in 1893 published his first book, *The Awkward Squads*. Most of Bullock's novels are set in the co. Fermanagh–co. Cavan borderland, drawing on family tradition and memories of his youth. Neither Dublin nor Belfast, nor even the county town of Enniskillen, feature in his work. His territory, overshadowed by 'My Lord the mountain' (Slíab Rushen, south co. Fermanagh) extends from Lisnaskea, co. Fermanagh ('Lismahee') to the market towns of 'Bunn' (Belturbet, co. Cavan) and 'Glann' (Cavan Town), with occasional visits to the seaside resort of Bundoran, co. Donegal ('Kyle') which had been opened up to rural holidaymakers by the railway. His characters are mostly Catholic and protestant small farmers poorer than his own family, though *The Squireen* (1903) depicts a big farmer with aristocratic pretensions. Landlords are glimpsed only in passing. His late memoir of childhood and upbringing, *After Sixty Years* (1931), describes a big house in the 1870s and 1880s, just before the final decline of Irish landlordism, seen from the community of estate workers which surrounded and serviced it.

Beside Thrasna River (1895), a semi-fictionalized account of his experiences caretaking at Killynick, co. Fermanagh, is his best regarded early work. The story collection *Irish Pastorals* (1900) is notable for descriptions of field labour. Subsequent Fermanagh novels have more highly developed plots, often focusing on a central character whose alienation from the community is viewed ambivalently, such as the successful returned emigrant *Dan the Dollar* (1905) and the protestant soldier of fortune who joins a nationalist uprising against his own community in the near future Ireland of *The Red Leaguers* (1904). Bullock also wrote three novels set in London, notably *Robert Thorne* (1907), a naturalistic account of a civil service clerk.

Bullock moved in London literary circles (he served on the Society of Authors' cricket team and made the acquaintance of J. M. Barrie and Thomas Hardy) but was never a full-time writer. His novels are very self-conscious about their inability to represent adequately the society they describe; he often portrays writers as irresponsible fantasists. His books were generally well reviewed but did not sell; he complained the Irish did not read novels, while the English were interested only in novels which confirmed preconceived views of Ireland. He later experimented with drama; two (unpublished) plays were performed by the Ulster Literary Theatre.

Bullock was emotionally attracted to 'the ragged Catholic' and criticized many aspects of Ulster protestantism (including the Orange order), but distrusted Irish nationalism as primitive and oppressive. (One story in *The Awkward Squads* gives a searing account of a harmless eccentric being driven mad by boycotting and intimidation.) His political views were Liberal Imperialist—radical in British terms, supporting the Liberals on most issues but opposed to home rule because he did not trust Irish party professions of loyalty to the crown. He admired the co-operative pioneer and Unionist politician Sir Horace Plunkett, and did some publicity work for him. Plunkett chose Bullock as official biographer of Thomas Andrews, designer of the *Titanic* (*Thomas Andrews, Shipbuilder*, 1912), and arranged for him to complete Emily Lawless's unfinished historical novel *The Race of Castlebar* (1913). After 1910 Bullock, like Plunkett, saw home rule as inevitable and opposed partition, believing Unionists should seek safeguards within an all Ireland settlement.

Bullock initially welcomed the First World War and John Redmond's support of the British war effort. His son, Sydney, an adventurous young man who spent some time as a cowboy in the United States before training as an engineer, served throughout the war in the Army Service Corps; in 1916 Bullock published anonymously a short account of his son's life and enlistment, *The Making of a Soldier*. In 1917–18 Bullock served on the secretariat of the unsuccessful Irish Convention, chaired by Plunkett, which tried to produce a compromise between Unionists and moderate nationalists. He was appointed MBE for this work.

Bullock was distressed by the post-war situation in Ireland and Britain (his son was unemployed after demobilization, his daughter was sacked to make way for ex-servicemen) and by the death of his wife in 1922, which inspired a small book of verse, *Mors et vita* (1923). This gloom underlies his last and best novel, *The Loughsiders* (1924), a bleak story about a farmer's manoeuvres to obtain his neighbour's land. He spent his last years in retirement in Surrey, brooding over his literary eclipse, watching his grandchildren, and editing a parish magazine. In 1931 he published his last book, *After Sixty Years*. In 1933 he was elected to the Irish Academy of Letters. He died on 27 February 1935 at Sutton and Cheam Hospital, Sutton, Surrey, after a long illness.

An undervalued writer, Bullock's subtle observations of life in rural Fermanagh never attracted the attention they deserve. He is now virtually forgotten outside Ireland, where he is seen as a founder of an Ulster regionalist literary tradition influenced by Hardy and including writers like Sam Hanna Bell and Michael MacLaverty.

PATRICK MAUME

Sources corresp. between Bullock and Sir Horace Plunkett, Plunkett Foundation, Long Hanborough, Oxfordshire • Queen's University of Belfast Library, Shan Bullock MSS • P. Maume, 'Ulstermen of letters', *Unionism in Ireland*, ed. R. English and G. Walker (1996), 63–80 • R. Greacen, 'Shan F. Bullock: laureate of Lough Erne', *Éire–Ireland*, 14/4 (1979), 109–24 • misc. Shan Bullock material, Fermanagh County Library, Enniskillen • N. Rodgers, 'Shan Bullock: his life and work', PhD diss., Queen's University of Belfast, 1983 • P. Maume, 'The papish minister: Shan Bullock, John Haughton Steele, and the literary portrayal of the nineteenth-century clergyman', *Ireland in the nineteenth century: regional identity*, ed. G. Hooper and L. Litvack (2000) • J. W. Foster, *Forces and themes in Ulster fiction* (1974) • B. Kiely, *Modern Irish fiction* (1950) • private information (2004) [Joan Bullock] • P. Maume, 'The margins of subsistence: labour and gender in the writings of Shan Bullock', *New Hibernia Review*, 2/4 (winter 1998), 133–46 • *CGPLA Eng. & Wales* (1935) • b. cert. • m. cert. • d. cert. • J. Darlington, ed., *The dilemma of John Haughton Steele* (1933), 48–51

Archives Fermanagh County Library, misc. material • Queen's University, Belfast, corresp. and literary MSS | Plunkett Foundation, Long Hanborough, Oxfordshire, corresp. with Sir Horace Plunkett

Likenesses D. O'Brien, oils, 1923, Queen's University, Belfast • photographs, Queen's University, Belfast • photographs, priv. coll.

Wealth at death £6674 2s. 9d.: probate, 9 May 1935, *CGPLA Eng. & Wales*

Bullock, William (d. 1342/3), administrator, is of unknown origins, and his early career is equally obscure. He is simply described in the sources as *capellanus* or *presbyterus* ('chaplain' or 'priest'), but his abilities seem to have been administrative and military. He first appears, probably at the end of 1333, as chamberlain to Edward Balliol, claimant to the Scottish throne. At this point Balliol, with English support, was trying to set up the basis of an administration, in which the chamberlain was, in Scottish practice, the principal financial official. Bullock, however, was also given charge of the royal castle of Cupar in Fife—as keeper he received wages from the English exchequer at latest from early 1336—and custody of the castle of St Andrews, which belonged to the bishopric, then vacant. In 1337 he successfully defended Cupar Castle against Sir Andrew Murray, the guardian for the young David II, though Murray was able to recover St Andrews Castle.

Scottish resistance to Balliol was growing and by 1339 his prospects must have looked slim. Probably in the summer of that year Bullock was approached by William Douglas, later known as Douglas of Liddesdale, who had come back from France to strengthen the siege of Perth, one of the few places remaining in the hands of an English or pro-English garrison. Douglas persuaded Bullock to transfer his allegiance and Cupar Castle to David II, in return, it is said, for 'a large reward in lands and possessions' (Bower, 7.141). From then on Bullock seems to have been an adherent of this William Douglas. The English government apparently did not discover Bullock's desertion for some time, since an advance payment on his wages for the next year was still being recorded in December 1339. At the siege of Perth he is said to have 'offered useful advice and brought appropriate help to the besiegers' (*Johannis de Fordun Chronica*, 364), particularly in suggesting moving their protective shelters closer to the walls to cover them from attack by crossbowmen. In 1341 he is credited with assisting in the cunningly executed seizure of Edinburgh Castle.

Bullock appears as chamberlain to David II from 22 May 1341, just before the king's return from France. His predecessor's account, covering the period 1334–8, showed an accumulated deficit of almost £2600. Bullock's first account, which he presented in 1342, struck an exact balance, after a number of complex allowances. This was mainly the result of a resumption of regular and efficient government, which points to Bullock's ability as a civil servant. He was clearly expert in balancing accounts. The fourteenth-century chronicler John Fordun describes him as 'outstanding among his contemporaries in prudence and in eloquence in his native tongue ... and famous for his experienced and penetrating counsel' (*Johannis de Fordun Chronica*, 364). But however much the turncoat's skill and advice were used, he was evidently not trusted. His wealth was envied, and apparently about the summer of 1342 he was accused of treason, though no details of the charges or names of the accusers are known. It is possible that his downfall was caused by a struggle for border lordship and engineered in retaliation for William Douglas's recent killing of Alexander Ramsay of Dalhousie. Bullock was arrested and imprisoned in a place called 'Malimoram', believed to be Mamore in Lochaber; he died 'of hunger and cold' soon after (Bower, 7.157).

BRUCE WEBSTER

Sources *Johannis de Fordun Chronica gentis Scotorum / John of Fordun's Chronicle of the Scottish nation*, ed. W. F. Skene, trans. F. J. H. Skene, 1 (1871), 364–5 · Andrew of Wyntoun, *The orygynale cronykil of Scotland*, [rev. edn], 3, ed. D. Laing (1879), 436, 451–2, 457–8 · W. Bower, *Scotichronicon*, ed. D. E. R. Watt and others, new edn, 9 vols. (1987–98), vol. 7, pp. 96–103, 140–43, 154–7 · R. Nicholson, *Scotland: the later middle ages* (1974), vol. 2 of *The Edinburgh history of Scotland*, ed. G. Donaldson (1965–75); repr. (1989), 138–41 · B. Webster, 'Scotland without a king, 1329–1341', *Medieval Scotland: crown, lordship and community: essays presented to G. W. S. Barrow*, ed. A. Grant and K. J. Stringer (1993), 223–38, esp. 230, 233, 238 · CDS, vol. 3, nos. 240, 251, 339 · G. Burnett and others, eds., *The exchequer rolls of Scotland*, 1 (1878), 499–574

Bullock, William (*b.* in or before **1667**, *d.* **1742**), actor, was probably from Yorkshire. Nothing is known of his parents, although a number of *The Spectator* by Richard Steele, who knew him personally, includes a letter asserting that Bullock was descended from Gabriel Bullock and Margaret Clark (17 March 1712). From his last benefit, on 6 January 1739, his birth date can be approximated, for the playbill carries a message from him:

> Bullock hopes his great age, upwards of threescore and twelve, will plead his excuse, that he cannot pay his duty to his acquaintance and friends, whose good nature may engage them to assist him in this decline of life, in order to make the remainder of his days easy and comfortable.

In fact, Thomas Davies says that he saw Bullock act his

William Bullock (*b.* in or before 1667, *d.* 1742), by Thomas Johnson, *c.*1710–20

part in this benefit—Dominic in *The Spanish Fryar*—when he was 'above eighty' (Davies, 3.463). Bullock and his wife, Margaret (*d.* 1729), had four children, Christopher *Bullock, Hildebrand, Henrietta Maria, and William, all of whom became actors and none of whose birth dates are certain.

Thomas Davies described Bullock as 'an actor of great glee and much comic vivacity ... in his person large, with a lively countenance' (Davies, 3.463). Addison commented on 'the Height and Gracefulness of his Person' (*The Spectator*, 6 Nov 1712), and he was reputed to be modest and hardworking. Steele remarked that he had 'much Wit and Ingenuity' along with his 'Talent of looking like a Fool' (*The Tatler*, 26 April 1709).

One of the very useful members of a theatre company who could play a variety of supporting roles and had some crowd-pleasing specialities, Bullock began his London acting career with Christopher Rich at Drury Lane in 1695 when he signed a contract guaranteeing him £1 per week. Described by knowledgeable theatre people as a master comedian to be ranked with James Nokes, William Pinkethman, and John Quick, he played famous ethnic parts such as Teague in Shadwell's *The Lancashire Witches* and Sauney in John Lacy's *Sauney the Scot*, and a series of fops, country innocents newly arrived in London, and parts that played on humours, such as Hothead in John Crowne's *Sir Courtly Nice* and Sir Amorous La Foole in Ben Jonson's *The Silent Woman* (*Epicene*). Towards the end of his career he played First Gravedigger in *Hamlet* and the Host in *Merry Wives of Windsor*. He was particularly famous for taking beatings and performing in what became formulaic comic scenes with Pinkethman. As Steele wrote:

> I cannot indeed sufficiently admire his Way of bearing a Beating, as he does in [Epsom Wells], and that with such a Natural Air and Propriety of Folly, that one cannot help wishing the Whip in one's own Hand: so richly does he seem to deserve his Chastisement. Skillful Actors think it a very peculiar Happiness to play in a Scene with such as Top their Parts. Therefore I cannot but say, when the Judgment of any good Author directs him to write a Beating for Mr. Bullock from Mr. William Pinkethman, or for Mr William Pinkethman from Mr. Bullock, those excellent Players seem to be in their most shining Circumstances. (*The Tatler*, 25 April 1709)

Steele's *Constant Couple* and *Tender Husband* include such scenes. In the latter Bullock, in one of his country parts, as Sir Harry Gubbin, says, 'My Business in Town is to dispose of an Hundred Head of Cattle, and my Son' (I.ii), and he and Pinkethman as his son Humphrey exchange farcical blows. In *The Constant Couple*, the roles had been reversed, with Pinkethman as the elder brother, an apprentice setting up for a beau, to Bullock as the brother educated in the country. Both Bullock and Pinkethman seem to have been inclined to ad lib, and the press could be hard on them for daring to 'mend a noble Play of *Shakspear* or *Johnson*' (*The Spectator*, 18 Nov 1712). Many playwrights wrote parts for Bullock, as George Farquhar did with the character Bullock in *The Recruiting Officer*. He also frequently played citizens, senators, innkeepers, and members of crowds. Two of his leading roles were the title parts in Dryden's *The Spanish Fryar* and D'Urfey's *The Fond Husband*, and he was a very successful Falstaff in *1 Henry IV*.

Bullock's first recorded performance was in September 1695, as the Landlady in Thomas Scott's *Mock Marriage*. Throughout his career he played what are known as transvestite parts, and many were written for him. As Sue Frowzy in John Dennis's *A Plot and No Plot* (1697) and Kate Matchlock in Richard Steele's *The Funeral* (1701) he played the 'campaigning whore', a woman who followed a company of English soldiers on the continent, 'marrying' a succession of them. In 1702 Bullock was tried and acquitted with the most prominent members of the Drury Lane company for taking part in performances of *Volpone*, *Sir Courtly Nice*, and Thomas Baker's *The Humour of the Age*, which the Society for the Reformation of Manners had complained against as containing 'Immoral Expressions'. Exploiting Bullock's now-proven skill in such roles and striking a blow at Jeremy Collier and the society, George Farquhar wrote for him the part of Mrs Midnight, the bawd and midwife in *Twin Rivals* (the character was Mrs Mandrake at Lincoln's Inn Fields performances, and some modern critics use that name). As Peter Holland has written, Mrs Midnight 'perverts her society; she is the perfect image of its confusion of roles on sex, just as Young Wou'dbe perverts its rules of primogeniture' (Holland, 90). Most of his transvestite parts were, of course, in the tradition that stretches from Nokes through Samuel Foote, where the characters were old, dowdy, or even misshapen and the objects of jokes and tricks, not effectors of active evil.

In 1703 Bullock, Pinkethman, and Thomas Simpson opened a booth at Bartholomew fair and by 1739 they claimed it was the largest there. Like most actors, Bullock moved from theatre to theatre throughout his career: for the 1706–7 season he moved from Drury Lane to the Queen's Theatre in the Haymarket; from 1707 through 1711 he performed at both Queen's and Drury Lane, and he and Rich engaged in suits and countersuits over alleged breaches of contracts; in 1710 he acted at Pinkethman's Greenwich theatre; from 1712 to 1715 he was at Drury Lane, and then he settled down at Lincoln's Inn Fields at Rich's theatre; he and his family acted there until in 1732 he followed Rich to Covent Garden, which kept him on its payroll, even after his last active season (1733–4), until his death. In his retirement Bullock performed rather regularly at booths at fairs and a few times at various theatres, including at Richmond (26 September 1734) and Lincoln's Inn Fields. His final performances were in 1739 at Covent Garden with his last at his booth at Bartholomew fair, when he played Judge Ballance in *The Escapes of Harlequin by Sea and Land* (23 August). He died in January 1742 and was survived by his daughter Henrietta Maria. His son Christopher had died in 1722; his wife was buried in Hampstead in November 1729; his younger sons Hildebrand and William had died within four months of each other in 1733.

PAULA R. BACKSCHEIDER

Sources Highfill, Burnim & Langhans, *BDA*, vol. 2 · W. Van Lennep and others, eds., *The London stage, 1660–1800*, 5 pts in 11 vols. (1960–68) · J. Milhous and R. D. Hume, eds., *A register of English theatrical documents, 1660–1737*, 2 vols. (1991) · S. B. Wells, ed., *A comparison between the two stages: a late Restoration book of the theatre* (1942) · T. Davies, *Dramatic miscellanies*, 3 (1784) · P. Holland, *The ornament of action: text and performance in Restoration comedy* (1979) · R. D. Hume, *The development of English drama in the late seventeenth century* (1976) · *The Tatler* · *The Spectator* · *Daily Courant* (1702–35) · Genest, *Eng. stage*, vol. 3 · *The works of George Farquhar*, ed. S. S. Kenny, 2 vols. (1988) · *The plays of Richard Steele*, ed. S. S. Kenny (1971)

Likenesses S. Harding, watercolour on wove paper, 1710–20 (after T. Johnson), Garr. Club · S. Harding?, watercolour, c.1710–1720 (after mezzotint by T. Johnson), NPG · T. Johnson, mezzotint, c.1710–1720, BM [*see illus.*] · C. Hall, mezzotint, pubd 1781 (after W. Hogarth), BM · S. Harding?, five engravings (after watercolour), BM · pen and grey ink (after stipple by A. Toedteberg), Harvard TC

Bullock, William (*b.* early 1780s, *d.* after 1843), naturalist and antiquary, was the son of William Bullock and Elizabeth, *née* Smallwood, the owners of a travelling waxworks, and brother of George *Bullock. He had two other brothers, James and Joseph. It is likely that William was born around the same time as George, that is in the early 1780s. The family probably came from Birmingham, where Elizabeth and George were in business at the turn of the century. By 1795 William was in Liverpool, where he lived at Church Street. In 1801, while trading as a jeweller and goldsmith, he published a descriptive catalogue of a museum which he had opened in that city in 1795. It contained works of art, armoury, objects of natural history, and curiosities brought by Captain Cook from the south seas partially acquired from Richard Green's Lichfield Museum and Sir Ashton Lever's collections. In 1809 Bullock moved to London, where his collection, still called the Liverpool Museum at 22 Piccadilly became extremely popular, especially after 1812 when placed in his newly erected Egyptian Hall, Piccadilly. Further enlarged from his own travels with Roman displays and memorabilia of Napoleon, Bullock's London Museum remained extremely popular and profitable until it was disposed of by auction in 1819. Altick suggests that Bullock was the first person in England to arrange a museum collection systematically and scientifically with imaginative back-cloths suggesting appropriate settings for the objects (Altick, 237). After selling his curiosities Bullock continued to let the Egyptian Hall for other exhibitions, notably Giovanni Battista Belzoni's Egyptian exhibition of 1821.

In December 1822 Bullock went to Mexico, where the Mexican government helped his research and ceded to him the silver mine of Del Bada near Themascaltpec. He was one of the first British travellers to visit Mexico, which was newly accessible to outsiders since its independence from Spain in 1821, and from his tour he brought home many valuable artefacts. These included plaster casts of the Aztec calendar stone known as 'Montezuma's watch', and of the 'sacrificial stone', thought to have been the Stone of Tizoc; plaster models of the pyramids at Teotihuacán; manuscripts and hieroglyphic documents sent to Montezuma to inform him of the transactions of the Spaniards; and a map of Tenochtitlan, said to be the original Aztec map made on the order of Montezuma for Cortés to send to the king of Spain. After his return to England in November 1823, Bullock opened in the Egyptian Hall in April 1824 an exhibition on ancient and modern Mexico, which contained his collection of ancient artefacts and casts, and illustrated the scenery, industry, art, minerals, and natural history of Mexico. His skill and imagination in displaying his objects in eye-catching but intelligent ways were again in evidence. Catalogues to the exhibition were published in 1823 and 1825. In 1824 he published *Six Months' Residence and Travels in Mexico* (facsimile edition, 1971), which included advice on the preservation of health in tropical climates.

After having disposed of his Mexican collection, partly to the British Museum, and having sold his lease on the Egyptian Hall, in 1827 Bullock again visited Mexico, continuing into the United States of America. He recorded his tour in *Sketch of a Journey through the Western States of North America* (1827) in which he and others praised Cincinnati, on the outskirts of which Bullock had bought The Elms, later Elmwood, an estate of some 1000 acres. He had commissioned the London architect John B. Papworth to draw a plan, included in the book, for a new town called Hygeia after the Greek goddess of health on this spot which was much later to become the site of Ludlow, Kentucky. The town was to contain cultural buildings, areas for agriculture and horticulture, houses for various classes of person, and a spacious house for Bullock, who retired there with his wife Margaret Latham and family in 1828, and who encouraged others 'of limited property' to follow him. Like so many other similar schemes, Bullock's failed, but the town plan and proposal were still being cited in

American works on town planning in the late twentieth century.

In 1830 Bullock sold Elmwood Hall, his new home on which he had spent much money, and most of his land, to move to a small cottage on the remaining land. In 1836 he sold this and returned to England. He is known to have been alive and in London in 1843. It has been suggested that he was the William Bullock, gentleman, who died at 14 Harley Terrace, Chelsea, on 7 March 1849, though this would make him substantially younger than other sources suggest. He was a fellow of the Linnean, Horticultural, Geological, Wernerian, and other learned societies, and published several pamphlets on natural history.

ELIZABETH BAIGENT

Sources R. D. Altick, *The shows of London* (1978) · F. Trollope, *Domestic manners of the Americans* (1832) · C. Lancaster, 'The Egyptian Hall and Mrs Trollope's Bazaar', *Magazine of Art* (March 1950), 94–112 · private information (2004) [John Ford] · S. Giles and J. Stewart, eds., *The art of ruins* (1989) · L. Boturini Benaduci, *Idea de una nueva historia general de la America septentrional* (Madrid, 1746) · *GM*, 1st ser., 94/2 (1824), 69–70 · F. F. Berdan and P. R. Anawalt, eds., *The Codex Mendoza*, 4 vols. (1992) · J. W. Reps, *The making of urban America* (1965) · J. B. Papworth, *Plan of a proposed rural town* (1965) · *DNB* · private information (2004) [Hugh Torrens]
Archives U. Edin. L., corresp. and papers relating to his natural history collection · Wellcome L., papers
Likenesses engraving, repro. in Altick, *Shows of London*

Bullock, William Edward (1877–1968), motor car manufacturer, was born on 14 March 1877 at Crockett Road, Handsworth, Birmingham, the son of William Bullock, smith, and his wife, Beatrice Caroline, née Barnett. He was educated at Smethwick Technical School, leaving at the age of fourteen for a job as a toolmaker's assistant with Denison and Wigley, of Handsworth. He went on to work for an electrical engineer for two years, and another toolmaker in the Birmingham area for a further two years, before joining the newly formed Wigley-Mulliner Engineering Company as foreman about 1897. After two years he became works manager. During the Second South African War the firm expanded, producing munitions. Bullock designed gun carriages, and when the firm became the nucleus of the Coventry ordnance works he moved to Coventry. In 1902 he married Nellie Elizabeth Parsons, moulder; they had one son (b. 1903) and one daughter. In 1907 Bullock was elected a member of the Institution of Mechanical Engineers.

In 1909 Bullock became works manager at Singer & Co., originally a cycle manufacturer founded in Coventry in 1876 by George Singer (d. 1909); the firm made its first motor cars in 1905, and by 1909 employed 600 workers producing four models of car. Following a brief vogue for cycle cars, Singer became the first British manufacturer to produce a small economy car, the Singer 10, launched at the 1912 Motor Show. Earlier, on the continent, small cars with limited engines had been produced: the Baby Peugeot had appeared in 1900, and the 4½ horsepower De Dion Bouton in 1901, but Singer was the first to produce a small car with a four-cylinder engine, a replica of a large car, with 10 horsepower, and to prove that a baby car was a practical proposition. Other motor manufacturers soon followed suit, and the Singer 10 had to face competition from the Morris Oxford and the Ford Model T, among others, but its success at the Brooklands trials 1912–14, where it reached 72 m.p.h., helped to publicize it. At £185 the Singer 10 appealed to those who could not afford a large car, and it became a best-seller. William Rootes was so impressed that he contracted to sell the whole first year's supply, and by 1913 the firm was making 1350 cars a year. During the First World War the factory concentrated on munitions production, but also supplied the armed forces with Singer 10s for the transport of junior army officers, and production continued after the war.

Bullock was appointed Singer's managing director in 1919 and in that year he was also a member of Coventry city council. After the war there was great demand for cars and the British motor manufacturing industry boomed, helped by the McKenna duties, first imposed in 1915, which protected British manufacturers from foreign competition, especially from the United States, which dominated the world market. Singer benefited from this and Bullock, advocating mass production for the popular market, began to acquire other companies in order to increase factory space, as the original factory site was hemmed in by housing and could not be expanded. In 1920 the firm acquired Coventry Premier Company Ltd, in 1922 Coventry Repetition Company, in 1925 Sparkbrook Manufacturing Company, and in 1926 the Calcott factory. In 1926 Singer was producing 9000 cars a year, 80 per cent of them Singer 10s. In 1927 a new car, the Singer Junior, was introduced to challenge the Austin 7, to be produced in Birmingham in an old BSA factory on the Coventry Road which had been bought by Singer the previous year. Despite additional competition from the Morris Minor, launched in 1928, the Singer Junior was very successful, with eight models listed in 1932. In 1929 Singer was one of the top three motor manufacturers in Britain, with 8000 employees and seven factories, producing 28,000 cars, but it was well behind Austin and Morris, which were responsible for 60 per cent of British car output whereas Singer had only 15 per cent of the market.

The fortunes of Singer nevertheless declined in the 1930s. Bullock had made some unwise purchases, including the acquisition of the large Hay Mills factory at Small Heath, Birmingham, bought from Daimler in 1928, into which he introduced new machinery and a moving assembly line, transferring assembly work from Coventry. The acquisition of the two Birmingham factories was a financial burden, despite the growth in popularity of small cars during the slump following the market collapse of 1929. In the 1930s the company struggled to survive: its rivals won the 10 horsepower market with the Hillman Minx and the Austin 10, while the Singer Junior was eclipsed not only by the Morris Minor and the Austin 7 but also, after 1932, by the Ford Model Y, which by 1934 had captured 56 per cent of the British market for cars of that class. In 1935 the Ford Popular, introduced at £100, went on to sell more than any other car in the United Kingdom before the outbreak of the Second World War.

A final blow came in 1935. In 1933 Singer had introduced its first sports car, the Singer 9, which finished thirteenth at Le Mans that year and was a serious rival to the MG, but in the 1935 Le Mans Tourist Trophy three of the four Singers crashed as a result of steering failures, and the fourth immediately withdrew. Singer never entered a team again, and the disaster did the company a great deal of harm. At the annual general meeting in May 1936 a loss of £129,292 was reported. Dividends had not been paid since 1931–2, and following criticism from the shareholders Bullock was not re-elected to the board. He resigned from the company shortly afterwards, together with his son, who had been general manager since 1931 and who had been in charge of the Birmingham factory.

From the beginning of his years with Singer, Bullock dominated the company, and as a vice-president of the Society of Motor Manufacturers and Traders in the 1920s was a leading figure in the motor industry. An advocate of mass production, he visited the United States in the 1920s to study ways of increasing production, and embarked on the acquisition of other factory sites to house the expanding moving assembly lines. His interest in technical and design improvements was wide-ranging: he was one of the first to introduce safety glass as standard equipment, low pressure tyres, and rear-mounted petrol tanks to reduce the risk of fire. However, he did not have a good grasp of financial matters: in the end the company was over-committed, and by the end of the 1930s Singer was no longer one of the top six motor manufacturers. In 1955 it was taken over by Rootes.

Bullock was small and energetic, with a prominent chin. He was always in the office by 8 a.m., and his main relaxation was gardening. After the death of his wife in 1934 he married, in 1936, Margaret F. Van Driest, *née* Whynant, a divorcée and daughter of a veterinary surgeon. This marriage ended in divorce. His third wife was Mrs Parsons, the widow of his first wife's brother.

After leaving Singer in 1936, Bullock worked for a time on the development of fire pumps. He left Coventry at the start of the blitz and spent the rest of the Second World War working on the farm in Warwickshire belonging to his daughter. He died on 17 March 1968 at Wootton Court, Leek Wootton, Kenilworth, Warwickshire.

ANNE PIMLOTT BAKER

Sources G. T. Bloomfield, 'Bullock, William Edward', *DBB* · K. Richardson and C. N. O'Gallagher, *The British motor industry, 1896–1939* (1977), 110–13 · G. S. Davison, *At the wheel: impressions of the leaders of Britain's greatest industry* (1931), 37–45 · R. Church, *Herbert Austin: the British motor car industry to 1941* (1979) · E. J. Appleby, 'The small car', *Autocar* (9 May 1930), 918–22 · G. N. Georgano, ed., *The complete encyclopedia of motorcars* (1969) · G. Maxcy and A. Silberston, *The motor industry* (1959) · R. Church and M. Miller, 'The big three: competition, management, and marketing in the British motor industry, 1922–1939', *Essays in British business history*, ed. B. Supple (1977), 163–86 · J. S. Foreman-Peck, 'The British motor industry before 1939', *Oxford Economic Papers*, 31 (1979) · K. Richardson, *Twentieth-century Coventry* (1972) · b. cert. · d. cert.
Likenesses photograph, repro. in Davison, *At the wheel*, facing p. 48 · photographs, repro. in Bloomfield, 'Bullock, William Edward'

Bullock, William Thomas (1818–1879), missionary, was born in London, the second son of John Bullock and his wife, Mary, *née* Soper. The family had been landowners in Leicestershire and Rutland for several generations, but his father and mother had settled in London. Bullock entered Magdalen Hall, Oxford, as a gentleman commoner, and took his BA degree in 1847, graduating fourth class. In the same year he was ordained deacon and licensed to the curacy of St Anne's, Soho, in London, where he remained until June 1850, when he was appointed assistant secretary to the Society for the Propagation of the Gospel (SPG). On 1 July 1862 he married Alice Oke Alford (*b.* 1837), the 25-year-old elder daughter of Henry Alford, dean of Canterbury. They had two daughters.

On the death of the Revd Ernest Hawkins in 1865 Bullock succeeded him as secretary of the SPG, an office which he held for the remainder of his life, though his appointment, according to *The Times*, was not without considerable controversy at the time. One of his first acts as secretary was to draw up a manual of missionary offices, sanctioned by Archbishop Longley, and to introduce a daily morning service into the routine of the society's London headquarters—a custom which continued long afterwards. In 1867 he was appointed chaplain to the royal household in Kensington Palace, where he occupied the chaplain's apartments, and in the following year he became honorary secretary of the Colonial Bishoprics Fund, a post he held until his death. In 1875 he was presented to the prebendal stall of Oxgate in St Paul's Cathedral.

Bullock helped to expand and reorganize the Society for the Propagation of the Gospel. No fewer than forty-two new sees were added to the colonial episcopate, and church operations were extended beyond the bounds of the British empire by the appointment of missionary bishops in the Niger territory, Honolulu, Ningpo (Ningbo), Madagascar, central Africa, and Melanesia. Missions, too, were opened in three new countries: independent Burma, China, and Japan. During this time the income of the society increased from £89,000 in 1850 to £145,000 in 1878. It was at Bullock's instigation that the society undertook the publication of the *Missionary Record*, the *Gospel Missionary*, and the *Mission Field*, which were conducted under his immediate supervision.

Apart from supervising the official publications of the society, Bullock found time amid the engrossing duties of his official life to pursue theological and biblical study. He was the author of at least seventy articles in *A Dictionary of the Bible* (1860, 1863), edited by W. Smith, and of one on the book of Ecclesiastes in F. C. Cook's edition of the Old Testament known as the Speaker's Commentary. He published, at the request of the archbishop of Canterbury, a sermon, 'Builders of the temple', which he had preached at the consecration of the bishop of Newfoundland on 1 May 1878. He left in manuscript a commentary on the book of Daniel, written for the Society for Promoting Christian Knowledge, and some months after his death his widow edited for publication a volume of sermons on missions and other subjects, most of which he had preached at Kensington Palace chapel.

In 1878 Bullock took an active part in the arrangements for the pan-Anglican synod (Lambeth conference), and the *Mission Field* records that 'his kindly hospitality and frank communication of wise counsels, and of the results of long experience, did much to further the objects of the assembly, especially in the direction of Missionary enterprise' (1 April 1879). By 1879 his declining health had compelled him to retire from active work and, having obtained six months' leave of absence, he went abroad. He died of a stroke at Menton, in France, on 27 February 1879, survived by his wife. *The Guardian* declared that:

> His singleness of purpose and unflinching devotion to duty, his suavity and patience, combined with his knowledge of the traditions of the Society to make him a most valued public servant, and to very many persons, who knew his worth and his graces, his loss will be as the removal of a dear friend.   (5 March 1879)

P. B. AUSTIN, *rev.* CLARE BROWN

Sources private information (1886) • Boase, *Mod. Eng. biog.* • *The Times* (4 March 1879) • *Mission Field* (1 April 1879), 137–40 • *The Guardian* (5 March 1879), 309 • Foster, *Alum. Oxon.* • *Annual Report* [Society for the Propagation of the Gospel] (1878–81) • C. F. Pascoe, *Two hundred years of the SPG*, rev. edn, 2 vols. (1901) • m. cert. • d. cert. **Archives** Bodl. RH, Society for the Propagation of the Gospel MSS • LPL, corresp. with Lady Burdett-Coutts • LPL, corresp. with A. C. Tait

Wealth at death under £14,000: resworn probate, Sept 1879, CGPLA Eng. & Wales

Bullokar, John (*bap.* 1574, *d.* 1627), physician and lexicographer, was born in St Andrew's parish, Chichester, Sussex, and was baptized there on 8 November 1574, the third of four known children of William *Bullokar (*c.*1531–1609) and his wife, Elizabeth, *née* Diggons (*d.* 1608). He initially continued to live, with his wife, Ellinor (*d.* in or after 1631), in the parish of his birth: at least two of their children, Thomas *Bullaker (*bap.* 2 November 1598) and Ellinor (*bap.* 29 October 1601), were born there. There is no record of the birthplace, in 1602 or 1604, of a second Thomas, but it may have been Midhurst, Sussex, where John held freehold property. Subsequently, the family moved from parish to parish in Chichester, possibly to avoid regular presentment for non-attendance at church.

The Bullokars were staunch Roman Catholics. In Elizabeth's reign female members of the Hampshire branch were sent to the house of correction at Winchester for harbouring priests. The Chichester branch too persisted in that faith, as a series of documents in the West Sussex Record Office and archives of Chichester council shows. John Bullokar and his wife were not only presented for recusancy but also excommunicated on a number of occasions. Between 1599 and 1604, John was also several times presented for being an unlicensed schoolmaster. His second son Thomas (also known as John Baptist Martyr) studied at the English colleges at St Omer, Flanders, and Valladolid, Spain, became a Franciscan, and, in 1642, was hanged, drawn, and quartered at Tyburn, having been arrested at the home of a member of the Montague family, where he was celebrating mass, and charged with high treason. It was presumably because of his religion that John himself obtained his MD degree overseas, at Caen, on 16 October 1612.

Bullokar was author of two publications, *An English Expositor: Teaching the Interpretation of the Hardest Words Used in our Language* (dedicated to Jane, Viscountess Mountague, and entered in the Stationers' register on 25 May 1610, but not published until 1616), and *A True Description of the Passion of our Saviour Jesus Christ*, a poem in six-line stanzas (dated by its author 2 November 1618, but not published until 1622). It is for the contribution to the development of the English dictionary made by the first of these that John Bullokar became known. The work of his 'younger yeares', a 'little Pamphlet' originally intended only for private use (J. Bullokar, *English Expositor*, 1616, epistle dedicatory), and written 'at the request of a worthy gentleman, one whose loue preuailed much with me' (possibly his father, who had himself planned to produce a dictionary), but subsequently put aside (*English Expositor*, 'To the courteous reader'), it has nevertheless over a thousand more lemmas than the 1613 edition of its immediate predecessor, Cawdrey's *Table Alphabeticall*, including a number of encyclopaedic entries and even a personal reference to a visit to London, where Bullokar reports having seen a crocodile 'brought thither dead, but in perfect forme, of about three yards long' (*English Expositor*, 'Crocodile'). A significant innovation is the marking of 'old words now grown out of use'.

Like other monolingual English dictionaries of the seventeenth century the *Expositor* was a 'hard-word dictionary' (dealing in large part with the Latin and Greek loanwords of Renaissance English). Its materials were taken from a wide variety of sources, ranging from Cawdrey's monolingual and Thomas's Latin–English dictionaries to specialist glossaries. It was not only drawn on freely by its competitors, from Cockeram onwards, but continued to be published in many editions (and after 1641 with constant enlargement) up to 1775. The most significant of the revisions, by 'A Lover of the Arts' (1663), adds both a 'reverse' dictionary, with the 'ordinary' equivalents set before the hard-word lemmas of the first part, and a nomenclature, 'containing a summary of the most memorable Things and famous Persons, whether Inventors and Improvers of rare Arts and Ingenuities, or others'. However, Bullokar lived to see only the second of these editions (1621): he died in 1627 and was buried in St Andrew's parish on 2 January 1628.   JANET BATELY

Sources T. J. McCann, 'The Catholic recusancy of Dr. John Bullaker of Chichester, 1574–1627', *Recusant History*, 11 (1971–2), 75–86 · *The works of William Bullokar*, ed. B. Danielsson and R. C. Alston, facs. edn, 1 (1966) · J. Schäfer, *Early modern English lexicography*, 1 (1989) · De W. T. Starnes and G. E. Noyes, *The English dictionary from Cawdrey to Johnson, 1604–1755*, new edn, ed. G. Stein (1991) · R. C. Alston, *A bibliography of the English language from the invention of printing to the year 1800*, 5 (1966) · RCP Lond., Innes-Smith MS 286a · parish register, Chichester, St Andrew, 8 Nov 1574 [baptism]

Bullokar, William (*c*.1531–1609), spelling reformer and grammarian, belonged to a landed family from west Sussex, and in three surviving legal documents is styled gentleman. His parents were William Bullokar and Elizabeth Bowyer, of Broadwater, Sussex. William the younger may have been born at Highden, Washington, Sussex,

where other Bullokars are recorded in the earlier sixteenth century; the little known of his early life is based on comments in his writings. In one of these he claims to have studied civil law; he was sufficiently well educated to be employed in the 1550s as a schoolmaster. He also claims expertise in agriculture and to have seen military service abroad in the reign of Queen Mary, when he served under the command of Sir Richard Wingfield and Sir Adrian Poynings as well as in a garrison under a Captain Turnor. On 30 January 1570 he married in Chichester Elizabeth (*d.* 1608), daughter of John Diggons, alderman, and he bought a house, which he retained until 1585, at the south gate of Chichester in the parish of St Peter the Great, the church where his eldest daughter, Katherine, was baptized on 28 January 1571. He later moved to the parish of St Andrew, in whose church his son John *Bullokar was baptized in 1574.

Bullokar's remarks in the *Booke at Large* (1580) reveal that his experiences as a schoolmaster made an unhappy impression on him. He explained that he was faced with serious difficulties in teaching children to read and write, which were due largely to the absence of a link between the names and the sounds of several letters, such as *h, y, w*. In addition, several letters were ambiguous because they represented more than one sound. He devised a reformed orthography (normalized here), which remained in manuscript until in 1573 he decided to lay aside his private business and devote himself entirely to the subject. In 1578, when his work was about to go to press, he learned of the proposed spelling reforms of Sir Thomas Smith (*d.* 1577) and John Hart (*c*.1501–1574); they shared his views on the deficiencies of English spelling but proposed different solutions, which introduced new letters. Bullokar disapproved, arguing that they would impose an intolerable strain on the memory, since children would have to learn both old and new orthographies if they were to read existing works in print.

Spelling reform was a controversial topic, so Bullokar prepared the ground for his proposals in the *Booke at Large*. First he distributed copies of a 'pamphlet' (probably the work which was later published in 1580 as *A Short Introduction or Guiding to Print, Write, and Reade Inglish Speech*) to 'men of understanding' in various places, inviting their comments on what was intended as a summary statement of his proposals. He also set up in the city of London, on 8 August 1580, posters advertising his reformed alphabet. The *Booke at Large* was followed by a revised version, in 1581, of the *Short Introduction* and then, in June 1583, by twenty 'brief articles', which he had printed for distribution in London and other places, which were 'of good skil and credit' (*Aesops Fablz*, 1585, sig. A3v).

A major problem was that there were, in Bullokar's reckoning, at least forty distinct 'divisions of the voice' but only twenty-four letters to represent them (*Booke at Large*, sig. Cjr). He attempted to clarify the sound values of existing letters by using diacritics, for example to indicate vowel length, while other diacritics were designed to demonstrate the etymology of a word. Occasionally Bullokar used ligatured forms, for example of *sh, th, gh*, and *oo*, although he eventually abandoned most of them on the advice of his printer. He demonstrates in verses in the *Booke at Large* the differences between the traditional and the new orthographies, which show how difficult it was to use his system; it is not surprising that Bullokar's work received no endorsement from his contemporaries.

Bullokar's overall plan was, apparently, to provide a complete course for the teaching of literacy. This would include a grammar, the purpose of which was to enable students to parse English 'for the perfecter wryting thaerof' (*Pamphlet for Grammar*, 1586, title-page); he hoped to teach his pupils to distinguish between compounds, 'declinatives' (grammatical inflections), and derivatives as an aid to correct orthography. Second, he intended to publish a set of readers in the new alphabet; and third, he exemplified manuscript forms of the alphabet in the various handwritings, such as secretary hand, then current. Finally he hoped to produce a dictionary providing different spellings for 'equivoces' (homophones).

Bullokar called his grammar *William Bullokarz pamphlet for grammar or rather … hiz abbreviation of hiz grammar for English, extracted out of hiz grammar at-larg*; the latter is no longer extant. The shorter grammar is noteworthy as being the first grammar of English ever to be published, but his description of English is heavily dependent on Latin grammar, known to Bullokar in William Lily's version which had been prescribed by royal decree for use in all schools. Bullokar's grammar was concerned mainly with classifying and describing the traditional eight parts of speech, and devoted little space to syntax. Nevertheless, while following Lily, Bullokar was perceptive enough to notice features of English not found in Latin. To quote only a few of his observations, he noted the use of 'do' as a substitute verb as in 'How do you think? As you do'; the use of 'do' with no function other than to mark tense, as in 'I did love'; the present tense with future meaning, as in 'I ride ten days hence'; and he made many other original comments.

Textbooks were an essential component of any course in literacy, the most important of them being the one known as the primer, consisting of an alphabet and a collection of prayers and used as the initial reading book in all schools. Bullokar often refers to his primer in his reformed spelling, of which no copy survives; nor do any copies of the psalter that he claimed to have published, nor of *Offices*, his translation of Cicero. The only surviving readers in Bullokar's orthography contain his own translations of *Aesops Fablz* and of the *Sentences* of Cato. Bullokar's remarks on translation reveal him as a conscientious teacher who is concerned that his translation is not always 'in the best phras' (*Aesops Fablz*, sig. Aivv) since, although English is capable of 'perfect sense', he wishes to help learners by making his translations as literal as possible. He is typically Elizabethan in his love for his native language explaining, for example, with reference to the verb 'deem', 'I am not ashamed of our olde wordes (deeme) and such like' (*Booke at Large*, 22). Nor does he object to the numerous monosyllables of English; on the contrary he praises them, pointing out that they say in

one syllable what other languages require 'divers' syllables to express.

Bullokar made a nuncupatory will on 3 March 1609, in favour of his daughter Agnes, and he died on the following day at Chichester. His son John produced a dictionary of English, *An English Expositor* (1616), which he claimed to have written at the request of 'a worthy gentleman' (probably his father). William's grandson Thomas became a Franciscan friar and in 1642 was executed in Ireland for his faith; there is some evidence that Bullokar himself was a Catholic. Bullokar's major achievement was to produce the first grammar of English to be published. However inadequate it was, it nevertheless reveals Bullokar's original observations on the language. It is a pity that such a dedicated scholar should have spent so much time and effort on the reform of English orthography, which has remained to this day a lost cause. VIVIAN SALMON

Sources W. Bullokar, *Bullokars booke at large, for the amendment of orthographie for English speech*, ed. J. R. Turner (1970) • W. Bullokar, *William Bullokarz pamphlet for grammar*, ed. J. R. Turner (1980) • V. Salmon, 'Orthography and punctuation', *The Cambridge history of the English language*, ed. R. M. Hogg, 3: *1476–1776*, ed. R. Lass (1999), 15–55 • *The works of William Bullokar*, ed. B. Danielsson and R. C. Alston, facs. edn, 1 (1966) • *Aesops fablz*, trans. W. Bullokar (1585); repr., ed. J. R. Turner (1969) • *DNB*

Bullough, Sir George, baronet (1870–1939). *See under* Bullough, John (1836/7–1891).

Bullough, James (1799–1868). *See under* Bullough, John (1836/7–1891).

Bullough, John (1836/7–1891), textile machinery manufacturer, was baptized at Blackburn on 10 December 1837, the third son of **James Bullough** (1799–1868) and his wife, Martha, *née* Mellor. In becoming a textile machinery maker, John Bullough had before him the example of his father, whose inventions greatly improved the powered weaving of cloth. James Bullough was born at Westhoughton, Lancashire, the son of Ann Bullough, and was put to the hand-loom when he was seven. The need to improve the clumsy power-looms of his youth stimulated his inventive genius and for most of his life he strove to make weaving more efficient. James Bullough is best remembered for the weft fork, which stopped the loom when the thread broke, thus preventing the shuttle from damaging the cloth. Controversy surrounded the invention, which Bullough and James Kenworthy, co-workers in a Blackburn mill, patented in 1841 (no. 8790); John Osbaldeston (c.1777–1842) also laid claim to it. Bullough, either alone or with others, took out patents covering all aspects of weaving. These included a roller temple that kept the woven cloth at its correct width and a loose reed that allowed the lathe to back away on encountering a shuttle trapped in the warp. With two employees, James Whittaker and John Walmsley, Bullough perfected a machine that sized two warps and wound them on two beams at the same time. Bullough managed and ran a number of small mills in Lancashire before joining John Howard in a textile machinery business at Accrington in 1856. Howard had begun three years earlier with four employees but with Bullough's backing expansion accelerated. The firm of Howard and Bullough specialized in machines for preparing and spinning cotton, and by 1866, the year of Howard's death, employed 300 workpeople. James Bullough died on 31 July 1868, leaving the business to his son John.

John Bullough studied at Queenwood College, Hampshire, and Glasgow University before joining his father's firm in 1859. Though he took out more than twenty patents, of which the electric stop motion, used in numerous machines, was the most important, he is best remembered for promoting the ring frame at a time when British spinners preferred the slower-moving mule. The machine, which had been developed in the United States, was a more efficient version of the throstle, itself an improvement on Sir Richard Arkwright's water frame. Bullough acquired the rights to a new type, the Rabbeth spindle, in 1879, and in the succeeding years kept the machines in the firm's expanding Globe Works running night and day to meet international demand. A technical school started by Bullough in 1881 was among the first of its kind.

The appointment of skilled managers to oversee the 2000 workpeople enabled Bullough to spend more time on his estate at Castle Meggernie, Perthshire, and on the island of Rum in the Inner Hebrides, both of which he bought in the 1880s. Throughout his life Bullough was an active Conservative and spoke regularly in support of self-help, *laissez-faire* capitalism, and union with Ireland. He married in 1868 Bertha Schmidlin, daughter of a Swiss cotton manufacturer. They had two children, George [*see below*] and Bertha. The marriage ended in divorce, after which, in 1884, Bullough married Alexandra Marion McKenzie, daughter of a Stornaway banker. The children of this marriage were John and Gladys. Bullough died at the Hotel Metropole, Westminster, aged fifty-three, on 25 February 1891, and was buried on Rum.

John Bullough's son **Sir George Bullough**, baronet (1870–1939), was born at Accrington on 28 February 1870 and was educated at Harrow School. As a young man he sailed round the world in his steam yacht, buying works of art, on one occasion outbidding the emperor of Japan for an ivory figure. His treasures found a home in Kinloch Castle, which he built on Rum in 1900–01 at a cost of £250,000. On the outbreak of the Second South African War Bullough converted his yacht into a floating hospital and sailed to South Africa, a service rewarded with a knighthood in 1901. He married in 1903 Monica Lilly, the eldest daughter of the fourth marquis de la Pasture. They had one daughter.

On his father's death George inherited half the equity of Howard and Bullough, of which he was chairman until his death. The setting up of a United States subsidiary in 1893 and the introduction of profit sharing in 1906 were highlights of his early years with the company. In 1931 the company took part in the merger that led to the formation of Textile Machinery Makers. Bullough left the day-to-day running of the business to others, preferring the racetrack and the hunting field to the board room, and in compiling his entry for *Who's Who* he made no reference to his business interests.

In 1908–11 Bullough served in the Scottish Horse imperial yeomanry and during the First World War he was superintendent of the remount department with the rank of major. He also made an interest-free loan of £50,000 to the government. For these services, he received a baronetcy in 1916. For fourteen years from 1908 he was master of Ledbury hounds. He served both the Jockey Club and the National Hunt Committee, and in 1917 his horse Ballymacad won the 'war' Grand National at Gatwick. Bullough died at the Château de Courcet in the Pas-de-Calais, France, on 26 July 1939; he was buried in the family mausoleum on Rum.   CHRISTOPHER ASPIN

Sources R. S. Crossley, *Accrington captains of industry* (1930) · R. Kirk, 'Bullough, John', *DBB* · R. M. Kirk, 'Bullough, Sir George', *DBB* · *Accrington Times* (15 Aug 1868) · *Accrington Times* (25 March 1891) · *Accrington Reporter* (8 Aug 1868) [James Bullough] · *Accrington Observer and Times* (29 July 1939) [Sir George Bullough] · C. Aslet, 'Kinloch Castle, Isle of Rhum', *Country Life*, 176 (1984), 380–84, 446–9 · *WWW*, 1929–40 [Sir George Bullough] · books of news cuttings (mostly undated), Accrington Public Library · J. Bullough, *Speeches and letters*, 3 vols. (1892) · *CGPLA Eng. & Wales* (1891) · *CGPLA Eng. & Wales* (1939) [George Bullough] · parish register, Blackburn, St John's [baptism, John Bullough], 10 Dec 1837 · d. cert. [John Bullough] · parish register, Westhoughton [baptism, James Bullough], 30 March 1799 · parish register, Bolton, St Peter's [marriage, James Bullough], 11 April 1824 · b. cert. [Sir George Bullough]

Archives Lancs. RO, Platt-Saco-Lowell archive, business records of Howard and Bullough

Likenesses photograph, *c.*1865 (James Bullough), Lancs. RO, Platt-Saco-Lowell archive · H. Rivière, oils, 1909 (Sir George Bullough), Kinloch Castle, Rum, Inner Hebrides · oils, Kinloch Castle, Rum, Inner Hebrides

Wealth at death £1,228,183 16s. 8d.: resworn probate, Jan 1892, *CGPLA Eng. & Wales* (1891) · £710,037 9s. 8d.—Sir George Bullough: probate, 3 Nov 1939, *CGPLA Eng. & Wales*

Bulman, Oliver Meredith Boone (1902–1974), geologist, was born on 20 May 1902 at Cheyne Walk Studio, Chelsea, London, the second of three children and younger son of Henry Herbert Bulman, artist, and his wife, Beatrice Elizabeth Boone (1864?–1946?), daughter of W. A. Boone, of Canterbury and Ramsgate, art master of King's School, Canterbury. Of the three Bulman children, only Oliver appears to have inherited any graphic ability, and he used it very effectively when making, with his left hand, the hundreds of drawings and diagrams illustrating his scientific papers, books, and lectures; some people even collected his 'doodles' after committee meetings.

Bulman went to Battersea grammar school in 1910, but an operation for a malignant cyst in his left femur kept him at home for a year when he was twelve years old. Wishing to study geology, which his school could not provide, he became an evening—and later a day—student at Chelsea Polytechnic as a pupil of A. J. Maslen. He gained the London University geology scholarship in 1920 and in 1921 he proceeded to Imperial College where he studied geology and zoology; he also attended vertebrate palaeontology lectures at University College, London. In 1923 he took a first-class BSc in geology, with zoology as the subsidiary subject, and also the ARCS.

Awarded a Beit scientific research fellowship, Bulman proceeded to a London PhD degree jointly with C. James Stubblefield with a thesis entitled 'The Shineton Shales of the Wrekin district, Shropshire' (1926). He spent the first year of an 1851 senior studentship (1925–6) at Imperial College where his fellow research students included Walter Frederick Whittard with whom he wrote a paper on Permian branchiosaurid amphibia. For the remaining two years of the studentship, he moved to Sidney Sussex College, Cambridge, to study dendroid graptolites under the supervision of Gertrude Lilian Elles at the Sedgwick Museum.

Bulman's researches were facilitated by following a technique devised by Gerhard Holm of using hydrochloric or hydrofluoric acid to dissolve the rock matrix from the graptolite and also by making serial sections by grinding, as W. J. Sollas had done for *Palaeospondylus*. Bulman produced two parts of the Palaeontographical Society's monograph *British Dendroid Graptolites* (1927 and 1928) which, with several subsidiary papers, earned him a Cambridge PhD degree (1928). Bulman was awarded the Imperial College Huxley memorial medal when he returned there in 1928 as a demonstrator in the zoology department. He moved in 1929 to a similar post in the geology department; then in 1931 he became a demonstrator in geology at Cambridge.

Whereas previously Bulman had been elucidating the structure of dendroid graptolites, he turned to true graptolites when E. H. O. Stensiö of Stockholm placed with him for description a series of South American graptolites, isolated from their matrices by Holm. Assisted by Holm's skilfully retouched photographs, Bulman produced a spectacular paper published in the *Arkiv för Zoologie*. This paper was followed by a seven-part study of Scandinavian graptolites, also published in the *Arkiv*. Bulman provided new information concerning the early growth stages of graptolite taxa which had a bearing on the interpretation of the evolution of particular groups. Appreciation of his views was helped by the wax enlargements made from serial sections of the fossils. He contributed the article on graptolithina to the *Handbuch der Paläozoologie* (ed. O. H. Schindewolf, 1938) but perhaps his most influential publication was the second edition (1970) of his *Graptolithina* volume (in part with R. B. Rickards) of the *Treatise on Invertebrate Paleontology* (ed. C. Teichert).

At Chelsea Old Church, London, in 1938 Bulman married Marguerite, the elder daughter of William George *Fearnsides FRS, professor of geology at Sheffield University, and his wife, Beatrix, daughter of Professor William Whitehead Watts FRS. They had a son and three daughters.

After W. B. R. King became Woodwardian professor at Cambridge in 1943, Bulman was made reader in palaeozoology (1944). When King retired in 1955 Bulman succeeded to his post and occupied the chair until he resigned in 1966, when he became emeritus professor. He retained editorship of the *Geological Magazine*, which he had taken up in 1934, until 1972. With W. G. Fearnsides he was author of the sixpenny Penguin *Geology in the Service of Man* (1944; 3rd edn, 1961).

Elected FRS in 1940, Bulman served on the Royal Society's council from 1952 to 1954 and as a trustee of the British Museum (Natural History) from 1963 to 1970. He was successively president of the geology section of the British Association (1959), the Palaeontological Association (1960–62), the Geological Society (1962–4), and the Palaeontographical Society (1971–4). He was a fellow of Sidney Sussex College (1944) and of Imperial College (1961). He received the Lyell medal of the Geological Society (1953) and an honorary DPhil of Oslo University (1965). He was ScD of Cambridge University (1936) and an honorary member of the Geological Society of Stockholm and of the Palaeontological Society of India. A volume of twenty essays on graptolites, by his students and friends, designed to form a Festschrift, but destined to be a memorial tribute to him, was published by the Palaeontological Association (1974) to which body he had given an inaugural address in 1958.

Bulman was 6 feet tall but sparsely built. Though he could strongly voice dislike of some, he was kindly and generous, and a staunch friend of others; he had a ready wit and was especially keen to help the careers of his students. He was a lucid and inspiring teacher. He died at his home, the White Cottage, Mount Pleasant, Cambridge, on 18 February 1974, and was cremated in Cambridge.

C. JAMES STUBBLEFIELD, *rev.* R. B. RICKARDS

Sources C. J. Stubblefield, *Memoirs FRS*, 21 (1975), 175–95 · *The Times* (20 Feb 1974) · R. B. Rickards and D. E. Jackson, 'Graptolite studies in honour of O. M. B. Bulman', ed. R. B. Rickards, D. E. Jackson, and C. P. Hughes, *Special Papers in Palaeontology*, 13 (1974), 1–17 · personal knowledge (1986) · private information (1986, 2004) · *Annual Report* [Geological Society of London] (1974)

Archives BGS · priv. coll.

Likenesses M. Bulman, ink and colour drawing, 1974, Sidney Sussex College, Cambridge · D. Palmer, sketch, repro. in R. B. Rickards, 'A century of graptolite research in Cambridge', *Geological Curator*, 7/2 (1999), 73

Wealth at death £35,029: probate, 15 July 1974, *CGPLA Eng. & Wales*

Bulmer [*née* Collinson], **Agnes** (1775–1836), writer and poet, was born in Lombard Street, London, on 31 August 1775, the third daughter of Edward Collinson (*d.* 1809) and his wife, Elizabeth, *née* Ball, of Lombard Street, London. She was a bright girl who left school at fourteen, but continued to study throughout her lifetime. Deeply religious, she was an active member of the Church of England, as well as participating in Methodist society. She corresponded with John Wesley, and is said to have been admitted by him into the Methodist congregation in December 1793. Also in 1793, she married Joseph Bulmer of London, who died in 1822 after a protracted illness.

Agnes Bulmer's publications include: *Memoirs of Mrs Elizabeth Mortimer* (1836), *Scripture Histories* (3 vols., 1837–8), and a long poem entitled *Messiah's Kingdom*, in twelve books, published in 1833. She also made many contributions to the Methodist publications *Youth's Magazine* and *Youth's Instructor*, as well as being an active letter-writer.

Agnes Bulmer fell ill while visiting the Isle of Wight and died there on 30 August 1836. Her remains were brought to London, and she was buried in her husband's family vault, in the Wesleyan Chapel burial-ground, City Road. A memoir by Anne Ross Collinson was published in 1837, and a collection of her letters appeared in 1842.

REBECCA MILLS

Sources A. R. Collinson, *Memoir of Mrs Agnes Bulmer* (1837) [incl. letters and poems] · *IGI* · Revd W. Bunting, *Select letters of Mrs Agnes Bulmer* (1842) · A. Bulmer, *Scripture histories*, 3 vols. (1837–8) · *Wesleyan Methodist Magazine*, 63 (1840) · *DNB* · PRO, PROB 11/1866, sig. 533
Archives JRL, Methodist Archives and Research Centre, letters to Jabez Bunting · JRL, poems and letters to W. B. Rawson
Wealth at death see will, PRO PROB 11/1866; probate, 1836

Bulmer, (George Henry) Bertram (1902–1993), cider manufacturer and business entrepreneur, was born on 30 August 1902 at Fair Oaks Cottage, Kings Acre Road, Hereford, the eldest of the three sons of Edward Frederick *Bulmer (1865–1941) [see under Bulmer, Henry Percival] and his wife, Sophie, née Rittner (1874?–1968), who was of German parentage but was born in Liverpool. Educated at Bedales School, Shrewsbury School, and King's College, Cambridge, he obtained a master's degree in modern languages before joining his father's family firm. H. P. Bulmer had been founded in Hereford in 1887 with a loan from Bertram's clergyman grandfather, the Revd C. H. Bulmer. Beginning as a small family organization, Bulmer's was for many years the largest employer in Hereford.

Fluent in both German and French, young Bulmer worked in every department of the firm and strongly believed that such experience was vital to understanding the nature of business. Appointed a director in 1924, he went to Normandy and Brittany to purchase apples at a time of company expansion. On 29 July 1933 he married, in King's College chapel, Christine Mary Frederica Laughton (1912–2000), who had been born in San Francisco. Then, with the repeal of prohibition, Bulmer went across to the United States to sell to Americans the concept of cider drinking. Company policy was to buy up small troubled cider factories, and in 1937 a 50 per cent interest was acquired in Bulmer, Magner & Co., along with W. Magner's extensive cider fruit orchards in the vicinity of Clonmel, co. Tipperary. During the Second World War Bulmer preferred to remain a sergeant in the Home Guard, unwilling to leave the ranks but enjoying the occasional romps inseparable from army life near to home. In the 1940s he served as a Liberal member of the Hereford rural district council, and in his younger days he had chaired the Hereford co-operative housing venture. Holidays were spent often in the company of Bancroft Clark, of the well-known firm of shoe manufacturers C. & J. Clark, of Street, in Somerset, or rough shooting and fly fishing for trout.

A profitable sideline was initiated with the establishment of a plant in Hereford to make pectin preservative for jam-setting from waste apple pomace, which until then had been dumped or sold to the pectin producers of the day. In the ongoing quest for citrus peel to improve the

(George Henry) Bertram Bulmer (1902–1993), by Bill Warhurst, 1984

quality of the firm's pectin base, the 1960s saw production companies set up in Ghana (since the 1940s a supplier of this peel) and Australia, the latter for cider brandy.

A director for sixty-three years, Bulmer succeeded his cousin Howard Bulmer as chairman from 1966 to 1973, when he handed over the chairmanship to the first non-family member, although he stayed on as a non-executive director until 1987. In 1970 he steered the company through a heady period of expansion leading up to stock-market flotation. He is best remembered, however, for reviving the art of apple brandy distillation—something not attempted in England for at least two centuries. Brussels was not amused, and thereupon a spirited fight was waged against European bureaucracy on methods of distillation and hostility to the notion of British brandy. In retirement Bulmer was in robust form, battling with the obfuscation and entrenched prejudice that tried to confine the term brandy to grape distillation. Eventually he won the right to be the first man in England since 1763 to be granted a customs and excise licence to distil apple brandy, using a Heath Robinson contraption of copper drum and curling pipes discovered in Normandy, to produce King Offa Cider Brandy. The queen and the prince of Wales conferred royal patronage on his cider and donated oaks from royal estates to make the maturation casks, and her majesty was rewarded with the first bottle of legitimate apple brandy at the firm's centenary in 1987. Bulmer held the queen's warrant for cider supply for many years and became a freeman of the city of Hereford. When buyers began to take the word 'offa(er)' too literally, the brand label was changed to Hereford Cider Brandy, although King Offa is still made available at the Cider Museum.

In retirement, Bulmer oversaw the Bulmer cider festival, and, after some years of planning, in 1973 he founded the Hereford Cider Museum Trust; the museum opened in 1981. Aged seventy, he opened the road race at the festivities of 1973 on a penny-farthing bicycle which he had learned to ride for the occasion. As was remarked at the time, there was no shortage of his own brew to steady the nerves. Such activity probably surprised and delighted the majority of the workforce, Bulmer's image being a microcosm of the paternal, punctilious employer of yesteryear, demanding respect, loyalty, and reliability in return for caring, compassionate, and structured stewardship of employees' livelihoods. Bulmer was honoured with the presidency of the National Association of Cider Makers and was life president of the European Cider Markets Association. He valued highly his election to membership of the Worshipful Company of Distillers and the French Calvados Connoisseurs' Association. Bulmer died at his home, Little Breinton, Breinton, Herefordshire, on 5 January 1993, survived by his widow, four sons, and a daughter. He was cremated. Christine Bulmer died on 30 September 2000 and was buried at Credenhill church, where many Bulmers lie.   GORDON PHILLIPS

Sources private information (2004) [family] · *The Times* (11 Jan 1993) · F. Jackson, *The Independent* (15 Jan 1993) · L. P. Wilkinson, *Bulmers of Hereford: a century of cider-making* (1987) · m. cert. · d. cert.
Archives King's Cam., family papers
Likenesses A. Connor, bronze bust, c.1980, Little Breinton, Herefordshire; copy, Hereford Cider Museum · W. Warhurst, photograph, 1984, News International Syndication, London [*see illus.*]
Wealth at death £3,488,988: probate, 10 Dec 1993, *CGPLA Eng. & Wales*

Bulmer, Sir Bevis (*d.* 1613), courtier and mining projector, whose origins are shrouded in mystery, was a close friend of both Queen Elizabeth and James VI and I. Stephen Atkinson, his refiner of ores and a constant companion after 1587, wrote an account of Bulmer's activities in 1619, describing him as an 'ingenious gent' (Atkinson, preface), and elsewhere Bulmer was referred to as 'Bulmer the Projector' (Surtees, pt 2, 78). He is known to have had a son, John, and two daughters, Elizabeth and Prudence.

Bulmer began his career at a group of mines near Clitheroe in the north of England, but his first major work was at Leadhills in Lanarkshire in 1576. His next project was established at Chewton minery in the Mendip hills, Somerset, in 1586, when Queen Elizabeth was one of his financial backers. The following year a silver-rich lead vein was discovered at Combe Martin in Devon, and Adrian Gilbert, one of the leaseholders and brother of Sir John Gilbert, the navigator, granted Bulmer a moiety of the lease. For the next two years each of the partners was reputed to have received £10,000 profit, but by 1590 this had declined to £1000. Bulmer also refined ore from the Irish mines of the Society of Mines Royal at Combe Martin.

In 1593 Bulmer began the construction of a horse-driven chain pump at Broken Wharf near St Paul's Cathedral to bring drinking-water from the Thames to the Cheapside area of London. To commemorate the pump's completion in 1595 he presented a tankard made from Combe Martin silver to Sir Richard Martin, master of the mint and lord mayor of London. This was engraved with a portrait of Bulmer and the following verse:

When waterworks in Broaken Wharf
  At first erected Weare,

And Bevis Bulmer with his art
  The waters 'gan to reare.
(Hoyle, 55–6)

This tankard was subsequently melted down, but three other dome-top tankards bearing the inscription 'the gift of Bevis Bullmer' were still in the Mansion House collection in the City of London some 400 years later.

In 1593 Bulmer obtained letters of recommendation from the queen to the Scottish government, who granted him a patent to search for gold and silver at Leadhills. For the next two years he prospected for alluvial gold in the Lowther hills and built a house at Glengonnar near Leadhills where, according to Atkinson, he lived in great splendour. It is his behaviour here, described by Atkinson, that provides an insight into his attitude to wealth. In Atkinson's words, 'he wasted much himselfe, and gave liberally to many, for to be honoured, praised, and magnified, else he might have bin a rich subject; for the least of these frugalities [*sic*] were able to robb an abbott' (Hoyle, 43). Bulmer later returned to London and presented a porringer made from Lowther gold to Queen Elizabeth, inscribed:

I dare not give, nor yet present,
But render parte of that's thine owne
My minde and hart, shall still invent
To seeke out treasure, yet unknown.
(ibid., 43)

This gift endeared him to the queen and he became a regular attender at court. In 1599 he was granted the farm of the duty on all seaborne coal and the duty on import of wines and he unsuccessfully tendered for the right of pre-emption of Cornish tin. He also received royal patents for two of his inventions: one in 1584 for a lighthouse and another in 1588 for a water-powered nail-making machine, which was used in a mill built at Dartford.

In 1603 King James devised with Bulmer a 'Plott' whereby they were to finance the search for gold in Scotland. The king would reward investors with a knighthood, and they would become one of the 'knights of the golden mines' or 'golden knights'. Unfortunately this scheme fell through owing to the interference of Robert Cecil. However, Bulmer was knighted in 1604, and after receiving £100 as a 'free gift' from the king (Jenkins, 402) along with £200 'to be employed about the gold mines in Scotland' (*CSP dom.*, 1603–10, 68) he returned to Scotland to hunt for gold in the Lowther hills. In 1606 he was granted a lease of all gold and silver mines in Scotland and received further gifts of £100 and £500 from the king in 1607 and 1608 respectively.

In 1608 a silver-rich mine was discovered at Hilderstone near Linlithgow, which the king had purchased from Sir Thomas Hamilton. Sir Bevis was granted £2419 16s. 10d. to finance the works and he was appointed master and surveyor; but after two years the venture proved a financial disaster for James. Bulmer then moved to Ireland and from 1611 to 1612 mined at Kilmore in co. Tipperary. After borrowing £340 from Atkinson he returned to England and died penniless at Randalholme, Alston Moor, Cumberland, in September 1613.

Despite his ignominious end, Sir Bevis Bulmer was one of the earliest British mining entrepreneurs to acquire a national reputation. His stature was such that he was caricatured in Ben Jonson's *Staple of News* (1625) in which a character asks:

Did I not tell you I was bred in the mines
Under Sir Bevis Bullion?
(quoted in Hobson, fol. 14)

LESLIE OWEN TYSON

Sources L. O. Tyson, 'Sir Bevis Bulmer: an Elizabethan adventurer', *British Mining* [Northern Mine Research Society memoirs] (1996), 47–69 • S. Atkinson, *The discoverie and historie of the gold mines in Scotland*, ed. G. L. Meason (1825) • R. W. C. Patrick, *Early records relating to mining in Scotland* (1878) • R. Jenkins, 'Bevis Bulmer', *N&Q*, 11th ser., 4 (1911), 401 • W. R. Scott, *The constitution and finance of English, Scottish and Irish joint-stock companies to 1720*, 3 vols. (New York, 1951) • P. F. Claughton, *The Combe Martin mines* (1992) • G. V. Irving and A. Murray, *The upper ward of Lanarkshire described and delineated*, 3 vols. (1864) • J. W. Gough, *The mines of Mendip* (1967) • J. W. Gough, *The rise of the entrepreneur* (1969) • *CSP dom.*, 1603–10 • R. Surtees, *The history and antiquities of the county palatine of Durham*, 1 (1816), 77–8 • W. D. Hoyle, *Historical notes of the baronial house of Bulmer and its descendants, AD 1042–1750*, ed. G. B. Bulmer (privately printed, 1896?) • M. A. B. Hobson, 'The Bulmer family chronicle from before 1050 to 1936', W. Yorks. AS, Leeds, Yorkshire Archaeological Society, MS 641 [cites Ben Jonson, *Staple of news* (1625), act I, scene iv]
Wealth at death penniless: Surtees, *The history and antiquities*

Bulmer, Edward Frederick (1865–1941). *See under* Bulmer, Henry Percival (1867–1919).

Bulmer, Henry Percival [Percy] (1867–1919), cider maker, was born on 28 January 1867 at the rectory, Credenhill, Herefordshire, the second son of Charles Henry Bulmer (1833–1918), rector of Credenhill, and his wife, Mary Grace Parnel Bulmer (*née* Cockrem). The rector was the son and grandson of Hereford wine merchants and cider makers, and himself won prizes for his bottled cider and perry. Bulmer, who was usually known as Percy, suffered from asthma as a child, and his interrupted education at Hereford Cathedral school between 1880 and 1886 gave him no chance of going to university. In 1887, at the age of twenty, he began to make cider out of the apples grown in his father's glebe orchard, borrowing the family pony and a neighbour's cider-mill for the purpose.

At that time most cider was made by farmers with ancient and primitive equipment out of any apples that came to hand, to be drunk as payment in kind by their thirsty but undiscriminating labourers. Bottled cider, carefully made from selected apples, for sale in hotels, public houses, and off-licences, was a rarity. It was this select market that Bulmer meant to supply. In the autumn of 1887 he moved to Hereford, where in his first full year of business he made forty casks (4000 gallons) of cider, that sold for a mere £157. His elder brother, **Edward Frederick Bulmer** (1865–1941), cider maker, born on 26 May 1865, at the rectory, Credenhill, lent a hand with the manual labour in the long vacations. Unlike Percy, Fred Bulmer went from Hereford Cathedral school to Shrewsbury School, and thence to King's College, Cambridge, with an exhibition in classics. On graduation in 1889, he joined his brother in the cider business. The brothers only had one employee at first, but, small though the firm was, it produced cider of excellent quality, winning prizes in Paris in 1888 and at the Royal Agricultural Show in 1889. These successes almost certainly reflected not only the rector's skill and experience, but also his financial support, as the brothers had little capital. They borrowed from some of Fred's Cambridge friends and from the local bank; the rector, by pledging his life insurance policy, raised a further £1760. With these funds they bought land, erected some buildings, and invested in equipment typical of the industrial age—a steam engine, hydraulic presses and pumps, and some large vats.

There was an informal division of labour between the two brothers: Percy Bulmer concentrated on production, organizing the factory, reading Pasteur on yeasts, visiting Rheims to learn the techniques of champagne making (transferable to cider), and Germany to study the handling of sugar beet (what was good for beet was good for apples). He also studied bottling at the works where the Apollinaris mineral water was produced. The firm consulted analytical chemists from time to time, and from 1905 had a small laboratory of its own, where important discoveries were made by H. E. Durham. Fred Bulmer undertook purchase and marketing, and was, *inter alia*, the commercial traveller. Affable and outgoing, he was equal to most situations. Confronted with a blunt Yorkshireman, who asked him who the hell he thought he was staring at, Fred replied 'The rudest bugger I ever saw' (Bulmer, *Early Days*, 10). The riposte won him a good order and a firm friendship. Nevertheless, he was happy to give up touting for orders when in 1896, with output not far short of 200,000 gallons a year, the firm appointed a full-time commercial traveller. The Bulmers owed their success not only to hard work, access to adequate funds, and a little science, but also to a flair for publicity. In an age well aware of the uses of advertising, they were skilful practitioners of the art: in brochures, by poster, and by the choice of such evocative brand names as Pomagne, Woodpecker, and Strongbow. The firm ran its business on advanced paternalist lines, instituting a superannuation scheme in 1898, and family allowances in 1938. It also built some workers' housing.

Percy Bulmer was chairman and managing director, and also the more single-minded businessman. He was secretary of the short-lived National Association of English Cider Makers, founded in 1894, and, as head of the largest firm of cider makers, was the natural choice as chairman when the association was refounded in 1920. He doubted the power of government to effect much social improvement, whereas Fred Bulmer was an ardent 'new Liberal', active in local politics. He was a local and a county councillor, and was twice mayor of Hereford. In later years, he moved to the right and in 1931 supported the National Government.

Percy Bulmer married a cousin, Susan Mildred Ball (*c*.1875–1968), in 1894, and they had four sons, and a daughter who died in infancy. Fred Bulmer married, in 1899, Sophie Rittner (1874?–1968), the daughter of a Liverpool merchant of German origin. They had three sons and three daughters.

The brothers ran the business as a partnership until 1918, when H. P. Bulmer & Co. was turned into a private company, as a result of Percy Bulmer's developing cancer; he died at the early age of fifty-two at his home, Long-meadow, Hereford, on 2 December 1919. His brother succeeded him as chairman. By then the firm was a soundly established concern with 200 employees, and produced some three-quarters of a million gallons of cider a year. When Fred Bulmer retired in 1938, the workforce had quadrupled, output was approaching 4 million gallons, and the firm was by far the largest cider maker in the country. Fred died on 2 September 1941 at his home, Adams Hill, Breinton, Herefordshire, at the age of seventy-six. Of contrasting characters and complementary talents, H. P. and E. F. Bulmer can fairly be regarded as joint creators of the firm that bears the younger brother's name. It became a public limited company in 1970.

B. W. CLAPP

Sources E. F. Bulmer, *Early days of cidermaking* (1937) · L. P. Wilkinson, *Bulmers of Hereford: a century of cider-making* (1987) · 'Report on the results of investigations into cider making carried out … from 1893 to 1902', *Parl. papers* (1904), 16.219, Cd 1868 · R. H. Bulmer, 'E. F. Bulmer: a man of unique capabilities', *Hereford Times* (9 June 1978) · R. H. Bulmer, 'Bulmer, Edward Frederick', *DBB* · b. cert. · d. cert. · *CGPLA Eng. & Wales* (1920) · b. cert. [Edward Frederick Bulmer] · d. cert. [Edward Frederick Bulmer] · *CGPLA Eng. & Wales* (1942) [Edward Frederick Bulmer]
Archives Hereford Cider Museum, Hereford · Herefs. RO | King's Cam., E. F. Bulmer and N. Wedd corresp.
Likenesses double portrait, photograph (with Edward Frederick Bulmer), Hereford cider museum, H. P. Bulmer Ltd
Wealth at death £35,769 7s. 11d.: probate, 27 Feb 1920, *CGPLA Eng. & Wales* · £48,369 5s. 9d.—Edward Frederick Bulmer: probate, 15 Dec 1942, *CGPLA Eng. & Wales*

Bulmer, William (*bap.* 1757, *d.* 1830), printer, was baptized in Newcastle upon Tyne on 13 November 1757, the seventh child of Thomas Bulmer (*bap.* 1716) and Esther Hodgson (1716–1798). He was apprenticed to Isaac Thompson, Quaker printer of Burnt House Entry, St Nicholas's Churchyard, Newcastle. While apprenticed he took proofs of early wood-engravings of Thomas Bewick, with whom he maintained a lifelong connection. Bulmer was admitted freeman of Newcastle by patrimony at the guild on 19 January 1778, but seems to have left the city by then, since he was not sworn until 13 September 1780. He is supposed to have worked in London for John Bell, then publishing his miniature editions, and may have spent time in Paris to improve his typographical skills.

By 1787 Bulmer was working for George Nicol, the king's bookseller, who was then starting work on the great edition of Shakespeare's plays, illustrated with engravings, that he had proposed in 1786 to John and Josiah Boydell. Nicol had also employed William Martin, brother of Robert Martin, Baskerville's foreman and successor, to cut a splendid transitional typeface for Bulmer's exclusive use until 1805, when it was used by the Liverpool printer John MᶜCreery for the first edition of his poem *The Press*. Bulmer established his Shakspeare [*sic*] Press in London at Cleveland Row, St James's, early in 1790, paying his first poor rate at Lady day, 1790. The folio Shakespeare was published in parts from 1791 to 1804. It was followed by the folio Milton (3 vols., 1794–7), and by perhaps his best work, the Boydells' *History of the River Thames* (2 vols., 1794–6), with coloured aquatints. All three used Martin's typeface very effectively.

By 1790 William Bulmer was a member of the Honourable Band of Gentleman Pensioners, which waited on the king; his elder brother Fenwick Bulmer, a druggist in the Strand and later knighted, probably helped him to purchase his commission. In December 1791, with the support of Sir Joseph Banks, president of the Royal Society, Bulmer was appointed printer to the society, printing the *Philosophical Transactions* from 1792 until his retirement in 1821. George Nicol seems to have been his 'sleeping' partner from the earliest years of the Shakspeare Press, and Bulmer's successor was George's son, William Nicol. Bulmer produced, as a venture at his own expense, the *Poems of Goldsmith and Parnell* (1795), with wood-engravings by Thomas and John Bewick, which caused some acrimony with the elder brother. His fine work was soon recognized, and he gained commissions from several leading London publishers, including William Miller and his successor John Murray II, the Boydells, George Nicol, Longmans, and Cadell and Davies. As well as the Royal Society work he also printed for the East India Company, the British Museum, the Board of Agriculture, the Royal Institution, and the Horticultural Society of London.

Although noted for his fine printing, Bulmer also produced 'jobbing' work such as the cheap pamphlets for the Society for Bettering the Condition and Improving the Comforts of the Poor, and a long run of auction catalogues for R. H. Evans, starting with the famous Roxburghe sale of May 1812. As an outcome of this sale the Roxburghe Club was established, and Bulmer printed sixteen books for the club between 1816 and 1820. He also earned the support of several prominent authors, including Shute Barrington, bishop of Durham, Frederick Howard, earl of Carlisle, Sir Richard Colt Hoare, T. J. Mathias, and T. F. Dibdin. In his *Bibliographical Decameron* (3 vols., 1817), printed by Bulmer, Dibdin writes of the Shakspeare Press that 'it has effectually contributed to the promotion of belles-lettres, and national improvement "in the matter of the puncheon and matrix"' (Dibdin, 396). Working as he did outside the City of London, Bulmer never became a member of the Stationers' Company, but was very active in the committee of London master printers negotiating with compositors and pressmen on piece-work rates over the years 1805–11, chairing the committee, of which Thomas Bensley was secretary, on several occasions. Bulmer retired to Clapham Rise, London, where he entertained Thomas Bewick in August 1828, and where he died on 9 September 1830, being survived by his wife Elizabeth. He was buried on 16 September in St Clement Danes in the Strand.

PETER ISAAC

Sources P. Isaac, *William Bulmer: the fine printer in context, 1757–1830* (1993) · R. Welford, *Men of mark 'twixt Tyne and Tweed*, 1 (1895), 431–6 · T. F. Dibdin, *The bibliographical decameron*, 2 (1817), 382–96 · J. Dreyfus and P. Isaac, 'William Bulmer's will', in J. Dreyfus and P. Isaac, *Studies in the book trade in honour of Graham Pollard* (1975),

341–9 • H. V. Marrot, *William Bulmer, Thomas Bensley: a study in transition* (1930) • [J. B. Nichols], *GM*, 1st ser., 100/2 (1830), 305–10 • [R. Pollard], 'Biographical sketch of three Newcastle apprentices', *Newcastle Magazine*, 9/10 (Oct 1830), 464–6 • *IGI*

Likenesses J. Ramsay, lithograph, pubd 1827, NPG • J. Ramsay, lithograph, pubd 1827 (after his portrait), NPG • P. Audinet, line print (after J. Ramsay), BM; repro. in Nichols, *GM* • engraving, repro. in Dibdin, *Bibliographical decameron*, 395 • engraving, repro. in Nichols, *GM*, facing p. 305

Wealth at death considerable wealth; money and property: will, PRO, PROB 11/1775

Bulstrode, Cecily (*bap.* 1584, *d.* 1609), courtier and subject of poetry, was baptized on 12 February 1584 at Beaconsfield, one of the ten children of Edward Bulstrode (*d.* 1595), landowner, and his wife, Cecily (*fl.* 1575–1608), daughter of Sir John Croke of Chilton, Buckinghamshire, and his wife, Elizabeth, and sister of Sir John Croke, recorder of London. Edward *Bulstrode (*c.*1588–1659) was her brother.

Members of the Bulstrode family had been minor courtiers in the fifteenth and sixteenth centuries, and Cecily Bulstrode followed them. In 1605 she was among the entourage of the countess of Bedford, her mother's first cousin and her father's second cousin. Her possession at that time of a copy of a surreptitiously circulated puritan text suggests that she shared Lady Bedford's godly religious inclinations. By 1607 she and her sister Dorothy were gentlewomen of the queen's bedchamber. She became the object of scandalous gossip at court. Two poems attributed to Sir John Roe, 'True Love Finds Wit' and 'Shall I go force an elegie?' are identified as about her in early manuscripts; the latter is about a woman's offer to have sexual intercourse once, and once only, with an admirer. Bulstrode has, on the basis of an obscure passage in a letter of Donne's, been seen as the lover of Roe's brother Sir Thomas. Ben Jonson attacked her as promiscuous, vain, and untrustworthy in his 'Epigram on the Court Pucell', a copy of which was stolen from him when he was drunk and given to Bulstrode. The subject of this poem associates with 'sermoneeres', but also with wits at court, and writes 'newes Equall with that, which for the best newes goes' (*Ben Jonson*, 8.222). This has been taken as evidence that the essays called 'newes' which were published with Sir Thomas Overbury's poem *A Wife* were composed by friends of Bulstrode's, and that she herself wrote the essay 'Newes of my Morning Worke', which is identified in *A Wife* as by 'Mris B'. Jonson's poem is, however, to some extent a formal exercise in satire, and it would be unwise to depend upon it as a biographical document.

Bulstrode fell ill in 1609, suffering great pain, sleeplessness, fever, and vomiting. Francis Anthony dosed her with potable gold, and claimed that this had helped her. She died on 4 August 1609 at the countess of Bedford's house, The Park, Twickenham, and was buried two days later at the church there. The title of a poem on her death by Edward Herbert (later Lord Herbert of Cherbury) states that she died 'non sine inquietudine spiritus et conscientiae' ('with an unquiet spirit and conscience'). Jonson also commemorated her in verse, as did Donne, in

the poems 'Death I recant' and 'Language thou art too narrow', which can be seen as products of Lady Bedford's patronage. Another elegy, 'Death be not proud', apparently a reply to 'Death I recant', has been ascribed to the countess herself.

In the 1990s Bulstrode was rediscovered by historians of women's writing. Although 'Newes of my Morning Worke' is very short, and dubiously ascribed to her, it has been admired by some critics, and it has been suggested that more witty pieces by her may lie undiscovered.

JOHN CONSIDINE

Sources J. Lee, 'Who is Cecilia, what was she?: Cecilia Bulstrode and Jonson's epideictics', *JEGP: Journal of English and Germanic Philology*, 85 (1986), 20–34 • *Liber famelicus of Sir James Whitelocke, a judge of the court of king's bench in the reigns of James I and Charles I*, ed. J. Bruce, CS, old ser., 70 (1858) • *Ben Jonson*, ed. C. H. Herford, P. Simpson, and E. M. Simpson, 11 vols. (1925–52) • *Calendar of the manuscripts of the most hon. the marquess of Salisbury*, 17, HMC, 9 (1938) • *VCH Buckinghamshire*, vol. 3 • B. K. Lewalski, *Writing women in Jacobean England* (1993) • R. W. Halli, 'Cecilia Bulstrode, "the court pucell"', *Subjects on the world's stage: essays on British literature of the middle ages and the Renaissance*, ed. D. G. Allen and R. A. White (1995), 295–312 • J. E. Savage, *The 'Conceited newes' of Sir Thomas Overbury and his friends* (1968) • L. Schleiner, *Tudor and Stuart women writers* (1994) • Blain, Clements & Grundy, *Feminist comp.*

Bulstrode, Edward (*c.*1588–1659), judge, was the second son of Edward Bulstrode (*d.* 1595) of Hedgerley and Upton, Buckinghamshire, and his wife, Cecily, daughter of Sir John Croke of Chilton, Buckinghamshire. Cecily *Bulstrode (*bap.* 1584, *d.* 1609) was his sister. He matriculated from St John's College, Oxford, on 27 January 1604 and was specially admitted two years later to the Inner Temple at the request of his uncle, the bencher George Croke, and his marriage to Margaret Chamberlain probably took place soon after. Despite close links to an extensive legal dynasty, together with the 'Favor and Care' (*The Seconde Part of the Reports of Edward Bulstrode*, 1658, sig. b2v) of his brother-in-law James Whitelocke, Bulstrode climbed the professional ladder only slowly. Called utter-barrister in 1614, he was not promoted to the bench of the Inner Temple until November 1629; some three years later he delivered a Lent reading on the statute 21 Hen. VIII c. 13 (pluralities).

In the 1620s and 1630s Bulstrode practised in the courts of chancery, king's bench, and Star Chamber, followed the midland and Oxford assize circuits, and occasionally appeared before the Warwickshire quarter sessions; from 1633 he also held a retainer to represent the council of the marches in Westminster Hall. He was not among the bar's leaders, which may account for the deletion of his name from a list of candidates recommended by the judges in 1637 for call as serjeants. This and other setbacks are referred to by his nephew Bulstrode Whitelocke, in noting the failure of an attempt to have his uncle 'made a Judge, who for his learning & integrity deserved it, butt was not fortunate in the world' (*Diary of Bulstrode Whitelocke*, 112). Efforts to gain a Welsh judgeship for Bulstrode the following year were also fruitless. His financial position may well have worried his relatives, not least those to whom he owed money, especially given the unprecedented downturn in legal business which he himself noted in a letter of November 1639 (Prest, 82).

Despite making a token contribution towards the king's expedition against the Scots early in 1640, and absenting himself from London throughout the civil war years, neither Bulstrode's family connections nor his godly religious zeal would have inclined him to the royalist cause. Yet an apparent lack of active commitment to parliament, coupled with military service in the king's army by his son Richard *Bulstrode (1617–1711), evidently prompted some attempted retaliation against his Warwickshire estates in 1647. Bulstrode was nevertheless regarded as sufficiently reliable to be successfully nominated by his nephew that same year to serve as second justice of the Anglesey circuit, an office confirmed by the Rump Parliament in 1649, as also to be appointed early next year to the commission of the peace for Warwickshire. In July 1653 Bulstrode became chief justice of north Wales.

Although Whitelocke failed to gain his uncle an Irish judge's place in 1656, Bulstrode's effusive gratitude for his nephew's past good offices was expressed in the dedicatory epistles to two books published in the last years of his life. *A Golden-Chain, or, A Miscelany of Divine Sentences* (1657) is a structured anthology of scriptural extracts, with special reference to the management of worldly afflictions. A more original and longer-lived compilation was the first of three substantial volumes of law reports which appeared successively between 1657 and 1659, and were reissued in 1688. Covering king's bench suits in 1610–17, and 1625–6, as well as some poor-law assizes cases from the early years of Charles I, these were translated by Bulstrode from his original law-French notes into English, the first reports to have been so published by their author. Edward Bulstrode was buried in the Temple Church on 4 April 1659. As with most other details of his personal life, it is unknown whether his wife survived him.

WILFRID PREST

Sources DNB · Foster, *Alum. Oxon.* · G. Lipscomb, *The history and antiquities of the county of Buckingham*, 4 vols. (1831–47), vol. 4, pp. 501–3, 572, 574–5, 620 · W. R. Williams, *The history of the great sessions in Wales, 1542–1830* (privately printed, Brecon, 1899) · *Liber famelicus of Sir James Whitelocke, a judge of the court of king's bench in the reigns of James I and Charles I*, ed. J. Bruce, CS, old ser., 70 (1858) · *The diary of Bulstrode Whitelocke, 1605–1675*, ed. R. Spalding, British Academy, Records of Social and Economic History, new ser., 13 (1990) · R. L. Lloyd, ed., 'Admissions to the Inner Temple to 1659', typescript, 1954, Inner Temple Library, London · F. A. Inderwick and R. A. Roberts, eds., *A calendar of the Inner Temple records*, 2 (1898) · W. R. Prest, *The rise of the barristers: a social history of the English bar, 1590–1640*, 2nd edn (1991) · *Warwickshire county records, quarter sessions order books*, vols. 1–3, 1625–1657, ed. S. C. Ratcliff and J. C. Johnson (1935–7) · Baker, *Serjeants* · register, London, Temple Church, 4 April 1659 [burial] · A. Hughes, *Politics, society and civil war in Warwickshire, 1620–1660* (1987) · V. M. Larminie, *Wealth, kinship and culture: the seventeenth-century Newdigates of Arbury and their world*, Royal Historical Society Studies in History, 72 (1995)
Wealth at death not well off: *The Diary of Bulstrode Whitelocke*, ed. Spalding, 112, 191, 511

Bulstrode, Sir Richard (1617–1711), diplomat and writer, probably born at Astley, Warwickshire, was the second

son of Edward *Bulstrode (*c.*1588–1659) of the Inner Temple and his wife, Margaret, daughter of Richard Chamberlain of Astley. In 1633 he wrote a poem to mark the birth of the duke of York, and he was admitted to the Inner Temple on 26 January 1634. He matriculated from Pembroke College, Cambridge, on 4 January 1640.

At the outbreak of the civil war Bulstrode stated: 'I was then in a labyrinth, not knowing well which way to go; but at last I resolved to go to Whitehall with some gentlemen of the Inner Temple, being then newly come thither from Cambridge' (Bulstrode, *Memoirs*, 2). According to his own, largely unsubstantiated, account, he fought for the king at Powick Bridge, losing his hat when his horse bolted towards the enemy, and then joined the prince of Wales's horse, in which he fought at Edgehill. There, 'I was wounded in the head by a person who turn'd upon me and struck me with his poleaxe' (Bodl. Oxf., MS Eng. hist. b.172, fol. 135); Bulstrode's life was saved by Sir Thomas Byron, who shot the assailant dead. He fought at Brentford, became adjutant to Lord Wentworth, and in 1643 took up the same post under Lord Wilmot. Again according to himself, in 1644 Bulstrode became adjutant-general of all the royalist cavalry, fighting at Lostwithiel, the second battle of Newbury, the siege of Taunton, and finally Langport.

With the ending of the civil war Bulstrode returned to the Inner Temple, being called to the bar on 12 May 1648. He married Joyce (or Jocosa) Dineley (*d.* 1677) on 21 February 1650. She was a daughter of Edward Dineley of Charlton, Worcestershire, and throughout the 1650s Bulstrode was greatly concerned with the management of the Dineley estate. His family and legal connections with moderate supporters of the Commonwealth (notably Bulstrode Whitelocke) led to a political rehabilitation as well: he seemingly became recorder of Reading in 1656 and served as steward of the borough twice between 1656 and 1658 thanks to the recommendation of Whitelocke and Charles Fleetwood. At the Restoration he was lodging in London at the house of Clarges the apothecary, whose sister was married to General George Monck, subsequently duke of Albemarle.

Unfortunately the absence of dates on a number of key sources makes it difficult to construct a satisfactory chronology and explanation for Bulstrode's actions between about 1665 and about 1669. His memoirs claimed that he was responsible for organizing Wentworth's funeral at Toddington, Bedfordshire, in 1667, that his outlay on the funeral was not repaid, and that he then fled to Bruges to avoid his creditors. However, in 1665 he was actually involved in two audacious thefts—first absconding to Ireland with £500 of plate belonging to Lady Wentworth (or so she claimed), then appropriating £600 belonging to the foot guards. The secretary of state's office ordered that he be tracked down at Bruges, and he certainly spent over two years in prison there. From his cell he petitioned Charles II to pardon him 'for his breach of trust in the place he conferred upon him'; imprisonment was 'a just punishment for his great fault … to the total ruin of himself and family, and the loss of one of his arms' (*CSP dom.*,

1653, 334—document wrongly calendared). While in prison he was converted to Roman Catholicism by Father John Cross, president of Douai College, and he subsequently engaged in a regular correspondence with Cardinal Howard and the duke of Norfolk.

On his release Bulstrode became auditor of a Scottish regiment serving in the Southern Netherlands, and on 14 July 1674 his official rehabilitation was completed when he was appointed English agent at Brussels. He was back in England in 1675–6, was knighted at Whitehall on 19 January 1676, and obtained the higher status of resident ambassador in James II's reign. His voluminous diplomatic correspondence survives, and is particularly important for the period of the Franco-Dutch war that ended in 1679 and for the reactions of the government in the Southern Netherlands to Louis XIV's policy of *réunion* in the 1680s. At some time after the death of his first wife on 24 September 1677, Bulstrode married the much younger Marie Stamford (*d*. after 1717), daughter of the duke of Neuburg's envoy to England, and began a second family.

Following the revolution of 1688 Bulstrode stayed on in Brussels and remained loyal to the old regime. In September 1689 Queen Mary of Modena requested and obtained lodgings for him and his family at the English Dominicans' convent in Brussels. He continued to serve as James II's agent there, sending regular letters of intelligence to St Germain and using the convent to shelter Jacobite deserters trying to reach the French lines. In 1694 his intelligence activities were discovered and he was forced to flee, leaving his family behind. In 1695–6 he was employed by the French to carry on correspondence in the Southern Netherlands, and at the completion of this mission the family was reunited at St Germain.

Bulstrode spent his last two decades of life in dire poverty, despite obtaining a pension from the queen of £166 (later reduced to £152). William III refused to pay his arrears; when he was ordered to move temporarily to Lier in 1691 his creditors confiscated and sold his goods; at his flight from Brussels in 1694 his remaining effects were confiscated; and during the bombardment of Brussels in 1695–6 his wife's properties there were burnt down. In 1694 he complained to his son Whitelocke 'how many children we have to provide for and how little we have to do it with', although the same letter also informed his 43-year-old son that Lady Bulstrode was pregnant again (BL, Add. MS 39923, fol. 13). In April 1703 Sir Richard wrote again to Whitelocke, stating that 'my present weakness and old age are sorely increasing', and requesting that Whitelocke's grant of £10 a year should be continued to Lady Bulstrode after his death. On 14 August 1700 he had been appointed a commissioner of the household at St Germain, and was reappointed by 'James III' on 6 December 1701. In 1706–7 he wrote to the duke of Marlborough to request the latter's protection for the convents in Lier and Brussels which then housed two of his daughters: Bulstrode described himself as 'the eldest, and I am sure the poorest with a numerous family that ever served the crown' who was 'obliged to spend my last days in studying

how to live, and not how to serve' (BL, Add. MS 61365, fol. 36).

Bulstrode died at St Germain on 3 October 1711 and was buried there two days later. Following his death his considerable literary output—composed chiefly in the last two decades of his life—was finally published, beginning in 1712 with Edward Bysshe's edition of letters from the early part of his Brussels residency. A volume of essays with a preface by Whitelocke Bulstrode was published in 1715, and his *Memoirs and Reflections*, concerning the reigns of Charles I and II, were published in 1721. A life of James II was also published at Rome. His essays reflected upon such themes as company and conversation, solitariness and retirement, and greatness of mind. Perhaps the most poignant, and one which Bulstrode was peculiarly well qualified to write, was an essay on old age:

> None can imagine how green and vigorous some men's minds are in old age, having a perpetual conflict with their bodies ... most men take care to live long, but few take care to live well ... life is to be measured by our actions, not by time. A man may die old at thirty, and young at eighty; the one lives after death, the other perished before he died. (Bulstrode, *Miscellaneous Essays*, 383–90)

The legends surrounding Bulstrode's longevity and virility began almost immediately after his death. In 1712 Bysshe stated that his subject had died at the age of 101; that he had seven living children (several under twenty) from his second marriage; that even when over eighty he often walked for 12 miles in the mornings; and that he would even have survived his last illness if his own doctor had been available. In his *Pedigrees of the Knights*, John Le Neve went further, claiming that Sir Richard had died at the age of 105 and had seventeen children, the eldest seventy-two, the youngest thirteen. These statements seem to have originated in a bizarre misreading of an unidentified source, perhaps the parish registers of St Germain. Le Neve, in particular, consistently exaggerated his numbers by ten—thus Bulstrode's age should have been given as ninety-five, the number of children (by the second wife only) as seven. Sir Richard himself stated that he was born in 1617 (BL, Add. MS 38855, fol. 130). His children from his first marriage were Edward (*c*.1650–1718), Whitelocke *Bulstrode (1652–1724), and Thomas (*d*. *c*.1661); the children from his second marriage were Charlotte (who married Dr Lawrence Wood), Mary (who married Sir Edward Hales), Anne (who married Colonel John Parker), Frances (who became a nun), and at least three sons, Benjamin, Joseph, and Richard, and possibly a James as well. The last child was born in the mid-1690s, leading Bulstrode to note with some pride and bemusement that there was an age difference of forty-four years between his eldest and youngest children. J. D. DAVIES

Sources R. Bulstrode, *Memoirs and reflections upon the reign and government of King Charles I and King Charles II* (1721) · R. Bulstrode, *Miscellaneous essays* (1715) · 'The chronicles of Bulstrode', compiled by Henry Wilton Bulstrode, 1936–9, BL, Add. MSS 47604–7 · miscellaneous papers, Bodl. Oxf., MS Eng. hist. b. 172 · Hodgkin papers, letters by Bulstrode, BL, Add. MS 38855 · E. Bysshe, *Original letters written to the earl of Arlington by Sir Richard Bulstrode*, 1712 · C. E. Lart, ed., *The parochial registers of Saint Germain-en-Laye: Jacobite extracts of births, marriages, and deaths*, 2 vols. (1910–12) · letter book of

H. Brown, 1690–91, BL, Add. MS 37662 • Bulstrode's letters to Marlborough, BL, Add. MS 61365, fols. 36, 113 • Jacobite letters, BL, Add. MS 39923 • *The manuscripts of J. Eliot Hodgkin … of Richmond, Surrey*, HMC, 39 (1897) • *Le Neve's Pedigrees of the knights*, ed. G. W. Marshall, Harleian Society, 8 (1873) • private information (2004) [Dr Edward Corp] • *Calendar of the Stuart papers belonging to his majesty the king, preserved at Windsor Castle*, 7 vols., HMC, 56 (1902–23), vols. 1, 7 • *CSP dom., 1653–67*, esp. 1653, p. 334, 1666, p. 237 • P. S. Lachs, *The diplomatic corps under Charles II and James II* (New Brunswick, New Jersey, 1965) • G. Hilton Jones, *Charles Middleton: the life and times of a Restoration politician* (1967) • W. A. Shaw, ed., *Calendar of treasury books*, [33 vols. in 64], PRO (1904–69), esp. vols. 7–8 [1681–5, 1685–1689] • PRO, SP 77/38–55 • letters to Bulstrode, BL, Add. MS 64950 • Bulstrode papers, BL, Egerton MSS 3678–84, esp. 3681 • Melfort's letter book, 1692, BL, Add. MS 37661 • letters to Bulstrode, BL, Add. MSS 62585–6 • letters to Bulstrode, Bodl. Oxf., MS Eng. hist. d. 154 • letters to Henry Coventry, Longleat House, Wiltshire, Thynne MSS • Venn, *Alum. Cant.* • G. M. Bell, *A handlist of British diplomatic representatives, 1509–1688*, Royal Historical Society Guides and Handbooks, 16 (1990) • W. A. Shaw, *The knights of England*, 2 (1906), 251 • G. Lipscomb, *The history and antiquities of the county of Buckingham*, 4 vols. (1831–47), vol. 4, p. 503 • Bulstrode pedigree, Bodl. Oxf., MS Rawl. B.53, fol. 163 • letters to Southwell, BL, Add. MSS 34341–4 • *Calendar of the manuscripts of the marquess of Ormonde*, new ser., 8 vols., HMC, 36 (1902–20), vols. 6–7 • *Report on the manuscripts of the marquis of Downshire*, 6 vols. in 7, HMC, 75 (1924–95), vol. 1 • F. W. Steer, ed., *Arundel Castle archives*, 1 (1968), 220–21, 226

Archives Bodl. Oxf., memoirs (fragment), MSS Eng. Hist. b172, d154 • NL Scot., corresp., MSS 420, 3418, 3830 | Arundel Castle, West Sussex, corresp. with duke of Norfolk • BL, Add. MSS, esp. 34341–34344, 37661–37662, 38847, 38855, 39923, 41832, 47899, 61365, 62585–62586, 64950; Egerton MSS, esp. 3678–3684 • BL, newsletters to first earl of Conway, Add. MS 40861 • Longleat House, Wiltshire, Thynne papers, letters to Henry Coventry • Yale U., Beinecke L., Osborn collection

Likenesses S. H. Harding, stipple, pubd 1795, BM, NPG

Bulstrode, Whitelocke (1652–1724), administrator and religious writer, was born on 25 September 1652, the second of three sons of Sir Richard *Bulstrode (1617–1711), diplomat, and his first wife, Joyce or Jocosa (d. 1677), daughter of Edward Dineley of Charlton, Worcestershire. He was named after his father's cousin, Bulstrode *Whitelocke. Whitelocke Bulstrode was specially admitted as a student of the Inner Temple on 27 November 1664 and called to the bar on 22 June 1702. The revolution of 1688 divided Bulstrode and his Jacobite father, who followed King James into exile. Bulstrode himself was a staunch whig and devout protestant, whose notebooks are full of religious reflections, particularly on occasions of taking the sacrament. He did, however, maintain communication with his Jacobite relatives.

Bulstrode's first publication was *An Essay of Transmigration, in Defence of Pythagoras, or, A Discourse of Natural Philosophy* (1692). This wide-ranging work of natural philosophy drew particularly on alchemical sources. Bulstrode was an admirer of Eirenaeus Philalethes, the pseudonym of the American alchemist George Starkey, whom he referred to several times as 'the great Eirenaeus'. Bulstrode argued that transmigration—the theory of the passage of the soul at death into another body—applied properly to vegetative and sensitive rather than rational souls, and that ancient mythology was an elaborately coded system of natural and experimental philosophy. The book

was republished in 1693. A Latin translation by Oswald Dyke was published in 1725.

Bulstrode married into his mother's family. His wife was Elizabeth, daughter of Samuel Dineley of Charlton. The couple had one son, Richard, and two daughters, Mary and Anne. Bulstrode established himself as a landowner in Hounslow, Middlesex, buying the manor of Hounslow from the heirs of Henry Sayer in 1706. He was the chief of nine subscribers who set up a charity school for twelve boys at Hounslow in 1708 (the school was last heard of in 1717) and donated a flagon, cup, and paten cover to Holy Trinity, Hounslow. He also was a leader of the local bench after being appointed a justice of the peace for Middlesex in 1709, serving several times as chair of quarter sessions. Bulstrode's morally reformist charges to the grand jury and other juries were published twice in 1718 and once in 1722. The charges were collected as *A compendium of the crown laws, contained in three charges given by Whitelocke Bulstrode, esq. at Westminster* (1723). Bulstrode, who had already served as solicitor to the excise, was appointed a commissioner of the excise by the whig government in 1709 on the retirement of Foote Onslow, keeping the extremely lucrative position (it paid £800 a year) with some difficulty through the subsequent tory government. The Hanoverian succession, while gratifying Bulstrode's public spirit, dashed his career, as despite frantic efforts he lost his position as commissioner to a client of Robert Walpole's. Still a whig advocate, following the Jacobite rising of 1715 he published under his favourite pseudonym of Philalethes, *A letter touching the late rebellion, and what means led to it, and of the Pretender's title, shewing the duty and interest of all protestants to be faithful to King George* (1717), and seized several crates of guns and swords headed for Bristol in 1716. He hectored the leaders of the new whig government with letters recounting his services and attempting to get a position for his son Richard.

Bulstrode composed a preface for a collection of his father's writings, *Miscellaneous Essays* (1715), which he dedicated to Charles Montagu, earl of Halifax. He also published an improved version of an exchange of letters he had had in 1709 and 1710 with Lawrence Wood, physician to James Stuart, the Old Pretender, and the husband of his half-sister, on the respective claims of the Roman and Anglican churches. This went through three editions in 1717 as *Letters between Dr. Wood, a Roman Catholic, the Pretender's physician, and Whitelocke Bulstrode esq., a member of the Church of England, touching the true church, and whether there is salvation out of the Roman communion* and one in 1718 as *The Pillars of Popery Thrown Down*. His last published work was a miscellaneous collection, *Essays, upon the Following Subjects* (1724). The frontispiece is an engraving after a portrait of Bulstrode by Godfrey Kneller.

Bulstrode died at Hatton Garden, London, on 27 November 1724, and was buried against the north wall of the chancel of the priory chapel at Hounslow. A monument was set up to his memory there.   WILLIAM E. BURNS

Sources DNB • W. Bulstrode, notebooks, Folger • *VCH Middlesex* • F. A. Inderwick and R. A. Roberts, eds., *A calendar of the Inner Temple records*, 1 (1896)

Archives BL, commonplace books, M/604 [copies] · Bodl. Oxf., letter-book · Folger · NYPL, Carl H. Pforzheimer collection, meditations, account books, and commonplace book · Yale U., Beinecke L., letter-book
Likenesses T. Cole, line engraving (after portrait by G. Kneller), repro. in W. Bulstrode, *Essays, upon the following subjects* (1724), frontispiece

Bulteel, Henry Bellenden (1800–1866), religious controversialist and seceder from the Church of England, was born on 14 September 1800 at Bellevue, Turnchapel, Plymstock, the fourth of the ten children of Thomas Hillersdon Bulteel (1766–1815) of Bellevue, and his wife, Anne, daughter of Christopher Harris of Radford, Plymstock. When the two eldest of Henry's six brothers died of their wounds after the attempted assault on Bergen op Zoom in 1814, his father (who never fully recovered from the shock) resolved against a military career for his younger sons. At Eton (1815–18) Henry lost the use of an eye in an accident, but at Brasenose College, Oxford, he was a great oarsman; he graduated BA in 1822, and was notorious for his rowdy behaviour during the Queen Caroline riots. In 1823 he was elected fellow of Exeter College and was ordained in 1824, taking a country curacy. On returning to Oxford in January 1826 as tutor and bursar at Exeter his lifestyle was more serious, and his Calvinist conversion in the summer caused some embarrassment to the rector of Exeter, John Collier Jones (d. 1838), especially when, as curate-in-charge of St Ebbe's from December 1826, his preaching attracted a following among undergraduates.

Bulteel vacated his fellowship on 6 October 1829 when he married Eleanor Sadler (1790–1878), the daughter of Thomas Blakeney Sadler, a pastry-cook in the High Street, Oxford, and the niece of James Sadler, pioneer balloonist. In 1830 Bulteel assisted in the efforts which removed J. H. Newman from the Church Missionary Society secretaryship at Oxford. His sensational 'Sermon on I Corinthians ii.12', preached before the University of Oxford in St Mary's on 6 February 1831, condemned the establishment's Erastianism and its widespread rejection of the doctrine of predestination as found in the articles, more specifically singling out the indiscriminate giving of testimonials for ordination candidates. It went through several editions and provoked some rejoinders. Having, in effect, anathematized the establishment, Bulteel joined William Tiptaft in a tour of the west country, preaching in dissenting chapels and in the open air. When, in August, his licence was withdrawn, he gathered several hundred of his former parishioners in his garden and destroyed the episcopal document of revocation, describing it as 'the act of an officer of Antichrist's Church' (*Jackson's Oxford Journal*). About a month later W. E. Gladstone, formerly an occasional worshipper at St Ebbe's, detected a 'soreness of spirit' (*Diaries*, 1.384). Impressed by the healings in Edward Irving's church in London, Bulteel began to teach Irving's doctrine of general redemption. Various healings occurred in Bulteel's congregation, details of which appeared in his *Doctrine of the Miraculous Interference of Jesus* (1832). In February 1832 he was baptized in James Hinton's Baptist meeting-house and in June a new chapel was opened for his congregation at the rear of Pembroke College, Oxford.

When in May 1833 Bulteel abandoned Irvingism some of his followers (known locally as 'Bulteelers') went elsewhere, but he continued to serve his independent congregation. At this stage they were loosely identified with the Brethren but in 1840 some of them seceded to form a separate Brethren assembly, probably because Bulteel was the chapel's only minister. By now his style was less controversial though his disapproval of the established church was unchanged. In 1844 he published a sermon delivered at the opening of a congregation of the Free Church of England in Exeter. When he moved to Plymouth after his mother's death in 1849 he worshipped with former Brethren, including his cousin J. L. Harris, in Ebrington Street Chapel; after 1862 he attended Compton Street Chapel where, with S. P. Tregelles, he preached occasionally. From February 1865 his health declined, and he died on 28 December 1866 at The Crescent, Plymouth. He was survived by two sons and by his widow, who died in Plymouth on 25 September 1878.

TIMOTHY C. F. STUNT

Sources J. S. Reynolds, *The evangelicals at Oxford, 1735–1871: a record of an unchronicled movement* (1953), 97–9 · T. C. F. Stunt, 'John Henry Newman and the evangelicals', *Journal of Ecclesiastical History*, 21 (1970), 65–74 · T. C. F. Stunt, *From awakening to secession: radical evangelicals in Switzerland and Britain, 1815–35* (2000) · H. H. Rowden, *The origins of the Brethren, 1825–1850* (1967), 61–9 · C. W. Boase, *Registrum Collegii Exoniensis*, 2 vols. (1879–94), 114–15 · Fellows' Registers and Library Register, Exeter College, A.I.7–8; D.IV.2 · C. E. Pitman, *The history and pedigree of the family of Pitman* (1920), 58–60 · C. Stapleton, Diary of Catherine Stapleton (née Bulteel), Plymouth Library, Acc. 381, introduction · *Jackson's Oxford Journal* (20 Aug 1831) · Gladstone, *Diaries* · S. P. Tregelles, Letter from S. P. Tregelles to B. W. Newton, 21 Feb 1865, JRL, 7181 · S. P. Tregelles, Letter from S. P. Tregelles to B. W. Newton, 30 March 1865, JRL, 7181 · *DNB* · Boase, *Mod. Eng. biog.*
Archives priv. coll., letters
Likenesses silhouette, Commercial Road Baptist Church, London; repro. in J. Betjeman, *An Oxford University chest* (1938), 133
Wealth at death under £8000: probate, 7 Feb 1867, CGPLA Eng. & Wales

Bulteel, John (bap. 1627, d. in or before 1692), writer and translator, was probably the second son and sixth child of John Bulteel (1584–1665), pastor of the Walloon church at Canterbury, and his wife, Marie Gabry: he was baptized there by his father on 26 August 1627. The Bulteels were even then an old family which first arose in Picardy and was first recorded in England in 1205. Many were wool merchants who traded with Flanders, where some of them settled: Bulteels are first recorded there in the mid-fifteenth century. Pastor John Bulteel was born in London in 1584, the third son of Gilles Bulteel and his wife, Marie, who had settled there in 1578. They were Walloons, French-speaking protestant refugees from Tournai in Flanders, who fled their home rather than face forced conversion to Rome under Spanish rule. Gilles died in London in 1603. At the time of the 1633–4 visitation of London Peter, the eldest of his four sons, was one of the wealthiest merchants in the City. His brother John Bulteel matriculated in March 1598 and entered Emmanuel College,

Cambridge, aged fifteen. In 1603 he went on to the University of Leiden, where he was ordained in 1610, returning to London in 1612. Soon afterwards he became a minister of the French church in Threadneedle Street where his family worshipped and another member of his family had been elected a deacon in 1578. By June 1618 Pastor John had moved to Canterbury where he was appointed minister of the Walloon church, in the crypt of Canterbury Cathedral. He resigned his position on 10 September 1640, moving a few years later to Dover as minister of another French church, and dying there in 1665.

Little is known of his son, the writer John Bulteel, who left Canterbury as a young man and seems to have settled in London where his eldest sister, Anne Guyot, was living. He must not be confused with his cousin, another John Bulteel, son of his uncle Peter Bulteel. That John Bulteel was secretary to the earl of Clarendon and a friend of Pepys, elected MP for Lostwithiel in 1661 and again in 1669. He died the same year.

John Bulteel the writer did not always sign his work or else merely put J. B. Gent.—sometimes only I. B.—so there is probably much more than has been identified. To confuse the issue his father published a number of translations of French theological works. The earliest identifiable work by the son is *London's Triumph, or, The Solemn and Magnificent Reception of that Honourable Gentleman, Robert Tichburn, Lord Mayor*. Dated October 1656, it is a eulogy on London, which he describes as a city 'where the rich live splendidly and the poorest are free from want'. Like his father, he was a linguist and made translations from both French and Italian as well as the classics. The best known of these was from Corneille's *Amour à la mode*. Rendered in heroic verse often close to doggerel, it was first published in 1665 as *The Amorous Orontus*. After being performed in London, it was reissued in 1675 as *The Amorous Gallant*. Bulteel also edited several collections of verse, to which he contributed himself, and numerous pamphlets. His last recorded work appeared in 1683 with the title *Apophthegmes of the Ancients, Taken out of Plutarch … and Others*.

Just when Bulteel married and died is unclear but Susan Bulteele (d. 1698, spelling varies), of Erith in Kent, made her will in 1692, being the 'widow' of John Bulteele, esquire, 'recently deceased'. One of her executors was her son, Peter, a merchant in Lisbon, the other her brother-in-law, Samuel Bulteel, who would act as sole executor during his nephew's absence overseas. Susan bequeathed property near Northfleet, Kent, where she wished to be buried: Pastor John Bulteel's descendants were connected with Northfleet for many years. She made special provision for 'my unmarried daughter Elizabeth', who was to have £250 from her own estate and £50 p.a. from the estate of her father, John Bulteel. A married daughter, Leah, and a grandchild, Susan, are also mentioned.

VIVIEN ALLEN

Sources private information (2004) [senior research archivist, Canterbury Cathedral; Jean-Marie Bultheel; R. Gwynne] • I. Scoloudi, ed., *Returns of strangers in the metropolis, 1593, 1627, 1635, 1639*, Huguenot Society of London, Quarto series, 57 (1985)

Likenesses J. Faber sen., engraving, 1699 (after earlier portrait?), NPG

Bultitude, Elizabeth (1809–1890), Primitive Methodist preacher, was born on 12 August 1809 at Hardwick, Norfolk, into a large and very poor family. She had no formal education. Her parents attended the nearby Wesleyan Methodist chapel, taking their children with them. When Elizabeth was thirteen her father died; the family was forced to search for work and so moved to Norwich, where they lived at starvation level. Primitive Methodist preachers held a camp meeting, led by Samuel Atterby, on Mousehold Heath, near Norwich, on 14 May 1826. Elizabeth recorded in her journal that she went without food that day, though it is not clear whether the fast was from choice or necessity. She was converted, but did not become a Primitive Methodist until 1829, when John Smith was stationed in Norwich as the denomination's itinerant minister.

It soon became evident that Elizabeth Bultitude had an aptitude for preaching and on 20 December 1830 she received a 'note' from Smith authorizing her to preach. For the first quarter she accompanied Elizabeth Fuller, assisting with her services, then in March she was appointed an exhorter and had to preach her trial sermon. She described the occasion: 'I broke down, but Mr. Smith helped me up. I preached it at Lakenham old chapel, which was full of people' (*Primitive Methodist Magazine*, 1891, 565). Becoming a local preacher 'on trial' in June, she was appointed to take forty-five Sunday services during the next four quarters. She became a travelling preacher in 1832, commencing her itinerancy on 22 July in the Norwich circuit, which 'pledged' her (undertook to take her back if she was deemed unsuitable) in 1833. Circuits in which she was stationed were Mattishall (1833); Lynn (1834, 1835); North Walsham (1836, 1837); Soham and Watton (1838, 1839); Wisbech (1840); Fakenham (1841); Peterborough (1842, 1843); Aylesham (1844—first six months) and North Walsham (1844—last six months); North Walsham (1845, 1846); Soham (1847, 1848); Fakenham (1849); Upwell (1850, 1851, 1852); Hinckley (1853, 1854); Aylesbury (1855, 1856); Wallingford (1857); Marlborough (1858, 1859); Farringdon (*sic*) (1860, 1861); and finally Norwich (1862–90) as a supernumerary.

In Soham and Watton she suffered persecution and was criticized for her clothes; she wrote, 'What money I had would not allow me to dress smart enough for the people' (*Primitive Methodist Magazine*, 1891, 565). On her retirement she summed up her ministry:

> Here ends thirty years' labour. In all the thirty years I only missed two appointments, one, when there was a flooding rain, and the other a heavy thunderstorm; and being planned out of doors, I did not think it wise to go. I have walked thousands upon thousands of miles during the thirty years. I have visited from ten to forty families in a day, and prayed with them. I have preached five and six times in the week, and three, and sometimes five times on the Sabbath. (ibid.)

On superannuation (1862) Elizabeth Bultitude received an annuity and settled in Norwich, where she continued to preach regularly, attend services and class meetings, and engage in private devotions. After a long, painful illness she died at her home, 70 Adelaide Street, Heigham, Norwich, on 14 August 1890, aged eighty-one, and was buried in the local cemetery. A memorial service, conducted by the Revd Jonathan Scott, was held in Queen's Road Chapel on 7 September. Elizabeth Bultitude was the last of the Primitive Methodist female travelling preachers and the longest-serving—twenty-eight years—but there is remarkably little information extant about her ministry, other than in manuscript minutes and accounts in local record offices, which chiefly record preaching appointments and salary payments. As she was the only female itinerant 'to die in the work' she alone has an obituary in the Primitive Methodist conference minutes. She was remembered as having a 'large round rubicund face in a poke bonnet', as using 'ejaculatory prayers with many fervent repetitions', and as a stickler for propriety: she would not allow 'any man to speak to her in chapel in her own pew; she would request him to go into the next seat' (Ritson, 152). E. DOROTHY GRAHAM

Sources *Primitive Methodist Magazine*, 72 (1891) · *Minutes of the annual conference of the Primitive Methodist connexion* (1891) · E. D. Graham, 'Chosen by God: the female itinerants of early Primitive Methodism', PhD diss., U. Birm., 1987 · E. D. Graham, *Chosen by God: a list of the female travelling preachers of early Primitive Methodism* (1989) · J. Ritson, *The romance of Primitive Methodism* (1909) · d. cert.
Likenesses portrait, repro. in H. B. Kendall, *The origin and history of the Primitive Methodist church*, 2 (c.1905), 217

Bulwer, Sir Edward Earle Gascoyne (1829–1910), army officer, was born on 22 December 1829 at Heydon in Norfolk, the second of the three sons of William Earle Lytton Bulwer (1799–1877) of Heydon Hall, who married on 11 December 1827 Emily (d. 1836), daughter of General Isaac Gascoyne, MP for Liverpool. Their eldest son, William, of the Scots guards, was wounded in the Crimea, and was later active in the volunteer movement. The third son was Sir Henry Ernest Gascoyne Bulwer (1836–1914), a colonial governor. Their father was elder brother of Sir William Henry Lytton Earle *Bulwer, Lord Dalling and Bulwer, and of Edward George Earle Lytton Bulwer-*Lytton, first Baron Lytton, the novelist.

Edward was privately educated, partly at Putney. Like his brothers he went, in 1848, to Trinity College, Cambridge, but decided to enter the army. On 21 August 1849 he joined the 23rd (Royal Welch Fusiliers). He purchased in December 1850 the rank of lieutenant, and spent the next few years in Canada and the United Kingdom. On 4 April 1854 he embarked with his regiment for Scutari, where it was placed in the 1st brigade of the light division. A company of his regiment were, on 14 September, the first British soldiers to land in the Crimea. On 20 September, on which day his elder brother was severely wounded, Edward Bulwer took part in the crossing of the Alma and the storming of the redoubt, which was much to the credit of the Royal Welch Fusiliers. Next day Bulwer was promoted captain.

The regiment endured great hardships and losses in the trenches, and maintained its reputation for valour until hostilities ended. It returned to England in July 1856.

Bulwer served for six months as aide-de-camp to the major-general commanding the eastern district.

By the treaty of Paris (1856) it was agreed to investigate the condition of the Danubian principalities. Bulwer was attached to the commission under his uncle, Sir Henry Bulwer, from September 1856 to September 1857.

In May and June 1857 Bulwer's regiment had sailed for service in China, but on news of the mutiny was diverted to India. Bulwer rejoined the regiment while it was travelling from Calcutta to serve under Sir Colin Campbell at Lucknow. It fought at the relief of Lucknow in November 1857, and in the operations which followed until the advance on Lucknow in March 1858, when it formed part of the attacking force under Sir James Outram. Bulwer, who had obtained his majority by purchase on 26 January 1858, marched in September, in the temporary absence of Colonel Pratt, with his regimental headquarters and six companies out of Lucknow to join Colonel Purnell's force.

The final capture of Lucknow had dispersed thousands of rebels, whom it was necessary to reduce to order before it was possible to re-establish the civil government. Bulwer especially distinguished himself on three occasions in command of a detached column, of which 180 men of the 23rd were a part. On 23 September he attacked and routed a rebel force near Salimpur on the River Gumti. Then, occupying the fort of Gosainganj, he cleared the neighbourhood of mutineers and pacified it, winning official praise from Brigadier-General Chute and from Lord Clyde. Again, at Jabrowli on 23 October and at Purwa on 29 October, Bulwer defeated much larger forces, leaving at the latter 600 Sepoys dead or wounded and capturing two guns. For his services during the mutiny Bulwer received a brevet lieutenant-colonelcy dated 26 April, and the CB in 1859. In July 1863 he married Isabella (d. 1883), daughter of Sir J. Jacob Buxton, bt, of Shadwell Court, Norfolk; they had one son and four daughters.

The rest of Bulwer's career was in staff appointments. He served as assistant inspector of reserve forces in Scotland (1865–70), and then as assistant adjutant-general for recruiting there in 1870. From 1873 to 1879 he was assistant adjutant-general, at headquarters, for auxiliary forces. Cardwell's new short-service system made it necessary to reorganize the infantry regiments and weld into a homogeneous whole the regular and auxiliary forces, as far as possible, as a county organization. During Bulwer's term of office, despite much opposition, this localization was begun.

On 1 October 1877 Bulwer was promoted major-general, and on 10 March 1879 was given command of the Chatham district. But in 1880 he was back at headquarters as inspector-general of recruiting (1880–86), taking an active part in the supply of troops for the Egyptian and Sudan wars and in carrying out the reforms of Hugh Childers, the secretary of state for war. In 1886 he was appointed KCB and became deputy adjutant-general to the forces (1886–7), being promoted lieutenant-general on 10 March 1887. He was also deputed in 1886 to serve on the commission of inquiry into the Belfast riots. From 1889 to 1894 he was lieutenant-governor and commander of the troops in Guernsey, serving also on the Wantage committee on terms and conditions of service in the army in 1891, and being promoted general on 1 April 1892. He retired from the active list in 1896.

In March 1898 Bulwer received the distinction which he most valued, colonel of the Royal Welch Fusiliers. In March 1898 he published his views on the army in the *National Review*. He was made GCB in 1905. He died after a long illness at his residence, 45 Hans Place, London, on 8 December 1910, and was buried on the 14th at Heydon, Norfolk.   WILLIAM LEE-WARNER, *rev.* JAMES LUNT

Sources M. Glover, *That astonishing infantry: three hundred years of the history of the Royal Welch Fusiliers* (1989) · *The Times* (10 Dec 1910) · *The Times* (12 Dec 1910) · A. W. Kinglake, *The invasion of the Crimea*, 8 vols. (1863–87) · T. H. Kavanagh, *How I won the Victoria cross* (1868) · R. Broughton-Mainwaring and R. Cannon, eds., *Historical record of the Royal Welch fusiliers, late the twenty-third regiment, or, Royal Welsh fusiliers … in continuation of the compilation … by R. Cannon* (1889) · Reports on annual recruiting presented to parliament · A. D. L. Cary, S. McCance, and others, eds., *Regimental records of the Royal Welch Fusiliers (late the 23rd foot)*, 7 vols. (1921–) · Burke, *Gen. GB* · *CGPLA Eng. & Wales* (1911)

Likenesses Walton, engraving, repro. in Cary and McCance, *Regimental record*, vol. 2, facing p. 226

Wealth at death £41,211 0s. 9d.: probate, 21 Feb 1911, *CGPLA Eng. & Wales*

(William) Henry Lytton Earle Bulwer, Baron Dalling and Bulwer (1801–1872), by Giuseppe Fagnani, 1865

Bulwer, (William) Henry Lytton Earle, Baron Dalling and Bulwer [*formerly* Sir Henry Bulwer] (1801–1872), diplomatist, was born at 31 Baker Street, Portman Square, London, on 13 February 1801. He was the second of the three sons of General William Earle Bulwer (1757–1807), of Wood Dalling, Heydon Hall, Norfolk, and his wife, Elizabeth Barbara Lytton (1773–1843), only child of Richard Warburton Lytton of Knebworth Park, Hertfordshire. His younger brother was the famous novelist Edward Bulwer-*Lytton (1803–1873).

Education and youth General Bulwer died in 1807 but it made little difference to his second son, who had already been informally 'adopted' by his maternal grandmother, Elizabeth, the daughter of Paul Joddrell of Lewknor, Oxfordshire, and was living with her at Upper Seymour Street, London. Elizabeth Lytton was a formidable woman, accustomed to driving her own phaeton between London and Bath, who had once worsted three highwaymen on Hounslow Heath. At the age of sixteen she had been married to the reclusive scholar Warburton Lytton, but subsequently obtained a judicial separation. She professed herself lonely when her only daughter married and subsequently demanded to be given charge of the second child, Henry. General Bulwer, calculating that Henry would cease to be a charge upon his estate, willingly agreed.

Henry was first sent to a bad school run by Dr Curtis at Sunbury and subsequently (from 1814) to Harrow School. He left Harrow in 1819 and spent a year with a tutor at South Mimms before entering Trinity College, Cambridge, in 1820. An illness delayed his return to Cambridge the following year and he transferred to the new Downing College. He had found Trinity too academic and preferred

Downing, which had the reputation of being the 'fastest' college in the university (Bulwer-Lytton, 1.228–30). His only interest at this time was in horses.

Bulwer had inherited a moderate fortune from his grandmother on her death in 1818, which would have been sufficient to have kept him in reasonable comfort if he had not adopted a very expensive lifestyle and gambled heavily. Like his younger brother, Edward, he frequented all the leading salons, and he formed friendships with, among others, Benjamin Disraeli. His gambling passed into legend. In 1829 he was said to have won between £6000 and £7000 at the tables in a single night in Paris without any sign of emotion and the following year in Berlin to have lost 500 louis on a single rubber of whist at Prince Wittgenstein's with equal indifference.

But, even as a young man, more serious ambitions were asserting themselves. On gaining full control of his inheritance when he came of age in 1822, Bulwer left Cambridge for Paris with letters of introduction that gave him an entry into French society. His nephew records that he arrived shy and awkward and left with the self-possession and charm that characterized him for the rest of his life (MS biography, Norfolk RO, Bulwer papers, BUL 1/421). He consciously set out to remedy the defects in his education and began to train himself in public speaking. At this time his ambitions were literary and he published a small volume of poetry in 1822.

In 1824, inspired by the example of his hero Lord Byron, Bulwer resolved to go to fight as a volunteer in the Greek war of independence, then raging. Instead he became embroiled in a somewhat murky episode. The London Greek Committee had raised a loan in London to aid the

Greek cause. Two large instalments, of £30,000 and £40,000 respectively, reached Zante in the Ionian Islands, then under British protection, in the spring and early summer of 1824. Disbursement should have been under the control of several commissioners, of whom Byron was one, but by this time Byron was dead and the other commissioners were unable or unwilling to travel out. In August the committee appointed two new commissioners, Bulwer and a former official of the Ionian government, James Hamilton Browne. Bulwer subsequently published an account of his mission in *An Autumn in Greece* (1826). Bulwer and Browne arrived in Nauplia, the temporary Greek capital, in October 1824 at about the same time as the *Florida*, under Captain Hodgson, arrived with the final instalment of the loan, £50,000 in gold. Bulwer's account, based on the letters he wrote at the time to a friend, C. S. Sheridan, the son of the playwright, show growing disillusionment. The first two instalments had already been handed over without authority. Bulwer, Browne, and Hodgson all became seriously ill with malaria and Hodgson died after a nightmare journey to Smyrna. They were rescued by the British consul and Bulwer was eventually shipped off to Malta, where he recovered, thanks to quinine, which he pronounced 'the most valuable drug in the Pharmacopoeia' (*An Autumn in Greece*, 130).

Diplomacy, politics, or literature? While still abroad Bulwer had been gazetted a cornet in the 2nd lifeguards on 19 October 1825. He exchanged as an ensign into the 58th foot in June 1826 and obtained an unattached ensigncy the following month. He was already considering a change to the diplomatic service and was appointed an attaché in Berlin in August 1827. While there he wrote two memoranda, one on the Prussian army, the other on how protestant Prussia governed Catholic Silesia and the Rhineland, drawing parallels with Ireland. They attracted the attention of the foreign secretary, Lord Aberdeen, if only for Bulwer's enterprise in writing them. He was transferred to Vienna in April 1829, and to The Hague in April 1830.

Bulwer's first important role was during the Belgian revolt against the Dutch. When the rising began in Brussels in August 1830, he was sent into Belgium to assess the situation. He arrived in Ghent just as trouble broke out. The commissionaire of his hotel was shot at his side in the Grande Place. He proceeded to Brussels and Ath, which the insurgents had just taken, and, by his own account, acquired very full information about the rebels' plans. To his indignation, his reports were not entirely believed in London because they conflicted with the official reports from The Hague, but when, after his return to England, they proved correct, Aberdeen sent him back to Brussels to continue to report. He wrote, anonymously, a sympathetic account of Belgian grievances in the *Westminster Review* (January 1831), which ended with a strong call for action in other oppressed countries.

Aberdeen had proved a useful patron and was to be so again, but he was now replaced by Lord Palmerston, whose more swashbuckling style exactly suited Bulwer.

Their fortunes became inextricably entangled, as Bulwer demonstrated in the official biography he wrote many years later of his former chief. He now felt that he was poised for a rapid take-off in the diplomatic service but, although he became an attaché in Paris in November 1832, he was still hesitating between a diplomatic, a literary, or a political career.

Bulwer contested Hertford unsuccessfully in 1826 but entered parliament for the pocket borough of Wilton in August 1830. The Wilton constituency was abolished by the Great Reform Act of 1832 and Bulwer was returned for Coventry in 1831 and 1833 and for Marylebone in 1835. During his seven years in the Commons he regularly commuted between London and his diplomatic postings to take part in debates, where he established some reputation as a radical speaker. In fact his views were 'liberal [rather] than democratic' (fragment of autobiography, Norfolk RO, Bulwer papers, BUL 1/410/1, 15). He voted for the total abolition of the corn laws but had doubts about the Great Reform Act itself. He could not identify with any one party. He thought the tories extreme and prejudiced on all questions but, like his friend Disraeli, he found the whigs a clique of aristocrats, who would not admit anyone else to their circle.

Bulwer wrote for the press and continued to publish: his substantial two-volume study *France: Social, Literary and Political* of 1834 was followed two years later by *The Monarchy of the Middle Classes*. His style was florid by modern standards but the work combines information and statistics with personal anecdotes and shrewd comparisons between British and French society, and retains its interest. Bulwer also commented on British politics in *The Lords, the Government and the Country* (1836).

First postings Bulwer confessed in his autobiography that he always craved 'adventure … a passion I have had all my life to keep under control' (Bulwer papers, BUL 1/410/1, 17), and in 1835 he was planning to join General Evans, the MP for Westminster, who was raising a British legion to help the liberal cause in Spain. But in November 1835 Palmerston offered him the post of secretary of legation in Brussels in a now independent Belgium. His chief, Sir Hamilton Seymour, was frequently absent and Bulwer was chargé d'affaires most of the time. He decided not to contest Marylebone in the general election caused by the death of William IV in 1837, partly because he had quarrelled with some of his constituents but also because he had now decided to become a full-time diplomat.

In August 1837 Bulwer was appointed secretary of embassy in Constantinople. Bulwer recorded his impressions of Constantinople and its cast of characters, including the grand vizier, General Husrev, and a later grand vizier, Mustafa Reshid Pasha, in his biography of Palmerston. At the time he wrote freely to Palmerston of his views (*Palmerston*, 2.273–80). The British ambassador, Lord Ponsonby, entrusted him with concluding a commercial treaty with Turkey and he brought the task to a triumphant conclusion in the summer of 1838.

In October 1838 Bulwer was appointed secretary of embassy at St Petersburg, at his own request, but he caught a fever just before leaving Constantinople, and when he arrived in London the government was embroiled in the 'bedchamber' crisis. As a result of these delays he never took up his Russian appointment and, instead, in June 1839, was appointed secretary of embassy in Paris. He acted as minister-plenipotentiary, in the absence of the ambassador, at various times in 1839, 1840, and 1841. Anglo-French relations became extremely bad in 1840 as a result of France's sympathy for their protégé Mehmet Ali, the rebellious pasha of Egypt, while Britain joined the three eastern powers, Russia, Austria, and Prussia, in shoring up the authority of the sultan.

Spanish difficulties   Bulwer was appointed minister-plenipotentiary to Madrid in November 1843. He tackled the job with his customary energy, and on one occasion went to Morocco to settle a serious dispute involving both France and Spain. For this service he was promised, and in June 1845 duly received, appointment to the privy council.

Other questions proved more difficult. Spain was a potential flashpoint in European diplomacy. The struggles between the conservatives and the liberals had resulted in great power intervention in the 1820s and 1830s. Britain and the Orleanist monarchy in France had united in defending the young queen Isabella against her absolutist uncle Don Carlos, who had the sympathy of the eastern powers, but British policy had also been swayed by a determination that French influence should not increase in the Iberian peninsula. During the period of the first *entente cordiale*, the British foreign secretary, Lord Aberdeen, and his French opposite number, François Guizot, entered into an informal agreement that Isabella's younger sister Maria Fernandez might marry one of the sons of King Louis Philippe, but only after Isabella had married and had at least one child. In return Britain promised to give no countenance to a Saxe-Coburg prince as Isabella's suitor.

Guizot began to regret the agreement and took advantage of the fact that Palmerston, when he replaced Aberdeen at the Foreign Office in 1846, wrote a dispatch to Bulwer, naming Prince Leopold of Saxe-Coburg and Gotha as a possible candidate, to regard it as void. The double wedding of Queen Isabella to her cousin the duke of Cadiz (who was generally regarded as impotent) and of her younger sister to Louis Philippe's son the duke of Montpensier swiftly followed. Anglo-French relations became very strained and Bulwer was caught in the fallout, accused of indiscreet support for the Coburg candidate.

Worse was to follow. In the great revolutionary year of 1848 there were liberal risings in Spain against the conservative government of General Narvaez. Bulwer was accused of being implicated and on 12 May was instructed by Narvaez to leave Madrid within forty-eight hours on the grounds that his life was in danger. Bulwer obviously believed in the reality of the danger (although sceptical of the direction from which it came) and left immediately for London; he arrived before the Foreign Office even knew of his expulsion. The incident caused an international sensation and Bulwer seems to have seriously expected the British government to make a military response.

The government was more cautious. Bulwer had no difficulty in disposing of the wilder charges against him: that he had dispensed 'foreign gold', sent secret agents to ferment provincial unrest, or summoned British warships laden with arms for the rebels, but his contacts with the opposition press had been indiscreet (Norfolk RO, Bulwer papers, BUL 1/74). The situation was not helped by the fact that only the intervention of friends had prevented him from fighting a duel with the Spanish foreign minister, the duke of Sotomayer, on a private matter.

Bulwer was saved because the opposition chose to concentrate their fire on his political chief, Lord Palmerston, and his policy. The court took the same line, the queen pointing out that Bulwer was '*her* Minister' and hence she had been insulted, but blaming Palmerston for the provocation (*Letters of Queen Victoria*, ed. A. C. Benson and Viscount Esher, 1907, 2.175).

Exile to Washington   Bulwer was now a diplomatic embarrassment. The government formally showed its support by making him a KCB and offered him a new post as minister-plenipotentiary in Washington since diplomatic relations with Spain had been broken off. Bulwer maintained that the government was duty-bound to find an equivalent post for him and only Washington happened to be vacant, but in reality it was a banishment and he recognized it as such. Only strong persuasion from his friends, including Disraeli, induced him to accept it.

In fact Bulwer's three years in Washington were among the most successful of his career. He liked America and regretted that, as a result of a number of incidents over the previous decade, Anglo-American relations were not good. He realized the importance of public opinion and was astute in discovering how to influence it. He became one of the wittiest and most popular after-dinner speakers in the States (Norfolk RO, Bulwer papers, BUL 1/97/1–2).

The serious issue between the United States and Britain at this time was Central America. When the Spanish empire had broken up in the 1820s, a number of independent states had emerged, among them Guatemala and Nicaragua. The Mosquito (Muchilos) Indians, however, denied that they had ever formed part of the Spanish empire and cited agreements with Britain in the seventeenth century. The Nicaraguans, refusing to accept such claims, occupied the Mosquito port of San Juan (Greytown) but were expelled with British help in January 1848. Bulwer was well aware that the United States was only interested in the issue because at that time the Mosquito Coast seemed likely to be the Atlantic entrance to a canal across the isthmus of Panama. He negotiated a treaty with the American secretary of state, John Clayton, signed 19 April 1850, which avoided disputes about territorial rights and concentrated on ensuring that there should be no barriers to the building of the canal, whoever had jurisdiction. Bulwer himself was very sympathetic to commercial developments in Central America and invested personally in projects, including coffee farming in Costa Rica.

Return to European diplomacy Nevertheless Bulwer found the Washington climate trying and wished to return to Europe. In 1852 he was appointed minister-plenipotentiary in Florence. Although Tuscany was then an independent state, it was something of a demotion. The pill was sweetened by the promise that he should also represent Britain in Rome and that this might make possible the opening of formal diplomatic relations with the papacy. It was hoped that the pope would bring his influence to bear in Ireland and that this would compensate for protestant irritation in Britain, but when Palmerston, who could not be accused of truckling to Rome, was replaced by Lord Granville, who chanced to be married to a Roman Catholic, the question was judged too sensitive and that part of Bulwer's instructions cancelled. He wished to resign but Spain had just protested at his appointment and withdrawal was therefore impossible.

Politically, Bulwer's mission to Florence was uneventful but persistent ill health compelled him to return home in 1854. When he went back, he was taken ill again and was granted a pension in April 1855. He suspected he had been poisoned, although a recurrence of malaria seems more likely. The illness may also have been partly psychosomatic.

On 9 December 1848 Bulwer had married at Hatfield House Georgiana Charlotte Mary Wellesley (1817–1878), the youngest daughter of Henry *Wellesley, first Baron Cowley, and the niece of the duke of Wellington. He complained to his brother that she was a 'fretful, unhappy companion' (Norfolk RO, Bulwer papers, BUL 1/109/2/1–5), and she admitted to her brother that she had 'an unhappy temper' (ibid., BUL 1/428a). In 1855 they considered a formal separation and he told a friend that the strain had reduced him to 'a nervous fever'. She rejoined him when he was ambassador in Constantinople but they were soon quarrelling again (ibid., 1/189/19–27).

Bulwer's pension had envisaged the possibility of future employment if his health improved, and from July 1856 to May 1858 he was in the Danubian provinces as a commissioner under article 22 of the treaty of Paris, concluded at the end of the Crimean War in 1856. The commission was to inquire whether Moldavia and Wallachia wished to be united and to supervise elections for this purpose. The first elections were so blatantly irregular that they had to be rerun but the two provinces were eventually united as Romania in 1862, although still at this time remaining part of the Ottoman empire.

Ambassador in Constantinople In 1858 Bulwer succeeded Stratford Canning as ambassador in Constantinople, and he remained there until his final retirement from the service in August 1865. In his autobiography he analysed fairly why he was not able to play the same role as the great Canning (Norfolk RO, Bulwer papers, BUL 1/410/1). Before the Crimean War Turkey had looked to Britain and her fleet for protection against Russia. After 1856 she had little to fear from Russia and had been much more impressed by the French than the British performance during the war. In his last years, in his attempts to get reforms accepted, Canning himself had overplayed his

hand. Bulwer had to move cautiously in trying to limit French control of the Suez Canal (completed 1869), which he believed Palmerston had been mistaken in opposing.

While in Constantinople Bulwer bought an island in the Bosphorus and ran an expensive yacht. He was an active freemason, master of the Oriental lodge and district grand master for Turkey. His lifestyle continued to be extravagant, but he was also a good businessman, keenly aware of new openings in developing economies from as early as the 1830s, when he had acted as agent for a number of the Australian colonies. Although his letters to his wife refer to some financial difficulties, unlike many contemporaries, he never seems to have been seriously embarrassed.

Retirement from diplomacy On his return to Britain Bulwer re-entered British politics by becoming Liberal MP for Tamworth in November 1868. Almost his last speech in the Commons was on the disestablishment of the Irish church (*Hansard 3*, 198.1018–26). His friends believed it to have been one of the ablest speeches on that thorny problem but unfortunately his physical frailty made it inaudible.

Bulwer also returned to literature. In 1870 he published the first two volumes of his biography of Palmerston. A third volume appeared posthumously but the work was still unfinished and was completed by Lord Ashley. Bulwer also published *Historical Characters*, studies of Talleyrand, William Cobbett, George Canning, and Sir James Mackintosh, based partly on personal recollections. Two further sketches, of Sir Robert Peel and Viscount Melbourne, were published posthumously.

Bulwer was raised to the peerage as Baron Dalling and Bulwer in the county of Norfolk on 21 March 1871. He died suddenly in Naples on 23 May 1872, while returning from a visit to Egypt. There were no children of the marriage and the peerage became extinct. He was immortalized as Mr Tremaine Bertie in Disraeli's *Endymion* and by the French writer Hortense Allart de Meritens (1801–1879), who had been his mistress in the 1830s, as Mr Henry Warwick in *Les enchantements de prudence* (1872).

MURIEL E. CHAMBERLAIN

Sources Norfolk RO, Bulwer papers · E. R. Bulwer-Lytton, first Earl Lytton, *The life, letters and literary remains of Edward Bulwer, Lord Lytton*, 2 vols. (1883) · Burke, *Peerage* · *FO List* · W. H. L. E. Bulwer, *The life of John Henry Temple, Viscount Palmerston*, ed. E. M. Ashley, 3 vols. (1870–74) · W. H. L. E. Bulwer, *An autumn in Greece* (1826) · J. Decrues, *Henry Bulwer-Lytton et Hortense Allart d'après des documents inédits* (1961) · E. B. D'Auvergne, *Envoys extraordinary* (1937) · K. Bell, 'The Constantinople embassy of Sir Henry Bulwer', PhD diss., U. Lond., 1961 · E. Jones-Parry, *The Spanish marriages* (1936) · R. Bullen, *Palmerston, Guizot and the collapse of the entente cordiale* (1974) · H. Reeve, *Memorandum on the diaries of the late Mr Charles Greville* (1865) · *The Times* (3 June 1872) · *Illustrated Review* (15 Aug 1872) · B. Disraeli, *Endymion* (1880) · H. Allart de Meritens, *Les enchantements de prudence* (1872) · *CGPLA Eng. & Wales* (1872)

Archives Duke U., Perkins L., corresp. · Herts. ALS, corresp. and papers · Hunt. L., letters and papers · Knebworth House, Hertfordshire, corresp. and papers · Norfolk RO, corresp. and papers · priv. coll. · PRO, corresp. | BL, corresp. with Lord Aberdeen, Add. MSS 43131, 43146–43147, 43163–43164, 43179–43180 · BL, corresp. with John Allen, Add. MS 52183 · BL, corresp. with A. J. Fraser, Add. MS 44913 · BL, corresp. with Lord Holland and Lady Holland, Add. MS

51614 • BL, corresp. with Sir Austen Layard, Add. MSS 38986–39120, *passim* • BL, letters to Princess Lieven, Add. MS 47376 • BL, corresp. with Ali Pasha, Add. MS 46695 • BL, corresp. with Sir Robert Peel, Add. MSS 40488–40609, *passim* • Bodl. Oxf., corresp. with Sir John Crampton; letters to Benjamin Disraeli; corresp. with Lord Kimberley • Coventry Archives, letters to William Hickling • Hants. RO, corresp. with Lord Malmesbury • PRO, corresp. with Stratford Canning, FO 352 • PRO, corresp. with Lord Cowley, FO 519 • PRO, corresp. with Lord Granville, PRO 30/29 • PRO, corresp. with Lord John Russell, PRO 30/22 • PRO NIre., letters to Lord Dufferin • U. Durham L., letters to Viscount Ponsonby • U. Southampton L., corresp. with Lord Palmerston • W. Yorks. AS, Leeds, corresp. with Lord Canning

Likenesses sketch, *c*.1825, BM • J. Doyle, pen-and-pencil caricature, *c*.1847 (*The mask of Comus*), BM • G. Fagnani, oils, 1865, NPG [*see illus.*] • O. Schoefft, photograph, *c*.1871–1872, repro. in *Illustrated Review* • Ape [C. Pellegrini], pencil caricature, NPG; repro. in *VF* (27 Aug 1870) • W. Sharp, lithograph (after Kreiger), NPG • sketch (aged twenty-four), repro. in Decrues, *Henry Bulwer-Lytton*

Wealth at death under £5000: probate, 3 Aug 1872, *CGPLA Eng. & Wales*

Bulwer, John (*bap.* 1606, *d.* 1656), medical practitioner and writer on deafness and on gesture, was the second and only surviving son of Thomas Bulwer (*d.* 1649), a London apothecary, and Marie (*d.* 1638), daughter of George Evans of St Albans, Hertfordshire; he was baptized at St Michael, Wood Street, London, on 16 May 1606. He married in 1634, his wife being named only as 'the widow Midleton'. The marriage appears to have been childless but his will refers to an adopted daughter, Chirothea Johnson. Urban London references often occur in his writings, and dedicatory verses suggest that he was part of a social circle centred on Gray's Inn, London. His friends Edward and Francis Goldsmith were members of the same circle, which identified with the strongly royalist high-church party supportive of Archbishop William Laud. Circumstantial evidence also points to Bulwer's having been educated at Oxford (a royalist stronghold) and John Harmer (1594?–1670), who became professor of Greek at Oxford, supplied dedicatory verses to his books *Chirologia* and *Philocophus*. These royalist sympathies occasionally surface in his published work.

Bulwer published four volumes exploring the theme of the human body as a medium of communication: *Chirologia* and *Chironomia* (as one volume, 1644, reprinted 1648), *Philocophus* (1648), *Pathomyotomia* (1649), and *Anthropometamorphosis, or, The Artificiall Changeling* (1650, a second edition of which appeared in 1653 and a third as *A View of the People of the Whole World* in 1654). Bulwer variously adopted the pseudonyms Philochirosophus (1644), The Chirosopher (1648, 1650), and Chirosophus (1649) in addition to his initials. Posterity has been unkind to Bulwer in that while each of his works is periodically rediscovered by writers in the specific modern disciplines to which they relate, their overall unity has rarely been recognized.

Chirologia comprehensively catalogues the meanings of hand gestures (illustrated by plates of 'chirograms'). Bulwer argued, in a colourful and rumbustious style which characterized all his work, that gestural language was universal and primary, with spoken language being

John Bulwer (*bap.* 1606, *d.* 1656), by T. Berry, pubd 1820 (after William Faithorne the elder)

but a gloss on gestural communication. This related to the widespread contemporary interest in the notion of universal languages, as well as curiously adumbrating later theories proposing that language evolved from gesture. *Chironomia* similarly surveys the 'Art of Manuall Rhetoricke', mentioning in passing a new rhetorical gesture of Bulwer's own invention. These works are complementary, the first treating of natural gesture, the second of its conscious deployment. Now accepted as a founding text of the English rhetoric tradition, its influence on subsequent seventeenth- and eighteenth-century works is nevertheless often covert (notably in Obadiah Walker's *Art of Oratory*, 1659).

As a result of this work Bulwer became known to the deaf mute Sir Edward Gostwicke and his similarly afflicted younger brother, William Gostwicke, who lived in Bedfordshire. Reflecting this, *Philocophus* is concerned with enabling deaf people to lip read, and most of it is a commentary on Sir Kenelm Digby's account of the successful treatment of the younger brother of the constable of Castile, whose name, not provided by Digby, was Don Luis Velasco. This had appeared in chapter 28, 'The sense of hearing', of Digby's *Two Treatises* (1644) which Bulwer reprinted virtually in full. Digby, writing twenty-one years after his Spanish visit, erroneously ascribed this treatment to a priest (Velasco's tutor was in fact a schoolmaster, Manuel Ramírez de Carrión) and referred in passing to a Spanish book on the topic without giving author or title. This was Juan Paolo Bonet's *Reducción de las letras y arte de enseñar a hablar los mudos* (1620, in which he claimed the credit for Ramírez de Carrión's method), which neither Digby nor Bulwer had read at this time. While he did append an engraved plate of manual sign language gestures, Bulwer concentrated on lip reading in order, as he explained, to enable deaf mute people to communicate with everyone else. This work contains a unique and particularly original mechanistic account of the senses couched in terms of the synaesthetic transfer of vibrations between modalities, hence Bulwer affirmed that a deaf mute man could, quite literally, 'Heare the sound of words with his Eie' (echoing a phrase of Digby's). Bulwer (and Digby) erred however in believing that lip reading could be taught without prior experience of attempting to speak. Bulwer subsequently obtained a copy of Bonet's treatise and developed his ideas further, as well as correcting this error, in 'The dumbe mans academie', an unpublished manuscript (BL, Sloane MS 1788) of about 1649. Although slightly unfinished this appears from its quality to have been intended for publication.

While it is unknown whether Bulwer directly treated any deaf mute patients, in *Philocophus* he describes a project to establish an academy for deaf people. His efforts on behalf of the deaf and dumb anticipated the better-remembered work by William Holder (whose efforts began in 1660), John Wallis (who presented a deaf mute youth to the Royal Society in 1662 and wrote a letter on the topic to Robert Boyle in 1670), and George Dalgarno, author of *Didascalocophus, or, The Deafe and Dumb Man's Tutor* (1680). That these never cite Bulwer is curious given that they almost certainly knew of his work. The explanation most likely lies in his political and social affiliations, the fact that he died prior to the Restoration, and his lack of social connections with Royal Society circles. Modern writers noticing the work have usually focused on this priority dispute aspect, overlooking Bulwer's distinct version of the mechanism concept and other aspects of his thinking.

Pathomyotomia is the scarcest and most crudely printed of Bulwer's books but in some ways the most ambitious, presenting a systematic head-to-toe survey of the physiological bases of human expressive behaviour and the relationship between sensation, images, and skilled actions. He skirts the philosophical issue of mind–body relations but conveys a picture of the entire body as a signifying system, its expressive motions 'answering in a kind of semblance and representative proportion, to the motions of the mind' (p. 4). Again the notion of mechanism used has distinct features. This unillustrated work has been the least discussed, despite being Charles Darwin's opening citation in *Expression of the Emotions in Man and Animals* (1872). *Anthropometamorphosis* surveys the artificial deformations of the body practised by various peoples, again from head to toe (with accompanying woodcuts

added in the 1653 edition), and ends with an attack on contemporaries for indulging in similar vanities. Unlike his other writings the moral agenda is uppermost here. Of particular interest is that for Bulwer the natural is morally superior to the artificial. This work is usually noticed by historians of anthropology. The 1650 edition has a somewhat cryptic frontispiece portrait. A less intriguing, but technically superior, replacement by W. Faithorne appears subsequently—although it seems to be based on the first rather than newly done from life. The 1653 edition is interesting in two other respects. The letters MD appear after Bulwer's name in several places, suggesting that he had only recently obtained this medical qualification; and it includes a closing Latin colophon in which he formally abandons the writing of books.

Bulwer's only other surviving text is BL, Sloane MS 805.6, 'Vultispex riticus, seu, Physiognomia medici', a densely written Latin medical text summarizing, once more from head to foot, the diagnostic meanings of bodily symptoms. It includes some astrological material, elsewhere entirely absent in his writings, and perhaps precedes his more creative published texts. This is listed, with seven other works 'accomplished by the Authour' (two also in Latin), at the end of *Anthropometamorphosis*, none of which, aside from 'The dumbe mans academie', are known to be extant. All relate either to gesture or to deaf mute people, and include 'Vox corporis, or, The morall anatomy of the body', the loss of which is particularly regrettable. Bulwer died in Westminster in October 1656.

Bulwer took Francis Bacon's plea for a 'science of man', as well as his inductive method, more literally than any other seventeenth-century savant, often referring to him by such epithets as 'the Verulamian oracle'. Indeed, his works more nearly approach modern psychology in character than those of his illustrious philosophical contemporaries. Despite his robust literary style, only at the end of the twentieth century did his long neglect as a serious thinker begin to be rectified.   GRAHAM RICHARDS

Sources J. Wollock, 'John Bulwer's (1606–1656) place in the history of the deaf', *Historiographica Linguistica*, 23, 1/2 (1996), 1–46 · J. Wollock, 'John Bulwer and his Italian sources', *Italia ed Europa nella linguistica del Rinascimento (Atti del convegno internazionale, Ferrara, 20–24 March 1991)*, ed. M. Tavoni, 2 (1996), 417–33 · J. W. Cleary, 'Editor's introduction', in J. Bulwer, *Chirologia, or, The natural language of the hand, and Chironomia, or, The art of manual rhetoric* (1974) · H. J. Norman, 'John Bulwer (*fl.* 1654), "The Chirosopher", pioneer in the treatment of the deaf and dumb and in psychology', *Proceedings of the Royal Society of Medicine*, 36 (1942–3), 589–602 · G. Richards, *Mental machinery part one, 1600–1850* (1992) · J. W. Cleary, 'John Bulwer: Renaissance communicationist', *Quarterly Journal of Speech*, 45 (1959), 391–8 · P. Morrel-Samuels, 'John Bulwer's 1644 treatise on gesture', *Semiotica*, 79 (1990), 341–53 · W. C. Metcalfe, ed., *The visitations of Hertfordshire*, Harleian Society, 22 (1886), 35 · C. Hoolihan, 'Too little too soon: the literature of deaf education in 17th-century Britain (part 1)', *The Volta Review* (1984), 347–53 · will, PRO, PROB 11/262, q. 70, fol. 151 [referenced in T. M. Blagg, ed., *Index of wills proved in the prerogative court of Canterbury*, vol. 8, 1936]

Archives BL, Sloane MSS 805.6, 1788

Likenesses T. Berry, line engraving, pubd 1820 (after W. Faithorne the elder), BM, NPG, Wellcome L. [*see illus.*] · W. Faithorne the elder, portrait, BM, NPG; repro. in J. Bulwer, *Anthropometamorphosis*, 2nd edn (1653), frontispiece • portrait, repro. in J. Bulwer, *Anthropometamorphosis*, 1st edn (1650), frontispiece

Bunbury, Sir (Thomas) Charles, sixth baronet (1740–1821), horse-racing administrator and politician, was born in Suffolk (probably at Mildenhall) in May 1740, the elder son of the Revd Sir William Bunbury, fifth baronet (*c.*1710–1764), and his wife, Eleanor Graham (*d.* 1762), daughter of Vere Graham of Wix Abbey, Essex; his brother was the caricaturist Henry William *Bunbury. The family had been prominent landowners in Cheshire for several centuries and his father, the vicar of Mildenhall, inherited estates in Suffolk also. He was educated at a school in Bury St Edmunds, at Westminster School, London, and at St Catharine's College, Cambridge, from where he matriculated in 1757 and graduated MA in 1765. He travelled to France and Italy on the grand tour in 1760–61.

Bunbury entered parliament as MP for Suffolk at the general election in 1761 and held his seat until 1812, apart from a break from 1784 to 1790. He held briefly the post of secretary to the lord lieutenant of Ireland, Lord Weymouth, from May to July 1765. He was a whig and later a supporter of Charles James Fox. Fox was a nephew of his first wife, Lady Sarah Lennox (1745–1826) [*see* Napier, Lady Sarah], whom he married on 2 June 1762. She was the daughter of Charles *Lennox, second duke of Richmond and Lennox (1701–1750), courtier, and Lady Sarah Cadogan (*d.* 1751). Lady Sarah, whose beauty had attracted the young George III, was unsuited to life with a good-natured but neglectful sporting gentleman who preferred the company of grooms and jockeys. She had several affairs and the daughter she gave birth to during the marriage was not her husband's but Lord William Gordon's. The union was dissolved by act of parliament on 14 May 1776.

Bunbury's main interest was horse racing and he regularly attended meetings at Newmarket, which was near his country seat at Barton Hall, Great Barton, Suffolk. He was co-founder of the Oaks (1779) as well as of the Derby. The story goes that he lost the toss of a coin with the earl of Derby for the privilege of having a new race at Epsom named after him. Ironically he won the first running of the Derby with his colt Diomed in 1780, and he owned two more winners of the race, Eleanor and Smolensko. He also bred Highflyer, the greatest stallion of the eighteenth century.

Bunbury was steward of the Jockey Club for the first time at the age of twenty-eight and for many years he ruled racing even when not in office. At first the club had authority only at Newmarket, but under his leadership it became the governing body of the turf throughout the country. He transformed the pattern of racing and helped to create the modern thoroughbred by replacing 4 mile heats with races that demanded greater speed and precocity. His determination to eradicate sharp practice in racing was shown in 1791 when he took action over the inconsistent running of Escape, a horse owned by the prince of Wales, who subsequently withdrew from racing at Newmarket.

Bunbury was a mild, kindly man but decisive in promoting the interests of the sport he loved. Little is known of his second wife, Margaret (1744?–1822), except that she was of humble origins and little education. He died at his London house in Pall Mall on 31 March 1821 and was buried in the family vault at Mildenhall ten days later, on 10 April. His widow died on 6 February 1822. He had no children and was succeeded in the baronetcy by his nephew Lieutenant-General Sir Henry *Bunbury (1778–1860).

JOHN RANDALL

Sources R. Mortimer, *The Jockey Club* (1958) • R. Mortimer, *The history of the Derby stakes* (1962) • *Sporting Magazine* (April 1821) • *Morning Herald* (11 April 1821) • GEC, *Baronetage*, vol. 4 • E. R. Curtis, *Lady Sarah Lennox* (1947) • *The life and letters of Lady Sarah Lennox*, ed. M. E. A. Dawson, countess of Ilchester and Lord Stavordale, 2 vols. (1901) • P. Napier, *The sword dance: Lady Sarah Lennox and the Napiers* (1971) • W. Vamplew, *The turf: a social and economic history of horse racing* (1976) • Burke, *Peerage* • *Racing Calendar* • Venn, *Alum. Cant.* • L. B. Namier, 'Bunbury, Thomas Charles', HoP, *Commons, 1754–90* • J. Ingamells, ed., *A dictionary of British and Irish travellers in Italy, 1701–1800* (1997), 155

Archives BL, diplomatic corresp., Add. MSS 38305, 38570 | BL, corresp. with Jeremy Bentham, Add. MSS 33541–33544, *passim*

Likenesses J. Reynolds, mezzotint, 1768 (after J. Watson), BM, NPG

Bunbury, Sir Charles James Fox, eighth baronet (1809–1886), naturalist and diarist, the oldest surviving son of Sir Henry Edward *Bunbury, seventh baronet (1778–1860), and his wife, Louisa Emilia Fox (1788?–1828), was born in Messina, Sicily, on 4 February 1809, while his father was stationed there as head of the quartermaster-general's department of the British army. His mother was a niece of Charles James Fox (1749–1806), hence his baptismal name. He was a sickly child. The family moved back to England to a house owned by the family in Mildenhall, Suffolk, in 1813 when Sir Henry was promoted to under-secretary of state for the war department; in 1824, three years after his father succeeded to the baronetcy, the family moved to the ancestral estate at Great Barton, Suffolk. During these years, young Bunbury visited many spas and seaside resorts for medical treatment and early on became very attached to botany. His mother taught him a great deal about this, in particular fostering an interest in scenery, his father meanwhile encouraging him in minerals and geology. From both parents he acquired markedly cultivated and varied tastes, and while still very young was introduced to some of the best-known experts in these fields as well as leading whig politicians and statesmen of the day. In 1829 he went to Trinity College, Cambridge, at the same time as his younger brother Edward. He became a scholar in 1831 but did not graduate.

By then Bunbury was showing much better health, and his father let him travel to Brazil, via Madeira, to work with his uncle Fox, who was minister in Rio de Janeiro. Bunbury lived there from 1833 to 1835, collecting plants and making notes on natural history. On his return he joined the Holland House circle and attended London's scientific societies, primarily the Linnean and Geological, where his accomplishments and remarkable memory stood him in good stead. With no need to work for a living, he pursued a gentleman's scientific and artistic occupations. In 1837 he stood unsuccessfully as a whig candidate for Bury St Edmunds. The following year he accompanied another uncle, Sir George Napier, to the Cape, where he collected plants assiduously, afterwards publishing a well-received *Journal of a Residence at the Cape of Good Hope* (1848); he also made a brief continental tour through France and Italy in 1842.

A turning point came, however, with Bunbury's connection (in quick succession) with the geologist Charles Lyell (1797–1875), followed by Lyell's friend and father-in-law, Leonard *Horner (1785–1864), and then Horner's unmarried daughter, Frances [*see below*], a keen botanist and linguist. Bunbury worked with increasing purpose in geology, becoming close friends with Lyell and others in the Geological Society, and specializing in fossil botany. He identified several of Lyell's coal deposit specimens and catalogued the Carboniferous fossils in the Geological Society museum. His relationship with Lyell and Horner was cemented in 1844 when he married Frances, on 30 or 31 May. Since Frances's older sister Mary was married to Charles Lyell, and her younger sister Katherine was married to Lyell's brother Henry, the two naturalists were now affectionately united as scientific brothers-in-law and shared many natural history excursions and personal experiences thereafter. This close family network gave a focus to Bunbury's endeavours. His letters to Horner and Lyell, and to others such as Charles Darwin, and the copious journal he began to keep at about this time, are full of detail about scientific societies, natural history excursions in Europe, the people he and Frances met, and the life they led in London and Suffolk. He enjoyed art exhibitions, visited historical sites and antiquities with enthusiasm, travelled, collected, and read widely. As well as this, he possessed an eager, enquiring mind that allowed him to accept Darwin's theory of evolution with equanimity, although he was a staunch, church-attending Anglican. Few other journals provide such an intimate view of mid-Victorian natural history. Extracts from the journal and letters were posthumously published in nine volumes, edited by his wife. In 1851 Bunbury was elected FRS.

Bunbury became eighth baronet when Sir Henry died in 1860 and he and Frances moved from Mildenhall to Barton Hall. Like Mary and Charles Lyell, they were childless. His botanical publications included papers on the influence of the chemical nature of the subsoil, the plants of South America and the Cape, and the characteristic features of leaves, using what he knew of fossil leaves to supplement traditional systems of classification. His geological papers were all on fossil plants. He also edited a *Memoir and Literary Remains* of his father in 1868. From 1868 he was high sheriff of Suffolk. Towards the end of his life Bunbury became depressed by the deaths of members of his close family circle. He died on 17 June 1886 at Barton Hall, and was buried on 24 June at Great Barton church. He was succeeded by his brother Edward *Bunbury, himself a keen geologist, and MP for Bury.

Frances Joanna Bunbury [*née* Horner], Lady Bunbury (1814–1894), was the second of five daughters of Leonard Horner and his wife, Anne Susan (or Susanna) Lloyd (1786–1862). Frances was a talented linguist, having been brought up in Bonn, and was capable enough as a botanist for Robert Brown to enjoy her company on family collecting excursions in Switzerland. Her father's parliamentary concerns and affability meant that she was from an early age a well-travelled and cultivated young woman. After her marriage to Charles James Fox Bunbury her life was fully taken up with the extended network created by her sisters, father, husband, and brothers-in-law. Although often an invalid, she usually travelled with her husband, and several of their natural history expeditions were made with her convalescence in mind. In 1849 she visited Edinburgh for extended medical attention, and at about that time she began work on *Life and Times of Dante Alighieri* (1852), a translation from Balbo's original. While in Edinburgh again in 1852 she became so ill that Bunbury feared to move her. However, he took her on a family expedition to Madeira in 1853, where she made barometric recordings for Lyell, and then in 1855 to Germany to see her sister Leonora Pertz. After her husband died she put his diaries and letters into publishable order, helped by her sister Katherine Lyell. A nine-volume set was privately printed at Mildenhall in 1890–93, and afterwards in three-volume form in 1894. A two-volume set was commercially published in 1906, after Frances's death, abbreviated by Katherine Lyell and with an introduction by their close friend Joseph Hooker. Lady Bunbury died on 21 July 1894 and was buried at Great Barton church. JANET BROWNE

Sources *Memorials of Sir C. J. F. Bunbury*, ed. F. J. Bunbury, 9 vols. (1890–93) · Mrs. H. Lyell, ed., *The life of Sir Charles J. F. Bunbury*, 2 vols. (1906) [incl. list of works] · C. J. F. Bunbury, *Journal of a residence at the Cape of Good Hope* (1848) · *Proceedings of the Linnean Society of London* (1886–7) · Burke, *Peerage* · J. D. H., *PRS*, 46 (1889), xiii–xiv · J. W. Judd, *Quarterly Journal of the Geological Society*, 43 (1887), 39–40 · M. Gunn and L. E. Codd, *Botanical exploration of southern Africa* (1981), 108–9 · *Life, letters, and journals of Sir Charles J. F. Bunbury*, ed. F. J. Bunbury, 3 vols. [1894]

Archives American Philosophical Society, Philadelphia, papers · GS Lond., Jurassic plant specimens · RBG Kew · Suffolk RO, Bury St Edmunds, corresp. and papers · U. Cam., department of plant sciences, notes and notebooks on herbarium · U. Cam., Sedgwick Museum of Earth Sciences, herbarium and fossil plants | Bodl. Oxf., letters to Lady Caroline Napier

Likenesses photograph, repro. in Lyell, ed., *Life of Sir Charles J. F. Bunbury*, vol. 2 · portrait, Hunt. L. · portrait (Frances Joanna Bunbury), repro. in Lyell, ed., *Life of Sir Charles J. F. Bunbury*, vol. 1, p. 186

Wealth at death £38,368 10s. 4d.: probate, 6 Sept 1886, *CGPLA Eng. & Wales*

Bunbury, Sir Edward Herbert, ninth baronet (1811–1895), classical scholar and author, was born on 8 July 1811 at Brighton, second of the six children (five sons followed by a daughter who died aged one) of Lieutenant-General Sir Henry Edward *Bunbury, seventh baronet (1778–1860), of Mildenhall and Barton Hall in Suffolk, and his first wife, Louisa Emilia (1788?–1828), daughter of General Henry Edward Fox (1755–1811). The family was a landed one renowned, as *The Times* (8 March 1895) said, for its 'brilliant social qualities and influential connexions', as well as for its art collection at Barton. Edward and his elder brother, Charles James Fox *Bunbury (1809–1886), were educated at home. The climax of the enlightened curriculum was an extended visit to Europe in 1827–9:

> Sir Edward's youthful memories were a changing kaleidoscope of rounds of Court gaiety, enlivened by an occasional *émeute*, of perils by flood and troubles at custom-houses; of the gems of art and the glimpses of scenery, of vessels stormbound by contrary winds, and of running the gauntlet of Salvator-like gorges, picketed by troops and ambushed by brigands. (*The Times*)

Bunbury matriculated at Trinity College, Cambridge, in 1829, and graduated as senior classic and chancellor's medallist in 1833; election to a fellowship followed in 1835. In 1833, however, he was admitted at the Inner Temple, and was called to the bar in 1841. From 1847 to 1852 he sat as Liberal MP for Bury St Edmunds, but both his attempts at re-election (in 1852 and 1868) proved unsuccessful.

Bunbury's obituary in *The Times* characterizes him as 'shy, self-contained, and almost painfully embarrassed in manner'. Perhaps the shyness amounted to little more than an aversion to small talk, because the writer goes on to remark that:

> his marvellous memory never failed him. As he got animated and excited he would gasp in his talk, and incident and reminiscence would crowd fast on each other, till he was almost apt to lose himself in a labyrinth of entertaining digressions.

Sir Clements Markham likewise described him as 'exceedingly fond of society, and in his later years he was a constant frequenter of the Athenaeum, where he enjoyed meeting and conversing with his numerous friends' (*GJ*, 499). He was noted for his grasp of disciplines as diverse as art, astronomy, and numismatics. He contributed occasionally to the *Numismatic Chronicle* and the *Quarterly Review*, and produced a revised edition (1846) of Sir William Gell's *Topography of Rome and its Vicinity*.

But Bunbury's most important work matched his classical training with his enthusiasm for geography and travel. As early as 9 December 1839 he was made a fellow of the Royal Geographical Society, and served on its council in 1846–7. It must have been from the 1840s that he became one of William Smith's principal collaborators in the preparation of his great classical dictionaries for John Murray—of geography above all. Bunbury's contributions were praised by E. A. Freeman and others as 'models of accuracy and of exhaustive erudition' (*GJ*, 499). This work laid the foundation for his major piece of scholarship and principal claim to fame, *A History of Ancient Geography among the Greeks and Romans from the Earliest Ages till the Fall of the Roman Empire*. Twelve years in the making, it runs to more than 1400 pages and was published in two volumes by John Murray in 1879, with a second edition following in 1883 and a reprint by Dover in 1959. Bunbury wrote to Murray from 35 St James's Street, his London residence, on 16 September 1878:

> I am fully aware that my work is not likely to be a pecuniary success and shall be quite satisfied for my own part if it proves as you express it a credit both to author and publisher. I need hardly add that I feel much gratified by the favourable opinion expressed by your referee.

Posterity has shared that opinion. As a thorough, balanced exposition of its challenging and fundamental subject, Bunbury's work remains unmatched in any language. It earned him a medal from the Royal Geographical Society in 1880, and continued to be cited as standard for a century.

Bunbury succeeded his brother as ninth baronet on 18 June 1886. He died unmarried at Apsley House, 148 King's Road, Brighton, from pneumonia on 5 March 1895, and was buried at Great Barton in Suffolk. His library and collection of Greek coins were sold at Sothebys in 1896.

RICHARD J. A. TALBERT

Sources *The Times* (8 March 1895) · *GJ*, 5 (1895), 498–500 · Mrs. H. Lyell, ed., *The life of Sir Charles J. F. Bunbury*, 1 (1906) · W. H. Stahl, 'Introduction', in E. H. Bunbury, *A history of ancient geography*, reprint (1959) · R. J. A. Talbert, 'Mapping the classical world: major atlases and map series, 1872–1990', *Journal of Roman Archaeology*, 5 (1992), 5–38 · letters, John Murray, London, archives · letters, RGS · *Memoir and literary remains of Lieutenant-General Sir Henry Edward Bunbury*, ed. C. J. F. Bunbury (privately printed, London, 1868) · *CGPLA Eng. & Wales* (1895) · Boase, *Mod. Eng. biog.*

Archives John Murray (Publishers) Ltd, London, letters · RGS, letters | Suffolk RO, Bury St Edmunds, letters to F. R. Matthews

Wealth at death £32,411 11s. 3d.: probate, 30 May 1895, *CGPLA Eng. & Wales*

Bunbury, Frances Joanna, Lady Bunbury (1814–1894). *See under* Bunbury, Sir Charles James Fox, eighth baronet (1809–1886).

Bunbury, Francis Ramsay St Pierre (1910–1990), army officer, was born on 16 June 1910 in Hong Kong, the only son of Lieutenant-Colonel Gerald Bruce St Pierre Bunbury, Indian army officer, of Wood View, Carlisle, and his wife, Frances Mary Olivia, *née* Dixon. Francis was educated at Rugby School (1924–8), where he was in the shooting eight, and at the Royal Military College, Sandhurst. He was commissioned second lieutenant in January 1930 into the Duke of Wellington's regiment (known as the Dukes), joined the 2nd battalion in India, and was promoted lieutenant in January 1933. On 27 April 1933 he married twenty-two-year-old Pamela Elizabeth Somers Liscombe (1910/11–1969), daughter of Francis Reginald Liscombe; they had a son, who later served in the Dukes, and a daughter. In 1935 Bunbury served on the north-west frontier in the Mohmand campaign. He returned in 1937 to become adjutant of the depot in Halifax, Yorkshire, was promoted captain in August 1938, and in 1941 attended staff college. He served with the 1st battalion, King's Own Royal regiment, in the 10th Indian division, in the Italian campaign, commanding the battalion from October 1944 to August 1945. Following actions at Pideura, Roversano, the River Senio, and Monte Grande he was awarded the DSO (1945). Promoted major in July 1946, he held a staff appointment. He commanded the 1st battalion, Duke of Wellington's regiment, from 1951 to 1954 in Germany, Korea, and Gibraltar, receiving promotion to temporary lieutenant-colonel in December 1951 and to lieutenant-colonel in February 1952.

Fighting in the Korean War (1950–53) was initially mobile, but from July 1951 involved static attritional trench warfare: when Lord Alexander visited the region it reminded him of Flanders. The 1st Duke of Wellington's regiment served in Korea from September 1952 to October 1953, as part of 29th brigade group, 1st Commonwealth division, in the US-commanded United Nations forces. In the static war hills were keys to the battlefield—and of symbolic and negotiating importance—and were scenes of heavy fighting. The 'Hook' was a tactically important horseshoe-shaped ridge west of the Samichon River and a few miles from the west coast, dominating the surrounding countryside and jutting forward into the Chinese lines, 'a sore thumb, bang in the middle of Genghis Khan's old route into Korea' (Hastings, 371–2), and much fought over. The 7th US marines had captured it, and in October 1952 had been driven off and then recaptured it. Its defences were barely 200 yards from the nearest Chinese position. It was held by the Commonwealth division, and the British lost more casualties there than on any other single battlefield in Korea.

The 1st Black Watch improved the American defences and by tactical 'defence in depth' repelled Chinese attacks in November 1952 and early May 1953. On 13 May 1953 the Dukes, commanded by Bunbury, took over the Hook. The battalion consisted mostly of young national servicemen (paid under £2 a week) lacking combat experience, but they had been well trained by Bunbury and his subordinates. With the Royal Engineers they repaired and improved the defences, and they prepared for another Chinese attack, of which they had been warned by a Chinese deserter. From the night of 20 May Chinese artillery and mortars bombarded the Dukes' position for seven days; and on the evening of 28 May, just after sunset, the bombardment lifted and waves of Chinese infantry attacked. The Dukes, heavily outnumbered but crucially supported by US and Commonwealth artillery, and tank fire, fought desperately at close quarters with grenades and sten guns. Bunbury was in the forefront of the battle, and his leadership, fighting spirit, and disregard of danger inspired his men. After midnight he ordered a final counter-attack to clear the Hook, and the Chinese withdrew. It had been 'a fine defence' (Hastings, 373). The Dukes had inflicted heavy casualties, for relatively light losses. They repaired the defences, and shortly afterwards were relieved by the 1st Royal Fusiliers. Bunbury was awarded a bar to his DSO (1953).

After Korea the Dukes served at Gibraltar. Promoted colonel in March 1955, Bunbury was an assistant adjutant-general at the War Office (1954–6), then commanded 50th independent infantry brigade in Cyprus (1956–9) in the emergency in the operations against EOKA, and was made CBE (1958). Promoted brigadier in April 1959, he was deputy adjutant-general, British army of the Rhine, from 1959 to 1961, and retired in 1962. He was a tall, slim, distinguished-looking man, whose principal hobby was shooting. He competed successfully for his battalion, and was especially proud of winning the army hundred cup at Bisley in 1950; he wrote that 'to my eyes this was my greatest achievement' (*Daily Telegraph*). He also played cricket, golf, and hockey and was a racing enthusiast. He died of bronchopneumonia and congestive cardiac failure on 28 April 1990 at his home, The Wilton, 2 Wood Road, Hindhead, Surrey.   ROGER T. STEARN

Sources *The Times* (2 May 1990) · *Daily Telegraph* (2 May 1990) · *WW* (1989) · m. cert. · d. cert. · *Army List* (1939–63) · A. H. Maude and A. Archer, eds., *Rugby School register, 1911–1946*, rev. edn (1957) · M. Hickey, *The Korean War: the west confronts communism, 1950–1953* (1999) · M. Hastings, *The Korean War* (1987) · A. Farrar-Hockley, *The British part in the Korean War*, Official History, 2 (1995) · J. M. Cowper, ed., *The King's Own: the story of a royal regiment*, 3 (1957) · H. Green, *The king's own royal regiment (Lancaster)* (1972) · J. Gooch, ed., *Decisive campaigns of the Second World War* (1990) · T. R. Moreman, *The army in India and the development of frontier warfare, 1849–1947* (1998)

Wealth at death £128,746: probate, 9 Oct 1990, *CGPLA Eng. & Wales*

Bunbury, Sir Henry Edward, seventh baronet (1778–1860), army officer, was born in lodgings in Pall Mall, London, on 4 May 1778, the younger of two sons of the artist and caricaturist Henry William *Bunbury (1750–1811) and his wife, Catherine (1754–1799), daughter of Captain Kane-William Horneck RE; his brother was Charles John Bunbury (1772–1798). The family claimed descent through the Norman St Pierre, who adopted the name Bunbury from the manor in Cheshire acquired after the conquest. Educated at a village 'humble school' at Mildenhall, a preparatory school near Eton, Buckinghamshire (from which he ran away), and at Westminster School, London, he became an ensign in the Coldstream Guards on 14 January 1795. He did not hold the rank of lieutenant before purchasing a captaincy in the 16th Queen's light dragoons on 16 August 1797. During the expedition to The Helder in the Netherlands in 1799, he served on the duke of York's personal staff and was present at the actions of 19 September and 2 and 6 October. He attended the newly formed Royal Military College at High Wycombe, Buckinghamshire, in 1800–01, secured a majority in the 9th West India regiment on 11 March 1802, and was appointed that year to a staff appointment as assistant quartermaster-general, serving in this capacity in the south-eastern district in 1803–4 when invasion seemed imminent. In 1803 he briefly went on half pay after his regiment was reduced. However, on 31 December 1803 he became lieutenant-colonel as a permanent member of the quartermaster-general's department, not holding a regimental commission. Having advanced to deputy quartermaster-general, he joined the Royal Newfoundland fencible infantry as lieutenant-colonel on 28 March 1805.

Bunbury acted as quartermaster-general, responsible for troop movements and deployment, with General Sir James Craig's expedition to support the kingdom of Naples in October 1805, and he withdrew with Craig to Sicily early the following year. He held the same post under Craig's successor, Major-General Sir John Stuart, when Stuart invaded Calabria in southern Italy, and was credited with issuing clear orders during the battle of Maida on 4 July 1806, after which he received a gold medal. During this encounter he recorded that a staff officer, confusing the dust of cattle with approaching French cavalry, embarrassingly ordered bathing troops out of the sea to stand naked to their arms. Bunbury remained in Sicily as quartermaster-general to the forces in the Mediterranean until 1809, that year taking part in another expedition to the Bay of Naples. Meanwhile, on 4 April 1807, he had married Louisa Emilia Fox (1788?–1828), the eldest surviving daughter of General the Hon. Henry Edward Fox, commander-in-chief of the Mediterranean forces and brother of the politician Charles James Fox. They had five sons and one daughter; only three sons survived their father, including Sir Charles James Fox *Bunbury, eighth baronet, naturalist and diarist, and Sir Edward Herbert *Bunbury, ninth baronet, classical scholar and author.

Early in 1809 Bunbury surrendered his Mediterranean appointment and sailed home. Nominally still a deputy quartermaster-general, shortly after reaching England he became military under-secretary of state for war in the duke of Portland's government (in which his wife's uncle was foreign secretary), retaining that position under Portland's successors until 1816. In the meantime, he had advanced to colonel, on 1 January 1812, and to major-general on 4 June 1814, when he ceased to be lieutenant-colonel in the Royal Newfoundland fencible infantry, and he was appointed KCB in 1814. In his official capacity Bunbury accompanied Admiral Lord Keith to Torbay, Devon, on 31 July 1815, where the government's decision that Napoleon should go to St Helena was read to him on the *Bellerophon*, provoking the former emperor's reaction that he would rather die than be exiled there. In December 1815, at Wellington's request, Bunbury travelled to St Jean de Luz, the duke's former Peninsular War headquarters, on a confidential mission. In March 1821 he succeeded to the baronetcy and estates of his uncle, Sir Thomas Charles Bunbury, sixth baronet (b. 1740), an MP for the county of Suffolk for forty-three years, who owned Barton Hall, near Bury St Edmunds, and Manor House at Mildenhall—both in Suffolk—and Stanney Hall in Cheshire.

In September 1828 Bunbury's first wife died, leaving him with four surviving sons: Charles James Fox Bunbury (1809–1886), later FRS, Edward Herbert Bunbury (1811–1895), Henry William St Pierre Bunbury (1812–1875), and Richard Hanmer Bunbury (1813–1857). On 22 September 1830 he married Emily Louisa Napier (d. 18 March 1863), daughter of Colonel the Hon. George Napier and his second wife, Lady Sarah Lennox, daughter of the second duke of Richmond. In 1830 he was also elected in place of the sitting tory as the second member for his late uncle's Suffolk seat, and he advanced to lieutenant-general on 22 July. A staunch whig, on 23 March 1831 he voted for the second reading of the first Reform Bill, which passed the Commons by a majority of one. In the following election he was again returned. However, he declined a post in Lord Grey's government on the grounds of ill health, did not contest the next election, and retired from the army in 1832. He was persuaded to stand for West Sussex at the 1837 general election: both whigs were defeated by a large majority.

Bunbury collected fossils and old Italian manuscripts, and acquired a fine library and art collection. A fellow of

the Society of Antiquaries, he published a paper in *Archaeologia* on Roman and British antiquities found at Mildenhall. He also wrote *Correspondence of Sir Thomas Hanmer, Bart, Speaker of the House of Commons* (1838), adding family sketches of this relative's life; and two military works: *Narrative of the Campaign in North Holland in 1799* (1849) and *Narrative of Certain Passages in the Late War with France* (1852). He was an improving landlord, with an active interest in the welfare of labourers. He provided allotments, and advocated them in the *Journal of the Royal Agricultural Society* (1845). From 1859, concerned at the French threat, he vigorously supported the establishment of the volunteers in Suffolk. Bunbury, who was renowned for his tact, dignified manner, and conscientiousness, died at his home, Barton Hall, Great Barton, near Bury St Edmunds, Suffolk, on 13 April 1860 and was succeeded in his title and estate by his eldest son, Charles James Fox Bunbury, who edited the *Memoir and Literary Remains of Lieutenant-General Sir Henry Edward Bunbury* (1868).   JOHN SWEETMAN

Sources Army List · H. Graham, *History of the sixteenth, the queen's, light dragoons (lancers)*, 2 vols. (privately printed, Devizes, 1912–26) · Burke, *Peerage* · Fortescue, *Brit. army*, vol. 5 · *DNB* · Boase, *Mod. Eng. biog.* · *Memoir and literary remains of Lieutenant-General Sir Henry Edward Bunbury*, ed. C. J. F. Bunbury (privately printed, London, 1868)
Archives BL, corresp. and papers, Add. MSS 37051–37052, 42863, 63106, 63108 · BL, memoir, RP 1921 [copy] · Suffolk RO, Bury St Edmunds, corresp., letter-books, and papers | BL, corresp. with Sir William A'Court, Add. MSS 41512–41513 · BL, corresp. with J. W. Gordon, Add. MS 49494 · BL, corresp. with Lord Holland and Lady Holland, Add. MS 51542 · BL, corresp. with Sir Hudson Lowe, Add. MSS 20108–20233, *passim* · BL, corresp. with Sir Charles Napier, Add. MSS 54529–54531 · BL, corresp. with Sir Robert Peel, Add. MSS 40221–40600, *passim* · Bodl. Oxf., letters to Napier family · NA Scot., letters to Sir Alexander Hope · NL Scot., corresp. with Lord Lynedoch · U. Nott. L., letters to Lord William Bentinck
Wealth at death under £90,000: probate, 5 June 1860, *CGPLA Eng. & Wales*

Bunbury, Henry William (1750–1811), artist and caricaturist, was born on 1 July 1750 at the Manor House, Mildenhall, Suffolk, the second son of the Revd Sir William Bunbury, fifth baronet (c.1710–1764) and vicar of Mildenhall, and his wife, Eleanor (d. 1762), daughter of Colonel Vere Graham, of Wix Abbey, Essex. His elder brother, (Thomas) Charles *Bunbury, later became an MP and a noted horse-racing administrator. Like his brother, Henry Bunbury was educated at Westminster School, London, where he began producing his characteristically humorous drawings, including *The Judgment of Paris* (1766; etching, 1771, BM 4920). This and other early compositions were etched by the artist himself, but after c.1771 all his published drawings were etched by professional engravers. On 30 January 1768 he was enrolled at St Catharine's College, Cambridge, and university life inspired works such as *The Hopes of the Family* (engraved by James Bretherton, 1774; BM 4727) and *Pot Fair, Cambridge*, exhibited at the Royal Academy in 1776 (engraved by Bretherton, 1777; BM 4729). A tour of France in 1767 had whetted his appetite for foreign travel, and in 1769 he abandoned his university studies to take the grand tour, travelling from Paris to Naples. Austin Dobson, writing in the *Dictionary of National Biography*,

Henry William Bunbury (1750–1811), by Thomas Ryder, pubd 1789 (after Sir Thomas Lawrence, c.1788) [notating his *Long Minuet*]

states that he studied drawing while in Rome, but this cannot be documented.

The tour resulted in a flood of works poking fun at foreigners, and particularly at the French; *La cuisine de la poste* was shown at the Royal Academy in 1770 (engraved by Harris; BM 4764) and won immediate acclaim, notably from the connoisseur and collector Horace Walpole, who subsequently heralded Bunbury as 'the second Hogarth', and avidly collected his works (H. Walpole, *Anecdotes of Painting in England*, 1762–71, 4.8). Other drawings from the tour, serious and humorous, were published by Mathew Darly, but thereafter until c.1781 nearly all drawings were etched by James Bretherton, who was particularly successful in capturing the sketchy but robust character of the originals. The drawings were composed in pencil, black or red chalk, and pen and ink, often enlivened with a monochrome wash or watercolour highlights; major collections are in the British Museum department of prints and drawings; Gainsborough's House, Sudbury, Suffolk; and the Manor House Museum, Bury St Edmunds, Suffolk. There are smaller holdings at the Lewis Walpole Library, Connecticut, and at the Courtauld Institute and Victoria and Albert Museum, both in London.

Although readmitted to Cambridge in February 1771, Bunbury seems never to have taken a degree. In August that year he married Catherine Horneck (1754–1799), and they settled in a house on his brother's estate at Great Barton, Suffolk. The couple shared a lively sense of humour and an enthusiasm for amateur theatricals; Catherine was nicknamed Little Comedy by their friend the author Oliver Goldsmith. Two sons were born to them: Charles John (1772–1798) and Henry Edward *Bunbury

(1778–1860), later to succeed to his uncle's title as seventh baronet.

Bunbury spent much of his time in London, where he and his wife enjoyed a convivial social life with friends drawn from the aristocracy and artistic and literary circles, including Garrick, Dr Johnson, and Sir Joshua Reynolds, who was godfather to his second son. As a result he was often in financial difficulties. His son later recorded: 'My father had embarrassed his circumstances by the generosity of his nature and a carelessness about money which did not befit a younger brother' (*Memoir*, 7). To augment his income he took the post of comptroller of army accounts, c.1775–1784, with an income of £750 per annum; he also served in the West Suffolk militia, rising to the rank of lieutenant-colonel. Drawings caricaturing military life were shown at the Royal Academy in 1779, with subsequent engravings by Thomas Watson and William Dickinson, such as *Recruits* (1780; BM 4766), while a series illustrating military costumes was published by Thomas Macklin in 1791.

A growing fashion for fanciful and sentimental subjects, initiated by Wheatley and Morland, encouraged Bunbury to produce works in similar vein, sometimes in round or oval formats. He also extended his range with illustrations from the works of popular authors, including Sterne and Goldsmith. Sketches for *The Arabian Nights* were exhibited at the Royal Academy in 1785, and issued in sepia and coloured stipple etchings. Of wider appeal were his depictions of the hilarious antics of inept and reckless horsemen. They include *Hints to Bad Horsemen* (1781; BM 5914–5917), and *An Academy for Grown Horsemen* (1787), which he wrote under the pseudonym Geoffrey Gambado esq (BM 7231–7242).

The design which proved to be the most successful in Bunbury's lifetime was another humorous work, *A Long Minuet as Danced at Bath*, engraved by Dickinson in 1787 (BM 7229). In the unusual format of a strip, 210 cm long (84 inches), it mocks the attitudes of both graceful and ungainly couples dancing. Its renown led to the speedy production of a similar composition, *The Propagation of a Lie* (engraved by Dickinson; BM 7230), in which eighteen men, each headed with an exclamatory comment, react in individual fashion to the spreading of a malicious rumour. These innovative story-telling designs were imitated by other caricaturists, such as G. M. Woodward, and were precursors of the modern comic strip. The esteem in which Bunbury was increasingly held led to his portrait by Sir Thomas Lawrence being issued as an engraving by Thomas Ryder in 1789 (NPG). He appears stocky, round-faced, in contemplative pose, but with a genial countenance, and his celebrity as an artist was evidently enhanced by his personal charm. The diarist and novelist Fanny Burney frequently encountered him while they were both employed in court circles, Bunbury having been appointed groom of the bedchamber to the duke of York, second son of George III, in 1787. She did not admire his character, but described him as 'entertaining and gay, full of talk, sociable, willing to enjoy what is going forward, and ready to speak his opinion with perfect unreserve' (*Diary and Letters*, 3.325). While he was in the duke's service, the Bunburys lived in fashionable residences at Whitehall and Richmond, and later moved to Weybridge when the duke took up his abode at nearby Oatlands Park.

In his later years Bunbury produced fewer humorous designs, but his earlier compositions continued to be reissued. Some were engraved by his distinguished contemporaries Rowlandson and Gillray; Gillray's *A Barber's Shop in Assize Time* (1818; BM 11779) is an elaborated version of a Bunbury original, and was the last plate he worked upon before he became incurably insane. A major commission towards the end of Bunbury's career, from Thomas Macklin, the printseller of Fleet Street, was for a series of forty-eight illustrations from Shakespeare's plays to be engraved by Bartolozzi and others. However, only half the drawings were completed, and the project ground to a halt in 1796; the artist may have found the elaborate designs tedious to work on, for they are largely uninspired, lacking dramatic power and his customary lively characterization.

In 1798 Bunbury's son Charles died, and then his wife in the following year. Their combined loss led to a decline in Bunbury's hitherto cheerful personality, and he seems to have turned to drink; he was disparagingly described by the diarist Joseph Farington in 1804 as 'living most of His time a sotting life at Bury in Suffolk' (Farington, *Diary*, 6.242). Thereafter he lived a retired life, chiefly at Keswick in the Lake District, where he began painting in oils; three compositions were exhibited at the Royal Academy in 1806; an example, *Rustics in a Landscape*, is at Gainsborough's House.

Alcohol perhaps hastened Bunbury's decline, and his death occurred at Keswick on 7 May 1811. He was buried in the churchyard at Keswick, and a memorial was placed in the family church at Great Barton. The eulogies heaped upon him by his contemporaries have subsequently been viewed as not altogether deserved, particularly when his drawings are compared with those of the more inventive and highly accomplished Gillray and Rowlandson; contemporary enthusiasm can be explained partly by his status as gentleman artist, and also by his gentle, burlesque style, eschewing malice and political topics, and offending nobody. In the twentieth century his individual qualities became more widely appreciated again, not only among print collectors, but also among historians, for whom he provides a diverse and illuminating portrayal of society in the mid- to late Georgian period.

CHRISTOPHER REEVE

Sources J. C. Riely, *Henry William Bunbury: the amateur as caricaturist* (1983) [exhibition catalogue, Gainsborough's House, Sudbury, Suffolk] • F. G. Stephens and M. D. George, eds., *Catalogue of prints and drawings in the British Museum, division 1: political and personal satires*, 11 vols. in 12 (1870–1954) • M. Clements, 'Henry William Bunbury, gentleman cartoonist', *Proceedings of the Suffolk Institute of Archaeology and History*, 34 (1977–80), 129–36 • J. C. Riely, 'Horace Walpole and "the second Hogarth"', *Eighteenth-Century Studies*, 9 (1975–6), 28–44 • *Memoir and literary remains of Lieutenant-General Sir Henry Edward Bunbury*, ed. C. J. F. Bunbury (privately printed, London, 1868) • L. Lambourne and J. Hamilton, eds., *British watercolours in the Victoria and Albert Museum* (1980) • H. Ewart, 'Henry Bunbury, caricaturist', *The Connoisseur*, 6 (1903), 85–9, 136–9 • *Diary and letters of Madame D'Arblay (1778–1840)*, ed. C. Barrett and A. Dobson, 6 vols. (1904–5), 3.304–31, 481–2; 4.59–67, 96, 405 • M. D. George, *Hogarth to Cruickshank: social change in graphic satire* (1967) • *GM*, 1st ser., 81/1 (1811), 501–2 • *DNB* • *IGI* • parish register, Mildenhall, St Mary and St Andrew, 25 July 1750 [baptism]

Archives Gainsborough's House, Sudbury, Suffolk, journals of a tour of Italy

Likenesses T. Patch, pen-and-ink caricature, *c*.1769–1770, Yale U. CBA • T. Lawrence, pastel drawing, 1789, NPG • T. Ryder, stipple, pubd 1789 (after T. Lawrence, *c*.1788), BM, NPG [*see illus.*] • H. R. Cooke, engraving, *c*.1812 (after T. Lawrence), NPG • T. Blackmore, mezzotint (after J. Reynolds; as a boy), BM • photograph (after oil painting by J. Reynolds, *c*.1764), NPG

Wealth at death £2000—administration: PRO, PROB 6/187, fol. 319r

Bunbury, Lady Sarah. *See* Napier, Lady Sarah (1745–1826).

Bunbury, Selina (1802–1882), novelist, was born at Kilsaran House, near Castlebellingham, co. Louth, Ireland, one of the fifteen children of the Revd Henry Bunbury and Henrietta Eleanor Shirley. Through her father she descended from a landed gentry family in co. Carlow, while on her mother's side she was related to the eleventh Earl Ferrers. Her father was non-resident rector of the nearby Mansfieldstown, co. Louth, from 1793 to 1815, after which he became treasurer of Ossory. Subsequently the family went to live at Beaulieu, outside Drogheda, on the banks of the River Boyne. Her father went bankrupt in 1819, and her mother had to move with the children to Dublin.

In Dublin, Selina taught in a primary school and began to write in secret, against her mother's wishes. She published her first work, *A Visit to my Birthplace* (1821), at the age of nineteen; the work went through twelve editions during her own lifetime. Her early work, which was published anonymously, consisted mainly of tales about protestant society in Ireland (for example *Cabin Conversations* of 1827), which she, unlike most Irish authors of the time, published in Dublin. She often, but not exclusively, used Ireland as a backdrop for religious fiction, which was written from a protestant point of view with a strong anti-Catholic message, as in *My Foster Brother* (1827) and *The Abbey of Innismoyle* (1828).

About 1830 the family moved to Liverpool, where Selina kept house for her twin brother. She returned to Ireland in 1842–3 to attend to her dying mother and then, after her brother's marriage in 1845, she began to travel throughout the continent of Europe, recording her experiences in many volumes, including *Rides in the Pyrenees* (1844). She also turned some of these travel diaries into fictional accounts such as *Evelyn, or, A Journey from Stockholm to Rome in 1847–48* (1849). One of her best-known novels, *Coombe Abbey* (1843), was set in England in the early seventeenth century, showing her predilection for writing historical religious fiction. She continued, however, to write about Ireland in works such as *Tales of my Country* (1833) and *Recollections of Ireland* (1839). Selina Bunbury later wrote juvenile fiction, including *Stories for Children* (*c*.1844) and *The*

Selina Bunbury (1802–1882), by Harriet Bunbury

Indian Babes from the Woods (1845?), and published pamphlets for the Religious Tract Society and the Society for Promoting Christian Knowledge. She was an early and frequent contributor to the *Dublin University Magazine*, and *Fraser's Magazine*. She wrote her last work, *Lady Flora*, while living at Lee, in Kent, in 1869. She was described as 'a petite little person, busy and bustling' by her niece in *The Irish Book Lover* (1916, 7.106), a volume which also shows her portrait. Selina Bunbury died, unmarried, at Cheltenham, Gloucestershire, on 8 September 1882, and was buried at Cheltenham cemetery, where a memorial was erected to commemorate her. She is not to be confused with the Selina Bunbury who wrote *Florence Sackville* (1851).

ROLF LOEBER and MAGDA STOUTHAMER-LOEBER

Sources Blain, Clements & Grundy, *Feminist comp.* · S. J. Brown, *Ireland in fiction*, new edn (1919) · B. McKenna, *Irish literature, 1800–1875: a guide to information sources* (1978) · P. Rafroidi, *Irish literature in English: the Romantic period*, 2 (1980) · *Irish Book Lover*, 7 (1915–16), 104–7

Archives BL, letters relating to grant application to the Royal Literary Fund, Loan no. 96

Likenesses H. Bunbury, miniature, repro. in *Irish Book Lover*, 104 [*see illus.*]

Bunce, Kate Elizabeth (1856–1927), painter, was born on 25 August 1856 at 312 Green Lane, Aston, Warwickshire, the daughter of John Thackray Bunce (1828–1899) and Rebecca Ann (*d.* 1891), daughter of Richard Cheesewright of Gosberton, Lincolnshire. Her father was the editor of the *Birmingham Daily Post* and a prominent local citizen closely associated with the new municipal museum and art gallery and Birmingham School of Art, and was granted the freedom of the city for his services to art. Two

other sisters having died in infancy, Kate (as she was baptized) grew up with Myra Louisa (1854–1919) and Edith, who died in early adulthood. She was educated at home.

Bunce 'inherited literary ability from her father' (*Birmingham Post*, 22 Dec 1927) and published a certain amount of verse (none has yet been traced) but her principal interest lay in painting, to which she devoted her career, making her exhibition début with the Royal Birmingham Society of Artists in 1874. With her sister Myra, a metalworker and watercolour artist, she trained at Birmingham School of Art through the 1880s, under its energetic principal Edward Taylor during a period when the Birmingham school of painting, illustration, and decorative art established its distinct identity. According to the Birmingham School of Art's historian, both Edward Burne-Jones and William Morris (who visited the school in 1880 and 1894) were interested in and hopeful of this generation of students, who included the painters Joseph Southall and Charles Gere, the embroiderer Mary Newill, and the illustrators and jewellery designers Arthur Gaskin and Georgie France (later Gaskin) (Catterson Smith, 294).

Bunce's earliest extant picture is a large watercolour, *The Sitting Room* (1887; Birmingham Museums and Art Gallery), produced in the same year as her Royal Academy début (with the unlocated *How may I, when he Shall Ask*—a title from D. G. Rossetti's poetry, a regular source of inspiration). Working mainly in oils and tempera, she exhibited regularly at the major English venues in Birmingham, London, Liverpool, and Manchester until 1912. In 1895 she furnished illustrations for *Fairbrass: a Child's Story* by T. E. Pemberton, and in 1903 she contributed to a volume of drawings for E. R. Taylor's retirement.

Artistically Bunce possessed a personally recognizable but not innovative style comparable to that of her Birmingham colleagues, and that of London-based Eleanor Fortescue Brickdale. Typically, she produced single-figure subjects on late romantic and religious themes, in which the secular female figures are pale and languid ('dyspeptic' in the *Athenaeum*'s view; 21 May 1892, 672) in a static manner more suited to sacred subjects. The chief stylistic development of her career was towards simpler forms and lighter tones, which may be attributed to the use of and influence of tempera. From 1888 she was an associate of the Royal Birmingham Society of Artists, and in 1901 a founder member of the Society of Painters in Tempera, although she never exhibited with them. In 1898 her young cousin Margaret Wright recorded how Bunce worked in the studio every morning, giving the rest of the day to social and cultural activities, including regular theatregoing (MS diary, priv. coll., Canada). In 1893 she was one of two female and eight male painters commissioned to produce large-scale historical works for Birmingham town hall; allocated two panels, her subjects were the medieval Guild of the Holy Cross and the early Tudor almshouses (all panels disappeared in the Second World War). She often painted on a heroic scale, such as the single figure *The Minstrel* (exh. RA, 1890; priv. coll.) and the four devotional pictures (*c.*1900) painted for Sts Mary and Ambrose, Edgbaston. Her most ambitious work is *The*

Chance Meeting (exh. New Gallery, London, 1907; formerly with Frost and Reed, London) showing the legendary encounter between Dante and Beatrice in a busy Florentine setting.

Bunce's work often received critical favour, *The Childhood of St Warburga* (1898; formerly with Christopher Wood, London) being described as 'frankly archaic in style but … charming in its delicate colouring and subtle suggestion of medieval illumination' (*The Artist*, Dec 1898). *The Keepsake* (exh. New Gallery, 1901; Birmingham Museums and Art Gallery) was chosen as 'Picture of the Year' by the *Pall Mall Gazette*. Medium-sized pictures like these and *Melody* (1901; Birmingham Museums and Art Gallery) are commonly strong in line and colour, with a wealth of decorative detail often directly linked to arts and crafts production. Several of her works either depict or are framed by Myra Bunce's metalwork, as, for example, multi-panel altarpieces at St Mary's, Longworth, Oxfordshire (1904; commemorating the artists' parents and sister Edith), and St Alban's, Bordesley, Birmingham (installed 1919). Bunce was a devout high-church Anglican, and her sacred art reflected her deep religious and spiritual temperament; picture titles suggest she especially revered English saints, while the deployment of stylized flat-planed figures whose gold leaf aureoles glow in rows is reminiscent of early Italian art and contemporary mural work such as that by Phoebe Traquair. In 1919 Bunce completed a war memorial diptych for Holy Trinity, Stratford upon Avon, and at the time of her death she was engaged on a picture of St Alban for the cathedral in Prince Albert, Saskatchewan, Canada.

Little is known of Bunce's personal life and opinions. She lived all her life in Edgbaston, with a considerable local acquaintance, and seems seldom to have travelled. It would appear that she was temperamentally reserved—family members recall a certain severity of aspect in old age—while her class position, private income, and religious faith precluded overt pursuit of artistic fame, although family papers attest to pride in the critical success of *The Keepsake*, which was also shown in 1903 at Manchester City Art Gallery and in 1905 at the Société National des Beaux-arts, Paris, the only known overseas exhibition of her work. Some works were sold to regional patrons, others being gifted to local institutions, for example, *The Puritan Maiden* (1893; priv. coll., USA) which was presented to Birmingham General Hospital.

After her sister Myra's death in 1919, Kate Bunce lived on at 10 Holly Road, Edgbaston, where she died, unmarried, on 24 December 1927. Still identified locally as the 'last surviving daughter' of J. Thackray Bunce, she was buried on 28 December at Edgbaston Old Church. In her will she bequeathed *The Keepsake* to Birmingham Art Gallery, with the residue of her estate (about £6000 after personal bequests) being divided between the gallery and Birmingham University.

While in her lifetime Bunce's work was generally well if not enthusiastically received, its old-fashioned style and subjects fell entirely from favour in the following half century; only subsequently has it been rediscovered, chiefly by curators at Birmingham Museums and Art Gallery and feminist art historians interested in the late Victorian period.   JAN MARSH

Sources A. Crawford, ed., *By hammer and hand: the arts and crafts movement in Birmingham* (1984) · J. Marsh and P. G. Nunn, *Women artists and the Pre-Raphaelite movement* (1989) · J. Christian, ed., *The last Romantics: the Romantic tradition in British art* (1989) [exhibition catalogue, Barbican Art Gallery, London, 9 Feb – 9 April 1989] · J. Marsh and P. G. Nunn, *Pre-Raphaelite women artists* (1997) [exhibition catalogue, Manchester, Birmingham, and Southampton, 22 Nov 1997 – 2 Aug 1998] · R. Catterson Smith, 'Birmingham Municipal School of Art', *Birmingham institutions*, ed. J. H. Muirhead (1911) · b. cert. · d. cert. · CGPLA Eng. & Wales (1928) · private information (2004) · *Birmingham Post* (27 June 1919) · *Birmingham Post* (27 Dec 1927) · *Birmingham Despatch* (28 Dec 1927)
Archives Birm. CL, papers · Birmingham Museums and Art Gallery, papers · Christies, papers, photographs · Courtauld Inst., Witt Library, papers, photographs · Sothebys, London, papers, photographs
Likenesses photograph, repro. in Marsh and Nunn, *Pre-Raphaelite women artists*, 145
Wealth at death £15,528 4s. 5d.: probate, 3 Feb 1928, CGPLA Eng. & Wales

Bundy [Bundy-Francklin], **Richard** (1693/4–1739), Church of England clergyman and translator, was born in 1693 or 1694, possibly in Devizes, Wiltshire. His parents may have been the Richard Bundy and Margery Flower who married at Southbroom St James, Wiltshire, in 1679. He matriculated at Christ Church, Oxford, on 22 March 1710 aged sixteen, and proceeded BA in 1713, and MA in 1716 as Richard Bundy-Francklin (Foster, *Alum. Oxon.*, 1.210). On 6 June 1723 he married Anne Gregory (*d.* in or after 1739) at Andover, Hampshire.

For several years Bundy translated scholarly works from French into English. First he published a translation of Lamy, *Apparatus biblicus, or, An Introduction to the Holy Scriptures* (1723), which essentially refers to the hermeneutic tradition of the four senses of scripture, and the biblical interpretation of the Catholic church. He then produced *The Roman History*, a translation of the Jesuit fathers Catrou and Rouillé (1727–38, 6 vols.), on account of which he had been engaged since 1725 in a pamphlet war with his competitor John Ozell, who had advertised a sample translation of the same text to be sold by subscription. On the other hand, it is now generally agreed that *A Plea for Divine Revelation* (1731), an anti-deistic and pro-trinitarian tract pertaining to another pamphlet war and the controversy about the respective roles of reason and religion, was wrongly attributed to Richard Bundy instead of John Jackson.

Bundy then embarked on a second career. In 1732 he was appointed as chaplain-in-ordinary to George II, whom he had already served when the latter had been prince of Wales (*Egmont Diary*, 3.349). Bundy was then selected to accompany the king on his visit to Hanover, and was created doctor of divinity by the archbishop of Canterbury for that purpose. On 9 June 1732 he was nominated a trustee to the society set up to establish the new colony in South Carolina to be known thereafter by the name of Georgia. He attended its board meetings regularly, and on 21 March 1733 he was promoted to its common council, from which he resigned on 26 February 1738 (*Egmont Diary*, 1.286–344 and 2.468). He was installed as prebendary of Westminster, London, on 2 October 1732, and became vicar of St Bride's, Fleet Street, later in the same year, and rector of East Barnet, Hertfordshire. He died on 27 January 1739, and was buried at Devizes. His wife, Anne, survived him. The following year two volumes of the posthumous *Sermons on Several Occasions, with a Course of Lectures on the Church Catechism* were published, followed by a third, possibly spurious, companion volume to the second edition (1750). FRANÇOISE DECONINCK-BROSSARD

Sources Foster, *Alum. Oxon.* • *GM*, 1st ser., 2 (1732), 777 • *GM*, 1st ser., 9 (1739), 47 • *ESTC* • *BL cat.*, [CD-ROM] • D. Lysons, *The environs of London*, 4 (1796), 17–18 • *CSP col.*, 39.138–9 • E. H. W. Dunkin, C. Jenkins, and E. A. Fry, eds., *Index to the act books of the archbishops of Canterbury, 1663–1859*, pt 1, British RS, 55 (1929) • *Fasti Angl.* (Hardy), 3.365 • will, PRO, PROB 6/115, fol. 28v • *Manuscripts of the earl of Egmont: diary of Viscount Percival, afterwards first earl of Egmont*, 3 vols., HMC, 63 (1920–23), vol. 1, pp. 286–344; vol. 2, p. 468; vol. 3, p. 349 • *IGI*

Wealth at death goods and chattels to widow: will, PRO, PROB 6/115, fol. 28v

Bungay, Thomas (*fl.* 1270–1283), Franciscan friar and theologian, may have entered the order at Norwich. His name suggests East Anglian origins. He was tenth lector to the Franciscans at Oxford in 1270, immediately preceding John Pecham (*d.* 1292), while from about 1272–5 he was eighth English provincial minister, being again succeeded by Pecham. Subsequently he was sent to Cambridge, where he was fifteenth Franciscan master in 1282–3. This seems to have been part of a policy pursued until the end of the thirteenth century, whereby experienced and able scholars were sent from elsewhere to bolster the Franciscan school at Cambridge.

Bungay had been a pupil of Richard of Cornwall (Richard Rufus; *fl.* 1250) and of John of Wales (*d.* 1285)—the fifth and sixth Franciscan lectors at Oxford, who between them held this post from 1256 to 1262. His commentary on the *Sentences* is now lost, although a copy was once in the library at St Augustine's, Canterbury. But extracts from his commentary on Romans can be found in the Biblioteca Classense, Ravenna, MS Bibl. Class. 472, and in the Biblioteca Comunale, Todi, MS Todi 59. Also extant, in the Biblioteca Comunale, Assisi, MS Assisi 158, are seventy or eighty questions discussed at Cambridge about 1280–82. Bungay's name appears more frequently than any other in these questions—more than thirty of them are or may be attributed to him—which are valuable above all in that they reveal his main interest to have been in the field of speculative theology.

However, Bungay also had an interest in mathematics, as demonstrated by his *De celo et mundo*, which survives in several manuscripts, for example Cambridge, Gonville and Caius College, MS 509 and Paris, Bibliothèque Nationale, MS Lat. 16144 (sec. xiii). This may help to explain why a tradition that goes back at least to the sixteenth century associates Bungay with Roger Bacon. No contemporary evidence to connect the two men has ever been found, but it seems probable that there was indeed some link, as they were contemporaries, both Franciscan friars, and with

interests in common. By 1600 Bungay appears alongside Bacon as a magician in vernacular histories. One of the most distinguished men of his order during his lifetime, Bungay retained a reputation as a worker of miracles long after his death; according to one chronicler, his aid was prayed for and granted during the battle of Barnet in 1471. The date of his death is unrecorded, but he is known to have been buried at Northampton. JENNY SWANSON

Sources Emden, *Oxf.*, vol. 2 • Emden, *Cam.* • A. G. Little and F. Pelster, *Oxford theology and theologians*, OHS, 96 (1934), 74, 105–8 • A. G. Little, *Studies in English Franciscan history* (1917), 220 • J. R. H. Moorman, *The Grey friars in Cambridge, 1225–1538*, The Birkbeck Lectures (1952), 157–8

Archives Biblioteca Classense, Ravenna, MS Bibl. Class. 472 • Biblioteca Comunale, Assisi, MS Assisi 158 • Biblioteca Comunale, Todi, MS Todi 59 • Bibliothèque Nationale, Paris, MS lat. 16144, sec. xiii • Gon. & Caius Cam., MS 509

Bunker, Henry James (1897–1975), microbiologist, was born in London on 27 April 1897, younger son and third child of Charles James Garibaldi Bunker (1864–1916), a pharmacist, and his wife, Kate Waterfield (1862–1944). He was educated at St Olave's Grammar School, London, from 1906. His schooling completed in 1915, he served in the First World War as an NCO and later a commissioned officer of the South Wales Borderers. Following demobilization in 1919 he went up to St Catharine's College, Cambridge, and took a degree in natural sciences with botany as his principal subject.

On 29 July 1922 Bunker married Pauline Rosemary (Pearl) Delahunty (*d.* 1950); they later had two sons and two daughters. It was also in 1922 that Bunker became assistant bacteriologist in a microbiology research group led by A. C. Thaysen at the Royal Naval cordite factory at Holton Heath, where he studied such practical problems as the fermentation of vegetable matter to produce fuel alcohol, and the microbial degradation of textiles and rope. Together with Thaysen he published a standard work on microbes. When the tomb of Tutankhamen at Karnak was opened by Howard Carter in 1924 Bunker was sent samples of the mummy's wrappings and other materials from the tomb, and he showed that, as far as current techniques could detect, no microbes survived.

In 1933 Thaysen's research group was transferred to the Chemical Research Laboratory, Teddington; its research interests had expanded. Bunker had now become interested in damage to materials caused by sulphur bacteria, especially the sulphate reducing bacteria. His 1936 review of these organisms was a seminal contribution to subsequent research. Nevertheless, he regularly attended to *ad hoc* problems involving microbes, such as the blackening of paint by fungi, taint in fish caused by bacteria, and microbial degradation of stored ropes. During the blitzkrieg of 1940–41 damage to wet fire hoses became a serious problem; Bunker showed that it was caused by sulphur bacteria forming acid from sulphur, a vulcanizing agent in the rubber, and was able to prescribe remedies. But during the Second World War the group's major project, to make edible yeast from waste molasses as a protein rich food supplement, largely displaced other research themes. It kindled in Bunker a long-lasting interest in yeast and food microbiology. At the end of the war he was one of many British scientists sent to defeated Germany to assess the state of its science and technology.

In 1944 Bunker left the Teddington group to set up and direct a research department for a London brewer, Barclay-Perkins. He found the practical microbiological problems of the industry, ranging from the fermentation process itself to washing-up glassware in public houses, of absorbing interest, and he published widely. However, in 1956 Barclay-Perkins was taken over by a larger firm and Bunker's laboratory was closed. Although of an age at which many might have retired, he used his wide professional experience to embark upon a new and highly successful career as a freelance consultant on microbiological problems in industry.

Bunker was one of the first British experts on microbial activities in non-medical contexts. Although he himself was mainly concerned with practical problems, he was a firm believer in the need for fundamental research. He played an important role in bringing about the recognition of microbiology as a distinctive discipline within biology. He became an influential figure in learned organizations concerned with both basic and applied microbiology; in 1945 he helped found the Society for General Microbiology; he became its first treasurer and was its president during 1952–5; he was also president of the Society for Applied Bacteriology, 1946–9. He represented microbiology at the inception of the Institute of Biology in 1950, was elected a fellow, and was president, 1967–9; he was also a fellow of the Institute of Food Science and Technology. He held forty-eight distinguished and honorific positions; he was especially pleased by a DTech conferred upon him in 1969 by Brunel University, and a DSc conferred by the Bath University of Technology in 1970. In all his offices he was notable for his tact, friendliness, and self-deprecating humour, yet as a chairman would display a firm and businesslike grasp of the discussion.

A popular after-dinner speaker who could draw upon a fund of comic anecdotes, Bunker was an outgoing and engaging man who enjoyed good food, drink, sociability, and travel. His cheerful personality sustained him through a persistent nephritis which, over the last thirty years of his life, resulted in his needing a number of quite serious kidney operations. On 21 April 1970, twenty years after the death of his first wife, Bunker married his companion, secretary, and friend, Marie Travers (née Currivan; d. 1992). He continued his consultancy work until his death from pancreatic cancer on 8 August 1975 at Teddington Memorial Hospital. He was cremated at south-west Middlesex crematorium on 13 August.

JOHN R. POSTGATE

Sources J. R. Postgate, *Journal of General Microbiology*, 93 (1976), 1–7 [incl. bibliography] · M. Ingram, *Journal of Applied Bacteriology*, 40 (1976), 125–7 · *Journal of the Institute of Biology*, 22 (1975), 163–4 · *The Times* (15 Aug 1975), 14 · various contributors, 'In memoriam', *The Olavian* [magazine of St Olave's Grammar School, Orpington], 76 (April 1976), 4–6 [special issue] · private information (2004)

Likenesses photographs, repro. in Postgate, 'Henry James Bunker, 1897–1975' · photographs, repro. in Ingram, *Journal of Applied Bacteriology*

Wealth at death £7584: probate, 20 Oct 1975, *CGPLA Eng. & Wales*

Bunn, Alfred (1796–1860), theatre manager and librettist, was born on 8 April 1796. In his autobiography, *The Stage: both Before and Behind the Curtain* (3 vols., 1840), he implied that he came from an upper-class family, but gave no details. He published some poetical works, written in a conventional vein, in 1816 and 1819. In the latter year he embarked on the sequence of positions as lessee and manager of various theatres that, together with writing opera librettos, occupied most of his career. From 1819 until 1824 he held the lease of the Theatre Royal, Birmingham. He married the actress Margaret Somerville [*see* Bunn, Margaret Agnes (1799–1883)], who was engaged at the theatre in 1819; apparently some scandal was attached to their marriage, but little is known of this or other personal details. Bunn may have been involved in the leasing of the Theatre Royal, Bath, from 1819 to 1823. He was stage-manager for R. W. Elliston at Drury Lane theatre during the season of 1823–4, and during 1830 he leased and managed theatres in Dublin and Cork.

In October 1830 Bunn returned to Drury Lane as stage-manager. Then, in 1833, he placed himself at the centre of the London theatrical world by taking the leases of both Drury Lane and Covent Garden. He soon plunged into controversy by successfully appealing to royalty and the House of Lords to reject Bulwer-Lytton's bill of 25 July 1833 to remove the patents enjoyed by these two theatres. He relinquished the Covent Garden lease in 1835, but remained lessee and manager of Drury Lane until 1839, while also leasing the English Opera House during 1837. He produced a wide range of works, including dramas by Shakespeare, Sheridan Knowles, Byron, and Joanna Baillie; ballet; lighter theatrical fare; and opera. Bunn was especially interested in the last. Among the noteworthy successes at Drury Lane during this period were *The Siege of Rochelle* (1835) and *The Maid of Artois* (1836), both composed by Michael Balfe. Bunn himself was the librettist of the latter work, which was intended as a vehicle for the soprano Maria Malibran, whom he engaged at £125 per week—an unprecedented fee, he claimed, at these houses. But he also offered lion tamers and tightrope acts, and he faced bitter hostility from the leading tragedians and their supporters among the London intelligentsia, who accused him of blatant disregard for dramatic standards. On 29 April 1836 this resulted in a brawl between Bunn and the actor W. C. Macready; in the ensuing court case judgement was given for the manager.

Bunn faced huge financial losses. In the 1838–9 season alone his expenditure was over £44,000, whereas his receipts were less than £29,000, and after meeting further expenses he was declared bankrupt in December 1839 with debts exceeding £23,000. Nevertheless he took short-term leases of the St James's, Prince's, Drury Lane, and Covent Garden theatres, and managed Vauxhall Gardens. In October 1843 he leased Drury Lane again, and overtly concentrated on opera and ballet, which he enhanced by highly admired staging. He produced eleven new operas by Balfe, Julius Benedict, Vincent Wallace, George Macfarren, and Louis Henry Lavenu. By far the most famous was Balfe's *The Bohemian Girl* (1843), one of the most successful of all English operas: the heroine's ballad 'I dreamt that I dwelt in marble halls' achieved extraordinary popularity. Again Bunn was the librettist. Throughout his career he wrote or contributed to eleven librettos, seven set by Balfe. As was common practice, he relied heavily on Parisian models.

Bunn could never command the aristocratic patronage or casts of international stars enjoyed by Her Majesty's Theatre in London or by the Opéra in Paris, whose government subsidy he envied; and, again, financial losses forced him to withdraw from management in May 1847. A particular blow was the decision of the immensely popular soprano Jenny Lind not to sing at Drury Lane in 1845. During the court action which Bunn took against her in 1848 for breach of contract, he claimed to have lost £10,000 as a consequence: he was awarded £2500 damages. By now he had frequently been pilloried by *Punch* as 'the Poet Bunn'. His response, *A Word with Punch* (1847), was virtuosically vituperative.

Thereafter Bunn took various short leases and managerial posts, including a final season at Drury Lane from October 1851 to May 1852, but he never regained his earlier preeminence. In 1852–3 he undertook a lecture tour of the United States. Later he moved to Boulogne, where, a convert to Roman Catholicism, and penurious, he died on 19 or 20 December 1860. He was buried in Boulogne.

Bunn was reviled by leading literary figures, including Dickens. The playwright J. R. Planché described his management as 'sheer gambling' and his taste as 'deplorable' (Planché, 2.200). Yet, for all their defects, his librettos are well written for singers, and, by bringing national composers to the fore, Bunn rendered signal service to English opera.   GEORGE BIDDLECOMBE

Sources A. Bunn, *The stage: both before and behind the curtain*, 3 vols. (1840) • G. G. Urwin, 'Alfred Bunn, 1796–1860: a revaluation', *Theatre Notebook*, 11 (1956–7), 96–102, 148 • F. H. W. Sheppard, ed., *The Theatre Royal, Drury Lane, and the Royal Opera House, Covent Garden*, Survey of London, 35 (1970) • G. Biddlecombe, *English opera from 1834 to 1864, with particular reference to the works of Michael Balfe* (1994) • *Punch*, 9 (1845), 87, 229 • A. Bunn, *A word with Punch* (1847) • C. H. Shattuck, ed., *Bulwer and Macready: a chronicle of the early Victorian theatre* (1958), 4, 18–19, 23, 29, 30 • J. R. Planché, *The recollections and reflections of J. R. Planché*, 2 (1872), 200–01 • *DNB* • *The Times* (18 Dec 1839), 6 • *The Times* (23 Feb 1848), 7–8
Archives Shakespeare Birthplace Trust RO, Stratford upon Avon, corresp. and papers | BL, letters to M. Barnett, Add. MS 43382
Likenesses R. J. Lane, lithograph, BM, NPG • prints, Harvard TC
Wealth at death under £200: probate, 2 May 1861, *CGPLA Eng. & Wales*

Bunn [*née* Murray], **Anna Maria** (1808–1889), writer, was born at Balliston, co. Limerick, Ireland, the second of three children and only daughter of Terence Murray (1776–1835), army paymaster, and his wife, Ellen (*d.* 1814), daughter of James Fitzgerald of Movida. Her parents were both Irish Catholics, and Anna Maria remained a member of the faith throughout her life. After her mother's early death Anna Maria was sent to the Ursuline convent in Cork. Illness caused her return to Limerick, where she attended Miss Dodd's school. On 26 November 1826 she sailed for Australia with her father, who had decided to retire there after spending many years stationed in Sydney. On 5 May 1828 she married George Bunn (1791–1834), a shipowner and merchant, at St James's Church, Sydney. Before his premature death in 1834, she had given birth to two sons as well as to a daughter who died in infancy.

In 1838 Anna Maria Bunn became the first woman to publish a novel in Australia, when *The Guardian: a Tale* was printed in Sydney under the pseudonym 'An Australian'. Only the second novel to appear in Australia, its authorship remained a mystery for many years. A highly Gothic tale involving Gypsies, incest, and blighted love, it is set in Bunn's Irish homeland, although with a significant number of mainly satirical references to Sydney. In 1994 it was reprinted by Mulini Press, Canberra. Although Bunn seems to have written no more fiction, numerous letters to family members are now in the National Library of Australia, along with many of her paintings of plants and insects. Small and slender, with auburn hair and blue eyes, she remained mentally active until her death on 23 September 1889 at her property, St Omer, near Braidwood, New South Wales. She was buried at Braidwood two days later.   ELIZABETH WEBBY

Sources G. Wilson, *Murray of Yarralumla* (1968) • P. Clarke, *Pen portraits* (1988) • D. Adelaide, *A bright and fiery troop* (1988), 53–67
Archives Mitchell L., NSW, MSS • NL Aus., MSS | Mitchell L., NSW, Murray MSS • NL Aus., Murray MSS
Likenesses watercolour, c.1838, repro. in Wilson, *Murray of Yarralumla* • photograph, 1889, repro. in Wilson, *Murray of Yarralumla* • A. M. Bunn, self-portrait, repro. in Clarke, *Pen portraits*; priv. coll.

Bunn [*née* Somerville], **Margaret Agnes** (1799–1883), actress, was born on 26 October 1799 at Lanark, Scotland, the eldest daughter of John Somerville, who later went to London and established himself as a biscuit baker in Marylebone. Margaret displayed an early talent for the stage, and at the age of eleven organized a tragedy, *Cato*, with her young friends in a hayloft in which she played Marcia. In 1815 she was introduced to the Hon. Douglas Kinnaird, a member of the Drury Lane committee of management. Her first audition, for which she gave the part of Belvidera (from Otway's *Venice Preserv'd*), was unsuccessful, but she persevered and after a second audition a year later, before Kinnaird and Lord Byron, she was taken on. She gave her first performance at Drury Lane on 9 May 1816, as Imogine in Maturin's tragedy *Bertram*, with Edmund Kean as Bertram. Kean—as was his wont—eased her out of many roles which she had rehearsed, saying that she was 'too big and o'ertowering a woman' for his figure. However, she remained at Drury Lane for three years, interspersed with provincial tours to Worcester, Lichfield, Shrewsbury, and Leicester. In January 1818 she was lent to the theatre at Bath, where she played Bianca in Dean Milman's *Fazio*, then being given for the first time. She resigned from Drury Lane later that year, considering herself underemployed. She played Bianca again at Covent Garden on 22 October 1818, and on 9 November was Alicia in Nicholas Rowe's *Jane Shore* to the Jane of Eliza O'Neill.

Margaret Agnes Bunn (1799–1883), by Frederick Christian Lewis senior, pubd 1816 (after Sir George Hayter)

In 1819 Margaret Somerville was in Birmingham, where she met and married Alfred *Bunn (1796–1860). Bunn was to be one of R. W. Elliston's 'triumvirate of management' at Drury Lane, at which theatre Margaret again repeated her role of Bianca on 27 October 1823. For the 1823 and 1824 seasons she continued at Drury Lane, creating the roles of Cornelia in Sheridan Knowles's *Caius Gracchus* and Queen Elizabeth in *Kenilworth*. After this she retired from the stage, having been regarded as the best Scottish-born tragic heroine of her day. W. C. Macready was critical of her performances, and her Lady Macbeth was described by another critic as 'even more monotonous than a church spout when it pours in wet weather'. Her marriage was not a happy one and led to much scandal: her husband was declared bankrupt in 1840 and died in 1860. Margaret Bunn died at Blue Earth City, Minnesota, in January 1883.

JOSEPH KNIGHT, *rev.* J. GILLILAND

Sources Mrs C. Baron-Wilson, *Our actresses*, 2 vols. (1844) · *Oxberry's Dramatic Biography*, 5/74 (1826) · *Theatrical Inquisitor* · Boase, *Mod. Eng. biog.* · *The biography of the British stage, being correct narratives of the lives of all the principal actors and actresses* (1824) · Genest, *Eng. stage* · *The Athenaeum* (3 Feb 1883), 163 · Hall, *Dramatic ports.* · *Dictionary of national portraiture* (1979) · W. C. Lane and N. E. Browne, eds., *A. L. A. portrait index* (1906)

Likenesses F. C. Lewis senior, stipple, pubd 1816 (after G. Hayter), NPG [*see illus.*] · engraving (as Elvira), repro. in *Oxberry's Dramatic Biography* · engraving (as Bianca), repro. in *Theatrical Inquisitor*, 14 (1819), facing p. 323 · nineteen prints, Harvard TC · prints, BM, NPG

Bunney, Herrick Cyril William (1915–1997), organist and conductor, was born on 12 May 1915 at 17 Elm Grove Road, Barnes, Surrey, the son of Cyril Herbert Herrick Bunney (1881–1969), electrical engineer and civil servant, and his wife, Ethel Letitia, *née* Ardley (1877?–1958). Educated at University College School, his first experience as an organist was at Hendon parish church as an assistant organist. While studying at the Royal College of Music he spent much of his spare time at the Temple Church watching George Thalben-Ball at work—even taking his future wife to a service there on their first date. At the same time he held various posts at London parish churches, eventually being appointed to All Souls, Langham Place, shortly before the outbreak of the Second World War.

During the war Bunney served in the Royal Corps of Signals and was posted to Edinburgh, where he came to know well St Giles's and its organist, W. Greenhouse Allt, playing at some services. Following his marriage to Dr Mary Howarth Cutting (*b.* 1918), a dermatologist, on 6 March 1943, he applied for the newly vacant position of organist. He was offered the post that was to become the focal point of his life, just prior to being demobbed in 1946. He and his wife thus settled permanently in Edinburgh, where they had a son and a daughter.

Bunney's appointment as Edinburgh University organist followed later in 1946. With Sydney Newman he established the highly popular annual carol parties, for which purpose the Edinburgh University Singers, which Bunney took over in 1952, had earlier been founded. Their performances of Bach's St Matthew passion soon became an annual occasion, including Peter Pears, among others, in the role of Evangelist. The St Matthew passion and the B minor mass, which became a regular festival event, were two examples of Bunney's devotion to the music of Bach: he performed four cycles of the complete organ works during his career at St Giles's, in both the fringe and international festivals. His arrival in Edinburgh coincided with the launch of the international festival, which from its inception in 1947 held its opening service in St Giles's Cathedral. He was co-opted as a member of the programme committee and appointed conductor of the Edinburgh Royal Choral Union in 1947.

The St Giles's Cathedral choir in 1946 was formed around a nucleus of a double quartet of singers who were paid a small honorarium. In the early 1960s the choir was reformed, with all thirty members having an equal status. With this choir, particularly with the development of St Giles's distinctive liturgy from the 1980s onwards by the minister, Gilleasbuig Macmillan, Bunney broadened the choral repertoire to include music from a variety of traditions. Renewed impetus was given to his final years at St Giles's by the installation in 1992 of a new Rieger organ, the result of a very generous gift by Alastair Salvesen. This magnificent 'beast', as Bunney affectionately called it, was to inspire his music making and the worship of St Giles's and provide a lasting monument to his fifty years of service as organist. His retirement in October 1996 was marked by the award of an honorary fellowship of the Royal College of Music, an honour that greatly pleased him.

Throughout his career Bunney sought to encourage young musicians. In addition to his teaching commitments at the Royal Scottish Academy of Music and the

Royal College of Music he was concerned to provide outlets for performance by young musicians. In 1962 he began a weekly series of Sunday evening recitals; his work as an adjudicator throughout the UK had convinced him that there was much young talent but little opportunity to perform. In 1964 he founded the Edinburgh Youth Orchestra, remaining its chairman until the mid-1980s.

Bunney became an institution in Edinburgh life, his courteous and courtly character being accompanied by a formidable presence as well as a wry sense of humour. He lived life at a hectic pace—for many years commuting to London on the King's Cross sleeper—but always managed to find time for his colleagues and friends. He was appointed MVO in 1964, and promoted LVO in 1984 and CVO in 1995. Following a long fight against cancer he died at St Columba's Hospice, Boswall Road, Edinburgh, on 17 December 1997, and was buried in Dean cemetery, Edinburgh, on 22 December. He was survived by his wife and two children. MICHAEL D. HARRIS

Sources *The Scotsman* (20 Dec 1997) · *Daily Telegraph* (31 Dec 1997) · *The Times* (1 Jan 1998) · personal knowledge (2004) · private information (2004) · b. cert.
Likenesses R. Henrikzen, oils, 1996, priv. coll. · photograph, 1996, repro. in *The Scotsman* · photograph, repro. in *The Times*
Wealth at death £294,187.11: confirmation, Scotland, 1998

Bunning, James Bunstone (1802–1863), architect, was born on 6 October 1802, in London, the son of Daniel James Bunning (d. 1819), surveyor. He left school at the early age of thirteen to enter his father's office, where he trained until, in 1821, he went to the Royal Academy Schools. About 1826 he was articled to George Smith, architect, and it was on his twenty-fourth birthday that he married Esther Basan, who was born in the West Indies of Italian parents. Between 1819 and 1848 several of his designs were exhibited at the Royal Academy; on the expiry of his apprenticeship he went into practice as an architect.

Bunning held in succession the offices of district surveyor, Bethnal Green, and surveyor for the Foundling Hospital estates; he was also surveyor to the London Cemetery Company (1839), in which capacity he designed the Egyptian Avenue in Highgate cemetery, the Haberdashers' Company, the London and County Bank (1840), the Thames Tunnel, and the Victoria Life office. He took great interest in the work of the Royal Humane Society, and designed their first receiving-house in Hyde Park. His success in competition for the City of London School in Milk Street, Cheapside, which was completed in 1837, brought him to public notice and secured his fortune in the city. He also prepared competitive designs for the Houses of Parliament and the Royal Exchange, and designed the mansion house at Lillingstone-Dayrell in Buckinghamshire, and the towers, since cut down, of Hungerford suspension bridge in London. His official works included the Bethnal Green union workhouse, built about 1840–42.

On 23 September 1843 Bunning was appointed clerk of the city's works, a post whose name was changed in 1847 to that of city architect. In this capacity he designed many works, including: in 1845, a new street from the west end of Cheapside to Carey Street; in 1846, the widening of Threadneedle Street, and the construction of New Cannon Street, opened in 1854; in 1848, the first plan for the raising of Holborn valley, a work first projected by Bunning, and in which he took great interest; in 1849, the coal exchange; in 1852, the City prison, Holloway; in 1853, the Freemasons' Orphan Schools, Brixton; in 1855, the metropolitan cattle market; in 1856, two new law courts in Guildhall; and in 1858, the interior of Newgate, a rearrangement that left Dance's building of 1788 outwardly untouched. At his death he also left a number of designs for various city improvements, such as one for lodging-houses for the poor, Victoria Street, and another for converting Farringdon market into baths; designs in 1858 for increasing the width of London Bridge; in 1860 for improvements in the library of Guildhall; and in 1861 for a new meat market at Smithfield.

Bunning was a fellow of the Institute of British Architects and of the Society of Antiquaries, in which latter capacity he took great care in preserving the remains of a Roman building found in excavating the site of the coal exchange. He died on 2 November 1863 at his home, 6 Gloucester Terrace, Regent's Park, and was buried in Highgate cemetery. His wife survived him. During his life and for some time afterwards Bunning's achievements were regarded as of the practical rather than the artistic order: his designs were often criticized for their 'sometimes vulgar aesthetic taste' (*The Builder*). More recently it has been recognized that his approach to the use of new materials means he deserves 'that recognition as a leading early Victorian architect posterity has so far denied to him' (Hitchcock, 316). Hitchcock noted that, in working for city men, Bunning's works expressed the taste of his sponsors: in his commercial adaptation of the design of an Italian palace, and in his use of an interior iron skeleton, his coal exchange 'is the prime City monument of the early Victorian period' (ibid.). Many of Bunning's important designs, now in the Corporation of London Records Office, were exhibited at the Victoria and Albert Museum in 1973 in *Marble Halls: Drawings and Models for Victorian Secular Buildings*, and were reproduced in the exhibition catalogue.

G. W. BURNET, rev. ANNETTE PEACH

Sources *The Builder*, 21 (1863), 782–3 · Colvin, *Archs.* · J. Physick and M. Derby, eds., *Marble halls: drawings and models for Victorian secular buildings* (1973) · H. R. Hitchcock, *Early Victorian architecture in Britain*, 2 vols. (1954) · *Catalogue of the drawings collection of the Royal Institute of British Architects: B* (1972) · Graves, *RA exhibitors* · S. C. Hutchison, 'The Royal Academy Schools, 1768–1830', *Walpole Society*, 38 (1960–62), 123–91 · *CGPLA Eng. & Wales* (1863) · *Dir. Brit. archs.*
Archives RIBA BAL, biography file · RIBA BAL, RIBA nomination papers, Fv2, p. 77
Likenesses J. Durham, bust, City of London School
Wealth at death under £70,000: probate, 15 Dec 1863, *CGPLA Eng. & Wales*

Bunny, Edmund (1540–1618), Church of England clergyman and theological writer, was born on 15 March 1540 at The Vache, near Chalfont St Giles in Buckinghamshire, the home of his maternal grandfather, Edward Restwold. He was the eldest son of Richard Bunny of Bunny Hall in Wakefield parish, Yorkshire, who served the crown as treasurer of Berwick under Henry VIII and Edward VI, and his wife, Bridget, *née* Restwold. His younger brother, Francis *Bunny, was also to become a clergyman and theologian.

Edmund Bunny went to Magdalen College, Oxford, at the age of sixteen and graduated BA four years later in 1560, whereupon he progressed to Staple Inn and Gray's Inn as his father intended him for a career in the law. He remained in London for at least two years but was determined to enter the church and in consequence was disinherited by his father. Proceeding MA from Oxford on 14 February 1565 he was made fellow of Merton College later that year. This appointment was chiefly due to his abilities as a preacher, for in the upheavals following Elizabeth's accession the college found itself without a fellow who could deliver the statutory sermons. Bunny remained at Merton for five years, taking the degree of BTh on 10 July 1570. Meanwhile he had gained the patronage of Edmund Grindal, bishop of London, who on 20 March 1565 collated him to the prebend of Oxgate in St Paul's Cathedral. Grindal ordained him deacon on the following 30 December, and on his elevation to the archbishopric of York in 1570 appointed Bunny one of his chaplains and took him north. He was appointed subdean of York Minster on 12 December that year. This post, having no pastoral responsibilities, enabled Bunny to preach at various places throughout a diocese where able protestant preachers were in short supply. In 1575 Bunny also acquired the prebend of Wistow in York Minster and was given the wealthy living of Bolton Percy, some 6 miles east of York.

Bunny took his parochial work seriously and was considerate to his poorer parishioners in the matter of tithe collection, concerning which he seems to have employed Christopher Saxton to make a detailed map of the parish in the course of a dispute with the resident gentry branch of the Fairfaxes. He resigned the subdeanery in 1576, and was made a canon of Carlisle Cathedral on 2 July 1585. He remained at Bolton Percy until 1600, by which time his fame as a writer had been established. He had published a catechetical text in 1576, *The Whole Summe of Christian Religion*, which was divided into two sections, one for the learned and one for the common multitude, in which he also extolled the virtues of singing in religious formation. There followed a Latin abridgement of Calvin's *Institutes* in 1579 with an English translation, by William May, in 1580. These were important if unexceptional works for a man of Bunny's views to produce in these years, but his reputation both then and subsequently was transformed by the publication in 1584 of his *A Book of Christian Exercise, Appertaining to Resolution*, which represented a radical departure from contemporary protestant devotional writing.

By the end of the century the book had gone into twenty-four full editions and six shorter versions, making it the most published work of protestant apologetic of the time and, in the words of the publisher's note to the second edition of 1584, 'one of the most vendible books ever issued in this country' (Milward, 73). Bunny's book was, in fact, a protestant version of the Jesuit Robert Persons's *Book of Resolution*, which sought to introduce Counter-Reformation devotional practices to English Catholics and had been published in Rouen in 1582. It was designed by Persons to inform English Catholics of continental developments and to combat the practice of church papistry, whereby Catholics attended services in their parish church. Bunny, working in a region in which Catholicism continued to have a strong hold among considerable sectors of the gentry and the people, recognized the merits of the book in the vigorous and attractive fashion in which it described the Christian way of life, and thought that a protestant version might serve equally well in inducing those church papists to give up their attachment to the Catholic mission, adding to the main text a 'Treatise of pacification' for that purpose. Thus, though the books share much common pastoral intent they were born of controversy, and Persons was furious at Bunny's emendations, halting the printing of his 1585 edition to insert a note at the end of chapter 5 referring to Bunny's 'infinite corruptions, maymes, and maylings, divers things shalbe noted in the margent' (Persons, chap. 5ff.). He also heavily annotated the succeeding chapters in addition to adding others of a more specifically Roman Catholic and controversial tone.

Surprised at the tone of Persons's attack, Bunny responded in 1589 with *A Briefe Answer, unto those Idle and Frivolous Quarrels of R.P.* in which he referred to Persons's 'moth eaten fragments of poperie' (fol. 2v). Thus with its combination of controversial and pastoral writing Bunny's book became a formative influence on the godly readership of the generation after 1590. The book stressed the need for an ordered Christian life and was said by Richard Baxter to have been instrumental in his conversion to godly ways when read by him as a teenager. Persons's work and Bunny's version of it thus became the most popular books of devotion among both Catholics and protestants in late Elizabethan and Jacobean England. Bunny's was also important in that it was among the first of the protestant controversial works to allow that the Church of Rome was indeed a true church, and here he departed from many of his Calvinist contemporaries such as William Perkins, who had denied that point in their writings. For Bunny, Rome had to be considered a church, albeit one that had been saved from her errors by the protestants, for both theological and controversial reasons. First it was necessary in order to establish the scriptural continuity of protestantism itself, but it was also necessary because, if Rome was not a church, then the pope could not be Antichrist. His views, although designed also to win over the recusants, were very influential on the character of controversy in Jacobean England, moving the debate on to a different ground in which the apostolic claims of the Roman church were acknowledged by many of its opponents.

Bunny's other published works included a political treatise, *The Scepter of Judah* (1584), a study of government in the Old Testament which, in true godly tradition, married monarchy with the role of the godly magistrate, and *The Coronation of David* (1588), in which the example of David was used to provide comfort for the troubles that the regime was experiencing from its foreign enemies, particularly Spain. In 1585 he also published *Certaine Prayers and Godly Exercises for the xvii November*, Elizabeth's accession day, which extended an earlier form introduced at York by Archbishop Grindal and subsequently formed the basis of the liturgy for the accession commemoration.

Bunny's contemporary fame also rested on his reputation as a preacher, an activity to which he devoted most of his energies in the years after 1600. He was a popular extempore preacher, invited to the pulpits of many market towns by their godly magistrates, and was a frequent visitor to Oxford, where he preached and catechized to large congregations in All Saints' Church and others in the vicinity. The impact of his preaching on the corporations of the towns he visited did not always meet with approval from the hierarchy at this time, and in 1602 he circulated among his friends a manuscript defence of his activities. He was said to have travelled 'over most parts of England like a new apostle' and was usually accompanied by 'two men in black liveries with horses' (Wood, *Ath. Oxon.*, 2.221–2). He was a close friend and contemporary of that other indefatigable and ageing preacher, Archbishop Tobie Matthew, and shared in his concern to establish a library at York Minster which would provide the basis for the intellectual defence and advance of the Reformation in the north of England. He was therefore a benefactor to the library which was being established there in these years. His friendship with Matthew ensured a base for him during his retirement at the archiepiscopal palace at Cawood, 10 miles south of York, and it was there that he died on 26 February 1618. Bunny was buried in York Minster where there is a fine painted memorial to him on the south wall of the choir which depicts him as a broad-faced and portly figure.   WILLIAM JOSEPH SHEILS

Sources A. Milton, *Catholic and Reformed: the Roman and protestant churches in English protestant thought, 1600–1640* (1995) · P. Milward, *Religious controversies of the Elizabethan age* (1977) · Wood, *Ath. Oxon.*, new edn, 2.219–24 · E. Bunny, *A book of Christian exercise* (1584) [see also later edns] · B. E. Gregory, '"The true and zealous service of God": Robert Persons, Edmund Bunny and the first *Booke of Christian exercise*', *Journal of Ecclesiastical History*, 45 (1994), 238–68 · V. Houlihan, 'Why Robert Persons would not be pacified: Edmund Bunny's theft of the *Book of resolution*', *The reckoned expense: Edmund Campion and the early English Jesuits*, ed. T. M. McCoog (1996) · R. Persons, *A Christian directory* (1585) · R. McNulty, 'The protestant version of Robert Parson's *The first booke of the Christian exercise*', *Huntington Library Quarterly*, 22 (1958–9), 271–300 · W. . Sheils, '"The right of the church": clergy, tithe and the courts of York, 1540–1640', *The church and wealth*, ed. W. J. Sheils and W. Wood, SCH, 24 (1987) · M. J. Harrison, 'Tithes, priest and people: aspects of the social history of the parish of Bolton Percy, 1580–1620', MA diss., University of York, 1990 · will, Borth. Inst., prob. reg. 34, fol. 867 · C. B. L. Barr, 'The Minster Library', in G. Aylmer and R. Cant, *A history of York Minster* (1977), 487–539 · monument, York Minster
Likenesses portrait (painted on monument), York Minster; repro. in Aylmer and Cant, *History*, 436

Bunny, Francis (1543–1617), Church of England clergyman and theologian, was born on 8 May 1543 at The Vache, near Chalfont St Giles in Buckinghamshire, the home of his maternal grandfather, Edward Restwold. He was the third son of Richard Bunny of Bunny Hall, Wakefield,

Yorkshire, and his wife, Bridget, and younger brother of Edmund *Bunny. The family were convinced protestants and his father had served as treasurer of Berwick until leaving the country at the start of Mary's reign, possibly for religious reasons but also to avoid prosecution for embezzlement. Francis entered Magdalen College, Oxford, in 1558, was admitted a demy the following year, graduating BA on 10 July 1562 and MA in 1567. He remained at Magdalen as a probationer fellow until 1572 and during his time there established a reputation as a preacher, having taken orders in 1567. His popularity brought him to the notice of the great patron of the first generation of puritan clergy, Francis Russell, second earl of Bedford, who made him his chaplain.

On 9 May 1572 Francis Bunny followed his brother north, being inducted to a prebend at the eighth stall in Durham Cathedral. From this position he was to be one of the preachers charged with bringing the Calvinist Reformation to the north of England and, like his brother at York, he set about this energetically. On 20 October 1573 he succeeded the former Marian exile Ralph Lever as archdeacon of Northumberland, continuing to preach throughout the diocese, as is indicated by a series of sermons on Joel, delivered during 1575 in and around Berwick where his father had formerly served. The manuscript is now lost. Bunny resigned the archdeaconry on being appointed to the substantial living of Ryton just outside Newcastle upon Tyne on 11 September 1578, and set about adding pastoral responsibilities among a populous but relatively poor community to his preaching activity. He was a conscientious pastor and, like his brother at Bolton Percy, was sympathetic to the needs of his people in matters of tithe during the economic difficulties of the mid-1590s. That sympathy, however, did not involve any relaxation of his spiritual standards and he was not averse to making critical comments on his parishioners when recording their burials if he thought it justified. He remained at Ryton until his death on 16 April 1617 and was buried in the chancel of his church where there is a brass memorial to him.

During his long incumbency, which he held with a canonry at Carlisle, Bunny produced in the 1590s a number of controversial works designed to refute Catholic claims to authority, including *A Survey of the Pope's Supremacie* (1590). This was directed against Cardinal Bellarmine and went to a second edition in 1595, the year in which he also published his more substantial *Truth and Falsehood, or, A Comparison betweene the Truth now taught in England, and the Doctrine of the Romish Church*. A further work of controversy followed in 1607 in reply to a petition from recusants 'in the north parts' affirming their loyalty to the crown following the oath of allegiance. In this he affirmed 'let the fift of November bee a witnesse whilest that daie shall be numbered in the Calenders, of the more than turkish crueltie of Poperie' (*An Answere to a Popish Libell*, 1607, preface, fol. 3v), and declared the current sufferings of the recusants to be small in comparison to the persecution of the protestants under Mary.

Thereafter Bunny devoted his energies to publishing

more pastoral works: *Of the Head Corner-Stone by Builders Still Overmuch Omitted* (1611), a treatise on the life of Christ; an exposition of the doctrine of justification by faith in 1616; and finally a more catechetical work set out in question and answer form, *A Guide unto Godlinesse* (1617), which was an exposition of the ten commandments. Originally brought north by Archbishop Edmund Grindal, Bunny later enjoyed the confidence and support of Archbishop Tobie Matthew, to whom he dedicated some of his works, and represented the tradition of godly conforming puritanism that was characteristic of the early Stuart church. He married Jane, a daughter of Henry Priestley, and they had five children, all of whom predeceased their father. By his will Bunny left £100 to Oxford University towards the building of a new school and £33 to his old college, Magdalen.   WILLIAM JOSEPH SHEILS

Sources F. Bunny, *An answere to a popish libell intituled 'A petition to the bishops, preachers and gospellers, lately spread abroad in the north partes'* (1607) · Wood, *Ath. Oxon.*, new edn, 2.200–01 · Foster, *Alum. Oxon.* · P. Milward, *Religious controversies of the Elizabethan age* (1977) · P. Milward, *Religious controversies of the Jacobean age* (1978) · M. Chayter, 'Household and kinship: Ryton in the late 16th and early 17th centuries', *History Workshop Journal*, 10 (1980), 25–60 · J. Freeman, 'The parish ministry in the diocese of Durham, 1570–1640', PhD diss., U. Durham, 1980 · monument, Ryton church

Bunsen, Sir Bernard de (1907–1990), educationist, was born on 24 July 1907 at Southacre, Trumpington, near Cambridge, the second of the three children of Lothar Henry George de Bunsen (1858–1950) and his second wife, Victoria Alexandrina (1874–1953), daughter of Sir Thomas Fowell *Buxton, third baronet (1837–1915). Lothar de Bunsen's mother was English: his father, Georg von Bunsen, son of Christian, Baron von Bunsen, liberal Prussian ambassador in London from 1842 to 1854, led the liberals in the Reichstag. Lothar was thoroughly English and a banker with Barclays: his second wife, from a notable Quaker family, was active in political and social causes; despite ill health she co-founded the Save the Children Fund after the First World War and worked for it for most of the remainder of her life.

Between Bunsens and Buxtons—high-minded Lutheran piety mated with missionary and internationalist evangelical politics—Bernard grew up sheltered and guided by his privileged, many-branched, widely influential, and often unconventional family connections. His became a socialist Christianity, a practical concern for others less fortunate. Educated at St George's School, Harpenden, he spent a year in Switzerland, before attending the Quaker Leighton Park school (1921–6). He then went up to Balliol College, Oxford, graduating BA in 1930. After a year's teacher training, he chose to teach for three years in elementary schools in Liverpool during the depression. His subsequent decision to seek a career of wider influence sprang naturally from his upbringing. Four years as assistant education officer in Wiltshire led to an invitation to join the national inspectorate: from 1938 to 1946 he served as an inspector of schools, at his own request back in the north of England. In August 1939 he accompanied

Sir Bernard de Bunsen (1907–1990), by Elliott & Fry, 1946

his Quaker uncle to Berlin in the unworldly hope of establishing grounds for a peaceful settlement with the Nazis. While Charles Roden Buxton had talks with Rudolf Hess and Heinrich Himmler, Bunsen put up a German aunt's blackout.

After the war, the contradictions in Bunsen's position were evident: pacific but not quite pacifist, he had accepted some shelter from war in his 'reserved occupation'; at ease with Quakers and tempted to join them, he remained in the broad Church of England, a practising believer with doubts and disbeliefs; by his own admission unacademic, he devoted himself to education. Yet his lack of dogmatism was a strength, and Christopher Cox, his perceptive friend who was educational adviser at the Colonial Office, persuaded him in August 1946 to take on the burden of director of education, Palestine. He proved able to deal evenly with Arabs and Jews and remained *en poste* through bombs and sniping, until the British mandate ended in May 1948.

Three weeks later Bunsen arrived at Makerere College, Uganda, flown out by the Colonial Office as reader and head of education. Although he had hoped to escape administrative responsibilities in Africa, the region, tumid with change, called for his capacities and held him, a presiding presence on Makerere Hill, for the next seventeen years. In 1949 he found himself acting principal as Professor Lamont resigned suddenly. The following year saw Bunsen confirmed as principal. Differences had arisen about the impending transformation of Makerere, then a mainly Ugandan training college, into the University College of East Africa, in special relation to the University of London and serving Kenya, Tanganyika, Uganda, and Zanzibar. It fell to the unacademic Bunsen, inexperienced in university affairs, to mediate and to soothe anxieties. He had to carry through the transformation, despite the suspicion of mission teachers, settlers, and many colonial civil servants (especially Edward Twining, governor of Tanganyika), many of whom were fearful of educated Africans. He nevertheless received strong backing from the Colonial Office, who provided financial support, from development and welfare funds, as did increasingly the Carnegie and Ford foundations. Above all, the fast growing, tribally diverse student body was keen to measure up internationally. Bunsen dealt firmly but sympathetically with a student strike in 1952, ostensibly about food. Despite political problems in Buganda and the Mau Mau uprising in Kenya, his astute leadership enabled the university college to function effectively: students were able to take their London degrees and to begin professional or academic careers.

Yet the great movement of opinion in Britain and beyond that had produced the university college would also destroy it. The 1950s saw separate stirrings towards independence in each of the territories. Indians in Kenya and government in Tanganyika set up their own universities, and Bunsen had to fight for Makerere's newly established identity. Early in the 1960s the rushed imposition of independence for Kenya, Tanganyika, Uganda, and Zanzibar allowed a temporary solution: in that colonial penumbra a University of East Africa, incorporating the new colleges together with Makerere, became politically possible for a time. Bunsen's character and skills came to the fore during this upheaval. Knighted in 1962, for his last two years in Africa (1963–5) he served as vice-chancellor of this independent university, still hoping to hand on the liberal principle of academic freedom and keep open for east African students their desired wider world.

Returning to Britain in 1965, Bunsen served for five years as principal of a Church of England training college at Chester. It proved, inevitably, something of an anticlimax. He retired to Hampstead in 1971 but remained president of various pro-African causes. On 25 October 1975 he married Joan Allington Harmston (b. 1913), a retired British Council librarian; and it was for her he wrote his autobiography, published as *Adventures in Education* (1995). He was dismayed by events in Africa and saddened when Africans whom he had respected behaved illiberally or worse; but he accepted that the ethos he had fostered at Makerere was being swept away by the fuller consequences of independence. Of a patient temperament, full of goodwill, he was humorously serious. In his African prime Bunsen was tall, stooped, short-sighted, thin, unathletic, and by turns vague and focused. He was a wise friend, and generous with his time. His characteristic evening walk, more a tentatively companionable shuffle, was stopped every few yards by a thought. Regarded by all as enigmatic, as somehow different from expectation, his behaviour gave rise, hence, to numerous anecdotes. He

died of tuberculosis at Coppetts Wood Hospital, Coppetts Road, Muswell Hill, on 4 June 1990, and was cremated five days later. His ashes were buried at St Thomas's Church, Upshire, Waltham Abbey, on 8 September 1990.

S. J. COLMAN

Sources B. de Bunsen, *Adventures in education* (1995) • personal knowledge (2004) • private information (2004) • S. J. Colman, *East Africa in the fifties: a view of late imperial life* (1998) • *The Times* (18 June 1990) • b. cert. • m. cert. • d. cert.
Archives priv. coll., MS Palestine diary | Bodl. RH, corresp. relating to Africa Bureau • Bodl. RH, corresp. with Margery Perham
Likenesses Elliott & Fry, photograph, 1946, NPG [*see illus.*] • F. Wilson, photograph, *c.*1953, repro. in Bunsen, *Adventures in education*, frontispiece • photograph, priv. coll.

Bunsen, Christian Karl Josias von, Baron von Bunsen in the Prussian nobility (1791–1860), diplomatist and scholar, was born on 25 August 1791 in Korbach, in the German principality of Waldeck, the only child of Heinrich Christian Bunsen (1743–1820), a regimental officer, and his second wife, Johannette Eleonore, *née* Brocken. Bunsen had two half-sisters through his father's first marriage; his family was not of aristocratic origin. After a grammar school education in Korbach (from 1798), Bunsen moved on to read theology and philology first in Marburg (in 1808) and later in Göttingen (from 1809). These studies culminated in a prize essay, the *Athenian Law of Inheritance*, for which the University of Jena granted him an honorary doctorate in 1812.

The years from 1812 to 1816 were a period of wide-ranging scholarly activities: Bunsen studied Persian, Icelandic, and Arabic in Munich, Leiden, Paris, and Copenhagen. During this time the idea of writing a universal history focusing on 'the Germanic nations, the ancient Greeks and Romans, and (for the earliest period) the Median-Persian-Indian race' (Bunsen, 1.88) also took shape in his mind. On the basis of work in comparative philology Bunsen intended his research to branch out into religion, literature, law, and philosophy. Early in 1816 this life-plan found the approval of the classical scholar Barthold Georg Niebuhr (1776–1831), to whom Bunsen paid a visit in Berlin at that time; Niebuhr's influence on Bunsen's life and work can hardly be overestimated.

When Niebuhr became Prussian envoy to the papal court in 1816 he succeeded in drawing Bunsen into the diplomatic service, even though Bunsen was more inclined to an academic career. He arrived in Rome in November 1816 and was quickly integrated into the vibrant community of German artists and intellectuals residing in the city. He also became friendly with Benjamin Waddington (d. 1828) of Llanofer, a country gentleman and magistrate who was spending the winter in Rome with his wife, Georgina Mary Ann, *née* Port (1771–1850), and his daughters. On 1 July 1817 Bunsen married Waddington's eldest daughter and coheir, Frances [**Frances von Bunsen**, Baroness von Bunsen in the Prussian nobility (1791–1876)], hostess and biographer, in the chapel of Niebuhr's residence, the Palazzo Savelli. The couple had ten children, five sons and five daughters, including the biblical scholar Ernest Christian Ludwig de *Bunsen. Born at Dunston Park, Berkshire, on 4 March 1791 and educated by her mother at Llanofer, Frances von Bunsen did not visit her native country for twenty-one years after her marriage. A dedicated mother, she shared her husband's strong Christian convictions. She also contributed to her husband's career: her British background allowed Bunsen to penetrate to the heart of the high-powered English community. Many of the friendships he and his wife built up in the early years of their marriage turned out to be of great importance in their later life.

Bunsen's appointment as secretary to the Prussian legation in 1818 marked the beginning of a new phase in his life: henceforth his scholarly ambitions had to compete with the demands of the Prussian civil service. In 1823 he succeeded Niebuhr as Prussian minister to the Vatican and held this position until he left Rome in 1838. Bunsen's twenty-two years in Rome were characterized by a variety of activities. His household in the Palazzo Caffarelli on the Capitol deserves to be mentioned as an international social meeting-point for artists and intellectuals. Visitors included, among others, the painter Johann Friedrich Overbeck, the sculptor Bertel Thorvaldsen, the poet and scholar Giacomo Leopardi, as well as Thomas Arnold, Julius Hare, Connop Thirlwall, Philip Pusey, and Sir Walter Scott from Britain. Bunsen managed to maintain his scholarly interests by co-authoring a work entitled *Description of Rome* (1830), which surveyed the city's ancient, medieval, and modern cultural treasures. He also developed an interest in Egyptian antiquities, which eventually led to the publication of *Egypt's Place in Universal History* (1848–67). Bunsen's 1828 proposal to found an archaeological institute can be perceived as an outcome of these endeavours. In addition he was closely associated with the establishment of a protestant infirmary. Both institutions outlived his stay in Rome.

Bunsen's concern with religious matters during his years in Rome had far-reaching consequences. In order to facilitate daily worship he wished to revive the hymns of German reformers and to provide for his countrymen a work comparable to the English Book of Common Prayer. His compilation of ancient hymns and prayers was first printed in 1833. Selections of this work were translated into English by Catherine Winkworth (1827–1878) in 1855 and became well known under the title *Lyra Germanica*; its various editions greatly influenced protestant worship in nineteenth-century England. Bunsen's involvement in religious questions also had a more political nature, which ultimately led to his departure from Rome. A diplomatic crisis between Berlin and the Vatican arose over the disagreement about the possibility of marriages between protestants and Catholics: while such 'mixed' marriages were allowed by Prussian law, the Vatican became increasingly determined to abolish them. The failure of Bunsen's mediating efforts in this matter led to his resignation in April 1838.

During a first sojourn in England from August 1838 to October 1839 Bunsen pursued his scholarly interests, visited many of the Englishmen he had met in Rome, and

saw a great deal of Elizabeth Fry, Frederick Denison Maurice, and William Ewart Gladstone. On 12 June 1839 Bunsen received an honorary DCL from the University of Oxford. In October of the same year he returned to the continent in order to become ambassador to Switzerland, where he and his family stayed until the spring of 1841. At that time Bunsen was summoned from Bern to Berlin in order to discuss the possibility of an Anglo-German bishopric in Jerusalem with Friedrich Wilhelm IV. Owing to his successful negotiations in London in this matter, this bishopric was controversially founded as the expression of a joint effort of the two great protestant powers in Europe to improve the situation of Christians in the Holy Land.

After this diplomatic success Bunsen was appointed Prussian ambassador to the court of St James in 1842. During his time in this office, which he held until 1854, Bunsen maintained close connections with Queen Victoria and Prince Albert. Bunsen's ambassadorial activities were wide-ranging, and included the organization of royal visits as well as the foundation of a German hospital in London in 1844. His fascination with the English parliamentary system was reflected in the advice he gave to Friedrich Wilhelm IV in constitutional matters. He also took a keen interest in educational and cultural issues, initiated translation activity, and increased his connections and his popularity in England by travelling extensively. As in Rome, Frances von Bunsen's active support of her husband's ambassadorial career, evidenced in the warm hospitality received by their many guests, put the couple at the centre of a wide social and cultural network: their London home in Carlton Terrace was a popular meeting-place for celebrities from many European countries.

On a scholarly level Bunsen promoted Niebuhr's innovative research in Roman history, which greatly influenced nineteenth-century English historiography. His enthusiasm was shared by three of his closest English friends: Thomas Arnold (1795–1842), Julius Hare (1795–1855), and Connop Thirlwall (1797–1875). Bunsen also kept up his interest in philological work and introduced his countryman Friedrich Max Müller to the scholarly resources in oriental studies in England. In the theological debates of his time Bunsen was a decided antagonist of the high-church party. As a result he was frequently associated with historicist German biblical criticism in the tradition of David Friedrich Strauss, and his research in this field was so widely known that a defence of his opinions by the broad-churchman Rowland Williams was included in *Essays and Reviews* (1860). The seven volumes of Bunsen's *Christianity and Mankind* (1854), which can be perceived as a development of the ideas about universal history presented to Niebuhr at the outset of his career, were published at the end of Bunsen's stay in England. In 1853 Bunsen received an honorary degree from the University of Edinburgh.

In a political context Bunsen supported the plans for German unification and did his utmost to foster English support for the union of Germany under the leadership of Prussia, thus aiming for an intimate alliance between the two countries. On two occasions, however, he could not reach an agreement between Prussian and English interests. In 1852 he was forced to sign a protocol about the abrogation of the constitutional independence of the duchies of Schleswig and Holstein from Denmark, which he had defended in a printed memoir presented to Lord Palmerston in 1848. A second political tension between England and Prussia arose at the outbreak of the Crimean War in 1853. Bunsen advised his king to join the western alliance of France and England. Friedrich Wilhelm IV, however, had an aversion to Napoleon III and mistrusted Palmerston's political principles. As a result he preserved neutrality towards Russia and accepted Bunsen's offer to resign his post as minister in London in April 1854.

After their return to Germany in June of the same year Bunsen and his wife settled in a villa near Heidelberg, where he passed most of his remaining years with literary work. The year 1855 saw the publication of the book translated into English as *Signs of the Times* (1856), which exercised a great influence in reviving the liberal movement in the German states after the failure of the revolution of 1848. In another important work (1868–70), translated as *God in History*, Bunsen explored how the progress of mankind is reflected in the conception of God formed within each nation. Bunsen's authorship was prolific and his output includes further books, articles, lectures, and political pamphlets within the wide scope of the interests covered in his major publications. Many of them appeared in German and English. During a visit to Berlin in September 1857 Friedrich Wilhelm IV raised Bunsen to the rank of baron and conferred upon him a life peerage.

In 1858 Bunsen's health began to fail and he suffered increasingly from the symptoms of chronic heart disease. The last two winters of his life were spent in Cannes, and in 1860, after having given up the house in Heidelberg, Bunsen and his wife arrived in their new home in Bonn, where he spent the last months of his life. As far as his health allowed, he still pursued his scholarly interests and was surrounded by his family and friends. Bunsen died on 28 November 1860 in Bonn and was buried there on 1 December 1860.

In response to one of her husband's last requests Frances von Bunsen wrote *A Memoir of Baron Bunsen, Drawn Chiefly from Family Papers* (1868), published in German and English and showing her linguistic and literary talent. After her husband's death she moved to Karlsruhe, where she looked after the children of her deceased daughter Theodora, Baroness von Ungern Sternberg. Her family and friends were dispersed in many European countries; she kept in touch with them in visits and letters, which showed her intimate knowledge of the political and cultural events of her time. She died in Waldhorn Strasse, Karlsruhe, surrounded by many of her children and grandchildren, on 23 April 1876, and was buried next to her husband in Bonn.   SUSANNE STARK

Sources F. Bunsen, ed., *A memoir of Baron Bunsen*, 2 vols. (1868) · *The life and letters of Frances, Baroness Bunsen*, ed. A. J. C. Hare, 2 vols. (1879) · W. Höcker, *Der Gesandte Bunsen als Vermittler zwischen Deutschland und England* (1951) · L. von Ranke, ed., *Aus dem Briefwechsel Friedrich Wilhelms IV mit Bunsen* (1873) · *Encyclopaedia* *Britannica*, 9th edn (1875–89) · *Encyclopaedia Britannica*, 11th edn (1910–11) · R. Pauli, 'Bunsen, Christian Karl Josias', *Allgemeine deutsche Biographie*, ed. R. von Liliencron and others, 3 (Leipzig, 1876), 541–52 · W. Bussman, 'Bunsen, Christian Karl Josias Frhr', *Neue deutsche Biographie*, ed. Otto, Graf zu Stolberg-Wernigerode (Berlin, 1953-) · K. D. Gross, 'Die deutsch–englischen Beziehungen im Wirken Christian Carl Josias von Bunsens, 1791–1860', PhD diss., Julius-Maximilans-Universität zu Würzburg, 1965 · F. P. Verney, 'Bunsen and his wife', *Contemporary Review*, 28 (1876), 948–69 · F. Förster, *Christian Carl Josias Bunsen: Diplomat, Mäzen und Vordenker in Wissenschaft, Kirche, und Politik* (Bad Arolsen, 2001)

Archives Bodl. Oxf., letters · Geheimes Staatsarchiv Preussischer Kulturbesitz, Berlin · NL Scot. · Sandon Hall, Staffordshire, Harrowby Manuscript Trust, letters and papers | BL, corresp. with Richard Cobden, Add. MS 43668 · BL, corresp. with W. E. Gladstone, Add. MS 44111 · BL, corresp. with Sir Robert Peel, Add. MSS 40491–40601, *passim* · Bodl. Oxf., corresp. with Lord Kimberley · Bodl. Oxf., corresp. with Friedrich Max Müller [in German] · Bodl. Oxf., corresp. with Sir Thomas Phillipps · Claydon House, Buckinghamshire, letters to Sir Harry Verney · Lpool RO, letters to fourteenth earl of Derby · NL Scot., letters to William Mure and others · NL Wales, letters to Waddington family · U. Southampton L., corresp. with Lord Palmerston · U. Southampton L., letters to the duke of Wellington · W. Sussex RO, corresp. with Richard Cobden

Likenesses lithograph, 1831, Bildarchiv Preussischer Kulturbesitz, Berlin · H. Adlard, engraving (after Richmond, 1847), Bildarchiv Preussischer Kulturbesitz, Berlin; repro. in Bunsen, *Memoir of Baron Bunsen*, vol. 1 · engraving (after J. Roeting, 1860), Bildarchiv Preussischer Kulturbesitz, Berlin; repro. in Bunsen, *Memoir of Baron Bunsen*, vol. 2 · portrait (Frances Bunsen), repro. in Hare, *Life and letters* · woodcut (after contemporary photograph), Bildarchiv Preussischer Kulturbesitz, Berlin · woodcut (after bust by Wolff, 1827), repro. in Bunsen, *Memoir of Baron Bunsen*

Bunsen, Ernest Christian Ludwig de (1819–1903), biblical scholar, was born on 11 August 1819 at the Villa Caffarelli, Rome, the second son in the family of five sons and five daughters of Christian Karl Josias von *Bunsen, Baron von Bunsen, a Prussian diplomatist and theological writer, and his wife, Frances von *Bunsen [see under Bunsen, Christian von], daughter of Benjamin Waddington of Dunston Park, Berkshire. Of his brothers, Henry (1818–1855) became a naturalized Englishman and was rector of Donnington, Wolverhampton; George (1824–1896) was an active politician in Germany; and Karl (1821–1887) and Theodor (1832–1892) worked in the Prussian and German diplomatic service. At the time of Ernest's birth his father was Prussian representative to the Vatican. Ernest was educated at home by his parents until 1834, and then at the school for cadets in Berlin.

In 1837 Bunsen became an officer in the Kaiser Franz regiment of grenadier guards. He subsequently served in the regiment of Emperor Alexander at Berlin, but after a severe illness he joined his parents in England in 1843 on long leave. He served under his father, who was Prussian minister in London from 1841 to 1854, as secretary of the Prussian legation and in 1848 he joined the entourage of the prince of Prussia, afterwards Emperor William I of Germany, during his visit to England. In 1849 he returned to Germany and served during the Baden campaign on the staff of the prince of Prussia, by whom he was decorated for distinguished service at the battle of Sedenburg. He left the German army shortly afterwards.

Bunsen then settled in England, and made his home at

Abbey Lodge, Hanover Gate, Regent's Park, London. This house he acquired on his marriage to Elizabeth (*d*. 1903), daughter of Samuel Gurney and niece of Elizabeth Fry. They married on 5 August 1845 at West Ham Church. They had at least two daughters and two sons, Fritz (the eldest child, who died in 1870) and Sir Maurice William Ernest de *Bunsen, who became British minister at Lisbon in 1905. During his father's lifetime Bunsen paid annual visits to Baden, and he also frequently went to Italy. During the Franco-Prussian War he helped in the hospitals on the Rhine (in 1870–71), and in 1871 he was made chamberlain at the court of William I.

Bunsen's main interests, however, were literary rather than military or diplomatic. In 1854 he published a German translation of Hepworth Dixon's biography, entitled *William Penn oder die Zustände Englands, 1644–1718*. Following in his father's footsteps, he also undertook research into biblical history and comparative religions. His main work, *Biblical Chronology* (1874), was an attempt to establish the dates of Hebrew history by comparing it with contemporary histories of Egypt, Babylonia, and Assyria. Later research questioned his conclusions, but he continued to write much on the theme in both German and English. His last years were absorbed by a work never finished, called 'The Transmission', which he hoped would ultimately unite the Orthodox and Catholic churches as well as the Lutheran and Anglican branches of the protestant church.

Bunsen, who had unusual musical talents, died four months after his wife, at Abbey Lodge on 13 May 1903, and was buried at Leytonstone churchyard. Among his other works were: *Hidden Wisdom of Christ* (1865), *The Keys of St Peter* (1867), *Die Einheit der Religionen in Zusammenhange mit den Völkerwanderungen der Urzeit und der Geheimlehre* (1870), *Das Symbol des Kreuzes bei allen Nationen* (1876), *Die Plejaden und der Thierkreis* (1879), *The Angel-Messiah of the Buddhists, Essenes, and Christians* (1880), *Die Ueberlieferung, ihre Entstehung und Entwicklung* (2 vols., 1889), *Essays on Church History* (1889), and *Die Rekonstruktion der kirchlichen Autorität* (1892). S. E. FRYER, *rev.* JOANNA HAWKE

Sources *The Times* (15 May 1903) · *The Times* (18 May 1903) · *The life and letters of Frances, Baroness Bunsen*, ed. A. J. C. Hare, 2 vols. (1879) · *Encyclopaedia Britannica*, 11th edn (1910–11) · F. A. Brockhaus, *Allgemeine deutsche Real-Encyclopädie für die gebildeten Stände: Conversations-lexicon*, 17 vols. (1864–73) · Meyer, *Conversations-lexicon* · private information (1912) · *CGPLA Eng. & Wales* (1903)
Likenesses double portrait, watercolour drawing (as a child, with his grandmother), priv. coll. · oils, priv. coll.
Wealth at death £737 1s. 9d.: probate, 19 Aug 1903, *CGPLA Eng. & Wales*

Bunsen, Frances von, Baroness von Bunsen in the Prussian nobility (1791–1876). *See under* Bunsen, Christian Karl Josias von, Baron von Bunsen in the Prussian nobility (1791–1860).

Bunsen, Sir Maurice William Ernest de, first baronet (1852–1932), diplomatist, was born in London on 8 January 1852, the second son of Ernest Christian Ludwig de *Bunsen (1819–1903), of Abbey Lodge, Regent's Park, London. He was the grandson of Christian von *Bunsen,

Baron von Bunsen, who was Prussian minister in England from 1841 to 1854, and the biographer Frances von *Bunsen [*see under* Bunsen, Christian von]. His father, a soldier, courtier, and mystical writer, became a British subject in 1849. His mother, Elizabeth Sheppard, daughter of Samuel *Gurney, was one of the Gurneys of Earlham and a remarkable character; she was a niece of Elizabeth Fry, with whom she travelled abroad.

De Bunsen was brought up with a Quaker background in the cultured and cosmopolitan atmosphere of Abbey Lodge, and was educated at Rugby School and Christ Church, Oxford. He entered the diplomatic service in 1877. In his third post, at Madrid, he was commended for his dignity and discretion when left in charge of the legation at a difficult time. After three years (1891–4) as secretary of legation in Japan, he was, in 1894, appointed chargé d'affaires and consul-general at Bangkok, where he was in the confidence of the king and the Siamese authorities in their struggle against French pressure. He was first secretary at Constantinople (1897–1902) in the days of Abdul Hamid and the Cretan troubles, and was then transferred to Paris as first secretary. He was appointed CB in 1895, CVO in 1903, and KCVO in 1905, in which year he went as minister to Lisbon.

In 1906 de Bunsen was sworn of the privy council and appointed KCMG, GCVO, and ambassador at Madrid, where he and his wife were popular and enjoyed the friendship and confidence of Alfonso XIII and his queen. Perhaps de Bunsen's most conspicuous diplomatic achievement was his unofficial mediation, in 1911–12, at the invitation of both parties, in the dispute over Morocco between France and Spain, which materially helped to bring about a peaceful settlement. He was appointed GCMG in 1909. In 1913 he succeeded Sir Fairfax Cartwright as ambassador at Vienna, where he kept the British government in close touch with the complicated political developments preceding the outbreak of war.

De Bunsen returned from Vienna on 14 August 1914 and served as assistant undersecretary in the Foreign Office from March 1915 to March 1918. He chaired an important committee, known as the de Bunsen committee, on the future of Britain's role in the Middle East, which reported in May 1915, adumbrating a British sphere of influence in Palestine to the exclusion of France. De Bunsen led a successful mission to seven South American states as ambassador on special mission, a post he held from April 1917 until October 1918, when he retired from the service. He was on 1 January 1919 created a baronet. He was subsequently active in the City and in the Royal Geographical Society and other such bodies.

De Bunsen's good looks and appearance went well with his courtesy, fearless character, and complete honesty. In the service he stood out among contemporary diplomatists for his ability to reconcile opposing parties and to bring the representatives of clashing interests to discuss their differences with reason and temper. He was looked upon as the ideal chief, for kindness, example, and hospitality. A keen sportsman and a good shot, he was also a lover of literature and well informed on many subjects.

His most notable accomplishment was in public and personal relationships and in the art of living.

De Bunsen's family life was a happy one. In 1899 he married Berta Mary, elder daughter of Armar Henry Lowry Corry, who was in the Foreign Office; she was a niece of M. W. Lowry Corry, Lord Rowton, Disraeli's secretary. They had four daughters. He died at his house, 43 Ennismore Gardens, London, on 21 February 1932, his wife surviving him.   GEORGE FRANCKENSTEIN, *rev.* H. C. G. MATTHEW

Sources *The Times* (22 Feb 1932) · E. T. S. Dugdale, *Maurice de Bunsen: diplomat and friend* (1934) · G. P. Gooch and H. Temperley, eds., *British documents on the origins of the war, 1898–1914*, 11 vols. in 13 (1926–38)
Archives Bodl. Oxf., corresp. and papers | BL, corresp. with Sir R. S. Paget, Add. MSS 51255 A, 51255 B, *passim* · BL OIOC, letters to Sir Evelyn Grant-Duff, MSS Eur. F 234 · Bodl. Oxf., letters to Lord Kimberley · Bodl. Oxf., corresp. with Sir Horace Rumbold · CAC Cam., corresp. with Sir Cecil Spring-Rice · Trinity Cam., letters to Sir Henry Babington Smith
Likenesses W. Stoneman, photograph, 1918, NPG
Wealth at death £10,365 1s. 4d.: resworn probate, 18 April 1932, *CGPLA Eng. & Wales*

Bunting, Basil Cheesman (1900–1985), poet, was born on 1 March 1900 at 27 Denton Road, Scotswood upon Tyne, Northumberland, the elder child of Thomas Lowe Bunting (1868–1925), physician and respected amateur scientist, and Annie Cheesman (1875–1968), daughter of a local mining engineer. One of his earliest memories was of the Northumbrian folksongs sung to him by his nursemaid. After early schooling on Tyneside, he was educated at the Quaker schools of Ackworth, Yorkshire, and Leighton Park, Berkshire. His holidays from Ackworth were spent with a schoolfriend in the west Yorkshire village of Briggflatts. At school he absorbed the elements of Quaker pacifism which led to his being imprisoned for conscientious objection at Wormwood Scrubs and subsequently Winchester from June 1918 until early in 1919. On his release from prison he threw himself into London literary and intellectual life, working in publishing, and with the Fabians. Through one literary contact, Nina Hamnett, he came across the latest work of Ezra Pound, *Homage to Sextus Propertius*, and this discovery was of crucial importance to his poetic development. From 1920 he studied at the London School of Economics, leaving without qualification in 1922 to work briefly as secretary to the MP Harry Barnes. In this role he visited Scandinavia, but failed to enter Russia.

By 1923 Bunting was in Paris, working for Ford Madox Ford on *Transatlantic Review* through the influence of Ezra Pound, who had become a close friend and mentor, and whom he followed to Rapallo in 1924. His earliest poems written at about this time show clearly the influence of modernism. In 1925 his father died and he returned to Newcastle, lecturing at Leamington Adult School in 1926. His first 'sonata', as he called most of his extended poems in acknowledgement of their musical form, was *Villon* (1925): admired by Pound, this poem won him some degree of recognition. Apart from drawing upon the work

of François Villon, the poem incorporates material from Bunting's growing experience of prisons, in England and later in Paris for drunken assault (he was extricated by Pound). For the next two years he made a living in journalism for a range of London weeklies, chiefly as music critic for *Outlook* and the *Town Crier*, before a benefactor, Margaret de Silver, enabled him to move back to Northumberland, living and writing in a shepherd's house in the Simonside Hills during 1928. Memories from this period of his life were recalled directly nearly four decades later in *Briggflatts*.

In 1929 Bunting travelled in Germany, before moving south to Rapallo again. He arrived in Rapallo by way of Venice, where he met Marian Gray Culver (1900–1982), daughter of Howard Leander Culver, a businessman from Eau Claire, Wisconsin, whom he married on 9 July 1930. They had two daughters, Bourtai and Roudaba, and a son, Rustam, who died in 1952. The children's names reflected Bunting's growing interest in Persian literature. From 1930 to 1933 he assisted Pound in Rapallo, contributing to the journal *Il Mare*, helping with concerts co-ordinated by Pound and Olga Rudge, meeting W. B. Yeats (who was able to recite one of Bunting's poems for him from memory, and recalled their meeting in his correspondence), and other writers including James Joyce and Louis Zukofsky. He also learned to sail, and sailed extensively on the Ligurian coast. His poetry began to be published, in anthologies edited by Pound and Zukofsky, and in a pamphlet, *Redimiculum Matellarum* (1930).

A photograph of Bunting taken about 1930 in Rapallo shows a strong, bespectacled profile of a wiry and sailorly man, with a fine goatee beard, apparently content with self and surroundings. He was growing in self-confidence as a poet, dropping the trappings of apprenticeship to reveal a sparse, modernist-classicist voice in which the teachings of Pound and others were moderated by an understanding of a range of older poetries. Though associated with Zukofsky's objectivists and Pound's 'Ezuversity' he was increasingly an individual, isolated to a degree which helped to delay his public notice for more than three decades.

In 1933 the Buntings moved to Santa Cruz de Tenerife—for economy, and perhaps to distance themselves from the increasingly strident Pound. Both were poor and unhappy, and Bunting wrote bitterly of his life there. One lasting and important friendship emerged at this time however, with the exiled German artist Karl Drerup: Bunting corresponded with Drerup at intervals for the rest of his life, and Drerup for his part painted one of the few portraits of Bunting. But the Buntings' marriage was over, and in 1937 Marian returned to America with their daughters and (unborn) son. They divorced in 1940. Bunting returned to Britain in 1937, buying a small boat, *The Thistle*, which he sailed on the south coast. He studied seamanship at Nellist's nautical school in Newcastle (1938), and lectured in Northumberland before the Second World War. In September 1940 he joined the RAF—with some difficulty, as his eyesight was already poor. Like many, his

Quaker principles of individual conscience led him to distinguish between the imperialist values of the First World War, in which he was an objector, and the Second World War, which he (and other objectivist poets such as George Oppen) saw as an important principled fight against fascism, in which he wanted to participate.

Bunting's war was an active and rewarding period of his life (retold, partially, in the sonata *The Spoils*, 1951). In 1942 he arrived in Tehran as an RAF interpreter (on the strength of his knowledge of classical Persian), where he undertook intelligence work and rose rapidly in rank, finishing the war as squadron leader. In peacetime he worked at the British embassy in Tehran, and subsequently as *The Times* correspondent there. He married Sima Alladadian (b. 1931) on 2 December 1948. They had a daughter, Sima-Maria, and a son, Thomas. Bunting's *Poems* (1950) was published in Texas, with little involvement from Bunting. *The Spoils*, his penultimate sonata, draws on his wartime experiences, and also on his love of Persia and respect for its people and culture: 'Sooner or later we must absorb Islam if our own culture is not to die of anaemia', he wrote at a later date (preface to *Omar Pound: Arabic and Persian Poems*, 1970, 5).

The family was ejected from Persia by Mossadeq in 1952, and returned to live in Throckley, Northumberland, with Bunting's mother. Bunting scratched a living for his family from local journalism for the *Newcastle Journal* and the *Newcastle Evening Chronicle*, and had little time for poetry. The poetry world, for its part, had, he thought, forgotten him. But in the early 1960s younger poets including Gael Turnbull and Jonathan Williams 'rediscovered' him, and in 1964 the young Tyneside poet Tom Pickard visited him, starting a friendship which led to the composition of Bunting's final sonata, *Briggflatts*, and its subsequent publication by Stuart Montgomery's influential Fulcrum Press.

With the exception of the few poems included in Pound's *Active Anthology* (1933), the work published by Fulcrum Press, including *Loquitur* (1965) and *Briggflatts* (1966), were Bunting's first British publications. *Briggflatts* is at once a modernist poem, cropped from an alleged 2000 lines to a compressed and often elliptical 700, and a romantic celebration of seasons, homecoming, and love, intensely musical both in its patterning of sound and in overall structure. It stands as the high point of Bunting's maturity, and as testimony to a career of long, often isolated development. After it, he was able to complete only a handful of fine poems. For a generation of younger poets it also stands as a unique achievement of English modernism, providing a link with the world of high modernism which had been lacking in British poetry.

Briggflatts was first performed at Morden Tower, the Newcastle reading venue established by Connie and Tom Pickard, in December 1965, the year in which Fulcrum Press published *Loquitur*, Bunting's first extensive collection published in Britain. In 1966 *Briggflatts* appeared in the Chicago magazine *Poetry*, and in a Fulcrum edition, which was greeted with widespread critical acclaim. Reviewing it, Cyril Connolly spoke for many:

I was quite unprepared for *Briggflatts* which seems to me one of the best poems I have read and reread for a long time ... In Bunting there is a lyrical note which he has been steadily compressing and which makes *Briggflatts* almost all lyric, or rather intensely musical; the words shine like hoarfrost. (*Sunday Times*, 12 Feb 1967)

Bunting's *Collected Poems* followed in 1968. Critical recognition in the USA and UK continued to grow, and in 1968 Bunting was appointed Northern Arts literary fellow at the universities of Durham and Newcastle, where he gave the series of lectures on poetry now published as *Basil Bunting on Poetry* (2000). Although further honours followed, including an honorary DLitt from Newcastle University in 1971, and the inevitable presidencies of the Poetry Society (1972) and of Northern Arts (1974–7), his reputation remained somewhat begrudged in Britain, and he lived the remainder of his days in poverty in his native Northumbria, dying in Hexham General Hospital, Northumberland, on 17 April 1985. Following cremation, his ashes were distributed at Briggflatts Quaker meetinghouse, Sedbergh. In these closing years of his life he performed two acts of editorial piety in the editing of *Selected Poems of Ford Madox Ford* (1971) and the Northumbrian pitman poet Joseph Skipsey (1976): this juxtaposition of modernist and local values says much about Bunting's intention, and his consistency.

Today Bunting's work has a steady readership, and is represented in most of the major anthologies; it is hard to imagine his work being out of print again. This has not always been the case: Bunting's late recognition in his own country was at once a product of his wandering life, a consequence of his outspoken criticism of the literary establishment in Britain, and due to a mistrust of his strong associations with the great modernists, after they ceased to be fashionable. He was unashamedly international in an age when much British poetry was arguably insular or parochial. Out of such elements, and knowledge of his poetic 'masters' Dante and Villon, and other Latin, Persian, Welsh, and classical writers, he constructed a human and evocative modernist poetry built upon the sound of words, intended to be read aloud, harking back to the oral traditions of his Northumbrian nurse: 'Poetry, like music, is to be heard', he insisted (Bunting, 'The poet's point of view', *Diary of North-Eastern Association for the Arts*, April–Summer 1966, 2).

RICHARD CADDEL

Sources B. Bunting, *Complete poems*, ed. R. Caddel (2000) · R. Caddel and A. Flowers, *Basil Bunting: a northern life* (1997) · *Basil Bunting on poetry*, ed. P. Makin (2000) · V. Forde, *The poetry of Basil Bunting* (1991) · P. Makin, *Bunting: the shaping of his verse* (1992) **Archives** Indiana University, Bloomington · Ransom HRC · State University of New York, Buffalo · U. Durham, corresp. and literary MSS · University of Chicago Library · Yale U. | U. Durham, letters to M. de Silver · U. Durham, letters to D. Goacher · U. Durham, letters to K. Drerup and others | FILM U. Durham | SOUND U. Durham **Likenesses** photograph, *c*.1930, U. Durham L., Basil Bunting poetry archive · K. Drerup, oils, 1937, U. Durham L. · J. Williams, photograph, 1980, repro. in Caddel and Flowers, *Basil Bunting* · J. Voit, photographs, 1982, repro. in R. Caddel, ed., 'Sharp study

and long toil', *Durham University Journal* [Basil Bunting issue] (1995) • photographs, U. Durham L., Basil Bunting poetry archive
Wealth at death under £40,000: probate, 30 Sept 1985, *CGPLA Eng. & Wales*

Bunting, Edward (1773–1843), collector of folk music, was born in February 1773 at Armagh, the youngest of the three children of a mining engineer at Dungannon colliery in Coalisland, co. Tyrone (originally from Shottle, Derbyshire), and his wife, Mary (*née* O'Quin). After his father's death, he went in 1782 to live, and to continue his musical education, with his organist brother Anthony in Drogheda, but in 1784 moved to Belfast as apprentice to William Ware, organist at St Anne's. He rapidly demonstrated his precocity, becoming deputy organist. While still a boy he coached many of Ware's adult pupils, but his already arrogant manner did not sit well with his youth, and on one occasion an indignant female pupil boxed his ears when reproached.

In Belfast, Bunting lodged for the next thirty-five years in Donegall Street with the McCracken family. In 1792 he was appointed to transcribe the tunes played at the Belfast Harpers' Festival. The festival had the aim 'to revive and perpetuate the Ancient Music and Poetry of Ireland', and to recover 'airs not to be found in any public collection'. Ten Irish harpers attended. The nineteen-year-old Bunting's imagination was fired by the experience, and he began an extended period of travelling the country, tracing harpers and noting their music. At the festival the blind Ulsterman Dennis Hempson, aged ninety-seven, impressed Bunting most. He alone played only ancient Irish music, and was the only performer to use long fingernails. Bunting visited him frequently after the festival; but his most fruitful collecting in the initial years was in Connaught. The result was the publication in 1796 of his *General Collection of the Ancient Irish Music*. Bunting's great hopes for it were dashed when a pirated edition was published within the year, denying him most of his profits.

Nevertheless, Bunting continued to collect. He mounted a major expedition in 1802–3, employing one Patrick Lynch to collect lyrics, as the 1796 volume had been criticized for the lack of words to its tunes. The results were not published until 1809, partly through Bunting's characteristic indolence, from which he was perhaps roused by the appearance in 1807 of a similar work, which used (unacknowledged) many tunes from Bunting's first collection, marrying them to lyrics in an immensely popular publication. Lynch's words were not used in the new volume, perhaps merely because lyrics and tunes were collected from different sources and often fitted together badly. Some have suggested, however, that the cause lay in the involvement of Bunting's landlords, the McCrackens, with the United Irishmen. Henry Joy *McCracken had been executed following the 1796 uprising, and in 1803 his associate Thomas Russell was hanged after Lynch turned king's evidence against him. Although the suggestion is plausible, there is no supporting evidence; Bunting apparently avoided political entanglements. The lyrics that Bunting substituted were poor

translations. Again he failed to profit from the enterprise, selling his rights to the publisher for a trifling sum. Meanwhile he continued his occupations as music teacher, agent for Broadwood's pianos, and organist at the Second Presbyterian Congregation in Rosemary Lane.

In 1819 Bunting moved to Dublin and married Mary Anne Chapman (1788–1863), formerly of Belfast. They lived at first with Mary's mother at 18 Leeson Street, but Bunting's difficult temperament caused the pair to move very shortly to 28 Baggot Street, where they lived until Bunting's final years, which they spent at 45 Baggot Street. In Dublin he was organist at St Stephen's, and later also a partner in a music warehouse. On 1 December 1827 he secured a well-remunerated position as organist at St George's. He did not publish more until, encouraged and aided by his wife, he commenced a third volume of his *General Collection*, which appeared in 1840. This contained a history of the Irish harp and a description of Irish technical terms.

Bunting's works have been criticized for their increasing remoteness, in successive volumes, from the strict reproduction of harp tunes: even the first volume lacked appropriate accompaniments, and many accompaniments in the last were unplayable on the harp. Despite his efforts to learn the relevant Irish words, Bunting's understanding of them was also deficient, and he lacked a notational basis for recording harp technique. However, without his work our knowledge of tunes and techniques would be immeasurably poorer.

Bunting's own musical abilities were considerable. In 1795, on Wolfe Tone's last night in Ireland, his rendition of 'The parting of friends' reduced the redoubtable Mrs Tone to tears. In 1815 he toured Europe. His music was well received but his large, portly, bespectacled form made him a rather comical 'John Bull' figure in French eyes: in Paris, after giving a performance of Irish music he exclaimed to the audience, slapping his thigh, 'Match me that!' (Petrie, 72).

In his later years Bunting derived much pleasure from family life, having three children. He apparently wore his religion lightly, being organist for both Presbyterian and Established congregations; he recorded that on Christmas day in 1820, 'I for the first time received the Sacrament at St Patrick's Cathedral [Dublin] … with my lady' (Fox, 65). On 21 December 1843, mounting the stairs at home, he suffered a heart attack and died within an hour. He was buried at Mount Jerome cemetery in Dublin.

MICHAEL HEANEY

Sources C. M. Fox, *Annals of the Irish harpers* (1911) • E. M. Dolan, 'The musical contributions and historical significance of Edward Bunting, 1773–1843', DMA diss., Catholic University of America, 1977 • C. Moloney, *The Irish music manuscripts of Edward Bunting (1773–1843): an introduction and catalogue* (2000) • M. McNeill, *The life and times of Mary Ann McCracken, 1770–1866: a Belfast panorama* (1960) • [G. Petrie], 'Our portrait gallery, no. XLI: Edward Bunting', *Dublin University Magazine*, 29 (1847), 64–73 [incl. plate] • G. Yeats, *The harp of Ireland* (1992) • F. O'Neill, 'Famous collectors of Irish music', *Irish Minstrels and Musicians* (1913), 136–49 • E. Bunting, *The Bunting collection of Irish folk music and songs*, ed. D. J. O'Sullivan and

[A. M. Freeman], 6 vols. (1927–39) | *Journal of the Irish Folk Song Society*, 22/23, 28/29) • B. M. Murphy, 'Edward Bunting', MA diss., Indiana State University, 1980 • T. M. Deane, '[Bunting genealogical tree]', 1906, Queen's College, Belfast, MS 4/35(38) • Queen's College, Belfast, MS 4/37(7)

Archives BL, collection of Irish airs, Add. MSS 41508–41510 • Queen's University, Belfast, notebooks and reports | NL Ire., D. 10086 • TCD, MS 4447

Likenesses W. Brocas, stipple, pubd 1811, NG Ire. • W. Brocas junior, etching, pubd 1811, BM, NPG • L. Sackville, engraving, 1811 (after J. Sidebotham), BL • H. Griffiths, engraving, 1847, repro. in Petrie, 'Our portrait gallery' • H. Griffiths, etching, pubd 1847, NPG • T. Smyth, engraving, repro. in 'Biographical notes of Irish musicians, III. Edward Bunting (1773–1843)', *Journal of the Irish Folk Song Society*, 2 (1905), 8 • photograph, daguerreotype, Queen's University, Belfast

Bunting, Jabez (1779–1858), Wesleyan Methodist minister, the only son of William Bunting of Monyash, Derbyshire, a tailor in Manchester, and his wife, Mary Redfern, was born in Manchester on 13 May 1779. The circumstances of Bunting's boyhood and youth suggested that he would develop in an entirely different direction from that which he finally took, and the later legends associating him personally with Wesley are in a high degree implausible.

Education and early ministry Bunting's mother was a model of Wesleyan piety, but his father was a radical who sent him to two Unitarian schools and then apprenticed him to Thomas Percival, a leading Unitarian doctor in the town. With Percival, who was quite prepared to give Bunting university training abroad and launch him in medical practice, he served for four years, retaining a lifelong gratitude for his 'truly paternal direction' (Ward, *Early Correspondence*, 8) and naming his third son and biographer after him. With his mother's support, however, he decided to offer for the Wesleyan ministry and was taken on trial in 1799. Here too the young Bunting was very different from what he soon became. He had been converted at the age of twelve under the ministry of Joseph Benson, a high Wesleyan and later one of the editors of Wesley's work, and now he began to preach among revivalists. He preached his trial sermon as a local preacher in the Manchester Band Room, a centre of revivalism maintained by the draper Broadhurst (whose following Bunting helped to turn out of the connexion in 1806), and he was still a practising revivalist during his time at Macclesfield, as late as 1802. It was in this appointment that his views changed fundamentally, for he had trouble with a group who were preparing to separate as Christian revivalists and link up with others of like mind in Leeds and Manchester. From this time onwards Bunting was a ferocious exponent of church order and discipline, and an implacable opponent of revivalism.

Bunting was a distinguished preacher in his own right, and one to whom his colleagues turned in 1812 for an authoritative exposition in sermon form of the doctrine of justification by faith. It was this preaching flair which launched him quickly into the most important circuits: Macclesfield (1801), London (1803), Manchester (1805), Sheffield (1807), Liverpool (1809), Halifax (1811), Leeds

Jabez Bunting (1779–1858), by David Octavius Hill and Robert Adamson, 1843–8

(1813), London (1815), Manchester (1824), Liverpool (1830), and, from 1833, to connexional offices in London. Bunting had already in Macclesfield revealed a capacity for administration; his transfer to London carried special responsibility for sorting out the muddled accounts of the foreign missions and the connexional book room, and he became assistant secretary to the conference in 1806, and secretary in 1814. Administration and discipline went closely together in Bunting's mind, and discipline 'equally with the dispensation of the word and sacraments [was] an institution of Christ' (*Sermons*, 2.375, 379). Nor was this simply a matter of securing an orderly and efficient church. In Methodism, as in society at large, peace and order were much affected by the trade cycle, and conditions of economic difficulty tended not only to kill the evangelistic appeal of the movement and raise problems of discipline, but to aggravate its internal problems.

A passion for order These problems were at their worst between the end of the Napoleonic Wars and Bunting's first presidency in 1821. The rapid multiplication of married preachers with claims to the support of wife and children, combined with the sudden increase in the real burden of chapel debts occasioned by post-war deflation, produced a tremendous financial crisis, which compounded the effects of social unrest and the suspicion of government. Discipline at every level of church life and discipline in society seemed to go hand in hand. Bunting, who had led the successful opposition to Lord Sidmouth's attempt to limit the Toleration Act in 1811 and had been an outspoken opponent of Luddism during his time at Halifax, made his way to the forefront of the Wesleyan ministry by his willingness to fight the battles of his fellow preachers, and his readily comprehensible solution to their problems. Order, including financial order enforced from the centre, together with discipline in the circuits enforced by the ministry, was to be the route to salvation.

This programme required ideals as well as pressure, and in Bunting's first presidency (1820) he secured in conference the Liverpool Minutes, which set out a detailed conception of the ministry: evangelical and evangelistic, pastoral and efficient, paternal in the double sense of kindly and firm, and in all things single-minded. It was Bunting's friends, and especially Richard Watson and John Beecham, who underpinned this conception doctrinally, by developing the high Wesleyan theory of the pastoral office. Appealing skilfully to scripture and Methodist history, but also to a priori assumptions about the sovereignty intrinsic to bodies politic, they perceived in conference the sovereign legislature of Methodism, in which Wesley had exercised his plenitude of power with the preachers, and to which he had bequeathed his authority to appoint them to their annual stations. The superintendent in each circuit exercised Wesley's general superintendence over the flock, and district committees acting on behalf of conference maintained his daily oversight over the connexion. This concentration of authority, it was maintained, was rooted in the New Testament. Christ had filled the whole pastoral office and transmitted his authority to his ministers. The pastor, wholly given up to the work, must feed and rule the flock; his authority was *sui generis* and could not be shared with those who were not pastors, even if, like local preachers or class leaders, they performed valuable spiritual functions. The concessions which had been made to the lay interest in the 1790s were simply (it was now held) procedural provisions designed to prevent abuse of ministerial authority.

While these developments in doctrine were incubating Bunting himself consolidated the status and enlarged the scope of the ministry. Seminary training (1834–5) and a mission house, both with Bunting at the head, were followed by ordination by imposition of hands (1836) and by some itinerants adopting the preaching gown; attempts were made in the 1840s to bring non-members who were adherents under ministerial authority, and ministers began gradually to celebrate weddings.

Role in Methodist disputes The result of these developments, theoretical and practical, was that those with grievances against connexional policy were driven to much more radical policies. As these issues came to a head in a number of great northern circuits which were crucial to connexional finance, and where subdivision of circuits both deprived the propertied of their influence in old city centre chapels and maximized the number of occasions for dispute, the representatives of the pastoral office found themselves thrown into the front line with not much besides the authority of office and Bunting's support from the centre of the connexion behind them. The first great conflict came in Leeds (1827–9), where disputes over the division of the Sunday school finally came to a head over the proposal to install an organ in the Brunswick Chapel. Connexional law relating to procedure in this matter was not absolutely clear, but Bunting's repeated intervention against all the local authorities except the trustees was certainly unwise and probably illegal, and resulted in the expulsion of large numbers of members, without trial, by a leaders' meeting which was not entitled to pass judgment on the matter. For these Leeds Protestant Methodists (as they became known) the older Methodist reform nostrums of a conference half-composed of lay representatives were not adequate; they needed safeguards to local and circuit rights. In their constitution the oversight of local societies was located in the circuit quarterly meeting, which also had the right to elect ministers (under the title of elders) for a year at a time. This arrangement was fatal to itinerancy as well as to ministerial authority, and it embodied a process of power rising from below rather than descending from above—unacceptable to the high Wesleyans. The more Bunting developed the outward trappings of church life the more the low Methodists, perceiving the root of the connexion's troubles in this very institutionalization, clung to the independence of the Sunday schools (many of which originated in the undenominational effort of the past), took up with teetotalism (another undenominational movement of moral reform with roots in artisan enterprise), retained the vision of Methodism as an evangelistic outpouring of grace, and signified their allegiance to the rising of the provinces against the central institutions of the England of their day by being much more wholeheartedly Liberal in their politics than was the Wesleyan community as a whole.

Was the pastoral office as Bunting conceived it tough enough to contain this alternative model of Methodism, which clearly had considerable social force behind it? The event proved that in important respects it was not. In the 1830s there were small secessions in defence of Derby faith (1831) and the disestablishment campaigner Joseph Rayner Stephens (1834), and a much larger one led by Dr Warren which began in a dispute over the theological institution and ended in the formation of the Wesleyan Methodist Association (1835). These divisions, however, seemed not to cripple the expansiveness of the Wesleyan Methodist denomination and the triumphant success of the Centenary Fund (1839) seemed to confirm the fruitfulness of Bunting's alliance with the lay grandees of the connexion. The social strains of the 1840s were a different matter. The old connexion seemed to run out of steam at a time when the Primitive Methodists were still expanding rapidly, and there was a pervasive sense of unease that new policies were called for, with no agreement as to what they might be. The result was that, when three ministers—Everett, Dunn, and Griffith—were expelled in 1849 on (doubtless well-founded) suspicions of pamphleteering against 'Dr Bunting's whole system of government' they took with them 50,000 members and scores of Sunday schools into a new reform connexion, and for a few years so damaged the morale of the old body that failure to sustain its regular recruiting reduced the total membership by one-third. Bunting, whose rise was built on his pugnacious willingness to fight the preachers' corner, was due for his fifth turn as president in 1852; but in this crisis it was politically impossible to throw him into the fray and he was hastily retired.

Family, decline, and death There is no doubt that the strain of exercising the authority he had assumed took its toll of Bunting's personal elasticity, as it wrecked the health of a number of his colleagues. He preached less often and less effectively in the 1830s; the old energy of conviction declined into mere vehemence, which he used as an instrument of policy in the conference to the extent that the commentators of his old age were apt to think that the troubles of the connexion were due to him personally. His wife, Sarah Maclardie, whom he married on 24 January 1804, and with whom he had three daughters and four sons, including William Maclardie *Bunting, Wesleyan Methodist minister, was a lively and much-loved young woman; she died in 1835 at the height of the Warrenite crisis. In August 1837 Bunting made a happy second marriage with a minister's widow, Mrs Robert Martin (née Green), but the life and soul of his family had now gone and the process by which his personality became absorbed in his office continued apace. He ceased to write, and his principal literary memorial consists in the huge collection of letters that preachers wrote to him.

Moreover, quite apart from the ultimate disaster of the reform secessions at the end of the 1840s, Bunting's policies for the decade ended in consistent failure. At the time of the great constitutional crisis Bunting staked much on the shrewd assumption that Catholic emancipation would be carried (1829), but that after the Reform Act (1832) the Church of England would not be disestablished, and that Methodism should keep out of the coalition of her enemies. But by the end of the decade Methodism was being venomously unchurched by the Tractarians. Still worse, Bunting had supported Thomas Chalmers in the hope of finding a subordinate role for Methodism under an evangelical establishment in Scotland, and at the time of the Disruption (1843) he forswore his past by wishing in conference that 'two thousand clergymen would leave the English Church in the same way'. He fought on protestant grounds to prevent the endowment of Maynooth (1845), and failed publicly again. On the question of national education Bunting was inhibited by his alliances with Irish Orange interests from support for any English version of the Irish national education scheme; in 1847, however, he bargained successfully with Lord John Russell, the usual supporter of such schemes, for Wesleyan schools to be approved for separate funding by the state. Wesleyanism, nevertheless, proved financially unable to develop a strong system of denominational schools, while the machiavellianism of the political bargain of 1847 did no credit to the reputation of a connexional administration which enforced a 'no politics' rule upon its Methodist critics. Repeated attempts to enforce a union of Canadian Methodists under English, as distinct from American, leadership ended in acrimony, the conference agreeing in

1840 that the union was dissolved. That Bunting made his power base in the Wesleyan Methodist Missionary Society was ostensibly a tribute to the ideal of the missionary church as understood in the early nineteenth century, but it was at best a paradox and at worst a contradiction that his main life's work was to transform Methodist preachers from evangelists into pastors. Indeed his doctrinaire attempt to substitute the pastoral office for older Methodist empiricism asked more of the pastoral office than it could provide.

After some two years of ill health (with a diseased throat and great pain in his arms) Bunting died on 16 June 1858 at his home, 30 Myddleton Square, Pentonville, London, and was buried by special permission of the home secretary in the graveyard beside City Road Chapel, London, on 22 June. Notable among the panegyrics at his death were tributes from the Wesleyan Missionary Society and the Evangelical Alliance.   W. R. WARD

Sources T. P. Bunting, *The life of Jabez Bunting DD*, 2 vols. (1858–87) · *The early correspondence of Jabez Bunting, 1820–1829*, ed. W. R. Ward, CS, 4th ser., 11 (1972) · *Early Victorian Methodism: the correspondence of Jabez Bunting, 1830–1858*, ed. W. R. Ward (1976) · W. R. Ward, *Religion and society in England, 1790–1850* (1972) · D. Hempton, *Methodism and politics in British society, 1750–1850* (1984) · J. C. Bowmer, *Pastor and people: a study of church and ministry in Wesleyan Methodism* (1975) · J. Kent, *Jabez Bunting: the last Wesleyan* (1955) · *Sermons by Jabez Bunting*, ed. T. P. Bunting, 2 vols. (1861–2)
Archives JRL, Methodist Archives and Research Centre, corresp.; memoranda book; papers; sermons · SOAS, Methodist Missionary Society archives · Wesley's Chapel, London, letters; notebooks; verses | Wesley College, Bristol, letters mainly to George Morley
Likenesses D. O. Hill and R. Adamson, calotype, 1843–8, NPG [*see illus.*] · W. Behnes, bronze, 1852, NPG · S. W. Reynolds jun., mezzotint, pubd 1855 (after J. Bostock), BM, NPG · J. Cochran, stipple, NPG · T. Thomson, stipple (after J. Jackson), BM, NPG · engraving (as a young man), repro. in Bunting, *Life of Jabez Bunting* · engraving (in middle age), repro. in Bunting, *Life of Jabez Bunting*
Wealth at death under £1500: probate, 22 Sept 1858, *CGPLA Eng. & Wales*

Bunting, John (1839–1923), sharebroker and cotton spinner, was born on 28 December 1839 at Carrington Field, Stockport, the son of John Bunting (1806–1853), a brick maker, and his wife, Kerenhappuch, née Hill. He grew up in the new railway town of Crewe, attended a private school in the village of Bunbury, and began work at the age of eleven. After the sudden death of his father in 1853 he migrated to Oldham, his mother's former home. The staple trades of Oldham were cotton spinning and engineering, in which the town established its world leadership during the 1850s and 1860s. Bunting became a blacksmith and engineer, and acquired a large practical knowledge of machinery. He was twice married and had two sons and two daughters. He first married, on 10 February 1862, Mary (1839–1865?), daughter of James Shaw, a cotton carder. After her death he married on 10 April 1871 Sarah (1844–1928), a dressmaker, and the daughter of James Jackson, a cotton spinner.

During the joint-stock boom of 1873–5 Bunting changed his trade from one of the oldest in the world to one of the newest. He became a sharebroker, and published his first advertisement for shares in 1875 (*Oldham Chronicle*, 14 Aug

1875, 4). He began his new career as one broker among many others in the town's new share market, but he succeeded in breaking out of the ruck, and became a mill owner in his own right. He began to compile a regular weekly survey of the share market, first for private circulation among his clients and then for public consumption in the local press, where it appeared for more than forty years (in the Saturday issues of the *Oldham Chronicle*, 13 December 1879–31 July 1920). In 1877 he became a member of the Manchester Royal Exchange, 'the parliament house of the lords of cotton' (W. C. Taylor, *Notes of a Tour in the Manufacturing Districts of Lancashire*, 1842, 9), and in 1880 he was a founder member of the Lancashire Sharebrokers' Association, of which he later became vice-president. In 1882 he extended his operations from the passive dealing in shares to their active promotion by undertaking his first independent issue of stock on behalf of a new spinning company. He also extended prudent loans against mortgage to mills in financial straits. From 1884 he began a new career as a company promoter and company director, extending his interests outside Oldham to Rochdale in 1890 and to Middleton in 1898. By then he had become a director of eight companies. From 1904 he established his primacy as the leading mill magnate of Lancashire by paying higher than average dividends and by embarking upon the construction of new first-class mills—the Bell Mill in 1904 and the Iris Mill in 1907. The latter was the first ring mill within his group and was built in the record time of four months, or one-third of the normal period, reputedly with a bricklayer working in every window-bottom of the multi-storeyed mill. In 1906 he decided to build Lancashire's largest mill, the Mammoth Mill (of 250,000 spindles, at a time when the newest mills averaged 100,000 spindles), at Hathershaw next to the Bell Mill, but he changed his mind about its location and instead built it (in 1907–8) at Middleton, as the Times Mill no. 2, with 160,000 spindles (by comparison, Arkwright's first mill at Cromford in 1771 had housed only 1000 spindles). The Times Mill was the largest single-unit mill ever built, driven by engines generating 2750 hp, and the Times Mill Company became the industry's most financially successful firm.

From 1910 Bunting achieved new success as a 'company doctor', and undertook the rescue of enterprises in difficulty, especially contractors' companies floated by firms with a direct material interest in the building and equipping of new mills. He bought up such companies cheaply at auction and then restored them to financial health by the issue of preference shares, so extending the range of financial techniques available to the industry. From 1912 he increasingly favoured the technique of high-speed ring spinning over the traditional Lancashire mule. In 1915 he established the Neva Mills Ltd at Middleton and re-equipped them with 99,600 ring spindles, so transforming the company into one of the largest of ring spinners. Thus he completed the construction of one of the earliest groups of mills within the industry. Such groups followed the example set from 1881 by the pioneer James Heap (1828–1892) of Rochdale and imitated by T. E. Gartside (1857–1941) of Royton. They began the process of rationalizing the structure of the industry, paving the way for the formal amalgamation of individual firms into large multi-unit corporations. Bunting had become the biggest individual mill owner in Lancashire and controlled, through separate companies united by the person of the chairman, twenty of the finest and most profitable firms in the industry. In 1916 his companies mustered in the aggregate 1.8 million spindles, or 8 per cent of the spindleage of the Oldham, Middleton, and Rochdale districts, and employed an estimated 7000 hands: 'No man was better known in the Lancashire cotton trade and no man played a bigger part in it during the last forty years … Almost everything he touched changed to gold' (*Oldham Standard*, 24 Feb 1923).

The secret of Bunting's success was to maintain high productivity and to exploit to the full the potential advantages offered by the use of loan capital, upon which most Oldham limited companies relied. An active director and chairman, Bunting reinforced his technical and financial ability by energy, industry, pertinacity, and shrewdness. In a town created by working men, he was reputed to work harder than any other person. He kept capital costs low by using large-scale units of production, by buying existing mills (or 'turnover' concerns), by re-equipping mills with the newest machinery, and by depreciating plant at the high annual rate of 6 per cent. By 1916 he employed more than double the proportion of ring spindleage than was customary in Oldham. He recruited good managers, employed the best operatives, paid the highest wages, and offered the best working conditions. He remained a stubborn opponent of employers' associations and a constant threat to their plans for united action. He always ran his mills full time so that he benefited by the competition of hands for employment and was rarely afflicted by strikes. He insisted that profits should be made only at the mill and avoided risky speculation in the raw cotton market. Above all, he became a master financier with a profound and permanent commitment to his client-investors, regarding himself simply as the steward or trustee of their capital. He sought to maximize the returns received by his shareholders while ensuring that loans retained a gilt-edged status, so that they might be serviced with a lower rate of interest than that paid by other companies. His fixed policy was never to accumulate large reserves for the benefit of posterity but always to pay out the maximum possible amount in dividends. Thus he won and maintained the confidence of both large capitalists and small loanholders. In particular he established close links with a clientele of wealthy investors, including a fellow Primitive Methodist, the jam manufacturer W. P. Hartley (1846–1922) in Aintree, and Hartley's son-in-law, the Congregationalist J. S. Higham (1857–1932), a cotton spinner and manufacturer in Accrington, who served with him as co-directors. From 1911 onwards Bunting perfected the financial management of his group; he no longer published balance sheets and used a very high ratio of loan to ordinary (or equity) capital in order to maximize the dividend paid on the ordinary shares. From 1912 his mills regularly paid out dividends which were almost double the Oldham average—22 per cent compared to 12 per cent. One company, the Iris, paid an average annual dividend of 86 per cent for eight years (1912–20). Another, the Bell, paid a dividend of 81 per cent for ten years (1910–20). The secret of those enormous dividends lay in the small proportion of ordinary capital upon which they were paid. Thus before 1919 Bunting called up only 5 per cent of the ordinary capital of the Times and Neva, only 15 per cent of that of the Bell, and only 20 per cent of that of the Iris. The Bell's true rate of profit was 17.5 per cent, but it could pay dividends five-fold that proportion by the extensive use of loan capital earning only a low fixed interest (*Oldham Chronicle*, 7 Aug 1920; 9 Oct 1920).

The post-war boom of 1919–20 carried the Bunting group to the heights of its success and fame. Bunting invested £150,000 in the 'victory loan' of 1919 on behalf of his mills, but avoided participating in the contemporary mania for recapitalization. Indeed, he condemned mill sales and company reconstructions because such operations could do nothing to increase dividends. He did, however, declare generous bonuses, preserving the reputation of his mills as the most profitable within the industry. During the climactic year of 1920 an average dividend of 86 per cent was declared by fourteen of his mills. Some began to announce dividends of 100, 200, and 400 per cent, while the Times Mill declared one of 600 per cent and the Bell one of 666.66 per cent (*Oldham Chronicle*, 7 Feb 1920, 14; 8 May 1920, 14; 7 Aug 1920, 14). Such dividends 'must make the mouths of the uninitiated water': inevitably they were misunderstood and provoked questions in the House of Commons (*Hansard 5C*, 129, 1920, 13–14; 138, 1921, 590). Such questions did not disconcert Bunting, whose group continued to declare spectacularly high dividends. His basic financial technique remained viable during his own lifetime and for three years thereafter, until 1926–7, when the industry reached its climacteric and loan capital began to flow out of the coffers of the Oldham limited companies on a large scale.

A staunch Conservative and a devout Primitive Methodist, Bunting dedicated himself to the work of his church, holding that it 'existed to make character, not merely to gather money' (*Oldham Evening Chronicle*, 25 Nov 1909, 7). He remained a lifelong supporter of the cause of temperance. He led the most frugal of lives, and controlled a vast industrial empire from a small terraced house at 115 Union Street, Oldham. His career was most unusual, insofar as he was born outside the ranks of the cotton trade but nevertheless made a fortune within it. He died at his home at the age of eighty-three on 22 February 1923 after a fall in Manchester while running to catch a tramcar, and was buried at Chadderton cemetery, Oldham. He left an estate of £658,190—one of the largest fortunes ever left by an Oldham cotton magnate. On his death his widow, Sarah, became one of the richest women in Lancashire.

D. A. FARNIE

Sources D. A. Farnie, 'Bunting, John', *DBB* · D. A. Farnie, 'The metropolis of cotton spinning, machine making, and mill building', *The cotton mills of Oldham*, ed. D. Gurr and J. Hunt, 3rd edn (1998), 4–11 · D. A. Farnie, 'The cotton towns of Greater Manchester', in M. Williams and D. A. Farnie, *Cotton mills in Greater Manchester* (1992), 13–47 · *Oldham Chronicle* (22 Feb 1923), 5 · *Oldham Chronicle* (26 Feb 1923), 6 · *Oldham Standard* (22 Feb 1923), 3 · *The Times* (27 Feb 1923), 14 · *The Times* (28 March 1923), 15 · *Primitive Methodist Leader* (1 March 1923), 139 · W. Tattersall, *Cotton Trade Circular* (1895–1923) · C. W. von Wieser, *Der finanzielle Aufbau der Englischen Industrie* (1919), 414–18 · W. A. Thomas, *The provincial stock exchanges* (1973), 150–55 · *Directory of Directors* (1921) · b. cert. · m. certs. · d. cert. · D. Gurr and J. Hunt, eds., *The cotton mills of Oldham*, 3rd edn (1998)

Likenesses portrait, in or before 1921 (framed); formerly at Henshaw Street School, Oldham · photograph, repro. in *Souvenir of the Primitive Methodist Chapel and Schools, Henshaw Street, Oldham* (1909), facing p. 38

Wealth at death £658,189 14s. 5d.: administration, 22 March 1923, *CGPLA Eng. & Wales*

Bunting, Sir Percy William (1836–1911), social reformer and journal editor, born on 1 February 1836 at Ratcliffe, near Manchester, was only son of Thomas Percival Bunting and his wife, Eliza Bealey. Bunting's father, third son of Jabez *Bunting, was a solicitor in Manchester. His sister, Sarah Maclardie *Amos (d. 1908), was active in many public causes.

After education at home, in 1851 Bunting became one of the first students at the newly founded Owens College, Manchester, graduating there as an associate in 1859. Meanwhile he obtained a scholarship at Pembroke College, Cambridge, and graduated BA in 1859, developing during his university career unusual musical gifts. Called to the bar in 1862 at Lincoln's Inn, he gradually acquired a large practice as a conveyancer and at the Chancery bar. In 1882 he was appointed examiner in equity and property law at London University, and grew less active in his profession in the presence of new interests. He finally retired from practice about 1895. Bunting married on 21 June 1869 Mary Hyett, daughter of John Lidgett of Hull, shipowner, and aunt of John Scott Lidgett, president of the uniting Methodist conference of 1932. They had two sons and two daughters. Mary Bunting was also an active participant in social reforming circles.

From an early age Bunting devoted himself to social reform, political Liberalism, and the welfare of modern Methodism. He was an active promoter of the Forward Movement in Methodism, and he aimed at the organization of nonconformity as a national religious force. In 1892 the National Free Church Council was founded at his house, and he was long the lay secretary of the committee of privileges (its legal adviser) for Methodism. He sought to stimulate the educational and social as well as the religious activity of the free churches, and was a founder in 1873 and thenceforth a governor of the Leys School at Cambridge. With Hugh Price Hughes he was a projector and founder in 1887 of the West London Mission, of which he acted as treasurer.

The promotion of moral purity, particularly at first the campaign against the Contagious Diseases Acts, was the social reform which engaged much of Bunting's adult

Sir Percy William Bunting (1836–1911), by unknown photographer, pubd 1910

energy. He frequently visited the continent in the cause, becoming an apt French and a moderately good German scholar. The repeal of the acts was finally achieved in 1886. From 1883 until his death Bunting was also chairman of the National Vigilance Association, which he helped to found, employing his continental influence to extend its operations to every capital in Europe.

In politics Bunting was a strong Liberal and admirer of Gladstone, serving on the executive committee of the National Liberal Federation from about 1880 until his death, and interesting himself in the National Liberal Club; in 1892 he unsuccessfully contested East Islington as a Gladstonian Liberal.

Meanwhile in 1882 Bunting became editor of the *Contemporary Review*, founded in 1862 by the publisher Alexander Strahan and first edited by Dean Alford, and subsequently from 1870 to 1877 by Sir James Knowles. Bunting remained editor until his death, conducting the *Review* on liberal lines. He enlisted the services of foreign contributors with whom his endeavours in social reform had brought him into touch, and he encouraged many new writers who could adequately present salient phases of contemporary theology, science, art, literature, and politics. He maintained in the *Review* a moderately advanced religious tone and gave topics of social reform a prominent place in its pages.

In 1902 Bunting succeeded Hughes as editor of the *Methodist Times* and carried on the work concurrently with the

Review until 1907. In his last ten years he wrote passionately on his favourite themes—of social reform in *The Citizen of Tomorrow* (1906) and on Christian unity in a chapter of *A New History of Methodism* (1909). As a leading free churchman, he joined a delegation to Lloyd George on the education issue, having written an article entitled 'Nonconformists and the Education Bill' in 1902.

A firm believer in international friendship, in 1907 Bunting joined other journalists, and in 1909 representatives of the churches, on visits to Germany, and he helped in the formation in the summer of 1911 of the Anglo-German Friendship Society. He was knighted in 1908. Subsequently his physical powers slowly failed, and he died somewhat unexpectedly on 22 July 1911 at 11 Endsleigh Gardens, his home in London. He was survived by his wife.   J. E. G. DE MONTMORENCY, *rev.* TIM MACQUIBAN

Sources *WWW* · W. J. Townsend, H. B. Workman, and G. Eayrs, *A new history of Methodism*, 2 vols. (1909) · *The Times* (24 July 1911) · *Contemporary Review*, 100 (Aug 1911) · *Manchester Guardian* (24 July 1911) · *Methodist Times* (27 July 1911) · *Methodist Times* (3 Aug 1911) · *Wellesley index* · private information (1912) · personal knowledge (1912)
Archives University of Chicago Library, corresp. and papers as editor of *Contemporary Review* | BL, corresp. with W. E. Gladstone, Add. MSS 44497–44525 · CUL, letters to Lord Acton · NL Scot., corresp. with Patrick Geddes
Likenesses photograph, pubd 1910, NPG [*see illus.*]
Wealth at death £8117 9s. 8d.: resworn probate, 26 Aug 1911, *CGPLA Eng. & Wales*

Bunting, William Maclardie (1805–1866), Wesleyan Methodist minister, the eldest son of Dr Jabez *Bunting (1779–1858), a Wesleyan Methodist minister, and his first wife, Sarah Maclardie (d. 1835), was born on 23 November 1805 at Manchester. He was educated at the Wesleyan schools at Woodhouse Grove, near Leeds, and Kingswood School, and at St Saviour's Grammar School, Southwark, under Dr William Fancourt. At the early age of eighteen he began his course as a preacher and wrote some of his hymns. In 1824 he was admitted a probationer minister, and in 1828 was received in full connection after serving in the Salford and Manchester circuits.

Bunting continued his itinerant ministry in circuits in Huddersfield, Halifax, Manchester, and London until 1841, when his health began to break down. He settled in London and became a supernumerary minister in 1849. For many years he was active in the Evangelical Alliance, and was one of its honorary secretaries. He held a similar post in the British Society for the Propagation of the Gospel among the Jews. He died at his home at 8 Highgate Rise in Kentish Town, London, on 13 November 1866, leaving a widow, Harriett. After his death, in 1870, a selection of his sermons, letters, poems, and hymns, of which the covenant hymn 'O God how often hath thine ear' was best known, was published with a biographical introduction by Thomas Percival Bunting, his younger brother.

C. W. SUTTON, *rev.* TIM MACQUIBAN

Sources *Minutes of conference of Wesleyan Methodist* (1867) · W. Hill, *An alphabetical arrangement of all the Wesleyan-Methodist ministers, missionaries, and preachers*, rev. J. P. Haswell, 10th edn (1866) · T. P. Bunting, *Memorials of the late Rev. W. M. Bunting* (1870) · *CGPLA Eng. & Wales* (1867)
Likenesses portrait, repro. in Bunting, *Memorials*

Wealth at death under £1500: administration, 29 Jan 1867, *CGPLA Eng. & Wales*

Bunyan, John (*bap.* 1628, *d.* 1688), author, was baptized on 30 November 1628 at Elstow, Bedfordshire, the eldest of the three children of Thomas Bunyan (*bap.* 1603, *d.* 1676), brazier, and his second wife, Margaret (*bap.* 1603, *d.* 1644), daughter of William Bentley and his wife, Mary (*née* Goodwin). Although Bunyan averred that his ancestry was 'low and inconsiderable', in 1542 William Bonyon, a direct ancestor, held part of the manor of Elstow from Henry VIII (Bunyan, *Grace Abounding*, 5). Subsequent generations of the declining family sold the land, leaving Bunyan's father poor but not destitute.

Youth and military service Although Bunyan's father apparently was unable to write, he sent his son to school to learn reading and writing. Bunyan later wrote contemptuously of his education, claiming he had neither studied Plato and Aristotle nor acquired a knowledge of Greek and Latin. Yet even his earliest works manifest an ability to write grammatically and coherently, so that he can hardly have forgotten what he had learned, as he professed. Whether he attended a grammar school for a time or taught himself what he knew, he took pains throughout his career to dissociate himself from dependence on the writings of others apart from the Bible and John Foxe's *Acts and Monuments*. Yet he read more than he admitted, acquiring an ability to use the theological language of academic discourse, a degree of legal knowledge, and a facility in writing verse and emblem literature. Before he married, he preferred to read newspapers, ballads, medieval romances, and possibly works on alchemy. He felt some guilt as he observed others reading pious books, but this did not deter him from a youth he later depicted as replete with profanity, vice, ungodliness, and illegal activities.

Near his sixteenth birthday, Bunyan enlisted or was conscripted into the New Model Army. The muster rolls for the garrison at Newport Pagnell, Buckinghamshire, though incomplete, list him as a member of Lieutenant-Colonel Richard Cokayne's company from 30 November 1644 to 8 March 1645, and of Major Robert Bolton's between 21 April and 27 May 1645; he probably served in Bolton's company until its disbandment in September 1646. Because the garrison was chronically behind in its pay and poorly equipped, Bunyan's experience must have been grim. Indeed some of the troops mutinied in February 1645. Bunyan would have learned to wield a sword and probably a musket and handgun. The garrison troops participated in the siege of Oxford and the defence of Leicester as well as periodic patrols, but there is no evidence to indicate whether Bunyan was engaged in the fighting. By June 1647 he had volunteered to serve in Captain Charles O'Hara's company, which was bound for Ireland to fight the rebels, but on 21 July parliament disbanded the regiment of which O'Hara's company was a part, thus terminating Bunyan's military career.

In addition to providing Bunyan with the military

John Bunyan (*bap.* 1628, *d.* 1688), by Thomas Sadler, 1684

imagery he used in some of his works, especially *The Holy War*, his service in the Newport Pagnell garrison exposed him to assorted religious views, including those of the presbyterians, especially after the governor, Sir Samuel Luke, imposed the solemn league and covenant in March 1645. Bunyan may have first learned Calvinist tenets from Luke's chaplain, Thomas Ford, and he probably heard the sectaries William Erbery and Paul Hobson preach; Bunyan would later espouse a doctrine of spirit-baptism akin to Erbery's. Nevertheless, none of these preachers had an immediate impact on Bunyan, who left the army without having made any noticeable religious commitment.

Spiritual turmoil Bunyan married at some time after he left the army, undoubtedly by October 1649, for his first child, a blind daughter named Mary, was baptized on 20 July 1650. He and his first wife had three other children, Elizabeth (*b.* 1654), John (*d.* 1728), and Thomas. He does not record his wife's name, but she was poor, bringing to the marriage only two books bequeathed to her by her pious father, Lewis Bayly's *The Practise of Pietie* and Arthur Dent's *The Plaine Mans Path-Way to Heaven*. Under her influence Bunyan outwardly reformed, attended the Elstow parish church, and revered its minister, Christopher Hall. The latter's sermon on sabbath observance impressed Bunyan, helping set the stage for the famous scene on a Sunday afternoon when an inner voice struck terror in him as he played the game of cat. The anxiety that had plagued him in his pre-adolescent years owing to nightmares of exclusion and punishment now returned, and he found himself in a spiritual maze whose false turnings and blind alleys would dominate much of his life for some nine years, until late 1657 or early 1658.

For approximately a year Bunyan sought spiritual comfort in outward conformity, though he was discomfited when a shopkeeper's wife castigated him for his swearing, and again when his fondness for bell-ringing stirred feelings of guilt. On a trip to Bedford to pursue his tinker's occupation he overheard three or four female members of John Gifford's separatist congregation discuss religion. What Bunyan heard triggered a spiritual awakening, prompting him to turn to Ranter works and the Bible, particularly the Pauline epistles. Before long he manifested signs of poor self-esteem and fatigue. Unrelieved anxiety and a growing fear that the day of grace had passed, leaving him without hope of salvation, probably led to chronic mild depression. Awash in feelings of guilt, he was overcome with doubt and anxiety for several years by his reckoning, experiencing only brief respites. Prone to blasphemy for a time, he was sorely tempted to commit the dreaded sin against the Holy Spirit, to 'sell' (abandon) Christ. Though Gifford's ministry and Martin Luther's commentary on Galatians provided temporary relief, the old fears returned, and in early or mid-1651 he succumbed to the temptation. 'Down I fell, as a Bird that is shot from the top of a Tree, into great guilt and fearful despair' (Bunyan, *Grace Abounding*, 43). Reading *A Relation of the Fearful Estate of Francis Spira* deepened his anguish, and he likened his plight to Esau's after he had sold his birthright. The combination of self-deprecation, a profound sense of shame, physical symptoms, diminished interest in other things, and difficulty sleeping suggest mild depression.

Bunyan was still wandering in this psycho-spiritual maze when, in 1655, he joined the separatist church in Bedford. Although still afflicted with profound spiritual doubts and a sense of doom, he began preaching approximately nine months later. 'I went my self in chains to preach to them in chains, and carried that fire in my own conscience that I perswaded them to beware of' (Bunyan, *Grace Abounding*, 85). His lengthy spiritual travail finally terminated in late 1657 or early 1658, after he had been preaching for two years. Hope dawned when he found himself able to reconsider the biblical passages that had caused him the most pain, especially Hebrews 6, 10, and 12. 'Now did my chains fall off my Legs indeed, I was loosed from my affliction and irons, my temptations also fled away' (ibid., 72).

Early writings and ministry While he was still troubled by anxiety and doubt, Bunyan learned about the Quakers, probably in late 1654 or early 1655. William Dewsbury had come to Bedfordshire in summer 1654, convincing John Crook of Beckerings Park and others to embrace the Quaker message. George Fox and other leading Friends met at Beckerings Park the following month, after which they held a series of debates with other protestants. Four times between April 1656 and January 1657 Bunyan engaged in these disputations, which provided the context for his first book, *Some Gospel-Truths Opened* (1656). His pastor, John Burton, provided a commendatory epistle in which he acknowledged Bunyan's lack of a higher education while insisting he had been trained in the heavenly university. Bunyan's primary audience consisted of

believers he feared might be misled by Quaker and Ranter teachings about Christ's person and work. Edward Burrough replied to Bunyan in *The True Faith of the Gospel of Peace Contended For* (1656), to which Bunyan responded in *A Vindication of … Some Gospel-Truths Opened* (1657). Burrough countered with *Truth (the Strongest of All)* (1657), and Fox briefly denounced Bunyan in *The Great Mistery of the Great Whore* (1659). At root, Bunyan and Burrough each insisted his antagonist was not enlightened by the Spirit; his words might be true, but his spirit was false. Substantive differences existed, though sometimes these were a matter of emphasis, as in Bunyan's stress on the Bible and Burrough's on the Spirit's primacy. Much of the debate revolved around Bunyan's accent on the external Christ in contrast to Burrough's focus on the Christ within everyone, and on Bunyan's sharp distinction between conscience and Christ's Spirit, a difference Burrough denied. Heated and at times offensive, the rhetoric reflected each man's belief that this was a duel between the forces of light and darkness.

For preaching at Eaton Socon, Bunyan was indicted at the assizes no later than February 1658. Nothing seems to have come of this, perhaps because of the Bedford church's willingness to seek legal counsel for him. This encounter with the state may have provided some of the impetus for his third book, *A Few Sighs from Hell* (1658), an exposition of Luke 16:19–31 probably based on sermon notes, in which he referred to his persecution at the hands of enemies who 'rage and threaten to knock me in the head' (*Miscellaneous Works*, 1.360–61). The work's primary thrust was a scathing attack on professional clergy and the wealthy, coupled with an exhortation to his readers to repent or be condemned to horrific everlasting punishment in a physical hell. Although this work, like many others of Bunyan's, included evangelical appeals implying people's right to choose their eternal destiny, he was a Calvinist. As enunciated in his next work, *The Doctrine of the Law and Grace Unfolded* (1659), an exposition of covenant theology, his views place him in the strict Calvinist tradition, with its stress on the promissory nature of the covenant of grace as distinct from the moderate Calvinists' emphasis on human responsibility in the covenant. This work also reflects Bunyan's indebtedness to Luther's commentary on Galatians, particularly the dichotomy between law and grace. Bunyan's denigration of the law led to charges of antinomianism by Richard Baxter, an accusation that cannot be sustained if one considers the total corpus of Bunyan's works.

Bunyan was also embroiled in other controversies. About the time he was writing *Law and Grace*, he preached in a barn at Toft, Cambridgeshire, sparking a debate with Thomas Smith, university librarian at Cambridge, who challenged his right to preach without formal ordination. The General Baptist Henry Denne came to Bunyan's defence in *The Quaker No Papist* (1659). The same year Bunyan became involved in a dispute over witchcraft, the reality of which he accepted, finding evidence for it in scripture. An anonymous tract, *Strange & Terrible Newes from Cambridge* (1659), recounted how one Margaret Pryor had been victimized by a Quaker witch who temporarily turned her into a mare. Bunyan wrote a pamphlet endorsing the allegation; no copy survives, but it was refuted by the Quaker James Blackley in *A Lying Wonder Discovered* (1659). Further controversy erupted when Bunyan preached in the parish church at Yelden, Bedfordshire, on Christmas day 1659 at the invitation of the rector, William Dell. Because of this, thirty of Dell's parishioners unsuccessfully petitioned the House of Lords for his ejection. In 1659 Bunyan married his second wife, Elizabeth (*d.* 1691), his first wife having died the previous year. He and Elizabeth had two children, Sarah and Joseph (*bap.* 1672).

Imprisonment: the early years At the Restoration the Bedford congregation to which Bunyan belonged lost its right to use St John's Church, though it continued to meet. However, when Bunyan went to the hamlet of Lower Samsell, near Harlington, to preach on 12 November, he was arrested under the terms of the 1593 Act against Sectaries. Warned of his impending apprehension, he eschewed flight, preferring to set an example for other nonconformists. Offered his release if he promised to cease preaching, he refused and was detained until the quarter sessions. In defending his position against a local minister, Dr William Lindale, Bunyan denounced the Church of England as false, thereby taking a more extreme stand than dissenters such as Philip Henry who were willing to worship in the established church. At the quarter sessions in January 1661, Bunyan and Sir John Kelynge (Keeling) argued over the former's right to preach as well as the nature of prayer and worship. Kelynge sentenced Bunyan to three months in prison, at which time he was to conform or be banished. Resolute, Bunyan stood his ground in April, refusing to renounce his right to preach if he were released. Unwilling to sue for pardon because it would entail an admission that the meeting at Lower Samsell had been illegal, he failed to benefit from the coronation pardon on 23 April. As Bunyan explains in *A Relation of my Imprisonment* (posthumously published in 1765), his wife thereupon went to London with a petition for his release, but Sir Matthew Hale and Thomas Twisden rejected her plea. Nevertheless, a sympathetic gaoler granted Bunyan a fair amount of liberty, enabling him to participate in the Bedford church's activities and even visit London in autumn 1661. When his enemies accused Bunyan of having gone to the city to plot an uprising and threatened to indict the gaoler, Bunyan was closely confined in late October.

While he was at liberty Bunyan had preached against the Book of Common Prayer, and he now expanded and published his sermon as *I will Pray with the Spirit* (*c.*1662). Expounding on 1 Corinthians 14:15, he insisted that true prayer is rooted in the Spirit's inner work, a profoundly intense uttering at the core of the Christian life. The Book of Common Prayer and other formal prayers are not only ineffectual, he averred, but unlawful human inventions. Those who enforced the established liturgy he likened to Edmund Bonner, the Marian bishop of London. The tract is an uncompromising denunciation of the Church of England as false and evil.

Bunyan passed some of his time in the Bedford county

gaol writing verse (and making shoelaces). His poetry reflects the influence of ballads, chapbooks, and broadsides, and probably of Sternhold's and Hopkins's metrical version of the Psalms. As Bunyan's poems improved over time, they marked a refinement of popular religious verse. His first volume, *Profitable Meditations* (1661), defended his use of poetry to convey the gospel message, reflected his conversion experience, and embodied the tension between the Calvinist doctrine of predestination and the preacher's call to repentance. Whereas the mood of *Profitable Meditations* was upbeat, Bunyan's *Prison Meditations* (1663) reflected his struggle to overcome the despair of seemingly interminable incarceration. The gaol, he concluded, was a school in which Christ teaches his disciples how to die. Now capturing Bunyan's emotional state, his verse has the capacity to move readers. Expecting to die in prison, he wrote *Christian Behaviour* (1663), intended as a final testament as well as a guide to Christian living. Essentially, it was a companion piece to *Law and Grace*, for it effectively repudiated the charge of antinomianism. Reflecting traditional protestant moral principles, Bunyan emphasized moderation as well as the subordination of wives to husbands, children to parents, and servants to masters. When he completed this book in June 1663, he thought death was imminent.

Reflections on the end times Separated from his wife and children, Bunyan went through another period of depression in late 1663 or 1664. Thoughts of the gallows haunted him, especially the fear of dying cravenly. Feeling 'empty, spiritless, and barren' when he was asked to address his fellow prisoners, he finally found inspiration in Revelation 21:11, with its depiction of a gleaming new Jerusalem. The full passage, Revelation 21:10–22:4, soon became the subject of a new book, *The Holy City* (1665), in which Bunyan set forth his understanding of church history and the end times. After the period of Christ and his apostles, church history's first age, the church entered into captivity. Near the end of this stage, according to Bunyan, two sub-periods occurred, the first of which, altar-work, extended from John Wyclif to Thomas Cranmer. The second sub-period, temple-work, in which Bunyan lived, featured the gathering of congregations of the manifestly godly, or 'visible saints'. Antichrist's fall marks the commencement of the final stage, the millennium, when the godly will build the new Jerusalem. Although Bunyan had almost certainly been attracted to Fifth Monarchist views at some point in the 1650s, in this work he does not call for the saints to expedite the millennium's arrival by taking up arms against the government. During this age, most monarchs will continue to serve the Mistress of Iniquity, though ultimately they will turn against her. Near the millennium's conclusion, Satan will mount a final, furious but unsuccessful assault, following which Christ will return to preside over the last judgment. Unlike some millenarian commentators, Bunyan refused to propose dates for these events, but he believed the millennium's onset was imminent. Writing this work, with its triumphal tone, heralded his emergence from the recurring depression and provided him with the assurance that enabled him to withstand nine more years behind bars.

Whereas Bunyan had decoded the book of Revelation's typology in *The Holy City*, in its sequel, *The Resurrection of the Dead* (1665?), he pursued a more traditional homiletic approach in explicating Acts 24:14–15. Again, the tone is exultant, the conviction of election certain, and the acceptance of persecution unwavering. Prison's terrors no longer daunted him; indeed, he used his temporal experience of torment as a model for the horrors that awaited the damned following the last judgment. In *The Holy City* Bunyan had dated that event at the conclusion of the millennium, but now he reversed his position, averring that the last judgment was impending. Much of the book is devoted to the great trials of the just and the unjust, the former in their spiritual, immortal bodies, unconstrained by the laws of physics, the latter in their physical but no less eternal bodies, subject to everlasting burning. These trials effectively reverse that of 1661, providing Bunyan with an opportunity to see the godly avenged. The same message, in verse form, appears in *Ebal and Gerizzim* (1665?), the sequel to *One Thing is Needful* (1665?), a poetic work that parallels *The Holy City*. Unlike Bunyan's earlier verse, which utilizes quatrains, *Ebal and Gerizzim* breaks new ground by adopting iambic pentameter couplets, probably influenced by his reading of other poets in prison.

About late 1665 or early 1666 Bunyan composed his spiritual autobiography, *Grace Abounding to the Chief of Sinners* (1666), six editions of which were published in his lifetime. This was to be a defence of his ministerial calling and an aid to his converts as they struggled to remain loyal to their nonconformist convictions. With its vivid recounting—and thus reliving—of his battle with spiritual doubt and depression, the book could only have been written once Bunyan had overcome the despair that threatened to engulf him during the early years of his incarceration. Although conventional in structure, *Grace Abounding* transcends contemporary examples of the genre in its depth of psychological experience, its riveting account of Bunyan's struggle to keep from succumbing to pervasive, numbing despair, and his agonizing wrestling with biblical texts. He was, of course, a prisoner of his memory no less than of the state, and his recollection of distant events and chronology is sometimes imprecise. Allowance must also be made for his undoubted tendency to exaggerate, as when he depicted himself as the greatest of sinners, a deliberate attempt to associate himself (here and elsewhere) with the apostle Paul. Indispensable as a source for Bunyan's early life and conversion, *Grace Abounding* also reveals much about Bunyan in the mid-1660s, especially his renewed triumph over despair and his state of spiritual assurance. In a telling analogy, he likened himself to David as he held Goliath's head in his hand.

The Heavenly Foot-Man and The Pilgrim's Progress Unless *A Pocket Concordance*, of which no copies are extant,

appeared between 1666 and 1672, Bunyan published nothing between *Grace Abounding* in 1666 and *A Confession of my Faith* in 1672 other than the second edition of his spiritual autobiography; he completed the third edition about 1672. However, some four years earlier he had begun to prepare 'The Heavenly Foot-Man', a sermon on the Christian life, for publication. Internal evidence suggests it may have been preached, or at least prepared for the pulpit, late in 1659 or in 1660. Directed to the spiritually indolent, the sermon urges people to repent before the day of grace has passed, a concern that played a prominent role in Bunyan's conversion experience. Using the metaphor of a race to portray the Christian life, Bunyan admonished his readers to begin promptly, cast off encumbrances, shun distractions and bypaths, and fight off fatigue. The message clearly implies an ability to choose to run this race, thus reflecting Bunyan's recurring tendency to suppress predestinarian doctrine in favour of pastoral evangelism. As he worked on his text, he became intrigued with the idea of writing a full-scale allegory on

> the Way
> And Race of Saints,

at last laying aside his manuscript to fall

> suddenly into an Allegory
> About their Journey, and the way to Glory.
> (Bunyan, *Pilgrim's Progress*, 1)

Thus was born the first part of *The Pilgrim's Progress*, though Bunyan, deterred by some of his friends' negative reaction to his allegorizing, delayed publication until 1678. Various biblical authors, he reasoned, use a similar methodology. *The Heavenly Foot-Man* lay unpublished until 1698.

One of the most popular books ever printed, *The Pilgrim's Progress* was composed by Bunyan partly as a distraction from 'worser thoughts', partly to allegorize his religious experience as a guide for others, and partly to add his voice to the great debate over conscience that raged especially between 1667 and 1672. A potent appeal for the primacy of conscience, *The Pilgrim's Progress* belongs with works by John Owen, Sir Charles Wolseley, John Locke, William Penn, Slingsby Bethel, and Andrew Marvell espousing liberty of conscience. The Vanity fair episode brilliantly makes the point that those who repress the godly in England are not the obviously evil but one's law-abiding, superficially religious neighbours, the same people whose worship found expression in the Book of Common Prayer. Christian's experience at Vanity fair echoes Bunyan's at the hands of Restoration magistrates and judges. More broadly, Bunyan drew on his military experience to craft an epic that creatively combined warfaring and wayfaring. Christian is both pilgrim and warrior, and the message of *The Pilgrim's Progress* is not only a call to embrace and persist in the Christian life, but also a summons to battle the forces of evil, if necessary by refusing to yield to the state's demands for religious conformity. Christian's 'Travels and Wars' brook no compromise (p. 248). Most of the work was probably in hand by autumn 1669, when Bunyan enjoyed modest liberty, and the rest was probably composed by early 1671.

Debating with Baptists and latitudinarians Bunyan was still in Bedford gaol when, on 21 January 1672, the Bedford congregation appointed him to the pastoral office. Following Charles II's promulgation of the declaration of indulgence, Bunyan emerged from prison in May at the hub of a network of five dissenting congregations that he and other imprisoned ministers had organized. Each of these churches—at Bedford, Keysoe, Cranfield, Stevington, and Newport Pagnell—had satellite meetings in surrounding communities. As a result of this organization, the churches were assured of an ample supply of preachers and teachers. In the ensuing years Bunyan preached widely, from Leicester to London and Southwark, at times engaging in the polemic characteristic of the period.

Bunyan had returned to debate while he was still in prison, having been motivated by Edward Fowler's *The Design of Christianity* (1671). The rector of Northill, Bedfordshire, Fowler admired the latitudinarians. In his book he argued that Christ purifies human nature, restoring believers to perfect righteousness rather than merely justifying them in God's sight; the design of Christianity will be accomplished in those who make Jesus's life the pattern by which to live. To Bunyan this amounted to an attack on the doctrine of justification by Christ's imputed righteousness, a thesis he expounded in *A Defence of the Doctrine of Justification*, finished on 27 February 1672 though not licensed until 21 November. Hoping to shame Fowler, Bunyan compared his views to those of the Jesuit Edmund Campion and the Quaker William Penn, and averred that Fowler's tenets contravened the Thirty-Nine Articles. Irate, Fowler or a defender replied in the anonymous *Dirt Wip't Off* (1672), denouncing Bunyan as a grossly ignorant antinomian who used inane arguments. Bunyan ignored such vituperation, though he later referred disparagingly to latitudinarians.

Another late prison work, *A Confession of my Faith* (1672), began with an epistle to an unnamed Baptist critic in which Bunyan defended his practice of communing with the godly who had not been baptized with water. His confession articulated his views on imputed righteousness, the Reformed doctrine of predestination, the Bible, and magistracy, but much of it argued for the right of the godly to participate in church fellowship, including communion, as long as they had been baptized by the Spirit. This work established Bunyan as an open-membership, open-communion Baptist with Reformed predestinarian views. His confession prompted attacks from the General (Arminian) Baptist John Denne in *Truth Outweighing Error* (1673), and the Particular (Calvinist) Baptist Thomas Paul in *Some Serious Reflections* (1673), with a preface by William Kiffin. Citing Henry Jessey for support, Bunyan retorted in *Differences in Judgment about Water-Baptism, No Bar to Communion* (1673). Paul issued a rejoinder in a work no longer extant, and Henry Denne appended a postscript to his *Treatise of Baptism* (1673), attacking Bunyan. Again Bunyan defended himself, this time in *Peaceable Principles and True* (1674), in which he complained that some of his critics had compared him to the devil while others had adjudged him insane. He chose not to respond to John Denne's *Hypocrisie*

Detected (1674) or Kiffin's *A Sober Discourse* (1681), a general critique of the open-communion position.

Evangelical concerns While Bunyan duelled with his opponents over the place of water-baptism in church life, Charles II, pressured by parliament, rescinded the declaration of indulgence in March 1673. Many dissenters, undoubtedly including Bunyan, continued to regard their licences to preach as valid, and numerous magistrates were reluctant to prosecute. Against this background, Bunyan focused on pastoral concerns, particularly his determination to give Calvinist theology a warm, evangelical face. His sermon on Luke 13:6–9, entitled *The Barren Fig-Tree* (1673), included a jeremiad warning England about the peril of being a nation of fruitless professors, but it was also directed to those members of gathered churches whose lifestyle brought disrepute on the godly. The easing of persecution had made religious complacency a matter of growing apprehension. For members of his congregation and the unconverted who had heard him preach, Bunyan wrote a catechism, *Instruction for the Ignorant* (1675). Although similar in form and matter to various contemporary works in the same genre, instead of the traditional sections on baptismal vows, the apostles' creed, the ten commandments, and the Lord's prayer, Bunyan's catechism is unique in devoting a full section to self-denial. His book is also rather atypical in the extent to which it reflects his personal experience. A reference to efforts to denigrate ministers by falsely accusing them of scandal recalls the controversy that erupted in 1674 when he infuriated Agnes Beaumont's father by carrying her to a meeting on his horse.

About the same time, Bunyan published *Light for Them that Sit in Darkness* (1675), a polemical work implicitly directed against Quakers and latitudinarians, who repudiated the doctrines of atonement by Christ's satisfaction and justification by his imputed righteousness. More broadly, Bunyan was attempting to reach those Christians who appeared to be succumbing to 'Fables, Seducing-Spirits, and Doctrines of Devils through the Intoxications of Delusions, and the Witchcrafts of false Preachers' (*Miscellaneous Works*, 8.49). Bunyan wrote amid heightened persecution, including a warrant for his arrest on 4 March 1675 for having preached at a conventicle. For his offence and subsequent refusal to appear in the archdeacon's court to answer the charges, he was excommunicated. He was almost certainly in London at this point, but some time after his return to Bedford he was arrested, probably in December 1676. He was released on a bond dated 21 June 1677, the result of an appeal to Thomas Barlow, bishop of Lincoln, by John Owen, minister of an Independent congregation at Leadenhall Street, London.

Bunyan published three more pastoral works in this period. In *The Strait Gate* (1676), an expanded sermon on Luke 13:24, he sought to awaken congregations and professing Christians to the gospel message, though much of the work reflects his opposition to the established church through his insistence that most professing Christians were bound for eternal damnation. Reflecting older controversies, he denounced latitudinarians and Quakers as well as Socinians, Arminians, libertines, formalists (Anglicans), and legalists. By June 1676 Bunyan had completed *Saved by Grace*, an exposition of Ephesians 2:5 in which he reiterated his belief that few would be saved, and assured the godly that they would persevere, notwithstanding persecution. Bunyan's most popular sermon, *Come, & Welcome, to Jesus Christ* (1678), six editions of which were published in his lifetime, was composed between the summer of 1677 and March 1678. An exposition of John 6:37, it dynamically reflected his refusal to let the logical ramifications of the Calvinist doctrine of predestination dim his enthusiastic appeal to his audience, urging them to respond to the offer of divine grace. The personification of Shall-come in this sermon is similar to the allegorical personages of Help, Good-Will, and Great-Grace in *The Pilgrim's Progress*, possibly reflecting Bunyan's decision to publish his allegory at this time. Both works beckon the unconverted to embrace the gospel, implying the sufficiency of divine grace for those who accept. Not surprisingly, *Come, & Welcome* echoes many of the themes and some of the imagery in *The Pilgrim's Progress*.

Coping with the Catholic threat When allegations of a popish plot caused consternation among many protestants, Bunyan used the atmosphere of fear to remind his audience of the imperative to fear God. *A Treatise of the Fear of God* (1679), apparently an expanded sermon on Revelation 14:7, explored the nature of godly fear, which prompts believers to revere God, seek mutual edification with other saints, observe such ordinances as the Lord's supper and prayer, practice self-denial, and distribute charity to needy believers. His condemnation of those who endeavour to overthrow the authority of the divine word was directed, *inter alia*, at Catholics. *Paul's Departure and Crown*, published posthumously but probably composed in the winter of 1678–9, also addressed the fears sparked by the Popish Plot, provided guidance for the godly in times of fierce persecution, and urged ministers to prepare to die for propagating the gospel. The Popish Plot was again in Bunyan's mind when he wrote *Israel's Hope Encouraged*, which was posthumously published. With its exploration of the theme of hope, it was the natural accompaniment of the virtually contemporary treatise on fear. Instead of placing their hope in God, the people of England, he complained, trusted in the king, parliament, London magistrates, and statutes to preserve them from the Catholic threat. He reminded his readers that the ordinary condition of the godly was to suffer persecution, especially at the hands of great men, whose 'Teeth, the Laws' terrorize saints (*Miscellaneous Works*, 13.14).

Throughout many of his works, Bunyan distinguishes between the suffering saints and the superficially religious. It was therefore natural for him to compose a sequel to the first part of *The Pilgrim's Progress* in which he recounted the story of someone who might have been a resident of Vanity fair; the sequel was published in 1680 as *The Life and Death of Mr Badman*. However, unlike most Vanity fair inhabitants, who are religious formalists, Badman is an atheist; indeed, he ridicules his wife's religious companions because of their hypocrisy. Like the youthful Bunyan, Badman is prone to swear, though unlike Bunyan he has inherited his father's wealth and acquired additional prosperity by marrying a rich bride. A dishonest businessman, Badman serves as a foil for Bunyan to moralize about appropriate standards of behaviour. Unlike Bunyan's pilgrim, whose end is perpetually in doubt, Badman's fate is clear from the beginning, and Bunyan recounts his story without exploring Badman's psyche. Devoid of drama, the book is nevertheless interesting because of Bunyan's incorporation of his observations of other people; the behaviour he describes, he says, has 'been acted upon the stage of this World, even many times before mine eyes' (p. 1). *Mr Badman* is a series of snapshots depicting the commonplace attitudes and practices against which Bunyan regularly preached. In addition to his own observations, he drew on Samuel Clarke's *Mirrour or Looking-Glass both for Saints & Sinners* (4th edn, 1671) as well as broadsides and newsbooks.

The succession crisis: holy war By the time *Mr Badman* was published, the country had plunged into a rancorous debate over the succession, the perceived threat to protestantism, and the role of parliament. Bunyan undoubtedly heard much about the controversy, particularly when he visited London, as in early 1682, when he preached to Richard Wavel's congregation at Pinners' Hall. An expanded version of the sermon, possibly inspired by the death of his stepmother, Anne, in September 1680, was published as *The Greatness of the Soul* (1682).

Bunyan addressed the political and religious crisis that gripped England in *The Holy War*. Using multiple levels of allegory, *The Holy War* deals simultaneously with the believer's justification and sanctification, Christian or world history from Satan's initial fall to the eve of Christ's conquest, and the contemporary crisis. The warfaring of *The Pilgrim's Progress* now becomes not only the dominant motif but the vehicle for Bunyan to address nonconformists and whigs concerned about the threat of Catholicism and arbitrary government. Bunyan wrote *The Holy War* in 1681 and early 1682, probably moved in part by the parliamentary dissolutions in January and March. The epic's violence—rape, arson, banishment, and murder, even of children—is a damning indictment of the tory regime. Bunyan's message was a call to resistance, but not insurrection, a summons to the faithful to stand resolutely for their faith in the face of a state determined to crush nonconformity and impose a Catholic sovereign on the country. Bunyan issued a shrill warning that arbitrary government and popery are the enemies of Emanuel; Mansoul is not only the soul of each believer and the allegorical personification of Christianity but the symbol of England itself. At the time Bunyan wrote this epic, he knew Owen, George Griffith, and probably Matthew Meade, all three of whom the duke of Monmouth and others subsequently implicated in the plotting now under way for an insurrection. Although there is no evidence that Bunyan knew of the conspiracy, some of his ministerial comrades in London had indisputably radical connections.

Among Bunyan's posthumous publications are two that were almost certainly composed during the succession crisis. One of these was the treatise *Of Antichrist, and his Ruine*, probably written in early 1682 and thematically related to *The Holy City*. Thoroughly millenarian, *Of Antichrist* was unmistakably anti-Catholic, with its denunciation of Rome, the 'great Babylon', for its witchcraft, blasphemy, spiritual prostitution, and myriad other offences. In a burst of patriotism, Bunyan lauded Henry VIII, Edward VI, and Elizabeth I for having eradicated Catholic worship in England. The Antichrist, Bunyan prophesied, would be overthrown by Christ through the agency of monarchs and the church. Bunyan's message was to resist evil, not topple the Stuart regime, God's interim agent in the war against Antichrist. He reiterated this theme in an unfinished work, *An Exposition of the First Ten Chapters of Genesis*, where his damning characterization of Nimrod, the instigator of absolute monarchy and the creator of an iniquitous state religion, as a Catholic tyrant can be read as a critique of Louis XIV or James, should he succeed Charles. Bunyan made the same point in depicting Cain as a tyrannical persecutor. In his commentary on Genesis Bunyan neither professed republicanism nor called for an insurrection to overthrow the Stuart regime, but he boldly castigated absolute monarchs and persecutory state churches.

Nonconformity in crisis The disclosure of the Rye House plotting and Monmouth's scheme for a general insurrection to exclude James triggered a widespread crackdown on nonconformists in summer 1683. In response to the revelations, Bunyan fiercely denounced the plotters, blaming their divisive work on Satan. In *Seasonable Counsel* (1684) he implicitly likened Monmouth to Absalom and advised the godly to follow Solomon's advice to shun those who schemed against the government. Evincing no pity for the plotters as they met their fate, he reserved his compassion for innocent dissenters assailed in the tory backlash, articulating an ethic of suffering designed to strengthen their resolve to persevere. Although Bunyan escaped persecution, perhaps owing to his unequivocal denunciation of the plotting, his heart clearly ached for nonconformists lashed by the whip of persecution.

Bunyan's other works during the tory reaction stress survival through Christian living, reliance on Christ's love, and a continuing denunciation of persecutors. Publication of *A Holy Life*, completed by August 1683, was delayed until the following year, probably because the printer, Benjamin Alsop, went into hiding following disclosure of the cabals. In *A Holy Life* Bunyan argued that godly living is the logical corollary of faith, and those who profess Christianity while living iniquitously are hypocrites. As the persecution deepened, Bunyan returned to verse to reach as many people as possible. His broadside, *A Caution to Stir up to Watch Against Sin*, published by early April 1684, strove to keep the godly 'from Enemies external' as well as internal, particularly by reminding them that sin is a prison capable of subjecting its victims to a

'living Death [that] will gnaw thee day and night' (*Miscellaneous Works*, 6.180, 182). The tyrant is no longer the monarch but sin. Bunyan also found space to lash out against those who boldly and audaciously engaged in what he regarded as vile, beastly behaviour. Likewise, in *The Saints Knowledge of Christ's Love*, also published posthumously but composed probably in late 1685, Bunyan combined comfort for the godly, expressed here through an exposition on the breadth of God's love through Christ, with a denunciation of the rage of men who endeavour to swallow up the church. In this context, Bunyan's mention of the king of Assyria was an implicit reference to the late Charles II or James II. To such rulers Bunyan's message was blunt and uncompromising: 'God is with us; God will overmatch and go beyond you' (ibid., 13.343). This may have been Bunyan's response to the 'bloody assizes' that followed Monmouth's revolt in 1685. To comfort the saints the posthumously printed *Christ a Compleat Saviour*, written probably in the spring and summer of 1686, discusses Christ's intercession with God on the elect's behalf. Alert to the fact that he might be incarcerated by the regime of the new Catholic king, on 23 December 1685 Bunyan transferred everything he owned to his wife, Elizabeth, through a deed of gift.

Women, the church, and pastoral matters Twice in the early 1680s Bunyan addressed the role of women in the church. On the first occasion he published *A Case of Conscience Resolved* (1683) in opposition to the practice of women regularly meeting alone for prayer or other acts of worship. Such a practice, he argued, had no scriptural precedent and was characteristic of the Quakers and Ranters. Bunyan's position rested on his fundamental belief in women's weakness and inferiority. For taking this stand he expected to be soundly chastised, and even 'to be sufficiently Scandalized, and counted a man not for Prayer', though there is no evidence this occurred (*Miscellaneous Works*, 4.296).

Addressing this issue may have contributed to his decision to write the second part of *The Pilgrim's Progress* (1684), in which Christiana and other female characters play prominent roles. On one level, women remain subservient in the sequel to men, but simultaneously Christiana is a type of the church, Christ's bride, and she and her companions represent an alternative, communitarian society that not only challenges but defeats its enemies. Their power, like the church's, is spiritual, not physical, but ultimately both Christiana and her co-pilgrims as well as the church are invincible. Although Bunyan does not relinquish his patriarchal attitude, his respect for women's religious prowess is manifest in Christiana's rigorous pursuit of the pilgrimage, the effective instruction of her children in doctrine, and the unplumbed depth of her piety. Yet Bunyan's traditionalism is evident in Christiana's reliance on male assistance—Great-heart's guidance—to navigate her journey successfully. As different as Christiana and Christian are, their pilgrimages traverse much of the same ground, underscoring the universality of the godly's religious experience. The sequel, however, also explores the church's communal life and worship. The two parts of *The Pilgrim's Progress* thus deal with much more than gender by pointing to varieties of religious experience, the dependence of churches on Great-hearts as pastoral guides, and the church's ultimate triumph over its foes. This is Bunyan's answer to the persecutory work of the tory reaction.

Although Bunyan described himself in his 1685 deed of gift as a brazier, he would have had little if any time to ply a trade given his ministerial responsibilities, prolific pen, and demand as a preacher, especially in London. Among his posthumously published works is *The Desire of the Righteous Granted*, which was based on a sermon to Stephen More's open-communion Baptist church at Southwark in 1685. During Bunyan's visits to London he learned about the Seventh-Day Baptists, probably because of Francis Bampfield's congregation, which shared Pinners' Hall with Wavel's church. Bampfield had died by the time Bunyan published his refutation of the sabbatarian Baptists, *Questions about the Nature and Perpetuity of the Seventh-Day-Sabbath* (1685). Generally less strident than his earlier polemical writings, this work nevertheless denounced those who rejected the primitive church's embrace of Sunday worship. Admitting that much had already been written on this subject, Bunyan joined the fray to address the common people. His simple approach differed sharply from the erudite treatises of Owen and Baxter. Bunyan's *Discourse upon the Pharisee and the Publicane*, also published in 1685, is unique in being the only book by a seventeenth-century author devoted solely to an exposition of the parable in Luke 18:10–13. Theologically, the book is significant because it reveals Bunyan's reversal of the traditional Calvinist sequence of faith preceding justification. Above all, the *Discourse* is evangelical in purpose, for Bunyan urges his readers to see themselves as either the self-righteous Pharisee or the penitent publican. In castigating the Pharisee's superficial piety Bunyan is again denouncing Church of England formalists. His pastoral concerns were also manifest in *A Book for Boys and Girls* (1686), a collection of parables or fables that use common actions and objects to make religious points. Bunyan drew on popular literature and, according to some scholars, the emblem poetry of George Wither and Francis Quarles. Bunyan's ability to make his points in a manner attractive to children sets him apart from writers such as James Janeway and Henry Jessey, who sought to scare children into repenting.

Last works   In Bunyan's final years the threat of arrest abated when James embraced a policy of toleration in summer 1686. As part of this policy he issued a declaration of indulgence in April 1687, seeking support from Catholics and dissenters. The anonymous author of 'A continuation of Mr Bunyan's life' (published with the seventh edition of *Grace Abounding* in 1692), claimed a prominent man had come to Bedford to offer Bunyan a position of public trust, but the latter refused to meet with him; this cannot be confirmed. According to the alderman John Eston, Bunyan expressed support for parliamentary candidates who favoured repeal of the penal laws and tests, and in March and April 1688 six members of his church were appointed

to the Bedford corporation. Such co-operation was consistent with Bunyan's conviction that monarchs would help overthrow Antichrist, but the anonymous biographer insisted Bunyan had zealously opposed the corporation's remodelling because of its potentially bad consequences. Given the fact that this author wrote in the aftermath of the revolution of 1688–9, he probably tried to distance Bunyan from the discredited James. Thus Bunyan likely favoured James's toleration policy.

By now Bunyan was drawing large crowds when he preached in London to the congregations of Cokayne, Wavel, More, Gammon, and possibly Griffith and Meade. His popularity fuelled demand for his works, including an eleventh edition of *The Pilgrim's Progress* in the year of his death. His final writings continued to reflect his evangelical pulpit oratory, as in *Good News for the Vilest of Men* (1688), an expository sermon on Luke 24:47 in which he argued that God offers mercy to the most heinous sinners first, and *The Water of Life* (1688), an exposition of Revelation 22:1 likening divine grace to a river. Addressed to the newly converted, *The Advocateship of Jesus Christ* (1688) casts Christ in the role of a barrister who pleads the cause of his clients, the saints, before the supreme judge in the heavenly court. The similitude suggests that Bunyan's audience primarily comprised people of substance in London and other urban areas; judging from this book, he had continued to acquire legal knowledge since his initial imprisonment in 1660. His interest in verse continued throughout this period, concluding with *A Discourse of the Building … of the House of God* (1688), in which he employed biblical and common imagery to explore the church's foundation, polity, and laws. A related work, *Solomon's Temple Spiritualiz'd* (1688), sought to unravel the temple's typological mysteries, finding multiple meanings in many of the types.

At a neighbour's request, Bunyan went to Reading in summer 1688 to mediate in a quarrel between father and son. Drenched in a rainstorm as he travelled to London, Bunyan became ill, though he preached on 19 August to Gammon's open-communion church. At the home in Snow Hill, London, of the grocer John Strudwick, a member of Cokayne's congregation, a high fever racked his body, finally claiming his life on 31 August 1688. He was buried at Bunhill Fields, Finsbury, on 3 September. He had brought the manuscript of his latest work, *The Acceptable Sacrifice*, to London, and this was published in 1689, as was *Mr John Bunyan's Last Sermon*, an exposition of John 1:13, explaining how people can ascertain if they have experienced spiritual rebirth. Cokayne's preface to *The Acceptable Sacrifice*, in which Bunyan affirmed the importance of a contrite heart, observed that this sermon was 'but a Transcript out of his own Heart' (*Miscellaneous Works*, 12.7). The ability to preach so effectively from his own spiritual experience was the key to Bunyan's success in the pulpit; in his own words, 'I preached what I felt, what I smartingly did feel' (Bunyan, *Grace Abounding*, 85).

Historical reputation   The popularity of Bunyan's major works brought a degree of international recognition during his lifetime. The Dutch publisher Johannes Boekholt issued five editions of *Eens Christens reyse* (*The Pilgrim's Progress*) between 1682 and 1687, three of *Het leven en sterven van Mr Quaadt* (*The Life and Death of Mr Badman*) between 1683 and 1685, and *Den heyligen oorlogh* (*The Holy War*) in 1685. The first, though incomplete, edition of Bunyan's works, edited by Charles Doe, appeared in 1692. A nearly complete edition, edited by Ebenezer Chandler (Bunyan's successor) and Samuel Wilson, followed in 1736–7, and the first complete edition, with George Whitefield's preface, was issued in 1767. Of subsequent editions, the most influential for more than a century was that of George Offor, first published, with evangelical commentary, in 1853. After J. B. Wharey planted the seed of the first critical edition with his *Pilgrim's Progress* in 1928, Roger Sharrock brought the work to fruition with a revised edition (1960) and new editions of *Grace Abounding* (1962), *The Holy War* (with James Forrest, 1980), *Mr Badman* (also with Forrest, 1988), and the collaborative thirteen-volume *Miscellaneous Works* (1976–94).

Bunyan's reputation has largely been driven by demand for *The Pilgrim's Progress*, the seventeenth century's most popular work of prose fiction. Its success is reflected in part by the appearance of imitations beginning in Bunyan's lifetime. According to Joseph Addison, Bunyan was as popular as Dryden and Tillotson by 1710, and Joseph Morgan drew inspiration from *The Pilgrim's Progress* and *The Holy War* in writing his allegorical *History of the Kingdom of Basaruah* (1715) for American colonists. Alexander Pope, Jonathan Swift, and John Wesley were complimentary about Bunyan, and Wesley even prepared an abridged edition of *The Holy War* in 1750. Bunyan's reputation suffered from about 1740 to 1830 as the upper classes tended to look disdainfully on popular culture. Edmund Burke contrasted Bunyan's inferior style with the *Aeneid*'s refined language, David Hume averred that no more equality of genius existed between Addison and Bunyan than between a mountain and a molehill, and John Dunlop castigated Bunyan for his coarse taste and execrable poetry. Even during this period Bunyan had his defenders, among them Laurence Sterne, Benjamin Franklin, James Boswell, and Horace Walpole. Although William Cowper thought highly of Bunyan, he recommended not mentioning his name lest it provoke sneers. Others looked on Bunyan's writings as little more than drivel, yet the Victorian emphasis on Bunyan's genius was foreshadowed in an anonymous article in the *Gentleman's Magazine* in 1765. Throughout this period evangelicals such as the Baptist historian Thomas Crosby and the Methodist preacher George Whitefield continued to express interest in Bunyan, sensing an affinity between their views and his.

The Romantic revival brought fresh appreciation of Bunyan's literary talent. Sir Walter Scott was the first British writer to allude to Bunyan in his works, and William Blake, Ralph Waldo Emerson, John Keats, and Nathaniel Hawthorne looked favourably on him. Robert Southey's critical edition of *The Pilgrim's Progress* and accompanying biography (1830) was a landmark in Bunyan scholarship, attracting attention from Scott, Thomas Babington Macaulay, and Samuel Taylor Coleridge.

Southey faulted Bunyan for his pessimistic view of human nature and intolerant attitude toward the Book of Common Prayer, but credited him for the mildness of his Calvinism and the catholicity of his spirit. Scholarly debate was now fully engaged, with most critics concluding that Bunyan was a literary genius. In Macaulay's opinion, Bunyan and Milton were the only two great creative minds in late seventeenth-century England. Yet Hawthorne, writing in 1836, worried that people were reading Bunyan mostly for entertainment, laughing rather than trembling as they read *Mr Badman*. The growing tendency to take Bunyan out of historical context was evident as apologists appropriated him to espouse evangelicalism, universalism, Anglicanism, nationalism, and liberalism. When Hawthorne's *Celestial Rail-Road* adapted *The Pilgrim's Progress* to satirize liberalism, the American Sunday-School Union quickly revised this for its own evangelical endeavours. American slaves found the allegory a ready source of metaphor to express their flights from slavery.

Bunyan's psychological state attracted the attention of John Ruskin (1845), who saw *Grace Abounding* as the product of a diseased mind. He contrasted George Herbert, who contemplated God cerebrally, with Bunyan, who supposedly viewed the deity through his liver. Ruskin labelled *Grace Abounding* a dangerous work that discredits religion and causes schism, heresy, and insanity. Half a century later Josiah Royce (1894) commented on Bunyan's morbidly insistent impulses, depression, and slow recovery. William James (1902) in turn thought Bunyan manifested a psychopathic temperament while a young man as reflected in his acutely sensitive conscience, melancholy, and subjection to sensory and motor automations. Never, he concluded, did Bunyan's mental health fully recover. Esther Harding's psychoanalytic approach (1956), indebted to Carl Jung, interpreted *The Pilgrim's Progress* as an archetype of humanity's quest for greatness.

The great outpouring of works at the tercentenary of Bunyan's birth generally extolled him, often uncritically, although Alfred Noyes harshly assessed his fear-dominated theology, style, and alleged vanity, asserting that *The Pilgrim's Progress* was the product of a defective, crude mind. William York Tindall (1934) and Christopher Hill (1988) returned Bunyan to his historical context amid enthusiasts and mechanic preachers. Some twentieth-century writers continued to appropriate Bunyan in expounding their ideologies. During the First World War, Rudyard Kipling adapted *The Holy War* to the allied cause in a poem of the same name accompanied by an illustration depicting the British pilgrim attacking the German Diabolus, and letters from British soldiers included many allusions to *The Pilgrim's Progress*. Jack Lindsay and Alick West appropriated Bunyan in defence of Marxism, and in 1940 Christopher Hollis cited Bunyan in depicting the struggle against the axis powers as a holy war. The resurgence of scholarly interest in Bunyan in the late twentieth century owed much to Roger Sharrock's work. By 2000 the major achievement of Bunyan scholarship was a critical edition of his works and a historical contextualizing of him without slighting his literary talent. The Bunyan of

Parnassus had at last been fully reconciled with the Bunyan of the conventicle.

The Pilgrim's Progress, twenty editions of which had been published by 1695 and at least 1300 by 1938, has been remarkably successful. It has been translated into more than 200 languages, with Dutch, French, and apparently Welsh editions appearing in Bunyan's lifetime. The New Zealand government commissioned its translation for the Maori in 1854, and the book has since sold well in the developing world. Musical settings date back to 1870, with the most famous being Ralph Vaughan Williams's, first performed at Covent Garden in 1951, the predecessor of his cantata 'Pilgrim's Journey'. The allegory has been adapted various times for enactment as a pageant. The most imaginative is a mystery play composed in 1928 featuring a dialogue between Cinderella and Bunyan using quotations from the latter's works. Among the literary classics that owe inspiration to Bunyan are Hawthorne's *Scarlet Letter*, Louisa May Alcott's *Little Women*, Herman Melville's *Moby Dick*, Charles Dickens's *Oliver Twist* and *The Old Curiosity Shop*, e. e. cummings's *The Enormous Room*, and Aleksandr Pushkin's *The Wanderer*. Of the artists drawn to Bunyan the most eminent was William Blake, who rendered twenty-nine watercolours of *The Pilgrim's Progress*. The unusual adaptations of the allegory include an eighteenth-century jigsaw puzzle, a 1000 foot canvas panorama exhibited in many American cities in the 1850s, and *Bob's Hike to the Holy City*, the tale of a boy scout and his sister on the road of life. Perhaps the most remarkable fact about Bunyan is that a work written amid bitter sectarian controversy has transcended internecine Christian rivalries and appeared in Catholic, Anglo-Catholic, and Unitarian versions.　　　　RICHARD L. GREAVES

Sources J. Bunyan, *The pilgrim's progress*, ed. J. B. Wharey and R. Sharrock (1960) · J. Bunyan, *Grace abounding to the chief of sinners*, ed. R. Sharrock (1962) · J. Bunyan, *The holy war*, ed. R. Sharrock and J. F. Forrest (1980) · *The miscellaneous works of John Bunyan*, ed. R. Sharrock and others, 13 vols. (1976–94) · J. Bunyan, *The life and death of Mr Badman*, ed. J. F. Forrest and R. Sharrock (1988) · J. F. Forrest and R. L. Greaves, *John Bunyan: a reference guide* (1982) · C. Hill, *A turbulent, seditious, and factious people: John Bunyan and his church* (1988) · M. A. Mullett, *John Bunyan in context* (1996) · R. L. Greaves, *John Bunyan* (1969) · R. L. Greaves, *John Bunyan and English nonconformity* (1992) · R. L. Greaves, *Glimpses of glory: John Bunyan and English dissent* (2001) · J. Brown, *John Bunyan (1628–1688): his life, times, and work*, rev. F. M. Harrison, rev. edn (1928) · N. H. Keeble, ed., *John Bunyan: conventicle and Parnassus, tercentenary essays* (1988) · A. Laurence, W. R. Owens, and S. Sim, eds., *John Bunyan and his England, 1628–88* (1990) · W. Y. Tindall, *John Bunyan: mechanick preacher* (1934) · H. G. Tibbutt, ed., *The minutes of the first Independent church (now Bunyan meeting) at Bedford, 1656–1766*, Bedfordshire Historical RS, 55 (1976) · D. Gay, J. G. Randall, and A. Zinck, eds., *Awakening words: John Bunyan and the language of community* (2000) · R. G. Collmer, ed., *Bunyan in our time* (1989) · T. H. Luxon, *Literal figures: puritan allegory and the Reformation crisis in representation* (1995) · T. L. Underwood, *Primitivism, radicalism, and the Lamb's war: the Baptist–Quaker conflict in seventeenth-century England* (1997) · K. M. Swaim, *Pilgrim's progress, puritan progress: discourses and contexts* (1993) · I. Rivers, *Reason, grace, and sentiment: a study of the language of religion and ethics in England, 1660–1780*, 1 (1991) · N. H. Keeble, *The literary culture of nonconformity in later seventeenth-century England* (1987) · R. Sharrock, *John Bunyan* (1954) · V. Newey, ed., *The pilgrim's progress: critical and historical views* (1980) · J. R. Knott, jun., *The sword of the spirit: puritan responses to the Bible* (1981) · V. J. Camden, ed., *The narrative of the persecutions of Agnes Beaumont* (1992) · J. Stachniewski, *The persecutory imagination: English puritanism and the literature of religious despair* (1991) · H. Talon, *John Bunyan: the man and his works*, trans. B. Wall (1951) · J. R. Knott, *Discourses of martyrdom in English literature, 1563–1694* (1993) · *Bunyan studies: John Bunyan and his times*, vol. 1 (1988)
Likenesses oils, 1673, Plimpton collection, New York · R. White, pencil drawing, *c.*1679, BL · T. Sadler, oils, 1684, NPG [*see illus.*] · R. Houston, mezzotint, 1685 (after T. Sadler), BM, NPG · van Hone, steel engraving, repro. in J. Bunyan, *The advocateship of Jesus Christ* (1688) · J. Sturt, engraving (after Sadler), BM, NPG; repro. in J. Bunyan, *The works of that eminent servant of Christ, Mr. John Bunyan*, ed. C. Doe (1692) · R. White, drawing, pencil on vellum, BM · R. White, engraving, Hunt. L.; repro. in J. Bunyan, *The pilgrim's progress* (1678) · R. White, line engraving, BL; repro. in J. Bunyan, *The pilgrim's progress* (1679) · line engraving (after R. White), BM, NPG
Wealth at death £42 19*s.*: registry of the archdeaconry of Bedford, Brown, *John Bunyan*, p. 388

Bunyard, Edward Ashdown (1878–1939), nurseryman and pomologist, was born on 14 December 1878 at 74 King Street, Maidstone, the eldest son of **George Bunyard** (1841–1919), nurseryman, and his wife, Katherine Sophia Ashdown. His father was born on 5 February 1841 at London Road, Maidstone, the son of Thomas Bunyard and his wife, Mary Ann Butler. He married Katherine Sophia (*b.* 1850/51), daughter of Charles Ashdown, paper maker, on 3 June 1873 and they had eight children. George Bunyard became one of Britain's foremost nurserymen, a leading fruit authority and head of George Bunyard & Sons Ltd, of Allington and Maidstone. His grandfather had founded a nursery at Maidstone in 1796 and George entered this business aged fourteen in 1855, before becoming partner and manager in 1869. Severe family and financial problems brought the firm to bankruptcy in 1879, but George was able to get the business back and begin again. His fortunes had changed with a contract in 1880–81 to supply half a million trees for Lord Sudeley's estate in Gloucestershire and the business continued to prosper with the enormous investment in fruit that occurred in the last decades of the nineteenth century as the modern British fruit industry was founded.

George Bunyard was at the centre of this activity. His nursery provided many of the trees for the new orchards and George was a key figure in the Royal Horticultural Society (RHS) and the Worshipful Company of Fruiterers—the main organizations that, through fruit shows and exhibitions, were encouraging the public to buy home-grown produce. George helped stage the historic National Apple Congress of 1883 and the Great Fruit Show at the Guildhall in 1896, for which he was made a freeman of the City of London, and he was among the first sixty to receive the prestigious RHS Victoria medal of honour in 1897. Throughout this period his firm was staging prize-winning exhibitions and he held many prominent positions on horticultural and trade societies: member of the RHS council, 1904–13; member of the fruit and vegetable committee from 1880 and chairman 1901–13; and master of the Worshipful Company of Fruiterers, 1906.

Bunyard was also a successful author: *Fruit Farming for Profit*, published in 1881, went into six editions and *The Fruit Garden* (1904), which he wrote with Owen Thomas,

Queen Victoria's head gardener, became the amateurs' bible. He contributed the fruit section to *The Century Book of Gardening* (1899), and wrote *A Book on Apples and Pears* (1910), *Handbook of Hardy Trees and Shrubs* (1907), and *England's National Flower*, on roses, his favourite flowers. He died at his home, The Crossways, Mereworth, near Maidstone, on 22 January 1919, survived by his wife.

Edward Bunyard was educated privately at home with his brothers and sisters, followed by a period in France with leading nurserymen, before he entered the family business in 1896. By the time he took over on his father's death it had become one of the foremost British nurseries, with an international reputation for fruit. He directed the business until 1939, when he retired and became librarian of the RHS's Lindley Library in London, and editor of the society's publications. He remained a bachelor. His main interest was in pomology, the study of fruit. He made many distinguished contributions through papers and books: *The Handbook of Hardy Fruits* (1920) and *Stone and Bush Fruits* (1925) cover the main cultivars of all the fruits then grown in Britain and remain standard reference works. He was acknowledged as Britain's leading pomologist, the successor to the great Victorian authority Dr Robert Hogg. In recognition of his work in systematic pomology, Bunyard was made a fellow of the Linnean Society in 1914, and sat on its council from 1924 to 1927. He was ideally placed to study fruit, with a wealth of material growing in the nursery around his home at Allington. The Bunyard nursery claimed '800 kinds true to name'. He was also a gifted bibliophile, and sought out rare books about fruit, creating an extensive library. His botanic and historical studies included many other plants and particularly roses. *Old Garden Roses* has inspired many gardeners to plant the 'older roses' since its publication in 1936.

Like his father, Edward Bunyard was a prominent figure in the horticultural world: council member of the RHS, 1924–39; chairman of its fruit and vegetable committee, 1930–39, and chairman of the library committee, 1925–39. He was closely involved with the work of the newly established government funded fruit research institutes—particularly East Malling Research Station, near Maidstone. In 1919 he founded, edited, and published the *Journal of Pomology*, which he ran for two years until it was adopted as the official organ of East Malling and Long Ashton Research Station. Bunyard was a member of the advisory committee to the national fruit trials formed in 1922, and also a key figure in setting up the associated national fruit collections, now internationally renowned and located at Brogdale, Faversham, Kent.

Edward Bunyard was a prolific writer, not only of scholarly works but also of lighter articles and books on the pleasures of the table. *The Anatomy of Dessert*, published in 1929, encompassed all the temperate fruits that could be enjoyed at the grand finale of dinner—the fresh fruit dessert—which was at its zenith in Victorian England. He wrote lyrically of the nuances of flavour to be found in fruit, especially the apple, and revived interest in many old favourites. The book was widely acclaimed and remains treasured by all fruit lovers. In the second (1933)

edition he included a section on the best wines to enjoy with fruit, and in 1937 wrote *The Epicure's Companion* in collaboration with his sister Lorna. Bunyard's delight in good food and wine led to his close association with the London dining clubs—the Wine and Food Society and the Saintsbury Club—to which he brought up baskets of fruit and nuts from the nursery, and organized tastings.

Bunyard had embarked on a career in broadcasting with the 'radio gardener', C. H. Middleton, shortly before his tragic death on 19 October 1939. It was said that he had become extremely depressed over the war and this had led to his taking his life. He shot himself in the RHS club, St James's, London, with the gun he used for frightening the bullfinches from the cherries at the nursery. Bunyard died on the way to St George's Hospital, London.

Edward's younger brother **(George) Norman Bunyard** (1886–1969), nurseryman and iris grower, was born on 21 October 1886 at London Road, Maidstone. Norman joined the family nursery in Kent on his return from the war in 1919. The business was still famous for its fruit trees and ornamental plants, especially roses, and he took over as its head on his brother's retirement in 1939. Under his direction the firm had begun an interest in irises in 1920 and Norman Bunyard raised a number of fine cultivars. He helped found the British Iris Society in 1922 and was its secretary in 1922–7 and for many years served on its committee. He married, and he and his wife, Dorothy Mary, had two daughters. Norman Bunyard died at home at 10 Faraday Road, Maidstone, on 9 February 1969.

JOAN MORGAN

Sources Desmond, *Botanists*, rev. edn • *CGPLA Eng. & Wales* (1940) • b. certs. • m. cert. • d. certs. • *CGPLA Eng. & Wales* (1919) [George Bunyard] • *CGPLA Eng. & Wales* (1969) [Norman Bunyard] • will [Norman Bunyard] • E. Wilson, 'If on fragrance we might thrive …', *Food and Wine*, 24 (1999), 66–9
Wealth at death £918 11s. 5d.: probate, Feb 1940, *CGPLA Eng. & Wales* • £19,268 8s. 3d.—George Bunyard: probate, 1919, *CGPLA Eng. & Wales* • £58,177—Norman Bunyard: probate, 1969, *CGPLA Eng. & Wales*

Bunyard, George (1841–1919). *See under* Bunyard, Edward Ashdown (1878–1939).

Bunyard, (George) Norman (1886–1969). *See under* Bunyard, Edward Ashdown (1878–1939).

Burbage, Cuthbert (1564/5–1636), theatre investor and entrepreneur, was baptized at St Stephen, Coleman Street, close to Guildhall, London, on 15 June 1565, the elder of the two surviving sons of James *Burbage (c.1531–1597) and his wife, Ellen, née Brayne (c.1542–1613). His younger brother, Richard *Burbage, was a leading actor of the day. James secured employment for Cuthbert with Walter Cope, a gentleman—knighted by James I in 1603—in the household of Queen Elizabeth's principal minister, the lord treasurer, Lord Burghley. Cuthbert came of age in June 1586, and supported his father in litigation after the death in August of John Brayne, James's brother-in-law and one-time financial backer of the theatre project in Shoreditch. Brayne's widow pursued his claim to half the theatre and its profits. The two men had fallen into debt, and in 1580 mortgaged the lease to John Hyde, a very prominent freeman of the Grocers' Company. Hyde intended to sell it to his father-in-law, but the Burbages sought help from Cuthbert's employer, and Cope duly wrote to Hyde saying it might be to his advantage in the future if he yielded up the property: this he reluctantly did, and on 7 June 1589 it was assigned to Cuthbert. The restoration of ownership to the Burbages is of great importance in stage history. Litigation, however, continued until Mrs Brayne's death in 1593.

Soon the Burbages were in more trouble. There seemed to be no prospect of renewing The Theatre's lease—due to expire early in 1597—with the ground landlord; James moved down from The Theatre to Blackfriars, and pledged the large sum of £600 for part of the former monastic complex, intending to have it converted to an indoor playing-place. A deed was signed with the previous owner early in 1596, James put down £100, and the rest was paid off by his sons on 23 July 1597. With James's death at the beginning of the year, and strong opposition to his theatre plan from influential residents of the precinct, the brothers now faced the imminent prospect of having no playing-place.

They found a site across the river in Southwark, and Cuthbert turned to the master carpenter Peter Street for help. The Street and Burbage families had known each other from the days when they were fellow parishioners of St Stephen, Coleman Street: John Street and James Burbage had both worked there as joiners (Burbage only briefly), and the terms of apprenticeship served within the Carpenters' Company by Street's son Peter and Burbage's younger brother or half-brother Robert had partially coincided. Robert completed his training in 1573, and James may have commissioned him to build The Theatre in Shoreditch in 1576: in 1598 Cuthbert commissioned Street to dismantle The Theatre and reuse the timbers for the Globe, which was built on Bankside in 1599.

On 8 July 1594 Cuthbert had married Elizabeth Cox, the daughter of John Cox, gentleman, by licence at St Mary-le-Strand. Their sons Walter and James, baptized at Shoreditch in 1595 and 1597, did not long survive. Cuthbert's sole heir, Elizabeth, was baptized there on 30 December 1601. Two damaged and incomplete Middlesex tax lists (E179/142/279 and 284) show that Cuthbert did not remain in Shoreditch for the rest of his life, as hitherto supposed. In the first, dated 1621–2, he appears as an assessor for Holywell Street, with Henry Hodge, a wealthy brewer and family friend, but he disappears from the second, for 1623–4. So far as one can tell from a third, very imperfect, tax list (E179/147/553, 1626), he had moved to Redcross Street, in the parish of St Giles Cripplegate, a fashionable part of the parish outside the City wall, with fine houses, gardens, and summer houses. The move must have been before 5 June 1623, when Nicholas Tooley was buried from the house of Cuthbert Burbage in Redcross Street, both entered in the register as 'gentleman'.

On 8 June 1620 Amyas Maxey, described as a gentleman of St Margaret's, Westminster, had secured a licence to marry eighteen-year-old Elizabeth Burbage. The marriage was to be at St Leonard, Foster Lane, off Cheapside, but as church and registers were destroyed in the fire of 1666, any relevant entries are lost. The couple had two children, Elizabeth and James. There was something dubious about Maxey: Tooley in his will describes him as Elizabeth's 'pretended' husband, and Cuthbert formally adopted their son, to be known as James Burbage Maxey. On 21 December 1630 Elizabeth was married at St Giles Cripplegate to George Bingley esquire, of a landed family in Nottinghamshire: he was much older than she, and probably a wealthy widower. He was a king's auditor, and appears in the state papers.

The 'sharers' papers' of 1635 provide invaluable information about the organization of the pre-eminent London theatre company the King's Men. Three of the younger actors petitioned to be admitted to share, as 'housekeepers', in the profits of the company's Blackfriars and second Globe playhouses; they argued that some of the existing housekeepers reaped most of the benefits 'without takeing any paynes themselves' (*Malone*, 2.364). During the hearing about 'sharers' in 1635, Cuthbert replied for himself, and his brother's widow and son William, about alleged unfair treatment of some younger actors: he argued that they should not be 'disabled' in their livelihoods by men 'so soone shott up' who were 'never bred from Children in the kings service' (*Malone*, 2.370, 371). The lord chamberlain ruled in favour of the petitioners.

At some stage Cuthbert had acquired a country house in the village of Hayes, close to Bromley in Kent: it was called The Heyes, and ranked second only to Hayes Place, later acquired and rebuilt by William Pitt the elder, earl of Chatham. Cuthbert and Elizabeth died there on 15 and 28 September 1636 respectively, and were buried at Shoreditch on 17 September and 1 October, in the chancel, beneath a flat stone with a Latin inscription. Evidence in wills of friends and professional associates, and their provision of a home for the fatherless actor Tooley and adoption of their grandson James, suggest that they were a kindly couple, and probably contributed to the remarkable cohesion, at a personal level, of the original members of the Chamberlain's (later King's) Men.

Cuthbert, who died intestate, had reached the age of seventy-one; when Elizabeth consulted the doctor Simon Forman on 7 July 1601 (Bodl. Oxf., MS Ashmole 411, fol. 79), he noted that she was thirty-two, so she would have been about sixty-seven at her death. Their son-in-law Bingley died, also intestate, at Hayes in 1652; his widow, Elizabeth, died there in 1672, and was buried at Shoreditch on 10 February. She left all her lands, houses, and tenements in Blackfriars to her daughter Elizabeth Maxey, and the rest of her estate to her son James, the last male descendant of the theatrical Burbage family. He died intestate at Hayes in 1677, and his widow was married by licence on 31 October at St Martin-in-the-Fields to Evan Lloyd, a gentleman of Gray's Inn.   MARY EDMOND

Sources C. W. Wallace, *The first London theatre: materials for a history* (1913) · W. Ingram, *The business of playing: the beginnings of the adult*

professional theater in Elizabethan England (1992) • M. Edmond, 'Yeomen, citizens, gentlemen and players: the Burbages and their connections', *Elizabethan theater: essays in honor of S. Schoenbaum*, ed. R. B. Parker and S. P. Zitner (1996), 30–49 • M. Edmond, 'Peter Street, 1553–1609: builder of playhouses', *Shakespeare Survey*, 45 (1993), 101–14 • Carpenters' Company records, GL • 'Sharers papers', *Malone Society Collections*, 2/1 (1913), 362–73, esp. 362–5, 370–72 • G. E. Bentley, *The Jacobean and Caroline stage*, 7 vols. (1941–68), vol. 1, p. 43 • PRO, lay subsidy rolls, class E 179 • *The visitation of London, anno Domini 1633, 1634, and 1635, made by Sir Henry St George*, 1, ed. J. J. Howard and J. L. Chester, Harleian Society, 15 (1880), 121 [Burbage pedigree] • E. A. J. Honigmann and S. Brock, eds., *Playhouse wills, 1558–1642: an edition of wills by Shakespeare and his contemporaries in the London theatre* (1993) • *The parish of St Leonard Shoreditch*, Survey of London, 8 (1992) • parish register, London, St Stephen Coleman Street, 15 June 1565, GL, MSS 4448, 4449/1 [baptism] • parish register, London, Shoreditch, St Leonard, 17 Sept 1636, GL, MS 7499/1 [burial] • parish register, London, St Mary-le-Strand, 8 July 1594, Victoria Library, London [marriage] • parish register, London, St Mary Magdalen, Old Fish Street, 31 Oct 1622, GL, MS 11529 [marriage: Winifred Burbage, sister-in-law] • parish register, London, St Giles Cripplegate, 5 June 1623, GL, MS 6419/2 [burial: Nicholas Tooley] • parish register, London, St Giles Cripplegate, 21 Dec 1630, GL, MS 6419/2 [marriage: Elizabeth Maxey, daughter, and George Bingley] • Bromley Central Library, MS P180/1/1 • will, 3 June 1623, proved 17 June 1624, PRO, PROB 11/143, sig. 53 [Nicholas Tooley] • will, PRO, PROB 11/338, sig. 25 [Elizabeth Bingley, daughter] • will, 1 July 1578; proved 10 Aug 1586, Commissary Court, 9172/12C [John Brayne, uncle] • will, 8 April, proved 3 May, commissary court, GL, MS 9172/16A [Margaret Brayne, aunt] • will, GL, Archdeaconry court of London, MS 9050/5, fol. 153v [Edmund Turner] • admin, PROB 6/16, fol. 26v • admin, PROB 6/52/123, 1677 [James Burbage Maxey, adopted grandson] • admin, PROB 6/27/101, 16 June 1652 [George Bingley, son-in-law]

Burbage, James (*c*.1531–1597), actor, is of unknown parentage. The family appear to have come not (as hitherto thought) from Hertfordshire but from Bromley in Kent. In the sixteenth century this was a small country place 10 miles south-east of London, within easy walking distance of the capital. Burbages are traceable to Kent at least as early as the fifteenth century, but the only cluster seems to have been in Bromley, apart from one property-owning family for a time at Boxley, near Maidstone. The surname persists up to 1700 and beyond. Surviving local tax returns include several Bromley Burbages liable to tax in the 1540s (PRO, E 179 series), most paying a few pence. The fact that James's elder son, Cuthbert, later had a country house in a village close to Bromley is a powerful argument in favour of the family's being from Kent.

Burbage married Ellen Brayne (*c*.1542–1613), the daughter of Thomas Brayne, a tailor and freeman of the Girdlers' Company, at St Stephen, Coleman Street, close to the Guildhall, on 23 April 1559. Girdlers' Hall was in the adjoining parish of St Michael Bassishaw, where Ellen's father had married Alice Barlow on 22 January 1541. Four of James's and Ellen's children survived to adulthood: Cuthbert *Burbage, baptized on 15 June 1565, Richard *Burbage on 7 July 1568, and Ellen on 13 June 1574, all at St Stephen; and Alice, baptized at St Leonard, Shoreditch, on 11 March 1576. Ellen was buried at St Anne Blackfriars on 13 December 1596 (register page wrongly dated 1595).

Burbage had been apprenticed in London as a joiner. There is a persistent but mistaken belief that the words 'joiner' and 'carpenter' were synonymous: both were craftsmen in wood, but while joiners were furniture-and-fittings men, carpenters were the highly trained men who put up buildings. Snug the joiner in *A Midsummer Night's Dream* is the most humble of the troupe that put on *Pyramus and Thisby*: their leader, Peter Quince, is a carpenter. Burbage is entered as a joiner just twice in the St Stephen's register, in 1559. That was the year in which Lord Robert Dudley (created earl of Leicester in 1564) granted his patronage to a small troupe of players. Perhaps Burbage was a founder member: by 1572, if not much earlier, he had become their leader. They then signed a letter to the earl, begging him not only to allow them to go on wearing his livery, but also to grant them a licence certifying that they were members of his household: they were not seeking 'any further stipend' (Ingram, 85–91). This was no doubt prompted by a proclamation renewing earlier statutes forbidding peers to grant livery to mere 'retainers'. On 10 May 1574 the first royal patent to players was issued to Leicester's men, licensing them to play in London and elsewhere, any ruling 'heretofore made, or hereafter to be made, to the contrarie notwithstandinge' (ibid., 120–21).

Years of touring had convinced Burbage of the need for a permanent playing-place as near to the capital as possible, and on 13 April 1576 he signed a twenty-one-year lease with the ground landlord, Giles Allen, of a site in Shoreditch, just north of the city and a short walk across Finsbury Fields. James presumably set his younger brother or half-brother Robert (who had completed his seven-year training within the Carpenters' Company on 16 June 1573) to build the theatre in 1576. In 1578 John Stockwood, master of Tonbridge School in Kent—preaching at Paul's Cross on 24 August—spoke of the 'gorgeous Playing-place erected in the fieldes', a tribute to the quality of the workmanship from an unexpected source: he naturally added that it was, like 'the olde heathenish Theatre at Rome, a shew place of all beastly & filthie matters'. Robert died in 1584; his will includes references to debts and duties owed to him by James and by John Brayne, his one-time associate in the theatre enterprise.

In 1583 the master of the revels had been required to choose twelve of the best actors from all groups to form a new company, the Queen's Men. They included three of Leicester's company; the rest disbanded. In 1584 James Burbage claimed the patronage of the queen's cousin Lord Hunsdon, who ten years later, as lord chamberlain, was to become first patron of the company of William Shakespeare and Burbage's son Richard. The recorder of London, William Fleetwood, in a report to Burghley dated 18 June 1584, said James at first rejected a summons to explain 'sundrye Broiles' near the theatre in Whitsun week: he would ride to his lord 'in the mornyng', but was sure no court would bind him, 'being a Counselers man' (BL, Lansdowne MS 41, no. 13, fol. 35v). Fleetwood described Burbage, in a much quoted remark, as 'a stubburne man'—mild words by Elizabethan standards.

Things had not been going smoothly at the theatre. Initially, Burbage's brother-in-law John Brayne, a freeman of the rich and powerful Grocers' Company, had backed him, but 'variance and controversy' soon developed.

Brayne died intestate in 1586, and his widow Margaret pursued his claim to a moiety (half) of the theatre and its profits, appointing Robert Miles, a freeman of the Goldsmiths' Company, as her agent. In November 1590 she secured a chancery order to sequestrate the playhouse and allow her the moiety pending litigation—an order which Cuthbert Burbage tried to block; and Miles moved to have father and son charged with contempt of court. Eventually it was ruled that the dispute over the theatre—'the cause'—and the contempt issue be taken together, and many witnesses were called. Miles recruited three unimpressive ones: his son Ralph and a friend, Nicholas Bishop, both soap makers of Whitechapel, and an actor employed at the theatre in 1590—John, the elder brother of Edward Alleyn. Attention has always focused on the events of 16 November 1590, when—according to the Brayne faction—James Burbage was guilty of the contempt of court and his son Richard of an assault with a broomstick. But Miles's witnesses were not heard until the first half of 1592, allowing plenty of time for fading memories and perhaps 'improved' depositions.

On 6 February 1592, Alleyn—speaking as though on stage rather than in court—claimed to have urged Burbage to allow the widow her rights, provoking the response: 'hang her ho^r [whore] … she getteth nothing here'; and when Alleyn spoke of conscience, Burbage allegedly retorted: 'godes blood what do you tell me of Conscience … yf ther were xx contemptes … he would withstand them all / before he wold lose his possession' (Wallace, 100–01). On 6 May, Alleyn said he thought these words had been spoken in the theatre yard 'about a yere past' (ibid., 127)—it was of course eighteen months. According to Bishop the soap maker, deposing on 6 April 1592, the Brayne party had gone to the theatre on 16 November 1590 and tried to show Burbage a copy of an old court order about contempt. Burbage dismissed this as 'A paper which he might wype his tale with' (ibid., 115). Then, according to the rather confused depositions, Burbage's wife and younger son, Richard (then twenty-two), fell upon Miles and Mrs Brayne (Richard's aunt Margaret) and drove them out of the theatre yard. It was a play day, and the affair probably provided some free entertainment for patrons arriving for the afternoon performance. John Alleyn, deposing on 6 May, did not even see it, but came upon Richard later, still holding the broomstick and claiming that he had sent them packing.

Robert Miles himself, speaking at length on 30 July, concentrated on what John Brayne had said before his death six years earlier. According to Miles, Brayne had insisted that he would never have backed the theatre but for Burbage's assurances that they would make great profits by being able to put on plays every week. Succumbing to the 'swete and contynuall persuasions' of his brother-in-law had led to his utter undoing, he claimed (Wallace, 139). A second accusation, that Burbage had had a key made to the box for the theatre takings, and for about two years stolen much of the money, is not credible. The company would have had a good idea of the size of each afternoon's audience, and could not have failed to notice how much they were missing.

Margaret Brayne died in 1593, and hearings ended. Soon the future of the theatre was in doubt. The ground landlord, Giles Allen, refused to extend the lease, due to expire in April 1597, and in 1596 the Burbages moved down from Shoreditch to Blackfriars. James spent £600 for part of an old stone building containing a former roofed playing-place, and a further £400 on having this converted to a handsome new one. In November distinguished residents of the precinct successfully petitioned the privy council to disallow his plan. Early in 1597, probably at the end of January, Burbage died, presumably at Blackfriars. His body was taken back to Shoreditch for burial in Holywell Street on 2 February, Candlemas. He may have been about sixty-six: he provided the only clue to his date of birth when he and Cuthbert deposed in court on 16 February 1591, describing himself as 'sixty or thereabouts' (Wallace, 61); Cuthbert thought himself about twenty-four, but was in his twenty-sixth year. Burbage died intestate, and his widow presented an inventory valued at £37: this modest sum gives no indication of his wealth, as he is said to have made deeds of gift of his personal property to Cuthbert and the Blackfriars property to Richard.

Burbage had been a man of some stature. He led Lord Leicester's small troupe of players, who often performed at court; was able to place his elder son in circles close to court and queen; and lived to see his younger son become a leading player in the pre-eminent company, the Chamberlain's Men. Late sixteenth-century London was a lively, overcrowded, noisy, and not especially orderly place. Burbage seems to have been a rumbustious character, but he was perhaps a representative Londoner rather than, as is often supposed, an exceptionally unruly one.

MARY EDMOND

Sources C. W. Wallace, *The first London theatre: materials for a history* (1913) · W. Ingram, *The business of playing: the beginnings of the adult professional theater in Elizabethan England* (1992) · M. Edmond, 'Yeomen, citizens, gentlemen and players: the Burbages and their connections', *Elizabethan theater: essays in honor of S. Schoenbaum*, ed. R. B. Parker and S. P. Zitner (1996), 30–46 · M. Edmond, 'Peter Street, 1553–1609: builder of playhouses', *Shakespeare Survey*, 45 (1993), 101–14 · Carpenters' Company records, GL · 'Sharers papers', *Malone Society Collections*, 2/1 (1913), 362–73, esp. 370–72 [letter to Leicester; unlawful retainers] · E. K. Chambers, *The Elizabethan stage*, vol. 2, p. 86; and vol. 4, appx D, p. 268, no. 19, 3 Jan, *Stat. realm*, 2.240, 522 [unlawful retainers] · *A sermon preached at Paules Crosse on Barthelmewe day, being the 24 of August 1578* (1578), C.94.a.3(1) · Fleetwood to Burghley, 18 June 1584, BL, Lansdowne MS 41, no. 13, fol. 35*v* · M. Eccles, 'Elizabethan actors, I: A–D', *N&Q*, 236 (1991), 38–49, esp. 43 · E. A. J. Honigmann and S. Brock, eds., *Playhouse wills, 1558–1642: an edition of wills by Shakespeare and his contemporaries in the London theatre* (1993) · *The visitation of London, anno Domini 1633, 1634, and 1635, made by Sir Henry St George*, 1, ed. J. J. Howard and J. L. Chester, Harleian Society, 15 (1880), 121 [Burbage pedigree] · parish register, London, St Stephen Coleman Street, 23 April 1559 [marriage] · parish register, London, Shoreditch, St Leonard, 2 Feb 1597 [burial]
Archives Folger, papers
Wealth at death widow presented inventory £37 · made deeds of gift of personal property to Cuthbert and Blackfriars property to Richard: Wallace, *First London theatre*, 25, and 158 for Court of Requests 1597

Burbage [Burbadge], **Richard** (1568–1619), actor, was baptized at St Stephen, Coleman Street, close to Guildhall, London, on 7 July 1568, the younger of the two surviving sons of James *Burbage (c.1531–1597) and his wife, Ellen, *née* Brayne (c.1542–1613). In 1635 his brother Cuthbert *Burbage stated that, 'for 35 yeeres paines, cost, and Labour', Richard had 'made meanes to leave his wife and Children, some estate' ('Sharers papers', 371). If this can be taken literally, and if it is assumed that Richard went on acting almost until his death, it indicates that he began his illustrious career about 1584, when he was sixteen. That was the year when his father declared himself to be Hunsdon's man—under the patronage of Queen Elizabeth's cousin Henry Carey, Lord Hunsdon. Ten years later, as lord chamberlain, Hunsdon became the first patron of the principal London company, with Richard Burbage as its leading actor. Perhaps father and son secured Hunsdon's patronage at the same time.

Small troupes of players had long been active in England, and in the sixteenth century some acquired noble patrons and began to arrive in the capital—the only place large enough to provide a market for what they had to offer—and often to settle there. They have been described as a 'new, experimental social group' (M. Bradbrook, *Rise of the Common Player*, 1962, vii), self-regulating, often on the move, not fully integrated into London society. Richard's father, James, had himself been a touring player, and well understood the need for a permanent playing place as near to London as possible, offering plays every weekday. In 1576, when Richard was eight years old, James opened The Theatre, just outside the north wall of the City.

The City of London, commercial and financial centre and major port, was largely puritan in sentiment and hostile to playing, which was seen as encouraging crowds and idleness. Within the queen's privy council, successive lord chamberlains, whose main duty was to provide good entertainments for the court, protected the players. Charles Howard, Lord Howard of Effingham and later earl of Nottingham, and his father-in-law, Hunsdon, who succeeded him, both helped the players to gain a foothold in the capital. In 1583 the Queen's Company was established, taking twelve of the best actors employed by assorted great lords outside London. A few years later the Queen's Company split into two touring groups, and in May 1594 Hunsdon and Howard replaced the monopoly with two companies (keeping their original titles of Chamberlain's Men and Admiral's Men) built respectively around Richard and his father at The Theatre in Shoreditch, and around Edward Alleyn and his father-in-law, Philip Henslowe, at the Rose Theatre on Bankside.

One small piece of information about Burbage's early days as a player survives at Dulwich College in London (founded by Edward Alleyn): it is the 'platt' (plot) dated about 1590–91 of part of a piece called *The Seven Deadly Sins*, written for the company of Ferdinando Stanley, Lord Strange, who died in April 1594. It is an abstract of the piece, written perhaps by the prompter, and lists 'R. Burbadge' as playing two of the main parts. He had probably begun with Strange's company as a 'hired man', and then

remained for a year or two. Speculation has also linked him later with a company sponsored by the third earl of Sussex; and he may have gone to Henslowe's Rose for a short time before becoming the leading actor of the Chamberlain's Men at his father's theatre in Shoreditch in 1594.

Burbage must have become closely associated with Shakespeare as soon as the latter arrived in London. Shakespeare may well have met Burbage's father for the first time when he was a young boy, since the small troupe of Lord Leicester's players led by James Burbage visited Stratford upon Avon on tour in 1573 and 1577. No doubt Shakespeare sought out the family when he arrived in London in the late 1580s; according to John Aubrey, in one of his scrappy notes for *Brief Lives*, Shakespeare actually lodged in Shoreditch for a time. Richard was at this point already well established in his career. Thus began a creative relationship of collaboration and friendship between the man who was an actor—for a time—as well as a playwright, and the actor who (unlike his rival Edward Alleyn) devoted his whole life to that career. Richard Burbage is one of only three men from his London life whom Shakespeare names in his will of 1616: he calls them 'fellows', then a strong word meaning friend and colleague.

The Chamberlain's Men, 1594–1603 The court celebrated the Christmas season of 1594–5 at Greenwich Palace, and at the end of December the company gave 'twoe severall comedies or Enterludes'—as usual in court records, no titles are mentioned. Shakespeare, aged thirty, and Burbage, twenty-six, were appointed payees and, with the comedian William Kemp, were deputed to receive payment of £20—the 'wage' of £13 6s. 8d., plus £6 13s. 4d. 'by waye of her Maties Rewarde' (Chambers, 4.164). The company never provided lists of its members, let alone cast lists. Ben Jonson, in the first folio of his *Works* (1616), included a dated list of plays which he had written for the company—always as a freelance. The first was *Every Man in his Humour*, acted in autumn 1598 by ten 'Principall Comoedians'—probably the complete membership—with Burbage named second after Shakespeare.

The Burbages had been in dire trouble over The Theatre since the beginning of 1596: the ground landlord had refused to renew their lease, due to expire in April 1597, and the family moved down to the river, to the parish of St Anne Blackfriars. James spent £600 for part of an old stone building containing a former roofed playing place used by a boy company, and £400 on having this converted to a handsome new one intended for use by his son Richard. The family's old friend and neighbour Peter Street also moved down to the river in 1596, to a parish adjoining Blackfriars, and this strongly suggests—although evidence is lacking—that it was he whom James and Cuthbert commissioned to build the Blackfriars roofed playhouse, no doubt to replace their ageing open-air theatre for all-year-round use. However, the plans were soon thwarted. James died at the beginning of 1597.

James had often used roofed City inns for playing in winter; but, as a result of bargaining between lord chamberlain and lord mayor, it had eventually been agreed that, while the Chamberlain's Men and Admiral's Men should enjoy exclusive rights to playing in their London suburban houses—then The Theatre and the Rose Theatre—the mayor was assured that there would be no more playing in City inns.

Distinguished residents of Blackfriars had successfully petitioned the privy council to forbid use of the new Blackfriars playhouse, and two months after James Burbage's death the owner of The Theatre in Shoreditch closed it. James's sons and inheritors thus were left with no playing place. Their £1000-worth of new and excellent house was now absolutely, and for all they knew permanently, unusable. They rented the Curtain Theatre at Shoreditch as a short-term measure while they thought what to do next.

Eventually they found a site on Bankside in Southwark and turned to Peter Street for help. At the end of 1598, while people were preoccupied with Christmas, he and his team dismantled The Theatre and transported the 'wood and timber' by way of Bishopsgate and Gracechurch streets to the bridge (then the only one in London) for carrying across the river to the south bank. The job required skilled work: the valuable framing timbers of The Theatre had to be extricated from lath and plaster and used to form the skeleton of the Globe Theatre on Bankside. Shakespeare, who is known to have been in Southwark at the time, and the brothers would have been able to ensure that their new playing place met their precise requirements—and especially those of Richard, who would grace its stage and that of its successor for the rest of his life.

Ben Jonson dates his second play for the company, *Every Man out of his Humour*, to autumn 1599, and it was probably one of the first new shows to be performed at the Globe (Burbage is listed here as first of the 'Comoedians'; Shakespeare is not listed). The Globe was financed, managed, and owned by leading members of the company, the first professional theatre for the specific use of one resident group. The system of management later caused resentment among some younger actors, who demanded more of the profits for players and less for investors.

Around this time, although the place and date are unknown, Richard Burbage married Winifred Turner (d. 1642): it must have been before 7 October 1601, when Simon Forman noted that 'Winfret Burbidg', aged twenty-five, had consulted him, complaining of 'moch pain head back belly shoulders' (Bodl. Oxf., MS Ashmole 411, fol. 150). Between 1603 and 1619 the couple had eight children (the last born posthumously to Richard) baptized at St Leonard, Shoreditch, all but one dying young. The survivor was William (*bap.* 6 Nov 1616), presumably named in memory of his father's oldest friend and colleague, who had died at Stratford upon Avon the previous April.

The King's Men James VI of Scotland, who on 24 March 1603 succeeded Queen Elizabeth as James I of England, was enthusiastic about plays and generous to players. By letters patent dated 19 May, the new company—the King's Men, the first company to enjoy the direct patronage of the sovereign—assumed their rights and title with unprecedented speed. The list of nine names was formally headed by Lawrence Fletcher, who had accompanied the king from the Scottish court, but the active list is headed by Shakespeare and Burbage. Jonson's third play for the company, *Sejanus*, was staged during the king's first Christmas in London, and the cast was headed by Burbage. In 1604 Burbage, Shakespeare, and seven other players were granted 4½ yards of red cloth each for their royal liveries to accompany the king on his progress through the City.

In January 1605 Sir Walter Cope wrote to Robert Cecil at court about the problems of entertaining the duke of Holstein, Queen Anne's brother, who was visiting London. Cope had spent the whole morning fruitlessly 'huntyng for players Juglers & Suche kinde of Creaturs', he said, and had left notes for them:

> burbage ys come, & Sayes ther ys no new playe that the queen hath not seene, but they have Revyved an olde one, Cawled Loves Labore lost which for Wytt & mirthe he sayes will please her excedingly … Burbage ys my messenger Ready attendyng yor pleasure.   (Hatfield House, Cecil papers 189/95)

On 31 May 1610 Burbage and John Rice (a former apprentice of John Heminges) took part in a water pageant honouring Prince Henry. The two 'rode upon the two fishes and made the speeches', spending the substantial sum of £17 10s. 6d. on their robes and other adornments. The city chamberlain ordered that they be reimbursed and allowed to keep the 'Taffety silke and other necessaries' (CLRO, aldermen's repertory 29, 5 June, fol. 232v).

Blackfriars Theatre regained, 1608–1609; the second Globe, 1614 In 1600, faced with competition from the Globe, Henslowe's rival company, the Admiral's Men, had commissioned Peter Street to build them a theatre, the Fortune, outside the north wall of the City, and left Bankside. The Burbages, no doubt short of cash after building the Globe, granted a twenty-one-year lease of the Blackfriars playhouse which they had been forbidden to use to a scrivener and entrepreneur, Henry Evans, for use by a boy company. Soon Evans had money troubles, surrendered the lease, and enabled the brothers to move in: they did so in 1608 and were open for business in 1609. It is not known who refurbished the place for them; Street had died in May.

On 29 June 1613, during a performance of Shakespeare's *Henry VIII*, the Globe was burnt down: as a contemporary 'Sonnett' has it:

> Out runne the knightes, out runne the lordes,
> And there was great a doe.
> Some lost their hattes, and some their swordes,
> Then out runne Burbidge too.
> (Chambers, 2.421)

The playhouse was rebuilt in 1614, 'in far fairer manner than before'—more expense for the company.

In the winter of 1612–13 the King's Men had been exceptionally hard worked by the court. During preparations for the wedding of Princess Elizabeth and Frederick, elector palatine, on 14 February 1613, they gave twenty performances at court, eight of Shakespeare's plays. At this period they were also approached by John Webster with his dark tragedy *The Duchess of Malfi*. They staged this successfully at the Blackfriars, probably in spring 1614, and then at the new Globe. Burbage played Ferdinand, the embodiment of evil, whose stated aim is to drive his twin sister to despair. Jonson, in his *Bartholomew Fair* (1614), provides a neat reference to Burbage's universal renown at this time. When the puppet master shows his little figures in a basket, a young gentleman asks: 'Which is your Burbage now?' James Burbage had always intended Blackfriars to be an all-year-round indoor playhouse: by now it was the place to see Burbage play Shakespeare, the Globe having become the secondary venue.

The only seventeenth-century description of Burbage the actor—in general terms—is by Richard Flecknoe (*d.* 1678?), who writes of 'a delightful Proteus, so wholly transforming himself into his Part, and putting off himself with his Cloathes, as he never (not so much as in the Tyring-house) assum'd himself again until the Play was ended' (Chambers, 4.370). Nothing is known of Burbage's appearance: a portrait now in Dulwich Picture Gallery is not safely identified as being of him. Queen Gertrude's description of Hamlet in act V, scene ii, of the play as 'fat' and breathless after the second bout of the fight with Laertes has caused puzzlement. All the plays have been fruitlessly scoured for a comparable usage, but the *Treatise* by Nicholas Hilliard (written at about the same time, *c.*1600) provides an example. Hilliard explains to aspiring miniaturists that a colour may not 'take' because 'some sweatye hand or *fattye* finger' has touched the parchment (N. Hilliard, *Treatise*, ed. R. K. R. Thornton, 1981, 98). (Gertrude clearly proffers a napkin to Hamlet to wipe his forehead and stop the sweat running into his eyes.) Audiences loved a good fight, and Shakespeare provided a carefully plotted and exciting one: a portly prince lumbering about the small stage would have provoked derision.

Death and reputation Burbage uttered his last words on Friday 12 March 1619: the nuncupative will (Honigmann and Brock, 17, 114–15) simply confirms Winifred as executrix. The seven witnesses included his wife, son, and daughter-in-law, and two fellow members of the King's Men, Nicholas Tooley and Richard Robinson. Burbage died on the following day, and the entry in the parish register of St Leonard, Shoreditch, in especially large letters, reads: 'Richard Burbadge Player, was buried the xvith of Marche'. He was in his fifty-first year. He was reported to have left more than £300—a very large sum—in 'land' (real estate). The available evidence strongly suggests that James and his sons all died intestate (or virtually so, in the case of Richard) deliberately: it seems that they were wealthy men, who preferred to conceal the facts. In the next local tax list after Richard's death Winifred is entered as the householder in Holywell Street. Her father, Edmund Turner of St Leonard, Shoreditch, who had presumably been living with her, died intestate in 1622, and letters of administration were granted to her on 6 August; on 31 October she was married by licence to Richard Robinson at St Mary Magdalen, Old Fish Street, and in the tax list of 1623–4 his

name replaces hers as householder. Winifred Robinson was buried at Shoreditch on 2 May 1642, and Robinson, 'a Player', at St Anne Blackfriars on 23 March 1648. Almost nothing is known of William, son of Richard and Winifred: his last appearance is in an indenture dated 25 May 1647, when he and Cuthbert's heir Elizabeth and son-in-law George Bingley sold a small plot of land in Blackfriars, for £80, to the adjoining Society of Apothecaries.

There were quantities of tributes to the great actor from theatre lovers, ranging from the constantly quoted 'Exit Burbadge' to an anonymous epitaph of turgid rhyming couplets more than eighty lines long, which does at least list some of the great parts he played. John Chamberlain, writing on 19 March to Sir Dudley Carleton, reported that all theatres were to remain closed until after the funeral of Queen Anne (who had died at the beginning of the month), 'to the great hinderance of our players … one speciall man among them Burbage is lately dead' (PRO, SP 14/107/43). Lord Pembroke, in a letter dated Whitehall 20 May 1619, wrote that he could not bear to attend a play performed after a great dinner for the French ambassador 'so soone after the loss of my old acquaintance Burbadg' (BL, Egerton MS 2592, fol. 81). This was William, the third earl, to whom, with his brother Philip, fourth earl, John Heminges and Henry Condell dedicated the Shakespeare first folio four years later. The only theatre man who seems to have contributed to the chorus of praise was the playwright Thomas Middleton, who was bold enough to imply that the prevailing sorrow was at the loss of player rather than queen. In a collection of poems published later, he produced some elegant lines:

> Astronomers and Stargazers this year
> Write but of four eclipses, five appear,
> Death interposing Burbage and there staying,
> Hath made a visible eclipse of playing.

But in general the tributes were notable for quantity rather than quality.

In 1634 Cuthbert Burbage, in a short family pedigree for the current visitation of London, entered his brother as 'the famous actor on the stage' (*Visitation of London*, 121). By benign providence, the lives of the greatest of playwrights and the first great English actor coincided almost exactly. It is not possible to list the many roles—mostly Shakespearian—that Burbage played (the records are hopelessly patchy and often non-existent), but it is known that he excelled in the tragedies, notably *Othello*, *Hamlet*, and *King Lear*; he also had a great success in the ever-popular *Richard III*. Playwright and player must have been in complete accord, and Burbage must have had a phenomenal memory. His was a life of constant learning of leading parts in newly written plays; morning rehearsals of current plays; afternoon performances for the public; many late-night command performances at court; and pressing invitations—probably often unrecorded—from the young lawyers at their inns of court in London, and from great houses in and away from the capital. In Flecknoe's words, the life of this actor was 'nothing else but action' (Chambers, 4.370); he did well to reach the age of fifty.   MARY EDMOND

Sources C. W. Wallace, *The first London theatre: materials for a history* (1913) • M. Edmond, 'Yeomen, citizens, gentlemen and players: the Burbages and their connections', *Elizabethan theater: essays in honor of S. Schoenbaum*, ed. R. B. Parker and S. P. Zitner (1996), 30–49 • M. Edmond, 'Peter Street, 1553–1609: builder of playhouses', *Shakespeare Survey*, 45 (1993), 101–14 • *The visitation of London, anno Domini 1633, 1634, and 1635, made by Sir Henry St George*, 1, ed. J. J. Howard and J. L. Chester, Harleian Society, 15 (1880), 121 • A. Gurr, *The Shakespearian playing companies* (1996) • lay subsidy rolls, PRO, E 179/142/279, E 179/142/284 • 'Sharers papers', *Malone Society Collections*, 2/1 (1913), 362–73 • C. C. Stopes, *Burbage, and Shakespeare's stage* (1913), 116–23 • E. K. Chambers, *The Elizabethan stage*, 4 vols. (1923) • G. E. Bentley, *The Jacobean and Caroline stage*, 7 vols. (1941–68) • M. Eccles, 'Elizabethan actors, I: A–D', *N&Q*, 236 (1991), 38–49, esp. 43–4 • E. A. J. Honigmann and S. Brock, eds., *Playhouse wills, 1558–1642: an edition of wills by Shakespeare and his contemporaries in the London theatre* (1993), 113–15 • parish register, St Stephen, Coleman Street, GL, MSS 4448/4449/1 [baptism] • parish register, Shoreditch, St Leonard, GL, MSS 7493 [baptism, marriage, burial] • parish register, St Mary Magdalen, Old Fish Street, GL, MS 11529 [marriage] • letters of administration, 6 Aug 1622, GL, archdeaconry of London, MS 9050/5, fol. 153v [Edmund Turner]

Burberry, Thomas (1835–1926), men's outfitter, was born on 27 August 1835 at Brockham Green, near Dorking, Surrey, the son of Thomas Burberry, farmer and nonconformist. Following an elementary education at Brockham Green village school, Burberry was apprenticed to a local draper's shop before opening his own outfitting business in 1856 in Westminster Street, Basingstoke. The shop expanded rapidly, benefiting from Burberry's knowledge of the retail trade and the requirements of the local farming community. He was particularly concerned with adapting the practical and watertight qualities of traditional linen farmers' smocks to a broader range of clothing products. With that aim in mind Burberry entered into experimental trials with British cotton manufacturers in order to produce a cheaper alternative weatherproof textile that would hold a strong appeal for the growing ranks of upper middle-class sportsmen and those following country pursuits, who made up the bulk of bespoke menswear consumers in the latter half of the nineteenth century.

In 1858 Burberry married Catherine Hannah, daughter of John Newman, currier, at the Salem Chapel, Strand, London. His second wife, named Mary, outlived him. The Basingstoke shop continued to prosper, employing eighty staff by 1871. These were later joined by Burberry's two sons, Thomas and Arthur, and in 1885 by R. B. Rolls who took on the position of marketing and retail manager. Experimentation with the design of wind- and rainproof textiles and garments continued into the 1880s, coinciding with a popular interest in rational and artistic dress reform. In 1884 Burberry's new 'gabardine', a hardwearing cloth waterproofed in the yarn before weaving and then closely woven and proofed again without the use of rubber, attracted approval at the International Health Exhibition in South Kensington, and in 1888 Burberry took out a patent for a new lighter material adapted for the garments of athletes.

From 1889 Burberry commissioned his youngest son, Arthur, to consolidate metropolitan patronage through giving fittings and taking orders from wealthy visitors at the Jermyn Street Hotel, Piccadilly. This led to the opening of a flagship London store at 30 Haymarket under the management of R. B. Rolls in 1891, a mill and workrooms in the East End in 1892, and a wholesale warehouse in Golden Square in 1900. All of these concerns were run under paternal principles, inspired by Burberry's strong Baptist beliefs. Development of the business also incorporated the fostering of overseas and colonial clients, and between 1900 and 1914 branches of the shop were opened in New York, Buenos Aires, Paris, and Montevideo.

In common with other clothing retailers, Burberry recognized the importance of promotion and publicity and ensured through R. B. Rolls, a partner in the firm by 1901, that the Burberry trade mark was associated in advertising and media coverage with specific 'heroic' personalities. Lord Kitchener and Lord Baden Powell both adopted Burberry weatherproofs from the time of the Second South African War, leading to commissions for uniforms from the army and the Royal Marines by 1906. Sir E. H. Shackleton, Captain Scott, and Roald Amundsen all proved high-profile customers in choosing Burberry textiles for kits and tents on their polar expeditions, and the pioneer aviator Claude Grahame-White provided a precedent for the Royal Flying Corps in its decision to use Burberry as a clothing supplier during the First World War.

Burberry retired to Abbots Court near Weymouth in 1917 and devoted his time to personal religious and humanitarian causes. His adherence to the principles of healthy living which had underpinned the philosophy of his clothing and textile design found outlets in sport, teetotal and anti-smoking campaigns, and support for the Sunday closing movement. Burberry's achievement lay in the marrying of these ethics to an astute understanding of the sartorial demands of the English gentleman. Individual items of Burberry clothing thus incorporated many concessions to the radical dress reform movement, such as the prioritizing of ease of movement and comfort, quality of manufacture, and the use of natural materials, while retaining the appearance of British traditionalism which Burberry clothes came to epitomize. Having witnessed the transition of the firm to a public company in 1920, Burberry died at Crossways, his home in Hook, near Basingstoke, on 4 April 1926.

CHRISTOPHER BREWARD

Sources 'In the Burberry tradition', 1981, Burberry Archives, London [unpublished publicity brochure] • M. Baren, *How it all began up the high street* (1996) • Company papers and brochures, Burberry Archive, London • *Men's Wear Journal* (c.1870–1926) • *Tailor and Cutter Journal* (c.1870–1926) • *Daily News* (7 April 1926) • *CGPLA Eng. & Wales* (1926) • m. cert. • d. cert.
Archives Burberry Archives, London
Wealth at death £69,443 9s. 11d.: resworn probate, 3 July 1926, *CGPLA Eng. & Wales*

Burbidge family (*per. c.*1870–1966), department store managers and directors, were managing directors and chairmen of Harrods from 1893 to 1959, through three generations. The first member of the family to enter the business was **Sir Richard Burbidge**, first baronet (1847–

1917), born on 2 March 1847 at Manor Farm, South Wraxhall, Wiltshire, the fifth of ten children of George Bishop Burbidge (1795–1861), farmer, and his wife, Elizabeth, *née* Clarke (1808/9–1873). Burbidge attended schools in Devizes, then spent two years at Dr Gilchrist's Spa Villa Academy in Melksham. On his father's death Burbidge was apprenticed to Jonathan Puckeridge, a grocer and wine merchant originally from Wiltshire then trading in Oxford Street, London. After his apprenticeship and a year as an assistant, Burbidge established his own successful grocery business in Marylebone. Burbidge's association with Wiltshire continued and he was president for many years of the Wiltshiremen in London society.

On 9 May 1868 Burbidge married Emily (*d.* 1905), youngest daughter of Jeremiah Woodman of Melksham, Wiltshire; they had two sons and four daughters. Burbidge enjoyed her help and support until her death. On 22 August 1910 he married his second wife, Lilian, youngest daughter of James Ambrose Preece, of Bartestree Court, Herefordshire. In his private life Burbidge was a devoted husband and father, and he kept in regular contact with his mother and siblings.

When Burbidge became aware that large department stores were coming into favour he worked for several, taking a post as superintendent for the Army and Navy Auxiliary, and as manager at Whiteleys and at the West Kensington Stores, before being appointed general manager at Harrods Stores Ltd in 1891, two years after its flotation on Charles Digby Harrod's retirement from his thriving family business in 1889.

Burbidge was appointed managing director of Harrods in 1893. The minutes of a board meeting held on 6 June 1917, immediately after his death, record that:

> It was resolved to record the Directors' very high appreciation of his uprightness of character and outstanding commercial ability during his many years with the Company … Under his Managing Directorship the trade has enormously expanded, until it now reaches to all parts of the world, while during this period the annual profit has increased from £16,071 to £309,227 before the War. The staff has increased from 200 to 6000, and the hours of employment have been substantially reduced and the working conditions improved all round. His was an attractive and charming personality; he endeared himself to all with whom he came into daily contact. His loss will be felt not only at Harrods but in wider circles outside.

Burbidge pioneered benefits for shop assistants. The store closed at 6 p.m., not 9, 10, or even 11 p.m. as was common. He instituted one day early closing long before the Shops Act came into force, set up a well-appointed staff sports club, organized training schemes, and established both provident and pension funds for staff. Burbidge himself, however, worked long hours. He rose at 5.30 a.m., rode in nearby Hyde Park from 6 to 6.45, left for Harrods at 6.55, and after a gruelling schedule of work, meetings, and decision making, returned home about 7 p.m.

Burbidge's success lay in anticipating and developing demand for services and products in Harrods. He had objected to lifts as 'new machines', but in 1898 he allowed a French company to install the first escalator in Britain. It attracted enormous publicity, and was a great convenience for customers. His refreshment rooms, with food at reasonable prices, encouraged ladies to linger shopping in the store, and 'retiring or dressing rooms' were provided for their comfort. The lavish decoration created between 1894 and 1911 was unrivalled. Burbidge held directorships in other stores including Dickins and Jones Ltd, the Hudson Bay Company, and Harrods (Buenos Aires) Ltd, which he founded in 1913.

Burbidge sat on government and charitable committees which benefited from his skills for organization and business. He was honorary treasurer of the tariff commission; a member of the commission looking into the wages of Post Office workers; one of the Crystal Palace trustees, a group that made possible the purchase of the Crystal Palace for the nation in 1913 (Burbidge donated £2500 publicly and £30,000 anonymously to the fund); and he served on the committees of the Discharged Soldiers' and Sailors' Association and the National Association for the Employment of ex-Soldiers. He gave aid, both personally and through his association with Harrods, to the Ministry of Munitions, and was chairman of the committee on the Royal Aircraft Factory and of the executive and war emergency committees for the provision of invalid kitchens. Burbidge provided premises and organized operations for Queen Alexandra's Field Fund Force, King Albert's Civilian Hospital Fund, and Lady French's Fund. He set up a successful scheme for training women, in reduced circumstances because of the war, to take up business careers. He was a religious man and had been a churchwarden. He was also a justice of the peace for London county. In 1916 he was awarded a baronetcy in the new year's honours list. He died at his London home, 51 Hans Mansions, Knightsbridge, after a full day at work on 31 May 1917 and was buried on 5 June at Littleton Park, Shepperton. He was survived by his second wife.

Burbidge was succeeded by his eldest son, **Sir (Richard) Woodman Burbidge**, second baronet (1872–1945), born on 7 December 1872 at 35 Upper George Street, Marylebone, London. Educated at St Marylebone Grammar School, he joined Harrods Stores Ltd in 1893, becoming general manager in 1901. On the death of his father in 1917 he became the second baronet, and was appointed managing director of Harrods Stores Ltd, by then the biggest store in the country. He became chairman in 1921, a post he held until his death in 1945, retiring as managing director in 1935. He also sat on the boards of Dickins and Jones Ltd, D. H. Evans Ltd, and Kendal Milne & Co., Manchester, which together formed the Harrods Group, as well as of Harrods (Buenos Aires) Ltd. He travelled frequently to North and South America on business.

Burbidge served on many committees including the Ministry of Munitions stores purchases advisory council, the Ministry of Munitions staff investigation committee, and the Empire Marketing Board, and he was treasurer of the Tariff Board. Burbidge was appointed CBE in 1919, a commander of the order of Leopold II of Belgium by King Albert in 1920, in recognition of organizing the construction, by Harrods Stores Ltd, of hospitals and airsheds behind the Belgian front line, and in 1917 he received the Marie Regina cross of Romania for organizing relief for Romanian refugees. Burbidge inherited his father's capacity for work, but also enjoyed sports such as coursing, horse-racing, and yachting.

On 2 September 1896 Burbidge married Catherine Jemima (1872–1964), daughter of Henry Grant of Sodbury House, Great Clacton, Essex; they had one son, Richard Grant Woodman Burbidge, and three daughters. Burbidge always affectionately referred to his wife as Mother when talking to staff, and they both took a great interest in the Harrodian Sports Club, Lady Burbidge presenting prizes at the Harrodian Club annual sports days long after her husband's death. Both ensured that staff amenities improved, providing a clinic, staff bank, and staff and buyers' councils. Burbidge was a religious man and he encouraged staff in religious studies, and he and Lady Burbidge regularly attended the staff Bible study group meetings.

Burbidge was involved in the building of the YWCA headquarters in London (completed in 1932), and the Purley Schools (for orphans of employees in the textile trade) benefited to the sum of £53,716 during his year as appeals chairman.

Burbidge died at his country home, Cisswood, Lower Beeding, Horsham, on 3 June 1945 and was buried at Littleton on 7 June. Queen Marie of Yugoslavia was represented among the large gathering at his memorial service at Holy Trinity Church, Brompton, on 11 June. He was succeeded by his son, **Sir Richard Grant Woodman Burbidge**, third baronet (1897–1966), who was born at 53 Stanhope Gardens, Kensington, London, on 23 June 1897. Burbidge was educated at Rugby School and commissioned into the army in 1914. He served in the RASC and saw action with the 47th division train, rising to the rank of captain. He trained in the retail trade in America in 1919 before joining Harrods Ltd in 1920. He succeeded his father as managing director in 1935, and was chairman from 1945 until 1959, when the Harrods Group was taken over by House of Fraser. He served for a while as managing director under Hugh Fraser but the two men did not get on. Burbidge later held directorships at British Home Stores Ltd and Maple & Co. Ltd. During the Second World War he was one of the civilians on the board of the Navy, Army and Air Force Institutes.

Burbidge married Gladys Amelia, eldest daughter of Charles Frederick Kearley, a contractor of Kensington, on 14 October 1925. They had a son and daughter. This marriage was dissolved, and on 6 December 1946 he married a widow, Joan Elizabeth Hamilton, *née* Mosley. Very much the traditionalist in his manner, he was well liked by his staff, most of whom he knew by name, and considered charming by all who knew him. Burbidge was appointed CBE in 1946. He died at his home, Walnut Tree Cottage, Ashampstead, Berkshire, on 2 February 1966. He was survived by his second wife.

Under the careful direction of the Burbidge family Harrods attained its status as the biggest, most elegant and best stocked of London's great department stores. The magnificent terracotta building became one of the capital's landmarks and the many departments, particularly the vast food halls, earned a worldwide reputation for quality.   N. HANSEN

Sources *The Sphere* (8 Jan 1916), 1 • A. C. B. Menzies, *Modern men of mark* (1921), 43–108 • *In memoriam* (June 1917), 1–12 [obit. booklet] • minute books, Harrods Ltd, 1891–1966, HS9.1.1–12 • *Harrodian Gazette* (July 1917), 141–3 • *Harrodian Gazette* (Nov 1914), 1–3 • *Harrodian Gazette* (June 1945), 227–31 • *Harrodian Gazette* (1960), 68–9 • *Harrodian Gazette* (1959), 507–11 • *Harrodian Gazette* (1964), 58 • *Harrodian Gazette* (1966), 3 • M. Moss and A. Turton, *A legend of retailing: the House of Fraser* (1989) • *The Times* (1 June 1917), 9e • *The Times* (4 June 1945), 6e • *The Times* (3 Feb 1966), 17a • m. certs. [Richard Burbidge] • d. cert. [Richard Burbidge] • d. cert. [R. G. W. Burbidge] • d. cert. [R. W. Burbidge] • d. cert. [George Bishop Burbidge] • d. cert. [Elizabeth Burbidge, *née* Clarke] • private information (2004) [E. McNeal]
Archives Harrods Ltd, London, company archives • LMA, papers | University of Sheffield, corresp. with W. A. S. Hewins
Likenesses J. H. Bacon, oils, 1909 (Richard Burbidge), Harrods Ltd, London • D. Jagger, oils, 1943 (Richard Woodman Burbidge), Harrods Ltd, London • P. Vincze, bronze and silver medallions, 1960 (Richard Grant Woodman Burbidge), Harrods Ltd, London • J. Gunn, oils (Richard Grant Woodman Burbidge), Harrods Ltd, London • Harrods Ltd, group portraits, photographs (Richard Woodman Burbidge and family), Harrods Ltd, London • Harrods Ltd, group portraits, photographs (Richard Grant Woodman Burbidge and family), Harrods Ltd, London • Harrods Ltd, photographs (Richard Burbidge), Harrods Ltd, London • Harrods Ltd, photographs (Richard Woodman Burbidge), Harrods Ltd, London • Harrods Ltd, photographs (Richard Grant Woodman Burbidge), Harrods Ltd, London
Wealth at death £186,262 9s.—Richard Burbidge: probate, 29 Aug 1917, *CGPLA Eng. & Wales* • £146,998 13s. 6d.—Richard Woodman Burbidge: probate, 30 Aug 1945, *CGPLA Eng. & Wales* • £122,518—Richard Grant Woodman Burbidge: probate, 15 Aug 1966, *CGPLA Eng. & Wales*

Burbidge, Edward (1839–1903), liturgical scholar, born on 9 August 1839 at Laura Place, Upper Clapton, London, was the younger son in the family of two sons and two daughters of William Smith Burbidge, distiller, of London, and his wife, Sarah Jane Peacock. Privately educated owing to delicate health, he was on 26 May 1858 admitted to Emmanuel College, Cambridge. In 1859 he was elected to a Whichcote scholarship and to an Ash and Browne exhibition. In 1860 he won a Thorpe scholarship, and graduated BA in 1862 with a second class in the classical tripos, proceeding MA in 1865. He was ordained deacon in 1863 and priest in 1864. After serving curacies at Aldbourne, Wiltshire (1863–8), and at Warminster (1868–73), he became in 1873 rector, and in 1882 vicar, of Backwell, Somerset. In 1887 he was appointed to a prebendal stall in Wells Cathedral. He married on 21 April 1869 Susan Mary, youngest daughter of William Topley Humphrey, vicar of East Stockwith, Lincolnshire. On resigning his living in October 1902, he retired to Weston-super-Mare where in his house, Adare, he died on 7 February 1903, and was buried at Backwell, survived by his wife, four sons, and three daughters.

Burbidge took an active interest in education, especially in the improvement of voluntary schools, and for many years he acted as diocesan inspector. But he was chiefly known as a zealous student of ancient liturgies. His *Liturgies and Offices of the Church* (1885), to which was prefixed a catalogue of the remains of Archbishop Cranmer's library, formed a scholarly commentary on the original sources of the Book of Common Prayer, and was a standard work in its day. Burbidge also published *The Parish Priest's Book of Offices and Instructions for the Sick* (1871), *A Plain Manual of Holy Communion* (1878; 2nd edn, 1882), and *Peace with God* (1880).   G. S. WOODS, *rev.* H. C. G. MATTHEW

Sources *The Times* (10 Feb 1903) · Crockford (1902) · private information (1912)
Wealth at death £20,305 16s. 10d.: probate, 30 March 1903, *CGPLA Eng. & Wales*

Burbidge, Frederick William Thomas (1847–1905), horticultural writer and explorer, was born at Wymeswold, Leicestershire, on 21 March 1847, the son of Thomas Burbidge, farmer and fruit grower, and his wife, Mary Spencer. He was educated at village schools and entered the gardens of the Royal Horticultural Society at Chiswick as a student in 1868, proceeding in the same year to the Royal Gardens, Kew. Here he showed skill as a draughtsman and was partly employed in making drawings of plants in the herbarium. Leaving Kew in 1870 he joined the staff of *Garden* where he stayed until 1877, writing under the pseudonym Veronica. He also wrote for *The Floral Magazine*. During this period he published a number of works including *Cool Orchids and How to Grow Them* (1874) and *Cultivated Plants, their Propagation and Improvement* (1877). These works drew much appreciation from contemporaries including Gladstone. Many of the plates included were drawn by Burbidge himself.

In 1876 Burbidge married Mary Wade (*d.* 1905); they had no children. In 1877 he was sent by the nursery firm James Veitch & Sons as a collector to Borneo. He was absent for two years, during which time he also visited Johore, Brunei, and the Sulu Islands. He brought back many remarkable plants, especially: pitcher plants, such as *Nepenthes rajah* and *N. bicalcarata*; orchids, such as *Cypripedium laurenceanum*, *Dendrobium burbidgei*, and *Aërides burbidgei*; and ferns, such as *Alsophila burbidgei* and *Polypodium burbidgei*. The chronicle of his journey was published in 1880 as *The Gardens of the Sun, or, A Naturalist's Journal on the Mountains and in the Forests and Swamps of Borneo and the Sulu Archipelago*. The first set of the dried specimens brought back by him numbered nearly a thousand species, and was presented by Veitch to the Kew herbarium. Sir Joseph Hooker named the scitamineous *Burbidgea nitida* 'in recognition of Burbidge's eminent services to horticulture, whether as a collector in Borneo, or as author of *Cultivated Plants, their Propagation and Improvement*, a work which should be in every gardener's library' (*Botanical Magazine*, 1879, tab 6403).

In 1879 Burbidge was appointed curator of the botanical gardens of Trinity College, Dublin, at Glasnevin, in which post he did much to encourage gardening in Ireland. In 1889 Dublin University conferred on him the honorary degree of MA, and in 1894 he became keeper of the college park as well as curator of the botanical gardens. While at Dublin he published *The Chrysanthemum: its History, Culture,*

Classification and Nomenclature (1883) and *The Book of the Scented Garden* (1905). In 1897 Burbidge became one of the first recipients of the Royal Horticultural Society's Victoria medal. He was also a member of the Royal Irish Academy. Though of only moderate ability as a cultivator, he was noted for his horticultural writings and expert draughtsmanship. Burbidge died from heart disease on 24 December 1905, and was buried in Dublin.

G. S. BOULGER, *rev.* ALEXANDER GOLDBLOOM

Sources Desmond, *Botanists*, rev. edn, 118 · A. M. Coat, *Quest for plants* (1969) · *Curtis's Botanical Magazine*, 3rd ser., 45 (1879), tab 6403 · *Journal of Botany, British and Foreign*, 44 (1906), 80 · *Gardeners' Chronicle*, 3rd ser., 38 (1905), 460 · *Gardeners' Chronicle*, 3rd ser., 39 (1906), 10 · *Bulletin of Miscellaneous Information* [RBG Kew] (1906), 392–3 · *Journal of the Kew Guild* (1906), 326–7 · J. H. Veitch, *Hortus Veitchii* (1906), 75–8, 235 · WWW
Archives NHM, botanical sketches · RBG Kew, mainly drawings · TCD, letters
Likenesses P. Haburgh, portrait, Hunt Botanical Library · portrait, repro. in *Gardeners' Chronicle*, 2 (1889), 212–13 · portrait, repro. in *Gardeners' Chronicle*, 1 (1896), 736 · portrait, repro. in *Gardeners' Chronicle*, 3rd ser., 38 (1905), 460 · portrait, repro. in *Garden*, 66 (1904), iv · portrait, repro. in *Garden*, 69 (1906), 16 · portrait, repro. in *Journal of the Kew Guild*

Burbidge, Sir Richard, first baronet (1847–1917). *See under* Burbidge family (*per. c.*1870–1966).

Burbidge, Sir Richard Grant Woodman, third baronet (1897–1966). *See under* Burbidge family (*per. c.*1870–1966).

Burbidge, Sir (Richard) Woodman, second baronet (1872–1945). *See under* Burbidge family (*per. c.*1870–1966).

Burbury, Charlotte Amy May (1832–1895). *See under* Kennedy, Marion Grace (1836–1914).

Burbury [*née* Hicks], **Edwina Jane** (1818/19–1870), writer, was the daughter of Edward Raymond Hicks and his wife, Frances Pickering. Nothing is known of her early life, but she married Thomas Potter Burbury (*bap.* 1815, *d.* 1868), solicitor, on 9 August 1841; they had at least two children, Thomas Raymond in 1842 and Florence Elizabeth in 1843. Her husband appears to have fallen into financial difficulties early in their marriage. In 1848 she published her first work, *How to Spend a Week Happily*, a religious tale for young people, the success of which led her to write a sequel, *Mabel Trevor*, in 1853. She became a contributor to *Sharpe's London Magazine* at the beginning of 1849 'for the support of herself and her young family'. In 1849 the editor, Frank Smedley, aware of her friendship with G. P. R. James, published *Seven Tales by Seven Authors*—a collection of short stories including one by James—with the aim of donating all the proceeds to Edwina Burbury. Her pecuniary difficulties do not seem to have been immediately alleviated, however; Charles Dickens's accounts show him 'contributing a subscription of £5 in favour of Mrs Burbury' in 1855. Burbury's own tale in this collection was 'The Trust', described in the 'Preface' as 'not actually "founded on fact"' but 'suggested by some of the bitter experiences of her own eventful career'; the story tells of the heroine's husband suffering severe financial losses and being imprisoned for bankruptcy, and of her children being taken into the care of her brother-in-law's family and one of them dying through neglect. How much of this is applicable to Burbury is, like so much of her life, a matter of conjecture. Of her contributions to periodicals and five works, she is most famous for her novel *Florence Sackville* (1853), which charts a woman's struggle for independence and love, and success in becoming an author, and was enjoyed by Charlotte Brontë. All her fiction has a strongly Christian emphasis. Her husband died on 15 March 1868 in Bewdley, leaving his wife 'debts' and his children his 'best love'. Edwina Burbury died in Wallingford on 17 February 1870 at the age of fifty-one, her occupation being listed merely as 'widow'. She is frequently confused in reference works with Selina Bunbury.

CATHERINE MALONE

Sources 'Preface', *Seven tales by seven authors, edited by the author of 'Frank Fairlegh'*, ed. F. E. Smedley (1849) · *The letters of Charlotte Brontë*, ed. M. Smith, 2 vols. (1995–2000), vol. 1 · *The letters of Charles Dickens*, ed. M. House, G. Storey, and others, 7 (1993), 636 · T. J. Wise and J. A. Symington, eds., *The Brontës: their lives, friendships, and correspondence*, 4 vols. (1933); repr. (1980) · d. cert. · m. cert.

Burbury, Samuel Hawksley (1831–1911), lawyer and mathematician, was born on 18 May 1831 at Kenilworth, the only son of Samuel Burbury, farmer, of Clarendon Square, Leamington, and his wife, Helen. He was educated at Kensington grammar school, Shrewsbury School (1848–50), and at St John's College, Cambridge. He was head boy at Shrewsbury, and at university he won distinction in both classics and mathematics, winning the Porson prize twice (1852 and 1853), the Craven university scholarship (1853), and the chancellor's classical medal (1854). He graduated BA as fifteenth wrangler and second classic in 1854, and became a fellow of his college in the same year. He proceeded MA in 1857. On 6 October 1855 Burbury enrolled as a student at Lincoln's Inn, and was called to the bar on 7 June 1858. He married Alice Ann, daughter of Thomas Edward Taylor JP, of Dodworth Hall, Barnsley, Yorkshire, on 12 April 1860, and became a partner in the family's linen manufacturing firm. The couple had four sons and two daughters.

From 1860 Burbury practised at the parliamentary bar, but increasing deafness compelled him to take chamber practice only. While engaged in legal work he continued to take part in advanced mathematical study, chiefly in collaboration with his Cambridge friend Henry William Watson, with whom he wrote two treatises, *The Application of Generalised Co-ordinates to the Kinetics of a Material System* (1879) and *The Mathematical Theory of Electricity and Magnetism* (2 vols., 1885 and 1889). In these works they explored Maxwell's natural philosophy from a more formal mathematical standpoint. Burbury also wrote independently of Watson; he contributed a number of papers to the *Philosophical Magazine*, including one on the second law of thermodynamics in connection with the kinetic theory of gases, in 1876, and another, on a theorem in the dissipation of energy, in 1882.

Burbury was elected a fellow of the Royal Society in 1890, and was awarded an honorary degree of LLD by St Andrews in 1911. He had a wide scientific correspondence—in which he displayed a notably forceful manner of

expression—and was in frequent contact with Ludwig Boltzmann, who appreciated his facility as a critic. He died on 18 August 1911 at his home, 15 Melbury Road, Kensington, and was buried at Kensal Green cemetery. He was survived by his wife.   D. J. OWEN, *rev.* ALAN YOSHIOKA

Sources *Nature*, 87 (1911), 281–2 · G. H. B., *PRS*, 88A (1912–13), i–iv · *Proceedings of the London Mathematical Society*, 2nd ser., 10 (1912), iv–v · R. Hesketh, 'The conspicuous merit of a Victorian scientist', *Times Higher Education Supplement* (20 April 1973), 11 · *Men and women of the time* (1899) · J. E. Auden, ed., *Shrewsbury School register*, 3rd edn, 1: 1798–1908 (1928) · J. Foster, *Men-at-the-bar: a biographical hand-list of the members of the various inns of court*, 2nd edn (1885) · *The record of the Royal Society of London*, 4th edn (1940) · *CGPLA Eng. & Wales* (1911) · Venn, *Alum. Cant.*

Archives St John Cam., letters to Sir J. Larmor · UCL, letters to Sir Francis Galton

Likenesses W. E. Miller, portrait, 1884, repro. in Hesketh, 'The conspicuous merit of a Victorian scientist' · Maull & Fox, photographs, RS

Wealth at death £42,927 5s. 9d.: probate, 15 Dec 1911, *CGPLA Eng. & Wales*

Burch, Cecil Reginald [Bill] (1901–1983), physicist and engineer, was born at 2 Museum Road, Oxford, on 12 May 1901, the fifth child of George James Burch (1852–1914) and his wife, Constance Emily Jeffries, otherwise Baker. Soon after birth Burch was nicknamed Bill by his family and friends. His father was professor of physics at Reading University from 1892 to 1909 and was elected FRS in 1900. His mother founded and ran Norham Hall as a women's residence for language students from overseas. Burch attended the Dragon School, Oxford from 1908 to 1915; in 1981 he wrote of the debt he owed to the school for teaching him the valuable art of public speaking and for persuading Oundle School to admit him without fee. Burch's family was suffering considerable financial hardship at that time due to the closure of Norham Hall caused by the travel restrictions brought about by the First World War. At Oundle (1915–19), in addition to the classics, he was taught manual skills and encouraged to carry out experiments such as the distillation of coal tar. In his 1943 article 'A technologist looks at the future' Burch described how these skills not only helped him in his later work but also allowed him to develop good personal relationships with many technicians and workmen.

In 1919 Burch and his brother Francis entered Gonville and Caius College, Cambridge, with a scholarship; both took the natural sciences tripos, graduating in 1922, and both joined the Metropolitan-Vickers Co. Ltd in Manchester as college apprentices. This was a very creative phase of Burch's life. In the eleven years that he worked for Metropolitan-Vickers Burch's name appears on twenty-eight patents. Initially he worked with complex electric circuits and was involved in early transatlantic radio transmissions with the BBC. Later, with his colleague N. R. Davis, he developed the technique of induction heating in order to avoid the contamination problems caused by other methods of melting metals. Burch and Davis went on to design large induction furnaces for commercial steel making. This work led Burch to write his only book, *An Introduction to the Theory of Eddy-Current Heating* (1928).

In 1927 Burch began to experiment with vacuum distillation, the work for which he is, perhaps, best known. He developed oils and greases with very low vapour pressures (apiezon oils). Using these oils Burch designed oil condensation pumps which were widely used to create vacuums in, for example, large thermionic valves. One of the most famous applications of Burch's research in this area was by J. Cockcroft and E. T. S. Walton who used Burch's high vacuum tubes for part of their work on high voltage proton acceleration at the Cavendish Laboratory, Cambridge, in 1932. Burch also found that vacuum distillation could be used on other organic compounds such as vitamin A which had previously been extremely difficult to distil.

In February 1933 Burch's brother Francis, with whom he lived and worked, died very painfully following blood transfusions given during an operation for peritonitis. Francis's death greatly affected Burch, and he felt unable to continue at Metropolitan-Vickers as every day was a constant reminder of his brother. He left Manchester to go to the physics department at Imperial College, London, in September 1933 as Leverhulme fellow in optics, but remained a paid consultant to Metropolitan-Vickers. At Imperial College Burch entered the second phase of his career. He began studying the optics of non-spherical surfaces and quickly developed a new way of testing mirrors called the wavefront shearing interferometer. He gained his PhD in 1936. In 1936 he went to Bristol as a research associate to continue his optical work. Soon after his arrival Burch met Enid Grace Morice (1899/1900–c.1980), the daughter of Owen Henry Morice; she was also a lecturer. They married on 5 April 1937; they had one daughter, Ann Lindsay. In Bristol Burch built the first Schwarzschild aplanatic aspheric reflecting microscope. He spent many hours, usually at night when vibration was at a minimum, polishing mirrors by hand.

During the Second World War Burch worked with the Ministry of Aircraft Production to enhance the lenses used for aerial photography. He also spent time working at Metropolitan-Vickers on war-related projects and mirrors for his microscopes. During the war years he patented two lens improvements and a machine to grind mirror surfaces. After the war Burch continued to work in Bristol on microscopes which he exhibited at the Physical Society exhibition in January 1947. As a result he was inundated with requests from research workers for him to make similar microscopes. Much against his better judgement Burch found himself taking on the responsibility of a production run of ten microscopes as well as supervising PhD students in Bristol. As a result of stress caused by his inability to turn down the job, and the drugs he took to keep himself awake, Burch suffered a perforated ulcer which required surgery in 1953.

While recuperating in Cornwall, Burch became interested in mineral dressing by gravity concentration and invented a mineral classifier to improve tin recovery from mines. During the last years of his career Burch worked on a wide variety of projects including stethoscopes, brazing torches, and mathematical analysis. During his long career he published fifty-six papers and one book, and was granted forty patents. He retired officially from Bristol in 1966 but retained his room in college and continued to work for the rest of his life. Burch was awarded the Physical Society's Duddell medal in 1943, was elected fellow of the Royal Society in 1944, was awarded the society's Rumford medal for achievement in 1954, and was made CBE in 1958.

Burch was tall and very slender. He was a loner who spent long, irregular hours on his work which sometimes affected his health. He died at his home, 2 Holmes Grove, Henleaze, Bristol, on 19 July 1983.   MARY CROARKEN

Sources T. E. Allibone, *Memoirs FRS*, 30 (1984), 1–42 · autobiographical notes, RS · 'Burch, Cecil Reginald', *McGraw-Hill modern scientists and engineers* (1980), 1.161–2 · J. G. Crowther, *The Cavendish Laboratory, 1874–1974* (1974) · C. R. Burch, letter to headmaster, Dragon School, Oxford, 7 Oct 1981, Bristol University, Burch MSS · C. R. Burch and N. R. Davis, *An introduction to the theory of eddy-current heating* (1928) · C. R. Burch, 'Oils, greases and high vacua', *Nature*, 122 (1928), 729 · C. R. Burch, 'A technologist looks to the future', *Nature*, 152 (1943), 523–5 · C. R. Burch, 'University physics: the challenge of technology', *PRS*, 288A (1965), 467–77 · b. cert. · m. cert. · d. cert. · private information (2004)
Archives RS, personal record · University of Bristol Library, corresp. and papers | University of Bristol Library, corresp. with Sir Charles Frank
Likenesses photographs, c.1928–1948, repro. in Allibone, *Memoirs FRS* · photograph, c.1943, repro. in *Proceedings of the Physical Society*, 55 (1943) · photographs, Bristol University · sketch, repro. in 'Burch, Cecil Reginald'
Wealth at death £114,165: probate, 1 Nov 1983, *CGPLA Eng. & Wales*

Burch, Edward (*bap.* 1730, *d.* 1814), gem-engraver, son of Andrew Burch and his wife, Hannah Roberts, was baptized on 30 October 1730 at St Botolph, Aldgate, in the East End of London. Originally a Thames waterman, he felt drawn towards the arts and taught himself seal engraving. On 7 November 1752 he married Ann Stockley; they had two sons. He was probably in his mid-twenties when he joined the St Martin's Lane Academy, which exerted a lasting influence on him through his studies in the life class, coupled with the anatomy lectures of Dr William Hunter; his fellow artists became lifelong influential friends.

In 1760 Burch took part in the first public exhibition by the Society of Artists; in 1763 he appears in Thomas Mortimer's *Universal Directory* as 'Engraver in Stone', with an address at 'The upper end of Red-Lion-Court, Fleet Street'. In the same year he received the first of three premiums for gem-engraving from the Society for the Encouragement of Arts, Manufactures, and Commerce; he subsequently exhibited annually until 1769 with the Society of Artists, as did his gifted former apprentice, Nathaniel Marchant. He exhibited engraved gems, wax models, and casts in sulphur and plaster. The subjects were the fashionable copies from the antique, heads of worthies favoured for seals (his *Shakespeare*, exhibited in 1765, was a favourite), and portraits of contemporary sitters; but a *Judith with the Head of Holofernes* (exh. 1764) and three 'emblematical pieces' show a more idiosyncratic spirit. Even among the antique subjects, many were not simply copies of ancient models, but were based on studies in the life room and proudly inscribed INV after Burch's signature. Figures of Hercules, which demonstrated his grasp of anatomy and mastery of modelling, were frequent; among them, an *Anatomical Figure* '[d]esigned as a reposing Hercules … introduced every external muscle which is requisite for a figure six feet high' (Burch, 15), on a stone measuring 26 millimetres. Among his subsequent works there were further biblical, especially New Testament, scenes, uncommon among neo-classical gem-engravings; but Burch was plausibly said to be of 'strong religious opinion' (Williamson, 47) and received commissions from members of the higher clergy. The list of his patrons was to be remarkable: George, duke of Marlborough, was among the earliest. According to his obituarist in the *New Monthly Magazine* 'Scarcely a potentate in Europe but possesses one of his beautiful performances' (1, March 1814, 193): while somewhat exaggerated, these high-flown words reflect his widespread fame at the height of his powers, all the more striking in the case of one who never left the shores of Britain.

In 1769 Burch resigned from the Society of Artists to follow his friends into the newly founded Royal Academy of Arts. He enrolled as a student, the following year was made an associate, and in 1771 became a full academician, among the first group of elected members. Burch's diploma work, a suitably allegorical *Neptune* 'resting on his trident after having crowned the British navy with victory', inscribed with the date, is signed BURCH RA. His election was a tribute to the contemporary status of gem-engraving, to his art, and to his popularity; he cut his fellow academicians' seals and they provided drawings and models for his use. He exhibited annually at the Royal Academy from 1770 until 1796, and after that sporadically until 1808; from 1788, having engraved two prize medals for Göttingen University and a portrait of the king's second son, he styled himself 'Engraver to His Majesty for medals and seals in stones and to H.R.H. the Duke of York'. He took a lively part in academy affairs and its social life, and was popular though 'often coarse in both manner and expression' (Williamson, 47). He figures prominently, cutting a half-ridiculous, half-lovable figure, seated at the feet of the model in Zoffany's painting of *The Life School at the Royal Academy of Arts* (Royal Collection). Both his sons became gem-engravers, but Henry Jacob, the elder, eventually became a successful miniature painter. Left a widower, on 24 December 1793 Burch married Mary Borckhardt at St Marylebone.

By then, however, Burch's life had taken a disastrous turn for the worse and he was slipping into dire poverty, partly caused by misfortune and improvidence, partly by failing powers; as his eyesight and the skill of his hands deteriorated, he tried his hand at miniatures. In the academy he badgered council and individuals for loans, and in 1794 was appointed librarian (virtually a sinecure) at a small stipend. However, he made himself unpopular by cantankerousness and by absurd pretensions, now sharpened by bitter rivalry with Marchant, who had become rich and famous during a sixteen-year stay in Rome. In 1795 Burch tried to retrieve his fortune by publishing one hundred casts from his gems, 'engraved in England'—a hit at Marchant—listing his prestigious patrons and including gems for sale. The semi-illiterate farrago of some of the captions contrasts markedly with the elegantly composed preface—perhaps written by his son, although expressing Burch's own opinions. He died in February 1814, in a cheap rented house in Kentish Town.

Burch's earlier fame had caused his gems to be widely dispersed: several, including an exquisite *Sacrifice to Minerva*, cut for Catherine the Great, are in the Hermitage; the minute *Time*, an extraordinary *tour de force* depicting the Belvedere torso in the grip of Chronos, is in the National Museum, Cracow; two beautiful intaglio heads on cornelian of *Sappho* and the *Apollo Belvedere* are among a group in the British Museum. Casts of his work can be found in the British Museum, the Victoria and Albert Museum, and Sir John Soane's Museum, London. When Burch began his career, there was no established English school of gem-engraving and he was self-taught in every sense. During the latter part of his life his images were too varied and too original to conform to the canons of neo-classical taste; yet his confident modelling based on a thorough study of the living body and his brilliant execution made him a worthy compeer of the outstanding European engravers of his day.   GERTRUD SEIDMANN

Sources G. Seidmann, 'Nathaniel Marchant, gem-engraver, 1739–1816', *Walpole Society*, 53 (1987), 1–105, 161 · G. Seidmann, 'Burch, Edward', *The dictionary of art*, ed. J. Turner (1996) · *New Monthly Magazine*, 1 (1814), 192–3 · *New Monthly Magazine*, 5 (1816), 417 · E. Burch, *A catalogue of one hundred proofs from gems* (privately printed, London, 1795) · M. Postle, 'The St Martin's Lane Academy', *Apollo*, 132 [i.e. 134] (1991), 33–8, pl.1, fig. 3 · G. Seidmann, 'A very ancient, useful and curious art', *The virtuoso tribe of arts and sciences*, ed. D. G. C. Allan and J. L. Abbott (1992), 120–31 · Graves, *Soc. Artists*, 43 · Graves, *RA exhibitors*, 1 (1905), 340–42 · Farington, *Diary* · T. Mortimer, *The universal director* (1763), 5 · G. Seidmann, 'An eighteenth-century collector as patron: the 4th duke of Marlborough and the London engravers', *Engraved gems: survivals and revivals*, ed. C. M. Brown (1997), 262–79, esp. 265–8 · G. C. Williamson, *John Russell, RA* (1894), 47 · *IGI* · G. Seidmann, 'A carnelian intaglio Antinous by Edward Burch', *Antiquaries Journal*, 73 (1993), 175–8, 188–91
Archives RA, catalogue | Keele University, Wedgwood corresp., 19551-106 · RA, Anderton collection of Royal Academy exhibition catalogues · RA, Northcote MSS · RA, Society of Artists MSS, corresp. · V&A, diary of John Russell
Likenesses attrib. J. Zoffany?, group portrait, oils, c.1761 (*An academy by lamplight*), RA; repro. in Postle, 'The St Martin's Lane Academy' · attrib. J. Zoffany?, group portrait, pen-and-ink, c.1761 (*Sketch key to An academy by lamplight*), BM · J. Zoffany, group portrait, oils, 1772 (*The life school at the Royal Academy of Arts*), Royal Collection · G. Dance, tinted black chalk drawing, 1793, RA · H. Singleton, group portrait, oils, 1794 (*The Royal Academicians in general assembly*), RA · A. Bengo, tinted engraving, RA, Anderton Royal Academy Catalogue (1798), fol. 150
Wealth at death died in poverty: Farington, *Diary*

Burchard [St Burchard, Burgheard] (*d.* 753), bishop of Würzburg, was a follower of Boniface (*d.* 754) who joined in the latter's work of church reform on the continent. It is not clear from what part of England he hailed: he may have come from the south-west like Boniface, or from Mercia. Boniface had had metropolitan status since c.732, but it was not until about ten years later that he appointed bishops in the area of his mission east of the Rhine. For the diocese covering northern Franconia, until recently in the territory of the dukes of the Thuringians, he established a see at Würzburg, and consecrated Burchard as bishop there on 21 October 742. In that year or the next Burchard was one of only seven bishops, all from the east Frankish kingdom of Austrasia, who participated in the first of Boniface's reforming councils, known as the Concilium Germanicum because its location is unknown. This marked the beginning of a concerted attempt to desecularize the Frankish church and to enforce a more rigorous observance of canon law in such matters as the celibacy of the clergy and the rules governing marriage. In 747 Burchard attended a synod of the whole Frankish church (again at an unknown location) which, as well as passing more reforming decrees, issued a formal profession of unity with Rome under the jurisdiction of St Peter. Burchard was designated to take this to Pope Zacharias (r. 741–52). He was also one of the signatories of the admonitory letter sent in 746 or 747 on Boniface's initiative to King Æthelbald of Mercia: his appearance there is the firmest indication that there is of his English origin.

Burchard's next journey to Rome in 750, when he was accompanied by Fulrad, abbot of St Denis, was a crucial stage in the process by which Pippin III, mayor of the Frankish royal palace, head of the Carolingian family, and *de facto* ruler of Francia, supplanted the last, powerless, king of the Merovingian dynasty, Childeric III. Burchard and Fulrad asked Zacharias whether it was right that a Frankish king should have no royal power, and whether he that did wield royal power should be called king. It remains uncertain whether they posed this question at Pippin's sole initiative or, as one contemporary text has it, 'with the consent and advice of all the Franks' (Wallace-Hadrill, 102). Either way, Zacharias gave the reply that Pippin sought, answering that it was better to call him king who had royal power, and commanding, 'by virtue of his apostolic authority' (*Annales regni Francorum*, s.a. 749), that Pippin be made king.

In a little over ten years, Burchard was able to build a secure infrastructure for his see. He founded the monastery of St Andrew as an adjunct of his cathedral and on 8 July 752 translated there the bones of the supposed seventh-century missionary to Franconia, the Irishman Kilian, an act which marks the beginning of that saint's veneration at Würzburg. Burchard may also have been responsible for bringing manuscripts to Würzburg. Most notably, he is associated with the so-called Burchard gospels (Würzburg, Universitätsbibliothek, MS M.p.th.f.68), a gospel book, originally written in Italy in the sixth century, which also includes twenty-three folios added in Northumbria in the late seventh century and has canon table decorations that are Frankish; and the *Homiliarium Burchardi* (Würzburg, Universitätsbibliothek, MS M.p.th.f.28), apparently Burchard's own compilation of sermons, chiefly taken from those of Caesarius of Arles (d. 543).

Burchard died on 2 February 753. His feast is celebrated on 14 October, the day in 986 on which the then bishop of Würzburg, Hugo, translated his relics to the monastery of St Andrew, which has consequently been called St Burkard's ever since. The earliest surviving life of Burchard was written about one hundred years after his death, by an author who knew very little about his subject. A second life, written between 1130 and 1156, erroneously makes him the brother of St Swithun (d. 863).

MARIOS COSTAMBEYS

Sources M. Tangl, ed., *Die Briefe des heiligen Bonifatius und Lullus*, MGH Epistolae Selectae, 1 (Berlin, 1916) • W. Levison, *England and the continent in the eighth century* (1946) • 'Vita sancti Burchardi episcopi', [*Supplementa tomorum I–XII, pars III*], ed. O. Holder-Egger, MGH Scriptores [folio], 15/1 (Stuttgart, 1887), 47–50 • F. Kurze, ed., *Annales regni Francorum*, MGH Scriptores Rerum Germanicarum, [6] (Hanover, 1895) • *The fourth book of the chronicle of Fredegar: with its continuations*, ed. and trans. J. M. Wallace-Hadrill (1960) • N. Netzer, *Cultural interplay in the eighth century: the Trier gospels and the making of a scriptorium at Echternach* (1994) • R. McKitterick, 'The diffusion of insular culture in Neustria between 650 and 850: the implications of the manuscript evidence', *La Neustrie: les pays au nord de la Loire de 650 à 850*, ed. H. Atsma, 2 (1989), 395–432 • G. Brown, 'Introduction', *Carolingian culture: emulation and innovation*, ed. R. McKitterick (1994) • *Lexikon des Mittelalters*, 10 vols. (1980–99)
Archives Universitätsbibliothek, Würzburg, MS M.p.th.f.28

Burchardt, Frank Adolf (1902–1958), economist, was born on 5 January 1902 at the schoolhouse, Barneberg, Magdeburg, Germany, the son of Franz Christian Burchardt (1867–1935), headmaster of Barneberg School, and his wife, Susanne Meta Spädte (1875–1961). His parents were protestant and he was baptized Franz Adolf Fritz on 19 February. With the aid of scholarships he attended the Unserer Lieben Frauen boarding-school in Magdeburg (1912–21) and went on (1921–4) to study philosophy and economics at the universities of Marburg, Heidelberg, and Kiel, his doctoral thesis at Kiel being on Schumpeter's concept of a stationary state. He became research assistant to Professor Adolf Löwe, research director at the Kiel Institut für Weltwirtschaft und Seeverkehr, and maintained his association with Löwe when the latter moved to Frankfurt University. Besides earning a reputation as a theorist by developing a model of cyclical growth, Burchardt showed his potential as a teacher in informal tutorials for advanced students. On 5 October 1932 he married Arnoldine (Arne) Helene Franziska Herren (b. 1906), a teacher, with whom he had a son and two daughters.

A study of the conditions of a steadily advancing economy was submitted for Burchardt's *Habilitation* and unanimously accepted by the faculty. Although not active in politics he had not attempted to hide his liberal opinions. Hitler came to power in January 1933 and the university senate refused to endorse the recommendation of the faculty, thereby abruptly terminating Burchardt's career as a scholar in Germany. He joined the editorial staff of the *Frankfurter Zeitung*, but in 1935 he was offered a research grant at All Souls College, Oxford. He joined the newly formed Oxford Economists' Research Group, denoting the shift in the emphasis of his own work from the theoretical to the empirical. The theme remained economic fluctuations, but now from the point of view of the use of public investment to regulate the British economy.

In 1940 Burchardt joined the Oxford University Institute

of Statistics, which was originally founded to promote the use of statistics in social studies but by the accident of war became a centre for employing a number of distinguished refugee economists from Poland, Germany, Austria, Hungary, and Czechoslovakia. He was to demonstrate once again his gift for unobtrusive intellectual leadership, contriving to elicit from these diverse, and in some cases temperamental, talents a remarkable programme of research in war economics. He was *de facto* the editor of the influential *Economics of Full Employment*, published in 1944. He had sought British citizenship soon after he had arrived in the country, but did not receive it until 1946: meanwhile, as were so many refugees, he was interned for a spell as an 'enemy alien' in 1940. Later in the war he became active in the re-education of German prisoners of war.

Burchardt became director of the Institute of Statistics at Oxford in 1948, and in the same year was elected a fellow of Magdalen College. He launched a programme of empirical studies in a number of fields. The survey of savings was the first to be undertaken in Britain, the methods adopted being later taken over by the government. A study of investment was deliberately confined to a few instances where the main elements of capital investment could be described in physical terms. The canvas for wages and earnings was broader, ranging from historical study of national statistics over long periods to in-depth studies of wage formation in a single industry. Burchardt brought over from the United States Lawrence Klein, the grandfather of econometric model building, to set up the first such model of the British economy. These programmes were beginning to bear fruit when Burchardt died of a stroke at the Churchill Hospital, Oxford, on 21 December 1958. He was cremated on 24 December and was survived by his wife. His second career thus ended as sharply as had his first. In the British stage of his career he wrote comparatively little under his own name, but, mainly through his contribution to the Institute of Statistics, he did more than anyone to establish Oxford as a leading centre of applied economics.   G. D. N. WORSWICK

Sources A. Lowe and G. D. N. Worswick, 'F. A. Burchardt', *Bulletin of the Oxford University Institute of Statistics*, 21/2 (May 1959), 59–71 · certificate of baptism, priv. coll. [copy held by widow] · d. cert. · m. cert.

Archives Bodl. Oxf., Society for the Protection of Science and Learning MSS; home office files

Likenesses photograph, repro. in Lowe and Worswick, 'F. A. Burchardt', facing p. 59

Wealth at death £3877 10s. 2d.: probate, 6 March 1959, *CGPLA Eng. & Wales*

Burchell, William John (1781–1863), explorer and naturalist, was born in Fulham on 23 July 1781, one of three children and the only son of Matthew Burchell (*d.* 1828), botanist and the owner of the Fulham nursery. He was educated at Raleigh House Academy, Mitcham, Surrey, and worked at Kew Gardens, becoming a fellow of the Linnean Society in 1803. In December 1805 he arrived on St Helena without the permission of the East India Company, but in February 1806 was nominated by the governor to be the island's schoolmaster. He took up the post in September, and in November 1806 was also appointed

William John Burchell (1781–1863), by Mary Dawson Turner (after John Sell Cotman, 1816)

superintendent of the botanic garden. He experimented with seeds and plants from South America, Africa, and the Far East brought by ships which used the island as a way station, and also studied the island's botany and geology. His botanical surveys provide a benchmark of the indigenous flora and its subsequent modification. In September 1808 he was appointed the company's naturalist in the island, responsible for surveying its natural resources, and gave up the job of schoolmaster.

Friction with a new governor, and contacts he had made in South Africa, resulted in Burchell's accepting an invitation to become 'botanist to Cape Colony'. He arrived in Cape Town in November 1810 and travelled locally for seven months. In June 1811 he set off on a major expedition into Cape Colony and Bechuanaland, which was to last four years and cover 4500 miles. The journey northwards was made by ox wagon and led by local guides. Travelling via Fraserburg and Prieska, it took Burchell three and a half months to reach Klaarwater (Griquatown). This was the base for several expeditions, the major ones being south-eastward along the line of the Brak River to Sneeberg and Graaff-Reinet, and north into Bechuanaland, via Kuruman and the Mashowing River, reaching lat. 26°2′ S. He finally left Klaarwater in January 1813 and travelled via Graaff-Reinet to Grahamstown and along the coast of the Indian Ocean, reaching Cape Town in April 1815. In August he sailed for England via St Helena, arriving on 11 November 1815.

Burchell brought to England some 63,000 specimens of plants, seeds, insects, fish, and animal skins and skeletons, which he had collected on his travels. This has been described as the largest collection made by one man ever to leave Africa. He had also made 500 field sketches and botanical, zoological, and ethnographic drawings, and kept detailed notes of his travels and observations of natural history. Between 1815 and 1819 he classified his specimens and cultivated the seeds and bulbs he had collected.

In June 1819, on the basis of his recent detailed knowledge of Cape Colony, Burchell was called before a House of Commons committee on the poor laws, to advise on the suitability of South Africa for British emigrants. He recommended the Albany district of the eastern Cape, and published a pamphlet, *Hints on Emigration to the Cape of Good Hope* (1819). In the same year he began to work on his *Travels in the Interior of Southern Africa*. The two volumes published (1822 and 1824; German trans., 1825) cover his journeys to August 1812, but a projected third volume never appeared.

During this period Burchell is reported to have been offered a pension by the Prussian government to move to Berlin with his collections. This he declined, and in 1825 joined a British diplomatic mission to Brazil. Travelling via Lisbon, Madeira, and the Canary Islands, he arrived in Rio de Janeiro in July 1825. He spent thirteen months collecting botanical, zoological, and geological specimens in the vicinity of the city, in the Serra dos Órgãos, and in southern Minas Gerais. Sketches he made of Rio de Janeiro formed the basis of a detailed panorama of the city by Robert Burford. In September 1826 he sailed to Santos and collected in the Cubatão area, before moving to São Paulo in January 1827. In July 1827 he travelled north across São Paulo province and the Triangûlo Mineiro into Goiás, claiming to be the first Englishman to visit it. He spent nine months in the town of Goiás and then, between August and November 1828, journeyed to Pôrto Real (Pôrto Nacional), where he waited five months until water conditions allowed him to sail 690 miles down the River Tocantins to the Amazon. He had earlier been advised of the illness of his father, but only after his arrival in Belém on 10 June 1829 did he learn that Matthew Burchell had died in July 1828. Burchell remained in Belém until February 1830, and arrived back in England on 24 March of that year.

Burchell spent the remaining three decades of his life in the labour of cataloguing his enormous collections. He has been described as a sensitive perfectionist, and his meticulousness meant that, working alone, this was a slow process. His material from Brazil, which totalled over 52,000 specimens, was not catalogued until 1860, and he published little on his collections from South Africa or Brazil (*Bulletin des Sciences*, 1817; *Zoological Journal*, 1824). He felt that he merited a government pension, but received little public recognition. He was appointed to the council of the British Association for the Advancement of Science in 1832, and awarded an honorary DCL by Oxford University in May 1834. A number of St Helena and South African plants, animals, and birds are named after him.

Burchell progressively withdrew from his scientific friends, and on 23 March 1863 he committed suicide at the family home, Churchfield House, Fulham. His sister Anna Burchell gave his botanical collections and manuscripts to the Royal Botanic Gardens, Kew, and his entomological materials to the Hope collection, University of Oxford. Some of his specimens, landscape drawings, and portraits are in Johannesburg.

A contemporary, William Swainson, described Burchell as one of the most learned and accomplished travellers of any age or country (Poulton, 45), and his *Travels* has been regarded as one of the best geographies ever written on South Africa. Burchell has also come to be recognized as a pioneer ecologist for developing what has become the common practice of recording the date and precise locality of specimens collected, their morphological features, and the characteristics of their habitats. Although his observations remain in manuscript form, his catalogues and collections are regarded by naturalists as basic sources of exceptional historical value on the botany of St Helena, South Africa, and Brazil.   JOHN DICKENSON

Sources H. M. Mckay, 'William John Burchell, scientist', *South African Journal of Science*, 32 (1935), 689–95 • E. B. Poulton, *William John Burchell* (1907) • H. M. Mckay, 'William John Burchell in St. Helena, 1805–10', *South African Journal of Science*, 31 (1934), 481–9 • M. Gunn and L. E. Codd, *Botanical exploration of southern Africa* (1981) • O. Fidalgo, 'Adicões à historia da micrologia brasileira II. Fungos coletadas por William John Burchell', *Rickia*, 6 (1974), 1–8 • L. B. Smith and R. C. Smith, 'Itinerary of William John Burchell in Brazil, 1825–30', *Phytologia*, 14 (1967), 495–506
Archives Oxf. U. Mus. NH, entomological corresp., notebooks, and papers • RBG Kew, notebooks, catalogues, and papers | Linn. Soc., letters to William Swainson • Oxf. U. Mus. NH, Hope MSS • RBG Kew, letters to Sir William Hooker
Likenesses M. Dawson Turner, etching, 1816 (after J. S. Cotman, 1816), NPG [*see illus.*] • J. S. Cotman, pencil drawing, 1818, V&A • T. H. Maguire, lithograph, 1854, NPG • photograph (after etching by Mrs Dawson Turner; after J. S. Cotman), Carnegie Mellon University, Pittsburgh, Hunter Archive
Wealth at death under £4000: probate, 24 June 1863, *CGPLA Eng. & Wales*

Burchett, Josiah (*c.*1666–1746), secretary of the Admiralty, was possibly the third son of John Burchett (*fl.* 1619–1666) of Sandwich, Kent, and his second wife, Katherine (*d.* 1681). The coat of arms used in George Vertue's 1720 engraved portrait was granted in 1589 to a Byrchett family of Rye, Sussex, and Goudhurst, Kent. The earliest surviving documents relating to Josiah Burchett are those associated with his employment as a clerk for Samuel Pepys, for whom he became a personal servant about 1680. He sailed with Pepys and Lord Dartmouth on the Tangier expedition in 1683 and probably became a clerk upon returning in May 1684. Burchett soon became Pepys's favourite clerk. By 1686 he was a confidant and companion as well as a virtual member of the Pepys household. In that year alone, Burchett accompanied Pepys on twenty trips from London to Windsor on Admiralty business, helping prepare for audiences with James II. In August 1687 he was abruptly dismissed by Pepys after more than seven years' service. The three earliest extant letters from Burchett are those to Pepys, denying the charge that he had accepted bribes while in Pepys's employment, seeking forgiveness, and asking for re-employment.

Burchett failed to reinstate himself, but he found temporary work with William Hewer, another of Pepys's former clerks. In September 1688 Burchett entered naval service in the *Portsmouth* (Captain George St Lo), after which he found favour with the earl of Dartmouth, commander-in-chief of the fleet, who was then quarrelling with Pepys. Burchett soon joined Dartmouth's flagship, the *Resolution*. There, he worked under Dartmouth's secretary and muster-master of the fleet, Phineas Bowles. Following him to the Admiralty, Burchett became a clerk in March 1689, and remained there after Bowles left in 1690.

In June 1691 Burchett left the Admiralty to serve with Admiral Edward Russell, his new patron, in the flagship *Britannia*; he probably witnessed the battle of Barfleur in May 1692. In June 1693 Burchett returned to the Admiralty, of which he was probably chief clerk from 18 July to 26 August. During the period 4 July 1693 to 18 August 1694 Burchett also served as deputy judge advocate of the fleet. He left the Admiralty to serve again with Russell in the Mediterranean from about 24 April 1694 until November 1695. During this period Russell was both commander-in-chief in the Mediterranean and first lord, and needed a loyal contact at the Admiralty to send him confidential information. Disappointed with Admiralty secretary William Bridgeman in this regard, Russell took advantage of the wartime need to increase the Admiralty's clerical staff and had Burchett appointed joint secretary with Bridgeman. The appointment was dated 26 September 1694, but it did not reach Burchett, who was with the fleet at Cadiz, until November. Sailing for England with the first available convoy, he reached Spithead on 11 January 1695.

Burchett was, at first, the junior secretary, and Bridgeman continued to sign all correspondence. Bridgeman had already begun a wide-ranging reorganization, and Burchett refined this, advancing further what Pepys had started. Among the changes were the abolition of fees for the issue of documents and the establishment of a fixed salary for the Admiralty secretaries. By the autumn of 1695 Burchett shared fully in all Admiralty business and was now paid £800 a year, the figure which remained his basic salary for the remainder of his career. He married Thomasina Honywood (d. 1713), the daughter of Sir William Honywood of Hampstead, on 24 December 1695, at St James's Church, Duke's Place, London; they had a son and two daughters.

From 24 June 1698, the time of Bridgeman's resignation, until May 1702, Burchett was the sole Admiralty secretary. At this time he added to his income by obtaining privy council approval for exemption from direct taxes for himself and his clerks; he received a refund for payments made since 1695. As Admiralty secretary he dealt with the full range of the Admiralty's administrative affairs, administering the preparations for the War of the Spanish Succession.

Burchett's patron, Admiral Russell (now earl of Orford), resigned as first lord in May 1699. In 1701 the Admiralty commissioners were superseded by Lord Pembroke as lord high admiral, and he was succeeded in 1702 by Queen Anne's consort, Prince George of Denmark. Pembroke

returned briefly (1708–9) before the office was returned to a commission, with Orford as first lord, in November 1709. Finally there was a total change of Admiralty commissioners with the accession of George I in 1714. In earlier years each such change would have brought a new Admiralty secretary, but Burchett demonstrated that his position was best filled by a knowledgeable civil servant rather than a temporary political appointee, exemplifying the independence of the administrative machinery of government.

Burchett served as Lord Pembroke's sole adviser during the five months of his tenure as lord high admiral in 1701. Without a board of senior officers Burchett was often the sole authority at the Admiralty. The weakness of this situation was readily apparent and, with Prince George's appointment in 1702, a new body was created called the lord high admiral's council. During the ensuing period Burchett joined the prince's private secretary, George Clarke, as joint Admiralty secretary. The prince paid Burchett, the senior of the two, an additional £200 a year. After Clarke's dismissal in 1705 Burchett became, once again, sole secretary, a position he was to hold until 29 April 1741. In 1717 Burchett obtained reinstitution of the additional £200 salary that had lapsed with Prince George's death in 1708, and a resumption of the practice of paying fees for commissions and warrants.

In 1703 Burchett published *Memoirs of Transactions at Sea during the War with France*, a naval history of the Nine Years' War, based on official reports in the Admiralty office. In the following year Colonel Luke Lillington attacked Burchett's credibility in a pamphlet; Burchett replied in a moderate tone that deflected the personal attack by channelling it into a discussion of current military and naval practices. In 1720 he incorporated his entire 1703 volume, with additions and corrections, in a much larger work, *A Complete History of the most Remarkable Transactions at Sea*. This volume is particularly important in the literature of naval history, not only as a narrative of naval operations in the Nine Years' War and the War of the Spanish Succession, but as the first general naval history written in the English language.

In May 1705 Burchett was elected to parliament as one of three members for Sandwich. A court whig, he remained in parliament until the 1713 election, when the property ownership requirements of the Qualification Act prevented him from standing for re-election. After his wife's death on 15 October 1713 he inherited property in Hampstead that enabled him to satisfy the requirement, but he did not return to parliament until 1721. He remained a member until May 1741, when, at the age of about seventy-five, he lost an election against three opponents.

On 22 July 1721 Burchett married for a second time, his bride being the widow of Captain Robert Arris, former resident commissioner of the navy at Plymouth. With the outbreak of war in 1739 Admiralty business increased at a time when Burchett's health became uncertain. His wife died in March 1740, and three months later he married Isabella Wood, the widow of a merchant who had traded with Spain. In April 1741 the Admiralty appointed Thomas

Corbett as joint secretary, and on 14 October 1742 Burchett retired, with a pension of £800, to his Hampstead property; he died there on 2 October 1746. His widow, Isabella, received a pension of £100 p.a. from 1747 until her death in 1756. Burchett was also survived by Elizabeth, his elder daughter from his first marriage, who married Sir Charles *Hardy (c.1680–1744); their son was the second Sir Charles *Hardy (bap. 1717, d. 1780). Burchett's son, George Anne, served as an Admiralty clerk for thirty-four years from 1727.

As an Admiralty secretary Josiah Burchett's greatest achievement was to convert his office from that of a political appointee to that of a civil servant; this brought enormous stability and cumulative expertise to the management of England's sea affairs. His monument lies in the mass of well-ordered Admiralty files in the Public Record Office and in his *Complete History*, the first naval history to be written from those files. JOHN B. HATTENDORF

Sources G. F. James, 'Josiah Burchett, secretary to the lords commissioners of the admiralty, 1695–1742', *Mariner's Mirror*, 23 (1937), 477–99 • J. B. Hattendorf, introduction, in J. Burchett, *A complete history of the most remarkable transactions at sea* (1720); facs. edn (1995) • J. C. Sainty, ed., *Admiralty officials, 1660–1870* (1975) • PRO, ADM 7/823 • PRO, PROB 11/750, fol. 19 • P. Watson, 'Burchett, Josiah', HoP, *Commons* • G. F. James, 'Josiah Burchett (1666?–1746): some additional notes', *N&Q*, 176 (1939), 56–8 • Monumental inscriptions of Bath Abbey, no. 814, R.215, section K • W. P. W. Phillimore and G. E. Cockayne, *London parish registers*, 4 vols. (1900–02), vol. 3

Archives PRO, ADM series | BL, letters to John Ellis, Add. MSS 28884–28892 • BL, letters to Lord Strafford, Add. MSS 31137–31139 • Hunt. L., letters to Cloudesley Shovell • Yale U., Beinecke L., letters to William Blathwayth

Likenesses J. Maubert, oils, Gov. Art Coll. • G. Vertue, line engraving (after J. Maubert), BM, NPG; repro. in Burchett, *Complete history* • miniature, repro. in James, 'Josiah Burchett, secretary to the lords commissioners of the admiralty', 489; priv. coll.

Wealth at death only a very inconsiderable personal estate, the whole mostly in pictures: widow's petition to privy council for a pension, PRO, privy council register, Nov 1747, quoted in James, 'Josiah Burchett, secretary'

Burchett, Richard (1815–1875), painter and art teacher, was born on 30 January 1815 in Brighton, Sussex. He was educated at the London Mechanics' Institution before entering the Government School of Design in Somerset House, set up in 1837 to train designers for industry. In 1845 he led a group of students who complained to the Board of Trade about the teaching system, which was based entirely on copying, and subsequently gave evidence to the parliamentary committee of inquiry into the situation at the school (1846–7). Appointed a master in 1845, he became headmaster in 1852, when Henry Cole became superintendent of all the government schools of design, under the new department of practical art (from 1855 the Department of Science and Art). The school moved to Marlborough House, and in 1857 to South Kensington, and was renamed the Central Training School for Art (from 1863 the National Art Training School). Its main purpose became the training of teachers for the branch schools of art, with the teaching of applied design of secondary importance. Burchett's pupils included Luke Fildes, George Clausen, Christopher Dresser, Gertrude

Jekyll, and Kate Greenaway. Author of several textbooks, including *Practical Geometry* (1855) and *Linear Perspective* (1856), which was translated into Chinese, Burchett remained in his post until his death, when he was replaced as headmaster by Edward Poynter.

As a painter, Burchett was known mainly for his large historical works in the Pre-Raphaelite style. He exhibited five paintings at the Royal Academy between 1847 and 1873, including *The Death of Marmion* (exh. 1847), *Sanctuary* (exh. 1867; Guildhall Art Gallery, London), and *The Making of the New Forest* (exh. 1873). Another of his well-known historical works was *Edward IV Withheld by Ecclesiastics from Pursuing Lancastrian Fugitives into a Church*. His only known landscape, *View across Sandown Bay, Isle of Wight*, probably painted in the mid-1850s, is in the Victoria and Albert Museum. Burchett also worked on several decorative schemes, including a series of Tudor portraits for the royal antechamber in the House of Lords (1855–9). He helped to decorate the dome of the building for the Great Exhibition of 1862, and he designed a mosaic of the thirteenth-century sculptor William Torrel for one of the niches in the south court of the South Kensington Museum (later the Victoria and Albert Museum). There is a window in Greenwich Hospital painted by him.

Burchett converted to Roman Catholicism in the mid-1850s, while living with the painter James Collinson, an earlier convert. He is said to have modelled St Oswald, in *The Death of St Oswald*, on Cardinal Manning. He was twice married: his second wife, Mary Eliza, was the niece of Sir Samuel Ferguson (1810–1886), poet and antiquary. An invalid for the last years of his life, Burchett died on 27 May 1875, in Samuel Ferguson's house, at 20 North Great George Street, Dublin, while visiting the city for the sake of his health. He was survived by his second wife. He was portrayed in Val Prinsep's *Distribution of Art Prizes* (1869), which decorated a panel in the national competition gallery of the Victoria and Albert Museum until its removal in 1939. ANNE PIMLOTT BAKER

Sources C. Frayling and C. Catterall, eds., *Design of the times: one hundred years of the Royal College of Art* (1996), chaps. 3–4 • J. Physick, *The Victoria and Albert Museum: the history of its building* (1982) • R. Parkinson, ed., *Catalogue of British oil paintings, 1820–1860* (1990) [catalogue of V&A] • C. Frayling, *The Royal College of Art* (1987) • G. Reynolds, *Victorian painting* (1966), 152–3 • A. Burton, *Vision and accident: the story of the Victoria and Albert Museum* (1999) • A. Staley, *The Pre-Raphaelite landscape* (1973), 80 • Wood, *Vic. painters*, 3rd edn • Graves, *RA exhibitors* • *The Graphic* (26 June 1875) • DNB • CGPLA Eng. & Wales (1875)

Likenesses G. Clausen and H. Montalba, sculpture, Royal College of Art, London; repro. in Frayling and Catterall, eds., *Design of the times* • woodcut, NPG; repro. in *The Graphic*

Wealth at death under £200: probate, 30 June 1875, CGPLA Eng. & Wales

Burckhardt, Johann Ludwig (1784–1817), traveller, was born at Lausanne on 25 November 1784 of a family which had long been settled at Basel. His parents were Johann Rudolf Burckhardt (1750–1813), ribbon manufacturer, and his second wife, Sara, née Rohner. The French invasion of Switzerland brought serious financial trouble to the family firm and divided the family members, with the father,

Johann Ludwig Burckhardt (1784–1817), by Angelica Clarke, pubd 1819 (after Slater)

sometime officer in the French army, obliged to live in retirement away from his family. Johann Ludwig spent two years at a school at Neuchâtel, and, after private tuition at the family house (the Kirschgarten) at Basel, went to Leipzig University in 1800 and four years later to Göttingen, where he studied natural science. Burckhardt has been described as popular among his fellow students at both universities, and respected for the talents and zeal for knowledge which he already displayed. Letters to his family reveal, however, that he got into debt and was not always an assiduous student. His family's reproofs bore witness to their straitened circumstances.

In July 1806 Burckhardt went to London, hoping initially for a position in the diplomatic service, which he hoped well-placed contacts could gain for him. Disappointment was exacerbated by shortage of money, and, reaching a crisis, Burckhardt turned to religion, promising his parents in a letter of 14 February 1808 to turn his back on his old life and lead a sober and godly life from then on. With a letter of introduction from the Göttingen naturalist Blumenbach, he contacted Sir Joseph Banks, at that time one of the chief supporters of the Association for Promoting the Discovery of the Interior Parts of Africa. He soon volunteered to carry on the work of exploration, particularly the search for the course of the Niger, and his offer was accepted. He received his instructions in January 1809 and sailed for Malta after attending lectures on chemistry, astronomy, and medicine, studying Arabic in London and Cambridge, and inuring himself to hardship by making long walks bareheaded, sleeping on the ground, and living on vegetables. At Malta he stayed seven weeks to improve his knowledge of Arabic and to equip himself as Ibrahim ibn Abdallah, a Muslim trader of Indian origin brought up in London, in which character he travelled in Syria, thus explaining imperfections in his speech which would reveal that he was not local. If he was asked to speak in Hindustani, he used to treat his Syrian auditors to an exhibition of Swiss-German, which completely satisfied them. He landed in Karamania, near Tarsus, reached Antioch, where his Indian disguise did not save him from some unpleasant treatment as a possible *giaour* (non-Muslim), and thence made his way with a caravan to Aleppo. There between two and three years' study not only made him a fluent Arabic speaker but gave him such a knowledge of the language that he was recognized to be more learned than the *ulema* (men with special knowledge of Muslim law and theology) themselves, and knotty points of interpretation were brought to him for solution by the doctors of the law at Aleppo. Burckhardt varied his long sojourn at Aleppo by a six-month journey (in 1810–11) to Palmyra, Damascus, Baalbek, Lebanon, and the Hauran, during which he was twice deserted by his guides and encountered numerous difficulties and dangers from the disturbed state into which the country had been thrown by the Wahabi revolt. In 1812, after a further course of Arabic study, he set off to Syrian Tripoli (Trablus) and the Hauran, journeyed through Palestine, visited Petra, where he sacrificed a goat at the grave of Aaron to corroborate his character as a pilgrim, and thence struck across the desert to Cairo, arriving in September 1812.

In Egypt Burckhardt's main object was to join a caravan to Fezzan, whence he intended to explore the sources of the Niger. He changed his disguise to that of a Syrian and, on occasion, that of a Turk looking for a missing relative. While waiting for a caravan he made an expedition up the Nile to see the monuments of ancient Egypt, which were then for the first time being revealed to Europeans. He started in January 1813, and before he returned to Aswan at the end of March he had explored the Nile valley as far as Mahas on the northern frontier of the province of Dongola. Being still delayed in his project of discovering the Niger sources by the unrest in the deserts, he made a lengthy stay at Esna, and then, in March 1814, succeeded in making his way through the desert by Berber and Shendi into Abyssinia, coming out at Suakin on 20 July. Thence he crossed over to Jiddah, where he suffered from fever, and found himself very short of money, since his ragged appearance after his desert hardships belied the credit which he should have obtained from his Egyptian bankers' letters. Fortunately, Mohammed Ali, the viceroy of Egypt, was at the time in the neighbourhood of Mecca, campaigning against the Wahabi, and, hearing of Burckhardt's proximity, summoned him to his presence and relieved him of his difficulties. Burckhardt expressed a wish to visit Mecca as a Muslim pilgrim, and the pasha, although he was aware of Burckhardt's nationality, consented, provided he could satisfy a competent committee of Muslim examiners. Two learned doctors of the law questioned him, and pronounced him not only a Muslim but an exceedingly learned one. After this Burckhardt dined with the kady, or chief religious judge of Mecca, said prayers with him, and recited a long chapter of the Koran; having thus placed himself on the best of terms with the authorities, he went as a pilgrim to Mecca, acquitting himself as a good Muslim. It is unlikely that any Christian or European had accomplished this feat before, and the penalty of discovery would probably have been death. Burckhardt, however, mixed freely with the pilgrims without being suspected, and spent September, October, and November of 1814 in Mecca, and in the following January joined a caravan to Medina in order to visit the prophet's tomb. Here he was again laid low by fever, probably malaria, until April, when he returned in an exhausted condition, via Yanbuʿ al-Bahr, to Cairo, arriving in June.

In Cairo Burckhardt spent some months revising and completing the journals of his several expeditions for the African Association. Still unable to pursue his Niger exploration, he occupied himself by helping the excavation then being carried on in Egypt by Giovanni Belzoni for Henry Salt, the British consul. He had not yet recovered from the hardships of his Arabian travels, and was compelled to seek the sea air of Alexandria for his health. When plague appeared in Cairo he started off on a fresh tour to Suez and Sinai in 1816, returning in June in the hope of carrying out the long-cherished Niger scheme. Months passed, however, spent in preparing his narratives of travels for the association and in writing valuable letters to England, and still the expedition was delayed. In 1817 he was attacked with dysentery after having eaten contaminated fish, and after eleven days' illness died on 15 October 1817. He was buried in the Muslim cemetery, under his eastern name of the pilgrim Ibrahim ibn Abdallah.

Burckhardt possessed the best qualifications for a traveller. He prepared meticulously for his voyages, obeying his maxim 'Eile mit Weile' ('more haste less speed'; Burckhardt to parents, 15 Oct 1812), even when this made it seem to contemporaries that he was slow and hesitant. Daring and yet prudent, a close and accurate observer with an intimate knowledge of the manners and language of the people among whom he travelled, he was able to accomplish feats of exploration which to others would have been impossible. He was zealous in his work, disinterested, generous and open-handed, an affectionate son and brother, and a staunch friend.

Burckhardt was a discriminating collector of artefacts, and left his valuable collection of oriental manuscripts to the University of Cambridge, because he there received his earliest lessons in Arabic and because he remained alienated from his home town, still dominated by the French. His journals, which were written with remarkable spirit in spite of the fact that he began to learn English only at the age of twenty-five, and that he had to jot down his observations secretly under his cloak or behind a camel for fear of exciting suspicion among his Arab guides and companions, were published after his death by the Association for Promoting the Discovery of the Interior Parts of Africa. They comprised *Travels in Nubia* (1819), *Travels in Syria and the Holy Land* (1822), *Travels in Arabia*

(1829), *Notes on the Bedouins and Wahabys* (1830), and *Arabic Proverbs* (1830). Many have been translated into other European languages. They contained few observations on the geography or natural history of the lands he visited, but numerous valuable and perceptive accounts of the people of the regions and their way of life. Other of his writings and translations remain unpublished.

STANLEY LANE-POOLE, *rev.* ELIZABETH BAIGENT

Sources T. Wollmann, *Scheich Ibrahim* (1984) · P. Hindeling, 'Scheich Ibrahim (Johann Ludwig Burckhardt), 1784–1817', *Beduinen aus Nordostafrika: Burkhardt-Sammlung zur Erinnerung an Scheich Ibrahim* (Basel, 1957), 5–12 [exhibition catalogue, Museum für Völkerkunde and Schweizerisches Museum für Volkskunde, Basel, 12 April – 30 Sept 1957] · K. Sim, *Desert traveller: the life of Jean Louis Burckhardt* (1969) · Otto, Graf zu Stolberg-Wernigerode, ed., *Neue deutsche Biographie* (Berlin, 1953–) · C. Burckhardt-Sarasin and H. Schwabe-Burckhardt, '*Scheik Ibrahim': Briefe an Eltern und Geschwister* (1956) · W. R. Dawson and E. P. Uphill, *Who was who in Egyptology*, 3rd edn, rev. M. L. Bierbrier (1995) · B. Meyer, *Sheikh Ibrahim: J. L. Burckhardt* (1990) · J. Sabini, *Armies in the sand: the struggle for Mecca and Medina* (1981) · *Historisches Lexikon der Schweiz*

Archives BL, corresp. and papers, Add. MSS 27620, 30239–30240, 52474

Likenesses A. Clarke, etching, pubd 1819 (after Slater), NPG [*see illus.*]

Burden, Harold Nelson (1860–1930), Church of England clergyman and health administrator, was born on 20 March 1860 at Hythe, Kent, the eldest of the three children of Thomas Burden (1829–1872), a grocer, and his wife, Sarah Ann (Sally) Munk (*c.*1833–1902). When he was twelve his father died, and he was probably brought up by his grandparents, who were farmers. Unfortunately he was not successful as a grazier and dairyman and was declared bankrupt in 1886. He then worked in the slums of the East End of London, where he met his first wife, Katherine Mary Garton (*c.*1854–1919), the daughter of Henry Garton, a tobacco manufacturer of Hull; she was a niece of the wife of George Huntington, rector of Tenby, and had worked with Octavia Hill, who praised her. They married on 26 September 1888 after Burden was ordained deacon in the Church of England; they then emigrated to Ontario, where they were missionaries for three years. Here their two children were born and died. Burden was ordained priest in 1891.

The Burdens returned on account of Harold's ill health and spent time in Shoreditch and Cambridge, where he wrote a well-received book on his missionary work, *Life in Algoma, or, Three Years of a Clergyman's Life and Church Work in that Diocese* (1894). This was followed by *Manitoulin, or, Five years of church work among Ojibway indians and lumbermen resident upon that island or its vicinity* (1895). In 1896 a novel and a set of sermons for 'busy clerics', *Duty's Call* and *Addresses on St Matthew's Gospel*, were published. At Cambridge, where he matriculated in Lent 1893 and served as chaplain of St Catharine's College (1893–5), Burden gained his English licence to be a priest. He also became a member of the Barbers' Company and a freeman of the City of London. From 1924 to 1926 he served as master of the Barbers' Company.

Burden moved to Bristol in 1895 as secretary of the

Church of England Temperance Society. With local support, he and his wife created a retreat for female 'habitual drunkards', the Royal Victoria Home, and later the first 'inebriate reformatory', the Brentry extension of the home. In 1902 they formed the National Institutions for Inebriates and two years later its 600 beds constituted two-thirds of the places in English establishments of that type. Because of this, and his good relationships with the Home Office, he was appointed to the royal commission on the care and control of the feeble-minded (1904–8).

From his experience on the commission, Burden set up Sandwell Hall, Birmingham, in 1906. This was the first industrial school for 'feeble-minded' children, and in 1909 he established another, at Stoke Park, Bristol. Partly on account of the low cost of his 'inebriate reformatories', the Treasury reduced its subsidy for these bodies in 1907, triggering the collapse of such institutions nationally. As a result the Burdens changed their reformatories into 'mental deficiency colonies'. Later they concentrated their efforts at Stoke Park and at Whittington, Chesterfield, operating the National Institutions for Persons Requiring Care and Control (NIPRCC).

Katherine Burden died in 1919, and on 12 May 1920 Burden married the superintendent of the Stoke Park colony, Rosa Gladys Williams (c.1873–1939), the daughter of the Revd John Williams. At the time of Katherine's death the incorporation of the NIPRCC operated more than 2000 of the 7000 beds in licensed institutions for mentally handicapped people in England. Burden's other innovation was the creation, just before his death, of the Burden Mental Research Institute (1929). He died on 15 May 1930 at his home, Clevedon Hall, Clevedon, Somerset, and was buried on 20 May at Clevedon parish church. His second wife in turn founded the Burden Neurological Institute in 1939. After their deaths the NIPRCC became the Burden Trust.

Harold Burden did well financially from running the institutions he created, leaving an estate of almost £150,000—although exactly how he managed to amass this wealth remains obscure. Although he engaged committees of the great and good to help him, Burden appears to have worked poorly with others and was autocratic. However, he undoubtedly benefited from the drive and support of his first wife. He was privately criticized by the Board of Education and fell out with several of the board's commissioners over the running of his establishments. Nevertheless, he created some of the first institutions to deal with alcoholism (as advocated by the temperance movement) and with mental handicaps (as proposed in the Mental Deficiency Act of 1913).

PETER CARPENTER

Sources P. K. Carpenter, A history of Brentry: house, reformatory, colony and hospital (2002) · P. K. Carpenter, 'Rev. Harold Nelson Burden and Katherine Mary Burden', Journal of the Royal Society of Medicine, 89 (1996), 205–9 · R. J. Berry, ed., Stoke Park monographs on mental deficiency and other problems of the human mind (1933) · Clevedon Mercury and Courier (24 May 1930), 3 · The Times (29 May 1930), 18 · Clevedon Mercury (8 Nov 1919) · The Times (13 Nov 1886) · Board of education report, PRO, ED 32/187 · C. E. Maurice, Life of Octavia Hill as told in her letters (1913), 265 · CGPLA Eng. & Wales (1930) · Venn, Alum. Cant.

Archives Bristol RO, Brentry deposit · Bristol RO, Burden Trust deposit · Bristol RO, Stoke Park deposit
Likenesses photograph, c.1901, Bristol RO; repro. in Forty views of Royal Victoria homes, Brentry · photograph, c.1920, repro. in J. Jancar, Research at Stoke Park, mental handicap (1930–1980) (1981) · Haines of London, photograph, c.1925, repro. in Berry, ed., Stoke Park monographs, frontispiece · Haines of London, photograph, 1925, repro. in Carpenter, 'Rev. Harold Nelson Burden and Katherine Mary Burden', 208; priv. coll.
Wealth at death £149,161 8s. 4d.: probate, 28 June 1930, CGPLA Eng. & Wales

Burden, Herbert Francis (1898–1915), soldier, was born on 22 March 1898 at 47 Silvermere Road, Lewisham, London, the son of Arthur Burden, gardener, and his wife, Charlotte Donaldson. Either he joined the army as a boy soldier or he lied about his age on enlistment. He later claimed that he had previously served with the Royal West Kent regiment in 1913, but certainly by 1915 he was a private with the 1st battalion, Northumberland Fusiliers. He probably served with this regiment in Britain before joining his battalion in the Ypres salient on 28 March 1915.

On 26 June 1915 Burden was warned for duty in a trench working party yet failed to attend roll-call at 7.00 p.m. on that day. Three witnesses from the Royal West Kent regiment later testified that he had been seen loitering by the lines near Dickebush over a period of three days, 26–8 June. When challenged Burden stated that he had had permission from the transport officer to visit a friend. He was returned to his regiment at 9.40 p.m. on 28 June by an escort from the Royal West Kents, and was subsequently charged with desertion, a crime punishable by death.

As was the customary practice in field general courts martial before 1917 Burden was not legally represented at his trial. His defence was confined to his own, very brief explanation of absence from duty on the days in question. He stated: 'I went to see a friend of mine in the Royal West Kent Regiment in which Regiment I served in 1913 and as I heard he had lost a brother I wanted to enquire if it was true or not' (PRO, WO 71/424). A witness from the Northumberland Fusiliers informed the hearing that Burden's service record showed a total of seven cases of absence, three miscellaneous offences on home service, and one case of absence while serving with the British expeditionary force in Belgium.

The court martial proceedings were then forwarded to Burden's battalion commander, Lieutenant-Colonel Clement Yatman, who was requested to comment on the soldier's character and behaviour. Yatman replied that Burden's platoon sergeant considered him 'a man you cannot trust' and that the defaulter sheet showed that he was 'much addicted to absence'. In addition Yatman was instructed to provide 'the Commanding Officer's opinion … or that of his officers, as to whether the crime was deliberately committed with the sole object of avoiding the particular service involved'. This request proved impossible to fulfil, since no officers of the company survived who knew Burden. Yatman wrote:

> In the absence of any officer who knows this man I do not feel justified in expressing an opinion. I know very little of

the man and it seems to me unfair to express an opinion with so little to back it up. (PRO, WO 71/424)

It may be the case therefore that a combination of previous misconduct and the fact that no officer remained in the company who could intercede on his behalf proved ultimately prejudicial to Burden's defence. On 2 July 1915 he was found guilty of desertion. He was executed by firing squad at 4.00 a.m. on 21 July 1915. He was seventeen and unmarried. The location of his grave is not recorded.

Private Burden was the youngest of over 300 British and Commonwealth troops shot for desertion or cowardice during the First World War. The Shot at Dawn campaign, launched in 1990 to secure official pardons for them, reflects changing perceptions of their deeds. A memorial to commemorate the soldiers was unveiled at the National Memorial Arboretum, Alrewas, Staffordshire, in 2001; it comprises an amphitheatre of 306 wooden stakes, each resembling an execution post, surrounding a 10 foot statue of a blindfolded youth modelled on Burden.

LESLEY COLLINS

Sources PRO, court martial papers, WO 71/424 · b. cert. · J. Putkowski and J. Sykes, *Shot at dawn: executions in World War One by authority of the British Army Act*, new edn (1992) · *The Independent* (22 June 2001) · *Daily Telegraph* (22 June 2001) · *The Guardian* (22 June 2001) · C. M. Corns and J. Hughes-Wilson, *Blindfold and alone: British military executions in the Great War* (2001)
Archives PRO, court martial papers, WO 71/424
Likenesses photograph, repro. in *The Guardian*

Burden, Jane. *See* Morris, Jane (1839–1914).

Burder, George (1752–1832), Independent minister, was born in Islington on 5 June 1752, the son of Henry Burder (1718–1788) and his first wife (1718–1762). He was educated at two schools in Hatton Garden, London, and trained as an engraver under Isaac Taylor. As a young man he heard a number of evangelical preachers, including John Fletcher, Rowland Hill, William Romaine, and Jonathan Scott. When he heard George Whitefield preach his last two sermons in London, he took them down by shorthand and published them. Soon after his conversion in 1776 Burder preached in the open air in Shropshire and Staffordshire. His father, who was against field-preaching, encouraged his son to attend a nonconformist academy before ordination. But Burder was unclear as to the denomination in which to be ordained. However, on a visit to the north-west of England, and although untrained, he was ordained on 29 October 1778 at the High Street Chapel, Lancaster. For the next three years he exercised an itinerant ministry, and supported the establishment of chapels in Lancashire, Cumberland, and Westmorland. Sometimes he accompanied John Wesley on his travels, and throughout his life maintained friendships across the denominational divide.

On 31 August 1781 Burder married Sarah Harrison (*d*. 1824) of Newcastle under Lyme, and they had a family of four boys and five girls. Two of their sons became Congregational ministers, one of whom, Henry Forster *Burder, was the chairman of the Congregational Union in 1844, and another became a doctor.

George Burder (1752–1832), by Henry Hoppner Meyer, pubd 1812 (after Henry William Pickersgill)

In August 1783 Burder was invited to become the minister of the West Orchard Chapel, Coventry. He began his ministry in November but was not inducted until May 1784. As the congregation increased galleries were added and the chapel enlarged (rebuilt in 1820 and destroyed in 1940–41). In Coventry he opened two branch chapels and was the originator of Sunday schools in the town. In this he tried to work with the Church of England clergy but without success. He encouraged the spread of nonconformity in Warwickshire and Staffordshire and promoted the erection of new chapels. He published three pamphlets in defence of the dissenters of Lichfield. Following the Birmingham riots of July 1791 the mob became active in Coventry, and Burder was caught up in the troubles, appearing in a contemporary cartoon, 'The devil amongst the saints, or, The revenge and journey to hell' (Reader collection, Bodl. Oxf.). In June 1793 Burder was a founding member of 'The Warwickshire Association of ministers for the spread of the gospel at home and abroad' (later known as the Warwickshire County Association). He was a keen supporter of the London Missionary Society: the first collection for the society took place in West Orchard Chapel and some of its early missionaries were from his congregation. He was one of the founders of the Religious Tract Society and supported the formation of the British and Foreign Bible Society. Although he had no formal education, he published a number of works and became 'a literary hack only less productive than John Wesley' (Ward, 300). Burder compiled three collections of popular sermons, 989,000 copies of which were published by the Religious Tract Society, and a Congregational hymnbook, which included four of his own compositions. The latter went through twenty-eight editions in forty-five years. He edited John Bunyan's *Pilgrim's Progress* and *Holy War* and abridgements of John Owen's *Justification by Faith* and his work on the Holy Spirit.

In 1796 Burder was invited to become the minister of York Street Chapel, Walworth, London, but declined. However in June 1803 he became the minister of Fetter Lane Chapel, London, where his father and brother had been deacons. During his ministry the congregation increased and the chapel was enlarged. As well as his pastoral duties Burder succeeded John Eyre as the secretary of the London Missionary Society (1803–27) and as editor of the *Evangelical Magazine* (1803–26), for which he remained treasurer until 1829. In 1806 he was elected one of the six preachers who delivered the Merchants' lecture. In 1825 he developed a cataract, and when he became blind in 1830 no longer accepted his minister's salary and employed an assistant minister, Caleb Morris.

During the first fifty years of his ministry Burder preached an estimated 10,000 sermons, some of which at Coventry were delivered to the crowds assembled for public executions. He preached plain, pious, evangelical sermons and was described as 'a serious man, employed about serious things' (Burder, 222). Burder died in Brunswick Square, London, in the home of his son, Dr Thomas Harrison *Burder, on 29 May 1832, and was buried in the family vault in Bunhill Fields burial-ground on his eightieth birthday, 5 June.   A. F. MUNDEN

Sources H. F. Burder, *Memoir of the Rev. George Burder* (1833) · J. Fletcher, 'Memoir of the late Rev. George Burder', *Evangelical Magazine and Missionary Chronicle*, new ser., 10 (1832), 333–42 · *DNB* · W. R. Ward, *Religion and society in England, 1790–1850* (1972) · B. Nightingale, *Lancashire nonconformity*, 6 vols. [1890–93], vol. 1 · A. P. F. Snell, 'George Burder and the Lichfield dissenters', *Transactions of the South Staffordshire Archaeological and Historical Society*, 13 (1971–2), 52–60 · A. F. Munden, 'George Burder: "an able minister of the new covenant"', *Warwickshire History*, 11/1 (1999), 37–53
Archives DWL, correspondence and MSS | Coventry Archives · SOAS, Council for World Mission Archive
Likenesses Ridley, engraving, 1800, repro. in *Evangelical Magazine*, 8 (1800), facing p. 265 · H. H. Meyer, mezzotint, pubd 1812 (after H. W. Pickersgill), BM, NPG [*see illus.*] · W. Holl, stipple, pubd 1824 (after J. R. Wildman), NPG · J. Andrews, engraving (after H. W. Pickersgill), repro. in Burder, *Memoir* · S. Russell, engraving (after drawing), Lancaster library

Burder, Henry Forster (1783–1864), Congregational minister, eldest son of the Revd George *Burder (1752–1832), whose *Memoir* (1833) he wrote, and his wife, Sarah Harrison (*d.* 1824) of Newcastle under Lyme, and brother of Thomas Harrison *Burder (1789–1843), was born on 27 November 1783 at Coventry. He was articled in 1798 to a wholesale firm with offices in Nottingham and London. In London he attended the Weigh-House Chapel, where John Clayton (1754–1843) was minister, and decided to enter the ministry. Accordingly he became a student in Hoxton Academy, and in 1804 entered the University of Glasgow, where his fellow students included George Payne and

Joseph Fletcher. He took his MA degree in 1807, and subsequently his DD.

After his graduation Burder became classical tutor at Wymondley Academy, resigning this appointment in 1808. From 31 October 1811 he was assistant to the Revd Samuel Palmer of St Thomas's Square Congregational Chapel, Hackney, and after Palmer's death Burder was ordained to his pastorate on 2 March 1814. His ministry at Hackney led to a marked increase in attendance at the chapel. He noted that, in general, many who filled the chapels were unwilling to be formal members of the Congregational churches and addressed this in his *Obligations to the Observance of the Lord's Supper* (1819). His ministerial work also led to his compiling *Psalms and Hymns, Principally for Public Worship* (1826), and to his publishing *Pastoral Discourses on Revivals in Religion* (1829) and a volume of *Sermons* (1854), among other writings. From 1810 he was also the tutor in philosophy and mathematics at Hoxton Academy, until its removal to Highbury in 1830. His tutorial work led to the publication of *Mental discipline, or, Hints on the cultivation of intellectual habits, addressed particularly to students in theology and young preachers* (1822), *Lectures on the Pleasures of Religion* (1823), and *Lectures on the Essentials of Religion, Personal, Domestic, and Social* (1825).

Burder remained at Hackney until 1852, when he delivered on 26 December, and afterwards published, *A Pastor's Farewell* (1853). His congregation presented him with £1000, which he used to establish a Burder scholarship at New College, London. He was a supporter of the temperance movement from 1830, and in 1834 helped to prepare a paper, submitted to the churches of the USA, criticizing the continuation of slavery there. Burder was prominent among the founders of the Congregational Union of England and Wales in 1831, and acted as its chairman in 1844. He advocated a Congregational approach to sabbatarianism in *Four Lectures on the Law of the Sabbath* (1831). Conscientious and precise, Burder's theology was conservative: opposed to 'all bold speculations', he was 'incapable of sympathy' (J. Stoughton, *Recollections of a Long Life*, 1894, 17).

Burder was twice married: first, on 14 June 1810, to Anne, eldest daughter of Joseph Hardcastle of Hatcham House, Deptford, London, who died in 1827 leaving a daughter and three sons; and secondly, on 17 April 1833, to Mary Tayler (*d.* 1859). In his later years he lived with his eldest son at Hatcham House, where he died on 29 December 1864; his body was interred in the cemetery at Stoke Newington.   ARTHUR H. GRANT, *rev.* ALAN ARGENT

Sources H. F. Burder, *Memoir of the Rev. George Burder* (1833) · J. Burder, 'Memoir of Rev. Henry Forster Burder', *Evangelical Magazine and Missionary Chronicle*, [3rd ser.], 7 (1865), 129–34 · *Congregational Year Book* (1866) · *GM*, 3rd ser., 18 (1865), 257 · *Daily News* (4 Jan 1865) · *The Nonconformist* (4 Jan 1865) · *The Patriot* (5 Jan 1865) · A. Peel, *These hundred years: a history of the Congregational Union of England and Wales, 1831–1931* (1931) · H. McLachlan, *English education under the Test Acts: being the history of the nonconformist academies, 1662–1820* (1931) · R. Tudur Jones, *Congregationalism in England, 1662–1962* (1962) · R. W. Dale, *History of English congregationalism*, ed. A. W. W. Dale (1907) · *CGPLA Eng. & Wales* (1865)
Archives DWL, corresp. and papers

Likenesses C. Baugniet, lithograph, 1845, BM, NPG · Andrews, portrait (of older man; after painting by Wildman), NPG · T. Blood, print (after J. Jackson), DWL · T. Blood, stipple (after J. Jackson), BM, NPG; repro. in *Evangelical Magazine* (Jan 1817) · J. Cochran, stipple (in later life; after E. B. Morris), BM, NPG · E. B. Morris, oils (of mature man), DWL

Wealth at death under £7000: probate, 1 Feb 1865, *CGPLA Eng. & Wales*

Burder, Samuel (1773–1836), Church of England clergyman, was the son of William Burder, and a relation of George Burder. In 1797 he was ordained as the first pastor of an Independent congregation in St Albans, but he subsequently conformed to the Church of England. In 1808 he was admitted to Clare College, Cambridge, but there is no evidence that he ever matriculated at the university. He was ordained in the autumn of 1808 by Bishop Barrington of Durham. He was morning preacher at St Margaret's, Lothbury, in London, curate and assistant preacher at St Dunstan-in-the-West, Fleet Street, and lecturer at Christ Church, Greyfriars. Before 1816 he was appointed chaplain to the duke of Kent, and in 1827 to the earl of Bridgewater. He died at Pentonville on 21 November 1836. He was the author of several works, including *Memoirs of Eminently Pious British Women* (1815) and three popular compilations, *Oriental Customs in Illustration of the Scriptures* (1802), *Oriental Literature Applied to the Illustration of the Sacred Scriptures* (1812), and *Oriental Customs* (1831); the first of these ran to several editions and a German translation.

DAVID HUDDLESTON

Sources W. Urwick, *Nonconformity in Hertfordshire* (1884) · *GM*, 2nd ser., 7 (1837), 215–16 · *Congregational Magazine*, new ser., 1 (1837) · *GM*, 1st ser., 97/1 (1827), 361 · *GM*, 1st ser., 102/2 (1832), 88 · Venn, *Alum. Cant.*

Burder, Thomas Harrison (1789–1843), physician, was born in Coventry, the son of George *Burder (1752–1832), a minister in the Independent church, and his wife, Sarah Harrison of Newcastle under Lyme. Henry Forster *Burder (1783–1864) was his brother. It was at first intended that Thomas should be a chemist and druggist, but after a while he decided to study medicine. After pursuing his studies for about five years in London he went to Edinburgh, in 1812, where he was elected one of the presidents of the Royal Medical Society, and where he took the degree of MD, in 1815. He decided to settle in London as a physician, and was for a time attached to the Westminster General Dispensary. However, he suffered from almost constant ill health, which made it extremely difficult for him to cope with the demands of medical practice, and forced him, during the nineteen years that he struggled on in London, to give it up sometimes for weeks, sometimes even for months together.

Burder was a contributor to the *Cyclopaedia of Practical Medicine* (1833–5), and his article 'Headache' was drawn largely from his own painful experience. Throughout his life Burder was from time to time inclined to devote himself entirely to ministerial work, and at one time had serious thoughts of joining the Church of England. He continued, however, to belong to the Independent church, though he did not formally become a member until he was nearly forty. Some time around 1828 Burder became acquainted with James Hope (1801–1841), and, when he later discovered that Hope shared similar religious feelings to his own, their acquaintance ripened into a warm friendship. After Burder had finally given up medicine a suggestion from Hope induced him to address to him three letters, which appeared in the *Evangelical Magazine* for 1836, under the title of 'Letters from a senior to a junior physician on the importance of promoting the religious welfare of his patients'; these were included in his *Memoir* and in the *Memoir of Dr Hope*, and also published in a separate form at Oxford in 1845.

Burder had married his cousin, Elizabeth Burder, in 1828, and his father had lived with them during the last four years of his life at their home in Brunswick Square; but after his death in 1832 Burder began to think seriously of leaving London altogether, and he did so in 1834. The change of air and his way of life improved, but it did not completely restore his health, and he died at Tunbridge Wells, Kent, in 1843, at the age of fifty-four. He left no children, and his widow died in the following year. Burder's 'Letters' (which he at one time had considered expanding) and the pattern of personal holiness exhibited in his correspondence published after his death are the only remains of a man of more than ordinary abilities.   W. A. GREENHILL, *rev.* MICHAEL BEVAN

Sources J. Burder, *A memoir of Thomas Harrison Burder* (1844) · W. A. Greenhill, *Life of Thomas Harrison Burder* (1845)

Burdet, Thomas (c.1425–1477), landowner, was the eldest son of Nicholas Burdet of Arrow, Warwickshire, and of Joan, sister and heir of Maurice Bruyn of Belne (Belbroughton) and Ab Lench (Fladbury, Worcestershire). His father having died in 1441, he succeeded his grandfather, another Thomas, in 1442 and was in the wardship of Humphrey, earl of Stafford, until c.1446, although active in local affairs from 1445. At this time the power of the Beauchamp earls of Warwick, centred on the west midlands, was largely in abeyance and, like several other men from this region with family traditions of service to the house of Warwick, Burdet gravitated towards the rising power of Lord Sudeley and Lord Beauchamp of Powick. However, in 1451 Burdet received a life annuity from Richard Neville, the Beauchamps' successor as earl—an association which probably accounts for Burdet's appointment as Warwickshire JP in 1453, and his election to the parliament held in 1455 after the battle of St Albans. Even so, like others who had been linked to Sudeley and Beauchamp, Burdet continued to flirt with these two for most of the decade. This facilitated his desertion of Warwick when the Yorkists were disgraced in 1459, though, judging by his exclusion from local commissions, he committed himself firmly to neither side.

From 1461 Burdet was embroiled in a dispute of increasing severity with a Warwickshire neighbour, John Rous of Ragley. Although apparently a less unstable character than his father or grandfather, who had been consistently involved in such episodes, when they were not warring with the French, Burdet was periodically engaged in local conflict, sometimes of a violent nature, throughout his adult life. The earl of Warwick's inability to settle the affair, despite the death of a minor participant in 1465, or to restrain Burdet's behaviour, was symptomatic of his loss of control of his midland affinity in the 1460s. It was probably Warwick who ensured that Burdet held no local office under Edward IV until 1468, when he was reappointed JP. By then Warwick's worsening relations with the king were forcing him to make friendly overtures to several of his estranged clients, but Burdet apparently remained too uncertain a quantity to hold office during the readeption. He was reappointed to the commission of the peace in December 1471 and remained on it almost continuously until 1475. In the 1470s he still served the house of Warwick, represented now by the duke of Clarence, although he continued to allow himself his earlier freedom of action, a course much simplified by Clarence's still more spectacular failure to control his political domain in the midlands.

In early 1477 Burdet made settlements to ensure the disinheritance of Richard, his son with his first wife, Agnes, daughter and coheir of John Waldeve of Alspath, Warwickshire. The marriage had been annulled by October 1456 on grounds of consanguinity, although a more lurid story alleges that Burdet had fallen for another woman and then tried not only to trap Agnes into adultery with a priest but to murder their young son. About 1456 Burdet had married Margaret, widow of John Hull and daughter of Sir John Rodney, both of Somerset, and by 1477 there were five under-age sons of this marriage (Nicholas, the eldest, John, Robert, George, and Edward). Later in 1477 Burdet was arrested for publishing seditious writings and, with Master John Stacy and Thomas Blake, both of Merton College, Oxford, encompassing the deaths of Edward IV and Prince Edward. If Burdet's treason and Clarence's were interlinked, as is often assumed, Burdet's role is puzzling, since he was by no means close to Clarence at this time. However, he had been alienating important local people, who perhaps denounced him to the king for loose talk, among them Sir Simon Mountford, who was given the wardship of the young heir which Burdet's untimely demise made available. Burdet was tried and then executed in London, at Tyburn, on 20 May 1477, protesting his innocence, while Clarence's further protests helped to seal his own fate. Burdet's widow married Thomas Woodhull and was living in 1495.

A protracted dispute over the Burdet inheritance between Richard, the son of the first marriage, and Nicholas, the eldest son of the second marriage, supported by his mother, followed Burdet's execution. Initially the second family was favoured, not surprisingly given their protection by so influential a local man as Simon Mountford. But, after Mountford's wardship of Nicholas was rescinded in November 1478, he changed sides and married his daughter to Richard Burdet, who was declared legitimate in 1482 and left in possession of almost the whole estate. The case was reopened under Richard III but the younger family, now represented by Nicholas's younger brother, John, gained little. In fending off the claim of the

Cokayns of Derbyshire and Warwickshire to Bramcote (Warwickshire), one of his few remaining properties, John was murdered in 1493.   CHRISTINE CARPENTER

Sources C. Carpenter, *Locality and polity: a study of Warwickshire landed society, 1401–1499* (1992) • M. C. Carpenter, 'The duke of Clarence and the midlands: a study in the interplay of local and national politics', *Midland History*, 11 (1986), 23–48 • Ancient Indictments, King's Bench Plea Rolls, Early Chancery Proceedings, PRO, KB 9, KB 27, C 1 • *Chancery records* • M. A. Hicks, 'False, fleeting, perjur'd Clarence': George, duke of Clarence, 1449–78 (1980) • *Reports of the deputy keeper of the public records*, 3 (1892) • W. Dugdale, *The antiquities of Warwickshire illustrated*, rev. W. Thomas, 2nd edn, 2 vols. (1730) • *VCH Warwickshire* • *VCH Worcestershire* • Inquisition post mortem, PRO, C 145/328/66 • Staffs. RO, D641/1/2/271
Archives Derbys. RO, Burdet of Foremark
Wealth at death £155 p.a. (Warwickshire lands only); also properties in Worcestershire: PRO, C 145/328/66

Burdett, Sir Francis, fifth baronet (1770–1844), politician, was born on 25 January 1770 at Foremark, near Repton, Derbyshire, second (but first surviving) son of Francis Burdett (1743–1794), country gentleman, and his wife, Eleanor, daughter and coheir of Sir William Jones of Ramsbury Manor, Wiltshire. He had two brothers and three sisters. He succeeded his grandfather Sir Robert Burdett (1716–1797) as fifth baronet on 13 February 1797, inheriting estates at Foremark and Bramcote, Warwickshire. In 1800 he inherited Ramsbury from his aunt. The Burdetts were an old midlands parliamentary family, lately tory, who had lived in England since 1066.

Education, marriage, and parliament Burdett was educated at Westminster School from 1778 until his expulsion following a rebellion in 1786, and then at Christ Church, Oxford, from 1786 to 1788. He later toured the continent for two years, before returning to Britain in 1791. On 5 August 1793 Burdett married Sophia (1775–1844), the youngest daughter and coheir of the London banker Thomas *Coutts (1735–1822). There were difficult relations with his wife and her parents, caused by the Burdett family's social prejudice, Burdett's own melancholia, pedantry, and quick temper, and Sophia's possessive attachment to him. In 1795–6 Burdett came close to separating from his wife, and discussed suicide. William Stevens, his family's chaplain, commented (18 August 1795) that 'He is too much a Philosopher to be happy or to make happy' (*Journal of the Rev. William Bagshaw Stevens*, 280). The marriage survived to produce six children. From an affair with Lady Oxford (Jane Elizabeth Harley), Burdett probably fathered one if not two children. When in London, the Burdetts lived at 1 Stratton Street (the home of Thomas Coutts) from 1793 to 1802, at 78 Piccadilly from 1802 to 1816, and at 25 St James's Place from 1816 to 1844. From 1796 Burdett also maintained a residence in Wimbledon.

Early in his adult life Burdett exhibited generous instincts, commenting in 1798 that 'The best part of my character is a strong feeling of indignation at injustice & oppression & a lively sympathy with the sufferings of my fellows' (Patterson, 1.34). He based his anti-establishment politics on the need to protect individuals put upon by those in power. Burdett stated frequently that country

Sir Francis Burdett, fifth baronet (1770–1844), by Sir Thomas
Lawrence, c.1793

gentlemen must help reclaim the ancient liberties of
Britons usurped by 'the undue influence of a junto of
nobility and placemen'. To counter the 'borough-
mongers' Burdett championed reforming the House of
Commons so as to represent even modest property-
owners. These principles he maintained through the
1820s, by which time many 'Burdettites' turned to other
political creeds. Yet his core idea, that political reform
would regenerate society, was later echoed in Chartism.

In 1796, to overcome his son-in-law's reclusive habits
and save his marriage (by keeping him from a threatened
move to France), Coutts purchased Boroughbridge, a
pocket borough of the dukes of Newcastle. As his own politics were more Jacobin than Jacobite, Burdett waited
until his grandfather's death to give his maiden speech in
parliament, in support of Fox's opposition to the government's Irish policy. His family chaplain termed him in
1795 'an implicit Follower of Robespierre' (*Journal of the
Rev. William Bagshaw Stevens*, 276), and on several occasions
Burdett spoke with admiration of Napoleon. He flirted
with revolutionary politics in both England and Ireland

through the early 1800s. In the 1796–1802 parliament Burdett voted consistently against Pitt on both domestic
issues and foreign affairs, and during the Foxite whig
secession emerged as a popular figure out of doors. He
almost always voted against fiscal and tax bills, aiming to
protect landowners and labourers alike from being overtaxed to support an unjust war abroad and 'manifold acts
of aggression against the constitution of the country'. Burdett also opposed repeated suspension of habeas corpus,
exclusion of reporters from the House of Commons, the
Combination Acts, and the Act of Union; in 1802 he moved
an inquiry into the Pitt regime.

Although more than one opponent was outraged by his
immoderate language, Burdett's parliamentary speeches
and public addresses were widely reported in the press,
often published as pamphlets, and were frequently
alluded to in satirical prints. His voice was crucial to the
survival of the reform movement in an era when pressure
from government and loyalists had driven parliamentary
reformers to secede and extra-parliamentary radicals to
gaol or silence. Burdett relentlessly inveighed against
those in power, helping make 'old corruption' an issue
that gained audience as the war against France dragged on
and domestic scandals arose. From 1796 Burdett was
understood to be a disciple of John Horne Tooke, although
Tooke confirmed rather than created the young baronet's
political philosophy, deepening an attachment to the
'ancient constitution' and to household rather than universal suffrage.

Westminster radical In December 1798 Burdett took up the
harsh treatment of prisoners at Cold Bath Fields prison,
having already raised the issue of prison conditions twice
that year. The effort forced a parliamentary committee
and later an ineffectual commission of inquiry. Frustrated
with politics, by 1802 Burdett seemed ready to abandon
his parliamentary career; earlier that year he had been
blackballed for membership in the Whig Club. But his
reputation as 'a dangerous but large-acred man' led in
1802 to an invitation to stand for Middlesex county,
Wilkes's old seat. Burdett's return after a tumultuous
campaign alarmed the government. The election was subsequently voided, and a new contest occurred in 1804.
Now Burdett emphasized parliamentary reform rather
than the treatment of political prisoners. Narrowly
defeated as a result of misconduct by the Middlesex sheriffs, the results were subsequently overturned and Burdett sat for Middlesex in 1805–6. The expense of the two
campaigns, which he bore himself, was enormous,
although nearer £60,000 than £100,000, as some believed,
and Burdett was forced to borrow on his estates. In the
general election of 1806 he refused to campaign or spend
money, and was soundly defeated for Middlesex. Here and
in his efforts at the borough of Westminster that same
election he began to sever his remaining ties to the
Foxites, 'these venal coalition Whigs' whom he denounced for having allied with the Grenvilles, 'those hateful
villains'. Burdett was now an independent: 'public principle', not the quest for office, 'is my God' (Burdett to
Thomas Sheridan, 14 Nov 1806, Bodl. Oxf., MS Eng. lett. c.

64). He sounded a theme that would be repeated over the next three decades: king and people had the same enemies, and they included the followers of both Pitt and Fox.

That Burdett spoke in parliament and acted in public for the rights of oppressed individuals and political reform made him attractive to radicals in the borough of Westminster. As in Middlesex in 1806, so in Westminster in 1807 he was not formally a candidate. If elected he would sit, but he would spend no money and make no speeches. Misunderstandings led Burdett to a duel with his erstwhile fellow candidate James Paull. The radical electors, now organized as the Westminster Committee, and most notably Francis Place, made enormous efforts on his behalf alone when following the duel they dropped their support of Paull. Burdett's lopsided victory achieved at a cost of less than £800 made Westminster the radical centre of London and indeed the kingdom. Place's subsequent analysis aside, that 'the people themselves have raised him to the pinnacle on which he stands' (*Authentic Narrative of the Events of the Westminster Election*, 1819, 51), the Westminster radicals won as much because of Burdett's prestige as their own hard work.

Frequent speeches in Palace Yard and the Crown and Anchor tavern kept Burdett continuously public in a way politicians had not been before. In 1808 he took up the abolition of flogging in the army, an issue he had first raised in 1798. Initially his efforts for political reform remained vague, based upon restoring the common law, Magna Carta, the Bill of Rights, and the Act of Settlement. But in 1809, outraged by the acquittal of the duke of York following a scandal over the sale of army commissions, Burdett offered the first comprehensive motion for parliamentary reform since 1797. The bill called for a ratepayer franchise, shorter parliaments, equal electoral districts, and single-day elections. Burdett was defeated in a small house, a sign that the man and the measure were deemed unimportant.

Imprisonment and parliamentary reform This changed when on 5 April 1810 Burdett was found guilty of breach of privilege by the House of Commons. He had used forceful language in a letter to the Westminster electors published in William Cobbett's *Political Register*, in which he condemned exclusion of reporters from the debates over the Walcheren expedition of 1809. The confrontation between the 'Man of the People' and the Perceval government had been building for some time, owing to Burdett's speeches about the unrepresentative character of the Commons, criticism of the war and the sale of army commissions, and tiresome lectures on the ancient constitution. On 6 April the Commons voted to commit Burdett to the Tower of London, whereupon he challenged the speaker's warrant and barricaded himself in his London house. Clashes followed between troops and the crowd, resulting in riots which one contemporary recalled as 'the most anxious day London has known since 1780'. Burdett was seized on the morning of 9 April, while along with friends and family he listened to his son, down from Eton, translating Magna Carta from Latin. Burdett was confined

to the Tower until the end of the parliamentary session on 21 June. The government was too afraid to expel him from the house, fearing a national outcry. Burdett's popularity reached its peak after the incarceration; three separate biographies of him were published during that spring. But he proceeded to disappoint his followers by preventing a procession through London on his release, fearing further riots and loss of life, or that he would be assassinated.

With the death of Horne Tooke in 1812 Burdett's political activities declined, and he began to move in circles that included Lord Byron and the princess of Wales. Once again he championed prison reform, as well as several matters concerning the navy. Alongside Major Cartwright, Burdett issued a call for county meetings at which landowning reformers would take the lead in canvassing the nation to boost reform. After 1815, however, some allies and followers turned to those radical politicians advocating universal suffrage. Burdett appeared aloof to many concerned by the country's increased urbanization and industrialization; he said little regarding the Luddites. To some plebeian radicals his brusque behaviour was read as condescending; Samuel Bamford found him 'civilly familiar', while others observed that the baronet was enervated in public and taciturn in private. A protracted conflict erupted at this time between Cobbett and Burdett, over Burdett's failure to assist prisoners condemned to die for the Pentrich rising of 1817, the 1818–19 elections in Westminster, and loans made to Cobbett by the baronet. This in turn was part of a complex struggle over political tactics among radicals within the borough of Westminster and elsewhere. The attempt in the spring of 1817, supported by Burdett, to flood parliament with petitions ended in failure, as did Burdett's motion that May for a select committee on representation. For those to Burdett's left, such as Henry Hunt, the baronet was trimming. For his part Burdett believed a reform bill which included universal suffrage and the ballot incapable of passing without the support of the whigs, and he questioned schemes, such as the Spa Fields meetings, which threatened insurrection.

In 1818 Burdett introduced a new reform bill, which joined arguments from utility and Burdett's ancient constitution, as Jeremy Bentham put it 'the most profound philosophy [uniting] with the greatest popularity of the time'. The bill called for manhood suffrage, annual parliaments, equal electoral districts, and the ballot. Although Burdett corresponded with Bentham on law reform, he remained less utilitarian than humanitarian. While soundly defeated in the house (2 June 1818), Burdett's effort preserved his position in Westminster against the charges of more radical reformers that he was 'a democrat in words, and an aristocrat in feeling' (*Cobbett's Weekly Political Register*, 12 June 1818). His reform motion of 1819 was the last he was to offer.

In response to the Peterloo massacre Burdett wrote to the Westminster electors on 22 August 1820 condemning the massacre, reminding the king of 1688, and using the phrase 'bloody Neroes'. He called on the gentlemen of

England to join the masses in protest meetings. Burdett was prosecuted for seditious libel, found guilty, sentenced to the Marshalsea prison for three months, and fined £2000. Although the episode and Burdett's role the same year in defending Queen Caroline helped recapture some of his standing, there were no Burdettite crowds this time, although he did finish at the top of the poll for the Westminster election held while his trial took place.

Richard Carlile spoke for many when in 1822 he suggested that 'the mind of the people has marched, and Sir Francis has not been disposed to march with it' (*The Republican*, 31 May 1822). Certainly by the mid-1820s Burdett's language was less violent and more vague; in an 1826 letter accepting the support of the Westminster Committee for his re-election he spoke of 'the great cause of the people—a full, fair, free, equal, and frequently-chosen representation in the Commons House of Parliament' (*Morning Chronicle*, 8 June 1826). For the first time Burdett paid part of his election expenses for Westminster, acting more like a normal candidate than 'Westminster's Pride and England's Glory'.

With the failure of reform in the 1820s Burdett moved to other issues. While his own pronouncements regarding religion suggest he was a rationalist, Burdett supported the established position of the Church of England. But tours of Ireland in the 1790s and 1810s led him to favour Catholic emancipation, and in February 1825 the Commons passed a relief bill introduced by Burdett which, however, was defeated by the Lords. His later bills in March 1827 and May 1828 helped lead to Catholic emancipation in 1829. Burdett supported two projects dear to Westminster radicals, the London Mechanics' Institute (now Birkbeck College of London University) and the West London Lancasterian Association. Burdett was one of the organizers in 1824 of the Greek Committee. In parliament in the 1820s he voted for repeal of the corn laws and the Combination Acts, against the London police, and for government interference regarding factory labour, emigration, the London water supply, and banking. His only publication was an edited version of *Annals of Banks for Savings* (1818).

Disillusionment and eclipse With the whigs in power after 1830 Burdett seemed, according to Denis Le Marchant, 'to oscillate between Democracy and Toryism'. Having chaired the moderate National Political Union, he quit the organization in February 1832; having been on the committee of the Parliamentary Candidates Society, which sought to extract pledges from potential candidates, Burdett denounced pledges during the 1832 election. New issues arose in politics which he could not make fit the principles he developed in the late eighteenth century. As he lost faith in 'the people' in the abstract, Burdett grew disillusioned. He spoke more of protecting the constitution from people led astray by demagogues than from objectionable laws and borough-mongers. Perhaps the greatest irony of his career as a reformer is that in 1832 he was eclipsed by men such as Lord John Russell. The Reform Act was a watershed: Burdett had argued that what he advocated was really a restoration; now he

believed his own rhetoric, that the ancient constitution had been resurrected.

After Grey retired in 1834, Burdett moved away from the whigs. Gout had plagued him for years, and ill health now made him more pessimistic; Daniel O'Connell irritated him, as did the poor law of 1834. In 1837 a meeting of electors asked him to resign his seat, which he did and thereupon stood in a by-election 'against an unnatural alliance … of Irish agitators, Popish priests, & paid patriots [and] a weak and vacillating Administration' (Patterson, 2.644). Having won the election, Burdett crossed the floor of the house. At the general election two months later he stood for North Wiltshire, which he represented until his death.

The Times in 1835 termed Burdett 'the head of the unenobled English Aristocracy'. He had lived simply, never seeking office and refusing peerages offered by Canning, Grey, and Melbourne. Politics was his only career, unless one counts fox-hunting and 'leisure, liberty & command of [my] own time, which', he wrote in 1804, 'are my Penates or household Gods' (Burdett to Thomas Coutts, 6 March 1804, Bodl. Oxf., MS Eng. lett. c. 61). Burdett subsidized a variety of people and causes: Paine, Cobbett, Fox's widow, Thomas Hardy, Horne Tooke, the Irish revolutionary Roger O'Connor, and various unfortunates in Westminster; the election campaigns of fellow radicals; John Wade's pro-trade union *Gorgon*; and London University.

Burdett died on 23 January 1844 at his residence at 25 St James's Place, two days short of his seventy-fourth birthday, from a pulmonary embolism; he may have met his death as a consequence of homoeopathic treatment. He was buried in the family vault in Ramsbury church together with his wife, who had died eleven days earlier. His daughter Angela Burdett-*Coutts erected and endowed St Stephen's, Rochester Row, Westminster, in memory of her father, which was consecrated on 24 June 1850.

Radical icon Burdett was one of the most caricatured politicians during the first two decades of the nineteenth century; his prominent aquiline nose and other patrician features appeared in well over 300 political cartoons beginning in 1798. Slogans such as 'Burdett and Liberty' and 'Burdett and Independence' were fixtures of early nineteenth-century political vocabulary. Burdett made appearances in literature from *Real Life in London* (1821) to Sir Fraunceys Scrope in Disraeli's *Endymion* (1880), and he was the subject of ninety pamphlets published during his half-century in parliament. As a genteel democrat in an age of oligarchy, Burdett was simultaneously revered and despised. He had one foot in the country party of the early eighteenth century, and the other in the strange birth of Liberal England in the early nineteenth. Historians, like contemporaries, have been sharply divided over his impact on politics, or even his political philosophy. As Burdett himself put it to John Cam Hobhouse in 1818,

In moderation placing all my glory
Tories call me Whig and Whigs a Tory!!

At least up to 1820 Burdett is generally recognized as the premier national figure of the radical reform movement. Scholars working on other individuals have seen Burdett through their subjects, so that he has been variously understood as an orthodox whig, a parliamentary liberal, and a revolutionary leader. In contrast with Paine's natural rights or Bentham's utilitarianism, Burdett offered an essentially antiquarian justification for reform. That his idea faded in the long run is no less significant than that it resonated deeply with English feelings during his lifetime. Strictly defined schools of radicalism obstruct the fluidity and pragmatism among early nineteenth-century radicals. Burdett was, according to Thomas Moore, 'neither very sensible, nor deeply informed upon any subject' (Moore, *Memoirs*, 2.158), which thus allowed him to blend Foxite rhetoric and radical anger with Enlightenment humanitarianism and tory paternalist instincts.   MARC BAER

Sources M. W. Patterson, *Sir Francis Burdett and his times (1770–1844)*, 2 vols. (1931) · M. H. R. Bonwick, 'The radicalism of Sir Francis Burdett (1770–1844) and early nineteenth century "Radicalisms"', PhD diss., Cornell University, 1967 · *Journal of the Rev. William Bagshaw Stevens*, ed. G. Galbraith (1965) · J. S. Jackson, *The public career of Sir Francis Burdett* (1932) · W. E. Saxon, 'The political importance of the Westminster Committee of the early nineteenth century, with special reference to the years 1807–22', PhD diss., U. Edin., 1958 · J. A. Hone, *For the cause of truth: radicalism in London, 1796–1821* (1982) · D. Miles, *Francis Place, 1771–1854: the life of a remarkable radical* (1988) · G. Cahill, 'Burdett, Sir Francis', *BDMBR*, vol. 1 · D. R. Fisher, 'Burdett, Sir Francis', HoP, *Commons* · J. R. Dinwiddy, *Radicalism and reform in Britain, 1780–1850* (1992) · W. Thomas, *The philosophic radicals: nine studies in theory and practice, 1817–1841* (1979) · P. Spence, *The birth of romantic radicalism: war, popular politics, and English radical reformism, 1800–1815* (1996) · C. S. Hodlin, 'The political career of Sir Francis Burdett', DPhil diss., U. Oxf., 1989 · *DNB*
Archives Bodl. Oxf., Burdett–Coutts MSS, corresp., letters, and papers · Derbys. RO, corresp. and papers relating to Derbyshire estates · JRL, Labour History Archive and Study Centre, letters · Wilts. & Swindon RO, corresp. and papers | BL, corresp. with Lord Broughton, Add. MS 47222 · BL, corresp. with J. C. Hobhouse, Add. MSS 36457–36470 · BL, corresp. with Lord Holland, Add. MS 51569 · BL, corresp. with Sir Robert Peel, Add. MSS 40345–40531 · BL, letters to Francis Place, Add. MSS 27823, 27842, 37949–37950 · Lpool RO, letters to Lord Stanley · NA Scot., corresp. with Thomas Cochrane · NRA Scotland, priv. coll., corresp. with Sir George Sinclair · U. Durham, letters to Earl Grey
Likenesses T. Lawrence, oils, *c*.1793, NPG [*see illus.*] · S. Percy, wax relief, exh. RA 1803, V&A · A. Cardon, stipple, pubd 1804 (after R. Cosway), BM, NPG · A. Buck, watercolour miniature, 1810, NPG · F. Chantrey, plaster bust, 1811, AM Oxf. · W. Sharp, line print, pubd 1811 (after J. Northcote), BM, NPG · W. Ward, mezzotint, pubd 1811 (after J. R. Smith), BM, NPG · R. Dighton, caricature, coloured etching, pubd 1820, NPG · J. Ternouth, marble bust, 1827, Palace of Westminster, London · Behnes, marble bust, 1832, Messrs Coutts & Co., London · J. Bruce, silhouette, *c*.1832, NPG · T. Phillips, oils, 1834, NPG · Ferneley, portrait, 1837, George Donald Collection, Canada · M. A. Shee, portrait, 1838, Westminster School, London · E. Landseer, portrait, *c*.1840, NPG · M. A. Shee, oils, 1843, NPG · W. C. Ross, miniature, exh. RA 1844, NPG · G. G. Adams, marble bust, *c*.1854, Westminster School, London · J. Doyle, caricatures, drawings, BM · G. Hayter, group portrait, oils (*The trial of Queen Caroline, 1820*), NPG · G. Hayter, group portrait, oils (*The House of Commons, 1833*), NPG · bronze token, NPG · caricatures, BL

Wealth at death under £160,000

Burdett, Sir Henry Charles (1847–1920), philanthropist and hospital reformer, was born on 18 March 1847 at Broughton, Northamptonshire, the son of Halford Robert Burdett (1813–1864), a clergyman in the parish of Gilmorton, Leicestershire, and his wife, Alsina, *née* Brailsford, from Lincolnshire. The Burdett family had enjoyed the living at Gilmorton since Elizabethan times, and the ethos of the country parsonage left the young man with strong religious convictions and an exceptional sense of social obligation. At school he earned a reputation for application and the nickname 'Bucket', after the single-minded, inquisitive detective in *Bleak House* (1853). He joined a bank in Birmingham at the age of sixteen, but soon developed an interest in medicine, administration, and politics. In 1868 he was appointed secretary to the Queen's Hospital, Birmingham, where he transformed the institution's management and finances. He and Joseph Chamberlain, the mayor of Birmingham (1873–5), were sometimes seen together on the same platform at the Edgbaston Debating Society, of which Burdett was the treasurer.

In 1874 Burdett registered at Guy's Hospital as a medical student. The following year he became house governor to the Seamen's Hospital in Greenwich, and on 5 August married Helen Shute (*d.* 1919), the daughter of Gay Shute FRCS, with whom he had four sons and two daughters. Burdett took the view that the voluntary hospitals must be run along commercial lines if they were to compete with the meritocratic public sector. At the Seamen's Hospital he dramatically increased revenue and reduced unit costs and earned a reputation as a highly professional hospital administrator. Meanwhile, he completed his training at Guy's, compiled comparative statistics on medical provision, and wrote widely on hospital affairs.

In 1881, in an exceptional change of career, Burdett joined the stock exchange as secretary to the shares and loan department. He remained there for seventeen years, producing what many investors used as the City bible: *Burdett's Official Intelligence*, a repository of information on British and American securities. Astonishingly energetic, he also found time to publish the four-volume *Hospitals and Asylums of the World* (1893) and to edit, from 1886 to 1920, *The Hospital*, a weekly journal of administrative medicine. He also made connections in the City of London which would help to bring to fruition the various schemes which his fertile mind devised. An avid sportsman and gambler, he was said to have broken the bank at the casino in Monte Carlo. He once placed a bet on the prince of Wales's lucky number and, characteristically, cabled the winnings to the prince.

Burdett admired voluntarism for its educative and humanizing influence, but he acted on a fundamental truth about charitable organization: it was not simply the nature of the campaign that determined its success, but who could be found to support it at the top. In 1889 he published *Prince, Princess and People*, in which he chronicled the patronage work of the prince and princess of Wales with

Sir Henry Charles Burdett (1847–1920), by Bassano, 1897

the same thoroughness that he applied to charitable institutions. He believed the royal couple to be uniquely placed to give a national prominence to charitable work while marking its local significance. Through the assiduous cultivation of palace officials, Burdett ingratiated himself at court. As a result the prince and princess began to seek his advice on patronage and consulted his *Year Book of Philanthropy* for information on worthwhile causes. In 1889 the royal couple agreed to become patrons of his National Pension Fund for Nurses, which proudly added the prefix 'Royal' to its title. In 1896 he persuaded the prince of Wales to join the Sunday Fund, a charity which co-ordinated and distributed church collections to the voluntary hospitals.

Apart from charitable administration and fund-raising, Burdett's hospital interests ranged from nursing and medical education to accounts and statistics. All of these concerns found expression in his most significant achievement, the foundation in 1897 of the Prince of Wales's Hospital Fund for London (renamed the King Edward's Hospital Fund for London in 1902). Established to commemorate Queen Victoria's diamond jubilee, the fund brought together the royal family and the middle classes in the cause of medical philanthropy. It soon established itself as the leading institution for the defence and development of London's voluntary hospitals. In its early decades it provided about 10 per cent of hospital income and acted as a central hospital board for the capital and a

forum for ideas on all matters dealing with medical administration. With royal support, Burdett also established the League of Mercy in 1898, a money-raising auxiliary of the Hospital Fund. It extended the fund's tendrils into the working-class districts of London and the home counties and assisted many of those much beloved cottage hospitals dotted around the country. For his charitable services he was appointed KCB in 1897 and KCVO in 1908.

An awesome presence in the charitable world, Burdett gave shape to the monarchy's social policy at the turn of the century. His intention was to bring the royal family and the City into philanthropic communion. Such a partnership would not only enliven the charitable establishment but would improve national efficiency, keep socialism at bay, and provide a humanitarian justification for the empire. (An imperialist from his days in Birmingham, Burdett stood unsuccessfully for parliament in 1906 as an independent Conservative.) His financial wizardry and City connections stood him in good stead. He brought financiers into palace circles and, along with his friend Ernest Cassel (1852–1921), advised the prince of Wales about investments. As one of Burdett's colleagues remarked, he was 'chosen as the medium through which these splendid gifts have been made to charity by the merchant princes and members of the Stock Exchange in the City of London' (memorandum, Burdett MSS).

Ardent, sanguine, and 'a little noisy', Burdett had the genius to persuade, indeed compel, others to join in his ambitious plans. His appearance—tall, well built, and handsome—was in keeping with his character: he steamrollered resolutely anyone audacious enough to disagree with him. To those who shared his outlook and kept pace with his exhausting demands, he could be the soul of kindness. He was on the best of terms with the caged birds in his study, if not always with his wife and colleagues. To royalty, in the accepted Edwardian manner, he was obsequious. This was due partly to his ingrained sense of social hierarchy, but also to the importance he attached to the voluntary cause. He distrusted state intervention in the hospital world because he believed it would substitute remote bureaucratic control for local initiative and individual responsibility. Arguably, he did more to defend and to expand voluntary hospital provision than anyone who had ever lived. His motto, which he never tired of repeating, was 'personal service to the sick in the days of health' (*The Hospital*, 8 May 1920, 130). He died at his home at The Lodge, 43 Porchester Terrace, London, of heart failure on 29 April 1920. FRANK PROCHASKA

Sources F. K. Prochaska, *Philanthropy and the hospitals of London: the King's Fund, 1897–1990* (1992) · F. Prochaska, *Royal bounty: the making of a welfare monarchy* (1995) · C. Maggs, *A century of change: the story of the Royal National Pension Fund for Nurses* (1987) · G. Rivett, *The development of the London hospital system* (1986) · H. C. Burdett, *Prince, princess and people* (1889) · *The Hospital* (8 May 1920) · *The Times* (30 April 1920) · *The Times* (10 July 1920) · Bodl. Oxf., MSS Burdett · m. cert. · b. cert.

Archives Bodl. Oxf., corresp. and papers · LMA, King's Fund archive · Royal National Pension Fund for Nurses, London · Warks. CRO, corresp.

Likenesses Bassano, photograph, 1897, NPG [*see illus.*] · cartoon, Wellcome L. · photograph, Wellcome L.
Wealth at death £26,682 8s. 8d.: probate, 6 July 1920 · £23,945—Personalty: *The Times* (10 July 1920), 16

Burdett [*née* Francis], **Jane**, **Lady Burdett** (d. **1637**), literary patron, was the only daughter and heir of William Francis of Foremark, near Repton, Derbyshire, and his wife, Elizabeth, daughter of William Francis of Ticknall. Details of her early life are unknown. In 1602 she married Thomas (1585–1646/7), son and heir of Robert Burdett (d. 1603) of Bramcote, Warwickshire, and his wife, Mary, daughter of Thomas *Wilson (1523/4–1581), scholar and secretary of state. Like her husband Jane may still have been a minor at the time of her marriage. On 6 May 1603 Burdett matriculated from Balliol College, Oxford, but he did not stay to take a degree. Once the couple had taken possession of their respective estates they lived mainly at Foremark. They had at least three daughters—Bridget, Dorothy, and Jane—and two sons, Francis (1608–1696) and Robert. Burdett served as sheriff of Derbyshire in 1610–11 and was created baronet on 25 February 1619. Despite his absenteeism he continued on the Warwickshire commission of the peace until 1625, and the following year was named a commissioner for the collection of the forced loan in the county.

The Burdetts were known as puritans but Lady Burdett also gained renown as an unusually learned woman at the hub of a circle of literary-minded gentry; she was, observed William Dugdale, 'a Ladie of singular endowments' (Dugdale, *Antiquities*, 2.1122). His report on 26 March 1637 to fellow Warwickshire antiquary Sir Simon Archer of 'sad news of that worthy Lady Burdett, our good friend, that she is eyther dead, or irrevocably sick' (*Life*, ed. Hamper, 163) postdated her death by five days. Her funeral address, delivered on 24 March by the family's chaplain, the godly minister Thomas Calvert, is a manifestation of conventional piety but over the following decade some of her former circle composed more striking elegies and epitaphs, which were published with the sermon in 1650 as *The Wearie Soules Wish, or, The Doves Wings*. Acknowledging 'her faith, her knowledge and her judgement sage' (p. 20) several contributors were at pains to emphasize Lady Burdett's participation as an equal in their conversations and literary endeavours. R. B. considered her 'a spirit masculine' (p. 26), while an anonymous versifier praised 'the female darling of the Aonian tribe' (p. 21), a 'Mentall Cosmographer' (p. 23), who not only 'did study to be most rationall', but succeeded. 'Great Reasons Quintessence', she:

> measured Women to so faire a span
> Of gifts and braines, as parallel to Man.
> (p. 21)

Sir George Gresley of Drakelowe (1580?–1651), whose son Thomas (d. 1642) had in 1622 married Lady Burdett's daughter Bridget, and who was himself a considerable patron of learning, celebrated in verse dated 23 March 1647 'So strong a Braine, ripe wit and well fraught head' (p. 18). Thomas Gresley's university friend John Newdigate

Jane Burdett, Lady Burdett (d. 1637), by unknown artist, c.1620 [with her husband, Sir Thomas Burdett, first baronet, and family]

(1600–1642), also a devotee of poetry and drama, paid tribute in metaphors of the law court and the tiltyard to a woman who both inspired and enlightened poets and debaters:

> She was the muse herself, Philosophie
> Fell from her in high raptures.

In composing his 'strong lines' he accepted her judgement entirely. 'Where she was summoned into other lists' she was equally active and commanding:

> She was the Schoolmans great Antagonist,
> The States-mans great Compeer; the Traveller
> Came to learn somewhat (he ne'er knew) from her.
> (p. 18)

Sir Thomas Burdett made his will on 13 June 1646, naming a second wife, Elizabeth, a son, Leicester, and three daughters in addition to his 'daughter Gresley' and other children from his marriage with Jane. He died some time before 22 May 1647, when his will was proved, and was buried at Repton. His widow is credited with giving shelter during the 1650s to the future archbishop Gilbert Sheldon. It was Jane's son Francis, second baronet and at the time sheriff of Derbyshire, who in 1650 was the dedicatee of *The Wearie Soules Wish*. In addressing him, and at least in partial reference to the literary circle at Foremark, Calvert regretted profoundly the passing of an age 'full of feastings, Masks and Comedies, the unruly Children of wanton peace'; now 'we … are come to act nothing but passively in sad and grave Tragedies' (p. 4).

VIVIENNE LARMINIE

Sources GEC, *Baronetage*, 1.119 · W. Dugdale, *The antiquities of Warwickshire illustrated*, rev. W. Thomas, 2nd edn, 2 (1730), 847–8, 1122 · W. Camden, *The visitation of the county of Warwick in the year 1619*, ed. J. Fetherston, Harleian Society, 12 (1877), 101 · A. Hughes, *Politics, society and civil war in Warwickshire, 1620–1660* (1987), 41, 54, 95–6, 347 · T. C. [T. Calvert], *The wearie soules wish, or, The doves wings*

(1650) • will, PRO, PROB 11/200, fol. 285r [Sir Thomas Burdett] • *The life, diary, and correspondence of Sir William Dugdale*, ed. W. Hamper (1827), 10, 127, 163 • 'Collections for a history of the Gresley family', Bodl. Oxf., MS Eng. hist. b. 159 • J. T. Cliffe, *The puritan gentry: the great puritan families of early Stuart England* (1984), 74

Likenesses group portrait, *c*.1620, priv. coll. [*see illus.*]

Burdett, Peter Perez

Burdett, Peter Perez (1734/5–1793), cartographer and draughtsman, was probably born in Eastwood, Essex, the only son of William and Elizabeth Burdett. His Christian names derive from his maternal grandfather, Peter Perez, vicar of Eastwood (1697–1748), from whom he inherited a small estate.

Of Burdett's first twenty-five years there is little record. By the early 1760s he lived in Derby and had launched a career as a cartographer. His map of Derbyshire at a scale of one inch to a mile, begun in 1763 and published in 1767, won him the £100 premium offered by the Society of Arts. His many talents in the arts and sciences brought him a wide circle of acquaintances in Derbyshire, especially the painter Joseph Wright, in several of whose paintings he appears, notably in *A Philosopher Giving a Lecture on the Orrery* (1776) where Burdett is seen sketching. In 1765 Wright painted a fine portrait of Burdett and his first wife, Hannah, which hangs in the Národní Galerie, Prague. Wright, who lent him money that he never repaid, continued to consult him on technical matters after he left Derby; Burdett in turn seems to have procured purchasers for some of Wright's pictures, including Washington Shirley, fifth Earl Ferrers, and Catherine the Great.

In 1768 Burdett moved to Liverpool and launched, in his impetuous way, several cartographic and artistic projects. His experiments with printmaking included aquatint, for which his claims to be the inventor are strong: he certainly published, in 1771, the first aquatint in England after a painting by his friend John Hamilton Mortimer, and, ever short of money and frequently in debt, sold the process to Paul Sandby, to whom it is usually credited, for £40. His interest in transferring aquatinted designs to pottery led him in 1771 to approach Josiah Wedgwood, who after considerable interest finally lost patience with the headstrong Burdett, who had hopes of years of lucrative work from his process. Frederick the Great of Prussia and Benjamin Franklin, with whom he corresponded over several years, were equally discouraging; Franklin remarked that the colonies were not yet ready for Burdett. A fine draughtsman and noted expert in perspective, he was the first president of the Liverpool Society of Arts and exhibited in London at the Society of Artists. His ambitious but financially unprofitable venture with George Perry, ironmaster for the Coalbrookdale Company, to publish views of Liverpool by Michael Angelo Rooker, a map (1769), and a history of the town was completed after Burdett withdrew to chase more promising interests, but his drawings of public buildings, engraved by Edward Rooker, appeared in the history, published in 1773.

Burdett's plan to survey Lancashire failed for lack of sufficient subscribers. His map of Cheshire, begun in 1774, must have been completed by assistants, for early in 1775 he entered the service of the margrave of Baden, leaving a

Peter Perez Burdett (1734/5–1793), by Joseph Wright of Derby, 1765 [with his first wife, Hannah Burdett]

wife, whose subsequent fate is unknown, with his considerable debts. He was engaged to conduct the official survey of the margravate, reaching the rank of major. From the school of surveyors and mathematicians he founded grew the Karlsruhe Technical School. On 11 June 1787 Burdett married Friedericke Kottewski. Their daughter Anne married Count Friedrich Nostitz. Burdett died in Karlsruhe on 9 September 1793. PAUL LAXTON, *rev.*

Sources B. Nicolson, *Joseph Wright of Derby: painter of light*, 2 vols. (1968) • P. Laxton and J. B. Harley, *A survey of the county palatine of Chester by P. P. Burdett 1777* (1974) • J. Egerton, *Wright of Derby* (1990) [exhibition catalogue, London; Grand Palais, Paris; and Metropolitan Museum of Art, New York, 7 Feb – 2 Dec 1990] • private information (1993) [D. Fraser; L. Slavicek] • Baden Generallandesarchiv, Karlsruhe

Likenesses J. Wright of Derby, double portrait, 1765, Národní Galerie, Prague [*see illus.*] • J. Wright of Derby, group portrait, 1776 (*A philosopher giving a lecture on the orrery*)

Burdett-Coutts. For this title name *see* Coutts, Angela Georgina Burdett-, *suo jure* Baroness Burdett-Coutts (1814–1906).

Burdon, John Shaw (1826–1907), bishop of Victoria, Hong Kong, and Chinese scholar, only son of James Burdon and Isabella, his second wife, was born at Auchterarder in Perthshire on 12 December 1826. After his father's early death he was brought up by an uncle, who kept a school at Liverpool, where he was overworked. From Liverpool he went to Glasgow. In 1850 he was accepted as a missionary by the Church Missionary Society (CMS), and he then spent two years at its training college at Islington, London. He was ordained deacon by the bishop of London on 19 December 1852. On 30 March 1853 he married Harriet Anne Forshaw.

Burdon and his wife sailed for Shanghai on 20 July 1853, but she died there on 26 September 1854, less than a fortnight before his ordination as priest by the bishop of Victoria, Hong Kong, on 8 October. Meanwhile the Taiping insurgents threatened imperial power in China. Shanghai was taken by them just before Burdon's arrival, and he occupied himself with long and very hazardous journeys into the surrounding country. There he preached, interviewed the iconoclastic and professedly half-Christian rebel leaders, and opened new mission stations. On 11 November 1857 he married Burella Hunter Dyer, who died on 16 August 1858.

From January to July 1859 Burdon stayed at Hangchow (Hangzhou); but the people proved inaccessible, and he returned to the coast. In 1860 he made a second attempt on Hangchow but was obliged to fall back on Shaohing (Shaoxing), where he worked until late in 1861. In December 1861 he was in Ningpo (Ningbo) when that city was captured by the rebels. Early in 1862 he went to Peking (Beijing) as pioneer of the Church of England at the capital, and after eleven years of hard work and domestic sorrow he returned to England on 22 May 1864. He married on 14 June 1865 his third wife, Phoebe Ester, daughter of E. T. Alder, vicar of Bungay; they had three sons, his earlier marriages having been childless.

In September 1865 Burdon was again in Peking, where he added to his other work the duties of chaplain to the British legation (from 1865 to 1872). In 1864 he had been appointed one of a committee of five eminent Chinese scholars to translate the New Testament into Mandarin. This work appeared in 1870–72 and was for long the foundation of all subsequent revisions. In 1872 appeared also a version of the Book of Common Prayer by Burdon and Bishop Samuel I. J. Schereschewsky, which also for long formed the basis of all the prayer books printed in Mandarin. Subsequently he prepared other editions of the prayer book (in 1879, 1890, and 1893), issued a revision of the New Testament translation with H. Blodget (in 1889), and from 1891 to 1901 was a member of a committee for revision of the Chinese Bible.

On his election as bishop of Victoria, Hong Kong, Burdon returned to England on 25 October 1873, and early in the following year he received the degree of DD from the archbishop of Canterbury. On 15 March 1874 he was consecrated third bishop of Victoria, a diocese which until 1883 included Japan as well as all of south China. At his own request his name was kept on the roll of CMS missionaries, and he had sometimes to insist on the fact that he was a missionary, as well as a colonial bishop. His episcopate was marked by ceaseless if unobtrusive work and boundless hospitality at Hong Kong, and by arduous visitations in Fukien (Fujian) and elsewhere. Burdon enjoyed the regard alike of the merchants of Hong Kong and the missionaries in Fukien. He resigned the bishopric on 26 January 1897 and retired to Pakhoi (Beihai), where his missionary life closed. His wife, Phoebe, died on 14 June 1898. Burdon left China in 1901, and his last years of failing health were spent with his youngest son, Edward Russell Burdon, in England. He died at Springfield House, Kempston, Bedford, on 5 January 1907, and was buried at Royston.   [ANON.], rev. H. C. G. MATTHEW

Sources private information (1912) · *Church Missionary Review*, 58 (1907), 227–36 · E. Stock, *The history of the Church Missionary Society: its environment, its men and its work*, 1–3 (1899) · G. E. Moule, *Notes on Hangchow past and present*, 2nd edn (1907) · M. Broomhall, *The Bible in China* (1934) · *CGPLA Eng. & Wales* (1907)
Archives Church Missionary Society Library, London, journals and letters to Church Missionary Society | LPL, corresp. with A. C. Tait

Likenesses photograph, NPG
Wealth at death £4394 2s. 9d.: probate, 8 Feb 1907, *CGPLA Eng. & Wales*

Burdon, William (1764–1818), writer, was born at Newcastle upon Tyne, the son of George Burdon of Newcastle upon Tyne. He was educated at Newcastle grammar school, then, from 1781, at Emmanuel College, Cambridge, graduating BA 1786 and MA 1788, when he was elected a fellow of his college. He resigned his fellowship in 1796 on declining to be ordained (but gave £100 towards rebuilding the college after a fire in 1811). He married in 1798 a daughter of Lieutenant-General Dickson; they had at least two sons. His wife died in 1806. Burdon was a wealthy man, owning coalmines at Hartford, near Morpeth, where he lived for a part of each year.

Burdon used his money to publish, often privately, his views on literature and politics. He wrote an *Examination of the Merits and Tendency of the Pursuits of Literature* (1799), *Various Thoughts on Politicks, Morality, and Literature* (1800), and *Materials for Thinking* (1803 and several later editions). He replied to T. J. Mathias's views of literature and Alexander Pope in two pamphlets in 1799; he wrote a life of Napoleon Bonaparte (1804), and translated A. Florez Estrada's book on the revolution in Spain (1811). He published several pamphlets on contemporary politics, which show him to have been a moderate reformer, and edited the *Memoirs of Count Boruwlaski* (published 1820). Burdon died at his London house in Welbeck Street on 30 May 1818.

H. C. G. MATTHEW

Sources *GM*, 1st ser., 88/2 (1818), 87 · Venn, *Alum. Cant.* · *DNB*
Archives Emmanuel College, Cambridge, corresp.
Likenesses C. Picart, stipple, pubd 1819 (after R. W. Satchwell), NPG · etching, pubd 1826, NPG

Burdy, Samuel (c.1760–1820), author, was born at Dromore, co. Down, the only son of Peter Burdy, a merchant of that town. The family was descended from a Huguenot who had fled to Holland and went to Ireland in the army of William III. Burdy obtained a sizarship by examination at Trinity College, Dublin, on 22 March 1777; he gained a scholarship in 1780, and graduated BA in 1781. He was ordained in 1783, and in the same year was appointed curate of Ardglass, a parish in co. Down. Burdy had been introduced to Bishop Percy of Dromore by Hely Hutchinson, the provost of Trinity College, and was welcomed into the bishop's household. He fell in love with the bishop's daughter, but Percy, who prided himself on belonging to the great Northumberland family, resented the possibility of an alliance with a curate, and for more than a year refused even to see Burdy. At the end of that time Burdy wrote a letter of apology, which shows that while he submitted to her father's wishes he remained in love with the daughter. The bishop ceased to be actively hostile, and used to lend books to Burdy, but the curate lived and died unmarried. He was only once promoted, and then to the perpetual curacy of Kilclief, a small preferment in co. Down. This was soon after 1800, and twenty years later he ended his life there.

In 1781 Burdy made the acquaintance of the Revd Philip Skelton, then in his old age. They were suited to one another, and became firm friends for the remaining six years of Skelton's life. Skelton lived in Dublin, and for three years Burdy used to visit him often. When the younger man left Dublin they corresponded until 4 November 1786. In February 1787 Burdy saw his friend again, and, as he says, 'parted for the last time from that dear and worthy man' (Burdy, 217). After Skelton's death Burdy set to work to record his friend's life and conversation. He visited co. Tyrone, Monaghan, and Donegal, to collect reminiscences of Skelton, and in 1792 he published at Dublin *The Life of the Late Rev. Philip Skelton, with some Curious Anecdotes*. The life was republished in London in two volumes, with the lives of Edward Pocock, Zachary Pearce, and Bishop Newton, in 1816. In 1824 a third edition appeared, prefixed to an edition of Skelton's works, edited by R. Lynam; but this edition was considered flawed, as the editor had altered the text of Burdy's biography. It was said by a contemporary that Macaulay gave the original work considerable praise. Soon after its publication the book was attacked for its provincial language, and the author defended himself with success (*A Vindication of Burdy's Life of Skelton*; 1795).

Before his life of Skelton, Burdy had published in 1792 *A Short Account of the Affairs of Ireland during the Years 1783, 1784, and Part of 1785*. In 1802 he published in octavo in Dublin *Ardglass, or, The Ruined Castles, also The Transformation, with some other Poems*. During his curacy at Ardglass he had often mused over the history of its five ruined castles—hence the poem. The poetry was not highly regarded, but now and then contains amusing glimpses of country life in Ireland. The Belinda who is several times the subject of praise and of lament is probably the bishop of Dromore's daughter. In 1817 Burdy published at Edinburgh *A History of Ireland*. It is not a work of great research, but gives a summary of affairs up to the union.

Burdy died on 7 March 1820. He was buried in Kilclief where his grave is marked by no monument.

NORMAN MOORE, *rev.* MYFANWY LLOYD

Sources *A new catalogue of living English authors: with complete lists of their publications, and biographical and critical memoirs* (1799) · D. J. O'Donoghue, *The poets of Ireland: a biographical dictionary with bibliographical particulars*, 1 vol. in 3 pts (1892–3) · S. Burdy, *The life of the late Rev. Philip Skelton, with some curious anecdotes* (1792) · Burtchaell & Sadleir, *Alum. Dubl.*

Burel, John (1565×8–1603), merchant and poet, was the son of Edinburgh's wealthiest flesher, Harry Burel (d. 1587), and his second wife, Isobel Abernethie (d. 1616), who were married in January 1565. Nothing is known of Burel's schooling, but he was a good Latinist. About 1592 he married Marjorie Mowbray (d. in or after 1626), one of the many daughters of John Mowbray of Barnbougall and his wife, Elizabeth Kirkcaldie, sister to Sir William Kirkcaldie of Grange. In the past the poet has been identified with a John Burel, goldsmith and temperer of the irons in the mint, traceable from March 1588 to his death in September 1632; this man was the second husband of the poet's elder half-sister Jonet (d. c.1600). Robert Birrell, schoolmaster and diarist, was also a relative.

Burel's poetry, though uneven, is interesting. A volume published in late 1590 or early 1591, whose title-page has not survived, was probably written at the behest of John Maitland of Thirlestane, chancellor of Scotland, to dissuade the dedicatee, James VI's favourite the sixteen-year-old Ludovick Stuart, second duke of Lennox, from pursuing his passion for Lylias Ruthven, a daughter of the late earl of Gowrie, and thereby aligning himself with aristocratic opposition to the chancellor. The book's centrepiece is a very fine translation of the twelfth-century verse drama *Pamphilus de amore*. The other poems in the book are a dedication to the duke, a translator's preface taking a distinctly post-Reformation view of the story of Pamphilus's seduction of Galathea, and an epilogue to *Pamphilus*, explicitly headed 'The aplication of the translater upon the purpose going before'. Divided in two by an elegant sonnet, the first part of the 'Aplication' condemns infatuated lovers like Pamphilus, whose irresponsible passion endangers whole societies. Its second part praises James VI's heroic matrimonial sea-voyage to Norway in 1589, urging this admirably responsible monarch to wield the sword of justice and 'gud men mentene, and punish that opres'. There follows a lively celebration, in near-doggerel, of Edinburgh town council's well-ordered commonwealth and its splendid welcome to Queen Anna on 19 May 1590.

Burel's book closes with an ambitious apocalyptic allegory, 'The Passage of the Pilgremer', which denounces Scottish society's lawless violence and irresponsible aristocracy, a major target being the earl of Huntly, an inveterate Catholic intriguer. Like the admonitions to the newly married king to 'let justice flourish in this land', these attacks echo those made by the Edinburgh minister Robert Bruce in his 'sermons on the sacrament' of 1589, and foreshadow John Napier's preface to his *Plaine Discovery of the Whole Revelatione* (1593). The poem ends very abruptly, and seems to have been written at high speed and left as an unrevised torso. It reveals Burel's close acquaintance with earlier and contemporary Scottish poets, notably Gavin Douglas and John Rolland, and with *The Cherrie and the Slae* of Alexander Montgomerie.

Burel's only other identifiable work is the broadsheet sonnet addressed to the diplomat Sir James Colville (distantly related to Burel by marriage) in October 1601, urging him to dispatch Burel's colourful Catholic brother-in-law Francis Mowbray, cadet of Barnbougall, a man deeply involved in espionage and counter-espionage. Accused in July 1601 of plotting to murder King James, Francis wrote to his erstwhile employer, Robert Cecil, that Burel 'has oft done me ignominious injury with his pen' (*CSP Scot., 1597–1603*, 13, no. 734), thus implying the existence of other verse by a poet of considerable interest both in his own right and as the voice of the rising bourgeoisie. Burel died at Edinburgh on 5 March 1603; Marjorie is found in documents of 1624 and 1626 alongside her eldest son, John, who was apprenticed to a goldsmith in 1608.

JAMIE REID-BAXTER

Sources J. Reid-Baxter, 'Politics, passion and poetry in the circle of James VI: John Burel and his surviving works', *A palace in the wilds*, ed. L. Houwen, A. A. Macdonald, and S. Mapstone (1999) · The

collected works of John Burel, ed. J. Reid-Baxter and R. Scheibe, STS [forthcoming] · P. Bawcutt, 'Pamphilus de amore in Inglis tongue', Medium Aevum, 64 (1995), 264–72 · A. H. Williamson, 'Scotland, Antichrist, and the invention of Great Britain', New perspectives on the politics and culture of early modern Scotland, ed. J. Dwyer, R. A. Mason, and A. Murdoch (1982), 44–58 · M. Lee, John Maitland of Thirlestane (1959) · CSP Scot., 1597–1603 [F. Mowbray to R. Cecil, 7 Nov 1601, 13, no. 734] · will, reg. 21/5/1603, NA Scot., Edinburgh testaments, CC8/8/37 · H. Burel's contract with brother John, 30/9/1580, NA Scot., register of deeds, RD1/19, fol. 83 · will, reg. 26/1/1591, NA Scot., Edinburgh testaments, CC8/8/22, fol. 181 [Harry Burel] · will, reg. 20/1/1597, NA Scot., Edinburgh testaments, CC8/8/31, fol. 110v [Marion Burel] · discharge by Isobel Abernethie, 11 Dec 1589, NA Scot., register of deeds, RD1/36, fol. 12v · obligation by Isobel Abernethie, 4 March 1590, NA Scot., register of deeds, RD1/33, fol. 359 · will, reg. 24/7/1633, NA Scot., Edinburgh testaments, CC8/56, fol. 153 [John Burel] · A. B. Calderwood, ed., The buik of the kirk of the Canagait, 1564–1567, Scottish RS (1961)
Wealth at death £2400 Scots: will, 21 May 1603, NA Scot., Edinburgh testaments, CC8/8/37

Burford, Robert (1791–1861), panorama painter and proprietor, was the son of John Burford, a panorama proprietor. Both Robert Burford and his father worked for Robert Barker (1739–1806), the inventor of the panorama, and then, after his death, for his son Henry Aston *Barker (1774–1856), at the Panorama, Leicester Square. In 1816 Henry Aston Barker and John Burford bought out the rival panorama establishment in the Strand, and managed it jointly until H. A. Barker's retirement early in 1824. The Leicester Square panorama and the Strand panorama were then managed by John and Robert Burford until the former's death in 1827. Thenceforth both institutions were managed by Robert Burford.

Robert Burford not only managed the two panoramas, he also produced many of the drawings and was in charge of the painting. Most of the panoramas of European cities that were exhibited had been drawn on the spot by him, as was New York. The drawings for Antwerp were taken by him personally in 1830 'during the last days of the siege' (descriptive booklet accompanying exhibition). While drawing Salzburg he was challenged for trespassing, and when drawing Vienna he found himself locked in the spire of the Karlskirche and had to be rescued by passers-by responding to his cries. Drawings for panoramas of more distant, exotic places were supplied by resident military officers and government officials—amateur artists in other words. The explorers Captain John Ross and Lieutenant William H. Browne provided drawings for Boothia and the polar regions respectively; and the artist, architect, and explorer Frederick Catherwood provided drawings for Jerusalem, Thebes, and Baalbek. Augustus Earle provided drawings for Hobart, Sydney, and the Bay of Islands, New Zealand; and David Roberts provided drawings for Cairo. Moscow was painted 'from drawings taken by Russian artists' (descriptive booklet accompanying exhibition). For panoramas created in the 1850s such as those of Sevastopol and Canton, Burford was able to make use of photographs.

Burford's principal artist, however, was Henry Courtney Selous who painted or contributed to more than forty panoramas beginning with Milton's Pandemonium (1829). From October 1833 until May 1834 Selous kept a diary describing life in Burford's painting room in Camden Town during the period when New York, Antwerp, and Boothia were being painted. (The aurora borealis and the stars on the latter attracted critical acclaim.) From Selous's journal (V&A NAL) emerges a picture of daily life at the painting room, and to a lesser extent at the Leicester Square panorama, with domestic gossip and occasional technical detail.

Burford was an alert and energetic showman, confidently providing London audiences with a seemingly never-ending sequence of sublime and topical patriotic spectacles. The sublime could be represented by foreign resorts visited normally only by the wealthy such as the Bernese Alps, Mont Blanc, or the Niagara Falls, or sensationally inaccessible quarters of the globe such as the Himalayas and the polar regions. The patriotic was catered for by the equivalent of twentieth-century newsreels or television news reports—royal visits, sieges, battles, and places in the news, all produced with commendable veracity and astonishing—sometimes almost uncanny—promptitude. Predictably, of the battles involving Britain, all were British victories except The Battle of Kabul in the Afghan War. Burford's sole venture into the field of literature was Pandemonium. It was not a success.

The profit rents on the Leicester Square panorama, the Strand Theatre (the converted Strand panorama), and the painting room in Camden Town were sold by Mr Robins at the auction mart opposite the Bank of England on 12 November 1857. Burford died at his residence, 35 Camden Villas in Camden Town, on 30 January 1861. He was succeeded by his son, Robert William, but the Leicester Square panorama, already very much in decline, was closed down on 12 December 1863.   RALPH HYDE

Sources S. B. Wilcox, 'The panorama and related exhibitions in London', MLitt diss., U. Edin., 1976 · R. D. Altick, The shows of London (1978) · S. Oettermann, The panorama: history of a mass medium (1997) · R. Hyde, Panoramania! the art and entertainment of the 'all embracing' view (1988–9) [exhibition catalogue, Barbican Art Gallery, 3 Nov 1988 – 15 Jan 1989] · H. C. Selous, journal, V&A NAL · descriptive booklets sold at the exhibitions, 1824–57, GL · descriptive booklets sold at the exhibitions, 1824–57, BM · private information (2004) [Grace Burford] · Art Journal, 23 (1861), 76
Wealth at death £8000: probate, 8 March 1861, CGPLA Eng. & Wales

Burford, Roesia [Rose] (d. 1329), merchant, was one of the four daughters of Thomas *Romeyn (d. 1313), a wealthy merchant and pepperer, mayor of London in 1309–10; her mother, Juliana Hauteyn, came from an old city dynasty. At an unknown date Roesia married her father's business associate John Burford (d. c.1322), a rich wool exporter and pepperer from Oxford, who from 1297 traded extensively in spices with the great wardrobe; he was alderman of Vintry ward in 1321–2. Roesia is best known as the recipient of 50 marks in 1317, part payment of 100 marks owed to her by Queen Isabella for an embroidered cope, a royal gift to the pope. The transaction has led many to identify Roesia as a London embroiderer of some standing. However, given her family's affluence and their links with the great wardrobe, it is more probable that she organized and financed the venture on the queen's behalf.

The commission is tentatively linked with two of the magnificent embroidered copes created at this time (generically referred to as *opus anglicanum*): a lost cope of 1315–35 only known through a seventeenth-century watercolour (now in the Walker Art Gallery, Liverpool), and more recently—and more probable—the cope presented to Pienza Cathedral in Tuscany by Pope Pius II in 1462 which is still preserved there. This latter cope is also dated to 1315–35, and has scenes from the lives of the Virgin, St Margaret, and St Catherine in three concentric zones. Richly embroidered copes of this kind were extremely expensive but nothing is known about the workshops where they were manufactured. They must have been designed by gifted professional artists and, clearly, were worked by a small team of highly skilled embroiderers. They were valuable diplomatic gifts much sought after by successive popes.

Roesia and John Burford apparently had a son Thomas, born before 1313 when he is mentioned in a document of expenses incurred by the executors of Thomas Romeyn; he did not survive to adulthood. There were two daughters, Joanna and Katherine, and then a further son, James, was born about 1320. On Romeyn's death in 1313 Roesia and John Burford inherited property in Aldermary.

When John Burford died *c.*1322 Roesia appears to have continued his business, and in 1324 is recorded selling sugar to the great wardrobe. She took John Lammas apprentice at about this time, and at her death in 1329 the apprenticeship was transferred to her son James. In due course Lammas became a leading pepperer and in 1345 was one of those who founded what became the Grocers' Company.

Roesia died in 1329. Her will, dated 25 March 1329, was made at her manor of Charleton in Kent. It reveals that Roesia had built a chapel on the south side of St Thomas the Apostle, London, where she now established a chantry for herself, her husband, and others. She left property in the London parishes of St Thomas the Apostle, All Hallows, Bread Street, and St Benet Sherehog to her young son James who also inherited her manors at Stockwell, Erith, and Combe. He and his sister lived at Charleton, under the guardianship of John Pulteney, a rich draper and alderman, who was later mayor of London. James did not become a merchant like his father, but instead lived as a gentleman on his country estates, and by 1358 was knighted. His sister Joanna was married to Thomas Betoyne, another pepperer. KAY STANILAND

Sources F. Devon, ed. and trans., *Issues of the exchequer: being payments made out of his majesty's revenue, from King Henry III to King Henry VI inclusive*, RC (1837), 133 • R. R. Sharpe, ed., *Calendar of wills proved and enrolled in the court of husting, London, AD 1258 – AD 1688*, 2 vols. (1889–90) • T. Stapleton, 'A brief summary of the wardrobe accounts of the tenth, eleventh and fourteenth years of King Edward the Second', *Archaeologia*, 26 (1836), 318–45, esp. 322 • PRO, E101/379/13 • Canterbury Dean and Chapter Library, Chart. Antiq. W.209a • G. A. Williams, *Medieval London: from commune to capital* (1963) • S. L. Thrupp, *The merchant class of medieval London, 1300–1500* (1948); repr. with new introduction (1989) • P. Nightingale, *A medieval mercantile community: the Grocers' Company and the politics and trade of London, 1000–1485* (1995)

Burford, Thomas (*b. c.*1710, *d.* in or after 1776), engraver and painter, was born about 1710. He seems to have been trained as both a painter and a mezzotint engraver, as his earliest known works, dating from 1741, include a portrait of Sir John Norris which was painted and engraved as well as published by him. From this same address—'the Golden Eagle in Villers Street, York Buildings'—he advertised in 1741 a portrait of Bishop William Warburton; in the same year he also engraved a set of *The Times of Day* after Nicolas Lancret for John Bowles.

Burford is now best remembered for numerous sporting plates, mainly of hunting scenes, but also of some shooting and racing events, and mostly engraved after works by James Seymour; more than sixty of them have survived. Some subjects were engraved in several different sizes—one hunting set appears in three sizes, as well as in a panoramic format—and some were completely re-engraved by Burford several times. His name also appears on a number of line-engraved copies of his sporting mezzotints. He engraved twenty-five portraits, many of them of British and foreign royalty, and about thirty decorative prints, among them sets after Lancret and Jacopo Amigoni. He appears to have published most of his prints himself: few other publishers' names appear on his work and he can be found advertising prints after Seymour in 1753, the year after the latter's death. Burford issued a set of seasons engraved by John Simon after Lancret in 1758, and was the retailer and possibly the part owner of John Dixon's much admired mezzotint print of a tigress after a work by Stubbs.

Burford's versatility and the rococo prettiness of his style were shown in the works he displayed at the Society of Artists, where he exhibited both drawings and mezzotints six times between 1762 and 1773 (by the latter date he was a fellow of the society). He also painted competent pastiches in oils of Seymour's works, but his whole-length portrait mezzotints, showing scant grasp of anatomy, betray the limitations of his talents. *The Twelve Months*, engraved after his own half-length drawings in 1745, have an elegance missing in much of his work. It is difficult to trace Burford's whereabouts during his career, but he clearly spent most of his working life in and about Broadway, Westminster, London. Advertised addresses include Cartaret Street in 1742 and the Golden Head, Chapel Street, in 1753 (this latter address was also the one given in the Society of Artists' catalogues from 1766 to 1768). From 1747 to 1774 Burford paid rates for addresses on the west and east sides of Broadway itself, and in 1774 he had premises in Bridge Street. He probably died in the late 1770s. Most of his sporting plates were then acquired by Robert Sayer, who with his partner, John Bennett, issued them in 1779 and again in his own name alone in 1787; many were still further reprinted by Sayer's successors, Laurie and Whittle, in 1794. Some of Burford's prints are held in the British Museum, London. C. A. LENNOX-BOYD

Sources J. C. Smith, *British mezzotinto portraits*, 1 (1878) · C. E. Russell, *English mezzotint portraits and their states*, 2 vols. (1926) · T. Dodd, 'Memorials of engravers practising in Great Britain, 1550–1800', BL, Add. MS 33394 · Graves, *Soc. Artists* · St Margaret's, Westminster, rate books, City Westm. AC · *Public Advertiser* (1741–53) · T. Mortimer, *The universal director* (1763) · M. A. Wingfield, *A dictionary of sporting artists, 1650–1990* (1992)
Wealth at death prosperous; approx. eighty copper plates; sixth share of important print

Burge, Hubert Murray (1862–1925), bishop of Oxford and headmaster, was born on 9 August 1862 at Meerut, India. He was the younger son of the Revd Milward Rodon Burge (1827–1874) and his wife, Mary Louisa Raffaella, daughter of Matthew Guerrin Price, of Guernsey. His father, a chaplain to the armed forces in India and later to the bishop of Calcutta, died in 1874, leaving his widow with little money. Burge briefly attended Marlborough College, before being sent to Bedford School as a day boy. In 1882 he went to University College, Oxford, as a scholar. He took a first in classical moderations in 1883 and a second in Greats in 1886.

After a period as a master at Wellington College, Burge returned to University College as fellow and tutor in 1890. He was a popular and effective college dean from 1895, and enjoyed a good rapport with young undergraduates, among them A. D. Lindsay, with whom he used to play golf. He was ordained priest in 1898, and in the same year he cemented his ties with University College by marrying Evelyn Isabel Franck, the youngest daughter of its master, Dr James Franck *Bright.

In 1900 Burge was elected headmaster of Repton School, but caused consternation by resigning after a year to become headmaster of Winchester College. As the first headmaster to be appointed by open competition, and the first non-Wykehamist for over a century, he was something of an experiment for the school, but he proved a triumphant success. He widened the syllabus, ending the stranglehold long enjoyed by classics, and built new buildings for science and music. Burge also made several astute appointments to the teaching staff and developed the prefectorial system. His great assets as a teacher were his humanity and his extraordinary memory for boys' names and details about them. He was particularly concerned to help those less academic boys traditionally neglected by the Winchester system. Later generations of Wykehamists looked back at his headmastership as a golden age, made the more poignant by the death of so many of his former pupils in the First World War.

A decade of strenuous effort at Winchester took its toll on Burge, whose broad frame and sporting demeanour belied a weak constitution stemming from childhood pleurisy. In 1910 illness forced him to spend two terms recuperating in south Africa. On his return he was offered the bishopric of Southwark by his friend H. H. Asquith. Burge's lack of parochial experience made him a controversial choice, but he confounded those detractors who feared a remote schoolmaster-bishop. He was assiduous in his pastoral duties and worked hard to establish a rapport with the people of south London. When a dock strike affected his diocese in 1912, he tried (unsuccessfully) to

Hubert Murray Burge (1862–1925), by George Harcourt, 1921

mediate in it, and raised money for dockers' families. He refused to use a car, travelling through his diocese by tram and bus in order to meet ordinary people. Such efforts again overtaxed his health, and he was relieved when translated to the less demanding diocese of Oxford as bishop in 1919.

Burge's religious faith was uncomplicated and undogmatic. His biographer, Lord Charnwood, described him as 'intellectually robust but nonetheless extraordinarily child-like' (*Discourses and Letters*, 16). As a bishop Burge defended the interests of liberal Anglicanism, and was courageous in supporting Hensley Henson in the row over his appointment as bishop of Hereford in 1917–18. But he eschewed church party, and rejected the extremism of many modernists in favour of a broad tolerance. He was responsible for setting up the Church of England doctrinal commission, of which he became the first president in 1922. Burge was also an early supporter of ecumenism, serving as president of the British Council of the World Alliance for Promoting International Friendship through the Churches. His international endeavours were continued after his death by the Burge memorial trust, which ran Anglo-German conferences in the 1920s and early 1930s.

Burge enjoyed politics, and was assiduous in attending the House of Lords. As a proponent of temperance reform he unsuccessfully introduced two bills in 1921–2 in support of the local option on licensing. In 1912 Asquith appointed him a member of the royal commission on the civil service, chaired by Lord MacDonnell. Burge was a Liberal supporter until the First World War, but thereafter moved towards Labour, under the influence of his close friend Lord Haldane.

Though not a prolific scholar, Burge was a lively, witty correspondent who set aside an hour a day for general reading. He also enjoyed outdoor pursuits, fishing, and making hay at his cottage in Northumberland.

As bishop of Oxford, Burge was *ex officio* chancellor of the Order of the Garter. He was also sub-prelate of the order of St John of Jerusalem in England, and clerk of the closet in ordinary to King George V. In June 1925, a week before his death, he was made KCVO. A keen cricketer, he was also a member of the MCC, I Zingari, and the Free Foresters.

Burge died of pneumonia at Cuddesdon, Oxfordshire, on 10 June 1925, and was buried in the village churchyard five days later. He was survived by his wife, and by a son and a daughter. MATTHEW GRIMLEY

Sources Lord Charnwood [G. R. Benson], 'Memoir of Burge', in H. M. Burge, *Discourses and letters of Hubert Murray Burge*, ed. Lord Charnwood (1930) · *The Times* (24 July 1925) · *The Times* (11 June 1925) · *Church Times* (12 June 1925) · *The Guardian* (19 June 1925) · J. D'E. Frith, *Winchester College* (1949) · J. Sabben-Clare, *Winchester College* (1981) · *Southwark Diocesan Chronicle* (1911–18) · *Burge memorial lecture, 1927–33* (1934) · D. Scott, *A. D. Lindsay* (1971) · O. Chadwick, *Hensley Henson: a study in the friction between church and state* (1983) · *CGPLA Eng. & Wales* (1925)
Archives Bodl. Oxf., letters to H. H. Asquith · NL Scot., letters to Lord Haldane · Wellcome L., letters to T. Barlow
Likenesses M. I. Cohen, oils, 1920–25, diocese of Oxford · G. Harcourt, oils, 1921 (after portrait), Winchester College · G. Harcourt, photograph, 1921, NPG [*see illus.*] · Spy [L. Ward], caricature, lithograph, NPG; repro. in *VF* (2 July 1903) · portrait, Diocesan House, Carshalton · portrait (posthumous), Cuddesdon College
Wealth at death £6758 4s. 6d.: resworn probate, 10 July 1925, *CGPLA Eng. & Wales*

Burgers, Thomas François (1834–1881), president of the South African Republic, was born on 15 April 1834 in Langfontein, Camdeboo, in the Graaff-Reinet district of Cape Colony, the youngest son of Barend Jacobus Burger or Burgers (1775–1845), a minister, and Elisabeth Magdalena Theron (1792–1867). He received his initial education at Graaff-Reinet, then went to Utrecht in the Netherlands to study for the ministry. It was while he was there, between 1853 and 1858, that he met Mary Bryson (1836–1929), a Scot, whom he married in 1858 and with whom he was to have ten children.

After being admitted as a minister in the Nederduits Gereformeerde Kerk (Dutch Reformed church) in Cape Town, Burgers became dominee at Hanover in the rural Karoo in 1859. The radical theology he had acquired in Utrecht from Professor Opzoomer and others soon revealed itself. He rejected much of the Bible as improbable, and did not believe in the bodily resurrection of Christ. In 1862 he was accused of rationalism and heterodoxy by his church, found guilty of deviation from its confession, and suspended as a minister. A strong-willed man, Burgers appealed to the Cape supreme court, which set aside the suspension in 1865. He was then able to return to his ministry. Two years later the supreme court's decision was upheld by the British privy council, the Cape's highest court of appeal.

Thomas François Burgers (1834–1881), by unknown photographer

Three brief sketches which Burgers wrote after a visit to the Transvaal were published first in the Cape Town journal *Volksblad* (1871) and then as *Schetsen uit de Transvaal* (1872). He found the Nederduits Hervormde Kerk in the Transvaal more congenial than his own branch of the Dutch Reformed church, and he impressed the white population of the Transvaal as one who would stand up to the British, then apparently seeking to encroach on Transvaal territory from Griqualand West. After President Brand of the Orange Free State had recommended Burgers as a man who would help extricate the Transvalers from their many difficulties, he was persuaded to run for president. Burgers was duly elected by a majority of 2964 votes, and sworn in on 1 July 1872. From the beginning he was opposed by the most conservative white burghers (citizens) of the Transvaal, led by Paul Kruger.

Burgers proved an idealistic but impractical president who failed to understand the people he ruled. Very seriously ill in 1874, he nevertheless worked hard to try to reduce the republic's isolation, and above all tried to launch a railway scheme to build a line from Pretoria to Delagoa Bay, a line which he believed would be the country's salvation. He sought to resist the interference of the British high commissioner, Sir Henry Barkly, who detested him, and he ignored the Keate award, which failed to grant the Transvalers the land they claimed in the south-west. On a fourteen-month visit to Europe he met

Lord Carnarvon, the colonial secretary, but was not persuaded to support the idea of a British-led federation. His goal was to put the Transvaal back on its feet, then lead it into a federation with the Orange Free State which would be the core of a future united South Africa with its own flag. He achieved very little in practice besides founding a newspaper in Pretoria in 1873 and establishing a museum, library, and botanical gardens. This last, in central Pretoria, is still known as Burgers Park.

Burgers's efforts for the Transvaal did not win him support there; instead the white burghers increasingly opposed him. They misleadingly claimed that his Education Act would remove the Bible from schools. When he sought to change the country's flag and coat of arms, in 1874, his attempt was reversed while he was absent. Tensions continued to grow as the burghers accused him of tactless behaviour. Burgers was often away from Pretoria and became increasingly isolated. His final failure came in 1876 when he led his burghers against the forces of Sekukuni of the Pedi, whose people were encroaching on land which the white Transvalers regarded as their own. For this war he drained the state's coffers, and this forced him to introduce a most unpopular war tax. The men who accompanied him in the field drifted away, and his campaign therefore failed.

Burgers's various failures as a leader gave Theophilus Shepstone, sent by Carnarvon to annex the Transvaal, the opportunity to claim that a majority of white Transvalers were in favour of British annexation. All Burgers could do was issue a note of protest when Shepstone proclaimed the annexation in April 1877. The following month he left for Cape Town, his political career at an end. He was then given a pension by the British from the Transvaal treasury on condition that he did not enter the territory. The Transvaal burghers accused him of treason for accepting it; he in turn blamed them for failing to reconcile themselves to British rule. He died poor, 'of a broken heart' (Appelgryn, 255), on 9 December 1881 at Richmond, Cape Colony, where he had been living, and was buried there. His remains were re-interred in the old cemetery, Pretoria, after the eventual opening of the Delagoa Bay Railway, his great dream, in 1895.   CHRISTOPHER SAUNDERS

Sources M. S. Appelgryn, *Thomas François Burgers: staatspresident, 1872–1877* (1979) · F. A. van Jaarsveld, 'Burgers, Thomas François', *DSAB* · T. F. Burgers, *Schetsen uit de Transvaal* (1872) · S. P. Engelbrecht, *Thomas François Burgers: a biography* (1946) · S. P. Engelbrecht, *Thomas François Burgers: 'n Lewenskets* (1933) · C. J. Uys, *In the era of Shepstone* (1933) · M. Macmillan, *Sir Henry Barkly* (1970)
Archives National Archives of South Africa, Pretoria, Transvaal archives depot · Nederduits Hervormde Kerk, Pretoria, archives
Likenesses photograph, repro. in J. Kotze, *Biographical memoirs and reminiscences* (1934) [see illus.] · photographs, repro. in Engelbrecht, *Thomas François Burgers* · sculpture, Burgers Park, Transvaal, South Africa

Burges, Cornelius (*d.* 1665), Church of England clergyman and ejected minister, was a native of Somerset. In 1611 he entered the University of Oxford, probably with the intention to study at Wadham College, which had been newly founded by Sir Nicholas Wadham and his wife, Dorothy, also of Somerset. He graduated BA from Wadham College on 5 July 1615. Some time in the middle of 1616 he migrated to Lincoln College, for on 9 November of the latter year, as a bachelor of arts of MA standing (from Lincoln), he was admitted as a reader to the Bodleian Library—a privilege he was gratefully to remember in the last days of his life. He proceeded MA from Lincoln on 20 April 1618.

Early career In the meantime Burges had been ordained and come under the patronage of Edward Russell, third earl of Bedford, who, Burges wrote in an epistle dedicatory to his *A Chaine of Graces* (1622), had condescended 'to admit me a meere stranger to the office of a Domestique Chaplaine in your Noble Familie'. It was through the 'gratious and effectuall mediation' of the countess of Bedford with Sir Charles Morison that Burges was instituted, 'with a setled comfortable abode, and a pastorall imployment', at the vicarage of Watford, Hertfordshire, on 21 December 1618. He was probably the Cornelius Burges who on 30 January 1618 or 1619 married Abigail Burges at Sutton Coldfield, Warwickshire. Forty years later, in a letter to Richard Baxter, the minister recalled his father-in-law, Dr Burges; John *Burges (1563–1635), who also moved in the Russell family orbit at this period, was rector of Sutton Coldfield from 1617 and had a doctorate in medicine.

In 1620, according to Arthur Wilson, Burges accompanied Sir Horatio Vere, the commanding general of the English volunteer forces, to the continent to fight in what was to become the Thirty Years' War, and was 'an instrument of much good to that Regiment' (Wilson, 138). At the encounter of the English forces with the Catholic army under the command of Ambrosio Spinola near the town of Altzi in the Palatinate, Burges gave encouragement to the English soldiers before battle. His stay on the continent was probably a brief one. He returned to England, perhaps with the earl of Essex, later in the year. It was also during these years that he was made one of the king's chaplains-in-ordinary, as he was to tell Charles II in the dedication to his *Prudent Silence* (1660) that he had 'had the honour to be a servant' to both 'your Royal Father' and 'your Majesties Grandfather King *James*'. In 1626 he was offered the rectory of St Magnus in the City of London, which was actually in the possession of the bishop of London. Burges proceeded DD at Oxford in June 1627 and in his divinity act he defended Calvinist positions on the certainty of salvation and perseverance.

Wood maintained that in this early period of his life Burges showed himself 'a zealous man for the Church of England, and it could never be thought in the least by those that knew him that he would have swerved from it' (Wood, *Ath. Oxon.*, 3.681). He probably preached a fast sermon before the House of Commons shortly after the convening of the parliament of 1628, but as the sermon was not published there is no way of establishing his views about the issues in that parliament. From the works which Burges published in the 1620s, however, it is clear he combined Calvinist theological predilections with conscious efforts to demonstrate that he was a loyal subject to the crown and a faithful son to the church.

Early publications Burges's first publication, *A Chaine of Graces* (1622), was a religious and pastoral treatise on such ethical topics as virtue, knowledge, temperance, patience, godliness, brotherly love, and charity. Educational and non-controversial in nature, the treatise was intended, as the title-page says, 'for reformation of Manners'. Interestingly, Burges expounded an empirical theory of knowledge: 'Though all knowledge be seated in the *Intellect*, yet it comes in thither by the *senses*' (p. 82), but it is doubtful that he was aware of its epistemological and theological implications. Only in a marginal note can his ambivalent attitude towards the word 'puritan' be detected. 'For such only were termed *Catharoi* in the Primitive Church', Burges wrote, 'who held themselves perfect. And this doth best agree to the scoffers of these dayes, who thinke themselves as good as need to be.' However, he made it clear that 'it can no way agree to honest godly sober men, who still acknowledge their wants, and goe on in their endevours' (p. 6).

In 1625 Burges published *The Fire of the Sanctuaries Newly Uncovered, or, A Compleat Tract of Zeale*. In spite of its seemingly radical title, this work, as Burges wrote in the preface, 'is *intended to* suppresse turbulence and all extremities'. Indeed, in dedicating the work to the earl of Pembroke he observed that 'Here is no ground for an *Utopian* Spirit to mould a new Common-Wealth: no warrant for *Sedition* to touch the *Lords Annointed*, so much as with her Tongue.' On the contrary Burges upheld, in one passage at least, the doctrine of divine right of kings in its unqualified claims. The Lord's annointed, Burges said, 'hath none betweene him and God, representing the Person of God, executing his office, and in this respect bearing his Name, to whom onely he is accountable for all his actions, by way of Summons and Commands' (pp. 262–3). Although this 'holy Fire of Zeale' was so important and useful for the Christian faith that 'he can be no good Christian who is without it' (p. 4), yet it should never stand 'with resistance, which is flat Rebellion. And no good cause calles Rebellion to aide' (p. 40). In 1625 Burges also published *A new discovery of personal tithes, or, The tenth part of mens cleere gaines proved due both in conscience, and by the lawes of this kingdome*. The publication of a treatise on tithes in 1625 is of special significance, for this was exactly the year when the puritan leadership, lay as well as clerical, began their scheme of feoffees for the purchase of impropriations, and the London clergymen, with the support of Archbishop William Laud, were soon to launch their lawsuit against the City for augmentation of their tithes. In any case, Burges presented an extremely broad claim to tithes and asserted that those who denied payment of 'what the Lawes of both God and Man have made due to the Pastor' violated 'six of the Ten Commandments' (Burges, *A New Discovery of Personal Tithes*, 1625, foreword). In 1629 Burges published *Baptismall Regeneration of Elect Infants* and dedicated it to Francis Russell, fourth earl of Bedford. It was a theological work based upon the scripture, and cited early church fathers as well as modern reformers. He devoted an entire chapter to the defence of the liturgy of the Church of England regarding the baptism of infants. Only briefly did he write against the Arminians in defence of 'the doctrine of Gods absolute election' and 'the comfortable doctrine of perseverance'—the two Calvinist doctrines which he had defended in his divinity act at Oxford in 1627. It may be noted, however, that the treatise originated in a series of lectures Burges had delivered during the Hilary term in 1627 at the parish church of St Magnus, for which, ironically, he had been accused 'not only of *Arminianisme*, but even direct Popery' (foreword and pp. 3–4, 18).

Ministry in the 1630s By 1630 Burges had become a prominent minister in London. When Sion College, a society of London clergymen, was founded in that year, Burges was elected one of its assistants. However, during the 1630s he appeared to become more and more alienated from the ecclesiastical establishment. Wood attributed this change of attitude to Burges's failure to procure 'that preferment confer'd upon him which he expected' (Wood, *Ath. Oxon.*, 3.681), but the intensifying vigour of the Laudian policy in the church and the personal rule of the king without calling a parliament must have been a factor. In February 1630, when Burges was invited to preach at Southwark Cathedral, he came into conflict with Bishop Richard Neile of Winchester, who insisted that Burges would have to read the prayer before his sermon. Upon Burges's refusal to comply, Neile refused to allow him to preach and expelled him from Southwark. In 1634 it was reported that he was one of the incumbents in the diocese of London who had refused to read the Book of Sports in church.

Yet in spite of these insubordinate actions, Burges seems to have maintained a friendly relationship with William Juxon, bishop of London, who in April 1635 appointed him to work with Brian Walton and other clergymen to promote the London clergymen's lawsuit for the augmentation of their tithes. On 28 January 1636 Burges was summoned to appear in the court of high commission for a Latin sermon he had preached before the clergy of London at St Alfege, London Wall, in which, according to Laud, he had 'uttered divers insolent passages against the bishops and government of the church' (*Works*, 5.338). However, although he declined to submit the notes of his sermon, which, he claimed, had been burned, no action appears to have been taken against him. In 1638 he signed the return of evaluations of the houses in the parish of St Magnus for the London clergy's lawsuit.

By the end of this decade he must have been in close touch with the puritan brotherhood. On 6 August 1640 he met with John Downham, Edmund Calamy, Arthur Jackson, and John Goodwin at Downham's house and at the Nag's Head tavern in Cateaton Street, London, to formulate a petition against the new canons which had been proclaimed two months before. Twelve days later warrants were issued by the privy council to search his houses at London Bridge and at Watford for arms. It was also said that he had carried the petition to York to present it to the king and that he had been to Scotland.

Religious reform and parliament, 1640–1642 It was with the meeting of the Long Parliament that Burges emerged as one of the most prominent and influential puritan divines in London. He had enjoyed the patronage of the earls of Bedford for many years and, through this connection, must have come to know John Pym as well. Besides, Pym was his countryman from Somerset. Years later, in a letter to Richard Baxter, Burges spoke of the early days of the Long Parliament when he and a small group of prominent puritan divines including John White of Dorchester, Stephen Marshall, and Edmund Calamy were appointed by the leaders of the parliamentary opposition—such as the earl of Warwick, Lord Saye and Sele, and Lord Brooke in the House of Lords, and John Pym and John Hampden in the House of Commons—to meet 'twice every week, at some of their lodgings' for deliberations on religious reform. Shortly after the opening of the Long Parliament, Burges and Stephen Marshall were invited by Pym to preach the first fast sermons before the House of Commons on 17 November 1640. In *The First Sermon* (1641) Burges, with adroit ingenuity, applied the prophecies of Jeremiah to the current situation in England. The 'Babylonian yoke' was used to symbolize the years of the Laudian oppression, while the Scots, whose rebellion had ended the Laudian rule, were cast into the role of the 'Northern Army' of the Medes and Persians. Now with the end of the Babylonian captivity, the English nation, like the Israelites, started their journey to return to Zion, and Burges urged the whole nation to enter into a holy covenant among themselves and with God. Although Burges made no greater request in this sermon than 'to provide a sound, godly, profitable and setled Preaching Ministry in every Congregation through the Land and the annexed Dominions' (Burges, *First Sermon*, 1641, 6, 41, 43, 78), he had set the basic tone of puritan preaching throughout the years of the English revolution.

On 23 January 1641 Burges presented to the House of Commons the so-called ministers' petition and remonstrance, a composite work from petitions of various counties with 700 to 800 signatures attached, and he acted as its spokesman, especially during the hearings before the committee for religion. Burges later protested that none of the ministers who appeared before the committee had ever spoken a word 'tending to the extirpicion of all Episcopacy; but only to reduce it to the Primitive' (Keeble and Nuttall, 1.409). However, what the ministers' petition and remonstrance requested was, if all its provisions were to be put into effect, not only that the bishops be deprived of their secular employments and temporal power but also that most, if not all, of their religious authorities and ecclesiastical jurisdiction be eliminated. The line between Burges's moderate position on church reform and the contemporaneous and more radical root-and-branch movement was, indeed, thin and often blurred. Speaking of Burges's testimonies before the committee Robert Baillie wrote that 'We did suspect him being too much Episcopal. Yet he has carried himself so bravely that we do repent of our suspicions' (*Letters and Journals of Robert Baillie*, 1.302). One Richard Floud, a minister, after 'having heard Dr. Burges speake touching the same remonstrance' on 17 February, said later in a tavern that 'he had

been amongst a companie of rouges ... who went about to pull downe Episcopacie, and ... he vowed to pistoll Dr. Burges with his own hande' (*Journal*, ed. Notestein, 369). In the following May Burges again appeared before the House of Commons to speak in favour of the suppression of the deans and chapters, though he agreed that it was sacrilegious to convert into secular hands what had been once consecrated to God. And after the rejection of the first Bishops Exclusion Bill by the House of Lords in early June, it was Burges who wrote in defence of the Commons' reasons against the votes of bishops in parliament.

As the political situation worsened, Burges appeared to be more personally involved—at times perhaps beyond his ministerial capacity. He did not shun the appearance of being associated with the City radicals such as John Venn or the London crowd. If the author of *Persecutio undecima* (1648) is to be believed, the London mob was 'led by Dr. *Burges* and Captain *Ven* to the Parliament doores to see that the *Godly party* (for so their Faction was called) in the House might not be out voted'. The author added that 'Dr. Burges said at the Parliament doores of the Multitudes and Tumults of the City rabble: These are my Band-Dogs. I can set them on, and I can take them off again' (*Persecutio undecima*, 1648, 56). What probably happened was that he was asked by the House of Commons to calm and pacify the crowd, as he did on 4 May 1641. But there can be no doubt that Burges was then trusted by the London populace as a godly divine, and the sequence of events does suggest some contrivance behind the scenes. On 3 May, amid the political crisis of the trial of Strafford and the fear of an army plot and a *coup d'état*, Pym introduced his controversial proposal for a 'protestation'. On the following day, while the crowd, some of them carrying swords and clubs, were gathering at Westminster, a petition by divers London captains and ministers in support of Pym's proposal was introduced to the House of Commons. Some of the captains and ministers were called in and told of the Commons' approval of their petition. Burges was thus on hand, and he was 'desired to acquaint the multitude with the Protestation, which both Houses had taken, which being read by him, and also made known unto them, that the Parliament desired, that they would return Home to their Houses, they forthwith departed' (J. Rushworth, *Historical Collections of Private Passages of State*, 8 vols., 1721–2, 4.250).

Family life and the civil war By this time Abigail Burges, if she was indeed Cornelius's wife, had been dead for some years; it is not clear whether the marriage produced any children. By 1634 Burges had married Elizabeth, whose other name is unknown; their son Daniel was baptized on 7 May that year at St Mary's, Watford. Four other children were baptized there between 1636 and 1641, the last, Elizabeth, on 6 September. Although Burges remained rector at Watford until 1645, the family seem thereafter to have lived in London as his role there expanded. Baptisms are recorded on 25 September 1643 for Benjamin, son of Cornelius and Elizabeth Burges, at both St Luke's, Chelsea, and (less surprisingly) St Stephen Coleman Street. Two further daughters, Mary and Abigail, were baptized respectively in 1646 and 1648 at St Anne Blackfriars.

Burges appears to have been financially affluent: in 1641–2, in addition to his contributions for the relief of protestants in Ireland, he invested £1000 in the Irish adventures. In June 1642, when the civil war was coming and parliament called for contributions of men and money, not only did Burges contribute himself, but it was through his efforts that 'the town of Watford in Hertfordshire … sent in 1200£ to lend upon the propositions and offered 150 foot volunteers and 50 horse and intended to make them up 60 horse' (Steele Young and Snow, 3.153). He was later said to have 'received out of the Irish store 20 great saddles, bridles and bits, 50 Carabines furnished, and 50 cases of pistol valued at 275 l. 5s od., which were borrowed for Watford troops, and satisfied by order of the Committee of Safety' (*CSP dom.*, 1644, 170). In 1642 Burges was also appointed chaplain to the earl of Essex's own regiment of horse.

In December 1643 Burges was appointed Sunday afternoon lecturer in St Paul's Cathedral with a salary of £400 a year—probably the highest ministerial stipend ever given to any puritan minister in this period—and he must have had other assets. He contributed large sums of money to the parliamentary cause. In October 1646, when the parliament had to raise £200,000 to pay off the Scottish army, the House of Commons, upon a paper from the common council of the City of London, offered, as an inducement for people to contribute, the system of 'doubling'—that is, if a person who had had standing unsettled loans and interests upon the security of the much discredited public faith was to loan the same amount, he would have the combined total value secured by the new excise tax and the bishops' lands. Although the scheme of doubling was proposed by the London common council, Baillie asserted that 'it was my dear friend Dr. Burgess's singular invention' (*Letters and Journals of Robert Baillie*, 2.411). In any case Burges took advantage of the doubling and had to his credit a total of £3400. 'Having a wife and ten children to provide for', Burges later explained in *A Case for the Buying of Bishops Lands* (1659), he decided 'to take out his money in Bishops' lands' (p. 2). In fact Burges made three purchases in 1649 and 1650 with a total of nearly £6000 and bought much of the property of the dissolved bishopric and dean and chapter of Wells.

Westminster assembly Notwithstanding his political activism, Burges remained moderate, and at times conservative, in religion and church polity. On 5 November 1641, in his Gunpowder Plot anniversary sermon before the House of Commons, later published as *Another Sermon* (1641), he urged the house to call 'a *free Synod* of Grave *Ministers*' to assist the Long Parliament to secure religion not only 'from Corruption in *Doctrine*, from Pollution in *Worship*, from superstition in *ceremonies*, from Exorbitancy and Tyranny in *Ecclesiasticall Government* and *Discipline*' but also 'from *Anarchy* and *Confusion* (under a false guide of *Christian Liberty*) which is farre worse than *Tyranny*' (foreword). Neither religious freedom nor toleration was part of his

vision for further reformation. 'To put all men into a course of *Order* and *Uniformity* in Gods way', he further advised the Commons, 'is not to force *conscience*; but to set up God in his due place, and to bring all people into the paths of righteousness and life' (pp. 63–4). The idea of calling a national synod must have been shared by John Pym, for it was included in the grand remonstrance to the king in the same month. On 20 December Burges further urged for it with a petition to the House of Commons, for which he had obtained numerous signatures from London ministers and said that he could have got more. On 30 March 1642, in another fast sermon to the House of Commons, later published in *Two Sermons* (1645), Burges boldly suggested, much to the offence and resentment of some members of the house, that the Irish rising, which had happened late in the year before, was God's divine punishment for the failure of the parliament to call a synod of divines. 'Do you not see, or hear daily of the disorders, sects, rents, and Schismes', he asked, 'that every where bud forth already, and threaten all Order, Unity and Government?' (p. 46).

When the Westminster assembly was eventually convened in July 1643 Burges, who had been appointed a member, was chosen one of its assessors. However, Baillie asserted that as Dr William Twisse, the prolocutor, was 'beloved of all, and highly esteemed; but merelie bookish and not much', and John White, the other assessor, 'hest keeped in of the gout', it was Burges, 'a very active and sharpe man', who 'supplies, so farre as is decent, the Proloquutor's place' (*Letters and Journals of Robert Baillie*, 2.108). For a time Burges appeared to have held onto his hope for a primitive episcopacy and objected, as he later told Richard Baxter, to 'that general expression of rooting out all Prelacy' in the first draft of the solemn league and covenant (Keeble and Nuttall, 1.410). But he was soon to embrace presbyterianism and took an active part in all the proceedings of the Westminster assembly in the establishment of a presbyterian church government and discipline.

Occasionally Burges appeared at the parliamentary pulpit again to give his exhortations. In a sermon before the Commons on 30 April 1645, published as *The Second Sermon* (1645), Burges, with an obvious reference to the rising sectaries in the newly formed New Model Army, advised his hearers not to listen to those 'Empiricks' who spoke of 'a necessity of complying with all sorts of Sectaries, yea, of trusting the sword in their hands, and to defer the settling of matters of Religion during the war, for fear of loosing the Godly party'. And he asked: 'What is this, but to teach God a new forme of Politicks' (p. 52). Later in the year, when he preached a fast sermon before the Lords, *The Necessity of Agreement with God* (1645), Burges pleaded for the fulfilment of the solemn league and covenant, which, he advised, 'should be publikely read in every Congregation, on every Fast day' (p. 34). He was elected president of Sion College in 1647 and 1648, and published in the latter year *Sion College what it Is, and Doeth* in answer to the charges of John Goodwin and Goodwin's disciple John Price. In *Prudent Silence* (1660), delivered early in 1649 on the eve of the trial of Charles I, he preached to the City magistrates at Mercers' Chapel against the City radicals' agitations for putting the king on trial: 'O ye Citizens … have no hand, nor joyn with any, in such a wicked Act' (p. 32). He also wrote the *Vindication of the Ministers in and about London* (1649).

Later career With the political crisis of 1648–9 came the end of Burges's influence and involvement in puritan politics. He is not known to have taken part in any religious or ecclesiastical decision under the Commonwealth and the protectorate, with the possible exception of testifying in favour of tithes before a committee of Barebone's Parliament. However, his life during the 1650s was hardly less controversial. From 24 April 1654 he was Dr White's lecturer at St Paul's, but payment for this was suspended from 12 February 1656, when the protector and council agreed on a salary of £200 a year for his preaching twice every Sunday at the cathedral church of St Andrew in Wells. However, purchases of former episcopal and dean and chapter lands there led to his long quarrel and litigation with the corporation of Wells, and his lectures at the cathedral church were frequently interrupted by disturbances of local people. In 1659 Burges published in his own defence *A Case Concerning the Buying of Bishops Lands* and *No Sacrilege nor Sinne to Aliene or Purchase the Lands of Bishops*.

At the Restoration Burges took no part in the conference between the presbyterians and the episcopalians for future religious settlement, although he is believed to be the author of *Reasons Shewing the Necessity of Reformation* (1660). It was also said that he was involved in a scheme to offer the king £500,000 in exchange for a lease of ninety-nine years for all the buyers of church lands. Eventually, however, he lost all the lands he had purchased. Having lost his position at Wells in 1660, he lived in poverty in the last years of his life. In May 1665, less than a month before his death, he presented to the Bodleian Library four rare volumes of the Book of Common Prayer. He died at Watford on 6 June, and was buried there on 9 June in the middle of the church. Administration of his goods and payment of his debts was granted to his widow, Elizabeth, together with 'Elizabeth Burges junior' on 5 March 1666.

TAI LIU

Sources Wood, *Ath. Oxon.*, 1st edn · Foster, *Alum. Oxon.* · Venn, *Alum. Cant.* · IGI [parish registers of Sutton Coldfield, St Mary, Watford, St Luke's, Chelsea, St Stephen Coleman Street, St Anne Blackfriars] · A. Wilson, *The history of Great Britain: being the life and reign of King James the First* (1653) · *The letters and journals of Robert Baillie*, ed. D. Laing, 3 vols. (1841–2) · *The journal of Sir Simonds D'Ewes from the beginning of the Long Parliament to the opening of the trial of the earl of Strafford*, ed. W. Notestein (1923) · A. Steele Young and V. F. Snow, eds., *The private journals of the Long Parliament*, 3: *2 June to 17 September 1642* (1992) · *The works of the most reverend father in God, William Laud*, ed. J. Bliss and W. Scott, 7 vols. (1847–60) · *Calendar of the correspondence of Richard Baxter*, ed. N. H. Keeble and G. F. Nuttall, 2 vols. (1991) · W. A. Shaw, *A history of the English church during the civil wars and under the Commonwealth, 1640–1660*, 2 vols. (1900) · *Calamy rev.* · J. Davies, *The Caroline captivity of the church: Charles I and the remoulding of Anglicanism, 1625–1641* (1992) · N. Tyacke, *Anti-Calvinists: the rise of English Arminianism, c.1590–1640* (1987) · D. Underdown, 'A case concerning bishops' lands: Cornelius Burges and the Corporation of Wells', *EngHR*, 78 (1963), 18–48 · R. S. Paul, *The assembly of the Lord:*

politics and religion in the Westminster assembly and the 'Grand debate' (1985) · T. A. Mason, *Serving God and mammon: William Juxon, 1582–1663* (1985) · *Persecutio undecima: the churches eleventh persecution* (1648) · administration and inventory, 10 June 1665, Herts. ALS, 101 AW21, A25/3717

Archives CUL, MSS of the Grounds of Divinity and sermons

Wealth at death £51 10s. 0d.: administration and inventory, 10 June 1665, Herts. ALS, 101 AW21, A25/3717

Burges, Francis (1675/6–1706), printer and newspaper proprietor, was the son of Francis Burges, clerk of the Tower liberties, in London. He was bound apprentice to the printer Freeman Collins on 7 November 1692, and was presumably one of the workmen involved in printing Edmund Gibson's edition of William Camden's *Britannia* in 1695. He became a freeman of the Stationers' Company on 4 December 1699, and married Elizabeth (d. 1708), who appears to have been the daughter of his former master, Freeman Collins. In 1695, following the final lapse of the 1662 Licensing Act, it became feasible to establish printing offices in provincial cities, and during the summer of 1701 Burges set up a press 'near the Red Well' in St Andrew's parish, Norwich, with the encouragement of Humphrey Prideaux, archdeacon of Suffolk. Freeman Collins may have helped fund the project, as he was associated with the press after the deaths of Burges and his wife. The first item to emerge from the press was a pamphlet written by Burges, seeking to justify his trade to the populace. *Some Observations on the Use and Original of the Noble Art and Mystery of Printing* was reprinted in the *Harleian Miscellany*. It was dated 27 September 1701, and claimed to have been the first work printed in the city, although unbeknown to the author there had previously been a printer there during the reign of Queen Elizabeth. Further printing commissions were forthcoming, from local booksellers, the Norwich corporation, and the cathedral authorities, but these were insufficient to maintain the press. In November 1701 Burges therefore established a weekly newspaper, the *Norwich Post*, which was probably the first English provincial newspaper. According to Thomas Tanner, this soon became his principal support, 'selling vast numbers to the country folk' (Cranfield, 13). Burges's business prospered over the next few years, and he also undertook some bookselling and publishing on his own account. There were more than fifty items surviving from his press dated between 1701 and 1706 (although many of these were lost in the Norwich Central Library fire in 1994). Francis Burges died on 2 November 1706, aged thirty, and was buried in St Andrew's Church. His death was the catalyst for the establishment of two competing printing offices in Norwich, each of which commenced printing its own newspaper. His widow also continued in business, until her death in September 1708. Thereafter the Red Well press was owned by Freeman Collins, using the imprint 'the Administrator of E. Burges' and operated by a succession of his apprentices, including Edward Cave.

DAVID STOKER

Sources D. Stoker, 'The establishment of printing in Norwich: causes and effects, 1660–1760', *Transactions of the Cambridge Bibliographical Society*, 7 (1977–80), 94–111 · D. Stoker, 'The Norwich book trades before 1800', *Transactions of the Cambridge Bibliographical Society*, 8 (1981–5), 79–125 • F. Burges, *Some observations on the use and original of the noble art and mystery of printing* (1745), 148–51 • D. Stoker, 'Printing at the Red Well: an early Norwich press through the eyes of contemporaries', *The mighty engine: the printing press at work*, ed. P. Isaac and B. McKay (2000), 29–38 • [J. Chambers], *A general history of the county of Norfolk*, 2 (1829), 1178, 1286 • G. A. Cranfield, *The development of the provincial newspaper press, 1700–1760* (1962) • R. M. Wiles, *Freshest advice: early provincial newspapers in England* (1965) • D. F. McKenzie, ed., *Stationers' Company apprentices*, [2]: *1641–1700* (1974)

Burges, George (1785/6–1864), classical scholar, was born in a remote station in Bengal. His father, Thomas, dying soon after his birth, he was sent to England, and educated at Charterhouse School under Matthew Raine. From there he proceeded in 1802 to Trinity College, Cambridge, where he gained a scholarship in 1803 and graduated BA in 1807 and MA in 1810. He obtained one of the members' prizes in 1808, and again in 1809. At Cambridge he acted for many years as a private tutor; he had a great reputation for his knowledge of Greek, and is said to have spoken it like a native. He once had considerable private property, but lost it through financial speculations and inventions. These included the construction of a machine for the aerial conveyance of passengers from Dover to Calais, and a new kind of stays called 'corsets à la Vénus'. He also ran a coach service along the New Road, London. In 1841, despite having been attacked with great acrimony by him, Bishop Blomfield procured for him, through Lord Melbourne, a pension of £100 a year for his services to Greek literature.

Burges was a tory, and his politics appear to have inspired some of his classical writing. When in 1840 Lord Brougham translated the *De corona* of Demosthenes, Burges met it with a long review in *The Times*, assailing Brougham as well as his translation with extreme virulence. In his own classical writings, although his learning was great and his criticism acute, Burges was led away by his arbitrary and querulous dissent from rival editors, and appeared to regard emendation more as an exercise of ingenuity than a means for restoring the original texts. He was a frequent contributor to A. J. Valpy's *Classical Journal*, and in its pages constantly attacked Blomfield, who replied in the *Museum Criticum*, each accusing the other of plagiarism.

Burges published the *Troades* of Euripides in 1807 and the *Phoenissæ* in 1809 when still in his early twenties. His editions of the *Supplices* (1821) and *Prometheus* (1831) of Aeschylus were an attempt to rival Blomfield. When these failed to gain the critical reception for which he had hoped, Burges turned to classical hack work (Clarke, 94). He translated the *Greek Anthology* (1852) and the bulk of Plato (1848) for Bohn's classical library, edited Poppo's *Prolegomena* (with criticisms) in 1837, translated the new readings in Hermann's posthumous edition of Aeschylus in 1848, and edited the *Fragment of Hermesianax* in 1839.

Besides these classical works Burges wrote and dedicated to Byron a play called *Erin, or, The Cause of the Greeks*, by 'An Asiatic Liberal', in 1823, and also wrote a pamphlet

on the use of native guano in 1848. Burges used to contribute to the *Gentleman's Magazine*, and for *The Era* he wrote a series of papers called 'Hungry handless', to show the social evils of excessive machinery. The latter part of his life he spent at Ramsgate, where poverty reduced him to keeping a lodging house. He died at 28 Hardres Street, Ramsgate, on 11 January 1864, aged seventy-eight. He has sometimes been confused with the Revd George Burges (d. 1853) of St John's College, Cambridge, the author of numerous polemical works.

ALFRED GOODWIN, rev. M. C. CURTHOYS

Sources Venn, *Alum. Cant.* • Boase, *Mod. Eng. biog.* • *GM*, 3rd ser., 10 (1861), 268–9 • *The Athenaeum* (23 Jan 1864), 124 • M. L. Clarke, *Greek studies in England, 1700–1830* (1945)
Archives Bodl. Oxf., papers • Chetham's Library, Manchester, papers, incl. annotated classical texts and MS notes • National Library of Greece, Athens | BL, letters to the Royal Literary Fund, loan no. 96 • Bodl. Oxf., letters to Walter T. Spencer
Wealth at death under £100: probate, 27 Feb 1864, *CGPLA Eng. & Wales*

Burges [*later* Lamb], **Sir James Bland**, first baronet (1752–1824), politician and poet, was born on 8 June 1752 in Gibraltar, where his father, George Burges (1725–1786), was deputy paymaster; his mother was Anne Whichnor Somerville, eldest daughter of the twelfth Baron Somerville, whom George Burges married secretly in 1748. George Burges had distinguished himself at Culloden by capturing the standard of Charles Edward Stuart's bodyguard and he had been aide-de-camp and military secretary to General Humphrey Bland during the pacification of Scotland; he later followed Bland to Gibraltar. Having won a reputation for integrity, George Burges was rewarded by the prime minister with a commission in the Scottish excise (1761–8); he was afterwards comptroller-general of Scottish customs from 1768 until his death on 16 March 1786. The father's dedication to the civil service and his loyalty to the house of Hanover set an example for a son similarly adept at tempering romance with prudence.

James Bland Burges spent his youth in Scotland. He was tutored by a cousin, the historian Thomas Somerville (1741–1830), and attended humanities classes at Edinburgh University before completing his education at Westminster School (1767–9) and at University College, Oxford (1770–73), where his tutor was William Scott, afterwards Lord Stowell, a distinguished maritime lawyer. Burges then travelled in the Low Countries, Germany, Switzerland, France, and Italy. He describes the tour, including an interview with Pope Clement XIV, in an amusing autobiographical fragment excerpted in his published correspondence. Burges studied law at Lincoln's Inn, where he was called to the bar in Easter term 1777. On 19 June that year he married Elizabeth Noel (1755–1779), second daughter of Edward Noel, first Viscount Wentworth, and Judith Lamb. After her death in childbirth two years later Burges married Anne (d. 1810), third daughter of Colonel Lewis Charles Montolieu, Baron de Saint Hypolite, on 16 December 1780. She became his political confidante and together they had a large family of five sons and two daughters. While a commissioner in bankruptcy

Sir James Bland Burges, first baronet (1752–1824), by Jean Laurent Mosnier, 1791

(1777–83) Burges made the acquaintance of his future political patrons, William Pitt and Francis Godolphin Osborne, duke of Leeds.

In 1787 Burges was elected to parliament for the borough of Helston in Cornwall. His maiden speech, made at the behest of Pitt, was a hapless response to one of Sheridan's brilliant attacks on Warren Hastings; Burges was astonished when the next day Pitt himself attacked Hastings. Over the objections of Burke, Burges successfully demanded an account of the money expended on the long-running trial; he was afterwards ridiculed when he tried a similar manoeuvre following Sheridan's famous speech on the begums of Oudh. Burges supported the anti-slave trade legislation put forward by Pitt's ally William Wilberforce. While commissioner for bankrupts Burges had published two pamphlets on the laws of insolvency; he now attempted to reform the laws through new legislation. His bill to relieve insolvent debtors was twice carried to a second reading and it was both times defeated by the opposition of Lord Chancellor Thurlow and the legal interest. In 1789 Burges published another pamphlet, *An Address to the Country Gentlemen of England and Wales*, protesting at the abuses in the legal profession. He was rechosen for Helston in 1790, but was deprived of his seat by a parliamentary commission as a consequence of irregularities in the election.

The previous year Burges had been appointed under-secretary of state by the duke of Leeds, who perhaps recognized the usefulness of a man who could remain on good terms with both Burke and Hastings amid all the fractiousness. He held this position from 1789 to 1795; like the government generally, he was at first slow to recognize the implications of the French Revolution and then was profoundly shocked by the terror. From the Foreign Office he kept Burke informed about unfolding events; he is said to have supplied the 'pattern dagger' that Burke brandished in parliament, declaring 'This is what you are to gain by an alliance with France' (Cobbett, *Parl. hist.*, 30, 1792–4, 189). Leeds was indifferent to routine business, and it fell to Burges to reorganize the management of the Foreign Office, which he did to such effect as to attract the notice and approval of the king. In 1792 he was a co-founder of *The Sun*, a newspaper supporting Pitt's policies with a circulation said to be 4000 copies. He contributed political verses, tales, and a series of essays published in 1792 as *Alfred's Letters: a Review of the Political State of Europe*. In 1794 he was appointed one of the three joint commissioners of the privy seal during Earl Spencer's absence. Lord Grenville retained Burges when he was appointed foreign secretary in 1791, but they were never close. In 1795, when Grenville decided to replace him, the under-secretary was offered a choice of going as minister to Copenhagen or Switzerland. On the prudent advice of his wife, Burges declined both offers. Eventually his friends came through handsomely, and the price of Burges's resignation finally amounted to a baronetcy, granted on 21 October 1795, the sinecure position of knight marshal of the royal household with remainder to his son, and a pension of £1500.

Burges was not averse to retirement; he declined an invitation to stand for parliament in 1796 and he looked forward to spending time with his growing family, composing poetry and music (he set William Collins's 'Ode on the Passions'), and purchasing and improving an estate. While in office Burges had cultivated acquaintances in the royal family and he exchanged verses with Princess Elizabeth; in 1796 he published *The Birth and Triumph of Love*, a Spenserian allegory written to illustrate a set of Elizabeth's drawings. He next began a more ambitious work, *Richard the First, a Poem: in Eighteen Books*, published in 1801. The design is modelled on Virgil's *Aeneid*: in the first part Richard retrospectively relates his adventures in Palestine, in the second he secures his sovereignty by defeating the forces of Philip of France. The political subtext of Burges's chivalric narrative is made manifest in book XII where Richard does battle with the Demon of False Philosophy. Although his friend Richard Cumberland marvelled at Burges's facility, the vast poem suffers from an excess of neo-classical propriety—every one of its more than 16,000 lines is end-stopped—and it was coldly received by the public, becoming something of a byword for ambitious failure.

The composition of an epic poem being no small thing, Burges none the less acquired status within the literary establishment, within which he could count as friends Cumberland, Christopher Anstey, William Beloe, William Boscawen, John Wilson Croker, Robert Nares, William Thomas Fitzgerald, William Sotheby, and the poet laureate Henry James Pye. Wordsworth sent Burges a copy of *Lyrical Ballads*, complimenting him on his 'pure and unmixed vein of native English' (W. Wordsworth, *The Letters of William and Dorothy Wordsworth, 1787–1805*, ed. E. de Selincourt, 2nd edn, 1967, 1.683). Appeals for patronage also came from less exalted quarters; in 1796 Burges had written the prologue for *Vortigern*, the Shakespeare forgery by William Henry Ireland, and in 1801 he was robbed by the child genius Thomas Dermody, already notorious for abusing his patrons. Despite these experiences Burges was active in the Literary Fund: through his influence £20 was contributed to relieve the necessities of Robert Burns's widow. In collaboration with Cumberland he published *The Exodiad*, a biblical epic on Moses (1807–8), which did not succeed.

Though Burges's limitations as a poet were by now apparent, he none the less continued to write. *Riches*, an adaptation of Massinger's *City Madam*, was produced at Drury Lane in 1810, followed by a comic opera, *Tricks upon Travellers*. Lord Byron, who had befriended Burges in his capacity as one of the executors of the Wentworth estate (Burges was Lady Byron's uncle), unsuccessfully tried to have additional plays by Burges produced by Drury Lane; two volumes of his dramas were eventually published in 1817. In 1818 Burges published *The Dragon Knight*, a verse romance in twelve cantos. Entering a new field of controversy, the following year he published *Reasons in Favour of a New Translation of the Holy Scriptures*, which drew a rebuttal from Henry John Todd, who had once praised *Richard the First* in his landmark edition of Spenser's works. Burges rounded out his literary career by contributing a preface to the tenth edition (1822) of his sister Mary Anne *Burges's *Progress of the Pilgrim Good-Intent in Jacobinical Times*.

Burges's later years were marked by personal misfortunes as well as literary failures. After the death of his beloved spouse in 1810, he married, on 18 September 1812, Lady Margaret Fordyce (*d.* 1814), widow of the banker Alexander Fordyce and daughter of James Lindsay, fifth earl of Balcarras, and Anne Dalrymple; she had been a childhood sweetheart four decades before and their first attachment had been commemorated in a well-known song, 'Auld Robin Gray', by Lady Margaret's sister, Lady Anne Barnard. The month following this marriage Burges's second son, Wentworth Noel, died heroically in the fifth assault at the siege of Burgos. Burges's third wife was never healthy and she died in December 1814; the next year another son, Somerville Waldemar, lost a leg to grapeshot at Waterloo while serving as a captain in the Grenadier Guards. It was to Burges, breaking the news of Wellington's victory, that Byron made his famous reply, 'I'm d—d sorry for it' (L. A. Marchand, *Byron: a Biography*, 3 vols., 1957, 2.533). In 1821 Burges changed the family name to Lamb as a condition of inheriting an estate left by his friend Sir James Lamb. Sir James Bland Lamb died on 13 October 1824.

Burges's obituary in the *Gentleman's Magazine* describes him as tall and handsome, dignified and personable. James Hutton, his Victorian biographer, praised him as a thorough English gentleman. An amateur in an age of professionals, Burges mixed easily with the famous statesmen and literary figures of his day while leaving very little reputation behind him. Political historians who have

examined the Burges manuscripts have acknowledged his managerial skill and respected his honesty as a witness to contemporary events. His literary tastes were those of the court: handling romantic subjects with neo-classical propriety, he followed Henry James Pye down the path to oblivion. As a politician and man of letters Burges exemplified the virtues prized in the age of George III: piety, charity, and amiableness; domestic affection, political loyalty, and unceasing industry. DAVID HILL RADCLIFFE

Sources *GM*, 1st ser., 58 (1788), 708–9 • *GM*, 1st ser., 95/1 (1825), 81–2 • J. G. Raymond, *Life of Thomas Dermody*, 2 vols. (1806) • R. Cumberland, *Memoirs of Richard Cumberland written by himself*, 2 vols. (1806–7) • Nichols, *Lit. anecdotes*, 8.127–9 • *Selections from the letters and correspondence of Sir James Bland Burges*, ed. J. Hutton (1885) • Foster, *Alum. Oxon.* • Burke, *Peerage* (1910) • *Old Westminsters*, vols. 1–2 • *The correspondence of Edmund Burke*, ed. T. W. Copeland and others, 10 vols. (1958–78) • *The later correspondence of George III*, ed. A. Aspinall, 5 vols. (1962–70) • A. Valentine, *The British establishment, 1760–1784: an eighteenth-century biographical dictionary*, 2 vols. (1970) • *Byron's letters and journals*, ed. L. A. Marchand, 12 vols. (1973–82) • P. Jupp, *Lord Grenville, 1759–1834* (1985) • *DNB* • M. Elwin, ed., *The Noels and the Milbankes: their letters for twenty-five years, 1767–1792* (1967)

Archives Bodl. Oxf., corresp. and papers | BL, corresp. with Lord Auckland, Add. MSS 34430–34450, *passim* • BL, corresp. with Lord Grenville, Add. MS 58968 • BL, letters to Sir Robert Murray Keith, Add. MSS 35542–35544, *passim* • BL, letters to first earl of Liverpool, Add. MSS 38223–38471, *passim*

Likenesses J. L. Mosnier, portrait, 1791, NPG [*see illus.*] • P. W. Tomkins, stipple, pubd 1796, BM • W. Ridley, stipple, 1801 (after Mosnier), BM, NPG; repro. in *Monthly Mirror* (1801) • F. P. Stephanoff or J. Stephanoff, drawing, 1821, V&A • P. W. Tomkins, engraving • plaster medallion (after W. Whitley), Scot. NPG

Burges [Burgess], **John** (1563–1635), Church of England clergyman and religious controversialist, was born in Peterborough, Northamptonshire, and baptized on 6 November 1563 in the parish church. He was probably the second of three known sons and perhaps seven daughters of John Burges (*fl.* 1561–1589) and his wife, Ales (*d.* 1588). He probably went to Peterborough grammar school and he continued his education at St John's College, Cambridge, where he graduated BA in 1584 and proceeded MA in 1587. At St John's he may have been influenced by the presbyterian-inclined fellow Henry Alvey and his faction. Apparently by 1589 he was incumbent of St Peter Hungate, Norwich, of which Sir William Paston was patron. This was a very poor living, where he was mainly dependent on voluntary contributions. On 4 November 1589 he married Ursula (*bap.* 1564), daughter of justice of the peace William Pecke (*d.* 1570?) and widow of a member of the Sotherton family. By 1605 they had ten living children.

Following the campaign of Archbishop John Whitgift and Bishop Edmund Scambler against the clandestine presbyterian movement, and much puritan debate about 'ceremonies', Norwich diocesan officials were enforcing the wearing of the surplice and use of the cross in baptism. Burges doubted if the sign of the cross was allowable, and many of his congregation thought surplice-wearing unlawful. When he told them he must wear the surplice or lose his place, they rejoined that they would not profit by his ministry if he wore it. Though he warned them that they would swiftly change their minds, they were obdurate; he was accordingly deprived in 1590. Subsequently they were said to have wished he had worn ten surplices rather than left.

In 1592 Burges was chosen town preacher of Ipswich, Suffolk, perhaps through the influence of Sir Robert Jermyn, one of the leaders of the 'godly' magistracy there, whose son, Sir Thomas, Burges described as his friend. There he was expected to preach thrice weekly, catechize the young, and visit the sick and troubled, for which he received £40 from the town treasury and an additional sum from the rates. In January 1602 he was elected for life, on condition he did not soon accept a cure of souls outside the town. By July, he had been replaced.

By October 1601 Burges had become resident vicar of the third part of Waddesdon, near Aylesbury, Buckinghamshire, whose patron was Sir Francis Goodwin. As this was worth only £15 a year this suggests either that he was already concerned about the separatist tendencies of churches such as the Ipswich one, or that he lectured in a nearby market town. By this time Burges was described as BD, and was preaching unlicensed. He was apparently tolerated by Bishop William Chaderton of Lincoln, who had a reputation for leniency. Since Sir Francis Bacon described Burges as a famous preacher, his reputation must have been high. Before the canons of 1604, compelling rigid conformity to the revised prayer book and ordinal, were authorized by James I on 16 July 1604, Burges was apparently taking a lead among the dissentients. Nevertheless, his contemporary at Cambridge, Dr James Montagu, dean of the Chapel Royal, invited him on 19 June to preach before the king at Greenwich. Burges, speaking with the boldness of some Old Testament prophets, urged James I to be gracious to his people, avoiding foolish flatterers and favourites' advice; and his servants to avoid harm 'by applying unwisely caustick to the sinews' (Burges, *Sermon*, 9). He pressed the need for Christian teaching and practical religion, and for unity in the face of the common Roman Catholic foe, with harmony and love between bishops and ministers. This implied avoidance of confrontation over ceremonies. The king, angered at his audacity, had Burges imprisoned in the Fleet. On 22 June he was summoned to explain himself before the privy council. He pleaded his duty, but this included speaking to those in power about relevant issues. He subsequently wrote an unrepentant letter to James I, urging that the enforcement of ceremonies and subscription could lead to the deprivation of between 600 and 700 of the ablest ministers. Later Richard Bancroft, bishop of London, and Montagu reprimanded him, urging him to subscribe to the three articles. Burges asked to be able to record his reservations. Bancroft regarded these as implicit, and agreed that only the king should know of his subscription lest Burges's ministry be diminished if he were thought to have complied from fear. He was soon discharged by the privy council even though he was only prepared to use ceremonies if they did not offend his congregation.

Nevertheless, on 3 October 1604 Burges was cited with others before the bishop of Lincoln's court for neither wearing the surplice nor using ceremonies, and given time to deliberate. This time was used by him and some thirty other ministers in the diocese to draw up for James I their objections to conformity, later printed as *An Abridgement of that Booke which the Ministers of Lincoln Diocese Delivered to his Majestie* (1605). Four of them presented the objections to James I at Hinchingbrooke on 1 December: the ministers selected Burges as a representative, but Montagu forbade this. Bishop Chaderton described them as standing all stiff in their former resolution. Mr Wilkinson, incumbent of the other two-thirds of Waddesdon, had taken the best legal advice that, as they were not seeking public office in the church, they should not be forced to subscribe, nor deprived for nonconformity over ceremonies, thus giving grounds for prolonged resistance. On 16 January 1605 both Wilkinson and Burges were deprived. Parish register evidence suggests that one or both may have remained at Waddesdon until 1607. As John Chamberlain commented in 1612 that Burges had left preaching, he may have continued an unofficial ministry after his deprivation.

In spring 1611 Burges departed for Leiden University in the United Provinces, where on 20 April he matriculated in the philosophy faculty. He graduated MD on 27 August of that year, defending a thesis on cholera (now in the British Library) dedicated to Sir William Paddie, president of the College of Physicians in London. It may have been at this time, and it was certainly before 1618, that one of his daughters married William Ames, a fellow minister in exile and chaplain to Sir Horace Vere, commander of English forces in the Netherlands. In 1612 Burges was incorporated MD at Cambridge and was practising in London. By June 1613 he had so impressed Sir Theodore Turquet de Mayerne, a royal doctor, when he treated Lucy Russell, countess of Bedford, that he was recommended to James I. The king, still angered by the 1604 sermon, protested to Cambridge University that it had allowed him to take his degree without subscribing. James also ordered Archbishop George Abbot to investigate: the latter forbade Burges to practise within 10 miles of London. He migrated to Isleworth, Middlesex, where soon Sir Ralph and Lady Winwood joined his clientele.

By June 1616 Gray's Inn was interested in appointing Burges as its preacher, and the countess of Bedford and James Montagu, then bishop of Bath and Wells, were working for his restoration as a minister, an effort which Sir Francis Bacon, Lord Verulam, honey-tongued, urged the king's favourite, Sir George Villiers (from August Viscount Villiers), to forward. By December they had succeeded, and Burges became preacher at Bishopsgate, London; in July 1617 he addressed a vast crowd at Paul's Cross. In August that year, through the influence of Lady Scudamore, he accepted from Robert Shilton the rectory of Sutton Coldfield, Warwickshire, said to be worth at least £250 a year. This, Burges claimed, was only worth a third of his medical income. In July 1620 he went as chaplain with the English volunteer force under Sir Horace Vere to the Palatinate to support the protestant cause in the Thirty Years' War. While there he managed to publish *The Popes Deadly*

Wound, a dissuasion from Roman Catholicism written by a parishioner whom he esteemed highly. Returning to London in July 1621, now a widower, on 8 November at St Antholin's, Budge Row, he married Sara (*d.* 1627), widow of Cleophas Smith and eldest daughter of Thomas *Wilcox (*c.*1549–1608). They were apparently childless.

Burges devoted his energies to a collected edition of Wilcox's biblical commentaries, published in 1624, and on 1 January 1625 Bishop Thomas Morton of Coventry and Lichfield collated him to Wellington prebend in Lichfield Cathedral. Subsequently he wrote *An Answer Rejoyned to … 'A Reply to Dr Mortons Generall Defence of Three Nocent Ceremonies'*, a riposte to his son-in-law William Ames. A manuscript of this existed by 1627. Burges expressed great perturbation about the divisiveness of disputes over ceremonies, which he saw as leading some to sectarianism and others to Roman Catholicism, praying that 'as [nonconformists] are true and zealous professors with us of the same Apostolicall *Faith*, so it may please God, by these my poor Labours, or any other good meanes, to reduce them to Uniformitie with us' (Burges, *Answer*, sig. A4). He argued that ceremonies were reconcilable with evangelical doctrine and devoted much academic proof to this. The work came to Charles I's attention, perhaps through Burges's patron Lord Coventry. The king in 1631 ordered him to show it to Bishop Morton, and commanded its publication. Perhaps this explains Burges's promotion to Hunsacre prebend on 5 August. By this time his health was worsening. He was unworried about defending his views: '… nor shall I bee troubled if once I get to heaven, about bookes written against mee on the earth' (ibid., 16). Elsewhere he writes of this time as the most troubled in his life—in the shadow of death. Compiling a further book, *The Lawfulness of Kneeling at the Lords Supper* (1631), was a medicine against a very bitter herb which had troubled him. This refers to the death in 1627 of his daughter Abigail, wife of Cornelius Burges (his fellow minister and probably the Cornelius *Burges who died in 1665), which was followed by that of Sara, John Burges's second wife, who was buried on 19 November 1627. Burges married again, and his wife, Dorothie, in January 1630 gave birth to a child which died soon after; Dorothie died a week later and was buried on 29 January. Burges died, according to Anthony Wood, on 31 August 1635; he was buried in the chancel of Holy Trinity Church, Sutton Coldfield, on 17 September that year. He was succeeded as rector by Anthony Burges, perhaps a relative. Burges's son John from his first marriage was a physician in Sutton Coldfield; his commonplaces survive in the British Library (Sloane MS 250). ELIZABETH ALLEN

Sources Venn, *Alum. Cant.* · N. Bacon, *The annalls of Ipswche*, ed. W. H. Richardson (1884), 368, 386, 409–11, 413 · J. Burges, *An answer rejoyned to … 'A reply to Dr Mortons generall defence of three nocent ceremonies'* (1631), title-page, sigs. A3r–v, A4, 16, 18, 118 · J. Burges, *A sermon preached before the late King James at Greenwich* (1642), 9, 21, 29, 38–9 · C. W. Foster, ed., *The state of the church in the reigns of Elizabeth and James I*, Lincoln RS, 23 (1926), 205, 273, 363–5 · *The letters of John Chamberlain*, ed. N. E. McClure, 2 vols. (1939), vol. 1, pp. 343, 470, 517; vol. 2, pp. 23, 86, 95, 408 · R. W. Innes Smith, *English-speaking students of medicine at the University of Leyden* (1932), 37 · *The letters and life of Francis Bacon*, ed. J. Spedding, 7 vols. (1861–74), vol. 5, pp. 372–3 · C. R. Markham, *The fighting Veres* (1889), 398, 406, 412 · *Calendar of the manuscripts of the most hon. the marquess of Salisbury*, 16, HMC, 9 (1933), 379 · parish register, Sutton Coldfield, Holy Trinity, Warks. CRO, vol. 1 [marriage] · parish register, Sutton Coldfield, Holy Trinity, Warks. CRO, vol. 1, 17 Sept 1635 [burial] · T. R. Tallack, transcript of the first register of St Michael at Plea, Norwich, 1892, Bodl. Oxf., MS G. A. Norf. c. 14, fols. 7, 49, 77 [marriage] · J. L. Chester and G. J. Armytage, eds., *The parish registers of St Antholin, Budge Row … and of St John the Baptist on Wallbrook*, Harleian Society, register section, 8 (1883), 38–9, 51–2, 56 · parish register, London, St Margaret Lothbury, GL, 8 Oct 1595 [marriage, Sara Willcocks and Cleophas Smith] · parish register, Peterborough, St John the Baptist, 6 Nov 1563, Northants. RO, 261p/46 [baptism] · J. Burges, *The lawfulness of kneeling in the act of receiving the Lords supper* (1631), 1 · *The works of that late Reverend and learned divine, Mr Thomas Wilcocks*, ed. [J. Burges] (1624), A3 · W. Covell, *A brief answer unto certaine reasons* (1606), 10 · *DNB* · Munk, *Roll* · *Fasti Angl.* (Hardy), 1.612, 627 · K. Fincham, *Prelate as pastor: the episcopate of James I* (1990), 290 · H. C. Porter, *Reformation and reaction in Tudor Cambridge* (1962), 187, 189, 192–5 · P. Collinson, *The religion of protestants* (1982), 186 · F. Blomefield, *History of Norfolk*, 4 (1806), 330–31 · *VCH Northamptonshire*, 2.203–9 · Waddesdon parish register, vol. 1, 1607 and 1608, Bucks. RLSS

Burges, John (*bap.* 1743, *d.* 1807), physician, the son of James Burges, apothecary, and his wife, Elizabeth, was baptized at St Paul's, Covent Garden, Westminster, on 14 August 1743. He was educated at Westminster School before matriculating from Christ Church, Oxford, in 1761, where he gained the following degrees: BA in 1764, MA in 1767, MB in 1770, and MD in 1774. He became a fellow of the Royal College of Physicians in 1775, was censor six times between 1776 and 1797, and an elect in 1797. He was physician to St George's Hospital from 1774 to 1787. As his health was delicate, he did not enter general practice but lived quietly with his two unmarried sisters, lecturing occasionally on scientific subjects.

Burges's main interests were in the study and the collection of materia medica. In forming his collection he received much assistance from his relative Sir James Bland *Burges, sometime under-secretary in the Foreign Office.

Burges died at his house in Mortimer Street, Cavendish Square, London, on 2 April 1807, leaving his collection of materia medica to E. A. Brande, a former pupil, who in 1809 presented it to the Royal College of Physicians.

[ANON.], *rev.* KAYE BAGSHAW

Sources Munk, *Roll* · Foster, *Alum. Oxon.* · E. A. Brande, memoir, RCP Lond. · P. J. Wallis and R. V. Wallis, *Eighteenth century medics*, 2nd edn (1988) · *IGI*
Archives RCP Lond., papers
Likenesses J. Gillray, etching with watercolour, 1795, Wellcome L.; repro. in M. D. George, *Catalogue of prints and drawings in the British Museum: political and personal satires*, 7 (1942), no. 8717
Wealth at death collection of materia medica to E. A. Brande

Burges, Mary Anne (1763–1813), writer, was born in Edinburgh on 6 December 1763, the youngest daughter of George Burges (*d.* 1786), of Berkshire gentry stock, comptroller-general of the customs, Scotland, and his wife, the Hon. Anne Whichnour Somerville. She was well educated and intelligent, and her accomplishments included Greek, Latin, French, Italian, and Spanish, with some Swedish and German. She was particularly interested in geology, was a friend of De Luc's, and took a large share in his last publication. She was proficient in botany, and she also prepared an exhaustive account of the British *Lepidoptera* (which does not seem to have been printed), illustrating it with her own hand. She was also a skilful musician. In 1800, while living in Devon, she brought out anonymously the book by which she is known, *The Progress of the Pilgrim Good-Intent*, which is in effect a continuation of *The Pilgrim's Progress*: Good-Intent is the great-grandson of Christian's eldest son, and in her preface Mary Anne Burges asks Bunyan to look with paternal regard on the labours of his descendant. It went through three editions in 1800, four more in 1801, with three in Dublin and two in Charlestown, USA, in the same year, and a third American issue, from Salem, in 1802. At this time Mary Anne Burges was living at her own house, Ashfield, near Honiton in Devon, and enjoyed an easy income. Shortly after the book's publication, however, she became very ill. She died at Ashfield on 10 August 1813, aged forty-nine, and was buried at Awliscombe, Devon. After her death her brother Sir James Bland *Burges (1752–1824) brought out a new edition of her *Good-Intent*, disclosing the authorship, and there was a tenth edition in 1822. Mary Anne Burges has sometimes been confused with Margaret Ann Burges (*née* Lindsay), her brother's third wife.   JENNETT HUMPHREYS, rev. REBECCA MILLS

Sources Blain, Clements & Grundy, *Feminist comp.* • *Selections from the letters and correspondence of Sir James Bland Burges*, ed. J. Hutton (1885)

Burges, William (1827–1881), architect and designer, was born on 2 December 1827, the eldest son of Elizabeth Green (*d.* 1855) and Alfred Burges (*d.* 1886), marine engineer. He was educated at King's College School, London, from 1839; there his near contemporaries included D. G. Rossetti and W. M. Rossetti. Their drawing master was probably J. S. Cotman. He stayed on at King's College to study engineering, but after one year as an undergraduate he left in 1844 to take up articles in the office of Edward Blore, surveyor to Westminster Abbey. Five years later he moved to Matthew Digby Wyatt as an 'improver', helping him also with preparations for the Great Exhibition of 1851. After that he formed an informal partnership with a fellow enthusiast for Gothic, Henry Clutton. This lasted until 1856, and produced at least one major design: their unexecuted scheme for Lille Cathedral (1855). But the influence of A. W. N. Pugin was stronger than any of these: Alfred Burges had presented his son with a copy of Pugin's *Contrasts* (1841) as early as his fourteenth birthday.

Like William Butterfield, Burges came from a nonconformist background. His family were prosperous builders, engineers, and contractors. His uncle John Leschallas was half-way to being a millionaire when he died in 1877. His father, a partner in Walker and Burges Ltd, was a leading government contractor in the field of civil engineering: he left £113,000. Burges himself—after a lifetime of aesthetic extravagance—left £40,000. From 1849 onwards the young architect was therefore able to travel regularly and extensively in Europe: northern and southern France,

William Burges (1827–1881), after Henry van der Weyde

Italy and Sicily, Greece and Turkey, Belgium, the Netherlands, Switzerland, Germany, and Spain. He also studied vicariously the arts of Japan, India, Scandinavia, and north Africa. During the 1850s and 1860s he built up an international reputation as a medieval archaeologist, though he lacked the systematic mind of Viollet-le-Duc; at the same time he developed a highly personal style, an eclectic compound chiefly based on French, Italian, Arabic, Japanese, Pompeian, and Assyrian sources. He was especially intrigued by the Islamic permeation of Gothic, and by pagan survivals in Christian art. The thirteenth century, in particular, was Burges's chosen field, and he modelled his style of draughtsmanship on the famous sketchbook of Wilars de Honecort in the Bibliothèque Nationale, Paris. For visionary drawings, however (notably his *St Simeon Stylites*, 1860), his model was Albrecht Dürer. The bulk of these drawings, as well as scores of architectural notebooks, are now preserved in three collections: at Cardiff Castle, in the drawings collection of the Royal Institute of British Architects, and in the prints and drawings department of the Victoria and Albert Museum.

Burges's career was diverse but brief. He secured his first major commission (St Fin Barre's Cathedral, Cork) in 1863 at the age of thirty-five; he died eighteen years later at the age of fifty-three. His style did not develop from commission to commission. Once established, after twenty years' preparation, his 'design language' had merely to be applied, and he applied and reapplied the same vocabulary with increasing subtlety and gusto. Apart from Lille Cathedral, several of his most ambitious schemes remained unexecuted or unfinished: his Crimea memorial church, in polychrome Italian Gothic, designed for

Constantinople in 1856; cathedrals in French Gothic style for Brisbane (1859), Edinburgh (1873), and Truro (1878); a multi-quadrangled campus for Trinity College, Hartford, Connecticut (1873); a multi-domed art school for Bombay in 'quasi-orientalizing Gothic' (1865); a controversial plan to make St Paul's Cathedral outdazzle St Peter's, Rome, by decorating its interior with polychrome marble and Byzantine mosaics (1870–77); and—most famously—a competition design for the new law courts in London (1866–7), a project which, in planning and silhouette, combined lucidity and drama to an exceptional degree. Such missed opportunities had their saving grace: Burges was rescued from Sir Gilbert Scott's prolixity, and from G. E. Street's overproduction. He was able to put his whole being into everything he undertook. At Cardiff Castle (1866 onwards) and Castell Coch, Glamorgan (1872 onwards), at Cork Cathedral (1863 onwards), at Christ the Consoler, Skelton (1870–76), and St Mary, Studley Royal (1870–78), both in Yorkshire, and in his own London home, Tower House, 9 Melbury Road, Kensington (1875–81), Burges managed to combine an unerring sense of mass with an insatiable relish for ornament. By assimilating the thirteenth century, mingling its features with Renaissance, Pompeian, Japanese, Assyrian, and Islamic work, then adding a touch of personal fantasy, he ended up—almost despite himself—with a new style. Contemporaries called it Burgesian Gothic.

Burges was friendly with most of the leaders of the Pre-Raphaelite movement, and he employed a number of peripheral Pre-Raphaelites in the production of mural decoration, stained glass, and painted furniture. William Morris was more a rival than a friend; but with E. W. Godwin, at least in the early days, he was very close. D. G. Rossetti, E. Burne-Jones, J. E. Millais, Simeon Solomon, N. H. J. Westlake, Albert Moore, Thomas Morten, Charles Rossiter, Frederick Smallfield, J. A. Fitzgerald, J. F. Yeames, E. J. Poynter, H. W. Lonsdale, W. Gualbert Saunders, Fred Weekes, Stacy Marks, Charles Campbell, Axel Herman Haig—all these worked at different times under Burges's direction. And quite a number—notably Burne-Jones, Poynter, Holiday, Westlake, Marks, and Campbell—acknowledged a considerable debt to Burges at the start of their careers. With the assistance of several of these artists, Burges conceived in 1858–9 the earliest and most striking examples of painted Gothic (or Pre-Raphaelite) furniture: the Yatman Cabinet, now in the Victoria and Albert Museum, and the Great Bookcase, now at Knightshayes, Devon. With the help of Saunders, Lonsdale, and Weekes, he produced in the 1870s (at Cork, Studley Royal, and Skelton) stained glass which in originality and brilliance matched the finest work of Morris & Co. He also excelled in two fields Morris never entered: jewellery and metalwork. Using several different silversmiths (Keith & Co.; Hart, Son, and Peard; Hardman & Co.; Barkentin and Krall), Burges inspired work—notably, silverware for his own use and for the third marquess of Bute—which anticipates in range and virtuosity the triumphs of the arts and crafts phase. Unlike the work of Pugin and Morris, Burges's designs for furniture, stained glass, and metalwork were never intended for commercial production. Many of the finest items are now in the Victoria and Albert Museum and the Cecil Higgins Art Gallery, Bedford.

Burges was a key member of several artistic coteries: the Hogarth Club, the Medieval Society, the Arts Club, and the Foreign Architectural Book Society. He was also a prominent—if eccentric—figure in a number of more obviously professional groups: the Royal Institute of British Architects, the Archaeological Institute, the Architectural Museum and Architectural Exhibition Society, the Architectural Association, and the Ecclesiological Society. For the last of these he organized the medieval court in the International Exhibition of 1862. His bohemian manners seem to have kept him out of the Royal Academy until just before his death—he was elected ARA in 1881—and he never joined the Society of Antiquaries. But he was much in demand as a lecturer. Besides numerous articles and essays he published *Art Applied to Industry* (1865) and *Architectural Drawings* (1870). He was an omnivorous, almost manic, collector, and bequeathed many items—armour, ivories, illuminated manuscripts—to the British Museum.

As an architectural pundit, Burges was vehement rather than original. Despite his engineering background, his aesthetic was essentially atectonic. 'The civil engineer', he admitted, 'is the real 19th century architect' (*The Ecclesiologist*, 28, 1867, 156). Like Ruskin, he knew that engineering alone could never be the same thing as architecture. In his early years he followed A. J. Beresford Hope's doctrine of 'progressive eclecticism'. Early French—rather than Italian or English Gothic—always seemed to him the most promising matrix for a new Victorian style. He especially admired its 'boldness, breadth, strength, sternness and virility' (*The Builder*, 19, 1861, 403). In the 1860s the excesses of popular Gothic dismayed him: the new style, he admitted in 1865, 'may perhaps take place in the 20th century, it certainly … will not occur in the 19th' (*Art Applied to Industry*, 8). During the 1870s, however, Burges refused to follow his contemporaries in rejecting Gothic for Queen Anne. 'I have been brought up', he announced, 'in the 13th century belief, and in that belief I intend to die' (*The Builder*, 34, 1876, 18). Towards the end of his life, therefore, he concentrated on decorative design, escaping in effect into a world of architectural fantasy.

To his friends he was always 'Billy' Burges: a crank, but a genius, and a really good fellow. As a schoolboy, W. M. Rossetti recalled, he was already 'excessively short-sighted', with 'a chubby face like a cherub on a tombstone' (*Some Reminiscences*, 1910, 155). Robert Kerr remembered his 'playful fanaticism'. In his miniature portrait of 1858 by Poynter, he wears a puckish look. In a *carte de visite*, dressed up in doublet, hose, and liripipe, he takes on the persona of a medieval court jester. 'He used to give the quaintest little teaparties', recalled Sir Edmund Gosse,

> the meal served in beaten gold, the cream poured out of a single onyx, and the tea strictured in its descent on account of real rubies in the pot … His work was really more jewel like than architecture, just because he was so blind, but he

had real genius I am sure.   (E. Charteris, *The Life and Letters of Sir Edmund Gosse*, 1931, 149)

Burges never ran a large office. Two of his assistants, however, Josiah Conder and Sir William Emerson, carried Burgesian eclecticism across the world, to Japan and India. Through his influence on H. H. Richardson, not a little of Burges's genius was exported to the United States. His leading patrons were Roman Catholics—such as the third marquess of Bute or the first marquess of Ripon—or else they were high Anglican, such as A. J. Beresford Hope. His own approach to religion was aesthetic rather than theological. As Robert Kerr put it, 'Butterfield was High Church, Scott Low Church, and Burges was no church' (*RIBA Transactions*, 1884, 232). He seems to have loved ceremony almost for its own sake. Hence perhaps the fact that he was an enthusiastic freemason, and may well have been a Rosicrucian. A lifelong bachelor, increasingly odd in appearance—he was known as 'Ugly Burges' to distinguish him from J. B. ('Pretty') Burgess the painter—he died unexpectedly in the same year as his rival G. E. Street. Like a number of the Pre-Raphaelite generation, he seems to have enjoyed opium and alcohol, and the intensity of his vision was perhaps diluted by a luxurious lifestyle. But no Gothic revivalist was more highly gifted, or better loved: 'Ugly Burges who designs lovely things', wrote Lady Bute; 'isn't he a duck' (Mount Stuart MSS, 1873).

On his last visit to Cardiff, 28 March 1881, Burges took a long ride in a dog cart and got very cold. Half paralysed for three weeks, he died at Tower House on 20 April. He was buried in Norwood cemetery, in the tomb he designed for his mother.   J. MORDAUNT CROOK

Sources J. M. Crook, *William Burges and the high Victorian dream* (1981) • J. M. Crook, ed., *The strange genius of William Burges* (1981) [exhibition catalogue, V&A and NM Wal., 1981] • J. M. Crook and C. A. Lennox-Boyd, *Axel Haig and the Victorian vision of the middle ages* (1984) • *CGPLA Eng. & Wales* (1881) • *The Builder*, 50 (1886), 471 • d. cert.
Archives Cardiff Castle, drawings and MSS • Mount Stuart, Isle of Bute, drawings and MSS • RIBA, drawings collection, drawings, and MSS • RIBA BAL, register relating to interior decoration of St Paul's Cathedral • V&A, department of prints and drawings, drawings and MSS • V&A NAL, estimate book | Essex RO, Chelmsford, plans for work at Waltham Abbey • Worcester College, Oxford, letters to C. H. O. Daniel
Likenesses A. Poynter, miniature, oils, 1858, V&A • Potts, photograph, c.1880, RIBA • wood-engraving, 1881 (after photograph by H. van der Weyde), NPG; repro. in *ILN* (30 April 1881) • H. van der Weyde, photograph, NPG [*see illus.*] • carte de visite, NPG; repro. in Crook and Lennox-Boyd, *Axel Haig*, 3 • watercolour over photograph (after H. van der Weyde), NPG
Wealth at death under £40,000: probate, 23 May 1881, *CGPLA Eng. & Wales*

Burgess, Anthony (d. 1664), clergyman and ejected minister, was born at Watford in Hertfordshire, the son of a local schoolmaster whose name is unknown. He matriculated as a sizar from St John's College, Cambridge, in 1623, graduating BA in 1627. He later migrated to Emmanuel College, where he was elected to the fellowship about 1629 and proceeded MA in 1630. Before leaving Cambridge in 1635 Burgess was the tutor of John Wallis, the future

Savillian professor of geometry, as well as the controversial presbyterian William Jenkyn.

Burgess left Cambridge to take up the cure of souls and was instituted as rector at Sutton Coldfield on 3 November 1635. With the coming of civil war he was forced to flee his parochial charge and became one of the chaplains to the parliamentary garrison at Coventry. Here he met with fellow godly ministers such as the young Richard Baxter. In 1644 Burgess was chosen as a delegate for Warwickshire to the Westminster assembly of divines and on 25 January 1645 he replaced the expelled Thomas Crane as vicar of the Guildhall church of St Lawrence Jewry, London.

Burgess received the favour of parliament and was invited to preach sermons to the Lords or Commons on six occasions. These sermons betray two themes in his thought: his biblical literalism and his desire to see the nation reformed through evangelical discipline. He was especially concerned with the policy of strict admission to holy communion. In a sermon entitled *The Reformation of the Church*, preached before the House of Lords on 27 August 1645, he exhorted the Lords to institute discipline in the church. The doctrine of this sermon was that 'a Commonwealth is made glorious, when it becometh holy and Christian' (Burgess, *Reformation*, 8).

Despite his support for reformation of the Church of England on a presbyterian model, Burgess was one of the less dogmatic members of the presbyterian camp. His sermons never specifically mention the presbyterian settlement to the prejudice of the congregationalists. He put his theory into practice, however, establishing a congregational presbytery at St Lawrence in 1645 and attending the meetings of the sixth London classis and the first two London provincial assemblies. In 1647 he joined with his fellow London presbyterian ministers in signing the *Testimony* of the London presbyterians against the toleration of heresy.

When the Westminster assembly finished its work in 1649 Burgess returned to Sutton Coldfield, where he was later chosen as one of the clerical assistants to the Cromwellian ecclesiastical commission for Warwickshire and Staffordshire in 1654. He also entered into a long disputation with Richard Baxter over the doctrine of justification. Baxter dedicated his first publication, *Aphorismes of Justification* (1649), to Burgess and his fellow minister Richard Vines. Nevertheless Burgess attacked the work for its Arminian tendencies in arguing for a process of justification involving human co-operation with grace. The dispute continued through a number of letters and printed works including Burgess's *The True Doctrine of Justification* (1654), which claimed that Baxter's retreat from predestination orthodoxy was tantamount to a Roman Catholic understanding of justification. Despite the heat of this debate Baxter and Burgess remained cordial friends and notwithstanding their substantial disagreements the two met in Birmingham to discuss the issue personally in September 1650. Baxter's respect for Burgess is shown by a letter addressed to Lord Chancellor Edward Hyde in November 1660, which recommended Burgess for a bishopric.

Burgess was ejected in 1662 for nonconformity; the

younger Edmund Calamy relates that 'He conformed before the wars, but was so far from the new Conformity, as settled at the Restoration, that upon his deathbed he professed great satisfaction at his having refused it' (*Non-conformist's Memorial*, 3.350). Burgess resisted the desire to form a conventicle and retired to Tamworth in Staffordshire, where he attended the ministry of his 'fast friend' Samuel Langley, a godly but conformist minister. He died in Tamworth in October 1664 and was survived by his wife, Sarah, a son, and three daughters: Mary, Abigail, and Ruth. His son, Anthony, followed his father into the church but as a conformist, serving St Bartholomew-the-Great in London as rector from 1663 until his death in 1709.

E. C. VERNON

Sources *Calendar of the correspondence of Richard Baxter*, ed. N. H. Keeble and G. F. Nuttall, 2 vols. (1991) • A. Laurence, *Parliamentary army chaplains, 1642–1651*, Royal Historical Society Studies in History, 59 (1990) • R. S. Paul, *The assembly of the Lord: politics and religion in the Westminster assembly and the 'Grand debate'* (1985) • Venn, *Alum. Cant.* • E. C. Vernon, 'The Sion College conclave and London presbyterianism during the English revolution', PhD diss., U. Cam., 1999 • *Calamy rev.* • *The nonconformist's memorial … originally written by … Edmund Calamy*, ed. S. Palmer, [3rd edn], 3 vols. (1802–3) • A. Burgess, *Romes cruelty and apostacie* (1645) • A. Burgess, *The reformation of the church* (1645) • A. Burgess, *Publick affections* (1646)

Burgess, Anthony. *See* Wilson, John Burgess (1917–1993).

Burgess, Daniel (1646–1713), Presbyterian minister, was born at Staines, Middlesex, the son of Daniel Burgess (1615/16–1679), clergyman, but soon moved to Sutton Veny, Wiltshire, where his father was rector by June 1646. Burgess senior became rector of Collingbourne Ducis, Wiltshire, in 1660 through the influence of his brother Isaac Burgess, high sheriff of the county, but was ejected following the Act of Uniformity in 1662 and retired to Marlborough. Burgess attended Westminster School in 1654, and on 21 February 1662 matriculated from Magdalen Hall, Oxford, as a commoner. He studied hard but did not graduate, declined to conform, and was not ordained. After leaving the university he returned to the neighbourhood of his father's old parish in Wiltshire, acting as domestic chaplain to Robert Foyle of Chute, and later to John Smith of North Tidworth, father of John Smith the politician.

In 1667 Roger Boyle, first earl of Orrery and lord president of Munster, took Burgess to Ireland, where he was appointed headmaster of the school built by Lord Orrery near his new house at Charleville, co. Cork, 'that I may myself inspect the education of the younge gentry, which I look on, as my duty' (Lynch, 127). Later Burgess acted as chaplain in the family of Sir Audley Mervyn, former speaker of the Dublin parliament, and his wife, Martha. He was ordained by the presbytery at Dublin and there, probably in 1674, married a woman surnamed Briscoe, perhaps Catherine Briscoe, daughter of Gabriel and Elizabeth Briscoe, although at the time of his death his wife, perhaps a second wife, was named Ann. He had two daughters, Katherine and Elizabeth, and a son, Daniel *Burgess, later a royal administrator.

It seems that Burgess was in England in 1669, when it

Daniel Burgess (1646–1713), by John Faber senior, 1707

was reported that he was preaching with his father to thirty or forty persons at Richard Pike's house in Collingbourne Ducis, but he did not return permanently until 1674 when he was preaching in Marlborough and surrounding villages; he was soon imprisoned in Marlborough gaol. In August 1675 he was living at Bayden near Marlborough, and may have remained there. In 1685 he was one of those canvassed by the Harleys for the living of Brampton Bryan, reportedly worth £80 per annum, but though Richard Baxter recommended his ability and the young Robert Harley preferred him, it seems that for Sir Edward Harley, Burgess's lack of episcopal ordination was decisive, and Thomas Oulton of Newcastle under Lyme was eventually preferred. Burgess therefore moved to London in the same year, and began to minister to a large congregation at a hired meeting-place in Brydges Street, Covent Garden. In July 1688 Sir John Rotheram, one of the new barons of exchequer, took him as his chaplain on the Oxford circuit and he was asked to prepare 'a short tract for instruction and admonition to such criminals as should be condemned in order to their preparation for death' (*Fifth Report*, HMC, 379). In 1695 Burgess preached the funeral sermon for the countess of Ranelagh. Among his other contacts were less elevated but important figures in the world of moderate dissent, including Richard Baxter (by now almost legendary), his publisher Matthew Sylvester, and William Bates of Hackney. A letter to Baxter, probably written after February 1687, contains an outline of Burgess's weekly routine:

> Mondays, I water my neophytes in an exercise. Tuesdays, I visit and enquire into the states of the families of my Congregation. Wednesdays, Thursdays and Fridays I Preach. Saturdays, I lock myself up. Visits of pleasure I make none: or if any, it's but of one, viz heavenly Dr [William] Bates, my

humble, condescending, helpful friend; and a near neighbour of my nearest kindred. Though it's rarely too, that I see even Hackney.   (Keeble and Nuttall, 2.285)

In 1695 Burgess and his congregation began to meet in Russell Court, Drury Lane, and in 1705 they had a new meeting-house built in New Court, Carey Street, Lincoln's Inn Fields. Burgess became famous as a preacher, but his use of pithy and humorous epigrams did not arouse universal approval. By no means everyone laughed at his assertion that Jews were called Israelites because God did not wish his people to be called Jacobites. Both in the Anglican church and among dissenters there was a growing trend towards dull and dutiful respectability among preachers; Burgess's humour was often seen as coarse; his perceived taste for combining ribaldry with unction drew criticism even from Jonathan Swift, and it provoked the high-church populists to fury. An apocryphal pamphlet had Burgess condemn the sermon of the high-church Henry Sacheverell before the mayor at St Paul's on 5 November 1709 as 'more fitted for a Billingsgate auditory than a Cathedral harmony' and designed 'to raise up the spirit of persecution' (*Dr Burgis's Answer to Dr Sacheverell's High Flown Sermon*, 1710?, 2, 7), and indeed on 1 March 1710 the Sacheverell mob smashed the widows of the Carey Street meeting-house, tore out the pulpit and pews, and burnt them in Lincoln's Inn Fields. (The attack later launched a famous tract, *The craftsman: a sermon … composed by the late Daniel Burgess, and intended to be preached by him in the high times, but prevented by the burning of his meeting house*, actually by the whig Thomas Gordon.) The government paid for the damage, estimated at £300, but Burgess and his followers still faced serious financial difficulties, for soon after the completion of the new building differences had arisen; many remained in the Drury Lane area and joined the congregation of Dr Jabez Earle, leaving the rest with unpaid construction costs of over £700. It seems that Burgess's congregation never recovered its former numbers or unity, and that his reputation suffered by these divisions. Despite all setbacks Burgess's wry sense of humour remained with him to the end. 'If I must be idle,' he remarked, 'I had rather be idle under ground than idle above ground.' He died at his house at Boswell Court on 26 January 1713 and was buried on 31 January in the church of St Clement Danes. Matthew Henry preached his funeral sermon.   STEPHEN WRIGHT

Sources M. Henry, *A sermon preached upon the occasion of the funeral of the Reverend Mr Daniel Burgess who died Jan 26 1712/3 in the 67th year of his age* (1713) • A. Gordon, ed., *Freedom after ejection: a review (1690–1692) of presbyterian and congregational nonconformity in England and Wales* (1917) • *Calamy rev.* • *VCH Wiltshire*, vols. 11, 15, 16 • J. T. Cliffe, *The puritan gentry besieged, 1650–1700* (1993) • W. Wilson, *The history and antiquities of the dissenting churches and meeting houses in London, Westminster and Southwark*, 4 vols. (1808–14) • *Calendar of the correspondence of Richard Baxter*, ed. N. H. Keeble and G. F. Nuttall, 2 (1991) • E. Calamy, ed., *An abridgement of Mr. Baxter's history of his life and times, with an account of the ministers, &c., who were ejected after the Restauration of King Charles II*, 2nd edn, 2 vols. (1713), vol. 2 • K. Lynch, *Roger Boyle, first earl of Orrery* (1961?) • D. Burgess, *Apokaradokia k'euchē hē Christianikē. Christians earnest expectation and longing for the glorious appearing of the great God* (1675) • will, PRO, PROB 11/531, sig. 27 • J. Caulfield, *Portraits, memoirs, and characters, of remarkable persons, from the revolution of 1688 to the end of the reign of George II*, 1 (1819) • *The life, death and character of Mr Daniel Burgess, later minster of the gospel: who departed this life at his house in Boswell Court, on Monday 26th of this instant January, 1713 in the 65th year of his age* (1713) • Foster, *Alum. Oxon.* • *Fifth report*, HMC, 4 (1876)
Archives Bodl. Oxf., commonplace book
Likenesses J. Faber senior, mezzotint, 1707, BM, NPG [*see illus.*] • J. Caulfield, portrait (Daniel Burgess?), repro. in Caulfield, *Portraits, memoirs, and characters*, 82 • J. Drapentier, line engraving, BM; repro. in D. Burgess, *Characters of a godly man* (1691) • G. Vertue, line engraving, BM; repro. in D. Burgess, *Psalms* (1714) • line engraving (after contemporary satirical print), BM, NPG
Wealth at death bequeathed income from £1000 in bonds, most of East India Company; plus house and chattels: will, PRO, PROB 11/531, sig. 27

Burgess, Daniel (d. 1747), royal administrator, was the son of the Presbyterian minister Daniel *Burgess (1646–1713) and his wife, the former Mrs Briscoe. His education is obscure but he probably trained for the Presbyterian ministry, as he seems to have signed the nonconformists' advices for peace at Salter's Hall on 10 March 1719. However, long before that date he had already entered the service of the house of Hanover. In his will his father left him only £20, with the comment that he had 'already had and received his portion and share and much more than any of the rest of my children can or will have' (PRO, PROB 11/531, sig. 27, fol. 204), which suggests that by 1713 he was already well established. He may have been English reader to the Electress Sophia in Hanover. In September 1714 Caroline, princess of Wales, appointed him her English secretary and tutor. Burgess thought that her English was in a poor state and the princess's abilities had been badly served by his predecessor, Miss Crow. He is credited with at least one pamphlet among the political propaganda of George I's reign, *A letter to the bishop of Salisbury, occasion'd by his son's letter to the earl of Hallifax, by a good friend to the late ministers* (1715). This distinguished between the prejudices of the Sacheverellite mob and the actions of the earl of Oxford, who was facing impeachment at the time, and his former colleagues; the author argued that the treaty of Utrecht had guaranteed the protestant succession. If Burgess was the author, its publication could be evidence of an early distancing between the courts of Caroline and George I. He ceased to be secretary to the princess some time after 1724; by 1727 he had become a pensioner.

Burgess was still secretary to the princess in 1723 when he proposed to Charles, Viscount Townshend, that an allowance from the Treasury be paid to the widows of dissenting ministers. Burgess became an intermediary, the annual grant of £500 being given to him and then passed on to a secret committee of leading nonconformists who reallocated the money to poor ministers and widows. This regular award gave the ministry a potential lever over Presbyterian ministers in seats which the Walpole and subsequent governments found difficult to win. Burgess certainly exerted his influence over Presbyterian congregations in the interests of the Walpole ministry in at least one election, that of 1733.

By 1733 Burgess was living in an apartment in Somerset House, London. He had a daughter, Katherine, and was probably married, perhaps to the sister of the Sarah Morris who received £10 in his will. He may also have had interests in Bristol, as he was a shareholder in the Bristol fire office. He left more than £200 in legacies, mainly to members of his family and household, and a further £1250 in various stocks. He died at his home on or about 11 February 1747.   MATTHEW KILBURN

Sources E. Calamy, *An historical account of my own life, with some reflections on the times I have lived in, 1671–1731*, ed. J. T. Rutt, 2 vols. (1829) · will, 8 Jan 1746, proved, 18 March 1747, PRO, PROB 11/753, sig. 26, fol. 103 · D. Burgess, letter to John Robethon, 18 Sept 1714, BL, Stowe MS 227, fol. 421 · D. Burgess, letter to Sir Hans Sloane, 24 Nov 1733, BL, Sloane MS 4053, fol. 95 · D. Burgess, letter to the duke of Newcastle, 7 June 1745, BL, Add. MS 32704, fol. 354 · will of Burgess's father, PRO, PROB 11/531, sig. 27, fol. 204 [proved 14 Jan 1714]
Archives BL, Sloane MSS · BL, Stowe MSS, letter to Robethon, Stowe 227, fol. 421 · BL, letter to duke of Newcastle, Add. MS 32704, fol. 354
Wealth at death over £1450; also plate: PRO, PROB 11/753, sig. 26

Burgess, Guy Francis de Moncy (1911–1963), spy, was born on 16 April 1911 at 2 Albemarle Villas, Devonport, the elder son of Commander Malcolm Kingsford de Moncy Burgess RN and his wife, Evelyn Mary, daughter of William Gillman, gentleman. Burgess's father died in 1924 and his mother subsequently married John Retallack Bassett, a retired lieutenant-colonel. Following a period at Eton College Burgess spent two years at the Royal Naval College, Dartmouth, but poor eyesight ended his naval prospects and he returned to Eton. He won an open scholarship to read modern history at Trinity College, Cambridge, in 1930, gained a first in part one of the history tripos (1932) and an aegrotat in part two (1933), and held a two-year postgraduate teaching fellowship. He became a member of the Apostles, home to the intellectual élite of the arts and sciences, and he was already well known for his drinking and homosexuality. His conversion to communism and his recruitment into Soviet intelligence remain unclear, but he joined the party while at university.

Marxism swept Cambridge in the autumn of 1933, and Maurice Dobb, a don and a communist and also a member of the Apostles, introduced Burgess to Kim *Philby, thus founding the Cambridge network of Soviet agents. In May 1934 Burgess met Arnold Deutsch, a Comintern officer and recruiter for Soviet intelligence, and began learning how to operate as a secret agent. That summer he visited Moscow. Philby asked Burgess to suggest other recruits, and he suggested Anthony *Blunt and Donald *Maclean; Blunt and Burgess later recommended John *Cairncross to the NKVD, the Soviet intelligence service. Burgess became a key member of the Cambridge network, including Kim Philby, Anthony Blunt, Donald Maclean, and John Cairncross, who secretly worked for the downfall of capitalism and the triumph of communism. How many people Burgess recruited or attempted to recruit is not known but Soviet intelligence valued him for his ability to meet useful people. In 1935–6 he was secretary to Captain Jack Macnamara, a Conservative MP, having joined the Anglo-

Guy Francis de Moncy Burgess (1911–1963), by Ramsey & Muspratt, 1930s

German Fellowship to mask his allegiance to communism.

In October 1936 Burgess accepted a prestigious post in the BBC's talks department, thereby gaining access to the British establishment. In March 1938 he was a courier between Chamberlain and Daladier, and in September he urged Churchill to repeat his warning against Hitler to Stalin; he received a signed copy of Churchill's *Arms and the Covenant* (1938). He invited friends such as Blunt, Roger Fulford, Lord Elton, E. H. Carr, David Footman, and John Hilton to broadcast. The BBC's internal hierarchy, together with effective political control from the Foreign Office, severely reduced Burgess's opportunities to influence opinion, although he enabled Ernst Henri, a Comintern agent, to boast about the Soviet intelligence service.

In December 1938 Burgess joined the British secret service. He was appointed to section D of MI6, dedicated to sabotage and subversion. He arranged pro-British and anti-Nazi broadcasts to Europe but his greatest achievement was to secure Philby's entry into MI6. In 1940 Burgess was charged for driving a War Office car while drunk, but the charge was dismissed, as he was carrying out confidential duties under the strain of working up to fourteen hours a day. He rejoined the BBC in 1941 and spent the next three years in the European propaganda department, liaising with Special Operations Executive (SOE) and the Secret Intelligence Service (SIS).

On 4 June 1944 Burgess joined the Foreign Office news

department. In December 1946 he became private secretary to Hector McNeil, then minister of state at the Foreign Office. Excitedly he told his Soviet controller about his rapid and sensational advance to the centre of British foreign and defence policy-making. Regarded as an expert on communism and with experience in propaganda, he was appointed to the information research department (IRD), a secret unit created to combat Soviet propaganda. Visiting European embassies to introduce IRD he was dangerously indiscreet and was peremptorily moved to the Far East department in November 1948. His arguments for recognizing communist China were possibly influential but many officials supported recognition to advance British strategic and economic interests.

In August 1950 Burgess was appointed second secretary to the Washington embassy. He shared accommodation with Philby and gained a reputation for dissolute and insulting behaviour. In the summer of 1951 he was sent home in disgrace, and was about to be discharged from the Foreign Office when he disappeared with Maclean on 25 May 1951, en route to Moscow. In a final theatrical flourish he had posed as Roger Styles to Maclean's wife, naughtily challenging MI5 officers to know two Agatha Christie novels: The Mysterious Affair at Styles (1921) and The Murder of Roger Ackroyd (1926). On 13 February 1956, at a press conference, Burgess and Maclean announced that they had left Britain to work for peace in the Soviet Union. Burgess contacted Tom Driberg, the Labour MP, to collaborate on a book that was the KGB's first attempt to use British defectors as vehicles for Soviet propaganda and psychological warfare. Philby became the KGB's preferred spokesman. Burgess worked in the Foreign Literature Publishing House while using the name Jim Andreyvich Fraser. Isolated in Moscow, where homosexuality was not officially tolerated, he turned to drink. He died from a heart attack in the Botin Hospital, Moscow, on 30 August 1963. His ashes were later interred in the churchyard at West Meon, Hampshire.

Burgess's defection had a devastating impact during the Korean War. Whitehall floundered in this unpleasant scandal of espionage, sex, and conspiracy. An anonymous series of articles in The People in 1957 depicted Burgess's life as a narrative of 'drunkenness, in addition to drugs, homosexuality and loose-living' (Mort, 112). The revelation that the author was Goronwy *Rees (1909–1979), fellow of All Souls and principal of the University College of Wales at Aberystwyth (and himself a member of the Wolfenden committee on homosexual offences), was another blow to the establishment. The revelations (like those of W. J. Vassall later) did much to prolong and accentuate repressive attitudes to homosexuality.

It was feared that Burgess and Maclean had passed over military secrets causing American casualties. This was not the case, but the myth was born. The defection struck at the heart of the 'special relationship' with America. US intelligence believed that MI5 and MI6 were incompetent and untrustworthy. Continued intelligence co-operation cost Philby's recall to London. The defection also delayed the renewal of atomic co-operation until 1954. The government tried to limit the damage by extending secrecy but this eroded trust within the British polity. One positive outcome was to reduce Foreign Office complacency about security, and positive vetting was introduced. Despite much fevered speculation about the damage that Burgess had caused there is too little evidence on the effects of his espionage and his influence upon international politics for a credible assessment to be feasible.

Guy Burgess achieved notoriety in British post-war history because he was a gifted son of the establishment who betrayed the realm by becoming a Soviet agent. His image has been etched onto Britain's collective memory by the ebb and flow of cold-war international politics and propaganda. Western perceptions of him underline his treachery and point to the damage that his espionage and subversion inflicted upon western interests and values. Soviet perceptions of him underline his loyalty to the communist revolution and point to his achievements in serving Soviet interests and values. History's final verdict must find some adjustment between these two dichotomous views, recognizing that the labyrinthine world of intelligence may never yield all its secrets. Burgess was intellectually brilliant but treacherous, ideologically committed but undisciplined; an ambitious extrovert but destructive when drunk, he remains a peculiarly English conundrum. His unhappy sojourn in Moscow and his eagerness to talk to visitors from London were memorably portrayed in Alan Bennett's 1983 BBC television play An Englishman Abroad.   SHEILA KERR

Sources C. Connolly, The missing diplomats (1952) · T. Driberg, Guy Burgess: a portrait with background (1956) · O. Tsarev and J. Costello, Deadly illusions (1993) · Y. Modin, My five Cambridge friends (1994) · O. Tsarev and N. West, The crown jewels: the British secrets at the heart of the KGB archives (1998) · C. Andrew and O. Gordievsky, KGB: the inside story of its foreign operations, from Lenin to Gorbachev (1990) · W. J. West, Truth betrayed (1987) · A. Boyle, The climate of treason: five who spied for Russia (1979) · V. Newton, The butcher's embrace: the Philby conspirators in Washington (1991) · R. Cecil, 'The Cambridge Comintern', The missing dimension, ed. C. Andrew and D. N. Dilks (1990) · S. Kerr, 'NATO's first spies: the case of the disappearing diplomats', Securing peace in Europe, 1945–1982, ed. R. O'Neil and B. Heuser (1991) · S. Kerr, 'British cold war defectors: the versatile, durable toys of propagandists', British intelligence, strategy and the cold war, 1945–1951, ed. R. J. Aldrich (1992) · b. cert. · G. Rees, A chapter of accidents (1972) · CGPLA Eng. & Wales (1963) · F. Mort, 'Mapping sexual London: the Wolfenden committee on homosexual offences and prostitution, 1954–57', New Formations, 37 (spring 1999), 92–113
Archives FILM BFI NFTVA, current affairs footage
Likenesses Ramsey & Musprath, bromide print, 1930–39, NPG [see illus.]
Wealth at death £6220—in England: administration, 19 Nov 1963, CGPLA Eng. & Wales

Burgess, (James John) Haldane (1862–1927), teacher and poet, was born in Burns Lane, Lerwick, Shetland, on 28 May 1862, the eldest son of John Burgess, a tailor, and his wife, Margaret, née Pottinger. A brilliant student at Miss Merrylees' private school, and at the Anderson Educational Institute, Lerwick, under its great headmaster John Allardyce, he won first place for Scotland in Glasgow University's bursary competition in 1881. After a year as a pupil teacher at the institute, and several as acting head-master on the small island of Bressay, he entered the University of Edinburgh. He seemed destined for great academic work, but while he studied his sight began to fail, and by the time he graduated he was completely blind.

Burgess had intended to enter the church, but he found it impossible to subscribe to certain matters of doctrine. He asked permission to proceed to the ministry without subscribing to those points, but was refused. 'The one quest for every man who thinks', he wrote later, 'is, of course, Truth. It is only in so far as dogma, or the Church, or any other institution or heritage from the past, embodies truth, that it merits consideration' (Graham, 14).

After graduating, Burgess returned to Lerwick, and for the rest of his life made his living there as an author and inspired teacher. His motto, expressed in the Shetland dialect in which he thought, was 'Ye can trivil an ye're blind' ('even if you are blind you can feel'). He taught classics and mathematics to private pupils, but his studies, especially in languages, were wide-ranging. He mastered most European languages, specialized in the Scandinavian ones, and dabbled in various Asian ones. Willing relatives and friends assisted him in this work by reading to him. His mother, for instance, helped him with Russian by describing the characters; she said that one was 'Like a frying pan, with the handle canted over to one side' (Scott, 15). When news of Esperanto came to Lerwick, in the 1890s, he learned it quickly, and became a lifelong practitioner and publicist of it. He learned Ido too, for good measure.

Burgess was considering his first book of verse when he overheard some sophisticated men say that great thought or feeling could not be expressed in dialect. He quickly produced *Rasmie's Büddie* (1891; 4th edn, 1979), his masterpiece, which contained such fine Shetland poems—some hilarious and some thoughtful—as 'Sensible ta da last', 'Boocin babbie', and 'Da restit fire'. In the long poem 'Scraana' he portrayed a Shetland crofter sparring with the devil, a plausible fellow like his counterpart in Max Beerbohm's 'Enoch Soames', who turns out to be the church in disguise. He was a prolific writer, tapping away on the typewriter whose keyboard he knew by heart. He produced historical fiction—including *The Viking Path* (1894) and *The Treasure of Don Andreas* (1903), and a sensitive novel about contemporary Shetland, *Tang* (1898), as well as masses of articles for the periodical press. A collection of his verse in English, *Young Rasmie's kit*, appeared posthumously in 1928.

When he wrote *Rasmie's Büddie*, Burgess was, to use his own formulation, 'an Ultra-Radical rapidly evolving into a Socialist' (Graham, 16). In the 1890s, under the influence of Robert Blatchford's popularizing work, and of young Shetlanders who had sampled the propaganda of the Social Democratic Federation in Edinburgh, he became a Marxist. In 1907 he wrote:

> I belong to the working class and my entire sympathy has always been with the working class—the only class that justifies its own existence. ... I believe that Social Democracy is the inevitable destiny of every nation, and that the way to

> that consummation will be short or long, smooth or rough, peaceful or bloody, in proportion to the state of the nation's economic development, and the extent to which the people as a whole understand the working of economic laws. (Graham, 16)

Burgess fraternized with youthful socialists in the town: he taught them languages and enchanted them with his conversation. He was an admirer of Shetland's Scandinavian past, and devised many of the Viking motifs for Lerwick's fire festival, Up Helly Aa, in conversation with its young organizers. His pupils marvelled at the disciplined way in which he planned his day: an hour of open-air exercise, during which he walked confidently with his stick through Lerwick's maze of lanes, a period of study, a portion of the day devoted to meetings and discussion, a session with his violin, and so on.

All classes warmed to Burgess. When he died, unmarried, in Lerwick on 16 January 1927, there was an outpouring of tributes. At a meeting of Lerwick Labour Party, Magnie Manson reckoned that 'had it not been for the great physical infirmity from which he suffered for so many years of a useful life, I have no hesitation in saying he would have been a world figure' (*Shetland News*, 27 Jan 1927). The Liberal *Shetland Times*, not known for poetry, became poetic: 'He was himself, unique, no one like him. ... He passed in his sleep into the light of the new day. Folding his tent he sped off to greet its wonders without a word of regret or sad farewell' (22 Jan 1927). A former pupil, the young communist Jack Peterson, called him 'the blind man who saw in the dark; who could not see across the road but saw across centuries; whose very bearing, gay and vivacious, invited passers-by to be of good cheer' (Peterson, 10).   BRIAN SMITH

Sources L. G. [Laurence Graham], 'J. J. Haldane Burgess', *New Shetlander*, 61 (1962), 14–16 · L. G. Scott, 'Reminiscences of Haldane Burgess', *New Shetlander*, 16 (1949), 15 · *Shetland News* (27 Jan 1927) · *Shetland Times* (22 Jan 1927) · J. Peterson, 'J. J. Haldane Burgess', *New Shetlander*, 164 (1988), 10 · corresp. and papers, Shetland Archives, Lerwick
Archives NRA, corresp. and papers · Shetland Archives, Lerwick, corresp. and papers

Burgess, Henry (1781–1863), financial journalist and businessman, was born on 7 July 1781 at Grooby Lodge, Railby, Leicestershire, the seventh of the eleven children of Joseph Burgess (1735–1807), farmer and grazier, and Sarah, daughter of Joseph and Sarah Airey of Strickland, Kirby Kendal, Westmorland. Brought up within the Society of Friends, he attended George Blaxland's school at Hitchin, Hertfordshire. Little is known about his early career, save that he visited Paris in 1803, and by about 1805 had married (outside the society) Frances Ridsdale (1784–1847). They had four sons.

Burgess became a cloth merchant in London during the wars against France, but in 1819 he sought to establish a new national postal service. Despite some governmental support, he faced mounting parliamentary opposition and was forced to discontinue his scheme, which left him with a hefty claim for compensation against the Treasury. In 1822 Burgess patented a lightweight coach—a residue of this project—and was also licensed to build ships on

William Annesley's principles. By 1826 he had returned to the woollen trade, this time in Leeds. Described as 'intimately connected with manufacturing and banking concerns' in the north of England, he also became one of the most forceful opponents of government economic policy. An early critic (as H. B.) of the resumption of cash payments in 1819 (effectively, a return to the gold standard), he contributed useful evidence to the 1826 committee on promissory notes, emphasizing the importance of bills of exchange in currency management. He did so primarily from the viewpoint of the country bankers suffering from the 'evils' of the return to cash payments, which Burgess believed harmed the productive classes of provincial England while benefiting the rentier classes of London. In 1827 he had established offices at 81 Lombard Street on behalf of the country bankers and set up, with himself as editor, the *Bankers' Circular*, in order to give them a more effective voice in the making of government policy. At this point Burgess, a tory by predilection, found himself in growing sympathy with Sir James Graham and the more 'liberal whigs', and the *Circular to Bankers* (as his journal became in September 1828) was to support the Reform Bill in 1831–2. His services to the whigs over reform did not receive the recognition he sought (the secretaryship to the factory commission or to the West Indian loan commission). Instead, Burgess became the secretary to the Country Bankers' Committee, giving evidence to the select committee on banking in 1832 and defending the country banks' interests on the renewal of the Bank of England's charter in 1833. With early losses on the *Circular* underwritten by the Quaker bankers Backhouse and Pease, he sought to widen its readership by a lower subscription in 1835, and thereafter it generally gave him an income of £1000 p.a. In common with Thomas Attwood and the Birmingham school, he staunchly promoted the interdependent interests of the country gentry, their bankers, and the provincial manufacturing interest against the injuries inflicted by an economic policy dominated by the financial interests of the Bank of England and its allies, the whigs.

But Burgess was to be no more a friend to the tories after 1841, for Peel's economic policies since 1819 had been anathema to him. As a result the *Circular* became in many ways the most effective and stringent critic of the Bank Charter Act in 1844 and of the repeal of the corn laws in 1846. Burgess, 'incorrigible' in his 'commercial heresies' (Porter to Burgess, 25 April 1846, Burgess papers), was a key figure supplying information on which the protectionists, above all Lord George Bentinck, sought to build their alternative economic policy. 'Few men', the *Morning Post* puffed, 'have rendered so great services to the cause of British productive industry' (20 July 1846). Burgess helped Bentinck to mastermind the select committee on the commercial crisis of 1847, a crisis he saw as the logical outcome of the misguided monetary policies of Peel's government. Disillusioned with free trade and banking policy, he retired as editor of the *Circular* in July 1850. He had completed single-handed all but two of its issues, in effect 1180 economic tracts for the times, one of which he

enlarged into *Reflections on the Designs and Possible Consequences of the Anti-Corn Law League* (1843). Although partly a vehicle for Burgess's own crotchets, the *Circular* also provided a genuine voice for the concerns of the country banking interest, and, in its combination of financial data and editorial opinion, set a precedent for journals such as *The Economist*. It has proved a considerable resource for economic historians, for example R. C. O. Matthews (*A Study in Trade Cycle History*, 1954), although it has been unaccountably neglected by historians of protectionist politics in the 1840s.

Burgess, never simply a financial journalist, also engaged in a variety of speculative ventures. In the early 1830s, for example, he had sought, with two of his sons, to pioneer trade with Persia. This proved ill-fated, for the elder son absconded in the 1830s with large debts, leaving the younger Charles in effect a permanent hostage. His father's tireless efforts eventually secured his release in 1855, only for him to die before leaving Persian territory. The youngest son, George, however, did successfully make his career as a merchant in New York. Burgess's personal misfortunes were compounded by estrangement from his wife in the early 1840s and by her death in 1847. Nor were his business ventures any more successful, despite his persuading Barings, the City's leading merchant bank, to join Charles Attwood and himself in setting up the Weardale Iron Company in 1845. This led to the building of the 'new' town of Tow Law in co. Durham but proved a failure in the short term, and Burgess sold his share in 1848. He then turned his hand to a variety of mineral speculations, importing in 1848 the white ore from Germany that played an important part in Robert Mushet's early development of steel. After retiring from the *Circular*, he redoubled his speculative efforts, buying and selling mines and shares, mostly in northern England, the Forest of Dean, and Cornwall. None of these proved lucrative, and by the early 1860s Burgess, then in extremely poor health, was forced to sell up his personal possessions for £120. He died on 6 June 1863 at his home, 29 St Swithin's Lane, London, and was buried at Winchmore Hill, Middlesex.   A. C. HOWE

Sources NYPL, Humanities and Social Sciences Library, Burgess family MSS, manuscripts and archives division · *Circular to Bankers* (1827–50) · D. J. Moss, '*Circular to Bankers*: the role of a prototypical trade journal in the evolution of middle-class consciousness', *Victorian Periodicals Review*, 25 (1992), 129–36 · B. Schwartz, *Letters from Persia: written by Charles and Edward Burgess, 1828–1855* (New York, 1942) · B. Austen, *British mail-coach services, 1784–1850* (1986) · biographical files, RS Friends, Lond. · *Bankers' Magazine*, 23 (1863), 557 · directories and letters
Archives NYPL, family corresp. and papers | U. Newcastle, Robinson L., letters to Sir Walter Trevelyan
Wealth at death poverty

Burgess, Henry (1808–1886), Church of England clergyman and scholar, was educated at Stepney College, where he was noted for his ability in Hebrew, Greek, and Latin. After ministering to a nonconformist congregation, he joined the Church of England, being ordained deacon in 1850 and priest in 1851. He took the degree of LLD at Glasgow University in 1851 and that of PhD at the University of

Göttingen in the following year. He failed in his application in 1854 to be rector of Edinburgh Academy. He held the perpetual curacy of Clifton Reynes, Buckinghamshire, from 1854 to 1861, when he was appointed by the lord chancellor to the vicarage of St Andrew, Whittlesey, Cambridgeshire, in recognition of his services to theological learning. That benefice he held until his death at Whittlesey on 10 February 1886, his wife, Eliza, and at least one son surviving him.

Burgess published widely and substantially, on the whole avoiding the clerical pamphlet warfare of his time. He translated from the Syriac the hymns and homilies of St Ephrem of Syria (2 vols., 1835) and *Festal Letters of St Athanasius* (1852; from a Syriac version). He wrote *The Reformed Church of England* (1869), *Essays, Biblical and Ecclesiastical* (1873), and *The Art of Preaching and the Composition of Sermons* (1881). He edited the second edition of Kitto's *Cyclopaedia of Biblical Literature* and was editor of the *Clerical Journal* (1854–68) and of the *Journal of Sacred Literature*.

THOMPSON COOPER, rev. H. C. G. MATTHEW

Sources *The Times* (16 Feb 1886) · Crockford (1882) · *CGPLA Eng. & Wales* (1886) · Allibone, *Dict.*
Wealth at death £1551 0s. 2d.: probate, 10 March 1886, *CGPLA Eng. & Wales*

Burgess, John. See Burges, John (1563–1635).

Burgess, John (1622/3–1671), clergyman and ejected minister, was the son of Walter Burgess, a poor clergyman, of Buckland in Dorset. In his boyhood he narrowly survived being bitten by an adder. He matriculated at Queen's College, Oxford, on 16 April 1641, aged eighteen, graduated BA on 15 December 1646, and proceeded MA on 14 July 1649. By 1650 he was in possession of the rectory of Ashprington, Devon, which had been sequestered from John Lethbridge by 1647. He was a member of the second classis of the Devon association of ministers formed in 1655. Burgess was deprived of his living by the bishop of London on 24 September 1662. Soon after, his patron, Edward Giles of Bowden, gave him the right to present the next rector, a right which Burgess sold for £500. He moved to Dartmouth, Devon, and there lived at the house of Allan Geare, the ejected minister of St Saviour's in that town, remaining for some time after Geare's death in December 1662 to comfort his widow. Nothing is known of his own marriage, but Calamy reported that Burgess had a daughter who married Thomas Brooks, the ejected minister of St Margaret's New Fish Street Hill, London.

Burgess eventually left Devon for London, where he ministered to a small congregation of about thirty families in Hackney, and kept a boarding-house for scholars of the popular academy in Clerkenwell run by Thomas Singleton, head of Eton College in 1655–60. Philip Henry was present at Burgess's funeral in Islington on 7 September 1671 with over a hundred ministers, including Thomas Senior, once lecturer at St Mary, Cambridge, and now a resident of Hackney, and Daniel Bull, former rector of Stoke Newington: 'I blest God that for one dead there were so many living, but it grieved me to see them divided, part staying [for] the office for the dead, part going out' (*Diaries and Letters*, 242).

ALEXANDER GORDON, rev. STEPHEN WRIGHT

Sources *Calamy rev.* · E. Calamy, ed., *An abridgement of Mr. Baxter's history of his life and times, with an account of the ministers, &c., who were ejected after the Restauration of King Charles II*, 2nd edn, 2 vols. (1713) · E. Calamy, *A continuation of the account of the ministers … who were ejected and silenced after the Restoration in 1660*, 2 vols. (1727) · Foster, *Alum. Oxon.* · *Diaries and letters of Philip Henry*, ed. M. H. Lee (1882) · J. Walker, *An attempt towards recovering an account of the numbers and sufferings of the clergy of the Church of England*, 2 pts in 1 (1714) · W. A. Shaw, *A history of the English church during the civil wars and under the Commonwealth, 1640–1660*, 2 vols. (1900)

Burgess, John Bagnold (1829–1897), painter, was born in Chelsea, London, on 21 October 1829, the son of Henry William Burgess (d. *c*.1844), landscape painter to William IV, and Sabina Stirling. His great-grandfather, Thomas *Burgess (*c*.1730–1791), was a teacher of art at Maiden Lane, Strand; his grandfather, William *Burgess (1748/9–1812) [*see under* Burgess, Thomas], was a renowned portrait painter, and he himself was the nephew of the artists John Cart Burgess (1798–1863) and Thomas *Burgess (1783/4–1807) [*see under* Burgess, Thomas]. His distinguished artistic family background led the *Magazine of Art* to write, 'he is a congenital talent; and he may be cited as a living argument in proof of the theory of heredity' (Weeks, 133).

Burgess was educated at Brompton grammar school under Dr Mortimer and after his father's death about 1844 his artistic education was continued by the miniature portrait painter Sir William Charles Ross RA, 'an intimate friend of his father' (Weeks, 134). He enrolled at James Matthew Leigh's School of Art in 1848 where his fellow students included Edwin Longsden Long and Philip Hermogenes Calderon. His ambition to make the transition to the Royal Academy Schools was achieved on 26 April 1849 when he enrolled as a student of painting. Burgess distinguished himself by winning a silver medal for the best painting from life in 1851. His early works, exhibited at the Royal Academy between 1850 and 1857, were portraits and English genre scenes. His first exhibit, *Inattention* (exh. RA, 1850), and subsequent works of this period received very little notice from the critics.

In 1858 Burgess made his first visit to Spain with Edwin Long. At this time depictions of Spain involving British painters were dominated by the artist John Phillip and inevitable comparisons between Burgess and Phillip followed; it was a comparison Burgess often complained about. Although Phillip did exert an influence over many painters of Spain in this period, including Burgess and Long, Burgess's work differed in showing a greater degree of realism and reflecting the harsher aspects of life. The *Magazine of Art* noted that while Phillip 'portrayed the gay, guitar twanging, castanet-playing, bolero-dancing, carnival-keeping, cigarette-smoking life of Seville', Burgess painted the 'rough, ragged, dirty, sheep-skin-clad, patched-up peasantry, gypsies, and contra-bandistas of the Sierra Morena' (Weeks, 134).

Spanish and Moroccan subjects, to which Burgess turned in the 1870s, dominated his work for the rest of his life. His first Spanish work sent to the Royal Academy, *Castilian Almsgiving*, was exhibited in 1859. The *Art Journal* described it as 'a felicitous study, carefully drawn, well painted, and strictly national' (*Art Journal*, 1859, 169). *Bravo toro!*, painted in 1865, was important for Burgess in showing originality and distinction in its depiction of Spanish spectacle despite its exhibition being slightly overshadowed by Phillip's *Murillo* of the same year. Burgess's painting shows the spectators of a bullfight and focuses on the variety of expressions of the crowd reacting to the action of the bullring. It has parallels with William Hogarth's *The Laughing Audience* in its focus on the spectators rather than the spectacle itself. For the vivid and various expressions this picture stands out distinctly from the rest of Burgess's works. However, the work was criticized by Ernest Chesneau in his *English School of Painting* (1885): 'what we complain of in most of these English pictures is, that a too great importance is paid to facial expression … As a study it may be remarkable, but as a picture it is horrible' (Chesneau, 277).

In 1869 Burgess visited Spain at a time of revolution and produced paintings of the scenes he observed. Although never entirely escaping from genre, his paintings did touch upon the social and political concerns of the period. *Licensing the Beggars in Spain* (1877; Royal Holloway College Picture Collection) was exhibited at the Royal Academy in 1877 and received very favourable attention, leading to his election as an associate Royal Academician. As was the case with most of his work, it was based on his studies and observations of Spanish life. He wrote that 'I made a lot of sketches of beggars there, and the room may be any sort of public room used for the purpose' (letter, 1887, Burgess MSS, Royal Holloway College archives).

In the early 1870s Burgess visited north Africa; he travelled with Edwin Long to Tangier about 1871 and then alone on an extended visit to Morocco in 1873. Several paintings resulted from these visits including a notable work of 1873: *The Rush for Water: a Scene during the Ramadan in Morocco* (exh. RA, 1873). Although his work was typical of the period he showed an unusual sensuousness, understanding, and 'realism' in his depictions of Spain and northern Africa that distinguished him from his contemporaries. The *Magazine of Art* mentioned 'his frank, firm, yet tender English manner … He works with industry, lovingly, diligently, but deliberately, as though he were revelling in the calm, warm atmosphere which he depicts' (Weeks, 135). In 1883 Burgess moved to St John's Wood, the centre of an established artistic community of genre painters. Five years later on 5 December 1888 he was elected a full Royal Academician, a further sign that he had reached the heart of the artistic establishment. In 1895 he started the St John's Wood Art Club with Dendy Sadler at 28 Finchley Road after most members of the St John's Wood clique had left. Members of the club included L. Alma Tadema, Arthur Hacker, and Onslow Ford.

From his youth Burgess had suffered from a hereditary valvular disease of the heart. It was a subject that had caused grave concern in connection with his marriage in 1860 to Sophia, daughter of Robert Turner of Grantham,

Lincolnshire, as he was unable to obtain life insurance. However, his condition did not prevent him from enjoying a good deal of exercise, including at one period rowing. Burgess died as a result of his heart condition and a bout of pneumonia on 12 November 1897 at his house, 60 Finchley Road, London. He was buried five days later in Paddington old cemetery at Kilburn after a service at St Mark's, Hamilton Terrace. He had made good provision for his widow by laying aside a certain portion of his income, leaving over £24,000. His studio sale took place at Christies on 25–6 March 1898. Collections of his work are held widely in British public collections, including the National Portrait Gallery, London, Walker Art Gallery, Liverpool, Aberdeen Art Gallery, and the Russell-Cotes Art Gallery and Museum, Bournemouth.   MARK BILLS

Sources *Art Journal*, 42 (1880), 297–300 · [C. J. Weeks], 'John Bagnold Burgess', *Magazine of Art*, 5 (1881–2), 133–7 · *ILN* (14 July 1877), 37 · *ILN* (20 Nov 1897), 719 · J. Chapel, *Victorian taste: the complete catalogue of paintings at the Royal Holloway College* (1982), 70–71 · A. Chester, 'John Bagnold Burgess R.A.', *Windsor Magazine*, 26 (Nov 1907), 613–28 · *Magazine of Art*, 22 (1897–8), 171 · *Studio sale of John Bagnold Burgess* (1898) [sale catalogue, Christies, 25–6 March 1898] · *Art Journal*, new ser., 18 (1898), 31 · E. Chesneau, *The English school of painting*, ed. J. Ruskin, trans. L. N. Etherington, 3rd edn (1887), 277 · R. Treble, ed., *Great Victorian pictures: their paths to fame* (1978), 94 [exhibition catalogue, Leeds, Leicester, Bristol, and London, 28 Jan – Sept 1978] · *Catalogue of pictures, Royal Holloway College* (1896), 8–9 · *Art Journal*, 14 (1852), 24 · *Art Journal*, 21 (1859), 169 · *IGI* · d. cert. · *DNB*

Archives RA · Royal Holloway College, Egham, Surrey

Likenesses J. B. Burgess, self-portrait, oils, 1884, Aberdeen Art Gallery · Bonnig & Small, photograph · E. O. Ford, bust · S. P. Hall, group portrait, chalk and wash (*The St John's Wood Arts Club*, 1895), NPG · M. Klinkicht, engraving, repro. in *Magazine of Art*, 5 (1881–2) · R. W. Robinson, photograph, NPG; repro. in *Members and associates of the Royal Academy of Arts, 1891* (1892) · W. C. Ross, group portrait, priv. coll. · engraving, repro. in *ILN* (14 July 1877) · engraving, repro. in *ILN* (20 Nov 1897)

Wealth at death £24,560 12s. 7d.: probate, 23 Dec 1897, *CGPLA Eng. & Wales*

Burgess, John Cart (1788/9–1863), landscape painter, was born in London, the second son of the portrait and landscape painter William *Burgess (1748/9–1812) [*see under* Burgess, Thomas]. Like his brothers Henry William and Thomas *Burgess (1783/4–1807) [*see under* Burgess, Thomas] he began his artistic career as a painter of flowers and fruit in watercolours, and first sent to the Royal Academy three flower pieces, in 1812, from the family home at 46 Sloane Street, Chelsea, London. In all he showed thirty-one works at the academy, including portraits and landscapes; he also exhibited thirteen oils at the British Institution and ten watercolours at the Society of British Artists. Burgess's flower pieces in particular were much admired for their brilliance and the beauty of their execution.

However, Burgess increasingly turned to landscape painting, and the first of a number of French and Italian scenes were exhibited in 1825. At least one trip to France is documented; an attractive study of Calais, now in the British Museum, is dated 1850. Burgess married Charlotte Smith (*bap.* 1792), daughter of the engraver Anker Smith, and they settled in Chelsea about 1813. Here Burgess developed a lucrative teaching practice, including among his pupils, it is said, several members of the royal family. He also published three drawing manuals: *A Practical Essay on the Art of Flower Painting* (1811); *An Easy Introduction to Perspective* (1814), which ran to several editions; and *Useful Hints on Drawing and Printing* (1818).

Burgess died, at the home of his son, the watercolour artist John Burgess, in Wellington Street, Leamington Spa, Warwickshire, on 20 February 1863, aged seventy-four. One of his daughters, Jane Amelia Burgess (*b. c.*1820), also exhibited as a flower painter.

L. A. FAGAN, *rev.* GREG SMITH

Sources Mallalieu, *Watercolour artists*, 2nd edn, 1.60 • Graves, *Brit. Inst.* • J. Johnson, ed., *Works exhibited at the Royal Society of British Artists, 1824–1893, and the New English Art Club, 1888–1917*, 2 vols. (1975) • *Art Journal*, 25 (1863), 64 • Graves, *RA exhibitors* • d. cert.

Burgess, Joseph Thomas (1828–1886), journalist and author, born at Cheshunt, Hertfordshire, on 17 February 1828, was the son of James Burgess, a bookseller at Hinckley, Leicestershire, and his wife, a native of that county. He was educated in Hinckley at the school of Joseph Dare, and subsequently at the school of C. C. Nutter, a Unitarian minister. While very young he became local correspondent of the *Leicestershire Mercury*, and was briefly in a solicitor's office in Northampton. In 1843 he was engaged as reporter on the *Leicester Journal*, a post he retained for eighteen months. He then became a wood-engraver at Northampton, and for some years divided his time among landscape painting, wood-engraving, literature, and journalism. In 1848 he went to London, but returned to Northampton in 1850 to study the arts.

Burgess had attained some proficiency as a landscape painter when he agreed to accompany David Alfred Doudney, an Anglican clergyman anxious to establish industrial schools in a depressed area of co. Waterford, to Ireland to found a printing school at Bunmahon. Subsequently, after a hasty marriage, Burgess became editor of the *Clare Journal* for six years, and distinguished himself as a champion of industrial progress. He also collected materials for a county history, with the title *Land of the Dalcassians*, but, though well subscribed for, only the legendary part was published, and it went speedily out of print.

In 1857 Burgess moved to Bury, where he became editor of the *Bury Guardian*. On 3 September 1864 he remarried, his second wife being Emma Daniell (*b.* 1825/6) of Uppingham. That year he moved to Swindon and became editor of the *North Wiltshire Herald* which terminated the following year, and Burgess, who had suffered serious financial loss, moved in April 1865 to Leamington Spa, where for thirteen years he was editor of the *Leamington Courier*. In 1878 he accepted a more lucrative appointment as editor of *Burrows's Worcester Journal* and of the *Worcester Daily Times*. While employed on these newspapers, Burgess also produced books on subjects as diverse as angling and dominoes; but his chief interest was in antiquarian subjects. He was elected fellow of the Society of Antiquaries

in 1876 and produced *The Last Battle of the Roses* (1872), *Historic Warwickshire* (1876), and a *Handbook to Worcester Cathedral* (1884). His *Warwickshire* was his best work, inspired by his friend the local archaeologist Matthew Holbeche Bloxam. In 1883, with his health failing, Burgess moved to London, where he spent three years, chiefly in researches at the British Museum. He died in the Warneford Hospital, while on a visit to Leamington Spa, on 4 October 1886. His second wife survived him.

E. I. CARLYLE, *rev.* ELIZABETH BAIGENT

Sources *Leamington Spa Courier* (9 Oct 1886) • J. Hill, 'Biography', in J. T. Burgess, *Historic Warwickshire* (1893), xvi–xx • C. R. J. Currie and C. P. Lewis, eds., *English county histories: a guide* (1994) • m. cert. • d. cert.

Archives U. Edin. L., letters to James Halliwell-Phillipps

Burgess, Richard (1796–1881), Church of England clergyman, of unknown parentage, was a convert from Roman Catholicism, who was ordained deacon in 1820 and priest in 1823 by Edward Vernon (later Harcourt), archbishop of York. Admitted at St John's College, Cambridge, in 1824 as a sizar, he graduated BD in 1835. In 1828 he was domestic chaplain to Lord Aylmer, and chaplain to the English residents at Geneva. In 1831 he became chaplain to a Church of England congregation in Rome, to whom his published *Lectures on the insufficiency of unrevealed religion, and on the succeeding influence of Christianity* (1832) were delivered. He also produced a *Description of the Circus on the via Appia Near Rome* (1828), *The Topography and Antiquities of Rome* (2 vols., 1831), and a diary of his excursion in Greece and the Levant (1835).

In 1836 Burgess was presented by the fourth Earl Cadogan to the rectory of Upper Chelsea, where by 1844 he had become identified as a low-churchman, keenly opposed to Tractarianism. He took a particular interest in the church's contribution to national education, producing several pamphlets on the subject between 1838 and 1846. From 1850 until his death he held the prebendal stall of Tottenhall in St Paul's Cathedral. Among his publications were a pastoral letter to his parishioners (1843), a review of the state of Church of England congregations in France, Belgium, and Switzerland (1850), *Sermons for the Times* (1851), *The Confessional* (1852), *Constantinople, and Greek Christianity* (1855), and *A City for the Pope, or, The Solution of the Roman Question* (1860). In 1861 his parishioners and friends presented him with a testimonial worth £1200.

Burgess was honorary secretary to the London Diocesan Board of Education and to the Foreign Aid Society. Having lectured to early meetings of the Institute of British Architects, founded in 1834, he was made an honorary member of the institute and became corresponding member of the Pontifical Archaeological Academy at Rome. In December 1869 Gladstone, on behalf of the crown, presented him to the rectory of Horningsheath-with-Ickworth, near Bury St Edmunds, Suffolk. Burgess died at Brighton on 12 April 1881.

JAMES MEW, *rev.* M. C. CURTHOYS

Sources *Men of the time* (1875) • Boase, *Mod. Eng. biog.* • Venn, *Alum. Cant.* • Bodl. Oxf., MS Add. C.290

Archives Hunt. L., letters, to John Arnold Rockwell • LPL, letters to A. C. Tait

Likenesses portrait, repro. in *ILN*, 26 (1855), 268

Burgess, Thomas (*c*.1730–1791), painter, lived and worked in London. Of his parents, nothing is known. He received his artistic training at the St Martin's Lane Academy, in London, and went on to specialize in historical and mythological subjects. In 1766 he became a member of the Incorporated Society of Artists, and sent to its exhibitions numerous portraits, drawings, and figure compositions. From 1770 to 1773 Burgess exhibited eighteen works at the Free Society including an engraving, after his portrait, *Isaak Polak* in 1770. In 1774–5 he exhibited four portraits in oils and chalks at the Society of Artists. In 1778, when living in Kemp's Row, Chelsea, London, he was represented for the first time at the Royal Academy by three pictures, *William the Conqueror Dismounted by his Eldest Son*, *Hannibal Swearing Enmity to the Romans*, and *Christ Appearing to Mary Magdalen*. In total he exhibited seventeen works at the Royal Academy between 1778 and 1791, mostly historical compositions, some mythical scenes and landscapes, and a self-portrait in 1782, which was reviewed in the *London Courant* of 13 May 1782, and lastly, in 1786, *The Death of Athelwold*. He died in 1791. As a teacher Burgess was highly regarded, and for some time kept a drawing school in Maiden Lane which had considerable success. His son **William Burgess** (1748/9–1812), painter, achieved his first success as early as 1761, when he was awarded a premium by the Society of Arts. 'He exhibited portraits and conversation-pieces with the Free Society of Artists in 1769 and 1771, and at the Royal Academy, commencing in 1774, portraits in chalk, small whole-lengths, groups, "Gipsy Boy and Girl", and occasionally landscape views. He last exhibited in 1799' (Redgrave, 62). He visited south Wales and the Wye in 1785. Like his father, he was probably better known as a successful teacher of drawing, in which occupation he made more money than by his pictures. In 1774 Burgess married Jane, with whom he had at least two sons. He died in Sloane Square, Chelsea, where he lived, on 12 May 1812. Examples of his topographical drawings are in the British Museum and Newport Art Gallery. His sons were H. W. Burgess, landscape painter to William IV, John Cart *Burgess (1788/9–1863), and **Thomas Burgess** (1783/4–1807), painter, who made his first appearance at the Royal Academy in 1802, when he exhibited *Market Gardener's House at Walham Green*. In 1803 he exhibited *Landscape and Flowers*; in 1804, *Ruins of a Fire in Soho*; and in 1805 and 1806, *Derbyshire and Devonshire Views*. He also made drawings of stormy beach scenes. Of a delicate constitution, he died of tuberculosis at his father's house in Sloane Square, Chelsea, on 23 November 1807. An artist of great promise, he was presumably unmarried. Examples of his work are in the British Museum.

HEATHER M. MACLENNAN

Sources Waterhouse, *18c painters* · Graves, *RA exhibitors*, 1 (1905), 348 · W. T. Whitley, *Artists and their friends in England, 1700–1799*, 2 vols. (1928) · Redgrave, *Artists* · B. Stewart and M. Cutten, *The dictionary of portrait painters in Britain up to 1920* (1997) · Mallalieu, *Watercolour artists* · Bryan, *Painters* (1903–5) · F. Lewis, *A dictionary of British historical painters* (1979) · Graves, *Soc. Artists* · DNB · GM, 1st ser., 82/1 (1812), 501

Likenesses T. Burgess, self-portrait, exh. RA 1782

Burgess, Thomas (1756–1837), bishop of Salisbury, was born on 18 November 1756 at Odiham, Hampshire, one of six children (three sons, of whom he was the youngest, and three daughters) of a respectable grocer in that town, William Burgess (1720/21–1787), and his wife, Elizabeth, *née* Harding (1729/30–1797). He received his early education at a dame-school and at Odiham grammar school before entering Winchester College in 1768. His biographer commented that he 'passed through the dangerous ordeal of a public school … uncontaminated' (Harford, 3). He gained a scholarship to Corpus Christi College, Oxford, whence he matriculated on 14 March 1775. At Oxford he devoted most of his time to the study of Greek and, while still an undergraduate, he produced a new edition of John Burton's *Pentalogia*, a textbook on five Greek tragedies, the first of well over a hundred publications. He took his BA in 1778, and in 1781 he won great scholarly praise for his edition of Richard Dawes's *Miscellanea critica*. Having taken his MA he was made tutor of his college in 1782 and fellow in 1783. College life suited this quiet and shy man, described by a contemporary as 'having, in youth, been, in person and manner, more like what he was in advanced life, than is often the case' (ibid., 67–8). After he was ordained deacon and priest in 1784 his scholarly interests turned to Hebrew and theology.

In 1785 Burgess was appointed examining and domestic chaplain to Shute Barrington, bishop of Salisbury, who became his principal patron. During summer vacations he lived at Salisbury, where he was treated as a member of the bishop's family and was appointed by Barrington to a prebendal stall in the cathedral. He refused the first stall offered to him because it was in too prominent a position in the choir but he later accepted a more secluded stall. He assisted the bishop in his scheme to increase the number of Sunday schools in the diocese, writing simple primers for Sunday scholars, and at Salisbury he met another promoter of Sunday schools, Hannah More, who described him as a 'tall, grave, and sensible young man, rather reserved and silent' (Harford, 112). He also published, in 1789, a treatise advocating the abolition of slavery and the slave trade.

When Barrington was translated to Durham in 1791 Burgess chose to move north with him and to leave, with great regret, his academic work in Oxford; he was awarded the BD in that year. Barrington rewarded his chaplain for his loyalty by presenting him to the first vacant prebendal stall in Durham Cathedral and, shortly afterwards, to a more valuable stall there, which Burgess held until appointed bishop of Salisbury. He gradually came to believe that he would be happier in the parochial ministry, and in 1795 the bishop appointed him rector of the 'sweet and delightful' rural parish of Winston, co. Durham (Harford, 174). On 1 October 1799 at St Mary-le-Bow, Durham, 'he relieved the solitude of his situation, effectually, by entering into the married state' (ibid., 197). His wife was Margery (*d*. 1842), daughter of John Bright of

Thomas Burgess (1756–1837), by William Owen, 1819

Pontefract, Yorkshire. There were no children of the marriage.

Burgess's quiet and retiring life was dramatically transformed in June 1803, a few days after he had taken his DD, when he was offered the see of St David's by the prime minister, Henry Addington, who had been his contemporary at both Winchester and Oxford. Burgess had visited Wales only once in his life; he now became bishop of a huge diocese that covered almost half the country and extended into Herefordshire. The episcopal palace was in the village of Abergwili, near Carmarthen, almost 50 miles from the cathedral. The new bishop found much need for reform in his diocese, which he himself called 'this dilapidated part of the Church of England' (Price, *Bishop Burgess*, 25). The church was financially impoverished and spiritually unimpressive, and nonconformity was growing rapidly. In 1804 Burgess indicated in his first episcopal charge his proposals for improving the condition of the diocese. Religious literature, free or at reduced prices, was to be made available to the faithful, libraries were to be established for the clergy, day schools and Sunday schools were to be set up, and the training of candidates for the ministry was to be improved. This last was Burgess's major concern, to which he devoted himself unstintingly: he set aside part of his income each year towards the proposed institution and he tirelessly appealed for contributions from others. After many vicissitudes he laid the foundation stone of St David's College, Lampeter, Cardiganshire, on 12 August 1822; the college opened on 1 March 1827, after Burgess had left the diocese.

Burgess attempted to learn Welsh, although he never became completely fluent in it; he refused however to institute into Welsh-speaking parishes clergy who could not speak Welsh. His interest in Welsh culture led him to encourage eisteddfods, and in 1819 he presided at that of Carmarthen, when the Gorsedd of Bards of the Isle of Britain was first brought into association with the eisteddfod.

In the wider church Burgess supported the interdenominational British and Foreign Bible Society, founded in 1804, the Church Missionary Society, and the London Society for the Promotion of Christianity among the Jews. He strenuously and consistently opposed Roman Catholic emancipation and he wrote tracts against unitarianism, strong in part of his diocese. He was also the first president of the Royal Society of Literature, for which he had written the prospectus in 1823, and wearied members with successive presidential addresses (in 1826, 1827, and 1828) on his reasons for believing that John Milton had not written *De doctrina Christiana*. His shyness meant that he seldom spoke in the House of Lords.

For over a century most of his predecessors in St David's had regarded the diocese as a stepping stone to a wealthier see in England but Burgess often said that he would be happy to remain in St David's until his death. In 1825, however, at the age of sixty-eight, he accepted translation to the see of Salisbury, which was much more compact in area than St David's and much nearer to London. It was also a wealthier diocese, which enabled him to resign his Durham stall, which had necessitated residence there for part of every year. Mrs Burgess was also finding Abergwili Palace too damp for her rheumatism, a factor that encouraged the move. Before he left St David's Burgess destroyed most of the papers relating to his episcopate. In spite of his failing eyesight, which led him to seek unsuccessfully to resign the see, he ruled his new diocese to the best of his ability, until his death at Southampton on 19 February 1837. His funeral was held on 27 February in Salisbury Cathedral, where he was buried in the south choir transept. Mrs Burgess died in 1842.

Hugh Pearson, dean of Salisbury, whose son had married Burgess's niece, expressed the opinion of many when he wrote that the diocese had not lost much with Burgess's death:

> He had some fine qualities, and some excellent dispositions, but they were rather such as would have adorned a more private station, such as that of a Greek Professor with a Canonry at Ch[rist] Ch[urch], rather than that of a Bishop … He was a profound Scholar, but neither a Preacher nor a Speaker, and very ill qualified to govern and direct a diocese. But the venerable Bishop was a good man, pious, blameless, munificent, placable, charitable. (Pearson, 132)

Bishop Burgess left his library of 8000 volumes to St David's College, Lampeter, together with money to enlarge the college library to house the collection. He also established four scholarships in the college.

D. T. W. PRICE

Sources J. S. Harford, *The life of Thomas Burgess* (1840) · D. T. W. Price, *Bishop Burgess and Lampeter College* (1987) · J. Ogden, 'Bishop Burgess and John Milton', *Trivium*, 32 (1997), 79–98 · H. N. Pearson,

'Family and personal memoirs', unpublished MS, c.1856, Salisbury Cathedral Library · D. T. W. Price, *A history of Saint David's University College Lampeter*, 1: *To 1898* (1977) · parish register, Odiham, Hampshire, 3 Dec 1756 [baptism] · parish register, Durham, St Mary-le-Bow, 1 Oct 1799 [marriage] · J. W. Walker, ed., *Yorkshire pedigrees*, 3 vols., Harleian Society, 94–6 (1942–4) · Foster, *Alum. Oxon.* · memorial, Odiham parish church [William Burgess; Elizabeth Burgess, *née* Harding]

Archives BL, corresp., mainly relating to classical subjects, Add. MS 46487 · Bodl. Oxf., corresp. and papers, Eng. lett. MSS. c. 133–40 | Glos. RO, letters to Samuel Viner · NL Wales, corresp. relating to Myddfai stone · Powys County Archives Office, Llandrindod Wells, corresp. with Richard Davies

Likenesses J. Russell, pencil and crayon drawing, c.1780, U. Wales, Lampeter · W. Owen, oils, 1819, CCC Oxf. [*see illus.*] · R. Cockle Lucas, miniature wax bust, c.1820, U. Wales, Lampeter · S. W. Reynolds, mezzotint, 1825, NPG · Thomson, stipple, pubd 1825, NPG · W. Owen, oils, c.1830; copy, U. Wales, Lampeter · silhouette, c.1830, U. Wales, Lampeter · G. Hayter, group portrait, oils (*The trial of Queen Caroline, 1820*), NPG · aquatint, BM; repro. in Harford, *Life of Thomas Burgess* · portrait, priv. coll. · wax bust, CCC Oxf.

Burgess, Thomas (1783/4–1807). *See under* Burgess, Thomas (c.1730–1791).

Burgess, Thomas (1791–1854), Roman Catholic bishop of Clifton, was born at Clayton-le-Woods, Lancashire, on 1 October 1791, the son of Thomas Burgess, a carpenter, and his wife, Cecily (*née* Gregson), whose parents were farmers. He was educated at Ampleforth, where he became a professed monk of the order of St Benedict on 13 October 1807, and was ordained priest in 1814. He was elected prior of Ampleforth at the 1826 chapter meeting.

The vicar apostolic of the western district, Bishop Peter Baines, had purchased the Prior Park estate, near Bath, in 1830, intending to establish there a boarding-school, a seminary, and, eventually, a Catholic university. Baines, Prior Burgess, Sub-Prior Rooker, and the procurator, Edward Metcalfe, all left Ampleforth and the Benedictine order to become secular priests and to start the venture at Prior Park in May 1830. Disagreement with Baines over his extravagant building schemes caused Burgess to leave Prior Park in January 1831 to become missioner at Cannington. He ministered there until February 1832, when he returned to Bath to the new chapel in Brunswick Place, where he served until 1835. Baines then asked him to move to the mission at Monmouth, where he served until 1851. In 1840 Wales was created a district separate from the western district. The new vicar apostolic of the Welsh district, Bishop Thomas Brown, appointed Burgess to be his vicar-general, an office he also held until 1851.

On the resignation of Bishop Hendren, the first bishop of Clifton, in June 1851 Burgess was elected to succeed him. He was consecrated bishop of Clifton at Southwark on 17 July 1851. He came to a diocese in serious financial difficulties. Prior Park was virtually bankrupt. To add to the financial problems confronting the new bishop, the establishment of the new dioceses after 1850 created further financial demands on the meagre funds of the Clifton diocese. Several missions that were in the western district in 1830 had lent large sums of money to Baines to assist in the building programme at Prior Park when its college

Thomas Burgess (1791–1854), by Henry Adlard

was founded. After 1850 these missions belonged to the new dioceses of Plymouth, Newport, and Shrewsbury—themselves in dire need of funds. Burgess was asked to return the money lent for building Prior Park, and it was a cause of great sorrow to him that, in spite of the pleas of his brother bishops, he could neither repay the loans nor even pay the arrears of interest.

In spite of his failing health, each year the bishop went on a fund-raising mission to the dioceses in the north of England. He found such 'begging-missions' as he called them very embarrassing, but he realized that this was the only way in which he could prevent the closure of his beloved Prior Park. Shortly after returning from one such mission in October 1854 he collapsed and he died at Westbury-on-Trym, Bristol, on 27 November. He was buried in the crypt of his pro-cathedral at Clifton. When the pro-cathedral ceased to be used in 1973, his remains were removed to the chapel of the Catholic cemetery at Arnos Vale in Bristol.

Almost exactly a year after Burgess's death the bailiffs moved into Prior Park; the school was closed and the assets auctioned. Prior Park College had lasted for less than twenty-six years.

THOMPSON COOPER, *rev.* JOHN CASHMAN

Sources *The Lancashire registers*, 4, Catholic RS, 23 (1922), 40 n., 106 n. · J. Gillow, ed., 'Records of the abbey of Our Lady of Consolation at Cambrai, 1620–1793', *Miscellanea, VIII*, Catholic RS, 13 (1913), 1–85, esp. 77–8, 14 · J. S. Roche, *A history of Prior Park College* (1931) · G. Oliver, *Collections illustrating the history of the Catholic religion in the counties of Cornwall, Devon, Dorset, Wilts. and Glos.* (1868) · *Ordo and Catholic Directory* (1860), 258–61 · *Ordo and Catholic Directory* (1854), 77 · *The Tablet* (2 Dec 1854), 760 · *The Tablet* (9 Dec 1854), 773 · *The Tablet* (16 Dec 1854), 788 · *GM*, 2nd ser., 43 (1855), 109

Archives Bristol RO, Clifton diocesan archives · Bristol RO, letters from Rome; papers

Likenesses H. Adlard, stipple, NPG [*see illus.*] · oils, St Ambrose, North Road, Bristol

Burgess, William (1748/9–1812). *See under* Burgess, Thomas (*c.*1730–1791).

Burgess, William (1754/5–1813), engraver, in conjunction with his son, Hilkiah, published a set of prints of twelve churches in Lincolnshire and Cambridgeshire (1800–05) and later of Lincoln and Ely cathedrals. To the profession of an artist he united that of a Baptist minister, and presided over a congregation of that sect at Fleet in Lincolnshire for twenty-two years. He was also the author of a controversial pamphlet on the works of Dr Adam Clarke. He died suddenly at Fleet on 11 December 1813, in his fifty-ninth year. GORDON GOODWIN, *rev.* ANNE PUETZ

Sources Redgrave, *Artists*, 2nd edn, 62 · *GM*, 1st ser., 83/2 (1813), 701 · 'Monuments in Fleet Baptist Church', typescript, London Society of Genealogists

Burgess, William Oakley (1818–1844), printmaker, was born in the parish of St Giles-in-the-Fields, London, the son of the parish surgeon. Little is known of his early life except that he studied under the mezzotint engraver Thomas Goff Lupton (1791–1873) until the age of twenty. Following this training he specialized principally in mezzotint, although his simple outline engraving of the Sistine Chapel ceiling, in Charles Eastlake's *Schools of Painting in Italy* (1837), is one exception. His highly refined mezzotints are characterized by their delicacy and graduated velvet tones, and this can be seen in reproductive portraits such as *The Duke of Wellington* or *Sir Robert Kerr Porter* (1843). In his short career the greater part of Burgess's output consisted of mezzotint portraits after the work of Sir Thomas Lawrence. These were published, periodically, in a series of fifty plates entitled *Engravings from the Choicest Works of Sir Thomas Lawrence P. R. A.* (1835–46). The last of these plates appeared after Burgess's untimely death, on 24 December 1844, caused by an 'abscess in the head' (Bryan, *Painters*, 22), which, it is thought, had developed from a blow he had received, many years earlier, while playing cricket. R. E. GRAVES, *rev.* LUCY PELTZ

Sources Bryan, *Painters* (1866); (1903–5) · Redgrave, *Artists*

Burgh, Benedict (*d.* in or before **1483**), clerk and translator, is known only from a few surviving scraps of information about his life. An Oxford MA, he rented a school from University College in 1432–3, and was granted letters testimonial by the university on 3 July 1433. In 1434 he was rector of Rendcomb, Gloucestershire. Thereafter he held a number of ecclesiastical offices in Essex and East Anglia: vicar of All Saints', Maldon, Essex (1440); rector of Sandon, Essex (1440–44); of Bildeston, Suffolk (until 1442); of Sible Hedingham, Essex (1450–77?); of Hitcham, Suffolk (1453–66?). Later records suggest a modest rise through the church hierarchy: he became a canon of Lincoln and prebendary of Empingham (July 1463–6?); archdeacon of Colchester (from February 1466); canon and prebendary of the king's free chapel of Bridgnorth, Shropshire (from April 1470); canon of St Paul's, London, and prebendary of Ealdland (February 1472 – June 1476); canon and prebendary of St Stephen's Chapel, Westminster (from June 1476; it was exchanged for another prebend in the same church in April 1479); dean of the king's free chapel in Hastings

Castle, Sussex (until 1481?); and chaplain to the king (April 1470).

Burgh is best known for his verse rendering of the distichs of Cato ('Cato major' with 'parvus Cato'), a collection of proverbial advice and a popular school-text, which was published by Caxton in three editions (1477–83), and for his completion of Lydgate's *Secrees of Old Philisoffres*. In the prologue to his own translation of a French version of Cato (after 23 December 1483), Caxton refers to Burgh's work, saying that it was done 'for the erudicion of my lorde Bousher', the son and heir of Henry Bourchier, first earl of Essex, and to Burgh as 'late Archedekene of Colchestre and hye chanon of Saint Stephens at Westmestre'. Burgh's translations do not show great literary talents, but belong to the tradition of educational and didactic verse which was popular with contemporary readers (the *Secrees* survives in over twenty manuscripts; the Cato in over thirty). He is almost certainly the 'Master Burgh' to whom is attributed a poem in praise of John Lydgate which expresses the wish to become his apprentice (BL, Add. MS 29729), written 'at th'abbey of Bylegh' (Beeleigh, near Maldon) with 'frosti fingers' in December. In the same manuscript a proverbial poem 'Kepe Well the Tonge' is also attributed to 'magister Benedict Burgh'. He may well be the 'maister Benet' who wrote 'A Christemasse Game' (BL, Harley MS 7333), a poem in which Christ welcomes each of the apostles and invites them to sit down with him in heaven, which sounds like a Christmas mumming. Much less certain is the attribution to 'mayster Benett' (in only one of a number of manuscripts) of the proverbial poem 'The ABC of Aristotle'. DOUGLAS GRAY

Sources Emden, *Oxf.*, 1.309 · M. Förster, 'Über Benedict Burghs Leben und Werke', *Archiv*, 101 (1898), 29–64 · E. P. Hammond, *English verse between Chaucer and Surrey* (1927) · *Lydgate and Burgh's Secrees of old philisoffres: a version of the Secreta Secretorum*, ed. R. Steele, EETS, extra ser., 66 (1894) · W. Caxton, *The book called 'Cathon'* (*c.*1483) · BL, Add. MS 29729

Archives BL, Add. MS 29729 · BL, Harley MS 7333

Burgh, Elizabeth de. *See* Elizabeth (*d.* 1327).

Burgh, Hubert de, earl of Kent (*c.*1170–1243), justiciar, has been wrongly said to have been the son of a brother of William fitz Aldhelm, steward of Henry II. It is possible, though doubtful, that his father was the Walter whose daughter Adelina, with her son William, owed 40 marks in the pipe roll of 26 Henry II (1179/80) for recognition of their right to a knight's fee at Burgh, Norfolk. His mother's name was Alice, for in his grant (*c.*1230) of the advowson of the church of Oulton to the prior of Walsingham, Hubert stated that the gift was 'for the soul of my mother Alice who rests in the church at Walsingham' (BL, Cotton MS Nero E.vii, fol. 91). His elder brother was William de *Burgh (*d.* 1206) who, in 1185, accompanied the king's youngest son, John, to Ireland, where he eventually became lord of Connacht; William's son would later refer to Hubert as uncle. Two younger brothers, Geoffrey and Thomas, became respectively archdeacon of Norwich (1202) and then bishop of Ely (1225), and castellan of Norwich (1215–16). Hubert has been said to have been born in

Hubert de Burgh, earl of Kent (*c.*1170–1243), drawing

John, as count of Mortain, at Tinchebrai in Normandy, and in another charter of the following 12 June he was styled chamberlain of John's household. When John became king in 1199, de Burgh was then chamberlain of the royal household. This office was one of the two most important domestic offices, in origin being that in charge of the chamber, including its finances; but it is uncertain how far, by 1199, it had become honorific. There is no evidence of de Burgh's domestic or financial duties at the time, but in 1202 he was one of the ambassadors sent by the king to the king of Portugal, to try to arrange John's marriage to the latter's daughter. While this embassy was still in Lisbon, however, John married Isabella (*d.* 1246), the young daughter of the count of Angoulême, and de Burgh and his companions had to make their way back. Towards the end of April 1200 de Burgh had tried to arrange a marriage for himself, to Joan, youngest daughter of William de Vernon, earl of Devon (*d.* 1217), whose dowry would be the Isle of Wight and the manor of Christchurch, Hampshire. The agreement was referred to in a charter of 28 April, issued at Portchester, and it provided that if Earl William's wife should bear a son, de Burgh was then to have £60 and the service of ten knights. The countess did bear a son, and the marriage agreement was apparently cancelled.

De Burgh's career in royal service was developing. At the beginning of 1201 he was sheriff of Dorset and Somerset, in the next year of Berkshire and Cornwall. In December 1200 the king had made him custodian of two important royal castles: Dover and Windsor. When John sailed for France in June 1201, having sent an important Welsh marcher baron, the earl of Pembroke, and Roger de Lacy, the constable of Chester, with 200 knights, ahead of him, de Burgh was made custodian of the Welsh marches at the head of 100 men-at-arms, and given the 'Three Castles' of Grosmont, Skenfrith, and Whitecastle 'to sustain him in our service'; this triangular group of fortresses dominated upper Gwent and the approaches to south Wales. At the same time the king granted him the manor of Cawston which adjoined Burgh, and the land of Emma, wife of Gilbert of Norfolk, at Creake. In November 1201 he was given seisin of the lands of Walter of Windsor, and on 28 April 1202 the barons of the Cinque Ports were ordered to render de Burgh the service they owed the king; both grants were presumably to sustain de Burgh as custodian of Windsor and Dover castles. As sheriff he had the baronies of Beauchamp and Dunster in Somerset in his hand. By 1202 de Burgh, as a royal servant, was becoming a significant and powerful figure.

Royal service and social advancement, 1202–1215 This English career was cut short in October 1202 when de Burgh was summoned to France, becoming constable of Falaise Castle, Normandy, and joint castellan of Chinon, Touraine, in the face of baronial rebellion and French attack. It was at Falaise, according to the chronicler Coggeshall, that de Burgh refused to blind and castrate the king's captured nephew, Arthur—an incident which, wrongly located, was a dramatic climax in Shakespeare's *King John*. If the story is true, de Burgh's failure to carry out John's order caused no detectable rift, for early in 1203 he was

1175, but if his brother William was of knightly age in 1185, a date some years earlier is more probable.

Early career to 1202 Hubert de Burgh's family was one of minor landholders. The manors of Burgh (South Erpingham hundred), Beeston (North Erpingham), and Newton (South Greenloe hundred), in Norfolk, and Sotherton in Suffolk, were described in 1232 as 'of his heredity'. Perhaps the neighbouring baronial family of Warenne, into which Hubert later married, introduced him into royal service, but his own brother was already in the service of Richard I's brother, John, whose son, the future Henry III, according to the unreliable chronicler Roger of Wendover, called de Burgh the faithful servant of his uncle King Richard from boyhood. If this is true, then de Burgh entered royal service during the justiciarship of Hubert Walter (1193–8), but there is nothing in the administrative record to show this.

On 8 February 1198 de Burgh witnessed a charter of

sent, jointly with Philip of Oldcotes, to hold the strategic-ally important castle of Chinon against the king of France, to whom he may have been an emissary in 1204. Hubert's stout defence of Chinon lasted a year, until in the summer of 1205, when the walls of the castle were said to have been levelled, he and his men rushed out to engage in a fierce fight in which he was wounded and captured.

Hubert de Burgh's captivity lasted for two years. Not surprisingly his absence from England saw alternative arrangements for his offices. In 1205 he was called chamberlain for the last time and he ceased to be a sheriff. His lands and his castles on the Welsh border were taken into the king's hand. In Norfolk and Suffolk the lands that he held of the count of Perche were granted to Gilbert of Stanford, while towards the end of the year the three Welsh castles were granted to William (III) de Briouze (d. 1211). King John nevertheless helped with de Burgh's ransom in 1207, for writs to the treasurer and chamberlains ordered them to pay William de Chayv 300 marks 'for the pledge of Hubert de Burgh' in February, and towards the end of the year to pay de Burgh £100.

With his return to England before the end of 1207 de Burgh again began to acquire lands and offices. In 1208 he paid £100 to be exempt from the much larger sum he owed from his time as sheriff of Somerset and Dorset, and for having the manor of Shepperton in Middlesex. On 28 May he was given custody of the castle and town of Lafford in Huntingdon. In the following year he married Beatrice de Warenne, who had succeeded to her father's barony of Wormegay. She was also widow of Doun Bardolf, and de Burgh became guardian of her young son, William, with land at Stowe and North Runcton in Norfolk, and Finborough in Suffolk. Beatrice died before 18 December 1214, but she was the mother of de Burgh's only son, John, probably before 1212, since in that year de Burgh was back in France on royal service, as deputy to the seneschal of Poitou, Ivo de Jallia. When the latter was summoned to England in 1213, de Burgh served as seneschal in association with Philip d'Aubigny and Geoffrey de Neville. By the time of his return to France de Burgh had re-established himself as a significant baron in England. He had bought two knights' fees near his hereditary lands, Beeston and Runton, and two carucates at Hindringham. King John granted him Corfe Mullen in Dorset, and he held Babcary and Stoke in that county of the honour of Mortain. By 1213 he had the Roumare honour of Camel in Somerset by royal gift. An inquisition of that year shows him holding more than fifty knights' fees in the East Anglian shires of Norfolk, Suffolk, Essex, and Cambridge, and in the south-western ones of Dorset and Somerset, with other lands in Buckinghamshire, Hampshire, Surrey, and Wiltshire.

During 1214 and early 1215 de Burgh, sometimes styled mayor of Niort (Deux Sèvres, France), probably because the town was his headquarters, was seneschal of Poitou during John's attempt to recover his lost dominions. After the defeat of Bouvines in 1214 he was one of the witnesses to the truce with the French king by which John retained his lands south of the Loire, but by late April or early May 1215 de Burgh was back in England; on 18 April he was ordered to dispose of the prisoners held in Poitou, while John fitz Robert, who on 25 June had been ordered to hand over his castles to John Marshal, on 24 July was instructed to surrender them to Hubert de Burgh. With the bishop of Coventry, de Burgh was then sent to John's half-brother, William (I) Longespée, earl of Salisbury (d. 1226), and to the mayor, sheriff, and knights of London, who were ordered to listen to what de Burgh and the bishop had to say with the strictest attention. The Londoners, however, admitted the rebellious barons, and John then ordered that anyone coming from overseas into his service should put themselves at the disposal of Hubert de Burgh who, with Philip d'Aubigny, gathered the royal forces at Rochester. The king came to terms with the barons, and in the preamble to Magna Carta de Burgh, called seneschal of Poitou, was listed eighth among the lay barons by whose advice the king said he had granted it. By 25 June 1215 de Burgh was being styled justiciar in official documents. According to Matthew Paris's later story, he had been appointed in the presence of Archbishop Stephen Langton (d. 1228), the earls of Warenne and Derby, and other magnates.

Civil war, 1215–1217 In Magna Carta Hubert de Burgh was always mentioned as the king's other self, who would take action if the king were abroad. There was no reference to the justiciar's usual role as president of the exchequer and as chief justice, whether the king were abroad or not. The office, which had been clearly established in Henry II's reign, had already somewhat changed its character. De Burgh succeeded the Poitevin bishop of Winchester, Peter des Roches (d. 1238), who had himself had no great experience of exchequer or judicial administration in England. Nor had de Burgh. His career had been more military than administrative, and as a sheriff he had often accounted by deputy. On the day he became justiciar, he became sheriff of Kent and Surrey, with custody of Canterbury Castle. He was also made castellan of Dover again. These offices look more like military precautions in the face of deteriorating relations between king and rebellious barons than normal administrative ones, precautions lent point when the barons invited Louis of France into England. In May 1216 Louis landed in Kent, captured Norwich Castle, ill-manned under Thomas de Burgh, and about 22 July laid siege to Dover, held by Hubert.

The justiciar had provisioned the castle well, and withstood a protracted siege, as he had earlier done at Chinon. Wendover and Paris have colourful later accounts of de Burgh's defiance, even when his captured brother Thomas was used as hostage. He was successfully defending the castle when King John died, on 19 October, and Louis abandoned the siege. No doubt his immurement at Dover accounts for the justiciar's not being named as an executor of John's will.

The young Henry III was crowned at Gloucester on 28 October 1216, when the papal legate Guala, representing the king's feudal suzerain, the pope, with Peter des Roches and loyal barons and bishops, made William Marshal, earl of Pembroke (d. 1219), regent, although briefly the chancery clerks called him justiciar in de Burgh's absence. Earl William used the title 'rector' of the king and kingdom. De Burgh was able to leave Dover to attend a council at Bristol on 11 November which reissued Magna Carta; he was named justiciar at the head of the lay barons who witnessed it. The king being a minor, government was by the council, with the rector and the legate at its head. Bishop Peter des Roches was the king's guardian. The justiciar therefore could not be the king's other self, and there was no normally functioning royal administration of justice and finance. There was a war in progress in England, and by February 1217 de Burgh was back in his vital castle of Dover, rebuilding and reprovisioning against a renewed siege, which began in April, and continued until the baronial defeat at 'the fair of Lincoln' on 20 May caused Louis to raise the siege and retire to London to await reinforcements.

On 24 August 1217 a French fleet with those reinforcements was routed off Sandwich by English ships from the Cinque Ports. Hubert de Burgh has sometimes been credited with this victory, entirely on the basis of Wendover's and Paris's later tales that the rector and Bishop Peter refused to sail out because they 'were neither sea-soldiers nor pirates' (Paris, *Chron.*, 3.28), and told the justiciar to go. It is not certain that de Burgh was in command. The decisive encounter with Eustace the Monk's ship was commanded by Richard, illegitimate son of King John, with Philip d'Aubigny prominent in the battle. However, de Burgh certainly kept the prisoners at Dover Castle.

Early years as justiciar, 1217–1224 With Louis's consequent withdrawal from England the civil war ended, but government was by council, of which de Burgh was not the most prominent member. From 1218 the new legate, Pandulf, and the rector, who took an active interest, were dominant, with Bishop Peter still the king's guardian. The legate issued orders and instructions to both bishop and justiciar, treating them as chief executive officers, while Earl William Marshal's seal was used for royal orders, until a royal seal was made in 1218. Only after the rector's final illness began in 1219 did Hubert de Burgh begin to attest royal orders, from 20 April, but on William Marshal's death it was the legate who succeeded to the latter's position, until he left England in 1221. Only in 1223, when the king was declared for some purposes of age, did the justiciar become the dominant figure, and even then under the restriction that no royal grants could be made in perpetuity.

With the departure of Pandulf in 1221 signs of partisan quarrels appeared. One of King John's foreigners, Peter de Mauley (d. 1241), was arrested, and lost his custody of Corfe Castle and of Eleanor of Brittany (d. 1241), Arthur's sister, together with the shrievalty of Dorset and Somerset. At Christmas 1221 the earl of Chester quarrelled with the justiciar and the earl of Salisbury. In August 1222 there was a riot in London which the justiciar and Falkes de Bréauté (d. 1226), another of John's mercenary captains, suppressed by hanging Constantine Fitzalulf, its leader, and two of his associates, without much of a trial, and then mutilating other arrested citizens. More serious disaffection followed the king's partial coming of age in 1223. A

general surrender of all royal castles was agreed by the council, and on 30 December de Burgh delivered his castles of Canterbury, Dover, Rochester, Norwich, Orford, and Hereford to the bishops of those places, castles that he held as sheriff of those shires, for the shrievalties too were to be handed back to the king as part of the re-establishment of royal government. As justiciar, this was the justiciar's responsibility, but, according to the St Albans chroniclers, it led to complaints of his oppressiveness. In fact he enjoyed Archbishop Langton's support.

The head of the government, 1224–1232 A major part of the complaints against the justiciar originated with Falkes de Bréauté. After Whitsuntide 1224 the itinerant justices sent out to hear cases of recent dispossession in Bedfordshire heard seventeen actions against Bréauté who neither appeared nor sent excuse; on 17 June he was outlawed. His brother, William, who held Bedford Castle for him, kidnapped one of the royal justices. The king, on the advice of the council, besieged the castle; de Burgh himself arrived on 20 June and issued a series of orders to neighbouring sheriffs to supply the besiegers for the eight weeks of the siege. When the castle was taken, Bréauté's brother and many of the defenders were hanged, and he himself was exiled. Thereafter he denounced both the justiciar and the archbishop of Canterbury as his persistent enemies. Bishop Peter des Roches may have sympathized with him; but the bishop went on crusade. With his departure Hubert de Burgh had no rivals, but as with any justiciar his position depended upon the king.

In September 1223 de Burgh and the young Henry III conducted a successful expedition against the Welsh, with de Burgh redesigning Montgomery Castle as part of it. With the three upper Gwent castles that he had recovered by a suit against Reginald de Briouze in 1219, he became a very powerful marcher lord, but the unsuccessful Welsh expeditions of 1228 and 1231, when the king was fully of age, coupled with his failure in the king's attempt to regain his lost dominions in France in 1230, must have destroyed royal confidence. Indeed, if Wendover can be believed, in 1229 when the ships assembled at Portsmouth were inadequate to transport all the troops, Henry III drew his sword against de Burgh, calling him an old traitor. In the previous year, however, the king had granted him the justiciarship for life, together with the castles of Dover, Canterbury, and Rochester, and the Welsh castles of Montgomery, Cardigan, and Carmarthen.

Given de Burgh's undoubted reputation as a soldier, military failure could obviously undermine his position and the king's confidence. So could administrative failure to provide the king with the money he needed. Justice was profitable, but the justiciar's mark upon the plea rolls was less than that of his predecessors in office. In part this may be the consequence of writs running in the king's name, not the justiciar's, for de Burgh was never regent in the king's absence, but the justiciar was less invoked by the justices to solve difficulties or doubts in their proceedings, either at Westminster or on eyre. Where the justiciar's authority was invoked, the occasions look political rather than judicial. The justices themselves, as their names appear in final concords, were men who specialized in this area of royal administration, with Martin of Pattishall (*d.* 1229) and Stephen of Seagrave (*d.* 1241) at their head. Hubert de Burgh neither sat regularly with the bench, nor regularly joined the itinerant justices. Nor did he regularly sit at the exchequer, presiding over the barons, as justiciars had done in the past. His interventions there were greater than those in judicial proceedings, and he was consulted more often, but his part in financial administration was conservative rather than innovative. When, for example, in 1224 there was a large-scale replacement of sheriffs, the practice of grouping debts owed to the king, which a reforming tendency had introduced into the accounts, was discontinued in favour of the old practice of listing individual debtors. The effort to raise more money to sustain the king was also met by reversion to old practice: the increment on the farm of the county was reintroduced.

Rivalries and resentments These conservative measures at the exchequer coincided with the removal of Peter de Rivallis (*d.* 1262), nephew (or perhaps son) of Bishop Peter des Roches, from his office in the wardrobe, the financial part of the king's chamber, which had provided the flexibility to meet the king's need for a ready supply of money. Whatever the personal factors in the relationship between Hubert de Burgh and Peter des Roches—it is impossible to know what these were from the surviving evidence—and whatever resentments there may have been about 'foreigners', the justiciar and the Poitevins had clear differences on administrative practices, most notably over the exchequer, the chamber, and the wardrobe. If the justiciar failed militarily, and his presidency of judicial and exchequer administration failed to meet the king's needs, then a reforming party like that led by Peter des Roches and Peter de Rivallis offered an alternative.

To these failures of an ageing justiciar were added other resentments against him. Wendover and Paris call him a *novus homo*, a new man unacceptable to the older baronial families, and cite the countess of Salisbury's indignant reaction to de Burgh's nephew Reimund's suit for her hand when her husband was believed dead at sea. Since Hubert de Burgh had more by inheritance than either Geoffrey fitz Peter or William Marshal, against neither of whom was such older baronial disdain evident, the chroniclers' account is doubtful. It is more likely that any resentment came from de Burgh's collection of lands and wealth as a consequence of his justiciarship and monopoly of the young king's favour.

When Hubert de Burgh became justiciar in 1215, King John had given him custody of the honour of Peverel, and a month later the honours of Rayleigh in Essex and Haughley in Suffolk. A month later still he was granted the lordship and hundred of Hoo in Kent. All these lands were taken into royal protection ten days before the king died. Then in 1217 de Burgh married the late king's divorced wife, *Isabella, countess of Gloucester, who was also the widow of Geoffrey fitz Peter's son and heir as earl of Essex. On 13 August 1217 the sheriffs of nine counties were ordered to give de Burgh custody of all her lands. She

died on 14 October, a few days after the wedding ceremony, her heir being her nephew Gilbert de Clare, whose son Richard was to marry the daughter of Hubert de Burgh and his third wife, *Margaret, sister of Alexander, king of the Scots. Their marriage was celebrated at York in June 1221. It brought no English lands to de Burgh, but in 1224 he became custodian of those of the earl of Arundel, and two years later of those of the earl of Norfolk. In 1227 he was made earl of Kent, granted £50 p.a. in lieu of the third penny of the county, to add to the £300 p.a. he had been granted in 1222 to sustain himself in the justiciarship, and the £1000 p.a. he had for the custody of Dover Castle. In late 1229 he was granted the honours of Knaresborough in Yorkshire and Eye in Suffolk. The succession to his earldom was conferred on the descendants of de Burgh and Margaret, who held many of his lands jointly with him. He had built up a great barony, but it was a widely scattered one which lacked the unity of a single honour, although he had a steward, Lawrence of St Albans, to administer all his lands. The daughter of de Burgh and Margaret, called Megotta, died before her father, and although John de Burgh, the son of his first marriage, inherited the justiciar's lands, the title of earl died with Hubert.

Fall from office and last years, 1232–1243 The growth of this great barony was cut short by Hubert de Burgh's fall from office in 1232. At the beginning of August 1231 Bishop Peter returned from crusade. In September Peter de Rivallis, who had formerly been a chamberlain and clerk of the wardrobe, was appointed treasurer of the chamber. Henry III kept Christmas at Winchester with his old guardian, Bishop Peter of Winchester. The St Albans chroniclers say that a plot was then hatched against the justiciar, and the occasion for its execution was the riots against Italian clerks appointed to English benefices. The justiciar was blamed for the riots, although not by the pope, and in 1232 Peter de Rivallis was given custody of the household finances and the shrievalties of twenty-one shires. On 15 June de Burgh was made justiciar of Ireland for life, but Peter de Rivallis was given custody of the king's small seal, the authenticating instrument for the chancery and exchequer great seals, for life. At the beginning of July the king stayed with Hubert de Burgh, and at the neighbouring shrine of the Holy Rood at Bromholm, the king by oath bound himself and his successors to observe all the charters and grants he had given to the Countess Margaret and de Burgh, the bishop of Carlisle, the royal steward Godfrey of Crowcombe, and Peter de Rivallis. De Burgh, the charter roll then records, took an oath at the king's order, to impede any royal invalidation of his oath. This may have been an attempt to reconcile different parties, but on 29 July de Burgh was dismissed from the justiciarship, stripped of all the royal castles he held, and had an account demanded of him for all receipts and payments while he was justiciar.

Most of the subsequent charges against Hubert de Burgh come from the St Albans chroniclers. It has been conjectured that Matthew Paris may have heard an account of his tribulations from de Burgh himself, or possibly from his steward, Lawrence of St Albans. Even if this were the case, it does not follow that the justiciar and his steward were good witnesses. In this account de Burgh was twice pulled from sanctuary—once at Boisars Chapel near his manor of Brentford, once from Devizes church—fettered as a royal prisoner on the first occasion, rescued by men of Richard Marshal, earl of Pembroke (d. 1234), on the second. The record evidence shows that on 25 August 1232 the king ordered de Burgh 'as he loved himself and all that was his' to leave the kingdom within fifteen days, but on 26 September told the sheriff of Essex not to allow the bishop of London and other clerks to go any further than the chapel at Brentford, nor was anyone to give or sell sustenance to de Burgh. On 7 October the sheriff was told that if Hubert left the chapel he was to be taken to the Tower of London, an order repeated on the 16th. If the Countess Margaret were to leave Bury St Edmunds she also was to be taken to the Tower, but on 13 November she and her daughter were given safe conduct to go into any lands of de Burgh's inheritance or purchase, other than those he held of the king. De Burgh's own small seal was to be broken and crushed to powder.

On 23 October the fallen justiciar had been ordered to appear before the king's court or be outlawed. De Burgh surrendered, delivered to the king the treasure he had stored with the templars, and threw himself on the king's mercy. His inherited and purchased lands were then restored to him on 10 November, although he was placed in the custody of the earls of Cornwall, Surrey, Pembroke, and Lincoln at Devizes Castle. And some of his lands, including Burgh, were given to Robert Passelewe (d. 1252) so that injured Italian clerks might be recompensed. However, de Burgh was released from Devizes by men of the earl of Pembroke, who had rebelled against the king, and was taken to Chepstow Castle, of which he became joint commander when the earl went to Ireland in May 1234. Pope Gregory IX (r. 1227–41) interceded for de Burgh in October 1233, and on 14 February 1234 his wife was given seisin of his hereditary manors, despite the grant to Robert Passelewe.

In April 1234 the indecisive king dismissed Peter de Rivallis and his associates, and on 25 May de Burgh was pardoned, together with the earl of Pembroke's heir; his hereditary lands were confirmed to him and the king 'undertook to do what grace he will' (CPR, 1232–47, 48), although not in excess of a sum to be determined. Henry did not, however, restore the lands formerly held of him in chief, while de Burgh undertook not to sue for the justiciarship. But in 1236 the knowledge of the secret marriage of Megotta to Richard of Clare, arranged by her mother, became public. The king had not known, nor had de Burgh himself, but in 1237 the 1232 charges of treason were revived, according to Matthew Paris, and rebutted by Lawrence of St Albans on de Burgh's behalf. The only record evidence of any further such trouble is that on 29 October 1239 de Burgh submitted himself to the king's liberality and grace, and yielded up the three castles in upper Gwent and the castle of Hadleigh in Essex which were then still

in his possession. De Burgh must certainly have been in his late sixties by then, but he lived on until May 1243, when he died at his Surrey manor of Banstead. He was buried in the house of the Blackfriars at Westminster, to whom he had been a benefactor and a neighbour in his own house in Westminster, which became the residence of the archbishop of York. Countess Margaret survived her husband, dying in 1259.

Reputation and significance Hubert de Burgh's career clearly shows the great rewards faithful royal service could bring to a man of minor landholding origins, and 'loyal' or 'constant' have been words applied to him by scholars. What is remarkable is that his loyal service did not make him unacceptable to the baronial opposition to John, and that he was able to serve Henry III within the limits set to royal government by Magna Carta. This was no mean achievement. Some earlier and some more recent scholars have also seen him as 'English' in his opposition to 'foreigners', relying on later chroniclers' statements about his actions against the Poitevins and the Italian clerks. It is likely that so nationalistic an interpretation is anachronistic for de Burgh's day. Contemporary hostility to Hubert de Burgh can be accounted for by resentment of his and his family's great acquisitiveness in office, but even more by the loss of the king's favour, both through military failure and through the growth of specialized branches of royal administration which made effective control by a single great minister impossible. Hubert de Burgh was the last of the great justiciars.

F. J. WEST

Sources PRO, ancient correspondence, special collections, SC 1 · PRO, exchequer, lord treasurer's remembrancer's memoranda rolls, E 368 · PRO, queen's remembrancer's memoranda rolls, E 159 · PRO, lord treasurer's remembrancer's pipe rolls, E 372 · T. D. Hardy, ed., *Rotuli litterarum clausarum*, 2 vols., RC (1833–4) · *Ann. mon.* · Paris, *Chron.* · *Rogeri de Wendover liber qui dicitur flores historiarum*, ed. H. G. Hewlett, 3 vols., Rolls Series, [84] (1886–9) · *Radulphi de Coggeshall chronicon Anglicanum*, ed. J. Stevenson, Rolls Series, 66 (1875) · W. W. Shirley, ed., *Royal and other historical letters illustrative of the reign of Henry III*, 2 vols., Rolls Series, 27 (1862–6) · PRSoc., new ser. (1925–) · Chancery records · C. Ellis, *Hubert de Burgh* (1952) · F. M. Powicke, *King Henry III and the Lord Edward: the community of the realm in the thirteenth century*, 2 vols. (1947) · F. J. West, *The justiciarship in England, 1066–1232* (1966) · B. Wilkinson, ed., *Angevin England, 1154–1377* (1978) [bibliographical handbook] · D. A. Carpenter, *The minority of Henry III* (1990) · *Curia regis rolls preserved in the Public Record Office* (1922–)

Likenesses drawing, BL, Royal MS 14 C.viii, fol. 119 [*see illus.*]

Wealth at death see PRO, special collections, ministers' accounts, SC 6, bundle 1117, no. 13

Burgh, James (1714–1775), educationist and author, was born late in 1714 at Madderty, Perthshire, one of the eleven children of Andrew Brugh (c.1677–1736) and Margaret Robertson (d. 1771), daughter of William Robertson of Gladney and an aunt of the historian William Robertson; James called Robertson his 'much esteemed friend and relation' (J. Burgh, *Political Disquisitions*, 1775, 3.15), although contact between the cousins is undocumented. Andrew Brugh, who spelled his name thus, received an MA from St Andrews University on 23 July 1697, was ordained in the Church of Scotland on 8 January 1701, and became the parish minister at Madderty. Both James and his elder brother John aspired to emulate their father's professional example; neither succeeded. John received a BA from St Andrews in 1721. He accepted a presentation at Foulis Wester without securing the congregation's approval and was censured by the Perth synod, which voided the appointment. Apparently he never secured another before his untimely death. Ill health forced James to withdraw from St Andrews University and abandon his ministerial aspirations. A substantial inheritance from John funded James's venture into the linen trade, but his business failed because of injudicious loans. Seeking a livelihood, James moved to London, probably early in the 1740s, and found work correcting the press for William Bowyer through whom he met 'several respectable friends who were highly serviceable to him in his future plans of life', including Arthur Onslow, speaker of the House of Commons (Nichols, *Lit. anecdotes*, 2.263). After a little more than a year Burgh sought more satisfying employment and he became an assistant in the free grammar school in Great Marlow, Buckinghamshire. The school prospered during his tenure, but the dearth of compatible company prompted Burgh, an enthusiastic conversationalist, to accept an assistant's position in 1746 at Mr Kenross's academy in Enfield, about 11 miles north of London. Impressed with Burgh, Kenross advised him to open his own academy and lent him funds to do so at Stoke Newington in 1747. The school's rapid success led Burgh to relocate in 1750 to larger premises at Newington Green, an enclave of dissenters. The eminent Arian Richard Price became minister at Newington Green Chapel in 1756; Burgh also became an Arian as well as lifelong friends with Price. Prospering, in 1751 the schoolmaster married Hannah Harding (*d.* 1788), a well-to-do widow four years his senior. Although childless, theirs was a model companionate marriage. A woman of 'excellent sense and character who zealously' supported her husband's 'laudable and useful undertakings' (Kippis, 3.14), Mrs Burgh later befriended Mary Wollstonecraft, financially assisting her and helping her to open a school at Newington Green in 1783.

The classroom first gave Burgh the opportunity to gratify his ministerial ambitions, but writing enabled him to reach a larger congregation. A 'bye-business' to his teaching responsibilities, Burgh's writing was unpolished, repetitive, and eclectic, but usually well received by the public and critics who complimented the substance and directness, if not the flourish, of his compositions and responded to the moral fervour that consistently infused his commentary. His thirty-year literary career was launched in January 1746 with the publication of *Britain's Remembrancer*; sales of six to eight editions in the British Isles exceeded 10,000 copies. Four editions were published in America, the first by Benjamin Franklin, who eventually became Burgh's friend. The tract was occasioned by the Jacobite rising of 1745 which the moralistic Burgh, a staunch anti-Jacobite, saw as a portent of divine retribution if the British did not overcome xenophobic rivalries

and curb the luxury and licentiousness that was ostensibly corrupting the moral fibre of the nation. Burgh's lifelong enthusiasm about Britain's growing commercial and imperial power was always tempered by his profound concern for the corrosive potential of affluence. He lauded the work ethic of the commercial classes and the prosperity made possible by the commercial revolution, while consistently lambasting the excessive materialism manifest in the consumer revolution.

Unsurprisingly, the schoolmaster's early publications focused on the importance of education in promoting individual and national probity and prosperity. Burgh shared John Locke's conviction in the critical importance of early education, but he vigorously disagreed with Jean-Jacques Rousseau's recommendation that fathers educate their sons. Instead, this responsibility should be entrusted to a professional who had the necessary objectivity and expertise to instruct youngsters in 'all the branches of useful and ornamental knowledge, suitable to their ages, capacities, and prospects' so that they would be 'useful in this life and secure the happiness of the next' (J. Burgh, *The Dignity of Human Nature*, 1754, 1.214–15). Rejecting corporal discipline and endorsing a practical curriculum, Burgh epitomized the progressive pedagogy characteristic of dissenting academicians. Burgh's appreciation of the persuasive power of the spoken word is reflected in his most significant educational tract, *The Art of Speaking* (1761), which had eight English and ten American editions. Scholars now recognize Burgh as one of the 'four early writers who gave the elocutionary movement its first distinctive framework' (Hargis, 275).

Two of Burgh's publications, *Thoughts on Education* (1747) and a pamphlet privately transcribed in 1749 for the edification of his students, but pirated and published in 1752 under the title *Youth's Friendly Monitor*, were used by Thomas Hayter, bishop of Norwich and preceptor to the princes in 1751–2, in the instruction of his royal pupils. Through Hayter, Burgh was introduced to Prince George and to Augusta, dowager princess of Wales. Burgh dedicated *The Dignity of Human Nature* (1754), a celebrated manual of 'maxims and homilies' reminiscent of *Poor Richard's Almanac* (Kramnick, 87), to the princess. Burgh also became acquainted with Stephen Hales, clerk of the closet to Augusta. Hales and Hayter enlisted Burgh in the successful campaign to limit legislatively liquor sales; *A Warning to Dram Drinkers* (1751) was the first of various polemical pieces Burgh penned as part of orchestrated campaigns to promote socially or politically significant causes.

Emboldened by these contacts, Burgh proposed the formation of a 'Grand Association' of prominent personages and peers who would underwrite a periodical dedicated to the promotion of '*virtue* and *truth*' (J. Burgh, *Crito*, 1767, 2.208). Hales and the princess endorsed the concept. Burgh co-ordinated a series of multi-authored essays published in the *General Evening Post* between 1753 and 1754 under the pseudonym T. Trueman. The project soon floundered, embittering Burgh, who retreated from public life until the accession of George III renewed his optimism that a crusade spearheaded by the righteous young sovereign could morally rejuvenate the nation. Burgh hastily transcribed 'Remarks historical and political' (1762) which exhorted George to be a 'patriot king' above party. There is no evidence that the monarch read this audacious manuscript.

The factionalism and political crises of the 1760s disillusioned Burgh about the likelihood of royal or aristocratic initiatives to solve national and imperial problems. Although he continued to urge the great to lead an association to redress political and social ills, he also encouraged all men of property, 'all persons who are on any tax book', to join an extra-parliamentary movement to restore the constitution (J. Burgh, *Political Disquisitions*, 1775, 3.428–9). Beguiled by the myth of the Gothic constitution, Burgh consistently spoke of restoring equilibrium to 'mixed' government that was imperilled by avaricious grandees, but his extra-parliamentary agenda for accomplishing this purportedly conservative goal and his endorsement of republicanism as theoretically the best form of government situated him on the radical fringe of the reform movement. He favoured annual parliaments, the secret ballot, the exclusion of placemen and pensioners from the House of Commons, term limits, reapportioning parliamentary seats to reflect a constituency's contributions to the nation's wealth, and universal manhood suffrage, or at least the enfranchisement of all males who paid direct taxes. Sustained by his association from the early 1760s with the Club of Honest Whigs, 'friends of liberty' such as Richard Price, Joseph Priestley, Benjamin Franklin, and William Rose (co-founder of the *Monthly Review*), who shared an interest in science and commitment to 'commonwealthmen' principles, Burgh became an important penman and propagandist for a radical network that, in the aftermath of the Stamp Act and the Wilkes controversy of 1768, included John Sawbridge, a founder of the Wilkite Bill of Rights Society; Sawbridge's celebrated sister, Catharine Macaulay (who was accused of publishing Burgh's essays posthumously under her own name, a charge she vigorously rejected); and colonial patriots such as Benjamin Franklin, Benjamin Rush, and John Adams. Burgh's reasoned tone in *An Account of the Cessares* (1764), a utopian model of good government, gave way in *Crito* (1766–7) to a caustic critique of public apathy in the wake of his failure in 1766 to organize an association to undercut the monopolists who had inflated meat prices in the metropolis. A growing sense of urgency infused the twenty Constitutionalist letters that alternated on the front page of the *Gazeteer and New Daily Advertiser* with those of Junius and Junius Americanus from July 1769 to May 1770. Burgh temporarily suspended this series, which promoted the Wilkite petitioning campaign, to lobby in the *Public Advertiser* as the Colonist's Advocate for the repeal of the Townshend duties. Kippis attributed the series to Burgh, but Verner Crane argued that Benjamin Franklin was the author. The evidence supports Kippis's theory. The failure of both initiatives determined Burgh to delineate the case for reform in a projected six-volume compendium of political disquisitions. Although only three volumes were published, the work was the most comprehensive exposition of the radical platform prior to the American War of Independence and it secured Burgh's place in the radical pantheon. Burgh did not live to enjoy the plaudits engendered by his *magnum opus*. Diagnosed with a stone in his bladder, he quit his academy and retired in 1771 to neighbouring Islington where he diligently worked on the *Political Disquisitions*, despite being in excruciating pain. He died in Islington on 26 August 1775 and was buried at Bunhill Fields, London. He left a 'competent though not a large fortune' (Kippis, 3.15) to his widow, who survived until 1788. She was interred at Bunhill Fields on 22 November of that year; she left specific bequests totalling £920 and the residue of her estate went to her nephew William Briggs.   CARLA H. HAY

Sources C. H. Hay, *James Burgh, spokesman for reform in Hanoverian England* (1979) • C. H. Hay, 'Benjamin Franklin, James Burgh, and the authorship of "The Colonist's Advocate" letters', *William and Mary Quarterly*, 32 (1975), 111–24 • C. H. Hay, 'The making of a radical: the case of James Burgh', *Journal of British Studies*, 18/2 (1978–9), 90–117 • I. Kramnick, 'Republicanism revisited: the case of James Burgh', *Proceedings of the American Antiquarian Society*, 102 (1992), 81–98 • D. Levering, 'James Burgh: moralist and reformer', PhD diss., Claremont Graduate School, 1974 • A. Kippis and others, eds., *Biographia Britannica, or, The lives of the most eminent persons who have flourished in Great Britain and Ireland*, 2nd edn, 3 (1784), 13–16 • Nichols, *Lit. anecdotes*, vol. 2 • O. Handlin and M. Handlin, 'James Burgh and American revolutionary theory', *Proceedings of the Massachusetts Historical Society*, 73 (1961), 38–57 • D. Hargis, 'James Burgh and *The art of speaking*', *Speech Monographs*, 24 (1957), 275–84 • W. Parrish, 'The burglarizing of Burgh, or, The case of the purloined passions', *Quarterly Journal of Speech*, 38 (1952), 431–4 • private information (2004)
Archives BL, 'Remarks historical and political collected from books and observations. Humbly presented to the King's most excellent majesty', King's MS 433
Wealth at death 'competent though not a large fortune': Kippis and others, eds., *Biographia Britannica*, vol. 3, p .15

Burgh [Borough], **John** (*fl.* 1370–1398), theologian, is first recorded as a master of arts at Cambridge in 1370, when he served as proctor of the university. He continued his studies at Cambridge, and was a doctor of theology by 1384. In that year he was appointed chancellor of the university, a post he held until 1386. He was probably the chancellor who in 1384 ordered the scrutiny for heresy and error of William Nassington's religious poem *Speculum vitae*. In 1388 he was rector of the church of Collingham, Nottinghamshire, and he still held that benefice when he was made vicar of Newark, Nottinghamshire, in 1398. On 12 January of the same year he was licensed to hear confessions in York diocese. It is not known when he died.

Some time probably between 1380 and 1385 Burgh composed a very influential work of pastoral theology entitled *Pupilla oculi*. It survives in more than forty manuscript copies and was printed at least four times before 1500. The *Pupilla oculi*, like the *Oculus sacerdotis* (1320–23) of William Pagula, of which it is an explicit adaptation, seeks to make available to parish priests the theological and canonical teachings necessary for administering competently the pastoral care of souls. Its first eight books treat the church's sacraments, and include an exposition of the mass and a guide to hearing confessions. Book 9 deals with such practical matters as tithes, residence, burials, and wills, and book 10 gives a programme of religious instruction—the fourteen articles of faith, the ten commandments, the seven sins, and so forth—such as was required by Archbishop John Pecham in the constitutions of Lambeth of 1281. *Pupilla oculi* may, indeed, have been partly intended to act as a restatement of orthodox doctrine in response to Wycliffite teachings circulating at the time of its composition.   JOSEPH GOERING

Sources Emden, *Cam.* · W. A. Pantin, *The English church in the fourteenth century* (1955) · L. E. Boyle, 'The *Oculus sacerdotis* and some other works of William of Pagula', *TRHS*, 5th ser., 5 (1955), 81–110; repr. in *Pastoral care, clerical education and canon law, 1200–1400* (1981) · M. W. Bloomfield and others, *Incipits of Latin works on the virtues and vices, 1100–1500 AD* (1979) · J. Hughes, *Pastors and visionaries: religion and secular life in late medieval Yorkshire* (1988)

Burgh, Sir John (1561/2–1594), soldier, was a younger son of William Burgh, fourth Baron Burgh of Gainsborough (1522–1584), and Katherine, daughter of Edward Clinton, earl of Lincoln. His elder brother, Thomas, fifth Baron Burgh (*d.* 1597), accompanied the earl of Leicester to the Netherlands in 1586, and served briefly as lord deputy of Ireland in 1597. John probably fought as a volunteer in Holland in the early 1580s with Sir John Norris, and raised a foot band in Lincolnshire in 1585 to join Norris in the Netherlands. He was wounded near Arnhem soon after his arrival, garrisoned Amersfoord, and was knighted by Leicester in 1586. He was appointed governor of Doesburg, and in 1588 deputized for his brother as governor of Brill. He served under Lord Willoughby, who had replaced Leicester, and like many English captains struggled to obtain the pay that was due to him. He wrote to Willoughby requesting his assistance in the payment of nineteen months' back pay. In 1589 he was involved in the preparations for the expedition against Lisbon which Sir John Norris and Sir Francis Drake were planning. He and a number of English captains initially opposed the use of experienced veterans from the Netherlands for the expedition, as they feared it would denude the remaining garrisons. None the less he reformed and re-equipped a horse band for the expedition at his own expense, but in the event did not participate in the operation.

In October 1589 Burgh commanded a regiment raised in Sussex, one of four that made up the expeditionary force sent to Normandy under Lord Willoughby's command, to assist Henri IV of France. The force performed well despite appalling conditions, and assisted in the capture of twenty towns. At the completion of the campaign they paraded before Henri IV, and Burgh became involved in an argument over precedence with Sir William Drury, the colonel of the regiment from Hampshire. The situation required the personal intervention of Willoughby, who forced the two men to promise to have no further dealings with each other until the campaign was over. The dispute came to a head as they prepared to re-embark for England, and Burgh and Drury fought a duel. Drury suffered a severe hand wound which developed gangrene and led to the amputation of his arm, rapidly followed by his death. Burgh wrote to Lord Burghley excusing his actions, and

his explanation seems to have been accepted at court. He did however remain in France with Henri IV, and as a result was the only Englishman to take an active part in the battle of Ivry (14 March 1590). His courage during the battle was recognized when the king knighted him and granted him permission personally to take the dispatch containing the account of the battle to the queen.

In 1592 Burgh joined Sir Walter Ralegh in a privateering venture which aimed to raid the West Indies. The consortium that financed the fleet also included the queen and the duke of Cumberland. Ralegh had hoped to command the force but the queen refused him permission. Command passed jointly to Burgh, who captained Ralegh's ship *Roebuck*, and the experienced mariner Sir Martin Frobisher, in the queen's ship *Garland*. Information was received that five Portuguese East Indiamen were expected to arrive at the Azores, and the fleet was instructed to intercept them. Frobisher stationed himself off the south coast of Portugal while Burgh headed for the Azores. The first East Indiaman evaded the fleet and ran itself aground, but a second carrack was close behind. Burgh deployed the fleet to intercept her, and the *Madre de Dios* was sighted at noon. At 1600 tons she was one of the largest ships afloat, referred to as the 'great carrack'. Burgh was anxious that she did not escape into the local harbour and the *Roebuck* and *Foresight* attacked and grappled her, but became entangled with each other. The *Roebuck* was sandwiched between the two ships, suffering considerable damage and losing thirty men. *Roebuck*, in danger of sinking, was forced to disengage, while *Foresight* remained attached to the carrack's bows, and forced her to slow down sufficiently for Cumberland's ships to catch up and board her. She surrendered after a struggle lasting one and a half hours. After hasty repairs Burgh returned to the carrack, which was being thoroughly plundered, and claimed the ship in the right of the queen, overruling the other captains. Much of the moveable wealth of the ship had already been looted, and Burgh and his crew received relatively little. The value of the carrack may have been as high as £500,000, but only £140,000 was recovered by the admiralty agents when Burgh brought the ship into Dartmouth harbour. Sent to investigate, Robert Cecil reported that Exeter and the west-country ports were awash with plunder and official recrimination followed. Burgh was investigated but cleared.

In 1593 Burgh made a second voyage to the West Indies, and attacked the pearl fisheries at La Margarita. He was heavily repulsed and had to leave several dead and wounded men ashore. This affront to his honour may have been the reason for his challenge to John Gilbert, Ralegh's stepbrother. The resulting duel, fought in London on 7 March 1594, caused Burgh's death from a rapier wound. He was buried in St Andrew's Chapel in Westminster Abbey. A tablet mourning his premature death, aged thirty-two, was erected in 1575, but has since disappeared. It was copied in 1711.   M. A. STEVENS

Sources *CSP dom.*, 1585–94 · *CSP for.*, 1585–94 · Burke, *Peerage* (1967) · J. Croll, *The antiquities of St Peter's or the abbey church of Westminster* (1711), 198 · S. Purchas, *Hakluytus posthumus, or, Purchas his*

pilgrimes, 4 (1625); repr. Hakluyt Society, extra ser., 16 (1906) • K. R. Andrews, ed., *English privateering voyages to the West Indies, 1588–1595*, Hakluyt Society, 2nd ser., 111 (1959) • *Boteler's dialogues*, ed. W. G. Perrin, Navy RS, 65 (1929) • J. K. Laughton, ed., *The naval miscellany*, 1, Navy RS, 20 (1902)

Burgh, Richard de (*d.* 1243), justiciar of Ireland, was the son of William de *Burgh (*d.* 1206) and his wife, the daughter of Domnall Mór Ó Briain, king of Thomond, who married in 1193. The de Burgh family came from Norfolk. William, the brother of Hubert de *Burgh, justiciar of England from 1215 to 1232, became involved in Ireland as a result of the visit of John, lord of Ireland, in 1185. About 1194 John granted him Connacht, but he made little progress in establishing himself there. Before 1201 he also held two knights' fees of Theobald Walter near Tullow, in Carlow, as well as land in Kilkenny, Tipperary, and Limerick. He died in 1206 and Richard, his heir, became a ward of the crown until 1214 when he received his inheritance. He later added to his property in Munster and also urged a regrant of Connacht. Between June and September 1215 Richard de Burgh served in the household of his uncle, Hubert de Burgh. On 13 September of that year Connacht was granted to its Irish king, Cathal Ó Conchobhair, but on the same day a secret grant of the province was also made to Richard, who in 1219 offered the crown money in return for a curtailment of Cathal's rights; this was rejected.

De Burgh was in Ireland in 1220 but appears to have made a pilgrimage to Santiago de Compostela in 1222. Before 1225 he married Egidia, daughter of Walter de Lacy and acquired with her the cantred of Eóghanacht Caisil with the castle of Ardmayle in Tipperary. In 1223 and again in 1225 he was appointed seneschal of Munster and keeper of the castle of Limerick.

De Burgh's grant to Connacht was executed in July 1226 after Áed, son of Cathal, was declared forfeit and in the following year de Burgh and Áed, son of Ruaidrí Ó Conchobhair, a rival to Cathal's son, plundered around Lough Mask. On 13 February 1228 de Burgh was appointed justiciar of Ireland, having previously been given custody of counties Cork and Waterford and all the crown lands of Decies and Desmond. In 1230 he made Fedlimid, son of Cathal, king of Connacht, but in the following year imprisoned him when he proved unco-operative and replaced him with Áed, son of Ruaidrí. In 1232 Hubert de Burgh fell from power and Richard was replaced as justiciar by Maurice Fitzgerald (*d.* 1257) and was ordered to release Fedlimid. Henry III was planning a campaign against Richard in 1233, but he distanced himself sufficiently from his disgraced uncle to reassure the king. In 1234 he was restored to favour and was one of the magnates of Ireland who opposed Richard Marshal on the Curragh on 1 April when Marshal was mortally wounded.

Richard de Burgh effectively conquered Connacht in 1235 and 1236. Of the thirty cantreds of the province the king was to have five centred on the Shannon and de Burgh the remaining twenty-five. De Burgh kept three of these cantreds for himself, all in Galway. His principal manor was in the barony of Loughrea where in 1236 he

built a castle. He also kept Galway town and the islands on Lough Mask and Lough Orben. The other cantreds were granted by him to magnates with existing Irish interests such as Hugh de Lacy, Maurice Fitzgerald, Richard de Carew, William Barrett, Jordan of Exeter, Peter of Bermingham and Adam of Staunton. De Burgh died early in 1243 when serving on Henry III's expedition to Poitou. He had three sons: Richard, his first heir, who died in 1248; Walter de *Burgh (*d.* 1271), his eventual heir, who in 1263 was created earl of Ulster; and William, who died in 1270 and whose descendants came eventually to control most of Connacht.　　　　　　　　　　　B. SMITH

Sources G. H. Orpen, 'Richard de Burgh and the conquest of Connacht', *Journal of the Galway Archaeological and Historical Society*, 7 (1911–12) • R. Frame, *Colonial Ireland* (1981) • J. Lydon, 'The expansion and consolidation of the colony, 1215–54', *A new history of Ireland*, ed. T. W. Moody and others, 2: *Medieval Ireland, 1169–1534* (1987), 156–78; repr. with corrections (1993) • Paris, *Chron.*, 4.199

Burgh, Richard de, second earl of Ulster [*called* the Red Earl] (*b.* in or after **1259**, *d.* **1326**), magnate, lord of Connacht, was the eldest son and heir of Walter de *Burgh, earl of Ulster (*d.* 1271), and of Avelina, daughter of *John fitz Geoffrey, justiciar of Ireland (1245–56).

Early career Following his father's death in 1271 he was conveyed to the king at Woodstock, and in December 1280 he was described as the king's groom. He was granted seisin of his inheritance on 5 January 1281, and paid a visit to Ireland as a result of which he was accused of having 'seized and destroyed the chattels' of William fitz Warin, former seneschal of Ulster, whom de Burgh replaced with a rival, Thomas de Mandeville (*Calendar … Ireland*, 2.1918). He married, before 27 February 1281, Margaret (*d.* 1304), said to have been the daughter of John de Burgh and a great-granddaughter of Hubert de Burgh, earl of Kent; in 1283 they were granted Ratoath, Meath, the former de Burgh property in Owney, Limerick, and the dower lands in Ulster of Hugh de Lacy's widow, by Queen Eleanor, who described Richard de Burgh as her cousin. He had returned to England by February 1282, was knighted by the king at Rhuddlan in Wales at Christmas 1283, and went to Ireland again after 1 July 1285, when the king pardoned him a half of his debts at the Irish exchequer 'for his laudable service', presumably in the Welsh war (ibid., 3.112).

The annals report that de Burgh led a campaign in Connacht in 1286, despoiling many churches and 'obtained ascendancy wherever he came and took the hostages of all Connacht' (*Annala Connacht*, 179); he then went to Ulster and obtained the hostages of Cenél Conaill and Cenéal Eóghain, deposing Domhnall Ó Néill in favour of his kinsman Niall Culánach. On 20 September, at Turnberry in Ayrshire, chief castle of the earldom of Carrick, he and Thomas de Clare, lord of Thomond, entered into a 'band' with a group of Scottish magnates, including members of the Bruce and Stewart families, whose support they enlisted for a campaign in Ireland; this was probably intended to secure Clare's succession to a share in the estate of his recently deceased father-in-law, Maurice fitz Maurice Fitzgerald (*d.* 1286), in the north-west of Ireland, in opposition to John fitz Thomas Fitzgerald (*d.* 1316), the leading surviving male Geraldine, an opponent of de Burgh. In 1288, when de Burgh marched to Roscommon to oppose the new king of Connacht, Maghnus Ó Conchobhair, the latter had the support of John fitz Thomas and a government army. At about this time he took possession of the Isle of Man, then part of the realm of Scotland, and handed the island over to Edward I before 4 June 1290. He returned to Ireland from England after 13 July, and on 6 August was granted custody of the heir of Toirdhealbhach Ó Briain, king of Thomond, perhaps out of concern for his estates there.

Campaigns in England and abroad With the appointment of William de Vescy as justiciar de Burgh's relations with the Dublin government improved, and both men led a campaign in Ulster against Ó hAnluain in 1291. In the same year de Burgh twice deposed Domhnall Ó Néill, and in 1291 and 1292 he campaigned against Maghnus Ó Conchobhair, on the latter occasion successfully. On 11 December 1294 his quarrel with John fitz Thomas came to a head when the latter imprisoned de Burgh in his castle of Lea, Laois, as a result of which, the annals state, 'all Ireland was disturbed' (*Annala Connacht*, 192). To secure his release the earl agreed on 12 March 1295 to surrender all his rights as overlord of John fitz Thomas in Connacht. Both men then took part in a successful campaign against the Irish of Leinster and de Burgh received £100 for his expenses in 'remaining in the mountains of Leinster on account of the war of the Irish, for 20 days' (*Calendar ... Ireland*, 4.273). The dispute with John fitz Thomas persisted, however, and the king wrote to both men on 18 October 1295 asking them to desist; the new justiciar, John Wogan, soon afterwards secured their agreement to a two-year truce. Both men served on King Edward's campaign of 1296 in Scotland, de Burgh receiving the highest rate of pay awarded any earl in the Scottish war, and on 5 September 1296 the king granted him a pardon 'for all homicides, robberies, and transgressions against the peace in Ireland, excepting those touching John fitz Thomas' (ibid., 4.315).

Some time before 10 October 1296 de Burgh's sister Egidia married James *Stewart [*see under* Stewart family], steward of Scotland, who received from the earl his castle of Roe, near Limavady, and its burgh and demesne lands. Richard acquired further lands in England following the death in 1297 without children of the heir of his maternal grandfather, John fitz Geoffrey. In May 1297 he was ordered to prepare for participation in the Flanders campaign and to be at London with horses and arms by 1 August, but he did not take part, the king finding the terms sought too harsh. On 30 March 1298, when the king was about to depart for Scotland, he asked the earl 'so to exert himself that peace and tranquility be firmly maintained in his lands' (*Calendar ... Ireland*, 4.506). However, John fitz Thomas complained to the king that 'the said earl and his men inflicted enormous transgressions and divers grievances on John against the form of the truce and the king's peace' (ibid., 4.514), and the justiciar was ordered on 11 April 1298 to summon the parties before him and to do justice to John. On 22 October Wogan finally

secured a settlement between them which saw John fitz Thomas surrender all his lands in Connacht and Ulster to de Burgh in return for lands of equal value belonging to the earl in Leinster and Munster.

In 1301 Edward I asked de Burgh 'to bear in mind that the king relies on him more than any other man in the land [of Ireland]', and that 'the earl should without bargain or covenant more quickly and willingly than any others in that country come to the king's service' in Scotland; de Burgh, however, refused to do so, and the justiciar was ordered 'that if the earl of Ulster does not come to the king's service in Scotland, the justiciar shall remain in Ireland' (*Calendar ... Ireland*, 4.849). He obtained special terms in return for his participation in the 1303 campaign in Scotland, leading the largest army to leave Ireland during the war (thirty-three of whom he knighted in Dublin Castle before departure), and was the principal negotiator of the terms of peace on the occasion. On 1 May 1304 he was given a grant of free chase in certain of his demesne lands in Ulster and elsewhere, on 22 July he was granted custody of the land and heir of Ralph Pipard, and on 15 August he was pardoned all his debts at the Irish exchequer 'for his service in Scotland' (ibid., 5.340), said to have exceeded £11,600, though Connacht alone was valued in 1305 at more than £1000 a year.

Irish affairs De Burgh's wife died in 1304, as did his eldest son, William, without children (another son, Thomas, died in 1316). The earl's second son, John, now heir, married Elizabeth de Clare, daughter of Gilbert de *Clare, earl of Gloucester (*d.* 1295); John and Elizabeth were thereby enfeoffed with manors in Ulster, Connacht, and Munster. His daughter Matilda married Elizabeth's brother, Gilbert de *Clare, earl of Gloucester, who was killed at Bannockburn. She was originally betrothed to John, son of Peter of Bermingham, later earl of Louth, but Gloucester's envoys picked her as she was fairer than her sister Avelina, whom Bermingham married instead. Another daughter, Elizabeth, married the future *Robert I of Scotland in 1302; Eleanor married Thomas Multon of Egremont; and, at Greencastle, Down, in 1312 a final reconciliation with the Geraldines was effected when de Burgh's daughter Joan married Thomas fitz John *Fitzgerald, son of John fitz Thomas *Fitzgerald, later earl of Kildare, and Catherine married Maurice fitz Thomas *Fitzgerald, later earl of Desmond.

In spite of his stature, or perhaps because of it, Richard de Burgh never held the Irish justiciarship (though his name sometimes precedes that of the justiciar in royal writs): he was *locum tenens* for John Wogan briefly in 1299 and, although he was appointed king's lieutenant on 15 June 1308, on the following day Piers Gaveston received a similar commission. Before July 1305 he sought a grant of Ó Conchobhair's core lands of Síol Mhuireadhaigh, Roscommon, and while a jury recommended it since the earl 'would be better able than another to chastise the Irish of that land' (*Calendar ... Ireland*, 5.437), it was granted instead to his cousin William Liath de Burgh, a close adherent. Having built one new castle at Ballymote, Sligo, in 1300, the earl built a second, the new castle of Inishowen (Northburgh or Greencastle, Donegal), in 1305, and in the same year purchased the manor of Carlingford, and lands in Cooley and Omeath, Louth, while before 1310 he obtained the city of Derry and other lands from the bishops of Derry and Raphoe.

Richard de Burgh was in England in August 1309 when, as king's commissioner, he unsuccessfully negotiated terms of peace with Robert I, king of Scots, being pardoned the yearly rent of 500 marks for his Connacht lands, and receiving custody for life of the royal castles of Roscommon, Randown, and Athlone (though he had been custodian of the last since 1304), and returned to Ireland on Christmas eve. In 1310 he rebuilt Sligo Castle and, in opposition to Richard de Clare, was involved the following year in Thomond, which he partitioned between rival members of the Ó Briain family.

The Bruce invasion and its aftermath In the summer of 1313 while Robert I was besieging the Isle of Man, the Dublin annalist records that he landed in Ulster 'by licence of the earl of Ulster' and made a truce (Gilbert, 2.342). But when Robert's brother Edward, earl of Carrick, invaded Ulster in May 1315, de Burgh gathered together an army at Roscommon, and by early July was marching to oppose him. He met with the royal army, led by the justiciar, at Ardee, Louth, and insisted on pursuing Bruce alone; he swore an oath at Dundalk that he would bring Edward Bruce back to Dublin dead or alive, but following a minor skirmish with him at Inishkeen, Monaghan, de Burgh was in the end decisively defeated by the Scottish army in a battle at Connor, Antrim, on 1 September, the annals commenting that he was 'a wanderer up and down Ireland all this year, with no power or lordship' (Annala Connacht, 241). In separate attacks, Aedh Ó Domhnaill and Ruaidhrí Ó Conchobhair destroyed several of his western castles, including Loughrea, the *caput* of his Connacht lordship. His failure to defeat Edward Bruce in the field, and his marriage alliance with Robert I, convinced many that the earl was colluding with the invaders, and, on 21 February 1317, when both Robert I and Edward Bruce were within sight of Dublin, the mayor and citizenry forcibly seized de Burgh in St Mary's Abbey, and imprisoned him in Dublin Castle. Edward II ordered an inquiry into his detention, and issued a safe conduct to England; the earl was finally released on 8 May, giving on 27 June an oath to repel the Irish and Scottish enemies of the king.

Though Richard de Burgh was at court in 1318 and obviously in royal favour, being one of the guarantors of the treaty of Leake and receiving a royal gift of a horse, on 17 March 1319 he was ordered to repair the royal castles in Connacht and, in spite of his life custody of them, to hand them over to Roger Mortimer, the new justiciar. His earldom may have been regarded as forfeit for a time since it was only in 1320 that the Dublin parliament restored his franchisal rights in Ulster. In 1322 he was ordered to levy a force from his own lands to take part in a proposed Scottish campaign and on 14 July he and William Liath de Burgh were described as 'coming to the king on the king's affairs', while in September Edward II announced that the earl had always been faithful to him and his father. In April 1323 de Burgh and William were again given safe conducts to travel to England for another proposed Scottish expedition, which likewise proved abortive.

Richard de Burgh went to parliament at Kilkenny in July 1326, described as infirm by the Dublin annalist (a confidential report compiled after his death stated that for a long time he had been so weak that his lordship in Ulster and elsewhere had deteriorated greatly). Having thrown a great feast for magnates and common people alike, he retired to the priory of Athassel, Tipperary (founded by his great-grandfather), where, on 29 July, he died, and where he was buried. Friar Clyn describes him as 'a knight prudent and witty, wealthy and wise, and full of years' (*Annals of Ireland*, ed. Butler, 18). The Irish annals call him 'the best of all the English of Ireland' (*Annala Connacht*, 261), and a bardic lament in Gaelic survives commemorating his death. Although he left at least one son, Edmund (d. 1338), he was succeeded by his grandson William de *Burgh, then in his fourteenth year, later known as the Brown Earl.   SEÁN DUFFY

Sources H. S. Sweetman and G. F. Handcock, eds., *Calendar of documents relating to Ireland*, 5 vols., PRO (1875–86) · *CCIR* · *CPR* · G. MacNiocaill, ed., *The Red Book of the earls of Kildare* (1964) · J. T. Gilbert, ed., *Chartularies of St Mary's Abbey, Dublin: with the register of its house at Dunbrody and annals of Ireland*, 2, Rolls Series, 80 (1884) · *The annals of Ireland by Friar John Clyn and Thady Dowling: together with the annals of Ross*, ed. R. Butler, Irish Archaeological Society (1849) · A. M. Freeman, ed. and trans., *Annála Connacht / The annals of Connacht* (1944); repr. (1970) · J. Stevenson, ed., *Documents illustrative of the history of Scotland*, 2 vols. (1870) · 'Do gabh Éire a húain cumhadh', Book of O'Conor Don, Library of the O'Conor Don, Clonalis, co. Roscommon · J. A. Claffey, 'Richard de Burgh, earl of Ulster, circa 1260–1326', PhD diss., National University of Ireland, 1970 · G. H. Orpen, 'The earldom of Ulster [6 pts]', *Journal of the Royal Society of Antiquaries of Ireland*, 6th ser., 3–11 (1913–21) · A. J. Otway-Ruthven, *A history of medieval Ireland* (1968) · J. Lodge, *The peerage of Ireland*, 1 (1754), 121

Burgh, Thomas, Baron Burgh (*c*.1430–1496), administrator and soldier, was the eldest son of Thomas Burgh and Elizabeth, daughter and coheir of Sir Henry Percy of Harthill, Yorkshire. He inherited his mother's estates, including Gainsborough (Lincolnshire) and a moiety of the Mitford barony in Northumberland, on her death in 1455, when he was said to be aged twenty-four and more. His early political affiliations were with the Staffords: he was a member of the household of the duke of Buckingham in 1456–7 and was one of the duke's feoffees in 1458. But after the duke's death at Northampton he appears to have made an early commitment to the victorious Yorkists, by whom he was made sheriff of Lincolnshire in autumn 1460. He was made an esquire of the body on 2 April 1461, just four days after the battle of Towton had confirmed Edward IV on the throne. He had been knighted by February 1463, and was master of the king's horse by February 1464. He was a knight of the body by 1466 and probably earlier. His rise in the king's service was accompanied by generous patronage, including forfeited land in Lincolnshire and elsewhere, and office within the duchy of Lancaster estates in Lincolnshire, notably the constableships of Lincoln Castle and of Bolingbroke.

Tensions created by Burgh's arrival as a force within the county contributed to the Lincolnshire rising of 1470. Unrest began with the sacking of Burgh's house at Gainsborough by Richard, Lord Welles, his son Robert and his brothers-in-law Sir Thomas de la Laund and Sir Thomas Dymmock, and escalated when it was rumoured that Edward planned to bring an army into the county to punish the offenders. Burgh was a crucial figure for Lincolnshire loyalties to the royal household under Edward IV, but his influence was eclipsed during the readeption of Henry VI until Edward's restoration in 1471 brought a return to power. In the French war his importance was reflected in his provision of 160 archers, no other knight of the body raising more than 100. Burgh transferred smoothly to the household of Richard III, retaining all his local offices. He received further patronage from the new king, including land worth £200, and was elected a knight of the Garter. But he was never one of those closest to the king and he probably avoided the battle of Bosworth. The accession of Henry VII brought the loss of his gains from Richard III and of several of his Lincolnshire offices, but he remained a royal councillor (a post he had held under both Yorkist kings) and in 1487 received a personal summons to parliament, although there is no evidence that he took his seat in the Lords and in his will he describes himself simply as 'Thomas Burgh knight'.

Burgh had married, by May 1464, Margaret, daughter of Thomas, Lord Ros, and widow of William, Lord Botreaux, who had died on 16 May 1462. She brought him extensive dower estates in Wiltshire, Somerset, and Dorset. She died on 10 December 1488. With her Burgh had two sons, Edward and Thomas, and two daughters, Elizabeth, who had married Richard, Lord Fitzhugh, by 21 May 1481, and Anne. In widowhood, Elizabeth was married in 1491 to Sir Henry *Willoughby (c.1451–1528) [see under Willoughby family (per. 1362–1528)]. Edward, Burgh's heir, was associated with his father in a grant of office in February 1469, and in 1477 married Anne Cobham, the widow of Edward Blount, Lord Mountjoy. By the time of his father's death Edward had three sons (Thomas, George, and Humphrey) and a daughter (Margaret). After a promising career he was judged lunatic in 1510 and died in 1528.

Burgh died on 18 March 1496 and willed burial in the new chapel he had built within the parish church of Gainsborough, where a perpetual chantry was to be founded for himself, his wife, and parents. He also endowed five bedesmen, to be chosen from his former servants, or, failing that, from his tenants in Gainsborough.

ROSEMARY HORROX

Sources Chancery records · GEC, Peerage · PRO, Prob. 11/10, fol. 240v · R. Somerville, History of the duchy of Lancaster, 1265–1603 (1953) · S. J. Gunn, 'The rise of the Burgh family, c.1431–1550', Gainsborough Old Hall, ed. P. Lindley (1991) · C. Rawcliffe, The Staffords, earls of Stafford and dukes of Buckingham, 1394–1521, Cambridge Studies in Medieval Life and Thought, 3rd ser., 11 (1978) · C. Ross, Edward IV (1974) · CIPM, Henry VII, 1, no. 1198

Burgh, Thomas (1670–1730), military engineer and architect, was the third son of Ulysses Burgh (d. 1692) of Drumkeen, co. Limerick, dean of Emly and later bishop of Ardagh, and Mary, daughter of William Kingsmill of Ballibeg, co. Cork. After education at Delany's school in Dublin he entered Trinity College, Dublin, on 22 November 1685, but does not appear to have taken a degree. Before the outbreak of the Williamite wars in 1688 he probably joined his father, who fled to London. Burgh may have returned to Ireland in King William III's army, as lieutenant in Lord Lovelace's regiment of foot. Pakenham-Walsh mentions that Thomas Burgh was appointed to the Irish engineers on 27 February 1691, but this remains unconfirmed.

After the war Burgh left for the continent, and received a commission as captain in 1692. He served at the battles of Steenkerke (1692) and Landen (1693) and the siege of Namur (1695). In 1697 he is mentioned (as Thomas Bourk) as one of the twenty-five engineers of the King's company of engineers, and in that year became third engineer on the Irish establishment, while keeping his former position. Burgh replaced the surveyor-general, William Robinson, on 10 July 1700, at a salary of £300 per annum. On 12 February 1701 he became barracks overseer in Ireland. Under his care the building of barracks was expanded greatly, the rebuilding of Dublin Castle (started by William Robinson) was advanced, and the Royal House at Chapelizod (co. Dublin) and Chichester House in Dublin were repaired. In addition he oversaw the improvement of numerous coastal fortifications, but did not build new forts. Both in the case of the alterations to fortifications and the building of barracks, it is difficult to determine whether Thomas Burgh or other engineers of the Irish ordnance were responsible for their design. In 1704 he was admitted as a freeman of the city of Dublin.

Burgh beautified Dublin with a number of large public buildings, notably the custom house (1704–6), Trinity College Library (1712–33), Dr Steevens' Hospital (1719), the Linen Hall (1722), and the Royal Barracks (1701 onwards), as well as smaller buildings. He was involved in the designing or rebuilding of several churches, including St Mary's and St Werburgh's. In 1721 he acted as a consultant to the city for creating a basin for the water supply and a pedestal for the statue of King George I on Essex Bridge. He carried out several unidentified public works for which, in 1723, he was awarded plate to a maximum value of £50. In 1704 he made a report on the lighthouses in Ireland and in 1707, as a member of the Dublin Philosophical Society, he presented a paper on the improvement of Dublin harbour. In 1725 the lord lieutenant and council ordered Burgh and Captain John Perry to take soundings and make a chart of Dublin harbour, but their resulting proposals were rejected by the ballast board. However, their map of the harbour was published in 1728. In 1729 he prepared an estimate for making a navigable passage from Newry to Lough Neagh to supply the city of Dublin with coals from co. Tyrone. Burgh's interest in coalmining dates from at least as early as 1721, when he and his partner the Hon. Richard Stewart received the first £2000 of a total of £8000 from the Irish government for their operation of a colliery at Ballycastle, co. Antrim.

Burgh was involved with several building operations for

private clients, although the exact nature of his involvement cannot be ascertained as most of the buildings have disappeared. For example, his part in rebuilding a residence for the O'Brien family—presumably at Dromoland, co. Clare about 1719—is rather vague. His architectural style was restrained, and was only notable chiefly for its massing on different planes, for arcading on the ground floor, and for the use of a central front of five bays often crowned by a large pediment as at the armoury (by 1714), the Royal Barracks (both Dublin Castle), Dr Steevens' Hospital, the custom house, the Linen Hall, and Ballyburley House. He did not introduce Palladian ideas into his buildings, except at his own country house, Oldtown, at Naas. For the layout of Dublin Castle he followed very closely the designs attributed to the former surveyor-general, William Robinson. In 1728 Burgh lost a commission to build the new parliament house in Dublin to Edward Lovell Pearce, and was forced to surrender to Pearce the position of surveyor-general.

Burgh's importance as an architect and engineer did not spread beyond Ireland. He combined a number of military appointments with civic functions. From 1706 to 1714 he was lieutenant of the ordnance of Ireland, which together with the surveyor-generalship made him the most influential officer in the Irish ordnance. He was granted the rank of lieutenant-colonel on 11 April 1706. In addition he was a captain in Brasier's regiment of foot from 1707 to 1714, high sheriff for co. Kildare in 1712, and MP for Naas from 1713 to his death in 1730. He became a governor of the Royal Hospital, Kilmainham, in 1707, and from 1717 onwards he acted as a trustee of Dr Steevens' Hospital. Burgh published a pamphlet entitled *A method to determine the areas of right-lined figures universally, very useful for ascertaining the contents of any survey* (Dublin, 1724), for which parliament granted him £1000 in 1723.

Burgh married on 10 July 1700 Mary, daughter of Rt Revd William Smyth, bishop of Kilmore, and with her had five sons (Thomas, Theobald, Ulysses, John, and Richard) and four daughters (Mary, Dorothea, Catherine, and Elizabeth). His town house was at 37 Dawson Street (now rebuilt) and he possessed a country estate at Oldtown, co. Kildare. Burgh dated his will 27 July 1726; he died on 18 December 1730, and the will was proved on 8 March 1731, but no copy has been located.   ROLF LOEBER

Sources R. Loeber, *A biographical dictionary of architects in Ireland, 1600–1720* (1981), 31–9 · W. P. Pakenham-Walsh, 'Lieutenant-Colonel Thomas Burgh, chief engineer of Ireland, 1700–1730', *Royal Engineers Journal*, new ser., 6 (1907), 69–74 · private information (2004) [E. McParland]
Likenesses portrait, repro. in Pakenham-Walsh, 'Lieutenant-Colonel Thomas Burgh', 6; priv. coll.

Burgh, Ulick Canning de, Lord Dunkellin (1827–1867). *See under* Burgh, Ulick John de, first marquess of Clanricarde (1802–1874).

Burgh, Ulick John de, first marquess of Clanricarde (1802–1874), politician, was born on 20 December 1802 in Belmont, Hampshire, the only son and second child in the family of one son and two daughters of John Thomas de Burgh, thirteenth earl of Clanricarde, army officer, and

Ulick John de Burgh, first marquess of Clanricarde (1802–1874), by Alfred, Count D'Orsay, 1847

his wife Elizabeth, daughter of Sir Thomas Burke, bt, of Marble Hill, co. Galway. The family had been settled in the west of Ireland from the early thirteenth century and on the death of his father in 1808 Ulick John de Burgh inherited, in addition to the earldom, 56,000 acres in co. Galway. In 1825 he married Harriet (1804–1876), the gifted daughter of George *Canning (1770–1827), foreign secretary and later prime minister. They had two sons and five daughters. Macaulay wrote of her: 'She is very beautiful, and very like her father ... she showed much cleverness and information, but, I thought, a little more of political animosity than is quite becoming in a pretty woman' (GEC, *Peerage*, 3.238). After his marriage it was rumoured he had been involved in a gambling scandal, but his father-in-law stood by him and it was largely through him that Burgh was created a marquess in the peerage of Ireland in 1825 and Baron Somerhill in the peerage of the United Kingdom in 1826.

Clanricarde was appointed under-secretary of state for foreign affairs in 1826, a post he resigned after Canning's death in 1827. A few years later he was accused of having speculated on the Paris bourse, using official information. This he vehemently denied. A Canningite, he became a whig. In 1830 he was appointed captain of the yeomen of the guard and in 1831 knight of St Patrick. In 1834 he resigned his office because he felt slighted by the ministry (another Irish peer, the second Marquess Conyngham, having been appointed postmaster-general). In 1838 he was appointed ambassador to St Petersburg. He served there until 1841, and, moving easily in Russian society, was a shrewd commentator on Russian social conditions, personalities, and policy.

From 1846 until 1852 Clanricarde was in Lord John Russell's cabinet as postmaster-general. He was an administrative reformer, working cordially with Rowland Hill, who was much pleased with 'his businesslike, straightforward manner' and his courageous willingness to follow 'a novel and decided course of action'. As a member of the cabinet which had to cope with the Irish famine, Clanricarde pressed hard for remedial measures, pointing out that from time to time 'an adherence to sound principle will cause an immediate sacrifice'.

Clanricarde was not included in Aberdeen's coalition cabinet in 1852. He took a strongly anti-Russian line in 1854, encouraging the government to war. In 1855 his name was opprobriously mentioned in the Irish case of *Hancock* v. *Delacour*, which attracted much attention. It was alleged that John Delacour, a minor, was Clanricarde's illegitimate son from a liaison with Josephine Hancock, the wife of William Henry Hancock, an Irish landowner, and that Clanricarde had schemed that Hancock's property should pass to Delacour. The case ended in a compromise. Clanricarde published long statements in which he denied the allegations and explained that he had become involved with the Hancock family's legal arrangements purely out of a good-natured wish to be of assistance. Nevertheless when Palmerston at the close of 1857 invited Clanricarde to join his cabinet, a large section of public opinion professed to be shocked. *Punch* published two harsh cartoons and, when at the end of February 1858 the government was defeated, *The Times*, with possibly a touch of exaggeration, declared that Clanricarde had been able by his 'mere presence' in the cabinet to destroy an exceptionally strong administration. He was the model for Trollope's Lord Brittleback.

For about forty years Clanricarde spoke frequently in the House of Lords on a wide range of subjects. Although it was said that his main contribution to debate was his sonorous 'hear, hear', his speeches, reflecting the outlook of a liberal-minded whig, were usually sensible and to the point. He seems to have possessed an ingenuous self-assurance which could get him into difficulties and arouse antagonism. In 1847 he was described as 'a tall, thin, aristocratic man, bald and bland, wearing ... tight pantaloons, striped silk socks, and pumps' (GEC, *Peerage*). He died at his home, 17 Stratton Street, Piccadilly, London, on 10 April 1874 and was succeeded in the marquessate by his second son, Hubert George Canning de Burgh.

Clanricarde's first son, **Ulick Canning de Burgh**, Lord Dunkellin (1827–1867), politician, was known lifelong as Lord Dunkellin (from a subsidiary title of his father's). He fought in the Crimea (being captured at Sevastopol) and was, after being military secretary in India in 1856, Liberal MP for Galway City, 1857–65, and for co. Galway, 1865–7; an Adullamite, he moved the famous amendment on the rating franchise which caused the resignation of Russell's government in 1866.

R. B. McDOWELL, *rev.* H. C. G. MATTHEW

Sources GEC, *Peerage* · H. E. Gower, *Letters, 1810–1845*, ed. F. Leveson-Gower, 2 vols. (1894) · Lord Holland [H. R. V. Fox] and J. Allen, *The Holland House diaries, 1831–1840*, ed. A. D. Kriegel (1977) · G. B. Hill and R. Hill, *The life of Sir Rowland Hill, and, The history of penny postage*, 2 (1880) · J. B. Conacher, *The Aberdeen coalition, 1852–1855* (1968) · F. B. Smith, *The making of the second Reform Bill* (1966) · M. Cowling, *1867: Disraeli, Gladstone and revolution* (1967)
Archives W. Yorks. AS, Leeds, corresp. and papers | Bodl. Oxf., corresp. with Lord Kimberley · Borth. Inst., letters to Sir Charles Wood · PRO, corresp. with Lord John Russell, PRO 30/22 · U. Durham L., letters to third Earl Grey · U. Southampton L., Broadlands MSS · U. Southampton L., corresp. with Lord Palmerston · W. Sussex RO, letters to duke of Richmond · W. Yorks. AS, Leeds, corresp. with Lord Canning · Woburn Abbey, Bedfordshire, letters to Lord George William Russell
Likenesses Count D'Orsay, pencil and chalk drawing, 1847, NPG [*see illus.*]
Wealth at death under £200,000: resworn probate, June 1875, CGPLA Eng. & Wales (1874)

Burgh, Ulysses Bagenal de, **second Baron Downes** (1788–1863), army officer, only son of Thomas Burgh (d. June 1810), comptroller-general and commissioner of the revenue of Ireland, and his wife, Anne, daughter of David Aigoin, was born in Dublin on 15 August 1788. He had two sisters. Burgh was the grandson of Thomas Burgh, bishop of Armagh, and second cousin of William Downes, lord chief justice of Ireland (1803–22), of Bert House, Athy, co. Kildare. Ulysses Burgh's family home was at Aghanville. Burgh attended Trinity College, Dublin (1803), and secured a commission as ensign in the 54th on 31 March 1804, advancing to lieutenant on 12 November 1804. He obtained a captaincy in the 60th foot (9 July 1806), but rejoined the 54th (9 October), serving with the regiment at Gibraltar before, in spring 1807, sailing for Jamaica. On 25 November 1808 he exchanged into the 92nd foot, and that month went with Lieutenant-General Sir John Cradock to Portugal as his aide-de-camp. When Lieutenant-General Sir Arthur Wellesley (later duke of Wellington), a friend of his father, succeeded Cradock in command in May 1809 Burgh joined him as aide-de-camp and assistant military secretary. He was wounded at Talavera (July 1809) and present at the battle of Busaco (29 September 1810), after which he carried Wellington's victory dispatch to England and was promoted major on 31 March 1811. On returning to the Peninsula he took part in the encounters at Fuentes de Oñoro (3–5 May 1811), El Bodon (September 1811), the storming of Ciudad Rodrigo (8–19 January 1812) and Badajoz (16 March – 6 April 1812), and the battle of Salamanca (22 July 1812). After Wellington entered Madrid (12 August 1812), he again carried a dispatch to England and consequently advanced to lieutenant-colonel (25 September 1812). Once more back with Wellington, he was at the battles of Vitoria (21 June 1813) and the Pyrenees (28–30 July 1813), the storming of San Sebastian (31 August 1813), the clashes on the Nivelle (10 November 1813)—where his horse was killed under him—and the Nive (10 December 1813). Burgh took part in the final encounter of the Peninsular War, Toulouse (10 April 1814), where he was once more wounded. His active service had now ended, although he became captain and lieutenant-colonel in the 1st or Grenadier Guards (25 July 1814), and briefly served with his company in Brussels shortly afterwards. For his services in the Peninsula he was appointed knight commander of the Portuguese order of the Tower and Sword and, on 2 January 1815, KCB. He also received a gold cross and one clasp for Vitoria, the Pyrenees, Nive, Nivelle, and Toulouse, and, once it became available in 1848, the Military General Service medal with bars for Talavera, Busaco, Fuentes de Oñoro, Ciudad Rodrigo, Badajoz, and Salamanca.

Burgh married on 20 June 1815 Maria (1792–1842), daughter and heir of the late Walter Bagenal of Athy, co. Kildare, and thereafter added Bagenal to his name. They had two daughters: Anne (b. 1818) and Charlotte (b. 1826). Burgh was tory MP for Carlow County (1818–26) and for Queenborough (1826–30). In March 1820 he became surveyor-general of the ordnance and an executive member of the Board of Ordnance, remaining in that post until 1830. Meanwhile he had progressed to colonel (27 May 1825), and on 2 March 1826 succeeded his cousin William in the Irish peerage as second Baron Downes, inheriting his residence in co. Kildare. As Downes he became a representative Irish peer in 1833, but was not politically active, although he did support Peel over repeal of the corn laws. He preferred the life of a country gentleman and spending some time in the Isle of Wight, where he had family connections. Downes advanced to major-general on 10 January 1837 and lieutenant-general on 9 November 1846. He was made colonel of the 54th foot (4 April 1845) then of the 29th foot (15 August 1850). Burgh married secondly, on 4 August 1846, Christopheria (d. 18 Oct 1860), widow of John Willis Fleming and daughter of James Buchanan. In 1848 he was authorized to take the name de Burgh, in lieu of Burgh. Downes acted as pallbearer on 28 July 1855 at the funeral of Lord Raglan, Wellington's military secretary in the Peninsula and more recently commander of British troops in the Crimea. Shortly afterwards the committee administering the Raglan Memorial Fund acquired the Kefntilla estate near Usk in Monmouth for the late field marshal's family. On behalf of the committee, Downes assured Raglan's son Richard that it was an 'excellent choice ... one I am sure your dear father would have highly approved of' (Sweetman, 333). Downes revealed to Richard that he had 'lately' reproached the architect for tardiness in carrying out agreed repairs and modifications, but Sir Matthew Digby Wyatt pleaded need to await completion of the railway from Monmouth to Usk for easy transportation of materials. Promoted general on 20 June 1854, two years later Downes received the Russian order of St Anne (second class), and was appointed GCB in May 1860. He died on 26 July 1863 at Bert House, Athy, co. Kildare. With no male heir, the peerage became extinct.

H. M. STEPHENS, rev. JOHN SWEETMAN

Sources Army List · Burke, Peerage · W. Stockdale, Peerage of the United Kingdom (1830) · H. Everard, History of the 29th foot, 1694–1891 (1891) · C. T. Atkinson, The Dorsetshire regiment, 2 (1947) · Records of the 54th West Norfolk regiment (1881) · C. G. Gardyne, History of the Gordon highlanders, 1714–1816 (1901) · F. W. Hamilton, The origin and history of the first or grenadier guards, 3 (1874) · J. Sweetman, War and administration: the significance of the Crimean War for the British army (1984) · GEC, Peerage · HoP, Commons · Dod's Peerage · DNB

Archives U. Nott. L., corresp. | PRO NIre., letters to John Foster · U. Southampton L., letters to the first duke of Wellington · W. Sussex RO, letters to duke of Richmond
Wealth at death under £9000: probate, 1 Oct 1863, CGPLA Eng. & Wales

Burgh, Walter de, first earl of Ulster (d. 1271), magnate and soldier, was the second son of Richard de *Burgh (d. 1243), lord of Connacht, and Egidia, daughter of Walter de Lacy, lord of Weobley and Meath. Richard de Burgh died early in 1243 while serving on Henry III's expedition to Poitou. His heir was his eldest son, Richard, who by December 1243 was attached to the king's household. He was granted his inheritance in 1247, and knighted by Henry III at Winchester at Whitsun 1248. He died the following November, shortly after being appointed constable of Montgomery Castle. He left no children but had a widow named Alice who, according to Matthew Paris, was from the king's continental circle. At the time of his brother's death Walter de Burgh was in Ireland and still under age. In October 1249 Henry paid his expenses in coming to England at his order, and the next few years saw de Burgh establish connections that were to be significant for his future career. Like Richard, he was attached to the royal household as a king's yeoman (valettus regis); in May 1250 he was granted his brother's lands, though his marriage was reserved to the king. Gifts and favours followed which, together with an absence of references to him in Irish annals, suggest that he was mostly outside Ireland until after the Gascon campaign of 1253–4, on which he served. Also in Gascony was *John fitz Geoffrey, the justiciar of Ireland, a key link between the court and the barons whose lands lay chiefly in Ireland. About 1257 de Burgh married John's daughter, Avelina, a union that at the end of the century was to bring his son, Earl Richard, a share of the Fitzjohn lands in England and Ireland.

By 1255 Walter de Burgh had plunged into the maelstrom of war and diplomacy in western Ireland that was his inheritance. Many of his deeds are recorded by the Gaelic Irish annalists, by whom he is often called Mac William Burke, a reference to his grandfather, William de *Burgh (d. 1206), who had first gone to Ireland with John in 1185. Between 1255 and 1263 the annals of Connacht tell of major campaigns against the Ó Conchobhair, and of constant negotiations. At Athlone in 1257 the justiciar brokered a settlement involving de Burgh and Fedlimid Ó Conchobhair, the king of Connacht, who had applied to Henry III for protection and received confirmation of his lands. This was followed by contacts and alliances between a number of native leaders in Ulster, Connacht, and Munster, including Fedlimid's son, Aodh, who seem to have been reacting against a fresh wave of English expansion which had been encouraged by grants made by Henry and the Lord Edward. After the indecisive end of a campaign in 1262, Walter and Fedlimid, whose families had contended for domination in Connacht since the 1190s, shared 'one room and one bed' (Annala Connacht, 139) in a symbolic reconciliation.

In July 1263 Walter de Burgh was with the Lord Edward,

to whom Henry III had granted Ireland in 1254, during military operations at Bristol. There he received a grant of Ulster, which had been in the king's hand since the death of Hugh de Lacy in 1242, to hold as Lacy had held it. In return he surrendered lands in south Tipperary. No formal instrument survives recreating the earldom, which Lacy had received by charter from King John in 1205; but Walter de Burgh is called earl of Ulster by the annals of Connacht in 1264 (*Annala Connacht*, 143), and he was addressed as earl by Henry III from 1266. The addition of Ulster to his existing lands in Connacht and north Munster made him, in theory (for much of the territory remained in the hands of Irish chiefs), holder of the biggest area of unbroken lordship in the British Isles. The grant may have arisen from royal concern about the recent vulnerability of the entire region both to alliances between Gaelic Irish leaders and to the intrusion of mercenary troops from western Scotland and the isles; but its timing reflected de Burgh's support for Edward during the early stages of the barons' war.

Walter de Burgh's sudden aggrandizement contributed to clashes with the successors of Maurice Fitzgerald (d. 1257), the former justiciar of Ireland who had expanded his family's power in Sligo and Donegal. During 1264 he seized the Connacht castles of the Fitzgeralds. There followed widespread disturbances, referred to in an Anglo-Norman poem, 'The Walling of New Ross'; these culminated in the capture and imprisonment of Richard de la Rochelle, Edward's justiciar, and other lords by Maurice Fitzgerald (d. 1268) and his uncle, Maurice fitz Maurice Fitzgerald (d. 1286). It is possible that these events reflected current party alignments in England; but they may simply have represented clashes over regional spheres of influence which ran out of control in a climate of political uncertainty. According to the Waverley annals, the leaders of both Irish factions arrived in England shortly after the battle of Evesham 'to assist the Lord Edward' (*Ann. mon.*, 2.365). De Burgh was certainly there during the early summer of 1266, when he was employed by the crown against contrariants in the midlands.

The remaining years of Ulster's life had an Irish focus, as he sought to dominate his vast lordships. In 1269 he imposed a fine of 3500 cattle on Aodh Buidhe Ó Néill, king of Tír Eoghain, exacted hostages from him, and made him swear that if he broke the arrangement 'the lord earl is entitled to expel me from the kingship, which I ought to hold of him' (*De L'Isle and Dudley MSS*, 1.31–2). In the same year Henry III reprimanded him for trying to assert jurisdiction over the archbishop of Armagh and his suffragans in Ulster. In 1270 a major conflict arose with Aodh Ó Conchobhair, who had succeeded his father in 1265. During negotiations the earl surrendered his brother, William, to Aodh as a pledge. When he heard that William had been imprisoned, he is said to have slain Toirdhealbhaigh Ó Briain, who was allied with the Ó Conchobhair, by his own hand. Aodh then defeated the earl's army at Áth an Chip, near Carrick-on-Shannon, and executed William. Earl Walter died at Galway on 28 July 1271 after a week's illness.

He was buried at the Augustinian priory of Athassel in Tipperary, which his grandfather had founded. His widow died in May 1274 and was buried at Dunmow Priory in Essex. In addition to his successor, Richard de *Burgh (d. 1326), Walter and Avelina had a son named Theobald (d. 1303), and a daughter, Egidia, who married James Stewart, the high steward of Scotland (d. 1309).   ROBIN FRAME

Sources *Chancery records* · H. S. Sweetman and G. F. Handcock, eds., *Calendar of documents relating to Ireland*, 5 vols., PRO (1875–86), vols. 1–2 · A. M. Freeman, ed. and trans., *Annála Connacht / The annals of Connacht* (1944); repr. (1970) · G. H. Orpen, *Ireland under the Normans*, 4 vols. (1911–20), vol. 3 · A. J. Otway-Ruthven, *A history of medieval Ireland* (1968) · K. Simms, 'The O Hanlons, the O Neills and the Anglo-Normans in thirteenth-century Armagh', *Seanchas Ardmhacha*, 9 (1978–9), 70–94 · R. Frame, 'Ireland and the barons' wars', *Thirteenth century England: proceedings of the Newcastle upon Tyne conference* [Newcastle upon Tyne 1985], ed. P. R. Coss and S. D. Lloyd, 1 (1986), 158–67 · GEC, *Peerage* · W. Heuser, *Die Kildare-Gedichte* (1904) · *Ann. mon.*, vol. 2 · *Report on the manuscripts of Lord De L'Isle and Dudley*, 1, HMC, 77 (1925) · A. Smith, ed., 'Annales de Monte Fernandi / Annals of Multifernan', *Tracts relating to Ireland*, Irish Archaeological Society, 2/2 (1842), 15

Burgh, Walter Hussey (1742–1783), politician and orator, was the son of Ignatius Hussey, barrister, of Donore, co. Kildare, and his wife, Elizabeth, daughter of Thomas Burgh of Oldtown in the same county. He was born in co. Kildare on 23 August 1742. After attending the school of a Mr Young in Abbey Street, Dublin, he entered Trinity College, Dublin, in 1758, and graduated BA in 1762. At university he showed considerable proficiency in classics and also distinguished himself by a poem written on the occasion of the marriage of George III. He adopted the additional name of Burgh on inheriting one half of the property of his maternal cousin, Richard Burgh of Drumkeen, who died in 1762. His connection with the Burgh family was strengthened even further when he married Anne Burgh (d. 1782), daughter of Thomas Burgh of Bert, co. Kildare, on 4 July 1767. After having entered the Middle Temple, London, on 13 October 1761, Burgh was called to the Irish bar in 1769. A career in the Irish parliament also began to take shape at this time. In November 1769 he was elected member for Athy borough, co. Kildare, through the influence of the duke of Leinster. At the next general election, in 1776, he was returned for Trinity College, Dublin.

Burgh's success as a barrister was almost unprecedentedly rapid, as within little more than a year he occupied a place in the very first rank. Among his close friends in his early years at the bar was Henry Grattan, with whom he afterwards became closely associated as a politician. As early as 1777 he was made prime serjeant, then the most important office open to a barrister in Ireland. In the same year he was sworn of the privy council. Although he was both amiable and prudent, his patriotism was much stronger than his love of peace or his love of office. A letter of his in reference to his candidature to represent Dublin University, subsequently published in *Anthologia Hibernica* (vol. 1, 1793), indicated the firmness and independence of his political views and his deep sense of the duties of a representative in parliament. He declined on principle to

Walter Hussey Burgh (1742–1783), by Hugh Douglas Hamilton

pledge himself to the particular course of action desired by some of his constituents, but he subsequently acted in accordance with his high principles. With Grattan he was chiefly responsible for securing the removal of Ireland's commercial disabilities.

Burgh also achieved rapid advancement in his early political career. The Irish viceroy, Buckinghamshire, entrusted the leadership of the government's party in the Irish House of Commons to him in 1777. However, there were early indications that his support for the free trade agitation was going to interfere with his new responsibilities. Two years later Burgh decided that he could no longer maintain his position and declined to continue as the leading government spokesman in the Commons. In a letter of 20 August 1779 to Lord George Germain, a British cabinet member, Buckinghamshire commented that Burgh sought freedom to 'press more earnestly for commercial indulgences'. He soon exerted his weight behind the free trade movement. On the opening day of the session Burgh, in concert with Grattan, moved an amendment to the king 'that it is not by temporary expedients but by a free trade alone that this nation is now to be saved from impending ruin' (*DNB*).

As the government gave no sign of compliance with the national demand for unrestricted free trade, Burgh allied himself to those in opposition. During the debates on the revenue bills in November 1779 he opposed the government even though he was still in possession of his legal post at the time. He also objected to John Foster's compromise proposal of rejecting new taxes provided the loan

duties were granted for the usual term of two years, stating that it was not right to limit the supplies granted to the king while making provision for the nation's creditors. It was during the debate on the loan duties that Burgh described the political situation in memorable words. Grattan's memoirs record him as saying: 'Talk not to me of peace; Ireland is not in a state of peace; it is smothered war. England has sown her laws like dragon's teeth, and they have sprung up as armed men' (Grattan, 1.403). His speech was received with great acclamation both inside and outside the Irish House of Commons. After concluding it he again rose and resigned the office he held under the crown.

When shortly afterwards the restrictive acts on the Irish trade were totally repealed Burgh advised Grattan, in view of the power of England, to adopt a more conciliatory attitude and not to press measures insistence upon which might tend to widen the breach between the two countries. As soon, however, as the question of Ireland's legislative independence was raised he strenuously supported the resolutions of Grattan that 'the king, with the consent of the parliament of Ireland, is alone competent to enact laws to bind Ireland, and that Great Britain and Ireland are inseparably united, but only under a common sovereign'. In supporting the resolutions he believed that he was cutting off all hopes of future promotion under the government. Grattan's memoirs report that after recording his vote Burgh said to a friend sitting nearby, 'I have now sacrificed the greatest honour an Irishman can aim at' (Grattan, 1.406).

After the adoption of the declaration of rights in 1782 Burgh again accepted his old office, and shortly afterwards he was appointed chief baron of the exchequer. While on circuit at Armagh he caught a cold which developed into fever, of which he died on 29 September 1783. He was buried in the cemetery of St Peter's Church, Dublin. His wife, Anne, had died the previous year, and on the motion of Grattan a grant of £2000 a year was voted to their five children.

Burgh's contemporaries placed great emphasis on the power of oratory and accredited him with possessing impressive oratorical skills. The 'Notes on the debates of the Irish House of Commons, 1776–89', compiled by parliamentarian Sir Henry Cavendish, who endeavoured to report speeches verbatim and followed strictly the order in which they were made, show clearly that Burgh was a frequent attender and speaker in parliament and that his words were listened to with great respect. Both as a man and as an orator he was equally popular at the bar, in the House of Commons, and among the great mass of the people. As a politician his noble and unselfish aims place him on a level with Grattan and fully justify the eulogy of Flood: 'He did not live to be ennobled by patent; he was ennobled by nature' (Grattan, 1.407). His chief weaknesses were a tendency to extravagance and a love of parade. He was accustomed to drive to court with six horses and three outriders, and although he both possessed a large professional income and inherited a considerable estate he was latterly deeply involved in money difficulties. It is not clear if his financial problems influenced his political outlook to any great extent. The least that can be said is that he was prepared to resign office in spite of them.

T. F. HENDERSON, rev. DAVID LAMMEY

Sources D. Lammey, 'A study of Anglo-Irish relations between 1772 and 1782, with particular reference to the "free trade" movement', PhD diss., Queen's University, Belfast, 1984 · H. Cavendish, 'Notes on the debates of the Irish House of Commons, 1776–89', PRO NIre., T 3435 and MIC 12 [transcript and microfilm of the Cavendish MSS, L. Cong.] · H. Grattan, *Memoirs of the life and times of the Rt Hon. Henry Grattan*, 5 vols. (1839–46), vol. 1, pp. 402–7 · C. Phillips, *Curran and his contemporaries*, 5th edn (1857), 38–44 · F. E. Ball, *The judges in Ireland, 1221–1921*, 2 (1926), 165–6, 219 · Burke, *Gen. GB* (1862) · J. Barrington, *Historic memoirs of Ireland*, 1 (1833), 36 · *GM*, 1st ser., 53 (1783), 893, 903 · J. R. O'Flanagan, *The Irish bar*, 2nd edn (1879), 30–42 · *Anthologia Hibernica, or, Monthly collections of science, belles lettres and history*, 4 vols. (1793–4), vol. 1 · *IGI* · E. M. Johnston-Liik, *History of the Irish parliament, 1692–1800*, 6 vols. (2002)

Archives TCD, corresp.; literary MSS · University of Kansas, Lawrence, Kenneth Spencer Research Library, corresp. and papers | L. Cong., Cavendish MSS · PRO NIre., letters to John Foster, D/562 (4562–4581)

Likenesses two line engravings, *c*.1779, NG Ire.; repro. in *Hibernian Magazine* (Dec 1779) · G. F. Joseph, oils, 1820 (posthumous), TCD · engraving, *c*.1833, repro. in Barrington, *Historic memoirs* · W. S. Barnard, mezzotint (after H. D. Hamilton), NG Ire., NPG · H. D. Hamilton, pastel drawing, NG Ire. [*see illus.*] · F. Wheatley, group portrait, oils (*The Irish House of Commons 1780*), Leeds City Art Galleries, Lotherton Hall · line engraving, NPG

Burgh, William de (d. 1206), baron, was the brother of Hubert de *Burgh, justiciar of England, father of Richard de *Burgh, lord of Connacht, and ancestor of the de Burghs, earls of Ulster. Closely associated with John, lord of Ireland, he probably accompanied him on his expedition to Ireland in 1185, and became John's principal agent in the conquest and organization of northern Munster. While other leading Anglo-Norman invaders are vividly described by Gerald of Wales, knowledge of this turbulent frontier lord has to be gleaned from hostile Gaelic sources or administrative records. Perhaps the best clue to his character lies in the study of the imposing sites of his castles at Kilfeacle, Carrigogunnell, and Shanid, among others, which reveals a powerful personality capable of impressing his authority on fiercely contested borders.

Although de Burgh's military ability undoubtedly accounts for his enduring achievement, he owed much to John's favour and, less certainly, a marriage alliance with the Ó Briain of Thomond. The concentration of his castles along the northern periphery of John's territories in Waterford and Lismore, chiefly at Tibberaghny, Kilsheelan, and Kilfeacle, suggests that John used him both to protect his demesne and to initiate the conquest of Tipperary in conjunction with Theobald Walter and Philip of Worcester. Much the same pattern is evident in Limerick, conquered in the closing years of the century, where the royal city of Limerick was protected in the west by de Burgh's castle at Carrigogunnell, and in the east by his castle at Castleconnell. Described in 1201 as *vicarius Momonie* ('seneschal of Munster'), de Burgh was the royal governor of the city until July 1203, when he was superseded by William (III) de Briouze. The measure of John's favour may also be gauged by the curious fact that among the tenants-in-chief of the honour of Limerick de Burgh alone was exempted from owing fealty to Briouze.

According to one Irish source de Burgh was married to a daughter of Domnall Mór Ó Briain, which is consistent with the fact that he was frequently accompanied by his Ó Briain allies, hereditary enemies of the Mac Carthaig and the Ó Conchobhair, in his numerous campaigns in Desmond and Connacht. Presumably this alliance gave him the means to prosecute his territorial interests in Desmond and Connacht, while leaving his castles on the Thomond frontier secure from attack. The erection of the de Burgh castle at Kilfeacle in 1193 brought a sharp response from Domnall Mac Carthaig, who destroyed it three years later. In 1199, 1201, and again in 1202 there were campaigns in Desmond led, in the latter years, by de Burgh with the assistance of the Ó Briain. The effect of these determined campaigns in the west and south left de Burgh freer to pursue his next priority, the conquest of the kingdom of Connacht, which he had been granted by John probably before 1195, when Cathal Croibdearg Ó Conchobhair, king of Connacht, launched a devastating attack on Anglo-Norman castles in Munster, including de Burgh's castle of Castleconnell. In 1200, 1202, and again in 1203 de Burgh intervened in the dynastic conflicts in Connacht, no doubt with a view to making good his territorial claims there, but in doing so he incurred the wrath of the justiciar, Meiler fitz Henry, who forced him to abandon Connacht and submit after besieging him in Limerick. De Burgh surrendered three castles and twelve hostages, besides a son and a daughter. Throughout the tangled dispute with Meiler he retained the king's confidence. As early as October 1203 the king commanded Meiler to restore de Burgh's castles of Kilfeacle and Askeaton, although he was to retain his other pledges in safe custody. The dispute was still not determined in September 1204, even though the king ordered that all of de Burgh's lands be restored, except for Connacht, which seems to have been the source of the trouble.

William de Burgh probably died in January or February 1206. On 7 April the king commanded Meiler to take his lands into the king's hand. Although he was married in or before 1193, there is no certainty about the identity of his wife. She may have been an unnamed daughter of Domnall Mór Ó Briain, but the authority for this statement rests solely on the evidence of a late medieval Gaelic genealogy. She is certainly not the Alienora, wife of William de Burgis, mentioned in the pipe roll of 1 Richard I. The order to Meiler on 5 October 1203 made reference to the sons of William de Burgh in his custody, which probably intended Richard, his heir, and Hubert, who became prior of Athassel and later bishop of Limerick (1224–50). The annals of Loch Cé refer in 1203 to an unnamed daughter, of whom nothing is known. De Burgh was almost certainly buried in his important foundation of Augustinian canons at Athassel, Tipperary.

C. A. EMPEY

Sources S. Ó hInnse, ed. and trans., *Miscellaneous Irish annals, AD 1114–1437* (1947) · *AFM* · W. M. Hennessy, ed. and trans., *The annals of Loch Cé: a chronicle of Irish affairs from AD 1014 to AD 1590*, 2 vols., Rolls Series, 54 (1871) · A. M. Freeman, ed. and trans., *Annála Connacht /*

The annals of Connacht (1944) • T. D. Hardy, ed., Rotuli litterarum patentium, RC (1835) • H. S. Sweetman and G. F. Handcock, eds., Calendar of documents relating to Ireland, 5 vols., PRO (1875–86) • J. MacCaffrey, ed., The Black Book of Limerick (1907) • J. Mills and M. J. McEnery, eds., Calendar of the Gormanston register (1916) • E. Curtis, ed., Calendar of Ormond deeds, IMC, 1: 1172–1350 (1932) • C. A. Empey, 'The settlement of the kingdom of Limerick', England and Ireland in the later middle ages: essays in honour of Jocelyn Otway-Ruthven, ed. J. Lydon (1981) • G. H. Orpen, Ireland under the Normans, 4 vols. (1911–20), vol. 2 • T. D. Hardy, ed., Rotuli de liberate ac de misis et praestitis, regnante Johanne, RC (1844) • J. O'Donovan, ed. and trans., The tribes and customs of Hy-Many, commonly called O'Kelly's country, Irish Archaeological Society (1843)

Burgh, William de, third earl of Ulster [called the Brown Earl] (1312–1333), magnate, was born on 17 September 1312, the only child of John de Burgh (d. 1313), son of Richard de *Burgh, second earl of Ulster (d. 1326), lord of Connacht, and his wife, Elizabeth de *Clare (d. 1360), sister and coheir of Gilbert de *Clare, eighth earl of Gloucester (d. 1314). He was the third and last earl of the de Burgh family. In 1327 he married *Matilda (d. 1377), a daughter of *Henry, third earl of Lancaster. William de Burgh was granted his grandfather's lands in February 1327, and was by far the biggest proprietor in Ireland. For most of his short life he was also heir to his mother's third of the Gloucester inheritance in England, Wales, and Ireland, and a figure of importance in the wider history of the British Isles. A report to Elizabeth from her council in Ireland during 1327 stressed the vulnerability of Ulster to the Scots, and the need for the young earl to come over to assert his authority there, and to provide a focus for the allegiance of his kinsmen and tenants in Connacht and Munster. The opportunity for his return was presented in 1328 by the treaty of Edinburgh between England and Scotland. Having been knighted by Edward III, the earl attended the wedding at Berwick of the future David II to Joan of England, after which *Robert I, who was his uncle by marriage, escorted him to Carrickfergus. During the years that followed he tried to reassert the position of dominance once held by his grandfather. He was drawn into disputes with the earl of Desmond in Munster (in 1330 the two earls were briefly placed in custody by the justiciar of Ireland), and with his cousin, Walter de Burgh, the most powerful figure in Connacht. These tensions were reflected in alliances with rival branches of the Ó Briain and Ó Conchobhair.

In 1331 Edward III, who intended to visit Ireland in 1332, appointed Earl William as his lieutenant. The earl and Anthony Lucy, the justiciar, brought an unusual ruthlessness to Irish baronial politics. Lucy arrested Henry de Mandeville, a former seneschal of Ulster, while the earl imprisoned Walter de Burgh in his castle of Northburgh on the Foyle, where he died in 1332. These events formed the background to Earl William's murder, which took place at 'Le Ford' (perhaps Belfast), near Carrickfergus, on 6 June 1333. The earl, who was preparing to lead an expedition to the renewed Scottish war, was killed as a result of a conspiracy involving some of his own men, among whom members of the Mandeville family were prominent. The Kilkenny annalist, John Clyn, attributed the chief blame to Egidia, wife of Richard de Mandeville and sister of Walter de Burgh; Richard de Mandeville subsequently fled to the Scots. When news of the murder reached Dublin, the justiciar, John Darcy, diverted the force he was preparing for the Scottish war to Ulster to punish the perpetrators, before crossing to Scotland as planned.

Earl William was known to native Irish annalists as the Brown Earl. Clyn describes him as 'of very subtle intellect, a lover of peace and of the common weal' (Annals of Ireland, ed. Butler, 25). His failure to recover the position in Irish society held by his grandfather may have had less to do with his personal abilities or English background than with the disruption caused in Ireland by the Anglo-Scottish wars and by the political turmoil of Edward II's reign and its aftermath. Upon his death his widow, who subsequently married Ralph Ufford, fled to England with his only child, an infant daughter whose marriage to *Lionel of Clarence was to carry the de Burgh lordships to the Mortimers and the house of York. Ulster and Connacht, which William de Burgh had struggled to manage, proved even less amenable to rule by absentee lords.

ROBIN FRAME

Sources Chancery records • PRO • J. T. Gilbert, ed., Chartularies of St Mary's Abbey, Dublin: with the register of its house at Dunbrody and annals of Ireland, 2, Rolls Series, 80 (1884) • The annals of Ireland by Friar John Clyn and Thady Dowling: together with the annals of Ross, ed. R. Butler, Irish Archaeological Society (1849) • G. H. Orpen, Ireland under the Normans, 4 vols. (1911–20), vol. 4 • R. Frame, English lordship in Ireland, 1318–1361 (1982) • G. O. Sayles, ed., Documents on the affairs of Ireland before the king's council, IMC (1979) • A. M. Freeman, ed. and trans., Annála Connacht / The annals of Connacht (1944) • A. J. Otway-Ruthven, A history of medieval Ireland (1968) • GEC, Peerage • CIPM, 7, no. 537 • G. H. Orpen, 'The earldom of Ulster', Journal of the Royal Society of Antiquaries of Ireland, 6th ser., 3–5 (1913–15) • G. H. Orpen, 'The earldom of Ulster', Journal of the Royal Society of Antiquaries of Ireland, 6th ser., 10–11 (1920–21) • H. T. Knox, 'Occupation of the county of Galway by the Anglo-Normans after 1237', Journal of the Royal Society of Antiquaries of Ireland, 5th ser., 11 (1901), 365–70
Wealth at death see CIPM; Orpen, 'Earldom of Ulster'; Knox, 'Occupation of … Galway'

Burgh, William (1741/2–1808), politician and theological writer, was born in Ireland, the eldest son of Thomas Burgh, MP and landowner, of Bert, co. Kildare, and Anne, daughter of Dive Downes, bishop of Cork and Ross. His grandfather was Ulysses Burgh, bishop of Ardagh, and his two sisters both married prominent politicians: Margaret Amelia (d. 1824) married John *Foster, speaker of the Irish House of Commons, and Anne (d. 1782) married Walter Hussey *Burgh, lord chief baron of the Irish court of exchequer. William Burgh owned considerable estates in Ireland and married into another Irish landowning family on his marriage c.1770 to Mary (d. 1819), daughter of George Warburton, but lived most of his life in York.

For most of his adult life Burgh was involved in politics and showed a keen interest in the liberty of the subject. He represented the borough of Athy, Kildare, in the Irish parliament of 1769–76. He later became a leading figure in the York association for parliamentary reform and was opposed to the war in America. He was a close friend of William Wilberforce and enthusiastically supported the campaign to abolish the slave trade. However, from its outset he denounced the French Revolution as a threat to liberty. Though applauded by his friend Edmund Burke, his views initially made him unpopular until the excesses of the revolution drove public opinion into alignment with his stance. Burgh's public utterances on liberty were matched in private life by a readiness to help and advise all who sought his assistance. It was said of him that 'his heart and his purse were open on all occasions' (*GM*, 612). Burgh is probably most celebrated for his defence of the doctrine of the Trinity against the Socinianism of Theophilus Lindsey. His case against Lindsey led him into a minute enquiry into the scriptural account of Christ's divinity, which resulted in the publication in 1774 of *A scriptural confutation of the arguments against the one Godhead of the Father, Son, and Holy Ghost produced by the Rev. Mr Lindsay*. A sequel entitled *An inquiry into the belief of the Christians of the first three centuries representing the one Godhead of Father, Son, and Holy Ghost* was published at York in 1778. His publications provoked the criticism of anti-trinitarians but received the approbation of many distinguished laymen, including Burke, and leading churchmen such as Bishop Thomas Newton. For his defence of trinitarian orthodoxy he was awarded a DCL by the University of Oxford in 1788. Burgh had intended writing a history of religious thought but nothing came of this project. His only other publication was an edition, with notes and commentary, of the poem *The English Garden* (1783) by his close friend William Mason.

After having lived in York for nearly forty years, Burgh died there in his house on the north side of Bootham Street on 26 December 1808, aged sixty-six. He was buried in the lady chapel of York Minster, where he is commemorated by a monument by Richard Westmacott, representing a woman holding in her left hand a book and in her right a cross, with a poetical inscription by J. B. S. Morritt of Rokeby. His wife outlived him by eleven years and on her death in 1819 was buried in the same vault with him. In compliance with Burgh's wish, 328 volumes from his library were added to the collections of York Minster Library. A fine miniature by Samuel Cooper, supposedly of John Milton but in fact a portrait of Cromwell's secretary, John Thurloe, was bequeathed to Morritt.

W. P. COURTNEY, rev. M. J. MERCER

Sources *GM*, 1st ser., 79 (1809), 611–15 · G. E. Aylmer and R. Cant, eds., *A history of York Minster* (1977), 463–4, 511 · B. Barr and J. Ingamells, eds., *A candidate for praise: William Mason, 1727–97, precentor of York* (1973), 16–17, 64–5, 76–7 [exhibition catalogue, York Art Gallery and York Minster Library, York, 16 June – 15 July 1973] · J. Hutchinson, ed., *A catalogue of notable Middle Templars: with brief biographical notices* (1902) · Allibone, *Dict.* · GEC, *Peerage*
Archives Bodl. Oxf., letters to W. Wilberforce · N. Yorks. CRO, corresp. with Christopher Wyvill
Likenesses J. R. Smith, mezzotint, pubd 1809, BM, NG Ire., NPG

Burgh, William George de (1866–1943), philosopher, was born at New Wandsworth, London, on 24 October 1866, the son of William de Burgh, barrister and civil servant, who died when de Burgh was twelve, and his wife, Hannah Jane, daughter of Captain Thomas Monck Mason RN. He went to Winchester College, thence as a postmaster to Merton College, Oxford, where he was awarded a

second class in classical moderations (1887) and a first class in *literae humaniores* (1889). Some difficult years followed in which he was briefly an assistant master at Derby School and, living at Toynbee Hall, was appointed in 1892 as censor of studies at Balliol House and Wadham House, university settlements in London. In 1896 he found his life work on appointment as lecturer in Greek and Latin in the University Extension College at Reading, where he remained until 1934. On 26 January 1897 he married Edith Mary, daughter of William Francis Grace, vice-consul at Mogador, with whom he had two daughters and one son.

For many years de Burgh's teaching burden was excessive; he soon added philosophy to his curriculum and became professor of the subject in 1907; he taught classics until 1910. His administrative cares were hardly less absorbing: from the first he had faith in the future of Reading, and he had the satisfaction of guiding the development of the college into a university (its charter was received in 1926). The credit for this achievement is generally ascribed to W. M. Childs, and de Burgh was willing that this should be so; but while the acquisition of the necessary funds was Childs's work, the academic statesmanship was de Burgh's. Childs, de Burgh (deputy vice-chancellor, 1926–34), and F. H. Wright, the registrar, 'formed a kind of inner cabinet' (Holt, 42) which ran the university's affairs.

The enforced leisure of 1914–18 was used by de Burgh to prepare work for publication, and *The Legacy of the Ancient World* (1924, rev. edn, 1947) proved the most successful of his books. Although his intellectual gifts were highly regarded by his pupils and by the Oxford philosophers who were his contemporaries and friends, their wider recognition was belated: he was Gifford lecturer at St Andrews (1937–8) and Riddell memorial lecturer at Newcastle (1938); not until 1938 was he elected to a fellowship of the British Academy. The reason for this may have lain in his disinterestedness; for himself he sought neither fame nor reward. He had a strong sense of duty as a categorical imperative, and in fulfilling his obligations the only standard he failed to satisfy was his own. Inflexible when any matter of principle was at stake, he was nevertheless warm-hearted and genial, an unfailing tonic to his friends. His sympathy with the young, his forensic gifts, and his vitality were the secret of his success as a teacher. He knew all the students in his faculty individually and was remembered for his influence upon them (Holt, 86).

Tall, slim, and erect, de Burgh made walking his only physical recreation; his other diversions lay in art, literature, light verse, and the complexities of the railway system. His radiance of personality had its roots in the religious faith expressed in his motto, *A cruce salus*, the keynote of his life. A student of scholasticism, yet much influenced by modern idealism, he endeavoured to construct a distinctively Christian philosophy by developing a philosophical argument to the truth of the gospel. His project was unfashionable at a time when protestant theologians were disparaging reason and when few philosophers were interested in religion, but his argument, based on the experience of a lifetime and elaborated by the resources of his vigorous mind, was found impressive by those in sympathy with his views. He suffered a stroke in the summer of 1942 while walking on the Dorset downs and died at his home, The Cottage, Toller Porcorum, Dorset, on 27 August 1943, survived by his wife. He was buried at Toller Porcorum on 30 August.

T. M. KNOX, *rev.* C. A. CREFFIELD

Sources A. E. Taylor, 'William George de Burgh', *PBA*, 29 (1943), 371–91 · J. A. R. Pimlott, *Toynbee Hall: fifty years of social progress, 1884–1934* (1935) · J. C. Holt, *The University of Reading: the first fifty years* (1977) · personal knowledge (1959) · private information (1959) **Archives** JRL, letters to S. Alexander
Likenesses C. Dodgson, portrait; priv. coll., in 1959 · J. Russell & Sons, photograph (aged about seventy), repro. in Taylor, 'William George de Burgh', facing p. 301
Wealth at death £7494 0s. 11d.: probate, 28 Jan 1944, *CGPLA Eng. & Wales*

Burghall, Edward (*bap.* 1600, *d.* 1665), clergyman and ejected minister, and schoolmaster, was baptized on 9 December 1600 at Beeston township in the parish of Bunbury, Cheshire, one of seven known children of Hugh Burghall (*d.* 1632) of Beeston, in Bunbury, a yeoman of an established local family, and his wife, Margaret. No certain details of his education are known, but by 1622 he was usher at the free grammar school at Bunbury. He married Joan Mason (*d.* 1668) in 1623; they had at least seven children, and lived in the township of Alpraham. Bunbury's noted puritan preacher and scholar William Hinde (*d.* 1629) no doubt influenced the young teacher. Burghall's headmaster, William Cole, died in 1632, and Burghall was certainly headmaster by 1637. That salary of £20 a year, plus a house and some land, no doubt insulated him from an obscure family quarrel over his father's estate. Burghall accepted a call in May 1644 to preach at Haslington chapelry in the parish of Barthomley, Cheshire, at £34 'paid' (*Memorials*, 126). He was appointed vicar of Acton, Cheshire, in 1646, with an augmentation by the committee for plundered ministers. Another schoolmaster was at Bunbury by 1648, but Burghall may not have moved from Alpraham immediately, as a child was baptized from there in 1645.

Burghall is best known because he 'left a MS. called *Providence improved; being remarks taken from his Diary*' (Palmer, 1.325). Any diary is lost, and the known text of 'Providence improved' is a copy made in 1778. It is well printed in J. Hall's edition of *Memorials of the Civil War* (1889) but earlier editions are inaccurate. 'Providence improved', a retrospective personal chronology from 1628 to 1663, has a place in the puritan autobiographical canon faintly paralleling, for example, the opening chapters of Richard Baxter's text. Burghall traces the evolution of godly puritanism and politics under Charles I into presbyterianism in the civil war, and then into the division, innovations such as Quakers, and uncertainty of the 1650s. Burghall felt betrayed by the outcome of the Restoration and deplored the 'severe' Act of Uniformity (*Memorials*, 235). 'Providence improved' ends with the illness of Queen Catherine in 1663, a judgment of a disapproving God. In that common puritan genre, God's judgment of

the central government, and of sin, illustrated from Bunbury parish register, is displayed. Accusations in Hall that Burghall's text for 1643–8 plagiarized Thomas Malbon's Nantwich-based annals of the civil war miss the point: Burghall was reviewing the events of his godly career, not writing an account of the war years.

'Providence improved' is reticent about Burghall's support for parliament at the start of the civil war, which may be significant given the early strength of neutralism in Cheshire. Although in June 1643 royalists tried to capture him, he did not refer to them as the enemy until August. He was plundered by royalists and driven from his house in the spring of 1644. Burghall signed the Cheshire attestation to the solemn league and covenant in 1648, did not engage, and took tithes, suggesting that he was presbyterian. In the 1650s his dinners with one of the important Cheshire magistrates probably indicate clerical influence in secular government. There are two extant sermons by Burghall, who was a well-regarded preacher: *The Perfect Way to Die in Peace* (1659), and *The Great Benefit of Christian Education* (1663). The latter was apparently given at the dedication of Acton grammar school in 1662. That year, having refused to conform, he was ejected from the vicarage of Acton, and returned to Alpraham.

Ejection brought loss of income and loss of the personal prominence enjoyed by Burghall in the 1650s. However, the excluded minister felt able to nominate two local gentry as supervisors of his will—his and his wife's probate inventories, and the 1664 hearth tax return, do not suggest, as Calamy does, that he was ejected into poverty. Burghall died at Alpraham on 8 December 1665 and was buried at Bunbury on 11 December.   C. B. PHILLIPS

Sources T. Malbon and E. Burghall, *Memorials of the civil war in Cheshire and the adjacent counties*, ed. J. Hall, Lancashire and Cheshire RS, 19 (1889) · Burghall's diary, copied in 1778, BL, Add. MS 5851, 105 · parish register, Bunbury, 1580–1676, Ches. & Chester ALSS [microfilm] · probate records, Ches. & Chester ALSS, W/Supra [index by year of probate, OS: Edward Burghall of Alpraham, clerk, 1665; Joan Burghall of Alpraham, widow, 1669; Hugh Burghall of Beeston, yeoman, 1632; Thomas Burghall of Bunbury, gent, 1647; Margaret Burghall of Beeston, widow, 1676; William Palin of Alpraham, yeoman, 1674; Thomas Mason of Haughton, 1647] · W. F. Irvine, ed., *Marriage licences granted within the archdeaconry of Chester in the diocese of Chester*, 2, Lancashire and Cheshire RS, 56 (1908), 190 · J. S. Morrill, *Cheshire, 1630–1660: county government and society during the English revolution* (1974), 241, 270 · *The nonconformist's memorial … originally written by … Edmund Calamy*, ed. S. Palmer, [3rd edn], 1 (1802), 324–5 · Wing, *STC* · W. A. Shaw, ed., *Minutes of the committee for the relief of plundered ministers and of the trustees for the maintenance of ministers … 1643–1660*, 1, Lancashire and Cheshire RS, 28 (1893), 45–6, 98, 238 · W. A. Shaw, ed., *Minutes of the committee for the relief of plundered ministers and of the trustees for the maintenance of ministers … 1643–1660*, 2, Lancashire and Cheshire RS, 34 (1896), 230 · lay subsidy returns, hearth tax returns, PRO, E. 179/86/145, for 1664 · Bunbury easter book for 1590, Ches. & Chester ALSS, Crewe of Crewe MSS, DCR, 27/3 · F. Gastrell, *Notitia Cestrienses, or, Historical notices of the diocese of Chester*, ed. F. R. Raines, 1, Chetham Society, 8 (1845), 200, 202, 219 · parish register, Acton, –1666, Ches. & Chester ALSS [microfilm] · *DNB* · R. C. Richardson, *Puritanism in north-west England: a regional study of the diocese of Chester to 1642* (1972)
Archives BL, diary, Add. MS 5851, 105 [copied 1778]

Wealth at death £79 1s. 11d.—personal estate: probate records, W/Supra: Edward Burghall of Alpraham, clerk, 1665, Ches. & Chester ALSS · at least two, and possibly three, tenements, incl. one leasehold: will, 1 Sept 1664

Burghers, Michael (1647/8–1727), engraver and draughtsman, was baptized in the Lutheran church in Amsterdam, and apprenticed as an engraver. He left the Netherlands soon after the capture of Utrecht by the French in 1672. In 1724 he told Thomas Hearne that he was seventy-six years old, and that he had worked for the University of Oxford for fifty-five years, part of the time as a journeyman under David Loggan (*Remarks*, 8.284). This would put his arrival in Oxford in 1673, at the age of twenty-five, when he would have assisted Loggan on his *Oxonia illustrata*, completed in 1675.

After Loggan moved to London in 1675 Burghers remained in Oxford, where for the rest of his career he had a virtual monopoly in engraving. After Loggan's death in 1692 Burghers was appointed (at the latest by 1694) to succeed him as *calcographus academicus*, an appointment that he held for the rest of his life.

Burghers engraved innumerable title-pages, plates, and ornaments for the publications of the Oxford University Press. His output includes plates of natural history (including 167 in the second volume of Robert Morison's *Historia plantarum* of 1680–1700, and sixteen of fossils in Robert Plot's *Natural History of Oxfordshire* of 1677); antiquities (including the plates for Hearne's edition of Leland's *Itinerary*); maps (including some of Oxford); and portraits (mostly after his own drawings). He made one mezzotint, a portrait of Anthony Wood, in 1712.

Burghers's best-known works are the Oxford almanacs, for which he engraved and designed most of the plates from the beginning of the series in 1676 until 1719, as well as several later ones. It has been observed that the designs were lifted from prints in the collection of Dean Aldrich, whose collection remains in Christ Church.

Hearne recorded that Burghers died on 9 January 1727, and noted that he 'was looked upon as the best general engraver in England' and that he had had 'a vast deal of business' until the past two or three years when his eyesight had declined (*Remarks*, 9.254–5). Although Burghers had made himself rich, after his wife's death he had handed his money to his daughter and her husband, Welman, a barber, who had treated him so badly as to hasten his death. He was buried on 12 January in St Peter-in-the-East, Oxford.　　　　　　　ANTONY GRIFFITHS

Sources Vertue, *Note books*, 1.98 · *Remarks and collections of Thomas Hearne*, ed. C. E. Doble and others, 11 vols., OHS, 2, 7, 13, 34, 42–3, 48, 50, 65, 67, 72 (1885–1921), vol. 8, p. 284; vol. 9, pp. 254–5 · H. M. Petter, *The Oxford almanacs* (1974) · H. Carter, *A history of the Oxford University Press*, 1: *To the year 1780* (1975), 201 · *Hist. U. Oxf.* 5: *18th-cent. Oxf.*, 641n., 763 · administration bond, Oxf. UA, hyp/B/37, fol. 219 · inventory, Oxf. UA, hyp/B/11, fol. 48

Burghersh. For this title name *see* individual entries under Burghersh; *see also* Fane, John, eleventh earl of Westmorland [*formerly* Lord Burghersh] (1784–1859).

Burghersh, Bartholomew, the elder, second Lord Burghersh (*d.* 1355), magnate and administrator, was a

Bartholomew Burghersh the elder, second Lord Burghersh (*d.* 1355), tomb effigy

younger son of Robert Burghersh (*d.* 1306), constable of Dover Castle and warden of the Cinque Ports, and Maud, sister of Bartholomew Badlesmere. Burghersh (after Burwash, Sussex) inherited the modest family estates in Kent and Sussex on the death of his elder brother, Stephen (*d.* 1310). By 1321 he had married Elizabeth Verdon (1305/6–1364), with whom he had at least three sons, Bartholomew *Burghersh, the younger (*d.* 1369), Henry (*d.* 1349), and Thomas, and a daughter, Joan. Elizabeth was one of four coheiresses of Theobald de Verdon (*d.* 1316) and Burghersh took part in a protracted struggle to overturn the division of the Verdon estates. In 1328 he achieved a favourable settlement, only to see his success diluted in 1332 following an accusation of corruption involving Roger Mortimer, earl of March, and Henry *Burghersh (*c.*1290–1340), bishop of Lincoln, Bartholomew's younger brother, who was at that time chancellor of England. However, under Edward III he acquired substantial wealth thanks to royal patronage. Furthermore, while at the siege of Vannes, Brittany, in 1343 he had all debts at the exchequer pardoned and by 1346 the king owed him almost £4000. Between 1349 and 1353 he had custody of the valuable Despenser lands at a farm of £1000 per year. He also inherited the land and goods of his brother Henry. In 1344 he was granted the stannary of Devon by Edward, the Black Prince. On his death he left substantial estates throughout the southern half of England and patronage continued with his estates being placed under royal protection and his debts at the exchequer again being cancelled.

In his early career Burghersh was closely associated with his uncle Bartholomew *Badlesmere (*d.* 1322), a Kent magnate active in the court of Edward II. However, Badlesmere became estranged from the court and in 1321 his wife refused Queen Isabella entry to Leeds Castle. Edward II laid siege to the castle and at its fall Burghersh, his wife, and his children were sent to the Tower of London and his estates confiscated. His wife and children were eventually released by order of 31 December 1325, but Burghersh was only freed by the mob when London was abandoned by Edward II during the invasion of Mortimer and Isabella in late 1326. By December he had been appointed to his father's office of constable of Dover Castle and warden of the Cinque Ports. He immediately petitioned parliament for the return of his estates and these were restored to him in February 1327. He lost his offices in October 1330, when they were given to William Clinton, later earl of Huntingdon, for his personal assistance to the king in the coup that toppled the minority regime of Mortimer and Isabella that month. Burghersh was compensated with an appointment as seneschal of Ponthieu (from October 1331 to September 1334) and then as keeper of the forests south of the Trent in 1335, an office he relinquished in late 1343 when he was again appointed constable of Dover Castle and warden of the Cinque Ports. Burghersh was also admiral of the western fleet (from August 1337 to November 1339), master of the household of Edward, the Black Prince (to whom he was a close adviser), the king's chamberlain (from 1347 to 1355) and, briefly, keeper of the Tower of London and one of the keepers of the realm during the king's absence in 1355.

Burghersh was an important royal councillor. He rapidly acquired expertise in diplomacy. In 1327 he went on a mission to the papal curia, and returned there in 1329 to negotiate for the king half the profits of four papal tenths levied on the English clergy, 1330–34. Thereafter he was closely involved in almost all negotiations between the king and the pope or his envoys, particularly concerning the war with France. Also in 1327 he went with William Clinton to accompany Philippa of Hainault to England for her marriage to the new king. He took part in negotiations with the king of France in 1329 concerning the homage of Edward III and in 1332 concerning a proposed crusade. Once war broke out with France in 1337 he was closely involved with negotiating support from allies and peace with the enemy. He also assisted in Edward III's struggle to raise finance for the war in its early years. He retained the confidence of the king in the crisis of 1340–41 and acted as a justice in the general commissions investigating the offences of officials and others that ensued. Burghersh's diplomacy also extended into domestic politics: in 1343 he addressed parliament to explain and gain support for the truce he had helped negotiate in Brittany. Two propaganda letters survive in his name from July 1346 recounting the course of the Normandy campaign (he fought in the vanguard at Crécy). That September the assembled parliament awaited the arrival of Burghersh and others bringing letters from the king at the siege of Calais. By his speeches in the parliament of 1351 and the great council of 1353 Burghersh assisted in securing duties on wool to finance the war, and in the parliament of 1354, following his address, the Commons acclaimed their approval for the king's pursuit of a permanent peace. In these, his later years, he spent almost half his days in personal attendance upon the king and his council.

Burghersh came from a pious family. He took the cross and in May 1344 received a papal licence to go on crusade, but in 1351 he received a dispensation to delay for three years and in 1355 another to delay a visit to Santiago de Compostela. In 1345 he established a chantry in Lincoln Cathedral with five chaplains for the benefit of the royal family, his own family, and his patron, Bartholomew Badlesmere. He died on 3 August 1355 and his eldest son

and namesake succeeded to his estates. Like his father, and Henry his brother, he was buried in Lincoln Cathedral. His canopied tomb is in the north wall but the effigy appears to be a late medieval replacement. At his head and feet are pairs of angels, one holding his shield and the other his soul in a napkin.   ANTHONY VERDUYN

Sources Chancery records · RotP, vol. 2 · Adae Murimuth continuatio chronicarum. Robertus de Avesbury de gestis mirabilibus regis Edwardi tertii, ed. E. M. Thompson, Rolls Series, 93 (1889) · M. C. B. Dawes, ed., Register of Edward, the Black Prince, 4 vols., PRO (1930–33) · J. R. Maddicott, Thomas of Lancaster, 1307–1322: a study in the reign of Edward II (1970) · G. J. Aungier, ed., Chroniques de London, CS, 28 (1844) · N. Pevsner, J. Harris, and N. Antram, Lincolnshire, 2nd edn, Pevsner (1989) · W. M. Ormrod, The reign of Edward III (1990) · CEPR letters, vol. 2 · W. H. Bliss, ed., Calendar of entries in the papal registers relating to Great Britain and Ireland: petitions to the pope (1896)
Likenesses tomb effigy, Lincoln Cathedral [see illus.]
Wealth at death uncertain but substantial: CIPM, 10.216–20; 469–74

Burghersh, Bartholomew, the younger, third Lord Burghersh (d. 1369), soldier and diplomat, was the eldest son of Bartholomew *Burghersh the elder (d. 1355) and Elizabeth Verdon (1305/6–1364). He married first Cicily de Wayland (or Weyland), the daughter of Richard Weyland, and second Margaret, a close relative of Bartholomew Badlesmere, his father's patron. He had, with Cicily, one daughter, Elizabeth (d. 1409), who married Edward, Lord Despenser (d. 1375). From an early age he was in contact with the court of Edward III through his father. As early as 1339 he accompanied the king in Flanders and he took part in the Brittany campaign of 1342–3. However, it was his service alongside Edward the Black Prince for which he became well known. He was part of the prince's retinue at Crécy in 1346 and took part in the siege of Calais the following year. In 1349 he accompanied Henry of Grosmont, earl of Lancaster (d. 1361), on the expedition to Gascony and in 1355 returned there with the Black Prince. While on this campaign Burghersh, along with Sir John Chandos and Sir James Audley, was leading twenty-four men to confirm the position of the French forces; he chanced upon 200 of the enemy and successfully captured thirty-two knights and esquires. Later, on a reconnoitring mission with a force of 200 men, he could not resist the temptation to launch a surprise attack on the French. Burghersh fought for the prince at Poitiers (19 September 1356) and, at the end of the campaign, he remained with a garrison at Cognac and raided into Anjou and Poitou. In 1359 Burghersh campaigned with Edward III in France. He led the successful siege of Cormicy, east of Rheims, and was commended by the surrendering garrison commander for his chivalry. He assisted the king in the negotiations for the treaty of Brétigny (8 May 1360). In 1364 he received and escorted King John of France at Dover when he surrendered himself back into captivity. He remained highly active in royal service, going on embassies to Flanders and the papal court at Avignon in 1364–5 as part of the doomed diplomatic effort to arrange a marriage between Edmund of Langley, Edward III's son, and the daughter of the count of Flanders.

For his services Burghersh received considerable patronage and honours from Edward III and the Black Prince. He was a founding knight of the Order of the Garter. The Black Prince made him constable of Wallingford Castle in 1351; two years later he was also appointed justice of Chester. In 1349 he inherited land from his brother Henry and in 1355 Burghersh not only inherited his father's substantial lands throughout the southern half of England, but was also granted the stannary of Devon that his father had held of the Black Prince. In 1357/8 he received 10,000 marks from Edward III for the capture of the count of Ventadour and in 1361 a share of the dower lands of the late widow of Theobald de Verdon, his grandfather. The high esteem in which he was held by the Black Prince was also illustrated by numerous smaller gifts of armour, silverware, and wine.

Burghersh seems to have been a man of conventional piety. In 1354 he seriously intended a visit to the Holy Land, an objective he shared with his father. Interestingly, Froissart states that Burghersh in 1361 quoted a prophecy contained in the *Brut* that the Black Prince would never become king of England. Burghersh wrote his will upon his deathbed in London on 4 April 1369. He died the following day. He sought burial in the chapel at Walsingham before the statue of the Virgin Mary, breaking the tradition of his grandfather, father, and uncle, who were all buried in Lincoln Cathedral. He gave detailed instructions for the carriage of his body and left his property in Wales and Wiltshire to his wife. In 1961 his tomb was excavated and revealed that at his death he was an upright man of 5 feet 10 inches, his right arm showing the strong physical development needed for martial pursuits but a twisted ankle and once broken ribs revealing the concomitant risks. He had a narrow face and nose with high-set eyes and a full, if very worn, set of teeth.

ANTHONY VERDUYN

Sources Chancery records · M. C. B. Dawes, ed., *Register of Edward, the Black Prince*, 4 vols., PRO (1930–33) · *Chroniques de J. Froissart*, ed. S. Luce and others, 15 vols. (Paris, 1869–1975) · *Adae Murimuth continuatio chronicarum. Robertus de Avesbury de gestis mirabilibus regis Edwardi tertii*, ed. E. M. Thompson, Rolls Series, 93 (1889) · *Chronicon Galfridi le Baker de Swynebroke*, ed. E. M. Thompson (1889) · C. Greene and A. B. Whittingham, 'Excavations at Walsingham Priory, Norfolk, 1961', *Archaeological Journal*, 125 (1968), 255–90 · N. H. Nicolas, ed., *Testamenta vetusta: being illustrations from wills*, 2 vols. (1826) · R. Barber, *Edward, prince of Wales and Aquitaine: a biography of the Black Prince* (1978) · *CEPR letters* · W. H. Bliss, ed., *Calendar of entries in the papal registers relating to Great Britain and Ireland: petitions to the pope* (1896)
Wealth at death uncertain but substantial: *CIPM*, 12.297–301

Burghersh, Henry (c.1290–1340), bishop of Lincoln, was a younger son of Robert, Lord Burghersh, and of Maud, daughter of Guncelin Badlesmere. His father, who held land at Burwash in Sussex (whence the family name was derived) and at Chiddingstone, Boughton Aluph, and Stowting, Kent, served as constable of Dover Castle and as warden of the Cinque Ports from 1299 until his death in 1306; he was summoned to parliament from 1303 to 1305. His mother was sister of Sir Bartholomew Badlesmere, of Badlesmere and Chilham Castle, Kent.

Family background and education The course of Burghersh's university career suggests a probable birth date of c.1290. He was one of a large family: in 1332 he had one surviving brother, Bartholomew *Burghersh (d. 1355), and three surviving sisters, Katherine, Margaret, and Joan, but a further five brothers (Stephen, Robert, Reginald, Guncelin, and John) and two sisters (Juliana and Cecily) had already died by that date. Stephen and Robert were certainly older than Henry, and Bartholomew probably younger. In 1320 Bishop Thomas Cobham of Worcester (d. 1327) noted that Henry Burghersh had studied at various universities for more than fifteen years. The place of his early studies is not known but there is strong indirect evidence linking his elder brother Robert with Oxford and it is possible that Henry too spent some time there. His studies were financed in part from the income of the church of Whitstable, Kent, to which he was instituted in 1311. By 1319 he had attained the degree of *magister*, and had embarked on the study of civil and canon law at the University of Angers.

Although Burghersh came from a minor baronial family, it is unlikely that this alone would have furthered his ecclesiastical career to any great extent. Of far greater importance was the influence of his maternal uncle, Sir Bartholomew *Badlesmere, who progressed from the retinue of the earl of Gloucester to the royal service and, during the years 1318–20, enjoyed the king's especial favour. Under Badlesmere's patronage the career of Burghersh blossomed. It was Badlesmere who presented him to Whitstable, and it was no doubt his influence that secured his appointment as a king's clerk some time before November 1316, in which month he obtained a royal grant of the prebend of Riccall in York Minster.

Bishop of Lincoln The exercise of Badlesmere's influence in favour of his nephew culminated in the elevation of Burghersh to the episcopate. Two attempts were needed for this. When Bishop John Sandale of Winchester died on 2 November 1319, the king, at Badlesmere's instigation, pressed the claims of Burghersh, but without success. Meanwhile the pope had reserved the provision of the see of Lincoln at the next vacancy. On the death of Bishop John Dalderby on 12 January 1320 the chapter of Lincoln elected first their dean (Henry Mamesfeld) and later their chancellor (Antony (II) Bek) but they were overruled by the earlier papal reservation. The king once more petitioned on behalf of Burghersh, who this time was accepted. The new bishop was consecrated at Boulogne on 20 July 1320.

The comments of contemporary chroniclers on this appointment were almost without exception unfavourable. They especially condemned the procedure by which Burghersh obtained the bishopric—the quashing of the election by the cathedral chapter, and in its place a provision by the pope at the urgent instigation of the king. Dark hints were made of a pecuniary transaction. At the same time the new bishop was held to be unsuitable for the position: it was said that he was too young and inexperienced for such high office. Such criticisms may, however, be viewed with reservation. The appointment of bishops by papal provision following nomination by the crown was at this date becoming standard procedure. If Burghersh was indeed technically too young for the episcopate, his putative date of birth would mean that he was only one year away from the canonically required age of thirty. He may have lacked experience of ecclesiastical administration, but he would appear to have been well grounded in learning.

The point on which Burghersh was most heavily criticized in the chronicles, however, was the charge that he turned against the king, to whom he was largely indebted for his promotion. In the rebellion of Thomas of Lancaster, which ended at the battle of Boroughbridge on 16 March 1322, the fortunes of Burghersh were inextricably linked with those of his uncle Badlesmere. The move by which Badlesmere in June 1321 turned against the king and joined the opposition, headed by Lancaster, may have come as a surprise to his nephew who, only a few weeks earlier, had ordered prayers to be said throughout Lincoln diocese for the king and for the repulse of his enemies. At the meeting of parliament in November 1321 Burghersh was still, with other bishops, attempting to mediate between the two sides but by the following month the king had convinced himself that the bishop of Lincoln, like his uncle, was now an enemy of the crown, and that he was using the revenues of the see to sustain the opposition. Furious royal letters were sent to the pope demanding Burghersh's removal from the bishopric and, from the beginning of 1322, the temporalities of the see began to be taken into the king's hands.

Outside the king's letters there is no evidence that Burghersh gave such active support to the rebels. The bishop's registers indicate that he remained in Lincoln, engaged on diocesan business, throughout the period of the rebellion. The king's reaction would appear to be exactly the kind of conspiracy theory that a man of Edward's personality would seize upon. Nevertheless, the events of 1322 were a personal tragedy for Burghersh—his temporalities confiscated, his brother Bartholomew imprisoned in the Tower of London, and his uncle (to whom the bishop had provided a refuge after Boroughbridge) seized and executed.

Involvements in politics The breach between Edward II and Burghersh was not to be healed. From the king's point of view any kinsman of the traitor Badlesmere must also be tainted with his betrayal. From the bishop's point of view the loss of his temporalities (they were not restored until March 1324) deprived him of a substantial part of his episcopal income and the position was exacerbated by the royal claim to present to benefices in the bishop's gift. On a personal level the continued imprisonment of Bartholomew Burghersh prevented any easing of the hostile relationship between king and bishop. It is not necessary, however, to argue from this, as did the chronicler Geoffrey Baker, that during these years Burghersh was engaged in a plot to remove Edward from the throne. The reasons for the disaffection of Queen Isabella from the king, and for her subsequent alliance with Mortimer, are largely to be found in her treatment at the hands of Edward and the Despensers. Burghersh's own movements during this period are shown by his registers to have been almost entirely within his diocese, where he was engaged in its administration. The suggestion that, on the landing of Isabella and Mortimer at Orwell, Suffolk, on 24 September 1326, Burghersh was among the first to hasten to their side derives originally from the chronicle of Adam Murimuth. The episcopal registers tell a very different story. When news of the invasion reached Burghersh, he was in Buckinghamshire, probably on his way to Biddlesden. His first instinct was to retreat to the protection of his castle at Banbury in Oxfordshire, and then, when the westward march of the queen's force brought it uncomfortably close, to withdraw further north to Daventry. These seem to be less the movements of one who had been engaged in a lengthy plot to engineer the invasion, than the reaction of a man who had learned from the traumatic events of 1322 the dangers of becoming involved in the politics of Edward II's reign.

Despite this initial hesitation it was not long before Burghersh decided to give his support to the invaders. He was with them at Gloucester on 20 October, and six days later at Bristol, when Prince Edward was appointed keeper of the realm. The deposition of the king and the assumption of power by Isabella and Mortimer opened the way for Burghersh to become involved in government. On 25 March 1327 he was appointed treasurer of the exchequer, a post that involved him in preparations for the forthcoming campaign against the Scots. On 12 May 1328, during the Northampton parliament at which the peace with Scotland was ratified, he was appointed chancellor.

This close involvement with Isabella and Mortimer brought with it the danger of becoming associated with the excesses of their regime. It was said that Burghersh was present with Mortimer when the surprise attack took place at Nottingham Castle on the night of 19 October 1330. The Bridlington chronicler inferred from this that the bishop, like Mortimer, was arrested and imprisoned. That this story is incorrect is demonstrated not only by the fact that Burghersh was not replaced as chancellor until 28 November, but also by the evidence of the episcopal registers which show him to have been at liberty throughout this period. Indeed, the king's attitude to Burghersh in the aftermath of the coup does not seem to have been unfavourable and, beyond relieving him of his office, he exacted no other penalty despite the 'envious whisperings' of some who had become hostile to the bishop through his association with Mortimer.

Administrator and bishop Unlike his father, Edward III was clearly determined not to alienate those he thought might prove to be useful in his service. Despite Burghersh's equivocal position after the Nottingham coup, less than four years later, on 1 August 1334, he was once more appointed treasurer, and held this post until 24 March 1337. He was then appointed to the first of a series of diplomatic missions to the Low Countries, whose aim was to seek offensive alliances against the king of France. He was to remain abroad, apart from two short visits to England, until his death at Ghent on 4 December 1340.

Burghersh seems to have been an efficient administrator; the fact that he held office under both Mortimer and Edward III indicates that his ability in the management of business was an attraction to whoever was in power. The suggestion that he used the office of chancellor for his own ends is based on the isolated complaint of a disgruntled candidate for a benefice in the king's gift; self-seeking was endemic in the Mortimer regime, but it seems unlikely that Burghersh would have been recalled to office in 1334 if he had been tainted in this way.

Burghersh's association with the Lancaster rebellion in 1322 and his lengthy periods in secular administration after 1327 have led to the conclusion that he was more of a politician than a bishop. His episcopal registers, on the other hand, reveal that he was at all times conscientious in the execution of diocesan business. To take but two instances: at Worcester as chancellor in 1330, and at Berwick as treasurer in 1335, he nevertheless found time to institute clerks to benefices, grant letters dimissory for ordination and licences for manorial chapels, and issue commissions for hearing ecclesiastical causes. Even when, in the later years of his life, he was out of the country altogether, he ensured that the administration of the diocese would continue to run smoothly by appointing as his vicar-general a man of the calibre of Simon Islip, the future archbishop of Canterbury (d. 1366). The character of Henry Burghersh is perhaps best summed up by the Leicester chronicler, Henry Knighton: 'a man of great distinction, wise in counsel, urbanely bold, of outstanding powers, and a shrewd manager of fighting men' (*Knighton's Chronicle*, 27–9).

After his death Burghersh's body was brought back to Lincoln Cathedral, where it was buried in a position of the greatest honour, beside the head shrine of St Hugh. The tomb chest, surmounted by the effigy of the bishop, remains; its canopy had been removed by the early nineteenth century. The chantry founded for his soul at the adjacent altar of St Katherine flourished until the dissolution.   NICHOLAS BENNETT

Sources N. H. Bennett, 'The beneficed clergy in the diocese of Lincoln ... 1320–1340', DPhil diss., University of York, 1989 · Lincs. Arch., episcopal registers nos. 4, 5, 5B · B. Wilkinson, 'The authorisation of chancery writs under Edward III', *Bulletin of the John Rylands University Library*, 8 (1924), 107–39 · *Knighton's chronicle, 1337–1396*, ed. and trans. G. H. Martin, OMT (1995) [Lat. orig., *Chronica de eventibus Angliae a tempore regis Edgari usque mortem regis Ricardi Secundi*, with parallel Eng. text] · *Chronicon Galfridi le Baker de Swynebroke*, ed. E. M. Thompson (1889) · *Adae Murimuth continuatio chronicarum. Robertus de Avesbury de gestis mirabilibus regis Edwardi tertii*, ed. E. M. Thompson, Rolls Series, 93 (1889) · C. W. Foster and A. H. Thompson, 'The chantry certificates for Lincoln and Lincolnshire', *Associated Architectural Societies' Reports and Papers*, 36 (1922)
Archives Lincs. Arch., episcopal registers nos. 4, 5, 5B
Likenesses tomb effigy, c.1300–1399, Lincoln Cathedral

Burghill [Burghull], **John** (c.1330–1414), bishop of Coventry and Lichfield, was the son of Thomas Burghill and his wife, Sibylla; heraldry links his father with the Burghills of Burghill, in Herefordshire; his mother's arms were a version of Peverel of Leicestershire. His family background is otherwise obscure. His will mentions two brothers (William and Thomas) and also two nephews, presumably the sons of at least one sister.

Burghill became a Dominican, being presumably a member of the Hereford house when ordained acolyte in March 1350 and priest in September 1354 by Bishop Trillek. These dates indicate that he was born in the early 1330s. His pre-episcopal career was tied to that of Thomas Rushook, warden of the Hereford Dominicans in the 1350s and later (having become confessor to Richard II) bishop of Llandaff, Chichester, and Kilmore. Burghill followed Rushook to the royal household, as his companion or chaplain. The early 1380s reveal him collecting corrodies, on the king's nomination, and receiving tithes from a forfeited alien priory. His Gloucester corrody caused litigation between 1388 and 1392, following an 'inadvertent' displacement which may have been a side-effect of political turmoil. In 1394 Burghill became king's confessor, and participated in Richard II's expedition to Ireland that year. On 12 April 1396 he was provided to the see of Llandaff, being consecrated at Rome.

Burghill's provision to Coventry and Lichfield on 2 July 1398 was probably fortuitous. On Richard Scrope's translation to York earlier that year, his intended successor was John Buckingham, the bishop of Lincoln. (Whether his move was being orchestrated to allow Henry Beaufort to acquire Lincoln is unclear.) Buckingham left Lincoln but declined Lichfield, and died later that year. Burghill was then nominated, obviously because of his familiarity with the king (who lent 1000 marks to cover his dues to the papacy), but probably not as a political act. His enthronement on 8 September 1398 was attended by Richard II, several nobles, and three archbishops (of York, Canterbury, and Dublin). Initially Burghill was an absentee, spending much of his time in attendance on the king, whom he accompanied to Ireland in 1399. That expedition gave the opportunity for Henry Bolingbroke's invasion and Richard II's removal from the throne, a revolution to which Burghill was probably an eyewitness.

Under Henry IV Burghill concentrated on his episcopal duties, rarely leaving his diocese. His principal residences were first Eccleshall and later Heywood, both in Staffordshire. This may have been a reaction to the events of 1399: Burghill remained loyal to Richard II's memory, being the sole bishop to attend his interment at Kings Langley on 14 March 1400. His own tomb became the new site for the chantry in Lichfield Cathedral that Richard Scrope had founded for himself and Richard II. However, his loyalty was pragmatic: he did not join any of the Ricardian plots of the early 1400s. From 1400 he had effectively retired from the national scene, possibly as a result of advancing age: he seems not to have attended any parliaments after 1399.

As bishop, Burghill fostered both his cathedral churches. At Coventry he promoted the cult of St Osberga, whose relics lay in the priory. To acknowledge his support an annual commemoration was established for him in 1409. He also supported Lichfield, making gifts of vestments and aiding the vicars-choral. By August 1409 his tomb had been constructed near the high altar, and here he was eventually buried. Burghill died in 1414, a grant of the temporalities *sede vacante* issuing on 20 May. His character is obscure, although Adam Usk calls him *vir avarissimus*. His will, made on 21 June 1412, scattered bequests widely, much going to religious houses. His arms in stained glass were depicted at several points in Lichfield Cathedral, with representations of himself and family members over the south door; but these have all disappeared.

R. N. SWANSON

Sources H. E. Savage, *Bishop John Burghull: an address given on the festival of St Chad, 1924* (1924) · register, Joint RO, Lichfield, B/A/1/7 · Canterbury Cathedral Archives, DCC/Reg. G. · *Chancery records* · R. G. Davies, 'Richard II and the church in the years of "tyranny"', *Journal of Medieval History*, 1 (1975), 329–62 · S. Shaw, *The history and antiquities of Staffordshire*, 1 (1798) · Joint RO, Lichfield, D30/I [Chapter Act Book] · C. F. R. Palmer, 'Fasti ordinis fratrum praedicatorum: the provincials of the friar-preachers, or Black friars, of England', *Archaeological Journal*, 35 (1878), 134–65 · R. G. Davies, 'The attendance of the episcopate in English parliaments, 1376–1461', *Proceedings of the American Philosophical Society*, 129 (1985), 30–81 · J. H. Parry, ed., *Registrum Johannis de Trillek*, CYS, 8 (1912) · *Chronicon Adae de Usk*, ed. and trans. E. M. Thompson, 2nd edn (1904)
Archives Joint RO, Lichfield, register, B/A/1/7
Likenesses stained glass, repro. in Shaw, *History and antiquities*
Wealth at death see will, Canterbury Cathedral Archives, DCC/Reg. G

Burghley. For this title name *see* Cecil, William, first Baron Burghley (1520/21–1598); Cecil, Mildred, Lady Burghley (1526–1589).

Burginda (*fl.* 7th–early 8th cent.), author, wrote a letter to an unnamed 'youth', which survives in a unique (non-autograph) copy in a manuscript formerly at St Bertin and now at Boulogne, Bibliothèque Municipale, MS 74 (82); the main item is an eighth-century southern English copy of Apponius's *Commentary on the Song of Songs*. Her name may be a latinization of an unattested Old English name Burgyth. The manuscript may have been written in the diocese of Worcester, to judge by its decoration, and possibly at Bath monastery, whence books seem to have travelled to St Bertin. Burginda herself should perhaps be located in Bath monastery: it is difficult to see why her poor letter would be copied far afield. Despite the weakness of its Latin, Burginda's letter is an important piece of early evidence for female education. In expressing her admiration for the 'illustrious youth' and urging him on to further spiritual endeavours, she shows herself familiar with current epistolary conventions, and quotes or echoes Virgil's *Aeneid* and *Georgics*, the anonymous *Carmen ad Flavium Felicem de resurrectione mortuorum et de judicio domini*, and the Christian Latin poet Arator. Her reading thus resembles that of Aldhelm of Malmesbury.

PATRICK SIMS-WILLIAMS

Sources P. Sims-Williams, *Religion and literature in western England, 600–800* (1990) · P. Sims-Williams, *Britain and early Christian Europe: studies in early medieval history and culture* (1995) · P. Sims-Williams, 'An unpublished seventh- or eighth-century Anglo-Latin letter in Boulogne-sur-Mer MS 74 (82)', *Medium Ævum*, 48 (1979), 1–22 · *Apponii: in canticum canticorum expositionem*, ed. B. de Vregille and L. Neyrand (Turnhout, 1986)
Archives Bibliothèque Municipale, Boulogne, MS 74 (82)

Burgis, Edward [*name in religion* Ambrose] (1673?–1747), Dominican friar, was a native of Bristol and the son of a clergyman of the Church of England, but nothing else is known about his origins. On becoming a Dominican friar at Naples in 1697 he assumed the name of Ambrose. He passed through the highest offices of his order with distinguished credit, and served as rector of Louvain during 1718–30 'with great prudence and ability' (Kirk, 38). He was elected provincial of his order in 1730, and was resident in London from 1730 to 1735. Installed as prior of Bornhem Abbey in 1741, he was vicar provincial and vicar-general for Belgium from 1746. Burgis wrote *An Introduction to the Catholic Church* (1709), as well as *The Annals of the Church* (5 vols., 1738). He died at Brussels on 27 April 1747.

THOMPSON COOPER, *rev.* ROBERT BROWN

Sources G. Oliver, *Collections illustrating the history of the Catholic religion in the counties of Cornwall, Devon, Dorset, Somerset, Wilts, and Gloucester* (1857) · H. Foley, ed., *Records of the English province of the Society of Jesus*, 7 vols. in 8 (1875–83) · J. Kirk, *Biographies of English Catholics in the eighteenth century*, ed. J. H. Pollen and E. Burton (1909) · C. F. R. Palmer, *Obituary notices of the friary preachers, or Dominicans, of the English province, from … 1650* (1884)

Burgo, Nicholas de (*fl.* 1517–1537), theologian and Franciscan friar, was a native of Florence and BTh of Paris. About 1517 he began to lecture in Oxford. He was incorporated BTh there in February 1523. After seventeen years' study in logic, philosophy, and theology, he supplicated for admission as DTh in January 1524. He asked to be released from paying his composition to the university since he was a foreigner, knew no English, and had publicly lectured for the past seven years virtually gratis. He incepted in August 1524.

De Burgo became lecturer in theology at Magdalen College, Oxford, for which he was paid £10 yearly between 1525/6 and 1535/6, by when he had resigned his lectureship. He was recruited by Thomas Wolsey as public reader in theology at Cardinal College, Oxford; his salary in 1529/30 was £20. In 1532 he was named reader in theology at Cardinal College's successor, King Henry VIII College.

Originally a client of Wolsey, on whose command he received £5 in November 1528, de Burgo also began to enjoy the king's favour from the summer of 1529. As 'one of the king's spiritual learned counsel', he received £6 13s. 4d. in July 'by way of reward' (*LP Henry VIII*, 5.313). The following month Henry asked Wolsey to arrange a benefice for de Burgo; in January 1530 he was admitted to the canonry and prebend of Timsbury in Romsey Abbey, Hampshire. He still held the benefice in 1535, when it was worth £35 12s. 8½d. On 25 January 1530 he received a grant of denization as well as a further sum of money from the king.

De Burgo was prominent in the campaign to secure Henry's first divorce. He was one of a group of scholars who were responsible for producing treatises in favour of the divorce, and for defending the king's case generally. In late 1529, when Thomas More asked to confer with those of Henry's learned counsel who had laboured most in the king's 'matter', Henry appointed de Burgo, along with Thomas Cranmer, Edward Foxe, and Edward Lee. In 1530 he was among the royal agents sent to Oxford to persuade the university to vote in favour of the divorce. So unpopular were de Burgo and another of the king's delegates, John Longland, bishop of Lincoln, that they were pelted with stones by the townswomen. When de Burgo complained, thirty women were imprisoned. He may also have been the Italian Franciscan, 'one of the chief writers in favour of the king', who in late 1531 was seen at court in conference with Robert Barnes (*LP Henry VIII*, 5, no. 593).

De Burgo's most significant contribution to the debate over the divorce was indeed as a writer. With Foxe and John Stokesley, he composed 'Henricus octavus', the treatise presented in the king's name to the second trial over his marriage in 1529. Much expanded and revised, this work was subsequently published, probably in the spring of 1531, as *Gravissimae, atque exactissimae illustrissimarum totius Italiae, et Galliae Academiarum censurae*. An English translation by Cranmer, *The determinations of the moste famous and mooste excellent universities of Italy and Fraunce*, appeared in November that year.

At the end of 1531, having disposed of his belongings in Oxford, de Burgo left for the London convent of his order and asked licence to return to Italy for his health. Longland advised Thomas Cromwell against allowing him to depart as he was so deeply involved in the divorce. In January 1533 de Burgo wrote to Cromwell, complaining that he had received neither remuneration for his duties as reader and his public lectures, nor the profits of his benefice; by June he had received £6 13s. 4d. from Cromwell. De Burgo was again in Oxford in August 1534 when he acted as vice-commissary of the university, but by October 1535 had with the king's permission returned to Italy. He hoped that he would retain his college place in Oxford and his benefice, which was worth, he said, £25 annually. In July 1537 he wrote again from Italy, repeating this request. Illness and trouble prevented him from coming to England but he promised to do so the following month. He does not appear to have returned, however, and it is not known when he died.   VIRGINIA MURPHY

Sources *LP Henry VIII*, vols. 4/3, 5–9, 12/2 · Register of Congregation and Convocation, 1518–35, U. Oxf. archives, NEP/*Supra*/Reg H, fols. 82v, 116v, 117r, 128r · A. G. Little, *The Grey Friars in Oxford*, OHS, 20 (1892) · Emden, *Oxf.*, 4.85–6 · *Reg. Oxf.*, 1.128 · *DNB* · E. Surtz and V. Murphy, eds., *The divorce tracts of Henry VIII* (1988) · Liber computi, 1525/6–1535/6, Magd. Oxf. · *CSP Spain*, 4/1 · W. Forrest, *The history of Griseld the Second*, ed. W. D. Macray, Roxburghe Club (1875) · H. Chitty, ed., *Registrum Thome Wolsey cardinalis ecclesie Wintoniensis administratoris*, CYS, 32 (1926), 63–6 · J. Caley, ed., *Valor ecclesiasticus*, RC, 2 (1814), 17 · exchequer, treasury of receipt, miscellaneous book, PRO, E36/104, fol. 9 · Chancellor's register, 1527–43, U. Oxf. archives, HYP/A/4, fols. 273, 274
Archives BL · PRO

Burgon, John William (1813–1888), dean of Chichester and biblical scholar, was born at Smyrna on 21 August 1813. His father **Thomas Burgon** (1787–1858), a Turkey merchant and member of the court of assistants of the Levant Company, moved from Smyrna to London in 1814 and settled at 11 Brunswick Square. His business declined after the Levant Company lost its monopoly in 1826, and it

collapsed altogether in 1841. An enthusiastic archaeologist and numismatist, Thomas Burgon was subsequently employed in the coin room of the British Museum, which had been enriched by the results of his excavations on Melos, and to which he now sold his collection of Greek antiquities. These included one of the earliest Panathenaic amphorae, which he had excavated near the Acharnian Gate at Athens in 1813. In 1847 he published in the *Transactions of the Royal Society of Literature* a seminal paper entitled 'An attempt to point out the vases of Greece proper which belong to the heroic and Homeric ages', which for the first time distinguished the geometric as a separate and universal stage in the development of Greek pottery, dating from the twelfth to the tenth century BC. Thomas Burgon's wife, Catherine Marguerite (1790–1854), was the daughter of the Chevalier Ambroise Hermann de Cramer, Austrian consul at Smyrna, and Sarah, daughter of William Maltass, a Turkey merchant. Sarah de Cramer's sister Mrs Jane Baldwin, *née* Maltass (1763–1839), was a celebrated beauty of her day, painted by Richard Cosway and Joshua Reynolds. The latter's portrait of her (1782) in Smyrniote costume, popularly known as 'The Fair Greek', became part of the marquess of Lansdowne's collection at Bowood.

Thomas and Catherine Burgon had two sons, John William being the elder, and four daughters. One of the latter, Sarah Caroline, married Henry John Rose (1800–1873), and another, Helen Eliza, married Charles Longuet Higgins (1806–1885). Catherine Burgon died on 7 September 1854; her husband died on 28 August 1858 at 3 Burton Crescent, St Pancras, London. Both were buried in Holywell cemetery, Oxford.

John William Burgon was only a few months old when the family returned to England. On the way they stopped at Athens, where their friend Charles Robert Cockerell (1788–1863) carried the infant up the Acropolis and playfully dedicated him to Athene. At the age of eleven Burgon was sent to a school at Putney kept by a brother of Alaric Watts (1797–1864), from which he transferred in 1828 to a private school at Blackheath. In 1829–30 he attended classes at London University, after which he entered his father's firm as a clerk. He shared his father's antiquarian tastes, and in 1832 published a translation of the monograph *On Panathenaic Vases* by the Danish archaeologist P. O. Brøndsted. Between 1837 and 1841 he contributed seven articles to John Yonge Akerman's *Numismatic Journal*. At his father's house he was introduced to a circle that included the architect Thomas Leverton Donaldson, the painter Charles Robert Leslie, and the poet Samuel Rogers. In 1836 he won a prize offered by the lord mayor of London for the best essay on Sir Thomas Gresham. This he subsequently extended into a two-volume *Life and Times* (1839), based on painstaking research into primary sources. While working at the Public Record Office he developed a close friendship with the Scottish historian Patrick Fraser Tytler (1791–1849), whose life he later wrote under the title *Portrait of a Christian Gentleman* (1859). In 1839 he began contributing to the *New General Biographical Dictionary*, edited by his brother-in-law Henry John Rose.

The collapse of Thomas Burgon's business in 1841 left his son free, with the financial aid of his friend Dawson Turner (1775–1858), to fulfil his long-standing wish to prepare himself for orders. John Burgon matriculated from Worcester College, Oxford, on 21 October 1841 and graduated BA in 1845 with a second class in classics. His disappointment at not securing a first class was counterbalanced by his success in winning the Newdigate prize the same year with his poem 'Petra'. Its much parodied couplet

Match me such marvel, save in eastern clime,
A rose-red city half as old as time

may owe something to a reminiscence of a line in Samuel Rogers's *Italy* ('By many a temple half as old as time').

Burgon's relative failure in the schools was partly attributable to overwork. Nor was he at ease in the role of undergraduate: he was set apart from his contemporaries by age and tastes, and nothing in his previous life had prepared him for the give and take of college society. Nature had intended him to be a don, and he achieved this state with his election to a fellowship at Oriel in 1846. He graduated MA in 1848 and was ordained priest on 23 December 1849. From 1849 to 1853, while still residing at Oriel, he served successive curacies at West Ilsley, Berkshire, and at Worton and Finmere in Oxfordshire. There he fulfilled his pastoral duties with immense conscientiousness.

At Oxford Burgon dedicated himself to biblical scholarship, while continuing his antiquarian pursuits. His interest in heraldry is displayed in the 'Historical notices of the colleges of Oxford', which he contributed to Henry Shaw's *Arms of the Colleges of Oxford* (1855). In 1860 he spent three months in Rome as acting chaplain to the English community there, and from September 1861 to July 1862 made a tour of Egypt, Palestine, and the Sinai peninsula, where he examined the manuscripts of St Catherine's. At Petra he was disconcerted to find 'nothing rosy'. On returning to Oxford he was appointed on 15 October 1863 as vicar of the university church of St Mary's. There for the next twelve years he occupied the pulpit made famous by J. H. Newman, whose afternoon services he revived. Henceforward he was an indefatigable champion of lost causes and impossible beliefs, though the vehemence of his advocacy somewhat impaired its effectiveness. A high-churchman of the old school, he was as opposed to Romanism and ritualism as he was to rationalism and every form of liberalism. In 1869 he denounced the disestablishment of the Irish church as 'the nation's formal rejection of God', and he was even more scandalized by the appointment of Frederick Temple (1821–1902) to the bishopric of Exeter in the same year. He was as irrepressible in pamphleteering as in preaching: wherever a breach was made in the battlements of tradition, he was in the forefront of the defence. Among the measures he opposed were the removal of the Athanasian creed from morning service and the suppression of its damnatory clauses, the reform of the lectionary, and the legalization of marriage with a deceased wife's sister. In 1872 he led the opposition to the appointment of Dean Stanley as select preacher.

In university politics Burgon was equally reactionary.

He opposed the abolition of religious tests as a condition of admission. The election of Eleanor Elizabeth Smith to the first Oxford school board in 1870 was made the occasion for a sermon entitled 'Woman's place', in which he deplored the appearance of women on public bodies and argued that their place, like Sarah's, was 'in the tent' (Genesis 18:9). The admission of women to university examinations in 1884 inspired a further outburst from the pulpit, subsequently published under the title *To Educate Young Women Like Young Men and with Young Men: a Thing Inexpedient and Immodest*. More positively, he urged the importance of a systematic study of ancient and medieval art, and in 1855 successfully advocated the establishment of a school of theology.

In November 1875 Disraeli offered Burgon the deanery of Chichester in succession to Walter Farquhar Hook. He accepted it, and was installed on 19 January 1876. He found Chichester to be, in his own words, a 'sleepy hollow', and his relations with the chapter were strained, largely on account of his abrasiveness. He continued to be prominent in controversy, waging a vigorous campaign against the Revised Version of the New Testament, published in 1881. His first work of biblical scholarship, published in 1871, had been a vindication of the last twelve verses of St Mark's gospel, and when the revisers threw doubt on the authenticity of these verses by placing them in brackets he attacked them for this and other delinquencies in a series of articles for the *Quarterly Review*, later published as *The Revision Revised* (1883). His criticism of the overreliance of the editors, B. F. Westcott and F. J. A. Hort, on the Vatican and Sinai codices for their recension has been sustained by more recent scholars, and his strictures on the style of the revised text were endorsed by Matthew Arnold. Burgon's attack seriously affected the popularity of the new version. He himself was a strenuous advocate of the doctrine of verbal inspiration and adhered to a strictly literal interpretation of scripture. His two posthumously published works in defence of the *textus receptus* of the New Testament (1896) are considered to be the most thorough exposition of the conservative view.

From Chichester Burgon continued to voice his opinions on university affairs. In 1876 he invited ridicule by attacking the lodging-house system as dangerous to undergraduate morals, alleging that some lodging-house keepers recruited servant girls from the local penitentiary. Lord Salisbury nominated him the same year to the parliamentary commission on university reform, but the appointment was greeted with such opposition that Burgon had to withdraw. Shortly before his death he completed what was to be his most popular work, the *Lives of Twelve Good Men* (2 vols., 1888), a revisionist account of the Oxford Movement which removed Newman from centre stage and presented a group portrait of loyalist Tractarians, pride of place being given to Hugh James Rose. Both provocative and evocative, the work is a classic of nineteenth-century ecclesiastical biography.

Burgon died unmarried at the deanery, Chichester, on 4 August 1888. His remains were conveyed to Oxford and buried in the family grave at Holywell cemetery on 11

August. He is commemorated at Chichester by a window in the lady chapel and a brass monument in the pavement of the south transept designed by Thomas Garner and G. F. Bodley. At Oxford his friends and admirers subscribed to a memorial window at the west end of St Mary's designed by C. E. Kempe. Burgon was portrayed by his enemies as a buffoon and a fanatic. In private he was warm-hearted and loyal, fond of the company of women and children. Impulsive, quixotic, and ingenuous, he inspired a grudging affection even in those who regarded his opinions as perverse.   G. MARTIN MURPHY

Sources E. M. Goulburn, *John William Burgon, late dean of Chichester: a biography*, 2 vols. (1892) · G. W. E. Russell, *The household of faith* (1902), 95–131 · W. R. Ward, *Victorian Oxford* (1965) · O. Chadwick, *The Victorian church*, 2nd edn, 2 (1972), 52–4 · R. M. Cook, *Greek painted pottery* (1960) · A. M. A. H. Rogers, *Degrees by degrees* (1938) · H. A. Morrah, *The Oxford Union, 1823–1923* (1923) · *The Times* (6 Aug 1888) · *The Times* (13 Aug 1888) · *CGPLA Eng. & Wales* (1888) · *CGPLA Eng. & Wales* (1858) [Thomas Burgon] · *The Athenaeum* (11 Sept 1858) **Archives** BL, collation of Greek gospel MSS and New Testament index, Add. MSS 33421–33436, 39317 · Bodl. Oxf., corresp., pamphlets, and sermons; glossary of Bedfordshire provincialisms; press cuttings of articles by him with notes and additions · GL, letters · Oriel College, Oxford, letters · Worcester College, Oxford, collections relating to Worcester College | BL, corresp. with W. E. Gladstone, Add. MSS 44375–44489, *passim* · BL, letters to Joseph Hunter, Add. MS 24866, fols. 84–218, 223–59 · Bodl. Oxf., letters to Benjamin Disraeli · Bodl. Oxf., letters to Samuel Wilberforce · Bodl. Oxf., letters mainly to Ella Monier-Williams · Keble College, Oxford, letters to H. P. Liddon · LPL, letters to Charles Golightly; corresp. with Roundell Parker · Pusey Oxf., letters to Robert Scott · Pusey Oxf., Swift MSS · Suffolk RO, Ipswich, letters to Lord Cranbrook · Trinity Cam., letters to Dawson Turner · U. Edin. L., letters to James Orchard Halliwell-Phillipps · UCL, letters to W. Sharpe **Likenesses** S. Hall, caricature, 1867, repro. in Morrah, *The Oxford Union*, 299 · W. E. Miller, crayon drawing, 1882, Oriel College, Oxford · photographs, repro. in Goulburn, *John William Burgon* **Wealth at death** £11,424 12s. 4d.: resworn probate, March 1890, *CGPLA Eng. & Wales* (1888) · under £300—Thomas Burgon: administration, 16 Sept 1858

Burgon, Thomas (1787–1858). *See under* Burgon, John William (1813–1888).

Burgoyne, Hugh Talbot (1833–1870), naval officer, only son of Field Marshal Sir John Fox *Burgoyne (1782–1871) and his wife, Charlotte (*d.* 1871), daughter of Hugh Rose of Holme, Inverness-shire, was born in Dublin in 1833. He entered the navy in 1847, was promoted lieutenant on 11 January 1854 and on 20 March was appointed to the *Boscawen*, in which he served for a few months in the Baltic. When the *Boscawen* returned to England, Burgoyne was appointed on 16 September to the *Swallow*, in which he went to the Mediterranean. The *Swallow* was attached to the fleet before Sevastopol, and on 29 May 1855, after Genichersk had been shelled, Burgoyne volunteered to land, with Lieutenant Cecil Buckley and a companion named Roberts, and burn the Russian stores. This was a dangerous service, and was rewarded with the Victoria Cross when it was instituted in the following year. Burgoyne was then appointed to the command of the dispatch gunboat *Wrangler*, in which he continued actively employed for the rest of the war.

Burgoyne was made commander on 10 May 1856, and on

16 July 1857 was appointed to the *Ganges*, bearing the flag of Rear-Admiral Baynes in the Pacific. He continued in the *Ganges* until she was paid off, then was promoted captain on 15 May 1861. In 1863 he accompanied Captain Sherard *Osborn to China, as second in command of the Anglo-Chinese flotilla. When Osborn resigned the appointment on a disagreement with the Chinese government, the post (with an unusually liberal pay) was immediately offered to Burgoyne, who, however, declined it, being no more disposed than Osborn to submit himself to the Chinese authorities. As the junior officers followed his example, the flotilla was broken up, and Burgoyne returned to England.

In 1864 Burgoyne married Evelyn Laura, daughter of Admiral Sir Baldwin Wake Walker: she survived her husband. Burgoyne was appointed on 27 September 1865 to command the *Wivern*, a small turret ship, in which he continued for the next two years, when he was appointed (22 October 1867) to the frigate *Constance* on the North American station.

Towards the close of 1868 the *Constance* was paid off, and Burgoyne was appointed to superintend the building, fitting out, and first commission of the *Captain*, the controversial low-freeboard, full-rigged turret ship designed by Captain Cowper Phipps Coles. In July 1870 she had a first cruise in the channel and the Bay of Biscay; she appeared to be an easy and comfortable sea-boat, and was spoken of as the steadiest platform for guns ever afloat. Burgoyne reported officially that the ship had 'proved herself a most efficient vessel both under sail and steam, as well as easy and comfortable'. In August she accompanied the Channel Fleet to Gibraltar.

On 6 September the fleet, on its return voyage, was off Cape Finisterre; Sir Alexander Milne, the commander-in-chief, visited the ship and was struck by her extreme lowness in the water, such that with a light breeze the water was washing over the lee side of the deck and striking the after turret to a depth of about 18 inches to 2 feet. He said to Captain Coles, who had come in a private capacity, 'I cannot reconcile myself to this state of things so very unusual in all my experience'. Still there was no thought of danger, and Sir Alexander went back to his ship puzzled rather than alarmed. That evening the wind rose. The ships were screened from each other's sight, but there had been plenty of warning, and the storm was of no alarming strength. About twenty minutes past midnight a fresh squall struck the ships; the *Captain* immediately heeled over, had no power of recovery, turned completely over bottom upwards, and sank. Most of her officers and men were below, and went down with her; of those who were on deck only eighteen managed to scramble into the launch, which had been thrown out when the ship was on the point of capsizing, and were saved. Burgoyne, with some few men, managed to climb onto the bottom of the ship's pinnace; and as the launch drifted near, the men jumped and were picked up. Whether from exhaustion, or from a determination not to survive the loss of his ship, Burgoyne refused to jump, and he was never seen again.

The loss of the *Captain* exposed the fragility of the Victorian fleet and the poor design of some of its capital ships. Burgoyne was not blamed by the subsequent court-martial and the various inquiries, and was commemorated, with his crew, by a plaque in St Paul's Cathedral.

J. K. LAUGHTON, *rev.* ROGER MORRISS

Sources R. W. O'Byrne, *The Victorian cross* (1880), 45 · *Minutes of the proceedings of the court-martial on the loss of HMS Captain, published by order of the lords commissioners of the admiralty*, PRO · G. Wrottesley, *Life and correspondence of Field Marshal Sir John Fox Burgoyne*, 2 (1873) · *Annual Register* (1870) · Burke, *Peerage* · Gladstone, *Diaries* · *CGPLA Eng. & Wales* (1871)
Wealth at death under £600: administration, 16 March 1871, *CGPLA Eng. & Wales*

Burgoyne, John (1723–1792), army officer, politician, and playwright, was born on 4 February 1723 at Park Prospect, Westminster, legally the son of Captain John Burgoyne (*d.* 1768) and his wife, Anna Maria, daughter of Charles Burneston of Hackney, but possibly fathered by Robert Benson, Baron Bingley (1675/6–1731), a Yorkshire politician who left Anna Maria an independent income and made Burgoyne, his godson, his heir should the issue of his legitimate daughter fail. He was educated at Westminster School, where he made friends with James Smith Stanley, Baron Strange (1717–1771), eldest son of Edward Stanley, eleventh earl of Derby. In 1737 a commission was purchased for him as sub-brigadier in the third troop of Horse Guards. He sold out in 1741, but returned in 1744 as a cornet in the 1st (Royal) Dragoons. He was promoted lieutenant in 1745, and purchased a captaincy in 1747. In 1751 he eloped with Strange's sister, Lady Charlotte Stanley (*d.* 1776), whom he married on 14 April. The oft-repeated statement that the couple eloped as early as 1743 seems to be without foundation; the promotions of 1744 and 1745 were not purchased with Derby's allowance to his daughter but were a new appointment and on grounds of seniority. Following his marriage Burgoyne sold his commission and the couple travelled in France and Italy until, with the birth of a daughter, they returned to England in 1755 and were reconciled with Lord Derby. In 1756 he purchased a captain's commission in the eleventh dragoons, and during the Seven Years' War, in 1758, distinguished himself in action in a landing near St Malo. For this William Pitt in 1759 named him lieutenant-colonel to recruit a new regiment, the sixteenth light dragoons. He proved an adept organizer and an enlightened disciplinarian. In 1762, with the local rank of brigadier-general in the campaign in Portugal, he dramatically captured Valencia de Alcántara, across the border in Spain, and then secured control of the Tagus River, thereby saving Lisbon from Spanish seizure. For this he was promoted full colonel.

Burgoyne was elected to parliament in 1761 from Midhurst, Sussex, through the patronage of his friend Sir William Peere Williams. With a deep-rooted reverence for the British constitution as a firm bulwark in the defence of the liberty of the British subject, he voted against the repeal of the Stamp Act in 1765 and supported the Declaratory Act of 1766 on the ground that neither measure threatened liberties of speech, religion, or the person.

John Burgoyne (1723–1792), by Sir Joshua Reynolds, 1766

Sensing the approach of war with France, he embarked on a scouting tour of European armies in order to enlarge his expertise as a claim to military promotion, and he submitted to Pitt a position paper advocating British development of cavalry second to none.

War, however, did not come, and Burgoyne, deprived of his parliamentary seat from Midhurst by the death of his patron, Williams, stood for a seat from the borough of Preston in 1768 with the support of Lord Derby. Contending with the corporation interest, which in previous decades had returned tory members rather than administration whigs such as Burgoyne, he campaigned in the streets with a pistol under one arm and another in his pocket. Violence erupted, and when the tory mayor disqualified more than 600 ballots for Burgoyne and his running mate, Sir Henry Hoghton, they appealed to parliament, which seated them, reinterpreting the 1661 resolution of parliament enfranchising the inhabitants of the borough to include all male residents rather than only the resident freemen. However, as a consequence of his armed campaign, Burgoyne was fined £1000 for inciting violence. He still hoped for war with France, and when France's ally Spain in 1770 seized the British naval station at Fort Egremont in the Falkland Islands he supported Chatham's ultimatum to which Spain, to their disappointment, yielded.

In 1772, during the North ministry, Burgoyne turned his attention to corruption in the East India Company. As chairman of an investigating committee, he attempted to obtain censure of Governor Robert Clive for illegally acquiring £234,000. He was not supported by North, and in the debate he was accused by the solicitor-general, Alexander Wedderburn, of the unproven charge by the anonymous 'Junius' of bribery and card-sharping.

Nevertheless, Burgoyne emerged as an advocate of the North ministry's decision for repression of the American colonies as punishment for their defiance of the Coercive Acts. He declared in parliament that 'the soldier draws his sword with alacrity'. He had enough, he said, of disputes over 'real and virtual representation, external and internal taxes, revenue and regulation, till one's head grows dizzy with distinctions' (Almon, 1.152). He requested a military assignment from the king and was appointed in February 1775, with Sir William Howe and Henry Clinton, to join General Thomas Gage, the commander in America, and spur him to energetic suppression of the rebels in Boston. All three were promoted major-general, but Howe had seniority. He commanded the troops at the battle of Bunker Hill, while Burgoyne, as the junior of the three, participated only by providing artillery cover from the mainland at Copp's Hill. Seeing little prospect of a significant command, he requested return home. On his arrival he found that the warlike Lord George Germain had replaced the conciliatory William Legge, second earl of Dartmouth, as secretary of state for the colonies. Burgoyne submitted to Germain 'Reflections upon the war in America', in which he proposed a campaign by mating armies from Canada and New York city to seal off New England from the other colonies. Germain decided to send 10,000 troops to rescue Sir Guy Carleton, commander in Canada, from the rebel army under Benedict Arnold at Quebec and to prepare for a Lake Champlain–Hudson River invasion of New York. Burgoyne was named second in command and promoted lieutenant-general. With the reinforcements, Carleton drove the rebels southwards on Lake Champlain and annihilated an American fleet under Arnold at Valcour Island on 11 October 1775, but turned back before the heavily garrisoned Fort Ticonderoga at the junction of Lake Champlain and Lake George. Burgoyne was disappointed at the invasion's abortion and requested return home.

In England, Burgoyne secured from Lord North appointment as head of the Canadian army, as against Germain's preference for Henry Clinton. He submitted to North his campaign plan, 'Thoughts for conducting the war on the side of Canada', calling for a main army of 8000 regulars (including Brunswick mercenaries), 2000 Canadian workmen, and 1000 or more American Indians. An auxiliary force under Colonel Barry St Leger of 200 British regulars, a corps of loyalists, and a body of Indians would provide a diversion by way of Lake Ontario to the Mohawk River. The main army would assault Crown Point and Ticonderoga, and then either proceed to Albany to join with an army under Sir William Howe coming northwards from New York city, or turn east and march down the Connecticut River to meet a British force coming from Rhode Island. Burgoyne preferred the latter option, as he was to maintain in the acrimony following his defeat at Saratoga. The king, however, authorized only the junction of Burgoyne with Howe at Albany. Germain chose to issue the orders to the commanders indirectly—to Burgoyne in a letter to Carleton, and to Howe in a copy of it. Burgoyne considered the orders so binding as to leave no room for deviation in the field. Howe ignored them and instead sailed south to take Philadelphia. Burgoyne received fewer men for his main force than he had requested: 4135 British regulars, 3116 German mercenaries, 150 unarmed French Canadians, and 500 American Indians. Carleton was to have provided land and water transport, but although a formidable flotilla had been assembled to navigate Lake Champlain, the supply of carts and horses was inadequate for transfer from Lake Champlain to the Hudson.

The expedition set out from St Johns on the Richelieu River on 13 June 1777. Burgoyne issued a bellicose proclamation to the Americans, threatening to loose the Indians on them if they did not desist, but the next day enjoined the Indian forces from harming aged men, women, and children, thus alienating both sides. He took Ticonderoga without a shot when the defending commander, Major-General Arthur St Clair, failed to protect his position against British encirclement from Sugar Loaf Hill at the south-west and Mount Hope at the north-west, and on 5 July escaped with his 2546 men across the lake to Vermont. Although briefly detained by his pursuers at Hubbardton, he reached Fort Edward on the Hudson, where his superior, Major-General Philip Schuyler, took charge. At Ticonderoga, Burgoyne elected not to use scarce horses and carts for transport of his troops across the portage to Lake George south to the Hudson. Supplies from Canada were not to be delayed. He sailed south with his men to Skenesboro and laboured 23 miles overland to Fort Edward, taking three weeks to build roads and bridges through the dense swamps. As he prepared to cross the Hudson, severing his supply line from Montreal, he dispatched the German Lieutenant-Colonel Friedrich Baum with a detachment of 750 to seize mounts from a Manchester supply depot. They were overwhelmingly defeated on 16 August, 4 miles outside of Bennington, by 2000 militia under Brigadier-General John Stark. Burgoyne, undeterred, collected twenty-five days' provisions and crossed the Hudson 2 miles above Saratoga on 11 September.

Waiting for Burgoyne was Horatio Gates's American army of more than 10,000 at Bemis Heights, a narrow defile between the Hudson and a spur of hills 3 miles north of Stillwater. He had replaced Schuyler, who was blamed for the loss of Ticonderoga and was unpopular with New Englanders. Burgoyne's army advanced on 19 September in three columns, converging on Gates's left. There they were met on the heights at Freeman's Farm by a corps of riflemen under Colonel Daniel Morgan, and then furiously assaulted by a brigade under Brigadier-General Benedict Arnold. By nightfall the outcome was inconclusive, but the British had lost 160 dead, 364 wounded, and 42 missing, while the American losses totalled 63 dead, 212 wounded, and 38 missing. Thousands of militia on the Hudson's east bank blocked the escape route while Burgoyne waited futilely for succour from Sir

Henry Clinton's army to the south. On 7 October Burgoyne attempted a last desperate stroke. With a 'reconnaissance' force, as he termed it, of 1723 drawn from every British and German regiment, he planned to surprise the Americans at Bemis Heights to the north and then bring up the rest of his army for a decisive stroke. He was overwhelmed, however, by the American army, now swollen to 13,065 effectives, half of them regular army continentals. Arnold, though without authorization, again led the troops and was wounded for the second time in his left leg. British losses were 184 killed, 264 wounded, and 183 taken prisoner. The Americans had about 30 dead and 100 wounded. Burgoyne had no choice but to surrender his entire army, and Gates agreed that it would be granted free passage to Britain on condition that it not serve again in North America. At the ceremony on 17 October Burgoyne told Gates, 'Your funds of men are inexhaustible. Like the Hydra's head, when cut off, seven more spring up in its stead' (Von Riedesel, 1.189–90). Of a grand total of 9074 men who had marched down from Canada, 5895 surrendered: 3018 British, 2412 Germans, and 465 auxiliaries.

Although the continental congress did not honour return of the prisoners, it did grant Burgoyne parole home to answer charges against him in parliament. Arriving on 13 May 1778, he requested but was denied an audience with the king and a court martial. When the House of Commons came to consider his conduct in May 1779 Burgoyne argued that his orders were peremptory to force his way to Albany, and that Germain had mismanaged the entire operation. He joined Charles James Fox in the opposition and came to oppose the American war and later even to side with the French Revolution. He voted for legislative autonomy for the Irish parliament, and with the formation of the second Rockingham ministry in 1782 was appointed commander-in-chief of the 15,000 man army in Ireland. His duties, however, were not political, which was the purview of the lord lieutenant of Ireland. As such, he felt able to continue in office under Shelburne and the Fox–North coalition. Following the accession of William Pitt the younger to power, Burgoyne resigned in 1784. His last significant political act was as a member of the prosecutorial committee in the unsuccessful India corruption trial of Warren Hastings that began in 1788.

Burgoyne returned to literary pursuits, having in 1774 authored a play, The Maid of The Oaks, a mix of concealed identities featuring a female advocate of women's equality. The play had been written in two acts as part of the lavish wedding celebrations for Edward Smith Stanley, later twelfth earl of Derby, and Lady Elizabeth Hamilton, held at Burgoyne's home, The Oaks, near Epsom in Surrey. It was later expanded to five acts by David Garrick and became a popular part of the Drury Lane repertory. Burgoyne also wrote political satire, and he achieved a success with a comedy, The Heiress, regarded by contemporaries and later critics as an authentic depiction of upper-class society of the period. Presented in London at the Drury Lane Theatre Royal in 1786, it ran for thirty performances and remained popular in England and on the continent

for half a century. Less successful was his libretto for Thomas Linley's adaptation of a French opera, Richard Coeur de Lion (1788).

Burgoyne's wife had died on 25 February 1776, but he had maintained close ties with the Stanley family. Beginning in 1782, he fathered four children, including Sir John Fox *Burgoyne, army officer, by a married actress, Susan Caulfield. The 1766 portrait of Burgoyne by Sir Joshua Reynolds reveals a handsome man. A bon vivant, he was nicknamed Gentleman Johnny by George Bernard Shaw in The Devil's Disciple. Burgoyne died at his town house, 10 Hertford Street, Mayfair, Westminster, on 4 August 1792; his death was attributed to gout. He was buried on 13 August in Westminster Abbey.   MAX M. MINTZ

Sources E. B. De Fonblanque, *Political and military episodes in the latter half of the eighteenth century derived from the life of … Burgoyne* (1876) · R. J. Hargrove jun., *General John Burgoyne* (1983) · G. Howson, *Burgoyne of Saratoga: a biography* (1979) · M. M. Mintz, *The generals of Saratoga: John Burgoyne and Horatio Gates* (1990) · J. Burgoyne, *A state of the expedition from Canada* (1780) · J. Almon, ed., *The parliamentary register, or, History of the proceedings and debates of the House of Commons*, 17 vols. (1775–80) · W. L. Stone, *The campaign of Lieut. Gen. John Burgoyne* (1877) · *Orderly book of John Burgoyne*, ed. E. B. O'Callaghan (1860) · F. A. Von Riedesel, *Memoirs and letters*, ed. M. Von Eelking (1868) · K. G. Davies, ed., *Documents of the American Revolution, 1770–1783*, 21 vols. (1972–81) · J. Burgoyne, *Dramatic and political works* (1808) · *Report on the manuscripts of Mrs Stopford-Sackville*, 2 vols., HMC, 49 (1904–10) · J. Brooke, 'Burgoyne, John', HoP, *Commons, 1754–90* · J. L. Chester, ed., *The marriage, baptismal, and burial registers of the collegiate church or abbey of St Peter, Westminster*, Harleian Society, 10 (1876), 463–5

Archives BL, corresp., Add. MSS 47568, 47582 · Boston PL, papers concerning expedition from Canada · HLRO, papers · PRO, Colonial Office papers · PRO, War Office papers | BL, corresp. with Major-General W. Heath, Add. MS 38343 [copies] · BL, corresp. with Charles Jenkinson, first earl of Liverpool, Add. MSS 38200, 38204, 38212, 38305–38306 · BL, letters to Lord Northington, Add. MS 33100 · PRO, letters to Lord Amherst, WO34/140, 144, 152–153, 167 · PRO, corresp. with Sir W. Howe, 30/55 · Sheff. Arch., corresp. with Edmund Burke · U. Mich., Clements L., corresp. with Lord George Germain and papers

Likenesses J. Reynolds, oils, 1766, Frick Collection, New York City [*see illus.*] · J. Sayers, caricature, etching, 1782, NPG · etching, 1782, NPG · J. Chapman, stipple, pubd 1801, NPG · T. Wallis, line engraving, pubd 1807 (after W. M. Craig), NPG · J. C. Armitage, line engraving (after H. Warren), NPG · portrait (after portrait by A. Ramsay, 1756), NPG · prints, NPG

Wealth at death approx. £7000: Chester, ed., *Marriage, baptismal, and burial registers*

Burgoyne, Sir John, seventh baronet (1739–1785), army officer, was the son of Sir Roger Burgoyne, sixth baronet (*bap.* 1710, *d.* 1780), MP for Bedfordshire, and his wife, Lady Frances Montagu (*d.* 1788), daughter of George Montagu, first earl of Halifax. Burgoyne was born into a family well established in Bedfordshire and Warwickshire, where they owned estates at Sutton Park and Wroxall. His younger brother, Montagu *Burgoyne, was a prominent Essex politician, while their cousin Sir John *Burgoyne (1723–1792), who also achieved fame for his military career, was commander at the British surrender at Saratoga in 1777.

Burgoyne entered the army at an early age. After serving

in the 7th fusiliers and other corps, he obtained the lieutenant-colonelcy of the 58th foot in Ireland in 1764. Some years later he was transferred to that of the 14th light dragoons (then on the Irish establishment); both appointments owed something to his political connections as well as his professional ability. In 1781 he was commissioned to raise a regiment of light dragoons (originally known as the 23rd dragoons) for service in India, the first European cavalry sent out to that country. Early in 1782 the regiment set sail on board the East India fleet commanded by Vice-Admiral Sir Richard Bickerton, landing at Madras towards the end of that year. Under its new name, the 19th light dragoons, the regiment won renown on Indian battlefields. Burgoyne himself was promoted to major-general on the Madras staff in 1782. Two years earlier he had succeeded as seventh baronet on the death of his father (31 December). He married Charlotte (*d.* after 1785), the daughter of General Johnstone of Overston, Northamptonshire; the couple had four daughters and three sons, of whom the eldest was Montagu-Roger Burgoyne [*see below*]. Burgoyne died in Madras in 1785 and was survived by his wife, who later married Lieutenant-General Eyre Power Trench.

Sir Montagu-Roger Burgoyne, eighth baronet (*d.* 1817), army officer, was, like his father, a cavalry officer who rose to the rank of major-general. He entered the army as cornet in the Scots Greys in 1789, and in 1795 became lieutenant-colonel of the 32nd light dragoon guards. He was afterwards an inspecting field officer of yeomanry and volunteer corps. On 1 November 1791 he married Catherine (1772/3–1855), daughter of John Burton of Owlerton, Yorkshire; they had three sons and three daughters. Burgoyne died at his mother's house on Oxford Street, London, on 11 August 1817, whereupon the baronetcy passed to his eldest son, John-Montagu Burgoyne (1796–1858). H. M. CHICHESTER, *rev.* PHILIP CARTER

Sources Burke, *Peerage* · *GM*, 1st ser., 87/2 (1817), 189 · R. S. Lea, 'Burgoyne, Roger', HoP, *Commons, 1715–54* · E. B. de Fonblanque, *Political and military episodes in the latter half of the eighteenth century derived from the life of the Right Hon. John Burgoyne* (1876)
Archives BL OIOC, corresp. relating to India · National Archives of India, New Delhi, official papers · Yale U., Beinecke L., letterbook | Bodl. Oxf., corresp. with Lord Macartney · NL Scot., corresp. with and about James Stuart · priv. coll., corresp. with Norman Macleod

Burgoyne, Sir John Fox, baronet (1782–1871), army officer, eldest of the four illegitimate children of Lieutenant-General John *Burgoyne (1723–1792) and the singer Susan Caulfield, was born on 24 July 1782. Baptized at St Anne's, Soho, on 15 August, he was named after his father and his sponsor, Charles James Fox. General Burgoyne left little money, so his children were brought up by their cousin Edward, earl of Derby (*d.* 1835), John being tutored privately by the Revd Maule at Cambridge before going to Eton College in 1794. Throughout his life he expressed 'the warmest affection and respect' (Wrottesley, *Life*, 1.5) for Derby and his wife. On 19 October 1796 Burgoyne entered the Royal Military Academy, Woolwich; he

Sir John Fox Burgoyne, baronet (1782–1871), by Ernest Edwards, pubd 1865

was appointed assistant engineer on 14 July 1798 and commissioned second lieutenant in the Royal Engineers on 29 August.

War in the Mediterranean and Peninsula, 1800–1814 Burgoyne first saw action during the siege of Valletta, in July–September 1800, and remained in Malta for six years until posted to Sicily. Meanwhile, he had been promoted first lieutenant (1 July 1800) and second captain (1 March 1805), and during leave in 1802 had visited Egypt, Turkey, and Greece. He sailed, on 6 March 1807, with Major-General Alexander Fraser's force to Egypt as commanding engineer, taking part in the capture of Alexandria and siege of Rosetta before briefly contracting ophthalmia. Having returned to Sicily in August 1807, in April 1808 he was appointed commanding engineer of Lieutenant-General Sir John Moore's expedition to Sweden, and later that year went with Moore to Portugal. When Moore assumed command of all British troops there, following the convention of Cintra, Burgoyne was superseded as commanding engineer. Attached to the light division, he destroyed crucial bridges during the retreat through northern Spain. While the main body fell back on Corunna the light division made for Vigo, and Burgoyne reached England in January 1809, later claiming that this campaign left him 'deaf for five years' (Wrottesley, *Life*, 1.335).

Burgoyne landed again in Portugal on 2 April 1809 to join Lieutenant-General Sir Arthur Wellesley, played an active role in transporting his army across the Douro, then reconnoitred the frontier province of Entre-Douro-e-Minho. He was promoted captain on 24 June 1809 and, although initially sent to repair it, under orders he blew up Fort Concepcion, near Almeida, on 21 July 1810. Prominent at the battle of Busaco (27 September 1810) he prepared several bridges for demolition as Wellesley (now Viscount Wellington) fell back on the lines of Torres Vedras. That winter (1810–11) he became regulating officer of the Bucellas district, responsible for sixteen redoubts and batteries with their integral fifty-nine cannon and protecting infantry. When Wellington advanced again in spring 1811 Burgoyne took part in the unsuccessful second siege of Badajoz (May–June 1811) before withdrawing to winter quarters in Portugal with the 3rd division. He acted as joint director of the attack at the capture of Ciudad Rodrigo (8–19 January 1812) and obtained a brevet majority on 6 February. He similarly served at the successful third siege of Badajoz (March–April 1812), becoming a brevet lieutenant-colonel on 27 April.

Burgoyne was commanding engineer at the capture of the forts of Salamanca and subsequent battle (July 1812), the following month with Wellington at Madrid, and during the unsuccessful siege of Burgos (September–October 1812), where he was twice wounded. At Vitoria (21 June 1813) he served with the 3rd division, having a horse 'wounded under me in three places' (Porter, 1.331); from Pamplona he went to San Sebastian, where (July–August) he became joint director of the attack. Severely wounded in neck and jaw, he nevertheless took over as commanding engineer when Lieutenant-Colonel Sir Richard Fletcher fell. In the latter stages of the Peninsular War Burgoyne acted as commanding engineer at the crossing of the Bidassoa (7 October), the passage of the Adour, and the blockade of Bayonne (February 1814), serving also with Lieutenant-General Sir John Hope at the battles of the Nive and Nivelle (November–December 1813). Because of an administrative error, in 1814 Burgoyne was not created KCB, but CB, which he refused to wear.

America, France, and Portugal, 1814–1828 Promoted lieutenant-colonel in the Royal Engineers on 20 December 1814, five days later Burgoyne landed in the Mississippi delta as commanding engineer with Major-General Sir Edward Pakenham's expedition to New Orleans. After the assault on that port had been abandoned he captured Fort Bowyer, at the entrance to Mobile Bay, on 12 February. Burgoyne reached England again on 30 May 1815 to find himself designated commanding engineer in Hull. At Wellington's instigation that posting was cancelled, but Burgoyne landed at Ostend on 6 July, too late for Waterloo. He served with the army of occupation in France until November 1818, then remained unemployed before successively becoming commanding engineer at Chatham (24 July 1821) and with Lieutenant-General Sir William Clinton's expedition to Portugal (1826–8). Meanwhile, on 31 January 1821, Burgoyne had married Charlotte (d. 1871), daughter of Colonel Hugh Rose from Holme in Inverness county, whom he had met during a shooting expedition to Scotland in September 1819. They had a son, Hugh Talbot (b. 19 July 1833), and seven daughters, including Margaret-Anne,

who married Burgoyne's biographer, Captain the Hon. George Wrottesley.

On arrival at Lisbon in January 1827 Burgoyne went to Elvas to watch for the expected Spanish invasion, and three months later undertook a similar uneventful mission to Portalegre. Once Clinton's force had been withdrawn Burgoyne became commanding engineer at Portsmouth, on 11 April 1828.

Ireland and invasion controversy, 1828–1852 Burgoyne advanced to brevet-colonel on 22 July 1830 before leaving the following year for a civil appointment in Ireland, as chairman of the new board of public works. While in this post Burgoyne produced a pamphlet, *Letters on the State of Ireland*, which perceptively forecast problems over the established church and excessive powers of landlords. More radically, in 1834, to the duke of Richmond's royal commission on the feasibility of administrative consolidation, he advocated 'uniting in one person the offices of Secretary at War, commander-in-chief, master-general under the title of "Secretary of State for the War Department"', dismissing objections as 'mere prejudices' (Wrottesley, *Life*, 1.398). Burgoyne became colonel in the Royal Engineers (10 January 1837) and major-general (28 June 1838), and was appointed KCB on 19 July 1838. In 1839 he was elected an honorary member of the Institution of Civil Engineers, but failed to secure appointment as under-secretary of state for Ireland in May 1840.

In 1844 Burgoyne produced a cogent analysis of measures necessary to secure Ireland against 'insurgents' which so impressed the master-general of the ordnance that the next year General Sir George Murray persuaded Burgoyne to resume his military career in England as inspector-general of fortifications. Apart from the defensive duties that his title implied, under the master-general Burgoyne would command the Royal Engineers (officers) and Corps of Royal Sappers and Miners (rank and file). He declined another civil position on the railway board in 1846, though a year later did agree to temporary appointment as president of a special commission to study the Irish famine and make recommendations 'for the adoption of further measures for the relief of the distress arising from the scarcity in that country' (Porter, 2.418). Burgoyne returned to the Ordnance in August 1847, with Treasury endorsement of his 'patient industry and never-failing sagacity … foresight and good management' (Porter, 2.323). He soon peppered the master-general, home secretary, and secretary of state for war and the colonies with a succession of papers highlighting the unsatisfactory state of coastal fortifications, many of which he declared 'defective', with protection of the dockyards so 'imperfect' that they had only 'a semblance of being fortified' (ibid., 2.213). This led him inadvertently to a serious contretemps with Wellington, after the duke summarized his own fears in a letter to Burgoyne on 9 January 1847, part of which appeared in the *Morning Chronicle* (4 January 1848). An embarrassed Burgoyne protested his innocence, but relations with Wellington were never fully repaired. In 1853 the acknowledged vulnerability of England to

French invasion prompted the home secretary, Palmerston, to call a series of meetings, which Burgoyne attended in his official capacity. He advanced to lieutenant-general (11 November 1851) and was appointed GCB (31 March 1852). After Wellington's funeral, in November 1852, Burgoyne had private discussions with the Russian general and later commander in the Crimea Prince M. D. Gorchakov, whom he considered able but a 'sly old fox' (Wrottesley, *Life*, 1.500).

The Crimean War, 1854–1855 As relations between Russia and Turkey worsened and military aid to the sultan became likely, Burgoyne pointed to the strength of Sevastopol, the Russian naval base in the Crimea, but doubted the wisdom of naval action against it without army support. When Russian troops advanced into Moldavia and Wallachia (modern Romania) the cabinet accepted 'with grateful thanks' his 'spirited and honourable offer' in January 1854 to inspect the area of 'the Bosphorus and Dardanelles with the utmost expedition'. Nevertheless, he was instructed not to 'go *beyond Constantinople*, but to turn his back on the Black Sea' (Wrottesley, *Life*, 2.7). *En route* Burgoyne visited Paris, where he met Napoleon III, the British ambassador (Lord Cowley), and senior French officers, being credited by Cowley with persuading Napoleon III to support 'a land expedition in case the last attempt at negotiation should break down' (Porter, 1.411). Once in Turkey he favoured a fortified line 'some ten or twelve miles in front of Constantinople, the right on the Black Sea, the left on the Sea of Marmora' defended by 30,000 entrenched troops (ibid., 1.410). Despite the cabinet's restriction Burgoyne did travel into Bulgaria to see the Turkish commander, Omar Pasha, but remained convinced that any allied force should man defences around Constantinople and not advance northwards.

War was declared in March 1854, British and French units quickly converged on Turkey, and in June the British commander (Lord Raglan) agreed to move into Bulgaria. Turkish troops then drove the Russians back from the Danube unaided, and the allied governments determined to invade the Crimea. When a seaborne reconnaissance of the western coast opted for landing at the mouth of the Kacha River, just north of Sevastopol, in London Burgoyne declared the plan 'impracticable'. None the less, he responded rapidly to an invitation to join Raglan's staff 'as a Lieut. General, … [who] in case of the absence of the commander of the Forces, would be in command of the army' (Porter, 2.425). Shortly after reaching Bulgaria, on 29 August Burgoyne outlined an alternative course of action: seize and fortify the small port of Eupatoria, 35 miles north of Sevastopol, and advance in strength on the Russian naval base as the Turks demonstrated along the south coast. He reiterated his opposition to the Kacha landing and joined Raglan on another reconnaissance of the coast (9–11 September), during which landing beaches close to Eupatoria were substituted. Having achieved an unopposed descent there shortly afterwards and defeated the Russians on the Alma River (where Burgoyne's horse was wounded), on 24 September the allied commanders

adopted Sir John's proposal to skirt Sevastopol to the east and assault it from the Khersonese plateau in the south. Once there Burgoyne discounted a swift assault and advised landing the heavy artillery. Rocky terrain slowed construction of the siege trenches, a bombardment in October failed, and by early November the strengthened Russian defences of Sevastopol were secure for the winter. On 22 November 1854 Burgoyne was appointed a colonel-commandant of the Royal Engineers.

With Raglan's staff being severely criticized in press and parliament for incompetence, on 24 February 1855 Lord Panmure, secretary of state for war, recalled Burgoyne. Panmure denied that Burgoyne was a political scapegoat: 'a man now far advanced in years [had been rescued] from the sufferings of a Crimean winter' (Porter, 2.427), which prompted Burgoyne whimsically to write home: 'I suppose you will expect to see me return with a tremulous, weak voice, without teeth, and on crutches' (ibid., 2.428). He did have the satisfaction, before he left the Crimea, of French agreement that the Malakhov fortification on the right of the allied line held the key to siege success. In London he discovered that the independent ordnance corps was about to be abolished, with the posts of master-general and lieutenant-general discontinued, and the engineers and artillery brought under the commander-in-chief of the army. Despite this major distraction Burgoyne retained close interest in the Crimea. On 18 April 1855 he attended a council of war at Windsor, presided over by the prince consort, at which he argued strongly against the allied forces being committed to field operations before the siege of Sevastopol had succeeded, expressing special reservation about a proposed French landing on the south coast. In August he inspected reinforcements for the front, and that same month was invited to Osborne by the queen to discuss the war's progress. On the anniversary of the battle of Inkerman (5 November 1855) he dined at Windsor. Meanwhile, one poignant duty had fallen to him on 28 July 1855, when he acted as pallbearer at Raglan's funeral.

Later life, 1855–1871 Already a juror of the Paris Exhibition, in 1858 Burgoyne travelled to the French capital on behalf of the queen for another purpose, in his own words to 'place at the disposition of the Emperor the funeral car which conveyed to his first tomb the remains of the illustrious founder of the Napoleon dynasty' (Porter, 2.431). At home he continued to highlight the parlous state of Britain's coastal defences, penning a critical memorandum, 'Remarks on the military condition of Great Britain', on 29 May 1859, and strongly supporting formation of the volunteers. Subsequently, he became honorary colonel of the 1st Middlesex and 1st Lancashire engineer volunteer corps. Burgoyne fought successfully to retain the specialist engineer train for transporting sapper equipment and ammunition, and he investigated reasons for unrest among cadets at Sandhurst and Woolwich, recommending greater accent on indoor and outdoor recreational competitions. Promoted general on 5 September 1855, Burgoyne was made constable of the Tower of London on 8 April 1865, retaining that appointment until his death.

He advanced to field marshal on 1 January 1868, with 'a special and exceptional' allowance of £1500 per year to mark 'the value of his services' (Wrottesley, *Life*, 2.426), and formally relinquished the post of director of works in the ordnance branch of the War Office (an appointment which replaced that of inspector-general of fortifications from 27 September 1862) on 20 January. He had previously been made a baronet (18 March 1856), freeman of the City of London, honorary DCL at Oxford, FRS, and honorary associate of the Institution of Naval Architects and of the Society of Arts.

Burgoyne's appointment to Raglan's staff, aged seventy-two, underlined enduring mental alertness (he wrote a well-argued letter to *The Times* about the abolition of purchase on 9 March 1871); and, whatever later commentators held, at the time the flank march around Sevastopol was declared an 'extraordinary movement, which claims rank with the greatest efforts of military science' (*Colburn's United Service Magazine*, 1854, pt 3, 435). In January 1868 he was described as 'still hale in body, and with an unclouded intellect' (Porter, 2.432), though in truth he was afflicted by deafness. An accomplished rider, he enjoyed field sports, and was an excellent shot and a good rackets player. He had a dry sense of humour and was particularly amused to read his own obituary, mistakenly published when Sir John Montagu Burgoyne died in 1858. Burgoyne composed several pieces of unpublished verse, which his son-in-law labelled '*jeux d'esprit* and epigrams' (Wrottesley, *Life*, 2.464).

Burgoyne's only son, Captain Hugh Talbot *Burgoyne RN, was lost when HMS *Captain* sank on 7 September 1870. Sir John never recovered from what he described as 'this melancholy disaster' (Wrottesley, *Life*, 2.439), and by mid-1871 'he was now a complete wreck of his former self' (ibid., 2.449). He died on 7 October 1871 at 5 Pembridge Square, London, and was buried in St Peter's Church, in the Tower of London, on 17 October; his wife died on 12 December 1871. Following a military subscription a statue of Burgoyne by Boehm was erected near the duke of York's column at Waterloo Place, London.

After the Peninsular War Burgoyne received a gold cross with one clasp for Badajoz, Salamanca, Vitoria, San Sebastian, and the Nive, and a silver medal with three clasps for Busaco, Ciudad Rodrigo, and the Nivelle. He also became a knight of the Portuguese order of the Tower and Sword. For his services in the Crimea he gained the Mejidiye (first class) and the decoration of grand officer of the Légion d'honneur. Besides numerous official and semi-official memoranda, circulated professionally, some of which were published in *The Military Opinions of General Sir John Fox Burgoyne* (1869), Burgoyne wrote articles on military subjects in journals such as the *Cornhill Magazine* and *Westminster Review*. He also served on a wide variety of committees and commissions about military and civil matters.

In his funeral oration the Revd G. R. Gleig described Burgoyne as 'brave, able, intelligent, upright, a humble Christian, a modest citizen' (Wrottesley, *Life*, 2.457). Wellington had previously observed: 'If Burgoyne only knew his own

value, no one would equal him' (ibid., 2.462); his biographer attributed 'timidity of manner and distrust of his own powers' (ibid., 1.5) to diffidence at family poverty after his father's death. Nevertheless, Napoleon III wrote to Burgoyne in 1870, following his own defeat by the Prussians: 'You are the Moltke of England' (ibid., 2.438).

JOHN SWEETMAN

Sources *Army List* · W. Porter, *History of the corps of royal engineers*, 2 vols. (1889) · G. Wrottesley, *Life and correspondence of Field Marshal Sir John Fox Burgoyne*, 2 vols. (1873) · R. F. Edwards, ed., *Roll of officers of the corps of royal engineers from 1660 to 1898* (1898) · J. Sweetman, *War and administration: the significance of the Crimean War for the British army* (1984) · E. Longford [E. H. Pakenham, countess of Longford], *Wellington*, 2: *Pillar of state* (1972); pbk edn (1975) · C. Hibbert, *The destruction of Lord Raglan* [1961] · J. Sweetman, *Raglan: from the Peninsula to the Crimea* (1993) · A. Sheppard, *Sandhurst: the Royal Military Academy and its predecessors* (1980) · T. W. J. Connolly, *History of the royal sappers and miners*, 2nd edn, 2 vols. (1857) · *Colburn's United Service Magazine* (1854–5) · A. D. Lambert, *The Crimean War: British grand strategy, 1853–56* (1990) · *The military opinions of General Sir John Fox Burgoyne*, ed. G. Wrottesley (1859) · m. cert.

Archives Royal Engineers Museum, Gillingham, corresp. and papers | BL, corresp. with Sir C. W. Pasley, Add. MSS 41961–41964 · BL, letters to Lord Strathnairn, Add. MS 42805 · Borth. Inst., letters to Sir Charles Wood · HLRO, corresp. with Thomas Greene and memoranda relating to new Palace of Westminster · Lpool RO, letters to E. G. Stanley · NA Scot., letters and memoranda to Lord Panmure · NAM, corresp. with Lord Raglan · PRO, letters to Lord Cowley, FO 519 · PRO, corresp. with Lord John Russell and memoranda on defence, PRO 30/22 · U. Nott. L., corresp. with duke of Newcastle · U. Southampton L., letters and memoranda relating mainly to Lord Palmerston · UCL, corresp. with Edwin Chadwick

Likenesses H. W. Phillips, oils, 1858, Royal Engineers, Chatham, Kent · D. J. Pound, stipple and line print, 1859 (after photograph by Mayall), BM, NPG; repro. in *Illustrated News of the World* (1859) · E. Edwards, pubd 1865, NPG [*see illus.*] · J. E. Boehm, bronze statue, 1874, Waterloo Place, London · J. Brown, engraving (after miniature), repro. in Wrottesley, ed., *Life and correspondence*, vol. 1, frontispiece · W. J. Edwards, stipple (after photograph by V. Plumier), BM; repro. in E. H. Nolan, *History of the war against Russia* (1855–7) · T. Heaphy, pencil and watercolour drawing, NPG · T. Heaphy, watercolour drawing, NPG · J. S. Templeton, lithograph (after photograph by G. F. Mulvany), NPG · photograph, repro. in Porter, *History of the corps of royal engineers*, vol. 1, frontispiece · portrait, repro. in Sweetman, *Raglan*

Wealth at death under £4000: probate, 13 Nov 1871, *CGPLA Eng. & Wales*

Burgoyne, Montagu (1750–1836), politician, was born on 19 July 1750, the second son of Sir Roger Burgoyne, sixth baronet (*bap.* 1710, *d.* 1780), politician, of Sutton, Bedfordshire, and Lady Frances Montagu (*d.* 1788), daughter of George Montagu, first earl of Halifax. His elder brother, Sir John *Burgoyne, seventh baronet (1739–1785), served in the British army in India; his cousin, also Sir John *Burgoyne (1723–1792), commanded the British forces at the surrender at Saratoga in 1777. After attending Henry Newcome's school at Hackney he was admitted to Trinity Hall, Cambridge, on 27 October 1768, graduating MA in 1774. During the North administration he served as chamberlain of the till office in the exchequer, a sinecure which provided him with an annual salary of £1660. He was in addition for many years a verderer of Epping Forest and was active in Essex local politics, although his bid in 1810 to become the county's MP ended, after a dogged campaign, with defeat by John Archer Houblon. Burgoyne offered his views of the event in his *Account of Proceedings at the Late Election for Essex* (1810). Other publications from this time included his *Letter on the Necessity of a Reform in Parliament* (1809) and *Speech to the Freeholders of Essex* (1812).

On 30 October 1780 Burgoyne married Elizabeth Harvey, daughter and heir of Eliab Harvey, MP for Dulwich. The marriage, a 'pattern of conjugal affection' (*GM*, 550), produced two sons, who died in infancy, and two daughters, Frances-Elizabeth (*d.* 1818) and Elizabeth (*d.* before 1836). Both husband and wife were described as well-respected members of the community near Mark Hall, Harlow, Essex, where they resided. Burgoyne later published a *Collection of Psalms and Hymns* (1827) and *An Address to the Governors of Public Charity Schools* (1830), in which he proposed improvements to the current system of charity education. In the same work he also advocated the allocation of land to the labouring poor of Bedford, Huntingdon, and Cambridge, part of a wider campaign which made him 'one of the earliest and most untiring friends' of the land allotment system (ibid.). He died at East Sheen, Surrey, where he was then living, on 6 March 1836, and was survived by his wife.   [ANON.], *rev.* PHILIP CARTER

Sources *GM*, 2nd ser., 5 (1836), 550 · Venn, *Alum. Cant.* · R. S. Lea, 'Burgoyne, Sir Roger', HoP, *Commons, 1715–54* · Burke, *Peerage*
Archives W. Sussex RO, letters to duke of Richmond

Burgoyne, Sir Montagu-Roger, eighth baronet (*d.* 1817). *See under* Burgoyne, Sir John, seventh baronet (1739–1785).

Burgoyne, Peter Bond (1844–1929), wine merchant, was born on 7 February 1844 at Dodbrook, Kingsbridge, Devon, the son of John Trist Burgoyne (*c.*1812–1856), beer and porter merchant, and his wife, Mary Ann Bond (*c.*1808–1854). Of his early years and education nothing is known, but in 1858, two years after his father's death, Burgoyne went to Newfoundland. He may have been apprenticed to Messrs Brooking & Co. of St John's, where he worked as a clerk, as he remained in the colony for no more than seven years. On his return to England in 1865 Burgoyne took employment as an estate agent before becoming a clerk to a London wine shipping firm of which he later became manager and where he was largely responsible for the introduction of Hungarian wines into England. In 1871 he set up in business on his own account, trading from offices and cellars at 50 Old Broad Street, London. On 28 March 1872 he married Marie Henrietta Johanna (1848/9–1934), daughter of Charles Achilles, artist of Acton.

Following an introduction to Dr Alexander Charles Kelly, manager and principal shareholder in the Tintara Vineyard Company of McLaren Vale in South Australia, Burgoyne agreed to represent the company, and the Tintara Vineyard Association was established in 1872. Existing prejudices for the wines of the Old World made sales difficult to secure, and by the end of year the agency

was relaunched as the Australian Vineyards Association, dealing in Australian wines generally. The difficulties experienced by those attempting to introduce Australian wines to the British public at this time were not easily overcome and the debts mounted up. In 1876 the Australian Vineyards Association was purchased by Walter Watson Hughes, a wealthy expatriate and owner of the Fairfield vineyard in South Australia's Clare valley. Wiping the slate clean, Hughes entered into partnership with Burgoyne, who reverted to selling European wines while the Australian wine trade was developed.

The greatest impediment to the trade was the duty structure which tended to penalize Australian wine merchants, who invariably had to pay a surcharge of 150 per cent over and above the standard duty of 1s. per gallon on wines above 26 degrees of proof spirit. In his evidence before the select committee on wine duties in May 1879, Burgoyne repeatedly stated that the natural wines of South Australia contained an average of 29 degrees of proof spirit, and claimed that vineyards in the colony were going out of production because of the high rate of duty in Britain. Not one to miss a marketing opportunity, he was quick to produce five samples of Fairfield wines for the committee to taste.

Burgoyne's fortunes took a turn for the better in 1886 when the duties were modified to accommodate colonial wine growers. This prompted a move to larger premises at Dowgate Hill, London, and the offer of a prize of 50 guineas to be awarded to the exhibitor of a claret style of wine at the Jubilee International Exhibition, to be held in Adelaide in 1887, and other prizes to be offered under the auspices of the South Australian Agricultural Society. In 1888 agents were appointed in Adelaide and Melbourne, and in 1893, on the first of several visits to the colonies, Burgoyne invested in vineyard and cellar accommodation in the Rutherglen district of north-east Victoria. Despite competition from the South Australian government's bonded depot in London, and other importers, Burgoyne soon became the leviathan of the trade selling half a million gallons of wine annually, mainly blends which were marketed under a number of registered brands.

In 1903 the business of P. B. Burgoyne was converted to a limited company. A publicity brochure from this period, 'The quality wines of the empire', quoted the chancellor of the exchequer, Sir Michael Hicks Beach, who remarked in the Commons in 1899 that 'Messrs. Burgoyne have annually during twenty-eight years paid more duty on Australian wines than all the rest of the trade put together'. The wines of the Cape were another departure for Burgoyne, whose name was commemorated by an award at the Western Province Agricultural Society's annual show for many years after his death.

Burgoyne died at his home, Broadlands, Ascot, Berkshire, on 4 September 1929. Numerous bequests were made to long-term members of his domestic and business staff, and a bequest of £1000 was made to the National Hospital for Consumption, Ventnor, Isle of Wight, which Burgoyne served for a total of thirty-eight years, twenty-six of them as chairman. The family business of P. B. Burgoyne & Co. Ltd was continued by Burgoyne's son Cuthbert John (1875–1955), and grandson John Fenner Burgoyne (c.1900–1976). GEORGE BELL

Sources *The Times* (7 Sept 1929) • *The Times* (10 Sept 1929) • *The Times* (17 Oct 1929) • *Adelaide Observer* (22 Feb 1902) • private information (2004) [Leslie A. Winsor, research officer, Newfoundland and Labrador Genealogical Society Inc.] • *Wine Trade Review* (June–Dec 1872) • P. B. Burgoyne, *Adelaide Observer* (1872–1910) • 'The quality wines of the empire', P. B. Burgoyne & Co. Ltd, [n.d.] [publicity brochure] • C. L. Leopoldt, *300 years of Cape wine*, 2nd edn (1974) • b. cert. • m. cert. • d. cert.
Likenesses photograph, repro. in *Australian Vigneron* [Melbourne] (April 1902), cover
Wealth at death £133,861: will, proved, 1929

Burgred [Burhred] (*d.* **874**?), king of the Mercians, succeeded to the kingship in 852, shortly after a serious Mercian defeat by a substantial viking force. It had been the West Saxon king *Æthelwulf who had managed to drive off the vikings who had assaulted Mercia; and the hallmark of Burgred's reign is his reliance on West Saxon support against his enemies. In 853 he joined with his witan in appealing to Æthelwulf for help against the Welsh. Accordingly, Æthelwulf 'went with his army across Mercia against the Welsh, and they made them all submissive to him' (*ASC*, s.a. 853). After Easter in the same year Burgred married Æthelwulf's daughter, in a ceremony in the West Saxon royal vill at Chippenham. Queen Æthelswith attests most of her husband's charters in a prominent position, and in two instances is presented as co-grantor; she makes one grant in her own name, probably of land which formed part of her own property. Ninth-century Mercian queens regularly played an important public role, and were clearly accorded a much higher status than their counterparts in Wessex; but it seems likely that Æthelswith enjoyed greater importance as a result of the vital West Saxon alliance.

The Anglo-Saxon Chronicle does not mention any further viking attacks on Mercia until 867–8, but it cannot be assumed that the kingdom was unthreatened during the interval. A chance reference in a charter of Burgred reveals an otherwise unknown incursion of the heathens into the territory of the 'Wrekin-dwellers' in what is now Shropshire in 855. All but one of Burgred's surviving charters belong to the period between 855 and 866; he followed the example of his predecessor Berhtwulf in occasionally granting privileges and exemption to various Mercian churches in return for cash payments and precious objects, but he seems to have been under less pressure than Berhtwulf to gather resources, and charters of this type are comparatively few. From about 860 the London mint, which had produced little since the viking sack of the city in 850–51, began a rapid expansion, and by the end of the reign some forty moneyers were working for the Mercian king; the rate of coin production seems to have been exceptionally high, and this may indicate that the Mercian economy was flourishing.

The last years of Burgred's reign were eventful. In late 865 'a great heathen army' landed in East Anglia and took up winter quarters there. The East Angles made peace and supplied them with horses, which enabled the vikings to take advantage of a civil war in Northumbria: both warring kings were killed and the vikings effectively became rulers of the kingdom. By the end of 867 they were poised to attack Mercia. They proceeded to Nottingham, where they wintered. Burgred was not prepared to confront them alone and appealed to Æthelred, the current king of Wessex. A joint West Saxon and Mercian force went to Nottingham and started a siege; eventually the Mercians agreed peace terms with the invaders, who left and returned to York. This successful operation bound the West Saxons and Mercians more closely together and in 868 a marriage was arranged between the atheling Alfred (King Æthelred's brother and the heir apparent) and a Mercian noblewoman named Ealhswith, daughter of a Mercian ealdorman and linked, through her mother, to the ancient Mercian royal dynasty. In the later 860s a number of very similar coins were struck for Burgred and Æthelred, which may indicate a degree of co-operation in this area—there is some evidence that the two kings were sharing moneyers.

For a few years after 868 the vikings seem to have left Mercia in peace, perhaps in accordance with the treaty agreed at Nottingham (although it is possible that the Anglo-Saxon Chronicle, the primary source for this period, neglects Mercian troubles in its concentration on West Saxon woes). In 869 the viking army passed through Mercian territory, presumably with the agreement of King Burgred, on its way to its final conquest of East Anglia. Subsequently Wessex bore the brunt of viking attacks, but in the winter of 871–2 the vikings settled themselves in London and forced the Mercians to buy peace: a charter of 872 refers to 'the great tribute of the barbarians, in the year when the vikings stayed in London' (*AS chart.*, S 1278). There was a repeat of this in the following winter, when the viking army occupied Torksey in the Mercian province of Lindsey; once more King Burgred and the Mercians 'made peace', no doubt at great cost. By now the vikings were well aware of Mercian weakness (it is possible that the West Saxon alliance had lapsed; certainly there is no record of Burgred coming to the West Saxons' aid in the battles of 870–71). In the winter of 873–4 the viking army moved to Repton in what is now Derbyshire, in the Mercian heartland. Burgred was helpless; he was deposed and driven into exile. He travelled as a pilgrim to Rome (he had previously been in correspondence with Pope John VIII, who was inclined to see the Mercians' troubles as the consequence of an unusual indulgence in fornication), where he died soon after his arrival; he was buried in Rome at Santa Maria in Saxia (that is, in the Saxon quarter), on the site of the present church of Santo Spirito in Sassia. The vikings established Ceolwulf II as their puppet king in Mercia, on condition that the kingdom should remain at their disposal; three years later they appropriated the northern and eastern half.

S. E. KELLY

Sources *ASC*, s.a. 853–74 [texts A, E] • *Asser's Life of King Alfred: together with the 'Annals of Saint Neots' erroneously ascribed to Asser*, ed. W. H. Stevenson (1904), 6–8, 24–5, 34–5 • *Alfred the Great: Asser's Life* *of King Alfred and other contemporary sources*, ed. and trans. S. Keynes and M. Lapidge (1983), 16–19, 69, 77, 82 • *AS chart.*, S 206–14, 1201, 1278 • *English historical documents*, 1, ed. D. Whitelock (1955), no. 220 • S. Keynes, 'King Alfred and the Mercians', *Kings, currency and alliances: history and coinage of southern England in the ninth century*, ed. M. A. S. Blackburn and D. N. Dumville (1998), 1–46 • P. Grierson and M. Blackburn, *Medieval European coinage: with a catalogue of the coins in the Fitzwilliam Museum, Cambridge*, 1: *The early middle ages (5th–10th centuries)* (1986), 308, 310–12

Burgwin [*née* Canham], **Elizabeth Miriam** (1850–1940), educationist, was born on 3 September 1850 at Occold, Suffolk, the second child of Samuel Canham, an agricultural labourer, and his wife, Miriam. After moving to London she attended the Practising School attached to Whitelands Training College before taking up a five-year pupil-teaching apprenticeship at St Luke's Parochial Girls' School, Chelsea, in 1864. Soon after completing this she married a London butcher, Thomas William Burgwin (*d.* in or before 1891), on 12 February 1870. Their only child, Thomas Lane, was born on 3 November in the same year.

From January 1872 to December 1873 Elizabeth Burgwin taught in West Ham, gaining her teacher's certificate by external examination in December 1872. In January 1874 she took up a post as head of Union Street Girls' School, Southwark, a newly established temporary school under the London school board, and it was from there that she and her fellow teachers moved to the new Orange Street Girls' School, also in Southwark, in June 1874. This was located in one of the poorest districts in London, and the pupils were unkempt and malnourished. Soon Mrs Burgwin, as headmistress, began to provide simple midday meals of bread and a hot drink. That led to the establishment of a small local organization to raise funds to supply food to pupils during the winter months. Early in the 1880s the venture received a major boost when she persuaded the journalist and author, George R. Sims, to publicize it in the column he wrote for *The Referee*, a leading sporting newspaper. That was repeated in subsequent years, with Elizabeth Burgwin acting as the fund's treasurer, and by the beginning of the twentieth century the Referee Children's Free Breakfast and Dinner Fund had become the largest agency for supplying free meals to scholars in London. In 1895 and 1899 she gave evidence to special committees of the London school board concerning underfed children. She also gave evidence to the Cross commission on the Elementary Education Acts on 26 November 1886, and to the inter-departmental committee on medical inspection and feeding of children on 23 May 1905, concerning her work to promote the welfare of her pupils.

Elizabeth Burgwin remained at Orange Street until her appointment in October 1891 as the London school board's first superintendent of schools for special instruction. By this time she was a widow, and prior to taking up the post she visited various institutions catering for mentally handicapped people in Britain, France, Germany, and Denmark. She opened the capital's first special classes in the summer of 1892. By 1897, when seven school boards in the country were providing classes for the 'feeble-minded', over a thousand of the 1300 pupils under instruction were taught in one of London's twenty-seven centres or classes, under Mrs Burgwin's direction. In 1905 she was described as having 'probably more experience of Special Schools than anyone else in the world', and the education authorities in Bristol, Brighton, and Birmingham sent their special-school teachers to her for training. She became one of the seven members of the departmental committee on defective and epileptic children in 1896–8. In 1898 she was involved in the establishment of a special school for the physically handicapped, and the provision of facilities for disabled children soon became an important aspect of her work. On 30 June 1905 she gave evidence to the royal commission on the care and control of the feeble-minded.

Elizabeth Burgwin was an enthusiastic supporter of the National Union of Elementary Teachers (or National Union of Teachers (NUT), as it became in 1889). In 1885 she was the first woman to be elected to its executive committee and remained a member of the executive until 1896. She was an enthusiastic and able supporter of the union's charitable activities and in 1878 was present at the inauguration of its Benevolent and Orphan Fund. She was a fund trustee from 1914 until 1936, and was closely involved in the work of the Boys' Orphanage.

Perhaps surprisingly, in view of her determined character and her general breaking of gender moulds, Elizabeth Burgwin was a strong opponent of the cause and tactics of the female suffrage movement; she was a member of the executive committee of the National League for Opposing Women's Suffrage. In 1912 she was an outspoken critic of a motion at the NUT annual conference in favour of votes for women. She was also opposed to the provision of sex education for elementary pupils, arguing in evidence to a London county council sub-committee in 1914 that it was the responsibility of parents rather than teachers to bring up their offspring 'in a healthy manner'.

Until her retirement in September 1916, Elizabeth Burgwin remained superintendent of London's special schools and as a sign of their regard, fellow teachers contributed a testimonial of £1000 to commemorate the occasion. She then took up a post with the Ministry of Labour, advising on the award of pensions to widows and children of officers killed in action during the First World War. For this she was made an OBE.

Elizabeth Burgwin died on 1 February 1940 at 147 Brixton Road, London. In an obituary *The Times* praised her as 'one of the outstanding authorities on the subject of the education of the mentally subnormal child and the technique of teaching which was developed was due in great measure to her initiative, her sympathy, and her understanding'. London's own pre-eminence in this field at the beginning of the twentieth century was a product of her hard work and commitment. *The Times* also paid tribute to the wit and good humour which had characterized her long association with London education.

PAMELA HORN

Sources *The Times* (15 Feb 1940) · *Schoolmaster and Woman Teacher's Chronicle* (8 Feb 1940) · *The Schoolmaster* (16 Feb 1895) · *The Schoolmaster* (13 April 1912) · P. Horn, 'Elizabeth Miriam Burgwin: child welfare pioneer and union activist', *Journal of Further and Higher Education*, 14/3 (1990) · application form for grant for Orange Street Girls' School, PRO, ED.7.78 · Orange Street Girls' School records, LMA · b. cert. · m. cert. · d. cert. · *CGPLA Eng. & Wales* (1940)
Archives LMA, records relating to Orange Street Girls' School and the feeding of schoolchildren
Likenesses photograph, 1870–89, repro. in T. Gautrey, *Lux mihi laus: school board memories* (c.1938), facing p. 137 · photograph (in old age), repro. in *Schoolmaster and Woman Teacher's Chronicle*
Wealth at death £10,247 13s. 8d.: probate, 11 April 1940, *CGPLA Eng. & Wales*

Burhill, Robert (*bap.* 1572, *d.* 1641), Church of England clergyman, baptized on 28 February 1572 at Dymock, Gloucestershire, was the son of George Burghill, descended from the armigerous family of Thinghill, Herefordshire, and his wife, Margaret. He entered Corpus Christi College, Oxford, on 13 January 1588, graduating BA on 5 February 1591 and proceeding MA on 12 December 1594. He was elected fellow on 20 March 1595 and took his BD on 7 July 1603. Burhill succeeded John Howson in a canonry of Hereford on 6 January 1604, and obtained rectories at Peterstow, Herefordshire, in 1604, and Holgate, Shropshire, the following year.

Esteemed for Greek and Hebrew scholarship, Burhill was consulted by Sir Walter Ralegh when he was writing *The History of the World*. Burhill himself wrote a preface to Miles Smith, *A Learned and Godly Sermon*, which he edited in 1602 without the author's permission, and contributed Latin verses to a number of works in 1602 and 1603. In 1606 he supported Howson's contention that remarriage of the divorced was unlawful against Thomas Pye with his *In controversiam inter Iohannem Howsonum & Thomam Pyum S.T. Doctores de novis post divortium ob adulterium nuptijs*, published with the second edition of Howson's *Thesis*. In 1611 he wrote *Pro tortura torti contra Martinum Becanum Jesuitam, responsio*, defending Bishop Lancelot Andrewes of Ely against Bellarmine. This was followed by the anti-papal *De potestate regia et usurpatione papali, pro tortura torti, contra parallelum Andreae Eudaemonioannis Cydonij Jesuitae, responsio* (1613) and by *Contra Martini Becani, Jesuitae Maguntini, controversiam Anglicanam, assertio pro iure regio* (1613), another defence against Bellarmine, this time of John Buckeridge, bishop of Rochester. Bishop Andrewes gave Burhill the rectory of Snailwell, Cambridgeshire, the same year. An enlarged edition of the last work appeared in 1614.

Also in 1614, Burhill was the king's candidate for the presidency of Corpus Christi College. He secured the votes of three of the seven senior fellows, but so did Thomas Anyan; the latter, favoured by the university's chancellor, Lord Ellesmere, was elected, with royal acquiescence, on the strength of the vice-president's casting vote after referral to the visitor, Bishop Bilson of Winchester. However, further modest preferment for Burhill came in 1622, when he obtained the rectory of Northwold, Norfolk.

Burhill's unpublished manuscripts include a Latin commentary on difficult passages in Job, in Corpus Christi Library, and a treatise supporting monarchy and episcopacy

and a long Latin poem, 'Britannia scholastica', dedicated to Sir Thomas Bodley, both in the Bodleian. He took his DD on 2 June 1632. Anthony Wood suggests that, 'upon the approach of the civil war' (Wood, *Ath. Oxon.*, 3.19), Burhill retired definitively to Northwold, where he died in October 1641 'or thereabouts' (ibid.); he was buried in the chancel of Northwold church. A monument was erected about 1740.   SIDNEY LEE, *rev.* A. J. HEGARTY

Sources Wood, *Ath. Oxon.*, new edn · Foster, *Alum. Oxon.* · T. Fowler, *The history of Corpus Christi College*, OHS, 25 (1893) · CCC Oxf., Fulman's collections, IX, MS 303 · *Fasti Angl., 1541–1857* · W. Ralegh, *The history of the world*, ed. W. Oldys, 2 vols. (1736) · F. Madan, *Oxford books: a bibliography of printed works*, 3 vols. (1895–1931); repr. (1964) · parish register (baptism), 28 Feb 1572, Dymock · Coll. Arms, G. 9, fol. 48
Archives Bodl. Oxf. · CCC Oxf.

Burhred. *See* Burgred (*d.* 874?).

Burke, Aedanus (1743–1802), jurist and politician in the United States of America, was born on 16 June 1743 in co. Galway, Ireland, of unknown parentage, although his parents were presumably Roman Catholics. He attended the English Jesuit seminary at St Omer, France, although later in life he was nominally a protestant.

In 1766 Burke was living in the vicinity of Fredericksburg, Virginia, and reading law in the large library of a prominent local resident, John Mercer. By 1775 he had arrived in Charles Town (later Charleston), South Carolina. Service in the local militia preceded a commission in the 2nd South Carolina regiment of the American continental army, which he resigned in February 1778 to become a judge of the local court of common pleas and general sessions. Elected to the South Carolina state legislature in 1779, he continued to represent the parishes composing Charles Town for most of the next decade. But when the British invasion of the state in 1780 disrupted regular governmental functions Burke returned to militia duty as a captain. The surrender of the city on 12 May made him and some 5000 others prisoners of war. Released in mid-1781 he joined the staff of the American patriot General Arthur St Clair; thus he was at Yorktown, Virginia, when General Charles, second Earl Cornwallis, surrendered his British army to American and French forces, effectively ending the War of American Independence.

Though offered the chief justiceship of Georgia in 1782, Burke declined it and returned to South Carolina, where he continued his service as a judge and member of the state house of representatives. When in 1782 the legislature debated punishing loyalists by banishment, confiscation of their property, or amercement, Burke unsuccessfully opposed these measures. Recognizing the need 'to reconcile to each other men whose fate it was to live together' (Barnwell, 26, 1925, 212), he believed that a general amnesty was the best policy, though his experience on the judicial circuit convinced him that making some examples was necessary to forestall vigilante justice. *An Address to the Freemen of South Carolina*, published in 1783, outlined his thinking on the subject for a wider audience.

During the 1780s Burke also wrote two other pamphlets

and participated in an attempt to codify state law. His publications reflected his concern about the political development of aristocratic oligarchies in America. The Order of the Cincinnati, a hereditary society established in 1783 by continental army officers, particularly alarmed him, and he attacked it in *Considerations on the Society or Order of the Cincinnati* (1783), which was reprinted in various forms in France, Germany, and England. *A Few Salutary Hints Pointing out the Policy and Consequences of Admitting British Subjects* (1786) added warnings to South Carolina against the insidious influence of wealthy British merchants. Appointed by the state's house of representatives in 1785 as one of three commissioners to revise and digest state law, Burke and his colleagues built on a compilation begun in the 1760s; some of their recommendations became statutory law or part of the state constitution of 1790.

Meanwhile Burke served as a member of both the state convention called to ratify the United States constitution and the first United States congress (1789–91) elected under it. In each case he represented predominantly rural districts and, like most residents of the interior of the state, he unsuccessfully opposed ratification of the constitution. After the convention approved the document on 23 May 1788, Burke favoured amendments that would further restrict federal power and bar the president from succeeding himself. In congress, despite some ambivalence on both subjects, he supported the assumption of state debts by the federal government and full payment to the current holders of United States securities. But he was against most other measures proposed by the secretary of the treasury, Alexander Hamilton, including the imposition of a federal excise tax and the establishment of a national bank. In discussions about port duties and slaves he championed the interests of his state. Tampering with slavery, he maintained, would sow 'the seeds of insurrection and public calamity' (Ward, 948). While in New York Burke developed a relationship with Isabella Murphy, a mantua maker, who bore an illegitimate child, George Burke, for whom Aedanus provided in his will.

Burke did not stand again for the national congress but returned to South Carolina, where he continued to serve as a judge. Early in 1791 the legislature considered but failed to choose him as chief justice. In 1798 he refused to be a candidate for the United States senate; but in 1799 the legislature named him to the court of chancery. He died on 30 March 1802 of unknown causes, presumably in Charleston, and was buried at the plantation of O'Brien Smith, in St Bartholomew's parish, near Jacksonborough, South Carolina. He was survived by his fiancée, Ruth Savage. His reputation was that of a good though somewhat eccentric judge; as a legislator he was an ardent republican and a champion of liberty but, especially on the national scene, a negative and ultimately marginal force.

ROBERT M. WEIR

Sources J. C. Meleney, *The public life of Aedanus Burke, revolutionary republican in post-revolutionary South Carolina* (1989) • H. M. Ward, 'Burke, Aedanus', *ANB* • 'Correspondence of Hon. Arthur Middleton, signer of the declaration of independence', ed. J. W. Barnwell, *South Carolina Historical and Genealogical Magazine*, 26 (1925), 183–213;

27 (1926), 1–29, 51–80, 107–55 • R. M. Weir, '"The violent spirit": the re-establishment of order and the continuity of leadership in post-revolutionary South Carolina', *The last of American freemen: studies in the political culture of the colonial and revolutionary south* (1986) • J. J. Nadelhaft, *The disorders of war: the Revolution in South Carolina* (1981) • R. N. Klein, *The rise of the planter class in the South Carolina backcountry, 1760–1808* (1990) • G. C. Rogers, 'Aedanus Burke, Nathanael Greene, Anthony Wayne, and the British merchants of Charleston', *South Carolina Historical Magazine*, 67 (1966), 75–83 • G. C. Rogers, *Evolution of a federalist: William Loughton Smith of Charleston, 1758–1812* (1962) • M. E. Stevens, 'Wealth, influence or powerful connections: Aedanus Burke and the case of Hezekiah Maham', *South Carolina Historical Magazine*, 81 (1980), 163–8 • W. B. Edgar, N. L. Bailey, and A. Moore, eds., *Biographical directory of the South Carolina house of representatives*, 5 vols. (1974–92), vol. 3 • J. B. O'Neall, *Biographical sketches of the bench and bar of South Carolina* (1859) • J. Haw, *John and Edward Rutledge of South Carolina* (1997)

Archives Hist. Soc. Penn., Pierre Butler papers • South Carolina Archives and History Center, Columbia, records of the general assembly

Likenesses portrait, Hibernian Society, Charleston, South Carolina; repro. in Meleney, *Public life*

Wealth at death not a man of great property: Meleney, *Public life*, 30–31

Burke, Sir (John) Bernard (1814–1892), genealogist and herald, was born on 5 January 1814 in London, the second of six children to survive infancy of John *Burke (1786–1848) of London, author of the *Peerage and Baronetage*, and his wife and cousin, Mary (1781–1846), daughter of Bernard O'Reilly of Ballymorris, co. Longford. He had three brothers and two sisters. A Roman Catholic, he was educated at Caen College in Normandy, where he obtained first prize in mathematics and prizes in Latin verses, Greek thesis, and history. He was admitted to the Middle Temple on 30 December 1835 and was called to the bar on 25 January 1839. He was listed in the 1840s in the same chambers as his brother Peter *Burke (1811–1881) at 2 Churchyard Court, Temple.

As early as 1838 Burke's name was joined with his father's as author of *A Genealogical and Heraldic History of the Extinct and Dormant Baronetcies of England*. Subsequent collaborations were the second (1840) and third (1846) editions of *A Genealogical and Heraldic Dictionary of the Peerages of England, Ireland and Scotland, Extinct, Dormant and in Abeyance*; *The Knightage of Great Britain and Ireland* (1841); the first three editions of *A General Armory of England, Scotland and Ireland* (1842, 1843, 1844); *Heraldic Illustrations* (3 vols., 1844–6); the ninth (1847) and tenth (1848) editions of *A Genealogical and Heraldic Dictionary of the Peerage and Baronetage*; the three-volume second edition (1843–9) of *A Genealogical and Heraldic Dictionary of the Landed Gentry of Great Britain and Ireland*; and the two-volume (1847 and 1851) *Royal Families of England, Scotland and Wales with their Descendants, Sovereigns and Subjects*. After his father's death in 1848 he continued to edit the principal genealogical works. The *Peerage and Baronetage*, which became an annual publication in 1847, was in its fifty-fourth edition at the time of Burke's own death in 1892, and he produced a further five editions of the *Landed Gentry* after 1849.

In 1853 Burke moved to Dublin on his appointment as Ulster king of arms and knight attendant on the Order of St Patrick in succession to Sir William Betham, who died

Sir (John) Bernard Burke (1814–1892), by Charles Clarkington

on 26 October 1853. On 22 February 1854 he was knighted and in 1855 made keeper of the Irish state papers. On 8 January 1856 at Westland Row Roman Catholic chapel, Dublin, he married Barbara Maria Frances (1827–1887), second daughter of James MacEvoy of Tobertynan, co. Meath. They had seven sons and one daughter, of whom the eldest, Sir Henry Farnham Burke (1859–1930), was deputy Ulster king of arms (1889–93) and Garter king of arms (1919–30). The fourth son, Ashworth Peter Burke (1864–1919), edited a number of the publications after his father's death.

A tribute in the *Irish Literary Gazette* of 14 November 1857 refers to Burke's urbanity, thorough kindness, genuine good nature, and lively disposition. Although a capable, businesslike, energetic, and ambitious man who brought order to the Irish state papers, Burke lacked critical scholarship. This was exposed in an anonymous pamphlet published in Edinburgh in 1865. Its reputed author, George Burnett (1822–1890), was appointed Lyon king of arms in 1866. The writer exposed the inaccuracies in Burke's *Peerage* and thought the majority of the pedigrees in the *Landed Gentry* 'utterly worthless'. In 1877 Edward Augustus Freeman, subsequently regius professor of modern history at Oxford, criticized Burke's scholarship and, writing in the *Contemporary Review*, showed the absurdity of the early ancestry claimed for such families as Fitzwilliam,

Leighton, Wake, and Stourton. He took particular exception to the fact that the pedigrees were given quasi-official approval through acceptance by an editor who held an official position. Much of the information on the origins of families came, if not from themselves, from the eighteenth-century peerages of Arthur Collins, and the uncritical acceptance of this material was a failing of both Sir Bernard Burke and his father before him. The reputation of their publications as far as the early history of families was concerned received a final blow from John Horace Round, who in books such as *Studies in Peerage and Family History* (1901) exposed their weaknesses. It was not until later in the twentieth century that the reputation of Burke's publications was rebuilt under the guidance of Sir Bernard Burke's son Sir Henry Farnham Burke (1859–1930), Garter king of arms. Even so, their value for information about nineteenth-century families, with their detail on children and their spouses, remains exceptional and allowed the British-property owning class to be the best referenced in the world.

In 1869, when three commissioners were appointed by the earl marshal to inquire into the College of Arms, Burke wrote suggesting that the College of Arms should become a government department with the fees going to the exchequer and the heralds receiving fixed salaries in lieu. He also suggested that he should be appointed garter. His recommendations were not adopted, although in 1867 the Lyon office had become a government department and Ulster's office became one in 1871.

Burke produced numerous popular books on heraldry and genealogy. *Anecdotes of the Aristocracy*, *Vicissitudes of Families*, and *The Rise of Great Families* are examples, all of which ran to a number of editions. He was appointed CB in 1868, having previously (1862) been made an honorary LLD of the University of Dublin. His *Times* obituary refers to the unfailing precision and effectiveness with which he arranged the order of precedence upon the arrival and departure of viceroys, the investitures of the Order of St Patrick, and other state events. Burke died on 12 December 1892 at his residence, Tullamaine House, Upper Leeson Street, Dublin, after several years' illness and was buried on the 15th at Westland Row Catholic chapel, Dublin. Thirty-three volumes of Sir Bernard Burke's Irish pedigrees and sixty-nine further volumes of his genealogical collections went with 184 volumes of Sir H. F. Burke's correspondence to the College of Arms after the latter's death.

THOMAS WOODCOCK

Sources A. Wagner, *Heralds of England: a history of the office and College of Arms* (1967), 511–13 · A. Wagner, *English genealogy*, 3rd edn (1983), 377–8, 388–93 · *Burke's family index* (1976) · J. J. Howard and F. A. Crisp, *Visitation of Ireland*, 1 (1897), 23–4 · J. H. Round, *Studies in peerage and family history* (1901) · J. H. Round, *Peerage and pedigree: studies in peerage law and family history*, 2 vols. (1910) · *New England Register*, 13 (1859), 3 · *The Times* (14 Dec 1892) · *N&Q*, 8th ser., 2 (1892), 500 · Boase, *Mod. Eng. biog.*, 4.545 · [G. Burnett], *Popular genealogists, or, The art of pedigree-making* (1865)

Archives Coll. Arms, genealogical collections | Bodl. Oxf., corresp. with Lord Kimberley · Leics. RO, letters to C. W. Packe · U. Leeds, Brotherton L., letters to John Torrens Kyle

Likenesses Spex, caricature, 1875 · C. Clarkington, photograph, NPG [*see illus.*] · line print, NPG · mezzotint (after engraving), NPG ·

portrait, repro. in *Burke's family index* · process block print (after painting), BM

Burke, Edmund (1729/30–1797), politician and author, was born in Dublin. His date of birth is not certain. 1 January 1729, according to the Julian calendar in force at the time, has generally been accepted but it is possible that the year was 1730. His mother, Mary (*c*.1702–1770), came from an impoverished but genteel Roman Catholic family, the Nagles of co. Cork. His father, Richard (*d*. 1761), was an attorney and represented the other Ireland, of prosperous, professional, protestant Dublin. It has been suggested that Richard was himself a convert and that the knowledge of his apostasy permanently afflicted his son with a sense of familial guilt. There was in any case no danger of the young Burke's being denied a knowledge of his Catholic roots. Portions of his childhood were spent away from the unhealthy air of Dublin with his mother's family in the Blackwater valley. His sister Juliana was brought up and remained a Roman Catholic.

Education and early writings In 1741 Burke was sent, with his elder brother Garrett and his younger brother Richard *Burke, to a very different environment, a Quaker school at Ballitore run by Abraham Shackleton. It provided him with a rigorous academic training and further exposure to the diversity of the Christian faith. Perhaps too, it gave him an alternative father figure in Abraham Shackleton. Richard Burke senior had a reputation for integrity and dependability; human warmth seems to have been beyond him. In 1744 Edmund returned to the parental home so that he could attend Trinity College by way of preparation for the law. There are indications that he found the formulaic curriculum tedious, and was at best a moderately conscientious student. On the other hand he read voraciously outside the syllabus, tried his hand as a poet, founded a debating club whose minutes reveal signs of his rhetorical skill, and contributed to a review periodical, *The Reformer*. In 1748 he graduated. What he did thereafter is unclear. It was a time when the populist Charles Lucas was making Irish politics more than usually turbulent. Scholars have enlisted the young Burke both for and against Lucas, but the evidence remains inconclusive.

In 1750 Burke set off for London and the Middle Temple, where he had been entered since 1747, with the intention of acquiring the training necessary to qualify for the Irish bar. He showed little taste for the law, and developed a lasting dislike for the narrowness of those who practised it. His health was not good, perhaps providing him with reasons for not studying too earnestly and also for discovering the English and Welsh countryside during summer breaks. An early companion at work and play was another young Irishman, William *Burke, whom Burke treated as a remote kinsman and whose fortunes were subsequently inseparable from his.

In 1756 he made his first widely noticed appearance in print. *A Vindication of Natural Society* was a riposte to the writings of Lord Bolingbroke, published posthumously three years before. Their somewhat dated deism provided a convenient target for orthodox pens. Burke shared the

Edmund Burke (1729/30–1797), by Sir Joshua Reynolds, 1767–9

revulsion but adopted an ironic mode of attack. Posing as a supporter of Bolingbroke's rational reductionism he argued that it could be employed as well in matters of government as of religion. 'The Professors of Artificial Law have always walked hand in hand with the Professors of Artificial Theology'. The history of civilized society was one of tyranny and slaughter. 'Dreams of Society' and 'Visions of Religion' should be abandoned together and we should 'vindicate ourselves into perfect Liberty' (*Writings and Speeches*, 1.173, 183). The *Vindication* was an artful work of demolition, but its reasonable tone carried such conviction that its satirical intent was easily lost from sight. In retrospect the work locates the author in an intellectual tradition that leads back to Berkeley and Swift. It also contains much that anticipates his later denunciations of the 'natural rights' school. But he plainly learned from its ambiguous reception. Irony was always to be a Burkean weapon, especially in his last years when it acquired an impressive savagery. But in future it was to be harnessed to a transparent argumentative purpose.

There followed in 1757 a work which earned Burke a less equivocal fame. *A Philosophical Enquiry into the Origin of our Ideas of the Sublime and Beautiful* shared the preoccupation of the time with the linkage between human psychology and cultural phenomena, in this instance aesthetic taste. It argued that the instinct for self-preservation was associated with apprehensions of pain and danger and thereby with a sense of the sublime. Instinctive sociability, by contrast, was associated with pleasure and a sense of beauty. On these simple foundations Burke erected a plausible account of various aspects of human sensibility, and obtained an appreciative audience which lasted well into the early nineteenth century. In Britain his doctrine of the sublime fuelled growing interest in the pictorial and literary appeal of landscape. His work also attracted attention on the continent. Kant described Burke as 'the foremost author' in 'the empirical exposition of aesthetic judgments' (*Writings and Speeches*, 1.187–8). His enduring achievement was to have tackled a difficult subject in a fashion accessible to any educated reader.

Philosophy was not the only discipline in which Burke sought to wear learning lightly but usefully. In 1757 he contributed to a joint publication with William Burke, *An Account of the European Settlements in America*. At a time when Britain and France were on the verge of their first great war for empire this caught a tide of interest not only in the commercial consequence of the West Indian and American colonies, but also in the history of their settlement and the manners of their native peoples. As a compilation of contemporary knowledge mixed with some telling appeals to British self-interest it was well received and continued to be read by subsequent generations. In more personal terms it should be placed alongside Edmund's thoughts of emigration to the New World at this time, William's success in obtaining a post in the administration of the French island of Guadeloupe when it was captured in 1759, and Richard Burke's appointment as collector of customs in Grenada in 1763.

Much of the *Account* was essentially history. There was seemingly more to come from Edmund's pen. In 1757 he contracted with his friend and publisher Robert Dodsley for a one-volume history of England from the time of the Romans. The manuscript was to be delivered by Christmas 1758, but Burke never got beyond Magna Carta. The portions of the text that he did draft were later published in his complete works as *An Essay towards an Abridgment of English History*. Its most striking feature is perhaps Burke's emphasis on the spirit of English customs as distinct from the letter of English law. From the conquest to the reign of John he discerned a fluctuation between freedom and servitude which finally, under a notably weak king, culminated in 'the grand revolution in favour of liberty' (*Writings and Speeches*, 1.550–51). The argument fits well with another and presumably related fragment, also published posthumously by his editors, as *An Essay towards an History of the Laws of England*. This remains interesting for its robust avowal of a tory position, to the effect that modern English law owed more to the Norman conquest than to the ancient Anglo-Saxon inheritance. But Burke denied what for tories was the principal advantage of this position, rejecting the notion that such a derivation would have made 'all our national rights and liberties' dependent on the will of the post-conquest monarchy (ibid., 1.324).

Posterity may regret that Burke did not complete his English history. Lord Acton thought that if he had persisted with it he 'would have been the first of our historians' (Chapman, 3). It was recognizably in the new philosophical style that marked the eighteenth century's self-conscious break with antiquarianism, and revealed its author's preference of rational conjectures to improbable relations. Burke believed that history as it had been handed down from the ancients was a poor instructor by comparison with contemporary discovery. As he later told another historian of the Americas, William Robertson, 'now the Great Map of Mankind is unrolld at once; and there is no state or Gradation of barbarism, and no mode of refinement which we have not at the same instant under our View' (*Correspondence*, 3.351).

Part of Burke's difficulty with the history was that he was also engaged on another literary venture for the same publisher. In 1758 he became editor of a new periodical, the *Annual Register*, until at least the mid-1760s writing much of what it contained himself. At £100 per volume his remuneration provided him with a powerful motive to ensure that publication took place on time. The matter also suited the experimental and wide-ranging nature of his intellectual interests. Like some other periodicals— the *Gentleman's Magazine* and *London Magazine*, for example—it contained a mixture of news and commentary designed to bring the general reader up to date with all kinds of expertise and learning. But unlike those, publication by the year rather than the month gave a more reflective tone to the discussion. Burke's 'characters', book reviews, selections of poems, and articles on new developments in science, all displayed his catholic taste and enlarged learning. But more than anything it was his survey of each year's history that made the *Annual Register* so successful. It quickly became the standard reference work of contemporary events.

By this time, as he approached thirty, Burke had acquired a family. On 12 March 1757 he had married Jane Mary Nugent (1734–1812), daughter of a Catholic physician who had treated him at Bath. His son Richard was born in February 1758. Another son, Christopher, died in infancy. The household also included Burke's father-in-law, Christopher Nugent, and at various times his elder brother Richard and his lifelong friend William Burke. The financial foundations of this little clan were to say the least unstable. Burke's writings brought in some funds, but hardly sufficient. If his legal ambitions had ever amounted to much they had long since evaporated, and with them his father's advances. Acquiring solid expectations meant employing his connections.

One of these yielded a significant opening. In 1759 Burke became private secretary to William Gerard Hamilton, a young MP of some promise who had ministerial office at the Board of Trade. In 1761 Hamilton was promoted to the office of chief secretary in Ireland, and made Burke his private secretary in this office. Their initial residence in Dublin coincided with an outbreak of Catholic peasant disturbances that was savagely repressed. The judicial murders of the Munster circuit appalled Burke. He was also dismayed by what he regarded as malicious attempts to implicate some of his Nagle relatives in subversive activities. At about this time he composed a piece on the treatment of Irish Catholics that was sufficiently strident to fit perfectly the debates of the 1790s and 1800s. It was eventually published by his editors as *Tract on the Popery Laws* in time to serve a contemporary purpose.

In 1763 Hamilton obtained further preferment: the chancellorship of the exchequer of Ireland. Burke accepted matching promotion in the form of a pension of £300 per annum, despite concern that it might place him in too personal a dependence on Hamilton. Soon afterwards Hamilton's star waned. In 1764 he had to resign his chief secretaryship, having alienated his superiors by his mismanagement. Burke himself grew restless as his aide. The past decade had seen him established as a substantial figure in the metropolitan culture. His network of relationships already included many notables of the age: Samuel Johnson, Arthur Murphy, David Garrick, Oliver Goldsmith, Joshua Reynolds, and Mrs Montagu. These were all to be lifelong friendships. In 1763 he became something of a patron himself when he met the Irish painter James Barry, who was sent to the continent at the expense of the Burkes. In 1764 too he was a founder member of the celebrated Club established by Reynolds and Johnson at the Turk's Head in Soho. His sense of his own merit must have become increasingly difficult to contain within a relationship that bound him to a lesser man. At the end of the year he and Hamilton quarrelled irretrievably, moving Burke to resign his pension. Throughout his life he combined intense loyalty to his friends with a prickly sensitivity where his perceived independence was concerned. Hamilton never succeeded in managing this combination. Had he been better at it Burke's future might have been very different.

A new identity Among the contacts that Edmund and William made at this time were two members of the whig opposition: William Fitzherbert and Lord John Cavendish. When a new ministry was formed in July 1765 they secured employment for both. William became undersecretary of state to Henry Conway, Edmund private secretary to the prime minister, Lord Rockingham. 'This little gleam of prosperity' as Edmund called it, was nearly doused at the outset. The old duke of Newcastle, who had his own candidate for the post, accused Edmund of being 'by birth and education a Papist, and a Jacobite' (*Charlemont MSS*, 2.281–2). If the charge had come from anyone but his meddling senior Rockingham might have taken notice of it. Instead he confirmed his new secretary in office. In December a further foothold was secured. Thanks to William's influence with a Buckinghamshire landowner, Lord Verney, Edmund was elected to the Commons for the borough of Wendover, taking his seat on 14 January 1766.

For a man with political ambitions, this was an advanced age at which to enter parliament. The moment was, however, propitiously dramatic for making an entrance. The American colonies were in uproar following the imposition of Grenville's stamp tax. British trade was imperilled by a retaliatory embargo on imports. Burke's first speeches were delivered on the ministry's answer to this crisis, a judicious mixture of firmness and concession which repealed the Stamp Act while asserting the mother country's sovereignty in the Declaratory Act. He made an immediate impression. From the outset the penetration and profundity that were to be his hallmarks

as a parliamentary performer were evident, and in his early speeches on America it is possible to discern the outlines of a mature imperial doctrine. What also counted for much was his skill in co-ordinating a campaign by merchants and manufacturers to convince a reluctant Commons of the wisdom of the government's policy. The experience confirmed his belief in the importance of 'out of doors' politics and provided him with valuable insight into its management.

Rockingham's ministry lasted only a year. The inexperience of its leaders, their suspicion of the king's inner core of courtiers, and the dominating and disruptive influence of William Pitt in the Commons deprived it of stability. When the king replaced Rockingham with Pitt himself in July 1766 Burke had ample opportunity to throw in his lot with his successors and would not have been blamed if he had done so. But he did not waver in his fidelity. Later in life he claimed that he made a visit to his native Ireland at this time to avoid the negotiations that would certainly have resulted in an offer of office. In part this may have been because he did not share in the adulation of Pitt. He had met him only once, in spring 1766, to discuss commercial policy, and had quickly recognized his intellectual shallowness, finding only a 'few rusty prejudices' (*Correspondence*, 1.251–2). The gulf between the two traditions of old whiggism widened. Burke, whatever he had been before, was now firmly and forever a Rockingham whig.

Burke's personal relationship with Rockingham, which ended only with the latter's death and is commemorated in an unfinished but evocative portrait by Reynolds, was not without difficulties. Burke had neither the wealth nor inherited status to aspire to equality or independence. As private secretary to a prime minister he had been remunerated by the crown. In opposition he received a salary from Rockingham, issued diplomatically in the form of loans which were to be cancelled in Rockingham's will. From 1771 to 1776 he was also employed by the provincial assembly of New York as its agent on a salary of £500 per annum. Beyond that his earnings were meagre.

It could certainly not be said that Burke's motives were mercenary. Lord North's offer in 1772 of a place on a commission to be sent to Bengal, generous to the extent that it could easily have been made to a ministerial placeman, less altruistic in the sense that it would have removed a formidable opposition speaker from the Commons, was rejected. Burke was never to enjoy financial security by making his career in politics. Moreover, acting as a great magnate's man of business could at times be unpalatable. 'This method of going hither and thither, and agitating things personally, when it is not done in chief, Lowers the Estimation of whoever is engaged in such Transactions', he wrote to his master in January 1773 (*Correspondence*, 2.408). There is a story of his arriving at Rockingham's house hot from the House of Commons and remaining in his sedan chair for a while in the hall in order to emphasize that he was not at anyone's beck and call (J. Taylor, *Records of my Life*, 2 vols., 1832, 2.190). Burke has been accused of subservience to the aristocratic leaders of his party. A letter to the duke of Richmond of November 1772 is often quoted:

> You people of great families and hereditary Trusts and fortunes are not like such as I am, who whatever we may be by the Rapidity of our growth and of the fruit we bear, flatter ourselves that while we creep on the Ground we belly into melons that are exquisite for size and flavour, yet still we are but annual plants that perish with our Season and leave no sort of Traces behind us. (*Correspondence*, 2.377)

This was one of Burke's numerous attempts to get the easily distracted leaders of his party to fulfil their duties. It did not in reality imply an undervaluing of himself. Indeed, it was Burke's sensitivity and fear of being patronized that made him somewhat detached from his supposed betters. He rarely joined in the country house visits that were employed for a mixture of business and pleasure, though frequently invited to do so. He boasted of never paying court to 'those that are called great'. On one occasion in the Commons, provoked by an attack on his origins by a tory country gentleman, he 'took to himself the appellation of a Novus Homo' and 'expatiated upon the Impropriety and danger of discouraging new Men' (ibid., 2.127–8).

When Burke sought to establish his own social identity it rather resembled that of the small propertied gentleman than the aristocratic hanger-on. There is evidence that as early as 1763 he involved himself in a farming venture at Theobald's Park in Middlesex, although the property was not his own but that of an Irish family whom he sought to assist. The experience, which made him the victim of sheep stealing and involved him in unpleasant litigation, did not put him off a more personal and extended commitment to rural life. In 1765 he inherited from his brother Garrett a small estate at Clogher in co. Cork, which he managed through his Nagle relatives and retained until 1790. He was soon to add to it in England. On 1 May 1768 he wrote to his friend Shackleton 'I have made a push with all I could collect of my own, and the aid of my friends to cast a little root in this Country' (*Correspondence*, 1.351). His new estate, once the home of the poet Edmund Waller, was Gregories, near Beaconsfield. By July 1768 his letters to Rockingham were featuring the state of the clover crop and the threat of rain to the harvest, alongside news of politics. His new home was close enough to London for frequent access, and provided him with an absorbing occupation as an agricultural improver capable of exchanging tips with Arthur Young. With his Irish friend Charles O'Hara his correspondence indeed came to suggest an equivalence in his 'pursuits, both in politics and farming' (Hoffman, 403). Gregories also satisfied something of his craving to be accepted as a country gentleman, though he never warmed to the society of the Buckinghamshire squires among whom he now dwelled.

The purchase price was £20,000. Most of it was borrowed, some from unidentified lenders who almost certainly included William Burke, and through him Lord Verney. Unfortunately, when the market for East India stock collapsed in 1769 both William and Verney were ruined, with consequences which inevitably affected

Edmund. Thanks to further borrowing, some of it from his friends, Burke and Gregories survived. Verney later accused his protégés of sharp practice in respect of these transactions, though nothing has been found directly to implicate Edmund himself. Even at the time there was unfavourable publicity about the financial affairs of the Burkes. William's involvement in East India speculations was well known. Richard Burke's part in some equally questionable dealings in the West Indies was to make matters worse. In the ministerial press the 'Hibernian orator' was exposed to unpleasant innuendo. The faint but distinct whiff of scandal, if only by association, still hangs over this phase of Burke's career.

The man of business Despite the financial crises and nervous strain that he endured during these years Burke threw himself into furthering his new cause. This was in some respects a thankless task, for Rockingham's leadership of his party was often perplexingly negative. Yet government during the late 1760s offered an inviting target. Pitt's physical and mental collapse left his cabinet colleagues to lurch from one crisis to another. In North America there was renewed controversy when regulatory duties imposed in 1767 were interpreted by the colonies as an infringement of their assumed right to tax themselves. The near bankruptcy of the East India Company moved parliament to take a controversial interest in the management of Britain's burgeoning Indian empire. Before long the disruptive activities of John Wilkes and his Middlesex electors also provided numerous openings for opposition. As Rockingham's man of business Burke ranked below more senior representatives of the party in the Commons, the former chancellor of the exchequer, William Dowdeswell, and Rockingham's Yorkshire comrade-in-arms, Sir George Savile. None the less much of the execution and not a little of the initiative came from Burke himself. By 1769 he had made himself indispensable.

Burke acquired credit with his new friends by his parliamentary performances. He quickly became the outstanding speaker in the Commons, the path cleared for him by Pitt's departure to the Lords in 1766 and Townshend's death in 1767. His only rivals in the parliament of 1768, to which he was re-elected for Wendover, were a past prime minister, George Grenville, and a future prime minister, Lord North. Neither could match his range of learning and rhetorical power. The magnetism of Burke's parliamentary presence and the majestic language that he seemed able to summon up without effort are well attested. Inside the house his growing authority was hard to challenge; outside, ridicule was resorted to. Burke suffered much on account of his Irish origins. In the press he was Edmund Bonny Clabber, the 'goose turned swan by the inspiring streams of the Liffey and the Shannon' (Mahoney, 30). Yet even hostile publicity raised his standing and by 1770 he was figuring in the prints as the British Cicero. This was not altogether inappropriate for an Irishman at Westminster. Cicero after all had been to his Roman enemies a *civis inquilinus* on account of his birth at Arpinum.

Many of Burke's auditors were overwhelmed by the richness of his discourse, though his gift for striking image and elaborate metaphor also made some of them suspicious of the substance. Yet his reputation owed as much to command of the debating style of the Commons as to high-flown oratory. His wit and humour (he was perhaps over-addicted to puns) were a more important part of his debating success than later accounts of his speeches would suggest. If sublime was a word much employed by those who heard him, there was often an earthiness about his language that disconcerted some. With back-bench MPs who valued solid reasoning more than sentiment Burke's attention to detail was tellingly effective. His training as a lawyer also stood him in good stead in an assembly that included many who practised the law and more who were familiar with its modes of argument. Burke's later reputation as the flowery orator who could make men weep but rarely obtained their votes obscures the tactical mastery that he displayed in these early years of his career when governments of the day were virtually guaranteed a parliamentary majority by the court and Treasury party. As his surviving manuscripts reveal, many of his performances were carefully prepared, but his debating skills went beyond set speeches. He customarily spoke late in debate in order to meet the full range of arguments put by opponents. It was this resourcefulness that was so impressive to seasoned debaters.

Burke was no less resourceful in print. He contributed a number of political articles to the newspaper press, probably more than can now be identified. He also published a succession of party tracts. *A Short Account of a Late Short Administration*, which appeared after Rockingham's dismissal in 1766, was a neat little essay purporting to describe 'plain facts; of a clear and public nature; neither extended by elaborate reasoning, nor heightened by the colouring of eloquence'. The facts chosen were naturally those most favourable to the reputation of the ex-ministers. Most interesting in retrospect is his emphasis on their alliance with commercial and manufacturing interests.

Burke's second major piece, of 1769, *Observations on a Late State of the Nation*, was written in response to a pamphlet penned by the Grenvillite William Knox, and reflected Burke's belief that the main obstacle to Rockingham's return to power was the respect that Grenville's record at the Treasury commanded. The argument was sufficiently weighty to challenge the prevailing view and to suggest that in the event of a vacancy in government the Rockingham party commanded fiscal expertise adequate to the task. Whether it was worth the undertaking must seem with hindsight doubtful. The question was not whether Rockingham or Grenville was better qualified to lead the country but whether either stood any chance of doing so. When the ministry did indeed collapse in January 1770 the king's chosen prime minister, Lord North, quickly restored order and morale by his amiable and persuasive style of management.

The timing of Burke's next political tract in May 1770, *Thoughts on the Cause of the Present Discontents*, was unfortunate in that the discontents described, principally those awakened by Wilkes, appeared to be subsiding. Fortunately, even at the time, the *Thoughts* were seen as transcending immediate concerns. They were penned self-consciously as 'the political Creed of our party', notwithstanding the doubts of some senior members of the party, who thought pamphlet warfare of this kind undignified and provocative (*Correspondence*, 2.136; *Writings and Speeches*, 2.246–7). Yet the tone could hardly be described as intemperate. Amid the ferocious polemics of the 1760s the *Thoughts* stood out as a beacon of calm, and, for many, conclusive reasoning about the political woes that beset Britain. Compared with the brutal invective of Junius, whom many contemporaries incorrectly identified with Burke, it was sedate and measured. Even its victims considered it 'gentlemanlike' (*Correspondence*, 2.139). The emphasis on the relationship between theory and practice also lent an air of statesmanship to what might otherwise look like mischief-making. 'It is the business of the speculative philosopher to mark the proper ends of Government. It is the business of the politician, who is the philosopher in action, to find out proper means towards those ends, and to employ them with effect' (*Writings and Speeches*, 2.318).

The argument, though hostile to the crown, displayed no personal animus against George III or even against Lord Bute. None the less, in identifying the growth of a court party which subverted the integrity of successive ministries, Burke developed a theme that passed into the mainstream of whig thought and informed much historical analysis well into the twentieth century. Modern historiography has preferred to treat it as at best propaganda and at worst downright invention, 'the most elaborate and famous of opposition fictions' (R. Sedgwick, *Letters from George III to Lord Bute*, 1939, xviii). Yet Burke and his friends were not alone in subscribing to the thesis of secret influence. And whatever its partiality it provided generations of whigs with a doctrine that sustained them in a long and hard fought war against executive power.

Burke's early success did not imply slavish adherence to his party. In 1767, when a cynical opposition appeal to voters forced government to reduce the land tax, he refused to cast his vote. There were matters of deep principle on which his opinions were quite remote from those of his friends. In 1772, though he supported dissenting ministers and schoolteachers who sought exemption from subscription to the established church he staunchly defended that church when it was threatened from within by unitarian clergy who wished to reform the Anglican creed. On that occasion he found himself voting alongside high tories against his whig colleagues.

Moreover Burke's general stance suggested rather the resigned patriotism of the old tory country party than the ruthless efficiency of whig power-mongers. In this he early captured something of the flavour of a party that was increasingly shorn of its natural courtiers. Casting his lot with the Rockinghams, Burke had a shrewd sense of the unlikelihood of preferment. As early as December 1766 he remarked that he saw a return to power at the End of a very long Visto. The View is dim and remote; and we do nothing in the world to bring it nearer, or to make it more certain. This disposition, which is become the principle of our party, I confess, from constitution and opinion, I like.   (*Correspondence*, 2.285)

Nor did he care for opposition for its own sake, though he lives in history as a remorseless harrier of governments and a formative influence on the development of party politics. He observed in October 1772 at a low point in whig fortunes:

there is no dignity in carrying on a teizing and vexatious sort of debate, without any other Effect, than fretting Ministers now and then, and keeping honest Gentlemen from their dinners; while we make triffling and ineffectual Divisions in the house, and the Nation quietly acquiesces in those measures which we agitate with so much eagerness. (ibid., 2.352)

Yet Burke remained a tireless speaker and campaigner. Between his parliamentary début in 1766 and the dissolution of 1774 he spoke in more than 200 debates. His pronouncements covered an enormous range of issues. In constitutional questions he from the beginning opposed parliamentary reform of the kind that Wilkite radicals advocated, including triennial parliaments and secret ballots. 'If no remedy can be found in the dispositions of capital people, in the Temper, spirit, (and docility too) of the Lower, and in the thorough union of both—nothing can be done by any alterations in forms' (*Correspondence*, 2.150). On the other hand he helped organize the petitioning movement which protested against the government's effective disenfranchisement of Wilkes's electors. He also advocated measures to limit the influence of the crown, including Savile's bill in 1768 to curb the legal inalienability of royal property, and Grenville's Controverted Elections Act of 1770. He favoured Dowdeswell's Jury Bill of 1771 which would have given juries the determination of seditious libel cases and supported the successful campaign of 1771 to force the House of Commons to concede the practice if not the principle of public reporting of its debates.

Some of his most interesting interventions on domestic issues found Burke enunciating doctrines in advance of contemporary opinion. In debates of the early 1770s he advocated freeing the grain trade several years before the publication of Adam Smith's *Wealth of Nations*. The act of 1772 repealing ancient legislation against free dealing in corn was passed at Burke's instigation. In 1774, in a passionate outburst against the poor laws, he denounced 'the amazingly mischievous tendency of them: their principle is nothing but slavery' (*Writings and Speeches*, 2.403). In imperial questions he repeatedly returned to the principle underlying the Rockingham policy of 1766 that, while parliament had a right to legislate for colonies and to tax them, it should in practice leave them free to run their own affairs while enriching the empire with their trade. In the East India crises of 1767 and 1773 he opposed growing state intervention in the East India Company as he opposed its meddling in the government of the American colonies. So far as India was concerned this stance was in later years to be considerably modified.

Meanwhile, from the time of the Boston Tea Party in 1773, it was the west rather than the east that was increasingly to command his attention.

MP for Bristol Events at Boston harbour precipitated the third and final crisis of Anglo-American relations. Earlier, in 1766 and 1770, it had been possible for government to make concessions without appearing to surrender to colonial blackmail. In 1774 there was a widely held view that the time had come to respond more vigorously. For the Rockingham party, which had always sought to distance itself from the wilder American claims, it would have been difficult to oppose a policy of carefully graduated coercion. Instead North, urged on by a bellicose cabinet and a surge of back-bench opinion, responded with draconian legislation punishing the port of Boston and remodelling the Massachusetts constitution. This hardened opinion on both sides of the Atlantic and led eventually to war. For Rockingham's friends the way was open to present themselves as the statesmanlike defenders of America's liberty and Britain's true interest.

Burke was the standard-bearer on this march into the annals of whig liberal imperialism. Without him it is hard to see how the Rockingham party could have survived as a coherent parliamentary force. Dowdeswell, its Commons leader, died in 1775. Lord John Cavendish, his nominal successor, was reluctant to put his parliamentary duties before his fox-hunting. A number of fair-weather friends deserted to a ministry that went from strength to strength and secured a substantial majority at the general election of 1774. The only important new recruit to the opposition, Charles James Fox, was tarnished by his earlier commitment to court policies, and for some years was accounted an unpredictable ally rather than a firm friend by the Rockingham whigs.

Burke's personal position was also strengthened by his election for the empire's second city, Bristol, in 1774. The invitation to stand there was timely, for he could not expect that his bankrupt patron Verney would renew his nomination for Wendover. Rockingham found a seat in his own pocket borough of Malton, but the call to Bristol came just as Burke was about to be elected there. The longstanding tory interest at Bristol was in some disarray, and whigs were short of a convincing candidate to run alongside Henry Cruger, an American-born merchant of radical views and little political experience. Richard Champion, the porcelain manufacturer, acted as campaign manager. He presented Burke to his friends as 'indisputably the first literary Character in the Kingdom' and 'a perfect Master of its commercial Interests' (*Correspondence*, 3.46). The new MP was elected with startling ease and at little expense to himself.

It could not be said that Burke was overwhelmed by a sense of dependence on his new constituents. A topic that featured in the election campaign, raised by Cruger himself, was the Wilkite demand for constituency instructions binding on MPs. Burke delivered what he called his 'poor sentiments on that subject' attacking any form of dictation which conflicted with the MP's duty to the public at large (*Writings and Speeches*, 3.68). Later, in 1791, he wrote:

> He was the first man who, on the hustings, at a popular election, rejected the authority of instructions from constituents; or who, in any place has argued so fully against it. Perhaps the discredit in which that doctrine of compulsive instructions under our constitution is since fallen, may be due, in a great degree, to his opposing himself to it in that manner, and on that occasion.   (ibid., 4.33)

Certainly his statement has generally been cited as the classic account of the nature of parliamentary accountability, often by those who have lacked the temerity to follow Burke and recommend it to electors from the hustings.

Burke's imperial thinking at this time is encapsulated in his two great American speeches. 'Taxation', which had been delivered on 19 April 1774, was not published until January 1775. 'Conciliation' was delivered on 22 March 1775 and published in May. In each he argued that the benefits of Anglo-American co-operation far outweighed any conceivable advantages to be derived from an insistence on the right to tax America. His own measures would have been the repeal of offending legislation, an abandonment of all attempts at taxation, and a return to what he took to be the benign mildness of whig government of the colonies. This made no appeal to a Commons bent on forcing to an issue the question of Britain's authority to tax. But Burke's exposition marked out important ground. His concept of empire was one of communities bound in partnership. Americans were Englishmen by another name, imbued with a strong sense of their ancient inheritance. 'An Englishman is the unfittest person on earth, to argue another Englishman into slavery' (*Writings and Speeches*, 3.130). For partners to dwell on rights rather than responsibilities was disastrous. On the face of it the Rockingham party's support for the Declaratory Act in 1766 seemed to contradict him. But Burke refused to be trapped into a commitment to taxation. In the British constitution there were numerous rights which it would have been folly to enforce. He thought it logically absurd to revoke what was a mere declaration, not an enactment, but as the war years passed he made it increasingly plain that he would not oppose such a repeal.

Burke was exasperated by those who persisted in thinking of constitutional principles rather than prudent practice. To his friend Charles O'Hara, who had read his 'Conciliation', he wrote:

> How could you imagine that I had in my thoughts any thing of the Theoretical seperation of a power of Taxing from Legislation. I have no opinion about it. These things depend on conventions real or understood, upon practice, accident, the humour or Genius of those who Govern or are governd, and may be, as they are, modified to infinity … I never ask what Government may do in *Theory*, except *Theory* be the *Object*; When one talks of *Practice* they must act according to circumstances.   (*Correspondence*, 3.181–2)

The American speeches mattered not only for their content but for their dissemination in printed form. It was not unknown for MPs to publish their own speeches, and by 1774 the public was becoming used to regular, if unreliable, newspaper reports of proceedings in parliament. But the care which Burke lavished on extended publication, from his own notes and from those of others in the Commons, was novel. Perhaps his strong Irish accent and the burden it imposed on parliamentary reporters lent urgency to this task. He was careful, however, not to be seen publicizing himself too openly. As Richard Burke told Champion when forwarding copies of *Taxation*,

> tho our Edmund *must* avow, what he cannot deny, that the Speech is his; yet he does not count it gracefull to be the publisher. You will therefore know nothing of this; and to whomsoever you give them, you will give them as from yourself, and by *no means as from him*.   (*Correspondence*, 3.93–4)

None the less Burke was the first parliamentarian to appeal to an extra-parliamentary audience in this way, and thereby the first politician to acquire not only a British but a European audience.

In 1775 American and British arms clashed. 'Blood has been shed', wrote Burke. 'The sluice is opend—Where, when, or how it will be stopped God only knows' (*Correspondence*, 3.160). As the breach widened opposition to the crown became increasingly difficult. Ridicule was perhaps the most effective weapon in these circumstances and Burke its most resourceful exponent. He denounced the government's convoluted definition of rebellion, based on the Boston Tea Party, as the drowning of tea 'like a puppy dog' (*Writings and Speeches*, 3.83). When North offered the colonies a formula for self-taxation that was mystifying in its imprecision Burke compared him with 'Nebuchadnezzar, who having forgot a dream of his, ordered the assemblies of his wise men, on pain of death, not only to interpret his dream, but to tell him what his dream was' (ibid., 3.88). When all else failed it was easy to raise a laugh at the minister's propensity to fall asleep in his place on the Treasury bench. 'Government is not dead, it only sleepeth', he declared on one occasion (ibid., 3.426). North was the most good-humoured of premiers, and there developed between the two a relationship in which the exchange of pleasantries often seemed to take precedence over the requirements of partisan hostilities.

In 1776 events threatened to reduce the parliamentary opposition to complete nullity. The American Declaration of Independence alienated moderate opinion in Britain. Military successes in New York and Pennsylvania brought the prospect of a decisive victory over the colonies and unleashed the full force of patriotic sentiment at home, appalling Burke by its implicit toryism. Both in private and in public he argued that the English national character itself was being transformed by an ugly outbreak of authoritarianism.

Full-scale war forced the Rockingham party to consider new tactics. Its answer was to cease participating in parliamentary debate about America. Secession of this kind was a rare but not unprecedented resort, simultaneously a recognition that opposition was pointless and a demonstration of disgust with government's conduct of affairs. The hidden undercurrent was the implied possibility of an

appeal to opinion beyond parliament. Burke saw secession as a formidable weapon and sought to maximize its
effect. He devised his 'Address to the king', to be presented
by leading peers in the hope that it would provoke
extreme measures. 'The Court may select three or four of
the distinguished among you for the Victims; and therefore nothing is more remote from the Tendency of the
proposed act, than any Idea of retirement or repose'. He
was aware that his plan involved martyrdom for others
rather than himself, 'as from my want of importance, I
can be personally little subject to the most trying part of
the consequences, it is as little my desire to urge others to
dangers, in which I am myself to have so inconsiderable a
share' (*Correspondence*, 3.312–13).

Rockingham and his colleagues showed little enthusiasm for the role in which Burke had cast them. The secession achieved nothing. It was not wholeheartedly
observed even by close friends. Moreover Burke found
himself under attack from his Bristol constituents for failing in his duty as an opposition MP to oppose. His self-
defence, published in April 1777 as *A Letter to the Sheriffs of
Bristol*, is memorable for its withering dismissal of any
notion that the war could yield profit to Britain, but less
convincing in vindicating the policy of secession. Matters
were made worse by the radical peer, Lord Abingdon,
whose riposte to the *Letter* demonstrated a lamentable
want of unity among the opponents of government.

When the party resumed its place at Westminster,
Burke moved to a bitter critique of the inhuman nature of
the war. He lashed the government for portraying this as
an honourable contest against natural enemies, especially when it enlisted the Anglican church in its cause. Of
the annual fast services held to solemnize the cause he
wrote 'Till our Churches are purified from this abominable service, I shall consider them, not as the temples of
the Almighty, but the synagogues of Satan' (*Writings and
Speeches*, 3.256). Ethnic distinctions featured largely in his
rhetoric. The enemy were 'the American English', 'our
English Brethren in the Colonies'. No opportunity was lost
to highlight the irony of a German-descended king
employing 'the hireling sword of German boors and vas-
sals' to deprive British colonists of their English liberties.
When the captured Fort Washington was renamed in honour of its captors Burke admitted: 'I have not yet learned
to delight in finding Fort Kniphausen in the heart of the
British dominions' (ibid., 300–01). In much of this there
was nicely calculated rhetoric. There was also authentic
horror. In a private letter of September 1775, after it had
been reported that the government was negotiating with
Catherine II to hire Russian troops, he wrote 'I am on
thorns. I cannot at my Ease see Russian Barbarism let loose
to waste the most beautiful object that ever appeared
upon this Globe' (*Correspondence*, 3.219).

Russian troops did not in the event find themselves
fighting for the British right to tax America, but other supposed barbarians did. Burke's oratorical onslaught on the
war makers culminated in his denunciation of the use of
Indian irregulars by the king's forces on 6 February 1778.

Horace Walpole called it 'the chef-d'oeuvre of Burke's orations' (H. Walpole, *Last Journals*, ed. A. F. Stewart, 1910,
2.104). It relied on his most characteristic skills, capturing
the attention and delight of the house by a sustained battery of good-humoured wit against the Treasury bench
that had ministers themselves in convulsions, and suddenly turning with dramatic effect to the savagery of
war:

> the Indians of America had no titles, sine-cure places,
> lucrative governments, pensions, or red ribbons, to bestow
> on those who signalized themselves in the field; their
> rewards were generally received in human scalps, in human
> flesh, and the gratifications arising from torturing,
> mangling, scalping, and sometimes eating their captives in
> war. (*Writings and Speeches*, 3.356)

The speech, like some of his later writings, also included
an excursion on the theme of abused and outraged
womanhood, in his painful account of the suffering of
Jane McCrea, the young woman slain and scalped by Britain's Indian allies. There were, of course, those among
North's supporters, such as the diplomat James Harris, for
whom all such performances were mock tragedy, more
plausible at Drury Lane. But parliamentary rhetoric was in
its nature theatrical, and the more so in an age when the
intended audience included readers as well as hearers. On
the continent indeed Burke was compared admiringly
with Europe's most celebrated actor, le Kain. The self-
conscious theatricality of Burke's writings during the
grand tragedy of the revolutionary 1790s is often noticed.
It was but a short step from much of his parliamentary
declaiming. He apparently intended to publish the Indian
speech in full, but what would have been an astonishing
triptych of American orations, 'Taxation', 'Conciliation',
and 'Savagery', remained incomplete.

In the real war Burgoyne's surrender at Saratoga in 1777
apparently vindicated North's opponents, confirming
what they had often said (without altogether believing it
themselves), that the war would not easily be won, and
forcing North to concede the principle of taxation which
had given rise to the conflict. But the effect was the reverse
in that Saratoga drew France and eventually Spain into
hostilities, turning a war of colonial repression into a war
of survival against Britain's historic enemies. The resulting tide of loyalism, not least in Burke's own constituency,
put the opposition in the awkward position of perpetually
having to explain that while they opposed hostilities in
America they supported them elsewhere.

The reformer On the other hand military escalation soon
produced strains that presented alternative opportunities
for critics of government. The conflict with America had
set Irishmen pondering their own relationship with Westminster. As the war grew more serious it offered them the
opportunity to resort to arms—nominally in defence of
the realm against its enemies, but increasingly with the
implied threat of action against the British themselves.
Initial demands were to free Irish overseas trade from the
shackles which English commercial hegemony had long
imposed. In 1780 North gave way, aware that the independence increasingly certain in America might soon be

practical politics in Ireland. Burke supported the resulting legislation but thereby offended his Bristol constituents, who saw Ireland's freedom to trade as their own slavery. In response he made one of his clearest statements about the underlying reasons for his dislike of protectionism.

> The Author of our Nature has written it strongly in that Nature, and has promulgated the same Law in his written Word, that Man shall eat his Bread by his Labour; and I am persuaded, that no man, and no combination of Men, for their own Ideas of their particular profit, can, without great impiety, undertake to say, that he *shall not* do so; that they have no sort of right, either to prevent the Labour, or to withhold the Bread. Ireland having received no *compensation*, directly or indirectly, for any restraints on their Trade, ought not, in Justice or common honesty, be made subject to such restraints. (*Correspondence*, 3.442)

By this time the spirit of independence was abroad in England itself. The apparent feebleness of an over-stretched navy brought pressure to bear on government. In January 1779, when a supporter of Rockingham's—Admiral Keppel—was triumphantly cleared of alleged incompetence in an inconclusive naval action off Ushant, there were riots in London recalling the patriotic mobs instigated by Wilkes. Keppel's defence at his court martial owed much to the hand of Burke, who was presented with Reynolds's portrait of the naval hero in gratitude.

The strains of war and the approach of a general election brought much lamentation on the parlous plight of a country which just twenty years before had been basking in the *annus mirabilis* of the Seven Years' War. Even friends of government believed that waste and inefficiency must surely explain the squandering of resources in a woefully unsuccessful war. More radical critics directly charged the crown with misusing the taxes it was voted to subvert the independence of parliament and the vigour of the war effort. The 'influence of the crown' was much exaggerated and misunderstood, but provided a convenient slogan and scapegoat for most parties.

Financial administration had never been Burke's favourite subject. As he remarked himself, 'I am not naturally an oeconomist' (*Writings and Speeches*, 3.473). In the mid-1770s he had pleaded for generous funding both of Sir William Chambers's Somerset House and the British Museum in opposition to Treasury penny-pinching. 'When the public money is spent on public works, the public spend it on themselves; they enjoy those works when elegant and magnificent; they pride themselves on the glory of their country possessing such' (ibid., 3.170).

None the less, more than anyone else Burke gave coherence and practicality to the campaign for economical reform. As in 1770 when the *Thoughts on the Present Discontents* had enraged the Wilkites he flatly opposed the more extreme demands. Triennial elections he roundly dismissed: 'Triennial Corruption, Triennial Drunkenness, triennial idleness, triennial fury, society dissolved, industry interrupted ruind' (*Writings and Speeches*, 3.596). But he warmed to the cause of administrative reform, bringing historical understanding and analytical rigour to a complex subject. Some of his targets were massed in the undergrowth of the crown's ancient administration, for example in the semi-autonomous fiefs of Wales, Lancaster, Chester, and Cornwall, which made England, as he observed, not so much a unified monarchy as a pentarchy. Others, such as his proposal to do away with the secretaryship of state for the colonies, were central to the governing process. Above all his determination to bring the crown's civil list under parliamentary control encroached on the royal prerogative and earned him the personal animosity of the king. Some of Burke's speeches rather unnecessarily went out of their way to condemn a supposedly reviving high tory monarchism. 'The King was only a trustee for the public. Property and subjects existed before Kings were elected' (ibid., 3.555).

During the parliamentary session of 1779–80 independent opinion in the House of Commons was sufficiently stirred to offer support. Eventually, when North conceded the establishment of a public accounts commission, Burke's bill was defeated by the narrowest of margins. For the moment, economical reform was dead, but it was not buried, and when the Rockingham whigs returned to power in 1782 it was resurrected as the centrepiece of their domestic legislation. In the nineteenth century Burke came to be seen as a pioneer in the cause of Gladstonian economy. In the twentieth century judgements emphasized the conservatism of his approach. Perhaps an appraisal more sensitive to the context in which Burke wrote and planned might grant that his carefully considered plan did indeed, as he put it, constitute 'radical, Systematick Oeconomy' (*Correspondence*, 4.219).

One of the less predictable effects of the war was the relief it brought to Roman Catholics. Awareness that Catholics might provide a valuable source of recruits gave impulse to the growing distaste for discrimination on account of creed. The result was the passage, in 1778, both in England and Ireland, of laws granting freedom of worship and education together with certain basic legal rights, including the ownership of landed property. Burke was much involved in the campaigning of the Catholic community and in the resulting negotiations with government. 'You are now beginning to have a Country', he told an Irish friend in August 1778 (*Correspondence*, 4.15). At the same time he was not behindhand in supporting additional relief for dissenting ministers and schoolmasters, in the process delivering a revealing remark about the nature of legal restraints. 'I think of Government as I do of every thing else made for the good of mankind—like their Cloaths made to fit them, not those who go by abstract rules to have their altitude taken by a quadrant and their solid content calculated by their cubick feet and inches' (*Writings and Speeches*, 3.432–3). More problematically he also sought to promote the Catholic cause in Scotland. Burke's exchanges with leading Scottish churchmen include some statements of his own position that have much interest in retrospect. He denied that he could ever be the 'Zealot of any National Church' and revealed that he considered the divisions of the Christian church as rather 'made for convenience and order, than Seperations, from a diversity of Nature, or from irreconcilable contradiction in principles'. He was infuriated by the bitterness of the Scottish opponents of Catholicism. 'I could not prevail on myself to bestow on the Synagogue, the Mosque or the Pagoda, the language which your Pulpits lavish upon a great part of the Christian world' (*Correspondence*, 4.85).

It transpired that these sentiments were controversial in England as well as Scotland. In June 1780 a protest movement led by the Scottish nobleman Lord George Gordon culminated in riots which threatened to reduce London to ashes. As a prominent supporter of Catholic relief Burke was particularly exposed. The crisis brought his characteristic courage and compassion to the fore. Having sent his wife and his papers to safety he dismissed the troops provided by government for his defence, and faced down the mob with sword in hand. 'He's a gentleman, make way for him', they shouted (*Correspondence*, 4.246). When order was restored he refused to join with those, including friends, who sought to appease popular opinion by a partial repeal of the offending legislation. Yet he had no stomach for the bloodbath of official vengeance that threatened the rioters. Seeing the prisoners at their trial he remarked 'The scene in Surrey would have affected the hardest heart that ever was in an human breast'. To Lord North he begged for at least 'a few lives less than first intended to be saved' as something that he would 'sincerely set down as a personal obligation'. But perhaps the abiding impression was of the champions of the people having to be protected by the crown. 'Saville House, Rockingham House—Devonshire House to be turned into Garrisons! Oh tempora!' (ibid., 4.257–8, 247).

The general election of 1780 found Burke at the height of his public reputation yet deprived him of his seat. It was not only the commercial concessions to Ireland that had lost him friends in Bristol. Catholic relief caused a backlash there as it did elsewhere. Burke's detestation of the slave trade, though expressed with caution, did not go down well in one of the great slaving ports of the empire. It incidentally yielded his unpublished 'Sketch of a negro code', which was later, in the 1790s, to play some part in the framing of slave trade legislation. There were other sources of irritation at Bristol. In 1777 Burke had supported the establishment of a theatre at Birmingham, observing that the question was not whether the English labourer was likely to be tempted to leave his workplace but rather 'shall he go to the Play or some Blacksmith's Entertainment?' (*Writings and Speeches*, 3.287). When Birmingham opponents urged their friends in Bristol to put pressure on Burke he withdrew his support, but the memory rankled with some of his constituents. Worse still, in 1780 he had supported Lord Beauchamp's bill for the relief of insolvent debtors, a measure guaranteed to arouse the ire of a mercantile community.

There was also Burke's failure to cultivate his constituency. He did not deny this, merely asserting that where the public interests of Bristol were concerned his record of assiduousness was unimpeachable. But courting what he called the 'private regards of the Citizens' had been beyond him. 'The Business of Parliament occupies me for a great part of the year; and the effects of it afterwards

make a residence at home necessary both to my health and my family affairs' (*Correspondence*, 4.219). Both his whig fellow member Henry Cruger and his tory opponents had the advantage in this respect.

On all these matters Burke defended himself with spirit. In private he did not, however, blame his downfall on them. In 1774 he had been the beneficiary of a freakish political situation at Bristol which left the local tories in turmoil and the local whigs unprepared. Circumstances had been ideal for the intrusion of a national figure at a time of national crisis. In 1780 the situation was quite different. Loyalist opinion had been strengthened by a reaction in favour of a government beset on all sides by ancient as well as modern enemies. A bitter contested election was inevitable and Burke lacked the resources to fight one. That his withdrawal was wise was confirmed by Cruger's humiliation at the poll.

Though this reverse was predictable it none the less dealt Burke a severe blow. Rockingham eventually found him a seat at Malton, not without difficulty. In the meantime he considered leaving public life altogether. His personal credibility was at stake. It was ironic, as he reflected, that as the proposer of the most popular of causes before the general election, economical reform, he had been voted out by the kingdom's second city. Returning to parliament for a close borough and engaging again in such a cause would look like 'a piece of Buffoonery' (*Correspondence*, 4.302). He also revealed in private his doubts about the political maturity and integrity of the electorate in great cities such as Bristol. 'If I had followd the humours of this town, which are called opinions, I should have been more frequently wrong, than even if I had been guided by the Court' (ibid., 4.274). The wound to his self-esteem was not superficial. In his manuscript notes for one of his first speeches in the new parliament he described himself as having been 'outlawed by the whole nation' (*Writings and Speeches*, vol. 4, February 1781). Not that his propensity for embracing unpopular humanitarian causes had been in any way inhibited. During the preceding parliament, in 1776, he had angered the landed interest by his campaign to make local ratepayers foot the bill for the plundering of vessels wrecked at sea by coastal communities. He had also joined critics of capital punishments to denounce 'the Butchery which we call justice' (*Correspondence*, 3.252–3). Most audaciously of all he had in 1780 challenged contemporary prejudice by taking up the case of a man convicted of sodomy who, condemned to stand in the stocks, was there killed by a mob.

Committeeman and minister One of Burke's duties in the new parliament was to sit on a select committee to consider the activities of the Calcutta supreme court established by North's Regulating Act of 1773. He quickly became the dominating presence on it and was instrumental in extending its brief to cover a range of Indian issues in 1782. On the eleven reports compiled by the committee he had extensive influence, in some instances amounting to authorship. One of these, the *Ninth Report*, was destined to become essential reading for the nineteenth-century student of India. It also announced a position which had evolved in unexpected directions from his stance on Indian matters during his early years in parliament. Then he had opposed interference in the affairs of the East India Company. Through Verney and William Burke he had been complicit in the defensive manoeuvres of the proprietors of the company. He had viewed with equanimity even those by-products of Indian empire that caused so much disquiet in other quarters. In 1773 he remarked that on seeing the parks and great houses of company servants who had returned from India enriched and 'rising with unequal'd grandeur, I think there is something of a divine providence in it' (*Writings and Speeches*, 5.2).

This posture changed markedly. One of the catalysts was William Burke's appointment as agent of the raja of Tanjore, whose lands had been seized by the company and its ally, the nawab of Arcot. Moreover, the governor of Madras, who had sought to restore Tanjore to its owner, was Lord Pigot, a follower of Rockingham's. When Pigot was deposed by his Madras enemies Burke's friends were quick to demand retribution. In a powerful oration in May 1777 Burke sought, not very fairly, to associate the ministry with these objectionable activities in India. 'Some people are great Lovers of uniformity—They are not satisfied with a rebellion in the West. They must have one in the East: They are not satisfied with losing one Empire—they must lose another—Lord North will weep that he has not more worlds to lose' (*Writings and Speeches*, 40).

Pigot died before he could be reinstated and the Tanjore question became part of an ever more complex web of intrigue at Madras. It had an impact on Burke, as his contribution to a tract published in 1779 by William Burke, *Policy of Making Conquests for the Mahometans*, reveals. The Tanjore business planted in his own mind a somewhat idealized picture of an Indian polity in its pre-colonial state. Tanjore was the Garden of Eden before an English-engineered fall. It had seemingly been a small independent state with a prosperous economy, a pious Hindu prince and a reputation for paternalistic government. This is not to say that Burke seriously considered the possibility of restoring Indian rule. He had too strong a sense of the forces released by Western expansion to suppose that any power could turn the clock back. Nor was he naïve enough to suppose that the East India Company was the only engine of change. Above all he never lost his faith in the energizing effects of European commerce. So he increasingly turned his mind to the means by which the company should be reformed and Indians provided with a share in its future prosperity.

Tanjore also gave Burke a new perspective on events elsewhere in India. At Calcutta the governor-general of British India had watched the proceedings at Madras with growing concern. Warren Hastings had no personal interest in the faction fighting there but the threatening aspect both of native and international politics made any dissensions in the English camp more worrying. His support for Pigot's enemies was a pragmatic manoeuvre in favour of the stronger party, and was designed to restore order in a territory likely to be in the forefront of a war with either Mysore or the French. He thereby became an enemy of the Burkes. By the same logic his own adversary on the council at Calcutta, Philip Francis, became their friend. Francis was to prove a highly partisan source of support and information. Burke himself insisted that he had not felt anything but 'a manifest partiality' for Hastings until much later, when his membership of the select committee had brought him a close acquaintance with the recent history of Bengal, but it is hard to believe that there was no connection at all in his mind between Tanjore and Calcutta (*Writings and Speeches*, 5.25).

Burke's early thinking as a member of the select committee revealed him rejecting the assumption that judicial and other institutions in India should be transplants from Britain. He saw an analogy with the crisis in the west. 'We must now be guided as we ought to have been with respect to America, by studying the genius, the temper, and the manners of the people, and adapting to them the laws that we establish' (*Writings and Speeches*, 5.140). But as his researches continued he moved from general predisposition to detailed analysis of what had gone wrong in India. The ninth report of the committee in June 1783 demonstrated the economic consequences of permitting merchants to become conquerors and governors. Throughout the reports there ran a critique of other consequences, especially of the abuse of power by those who found themselves exercising authority on the ground. The last, eleventh report, examined the taking of bribes by British officials, including the governor-general himself. This theme was the richest of all those he illuminated in the breadth of its consequences, linking corruption in England with vice in India. Its underlying force derived from his profound disgust at the activities of a whole class of Britons whom fate had entrusted with responsibility for many millions of oriental subjects. This is not to say that he necessarily blamed them as individuals. 'There is nothing in the boys we send to India worse than the boys whom we are whipping at school, or that we see trailing a pike, or bending over a desk at home'. None the less this was an invasion that brought no benefits to those invaded, only misery.

> Animated with all the avarice of age, and all the impetuosity of youth, they roll in one after another; wave after wave; and there is nothing before the eyes of the natives but an endless, hopeless prospect of new flights of birds of prey and passage, with appetites continually renewing for a food that is continually wasting.

Even the Tartars had incidentally carried with them some advantages to those they conquered. The commercial conquest of the English had created no arts, no architecture, no charity, no education, no monuments to their own superiority. 'Were we to be driven out of India this day, nothing would remain, to tell that it had been possessed, during the inglorious period of our dominion, by any thing better than the ouran-outang or the tiger' (ibid., 5.402–3).

Later reformers were to address this bleak diagnosis of the ills of imperial rule. When they did so, evolving a new form of Indian governance, they sometimes looked back to Burke as the pioneer of their cause. Yet Burke seems not to have viewed his role in this light. Rather he saw himself as a scourge of rottenness in the English state as it comported itself in India. Reform was indeed about institutional regeneration, to the forms of which Burke gave much thought. But it was even more about the extirpation of vice, a benevolent British parliament uniting in a moral and social community with remote and alien cultures. Such aspirations, it has been remarked, 'belonged to the world of Cicero and perhaps of the great debates set off by the Spanish conquest of Indian peoples. They were already beginning to look irrelevant to the British empire of the 1790s' (P. J. Marshall, introduction to *Writings and Speeches*, 6.36).

Even in Burke's terms it might be thought that there was something unfair about identifying Hastings as the supreme villain and victim in this cause. For he too was one of that class of young men who had set out for India fresh from boarding-school largely unprepared for the duties they must undertake. Moreover Burke's cosmology did not generally allow for the identification of any one human being as uniquely or comprehensively evil, though his more extravagant language sometimes gave the impression that it did. On the other hand if there had to be a sacrificial victim Hastings certainly lacked an obvious rival for the honour. As Burke's researches took him deeper into recent events in India he encountered him at every turn. And the same logic of imperial crisis and war that had driven Hastings to questionable expedients exposed him the more to censure. The situation that made Hastings for himself and for many others the saviour of British India made him for Burke a kind of Antichrist, the pattern of everything that was unjustifiable in British rule. It is ironic that Hastings placed such emphasis on the practical necessity of the measures he took, for Burke saw pragmatism as central to what he called the 'science of government'. But although he considered morality itself a subject for discriminating analysis he did not hold that moral goods as such could be sacrificed in the cause of pragmatism. He was perhaps fortunate that he was rarely placed in a public position where such choices had to be made.

Burke's growing investment in knowledge of India did not distract him from other business. In the 1781 session he unsuccessfully renewed his motions in favour of economical reform, and launched a forceful attack on the increasingly desperate fiscal measures to which North was reduced (comparing him unfavourably with Louis XVI's finance minister, Necker). He also returned to a favourite theme of the preceding parliament: the cruelty of war. Admiral Sir George Rodney's capture of the Dutch island of St Eustatius was followed by confiscation of the effects of its merchants. Burke denounced this as 'a cruelty unheard of in Europe for many years, and such as he would venture to proclaim was a most unjustifiable, outrageous, and unprincipled violation of the laws of nations'. In one passage of this speech he dwelt on the uprooting of the island's Jewish community.

> From the east to the west, from one end of the world to the other, they are scattered and connected; the links of

communication in the mercantile chain; or to borrow a phrase from electricity, the conductors by which credit was transmitted through the world. Their abandoned state, and their defenceless situation calls most forcibly for the protection of civilized nations.

This was no casual political manoeuvre. For Burke the St Eustatius affair raised deep questions of international law and morality which he was to revisit during the ideological battles of the 1790s (*Writings and Speeches*, vol. 4, 14 May 1781).

America remained centre stage in parliament. It was Burke's later view that in the last years of the war of independence the opposition's harrying of North caused the collapse of his support in the Commons. Historians argue rather that the surrender of Cornwallis at Yorktown in 1781 destroyed British sovereignty in America and North's government together. Yet it was the loss of some of his key independent supporters that forced North to resign, and these men were peculiarly open to persuasion by debate. In any event in March 1782 Rockingham's friends returned to power for the first time in sixteen years. Burke was installed as paymaster-general of the army, without a seat in the cabinet. His exclusion is generally attributed to his lowly social origins but may equally have resulted from his friends' sense of his uncompromising independence of mind and behaviour.

The ministry was brought to a premature end by the death of Rockingham himself on 1 July. For Burke the months in office were none the less important in that they enabled him finally to carry a number of those economical reforms which he had championed since 1779. His protestations of loyalty to the crown verged on the excessive in the circumstances. In the Commons on 15 April 1782, for example, he declared, 'This was one of the blessed effects of a change of Administration; that mist which was raised between the Prince and his people was now cleared away—he now saw with his own eyes, and felt with his own heart' (*The Gazetteer*, 16 April 1782). The truth was that Burke's insistence on a parliamentary regulation of the civil list made it harder than ever for George III to warm to the whigs.

It was not only in England that the Rockingham ministry brought about constitutional change. In a major revision of Anglo-Irish relationships it repealed the legislation which effectively subordinated the Dublin parliament to Westminster and the British privy council. For Burke this was not the straightforward triumph of reason that his colleagues considered it. His sympathy with the plight of Irish Catholics had never taken the form of seeking greater independence for Ireland. In 1773 he had strenuously opposed proposals for a tax on absentee landlords which would have had the effect of penalizing those, like his own leader, who influenced the politics of both countries while residing almost wholly only in one. In 1782 his support for the new settlement was at best lukewarm. Empowering the protestant minority in Ireland would not necessarily strengthen the ties that bound it to Britain, nor, for all the liberal intentions of Fox's friends in Dublin, would it necessarily improve the lot of the Catholic majority.

Rockingham's death was a devastating blow, removing the one political and personal connection that, when all else failed, could command Burke's allegiance. Whether Rockingham could have prevented those subsequent excesses which gave even close friends cause for concern is debatable, for Burke had increasingly set his own course, especially where Indian affairs were concerned, and it is hard to believe that any human agency would have diverted him. In the short run, in any case, he remained a staunch supporter of Rockingham's political heirs, led by Fox. The successor to Rockingham's estates, the Earl Fitzwilliam, had a particular lien on Burke, as the owner of the borough for which he sat in parliament. Only shortly before Rockingham's death, in March 1782, Burke had been elected a member of Brooks's, the sanctum sanctorum of whig sociability.

Rockingham's death occasioned the definitive split between those whigs who had once followed Pitt (later earl of Chatham), now led by the earl of Shelburne, and those who remained loyal to Fox. Shelburne was much preferred by the king, but the peace that his ministry was compelled to negotiate was hugely unpopular. The easy line of attack was to concentrate on the concessions made, especially in North America, where the independence of the new United States was granted on terms more generous than those required by the military and diplomatic context. Burke's contribution was to seek recognition that the peace of 1783 was no mere diplomatic conjuncture but a redrawing of international realities. In a manuscript draft of this time he wrote,

> A great revolution has happened. A revolution, made not by chopping and changing of power in existing States; but by appearance of a *new State* among Mankind of a *new* species in a new part of the Earth. It has made as great a change in all the relations and ballances and gravitations of power as the appearance of a New planet would in the System of our Solar World. (Wentworth Woodhouse Muniments, Sheffield City Libraries, 6.165)

In February 1783 Shelburne fell, partly because his ministry failed to carry independent opinion, but more because of the alliance contracted between the Foxite whigs and their former enemies, North's followers. In the resulting coalition Burke resumed the office of paymaster-general, expecting that he would complete the reform of his office and transform the paymastership from a notorious source of corruption to an efficient instrument of government. This ambition was hampered by his defence of two of his senior officials, John Powell and Charles Bembridge, who had been removed from office by Shelburne on suspicion of serious misdemeanours, and whom Burke restored on his own authority. He insisted that the two must be treated as innocent until proven guilty and also that the reforms which he had introduced could not be carried through without the benefit of their professional experience. The Commons gave him a rough time. In a speech that strongly conveyed his own discomfiture, he described in comical terms his

roasting by the 'bons rotisseurs' of the opposition and dismissed Caesar's wife as a lady with whom he had no acquaintance. For once Burke's wit failed of its effect, and tempers rose. Burke ended by apologizing to the house for his warmth. Powell committed suicide and Bembridge was duly convicted. The episode may have reflected Burke's generosity of spirit. It did not enhance his reputation for sound judgement.

Burke's reforming zeal in the pay office did not inhibit him from playing a larger role in the ministry's activities. The framing of the East India measures that ultimately brought the Fox–North coalition down, though often described as Fox's, were in reality largely Burke's. One was a prescription for the better government of Britain's Indian possessions, drawing on Burke's select committee experience. The other offered a radical alternative to the supervision of those possessions from Britain, proposing two new statutory commissions, one for the direction of the company's commercial affairs, the other to take over its political functions. This latter was controversial, for it entrusted the places of power to Foxite whigs and appeared to entrench them in a position from which the crown would be unable to dislodge them. Burke's principal remarks on the subject, delivered on 1 December 1783 and subsequently published by Burke himself, vigorously defended the principle and justified the bill 'as destroying a tyranny that exists to the disgrace of this nation' (*Writings and Speeches*, 5.451). But to many it looked like a hypocritical attempt by the whigs to lay hold of the Indian patronage that they had so resisted in the hands of others. The king used his friends in the Lords to defeat the bill, dismissed his ministers and placed the young William Pitt in office. Three months later, in March 1784, a general election was held which overwhelmingly registered a popular verdict on the side of the crown.

Inquisitor and prosecutor As the personal nominee of Fitzwilliam, Burke retained his seat for Malton notwithstanding the electoral debacle. None the less he regarded it as a political landmark of fearful significance. He wrote in June 1784:

> I consider the House of Commons as something worse than extinguishd. We have been labouring for near twenty years to make it independent; and as soon as we had accomplishd what we had in View, we found that its independence led to its destruction. The people did not like our work; and they joind the Court to pull it down. The demolition is very complete.

And a little late, perhaps influenced by an impudently daring burglary of Gregories, he remarked, 'Lord! how they will rail at the abominable degeneracy of the age in the reign of George the fifth' (*Correspondence*, 5.154, 169).

Burke constructed an analysis of the ills that must flow from the crown's victory and presented it to the new parliament in a formal 'Representation to the king'. He identified a ministerial plot to create a double Commons (recalling the double cabinet of the *Thoughts on the Cause of the Present Discontents*), one sitting at Westminster, the other consisting of a court party that led popular opinion into all kinds of errors. Overall his conclusion was that the events of 1784 had turned the clock back a century, undoing what had been achieved in spirit if not in form by the revolution of 1688. The parallel was reinforced by the commercial vigour of each period and the blindness it induced in its beneficiaries. 'The Nation is rich; and Trade flourishes as it did at the End of Charles the Seconds reign; and as then people say little of any thing else' (*Correspondence*, 5.296).

In summer 1784 Burke's language suggested a degree of agitation unusual even by his standards. In parliament his friends were embarrassed and less than wholehearted supporters of his activities. Something akin to madness was hinted at. The new Commons was not only dominated by government supporters but contained a high proportion of new members, many of them young and irreverent. Their noisy refusal to listen to Burke somewhat nonplussed him for the first time in his parliamentary career. He was reduced to deploring their bad manners or criticizing their youth.

For the resulting frustration there had to be an outlet. Hastings was the unfortunate recipient of this energy. This is not to say that there was any want of logic in the vigour with which Burke renewed his assault on the governor-general. In his programme for Indian reform an exemplary inquisitorial prosecution had always seemed highly desirable. The entanglement of Indian questions in the constitutional crisis that had brought down the Fox–North coalition made its remedial value all the more evident.

The winding up of parliament's involvement in the tortuous affairs of the nawab of Arcot, whose debts to the men who had brought down Pigot and the raja of Tanjore were now to be underwritten by the British taxpayer, provided Burke with an opportunity to signal his intentions. His devastating speech of 28 February 1785 in which he linked the guilty parties both with Hastings and with the corruption that had supposedly triumphed in the election of 1784 was not so much a diversion as a preparation for the greater task ahead. A significant link was also provided through Pitt's refusal to assist by providing official papers on the subject. 'Here, in the very moment of the conversion of a department of British government into an Indian mystery, and in the very act in which the change commences, a corrupt, private interest is set up in direct opposition to the necessities of the nation' (*Writings and Speeches*, 6.491). The speech was published. Viewed in Burke's Victorian heyday as a model of majestic prose, it came to be seen by some as the finest of all his writings.

Early in the next session Burke determined on a formal impeachment as the means of prosecuting Hastings. Impeachment was a parliamentary proceeding requiring a decision to lay charges by the Commons followed by a trial before the Lords. It had the advantage of keeping the matter clear of the crown's courts. Prosecuting Hastings for offences committed at such a distance would in any case have been difficult by ordinary process. Through winter 1785–6 Burke laboured on the preparation of materials; on 4 April 1786 he laid the articles of charge before the Commons. At this stage he did not expect success. His

bleak view of the abyss into which parliament had descended in 1784 took for granted a wellnigh invincible nexus of corrupt interests uniting crown, company, and Calcutta. His mood was grimly self-vindicatory. He saw himself in ancient mould, 'the noble character of an accuser in Rome'. He strenuously denied, however, that he was actuated by malice.

> Not all the various occurrences of the last five years, neither five changes of administration, nor the retirement of summer, not the occupation of winter, neither his public nor his private avocations, nor the snow which in that period had so plentifully showered on his head, had been able to cool that anger, which he acknowledged to feel as a public man, but which, as a private individual, he had never felt one moment. (*Writings and Speeches*, 6.104, 106)

In May 1786 Hastings appeared in person before the Commons and did his own cause much damage, partly through the incoherence and inaccuracy of his defence, but more by his insistence that there was no case to answer. An admission that at times the interests of the empire had driven him to exceptional but justifiable measures might have earned him much sympathy. Instead his seeming arrogance squandered that which he already possessed. Even so, the prospects were not encouraging for his opponents. The first charge, concerning Hastings's treatment of the Rohilla tribes of Oudh early in his governorship, failed on 2 June by 119 votes to 67. The second charge concerned Chet Singh, the ruler of Benares, who had found himself wedged between Hastings and his Maratha enemies at a moment of extreme peril for the British. His expropriation and dethronement were considered by Burke as clear instances of the mentality that he had first glimpsed in the sufferings of the raja of Tanjore. Fox himself laid the case before the Commons on 13 June; it was approved by 119 votes to 79. The support of Pitt, who was perhaps not averse to encouraging the opposition to focus on matters that did not implicate his own administration, was material.

Whatever the cause, not only was the effect heartening for Burke himself, but his political tactics changed markedly. Instead of being the tireless opponent of a supposedly degenerate court, he now looked for every opportunity to co-operate with Pitt and his minister for Indian affairs, Henry Dundas. To the latter on 26 March 1787, he wrote 'if ever there was a common National Cause totally separated from Party it is this' (*Correspondence*, 5.314). He also partially revised his view of the constitutional gravity of what had happened in 1784. Parliament, he remarked in July 1787, 'has prosecuted the very delinquent which it was (very near expressly) chosen to protect and exalt. In other things this Parliament is faithful to the principles of its institution. In this respect it has certainly failed' (ibid., 5.341).

Thus encouraged, Burke expected a speedy conclusion, predicting to Adam Smith in December 1786 that 'This Session will finally dispose of the affair' (*Correspondence*, 5.296). In fact proceedings were not completed until April 1795. It took two full sessions to secure Commons agreement on the charges, and the trial before the Lords did not begin until 13 February 1788. The first stages of the impeachment itself turned into a grand state occasion which attracted extraordinary interest but did not promote the gravity that Burke sought. The great orations that introduced each of the major charges, including his own four-day peroration at the commencement, were indeed hailed as feats of rhetoric worthy of the classical models that the orators certainly had in mind. Yet the atmosphere of high drama that prevailed was not to be taken for endorsement of their case. Indeed the highly wrought appeals to sensibility in which Burke indulged himself came close to serious misrepresentation of the facts. His emotive allegations of torture by agents of Hastings, in particular, were in some instances based on questionable sources later used against him.

There was also the question of the rules by which Hastings was to be prosecuted. From the outset Burke saw the danger presented by a trial in England before English authorities, presided over by a lord chancellor, Edward, Lord Thurlow, who was known for his judicial conservatism and predisposition in favour of his former school colleague, the defendant. Burke considered impeachment a matter solely for parliament and preferably one that dealt in terms of equity rather than precedent or 'municipal maxims', such as the common lawyers produced. 'You are not bound by any rules whatever except those of natural, immutable and substantial justice', he told the Lords (*Writings and Speeches*, 7.276). The judges who counselled the Lords usually rejected Burke's interpretations and made a conviction increasingly unlikely.

None the less Burke continued the fight. Nor while doing so did he entirely neglect other concerns. On two major questions of economic regulation he demonstrated that he was by no means an unqualified supporter of free trade. He opposed Pitt's commercial propositions for Ireland, to which Burke paid his last visit in 1786, on the grounds that the financial burdens which they incidentally imposed were oppressive. He also joined in the opposition's attack on Pitt's commercial treaty with France, though he accepted that Britain could outdo France in the manufacture of marketable goods. The driving force of Britain's commercial supremacy, he rather contentiously argued, was the huge infrastructure for capital accumulation created by the national debt and its associated government establishments.

> It was by keeping it dammed up from France, that this general partnership, within the nation subsisted. The moment we admit France, she will immediately begin to insinuate herself into the partnership, and, in the end, come in for a share of the capital. (*The World*, 22 Feb 1787)

During the mid-1780s Burke's stock recovered from the low point it had registered in the aftermath of the election of 1784. In 1788–9 however, his reputation sank once more when he fiercely supported the Foxite line during the regency crisis. The breakdown of the king in November 1788 found the whigs arguing for his son's hereditary right to exercise the powers of the crown in full. Burke's own views were among the more extreme, taking it for granted that the ministers of a king evidently insane lost

all official status and must give way at once to the nominees of his heir. Not that he was an uncritical supporter of the prince regent. His own recommendation was that the prince's sexual adventures should come to an end. 'No Prince appears settled unless he puts himself into the situation of the Father of a Family' (*Correspondence*, 5.444–5). Burke achieved the rare feat of alienating royal father and royal son at the same time.

One way and another his friends were not pleased. In the projected whig ministry that was to follow the prince's taking of power Burke was to be offered the paymastership once more, notwithstanding claims that he might have had to the chancellorship of the exchequer. Even in Indian matters he was to be awarded at best a place on the Indian Board of Control while Fox himself took the lead. In the event the king's recovery exploded all such castles in Spain. Burke was well aware of his increasing isolation, and exasperated by its causes. Fox's 'tone of calm reasoning' implied a gentlemanly exchange of views with Pitt prior to a coalition. Burke considered it both mistaken tactics and betrayal of the party (*Correspondence*, 5.438).

There were other signs of strain. In May 1789 the dissenters pressed their case for the repeal of the Test and Corporation Acts, a cause that Burke had supported in the past, notably in 1773. On this occasion he absented himself, citing illness as his excuse, though in 1790 he explained that he had evaded the issue because unable to make up his mind. The fact was that for several years Burke had entertained doubts about dissent as it was developing in the 1780s. One thing that rankled was its leaders' desertion of the whigs in the constitutional crisis of 1784, something which seems to have offended Burke more than Fox. But increasingly he was also disturbed by what he took to be the impious and seditious dogmas of a new strain of 'rational' or Unitarian dissent. At the same time, in May 1789, he came under severe criticism for words that he had used at the impeachment, accusing Hastings directly of the judicial murder of one of his native enemies in Bengal, Nandakumar. The Commons contented themselves with censuring Burke and allowed the prosecution to continue. But Fox would have been happy to settle for its abandonment. Burke was becoming more and more of an embarrassment.

The prophet All this preceded the sensational events of the summer of 1789 in France. To Lord Charlemont on 9 August Burke wrote of 'the wonderful Spectacle which is exhibited in a Neighbouring and rival Country—what Spectators and what actors! England gazing in astonishment at a French struggle for Liberty and not knowing whether to blame or to applaud' (*Correspondence*, 5.10). Very soon Burke himself knew whether to blame or applaud. By late September 1789 France was 'a Country where the people, along with their political servitude, have thrown off the Yoke of Laws and morals' (ibid., 5.25). By November they had made a 'Revolution but not a Reformation' (ibid., 5.46). This rapid process of alienation contrasted strikingly with the enthusiasm that marked the reaction of his whig friends to events in France. It is possible to imagine a Rockingham holding this tension in check. Fox venerated Burke, but he was no Rockingham.

In February 1790 Burke publicly revealed what a gulf now separated him from his friends. The occasion was a routine debate on the army estimates, which he used to raise the issue of the French Revolution as a threat to European security. He could have let the moment pass, but chose not to do so. Lest there remain any misunderstanding he published his own version of the speech. The French were a people whose 'character knew no medium' between despotism and anarchy. Their declaration of the 'rights of man' was 'a sort of *institute* and *digest* of anarchy, … in such a pedantic abuse of elementary principles as would have disgraced boys at school'. He was himself 'no enemy to reformation' but 'any thing which unnecessarily tore to pieces the contexture of the state' was guaranteed not to establish reform but to make it more necessary. Fox pronounced himself hurt by this outburst but sought to mollify Burke. By contrast, Fox's ally, Richard Brinsley Sheridan, went out of his way to condemn his remarks, leading Burke instantly to announce their separation. Pitt naturally took the opportunity to pour oil on these flames.

This was on 9 February. Three weeks later, on 2 March, there took place a further motion for the repeal of the Test and Corporation Acts, which found Burke clashing openly with Fox, the mover. He did not deny that the sacramental test was a repugnant tool of policy but objected to a wholesale repeal that would expose the state to subversion by republicans and atheists.

By this time there was already in existence a draft of the *Reflections on the Revolution in France*, written formally as a public reply to a young Frenchman, Charles Depont, who had earlier met Burke in England and now sought to convince him of the moderation of the revolution. In reality it was an attack on those radical dissenters, such as Richard Price, who sought to stimulate radical change in England. Burke's whig friends were in many instances dismayed. Francis, who was shown the draft, lectured him on the extravagance of his language and the incorrectness of his prose, and also warned him of his folly. 'The mischief you are going to do yourself is, to my apprehension, palpable. It is visible. It will be audible. I snuff it in the wind. I taste it already' (*Correspondence*, 6.85–7). Francis chided Burke for what was to be one of the most famous passages in the *Reflections*, that in which Burke rhapsodized about the queen, whom he had seen himself in France in 1773 as dauphiness. Francis dismissed it as foppery. It was also to occasion a much quoted remark in Tom Paine's response to the *Reflections*, the *Rights of Man*, when Paine observed that Burke 'pities the plumage, but forgets the dying bird'.

The *Reflections* began with a frontal assault on the sermon which Price had preached on 4 November 1788, the hundredth anniversary of William of Orange's appearance in Torbay. Price had argued that the revolution of 1688 had asserted the fundamental and wide-ranging rights of the people of England over their governors.

Burke insisted that it had been no more than a constitutional adjustment, securing an ancient inheritance against a tyrannical monarch. The revolutionaries of France had recently been offered a similar opportunity to restore their constitution by well-tempered reform. Instead 'you [Price] chose to act as if you had never been moulded into civil society, and had every thing to begin anew' (*Writings and Speeches*, 8.86).

The destruction thereby unleashed on monarchy, aristocracy, and church, much of which had yet to occur when Burke was writing (but which he foretold with notable percipience), followed naturally from this spirit of supposedly rational but in reality mindless innovation. At the root of the evil was a doctrine of natural rights that entrusted the so-called representatives of the people, in the case of France newly elected from the third estate, a class lacking any of the qualifications to reshape its country's future, with unlimited power. It was this same doctrine that Price and his comrades were now advocating for application in their own country.

Against it Burke set out his own statement of contrary values: of inherited manners that conferred honour and utility on institutions that might seem otherwise outmoded, of religious beliefs that were deeply ingrained in any civil society worthy of the name, of prescriptive customs and institutions, including property itself, that required protection against untried and arbitrary ideas of rationality. He also conducted a critique of what had been done in France in 1789 and 1790, 'especially the puerile and pedantic system, which they call a constitution', its devastating impact on the fabric of French society, government, and religion, its utter invalidity as a template for use in Britain (*Writings and Speeches*, 8.263). He ended by proclaiming the virtues of Britain's own constitution, and the happiness it brought 'owing in a great measure to what we have left standing in our several reviews and reformations, as well as to what we have altered or superadded' (ibid., 292).

Published in November 1790, the *Reflections* generated enormous interest and numerous replies. To the most celebrated, that of Paine himself, Burke did not deign to respond. In a sense Burke never did argue systematically against Paine's doctrines; he simply dismissed them as based on a false premiss—that it was possible to derive practical rights and duties from a wholly artificial notion of nature. His own conception of natural rights that could be built upon in civil society was restricted to those which conveyed an entitlement to justice and the fruits of one's labours. Equality of property or equality in the 'management of the state' he considered an infantile fantasy. His own position depended crucially on rights that were prescriptive, judgements that derived from the inherited reason of the ages, and a deep scepticism about the wisdom of the human mind when released from reliance on faith in a spiritual creator. Of one Enlightenment Burke was manifestly a child, but much of what was in retrospect to pass under that heading he did not so much confute as treat as below contempt. He also had a low opinion of his adversary in this case. He wrote in July 1791 that Paine 'is utterly incapable of comprehending his subject. He has not even a moderate portion of learning of any kind. He has learnd the instrumental part of literature, a style, and a method of disposing his ideas, without having ever made a previous preparation of Study or thinking—for the use of it' (*Correspondence*, 6.303). For his part Paine was genuinely shocked by what he saw as the treachery of one whose reforming activities he had once admired, and with whom he claimed somewhat exaggeratedly to have been 'in some intimacy' (Lock, *Burke's 'Reflections'*, 158).

It is remarkable in retrospect that Burke remained nominally a member of Fox's party for so long. Each avoided provoking the other in parliament, where a personal rift was bound to be damaging. They also collaborated to the extent that was necessary to sustain the impeachment proceedings against Hastings into the new parliament that commenced in November 1790. But Burke's own political evolution was no longer in doubt. On 3 February 1791 he crossed something of a Rubicon by attending a royal levee. Face to face with George III and in a subsequent correspondence with the king's son, the duke of Clarence, he received the royal thanks for supporting 'the cause of the Gentlemen' (*Correspondence*, 6.238–9).

On 15 April 1791 Fox praised the revolution in the Commons in terms that Burke could not ignore, though a hostile house prevented him from replying at once. There followed a private meeting in which Fox sought to dissuade Burke from a response. But the Quebec Bill, which altered the constitution imposed on Canada in 1774 and made possible some rather contrived debate about the desirability or otherwise of French and English models of government, offered an opportunity which Burke would not resist. In a series of fraught confrontations the two drew apart, notwithstanding attempts at mediation by friends. On 6 May Fox charged Burke with inconsistency in having previously supported the American rebels and numerous reforming causes, while Burke accused Fox of stage-managing his friends' hostile manoeuvres against him. At the height of this emotional exchange Burke pronounced their friendship at an end. Fox, tears and all, urged him to reconsider, but made matters worse by expressly condemning Burke's *Reflections*. There remained one further debate, on 11 May, when this historic rupture was revisited, but the outcome was no different. Pitt was left rejoicing and the two most influential whigs of their day were forever divided.

Burke's separation from his party is frequently portrayed as a personal and political tragedy. If so it was a remarkably liberating one, opening a period of intense activity and creativity, not least with his pen. His *Letter to a Member of the National Assembly*, published with his consent in Paris in April 1791 included a devastating onslaught on the philosopher hero of the revolution, Rousseau, whose preposterous egomania Burke well recalled from the time when Rousseau had visited England in 1766. It prophesied too the utter humiliation of the king and queen and the effective ruin of the French monarchy.

With the *Appeal from the New to the Old Whigs*, published in August 1791, Burke turned again to party politics, and

item by item responded to Fox's remarks on 6 May. Convincing though it might be as a systematic rebuttal of charges which Burke regarded as highly offensive, its initial effect was to alienate moderate whigs, led by the duke of Portland. It was not abuse of former colleagues, however justified, that would bring them over. Only Fitzwilliam of the old Rockingham whigs remained unequivocally (and then not very publicly) his friend.

By now Burke enjoyed something of the stature of an international statesman. After approaches by leading French émigrés he sent his son Richard to the exiles' base at Koblenz in August 1791, corresponded with members of the French royal family and sought to instil energy into those who pressed the great powers of Europe to make war on revolutionary France. These were inherently futile activities, given the divisions of the émigrés themselves and the understandable caution of continental governments. Another mission on which Richard was dispatched, to Dublin, promised only a little better. Richard became the paid agent of the Catholic Committee in Ireland, dedicated to improving upon the relief obtained for Catholics during the American war. His father's own contribution, in January 1792, was a tract in the form of a letter to an old protestant friend, Sir Hercules Langrishe, arguing for fully fledged Catholic enfranchisement. Richard's was to become enmeshed in the far from eirenic deliberations of the Catholic Committee. Both used their persuasive powers on Pitt, Dundas, and ministers in Dublin, though to limited effect.

With the onset of the French revolutionary wars Burke flung himself into supporting the allied powers and advocating Britain's joining them as soon as possible. 'The Duke of Brunswick is as much fighting the Battle of the Crown of England as the Duke of Cumberland did at Culloden', he wrote (*Correspondence*, 8.177). The September massacres brought Burke to fever pitch and led him to give up any pretence of remaining within the whig camp. Henceforth he was an open supporter of Pitt's government. His search for evidence of subversion and sedition at home became almost obsessive. In a debate on the Aliens Bill on 28 December 1792 he produced a dagger, which he melodramatically flung on the floor of the house, as evidence of the manufacture of weapons of revolution in Britain.

War between Britain and France in January 1793 confirmed Burke's reputation as a prophet but distanced him further from his former friends as he worked to bring over the more moderate of them to government. 'Party ought to be made for politicks; not politicks for Party purposes' (*Correspondence*, 7.318). In September 1793 he directed to the duke of Portland his 'Observations on the conduct of the minority', the most direct attack on Fox to date. Portland's initial response was discouraging but the final breach in the whig party for which Burke had worked unremittingly was not long delayed. By January 1794 the Portland whigs had given up any hope of persuading Fox to join in a patriotic union against the French republic. In July they took office in Pitt's administration.

By this time another of Burke's long-standing concerns,

the impeachment of Warren Hastings, was reaching resolution. His 'Speech in reply' to the defence, spread across nine days between 28 May and 16 June 1794, ranged widely over the matter that had now occupied nine years of parliamentary time and culminated in a direct comparison between Hastings and the Jacobins in France. He warned the Lords of their close resemblance to the *parlement* of Paris on the eve of the French Revolution. 'My Lords, your house yet stands. It stands as a great edifice, but let me say that it stands in the midst of ruins, in the midst of ruins that have been made by the greatest moral earthquake that ever has convulsed and shattered this globe of ours' (*Writings and Speeches*, 7.692–3). Failing to convict Hastings was to invite the Jacobins in England to slaughter the aristocracy of England as they had already slaughtered the aristocracy of France. On 20 June Burke received the thanks of the Commons for his long service as a prosecutor and immediately resigned his parliamentary seat. Judgment was not pronounced until April 1795 but the outcome was not eagerly awaited. The Lords found for Hastings on every charge.

By that time Burke had suffered a personal tragedy. When he retired from the Commons, Richard took his seat at Malton. It is hard to believe that Burke was unaware of the reservations that even his friends entertained about his heir. Richard's arrogance and assertiveness had made many enemies, but his father seems to have expected that the opportunity to shine in parliament, which he entered at much the age he had himself been first elected, would allow his talents to have their full effect. This was not to be. Shortly after his election Richard fell ill. The family moved to provide him with country air in South Kensington but he died within days, on 2 August 1794. The grief of the parents was almost uncontrollable. It did not weaken Burke's commitment to politics, but it must surely have sharpened the intensity of his emotion on behalf of the public in the years that remained to him. From the time of Richard's death he considered himself 'marked by the hand of God' (*Correspondence*, 8.90). In Wolfe Tone's *Life* there is an anecdote relating Paine's belief that Burke's grief was in reality occasioned by his powerlessness before the arguments of the *Rights of Man*. Tone remarked: 'Paine has no children!' (O'Brien, 572).

Final years In Burke's last years his diverse anxieties came together in what seemed a unified mosaic of evil. 'I think I can hardly overrate the malignity of the principles of Protestant ascendancy, as they affect Ireland; or of Indianism, as they affect these countries, and as they affect Asia; or of Jacobinism, as they affect all Europe, and the state of human society itself' (*Correspondence*, 8.254). The exoneration of Hastings was a predictable blow but the evident failure of the war with France was more disappointing. For some the installation of the Directory in Paris might have taken the edge off the social radicalism of the revolution, but for Burke one regicide was much like another and merely heightened the horrors of any conceivable peace with a republican regime. In Ireland,

where Fitzwilliam was installed as lord lieutenant and liberal whig rule promised the possibility of reform, disaster struck in the form of a premature demand for Catholic admission to parliament. Fitzwilliam supported it, thereby provoking Pitt to remove him from office. Burke had never regarded the concession of Catholic parliamentary emancipation as of much significance in itself, unless the property franchise were lowered. But such a public humiliation for the whig supporters of government was disturbing. And the crisis left Ireland on a course for polarization that would result in the rising of 1798.

During his last years Burke's financial difficulties intensified. As an MP, his legal immunity had rendered his debts embarrassing but not disabling. Leaving the Commons exposed him to the full force of the law. On the other hand, by joining government he was well placed to secure the rewards which a lifetime of public service might justify. Originally he seems to have envisaged a peerage as well as a pension, the former with a view to his son's future prospects, the latter in order to satisfy his creditors and provide his wife with financial security. His friends expected the title to be Beaconsfield, anticipating Disraeli's ennoblement. It is not clear that Pitt ever endorsed the suggestion of a peerage. He may have considered that Burke's support in parliament would be far from an unmixed blessing. After Richard's death the peerage became a secondary consideration and negotiations focused on the financial arrangements. These were complicated but eventually secured Burke's objectives.

They also gave rise to controversy. Burke as a pensioner was exposed to some ridicule. Contrary to a popular impression, he had never opposed pensions nor indeed had he objected to the use of sinecures as a form of public reward. It was their employment for purposes of political bribery that had attracted his ire. Even so his own acceptance of a pension exposed him to the charge of sacrificing his convictions to his comfort, a ludicrous suggestion to anyone who knew him well but one that sprang readily to the lips of Fox's friends. Two of these, the duke of Bedford and the earl of Lauderdale, raised the matter in the House of Lords. The result, in February 1796, was Burke's *Letter to a Noble Lord*, a scorching exposure of the self-serving history of the house of Bedford and of the naïvety and folly of its current representative. It was the rebuke of an 'old man with very young pensions' to a 'young man with very old pensions', and gave Burke a magnificent opportunity to picture the likely fate of this revolutionary duke if England experienced the political upheaval he apparently recommended (*Writings and Speeches*, 9.165).

At the same time Burke was writing what became his last piece on political economy. 'Thoughts and details on scarcity', drafted for several correspondents, including the prime minister, was his response to the famine conditions which occurred in 1795. Published after his death they revealed his continuing commitment to the market. They also included a definition of what lay within the purview of government, in sharp contradistinction to Paine's vision of a state dedicated to social welfare. The religious establishment, the judiciary, military forces, and those legal entities that it created for specific purposes must be its prime concerns. Statesmen should know the difference between 'what belongs to laws, and what manners alone can regulate' (ibid., 9.144).

Burke's pen was also employed in criticizing the government which he now supported. Pitt had never seen the war as an ideological crusade against France but rather as a matter of national interest. After three years of warfare that showed signs of hurting Britain more than France he displayed increasing interest in the possibility of a negotiated peace. Burke's *Two Letters on a Regicide Peace*, published in October 1796, was directed against what its author regarded as signs of dangerous appeasement on the part of government. The letters included one of Burke's most interesting expositions of the history of his own century, emphasizing how far Britain's interests and those of Europe as a whole coincided. They also hammered home the unique character of the French threat, based ultimately on the 'systematick unsociability of this new-invented species of republick', a barbarous form of polity which could not co-exist with a civilized order. The enemy was not the familiar one in the history of Anglo-French warfare. 'It is not France extending a foreign empire over other nations: it is a sect aiming at universal empire, and beginning with the conquest of France' (*Writings and Speeches*, 9.257, 267). There were two other letters on this theme: one published without authority in October 1797, soon after Burke's death; the last, which had actually been drafted before the others but was overtaken by events, not until 1812. Readers who found the Burke of the 1790s exasperating found these pieces the most exasperating of all. But this was in large measure a matter of language and tone. There is nothing in them inconsistent with his earlier position, and as a matter of historical fact when Europe was restored to something resembling a lasting peace, the government of France was once more in the hands of the Bourbon dynasty on whose restoration Burke had so unfashionably insisted.

Burke died at Gregories on 9 July 1797 after a prolonged illness. For more than a year he had been aware that his stomach was 'irrecoverably ruin'd' (*Correspondence*, 10.76–7). In the interim there had been visits to Bath and an acceptance that he had not long to live. He died at a time of dire national crisis, never railing at his own or his country's fate, but depressed by the darkening horizon. He was buried alongside his son and brother at Beaconsfield on 15 July. His wife survived him by nearly fifteen years. His estate was sold shortly before her death. His home burnt down soon afterwards, in 1813.

Personal legacy The Burke of the 1790s was not readily recognizable to those who knew the Burke of earlier days. Some thought him close to breakdown. Images of age and mortality occurred with growing frequency in his speeches and writings during the late 1780s and the 1790s. But this rhetoric of declining powers was misleading, for his energy was undiminished until the very last months of his life. Moreover, the intellectual turmoil that he experienced combined with much personal anguish to lift him on to a new plane of emotional intensity. He has been

memorably described as living at this time in 'a kind of mental thunderstorm' (A. P. Thornton, *The Habit of Authority*, 1966, 78).

In these years, too, Burke was addressing audiences that no other single figure of the age commanded, either in Britain or elsewhere. Oliver Goldsmith had said famously of his friend that he had given up to party what was meant for mankind but Goldsmith did not live to see Burke during these last years when he cast party off without compunction or even much regret. All his life he had sought to address the public and nobody could doubt how directly he was now in touch with it. William Hazlitt remarked that he seemed 'to have a fuller possession of his faculties in addressing the public, than in addressing the House of Commons' (W. Hazlitt, *The Complete Works*, ed. P. P. Howe, 1930–34, 21 vols., 7.302). Hazlitt underrated Burke's earlier mastery of parliamentary debate but clearly grasped that he had taken flight to previously unexplored regions of personal experience and public discourse.

There were disadvantages. The Burke who reached readily for hyperbole, whose rhapsodies revealed to more literal-minded men such as Pitt 'much to admire, and nothing to agree with', was much in evidence at this time (Ayling, 260). His prose was never uncontrolled but in younger days it had certainly been more restrained. Nineteenth-century admirers often preferred his earlier work, though that was in part because liberal whigs were discomforted by the uses to which his later writings had been put. But it was also because they were appalled by the words he coined, the metaphors he constructed and the tasteless rhetoric he relished, 'as though he strained against the limits of language itself, as if he had abandoned all care for propriety in a desperate effort to shock his readers' (Chapman, 236).

Manners were at stake, too. The generation growing up at this time was increasingly bred to a code of decorum and self-restraint. Burke represented an older tradition and never did regard temper as something that must be kept perpetually under control. On one occasion, the young whig reformer Charles Grey spoke in a parliamentary debate with a vehemence that led him to remark to his neighbour Burke, '"I hope I have not shown much temper." "Temper!" replied Mr. Burke, "temper, sir, is the state of mind suited to the occasion!"' (E. Hodder, *The Life of Shaftesbury*, 3 vols., 3.160–61). It seems likely that Burke's displays of passion were indeed more carefully regulated than its victims assumed. Political duels were a feature of the late eighteenth century but Burke came close to one only once—in December 1777, when an exchange with the attorney-general, Alexander Wedderburn, took him to the brink of a challenge. News of a peaceable resolution resulted in a heartfelt note from the normally unemotional Rockingham.

My dear Burke
My heart is at ease
Ever yours
Most affectionately

It is remarkable not that Burke quarrelled but that those with whom he quarrelled were so few. In 1791 he boasted in the Commons 'that he had sat six and twenty years in that House, and had never called any man to order in his life' (*Writings and Speeches*, vol. 4).

Throughout his life Burke's personal magnetism was an acknowledged, even overpowering force. He always commanded the admiration of many of his own and older generations, and when he grew old acquired a considerable younger following that was not only inspired by his prophetic wisdom but touched by his personal warmth. Burke had no Boswell and there is hardly any systematic record of his casual wit and wisdom, aside from some jottings by friends such as the whig hostess Frances Crewe. Boswell did indeed seek to capture Burke's conversation but rarely succeeded. Contrasting Burke with Johnson, Coleridge thought the latter's 'bow-wow' manner might have made him the easier to record.

> Burke, like all men of genius who love to talk at all, was very discursive and continuous, hence he is not reported; he seldom said the sharp short things that Johnson almost always did, which produce a more decided effect at the moment, and which are so much more easy to carry off. (Copeland, 13)

Whatever the truth of this, the engaging nature of Burke's personality is widely attested. This was true as much in a family setting as elsewhere. Independent onlookers tended to think of Burke's kin, the two Richards and William, as a millstone around his neck. But in their company as a group most found pleasure and almost all found Burke himself and his wife, Jane, truly delightful. Elsewhere those who met him for the first time were charmed by his infectious bonhomie. The organist Richard Stevens was startled on meeting him at a Royal Academy dinner in 1789 'by the Fun, frisk, and Anecdote of Mr. Burke's conversation: I never heard anything so animated or captivating in my life; and, perhaps, I never shall: we laughed immoderately for nearly (two) hours at his eccentric and witty conversation' (R. Stevens, *Recollections of R. J. S. Stevens*, ed. M. Argent, 1992, 67). Much of Burke's life, more than would be obvious from his public pronouncements, was filled with laughter. His potential for biting sarcasm is not in doubt where the printed word was concerned, but in conversation his badinage was always good-humoured. If he was criticized it was usually for the crudeness of his humour. Significantly Johnson, who crossed swords with Burke without ever falling out with him, was extravagant in his praise of his wisdom but not of his wit. And it was conceded by his friends that Burke could also be a little overbearing in conversation.

As a young man Burke had struck Horace Walpole, at first meeting, as somewhat affected and pompous, with more than a tinge of authorial self-importance. It is not an impression confirmed by others, then or later. As a politician Burke denied any literary pretensions and confined himself to the role of patron, in some cases with notable results. It was he who discovered the poet George Crabbe in 1781 and shepherded him to social acceptance, professional advancement, and literary success. Of Fanny Burney he was a formidable early champion. Throughout his life he was bombarded by budding authors whose works

he customarily treated with kindly but candid criticism. He seems never to have acquired the habit of commenting on them without having read them.

Perhaps the older Burke was sterner and less tolerant than he had once been. There was a certain ruthlessness that grated with some even of his admirers. The obsessive hunt of Warren Hastings left friends trailing despairingly in his wake or abandoning the chase altogether. Burke's refusal to recognize any good at all in Hastings, though they shared an interest in Hindu culture and its preservation, was hard to defend. The unequivocal and unforgiving break with Fox seemed to come oddly from a man who had on occasion got himself into trouble on behalf of some rather dubious friends or even acquaintances. On his deathbed Burke refused to see Fox. The most chilling feature of the refusal was Burke's insistence that what was at issue was the way it would be publicly perceived: 'that his principles remain the same … and that these principles can be enforced only by the general persuasion of his sincerity' (Prior, 2.397). Gillray's savage portrayal of Burke as the grand detector of conspiracies, unconsciously mimicking those prosecutors of enemies of the state that flourished in the republic of virtue, seemed to fit rather well with this increasingly evident streak of harshness.

Yet Burke's humanity remained manifest. He had always been prone to over-fierce self-vindication when threatened and equally prone to over-generous allowance when not. And in his acute sensitivity to the sufferings of those less fortunate than himself nothing ever hardened him. Pictures treasured by those who knew or heard of him were of Burke personally preparing pills at the dispensary for the poor that he instituted at Beaconsfield, or Burke minutely regulating the school for the sons of French refugees that he established at Penn, or Burke providing a greenhouse for the preparation of food by two visiting Brahmans, or Burke as ever bestowing money that he could ill afford on those who sought his charity. Humanity was indeed the core of his politics as of everything else, and certainly not less so during the last years, even if it seemed to acquire a harder edge. Then indeed Burke saw with a fearful clarity what seemed to him the ultimate obscenity of a creed, the 'rights of man', that degraded humanity while professing to serve it. A favourite phrase employed of Jacobinism, 'the cannibal philosophy', encapsulated this vision not simply because there were examples of cannibalism in the French Revolution, eagerly sought out by Burke, but because this was taken to be a kind of substitute religion that fed on slaughter and destruction. What linked this nightmare vision with the politics of his entire lifetime was his systematic critique of the abuse of power. Faced by unchallengeable evidence of what human nature was capable when those in power were unrestrained by humanity, Burke was indeed merciless.

Burke's personal dreams for himself and his kin came to nothing. The Burke family did not take root among the gentlemen of England. His sons and his brothers predeceased him. If he had sought fortune in material terms, he certainly did not achieve it, leaving sufficient only to sustain his widow. He cannot be said to have died loaded with honours. He had taken pleasure in his election as lord rector of Glasgow University in 1783 and used it to acquaint himself with Scotland. Trinity College, Dublin, had honoured him in 1790. Oxford refused to do so at the same time; when later it changed its mind Burke declined to be propitiated but eventually compromised by permitting his son to be awarded a degree. By his own desire, the honour of an Abbey burial was turned down.

Irishmen of minor gentry or professional background were conventionally portrayed in England as fortune-hunters and Burke sometimes among them. In his case it was a particularly absurd charge, for at all the critical points in his career he had turned his back on promotion for its own sake. None the less the adversities of the 1790s sorely tried him, and he was thrown back on his belief in an omnipotent God. That belief has sometimes been found puzzling. There is little in the surviving sources about Burke's life as a worshipper. He lacked the kind of studied introspectiveness that might yield insights into the nature of his devotions or even his beliefs. Moreover he seemed uneasy with the dogmas that sustain most believers, and sometimes spoke and wrote as if religious creeds were primarily matters of political convenience. If fervour were needed to defend them it was fervour on behalf of a sane society. Yet there is no doubting Burke's commitment. For many of his generation the deity of the early Enlightenment was little more than a stage prop in a rationally ordered existence. For Burke it was an intense and all-pervading spiritual reality.

Burke lived on in the extraordinary public impact that he achieved in his later years through several generations of men and women, especially those prominent in public life who, like Canning, hung onto his words as 'the manual of my politics' (G. Canning, *Some Official Correspondence of George Canning*, ed. E. J. Stapleton, 2 vols., 1887, 1.23). Beyond that it is his writings that have kept him in the mainstream of the Western political and intellectual tradition. They were ably edited by two of his followers, Walker King and French Laurence, who had assisted him with the *Annual Register*, the impeachment, and other concerns. Publication commenced in Burke's own lifetime, in 1795, and concluded many years later in 1827. A number of Burke's less finished writings and drafts appeared alongside those which were a recognized part of his canon. This edition has since been reprinted and cannibalized in numerous versions and employed for all kinds of purposes. It will be fully supplanted only when the Clarendon edition of *Writings and Speeches*—which draws heavily on Burke's personal archive among the papers of the Fitzwilliam family, and also on close study of his parliamentary speeches as reported in the contemporary press—is completed. Publication of this edition in ten volumes began in 1981.

The uses to which Burke's writings have been put indeed indicate the richness of his thought and the many-sidedness of his talent. To Victorians especially, he appeared 'to be in the political what Shakespeare was in the moral world' (H. Reeve, ed., *The Greville Memoirs*, 3rd edn, 3 vols., 1875, 3.209). He defied party political classification and remained a source of inspiration as well as argument to generations of Conservatives and Liberals. Matthew Arnold attributed this to Burke's unique capacity to marry the mind of the thinker to the actions of a politician. 'His greatness is that he lived in a world which neither English Liberalism nor English Toryism is apt to enter;—the world of ideas, not the world of catchwords and party habits' (Ritchie, 27).

Hazlitt and Leslie Stephen considered Burke the greatest prose writer in the English language. His impact on Romantic and organic trains of thought was marked not only in Britain where it was transmitted through the Lake poets, but in Germany, where his followers included some of the most influential in this genre, Justin Möser, Adam Müller, Novalis. His remarkable ability to bring historical imagination to bear on all kinds of contemporary and controversial questions fired the enthusiasm of generations of historically minded Victorians. As Macaulay memorably put it, 'he had, in the highest degree, that noble faculty whereby man is able to live in the past and in the future, in the distant and in the unreal' (T. B. Macaulay, 'Warren Hastings', in *Critical and Historical Essays*, 3 vols., 1843, 3.433).

Burke continued to be read and admired throughout the twentieth century, though some historians were more dismissive of his talents than any of the preceding century had been. Sir Lewis Namier, who regarded the whig creed and the whig version of history as nothing more than covers for aristocratic self-interest, thought Burke the most pernicious exponent of each. Such scepticism was rarer beyond Britain and purely British affairs. Both world wars in different ways revived interest in his defence of civilized values against the beast within and without. The search for an international order brought recognition of his faith in an overriding principle of natural justice by men of widely differing opinions. A. V. Dicey saw in his defiance of Jacobin France a template for application to Bolshevik Russia. Harold Laski wrestled with his ideas and came to have a profound respect for them. The turbulent politics of the second half of the twentieth century reinforced the appeal of Burke's invocation of prescriptive practices, values, and institutions. In the hands of American admirers such as Peter Stanlis and Russell Kirk—who glimpsed in Burke a direct link to ancient Christian, indeed Catholic natural law tradition—his thought became almost as potent a weapon in the cold war against communism as it had been nearly two hundred years before in the wars of the French Revolution.

On the whole, what is most striking about Burke's influence is its variety. Quite different positions have been supported by Burkean wisdom, and proponents of new ones continue to find vindication in citing it. No other member of parliament in the country that invented the parliamentary tradition has exerted such influence over such a diverse and enduring audience. His legacy extends beyond the community of scholars, and beyond the shores of his own and his adopted country. No single tradition or party has succeeded in monopolizing it.

PAUL LANGFORD

Sources *The writings and speeches of Edmund Burke*, ed. P. Langford, 9 vols. (1981–) • *The correspondence of Edmund Burke*, ed. T. W. Copeland and others, 10 vols. (1958–78) • F. Crewe, 'Extracts from Mr. Burke's Table-Talk, at Crewe Hall', ed. R. M. Milnes, *Miscellanies of the Philobiblon Society*, 7, pt 5 (1862–3) • A. P. I. Samuels, *The early life, correspondence and writings of the Rt. Hon. Edmund Burke, LL. D.* (1923) • *The manuscripts and correspondence of James, first earl of Charlemont*, 2 vols., HMC, 28 (1891–4) • *The manuscripts of J. B. Fortescue*, 10 vols., HMC, 30 (1892–1927) • G. Thomas, earl of Albemarle [G. T. Keppel], *Memoirs of the marquis of Rockingham and his contemporaries*, 2 vols. (1852) • *Life and letters of Sir Gilbert Elliot, first earl of Minto, from 1751 to 1806*, ed. countess of Minto [E. E. E. Elliot-Murray-Kynynmound], 3 vols. (1874) • *The journal and correspondence of William, Lord Auckland*, ed. [G. Hogge], 4 vols. (1861–2) • *Memoirs of Sir Philip Francis*, ed. J. Parkes and H. Merivale, 2 vols. (1867) • *Correspondence of William Pitt, earl of Chatham*, ed. W. S. Taylor and J. H. Pringle, 4 vols. (1838–40), vols. 1–2 • *Sir Henry Cavendish's Debates of the House of Commons during the thirteenth parliament of Great Britain*, ed. J. Wright, 2 vols. (1841–3) • Walpole, *Corr.* • J. Prior, *Life of the Right Honourable Edmund Burke*, 5th edn (1854) • C. C. O'Brien, *The great melody: a thematic biography and commented anthology of Edmund Burke* (1992) • F. P. Lock, *Edmund Burke* (1998) • T. W. Copeland, *Six essays* (1950) • N. K. Robinson, *Edmund Burke: a life in caricature* (1996) • H. V. F. Somerset, ed., *A note-book of Edmund Burke* (1957) • D. C. Bryant, *Edmund Burke and his literary friends* (1939) • R. J. S. Hoffman, *Edmund Burke: New York agent* (1956) • D. Wecter, *Edmund Burke and his kinsmen: a study of the statesman's financial integrity and private relationships* (1939) • T. H. D. Mahoney, *Edmund Burke and Ireland* (1960) • P. J. Marshall, *The impeachment of Warren Hastings* (1965) • C. B. Cone, *Burke and the nature of politics*, 2 vols. (1957–64) • S. Ayling, *Edmund Burke: his life and opinions* (1988) • G. W. Chapman, *Edmund Burke: the practical imagination* (1967) • C. Parkin, *The moral basis of Burke's political thought* (1956) • C. P. Courtney, *Montesquieu and Burke* (1963) • T. O. McLoughlin, *Edmund Burke and the first ten years of the 'Annual Register'* (1975) • J. T. Boulton, *The language of politics in the age of Wilkes and Burke* (1963) • C. Reid, *Edmund Burke and the practice of political writing* (1985) • A. Cobban, *Edmund Burke and the revolt against the eighteenth century*, 2nd edn (1960) • F. P. Lock, *Burke's 'Reflections on the revolution in France'* (1985) • P. Stanlis, *Edmund Burke and the natural law* (1958) • B. Taylor Wilkins, *The problem of Burke's political philosophy* (1967) • F. de Bruyn, *The literary genres of Edmund Burke* (1996) • S. Blakemore, *Burke and the fall of language: the French Revolution as linguistic event* (1988) • R. Kirk, *Edmund Burke: a genius reconsidered* (1967) • D. E. Ritchie, ed., *Edmund Burke: appraisals and applications* (1990) • T. Furniss, *Edmund Burke's aesthetic ideology: language, agenda and political economy in revolution* (1993) • F. A. Dreyer, *Burke's politics: a study in whig orthodoxy* (1979) • M. Freeman, *Edmund Burke and the critique of political radicalism* (1980) • F. P. Canavan, *The political reason of Edmund Burke* (1960) • H. C. Mansfield, *Statesmanship and party government: a study of Burke and Bolingbroke* (1965) • F. O'Gorman, *Edmund Burke: his political philosophy* (1973) • S. Murphy, 'Burke and Lucas: an authorship problem re-examined', *Eighteenth-Century Ireland*, 1 (1986), 143–56 • L. S. Sutherland and J. A. Woods, 'The East India speculations of William Burke', *Proceedings of the Leeds Philosophical and Literary Society*, 11 (1966), 183–216 • M. Fuchs, 'Edmund Burke et Augustus Keppel', *Études Anglaises*, 18 (1965), 18–26 • P. T. Underdown, 'Henry Cruger and Edmund Burke: colleagues and rivals at the Bristol election of 1774', *William and Mary Quarterly*, 15 (1958), 14–34 • L. S. Sutherland, 'Edmund Burke and the relations between members of parliament and their constituents', *Studies in Burke and his Time*, 10 (1968), 1005–21 • P. T. Underdown, 'Edmund Burke, the commissary of his Bristol constituents, 1774–1780', *EngHR*, 73 (1958), 252–69 • E. A. Reitan, 'Edmund Burke and the civil list, 1769–1782', *Burke Newsletter*, 8 (1966), 604–18 • J. G. A. Pocock,

'Burke and the American constitution', *Politics, language, and time* (1971), 202–32 • P. Lucas, 'On Edmund Burke's doctrine of prescription, or, An appeal from the new to the old lawyers', *HJ*, 11 (1968), 35–63 • J. E. Tierney, 'Edmund Burke, John Hawkesworth, the *Annual Register*, and the *Gentleman's Magazine*', *Huntington Library Quarterly*, 42 (1978), 57–72 • T. O. McLoughlin, 'Edmund Burke: the post-graduate years, 1748–50', *Studies in Burke and his Time*, 10 (1968), 1035–40 • T. O. McLoughlin, 'Edmund Burke's *Abridgement of English history*', *Eighteenth-Century Ireland*, 5 (1990), 45–59 • T. W. Copeland, 'Edmund Burke's friends and the *Annual Register*', *The Library*, 18 (1963), 29–39 • I. Hampsher-Monk, 'Burke and the religious sources of skeptical conservatism', *The skeptical tradition around 1800*, ed. J. van der Zande and R. H. Popkin (1998), 235–59

Archives Bodl. Oxf., library catalogue • Bristol RO, letters • CUL, letters • Harvard U., Houghton L., corresp. and papers • Harvard U., Houghton L., papers by and about him • Hunt. L., letters • NL Ire., corresp. and papers • Sheff. Arch., Wentworth Woodhouse Muniments, corresp. | BL, corresp. with Lord Grenville, Add. MS 69038 • BL, corresp. with first earl of Liverpool, Add. MSS 38191, 38227, 38308, 38310, 38404 • BL, corresp. with William Windham, Add. MS 37843 • BL OIOC, letters to Sir Philip Francis, MS Eur. F 6 • Bodl. Oxf., corresp. with Lord Macartney • CKS, letters to William Pitt • Devon RO, corresp. with Lord Sidmouth • Herts. ALS, corresp. with William Baker • N. Yorks. CRO, corresp. with Christopher Wyvill • NL Ire., corresp. with Charles O'Hara • NL Scot., letters to Henry Dundas • NL Scot., Minto MSS • NL Scot., corresp. with Charles O'Hare • Northants. RO, Fitzwilliam MSS, corresp. and papers • PRO, letters to William Pitt, PRO 30/8/118/1/86–111 • Royal Irish Acad., corresp. with Lord Charlemont • Sheff. Arch., Wentworth Woodhouse Muniments, Rockingham MSS • Sheffield Central Library, corresp. with Lord Fitzwilliam • U. Nott. L., Portland MSS • Yale U., Beinecke L., corresp. with James Boswell • Yale U., Beinecke L., Osborn collection, letters to Walter King, bishop of Rochester • Yale U., Beinecke L., letters to Richard Shackleton, etc.

Likenesses J. Reynolds, double portrait, unfinished sketch, 1766–8 (with Lord Rockingham), FM Cam. • J. Reynolds, portrait, 1767–9, priv. coll. [see illus.] • J. Jones, mezzotint, pubd 1770 (after G. Romney), BM, NPG • J. Watson, mezzotint, pubd 1770 (after J. Reynolds, 1767–9), BM, NPG • J. Barry, oils, 1771, NG Ire.; copy, NPG • studio of Reynolds, oils, 1771, NPG • J. Reynolds, oils, exh. RA 1774, Scot. NPG; on loan to NG Ire. • J. Sayers, etchings, pubd 1782–96, BM, NPG • T. R. Poole, wax medallion, 1791, NPG • J. Opie, oils, 1792, Knole, Kent • J. Hoppner, oils, 1795–1801, TCD • H. Kingsbury, mezzotint, pubd 1798, BM, NPG • S. W. Reynolds, mezzotint, pubd 1820 (after J. Reynolds), BM, NPG • J. Barry, group portrait, oils (*The Society for the Encouragement of the Arts*), RSA • J. Gillray, caricature, BM, NPG • J. Hickey, bust, TCD • T. Hickey, double portrait, oils (with Charles James Fox), NG Ire. • W. Holl, stipple (after unknown artist), NPG • J. Jones, engraving (after G. Romney, 1776), repro. in W. Bellenden, *De stato libri tres* (1787) • J. Nixon, caricature, Palace of Westminster, London • J. Reynolds, oils, Scot. NPG • J. Sayers, caricature, BM, NPG • bust, TCD • plaster medallion (after W. Tassie), Scot. NPG • plaster medallion (after Wedgwood medallion by J. C. Lochée), Scot. NPG

Burke, Edmund Plunkett

Burke, Edmund Plunkett (1802–1835), judge, was born of Irish parents at Lisbon, Portugal. He was brought to England as a child and was educated at home and by an able schoolmaster, Dr Robertson. At fifteen he attended the lycée at Caen, Normandy, where he studied for three years. He then entered Caius College, Cambridge, but disliked mathematics, and so did not take a degree. He showed early talent in the study of civil law: as an undergraduate he wrote an *Essay on the Laws and Government of Rome; Introductory to the Civil Law*, a surprisingly mature work for his years which attracted attention in Cambridge. In 1830 he published a second edition under his own name. He joined the Inner Temple and was called to the bar. Disaster then struck. He lost his private means through the imprudence of a relative, which left him too poor to buy books or pay fees for reading in counsel's chambers. He was too proud to borrow money from friends. Though diligent in research, he was dilatory and unsystematic, and did not make much progress in his profession at this time. He wrote poorly paid biographical notices for the *Law Magazine*, but found it difficult to meet deadlines and work efficiently. Rescue came in 1832 when, because of the reputation of his book and his knowledge of French, he was appointed a judge in St Lucia, West Indies. In 1833 the governor of the West Indies, General Farquhar, promoted him to the position of judge of the admiralty court. He died in 1835 of an injury received during a hurricane in St Dominica.

J. A. HAMILTON, *rev.* HUGH MOONEY

Sources *Law Magazine*, 13 (1840), 532
Archives UCL, letters to Society for the Diffusion of Useful Knowledge

Burke, John (1786–1848), author and genealogist, was born on 12 November 1786 at Parsonstown, King's county, Ireland, the eldest of three children of Peter Burke (1756–1836) of Elm Hall, co. Tipperary, JP for that county and for the King's county, and his first wife, Anne (*d.* 1818), second daughter and coheir of Matthew Dowdall MD of Mullingar, co. Westmeath. Burke married on 6 May 1807 at Longford, co. Longford, his first cousin Mary (1781–1846), daughter of Bernard O'Reilly of Ballymorris, co. Longford, and his wife, Mary, daughter and coheir of Dr Matthew Dowdall, and had with her four sons and two daughters who survived infancy. By the time his eldest child, Peter *Burke, serjeant-at-law, was born in 1811 Burke had moved to London; according to one source, 'to devote himself to literary pursuits', having received 'a good classical education' (Waller). The same source asserts that he wrote for *The Examiner* and published a volume of poetry prior to 1826, when he produced the first of his most important series of genealogical books, entitled *A General and Heraldic Dictionary of the Peerage and Baronetage of the United Kingdom*.

Burke was responsible for the first eight editions and edited the ninth and tenth editions of 1847 and 1848 jointly with his son (John) Bernard *Burke (1814–1892), subsequently Ulster king of arms. This book, better known as *Burke's Peerage*, was (with the exception of the years 1918–20) produced annually from 1847 until 1940; in the following half-century there were seven editions. Previous printed peerages such as those of Arthur Collins (*d.* 1760) and John Field Debrett (1753–1822) not only divided the peerages of England, Scotland, and Ireland, but listed them in order of precedence. In 1825 Nicholas Harris Nicolas (1799–1848) had produced *A Synopsis of the Peerage of England*, with an alphabetical arrangement. The strength of Burke's work was that it not only listed all titles alphabetically irrespective of rank, but also included baronets and the entire peerage of the United Kingdom. Its ease of use brought popularity, and in 1840 Debrett's *Peerage* too adopted an alphabetical format. The first four editions of

1826, 1828, 1830, and 1833 were all printed on paper of the same octavo size, and the number of pages of pedigrees increased from 359 in 1826 to 683 in 1828, 845 in 1830, and 1300 in 1833. In the first edition Burke stated that he was 'deducing the lineage of each house from the founder of its honors'; thereafter he was 'deducing the genealogical line of each house from the earliest period'. It was in this expansion of material in and after 1828 that his weakness lay, as he accepted uncritically fictional and inaccurate information on the origins of families, some of which was supplied by the subjects, and much of which had been printed by Collins.

Many peerages had been published prior to Burke's, but there was no precedent for his *Landed Gentry*, which was first published as *A Genealogical and Heraldic History of the Commoners of Great Britain and Ireland, Enjoying Territorial Possessions or High Official Rank* in three volumes (1833–5), with a fourth volume in 1838. In the second edition, which like all his later works was co-edited with his son (John) Bernard Burke, the title was changed to *A Genealogical and Heraldic Dictionary of the Landed Gentry of Great Britain and Ireland* (3 vols., 1843–9). The closest to a forerunner was the *Baronage of Scotland; containing an historical and genealogical account of the gentry of that kingdom* (1798), a posthumous work of Sir Robert Douglas (1694–1770). Burke's *Landed Gentry*, of which there were eighteen editions between 1833 and 1972, was the first printed national record of the untitled aristocracy or county families of Great Britain, whose genealogies were otherwise to be found in the county histories and heralds' visitations of the sixteenth and seventeenth centuries. In addition to an alphabetical format, which was adopted from the second edition onwards, the pedigrees of the families were laid out as in the *Peerage* in a narrative style, which has since become a model for many similar pedigrees. But the *Landed Gentry* was marred by the same lack of attention to detail as the *Peerage*. In his anonymous pamphlet of 1865 entitled *Popular Genealogists, or, The Art of Pedigree-Making*, George Burnett (1822–1890) attacked the inaccuracy of both works, and described the majority of pedigrees in the *Landed Gentry* as 'utterly worthless'. This criticism was not isolated: John Horace Round (1854–1928) notably drew attention to Burke's errors, mis-statements and absurdities in an article on the *Peerage* contributed to the *Quarterly Review* in 1893.

In collaboration with his son, Burke produced *A General Armory of England, Scotland and Ireland* (1842), of which there have been three further editions and a number of reprints. Manuscript and printed collections of armorial bearings arranged alphabetically by surname had existed since the seventeenth century; this, however, was far more comprehensive than any of its predecessors. But it contained true and false arms inextricably mingled, and has since been used as a work of reference by purveyors of bogus armorial bearings.

Burke's other output was considerable. In 1831 he produced *A General and Heraldic Dictionary of the Peerages of England, Ireland and Scotland, Extinct, Dormant and in Abeyance*, of which there were further editions under variant titles in

1840, 1846, 1866, and 1883. There was no continuation of *The Official Kalendar for 1831*. Another non-genealogical work was *The portrait gallery of distinguished females, including beauties of the courts of George IV and William IV* (1833). With his son, he was co-author of *A Genealogical and Heraldic History of the Extinct and Dormant Baronetcies of England* (1838), with a second edition in 1841; of *The Knightage of Great Britain and Ireland* (1841); of *Heraldic Illustrations* (3 vols., 1844–6); and of *Royal Families of England, Scotland and Wales with their Descendants, Sovereigns and Subjects* (2 vols., 1847 and 1851). He also edited from May 1846 to March 1848 a short-lived periodical entitled *The Patrician*, which his son continued from April to October 1848.

Although overshadowed by his son Sir Bernard Burke, John Burke was the founder of the most widely known and extensive series of genealogical reference books relating to the titled and landed classes of the United Kingdom, and was the progenitor of a dynasty which oversaw their publication until the death of his grandson Sir Henry Farnham Burke (1859–1930), Garter king of arms.

Burke, who was a Roman Catholic, lived at a number of addresses in London and latterly at 25 Gower Street, Bedford Square. He died at Aix-la-Chapelle on 27 March 1848, and was buried there. He was survived by his two eldest sons, Peter Burke and Sir Bernard Burke.

THOMAS WOODCOCK

Sources *DNB* · A. Wagner, *Heralds of England: a history of the office and College of Arms* (1967), 511–13 · A. Wagner, *English genealogy*, 3rd edn (1983), 377–8, 388–93 · [H. Montgomery-Massingberd], ed., *Burke's family index* (1976) · J. J. Howard and F. A. Crisp, eds., *Visitation of Ireland*, 1 (1897), 23–4 · J. H. Round, *Peerage and pedigree: studies in peerage law and family history*, 2 vols. (1910) · J. F. Waller, ed., *The imperial dictionary of universal biography*, 3 vols. (1857–63) · J. H. Round, *Studies in peerage and family history* (1901) · J. B. Burke, ed., *The Patrician*, 5 (1848), 501–3
Archives V&A, Forster collection, corresp. and MSS relating to peerage | Bodl. Oxf., MSS Phillipps-Robinson, corresp. with Sir Thomas Phillipps
Likenesses portrait, repro. in *Engraved Brit. ports.*, vol. 6

Burke, Kathleen. *See* Hale, Kathleen (1887–1958).

Burke, Peter (1811–1881), serjeant-at-law, was born on 7 May 1811 in London, the eldest son of John *Burke (1786–1848) of Elm Hall, co. Tipperary, the originator of *Burke's Peerage*, and his wife, Mary (1781–1846), daughter of Bernard O'Reilly of Ballymorris. His brother was Sir (John) Bernard *Burke, genealogist and Ulster king of arms. Peter Burke was educated at the college of Caen in Normandy. Having been called to the bar at the Inner Temple in 1839, he joined the northern circuit and the Manchester and Lancashire sessions. He afterwards practised at the parliamentary bar, and appeared before the House of Lords in several important peerage cases. He was made a queen's counsel of the county palatine of Lancaster in 1858 and a serjeant-at-law in 1859. He was elected director or chief honorary officer of the Society of Antiquaries of Normandy for 1866–7. He died at his home, 7 Coleherne Road, South Kensington, London, on 26 March 1881.

In addition to some legal works Burke published

between 1851 and 1866 several volumes of anecdotal material on the subject of famous trials and two works on the life and writings of Edmund Burke.

THOMPSON COOPER, *rev.* CATHERINE PEASE-WATKIN

Sources *Men of the time* (1879) · *ILN* (2 April 1881) · *CGPLA Eng. & Wales* (1881) · d. cert.
Wealth at death under £10,000: probate, 11 April 1881, *CGPLA Eng. & Wales*

Burke, Richard, fourth earl of Clanricarde and first earl of St Albans (1572–1635), politician, was the eldest surviving son of Ulick Burke, third earl of Clanricarde (*d.* 1601), and his wife, Honora (*b.* 1534/5, *d.* in or after 1615), daughter of John Burke of Clogheroka. Styled baron of Dunkellin, his father's subsidiary title, Burke was of the first generation of the family to be brought up completely under the influence of English culture. He was raised in England, spending much of his boyhood in the household of the earl of Essex. In December 1584 he matriculated from Christ Church, Oxford, and he was created MA in July 1598. In the last years of the campaign against the earl of Tyrone he served in the English forces, helping to defend the province of Connaught and the vicinity of Galway in 1599–1600 against attack by the insurgents. It was in December 1601 at Kinsale that he won a reputation for outstanding valour. He was knighted on the battlefield by Lord Deputy Mountjoy for his leading role in the defeat of the Irish confederates and their Spanish allies, and he enjoyed thereafter the sobriquet Richard of Kinsale.

By that time Burke had become fourth earl of Clanricarde on the death of his father in May 1601. Before April 1603 he married Frances (1567–1632), the widow successively of Sir Philip Sidney and Robert Devereux, second earl of Essex, and daughter of Queen Elizabeth's secretary of state, Sir Francis Walsingham. They had a son, Ulick, and two daughters. Given his important courtly and aristocratic connections, it is unsurprising that he lived for most of the rest of his life in England. He appointed his principal residence at Somerhill, built for Frances and himself in 1609, near Tonbridge, in Kent. In 1624 he was created an English peer with the titles of baron of Somerhill and Viscount Tunbridge.

Despite his increasing involvement with the English aristocracy from the early Jacobean period Clanricarde remained fully engaged in Irish affairs and continued to play a prominent part in the political and social life of Connaught down to his death. In 1604 James I appointed him president of the province, notwithstanding his unashamedly Catholic convictions, for which he gained legal immunity from both James and Charles I. He was popular as provincial ruler, a position he held until 1616. In that year he petitioned the king to be allowed to relinquish the presidency and to have instituted for himself instead the office of governor of the city and county of Galway. Thenceforth these were free from the jurisdiction of the Connaught president, a factor that proved of major significance for Galway during the warfare of the 1640s.

The earl also paid close attention to his vast estates in the western province, centred on his residences at Portumna and Loughrea in co. Galway. During the years of his extended absences he supervised the management of his properties mainly through the agency of his friend Henry Lynch, a merchant of Galway city. In letters sent from England over a twenty-year period Clanricarde dealt with the minutiae of running his Irish estates and with the petitions of his tenants. It is evident that he needed a sure income from Galway to maintain his lifestyle in Kent. Also of concern to him were the fortunes of his immediate and extended family and the friends and followers of his house. Frequently bemoaning his absenteeism, the earl expressed his wish to return to live in Ireland and hoped that his son would settle on his estates there.

Although enjoying the patronage of powerful friends such as the duke of Buckingham at the royal court, Clanricarde was faced with challenges to his position during the last decade of his life. A dispute broke out in 1626 with the earl of Thomond over the right to precedence in the Irish nobility, the issue being resolved to Clanricarde's satisfaction in 1628, when, owing to royal favour, he was awarded the titles of earl of St Albans, baron of Imanney, and Viscount Galway. The threat to the security of landholders in Connaught, raised periodically since the late sixteenth century, became acute during the lord deputyship of Thomas, Viscount Wentworth. The latter planned a plantation of Connaught, titles to lands in the province never having been confirmed in the Elizabethan composition. In 1635 a commission of inquiry sat in the counties of the provinces, taking evidence from juries. The jurors under the influence of Clanricarde obstructed the proceedings for Galway, held at Portumna. The resulting trials and punishments of recalcitrant jurors caused Clanricarde a great deal of anguish, and it was widely believed that his death in Kent on 12 November 1635 was hastened by his despair at the prospect of the confiscation of the Connaught lands (which never materialized). He was buried that year in Tonbridge beside his wife, and was succeeded by his son, Ulick.   COLM LENNON

Sources Burke, *Peerage* · GEC, *Peerage*, new edn · B. Cunningham, 'Clanricard letters', *Journal of the Galway Archaeological and Historical Society*, 48 (1996), 162–208 · M. D. O'Sullivan, *Old Galway* (1942) · H. Kearney, *Strafford in Ireland, 1633–41: a study in absolutism* (1959) · B. Cunningham, 'A view of religious practice and affiliation in Thomond, 1591', *Archivium Hibernicum*, 48 (1994), 13–24 · J. J. Silke, *Kinsale: the Spanish intervention in Ireland at the end of the Elizabethan wars* (1970) · *DNB* · Foster, *Alum. Oxon.*
Archives NL Ire., letters, MS 3111

Burke, Richard (1733–1794), political writer and lawyer, was born in Dublin on 18 December 1733, the sixth of the eleven children of Richard Burke (*d.* 1761), attorney, and his wife, Mary, *née* Nagle (*c.*1702–1770), daughter of Garrett Nagle. Both his parents were Irish. Among his elder brothers was the politician and writer Edmund *Burke.

From 1741 Richard Burke, alongside his brothers Garrett and Edmund, attended Abraham Shackleton's school at Ballitore. In 1752 he went to London to train in commerce, and in 1759 he travelled to Grenada. His first published political writing may have been a contribution to *Remarks on the Letter to Two Great Men* (1760). This has been attributed to his kinsman William *Burke on the basis of

stylometric analysis by George C. McElroy, but was considered by earlier commentators to be the work of Charles Townshend. The section warning that colonies with no fear of the French were more likely to seek independence gained most attention, and McElroy has argued that this section, written in short pointed sentences, was Richard's. Richard Burke's writings have been difficult to identify as he always wrote anonymously or pseudonymously and mostly in collaboration with Edmund or William Burke. He may have written the accounts of the fighting in India for the *Annual Register* in 1760 and 1764 and the review in the latter of volume 1 of Robert Orme's *History of the Military Transactions of the British Nation in Indostan*, suggesting that he, not Edmund, was the first Burke to become interested in Indian government. He continued to contribute small items to the *Annual Register*, particularly concerning Edmund's speeches and actions, after Edmund handed over the editorship to Thomas English.

Burke was in Liverpool in 1762, when he successfully urged traders to address the crown in protest against the anticipated return to France of islands in the West Indies captured during the Seven Years' War. In 1763 he was appointed collector of customs in Grenada, but was given a leave of absence because of ill health two years later. If he was the author of a series of pro-Rockingham letters from 'A Spitalfields Weaver' in the *Public Advertiser* that year, he had returned to London by July. He was probably one of the many writers who contributed letters in support of the Rockingham administration, behind pseudonyms such as Tyro, Liber, Vindex, Idem, Tranquilius, Thersites (in the case of the principal series supporting the administration), and 'A Disappointed Tory'. The sentence constructions associated with Richard Burke appear less frequently after the fall of the Rockingham ministry, but probably contributed to several articles critical of the government and defending his brother Edmund Burke. In 1768 Edmund Burke sought for him a parliamentary seat, without success.

Burke returned to Grenada in 1769, but his career there was again marred by health problems. In 1770 he purchased land in St Vincent from the Caribs, but the government opposed his purchases and those made by other adventurers, and the purchases were declared illegal by act of parliament in 1771. He had returned to Britain by 12 November 1771, when he entered Lincoln's Inn. He continued to attempt to validate his purchases in St Vincent, and a ruling from the commissioners for trade in July 1772 disallowed the 1771 act, but his claim was decisively rejected by the Treasury board in November 1775. In September that year he was removed from his office in Grenada following a breach of government orders by his deputy William Senhouse. He also assisted his brother in electoral politics, writing Edmund Burke's farewell letter to the electors of Wendover for him in 1774, and represented him in October 1774 during the election in Bristol. He was called to the bar in 1777, and travelled the western circuit.

During this period Burke probably wrote reports of his brother's speeches in the press, and wrote acidly against the ministry's American policy. As early as 15 April 1769, 'O. C.', arguably a collaboration between Richard and Edmund Burke, had derided an assertion by James Macpherson ('Seneca') that the Grafton ministry had extinguished American discontent, and that the colonists could soon be expected to take up arms. When this occurred, from 23 September 1775 he pursued a high-spirited, satirical attack on the ministry and its American actions in a series of fourteen letters from Valens in the *London Evening-Post* (several of which were reprinted in *The Gazetteer*), which the *Post* treated as a special feature. When the letters were published in pamphlet form by John Almon in 1777, Edmund Burke wrote the preface, but Almon believed that most of the letters were written by Richard. The styles of William and Edmund Burke can be identified in the latter seven of the series from other sources; the author of the first seven letters and most of the last three may therefore have been Richard Burke.

Richard Burke, like his brother, was active in the Buckinghamshire meeting of 1780 which called for economical reform. He also appeared in two legal cases that were important to the opposition. On 29 August 1780 he was a counsel for Captain John Caton, a Bristol merchant who opposed the American War of Independence, and had been seized by the press gang, allegedly for political motives, and subsequently released when it was confirmed that he no longer owned any merchant ships that could be commandeered by the navy. Burke successfully pursued Caton's claim for damages, but won only £150 instead of the hoped-for £5000. That year he was also counsel for General John Burgoyne in the successful defeat of the petition by government supporters against Burgoyne's election as MP for Preston. During the second Rockingham administration, Richard Burke was briefly secretary to the Treasury, from 6 April to 15 July 1782. He resumed that office a year later under the Fox–North coalition. He may have been the author of *A brief and impartial review of the state of Great Britain at the commencement of the session of 1783*, actually an overview of the coalition ministry's proposed legislative measures, although the section urging the Irish to be content with their recent gains was written in a style more like that of Edmund Burke. The section on India not only addressed topics that would reappear in Edmund's India Bill speech, but outdid anything Edmund had yet said of Warren Hastings and his supporters: British misfortunes in India 'originated solely and exclusively from the wild ambition of one man, supported by a corrupt confederacy at home, unchecked by directorial or parliamentary control' (p. 45). If this opinion was Richard Burke's, no wonder that during the Hastings impeachment, for which he was retained as counsel by the prosecution, it was he, not Edmund, who was impersonated by the actress Mary Stephens (Becky) Wells.

In 1783 Richard Burke was appointed recorder of Bristol. The post did not fully compensate for his debts, many of which had been incurred in 1769 when he, William Burke, and others had lost thousands of pounds when East India Company futures collapsed on the Amsterdam stock exchange. From November 1787 to April 1788 he lived in Paris while his brother and friends arranged for the payment of his creditors. His last published writing was his charge to the Bristol grand jury, delivered in April 1793, less than a year before he died, which the jurors agreed should be printed as a pamphlet at their expense. The reason was not his businesslike and humane recommendation that the jurors, conscious of the rise in criminal gangs, should be cautious of indicting anyone without truly convincing evidence, but the lengthy adjuration added to the speech by Edmund Burke against subversive doctrines, with a stinging contrast between the proclaimed goals of the French revolutionaries and the contrary results.

As the younger brother of Edmund Burke, Richard Burke suffered by comparison. His good-natured sense of humour and the debts he accumulated in East India stock and through land speculations on the island of St Vincent added to the perception of him as an intellectual lightweight who was a millstone around his brother's neck. James Boswell described him as rough and wild, but others, such as Oliver Goldsmith and Fanny Burney, remarked upon and appreciated his wit and good spirits. David Garrick and Sir Joshua Reynolds readily assisted him financially. Both John Almon and Robert Bisset praised his abilities as a writer.

Richard Burke never married, but his devotion to Edmund's wife, Jane, and to his nephew, also named Richard, gave him a rich family life. Following a period of ill health, he died unexpectedly on 5 February 1794 at Lincoln's Inn, London (where he had lived for some years), after a coughing fit. He was buried on 10 February 1794 in the parish church of St Mary All Saints, Beaconsfield, Buckinghamshire.

George C. McElroy and Elizabeth R. Lambert

Sources *The correspondence of Edmund Burke*, ed. T. W. Copeland and others, 10 vols. (1958–78) · A. P. I. Samuels, *The early life, correspondence and writings of the Rt. Hon. Edmund Burke, LL. D.* (1923) · C. Dilke, *The papers of a critic* (1875) · *Boswell: the applause of the jury, 1782–1785*, ed. I. S. Lustig and F. A. Pottle (1982), vol. 12 of *The Yale editions of the private papers of James Boswell*, trade edn (1950–89) · *Boswell: the English experiment, 1785–1789*, ed. I. S. Lustig and F. A. Pottle (1986), vol. 13 of *The Yale editions of the private papers of James Boswell*, trade edn (1950–89) · *Boswell, laird of Auchinleck, 1778–1782*, ed. J. W. Reed and F. A. Pottle (1977), vol. 11 of *The Yale editions of the private papers of James Boswell*, trade edn (1950–89) · E. E. E. Elliot-Murray-Kynynmound, countess of Minto, *Life and letters of Sir Gilbert Elliot*, Memoirs of the American Philosophical Society, 41 (1954) · R. J. S. Hoffman, *Edmund Burke: New York Agent* (Philadelphia, 1956) · D. Nester, *Edmund Burke and his kinsmen* (Boulder, 1939) · G. McElroy, 'Edmund, William, and Richard Burke's first attack on Indian misrule, 1778', *Bodleian Library Record*, 13 (1988), 52–65 · J. Maclean, *Renard is secondary* (1963) · *Public Advertiser* (1765–76) · *London Evening-Post* (1775) · *The Gazetteer* (1775)

Archives BL, letters to Sir Frederick Houldimand, Add. MSS 21706–21707 · BL OIOC, Francis papers · Bodl. Oxf., Macartney papers · Northants. RO, corresp. with Edmund Burke · Sheff. Arch., corresp. with Edmund Burke

Burke, Robert O'Hara (1820–1861), explorer in Australia, was born at St Clerans, co. Galway, Ireland, the second of three sons of James Hardiman Burke, army officer, and his wife, Anne, *née* O'Hara. The Burkes were protestant gentry and landowners. He was educated at Woolwich Academy, entered the Austrian army in 1840, and served as a lieutenant in a cavalry regiment. In 1848 he joined the Irish constabulary, and in 1853 emigrated to Australia, becoming an inspector, and later a superintendent, of police in Victoria. In 1860 he was appointed to the command of an exploring expedition dispatched for the purpose of crossing the Australian continent from south to north, which had originated in Ambrose Kyte's contribution of £1000 and had been liberally supported by private subscriptions and government aid. Burke undertook the expedition partly out of a sense of adventure, partly for financial reasons, and partly to further his career. One novel feature was the employment of camels, specially imported from India, from which great results were expected.

The expedition left Melbourne on 20 August 1860. Dissensions soon arose, and several members of the party returned. Burke reached Cooper's Creek on 11 November, and after waiting for reinforcements (which from mismanagement failed to arrive) made a dash for the Gulf of Carpentaria on 16 December, leaving the bulk of his stores in charge of an assistant, William Brahe, with directions to await his return for three or four months. Although not actually coming within sight of the sea, Burke and his associate William Wills reached the tidal waters of the Flinders River, and won the reputation of being the first white men to cross the Australian continent. But on their return to Cooper's Creek on 21 April, exhausted with hardships, they found that Brahe, interpreting his instructions too literally, and discouraged by disease among his companions, had abandoned his post that very day, leaving only a small stock of provisions behind him. Contrary to the advice of Wills, who urged following in Brahe's track, Burke unfortunately determined to strike for the South Australian stations, which he had been misled into believing much nearer to Cooper's Creek than was actually the case. Want of water drove him back, and, too weak to make another attempt, he remained at Cooper's Creek, subsisting mainly on the food casually obtained from friendly Aborigines. Burke died there of starvation about 28 June 1861, and Wills at about the same time. John King, their only surviving companion, managed to exist with the Aborigines until rescued on 21 September by a relief expedition, under the command of Alfred Howitt, dispatched in quest of the explorers, whose failure to return had been reported by Brahe. Another expedition, also commanded by Howitt, was sent to bring back the remains of the unfortunate travellers; and, after making several important discoveries, returned with them to Melbourne on 28 December 1862. The public funeral took place on 21 January following, and memorial statues, the work of Charles Summers, were erected in the principal street of Melbourne.

Although undoubtedly a brave man, Burke was also impulsive, quick-tempered, and arbitrary. The object of his journey was achieved, but he did not possess all of the skills which were needed to lead an exploratory expedition of this nature.

RICHARD GARNETT, *rev.* DAVID CARMENT

Sources T. Bonyhady, *Burke and Wills: from Melbourne to myth* (1991) · A. Moorehead, *Cooper's Creek: the story of Burke and Wills* (1963) · K. Fitzpatrick, 'Burke, Robert O'Hara', *AusDB*, 3.301–3 · F. Clune, *Dig!* (1944) · C. M. H. Clark, *A history of Australia*, 4 (1978)
Archives Royal Society of Victoria, Melbourne, archives · State Library of Victoria, Melbourne, La Trobe manuscript collection | State Library of Victoria, Melbourne, La Trobe manuscript collection, Wills MSS
Likenesses W. Strutt, oils, 1862, priv. coll. · C. Summers, statue on monument, 1865, Collins Street, Melbourne, Australia · E. Gilks, lithograph, NPG

Burke, Thomas (1709/10–1776), historian and Roman Catholic bishop of Ossory, was born in Dublin of gentry stock from near Loughrea, co. Galway. The names of his father and mother have not been preserved.

No account of Burke's early education has survived. In these years the penal code was rigorously enforced, although even then the Dominicans in Dublin had some kind of community existence in Bridge Street, and he may have received his first education there. In 1723 he went to Rome, aged thirteen. The following year he was received into the Dominican community at the Irish convent of San Sisto. That same year his great-uncle and namesake, also a Dominican, died in Rome, where he had gone when he left Ireland after the Banishment Act in 1697. Also in 1724 a Dominican was elected pope as Benedict III; he showed much kindness to the exiled Irish Dominican community. The Stuart claimant to the English throne had settled in Rome in 1718, and it was unsurprising that Burke became a committed Jacobite.

Burke pursued the usual course of ecclesiastical studies and was ordained priest on 28 February 1733. He then taught theology in the Irish Dominican house. In 1740, at the request of the Irish bishops, he began the work of restoring the commemoration of Irish saints to the liturgical calendar, from which they had been excluded since the imposition of a uniform Roman missal in the sixteenth century. In 1742 he received the Dominicans' highest academic distinction, the master's degree in theology (STM). In the same year he set out for Ireland, where he arrived late in 1743 and joined the Dominican community in Bridge Street, Dublin. The chapels were closed in 1744 by reason of the Jacobite scare, but they reopened in 1745, and thereafter the laws against religious practice were by and large not enforced, even though they were not to be repealed until much later in the century.

The general chapter of the Dominican order held at Bologna in 1748 ordered each province to appoint a historiographer. Because of difficulties of communication it was only in 1753 that the Irish provincial chapter appointed Burke to write its history. He faced a difficult task. Because of its disturbed history, the Irish province had little or nothing in the way of archives. His Dominican colleagues were unco-operative and not very interested. He was forced to rely heavily on printed works and on, of course, his growing personal experience. None the less the finished work was presented to the provincial chapter of 1757, approved in Rome in 1759, and published in 1762 with the title *Hibernia Dominicana, sive, Historia provinciae Hiberniae ordinis Praedicatorum*. The imprint gave Cologne as the place of publication, but in fact Kilkenny seems more probable: at least one copy is known with the imprint of a Kilkenny printer, 'James Stokes at the Tholsel (*iuxta Praetorium*)'. Burke published several other works, including an edition of George Touchet's *Historical Collections out of Several Eminent Protestant Historians* (1758), but the treatise entitled *Catechism Moral and Controversial* has been wrongly attributed to him. The author was another Irish Dominican with a similar name, Thomas Myles Burke, who published the work in Lisbon in 1752.

Burke was appointed bishop of Ossory by papal brief dated 9 January 1759; he lived in Kilkenny. He had already shown himself a man of uncompromising Stuart loyalties in the divisive debates among Irish Roman Catholics on how agreement might be reached with the protestant Hanoverian dynasty now that the events of 1745 and the following years had shown that the Jacobite cause was finally lost. James III, the Pretender, was to linger in Rome until he died in 1766, and until his death he formally nominated the Roman Catholic bishops of Ireland.

Burke was consecrated bishop of Ossory on 22 April 1759 by Anthony Blake, archbishop of Armagh, in the convent of the Dominican nuns in Drogheda. He took possession of his diocese immediately, but as a bishop coming from outside he faced some difficulties. He had problems with some of his clergy, but was largely successful in resolving them. There were problems arising from the social unrest among the poorer classes that passed under the name of Whiteboyism. The bishop felt constrained to oppose this movement, although he refrained from harsh condemnation or censure. This attitude brought him into contention with some of the few surviving Catholic gentry families, notably the Butler family of Ballyraggett, who also challenged his authority by their claim to the right to nominate their parish priest.

In 1769 Burke set out for Rome to make the *ad limina* visit prescribed for Roman Catholic bishops. He used a lengthy journey, lasting nearly two years, to collect material for Irish Dominican history. In Rome he received much help from a younger colleague, John Thomas Troy, who was to succeed him as bishop of Ossory and who later became archbishop of Dublin. Burke's researches were published in 1772 as *Supplementum Hiberniae Dominicanae*.

In 1774 parliament passed 'An Act to enable His Majesty's subjects of whatever persuasion to testify their allegiance to him'. Burke opposed the development, but he was in a minority. The bishops of the ecclesiastical province of Cashel, led by Archbishop James Butler, denounced him and his historical work for alleged Jacobitism. Butler, of the family of Ballyraggett, was young, abrasive, and of marked Gallican tendencies. Burke refused to be intimidated and planned a revised edition of *Hibernia Dominicana*. He died at his home in Maudlin Street, Kilkenny, on 25 September 1776 after what appears to have been a brief illness, and was buried in the cemetery attached to St John's Church, Maudlin Street.

PATRICK J. CORISH

Sources W. Carrigan, *The history and antiquities of the diocese of Ossory*, 1 (1905), 158–79 · H. Fenning, *The Irish Dominican province,* 1698–1797 (1990) · A. Coleman, 'Thomas de Burgo, author of the *Hibernica Dominicana* and bishop of Ossory', *Irish Ecclesiastical Record*, 3rd ser., 13 (1892), 587–600, 707–19, 828–41, 1010–25 · *DNB*
Archives Archives of Irish Dominican College, San Clemente, Rome · Dublin Roman Catholic archdiocese, archives · Kilkenny Roman Catholic diocese, archives
Likenesses oils, St Kieran's College, Kilkenny, Ireland; repro. in Carrigan, *History and antiquities*, facing p. 158
Wealth at death £2 8s. 3d. to sister; £2 5s. 6d. to niece; residue to John O'Connor (Irish Dominican provincial): will, 16 July 1776, W. Carrigan, *Archivium Hibernicum*, 4 (1915), 92–3

Burke, Thomas (*c.*1744–1783), physician and politician in America, was born in co. Galway, Ireland. He was the son of Ulick Burke, a man of some education and of an Anglo-Irish protestant family that had lived in Ireland since the time of Henry II, when they were granted land in the province of Connaught, Connacht, and Letitia Ould, a sister of Sir Fielding *Ould, a physician. Sir Fielding, with whom Burke enjoyed a close relationship, was master of the Dublin Lying-in Hospital and author of a treatise on midwifery, and was knighted in 1760 by the lord lieutenant of Ireland. When Thomas was growing up in Dublin, he lost, for causes now unknown, the sight of his left eye; the remaining one, however, was later said by his daughter to have been a fine expressive blue. He also was said to have been 'of middle stature well formed', but his face was pockmarked by smallpox.

Unfortunate circumstances left the family in such straits that young Burke felt it necessary to make a choice between indolence and departing the country. He clearly was a serious young man intent on directing his own future; in a letter to his uncle he described himself as void of 'vices' and 'levity'. Perhaps through the good offices of his uncle, with whom he lived for a time, he had already received some medical training, and after study and the customary examination the young Burke was licensed to practise medicine. How much of Burke's training took place in Dublin and how much elsewhere is not known, but he apparently was about fifteen years of age when he set off for America.

Going by way of Philadelphia, he appeared on the eastern shore of Virginia, where Northampton county records locate him by 1760; in 1763 he was practising medicine and being referred to as Dr Burke. It is evident that he was an eager reader and a quick learner, with no patience for slow mental response. His active mind directed his thoughts into other channels. He first jotted his literary thoughts in shorthand, fearing to be deemed an idler. Essays and poems by Burke began to appear in the *Virginia Gazette*, suggesting a rising interest in political events, the beauties of nature, and an awareness of women in his presence.

After a while Burke apparently decided that medicine practised in an isolated setting was unlikely to gain him either wealth or social standing. He moved to Norfolk, Virginia, studied law, and was licensed to practise, but he continued to be referred to as doctor and offered his services *pro bono*. He was acquainted with the editors of newspapers, merchants, and local officials, and clearly found acceptance in Virginia. There he was married, in March

1770, to Mary Freeman (1752–1836), a teacher; theirs was an often uneasy relationship during which he was away for long periods of time as an office-holder.

In the spring of 1772, when Burke planned to leave Virginia, he bought 591 acres 2½ miles north of the town of Hillsborough, North Carolina, in a region of small farms. He named his new estate Tyaquin, after the home he had known in Ireland when he was a child, and here he made his home. His legal practice grew; it consisted mainly of debt collection for merchants. He also was aware of the larger scene and kept abreast of developments in Boston, New York, and Philadelphia as well as in North Carolina. Nor did he lose sight of events in London. The regulator disturbances during this period in Burke's new neighbourhood, though tied to disputes with colonial government rather than British rule, at least sharpened his understanding of the mood of Americans. He surely anticipated the break between Britain and the colonies: in 1766 he had composed a poem, 'Triumph America', to mark the repeal of the Stamp Act, which had attempted to introduce British taxation on internal American trade. When the opportunity for political activity arrived, he was available. He represented Orange county in the four provincial congresses that met in New Bern, Hillsborough, and Halifax in 1775 and 1776, providing a revolutionary government for North Carolina. Burke played significant roles in the debates, served on the small committee that prepared North Carolina's constitution, and became better acquainted with important leaders. In the spring of 1777 he represented his county in the first state legislature and again in the longer autumn session that year. Also in 1777 a new county was created in the foothills of the mountains and named Burke in his honour. The next call to serve took him to Philadelphia as a member of the continental congress from 1777 to 1780. As a member of the congress Burke was the leading proponent of the doctrine that came to be known as states' rights, and this ideal came to be incorporated in the tenth amendment to the constitution. He was also a representative in the legislature in 1783.

Burke's peak position was attained on 26 June 1781, when the legislature elected him governor. This was in the midst of a period of military activity in North Carolina when both regular British troops and roaming bands of loyalist irregulars were active. The notorious David Fanning led a raid into Hillsborough on 12 September 1781, and took about 200 prisoners—including Burke. The governor was sent to British-occupied Charlestown, South Carolina. There he was restricted to an area occupied by loyalist refugees from North Carolina, who blamed Burke for their situation. He was not secure there: his quarters were fired upon and an occupant of his room was killed. Lacking proper protection, he broke parole, returned home, and resumed his duties as governor. Soundly condemned by both the British and his own people for this dishonourable act, Burke was humiliated. He withdrew from public life, and died on 2 December 1783, separated from his wife, at the age of about thirty-nine. It has been said that he died of a broken heart. He was survived by his wife and a ten-month-old daughter, Mary Williams, who lived until 1869 unmarried. He was buried in a solitary grave at the family cemetery at Tyaquin, North Carolina.

WILLIAM S. POWELL

Sources J. S. Watterson, *Thomas Burke, restless revolutionary* (1986) · J. S. Watterson, 'The ordeal of Governor Burke', *North Carolina Historical Review*, 48 (1971), 95–117 · R. Walser, *The poems of Governor Thomas Burke* (1961) · W. L. Saunders and W. Clark, eds., *The colonial records of North Carolina*, 30 vols. (1886–1907), vols. 10–24 · A. Henderson, 'Address at the dedication of marker at Burke's grave in Orange County, N.C.', *Congressional Record*, 90/166 (30 Nov 1944) · E. P. Douglass, 'Thomas Burke, disillusioned democrat', *North Carolina Historical Review*, 26 (1949), 150–86 · W. S. Powell, ed., *Dictionary of North Carolina biography*, 6 vols. (1979–96)

Archives North Carolina Division of Archives and History, Raleigh, personal and official papers · University of North Carolina, Chapel Hill, Southern Historical Collection, personal and official papers

Burke, Thomas (1749–1815), engraver, born in Dublin, is said to have been a pupil of John Dixon. Dixon presumably taught Burke to scrape mezzotints and may have brought Burke with him when he moved from Dublin to London in 1765. Most of Dixon's early mezzotints, and most of Burke's, were published by William Wynne Ryland. They include some portraits, but both engravers were better known for 'history' pictures and Burke scraped *A Dutch Peasant* after Brouwer (1771) and an *Infant Jesus and St John* after Van Dyck (1772) as well as George Stubbs's portrait of the great racehorse Eclipse (1772).

Ryland became Burke's principal employer and for him between 1772 and 1775 Burke scraped a series of eight mezzotints after paintings by Angelica Kauffman, beginning with a portrait optimistically entitled *Queen Charlotte Raising the Genius of the Fine Arts* (1772). Between 1775 and 1779 Burke did not sign a single plate and it has been suggested that during this period he was working for Ryland on stipple engravings, perhaps being taught the niceties of the new process by the French-trained master. In 1779 Burke's name again appeared on plates published by Ryland and, after 1782, by other printsellers. For John Raphael Smith he engraved Henry Fuseli's notorious painting *The Nightmare* (1783), which showed an incubus perched on the body of a sleeping woman. This print immediately became a best-seller throughout Europe. After Ryland was hanged for forgery in 1783 Burke completed his plate of *The Battle of Agincourt* (1784) for Jane Mortimer, the painter's widow. From now on he sometimes published or took a share in the publication of his own plates: he was owed 108 livres by the leading French printseller François Basan in 1788. He had inherited Ryland's mantle as Angelica Kauffman's preferred interpreter and engraved some twenty-eight stipples after her designs between 1779 and 1795. Beyond this specialization he worked after a wide variety of designers for a variety of publishers, producing numerous small stipple portraits as well as larger scenes drawn from sentimental literature and genre.

By 1797 Burke had been appointed engraver to his serene highness the landgrave of Hesse-Darmstadt, a title proudly engraved on *Saturday Morning* and *Saturday Evening* after William Redmore Bigg. His mezzotints have exceptional richness and depth and his work in stipple is elegant and delicate. Burke's last dated work was a portrait of the duke of Wellington (1815). He died in London on 31 December 1815.

TIMOTHY CLAYTON and ANITA MCCONNELL

Sources W. G. Strickland, *A dictionary of Irish artists*, 1 (1913); repr. with introduction by T. J. Snoddy (1989), 128–9 · D. Alexander, 'Kauffman and the print market in eighteenth-century England', *Angelica Kauffman: a continental artist in Georgian England*, ed. W. W. Roworth (1992), 141–89 · C. F. Weisse, ed., *Neue Bibliothek der schönen Wissenschaften und der freyen Künste*, 60 vols. (Leipzig, 1765–1806) · J. H. Slater, *Engravings and their value*, 4th edn (1912), 232–4 · J. C. Smith, *British mezzotinto portraits*, 1 (1878), 133–6 · *Engraved Brit. ports.* · T. Clayton, *The English print, 1688–1802* (1997), 279 · D. Alexander, 'The Dublin group: Irish mezzotint engravers in London, 1750–75', *Quarterly Bulletin of the Irish Georgian Society*, 16 (1973), 73–92 · J. Hoffmeister, *Gesammelte Nachrichten über Künstler und Kunsthandwerker in Hessen seit etwa 300 Jahren* (Hannover, 1885)

Burke, Thomas Henry (1829–1882), civil servant, born on 29 May 1829, was the second son of William Burke (1794–1877) of Knocknagur, co. Galway, and Fanny Xaveria (*d.* 1874), only daughter of Thomas Tucker of Brook Lodge, Sussex, and his wife, Maryanne, sister of Nicholas, Cardinal Wiseman. He was educated in Belgium, Germany, and at Trinity College, Dublin.

Burke, a Catholic, was appointed a supernumerary clerk in the Irish chief secretary's office, Dublin Castle, in May 1847, and was placed on the permanent staff there in July 1849. He acquired an early unpopularity for his part in searching the private papers of William Smith O'Brien. In April 1851 he was appointed private secretary to Sir Thomas Redington, then under-secretary for Ireland. Burke subsequently served in the various departments of the chief secretary's office, including the Irish Office, London. He acted as private secretary to the chief secretaries Edward Cardwell, Sir Robert Peel, and Chichester P. Fortescue, and in May 1869 was appointed under-secretary.

While not unsympathetic to tenant demands during the Land War (1879–82), Burke was a consistent advocate of coercive measures against the Land League. On 1 May 1882 his letter opposing the abandonment of the suspension of habeas corpus was read to the cabinet; its rejection provoked the resignation of Burke's ally the chief secretary, W. E. Forster. On 6 May 1882 Lord Frederick Cavendish arrived in Dublin, and was formally installed as the new chief secretary. Early that evening Cavendish and Burke, while walking in Phoenix Park, Dublin, were assassinated by a Fenian splinter group calling themselves the 'Irish National Invincibles'. Published allegations that Burke's murder had been condoned by Charles Stewart Parnell were later proved to have been based on forged documents.

Burke was interred in Glasnevin cemetery, and the viceroy, Earl Spencer, erected a memorial window to him in

Thomas Henry Burke (1829–1882), by Walter Frederick Osborne (after Augustus Burke and photographs)

the Dominican church, Dublin. Burke's services as an official were, on his death, publicly commended in parliament, and a pension was conferred by the government on his sister. (For an account of the subsequent detection of the murderers *see* Carey, James.)

J. T. GILBERT, *rev.* PETER GRAY

Sources T. Corfe, *The Phoenix Park murders: conflict, compromise and tragedy in Ireland, 1879–1882* (1968) · P. Bew, *Land and the national question in Ireland, 1858–82* (1978) · A. B. Cooke and J. R. Vincent, 'Lord Spencer on the Phoenix Park murders', *Irish Historical Studies*, 18 (1972–3), 583–91 · D. Cosgrove, 'The true history of the Phoenix Park murders', *New Ireland Review*, 25 (June 1906), 225–36, 274–87 · *Annual Register* (1882) · Ward, *Men of the reign* · *The Times* (8 May 1882) · Burke, *Peerage* · Gladstone, *Diaries*
Archives BL, W. E. Gladstone MSS · Chatsworth House, Derbyshire, letters to Lord Hartington · CUL, letters to duke of Marlborough · Glos. RO, corresp. with Sir Michael Hicks Beach
Likenesses A. Burke, oils, NG Ire. · W. F. Osborne, pencil drawing (after A. Burke and photographs), NG Ire. [*see illus.*] · engraving, repro. in *ILN*, 80 (1882), 453 · engraving, repro. in *The Graphic*, 25 (1882), 464
Wealth at death £1901 11s. 4d.: probate, 7 June 1882, *CGPLA Ire.*

Burke, Thomas Nicholas [*formerly* Anthony Nicholas] (1830–1883), Dominican friar and preacher, was born in Kirwans Lane in the town of Galway on 8 September 1830, the third son of Walter Burke, a baker, and his wife, Margaret Macdonagh of Moycullen. He was christened Anthony Nicholas. His two elder brothers had died young; he had three elder sisters. He was educated in local schools. He early acquired a reputation as a prankster, and was often severely disciplined by his mother. It was probably her piety which inspired him, at the age of seventeen, to join the Dominican order. He went to Rome, and then to Perugia, where he was admitted on 29 December 1847 to the noviciate of the Irish province, and witnessed the 1848 risings. He was professed on 30 November 1848, and took the name of Thomas, after Thomas Aquinas. On 30 January 1850 he was sent to Rome to study theology at the college of the Minerva and Santa Sabina. In 1851 he was sent to England to organize the noviciate of the Dominican house at Woodchester, and was ordained priest on 26 March 1853. His gift for preaching was soon recognized, while his fondness for practical jokes and puns enlivened the otherwise austere life of the house.

In 1855, Burke was sent to Ireland to found a noviciate and house of studies for his order at Tallaght, near Dublin. For the next nine years he was busily employed in this task, and in preaching missions in different parts of Ireland and England. He succeeded W. H. Anderdon as popular preacher at the church of the Catholic University at Dublin, formed close links with the sisters at Rathfarnham Abbey, where he acted as confessor, and became the friend and jester of Cardinal Cullen. In September 1864 he returned to Rome to be a prior of the Irish Dominican house at San Clemente. After the death of Cardinal Wiseman, Burke succeeded Manning as preacher of the Lenten sermons in English in the church of Santa Maria del Popolo. Upon his return to Ireland in 1869 he was attached to St Saviour's Dominican church in Dublin. In the May of the same year he preached the sermon at the reinterment of the remains of O'Connell in the crypt of the tower at Glasnevin. He was chosen by the bishop of Dromore to accompany him as his theologian to the Vatican Council, where Burke supported the 'inopportunist' cause.

In 1872 Burke visited the United States, as visitor for his order. He delivered sermons and lectures—on subjects ranging from the inadmissibility of divorce to the character of the Irish people—in all parts of the country, and acquired considerable popularity as an orator. The sum collected for American charities by his sermons was said to have reached £100,000. His passionate but partisan speeches in reply to J. A. Froude's lectures on the historical relationship between England and Ireland provoked great excitement: Burke's life was threatened and he was forced to retain a special guard. His lectures were published in New York in 1873.

On Burke's return from this tour, which seems to have damaged his health, he lived mainly in the Dominican houses in Rutland Square, Dublin, and at Tallaght. He continued, however, to lecture and conduct retreats throughout the British Isles. He declined several invitations to be raised to the episcopate, and the chance to be provincial of his order. In June 1883, after preaching a sermon in aid of the destitute children of Donegal, he collapsed. He died at Tallaght, probably of a stomach ulcer, on 2 July, and was buried there two days later.

Father Tom, as he was popularly known, was ugly in appearance, with prominent ears, which he ascribed to his mother's habit of pulling them as a punishment. He was best known as a compelling preacher: listeners thought him adept at conjuring up images, and remarked on the expressive gestures that enhanced the impact of his oratory. In private life he was a great raconteur and mimic. But, despite his sense of fun, he was known to be very strict, both with his novices and in the confessional. He was as fervent an Irishman as he was a Roman Catholic, and seemed almost to consider the two to be synonymous. ROSEMARY MITCHELL

Sources W. J. Fitzpatrick, *The life of the Very Rev. Thomas N. Burke*, 2 vols. (1885) · *The Tablet* (7 July 1883), 26 · W. H. Dunn, *James Anthony Froude: a biography*, 2 vols. (1963), 2.377–83

Likenesses G. F. Mulvany, portrait, c.1880, NG Ire. · Chancellor, photograph, repro. in Fitzpatrick, *Life of the Very Rev. Thomas N. Burke*, vol. 1, frontispiece · lithograph, NG Ire.

Burke [de Burgh], **Ulick, marquess of Clanricarde** (1604–1658), landowner and politician, was the only son of Richard de Burgh, fourth earl of Clanricarde (1572–1635), and his wife, Frances (d. 1632), daughter and heir of Sir Francis Walsingham and widow of Sir Philip Sidney and of Robert Devereux, earl of Essex, who was executed in 1601. Despite Ulick's later claims that 'I was born in Clanricarde-house, Great Queen Street, Lincoln's-inn-fields, London', a letter from Sir John Davies proves otherwise (Clanricarde, *Memoirs and Letters*, 68). Writing in December 1604, Davies noted that he had spent the past two months in Connaught with the fourth earl at Galway and then at Athlone, 'where his lady, being then big with child, and now delivered of a son, then lay' (*CSP Ire.*, *1603–6*, 215). Despite his prominence as an Irish lord, the fourth earl spent most of his life in England, where he reared his son, Ulick, and daughters, Margaret and Honoura, delegating the running of his vast Connaught patrimony to his trusted friend and agent Sir Henry Lynch. Aged eighteen (their post-nuptial settlement dates from February 1623), Ulick married Lady Anne Compton (d. 1675), the only daughter of William, earl of Northampton, and in 1628 he took his seat in the English House of Lords as Lord Burgh.

Achieving privilege at court With his father's death in November 1635 Clanricarde inherited his titles—becoming fifth earl of Clanricarde and second earl of St Albans—his English mansion at Somerhill and estate in Kent, together with Irish lands (in co. Galway, Westmeath, co. Mayo, co. Roscommon, and King's county) allegedly worth £29,000 p.a. (special license to his inheritance was granted on 26 January 1636). His father also bequeathed him debts in the region of £25,000, largely secured on the Irish lands, and in 1637 Clanricarde was forced to mortgage his estate in Kent for seven years to underwrite these and other debts and sureties of £20,000 (*To the parlament of the common-wealth of England, Scotland and Ireland. The humble petition of … creditors of Ulick earl of St. Albans, and Clanricard*, 1654). As an Anglicizing earl and Irish lord, Clanricarde, like his father before him, consolidated his power base in Ireland by improving his estates (introducing English tenants, innovative farming techniques, and economic initiatives) and by checking local lords who threatened to provide alternative focuses to his authority in Connaught. Two additional factors helped Clanricarde to secure his

Ulick Burke, marquess of Clanricarde (1604–1658), by unknown artist

position as an influential figure in both Ireland and England. First, he manipulated the common law process in order to further his personal and dynastic agendas: he cultivated strong links with the members of the inns of court (becoming in March 1640 an 'honorific' member of Lincoln's Inn), continued his father's patronage of Galway entrants, especially to the Middle Temple, and regularly employed the leading lawyers, including Richard Hadsor, to secure his tenurial and other interests. Second, Clanricarde's prolonged residence at court and his kinship, marriage, and clientage links afforded him direct access to influential patronage networks and, more importantly, to the king himself. Through his mother he was allied to the late duke of Buckingham and to the earl of Essex (his stepbrother and general of the English parliamentary army in 1642–6). He enjoyed close friendships with the earl of Bristol, the earl of Northampton (his father-in-law), the Catholic marquess of Winchester (his brother-in-law), the earl of Holland, a prominent member of the queen's court, and the duke of Lennox (and Richmond), the king's cousin and a great royal favourite. His privileged position at court also enabled him to practise his Catholicism without fear of persecution though he attracted the venom of an anonymous poet–priest who visited him at Somerhill only to be denied hospitality:

> I thought that in that mansion there would be
> A welcome for me for the sake of God;
> … When of the house the denizens
> Me recognised, they threw me out,
> Saying to me 'Come not again
> Into this house'—that's what stung me.
> (C. O Lochlainn, *Irish Chiefs and Leaders*, Dublin, 1960, 134–5)

Clanricarde used his English connections to great effect

as he spearheaded the opposition to Lord Deputy Wentworth's attempts to plant Connaught. Ultimately, the entire initiative foundered when the king granted Clanricarde an exemption from the scheme, much to Wentworth's fury. After serving the king in the first bishops' war Clanricarde took his seat in the English Lords in 1640 (Ormond held his proxy in the Irish parliament) and worked closely with men determined to secure Wentworth's downfall. Presumably it was Clanricarde who ensured that Thomas Bourke and Nicholas Plunket enjoyed private access to the king during their negotiations on behalf of the Irish parliament in the spring of 1641, about the time when he was added to the English privy council.

These efforts to influence politics in London should not obscure the political clout that Clanricarde enjoyed in Ireland. Despite his absenteeism, Clanricarde—thanks to his status as governor of the town and county of Galway—was the most influential figure in Connaught, and marriage linked him to many members of prominent local families, including Viscount Mayo and the Bourkes of Brittas, of Clanmorris, and of Castle Connell, together with other Irish aristocratic houses (the Butlers of Ormond, lords Slane and Fermoy). The quality of his associations in the Irish House of Commons was exceptional and included at least six prominent lawyers (Sir Richard Blake, Sir Valentine Blake, Geoffrey Browne, Patrick Darcy, Roebuck Lynch, and Richard Martin), who played a critical role in shaping developments in the later sessions of 1641, and his nephew Thomas Bourke, an active member of the Irish parliamentary delegation to London. Thus Clanricarde served as an essential human link between the opposition groups in the Irish and English parliaments and played a key, albeit discreet, role in the fall of Wentworth.

Royalist support In September 1641 Clanricarde returned to Ireland to live in the grand fortified mansion that his father had built at Portumna, near Galway. Like so many of his peers, he was horrified by the outbreak of the Irish rising—that 'strange madness', as he dubbed it—the following month (Clanricarde, *Memoirs and Letters*, 2). He immediately tried to rally the local grandees for the king, and raised a regiment of foot; by this means, and to 'the generall affection borne to his family', he managed to preserve Galway for the crown, maintain law and order on his estates, and protect local protestants or bring them under his personal protection (*Irish Confederation*, ed. Gilbert, 1.54). By the spring of 1642 he came under pressure, particularly from the lords of the pale, to join the insurrection. They appealed to his Catholicism, reminded him of his Irish lineage, and invited him to help them 'to vindicate the honour of our sovereign' (Clanricarde, *Memoirs and Letters*, 171). Unable to embrace their cause publicly, Clanricarde worked covertly and closely with his Galway associates (especially the lawyers Patrick Darcy and Richard Martin) and suggested 'a model for a form of government' which involved establishing a national supreme council and subordinate provincial and county councils (TCD, MS 816, fol. 44). He also offered to mediate a truce directly with the Dublin administration or with the king. To this end Charles I nominated him in January 1643 as a commissioner to meet the representatives of the confederate Catholics, and at a meeting at Trim, Meath (17 March 1643) he received their 'Remonstrance of grievances'.

The fall of Galway town to the confederates (April 1642), followed by the fort (June 1643) and the defection of many of his kinsmen to the Catholic cause, combined with his failure to secure either a senior military command or the lord presidency of Connaught, left Clanricarde in a particularly vulnerable and isolated position. To make matters even worse his Irish estates lay 'spoiled and pillaged by both English and Irish, what one left always destroyed by the other', while the parliamentary occupation of his English estates (albeit by his stepbrother Essex) denied him any revenue from them (Lowe, 38). Ill health—'my old diseases of the stone and cholick' and 'bloody waters' caused by gallstones—added to his misery (Clanricarde, *Memoirs and Letters*, 256, 356). In February 1644 he articulated his predicament to a friend in England:

> a vast debt and a constant growing charge upon me, no estate, no pay nor entertainment, nor no forces, nor powder trusted to me … forsaken or forgotten by my friends in England, suspected and discountenanced formally by the State here, hated and scorned by the natives for my opposition to their ways, and nothing regarded for it by others. (Lowe, 40)

Only in February 1645 did the king finally recognize his loyalty by conferring a marquessate on him and then, in May, making him an Irish privy councillor and commander of a regiment of foot and troop of horse in the royalist standing army.

Throughout these years Clanricarde remained determined to be 'freed from the violent pursuits of two extremes, the covenant and the association' and to secure a moderate constitutional settlement that ensured that Catholics enjoyed 'places of honour, profit and trust in the civil government' as well as in the army and the judiciary, together with the right to worship freely (Lowe, 458, 192). Using his excellent contacts within the confederate association, with Ormond, and at the Stuart court, he promoted a peace treaty with Charles I in 1646, and, after its rejection by the Irish, endeavoured to have negotiations reopened (Lowe, 458). In the autumn of 1646 he accompanied the Leinster army as it moved against Dublin in a last-ditch attempt to broker a peace. However, the arrival of parliamentary troops in Dublin in November 1646 and Ormond's subsequent handover of the capital in June 1647 effectively discredited his efforts and brought him into direct conflict with the papal nuncio Rinuccini and the extremists at Kilkenny.

Having consistently refused to join the confederates, Clanricarde wholeheartedly supported the Inchiquin truce (May 1648) and the pan-British royalist coalition of which it formed a critical component. In a public statement, published in June 1648, he highlighted the dire nature of the king's cause in Ireland 'as by the sad effects of civill discord' and argued that, if the Irish failed to unite quickly behind the king, their enemies 'will soon root out

religion, divert the due course of loyalty, and instead of just liberty bring slavery on the subjects; besides all kinde of incident losses and miseries' (Clanricarde, *A Declaration of the Resolutions of his Majesties Forces*, 1648, 3). In the event this anti-parliamentarian coalition failed to win the war in Ireland for the king. When a series of crushing defeats at the hands of Oliver Cromwell and internecine quarrels among his Irish allies forced Ormond into exile, Charles II, in December 1650, appointed Clanricarde as his replacement. Clarendon recorded Clanricarde's reluctance to accept the post and attributed it to ill health:

> a man, though of unquestionable courage, yet of an infirm health, and who loved and enjoyed great ease throughout his whole life, and of a constitution not equal to the fatigue and distresses that the conducting such a war must subject him.

Ultimately Clanricarde's friendship with Ormond and his sense of loyalty to the crown, combined with pressure from the Irish nobility, especially the earl of Castlehaven, and the clergy 'that he would preserve his nation' won him over (Clarendon, *Hist. rebellion*, 5.220). However, his efforts against the parliamentarians proved ineffective, as did his lengthy negotiations with the duke of Lorraine to secure foreign backing for the war effort, and in April 1652 he surrendered the last major Catholic stronghold of Galway to the Cromwellians. The anonymous chronicler of the *Aphorismical Discovery of Treasonable Faction* lambasted him for agreeing to this, claiming that his 'acte was really the betrayinge of a whole nation, a whole kingdome, the three deerest interests of rationall creatures, religion, lives, and best fortunes' (Gilbert, *Contemporary history*, 3.123).

In August 1652 the king gave Clanricarde permission to retire to England, and on 6 September he concluded articles with the Cromwellians, which protected him from arrest for his debts as he travelled through England *en route* for the continent. In the event his poor health prevented him from joining the royalist court in exile, and instead he travelled in March 1653 to London, where he was 'civilly treated by all men, as a man who had many friends, and could have no enemies but those who could not be friends to any' (Clarendon, *Hist. rebellion*, 5.272). The following year Cromwell awarded him £600 and agreed that his wife should receive 4000 acres of profitable land from her husband's estate in Ireland (Clanricarde himself was exempted from pardon and estate by the Act for the Settling of Ireland, 12 August 1652: (PRO, SP 25/77/441)). The precise date of Clanricarde's death is uncertain. Clarendon misleadingly stated that he died in 1653 owing to 'the unnatural fatigues and distresses he had been exposed to' in Ireland (Clarendon, *Hist. rebellion*, 5.272). Other sources, including the *Dictionary of National Biography*, suggest July 1657, whereas he appears to have died in late April (as government records suggest) or possibly early May 1658 (*CSP dom.*, 1658–9, 237–8). On 4 May the state contributed £100 towards his funeral expenses and on 7 May, according to the burial book of Tonbridge church, he was interred alongside his father (PRO, SP 25/78/596). On his death his titles became extinct and the earldom of

Clanricarde and barony of Dunkellin devolved on his first cousin Richard (*d.* 1666), eldest son of his uncle who had married Elizabeth, a sister of the duke of Ormond. An active confederate, Richard had 'endured many yeeres imprisonment in the Tower' for his involvement in royalist plots before escaping to serve the king abroad until the Restoration (PRO, SP 63/345/59, fol. 73*v*). While the earldom passed to Richard, Clanricarde's only daughter, Margaret, Lady Muskerry, inherited his English estates together with some of his Irish ones (though Richard disputed her right to these).

Reputation Excoriated by the anonymous chronicler of the *Aphorismical Discovery of Treasonable Faction* as a traitor to the Irish cause, Clanricarde was praised by other commentators for his loyalty, his integrity, and his devotion to religion. Clarendon described him as:

> a person of unquestionable fidelity, and whom the king would without any scruple trust, and whom the Irish could not except against, being of their own nation, of the greatest fortune and interest amongst them, and of the most eminent constancy to the Catholic religion of any man in the three kingdoms. (Clarendon, *Hist. rebellion*, 5.219)

Certainly Clanricarde's reputation as a loyal servant of the crown—who allegedly contracted debts of £60,000 in royal service—has withstood the test of time. In view of his reputation as one of the most astute minds of his day and as a major statesman, it is remarkable that Clanricarde has not attracted a serious biographer, especially given that so much of his archive has survived (a large portion of which is available in print). His papers include his extant letter-books for the period of the civil wars (except for the period September 1647 to February 1650, for which the letter-book is missing); he probably compiled these after he left Ireland with a view to writing his own version of events. The bulk of these letters are political (certainly, they contain relatively little detail on his domestic relationships or the management of his financial and landed affairs) and they provide invaluable insights into the running of local affairs in Connaught and the machinations of confederate and royalist politics during the 1640s. Equally importantly they help to recapture Clanricarde's mindset and the values that underpinned it: his sincere religious beliefs, his finely tuned sense of honour and justice, and his keen awareness of his status, role, and position within Stuart society. Moreover his personality begins to emerge from these letters: his devotion to and concern for his wife, family, servants, and followers, his sharp sense of humour, his fortitude as he grappled with chronic ill health and disability, and the very real personal dilemmas that he faced as he struggled to reconcile his loyalty to his king, to his faith, and to his kin and countrymen.   JANE OHLMEYER

Sources J. Smyth, eleventh earl of Clanricarde, *The memoirs and letters of Ulick, marquis of Clanricarde, and earl of Saint Albans* (1758) • [U. de Burgh, earl of Clanricarde], *Letter-book of the Earl of Clanricarde, 1643–47*, ed. J. Lowe, IMC (1983) • T. O'Sullevane, ed., *Memoirs of the marquis of Clanricarde* (1722) • B. Cunningham, 'Clanricard letters: letters and papers, 1605–1673, preserved in the National Library of Ireland manuscript 3111', *Journal of the Galway Archaeological and Historical Society*, 48 (1996), 162–208 • B. Cunningham, 'Political and social change in the lordships of Clanricard and Thomond, 1596–1641', MA diss., National University of Ireland, Galway, 1979 • P. Little, 'The earl of Cork and the fall of Strafford, 1638–41', *HJ*, 39 (1996), 619–35 • P. J. S. Little, 'Family and faction: the Irish nobility and the English court, 1632–42', MLitt diss., TCD, 1992 • *History of the Irish confederation and the war in Ireland ... by Richard Bellings*, ed. J. T. Gilbert, 7 vols. (1882–91) • J. T. Gilbert, ed., *A contemporary history of affairs in Ireland from 1641 to 1652*, 3 vols. (1879–80) • M. Ó Siochrú, *Confederate Ireland, 1642–1649* (Dublin, 1999) • Clarendon, *Hist. rebellion* • [T. Carte], *The life of James, duke of Ormond*, new edn, 6 vols. (1851) • *CSP Ire.*, 1603–6; 1633–47 • *CSP dom.*, 1658–9 • *DNB* • GEC, *Peerage* • J. Lodge, *The peerage of Ireland*, rev. M. Archdall, rev. edn, 7 vols. (1789)
Archives BL, memoirs, Add. MS 42063 • NL Ire., letters and papers, MS 3111 | BL, letters to Lord Essex, Add. MS 46188 • Bodl. Oxf., Carte MSS • PRO, state papers, Ireland • Sheffield Archives, Strafford MSS • TCD, 1641 depositions
Likenesses Ravenet, engraving, probably NL Ire. • engraving, probably NL Ire. • oils, NPG [*see illus.*] • portrait, Westport House, Co. Mayo
Wealth at death allegedly £60,000 in debt

Burke, Ulick Ralph (1845–1895), Spanish scholar, eldest son of Charles Granby Burke (*b.* 1814), of St Philip's, Milltown, co. Dublin, master of the court of common pleas in Ireland (1852–82), and his first wife, Emma Jane (*d.* 1869), daughter of Ralph Creyke of Marton, Yorkshire, was born at Dublin on 21 October 1845. He was educated at Trinity College, Dublin, where he graduated BA in 1867; he had previously been entered as a student of the Middle Temple on 28 January 1865, and was called to the bar on 10 June 1870. On 9 July 1868, he married Katharine (*d.* 1933), daughter of James Bateman; they had one son and two daughters. A tour in Spain led Burke, on his return, to bring out in 1872 (in the same year as his *Handbook of Sewage Utilization*) an annotated collection of the proverbs in *Don Quixote*. Thenceforth his interests were to a large extent concentrated upon the Spanish language, literature, and history. In 1872, he published a collection of *Sancho Panza's Proverbs*, with a literal English translation and notes; enlarged and revised editions of this work were published in 1877 (under the title *Spanish Salt*) and 1892.

In 1873 Burke went to India, and practised as a barrister at the high court of the North-Western Provinces until 1878. While there he put together a short biography of Gonzalo Fernández de Córdoba, which he entitled *The Great Captain: an Eventful Chapter in Spanish History* (1877). On his return to England, Burke published two novels, *Beating the Air* (1879) and *Loyal and Lawless* (1880), in which he evinced a measured but critical interest in Anglo-Indian and Anglo-Irish social attitudes and political relations. In 1880 he unsuccessfully contested Calne for the Conservative Party. Subsequently a journey to Brazil in 1882 led to his publishing, with Robert Staples, Jr, *Business and Pleasure in Brazil* (1886), consisting of letters written home during the journey and giving 'a plain, unvarnished statement of facts and experiences'. From 1885 to 1889 he practised his profession at the bar in Cyprus. After that he acted as clerk of the peace, co. Dublin, and registrar of quarter sessions. He contributed chapter 8, on the early buildings, to the tercentenary *Book of Trinity College, Dublin* (1892). In 1894 he brought out an admiring and highly readable *Life of Benito Juárez, Constitutional President of Mexico*, and early in 1895 the two-volume *History of Spain from the Earliest Times to the Death of Ferdinand the Catholic*, at which he had been working for over four years. A corrected second edition appeared in 1900 with additional notes, limited rearrangement, and an introduction by M. A. S. Hume, who—with fewer caveats than the reviewer of the first edition in *The Athenaeum*—declared it 'a work which I hope may be regarded as a classic'.

In May 1895 Burke was appointed agent-general to the Peruvian Corporation, which in return for large concessions had recently taken over the Peruvian government's foreign debt. He had been on the point of setting out on a visit to Santiago in Spain, but rapidly changed his destination and embarked for Lima. Early in the voyage he fell a victim to dysentery and died on 17 July 1895. His notes and glossary for George Borrow's *The Bible in Spain*, which contained some of his best work, were completed by his friend Herbert W. Greene, fellow of Magdalen College, Oxford, and issued with Murray's 1896 edition of Borrow's book (and again in 1899 and 1907).

THOMAS SECCOMBE, *rev.* R. W. TRUMAN

Sources *The Times* (20 July 1895) · *The Times* (30 July 1895) · *The Athenaeum* (27 July 1895) · J. Foster, *Men-at-the-bar: a biographical hand-list of the members of the various inns of court*, 2nd edn (1885) · Burke, *Gen. GB* [Bateman] · Burke, *Peerage*
Wealth at death £6656 16s. 10d.: probate, 1895, *CGPLA Eng. & Wales*

William Burke (1728x30–1798), by Sir Joshua Reynolds, *c.*1778

Burke, William (1728x30–1798), political writer and administrator in India, was the eldest son of John Burke (*d.* 1764), attorney, of St Marylebone, London, and Plaistow, Essex, and his first wife, Elizabeth, daughter of Thomas Burke, a London vintner. He entered Westminster School in September 1742, when he was described as being thirteen years of age, although reports of his age throughout his life are inconsistent. He was elected king's scholar in 1743. While at Westminster he won the notice of the headmaster, William Markham, afterwards archbishop of York. On 26 June 1747 William matriculated from Christ Church, Oxford, and on 26 May 1750 he began law studies at the Middle Temple, London. A fellow student, lodging with his father, was Edmund *Burke, and the young Burkes, including Edmund's brother Richard *Burke, became lifelong friends. But, as William Burke put it in a verse exchange with Edmund:

> Your word, dear Friend, has been my guiding Line,
> Your Conduct was, and is the Rule of mine;
> (*A Notebook of Edmund Burke*, 27)

Edmund Burke referred to William as his cousin, and said that their fathers had done so, but research has been unable to establish a blood connection. Edmund sketched 'Phidippus' (William) as having sudden violent, unopposable, but short-lived passion-fits. His understanding was 'strong and Quick but ... not steady'; he saw things plainly, but not for long enough in the same posture to make the best judgment. Edmund suggested that William be employed where penetration into character was needed to seize 'an opportunity never to be retrieved', but should not be relied upon where 'attention, care, and power of comparing various and discordant matters' were

needed. He 'would make an excellent ambassador', and had the aspect and demeanour of a gentleman (ibid., 57–9).

In 1755 William Burke graduated BCL from Oxford University, and on 28 November was called to the bar, but he never practised. Instead, he pieced together *An Account of the European Settlements in America*, published by Robert Dodsley in 1757, which had appeared in six editions by 1777. Stylometric analysis suggests that Edmund Burke contributed a history of puritanism in old and new England to the *Account*, but the rest was probably by William Burke. Works by any one of the Burkes usually included contributions from one or both of the others.

Burke easily made friends; one was Henry Fox, paymaster-general, who in 1759 may have helped get Burke the post of secretary and register of newly conquered Guadeloupe. Before going, he wrote a pamphlet published that year, *Remarks on a Letter to Two Great Men*. This replied to an earlier pamphlet, which had proposed that for peace Britain should re-cede Guadeloupe, and keep Canada. The *Remarks* argued that sugar-rich Guadeloupe was more valuable than barren Canada; the style suggests that Edmund Burke contributed a substantial portion. The *Monthly Review* (January 1760) thought that 'the hand of a master' was evident; the *Critical Review* (January 1760) thought it written 'with uncommon elegance ... in the most polite terms', an opinion shared by Benjamin Franklin.

Burke resided on Guadeloupe for a year (1760–61). The governor, Campbell Dalrymple, liked his company, but disliked private trading by Burke and other officials. When an abortive peace negotiation in 1761 did propose re-ceding Guadeloupe, Burke, who had returned to England, wrote *An examination of the commercial principles of the late negotiation between Great Britain and France in 1761* (1762), arguing that the return of Guadeloupe to France was unnecessary. He argued his case unsuccessfully with the prime minister, John Stuart, third earl of Bute; and his friend Fox, who was working to have the peace treaty approved by parliament, complained that the pamphlet had helped opposition. Burke compensated by persuading his rich friend Ralph Verney, second Earl Verney, MP for Buckinghamshire and a borough patron, to support the peace.

Fox supported Burke's bid to become governor of a colony, but in 1763 moved to the Lords as Baron Holland of Foxley, and without the powerful leadership of the Commons was unable to help Burke's career further, though Burke still thought Holland his 'great north star' (Brooke) in politics for many years. Early in 1765 Burke joined Edmund Burke and others in writing newspaper letters from 'A Country Tory', which satirized George Grenville's ministry with spoof praise for its 'tory' policies. In the next decade Burke may have been the sole author of at least six substantial newspaper letters and joint contributor of over forty-five others, stylometric analysis suggesting that his most frequent collaborator was Richard Burke. Among these are four in the series of six from an 'Occasional Writer' that appeared in *The Gazetteer* early in 1765, justifying the removal of the Grenville ministry and arguing that the Rockingham ministry was not Bute's tool; the other two may be ascribed to Edmund and Richard Burke.

In July 1765, at the formation of the Rockingham ministry, Burke became under-secretary of state to General Henry Seymour Conway, secretary of state for the southern department. Burke was offered a parliamentary seat at Wendover, Verney's pocket borough, but instead he insisted it should go to Edmund Burke, who was seated just in time for the stamp tax debate. Verney eventually secured William Burke a seat at Great Bedwyn, where he was returned on 16 June 1766. He spoke frequently in the Commons, but made no remarkable speeches. He remained in office under the Chatham administration, but moved with Conway to the northern department. However, Edmund Burke was now in increasingly bitter opposition; William Burke joined in writing letters against his own administration, then resigned in February 1767 to join his fellow Rockingham whigs in opposition. He was returned by Verney for Great Bedwyn at the 1768 election. According to John Brooke's article on Burke for the History of Parliament, Burke spoke 173 times in the 1768–74 parliament, becoming one of the twenty most frequent speakers in the Commons.

Burke was out of office, but thought himself financially independent, because the Burkes' friend Lauchlin Macleane had organized a group, including William Burke, Richard Burke, Lord Verney (who advanced the capital), and Laurence Sulivan, head of the faction in the East India Company opposed to Robert Clive, to speculate on India stock futures—which was illegal in England—on the Amsterdam stock exchange. The stock price rose steeply until the great slump of mid-1769, when the speculators were ruined. Burke, Macleane, and Sulivan were never again solvent, and Verney was nearly bankrupted. At the 1774 election, Burke was unable to pay Verney the sum required to retain the Commons seat at Great Bedwyn, and Rockingham refused to help him. He stood for Haslemere, but was defeated at the poll, and his petition against the result was rejected. Without a seat, he had lost his parliamentary immunity from his creditors.

The cure for insolvency was India. Macleane was sent to Bengal by Sulivan to earn the £10,000 he owed, and in 1774 returned to Britain as agent for Warren Hastings, governor of Bengal, and for the nawab of Arcot. Burke, who owed Sulivan £6000, applied vainly to replace Macleane in Bengal. In late 1776 came news from Madras that the governor, George, Baron Pigot, had been arrested by a military commander, and his supporters excluded from the council of the company at Madras.

The coup against Pigot opened a new possibility for Burke. Edmund Burke and Lady Rockingham rounded up votes for a company general court to reinstate Pigot and recall his opponents. William Burke won the job of taking out the orders restoring Pigot, and Rockingham suggested, in a letter for him to take to Pigot, that he become agent for the raja of Tanjore, whose interests Pigot had tried to protect before the coup, to counter the nawab's virulent spokesmen, Macleane and James and John Macpherson.

Pigot died before Burke arrived at Madras in August 1777, but Pigot's friends secured Burke the post of agent that he sought. He came home 'with uncommon rapidity' (*Correspondence*, 4.352) and was the effective ambassador Edmund Burke had predicted. He disabused Lord North of James Macpherson's imaginative slanders of the raja, and with Edmund's help wrote representations to the directors of the East India Company and to the king. All three Burkes may have combined on an unpresented protest against the nawab's ambitions, the debts which gave company officials an incentive to serve them, and the threat to Tanjore. In answer to a Macpherson pamphlet, it was expanded into *Considerations on the policy of making conquests for the Mahometans in India by the British arms* (1779), about half of which may be attributed to Edmund and half to William on stylistic grounds.

The Burkes' friend William Hickey had returned from Calcutta bearing a petition from British inhabitants against their new 'supreme court', with money to support it. He hired Burke to write an anti-court pamphlet, *Observations upon the administration of justice in Bengal; occasioned by some late proceedings at Dacca*, but its authorship was kept secret lest it offend ministerial lawyers needed to help the raja. Burke left it half finished when he received the all-important royally commanded letter to the raja—bland, but implicitly recognizing his independence from Arcot—and left for India with the letter in September 1780, leaving Edmund Burke to deal with the ministry, take over his proprietor's qualification of India stock, and argue in the court of proprietors against the nawab's ambition and his creditors. Edmund Burke may also have finished the *Observations* for publication.

In India the raja paid slowly; Burke, not being in company service, found a scheme for better employment dutifully vetoed by his old friend George, Baron Macartney, governor of Madras from 1781. When Edmund Burke was briefly paymaster-general in the Rockingham administration, he made William Burke deputy paymaster with responsibility for the British forces in India, a new job that Charles, first Marquess Cornwallis, governor-general of India from 1786, would call 'most unnecessary' (*Correspondence of … Cornwallis*, 1.465), and for which William Burke, wretched at calculations, was unfit. His deputies calculated while Burke dreamt hopeless schemes to make a fortune and pay debts. In 1784 Verney calculated that William Burke owed him £20,000. The regime of Governor-General Cornwallis, installed by William Pitt the younger, was unsympathetic to Burke, whom it regarded as superfluous. None the less, Burke attempted to show his devotion to his office, and in December 1790 joined Cornwallis at the governor-general's headquarters during the third Anglo-Mysore war.

Meanwhile, in Britain, Burke's salary payments were drawn by the younger Richard Burke, Edmund's son, and devoted to drawing down Burke's debts until, in May 1792, Richard wrote to Burke in India to say that it was safe for him to return to Britain. He did so in 1793 and tried to return to writing, and in 1794 translated for Edmund an address by Jacques-Pierre Brissot, but his out-of-date French needed much correction. By autumn 1795 his health was in decline, and in December he was arrested for the remains of his debt to Verney, who had died in 1791. Edmund Burke arranged for him to be released on a bond and for his salary and effects to be used to pay the Verney trustees, but Edmund remained uncertain of the extent of his debts and in late 1796 smuggled him to the Isle of Man, where debts from outside the island could not be collected. By this time Burke was helpless from two strokes, but he lingered on Man until his death in August 1798. He was buried on the Isle of Man. He was unmarried.   GEORGE C. MCELROY

Sources *The correspondence of Edmund Burke*, ed. T. W. Copeland and others, 10 vols. (1958–78) · *Correspondence of the Right Honourable Edmund Burke*, ed. Earl Fitzwilliam and R. Bourke (1844) · D. Wecter, *Edmund Burke and his kinsmen* (1939) · W. B. Todd, *A bibliography of Edmund Burke* (1964) · L. Sutherland, *The East India Company in eighteenth-century politics* (1952) · G. C. McElroy, 'Edmund, William, and Richard Burke's first attack on Indian misrule, 1778', *Bodleian Library Record*, 13 (1988), 52–65 · W. Burke, letters to Lord Macartney, Koninklijke Bibliotheek, The Hague · Macartney MSS, Bodl. Oxf. · BL, Macartney MSS · Sheffield Central Library, Wentworth–Fitzwilliam MSS · BL OIOC, Francis MSS · F. P. Lock, *Edmund Burke*, 1: *1730–1784* (1998) · J. Maclean, *Reward is secondary* (1963) · *The memoirs of William Hickey*, ed. A. Spencer, 4 vols. (1913–25) · P. D. G. Thomas, 'Check list of MPs speaking in the House of Commons, 1768–1774', *BIHR*, 35 (1962), 220–26 · *Correspondence of Charles, first Marquis Cornwallis*, ed. C. Ross, 2nd edn, 3 vols. (1859) · H. A. C. Sturgess, ed., *Register of admissions to the Honourable Society of the Middle Temple, from the fifteenth century to the year 1944*, 1 (1949), 342 · J. Brooke, 'Burke, William', HoP, *Commons, 1754–90* · *Old Westminsters*

Archives BL, dispatches relating to raja of Tanjore, Add. MS 39856 · Koninklijke Bibliotheek, The Hague · Northants. RO, corresp. · Sheff. Arch., corresp. | BL, Macartney MSS · BL OIOC, Francis MSS · Bodl. Oxf., Macartney MSS · NL Ire., letters to Charles O'Hara · Sheffield Central Library, Wentworth–Fitzwilliam MSS · U. Nott. L., letters to the third duke of Portland

Likenesses J. Reynolds, oils, *c.*1778, priv. coll. [*see illus.*]

Wealth at death in debt: *Correspondence of Edmund Burke*

Burke, William (1792–1829), murderer, and his accomplice, William Hare [*see below*], were Irish immigrants whose activities in Edinburgh made theirs perhaps the best-known pair of names in Scottish history. William Burke was probably born in the parish of Urney, near Strabane, co. Tyrone. His mother, formerly a Miss Docherty, and his father, Neil Burke, were respectable married cottars who were Roman Catholics; they gave their family a better education than most people in their situation. William worked as a servant to a Presbyterian minister, then as a baker and a weaver, and at nineteen joined the Donegal militia as a fifer and an officer's servant, his brother Constantine being an NCO with the same unit. He served seven years, during which time he married a woman from Ballina, co. Mayo, and had at least two children. He had a dispute with his father-in-law over a piece of ground, and in 1818 left for Scotland without his wife, who refused to emigrate. He was at this time about 5 feet 5 inches tall, stoutly made, with a round face and high cheekbones, grey eyes, and light sandy hair.

Burke became a labourer on the Union Canal at Polmont and lived at Maddiston, where he met a Scottish Presbyterian named Helen (Nelly) McDougal, with whom he lived for the rest of his life. They never married as both had living spouses. Burke was excommunicated because of this liaison. They moved to Peebles in 1825 and then to Leith, where their landlord taught him to cobble shoes. In 1827 they were at Portsburgh, Edinburgh, at a lodging house called the Beggars' Hotel owned by Micky Culzean, selling old shoes and other used articles to the poor, Burke being described as 'a happy man, given to music and singing'. These lodgings burned down and Burke lost everything including, perhaps surprisingly, some books. His brother Constantine at that time also lived in Edinburgh, employed as a scavenger by the Edinburgh police establishment. Next Burke and Nelly McDougal were to be found at Brown's Close, off the Grassmarket, when their relationship had become rowdy, due, it was said, to drink and to Burke's constant infidelity. They went temporarily to the harvest at Penicuik where they met William Hare. A friendship developed, and Burke and McDougal went to lodge with Hare and his wife, Margaret (Maggie), at Tanner's Close, the four forming a riotous group known for hard drinking.

On 27 November 1827 an army pensioner named Donald died in the house at Tanner's Close, owing Hare £4. In order to recoup the debt Hare, assisted by Burke, decided to sell the body to Professor Robert Knox (1791–1862), the surgeon, for dissection. The coffin was filled with bark and the body removed in a sack. They received a sum of £7 10s.

William Burke (1792–1829), by Benjamin William Crombie, pubd 1829 [on the day before his execution]

for this transaction. Seeing how easily money could be gained in this way, Hare was the prime mover in suggesting and carrying out a series of at least fifteen murders over the following months. Burke generally acted as the decoy, as he was literate, cunning, and plausible. The pair were actively assisted by their female partners, who were, however, apparently never present at the moment of murder. The victims were invited to the lodging house with a promise of accommodation, made drunk, and suffocated by a method which left no marks on the victim—Hare holding the lips and Burke pressing his own 12 stone weight onto the chest. Professor Knox bought the corpses for sums varying from £8 to £14. His part in these dubious transactions was the subject of much fierce discussion in public and medical circles, but the aloof anatomist refused to acknowledge any practical or moral accountability for these dire deeds. At one point Maggie Hare suggested that they should do away with McDougal, perhaps for religious reasons, the other three being Roman Catholics. Burke did not fall in with the plan and, angered that Hare had apparently committed another murder during his absence without paying him a share of the proceeds, moved to the house of John Broggan in the West Port.

On 31 October 1828 Burke and Hare murdered a poor old woman named Margery Campbell or Docherty, who may have been a distant relative of Burke, and disposed of the body in the usual way. The suspicions of neighbours being on this occasion aroused, the police were informed and the corpse was found in a box in the cellar of Professor Knox's house. Burke and McDougal were immediately arrested and arraigned on 8 December, the Hares being

arraigned soon afterwards. They were charged with three murders, those of Mary Paterson, killed in Constantine Burke's house probably without his knowledge, James Wilson ('Daft Jamie'), a well-known local character whose corpse Knox must have recognized, and Margery Docherty, whose body had been seen in Burke's room by the neighbours. Hare turned king's evidence, and, although he was clearly guilty, was eventually released. Burke wrote a full confession during his period awaiting trial. This took place on 23 December 1828 before the lord justice clerk, Lord Boyle, in the high court of justiciary, at Parliament Hall. There was a tradition in the Scottish legal profession of accepting paupers' briefs and Burke had the best counsel available: the dean of the faculty, Sir James Moncrieff. The famous Henry Cockburn appeared for McDougal. Fifty-five witnesses were examined. The charges against McDougal were dismissed as not proven and 'Lucky' Hare was also exonerated; they went respectively to England and back to Ulster, Maggie Hare possibly reappearing in Paris in 1850. The trial evoked immense public interest, Sir Walter Scott, for example, following the evidence and outcome with fascination. Burke was sentenced to death and taken to the Calton gaol, where he was chained to an iron gaud (or goad), and from there to the Lawnmarket, where he was hanged on 28 January 1829, attended by four priests, two Catholic and two Presbyterian, and watched by Sir Walter Scott and a large crowd. Three stones later marked the spot where the gallows stood.

Lord Boyle had expressed regret that Burke's body could not be gibbeted, and decreed that he was to be publicly dissected and the skeleton, if possible, preserved. The dissection was carried out by Knox's rival Sir Alexander Monro and the body viewed by 30,000 people, including various distinguished persons of Edinburgh intellectual society, who also acquired pieces of his pickled skin. Burke's skeleton was displayed in the anatomical museum of Edinburgh University, where it has remained.

Robert Louis Stevenson was inspired by the case to write *The Body-Snatcher*, a short story about students who worked for Knox (written in 1881, then laid aside 'in a justifiable disgust', and published in 1884). But the activities of Burke and Hare were very different from those of body-snatchers; nor were they Resurrectionists, who dealt in already dead bodies and whose trade was finally extinguished by the construction of bars or mortsafes over graves to prevent the removal of corpses.

William Hare (*b*. 1792/1804), murderer, was born in Ireland, either in Newry, co. Armagh, or Londonderry; the year of his birth is variously given as 1792 and 1804. His father was a protestant and his mother a Catholic. It is likely that he was a farm worker, but no further details have been found of his early life. He is known to have landed from Ireland at Workington and gone to Newcastle, and to have worked on the Union Canal in Scotland for about seven years, on a portion of the waterway further east than Burke. He was a quarryman for a further two years. He was described as appearing to be a simpleton, 5 feet 6 inches in height, weighing 10 stone, illiterate, with dull, black, reptilian eyes, a coarse-lipped mouth, and high cheekbones. He became a huckster and took lodgings with Logue or Log and his wife, Margaret (Maggie) Laird, in Tanner's Close in Edinburgh. It has been suggested that he murdered Log before moving in with the widow in 1826. There is no evidence that they ever formally married, but under Scots law their union was recognized by habit and repute; they had one child. Hare succeeded to the business of the lodging house, which had eight beds let out nightly at 3d. each with two or three people to a bed. He was a more violent character than Burke, and was quarrelsome and brutally callous about his part in the murders which the two carried out. After Burke's arrest Hare turned king's evidence and gave details of their activities to the police, which led to his dismissal from the case.

After the trial Hare was removed from the Tolbooth to the prison at Dumfries for his own safety, as the mob was anxious to 'burke' him as well. Relatives of 'Daft Jamie', one of the victims, averred that the decision of the crown was not binding on them and they tried to have Hare brought to trial. However, after legal proceedings he was released in February 1829. It is reported that he then obtained employment at a lime kiln; when his identity became known his fellow workers threw him into the lime, from which he emerged blinded. He was last heard of making for Carlisle and probably changed his name. A blind beggar with a dog who frequented Oxford Street in London was later pointed out as the notorious William Hare. It has also been suggested that he went either to Ireland or America and that he survived his confederate by over forty years. No record of his death has been traced.

J. GILLILAND

Sources D. Roughead, *The West Port murders* (1829) · G. Macgregor, *History of Burke and Hare* (1854) · J. J. Bell, *The glory of Scotland* (1932), 49 · J. Grant, *Cassell's old and new Edinburgh*, 3 vols. [1880–83] · W. Roughead, ed., *Burke and Hare*, 2nd edn (1921) · H. L. Adam, *Burke and Hare* (1913) · H. Douglas, *Burke and Hare, the true story* (1973) · O. D. Edwards, *Burke and Hare* (1981) · *The Times* (2 Feb 1829) · J. B. Atlay, *Famous trials of the century* (1899) · 'Noctes ambrosiana', *Blackwood*, 25 (1829), 371 · E. Byrd, *Rest without peace* (1974) · *The letters of Robert Louis Stevenson*, ed. B. A. Booth and E. Mehew, 8 vols. (1994–5) · R. Richardson, *Death, dissection and the destitute*, pbk edn (1988)
Likenesses B. W. Crombie, etching, pubd 1829, Scot. NPG [*see illus.*] · group portrait, 1829 (*Life and transactions of the murderer Blake and his associates*), BM · A. Edouart, paper silhouette, Scot. NPG · etching, BM · group portrait, cartoon (with Peel and Wellington as Burke and Hare) · seven coloured lithographs · sketches, repro. in Roughead, *West Port murders*

Burkhead, Henry (*fl.* 1645–1646), playwright, was described as a merchant in one of the commendatory verses published with his play, *A Tragedy of Cola's Furie, or, Lirenda's Miserie* (1646). Wood calls him 'no Academian, only a Merchant of Bristol', but nothing is definitely known of his origins or background (Wood, *Ath. Oxon.*, 2nd edn, 1721, 2.1007). He has sometimes been confused with both Henry Birkhead and Sir John Birkenhead (Coughlan, n. 3). The play yields strong circumstantial evidence that he was a Catholic who very decidedly supported the confederation of Kilkenny, the uneasy alliance during the 1640s between Catholics whose backgrounds ranged from Gaelic through Hiberno-Norman to later English arrivals. There are commendatory verses by Paul Aylward and William Smyth, members of two Old English families who were prominent as lawyers and merchants in south-eastern Ireland. The dedication to Edward Somerset, in 1646 created earl of Glamorgan, refers glowingly to his embassy to the confederation from Charles I in summer 1645, seeking support in the form of troops against parliament after Naseby.

The play's action rehearses events during the Irish wars up to the Ormond cessation of 1643. The confrontation between the armies of Angola (England) and Lirenda (Ireland) is shown in a series of skirmishes, interspersed with a small massacre and three torture scenes, songs, dances, a short masque of gods, a haunting featuring a retributive Revenge-figure, and several summary deaths on stage and off. The concluding cessation is divinely sanctioned via a dream but unwillingly accepted by some Lirendeans.

Most of Burkhead's main dramatis personae are identifiable as historical figures. Sir Carola Cola, hero–villain on the Angolean side, represents Sir Charles Coote Senior, notorious for atrocities committed near the outset of the rebellion, notably in co. Wicklow. Cola is characterized by Senecan ranting speeches. In act IV he is killed after a headlong career through torture and mass destruction, an event presented as the product of divine intervention. The play's hero Abner is a rosy view of the actually unimpressive Sir Thomas Preston, who had returned from continental Europe to be a confederate general. Other historically decodable characters include Theodorike (Owen Roe O'Neil), who is represented with dignity but not given the leading role—clearly indicating that Burkhead's allegiance lay with the Old English party among the confederates—Osirus (Ormond), and the lords justices Pitho and Berosus (Parsons and Borlase), who aid and abet the murderous Cola.

There are also low soldiers, a bewildered Gentleman whose avowed protestantism does not spare him the loss of his money, peasants speaking snatches of Irish, a servant–maid—whose robust character deters a rape attempt by the rapacious soldiers—and some Lirendean gentlewomen who duly sustain their menfolk by praise and steadfastness. Burkhead's play is loose in texture and generically somewhat uncertain, like much of the English drama of the 1640s, but thematically of great interest and worth further study. Though we do not know whether it was performed, in writing it Burkhead may have been drawing on the Kilkenny theatre traditions of an annual civic miracle play and some drama at the 1642 Jesuit college (P. Kavanagh, *The Irish Theatre*, 1946, 47–55).

PATRICIA COUGHLAN

Sources H. Burkhead, *A tragedy of Cola's furie, or, Lirenda's miserie* (1646) · P. Coughlan, '"The modell of its sad afflictions": Henry Burkhead's *Tragedy of Cola's furie, or, Lirenda's miserie*', *A kingdom in crisis: the confederates and the Irish civil wars*, ed. M. Ó Siochrú (Dublin, 2000) · *History of the Irish confederation and the war in Ireland ... by Richard Bellings*, ed. J. T. Gilbert, 1 (1882) · G. C. Duggan, *The stage Irishman* (1937) · P. J. Corish, 'The rising of 1641 and the Catholic confederacy, 1641–5', *A new history of Ireland*, ed. T. W. Moody and others, 3:

Early modern Ireland, 1534–1691 (1976) • P. J. Corish, 'Ormond, Rinuccini, and the confederates, 1645–9', *A new history of Ireland*, ed. T. W. Moody and others, 3: *Early modern Ireland, 1534–1691* (1976), 317–35 • M. Ó Siochrú, *Confederate Ireland, 1642–1649: a constitutional and political analysis* (1999) • D. B. J. Randall, *Winter fruit: English drama, 1642–1660* (1995), 88–92 • C. P. Meehan, *The confederation of Kilkenny* (1905) • J. Lowe, 'Some aspects of the wars in Ireland, 1641–1649', *Irish Sword*, 4 (1959–60), 82–7 • S. Wiseman, *Drama and politics in the English civil war* (1998) • A. Harbage, *Annals of English drama, 975–1700*, 2nd edn, ed. S. Schoenbaum (1964) • M. Butler, *Theatre and crisis, 1632–1642* (1984) • G. E. Bentley, *The Jacobean and Caroline stage*, 7 vols. (1941–68), vol. 3

Burkill, (John) Charles (1900–1993), mathematician and college head, was born on 1 February 1900 at Holt, Norfolk, the only child of Hugh Roberson (Rob) Burkill (1867–1950), a schoolmaster, and his wife, Bertha, *née* Bourne (1866–1937). His father's family had farmed for generations in the Winteringham area of Lincolnshire; his mother came from a family of farmers and builders in Woodchurch, Kent. From 1911 to 1914 he attended Richmond county school, and from 1914 to 1918 St Paul's School, to which he won a scholarship. Though he later averred that it was a howler in his Latin prose which steered him into the mathematical stream, he was in fact a good Greek and Latin scholar: his recreational reading in later life included the preface to A. E. Housman's great edition of Manilius. He was always deeply grateful for the superb teaching he received at St Paul's in what has been described as the university atmosphere inspired by F. S. Macaulay FRS and maintained by his successors; and his election as a governor of the school in 1940 gave him much pleasure. In 1917 he won a scholarship to Trinity College, Cambridge. After leaving school in 1918 he joined the Royal Engineers, but he was demobilized shortly after being commissioned and went up to Trinity in January 1919. In the mathematical tripos he was placed in the first class in part one in 1919, and in 1921 he was a wrangler in part two, with distinction in his special subject in schedule B. In 1922 he was elected to a research fellowship at Trinity on the strength of a dissertation on surface areas, and in the following year was awarded a Smith's prize for an essay on 'Functions of intervals and the problem of area'.

In 1924 Burkill was appointed to the chair of pure mathematics in the University of Liverpool, where soon after his arrival he secured the appointment to his staff of A. S. Besicovitch, later himself a fellow of Trinity and Rouse Ball professor. On 9 August 1928 Burkill married Margareta (Greta) Braun [**Margareta Burkill** (1896–1984)]. They had a son and two daughters. A hint of the part that she was to play in his life is evident in the fact that from their marriage and at her insistence he was always known as Charles; hitherto he had been Charlie in the family, John outside it. In contrast to his completely English origins and upbringing, her background was comprehensively European. She was born on 1 December 1896, in Germany; her grandfather was an Austrian railway engineer, her father, Adolf Braun, a journalist in Germany, her mother a Russian, her mother's second husband an Englishman. Her schooling reflected this diversity: first in Germany

and Russia, then at Harrogate Ladies' College and Newnham College, Cambridge (1917–20), where she read modern languages and economics. Her experiences at school in Nuremberg, where she was exposed to persecution because of her father's left-wing politics, bred in her a lasting sympathy with the underdog. This manifested itself both in her work for prisoners and refugees and later in the Burkills' joint efforts to improve the lot of those they saw as the underprivileged sections of Cambridge academic society, graduate students and visiting scholars. From 1933 onwards she helped to bring out of Germany and settle in England many hundreds of refugee children, and the Burkills themselves took into their family and assumed responsibility for the education of a German and an Austrian boy, who both went on to achieve positions in university departments of mathematics: (Gerd Edzard) Harry *Reuter at Manchester, Durham, and Imperial College, London; Harry Burkill at Sheffield. Several other children became for a time in effect members of the Burkill family while being helped to build new lives.

In 1929 the Burkills had returned to Cambridge on Charles Burkill's appointment to a university lectureship in mathematics and election to a fellowship and lectureship at Peterhouse. He was also appointed assistant tutor to the redoubtable P. C. (Paul) Vellacott, and when Vellacott became headmaster of Harrow School in 1934 he succeeded to the senior tutorship, which he held until 1948 and again briefly during an emergency in 1953. During the Second World War he was one of the four resident fellows who were in effective charge of the college while Vellacott, now master, was away on war service. He also joined the university senior training corps with his demobilization rank of second lieutenant, rising by the end of the war to command the Royal Engineers section of the corps with the rank of major. Release from these administrative responsibilities allowed his creative energies to be redirected into mathematics, and the flow of his publications, arrested after 1936, resumed in 1948. Recognition of the quality of his work was forthcoming in the shape of an Adams prize for 1947–8 for an essay on integrals and trigonometric series, and election to fellowship of the Royal Society in 1953. In 1961 he was appointed university reader in mathematical analysis (becoming emeritus reader on his retirement in 1967).

The deep respect felt for Burkill by his colleagues at Peterhouse was strikingly demonstrated on his retirement. Sir Herbert Butterfield had announced his intention of retiring as master in 1968, and though under the existing statutes of the college Burkill's age debarred him from election, a rapid—not to say opportunistic—amendment made it possible to offer him the position. He was genuinely surprised by the offer, and accepted with some hesitation. In the event his tenure was notably successful. The Peterhouse statutes give the master the alternative title of keeper (*custos*), and it was as keeper of the college and its traditions that Burkill saw his role. Coming to office at a time of widespread student unrest, he took a far-sighted view of its eventual course, and devised effective machinery for consultation and dialogue with junior members without saddling the college with a statutory commitment to full participation in its government more easily incurred than shed. His relationship with the fellows was also based on consultation, and in particular on cultivating a spirit of trust and co-operation between the master and the tutors—something which his own relationship with Vellacott had taught him to appreciate. In the master's lodge the Burkills entertained generously, understanding its importance as a place where all sections of the society could meet on common ground. His memory was perpetuated in the college by the annual award of a Burkill prize for mathematics.

In 1948 Burkill had put on record a policy of keeping undergraduate numbers at about their existing level (about 180) and increasing the number of fellows and research students. The college adhered broadly to this intention; and when he became master Burkill acted to assist graduate students by securing the abolition of college fees, for which they received little or nothing in exchange, and providing more and better accommodation for both married and unmarried graduates. In the university context both the Graduate Society, which ultimately developed into the University Centre, and the Society for Visiting Scholars were established largely on Greta's initiative. The idea of the Society for Visiting Scholars had originated during a visit to the Princeton Institute for Advanced Study in 1947, when the Burkills were forcibly struck by the contrast between the hospitality on offer there and the lack of any such provision in Cambridge; that of the Graduate Society was inspired by the feeling of isolation which they had encountered in graduate students whom they had taken into their own home. Other related initiatives with which Greta was closely associated included the foundation of New Hall, Cambridge's third women's college, and of University (later Wolfson) College, for graduates and holders of university posts without college fellowships. She was also active in fund-raising for her own college, Newnham. In all these activities her restless drive and determination, and her often outspoken intolerance of bureaucracy and red tape, were complemented by her husband's imperturbable patience and solid judgement.

Burkill's mathematical publications were distinguished by quality rather than volume. His most important legacy was in the field of integration. Examples are his Adams prize work, in which he elegantly solved a long-standing problem in the theory of Fourier series, and his strikingly original contribution to the notoriously difficult notion of surface area; it was here that the 'Burkill integral' featured (though in fact it was not so called by him). In addition he produced a series of papers on less closely related topics and a number of textbooks which for many years ranked as standard works. 'These all display … not only his mastery of the field but a lucidity and elegance that encourage his readers to appreciate the profound aesthetic quality of good mathematics' (Pitt, 59).

Brevity, precision, and conciseness were as characteristic of Burkill's conversation as of his written style, and his silences could be eloquent. He was an accomplished mimic. As a boy he had been given to practical joking, and though in later life his sense of humour was well under control it was never far from the surface. Fellows of Peterhouse were familiar with (and were indeed known to imitate) the slight sideways vibration of the body which betokened amusement and often preluded a mildly ironical or deflationary quip. The uncompromising austerity of the moral standards that he set himself and expected of others could make him sometimes appear hard; but although he begrudged what he thought unnecessary expenditure of money of which he was a trustee, from his own resources he was unfailingly generous to those in need. It was typical of him that on retiring as master in 1973 he became editor of the *Mathematical Proceedings of the Cambridge Philosophical Society* on the grounds that his younger colleagues should be left free to concentrate on their research. The journal's high reputation when he eventually stood down reflected his own exacting standards.

In retirement Burkill continued to be active so long as his health permitted. Before the war, skiing had been a favourite recreation, and he was a keen walker until his eighties. Greta Burkill died of heart failure at their home, 2 Archway Court, Barton Road, Cambridge, on 14 June 1984. After her death Charles Burkill put in order her voluminous papers on her refugee work and secured their safe deposit in the Cambridge University Library. He died on 6 April 1993 in a Sheffield nursing home of bronchopneumonia and Alzheimer's disease. He was cremated and his ashes buried at the Hutcliffe Wood crematorium in Sheffield. He was survived by his son and by Harry Burkill, his two daughters and Harry Reuter having predeceased him.   E. J. KENNEY

Sources J. C. Burkill, autobiographical notes, priv. coll. • H. Pitt, *Memoirs FRS*, 40 (1994), 43–59 • *The Independent* (24 April 1993) • *The Times* (13 April 1993) • *Daily Telegraph* (14 April 1993) • W. O. Chadwick, 'Address at funeral of Greta Burkill', *Cambridge Review* (20 Nov 1984) • *Cambridge News* (3 June 1964) [Margareta Burkill] • *The Times* (14 July 1984) [Margareta Burkill] • [A. B. White and others], eds., *Newnham College register, 1871–1971*, 2nd edn, 1 (1979) • *WWW*, 1991–5 • personal knowledge (2004) • private information (2004) [Harry Burkill, K. Chandrasekharan, H. Croft] • b. cert. [John Charles Burkill] • m. cert. [John Charles Burkill and Margareta née Braun] • d. certs. [Hugh Roberson Burkill, John Charles Burkill, Margareta Burkill]

Archives priv. coll., autobiographical notes [typescript] | CUL, papers of Mrs M. Burkill, Add. MS 8433

Likenesses photograph, 1922, Trinity Cam. • W. Bird Studios, photograph, 1953?, RS; repro. in Pitt, *Memoirs FRS*, 42 • M. Noakes, drawing, 1961, Peterhouse, Cambridge • J. Ward, oils, 1972, Peterhouse, Cambridge • G. Dubrovsky, photograph, 1984 (Margareta Burkill), repro. in *Cambridge Review* • photograph, repro. in *The Times* • photograph, repro. in *The Independent* • photograph (Margareta Burkill), repro. in *Cambridge News*

Wealth at death £330,582: probate, 9 July 1993, *CGPLA Eng. & Wales*

Burkill, Margareta (1896–1984). *See under* Burkill, (John) Charles (1900–1993).

Burkitt, Denis Parsons (1911–1993), surgeon and geographical epidemiologist, was born at Alexander Terrace, Enniskillen, co. Fermanagh, Ireland, on 28 February 1911,

Denis Parsons Burkitt (1911–1993), by Godfrey Argent, 1973

the elder of the two sons of James Parsons Burkitt (1870–1959), an engineer and county surveyor for Fermanagh, and his wife, Gwendolyn Hill (1879–1960), from the city of Cork. He started his education at Portora Royal School, Enniskillen, but at the age of eleven an accident led to the loss of his right eye. After he recovered he was sent to Tre-Arddur Bay School in Anglesey, north Wales, and then to Dean Close School in Cheltenham, Gloucestershire.

In 1929 Burkitt entered Trinity College, Dublin, to study engineering. He came from a deeply religious family and during Bible readings in his first year became convinced he had received a divine call to become a doctor; he therefore transferred to the medical faculty. He was placed second in his final qualifying examinations in 1935 and won the Hudson prize and a silver medal, but the house job he expected at the teaching hospital went to a rugger international. Instead, Burkitt took various provincial house jobs and finally became senior resident surgical officer at Poole in Dorset. After this he went to Edinburgh for a six months' course preparing for the Edinburgh Royal College of Surgeons fellowship examinations, which he passed in 1938.

To consider his future Burkitt became ship's surgeon on the SS *Glen Shiel* bound for north-east China, and during the voyage he came to believe that he should ultimately work in the developing world. Meanwhile he took employment as resident surgical officer at the Prince of Wales Hospital in Plymouth, Devon, where he remained during the early part of the Second World War and where he met Olive Elsie Lettice Mary Rogers (*b.* 1920), a nurse,

daughter of Rupert Rogers, an education officer; she had a similar religious background to his own.

At the time of the Dunkirk evacuation in 1940 Burkitt volunteered for the Royal Army Medical Corps (RAMC) but was rejected. Early in 1941 he applied to the British Colonial Office for appointment to its medical service in west Africa, but this was also unsuccessful. However, Burkitt was sure he should serve somewhere and immediately tried again to join the RAMC; he was accepted and commissioned, and for the next two years was attached to 219 field ambulance in England. On 28 July 1943 he married Olive Rogers. Shortly afterwards he was posted to serve with African troops in Kenya and Somaliland, and he also visited Uganda on local leave. The absence of settlers in Uganda spared the country from racial problems but it did have much Christian activity and Burkitt decided his vocation would lie in helping the people of Uganda; he returned to the UK for demobilization in 1946 with the firm belief he had been called to do this.

Accordingly, Burkitt applied to the Colonial Office once more, this time for medical service in Uganda. He was successful and soon found himself at Lira, Lango district, in sole medical charge of 300,000 people with only a 100 bed bush hospital to cover all aspects of medicine and surgery. Eighteen months later he was moved to Mulago Hospital in Kampala, the Ugandan capital, to take charge temporarily of the surgical division during the illness of the chief specialist, and he remained there until he left the colonial service in 1964.

In the twenty years after qualification Burkitt published only eleven brief papers, either case reports or accounts of simple orthopaedic devices suitable for the many amputees in Uganda. He also published an additional paper on 200 of his Lira patients with hydrocele, a collection of fluid in the testicular membranes, with which he made his first contribution to the geography of disease by recording that most cases came from east Lango district; almost none came from west Lango. This was later explained by others to be caused by the distribution of filarial parasite infection.

However, in 1957 at Mulago Hospital, Burkitt made the seminal observations which gave him fame when a colleague consulted him over a child with swellings in all four angles of the jaw. This made no sense either as cancer or infection, but Burkitt kept characteristically careful clinical notes and photographs. By chance, shortly afterwards Burkitt noticed another child with swellings affecting all four jaw angles and immediately realized that this was something special; as he said later, 'a curiosity can occur once, but two cases indicated something more than a curiosity'. This boy had an abdominal tumour as well. With his data on the two cases Burkitt studied the hospital's records on children's cancer and found that jaw tumours were common, that they were often associated with multiple tumours at unusual sites, and that the latter sometimes presented without jaw tumours. He concluded that these seemingly different childhood cancers were all facets of a single, hitherto unrecognized, tumour complex which was exceedingly common in Uganda.

The first publication on the tumour, Burkitt's 'A sarcoma involving the jaws of African children' (*British Journal of Surgery*, vol. 46, 1958, pp. 218–23) failed to attract attention at the time; however, it became a citation classic (a paper in biomedical science cited in more than 400 publications) twenty-five years later. Only when Burkitt involved pathologist colleagues who established that the tumour was a lymphoma (cancer of lymphatic cells) unlike any other of this kind did their joint publications arouse interest. Burkitt had identified a unique new cancer, which soon became known as Burkitt's lymphoma, and most researchers would have been satisfied with such a major discovery. But prompted by his geographical observations on hydrocele in Lira, Burkitt went on to make a second outstanding contribution by mapping the distribution of the tumour. He did this with the most primitive resources; a £25 grant allowed him to circulate a questionnaire to hospitals throughout Africa asking if aspects of the lymphoma were seen, and with £250 from the UK Medical Research Council (MRC) he undertook a 10,000 mile trip in an old station-wagon to confirm the replies from the east of the continent and relate them to climate.

The findings on the distribution of the tumour were crucial because a bizarre cancer dependent on conditions of temperature and rainfall suggested a biological agent was involved and raised the possibility of a tumour-inducing virus spread by a climate-dependent insect or other similar vector. Although this hypothesis subsequently required revision it stimulated the search for a viral cause and had a profound influence on theories of human cancer initiation by focusing the attention of the world biomedical community on the possible role of viruses in other cancers in humans. Between 1958 and 1966 Burkitt reported on the lymphoma in some twelve original papers, six reviews, and a comprehensive survey in leading international journals; other publications dealt with chemotherapy, and a multi-author monograph was edited later.

When the painstaking mapping of the lymphoma had been completed and after his first visit to the United States, Burkitt devised a programme on the geography of disease which resulted in his leaving the colonial service and joining the MRC external scientific staff. From April 1964 he was based in Kampala as an MRC scientist examining the distribution of cancer and other diseases in Africa by travel and correspondence, and he then transferred the work in 1966 to MRC offices in London. Useful methods for assessing the incomplete information available in Africa were elaborated.

Shortly after returning to Britain, Burkitt became greatly influenced by the retired Surgeon-Captain T. L. Cleave RN, who believed strongly that modern processed diets were responsible for many illnesses of the developed world. Burkitt set about comparing the pattern of the latter with the pattern of disease in the hundreds of African hospitals with which he was in contact and concluded that diabetes, coronary disease, diverticulosis, colon cancer, appendicitis, varicose veins, and haemorrhoids, so common in the West and rare in Africa, were, as Cleave suggested, the result of diet and especially due to a lack of fibre.

From then on Burkitt became fascinated with the role of fibre. In 1972 at a meeting in Edinburgh he met a small group of other enthusiasts and provided them with novel geographical epidemiological data and authority arising from his lymphoma fame. With Cleave and H. C. Trowell, the hypothesis on dietary fibre and disease was developed and Burkitt spent the rest of his life tirelessly advocating the value of the fibre content of food. His paper claiming that colon cancer resulted from a deficiency of dietary fibre, entitled 'Epidemiology of cancer of the colon and rectum' (*Cancer*, vol. 28, 1971, 3–13), became a second citation classic within ten years. Burkitt promoted these hypotheses in some 200 articles, for the most part as reviews or in minor journals and the semi-scientific press. A book for laymen, *Don't Forget Fibre in your Diet* (1975), was an international best-seller.

Much of this work relied on anecdote rather than the detailed epidemiology applied to the lymphoma, and no scientific link was established between dietary fibre and the various diseases to which Burkitt and his colleagues connected it. The contrasts cited between African and Western populations were made without age controls or modern diagnostic techniques, and the definition of fibre and proper methods to measure it were never established. Yet Burkitt's unflagging speaking and writing on the association of fibre deficiency with disease held a strong element of truth and engendered new studies and an expanding interest which changed the management of diabetes mellitus and colonic diverticulosis by increasing the fibre content of diet.

In 1976 Burkitt retired from the MRC and took up an honorary appointment at St Thomas's Hospital medical school in London, where a former colleague from Uganda (M. S. R. Hutt) had become professor of geographical pathology. From this base Burkitt continued to write, travel, and lecture on dietary fibre. He formally withdrew from professional work in 1984, but in reality he pursued his activities as before, until almost the day he died.

Burkitt was a kind man with unwavering determination and an unshakeable faith in the divine ordering of life. Because of his faith he took the bad with the good, and his persistence with a career in surgery despite the loss of an eye exemplified his attitude. He was enormously enthusiastic, brimming with energy, and an amusing and voluble talker. He enjoyed a happy home life, supported in everything by his wife, Olive, and was devoted to his three daughters and nine grandchildren.

Burkitt was appointed CMG in 1970, elected to the Royal Society in 1972, and received numerous prestigious awards including ten major international prizes, seven honorary degrees, four gold medals, and five honorary fellowships. Yet he was always self-deprecatory and generous with acknowledgements to others, sometimes even where these were not due. Burkitt never laid claim to being a scholar or a scientist, and was proud he had never spent a day in the laboratory but had always worked as an epidemiologist. In the conventional scientific settings of meetings and lectures Burkitt, with his unsophisticated experiences in remote parts of Africa and his austere religious faith, was rather a phenomenon. His lectures were sensational and always packed, because of both their content and their somewhat unusual presentation—in lay-preaching manner. However, they were enlivened with unexpected jokes, arresting slides of outstanding scientific material, and line-drawing cartoons in the religious tract mode to underline almost every point.

Burkitt carried his old-fashioned evangelical beliefs into the modern scientific world; he was active in the Christian Medical Fellowship and wrote frequently on religion in the service of medicine and on the influence of religion in shaping his life. He was a remarkable person who by his contributions altered current thought in two quite distinct fields of medical science. In February 1993 he suffered a stroke at his home in Bisley, Gloucestershire, a few weeks after returning from a scientific visit to the USA. He died shortly afterwards on 23 March 1993 in Gloucester Royal Infirmary, and was buried in Bisley.

ANTHONY EPSTEIN

Sources B. Glemser, *Mr. Burkitt and Africa* (1970) · A. Epstein and M. A. Eastwood, *Memoirs FRS*, 41 (1995), 87–102 · D. Coakley, 'A great twentieth century Irish doctor', *Irish masters of medicine* (1992), 333–44 · *The Times* (27 March 1993) · *Daily Telegraph* (27 March 1993) · *The Guardian* (27 March 1993) · *The Independent* (3 April 1993) · *Irish Times* (4 April 1993) · *The Lancet* (10 April 1993) · *BMJ* (10 April 1993), 996 · m. cert. · private information (2004) [O. Burkitt; Dr R. Burkitt]
Archives TCD, MSS · Wellcome L., papers; photograph albums; research notes | Wellcome L., corresp. with Sir Ernst Chain |FILM Oxford Brookes University Medical Sciences Archive, 3 VTR tapes (interviews); 1 VTR tape (interviews by Sir Anthony Epstein) · RCP Lond., 3 VTR tapes (interviews); 1 VTR tape (interviews by Sir Anthony Epstein)
Likenesses G. Argent, photograph, 1973, RS [*see illus.*] · photographs, Wellcome L.
Wealth at death £187,936: probate, 27 Aug 1993, *CGPLA Eng. & Wales*

Burkitt, Francis Crawford (1864–1935), biblical scholar, was born in London on 3 September 1864, the only child of Crawford Burkitt and his wife, Fanny Elizabeth Coward. Burkitt's grandfather had migrated to London from Sudbury in Suffolk, and founded the business which his father carried on so successfully that the son had no need to make a living for himself. This grandfather married a sister of the philanthropist William Crawford, whose unworldliness and reforming spirit were seen again in some measure in his great-nephew.

Burkitt was sent to a day school near his home. In 1878 he went to Harrow School, on the modern side, and in 1883 entered Trinity College, Cambridge, of which he was elected a scholar in 1885. He graduated as a wrangler in part one of the mathematical tripos of 1886, but he turned at once from mathematics to the theological tripos. This involved a course of scientific study of the Old and the New Testament and the early history of Christian thought and institutions, which gave him a good foundation for his later work in the domain of the beginnings of Christianity. He won several university prizes, the second Tyrwhitt scholarship (1889), and in 1888 was placed in the first class in part two of the tripos.

Burkitt married Amy Persis, daughter of William Parry, rector of Fitz, Shropshire, and granddaughter of Sir Edward Barnes, also in 1888. They settled down in Cambridge and had one son, the archaeologist Miles Burkitt. It was not until 1903 that he held any academic office—a university lecturership in palaeography previously held by James Rendel Harris—and it was not until after the promulgation of the university statutes of 1926 that he was elected a fellow of Trinity, although he had been Norrisian professor of divinity (combined with the Hulsean professorship in 1934) since 1905. So he had his whole time at his own disposal and he set to work to study other oriental languages, Syriac in particular. It was as a Syriac scholar that he first became widely known, especially in connection with the textual criticism of the gospels. He was the first to recognize the importance of the Syriac palimpsest of the four gospels in the convent of St Catherine on Mount Sinai and was one of the party that transcribed it in 1893. The two-volume edition of the old Syriac gospels which he published in 1904 with the title *Evangelion da-Mepharreshe: the Curetonian version of the four gospels, with the readings of the Sinai palimpsest and the early Syriac patristic evidence edited, collected and arranged* has proved indispensable to students of the Syriac versions of the New Testament.

Burkitt also contributed to Old Testament scholarship. His article 'Text and versions' in the *Encyclopaedia Biblica* (1903) was a masterly survey. He lived through the years when the new literary and historical criticism of the Old Testament was fighting its way, and was active in expounding its main results. But it was in the critical study of the New Testament that his own chief contributions were made. In this sphere Burkitt was, for English students at least, one of the pioneers, especially by his book *The Gospel History and its Transmission* (1906), but scarcely less so by his acceptance of the teaching of Johannes Weiss as to the meaning of 'the kingdom of God' in the message of Jesus. Burkitt made himself at once the champion in England of the 'eschatological', 'apocalyptic', interpretation of the aims and teaching of Jesus. It was mainly at his instigation also that Albert Schweitzer's great book *Von Reimarus zu Wrede* (1906) was translated by William Montgomery and was made known to English readers under the title *The Quest of the Historical Jesus* (1910).

In addition Burkitt took a lead in showing the inadequacy of the liberal protestant ideas of the nineteenth century as regards Jesus and his gospel, and recalled students to the fact that Jesus shared the apocalyptic conceptions current among some religious Jews in his time and to acknowledging that his teaching never envisaged a future for human society such as was later realized. Burkitt's mastery of the conditions of the transition from the reformed religion of Israel to the Jewish-Christian conditions of the first century AD was shown in his

Schweich lectures for 1913, *Jewish and Christian Apocalypses* (1914).

In common with other students Burkitt held that the Christ of the Catholic creeds and institutions was the product of epigenesis, in the course of which the historical figure had been transformed. But he was convinced that really scientific criticism applied to the gospels revealed a historical person with a *substratum* of his actual doings and sayings adequate to account for the origin and the later developments of the Christian church. So he found the new school of 'form criticism' unacceptable as leaving one of the greatest of historical phenomena—the rise of Christianity—in the air, without foundation in events and happenings in actual human experience (*Jesus Christ: an Historical Outline*, 1932).

Burkitt made valuable contributions also to Franciscan studies (notably in his essay, 'The study of the sources of the life of St Francis', in the volume *St Francis of Assisi* edited by Walter Seton in 1926), and to the history and significance of Christian worship in *Eucharist and Sacrifice* (1921) and in volume 3 (1930) of *The Christian Religion: its Origin and Progress*, edited by J. F. Bethune-Baker, as well as in numerous articles on special points. His books on Manicheism and gnosticism, *The Religion of the Manichees* (1925) and *Church and Gnosis* (1932), were fresh and original surveys of well-worn themes.

A list of Burkitt's published writings (books, pamphlets, and articles in various magazines) occupies ten pages of small print in the *Journal of Theological Studies* for October 1935. Such a list shows the wide range of Burkitt's learning. All his writings bore the mark of a mind of unusual acumen as well as equipment. Burkitt received honorary degrees from the universities of Edinburgh and Dublin (1907), St Andrews and Breslau (1911), Oxford (1927), and Durham (1934). He was elected a fellow of the British Academy in 1905.

Burkitt's was a vivid and attractive personality, full of interests other than those of the mere scholar—an eager fisherman and occasional gardener, a skilled pianist and musician (with Bach as his standard of perfection), a player of patience and other such games, and a rapid solver of the crossword puzzles in *The Times*. In addition, he was a practising member of the Church of England of the modernist school, and regularly read the lessons at a liberal evangelical church near his home.

Burkitt remained alert and active in retirement, but died suddenly at his home in Cambridge, 1 West Road, on 11 May 1935.   J. F. BETHUNE-BAKER, *rev.*

Sources J. F. Bethune-Baker, 'Francis Crawford Burkitt, 1864–1935', *PBA*, 22 (1936), 445–84 · E. C. Ratcliffe, 'Francis Crawford Burkitt', *Journal of Theological Studies*, 36 (1935), 22–53 · personal knowledge (1949) · F. L. Cross, ed., *Oxford dictionary of the Christian church*, 3rd edn, ed. E. A. Livingstone (1997) · *CGPLA Eng. & Wales* (1935)
Archives CUL, corresp., lectures, articles, and papers · JRL, lecture | BL, letters to W. E. Crum, Add. MS 45682 · CUL, letters to H. F. Stewart
Likenesses W. Stoneman, photograph, 1921, NPG · Proffit, portrait, priv. coll.
Wealth at death £62,806 7s. 2d.: administration, 15 July 1935, *CGPLA Eng. & Wales*

Burkitt, William (1650–1703), Church of England clergyman and devotional writer, was born on 25 July 1650 at Hitcham, Suffolk, the son of Miles Burkitt (1609/10–1669), the rector there, and his wife, Rebecca Sparrow. Miles Burkitt had clashed repeatedly with the Laudian authorities in Northamptonshire in the 1630s over his puritanism when vicar of Pattishall. He was ejected from Hitcham at the Restoration, and within a year from the Norfolk living of Irstead with Nettlestead to which he was collated in April 1661.

William Burkitt was first taught by Mr Goffe at Bildeston, Suffolk, before attending school at Stowmarket and the Perse School, Cambridge. He was admitted sizar at Pembroke College, Cambridge, on 28 January 1665, graduating BA in 1668 and proceeding MA in 1672. William Burkitt's biographer and brother-in-law, Nathaniel *Parkhurst, had access to a devotional diary maintained by Burkitt. From this source it is known that Burkitt suffered smallpox as a child, and while at Cambridge he saw the plague mortality of 1665. Burkitt developed a sense of living in the midst of death and resolved to a regular pattern of private and family prayer. He was ordained deacon at Norwich on 27 August 1669, as curate of Bildeston, Suffolk, where he was also chaplain at Bildeston Hall. He was ordained priest on 15 March 1672, as curate of Milden, near Lavenham, Suffolk. He served there as curate until his institution as rector in 1679. He married Martha (d. 1698), the daughter of Henry *Wilkinson, the former principal of Magdalen Hall, Oxford, who following his ejection had settled in north Essex and south Suffolk. Wilkinson was buried in his son-in-law's parish in May 1690. Following Martha's death in October 1698, Burkitt married Mary, daughter of Samuel Cox, the presbyterian minister at Ealing, Middlesex.

In 1692 Burkitt became vicar of Dedham in Essex. He retained the rectory at Milden, and returned to preach there from time to time and to inspect the work of his curates. He retained Milden not for any profit—little enough after expenses—but because he hoped that he would be able to withdraw there when the work at Dedham, a large market town, became too great a burden for him as he aged. Burkitt was, Parkhurst recalled, honoured to receive 'such a unanimous and affectionate call' from Dedham, 'a place that had been so long blest with the preaching of the Word, and had been noted for so many eminent professors of Christianity in it' (Parkhurst, 47): a comment which suggests his strong sympathy for the puritan traditions of the town, whose pastoral commitment his own activities echoed so strongly. On arrival at Dedham, he resolved, as a model of parish ministry, that he would pray for his people regularly, preach three times a week, and administer the Lord's supper six times a year, catechize the youth at church, and visit 'house to house through the Town, warning and directing'. Very soon, Dedham was visited by smallpox, and Burkitt ministered faithfully and supportively. In a time of dire need at Christmas 1696 he persuaded the wealthy of Dedham to forgo feasting and instead to feed the starving in the town. He also worked for years for the relief of destitute Huguenots in Suffolk and Essex.

As part of his strategy of ministry, Burkitt turned to writing. This work was undertaken specifically to complement his ministry so that there would not be any lack of resources to support people in their faith. His writing was geared to the ordinary people that he knew and served. Two of his books, *The Poor Man's Help and Young Man's Guide* (2nd edn, 1694) a volume of godly instruction, catechism, and prayers, and the closely printed double-column folio *Expository Notes, with Practical Observations, on the New Testament* (originally issued in two parts in 1700), were reprinted repeatedly for over a hundred years. The former had reached its twenty-second edition by 1736.

Burkitt was characterized as a peacemaker, and he was respected for his care and concern for the needy. When a Baptist tried to create an alternative congregation near Milden, he was as much pained at the breach of unity within the community as at their castigations of Anglican practice. He evinced great pastoral concern that some of his flock had been misled by someone who Burkitt felt was clearly misguided, and the incident caused him to write *An Argumentative and Practical Discourse of Infant-Baptism* (1692; 2nd edn, 1695). Burkitt's concern for Independents was also expressed in one of his two extant manuscript letters addressed to his publisher, John Wyat (BL, Add. MS 4275, fols. 70–71).

Parkhurst's funeral sermon, delivered on 2 November 1703, emphasized how as he was a minister of the church of England, 'conformable to her doctrine, discipline, and ceremonies', Burkitt had kept the parish firm to their public services, 'free from those rents and divisions that are to be seen in many numerous parishes'. As he was a member of the church universal, 'he held a good respect and esteem for many of our dissenting brethren that are sound in the faith, and holy and exemplary in their lives, tho' they had different sentiments from him in matters of lesser moment' (Parkhurst, 49–50). His own family connections, his respect for his puritan predecessors at Dedham, and the fact that his major devotional works were published by the leading presbyterian publisher Thomas Parkhurst all lend weight to this portrait of the breadth of Burkitt's protestant sympathies.

The depth of Burkitt's commitment to his parishes is clearly articulated in his will. He asked to be buried 'amongst my beloved and loving parishioners' on the south side of Dedham Church. His will reveals him to have been a man of substance who sought in death to use his wealth for the benefit of three groups: first, the poor of Dedham, Milden, Lavenham, and Bildeston; second, his wife and various relatives; and third, the town of Dedham. He left a house in Dedham with lands to ensure the perpetuity of the office of lecturer so that there would continue to be addresses on Sunday afternoons and Tuesday mornings at the parish church. Burkitt had recognized that the town of Dedham could no longer maintain a lecturer from voluntary contributions and he had raised funds from dignitaries and benefactors that enabled the lecturer's house to be purchased and put in trust through

his will. The provision of this lectureship defied the usual attrition of time. The office of lecturer was not combined with the tenure of the living until 1918; the Dedham Ecclesiastical Lectureship Charity was still operational in 2000 (registered charity 216907). Burkitt's will also reveals a depth of scholarship: two folio volumes by the Hebraist and rabbinical scholar Dr John Lightfoot and a six-volume polyglot Bible are mentioned. The remaining books were bequeathed to be set up as a library in the parsonage at Milden for the benefit of his successors in office and the surrounding incumbents.

Burkitt collapsed while officiating at the holy communion on Sunday, 17 October 1703. After a week of high fever, he died on 24 October, at Dedham, where he was buried. His second wife survived him. Burkitt's importance rests on the example that he offered as a minister. His appeal stretched far beyond Dedham. His *Poor Man's Help* concluded with 'An earnest exhortation unto all Christians to the love and practice of universal holiness'.

RICHARD J. GINN

Sources N. Parkhurst, *The life of the Rev. W. Burkitt* (1704) · H. Mackeon, *An inquiry into … William Gurnall … a biographical sketch of William Burkitt* (1830) · G. H. Rendall, *Dedham in history* (1937) · *DNB* · will, PRO, PROB 11/473, sig. 232, fols. 218, 221 · letters of William Burkitt to John Wyat, BL, Add. MS 4275, fols. 70–71 · *Calamy rev.* · Venn, *Alum. Cant.* · I. Green, *Print and protestantism in early modern England* (2000)
Archives Pembroke Cam., commonplace book
Likenesses R. White, line engraving, 1703, BM, NPG; repro. in W. Burkitt, *Expository notes, with practical observations, on the New Testament*, 3rd edn (1707)

Burlamachi, Philip (d. 1644), financier, was born in Sedan, France, of Italian stock. Before settling in London around 1605 he had been active in the Netherlands. He became an English denizen in 1614, and was naturalized by statute in 1624. His marriage to Elizabeth Calandrini cemented important business ties with her family, and one of her brothers, Philip Calandrini, was to be particularly closely associated with him, acting frequently as his agent in Amsterdam in a variety of business, including the pawning of jewels for Charles I in 1625.

Burlamachi's prime corresponds with the period of more active English involvement in continental affairs from about 1618 to 1630. Both the scale of his operations and the degree of his specialization in financial business made him a unique figure in early Stuart England, though he did have a few other economic irons in the fire: among these were a share in the tobacco monopoly, the export of iron ordnance in the 1620s, and huge purchases of East India Company pepper in 1623 and 1628. In 1619, together with other merchants of alien extraction, he was fined in Star Chamber for illegally exporting gold. Both the smallness of his fine of £2000 and the fact that it was later remitted in return for a loan of £10,000 to James I provide early testimony of his value to the government. Beginning with a modest advance of £6000 to James I in 1613, his formal loans culminated in his truly massive advances of the war years 1624–9, amounting to more than £127,000, much of it to finance English and foreign military operations; and this sum does not include the £55,000 which he and the Russia Company magnate Sir Ralph Freeman advanced in 1624. His last recorded loan was £5000 in July 1631.

Impressive though the scale of such formal loans was, they were not the most substantial of Burlamachi's financial services. Hardly less important was his willingness to lend his credit to the government by standing security for its borrowings. Here, his skill in playing the bill market was often of crucial importance, as it was in providing funds abroad for such purposes as the payment of English ambassadors, the purchase of art treasures for the Royal Collection, and, above all, the transmission of subsidies for Charles I's foreign allies. Most spectacular of all were Burlamachi's services as a sort of unofficial paymaster, notably of English and English-financed expeditions abroad, which provided the occasion for a multitude of ways and means advances in anticipation of slowly and irregularly mobilized government funds. His occasional demands for 'surplusage' respecting the extent to which his disbursements exceeded his receipts on particular accounts are eloquent illustrations of the scale of these activities: for example, £26,000 for operations in the Palatinate in 1624, and £30,000 on another account in 1630. Both sums were repaid, but by 1631 a further 'surplusage' of £12,000 had arisen on the latter account.

By this time the coming of peace had ended Burlamachi's usefulness to the government, but not his own indebtedness, notably for recurring interest, reckoned by him at £14,763 in 1632. His bankruptcy in 1633 was the result of his inability to meet such charges due to the failure of the undertaking from the lord treasurer, Richard Weston, first earl of Portland, to keep up payments due to him. In the meantime he was accorded royal protection from his creditors and the crown's principal debt to him was discharged in 1637. Interest and miscellaneous expenses were, however, quite a different matter, and the fact that it had been in the nature of his employment to disburse vast and unspecified amounts, as he put it, 'upon the simple word of the treasurer', who had died in 1635, did not help matters. He was ultimately allowed £49,752 of such 'pretences', but as an *ex gratia* payment which did not take in further claims of £46,803. It is perhaps ironic that a financier whose fortunes had foundered on the unreliability of the royal credit should have busied himself three years after his bankruptcy with devising a project for a national bank, the impracticability of which his own fate had spectacularly demonstrated. In 1640 he was given the minor office of master of the posts, but did not retain it beyond 1641, at the end of which year he suffered a short spell of prison for alleged defiance of a parliamentary order. He died in penury in 1644, and it was said that his daughters had to enter into service as paid gentlewomen in order to live.　ROBERT ASHTON, *rev.*

Sources A. V. Judges, 'Philip Burlamachi: a financier of the Thirty Years' War', *Economica*, 6 (1926), 285–300 · R. Ashton, *The crown and the money market, 1603–1640* (1960) · R. Ashton, 'The disbursing official under the early Stuarts', *BIHR*, 30 (1957), 162–74 · State papers, PRO · Exchequer records, PRO
Archives CKS, letters and accounts relating to business dealings with Lionel Cranfield

Burland, Sir John (1724–1776), judge, was born at Wells, Somerset, on 10 July 1724, the eldest surviving son of John Burland (1696–1746) and Elizabeth (1692/3–1760), daughter of Dr Claver Morris of Wells. The Burlands were an old Somerset family who held the manor of Steyning. Burland had three brothers and two sisters. From Sherborne School he went up to Balliol College, Oxford, in February 1740 but left without taking a degree, though he was awarded an honorary DCL in 1773. He was admitted to the Middle Temple on 11 April 1743 and was called on 23 January 1746. On 29 October 1747 he married Laetitia, daughter of W. B. Portman of Orchard Portman and Anne, only daughter of the speaker, Sir Edward Seymour.

Burland evidently practised law with some success. In January 1762 he was made a serjeant and in May 1764 a king's serjeant. He also became recorder of Wells, but in 1767, after he had held the post for some years, he had to resort to the court of king's bench when the corporation attempted to remove him. Lord Mansfield felt that Burland's case was so strong that he did not need to call upon his counsel, and 'the friends of freedom' (*Pope's Bath Chronicle*) celebrated the verdict with festivities and bonfires. By 1770 he had become one of the leaders in the common pleas (D. Lemmings, *Professors of the Law*, 2000, 349). On 8 April 1774 Burland was made a baron of the exchequer and knighted. It is said that he was appointed purely on merit and on the king's personal recommendation. However, he had little opportunity to show his worth, for on 29 February 1776 he died in London of a brain haemorrhage and was buried in Westminster Abbey on 7 March.

Since Burland's wife (who survived him and died in 1779) had an ample income following the death of her brother, he left his lands and most of his goods to their only child, John (1754–1804), subsequently member of parliament for Totnes from 1802 to his death.

PATRICK POLDEN

Sources Foss, *Judges*, vol. 8 · J. Hutchins, *The history and antiquities of the county of Dorset*, 3rd edn, ed. W. Shipp and J. W. Hodson, 4 (1861); 4 (1874) · A. J. Jewers, *Wells Cathedral, its monumental inscriptions and heraldry* (1892) · J. L. Chester, ed., *The marriage, baptismal, and burial registers of the collegiate church or abbey of St Peter, Westminster*, Harleian Society, 10 (1876) · *GM*, 1st ser., 37 (1767) · *GM*, 1st ser., 46 (1776) · J. Collinson, *The history and antiquities of the county of Somerset*, 1 (1791) · H. A. C. Sturgess, ed., *Register of admissions to the Honourable Society of the Middle Temple, from the fifteenth century to the year 1944*, 1 (1949) · Foster, *Alum. Oxon.*, 1715–1886, vol. 1 · Sainty, *King's counsel* · Sainty, *Judges* · Baker, *Serjeants* · HoP, *Commons, 1790–1820* · *The Sherborne register*, 3rd edn (1937) · *VCH Somerset*, vol. 6 · *Pope's Bath Chronicle* (7 Feb 1767) · will, PRO, PROB 11/1017, fol. 110 · W. A. Shaw, *The knights of England*, 2 vols. (1906)
Wealth at death lands, incl. manor of Steyning to son: will, PRO, PROB 11/1017, fol. 110

Burleigh, Bennet Gordon (c.1840–1914), journalist and soldier, was born in Glasgow. Little is known about his early life: in his later years he concealed his age, and his father has been variously described as a timber merchant and as a master mechanic. At the time of the Civil War, Burleigh went to the United States and served with the Confederates. By his own account he was involved in daring adventures—being captured, twice sentenced to death, and twice escaping—and was promoted captain.

He worked as a journalist in the United States and, from about 1878, in England. Reporting the Bradlaugh affair, he once gained admittance to the lobby of the House of Commons by disguising himself as a gas fitter.

In 1882 Burleigh was employed by the British news agency Central News as a war correspondent in Egypt. He successfully reported the campaign there, achieving a notable scoop on the capture of Cairo. He was then hired for the *Daily Telegraph* by its managing editor, John Merry Le Sage. This was the turning point of Burleigh's career: he worked for the *Telegraph*, reporting over twenty campaigns, until he belatedly retired in 1913. In the 1880s and early 1890s, before it was overtaken by the *Daily Mail*, the *Telegraph* had the largest daily-paper circulation, and its profits enabled it to provide Burleigh with the resources which made possible his further success as a war correspondent.

In 1884 in the Sudan, Burleigh reported Major-General Graham's Suakin campaign. In February he reported the battle of al-Teb and scooped his rivals. At the battle of Tamai, in March, the Hadendowa broke one of the British squares. Burleigh fought and helped rally the troops. His admirers later claimed he should, if eligible, have been awarded the Victoria Cross. In his reporting he criticized faulty British weapons. Later that year and in 1885 he reported the Gordon relief expedition. He fought at Abu Klea and Gubat, was wounded, mentioned in dispatches, and lost his kit in the Nile. In February 1885 he achieved an outstanding scoop by his report on the safe withdrawal of the desert column: the *Telegraph* published a special Sunday edition. In his reporting he again criticized faulty weapons and ammunition. This contributed to public concern and questions in parliament, followed by an official inquiry and the introduction of improved weapons. Following the precedent set by W. H. Russell and Archibald Forbes, he compiled books—six in all—from his war correspondence, starting with *Desert Warfare* (1884) on the eastern Sudan campaign.

Like other war correspondents Burleigh also reported manoeuvres and other military events, and cultivated his military acquaintance. He was married—his wife, Bertha, was a sculptor—with five sons and three daughters. They lived in Brixton and later at 4 Victoria Road, Clapham, both areas favoured by journalists, and he was a member of the Savage Club. Despite working for a Conservative paper he was a self-declared advanced radical and socialist. He stood in Lanarkshire and Glasgow constituencies— in 1885 as Liberal-Labour candidate, in 1886 as Liberal Unionist, and in 1892 for the Scottish Parliamentary Labour Party, always unsuccessfully.

In the 1890s Burleigh reported the French invasion of Madagascar, the 1896 Asante expedition, the Spanish Riff war in Morocco, and the Graeco-Turkish War. In 1896 he published *Two Campaigns: Madagascar and Ashantee*. In 1898, a veteran and doyen of correspondents, he reported the Sudan War. Again he was successful and, when one of the *Times* correspondents was wounded and the other killed, *The Times* used Burleigh's *Telegraph* report on the battle of Omdurman. In the controversy over the killing of Mahdist wounded and the treatment of the Mahdi's corpse, he defended Kitchener. He again criticized the War Office, and faults of weapons, ammunition, and equipment. Despite the controls and censorship he managed to outstrip his rivals and win the *Telegraph* more scoops. He evaded Kitchener's attempted news embargo on the Fashoda affair, reporting it from leaked information. In 1898 he published *Sirdar and Khalifa*, and in 1899 *Khartoum Campaign, 1898*.

At the height of his reputation Burleigh reported the 1899 South African crisis and the opening Natal battles of the Second South African War. When Sir George White withdrew into Ladysmith and the siege was imminent the other correspondents decided to remain there. Burleigh, knowing he could report more elsewhere, left. He reported Sir Redvers Buller's campaign until after the failure at Vaal Krantz in February 1900, then Roberts's offensive and later the guerrilla war. In his reporting he included—insofar as the censor permitted or could be evaded—criticism of the War Office, and British generalship, tactics, and *matériel*. He emphasized the horror of Spion Kop and demanded an inquiry into the disaster. In 1900 he published *Natal Campaign*. At the end of the war he achieved another scoop, reporting by an apparently innocent cable the agreement on peace terms.

Burleigh next reported the war in Somaliland against Muhammad bin Abdullah, the 'Mad Mullah'. In 1904 he reported the Russo-Japanese War, resenting the Japanese restrictions and censorship, and praising their military qualities. He demanded military training, as in Japan, in British state-aided schools. From this war correspondence he compiled *Empire of the East* (1905). He reported the Balkans, where his pro-Serbian sympathies offended the Austrian authorities. In 1909 he was seriously ill and thereafter, old and weakened, he lacked his former energy and aplomb. He reported the 1911 Tripoli campaign with the Italian forces, and the 1912 Balkan war with the Bulgarian forces—his last campaign. He died at the Bell Hotel, Bexhill, Sussex, on 17 June 1914.

Burleigh was a big, heavy man—brown-haired, blue-eyed, walrus-moustached, and with a loud and strident voice. Until his 1909 illness he was physically strong, with a tough constitution and exceptional endurance. He was aggressive, argumentative, and opinionated, 'as if his judgement was authoritative' (Bullard, 230), and alternated boisterous bonhomie and morose disagreeableness. He had the qualities then conducive to success as a war correspondent: he was brave—repeatedly risking death— enterprising, competitive, cunning, unscrupulous, and deceitful. Apparently on occasion he faked reports. Self-publicizing, he was not modest in describing his own adventures and achievements. He wrote vividly and acceptably—though owing much to Edwin Arnold's editing of his copy—identifying with the British troops and the imperial cause. He enjoyed war and war reporting, and, as his *Daily Telegraph* obituary stated, 'embraced the career with the ardour of a lover'. He was proud he was a professional correspondent and defended his profession against criticism, and asserted 'the clear right of the

British public under our free institutions to have news dealing with the progress of their arms rapidly transmitted home' (Burleigh, *Khartoum*, 65–6).

Burleigh was a controversial figure. Those who liked and praised him included Sir Evelyn Wood and the special artists Melton Prior and Frederic Villiers. He was not popular with his colleagues and was disliked and criticized by his rivals on other papers, 'largely because he was fiercely, and sometimes in their view, unscrupulously competitive' (Burnham, 66). Rivals who disliked and criticized him included the Liberal journalists Ernest N. Bennett and Henry W. Nevinson. According to Lord Burnham (65) he was 'possibly the greatest of all war correspondents'. In fact his achievements were inferior to those of W. H. Russell or Archibald Forbes, and neither in methods nor copy was he essentially original. Nevertheless he was outstandingly successful in his profession, and one of the leading war correspondents of the era. He was one of the last of the Victorian school of picturesque, adventurous war correspondents.   ROGER T. STEARN

Sources R. T. Stearn, 'Bennet Burleigh: Victorian war correspondent', *Soldiers of the Queen*, 65 (1991) • *Daily Telegraph* (18 June 1914) • F. L. Bullard, *Famous war correspondents* (1914) • Lord Burnham [E. F. L. Burnham], *Peterborough Court: the story of the Daily Telegraph* (1955) • B. Burleigh, *Desert warfare: being the chronicle of the eastern Sudan campaign* (1884) • B. Burleigh, *Two campaigns: Madagascar and Ashantee* (1896) • B. Burleigh, *Sirdar and Khalifa* (1898) • B. Burleigh, *Khartoum campaign, 1898, or, The re-conquest of the Soudan* (1899) • B. Burleigh, *The Natal campaign* (1900) • B. Burleigh, *Empire of the east, or, Japan and Russia at war, 1904–1905* (1905) • M. Prior, *Campaigns of a war correspondent*, ed. S. L. Bensusan (1912) • L. S. Amery, *My political life*, 1: *England before the storm* (1953) • *CGPLA Eng. & Wales* (1914) • d. cert. • Graves, *RA exhibitors*, vol. 8
Archives Hove Central Library, Wolseley MSS
Likenesses B. Burleigh, bust, exh. RA • photograph, repro. in Burleigh, *Natal campaign* • photograph, repro. in Bullard, *Famous war correspondents*
Wealth at death £1331 3s. 10d.: probate, 7 Nov 1914, *CGPLA Eng. & Wales*

Burley, Adam (*d.* 1327/8), schoolman, was of unknown origins, though he may have been related to his older contemporary, the schoolman Walter Burley (*d.* 1345)—both, for instance, occupied positions vacated by James Berkeley, bishop of Exeter, and were granted these benefices by papal provision on the same day. Adam Burley was a fellow of University College, Oxford, from 1307 until at least 1311, probably becoming MA during this period. He then acquired a succession of benefices: in March 1317 he became rector of Fifehead Neville, Dorset; in 1318 rector of Chew, Somerset; in June 1324 rector of Aldington, Kent; and in May 1327 canon and prebendary of Wells. The rectories of Aldington and Chew, at least, were held simultaneously with his position at Wells. These sources of income enabled him to continue his studies and in 1320 he was given a year's study leave from his rectorate at Chew. By 1327 he was styled doctor of theology. He died between 1 May 1327 and 21 August 1328, when there is record of a payment arising from his will.

Burley's work is represented in a single manuscript, Cambridge, Gonville and Caius College, MS 668*/645, where it appears alongside that of Walter Burley and four

other Oxford masters, with at least two of whom, Richard Campsall and Peter Bradele, he had been acquainted during the period of his residence at Oxford. It is thus most likely that the manuscript was written when Burley was at Oxford, perhaps before 1306/7. Burley is responsible for two question commentaries in this manuscript. The first (fols. 9r–13v) is a set of four questions on the *Liber sex principiorum*, the anonymous medieval expansion of the Aristotelian *Categories*; the second (fols. 150r–159v) is a set of fourteen questions on Aristotle's *De anima*. As Synan and Lewry have noted, the first commentary is of particular interest, though at times it retains only a tenuous connection to the *Liber sex principiorum*. Burley's commentary uses the text as a framework upon which to hang an analysis of current philosophical controversies. The first two questions concern the problem of the 'intension and remission of forms'—that is, whether the Aristotelian categories admit of degree. Characteristically, Burley finds a middle way between two opposing positions, and furthermore, shows that the extreme stances can be held only by insisting upon a single interpretation of an ambiguous term. The same caution is apparent in the third question, dealing with the more celebrated problem of universals. When we recognize a horse (to use one of his examples) as a horse, is this because the universal 'horseness' exists in our minds? Or is the universal a thing existing outside our minds, in the horse itself? To Burley, both these positions can easily be refuted. In his last question, asking whether an action is caused by an agent, Burley takes a firm stand against some of his more materialist contemporaries, who were content to explain physical actions by other physical actions. An action requires an agent; and, implicitly, he leaves the door open for the First Agent ultimately responsible for all actions, namely God. His arguments again examine the difficulties inherent in the framing of the question: especially the assumption that the terms 'action', 'agent', and caused 'by', are terms of obvious, fixed, and philosophically uncontroversial meaning.
R. D. GOULDING

Sources Emden, *Oxf.* • E. A. Synan, 'Four questions by Adam Burley on the *Liber sex principiorum*', *Mediaeval Studies*, 32 (1970), 60–90 • E. Hobhouse, ed., *Calendar of the register of John de Drokensford, Bishop of Bath and Wells*, Somerset RS, 1 (1887), 227, 291, 306 • *CEPR letters*, 2.175, 258 • H. E. Salter, ed., *The Oxford deeds of Balliol College*, OHS, 64 (1913) • C. H. Lohr, 'Medieval Latin Aristotle commentaries', *Traditio*, 30 (1974), 119–44, esp. 119 • P. O. Lewry, 'Grammar, logic and rhetoric, 1220–1320', *Hist. U. Oxf.* 1: *Early Oxf. schools*, 401–33 • *The works of Richard of Campsall*, ed. E. A. Synan, 1 (1968)
Archives Gon. & Caius Cam., 668*/645

Burley, John (*d.* 1332), Carmelite friar and logician, joined the order in Stamford, and studied at Oxford University, where he incepted as DTh. In 1303 he was one of the Carmelite doctors who supported the provincial William Ludlington in his resistance to the decision of the general chapter establishing the Irish and Scottish houses as a separate province. At the provincial chapter in 1305, presided over by two German Carmelites sent by the prior-general, Ludlington and his supporters were banished to other Carmelite houses in Europe. Burley, because of his age, was allowed to remain in England, but was transferred to another community. He died and was buried at the order's house in Stamford in 1332. Some have claimed that he was involved in the brief breakaway from Oxford University at Stamford in the 1330s, but there is no evidence and it is unlikely. Bale lists eight works on logic under his name, but these are almost certainly by Walter Burley (d. 1344/5).   RICHARD COPSEY

Sources J. Bale, Harley MS, BL, 3838, fols. 27v–28, 57v–58, 166–166v [some parts of 27v–28 are transcribed in B. Zimmerman ed., *Carmelitana*, 1907, 1. 225–7] • Bale, *Cat.*, 2.42 • J. Bale, Bodl. Oxf., MS Bodley 73 (SC 27635), fol. iv • Emden, *Oxf.*, 1.311–12 • F. Peck, *Academia tertia Anglicana, or, The antiquarian annals of Stanford* (1727), 27–8, 49–50

Burley, John (d. 1649), royalist naval and army officer, belonged, according to the earl of Clarendon, to a good family in the Isle of Wight. He served as captain of the *Antelope* but was put out of his command when the fleet rebelled against the king in 1642. He then joined the army, in which he became a general of ordnance. In 1646 he was appointed governor of Pendennis Castle by Ralph Hopton.

At the end of the war he moved to the Isle of Wight, where he led a minor and abortive effort to rescue Charles I from his imprisonment at Newport on 29 December 1648. He tried to raise a crowd in the town to storm Carisbrooke Castle, but those who gathered were quickly dispersed by the mayor, who demanded the return of the town drum they were beating. Burley was tried by a special commission of oyer and terminer presided over by Serjeant Wylde at Winchester, found guilty of high treason, and condemned to death. He was accordingly executed on 10 February 1649. Royalists regarded him as a martyr to the cause; some claimed that a spring of blood had risen on the spot where he was quartered.

                                    T. F. HENDERSON, *rev.* SARAH E. TROMBLEY

Sources P. R. Newman, *Royalist officers in England and Wales, 1642–1660: a biographical dictionary* (1981) • *CSP dom.*, 1648–9 • Clarendon, *Hist. rebellion*, vols. 2, 4 • E. Peacock, ed., *The army lists of the roundheads and cavaliers*, 2nd edn (1874) • W. Winstanley, *The loyall martyrology* (1665) • J. D. Jones, *The royal prisoner* (1965) • R. Ashton, *Counter-revolution: the second civil war and its origins, 1646–8* (1994)
Likenesses print, repro. in Jones, *Royal prisoner*, facing p. 15

Burley, Sir Simon (1336?–1388), soldier and courtier, was the second of at least three sons of a minor Herefordshire landowner, perhaps Roger Burley (*fl.* 1322–1331); Simon's nephew was also named Roger. Simon's elder brother Sir John Burley, and John's son Sir Richard, were both knights of the Garter. It was once said that Simon and Prince Edward (the Black Prince) studied together under Walter Burley, supposedly Simon's kinsman, and Simon's start in life was attributed to this connection with the prince. But in fact, Walter Burley probably derived his name from Burley in Yorkshire, and it is likely that it was Sir John who launched Simon's career.

Simon Burley began his military career in the sea battle off Winchelsea in 1350, and then served Prince Edward in Aquitaine and Spain. In 1367, by which time he had been knighted, he took part in a night raid on the Spanish camp

before Nájera. When the prince's government in Aquitaine collapsed in the face of a French invasion in 1369 Burley was captured near Lusignan, but he was exchanged in the following year, in time to join the prince's last expedition against Limoges.

Thereafter Burley became one of the tutors to Prince Edward's son Richard, and on Edward's death in 1376, became chamberlain to Richard as prince of Wales. Representing the prince's mother, Joan, he tried to calm anti-Lollard riots in London in 1377, and when the boy was crowned Richard II in 1377, he carried the young king on his own shoulders. Since the new king's hereditary chamberlain (Robert de Vere, earl of Oxford) was a minor, Burley became vice-chamberlain. He was also master of the king's falcons, and spent substantially on the mews. Several grants he had received earlier were now confirmed, notably the lordship of Llansteffan in Wales, and he was constable of Windsor as well.

From August to December 1380 Burley was in Germany to discuss Richard's marriage to Anne of Bohemia. After a brief return, he was authorized to go again on 12 May 1381. This fact casts some doubt on the *Anonimalle Chronicle*'s story that his arrest of a fugitive serf on 3 June at Gravesend provoked the peasants to storm Rochester Castle to free the prisoner. A prisoner was freed there during the revolt, and Burley might have ordered his arrest while *en route* for the coast, but he was absent during the main peasants' revolt. His successful arrangement of Richard's marriage was rewarded by the Order of the Garter and also by the grant of Newcastle Emlyn for life in 1382, which spoke warmly of his long service. This in turn was followed by several wardships from the Mortimer estates, concentrating his influence in Wales.

On 24 January 1384 Burley was made constable of Dover and warden of the Cinque Ports for life, an appointment which solidified a second group of interests in Kent. A third group began in Herefordshire, where he obtained the right to hold a market at Lyonshall, granted on 26 June 1384, but an agreement with the widow of his nephew Sir Richard, under which he would acquire her life interest in the family estates in Herefordshire, Southampton, and Gloucestershire, was forestalled by political events in 1387.

By now Burley was resented as leader of an exclusive clique monopolizing royal favour. His ally Michael de la Pole, earl of Suffolk, had been impeached in 1386, but was entrusted to Burley's keeping and soon released. Then in November 1387, Thomas of Woodstock, duke of Gloucester, Richard (III) Fitzalan, earl of Arundel, and Thomas Beauchamp, earl of Warwick, brought an appeal of treason against Robert de Vere, Michael de la Pole, and three others of Burley's allies. While de Vere raised an army in Cheshire, Burley tried to persuade the Cinque Ports to provide 1000 men. But de Vere's army was defeated by the appellants (now joined by Henry Bolingbroke, earl of Derby, and Thomas (I) Mowbray, earl of Nottingham) at Radcot Bridge on 20 December [*see* Lords appellant]. The victors entered London and arrested Burley and others. In the Merciless Parliament which followed, several of Burley's allies were condemned before his trial, which took place between 12 March and 5 May 1388. He was charged with abusing his influence over the young king in various ways, but convicted on the eighth article which accused him of plotting to destroy the appellants. For this, after many protests, he was sentenced to death. The king's uncle, Edmund Langley, the duke of York, and the younger appellants Derby and Nottingham, favoured sparing him, and the queen begged on her knees for his life. The king himself later maintained that he had plainly said Burley was not guilty. None the less, on the insistence of the three senior appellants, Burley was beheaded on Tower Hill on 5 May 1388, his properties being forfeited.

Three religious houses now dared to come forward and claim lands left them by Edward III, which Burley had occupied by letters patent. Despite such abuses, the king never forgot Burley. In 1392 Richard built him a tomb in the abbey church of St Mary Graces, London, to which John of Gaunt, the duke of Lancaster, contributed, while Burley's nephew Baldwin Raddington paid for prayers to be said for him.

When the king took his revenge on the appellants in 1397 the earl of Arundel was executed on the spot where Burley died. Even after the revenge had been reversed by Henry IV's deposition of Richard II, Henry restored Burley's rights to his great-nephew John, the son of Roger Burley. Simon Burley was married to Marguerite de Beausse, who was with him in Poitou in 1366. Neither she nor any child survived him. He may also have married a member of the Ros family, though confirmation is lacking. The hostile Walsingham called him an adulterer, but no illegitimate children are known. He was certainly a man of some culture, who left a number of books, including nine French romances, a *Brut* chronicle, and other works on philosophy, theology, and political theory.

Burley's general reputation has risen and fallen with his master's. Whigs later saw Richard II as a tyrant and Burley as his unworthy favourite. When Richard was rehabilitated Burley became a martyred statesman. Since then evidence of his domineering opportunism has darkened the picture again. In his day he was respected for long service, but disliked for showy clothes and haughty ways unsuited to a mere knight. Many wished to see his powers restricted, but far fewer endorsed his death. The decision to carry out the sentence of death crucially intensified the hostility between the king and the elder appellants, successively destroying Burley, the appellants, and the king.

JOHN L. LELAND

Sources Chancery records · ancient correspondence, PRO, SC 1 · ancient petitions, PRO, SC 8 · exchequer of receipt, issue rolls, PRO, E 403 · accounts various, duchy of Lancaster, PRO, DL 28 · Rymer, *Foedera* · J. Froissart, *Chronicles of England, France, Spain, and the adjoining countries*, trans. T. Johnes, 2 vols. (1874) [incl. a passage on Burley's embassy to Bohemia not preserved in the Fr. edns] · *RotP*, vol. 3 · N. Saul, *Richard II* (1997) · J. A. Tuck, 'Richard II's system of patronage', *The reign of Richard II: essays in honour of May McKisack*, ed. F. R. H. Du Boulay and C. Barron (1971), 1–20 · N. H. Nicolas, ed., *The Scrope and Grosvenor controversy*, 2 vols. (privately printed, London, 1832) · R. A. Griffiths and R. S. Thomas, *The principality of Wales in the later middle ages: the structure and personnel of government*, 1: South Wales, 1277–1536 (1972) · *Thomae Walsingham, quondam monachi S. Albani, historia Anglicana*, ed. H. T. Riley, 2 vols., pt 1 of *Chronica monasterii S. Albani*, Rolls Series, 28 (1863–4) · M. B. Lewis, 'Simon Burley and Baldwin of Raddington', *EngHR*, 52 (1937), 662–9 · R. P. Dunn-Pattison, *The Black Prince* (1910) · C. D. Ross, 'Forfeiture for treason in the reign of Richard II', *EngHR*, 71 (1956), 560–75 · A. Réville, *Le soulèvement des travailleurs d'Angleterre en 1381*, ed. C. Petit-Dutaillis (1898) · M. V. Clarke, *Fourteenth century studies*, ed. L. S. Sutherland and M. McKisack (1937) · G. B. Stow, ed., *Historia vitae et regni Ricardi Secundi* (1977) · Emden, *Oxf.*, vol. 1 · Chandos herald, *Life of the Black Prince by the herald of Sir John Chandos*, ed. M. K. Pope and E. C. Lodge (1910) · HoP, *Commons* · G. A. Holmes, *The estates of the higher nobility in fourteenth-century England* (1957) · A. Tuck, *Richard II and the English nobility* (1973) · F. S. Haydon, ed., *Eulogium historiarum sive temporis*, 3 vols., Rolls Series, 9 (1858–63) · *Chronicon Henrici Knighton, vel Cnitthon, monachi Leycestrensis*, ed. J. R. Lumby, 2 vols., Rolls Series, 92 (1889–95), vol. 2 · R. Barber, *Edward, prince of Wales and Aquitaine: a biography of the Black Prince* (1978) · *Chronicon Adae de Usk*, ed. and trans. E. M. Thompson, 2nd edn (1904) · J. J. N. Palmer, *England, France and Christendom, 1377–99* (1972) · P. E. Russell, *The English intervention in Spain and Portugal in the time of Edward III and Richard II* (1955) · T. Plucknett, 'Impeachment and attainder', *TRHS*, 5th ser., 3 (1953), 145–58 · R. H. Jones, *The royal policy of Richard II: absolutism in the later middle ages* (1968) · A. Goodman, *The loyal conspiracy: the lords appellant under Richard II* (1971) · M. McKisack, ed., 'Historia, sive, Narracio de modo et forma Mirabilis Parliamenti apud Westmonasterium', *Camden miscellany, XIV*, CS, 3rd ser., 37 (1926)
Likenesses W. Hollar, etching, NPG, V&A; repro. in W. Dugdale, *The history of St Paul's Cathedral* (1658)
Wealth at death property forfeited: Ross, 'Forfeiture for treason'; Clarke, *Fourteenth century studies*

Burley, Walter (*b.* 1274/5, *d.* in or after 1344), philosopher and commentator on Aristotle, was born (on the evidence of a note in one of his own works which records his age as sixty-two in 1337) in 1274 or 1275, possibly either at Burley in Wharfedale or Burley, near Leeds, Yorkshire. A manuscript describing him as 'Master Walter Burley, Englishman, best of logicians, renowned natural philosopher and subtle theologian', also provides the locations of the two parts of his strictly academic career: 'for many years he was regent in arts at the University of Oxford and finally at Paris in the faculty of theology' (LPL, MS 70, fol. 109vb). Two later phases of his scholarly, if non-academic, career can be distinguished: his connection with Richard Bury and the English crown, and his years spent mainly abroad in southern France and Italy.

Oxford, 1294?–c.1309 As far as Burley's years at Oxford are concerned, there are two dates which can be established with certainty: 1301, when he is called a master of arts, and 1305, when he is called a fellow of Merton College. Merton was founded in 1274 as a lodging for scholars of the arts who were expected to continue on to higher studies in theology or canon law after their necessary regency in arts, which was a course of three years. Fellows were elected while bachelors in arts for a probationary term of one year. Burley would therefore have had to be elected no later than the academic year of 1300–01, which would place the beginning of his studies at Oxford *c.*1296.

It is clear from Burley's own words, that he heard John Duns Scotus ('a certain very subtle doctor'; *In physicam*, bk

7, 1501, fol. 198ra) lecture on the *Sentences* at Oxford, probably in the academic year 1298–9. Indeed, there are important Scotistic positions which Burley adopts in later works: that being *qua* being is the primary and adequate object of the intellect, and that the intellect understands the singular as singular. If Burley followed the pattern for Merton fellows, and began to study theology at Oxford, he and William Ockham, whose studies began c.1307–8, may have been fellow students.

Burley's writings from this period cover the whole field of logic as it was then understood. He produced commentaries on almost all the books of the 'old logic', for example *Quaestiones* on the *Perihermenias* (ed. S. F. Brown, 1974), and the 'new logic', for example *Quaestiones* on the *Posterior Analytics* (ed. M. Sommers, 2000), as well as treatments of specific topics, his *De suppositionibus* (ed. S. F. Brown, 1972), for example, and *De consequentiis* (ed. N. J. Green-Pedersen, 1980). There are commentaries on Aristotle's natural philosophy as well, including *Quaestiones* on *De anima*, volume 3 (ed. E. A. Synan, 1997).

Paris, c.1309–1327 Some time between 1307 and 1309 Burley resigned his fellowship at Merton and left for Paris. It is known that Walter Burley, 'acolyte', was instituted as rector of Welbury, Yorkshire, on 15 June 1309, and was given leave of absence for the purpose of study for seven years, and dimissorial letters for reception of holy orders abroad. His benefice was in the gift of Archbishop William Greenfield, who in 1310 instructed his agents to pay £60 to his nephew Baldwin St Albans and Master Walter to cover the expenses of Baldwin's inception as a master of arts at Paris.

If Burley had begun to study theology at Oxford, his studies at Paris need not have consumed the statutory sixteen years. A plausible chronology would be that between 1309 and 1314 Burley was an *auditor* of lectures on the scriptures and the *Sentences* of Peter Lombard; from 1314 to 1317 a *biblicus* (lecturer) on the scriptures; and from 1317 to 1318 a *sententiarius*. Burley's lectures on the *Sentences* have never been identified, so with the exception of his account in the *Tractatus primus* of the controversy with his master, Thomas Wilton, on accidental form, which arose out of his *principium* on book 4, there is no record of the major exercise of his career as a theologian. His arguments there for the last of four conclusions that his opponents, including Wilton, found 'doubtful or false', show a layering of logic and physics, in a way that makes him a precursor of the Oxford 'calculators', like Richard Swineshead and John Dumbleton. In support of his claim that contrary forms, like hot and cold, belong to the same ultimate species, he argues first 'from logic' that things equidistant from an extreme are of the same species. Then, 'from Aristotle in natural philosophy', he argues that if a cooled body is immediately reheated, at some instant (B) preceding the first instant the body is cold (A) it will have a degree of heat, and at some instant (C) succeeding A it will have a degree of cold, both of which degrees will be formally equidistant from maximum heat and thus in the same species. This argument also reflects contemporary debates, over first the 'latitude' of forms, the

intensive range of possible degrees that an instance of a species of quality may possess, and, second, the 'first and last instants' of change.

In October 1318 Burley made a return trip to England to swear obedience to John Dalderby, bishop of Lincoln, for his new rectorship at Pytchley, Northamptonshire. Described as *presbyter*, he received his last leave of absence for two years of study in 1321, so it is reasonable to assume that he completed his studies by the end of 1323 at the latest. He is referred to as 'doctor of sacred theology' in 1324, and subsequently held a *disputatio* at Toulouse, *De primo et ultimo instanti* (ed. H. and C. Shapiro, 1965). His teaching career was short, since he had left Paris by the beginning of 1327.

Burley and Ockham Perhaps in the same year (1317–18) that Walter Burley was lecturing on the *Sentences* at Paris, William Ockham was doing likewise at Oxford. It is clear that from his first exposure to Ockham's *Sentences* commentary, Burley found it necessary to oppose the Venerabilis Inceptor on a number of important issues in logic and natural philosophy. It was not a one-sided engagement. Ockham borrows from Burley's *Tractatus primus* (before 1324) in his *Quaestiones* on the *Physics*, which Burley in turn criticizes in his own final commentary on the *Physics*, the first six books of which were written after 1324–7 (1501). In the *Summa logicae* Ockham both uses and attacks Burley's *De suppositionibus*. Burley counter-attacks in his second version (after 1323) of *De puritate artis logicae* (ed. P. Boehner, 1955). While Ockham's *Logic* is organized in the traditional way around terms, propositions, and arguments, Burley's is organized around the general rules of consequences, thus giving priority to propositional logic.

Burley's explanation of the supposition of terms differs from Ockham's, who holds that, first, universals do not exist *in re*, and, second, that they are not constitutive parts of the essence of individuals. On the contrary, Burley holds that universals do exist *in re*, although not apart from singulars. Therefore, according to Burley, when the term 'human' in a sentence has 'simple supposition' or 'stands for' what is common or universal, it stands for what it primarily signifies, the humanness in Socrates or Plato. For Ockham, however, when 'human' has simple supposition, it stands for a common concept, humanness in the mind. The only thing a term can signify or refer to is the individual, for instance when 'human' supposits 'personally' for Socrates, Plato, and so on. Burley eventually ceded ground to Ockham on the issue of universals as constitutive parts, holding that the universal form merely discloses the individual's essence (for instance, 'human'). Ockham's position that universals are only general concepts implies that science, which is of the universal, must be about spoken, written, and mental propositions, while for Burley, science is founded on 'real propositions', that is, propositions whose subjects and predicates are real entities, either singular or universal, but whose copulas are purely mental.

As well as resisting Ockham's reduction of *res* to singular things, Burley objects to Ockham's reduction of Aristotle's categories to substance and quality. In his *De formis* (c.1324–6, ed. F. J. D. Scott, 1970), he holds that quantity is a form separate from the quantified body, and elsewhere he argues that motion is a form over and above the body in motion, increased and decreased by a succession of specifically distinct forms (*De intensione et remissione formarum*, Venice, 1496; written after 1323). This explanation, which can be called a 'succession' theory, extends to all changes in the degree of a quality a thing may possess: how the just person comes to have more justice, or that something cold becomes somewhat hot. Every increase in justice or heat, every acceleration of motion results from the acquisition of a new, more perfect form and the loss of the old, less perfect form. Also dating from this period are the *De potentiis animae* (ed. M. J. Kitchel, 1971), and *Expositiones* of *De anima* (Oxford, Balliol, MS 92; Vatican City, Biblioteca Apostolica Vaticana, MS Vat. lat. 2151) and *Posterior Analytics* (1497).

England, 1327–1341 Burley's departure from Paris was followed by a connection with the English government which began immediately after the coronation of Edward III. Among the first initiatives of the new government was to pursue the cause of the canonization of Thomas of Lancaster, executed in 1322 after the barons' defeat by Edward II at the battle of Boroughbridge. Master Walter Burley was sent to Avignon in February 1327, along with Sir William Trussell, and Master John Thoresby, clerk, to recommend to the pope the king's request for an inquiry into Earl Thomas's sanctity. Burley and Thoresby, who would later become chancellor of England, repeated this mission in 1330, when Burley is described as one of the king's 'beloved clerks'. These were men in the royal service, usually of humble beginnings, who were most often trained in civil and canon law, frequently acting as the king's agents on diplomatic missions. It is perhaps no accident that the most notable doctrine to emerge from Burley's commentary on Aristotle's *Politics* (Oxford, Balliol, MS 95, fols. 161r–232r), that of the 'co-rulership' of kings with those who are 'their friends and the friends of the government' (Oxford, Balliol, MS 95, fol. 186r), should have had some affinity with the ordinances of 1311 that Thomas of Lancaster had died defending.

Burley's academic career had come to an abrupt halt when he left Paris, nor does it seem that he had any significant scholarly projects in hand during the next seven years. However, he was able to improve his ecclesiastical position, perhaps by virtue of his service to the king, or as a result of the contact with the papal court at Avignon which this service provided. He received a canonry at Chichester, with the prebend of Waltham, by papal provision on 1 May 1327, and in 1332 exchanged these for a canonry at Wells with the prebend of Shalford. Wells may have been where Burley met Richard Bury, who was also a canon and prebendary of Wells. Bury would become the patron of 'seven years of plenty' (1334–40) in Burley's renewed career as a scholar.

Some time after Bury was enthroned as bishop at Durham in 1334, Burley became a member of the household of this churchman, who 'took great delight in the company of clerics' (Raine, 128). Bury's household at Durham

included other doctors of theology: Thomas Bradwardine (later archbishop of Canterbury), John Maudith, Richard Fitzralph (later archbishop of Armagh), Richard Kilvington, and the Dominican Robert Holcot; civil servants Richard Bentworth (later bishop of London), and Walter Seagrave (later dean of Chichester), and probably the canonist John Atton. This roll certainly supports Burley's description of Bury as one who so loved scholarship that he directed his clerks, doctors in every faculty, 'to work at those studies which they knew best and to put into writing the best and most useful of their thoughts' (All Souls College, Oxford, MS 86, fol. 1r).

Indeed, there were many writings during his residence with Bury that Burley could truly attribute to 'your money and my labour' (Burley, *Politics*, Munich, MS Clm. 8402, fol. 135v). Between 1334 and 1337 he completed a commentary on books 1 to 6 of the *Ethics*, added books 7 and 8 to his final commentary on the *Physics*, and revised his commentary on the *Ars vetus* (Venice, 1497). Again, when Burley accepted the project of revising the commentary on *Ethics* 1 to 6, and adding a commentary on 7 to 10 (Venice, 1481) from Richard Bentworth, bishop of London (1338–9), it was Bury's patronage that saw the task to its conclusion. The *Politics* commentary shows the same pattern of initiative from Bentworth and completion with Bury's support, possibly because of Bentworth's untimely death. In the commentaries on the *Physics* and *Ars vetus* are found Burley's references to the *moderni*, those thinkers encountered first during his Paris years, who threaten the purity of the font of all philosophy: Aristotle. The doctrines that Burley identifies as being those of the *moderni* are not confined to any single philosophical discipline, and appear, by Burley's account, to form a systemic threat to philosophy itself.

On one occasion at least, Bury's influence was exerted on Burley's behalf in a more mundane matter. In the winter of 1336 certain of Burley's rivals caused him to be imprisoned for cutting down two oaks in Rockingham forest. The oaks were said to be a gift granted to Master Walter Burley, the king's clerk, by Queen Philippa, which gives some support to Holinshed's claim that Burley was appointed almoner to the queen upon her marriage to Edward III in 1328. Bury procured a 'pardon for all trespasses of vert and venison' (*CPR, 1334–8*, 341). It was probably to join Bury, who was with the king in the Rhineland, that 'Master Walter de Burleye, parson of Pyghtesleye, going beyond the seas on the king's service' was granted royal protection from 7 September 1338 until Easter 1339 (*CPR, 1338–40*, 123).

Upon completion of the four expositions of Aristotle (c.1340), Burley, who was now in his mid-sixties, appears to have sought some disengagement from the rigours and antagonisms of scholarly life. In dedicating his *Ethics* to Bury, he acknowledges sluggishness and a waning of skill: while in his youth he confidently offered the treasures of his writing to others, he is now diffident, even embarrassed to publish his work. It is not, therefore, fanciful to see Burley's journey to Italy, probably in 1341, as a kind of retirement. He perhaps found it impossible to resist, at close quarters, the urging of a patron as generous and encouraging as Richard Bury to undertake still another project.

Southern France and Italy, 1341–1344 Retirement, if such it was, did not mean inactivity. In 1341 Burley engaged in a *disputatio de quolibet* in the arts faculty at Bologna, an event that has been connected with his supposed Averroism. If, however, an Averroist is a thinker who, on the authority of Averroes, adopts positions contrary to the Christian faith, then Burley was not an Averroist. This is clear from the beginning of his career in his questions on *De anima*, where he concludes that 'neither is the material intellect one in all, nor also the agent intellect' (ed. Synan, 3.44). Then in Paris, where his master was the Averroist Thomas Wilton, his short work *De potentiis animae* reiterates this position.

The *De vita et moribus philosophorum* (ed. H. Knust, 1866), which survives in more than 270 MSS and twelve incunabula editions, has also been assigned to this period, in the light of solid evidence for the work's inception in southern Europe. However, large sections from the *De vita et moribus* are found in a manuscript dated 1326, when Burley was in Paris, and this, together with the claim that no attribution of the work to him is recorded before the fifteenth century, has led to a presumption against Burley's authorship. Nevertheless this evidence is not conclusive, and given his habits of appropriating large amounts of text from other authors and frequently reworking his own writings, it may yet be found that the *De vita et moribus* passed through Burley's hands at some point in its history.

This new environment occasioned changes in Burley's ecclesiastical holdings, a number of which centred around the papal court at Avignon, where the Benedictine Pierre Roger, who had incepted as a master in theology in Paris in 1323, reigned from 1342 to 1352 as Clement VI. On 23 November 1343 Burley was in Avignon to present a copy of his commentary on the *Politics* (Vatican City, Biblioteca Apostolica Vaticana, Borghese MS 129) to his old acquaintance. This gift, complete with an elegant letter and a miniature showing the presentation, could have been both in appreciation and expectation of further favours. Nor were Burley's efforts only for himself: in a petition of August 1342 he requested appointments for four of his kinsmen. In January 1344 he obtained papal favours for his nephew, Nicholas Borbache, 'light of his eyes and staff of his old age' (*Calendar*, ed. Bliss, 1.34), his clerk, and two servants. Whether, having made these provisions for his dependants, Burley returned to England to spend his last days in the rectory at Great Chart, Kent, obtained on 19 June 1344, or died abroad is not known. Nor is the date of his death recorded.

Influence and significance Walter Burley exerted considerable influence, both on his contemporaries and on philosophical thought into the sixteenth century, as may be deduced from the number of printed editions of his commentaries on Aristotle which appeared in the years on either side of 1500, especially at Venice. This owes something to both the originality and the clarity of the arguments he advanced in the philosophical controversies of his day, and to his skill at the traditional exercise of commentary on Aristotle. His contributions to the debates on supposition theory, consequences, and *sophismata* ensured the notice, not always friendly, of his contemporaries and the wide diffusion of his logical works. This pattern holds as well in natural philosophy, where, for example, the 'succession' position which he defends in his 'classic work', *On the Intension and Remission of Forms*, is frequently cited, being both opposed and defended, into the sixteenth century, even by the young Galileo.

Burley also occupies a pre-eminent position as a commentator on Aristotle. In glossed Latin manuscripts of Aristotle and Averroes, he is one of the commentators most frequently cited, especially in connection with the *Ethics*, *Politics*, *Physics*, and logical works of Aristotle. In addition, manuscripts of Burley's commentaries on these works had a wide circulation. Early printed editions of an important collection of *auctoritates* of Aristotle and other philosophers carry his textual comments, along with those of Averroes, Grosseteste, Albert the Great, and Thomas Aquinas. In recent times there has been abundant interest in his thought, particularly his logic and natural philosophy, and earlier assessments of him as an unworthy opponent of Ockham have not survived a closer study of his work, which has revealed its originality and depth.

M. C. SOMMERS

Sources LPL, MS 70 · Balliol Oxf., MS 95 · All Souls Oxf., MS 86 · Bayerische Staatsbibliothek, Munich, MS Clm. 8402 · Biblioteca Apostolica Vaticana, Vatican City, MS Borghese 129; MS Lat. 2146 · *CPR, 1334–40* · W. H. Bliss, *Calendar of entries in the papal registers relating to Great Britain and Ireland: petitions to the pope* (1896) · *Historiae Dunelmensis scriptores tres: Gaufridus de Coldingham, Robertus de Graystanes, et Willielmus de Chambre*, ed. J. Raine, SurtS, 9 (1839) · Emden, *Oxf.*, 1.312–14 · C. Martin, 'Walter Burley', *Oxford studies presented to Daniel Callus*, OHS, new ser., 16 (1964), 194–230 · A. Una Juárez, *La filosofía del siglo XIV: contexto cultural de Walter Burley* (1978) · J. A. Weisheipl, 'Ockham and some Mertonians', *Mediaeval Studies*, 30 (1968), 174–88 · J. A. Weisheipl, 'Ockham and the Mertonians', *Hist. U. Oxf. 1: Early Oxf. schools*, 607–58 · J. A. Weisheipl, 'Repertorium Mertonense', *Mediaeval Studies*, 31 (1969), 174–224, esp. 185–208.7 · R. Wood, 'Studies on Walter Burley, 1968–1988', *Bulletin de Philosophie Médiévale*, 30 (1988), 233–50 · G. Krieger, 'Studies on Walter Burley 1989–1997', *Vivarium*, 37 (1999), 94–100 · J. Ottman and R. Wood, 'Walter Burley: his life and works', *Vivarium*, 37 (1999), 1–23 · N. Kretzmann, A. Kenny, and J. Pinborg, eds., *The Cambridge history of later medieval philosophy: from the rediscovery of Aristotle to the disintegration of scholasticism, 1100–1600* (1982) · A. D. Conti, 'Ontology in Walter Burley's last commentary on the *Ars vetus*', *Franciscan Studies*, 50 (1990), 120–76 · J. M. Fletcher, 'The faculty of arts', *Hist. U. Oxf. 1: Early Oxf. schools*, 369–99 · C. J. Nederman, 'Kings, peers, and parliament: virtue and corulership in Walter Burley's *Commentarius in VIII libros politicorum Aristotelis*', *Albion*, 24/3 (1992), 391–407 · A. Maier, 'Zu Walter Burleys Traktat *De intensione et remissione formarum*', *Franciscan Studies*, 25 (1965), 293–321 · E. D. Sylla, 'Medieval concepts of the latitude of forms: the Oxford calculators', *Archives d'Histoire Doctrinale et Littéraire du Moyen Âge*, 40 (1973), 223–83 · E. D. Sylla, 'Infinite indivisibles and continuity in fourteenth-century theories of alteration', *Infinity and continuity in ancient and medieval thought*, ed. N. Kretzmann (Ithaca: Cornell University Press, 1982), 231–57, 322–30 · L. M. De Rijk, 'Burley's so-called *Tractatus primus*, with an edition of the additional quaestio *Utrum contradictio sit maxima oppositio'*, *Vivarium*, 24 (1996), 161–91 • M. Grignaschi, 'Lo pseudo Walter Burley e il *Liber de vita et moribus philosophorum'*, *Medioevo*, 16 (1990), 131–90 • J. Prelog, '"De Pictagora phylosopho": die Biographie des Pythagoras in dem Walter Burley zugeschriebenen *Liber de vita et moribus philosophorum'*, *Medioevo*, 16 (1990), 191–252 • R. Holinshed and others, eds., *The chronicles of England, Scotland and Ireland*, 2nd edn, ed. J. Hooker, 3 vols. in 2 (1586–7) • S. F. Brown, 'Walter Burleigh's treatise *De suppositionibus* and its influence on William of Ockham', *Franciscan Studies*, 32 (1972), 15–64 • *Walter Burley's treatise 'De formis'*, ed. F. J. Scott (Bayerische Akademie der Wissenschaften, Munich, 1970) [partial edn] • *Gualterii Burlaei 'Liber de vita et moribus philosophorum'*, ed. H. Knust (Tübingen, 1866); repr. (1964)

Archives Biblioteca Apostolica Vaticana, Vatican City • Bibliotheca Amploniana, Erfurt • Gon. & Caius Cam. • LPL

Likenesses miniature, 1343, Bibl. Vat., Borghese MS 129 • group portrait, manuscript illumination, 15th cent., Yale U., Beinecke L., Marston MS 91, fol. 1r; repro. in C. E. Lutz, 'Walter Burley's *De vita et moribus philosophorum'*, *Essays on manuscripts and rare books* (1975), 50

Burley, William (*d.* 1458), administrator and speaker of the House of Commons, was the eldest son of John Burley of Broncroft, Shropshire, and his wife, Juliana. John Burley had been six times member of parliament for Shropshire between 1399 and 1411. Apparently of age (and legally qualified) on John's death in 1415 or 1416, William was already following him in service to Thomas Fitzalan, earl of Arundel (*d.* 1415), acting as one of the earl's executors, and also to Shropshire's other two leading families—he served as steward for the Arundel lordship of Oswestry, the Stafford lordship of Caus, and the Talbot lordship of Blackmere. By 1426 he was also steward of the town of Shrewsbury. In 1428 Humphrey, duke of Gloucester (1390–1447), made Burley a deputy justiciar for Chester and north Wales; in 1440 the place was confirmed by William de la Pole, earl (later duke) of Suffolk (*d.* 1450), while Gloucester took him to south Wales on an oyer and terminer commission.

Burley was elected member of parliament for Shropshire in 1417, and on eighteen further occasions until 1455—nearly all those possible. In 1426 he held instead the office of sheriff. He became speaker for nine days in 1437 when Sir John Tyrell (*d.* 1437) fell ill, and was also elected speaker in 1445, when he lauded Suffolk's negotiation of peace with France and helped to procure satisfactory grants of taxation. In 1442 he received a life annuity of £40 from the crown for parliamentary work.

In spite of his association with Suffolk—on whose death his henchmen Sir Thomas Tuddenham (*d.* 1462) and John Heydon turned to Burley for help—Burley became an open supporter of Richard, duke of York (*d.* 1460). By 1442 he was his steward for Denbigh and Montgomery; by 1448 he was receiving some £100 a year from him in fees and land grants. This allegiance excluded Burley from the parliament of 1453 and even briefly from the Shropshire peace commission. Returned to the Commons in 1455, however, he was chosen to lead a deputation—bypassing the speaker, John Wenlock (*d.* 1471)—to press the Lords to appoint a protector (the duke of York) to check disorder. Burley never saw the crisis of Yorkist ambitions, but

died on 10 August 1458 (intestate, despite his legal training). He was twice married, first to Ellen Brown (*née* Grendon) of Lichfield, then (by 1444) to Margaret Parys of Ludlow, who survived him, dying in or after 1465. His heirs were his daughter Joan, who married as her second husband her father's fellow lawyer Thomas Littleton (*d.* 1481), and his grandson William Trussell, the son of Burley's other daughter, Elizabeth.   JULIAN LOCK

Sources J. S. Roskell and L. S. Woodger, 'Burley, William', HoP, *Commons* • J. S. Roskell, 'William Burley of Broncroft, speaker for the Commons in 1437 and 1445–6', *Transactions of the Shropshire Archaeological Society*, 56 (1957–60), 263–72; repr. in J. S. Roskell, *Parliament and politics in late medieval England*, 3 (1983), 343–52 • J. S. Roskell, *The Commons and their speakers in English parliaments, 1376–1523* (1965) • R. A. Griffiths, *The reign of King Henry VI: the exercise of royal authority, 1422–1461* (1981) • J. R. Lander, *The Wars of the Roses* (1965) • L. S. Woodger, 'Burley, John I', HoP, *Commons* • J. C. Wedgwood and A. D. Holt, *History of parliament*, 1: *Biographies of the members of the Commons house, 1439–1509* (1936) • H. T. Weyman, 'The chantry chapels in Ludlow church', *Transactions of the Salop Archaeological Society*, 3rd ser., 4 (1904), 331–70 • E. Martin, 'Broncroft and its owners', *Transactions of the Salop Archaeological Society*, 4th ser., 6 (1916–17), 223–76

Burlington. For this title name *see* Boyle, Richard, first earl of Burlington and second earl of Cork (1612–1698); Boyle, Richard, third earl of Burlington and fourth earl of Cork (1694–1753); Boyle, Dorothy, countess of Burlington (1699–1758).

Burlowe, Henry. *See* Behnes, Henry (1801/2–1837).

Burman, Thomas (1617/18–1674), sculptor and metal-engraver, was born, according to an inscription on his tomb, in 1617 or 1618. He was apprenticed to Edward Marshall under the auspices of the Masons' Company of London in 1632 or 1633. From 1649 onwards he is recorded as living in Drury Lane, London. During the Commonwealth he is said to have suffered poverty but by the time of his death he seems to have become prosperous with a considerable amount of real estate to his name and a workshop staffed by at least five apprentices. His widow, Rebekah, appears to have carried on his workshop after his decease.

Burman's first known works were the funeral effigy of Robert Devereux, third earl of Essex, and the engraved armorial brass plate that was fixed to the earl's coffin (1646). In 1651–2 he supplied designs for the family monument that Sir Ralph Verney intended to erect at Middle Claydon, Buckinghamshire, but the commission went instead to his former master. The latter year, 1652, saw him complete a carved head which had been roughed out by another sculptor and was then supplied by a third artist, John Stone, to a Norfolk gentleman, Sir William Paston. In the post-Restoration period Burman is known to have been paid for two chimneypieces, one of which was installed in the king's bedchamber at Whitehall Palace in 1661 while the other was made for Alderman Clayton's banking house in Old Jewry in the City of London (1671).

Nothing of the above is known to survive, but three authenticated works by Burman are extant: the statue of

Mary, countess of Shrewsbury, at St John's College, Cambridge (1671), and two church monuments, one of which is signed and the other documented. The signature appears on John Dutton's memorial at Sherborne, Gloucestershire (1661), which follows the contemporary fashion for standing effigies wearing shrouds. Payments are recorded for commemorating Bartholomew Beale and Katharine, his wife, at Walton, Buckinghamshire, in 1672; here the deceased are represented by portrait busts in hemispherical niches with an imposing architectural surround.

Burman died on 17 March 1674 in the parish of St Paul's, Covent Garden, London, and was buried three days later in the parish churchyard. Early in 1675, about a year after Thomas's death, Rebekah Burman submitted an invoice to William Russell, the future first duke of Bedford, for repairs to the tombs of his ancestors in the family chapel at Chenies, Buckinghamshire, and for a new tomb to stand beside them, almost certainly that of the patron's grandmother Frances, Lady Chandos. The work was evidently done in the Burman family workshop, probably by Thomas himself. A number of further monuments can be attributed to him, including the handsome sarcophagus erected in 1659 to Henry Bourchier, sixth earl of Bath, at Tawstock, Devon.   ADAM WHITE

Sources A. White, 'A biographical dictionary of London tomb sculptors, c.1560–c.1660', *Walpole Society*, 61 (1999), 1–162, esp. 13–17 · L. Stone, 'The Verney tomb at Middle Claydon', *Records of Buckinghamshire*, 16 (1953–60), 67–82, esp. 67–71, 74, 76–7 · M. Whinney, *Sculpture in Britain, 1530 to 1830*, rev. J. Physick, 2nd edn (1988), 95, 440 n. 12 · 'A bill for the right honourable the earle of Bedford, 1674/5', Beds. & Luton ARS, Russell, box 262 · GL, Masons' Company of London MSS · parish register, London, St Paul's, 20 March 1674 [burial]

Burn, Andrew (1742–1814), marine officer and religious writer, was born in Dundee on 8 September 1742, the son of George John Burn and Christian Donie. When business failure induced his father to become a naval purser the sixteen-year-old Andrew accompanied him as an assistant clerk on active service in the North Sea and West Indies. Through the good offices of a family friend he obtained a commission in the marines at Chatham in 1761. With the coming of peace in 1763 Burn went on half pay and spent the next six years in France as tutor to a young man. He returned home bankrupt from gambling and with the piety of his upbringing undermined by deistic philosophy. He was brought to face the emptiness of his life by the death of his brother, and in 1772 he experienced an evangelical conversion. He became a keen student of the Bible, a man of disciplined prayer, and, through the medium of a detailed journal, a sharply introspective critic of his own shortcomings.

During the American War of Independence, Burn experienced active service off North America and a posting to the East Indies, but with his health permanently damaged by tropical disease he was allowed to return to home waters. On 11 February 1771 Burn had married Mary Southerden (d. 1785) at Rochester. After her death he married Sarah Grigg (1763x6–1828) also at Rochester on 2 February 1786. Both unions produced several children.

In the French Revolutionary War, Burn took part in the capture of the Cape of Good Hope from the Dutch in 1796, served under Admiral Sir John Jervis in the Mediterranean in the *Goliath* (74 guns), and was senior marine officer at the battle of Cape St Vincent in 1797. After his promotion to lieutenant-colonel in the army and major in his own corps, Burn's military service was in administration, training, and garrison duties, most notably as colonel commandant of the Woolwich division (1808–14). His final promotion was to major-general on the army list in July 1810 before his retirement in 1814 after 53 years in the marines. With ten sons and daughters to support on his military pay he was never a wealthy man. Contemporaries recalled his integrity and kindness, but his lasting reputation rests upon his religious writings.

In 1789 Burn published *The Christian Officer's Panoply*, retitled *Complete Armour* for the second edition in 1806. Burn's thesis is that reason alone cannot lead to knowledge of God which must come by divine revelation. His next work, *Who Fares Best, the Christian or the Man of the World?* (also 1789) used dialogue to compare (in the words of the subtitle) 'the advantages of a life of real piety to one of fashionable dissipation'. Burn sought to demonstrate that the Christian believer enjoyed all the rational joys of life enriched by daily fellowship with God in prayer, and fortified in the face of death with the assurance of eternal glory in the presence of his Saviour. These are substantial little works, reflecting a well educated mind and a secure grasp of basic Calvinist theology. In addition he wrote an evangelistic tract for a military readership and a pamphlet in support of the Bible Society.

Burn died at Gillingham, Kent, on 18 September 1814 and was buried on 22 September at St Margaret's, Rochester. Published in 1815, his posthumous memoirs are edited extracts from his publications and personal journals, richer in spiritual introspection than factual detail, and unlikely to appeal far beyond his own day.

For one at the top of his profession Burn made surprisingly little impact upon the history of his famous corps, with but passing notice in officer lists and routine papers and little contact with the wider evangelical world. Such straitened recognition would scarcely have troubled the Burn who emerges from his writings: an unassuming character uncomfortable with rank and eminence, a soldier of proven courage who had no love for war, and a writer indifferent to fashionable opinion so long as he could commend the Christian gospel to his readers.

                                                    RICHARD C. BLAKE

Sources A. Burn, *Memoirs of the life of the late Major General Andrew Burn of the royal marines: collected from his journals, with copious extracts from his principal works on religious subjects*, 2 vols. (1815) · M. F. Conolly, *Biographical dictionary of eminent men of Fife* (1866) · [J. Watkins and F. Shoberl], *A biographical dictionary of the living authors of Great Britain and Ireland* (1816) [for list of his works] · J. Philippart, ed., *The royal military calendar*, 1 (1815), 310 · P. H. Nicolas, *Historical record of the royal marine forces*, 2 (1845) · *Army List* · *Navy List* · *Marine Officers Lists* · parish registers, Medway Archives and Local Studies Centre, Rochester, Kent · J. A. Lowe, ed., *Records of the Portsmouth division of marines, 1764–1800* (1990)

Archives Royal Marines Museum, Eastney barracks, Southsea, Hampshire, MSS | Medway Archives and Local Studies Centre, Rochester, Kent • PRO, ADM, MSS
Likenesses engraving, repro. in Burn, *Memoirs*

Burn, Andrew Robert [Robin] **(1902–1991)**, historian and classical scholar, was born on 25 September 1902 at the rectory, Kynnersley, Shropshire, the son of Andrew Ewbank Burn (1864–1927), rector of Halifax and dean of Salisbury, and his wife, Celia Mary (1866–1959), daughter of Edward Richardson. From Uppingham School (1916–1921) he proceeded as a scholar to Christ Church, Oxford, where his tutor was R. H. Dundas. After graduating with a first in *literae humaniores* in 1925 he returned to teach in his old school, Uppingham, where he was senior classical master from 1927 to 1940. On 31 December 1938 he married Mary Wynn Thomas (*b.* 1910), daughter of Wynn Thomas, until her marriage assistant keeper in the Victoria and Albert Museum and a part-time teacher of Greek and Byzantine art.

In 1940 Robin and Mary Burns moved to Athens, where Robin was British Council representative until 1941. On 22 April 1941, as the German army advanced, they left Athens on the last civilian boat, and travelled via Crete to Egypt, where Burn was commissioned in the intelligence corps at general headquarters Middle East in Cairo. In 1942 he was involved in cipher-breaking German intercepts at an 'outstation' of Bletchley Park at Heliopolis. In 1943 he was posted to Aleppo to interrogate escapers, mainly Greek, from Europe. The following year he was appointed second secretary in the British embassy to the Greek government in exile in Cairo, and worked briefly in Caserta for Harold Macmillan, at that time resident minister in the Mediterranean. After the liberation of Greece he returned with the embassy to Athens, where he experienced the communist rising and the siege of central Athens and the embassy. At Christmas 1944, in a time of emergency, he met Churchill and Eden on their visit to Athens. He never lost his love for Greece, its landscape, its culture, and its people, and the Greek government recognized this when it honoured him in 1970 with the silver cross of the royal order of the Phoenix.

In 1946 Burn returned to academic life when, on the invitation of A. W. Gomme, he accepted the post of senior lecturer in ancient history in the University of Glasgow. He remained there until his retirement in 1969, being promoted to reader in 1965. After his retirement the teaching of ancient history at Glasgow was incorporated in the departments of humanity (Latin) and Greek (later to be incorporated in a single department of classics), but before then history was still regarded as somewhat peripheral to the studies of classics students, and Burn was in effect a self-contained one-man department, with sole responsibility for the teaching of both Greek and Roman history at all levels. From 1958 to 1959 he was visiting Gillespie professor of the College of Wooster, Ohio, and from 1961 to 1962 he was a member of the institute of advanced studies at Princeton. From 1966 to 1969 he served as president of the Glasgow Archaeological Society.

Burn was a highly congenial teacher and colleague, and many newly appointed lecturers were grateful to him and his wife for the hospitality and encouragement which they provided in their Glasgow flat. He was noted for his fund of anecdotes, and for his dry humour.

In 1969 he retired from his Glasgow post to spend his final three teaching years as visiting professor at the American 'College Year in Athens', thus appropriately combining his love of teaching with his love of Greece. His last years were spent with his wife, Mary, in retirement in Oxford, where 'he was already a legend' when he arrived (*The Independent*, 27 June 1991). In 1979 he was elected a fellow of the Society of Antiquaries, and in 1982 Oxford awarded him the degree of DLitt. He continued to play an active part at seminars and meetings until his death of heart failure and old age at the Radcliffe Infirmary, Woodstock Road, Oxford, on 17 June 1991. After cremation on 21 June his ashes were interred at St Michael's Church, Summertown, Oxford, on 8 October 1991.

Apart from journal articles and reviews Burn published a large number of books. Indeed, he used to say that writing books was his hobby. Already, as a schoolmaster at Uppingham, he produced *Minoans, Philistines and Greeks, 1400–900 B.C.* (1930), *The Romans in Britain: an Anthology of Inscriptions* (1932), and *The World of Hesiod: a Study of the Greek Middle Ages, c.900–700 B.C.* (1936). During the war years he found time to publish two small books, *This Scepter'd Isle: an Anthology of English Poetry* (1940) and *The Modern Greeks* (1942). His Glasgow years saw the appearance of *Alexander the Great and the Hellenistic Empire* (1947), *Pericles and Athens* (1948), *Agricola and Roman Britain* (1953), *The Lyric Age of Greece* (1960), *Persia and the Greeks: the Defence of the West, c.546–478 B.C.* (1962), *A Traveller's History of Greece* (1965), and *The Warring States of Greece: from their Rise to the Roman Conquest* (1968). After retirement he published, with his wife, Mary, *The Living Past of Greece: a Time-Traveller's Tour of Historic and Prehistoric Places* (1980). Many of these books were to be revised and reprinted, some under different titles. All were highly readable, and many remained for many years standard in their field, and figured prominently in students' reading lists. They ranged widely over ancient and modern, political and military, Greek, Roman, and oriental history, literature, archaeology, and topography, and combined sound scholarship with exceptional skill in communicating it to specialist and non-specialist alike. Burn was a popularizer in the best sense of that word. He enjoyed reading as much as he enjoyed writing. At the age of eighty-six, in accepting an invitation to review a book for the *Classical Review*, he wrote to the editor, 'I love reviewing now that I do no more serious work! Send me anything you think fit' (personal knowledge). Throughout his life he was a committed member of the Church of England, and, during his Glasgow period, of the Scottish Episcopal church.   A. F. GARVIE

Sources WWW, 1991–5 • *The Independent* (27 June 1991) • *The Times* (9 July 1991) • personal knowledge (2004) • private information (2004) • *The Writers Directory* (1988–90) • Uppingham school register • register, Christ Church Oxf. • register of the Society of Antiquaries • d. cert.
Archives U. Glas. L., corresp. and papers | Bodl. Oxf., corresp. with J. L. Myers

Likenesses photograph, repro. in *The Times*
Wealth at death £43,895: probate, 17 Oct 1991, *CGPLA Eng. & Wales*

Burn, Duncan Lyall (1902–1988), economist, was born on 10 August 1902 at Holloway, London, the younger child and younger son of Archibald William Burn, engineer, and his wife, Margaret Anne Mead, who, prior to her marriage, worked as a nanny. He was taught history at Holloway county school by Arthur Bryant and won a scholarship to Christ's College, Cambridge, where he took a first class (division two) in both parts of the history tripos (1923 and 1924). On graduation he won a Wrenbury scholarship, which enabled him to spend a year (1924) as a bachelor research scholar at Christ's. After two years at Liverpool as a university lecturer in economic history (1925–6) he returned to Cambridge in 1927 in the same capacity. There he remained until the outbreak of the Second World War in 1939, living out of Cambridge and with no college attachment. During that time he completed his authoritative study of the British steel industry, *The Economic History of Steelmaking, 1867–1939* (1940). He was also a kindly and rigorous supervisor, some of whose students maintained a lifelong friendship with him.

A self-taught economist, Burn never ceased to be an academic, pursuing research in industrial economics throughout his life. He was not much interested in macroeconomics, dismissing demand management after the war as 'penny-in-the-slot-economics'. Throughout the war he served with Robert Shone in the iron and steel control of the Ministry of Supply, taking part in the later stages in government planning for the post-war steel industry. In 1946 he did not return to Cambridge but joined *The Times* as leader writer and industrial correspondent, continuing in that capacity for the next sixteen years, and displaying an impressive knowledge of industry in Britain and abroad. He won a high reputation in the main industrial countries and maintained close and frequent contact with Jean Monnet, the French economist and politician. He was a natural choice to edit a two-volume study of British industry (*The Structure of British Industry*, 1958), and contributed to it chapters on oil and steel, as well as an analytical survey. He continued to write on the steel industry, producing in 1961 a sequel to his earlier book, *The Steel Industry, 1939–59*. When re-nationalization was under debate he argued (in *The Future of Steel*, 1965) that the proposal misconceived the problems of the industry and misjudged the likely effects. 'More scope', he maintained, 'must be given to rebels in management', who backed far-sighted but unfashionable or unpopular projects.

In 1962 Burn left *The Times* and adopted a third career as an industrial consultant, acting for three years as director of the economic development office set up by four leading manufacturers of heavy electric generators. This increased his interest in nuclear energy, on which he wrote extensively over the next fifteen years, beginning with a lengthy study in 1965, after a visit to America, entitled *The Significance of Oyster Creek*, the first large boiling water reactor to be ordered. He also acted as consultant to firms in the aircraft and chemical industries, and wrote *Chemicals under Free Trade* (1971). He served on a number of official and academic committees such as the economic committee of the Department of Scientific and Industrial Research (1963–5), and had two further spells of academic life as visiting professor at the University of Manchester (1967–9) and the University of Bombay (1971). At his death he had been working for a number of years on his book *The Public Interest*.

In 1967 Burn developed his criticisms of British plans for a programme of gas-cooled reactors (AGRs) in *The Political Economy of Nuclear Energy*, maintaining that the AGR was well behind light water reactors in performance and likely to fall further behind. By the time he published *Nuclear Power and the Energy Crisis* in 1978 it was apparent that, instead of Britain leading the world in nuclear energy as ministers claimed even in the mid-1960s, no British nuclear reactors had ever been built abroad. Burn continued to interest himself in nuclear energy, acting from 1980 until his death as specialist adviser to the House of Commons select committee on energy.

The distinguishing feature of Burn's work was his deep interest in what made for successful industrial and technological development. He stressed the contribution made by competition in encouraging a variety of approaches and allowing scope for differences of opinion. His research was meticulous and quantitative, and aimed to single out the key elements in competitive success. He had many contacts in industry and, as he was a good listener with a retentive memory, he came to have a rare knowledge of expert industrial opinion as well as its divisions and weaknesses. In expressing his own views he was never daunted by the authority or eminence of those from whom he differed. He could be scathing in his criticisms, but his views were well documented and carefully argued.

Burn was short in stature and clean-shaven, with blue eyes and a slightly puckered face. He spoke slowly and quietly, but with assurance, and he enjoyed an argument. Normally serious-minded, he did not lack a sly humour and was given to an occasional quip and twinkle of the eye. On 30 December 1930 he married Jessie Mabel (Mollie), four years his senior and daughter of William Louis White, a chemist who worked in a retail pharmacy. It was an extremely happy marriage, producing two daughters and lasting for nearly sixty years until his death from heart failure on 9 January 1988 in the Royal Free Hospital, London.   ALEC CAIRNCROSS, *rev.*

Sources personal knowledge (2004) · *The Times* (13 Jan 1988) · *WWW* · *CGPLA Eng. & Wales* (1988)
Archives BLPES, papers
Wealth at death £134,086: probate, 13 May 1988, *CGPLA Eng. & Wales*

Burn, Edward (1762–1837), Church of England clergyman and theological writer, was born on 29 November 1762, the son of Charles Burn of Killyleagh, co. Down. He was educated for the ministry at the countess of Huntingdon's college at Trefeca, and, after taking orders and obtaining a Birmingham curacy, he matriculated at St Edmund Hall, Oxford, on 26 May 1784, graduating BA on 20 February

1790, and MA on 22 June 1791. In 1785 he became curate and lecturer at St Mary's Chapel, Birmingham. He retained this position until his death and was 'justly celebrated for extemporary oratory'. Burn's first appearance as an author was in opposition to the unitarian radical Joseph Priestley, with whom he was personally acquainted. Their dispute, which took the form of a correspondence, and which Burn published as *Letters to Dr Priestley on the infallibility of the apostolic testimony concerning the person of Christ* (1790), dissolved the friendship. The initiative was with Burn, who received the thanks of Beilby Porteus, bishop of London. Burn's later judgement, as he told the American traveller F. W. P. Greenwood, was that Priestley 'handled him much too roughly' (Greenwood, 45). This applied particularly to Burn's and Priestley's subsequent encounter on the subject of the Birmingham riots of 14 July 1791 in which Priestley's house had been destroyed by a mob. Priestley attacked the act in his *Appeal to the Public* (1792). Burn responded in *A Reply to the Revd Dr Priestley's Appeal* which criticized the mob but claimed that it had been incensed by Priestley's controversial defence of the French Revolution. Burn, as he grew older, became a liberal in politics, and was willing to act with unitarians on the local committee of the Bible Society. He was one of the founders of the Birmingham Association of the Church Missionary Society, and its first secretary. It is greatly to his honour that in October 1825 he went out of his way to express regret (at the Birmingham low bailiffs' annual dinner) for his asperity against Priestley. In 1830 Burn is mentioned as minister of St James's Chapel, Ashted, Birmingham, and at the time of his death he held, with St Mary's, the rectory of Smethcott, Shropshire. His later works include *Serious Hints to the Clergy* (1798) and *Pastoral Hints, or, The Importance of a Religious Education* (1801). He was married with children, though no details are known. Burn died at Birmingham on 20 May 1837; his funeral was attended by churchmen of many denominations.

ALEXANDER GORDON, *rev.* PHILIP CARTER

Sources F. W. P. Greenwood, *Miscellaneous writings* (1846) · Foster, *Alum. Oxon.* · *Anything, or, From anywhere: otherwise some account of the life of the Revd Secretary Turnabout, the great high priest* (1792) · *Birmingham Journal* (29 Oct 1825) · *Life and correspondence of Joseph Priestley*, ed. J. T. Rutt, 2 vols. (1831-2)
Likenesses A. Cardon, stipple, pubd 1837 (after Hancock), NPG

Burn, John (1743/4–1802), magistrate and legal editor, the son of Richard *Burn (1709–1785), vicar of Orton and chancellor of the diocese of Carlisle, was born at the family home, Orton Hall, Westmorland. Although trained for the legal profession Burn did not practise, but his legal knowledge stood him in good stead in his capacity as a magistrate in the counties of Westmorland and Cumberland. The duties of this position he is said to have performed with 'great intelligence and activity' (Britton, 149).

Although Burn produced no original work he devoted himself to editing, correcting, and continuing his father's legal writings. In 1788 he published in four volumes the sixteenth edition of *The Justice of the Peace and Parish Officer*, published originally in two volumes in 1755 and for long

recognized as the standard legal text on the role and duties of the justice of the peace. He published three further editions; to the seventeenth edition he added in 1795 an appendix containing all the new laws introduced since the outbreak of war with France in February 1793 that related to the office of justice of the peace, including laws regarding the militia, the treatment of aliens, and, on the suggestion of the lord chief justice, a new set of precedents respecting the excise laws. He also updated his father's *New Law Dictionary* in 1792.

Burn died at Orton Hall on 20 January 1802, aged fifty-eight, and was buried in the churchyard at Orton. A monument to his memory was erected in Orton church.

AGNES MACDONELL, *rev.* M. J. MERCER

Sources J. Britton, E. W. Brayley, and others, *The beauties of England and Wales, or, Delineations topographical, historical, and descriptive, of each county*, [18 vols.] (1801–16), vol. 15, pt 2, pp. 148–9 · *A new catalogue of living English authors: with complete lists of their publications, and biographical and critical memoirs* (1799) · [J. Watkins and F. Shoberl], *A biographical dictionary of the living authors of Great Britain and Ireland* (1816) · W. Whellan, ed., *The history and topography of the counties of Cumberland and Westmoreland* (1860), 762–3

Burn, John Southerden (1798–1870), antiquary, was born on 7 July 1798 at Maidstone, Kent, the son of John Burn and his wife, Ann. He qualified as a solicitor in 1819, when he began to practise at 11 Staples Inn, Holborn. In 1820 he moved to 11 King's Bench Walk, Temple, and in 1822 to 27 King Street, Cheapside. In the following year he formed a partnership with Samuel Woodgate Durrant, which lasted until 1828, when he moved to 25 Tokenhouse Yard. Finding that his professional duties involved frequent consultation of parish registers, Burn started to collect information relating to them, and in 1829 he published his *Registrum ecclesiae parochialis*, a history of English parish registers, with some comments on foreign equivalents. It was the first work concentrating exclusively on these records since Ralph Bigland's *Observations on Parochial Registers* of 1764. In 1831 Burn published, with biographical notes, the *Livre des Anglois à Genève*, the register of the English church in Geneva from 1554 to 1558, which had been sent to him by Sir Samuel Egerton Brydges too late to be included in the *Registrum*.

In 1831 Burn was appointed registrar of those marriages which had taken place at chapels before 1754, and in 1833 he published *The Fleet Registers*, containing a history of Fleet marriages; it reached a third edition in 1836. In the same year he edited *The Marriage and Registration Acts (6 and 7 William IV)*, and became secretary to a commission investigating non-parochial registers, a post that he retained until 1841. In that year he moved to 1 Copthall Court, Throgmorton Street, and entered a partnership with Stacey Grimaldi and Henry Edward Stables, which lasted until Grimaldi's retirement in 1847. In 1854 a new partner, Charles Tayler Ware, joined the firm, but the following year, after Stables's death on 13 October, Burn retired from practice.

In 1846 Burn issued his most important work, *The history of the French, Walloon, Dutch, and other foreign protestant refugees settled in England*, which he compiled mainly from the registers of the refugees' places of worship. Although little more than a series of notes on the subject, it contained a valuable summary of the facts to be found in the records of the foreign congregations in England.

After retiring from the practice of law, Burn lived at The Grove at Henley-on-Thames, and in 1861 he published *A History of Henley on Thames*. In 1865 he produced *The High Commission*, a collection of notices of the court and its procedure, and early in 1870 he published a similar but more elaborate work, *The Star Chamber*, which also contained some additional notes on the court of high commission. Burn died at The Grove on 15 June 1870. His wife, Jane Burn, survived him.

E. I. CARLYLE, *rev.* NILANJANA BANERJI

Sources *N&Q*, 4th ser., 5 (1870), 611 · *Law List* · *CGPLA Eng. & Wales* (1870) · baptism register, Week Street Independent Chapel, Maidstone, PRO, RG 4/1010
Archives BL, corresp., Add. MSS 24886, 34189, 40515 · Bodl. Oxf., corresp. with Sir Thomas Phillipps
Wealth at death under £50,000: probate, 15 July 1870, *CGPLA Eng. & Wales*

Burn, Richard (1709–1785), legal writer and Church of England clergyman, the son of Richard Burn, was born in Winton, in the parish of Kirkby Stephen, Westmorland. He matriculated at the Queen's College, Oxford, in 1729, was awarded a BA in 1734, and was in 1736 elected, presented, and instituted to the vicarage of Orton in Westmorland. He became a justice of the peace for the counties of Westmorland and Cumberland. In 1762 he was made a DCL by Oxford, and in 1765 Bishop Lyttelton appointed him chancellor of the diocese of Carlisle. He died at Orton on 12 November 1785, and was succeeded in the chancellorship of Carlisle by his friend William Paley.

Burn's publications reveal a man fascinated by the structures within which he lived and worked. His first book, *The justice of the peace and parish officer, upon a plan entirely new, and comprehending all the law to the present time* (2 vols., 1755), became a classic because it fulfilled the promise of its title. Before Burn, justices' manuals had arbitrarily subdivided the myriad matters with which justices dealt, and then simply listed the laws uniquely concerned with each arbitrarily defined topic. Burn instead constructed coherent categories for the discussion of the matters subject to the powers of justices and parish officers; and within each category he presented, in the order in which they arose in the performance of the justice's or officer's duty, the steps a justice or officer would take in dealing with each matter, and the law relevant to each step. For instance, in his section on the poor rate Burn began by explaining what the rate was, what purposes it served, who was assessed for the rate, and on the basis of what wealth. He then proceeded to the allowance of the rate by the justices, the procedure for appeal against the rate, and finally the methods of collecting the rate from those who refused to pay. His presentation included the form used to levy distress on the goods of recalcitrant ratepayers. The manual was immediately recognized as authoritative. Sir William Blackstone added a note to his *Commentaries on the Laws of England* declaring that Burn's *Justice* contained 'every thing

relative to this subject, both in ancient and modern practice, collected with great care and accuracy, and disposed in a most clear and judicious method' (bk 1 c.9 iii [354 (1771)]). The thirtieth and last edition of *The Justice* was published in 1869.

In 1760 Burn published two works which again deployed his unique and helpful methods of categorization and explication. *A Digest of the Militia Laws* explained all phases of the organization and production of a county militia as specified by the new Militia Act of 1757 (30 Geo. II c.25) and its subsequent revisions. *Ecclesiastical Law* (2 vols.), which like his justices' manual was a great success, presented the law relevant to matters arising in ecclesiastical courts. This manual reached its ninth and final edition in 1842.

In his later years Burn published a number of lesser works: *A History of the Poor Laws* (1764), which suggested alterations in both the poor laws and other laws relevant to local government, and *Sermons on Practical Subjects* (4 vols., 1776). In 1777, in collaboration with Joseph Nicolson, he published *The History and Antiquities of the Counties of Westmorland and Cumberland* (2 vols.), a work based in part on the collections made by Nicolson's uncle, Dr William Nicolson, bishop of Carlisle. Burn was responsible for compiling the very full account of Westmorland; and his general introduction to Westmorland has been described as 'particularly wide-ranging, containing information on housing, clothing, tenures, and communications' (Currie and Lewis, 97). In 1783 he published a new and ninth edition of Blackstone's *Commentaries* (4 vols.), and subsequently also produced the tenth and eleventh editions. Burn's last publication was posthumous—*A New Law Dictionary* (2 vols., 1792), edited by his son John *Burn (1743/4–1802), magistrate and legal editor, who also edited editions sixteen to nineteen of Burn's *Justice of the Peace*.

NORMA LANDAU

Sources J. Nicolson and R. Burn, *The history and antiquities of the counties of Westmorland and Cumberland*, 1 (1777), 484 · Foster, *Alum. Oxon.* · *GM*, 1st ser., 55 (1785), 922 · Holdsworth, *Eng. law*, 12.333–4, 339, 415, 612 · Nichols, *Illustrations*, 3.586–8 · W. Blackstone, *Commentaries on the laws of England*, 4th edn, 1 (1771), 354 [Book 1 c.9 iii] · C. R. J. Currie and C. P. Lewis, eds., *English county histories: a guide* (1994) · *DNB*
Archives Bodl. Oxf., corresp. | BL, letters to T. Cadell and Charles Lyttelton, Add. MSS 754, 28104, 28167, 34417 · Lancs. RO, corresp. with Thomas West
Likenesses T. Trotter, line engraving, 1791, BM, NPG · engraving?, repro. in H. Bromley, *Catalogue of engraved British portraits* (1793), 358 · engraving?, repro. in E. Evans, *Catalogue of a collection of engraved portraits*, 2 vols. (1836–53)

Burn, Robert (1829–1904), classical scholar and archaeologist, was born at Kynnersley, Shropshire, on 22 October 1829, the second son of Andrew Burn (1790/91–1874), rector of Kynnersley, and his second wife, Mary Harris. He entered Shrewsbury School under B. H. Kennedy in 1843 and Trinity College, Cambridge, in 1849. He had remarkable skill in the writing of Latin hexameter verse. He was senior classic in 1852, and took a second class in natural science in 1853. He was elected a fellow of Trinity in 1854, and spent the rest of his life at Cambridge. He was ordained deacon in 1860 and priest in 1862. For many years he lectured on classical subjects; from 1856 to 1872 he was a tutor of Trinity, and discharged the duties of that office with conspicuous success. He vacated his fellowship on his marriage in 1873 to Augusta Sophia (*née* Prescott), a descendant of Oliver Cromwell. Re-elected fellow in 1874, he was also praelector in Roman archaeology from 1873 to 1885.

Burn, who frequently visited Rome and its neighbourhood during his vacations, was one of the first Englishmen to study the archaeology of the city and the Campagna, and he published several works dealing with it, including *Rome and the Campagna* (1871); *Old Rome* (1880); *Roman Literature in Relation to Roman Art* (1888); and *Ancient Rome and its Neighbourhood* (1895). In 1881 he was president of the Cambridge Antiquarian Society. He received an honorary degree from Glasgow University in 1883.

A member of the Alpine Club, Burn was a distinguished athlete in his youth and a good real tennis player up to middle age. He was one of the first captains of the Cambridge University rifle corps, and he was among the committee of Trinity men who drew up the Cambridge University rules for football in 1863. During the last twenty years of his life he was an invalid confined to a bath chair. He died on 30 April 1904 at his home at St Chad's, Cambridgeshire, and was buried in St Giles's cemetery at Cambridge. There is a brass to his memory in the ante-chapel of Trinity College.   J. D. DUFF, rev. M. C. CURTHOYS

Sources Venn, *Alum. Cant.* · *Cambridge Review* (5 May 1904) · *The Times* (4 May 1904) · P. M. Young, *A history of British football* (1968) · *CGPLA Eng. & Wales* (1904)

Likenesses A. Legros, oils, 1880, FM Cam.

Wealth at death £17,024 0s. 2d.: probate, 17 May 1904, *CGPLA Eng. & Wales*

Burn, William (1789–1870), architect, was born in Edinburgh on 20 December 1789, the fourth and eldest survivor of the sixteen children of Robert Burn (1751–1815) and his wife, Janet Laing (*bap.* 1765). The elder Burn was an architect–builder of the Adam school, with a good practice in medium-sized country houses and a marble works in Leith Walk. Not less importantly, he was also a minor landowner with an estate called Jessfield in North Leith parish. This gave the son an entry to society, and a profound understanding of the landed gentry who were to be his principal clients: as T. L. Donaldson recalled, 'no one could tell with greater spirit many a good story about the auld Scotch lairds and their vagaries' (Donaldson, 122). A father-and-son double portrait (priv. coll.) showing Robert at an easel and William with a portfolio well records the son's slight build and sharp, alert features.

Education and early works Burn was educated at the Royal High School, Edinburgh, and trained as an architect with his father. In 1808 he obtained a place in Sir Robert Smirke's office in London, where he worked on the drawings of Lowther Castle alongside C. R. Cockerell, Henry Roberts, and Lewis Vulliamy. There they received what they later described as 'important lessons', not least the art of dealing with the great landowners and their agents. In Burn's case the lessons also included the business of

building: he was site architect at Covent Garden Theatre, where instructing the contractor Alexander Copeland, one of the giants of the London building world, proved an abrasive experience which was to steel him for the responsibility of having as many as a dozen houses under construction in any one year.

In 1811 Burn returned to Scotland in a similar capacity at Smirke's Kinmount in Dumfriesshire, the plan of which was strongly to influence that of several of his early country houses. His first commission in independent practice was in Renfrewshire. He designed the exchange assembly rooms at Greenock in 1812, but lost the commission for the town hall at Port Glasgow to David Hamilton in 1813. But in the same year his father—as one of the heritors of the parish—managed to change his role from competitor to assessor and awarded him the commission for the very large parish church of North Leith. With its Greek Ionic portico and elegant spire it was the most ambitious classical church built on either side of the border for a decade past and it instantly made his reputation, enabling him to establish an office independent of his father's at 78 (later 131) George Street and, on 3 August 1815, to marry Elizabeth (Eliza) MacVicar. The marriage is said to have been happy, but was saddened by the loss in infancy of two of their seven children. This led to Burn's renting Hermiston on the Riccarton estate for his wife and surviving children; there, as business permitted, he pursued the life of a country gentleman.

Major works In 1816 Burn was among those invited to enter the competition for the completion of Robert Adam's Edinburgh University buildings. He was only narrowly defeated by William Henry Playfair, who had the influential support of his uncle Professor John Playfair. Although Playfair's success was by no means undeserved, the affair left Burn with an abhorrence of competitions and a lifelong dislike of Playfair which became mutual. Their differences were in part political, with Burn being very much the architect of the tory landed gentry and their legal agents and Playfair that of the whig advocates: Burn seldom missed an opportunity of causing him annoyance. Nevertheless, in that same year Burn won a further competition, that for the Merchant Maiden Hospital in Edinburgh, and secured the commission for the custom house at Greenock. At the time the Greek purity and logic of these buildings were revolutionary in the Scottish post-Adam architectural scene, and were paralleled in Edinburgh only by Archibald Elliot's county buildings.

Burn's long career as a country house architect had a rather slower start. In 1814 Dugald Campbell, a schoolfriend, commissioned him to design Gallenach, Argyll, plain post-Adam castellated and little different from his father's houses. But at Craigielands, Dumfriesshire (1817), for William Younger, and the larger Adderston, Northumberland (1819), for Thomas Forster, he designed two very stylish neo-Greek houses with top-lit central saloons on the Kinmount model. The design of

Adderston was further developed at Camperdown, Forfar-shire (1820–26), for the second Viscount Duncan, the elevations of which were simplified Ionic versions of those for William Wilkins's Grange Park, Hampshire. Although Greek revival houses on this scale were to be rare after 1820, Camperdown was a landmark in Scottish, and indeed British, country house design. The private apartments—family bedroom, bathroom, dressing-rooms, breakfast room, and private sitting-room—now formed a clearly identified private wing *en suite* with the garden hall, drawing-room, library, and dining-room, and were carefully ordered in the sequence in which they would be used.

In these same years Burn developed the mastery of Gothic detail he had acquired on the drawings for Low-ther. In 1816 he received the commission to design Bishop Sandford's episcopal chapel of St John on Edinburgh's Princes Street, a neo-Perpendicular church with a west tower and fan-vaulted interior. Equally advanced was the cruciform New Abbey Church at Dunfermline (1818), which recovered something of the lost profile of the medieval abbey. There the principal heritor was the seventh earl of Elgin, who had his forebear Robert the Bruce proudly commemorated in the lettering of the parapet.

In parallel with these Burn designed Dundas Castle, Midlothian (1818), for James Dundas, which still had rather plain Smirke castellated elevations but within had an excellent scheme of public and private apartments arranged round a rib-vaulted hall-corridor. Much bolder was the giant Saltoun, East Lothian (1818–26), for Andrew Fletcher, the lantern-towered main block of which challenged comparison with Taymouth in the stronger, Smirke-inspired cubic forms of its massing, and in the richness and spatial qualities of some of the interiors. But in his succeeding houses Burn again looked more to Wilkins for inspiration. In 1820–21 he designed first Blairquhan, Ayrshire, for Sir David Hunter Blair and then Carstairs, Lanarkshire, for Sir Henry Monteith, large neo-Tudor houses with details fairly closely modelled on those of Wilkins's Dalmeny, Midlothian, and its prototype, the fifteenth-century East Barsham in Norfolk.

In these houses Burn developed with ever-increasing skill a system of composition in which a slightly asymmetrical two-storey main block with a tower was balanced by a lower service wing: in the largest houses there was usually a secondary tower and sometimes a turret as well, which marked that important convenience the luggage entrance. The neo-Tudor of Carstairs was perfected at Garscube, Dunbartonshire (1826), for Sir Archibald Campbell and then developed into neo-Jacobean at Fettercairn, Kincardineshire (1827), for the banker Sir William Forbes, the huge Dupplin, Perthshire (1828), for the eleventh earl of Kinnoul, and St Fort, Fife (1829), for A. C. Stewart. With details taken from Westwood, Worcestershire, and Aston Hall, Warwickshire, the last two were the most accomplished neo-Jacobean houses built in the United Kingdom before 1830, but their importance lies as much in the development of Burn's plan-forms, which became ever more concerned with domestic comfort. His houses were now seldom higher than two storeys and attic, and high galleried central saloons were given up in favour of hall-corridor plans, often single-aspect with symmetrically arranged principal apartments completely out of sight from the entrance. The private wing was either stepped forward or, more usually, back to create sheltered private garden areas; and the service wing or stable court deployed at right-angles to the main block to form an equally sheltered forecourt. In these houses the service areas developed ever greater sophistication, with male and female lines of communication kept strictly separate, the juxtaposition of rectangular rooms, corridors, and stairs fitting together, as Jill Franklin observed, 'as neatly as the cells in a beehive both in vertical and horizontal relationships' (Franklin, 153). The principal interiors tended to be relatively simple, with good Louis Quinze chimney-pieces, more designed for hanging pictures than architectural display, though Dupplin had particularly good Jacobean ceilings.

Burn's skills were not confined to new houses. Much of his reputation was based on his resourceful rearrangement of older houses to achieve contemporary standards of comfort and service; his work at Castle of Mey, Caithness (1819), for the twelfth earl of Caithness is a very early example, which led to fairly tactful additions at Pinkie (1825) for Sir John Hope and the complete reconstruction of the great medieval castle of Dalhousie (1826) for the tenth earl of Dalhousie, both in Midlothian.

A similar reconstruction at Freeland, Perthshire (1825), for Lord Ruthven, brought Burn into contact with Edward Blore, who was then pioneering the Cotswold Tudor revival at Corehouse, Lanarkshire (1824–7). In Corehouse, Burn saw the answer to the design of the smaller picturesque country house and built several 'cottage houses' in Perthshire, all set on picturesquely wooded hillside sites, the best of which was Snaigow (1827) for Mrs Keay. Although Lord Cockburn, who had rejected Burn's designs for one at Bonaly in favour of a Scots tower-house by Playfair, disapproved of cottage-houses in his *Circuit Journeys*, observing that none were 'in keeping with a rough climate and situations of romantic wilderness', the Burn cottage-house in plain sash-windowed form proved very popular and in the hands of his pupils was to become a universal Scottish house-type throughout the 1840s and 1850s.

Throughout the 1820s Burn designed a considerable number of churches and repaired or restored several others. The most notable instance was the controversial refacement of St Giles, Edinburgh (1829–32), which was, however, necessary to save the building from at least partial collapse. In 1824 he replanned the central area of Dundee, and his proposals for new streets were implemented between 1827 and 1844 under an Improvement Act of 1825. Major public buildings included the Greek Doric Edinburgh Academy (1823–36) and John Watson's Hospital (1825–8), both in Edinburgh, and a number of provincial bank offices, mainly for the Bank of Scotland; he also became a specialist in the design of mental institutions, beginning in 1825 with the Murray Royal at Perth, the basic design of which was later developed at the Crichton Institution at Dumfries (1835) and Edinburgh's West House (1839). At Tanfield, Edinburgh, in 1824 he designed a very remarkable Italianate gasworks which drew the admiration of Karl Friedrich Schinkel, and still more importantly brought him into contact with Sir Walter Scott, through whose influence he secured the patronage of the fifth duke of Buccleuch in 1828. In doing so, Burn forestalled Atkinson's planned remodelling of the late Stuart palace of Drumlanrig, Dumfriesshire, the interior of which he tactfully adapted. For the duke Burn also designed a great many buildings on the Buccleuch estates, most notably the fine churches at Dalkeith, Morton, and Langholm, additions at Bowhill, Selkirkshire, and a complete town at Granton Harbour in 1838.

Scott's guidance also resulted in a change of approach to the remodelling of old Scots houses. At Riccarton, Midlothian (1823), for Sir William Gibson Craig the ancient tower-house had been Tudorized, but at Lauriston, Midlothian (1827), for Scott's friend Tom Allan, the old tower-house was respected for what it was with a restored roof-line. By 1829 at Milton Lockhart, Lanarkshire, his neo-Jacobean houses were acquiring Scottish features and by 1836 he was designing additions in an accomplished late sixteenth-century turreted idiom to complement houses of that date at Stenhouse, Stirlingshire, and Castle Menzies, Perthshire.

The average Burn house of the earlier 1830s was, however, simple two-storey neo-Jacobean with fairly standard plan-forms and elevations enlivened by handsome mannerist or baroque doorpieces, and window, gable, and chimney-head details which varied according to the means of the client. Very few were turreted, but even the plainest had a gentlemanly look about them. His one really large country house commission of the earlier 1830s, the neo-Jacobean scheme for the remodelling of Dalkeith (1831 onwards), which was clearly commissioned to remind the duchess of her parents' Longleat, never got beyond the splendid model made by George Meikle Kemp: the baroque palace of 1702–10 was adapted for modern living in the same low-key way as Drumlanrig. But in 1838 Burn was called upon to complete Harlaxton, Lincolnshire, Salvin's great neo-Jacobean palace for Gregory Gregory. To what extent he inherited arrangements already made for its continental baroque interiors remains a mystery, but his experience there led directly to a magnificent series of neo-Jacobean houses: Falkland, Fife, for Mrs Tyndall Bruce, Whitehill, Midlothian, for Wardlaw Ramsay, and Muckross, Kerry, for H. A. Herbert (all begun in 1839); Stoke Rochford (1841) for Christopher Turner, South Rauceby (1842) for Anthony Willson, and Revesby (1844) for J. Banks Stanhope (all Gregory's Lincolnshire neighbours); and Dartrey, co. Monaghan (1844–6), the largest of the series, for Lord Cremorne, later first earl of Dartrey. Except for the last, all of these houses had basically similar plan-forms reversed or rearranged according to the site and the needs of the client, but their rich repertory of Jacobean detail and resourceful interchange of gables, towers, and oriels avoided any one house having too close

a resemblance to another. All had great formal gardens with parterres, elevated above the surrounding landscape.

Throughout the 1830s Burn had maintained a general practice. He was never so original a Greek revivalist as Playfair, and a visit to London in 1833 to survey the London club-houses in connection with his commission to design the New Club, Edinburgh (1834), made him realize that neo-Greek was shortly to be superseded by the Italian Renaissance of Charles Barry and his circle. The palazzo formula for the club quickly spread to Scottish bank, insurance, hotel, and other commercial buildings, notably at Burn's own Granton Square (1838) and North British and Edinburgh Life Insurance offices in Edinburgh (1841 and 1843); but in some of his provincial public buildings Burn broke with the classical tradition and adopted the neo-Jacobean idiom of his country houses, as at the county buildings, Haddington (1833), and the outstanding Madras College, St Andrews (1832). Very exceptionally, the county buildings at Inverness Castle were castellated in response to the site, their style taken from Smirke's citadel at Carlisle.

London practice With the remodelling of Raby Castle, co. Durham (1843–7), in hand for the second duke of Cleveland, and Prestwold, Leicestershire (1843), being recast as a palazzo for C. W. Packe, the balance of Burn's practice had shifted southwards. In 1844 he moved house and office to 6 Stratton Street, Piccadilly, leaving David Bryce, his partner since 1841, in charge of the Scottish practice at 131 George Street. In London he sought out Robert William Billings and advanced £1000 to induce him to undertake *The Baronial and Ecclesiastical Antiquities of Scotland* (4 vols., 1845–52), which was to be the source book for the Scottish baronial revival for the next half-century. Problems soon arose with both partnerships, and that with Bryce was closed in 1850. The reasons for the break-up of the Bryce partnership were complex and in part related to problems at the duchess's chapel at Dalkeith: but the more fundamental reasons appear to have been that in London, Burn concentrated exclusively on domestic work, suggesting others of whom he approved for such public and commercial commissions which came his way, most notably that for Wellington College, where he recommended John Shaw. In Edinburgh, by contrast, Bryce was continuing to run a general practice which was more profitable than the London one. Moreover, the partners were now being separately commissioned to design houses in Scotland, which inevitably led to friction, and the volume of English and Irish commissions for completely new houses was not sustained after 1846. Burn's London career was more notable for its clientele than for actual building, a roll-call of dukes, marquesses, earls, viscounts, and baronets, for whom some forty houses were made more comfortable, commodious, and better-serviced for the constant round of house guests. The more important of these commissions were the short-lived reconstruction of Eaton Hall, Cheshire (1846–51), for the second marquess of Westminster, the very successful neo-Tudor reconstruction of Taplow Court, Buckinghamshire

(1855), for C. Pascoe Grenfell, and the stylish Italianization of Somerley, Hampshire (1868–74), for the earl of Normanton.

Burn's London career had in fact commenced much more auspiciously. The mighty Franco-Scottish château he planned at Fonthill, Wiltshire, for the marquess of Westminster in 1847–9 would have been the finest building of his whole career, but it was cancelled in 1856 in favour of a more modest house. The grandest of his later neo-Jacobean houses should have been Eastwell, Kent, for the tenth earl of Winchilsea (1848), but the main block was never constructed. The only neo-Jacobean houses built south of the border to approach those of the earlier 1840s were Amport, Hampshire (1855), for the marquess of Winchester, and Lynford, Norfolk (1859), for S. Lyne Stephens, the latter with a particularly fine garden by W. A. Nesfield. Idsworth, Hampshire (1848), for Sir J. Clarke-Jervoise, Sandon, Staffordshire (1852–5), for the earl of Harrowby, and the very similar Rendlesham, Norfolk (1868–71), for Lord Rendlesham represented a different line of approach to neo-Jacobean design with plate glass rather than mullioned windows, very much on the model of some of the Scottish houses of the 1830s. Of the same type would have been Watcombe, Devon, designed in 1854 for Isambard Kingdom Brunel and abandoned just above foundation level in 1859. Unsurprisingly, some of the best houses of these later years were either in Scotland or for Scottish clients: Poltalloch, Argyll (1849), for Neil Malcolm, one of his best Jacobean houses; Dunira, Perthshire (1851–2), for Sir David Dundas; and Buchanan, Stirlingshire (1854–8) for the fourth duke of Montrose, where the concept of the first Fonthill scheme was partly realized. Easily the finest building of these later years was the duke of Buccleuch's great château of Montagu House, Whitehall, where Burn deployed all his architectural and decorative skills in a vain attempt to win the favour of the duchess.

The loyalty Burn commanded from his clients, even in such difficult circumstances as the duke's, was very much based on his personal qualities: he was, again in Donaldson's words,

> frank and plain spoken, occasionally even to roughness … no flatterer … somewhat impulsive and gifted with great shrewdness and common sense … he was a man of the highest integrity and independence, and so far from leading his clients into any needless or extravagant outlay, he would demur at any expense beyond his employers' means. (Donaldson, 124)

Not less importantly, he respected the privacy of his clients. Although he accepted election as a fellow of the Institute of British Architects in 1835, and co-founded the Institute of Architects in Scotland, with the duke of Buccleuch as president in 1840, he never allowed his work to be published and had refused election to the Royal Scottish Academy in 1829 rather than exhibit. All knowledge of the planning of his houses was strictly confined to those who commissioned them and those who worked on them: the unauthorized publication of the plans of Buchanan in

Robert Kerr's *The Gentleman's House* resulted in a strongly worded letter of complaint to the Royal Institute in 1865. Yet for all his reticence he was prepared to undertake public duties if asked. On the retirement of Edward Blore in 1849 he became consulting architect to the government in Scotland and in that capacity advised on the rebuilding of King's College, Aberdeen, in 1854 and designed the short-lived Glasgow post office of 1855. More important, he was the key juror in the Whitehall competitions of 1857 and 1858, and having himself placed George Gilbert Scott second in both competitions, concluded that the commission for the combined project should be Scott's, observing that the issue of style 'did not operate' in his mind, only that the plans 'were the best and most suitable' (Port, 198).

Those brief comments summed up Burn's attitude to design. However sensitive he may have been to changing fashions, his buildings were essentially about fitness for purpose: no architect before him had thought quite so profoundly about how buildings should function, and the sheer logic of his planning, with its neat resolutions of all manner of complexities and pioneer elements of standardization, testifies to his formidable intellect. His office had an important teaching role. Many of the leading Scottish architects in the period 1840–80 had spent time in his office, and spread his plan-types throughout the land. In London his pupils included Richard Norman Shaw, William Eden Nesfield, and the architect–historian David MacGibbon.

Burn died at home at 6 Stratton Street on 15 February 1870 and was buried at Kensal Green on 19 February. His wife survived him. The practice was continued by his wife's nephew John MacVicar Anderson (1835–1915), with the continued assistance of Burn's chief clerk, William Bunn Colling (1813/14–1886).　　DAVID M. WALKER

Sources T. L. Donaldson, 'Memoir of the late William Burn, fellow', *Transactions of the Royal Institute of British Architects* (1869–70), 121–9 · *The Builder*, 28 (1870), 189, 231 · J. Cunliffe, 'The relationship between architect builder and client with particular reference to William Burn's early practice', diss., U. Edin., 1976 · I. Ozols, 'Aspects of urban development and public buildings in Dundee, circa 1820–34', diss., U. St Andr., 1983 · D. Walker, 'William Burn and the influence of Sir Robert Smirke and William Wilkins on Scottish Greek revival design, 1810–1840', *Scottish pioneers of the Greek revival*, ed. N. Allen (1984), 3–35 · D. Walker, 'William Burn: the country house in transition', *Seven Victorian architects*, ed. J. Fawcett (1976) · D. Walker, 'William Burn', *The Victorian great house*, ed. M. Airs (1990) · V. Fiddes and A. Rowan, *Mr David Bryce: David Bryce, 1803–76* (1976) · M. Girouard, *The Victorian country house*, rev. edn (1979) · J. Franklin, *The gentleman's country house and its plan, 1835–1914* (1981) · Colvin, *Archs.* · M. H. Port, *Imperial London: civil government building in London, 1850–1915* (1995) · CGPLA Eng. & Wales (1870) · private information (2004)

Archives Lpool RO, letters to the fourteenth earl of Derby · NA Scot., letters to the duke of Buccleuch · NL Scot., corresp. relating to the national monument

Likenesses T. Campbell, marble bust, 1834, Royal Incorporation of Architects in Scotland, Edinburgh · plaster cast, 1836 (after T. Campbell, 1834), RIBA, drawings collection · double portrait (with Robert Burn), priv. coll. · photograph, Madras College, St Andrews · photographs, RIBA

Wealth at death under £40,000: probate, 25 March 1870, CGPLA Eng. & Wales

Burn, William Laurence (1904–1966), historian and lawyer, was born on 15 October 1904 at Bombay House, Angate Street, Wolsingham, co. Durham, the only son of Laurence Burn (1864–1920) and his wife, Annie (1871–1931), daughter of William Coates of Oakcroft, Wolsingham. Burn's father was a minor landowner and tradesman, possessing a local quasi-patriarchal position which his son was to inherit. Burn was educated at Wolsingham grammar school (1914–19), Durham School (1919–22), and Merton College, Oxford (1922–5). He graduated with a second-class degree in modern history in 1925 and was appointed assistant in history at the University of St Andrews. In 1929 he became assistant lecturer in colonial and American history. While a Rockefeller fellow in America in 1932–3 he married (in the latter year) Alice (1902–1970), eldest daughter of John Proud of Wolsingham. Their son, Nicholas, was born in 1936. In 1932 Burn was called to the bar (Inner Temple), and for the remainder of his life historical scholarship and the law provided twin strands to his career.

During his ten years at St Andrews, Burn established himself as a historian. His main achievement there was the publication in 1937 of *Emancipation and Apprenticeship in the British West Indies*. Many years later this was still seen as 'a scholarly monograph and the definitive work on apprenticeship' (E. Williams, *From Columbus to Castro*, 1970, 545). Already a distinctive quality which combined his two main interests, history and law, was apparent, for his starting point was the act of 1833 which emancipated the slaves. He posed the questions, 'How does the statute emerge, in the end, from the mill of human obstinacy, apathy and selfishness? Are its results such that, had they been accurately foreseen, it would ever have been passed?' (*Emancipation and Apprenticeship*, 7).

Nevertheless, despite scholarly distinction, Burn's years at St Andrews were not entirely congenial. The role of junior staff at Scottish universities was distinctly subordinate. Initially he was essentially an assistant to the lecturer in modern history, and even after his position improved in 1929 he 'filled in the many gaps left by the Professor'. Moreover, that academic community was far from harmonious. Burn made many friends and earned a reputation as an excellent teacher, but he also experienced what he later described as 'old rancour' there (letter to Knox, 20 Dec 1938). In 1937 he resigned and returned home to practise as a barrister on the north-eastern circuit and in the Durham chancery court. This did not involve abandoning his historical interests, and he always envisaged a return to academic life.

In the years immediately before the Second World War Burn clear-sightedly appreciated that war was coming, and enlisted in the army reserve. In 1940 he was called up as a second lieutenant in the Royal Army Service Corps, but his army service proved short-lived. Injured during a parachute descent early in 1941 he contracted phlebitis. He was invalided from the army but was seconded to work in the research department of the Foreign Office. He was one of several distinguished historians employed there, and late in 1943 some of them, including Arnold Toynbee, backed him strongly for a history chair at King's College, Newcastle, in the University of Durham. He hesitated before deciding to accept, but in 1944 took up the chair which he held for the rest of his life.

Burn made a major contribution to what became, in 1963, the University of Newcastle upon Tyne, by his teaching, his research and publications, and his administrative services. He was largely responsible for the key decision to constitute the senate of the new university as a small body capable of effective executive action rather than as a large and unwieldy assembly. Perhaps even more important, he informally provided counsel to many colleagues. As head of department he was respected and liked by colleagues and students alike. His lectures were popular, interesting, and perceptive. He was a sought-after external examiner, and held visiting appointments at places as diverse as University College, Ibadan, and Johns Hopkins University. He served on the council of the Royal Historical Society from 1954 to 1957, and also on several government commissions.

During his Newcastle tenure Burn consolidated a reputation as a distinguished scholar, although now his interests had moved to mainstream British history. He was in frequent demand as a reviewer and contributor to historical journals. In a review article in 1953 he wrote of Britain after 1832 that

> There was always plenty, perhaps a majority, of competent, business-like, not too sensitive or scrupulous persons, who took the world as they found it and set themselves to squeeze money or power or position out of it. They were not, perhaps, the most admirable of mankind but they conducted into safer channels feelings which, if left to themselves, might have disrupted society. (*Twentieth-Century*, 144.127)

His most significant publication was *The Age of Equipoise: a Study of the Mid-Victorian Generation* (1964), described by one scholar as 'full of learning, sympathy, insights and wisdom' (D. E. D. Beales, *Historical Journal*, 8, 1965, 418). Another distinguished writer commented:

> To capacious reading, wise discernment, and a scholar's handling of evidence, are added the less usual accompaniments of lightness of touch, visual imagination, and an occasional use of almost impressionistic technique which few professional historians could have devised and fewer would have attempted. (N. Gash, *Alumnus Chronicle*, St Andrews, June 1964, 24.5)

It was an idiosyncratic work, and the author's command of the law as well as of history was evident. The breadth of coverage involved reflected an immense amount of reading in primary sources (a personal affection for Surtees and Trollope was part of his make-up). The book's title was expanded by the appreciation that 'If there was equipoise it was not deliberately planned or contrived. It was the outcome of a temporary balance of forces, but of forces, struggling, pushing, shoving to better their positions' (*Age of Equipoise*, 82). At the time the left-wing 'labour history' approach associated with authors like E. J. Hobsbawm and E. P. Thompson was at its height, and *The Age of Equipoise*, together with works by such historians as G. Kitson Clark, O. MacDonagh, and D. Roberts, provided useful balancing factors. Burn's sudden death in 1966 was a blow to historical scholarship, involving the loss of two important projects to which he had turned, one a replacement of the volume for 1870–1914 in the *Oxford History of England* and the other a major study of Anglo-Irish relations. The president of the Royal Historical Society offered this tribute:

> He brought to his historical studies a first-hand knowledge and understanding of the law, of local government, of public administration, and of county or country society at all levels. He brought also a broad humanity, a sturdy common sense, an ironic wit, an aversion from humbug, and a profound insight into the complexities of human nature and of social and intellectual life. (*The Times*, 19 July 1966)

Burn's university work was only part of a busy and varied life. Under the pen-name Richard Sheldon, he wrote two detective novels, *Poor Prisoner's Defence* (1949) and *Harsh Evidence* (1950). The latter is much the better of the pair, being written around an imaginary murder trial of 1874; suspense is skilfully built up and lasts until the final verdict at the end. In his early years at Newcastle University commitments still allowed a parallel part-time career as a judge. A Durham county magistrate from 1946, he became deputy chairman of quarter sessions in 1953 and chairman in 1958. This was an important part of his contribution to his home region, but he also served on a variety of local government, farming, and public service institutions. As time went by his commitments became increasingly onerous. The university needed more of his time, and judicial duties grew even more. An observer noted that 'He often looked exhausted, as he sat, by the hour, patiently listening to the crimes of the county paraded before him day by day' (*Northern Echo*, 12 July 1966). His health was increasingly threatened, and on 11 July 1966 he died at Dryburn Hospital, Durham, following a sudden heart attack while on his way from his home to Newcastle. His funeral in Wolsingham parish church on 14 July was a most impressive demonstration of the respect and affection felt for him over a wide range of the region's society. He was buried in the churchyard.

Burn was a devout Anglican, and a churchwarden for many years. In politics he was a staunch Conservative, resigning from a local hospital board after the minister of health, Aneurin Bevan, made a notorious speech describing Conservatives as 'vermin'. He distrusted the state, noting in 1938 that it was 'surely the proper initial step, to believe the government wrong and to resolve upon minimizing whatever amount of power over yourself you are obliged to hand over to them' (Burn to Knox, 13 March 1938). In late 1941 he wrote that 'One great fear that I have is the spread of what I call democratic totalitarianism—the totalitarianism of Bevin and Morrison—in this country after the war' (Burn to Knox, 22 Dec 1941). His writings and his conversation were spiced with a pleasing dry wit, and he was a very agreeable companion.

NORMAN MCCORD

Sources *The Times* (12 July 1966) · *The Times* (15 July 1966) · *The Times* (19 July 1966) · *Gazette* [U. Newcastle] (Aug 1966) · *Northern Echo* (12 July 1966) · N. Gash, 'A Victorian miniaturist', *Alumnus Chronicle* [U. St Andr.], 55 (1964), 24–5 · J. Hart, 'Nineteenth-century social reform: a tory interpretation of history', *Past and Present*, 31 (1965), 39–61 · *The Phoenix* [Wolsingham grammar school magazine] · W. L. Burn, letters to Sir T. M. Knox, U. St Andr. L. · personal knowledge (2004) · private information (2004) [N. Gash; B. W. Beckingsale; J. M. Taylor; R. Hopkinson; L. Lister] · *WWW*, 1961–70 · b. cert. · d. cert. · *CGPLA Eng. & Wales* (1966) · tombstone, Wolsingham parish church
Archives U. Newcastle | U. St Andr. L., letters to Sir T. M. Knox · Wolsingham grammar school, co. Durham, school records
Wealth at death £31,999: probate, 16 Nov 1966, *CGPLA Eng. & Wales*

Burnaby, Andrew (1732–1812), Church of England clergyman and traveller, was born at Asfordby, Leicestershire, on 16 August 1732, the eldest son of Andrew Burnaby (1702–1776) of Brampton Manor, Huntingdonshire, and his wife, Hannah (*d.* 1757), daughter of George Beaumont of Darton, Yorkshire. His father was one of several members of the Burnaby family who were rectors of Asfordby, and later became also a prebendary of Lincoln Cathedral. Andrew was educated at Westminster School and at Queens' College, Cambridge, where he received the degrees of BA (1754), MA (1757), and DD (1776). He was ordained deacon (1755) and priest (1756) by the bishop of Lincoln. As a young man he travelled widely, and in later years produced two books giving accounts of his travels. The first, published in 1775, was entitled *Travels through the middle settlements in North America in the years 1759–60, with observations on the state of the colonies*. This book, which Burnaby considerably enlarged for a third edition in 1798, gave much information on the animals and birds of North America and its climate, but as regards the political situation Burnaby was to be proved a false prophet: he thought a permanent union of the colonies would be impossible because of their disagreements and mutual jealousies.

From about 1762 to 1767 Burnaby was chaplain to the British factory at Leghorn, in the grand duchy of Tuscany. He was also acting as pro-consul there in the absence of the consul, Sir John Dick, when in 1767 the Jesuits were expelled from Naples, and ships transporting them were caught in heavy storms off Leghorn. The grand duke had given orders that they should not land in his territory, but Burnaby, who was horrified by their treatment, interceded on their behalf and they were permitted to do so until the storms had abated. From Leghorn, Burnaby toured Italy, and in 1766 visited Corsica with Frederick Augustus Hervey, commencing a lifelong interest in Corsican affairs and a friendship with the patriot leader Pasquale Paoli, though it was not until 1804 that he published his second book, *Journal of a Tour to Corsica in the Year 1766*. He wrote descriptively, even giving details of the numerous local wines, and with touches of humour, but the actual journal accounted for only 32 pages of the volume, as 125 pages consisted of Paoli's letters to the author over the intervening years. Besides his two books, several of Burnaby's sermons (one of which, in 1777, bore the title 'Moral advantages to be derived from travelling in Italy') were printed, and a collected volume of his sermons and charges appeared in 1805.

After his return from Italy, Burnaby received from the crown in 1769 the vicarage of Greenwich, which he retained until his death. He married, on 26 February 1770, Anna (*bap.* 1735, *d.* 1812), daughter and heir of John Edwyn of Baggrave Hall, Hungarton, Leicestershire. They had four sons and one daughter; their eldest son was the grandfather of the traveller Frederick Gustavus Burnaby and the great-great-great-grandfather of Queen Elizabeth, the consort of King George VI. Burnaby inherited property in Huntingdonshire when his father died in 1776, but resided mostly at Baggrave or at Blackheath, near Greenwich. In 1786 he was appointed archdeacon of Leicester by Bishop Thurlow of Lincoln. He carried out thorough visitations in his archdeaconry and acted as spokesman for the local clergy in opposition to the slave trade. Andrew Burnaby died at Blackheath on 9 March 1812. His wife survived him only ten days, and they were both buried at Hungarton parish church, near Baggrave Hall, on 31 March. A memorial tablet with a long epitaph was erected in St Alfege, Greenwich.   T. Y. COCKS

Sources J. Nichols, *The history and antiquities of the county of Leicester*, 1 (1795–1815), 466; 2 (1795–8), 288 · Venn, *Alum. Cant.* · 'The archdeacons of Leicester, 1092–1992', *Leicestershire Archaeological and Historical Society Transactions*, 67 (1993) · *GM*, 1st ser., 82/1 (1812), 301–2 · *Old Westminsters* · *DNB* · Burke, *Gen. GB* (1952) · parish register, Asfordby, All Saints, 31 Aug 1732, Leics. RO [baptism] · parish register, Hungarton, Leics., 15 Oct 1735, Leics. RO [baptism] · parish register, Hungarton, Leicestershire, 31 March 1812 [burial]
Likenesses oils, 1789, Leicester City Museum, Leicester

Burnaby, Frederick Gustavus (1842–1885), army officer and traveller, was born at the old rectory, St Peter's Green, Bedford, on 3 March 1842, the elder son of the Revd Gustavus Andrew Burnaby (1802–1872) of Somerby Hall, near Oakham, Rutland, rector of St Peter's, Bedford, and chaplain to the duke of Cambridge, a wealthy land-owning tory 'squarson', 'a fox-hunting parson of the old school' (Wright, 2), and his wife, Harriet (*d.* 1883), daughter of Henry Villebois of Marham House, Norfolk. Both Burnaby's godfathers were masters of foxhounds. He claimed descent from King Edward I, his hero. Burnaby's family wealth made possible his career and adventures.

Burnaby, called Fred by family and friends, was educated at Bedford grammar school, the Revd Charles Arnold's school at Tinwell near Stamford (1852–5), Harrow School (1855–7), Oswestry School (1857–9), and privately at Dresden, where he studied languages, for which he had shown exceptional aptitude at school. In later years he was proficient in the main European languages and Russian, and could speak some Arabic and Turkish.

At the age of sixteen Burnaby passed the army examination, and on 30 September 1859 became by purchase—the regulation price was £1200—a cornet in the Royal Horse Guards (the Blues). He became, also by purchase, lieutenant in 1861 and captain in 1866. Household Cavalry officers enjoyed much leave, which enabled him to travel far. As a young man he was 'the modern Hercules': of exceptional size—6 feet 4 inches tall with a 46 inch chest—and strength. He was probably the strongest man in the army, and excelled at gymnastics, weight-lifting, fencing, and boxing. His regimental nickname was 'Heenan', after the prizefighter, and various stories were told of his feats of strength. Although he was proudly English, his appearance—with his sallow complexion, dark hair, and moustache—was that of 'an Italian baritone'

Frederick Gustavus Burnaby (1842–1885), by James Tissot, 1870

with 'a suggestion of the Hebrew physiognomy' (Ware and Mann, 337). He disliked his own appearance, and his voice was thin and piercing. His health was poor and he suffered from liver trouble, apparently exacerbated by excessive, unwise exertion, diet—including one of fat bacon for a month—and strong cigars.

Burnaby's tastes were relatively bohemian, and his civilian clothes slovenly: one contemporary wrote 'Perhaps there is no man in the Service who off parade looks less like a British cavalry officer' (Alexander, 82). The 1870 Tissot portrait (later in the National Portrait Gallery) shows an atypical elegance and atypical waxed moustache. His friends and acquaintances included journalists, notably his great friend Thomas Gibson Bowles, whom in 1868 he helped found the weekly *Vanity Fair*, and Edmund Yates. Burnaby contributed intermittently to the press, despite the disapproval of the duke of Cambridge and other senior officers.

In 1868 Burnaby visited Spain and Tangier, and in 1870 Russia. In 1873 he contracted typhoid in Naples and was saved, apparently, by his mother who travelled out to nurse him. In 1874, accredited as a *Times* correspondent, he visited the Spanish Civil War and reported on the Carlists, beginning a lasting friendship with Don Carlos. In early 1875, again accredited as a *Times* correspondent, he travelled to Khartoum and then to Sobat, where he briefly met Gordon, who disliked journalists and did not welcome him.

In 1875, on leave again, Burnaby departed from London on 30 November and in the winter travelled through Russia and central Asia, enduring intense cold and frostbite. Evading Russian officials, and accompanied by a dwarf Tartar servant, in January 1876 he reached Khiva and was welcomed by the khan.

Back in England Burnaby was lionized, and summoned by the queen to dinner at Windsor. He published *A Ride to Khiva* (1876), which he sold outright for £750. It was a vivid, lively travelogue, proudly British, in which he warned against Russian aggressive expansion through central Asia towards India, and denounced Russian rule as despotic, corrupt, and cruel. The book, vigorously advertised, sold well and was reprinted and translated. His journey and book made Burnaby a celebrity. From then on he was repeatedly featured in the gossip columns and in cartoons, often with a box of Cockle's pills, which he had praised in his book as 'a most invaluable medicine, and one which I have used on the natives of Central Africa with the greatest possible success' (Burnaby, *Khiva*, 13). Messrs James Cockle & Co. sent him a cheque for £100, which he gave to charity, and for years afterwards quoted him in their advertisements.

At the time of controversy in Britain over the Eastern question, in the winter of 1876–7, Burnaby, on leave, travelled in Turkish-ruled Asia Minor. With his faithful soldier-servant George Radford, he went from Constantinople via Angora to Kars and Batumi. He was welcomed by Turkish officials and others, hoping for British support against Russia. He wrote *On Horseback through Asia Minor* (2

vols., 1877). Another proudly British travelogue, its message was pro-Turkish and anti-Russian, asserting that, despite faults, Turkish rule was better than Russian, and that Russia was a threat to India. While he was writing the book the Russo-Turkish War began, and he demanded British support for Turkey. The publisher paid him £2500 plus further royalties and, despite radical criticism, his 'panegyric upon the pashas' (Alexander, 93) sold well.

Determined to see the Russo-Turkish War, later in 1877 Burnaby obtained accreditation as a 'travelling agent' of the Stafford House committee (formed by the duke of Sutherland and others to provide medical services for the Turks). He went to Bulgaria, originally intending to reach Plevna. He joined his friend Valentine Baker, a major-general in the Turkish army, and in the bitter winter accompanied him on the retreat through the Balkan Mountains, at the battle of Tashkesan (31 December 1877), and on the retreat over the Rhodope Mountains, suffering from cold and harsh conditions, to the Aegean coast. Baker and Burnaby stayed at the house of the Greek archbishop at Gumurdjina and were poisoned with arsenic, apparently by a Bulgarian acolyte, but were saved by Baker's British doctor, Dr Gill. By the time they reached Constantinople an armistice had been declared. Burnaby wrote to his brother on 17 February 1878, 'And so England does not mean to fight for Constantinople after all! What a lot of shopkeepers we are! The country would seem to have lost all its backbone!' (Alexander, 111).

Burnaby returned with Radford to England. Radford, weakened by the hardships of the retreat, had contracted typhus, and died in Burnaby's arms at Dover on 22 February 1878. Burnaby's widow later wrote that Burnaby 'felt deeply the death of one who had been rather a friend than a servant' (Le Blond, 50). After Radford's death Burnaby reportedly 'never quite recovered his gaiety' (Ware and Mann, 167). Burnaby made repeated, but unsuccessful, attempts to obtain Baker's reinstatement in the British army. His trust in Baker was shown by him later, in his will, nominating Baker the guardian of his son in the event of his widow's death.

On 25 June 1879 Burnaby married, at St Peter's Church, Onslow Gardens, London, Elizabeth Alice Frances (*d.* 27 July 1934), only child of Sir St Vincent Bentinck Hawkins-Whitshed, bt, of Killoncarrick, Greystones, co. Wicklow. She was an eighteen-year-old Irish landowning heiress of 'piquant beauty', and related to the dukes of Portland. She and Burnaby had one child, Harry Arthur Gustavus St Vincent, born on 10 May 1880. She suffered from lung trouble, diagnosed as consumption, and so lived apart from Burnaby in Switzerland: during their married life they spent only about one year together. After Burnaby's death she twice remarried, and was best known as Mrs Aubrey Le Blond [*see* Le Blond, Elizabeth Alice Frances]. That she was an Irish landowner may well have influenced Burnaby's attitudes to Irish policy.

Adventurous and excited by danger, Burnaby became an enthusiastic balloonist. He made his first ascent in July 1864, and reportedly made nineteen in all. He was an early member of the Aeronautical Society (founded 1866) and became a member of its council. On 23 March 1882 he crossed the channel in the gas balloon *Eclipse*, from Dover to Normandy, gaining much publicity. He described his flight in a shilling publication *A Ride across the Channel* (1882), for which the publisher paid him £250. In this, and in his May 1884 *Fortnightly Review* article, 'Possibilities of ballooning', he advocated the military use of observation balloons, and claimed that the future of aviation lay with heavier-than-air craft.

Burnaby inherited his father's toryism, and this was strengthened by his admiration of Disraeli's foreign and imperial policy, and his loathing of Gladstone's, which he believed weak, contrary to British imperial interests, and pro-Russian. He sent Disraeli copies of his Khiva and Asia Minor books. Attempting to enter parliament, he chose to contest the radical stronghold of Birmingham, whose MPs included Bright and Chamberlain. Adopted as a candidate in July 1878, he appealed to 'tory democracy' and claimed, 'with the help of the Conservative working man I shall yet carry Birmingham' (Wright, 153). In the 1880 election he campaigned vigorously, against violent opposition, and attacked Gladstone and his supporters as friends of Russian despotism. He was not elected, but gained 15,735 votes. From then on he alternated political campaigning with his other activities.

Burnaby's politics mixed an idiosyncratic, populistic, pugnacious and opportunist 'tory democracy' similar to and presumably influenced by that of Lord Randolph Churchill, with traditional right-wing landed toryism. He repeatedly attacked Gladstone who, he alleged, 'calls black one day what he calls white another' (Ware and Mann, 235). He favoured protection, purchase of commissions, and army flogging, though on that emotive issue he was evasive in public. He demanded martial law and crown colony government in Ireland. Like Churchill, he denounced the 1882 Egyptian campaign as 'solely on account of the bondholders' (Ware and Mann, 193), though apparently he did not know of Gladstone's own large holding of 'Egyptian' bonds, which would have strengthened his case. In 1883 he was one of the pioneers of the Primrose League, opposing Churchill's proposal that it be a semi-secret society, and he and Churchill agreed to jointly contest Birmingham. In 1884 he was elected to the councils of both the Primrose League and the National Union of Conservative Associations. He demanded a Gordon relief expedition and alleged that 'Gordon may die in order to let Mr Gladstone's Government live' (Ware and Mann, 285). When attending the sometimes violent political meetings Burnaby carried a large stick, and it became the custom for his admirers to present him with sticks, some inscribed. He accumulated a large collection.

Burnaby was promoted major in July 1879, lieutenant-colonel in September 1880, and colonel in September 1884. In 1881 he was promoted regimental lieutenant-colonel, commanding the Blues. In 1882 he wanted to serve in the Egyptian campaign, but was disappointed. In January 1884 he joined Valentine Baker at Suakin, as a private volunteer. At the battle of al-Teb (3 February) Baker's force of reluctant and demoralized Egyptians was attacked by a smaller force of Mahdist warriors, and panicked and fled. Burnaby shot some, but he and Baker were unable to stop the rout and withdrew with the remnants to the coast. When the British force under Major-General Sir Gerald Graham arrived at Suakin later in February, Burnaby and Baker were appointed intelligence officers and accompanied it. Burnaby fought at the second battle of al-Teb (29 February), using a double-barrelled twelve-bore shotgun borrowed from a naval officer, and was wounded. He returned to England in March. His use of the shotgun was condemned by some of his political opponents, but defended by those who had experienced the Mahdists.

To the British press and public Burnaby was a colourful celebrity, 'Freddy the Khivan Kove, otherwise Horatius Cockles, otherwise Balloonatic Bunsby' (Alexander, 176). Yet, behind the image, Burnaby's last years were apparently largely unhappy. His health deteriorated, his weight increased, and he lived much as an invalid. He suffered from liver and lung ailments, and from a heart condition he knew might kill him at any time. He had been one of the prince of Wales's set, but his relations with the prince had deteriorated. He had offended the prince by his claim of royal descent, his jokes at the expense of the prince and his friends, and his refusal to advance the prince's favourites among the officers of the Blues, of which the prince was colonel-in-chief. By 1885 Burnaby was reportedly 'under the ban of royal disapprobation' (Ware and Mann, 315). Moreover, some of his senior officers were hostile, partly because of a quarrel between him and Major-General Owen Williams. Burnaby's marriage, if not a sham, was presumably scant consolation. Some who knew him believed that when, in November 1884, he left for the Sudan, he hoped to die there. The evidence is inconclusive: possibly he was ambivalent.

As public concern increased at the fate of Gordon, in 1884 Burnaby and Mark Napier proposed that a camel-mounted force of big-game hunters ride from Suakin to rescue Gordon. When Gladstone's government belatedly decided to send a relief expedition, Burnaby wanted to join it but was not permitted to. However Wolseley—who believed him 'clever and as brave as a lion' (Symons, 145)—suggested privately that he come unofficially. Burnaby, having indicated he was going to Bechuanaland, in November went to Egypt. Wolseley gave him a staff appointment and used him on the line of communication, though he wrote that Burnaby's employment 'will raise the devil's own row at Marlborough House' (Preston, 73).

In January 1885 Burnaby joined the desert column commanded by Brigadier-General Sir Herbert Stewart, and was designated his successor if necessary. At the battle of Abu Klea (17 January) the Mahdists attacked the British square. Burnaby's orders unintentionally contributed to the breaking of the square. Fighting with his sabre, he was speared in the throat then cut with swords, and died soon after. His wife wrote that 'he died as he would have wished, facing the foe' (Le Blond, 86). He and the other

British dead were buried near where they fell. Wolseley wrote, 'How delighted the Prince of Wales & the Duke of Cambridge will be that poor Burnaby is killed' (Preston, 122). To most of the British public and to the Primrose League Burnaby was a hero. He was commemorated in verse, song, and Staffordshire pottery. He was a brave fighting soldier, but not a military thinker or innovator. In his last years his public persona hid a private life that was sad, even tragic. ROGER T. STEARN

Sources T. Wright, *The life of Colonel Fred Burnaby* (1908) · J. R. Ware and R. K. Mann, *The life and times of Colonel Fred Burnaby* (1885) · M. Alexander, *The true blue: the life and adventures of Colonel Fred Burnaby, 1842–85* (1957) · E. A. Le Blond, *Day in, day out* [1928] · F. Burnaby, *A ride to Khiva* (1876) · F. Burnaby, *On horseback through Asia Minor*, 2 vols. (1877) · F. Burnaby, *A ride across the channel* (1882) · F. Burnaby, 'Possibilities of ballooning', *Fortnightly Review*, 41 (1884), 668–76 · F. Burnaby, *Our radicals: a tale of love and politics*, 2 vols. (1886) · L. E. Taylor, *The irrepressible Victorian: the story of Thomas Gibson Bowles* (1965) · *In relief of Gordon: Lord Wolseley's campaign journal of the Khartoum relief expedition, 1884–1885*, ed. A. Preston (1967) · J. Symons, *England's pride: the story of the Gordon relief expedition* (1965) · *Annual Register* (1885) · M. Pugh, *The tories and the people, 1880–1935* · F. Burnaby, letters to Disraeli, Bodl. Oxf., Dep. Hughenden · private information (2004) · *Hart's Army List* (1885) · Venn, *Alum. Cant.* · R. R. Oakley, *A history of Oswestry School* (1964) · B. Robson, *Fuzzy-wuzzy: the campaigns in the eastern Sudan, 1884–85* (1993)
Archives King's Lond., Liddell Hart C., papers | Bodl. Oxf., letters to Disraeli · Hove Central Library, Sussex, letters to Viscount Wolseley · Palestine Exploration Fund, London, letters to Palestine Exploration Fund
Likenesses J. Tissot, oils, 1870, NPG [*see illus.*] · H. Furniss, pen-and-ink caricature, *c.*1880–1910, NPG · E. A. Armstrong, etching (after M. Reed), BM · R. Corder, miniature, repro. in Le Blond, *Day in, day out* · Donovan, carte-de-visite, NPG · Lock & Whitfield, Woodburytype photograph, NPG; repro. in T. Cooper, *Men of mark: a gallery of contemporary portraits* (1877) · Spy [L. Ward], chromolithograph caricature, NPG; repro. in *VF* (2 Dec 1876) · medallion on obelisk, St Philip's churchyard, Birmingham · photograph, repro. in Burnaby, *On horseback*, frontispiece · photographs, cartoons, and drawings, repro. in Alexander, *True blue*
Wealth at death £18,638 15s.: resworn probate, June 1886, *CGPLA Eng. & Wales* (1885)

Burnaby, William (1673–1706), playwright and translator, was the second son of William Burnaby (1643–1693), brewer, and Isabella (d. 1693), who settled in the parish of St Clement Danes, London. The younger William entered Merton College, Oxford, in 1691, where he was a contemporary of Richard Steele, but he left abruptly on his father's death in April 1693 and was entered at the Middle Temple that same year. Burnaby, together with an anonymous collaborator, translated from Latin the *Satyricon* of Petronius Arbiter, giving it an idiomatically Restoration flavour. This work was published in 1694. He left the Middle Temple but frequented Will's Coffee House, exchanging banter with such littérateurs as William Wycherley, William Congreve, John Vanbrugh, and Nicholas Rowe.

Burnaby's comedy of manners *The Reform'd Wife* was staged with a strong cast at Drury Lane in 1700. But public taste was changing, prompted by Jeremy Collier's *A Short View of the Immorality and Profaneness of the English Stage*. Audiences were in no mood to countenance a plot in which a self-satisfied husband instructs a soldier newly returned from Flanders in the art of seduction only to find that the lesson is applied to his own wife. With an even stronger cast, headed by Mrs Bracegirdle in a breeches part, *The Ladies' Visiting Day* (1701) was nevertheless a failure. Here a husband conspires with a gallant whom he believes impotent to pay court to his wife, in order to distract her from his own amatory affairs. The resemblance in plot to Wycherley's *The Country Wife* is obvious, though it has its moments of wit: 'A Woman's Character is not compleat before she has been in a Lampoon, and had a Fellow or two kill'd for her'. The Restoration mood, however, had melted away. *The Modish Husband* (1702) with Colley Cibber in the lead, covered much the same ground, of cuckolds and flirts, while Burnaby's brief career as a dramatist concluded in 1703 with *Love Betray'd*, a misguided adaptation of Shakespeare's *Twelfth Night*.

The remaining three years of Burnaby's life were sustained by manipulating a fortune entrusted to his care by Mary Holmes. This financed a vain research, conducted by his friend Steele, into converting base metals to gold. He managed to procure a post under the Admiralty, first as sub-commissioner for prizes at Hull, then as agent for prizes with the West Indies fleet, but was dismissed. Burnaby, who never married, died, penniless, in London on 8 November 1706. He was buried in Poets' Corner at Westminster Abbey on 14 November. PHILIP HOBSBAUM

Sources *The dramatic works of William Burnaby*, ed. F. E. Budd (1931) · *Letters of wit, politicks and morality* (1707) · [D. Manley], *Secret memoirs and manners of several persons of quality of both sexes, from the New Atalantis*, 2 vols. (1709) · parish register, Manton, 1643 [baptism; William Burnaby, father] · parish registers, St Clement Danes, City Westm. AC, April, Sept 1693 [burial; William Burnaby, father; Isabella Burnaby] · parish register, Westminster Abbey, 14 Nov 1706 [burial]
Wealth at death see will, PRO, PROB 11/491, sig. 229, repr. in *Dramatic works*, ed. Budd, 71

Burnaby, Sir William (c.1710–1776), naval officer, of Broughton Hall, Oxfordshire, was the son of John Burnaby of Kensington, and Clara, daughter of Sir Edward Wood. He was the third of four surviving sons: John, who became minister to the Swiss cantons and secretary to Earl Waldegrave when ambassador-extraordinary at the court of France; Edward, one of the chief clerks of the Treasury; and Daniel, rector of Hanwell and fellow of St John's College, Cambridge. He also had a sister, Caroline. He married first Margaret (d. 1757?), widow of Tim Donovan of Jamaica; they had a son, Sir William Chaloner Burnaby, and a daughter, Elizabeth. His second wife was Grace, daughter of Drewry Ottley of Bedford Row, London, whom he married at St Benet Paul's Wharf, London, on 6 October 1757; they had six children, including Edward, who followed his father into the navy.

Burnaby entered the navy and was promoted lieutenant on 16 December 1732. In August 1741 he was given command of the bomb-ketch *Thunder* and posted to Admiral Vernon's squadron in the West Indies. An anecdote is told of his arrival there. Burnaby had the reputation of being a dandy while Vernon was said to be so slovenly in dress as to disgrace any officer. As was customary Burnaby made a formal visit to the commander-in-chief to report his arrival. He boarded the flagship clad in silk much ornamented with gold lace. After some delay he was admitted to Vernon's presence and the admiral solemnly apologized for keeping him waiting, his reason for doing so being that he had thought Burnaby was a dancing-master (Charnock, 5.132).

On 9 December 1742 Burnaby was promoted captain in the *Lichfield* (50 guns). He was mentioned in a dispatch for his cruise off Puerto Rico in October 1743 which reported that Burnaby had captured two privateer sloops, destroyed a privateer off the east end of Hispaniola and another off the west end of Puerto Rico, burnt a sloop in Aquada Bay, and destroyed a shore battery of four guns. There is little further mention of his service in the West Indies except for his appointment to the *Cumberland*, flagship of Sir Chaloner Ogle, with whom he returned to England in 1744. It is reasonable to think that Burnaby's eldest son was named after his commander-in-chief.

On 9 April 1754 Burnaby was knighted, and in 1755 he became sheriff for the county of Oxford. With the threat of war with France he was, in October 1755, appointed captain of the *Jersey*, and in July 1757 he was moved to the *Royal Anne*, a first-rate which, due to her great age, was employed as a guardship. At this time Burnaby was corresponding with the Admiralty about a sum of £109 relating to false pay tickets which he admitted signing. A compromise was reached in which Burnaby received his pay but undertook to pay any legal costs which might arise from the discussion.

On 21 October 1762 Burnaby was promoted rear-admiral of the red. In June 1763 he was appointed commander-in-chief of a squadron ordered to the West Indies, and hoisted his flag in the *Dreadnought*. He reached Jamaica on 2 January 1764 and found the naval yards in a poor state of repair. His orders required the charting of the coasts of the islands and of Florida and the protection and exploitation of trade. The two persistently difficult tasks that took his attention were the dispute of the loggers of Honduras with the governor of Yucatan, and the French claim to the Turks Islands; each presented a delicate problem of diplomacy and each was successfully negotiated.

Burnaby's command brought him numbers of suitors for his patronage. Particularly persistent was Lady Cornwallis, who pressed him to make her son William a post captain. She claimed that Burnaby had given her an absolute promise of advancing her son. With the change of ministry in 1762 Burnaby backed away from his earlier promise, telling Lady Cornwallis that he would need to defer to any different preferences of Lord Egmont, who was now at the Admiralty. Even so, in the list of promotions for 22 November 1764 the Hon. William Cornwallis was made captain in the *Prince Edward*. Burnaby promoted his son William Chaloner Burnaby three times during his West Indian command.

Sir William returned to England in the autumn of 1767 and on 31 October was made baronet. He was promoted vice-admiral of the white on 20 October 1770 and vice-admiral of the red on 24 October. At the end of 1771 he was appointed commander-in-chief in Jamaica but quickly made way for Sir George Rodney. He died intestate in 1776, and was succeeded by his son Sir William Chaloner Burnaby.

KENNETH BREEN

Sources Burnaby dispatches, PRO, ADM 1/258 · Vernon and Ogle dispatches, PRO, ADM 1/233 · muster books, PRO, ADM 1/4313 · D. Syrett and R. L. DiNardo, *The commissioned sea officers of the Royal Navy, 1660–1815*, rev. edn, Occasional Publications of the Navy RS, 1 (1994) · navy board correspondence, NMM, ADM /B/149 · correspondence of Lady Cornwallis and Burnaby, NMM, COR/56 · J. Charnock, ed., *Biographia navalis*, 6 vols. (1794–8) · PRO, PROB 6/152, fol. 111 · Burke, *Peerage* · T. Wotton, *The baronetage of England*, ed. E. Kimber and R. Johnson, 3 vols. (1771)
Archives PRO, dispatches, ADM 1/238 | NMM, corresp. of Lady Cornwallis
Wealth at death see administration, PRO, PROB 6/152, fol. 111

Burnand, Sir Francis Cowley (1836–1917), playwright and humorist, was born in Mortimer Street, London, on 29 November 1836, the only son of Francis Burnand, a London stockbroker of protestant Savoyard descent, and his first wife, Emma Cowley, who died eight days after her son's birth. Young Frank was educated at Eton College and at Trinity College, Cambridge, from 1854 to 1858, where he wrote plays, acted in them under the name of Tom Pierce, and founded the Cambridge Amateur Dramatic Club described in his *Personal Reminiscences of the A.D.C.* (1880). He submitted drawings to *Punch*, one or two of which were published after revision by one of the artists on its staff. Burnand began to prepare first for law and then for the Anglican ministry, but in 1858 he converted to Roman Catholicism under the influence of John Henry Newman's *Doctrine of Development*. His infuriated father cut him adrift, and after a brief career as a barrister Burnand turned to the stage. For a short time he was an amateur actor and later managed a theatre; he sold the burlesques he had written for the Cambridge Amateur Dramatic Club to a theatrical publisher. On 31 March 1860 he married an actress, Cecilia Victoria Ranoe (1843?–1870), daughter of James Ranoe, a clerk; the couple had five sons and two daughters. In 1874 he married her sister Rosina (also an actress), the widow of Paysan Jones, in a ceremony on the continent, such marriages being illegal in England at that time. They had two sons and four daughters.

In the 1860s Burnand became a comic journalist. He edited *The Glow-Worm*, a transient periodical, joined the staff of *Fun*, and, when its proprietor rejected his 1863 proposal for 'Mokeanna', a parodistic serial, he took it to the more receptive *Punch*. With its success, he severed his connection with *Fun* and became in due course a staff writer for *Punch* and in 1880 its editor. His predecessor, Tom Taylor, had allowed the paper to become heavy, but Burnand's rackety leadership brightened it. His own series, 'Happy Thoughts', begun in 1866, gave a catchword to the language and initiated a new style of narrative in which the speaker is perpetually the comic victim of some minor crisis or small disaster. His greatest editorial coup along these lines, however, was his publication of *The Diary of a Nobody* (1888) by George and Weedon Grossmith, still in print more than a hundred years later. Burnand, who declared himself hostile to no man's religion, banned *Punch's* earlier sharp attacks on Catholicism,

Sir Francis Cowley Burnand (1836–1917), by Walery

though he proved unable to remove antisemitic jokes. His own style became increasingly prolix and anecdotal, devoted to more and more far-fetched, sometimes almost unintelligible, puns.

Meanwhile, Burnand was concurrently pursuing the profession of comic playwright, occasionally collaborating with Montagu Williams in the 1860s. In 1865 he and a theatre musician, Frank Musgrave, produced the first attempt at English *opera buffe*: *Windsor Castle*. For the most part, however, his dramatic output consisted of burlesques, extravaganzas, and farces, with some librettos, comedies, and a few serious plays. Characteristic titles included *Helen, or, Taken from the Greek* (1866) and *Fowl Play, or, A Story of Chicken Hazard* (1868). Word play rioted in his dramatis personae and texts; for example, Whiskitoddikos appears as a high priest in *Ixion Rewheel'd* (1874), and *The Rise and Fall of Richard III, or, A New Front to an Old Dicky* (1868) contains the lines:

I can look back on several ginny-rations,
… my ancestors, they never fought
With greater spirit than at A-gin-court.

Burnand's real superiority, however, lay in his invention of absurdly funny 'stage business'. Unfortunately he had little sense of form, his dramatic structures being loosely supplied by the works he parodied or adapted. For example, his best burlesques, *The Latest Edition of Black-Eyed Susan* (1866) and *Dora and Diplunacy* (1878) were based on very popular serious plays. Egotistically he asserted that he merely imitated Shakespeare in appropriating sources. His best comedy, *The Colonel* (1881), was a farcical adaptation of Morris Barnett's *The Serious Family*, itself taken from

Le mari à la campagne, both satirizing religious mania. He turned the subject to the aesthetic movement, which *Punch* was then heavily attacking, and pitted a fake professor of 'aesthetics' against a practical American colonel. The play ran for 550 performances, continued in the provinces for years, and was performed privately before Queen Victoria.

As a librettist Burnand had one lasting success in *Cox and Box*, with music by Arthur Sullivan, first given by amateurs (1866, 1867) and then professionally at the Gallery of Illustration, London (1869). Still performed in the twentieth century, this musical triumveretta was based on John Maddison Morton's farce *Box and Cox* (1847). In 1867 Burnand and Sullivan also collaborated on the moderately successful *The Contrabandista* and in 1870 on *The Miller and his Men*, a Christmas extravaganza for amateurs. These early works convinced Burnand that he, not W. S. Gilbert, should have been Sullivan's librettist. His jealousy led to antagonistic reviews of Gilbert in *Punch*, but when at last Burnand revised *The Contrabandista* for Sullivan to set as *The Chieftain* in 1894, it ran for only ninety-seven performances despite first-night enthusiasm and *Punch's* adulatory review. His last libretto, *His Majesty* (1897), a collaboration, with music by Sir Alexander Mackenzie, was a failure. His work on *Punch*, rather than his dramatic output, earned him a knighthood in 1902. By that time he had lost interest in practical editorship and left it to a deputy. An attempt had been made to replace him as early as 1891, but he was not forced into unwilling retirement until 1906. After a winter of bronchitis he died unexpectedly at his home, 18 Royal Crescent, Ramsgate, Kent, on 21 April 1917, and on 25 April he was buried in the cemetery attached to St Augustine's Abbey church there. He was survived by his second wife.   JANE W. STEDMAN

Sources F. C. Burnand, *Records and reminiscences, personal and general*, 2nd edn, 2 vols. (1904) • R. G. G. Price, *A history of Punch* (1957), 122–77 • K. Gänzl, *The British musical theatre*, 1 (1986), 1–6 • *The Athenaeum* [reviews] • *The Theatre* [reviews] • *The Era* [various reviews] • *Theatrical Journal* [reviews] • *The Times* [reviews] • Q [T. Purnell], *Dramatists of the present day* (1871), chap. 4 • *Punch*, 78–119 (1880–1900) • A. Jacobs, *Arthur Sullivan: a Victorian musician* (1984) • M. H. Spielmann, *The history of 'Punch'* (1895) • W. Archer, *Pall Mall Budget* (20 Dec 1894) [review] • A. Nicoll, *Late nineteenth century drama, 1850–1900*, 2nd edn (1959), vol. 5 of *A history of English drama, 1660–1900* (1952–9), 287–92 • m. cert. [F. C. Burnand and C. V. Ranoe] • d. cert. • *CGPLA Eng. & Wales* (1917) • J. P. Wearing, *American and British theatrical biography* (1979) • F. C. Burnand, ed., *The Catholic who's who and yearbook* (1908)

Archives Theatre Museum, London, corresp. incl. family corresp. | BL, corresp. with William Archer, Add. MS 45290, fols. 324–9 • BL, letters to T. H. S. Escott, Add. MS 58776 • BL, corresp. with Macmillans, Add. MS 55041 • Bodl. Oxf., letters to John Callcott Horsley • Hove Central Library, letters mainly to Viscount Wolseley • Morgan L., Gilbert and Sullivan collection • NRA, MSS • U. Leeds, Brotherton L., letters to Bram Stoker

Likenesses L. Sambourne, sketch, 1891, repro. in A. Prager, *The mahogany tree: an informal history of Punch* (1979) • W. H. Barrett, carte-de-visite, 1902, NPG • Ape [C. Pellegrini], caricature, NPG; repro. in *VF* (8 Jan 1881) • H. Furniss, two pen-and-ink drawings, NPG • H. von Herkomer, oils, repro. in Burnand, *Records and reminiscences*, frontispiece • F. T. Palmer, photograph, repro. in Spielmann, *History of 'Punch'* • J. Russell & Sons, print, NPG • Walery, photograph, NPG [see illus.] • group portrait (*Editors of Punch*), BM,

NPG; repro. in *ILN* (18 July 1891) • photograph, NPG • photographs, repro. in Burnard, *Records and reminiscences* • woodburytype photograph, NPG
Wealth at death £18,176 6s. 7d.: probate, 3 July 1917, *CGPLA Eng. & Wales*

Burnard, Neville Northey (1818–1878), sculptor, was born on 11 October 1818, at Penpont, Altarnun, Cornwall, where he was baptized on 1 November, the eldest of the two sons and a daughter (Jane) of George Burnard (b. 1787), a stonemason, and his wife, Jane, *née* Northey, whom he had married on 1 December 1817. Burnard received his education from his mother, who kept a dame-school, and then served as mortar boy to his father. At fourteen he cut a tombstone to his grandfather George Burnard (b. 1753) which remains in Altarnun churchyard, together with others also carved by Burnard and his brother, George (b. 1828), who also became a sculptor. At sixteen Burnard carved a head of John Wesley, still *in situ* over the porch of the old Methodist meeting-house in Penpont. That same year he also carved a slate bas-relief *Laocöon* after a woodcut he had seen in the *Penny Magazine*, using a French burr and some tools of his own making. In 1834 he sent the carving to the exhibition of the Royal Cornwall Polytechnic Society at Falmouth where this remarkable work was awarded the society's silver medal. In 1841 he was again awarded the society's silver medal for three portrait medallions.

From Altarnun Burnard went to Fowey where he received the encouragement and assistance of Sir Charles Lemon, bt, president of the Cornwall Polytechnic Society. Lemon introduced him to the celebrated sculptor Sir Francis Chantrey, who took him on as a carver in his London atelier where he worked alongside Henry Weekes, who took over his master's studio on Chantrey's death in 1841. Again with an introduction from Lemon, Burnard was given access in 1847 to Buckingham Palace to model a bust of HRH Albert Edward, duke of Cornwall, later prince of Wales; it was exhibited at the Royal Academy in 1848 and, with Queen Victoria's approval of the likeness, subsequently sent to Osborne House on the Isle of Wight. Burnard was commissioned to produce a marble copy of the bust for the Polytechnic Hall in Falmouth, exhibited in 1873 in Truro town hall. This royal favour led to further work in the studios of E. H. Baily, W. C. Marshall, and J. H. Foley.

A large, tall man with an enormous head, Burnard married Mary Ann Nicholson on 7 November 1844 at All Souls, St Marylebone, Middlesex. They lived at 36 Hugh Street, Pimlico, and had two sons and two daughters, of whom the elder son, Thomas, also became a sculptor. There remains at Penpont House a small, plaster self-portrait of Burnard carved in relief. A friend of the Cornish diarist Caroline Fox, Burnard was described in her *Memories of Old Friends* as 'a great powerful pugilistic looking fellow at twenty nine, a great deal of face, with all the features massed in the centre, mouth open and all sorts of simplicities flowing out of it' (Fox, 2.89). She also transcribed an extract of a letter from Thomas Carlyle to 'my "gigantic countryman"' in which he encouraged Burnard to 'Persist in your career with wise strength, with silent resolution, with manful, with patient, unconquerable endeavour' (ibid., 2.109).

In 1852 Burnard was commissioned to make a statue for the column erected in Truro in honour of the explorer Richard Lemon Lander. This was followed in 1854 by his bronze statue in memory of 'the Corn Law Rhymer' Ebenezer Elliott, on whom Burnard had published a commemorative poem in the *West Briton* (30 January 1852). A subscription of £600 was raised for the statue by the working men of the town for the market place in Sheffield (since moved to Weston Park). Burnard's modest background and association with the Chartist movement later led to commissions for memorials of several radical politicians. He was also commissioned to make portrait busts, exhibited at the Royal Academy between 1848 and 1873, of many eminent men, including the discoverer of the planet Neptune, John Couch Adams (marble, exh. RA, 1849; Royal Astronomical Society, London), the botanist Edward Forbes (exh. RA, 1867; Douglas, Isle of Man), and the novelist William Makepeace Thackeray (marble, c.1867). The latter was given by the sculptor to Plymouth Library and Cottonian Museum, and a marble version was given by Sir Theodore Martin to the National Portrait Gallery in 1885. Other notable busts included those of Sir Charles Lemon (exh. RA, 1849); Beethoven (1851); Harriet Beecher Stowe (c.1853), subscribed by the British and Foreign Anti-Slavery Society the year after her publication of *Uncle Tom's Cabin*; Lord Macaulay (1859; Westminster Abbey); Richard Cobden (exh. RA, 1866; unfinished); John Bright (exh. RA, 1869), and W. E. Gladstone (exh. RA, 1871). Mary Martin recorded that 'Burnard also sculpted in marble the hand of Richard Cobden [resting] on an open Bible and pointing to the words "Give us this day our daily bread"' (Martin, 32).

Burnard's eleven-year-old daughter, Charlotte (Lottie), died of scarlet fever on 7 March 1870. Her father carved a relief of her head on the tombstone in St Nicholas's churchyard, Weymouth, which she shares with her uncle Thomas, who died the following day of the same disease. Around this time Burnard also 'lost his wife' (Gould, 189), a comment interpreted in later accounts as a reference to her death, although, as his executor, Mary Ann Burnard, then living at 11 Hugh Street, Pimlico, was granted letters of administration of Burnard's small estate in 1879. Following the last exhibition of his work at the Royal Academy in 1873, Burnard's private life deteriorated rapidly and he began to drink heavily. Unable to fulfil commissions, he also lost many London friends. Towards the end of his life, and living like a tramp, he made periodic visits to Altarnun, making sketches and drawing portraits at farms and public houses. He lived by his wits, writing articles for local newspapers, and election squibs for either side. During his last visit to Altarnun in 1875 he was still drawing pencil portraits with a firm hand, and composed a long dignified poem on the death of an old friend. He died in the union workhouse at Illogan, Cornwall, on 27 November 1878.

ANNETTE BURNARD and ANNETTE PEACH

Sources private information (2004) [Alfred Douglas Burnard] · IGI · CGPLA Eng. & Wales (1879) · M. Martin, *A wayward genius: Neville Northy Burnard* (1978) · S. B. Gould, *Cornish characters and strange events* (1909) · R. Gunnis, *Dictionary of British sculptors, 1660–1851* (1953); new edn (1968) · Graves, *RA exhibitors* · B. Read, *Victorian sculpture* (1982) · C. Fox, *Memories of old friends* (1882) · R. Ormond, *Early Victorian portraits*, 2 vols. (1973)
Likenesses N. N. Burnard, self-portrait, bas-relief, repro. in Gould, *Cornish characters*, facing p. 186 · N. N. Burnard, self-portrait, carved plaster cameo, Penpont House, Altarnun, Cornwall · N. N. Burnard, self-portrait, drawing, repro. in Martin, *Wayward genius*
Wealth at death under £50: administration, 1879

Burne, Nicol (*fl.* 1574–1598), Roman Catholic controversialist, was probably born in the late 1550s. Little is known of his family or early education, except that he was (he said) brought up as a Calvinist and that his brother George (*d.* 1596) lived at Gogar, near Stirling. Burne matriculated at St Andrews (St Leonard's College) in 1574 and graduated MA in 1578. He then became a college regent in arts ('Professor of philosophie' is his self-description). The university was, at just that time, under parliamentary investigation for suspected Roman Catholic influence: two notable teachers during, or just before, Burne's time at St Andrews were reconverted to Catholicism in the mid-1570s, both destined to play a part in doctrinal controversy. Burne's teaching career was seemingly cut short by his turning to the old religion, which makes him one of the earliest recorded people in Scotland to convert to Roman Catholicism from an entirely protestant formation. He ascribes his conversion to reading Catholic writers, two of whom (Domingo de Soto and Jean Garet) are cited in his *Disputation Concerning the Controversit Headdis of Religion* (1581).

The published text of Burne's work originated in a brief but energetic career in confrontational polemics in 1580. The first episode in this was, probably, Burne's interview at Dalkeith with the former regent of Scotland, the earl of Morton. This was followed by a discussion in Paisley with Thomas Smeaton, a leading figure in the kirk, who, according to Burne, having agreed the conditions for a more formal disputation, took steps to have Burne apprehended and detained. Despite enjoying the protection of James VI's favourite Esmé Stuart, earl of Lennox, Burne was a prisoner from mid-October 1580 in the Edinburgh Tolbooth, where the general assembly was to meet at much the same time. Burne was interrogated at length by Andrew Melville and other prominent churchmen. Although an attempt to have him tried for treason failed, his adversaries did eventually procure his banishment—pending which, security for his abstaining from further controversy was provided by his brother George, together with 'Andrew Burne in Leith'.

At the end of January 1581 Nicol Burne left Scotland for Paris, where he prepared his *Disputation* for its publication in October. Although elaborately equipped with marginal references, scriptural and patristic, and plainly the work of a young man who had made himself knowledgeable in the ways of controversy, this is not a work of sophisticated theological argument. It is, rather, a piece of vigorous polemical writing, shrewd, scurrilous, and occasionally obscene. Some copies are bound with an anonymous verse, *Admonition to the Unchristian Ministers in the Deformed Kirk of Scotland*—a clumsy and laboured performance, sometimes (but perhaps improbably) attributed to Burne. Little is known of his later life. After studying, presumably theology, at the Scots College attached to the Jesuit university at Pont-à-Mousson in Lorraine, Burne joined the order of Preachers and was said in 1598 to be then 'a Dominican in Spain'. His date of death is unknown.

J. H. BURNS

Sources N. Burne, *The disputation concerning the controversit headdis of religion* (1581) · T. Thomson, ed., *Acts and proceedings of the general assemblies of the Kirk of Scotland*, 3 pts, Bannatyne Club, 81 (1839–45), pt 2, pp. 434–7, 464, 472 · A. I. Dunlop, ed., *Acta facultatis artium universitatis Sanctiandree, 1413–1588*, St Andrews University Publications, 56 (1964), 448, 450–51 · *CSP Scot., 1574–81*, 555 · *Reg. PCS*, 1st ser., 5.328, 355 · P. J. Anderson, ed., *Records of the Scots colleges at Douai, Rome, Madrid, Valladolid and Ratisbon*, New Spalding Club, 30 (1906), 1–2 · *DSCHT* · J. M. Anderson, ed., *Early records of the University of St Andrews*, Scottish History Society, 3rd ser., 8 (1926), 175, 179, 285

Burne, Sir Owen Tudor (1837–1909), army officer and administrator in India, was born at Plymouth on 12 April 1837, the eleventh of the nineteen children of the Revd Henry Thomas Burne (1799–1865), and his wife, Knightley Goodman (1805–1878), daughter of Captain Marriott, Royal Horse Guards. In 1835 his father had converted from the Church of England to the Holy Catholic Apostolic church, founded by Edward Irving, in which faith his children were brought up. His eldest brother was Colonel Henry Burne, and another brother, Douglas, was manager of the Bank of Bengal.

Burne was educated at home by his father, and at the Royal Military College, Sandhurst. He was commissioned in the 20th (East Devonshire) regiment (later the Lancashire Fusiliers) on 15 May 1855, and served for several months at its depot at Parkhurst on the Isle of Wight before joining his regiment in the Crimea, in charge of a draft of 200 recruits, on 3 April 1856, following the cessation of hostilities. In June he returned home, and after a year at Aldershot, on 5 August 1857, embarked for India to assist in suppressing the uprising there. After it landed at Calcutta, in November 1857, his regiment was sent to Oudh to deal with mutinous Sepoys gathered between Benares and Lucknow. As Burne had learnt Hindustani aboard ship, he was given a staff appointment as brigade major to Brigadier Evelegh, commanding a brigade in the 4th infantry division (Brigadier Franks). Burne first saw action on 19 February 1858 at Chanda, near Sultanpur in Oudh, where several artillery pieces were captured from the enemy; after several difficult engagements, on 4 March his division joined Sir Colin Campbell's army besieging Lucknow, which was held in strength by the rebels. His brigade was initially deployed under heavy fire in outworks near the Dilkusha palace on the outskirts of the city, where it was exposed to a heavy fire. For a feat of gallantry on 11 March, when Burne carried out a dangerous reconnaissance mission to discover the whereabouts of units deployed on the flanks of his brigade and during which he rallied some shaken Nepalese troops, he was unsuccessfully recommended for promotion and for the

Victoria Cross. When the 4th division attacked the *kaisarbagh* and *imambara*, the keys of the enemy's position, on 14 March, Burne was brigade major of the attacking column, and was one of the first to enter the gate of the heavily defended *kaisarbagh*. Until Lucknow fell on 21 March Burne participated in the heavy fighting in the city. On 10 April 1858 he was promoted lieutenant and served with Evelegh's brigade, engaged in clearing the country near Lucknow of rebels in spite of widespread outbreaks of cholera and the intense heat. Burne later rejoined as adjutant the 20th regiment, which now formed part of Sir John Campbell's field force operating in northern Oudh. He served in 1859 as a staff officer with Brigadier Holdich's column in the final operations in Oudh under Sir James Hope Grant's command. Burne was mentioned in dispatches on several occasions, received the medal with clasp for Lucknow, and was later promoted captain (9 August 1864) and brevet major (January 1865) for his services in the uprising.

Burne's efficiency as adjutant while the 20th (East Devonshire) regiment was stationed at Goudah greatly impressed Sir Hugh Rose, the commander-in-chief in India, when he inspected the regiment on 14 December 1860. Despite his low rank Burne was unexpectedly appointed Rose's military secretary the following spring. Although this appointment was later confirmed in England, as a result of friction between the duke of Cambridge, the commander-in-chief there, and Rose over the choice of such a junior officer, Burne resigned his post at the end of 1862; he was instead appointed Rose's private secretary. He occupied this post during the debate about reconstruction of the Indian army following the uprising of 1857, and participated in various consultations between Rose and Lord Canning. During these deliberations Burne demonstrated his administrative ability and detailed knowledge of the military profession. Burne accompanied Rose when he returned to England at the end of his tenure as commander-in-chief in India, and then to his new command in Ireland where he became one of his aides-de-camp. For his assistance in suppressing the 1867 Fenian conspiracy Burne received the thanks of the government. On 20 November 1867 he married Evelyne, daughter of Francis William Browne, fourth baron of Kilmaine; the couple had three sons and two daughters. His first wife died on 22 April 1878 and on 9 August 1883 he married Lady Agnes Charlotte Douglas, youngest daughter of the nineteenth earl of Morton.

Burne returned to India in December 1868 as private secretary to Lord Mayo, the newly appointed viceroy, with whom he enjoyed a close friendship and whose political views he shared. Burne was with Mayo during a visit to the Andaman Islands when on 6 February 1872 the viceroy was assassinated by an Afridi convict. He briefly remained at Calcutta as private secretary to Lord Napier and Ettrick, governor of Madras, who temporarily acted as viceroy, but departed for England when Lord Northbrook arrived in May 1872.

On 1 June 1872 Burne was created a CSI and early in August he visited Queen Victoria at Osborne on the Isle of Wight, to give a personal report on the exact details of Mayo's death. Also in August he was appointed to the new post of political aide-de-camp to the duke of Argyll, secretary of state for India. His duties included overseeing all visiting Indian dignitaries and embassies and advising the India Office generally on its dealings with the Indian people. In the summer of 1873 he assisted Sir Henry Rawlinson in entertaining the shah of Persia during his visit to England. In April 1874 Burne was appointed assistant secretary to the foreign department of the India Office, which was generally responsible for overseeing British India's external relations, both in Asia and in Europe. He was promoted lieutenant-colonel on 16 July, and in October succeeded Sir John Kaye as secretary and head of the foreign department. In this capacity he wielded considerable personal influence, and he closely consulted with the marquess of Salisbury, secretary of state for India, on central Asian and Afghan questions.

Burne returned to India in April 1876, and served for two years as private secretary to Lord Lytton, the new viceroy. The successful ceremonial proclamation of Queen Victoria as empress of India at the imperial assemblage at Delhi on 1 January 1877 was in large part due to Burne's work, although he was primarily interested in Afghan and central Asian policy. A year later, on 1 January 1878, Burne was created a CIE. He returned to England shortly afterwards as his wife was ill. Lytton wrote to him: 'You have done for me, and been to me, all that one man could have done or been.' Burne returned once again to the India Office in February and was promoted KCSI in July 1879; shortly afterwards he reached the rank of colonel. From 1879 he regularly contributed to *The Times*, as well as writing several magazine articles and books on British India. In 1880 Burne helped negotiate a highly satisfactory settlement for the Indian exchequer with the nawab nazim of Bengal, and supervised the affairs of Maharaja Duleep Singh. Burne joined the Council of India—an advisory body to the secretary of state composed of men with extensive experience of the subcontinent—in December 1876, and was promoted major-general in 1886. In 1894 he retired from the army, although he continued to work, and served as vice-president of the Council of India in 1895 and 1896. He finally retired from this post on 31 December 1896, when he was also made a GCIE.

Following his retirement, Burne was busily occupied in various philanthropic, mercantile, and other public work, acting as chairman of the council of the Society of Arts (1896–7) and as a member of the advisory committee of the Board of Trade (1903). He died after a long illness at his home, 132 Sutherland Avenue, Maida Vale, London, on 3 February 1909. He was buried with military honours six days later at the priory church, Christchurch, Hampshire. He was survived by his second wife.   T. R. MOREMAN

Sources O. T. Burne, *Memories* (1907) · *The Times* (4 Feb 1909) · *The Times* (9 Feb 1909) · *The Times* (10 Feb 1909) · BL OIOC, Burne MSS · BL OIOC, MS Eur. D 951 · B. Balfour, *History of Lord Lytton's Indian administration, 1876–1880* (1899) · S. N. Sen, *Eighteen fifty-seven* (Delhi, 1958) · C. Hibbert, *The great mutiny, India, 1857* (1978) · CGPLA Eng. & Wales (1909)

Archives BL OIOC, corresp. and papers, MS Eur. D 951 | Balliol Oxf., letters to Sir Louis Mallet • BL OIOC, corresp. with Sir Alfred Lyall, MS Eur. F 132 • BL OIOC, letters to Sir Lewis Pelly, MS Eur. F 126 • Bodl. Oxf., letters to Lord Kimberley • Bodl. Oxf., letters to Sir Matthew Nathan • CUL, corresp. with Lord Mayo
Likenesses Isca, coloured lithograph, BL OIOC, W2990(40); repro. in *Indian Chaiavari album* [n.d., *c*.1875], no. 40 • photograph, BL OIOC, photo 295(31) • portrait (after L. Melville), repro. in Burne, *Memories*, frontispiece
Wealth at death £15,619 13s. 1d.: probate, 6 April 1909, *CGPLA Eng. & Wales*

Burne, Robert (1755?–1825), army officer, details of whose parents and upbringing are unknown, entered the army in 1773 as an ensign in the 36th regiment where he remained until 1811. In 1783 he went to India with the regiment and, in the following year, was promoted captain, and commanded the grenadiers of the 36th regiment throughout the campaigns of 1784–6 against Tipu Sultan, ruler of Mysore. He served at Sattimungulum, at Showera, and was present at the capture of Bangalore, the storming of the hill fortress of Nandidroog, and the siege of Seringapatam. In 1793 he played a conspicuous part at the siege of Pondicherry, and on 1 March 1794 was promoted brevet major as a consequence. Two years later he purchased a majority in the regiment. In 1798 he was promoted lieutenant-colonel by brevet, and the same year the officers and headquarters of the regiment returned to England.

On reaching England in 1799 Burne became lieutenant-colonel of the 36th. In 1800 he accompanied the regiment to Minorca. In 1802 he rejoined it in Ireland after a brief period of leave. He served in the expedition to Hanover in 1805, and in the attack on Buenos Aires on 5 July 1807, where his services so impressed his fellow officers that he was presented by them with a sword of honour and 120 guineas. In April 1808 he was promoted colonel, and in July accompanied Sir Arthur Wellesley (later first duke of Wellington) to Portugal. Burne, after doing good service at Roliça, received special notice in Wellesley's report to Sir Harry Burrard on the battle of Vimeiro (Wellesley, 3.92). Sir Arthur also wrote to Lord Castlereagh:

> You will see in my despatch that I have mentioned Colonel Burne of the 36th regiment in a very particular manner; and I assure you that there is nothing that will give me so much satisfaction as to learn that something has been done for this old and meritorious soldier. The 36th regiment are an example to this army.   (ibid., 3.95)

Burne, in consequence, was appointed governor of Carlisle Castle. He remained in the Peninsula after Wellesley returned home, and served under Sir John Moore in the retreat to Corunna and in the battle.

In 1809 Burne commanded the 36th at the capture of Flushing, and was made a colonel on the staff until the evacuation of the island. Two years later he was made major-general, and sent out to the Peninsula from where he was posted to the command of a brigade in the 6th division, with which he was present at the battle of Fuentes de'Onoro. His health now declining, he returned to England, where he commanded the camp at Lichfield (1812–13) and Nottingham (1813–14). Burne was completely passed over when rewards were liberally heaped on the

Peninsula officers in 1814. However, he was promoted lieutenant-general on 19 July 1821, and died at Berkeley Cottage, Stanmore, on 16 June 1825.
                              H. M. STEPHENS, *rev.* PHILIP CARTER

Sources J. Philippart, ed., *The royal military calendar*, 3 vols. (1815–16) • [A. Wellesley, duke of Wellington], *The dispatches of … the duke of Wellington … from 1799 to 1818*, ed. J. Gurwood, 3: *India, 1794–1805* (1835), 92

Burne-Jones. For this title name *see* Jones, Georgiana Burne-, Lady Burne-Jones (1840–1920) [*see under* Macdonald sisters (*act.* 1837–1925)].

Burnell, Arthur Coke (1840–1882), Sanskritist and expert on southern Indian language and literature, was born at St Briavels, Gloucestershire, on 11 July 1840, the eldest son of Arthur Burnell, of the East India Company's marine service and great-nephew of Sir W. Coke, chief justice of Ceylon, and his wife, Mary Agnes, *née* Coke. He was sent to King's College, London, where he met Professor V. Fausböll of Copenhagen, who seems to have turned towards Indian studies a mind that had already shown a keen interest in languages and linguistic science. This interest was also stimulated by Burnell's early contacts with the writer and traveller George Borrow. He passed the Indian Civil Service examination in 1857, the fourth year of the competitive entry system. After a course of Sanskrit (under Professor Theodor Goldstücker) and Telugu, in which he passed with credit at the final examination, he went to Madras in 1860.

In the Malabar, Tanjore, Chingleput, Cuddapah, and Nellore districts, where he successively filled the usual subordinate offices of the civil administration in the Madras presidency, Burnell lost no opportunity of acquiring or copying Sanskrit manuscripts, and thus formed a splendid collection. In 1868 he was compelled to return on sick leave, and travelled through Arabia, Egypt, and Nubia. While in England he published part 1 of his *Catalogue of a Collection of Sanskrit MSS* (1869), dealing with Vedic manuscripts, and then presented the whole collection (350 in number) to the India Library. After returning to India in 1870, he served successively at Mangalore and at Tanjore as judge. His greatest work is the *Classified Index to the Sanskrit MSS in the Palace at Tanjore*, printed for the Madras government in 1880. Burnell had been deputed by Lord Napier, the governor of Madras, to report on this huge collection, and his catalogue, which describes many of the well over 12,000 manuscripts which he listed, represents an enormous amount of labour and learning, and affords a pioneering conspectus of the Sanskrit literature of southern India. The work was revised and supplied with valuable indexes by Dr R. Rost in London, who commented:

> The mere arranging and classifying of such a vast number of manuscripts—most of them written on palm-leaf and in the various sets of characters used for writing Sanskrit in South India—must have been a work of untold labour, which no other Sanskrit scholar could so successfully have accomplished.

Burnell also did for south Indian writing what James

Prinsep had attempted forty years before for the palaeography of the north, and his *Elements of South Indian Palaeography* (1874; 2nd edn, 1878), was the first monograph published on the subject, and deservedly won for him the honorary doctor's degree of the University of Strasbourg. Originally intended as an introduction to the Tanjore catalogue, it opened, in the words of Professor Max Müller, 'an avenue through one of the thickest and darkest jungles of Indian archaeology, and is so full of documentary evidence, that it will long remain indispensable to every student of Indian literature'. The work has been built upon and in part superseded by later studies, but is still frequently cited by scholars of Indian palaeography and epigraphy.

Among Burnell's other works (most of which were printed at Mangalore) were a translation of the section on inheritance from Madhava's *Commentary on the Parâsarasmriti* (1868) and *The law of partition and succession, from the manuscript Sanskrit text of Varadarâja's Vyavahâranirṇaya*, which won praise for its erudition from Dr Rost. In 1875 Burnell published a brief summary of Hindu law of inheritance and partition, in the preface to which he commented severely upon the character of the then current English manuals on Hindu law. Between 1873 and 1878 he brought out a series of five Samaveda-Brahmanas, without translations but with the commentary of Sayana, indexes, and elaborate introductory essays of the greatest value to scholarship at that time, especially that to the Vamsbrahmana which gives a full account of Sayana's literary life. These were followed, in 1879, by one of the Samaveda-pratisakyas, also with an essay. In 1878 he published an extract, with translation, of the Talavakara, one of the Brahmanas, as a specimen of its legendary lore. He also issued, in a succession of small pamphlets (1873–8), *Specimens of South Indian Dialects*; and an edition, prepared from the author's own manuscript, of Beschi's celebrated work on High Tamil and on Tamil poetry and rhetoric, which bears the title *Clavis humaniorum litterarum sublimioris Tamulici idiomatis* (1876). His essay *The Aindra School of Sanskrit Grammarians* (1875) put forward a theory on the development of grammatical science in ancient India. It failed to meet with general acceptance, but contributed to scholarly debate in this field of technical literature. Many minor communications were also addressed by him to the *Indian Antiquary*.

Burnell's health had from childhood never been strong, and his excessive exertions, extended over many years, in trying to combine heavy official work with studious labour in the most exhausting of Indian climates, broke him down. He had gone through a severe attack of cholera, followed at a later date by partial paralysis, before his last return to Europe in 1880, and he suffered besides from other constitutional illness; yet he had so far recovered that his friends began to hope that, although taxing work and a return to India were out of the question, he might still complete some of the tasks that he had begun. His last two winters were spent at San Remo. He returned from Italy in the early summer of 1882, and while staying at his brother's house at West Stratton, near Micheldever,

Hampshire, he was struck with a chill, which brought on inflammation of the lungs. He died there on 12 October and was buried in Micheldever churchyard.

An almost complete list of Burnell's major publications is appended to the obituary notice in the *Annual Report of the Royal Asiatic Society*. Of the works he left unfinished two were later published. The half-completed *Translation of the Ordinances of Manu* was finished by the American scholar E. W. Hopkins and published by Trübner & Co. (Oriental Series, 1885). A reprint of the old English version of Linschoten's *East Indies*, with interesting notes by Burnell, was half done in typescript, and having been completed by P. A. Tiele of Utrecht, was issued by the Hakluyt Society (2 vols., 1885). Another work, undertaken jointly by Burnell and Henry Yule, had been the occasional occupation of both scholars for many years, and Burnell's part in it was nearly completed. It appeared in 1886 (new edn, 1903) as *Hobson-Jobson, being a Glossary of Anglo-Indian Colloquial Words and Phrases*. This has remained in print and is still an invaluable and highly entertaining source for Anglo-oriental lexicography and historical folklore.

During the last years of his life Burnell took great interest in the history and literature of Portuguese India, and he collected many valuable books on the subject, which would probably, had he lived longer, have formed the foundation of scholarly writings. Preliminary labours of love in this connection were his *Tentative List of Books and some MSS Relating to the History of the Portuguese in India Proper* (1880) and a reprint (like the previous, for a few friends only) in a very handsome form, with preface and notes, of a rare and curious Italian version of a letter of King Emanuel of Portugal to Ferdinand of Spain, giving an account of the voyages and conquests in the East Indies between 1500 and 1505, originally printed at Rome in the latter year.

Burnell, in addition to his profound knowledge of Sanskrit and wide acquaintance with the vernaculars of southern India, had some knowledge of Tibetan (which he had studied with H. A. Jäschke when a fellow passenger from India in 1868), of Arabic (the language in which he passed in the competitive examination for the civil service), of Kawi, Javanese, and Coptic. Pali had been an eager object of study before he went to India, and perhaps remained so for a time, though his collectanea on Pali are all of early date. His last love in study was given to the Italian writers of the Renaissance, and especially to Cardinal Pietro Bembo, his intense admiration of whom was not widely shared among his correspondents either in England or in Italy. His circle of friends was small but close. An ardent bibliophile, he spent liberally on books, and was generous in lending them to other scholars. Likewise he would readily lend manuscripts and photographs, and gave freely of his time to answer requests for particular information. After the presentation of his manuscript collection to the India Library in 1870, he recommenced collecting on his return to India, and had gathered about 350 more. These were purchased from his heirs by the secretary of state in council for the same library.

STANLEY LANE-POOLE, *rev.* J. B. KATZ

Sources R. Rost, *The Athenaeum* (28 Oct 1882) · F. M. Müller, *The Academy* (21 Oct 1882), 295 · H. Yule, *The Times* (20 Oct 1882) · *Journal of the Royal Asiatic Society of Great Britain and Ireland*, new ser., 15 (1883), iv–xi [incl. list of published works] · *CGPLA Eng. & Wales* (1883) · b. cert.
Archives BL OIOC, commonplace book containing notes on south Indian languages and religions, etc. · JRL, corresp. | BL OIOC, Temple MSS · JRL, Melville MSS, Eng. MS 740
Likenesses photograph, BL OIOC · portrait, repro. in H. Yule and A. C. Burnell, *Hobson-Jobson* (1886)
Wealth at death £2129 9s. 1d.: probate, 23 Jan 1883, *CGPLA Eng. & Wales*

Burnell, Charles Desborough (1876–1969), oarsman, was born at Notting Hill, London, on 13 January 1876, the only child of George Edward Burnell, stockbroker, of Notting Hill, and his wife, Harriet Desborough. He was educated at Eton College and Magdalen College, Oxford, before becoming senior partner in the stockbroking firm of Wise and Burnell. A giant of a man, he showed exceptional promise as a schoolboy oarsman and won the ladies' plate at Henley royal regatta in 1894; at Oxford he was a member of four consecutive winning crews in the Oxford–Cambridge boat race from 1895 to 1898. In 1896 conditions for the race were appalling and Oxford, having lost the toss, chose to tuck in behind Cambridge rather than attempt to race alongside them on the outside of the Hammersmith bend. Though they were at one time a length and a half behind, they overlapped at Barnes Bridge and then, forcing Cambridge out into the rougher water, won by two-fifths of a length, at that time the closest finish in the history of the race except for the 1877 dead heat.

Burnell won the Grand Challenge Cup each year from 1898 to 1901, rowing for his college in 1899 and for Leander on the other occasions. In all but the last of those four years he also won the stewards' challenge cup, the premier prize for coxless fours. Still in Leander colours, he won the Cork international eights in 1902 and 1903. He was persuaded to come out of retirement to join the Leander eight which represented Great Britain in the 1908 Olympic regatta at Henley-on-Thames; the eight beat Belgium in the final to win the gold medal—a feat equalled by Burnell's son Richard, also at Henley, in the 1948 Olympics. Don (as Burnell was called by rowing men) used to say that in the fully forward position he rubbed the outside of his shoulders against the inside of his knees, an extraordinary illustration of how widely styles differ. Steve Fairbairn, the ultimate advocate of the unorthodox, once described Burnell as the best oarsman he had ever seen.

After the First World War, in 1919 Burnell was elected a steward of the royal regatta; he joined the committee of management the following year and umpired at the regatta for over forty years. He umpired the university boat race from 1927 to 1930 and was president of Leander and of the Henley Rowing Club: he held the latter office until his death.

Burnell joined the London rifle brigade as a territorial in 1894 and retired with the rank of major in 1913. After rejoining the army on the outbreak of war, as a captain, he commanded a company in France and was wounded at the second battle of Ypres and on other occasions. He commanded the 1st battalion of the regiment between 1917 and 1919, was twice mentioned in dispatches, and appointed DSO (1919) for services in France and Flanders. During the Second World War he served as a major in the upper Thames patrol of the Home Guard. He played a major part in local government, initially as vice-chairman of Walton and Weybridge urban district council and for over thirty years as chairman of the Wokingham rural district council. He became a JP in 1934 and was deputy lieutenant of the county of Berkshire in 1936. He was appointed OBE in 1954 for services in Berkshire.

Burnell married in 1903 Jessie Backhouse (d. 1966), daughter of Dr Frederick Thomas Hulke. They had two sons and two daughters. One daughter, Mary Balding, was appointed MBE in 1978. One of Burnell's grandsons (Peter, the son of Richard) gained an Oxford blue in 1962. The family was only the fourth to have had a father, son, and grandson row in the university boat race, all for Oxford. A special parade was held in the Guildhall, London, in 1964 'to mark the seventieth anniversary of his entry into the London rifle brigade and as a token of the universal esteem in which he is held'. Burnell died at Blewbury, Berkshire, on 3 October 1969.   DESMOND HILL, *rev.*

Sources *The Times* (6 Oct 1969) · personal knowledge (1981) · private information (1981)
Wealth at death £6250: probate, 9 Jan 1970, *CGPLA Eng. & Wales*

Burnell, Edward (*fl.* 1542–1565?), classical scholar, was reported by Thomas Tanner to have been professor of Greek literature at Rostock, Germany, where in 1542 he published a Latin study, *Epitomen dialectices*, for the use of the students. He had almost certainly left Rostock before 1560, and may very well be the man of that name who was vicar of Meopham, Kent, from 1550, and who resigned in 1553. This might suggest protestant convictions. Edward Burnell of Meopham was appointed as one of the six preachers of Canterbury Cathedral in 1557, and was in occupation of his position in September 1560. It was probably he who in 1565 contributed a short prefatory Latin verse to *The Poore Man's Library*, by William Alley, the unambiguously protestant bishop of Exeter. The Rostock professor cannot have been the Edward Burnell, gentleman, reported by Strype as imprisoned as a papist in the Marshalsea in 1581, not least since the age of the prisoner is given as about forty years.   STEPHEN WRIGHT

Sources Tanner, *Bibl. Brit.-Hib.* · J. Strype, *The life and acts of Matthew Parker*, new edn, 3 vols. (1821), vol. 1, p. 144 · J. Strype, *Ecclesiastical memorials*, 3 vols. (1822), vol. 3, p. 478 · D. I. Hill, *The six preachers of Canterbury Cathedral* (1982) · J. Posselius, *Scripta in academia Rostochiensi publice proposita* (1565) · J. Strype, *Annals of the Reformation and establishment of religion … during Queen Elizabeth's happy reign*, new edn, 2/2 (1824), 661

Burnell, Henry (*fl.* 1640–1654), playwright, appears to have been the son and heir of Christopher Burnell of Castleknock, near Dublin. The Burnells, of Old English Catholic descent, held considerable estates in Leinster and served as judges and legal officials in the fifteenth and sixteenth centuries. Burnell's grandfather Henry Burnell (d. 1614) was imprisoned for his organization of legal resistance to taxes levied on recusants under Elizabeth I. Burnell married Lady Frances Dillon (*d.* 1640), daughter of James Dillon, first earl of Roscommon. This extended family circle connected Burnell to the influential Barnewall and Wentworth families. His only known play is *Landgartha. A tragie-comedy, as it was presented in the new theater in Dublin, with good applause, being an ancient story, written by H. B.* (Dublin, 1641). The prologue suggests that Burnell had already produced one unsuccessful play. Harbage linked the lost plays *The Toy* and *The Irish Gentleman*, for which only James Shirley's prologues are extant, to Burnell but there is no evidence for this (A. Harbage, *Annals of English Drama, 975–1700*, 1940). The British Library catalogue ascribes *The World's Idol, or, Plutus the God of Wealth* (1659), a translation from Aristophanes 'by H. H. B.', to Burnell, but there is, again, no evidence for this.

Burnell's prologue '*delivered by an* Amazon, *with a Battle-Axe in her hand*' states that the play was written 'with the expense / Of lesse then two Moneths time'. He took his plot from Saxo Grammaticus. The Amazon queen, Landgartha, aids Reyner, king of Denmark to invade Norway, defeating and killing its ruler King Frollo of Sweden. Reyner persuades the reluctant Landgartha to marry him, but he deserts his pregnant wife for Vraca, a lover in Denmark. Landgartha nevertheless saves Reyner from invasion and he repents his adultery. There is, however, no final scene of reconciliation and the play ends with another speech by an Amazon '*with her Sword and Belt in her hand*'. In a definition of tragicomedy, rare for the period, Burnell wrote in his epilogue: 'a Tragie-Comedy sho'd neither end Comically or Tragically, but betwixt both: which Decorum I did my best to observe … To the rest of the bablers, I despise any answer'. Clark described *Landgartha* as 'the first play written by an Irishman with Irish local colour' (Clark, 37). The only Irish character is the Amazon Marfisa, who wears 'an Irish Gowne tuck'd up to mid-legge, with a broad basket-hilt Sword on, hanging in a great Belt, Broags on her feet' (act III).

Landgartha was performed at the Werburgh Street Theatre, founded by John Ogilby and home for some years to James Shirley. Indeed it was probably a reply to Shirley's *St Patrick for Ireland: the First Part* (1640). Contrary to Shirley's vision of St Patrick's civilization of Ireland by conversion, Burnell's play offers a more military version of conquest. *Landgartha* was 'first Acted on S. Patricks day, 1639', the day after the opening of the Dublin parliament. Fletcher suggests that Burnell intended the play to influence opinion in the debates scheduled on the Act for the Repealing of the Statute of Bigamy. According to Chetwood, *Landgartha* was 'the last [play] that was performed … before the Rebellion' (Fletcher, 52). The published version includes dedicatory poems by Burnell's daughter Eleonora, an unidentified 'Philippus Patricius', and by an English cousin, one 'Io. Bermingham'. This last compares Burnell to Ben Jonson:

> And though thou *England* never saw'st …
> thou art farre more like to *Ben*: then they
> That lay clayme as heires to him, wrongfully.

Burnell joined the Catholic confederation, established in 1642. The state papers record orders for payments for military service in 1645 and 1646, and payment for outstanding rents in 1647 (*CSP Ire.*, 1633–47, 643, 713). The date and cause of Burnell's death are unrecorded. He is last glimpsed in a 1654 petition to the Cromwellian administration requesting, 'for his tedious and languishing sickness' (Prendergast, 41), a dispensation from the order to transplant to Connaught.   DEANA RANKIN

Sources J. T. Gilbert, *A history of the city of Dublin*, 3 vols. (1854) • J. T. Gilbert, *History of the confederation and war in Ireland*, 7 vols. (1882) • *DNB* • *CSP Ire.*, 1633–47 • Genealogical Office, Dublin, MSS 72, 172 • J. P. Prendergast, *The Cromwellian settlement of Ireland* (1865) • A. Fletcher, *Drama, performance and polity in pre-Cromwellian Ireland* (2000) • W. S. Clark, *The early Irish stage* (1955) • F. H. Ristine, *English tragicomedy, its origin and history* (1962) • W. R. Chetwood, *A general history of the stage, from its origin in Greece to the present time* (1749) • R. Gillespie, 'Political ideas and their social contexts in seventeenth-century Ireland', *Political thought in seventeenth century Ireland: kingdom or colony?*, ed. J. Ohlmeyer (2000), 107–27 • C. Shaw, 'Landgartha and the Irish dilemma', *Éire–Ireland*, 13/1 (1978), 26–39 • B. McGrath, 'A biographical dictionary of the membership of the Irish House of Commons, 1640–41', 2 vols., PhD diss., TCD, 1997 • *The works of Sir James Ware concerning Ireland revised and improved*, ed. and trans. W. Harris, rev. edn, 3 vols. (1739–46)

Burnell, Robert (*d.* 1292), administrator and bishop of Bath and Wells, came from a family that by 1198 had given its name to Acton Burnell in Shropshire.

Family and early career Robert was probably the son of Roger Burnell, last heard of in 1259, from whom he would have inherited the half of the manor of Acton held of the Corbets of Caus. He had two brothers who were killed in 1282 fighting against the Welsh at the Menai Strait, and another, Hugh, who died in 1286 leaving a son named Philip to be Robert's heir. After the outlawry and death of William Burnell, the representative of the senior branch of the family, for a double murder committed in 1248, the other half of Acton, and Burnell lands in nearby Ruckley and Langley, held from the crown in serjeanty for the service of going into Wales with the king for forty days in time of war, were granted in fee to William de Gardinis. By 1266 Robert had bought them back, and was consolidating his estates with a single-mindedness that culminated in the building at Acton Burnell of the fortified manor house, the ruins of which still survive. When permission was given for the embattlement of the house in 1284, Edward I remarked on the affection that he had long observed the bishop of Bath and Wells to entertain 'towards his native place of Acton Burnell, whence he derived his origin, and towards the people of those parts' (Eyton, 6.132).

Robert Burnell would have been about the same age as Edward, and it was service to him as prince and king that made possible the redemption and development of the Burnell inheritance, a service that must have begun soon after the prince's acquisition in 1254 of great estates in the marches and of a household to administer his apanage. In April 1257 Robert Burnell appeared in a witness list with known members of Edward's council, and in November 1260 he went to France with the prince. He was rewarded in 1266 by permission to impark his land within the royal forest, and in 1269 by the grant of a weekly market and two annual fairs at Acton. His standing as the senior clerk in Edward's entourage was spectacularly revealed in 1270 by the prince's attempt to get him elected to the see of Canterbury, following the death of Archbishop Boniface of Savoy, the queen's uncle. The attempt, which was ended by the pope's appointment of Robert Kilwardby (d. 1279), was no doubt intended to seal Edward's arrangements for the safeguarding of his interests while he was on crusade. Burnell had vowed to accompany the prince to the East, but instead he replaced Henry III's veteran servant, Robert Walerand (d. 1273), as one of the four 'lieutenants of the Lord Edward', along with Walter Giffard, archbishop of York (d. 1279), Philip Basset (d. 1271), and Roger Mortimer (d. 1282). On their behalf, and soon with the title of archdeacon of York, he is found issuing mandates to the justiciar of Ireland and others under the Lord Edward's seal. In August 1272, three months before Edward's accession as king, and two years before his return to England, Burnell bought a house at Westminster immediately to the north of the palace. With the other lieutenants he oversaw the transition to the new reign, calling a parliament and receiving oaths of fealty. He also transacted wardrobe business, receiving money loaned by Italian bankers for the furtherance of the king's affairs and, with the treasurer, the proceeds of a clerical tenth.

The chancellor and the statutes   Immediately after Edward's coronation in September 1274 Burnell replaced the veteran Walter of Merton (d. 1277) as chancellor and became the leading figure of a new government. In the following January the king at last saw him elected to a bishopric at Bath and Wells. Edward's later chancellors were not promoted as vigorously as Burnell: he seems to have had unique importance by reason of his intimacy with the king and his ability to supervise the whole administration. Because he was so constantly with Edward, there is little written evidence of his relationship with the king, or of his part in the genesis of the great administrative and legal measures of the first half of the reign. It is significant, however, that Burnell's chancellorship coincided exactly with the period of Edwardian statute making, and no one but the chancellor could have had responsibility for instituting the series of administrative inquiries and handling the growing stream of petitions to the crown that together provided the basis for legislation in parliament.

The chroniclers remark on Burnell's determination that chancery should have a fixed base in London, so that petitioners would know where to find a remedy. In 1280 a chancery memorandum gave to the chancellor, in collaboration with other chief ministers, the responsibility of sorting the multitude of petitions that were arriving at parliament time, and of passing only the most urgent to king and council. Magnates and royal officials wrote to Burnell constantly, seeking favours or asking administrative questions. The bishop of Exeter sought his help in a dispute with Ralph Hengham (d. 1311), who may have owed to the chancellor his own promotion to be chief justice of king's bench. When the earl of Gloucester was kept

from court by the illness of one of his children he asked Burnell to make his excuses privately to the king. Queen Eleanor, the king's mother, wrote requesting him to obtain a pardon for John de Beauchamp, the bearer of her letter, for not having performed his service in one of the Welsh campaigns. And the king's justices in Devon wrote pressing him to suspend the eyre, because they would be needed at a parliament and did not want to stay on in the south-west where the corn had failed. The issuing of judicial commissions and the direction of the justices' circuits was a particular responsibility of the chancellor, wherever he happened to be.

On 11 October 1274, within a month of Burnell's receipt of the great seal and his starting to sign writs 'of course as well as by command', commissions were issued for inquiries in each county concerning royal rights and liberties, the behaviour of sheriffs and bailiffs, and other matters affecting 'the state of the king and the state of the community of the said counties' (Rymer, *Foedera*, 4, 1, pt 2, 517). In the following April 'the first general parliament' of the reign was called so that the king might 'set to rights the state of his kingdom' (*Statutes of the Realm*, 1.26), and the fifty-one 'establishments' known as Statute of Westminster I were issued. But the problems of Wales and Gascony soon intruded upon the administration of England.

Welsh and Gascon affairs   In November 1276 Burnell took part in the council at Westminster that judged Llywelyn ap Gruffudd (d. 1282) a rebel and disturber of the peace, and in the late summer and autumn of 1277 the chancellor was at Chester or Shrewsbury, providing safe conducts for merchants bringing supplies for the army fighting Edward's first Welsh war as well as issuing routine commissions for the whole realm. On 13 August he celebrated mass before the king and nobility at the laying of the foundations of Edward's abbey of Vale Royal in Cheshire. After the imposition on Llywelyn in November of the humiliating treaty of Aberconwy, the chancellor conducted him to Westminster to do homage to Edward. He must have had a part in devising the commission to a party of justices, headed by another Shropshire man, Walter of Hopton, to hear and determine cases in the marches and in Wales itself, a challenge to native law that helped to provoke the Welsh revolt of 1282 and the final conquest of the principality. Burnell and Sir Otto Grandson (d. 1328), his neighbour in Westminster and Edward's other close friend, were in Paris on their way to pacify the Gascons, when the king reported to them—too complacently— that Llywelyn was submitting to his justice 'in the most agreeable manner' (Powicke, 672). This letter of March 1278 commended the envoys for their efforts: no one, not even the king himself, knew better than they what needed to be done in Gascony. Their negotiations led to Burnell's return to France in the spring of 1279, this time with the king, for the sealing of the treaty of Amiens.

From August 1282 Burnell was again on the Welsh front, directing chancery business from Rhuddlan or, as the second Welsh war moved to a climax, from Conwy or Caernarfon. At Rhuddlan on 19 March 1284 there was sealed the statute that laid down the form of government of the conquered principality and prescribed the chancery writs that should run there. The years of the conquest of Wales and the ringing of Snowdonia with castles were also the years when Burnell was receiving gifts of oaks from the royal forest for the embattlement of his manor house at Acton, easily accessible from north Wales, and of deer in preparation for the entertainment there of Edward himself or his children. In October 1283 a parliament begun at Shrewsbury was completed at the chancellor's house, and the Statute of Acton Burnell issued.

Financial and family business It was appropriate that the first of the two Edwardian statutes designed to expedite the recovery of mercantile debts should have been promulgated at Burnell's house, for the majority of references to the chancellor in his own rolls concern his financial transactions, most often acknowledgements of debts to him ranging from a few marks to 500 marks or more. Public and private finances were intermeshed. Burnell arranged and audited loans to the king by the merchants of Lucca, and himself lent more than 3000 marks to Edward between 1282 and 1285. For his own profit and that of Hugh Burnell he engaged in the trade in Jewish mortgages, and 'in consideration of the service he had rendered the king from his earliest years' (*CPR, 1281–92*, 228) the brothers were allowed to take timber freely from their woods in Shropshire although they were part of the royal forest. He bought the barony of Castle Holgate in Shropshire, property in Bristol (while the chancery was in the town), lands in the Isle of Ely, and the manor of Sheen in Surrey, the last of which he then sold to Otto Grandson. As bishop he was allowed his liberties with little question. He was also permitted to enclose the churchyard and canons' precinct of Wells Cathedral with a stone wall and to crenellate it for better security. But provision for his family seems to have been his chief concern. In June 1283 he purchased from the abbot of Vale Royal the custody of some of the lands of Richard (I) Fitzalan (*d.* 1302) during his minority, gaining temporary possession not only of the honour of Whitchurch but also of the castle and honour of Arundel. This gave him the opportunity to arrange a marriage between Philip Burnell and Richard Fitzalan's sister Matilda.

By repute Robert Burnell had several bastard children of his own to provide for. His daughter Amabilla married Andrew Hengham, of the chief justice's family. By a deed of 1275 witnessed by Otto Grandson, William of Greystoke in Cumberland (where Burnell had one of his numerous livings) undertook to pay the bishop of Bath and Wells and Joan Burnell £500 if his son and heir did not marry Joan within five years; fifteen years later the bond of Ralph of Grendon in Warwickshire that he would marry Joan was enrolled in chancery. A Master William Burnell became dean of Wells and was one of the bishop's executors. Edward tried to get his chancellor, despite his reputation, translated from Bath and Wells to Canterbury in 1278, and to the rich see of Winchester in 1280, but the pope quashed both appointments after inquiries into the bishop's morals. On the latter occasion John Pecham (*d.* 1292), whom the pope had made archbishop in 1278,

begged the Roman curia to deny that he reported unfavourably about Burnell, but he certainly believed that the bishop used spiritual censures to enforce the payment of debts to merchants who were useful to the government.

Burnell was assiduous in caring for his cathedral church, however, bought advowsons to give to monasteries, and generally co-operated with other prelates in the interests of church as well as state. The chancery rolls record his retirement from court to his diocese at the beginning of each Lent, after depositing the great seal in the wardrobe. As chancellor he sent in clerks to restore debt-ridden abbeys to solvency. Otto Grandson and other magnates gave him power to appoint to livings in their patronage during their absence from the country, and Pecham chose him to be his vicar-general when he went to Aber in 1282 to try to mediate between Edward and Llywelyn. The king left him to receive the grievances of the clergy in the Easter parliament of 1285, and he seems to have suggested the mechanism that implemented the eventual compromise between the two jurisdictions by which the chancellor or chief justice would have the power to send back to the church courts clearly spiritual cases.

Foreign affairs and last years The parliament of 1285 produced another great statute, Westminster II, which made detailed regulations about the writs obtainable in chancery and defined the power of the clerks to frame new writs. But within a year the chancellor was again on the way to Gascony, this time travelling in the company of the king and taking the great seal and the wardrobe with him. At the French court Burnell made a speech on Edward's behalf, setting out the English interpretation of Anglo-French relations since the treaty of Paris of 1259. In Gascony he sat on a powerful tribunal to try the seneschal and had a *bastide* named after him. He returned to England with the seal in August 1289, a few days before the king, and was quickly engaged on an inquiry into widespread allegations of misdeeds by some of the royal servants who had stayed in England. Scottish affairs then became the major preoccupation. At Salisbury in early November 1289 the chancellor oversaw a formal exchange of letters from the keepers of the realm of Scotland on the one hand and the king of Norway on the other, appointing ambassadors to negotiate about the affairs of Erik's daughter Margaret, 'the Maid of Norway', and setting out Edward's terms for arranging her passage from Norway. In February 1290 further letters concerning the matter were sealed in secrecy at Burnell's house in London.

But plans for a marriage between Margaret and Edward's son were dashed by the death of Margaret in the autumn of 1290 on her way from Norway, and then in November Edward's own queen, Eleanor, died. Edward depended even more heavily on Burnell, who was one of the queen's executors, and in May 1291 he baptized the king's grandson, Gilbert de Clare (*d.* 1314). Early in June he was at Norham on the Scottish border, where on Edward's behalf (though the king was present) he required each of the claimants to the Scottish throne to acknowledge English overlordship of Scotland before the hearing of the Great Cause commenced. In the following year he received a grant of 158 oaks from the forest of Cannock for works at his manor of Wolverhampton, but by the autumn he was back in the borders with Edward, considering the claims of John Balliol and Robert Bruce to the Scottish crown; he died at Berwick on 25 October 1292. William of Hambleton (d. 1307), archdeacon of York and the bishop's long-serving attorney, placed the seal in the hands of the keeper of the wardrobe, Walter Langton (d. 1321), Burnell's old clerk and Edward's most trusted servant for the remainder of his reign, and set out with his master's body for burial at Wells.

Philip Burnell was heir to the eighty-two manors the chancellor had amassed in nineteen counties, twenty-one of them in Shropshire, another thirteen in a belt stretching around south London. But Philip died in 1294 leaving extensive debts, and although two of his descendants were summoned to parliament as barons, the chancellor founded no great dynasty.   ALAN HARDING

Sources CIPM, 3, no. 65 · Chancery records · R. W. Eyton, Antiquities of Shropshire, 12 vols. (1854–60), vol. 6 · VCH Shropshire, vol. 8 · Ann. mon., vols. 2, 3, 4 · Registrum epistolarum fratris Johannis Peckham, archiepiscopi Cantuariensis, ed. C. T. Martin, 3 vols., Rolls Series, 77 (1882–5) · D. L. Douie, Archbishop Pecham (1952) · E. L. G. Stones and G. G. Simpson, eds., Edward I and the throne of Scotland, 1290–1296, 2 vols. (1978) · M. Prestwich, Edward I (1988) · F. M. Powicke, King Henry III and the Lord Edward: the community of the realm in the thirteenth century, 2 vols. (1947) · Rymer, Foedera, new edn, 4, 1, pt 2 · A. Luders and others, eds., Statutes of the realm, 11 vols. in 12, RC (1810–28), vol. 1 · RotS, vol. 1 · CPR, 1281–92
Wealth at death see CIPM

Burnes, Sir Alexander (1805–1841), political officer in India and explorer, fourth of the five sons of James Burnes (1780–1852), provost of Montrose, and his wife, Elizabeth, daughter of Adam Glegg, chief magistrate of Montrose, was born on 16 May 1805 in Montrose. Sir James *Burnes (1801–1862) was his brother. He was educated at Montrose Academy and in 1821, aged sixteen, sailed for Bombay to take up a cadetship in the Bombay army.

Immediately upon arrival Burnes began learning Hindustani and Persian and within a year was made regimental interpreter to the 1st Bombay native infantry (Bombay Grenadiers) at Surat. In 1825 he was appointed Persian interpreter, and thereafter quartermaster, to the Cutch field force. In 1828 he was transferred to Bombay as the assistant quartermaster-general of the army and in 1829 he became assistant to the British resident in Cutch.

Burnes excelled at political work. His linguistic ability combined with adventurousness, boundless self-confidence, and a certain diplomatic guile earmarked him for delicate political duties. In January 1831 he was dispatched on a double-edged mission up the River Indus to Lahore. His stated object was to present five dray horses from William IV to Ranjit Singh, but he was also instructed to conduct a detailed survey of the river and the countries bordering it—a duplicitous scheme which Sir Charles Metcalfe criticized as a foolhardy and underhanded approach to foreign relations. The amirs of Sind,

wary of Burnes's intentions, delayed his progress upriver for several months, but he finally reached Lahore in July, where he was greeted cordially by Ranjit Singh. From Lahore Burnes travelled to Simla to present his report to the governor-general, Lord Bentinck, and while there proposed a much grander expedition across central Asia to Bukhara and beyond. His suggestion was well timed. Political opinion in London and Calcutta worried increasingly about Russian expansion in central Asia and Burnes seemed the ideal man to gather information about the region.

In January 1832 Burnes set out from Ludhiana accompanied by Dr James Gerard of the Bengal army; an Indian surveyor, Muhammad Ali; and a young secretary of Kashmiri descent, Mohan Lal. The party travelled modestly, always in local dress, and variously represented themselves as Englishmen, Armenians, pilgrims, merchants—whatever the often hazardous circumstances seemed to require. They reached Bukhara in June and then travelled across the Turkoman desert to Mashhad, on to the Caspian Sea, down to Tehran, and finally back by sea to Bombay. The journey took thirteen months and so captured the public's imagination that Burnes was welcomed back to England in 1833 as a hero. He received the gold medal of the Royal Geographical Society, was elected a fellow of the Royal Society and honorary member of the Royal Asiatic Society, and enjoyed a flattering audience with William IV. In 1834 he published an officially sanctioned account of his journey, which also included a narrative of the earlier voyage up the Indus. The book, Travels into Bokhara; being the account of a journey from India to Cabool, Tartary, and Persia, was an instant success, selling 900 copies on the first day. It is noteworthy for the freshness and acuteness of its descriptions and, given the times, the relatively cosmopolitan outlook of its author.

In 1835 Burnes returned to his post as political assistant in Cutch. At the end of 1836 Lord Auckland dispatched him on a commercial mission to Kabul. Inevitably, however, political concerns about Afghanistan's position as a buffer between the British and Russian empires dominated the mission. Burnes reached Kabul in September 1837 and was warmly welcomed by the amir, Dost Muhammad Khan, who was desperately seeking an ally to help fend off Sikh and Persian aggression. Burnes, who had formed a favourable impression of him when they had met in 1832, wanted to offer him British support, but his hands were tied. Lord Auckland and his counsellors mistrusted Dost Muhammad's independence and proposed instead to restore a former amir, Shah Shuja, to the Afghanistan throne and hence have their own man in Kabul. Burnes swung into line behind this policy although he had little faith in it; he had met Shah Shuja in exile in 1831 and thought him an ineffectual leader. In the summer of 1838 Burnes was sent ahead of the army of the Indus to smooth its passage through Sind and Baluchistan en route to Afghanistan. In August 1839 he was one of the three British officers who escorted Shah Shuja into Kabul but, to his disappointment, the top job of envoy went to William Hay Macnaghten, one of the architects of Shah Shuja's restoration. In 1838 Burnes learned that he had been knighted and granted the brevet rank of lieutenant-colonel, but this was inadequate compensation for the boredom and inactivity he endured as the second political officer in Kabul. Towards the end of 1841 the political situation deteriorated and Burnes, although aware of the unpopularity of Shah Shuja's government, was unprepared for the ferocity of the Afghan revenge. On 2 November 1841 an infuriated crowd besieged his house in Kabul and murdered him, along with his younger brother Charles and Lieutenant William Broadfoot. It marked the beginning of Britain's disastrous retreat from Afghanistan. Ironically, in the ensuing search for scapegoats it was Burnes's reputation which suffered most, even though he had been a severe and well-informed critic of the policy of intervention. *Cabool: being a personal narrative of a journey to, and residence in that city in the years 1836–38* was published posthumously in 1842. KATHERINE PRIOR

Sources J. W. Kaye, *Lives of Indian officers*, new edn, 2 (1904) · J. Lunt, *Bokhara Burnes* (1969) · *GM*, 2nd ser., 17 (1842), 434–6 · A. Burnes, *Travels into Bokhara*, 3 vols. (1834) · C. E. Buckland, *Dictionary of Indian biography* (1906) · *DNB* · Bombay army records, BL OIOC
Archives PRO, embassy and consular archives, foreign office documents · Worcester College, Oxford, journal to Kabul | BL OIOC, Masson MSS · NA Scot., Dalhousie MSS · RGS, letters to Sir Henry Rawlinson and papers
Likenesses W. Brockedon, chalk drawing, 1834, NPG · D. Maclise, oils, 1834, priv. coll. · E. Finden, stipple, pubd 1835 (after D. Maclise), NPG

Burnes, Sir James (1801–1862), surgeon, son of James Burnes (1780–1852), provost of Montrose, and his wife, Elizabeth, daughter of Adam Glegg, chief magistrate of Montrose, was born at Montrose on 12 February 1801. He belonged to the same family as Robert Burns. After medical training at Edinburgh University and at Guy's and St Thomas's hospitals, London, he arrived at Bombay with his brother Alexander *Burnes, in 1821. He filled various minor posts in the Indian Medical Service (IMS), and was successful in the open competition for the office of surgeon to the residency of Cutch. He volunteered to accompany the force which, in 1825, expelled the Sindians who had devastated Cutch and forced the British brigade to retire to Bhuj. The amirs of Sind then invited him to visit them as 'the most skilful of physicians and their best friend, and the cementer of the bonds of amity between the two governments', and on his return he was complimented by the government on the zeal and ability he had displayed at Cutch and Hyderabad. His account of his visit to Sind, written as an official report to the resident at Cutch, is an excellent account of the country, and was a valuable contribution to the geography of India. It was published with the title *Narrative of a Visit to Scinde*, in 1830. In 1829 Burnes married, in Bombay, Sophia, the second daughter of Major-General Sir George Holmes. They had nine children. In June 1862 Burnes married Esther Pryce, in London.

During a visit to England on sick leave in 1834 Burnes was made LLD at Glasgow University and a fellow of the Royal Society, and received the knighthood of the Royal Guelphic Order from William IV. On his return to India in 1837 he was at once appointed garrison surgeon of Bombay; afterwards he became secretary of the medical board, superintending surgeon, and finally physician-general on 17 September 1849. He was also a member of the board of education and a trustee of the Oriental Bank. Ill health compelled Burnes to retire on 20 November 1849, and to return to Britain. He served as a justice of the peace in Forfarshire and in Middlesex.

Burnes was an enthusiastic freemason and held the office of grand master for western India. In December 1844 he established the Rising Star masonic lodge for native Indians in Bombay. Burnes died in London on 19 September 1862.

STANLEY LANE-POOLE, *rev.* JAMES MILLS

Sources W. A. Laurie, 'Memoir of James Burnes', *Notes on his name and family*, ed. J. Burnes (1851) · D. G. Crawford, ed., *Roll of the Indian Medical Service, 1615–1930* (1930) · *Men of the time* (1862)

Burneston, Simon. *See* Boraston, Simon (*fl.* 1311–1338).

Burnet, Alexander (1615–1684), archbishop of St Andrews, was baptized in Edinburgh on 6 August 1615, the younger of two sons of James Burnet, minister of Lauder from 1615, and his wife, Christian, daughter of George Dundas of that ilk, and kin to the Traquair family. His grandfather William Burnet of Barns in the parish of Manor in Tweeddale, known as the Hoolet o' Barns, was a notorious border raider; ironically several of his sons rose to eminence in Scottish legal circles. Burnet studied at the University of Edinburgh, graduating MA on 22 June 1633. Instead of assuming a parochial charge he entered the family of John Stewart, first earl of Traquair, as chaplain and tutor. Charles I presented him to Coldingham on 10 January 1639, but this was after the national covenant and the Glasgow general assembly and nothing could come of this for an episcopalian sympathizer. Burnet's father, who had become minister of Jedburgh in 1635, was deposed in April 1639 for the same opinions. It may have been about this time that Burnet married Elizabeth Fleming, daughter of George Fleming of Kilconquhar, Fife. They had a son and two daughters.

On 15 April 1641 Alexander entered the living of Burmarsh, Kent, one of a number of Scottish episcopal refugees to find work in the English church, and received ordination there. His royalism led to his ejection in 1650, though an A. Burnett is found as minister of Tenham, Kent, on 22 January 1657. He went to the continent and acted as a courier for Charles II. Following the Restoration, Burnet became rector of Ivychurch, Kent, and chaplain to his father's cousin General Andrew Rutherford, governor of Dunkirk. Burnet's duties in Dunkirk, where his elder brother, Robert, was a physician, included ministry to the English congregation, hence his title in one source, 'Dean of the City of Dunkirk'. He desired to build 'a handsome and convenient chappell' (Sheldon MSS, first letter, 20 Nov 1661) for the congregation, imploring English aid through Bishop Gilbert Sheldon. He is reported to have preached to parliament on 16 June 1663 on 2 Chronicles 19: 6, 'And [King Jehoshaphat] said to the judges, "Take heed what ye do: for ye judge not for man, but for the Lord'".

In 1663 Burnet returned to Scotland after an absence of nearly twenty-five years, and on 18 September was consecrated bishop of Aberdeen by the archbishop of St Andrews, James Sharp, and some others. He quickly succeeded Andrew Fairfoul in the archiepiscopal see of Glasgow on 18 January 1664, and was installed on 11 April; Gilbert Burnet (no relation) alleged the influence in both appointments of General Rutherford (from 2 February 1663 earl of Teviot). Burnet was sworn of the privy council on 26 April 1664 and became an extraordinary lord of session in November; that year he preached at the earl of Glencairn's funeral.

In Glasgow this convinced episcopalian had to wrestle with the deteriorating situation in the west of the country of radical presbyterians refusing to attend regular parochial services and resorting to conventicles. Burnet had no patience for this behaviour, and it was reported that he said 'that the only way to deal with a fanatic was to starve him' (R. Wodrow, *History of the Sufferings of the Church of Scotland*, 1.429). He was inclined to take the worst view of affairs and behaved provocatively, quickly ordaining, according to Robert Wodrow, five or six curates using 'the English pontifical' (ibid., 2.8). He was vigorous in proceeding against nonconforming ministers whom his predecessor had left alone, to the extent that even some of his co-religionists were provoked. Burnet was a leader in acting against the rebels of the Pentland rising in 1666, and in a letter to Archbishop Sheldon on 17 November he urged that 'all persons of interest in this kingdom be forthwith requyred to sign the declaration appointed by Act of Parliament concerning the covenant' (Airy, 36, appx 39).

However, with the failure of repression came toleration for those nonconforming ministers who would behave peaceably, beginning with the indulgence of 7 June 1669 which permitted the restoration of forty-two presbyterian clergy to their parishes. This represented a rejection of Burnet's policy, but of more immediate impact in effecting his downfall was the culmination of his agitation against the conduct of the earl of Lauderdale and other nobles who he believed were sabotaging royal policy in Scotland. Beginning in 1667 he had reported to the king about his concerns; in October 1668 a synod held at Peebles, which he attended, proposed to address the king directly, circumventing council, about 'the griwancis of the chirch through the increas of popery & qwakerisme, the frequency of conventticles, & the not putting the laws in wigorous executione agains disorderly persons' (Airy, 38.121), and in mid-September 1669 he endorsed the remonstrance of the synod of Glasgow. This document complained about the new policy of leniency, which, it alleged, encouraged nonconformity and eroded the position of the episcopal party, 'so that being placed without the reach of our censures they value not any thing that is our Interest as a constituted Church' (ibid., 36, appx 65). Sir Robert Moray thought 'that this damned paper shewes Bishops & Episcopall people are as bad on this chapter as the most arrant Presbyterian or Remonstrator'

(ibid., 36.139). The king was not prepared to suffer this public assertiveness, which undermined his determination to keep Scotland quiet, and thus he acted to force the archbishop out. The privy council learned on 6 January 1670 that Burnet had resigned on 24 December 1669, telling Archbishop Sheldon that '[I] am so legally divested of a very weighty and comfortlesse charge ... Now I am laid aside as ane uselesse and unprofitable person' (ibid., 2, appx 68).

Burnet retired to England, reserving a pension of £300 from the diocesan revenues. He was replaced by Robert Leighton of Dunblane first as commendator and then formally as archbishop in 1671, though Burnet believed that Leighton 'was never legally translated ... as the Canons require' (*Historical Notices*, 1.165); but after several years Leighton had had enough and on 17 December 1674 he too resigned and went to England. Burnet had already been reappointed by Charles on 16 September 1674 and then by the privy council on 29 September. Wodrow believed that simony was behind the restoration, but John Lamb wrote that it was political: Lauderdale was now reverting to more rigorous methods, and his move was seconded by those who upheld the episcopal government of the church. Though Sir John Lauder of Fountainhall wrote that after his dismissal and return to Glasgow 'he was a man of much moderation and temper' (Lauder, *Historical Observes*, 1840, 136), rather like Gilbert Burnet would write, Archbishop Burnet was soon once again on the attack, petitioning Lauderdale in February 1676 about the audacity of the indulged and the conventiclers. Burnet reported to the king on 25 April 1678, and returned the next year to London. He succeeded James Sharp in the see of St Andrews on 13 August 1679. He wrote to the Aberdeen magistrates to vacate the charges of those clergy who refused the test.

Burnet took sick the same night he assisted in the consecration of Alexander Cairncross as bishop of Brechin, 10 August 1684, and died at St Andrews on 22 August 1684. He was buried there on 2 September in St Salvator's Chapel 'besyde Bischop Kennedy' (James Kennedy, c.1408–1465), but there is no longer any sign of his burial. The sermon was preached by Bishop John Paterson of Edinburgh. His son was already dead; his daughter Anne had married first, on 10 September 1667, Alexander Elphinstone, seventh Lord Elphinstone (d. 1669), and second, on 20 August 1674, Patrick Murray, third Lord Elibank; his daughter Margaret had married, on 28 April 1674, Roderick Mackenzie of Prestonhall. Burnet's estate was valued at £41,470 Scots, including two coaches worth £300, silver plate worth £923, and books worth £1050. His beneficiaries included a nephew, Robert Burnet, and Joan Fleming, who was the widow of James Smith, minister of Eddleston, presumably the archbishop's sister-in-law. He also made provision for the poor of his archiepiscopal see, namely a plot of land worth an annual rental of £5 10s., called the Bishop's Rig or Bishop Burnet's Acre. In 1668 he had inherited one half of the estate of Woodhouse in Manor; the value of its rental in 1649 was £164 18s., and upon his death was shared by his daughters.

There is no surviving portrait of Burnet: the Lauderdale correspondence refers to him as Longifacies and Long Nez. In the dedication to his only published work, *The Blessedness of the Dead* (1673), his funeral sermons for the second marquess of Montrose, and for the marchioness, he wrote of 'this age which looks upon me with more prejudice than impartial Posterity will (I hope) think I have deserved', and indeed Gilbert Burnet thought that while he was a good and sincere man, he was 'much in the power of others' and 'not cut out for a Court, or for the Ministry' (*Bishop Burnet's History*, ed. Burnet and Burnet, 1.160). On the final letter sent to him by Burnet, Archbishop William Sancroft wrote with words borrowed from Horace: 'Multis ille bonis flebilis occidit: Nulli flebilior quam tibi, Scotia' ('Many lament his passing, but none more than thee, Scotland').

DAVID GEORGE MULLAN

Sources J. A. Lamb, 'Archbishop Alexander Burnet, 1614–84', *Records of the Scottish Church History Society*, 11 (1951–3), 133–48 · J. Buckroyd, *Church and state in Scotland, 1660–1681* (1980) · J. Buckroyd, 'The dismissal of Archbishop Alexander Burnet, 1669', *Records of the Scottish Church History Society*, 18 (1972–4), 149–55 · *The Lauderdale papers*, ed. O. Airy, 3 vols., CS, new ser., 34, 36, 38 (1884–5); repr. (New York, 1965) · *DNB* · I. B. Cowan, *The Scottish covenanters, 1660–1688* (1976) · *Fasti Scot.*, new edn, 7.327–8 · Bodl. Oxf., Sheldon MSS, MS Add. c. 306 · *Bishop Burnet's History of his own time*, ed. G. Burnet and T. Burnet, 2 vols. (1724–34) · J. Lauder, *Historical observes of memorable occurrents in church and state, from October 1680 to April 1686*, ed. A. Urquhart and D. Laing, Bannatyne Club, 66 (1840) · *Historical notices of Scotish affairs, selected from the manuscripts of Sir John Lauder of Fountainhall*, ed. D. Laing, 2 vols., Bannatyne Club, 87 (1848)

Archives U. Edin., corresp. | BL, letters to duke of Lauderdale, Charles II, etc., Add. MSS 23122–23138, 23242–23247 · Bodl. Oxf., Sheldon MSS, letters to Sheldon, MS. Add. C. 306 · NL Scot., letters to duke of Lauderdale · priv. coll., corresp. with duke of Lauderdale

Burnet [*née* Blake; *other married name* Berkeley], **Elizabeth** (1661–1709), religious writer, was born on 8 November 1661, the elder daughter of Sir Richard Blake, of Easterton, Wiltshire, and Elizabeth, daughter of Dr Bathurst, a London physician, who may have been John *Bathurst MD (d. 1659). After a puritan upbringing she was married in Westminster Abbey on 11 March 1678 to Robert Berkeley (1650–1694), landowner, of Spetchley, Worcestershire, son of Robert Berkeley and Anne Darell, and the ward of her godfather, John Fell, bishop of Oxford. Since Berkeley's mother was a Roman Catholic, his wife had the task of maintaining the young couple's protestantism while taking care that her husband, who was much under his mother's influence, would not be disturbed with disputes about religion. On the death of Dr Fell and the accession of James II she persuaded him to travel to the Netherlands, and settle near the court of William of Orange at The Hague, where they became acquainted with Gilbert Burnet and his second wife, Mary Scott.

After the revolution of 1688, of which Elizabeth Berkeley was a passionate supporter, they returned to Spetchley, where they lived 'with a great deal of innocency', devising projects for gardening and charity (Elizabeth

Elizabeth Burnet (1661–1709), by Sir Godfrey Kneller, 1707

Packer to Mary Evelyn, 21 Dec 1689, BL, Evelyn MSS). She formed close friendships with a number of the cathedral clergy, including Bishop Stillingfleet, who was heard to say 'that he knew not a more considerable Woman in England than she was' (Burnet, *Method of Devotion*, viii). In 1694 Robert Berkeley died and his widow, who had remained childless, moved to London to live with her sister Mary, wife of Robert Dormer, in Lincoln's Inn. There she was the neighbour of John Locke, whose writings on government she admired, and in 1696 she began a protracted correspondence with him, arising from his controversies in print with Bishop Stillingfleet.

In May or June 1700 Elizabeth Berkeley married Gilbert *Burnet (1643–1715), bishop of Salisbury, whose former wife had died having recommended her to him as a successor and stepmother of their five children. Although not in favour of second marriages, she thought the bishop too naive to engage in court politics unsupported, and herself capable of 'preventing sometimes too hasty impressions of others, or errors of inconsideration which ill-designing men might unwarily engage him in' (Bodl. Oxf., MS Rawl. D. 1092, fol. 135). Burnet allowed her the disposal of her own income, estimated at £800 a year, of which she devoted the greater part to the education of poor children in Worcester and Salisbury. Her two daughters of this marriage died in infancy.

In 1708 Elizabeth Burnet published her religious manual, *A Method of Devotion*, first drafted in her widowhood. This work, together with the memoir written by Timothy

Goodwyn, bishop of Cashel, to her husband's instructions—Goodwyn's work preceded later editions of Burnet's—gives the impression of an unworldly woman, wholly occupied with piety and good works: 'the last of a long line of seventeenth century "devout ladies"' (Kirchberger, 18). But even her husband adds that 'her zeal for the Publick Good … was the single thing he had ever observed in her that looked like Excess; which as it preyed upon her own Spirits, so on some occasions it might set too great an Edge on them' (Burnet, *Method of Devotion*, xxiv). In fact her correspondence shows her to have been a highly politicized woman and a determined whig lobbyist. In letters to her moderate tory acquaintance Sir William Trumbull, which have gone unidentified because they are unsigned, she inveighs against high tories, 'a company of unjust & extravagant men who have no good end', and urges Trumbull to 'try all your skill and interest to persuade all you have hope of to break from that insolent party' (BL, Add. MS 72539; 15 Dec 1703, *Downshire MSS*, 1.817). A longer sequence of letters written to Sarah, duchess of Marlborough, shows her using this friendship at the instigation of her brother-in-law, Robert Dormer, and his fellow whig MPs to bring pressure to bear on the Marlborough–Godolphin ministry in favour of whig elections and appointments.

In 1707 Elizabeth Burnet travelled to the continent for the benefit of her health and her stepchildren's education. The resulting journal contains much acute observation concerning matters as diverse as shopping, the intellectual pretensions of the electress of Hanover, and the motivation of women in religious communities. During the bitter winter of 1708–9 she succumbed to pleurisy; she died in London on 3 February 1709, and was buried at Spetchley in accordance with a promise made to her first husband.   FRANCES HARRIS

Sources T. Goodwyn, 'Memoir', in E. Burnet, *A method of devotion*, 2nd edn (1709) • E. Burnet, journal and other writings, Bodl. Oxf., Rawl. MS D. 1092, fols. 111–203 • C. Kirchberger, 'Elizabeth Burnet, 1661–1709', *Church Quarterly Review*, 148 (1949), 17–51 • *A supplement to Burnet's History of my own time*, ed. H. C. Foxcroft (1902) • BL, Evelyn MSS, Elizabeth (Packer) Geddes to Mary Evelyn, 1682–1704 • Robert Berkeley to John Evelyn, 1684–1693, BL, Add. MS 15857, fols. 42–59 • *The correspondence of John Locke*, ed. E. S. De Beer, 8 vols. (1976–89) • unsigned autograph letters of Elizabeth Burnet to Sir William Trumbull, 1703–4, BL, Add. MS 72539; partly printed in *Report on the manuscripts of the marquis of Downshire*, 6 vols. in 7, HMC, 75 (1924–95), vol. 1, pt 2, pp. 817–18 • letters of Elizabeth Burnet to Sarah, duchess of Marlborough, 1701–1708, BL, Add. MS 61458, fols. 1–97 • T. Nash, *Collections for the history of Worcestershire*, 2 (1782), 362 • PRO, PROB 11/506/26 • monumental inscription, Spetchley parish church, Worcestershire

Archives Bodl. Oxf., journal and other writings, MS Rawl. D. 1092, fols. 111–203 | BL, Blenheim MSS, Add. MS 61458 • BL, Trumbull MSS, Add. MS 72539 • Bodl. Oxf., corresp. with John Locke

Likenesses G. Kneller, oils, 1707, NPG [*see illus.*] • M. Vandergucht, engraving, 1709 (after G. Kneller), BM, NPG; repro. in E. Burnet, *Method of devotion*, 2nd edn (1709), frontispiece

Wealth at death approx. £800 p.a.: *Supplement to Burnet's history*, ed. Foxcroft, 509n.

Burnet, Sir Frank Macfarlane (1899–1985), virologist and immunologist, was born on 3 September 1899 in Traralgon, Gippsland, Victoria, Australia, the second of seven

Sir Frank Macfarlane Burnet (1899–1985), by Walter Bird, 1958

children of Frank Burnet (*b*. 1856), a banker of Scottish descent, and Hadassah Pollock Mackay (*b*. 1872), the daughter of a schoolteacher who had also emigrated from Glasgow to settle in Australia. As a child Burnet was clever, but shy and diffident. He was educated at Terang state school, and from 1913 at Geelong College, where his interest in natural history soon made itself felt in explorations of local habitats and in the collection and classification of beetles. He was pleased to find out that Charles Darwin, his hero, had also been a coleopterist in his youth, and that Darwin, following his cousin Francis Galton, believed in the likelihood of genetically determined qualities. In 1917 Burnet was admitted to the faculty of medicine at the University of Melbourne and went into residence at the Presbyterian Ormond College. He did very well at university but continued to suffer from doubt and depression, as well as from an inability to make close contact with other people. In 1922 he graduated MB BS and moved into residencies in surgery and clinical neurology at Melbourne Hospital. In 1923 he was appointed pathological registrar at the Walter and Eliza Hall Institute, where he was to spend the rest of his career; the director, Charles Kellaway, encouraged Burnet, and eventually groomed him as his successor.

In 1925, the year after he had been awarded his MD degree, Burnet left for London. Kellaway had arranged a position for him as assistant curator of the national collection of type cultures at the Lister Institute, while he worked on a thesis on the immunological response of mice to bacteriophage. There he renewed his acquaintance with Edith Linda Marston Druce, a graduate of Melbourne University and teacher at Geelong preparatory school, and began to write long personal letters to her. In December 1927, after submitting his PhD dissertation, he returned to Melbourne, where they married on 10 July 1928. It was a long and successful marriage, which ended with her death from leukaemia in 1973. There were three children, Elizabeth, Ian, and Deborah.

The first few years of Burnet's working life were spent on the problem of the bacteriophages and their relation to the host bacterium. Burnet was able to reconcile the views of Jules Bordet and Felix d'Herelle—the one arguing that lysogeny in bacteria was inherited, the other that it was due to an infection—and in 1929 he and his co-workers managed to show that it was both: that the infecting particle became 'physiologically co-ordinated in the hereditary constitution of the bacterial strain', and that the bacterial wall carried a specific receptor that rendered it susceptible to infection by a specific phage (*Australian Journal of Experimental Medicine*, 6, 1929, 277–84).

In November 1931 Burnet was invited by Sir Henry Dale to spend two years at the National Institute for Medical Research at Hampstead, London, working on animal viruses. Here he made his first attempts to grow virus on the chorioallantoic membrane of the chick embryo, on which many viruses produce a small white pock or clone of infected cells. It was a technique in which he was soon the acknowledged expert. He used it to estimate the number of infecting particles in the starting material, and as such it was an important means of quantification. Working at the bench with these biological methods also introduced Burnet to techniques of cloning and limit-dilution to obtain pure cultures of virus, and helped him to think in terms of cells and organisms rather than biochemistry. On his return to the Hall Institute in 1933, Burnet was provided with support by the Rockefeller Foundation to set up a virus research laboratory. The technique on which the research was to be based was that of growing virus on egg membranes. The laboratory worked on polio, influenza, and herpes, as well as the rickettsias psittacosis, Q fever, and scrub typhus. In 1942 Burnet was elected to a fellowship of the Royal Society. In 1944 he travelled in the United States, visiting departments and giving the Dunham lectures at Harvard. He was offered a chair at Harvard, but loyally decided to turn it down. In the same year he succeeded Sir Charles Kellaway as director of the Hall Institute. Burnet was knighted in 1951, and in 1958 he received the Order of Merit.

Burnet's period as director was marked by major changes in virology. By the mid-1950s cell culture was replacing the egg-membrane technique as the preferred method for the cultivation of virus and had already been successfully adopted by Frank Fenner at Australian National University in Canberra. Molecular biology, too, was on the horizon. Younger colleagues noted that Burnet disliked biochemistry and its sophisticated equipment, and always preferred to work with biological methods and simple techniques. The result, however, was that the institute's workers did not have access to the latest equipment, the electron microscopes and ultracentrifuges that were in use elsewhere: things would have to change if they were not to fall behind. In 1957 Burnet took the astonishing step of ending all of the institute's work in virology, both his own and that of others, and converting to immunology. He himself wrote—not entirely as a joke— that this was the only way he could continue working on his chick embryos.

In fact Burnet had already made the transition to immunology. He had been thinking about the problem of how the organism distinguished self from not-self for some time. His initial use of the terms had occurred in 1940 in his first book of biological philosophy, *Biological Aspects of Infectious Diseases*, where he used it to account for the way that mixed cells from two different species of sponge managed to sort themselves out and come together again in the right species. In the book's second edition, in 1949, he developed the idea further as an explanation of immunological tolerance. Burnet was not the first to notice that chick embryos inoculated with virus did not produce any antibodies, but he made the connection between this and reports of blood-group chimaeras in twin cattle, and an earlier report that if mice were infected with virus before birth they did not react to it. He suggested that a state of immunological tolerance could be induced in animals if they were exposed to an antigen before birth, when a foreign antigen might be accepted as self. He failed to demonstrate it using either virus or red cells, but in 1956 Peter Medawar and his group in London managed to induce tolerance using nucleated cells that persisted in the animal body. Medawar and Burnet were to share a Nobel prize for this work in 1960.

It was the problem of tolerance that led Burnet and Frank Fenner to question the current instructional theory of antibody production, originally proposed in 1930 by the biochemist Felix Haurowitz, then working in Prague. According to this, antibody was formed by assembling the globulin molecule using the antigen as a template. The theory did not, however, account very well for either tolerance or the more rapid response to antigen on second exposure. In 1955 Niels Kaj Jerne of Copenhagen proposed an alternative: that globulin molecules with innumerable antibody specificities were continually being produced by the body. When an antigen appeared that bound to one of them, a complex was formed that was engulfed by a phagocyte, which set up further production of the same specificity of antibody. It was a selection rather than an instruction theory, very close to that proposed by Paul Ehrlich at the turn of the century. Jerne's paper was discussed in a review in 1957 by an American immunologist, David W. Talmage, who noticed that when replicating myeloma cells produced globulin it was strikingly homogeneous: antibody production must involve the replication of cells, not free molecules as Jerne had it. Burnet too, rejected Jerne's phagocytic mechanism. Using concepts familiar from his work with virus-infected clones of cells, he suggested that Jerne's free antibody molecules should be replaced by antibody-producing cells. When an antigen selected one of them, that cell then reproduced to form an expanding clone which produced antibody. According to the new theory, a single cell made only one specificity of antibody, but the population of lymphocytes taken together were capable of making all possible specificities. Tolerance was the result of the absence of clones with receptors that reacted with self or with the antigen to which the animal had been made tolerant. Burnet called them 'forbidden clones'.

Initial reactions to the new theory were cool—the template theory was very thoroughly entrenched, making use of well-supported concepts of immunochemistry, especially modern views on charge and Linus Pauling's work on types of chemical bond. Burnet's suggestions were based on the activities of populations of cells, and were less attractive to an audience attuned to biochemical explanations. Over the next ten years, however, support gradually accumulated. One of the most important contributions came from Gustav Nossal and the American bacterial geneticist Joshua Lederberg, working at the Hall Institute. Lederberg had come to Melbourne to discuss viral genetics with Burnet, but found when he arrived that virology was no longer allowed. He and Nossal set up a project to micromanipulate single cells from an animal immunized with two antigens. They found that of sixty-two cells tested, not one produced both antibodies. The experimental procedure was extremely difficult to reproduce: it could only be learned from one of the two authors. This changed when Jerne introduced his haemolytic plaque technique, which was simple and reproducible. It was soon widely agreed that one cell produced only one antibody.

Nossal said that perhaps the greatest force for acceptance of the theory was in the end the unravelling of the chemistry of the globulins, but Burnet cared very little about this aspect or about the genetic problem of the generation of diversity in the cellular repertoire. Molecular questions did not interest him. Introducing his theory in 1959 he emphasized his trust in 'the simple concepts of biology—reproduction, mutation … and selective survival'. For Burnet, the immune response was a kind of Darwinian microcosm: clonal selection was natural selection in miniature, and from the evolutionary point of view, the recognition of self and non-self had preceded defence as the function of immune competence.

Burnet's theory exerted a powerful heuristic effect on the field of immunology. The vast outpouring of work that occurred from about 1967 onwards was broadly the result of the acceptance of the theory with its focus on the activities of lineages of cells, in contrast to the dominance of biochemistry typical of the era now ending. Burnet himself proclaimed in his Nobel lecture that 'the new immunology … has far greater potentialities, both for practical use in medicine and for the better understanding of living processes, than the classical immunochemistry [of Karl Landsteiner and his generation] which it is incorporating and superseding'. Its success may be measured by the proliferation since 1970 of dozens of specialist journals dealing with the cellular aspects of immunity. It guided work on transplantation and immune suppression, and in the 1980s on the elucidation of the effect of the AIDS virus on the cells of the immune system, as well as the development of monoclonal antibody and techniques for separating different lineages of antibody-producing cells. In 1991 Anne Marie Moulin suggested that the view of immunity as mediated by a system (as the circulation is mediated by the cardiovascular system) dates from the acceptance and development of the clonal selection theory. The Soviet Russian immunologist R. V. Petrov has called this the period of the dictatorship of the lymphocyte.

Burnet retired from his directorship in 1965, and thereafter took up a series of positions in which he represented both science and Australia. His first such post was as president of the Australian Academy of Science; from 1966 to 1969 he served as first chairman of the Commonwealth Foundation; and from 1962 to 1969 he chaired the Medical Research Advisory Committee for Papua New Guinea. His appointment to the consultative council of the Eugenics Society in London dated from the late 1950s. This was the time when he began to draw together his thoughts to form an articulated philosophy, an effort which produced no less than sixteen books written after his retirement, between 1966 and 1979.

Burnet's biological view of life had been formed in his early youth, as he read Darwin and classified beetles in the bush before the First World War. It was an approach that affected not only his science but also his view of society. Like other biological thinkers of his time he embraced some of the less attractive aspects of that view: his research was carried on through the years with a series of female assistants who were not encouraged to become independent workers, for in Burnet's opinion women who demanded equality were simply resentful of their genetically determined role. As a sociobiologist he felt that the era of the hunter-gatherer society had permanently fixed male and female social roles at a genetic level, though he accepted that special abilities in either sex should be allowed equal opportunities. As a genetic determinist he was attracted by the ideas of eugenics, and he enjoyed Francis Galton's élitist positive eugenics of the healthy and intelligent, emphasizing the effect of his own lineage in his scientific success. In 1978 Burnet advocated the abortion of defective foetuses, infanticide of children with severe genetic disorders, euthanasia for patients with incurable diseases, and the death penalty, discreetly administered, for those who were a danger to society. These opinions appeared at a time when such views were generally unaccepted, and the reviewers told him so.

In 1973, after his wife's death, Burnet returned to live in Ormond College as a senior fellow. There he met Hazel Jenkin, a widow in her seventies, who had been a distinguished singer and was then working as an honorary librarian in the college. In January 1976 they married. Burnet died of cancer on 31 August 1985, at his son's farm in Port Fairy, Victoria. He was buried at Tower Hill cemetery, near Port Fairy.   PAULINE M. H. MAZUMDAR

Sources M. Burnet, *Changing patterns: an atypical autobiography* (1968) · G. L. Ada, 'The conception and birth of Burnet's clonal selection theory', *Immunology, 1930–1980: essays on the history of immunology*, ed. P. M. H. Mazumdar (1989), 33–40 · A. Cambrosio and P. Keating, *Exquisite specificity: the monoclonal antibody revolution* (1995) · A. M. Moulin, *Le dernier langage de la médecine: histoire de l'immunologie de Pasteur au SIDA* (1991), 263–339 · G. Nossal, 'The coming of age of the clonal selection theory', *Immunology, 1930–1980: essays on the history of immunology*, ed. P. M. H. Mazumdar (1989), 41–50 · R. V. Petrov, *Me and not-me: immunological mobiles* (1987) · C. Sexton, *The seeds of time: the life of Sir Macfarlane Burnet* (1991) [incl. list of Burnet's pubns] · A. I. Tauber, *The immune self: theory or metaphor?* (1994) · A. I. Tauber and S. H. Podolsky, 'Frank Macfarlane Burnet and the immune self', *Journal of the History of Biology*, 27 (1994), 531–73 · F. J. Fenner, *Memoirs FRS*, 33 (1987), 99–162
Archives University of Melbourne
Likenesses W. Bird, photograph, 1958, NPG [*see illus.*] · M. Strizic, photograph, 1968, priv. coll. · A. Bonett, bronze, 1979, Australian Academy of Science, Canberra · W. Bird, photograph, RS; repro. in Fenner, *Memoirs FRS* · D. Faingold, photograph, Wellcome L.

Burnet, Gilbert (1643–1715), bishop of Salisbury and historian, was born in Edinburgh on 18 September 1643, the youngest child of Robert Burnet (*d.* 1661), a judge of the court of session as Lord Crimond, and Rachel Johnston, sister of Archibald *Johnston, Lord Wariston. Sir Thomas *Burnet (1638–1704) was one of his elder brothers.

Early years and education Robert Burnet was a lawyer of great integrity. His personal life was so strict and he was on such bad terms with the Scottish bishops that many reckoned him a puritan; yet in reality he was 'very well satisfied with Episcopacy and the Common Prayer' (Burnet, 'History', 1, fol. 4a). As such, in 1643 when the Scottish rebels drew up the solemn league and covenant to conclude an alliance with the English parliament Robert Burnet could not support it. When an ordinance was issued on 22 October by the committee of estates obliging everyone to sign the solemn league and covenant Robert Burnet refused. He was ordered to leave Scotland, and spent the next five years in France and the Netherlands. This left the young Burnet with his mother, who was, according to him, tender-hearted and charitable, as well as meddlesome, credulous, and indiscreet. The same could be said for her son. Rachel Johnston was also 'Presbyterian to the highest degree'. Burnet blames the fact that he had a 'good deal of the heat of my mother's family' on those first five years wholly under his mother's care.

Robert Burnet returned in 1648, but found that his enemies were still determined to punish him. He was obliged to retire for some months to Dalkeith, just outside Edinburgh, and he took young Gilbert with him. For the next four years, first at Dalkeith and then at his estate at Crimond in Aberdeenshire, Robert Burnet devoted his time to educating his youngest son. The result, Burnet recalls, was that before the age of ten 'I was master of that tongue [Latin] and of the Classick Authors' ('Burnet's autobiography', 454). He had also memorized the Bible 'so exactly that afterwards my Father grew proud of it' (Burnet, 'History', 1, fol. 8b). At the tender age of nine Burnet was sent to Marischal College, Aberdeen, to continue his education. Yet he remained under the harsh discipline of his father. He continued to live at home, with his father

Gilbert Burnet (1643–1715), by Sir Godfrey Kneller, 1693

acting as his 'chieff tutor' ('Burnet's autobiography', 454). He was at Marischal College for five years, graduating MA in early 1657, six months before his fourteenth birthday, 'which was a thing not ordinary' (Burnet, 'History', 1, fol. 11a). Upon graduation Burnet chose to follow his father into the legal profession, but after a year of legal studies at the court of justice in Edinburgh he changed to divinity, much to the delight of his father who 'had always designed me for the Church' (ibid., fol. 12a). He studied divinity at home until early 1661, when he underwent three months of trials as an expectant preacher in the Scottish church. He passed these trials some months before his eighteenth birthday and was given a licence to preach.

In that same year, on 24 August 1661, Robert Burnet died. With his father's death Burnet lost the person who had been the dominant force in his life to that point. The relationship between Burnet and his father was complex. On the one hand the attention which the elder Burnet had paid to his son's upbringing and education had given them a closeness which inspired in the younger Burnet a genuine love for his father. On the other hand the severe discipline of his father caused Burnet, at times, to hate him and to come close to 'taking desperate methods' ('Burnet's autobiography', 454). It is not surprising, then, that Burnet experienced mixed emotions on the death of his father.

Following his father's death Burnet began a process of re-evaluating all that he had learned under him. It was in the middle of this re-examination of himself and his notions that Burnet met and became friends with James Nairn, minister of the Abbey Church in Edinburgh, who was to have a profound effect on his intellectual development. Nairn was a 'very easy and cheerful man', who had 'the softest and yet the chiefest eloquence' (Burnet, 'History', 1, fol. 49b) that Burnet had ever heard—characteristics that Burnet's own stern, humourless father had lacked. Nairn encouraged him to abandon the books of his youth—'systematical divine books of controversy and tedious commentaries on the scripture together with the schoolmen' (ibid.)—in favour of works of moral philosophy. Burnet's discoveries included Richard Hooker's *Laws of Ecclesiastical Polity*, as well as the books of Plato and the Neoplatonists, and the writings of the Cambridge Platonists. In his *History* and his autobiography Burnet openly acknowledged the debt that he owed to the Cambridge Platonists and their followers. He recalled how, after meeting Benjamin Whichcote, John Wilkins, Henry More, John Tillotson, and Edward Stillingfleet on his first visit to England in 1663, 'I easily went into the notions of the Latitudinarians' (Burnet, 'History', 1, fol. 76a).

Burnet's journey to England was occasioned by the arrest in France of his uncle Lord Wariston. Wariston was taken to London and imprisoned in the Tower, and as soon as the news reached Edinburgh Burnet's mother begged him to go to London to do what he could for his uncle. It quickly became clear that nothing could be done for Wariston, and so Burnet occupied himself by making connections in England. The two most important were with Sir Robert Moray, first president of the Royal Society, and Patrick Drummond, a presbyterian minister, both Scotsmen who were then resident in London. He became acquainted with 'the more select of all parties' (Burnet, 'History', 1, fol. 76a) among the London ministers, and travelled to both universities where he was introduced to numerous divines, as well as the mathematician John Wallis and the chemist Robert Boyle. Burnet returned to Scotland in June 1663 at the same time that Wariston was sent back and condemned to die by the Scottish parliament. Burnet walked with his uncle to the scaffold.

In February 1664 Burnet embarked on an extended journey. He spent some time in London, and while there was elected a fellow of the Royal Society (16 March 1664) through Moray's influence. Two months later he crossed over to the Netherlands, where he met Arminians, Lutherans, Anabaptists, Brownists, Catholics, Unitarians, and Socinians. He was particularly impressed with the Arminians, who had a spirit of 'mutual forbearance' ('Remaining fragments') or tolerance, which he vowed to emulate in his own life and career. He then proceeded through the Southern Netherlands to France where he met, through the introduction of Moray, leaders of the Huguenots. They did not make a favourable impression on him. The Roman Catholics were no better, except for the preaching of their

secular clergy, which he tried to emulate. After six weeks in Paris he returned to England where he remained for three months studying algebra with a tutor before heading back to Scotland towards the end of September 1664.

Scottish career, 1664–1674 After his return to Scotland, Burnet lived in the house of Sir Robert Fletcher in Saltoun, about 15 miles east of Edinburgh, where he instructed both Sir Robert and his two eldest sons in algebra. In January 1665 Sir Robert died. Burnet preached the funeral sermon, and then, apparently without the knowledge or consent of Fletcher's family or friends, had the sermon published. Although Sir Robert's brother was said by John Cockburn to have been disgusted with the sermon it does not seem to have upset Lady Fletcher, for Burnet continued to live in her house for another year directing the education of her children. He was instituted as minister in the parish of Saltoun in June 1665, and spent much of his time ministering to his new parishioners. He was clearly a conscientious minister.

While at Saltoun Burnet continued his studies. Of particular interest at this time was the history of the church in the first three centuries. Burnet became concerned about the differences between the bishops of the early church and those of the recently reinstated Scottish episcopate. Although he staunchly approved of episcopal church government he was indignant at the Scottish bishops for their extravagance, pompous lifestyle, and mismanagement of ecclesiastical affairs. In 1665 he drafted *A Memorial of Divers Grievances and Abuses in this Church* and sent copies to the archbishops of St Andrews and Glasgow, and the bishops of Edinburgh, Dunblane, and Aberdeen. The bishops were shocked by such a brutally frank indictment of their conduct by a 23-year-old cleric, and Burnet was summoned to Edinburgh to explain himself. At this meeting with the two archbishops and the bishops of Edinburgh and Aberdeen Burnet refused to submit to his ecclesiastical superiors and ask their pardon. Incensed by his insolence James Sharp, archbishop of St Andrews, proposed to his colleagues that he be deprived of his living at Saltoun and excommunicated. The other bishops, however, were not prepared to act so boldly. As Burnet later remarked, 'they told him I had great friends' (Burnet, 'History', 1, fol. 113a). They were right. Burnet's patron at that time was John Maitland, second earl of Lauderdale, Charles II's powerful secretary of state in Scotland, whom Burnet had come to know in summer 1663. Lauderdale was apparently delighted with the *Memorial*, and had even given the king an account of it, 'who was not ill pleased at it' (*Bishop Burnet's History*, 147). With the support of such great friends it is not surprising that 'after three or four weeks stir about it the whole thing was let fall' (Burnet, 'History', 1, fol. 113a). Following this episode Burnet resolved to retire as much as possible from the world and live an ascetic course of life. By his own account he kept to this new lifestyle for about two years, but finally abandoned it after a severe illness.

About the time that he relinquished his attempt at asceticism in the middle of 1667, a change of government in Scotland occurred which brought Burnet into an active role in promoting a new church policy. Even though episcopacy had been restored in Scotland in 1660 nonconformity flourished. In 1667, after a period of severity against the dissenters that had only produced rebellion, Lauderdale embarked on a policy of moderation. Lauderdale's idea was to split the nonconformists into two camps: the peaceable dissenters would be 'indulged' in an effort to reclaim them into the national church, whereas the 'willful opposers' would be punished. The indulgence was to be based on a scheme of accommodation proposed by Burnet's friend and mentor Robert Leighton, bishop of Dunblane. The concessions that Leighton proposed were extensive and, if adopted, would have significantly altered the nature of the Church of Scotland. As such they were highly controversial. Burnet, as Leighton's protégé, was heavily engaged in the indulgence. Apparently Leighton 'made no step without talking it over to me' (*Bishop Burnet's History*, 185). Burnet was delegated in summer 1667 to propose the scheme to George Hutcheson, one of the leading presbyterian ministers, with whom he was acquainted. Nothing came of those early meetings, however, and the scheme floundered for close to a year and a half.

Early in 1669 Burnet submitted a paper to John Hay, second earl of Tweeddale, entitled 'The constitution and present condition of the Church of Scotland'. In it he suggested, apparently on the advice of Anne, duchess of Hamilton, a presbyterian, and her friends, that the more moderate of the presbyterian ministers be readmitted to their former parishes. Tweeddale was impressed with Burnet's assessment and passed the paper to Lauderdale in London, who may well have read it to the king. Whatever the case Lauderdale and the king clearly approved of the idea, and in summer 1669 the king wrote to the Scottish privy council ordering them to indulge those presbyterian ministers who were peaceable and loyal. However, owing to the implacable opposition of all the bishops save Leighton, and many of the nonconformists themselves, by the end of 1669 the indulgence was in shambles.

The indulgence fiasco exasperated Burnet and he placed the blame for its failure squarely on the shoulders of the dissenters, for whom he now expressed a great aversion. It was out of this disappointment, and of a desire to salvage his reputation among the episcopal clergy, that in the latter half of 1669 he wrote a scathing attack on the dissenters entitled *A Modest and Free Conference betwixt a Conformist and a Non-Conformist*. In the first of six dialogues the conformist berates the nonconformist for breaching the unity of the catholic church, 'which is not to be broken, but upon a matter of great certainty and weight' (*Modest and Free Conference*, 4). In the succeeding five dialogues the conformist demonstrates to the nonconformist that the points on which he takes issue with the established church, such as worship, ceremonies, and church government, are neither certain nor weighty. It was hardly a tolerant or sympathetic work. Burnet later described it as 'the wittiest book I ever yet writ, in which I made a Nonconformist appear a very ridiculous and contemptible creature' (Burnet, 'History', 2, fol. 6b).

While visiting the duchess of Hamilton at Hamilton Palace in 1669 Burnet met James Ramsay, rector of the University of Glasgow (afterwards bishop of Dunblane and bishop of Ross), who, later that year, obtained for him the professorship of divinity there. In December 1669 Burnet left Saltoun to take up his new position. He was now in the thick of western Scottish affairs and continued, in spite of his distaste for the dissenters, to labour, unsuccessfully, in the cause of accommodation.

Despite the failure of the accommodation between 1669 and 1671 Burnet was at the height of his favour with Lauderdale in 1671. He had apparently been offered a bishopric before, but in late 1671 Lauderdale offered him his choice of four vacant dioceses, of which Edinburgh was one. Believing that he was too young for a bishopric he declined. Such high favour, however, came at a price. Lauderdale was a strong character who at times exercised an enormous influence over the young Burnet. One such occasion was in early 1671 when Lauderdale divulged to Burnet the secret that James, duke of York, the king's brother, had converted to Roman Catholicism, and then proceeded to question him about the king's barren marriage. Divorce, and even polygamy, had been floated among the king's advisers as possible solutions to the problem of a Catholic heir, and Lauderdale asked Burnet to give his opinion. Eager to be helpful he gave his reply in the form of a paper entitled *Resolution of Two Important Cases of Conscience*. In it he addresses two questions: is a woman's barrenness a just ground for divorce? and, is polygamy in any case lawful under the gospel? Astonishingly he answered both in the affirmative. It was a foolish paper that Burnet would quickly come to regret. His later enemies, including Lauderdale himself, never let him forget his early indiscretions.

Although Burnet thought the presbyterians peevish and stiff for not taking up the accommodation, he continued to push for moderation, this time in the form of a second indulgence which he suggested to Lauderdale in the latter half of 1672. It was no more successful than the first. It was also in the latter half of 1672 that Burnet vigorously defended in print Lauderdale's moderate church policy. Burnet later claimed that his *Vindication of the Authority, Constitution, and Laws of the Church and State of Scotland* (1673) was meant to counter a recent presbyterian reply to his earlier work, *A Modest and Free Conference*. Notwithstanding this declaration, the size and scope of the *Vindication* clearly indicate an additional motive for its composition. In order to push through his indulgence against the will of the bishops, Lauderdale had presented to parliament, in October 1669, an Act of Supremacy that would affirm the king's sole right to dispose of the external government and policy of the church. Three years later, with the policy of indulgence in ruins, Burnet probably felt it necessary to defend royal supremacy in ecclesiastical affairs from the calumnies of both the presbyterians and the episcopal clergy. The fact that the *Vindication* was dedicated to Lauderdale with 'much indecent flattery' suggests that it was written with this view in mind. What is certain is that the *Vindication* does provide a theoretical basis for the model of church government found in the 1669 act. Yet the second indulgence proved to be the last attempt by Lauderdale's administration to win over moderate dissent. From 1672 Lauderdale drifted away from moderation towards policies of repression. As he drifted he gradually abandoned his old allies Moray, Tweeddale, Leighton, and Burnet, and replaced them with 'high flying' episcopal men. The second indulgence marks the last time that Burnet had any influence over Scottish affairs.

Although these various accommodation schemes occupied much of Burnet's time between 1668 and 1672 it was by no means all that he was engaged in. From late 1669 he was diligently carrying out his duties as professor of divinity at the University of Glasgow. It was also at this time that he first became engaged in historical writing. In 1671 Burnet became a frequent guest at Hamilton Palace, about 8 miles from Glasgow. During one of these visits he was shown the family papers, and he conceived the idea of writing a memoir of the first two dukes of Hamilton. Shortly after it was finished Burnet formulated a more ambitious plan. He decided that he would expand its scope to give a general account of Scottish affairs from 1638 to 1651, and in that way make it a continuation of John Spottiswoode's *History of the Church and State of Scotland*. The final version of the *Memoirs of the Dukes of Hamilton*, finished in 1673 but not published until 1677, presents both the two dukes and Charles I in a very favourable light. Indeed Burnet later conceded that his character of Charles I was too flattering, and confessed that he had suppressed some passages in the king's letters that illustrated his poor judgement, understanding, and temper. In the 1670s the omissions seemed perfectly justified to the young royalist.

Burnet's frequent visits to Hamilton brought him into close contact with Lady Margaret Kennedy (*d.* 1685) [*see* Burnet, Lady Margaret], eldest daughter of John *Kennedy, sixth earl of Cassillis, and the duchess of Hamilton's cousin, who often lived at Hamilton. Although she was at least thirteen years older than Burnet he was attracted to her intelligence, generosity, virtue, and piety, and he courted her for about two years. Finally, about 1672 or 1673, they married. The marriage was kept a secret, probably at Kennedy's insistence. Burnet later commented that Kennedy thought the inequality of the match would much lessen her. He also adds that in order to avoid the accusation that he had married her for her considerable fortune, 'I prepared a deed which I delivered to her before our marriage by which I renounced all pretensions to it' ('Burnet's autobiography', 481).

In summer 1673 Burnet journeyed to London for the purpose of obtaining a licence to publish his *Memoirs of the Dukes of Hamilton*. He was received with great kindness by Lauderdale, who presented him to the king. Charles was favourably impressed: he read Burnet's book, asked him to preach before him, and made Burnet a royal chaplain. Burnet was treated with even greater favour by the Catholic James, duke of York. The two shared a love of religious debate, and they apparently spent many hours discussing their differences in religion. Burnet's encounter with the duke of York piqued his interest in Roman Catholicism and prompted him to publish two anti-Catholic tracts in London in 1673. One was a republication of his *The mystery of iniquity unvailed* which had originally been published in Glasgow the year before. Although he passed this work off as his own Burnet had in fact lifted it entirely from Henry More's *Modest inquiry into the mystery of iniquity* (1664). The second was *Rome's glory, or, A collection of divers miracles wrought by popish saints … with a prefatory discourse, declaring the impossibility and folly of such vain impostures*. The royal favour that Burnet had received, however, made Lauderdale jealous. Lauderdale's displeasure with his young protégé was increased when he became convinced that Burnet was actively involved with the duke of Hamilton and the opposition in Scotland. Burnet now thought it prudent to resume his duties in Glasgow and lie low for a while.

In June 1674 Burnet returned to London, ostensibly to fulfil his duties as royal chaplain for July. On his arrival in London he discovered that, owing to Lauderdale's influence, he was no longer in favour with the king. He was struck off the list of royal chaplains and told by the king to go home to Scotland and be quiet. However, the duke of York, who was still friendly, warned him that if he did go home without first having reconciled with Lauderdale, 'I would certainly be shut up in a close prison, where I might perhaps lie too long' (*Bishop Burnet's History*, 247). Deciding that peace with Lauderdale was no longer possible, and fearing for his life if he went back, Burnet resigned his professorship at Glasgow in September 1674 and remained in London. So ended his Scottish career. He would never return to his homeland.

London, 1674–1685 Burnet's prospects in London were bleak. Lauderdale, his former patron, was now his implacable foe, and he had alienated the king and others who might have helped him. Towards the end of 1674 he was forbidden at court. Yet in spite of this Burnet was anxious to demonstrate his loyalty, and so on 6 December 1674 he preached a sermon entitled *Subjection for Conscience Sake Asserted*, followed on 31 January 1675 by *The Royal Martyr Lamented*. In the former he set out the case for state supremacy in church affairs. In the latter he delivered a panegyric on Charles I, comparing him favourably to Saul. Neither succeeded in mollifying Lauderdale or the king. Just as Burnet was anxious to prove his loyalty to the king, so too was he eager to defend his newly adopted church against its Roman Catholic foe, resulting in *A rational method for proving the truth of the Christian religion, as it is professed in the Church of England* (1675).

In spite of his best efforts to ingratiate himself with the court it was not long before Burnet was in trouble again. When parliament reconvened in April 1675 the House of Commons appointed a committee to formulate a demand for Lauderdale's dismissal. Burnet, ever loquacious and indiscreet, had let it be known to many that he had some damning evidence against Lauderdale. As a result he was summoned to appear before both the committee and the whole house to tell all that he knew. At first he resisted, but eventually he yielded and testified. His information failed to damage Lauderdale, but Burnet's conduct brought him a great deal of criticism. In his autobiography he candidly admits his error. It made his breach with Lauderdale permanent, and it soured his relations with the duke of York.

Such powerful enemies, however, did not stop Burnet from obtaining two prominent positions in 1675. The first was his appointment as chaplain to the Rolls Chapel, which was conferred on him, much against the wishes of the court, by Sir Harbottle Grimston, master of the rolls. The second was his appointment as Thursday lecturer at St Clement Danes. Neither position had cure of souls attached to them, and so Burnet was free to devote himself over the next ten years to preaching and writing. For the next few years life passed, as he himself remarked, in a 'very easy manner' (Clarke and Foxcroft, 142). He quickly obtained a reputation as one of the best extempore preachers in London. During term time he drew large crowds to the Rolls Chapel, and in vacation time he was in great demand as an occasional preacher. From his two posts and his writing he made enough money to live comfortably in a house in the fashionable area of Lincoln's Inn Fields. His next-door neighbour there, Sir Thomas Littleton, was a leading member of the opposition. For the next six years (1675–81) the two were on very intimate terms, and it was through Littleton that Burnet came to know the leaders of the opposition, particularly the more moderate ones, like Sir William Coventry and George Savile, earl of Halifax. He was also able to cultivate friendships with some of the leading latitudinarians who held benefices in London at the time—William Lloyd, rector of St Martin-in-the-Fields, John Tillotson, dean of Canterbury and canon of St Paul's, and Edward Stillingfleet, archdeacon of London from 1677. Like Burnet all were disciples of Cambridge Platonism, and all became his close friends and allies from this time until their deaths.

Given his close relationship with the leading latitudinarians in London it appears rather surprising that Burnet launched an attack on the book *The Naked Truth* (1675) in which Herbert Croft, bishop of Hereford, set forth proposals for a comprehension with the dissenters in England. It is a work with which Burnet should have sympathized, and yet in May 1676 he wrote a stinging reply to it entitled *A modest survey of the most considerable things in a discourse lately published entitled 'Naked truth'*. The *Modest Survey* is a work that has puzzled Burnet's biographers. They speculate that perhaps it was the result of a first flush of enthusiasm for the Church of England, or of his disappointment with the failure of the Scottish accommodation scheme. The second explanation is more likely. One of Burnet's frustrations with his Scottish experience was that the dissenters consistently refused to state explicitly what concessions would bring them into the established church. This put the onus on the established church to offer concessions, which could then be construed as a tacit admission that the church required further reformation. Furthermore it opened the church to humiliation if the proposals were ultimately rejected, as they were in Scotland. Simply offering concessions, Burnet insisted, served

only to 'expose the dignity of the Church' (*Modest Survey*, 7). Also, fear of popery was at least partly responsible for the *Modest Survey*. The presence of a prominent popish party in England was one of the features that distinguished the English religious scene from the Scottish, and anti-Catholicism became something of a passion for Burnet in the latter half of the 1670s. He was particularly sensitive to the papists' charge that the Church of England was not a true church. For this reason he was reluctant to offer too much, for

> what occasion would be given them to insult, and say we had changed the boundaries and land-marks our Predecessors had left us: and were making a new hotch potch of a Church, to take in all Hereticks? How the Church of Rome triumph, and say that our Faith was indeed temporary, and changed with the fashion. (*Modest Survey*, 4)

The legitimacy of the Church of England was also challenged in *De origine et progressu schismatio Anglicani libri tres* by Nicholas Sanders, originally published in 1585 but reissued in a new French translation in the mid-1670s. It caused a stir in continental religious circles and some English churchmen were anxious to have it rebutted. Sanders argued that the English Reformation was illegitimate because it was purely a political act of state carried out by a corrupt king. Many of Burnet's friends urged him to answer Sanders, so late in 1677 he began researching his *History of the Reformation of the Church of England*. The first volume, covering the reign of Henry VIII, was published in 1679, followed by a second volume on the progress of the Reformation down to the Elizabethan settlement, which appeared in 1681. A supplemental third volume containing additions and corrections was not published until 1714. In his *History of the Reformation* Burnet concurred that Henry VIII was a man of many faults, but argued that even ill princes could be the instruments of God's providence, such as King David or Constantine the Great. In the case of the English Reformation, Burnet argued, it could not have been achieved without a man of Henry's temper as king. So what seems to have been a political act of state was in fact the unfolding of God's will. Burnet then went on to defend the idea of a national church and the fundamental doctrines of the Reformation.

The History of the Reformation was the first attempt to write an account of the English Reformation from authentic sources. Although his early researches were hampered by Lauderdale, who convinced the antiquarian Sir John Cotton to deny Burnet access to his library, which contained many Reformation manuscripts, after the publication of the first volume Sir John relented. As a result the documentary evidence that Burnet collected is impressive. Unfortunately, as he himself later admitted, he was too impatient to commit the time and attention to detail that was required for such a large historical work, and so it is marred by countless mistakes, as his contemporary critics gleefully pointed out.

While Burnet was at work on the first volume of his *History of the Reformation* revelations about a Catholic plot to assassinate the king and bring the duke of York to the throne came to light. In his lengthy account of the Popish

Plot in the first draft of his *History*, written some seven years after the fact, Burnet endeavoured to maintain a detached and objective tone. He expressed his disbelief in the evidence and deprecated 'the shedding of blood upon such a testimony' (Burnet, 'History', 2, fol. 44a). He concluded: 'I do not doubt but there was a good measure of truth in what they had sworn, though it was so mixed and dressed up that there was no relying on anything they said' (ibid., fol. 48a). Burnet's biographers are sceptical, and see his memoirs as 'defective' and 'anachronistic'. They maintain that Burnet, like so many others, 'certainly lost his head' (Clarke and Foxcroft, 155). As proof they point to the fact that during the course of the plot crisis he published anonymously four anti-Catholic pamphlets, which were 'obviously inflammatory' (ibid.). This is true, but this cannot be equated with his belief in the plot. Despite his scepticism he was not above using the plot as a stick with which to beat the papists. Burnet made a distinction between employing the dubious plot as a weapon against popery in general, which was acceptable, and perverting it to shed the blood of innocent individuals, which was not. By November 1678 his reputation as a sceptic was such that the king asked to see him. Apparently he waited on the king often throughout December 1678, and they spoke at length about the plot. According to Burnet, 'we were both of one mind, that the greatest part of the plot was a contrivance' (Burnet, 'History', 2, fol. 45a). He maintained that his aim in meeting the king was:

> to try, on the one hand if I could soften him, and if on the other hand I could have moderated the heat that was in the nation, and have turned it to a total extirpation of Popery, without drawing on us the guilt of innocent blood.
> (ibid., fol. 45b)

There seems to be no reason, then, to doubt Burnet's account of his reaction to the plot.

A few months later, on 23 May 1679, Burnet's first volume of his *History of the Reformation* was licensed and published. The timing could not have been better. Such a vigorous defence of the English Reformation would have been welcome at any time, but in the midst of the revelations of the Popish Plot it was greeted with wild enthusiasm. Both houses of parliament voted to give him their thanks, and requested that he finish the work. In October 1680, at the instigation of Archbishop William Sancroft, the University of Oxford conferred on Burnet the degree of doctor of divinity.

As Burnet basked in the glory of his *History of the Reformation* a new political crisis emerged out of the Popish Plot. Some of the country opposition, led by Anthony Ashley Cooper, first earl of Shaftesbury, were anxious to use the plot as an excuse to exclude the duke of York from the succession. However, the more moderate among the opposition, like Burnet's friend and patron Halifax, preferred to limit by legislation the powers of any future popish king. In the ensuing exclusion crisis Burnet at first sided with the moderates, and he used whatever credit he had gained from his *History of the Reformation* to win support among the country opposition for limitations. Although Charles initially seemed in favour of limitations, by January 1680 he no longer supported them, and Halifax and four other privy councillors from the country opposition resigned their places in disgust.

Burnet now believed that the king was facing a crisis and he resolved to advise him on how to extricate himself from his troubles. On 29 January 1680 Burnet addressed to Charles II a letter scolding him for his immoral personal life. The answer to his political troubles 'is not the change of a minister or of a council, a new alliance or a Session of Parliament, but it is … a change of your own heart, and of your course of life' (Clarke and Foxcroft, 159). The king read this extraordinary and unsolicited letter over twice and, without a word, threw it into the fire. While he never acknowledged receipt of the letter, he subsequently spoke of Burnet 'with more than ordinary sharpness' (Burnet, 'History', 2, fol. 60a).

Meanwhile the exclusion crisis continued. Burnet, with most of the country party, became an exclusionist. His conversion was due largely to the influence of William Russell, Lord Russell, and Arthur Capel, first earl of Essex, both of whom were now on close terms with him. His support for exclusion brought him into great favour with the House of Commons, and on 22 December 1680 he was asked to preach before the house on a solemn fast day. Burnet's favour with the exclusionists, however, did not last, and by the final vote he was supporting a regency plan.

About January 1682 Burnet left his house near Lincoln's Inn Fields and moved to Greville Street, near Furnivall's Inn, where he threw himself into the study of natural philosophy and chemistry. In early 1682 he also published two books, *The Life and Death of Sir Matthew Hale* and *The History of the Rights of Princes in the Disposing of Ecclesiastical Benefices and Church-lands*. The latter was written in defence of Louis XIV in his dispute with the pope over his claim of a royal right to the temporalities of vacant sees. His motive in writing such a book was probably a mixture of wishing to foment discord in the Roman Catholic church and endeavouring yet again to defend his views on the state's authority over the church.

The revelation in June 1683 of the Rye House plot, which sought to kill Charles II and the duke of York and put Charles's illegitimate son James Scott, duke of Monmouth, on the throne, implicated Burnet's friends Essex and Russell and Burnet's cousin Robert Baillie. Burnet was at first convinced that the charges, at least against Russell and Essex, were false, and he immediately offered his services to Lady Russell. To his cousin, however, he was less helpful, possibly because he was less certain of Baillie's innocence. Although Burnet sent money to his gaoler to provide him with all possible comforts, when Baillie was threatened with a trial and sent for his cousin to stand by him, he refused. On 13 July Essex committed suicide in the Tower. Such an action seemed to confirm his and Russell's part in the plot, and Russell was found guilty that day. This sudden turn of events had a profound effect on Burnet. He too seems to have now believed that Essex and Russell were guilty, and his first thought was to protect himself against suspicion of complicity. In a rather grovelling letter of appeal to Halifax and the king Burnet made ardent protestations of both his complete ignorance of the plot and of his loyalty to the king. Yet anxious as Burnet was to save his own skin he did attend Russell in the Tower, though he and John Tillotson spent much of their time in an unsuccessful attempt to induce Russell to recant the doctrine of resistance. He did, however, attend Russell on the scaffold, and received his watch as a parting present. While awaiting execution Russell wrote a paper in justification of himself which his wife had printed and was selling in the streets within an hour of his death. The king and court were offended with the paper, and Burnet and Tillotson were summoned before the cabinet council to explain themselves. Burnet was questioned at some length because he was suspected to be the author of the paper. Eventually the matter was dropped, but by now Burnet had incurred the everlasting enmity of the king and the duke of York.

Finding that he was now under a cloud in London, Burnet decided to travel to France at the end of August 1683. His reception at the French court was nothing short of astonishing. There were two reasons for this. In the first place, Lady Russell was the niece of Henri de Massue, marquis de Ruvigny, who, Burnet remarked, 'upon his niece's account, set himself much to procure me great respect there' (Burnet, 'History', 2, fol. 77b). Second, and more important, his *History of the Rights of Princes* had pleased Louis XIV and the French king was happy to use Burnet's visit to send a message to the papal nuncio. Burnet was therefore granted unprecedented access to the king, much to the disgust of Richard Graham, first Viscount Preston, the English envoy in Paris. Burnet also met many of the most important figures in church and state in France. Preston complained bitterly to the English court, and both the king and the duke of York protested to the French ambassador in London. As a result, as Burnet noted, 'if I had stayed longer there I believe I would have been forbid coming to Court' (Burnet, 'History', 2, fol. 78b).

Burnet returned to London in November 1683 to find that he had been dismissed from his lectureship at St Clement Danes by order of the king. He was also removed from his post at the Rolls Chapel after preaching a particularly vehement anti-Catholic sermon on 5 November. Now deprived of all employment Burnet settled down to work on several literary projects. One was apparently 'a large book concerning the truth of religion and the authority of the … scripture' (Clarke and Foxcroft, 201) which was never published, and the manuscript has been lost. Another was an anonymous translation of Thomas More's *Utopia* (1685) to which he attached a preface praising More. Finally, there was *The Life of William Bedell* (1685), formerly bishop of Kilmore, which was based entirely on an account of Bedell written by his son-in-law, who had asked Burnet some years earlier to rewrite it.

On 6 February 1685 Charles II died and was succeeded by the duke of York as James II. Burnet was apprehensive about the new king. In addition, his own position was precarious. He was so much out of favour that he was even denied permission to come and kiss the new king's hand. Furthermore he was often visited by those who were beginning to hatch a rebellion in favour of the duke of Monmouth. Clearly Burnet was not involved in Monmouth's rebellion in any way, but he seems to have suspected that something was afoot. It was at least partly to avoid suspicion of complicity that he pressed Halifax to ask the king to let him go abroad. James apparently assented to this request 'with all his heart' (Burnet, 'History', 2, fol. 90a).

Burnet wanted to leave as early as the end of February or the beginning of March, but his wife 'was languishing, and likely to die every day' (Burnet, 'History', 2, fol. 90a), so he remained until May. By then he was becoming increasingly nervous so he made arrangements to have his wife looked after. On the night of 10 May James Hamilton, earl of Arran, the duke of Hamilton's son, visited Burnet and warned him that the king had just received word that Archibald Campbell, ninth earl of Argyll, had set sail for England. Burnet made his will and sailed for France the next day. He reached Paris towards the end of May. At about the same time Lady Margaret died.

Exile, 1685–1688 Burnet chose France on the assumption that it was his safest retreat. Prior to leaving England he had obtained assurances from Barrillon, the French ambassador in London, that he would be safe there. Moreover, he wished to avoid the Netherlands so as not to come into contact with any of Monmouth's party. He took a house in Paris and lived there by himself for two months, resolving to stay until the rebellions had been defeated and all the trials were over in order to avoid suspicion of his complicity. He left Paris in early August 1685, and with a French protestant officer, Colonel Stouppe, he travelled south through France into Switzerland, and from there into Italy. At Rome he was treated with astonishing civility. Pope Innocent XI even offered Burnet an audience, which he prudently declined on account of his poor Italian. He did, however, converse quite frequently with Cardinal D'Estrees and the English Cardinal (Philip) Howard, both of whom treated him 'with great freedom' (*Bishop Burnet's History*, 423). Eventually this freedom began to be taken notice of and Prince Borghese advised him that it was time to move on. He journeyed back through the southern provinces of France where he encountered at first hand the barbarity and cruelty produced by the revocation of the edict of Nantes, which had taken place while he was in Italy. It merely served to confirm all the worst that Burnet had ever thought about Roman Catholicism. He passed three or four months in Geneva in the winter of 1685–6; then from Geneva he journeyed through Switzerland, the German states, and back to the Netherlands, arriving in Utrecht about May 1686. In all he had been rambling for about ten months.

In 1687 Burnet revised and published a series of five letters that he had written to Robert Boyle at various intervals during his trip. *Some Letters, Containing an Account of what Seemed most Remarkable in Switzerland, Italy, etc* proved to be one of Burnet's most popular works. But it was far from a conventional travelogue. He rarely described buildings or scenery, nor was he enthusiastic about art. What really interested him were politics, religion, commerce, and learning. The underlying theme of the letters, however, was anti-Catholic: 'my chief design was to lay open the misery of those who lived under an absolute government and a devouring superstition' (Burnet, 'History', 2, fol. 15b).

When Burnet arrived in Utrecht in May 1686 he was presented with letters from the court of William, prince of Orange, inviting him to live in The Hague. Both the prince and the princess of Orange (Mary, daughter of James II) were favourably disposed towards him and for a time he had free access to them. They often discussed English affairs, and Burnet even claims in his *History* that he was responsible for reconciling the estranged prince and princess, and for convincing Mary that if she ever became queen of England she should undertake to place all power into William's hands. Whether this is true or not is unknown. Nevertheless, the favour shown to Burnet by the prince and princess outraged James II, who threatened a breach if they did not dismiss Burnet from their court. This was done, though Burnet remained in The Hague and continued to be in touch with the prince and princess through the medium of Hans Willem Bentinck.

The issue that engaged Burnet the most throughout 1687 was James's attempt to abolish the Test Acts and to introduce a liberty of conscience in Scotland and England. Both the marquis d'Albeville and William Penn were sent over to The Hague to convince the prince and princess to assent to the repeal of the Test Acts. They declined, apparently after consulting Burnet. Furthermore, Everard van Dyckveldt was dispatched to England to talk to James and other prominent Englishmen about the tests and the indulgence, and Burnet was ordered to draw up his instructions. He also published in 1687 his *Reasons Against the Repealing the Acts … Concerning the Test*, in answer to Samuel Parker's defence of their repeal, as well as reflections upon the declarations for liberty of conscience issued by James in both Scotland and England. Although these works were published anonymously Burnet knew that James 'suspected me to be the author, as I was indeed, though he could never find proofs of it' (Burnet, 'History', 2, fol. 115b). They earned for Burnet the epithet of 'Captain of the Test' from John Dryden. They also served to fuel James's hatred for him.

At the same time Burnet became engaged to Mary Scott (1659/60–1698), a young woman whose family was of Scottish heritage but had been settled in the Netherlands for some time. She was twenty-seven, very accomplished and 'well-shaped'. She was also the sole heir to one of the best fortunes at The Hague. News of Burnet's impending marriage to a wealthy heiress was the final straw for James. In Burnet's opinion it was in order to break his engagement to Mary that James launched a prosecution for high treason against him in Scotland 'for having had a correspondence with Argyle and for having conversed with some that were condemned of high treason' (Burnet,

'History', 2, fol. 115b). The criminal letters were issued at Edinburgh on 19 April 1687. In an attempt to protect him it was proposed that he should petition the states of Holland to be naturalized. This was passed with no opposition the next day. Nevertheless Burnet felt compelled to justify himself in several letters that he wrote to James's secretary of state, Charles Middleton, second earl of Middleton. He wrote in his first letter that his recent naturalization had transferred his allegiance from the king to the states, and added that if a sentence should be passed against him he might be forced to 'give an account of the share which I had in affairs these twenty years passed, in which I might be led to mention some things that … might displease the King' (ibid.). All that this accomplished was to bring on a new suit against him in June for a traitorous transfer of allegiance and a threat to reveal royal secrets. On 29 August 1687 a sentence of outlawry was passed against him and his extradition was demanded. The states refused. If James was really hoping that the treason charges against Burnet would scare off Mary Scott he was mistaken. The marriage went ahead about the end of May 1687. In March 1688 Mary gave birth to their first child, who was named William [*see* Burnet, William], presumably after the prince of Orange. The prince and princess stood as sponsors at the baptism of young William on 2 April 1688.

Of the political intrigues carried on by the prince with the English opposition Burnet knew very little. No one trusted him to be able to keep a secret. Apparently he was not even informed of the prince's intention to invade England until July 1688. Even then it is likely that he was told only because his literary services were in demand. He was asked to translate into English the prince's *Declaration* that had been written in Dutch by Gaspar Fagel. More important from a propaganda standpoint was Burnet's *Enquiry into the measures of submission to the supream authority, and … the grounds on which it may be lawful or necessary for subjects to defend their religion, lives, and liberties*, which had been written for the princess as early as 1687. It was now rewritten and printed by order of the prince. It was to be distributed by his troops upon arrival in England.

As preparations advanced Burnet offered to go along with the prince on the expedition to England. The offer was accepted, and he was installed as chaplain to the prince of Orange just before the fleet set sail. As the time for departure drew near he composed his 'Meditation on my voyage for England', which was meant as his last words in case he should perish in the expedition. In it he denied that he was 'contributing to procure a revolution in England' for any personal gain. Neither was he filled with animosity for Roman Catholics, with the exception of the Jesuits. He then went on to summarize the arguments that he put forward in his *Enquiry*, insisting that they were entirely consistent with 'all that I ever writ or preached on the subject'. Finally he left directions for the posthumous publication of various manuscripts. On 29 October 1688 NS, the expedition sailed.

The revolution of 1688 The invasion fleet landed at Torbay on 5 November 1688. The extraordinary weather which aided the Dutch fleet and hindered the English one served to strengthen Burnet's belief that the expedition was not only just but also had divine sanction. In the subsequent march to London, Burnet played a variety of roles. As the prince's chaplain he was charged with the general task of trying to conciliate the English clergy. As an author of some repute his writing talents were also put to use. He drafted the 'Association', which bound all the prince's supporters to unite in pursuit of the goals of the *Declaration*, to protect him, and to revenge him if he should be attacked. His *Review of the Reflections upon the Prince of Orange's 'Declaration'* was composed while at Exeter. Finally, his previous connection with Halifax proved to be useful when the latter, along with Sydney Godolphin, Baron Godolphin, and Daniel Finch, second earl of Nottingham, were sent by the king to negotiate terms with the prince. In addition to these roles he was also more than ready to offer his advice to the prince. Just before William reached London, about the middle of December 1688, Burnet drew up a memorandum of his opinions on ecclesiastical affairs. The first part was devoted to recommendations of suitable candidates for high ecclesiastical office. He advised the prince to refuse to see bishops Nathaniel Crew of Durham, William Lloyd of Oxford, and Thomas Watson of St Davids because they were 'deserving to be proceeded against' (*Diary of … Sidney*, 2.286). He recommended that the prince dismiss all the royal chaplains and consult Henry Compton, bishop of London, about their replacements. Finally he counselled the prince to revoke all King James's ecclesiastical appointments and to reappoint only those who merited their positions. The second portion contained recommendations on more general topics, such as: suppressing drunkenness and vice; keeping English troops in order; the singing of a *Te Deum* in Whitehall Chapel when the prince reached London; and regular attendance by the prince at 'prayers in the lobby' (*Diary of … Sidney*, 2.288).

Late in December 1688 or early January 1689, after the prince had arrived in London, Burnet drew up another memorandum, this time on the subject of how to proceed now that James had successfully fled. In it he proposed that James be induced to settle in Italy with a substantial pension and that his duties in England be assumed by a regent. The problem with this argument was that the prince of Orange had no intention of accepting a regency. This fact must soon have been made abundantly clear to Burnet because in very short order—certainly before the Convention Parliament met on 22 January 1689—he wrote and published anonymously *An Enquiry into the Present State of Affairs* in which he argued against a regency. James II, by his subversion of government and law, and by his desertion of his kingdom, had dissolved the allegiance owed to him by his subjects. It was the plain right of the English nation to preserve itself in cases of extreme necessity against the violent invasions of the crown. If the king ceased to be king then the throne must pass to the next lawful heir. But if, as in this case, that heir was a woman, then by the 'laws of nations' which transferred the rights

of the wife to her husband, 'this is likewise communicated' (*Enquiry*, 10). Without doubt Burnet's *Enquiry* reflected the views of the prince. And when the time came for the Convention to discuss the matter of the crown William made it clear that he would not consent to being a regent or a consort to his wife. However, he went even further to insist that the crown be vested in himself alone. This shocked many, including Burnet. Eventually a compromise was reached in the convention and on 13 February 1689 William III and Mary II were proclaimed king and queen. Burnet was chosen to preach their coronation sermon on 11 April 1689.

Burnet's political theory Burnet's enthusiastic support of William's armed intervention in English politics produced much derisive comment from his contemporary critics. They did not fail to accuse the man who had once so passionately preached obedience to the authority of the sovereign monarch of suddenly, and opportunely, becoming a revolutionary. Subsequently historians have also accepted that Burnet's abandonment of nonresistance theories occurred abruptly, and suspiciously, some time just before the revolution. While there is no doubt that between 1673 and 1688 his views on the power of princes changed, a close reading of his writings in this period suggests that the transformation that occurred was not as sudden, or even as drastic, as has previously been thought. The most important feature to remember about Burnet's political philosophy is the fact that it was arrived at not for a political purpose, but for an ecclesiological one. His foray into the realm of political theory was strictly for the purpose of proving that ultimate ecclesiastical authority lay in the hands of the secular authority and not in the hands of the clergy. Burnet was a thoroughgoing Erastian in the tradition of Hugo Grotius and John Selden, as already demonstrated by his *Vindication of the Authority, Constitution, and Laws of the Church and State of Scotland* in 1673. Yet four years later in his *Vindication of the Ordinations of the Church of England* he opened the door to the possibility of resistance to the English king if he failed to govern 'legally and by the Councils and their Parliaments'. Thus in the 1670s he had put forward both a conservative and a radical theory of natural rights. There remained much ambiguity and even contradiction on the subject of natural rights in Burnet's writings and sermons over the next few years. This should come as no surprise, since Burnet had never attempted to formulate a completely coherent political philosophy; he was merely trying to construct an Erastian model of church government. The ambiguity that plagued his political thought would work itself out only after the accession to the thrones of England and Scotland of James II and VII in 1685. The process began with his *Reflections on his Majesty's Proclamation of 12th February 1687 for a Toleration in Scotland* and culminated in his final commitment to a radical natural rights theory in his *An Enquiry into the Measures of Submission to the Supream Authority* in summer 1687.

That having been said Burnet was well aware that intricate legal and philosophical reasoning might not be acceptable to the vast majority of the English clergy, and he was not averse to making use of any argument that might convince them to take the new oaths to William and Mary. It was for this reason that, in the middle of May 1689, Burnet, newly consecrated as bishop of Salisbury, published *A Pastoral Letter* in which he argued, on the basis of biblical and historical principles, that allegiance was owed to those who were in actual possession of the throne. Although this position may well have persuaded many clerics, it clearly offended both dynastic legitimists and 'original contract' whigs. Later on his enemies, both tory and whig, combined to attack the *Pastoral Letter* in parliament, and on 25 January 1693 it was burnt by the common hangman by order of the House of Commons.

Bishop of Salisbury under Mary II and William III, 1689–1702
Now that William had achieved his ambition of gaining the English crown it was clear that his principal supporters would have to be rewarded. Almost immediately Burnet was appointed a royal chaplain and clerk of the royal closet, and it looked for a time as if he might be elevated to the wealthy and prestigious see of Durham. The incumbent, Nathaniel Crew, one of the bishops who, Burnet had told William, ought to be proceeded against, was contemplating retirement. He made it known that he would resign in Burnet's favour if the latter would agree to give him £1000 a year out of the episcopal revenues. Burnet refused, largely because the arrangement struck him as simonical. There was also the strong possibility that Crew would resign anyway. In the end, however, Crew decided to hang on when it became apparent that Henry Compton, bishop of London, whom he hated, was the likely candidate to succeed him. Meanwhile, the see of Salisbury lay vacant following the death of Seth Ward in January 1689. William gave it to Burnet. The archbishop of Canterbury, William Sancroft, at first refused to consecrate him. However, when it was pointed out that this could bring a *praemunire* charge against him he resorted to the rather unusual expedient of granting a commission to the bishops of his province to do it for him. On Easter day 1689 Burnet was consecrated bishop of Salisbury by bishops Henry Compton of London, Peter Mews of Winchester, William Beaw of Llandaff, William Lloyd of St Asaph, and Thomas Smith of Carlisle. Anthony Horneck preached the consecration sermon. Three days later he was sworn in as chancellor of the Order of the Garter, a post that came to him as Windsor, the headquarters of the order, was then within the bounds of his see.

Although he had in his earlier years criticized bishops for their meddling in secular affairs Burnet now embraced his new role as a political bishop. The Lords' *Journals* confirm that he was one of the most assiduous attenders of the house from the episcopal bench. Politically Burnet was a whig. On most party issues that arose between 1689 and 1715 he is reported to have sided with the whigs. Yet this was not always the case. For all his political partisanship there was still the odd time when even he was obliged by his conscience to refuse to support the party line.

Yet for all of his interest in political affairs Burnet proved to be an energetic and active bishop who took his diocesan responsibilities seriously. His first concern was with residence. As his diocese consisted of the two counties of Wiltshire and Berkshire he resolved at the outset to divide his year between them. The former was a bigger county, and the seat of his see, so he intended to be in Salisbury eight months of the year, and four at Windsor. Once a year he planned to spend some weeks visiting parishes in his diocese where he would preach and confirm. By fifteen months he had already preached and confirmed in fifty churches. After twenty-one years that number had risen to 275, many of them more than once. His other great concern was with the quality of the clergy in his diocese. Although he acknowledged that he had not met with much scandal among them, he did think that many of them were ignorant, had no great sense of devotion, and 'none at all of the pastoral care' (Burnet, 'History', 2, fol. 141b). In an effort to raise the level of the existing clergy he initiated the practice of holding conferences with them. The idea for these may have come from Bishop Compton, who held similar meetings in his diocese. These conferences would begin with a discourse of about two hours in which Burnet would expound on a subject of doctrinal or pastoral interest. This would be followed by a discussion. Four of these discourses were collected and published in 1694. However, he found that 'the clergy were not much the better for them, and false stories were made and believed of what I delivered in those conferences', and so he eventually abandoned them ('Burnet's autobiography', 499). He was also concerned with the education of future ministers. He had little respect for the education that they received in the universities, so he conceived a scheme to train students in divinity at Salisbury. He offered students £30 a year to go to Salisbury to study 'matters of learning and piety, and particularly of such things as related to the pastoral care' (Burnet, 'History', 2, fol. 141a). However, owing to the hostility of the universities and disappointing quality of the students he let the project fall after five years. When it came to ordaining clergy he resolved 'to ordain no persons without knowing them well, and examining them strictly myself' (ibid., fol. 141b). This was not entirely successful either: it simply had the effect of drastically reducing the number of candidates that approached him. He also attempted to reform the bishop's court at Salisbury by attending frequently in person, but after some years he gave up all hope of doing any good there and stopped attending.

In addition to his episcopal duties Burnet also dispensed substantial sums of money in charity, much of it to his own clergy. By his own reckoning he spent £3000 'in larger sums among them, besides smaller ones that occur daily' ('Burnet's autobiography', 500). An ardent proponent of the charity school movement he set up a school for fifty poor children at Salisbury who were taught and clothed at his expense. He also assisted promising but poor young men in obtaining a university education.

Yet in spite of all of this activity Burnet doubted, probably rightly, whether he was having much of an impact on the church. After twenty-one years he admitted that he was likely 'doing little good with all this agitation' (*Bishop Burnet's History*, 501–2). He was ineffectual partly because he lacked the charm and tact required of great leaders. Much more important, however, was the huge gulf that existed between his political and ecclesiastical opinions and those of the vast majority of his clergy. He was a whig and a latitudinarian, whereas most of his clergy were sympathetic to the tory and high-church party.

That Burnet's views were out of sympathy with the 'whole body of the clergy' is illustrated best in the controversy that took place over the toleration and comprehension bills introduced into the House of Lords in February and March 1689. While both the whig latitudinarians and tory high-churchmen could support toleration, the latter were 'much offended with the bill of comprehension' (*Bishop Burnet's History*, 531). A commission was issued to a diverse group of clergy (including Burnet) empowering them to meet and prepare a draft of alterations and amendments to the liturgy and canons which would be presented to convocation. But the high-church party opposed the whole idea of altering the liturgy and canons. They thought that too much had already been done for the dissenters in the Toleration Act, and they would do nothing to make things even easier for them. Moreover, by offering these alterations they thought the church was tacitly admitting that it had previously been in error. This would cause division, and people would then lose their esteem for the liturgy if they thought that it needed correction.

These were difficult charges for Burnet to answer. Indeed, he had made the same points in his *Modest Survey* back in 1676. This time his response was that ritual matters were of their own nature indifferent and had always been declared to have been so. This in no way implied that the Church of England was anything less than it ought to be; but it would be unreasonable to deny any modification of that liturgy if it would go some way towards healing the wounds of the church. Of course it was possible that the liturgical alterations might not be acceptable to the vast majority of dissenters. In this case, he argued, 'if some more sensible objections were put out of the way, we might well hope that it would have a great effect upon the next generation' (*Bishop Burnet's History*, 543). The fact that the toleration was now in place made the comprehension project all the more urgent:

> the toleration now granted seemed to render it more necessary than formerly to make the terms of communion with the church as large as might be, that so we might draw over to us the greater number from those who might now leave us more safely. (ibid.)

The Toleration Act did nothing to heal the separation, for it offered nothing to the moderate dissenters to encourage them to return to communion with the established church. But in the end the majority of the lower clergy in convocation disapproved of what the commission proposed and the project failed.

Encouraging dissenters back into the Church of England was one of the motivations behind *A Discourse of the Pastoral Care*, written in late 1691 or early 1692. The passing of the Toleration Act meant that the dissenters could 'no more be forced' to conform (*Pastoral Care*, 101). Although,

Burnet argued, it did not absolve the dissenters from the obligation laid upon them by the laws of God and the gospel to maintain the unity of the church, it was now up to the Church of England to win them back. The best way to achieve this was if the clergy 'were stricter in our lives, more serious and constant in our labours, and studied more effectually to Reform those of our Communion, than to rail at theirs' (ibid.). Burnet set out the function and character of the clerical profession as described in scripture, the primitive church, and the Church of England. He suggested a number of books which young men ought to read in preparation for ordination. He then stated the appropriate labours of a clergyman, and ended with a short discussion about preaching. The *Pastoral Care* is unquestionably one of Burnet's finest works. Archbishop John Tillotson praised it as 'perfect in its kind' (Clarke and Foxcroft, 310), and Queen Mary, to whom it was dedicated, heartily approved of it. Burnet, too, preferred it to his other writings. It is simply written, yet passionate and sincere, and next to his *History* was his most popular work throughout the eighteenth and nineteenth centuries.

Despite William's quickness to reward Burnet with a bishopric before any other clergy the two began the new reign on very poor terms. Halifax commented in early 1689 that he never heard the king say a kind word of Burnet, and about the same time Dyckveldt apparently heard the king refer to Burnet as a wretched Tartuffe. With Queen Mary, however, Burnet had a much better relationship. She was much more forgiving of his garrulity and lack of tact, and he for his part 'never admired any person so entirely as I did her' (Burnet, 'History', 2, fol. 162b). In fact it appears that the queen relied quite heavily on Burnet's advice on religious matters. He suggested a string of fasts and thanksgivings for the war, which she organized while William was away fighting, and he was always her preferred preacher to perform on these occasions at court. This is why Mary's death on 28 December 1694 so affected him. Three months later he wrote, 'I never felt myself sink so much under anything that had happened to me' (ibid.); and early in 1695 Burnet eulogized Mary in *An Essay on the Late Queen*.

During her life Mary had controlled the administration of ecclesiastical affairs; following her death William put all ecclesiastical patronage into the hands of an ecclesiastical commission that comprised archbishops Thomas Tenison of Canterbury and John Sharp of York, bishops William Lloyd of Lichfield, Edward Stillingfleet of Worcester, Simon Patrick of Ely, and Burnet. They were to recommend to the king one or more suitable candidates for all major ecclesiastical appointments (including bishoprics), and during the king's absences abroad they even presented to all livings under the yearly value of £140. Such a commission was terribly unpopular with the vast majority of the clergy because, aside from the moderate tory high-churchman Sharp, the rest of the membership was firmly whig latitudinarian.

Equally unpopular was Burnet's appointment in early summer 1698 as preceptor, or tutor, to the eight-year-old

William, duke of Gloucester, the only surviving child of Princess Anne. It was a surprising appointment, given the fact that Princess Anne loathed Burnet. Undoubtedly his previous experience in education and his intellectual abilities were a factor in the king's choice, but his whig political sympathies likely also played a part. Aware of Anne's hostility, however, Burnet was reluctant to accept the post. It was only after interventions by the earls of Godolphin and Marlborough that Burnet was induced to acquiesce. He held the post until the death of Gloucester on 24 July 1700.

Just as Burnet was about to assume his duties as preceptor, his second wife, Mary Scott, died. She left England on 29 May 1698 for the United Provinces to conduct business relating to her property, estimated at £30,000, which was invested in Dutch securities. Shortly after her arrival in Rotterdam she contracted smallpox and died very quickly on 18 June 1698. Burnet seemed genuinely distressed at her death: their eleven-year marriage had apparently been a happy one. She had borne seven children, five boys (two of whom died very young) and twin girls. Her premature death now left Burnet a widower with a young family. However, before leaving for the United Provinces, Mary, who had a sense of her impending demise, had suggested to her husband that in the event of her own death he should take their friend Elizabeth Berkeley (1661–1709) [see Burnet, Elizabeth] as his new wife and 'her children's mother' (Clarke and Foxcroft, 353). With five children, all under ten, Burnet certainly saw the need 'to provide a mistress to my family, and a mother to my children' (ibid., 379). Elizabeth Berkeley was also, according to Burnet, 'one of the most extraordinary persons that has lived in this age'. The fifty-seven-year-old bishop and his thirty-nine-year-old bride, who was the elder daughter of Sir Richard Blake, of Easterton, Wiltshire, and Elizabeth Bathurst, were married in May or June 1700.

The 1690s proved an extraordinarily busy decade for the energetic and active Burnet. In addition to his political and pastoral responsibilities as a bishop, as well as his rather full personal life, Burnet became embroiled in two major controversies that erupted in the Church of England in the last decade of the seventeenth century.

Trinitarian controversy Although the general charge of anti-trinitarianism against the latitudinarians first appeared in their controversies with the Catholics, it was in the 1680s and 1690s that the high-church party adopted it as a stick with which to beat their latitudinarian enemies. For a variety of reasons Burnet's own orthodoxy came under suspicion. Towards the end of 1693 he collected several of his diocesan discourses and had them published as *Four Discourses Delivered to the Clergy of the Diocese of Sarum* (1694). The second of them, 'Concerning the divinity and death of Christ', was meant to clear the air and to put an end to speculation about his views on the Trinity. The effect was quite the opposite. Far from allaying the fears of some of the clergy, Burnet exacerbated them.

Under constant attack from the papists and high-church

party for denying all mysteries, Burnet, in the discourse, developed his notion of mystery further, and gave it more prominence than ever before. Concomitant to this was a corresponding reduction in the stress he had once placed on the clarity and distinctness of scriptural doctrine. Under rationalist pressure from the anti-trinitarians he was also forced to reduce the role of reason in determining doctrine. The result, however, was far from satisfactory to his opponents. By arguing that the Trinity was a mystery which scripture and reason did not fully reveal he left too much room for latitude in explaining its intricacies. In the view of his critics he had put forward in the discourse an account of the Trinity that was both unclear in its language and unorthodox in its rejection of traditional patristic learning.

Convocation controversy Yet there was more to the trinitarian debate between the high-church party and the latitudinarians than pamphlet warfare. From very early on the high-churchmen made it clear that they were not content to leave the question of trinitarian orthodoxy to be settled in the popular press. Throughout the 1690s the high-church clergy campaigned for a convocation of the clergy of the ecclesiastical province of Canterbury to be called in order to settle once and for all the Anglican definition of the Trinity.

In the meantime, in autumn 1699 Burnet had published *An Exposition of the Thirty-Nine Articles of the Church of England*. The *Exposition* could be considered the logical extension of Burnet's discourse on the Trinity. In it he applied a latitudinarian epistemology not just to the Trinity, but to all the doctrinal articles of the church. It was also intimately connected with his *History of the Reformation*. If his *History of the Reformation* was an attempt to rewrite English church history from the perspective of a late seventeenth-century latitudinarian divine, then his *Exposition* was its theological counterpart. Burnet himself described his *Exposition* as a 'proper addition to the History of the Reformation, to explain and prove the doctrine that was then established' (*Bishop Burnet's History*, 658). As the logical extension of both his *Four Discourses* and his *History of the Reformation*, the *Exposition* was one of Burnet's most important works, and one which the high-church party could hardly ignore for long.

When convocation was finally called and allowed to sit in 1701, the high-church dominated lower house proceeded to establish a committee on heretical and scandalous books which produced censures on both John Toland's *Christianity not Mysterious* (1696) and Burnet's *Exposition*. The committee objected to Burnet's whole approach to doctrine. The avowed aim of the *Exposition* was to help heal the breaches, both within the Church of England, and between Anglicans and other protestants. In his zeal to foster a mutual forbearance of diversity Burnet was accused of introducing a latitude and diversity of opinions that utterly misrepresented the true state of Anglican doctrine. His latitudinarianism had led him to heterodoxy. Much worse, however, he was charged with deliberately downplaying the differences in religion in

England with the intent of laying a platform for comprehension with the dissenters. The high-church party had not forgotten, or forgiven, Burnet's role in the ill-fated comprehension scheme of 1689.

Accession of Queen Anne and occasional conformity, 1702 Both Burnet and Tenison attended William III on his deathbed, and were present when he died on 8 March 1702. With William's passing came a substantial change in Burnet's influence in ecclesiastical affairs and in his position at court. The staunchly high-church Queen Anne had no intention of leaving church patronage in the hands of a pack of latitudinarian bishops. She promptly revoked William's ecclesiastical commission. On a more personal level Anne publicly displayed her abhorrence for Burnet by ejecting him from his lodgings in St James's Palace and handing them over to Compton. Burnet had lost the royal favour that had allowed him to play such a prominent role in ecclesiastical affairs throughout the 1690s, but the change in circumstances did nothing to alter his commitment to defending his latitudinarian principles. It was not long before he was in the thick of religious controversy again.

It was the issue of comprehension of dissent that was also at the bottom of the occasional conformity controversy that erupted in 1702. Following the revolution an increasing number of dissenters were noticed taking communion in an Anglican church just often enough to qualify, according to the Test Act, for public office. In order to put a stop to this a bill was introduced into the House of Commons in November 1702 to prevent occasional conformity. Burnet spoke and voted in the House of Lords against the Occasional Conformity Bill. This was largely because he and his fellow latitudinarians fully accepted the principle of occasional communion as a sign that the dissenters had not closed their minds to the possibility that the Church of England was a true church. This gave him cause to believe that a great number of dissenters could yet be persuaded to come back into the fold of the established church. Yet this position was not exclusive to those who opposed the bill. Few high-churchmen were prepared to condemn every act of occasional communion. And the bill itself did not prohibit occasional communion; it merely prevented those who had practised it from holding public office. This was the crux of the matter. The Corporation and Test Acts offered only moderate dissenters, who had no objection to taking communion in the Church of England, a full toleration in exchange for their occasional attendance at communion in a parish church. To Burnet this was a fair exchange, for it preserved the principle that moderate and separatist dissenters ought to be treated differently. Moderate dissenters must be encouraged 'to come as near the Church as they could, and to do all that they could do with a Good Conscience' (*The Bishop of Salisbury's Speech … upon the Bill Against Occasional Conformity*, 6). By denying full social and political rights to separatist and moderate dissenters without distinction the bill was abandoning what Burnet insisted was a fundamental principle of the policy that the church had traditionally applied to the dissenters. He feared that the Occasional Conformity Bill would drive into a total separation from the church those who were most likely to respond to a comprehension scheme.

Bishop of Salisbury under Anne and George I, 1702–1715 Despite his diminished influence in ecclesiastical matters under Anne, Burnet did manage to convince the queen to agree to a scheme that he had been promoting since early 1696. Concerned with the poor endowment of some parish livings, particularly in market towns, he had proposed to William that the crown's income from the first fruits and tenths be used to supplement poorer livings. Nothing came of it in William's reign; however, Anne was far more favourable to the idea. In February 1704 she announced in a speech to parliament, in which she publicly admitted Burnet's responsibility, the creation of Queen Anne's Bounty.

On 3 February 1709 Elizabeth Burnet died. Burnet was greatly affected by her death. As a tribute to her memory he immediately arranged for her *Method of Devotion*, written before their marriage but not published until 1708, to be reprinted. Attached to this new edition was a biographical preface, supposedly written by Dr Timothy Goodwin, but which Burnet later admitted that he had largely dictated. Following his wife's death Burnet seems to have withdrawn somewhat from society. In her will Elizabeth Burnet had bequeathed to her husband a life interest in her estate at St John's, Clerkenwell, and from this time on, whenever he was in town he lived in this secluded dwelling on the edge of London. Visits there tended to be confined to a few select and intimate acquaintances, including the Marlboroughs, Godolphin, John, Baron Somers, William, Baron Cowper, George Baillie of Jerviswood, and other members of the more moderate wing of the whig party.

Towards the end of that year, on 5 November 1709, the tory high-churchman Henry Sacheverell preached his notorious sermon in St Paul's Cathedral in which he launched a tirade against those 'false brethren' who had 'shamefully betrayed and run down' the principles and interests of the Church of England. He included among the false brethren those who modified its doctrines, discipline, and worship (here he plainly alluded to Burnet and his *Exposition*), and those who advocated resistance to the supreme power. In setting out his own non-resistance theories Sacheverell cleverly used citations from Burnet's early works. Yet although he had been personally insulted in the sermon Burnet did not approve of the subsequent attempt by the current whig ministry to have Sacheverell impeached in parliament for high crimes and misdemeanours. He believed, quite rightly, that it would serve only to excite sympathy among high-churchmen for the persecuted priest. The passions aroused in support of Sacheverell were such that on the night of 1 March 1710 tory high-church mobs attacked six dissenting meeting-houses in London, including the chapel in St John's Court where Burnet lived. A man was killed right in front of his house. Apparently only the arrival of troops saved Burnet's house from demolition by the angry mob. Despite his objection to the impeachment, however, when the proceedings eventually reached the House of Lords in March 1710 Burnet attended and made a speech attacking Sacheverell which was later published. In the end, he voted with the majority in condemning Sacheverell.

The three issues that excited Burnet's passions most in the last few years of his life were the war, of which he was staunchly in favour, the toleration, which he was determined to defend against the attacks of the tories, and the protestant succession. He saw the conclusion of war at the end of March 1713 with the treaty of Utrecht, although like the rest of the whigs he deplored the treaty as a breach of solidarity with Britain's allies. Before his death the other two issues would be more satisfactorily concluded. The toleration was intact and as secure as possible. And on 1 August 1714, the day Queen Anne died, George, elector of Hanover, was proclaimed King George of Great Britain. Burnet preached to the new king on 30 October, ten days after his coronation. In January 1715 the third and last volume of his *History of the Reformation* finally appeared, with a dedication to the new king. It was the last of his works to be published during his life.

Death Two months later, in March 1715, Burnet caught a chill that advanced into a pleuritic fever. After three days of illness he died, on 17 March 1715, in his house in St John's Court, Clerkenwell, London. According to his son Thomas he approached his imminent death with 'calm resignation to Providence' (Clarke and Foxcroft, 473). He apparently retained full consciousness to the last, and took leave of his family with 'the utmost tenderness [and] firmest constancy of mind' (ibid.).

Burnet had stated in his will, dated 24 October 1711, that if he died away from Salisbury he was to be buried in his London parish church of St James, Clerkenwell, and he was interred there soon after his death. St James's was later rebuilt, but his burial site is still marked by a stone beneath the altar, and a tablet erected in his memory by the parishioners remains in the vestibule of the church. Burnet was a controversial figure to the end: his funeral cavalcade was stoned by a tory and Jacobite mob, and numerous satires and lampoons on his life were published.

According to the terms of his will, of which his eldest son, William, was executor, his entire estate (specific bequests excepted) was to be divided into six shares, two of which were to go to William and the other four to each of his remaining children. William was also to receive some plate and furniture, all his father's works bound in red Turkey leather, mathematical instruments, windpump and glasses, and, after James Johnston's death, the reversion of his portrait painted in 1693 by Sir Godfrey Kneller. He left legacies to Marischal College, Aberdeen, and the parish of Saltoun amounting to £2222 3s. 6d. To his successor at Salisbury he left the furniture of the chapel and of the great upper room in the bishop's palace. To the town of Salisbury he gave £20 for the poor and six months' salary in advance to the master of the charity school. Each of his servants was given six months' wages. A codicil was later added which bequeathed his papers to his second son, Gilbert *Burnet (1690–1726), to use as he pleased. The

two exceptions were his manuscript *Essays and Meditations on Morality and Religion*, which Gilbert was directed to publish (he never did, and the manuscript has been lost), and his *History of his Own Time*, which was also to be published, but only after a period of six years. In 1724 Gilbert published the first (pre-revolution) volume. Ten years later Burnet's third son, Thomas (1694–1753) [see Burnet, Sir Thomas] issued the second volume (Gilbert having died in 1726). Neither was published verbatim from the final text, as Burnet had instructed in his will. As well, an autobiographical appendix was suppressed and substituted with a short biographical sketch written by Thomas.

The *History of his Own Time* The origin of Burnet's 'secret history', as he called it, goes back to 1683 when, in the fortieth year of his age, he resolved both to 'let the world see truly the good and bad that has been in me' and to 'discover all I know of the world, that I think may be of use to mankind' (Burnet, 'History', 1, fol. 1b). He worked on it from 1683 until his departure from England for the safety of the continent in May 1685. He seems to have kept a running account of events in England during the reign of James II from his vantage point in The Hague, where he spent the bulk of his exile. In October 1688, just before embarking on William's invasion of England, Burnet brought his 'secret history' up to date. Anticipating possible disaster on the impending expedition he left directions in his will for its posthumous publication. After the revolution he worked intermittently on it from 1691 through to 1703. In spring 1703 he decided to recast substantially what he had already written. He had recently read Jacques-Auguste De Thou's *Historia sui temporis* and had been impressed with its literary style, and particularly with its attempt at impartiality. Inspired by De Thou's example Burnet sought to expunge his *History* of its more personal and autobiographical elements and to transform it from a memoir into a more strictly historical work. He was likely also have been influenced by the publication in 1702 of the first volume of Edward Hyde, first earl of Clarendon's *History of the Rebellion*. Like Burnet, Clarendon had originally set out to write a life of himself, but had thought better of it and had written a formal history instead. Its success, and Burnet's admiration for it, must have spurred him on in his resolve to alter his own work. By 15 September 1704 he had completed his recast narrative, and in May 1705 he resumed his *History* from where he had left off. He worked on it on and off until 1713 when the *History* reached its conclusion with the treaty of Utrecht. The final two years of Burnet's life were taken up revising these latter portions.

Ever since the appearance of *Bishop Burnet's History of his Own Time* it has been the subject of great controversy. It engendered much excitement and clearly sold well in England, each volume going through a number of editions. In the following years several Dutch and French translations were published on the continent. Not all the attention was favourable, and Burnet's critics, of whom there were many, fell over themselves to excoriate it. The margins of Jonathan Swift's personal copy of it are filled with vitriolic comments such as 'dunce' and 'Scotch dog'.

The nonjuring Jacobite John Cockburn called it 'a History full of Errors and Falsehoods'. Yet even his enemies were far from united in this opinion. Francis Atterbury, the tory high-church cleric who eventually turned Jacobite, and who had clashed with Burnet in the convocation controversy of 1702, exclaimed in frustration: 'Damn him, he has told a great deal of truth, but where the devil did he learn it?' (Clarke and Foxcroft, xxxv).

Even his severest critics had to admit, however reluctantly, that Burnet was well suited to writing a history of his own time. Cockburn, who claimed to have loathed Burnet from the first time that they met when the former was only ten, grudgingly conceded that no one was

> more qualified for writing the History of His Own Times, for he was Curious and Inquisitive, and had a large Acquaintance, and the Opportunity of conversing with all sorts of Persons, of all Ranks, from the Throne downwards. He never heard of any Person of Note, whether at home or abroad, whom he did not take some Opportunity of visiting and if they were not of themselves ready to declare what they knew, he endeavoured to draw them into it by his curious Questions, as I have been informed by those who know his ways; so that without Question, there were few who could know more, or so much of the Transactions of those Times he writes of.   (Cockburn, 66)

The earl of Dartmouth concurred: 'Bishop Burnet was a man of the most extensive knowledge I ever met with; had read and seen a great deal, with a prodigious memory' (*Burnet's History*, ed. Airy, 1.xxxiii).

Burnet had the personality of a journalist: he was voracious in his appetite for news. His problem came not in collecting information, but in sifting through the chaff to find the seed. He had little sense of judgement. As Cockburn added, he was 'too volatile for exercising a Judgement, and penetrating into the Depth of Things' (Cockburn, 28). Dartmouth, in his own character of Burnet, also noted his poor judgement:

> he was extremely partial, and readily took every thing for granted that he heard to the prejudice of those he did not like: which made him pass for a man of less truth than he really was. I do not think he designedly published any thing he believed to be false.   (*Burnet's History*, ed. Airy, 1.xxxiii)

Although Burnet was a journalist he was not a discriminating one, and his *History*, although a valuable source for the history of the period, needs to be used with some caution.

Historical significance Burnet's critics often accuse him of overstating, in his *History* and elsewhere, his own importance in the events of his time. While it is true that Burnet was an egomaniac, and he undoubtedly expected future historians to study him, there is much truth to his assertions. His career can be evaluated by dividing it into two, sometimes overlapping, spheres: his engagement in public affairs and his vocation as an author. In public affairs there were two periods in his life when he really was of some importance. The first was as a young cleric in Scotland. His very close relationship with the powerful earl (later duke) of Lauderdale drew him into the thick of

Scottish ecclesiastical affairs, when Burnet played a prominent role in promoting Lauderdale's policy of accommodation between 1668 and 1672. The second period of influence resulted from his close association with William III and Mary II. Burnet was invited by them to live at The Hague in 1686. While he was not involved in any way with planning and preparing for William's invasion of England, he did accompany William over as his personal chaplain, and he did provide William with much useful advice on ecclesiastical affairs in England. Furthermore William did not hesitate to use Burnet's writing skills in the service of his cause. Burnet was rewarded for his loyalty and service with the bishopric of Salisbury in 1689. Although his personal relationship with William was never warm, he and Queen Mary got along very well. It was Mary who had control over church matters in the first half of the 1690s, and Burnet was undoubtedly one of her trusted advisers. After her death at the end of 1694 Burnet retained his influence in ecclesiastical matters. His place on William's ecclesiastical commission from 1695 until 1702 is the most obvious illustration of this. As an author Burnet can be reckoned as one of the most prolific and substantial of his day. In his lifetime he published more than 140 works, ranging from sermons and short polemics to major works of theology, biography, and history. More important, unlike most authors his works were rarely ignored. Sometimes the reaction was positive, as with his *History of the Reformation*, which brought him votes of thanks from both houses of parliament and the degree of doctor of divinity from the University of Oxford. On other occasions the reaction was negative, as with his *Exposition of the Thirty-Nine Articles* which brought him the censure of the lower house of convocation. Yet other works, such as his *Letters* on his trip through western Europe and his *Pastoral Care*, were clearly popular, both going through several editions in his own lifetime. Moreover Burnet was one of the few British writers of his time who could boast of a European reputation. Many of his works were published on the continent in French, Dutch, and even German translations. Louis XIV was obviously well aware of his *History of the Rights of Princes*. Bishop Jacques Bossuet, tutor to the dauphin and one of the most celebrated of French theologians of the day, considered Burnet one of the three principal champions of protestantism. Burnet also corresponded with several notable continental figures in religious and intellectual circles, including Daniel Le Clerc, Philippus van Limborch, and Gottfried Wilhelm Leibniz. Finally, some of his books continued to be published throughout the eighteenth and nineteenth centuries and were clearly still considered to be important works. For example, Richard Hurrell Froude, the noted nineteenth-century tractarian, recalled how he had studied Burnet's *History of the Reformation* 'a good deal', even though he utterly disagreed with Burnet's interpretation of it. In both spheres of his public career, then, Burnet was indeed a man of great significance.   MARTIN GREIG

Sources G. Burnet, 'The history of my own life and of the most remarkable things that I have known and observed in the world', 1683–1715, BL, Add. MSS 63057a–b · *Bishop Burnet's History of his own*

time, new edn, 2 vols. (1838) · G. Burnet, 'Autobiography', in *A supplement to Burnet's History of my own time*, ed. H. C. Foxcroft (1902), 451–514 · T. E. S. Clarke and H. C. Foxcroft, *A life of Gilbert Burnet* (1907) · M. Greig, 'The reasonableness of Christianity? Gilbert Burnet and the trinitarian controversy of the 1690s', *Journal of Ecclesiastical History*, 44 (1993), 631–51 · M. Greig, 'Heresy hunt: Gilbert Burnet and the convocation controversy of 1701', *HJ*, 37 (1994), 569–92 · M. Greig, 'Gilbert Burnet and the problem of nonconformity in Restoration Scotland and England', *Canadian Journal of History*, 32 (1997), 1–24 · J. Buckroyd, *Church and state in Scotland, 1660–1681* (1980) · W. A. Speck, *Reluctant revolutionaries* (1989) · G. Every, *The high church party, 1688–1718* (1956) · G. U. Bennett, *The tory crisis in church and state, 1688–1730* (1975) · C. Rose, *England in the 1690s* (1999) · G. Holmes, *Politics, religion and society in England, 1679–1742* (1986) · M. Goldie, 'The nonjurors, episcopacy, and the origins of the convocation controversy', *Ideology and conspiracy: aspects of Jacobitism, 1689–1759*, ed. E. Cruickshanks (1982), 15–35 · G. S. Holmes, *British politics in the age of Anne*, rev. edn (1987) · 'Remaining fragments of Bishop Burnet's original memoirs', *A supplement to Burnet's 'History of my own time'*, ed. H. C. Foxcroft (1902), 1–450 · *Diary of the times of Charles the Second by the Honourable Henry Sidney (afterwards earl of Romney)*, ed. R. W. Blencowe, 2 vols. (1843) · *Burnet's History of my own time*, ed. O. Airy, new edn, 2 vols. (1897–1900) · J. Cockburn, *A specimen of some free and impartial remarks on publick affairs and particular persons, especially relating to Scotland; occasion'd by Dr Burnet's history of his own times* (1724)

Archives BL, family and estate corresp. and papers, Add. MSS 11403–11404 · BL, memoirs of the dukes of Hamilton and corresp., Sloane MSS 1007–1008, 1685 · Bodl. Oxf., corresp. and papers · NL Scot., letters and papers · NRA, priv. coll., papers relating to his lives of the dukes of Hamilton · PRO, sermons, PRO 30/26/66 | BL, Add. MSS 4236, 4238, 63057a, 63057b, SC 283; Lauderdale MSS · BL, letters to Admiral Herbert, Egerton MS 2621 · Bodl. Oxf., MSS Add. A 191, D 23, Eng. lett. d. 184, St Edmund Hall 14 · Chatsworth House, Derbyshire, letters to Lady Russell · Christ Church Oxf., MS Arch W Epist, vols. 1 and 17 · LPL, Gibson papers, corresp., vols. 929–42, *passim* · NL Scot., letters to Lord Tweeddale · TCD, corresp. with William King · U. Nott. L., letters to Lady Russell

Likenesses miniature, c.1680–1688, Crathes Castle and Garden, Aberdeenshire · oils, 1681, Scot. NPG · by or after J. Riley, oils, c.1689–1691, Scot. NPG; version, Crathes Castle and Garden, Aberdeenshire; version, NPG · M. Beale, oils, c.1690, LPL · G. Kneller, oils, 1693, Wimpole Hall, Cambridgeshire [*see illus.*] · G. Vertue, line engraving, 1723 (after S. Hoadley), BM, NPG · R. White, line engraving (aged forty-four), BM · line engraving, caricature, NPG

Burnet, Gilbert (1690–1726), writer on religious and moral subjects, was born in Salisbury on 15 November 1690, the second son of Gilbert *Burnet, bishop of Salisbury (1643–1715) and his second wife, Mary Scott (1659/60–1698). William *Burnet (1688–1729) and Sir Thomas *Burnet (1694–1753) were his brothers. His mother, who was Dutch, of Scottish ancestry, died on a visit to Rotterdam with her son on 18 June 1698. Burnet was educated at Merton College, Oxford, from where he matriculated on 6 July 1703 (BA 1706); at the University of Leiden, 1706–7; and at Peterhouse, Cambridge (MA 1713). He was ordained a priest at Ely on 13 March 1715, and collated prebendary at Salisbury for Beminster Secunda on 1 July 1715 and Gillingham Major on 24 February 1721. He was appointed chaplain to George I in 1718 and elected fellow of the Royal Society in 1723. From 1719 to 1726 he was rector of East Barnet, Hertfordshire.

Burnet was an able and energetic defender of Benjamin Hoadly in the Bangorian controversy. He wrote pamphlets in answer to Dr Andrew Snape, William Law, and the Revd Joseph Trapp in support of Hoadly's identification of the church with the kingdom of Christ. It followed from this identification, Burnet wrote, that Jesus Christ is 'the sole Law-giver, King and Judge in his Church', and that 'Christ left behind him no Vicegerent who can be said properly to supply his Place' (*A Vindication of the Honour and Prerogative of Christ's Church … being an Answer to the Cavils of Dr. Snape*, 1717, 24). He challenged the right of any church or assembly or succession of clergy to legislate for Christians; Christ had given no such authority to the apostles; it was a derogation of the 'sole Priesthood and Mediatorship' of Christ to invest authority in fallible men: 'Christ himself, in his own Person, is the sole Christian Priest, properly so-called' (*A full examination of several important points relating to church-authority, the Christian priesthood, etc. … in answer to the notions and principles contained in Mr. Law's Second Letter to the Lord Bishop of Bangor*, 1718, iv, 137, 293). He considered that the direct subjection of Christians to Christ alone permitted individuals the right of private judgement in matters of religion. The great achievement of the Reformation of the Church of England was that it secured this right of judgement; wherever this right is denied, 'there Popery still remains, though it pass under the name of Protestantism' (*An Abridgment of the Third Volume of the History of the Reformation of the Church of England*, 1719, vii–viii).

Burnet also wrote for weekly journals. He contributed at least eight articles anonymously to *The Free-Thinker* in 1718–19 on atheism, superstition, and enthusiasm. In contrast with 'the perpetual Anxieties of the Superstitious, the wild Perturbations of the Enthusiast, the comfortless Prospects of the Atheist', the truly religious man will reason from 'the Beauty, Order and Design which appears in the Universe, to the Belief of an Eternal, Powerful, Wise and Beneficent Agent' (*The Free-Thinker*, 22, 1718, 8). He distinguished between vicious atheists who make no use of reason, and virtuous atheists, who delight in everything sensible and beautiful, but remain atheists because they confuse religion with superstition or enthusiasm. He discovered the causes of superstition in weakness of mind, in imagining that the deity will be pleased by outward displays of pomp and ceremony (no. 34). He traced the causes of enthusiasm to an opposite weakness of mind, to the extravagant belief that one has been singled out by divine providence for a particular mission (nos. 71 and 77). Both of these aberrations of true religion, he argued, were directly destructive of morality and society (no. 96).

Burnet engaged in an exchange of correspondence with Francis Hutcheson in the *London Journal*, from 10 April to 15 December 1725, on the subject of virtue or moral goodness. Burnet's contributions are found in numbers 298, 314, 315, 331, and 335. He argued (using the name Philaretus) in opposition to Hutcheson (Philanthropus) that the dependence of virtue on a moral sense, however cultivated or refined, left moral life without an adequate foundation. Burnet maintained, following the reasoning of Samuel Clarke and William Wollaston, that moral distinctions depend upon the ability of reason to apprehend what is right or true. His controversy with Hutcheson was reprinted in *Letters between the late Mr. Gilbert Burnet and Mr. Hutchinson, concerning the true foundation of virtue or moral goodness* (1735). There is also a letter to the *London Journal* for 18 September 1725 (no. 321) which is subscribed Philaretus but is not concerned with Hutcheson; the letter complains of a lack of delicacy and good breeding in the publication of the details of trials in the sessions papers. Burnet died on 17 June 1726 and was buried in East Barnet.

JAMES MOORE

Sources *Bishop Burnet's History of his own time*, ed. G. Burnet and T. Burnet, 2 vols. (1724–34) · A. Kippis and others, eds., *Biographia Britannica, or, The lives of the most eminent persons who have flourished in Great Britain and Ireland*, 2nd edn, 3 (1784), 39 · T. E. S. Clarke and H. C. Foxcroft, *A life of Gilbert Burnet, bishop of Salisbury* (1907) · Foster, *Alum. Oxon.* · Venn, *Alum. Cant.* · Fasti Angl. (Hardy) · *Fasti Angl., 1541–1857,* [Salisbury] · T. Herne, *An account of all the considerable pamphlets that have been published on either side in the present controversy between the bishop of Bangor and others, to the end of the year MDCCXVIII* (1719) · T. Herne, *A continuation of the account of all the considerable pamphlets that have been published on either side in the present controversy between the bishop of Bangor and others, to the end of the year MDCCXIX* (1720) · L. Stephen, *History of English thought in the eighteenth century*, 2 (1876), 156–66 · G. Rupp, *Religion in England, 1688–1791* (1986), 88–101 · F. Hutcheson, *Illustrations upon the moral sense*, ed. B. Peach (1971) · *London Journal* (25 June 1726)

Burnet, James M. (1788–1816), landscape painter, was born in Musselburgh, Edinburghshire, the son of George Burnet, surveyor-general of excise for Scotland, and his wife, Anne Cruikshank. His elder brother was the painter and engraver John *Burnet. He was first apprenticed to a woodcarver, but also attended evening classes held by John Graham at the Trustees' Academy in Edinburgh. Burnet soon established a reputation in Edinburgh as a cattle painter but in 1810 decided to join his brother John in London. When James arrived in London John Burnet was engraving Wilkie's *Blind Fiddler*. James was delighted with this painting and his knowledge of it led him to study the Dutch seventeenth-century art that had been Wilkie's inspiration. Burnet did not turn to genre scenes, however, but—now strongly influenced by Paulus Potter and Aelbert Cuyp—he continued to specialize in paintings of cattle. In London Burnet worked directly from nature. Living in Chelsea, he found his subjects in what was then open pasture around Battersea and Fulham. In 1812 he first exhibited at the Royal Academy with *Evening: Cattle Returning Home*. The next year he contributed *Midday, The Return in the Evening*, and *Early Morning*, and in 1814 *The Ploughman Returning Home*.

Burnet suffered from tuberculosis and, in an attempt to alleviate the symptoms of the disease, moved to Lee in south London, but this proved futile and he died there, apparently unmarried, on 27 July 1816. He was buried in Lewisham churchyard. Burnet's death was much regretted by his fellow artists, who admired his use of rich and brilliant colour and the luminous lighting effects that he created in his landscapes, the best-known of which is probably *Taking Cattle to Shelter during a Storm* (NG Scot.). His brother John engraved some of his work and used the plates to illustrate a book on landscape and painting entitled *Painting in Oil Colours* (1849). The character of Knox in John Burnet's novel *Progress of a Painter in the Nineteenth Century* (1854) was loosely based on his brother, a characterization that increased the fame of James after his death. This fame was endorsed when Allan Cunningham devoted an entire chapter to James Burnet in his *Lives of the most Eminent Painters* (1829–33). In this book Cunningham reveals Burnet's detailed study of cloud formations and lighting effects. Writing in 1906 W. D. McKay could not understand such devotion although he had apparently seen only one of the artist's paintings. A more measured view was expressed by Irwin and Irwin in 1975, when they pointed out how a painting such as *Old Chelsea Bridge* (Aberdeen Art Gallery) illustrated Burnet's ability to convey atmosphere and lighting effects, but that his clumsy grouping of the cattle and his inability to envelop them in the same light as the landscape revealed weaknesses in his artistic abilities.

ERNEST RADFORD, *rev.* JENNIFER MELVILLE

Sources D. Irwin and F. Irwin, *Scottish painters at home and abroad, 1700–1900* (1975) · P. J. M. McEwan, *Dictionary of Scottish art and architecture* (1994) · W. D. McKay, *The Scottish school of painting* (1906) · J. L. Caw, *Scottish painting past and present, 1620–1908* (1908) · Graves, *RA exhibitors* · IGI

Burnet, John (1784–1868), painter, engraver, and writer on art, was born in Musselburgh, Edinburghshire, on 20 March 1784, the elder son of George Burnet, surveyor-general of excise for Scotland, and his wife, Anne Cruikshank. His younger brother was the landscape artist James M. *Burnet. After receiving instruction from Mr Leeshman, the master of Sir Walter Scott, he was apprenticed to the engraver Robert Scott (who was the father of the artists David Scott and William Bell Scott). In 1803 Robert Scott produced a series of aquatints, *Edinburgh Cries*, which were based on drawings of street criers by his young apprentice John Burnet. While serving a full seven-year apprenticeship with Scott, Burnet continued to paint in his free time and studied painting under John Graham at the Trustees' Academy in Edinburgh, where his fellow pupils included William Allan and David Wilkie.

In 1806 Burnet sailed to London. There he made contact with his friend Wilkie, who was then painting *The Blind Fiddler* (Tate collection). Wilkie had arrived in London the previous year and had already found favour with *The Village Politicians*. Soon a circle of Scottish friends and admirers had formed around Wilkie. This group included Alexander Fraser, Andrew Geddes, Alexander Carse, and John Burnet. Burnet was also a friend of Richard Parkes Bonnington. After working for some years at small plates for *The Beauties of England and Wales* by J. Britton and E. W. Brayley, Mrs Inchbald's *British Theatre*, and other works, in 1810 Burnet produced his first large plate, of *The Jew's Harp* by Wilkie. This was the first picture by Wilkie to be engraved. The success of Burnet's print led to the publication of others, the first of which was *The Blind Fiddler*, for which he abandoned his earlier, precise style which had been influenced by James Heath and Philippe Le Bas and instead adopted the larger, bolder, and more expressive style of Cornelius Visscher. The plate, however, pleased neither David Wilkie nor the owner of the painting, Sir George Beaumont. Consequently Burnet reworked it after the proofs had been struck off, so that there are now two sets of proofs to this engraving. The engraving proved to be popular and a companion, of Wilkie's *The Village Politicians*, was proposed, but because of a dispute over terms Abraham Raimbach executed it instead. The disagreement was overcome and Burnet went on to engrave many more of Wilkie's works. These included *The Reading of the Will*, *Chelsea Pensioners Reading the Gazette of the Battle of Waterloo* (which was published by Boys and Graves of Pall Mall, London, in 1829), *The Rabbit on the Wall*, *The Letter of Introduction*, *Sir David Baird Discovering the Body of Tippoo Saib* (which was published by F. G. Moon in 1843), and *The Village School*. Burnet's fame rests largely on these engravings of the paintings of David Wilkie, although he also engraved works by other artists such as William Allan, Edwin Landseer, John Faed, and J. M. W. Turner.

After the peace of 1814 Burnet spent five months in Paris copying the masterpieces in the Louvre that Napoleon had brought from all parts of Europe. Shortly afterwards he engraved several plates of works by artists including Metsu and Rembrandt, for Edward Foster's *The British Gallery of Engravings* (1807–[1813]). He then engraved works by Rembrandt for an association of engravers that brought out a series of engravings from pictures in the National Gallery. He also engraved *The Battle of Waterloo*, after Atkinson, and the same subject after Arthur William Devis, as well as some of his own pictures, including *The Draught-Players*, *Feeding the Young Bird*, *The Escape of the Mouse*, *Christmas Eve*, *The Valentine*, and *Greenwich Pensioners Commemorating the Anniversary of the Battle of Trafalgar*.

Burnet also devoted some time to the improvement of the mechanical processes of engraving, with a view to the cheap reproduction of works of art. He produced some engravings of Raphael's cartoons at a low cost, but the venture failed. Burnet's best-known, largest, and most important oil painting is *Greenwich Pensioners Commemorating the Anniversary of the Battle of Trafalgar* (Apsley House, London). This was intended to be a naval version of Wilkie's painting of army veterans, *Chelsea Pensioners Reading the Gazette of the Battle of Waterloo*, which was then already in the possession of the duke of Wellington. Burnet exhibited his painting at the British Institution in 1837 under the title *Greenwich Hospital and Naval Heroes* and invited the duke of Wellington to view the painting with a view to it becoming a companion picture to that of Wilkie. Clearly it pleased the duke, who paid Burnet 500 guineas for it. Its close proximity to Wilkie's picture, however, reveals its flaws of composition and lack of drama when compared to the earlier work. Wilkie's compositions were again drawn upon when Burnet painted a rare historical work, *The Trial of Charles I*, which resembles closely Wilkie's *Preaching of Knox*. Burnet exhibited work at the British Institution and, less often, at the Royal Academy. In 1808 he exhibited at the Royal Academy *The Draught-Players* and in 1816 *Cowherd and Cattle* and *Crossing the Bridge*. Like Alexander Fraser he could paint comical scenes, such as *The Humorous Ballad*, which was exhibited at the Royal Academy in 1818 and Wilkiesque genre subjects like *The Card Players* (Guildhall, London), but generally he is considered

at his best when painting landscapes such as *A Windy Day*, which he exhibited at the Royal Academy in 1823. Like those of his brother James, John Burnet's landscapes often feature cattle and the influence of Dutch seventeenth-century art, particularly the paintings of Aelbert Cuyp, is clear in works such as *Cows Drinking* (1817; Sheepshanks collection, V&A).

Burnet was a highly respected writer on art. His best-known works include *Practical Hints on Composition* (1822), *Practical Hints on Light and Shade* (1826), and *Practical Hints on Colour* (1827). These were published together as *A Practical Treatise on Painting*, in three parts, in 1827. In 1836 Burnet gave valuable evidence before the select committee of the Commons on arts and manufactures. The following year he published *An Essay on the Education of the Eye*, which was added to and published with his previous three publications as *A Treatise on Painting*, in four parts. He also wrote *Discourses of Sir Joshua Reynolds* (1844); *Letters on Landscape-Painting in Oil* (1848); *Practical Essays on Various Branches of the Fine Arts and an Enquiry into the Practice and Principles of the Late Sir David Wilkie, R.A.* (1848); *Rembrandt and his Works* (1849); *Hints on Portrait-Painting* (1850); *Turner and his Works* (1852) and a novel: *Progress of a Painter in the Nineteenth Century* (1854). Burnet illustrated most of these works with etchings, including 130 prints for the four parts of the *Treatise on Painting*. Throughout the latter part of the nineteenth century this treatise was reprinted, as were many of his other works.

Burnet was elected a fellow of the Royal Society, and in 1860, at the recommendation of the prime minister, Lord Palmerston, he received a pension from the civil list and retired to Stoke Newington, where he died at his house in Victoria Road on 29 April 1868.

W. C. MONKHOUSE, *rev.* JENNIFER MELVILLE

Sources D. Irwin and F. Irwin, *Scottish painters at home and abroad, 1700–1900* (1975) · J. L. Caw, *Scottish painting past and present, 1620–1908* (1908) · W. D. McKay, *The Scottish school of painting* (1906) · Graves, *RA exhibitors* · D. Macmillan, *Scottish art, 1460–2000* (2000) · R. K. Engen, *Dictionary of Victorian engravers, print publishers and their works* (1979) · CGPLA Eng. & Wales (1868) · IGI
Likenesses W. Simson, oils, 1841, NPG · S. P. Denning, watercolour and charcoal drawing, Scot. NPG · J. Watkins, photograph, carte-de-visite, NPG · wood-engraving (after photograph by J. Watkins), NPG; repro. in *ILN* (1868) · woodcut (after self-portrait?), NPG; repro. in *Art Journal* (1850)
Wealth at death under £100: probate, 25 July 1868, CGPLA Eng. & Wales

Burnet, John (1863–1928), Greek scholar, was born at Edinburgh on 9 December 1863, the eldest child of John Burnet, advocate, and his wife, Jessie, daughter of Dr James Cleghorn Kay RN. He was educated at the Royal High School, Edinburgh, and was also for a few months at a school near Geneva. In October 1880 he matriculated at the University of Edinburgh, where he pursued the study of Latin and Greek, and began that of Sanskrit. He won there the Vans Dunlop scholarship in classics, and a little later the first open classical scholarship at Balliol College, Oxford. After paying a short visit to Paris, where he attended lectures at the Sorbonne and the Collège de France, Burnet went into residence at Oxford in October

John Burnet (1863–1928), by Walter Stoneman, 1917

1883. There, besides being placed in the first class in classical moderations (1884) and in *literae humaniores* (1887), he won the Taylorian scholarship in French (1885) and was *proxime accessit* for the Boden scholarship in Sanskrit. While he was an undergraduate he preferred to follow his own lines of study, even at the risk of leaving considerable gaps in the conventional programme of preparation for the final examinations. Like many of his contemporaries he was specially influenced by Richard Lewis Nettleship, but he showed no particular interest in philosophy.

Burnet's first attempt to win a fellowship was not successful, and he left Oxford in 1887 in order to become private assistant to Lewis Campbell, professor of Greek at the University of St Andrews. With his work there under Campbell began his lifelong concern with the philosophy of Plato. Campbell was a pioneer in the attempt to determine, largely upon 'stylometric' considerations, the chronological order of the Platonic dialogues, and Burnet became convinced not only of the rightness of Campbell's methods, but of the correctness in the main of the results attained by them. After five months at St Andrews he made a brief trial of teaching at Harrow School (1888), but did not find the work congenial. Fortunately, he was soon after elected to a prize fellowship at Merton College, Oxford, and entered into residence there in 1889. The leisure which the position gave him was employed in increasing his knowledge of Aristotle, partly under the guidance of Ingram Bywater, and in planning a commentary on the *Nicomachean Ethics*, which he did not complete until considerably later (1899).

After some temporary teaching posts at the universities of Edinburgh and St Andrews in 1890 and 1891, Burnet was elected professor of Greek at the latter university in 1891 upon the resignation of Campbell, and occupied the chair there until he resigned it in 1926. He married in 1894 Mary, daughter of John Farmer, organist at Harrow and at Balliol College; they had one daughter. He lived and worked at St Andrews until his death. From the time of a grave illness in 1923 his health grew worse in spite of occasional rallies. In 1926 he was able to fulfil an engagement to deliver the Sather lectures in classical literature in the University of California (published in 1928 under the title *Platonism*); but the summer heat of Chicago, where he also lectured, exhausted his strength, and on his return to St Andrews he was unable to continue his work as professor. He died at St Andrews on 26 May 1928; he was survived by his wife.

During the whole tenure of his chair Burnet proved himself an exceptionally inspiring and successful teacher by his striking personality and his command of his whole subject, winning the affectionate admiration of generations of his students. He took a large part in the work of university administration. He had a wide knowledge of the systems of higher education in other countries, and held clear and firm views upon the proper methods of its organization. He occupied several important posts upon educational committees and boards, and was active in promoting the popularization of humanistic culture in Scotland through the Classical Association of Scotland, which he helped to found. His services to education were not diminished by his occasional failures to secure the adoption of some of the policies which he advocated.

To the world of scholarship in the narrower sense Burnet's greatest contribution was his critical edition, in the Oxford Classical Texts series, of the whole text of the works of Plato (1900–08; rev. 1905–13); this superseded all previous editions. It was based on a wide foundation of the manuscript evidence, and guided by a close knowledge of Platonic vocabulary, idiom, and style. Burnet's judgements on disputed points were sober and sane, and the text was fairly conservative. More detailed work on the textual transmission has, however, revealed some shortcomings in the edition, not all of which can legitimately be counted against him. His commentaries on the *Phaedo* (1911), *Euthyphro*, *Apology*, and *Crito* (1924) were models of conciseness and lucidity, full of original observations upon Platonic usages. He designed a new *Lexicon Platonicum*, but although he laboured at it, did not proceed far in its construction. His commentary on Aristotle's *Nicomachean Ethics* contained much that was fresh and enlightening, but his work on Aristotle, of whose philosophy he never acquired the same wide and intimate knowledge as he had of Plato's, perhaps scarcely reaches the same level as his work on Plato.

In his *Early Greek Philosophy* (1892; rev. edn, 1908; 4th edn, 1945) Burnet did not carry his detailed study down beyond Aristotle, and indeed he gave no systematic account of the philosophy of Aristotle. On the other hand, he several times revised and restated his views on the pre-Socratics, withdrawing some of his more venturesome specula-tions, but repeating his general results in a form which won the acceptance of most scholars. In his account of these thinkers he keeps steadily in view and vividly expresses the historic background of their lives and thoughts. For the English reader he superseded previous accounts, and effectively removed the misleading veil which had been cast over them by Hegel and the Hegel-ians. He utilized the contributions to this work of correc-tion and interpretation made by Tannery, Baeumker, and Diels, but his agreement with them is the result of his own independent investigation of the evidence.

Burnet's *Greek Philosophy: Part I, Thales to Plato* (1914) adds to a summary statement of his views on these early cosmological thinkers an equally original account of the sophists, Socrates, and Democritus. But its most valuable part is its masterly account of the life, character, and whole philosophy of Plato. It is brilliantly written, and was in its day incomparably the best treatment in English of its subject. Burnet accepts as trustworthy evidence for the career and thought of Plato most of the letters, and assumes as now ascertained facts the dates of compos-ition of most of the dialogues. In his account of the devel-opment of Plato's thought he draws a firm line between a Socratic period and a later period in which Plato is expounding his own philosophy; and he attributes to Plato a consciousness and acknowledgement of his pas-sage from discipleship to independence. But his view of the historical Socrates as the source of fundamental Pla-tonic doctrines concerning 'separate forms' and 'recollec-tion' has been challenged. He regards Plato as in his later works criticizing his master's teaching on physics, theory of knowledge, metaphysics, and politics.

Burnet's title to the fame which his work enjoys both at home and abroad rests securely upon his inspiring force as a teacher, upon his edition of the text of Plato, upon his classic and convincing account of the beginnings of Greek science and philosophy, upon his minute acquaintance with and vivid sense of the niceties of Platonic vocabulary and idiom, upon his long and deeply meditated presenta-tion of the philosophy of Plato, whom he admired and loved above all writers and thinkers, and upon the fresh-ness of view and the distinction of style which mark all his writings.   J. A. Smith, *rev.* N. G. Wilson

Sources W. L. Lorimer and A. E. Taylor, 'John Burnet, 1863–1928', *PBA*, 14 (1928), 445–70 · Lord Charnwood [G. R. B. Charnwood], 'Memoir', in *Essays and addresses by John Burnet* (1929) · personal knowledge (1937) · *CCI* (1928)
Likenesses W. Stoneman, photograph, 1917, NPG [*see illus.*] · photograph, repro. in *Essays and addresses*, frontispiece
Wealth at death £2659 12s. 9d.: confirmation, 24 July 1928, *CCI*

Burnet, Sir John James (1857–1938), architect, was born in Glasgow on 31 March 1857, the youngest of the three sons of John Burnet (1814–1901), a successful architect, and his formidable wife, Elizabeth Hay Bennet. He was educated at the Western Academy, Glasgow, and at Blair Lodge. In 1874 he joined the atelier of Jean-Louis Pascal in Paris and in 1875 was the first of several Glasgow architects to enrol at the École des Beaux-Arts. He gained the Diplôme du Gouvernement in 1877 and toured Italy thereafter. On his return he won the competition for the Glasgow Institute of Fine Art with a sophisticated design combining 'Greek with modern French Renaissance'. It demonstrated the absolute mastery of plan and elevation, the precise stonecutting, and the love of sculpture which were to dis-tinguish almost all his work.

In 1882 Burnet's father took him into partnership. Four years later another Pascal *élève*, John Archibald Campbell (1859–1909), rejoined them, and the firm became Burnet, Son, and Campbell: the work of the two younger partners was to remain indistinguishable until Campbell set up on his own in 1897. The major works of these earlier years were all very Beaux-Arts in style: the Clyde Navigation Trust (1883–6), the Athenaeum (1886), Charing Cross Man-sions (1891), all in Glasgow, and the Edinburgh Inter-national Exhibition of 1886. But in 1891 at Glasgow's Athenaeum Theatre Burnet began introducing the American elevator building types which were to be copied by others throughout central Glasgow, and moved into a Norman Shaw type of neo-baroque. American and Shaw influences had already been in evidence in his domestic work, notably at Kilneiss, Moniaive, Dumfriesshire (1884), and Corrienessan, Loch Ard, Perthshire (1887).

Burnet's Gothic work was also of exceptional quality: his tall first-pointed Barony Church, Glasgow (1886–99), was among the finest of the period. More innovative, how-ever, were the low-profiled, rather American churches with broad unbuttressed towers, sweeping roofs, and mixed late Gothic and Romanesque motifs first intro-duced at St Molio's, Shiskine, Arran, in 1886, the finest of which was the Gardner Memorial at Brechin, Forfarshire, built ten years later. In the same period Burnet designed several buildings at Glasgow University and the associated Western Infirmary, mostly in a Scottish Renaissance idiom, for which he was rewarded with the honorary degree of LLD in 1910. In 1913 the university commis-sioned its tall and magnificent chapel, built as its war memorial in 1923–7.

In 1896 Burnet made the first of several visits to the United States of America (where his brother-in-law James Marwick had useful connections in Illinois and New York), primarily to study laboratory and hospital design. It quickly had wider consequences: his reconstruction of his father's Savings Bank, Glasgow (1898), continuing a pro-gramme of aggrandizement begun with the superb bank-ing hall of 1894, reflected his acquaintance with Charles Follen McKim; but his subsequent seven-storey commer-cial blocks, Atlantic Chambers and Waterloo Chambers (both 1899) and the McGeoch warehouse (1904–6), all in Glasgow, were pioneer buildings of their kind in Britain and demonstrated a wider range of influences, particu-larly those of Daniel Burnham and Louis Sullivan. These were followed by two Edinburgh department stores, the Civil Service and Professional Supply (1903–7) and Forsyths (1906–10), the latter of which was the first Scottish building to be fully steel-framed. All of these were vigorously neo-baroque in style, with deeply shadowed eaves galleries. They launched the careers of a number of important sculptors, notably George Frampton, Albert Hodge, Phyllis Archibald, William Reid Dick, and Archibald Dawson.

Burnet's domestic commissions of the late 1880s, 1890s, and early 1900s were mostly terraced houses, principally in his University Gardens, Glasgow (from 1887), or remodellings of existing houses, notably Carronvale, Larbert, Stirlingshire (1897), and Finlaystone, Port Glasgow, Renfrewshire (1898–1903), both with sumptuous interiors. The three large houses he built completely anew—Garmoyle, Dumbarton, and Baronald, Lanark (both 1889–90), and Fairnilee, Selkirk (1904–6)—were in an innovative early seventeenth-century Scottish manner: Garmoyle anticipated Lorimer in its arts and crafts masonry. At the Marine Hotel, Elie, Fife (1903), however, an asymmetrically gabled Anglo-American arts and crafts idiom was adopted. At Duart, Mull, Argyll (1911–16), the ancient fortress was re-roofed and skilfully adapted within its existing profile for Sir Fitzroy MacLean.

In 1903–4 the office of works and the trustees of the British Museum selected Burnet to design the Edward VII galleries. Burnet's scheme adopted the Ionic order of Sir Robert Smirke's colonnades but reflected contemporary French and American Beaux-Arts ideas. His giant colonnade of twenty attached columns stretched between pylons demonstrated every possible subtlety of varying diameters, intercolumniations, and inclination of verticals to achieve absolute refinement and repose. Within, the stair was unmatched for its scale and originality. The completion of the galleries in 1914 brought Burnet a knighthood and the bronze medal of the Paris Salon, followed by the gold in 1922; the Royal Institute of British Architects conferred on him its royal gold medal in 1923. In parallel with this cascade of honours Burnet, who had been an associate of the Royal Scottish Academy since 1893, was elected Royal Scottish Academician in 1914, associate of the Royal Academy in 1921, and Royal Academician in 1925.

To build the Edward VII galleries Burnet had established a London office in 1905, taking with him Thomas Smith Tait and recruiting a trusted former assistant, the classical scholar David Theodore Fyfe. The Glasgow office continued separately, from 1909 in partnership with the Paris-trained Norman Aitken Dick (1883–1948). The major London commissions of the pre-war years were the baroque General Accident Building, Aldwych (1909–11), and the classical modern Kodak Building, Kingsway (1910–11), in the latter of which Tait had a hand, and which set the pattern for a great many inter-war commercial buildings. Kodak showed the influence of the American architect Albert Kahn, even more strongly reflected in Glasgow at the Wallace Scott Tailoring Institute of 1913–22.

Tait was taken into partnership after the war. Together Burnet and Tait did much work for the Imperial War Graves Commission in the Middle East, notably at Port Taufiq, Cape Helles, Gallipoli, and Jerusalem. In London they designed the very American Adelaide House, London Bridge (1921–5), the modern French classical Vigo House,

Regent Street (1920–25), and the more conservatively Corinthian Lloyds Bank, Cornhill (1925–7), and Unilever House (1929–32). Burnet exercised tighter design control in Glasgow, notably at the city's war memorial, the university's zoology building (1923), and the giant American palazzo of the North British and Mercantile Company (1925–7). In 1926 he was appointed to the original international jury for the League of Nations Building: he voted for the Roman architect Giuseppe Vago. The second jury (1927–9) voted for the design by Burnet's friend and mentor at Pascal's, Henri-Paul Nénot, but appointed him in association with Vago and two other prize-winners, Carlo Broggi and Camille Lefevre; Nénot consulted with Burnet on the radically revised design which resulted from this complex arrangement.

In person Burnet was a courteous Frenchified Scot with a firm belief in the Beaux-Arts 'essentials' and 'classics', and his international outlook was reflected in numerous corresponding memberships. The last decades of his life, and that of his wife, Jean Watt (1864–1949), the daughter of Sir James David Marwick, whom he had married on 18 February 1886, were somewhat difficult. Although possessed of great charm, Lady Burnet was a hypochondriac, and the couple had no children. Burnet suffered acutely from eczema and had to wear a skull-cap and gloves. War, perfectionism, a major theft of sums held on behalf of contractors, and a structural error (the last two both in the Glasgow office) had seriously damaged his finances when ill health obliged him to retire in 1930. Thereafter he moved to Woodhall Cottage, Woodhall Road, Colinton, Edinburgh, where he died on 2 July 1938. He was cremated at Warriston crematorium, Edinburgh, on 5 July 1938. His wife survived him. A bronze bust of Burnet by Sir William Reid Dick is in the possession of the Royal Incorporation of Architects in Scotland.   DAVID M. WALKER

Sources H. S. Goodhart-Rendel, 'The work of Sir John Burnet, royal gold medallist', *Architects' Journal* (27 June 1923), 105–10 · *Builders' Journal*, 14 (1901), 138–47 · *Sir John Burnet and Partners*, E. J. Burrows & Co. (1924), pts 1 and 2 of *Modern Architectural Art* · *The Architectural Work of Sir John Burnet and Partners*, Masters of Architecture Series (1927) [Geneva] · A. Service, *Edwardian architecture and its origins* (1975), 192–215 · J. Frew and D. Jones, *Scotland and Europe* (1991), 15–40 · *The Times* (4 July 1938) · *Glasgow Herald* (4 July 1938) · *The Scotsman* (4 July 1938) · L. Eaton, *American architecture comes of age* (1972), 38–55 · private information (2004) [family and former staff] · *CGPLA Eng. & Wales* (1938) · will, NA Scot., SC 70/4/746, fols. 201–4 · A. N. Paterson, *RIBA Journal*, 45 (1937–8), 893–4 · T. S. Tait, *RIBA Journal*, 45 (1937–8), 894–5 · T. Fyfe, 'Sir John Burnet', *RIBA Journal*, 45 (1937–8), 941–3 · 'The new architectural RA', *Architects' Journal* (4 May 1921), 553 · P. Waterhouse, 'The royal gold medal: presentation to Sir John J. Burnet', *RIBA Journal*, 30 (1922–3), 509–16 [incl. Burnet's reply] · W. J. Smith, 'An architectural anthology: Greek Thomson, Burnet and Mackintosh', *Quarterly Journal of the Royal Incorporation of Architects in Scotland*, 85 (Aug 1951), 56–60 · R. B. Rankin, 'Sir John J. Burnet RA, RSA, LLD and his works', *Quarterly Journal of the Royal Incorporation of Architects in Scotland*, 84 (Nov 1953), 27–40 · *The Bailie* (7 April 1886), 1–2 · *The Bailie* (6 May 1914), 1–2 · *The Bailie* (4 May 1921), 3 · m. cert. · b. cert. [Jean Watt Marwick]
Archives Berkshire War Graves Commission, deposits · BM, deposits · Commonwealth War Graves Commission, deposits · Maidenhead War Graves Commission, deposits | priv. coll., papers from London office

Likenesses photograph, *c.*1910, National Monuments Record of Scotland · C. Buchel, watercolour drawing, priv. coll. · W. R. Dick, bronze bust, Royal Incorporation of Architects in Scotland, Edinburgh

Wealth at death £13,725 11*s*. 1*d*.: Scottish action sealed in London, 11 Nov 1938, *CGPLA Eng. & Wales*

Burnet [*née* Kennedy], **Lady Margaret** (*d.* 1685), religious and political adviser, was the eldest daughter of John *Kennedy, sixth earl of Cassillis (1601x7–1668), and his first wife, Lady Jean Hamilton (1607–1642). Known as 'the grave and solemn Earl', John Kennedy was, according to his son-in-law Gilbert *Burnet (1643–1715), 'the strictest Presbyterian that I have ever heard of' (Burnet, 'History', vol. 1, fol. 32a), and his daughter inherited her father's rigid presbyterianism. She was also well known and widely regarded both for her learning and her character. Charles II told his brother that 'she was a most extraordinary woman' (ibid., fol. 29a), and Sir Robert Moray wrote to the earl of Lauderdale (Scottish secretary, 1663–80) that there was 'not more nobleness nor virtue in any breast than in hers' (Airy, 2.38). She was on such close terms with Lauderdale and Moray that they often referred to her in letters as 'our wife', or 'one of our wives', the other being her cousin, Anne Hamilton, duchess of Hamilton, with whom she frequently resided.

After 1660 Lady Margaret used her intimacy with Lauderdale to urge him towards a policy of concessions towards the dissenters. In 1667 Lauderdale did embark on a new policy of moderation, and in this indulgence Lady Margaret was his ally. She corresponded regularly with Lauderdale about Scottish affairs, and in 1670 the earl of Tweeddale asked her if she and the duchess of Hamilton would use their influence among the moderate dissenters to get them to accept a proposal for accommodation. Both she and her future husband, Gilbert Burnet, from 1665 to 1669 minister of Saltoun, and from 1669 professor of divinity at Glasgow University, laboured for the accommodation, but without success.

The exact date of Lady Margaret's marriage to Burnet is uncertain because they were married privately by Burnet's friend Laurence Charteris, under licence from Alexander Young, bishop of Edinburgh, in the presence of only two witnesses. In his *History* Burnet mentions that he was married to her for thirteen years, which would place the marriage in 1672. Elsewhere he states that the marriage remained secret for two years, and as the news became public the same week as his appointment to the Rolls Chapel in the Easter term of 1675, this would place the marriage in 1673. Whatever the case, the marriage was kept a secret, probably at the bride's insistence. According to Burnet, Lady Margaret thought the inequality of the match would much lessen her social status. Why she would agree to such a mismatch is not clear, but in his memoirs Sir George Mackenzie states that she did so to revenge herself on Lauderdale who, after his first wife's death, married the countess of Dysart instead of her.

Before news of the marriage became public, Burnet's formerly close relationship with Lauderdale began to deteriorate. In July 1674 Burnet fled to London. It is unclear when Lady Margaret joined him there. Apparently she had been living with the duchess of Hamilton, but 'retired to Edinburgh' in 1675 after news of her marriage became public (Law, *Memorials*, 65). By the early 1680s she seems to have been living with Burnet in London, but by then she had fallen 'under such a decay of memory and understanding that for some years [before her death] she knew nothing and no body' (Burnet, 'Autobiography', 481). She died towards the end of May 1685.

MARTIN GREIG

Sources *Letters from Lady Margaret Burnet to John, duke of Lauderdale* (1828) · G. Burnet, 'Autobiography', in *A supplement to Burnet's History of my own time*, ed. H. C. Foxcroft (1902) · G. Burnet, 'History of my own life', BL, Add. MS 63057b · *DNB* · *The Lauderdale papers*, ed. O. Airy, 3 vols., CS, new ser., 34, 36, 38 (1884–5) · GEC, *Peerage*
Archives Buckminster Park, Grantham, corresp. with duke of Lauderdale · NL Scot., letters to duke of Lauderdale

Burnet, Thomas (*c.*1635–1715), natural philosopher and headmaster, was born at Croft in Yorkshire, the son of John Burnet, and educated at the free school of Northallerton under Thomas Smelt, who held him up as an example to his later pupils. He was admitted as a pensioner at Clare College, Cambridge, on 26 June 1651. Officially a pupil of William Owtram, and also under the care of John Tillotson, he was inspired by the Platonic and Cartesian ideas of Ralph Cudworth. In 1654 Cudworth gave up the mastership of Clare College for that of Christ's College and, on 28 September 1655, Burnet, who had proceeded to his BA, was admitted as a pensioner there. He became a fellow of Christ's in 1657, and took his MA in 1658. He was senior proctor in 1667–8. According to his namesake Gilbert Burnet, he was at this time 'the most considerable among those of the younger sort' of followers of the philosophy of Descartes and Henry More (Foxcroft, 463–4).

Burnet was prominent in the teaching of the new philosophy at the university, despite increasing complaints about periods of absence from college. From 1671 he travelled on the continent as tutor to Lord Wiltshire, son of the marquess of Winchester and later second duke of Bolton, and his portrait was painted at Rome by Ferdinand Voet in 1675. He later returned to England, he received his last payment as a fellow of Christ's in Michaelmas 1678, and lived subsequently in London. In 1681 he was recommended by Tillotson, then dean of Canterbury, to the duke of Ormond as a tutor for his grandson, the earl of Ossory. After initial problems regarding his employment, in particular concern over the propriety of Burnet's accepting such a secular position despite being in holy orders, he was taken on and continued to retain links with the Ormond household thereafter. In a letter to Fitzpatrick, Ormond described him as 'a discreet and sober man' (*Ormonde MSS*, 248–9), and was his principal supporter among the governors in the election to the mastership of Charterhouse School which took place on 29 May 1685. 'The duke being satisfied that his conversation and manners were worthy of a clergyman in all respects', it was possible to overcome the complaints of the archbishops of Canterbury and York and the bishop of London that

Thomas Burnet (c.1635–1715), by Sir Godfrey Kneller, c.1693

'though he was a clergyman, he went always in a lay-habit' (Carte, 4.683).

Master of Charterhouse As master, Burnet played a substantial role in the resistance of the governors of Charterhouse, led by the earl of Danby, to James II's demands, initially made in December 1686 and reiterated in March 1687, that they appoint a Catholic, Andrew Popham, as a pensioner of the hospital without tendering the necessary oaths or requiring his conformity to the doctrine and discipline of the Church of England. Despite the efforts of Lord Chancellor Jeffreys, one of their number, a majority of the governors defied the king's wishes at two meetings on 17 January and midsummer's day 1687. Burnet's involvement in this action in defence of the authority of the Church of England and the liberty of Charterhouse helped to place him in line for preferment after the revolution of 1688. Benefiting from the patronage of his former pupil, now the second duke of Ormond, and of Tillotson, newly promoted archbishop of Canterbury, Burnet was appointed chaplain-in-ordinary and clerk of the closet to William III in Tillotson's place, taking up his preferments in November 1691. He was mentioned as a possible successor to Tillotson in the primacy, but changing political circumstances, and increasing doubts about the orthodoxy of his beliefs, ended Burnet's hopes of further advancement. By November 1695 he had retired from his court offices, spending the remainder of his years uneventfully at Charterhouse.

Apart from his brief moment of political fame in 1687, Burnet's importance derives from his publications and the debates which they engendered. Burnet was certainly aware of the enhancement which his writings might bring to his career, dedicating the first part of *Telluris*

theoria sacra (1681) to one of his pupils, the earl of Wiltshire, and the second part (1689) to another, the second duke of Ormond. An English translation of the first part of *The Theory of the Earth* was dedicated to Charles II as 'the Defender of our *Philosophick Liberties*' in 1684, and the English translation of the second part was offered to Queen Mary in 1690. William III, whom Burnet lauded as 'Hercules', was the recipient of the dedication of *Archaeologiae philosophicae* in 1692. His skilful use of these works to seek and reward patronage was matched by his achievement in them as a literary stylist. Both Joseph Addison, in a Latin ode in the style of Horace, addressed to Burnet, which he composed in 1699, and Richard Steele, in number 146 of *The Spectator* (1711), drew attention to the sublime manner in which Burnet had matched his writing to the tragic fate of the earth, whose past destruction at the flood and future demise through conflagration had been described in scripture and formed the subject of the two parts of *The Theory of the Earth*.

Theories of the earth Many of those who disagreed with the arguments in *The Theory of the Earth* were natural philosophers who were prompted to consider questions relating to the formation and development of the earth by his writings, but whose assumptions, methods, and conclusions differed markedly from those of Burnet. The first two books of Burnet's *Telluris theoria sacra* (1681), which treated the deluge, the dissolution of the earth at the flood, the primaeval earth, and paradise, had drawn to some extent on the account of the creation and form of the earth given by Descartes in his *Principia philosophiae* (1644). Although several parts of Burnet's theory of the earth were not to be found in Descartes, most notably his separation of the history of the earth from that of the older universe, his preservation of the traditional four elements, and his consideration of the role of the deluge in reshaping the form of the earth, numerous readers noted the similarities between the two authors. For Roger North, Burnet's work was 'meer Cartesian' (BL, Add. MS 32546, fol. 221v), despite its clear homage to other authorities, notably Plato and other classical authors, the Bible, and the fathers. Burnet claimed that the original surface of the world had been smooth and uniform, that it had been oval in shape, but flattened out on two sides so as to resemble an egg. Prior to the flood, it had been particularly suited to sustaining life, being covered with a moist, oily earth. The earth's axis had been aligned differently, so that there was perpetual spring in paradise, and vapours condensing out of the warmer parts of the earth fell as rain at the poles, forming rivers which flowed towards the equatorial regions. All this had been changed at the deluge, when the surface of the earth had been fractured, liberating the waters of the abyss beneath, and creating in time the corrupted modern world, marked by its mountains and seas. Burnet's account of the physical processes of the flood encouraged several natural philosophers, notably John Beaumont (*Considerations on a Book, Entituled the 'Theory of the Earth'*, 1693), to address the problem of the volume of water needed to cover the earth. Johann Caspar

Eisenschmidt defended Burnet's idea of an oval earth in his *Diatribe de figura telluris* (1691). Other critics, in particular Herbert Croft, bishop of Hereford (*Some Animadversions upon a Book Intituled the 'Theory of the Earth'*, 1685), drew attention to Burnet's apparent preference for the account of the earth given in 2 Peter over that of Genesis.

Burnet had discussed various aspects of his theory with Isaac Newton, in a correspondence conducted in the winter of 1680–81, where he made explicit his view that the account of the creation given in Genesis was a simplified one, adapted by Moses in order not to bother the primitive Israelites with philosophical truths which were not immediately apparent to vulgar observation. Although Newton was generally respectful towards Burnet's ideas, he did take issue with this criticism of the veracity of Genesis, and several of his followers, particularly Halley and Whiston, whose *New Theory of the Earth* appeared in 1696, debated other topics arising from *Telluris theoria sacra*. The second part of Burnet's theory, containing the third and fourth books, was completed by May 1688 and published in the following year along with a reprint of the first two books. In it Burnet discussed the completion of the sacred history of the earth in the coming conflagration of the world and the creation from it of a new heaven and a new earth, similar in form to the original, pristine world, which would last for a thousand years in which the saints would practise devotion to and contemplation of the divine. After the day of judgment, the earth's final state would be that of a star, like the sun. Despite the stirring times in which he was writing, Burnet did not attempt to set any clear timetable for the arrival of the millennium, remarking that:

> the difference there is betwixt the *Greek*, *Hebrew*, and *Samaritan* Copies of the Bible, makes the Age of the World altogether undetermin'd: … Seeing therefore we have no assurance how long the World hath stood already, neither could we be assur'd how long it hath to stand. (*The Theory of the Earth*, the two last books, 1690, 31)

Burnet published a *Review of the Theory of the Earth* in 1690. The completion of his work occurred at a time of widespread discussion of many of its themes, notably in papers being given by Robert Hooke to the Royal Society. Its publication prompted a long-running debate in print which soon embraced issues independent of those raised by Burnet's own work. Among those who contributed to these exchanges were John Edwards, John Flamsteed, Melchior Leydekker, Edward Lhwyd, Archibald Lovell, Matthew Mackaile, William Nicholls, John Ray, Robert St Clair, and John Woodward. Burnet did not seek to reply in detail to all his critics, but he did answer Erasmus Warren's *Geologia* (1690), and subsequent replies by Warren, and John Keill's *An Examination of Dr. Burnet's Theory of the Earth* (1698). A new edition of *The Theory of the Earth* came out in 1697, and further editions, bearing the title *The Sacred Theory of the Earth*, were published between 1719 and 1759, when the seventh edition appeared, with a life of the author by Ralph Heathcote, written at the request of Whiston. A German edition was published in 1703.

Accounts of creation One of the most controversial aspects of Burnet's work was his argument that Moses had simplified the language and concepts to be found in Genesis to suit the comprehension of an ignorant people. This argument had its origin in the writings of St Augustine, but a sense of the inadequacies of its assumptions may have helped to encourage Burnet to publish his second major work, *Archaeologiae philosophicae*, which was registered in November 1692. A major part of Burnet's purpose was to demonstrate that his theory of the earth was also compatible with what could be known of ancient accounts of creation. In the process of showing this, however, he also reconstructed a history of the progress of human knowledge about divine moral teaching. Thus, Burnet moved from an interpretation of Moses the historian to one of Moses the lawgiver. He discussed the transmission through the gentile world of the precepts of morality which had been known to Noah and his children, as well as the Mosaic account of the fall. In this account, he argued for the importance of Egyptian civilization as a vector for the transmission of knowledge about nature and morality, from which both the Israelites and the Greeks had learned. He suggested the similarities between the account of the origin of morality given by Moses and the fables told by other lawgivers, for example Orpheus, in order to establish their authority. He also maintained that knowledge of the original principles of Noah had been preserved best among northern peoples, in the teachings of the druids.

Despite its idiosyncrasies, *Archaeologiae philosophicae* was both a serious work of history which drew, for example, on the findings of contemporary scholars of Judaism, such as John Spencer, and an attempt to interpret difficult passages of scripture in accordance with the teaching of the fathers and of the Church of England. Politically, it was, however, a serious mistake. The work was taken up immediately by deist authors. Burnet's parodic retelling of the encounter in Eden between Eve and the serpent was translated in Charles Gildon's edition of Charles Blount's *The Oracles of Reason* (1693) and, by 1698, was being circulated as part of a verse libel, which also attacked William Sherlock and Robert South. Burnet was accused of believing:

> That all the books of Moses
> Were nothing but supposes

and:

> That as for father Adam,
> With Mrs. Eve his madam,
> And what the serpent spoke, Sir,
> 'Twas nothing but a joke, Sir,
> And well-invented flam.
> (W. King, *The Original Works*, 1776, 221–2)

The words of Burnet's dedication to William III were turned into an attack on the Erastianism of his late patron, Tillotson, by the non-juror George Hickes (*Some Discourses upon Dr. Burnet and Dr. Tillotson*, 1695, 56). *Archaeologiae philosophicae* fared little better on the continent, where it was published along with *Telluris theoria sacra* in one volume in 1694 by the Amsterdam bookseller

Johannes Wolters. This edition was reprinted in 1699. It was read and cited by freethinkers such as Henri de Boulainvilliers, attacked by several authors, notably Jean Graverol (*Moses vindicatus*, 1694), who falsely suspected Burnet of Socinianism, and prompted Christiaan Huygens to express amazement at the temerity of its author. Although he wrote two letters 'ad virum clarissimum A.B.', clarifying his writings, and attempted to persuade Wolters to add a footnote to the work, giving reputable sources for the contentious dialogue between Eve and the serpent, the reception of *Archaeologiae philosophicae* left Burnet exposed to changes in political fortune and was widely credited with precipitating his retirement from the court. Other reasons may, nevertheless, have contributed to this decision. Robert Hooke commented that Burnet had originally intended:

> to have written a generall Body of Philosophy, but the sense of his Age and approaching Death seems to have made him desist, & to satisfy himself with what he hath hitherto perform'd in the preceding Books, and in this which he seems to make the seal and consummation of the former. (Bodl. Oxf., MS Eng. misc. c. 144, fol. 239)

Archaeologiae philosophicae did, in effect, mark the end of Burnet's public career as an author. He instructed its publisher, Walter Kettilby, not to reprint, abridge, or translate the book. He published *Remarks* (1697) on Locke's *Essay Concerning Humane Understanding*, following these up with *Second Remarks* (1697) and *Third Remarks* (1699), but they were all anonymous. In these pamphlets, Burnet criticized Locke's attack on the doctrine of innate ideas, particularly concentrating on the natural philosophical assumptions made by Locke's arguments, and suggested that his work might lead to atheism. Locke replied to Burnet's *Remarks* in an appendix to his answer to Stillingfleet (1697), and a fuller response was prepared by Catherine Cockburn in 1702. Burnet died, unmarried, at Charterhouse on 27 September 1715 and was buried in the chapel.

Posthumous reputation Burnet composed two other books, *De statu mortuorum*, which argued against belief in the endless punishment of the wicked although accepting its usefulness for ensuring popular compliance with moral standards, and *De fide et officiis Christianorum*, which rejected the Calvinist notion of original sin and attacked the Catholic theology of the sacraments. Both of these developed the Arminian theology and respect for natural religion which Burnet inherited from the Cambridge Platonists and which he had already displayed in his earlier works. Burnet printed a small number of copies of *De statu mortuorum* for distribution to his friends, one of which was bought at auction by Richard Mead. Mead had *De statu mortuorum* reprinted in 1720, and several other unauthorized editions appeared thereafter, some with additional emendations from the author's copies. The earl of Macclesfield persuaded Francis Wilkinson of Lincoln's Inn, a lawyer retained by Burnet's brother and executor, George, to allow him to publish an edition of *De fide* in 1722, and in October 1727 Wilkinson issued his own edition, with an account of the affair. In June of that year Wilkinson also published an edition of *De statu mortuorum*, to

which was appended a hitherto unpublished dissertation by Burnet on the future restoration of the Jews. In 1728 a second edition of *Archaeologiae philosophicae* was issued by Wilkinson's bookseller, J. Hooke. Wilkinson had acted for George Burnet in a suit against William Chetwood, John Watts, and others on 12 October 1720, in order to prevent the publication of a translation of *De statu mortuorum*. In the end, attempts to hinder the dissemination, translation, and misrepresentation of Burnet's works proved impossible. Curll printed a translation of *De statu mortuorum* 'with an answer to all the heresies therein' by Matthias Earbery in 1727, with a second edition in 1728. *Archaeologiae philosophicae* was translated by Foxton and published by Curll in 1729, as was Burnet's work on the restoration of the Jews, and further unauthorized translations of books or parts of books by Burnet appeared frequently during the 1730s. More faithful and accurate translations were prepared by John Dennis and published by Hooke. *De fide* came out in 1728, with a dedication to Queen Caroline, and *De statu mortuorum* in 1730. Despite his wish for anonymity and retirement, the lively and controversial nature of Burnet's writings thus ensured that his name remained in the public eye for some years after his death. SCOTT MANDELBROTE

Sources M. Pasini, *Thomas Burnet* (1981) • T. Birch, *The life of the Most Reverend Dr John Tillotson, lord archbishop of Canterbury* (1752), 277–9 • *Calendar of the manuscripts of the marquess of Ormonde*, new ser., 8 vols., HMC, 36 (1902–20), vol. 6 • T. Carte, *An history of the life of James, duke of Ormonde*, 3 vols. (1735–6); new edn, pubd as *The life of James, duke of Ormond*, 6 vols. (1851), vol. 4, p. 683 • Chancery Cases, PRO, C33/335, fol. 350b • *CSP dom.*, 1691–2, 20; 1695, 110 • *The correspondence of Isaac Newton*, ed. H. W. Turnbull and others, 2 (1960), 319, 321–35 • [R. Heathcote], 'An account of the life and writings of the Rev. Thomas Burnet, LL. D', in T. Burnet, *The sacred theory of the earth*, 7th edn, 2 vols. (1759), vol. 1, pp. xvii–xxv • *Œuvres complètes de Christiaan Huygens*, ed. Société Hollandaise des Sciences, 22 vols. (1888–1950), vol. 10, pp. 455–6 • Nichols, *Lit. anecdotes*, 4.717; 6.221 • Charterhouse assembly orders, vols. C–D, LMA, ACC/1876/G/02/03–04 • J. Addison, *Poems on several occasions* (1713), 7–16 • *A supplement to Burnet's History of my own time*, ed. H. C. Foxcroft (1902)

Archives CUL, corrections to *Telluris theoria sacra*, Adv. c. 27. 4 | BL, corresp., Add. MS 28104 • BL, corresp., Add. MS 10039 • Bodl. Oxf., MS Tanner 26, fol. 44 • King's Cam., letters to Newton [copy in CUL, Add. MS 4007]

Likenesses attrib. F. Voet, oils, 1675, NPG • G. Kneller, oils, c.1693, Charterhouse School, Godalming, Surrey [*see illus.*] • R. White, line engraving, 1697 (after G. Kneller), BM, NPG; repro. in T. Burnet, *The theory of the earth*, 3rd edn (1697)

Wealth at death over £600: will, PRO, PROB 11/548, sig. 186; [E. Curll], *The last wills and testaments of J. Partridge and Dr. Burnett* (1716)

Burnet, Sir Thomas (1638–1704), physician, was the son of Robert Burnet, an advocate of Edinburgh, and was thus brother of Gilbert *Burnet, bishop of Salisbury. His mother was Rachel, the sister of Archibald Johnston, Lord Wariston. He studied and graduated in medicine at Montpellier, being already MA, and the theses which he defended for his degree on 26–8 August 1659 show that his medical knowledge was mainly based upon Galen and Hippocrates. He returned to Edinburgh and practised there. Burnet is named in the original charter of the Royal College of Physicians of Edinburgh, granted in 1681, as a fellow. He was president of the college from 1696 to 1698. He was physician to Charles II, and apparently to James II, certainly also to Queen Anne. Burnet was knighted some time before 1691 and died in 1704. His son Thomas Burnet graduated MD at Leiden in 1691.

Burnet was an eminent physician in his day, and his reputation was spread all over Europe by his books, especially by the *Thesaurus medicinae*, which was very often reprinted, and was evidently a useful compendium of the knowledge of the time. An abridgement was published by the author himself in 1703. His *Hippocrates contractus* (1685) is an abridgement in Latin of the most important works of Hippocrates. To obtain his licence he wrote: *Currus Iatrikus triumphalis, … ad Apollinarem laudem consequendam* and for his doctor's degree *Quaestiones quatuor cardinales pro suprema Apollinari daphne consequenda* (both Montpellier, 1659).   J. F. Payne, rev. Michael Bevan

Sources W. S. Craig, *History of the Royal College of Physicians of Edinburgh* (1976) • *Bishop Burnet's History*, vol. 2
Likenesses R. White, line engraving, 1697 (after G. Kneller), Wellcome L. • G. Vertue, line engraving, 1726 (after G. Kneller), Wellcome L. • J. Faber, mezzotint, 1752 (after G. Kneller, 1697), Wellcome L.

Burnet [Burnett], **Thomas** (d. **1750**), theologian, was possibly the Thomas Burnett from Essex who matriculated from Queens' College, Cambridge, in 1687, and graduated BA in 1691 and MA in 1694 (Venn, *Alum. Cant.*, 1.261). He received his DD from New College, Oxford, in 1720. Following his ordination, he was appointed to the living of West Kington, Wiltshire, in 1706, which he held until his death. He was prebendary of Salisbury from 1711 to 1750 and was also rector of Littleton Drew, Wiltshire, from 1715 to 1730, and rector of Dodington, Gloucestershire, from 1738.

Burnet delivered his sermons, *The Demonstration of True Religion* (1726), as the Boyle lectures. He wrote several explicatory works on Christianity, including *The Scripture-Trinity Explained* (1720), *The Sacrament of the Lord's Supper* (1731), and *The Scripture Doctrine of the Redemption* (1737), in which Burnet, a fair and candid though uninteresting writer, attempts to mediate between orthodox and Arian views. In the 'Dedication' of the *Scripture-Trinity* to his bishop, Burnet says the work was written 'by broken snatches, and at such leisure time as I could steal from a life encumbered with disagreeable business, and embarrassed with care and difficulties'.

Burnet also wrote essays which attempt to reason logically from propositions assumed as axiomatic, including *On Government* (1716) and *On the Power of Human Reason* (1732), appended to the second instalment of his *The Argument Set Forth* (1730–32), a response to Matthew Tindal's *Christianity as Old as the Creation* (1730). His Christian guide for children was published in 1752 after his death on 28 May 1750. In his will, he bequeathed his books, papers, and manuscripts to his son Robert Burnett, clerk, as well as the rents from his property in Fremington and Grinton in Yorkshire.

Richard Garnett, rev. Adam Jacob Levin

Sources Foster, *Alum. Oxon.* • A. Kippis and others, eds., *Biographia Britannica, or, The lives of the most eminent persons who have flourished in Great Britain and Ireland*, 2nd edn, 5 vols. (1778–93) • Venn, *Alum. Cant.* • *GM*, 1st ser., 20 (1750), 284 • will, PRO, PROB 11/787, sig. 133 • R. Bigland, *Historical, monumental and genealogical collections, relative to the county of Gloucester*, 2 (1792), 236
Archives priv. coll., MSS
Wealth at death see will, PRO, PROB 11/787, sig. 133

Burnet, Sir Thomas (1694–1753), judge, was born in London on 19 February 1694, the third son of Gilbert *Burnet (1643–1715), the celebrated whig bishop of Salisbury, and his second wife, Mary Scott (1659/60–1698)), a Dutch woman of Scottish family origins. William *Burnet (1688–1729) and Gilbert *Burnet (1690–1726) were his brothers. After study under a private tutor in his father's household, on 12 November 1705 he entered Merton College, Oxford, and in 1707 went on to the University of Leiden, where he remained until 1710. He was a grandson of Robert Burnet, Lord Cramond, a Scottish judge, and by his own choice he was intended for the law, having been admitted to the Middle Temple in 1709. But although he took up residence at the Temple in 1711, after returning from a brief tour of Germany, Switzerland, and Italy he was distracted from study by politics and the gay life affected by many law students, and spent much of his time in coffee houses and taverns. His parentage made his bouts of drunkenness and debauchery notorious, although he denied the talk of the town that he was one of the young Mohocks who were said by Swift to roam the streets of London committing mayhem, and particularly looking for tories. It is probable that the slur was politically motivated, because in 1712 and 1713 Burnet published several pamphlets attacking the tory ministry's policy of peace with France and indicting its leaders as crypto-Jacobites. Bolingbroke initiated a prosecution for libel after the publication of *Some New Proofs by which it Appears the Pretender is Truly James III* (1713), which included a preface comparing him with Cato and insinuating that he had accepted favours from the king of France, and Burnet escaped imprisonment only after his father intervened on his behalf with the queen.

Although the experience seems to have cooled his party ardour for a while, Burnet returned to the fray with vigour after the Hanoverian succession restored the whigs to favour. In October 1714 he was associating with Charles Montagu, first earl of Halifax, and the king's principal German minister, Baron Andreas Gottlieb von Bernstorff, and early the following year he published his most important pamphlet, *The Necessity of Impeaching the Late Ministry, in a Letter to the Earl of Halifax*, which was sponsored by the government and ran to several editions. About the same time Burnet also published *A Second Tale of a Tub* (1715), a satire targeted at Robert Harley, first earl of Oxford, and *Homerides* (1715), a sarcastic attack on Pope written with his friend and literary collaborator George Duckett, which ultimately secured them both places in *The Dunciad*. At the same time they collaborated on a periodical, *The Grumbler*. After such sterling political service Burnet was confident of a reward, but his prospects were damaged by his father's death in 1715, and over the next few years he was forced to solicit at court in hope of a place. He had published a character of his father on the bishop's decease, but thereafter his literary output slowed, and besides his 'cursed Court Attendance' (*Letters of Thomas Burnet*, 153) he made himself useful by assisting with government proceedings against suspected Jacobites. Eventually, in 1719 he was appointed British consul at Lisbon, and he remained there for eight years, although after his death a story circulated that he had quarrelled with the ambassador, Charles O'Hara, first Baron Tyrawley, and humiliated him at the Portuguese court. In 1728 Burnet returned to England, where after so long an absence he found himself without interest at court, and as he said in a letter of appeal to the duke of Newcastle 'find myself under a necessity of returning to the study of the Law, which I had quitted for nine years, after having spent the flower of my youth in the royal service' (ibid., 180).

Burnet was called to the bar and admitted to a chamber at the Middle Temple in February 1729, twenty years after first admission, and followed the western circuit, which included his late father's see. In September his troubles were increased by the death in embarrassed financial circumstances of his elder brother William, the governor of Massachusetts Bay, whose children were left to his care. But a government pension was obtained with the help of Sir Philip Yorke, the attorney-general, and his bar practice seems to have advanced rapidly with Yorke's subsequent promotion. He became a serjeant-at-law at the last general call of serjeants in 1736, and received a patent as king's serjeant in 1740, after applying to Yorke, now Lord Chancellor Hardwicke. At that time he was one of the busiest serjeants in the court of common pleas, and in 1741 Hardwicke promoted him to the bench of that court, in succession to Sir John Fortescue-Aland. He sat there for over eleven years, and was knighted with several other judges and lawyers at the time of the 1745 rebellion, on the occasion of the legal profession's loyal address to the crown. A modest application to become master of the rolls was unsuccessful, and he died 'of the gout in his stomach' (*GM*, 23.51) on 8 January 1753 at his house in Lincoln's Inn Fields and was buried at St James's Church in Clerkenwell. He never married, but his patron Hardwicke's son said of him 'a better and more agreeable man there never was than this worthy judge. He was a zealous and sincere friend' (BL, Add. MS 35591, fols. 3–4). At the last he returned to the provocative style of his youth, however, declaring in his will 'I trust I shall die, in the true faith of *Christ* as taught in the scriptures; but not as taught or practiced [*sic*] in any one visible church I know of, tho' I think the church of *England* is as little stuff'd with the inventions of men as any of them' (*GM*, 23.98).   DAVID LEMMINGS

Sources *The letters of Thomas Burnet to George Duckett, 1712–1722*, ed. D. N. Smith (1914) · E. Foss, *Biographia juridica: a biographical dictionary of the judges of England … 1066–1870* (1870) · *DNB* · Foster, *Alum. Oxon.* · BL, Add. MS 35586, fols. 220, 310; Add. MS 35590, fol. 450; Add. MS 35591, fols. 3–4 (Hardwicke MSS) · A. Pope, *The Dunciad*, ed. J. Sutherland, rev. edn (1953), vol. 5 of *The Twickenham edition of the poems of Alexander Pope*, ed. J. Butt · *GM*, 1st ser., 23 (1753) · *GM*, 1st ser., 49 (1779) · Baker, *Serjeants* · P. C. Yorke, *The life and correspondence of Philip Yorke, earl of Hardwicke*, 3 vols. (1913) · Sainty, *Judges* · *Report on the manuscripts of the marquis of Downshire*, 6 vols. in 7, HMC, 75 (1924–95), vol. 1, pp. 905–8 · W. A. Shaw, *The knights of England*, 2 (1906), 287

Archives BL, entry-books of dispatches and letters as consul at Lisbon, Add. MSS 11569–11570 · Lincoln's Inn, London, legal notebooks | BL, letters to George Duckett, Add. MS 36772 · BL, letters to first earl of Hardwicke, Add. MSS 35586, 35590–35591, *passim*

Likenesses J. Faber junior, mezzotint (after A. Ramsay), BM, NPG

Wealth at death inherited approx. £1000 from father in 1715; also money from mother's estate: letter to Sir William Trumbull, *Downshire manuscripts*, vol. 1, p. 907, 26 March 1715

Burnet, William (1688–1729), colonial governor, was born in March 1688 in The Hague, the Netherlands, the son of Gilbert *Burnet (1643–1715), bishop of Salisbury, and his second wife, Mary Scott (1659/1660–1698). Gilbert *Burnet (1690–1726) and Sir Thomas *Burnet (1694–1753) were his brothers. William Burnet was named after his godfather, William of Orange, who became William III after the revolution of 1688. Burnet entered Trinity College, Cambridge, in March 1698, but was later expelled and then tutored at home. He was admitted to the bar and in May 1712 married a daughter of Dean Stanhope (name unknown); she died three years later. In 1722 Burnet married a New Yorker, Anna Maria van Horne (d. 1728); they had three children.

In 1714, shortly after the accession of George I, Burnet, a loyal whig, was named comptroller of customs. He served until 1720, when he exchanged posts with Robert Hunter, governor of New York and New Jersey. On arrival in New York, Burnet allied with Hunter's old 'court' party, composed largely of landowners. Merchants, who comprised the opposition, or 'country' party, soon criticized Burnet because the governor, on Hunter's advice, did not dissolve the existing assembly, elected during Hunter's administration. This body, composed largely of landowners, proved their loyalty to the new governor by voting for a five-year revenue.

Controversy between landowners and merchants escalated when Burnet and the landowner-dominated assembly banned the lucrative Albany–Montreal trade, which was enriching the French in Canada. New York merchants, concerned only with the immediate loss of business, promptly complained to officials in London that Burnet was interfering with trade. Burnet then tried to weaken merchant influence on the assembly by refusing to administer the oath of office to a French-born merchant, Stephen DeLancey, who had been naturalized by a 1715 act. The assembly, indignant that the governor should judge the qualifications of its members, voted unanimously in September 1725 that DeLancey was eligible to serve. Burnet's actions caused most of the formerly loyal assembly to abandon Burnet and swing their support to the DeLancey faction. The result was that instead of voting another five-year revenue in 1725, the assembly voted only two years' support.

Burnet also faced assembly opposition in New Jersey. Here he favoured the interests of the proprietary party, or large landowners, who had land grants from the crown. His assembly opposition consisted of the anti-proprietary interests, or those landowners who had received their land patents from the first governor of New York, Richard

Nicolls, not the crown. Burnet called for assembly elections in 1722 and achieved a more agreeable body, dominated by large landowners, which provided five-year support for the government.

In 1727 Burnet was transferred from the governorship of New York and New Jersey to that of Massachusetts and New Hampshire. His transfer was primarily to make way in New York for the appointment of the king's placeman, John Montgomerie. It may also have been the result of rising opposition in New York and Britain to Burnet's anti-mercantile policies, which conflicted with the commitment to trade of the first lord of the Treasury, the prime minister, Sir Robert Walpole.

Burnet arrived in Boston on 13 July 1728 and called his first assembly. He met opposition when the assembly refused to commit itself to paying him a fixed salary. Rather than compromise, Burnet refused to accept any salary, living off the charity of friends. The assembly baulked when Burnet tried to raise money for government expenses by imposing a fee on shipping. At Burnet's suggestion, the ministry asked parliament to intervene in the salary dispute. Before the Massachusetts issue was considered by parliament, the governor contracted a fatal fever following a carriage accident, and died in Boston on 7 September 1729. His will stipulated that he be buried next to his wife in New York city.

Burnet was noted for his competence, intelligence, and honesty. These attributes won him the respect of many colonists, as did his commitment to protecting the royal prerogative and to furthering Britain's imperial interests. His administrations in New York and New Jersey are generally not considered as successful as those of his predecessor Robert Hunter, but Hunter's longer tenure gave him more time to solve problems. Hunter's conciliatory nature also made him a more effective governor, while Burnet himself admitted that he was stubborn and inflexible. Though a committed whig in Britain, Burnet, like all other royal governors, did not apply whig theories of government to the colonies, and could not condone rising republican tendencies in Britain's provinces.

MARY LOU LUSTIG

Sources board of trade MSS, 1696–1786, BL, Add. MS 14304 · BL, Clarendon MSS, Add. MS 15895 · BL, Newcastle MSS, America and West Indies, 1701–1802, Add. MSS 33028–33030 · PRO, Admiralty MSS, ADM 1/231 · PRO, colonial office MSS, Board of Trade MSS, Class 5, vols. 1050–1058 · New York State Library, Albany, New York, colonial MSS, vols. 61–2 · PRO, colonial office MSS, Secretary of State MSS, Class 5, vols. 1090–1093 · New York Historical Society, New York, Cadwallader Colden MSS · New York Historical Society, New York, Rutherfurd Collection · *CSP col.*, vols. 31–40 · W. Nelson, ed., *Original documents relating to the life and administrations of William Burnet, governor of New York and New Jersey, 1720–1728* (1897) · E. B. O'Callaghan and B. Fernow, eds. and trans., *Documents relative to the colonial history of the state of New York*, 15 vols. (1853–87) · W. A. Whitehead and others, eds., *Documents relating to the colonial, revolutionary and post-revolutionary history of the state of New Jersey*, 1–10 (1880–86) · *Minutes of the common council of the city of New York, 1675–1776* (1905) · C. Colden, *Letters on Smith's History of New York* (1868) · *The letters and papers of Cadwallader Colden*, 1 (1918) · W. Smith, *The history of the province of New-York* (1757); repr. M. Kammen, ed., 2 (New York, 1972) · T. Hutchinson, *The history of the colony of Massachusetts-bay*, 2nd edn, 3 vols. (1764–1828); repr. (New York, 1972) · P. A. Stellhorn and M. J. Birkner, eds., *The governors of New Jersey, 1664–1974* (1982) · J. J. Adams, 'Burnet, William', *DAB* · M. L. Lustig, 'Burnet, William', *ANB* · Venn, *Alum. Cant.*

Likenesses attrib. J. Watson, oils, 1726, Colby College Art Museum, Waterville, Maine

Burnett, Sir Charles Stuart (1882–1945), air force officer, was born at Brown's Valley, Minnesota, United States of America, on 3 April 1882, the second of the four sons of John Alexander Burnett (1852–1935), a landowner, of Kemnay, Aberdeenshire, and his wife, Charlotte Susan, *née* Gordon (d. 1925). Admiral Sir Robert Lindsay *Burnett was his younger brother. After attending Bedford School, at the age of seventeen Burnett enlisted to fight in the Second South African War, claiming to be a year older than he was. He joined the 8th company of the imperial yeomanry, from which he was discharged in 1901 to enable him to take a commission in the Highland light infantry. He was then employed with the imperial yeomanry once more, before secondment in 1904 to the West African frontier force; he fought in Northern Nigeria, and was twice mentioned in dispatches. In October 1907 he was promoted lieutenant, but resigned his commission in 1909 to run a small retail business in Portuguese Guinea. This venture was not particularly successful, and Burnett entered government service in 1911, serving as the assistant resident in Northern Nigeria.

On the outbreak of the First World War Burnett rejoined the army, but not with his old regiment, choosing instead to become a member of the Royal Flying Corps (RFC). He qualified as a pilot in November 1914, and before his first posting married, on 30 November, Sybil Maud Pack-Beresford (b. 1882/3), whose previous marriage had been dissolved; she was the daughter of John Bell, an ironmaster of Saltburn, Yorkshire. Burnett was sent to 17 squadron in the Middle East, and in February 1915 became a flight commander. Command of a squadron followed in April 1916, this time with 12 squadron in France. Promotion to temporary lieutenant-colonel in October 1917 saw Burnett take command of the RFC's fifth wing in Palestine. Burnett was appointed to the Distinguished Service Order following the capture of Jerusalem in December 1917, and was made a CBE in 1919. He was offered, and accepted, a permanent commission as a wing commander in the Royal Air Force.

In 1920 Burnett commanded the RAF in Iraq, then returned to the United Kingdom the following year for a variety of appointments, beginning as station commander, with the rank of group captain, at RAF Leuchars. A spell at the Air Ministry as deputy director of operations and intelligence was followed by command of the Central Flying School for two years from January 1927. Once this posting was completed, Burnett returned to Iraq for another two years' duty, this time as the senior staff officer in the country, leading a return flight from Basrah to Muscat, in flying boats, in May 1929. In January 1931 he was again in the United Kingdom to take up the position of director of operations and intelligence at the Air Ministry, at the same time becoming deputy chief of the air staff. Promotion to air vice-marshal followed in July 1931, but his time in Britain was relatively brief, since in November 1932 he was sent to become air officer commanding, British forces in Iraq. The period was marked by the need to suppress various tribal incursions near Kuwait, during the course of which Burnett was wounded. He returned to Britain in 1935, taking command of the Inland Area. A major reorganization of the RAF in 1936 saw the Inland Area become Training Command: Burnett was promoted air marshal in January 1936 and became air officer commanding-in-chief in May 1936, when he received a knighthood (KCB). As the threat from Hitler's Germany increased, the demands placed upon Training Command were notable. Burnett was posted out of that key position in July 1939, when he was made inspector-general of the RAF.

By the outbreak of war Burnett's health had declined, and he was due for retirement; this was postponed as a result of events in Australia. The Australian prime minister, Robert Menzies, decided that a British officer should take over as chief of the air staff of the Royal Australian Air Force (RAAF). After some discussions with the British government, it was agreed to appoint Burnett to this post, in the rank of air chief marshal. The decision to appoint a British officer ahead of an Australian one was particularly controversial, and this did not help Burnett's cause. Many members of the RAAF were openly resentful of his appointment, and Burnett's actions while in post were the source of some controversy later.

Burnett saw his prime task as being to increase the ability of the RAAF to provide aircrew to the RAF. He sought to do this through the medium of the empire air training scheme. The scheme was enormously successful in producing trained aircrew, but proved controversial. Many Australians felt that the scheme would undermine their nation's identity. Burnett was not persuaded, however, taking the view that victory in Europe demanded the exploitation of the whole British empire; as a result, he set about creating a structure that would produce 50,000 men by March 1943. The focus on Europe meant that the RAAF was lacking in numbers when facing the threat of invasion by the Japanese.

This situation did little to commend Burnett to the newly appointed Australian minister for air, A. S. Drakeford, and their relationship was particularly stormy. Burnett's proposed major organizational changes to the RAAF, most notably the abolition of the RAAF's air board, proved to be too much for the Australian government, and Burnett was replaced in May 1942 as the threat from the Japanese increased. Despite the criticisms levelled against him, Burnett had overseen an enormous expansion in the strength of the RAAF—the service had just 3489 men before the start of the war, while by the time of Burnett's departure there were nearly 80,000 service personnel. This achievement has been largely overshadowed by the controversial nature of Burnett's tenure. Not only was he imposed upon the RAAF when it appeared that equally capable Australian alternatives existed, but Burnett's focus upon the empire air training scheme has

added to the generally ambivalent—and sometimes hostile—attitude towards him in histories of the RAAF.

After his departure, Burnett was placed on the retired list, as had been planned, but in 1943 he was recalled to duty as the commandant of the Air Training Corps. He continued to serve the air force, even though his health was declining. On 9 April 1945 he died of coronary thrombosis while in the Princess Mary Hospital at Halton Camp, Wendover, Buckinghamshire. He was survived by his wife and four daughters.   DAVID JORDAN

Sources DNB · AusDB · A. Stephens, *The Royal Australian Air Force, 1921–1939* (2001) · C. D. Coulthard-Clark, *The third brother: the Royal Australian Air Force, 1921–1939* (1991) · A. Stephens and J. Isaacs, *High fliers: leaders of the Royal Australian Air Force* (1996) · Burke, *Peerage* (1939) · Burke, *Gen. GB* (1937) [Burnett of Kemnay] · m. cert. · d. cert.
Wealth at death £5886 18s. 6d.: probate, 17 July 1946, *CGPLA Eng. & Wales*

Burnett, Frances Eliza Hodgson (1849–1924), children's writer and novelist, was born on 24 November 1849 in Cheetham Hill, Manchester, the third child and eldest daughter in the family of two sons and three daughters of Edwin Hodgson (1816–1854) and his wife, Eliza, *née* Boond (1815–1870). Edwin Hodgson, wholesaler of decorative ironmongery, died aged thirty-eight. His widow struggled to run the business herself until her brother, who had established a dry-goods store in Knoxville, Tennessee, USA, persuaded her in 1865 to emigrate with the children. The early years in Tennessee were hard and the family was frequently hungry, but in 1868 Frances, who from her earliest childhood had been a compulsive inventor of romances, sold her first two stories to *Godey's Lady's Book*, raising the money for paper and postage by selling wild grapes. Until her marriage she supported the family by a constant stream of magazine stories, her only object, as she said herself, being remuneration.

On 19 September 1873 Frances Hodgson married an ophthalmologist Swan Moses Burnett (c.1847–1906), the son of John Burnett, a Tennessee physician, and his wife, Lydia Peck. They lived first in Knoxville, and moved to Washington, DC, in 1877. There were two sons, Lionel (b. 1874) and Vivian (b. 1876). Mrs Burnett took her marital duties lightly, and though she did not formally end the marriage until 1898, from early days she made a practice of absenting herself from her family, often for months on end, travelling in North America and Europe, and spending long periods in England, where she moved in high society and had many literary friends, Henry James and Israel Zangwill among them. In spite of frequent and prolonged separation from them, she was devoted to her sons and they to her, and the death of Lionel, from tuberculosis, in 1890 was a shattering blow. Early in 1900 in Genoa, Italy, she married Stephen Townesend (1859–1914), a young physician with stage aspirations whom she had tried to help, and who in his turn assisted her in her business affairs. Ten years younger than his wife, he was the youngest son of the Revd George Fyler Townesend and grandson of the Revd George *Townsend (1788–1857), a redoubtable cleric who had travelled to Italy in 1850 to try

Frances Eliza Hodgson Burnett (1849–1924), by Barraud, pubd 1888

to convert the pope. They were divorced in the following year, and she continued to publish under her first married name.

Frances Hodgson Burnett had early had to turn herself into 'a pen-driving machine' (Burnett, 75) to support the ever-increasing opulence of her lifestyle, and her adult fiction (she wrote more than twenty novels and innumerable short stories) for the most part is facile and superficial. She was never to equal her first novel, *That Lass o' Lowrie's* (1877), a robust account of a Lancashire mining community in which she had taken great care with background and dialect, though *Through One Administration* (1883), a study of a failed marriage against a turbulent background of Washington political life, was noteworthy, and the much shorter *The Making of a Marchioness* (1901) is an effective indictment of Edwardian society. She adapted many of her novels, including the first, for the stage, with mixed success.

Frances Hodgson Burnett's first children's book, *Little Lord Fauntleroy*, appeared in 1886. This account of how a sturdy and friendly young American wins the heart of the irascible and hostile earl of Dorincourt, the grandfather who has hitherto refused to see him, acquired a largely undeserved reputation for sentimentality. This was in part due to Reginald Birch's illustrations which kept the boy always in black velvet and lace, even when he was riding his pony, and in part to the intense relationship between mother and son; Frances Hodgson Burnett here

had in mind herself and her son Vivian, upon whom Fauntleroy himself was modelled. It was a huge success, stage and film versions were made of it, and it led to thousands of unwilling boys being dressed in black velvet suits. When E. V. Seebohm presented it as a play in London in 1888 without her permission, she challenged him in the courts and succeeded in getting the current copyright laws changed.

'She wanted to be in the land of make-believe as often and as long as possible' (Burnett, 331), her son Vivian said of her. In her books this is to be found at its most extreme in *Sara Crewe* (1888)—expanded, following the stage version, as *The Little Princess* (1905)—a Cinderella story where a bullied little drudge at a girls' school is restored to riches and esteem and the tyrannical headmistress humiliated. Her finest book was undoubtedly *The Secret Garden* (1911), which achieved classic status. This describes how two disagreeable and unloved children are transformed by the discovery of a hidden garden which they appropriate and which they watch springing into life as the year advances. The garden depicted with such passionate intensity is based partly on an abandoned one she had seen near her Manchester home when she was a child, and partly on the rose garden at Maytham Hall, Rolvenden, near Tenterden, Kent, a house she rented for many years and last visited in 1907.

Frances Hodgson Burnett had to the last a youthful enthusiasm, an erect carriage, and a firm step. Stocky in childhood, she became stout in middle age and the auburn of her hair was maintained by henna. She always loved clothes and dressing-up, particularly in 'clinging, trailing chiffon things with *miles* of lace on them' (Thwaite, 212). She took American citizenship in 1905. A libel action brought by her nephew's wife brought her much unpleasant notoriety in 1918. 'She has shattered the mirrors which might betray her to herself' was one of the milder comments. The last years of her life were divided between Bermuda and Plandome, Long Island, New York, USA, where she built herself an Italian-style villa and where she died on 29 October 1924. She was buried at God's Acre, Roslyn, Long Island, and a memorial to her was placed in Central Park, New York city, consisting of statues of a boy and girl.   GILLIAN AVERY

Sources A. Thwaite, *Waiting for the party* (1974) · V. Burnett, *The romantick lady* (1927)
Archives BL, literary MSS, Add. MSS 41678–41681
Likenesses Barraud, photograph, NPG; repro. in *Men and Women of the Day*, 1 (1888) [*see illus.*]

Burnett, George (1776?–1811), writer, was born at Huntspill, Somerset, the son of John Burnett (*d.* 1799), a respectable farmer. After a suitable introduction to classical literature under the care of a clergyman in the neighbourhood, he was sent to Balliol College, Oxford, where he matriculated on 21 March 1793 with a view to taking orders. It was there that he met Southey and the two became fast friends, often visiting one another's rooms or ambling about on walking tours together. Southey and Coleridge met for the first time in 1794, and Burnett, increasingly disenchanted with college life, took part with them in the well-known utopian scheme of 'panti-socracy'. Since Southey and Burnett were fellow inmates at Balliol and probably in direct contact with one another, it is highly likely that the pair were more intimate co-agitators in the preliminary formulations of the pantisocratic vision, which originated at Oxford in June 1794. According to a letter from Burnett to Nicholas Light-foot, dated 22 October 1796, the original scheme had contained no plan to emigrate to America, and the idea to emigrate had originated while Southey and Burnett were on a walking tour. Burnett's letter further suggests that he was the most politically radical of the pantisocratics, for he believed that the core of the utopian society lay in the total community of property and the abolition of private property.

While Southey and Coleridge courted and eventually married Edith and Sara Fricker, respectively, Burnett, who was supposed to complete the triumvirate by marrying another of the Fricker sisters, Martha, found his advances rebuffed. When plans to emigrate to America began to fall apart, Burnett acted as an emissary between Southey and Coleridge, and was supposed to go with Thomas Southey to north Wales in early 1795 to reconnoitre a suitable spot for plan B for the pantisocratic society. After this scheme also collapsed, Burnett lingered about for a year or so, dependent on an allowance from his father, and finally obtained admission as a student into the dissenting college at Manchester. In 1797 Burnett was appointed pastor of a Unitarian congregation at Yarmouth and also became the tutor of Southey's younger brother Henry Herbert. Burnett also became, for a short time, a student of medicine at the University of Edinburgh. He worked in London in 1801 as an assistant to Rickman, the census-taker, and later did some hack writing for Phillips the publisher, by contributing some filler to Mavor's *Universal History*. Unfortunately, by all accounts, Burnett thought that he was above the common sorts of employment, and though friends such as Rickman, Lamb, Southey, and Coleridge all persevered over the years in trying to find him suitable employment, Burnett, through either incompetence or pride, and to the consternation of his friends, was never able to keep a job.

Through the influence of friends, in 1802 Burnett was appointed domestic tutor to two sons of Lord Stanhope, but had scarcely entered on his charge when both his pupils—though not through any fault of his—left their father's house. Lord Stanhope kept Burnett on a bit longer as an assistant (sent to do any 'fiddle-faddle errand', said Lamb in a letter to John Rickman on 14 February 1802; *Letters of Charles and Mary Lamb*, 302) and eventually paid £200—a year's salary—to Burnett, who later repaired to London, where he probably began taking opium. In a letter of January 1803 Southey complained to Rickman that not only was Burnett continuing in his shiftless ways, but that he had also accused Southey and Coleridge of treating him shabbily. By July 1803, however, Burnett had apparently decided to mend his ways. He sent a circular to his friends saying that he had recovered from his 'mental

distortion', and that he was going to become a naval surgeon. He nevertheless angered Southey once again by asking a complete stranger for money in Southey's name so that he could procure his military accoutrement. He did by December 1803 become an assistant surgeon in a militia regiment, but he soon resigned this post. By December 1804 Burnett was in Poland with the family of Count Zamovski, as English tutor, but in 1805 returned to England, without any employment, and apparently in love with a Polish princess. In 1806 Burnett converted to Methodism and attempted to convert his family as well.

By 1807 Burnett settled down to a few productive years. He contributed to the *Monthly Magazine* a series of letters which were subsequently published under the title of *View of the Present State of Poland* (1807). He next published *Specimens of English prose writers, from the earliest times to the close of the seventeenth century; with sketches biographical and literary; including an account of books, as well as of their authors, with occasional criticisms* (3 vols., 1807). This judicious compilation, forming a companion to George Ellis's *Specimens of the Early English Poets*, is exemplary of the rising interest of the time in the history of English literature, as evidenced by the proliferation of anthologies arranged by historical period with accompanying commentaries. His last production, *Extracts from the Prose Works of Milton*, with new translations and an introduction (2 vols., 1809), was completed at Huntspill in 1808–9, and dedicated to Lord Erskine. On its completion, however, he left his native place; and by February 1810 Rickman communicated to Southey that he had received from Burnett a few letters begging for support, but it was Rickman's opinion that Burnett was completely dissolute and beyond hope. When his application for the position of assistant librarian at the London Institution fell through, Burnett preferred to stay in London though without any means to support himself. It is not known how he subsisted from November 1809 until his death, which took place in the Marylebone Infirmary in February 1811.

THOMPSON COOPER, rev. DAVID KALOUSTIAN

Sources R. Williams, 'Sketches in a tour. Letter IV', *Monthly Magazine*, 42 (1 Nov 1816), 310–13 · J. Cottle, *Reminiscences of Samuel Taylor Coleridge and Robert Southey* (1848) · *The life and correspondence of Robert Southey*, ed. C. C. Southey, 6 vols. (1849–50) · Watt, *Bibl. Brit.* · W. T. Lowndes, *The bibliographer's manual of English literature*, new edn, ed. H. G. Bohn, 5 vols. (1858–68), vol. 1, p. 325 · [J. Watkins and F. Shoberl], *A biographical dictionary of the living authors of Great Britain and Ireland* (1816) · G. Burnett, *Specimens of English prose—writers from the earliest times to the close of the seventeenth century*, 2nd edn, 3 vols. (1813) · G. Burnett, *View of the present state of Poland* (1807) · M. Storey, *Robert Southey: a life* (1997) · *Collected letters of Samuel Taylor Coleridge*, ed. E. L. Griggs, 6 vols. (1956–71) · *New letters of Robert Southey*, ed. K. Curry, 2 vols. (1965) · O. Williams, 'A study in failure', *Blackwood*, 189 (1911), 324–33 · O. Williams, *Lamb's friend the census-taker: life and letters of John Rickman* (1912) · C. Lamb, *The life, letters and writings of Charles Lamb*, ed. P. Fitzgerald, 6 vols. (1971) · *Letters of Charles and Mary Lamb*, ed. E. V. Lucas, 1 (1968) · N. Roe, *The politics of nature: Wordsworth and some contemporaries* (1992)
Archives Bodl. Oxf., letter MSS

Burnett, George (1822–1890), genealogist, born on 9 March 1822, was the third son of John Burnett of Kemnay, an estate in central Aberdeenshire, and Mary, daughter of

Charles Stuart of Dunearn. Educated partly in Germany, he acquired a taste for art and became an enthusiastic amateur musician; he was for many years music critic for *The Scotsman*. He was called to the Scots bar in 1845, but did not practise much, devoting himself to literary pursuits, particularly genealogy. Burnett became well acquainted with leading figures of the Spalding Club, including John Hill Burton, George Gibb, Joseph Robertson, Cosmo Innes, and its secretary, John Stuart, as well as with W. Forbes Skene, the Celtic scholar.

In Scottish genealogy and peerage law Burnett was one of the foremost lawyers of his time. In 1863 he entered the Lyon office as Lyon depute, and three years later, when the office was reorganized on the death of the earl of Kinnoull, he became Lyon king of arms. Through his efforts he restored this position from an honorary and titular office to a working one, ably supported by Stodart, the Lyon clerk depute, an accomplished genealogist. In 1865 Burnett published *Popular Genealogists, or, The Art of Pedigree-Making*, which exposed several mythical pedigrees that had appeared in other genealogical volumes. Burnett's principal historical work was his edition of the exchequer rolls from 1264 to 1507, published under the control of the lord clerk register, which he undertook on the death of John Stuart (1813–1877). He edited twelve volumes between 1878 and 1890. The prefaces to these volumes were considered valuable commentaries on the history of Scotland during the period to which they relate. Burnett also published *The Red Book of Menteith Reviewed* in 1881, and his manuscript *Treatise on Heraldry, British and Foreign* was completed in 1891 by the Revd John Woodward, who was subsequently criticized for the alterations he had made to Burnett's text.

On 11 August 1870 Burnett married in Dresden his cousin Alice, youngest daughter of John Alexander Stuart (son of Charles Stuart of Dunearn). They had a son, John George, and a daughter, Alice Christina. Burnett received the degree of LLD in 1884 from Edinburgh University. He died on 23 January 1890 at his residence, 21 Walker Street, Edinburgh. His wife died on 5 July 1908.

A. J. G. MACKAY, rev. MYFANWY LLOYD

Sources Boase, *Mod. Eng. biog.* · J. Allardyce, ed., *The family of Burnett of Leys: with collateral branches*, New Spalding Club, 22 (1901) · Burke, *Gen. GB* · Brown & Stratton, *Brit. mus.* · CCI (1890)
Wealth at death £2806 6s. 9d.: confirmation, 19 March 1890, CCI

Burnett, Gilbert Thomas (1800–1835), surgeon and botanist, was born in London on 15 April 1800, one of three children of Gilbert Burnett, surgeon, and his wife, Ann. He was reputedly a descendant of Bishop Gilbert Burnet (1643–1715). Educated by Joseph Benson (1778?–1861) at Hounslow Heath, he was apprenticed to a Mr Ewbank in 1815 as surgeon and apothecary, and studied anatomy with Joseph Carpue (1764–1846). When qualified he continued his late father's practice. Burnett developed an expertise in medical botany and lectured widely and frequently, popularly at the Royal Institution on general botanical topics, and professionally at, among others, St George's Hospital and the Medico-Botanical Society, to which he was honorary professor. He was appointed as the

foundation professor of botany in King's College London on 15 April 1831, and in 1835 as professor of botany to the Society of Apothecaries, to which he delivered one series of lectures before his death. Burnett saw the society's Physic Garden at Chelsea as an important resource, hoping that 'what the hospital is to the students of medicine and surgery, this garden may become to students of botany' ('A lecture delivered in Chelsea Garden on April 21 1835'). He was elected a fellow of the Linnean Society on 21 February 1831, on the nomination of J. L. Wheeler, demonstrator in botany at the Chelsea Physic Garden, and six other, mostly medical, supporters.

Burnett was predominantly a synthesizer and compiler and published no major works based on original research. His first major work was an edited edition of Stephenson and Churchill's *Medical Botany* (1834–6). Only the first of the two volumes of *Outlines of Botany* (1835), 'a considerable collection of botanical information' (Lindley, 517), had appeared before his death, from pneumonia, on 27 July 1835. *Plantae utiliores, Illustrations of Useful Plants Employed in Medicine &c*, illustrated and edited by his sister, Mary Ann Burnett, appeared in 1839–40, and a catalogue of the plants of China also appeared posthumously. John Lindley commemorated him in 1840 by the Tasmanian orchid genus *Burnettia*.

Described by his anonymous obituarist as 'delicate and slender, … handsome and intellectual, [with] eyes dark, sparkling and expressive', Burnett, the excellent lecturer who imparted knowledge 'with ease and with elegance' (*Annual Biography and Obituary*) was widely mourned. He was survived by his mother and sister, and stated in his will that his 'greatest temporal grief is that my dearest mother and sister are not … well provided for'. He was buried in St Marylebone churchyard on 1 August 1835.

A. M. LUCAS

Sources *Annual Biography and Obituary*, 20 (1836), 264–75 · F. A. Stafleu and E. A. Mennega, *Taxonomic literature: a selective guide*, suppl. 3, Regnum Vegetabile, 132 (1995), 258 · J. Lindley, *The genera and species of orchidaceous plants* (1830–40), 517 · King's College council minutes, 15 April 1831, King's Lond., vol. B. 68 · E. Bretschneider, *History of European botanical discoveries in China*, 1 (1898), 279–80 · H. Murray, J. Cawfurd, T. Lynn, W. Wallace, and G. Burnett, *A historic and descriptive account of China* (1836) · *Catalogue of scientific papers*, Royal Society, 1 (1867), 735 · private information (2004) · Linnean Society election certificates, Linn. Soc. · PRO, PROB 11/1854/691, fol. 332 · parish register (burial), London, St Marylebone, 1 Aug 1835
Archives King's Lond.
Wealth at death see will, PRO, PROB 11/1854/691, fol. 332

Burnett, Dame Ivy Compton- (1884–1969), novelist, was born on 5 June 1884 at 2 Onslow Gardens, Pinner, Middlesex, the seventh of the thirteen children of Dr James Compton Burnett (1840–1901), a distinguished and crusading homoeopath, and first child of his second wife, Katharine (1855–1911), daughter of Rowland Rees, civil engineer and mayor of Dover. Until the age of fourteen Ivy Compton-Burnett was educated at home by a governess and tutors, alongside her younger brothers, Guy (1885–

Dame Ivy Compton-Burnett (1884–1969), by Howard Coster, 1942

1905) and Noel (1887–1916), to whom she was passionately attached. In 1891 her family moved to Hove, then a new and developing suburb of Brighton, and from 1898 to 1901 she was a day pupil at the nearby Addiscombe College, where she took university matriculation. In 1901–2 she spent two terms as a boarder at Howard College, Bedford, in preparation for living away from home; and in 1902 entered Royal Holloway College, Egham, where she studied classics, graduating in 1906. Nothing suggests that she enjoyed school; her university contemporaries recall her only as shy and withdrawn; educational institutions later provided an enclosed setting and hothouse atmosphere for several of her novels.

Compton-Burnett's father died suddenly in 1901 and there followed a series of misfortunes that brought increasing bleakness to her life. Her mother was already inclined to social posturing—the hyphenated form of the family name was her invention—and entered into extravagant mourning, which she sustained for ten years and imposed to the extent that even the baby in her pram was bedecked with black ribbons. In widowhood Compton-Burnett's mother provided her with an early model for the line of outrageous domestic bullies that appear in her novels, anticipating the grief-stricken and over-demanding Sophia Stace (*Brothers and Sisters*, 1929) and the more shamelessly lucid Harriet Haslem (*Men and Wives*, 1931), who declares candidly: 'I see my children's

faces, and am urged by the hurt in them to go further, and driven on to the worse'.

When her brother Guy died of pneumonia in 1905, Compton-Burnett became indifferent to her studies, and graduated without the first-class degree which had been expected for her. Back in Hove she was set to tutoring her four younger sisters, a duty she conducted lackadaisically. She was, however, observing, and from the mid-1930s her novels would more and more feature groups of put-upon children whose only independence in otherwise miserable confinements is their outspokenness. Intermittently encouraged by her brother Noel—for whom boarding-school and Cambridge were an escape from the Hove household—she wrote a novel about self-abnegation, *Dolores* (published in 1911), a book influenced by the work of George Eliot which she later dismissed as a false start. After her mother's death from protracted cancer in 1911, Compton-Burnett became head of the household, and in taking over her mother's role she took on too its rigour and despotism. She explored domestic tyranny with herself as its practitioner, until in 1915 her sisters mutinied, setting up home in London with the pianist Myra Hess, and leaving her alone and largely friendless. She was not, however, poor: her father had invested extensively in property, and after her mother's death Compton-Burnett managed his estate and trusts, which she administered judiciously and profitably over the next fifty years.

In 1916 Compton-Burnett's brother Noel was killed on the Somme, and his young wife attempted suicide. Though there was little liking between them, Compton-Burnett grimly set about nursing her brother's widow back to health. Late in 1917 her two youngest sisters were found in a locked bedroom, dead from a self-administered overdose of veronal. Considerably enervated after the inquest into their deaths, she fell victim to the influenza epidemic that swept England in 1918, and was herself for a time near death. Her luck changed in 1919, when the writer Margaret *Jourdain (1876–1951) moved into Compton-Burnett's flat in Bayswater, London, beginning a lifelong relationship. Under Margaret's indulgent care Ivy slowly returned to brighter spirits, and in 1925 published *Pastors and Masters*, her second novel, and the first of her nineteen avant-gardist novels composed almost entirely in brisk dialogue.

These are witty and often demanding novels, peopled with alert sceptics who are devoted to epigrammatic talk and edgily precise analysis of talk. 'Dear, dear, how you overwork your words! I feel quite sorry for them'—says a governess to her charges in *The Mighty and their Fall* (1961). Set in the home county residences of a *fin de siècle* gentry, they are claustrophobic in mood and concerned with the tyranny of family life; they are also often melodramatic. Elizabeth Bowen described the intensity of the characters' lives and the novelist's reliance on dialogue in her analysis of the novels printed in the *Cornhill Magazine* in 1944:

> In space they move about very little: they go for short walks, which generally have an object, or advance on each other's houses in groups, like bomber formations. They speak of

what they will do, and what they have done, but are seldom
to be watched actually doing it.   (Burkhart, *Art*, 62)

This dialogue method moved against the emphasis on seg-regated subjectivity favoured by writers such as Virginia
Woolf, and instead foregrounded interaction and group
dynamics, the territory of W. R. Bion and transactional
analysis. Her probing into the springs of utterance is often
kindred to the linguistic enquiries of Jacques Lacan's
psychoanalytic studies, but is without parallel among her
British contemporaries. Moralizing is largely absent,
unless to be exposed as a ludicrous cover for low impulses
that it could never itself sanction.

Jourdain was a freelance writer who specialized in the
history of Regency furniture. She was vigorous and gre-garious, and brought to their household a lively social
circle, in which Compton-Burnett was mostly content to
play second fiddle and pour tea. Neither woman married,
and in 1934 they moved to a flat in 5 Braemar Mansions,
Cornwall Gardens, Kensington, London, which remained
Compton-Burnett's home until her death. Whether they
enjoyed a lesbian partnership is disputed. 'We are neu-trals', was how Compton-Burnett described herself and
Margaret to one friend, and the biographer Hilary Spurl-ing accepts this as meaning that theirs was not a sexual
relationship. However, Herman Schrijver, a close friend
who looked after Compton-Burnett on the day of
Jourdain's funeral and the last friend to spend time with
Compton-Burnett before her own death, had no doubt
that in every way 'their relationship was a *marriage*'
(Burkhart, *Three Lives*, 76). A fearless and very positive
account of both lesbian and male homosexual relations
recurs in Compton-Burnett's novels, as does mockery of
conventional marriage. After Jourdain's death Compton-Burnett openly mourned her with an intensity not unlike
that of her mother for Dr Burnett.

Compton-Burnett's persistent habit of setting her
novels in an isolated country-house milieu, somewhat
like Agatha Christie transposed back to the late years of
Queen Victoria, did not, however, make her an anachron-ism to her younger contemporaries. On the contrary.
Elizabeth Bowen, reviewing *Parents and Children* (1941),
wrote that 'to read in these days a page of Compton-Burnett dialogue is to think of the sound of glass being
swept up, one of these London mornings after a blitz'
(Burkhart, *Art*, 55). In an obituary notice Angus Wilson
argued that 'In the age of the concentration camp … no
writer did more to illumine the springs of human cruelty,
suffering and bravery' (ibid., 192). The French novelist
Nathalie Sarraute, writing in the *Nouvelle Revue Française* in
1956, singled out Compton-Burnett as 'one of the greatest
novelists that England has ever had', praising especially
her location of dialogue 'somewhere on the fluctu-ating frontier that separates conversation from sub-conversation' (ibid., 154–5). In 1951 Compton-Burnett was
appointed CBE, and in 1967 DBE.

Like Margaret Jourdain, and most of her characters who
are not fools or knaves, Ivy Compton-Burnett was a firm
atheist, dismissing religion because 'No good can come of

it' (Spurling, *Ivy when Young*, 77). She died peacefully, at her
home in Kensington, from bronchitis, on 27 August 1969,
and was cremated at Putney Vale crematorium.

PATRICK LYONS

Sources I. Compton-Burnett, *Collected works* (1972) · H. Spurling, *Ivy when young: the early life of I. Compton-Burnett, 1884–1919* (1974) · H. Spurling, *Secrets of a woman's heart: the later life of I. Compton-Burnett, 1920–1969* (1984) · C. Burkhart, *Herman and Nancy and Ivy: three lives in art* (1977) · C. Burkhart, ed., *The art of I. Compton-Burnett* (1972) · B. Bałutowa, *Nowe formy powieści: twórczość Ivy Compton-Burnett* (Wrocław, 1975) · A. Light, *Forever England: femininity, litera-ture and conservatism between the wars* (1990) · W. Iser, *The implied reader* (1974), 152–63 and 234–56
Archives King's AC Cam., corresp., engagement diaries, literary MSS, radio broadcasts · NRA, letters and literary MSS · Washing-ton University, St Louis, letters and literary MSS | BL, corresp. with Society of Authors, Add. MS 63222 · Bodl. Oxf., letters to J. R. Liddell · Bodl. Oxf., corresp. with Barbara Pym · Wightwick Manor [NT], Wolverhampton, letters to Lady Rosalie Mander | SOUND BBC WAC
Likenesses H. Coster, photograph, 1942, NPG [*see illus.*] · B. Brandt, photograph, 1949, NPG · four photographs, 1955, Hult. Arch. · H. Beacham, photograph, 1960–69, repro. in Spurling, *Secrets of a woman's heart*, following p. 240 · J. V. Brown, photo-graph, 1960–69, repro. in Spurling, *Secrets of a woman's heart*, jacket · W. Bird, photograph, NPG · H. Coster, photographs, NPG · F. Topolski, portrait, NPG
Wealth at death £86,570: probate, 24 Oct 1969, *CGPLA Eng. & Wales*

Burnett, James, Lord Monboddo (*bap.* 1714, *d.* 1799), judge
and philosopher, was born at Monboddo, near Fordoun,
Kincardineshire, and baptized on 25 October 1714. He was
the eldest surviving son of James Burnett (*b.* 1688), third
laird of Monboddo, and Elizabeth (1690–1765), his wife,
only daughter of Sir William Forbes of Craigievar, bt. Of
his sixteen siblings only his younger brother William and
sisters Margaret and Eliza survived childhood.

The Burnetts were a cadet branch of the Burnets of Leys,
Deeside—a connection reinforced by the marriage of the
second laird, Alexander, to his cousin Margaret, daughter
of Sir Alexander Burnet of Leys. Both families were
staunchly Jacobite and Episcopalian, and the estates of
James Burnett the elder were depleted after he was
imprisoned for his part in the 1715 rising. But the family's
misfortunes had begun with the early death of his father,
and his mother's subsequent marriage to the Revd
Andrew Burnett MD, who, about 1700, in accordance with
Scots law, was appointed the second tutor of Monboddo in
charge of James and his properties. Andrew Burnett was a
controversial figure, twice deposed from his ministry
(1695 and 1716), and once banished from Scotland for his
Jacobitism. On his death the claims of James's half-siblings to the estates caused legal and financial difficul-ties inherited by James's son. Not until 1782, after mortga-ging his properties for £3000 to pay debts, was James Bur-nett the younger (now Lord Monboddo) finally recognized
as heir, not to his father but to his grandfather.

Burnett was tutored at home, principally by Dr Francis
Skene (afterwards professor of civil and natural history at
Marischal College, Aberdeen), but he also attended Laur-encekirk parish school. From 1728 to 1732 he studied at

James Burnett, Lord Monboddo (*bap.* 1714, *d.* 1799), by John Brown

King's College, Aberdeen. Excelling in Greek, he was influenced by the primitivist Thomas Blackwell (1701–1757), professor of Greek at Marischal, a devotee of the third earl of Shaftesbury's Hellenism whose interests included the history of society and the origin of language. Before going to study Roman law in the Netherlands—at Groningen, where he registered on 20 September 1733, and possibly also at Leiden—Burnett was evidently tutored by Thomas Ruddiman, keeper of the Advocates' Library, Edinburgh, and formerly schoolmaster at Laurencekirk. After his return to Scotland he passed the civil law examination on 12 February 1737, and was admitted to the Faculty of Advocates on 17 February.

During the Jacobite rising of 1745–6 Burnett went to London, and made friends with the Scottish poets James Thomson, David Mallet, and John Armstrong, and with Shaftesbury's nephew James 'Hermes' Harris, who was to be a major influence. In his later years he visited London regularly during the spring vacation, becoming a celebrity in literary circles. He was received at court and made many distinguished friends with whom he corresponded, among them Bishop Samuel Horsley, Richard Price, Sir George Baker, Sir Joseph Banks, and Sir William Jones. He also sometimes visited Oxford, where his disciples included Thomas Burgess and George Isaac Huntingford.

After the 'Forty-Five, as the Scottish Enlightenment unfolded and Scottish jurisprudence entered its classical period, Burnett distinguished himself in the social and intellectual life of Edinburgh. A brilliant controversialist, he became known for his wit, learning, eloquence, and

eccentricity in social and literary clubs, and, later, for his 'learned suppers' in emulation of the ancients at 13 St John Street, Canongate. Regular guests included friends such as Joseph Black, Dr John Hope, James Hutton, William Smellie, Dugald Stewart, and James Boswell. As a curator of the Advocates' Library (1751–6), he removed examples of French *belles-lettres* ordered by David Hume as unworthy of a 'learned library'. In the same year, 1754, he became a founder member of the leading literary club, the Select Society, which included Adam Smith, William Robertson, Burnett's literary rival Lord Kames, and David Hume, his philosophical adversary.

Burnett was preoccupied with his health, and, like other primitivists, also with what he saw as modern luxury and decadence. Extremely abstemious, he exercised naked in the open air, took cold baths, and—as the ancients did not use coaches—rode to London regardless of the weather. Every autumn he visited Monboddo, dressed as a farmer, and lived frugally like his ancestors, 'who were better men than we', as he told Dr Johnson during his visit with Boswell in 1773 (*Boswell's Journal*, 53–8). He did his best to improve his meagre estates, but was more concerned for his tenants than for his annual rent roll, which apparently never exceeded £300.

On 1 May 1758 Burnett married Elizabeth, daughter of Lieutenant Farquharson and evidently a relative of the Keith family, earls Marischal. Tragically, Elizabeth died after giving birth in 1766, and their son Arthur died aged eleven in 1774. In 1780 their elder daughter, Helen (*d.* 1833), eloped with Burnett's clerk, Kirkpatrick Williamson, later keeper of the outer house rolls in the court of session. Their younger daughter, Eliza (1766–1790), was a famous beauty celebrated by Robert Burns in his 'Address to Edinburgh' and in an elegy on her early death (R. Burns, *Works*, 1871, 1.181, 2.154–5).

Between 1762 and 1767 Burnett made his name in the controversial Douglas cause. He three times visited Paris to gather evidence and his persistence was largely responsible for the final success of the Douglas family (to which he was related) on appeal to the House of Lords. On 12 February 1767 Burnett—already sheriff of Kincardineshire since 5 August 1760—was raised to the bench as an ordinary lord of session, taking the title Lord Monboddo.

The large collection of Monboddo papers in the National Library of Scotland reveals that the six volumes of his uncompleted major work, *Of the Origin and Progress of Language* (1773–92), owe much to the Advocates' Library, Scottish humanist jurisprudence, Select Society debates, and his visits to Paris where he saw Buffon's stuffed chimpanzee and interviewed a celebrated 'wild girl'—interviews described in his introduction to *Account of a Savage Girl Caught Wild in the Woods of Champagne* (1768), a translation by his clerk, William Robertson, of Charles-Marie de la Condamine's account of her. In Paris Monboddo also borrowed books on 'barbarous' languages and read Charles de Brosses's influential *Traité de la formation méchanique des langues* (1765), which prompted him to refute its Lockian theories by adopting the same historical method to reinstate Aristotle's unfashionable philosophy in a Platonized form.

Inspired by Rousseau's *Discours sur l'inégalité* (1755), Monboddo's first volume (1773) traces the natural history of man using data from travel books, Buffon's *Histoire naturelle* (1749–1804) and, in his second, revised, edition (1774), from Edward Tyson's *Orang-Outang* (1699). His controversial claims about men with tails and the humanity of the 'orang-outang' (chimpanzee) were ridiculed by Dr Johnson and Lord Kames, among many others. Monboddo argued that language was invented and that man was a wild animal until humanized by civil society and the arts. By means of the faculty of abstraction, man's mind and language gradually transcended sense and matter, finally reaching the Aristotelian categories—which enabled philosophers to invent Greek and Sanskrit, the only languages completely free from barbarity. Volume two (1774; 2nd edn, 1809) is an Aristotelian universal grammar influenced by James Harris's *Hermes* (1751). Possibly anticipating the research of his correspondent Sir William Jones, it recognizes the affinity of Greek and Sanskrit, identifying Egypt as the cradle of civilization and their ultimate source. The four remaining volumes constitute an Aristotelian philosophical rhetoric based on Cicero. Volume three was published in 1776 (2nd edn, 1786), volume four in 1787, volume five in 1789, and volume six in 1792.

Essentially an attack on Locke's fashionable theory of ideas as the source of scepticism and materialism in Hume and the French Enlightenment, Monboddo's work was recognized in France, Italy, and Germany. It was translated in part into German by E. A. Schmidt (1784–6) and praised by J. G. von Herder, who attributed the British notices of the first volume to a conspiracy in defence of Locke. British criticisms, which included vicious attacks in the *Edinburgh Magazine and Review* (1773–6) and in *Dissertations: Moral and Critical* (1783) by his friend James Beattie, culminated in John Horne Tooke's Lockian assault on Monboddo and Harris in *The Diversions of Purley* (1786). A century later, the ninth edition of the *Encyclopaedia Britannica* (1875–89) found neo-Kantianism implicit in Monboddo's 'intimate knowledge of Greek philosophy' and Darwinism in 'His idea of studying man as one of the animals, and of collecting facts about savage tribes to throw light on the problems of civilisation' (*DNB*).

With the growing interest in the Scottish Enlightenment, particularly since the 1960s, appreciation of Monboddo's anthropological and proto-evolutionary speculations has increased. And although his Aristotelianism made him exceptional among the Scottish philosophical historians, modern historians of linguistics have seen his work as the major British contribution to the Enlightenment debate on the origin of language. Monboddo's other work, *Antient Metaphysics* (6 vols., 1779–99), a critique of the philosophical implications of Newtonian science in the light of Greek philosophy, has, despite Herder's approval, been largely ignored.

Fastidious in dress, Monboddo was under 5 feet tall with a lively expression and a long, aquiline nose. The best likenesses are the pencil portrait by John Brown (1752–1787) in the Scottish National Portrait Gallery, and the spirited engraving by C. Sherwin based on it. There is also a pencil portrait supposedly by or after Sir Joshua Reynolds, and John Kay's *Original Portraits and Caricature Etchings* (3rd edn, 1877) contains four brilliant caricatures.

Monboddo died at his home, 13 St John Street, after a paralytic stroke, on 25 or 26 May 1799, in his eighty-fifth year, and was buried in Greyfriars churchyard, Edinburgh. According to a deed in the National Archives of Scotland dated 22 June 1796, he left his properties, which had been mortgaged in 1781, to his only surviving child, Helen, and her husband, Kirkpatrick Williamson, on condition that he took the 'surname, arms and designation of Burnett of Monboddo' (Scot. RO, RD3/285/fol. 548).

IAIN MAXWELL HAMMETT

Sources NA Scot. · E. L. Cloyd, *James Burnett, Lord Monboddo* (1972) · I. M. Hammett, 'Lord Monboddo's *Of the origin and progress of language*: its sources, genesis and background, with special attention to the Advocates' Library', PhD diss., U. Edin., 1985 · W. Knight, *Lord Monboddo and some of his contemporaries* (1900) · J. Allardyce, ed., *The family of Burnett of Leys: with collateral branches*, New Spalding Club, 22 (1901) · old parish registers (Fordoun and Edinburgh), General Register Office for Scotland, Edinburgh · *DNB* · *Scots Magazine*, 61 (1799), 352 · *Scots Magazine*, 61 (1799), 727–31 · A. Tayler and H. Tayler, eds., *The house of Forbes*, Third Spalding Club, 8 (1937) · *Boswell's journal of a tour to the Hebrides with Samuel Johnson*, ed. F. A. Pottle and C. H. Bennett (1963), vol. 9 of *The Yale editions of the private papers of James Boswell*, trade edn (1950–89)

Archives NL Scot., personal and family corresp.; legal papers; literary MSS | Birm. CL, Hagley MSS, corresp. with Lord Lyttelton · Bodl. Oxf., corresp. with Thomas Burgess, Eng. Letters MSS, c.133, fols. 136–89; c.140, fol. 46 · General Register Office for Scotland, Edinburgh, letters relating to the Douglas cause · priv. coll., letters to earl of Southesk · U. Aberdeen, King's College, Beattie corresp. · U. Edin., Grim Thorkelin corresp.

Likenesses C. Sherwin, engraving, 1787 (after J. Brown), BM · R. Stanier, engraving, 1790 (after J. Brown), Hult. Arch., BM, Scot. NPG · W. Ridley, engraving, 1799 (after J. Brown), BM · J. Edgar, group portrait, wash drawing, c.1854 (*Burns at an evening party of Lord Monboddo's*, 1786), Scot. NPG · T. R. Spence, stained glass, 1895, Marischal College, Aberdeen · J. Brown, pencil drawing, Scot. NPG [*see illus.*] · J. Kay, caricatures, etchings, Scot. NPG; repro. in J. Kay, *Original portraits and caricature etchings*, 3rd edn (1877), 4 · J. Reynolds?, pencil drawing, repro. in C. H. Burnett, *The Burnett family* (1950), 46; formerly at Crathes Castle, Banchory, Kincardineshire, Scotland · W. S. Watson, group portrait, oils (*The inauguration of Robert Burns as Poet Laureate of the Lodge of Canongate, Kilwinning*, 1787), Scot. NPG · chalk and wash drawing (after Stanier), NG Scot. · engraving (after pencil drawing by Sir Joshua Reynolds?), repro. in Knight, *Lord Monboddo*, frontispiece · miniature, V&A

Burnett, John (1729–1784), philanthropist, was born in Aberdeen, the son of a city merchant; after education in Aberdeen, Burnett himself began a career in trade in 1750, shortly after the failure of his father's business due to a fall in prices—a result of Britain's involvement in the War of the Austrian Succession. Burnett enjoyed success, and was involved chiefly in fisheries and manufacturing. In 1773 his brother returned to Scotland from India, having acquired some wealth. The brothers then paid off their father's debts of £7000–£8000, each paying half. Burnett was known as a shrewd businessman, but returned any profits which exceeded his expectations. In adult life he gave up the Episcopal church, in which he had been raised, but continued to provide religious instruction to his servants, and insisted that they go to church even if he did not. His personal religious views appear to have been deistic.

Burnett may have been influenced by the example of John Howard, the philanthropist, whom he probably met in 1776 in Scotland, and took an interest in various charitable movements. Burnett is said to have given £300 annually to the poor, and devoted two hours a day to listening to their appeals. He died unmarried on 9 November 1784. He directed that part of his estates should be applied for the benefit of the poor of Aberdeen and the neighbourhood, as well as that of prisoners and lunatics, and part to a fund for inoculation (the last was afterwards applied to vaccination). The remaining income was to accumulate for a period, and then to be given as a first and second prize for essays in proof of the existence of a supreme creator, upon grounds both of reason and revelation. In 1815 the first prize was won by the principal of Aberdeen University, William Laurence Brown, who prefaced his essay with a biographical sketch of Burnett. The second prize in this inaugural year was awarded to John Bird Sumner, later archbishop of Canterbury. The use of the funds was later expanded to support lectures on aspects of science, history, or archaeology for the purpose of illustrating natural theology, and were first delivered at Aberdeen in November 1883.   [ANON.], rev. ALEXANDER DU TOIT

Sources W. L. Brown, 'Memoir relating to John Burnett Esq of Dens', *An essay on the existence of a supreme creator* (1816) · 'Royal commission on endowed institutions in Scotland: second report', *Parl. papers* (1881), 36.237, C. 2790 · L. R. Timperley, ed., *A directory of land-ownership in Scotland, c.1770*, Scottish RS, new ser., 5 (1976) · *Daily Free Press* [Aberdeen] (6 Nov 1883)

Wealth at death £683 18s. 4d.; estates of Dens and Knock in Aberdeenshire; plus estate in Buchan; also charitable bequests: Brown; Timperley

Burnett, John (1764?–1810), judge, was born in Aberdeen, where his father, William Burnett, was procurator-at-law. He was admitted advocate at Edinburgh on 10 December 1785, and was appointed advocate-depute in 1792 and sheriff of East Lothian in October 1803. In April 1810 he became judge-admiral of Scotland. He was also for some time counsel for the city of Aberdeen. He died on 8 December 1810 while his work, *Criminal Law of Scotland* (1811), was being prepared for publication; though in certain respects considered imperfect and misleading, it was none the less held to be a work of great merit, especially since it was one of the earliest attempts to form a satisfactory collection of decisions in criminal cases.

T. F. HENDERSON, rev. ERIC METCALFE

Sources Irving, *Scots.* · *Catalogue of the printed books in the library of the Faculty of Advocates*, 7 vols. (1863–79) · W. Anderson, *The Scottish nation*, 3 vols. (1866–77)

Wealth at death £4350 2s. 1d.: inventory, SC 70/1/2, 1812, Scotland

Burnett, John (1842–1914), trade union leader and civil servant, was born on 21 June 1842, at Alnwick, Northumberland, of unknown parentage. He was educated at the school in Alnwick endowed by the duke of Northumberland. Orphaned at the age of twelve, he went to live with an uncle on Tyneside, where he worked as an errand-boy before becoming an engineering apprentice when he was fourteen. During that time he also attended evening classes and became prominent in the Newcastle Mechanics' Institute. In early manhood, while employed in the engineering works first of Sir Charles Mark Palmer and then of Sir William Armstrong (1810–1900), Burnett became a leader among the skilled workers on Tyneside. In 1864 he took a prominent part in the local campaign for the Saturday half-holiday and two years later in abortive attempts to secure a reduction in the engineering workers' working week. His local reputation was enhanced during the campaign for parliamentary reform in 1866–7.

In 1871 growing industrial prosperity produced renewed demands for a shorter working week, a theme that had the advantage of avoiding sectional differences between skilled and unskilled workers. A successful campaign on Wearside secured a reduction to fifty-four hours, and acted as the curtain-raiser to a more prolonged and intense struggle on Tyneside, in which Burnett was the principal leader and spokesman of the Tyneside engineering workers. Employers' intransigence led to a major strike, lasting from May until October 1871, in which the Tyneside engineering workers, organized in the Nine Hours League, achieved a considerable victory. The strike's leadership was cleverer than that of the employers, headed by Sir William Armstrong, whose prolonged refusal to negotiate and tactics of intimidation alienated public opinion. The strike's leaders managed to raise some £20,000 to maintain their followers during the strike, and this task was eased by the willingness of engineering employers elsewhere to recruit many of the strikers. Burnett was largely responsible for the strikers' public image of moderation and law-abidingness, while in practice the employers' attempts to break the strike by importing blacklegs was frustrated by efficient strong-arm tactics on the part of the strikers and their supporters.

The employers found themselves isolated and heavily criticized in both the local and national press. Joseph Cowen, a wealthy local radical MP and owner of the principal Tyneside newspaper, gave the strike invaluable support. Although the strike leaders were keen unionists, only a small minority of Tyneside engineering workers were union members and the control of the strike was always firmly in the hands of the local leadership headed by Burnett. After five months the resistance of the employers crumbled and the shorter working week was won. The strike provoked widespread interest and served as an important symbolic victory for labour, as well as encouraging attempts to obtain cuts in working hours in other spheres.

After the reluctant climb-down by the engineering employers, it was inexpedient for Burnett to return to Armstrong's works. For some time he was employed by Cowen and then in 1875 he succeeded William Allan as general secretary to the Amalgamated Society of Engineers (ASE) and as treasurer of the parliamentary committee of the Trades Union Congress which entailed a move to

London. His period of office at the ASE was marked by friction with some of the union's militant sections and by continual overwork. In the spring of 1886, the Liberal government, recognizing its lack of effective machinery to deal with labour questions, set up a small labour bureau within the Board of Trade. Burnett was involved in the discussions preceding this decision. The minister responsible, A. J. Mundella, had come to know and respect him during the 1871 strike on Tyneside, and appointed him as the first official labour correspondent. When the bureau was expanded into a larger labour department in 1893, Burnett was promoted to be its first chief correspondent. These were Liberal appointments, but it was a Conservative administration that appointed him to the important royal commission on labour in 1891.

In his new role as a senior civil servant, Burnett produced perceptive reports on labour conditions and associated topics. His own annual report for 1900 provided a mass of information on trade union membership and finances. He was much in demand as a successful mediator in industrial disputes. Like contemporary leaders of the Northumberland and Durham miners' unions, such as Thomas Burt, Charles Fenwick, John Wilson, and William Crawford, Burnett was something of a show-piece working man of the late Victorian establishment, often referred to as proof that a worker could rise to a position of considerable respectability and public responsibility. He exemplified an important strand in labour leadership. Although a loyal and devoted trade unionist, capable of tough bargaining and sophisticated industrial tactics, he believed in the existence of a national consensus in both political and industrial relationships. While he was never a revolutionary, his services to the labour movement in Britain were considerable, though it may be that his greatest achievement was his leadership of the great Nine Hours strike on Tyneside in 1871.

Burnett retired in 1906, but remained active in the labour movement until his sudden death in Woodlands Road, Putney, on 30 January 1914, an event marked by many tributes to his abilities, his life of service, and his essential good sense and moderation. He was buried at Nunhead cemetery. He was survived by his wife, Jean, and three children.   NORMAN MCCORD

Sources E. Allen and others, *The north-east engineers' strikes of 1871: the Nine Hours' League* (1971) • *The Times* (2 Feb 1914) • *Newcastle Weekly Chronicle* (7 Feb 1914) • *Newcastle Weekly Chronicle* (14 Feb 1914) • *Newcastle Weekly Chronicle* (21 Feb 1914) • J. A. M. Caldwell, 'The genesis of the ministry of labour', *Public Administration*, 37 (1959), 371–82 • R. Davidson, 'Llewellyn Smith, the labour department and government growth, 1886–1909', *Studies in the growth of nineteenth-century government*, ed. G. Sutherland (1972), 227–62 • *DLB*, vol. 2 • J. Burnett, *Nine hours movement: a history of the engineers' strike, Newcastle and Gateshead* (1872) • d. cert.

Likenesses photograph, repro. in *Newcastle Weekly Chronicle* (7 Feb 1914)

Wealth at death £6000 11s. 5d.: probate, 12 Feb 1914, *CGPLA Eng. & Wales*

Burnett, Dame (Annie) Maud (1863–1950), local politician, was born at 10 Prior's Terrace, Tynemouth, Northumberland, on 27 February 1863, the second daughter in the family of two daughters and two sons of Jacob Burnett (1825–1896), and his first wife, Annie Daglish (1830–1866); there were a further daughter and son from his second marriage. Her father, the last of the Tyneside alkali manufacturers and a shipowner, was also a patron of the arts and a collector of pre-Raphaelite paintings, who had moved to Tynemouth by 1861. Maud was educated first at Miss Baker's school and then at Miss Hoald's school, both in Tynemouth, and completed her education at Vevey, Switzerland. She honed her public skills with work at the church of the Holy Saviour, Tynemouth, a Bible class in North Shields, and voluntary welfare work of various kinds. Though said to espouse no particular party she followed her family's political sympathies and was honorary secretary of the Tynemouth Women's Liberal Federation from 1895 to 1910, assisting at three parliamentary general elections.

When in 1902 it became necessary for there to be two women on municipal education committees Maud Burnett was co-opted onto that for Tynemouth. In 1907 she founded a branch, at Tynemouth, of the Women's Local Government Society (WLGS) and in 1909 she stood unsuccessfully as an independent candidate for election to Tynemouth council. She was returned in the following year, with Liberal support, for the Dockray ward, becoming the first woman in the north of England to become a municipal councillor, following the passage in 1907 of the WLGS's bill allowing women ratepayers to be elected. She was immediately placed on the committees for health, finance, small-holdings and allotments, public libraries, education, local pensions, and distress. In 1915 she was made deputy chairman of the committee for the care of the mentally defective. She also concerned herself with the provision of welfare for mothers and babies (including play centres) and with the issue of women's employment. Described as a 'charming suffragette' (*Tyneside Weekly News*, 1 Jan 1909) she supported the non-militant campaign for women's parliamentary suffrage.

During the First World War Maud Burnett was president of the War Savings Association in Tynemouth and chairman of committees concerned with war aims, food control, and food economy. She served on the YMCA committee on comforts for the forces, and on the naval and military war pensions committee. For her war work she was created DBE in 1918. She was appointed a JP on 28 August 1920 and retired from Tynemouth council in 1921 to resume voluntary work within the town. She was re-elected to the council in 1926, and served as mayor of Tynemouth in 1928–9 and 1929–30, being the first woman to hold that office. She finally retired from the council in 1934. Comparing her municipal record with the rest of Tyneside there were women councillors at Newcastle upon Tyne by 1919 and in Gateshead by 1920, the latter being in 1929 the first Tyneside municipality to raise a woman to the aldermanic bench.

Indomitable in old age, Dame Maud Burnett ruled the women's organizations of Tynemouth village with a rod of iron. In her seventies, when she lost her eyesight, she learned Braille and took up blind welfare. She died at her home, Collingwood House, Collingwood Terrace, Tyne-mouth, on 17 November 1950 and was buried at Preston cemetery, North Shields, on 21 November.

C. M. FRASER

Sources *Shields Evening News* (17 Nov 1950) · newspaper cuttings file, North Tyneside Central Library, Local studies · *WWW* · b. cert. · d. cert. · P. Hollis, *Ladies elect: women in English local government, 1865–1914* (1987) · D. S. Macleod, 'Avant-garde patronage in the north east', *Pre-Raphaelites: painters and patrons in the north east* (1989) [Laing Art Gallery, Newcastle upon Tyne] · Ward's Trade Director-ies, 1909–1935 · census returns, 1871, 1881
Likenesses F. Eastman, portrait
Wealth at death £3237 5*s.* 6*d.*: probate, 31 March 1951, *CGPLA Eng. & Wales*

Burnett, Sir Robert Lindsay (1887–1959), naval officer, was born at Old Deer, Aberdeenshire, on 22 July 1887, the fourth son of John Alexander Burnett, of Kemnay, Aber-deenshire, and his wife, Charlotte Susan, daughter of Arthur Forbes Gordon, of Rayne, Aberdeenshire. Sir Charles Stuart *Burnett, air chief marshal, was an elder brother. At the early age of seven he announced his inten-tion of joining the navy, and after education at Bedford School and Eastman's he entered the *Britannia* in 1903. His academic progress was undistinguished, but he showed great promise as an all-round athlete, and after reaching the rank of lieutenant in 1910 he qualified as a physical training instructor. In the ensuing eight years he served mainly in small ships, saw action in the Heligoland bight and at the Dogger Bank engagement, gained his first com-mand (a torpedo boat) in 1915, and subsequently went on to command destroyers with the Grand Fleet until 1918. In 1915 he married Ethel Constance, the daughter of R. H. Shaw. They had no children.

With subsequently only one break of two years in com-mand of a sloop on the South Africa station, Burnett was continually employed until 1928 in physical training appointments, being promoted commander in 1923 while acting as secretary to the Sports Control Board. He did much in this period towards reorganizing the physical training branch of the navy. He himself also won the sabre championship at the royal tournament and became a qualified referee for association and rugby football, hockey, water polo, and boxing. In addition, he developed his admirable bent as a producer of amateur theatricals.

Burnett gained his second selective promotion, to cap-tain, in December 1930 at the conclusion of a successful commission as executive officer of the *Rodney*. In the ensu-ing eleven years in that rank he commanded a destroyer flotilla on the China station, did two years as the director of physical training and sports, commanded the cruiser flagship of the South African squadron, and finally was appointed commodore of the royal naval barracks at Chat-ham in 1939, where he had the arduous task of mobilizing the personnel of the east country manning port for war.

Although Burnett himself had more than once in his time as a captain expressed surprise at his progressive pro-motions, his superiors fully appreciated his zeal, energy, and ability, and after only eighteen months at Chatham he was specially promoted to the acting rank of rear-admiral

Sir Robert Lindsay Burnett (1887–1959), by Walter Stoneman, 1942

in November 1940 (confirmed two months later) on appointment as flag officer of the Home Fleet mine-laying squadron engaged on the hazardous task of laying the deep minefield in northern waters. On completion of this task in 1942 he became flag officer, Home Fleet destroyer flotillas, and a year later flag officer, 10th cruiser squad-ron, continuing in this appointment on promotion to vice-admiral (1943) until he left the fleet in mid-1944 to become the commander-in-chief, south Atlantic, respon-sible for the security of the sea route round the Cape.

It was especially during those fateful years of 1941 to 1944, when a hard-pressed Royal Navy faced its greatest challenge, that Burnett rendered outstanding service and played a leading part in the saga of the Arctic convoys, when the enemy could choose its own time and place at which to bring superior force to bear upon the lifeline to Russia. These circumstances called for the physical endur-ance, capable leadership, and readiness to fight back whatever the odds which Burnett notably possessed. His indomitable spirit and simple philosophy of immediate aggressive tactics inspired others and gained for him the trust and loyalty of those who served under him in the course of these exhausting operations to reach north Russia and return.

There were occasions on which Burnett's determination was particularly put to the test. In September 1942 he fought a convoy of forty ships through in the face of four days of sustained submarine and massed air attack for a loss of thirteen merchantmen, and then saw the returning empty convoy back. On new year's eve 1942, in the Barents Sea, his covering force of two cruisers finally managed to reach another convoy with such an offensive impact that the greatly superior enemy surface force retired in disorder and the merchant ships reached port unscathed. On Boxing day a year later, off North Cape, again in midwinter, he so skilfully handled his covering force of three cruisers that the *Scharnhorst* was twice forced to turn back from the convoy without achieving any success, and was finally delivered up to destruction by the commander-in-chief's flagship.

Burnett was promoted admiral in 1946 and in the following year took up his last appointment, the Plymouth command, which he held for three years, being placed on the retired list in May 1950. He was subsequently chairman of the White Fish Authority for four years.

Throughout his service Burnett was sustained by a firm religious belief from which he got much help and comfort, and he expected others to try to measure up to his own high moral standards and example of officer-like behaviour and appearance. He loved the navy, was easily moved to emotion, and was a first-class speaker in a manner which carried conviction. He died suddenly at 116 Pall Mall, Westminster, London, on 2 July 1959, his wife surviving him.

During his career he was successively appointed OBE (1925), CB (1942), to the DSO (1943), KBE (1944), KCB and CStJ (1945), and GBE (1950). He received an honorary LLD from Aberdeen (1944) and high orders from the Soviet Union, Greece, and the Netherlands.

A. W. CLARKE, rev.

Sources S. W. Roskill, *The war at sea, 1939–1945*, 3 vols. in 4 (1954–61) · private information (1971) · personal knowledge (1971) · *WWW* · *The Times* (3 July 1959) · *CGPLA Eng. & Wales* (1959)

Archives IWM · priv. coll., corresp. and papers | FILM BFI NFTVA, news footage · IWM FVA, news footage | SOUND IWM SA, Naval operations, IWM, 20 Feb 1991, 11895

Likenesses W. Stoneman, photograph, 1942, NPG [*see illus.*] · E. Rowarth, oils, 1950, NMM · W. Stoneman, photograph, 1953, NPG · W. Dring, pastel drawing, IWM

Wealth at death £2416 1s. 5d.: probate, 9 Sept 1959, *CGPLA Eng. & Wales*

Burnett, Sir William (1779–1861), naval physician, was born on 16 January 1779 at Montrose. He was educated at Montrose grammar school, and was apprenticed to a local surgeon, Dr Hunter. He then went to Edinburgh to pursue his medical studies but, soon after, entered the navy as surgeon's mate on board the *Edgar*. Later he served as assistant surgeon in the *Goliath* under Sir John Jervis, and in 1798 he was promoted surgeon. Burnett was present at St Vincent, and the siege of Cadiz. He served with distinction at the Nile and at Trafalgar, and received a CB and four war medals for his services.

From 1805 to 1810 Burnett was in charge of the hospitals for prisoners of war at Portsmouth and Forton. In 1807 he married Maria (1784–1859), only daughter of Isaac and Elizabeth Baker; they were to have a son and four daughters. In 1810 Burnett was appointed physician and inspector of hospitals to the Mediterranean Fleet and was awarded his MD by St Andrews University; in 1825 he also became MD at Aberdeen.

Burnett returned to England towards the end of 1813 owing to poor health, but in March 1814 he was able to undertake the medical charge of the Russian fleet in the Medway, which was suffering severely from fever. In the same year he published *An Account of the Bilious Remittent Fever in the Mediterranean Fleet of 1810–13*. He combined with this the charge of prisoners of war at Chatham, among whom a virulent fever was raging. His account of this epidemic appeared in 1831.

Burnett then settled at Chichester where he was physician to the general dispensary. In 1822 Lord Melville offered him a seat on the victualling board of the navy. Later Burnett became physician-general of the navy, and in this capacity he introduced a number of reforms: he required regular classified returns of diseases from each naval medical officer, thus rendering it possible to obtain accurate information about the health of the navy; he urged that a hospital be built at Chatham to replace the hospital ship then in use; and he introduced the humane treatment of naval 'lunatics' at Haslar. The codes of instructions to naval medical officers of hospitals and ships were also revised and improved by him and he was instrumental in improving the status of assistant surgeons. In 1841 the naval medical corps expressed their gratitude to Burnett for his work on their behalf when they presented him with his portrait, painted by Sir Martin Shee.

Burnett retired from service in 1855. During his career he received a number of honours: he was knighted in May 1831 and appointed physician-in-ordinary to King William IV in 1835; he was made KCH in 1835, and KCB in 1850; and he was FRCP, FRCS of Edinburgh and Dublin, and FRS in 1833.

Although Burnett was regarded as a sound administrator, his career was not without controversy. He clashed with Sir William Pym over the nature of yellow fever, Burnett maintaining that the disease was not contagious and that quarantine measures were inappropriate. Additionally, his commercial involvement in the patenting of a solution of zinc chloride for use as a preservative and disinfectant was found distasteful by many of his colleagues.

Burnett died on 16 February 1861, at Chichester, and was buried at Boxgrove, Sussex. A memorial to Burnett and his wife was erected at Boxgrove by their son, William, vicar of the same.

G. T. BETTANY, rev. CLAIRE E. J. HERRICK

Sources H. D. Rolleston, 'Sir William Burnett, KCB, KCH, MD, FRS, FRCP, the first medical director-general of the Royal Navy', *JRNMS*, 8 (1922), 1–10 · 'Biographical sketch of Sir William Burnett … director-general of the medical department of the navy', *The Lancet* (16 Nov 1850), 558–63 · *Medical Times and Gazette* (2 March

1861), 240–41 • Munk, *Roll* • *BMJ* (23 Feb 1861), 213 • S. Jenkinson, 'Sir William Burnett, KCB, KCH, MD, FRS', *JRNMS*, 26 (1940), 3–15 • *Medical Times and Gazette* (23 Feb 1861), 214 • J. J. Keevil, J. L. S. Coulter, and C. Lloyd, *Medicine and the navy, 1200–1900*, 4: *1815–1900* (1963) • J. Shepherd, *The Crimean doctors: a history of the British medical services in the Crimean War*, 2 vols. (1991) • *The Lancet* (23 Feb 1861)

Archives W. Sussex RO, letters to duke of Richmond

Likenesses H. Cousins, engraving, 1844 (after M. A. Shee, 1841), repro. in Jenkinson, 'Sir William Burnett', 2 • Mayall, daguerreotype and crayon, 1850, repro. in 'Biographical sketch of Sir William Burnett', 559 • T. Bridgeford, lithograph, Professional Scientific and Literary Portrait Gallery

Wealth at death £5000: resworn probate, May 1864, *CGPLA Eng. & Wales* (1861)

Burney, Sir Cecil, first baronet (1858–1929), naval officer, was born in Jersey on 15 May 1858, the second son of Captain Charles Burney RN, for many years superintendent of Greenwich Hospital school, and his wife, Catherine Elizabeth, daughter of Charles Jones, of La Ferrière, Jersey. He was educated at the Royal Naval Academy, Gosport, and entered the *Britannia* as a naval cadet in July 1871. He went to sea as a midshipman in October 1873, served for three years in the flagships of the Pacific and American stations, and was promoted sub-lieutenant in October 1877. The next three years were spent in educational courses and in short appointments in the troop ship *Serapis* and in the royal yacht, from which he was promoted to the rank of lieutenant. He then joined the corvette *Carysfort*, one of the vessels of Lord Clanwilliam's detached squadron, which was afterwards merged into the Mediterranean Fleet during the Egyptian campaign of 1882. This gave Burney an opportunity of war service ashore, and he was in charge of a Gatling gun at the actions of Tell al-Mahuta and Qassasin in August 1882. In the same year he accompanied the mission led by Charles Warren across the desert in order to capture the Arabs who had seized and murdered Professor Edward Henry Palmer, Captain William John Gill, and Lieutenant Harold Charrington; he also took part in the operations against Osman Digna near Suakin in 1884.

Burney next spent two years in the gunnery schools at Portsmouth and Devonport. Then followed over five and a half years' service as gunnery lieutenant in the North American, reserve, and channel squadrons. On promotion to commander in January 1893 he was appointed to the *Hawke* and served in the Mediterranean for three years; and in 1896 he went to Portland in command of the boys' training establishment in the *Boscawen* and *Minotaur* for three and a half years until September 1899. He was promoted captain in January 1898. After commanding the *Hawke* in the naval manoeuvres of 1900, he commissioned the *Sappho* for service on the south-east coast of America, but was soon transferred to the Cape station during the Second South African War. His ship struck the Durban bar when in the charge of a pilot on 3 May 1901, and Burney had to bring her home. In May 1902 he became flag-captain to Rear-Admiral Atkinson-Willes in the Home Fleet, and remained with him and his successor, Rear-Admiral Poë, until June 1904. He then spent a year (1904–5) in command of the ex-Chilean battleship *Triumph* in the

Channel Fleet. His successful work in training boys at Portland led to his appointment in July 1905 to the *Impregnable* as inspecting captain of all boys' training ships, a post that he held until his promotion to flag rank in 1909. He thus spent, in all, six years in supervising the training of boys.

Burney's first appointment to flag rank was in the Plymouth division of the Home Fleet for one year. From February 1911, when he took command of the 5th cruiser squadron, he was continuously on full pay for nine years. At the end of 1911 he took command of the Atlantic Fleet, with the acting rank of vice-admiral; he transferred to the 3rd battle squadron in 1912, shortly before reaching confirmed vice-admiral's rank. This squadron was on special service in the Mediterranean, and the disturbances that arose in Montenegro and Albania at the close of the second Balkan war led to the dispatch, arranged by the British foreign secretary, Sir Edward Grey, of an international naval force to Antivari on the Montenegrin coast in April 1913. Burney's squadron was sent in order to secure that an Englishman should be senior officer of the combined fleet. Burney took command and handled the highly delicate and difficult situation, in which his firm manner and rugged mien stood him in good stead, with great ability, and he received a special commendation both from the Foreign Office and from the Admiralty. He had to secure unanimity of action between the naval forces of the five powers represented, as well as resolve the differences between the turbulent Balkan states ashore. He established a pacific blockade of the coast during April and May of 1913, and then from May to November commanded the international force occupying Scutari, which the Montenegrins had captured, until the trouble was finally settled by the conclusion of peace. He was created KCB in the summer of 1913, and on the termination of the Scutari affair he was gazetted KCMG.

On his return to England at the end of 1913 Burney took over the command of the Second and Third fleets, then in partial reserve, and the early part of 1914 was occupied in preparing for the test mobilization of that summer. On the outbreak of the First World War in August these fleets were organized as the Channel Fleet, with the duty of protecting the channel from enemy raids. In December 1914 Burney went to the 1st battle squadron of the Grand Fleet, as second in command under Lord Jellicoe. At the battle of Jutland (31 May 1916) his squadron was the rear of the line, and was more heavily engaged than the rest of the battleships of the main fleet. His flagship, the *Marlborough*, was torpedoed, and during the night he transferred his flag to the *Revenge*. He was promoted admiral a few days after the battle of Jutland, and was made GCMG for his services in the action. Jellicoe had complete confidence in Burney, but that confidence was not shared by many other flag-officers, who were apprehensive that Burney might succeed to command of the Grand Fleet. He was regarded as overcautious, lacking in initiative, and burdened by ill health.

In November 1916, when Jellicoe was appointed first sea lord, Burney joined the Board of Admiralty as second sea lord. However, the prime minister, Lloyd George, and Sir Eric Geddes, who became first lord in July 1917, grew anxious to replace him by a younger, and in their opinion more efficient, man. Consequently, and despite Jellicoe's effort to keep him, when the board was reorganized the following September, Burney was relieved. Shortly afterwards he was appointed commander-in-chief, coast of Scotland at Rosyth; there he remained until appointed in March 1919 to be commander-in-chief at Portsmouth. A year later, owing to prolonged ill health, he was relieved of the command at his own request. He was promoted admiral of the fleet in the following November, created a baronet for his war services in January 1921, and promoted to GCB in 1922. He died at his home, Upham House, Upham, Hampshire, on 5 June 1929. He was buried at Brookwood cemetery five days later.

Burney married in 1884 Lucinda Marion (d. 1944), second daughter of George Richards Burnett, of London; they had one son and two daughters. His son, Commander Charles Dennistoun *Burney RN (1888–1968), who succeeded to the baronetcy, invented during the First World War the paravane, a device for protecting ships against mines, and subsequently was a major supporter of projects for the commercial development of airships. His daughter Sybil Katherine Neville-*Rolfe (1885–1955) was founder of the Eugenics Society.

Burney was a fine seaman of the old school, with a deep sense of loyalty to his chiefs. In handling ships and fleets he had the natural ease and confidence of a born sailor. A man of powerful physique, in his early days he excelled in boxing and feats of strength. Although of somewhat austere demeanour, his patent sincerity won him the complete confidence and affection of many who served under him throughout his long sea service. There were others, particularly his fellow flag-officers, who tended to regard him as lacking in the qualities of personality and initiative necessary for the highest command, and as a trusted second in command to Jellicoe Burney probably reached the peak of his potential.

V. W. Baddeley, rev. Paul G. Halpern

Sources official records (1937) · private information (1937) · A. J. Marder, *From the Dreadnought to Scapa Flow: the Royal Navy in the Fisher era, 1904–1919*, 5 vols. (1961–70) · *The Times* (6 June 1929) · *The Jellicoe papers*, ed. A. T. Patterson, 2 vols., Navy RS, 108, 111 (1966–8) · *The Beatty papers: selections from the private and official correspondence of Admiral of the Fleet Earl Beatty*, ed. B. Ranft, 1, Navy RS, 128 (1989) · Burke, *Peerage* · G. Bennett, *Naval battles of the First World War*, rev. edn (1974) · WWW · H. C. Meyer [Charles Dennistoun Burney], *Airshipmen, businessmen and politics, 1890–1940* (1991) · *The Times* (7 June 1929)
Likenesses F. Dodd, charcoal and watercolour drawing, 1917, IWM · W. Stoneman, photograph, 1917, NPG · A. S. Cope, group portrait, oils, 1921 (*Naval officers of World War I, 1914–1918*), NPG · J. Lavery, oils, IWM
Wealth at death £2334 4s. 5d.: probate, 27 Dec 1929, *CGPLA Eng. & Wales*

Burney, Charles (1726–1814), musician and author, was born on 7 April 1726 in Raven Street, Shrewsbury, the fourth of six children of James Macburney (1678–1749), dancer, musician, and portraitist, and his second wife, Ann Cooper (c.1690–1775).

Charles Burney (1726–1814), by Sir Joshua Reynolds, 1781

Early career Little is known of Charles Burney's early life (the prefix Mac was dropped by the family about the time of his birth). For reasons that remain unknown, he and his brother Richard (1723–1792) were early on sent to the village of Condover near Shrewsbury and placed in the care of a Nurse Ball. While there, about 1737 Burney became a pupil at Shrewsbury Free School. Both boys remained with Ball until 1739, when Richard was sent to London and Charles joined his father in Chester. He began studies at Chester Free School on 25 December 1739. His talent for music had already manifested itself at Shrewsbury. His early musical training evidently did not include much music theory, as he later recollected being taught to play a chant on the Chester Cathedral organ by the organist, Mr Baker, 'before he knew his Gammut or the names of the keys' (*Memoirs of Dr Charles Burney*, 23). But his progress thereafter was such that in 1742 he returned to Shrewsbury as assistant to his half-brother James (1710–1789), organist at St Mary's Church. Although this work did not rise above a low level, Burney's experience of organ recitals given at Shrewsbury by William Felton of Hereford Cathedral and by William Hayes of Oxford University seems to have awakened a musical enthusiasm and ambition that led him to feverish study. None the less, in 1743 he returned to Chester, whose musical life was periodically enhanced by London musicians passing through on journeys to or from Ireland. Burney had already encountered Handel on such a journey in 1741, and in August 1744 Thomas Arne, London's leading composer save for Handel, likewise visited Chester: Burney was brought to his attention, and subsequently became his apprentice. In this role Burney gave lessons to Arne's pupils and wrote out scores and parts for, and occasionally played in, the orchestra of the Drury Lane theatre. Through Arne he met such composers as John Christopher Pepusch and literary men including David Garrick; but at a personal level Burney soon became discontented with Arne, whom he described as 'selfish and unprincipled' (ibid., 50) and despised for his womanizing. Perhaps fortunately, in the summer of 1746 he met the aristocrat Fulke Greville, following Greville's challenge to the harpsichord maker Jacob Kirkman to find him a musician of intellect as well as technical competence. Greville adopted Burney as a musical companion from 1746, regularly taking him to Bath and to his country seat of Wilbury in Wiltshire; and he subsequently paid Arne £300 at Michaelmas 1748 to release Burney from the remainder of his apprenticeship. In the event this brought Greville little benefit, since Burney was formally in his service for only a few months.

In late 1748 or early 1749 Greville was planning a long stay on the continent, and naturally expected Burney to go too. Burney had meanwhile fallen in love with Esther Sleepe (*bap.* 1725?, *d.* 1762), whom he had met through his brother Richard, and was not keen to leave her for such a long period as she was pregnant with their first child, Esther, who was born before the couple married, at St George's, Mayfair, on 25 June 1749. He accordingly asked, successfully, to be released from Greville's employ. His freedom left him without money or lodging, and in 1749 he applied to become organist of St Dionis Backchurch in Fenchurch Street, London, securing the vote for the position by a large majority in October that year. In addition to providing an income of £30 per annum, the post was useful for obtaining pupils and for establishing Burney as a performer on the organ. He also succeeded John Stanley at concerts held at the King's Arms tavern, and renewed his acquaintance with Handel at this time. These connections helped Burney sustain his growing family, which included James *Burney (1750–1821); Charles (1751–1752); Frances (Fanny) *Burney (1752–1840); Charles (*d.* 1754); and later Susanna (or Susan) Elizabeth (1755–1800).

Composer and teacher Burney's activities as a composer had until this point been fairly limited, and it is not for his compositions that he has been remembered by posterity. He performed an organ concerto of his own composition at the King's Arms concerts, and had published *Six Sonatas for Two Violins, with a Bass for the Violoncello or Harpsichord* in 1748 (a copy is depicted in Toms's 1754 portrait of Burney). Composition continued in earnest until the 1760s, and sporadically thereafter. The catalyst for a burst of music writing late in the 1740s was Burney's friendship with the violinist and publisher James Oswald (1711–1779), who issued Burney's *Six Songs with a Cantata* op. 2, plus the works of a group known as the Society of the Temple of Apollo. It seems that this 'group' consisted at least mainly, and quite possibly solely, of Burney and Oswald, and that its existence was a device for obtaining commissions from Garrick at Drury Lane. Outside the Temple of Apollo Burney wrote two further works for the stage: some songs for *A Midsummer Night's Dream* in 1763, and a setting of Jean-Jacques Rousseau's *Le devin du village*, published as *The Cunning Man* in 1766.

Whether or not the continuation of such work was Burney's ambition, his plans were thrown into disarray by a serious fever early in 1751 that confined him to bed for thirteen weeks. On medical advice he moved to Canonbury House in Islington, but he showed only a small improvement. Consequently his doctor, John Armstrong (1709–1779), suggested that he leave London altogether, and brought a proposal from Sir John Turner, MP for King's Lynn, that he accept the post of organist of St Margaret's Church there. In September 1751, therefore, Burney left London for King's Lynn, his wife, daughter, and son joining him some months later. Acquaintances made in King's Lynn included William Bewley, who although a surgeon and apothecary by trade was equally appreciated by Burney for his love of music, books, and fun; and Stephen Allen, whose wife, Elizabeth, Burney admired for her beauty and education and was later to marry.

Although his time at King's Lynn was very settled, the fact that Burney visited London each winter hints at an ambition eventually to return there for good, and this took place in 1760. He had little trouble finding new pupils, owing partly to his own reputation and also to that of his daughter Esther, exhibited as a prodigy on the harpsichord in April 1760. Esther and her sister Susan were later taken to France to further their education. In September 1762 Burney was widowed, Esther Burney having died following a long illness. He wrote movingly of this loss in his memoirs. Among their surviving children was Charles *Burney (1757–1817), schoolmaster and book collector. Burney remained in widowhood for just over five years before marrying Elizabeth Allen (1728–1796) at St James's, Westminster, on 2 October 1767. There has been much debate over how much money Elizabeth brought to the marriage, Burney himself claiming that she had lost almost all that she had inherited on the death in 1763 of her husband, Stephen Allen, by an unwise loan to an English merchant based in Russia. However, the fact that Burney was, only three years after the marriage, able to undertake extensive tours in Europe—no doubt requiring sufficient funds to cover his expenses plus any loss of income from teaching while he was away—may indicate otherwise: Slava Klima, Garry Bowers, and Kerry S. Grant have suggested in their edition of his *Memoirs* that he was earning between £30 and £100 per month in the London season. This was enough to sustain his still growing family: Charlotte Ann (1761–1838), his last child with Esther, was followed by two with Elizabeth, Richard Thomas (1768–1808) and Sarah Harriet *Burney (1772–1844). The decade ended with Burney receiving the degree of DMus from Oxford University (June 1769) with the ode *I will Love thee, O Lord my Strength*, later performed in Hamburg under Carl Philipp Emanuel Bach's direction. He also published an *Essay on Comets*, a manifestation of a lifelong interest in astronomy that later revealed itself in a long poem on the subject, begun in 1797 but later destroyed.

Writing *A General History of Music* In the 1770s Burney established himself as a literary man, no longer simply the music teacher to the upper classes. In 1770 he undertook a tour of France and Italy to collect material for what later became his *A General History of Music* (4 vols., 1776–89), but which was published separately as *The Present State of Music in France and Italy* in May 1771. This was widely acclaimed, doubtless partly because he had efficiently taken steps to ensure favourable reviews in London's literary monthlies. A further volume, covering Germany and the Netherlands, followed in 1773. Perhaps on the strength of his first volume he was elected FRS in 1772. Following the success of both books of tours, which guaranteed him a welcome in noble circles, Burney immediately issued an invitation to subscribe to his *History*. He initially found few takers, because many potential purchasers had already left London; but with the start of the new season the subscription list grew satisfactorily. The first volume, originally advertised for summer 1774, finally appeared in January 1776. The five-volume *General History of the Science and Practice of Music* of Sir John Hawkins appeared, complete, in November that year; and although Burney did not finish his own history until 1789, his elegant writing style, already known to the public through the books of tours, seems to have led to his history being preferred from the outset to that of Hawkins, who was up to that point known mainly as a lawyer and as editor of several editions of Izaak Walton's *Compleat Angler*. Hawkins, unlike Burney, had the disadvantage of not being a practising professional musician; and his fondness for the music of earlier centuries at the expense of his own may have worked against him in the minds of readers of fashion. Burney (who avoided Hawkins's latter problem by giving much space to discussion of the music, especially opera, of his own century) once again went out of his way to secure favourable reviews for his own book, and it appears that he may have had a hand—albeit indirectly—in press criticism of Hawkins's work. Burney certainly was sufficiently irked by Hawkins to write a poem, 'The Trial of Midas the Second', in 1777 that was deeply unflattering to his rival, and he encouraged his friend Bewley to criticize Hawkins in print in the *Monthly Review*. For all his well-attested geniality, Burney was not above *schadenfreude*.

While the next thirteen years are linked by the common thread of Burney's *History*, they were not exclusively given over to this project. Burney continued to spend most of his day giving music lessons, a feature of his life that ended only in 1804. In 1779 he read a paper (subsequently published) to the Royal Society concerning the musical prodigy William Crotch. His friendship with Samuel Johnson, falteringly begun in the mid-1750s with his subscription to six copies of Johnson's *Dictionary*, developed and continued to blossom up to the time of Johnson's death in 1784: their friendship was sufficiently strong to lead Johnson to supply the dedicatory preface for the *History*, and for Burney to become a member of Johnson's Literary Club. Burney's obituary in the *Gentleman's Magazine* (possibly contributed by a family member) notes that he had planned to write a biography of Johnson after the latter's death, but had eventually decided against it after learning that others were planning their own publications—had he done so he would again have been directly pitted against Hawkins, who was one of Johnson's executors and

published his own *Life of Johnson* in 1787. He was appointed organist at Chelsea College from Christmas 1783; and in 1785 he published an account of the Handel commemoration festival of the previous year.

Burney also had ambitions at court. He had dedicated the first volume of his *History* to Queen Charlotte, wife of George III, formally presenting it to her in January 1776. He was enormously proud when his daughter Fanny was appointed second keeper of the robes to the queen in 1786, even though Fanny herself seems to have felt thoroughly wretched throughout this employment. But in general Burney's dealings with the king and queen brought him more disappointment than satisfaction. His attempt to write a brief account of the 1784 Handel commemoration festival was made more difficult by the king's attempts to interfere; he had been passed over as master of the king's band in 1779 in favour of John Stanley, and again on Stanley's death in 1786 in favour of William Parsons. It seems likely that Fanny's appointment was intended in some way to make up for this latter snub.

Although the publication of the final volumes of the *History* in 1789 probably marked the peak of Burney's literary success, his career as a writer was by no means over. He continued to contribute pieces to the *Monthly Review* as he had done since 1785; he published a three-volume *Memoirs of the Life and Writings of the Abate Metastasio* in 1796; and he contributed a large number of articles to Abraham Rees's *Cyclopaedia* from about 1802 until 1805, for which he earned £1000. Fanny wrote that the Metastasio book lacked 'that brightness of popular success which had flourished into the world the previous works of the Doctor' (*Memoirs of Doctor Burney*, 3.212), but blamed the fact that Metastasio was not a subject of such general interest as the books of tours or the *History*. The fact that Burney was sixty-three when the *History* was finished and became increasingly prey to illness during the 1790s and after may also partially explain the diminished sparkle of his work. His spirits suffered at news of the French Revolution; a severe attack of rheumatism (a condition from which he had long suffered) caused him to visit Bath in 1793; and his second wife died on 20 October 1796. Because Fanny was living in France from 1802 to 1812 she gives far fewer details of this last period than of earlier ones in her published memoirs, and quotes quite extensively and without interference from Burney's own diaries. The principal events of Burney's life after 1800 were his giving up of teaching activities at the age of seventy-eight, his receipt of a royal pension of £300 per year from 1805, and his election as a corresponding member of the Institut National de France late in 1810. These signs of recognition were counterbalanced by frequent news of the death of various friends; he was particularly affected by the passing of his long-time correspondent Thomas Twining, who had helped with the first volume of the *History*. In 1807 Burney suffered a stroke that paralysed his left hand and necessitated another trip to Bath. While the visit had a positive outcome, he had become sufficiently concerned about the event to draw up his will. In fact he lived for a further seven years, although from 1813 he was increasingly confined to his rooms at Chelsea College. He died there on 12 April 1814, and on 20 April was buried in the grounds, as his second wife had been. A memorial was later installed in the north aisle of Westminster Abbey, and bears a long epitaph from Fanny.

Reputation The unsigned obituary in the *Gentleman's Magazine* of 1814 describes Burney as an 'excellent scholar' (*GM*, 421) and an exemplary husband, father, and friend. Hester Lynch Thrale called him 'In professional Science a second to none, In social—if second—thro' Shyness alone' (*Thraliana*, 1.475). Lonsdale, whose painstaking biography was the first to take account of new materials that became available only in the 1950s, claimed that Burney was 'not a great man, for he was limited by his pursuit of social and literary success' (Lonsdale, 481); and suggested that his death went largely unnoticed by a public more interested in the figures of its own century than in those perceived as belonging more to the previous one. The nineteenth century knew Burney chiefly through the three-volume *Memoirs of Doctor Burney* by his daughter Fanny, published in 1832. It is an account distorted by frequent inaccuracy and by Fanny's attempt, surely prompted by an over-zealous sense of duty, to paint her father in the best possible light. Almost from the moment of publication, the *Memoirs of Doctor Burney* was dismissed as a factual account, notably by John Wilson Croker in the *Quarterly Review* of 1833 (pp. 97–125). The works of Joyce Hemlow and of Percy Scholes have made some attempt to moderate this viewpoint. None of Burney's own publications was reprinted in the nineteenth century; even the *History* had to wait until 1935 for a new edition, being regarded by the nineteenth century as second to Hawkins's history as a factual account of music (Hawkins's work enjoyed new editions in 1853 and 1875). Studies of the Burney family shifted their focus away from Charles Burney towards the life and work of Fanny Burney as an interesting early example of a female novelist. In the twentieth century a more rounded view of Charles Burney emerged via the publication of the contents of the surviving fragments of his memoirs, scattered in the UK and USA, in 1988, and by the initiation of a scholarly edition of his letters.

JOHN WAGSTAFF

Sources *Memoirs of Dr Charles Burney, 1726–1769*, ed. S. Klima, G. Bowers, and K. S. Grant (1988) · *The letters of Dr Charles Burney*, ed. A. Ribeiro, 1 (1991) · P. A. Scholes, *The great Dr Burney: his life, his travels, his works, his family and his friends*, 2 vols. (1948) · R. Lonsdale, *Dr Charles Burney: a literary biography* (1965) · Madame D'Arblay [F. Burney], *Memoirs of Doctor Burney*, 3 vols. (1832) · R. B. Johnson, ed., *Fanny Burney and the Burneys* (1926) · C. Hill, *The house in St Martin's Street: being chronicles of the Burney family* (1907) · J. Hemlow, J. M. Burgess, and A. Douglas, *A catalogue of the Burney family correspondence, 1749–1878* (1971) · *GM*, 1st ser., 84/1 (1814), 420–21; 1st ser., 84/2 (1814), 93–4 · 'Memoirs of Charles Burney', *The Harmonicon*, 10 (1832), 215–17 · 'Some account of the life and writings of Dr Charles Burney', *European Magazine and London Review*, 7 (1785), 163–4 · *Thraliana: the diary of Mrs. Hester Lynch Thrale (later Mrs. Piozzi), 1776–1809*, ed. K. C. Balderston, 2nd edn, 2 vols. (1951) · BL, Add. MS 37916, fol. 16

Archives BL, part of autobiography, Add. MS 48345 · BL, corresp. and musical papers, M440, 490–91 [microfilm] · BL, journal of tour in France and Italy, Add. MS 35122 · BL, papers relating to his dictionary of music, Add. MSS 27651–27686 · BL, papers relating to early musical writers, Add. MSS 11581–11591 · BL, personal and family papers, Egerton MSS 3690–3708 · JRL, notebook | BL, corresp. with Twining family, Add. MSS 39929–39936 · BL, letters to Arthur Young, Add. MSS 35126–35130, *passim* · Bodl. Oxf., letters to Edward Malone · Cumbria AS, Carlisle, letters to first earl of Lonsdale · JRL, letters to Mrs Thrale, etc. · King's Lond., letters to Mrs Chambers · NMM, letters to Lord Sandwich · NYPL, Henry W. and Albert A. Berg collection of English and American literature · RAS, letters to Sir William Herschel

Likenesses P. Toms, oils, 1754, Yale U., J. M. and M.-L. Osborn collection; repro. in *Memoirs*, ed. Klima, Bowers, and Grant, frontispiece · J. Barry, group portrait, oils, 1776–9 (*The triumph of the Thames*), RSA; repro. in Scholes, *The great Dr Burney* · J. Reynolds, oils, 1781, NPG; copy, U. Oxf., faculty of music [*see illus.*] · C. L. Smith, caricature, pubd 1782, BL; repro. in *Letters*, ed. Ribeiro, vol. 1, p. 351 · F. Bartolozzi, stipple, pubd 1784 (after J. Reynolds), BM, NPG · G. Dance, pencil drawing, 1794, NPG · J. Nollekens, marble bust, 1801, BM · S. Gahagan, tablet, 1819, Westminster Abbey · A. Wivell, stipple, pubd 1819 (after J. Nollekens), NPG · D. G. Thompson, group portrait, stipple and line engraving, pubd 1851 (*A literary party at Sir Joshua Reynolds's*; after J. E. Doyle), NPG · J. Nollekens?, pencil drawing (*Dr Burney at Calis in the year 1770*), Yale U., J. M. and M.-L. Osborn collection · J. Scott, mezzotint (after J. Reynolds), NPG · engraving, repro. in Scholes, *The great Dr Burney*, for *European Magazine and London Review* (1785) · silhouette (*The Burney family*), priv. coll.

Wealth at death £7800 in money; music library sold for approx. £1415; also paintings, instruments, and other effects: Scholes, *The great Dr Burney*, vol. 2, pp. 261–73

Burney, Charles (1757–1817), schoolmaster and book collector, was born on 4 December 1757 in King's Lynn, the fifth surviving child and second surviving son of Dr Charles *Burney (1726–1814), music historian, and his first wife, Esther Sleepe (*bap.* 1725?, *d.* 1762). He was admitted in February 1768 to the Charterhouse on the nomination of George Spencer, fourth duke of Marlborough. In January 1777 he was admitted a pensioner at Gonville and Caius College, Cambridge. The following October occurred the event which would colour the remainder of Burney's life. As reported by William Cole, the Cambridge antiquary, he was discovered to have secreted 'in a dark Corner' of his room 'about 35 Classical Books' from the university library 'which he had taken the University Arms out of, & put his own in their Place' (Walker, 314). It was soon learned that he had been sending books, 'cheifly classical Books of Elzevir Editions', to London as his own and selling them to book dealers. In later years his sister Frances (Fanny) *Burney tried to explain away the theft as due to a 'MAD RAGE for possessing a library' (*Journals and Letters*, 10.795) and his selling them as due to his fear of being found out. But it is much more probable that Burney's love of gaiety and extravagant living caused him to incur heavy debts aggravated by gambling, and that he sold the books to cover these debts without his family's knowledge.

In any event, Cambridge immediately dismissed Burney in disgrace. His furious father considered disowning him and forcing him to change his name. At first he was banished to the provincial town of Shinfield in Berkshire. Then admission was obtained for him to King's College, Aberdeen, where he was able to pursue the classical studies for which he had shown a bent. At Aberdeen he

Charles Burney (1757–1817), by Sir Thomas Lawrence, 1802

appears to have applied himself diligently to his studies, but he also continued his gambling, heavy drinking, and association with high-born and possibly profligate friends, most notably the earls of Fife and Lindlater. He also pursued his penchant for romance, falling in love with Jane Abernethie, a cousin of Fife's, who did not return his passion.

Burney went back to London in July 1781, having received the degree of MA from Aberdeen the preceding March. Efforts were made to obtain a curacy for him, but the scandal of the Cambridge theft and continuing doubts about his character made such an appointment impossible. Instead he settled into the career of a schoolmaster. At first he taught at Highgate School, and then became assistant master in Dr William Rose's private school at Chiswick. He there fell in love with Rose's daughter Sarah Rose (1759–1821), whom he married on 24 June 1783.

On 4 July 1786 Rose died, and Burney succeeded him as headmaster and moved the school from Chiswick to Hammersmith. His only child, Charles Parr Burney (1785–1864), had been born the preceding year. Now almost thirty years old, the headmaster, husband, and new father, no doubt recalling all too well the sins of his own youth, became a strict disciplinarian. He continued adding to his credentials as a Greek and Latin scholar by publishing translations, commentaries, editions, and reviews. In time his reputation as a scholar would rival those of Samuel Parr (his classical mentor and godfather of his son) and Richard Porson, though it declined precipitously after his death.

Through the influence of his friends in Scotland, Burney was able to obtain honorary doctorates in law from King's College, Aberdeen, and the University of Glasgow in 1792.

In 1793 he moved his flourishing school to Greenwich. His redemption in the eyes of society was completed in 1807 when he was finally ordained a deacon in the Church of England. Through the efforts of Parr's friend and former pupil Martin Davy, who had become master of Gonville and Caius College, he was reinstated at Caius in 1807 and granted the degree of MA by royal mandate in July 1808; he had been ordained priest the preceding month. The blot at Cambridge thus removed, advancement in the church came rapidly. Appointed a chaplain to the king in 1810, he was named vicar of Herne Hill, Surrey, and rector of Little Hinton, Wiltshire, and of St Paul's, Deptford, Kent, in 1811. After proceeding DD (Lambeth) in 1812 he received the rectory of Cliffe-at-Hoo, Kent, in place of the Herne Hill living in 1815, and was collated prebendary of Lincoln for Sutton in the Marsh in 1817. He also continued to accrue scholarly honours. Elected a fellow of the Royal Society in 1802, he was appointed professor of ancient literature at the Royal Academy in 1810, and the same year elected to the Literary Club. He was also a fellow of the Society of Antiquaries. In 1813 he retired from the school at Greenwich in favour of his son, Charles Parr Burney, who until then had been his assistant.

Burney died of an apoplectic stroke at Deptford on 28 December 1817, having just passed his sixtieth birthday. He was buried in St Paul's churchyard, Deptford. His contemporary reputation as a classical scholar is attested by the bust of him in Westminster Abbey, over a lengthy inscription in Latin by Parr. His portrait by Sir Thomas Lawrence was engraved in 1817 by William Sharp. Both bust and engraving show him with a rather fleshy face and supercilious expression. The features display perhaps (in softened manner) the ruined constitution attributed by a latter-day contemporary to Burney's intemperance as a youth; to the end of his days he kept a notable collection of vintage wines. The superciliousness (like his disciplinarian streak) was perhaps acted or acquired; family and friends alike attested to his essential good nature and warm-heartedness.

Burney's principal published works include: *Appendix ad lexicon Graeco-Latinum a Joan. Scapula constructum* (1789); *Remarks on the Greek Verses of Milton* (1790); *Richardi Bentleii et doctorum virorum epistolae* (1807); *Tentamen de metris ab Aeschylo in choricis cantibus adhibitis* (1809); and *Philemonos lexikon technologikon* (1812). He contributed articles to the *Monthly Review* and was editor of the *London Magazine*. His holograph familiar letters, occasional verses, and other manuscripts are chiefly to be found in the James Marshall and Marie-Louise Osborn collection at Yale University.

Burney's main legacy consists of the huge private library which he amassed during a lifetime of passionate and assiduous collecting. In 1818 the House of Commons granted £13,500 to the trustees of the British Museum to purchase this library. By this acquisition the museum gained over 13,000 printed books, mostly of classical editions, including 47 editions of Aeschylus, 102 of Sophocles, 166 of Euripides, and over 500 manuscript volumes. It also acquired nearly 400 volumes of materials relating to the English stage, consisting of notes, newspaper cuttings, prints, and playbills. Burney had hoped to write a history of the stage from his collection, and his love of the theatre stemmed from his early youth, when the Burney household received the visits of such luminaries as Richard Brinsley Sheridan, Arthur Murphy, and David Garrick. The third major part of the purchase was an extensive collection of newspapers (the Burney Collection of Early English Newspapers), which he had begun on his return from Aberdeen in 1781, when he started gathering the old newspapers from a coffee house (Gregg's) managed by his maiden aunts.   LARS TROIDE

Sources *The early journals and letters of Fanny Burney*, ed. L. E. Troide, 1: *1768–1773* (1988); 2: *1774–1777* (1990) • *The journals and letters of Fanny Burney* (*Madame D'Arblay*), ed. J. Hemlow and others, 12 vols. (1972–84) • P. A. Scholes, *The great Dr Burney: his life, his travels, his works, his family and his friends*, 2 vols. (1948) • R. S. Walker, 'Charles Burney's theft of books at Cambridge', *Transactions of the Cambridge Bibliographical Society*, 3 (1959–63), 313–26 • M. L. Clarke, *Greek studies in England, 1700–1830* (1945), 77–8 • C. O. Brink, *English classical scholarship: historical reflections on Bentley, Porson, and Housman* (1986), 85, n. 5 • E. Miller, *That noble cabinet: a history of the British Museum* (1974), 109–10 • Venn, *Alum. Cant.* • *GM*, 1st ser., 89/1 (1819), 294–6, 369–73
Archives BL, corresp., M/440, M/445, M/460 [microfilm copies] • BL, corresp. and papers, Add. MSS 59902–60165, 65162–65177, 70857–70886; Egerton MSS 3690–3708 • BL, materials collected for a history of Greek drama, Add. MSS 65162–65177 • BL, Burney MSS, MS collections • BL, notes and indices relating to Terantianus Maurus, Add. MSS 62582–62584 • LPL, description of MSS and collections of St Mark's gospel, MSS 1223–1224, 1255, 1259 • Yale U., Beinecke L., corresp. and papers | BL, letters to Thomas Burgess, Add. MS 46847
Likenesses G. Dance, pencil drawing, 1794, BM • T. Lawrence, oils, 1802, priv. coll. [*see illus.*] • W. Sharp, line engraving, 1817 (after T. Lawrence), BM, NPG • L. A. Goblet, bas-relief medallion bust, 1818, St Paul's Church, Deptford, London • L. A. Goblet, relief bust on monument, 1818, Westminster Abbey • H. Edridge, pencil drawing, BM • J. Nollekens, bust, BM • D. Turner, etching (after T. Phillips), BM, NPG
Wealth at death £25,000—'goods, chatels and credits' valued at this amount: administration, 1818, PRO, PROB 6/194, fol. 181

Burney, Sir (Charles) Dennistoun, second baronet (1888–1968), marine and aeronautical engineer, was born in Bermuda on 28 December 1888, the only son among the three children of Sir Cecil *Burney, first baronet (1858–1929), later admiral, and second in command of the Grand Fleet at Jutland, and his wife, Lucinda Marion, second daughter of George Richards Burnett, of London. He received a formal naval education, starting his training at the *Britannia* in 1903, and joining the battleship *Exmouth* as midshipman in early 1905.

Burney joined the destroyer *Afridi* in 1909, and soon afterwards the *Crusader*, used for experimental work by the anti-submarine committee, of which his father was the first president. Burney became very interested in the experiments then in progress for destroying this, then novel, craft by towing explosive charges. He was also quick to see the potential of another recent invention, the aeroplane, as a means of spotting submarines, and this sparked off his interest in aeronautics. In September 1911 he went on half pay so that he could continue his researches at the Bristol aviation works of Sir George White. His work there was interrupted by appointments

to the battleship *Venerable* and the cruiser *Black Prince*, but in each ship he remained only long enough to apply for half pay and return to Bristol. In August 1912 he commenced a one-year gunnery course, and on its completion the Admiralty allowed him to continue his anti-submarine work and seaplane construction. At this time Burney made the far-reaching suggestion that aircraft fitted with wireless for hunting and attacking submarines should be carried by ships. For this purpose, he and F. S. Barnwell developed at Bristol a seaplane which the Admiralty afforded facilities for trials at Burney's expense, but the outbreak of the First World War halted this work. Seaplanes were indeed used during the war for tracking down submarines. They were fitted with hydrophones (a form of underwater microphone), which allowed them to listen for submerged submarines underway. However, these flimsy craft could be used only in calm weather.

When the First World War broke out, Burney was given command of the destroyer *Velox*, but soon afterwards he joined the *Vernon*, the Portsmouth torpedo school, where up to that time much of the navy's scientific research and development had taken place. At *Vernon* he was primarily responsible for the development of the explosive paravane. He was able to make good use of his knowledge of aircraft design, as this device, towed astern, was essentially a small underwater aeroplane, consisting of a torpedo-shaped body fitted with fins and a rudder to keep it at any depth. He described its basic uses in a secret patent taken out in 1915. These included destroying submarines on impact, and cutting the moorings of underwater mines by means of serrated cutters attached to the nose, allowing the mines to be destroyed on the surface. Trials with this device started in the spring of 1915, and in June Burney was appointed to organize a new paravane department at *Vernon*. In the following year he took out another ten patents dealing with paravanes and associated gear, such as davits and towing cables. In 1920 the Royal Commission on Awards to Inventors gave Burney the main credit for this invention, but recommended that, as he had received some £350,000 for patent rights for its use by merchant vessels and abroad, no further payments should be made to him. He had received no payment for the navy's wartime use of this device, but he had been rewarded in the 1917 birthday honours by his appointment as CMG, an honour rarely given to a lieutenant. In 1920 Burney retired from the navy as a lieutenant-commander, and on reaching the age of forty, he was promoted on the retired list to commander. In 1921 he married Gladys, the younger daughter of George Henry High, of Chicago; they had a son. Burney succeeded his father in the baronetcy in 1929.

After the war, Burney took out a series of patents relating to precast concrete as a building material, and he joined Vickers Ltd as a consultant. He realized that the new developments in aviation held both economic and political implications. Communications in the British empire would be greatly improved by a comprehensive system of air travel: airships to operate the main trunk routes over the oceans; large flying boats for the eastern routes, serving Egypt, India, and the Far East, feeding the trunk routes; and smaller land planes for shorter routes, feeding the flying boats. These ideas were set out in his *The World, the Air and the Future* (1929), and to further them he entered parliament as a Unionist member for Uxbridge in 1922, and held his seat until 1929. Burney was keen to start his airship service using the German Zeppelins surrendered to Britain at the cessation of hostilities, but these were found to be too corroded. After lengthy negotiations with Vickers and the government, Burney formed the Airship Guarantee Company, appointing Barnes *Wallis as chief designer in 1923, and soon after Nevil Shute *Norway, who became a novelist, as chief calculator. An order for a new airship, the R.100, was placed with Burney's firm, but the government decided that competition was healthy and put together its own design team at the Air Ministry (consisting mainly of members already discarded by Burney for his board on the advice of Barnes Wallis), to develop the R.101 at the Royal Airship Works at Cardington. This resulted in an unhealthy race between the two projects that eventually ended with the crashing of the R.101 on 5 October 1930 at Beauvais in France, killing forty-eight of the fifty-four people on board, including Lord Thomson, the secretary of state for air who had instituted this project, and the design team. This destroyed the British rigid airship programme for all time. The R.100, which had made a successful acceptance flight to Canada and back in July–August 1930, on which both Burney and Nevil Shute Norway were present, was dismantled in 1931, its valuable remains crushed by a steamroller.

In the late 1920s Burney designed a streamlined rear-engined saloon car, the prototype of which is in the Montagu motor car museum at Beaulieu. Its novel features were the subject of a number of patents taken out in 1929–33, and included independent suspension and hydraulic brakes. It was supplied with either a six-cylinder Crossley or an eight-cylinder Beverley Barnes engine. The prince of Wales bought one, but at £1500 it was not an economic proposition and very few were sold. In 1933 this unconventional design was taken up by Crossley but they, too, could not make it a commercial success.

During the Second World War Burney was employed by the War Office on secret experimental work, the scope of which can be surmised by a large number of patents that began to appear in the early 1950s relating to, among other matters, aerial gliding bombs and marine torpedoes with gyroscopically controlled aerofoils, gun-fired rocket projectiles, and a non-recoil gun. After the war, he became interested in improving fishing trawlers. He designed a catamaran trawler, apparatus to facilitate trawling and landing the catch, an otter or 'porpoise' (a kind of paravane) incorporating sonar to detect fish shoals, and plants for freezing fish either on board or ashore. In all, Burney took out more than one hundred patents during the period from 1915 to 1962. Among these were six with Barnes Wallis and one with Wallis and Nevil Shute Norway on aspects of airship design. In 1947, acting for British iron and steel interests, he secured a concession in Northern Rhodesia for iron and coal prospecting, and consequently maintained two homes: one in Rhodesia and the other in Bermuda.

Burney could be a difficult taskmaster and his relations with his colleagues were sometimes uneasy. One of them described him as 'a man of whom one could believe that no situation could be so awful as actually to daunt him' (private information). He died on 11 November 1968 in Hamilton, Bermuda. His son, Cecil Dennistoun Burney (*b.* 1923), succeeded to the title.   W. D. HACKMANN, *rev.*

Sources *The Times* (14 Nov 1968) • *The Guardian* (14 Nov 1968) • N. Shute, *Slide rule: the autobiography of an engineer* (1954) • J. E. Morpugo, *Barnes Wallis: a biography* (1972) • private information (1981) • *WWW* • *WWBMP*, vol. 3
Archives BL, papers | Nuffield Oxf., corresp. with Lord Cherwell | FILM BFI NFTVA, news footage

Burney, Edward Francisco (1760–1848), artist, the son of Richard Burney (1723–1792), a dancing-master, and Elizabeth Humphries (*c.*1720–1771), was born in Worcester on 7 September 1760. He was an accomplished amateur violinist, while his brother Charles Rousseau Burney (1747–1819) was a distinguished if impecunious professional on violin and keyboard. He was the nephew of the music historian Dr Charles *Burney (1726–1814) and a favourite cousin of the novelist Frances (Fanny) *Burney (1752–1840).

Burney enrolled at the Royal Academy Schools in 1776, studied there from 1777, lodged with his Burney cousins while there, and left in the 1780s. He exhibited at the Royal Academy in 1780–1803, showing portraits of family and friends (he was too shy to paint other sitters) and history pieces. (A watercolour drawing of his brother playing the violin is in the National Portrait Gallery, London.) He made good copies after Sir Thomas Lawrence and Sir Joshua Reynolds (for example, the fine *Miss Mary Horneck*, ex Sothebys, London, 9 July 1980, lot 114). His best portrait in oils is probably *Fanny Burney* (1782; NPG), which uses a bright rococo palette and flat tones to striking effect. He worked chiefly, however, as an illustrator, and exhibited stained drawings for Fanny Burney's *Evelina* at the Royal Academy in 1780, in which year he is described as living in York Street, Covent Garden, probably at Gregg's (or Grigg's) coffee house, which seems to have been part owned by Dr Burney, whose two sisters, Becky (Rebecca) and Nancy (Ann), ran it. Illustrations for *Paradise Lost*, in a manner of controlled reflection of the style of Henry Fuseli, are in the Huntington Library, California, and a pleasant group of drawings, chiefly landscapes, is in Nottingham Castle Museum.

Burney's most original works are four remarkable large-scale watercolour compositions of a sharply satirical nature: *The Waltz* and *The Elegant Establishment for Young Ladies* (V&A), and *Amateurs of Tye-Wig Music* and *The Glee Club, or, The Triumph of Music* (Yale U. CBA). A version in oil of *Amateurs of Tye-Wig Music* (*c.*1820; Tate collection) with the particular theme of modern versus traditional taste in music, is painted with verve and precision, and the group suggests that Burney had formed plans to develop his satires and their publication along the lines pioneered by Hogarth. Burney relies upon caricature to a degree which

Hogarth would never have allowed, although his targets—society in general and musical life in particular—are similar. Burney exploits an extravagantly swooping line that lends his works a distinctive edge. For whatever reason, the other compositions in this group appear not to have been painted, and none was published as an engraving.

Another group of drawings now firmly attributed to Burney (BM, 1904-1-1-1 ff.) shows the hang of the Royal Academy exhibition in 1784, and the pictures thus predate the famous 1787 illustration by J. H. Ramberg, to whom these drawings were previously given. Another important record of contemporary life is Burney's drawing of De Louterbourg's famous Eidophusikon (1782; BM). Even slight sketches by Burney can provide rare insights, and *A Tragic Actress* (Tate collection) reveals more than many verbal records about contemporary theatrical style. Burney died in London on 16 December 1848; he was unmarried.

ROBIN SIMON

Sources K. Chisholm, *Fanny Burney* (1999) · C. Harman, *Fanny Burney* (2000) · www.tate.org.uk, 25 Feb 2002 · P. Crown, *Drawings by E. F. Burney in the Huntington collection* (1982) · P. Crown, 'Visual music: E. F. Burney and a Hogarth revival', *Bulletin of Research in the Humanities*, 83/4 (winter 1980), 435–72 · Graves, *RA exhibitors* · Waterhouse, *18c painters* · D. H. Solkin, ed., *Art on the line* (2001) · H. Hammelmann, *Book illustration in eighteenth-century England*, ed. T. S. R. Boase (1975)

Burney [*married name* Wood], **Fanny Anne** (1812–1860), diarist, eldest in the family of two sons and four daughters of the Revd Charles Parr Burney and his wife, Frances Bentley Young, daughter of George Young of Blackheath, was born on 29 April 1812 at 61 Crooms Hill in Greenwich, where her father directed a school. She was the grand-daughter of Charles *Burney (1757–1817), and great-niece of the novelist Fanny Burney. In the summer of 1830, during one of the family's frequent trips to Europe, she began the diary which she was to keep for twenty-five years, and extracts of which, edited by her granddaughter, were later published. The family was a close one, and Fanny Anne was to remember her years at home with nostalgia. On 1 July 1835 she married Major James Wood (b. 1797) of the 5th dragoon guards, a descendant of the ancient Scottish Wood family of Largo and fifteen years her senior. The couple settled at Tunbridge Wells, and her husband's wards, Margaret and Jane Wood, then thirteen and sixteen years old respectively, came to live with them. On 7 January 1837 the Woods' only child, christened Fanny Paulet, was born. In April 1838 Jane Wood's consumption led the family to move first to Torquay, then in September to Funchal, Madeira. Jane died in February 1839 and they returned to England to live at Blackheath.

When her famous great-aunt's diaries began publication in 1842, Fanny Anne was unimpressed, opining that Fanny Burney was too receptive to flattery and that the work needed much pruning: 'As to six Volumes of these journals, one yawns at the bare idea!' (*Journals and Letters*, 337). Her own diary style was more inhibited as is evidenced by her lengthy description of her wedding in which the closest she comes to an allusion to the groom is in a single use of 'we' (ibid., 61). Her restrained diaries are largely impersonal, taken up with descriptions of places (especially fine homes and their grounds) and of nature, in which she took an amateur naturalist's interest; with anecdotes about famous people; and with plentiful lore about local customs and curiosities. Introspection, reflection, and emotional relief play little part in them. Yet a sense of her personality does emerge as she intersperses her accounts with her own responses—her dislike of novelty, her sense of family loyalty and love of her daughter, her musical tastes, and her conventional piety—and a miscellany of bits and pieces collected by her magpie mind. She died at the age of forty-eight on 2 May 1860 at 10 Cleveland Terrace, Kensington, from a disease of the spine which had afflicted her for more than twenty years.

HARRIET BLODGETT

Sources *A great-niece's journals: being extracts from the journals of Fanny Anne Burney*, ed. M. S. Rolt (1926) · d. cert.
Likenesses Richmond, crayon drawing (aged twenty-three), repro. in Rolt, ed., *Great-niece's journals*, facing p. 60 · drawing (aged seventeen or eighteen), repro. in Rolt, ed., *Great-niece's journals*

Burney [*married name* D'Arblay], **Frances** [Fanny] (1752–1840), writer, was born at King's Lynn, Norfolk, on 13 June 1752, and baptized in the chapel of St Nicholas on 7 July. She was the third child of Charles *Burney (1726–1814), musician and author, and his wife, Esther Sleepe (*bap.* 1725?, *d.* 1762), musician, who may have been the daughter of Richard Sleepe, leader of the lord mayor's band, and his wife, Frances. The Sleepe family were of French origin and lived in the parish of St Mary-le-Bow. Charles and Esther were married in London on 25 July 1749. A daughter, Esther, was born in May 1749 prior to the marriage, and a son, James *Burney (1750–1821), followed in June 1750. The family moved to King's Lynn where Charles Burney became organist of St Margaret's Church in the autumn of 1751. Later children who survived from this marriage were Susan, born in 1755; Charles *Burney (1757–1817); and Charlotte, born in 1761. It was a close-knit family and Frances Burney's siblings were to be important to her throughout her life.

Within the household Frances Burney was always known as Fanny, except when she acquired the nickname 'the Old Lady' about the age of eleven because of her grave demeanour. Small and slender, she had also to cope from childhood with short sight, which may have helped to make her shy in company as an adult. Surprisingly, she was, according to her father, 'wholly unnoticed in the nursery for any talent or quickness of parts'; educated at home, she did not know her letters at eight years old, and was teased by her brother James on this account (*Memoirs of Dr Charles Burney*, 141–2). However, her mother's example began to induce a taste for reading, and she claims to have learned partly by overhearing her sister Esther as she recited passages from Pope 'many *years* before I read them myself' (Hemlow, *History of Fanny Burney*, 8). By the time she was ten she had acquired her life-long addiction to writing, and she composed a novel

Frances Burney (1752–1840), by Edward Francisco Burney, *c.*1784–5

entitled 'The History of Caroline Evelyn', which is lost. The story was probably burnt on her fifteenth birthday, when in an attempt 'to combat this writing passion' she consigned to a bonfire her collected works up to this time, including 'Elegies, Odes, Plays, Songs, Stories, Farces— nay Tragedies and Epic Poems' (*Memoirs*, 2.124–5). It has been suggested that this was at the insistence of her father or her future stepmother.

Youth Frances underwent two major childhood experiences in quick succession. The first was a move from King's Lynn back to London about October 1760, when her father took up a career as a music teacher. The family took up residence in Poland Street, a road leading southwards from Oxford Street into modern Soho. Her father soon acquired a number of pupils of rank and distinction; his personal acquaintances already included Samuel Johnson and David Garrick, who were to remain close family friends. Frances settled happily into life in the capital, which was her principal home for the next quarter of a century.

The second event was the death of her mother on 29 September 1762, after a lingering consumption which 'baffled all medical skill from the beginning' and had been only briefly alleviated by a visit to Bristol Hotwells (*Memoirs*, 1.143). The painful last hours of Esther Burney, attended by Dr William Hunter, made a huge impact on Frances, who clung to the memory of her mother ever afterwards. Her father and the other children were initially prostrated, and they rallied only with the help of friends such as Garrick and the cultivated bachelor Samuel *Crisp, another lasting presence in the life of Frances.

Crisp lived in an isolated and old-fashioned house at Chessington in Surrey, where the Burneys were frequent visitors. They called it 'Liberty Hall'. The strong family ties were temporarily broken in June 1764, as Charles Burney senior took two of his daughters, Esther and Susan, to be educated in Paris. Frances was left behind, allegedly because Susan's weak lungs would benefit more from a warmer climate, but also because there was felt to be a danger she might fall under the influence of some 'zealot' who would convert her to Catholicism (she was close to her maternal grandmother who was Roman Catholic). At home Frances appeared to have taught herself French and was able to undertake a version of Bernard le Bovier Fontenelle's *Entretien sur la pluralité des mondes*, 'murdered into English by Frances Burney' (MS in Berg, New York Public Library; Hemlow, *History of Fanny Burney*, 16).

On 2 October 1767 Charles Burney married Elizabeth Allen (*c.*1728–1796), formerly a celebrated beauty of King's Lynn, who had been married to Stephen Allen (1725–1763), a prosperous merchant. The Allens were among the closest friends of the Burneys during their time in Norfolk. After Elizabeth lost her husband in 1763 she was ardently courted in the following years by Charles. Strangely, the new Mrs Burney kept her home in King's Lynn for at least two more years, together with her two daughters and one son. There were regular visits by each side of the family to the other, and the two sets of children got on well: the teenage Maria Allen was especially fond of Frances, who was her junior by one year. It is about this time that Frances Burney's first extant diary begins (the opening entry is dated 27 March 1768). As a teenager Frances habitually sent letter-journals to Crisp, and to Susan who would sew them into notebooks. In these Frances experimented with different literary styles. It also emerges from the diaries that the Burney children gradually became estranged from their stepmother, whom they regarded as moodily neurotic and insecure. This was despite the fact that the family welcomed the arrival of a baby son Richard, born to Elizabeth and Charles in King's Lynn in November 1768.

The year 1770 brought a series of significant events in the household. In September the eldest sister, Esther, married her cousin Charles Rousseau Burney (1747–1819), a harpsichordist and like his uncle a music teacher. Indeed it was he who took over the pupils when Frances's father (by now the recipient of a DMus degree from Oxford) left on the first of his celebrated musical tours. In the meantime Elizabeth Burney had bought a new family house: it stood on the south side of Queen Square, Bloomsbury, an impressive early Georgian development which was still open to the north and commanded an uninterrupted view of Hampstead and Highgate. On reaching her new home in November, Frances found it 'a charming House' with 'a delightful Prospect' (*Early Journals*, 1.141). One factor behind the move was the desire to unite the Burney and Allen families: Elizabeth was finally able to give up her home in King's Lynn and brought her children to the larger residence in Queen Square.

The next few years were comparatively uneventful. Frances enjoyed the success which greeted the account of

Dr Burney's tour when her father published *The Present State of Music in France and Italy* (1771). In the same year she welcomed back her brother James, a midshipman, from a voyage to the Far East, and in July 1772 she felt a glow of pride when he embarked on the *Resolution*, commanded by James Cook. This was the start of Cook's second expedition; James was shortly promoted second lieutenant of the sister ship *Adventure*, on which he returned safely in 1774. He had befriended the Tahitian Omai, who was brought back to England as a living specimen of the noble savage. Omai was lionized at a variety of social gatherings; and Frances was pleased to see her brother mixing in such company, when he was marked out as speaking 'more Otaheite than any of the ship's *Crew*' (*Early Journals*, 2.41). Frances remained shy in company, but she inevitably came into contact with a wider world as her father's reputation grew. His second tour, undertaken between July and November 1772, resulted in the publication in the following year of a second narrative, which was again well received. Frances had acted as his amanuensis on this project, and was now busily involved with the full-scale history of music which Dr Burney planned. The main domestic episode was the birth in August 1772 of a stepsister for Frances, Sarah Harriet *Burney (1772–1844), who subsequently also gained fame for her novels. As an infant she seemed to Frances 'one of the most innocent, artless, *queer* little things you ever saw' (ibid., 1.163).

Family and social life   The Burneys moved again in October 1774, and once more Elizabeth Burney seems to have handled the arrangements while her husband and stepdaughter rusticated at Crisp's home in Surrey. This time they were to occupy a house of historic interest, built in the 1690s for Sir Isaac Newton, and standing on the east side of St Martin's Street, near Leicester Square. At the attic level, above the three main storeys, could be found Newton's observatory, which was shown to all visitors, as Frances put it, 'as our principal Lyon' (*Early Journals*, 2.52). She shared a bedroom on the second floor with her sister Susan; on the first floor was a small study used by Newton, which Dr Burney took over for his literary work, together with the large library, where the family entertained and held musical parties. Among the visitors was Omai, still a glamorous society figure when he came to St Martin's Street in December 1774; Frances was impressed by the Tahitian's civility when she sat next to him at dinner. Soon afterwards Frances went to the house of Sir Joshua Reynolds, who lived barely 50 yards from the Burneys in Leicester Fields, and admired the 'ease and elegance' of his paintings. She often heard performances by eminent musicians, as when the young keyboard virtuoso Muzio Clementi demonstrated a new compound harpsichord. He was 'a very good player', Frances observed, 'Indeed, Mr [Charles Rousseau] Burney excepted, I do not recollect ever hearing a better' (ibid., 2.67–8). The young woman's growing acquaintance with an array of distinguished men and women did not lead her to underrate the talents of her own family.

For Frances, the most significant new contact came when her father was introduced to the brewer Henry Thrale at a dinner given by Joshua Reynolds in 1776. By the end of the year Dr Burney had met the memoirist Hester Thrale (later Piozzi), visited the couple's home at Streatham, and begun to give weekly music lessons there to their eldest daughter Queeney. Frances became a *habituée* of this circle after the Thrales attended a morning party at St Martin's Street in March 1777; another guest on this occasion was Samuel Johnson, who now began to figure more largely in the life of the Burney family. Frances and the elderly man of letters soon became attached to one another, while she was impressed by the polished and self-confident Hester Thrale. For her part, Hester considered the Burneys 'a very low Race of Mortals' (Hemlow, *History of Fanny Burney*, 109), but she gradually took to Frances and for the next few years the two women retained an outwardly warm friendship.

Domestically, a quiet period followed the move to St Martin's Street. Frances resisted without much difficulty the attentions of a young man named Thomas Barlow, who fell in love with her in May 1775, although she thought it worth consulting 'Daddy' Crisp. Her suitor was stiff and inept in company, even if inoffensive otherwise, and he was quickly rejected. Relations with her stepmother remained a source of strain for Frances, and within the household there were other troubles, something which always caused the family to close ranks and devise stratagems for secrecy. Both Elizabeth Burney's daughters by her first marriage had eloped to the continent: the elder, Maria, had married her lover, Martin Rishton, in 1772, while the younger, Bessy, ran off with an adventurer named Samuel Meeke before marrying him in Belgium in October 1777. Initially Frances found Maria's escapades 'romantic', but she came to regard Bessy's conduct as shameless and shocking, and she played her part in editing out these events from family history in later life. It was also in October 1777 that a more extensive cover-up was required in the case of Charles junior, who had transferred from Charterhouse to Cambridge. Not long after taking up his place at Caius College, Frances's brother was caught stealing books from the university library and sent down by the authorities. He may have been actuated by 'a MAD RAGE for possessing a library' (*Journals*, 10.795), as Frances told the offender's son forty years later (the Burney machine had operated so efficiently that this son only learned what had happened when his father died in 1817). In later years Charles did indeed amass a splendid collection of books and newspapers, much of it preserved in the British Library. However, it seems likely that young Charles had quickly run up debts in Cambridge by gambling and high living, with the result that he sold the stolen items to London booksellers to recoup money. Elaborate schemes were put in place to hush up the matter, as well as to find an alternative route for Charles now that his intended career in the church was blocked. Frances tried to give him good advice, which he good-humouredly accepted, but she destroyed all references to the episode in her journals.

Fame   In the light of this, it is not surprising that the novel *Evelina* which made 'Miss Burney' into a celebrated name emerged in circumstances of extreme secrecy. Virtually nobody outside the most intimate members of her family knew that she was engaged in any form of serious writing. It is not certain exactly when Frances embarked on her first mature work of fiction. *Evelina* was composed partly of 'disjointed scraps and fragments' she had assembled in 1772, as a sequel to 'The History of Caroline Evelyn'. Most of the writing was probably carried out in 1776, when a number of family absences gave her unaccustomed leisure. Moreover, her extensive unpaid labour on behalf of her father could ease up, since the first volume of Dr Burney's *History of Music* had been completed at the end of 1775 and published on 31 January 1776. At last Frances had a respite from her usual tasks, finding herself 'at large and at liberty!' through most of the summer (*Early Journals*, 2.208). Probably she never again enjoyed quite such a freedom from distractions to pursue her writing career. Further progress was made on the later sections of the novel during a long visit to Samuel Crisp at Chessington early in 1777. Substantial revision was carried out on the early drafts, and a fair copy made in a disguised hand, to prolong the mystification. Even the approach to a publisher was made in a preposterously clandestine manner, using a non-existent 'Mr King' as intermediary. After an unsuccessful application to James Dodsley, Frances and her young confidants (who included her siblings and her cousin Edward Francesco *Burney (1760–1848), later the well-known artist and illustrator) decided to approach the Fleet Street bookseller Thomas Lowndes. About Christmas 1776 her brother Charles carried the first instalments of the novel to Lowndes 'in the dark of the evening', muffled up in an old greatcoat and hat, 'to give him a somewhat antique as well as vulgar disguise' (*Memoirs*, 2.129). On 11 November 1777 Lowndes agreed to publish the work and offered 20 guineas, duly accepted by Frances. *Evelina, or, A Young Lady's Entrance into the World* made its appearance about 29 January 1778. Since Frances had served as her father's amanuensis she may have feared that her writing would be recognized. Certainly her father had no idea of the book's authorship when it appeared, despite hints from his daughter that she had a literary work in hand; and her anonymity survived much longer in the wider world, as unlikely guesses were made as to the identity of the author.

The book soon achieved considerable popularity and received favourable notices in the *London Review* and *Monthly Review*. Its fame naturally spread in the circles frequented by Dr Burney and his children; by the middle of summer the novel had reached the attention of Reynolds, Edmund Burke, and even Johnson, as Frances's father learned when visiting the Thrales at Streatham. He had only recently been let into the secret of the book's authorship by Susan, and he passed the evidently astonishing news to his wife. Further information came from Hester Thrale, to the effect that Johnson was full of praise after borrowing a copy of *Evelina*; the great critic later asserted that the book contained effects beyond the reach of either Henry Fielding or Samuel Richardson. Mrs Thrale also

reported that Reynolds 'had been fed while reading the little work, from refusing to quit it at table! and that Edmund Burke had sat up a whole night to finish it!!!' (*Memoirs*, 2.148). The identity of the author was eventually exposed in a satire by George Huddesford (published late in the year), when 'dear little Burney' was named as the writer, much to her distress. For many months the novel remained a favourite talking point in society, as further editions appeared, the second on 26 October 1778 and two more by the end of 1779, bringing the combined print run to well over 2000 copies. Booksellers in London and the fashionable spas were unable to keep up with the demand.

Even those who professed themselves unwilling to read fiction in general found in *Evelina* social truth, along with humour, entertainment, realistic characterization, and an expressive style. The novel was cast in the form of letters, allowing extensive treatment of the leading public resorts and places of amusement in London and Bristol—familiar locations which must have helped the book become so popular. The plot enacted the archetypal Cinderella-like story of a pseudo-orphan who was ultimately revealed as an heiress. There was pathos along with broad humour at the expense of vulgar *nouveaux riches*. Hester Thrale noted most of these features, as well as 'an infinite deal of fun in it', and when she discovered that Frances was the author demanded that her father should bring her on a visit (Hemlow, *History of Fanny Burney*, 105). Late in July 1778 the blushing author was duly presented at Streatham, on what she described with no intention of hyperbole as 'the most *Consequential* Day I have spent since my Birth' (*Early Journals*, 3.66). By the end of the year Mrs Thrale had begun to correspond regularly with Frances, having overcome her snobbish dislike of what she now called 'the Burneian system'. Thus, by means of *Evelina*, Frances achieved widespread celebrity as a writer, especially among the upper echelons of society. She also gained entrée personally to the leading intellectual circles of the day, which included the bluestocking group headed by women such as Elizabeth Montagu and Hannah More, as well as the illustrious figures who surrounded Johnson in the Literary Club.

During the next few years Frances spent many hours in this distinguished company. The pages of her diary which relate these meetings have long been classics, on account of the intrinsic historic interest of the material as well as the skill with which it is deployed in the journal. Quite often the narrative can be checked against parallel reports of the same events, by Hester Thrale, James Boswell, Hannah More, and others; the recital by Frances loses nothing by comparison, in terms of accuracy or of vigour in presentation. She often shows Johnson in a more intimate vein at Streatham than his usual appearance in the pages of Boswell. (Frances met the biographer in this period, but never overcame a dislike of his pushy ways.) A characteristic set piece from about 1778 describes the occasion when Dr Burney invited a mixed gathering to St Martin's Street, including Johnson and the Thrales. A musical entertainment was provided by the Italian singer Gabriel Piozzi; in her account Frances brilliantly evokes the scene as Mrs Thrale mocked the man who was to be her future husband behind his back (this was the basis of 'Dr Burney's Evening Party', a famous essay by Virginia Woolf). By this time Frances had another rival in the person of her sister Susan, who wrote an almost equally vivid description of an episode in 1780 when Johnson and the Thrales visited Crisp and Frances at Chessington.

Other literary projects were now under way. Frances was told by several people, including Richard Brinsley Sheridan, Reynolds, and Arthur Murphy, that the powers of writing dialogue she had displayed in her novel ought to be put to dramatic use. Johnson even made the joking suggestion that she should produce a work entitled 'Streatham: a Farce', and it was Hester Thrale who was most persistent in urging Frances to write a comedy. Accordingly about August 1778 she began a play entitled *The Witlings*, satirizing the literary world and especially the *précieuses ridicules* who were to be found on the fringes of the bluestocking group. By the following May this work was completed. However, the timid Dr Burney feared that one of the leading characters, Lady Smatter, would be identified with Mrs Montagu (others have detected certain lineaments of Elizabeth Burney). Together with the equally old-maidish views of Samuel Crisp, her father's discouragement was enough to deter Frances. Writing from Chessington on 29 August 1779 he recommended that she turn her attention to some other branch of writing, so as to avoid the dangers of stage productions; his views were seconded by Crisp in a letter to his 'dear Fanni-kin'. Soon afterwards, in response to the arguments of her true father and her beloved 'Daddy', Frances abandoned her plan, and wished a sad farewell to 'the poor *Witlings*—for ever, and for ever, and for ever' (*Early Journals*, 3.345). Most modern commentators believe that *The Witlings* would have been able to succeed on the stage, especially if Sheridan had been given the opportunity to present it at Drury Lane.

Some time in 1780 Frances began serious work on her second novel, this time with the active encouragement of Samuel Crisp. By early 1781 she had completed a draft of the first volume of *Cecilia*, a much longer work than *Evelina*. Progress was more than once delayed by illness, and the writing caused Frances more anxiety than before: revision and copying went on after the first part had been set in type. *Cecilia, or, Memoirs of an Heiress* was published in five volumes on 12 June 1782 in an edition of 2000 copies, which quickly sold out. The publishers, Thomas Payne and Thomas Cadell, had paid her £250 for the rights; even though this contract may have been negotiated by Johnson, it was a favourable one for the booksellers, since the first edition enjoyed a quick sale. *Cecilia* was highly popular in circulating libraries, whose readers seemed to relish its broad canvas, and its often unflattering picture of life in high society. The book contained passages of drama—even melodrama—as well as pathos and humour, but it was Cecilia's guardians, the snobbish Mr Delville and his proud wife, who brought a note of moral ambiguity and who excited the most interest and admiration.

One of the early devotees of the novel was Edmund Burke, whom Frances met for the first time at a dinner party given by Reynolds about the same time as *Cecilia* came out. Other guests included Edward Gibbon, who made a much less pleasing impression on Frances. Burke complimented the author on her writing, and declared that this was now 'the age for women'. For Johnson, the 'grand merit' of *Cecilia* lay 'in the general Power of the whole' (Hemlow, *History of Fanny Burney*, 151). Throughout the process of composition Hester Thrale had been a strong supporter, and the two women remained on friendly terms despite the death of Henry Thrale in 1781, which led to the dissolution of the old Streatham set. At home, Frances had greeted her brother James back from his service on Cook's last, fatal voyage; she then welcomed another hero of this expedition into the family, in the person of Molesworth Phillips (1755–1832), a lieutenant in the marines, who married Susan Burney on 10 January 1782. Frances was with her sister for the birth of a daughter named in her honour during the following October.

The year 1782 also saw the publication of the second volume of Dr Burney's *History of Music*, which delighted Frances partly because she now had more of her father's company than she had enjoyed for a long time. In the early 1780s Frances was half-heartedly pursued by the clergyman George Cambridge but the relationship petered out. Her friendship with Hester Thrale also suffered. Hester Thrale's second marriage to Gabriel Piozzi drove a wedge between Frances and her old friend, as it estranged almost all the bluestockings and former members of the Streatham set. Frances made little secret of her distaste for the match, and when it took place in July 1784 the break was irrevocable. Hester thought that Frances had secretly abetted her daughter Queeney in scheming against Piozzi, and rightly judged that the socially insecure Burney clan were embarrassed by the prospect of a misalliance. The two women did not meet again until 1815, when Frances called on the widowed Mrs Piozzi in Bath; Hester claimed to have perfectly forgiven 'l'aimable traitresse', but it was too late to resume cordial relations. Equally upset by the marriage was Samuel Johnson, whose death in December 1784 removed one of Frances's most beloved and supportive friends. A year previously, Frances had gone down to Chessington to provide last offices for Samuel Crisp, who died on 26 April 1783.

Drudgery at court In the middle of the 1780s, however, Frances seemed in a comfortable situation. The success of her novels had brought her renown and some modest financial success. Now enjoying the acquaintance of Elizabeth Montagu, she also became intimate with the writer and artist Mary Delany, who had known Jonathan Swift and other great figures from the early part of the century. Family affairs prospered. On 17 February 1784 Dr Burney was elected to Johnson's Literary Club, an honour he valued beyond any other for the rest of his life; Frances was equally proud of his elevation into the ranks of the nation's most distinguished intellectual figures. Four months later came the Handel commemoration, one of the major musical events of the century in England, and again Frances derived deep satisfaction from the prominent role which her father took in the proceedings.

Through her contacts with Mary Delany, a court favourite at Windsor, Frances was presented to the king and queen, and soon afterwards received an offer to serve as second keeper of the robes to Queen Charlotte. The salary of £200 per year, along with provision of a footman and a maid, was far from stingy, but Frances recoiled from the prospect: as she wrote to her sister Esther in June 1786, 'The separation from all my friends and connections is so cruel to me—the attendance, dress, confinement, are to be so unremitting' (Hemlow, *History of Fanny Burney*, 196). Her father, flattered by this mark of royal favour, urged her to accept. She may have agreed partly to escape from her increasingly strained relations with her stepmother. The home in St Martin's Street no longer served as a refuge of the nuclear family, especially after Charlotte married Clement Francis (*c*.1744-1792), an East India Company surgeon, in February 1786. Dr Burney was himself poised to move house, when he took up a post as organist at Chelsea Hospital. Other support systems had failed, with the dissolution of the Streatham circle and the loss of Crisp and Johnson in quick succession. Frances understood well enough the prison she would be entering at court, and she lamented the end of many dreams for her future. But she was an unmarried woman approaching her mid-thirties, and her choices were severely limited. Eventually on 17 July 1786 she set out for the Queen's Lodge at Windsor Castle, and by her own account almost staggered into her new apartments, pale and sick with apprehension. Even her father perceived her distress, in spite of his instinct to support what he saw as social advancement for the family.

The next five years contained little but refined servitude. Frances was compelled to work long hours, to attend her royal mistress through uneventful days and nights, and to live a life of dull routine, menial activity, and rigid protocol. Her journals chronicle this dismal succession of uneventful days at Windsor and Kew, in the company of a narrow circle of unexciting people. She had to defer to her immediate superior, Madame Elizabeth Schwellenberg, whom she found the 'exactest fellow' of her stepmother, 'gloomy, dark, suspicious, rude, reproachful' (Hemlow, *History of Fanny Burney*, 36). This uneventful tenor of living was finally shattered by the onset of the king's first serious attack of mental illness in 1788. The episode prompted some striking passages in the diary, exhibiting George III in a variety of comic and pathetic guises, including pursuing Frances around Kew Gardens, but it made Frances's duties even more stressful. After the king recovered in 1789, she was able to accompany the royal party on a trip to south-west England, but all too soon she had to return to Windsor, her heart sinking as she entered the apartments of Madame Schwellenberg. She wrote a number of tragic dramas while at Windsor, but by this time her health was giving way under the strain, and members of the Literary Club led by William Windham organized a conspiracy to allow her to escape from her captive role. As Boswell told Frances after intercepting her at Windsor, the matter had been 'puissantly discussed' at the club (*Memoirs*, 3.116). Pressure continued to be put on Dr Burney by a group including Burke and Reynolds, and eventually Frances was allowed to draft a petition to the queen, asking permission to resign her post on grounds of ill health. It took another six months before she was permitted to retire on half-pay, so that she could leave office on 7 July 1791.

Marriage Frances Burney's health now improved rapidly. After entering once more into the intellectual society she had missed so much, she embarked on a holiday to the south-west in the company of the bluestocking Anna Ord. On her return to London, where she took up residence with her father at Chelsea Hospital, she visited the Locke family at Mickleham in Surrey. Frances had known Frederica Locke (1750-1832) and her husband, William (1732-1810), for several years, but it was only now that she was able to keep regular contact with the couple, who lived opulently in a newly built mansion at Norbury Park. On the edge of the estate near the River Mole stood a cottage where Susan Phillips had been living since 1784: Susan enjoyed the society of the cultivated Lockes, and even named her son (born in 1785) Norbury in their honour. It was Susan who reported to her sister in October 1792 the arrival of 'a little colony of unfortunate … French noblesse in our neighbourhood' (Hemlow, *History of Fanny Burney*, 226). This event transformed Frances's life.

The émigrés settled at Juniper Hall, across the valley from the Locke estate. A little later they were joined by Charles Maurice Talleyrand and the writer Germaine de Staël, but initially the party included the comte de Narbonne, at this time de Staël's lover, along with his friend Alexandre-Jean-Baptiste Piochard D'Arblay (1754–1818), a career soldier and former adjutant to the marquis de Lafayette. Frances was interested to learn of the doings of this émigré group, though she found them unexpectedly liberal in political outlook. As aristocrats they had naturally fallen foul of the Jacobins, but they were constitutional reformers rather than royalist ultras. By this date the Burney circle had been persuaded by Edmund Burke of the iniquities surrounding the French Revolution and Charles Burney had renounced his former whiggish and even radical views. As the terror progressed in Paris, the situation of the refugees became more exposed, and they drew more closely to their sympathetic neighbours, the Locke and Phillips families. Frances met the group for the first time in January 1793, at the time of the execution of Louis XVI, and she naturally found them in a confused and disheartened state. Even D'Arblay, with his fine figure and handsome face, had changed overnight into a black and mournful spectre. While the sly Talleyrand repelled Frances, she was at first favourably impressed by Mme de Staël, who had made warm overtures of friendship. She seemed to Frances 'one of the first women I have ever met with for abilities and extraordinary intellects' (*Journals*, 2.10). Before long, however, Frances became uncertain about establishing intimacy with someone who was not only a freethinker but also a free liver, noted for her promiscuity.

Cautiously she retreated and distanced herself from de Staël, partly it may be to make a clear distinction between this extreme personage and the respectable d'Arblay, with whom she was now conducting a decorous romance.

D'Arblay visited Frances at Chelsea several times in the spring of 1793, and even Dr Burney was charmed by his appearance and manner, despite his comparatively advanced political opinions. Frances began the process of softening up her father, who was dismayed by the prospect that she might marry a penniless foreigner, as her pension of £100 represented almost the whole of the couple's joint income and could be withheld at any time. And he did not wish to lose his daughter, such was his habitual reliance on her. Mrs Burney stayed out of the matter. In the end resistance was worn down, but her father declined to attend the wedding. When this took place at St Michael's Church, Mickleham, on 28 July 1793, the entire party consisted of the couple, James (who gave the bride away), the Lockes, and the Phillips. D'Arblay was Roman Catholic and two days later the ceremony was repeated in the Sardinian Chapel in Lincoln's Inn Fields, London (this was another feature which dismayed the elder Burneys). As has been pointed out by Joyce Hemlow, it took immense courage for a woman of forty-one, with few resources of her own, to defy prejudice and opposition in this way. The match proved extremely happy: Frances had previously encountered admirers who were unsuitable, like the hapless Thomas Barlow, or irresolute, like George Cambridge. Now she had found a mature man, who had experienced an adventurous past, and who possessed an outlook broader than that of the weak-kneed socialites who had courted Frances previously. Cultivated, widely travelled, and experienced, D'Arblay must have impressed her with his military prowess and his refined bearing.

The newly married couple settled at Phoenice, a farmhouse near Bookham to the west of Norbury Park. In November 1793 they moved into an adjoining property known as The Hermitage. The D'Arblays read and wrote together: Frances sewed while her husband gardened or studied English. A happy start to the marriage was confirmed when their son, Alexander Charles Louis Pichard, was born on 18 December 1794. After years of tending nieces and nephews, Frances had her own child for the rest of the family to admire. It brought the brothers and sisters closer together again, although Charlotte had been left a widow with three young children when her husband Clement died suddenly in 1792. Susan, too, although a close neighbour, was suffering hardship as her husband grew increasingly capricious and unpredictable.

In time Frances resumed her writing career. *Edwy and Elgiva*, one of the tragic dramas she had composed during her service at Windsor, was the first, and as it turned out the only one, of her plays to be performed in her lifetime. Based on the tenth-century conflict between a king of the west Saxons and the contentious abbot of Glastonbury, Dunstan, the play's mood is sometimes gloomy and Gothic, and sometimes sweetly plangent. It was her brother Charles who had taken the initiative in mounting the play at Drury Lane after consulting John Philip Kemble and Sheridan. It was performed only once, on 21 March 1795, and even an impressive cast headed by Kemble and his sister Sarah Siddons could not save the day as the audience gave vent to their disapproval. Frances herself asked for the play to be withdrawn. Few commentators have judged this hostile verdict unfair, although the tepid reception for this play owes most to a lingering distaste for verse tragedy in its full histrionic panoply.

Soon after this set-back, Frances achieved her most spectacular success in commercial terms. She began what she called her '*grand ouvrage*', a new novel entitled *Camilla*, just before the birth of her son. Progress was surprisingly quick in view of the many distractions in her life: this time she had the assistance of her husband as amanuensis, in a reversal of previous Burney roles, and a fair copy survives in his hand, running to over 1300 pages. Even with substantial revision, the manuscript took little over a year to complete. *Camilla, or, A Picture of Youth* was published on 28 June 1796 by Payne (whose daughter Sarah was now married to James Burney), but on this occasion the Burneys had resolved to reap the profits for the family. An elaborate subscription campaign was mounted, with the help of leading figures in society including Frances Boscawen, Frances Crewe, and Frederica Locke. Three hundred subscribers at a guinea and a half for the three volumes included great national potentates and church dignitaries, with many multiple sets listed (fifteen for Burke, and ten for Elizabeth Montagu). The bluestockings were present in numbers, along with surviving members of the Johnson circle like Bennet Langton; even Hester Thrale, by now thoroughly removed from Frances, entered her name. Other women writers among the subscribers were Anne Radcliffe, Hannah More, Maria Edgeworth, and Jane Austen, then an unknown twenty-year-old, who thus publicly announced her discipleship to Frances for the first time. Though the novel was greeted less warmly than its predecessors, the author was paid £1000 for the copyright and gained at least as much again from the subscription. The sale was even more rapid than it had been for *Cecilia*, with almost all the 4000 copies disposed of by November 1796. The work acquired further éclat from its dedication to the queen.

Students of the novel have discovered more autobiographical references in *Camilla* than in previous works. Among those who allegedly appear in the text are individuals from the Norbury Park group (especially Mrs Locke), visitors to St Martin's Street, and even (heavily disguised) members of the Burney family itself. One clear reference is to Mary Ann Port (1771–1830), a relative of Mary Delany who lived with the old lady until her death in 1788; Frances was a confidante who had learned of Mary Ann's unhappy affair with the dashing heir of Norbury, William Locke (1767–1847), later well known as an artist. The main story concerns the education of the heroine as she encounters a wide range of more or less plausible role models and love objects. While satire and comedy have not disappeared, *Camilla* as a whole is more overtly moralistic than the earlier books, and its language has acquired some of the latinate pomp which marks the author's later work. It has consequently never been her most popular novel, although recent critics have commended its rich portrayal of female difficulties in an age which also saw the appearance of books on this theme by writers such as Mary Wollstonecraft and Mary Hays.

Home and abroad The profits from this literary work enabled the D'Arblays to build their own house on a site which William Locke had set aside on his estate. They occupied Camilla Cottage, as it was called, in November 1797, and Frances must have looked forward to a period of quiet prosperity. Events were to dictate otherwise. The first blow came when Susan was carried off from Mickleham to Ireland by her undependable husband Molesworth Phillips, to the great distress of Frances. The marine resigned his commission, contracted debts all round, and pursued women; Susan's health began to suffer under this strain. Then, on 20 October 1796, Elizabeth Burney died after severe lung haemorrhage; Frances had never found her stepmother easy, but she pitied her father's grief as he was again widowed. The old man remained true to his colours when he refused permission for Charlotte to make a second marriage with Ralph Broome (1742–1805), a man of middle age who appeared from the Burney perspective to be wild and immature. The marriage ultimately took place in February 1798, but despite attempts by Frances to reach a settlement on money and other difficulties, Dr Burney refused the couple his blessing. It was the repetition of a pattern with which Frances was all too familiar.

As the century neared its close, problems continued to crowd in on the Burneys. The cruelty of Molesworth Phillips prompted the family to rescue Susan and bring her home, but Charles's journey to meet her was in vain: Susan's fragile health could not withstand the strain of travel, and she died on 6 January 1800, a few days after landing in England near Chester. To Frances Susan was the closest of her sisters, and she never forgave Phillips for his conduct; the shadow of this catastrophic turn of events haunted her for the rest of her life. The depth of this grief can be seen in the *Memoirs* of her father, published long afterwards. Another tumultuous development left no trace, however, and indeed its existence was censored so effectively that the truth became fully apparent only in recent years. In 1798 Frances was forced along with Dr Burney to accept a startling revelation: her brother James, who had left his wife, was now living with his half-sister Sarah. It has been suggested that the liaison was probably sexual, although it had to be conducted in squalid retirement. For the next few years Frances attempted to convince herself that her brother's behaviour was 'dark—dark!' but not, she hoped, 'black!' (*Journals*, 4.216). In 1807 Sarah eventually returned to Dr Burney's house, but by that time Frances was living abroad.

At the same time the affairs of Monsieur D'Arblay were giving almost equal concern. After the rise of Napoleon he had travelled to Holland with the aim of settling his affairs in France. In 1801 he returned to his native land and became deeply embroiled in efforts to retrieve his former

property. At first Frances remained at home with little Alex, and she managed to get Covent Garden Theatre to accept a comedy entitled *Love and Fashion*, but again Dr Burney was unenthusiastic and the play was never put on. Another comedy, *The Woman-Hater*, was written about 1800–02; it may have been intended for Drury Lane, but it suffered the same fate as other plays by Frances, as it had to wait until recent years before reaching print. This is also true of *A Busy Day*, generally considered her most impressive achievement as a writer for the stage. This play too may have been composed about 1801, when Frances was waiting for news of D'Arblay on his Parisian quest.

Later years In April 1802 the peace of Amiens enabled Frances to join her husband. When hostilities resumed a year later, the couple and their son were effectively trapped in France. D'Arblay was eventually awarded a small pension and took up a minor official post. The family spent the next ten years living in and around Paris. In September 1811 Frances had a cancer diagnosed in her right breast and underwent a painful mastectomy, performed by Dominique-Jean Larron, military surgeon to Napoleon. In her correspondence she left a much consulted and graphic account of this operation, carried out with no anaesthetic. A year later she was allowed to return to England with Alexander, who was now seventeen, and soon to begin studies at Cambridge. In March 1814 she published her last novel, *The Wanderer, or, Female Difficulties*, which drew on her own experiences as well as those of family members in describing the adventures of a penniless spinster buffeted from pillar to post. The book was eagerly awaited, and Frances received £1500 for the first edition of 3000 copies, with further sums for subsequent editions. Unfortunately the sales did not exhaust even a second edition, and the work quickly fell into obscurity. Frances nursed her father in his last illness. Dr Burney died on 12 April 1814, a week before his eighty-eighth birthday, and Frances began to assemble the manuscripts she needed for a planned biography.

Frances returned to Paris after the fall of Napoleon in November 1814, when her husband regained his position in the army. D'Arblay took an active military role during Peel's 'hundred days', and Frances rejoined him in Brussels in time to witness events leading up to Waterloo (it is likely that William Makepeace Thackeray made some use of her journal entries in *Vanity Fair*). Her husband received an injury during the campaign which forced him to retire from the army. In October 1815 the couple returned to England for good, apart from occasional visits to France by M. D'Arblay, who had been promoted to general but was denied his half-pay. They settled in Bath. Frances grew increasingly frustrated by her son's failure to advance his career at Cambridge, although his dissipations took no stronger form than an obsession with mathematics and chess, activities in which he was joined by the computer pioneer Charles Babbage and the astronomer John Herschel.

The next few months were distressing. In October 1817

Frances joined her son for a reading party at Ilfracombe; caught on the rocks by the tide, she spent several hours alone and almost drowned. On 28 December 1817 her brother Charles succumbed to a stroke, and then on 3 May 1818 her husband died after a long and painful illness which may have been cancer of the colon. Grief-stricken at first, Frances slowly gained strength with the support of her sisters, and showing true Burney resilience she moved back to London and managed to survive further afflictions. These included the loss of her brother-in-law Charles Rousseau in 1819, followed by the sudden death of James, who had ended up as an admiral, in November 1821. Frances was deeply disappointed by the continued irresolution of her son Alex, even after strings had been pulled to gain him ordination and a curacy at Camden Town. Much of her time was devoted to assembling the *Memoirs* of her father, ultimately published in three volumes in 1832. Although the project involved much tactical rewriting of history, and constitutes in some measure an apologia for the author's own conduct, it remains an absorbing compilation of first-hand recollections. Not all the relatives were pleased by this act of family piety; Frances had to face complaints from her long-lived half-brother, the Revd Stephen Allen, that she had been unfair to the second Mrs Burney.

The last years followed a familiar downward curve, even though Frances retained her faculties to an advanced age. She naturally had to face bereavements, notably when the death of Esther occurred on 17 February 1832, quickly followed by that of her devout and multi-talented niece Marianne Francis. Last came that of Charlotte on 12 September 1838. These events brought to an end a lifelong history of shared intimacies, but they were easier for Frances to bear than the loss of her son Alex, whose enigmatic and unfulfilled career, marked by bouts of ill health and depression, was cut short by a sudden fever on 19 January 1837. Frances herself died in London at her home, 29 Lower Grosvenor Street, on 6 January 1840. She was buried alongside her son at St Swithin's, Walcot, Bath, on 15 January. Among the older generation of Burneys, only Sarah outlasted her half-sister, living for another four years. Frances bequeathed Sarah, with whom she had a complicated but close relationship, £200 per year. Her niece Fanny Phillips (later Raper) survived until 1850, and true to the Burney tradition she left extensive manuscripts including a short character sketch of her aunt, written after the latter's death, stressing her warm heart and generous nature.

Frances Burney became better known to the world in stages as successive portions of her journals were published after her death. The first instalment, brought out by her niece Charlotte Barrett in 1842–6, elicited a famous essay by Thomas Macaulay in the *Edinburgh Review*. For the next century she lived in the eyes of posterity mainly through these vivid portrayals of the life of late Georgian England and post-revolutionary France. In the first half of the twentieth century Virginia Woolf resuscitated Burney's reputation as a novelist by calling her the mother of English fiction. Burney was identified as one of the first successful female novelists and recent decades have witnessed growing esteem for her contribution to the development of the novel, especially in the creation of a genre in which women were portrayed in realistic social settings, which significantly influenced Maria Edgeworth and Jane Austen. While *Evelina* remains Burney's most widely read work of fiction much more attention has been paid to the later works, especially to *The Wanderer* with its darker mood and bitter insights into the experience of women, particularly the heroine struggling to attain independence and identity. Her plays have been lifted out of obscurity. A scholarly edition of *A Busy Day* appeared in 1984, and a successful performance was mounted in 1993 above a pub in Bristol. It moved to the Old Vic in Bristol and then to London's West End. *The Witlings* has also been recently published, performed, and greeted as a considerable addition to the repertoire of eighteenth-century comedy. Joyce Hemlow's *The History of Fanny Burney* (1958) was the major biography for forty years. The 1980s and 1990s saw increased interest in Burney particularly as part of feminist scholarship, and two significant biographies have been published by Kate Chisholm and Claire Harman. The journals have been re-edited to illuminate previously suppressed aspects of the Burneys' story. As a writer and a human being, Frances was deeply conditioned by her place in a complex family plot, and it is now easier to appreciate the intricate means by which these materials were used to nurture her own art.

A memorial window to Frances at Poets' Corner in Westminster Abbey was unveiled by her great-great-great-great-nephew Charles Burney at a service on 13 June 2002.   PAT ROGERS

Sources The journals and letters of Fanny Burney (Madame D'Arblay), ed. J. Hemlow and others, 12 vols. (1972–84) · The early journals and letters of Fanny Burney, ed. L. E. Troide, 3 vols. (1988–94) · F. Burney, Memoirs of Dr Burney: arranged from his own manuscripts, from family papers, and from personal recollections, 3 vols. (1832) · J. Hemlow, The history of Fanny Burney (1958) · Diary and letters of Madame D'Arblay, ed. [C. Barrett], 7 vols. (1842–6) · J. Hemlow, J. M. Burgess, and A. Douglas, eds., A catalogue of the Burney family correspondence (1971) · Memoirs of Dr Charles Burney, 1726–1769, ed. S. Klima, G. Bowers, and K. S. Grant (1988) · The complete plays of Frances Burney, ed. P. Sabor, 2 vols. (1995) · M. Doody, Frances Burney: the life in the works (1988) · C. Hill, The house in St Martin's Street (1907) · The letters of Dr Charles Burney, ed. A. Ribeiro, 1 (1991) · R. Lonsdale, Dr Charles Burney: a literary biography (1965) · P. Scholes, The great Dr Burney, 2 vols. (1948) · Thraliana: the diary of Mrs. Hester Lynch Thrale (later Mrs. Piozzi), 1776–1809, ed. K. C. Balderston, 2nd edn, 2 vols. (1951) · J. L. Clifford, Hester Lynch Piozzi (Mrs Thrale), 2nd edn (1961) · The Piozzi letters, ed. E. A. Bloom and L. D. Bloom, 5 vols. to date (1989–) · The letters of Sarah Harriet Burney, ed. L. Clark (1997) · C. Harman, Fanny Burney: a biography (2000)

Archives BL, corresp. and family papers, Egerton MSS 3690–3708 · BL, corresp. and literary MSS, M/440, 445, 460, 462, 484, 490–1600 [microfilm copies] · JRL, travel journals and papers · Morgan L., corresp. and papers · priv. coll. · Yale U., Beinecke L., corresp. and papers; part of a diary | Armagh Public Library, Susan Burney papers · Bodl. Oxf., Malone MSS · JRL, Thrale MSS, letters to Hester Piozzi · NYPL, Berg collection, diary

Likenesses E. F. Burney, portrait, c.1782–1785, Parham Park, West Sussex · J. Bogle, portrait, c.1783, priv. coll. · E. F. Burney, oils, c.1784–1785, NPG [see illus.]

Wealth at death see will, 6 March 1839, PRO, PROB 11/1922, sig. 88

Burney, Frances (1776–1828), governess and poet, was born in London in January 1776, the fourth child and second daughter of cousins Esther (Hetty) Burney (1749–1832) and Charles Rousseau Burney (1747–1819), and niece of the novelist and diarist Frances Burney, Madame D'Arblay. Her parents were both talented musicians: Esther had been a child prodigy and had made her musical début playing the harpsichord before a select audience at the Little Theatre, Haymarket, in 1760, while Charles Rousseau was an acknowledged virtuoso of both the harpsichord and the violin. Despite their talent, the couple—and their eight children—were dogged by poverty, and in 1794 Frances was obliged to take up her first post as governess in the household of Lord Beverley. Thereafter family connections helped her to secure positions in a number of eminent households, her employers including the attorney-general Sir Thomas Plumer (1753–1824) and Sir Henry Russell (1751–1836), chief justice at Bengal.

In spite of the gruelling nature of her work and chronic ill health, Burney pursued her education and gradually acquired a library that included books in French, German, Latin, Greek, and Italian. In 1818 she published *Tragic dramas; chiefly intended for representation in private families: to which is added, Aristodemus, a tragedy, from the Italian of Vincenzo Monti*. The tragedies themselves, 'Fitzormond, or, Cherished Resentment' and 'Malek Adhel, the Champion of the Crescent', are overblown and melodramatic, and the style and tone can be gleaned from a short quotation from 'Fitzormond':

> Lady Fitzormond: 'My taper's spent, yet I am loth to quit
> The deep'ning gloom of this sequester'd scene'

It is telling that the very title of these plays assures readers that they are meant for private performances only—Frances had clearly been affected by the concerns of her grandfather Charles Burney (1726–1814) about the potential impropriety of the stage, particularly for female dramatists. Burney's preface to *Tragic Dramas* similarly recalls her aunt's preface to *Evelina* (1776) in expressing feminine diffidence at publishing:

> Various motives … having combined to induce the Writer of the following pages to bring them before the public, she is desirous, by stating a few of them, to obviate as much as possible, the imputation of temerity to which the publication of them may subject her. (p. 1)

Burney suffered attacks of jaundice throughout her life, and on Friday, 28 March 1828, 'wasted to a skeleton' (*Journals and Letters*, 11.712), she succumbed to the disease at her mother's home in King Street, Bath. She was buried on 4 April at Batheaston church, where her father's remains were also interred. Though a letter to Esther from Frances Burney, Madame D'Arblay, in 1824 had rather petulantly complained of what she saw as her niece's neglect: 'I once thought I had caught a bit of her heart—& I *tried* for it, 3 or 4 years ago—but I see, & am sorry to see, my mistake' (ibid., 11.566), Burney's pupils evidently loved their old governess who was a regular visitor and guest

(ibid., 11.371). As her aunt observed, in spite of an onerous profession and repeated illness, 'her spirits seem never failing' (ibid.). EMMA PLASKITT

Sources J. R. de J. Jackson, *Romantic poetry by women: an anthology, 1770–1835* (1993), 45 · R. Brimley Johnson, *Fanny Burney and the Burneys* (1826); repr. (1926), 366–71, 400 · *The early journals and letters of Fanny Burney*, ed. L. E. Troide, 3 vols. (1988–94) · *The journals and letters of Fanny Burney (Madame D'Arblay)*, ed. J. Hemlow and others, 12 vols. (1972–84), vols. 11–12 · K. Chisholm, *Fanny Burney: her life, 1752–1840* (1998)
Likenesses E. Burney, portrait (as child), repro. in Brimley Johnson, *Fanny Burney*
Wealth at death £100 in the stocks to mother; £25 each to aunts; £30 severally to brother and surviving sisters; library, incl. grammars and books in French, Latin, Italian, Spanish, German, Greek, MS works of her own (both music and poetry): will, PRO, PROB 11/1740/259

Burney, James (1750–1821), naval officer and writer, was born on 13 June 1750 in London, the second child of Charles *Burney (1726–1814), music historian, and his first wife, Esther (*bap.* 1725?, *d.* 1762), who may have been the daughter of Richard Sleepe, a leader of the lord mayor's band, and his wife, Frances. When he was ten his father sent him to sea as a captain's servant in a man-of-war, the *Princess Amelia*. At fifteen he began a tour of the Mediterranean as midshipman in the frigate *Aquilon* (28 guns). Upon the *Aquilon*'s return to England after three years in 1769 the Burney family were dismayed to learn that Jem, as he was known, had been disciplined for insubordination, which was to be a continuing problem.

In 1772 Burney's father used his influence with his friend John Montagu, fourth earl of Sandwich, first lord of the Admiralty, to procure James a berth as able seaman in Captain James Cook's ship, the *Resolution*, on Cook's second voyage of discovery to the south seas. Cook's expedition departed in June, and in November Burney was transferred to the *Resolution*'s sister-ship, the *Adventure*, as second lieutenant, his first commission. Returning to England in 1774, he acted as interpreter for Omai, the first Tahitian to visit Britain. From 1776 to 1780 he sailed on Cook's third voyage of discovery, and witnessed Cook's killing by Hawaiians in 1779. During the voyage he was several times passed over for promotion because of an early altercation with his immediate superior, Captain Charles Clerke, commander of the *Discovery*. Only at the very end of the voyage was he promoted from first lieutenant to command of the *Discovery*, after Clerke's death.

In June 1782 Burney was commissioned captain of the *Bristol* (50 guns), which convoyed twelve East India Company ships to Madras. As part of Sir Edward Hughes's squadron the *Bristol* saw action in the final engagement with the French fleet off Cuddalore on 20 June 1783. At the end of 1784 Burney fell seriously ill and departed for England. This was the end of his active naval career. While convoying the East India fleet in 1782 he had directly disobeyed orders, a final act of insubordination which meant his forced retirement on the half pay list after leaving the *Bristol*. Repeated petitions for a new command were rebuffed, in part because of his openly republican political views. Only in July 1821, aged seventy-one, did he receive a promotion to rear-admiral on the retired list, and then only because of the personal intervention of the duke of Clarence (later William IV), admiral of the fleet.

While waiting in vain for a new command Burney turned to his second career, that of author (mostly on exploration), following the examples of his father and his sister, the novelist Frances (Fanny) *Burney. His first (anonymous) effort was an edition of William Bligh's *A Voyage to the South Sea in HMS Bounty* (1792). His *magnum opus* was *A Chronological History of the Discoveries in the South Sea or Pacific Ocean*, 5 vols. (1803–17), which describes the discoveries up to but not including Cook's. This work, carefully researched and clearly and concisely written, long remained the standard on its subject. He was elected a fellow of the Royal Society in 1809.

In his early years Burney enjoyed the friendship of Samuel Johnson and other social and literary luminaries. Later he became a crony of Charles Lamb, William Hazlitt, Robert Southey, and Henry Crabb Robinson, all of whom would repair to his home in James Street, Westminster, to enjoy an evening of their favourite game, whist. Sir Joseph Banks the naturalist was a lifelong friend.

A convivial and entertaining man in society, Burney was decidedly unconventional in his private life. While in the south seas, he, like many of his mates, enjoyed the sexual favours of the native women. On 6 September 1785 he married Sarah Payne (1759–1832), daughter of Thomas Payne, one of his sister's publishers, in the parish church of Chessington, Surrey. In 1798 he left his wife and two children to set up house with his half-sister Sarah Harriet *Burney (1772–1844). He was forty-eight and she twenty-six. It is moot whether the arrangement was sexual. His marriage was unhappy, but he returned to his wife in 1803.

Rear-Admiral James Burney died suddenly of an apoplectic stroke at his home, 26 James Street, Westminster, on 17 November 1821, at the age of seventy-one, four months after his last promotion. He was buried in the churchyard of St Margaret's, Westminster. Charles Lamb wrote to William Wordsworth: 'There's Captain Burney gone!—What fun has whist now?' (*Letters of Charles Lamb*, 2.319). LARS TROIDE

Sources *The early journals and letters of Fanny Burney*, ed. L. E. Troide, 1: *1768–1773* (1988) • *The early journals and letters of Fanny Burney*, ed. L. E. Troide, 2: *1774–1777* (1990) • *The journals and letters of Fanny Burney (Madame D'Arblay)*, ed. J. Hemlow and others, 12 vols. (1972–84) • *The letters of Sarah Harriet Burney*, ed. L. J. Clark (1997) • *Memoirs of Dr Charles Burney, 1726–1769*, ed. S. Klima, G. Bowers, and K. S. Grant (1988) • J. Burney, *With Captain James Cook in the Antarctic and Pacific*, ed. B. Hooper (1975) • *The journals of Captain James Cook*, ed. J. C. Beaglehole, 4 vols. in 5, Hakluyt Society, extra ser., 34a, 35, 36a–b, 37 (1955–74) • G. E. Manwaring, *My friend the admiral: the life, letters, and journals of Rear-Admiral James Burney* (1931) • *The letters of Charles Lamb: to which are added those of his sister, Mary Lamb*, ed. E. V. Lucas, 3 vols. (1935)

Archives BL, journal, Add. MS 8955 • British Columbia Archives and Records Service, papers, incl. admiralty instructions • Morgan L. • NL Aus., journal | Mitchell L., NSW, journal • Morgan L., corresp. with Fanny Burney • NYPL, Berg collection • PRO, Admiralty records

Likenesses R. H. Dyer, engraving (after bust), NMM • charcoal drawing (after bust), NYPL, Berg collection, scrapbook, 'Fanny Burney and family, 1653–1890' • silhouette, NPG

Wealth at death owned Beldawe House, Mickleham, Surrey; house at 26 James Street, Westminster; furniture and books; £100 in stock; made bequests of 50 guineas, 5 guineas (twice): will, 1821, Principal Registry of the Family Division, London, Herschell, 1822, extract in Manwaring, *My friend the admiral*, 285–6

Burney, Sarah Harriet (1772–1844), writer, was born on 29 August 1772, probably in King's Lynn, Norfolk, the youngest of two children of Charles *Burney (1726–1814), musician, and his second wife, Elizabeth, *née* Allen (1728–1796), widow of Stephen Allen, a merchant of King's Lynn. She was much younger than the six children from her father's first marriage who included Frances (Fanny) *Burney (1752–1840), circumnavigator James *Burney (1750–1821), and Charles *Burney (1757–1817), classical scholar and bibliophile. Tension seems to have arisen from these imperfectly blended families.

Sarah Harriet Burney probably spent her earliest years in King's Lynn, joining her father's lively household in London in 1775 when Dr Burney was rising to eminence in his profession. She spent two years (1781–3) in Switzerland learning French and later studied Italian, drawing, and some music. Largely self-taught, she became an avid reader. The only child left at home by 1787, and isolated even more by her mother's death in 1796, she experienced conflict with her father and left him in 1798 to live with her half-brother James. Any suspicion of incest appears to be unwarranted, but the household was unsettled and financially insecure.

In 1803 Burney took a post as governess with a Cheshire family but returned home in 1807 to the Royal Hospital, Chelsea, to care for her elderly father. She remained in Chelsea after his death in 1814 left her in straitened circumstances. After serving briefly as companion to a young invalid, she was asked in 1822 by Lord Crewe to oversee the education of his granddaughters, a position she resigned in 1829. She left soon after for Italy, spending some months in Rome and three lonely years in Florence before returning to England in 1833, where she retired to a boarding house at Bath (1834–41) and later Cheltenham (1841–4).

Burney's letters show intelligence, humour, and a yearning for intellectual companionship. Somewhat unconventional, she preferred the company of men; although unattractive physically (slight of build with a sharp nose but luxuriant hair), she could charm those who, like Henry Crabb Robinson, admired her abilities. Sometimes isolated in her own family, she retained the affectionate loyalty of her pupils. She read widely (partly from loneliness), and showed critical acumen; of her contemporaries, she preferred Sir Walter Scott and Jane Austen, *Pride and Prejudice* especially.

Burney's literary preferences are reflected in her fiction. *Clarentine* (1796) is a novel of manners with a variety of characters and scenes both sentimental and comic. *Geraldine Fauconberg* (1808), epistolary, features an overly scrupulous hero and a Gothic subplot set in picturesque Wales. These novels, published anonymously, were well received, but her third, published by Henry Colburn (under her own name) sold out within four months. *Traits of Nature* (1812) is a lively five-volume work in which lovers are caught between hostile families and the heroine seeks the approval of a tyrannical father. Buoyed by its success, Colburn offered Burney £100 a volume for her next. *Tales of Fancy*, in three volumes, comprises *The Shipwreck* (1816), a one-volume tale about castaways on a tropical island, and *Country Neighbours* (1820), in which an acerbic spinster is narrator; the heroine inspired a sonnet by Charles Lamb. Finally, *The Romance of Private Life* (3 vols., 1839), includes *The Renunciation*, which draws on Burney's travel experiences, and *The Hermitage*, a melodrama involving a ruined country maiden and a murder.

Burney's writing provided a welcome source of income but also offered a release. Suggestive motifs recur: orphaned children, implacable fathers, harsh mothers, spiteful sisters, and domineering brothers. A sense of isolation pervades, as heroines experience rejection, loss, grief, and abandonment, and unsupportive families often provide a source of conflict.

Sarah Harriet Burney died at Belgrave House, the Promenade, Cheltenham, on 8 February 1844; she was buried at St Mary's new burial-ground, Cheltenham, a week later. Her contemporary and posthumous reputation suffered by comparison with that of her more famous sister novelist, Mme D'Arblay, and her work, about which she herself was diffident, has been too much undervalued.

LORNA J. CLARK

Sources *The letters of Sarah Harriet Burney*, ed. L. J. Clark (1997) · *The journals and letters of Fanny Burney (Madame D'Arblay)*, ed. J. Hemlow and others, 12 vols. (1972–84) · *The early journals and letters of Fanny Burney*, ed. L. E. Troide, 3 vols. (1988–94) · J. Hemlow, J. M. Burgess, and A. Douglas, *A catalogue of the Burney family correspondence, 1749–1878* (1971) · *Diary, reminiscences, and correspondence of Henry Crabb Robinson*, ed. T. Sadler, 3 vols. (1869) · H. C. Robinson, travel journals, 25 Nov 1829–7 Oct 1831, DWL · H. C. Robinson, diaries, 14 Oct 1831–18 Feb 1844, DWL · R. Lonsdale, *Dr Charles Burney: a literary biography* (1965) · J. Hemlow, *The history of Fanny Burney* (1958) · parish register, St Nicholas, King's Lynn, Norfolk, 25 Sept 1772 [baptism] · parish register (death), district of Cheltenham, 8 Feb 1844 · parish register (burial), district of Cheltenham, 15 Feb 1844

Archives BL, corresp., Egerton MSS 3699–3705 · Bodl. Oxf. · DWL, letters and MSS · Morgan L. · New York University, Elmer Holmes Bobst Library · New York University, Fales Library · NL Wales, manuscript collections · priv. coll. · priv. coll. | BL, Ayrton collection · BL, Barrett collection of Burney papers, letters and MSS · DWL, letters to Henry Crabb Robinson · Four Oaks Farm, Somerville, New Jersey, Hyde collection · NYPL, Henry W. and Albert A. Berg collection, letters and MSS · NYPL, Carl H. Pforzheimer Collection of Shelley and His Circle · Smith College, Northampton, Massachusetts, New England Hospital collection, Sophia Smith collection · Yale U., Beinecke L., James Marshall and Marie-Louise Osborn Collection, letters and MSS

Likenesses E. F. Burney, portrait, *c.*1782–1785, Parham Park, Sussex · E. F. Burney, portrait, *c.*1784–1785, NPG · J. Zoffany, oils (of Burney?), repro. in R. B. Johnson, *Fanny Burney and the Burneys* (1926) · photograph (of Burney?; after portrait by J. Hoppner), repro. in M. A. Doody, *Frances Burney: the life in the works* (1988)

Wealth at death under £6000; bank balance of £336 12s. 3d. and holdings totalling £5731 1s. (comprising £1991 19s. invested at 3.5 per cent, a £500 exchange bill, and £3239 2s. in consols); £1202 1s. 10d. paid out in various sums during the year following her death; £63 0s. 2d. paid to each of her beneficiaries; £200 to a Mrs Ann Hart Cooper (possibly her servant), and some personal bequests of books, jewellery, a shawl, and some drawings; entire estate left in trust to John Thomas Payne, with interest shared by her nephew and niece (who would inherit whole estate at demise of nephew): will, PRO, PROB 10/6242; bank account SHB, 1801–1845, Coutts & Co., London

Burneyeat, John. *See* Burnyeat, John (1631–1690).

Burnham. For this title name *see* Lawson, Edward Levy-, first Baron Burnham (1833–1916); Lawson, Harry Lawson Webster Levy-, Viscount Burnham (1862–1933); Lawson, Edward Frederick, fourth Baron Burnham (1890–1963).

Burnham, Frederick Russell (1861–1947), scout and prospector, was born on 11 May 1861 in Tivoli, Minnesota, the elder son of Edwin Otway Burnham (d. 1873), Congregational minister and missionary, and his wife, Rebecca, *née* Russell, both of English descent. The family moved to Los Angeles, California, in 1871. Obliged to fend for himself after his father's death, Burnham worked as a mounted messenger for the Western Union Telegraph Company, and underwent a rigorous apprenticeship in scouting from veterans of campaigns against the American Indians of the south-west. Soon afterwards he was caught up in one of Arizona's vicious cattle ranching feuds and with a price on his head abandoned regular employment for hunting and prospecting for gold. An initial lucky strike in December 1883 (followed by a succession of failures) was sufficiently rich to allow Burnham to establish his mother and brother in California and to marry, in 1884, Blanch Blick, of Clinton, Iowa, second daughter of J. S. Blick. They had three children: Roderick, born in 1886, Nada, born in 1893, and Bruce, born in 1899. Hoping to make his fortune in the sprawling African territories of Cecil Rhodes's British South Africa (BSA) Company, in January 1893 Burnham, with his wife and son, sailed from New York via Liverpool to Durban, eventually reaching Fort Victoria in Mashonaland shortly before the start in October 1893 of the campaign against the Matabele (Ndebele).

By his own account, Burnham had a good war. Like all the other white volunteers in the Victoria column, he was promised a 6000 acre farm, twenty gold claims, and a share of any cattle looted from the Ndebele. Among the first troopers to enter Bulawayo in November 1893 after Lobengula abandoned it, Burnham was subsequently a member of Major Allan Wilson's ill-fated Shangani patrol, the small mounted detachment that in December pursued Lobengula. Burnham was one of the patrol's few survivors. As he told it, he and two other scouts were ordered by Wilson to break through the surrounding Ndebele to summon reinforcements. Others were convinced that the flamboyant Burnham and his companions had 'cleared off of their own accord' (O'Reilly, 77). Whatever the truth of that particular incident, the next eighteen months were prosperous ones for Burnham and his family, which now included a baby daughter and two brothers-in-law.

Frederick Russell Burnham (1861–1947), by Elliott & Fry, 1901

Towards the end of 1895 he and his wife left from Beira in Mozambique on an extended holiday planned to take in Cairo, London, and Paris. In Paris they heard news that sent Burnham hurrying back to Africa. Jameson's raid into Transvaal had ended in ignominious surrender. With southern African politics entering a new and ominous phase, the continued success of Burnham's hard won Rhodesian interests required him to be on the spot.

By the time Burnham's ship had docked in Cape Town in March 1896 Matabeleland was in flames. Taking advantage of Jameson's imprisonment in Pretoria along with the larger part of the BSA Company's armed forces, the Ndebele had risen up against chartered rule. Slipping back into Bulawayo, Burnham immediately set to work. His scouting talents greatly impressed Baden-Powell: 'Burnham a most delightful companion … amusing, interesting and most instructive. Having seen service against the Red Indians, he brings quite a new experience to bear on the scouting work here' (Baden-Powell, 26). Baden-Powell also described him as 'a sort of better class Buffalo Bill' (Jeal, 188), and they corresponded as late as 1940. Baden-Powell learned from Burnham, who thus contributed to the accumulation of ideas from which Baden-Powell developed the Boy Scout movement. Burnham's talents also found favour with the fourth Earl Grey, the hard-pressed acting administrator of Matabeleland.

Under the impression that the rising had been instigated by a religious figure called the Mlimo, actually a high-god at the apex of a cult approached through the intercession of priests in cave shrines, Grey agreed to a plan whereby Burnham and Bonner W. Armstrong, native commissioner, Mwange, would capture or kill the Mlimo, so ending the fighting.

There followed an adventure, as described by Burnham, worthy of his Wild West background. According to Burnham, he and Armstrong made their way stealthily to the cave, and despite the presence of a large number of Ndebele, they hid in its shadows unobserved. Ahead of the worshippers a solitary figure approached the cave, pausing to make cabalistic signs and utter prayers. When he entered, Burnham 'made a slight sound and gave him his last chance to turn the white man's bullet to water … [before putting] the bullet under his heart' (Burnham, *Scouting on Two Continents*, 257). The two men then had a furious ride and a running fight for several hours, 'until we were nearly exhausted, but the savages abandoned the chase after we had crossed the Shashani River' (ibid., 258). Their deed was highly commended in Bulawayo, where it was hoped that 'the killing of the Mlimo' might quickly end the war, and they were each presented by the board of the BSA Company with a gold watch.

But as the conflict showed no signs of abating, doubts began to emerge about Burnham's version of events. An inquiry held at Rhodes's insistence, by Judge J. P. F. Watermeyer of the High Court, found that while Burnham and Armstrong had indeed murdered a cult priest, much of their story had been fabricated. Scoffed one contemporary, 'they shot a country curate and claimed to have killed God' (O'Reilly, 38). The priest (Jubane Hlabanga) they killed, near Mwange, was hostile to the rebellion, and the killing came near to pushing the most important 'loyalist' group in Matabeleland into joining the insurgents. Not wanting a scandal, which would adversely affect settler morale and be used by the BSA Company's enemies in Britain, the company let Burnham go quietly. Ruined if not publicly disgraced, he joined the Klondike gold rush in Alaska where the rest of his career might have passed in obscurity but for the Second South African War. Boer victories in December 1899 led to the appointment as British commander-in-chief in South Africa of Lord Roberts, whose urgent need for field intelligence caused him to invite Burnham to become his chief of scouts. Burnham accepted with alacrity, and fought with distinction. Wounded, captured, and promoted major, in 1900 he was invalided back to Britain where he was received by Queen Victoria and awarded the DSO (1900), the highest honour won by an American in the Second South African War.

His reputation now eminently marketable, Burnham for a time found ready employment at the head of African exploration syndicates of the sort then fashionable in the City of London. He also worked for the Guggenheims in Mexico, but by 1914 was once again nearly penniless. Before the United States entered the First World War, he worked with pro-British groups in America to mobilize support for the allied cause. After the war he enjoyed a characteristic stroke of luck when he discovered oil in Dominguez Hills, California. Able to retire in some comfort, he and his wife were prominent citizens of southern California in the 1930s and devoted themselves to good causes, including the Boy Scout movement. They had earlier lost two of their children: their daughter 'from the hardships of the [Ndebele] siege [of Bulawayo]' (Burnham, *Scouting on Two Continents*, 248) in 1896; and their younger son by drowning in the Thames in 1905. Burnham published two volumes of memoirs, *Scouting on Two Continents* (1926)—repeating his false account of the 'Mlimo' episode—and *Taking Chances* (1944). He died in Santa Barbara, California, on 1 September 1947. In 1952 the United States department of the interior named a mountain peak east of Pasadena after him, an oddly inappropriate monument to so restless an individual.   IAN PHIMISTER

Sources O. Ransford, *Bulawayo: historic battleground of Rhodesia* (Cape Town, 1968) · J. O'Reilly, *Pursuit of the king: an evaluation of the Shangani patrol* (Bulawayo, 1970) · A. Keppel-Jones, *Rhodes and Rhodesia: the white conquest of Zimbabwe, 1884–1902* (1983) · F. R. Burnham, *Scouting on two continents* (1926) · B. Farwell, 'Taking sides in the Boer War', *American Heritage*, 27/3 (1976) · S. Crompton, 'Burnham, Frederick Russell', *ANB* · R. S. S. Baden-Powell, *The Matabele campaign, 1896* (1897) · H. M. Hole, *The making of Rhodesia* (1926) · F. R. Burnham, *Taking chances* (New York, 1944) · T. O. Ranger, *Revolt in Southern Rhodesia, 1896–1897: a study in African resistance* (1967) · *WW* · R. Blake, *A history of Rhodesia* (1977) · T. Jeal, *Baden-Powell* (1989)
Archives Yale U., papers, MSS, archives | National Archives, Harare, Zimbabwe, Hist. MSS, Hugh Marshall Hole papers, notes by H. M. Hole, HO 1/4/6 · National Archives, Harare, Zimbabwe, BSA Company London Office MSS, LO 5/6/1–2 [especially report by Burnham and Armstrong, 25/6/1899, in LO 5/6/1]
Likenesses Elliott & Fry, photograph, 1901, NPG [*see illus.*] · R. S. Baden-Powell, sketches and drawings, repro. in Baden-Powell, *The Matabele campaign, 1896* · photographs and illustrations, repro. in Burnham, *Scouting on two continents*
Wealth at death wealthy from oil: Crompton, 'Burnham, Frederick Russell'

Burnham, Richard (1709–1752), writer, was born at Guildford, Surrey, on 18 December 1709 and probably baptized at either Black Horse Lane or Chapel Street Independent chapel, Guildford, of pious parents, George and Elizabeth Burnham. He collected the dying sayings of more than a hundred pious persons, with some account of their lives and last hours. He died on 4 June 1752, and in the following year was published *Pious Memorials, or, The Power of Religion upon the Mind in Sickness and at Death*, by the Revd Richard Burnham, with a recommendatory preface by the Revd James Hervey, author of *Meditations*. Besides the preface, Hervey added in an appendix an account of Burnham, by which it appears he preached for a few years to a small congregation. When he was dying, seeing his wife 'in a flood of tears', he said, 'My dear, don't let us part in a shower.' *Pious Memorials* was translated into German in 1765, reprinted at Paisley in 1788 with additions, enlarged in 1789, reprinted with a continuation by the Revd George Burder in 1820, and reprinted in 1856 under the title *Records of Good Men in Sickness and in Death*.

J. H. THORPE, rev. ADAM JACOB LEVIN

Sources J. Hervey, 'Appendix', in R. Burnham, *Pious memorials*, 2nd edn (1754), 367–75 · *IGI* · *National union catalog*, Library of Congress
Likenesses J. Dean, mezzotint (after W. Smith), NPG · Rothwell, line and stipple (after Peat), NPG

Burnham, Richard (*bap.* 1749, *d.* 1810), Particular Baptist minister and hymnodist, son of William and Ann Burnham, was baptized at the parish church, High Wycombe, Buckinghamshire, on 22 April 1749. Burnham later embraced Baptist views and joined the Particular Baptist church at Reading.

Without any formal training Burnham was ordained by the Baptists in 1778 and first led a small congregation at Staines in Middlesex. From 1780 he served a Baptist church in London, which first met at Green Walk, near Blackfriars Bridge, but was troubled by divisions. One group left with Burnham in 1782 to meet at Gate Street, Lincoln's Inn Fields. In 1787 another split erupted after the misconduct of Burnham, a new group accepting his repentance and supporting him. This group met in a chapel at Edward Street, Soho, from 1790 and relocated in 1795 to a chapel on Grafton Street, Westminster. Burnham established a popular ministry although he was viewed with disdain by some dissenting ministers, as acerbic comments by the historian Walter Wilson clearly reveal (Wilson, 4.25–9).

Burnham was more widely known for his hymns, which reveal an intense Calvinistic theology. In 1780 he published *New Hymns on Divers Subjects*, which contained 117 hymns. Various enlarged editions appeared, the sixth and last in 1803, retitled *Hymns Particularly Designed for the Use of the Congregation at Grafton Street, Soho* and containing 452 hymns by Burnham. This represents a remarkable achievement, and while none of his hymns is in common use today many were much appreciated within Baptist Calvinistic churches during the nineteenth century. Burnham also published various sermons, an autobiographical account in *The Triumphs of Free Grace* (1787), defences of believers' baptism and Calvinist theology, and broadside elegies on Lord Nelson and Baptist minister Andrew Gifford. Burnham, who had a son, William, died on 30 October 1810 and was buried in the burial-ground at Tottenham Court Chapel, London.

J. H. THORPE, rev. KEN R. MANLEY

Sources T. Wright, *Richard Burnham* [n.d., *c.*1910] · W. Wilson, *The history and antiquities of the dissenting churches and meeting houses in London, Westminster and Southwark*, 4 vols. (1808–14) · J. Julian, ed., *A dictionary of hymnology*, rev. edn (1907) · 'Burnham's group of churches', *Baptist Quarterly*, 3 (1926–7), 327–9 · E. A. Payne, 'An elegy on Andrew Gifford', *Baptist Quarterly*, 9 (1938–9), 54–7 · W. T. Whitley, ed., *A Baptist bibliography*, 2 vols. (1916–22) · W. Crawford, *Funeral sermon for Rev Richard Burnham* (1810) · R. Burnham, *The triumphs of free grace* (1787) · private information (2004) [D. J. B. Vesey]
Likenesses engraving, *c.*1790 (after portrait formerly at Baptist Chapel, Shaftesbury Avenue, London), repro. in Wright, *Pocket series* · R. Woodman, stipple, pubd 1811 (after portrait), repro. in Wright, *Pocket series*; formerly at Baptist Chapel, Shaftesbury Avenue, London · J. Dean, mezzotint (after W. Smith), NPG · H. Kingsbury, stipple, BM · Rothwell, line print and stipple (after Peat), NPG · W. Smith, mezzotint (after J. Dean), NPG

Burns, Sir Alan Cuthbert Maxwell (1887–1980), colonial governor, was born on 9 November 1887, at Basseterre, St Kitts, the fourth son and fifth child of James Burns (1852–1896), treasurer of the presidency of St Christopher-Nevis and member of the executive council of the Leeward Islands, and his wife, Agnes Zulma Delisle (1854–1914). One of his brothers, Cecil Delisle, was an academic; another, Robert Edward Burns, like their father and grandfather, was in the colonial service; and a third, Emil, was a leading British communist. He was educated at St Edmund's College, Ware, the oldest Catholic school in England, but had to leave early because his family could not pay the fees. Aged only seventeen, Burns was appointed to the treasury and customs department of St Kitts in 1905. His appointment in 1909 as clerk to the magistrate of Basseterre was followed by that of deputy coroner and justice of the peace for St Kitts, magistrate on Anguilla, and in 1912 clerk and provincial secretary to the administrator of Dominica.

In 1912 Burns became supervisor of customs in Nigeria, and served in Koko and Lagos. No sooner had he earned promotion to the central secretariat cadre than he enlisted in the Nigeria regiment. In 1914 he married Kathleen (Kate) Fitzpatrick (d. 1970), daughter of Robert Altman Hardtman, an Antigua sugar planter, and his wife, Alice; they had two daughters. He saw service in the Cameroons campaign, became adjutant of the Nigeria land contingent, and took part in the Egbe expedition of 1918. As private secretary to Sir Frederick Lugard and then to Sir Hugh Clifford, Burns (like the latter, a Roman Catholic) confirmed his reputation as a highly efficient staff officer, and he was soon mounting the promotional secretariat ladder for colonial service high-climbers. A proving period as colonial secretary of the Bahamas from 1924 to 1929, during which he acted as governor, was followed by his return to Nigeria, for further grooming for high office, as deputy chief secretary. In 1934 he was given his first governorship, British Honduras.

In 1940 Burns was seconded to the Colonial Office on special duty in the rank of assistant under-secretary, as part of the wartime experiment of bringing a serving governor into Whitehall. He became governor of the Gold Coast in 1941, and acted as governor of Nigeria for five months in 1942. At his initiative, and to his unending pride, in 1942 he persuaded a reluctant Colonial Office to admit Africans on to the executive council of the governor of the Gold Coast, and to sanction the appointment of Africans as district commissioners there. He also inspired the constitutional advances of 1946, which provided for an unofficial majority in the Gold Coast legislative council. The fact that the Watson commission inquiring into the Accra riots of 1948 stigmatized the Burns constitution as outmoded at birth perhaps reflects more on the Gold Coast's capacity for political pioneering than on Burns's foresight. His last year in Accra was marred by the so-called 'juju' Kyebi murder case. The confusion and dithering in London—Rathbone's 'grisly minuet' (Rathbone, 132)—over his exercise of the royal prerogative prompted Burns to offer his resignation. In 1945 his name

had been put forward by the Colonial Office for the governorship of the new Malayan Union, but the colonial secretary's nomination was not accepted by Downing Street. From 1947 until his retirement in 1956 Burns, following the pro-consular footsteps of his old master Lugard after the First World War, became Britain's representative on the Trusteeship Council of the United Nations. At the age of seventy-two he accepted the chairmanship of an inquiry into land resources and population problems in Fiji.

Burns was a typical example of a scholar–administrator. A scrupulous and hard-working official, he also delved into African history, so that his well-travelled career was marked by a number of authoritative books. His first contained an index to the laws of the Leeward Islands. In 1917 he began a comprehensive annual review, the *Nigeria Handbook*; he also initiated the *Nigeria Civil Service List*. His *History of Nigeria*, first published in 1929, reached its eighth revised edition in 1972. After his retirement from the colonial service he published four books: *Colour Prejudice* (1948), originally written when he was governor of British Honduras; *History of the British West Indies* (1954); the autobiography *Colonial Civil Servant* (1949); and *In Defence of Colonies* (1957), a riposte to the positive anti-colonialism of the United Nations which he had found so disillusioning. On completion of his Fiji mission, he published a volume on that country in the Corona series (1963), and in his nineties he contributed to the BBC series of reminiscences *Tales from the Dark Continent*.

Burns's recreations were cricket, writing, ornithology (he maintained an aviary in Christiansborg Castle), and bridge (at one time in the 1920s he was bridge correspondent of the *Daily Telegraph* and he wrote a book on the game). He served as a purposeful president of the Hakluyt Society, chairman of the Royal Commonwealth Society library committee, and as a council member of the Zoological Society. He had an assertive humanity, 'a way of going to see for himself, cutting out red tape, and getting on with things' (Parkinson, 108), and an ever ready humour. Sparing with words, he was never short on kindness or courtesy. In character and the stout expression of his opinions he was a big man, straight dealing, and impatient of cant. Burns was appointed CMG in 1927, KCMG in 1936, and GCMG in 1946. He was made a knight of the order of St John of Jerusalem in 1942. He died on 29 September 1980 at the Westminster Hospital, London.

A. H. M. KIRK-GREENE

Sources A. Burns, *Colonial civil servant* (1949) · *The Times* (1 Oct 1980) · R. Rathbone, *Murder and politics in colonial Ghana* (1993) · D. H. Simpson, *Royal Commonwealth Society Library Notes*, 239 (1980) · *West Africa* (20 Oct 1980) · interview (transcript), 14 Sept 1967, Bodl. RH · transcript of interview, for *Tales from the dark continent*, 1979, BL NSA, BBC sound archive · F. M. Bourret, *Ghana: the road to independence* (1960) · A. H. M. Kirk-Greene, *A biographical dictionary of the British colonial governor* (1980) · C. Parkinson, *The colonial office from within* [1947] · *CGPLA Eng. & Wales* (1981) · *WWW* · d. cert. · private information (1986)
Archives Bodl. RH | SOUND BL NSA, BBC sound archive
Likenesses photograph, 1947, Bodl. RH, Afr. MS s. 1755/25 · photograph, repro. in Rathbone, *Murder and politics*, 105

Wealth at death £56,537: probate, 24 Feb 1981, *CGPLA Eng. & Wales*

Burns, Allan (1781–1813), anatomist, was born in Glasgow on 18 September 1781, one of the sons of the Revd John Burns (1744–1839), minister of Barony parish, Glasgow, and his wife, Elizabeth Stevenson. Family interests connected the professions and commerce: his brother George *Burns was a founding partner of the Cunard Line and his brother James *Burns was a shipowner. However, Allan was most associated with his brother John *Burns. From at least the age of fourteen Allan studied medicine under his brother John, who later became professor of surgery at Glasgow University after a career in private teaching and lecturing in surgery and anatomy. The city of Glasgow was home to the College Street medical school where John Burns, among others, had taught. In this period attendance at the school eliminated the need to attend university based medical classes to gain a medical education. The medical school, established in the eighteenth century, provided inexpensive medical training and drew students from across the United Kingdom and beyond. Working with John in his private anatomy and surgery classes at College Street, near to the university buildings on High Street, he was placed in charge of the dissecting rooms by the age of sixteen. Burns's working association with his brother allowed him access to the anatomical materials from which he built up a major collection of preserved specimens, focusing especially on the vascular system. Burns is noted as having changed the manner of injecting preservatives into bodies and it was said that his vascular preparations were 'superior to any other in the world'.

Having no formal qualifications, Burns travelled to London in 1804 with the intention of entering the Army Medical Service. To that end he obtained the diploma of membership of the Royal College of Surgeons in London by examination on 21 December 1804. However, he did not enter the army service but, on the recommendation of a Dr Creighton, who had international contacts, he accepted a position in St Petersburg. The position, from the Empress Catherine, was to run a hospital there on the 'English plan'. After a six-month trial period, during which he was apparently repelled by 'Asiatic pomp and Scythian barbarism' in Russia, he returned to Glasgow. A diamond ring presented by the empress was still held by Burns's relations in the late nineteenth century. Back in Glasgow Burns did not enter practice but worked with John in the private medical classes that formed part of the Glasgow medical school. The proximity of their school to the Ramshorn burial-ground was convenient for resurrectionists to acquire the corpses required to stock the anatomy classes. John Burns's association with grave robbing resulted in a deal between him and the Glasgow magistrates. This meant that he worked on classes in surgery while Allan, conveniently, took over the classes in anatomy. The Burns brothers built up a considerable museum which provided material for teaching. The museum was eventually bought by Granville Sharp Pattison; some of the exhibits found their way to Philadelphia.

Allan Burns's publications included: *Observations on some of the most frequent and important diseases of the heart: or aneurism of the thoratic aorta; or preternatural pulsation in the epigastric region; and on the unusual origin and distribution of some of the large arteries of the human body* (1809) and *Surgical Anatomy of the Head and Neck* (1812). These were quickly translated into German and were published concurrently in the United States. He also published papers in the *Edinburgh Medical and Surgical Journal*. His writings were seen as clear and systematic, and he presented information in a new and illustrative format. His work on vascular pressure systems and on heart disease were seen as pioneering and were long in print.

Burns died in Glasgow on 22 June 1813. His health and work had been affected for over two years by an abscess, which may have been recurring appendicitis. This abscess ruptured into his bowel and he died quickly of the resultant complications. His early death meant that his contributions were somewhat overshadowed by those of his brother John. Nevertheless, the work of Allan Burns was a contribution of major importance in anatomy, surgery, and medicine.　　　　　　　　　　　　Campbell F. Lloyd

Sources Chambers, *Scots.*, rev. T. Thomson (1875) · J. B. Herrich, 'Allan Burns, 1781–1813: anatomist, surgeon and cardiologist', *Bulletin of Society of Medical History of Chicago*, 4 (1928–35), 457–83 · A. Duncan, *Memorials of the Faculty of Physicians and Surgeons of Glasgow, 1599–1850* (1896) · RCSL examinations list, 1804, RCS Eng. · J. Finlayson, *Queen Margaret College Medical Club opening lecture* (1896) · *DNB* · P. Mathias and A. W. H. Pearsall, eds., *Shipping, a survey of historical records* (1971), 34–5 · F. L. M. Pattison, *Granville Sharp Pattison: anatomist and antagonist, 1791–1851* (1987) · D. W. Richards, introduction, in A. Burns, *Observations on some of the most frequent and important diseases of the heart* (1964) · Irving, *Scots.*

Burns, (James) Dawson (1828–1909), temperance reformer, born at Southwark in London, on 22 January 1828, was the younger son of Jabez *Burns, DD (1805–1876), Baptist minister of New Church Street Chapel, Marylebone, for forty-one years, and a popular religious writer and temperance advocate. His mother was Jane, the daughter of George and Ann Dawson of Keighley.

In 1839 Burns took the pledge and addressed the young members of his father's congregation in New Church Street. During his teenage years he wrote *A Plea for Youths' Temperance Societies*, held a public discussion, and contributed articles to the *Weekly Temperance Journal* and the *National Temperance Advocate*. In February 1845 he became assistant secretary to the National Temperance Society, and a year later joint secretary, besides managing its monthly organ, the *Temperance Chronicle*. He was official reporter of the world's convention held in August 1846, in which his father took a prominent part.

From September 1847 to 1850 Burns studied at the General Baptist College, which was then at Leicester, and in September 1851 became pastor of the Baptist chapel at Salford. In 1853 he helped Nathaniel Card, a Quaker, to found in Manchester the United Kingdom Alliance with a view to influencing the licensing laws. He was in London in March 1853 as metropolitan superintendent, and was enrolled the sixth member on 1 June 1853.

Burns lived in north London, where he worked energetically for the cause and exercised considerable influence on policy. From March 1856 he wrote a 'London Letter' for the weekly *Alliance News* and published numerous books and pamphlets. He was made an honorary MA of Bates College, Maine, in 1869 and afterwards DD. He edited *Graham's Annual Temperance Guide* from 1867 to 1876. At his father's death in 1876 he took over the pastorate of New Church Street Chapel, where he had lately assisted, but resigned it in 1881 to devote himself entirely to temperance work.

Burns represented the Baptist New Connexion at the centennial conference in America in 1880, acted as secretary to the Temperance Hospital opened in 1881, and was president of the Association of General Baptists held at Norwich in the same year. He was active in promoting temperance legislation, holding that the law should protect the public and not the liquor trade. In a series of annual letters to *The Times* (1886–1909), on the national drink bill, he showed a notable grasp of facts and statistics.

Burns was also a director of the Liberator Building Society, which his brother-in-law, Jabez Balfour, founded in 1868 and of which Balfour was chairman. Owing to disapproval of the increase of directors' fees, Burns resigned before the society's failure in October 1892. Subsequently Balfour and other directors were convicted of fraud and sentenced to long terms of imprisonment. Because of this embarrassment the United Kingdom Alliance asked Burns to resign as metropolitan superintendent. When he refused, the post was discontinued.

On 22 December 1853 Burns married Cecile, the only daughter of James and Clara Lucas *Balfour. His wife died at Battersea on 27 March 1897; of his five sons and a daughter, only two sons survived him. He wrote memoirs of his wife (1878) and of his third son (1886), **Edward Spenser Burns** (1861–1885), who died on 1 March 1885 at Leopoldville, Stanley Pool, on the Lower Congo, after opening up a new route towards the Niadi River, and constructing charts. Burns himself died at his home in Foxmore Street, Battersea Park, on 22 August 1909, and was buried at Paddington on 26 August. Two of his many temperance publications deserve special mention: *The Temperance Bible Commentary* (1868), which he wrote with F. R. Lees, went through six English editions, and his two-volume *Temperance History* (1889–91) established his reputation as the movement's best historian.

CHARLOTTE FELL-SMITH, *rev.* MARK CLEMENT

Sources P. T. Winskill, *The temperance movement and its workers*, 4 vols. (1891–2), vols. 2–4 • B. Harrison, *Dictionary of British temperance biography* (1973) • A. E. Dingle, *The campaign for prohibition in Victorian England: the United Kingdom Alliance, 1872–1895* (1980) • *The Times* (23 Aug 1909), 9 • *The Times* (27 Aug 1909), 11 • B. Harrison, *Drink and the Victorians: the temperance question in England, 1815–1872*, 2nd edn (1994) • H. Carter, *The English temperance movement: a study in objectives* (1933)

Burns, Edward Spenser (1861–1885). *See under* Burns, (James) Dawson (1828–1909).

Burns, Sir George, first baronet (1795–1890), shipowner, was born on 10 December 1795 in Glasgow, the youngest of four sons of the Revd Dr John Burns (1744–1839), minister of the Barony parish, Glasgow, and his wife, Elizabeth, *née* Stevenson. While his elder brothers John *Burns and Allan *Burns pursued distinguished careers as surgeons, George and his brother James *Burns turned their attention to trade. In 1818 they set up as general merchants in Glasgow, and, in 1824, they associated with Hugh Mathie of Liverpool to establish a small shipping line of six sailing vessels trading between Glasgow and Liverpool. Steamers quickly replaced these ships, and in 1830 the firm G. and J. Burns in Glasgow joined with two Liverpool-based Scots, David and Charles MacIver, forming the Glasgow Steam Packet Company to develop steamer services between Glasgow, Liverpool, Belfast and Londonderry.

George Burns was the main link with the MacIvers in Liverpool and he travelled regularly between the two ports to conduct their business, much of which they placed with Robert Napier for the ships' engines. It was through Napier that Burns came into contact with Samuel Cunard, who came to Britain from Nova Scotia in 1839 seeking partners, and financial support, to develop a transatlantic steamer service to compete for the Admiralty's invitation to tender for carrying the American mails. Disappointed in London, Cunard travelled north to Glasgow with a letter of introduction to Robert Napier, who introduced him, in turn, to Burns. Like Cunard, Burns recognized the opportunity and quickly succeeded in raising £270,000 in subscriptions of £100 shares to back the tender to the Admiralty. The application succeeded and the signatories on the contract were George Burns, David MacIver, and Samuel Cunard. The British and North American Royal Mail Steam Packet Company was born, the forerunner of the Cunard Line. Cunard based himself in London to manage the business there and in North America, while David MacIver controlled operations from Liverpool, and George Burns travelled regularly between Glasgow and Liverpool to confer with MacIver in the development of their business interests. The original shareholders were gradually bought out, and the transatlantic shipping enterprise came to be controlled by the three families of Cunard, Burns, and MacIver. George Burns was particularly involved with the ordering and building of the ships, which developed a high reputation for technical innovation and for the quality of service.

Burns had married in 1822 Jane, eldest daughter of Dr James Cleland of Glasgow. They had seven children, of whom only two sons survived. In 1860, at the age of sixty-five, he retired from active involvement in his businesses in Glasgow and Liverpool, his son John *Burns (1829–1901) taking his place. On his retirement Burns purchased the estate of Wemyss Bay overlooking the Clyde estuary and the Cowal hills, where he spent the remainder of his life. He took a lively interest in local affairs and was a member of the Episcopal church in Wemyss Bay. He was created a baronet in May 1889, a year before his death. He retained a keen interest in scientific and religious affairs, and this occupied him for many hours each day; to the end he could read and write without the aid of spectacles. He died at his home, Wemyss House, Wemyss Bay, Renfrewshire, on 2 June 1890, having survived his wife, Jane, by thirteen years; his elder son, John, succeeded to the title. He was buried at Wemyss Bay.

J. K. LAUGHTON, rev. ANTHONY SLAVEN

Sources E. Hodder, *Sir George Burns, Bart: his times and friends* (1890) · *The Engineer* (6 June 1890), 458 · *Engineering* (6 June 1890), 682 · Calendar of Confirmations, 29/9/1890 · d. cert. · *The Times* (6 June 1890)
Likenesses A. Edouart, silhouette, Scot. NPG
Wealth at death £91,357 8s. 10d.: confirmation, 27 Oct 1890, CCI

Burns, Islay (1817–1872), Free Church of Scotland minister, was the sixth son of William Hamilton Burns (1779–1859), then minister of Dun and later of Kilsyth, and his wife, Elizabeth (d. 1879), daughter of James Chalmers, proprietor of the *Aberdeen Journal*. He was the brother of the missionary William Chalmers *Burns (1815–1868) and the Roman Catholic publisher James Burns (1808–1871). Burns was born at the manse at Dun on 16 January 1817, and was educated at Kilsyth parish school and Aberdeen grammar school. He then studied at Marischal College and the University of Aberdeen, distinguishing himself in classics and mathematics, before moving on to Glasgow University to study theology. He was licensed by the presbytery of Glasgow, and served as a missionary minister in Edinburgh before being appointed in 1841 as missionary in Bothriphnie, one of the parishes from which the notorious ministers of Strathbogie had been suspended by the general assembly. Having thus aligned himself with the non-intrusionists, he joined the Free Church at the Disruption, and in June 1843 succeeded the popular minister Robert McCheyne at St Peter's Free Church, Dundee. In 1845 he married his cousin Catharine Sarah, eldest daughter of William Brown of Aberdeen; they had four sons and four daughters.

As his ministry lacked the evangelistic appeal of McCheyne's, Burns found that his congregation declined slightly. It still remained large, however, as Burns proved to be a hard-working pastor, whose sermons were 'marked by a solid, substantial richness and power' (Blaikie, xix). Burns's mind was 'essentially broad and catholic' (ibid., xxiv): papers published in the *Free Church Magazine* in 1850–51 and later in the *British and Foreign Evangelical Review* showed his interest in the Oxford Movement, and his appreciation of attempts to use architecture and music as aids to worship. These views aroused the suspicion of some of his contemporaries: after running a close rival to Robert Rainy for the professorship of church history at the Free Church college in Edinburgh, in 1864 Burns stood as a candidate for the college professorship of theology in Glasgow and found himself under attack for his latitudinarian opinions. Nevertheless he was elected to the post, which he held until his death. He was active in local and church affairs: he was one of the chief promoters of the Glasgow Foundry Boys' Society, and supported a union between his own and the United Presbyterian church. In addition to contributions to journals, Burns

also published a *History of the Church of Christ* (1862) and memoirs of his father (1860) and brother (1872). He received a DD from the University of Aberdeen in 1864. He died after a haemorrhage on 20 May 1872 at 4 Sardinia Terrace, Glasgow, and was survived by his wife and six of their children.

ROSEMARY MITCHELL

Sources W. G. Blaikie, 'Memoir', in *Select remains of Islay Burns*, ed. J. C. Burns (1874), ix–xlvii · H. Scott, *Fasti ecclesiae Scoticanae*, new edn, 3, 480 · Boase, *Mod. Eng. biog.* · d. cert.
Likenesses engraving (after W. H. Mote), repro. in Burns, ed., *Select remains*, frontispiece

Burns, Jabez (1805–1876), General Baptist minister, was born on 18 December 1805 at Oldham, Lancashire, where his father, Joseph, was a chemist. He was educated at a school at Chester and at the grammar school in Oldham, which he left in 1820 to become a draper's assistant in York. His mother, Mary, who died in his early childhood, was a Wesleyan, and named him after Dr Jabez Bunting. In York Burns was converted by the Wesleyans, and delivered his first public address in a Methodist house when he was about sixteen. Work later took him to Bradford, then to Keighley, where for some three years he managed a bookselling business. During this time he began to preach more often, settling with the Methodist New Connexion. Feeling his lack of formal education, he developed a passion for books. In 1824 he married Jane, the daughter of George and Ann Dawson of Keighley, and in 1826 he moved to London in search of work. Here, in some poverty, he began his career as a religious writer by compiling the *Christian's Sketch Book* (1828), of which a second volume with the same title was issued in 1835, and *The Spiritual Cabinet* (1829).

From about the time that he left Yorkshire Burns had been convinced of the scriptural basis of believer's baptism, and in London he was baptized by John Farrent, the pastor of a General Baptist congregation at Suffolk Street Chapel. He was, however, uncomfortable with the General Baptists' views on strict communion, and so kept his links with the Methodist New Connexion. From late 1829 Burns was engaged in mission work for the Christian Union Mission, briefly in Edinburgh and Leith, then in Perth from 1830 to 1835. In June 1835 he returned with his family to London, having accepted a call to the pastorate of the General Baptist congregation at Aenon Chapel, New Church Street, Marylebone. His congregation was small at first, but increased greatly during his time as pastor. Debts were paid off, and the buildings were enlarged and improved.

Burns was a popular and influential preacher and an energetic public speaker, especially on temperance. In Scotland he had joined a society which opposed the consumption of spirits, but in 1836 he became a total abstainer. He is said to have been the first minister of any denomination to preach teetotalism from the pulpit. Beginning on 16 December 1839 he delivered thirty-five annual temperance sermons, many of which were published, and in 1853 preached the inaugural sermon for the prohibitionist United Kingdom Alliance. He was one of the earliest members of the Evangelical Alliance, formed in 1846, and held the chair of the Baptist Union in 1850. In 1847 he paid his first visit to America as one of the two delegates from the General Baptist Association of England to the triennial conference of the Freewill Baptists of the United States. He published *Notes of a Tour in the United States and Canada in the Summer and Autumn of 1847* (1848). In later life he travelled widely. In 1869 he visited Egypt and Palestine on the first tour of the region arranged by Thomas Cook, subsequently preparing a *Help-Book for Travellers to the East* (1870). In 1846 the Wesleyan University of Middletown, Connecticut, conferred on Burns the honorary degree of DD, and on a second visit to America in 1872 the faculty of Bates' College, Lewiston, Maine, awarded him the LLD. Both degrees were an acknowledgement of his books' popularity in America. Burns died at his home in Porteus Road, Paddington, on 31 January 1876, and was buried at Paddington old cemetery, Kilburn. Of his four children, two, George Burns and Dawson *Burns, survived to adulthood.

Burns was a prolific author, averaging two or three volumes a year for about thirty years. His publications, many of which ran into several editions, consisted mainly of sermon outlines (designed to help preachers, and especially lay preachers, who had not had the benefit of a college education) and popular devotional works for family and private use. Notable in the first category was the four-volume *One Hundred Sketches and Skeletons of Sermons* (1836, 1839), an additional volume entitled *Sketches of Discourses for Sunday Schools and Village Preaching* (1838, later revised and enlarged), and his four-volume *Pulpit Cyclopaedia and Christian Minister's Companion* (1844). Popular devotional works included: *The golden pot of manna, or, Christian's portion, containing daily exercises on the person, offices, work and glory of the redeemer* (2 vols., 1837), renamed in its fifth edition *The Christian's Daily Portion* (1848); *Christian Exercises for every Lord's Day, Morning and Evening, in the Year* (1858); and, on a smaller scale, *Light for the Sick-Room: a Book for the Afflicted* (1850) and *Light for the House of Mourning: a Book for the Bereaved* (1850).

Other works by Burns included *Christian Philosophy, or, Materials for Thought* (1845); *Mothers of the Wise and Good, with Select Essays on Maternal Duties and Influence* (1846); *Doctrinal Conversations* (1849); and an autobiographical *Retrospect of Forty-Five Years' Christian Ministry* (1875). In addition to the *Christian Miscellany* which he edited while in Perth, Burns edited *The Preachers' Magazine and Pastors' Monthly Journal* (1839–44), which he founded, the *London Temperance Journal*, and, for a time, the *General Baptist Magazine*. He wrote several books in verse for children (of whom he was very fond), together with some early and popular temperance hymns.

ARTHUR H. GRANT, *rev.* ROSEMARY CHADWICK

Sources J. Burns, *Retrospect of forty-five years' Christian ministry* (1875) · D. B., 'Memoirs of Baptist ministers deceased', *Baptist Hand-Book* (1877), 354–6 · J. C., 'Memoirs of deceased ministers and missionaries', *Baptist Handbook* (1910), 476–8 · *General Baptist Magazine*, 58 (1876), 81–7 · *General Baptist Magazine*, 75 (1882), 25–6 · *The Baptist* (4 Feb 1876) · *The Baptist* (11 Feb 1876) · *Christian World* (4 Feb 1876) · *Christian World* (11 Feb 1876) · *The Freeman* (4–11 Feb 1876) · P. T. Winskill, *Temperance standard bearers of the nineteenth century: a biographical and statistical temperance dictionary*, 2 vols. (1897–8)
Likenesses R. Dale, mezzotint (after R. James), NPG · D. J. Pound, line print (after photograph by Mayall), NPG; repro. in D. J. Pound, *Drawing room portrait gallery* (1861)
Wealth at death under £3000: probate, 29 Feb 1876, CGPLA Eng. & Wales

Burns, James (*fl.* 1644–1661), merchant and writer, may have been the son of one Robert Burns who is mentioned in John M'Ure's *A View of the City of Glasgow* (1736) and whose name appears in the 'List of Linen and Woollen Drapers, commonly called English Merchants, since the year 1600'. James Burns was a merchant and for a time he was the bailie of the river and frith (that is, firth) of Clyde, being a municipal officer and magistrate of Glasgow with jurisdiction in matters of debt, services, and questions of possession between citizens, and holding rank next to the lord provost, who was the head of the burgh.

Burns produced a memoir 'of the Civil War and during the Usurpation' which chronicles political and military events in Scotland between 1644 and 1661. The manuscript of the memoirs, once held by the Faculty of Advocates, is now lost, but a transcript of them, evidently much mutilated, by George Crawford, the historian of Renfrewshire, was published as *Memoirs by James Burns, Bailie of the City of Glasgow, 1644–1661* (1832).

LEONARD W. COWIE

Sources A. Stevenson, *The history of the church and state of Scotland from the accession of Charles I to the restoration of Charles II*, 3 vols. (1753–7) · *Memoirs by James Burns, bailie of the city of Glasgow, 1644–1661*, ed. J. Maidment (1832) · DNB

Burns, James (1789–1871), shipowner, was born in Glasgow on 9 June 1789, the third son of the Revd Dr John Burns (1744–1839), minister of the Barony parish of Glasgow, and his wife, Elizabeth, *née* Stevenson. His eldest brother, Dr John *Burns FRS, became the first professor of surgery in the University of Glasgow, and his second brother, Allan *Burns, became physician to the empress of Russia at St Petersburg.

Unlike his older brothers, James Burns turned to commerce, and was joined by his younger brother, George *Burns (1795–1890), in 1818, setting up as G. and J. Burns, general merchants in Glasgow. After six years, the two brothers moved into shipping, joining with Hugh Mathie of Liverpool to establish a small shipping line of six sailing vessels plying between the two ports. The Clyde was then the leading waterway for steam navigation; within a year James and George Burns had ordered their first steamer, and they quickly replaced all their sail ships by steamboats. While George was mainly interested in the technical aspects of the ships, it was James who was the chief commercial influence in the business, supervising the day-to-day transactions, the negotiation of cargoes and contracts.

The Mathie connection with Liverpool was replaced in 1830 by a new arrangement with two Liverpool-based Scots, David and Charles MacIver, to form the Glasgow Steam Packet Company. This arrangement allowed James and George Burns to extend their steamship business to

Londonderry, Larne, and Belfast. As before, George concentrated on the shipping department, while James was mainly responsible for the mercantile side of the business.

While the Irish Sea trade was their first and main business, two other avenues opened up to James and George Burns. In 1839 the Liverpool connection was greatly strengthened when George Burns was introduced to Samuel Cunard and raised £270,000 in subscriptions to establish the British and North American Royal Mail Steam Packet Company. This company secured a seven year contract from the Admiralty to carry the American mails by steamship. James and George, with the MacIvers, were founding partners and shareholders with Cunard in the new venture. While this took George's attention south to Liverpool, James concentrated on the Glasgow business, and in 1845 G. and J. Burns acquired an interest in the developing west highland steamer services by purchasing the Castle Line. This however was quickly re-sold to their nephew David *Macbrayne, their shipping clerk David Hutcheson, and his brother Alexander.

Burns was married twice: first, to Margaret Smith and, second, to Margaret Shortridge, who predeceased him. He retired from active business and developed an interest in estate improvement, acquiring the estates of Kilmahew, Cumbernauld, and Bloomhall in Dunbartonshire. He spent much time on improvements and was a liberal supporter of religious and philanthropic enterprises. He died on 6 September 1871 at Kilmahew Castle, Cardross, Dumbarton, and was succeeded in his estates by his only son, John William Burns.

T. F. HENDERSON, rev. ANTHONY SLAVEN

Sources *Glasgow Herald* (8 Sept 1871) · *The Engineer* (6 June 1890), 458 · d. cert.
Likenesses E. Burton, mezzotint (after D. Macnee), BM

Burns, James Drummond (1823–1864), Free Church of Scotland minister and poet, was born in Edinburgh on 18 February 1823 and educated at Heriot's Hospital, a charitable foundation. A boyhood accident deprived him of the sight in his left eye 'and somewhat marred the beauty of a very noble countenance' (*Free Church of Scotland Monthly Record*, 734). He was one of three boys who, having exhausted the curriculum at Heriot's, were sent to attend the rector's class at Edinburgh high school. In November 1837 he entered the arts classes in Edinburgh University as a Heriot bursar, progressing to the study of divinity under Thomas Chalmers and David Welsh. Burns adhered to the Free Church at the Disruption of 1843 and finished his theological training at the New College in Edinburgh, where he excelled as a public speaker. Such was the demand for ministers that he had scarcely completed his course before he was heard by the congregation of Dunblane, Perthshire. Although he 'stuck' in the morning sermon, he was called and ordained in August 1845.

In delicate health as a student Burns soon developed alarming signs of pulmonary disease, and he was induced to accept an offer from the Free Church Colonial Committee to take temporary charge of a congregation in Funchal, Madeira, where he arrived in September 1847. He returned to Scotland the following year but accepted that he must leave Dunblane, and by November 1848 he was again in Funchal. There had recently been disturbances in Madeira on account of the missionary activities of Robert Reid Kalley and protestant converts had been forced to leave the island. Burns found the resurgence of Catholicism distasteful but his ministry was otherwise uneventful. The failure of the vintage, together with a diminished flow of invalids, reduced his congregation and he decided to return to Britain. In the autumn of 1853 he ministered briefly to a presbyterian congregation in Brighton and the following year served a church in St Helier, Jersey. Burns was reluctant to commit himself to a congregation in case of a renewed breakdown in his health, but the offer of a smallish congregation at Well Walk in Hampstead was deemed appropriate and he was admitted on 22 May 1855. In 1862 a new and larger building, Trinity Presbyterian Church, was opened.

In 1854 Burns published *The Vision of Prophecy, and other Poems*, which went to a second edition in 1858. He produced two volumes of meditations, interspersed with devotional poetry, *The Heavenly Jerusalem, or, Glimpses within the Gates* (1856) and *The Evening Hymn* (1857). For the eighth edition of the *Encyclopaedia Britannica* he prepared the article on hymns and he contributed a series of articles on the cities of the Bible to the *Family Treasury of Sunday Reading*, edited by Andrew Cameron. On 2 November 1859 Burns married Margaret, daughter of Major-General John Macdonald of the Bengal army and widow of Lieutenant Archibald Procter. There were three children of the marriage.

Habitually pensive, Burns's personality was marked by an awareness of the nearness of death. Illness induced anxiety and sensitivity to a degree greater than might have otherwise occurred, and his gentleness, meekness, and diffidence were perhaps determined in part by his bodily weakness. Physical frailty only increased the devotion of those close to him and never eclipsed his playful sense of humour. He returned from attendance at the Free Church of Scotland general assembly of 1863 with a cold, and more severe symptoms followed. In an effort to regain his health Burns travelled to Menton in France the following January. He spent the summer in Switzerland before returning to Menton, where he died on 27 November 1864. His body was brought back for burial in Highgate cemetery in December.

LIONEL ALEXANDER RITCHIE

Sources J. Hamilton, *Memoir and remains of the Rev. James D. Burns MA of Hampstead* (1869) · 'Reminiscences of the late Rev. James D. Burns MA of Hampstead', *Weekly Review* (17 Dec 1864) · *British and Foreign Evangelical Review*, 14 (Jan 1865), 198–205 · *Free Church of Scotland Monthly Record*, 31 (Feb 1865), 734–5 · *GM*, 3rd ser., 7 (1859), 640 · *GM*, 3rd ser., 18 (1865), 120 · *DNB*
Likenesses engraving, repro. in Hamilton, *Memoir and remains*, frontispiece

Burns, John (1774–1850), surgeon, born in Glasgow, was the eldest of the sons of John Burns (1744–1839), minister of the Church of Scotland's Barony parish in Glasgow, and his wife, Elizabeth Stevenson, and was grandson of John

Burns, the author of *Burns's English Grammar*. His brothers George *Burns and James *Burns both entered the ship business. John's career in medicine commenced when he was appointed surgeon's clerk at the opening of the Glasgow Royal Infirmary in 1792, having been first licensed by the Faculty of Physicians and Surgeons of Glasgow. He began lectures on anatomy, in extramural courses, and became the first private anatomy teacher in Glasgow, extending the repute of Glasgow as a centre of medical studies. With his brother Allan *Burns (1781–1813), who had returned from Russia, he set up lecture rooms near the university buildings on the High Street. Their work was jeopardized when John's association with grave robbing became known to the city magistrates. Grave robbing and the supply of bodies for dissection had led the city authorities to appoint guards in kirkyards by the 1820s. Burns's ability to negotiate his way out of a prosecution gives some credence to the comments of Ruth Richardson in *Death, Dissection and the Destitute* (1987) on the situation favouring anatomists before the Anatomy Act of 1832. Burns negotiated instead to lecture in surgery while Allan lectured in anatomy.

In 1799 Burns published his *The Anatomy of the Gravid Uterus*, and was appointed professor of anatomy and theory of surgery at Anderson's University in Glasgow. He married in 1801 Isabella Duncan, the daughter of John Duncan, minister of Alva, Stirlingshire. She died in 1810, shortly after the birth of their fourth child, Allan. A skilled surgeon at the Royal Infirmary, Burns lectured at Anderson's University on the principles of surgery, midwifery, and women's and children's diseases. He was appointed town's surgeon in 1808 and in 1815 was appointed to the newly created chair of surgery at Glasgow University, having been nominated by the duke of Montrose, who was hereditary chancellor of the University of Glasgow and to whom Burns dedicated his *Principles of Midwifery* (1809). Alongside this position Burns maintained a private practice and was elected as a physician to the Royal Infirmary in the 1840s. Glasgow University awarded him the degrees of CM (1817) and MD (1828). He remained as professor of surgery at Glasgow University for the rest of his life. However, he withdrew from some aspects of his work after the death of his son Allan in 1843.

Burns typifies some of the aspects of the Scottish medical community of the period, in terms of the wide-ranging scope of its members' business, teaching, and intellectual skills. Burns's works on abortion and midwifery were read on the European mainland, being translated into several languages. They were also published several times in the United States. They give an indication of his early influences. He dedicated the *Anatomy of the Gravid Uterus* to Robert Cleghorn, lecturer on materia medica and chemistry at Glasgow University and sometime physician at Glasgow Royal Infirmary, and to James Muir, a Glasgow surgeon who initiated lectures on midwifery for women in 1759. He prefaced and dedicated the 1799 version 'as a small testimony of the respect which I bear to your professional eminence, as well as of the sense which I entertain

of the friendship with which you have hitherto honoured me'. He also carefully noted the earlier work of William Hunter, but pointed out that his own work aimed to make clear 'those practical inferences and conclusions which are so essential to the student' (Burns, *Anatomy of the Gravid Uterus*, preface). In 1811 he published *Popular Directions for the Treatment of the Diseases of Women and Children*, which was well received. However, his *Principles of Surgery* (1830) met with less success. It should, though, be borne in mind that throughout his publishing career Burns was aiming to produce texts for students which were clear, well laid out, and accessible. He mixed theory with notes of experience and observation. As the third edition in 1814 of *The Principles of Midwifery* noted: I 'have endeavoured to proceed as much as possible upon the method of induction'. His level of commitment to improve the standard of his books in the face of developments in medicine partly explains the continued success of his books over many years. He continued to revise and enlarge, as the tenth edition of 1843 stated, and they remained on the list of prizes awarded by his colleagues into the late 1840s.

Burns spent a great deal of his time lobbying on behalf of Glasgow University, giving evidence to parliamentary commissions, and often travelling to London. There he defended Glasgow University's interest in the medical reform bills before parliament. In the run up to the Anatomy Act of 1832 Burns worked hard to promote the regulation of the supply of bodies. This was an ongoing sore in relations between the public and the medical teaching profession and it had affected his own medical practice. He and Professor Jeffray of Glasgow University memorialized the government criticizing Warburton's Anatomy Bill of 1830. Burns was elected a fellow of the Royal Society in 1830.

Although born into the Church of Scotland, Burns became a member of the Scottish Episcopal church. A high tory, his move to the more ritual-based church was not peculiar in Scotland after the Disruption in 1843. Alongside his work in medicine Burns published works on religious matters, such as *The Principles of Christian Philosophy* (1828). His business interests included holding shares in the Forth and Clyde Canal and in the development of fresh water supplies. Burns drowned on 18 June 1850, along with his niece, on the wreck of the *Orion*, which foundered off Portpatrick on his way back to Glasgow from London. The *Orion* belonged to the Cunard Line, of which Burns's brother George was a part owner, and through marriage he was also related into the MacBraynes shipping-line family. Burns was therefore associated with an influential business and philanthropic circle with interests in the Clyde area.   CAMPBELL F. LLOYD

Sources *Glasgow Herald* (21 June 1850) · *Glasgow Herald* (24 June 1850) · *Glasgow Herald* (28 June 1850) · senate minutes, U. Glas., Archives and Business Records Centre, 1/1/3-6 · Irving, *Scots.*, 53 · A. Duncan, *Memorials of the Faculty of Physicians and Surgeons of Glasgow, 1599–1850* (1896) · [L. Hamilton], ed., *Pioneers and patrons* [1996], 14 · NA Scot., SC 36/48/37, pp. 496–7 · *Old Glasgow exhibition 1894* (1894), 79–80 · J. D. Marwick, ed., *Extracts from the records of the burgh*

of Glasgow, 9–11 (1914–16) · *DNB* · P. Mathias and A. W. H. Pearsam, eds., *Shipping, a survey of historical records* (1971), 34, 35 · R. Richardson, *Death, dissection and the destitute* (1987)
Likenesses J. G. Gilbert, oils, 1848, U. Glas. · J. Faed, mezzotint, pubd 1851 (after J. G. Gilbert), BM · W. & D. Downey, photograph, Wellcome L.; also in U. Glas. · L. Ghémar, lithograph (after S. Watson), BM, Wellcome L. · L. Ghémar, lithograph, BM · pen drawing, Wellcome L. · photograph, Wellcome L. · photograph (after lithograph), Wellcome L.
Wealth at death £29,643 8s. 6d.: NA Scot., SC 36/48/37, p. 496

Burns, John, first Baron Inverclyde (1829–1901), shipowner, born in Glasgow on 24 June 1829, was the elder of two surviving sons of seven children born to Sir George *Burns (1795–1890), shipowner, and his wife, Jane Cleland (d. 1877?). After school he attended Glasgow University and took the general arts degree before joining the family firm about 1850. By that time his father and uncle James *Burns (1789–1871) were well established as prominent shipowners, operating as G. and J. Burns with steamer services to Liverpool, Larne, Londonderry, and Belfast, and in association with the MacIvers and Samuel Cunard as partners in the British and North American Royal Mail Steam Packet Company, later the Cunard Line.

When his father retired from active business in 1860, John Burns stepped into his roles in both G. and J. Burns and in the management and development of the Cunard Line. Although the three families, Cunard, MacIver, and Burns, owned the business, the death of Samuel Cunard in 1865 left the major influence in the hands of the MacIvers and the Burnses. By then Charles MacIver in Liverpool and John Burns in Glasgow were in effective command. John Burns, like his father, was greatly interested in improving the ships, and under his influence in the 1860s, Cunard began to replace its fleet of wooden paddle steamers with iron ships, first paddle driven, but increasingly employing the screw propeller. The first iron screw steamer was the *China* in 1862. Burns was particularly keen on economy, and the Cunard Line quickly adopted the new compound engine with the *Batavia* in 1870. Cunard, under Burns, was also quick to order a steel vessel, the first in their service being the *Servia* in 1881, which, apart from the *Great Eastern*, was the largest liner afloat.

The costs of this expansion motivated the partners to reconstruct the partnership in 1878 as a limited company with a nominal capital of £2 million, of which £1.2 million was issued and taken up in entirety by the three founding families in part payment for the assets transferred to the company. A prospectus and shares were not offered to the public until 1880, when the balance of the capital was offered for subscription and was quickly taken up. The Cunard, Burns, and MacIver families retained their £1.2 million holding and their control, and John Burns was elected chairman of the board. With new resources and undiminished energy he pursued a growth policy of constructing successively larger, more powerful, and increasingly luxurious liners to keep Cunard ahead of competitors on the north Atlantic. Like his father he built for quality, reliability, and safety, and he was proud of Cunard's

(questionable) claim never to have lost a passenger through accident.

While John Burns devoted much time to his responsibilities with Cunard, he was also proprietor and in control of the Glasgow-based family firm of G. and J. Burns, which continued to trade successfully and extensively in the Irish Sea. In 1860, on taking over his father's position in G. and J. Burns, he had married Emily (d. 1901), daughter of George Clerk Arbuthnot, with whom he had two sons and three daughters. His sons George Arbuthnot Burns and James Cleland Burns first joined their father in the Glasgow business of G. and J. Burns, allowing John Burns time during the 1880s to develop his interests in maritime affairs more generally. As a young man he had been in the Crimea at the fall of Sevastopol in 1855, and had subsequently been an advocate both of good coastal defences and of constructing merchant ships capable of rapid conversion for war purposes. In 1887 he wrote and published a study on the *Adaptation of Merchant Steamships for War Purposes*. His business allowed him to travel widely and his interest in distant lands involved him with the Royal Geographic Society, of which he became a fellow.

By the end of the 1880s John Burns was less involved in the day-to-day operation of Cunard and G. and J. Burns. In Liverpool the deputy chairman of Cunard, David Jardine, took on more of the responsibility, while in Glasgow his elder son George A. Burns ran the Scottish and Irish mail services, although he had by then also trained extensively in the Cunard office in Liverpool. The younger son, James C. Burns, was widely involved in Clyde shipping circles and became chairman of the Glasgow Shipowners' Association at that time.

In spite of a very full business life John Burns fulfilled extensive public duties. He was a deputy lieutenant of Renfrewshire, of Lanarkshire, and of the county of the City of Glasgow. He was also a justice of the peace in Renfrewshire. He was an enthusiastic yachtsman, member of all the leading Clyde clubs, and an honorary lieutenant in the RNVR. He was active in support of youth training, and in large part it was his efforts that saw the training ship scheme established. In his will he made ample provision for the Eastpark Children's Home in Glasgow, and also for the Training Home for Nurses, as well as supporting his own St Silas Episcopal Church. Like his father he was an active Episcopalian; he also shared his father's support for the Liberals in politics.

When his father died in 1890, John Burns inherited the family estate at Wemyss Bay and the baronetcy. In 1897 he was created a baron on the occasion of Queen Victoria's Jubilee, taking the title Lord Inverclyde. He enjoyed his distinction only briefly, for he died on 12 February 1901; his wife Emily, tragically, died only two days later. His elder son, George A. Burns, succeeded him as the second Lord Inverclyde, and when David Jardine, who had succeeded John Burns as chairman of Cunard, retired in 1902, George A. Burns followed as Cunard chairman, as well as being partner and director of G. and J. Burns Ltd. He survived his father by only four years, the title then passing to his younger brother, James C. Burns, in 1905. These two deaths in quick succession diminished the Burns role in Cunard, and reconcentrated the family interests in the family firm of G. and J. Burns.   ANTHONY SLAVEN

Sources *DSBB* · *The Engineer* (15 Feb 1901) · *Engineering* (15 Feb 1901) · *The Times* (15 Feb 1901) · *Glasgow contemporaries at the dawn of the twentieth century* [1901] · inventory of estate, SC 53/41/11 · will, SC/53/47/8 · *Glasgow Herald* (15 Feb 1901) · *WWW*
Likenesses photograph, repro. in D. Pollock, *Modern shipbuilding and the men engaged in it* (1884), facing p. 2 · photograph, repro. in *Glasgow contemporaries*, 216
Wealth at death £886,545 15s.: confirmation, 3 June 1901, *CCI* · £222 8s. 9d.: additional estate, 24 June 1902, *CCI*

Burns, John Elliott (1858–1943), labour leader and politician, was born in South Lambeth, London, on 20 October 1858, the sixteenth child of Alexander Burns, a Scottish fitter, and Barbara Smith. He left St Mary's national school when he was about ten and after a series of short-term jobs was apprenticed as an engineer.

Burns spent his childhood in relative poverty. Apparently deserted by his father, his mother took in washing and the family moved to a basement dwelling in Battersea. Despite his brief schooling Burns attended night classes and became an avid consumer of radical literature. A useful boxer, he was a pugnacious and combative individual, and insubordination twice resulted in the cancellation of his indentures by irate employers before he finally completed his apprenticeship at Mowlems, a major London contractor. There he came under the influence of Victor Delahaye, an exiled former communard and member of a French Marxist group, committed to the view that in the absence of effective physical force and organization, the working class could throw off capitalism only through the ballot box. In 1878 Burns had his first encounter with the law when he was arrested for holding a political meeting on Clapham Common in defiance of a police prohibition. More than a year spent working for the Niger Company in west Africa further strengthened his belief in the exploitative nature of imperialism and capitalism. It was there, too, that he read Mill's *Political Economy*, the book which, he said, converted him to socialism.

Labour leader On his return to England in 1881 Burns settled in Battersea, London. In July 1882 he married Martha Charlotte Gale, daughter of a Battersea shipwright. They had one son, Edgar. Burns threw himself energetically into the radical movement. His impeccably proletarian origins and popular interests (he enjoyed cricket and played football for Wandsworth Clarence Rovers) made him a welcome recruit for the Democratic Federation (later the Social Democratic Federation, or SDF), a Marxist organization with a predominantly middle-class leadership. So, too, did his remarkable gift for public speaking which enabled the federation to use him as 'a sort of giant gramophone' (Burgess, xiv). By 1884 his dynamic and colourful oratory—it was Burns who on a later occasion described the Thames as 'liquid history' (Hughes, 283)—had earned him a place on the party's executive. When the federation split over strategy, he stood firmly with the advocates of parliamentary action, opposing William

John Elliott Burns (1858–1943), by John Collier, 1889

Morris, who broke away to form the Socialist League. In 1885 Burns unsuccessfully contested Nottingham West in the general election, but his 598 votes dwarfed the total of 59 cast for the two SDF candidates in other constituencies. Furthermore, they were secured without any of the finance offered by the tory party in the hope of dividing the anti-Conservative vote. Throughout his public life Burns had the highest standards of personal integrity and was scathing of all who did not, whatever their social standing.

In the course of 1886 Burns was arrested and charged with sedition and conspiracy following his involvement in an SDF unemployment march that deteriorated into a riot. As 'the man with the red flag' he conducted his own defence so ably that he was discharged. Early in the following year he was again arrested when, in company with the radical MP, R. B. Cunninghame Graham, he led the crowd's attack against the police cordon set up to enforce a ban on public meetings in Trafalgar Square. He received a six-week sentence. The language Burns used at this time was often cited later as evidence of his revolutionary aspirations, but he was sometimes tempted into excesses because he so revelled in his ability to inspire adulation in a crowd, and many of his words were subsequently taken out of context. Fundamentally, he never wavered in his conviction that social change was the priority, the method of achieving it a secondary consideration. Even before his imprisonment he had shown signs of disenchantment with the SDF's chronic internecine bickering and its desire to engage in class warfare in the House of Commons, rather than seeking some tangible benefits for ordinary people. In 1889 Burns's popularity and record as a Labour militant enabled him to win one of the two Battersea seats on the newly established London county council.

On the London county council Barely had the new council begun its work when Burns's attention was diverted to the London dock strike. Although the dock gates had long been a favourite stamping ground he did not initiate the strike, and many other leading labour figures, especially Tom Mann and Ben Tillett, were prominently involved. Even so, the short, powerfully built, and bearded figure of Burns, sporting a straw boater for ease of identification, eclipsed them all. While he negotiated skilfully with intractable employers and organized picket lines tirelessly, Burns's major contribution was his oratory which sustained the strikers with its vision of 'the full round orb of the docker's tanner' (Smith and Nash, 147). The long-drawn-out stoppage and its successful outcome made Burns an internationally known figure. Everywhere his support was coveted to boost the ensuing surge of trade union organization and in 1890 he was elected to the parliamentary committee of the TUC. Burns's moderation in conducting the dock strike earned it considerable sympathy from the wider public and did much to dispel the militant reputation he had acquired in 1886 and 1887—so much so that Battersea Liberals solicited his parliamentary candidature.

Burns's election prospects were considerably enhanced by his performance in the London county council where for two or three years he was a dominant figure. He was an assiduous worker, diligently attending the numerous committees on which he served, visiting many of the council's projects, talking to technical experts, and generally bringing the force of his powerful personality to bear on behalf of municipal enterprise and improvement. In particular, he led the campaign which resulted in council work going only to those contractors who observed trade union rates and conditions. Eventually and with help from other Progressives, notably John Benn, he masterminded the establishment of the council's own works department, demanding of it the same rigorous standards of behaviour and performance he had required of private firms. Later he was instrumental in steering through the House of Commons the legislation that gave London its municipal steamboat service. From the middle 1890s until he finally left the council in 1907, however, Burns's influence diminished somewhat. This was partly because the growing hold of party politics made it difficult for him to preserve the freedom of action which he cherished, partly because in 1892 he was elected as MP for Battersea, winning the seat by 5616 votes to 4057.

In parliament At Westminster Burns generally eschewed larger political issues and concentrated on matters close to his heart, such as working conditions, corruption, public amenities, and the eight-hour day. As had happened in the London county council, these interests inevitably

drew him into informal co-operation with the radical wing of the Liberal Party but Burns insisted on his independence. He rejected offers of Liberal financial support in his constituency, relying instead on the salary provided by his own Battersea Labour League. While he emerged as the natural leader of the small group of Labour MPs in the Commons, he was profoundly suspicious of attempts to turn this into anything more structured. This brought him into conflict with Keir Hardie, a leading force behind the establishment of the Independent Labour Party (ILP) in 1893. Beatrice Webb oversimplified this clash in attributing it to Burns's immense egotism. Reared in the secular tradition of metropolitan radicalism, Burns could never come to terms with Hardie's more mystical version of socialism, couched as it was in terms of the New Testament. He also found irritating Hardie's penchant for parliamentary histrionics and his indifference to procedure. Above all, Burns had reaped handsome dividends in the county council by remaining free of party commitments and co-operating widely for the advancement of specific causes. He did not, therefore, share Hardie's view that within a broad progressive alliance, Labour should have a separately organized political identity. Fearing that the ILP was merely a northern version of the SDF and would divert Labour into narrow sectarianism and a political dead end, Burns supported—though contrary to received opinion he did not initiate—moves to emasculate its influence in the TUC. Although he attended the foundation conference of the Labour Representation Committee (LRC) in 1900 he declined to lend his support to an organization that demanded allegiance to a party programme exclusively geared towards the interests of a specific class. He maintained this position in the face of Hardie's several later attempts to win him over.

Once the major trade unions began to turn to the LRC in the aftermath of the Taff Vale judgment which threatened to expose their funds to legal action, Burns became increasingly isolated within the broader labour movement, even though his own Battersea base remained secure. At the same time his opposition to British involvement in the Second South African War reinforced his links with the radical wing of the Liberal Party, though he held aloof from the formal anti-war movement, once again preferring to conduct an independent campaign. Burns was also a convinced free-trader and when Joseph Chamberlain launched his tariff reform campaign in 1903 Liberal leaders appreciated the political advantage of having on their platforms a genuine working man who was not afraid to attack Chamberlain as a 'fiscal pervert' (*The Times*, 3 Jan 1906). When Campbell-Bannerman formed his administration in 1905 Burns was offered the presidency of the Local Government Board, the first working man to achieve cabinet rank.

At the Local Government Board Burns's acceptance of office has often been portrayed as the first in a long line of betrayals by Labour politicians. Yet Burns had long resisted the notion of an independent working-class party. The flexibility and independence of action that he preferred could be maintained in a Liberal government where the onus for legislative initiatives lay with individual ministers, not a party manifesto. His position was vindicated almost immediately after the general election of 1906 returned the Liberals to power with a huge majority. Faced with a hostile Labour Party reaction to his own Trades Disputes Bill, Campbell-Bannerman threw over the views of most legal experts, a royal commission, and his own senior cabinet colleagues by announcing that it would be amended to confer on union funds total immunity from legal action. It seems probable that the major influence behind this sudden volte-face was Burns. He had long been Campbell-Bannerman's unofficial adviser on trade union affairs, and had previously introduced the TUC's own bill granting total immunity.

It has been generally concluded that Burns's eight years at the Local Government Board were barren. Behind this judgement lies the view, originally propagated by Beatrice Webb, that Burns's civil servants played on his personal vanity, flattering him into becoming an ineffective and reactionary minister. Burns's vanity is not in doubt: when Campbell-Bannerman offered him the Local Government Board, Burns is alleged to have replied that the prime minister had never done a more popular thing. But Mrs Webb's views were heavily influenced by the fact that Burns was the rock on which her ambitious plans for restructuring the poor law foundered. He had long believed that poverty and its related problems were the combined outcome of individual failure and an inadequate social environment. This was reinforced by a strong streak of puritanism which expressed itself in his opposition to smoking, drinking, and gambling. He was not flattered either into holding an inquiry into the administration of the Poplar poor-law union in 1906. Rather he was disturbed by the possibility that public money might have been dispensed in a corrupt way. In similar fashion, his hostility to the Webbs' plans for the poor law owed less to the conservatism of the Local Government Board than to his own fear of undermining individuality by regimentalizing pauperism.

Other aspects of Burns's character were important in determining his performance at the board, however. His insistence on being personally involved in relatively trivial matters often caused him to lose sight of the president's strategic role. What had just about been possible in London was not practical on a national scale. He lacked many constructive ideas of his own, most obviously in the area of unemployment policy. Intellectual limitations forced him, as the wife of one colleague remarked, to spend most of his official life struggling with 'things he did not fully understand and bluffing to hide the fact' (Masterman, 205). In this regard he was not helped by the operational deficiencies of a department enmeshed in red tape. More particularly, the absence of a statistical section hampered the development of a programme to deal with unemployment, while the poor law section was wedded to the principles of 1834. As the Cinderella of Whitehall, the Local Government Board did not attract high quality civil servants. Burns's parliamentary draftsman was particularly incompetent and must bear much of the blame for the failure of at least two important legislative measures concerning rating and the municipal milk supply to reach the statute book. Burns's diaries (now in the British Library) indicate his frustration with this situation, though ultimately he seems to have given up his struggle to introduce a more dynamic ethos. He came to tolerate the problems because neither his pride nor his conviction that he was somehow called to represent the people would allow him to admit defeat and give up his office.

The one significant piece of legislation Burns did oversee, the Housing and Town Planning Act of 1909, was a major achievement, introducing for the first time the principle of municipally owned housing and conferring wide planning powers on local authorities. In general, however, Burns found the legislative process tedious and he preferred to implement change through administrative means. Even the Webbs conceded that he did much to humanize the operation of the poor law. Equally significant in his attempts to improve the general social environment were the compulsory notification of pauper tuberculosis and his crusade against infant mortality. This administrative record has been largely overlooked, although it helps to explain why Burns was retained in the cabinet when H. H. Asquith replaced Campbell-Bannerman as prime minister in 1908. It also lay behind his transfer to the Board of Trade on 12 February 1914. After the stream of radical legislation produced by its previous heads, Churchill and Lloyd George, its paramount requirement was for an administratively competent president.

On broader political issues Burns was never as significant a figure within the cabinet as his diary entries suggest. He was consistently opposed to high military expenditure, took a dim view of colleagues like Lloyd George who appeared to flout his own high standards of public behaviour, and was unswervingly loyal to Asquith. However, that support did not survive the outbreak of war in 1914. Despite his stand against the Second South African War, Burns was not a principled pacifist and as a confirmed home-ruler had advocated strong action against the Ulster Unionists. But he was essentially a little Englander and when it became clear on 2 August 1914 that Britain was committed to support France in the event of a conflict with Germany, he resigned from the government, rejecting Asquith's last minute plea to remain.

Retirement and old age This was the effective end of Burns's political career although he did not leave the House of Commons until 1918. There was no obvious political home for him in post-war Britain. He had forfeited the support of the Asquithian Liberals through his anti-war stance and he would not consider supporting Lloyd George, for whom he had a deep antipathy. But neither could Burns, despite a few fanciful entries in his diary, contemplate a return as a Labour candidate, for his stewardship of the Local Government Board, particularly his handling of unemployment and the Poplar poor-law inquiry, had closed that particular door. Any lingering inclination to return was finally extinguished by the sudden death in 1922 of Edgar, the son on whom he doted.

Thereafter, supported by a Carnegie pension worth about £1000 a year, Burns retreated from public life, browsing in bookshops, emerging occasionally to receive academic or civic honours and—more frequently—to watch cricket or to attend to his one remaining public duty as a trustee of the Strathcona leper colony. His wife died on 30 October 1936.

By the end of 1941 Burns was practically bedridden, as a result of a combination of old age which had finally conquered his robust health, and of a nearby bomb blast which had thrown him heavily to the ground. He died of heart failure and senile arteriosclerosis at the Bolingbroke Hospital in Wandsworth on 24 January 1943, and was buried in St Mary's churchyard, Battersea. He left an estate valued at £15,137 3s. 7d.

KENNETH D. BROWN

Sources K. D. Brown, *John Burns* (1977) • W. Kent, *John Burns: labour's lost leader* (1950) • G. D. H. Cole, *John Burns* (1943) • H. Haward, *The London county council from within* (1932) • A. G. Gardiner, *John Benn and the progressive movement* (1925) • A. P. Grubb, *From candle factory to British cabinet: the life story of the Right Hon. John Burns* (1908) • J. Burgess, *John Burns: the rise and progress of a right honourable* (1911) • G. H. Knott, *Mr John Burns MP* (1901) • C. J. Wrigley, 'The myth and the facts in the life of Honest John', *South Western Star* (4 Sept 1970) • R. Donald, 'Mr John Burns the workman minister', *Nineteenth Century and After*, 59 (1906), 191–204 • S. L. Hughes, *Press, platform and parliament* (1918), 283 • H. L. Smith and V. Nash, *The story of the dockers' strike* (1889), 147 • *The Times* (3 Jan 1906) • L. Masterman, *C. F. G. Masterman* (1939), 205 • *The Times* (31 Oct 1936)

Archives Battersea Public Library • BL, corresp. and papers incl. diaries, Add. MSS 46281–46345, 59669 • California State University, Northridge, letters • HMC, priv. coll., letters and papers • LMA • LUL | BL, Campbell-Bannerman MSS • BL, letters to Lord Gladstone, Add. MSS 46055–46085 • BLPES, corresp. with E. D. Morel • BLPES, Fabian Society Archives, corresp. with Fabian Society • BLPES, Passfield MSS • Bodl. Oxf., corresp. with Herbert Asquith • Communist Party Library and Archive, Manchester, Communist MSS • HLRO, letters to Herbert Samuel • HLRO, corresp. with John St Loe Strachey • LMA, corresp. with the Central Unemployed Body for London • U. Newcastle, Robinson L., corresp. with Walter Runciman

Likenesses A. Furniss, pen-and-ink, *c.*1880–1910, NPG • J. Collier, portrait, 1889, NPG [*see illus.*] • W. & D. Downey, woodburytype photograph, 1893, NPG • A. J. Finberg, portrait, 1897, Battersea Library, London • G. F. Watts, portrait, 1897, Watts Library, Compton, Surrey • B. Stone, photographs, 1897–1905, NPG • G. C. Beresford, photograph, 1902, NPG • H. Speed, pastel, 1907, NPG • F. C. Gould, ink, 1908, NPG; repro. in *Pall Mall Gazette* (1908) • H. Speed, portrait, 1909, National Liberal Club, London • M. Beerbohm, watercolour, NPG • S. P. Hall, pencil, NPG • G. W. Leech, portrait (posthumous), Battersea Town Hall, London • L. Ward, chromolithograph, NPG; repro. in *VF* (15 Oct 1892) • photographs, NPG

Wealth at death £15,137 3s. 7d.: administration with will, 12 July 1943, *CGPLA Eng. & Wales*

Burns, Robert (1759–1796), poet, was born on 25 January 1759 in a two-room clay cottage built by his father (and now restored as Burns's Cottage) at Alloway, Ayrshire, the eldest of the four sons and three daughters of William Burnes (1721–1784), gardener and tenant farmer, and his wife, Agnes Brown (1732–1820), of Maybole, Ayrshire.

Ancestry and childhood Burns's grandfather Robert Burnes (*c.*1685–*c.*1760) had worked as gardener to the Earl Marischal at Inverugie Castle, Aberdeenshire. Burns believed that this Robert Burnes had suffered for his Jacobite sympathies at the time of the 1715 Jacobite rising; afterwards

Robert Burns (1759–1796), by Alexander Nasmyth, 1787

he became a struggling farmer in Kincardineshire, and his third son, William (born at Clochnahill farm, Dunnottar, Kincardineshire), headed south, working as a gardener first in Edinburgh and then in Ayrshire. In 1754 William engaged himself for two years to work as gardener for John Crawford of Doonside House, near Alloway, 2 miles south of Ayr. By 1756 he had feued from Dr Alexander Campbell of Ayr 7½ acres of land near Alloway with the intention of setting up a market garden. There he began to build his cottage while also working as head gardener for Provost William Fergusson of Doonholm, Alloway. In the summer of 1756 William Burnes met Agnes Brown at Maybole fair; they married on 15 December 1757. William Burnes was comparatively well educated for a Scottish peasant. He valued learning and sought to procure education for his sons and daughters; later he prepared a short catechism for the instruction of his children, and instigated attempts to care for the historic local church, Kirk Alloway. Agnes Brown could not write but had a good knowledge of ballads and songs, having come from an extended family in which such lore was valued.

Burns was born into a small, Scots-speaking, west-of-Scotland rural community in which vernacular culture was strong. Betty Davidson (widow of Agnes's cousin) lived with the Burnes family and, as the poet put it later, 'cultivated the latent seeds of Poesy' in the wee boy Robert (*Letters*, 1.135). Superstitious and unlettered, Betty entertained the children with what Burns recalled in his 1787 autobiographical letter to the London Scottish novelist Dr John Moore as 'the largest collection in the county of tales and songs concerning devils, ghosts, fairies, brownies, witches, warlocks, spunkies, kelpies, elf-candles, dead-lights, wraiths, apparitions, cantraips, giants, inchanted towers, dragons and other trumpery' (ibid.). Such accounts preoccupied the young boy, who also heard from his mother frankly erotic traditional Scots songs and ballads. Although local vernacular culture was strong the community was linked to the wider world and to English-language culture through church, education, and other channels. William Burnes became a private subscriber to Ayr Library (founded in 1762). Moreover William and Agnes were friendly with, for instance, William Paterson, Latin master of Ayr's grammar school, and with that school's writing master, while William Dalrymple, the young Ayr minister who baptized Robert on 26 January 1759, went on to become moderator of the Church of Scotland. By the age of seven Robert had been taught some reading and writing, having been enrolled by his father in William Campbell's short-lived school at Alloway Mill in 1765; when Campbell left William Burnes obtained a tutor for his children and those of four other local families. This was John Murdoch (1747–1824), an Ayr man, who worked with William Burnes to teach Robert to comprehend and to commit to memory passages of English. Robert was sometimes punished by Murdoch for pranks, but he and his younger brother Gilbert (1760–1827) were usually near the top of Murdoch's class in spelling and parsing. Murdoch recalled how he taught his young pupils 'to turn verse into its natural prose order; and sometimes to substitute synonimous expressions for poetical words' (Mackay, 34). Among the schoolbooks used were the Bible and Arthur Masson's *A Collection of Prose and Verse, from the Best English Authors*, in which Robert particularly enjoyed passages of Addison. He also read 'in private' for the first time, devouring accounts of Hannibal and of Sir William Wallace, whose narrative 'poured a Scottish prejudice in my veins' (*Letters*, 1.135–6).

Late in 1765 Burns's father, seeking a larger house, took out a lease on Provost Fergusson's farm at the more isolated, less easily cultivated Mount Oliphant, near Alloway, but William Burnes had to keep paying the lease of his Alloway land too, since he could find no taker for it. So began a series of financial struggles that were to affect the Burnes family. By 1768, when John Murdoch moved to Dumfries, William and Agnes Burnes were living at Mount Oliphant with five children and no school nearby. William worked on the farm by day and taught the children arithmetic by candlelight, talking to his sons as if they were fellow men. In 1768 John Murdoch visited and reduced the family to tears with his reading from *Titus Andronicus*. Robert's father borrowed and passed to his sons such improving volumes as William Derham's *Astro-Theology* (1714) and John Ray's *Wisdom of God Manifest in the Works of Creation* (1691). The young boy began to take a sometimes puzzled and sceptical interest in questions of Calvinist theology, much debated in the local area, where (as elsewhere in Scotland) the more extreme faction of Auld Licht presbyterians was in contention with the more moderate New Licht wing of the Church of Scotland; he also devoured a collection of 'Letters by the most eminent

writers' and was inspired to imitate their English-language eloquence (Mackay, 43).

By his early teens Burns was familiar with the work of ploughing, though for a time his father also sent him and Gilbert 'week about during a summer quarter' to the parish school of Dalrymple, near Maybole (Mackay, 45). About this time Robert also encountered a version of Richardson's *Pamela* and some fiction by Smollett. By 1772 he had access to the *Edinburgh Magazine* and (thanks to a gift from Murdoch) the works of Pope. In 1773 his father sent him to Ayr for some sporadic teaching from Murdoch, including lessons in French and an amount of Latin. He was also acquainted with the more vernacular chapbooks and broadsheets of printed ballads sold by rural hawkers. Like several other Scottish writers Burns was in important ways bicultural, brought up on traditional (largely oral) Scots-language songs and narratives, as well as on English-language book culture.

Early compositions By 1774 Burns was beginning to compose songs. In his autobiographical letter to Dr Moore in 1787 he recalled that in his 'fifteenth autumn' he 'first committed the sin of RHYME' by making a song for a 'bewitching' girl with whom he had been partnered at harvest time, and for whom he had conceived a reciprocated passion: ''twas her favourite reel to which I attempted giving an embodied vehicle in rhyme' (*Letters*, 1.137). Though Burns lacked any formal musical education the sense here of a traditional Scottish tune underlying the poet's words, which become an 'embodied vehicle' for it, is important to much of his work, as is his linking of poetry with the 'bewitching', the erotic, and a mercurial consciousness of 'sin'. His earliest songs were not 'like printed ones, composed by men who had Greek and Latin' but were suited to those 'living in the moors' (ibid., 137–8). This may have been so but Burns's first poems often appear exercises in the rhetoric of eighteenth-century book-verse:

> Avaunt, away! the cruel sway,
> Tyrannic man's dominion.
> (R. Burns, 'Song, Composed in August')

By 1775 Burns was at school again, for a time studying 'Mensuration, Surveying, Dialling, &c.' under Hugh Rodger (1726–97), the parish dominie in Kirkoswald, not far from the farm of Shanter, in Carrick, on the Firth of Clyde (*Letters*, 1.140). There he had a passionate encounter with a local girl, thirteen-year-old Peggy Thomson, with whom he kept in touch for some years; he also larked, and debated Calvinist theology with local lads. In Kirkoswald he read Thomson and Shenstone, and developed his own, studied epistolary eloquence.

Dr Fergusson, William Burnes's landlord, died in 1776 and the struggling Burnes moved inland from Mount Oliphant to the windswept, boggy 130-acre farm of Lochlie, in the nearby parish of Tarbolton. There the young Burns romanced local girls and read the works of Allan Ramsay, alongside a collection of English songs, while he developed his own poetic gifts in the composition of songs to local girls and celebrations of the local terrain. As a young man he developed a great fondness for dancing and assumed a slightly dandified appearance. His teenage friend David Sillar recalled the young Burns attending kirk in Tarbolton regularly with his family, when he 'wore the only tied hair in the parish; and in the church, his plaid, which was of a particular colour, I think *fillemot*, he wrapped in a particular manner round his shoulders' (Mackay, 76). Reading theology and (by 1781) *Tristram Shandy*, confident with women, and maturing as a poet, Burns was sociable and popular in the local community. Working hard on his father's farm, he also found time to practise the fiddle. Though he never became adept at this instrument he learned to read music with some competence, and later attempted to play the German flute. As well as Scots songs addressed to various sweethearts the young Burns was turning verses of the psalms into quatrains, and several early English-language poems reflect a concern with the precariousness of existence ('To Ruin', for instance, and 'A Prayer, under the Pressure of Violent Anguish'). While such works may have the quality of exercises they represent a fear of despair that dogged Burns, counterpointing his normal joviality. So among his early works the dark and the jaunty are often hand in hand.

On 11 November 1780 in a top-floor room in John Richards's alehouse in the Sandgate, Tarbolton (a room also used for masonic meetings), Burns founded the Tarbolton Bachelors' Club, perhaps the earliest Scottish rural debating society. This all-male fraternity, whose rules were drafted by Burns, swore its members to secrecy and demanded that each 'must be a professed lover of one or more of the female sex'. Swearing was forbidden, social drinking encouraged, and haughtiness prohibited, so that 'the proper person for this society is a cheerful, honest-hearted lad'. Topics debated by the club included suitable marriage partners and 'Whether is the savage man or the peasant of a civilized society in the most happy situation' (Mackay, 82–3). Such a topic is at one with the Scottish Enlightenment interest in the progress of 'civil society', and it is evident that the young Burns was developing an interest in such works as Adam Smith's *Theory of Moral Sentiments* (1759), with its ethic of sympathy as a social bond. By 1781 he was also praising Henry Mackenzie's novel of sympathetic sentimentality, *The Man of Feeling* (1771), which he carried so frequently on his person that his copy disintegrated and had to be replaced. In 1783 he described Mackenzie's novel as 'a book I prize next to the Bible' (*Letters*, 1.17).

Sometimes happy, but also sometimes hurt and rebuffed in his own affairs of the heart, Burns in 1781 decided to strike out in a new direction and become a flax-dresser in the Ayrshire town of Irvine; this venture failed, the shop in which he worked burned down, and Burns suffered a bout of depression in late 1781. At this time he also read with great appreciation the Scots and English poems of Robert Fergusson (1750–1774), who had died in Edinburgh's madhouse. While in Irvine, Burns enjoyed a very close 'bosom-friendship' with the sailor Captain Richard Brown (1753–1833), with whom he walked in Eglinton

Woods, where Brown suggested to the still unpublished poet that he send his poems to a magazine (*Letters*, 1.142). Though Burns does not seem to have acted on this suggestion he sent Brown one of the very few personal presentation copies of the first, Kilmarnock, edition of his poems when that volume appeared in 1786.

During 1781 Burns had also become a freemason, having been 'entered an Apprentice' in the combined Lodge St David, Tarbolton, on 4 July (Mackay, 119). He became an active mason, rising to depute master of St James Lodge, Tarbolton, by 1784. During Burns's deputy mastership Professor Dugald Stewart of Catrine, who later championed the poet's work, was made an honorary member of the lodge. Through masonic contacts Burns also came to know Sir John Whitefoord (1734–1803), the agricultural improver, whose own contacts were later of use to the aspiring poet. Burns returned to Lochlie in 1782 to find matters there deteriorating. Struggling with the farm's acidic soil, William Burnes was facing severe financial problems. By 1783 his property had been sequestrated, and he was being pursued through the courts for rent arrears. Bad summers in 1782 and 1783 added to William's troubles and, though he succeeded in winning his law case before Lord Braxfield, the disastrous harvest of 1783 saw him a broken man, fighting tuberculosis; he died on 13 February 1784, and his body was taken for burial at the ruined Kirk Alloway. Burns's admiration for his father was great and is reflected in 'The Cotter's Saturday Night', with its portrait of noble paternal concern and undaunted domestic virtue.

In April 1783 Burns at Lochlie began to keep a commonplace book of 'Observations, Hints, Songs, Scraps of Poetry, etc.', including his own shrewd critical appraisals of his verse. He was conscious of the curious interest that a ploughman's literary concerns might have for future readers. As well as reworking comic and erotic song and ballad materials he composed several poems relating to his father's death; a strange fusion of the comic and elegiac is evident in 'The Death and Dying Words of Poor Mailie, the Author's Only Pet Yowe: an Unco Mournfu' Tale', which builds on earlier works such as 'The Last Dying Words of Bonnie Heck' (a greyhound) by Allan Ramsay's friend William Hamilton of Gilbertfield (*c*.1665–1751). Appearing in his commonplace book along with several mock epitaphs, Burns's poem treats with a tenderly comic voice the anxieties of death and the agricultural grind; at once mock-elegy and genuine lament, this poem led to another, 'Poor Mailie's Elegy' (composed about 1785), which uses the six-line 'Standard Habbie' verse form inherited from the comic elegy 'The Life and Death of Habbie Simson, the Piper of Kilbarchan' by Robert Sempill of Beltrees (*c*.1595–*c*.1665). Burns's verse artistry led him to give new life to several Scottish stanza forms, making them 'crucial to the national spirit of his poetry' (Crawford, 84). He made such great use of the Standard Habbie stanza form in such works as 'Holy Willie's Prayer' (1785), which mocks Calvinist hypocrisy, and in his verse letters that it acquired the name 'Burns stanza'. Its flicking short lines towards the end of each stanza lend themselves to speedy nods and winks:

> Maybe thou lets this fleshy thorn
> Buffet thy servant e'en and morn,
> Lest he o'er proud and high should turn,
> 　　That he's sae gifted;
> If sae, thy hand maun e'en be borne
> 　　Untill thou lift it.
> (R. Burns, 'Holy Willie's Prayer')

Burns comes to use this stanza form in the period in the mid-1780s when he clearly blossoms as a poet. The form, already over a century old, transmits metrically an impulse to fuse the solemn and the lightly risible, the dark and the boisterous, which Burns inherited, developed, and transmitted with mischievous grace. Many of his finest poems delight in juxtaposing or blending uneasily defended respectability with gleefully subversive energy. His commonplace book functioned as a literary laboratory in this regard, and by about 1785 most elements of his literary personality had been assembled, including a humorous and purposeful tendency to view himself as what Robert Fergusson had called a 'Bardie'—at once an ambitious poet of his people in full flight and a snook-cocking belittler of the grandiose tendencies in himself and others.

Burns knew about bards from his enthusiastic reading of the poems of Ossian, but his own mundane struggles were far removed from the nobly misty realms of that bard. In 1784, following their father's death, Gilbert and Robert took a lease on another farm, at Mossgiel, in the neighbouring parish of Mauchline. Drainage there was poor, and for all the brothers' efforts they were beset with problems of bad seed, hard frosts, and late harvests. During that summer and autumn, troubled by 'a kind of slow fever' and 'langor of my spirits' (*Letters*, 1.23), Burns seems to have suffered another bout of depressive or psychosomatic illness, though he was also enjoying the 'honours masonic' and the 'big-belly'd bottle' of the lodge (R. Burns, 'No churchman am I'). On 22 May 1785 an uneducated servant woman in her early twenties, Elizabeth Paton, gave birth to Burns's daughter Elizabeth (1785–1817)—'Dear-bought Bess' (Mackay, 137). Burns had made no promise to wed his lover, who later married a farmworker and widower, John Andrew, in 1788, after the poet and 'handsome Betsey' had apparently paid a fine and done penance for fornication before Tarbolton Kirk Session (R. Burns, 'The Fornicator'). Burns's poem 'The Fornicator' details these events, but was not published in his lifetime.

Styling himself Rab Mossgiel, Burns wrote flirtatious as well as satirical verse at this time, when he was paying court to Jean Armour (1765–1834), the literate daughter of a Mauchline stonemason, though he also dallied with other local girls. By summer 1785, recovered from his illness and fired up by the poetry of those whom he called in his first commonplace book 'the excellent Ramsay, and the still more excellent [Robert] Fergus[s]on', Burns was committing himself to a concentrated and ambitious aesthetic of the local, eager to write poems that celebrated his native ground (Mackay, 156). His sense of himself as a

Scottish poet was developing, and Gilbert was encouraging him to go into print, though the shock of the death of his youngest brother, John (aged sixteen), on 1 November 1785 meant that his awareness of tribulation also remained heightened. To this period belong some of Burns's major verse epistles as well as 'Holy Willie's Prayer', a spirited and sly dramatic monologue that satirizes the Calvinist doctrine of predestination and its hypocritical exponent William Fisher (1737–1809), an elder in the parish of Mauchline who had been involved in a series of vigorously prosecuted kirk disputes with Burns's Mossgiel landlord and friend, the lawyer Gavin Hamilton (1751–1805). In his prefatory headnote, setting out the argument of 'Holy Willie's Prayer', Burns describes Holy Willie as 'justly famed for that polemical chattering which ends in tippling Orthodoxy, and for that Spiritualized Bawdry which refines to Liquorish Devotion'; the poem that follows is equally devastating. This work is one of a group of contemporary satires on local kirk politics and arguments featuring neighbouring ministers and worthies; these poems include 'The Holy Fair', 'The Twa Herds, or, The Holy Tulzie', and 'Death and Dr Hornbook'. 1785 was also the year of the composition of Burns's 'Address to the Deil', in which the devil (hailed variously as 'auld Cloots', 'Hornie', and 'Nick') is spoken to with confident wonder as well as familiar vernacular directness; as in 'Hallowe'en' this is one of the poems in which Burns clearly delights in his repertory of folklore and superstitious tales. A mischievously confident tone married to a sense of inexhaustible and undeflected purposefulness characterizes these poems, as it does such different works as 'The Twa Dogs: a Tale' (about social inequality), 'The Vision' (presenting Burns's local muse in Ossianic 'duans'), and a superb series of verse epistles in Standard Habbie. These poetic letters were actually sent, and should be seen as reinforcing Burns's emphasis on vernacular communion and on the local as paramount. This poetic outpouring in 1785 shows a determined confidence, though poems of the same period such as 'To a Mouse' demonstrate a continuing sense of vulnerability and the need for social sympathy.

By early 1786, when Burns was composing such works as 'The Cotter's Saturday Night' (that pious celebration of impoverished domestic virtue), it became evident that Jean Armour was going to have Burns's child. He was reluctant to marry her but seems to have given her some documentary assurance (now lost) that he would stick by her. Jean Armour's father reacted angrily, had resort to law, and had this 'unlucky paper' mutilated, sending off his daughter to Paisley (*Letters*, 1.30). While the kirk investigated the affair Burns was well advanced with arranging for the publication (by subscription) of his first volume of poems. With Jean in Paisley he made eyes at Margaret Campbell ('another wife', who appears to have died young and is remembered as the shadowy 'Highland Mary'), though when Jean returned in early summer 1786 Burns protested that he adored her and had tried to forget her by running into 'all kinds of dissipation and riot, Mason-meetings, drinking matches, and other mischief' (ibid., 37, 39). Emotionally upset, he resolved to sail as an emigrant to Jamaica ('farewel dear old Scotland, and farewel dear, ungrateful Jean'), but was called to do public penance on the stool of repentance ('the creepy chair') at Mauchline kirk on 25 June 1786, with further public rebukes on 23 July and on 3 August, when Burns, Jean Armour, and three other fornicators were 'absolved from scandal' by the Auld Licht minister, the Revd William ('Daddy') Auld (ibid., 39; Mackay, 191). On 22 July Burns had made over his share in Mossgiel and all his property to his brother Gilbert. Jean Armour's father took out a writ for damages against Burns, threatening him with imprisonment. Burns fled towards Kilmarnock, wrote letters to friends about his forthcoming volume of poems, and planned his emigration to Jamaica on 1 September. Backed by local Kilmarnock businessmen and published by John Wilson of Kilmarnock, Burns's *Poems* appeared at the end of July, and during August he collected money from subscribers to the book. His departure for Jamaica from Greenock was now rescheduled for the end of September. On 3 September he received news of the birth of his twins: a son, Robert, and a daughter, Jean. Paternal emotions and the possibility of a second edition of his book seem to have led him to abandon his Jamaica plans, though he arranged for a ticket that would have allowed him to emigrate in October.

Book publication and visits to Edinburgh Burns's preface to the 240-page Kilmarnock *Poems, Chiefly in the Scottish Dialect*, published in 1786, presents the author as one who lacked 'all the advantages of learned art' and who, being 'Unacquainted with the necessary requisites for commencing Poet by rule', instead 'sings the sentiments and manners, he felt and saw in himself and his rustic compeers around him, in his and their native language'. The book, published in an edition of just over 600 copies, contained forty-four poems, in Scots and in English, including such substantial recent works as 'Scotch Drink', 'The Twa Dogs', 'The Vision', and 'The Cotter's Saturday Night'. Thanks not least to the large number of subscribers obtained by Gilbert Burns and the poet's friends, the edition sold out in a month, making Burns a profit of over £50. John Wilson wished Burns to advance money for a second edition, but the poet was reluctant to hazard this. The book had won him intense local admiration among the common people and gentry. A local minister, the Revd George Lawrie of Loudoun, sent Burns's *Poems* to an Edinburgh literary friend, the blind poet the Revd Thomas Blacklock, who asked his friend Professor Dugald Stewart to read some of the poems aloud to him. Blacklock wrote enthusiastically to Lawrie, hoping that there would be a second edition of the poems, and his letter was passed on to Burns, who soon gave up his emigration plans. In autumn 1786 he visited the Lawries, lent George's son Archibald a two-volume edition of Ossian and some books of songs and Scottish poetry, and got on well with the family. By 23 October he was dining with Lord Daer (recently returned from France, where he had met leading revolutionaries) and Dugald Stewart at the latter's house near

Mauchline. Stewart recalled Burns then and later as 'simple, manly, and independent', noting that:

> Nothing, perhaps, was more remarkable among his various attainments than the fluency, and precision, and originality of his language, when he spoke in company; more particularly as he aimed at purity in his turn of expression, and avoided, more successfully than most Scotchmen, the peculiarities of Scottish phraseology. (Mackay, 243)

Burns and his poetry also appealed to other local figures, including the widowed grandmother Frances Anna Wallace, Mrs Dunlop of Dunlop, who began to correspond with the poet. By November, encouraged by his new acquaintances, Burns was proposing to visit Edinburgh, with plans for a second edition of his poems to be published there. He was also exploring the possibility of earning his living as an excise officer, a plan that would later bear fruit.

Late in November 1786 Burns rode to Edinburgh, feted along the way by lowland farmers who had read his verse. On arrival he shared lodgings in the house of a Mrs Carfrae ('a flesh-disciplining, godly Matron') in a tenement, now demolished, at Baxter's Close, Lawnmarket (*Letters*, 1.83). Using his network of masonic connections, as well as other supporters, Burns investigated the likelihood of a new edition of his *Poems*. Dugald Stewart had given a copy of the Kilmarnock edition to the novelist and Edinburgh man of letters Henry Mackenzie, who reviewed the book in his magazine, *The Lounger*, on 9 December 1786, calling attention to Burns as a 'Heaven-taught ploughman' whose 'neglected merit' Scotland should recognize. Other Edinburgh reviewers also praised Burns in November and December 1786, while the influential earl of Glencairn secured the agreement of the hundred or so gentlemen of the Caledonian Hunt that they would all subscribe to a second edition of Burns's *Poems*, which (with its dedication to the Caledonian Hunt) was published by subscription on 17 April 1787 by the famous and tight-fisted Edinburgh bookseller William Creech, who eventually paid Burns £100 for the copyright. The typesetter was William Smellie, one of the founders of the *Encyclopaedia Britannica*; he introduced Burns to the all-male club that he had founded, the Crochallan Fencibles, for which Burns collected bawdy songs and where he met several of his fellow masons. Published in an edition of about 3000 copies, the 408-page Edinburgh volume of his poems was an immediate success, with ploughman Burns cannily presenting what his preface called 'my wild, artless notes'. Among the new poems added to the volume were the vigorous, slyly modulated Scots poems 'Address to the Unco Guid' and 'Death and Dr Hornbook', as well as the 'Address to Edinburgh', in which Burns on his best behaviour delivers a paean to 'Edina! Scotia's darling seat!'

During winter 1786–7 Burns seems to have engaged in several dalliances (resulting in at least one child) but also met many of Edinburgh's distinguished literati, and was given star treatment. At the house of the philosopher and historian Professor Adam Ferguson (1723–1816) he met the scientists James Hutton and William Black, along with the playwright John Home and the sixteen-year-old Walter

Scott. Scott recalled that Burns wept on seeing a print of a soldier lying dead in the snow beside his widow, with a child in her arms. According to Scott the twenty-eight-year-old Burns (5 feet 10 inches tall) 'was strong and robust: his manners rustic, not clownish'; he had 'a sort of dignified plainness and simplicity' that made Scott think of:

> a very sagacious country farmer of the old Scotch school—*i.e.* none of your modern agriculturists, who keep labourers for their drudgery, but the *douce gudeman* who held his own plough. There was a strong expression of sense and shrewdness in all his lineaments; the eye alone, I think, indicated the poetical character and temperament. It was large, and of a dark cast, and glowed (I say literally *glowed*) when he spoke with feeling or interest.   (Lockhart, 115–17)

Scott recalled also that Burns, who talked of Allan Ramsay and Robert Fergusson 'with too much humility as his models', was at that time 'much caressed in Edinburgh, but (considering what literary emoluments have been since his day) the efforts made for his relief were extremely trifling' (ibid.). For the young Scott, Burns's conversation:

> expressed perfect self-confidence, without the slightest presumption. Among the men who were the most learned of their time and country, he expressed himself with perfect firmness, but without the least intrusive forwardness; and when he differed in opinion, he did not hesitate to express it firmly, yet at the same time with modesty … his dress corresponded with his manner. He was like a farmer dressed in his best to dine with the laird … his address to females was extremely deferential, and always with a turn either to the pathetic or humorous, which engaged their attention particularly.   (Mackay, 267)

The Revd Hugh Blair, the elderly professor of rhetoric and belles-lettres at Edinburgh University, pronounced himself 'a great friend to Mr. Burns's Poems' and made suggestions about what Burns should include and exclude from his second, Edinburgh, edition, judging that his rollicking cantata 'Love and Liberty' ('The Jolly Beggars') was 'too licentious' and 'altogether unfit' for publication (Low, 82). This spirited work of 1785 is set in Poosie (that is, Pussy) Nancie's doss-house (then disreputable, now splendidly preserved) for the 'lowest orders' in Mauchline, and it is hard to think of Hugh Blair warming to a text one of whose boozy singers proclaims:

> A fig for those by LAW protected
> LIBERTY's a glorious feast!
> COURTS for Cowards were erected,
> CHURCHES built to please the Priest.

Burns excluded 'Love and Liberty' from the Edinburgh edition, and it was not published until 1799. While he respected Blair, Burns got on better with Blair's younger colleague and professorial successor, the Revd William Greenfield, who became moderator of the Church of Scotland but was later dismissed after a homosexual scandal. Promoted in Edinburgh society by such figures as the duchess of Gordon, Burns was also toasted at Edinburgh's St Andrew's masonic lodge as 'Caledonia's bard, brother Burns' (*Letters*, 1.83). In Edinburgh he made friends not only with noble patrons but also with people such as the printer Smellie and the borders law clerk Robert Ainslie (1766–1838), who became a close companion and confidant.

Burns composed comparatively little verse during his six-month stay in Edinburgh, but one of his most revealing acts was to write to the bailies of the Canongate to complain that the remains of the poet Robert Fergusson, 'a man whose talents for ages to come will do honor to our Caledonian name', lay buried in the Canongate churchyard 'unnoticed and unknown'; the bailies granted Burns permission to erect a headstone on Fergusson's grave (ibid., 90). Though the clerkly Fergusson, educated at St Andrews University, came from a background rather different from that of Burns he was the Scottish poet to whom Burns felt closest. Early in 1787 Burns wrote three poems to Fergusson's memory, calling him:

> my elder brother in Misfortune,
> By far my elder Brother in the muse.

Fergusson's vivid vernacularity, his poetically vigorous championing of Scots language and of Scottish culture, and his depressive decline all struck chords with Burns, who modelled several of his poems, including 'The Cotter's Saturday Night', on Fergusson's originals. Burns recognized in Allan Ramsay and in Fergusson channels of vernacular skill and poetic vitality; his own verse launches out from such Scottish examples. Early in 1787 he wrote to his admirer Mrs Dunlop that 'The appelation of, a Scotch Bard, is by far my highest pride', and that he hoped to visit patriotic sights, making 'leisurely pilgrimages through Caledonia' (*Letters*, 1.101). Several works of this period celebrate peculiarly Scottish subjects. Where Fergusson had dreamed of feeding haggis to Samuel Johnson, Burns celebrated that Scottish delicacy with humorously patriotic glee in his address 'To a Haggis', apparently the first of his poems to be published in a newspaper; celebrating the 'honest, sonsie face' of the 'Great Chieftain o' the Puddin-race', it appeared in the *Caledonian Mercury* in December 1786.

Several portraits of Burns were painted during his first Edinburgh visit. The first, by the coach painter and sign writer Peter Taylor, is in the Scottish National Portrait Gallery. Alexander Nasmyth, commissioned by Creech to paint a portrait of Burns from which John Beugo made an engraving for the Edinburgh edition of the *Poems*, became a walking companion of the poet. In entries from his second commonplace book that date from this period Burns recorded with a certain self-mocking tone comments on some of the people whom he encountered, including Blair, Greenfield, and the Creech who was slow to pass on to the poet profits from the Edinburgh edition. Reviews of this, published on 17 April 1787, were generally laudatory, and on 5 July the first London edition was published by Cadell, followed later in the year by pirated editions in Belfast, Dublin, Philadelphia, and New York.

Acclaimed, and fired by poetic and patriotic ambition, Burns embarked on a series of tours in Scotland and northern England in 1787. First, with his friend Ainslie, he set off for the borders on 5 May, visiting Duns, then crossing the border at the Coldstream bridge before returning to Scotland and progressing to Kelso, Melrose, Innerleithen, Berwick, Alnwick, and sites famous from the border ballads and Scottish songs. At Carlisle on 1 June 1787 Burns wrote to his friend William Nicol, classics master at Edinburgh High School, his only surviving letter in Scots; he then proceeded to Dumfries, where he was awarded the freedom of the burgh, and to Dalswinton, where he met his admirer Patrick Miller, before returning to Mauchline (where he was warmly reunited with Jean Armour) and Mossgiel. At this time Burns was reading Milton and admiring 'the desperate daring, and noble defiance of hardship, in that great Personage, Satan' (*Letters*, 1.123). Later in June he set off on a west Highland tour that took in Argyll and Loch Lomond; he returned, having resolved not to marry Jean Armour, though he resumed his affair with her. By August he and the Jacobite William Nicol were on another highland tour, setting off via the battlesite of Bannockburn associated with 'glorious Bruce' and heading north to Glenlyon (where Burns was fascinated by a supposed druids' temple) and Dunkeld, where he met the 'honest highland figure' of the great fiddler Niel Gow (1727–1807), whose 'kind open-heartedness' appealed to him (Mackay, 334). The forthright Jacobite Nicol and Burns went on to Crieff, Glen Almond, and the supposed site of Ossian's grave; at Blair Castle, Burns was a guest of the duke of Atholl, before he and Nicol headed for Aviemore, Cawdor, Inverness, Loch Ness, and Culloden; *en route* Burns collected some highland ballads and wrote some short poems celebrating his time 'Among the heathy hills and ragged woods' (R. Burns, 'Written with a pencil, standing by the fall of Fyers, near Loch-Ness'). Returning south via Aberdeen, where he encountered some local writers and academics, Burns met some of his Kincardineshire relatives at Stonehaven in mid-September, then visited his cousin James in Montrose. Burns and Nicol sailed from the fishing village of Auchmithie to Arbroath, visited Scone Palace, near Perth, on 15 September, then headed to Edinburgh.

Burns's last tour of 1787 was to Stirlingshire, in October; there, though Jean Armour was again pregnant by him, he pursued Margaret Chalmers and visited local historical and patriotic sites. While they may have had a business angle (since he visited some of his subscribers), Burns's 1787 Scottish tours developed and confirmed his interest in lowland ballad and song culture, as well as Ossianically refracted highland lore; the tours suggest his wish to assemble a sense of different Scotlands that would nourish him in his role as 'Caledonia's bard', and they undergird his developing work as a collector and remaker of songs and folk poetry.

By October 1787 Burns was back in Edinburgh, renting a room in what is now part of Register House, overlooking St Andrew Square, in the New Town. Robert Ainslie, Alexander Nasmyth, John Beugo, and Burns's new friend the law student Alexander Cunningham (1763–1812) were near neighbours. At this time Burns seems to have suffered some depression ('bitter hours of blue-devilism', as he called it, in Fergusson's phrase), which may be connected with the fact that his baby daughter, Jean, died on 20 October, though Burns, miles away in Edinburgh, refers to the child's death almost glancingly; as is often the case, it is hard to gauge accurately his innermost emotions, since his correspondence exhibits not infrequently notes of self-protective bravado (see *Letters*, 1.166). He examined himself closely (as in his long autobiographical letter of summer 1787 written to the London Scottish novelist Dr John Moore in a 'miserable fog of Ennui'), yet he also liked to adopt protean poses in his highly readable correspondence (ibid., 133). Sympathetic to the 'honest Scotch enthusiasm' of the Edinburgh engraver James Johnson, who was collecting 'all our native Songs' (ibid., 163) for a large, six-volume anthology with music, Burns had contributed work that he had collected to Johnson's *Scots Musical Museum*, the first volume of which appeared in May 1787 and the last in 1803. Burns was for the rest of his life *de facto* editor of this publication, contributing well over 150 of his own songs and reworking others that he collected. Mixing his own voice with the inherited and contemporary voices of Scottish popular poetry and song, he achieved some of his finest, world-class work, by turns piercingly lyrical, challenging, and playfully companionable. These are songs such as the male-voiced 'O my luve's like a red, red rose' or the female-voiced 'John Anderson my jo' that sound warmly direct. Yet any autobiographical matter that they contain is subsumed into a nurturing traditional form, so that the poet appears at least as much a transmitter, editor, or bearer of tradition as a creator who imposes his own personality on the material. Repeatedly Burns intensified the emotional charge of the work that he collected and remade, but he did this through instinctive and calculated artistry rather than through direct revelation.

On 4 December 1787, at an Edinburgh tea party, Burns met Mrs Agnes *Maclehose (1758–1841), who had separated from her rakish husband. Writing as 'Sylvander' and 'Clarinda', Burns and Mrs Maclehose began a remarkable, intense, and mannered epistolary affair, one made all the more heated by the fact that for some of the time Burns was housebound with a dislocated kneecap and suffered depressive episodes. While conducting this passionate correspondence he was also applying for a post as an excise officer, and was made anxious by news from Gilbert that the farm at Mossgiel was doing badly and that Jean Armour's parents had expelled their pregnant daughter from their house. In mid-February Burns returned to Ayrshire, saw Jean Armour, and made arrangements to move to another, run-down, farm at Ellisland, in Dunscore parish, on the River Nith, north of Dumfries, which he would lease from his literary admirer the inventor Patrick Miller of Dalswinton. Burns meanwhile was still corresponding amorously with Clarinda, and had got with child her maidservant Jenny Clow of Newburgh (1768–1792), whose son Robert Burns was born in November 1788. His dalliance with Clarinda did not stop Burns making love to the pregnant Jean Armour early in 1788 ('I took the opportunity of some dry horse litter, and gave her such a thundering scalade that electrified the very marrow of her bones'; *Letters*, 1.251). Shortly afterwards Jean gave birth to twins, who lived only a few days. Burns returned to Edinburgh in March, was inducted into the excise, and ended his affair with Clarinda.

Exciseman and farmer In spring 1788 Burns was trained as an excise officer by James Findlay, the Tarbolton exciseman. He also began to refer to Jean Armour as his wife, having apparently married her privately in a civil ceremony at the office of his Mauchline lawyer friend Gavin Hamilton. In mid-June Burns moved into Ellisland; on 14 July 1788 his excise commission was issued; and in August, having admitted to 'Daddy' Auld the irregularity of their marriage, Burns and Jean Armour were rebuked by Mauchline Kirk Session, who 'took them solemnly bound to adhere to one another as Husband & Wife all the days of their life' (Mackay, 427). Burns ordered for Jean 15 yards of 'black lutestring silk' (*Letters*, 1.304).

After Edinburgh, Burns felt 'at the very elbow of Existence' on the demanding, 170-acre farm of Ellisland, and complained that the locals had 'as much idea of a Rhinoceros as of a Poet', though he continued to collect songs and made friends with some of his country gentlemen neighbours, such as the amateur musician Robert Riddell of Glenriddell, for whom he prepared a two-volume collection of his unpublished poems and letters (now the Glenriddell Manuscripts in the National Library of Scotland) and whose interleaved copy of *The Scots Musical Museum* (now in the Burns birthplace museum, Alloway) Burns annotated (*Letters*, 1.311–12). By the end of 1788 Jean Armour had joined Burns at Ellisland, though work on their farmhouse there (paid for by Patrick Miller) was not completed until the following year. Burns at Ellisland was to switch from arable to dairy farming, taking some interest in milk yields. William Clark, one of his hired ploughmen, recalled him in 1789 wearing at home 'a broad blue bonnet, a blue or drab long-tailed coat, corduroy breeches, dark-blue stockings and cootikens, and in cold weather a black-and-white-checked plaid wrapped round his shoulders' (Mackay, 442). On 18 August 1789 Jean gave birth to Burns's son Francis Wallace, and on 1 September Burns began work as exciseman for the Dumfries first itinerary, at a salary of £50 per annum. This work involved riding often 30 or 40 miles a day, four or five days a week, searching for contraband materials; attempting to combine this work with farming exhausted Burns, who suffered from headaches and depression that winter. However, in July 1790 he was promoted to the Dumfries third foot-walk division, at a salary of £70 per annum; there his duties demanded only a walk around the town of Dumfries. At The Globe inn he had an affair with the barmaid, Ann Park, who gave birth to his daughter Elizabeth on 31 March 1791, nine days before William Nicol Burns was born to Jean Armour. She went on to raise both children.

At Ellisland Burns wrote a good deal of poetry, including the erotic lyrics 'I love my Jean' and 'O, were I on Parnassus hill'. As a collector of songs and ballads he reworked many traditional lyrics, including 'My Heart's in the Highlands' and—perhaps his most widely known work—'Auld Lang Syne', a poem of healing sociability. Having found a 'kind funny friend' in the English antiquary, relisher of slang,

and bon viveur Captain Francis Grose (1731–1791), 'a cheerful-looking grig of an old, fat fellow' who was researching his *Antiquities of Scotland*, Burns in 1790 wrote for Grose 'Tam o' Shanter: a Tale', which accompanies the account of Kirk Alloway in the second volume (1791) of Grose's work (*Letters*, 2.52, 1.423). This substantial, carnivalesque, mock-heroic narrative poem begins with Tam (minus wife) and his male 'drouthy cronies' in the pub, then sends its drunken protagonist on a storm-swept night ride to Kirk Alloway, where he sees 'Warlocks and witches in a dance'. Excited by a witch in a short shirt ('cutty sark'), Tam cries out and is chased by all the 'hellish legion', but his 'grey mare, Meg' rescues him, at the cost of losing her own tail to a pursuing witch; the poem ends with a po-faced mock-moral. Varying pace and diction, and characterized by power surges of excitement and reeling humour, this poem in Hudibrastic couplets is one of Burns's greatest achievements.

In the late summer of 1791 Burns extricated himself from the Ellisland lease, sold his crops in a roup, and then in November moved with his family to a tenement in the Wee Vennel (now 11 Bank Street), Dumfries. Almost immediately he needed to visit Edinburgh, where he had to deal with Jenny Clow, who was dying of tuberculosis, and where he and Agnes Maclehose exchanged locks of hair and the final, parting kiss; this appears to have given rise to Burns's slow and tender song beginning:

> Ae fond kiss, and then we sever;
> Ae fareweel, and then for ever!

Though Burns and Agnes Maclehose exchanged further letters early in 1792, she sailed to Jamaica at the end of January in a failed attempt at rapprochement with her husband, after which she returned to Scotland.

Back in Dumfries Burns joined the Dumfries St Andrew's masonic lodge on 27 December 1791; as an exciseman he was involved early in 1792 in the capture of a smuggling schooner in the Solway Firth, and in April was appointed to the Dumfries first foot-walk. On 10 April 1792 he received his diploma as a member of the Royal Archers of Scotland, the monarch's ceremonial bodyguard. Nevertheless about this time, in poems such as 'Here's a health to them that's awa', and 'Address to General Dumourier', as well as in his correspondence, Burns displayed sympathies with political radicalism and with the republican cause in France, though Britain was soon at war with that country. When his employer, the board of excise, began to investigate his political loyalties he anxiously protested that 'To the British Constitution, on Revolution principles, next after my God, I am most devoutly attached!' (*Letters*, 2.169). Despite such protestations his politics, as articulated in verse, are more complex. As a poet he participated energetically in local election contests, but he was also very alert to larger issues. While in 1795–6 he wrote the seemingly loyal sentiment 'Does haughty Gaul invasion threat' (R. Burns, 'The Dumfries Volunteers'), in 1793 he had celebrated the overthrowing of 'Chains and Slavery' in 'Robert Bruce's march to Bannockburn', and earlier had cursed the loss of Scottish political independence: 'Such a parcel of rogues in a nation'. In 1795 he published in the *Glasgow Magazine* the song 'For a' that', which celebrates universal brotherhood and concludes with a stanza that Marilyn Butler calls 'probably the closest rendering in English of the letter and spirit of the notorious Jacobin "Ça ira"' (Crawford, 102). Its last two lines express the hope:

That Man to Man the warld o'er,
Shall brothers be for a' that.

The scale of Burns's song-collecting activities is obvious from the publication of the fourth volume of *The Scots Musical Museum*, in August 1792; Burns composed or at least revised some sixty of the hundred songs in the book, while in the following month he agreed to contribute to the *Select Collection of Original Scotish Airs* being planned by the fussily genteel Edinburgh amateur musician George Thomson. Burns sought no pay for this work and intended that his contributions would contain 'at least a sprinkling of our native tongue' (*Letters*, 2.149). He contributed over a hundred songs to the *Select Collection*, which appeared in six volumes between 1793 and 1841 and for which settings were written by Haydn, Beethoven, Weber, and Hummel.

On 21 November 1792 Jean Armour gave birth to Elizabeth Riddell Burns (who died while still a toddler), and on 30 November Burns was elected senior warden of the Dumfries St Andrew's masons. In mid-December he travelled to Ayrshire to spend a few days with his friend and patron Mrs Dunlop, who worried that he was drinking too much. He was acquiring something of a reputation as a drinker, though this was probably exaggerated by his early biographers. Like his father he showed considerable care for his children's education, one Dumfries friend recalling him explaining English poetry to his nine-year-old son. February 1793 saw the publication of the second Edinburgh edition of his *Poems* (including twenty new pieces) and May the publication of the first set of Thomson's *Select Collection*. Also in May the Burns family moved to a larger house, 24 Mill Hole Brae (now Burns Street), Dumfries, the poet's last home and one that was occupied by Jean Armour until her death, in March 1834. In summer 1793, excited by his friend Thomas Fraser playing the air 'Hey Tutti Taitie' on the oboe, Burns, familiar with the tradition that this tune had been Robert Bruce's march at the battle of Bannockburn, warmed 'to a pitch of enthusiasm on the theme of Liberty & Independance' and composed the lyric that begins:

SCOTS, wha hae wi' WALLACE bled,
SCOTS, wham BRUCE has aften led …
(R. Burns, 'Scots wha hae')

Burns confessed to Thomson that his thoughts of 'that glorious struggle for Freedom' were also linked to other struggles 'not quite so ancient' (*Letters*, 2.235–6). Another account links the composition of this song to the poet's tour of Galloway with his friend John Syme in late July and early August 1793. That December a drunken Burns appears to have been one of a number of gentlemen who took part in a mock re-enactment of the rape of the Sabine women, during which Burns grabbed his admirer and

friend the young poet and mother Maria Riddell. Though he was later stricken with awkward remorse the Riddell family broke off relations with him and ignored his efforts to atone. Burns attempted to exact revenge in several poems, and eventually achieved a measure of reconciliation with Maria, with whom he was again corresponding by December 1794.

Last years Early in 1794 Burns again suffered 'low spirits & blue devils', yet he managed to propose a somewhat self-interested reorganization of the Dumfries excise divisions (the plan was not adopted) and to send James Johnson forty-one songs that he had collected or composed (*Letters*, 2.280). That summer he toured south-west Scotland and was at work on his 'Ode for General Washington's Birthday', another celebration of a struggle for liberty. Drinking too much and feeling maudlin, he resumed his correspondence with Agnes Maclehose and addressed a number of poems to Jean Lorimer ('Chloris'). Jean Armour gave birth to Burns's son James Glencairn on 12 August. Though tempted by an offer of work on the *Morning Chronicle*, which would have paid him 1 guinea a week, Burns resolved to stay with the excise; he seems to have been worried about deteriorating health and comforted by the thought that in the event of his death the excise would pay a pension to his dependants. In December 1794 he was promoted acting supervisor in the excise service.

Burns's last eighteen months were marked by illness, family bereavement, and a falling-out with one of his oldest admirers. In late 1794 he sometimes worked fourteen-hour days, visiting the excise's Sanquhar division. These long hours worked by Supervisor Burns continued into early 1795, a particularly harsh winter of intense blizzards and 30 foot snowdrifts. At the very start of 1795, aged thirty-six, he was complaining about 'stiffening joints of Old Age coming fast o'er my frame' (*Letters*, 2.333). That January Mrs Dunlop took offence at his description of Louis XVI and Marie Antoinette as 'a perjured Blockhead & an unprincipled Prostitute' and broke off relations with him, despite his pained attempts to revive their correspondence during the months before his death (ibid., 334). From May 1795 onwards Burns suffered several bouts of illness. Continuing his long interest in local politics, he wrote in 1795 a series of poems in support of the successful whig candidate for the stewartry of Kirkcudbright by-election, Patrick Heron. Despite his radical sympathies, and his close friendship with his doctor, William Maxwell of Kirkconnell (1760–1834), a Jacobin who had been involved in founding the London Correspondence Society, Burns also played a considerable part in organizing the Dumfries Volunteers. This uniformed band protested their loyalty to the crown and exercised locally with their weapons in the Dock Park, Dumfries. In November 1795 Burns helped to draft the volunteers' address to the king celebrating the 'lasting fabric of British Liberty' (Mackay, 595). Prolonged ill health (perhaps rheumatic fever) in 1795 resulted in Burns's 'Address to the Toothache' ('My curse on your envenom'd stang'); then, when he was recovering from illness, in September his daughter Elizabeth Riddell died during a visit to Mauchline. After her death Burns, unable to travel to her funeral, suffered a severe depressive illness, which seems to have continued throughout the winter, though some visitors noted his animation in conversation, ability to hold his drink, and apparent health.

By February 1796, however, when there was unrest in Dumfries, Burns was back at work for the excise and collecting songs for Thomson, but that same month saw further rheumatic attacks, which made him unfit for work. Burns may have rallied in the early spring (he attended a masons' meeting on 14 April) but was soon complaining in a letter to his musical friend George Thomson of 'the heavy hand of SICKNESS; & [I] have counted Time by the repercussions of PAIN! Rheumatism, Cold & Fever' (*Letters*, 2.378). Gravely ill, he presented a set of *The Scots Musical Museum* to his seventeen-year-old nurse, Jessie Lewars, having written verses for her in the flyleaf. Worried about money and complaining that sickness reduced an exciseman's salary from £50 to £35, he called in loans that he had made; he reacted with fearful gratitude to an offer of financial aid from his cousin James Burness of Montrose. He complained of 'excruciating rheumatism' and followed the advice of 'Medical folks' (among them Dr Maxwell) that his 'last & only chance is bathing & country quarters & riding' (ibid., 385). Under advice the ailing Burns practised regular sea-bathing in the cold spring tides of the Solway at Brow, in the parish of Ruthwell. When the spring tides abated the rheumatic Burns returned to Dumfries, feeling no better. For Jessie Lewars he wrote his last song, 'Oh wert thou in the cauld blast', and on 18 July returned from Brow to Dumfries; on the same day he wrote to his father-in-law, begging help for Jean Armour, who, about to be left with his five children, was in the last stages of pregnancy. Burns died at home, in Dumfries, on 21 July 1796, most probably of rheumatic heart disease complicated by bacterial endocarditis. On 25 July the Dumfries Volunteers fired over Burns's coffin at his burial, under a plain slab in St Michael's churchyard, Dumfries; on that same day his son Maxwell was born, but lived for only thirty-three months.

Posthumous reputation After Burns's death there were published several volumes of work that had circulated only in private during his lifetime. These included *The Jolly Beggars* (1799), *The merry muses of Caledonia: a collection of favourite Scots songs, ancient and modern, selected for use of the Crochallan fencibles* (c.1800; a collection of bawdy verses), and *Letters Addressed to Clarinda* (1802). James Currie's *Works of Robert Burns, with an Account of his Life* (1800) and Robert H. Cromek's *Reliques of Robert Burns* (1808) assembled more poems and documents, Currie censuring Burns for drunkenness. Burns's attitudes to drink, poetry, politics, and women have been argued over in a succession of biographies, distinguished among which are those by his friend Allan Cunningham (1834); by Robert Chambers (1851), Catherine Carswell (1930), and Franklyn Snyder (1932); and by David Daiches (1952), James Mackay (1992), and Ian McIntyre (1995).

Within a few years of the poet's death a number of clubs had been formed to honour his memory. The first was Greenock Burns Club (1801), which was soon followed by Paisley Burns Club (1805) and, as the century wore on, by literally hundreds of other Burns clubs in Scotland, Britain, and overseas. Accepted since his death as Scotland's national bard, Burns was the first poet of the English-speaking world to be honoured by a network of clubs dedicated to celebrating his life and works. The clubs were originally all-male and can be seen as drawing on masonic traditions as well as on the legacy of such associations as the Tarbolton Bachelors' Club, the Crochallan Fencibles, and other clubs to which the poet belonged. An international network of Burns clubs is now co-ordinated by the Burns Federation, which publishes the *Burns Chronicle* and encourages the holding of Burns suppers around the world on 25 January each year. Sites associated with the poet in south-west Scotland are known collectively as 'the Burns country', and the Burns Mausoleum, in St Michael's churchyard, Dumfries, erected in 1815 to provide a grander memorial to the poet (whose remains were moved to a vault below it in 1815), is one of several destinations for tourists and literary pilgrims to the Burns country. Among the earliest of these were several of the Romantic poets, including Wordsworth, Coleridge, and Keats, for whom Burns was an important exemplar. Burns was read enthusiastically throughout the British empire, and in America, where he mattered to poets as different as Whitman and Whittier.

Though the reputation of some poems, such as 'The Cotter's Saturday Night' (much admired in the nineteenth century), has declined, Burns has remained widely admired. In his essay 'The study of poetry' (1880) Matthew Arnold complained that Burns lacked 'high seriousness' and 'a beautiful world', but T. S. Eliot, in *The Use of Poetry*, thought Arnold's attitude to Burns 'patronising' (p. 106). In the twentieth century Burns has interested Robert Frost, D. H. Lawrence, Hugh MacDiarmid, Seamus Heaney, and Les Murray, among other poets. The modern scholarly edition of the verse is James Kinsley's three-volume *Poems and Songs of Robert Burns* (1968), while the letters were edited by J. De Lancey Ferguson (second edition by G. Ross Roy, 2 vols., 1985). A full, musicologically researched edition of *The Songs of Robert Burns* was edited by Donald A. Low in 1993. Burns has remained a genuinely popular poet, though not always one widely taught in universities. His work has been translated into most major and many minor languages, and his songs, still sung in Scotland and abroad, are available in a variety of recordings.

ROBERT CRAWFORD

Sources J. Mackay, *Burns: a biography of Robert Burns* (1992) • *The letters of Robert Burns*, ed. J. de Lancey Ferguson, 2nd edn, ed. G. Ross Roy, 2 vols. (1985) • *The poems and songs of Robert Burns*, ed. J. Kinsley, 3 vols. (1968) • R. Crawford, ed., *Robert Burns and cultural authority* (1997) • R. Burns, *Poems, chiefly in the Scottish dialect* (1786) • D. A. Low, ed., *Robert Burns: the critical heritage* (1974) • *DNB* • J. G. Lockhart, *Memoirs of Sir Walter Scott*, 5 vols. (1900), vol. 1 • M. Arnold, *Complete prose works*, ed. R. H. Super, 11 vols. (1973), vol. 9 • T. S. Eliot, *The use of poetry and the use of criticism* (1933) • R. Burns, *The merry muses of Caledonia*, ed. J. Burke and S. G. Smith, 2nd edn (1982) • R. Brown, *Paisley Burns clubs* (1893)

Archives BL, letters and songs, Add. MS 22307, Egerton MS 1656 · Burns Cottage Museum, Mauchline, Ayrshire, corresp. and literary MSS, letters and verses · Hunt. L., letters; literary MSS · Mitchell L., Glas., poems, letters, and papers · NL Scot., corresp. and papers · NL Scot., corresp., verses, etc., family papers · U. Edin. L., letters and MS poems · U. Nott. L., transcripts; notes for edition of collected poems · University of Strathclyde, Glasgow, archives, MSS · Writers' Museum, Edinburgh, letters, MSS, etc. · Alloway, Ayrshire, Burns Cottage collection | BL, Hastie MSS · BL, autobiography in letter to John Moore, Egerton MS 1660 · Burns Monument, Kilmarnock, Ayrshire, holograph MSS · Morgan L., corresp. with Frances Dunlop · Morgan L., letters to Peter Hill · Morgan L., letters to George Thomson · NL Scot., Cowie collection, corresp. and poems · NL Scot., Glenriddell MSS · NL Scot., Watson MS

Likenesses A. Nasmyth, pencil drawing, 1786, Scot. NPG · P. Taylor, oil on panel, 1786, Scot. NPG · by or after J. Miers, ink silhouette, 1787, Scot. NPG · A. Nasmyth, oils, 1787, Scot. NPG [see illus.] · A. Nasmyth, pencil sketch, 1787, Irvine Burns Club; version, Scot. NPG · A. Reid, miniature, oils, 1795, Scot. NPG · A. Reid, watercolour on ivory, 1795–6, Scot. NPG · A. Skirving, chalk drawing, 1796–8 (after Nasmyth?), Scot. NPG · medallion, plaster replica, 1801 (after W. Tassie), Scot. NPG · J. Henning, plaster medallion, 1807, Scot. NPG · J. Flaxman, marble statue, begun 1824, Scot. NPG; on loan from the City of Edinburgh District Council · A. Nasmyth, oil on panel, 1828 (posthumous), Scot. NPG · D. Dunbar, plaster cast of skull, 1834?, Scot. NPG · J. Edgar, group portrait, wash drawing, c.1854 (Robert Burns at an evening party of Lord Monboddo's, 1786), Scot. NPG · J. Beugo, copperplate engraving (after unfinished portrait by A. Nasmyth; from life), repro. in R. Burns, Poems (1787), frontispiece · by or after P. Taylor, oils, Scot. NPG · S. Watson, group portrait, oils (The inauguration of Robert Burns as poet laureate of the lodge Canongate, Kilwinning, 1787), Scot. NPG · H. W. Williams, watercolour, Scot. NPG · portrait (after watercolour on ivory), Scot. NPG

Wealth at death £15 in drafts; £90 in library valuation; £183 16s. in debts owed to Burns: Mackay, Burns, 632

Burns, Robert (1789–1869), Canada Presbyterian church minister, was born on 13 February 1789 at Bo'ness, Linlithgowshire. He was one of the eight sons and at least one daughter of John Burns, a merchant and customs officer, and his wife, Grizzell Ferrier. He attended the parochial school at Bo'ness from 1795 to 1801, when he entered the University of Edinburgh. He was licensed as a probationer of the Church of Scotland in March 1810, and ordained minister of St George's, Paisley, in July 1811. His marriage on 8 July 1814 to Janet (d. 1841), daughter of John Orr, a local manufacturer, brought them six sons and a daughter.

Burns proved to be an energetic and hard-working minister, organizing Sabbath schools and Bible and tract societies, and acting as editor for the Edinburgh Christian Instructor from 1838 to 1840. The poverty and unemployment of the weavers of Paisley led him to encourage emigration to North America, and in 1825 he was instrumental in the foundation of the Glasgow Colonial Society, which aimed to meet the religious needs of emigrant Scots. He remained the mainspring of this society for fifteen years, dispatching over forty missionaries, making many fund-raising tours, and encouraging the foundation and expansion of Presbyterian colleges in Canada. In 1828 the University of Glasgow awarded him a DD in recognition of his literary and philanthropic endeavours. It was during this time, too, that Burns produced all his publications, which included Plurality of Office in the Church of Scotland (1824) and

A Plea for the Poor of Scotland and for an Enquiry into their Situation (1841).

At the Disruption in 1843, Burns led his congregation into the Free Church of Scotland, but he did not long remain minister of the newly established St George's Free Church. His wife had died on 14 November 1841 and in 1844 he married, on 12 December, Elizabeth Bell (d. 1882), daughter of Thomson Bonar of Grove. In the same year he was sent to the eastern United States, as one of five ministers deputed by the general assembly to raise funds and sympathies among the transatlantic churches. His vigorous defence of Free Church principles probably contributed to the 1844 formation of the Presbyterian Free Church in Canada. The reputation which he had made for himself led to several calls to Canadian Free Church parishes, and in 1845 Burns accepted an invitation to be minister of Knox Church, Toronto, with an interim professorship of divinity at Knox College. In 1845–6 he was moderator of the Canadian Free Church general assembly, where his vehement opposition to slavery, voiced in a letter to the United Presbyterian churches of the United States, caused some controversy.

In the 1840s and 1850s Burns undertook a series of missionary tours to investigate the state of religious opinion in Canada and North America. He opposed any union with the United Presbyterian Church of Canada, and remained a dedicated exponent of Free Church anti-voluntarism. His concern for the disadvantaged continued: he became an officer of the Anti-Slavery Society of Canada, and an important supporter of the Elgin Association, which was established in 1849 to aid communities of fugitive slaves living in Canada. He supported educational improvements in Canada, favouring a non-sectarian state-supported system.

Burns's many commitments, however, led him to neglect his congregation in Toronto, and an argument with the superintendent of the Knox Church Sunday school, G. A. Piper, seriously split the congregation in 1855. He had already experienced problems at Knox College in 1847, when he was involved in a controversy over his plurality of office which led to his resignation. Nevertheless, he maintained ties with the college, and in 1856 he was appointed professor of history and apologetics. As he grew older Burns's fiery nature mellowed, and he avoided appointments which might have led to controversy. His last public post before his death in Toronto on 19 August 1869 was as representative of the Canada Presbyterian church at the Scottish general assemblies of 1868 and 1869. His second wife outlived him, dying in August 1882.

ROSEMARY MITCHELL

Sources H. J. Bridgman, 'Burns, Robert', DCB, vol. 9 · R. F. Burns, ed., The life and times of the Rev. Robert Burns (1872) · Fasti Scot. · J. A. Wylie, Disruption worthies: a memorial of 1843, ed. J. B. Gillies, new edn (1881)

Archives NA Canada · NA Scot., Church of Scotland records · United Church of Canada Central Archives, lecture notes and sermons | NL Scot., Lee MSS · U. Edin., New College, letters to Thomas Chalmers

Likenesses J. Swan, line engraving, NPG

Burns, William Chalmers (1815–1868), missionary in China, was born at the manse of his father, William Hamilton Burns (1779–1859), at Dun, Forfarshire; his mother, Elizabeth, *née* Chalmers (*d.* 1879), came from Aberdeen. The family moved to Kilsyth, near Glasgow, about 1817, and later Burns attended Kilsyth parish school. On an uncle's initiative he next attended Aberdeen grammar school for a year; afterwards he entered Marischal College, Aberdeen, which he left in 1831. His first training was in the office of Alexander Burns, an Edinburgh lawyer, but in 1832 he felt called to be a minister of the gospel and returned to the university. He graduated from Aberdeen in 1834 and began to study divinity at Glasgow University. In 1839 he was licensed as a probationer by the presbytery of Glasgow. His purpose was to be a missionary abroad, but, there being then no vacancy in the mission field, he accepted temporary occupation at home.

Burns first took charge of the congregation of the Revd R. M. McCheyne in Dundee during the latter's absence in Palestine. He preached with extraordinary earnestness and depth of conviction; a great revival of religious life followed, much as in the days of Whitefield and Wesley. Burns then spent some years visiting different parts of Scotland and the north of England, and with corresponding results. The Kilsyth revival, in 1839, which he conducted with his father and his brother Islay *Burns, was one of the most dramatic moments in Scottish evangelicalism. Burns tried Dublin, but had little success there. In 1843 he left the Church of Scotland for the Free Church. In 1844 he visited Canada, and made a great impression, especially in areas of Scottish settlement, but the scenes did not equal those that had taken place in his native land.

In November 1847, as a missionary under the auspices of the English Presbyterian Church Missionary Committee, Burns reached Hong Kong. His first efforts among the Chinese were very discouraging, with no converts in his first seven years. But by 1854, at Pechuia, near Amoy (Xiamen), he had established an effective ministry. Many native congregations of Christians were formed in the neighbourhood; however, it was his practice to leave these to the care of others, and always to press forward to occupy new ground. He returned briefly to Scotland in 1854. After returning to China, he went to Shanghai, Swatow (Shantou), and then in 1864 to Peking (Beijing) and Newchwang (Yingkou). Burns translated John Bunyan's *The Pilgrim's Progress* and many British hymns into Chinese. He began a translation of the Psalms. On his mission tours he took little with him but tracts and Bibles, trusting to the hospitality of the people. Often he was annoyed, once arrested and imprisoned, and sometimes robbed. To avoid being stared at as a foreigner, he ultimately adopted Chinese dress and ways of life. Having caught a chill at Newchwang, where he had gone in 1867 to try to establish a mission in Manchuria, he died there on 4 April 1868.

Burns was exceptional in an age of exceptional missionaries and was one of the most remarkable figures in the

William Chalmers Burns (1815–1868), by William Henry Mote, pubd 1870

nineteenth-century Scottish church. Asked if he knew Burns, a fellow missionary exclaimed: 'All China knows him! He is the holiest man alive' (Miller, 168).

W. G. BLAIKIE, *rev.*

Sources I. Burns, *Memoir of the Rev. Wm. C. Burns, M.A.*, 3rd edn (1870) • R. S. Miller, 'William C. Burns', *Five pioneer missionaries*, ed. S. M. Houghton (1987), 95–169 • K. S. Latourette, *A history of Christian missions in China* (1929)
Archives SOAS, letters, writings, etc. | U. Edin., New College, letters to R. M. McCheyne
Likenesses Dalziel, woodcut, BM • W. H. Mote, engraving, repro. in Burns, *Memoir* [*see illus.*] • portrait, repro. in S. M. Houghton, ed., *Five pioneer missionaries* (1965)

Burnside, Robert (1759–1826), Seventh Day Baptist minister, was born in the parish of Clerkenwell on 31 August 1759, one of two sons of a putative John Burnside. He was educated at Merchant Taylors' School from 1770 and at Marischal College, Aberdeen, the sixth scholar supported by Dr John Ward's Trust. Called to the ministry on 17 June 1780 by the Seventh Day Baptist Church, Curriers' Hall, London, on 1 July he was appointed afternoon preacher there, and on 25 May 1785 was ordained pastor of that congregation, which moved in 1799 to Redcross Street and thence in 1812 to Devonshire Square. He associated with other Baptist ministers in London, both in the General Body (Baptist Board), to whose committee he was elected on 11 March 1794, and in the Baptist Monthly Association, one of his sermons to which was published as *The Fruits of* the Spirit, the Ornament of Christians (1805). His two-volume *The Religion of Mankind, in a Series of Essays* (1819) and three-volume *Tea-Table Chat* (1820–22) won renown, and in *Remarks on the Different Sentiments Entertained in Christendom Relative to the Weekly Sabbath* (1825) he advocated the seventh-day sabbath. His prowess as a teacher of languages, in which he amassed a considerable fortune, said to be nearly £10,000 at his death, found expression in *The Theory of Composition* (1824). He never married, and died in Snow's Fields, Bermondsey, on 19 May 1826 after a short illness, in the same house in which he had lived from early childhood, and was buried on 25 May in the Mill Yard meeting burial-ground, Goodman's Fields.

SUSAN J. MILLS

Sources J. B. Shenston, *A small tribute to the memory of the late pious, learned, and Rev. Robert Burnside, AM* (1826) • J. Ivimey, *A history of the English Baptists*, 4 vols. (1811–30), vol. 4, pp. 326–7 • C. J. Robinson, ed., *A register of the scholars admitted into Merchant Taylors' School, from AD 1562 to 1874*, 2 (1883), 134 • E. J. Tongue, *Dr. John Ward's Trust* (1951), 15 • W. Wilson, *The history and antiquities of the dissenting churches and meeting houses in London, Westminster and Southwark*, 4 vols. (1808–14), vol. 2, p. 608 • 'Non-collegiate studies, 1779: a letter from Robert Burnside to Dr. Samuel Stennett, Aberdeen, Dec. 23, 1779', *Baptist Quarterly*, 9 (1938–9), 424–6 • *Seventh Day Baptists in Europe and America*, 2 vols. (1910), vol. 1, pp. 71–2 • W. T. Whitley, *The Baptists of London, 1612–1928* (1928), 119 • minutes of a society of ministers of the Baptist Particular persuasion meeting at the Gloucester Coffee House, 1723–1817, Regent's Park College, Oxford, Angus Library MS • minutes of meetings of the ministers and deputies of the Particular Baptist churches held by adjurnment at Blackwell's (later Jamaica) Coffee House, 1748–1829, Regent's Park College, Oxford, Angus Library MS

Archives Regent's Park College, Oxford, Angus Library, minutes of Baptist meetings at Gloucester Coffee House • Regent's Park College, Oxford, Angus Library, minutes of Particular Baptist meetings at Blackwell's (later Jamaica) Coffee House

Wealth at death under £10,000: Tongue, *Dr. John Ward's Trust*, 15; Ivimey, *History of the English Baptists*, 327

Burnside, William (1852–1927), mathematician, was born at 7 Howley Place, Paddington, Middlesex, on 2 July 1852, the elder son of William Burnside, merchant, of that address, and his wife, Emma Knight. His father was of Scottish ancestry; his grandfather had settled in London, and was a partner in the bookselling firm of Seeley and Burnside.

Left an orphan at the age of six, Burnside was educated at Christ's Hospital—then situated in Newgate Street—and achieved distinction in both the grammar school and the mathematical school. He won a mathematical scholarship at St John's College, Cambridge, and began residence there in October 1871. In his day, all able mathematical students in the university were prepared for the tripos by private coaches, and Burnside's was W. H. Besant, one of the few rivals of the well-known Edward John Routh. In April 1873 Burnside migrated to Pembroke College. In the mathematical tripos of 1875 he was bracketed second wrangler with George Chrystal (1851–1911); in the immediately subsequent examination for the Smith's prizes, Burnside was first and Chrystal second.

Burnside was elected a fellow of Pembroke and appointed a lecturer at the college in 1875; he continued to be a fellow until 1886. College teaching at that time had slight influence upon the most capable students. However, in addition to the usual college courses, Burnside also lectured on hydrodynamics, a subject then developing into importance. He took a few private pupils and examined occasionally for the tripos, but it soon became apparent that he was devoting himself to mathematical studies beyond the organized range of the tripos.

As an undergraduate, Burnside had proved an expert oar. After leaving Cambridge his main recreation was found in fishing during holidays in Scotland, and in this also he developed marked skill. Through all his years his lithe frame retained an unusual power of physical endurance. In 1885 he was appointed professor of mathematics at the Royal Naval College at Greenwich, and the rest of his teaching life was spent in that post.

On 25 December 1886 Burnside married Alexandrina Urquhart (*b.* 1854/5), of Poolewe in the county of Ross, Scotland. His wife's father, Kenneth Urquhart, was a crofter. The couple had two sons and two daughters. Burnside retired in 1919. His old college at one time invited him to return as tutor and, on the death in 1903 of Sir George Gabriel Stokes, Pembroke invited him to return as master. Both invitations were declined, mainly because (outside his teaching) the administrative and social details of official duty were irksome to his temperament.

At Greenwich Burnside worked in three areas, being concerned with ballistics, for gunnery and torpedo officers, with mechanics and heat, for engineer officers, and with dynamics (especially hydrodynamics), for naval constructors. He was elected a fellow of the Royal Society in 1893, served on the council of the society from 1901 to 1903, and was awarded a royal medal in 1904. He was president of the London Mathematical Society from 1906 to 1908, having received its De Morgan medal in 1899. In 1900 he was elected an honorary fellow of Pembroke College. He received the honorary degrees of ScD from Dublin University and of LLD from Edinburgh University.

Burnside is remembered for his original contributions to mathematics. He published over one hundred and fifty papers. His book, the *Theory of Groups* (1897), is now an acknowledged classic and did much to establish group theory as a subject in its own right and with its own methods. He left a long manuscript of the *Theory of Probability*, which was published in 1928, after his death. His range of subjects, mainly in pure mathematics (although applied mathematics had been the Cambridge vogue of his earlier years), was extensive. As a writer he was clear and definite in argument, lucid and terse in exposition. Each of his papers dealt with a definite issue: nothing was elaborated beyond a main result, and subsidiary developments were avoided. He wrote on hydrodynamics and on potential theory, combining the established methods with the new analysis based on the use of complex variables. Several papers were devoted to elliptic functions and several to differential geometry, at a time when the subject was receiving little attention in England. He passed from the automorphic functions and their groups of transformations, where he was one of the first to understand

Poincaré's ideas which had opened up the area of geometrical function theory, to the general theory of discontinuous groups of finite order: on this subject he produced some fifty papers, each of them containing some definite contribution to the theory, and marked by clarity and terseness.

The outbreak of war in 1914 slowed down Burnside's output of papers: the end of hostilities found him interested in the theory of mathematical probability, and he continued to produce fresh investigations. Ultimately failing health interfered with creative work, but it did not cramp active interest, and he was able to draft an exposition of his views on this subject.

Burnside died at Cotleigh, West Wickham, Kent, on 21 August 1927, and was buried in the churchyard there. His wife survived him.   A. R. FORSYTH, *rev.* J. J. GRAY

Sources A. R. F., *PRS*, 117A (1928), xi–xxv · personal knowledge (1937) · J. J. Gray, 'Geometry in complex function theory', *Companion encyclopedia of the history and philosophy of the mathematical sciences*, ed. J. Grattan-Guinness, 1 (1994), 432–9 · b. cert. · m. cert. · d. cert. · *CGPLA Eng. & Wales* (1927)

Archives St John Cam., Larmor MSS

Likenesses W. Stoneman, photograph, 1917, NPG · Maull & Fox, photograph, RS · photograph, repro. in *PRS*, facing p. xv · photograph, RS

Wealth at death £12,160 13s. 9d.: probate, 29 Oct 1927, *CGPLA Eng. & Wales*

Burnyeat, John (1631–1690), Quaker minister, was born at Crabtreebeck, near Loweswater, Cumberland. Beyond his occupation as a farmer, little is known of his life before George Fox convinced him of Quakerism in 1653.

Until 1657 John Burnyeat limited his religious activities to attending meetings and occasionally speaking publicly, then became more active by disrupting Anglican services to espouse the Quaker faith. In 1658 he tried unsuccessfully to spread Quakerism in Scotland, and was gaoled several times on a subsequent missionary journey to Ireland. He travelled in 1664 to Barbados, then Maryland, Virginia, and New England, where he combated the schismatic efforts of John Perrot, an Irish Friend who condemned George Fox's leadership. Perrot initially opposed the rule that men should remove their hats when others preached in Quaker meetings, then denounced the scheduling of religious worship altogether. Burnyeat left New England in 1667 without fully eradicating Perrot's influence, even though Perrot had died two years earlier. Burnyeat resumed his public testimony in England, Wales, and Ireland, and like other 'public Friends' was gaoled and fined for his refusal to conform to the established church. In 1669 William Penn, who founded the colony of Pennsylvania in North America twelve years later, noted that Burnyeat spoke at a Quaker meeting in Dublin, 'a good meeting it was in the powr of the allmighty' (*Papers of William Penn*, 1.108).

In 1670 John Burnyeat sailed again to America, where he prepared the way for George Fox's visit the next year. Their primary goal was to establish the disciplinary meeting structure among Friends in the colonies that Fox and his allies had developed in England during the 1660s. In part through Burnyeat's efforts, American Quakers gave Fox an enthusiastic welcome, drew large audiences of Friends and non-Friends, and set up monthly meetings for discipline. In Maryland, for example, Burnyeat organized a four-day meeting at West River. Fox related in his journal,

> there came to it five or six justices of the peace and he that was Speaker of the Assembly and one of the Council and many considerable people of the world and a glorious meeting we had. After the public meeting there were men's and women's meetings and I opened to Friends the service thereof and all were satisfied.   (*Journal of George Fox*, 616)

In New England in 1672 Burnyeat left Fox among Friends in Rhode Island and went to Massachusetts, where resistance to Fox's meeting structure was especially strong. Burnyeat reported that one group of Friends 'pretended to be against all Forms' (Burnyeat, 52); many of these opponents were women who had joined Quakerism very early and believed the separate men's and women's meetings for discipline would undercut their authority within the sect. In Rhode Island, Burnyeat, William Edmundson of Ireland, and John Stubbs of England disputed with the colony's founder, Roger Williams, whose challenge to George Fox to a theological debate reached Fox after he had left the colony. Williams published his side of the Newport and Providence debates in *George Fox Digg'd out of his Burrowes* (1676). Burnyeat and Fox collaborated in a widely read response entitled *A New-England Fire-Brand Quenched* (1678). As reported in these publications, Williams accused the Quakers of heresy, in that they placed their faith in the inner light instead of emphasizing scripture and the historic Christ. Burnyeat, Stubbs, and Edmundson countered that they did believe in the historic Jesus, and were neither papists nor ranters.

John Burnyeat departed the colonies in 1673 and returned to England, where he soon became involved in a serious dispute within the Society of Friends, the Wilkinson–Story controversy. A loyal, consistent supporter—with William Penn, George Whitehead, and others—of Fox's institutionalization of Quakerism, Burnyeat tried to convince the faction of Quakers led by John Wilkinson and John Story of Preston Patrick meeting in Westmorland to abandon their resistance to men's and women's meetings for discipline. The Wilkinson–Story party particularly opposed certain powers of the new meetings, including the authority to discipline members who paid tithes or worshipped secretly when threatened with persecution, and the right of women's meetings to participate in supervising marriages. When the Wilkinson–Story faction established a separate meeting by May 1675, Burnyeat, Whitehead, Penn, and three other leaders of the London yearly meeting of ministers signed a fundamental statement of Quaker discipline addressing the main issues under debate as well as less controversial rules. The considerable efforts of Burnyeat and other leaders to heal the breach came to naught: Wilkinson and many of his followers separated permanently from orthodox Friends. John Story did express regret and returned to the Society of Friends in 1679.

Burnyeat purchased land in Pennsylvania but did not

migrate to the colony. Instead he travelled to Ireland, where he married in 1683. His missionary work there met such success that the number of Quaker adherents increased rapidly. He was imprisoned for holding a Quaker meeting in Dublin, but released after two months by the earl of Arran, a friend of William Penn and favourably disposed toward Quakers. Burnyeat's wife died in 1688 and he apparently continued to live primarily in Ireland, where he preached without further persecution. He died in 1690 in or near Dublin and was buried at New Garden burial-ground near Dublin. A Quaker testimonial described Burnyeat as a man

> whose innocent deportment and blameless conversation preached wherever he came; gravity and patience was with him [and] moderation in meat, drink and apparel, ... in all his travels, into whose house he entered, he was content with what things were set before him, were they never so mean, which was great satisfaction to many poor, honest Friends amongst whom his lot was cast. (Braithwaite, *Second Period*, 366–7)

Burnyeat's writings are few compared with other leading Friends of his generation, and most are co-authored. A collection of his works and testimonies about him was published in 1691 with the title *The truth exalted in the writings of that eminent and faithful servant of Christ, John Burnyeat*. He left one son, Jonathan, who served as a Quaker minister and died in Cumberland in 1723.

JEAN R. SODERLUND

Sources J. Burnyeat, *The truth exalted in the writings of that eminent and faithful servant of Christ, John Burnyeat* (1691) · *The journal of George Fox*, rev. edn, ed. J. L. Nickalls (1952) · *The papers of William Penn*, ed. M. M. Dunn, R. S. Dunn, and others, 1–2 (1981–2); 4 (1987) · W. C. Braithwaite, *The second period of Quakerism*, ed. H. J. Cadbury, 2nd edn (1961) · *DNB* · A. J. Worrall, *Quakers in the colonial northeast* (1980) · C. Pestana, *Quakers and Baptists in colonial Massachusetts* (1991) · H. L. Ingle, *First among Friends: George Fox and the creation of Quakerism* (1994) · W. C. Braithwaite, *The beginnings of Quakerism* (1912)

Burr, Aaron (1716–1757), Presbyterian minister and college head, was born on 4 January 1716 in Upper Meadows, near Fairfield, Connecticut. He was the last son of Daniel Burr and Elizabeth, *née* Pinkney, his third wife. His grandfather, of Celtic ancestry, had come to Massachusetts Bay with John Winthrop's fleet in 1630, settled first in Roxbury, helped to found Springfield, and moved to Fairfield. His father was a well-off farmer and landowner in the area. Little is known about Aaron Burr's youth and early schooling.

In the early 1730s Burr enrolled at Yale College, where he excelled in languages and the sciences. After graduating in 1735 he was provided with an additional year by the Berkeley Foundation. The revival of religion that had developed in Northampton, Massachusetts, under the preaching of Jonathan Edwards spread to New Haven and affected several students, including Burr. His religious experience caused him to accept the Calvinistic view of God's absolute sovereignty, as a result of which he determined to enter the ministry. His early preaching attracted the attention of Newark's Presbyterians, who invited him

in 1736 for a trial year and then asked that he be ordained and installed as their regular pastor.

Burr's ministry in Newark was obviously successful. In the summer of 1739, and again in the winter of 1740, revivals broke out in his congregation and spread through Newark. Although Burr sympathized with Gilbert Tennent and George Whitefield, noted revivalists, he opposed the emotional excesses and censoriousness that characterized their followers. In addition to his pastoral duties, he had begun to teach local youths the fundamentals of Greek and Latin. Despite his success in the pastorate, he became best-known as an educator.

Middle colony Presbyterians who favoured revivals, so-called New Siders, lacked an institution in which to train a sufficient number of ministers. The other colleges in British America were hostile or indifferent. Consequently, several New Sider ministers, including Burr, began to plan a college of their own. They overcame the hostility of 'Old Side' Presbyterians and Anglicans, solicited funds broadly, and in 1746 obtained a charter. The College of New Jersey was to be a genuine institution of higher learning for all men, not only those aspiring to the Presbyterian ministry. The trustees chose John Dickinson, minister at Elizabethtown, as president. In May 1747 nearly a dozen students gathered in Dickinson's home. Four and a half months later, Dickinson died.

Burr volunteered to assume leadership of the new college, and in November 1748 he was formally elected president by the trustees. Students moved from Elizabethtown to Newark. The trustees had chosen wisely. Burr was young, had a pleasant personality, was popular with members of his congregation and the students, was an inspiring teacher and preacher, was an outstanding scholar, and had unbounded energy. He became directly involved in all phases of the college's life, regularly teaching classes, supervising tutors, and raising funds. In addition he continued to serve his Newark congregation. Because the enrolment had increased under his leadership to about fifty by 1751, the trustees decided to move the college to more spacious quarters in Princetown (Princeton). There Burr supervised the construction of the president's house and college building, Nassau Hall, which was completed by late 1756.

During the early years of Burr's presidency he served without a salary, a problem that the college's trustees eventually solved. Then unmarried, Burr was recommended by a ministerial colleague to court Esther (1732–1758), daughter of the theologian Jonathan *Edwards (1703–1758). According to hearsay, he had spotted her on previous visits to the Edwardses' home and was waiting for her to reach marriageable age. At twenty she was pretty, pleasant, and smart. After visiting her for three days the 36-year-old Burr won her consent to the marriage, which took place in Newark on 29 June 1752. Although he did not record his thoughts on conjugal bliss, she did. According to her revealing diary that she kept between 1754 and 1757, she was pleased with her husband and would not have traded him for any other. The couple had two children: a daughter, Sarah, who married the noted jurist Tapping Reeve, and a son, Aaron, who became a soldier, senator, vice-president, and political adventurer. Unfortunately, Burr did not have much time to enjoy his family.

Exhausted by overwork and weakened by a fever, Burr died on 24 September 1757 at Princeton, where he was buried. Not as well known as his famous father-in-law, Jonathan Edwards, or his infamous son, Aaron Burr jun., he deserves credit in his own right. As a New Side Presbyterian minister, he helped to found the College of New Jersey. When he became its second president he placed it on a firm footing, enabling it to become Princeton University, one of the most outstanding educational institutions in the United States.   JOHN B. FRANTZ

Sources W. B. Sprague, 'Aaron Burr, 1736–1757', *Annals of the American pulpit*, 3 (1859), 68–72 • F. B. Dexter, 'Aaron Burr', *Biographical sketches of the graduates of Yale College*, 1 (1885), 530–34 • S. D. Alexander, *Princeton College during the eighteenth century* (1872) • *The diary of Esther Burr, 1754–1757*, ed. C. F. Karlsen and L. Crumpacker (1984) • T. J. Wertenbaker, *Princeton, 1746–1896* (1946) • M. Lomask, *Aaron Burr: the years from Princeton to vice president, 1756–1805* (1979) • L. J. Trinterud, *The forming of an American tradition: a re-examination of colonial Presbyterianism* [1949] • B. F. LeBeau, *Jonathan Dickinson and the formative years of American Presbyterianism* (1997) • J. McLachlan, *Princetonians, 1748–1768: a biographical dictionary* (1976) • M. A. Noll, 'Burr, Aaron', *ANB*

Archives Hist. Soc. Penn. • Presbyterian Historical Society, Philadelphia • Princeton University Library, New Jersey

Likenesses print, repro. in Wertenbaker, *Princeton*, facing p. 24

Wealth at death left little estate: Wertenbaker, *Princeton*, 31

Burra, Edward John (1905–1976), painter, was born at 31 Elvaston Place, South Kensington, London, on 29 March 1905 (he had two younger sisters, one of whom died young, in 1929), the son of Henry Curteis Burra of Rye, Sussex, a barrister who also sat as a JP and was at one time chairman of East Sussex county council, and his wife, Ermentrude Ann, daughter of J. S. O. Robertson-Luxford of Salehurst, Sussex.

Burra went to Northaw Place preparatory school, Potters Bar, but had to be withdrawn on account of ill health. He suffered all his life from anaemia. He was at Chelsea Polytechnic school of art 1921–3 and the Royal College of Art 1923–5. In his early paintings of figures in landscapes he used bright colours decoratively in a manner recalling the designs of Leon Bakst and others for the Russian Ballet and also contemporary book illustration.

Burra's sardonic commentaries on the inhabitants of Mediterranean resorts and port cities started in 1925, when he accompanied his mother on a visit to Bordighera on the Italian riviera. He wrote to his friend the dancer William Evelyn *Chappell (Billy) in what was to become his typical manner of communicating with his friends in letters that were unpunctuated and often illustrated with sharp observations on styles and manners:

> we came back from Bawdi in the Blue train which is *sposed* to be ever so mondaine but all I saw was ancient invalids and a couple with a baby that looked as if it came off Margate Sands there were a few mondaines tho to lighten the gloom … the native population are too beautiful and wear such exotic garments speshly the men I saw some exotic shirts with Kubismus decorations all over them … its just like an

Edward John Burra (1905–1976), by Maurice Ambler, *c.*1950

enormous Berwick St only more so…   (Chappell, *Well Dearie!*, 16)

From 1926 Burra made regular trips to Paris, visiting night-clubs and music halls as well as the art galleries. As an artist he was occupied in the next few years with the seamier side of life in the sailors' bars and clubs of Marseille and Toulon and the crowded dance floors of Paris clubs. Sitting quietly at the edge of the action, Burra would absorb the goings-on around him. His sharp eye for human eccentricities and an excellent visual memory enabled him to capture, without elaborate sketching, scenes, poses, and styles of dress which he would recreate, subtly satirized, in the studio. Though he was aware of the tradition of French urban realism from Toulouse-Lautrec to Fernand Léger, Burra's linearity and obsessive detail mark his Englishness.

In 1931 he met in Rye the American poet Conrad Aiken, who shared Burra's attraction to low-life subjects. Burra's watercolour *John Deth* (1931; Whitworth Art Gallery, Manchester University) is based on Aiken's poem of the same title and is a tongue-in-cheek satire, somewhat in the style of the German George Grosz, on gluttony, base sexuality, and corruption. *John Deth* typifies Burra's dislike of moral (or any kind of) earnestness and his apparently easy-going acceptance of human weakness. In 1933–4 Burra made the first of at least four visits to America (others were in 1937, 1948, and 1955), spending part of his time in Harlem where he observed African-American life with a mixture of amused curiosity and detachment. Settling at once in Harlem, he described the scene to his photographer friend Barbara-Ker Seymer in October 1933:

New York would drive you into a fit. Harlem is like Walham Green gone crazy we do a little shopping on 116th St every morning and there are about 10 Woolworths of all sorts also 40 cinemas & Apollo burlesk featuring Paris in Harlem which I am plotting to go to It must be seen to be believed. Sophie [Fedorovich, dancer and painter, with whom he was travelling] and I go out and have breakfast at different quick lunches we hope to try the Arabian nights luncheonette tomorrow the food is delish 40000000 tons of hot dogs and hamburgers must be consumed in N. Y. daily … (Chappell, *Well Dearie!*, 83)

From the beginning Burra worked chiefly in watercolour, but made a number of small oil paintings between 1927 and 1931, and a few collages, reminiscent of the work of the Berlin Dadaists, in 1929–30. Also in the early years he made numerous ink drawings, on large sheets of paper and unrelated to paintings, of people dancing and partying, a practice he later discontinued. His paintings, especially from the mid-thirties, were often unusually large for the watercolour medium, and frequently consist of more than one sheet of paper joined together. Burra liked to work on a flat table-top, drawing the design in lightly in pencil and completing the picture section by section in a manner that recalls the Pre-Raphaelites.

Burra had his first one-man shows at the Leicester Galleries, London, in 1929 and 1932. Encouraged by Paul Nash, a friend and neighbour at Rye, he joined in 1933 the avant-garde Unit One, the only artists' group he was ever a member of. In 1936 he showed at the International Surrealist Exhibition in London, and in 1937 in 'Fantastic art, Dada, surrealism' at the Museum of Modern Art, New York. Though influenced by a number of painters in the Surrealist circle—Giorgio de Chirico, Max Ernst, and Salvador Dalí, in particular—Burra was not in the truest sense a Surrealist. The more conservative side of his temperament shared with Percy Wyndham Lewis, whom he admired, a notion of realism founded on rigorous outline drawing which ran counter to the more anarchic aspects of Surrealism.

The Spanish Civil War and the Second World War stimulated important changes in Burra's art: while a strong fantasy element persisted, Burra became less the wry, uncommitted observer, his designs were strong and clear, and his imagination responded to the violence with images of brutish soldiers, weird, hooded skeletons, and predatory monsters in bird-like masks. Burra showed these pictures at the Redfern Gallery in 1942, his first exhibition for a decade. He was beginning to receive more recognition. Five of his paintings entered the Tate Gallery's collection between 1939 and 1942. These include his bizarre, underworld vision *Dancing Skeletons*, one of his best-known Harlem scenes (1934) with characteristic exaggerated figures lounging and gossiping on doorsteps, and the massive and baroque *Mexican Church* (c.1938), inspired by a visit to Mexico in 1937 with Aiken to see the novelist Malcolm Lowry at Cuernavaca. In 1945 Burra was the subject of a monograph in the Penguin Modern Painters series with an introduction by John Rothenstein. Later he was fortunate in developing a particularly happy relationship with the Lefevre Gallery where he showed more or less biennially

from 1952. The public and critical response to the exhibitions, though generally favourable, was modest and it was not until the retrospective exhibition at the Tate in 1973 that his work began to be widely appreciated. He was made a CBE in 1971.

Latterly Burra turned increasingly to landscape for his subjects, liking especially lonely places such as the west of Ireland, the Yorkshire moors, north Wales, and parts of the Lake District. In immediate appearance his pictures were calmer than before, but he continued none the less to imbue his landscapes, and even arrangements of flowers and other still-life subjects, with a menacing aspect. Parallel with his other work Burra was involved in designing for the theatre. Starting with sets and costumes for Sir Frederick Ashton's production in 1931 of the ballet *Rio Grande*, Burra worked between then and the late 1950s on six ballets, an opera, and a musical play.

Except when he was at art school Burra lived in or near Rye all his life. He has been called a recluse, but this is not true. Though a private man and not one for casual acquaintances, he had long-standing and valued friendships, several of them dating from his art school days. The range of his activities was circumscribed by his poor health. He loved travelling and discovering new places, and he read widely, if not systematically, in French and Spanish as well as English literature, including poetry. All his life Burra made regular visits to London to stay with friends, visit the art exhibitions, and, above all, the cinema.

Burra was unmarried. He died in hospital at Hastings on 22 October 1976. There was a posthumous exhibition of his work at the Hayward Gallery in 1985.

ANDREW CAUSEY

Sources A. Causey, *Edward Burra* (1985) · G. Melly, A. Causey, and others, *Edward Burra* (1985) · W. Chappell, ed., *Edward Burra: a painter remembered by his friends* (1982) · J. Rothenstein, *Edward Burra*, Penguin Modern Painters (1945) · *Well, dearie! The letters of Edward Burra*, ed. W. Chappell (1985) · J. Rothenstein, *Edward Burra* (1973) · *The Times* (26 Oct 1976)
Archives Lefevre Gallery, London, MSS · Tate collection, corresp., notebooks, diaries, MSS, and artwork | Hunt. L., letters to Conrad Aiken · Tate collection, corresp. with John Banting · Tate collection, letters to Seymour Lawrence · Tate collection, letters to Paul Nash
Likenesses M. Ambler, photograph, c.1950, priv. coll. [*see illus.*] · portrait, Tate collection
Wealth at death £272,245: administration, 17 Jan 1977, *CGPLA Eng. & Wales*

Burrant, Robert (*fl.* 1546–1553), translator, was an Englishman, as is evident from his preface to Sir David Lindsay's poem, which also reveals his strongly pro-Reformation opinions. There seems to be no reason to support Tanner's citing of Burtant as an alternative form of his name, or his doubts as to whether Burrant was the author of both the works mentioned in this article.

About 1548 Burrant published an edition of Sir David Lindsay's *Tragical death of David Beaton, bishoppe of Sainct Andrewes in Scotland: whereunto is joyned the martyrdom of Maister George Wyseharte, gentleman … for the blessed gospels sake*. This Anglicized edition is the oldest extant text of the poem and is very probably based on a lost earlier edition in Scots, possibly published by John Scot in Edinburgh in 1547. Burrant prefaces Lindsay's poem with a long epistle from 'Roberte Burrante to the Reader' and appends an account of the trial and death of Wishart, possibly also by Burrant, both in prose. The preface indicates that Burrant was in Scotland at the time of Wishart's execution (about 31 March 1546) and Beaton's murder (29 May 1546). The prose material elaborates upon Lindsay's stress on Beaton's enmity against the gospel and England, and lays special emphasis on the condemnation of Wishart as the summit of Beaton's vice. The smaller typeface in which Lindsay's poem is printed suggests that it is his own additional material that Burrant wished to highlight. Burrant's extremely rare edition is in the Grenville collection in the British Library.

In 1553 Burrant published his translation the *Preceptes of Cato, with Annotacions of D. Erasmus of Roterodame, Very Profitable for All Menne*, dedicated to Sir Thomas Caverden. Burrant says of Cato that nothing was wanting in him 'to the perfeccion of Christes religion, savying the hope and faithe that a Christian man ought to have'.

J. K. MᶜGINLEY

Sources Tanner, *Bibl. Brit.-Hib.*, 143 • preface, D. Lindsay, *Tragical death of David Beaton* [n.d., 1548?] • *STC, 1475–1640* • D. Hamer, 'The bibliography of Sir David Lindsay (1490–1555)', *The Library*, 4th ser., 10 (1929–30), 1–42 • *DNB*

Burrard, Sir Harry, first baronet (*bap.* **1755**, *d.* **1813**), army officer, was born at Vinchelez de Haut, Jersey, and baptized there at St Ouen's Church on 1 June 1755, the eldest son of George Burrard (1718–1768) (the third son of Paul Burrard, MP for Lymington, 1705–13, 1722–7), formerly of Lymington, Hampshire, and an officer of the Jersey militia, and his wife, Magdelaine Anne (*d.* 1812), the daughter of Jean Durell, attorney-general, and heir of Longueville. He entered the Royal Military Academy, Woolwich, as a cadet in 1768 and joined the Royal Artillery as a second lieutenant in 1772. In 1776 he accepted a lieutenancy in the 60th regiment and in 1777 he was promoted captain; he served in the Floridas during the American War of Independence. The Burrard family had a very strong interest in the freeman-franchise parliamentary borough of Lymington, which usually gave them the recommendation to both seats. In 1780, through his uncle Sir Harry Burrard, Burrard was returned in his absence for the parliamentary borough of Lymington. He represented the constituency almost continuously until 1791, and again in 1802, but made no mark. He was appointed governor of Calshot Castle, Isle of Wight, in 1787 and riding forester of the New Forest in 1791, both of which positions he retained until his death.

Having in 1786 received his majority in the 14th foot, in 1789 Burrard transferred to the 1st foot guards as a captain and lieutenant-colonel. On 20 February 1789 he married Hannah, the daughter of Harry Darby, a London merchant; they had seven children. Burrard served with his regiment in Flanders during 1794 and 1795, rising to colonel. In 1798 he was promoted major-general and appointed second in command of an expedition to destroy the locks of the Ostend–Bruges Canal. On 19 May, 1300 troops landed and accomplished their mission, but as bad weather prevented their re-embarkation they had to surrender the following day. Burrard was a prisoner of war at Lille for six months until exchanged. In 1799 he commanded a brigade during the expedition to The Helder in north Holland. This time he was part of an army that was able to re-embark only after the conclusion of an armistice. In 1804 he became a regimental lieutenant-colonel, and in 1805 he was promoted lieutenant-general. He was second in command to Lord Cathcart for the expedition to Copenhagen in 1807, and for his services was created a baronet.

In 1808 the government sent Sir Hew Dalrymple—with Burrard as his second in command—to supersede Sir Arthur Wellesley in Portugal. Burrard arrived off the Portuguese coast before Dalrymple and on 20 August instructed Wellesley to halt his advance on Lisbon. The next day, however, before he had disembarked, the French attacked the British army at Vimeiro, and by the time Burrard appeared on the battlefield the fighting was well advanced. He asserted his authority only once the French attacks had been repulsed, overruling Wellesley's wish to pursue the beaten enemy towards Lisbon. He then relinquished command upon Dalrymple's arrival from Gibraltar the following day. Although a signatory to the convention of Cintra, which allowed the hard-pressed French to be evacuated from Portugal in British ships, Burrard played no active part in its negotiation, and when in response to a public outcry those involved were recalled and an inquiry held at the Royal Hospital, Chelsea, the only question he had to answer was why he had forbidden an advance after Vimeiro. He argued that the numbers of the French had been uncertain, that the British were short of cavalry, and the commissariat disorganized. He also claimed to have seen a French reserve covering their retreat. Yet no witness—apart from General Brent Spencer—could corroborate this statement. Wellesley was perplexed: '"Why, Spencer, I never heard of this reserve before. How is it you only mention it now?" "Oh," said he, "poor Burrard has so large a family"' (*The Croker Papers*, ed. L. J. Jennings, 1884, 2.123). Those who knew the amiable Burrard liked him too much to wish to be unkind. Even Wellesley, although in private highly critical of the timidity of 'Betty Burrard', in the end did his best to shield him.

On 22 December 1808 the court of inquiry absolved Burrard—who was supposed to enjoy the king's protection—and concluded that there were fair military grounds for his decision not to order a pursuit. Historians are more critical. Burrard's experiences at Ostend and The Helder, they consider, left him unduly fearful that, should events in Portugal miscarry, he would face another evacuation by sea. He returned to a staff appointment in London. Of his five sons, all of whom served in either the army or the navy, two were killed in 1809. The loss of a third at San Sebastian affected Burrard so badly that, upon the news of it, he died of grief at Calshot Castle, Isle of Wight, on 17 October 1813. He was buried in Lymington churchyard; his wife survived him. He was succeeded as baronet by his third son, Charles (1793–1870), a naval officer (retired admiral, 1863), who had six daughters and on whose death on 12 July 1870 the baronetcy of Lymington became extinct.   ALASTAIR W. MASSIE

Sources Burrard's statement of service, 1809, PRO, WO25/744B pt 1, fol. 13 · *The whole proceedings of the court of enquiry upon the conduct of Sir Hew Dalrymple* (1808) · M. Glover, *Britannia sickens: Sir Arthur Wellesley and the convention of Cintra* (1970) · G. R. Balleine, *A biographical dictionary of Jersey*, [1] [1948] · S. G. Burrard, *The families of Borard and Burrard* (1892) · *Supplementary dispatches … of Field Marshal Arthur, duke of Wellington, K.G.*, ed. A. R. Wellesley, second duke of Wellington, 6: *Expedition to Denmark; plans for conquest of Mexico; expeditions to Portugal in 1808 and 1809; and the first advance of the British army into Spain* (1860) · Fortescue, *Brit. army*, vols. 4, 6 · *The manuscripts of J. B. Fortescue*, 10 vols., HMC, 30 (1892–1927), vol. 9 · C. T. Atkinson, ed., *Supplementary report on the manuscripts of Robert Graham esq. of Fintry*, HMC, 81 (1940) · F. W. Hamilton, *The origin and history of the first or grenadier guards*, 2 (1874) · R. Muir, *Britain and the defeat of Napoleon, 1807–1815* (1996) · S. Burrard, *The annals of Walhampton* (1874) · HoP, *Commons* · *GM*, 1st ser., 83/2 (1813), 507 · Burke, *Peerage* (1924) · Boase, *Mod. Eng. biog.*
Archives Hants. RO, family MSS
Likenesses portrait, *c*.1790–1795, NG Scot.; repro. in Glover, *Britannia sickens*

Burrel, John. *See* Burel, John (1565x8–1603).

Burrell family (*per. c.*1800–1929), agricultural machinery manufacturers, came to prominence with three brothers who were partners in a small engineering business at Thetford in Norfolk. These were Joseph Burrell, William Burrell (1766–1832), and James Burrell (1770–1837).

Joseph Burrell (1759–1831) is generally regarded as the founder of the firm, and he was certainly in business on his own account by about 1790, repairing agricultural implements. Within a few years he was beginning to make implements as well. He first attracted notice in 1803 when, at the annual Holkham sheep shearing, he exhibited a seed and manure drill of his own design. The following year he filed a patent for an improved threshing machine, and in 1805 he showed a mowing machine at Holkham. On these foundations the business run by the three Burrell brothers was able to develop. James Burrell managed the business alone after his two elder brothers died, and on his death in 1837 control passed to his second son, aged only twenty. This was **Charles Burrell** (1817–1906), who was to play a key role in the transformation of the firm. He changed the name of the business to Charles Burrell, engineers and agricultural machinists, and later to Charles Burrell & Sons.

Charles Burrell had an engineer's mind that was inventive and ready to explore new ideas. His was one of the earliest firms to make portable steam engines, the first device being made in 1846, and in 1848 he produced the first threshing machine that also dressed the grain. This type of combined threshing and dressing machine soon became the standard in farming, except where the smallest machines were required.

In the 1850s Burrell concentrated his technical abilities on the development of self-moving steam engines. In particular he collaborated with James Boydell, patentee of an 'endless railway' mechanism. This consisted of a series of flat feet attached to the outside of the engine's wheels. They were hinged in such a way that as the wheel revolved each succeeding foot would lie flat in contact with the ground, thus spreading the weight of the engine. The idea was that this arrangement would be more efficient for road-haulage engines, enabling them to deal with poor road surfaces. Burrell became the licensed manufacturer of Boydell engines in 1855, and from 1856 to 1862 he made several types of machine for use on the roads and for ploughing by direct traction.

Boydell engines proved to be unsuccessful, both technically and commercially, and Burrell turned instead to the development of conventional wheeled traction engines. In this he had considerable achievements, and his firm came to be known mainly for its traction engines and road locomotives. In the 1870s he worked with R. W. Thompson in the production of his road steamers—steam tractors designed to haul passenger and goods vehicles on the roads. A number of these were built for export. Burrell improved and adapted the design.

In 1846 Charles Burrell married Elizabeth Cowen (*d. c.*1895), daughter of Robert Cowen, owner of Beck Foundry, Nottingham. The couple had five sons and two daughters. Charles Burrell served on Thetford council's navigation committee for the River Ouse. He was a justice of the peace for the county, appointed in 1877. In 1884 the family business was incorporated as Charles Burrell & Sons Ltd. Charles Burrell remained as chairman, though by now he was not so actively engaged in day-to-day management. In 1904 he retired completely. He died at Thetford on 28 June 1906.

Burrell was succeeded as chairman of the company in 1904 by his eldest son, **Charles Burrell** (1847–1929), one of three sons who entered actively into the business in the 1870s. The younger Charles went to Thetford grammar school, and received some technical education at King's College, London. After initial training in the firm he became a general manager, steadily taking over more and more responsibility from his father. Under his leadership the firm grew from about 200 employees in 1870 to 400 in 1913, comfortably the largest employer in Thetford. Charles Burrell was a highly regarded local figure and, like his father, was engaged in the civic life of Thetford. He was elected to the council in 1874 and served continuously for the fifty-five years until his death, in later years as an alderman. He was mayor seven times, and was a justice of the peace for the borough and the county. He was a member of the Institution of Mechanical Engineers, and of the council of the Smithfield Club from 1916 to 1925. He was married twice, in 1873 to Sarah Annie Thomas (*d.* 1910) and in 1912 to Annie Phillis Wilberforce (who survived her husband). He died at Thetford on 12 November 1929.

His younger brother **Robert George Burrell** (1849–1904) was sales director for the family firm and travelled extensively throughout Europe and Russia between 1875 and the 1890s, when heart disease began to restrict his activities. He was also active in the town, and was elected to the borough council in 1882. Robert Burrell served as mayor for three years consecutively (1888–91) and became an alderman in 1901. He was a justice of the peace for the borough, and a major in the Norfolk Volunteers. He was president of the local Conservative association from 1885 to 1898, and his involvement in local charities included the governorship of Thetford School and the hospital foundation. In 1882 he married Ellen Alborough Cockayne (who survived her husband). Robert Burrell died from a heart attack on 7 September 1904.

Frederick John Burrell (1855–1927) was the third son of Charles Burrell the elder to become active in the firm, and he was the one who inherited the family's technical genius to fullest measure. Most of the technical developments and soundness of the engineering of Burrell products in the 1880s and 1890s were due to him. His inventiveness was not confined to his own firm's products. Among the patents registered in Frederick's name were those for a machine for freezing ice cream, a bacon-slicing machine, and burglar-proof fasteners for sash windows. He was a member of the Institution of Mechanical Engineers. He had an unhappy marriage, and from the late 1890s his health deteriorated. His involvement with the management of the firm ceased about 1900, and he died of pneumonia on 15 October 1927, at St Andrew's Hospital, Thorpe, Norfolk.

From modest beginnings as a country firm repairing agricultural implements, Charles Burrell & Sons Ltd had, by the end of the nineteenth century, become an important manufacturer of agricultural machinery. The steam engines developed by Charles and his sons were well known throughout Europe, and their traction engines and road locomotives were especially popular with travelling showmen. However, Burrells remained a modest enterprise compared with such competitors as Aveling and Porter Ltd and John Fowler & Co. (Leeds) Ltd; and the retirement of Charles Burrell the younger, soon after the end of the First World War, led to the firm's being taken over by Agricultural and General Engineers Ltd.

JONATHAN BROWN

Sources M. Lane, *The story of St Nicholas works* (1994) · 'The late Mr. Charles Burrell of Thetford', *Implement and Machinery Review*, 32 (1906–7), 448 · 'Charles Burrell', *The Engineer* (6 July 1906), 10 · R. H. Clark, *The steam engine builders of Norfolk* (1988) · 'The late Mr. R. G. Burrell of Thetford', *Implement and Machinery Review*, 30 (1904–5), 659 · 'Mr. Charles Burrell, JP', *Implement and Machinery Review*, 55 (1929–30), 807 · *DBB* · d. cert. [Charles Burrell the elder] · d. cert. [Charles Burrell the younger] · d. cert. [Frederick John Burrell] · d. cert. [Robert George Burrell] · b. cert. [Robert George Burrell] · *CGPLA Eng. & Wales* (1904) · *CGPLA Eng. & Wales* (1906) · *CGPLA Eng. & Wales* (1928) · *CGPLA Eng. & Wales* (1930)
Archives Burrell Museum, Thetford, business records of firm
Likenesses photographs, repro. in Lane, *Story of St Nicholas works*, frontispiece, fig. 141
Wealth at death £13,546 6s. 9d.—Charles Burrell the elder: probate, 27 Nov 1906, *CGPLA Eng. & Wales* · £8344 15s.—Charles Burrell the younger: probate, 12 March 1930, *CGPLA Eng. & Wales* · £3574 17s.—Robert George Burrell: probate, 10 Oct 1904, *CGPLA Eng. & Wales* · £1948 8s. 6d.—Frederick John Burrell: probate, 17 May 1928, *CGPLA Eng. & Wales*

Burrell, Charles (1817–1906). *See under* Burrell family (*per.* c.1800–1929).

Burrell, Charles (1847–1929). *See under* Burrell family (*per.* c.1800–1929).

Burrell, Frederick John (1855–1927). *See under* Burrell family (*per.* c.1800–1929).

Burrell, John Percy (1910–1972), theatre director, was born on 6 May 1910 in Naini Tal, north India, the younger of the two sons of Percy Saville Burrell (1871–1958), teacher and headmaster in the Indian education service from 1904 to 1926, and his wife, Ethel Marion Jane Bilton (d. 1945). As a young boy he contracted poliomyelitis. He was educated at Shrewsbury School, where his father had become headmaster, and from 1928 to 1934 he studied painting, sculpture, and stage design at the Royal College of Art. He also became involved in production, and in 1930 he founded the Royal College of Arts Theatre Group.

From 1933 to 1937 Burrell was producer and director at the Barn Theatre, Shere. He then joined the staff of the London Theatre Studio as producer and director of décor. The studio was founded by Michel Saint-Denis, the former director of the celebrated Compagnie des Quinze, as a centre of drama study and as a training ground for actors. On 6 August 1936 Burrell married Margaret Souttar (1914–1987), a painter and sculptor, the daughter of William George Westerbery Souttar, of the Indian police force. They had studied together at the Royal College of Art, and they had two sons.

In 1939 Burrell was appointed director of drama at Toynbee Hall in the East End of London. He served in the War Office until 1941, and then moved to the BBC as a drama producer, where his programmes included adaptations of *Pilgrim's Progress* and *Don Quixote*. He also worked with Tyrone Guthrie on his production of Henrik Ibsen's *Peer Gynt*, with Ralph Richardson in the title role. He remained with the BBC until 1944, having made his début as a theatre director in 1943 at the Cambridge Theatre in London, with a successful revival of George Bernard Shaw's *Heartbreak House*, with Edith Evans, Robert Donat, and the young Deborah Kerr.

In 1944 Burrell was invited by Ralph Richardson and Laurence Olivier to join them as newly appointed directors of the Old Vic company, temporarily displaced to the New (later Albery) Theatre from its bombed-out home on the Waterloo Road. Rehearsals were held in evacuated rooms in the National Gallery, and a legendary company of performers was recruited, including Olivier and Richardson, Sybil Thorndike, Nicholas Hannen, Harcourt Williams, Joyce Redman, Margaret Leighton, and in later seasons Alec Guinness, Celia Johnson, and Trevor Howard. In the first and most successful season Burrell directed Shaw's *Arms and the Man* and Anton Chekhov's *Uncle Vanya*, as well as Olivier's historic performance of *Richard III*, and in subsequent seasons both parts of *Henry IV* (1945), with Richardson a definitive Falstaff and Olivier doubling as Hotspur and Shallow, Ben Jonson's *The Alchemist* (1946), Shaw's *Saint Joan* (1947), Gogol's *The Government Inspector* (1947), and William Congreve's *The Way of the World* (1948), with Dame Edith Evans, who had been the Millamant of the 1920s, now playing Lady Wishfort. At the time some thought that Burrell 'hadn't got the guns', that he was overshadowed by Olivier and Richardson, and that he was little more than an 'office boy' and a 'timekeeper'. But he was a man of huge determination and ambition, and his work in the early seasons refutes this view. This was the first time in London that a classical repertory had been supported by the British public, and it proved an essential blueprint for the formation of a national theatre company. Despite the joint success of the triumvirate, however, their contracts were not renewed.

The polio Burrell had contracted as a small boy, which in many ways shaped his life, proved no obstacle to the physical rigours of rehearsal. His legs were severely wasted, and, with one leg in irons and a surgical boot on the foot of the other, he needed sticks for support, but would haul himself up ladders and on to the stage by the strength of his forearms alone. A favourite trick of his was to ride a bicycle, using his hands to work the pedals, his body across the saddle and his legs dangling off the back. It is tempting to think that Olivier's dynamic performance as Richard III might have been influenced by observing Burrell's infirmity.

After his peremptory dismissal by the Old Vic board, Burrell went on to direct John Burgoyne's *The Heiress* (1949) with Richardson and Peggy Ashcroft at the Haymarket, but his confidence and energy had been affected and with his own loss of confidence went that of the two stars and the producer, Hugh Beaumont. He was dismissed and replaced by John Gielgud.

After these setbacks Burrell left for America, where he remained for the rest of his life. On Broadway in 1950 he directed Jean Arthur and Boris Karloff in a hugely successful revival of James Barrie's *Peter Pan*, with incidental music by Leonard Bernstein. He was a founder of the American Shakespeare Festival Theatre and Academy at Stratford, Connecticut, where he also taught acting, and which opened its first season in July 1955. He was then executive artistic director for CBS TV in New York, and was credited with revolutionizing design on television. His final post was as a drama professor at the University of Illinois.

Burrell died from a heart attack on 28 September 1972, at Champaign, Illinois, USA.   ALEX JENNINGS

Sources F. Gaye, ed., *Who's who in the theatre*, 14th edn (1967) · *WW* · *WWW* · H. Williams, *Old Vic saga* (1949) · *The Times* (4 Oct 1972) · G. O'Connor, *Ralph Richardson: an actor's life* (1982) · T. Guthrie, *A life in the theatre* (1960) · m. cert. · private information (2004)
Likenesses F. Man, group portrait, photograph, 1944 (*Thespian talk*), Hult. Arch.

Burrell, Joseph (1759–1831). *See under* Burrell family (*per. c.*1800–1929).

Burrell, Litellus (1753–1827), army officer in the East India Company, was born in 1753. Nothing is known of his parents (it is just possible that he was related to the Litellus Birrell born in Edinburghshire in 1712) or his life until he was 17, when he set off for India. He apparently arrived there with little money and few contacts, since it was as a private soldier that he entered the Bengal army. Yet he was

fortunate to arrive in India when he did, for British military campaigns against Indian states had forced the East India Company to expand its armies. This meant that not only were there plenty of vacancies in the Bengal army, but there were also occasional opportunities for a few soldiers to be promoted to officers. This was easier to accomplish in the East India Company's armies than it was in the royal army, since the company did not employ the purchase system for promotion, and it also tended to take a more relaxed view of the social status of its officers. Burrell, however, was unusual: not only was he promoted from the ranks, but he eventually rose to the rank of major-general.

Burrell began as a volunteer in Captain Rawstorne's company of the 2nd battalion 2nd Bengal Europeans, in which he became a corporal in 1771 and sergeant in 1772. In 1774, on the recommendation of his captain, he was transferred to the 18th native infantry regiment. He served at the battle of Katra (23 April 1774), which resulted in the defeat of the Rohillas and the cession of Rohilkhand to Britain's ally, Oudh. He became sergeant-major of the corps in 1775, and remained with it until 1779, when he was nominated to a Bengal cadetship by Warren Hastings. In October of the same year he obtained a commission as ensign, and was posted to a battalion of sepoys that comprised part of the force under Captain Popham which had been dispatched to reinforce General Goddard's army in western India. Burrell was present at the capture of Gwalior, widely thought to be one of India's most impregnable forts. His battalion of sepoys, which was first numbered the 40th native infantry and then the 33rd native infantry, next joined the forces under colonels Camac and Muir in their campaigns in Malwa against the Maratha leader Mahadji Sindhia, whose baggage train and artillery park were at one point captured by a force including Burrell's battalion. In 1785 Burrell joined the 2nd native infantry, where he served as regimental adjutant until 1797, when, in anticipation of the possibility of action against a threatened invasion of Zaman Shah of Kabul, he transferred to the 3rd native infantry. He became brevet captain in 1796, captain-lieutenant in 1797, and substantive captain in 1798, in which year he was transferred to the 2nd battalion 5th native infantry at Lucknow.

At this time the government called for 3000 sepoy volunteers from the Bengal infantry to proceed by sea to reinforce Madras in its war with Tipu Sultan of Mysore, and Burrell, who had come down the Ganges to Calcutta in charge of the volunteers of his regiment, was appointed to command the 3rd battalion. The three battalions of Bengal Volunteers proceeded to Madras, and joined General Harris's army, in which, as the 4th native brigade, under command of Colonel John Gardiner, they fought at Malavalli and at the storming and capture of Seringapatam. They were next employed under Colonel Arthur Wellesley in subjugating the chieftains of Mysore and in mopping up disbanded units of Tipu Sultan's army. Subsequently the volunteers were sent home overland, having put down some disturbances at Pallavaram *en route*. Burrell, during his absence, had been appointed to the 15th native infantry, which had been raised in Bihar and added to the Bengal army in 1798. He joined them in Oudh in 1801, and saw service in Lord Lake's 1803 campaign against the armies of the Maratha leader Daulat Rao Sindhia. Burrell was present at the battles of Delhi, Agra, and Laswari: at Laswari, after which Sindhia was forced into a peace treaty, Burrell commanded the lead units of the advance column. In 1804 he was promoted to the rank of major and, continuing with the 15th native infantry, he participated in Lake's campaigns against the other great Maratha general Jaswant Rao Holkar. Burrell was at the successful siege of Dig as well as at the several unsuccessful attempts to take the Jat fort and city of Bharatpur, which was then allied to Holkar. British failures at Bharatpur largely resulted from their lacking sufficient guns and personnel to besiege such a large fort. Burrell's health broke down during these campaigns and he was forced back to Bengal to convalesce.

Burrell became brevet colonel in 1814, and in 1817 was appointed to the command of the 3rd brigade of the grand army under Lord Hastings, then in the field against the Pindaris (gangs of disbanded soldiers and mercenaries from India and central Asia). At the end of the campaign he rejoined his regiment, and in 1818 was appointed to command all the East India Company's forces in the territory of the nawab of Oudh. In 1819 he succeeded to a regiment on the Bengal establishment, and in 1821 was promoted to the rank of major-general on the occasion of the coronation of George IV. He remained in Oudh until 1820, when severe illness sent him back to Bengal. Having benefited by the change, he was appointed to a command at Cuttack in 1821. Failing health, however, compelled him to retire and return to Britain. He died in Notting Hill on 30 September 1827, having suffered a series of strokes over the past four winters.

Contemporary opinions of Burrell emphasized that he was particularly adept at managing the internal discipline of a regiment; perhaps this was owing to his having experienced regimental life as both a soldier and an officer. He was also respected for his sensitive handling of Indian soldiers; this no doubt played a role in his being appointed on several occasions to the office of battalion adjutant. Disciplinary problems in units under his command were apparently very rare, morale was generally high, and he was more successful than many of his contemporaries in securing sepoy volunteers for distant and foreign service.   DOUGLAS M. PEERS

Sources J. Philippart, *East India military calendar*, 2 (1824), 218–29 · *GM*, 1st ser., 97/2 (1827), 640–43 · *The Times* (2 Oct 1827) · Dodwell [E. Dodwell] and Miles [J. S. Miles], eds., *Alphabetical list of the officers of the Indian army: with the dates of their respective promotion, retirement, resignation, or death … from the year 1760 to the year … 1837* (1838) · J. Williams, *An historical account of the rise and progress of the Bengal native infantry, from its first formation in 1757 to 1796* (1817) · F. G. Cardew, *A sketch of the services of the Bengal native army to the year 1895* (1903) · Fortescue, *Brit. army*, vols. 3–5 · C. E. Buckland, *Dictionary of Indian biography* (1906) · G. Bryant, 'Officers of the East India Company's army in the days of Clive and Hastings', *Journal of Imperial and Commonwealth History*, 6 (1977–8), 203–27 · H. T. Prinsep, *History of the political and military transactions in India during the administration of the marquess of Hastings, 1813–1823* (1825) · 'List of the Bengal army, corrected to 31 December 1821', BL OIOC, L/Mil/17/2/5

Burrell, Peter, first Baron Gwydir (1754–1820). *See under* White Conduit cricket club (*act.* c.1785–1788).

Burrell, Robert George (1849–1904). *See under* Burrell family (*per.* c.1800–1929).

Burrell [*née* Raymond], **Sophia**, Lady Burrell (1753–1802), poet and playwright, was born on 11 April 1753, the eldest daughter of the wealthy banker Charles Raymond (1713–1788) of Valentines, Ilford, Essex, and Sarah (d. 1778), daughter of Thomas Webster of Bromley. On 13 April 1773 she married William *Burrell (1732–1796) of Beckenham, advocate, member of parliament for Haslemere (1768–74), director of the South Sea Company (1763–75), and commissioner of the excise (1774–91), with whom she had five sons (of whom two died in infancy) and two daughters, and came into possession, it is said, of £100,000. A baronetcy was granted to her father on 3 May 1774, the year after her marriage, with remainder to her husband and their male heir, Charles Merrik Burrell (b. 24 May 1774). From 1773 to 1782 Sophia Burrell's pen was employed on *vers de société*, varied by such heavier matter as *Comala*, from Ossian, in 1784. In 1787 her husband had a stroke and in 1791 they retired to The Deepdene near Dorking in Surrey. Lady Burrell circulated most of her work in manuscript before publishing two volumes of her collected *Poems* anonymously in 1793, followed in 1794 by the *Thymriad* from Xenophon and *Telemachus*, with her name attached. Sir William Burrell died on 20 January 1796, and was buried at West Grinstead, Sussex. On 23 May 1797 Lady Burrell was married at Marylebone church by the bishop of Kildare to William Clay, Church of England priest, the second son of Richard Augustus Clay of Southwell, Nottinghamshire, with whom she lived intermittently at The Deepdene. Also in 1797 she published, anonymously, her only novel, *Adeline de Courcey*. In 1800 Lady Burrell produced two tragedies. The first was *Maximian*, taken from Corneille, dedicated to William Lock; the second was *Theodora, or, The Spanish Daughter*, dedicated by permission to Duchess Georgiana of Devonshire. *Theodora* was reprinted in 1814 in volume 1 of *The New British Theatre*, a collection of rejected dramas. Lady Burrell retired with her second husband to West Cowes, Isle of Wight, where she died on 20 June 1802.   JENNETT HUMPHREYS, *rev.* REBECCA MILLS

Sources R. Lonsdale, ed., *Eighteenth-century women poets: an Oxford anthology* (1989), 340–45 · Blain, Clements & Grundy, *Feminist comp.* · J. Todd, ed., *A dictionary of British and American women writers, 1660–1800* (1984) · D. E. Baker, *Biographia dramatica, or, A companion to the playhouse*, rev. I. Reed, new edn, rev. S. Jones, 1 (1812), 79 · Burke, *Peerage* · Nichols, *Lit. anecdotes*, 9.797 · *GM*, 1st ser., 66 (1796), 86 · Allibone, *Dict.* · IGI
Archives BL, MSS
Likenesses portrait, repro. in T. W. Horsfield, *The history and antiquities of Lewes and its vicinity*, 1 (1824), facing p. 328
Wealth at death presumed wealthy; acquired £100,000 on first marriage

Burrell, Sir William, second baronet (1732–1796), antiquary, was born on 10 October 1732 in Leadenhall Street, London, the third son of Peter Burrell (1692–1756), merchant and MP, of Mark Lane, London, and Kelsey in Beckenham, Kent, and Amy (1699/1700–1789), daughter of Hugh Raymond, merchant, of Stepney and Saling Hall, Essex, and Langley in Beckenham. He entered Westminster School in January 1743, proceeded to St John's College, Cambridge, in June 1749, and graduated LLB in 1755. Under the influence of his tutor, Dr John Taylor (1704–1766), in 1760 he graduated LLD and was admitted as an advocate in the Canterbury court of arches and as a fellow of Doctors' Commons. He practised chiefly in the ecclesiastical courts, but also in the Admiralty courts. He was appointed chancellor of the diocese of Worcester in July 1764, through the influence of the duke of Newcastle, and of Rochester in November 1771, and continued in both offices until his death. Elected MP for Haslemere in March 1768 on the family interest, he steadily supported the administration. His most prominent contribution to parliamentary business was in November 1772, seconding the investigation into the East India Company and serving on the secret committee—probably at the prompting of his future father-in-law, leader of the East India shipping interest and a critic of the directors.

On 13 April 1773 Burrell married Sophia (1753–1802), poet and dramatist [see Burrell, Sophia, Lady Burrell], daughter of Charles Raymond of Valentines, Ilford, Essex, and Sarah, daughter of Thomas Webster of Bromley, Kent. They brought up at 71 Harley Street, Marylebone, London, five sons, of whom two died in infancy, and two daughters. Although his wife's fortune was said to be the great sum of £100,000, he needed a secure income—which came from appointment as a commissioner of the excise in March 1774, whereupon he resigned from parliament and from Doctors' Commons. He was a director of the South Sea Company (as his father had been), from 1763 to 1775, and (in place of Charles Raymond) of Sun fire insurance, 1773–95. His father-in-law was made a baronet with remainder to Burrell in 1774, and he succeeded to the title in 1788.

Burrell was elected a fellow of the Society of Antiquaries in 1754, as an adjunct to his legal training. Despite his upbringing and career within the London-based mercantile governmental nexus, by 1770 he was working on the history of Sussex. His great-grandfather's Sussex estate had mostly passed out of the main line, but the remnant had unexpectedly devolved on his grandfather, the ninth son, and his father, and his uncle Merrik Burrell had bought back the rest. The latter, a governor of the Bank of England, greatly augmented his holding and rebuilt West Grinstead Place; he may have prompted his studious nephew to embark on the project, which was to be a deduction of the landed property from the Norman conquest, in the manner of Dugdale's *Warwickshire*. Burrell transcribed documents, often initialling the original, in the keeping of the great landowners, stewards, lawyers, and clergy, as well as copies made by Sussex antiquaries such as John Elliot. He visited at least two-thirds of the churches, mainly in 1773–8, to transcribe the monumental inscriptions and make extracts from the parish registers, and elsewhere the clergy responded to his enquiries. Over 1300 views of Sussex antiquities and gentry houses were commissioned from James Lambert (1725–1788) and his nephew James (1744–1799), in 1776–84, and S. H. Grimm (1733–1794), in 1780–91.

Burrell suffered a stroke in August 1787 and, though he recovered his speech, lost the use of his left arm. Wealth cascaded onto him at his father-in-law's and mother's deaths, but too late to buy leisure for research. He resigned from the commission of excise in September 1789, and in 1791 retired to The Deepdene, Dorking, Surrey. His active researches now ended, he offered his collections to John Nichols, but Nichols declined to print them and the principal drawings at his own risk, for he was committed to his own history of Leicestershire. So Burrell bequeathed them, by his will of November 1790, to the British Museum library (BL, Add. MSS 5670–5711).

Burrell was exceptionally diligent in collating his materials. What he bequeathed, in several series of volumes arranged mainly by parish within rape in Sussex, were fair copies in his own or a clerk's neat hand. The systematic arrangement has greatly assisted later historians of Sussex to quarry his work for their own. Few working notes or private or business papers have survived, probably being lost by fire in 1904 at Knepp Castle, Shipley, Sussex, the family seat his eldest son built on the estate Burrell had acquired through his father-in-law.

Burrell died at The Deepdene on 20 January 1796 and was buried on the 28th in the family vault at West Grinstead, Sussex, where his second surviving son held the remainder of Uncle Merrik's estate. Simple monuments by Flaxman are both there and at Cuckfield. Burrell's widow married the Revd William Clay in May 1797 and lived intermittently at The Deepdene until her death on 20 June 1802. William Cole, a fellow antiquary, described Burrell as 'an active, stirring, man, and a good antiquary. He is rather low, and squints a little; but very ingenious, and scholar-like' (BL, Add. MS 5864, fol. 69).

JOHN H. FARRANT

Sources J. H. Farrant, 'The family circle and career of William Burrell, antiquary', *Sussex Archaeological Collections*, 139 (2001), 169–85 · J. H. Farrant, *Sussex RS, 85 (2001), 32–9, 115–36*
Archives BL, Add. MSS 5670–5711 | NL Scot., MS 2911 [travel journal] · W. Sussex RO, estate records
Likenesses A. Plimer, miniature, 1786–9 (after R. Cosway?), repro. in G. C. Williamson, *Andrew and Nathaniel Plimer, miniature painters: their lives and their works* (1903), 47 and plate · R. Laurie, mezzotint engraving, before 1788 (after R. Cosway or A. Plimer), BM; repro. in O. Manning and W. Bray, *The history and antiquities of the county of Surrey*, 1 (1804), facing p. 562 · P. Audinet, engraving, 1824–30 (after R. Cosway or A. Plimer), repro. in E. Cartwright, *History of the western divisions of the county of Sussex*, 2/2 (1830), facing p. 296 · P. Audinet, mezzotint engraving (after R. Cosway), repro. in E. Cartwright, *History of the western division of the county of Sussex*, 2 (1830), facing p. 296 · F. Pollard, lithograph (after R. Laurie), repro. in T. W. Horsfield, *The history and antiquities of Lewes and its vicinity*, 1 (1824), facing p. 328
Wealth at death see will, PRO, PROB 11/1271

Burrell, Sir William (1861–1958), art collector, was born at 3 Scotis Street, Glasgow, on 9 July 1861, the third son of William Burrell (1832–1885), a shipowner, and his wife, Isabella Duncan Guthrie (d. 1912), and grandson of George Burrell, the founder of the shipping firm later known as Burrell & Son, which Burrell joined when he was fifteen. He was educated at a boarding-school at St Andrews. In 1877 one of the firm's ships salvaged Cleopatra's Needle, which had been lost in the Bay of Biscay on its passage to England. For many years Burrell managed the family business in conjunction with his eldest brother, and the firm greatly prospered under his vigorous direction; it reached its peak activity in 1915, when it owned thirty ships all of over 4000 gross tonnage. Burrell, however, determined to devote the remainder of his long life to art, and by 1917 almost the entire fleet had been sold.

Burrell's interest in art had shown itself, he used to recall, as a boy when, to his father's annoyance, he had used his pocket money to buy not a cricket bat but a picture. Realizing that it was not very good he later sold it to buy a better one. By 1901 he already owned a considerable collection, not only of pictures (including works by Géricault, Daumier, and Manet), but of tapestries, stained glass, Iranian carpets, furniture, metalwork, and carvings in wood and ivory. In that year he lent over 160 works of art to the International Exhibition in Glasgow, for which he was an active committee member. Also in 1901 Burrell married Constance Mary Lockhart (d. 1961), daughter of James Lockhart Mitchell, merchant; they had one daughter.

At this time Burrell's interests were by no means confined to shipping and art. He served in the corporation of Glasgow as a representative of the tenth ward (1899–1906) and became convener of a sub-committee on uninhabitable houses, back lands, and underground dwellings—retiring, it is said, because the policy of slum clearance he advocated was not followed. Until 1906 he also acted as consul at Glasgow for Austria–Hungary.

In 1916 Burrell acquired Hutton Castle near Berwick upon Tweed, previously the home of Lord Tweedmouth, who had largely rebuilt and added to the ancient castle. Burrell made further additions to the structure and entirely remodelled the interior. He and his wife lived there from about 1926, by which time the castle was sumptuously furnished throughout with works of art, many of which were built into the fabric of the rooms. As the collection continued to grow, it soon outstripped the accommodation available in the castle and for many years much of it was widely dispersed on loan to many different art galleries, museums, and cathedrals, including the national galleries of Scotland, England, and Wales. In 1925 Burrell presented over sixty paintings and drawings to the Glasgow Art Gallery, and for several years a large number of his pictures were on loan to the Tate Gallery. Donations were also made to other galleries.

In 1944 Burrell presented to the city of Glasgow a great art collection to which he added lavishly every year until the end of his life. This diverse collection contained works of art of ancient civilizations, including Sumer, Egypt, Greece, and Rome; oriental art of the Far and Near East including Chinese pottery, bronzes, and jades, and Iranian carpets, pottery, and metalwork; European art of the medieval and post-medieval periods including tapestries, stained glass, furniture, stone, wood, and ivory carvings, embroideries and lace, pottery, arms and armour, glassware, treen, silver and metalware; and between 700 and 800 paintings, drawings, and engravings, chiefly by European artists of the fifteenth to the nineteenth centuries. The collection also included the largest single assemblage of works (132) by Joseph Crawhall (1861–1913), a large number of drawings by Phil May, and a quantity of Japanese prints.

Burrell's most abiding interest probably centred in the art of the later Middle Ages and Renaissance. The collection of Franco-Flemish, German, Swiss, and English tapestries of the fourteenth to sixteenth centuries has been considered the finest of its kind; that of English, French, German, Dutch, and Swiss stained and painted glass of the twelfth to seventeenth centuries is even more extensive and hardly less remarkable. Largest of all is the collection of Chinese pottery and porcelain which comprises a magnificent range of wares dating from the earliest known neolithic vessels to the brilliantly enamelled vessels and figures of the reign of Kangxi (1662–1722). The furniture, silver, and needlework is chiefly English of the sixteenth and seventeenth centuries.

Beginning in 1911 the twenty-eight notebooks in which Burrell recorded his acquisitions and payments continue in unbroken sequence until a few months prior to his death. They show that for almost half a century he was spending on average at least £20,000 a year on acquiring works of art. After 6 April 1944, when the collection as it then stood became the property of Glasgow, he continued to acquire on an equally grand or even grander scale. The year 1948, when he spent over £60,000, probably represents his highest expenditure in any one year, except for 1936 when he spent almost £80,000.

To his great gift to Glasgow Burrell added £450,000. This was to build a new museum for housing the collection in an area of the Scottish countryside not less than 16 miles from the centre of the city and within 4 miles of Killearn. This condition proved difficult to honour, and apart from the selections on permanent or changing display in the municipal art gallery and museum at Kelvingrove, the collection remained in store. The tapestries and other textiles could not at first be exhibited in Glasgow being susceptible to damage from polluted air. But in 1966 Pollok House and Estate on the southern outskirts of the city were presented to Glasgow, and a museum was built to house Burrell's collection on the estate. The project finally came to fruition with the opening of the award-winning building, designed by Barry Gasson, John Meunier, and Brit Andreson, in 1983.

Burrell was reserved by temperament, and in the midst of the beautiful objects which filled his home he led a comparatively frugal existence. Starting as a private collector, he became during thirty or more years a collector for posterity rather than for himself. Yet in spite of its size he always preserved a keen intellectual and artistic interest in his collection, about which he had read widely and for whose details his memory was excellent. By nature he was clearly attracted by vigour of form and colour rather than by elegance, so the collection is rich in works of the sixteenth and seventeenth centuries but deficient in those of the eighteenth. Numbering about 8000 objects, the collection was probably one of the largest ever assembled by one man, and certainly the largest given to a municipality.

For many years Burrell was a trustee of the Tate Gallery and from 1923 to 1946 of the National Gallery of Scotland. He was knighted in 1927 for his services to art; he received the freedom of the city of Glasgow in 1944, and the St Mungo prize in 1946. He died at Hutton Castle on 29 March 1958, and was buried in early April at Largs cemetery, Ayrshire. WILLIAM WELLS, *rev.* RICHARD MARKS

Sources *The Times* (31 March 1958) · *Glasgow Herald* (31 March 1958) · D. S. Leslie, *Notes on Hutton parish* (1934) · personal knowledge (1971) · private information (1971, 2004) · purchase books, correspondence, Glasgow Museums, Archives of the Burrell Collection · R. Marks, *Burrell: a portrait of a collector*, rev. edn (1988)
Archives Glasgow Museums, Archives of the Burrell Collection | Tate collection, corresp. with Lord Clark rel. to his art collection
Likenesses T. & R. Annan, photograph, c.1920
Wealth at death £312,035 1s. 9d.: confirmation, 21 June 1958, *CCI*

Burrington, George (c.1685–1759), colonial governor, was most likely born in Devon, where the name has been known since the Domesday Book of the eleventh century, the son of Gilbert Burrington. His mother's name is unknown, and there is no record of his precise birthplace or education. His family is said to have been early supporters of William of Orange. At about the age of seventeen Burrington received a commission in the army. It is likely that this appointment, as well as subsequent ones and his rise to the rank of captain, came because he was recommended by 'my noble patron', Thomas Pelham-Holles, duke of Newcastle, secretary of state for the southern department, which had oversight of the colonies in America.

Burrington was named governor of North Carolina by the lords proprietors on 3 June 1723, and sworn in on 15 January 1724. The colony as a whole was sparsely settled, but in the southern portion, where land could be acquired only through London, there were even fewer settlers. Soon after his arrival Burrington went to South Carolina for a brief time and along the way was excited by the fine land he saw and the possibility of commerce on the Cape Fear River. He spent months exploring the region, often with only a servant to accompany him and limited supplies—a single biscuit in one three-day period, for example. He measured the depth of the river, determined where the channel flowed, and explored some of its tributaries.

After Burrington had been on the scene only a short time, unsubstantiated rumours about him arose. It was reported that he had been imprisoned in England for beating an old woman. Soon a quarrel between Chief Justice Christopher Gale and the governor became so violent that, it was said, Burrington attempted to blow up Gale's house. It is not clear who stepped in to stop such careless talk, but Burrington was removed from office before 7 April 1725. Since he had many loyal supporters in North Carolina, he stayed a while longer and even represented Chowan county in the assembly for two sessions (1–2 November 1725 and again 5–13 April 1726) while Sir Richard Everard was governor. It may be impossible ever to understand the charges and denials concerning Burrington, but he apparently was temperamental on occasion and kind-hearted on others.

In 1729 the crown purchased the proprietors' interest in Carolina and on 15 January 1730, to the satisfaction of many, Burrington was again appointed governor—this time by the crown. He took office on 25 February 1731 and remained in office until November 1734. At the request of the new governor, Mrs Edmund Porter lent her chaise and the use of a servant 'to fetch his big bell[i]ed wife (as he termed her) out of Virginia'. Neither the wife nor the expected child is further identified.

During the sixteen months of his first term Burrington had taken the initiative, contrary to instructions from London, and began issuing warrants for the occupation of land in the Lower Cape Fear region in expectation that formal grants would soon be authorized. He pursued this policy in his second administration and was responsible for the opening of a road from the Albemarle region in the northern part of the province to Cape Fear in the south. As newcomers settled in communities it was Burrington's practice to visit them and enquire after their welfare. He often distributed his personal resources among them, even to the extent of denying himself to the point of poverty. He inspected new roads and bridges to determine that they were adequate and safe. His appreciation for the potential of the region that he knew so well was great and may have been the source of envy among those who wanted to benefit personally from the land. Burrington was hard on his old enemies, purging them from office and packing in his own supporters. Following the orders of the Board of Trade he pressed the colony's assembly to require registration of previously claimed land so that quitrents could be collected. When it refused, Burrington gained further enemies when he threatened to implement stricter rules for obtaining land. Complaints about the governor multiplied and his successor was appointed in 1734.

Formal letters and reports sent by Burrington to his superiors in England were informative and well written as were three publications by him. In 1743 he wrote on the possibility of war with France in America. A contribution by him to the *Gentleman's Magazine* in 1745 offered advice on the defence of the Carolina region in case a threatened French invasion materialized. Both reflect his earlier military activity. In 1757 a discourse on the population of London contained observations on birth control, employment opportunities, and resettlement of the population that would have been understood in the twentieth century.

Burrington's body was found on 22 February 1759 in a canal near Birdcage Walk in St James's Park in London. He was elegantly dressed, firmly holding his walking cane, and there was evidence of a struggle, implying murder. He had been robbed, as his pockets were turned inside out. His will, dated 8 December 1750 in the parish of St Martin Ludgate, London, left all his property in North Carolina and all other real estate and personal property in America and England to his twelve-year-old son George, 'who lives with me'. By 23 March 1759, when administration of his estate was granted, his residence had changed to the parish of St John the Evangelist, Westminster. As Burrington suggested in his will, Paul Whitehead (noted poet and satirist of London) was named guardian of George. On 14 May 1762 when his ward was about twenty-four and an officer in the army, Whitehead relinquished his role to Frederick Gregg of Wilmington, North Carolina, whose primary duty was to assist with management of the property in America. Stag Park, Burrington's estate in North Carolina, was sold soon afterwards.	WILLIAM S. POWELL

Sources R. J. Cain, ed., *The Church of England in North Carolina: documents, 1699–1741* (Raleigh, NC, 1999) · *CSP col.*, vols. 33–4, 36–8, 41–2 · J. L. Cheney, ed., *North Carolina government, 1585–1979: a narrative and statistical history*, 2nd edn (1981) · A. R. Ekirch, 'Poor Carolina': politics and society in colonial North Carolina, 1729–1776 (1981) · 'Ex-governor George Burrington's attack on Governor Richard Everard and others in Edenton, North Carolina, 1725', *North Carolina Historical and Genealogical Register*, 3 (1903), 229–37 · H. P. R. Finberg, 'Childe's tomb', *Report and Transactions of the Devonshire Association*, 78 (1946), 265–80, esp. 279 · *GM*, 1st ser., 15 (1745), 29–31 · M. D. Haywood, *Governor George Burrington, with an account of his official administration* (1896) · J. A. Henretta, *Salutary neglect: colonial administration under the duke of Newcastle* (1972) · L. Lee, *The Lower Cape Fear in colonial days* (1965) · W. S. Price, 'A strange incident in George Burrington's royal governorship', *North Carolina Historical Review*, 51 (1974), 149–58 · B. P. Robinson, *The five royal governors of North Carolina, 1729–1775* (1963) · W. L. Saunders and W. Clark, eds., *The colonial records of North Carolina*, 30 vols. (1886–1907), vols. 2–3 · J. Sprunt, *Chronicles of the Cape Fear River*, 2nd edn (1916)
Wealth at death substantial lands in North Carolina

Burrough, Edward (1633–1663), Quaker activist and writer, was born at Underbarrow, near Kendal, on 1 March 1633 and baptized in Kendal on 3 March, the son of James Burrough (d. 1658), a farmer from Underbarrow. Nothing is known of his mother, except that she died in 1658, or of his other siblings. Of Burrough's family, Francis Howgill stated, '[they were] honest parents who had a good report among their neighbours for [their] upright and honest dealing' (Howgill, 4). The family were conventionally religious, and appear to have brought up Burrough to follow the established religion. The Burroughs' godliness encompassed prayer, reading of the scripture, hearing sermons, and singing hymns—practices Burrough later described somewhat indifferently as the 'Customes and Traditions of this Nation' (*A True Description of my Manners of Life*, 1663, 1). Indeed, Burrough's religious enquiries would progressively separate him from the religion of his childhood. Between the ages of twelve and sixteen, Burrough began travelling throughout Westmorland to hear presbyterian speakers. Yet this religious search produced a greater sense of isolation—both from God and from his friends.

He was proud, he remembered in a 1654 account of his early life, separated from the 'vain waies of the world', and consequently became an object of ridicule: 'some of my former acquaintance began to scorn me, calling me a Round-head', he recalled (*A Warning … to the Inhabitants of Underbarrow*, 1654, 32, 31). This severance from the world of his childhood only increased when, in 1652, hearing George Fox speak, Burrough became a Quaker. His parents disowned him and the relationship may still have been strained at the time of their deaths in 1658, since there is no love lost in Edward's terse observation that 'the old man and old woman […] according to the flesh, is both departed' (Brockbank, 132).

By the time of his parents' death, Burrough's ministry had been established throughout England, Ireland, Scotland, and, most concentratedly, London. *First Publishers of Truth* shows his effect on Quaker communities in the north—for instance Cheshire and Durham—and gives an indication of Londoners' first impressions of the 'plaine north cuntry plow men' who evangelized in the capital from 1654 onwards (Penney, 16, 89–90, 163). William Crouch remembers Burrough and his close companion Francis Howgill as 'the Apostles of this City in their Day', and it seems that their apostleship was based partly on the successful conversion of many to Quakerism, as well as the management of the movement in this turbulent city which in 1655 became the centre for the enthusiastic and irreverent followers of the Quaker James Nayler (Crouch, 16). Burrough and Howgill spent the winter of 1655–6 in Ireland, making friends of people such as John Perrot, and an enemy of Henry Cromwell, who imprisoned and then banished them. Cromwell considered the Quakers his 'most considerable enemy', but on their return to the divided Quaker community in London, Burrough and Howgill found that their enemy was within (Kilroy, 85). Both Burrough and Howgill were involved in the disciplining of James Nayler and his followers—though their actions were as nothing in comparison to the state's punitive response to the charges against Nayler for blasphemy later in 1656.

Nayler had been the Quakers' most prolific writer until 1656, but his abeyance was Burrough's rise; the latter became their leading publicist by 1659. Despite being a man of 'no great learning', Burrough had read the Bible conscientiously as a youth, and his work is saturated with biblical knowledge (*A Testimony Against a Great Idolatry*, 1658, 10). Indeed, a nice vignette of Burrough preaching to London audiences describes him standing 'upon a Bench, with his *Bible* in his Hand … speaking to the People with great Authority' (Crouch, 26). Burrough's writing did elicit the unwanted attention of the licensing authorities for some passages that had caused offence, and the publisher, Giles Calvert, was called to account. Perhaps the two unprinted broadsides of 1659 by Burrough were also thought too confrontational to publish. However, it would seem that Burrough was generally able to use his position in London to publish widely.

Burrough's personal sufferings were few, at least in comparison to those of other Friends. Beaten by a mob in

Durham (1653), and banished from Bristol (1654), Ireland (1656), and Dunkirk (1659), he endured his most extended imprisonment during the Commonwealth in Kingston upon Thames. *A Short Account of the Unjust Proceedings* (1658), written from gaol in Kingston, describes how his refusal to swear the oath of abjuration led to his being fined £100—though a technical flaw in the case against him meant that he escaped payment, and he was released after seven months. Burrough was not one to accept the strictures of others, as evidenced by his return to Ireland between late 1660 and February 1661.

Burrough's Quakerism was of a particularly confrontational kind; indeed he is described on the title-page of the posthumously published works as a 'son of Thunder and Consolation'. The thunder was directed mostly at those Quaker enemies whom Burrough regarded as ungodly, including John Bunyan and Richard Baxter, the 1650s parliaments, the army, and (after the restoration of monarchy) Charles II. Bunyan is characterized as an iniquitous sinner, whose arguments reveal only envy and confusion, while Baxter, whom Burrough engaged with in 1657, was equally derided. Far less capable opponents were also given short shrift: ministering in Durham, Burrough declared to the local priest that 'he [Burrough] was a messinger sent from ye Lord to declare unto him yt he was one yt God never sent' (Penney, 90). Burrough's religious certainty also made him critical of parliament and king alike. In *A Message to the Present Rulers of England* (1659), for instance, he told the army's leaders that if they continued in their treachery, God would judge them. His impolitic statements to Charles II include the observation that the parliamentarians had been raised by God, who was 'clearly on their side', to judge 'your iniquities, which were many and great against God' (*A Presentation of Wholesome Informations*, 1660, sig. Bv). Burrough was no obsequious opponent; he had been too young to fight in the civil wars, yet for him the battle continued.

Burrough's theological messages were often bombastic denunciations of corruption and vice. His sense of the inherent sinfulness of humankind made him visualize the 1650s as a time of cosmic struggle, and the language he used retained traces of his earlier Calvinism. Having criticized just about everyone in *A Trumpet of the Lord* (1654), Burrough advised the 'elect and chosen' to 'tread down the fenced Cities, and enlarge your Dominion' (p. 37). Casting off sin did not have merely personal implications: it would change society as a whole. In Burrough's view, the providential God was giving power to his saints to 'bind Kings in chains and Nobles in fetters of iron, ... to execute upon the heathen all the judgements written' (*The Wofull Cry*, 1657, 18). Indeed, his work often seems to assume an inbuilt resistance to God in human nature. He was a 'breaker of stony hearts', one writer observed, when retelling a particularly colourful incident when Burrough, coming across a wrestling match, stepped into the ring and 'fought against spiritual wickedness' (Sewell, 1.105). According to the millenarian position that Burrough occupied, the rule of God had overthrown the vices associated with the whore of Babylon, and his language

here is, at a literal level, often highly misogynistic. As one of the leading spokesmen for Quaker faith and politics, he also wrote one of the most comprehensive accounts of their theology in *A Declaration of All the World of our Faith* (1659). In reality, though, Burrough was looking for a new earth as well as a new heaven.

The Restoration was a dangerous time for radicals, whose position was particularly unstable after the 1661 Fifth Monarchy uprising. Burrough attempted to define the Quakers in terms that offered the authorities some comfort, but he never retreated from the idea that he owed loyalty not to temporal powers but to God. Even when addressing Charles II directly in an appeal for clemency towards Quakers in New England, Burrough could not fully mask his objection to secular authority: 'we are not Enemies to Government itself ... but it is *our Principle*, ... and is *our Practice* to be subject to whatsoever Government is set up over us, either by doing or suffering' (*A Declaration of the Sad and Great Martyrdom*, 1661, 7–8). Though the Quakers more generally embraced peaceful measures in the Restoration period, Burrough's work seems charged with a militaristic sense of spiritual battle. Quaker legend has it that Burrough sought his final arrest: allegedly he intended, on his return to London from Bristol, to 'lay down my Life for ... Truth' (Howgill, 11). Burrough was duly taken while attending a Quaker meeting at their headquarters, the Bull and Mouth, London, on 1 June 1661. Rosemary Moore argues that the authorities considered him too dangerous to be set free and, though a special order was signed for his release, Burrough was to die, unmarried, in Newgate prison on 14 February 1663 aged twenty-nine, and was buried at Bunhill Fields. The administration of the estate of an Edward Burrowes of London was granted on 10 July.

By the time of Burrough's death, this 'son of Thunder and Consolation' had indeed delivered both words of condemnation to the unjust, and encouragement to the 'seed' of God. His great friend Francis Howgill wrote of the companionship they had shared, observing that they were 'bound up in unity and peace' (Howgill, 8). Though Howgill was several years Burrough's senior, the authoritative style of Burrough's writing and leadership led to the observation that his 'knowledge and understanding did far exceed his years' (ibid., 4). Less hagiographic was Thomas Ellwood's impression of a 'brisk young man of ready tongue', which probably comes near the mark (Ellwood, 26). Burrough was a prolific writer, a powerful preacher, and, in Crouch's view, a man of 'Undaunted Courage' (Crouch, 26). Burrough saw God working in England to bring in a new era: the millenarian dream was, for Burrough, both personal and political: 'the old is done away, and a new heart given, and all things are become new' (*A Standard Lifted Up*, 1657, 24).   CATIE GILL

Sources E. Backhouse and T. Backhouse, *Biographical memoirs* (1854) • J. Besse, *A collection of the sufferings of the people called Quakers*, 2 vols. (1753) • W. C. Braithwaite, *The beginnings of Quakerism*, ed. H. J. Cadbury, 2nd edn (1955); repr. (1981) • E. Brockbank, *Edward Burrough: a wrestler for the truth, 1634–1662* (1949) • W. Crouch, *Posthuma Christiana* (1712) • 'Dictionary of Quaker biography', RS Friends, Lond. [card index] • T. Ellwood, *The history of the life of Thomas*

Ellwood, ed. J. Wyeth, 6th edn (1855) [incl. suppl.] • P. Kilroy, *Protestant dissent and controversy in Ireland, 1660–1714* (Cork, 1994) • R. Moore, *The light in their consciences: the early Quakers in Britain, 1646–1666* (University Park, Pennsylvania, 2000) • N. Penney, ed., *First publishers of truth* (1907) • *The journal of George Fox*, ed. N. Penney, 2 vols. (1911) • B. Reay, 'The Quakers and 1659: two newly discovered broadsides by Edward Burrough', *Journal of the Friends' Historical Society*, 54 (1976–82), 101–11 • W. Sewell, *The history of the rise … of the Christian people called Quakers*, 2 vols. (1834) • J. Smith, *A descriptive catalogue of Friends' books*, 2 vols. (1867) • F. H. [F. Howgill], *A testimony concerning the life, death, travels, and labours of Edward Burrough* (1663) • administration, PRO, PROB 6/38, fol. 78r

Archives RS Friends, Lond., letters and papers | RS Friends, Lond., Swarthmore MSS

Burrough, Sir Harold Martin (1888–1977), naval officer, was born at the rectory, Eaton Bishop, Herefordshire, on 4 July 1888, the ninth son of the Revd Charles Burrough, rector of Eaton Bishop, and his wife, Georgina Long. He entered HMS *Britannia* as a naval cadet in 1903 and went to sea in 1904 in HMS *Good Hope*. He specialized in gunnery in 1912. He served in seagoing ships throughout the First World War. At the battle of Jutland in 1916 he was gunnery officer of the cruiser *Southampton*. In 1914 Burrough married Nellie Wills (d. 1972), daughter of C. W. Outhit of Halifax, Nova Scotia; they had three daughters and two sons.

Promoted to commander in 1922, Burrough served in the Chatham gunnery school, the Admiralty and HMS *Barham*, a battleship of the Mediterranean Fleet. He was promoted to captain in 1928 and in that rank commanded the cruiser *London*, the tactical school at Portsmouth, the fifth destroyer flotilla, and HMS *Excellent*, the Royal Navy's gunnery school. In both seagoing commands he was occupied in protecting British and humanitarian interests, during a revolution in Madeira and the Spanish Civil War respectively. On the outbreak of the Second World War Burrough, newly promoted to rear-admiral, was assistant chief of naval staff (trade). In April 1940 he was appointed to command the 10th cruiser squadron. This exacting appointment ranged widely in both role and location. The main task of the squadron and its attached destroyers was the escort of convoys threatened with air attack. This duty was necessary not only for convoys to Malta but, from mid-1941, to Russia also.

Burrough's first Malta convoy, Operation Halberd, was in September 1941. The very strong main escort turned back for Gibraltar, as planned, on approaching the Sicilian narrows, leaving Burrough's force to see the twelve merchant ships through to Malta. This was accomplished with the loss of only one ship. Returning to northern waters, Burrough's force escorted an early Arctic convoy, PQ 3, to Murmansk in November 1941. He spent several weeks in Russia, establishing good relations with the Soviet navy and carrying out with them a bombardment of Vardo, before escorting the return convoy QP 3. On 27 December, after careful planning, Burrough executed a copybook raid on the German-occupied island of Vaagso. 16,000 tons of shipping and many shore installations were destroyed by the joint naval, army, and air forces, and some 100 prisoners taken. Burrough was awarded the DSO for his leadership in this operation.

Further Arctic convoy operations followed in February and March 1942. By now highly experienced in this field, Burrough was able to advise higher authority on improvements and these bore fruit in the later convoys PQ 15 and 16. These, though heavily opposed, got most of their ships through. His greatest test now arrived, in the Mediterranean operation Pedestal in August 1942. This critical convoy, on which Malta's survival depended, was very heavily opposed by submarine, air, and light surface forces. Burrough's through escort suffered greatly, as did the escorted merchantmen, but through prodigious efforts five ships of the convoy reached Malta. Later that year Burrough was created KBE for his 'bravery and dauntless resolution'.

Some months later Burrough was in charge of operations at Algiers during the north Africa landings, and received a bar to his DSO for this service. In 1943 and 1944 he was flag officer, Gibraltar and Mediterranean approaches, but was recalled in January 1945 to be allied naval commander, expeditionary force, in place of Sir Bertram Ramsay who had died in an air crash. For the last few months of the war, therefore, Burrough was responsible for the sea supply of allied forces in Europe. After the armistice he became flag officer, Germany, and in 1946 commander-in-chief, the Nore. He retired in 1949, being created GCB that year. A committed Christian, he remained active in local and church affairs in Hampshire for many years. He died on 22 October 1977 from pneumonia at the Moorhouse Nursing Home, Hindhead, Surrey.

RICHARD HILL

Sources private information (2004) • H. M. Burrough, 'A parson's son', private autobiography, c.1970 • *The Times* (25 Oct 1977) • *WWW*, 1981–90 • record of service supplied by the naval secretary, Ministry of Defence • S. W. Roskill, *The war at sea, 1939–1945*, 1 (1954), 492, 513–14; 2 (1956), 218–33, 302–8; 3/1 (1960), 267–72 • P. C. Smith, *Pedestal: the Malta convoy of August 1942* (1970) • b. cert. • d. cert. • *CGPLA Eng. & Wales* (1978)
Archives IWM, papers relating to the battle of Jutland and the Second World War [microfilm] | FILM BFI NFTVA, news footage • IWM FVA, actuality footage • IWM FVA, news footage | SOUND IWM SA, oral history interview
Wealth at death £17,751: probate, 14 Feb 1978, *CGPLA Eng. & Wales*

Burrough, Sir James (1691–1764), architect and college head, was born on 1 September 1691, the son of Dr James Burrough, a physician at Bury St Edmunds, Suffolk, and his wife, Amy. He was educated from 1700 at Bury grammar school, and in March 1708 entered Gonville and Caius College, Cambridge, where he proceeded MA in 1716; he became a senior fellow in 1719, and one of the esquire bedells of the university in 1727. As a tutor and president of Caius for many years, he had already played a central role in the educational and administrative life of the college before his appointment as master in 1754.

Burrough was closely associated with the creation of the Senate House at Cambridge, originally intended to be one element in a more ambitious forum of university buildings. His design for the Senate House was sent to the architect James Gibbs, whose own executed design was said to be partially based on it. A member of the syndicate responsible for its erection, Burrough supervised its construction in 1722–30. Its high-quality carved woodwork was the work of James Essex the elder, a Cambridge joiner, whose son became an architect and was much indebted to Burrough for his promotion in Cambridge.

In 1752 Burrough made a design for rebuilding the east front of the university library adjacent to the Senate House. However, the chancellor, the duke of Newcastle, had his own architect, Stephen Wright. By promising the syndics £500 towards the execution of Wright's design, Newcastle persuaded them to adopt it rather than Burrough's design. The controversy had political as well as architectural dimensions, for the duke was a whig and Burrough a tory. Some considered that the duke's successful petition for Burrough to be knighted in 1759 was in partial compensation for the rejection of his designs for the library.

The loss of this commission did not affect Burrough's standing as an architectural adviser in Cambridge, where his finest executed designs are Burrough's Building at Peterhouse and the chapel at Clare College. The former is a handsome block of fellows' chambers, designed in 1736 and built in 1738–42, an elegant echo of Palladio's Palazzo Iseppo Porto in Vicenza. For this work he was rewarded with £50 and a piece of plate. The chapel at Clare, begun in 1763 and completed by James Essex in 1764–9 after Burrough's death, has a more neo-classical flavour than Burrough's earlier work, which veered between Palladianism and Gibbsian baroque: a dark passage leads dramatically into the top-lit, octagonal, ante-chapel, with a coffered dome and lantern. The chapel proper, a monument to the Age of Reason, is flooded with light from five large windows on each side. The plasterwork, masonry, and woodwork, including the stalls, are all of the high quality associated with the Essex family firm.

Less successful was Burrough's treatment of the decaying medieval façades of several colleges, including Trinity Hall in 1742–5, his own college in 1751–4, and Peterhouse in 1754–6. These he refaced with neat ashlar and small Georgian sash windows, thus justifying Pevsner's claim that Trinity Hall, after Burrough's attentions, 'is comfortable and a little phlegmatic, an excellent visual representation of what the University then was' (Pevsner, *Cambridgeshire*, 179). He also prepared schemes for largely rebuilding Trinity Hall and Peterhouse in unadventurous Palladian styles, the former engraved for him by James Essex. However, his internal classicizing of the halls at Queens' College (1732–4), for which he was paid 25 guineas, at Trinity Hall (1742–5), and at Sidney Sussex (1749–52), was considerably livelier.

Consulted about most of the architectural changes, both large and small, which were made in Cambridge in his lifetime, he was also asked to advise on projects outside the university, including the erection of a new bridge at Wisbech in 1757. He designed a classical altarpiece for Canterbury Cathedral in 1733 (removed 1820), the manor house (now the museum) at Bury St Edmunds for the countess of Bristol in 1736–8, and interiors in the assembly rooms at Norwich built by Thomas Ivory in 1754.

A genial figure, corpulent through not taking exercise, Burrough seems to have been universally popular. Elected a fellow of the Society of Antiquaries in 1740, he was an enthusiastic collector of prints, pictures, and books, as well as of Greek and Roman coins and medals, which he left to his college. He was a friend of the antiquaries and architects who, by the 1760s, made Cambridge a centre of architectural scholarship, notably William Cole, Thomas Gray, William Mason, and James Essex. He died unmarried at Caius on 7 August 1764 and was buried in the ante-chapel of his college on 10 August.   DAVID WATKIN

Sources J. Venn and others, eds., *Biographical history of Gonville and Caius College*, 3: *Biographies of the successive masters* (1901) · R. Willis, *The architectural history of the University of Cambridge, and of the colleges of Cambridge and Eton*, ed. J. W. Clark, 3 (1886), 43–70, 536–40 · C. N. L. Brooke, *A history of Gonville and Caius College* (1985) · T. Cocke, ed., *The ingenious Mr Essex, architect, 1722–1784* (1984) [exhibition catalogue, Fitzwilliam Museum, Cambridge, 17 July – 2 Sep 1984] · *DNB* · *IGI*

Archives BL, corresp. with duke of Newcastle, Add. MSS 32898–32912 · Bury St Edmunds Cathedral Library, Collectanea Buriensia

Likenesses attrib. D. Heins, oils, Gon. & Caius Cam.

Burrough, Sir James (1749–1837), judge, was born in August 1749 at Abbotts Ann in Hampshire, the seventh child of the Revd John Burrough and his wife, Sarah. He was admitted into the Inner Temple in February 1768, and was called to the bar in November 1773, after practising for some time as a special pleader. After his call he attended the Hampshire sessions and the western circuit, where he acquired a good practice. His profits at a single sessions often exceeded 100 guineas. In 1792 he was made a commissioner of bankrupts; such was his skill in that position that he was frequently consulted on practical points by Lord Eldon when lord chancellor. In 1794 he was appointed deputy recorder in Salisbury, and was subsequently made recorder of Portsmouth. In 1808 he was elected a bencher of his inn. Burrough married at some point before May 1785, and he and his wife, Anne, had four children.

In May 1816 Burrough was appointed a judge of the common pleas, when Charles Abbott was removed into the king's bench. Abbott always believed that the sole reason for his removal was because Eldon wished to make a judge of Burrough, who—in part because of his age—would not pass muster in the king's bench. He was knighted when appointed to the bench. As a judge, Burrough was noted for his unpretentious manner: it was said that on his elevation he made it a formal request to the bar not to call him Jemmy in court. He had the facility for explaining legal ideas in simple language to a jury, as well as a memorable turn of phrase when elaborating the law. It was Burrough who famously observed, when arguing for caution in grounding legal arguments on public policy, that 'it is a very unruly horse, and when once you get astride it you never know where it will carry you' (*Richardson* v. *Mellish*, 1824). His down-to-earth common sense manifested

Sir James Burrough (1749–1837), by Thomas Goff Lupton (after Thomas Phillips, 1826)

itself in another case, when counsel attempted to question the validity of an indenture on the grounds that the paper on which it was written had not been cut at the top: Burrough asked to look at the deed, took scissors out of his pocket, cut a zigzagged line on the deed, and returned it, pronouncing it valid. Though appointed late in life, Burrough stayed long on the bench, retiring only in January 1830. He remained popular with the bar, but it was felt that he had stayed too long. By then, he had begun to suffer seizures in court, and there was a general view that 'he is wholly incompetent, for he has neither Eyes or Ears or Voice' (Hobhouse to Peel, Peel papers, BL, Add. MS 40399, fol. 309). Burrough died on 25 March 1837 at his London home, 16 Bedford Row, and was buried in the Temple Church. His only surviving daughter, Anne, erected a monument to his memory in the church of Laverstock, Wiltshire. MICHAEL LOBBAN

Sources Foss, *Judges*, vol. 9 · John, Lord Campbell, *The lives of the chief justices of England*, 3 (1857) · *Law Magazine*, 3 (1830), 299 · *Legal Observer*, 13 (1836–7), 450 · *The Times* (28 Sept 1826) · F. A. Inderwick and R. A. Roberts, eds., *A calendar of the Inner Temple records*, 5 (1936) · Sainty, *Judges* · *GM*, 2nd ser., 8 (1837), 211 · *IGI* · *DNB* · BL, Add. MS 40377 fol. 185
Likenesses T. G. Lupton, mezzotint (after T. Phillips, 1826), BM, NPG [*see illus.*] · monument, Laverstock church, Wiltshire

Burroughes, Jeremiah (*bap.* 1601?, *d.* 1646), Independent minister, was perhaps the son of Francis Borroughe baptized on 10 June 1601 at St Nicholas, Colchester, Essex. In 1617 he was admitted pensioner to Emmanuel College, Cambridge, where he graduated BA in 1621 and proceeded MA in 1624; his tutor was Thomas Hooker. While he was at

university he went to Essex 'on purpose to observe the Ministers in that County' (Mather, 3.46) with Thomas Goodwin and William Bridge, being particularly impressed by John Wilson at Sudbury, just over the border with Suffolk. In the mid-1620s he was among a number of godly ministers who joined in spiritual exercises with Hooker at Chelmsford, Essex. There was an attempt to establish him as minister at Pontisbright, Essex but this failed. In 1627 he became lecturer at Bury St Edmunds, Suffolk, a post for which he was recommended by Hooker and where he assisted Edmund Calamy. He was a very popular preacher, it seems, and thereafter contributed sermons to the combination lectures at Mendlesham, Suffolk, and at St George's Tombland, Norwich. In 1631 he acquired his first benefice, becoming rector of Tivetshall, Norfolk, a post in the gift of Jane, Lady Bacon.

Burroughes came to the attention of the ecclesiastical courts when Matthew Wren became bishop of Norwich in July 1635. Wren's chancellor, Clement Corbett, noted that Burroughes was 'though but young, yet ancient in his nonconformity, & universally followed as a popular Patriarck' (Webster, 211). However, the context of Burroughes's later attestation that he generally conformed early in his career, refusing only the rituals of the new Laudian regime, modifies Corbett's judgement. Burroughes claimed, with some justification, that there was no minister in the diocese 'who was so eyed as I was' (Burroughes, 17). He refused to read the Book of Sports and then, under close observation, refused to read prayers rather than deliver them extempore and to bow at the name of Jesus. Despite the best efforts of his patron, of Henry Rich, earl of Holland, and others to secure his departure without censure, he was suspended in 1636 and deprived in 1637. He then led a fairly peregrine life, being a visiting preacher at Little Leighs, as guest of Robert Rich, earl of Warwick. He came to the attention of the court of high commission in August 1638 following a report of a conversation there in which he seemed to have justified Scottish actions and general resistance to the king. His activities and contacts are difficult to reconstruct in detail. He sheltered Thomas Shepard while he was waiting for a ship to New England and is known to have preached in London. He seems to have made his first visits to the Netherlands; in 1637 he was reported to have been working with William Greenhill smuggling John Bastwick's *Letany* from the Netherlands. Both deprived ministers were disguised as soldiers.

Dutch contacts became formalized when Burroughes received a call in January 1639 to join the English Reformed church in Rotterdam as teacher. This was probably the crucial element which encouraged his migration. Here he joined William Bridge. Sidrach Simpson established a second church in the city. This brought together three future dissenting brethren, the propagandists of congregationalism in the 1640s, although it should be noted that Burroughes was called during a dispute between Bridge and Simpson over clerical authority in the first church. It may have been at this time that his congregational convictions became fine-tuned but his earlier contacts with Hooker and John Cotton should be noted.

Ætatis Suæ. 45.   *June. 1. 1646*

Printed by Pet.ʳ Cole   *In Leaden-Hall*

JEREMIAH BVRROVGHES
Gospell = Preacher
To two of the greatest Congregations in England Viz:
Stepney and Cripplegate London   *Crosse Sculpt:*

Jeremiah Burroughes (*bap.* 1601?, *d.* 1646), by Thomas Cross, 1646

Indeed, of all the dissenting brethren, Burroughes seemed closest to the presbyterians, taking his moderate model from the Massachusetts and Connecticut practices of Congregationalism.

Burroughes returned to England in the winter of 1640 and immediately started working for godly reform. His goals were dual. He wanted to keep the disparate puritan parties presenting a united face to their adversaries and to keep parliamentary attention on religious reform. The latter was an important element in the sermons he preached to the houses of parliament at their fasts. The former is present in a cross-party response to a pro-episcopacy petition which he co-authored with Thomas Goodwin and Alexander Henderson. This ethos was formalized in a meeting at Edmund Calamy's house in November 1641 and was still present when Burroughes signed an attempt to dissuade people from establishing new gathered churches in 1643. It was the dominant theme in one of his last works, *Irenicum* (1646), which called for a toleration, albeit a limited one. A great deal of his time, however, was still spent on practical divinity. He was welcomed to pulpits across London but was best-known as the lecturer of Stepney, where he delivered the morning sermons at 7 a.m. in tandem with Greenhill's preaching at 3 p.m.

Burroughes is remembered for his activity in the Westminster assembly of divines. Throughout he walked the difficult line of promoting the congregational cause of the dissenting brethren while maintaining accommodation with the more moderate presbyterians. In November 1643 he reassured his colleagues that he recognized the Church of England as a true church on the grounds that its members included members of the elect, a very traditional line, but he also worked hard to limit the powers of the classis beyond the particular church. However, this produced a constant strain. Things came to a head in January 1644 when he co-authored *An Apologeticall Narration*, a short and careful account under the names of Burroughes, Goodwin, Simpson, Bridge, and Philip Nye. From that point he was an important figure in the assembly, using frustrating delaying tactics, recognizing that the interests of the congregationalists were best served by the growing influence of the army and their allies in the parliament, allowing a greater emphasis on their Erastianism, and slowly turning the assembly's blueprint for presbyterianism into a dead letter. He received acerbic criticism from Thomas Edwards, responding with his *A Vindication of Mr Burroughes Against Mr Edwards* (1646) setting out his experience and giving the clearest definition of the congregational order that he and his like-minded colleagues published.

Early in November 1646 Burroughes fell from his horse. The resulting bruise seems to have become infected, and he died in London on or about 13 November 1646. His long-term reputation as a writer of practical divinity was ensured by the efforts of his friends to publish many of his sermons and they continued to appear towards the end of the century. He is particularly known by Richard Baxter's aphorism that accommodation could have been reached if all the episcopalians had been like James Ussher, all the presbyterians like Stephen Marshall, and all the congregationalists like Burroughes and by the Latin phrase said to be over his study door which translates as 'Variety of opinions and unity of opinion are not incompatible.'

TOM WEBSTER

Sources J. Burroughes, *A vindication of Mr Burroughes against Mr Edwards* (1646) · R. S. Paul, *The assembly of the Lord: politics and religion in the Westminster assembly and the 'Grand debate'* (1985) · T. Webster, *Godly clergy in early Stuart England: the Caroline puritan movement, c.1620–1643* (1997) · K. Sprunger, *Dutch puritanism* (1982) · J. Reid, *Memoirs of the Westminster divines*, 2 vols. (1811) · C. Mather, *Magnalia Christi Americana*, 3 vols. (1704) · Tai Liu, *Discord in Zion: the puritan divines and the puritan revolution, 1640–1660* (1973) · J. Browne, *A history of Congregationalism and memorials of the churches in Norfolk and Suffolk* (1877) · IGI
Likenesses T. Cross, engraving, 1646, NPG [*see illus.*]

Burroughs, Sir Frederick William Traill- (1831–1905), army officer, was born on 1 February 1831, the eldest of the seven children of Major-General Frederick William Burroughs (*d.* 1879) of the Bengal army. His grandfather, Sir William Burroughs of Castle Bagshaw, co. Cavan, was advocate-general of Bengal under Marquess Cornwallis. His mother, Caroline (*d.* 1863), only daughter of Captain Charles Adolphus Marie de Peyron of the Bengal light cavalry, was granddaughter of Chevalier Charles Adrien de

Peyron, who was killed in a duel in Paris in 1777 by the Comte de la Marck.

After education at Kensington grammar school, at Blackheath proprietary school, and at Hofwyl in Switzerland, Burroughs was commissioned ensign in the 93rd highlanders on 31 March 1848. Promoted lieutenant on 23rd September 1851, he became captain on 10 November 1854 and major on 20 July 1858. On his twenty-first birthday, in 1852, Burroughs succeeded to the Scottish estates of his grand-uncle, George William Traill of Viera, Orkney, and assumed the surname of Traill-Burroughs. He served with the 93rd under Sir Colin Campbell throughout the Crimean War, and was at the battle of the Alma and at Balaklava, when he commanded the left centre company of his regiment, the 'thin red line'. Traill-Burroughs took part in the expedition to Kerch and Yenikale, the siege and fall of Sevastopol, and assaults of 18 June and 8 September. He was awarded the Mejidiye (fifth class).

During the Indian mutiny Traill-Burroughs was engaged again under Campbell, now Lord Clyde, in the fighting before the relief of Lucknow and in the storming of the *sikandarabagh* and of the Shah Najaf mosque (both outer defences of Lucknow). He was the first through the breach at the *sikandarabagh*, and with some dozen men overpowered the gate guard. For this action, in which he received a slight wound, he was recommended for, though not awarded, the Victoria Cross. For his conduct at the battle of Cawnpore on 6 December, and the pursuit to Serai Ghat at the action of Khudaganj, the storming of the Begfam Kuthi, and the siege and capture of Lucknow, he was mentioned in dispatches, and received a brevet majority (29 July 1858). The wounds he received during the mutiny campaign disabled him for two years, and it was not until 1860 that he rejoined his regiment. In 1862 he succeeded to the temporary command of the 93rd highlanders, which had lost two commanding officers from cholera.

Traill-Burroughs accompanied the Yusufzai field force, under Sir Neville Chamberlain, in the campaign against the Hindustani fanatics and other groups on the north-west frontier in December 1863, commanded the 93rd in the action at Ambela, and was mentioned in dispatches (1864).

Promoted lieutenant-colonel on 10 August 1864, Traill-Burroughs became full colonel on 10 August 1869. On 4 June 1870 he married Eliza D'Oyly, youngest daughter of Colonel William Geddes, Bengal horse artillery, JP and deputy lieutenant of Midlothian (d. 1879), and Emma, daughter of Edward D'Oyly of Zion Hill, Yorkshire; they had no children. Retiring from the command of the 93rd highlanders in 1873, he was promoted major-general on 16 March 1880 and lieutenant-general (retired list) on 1 July 1881. He commanded the Orkney volunteer artillery, 1873–80. In 1904 he was transferred from the colonelcy of the Royal Warwickshire regiment, which he had held since 1897, to that of the Argyll and Sutherland Highlanders. He was appointed CB on 24 May 1873 and KCB in 1904. He owned about 12,000 acres; his seat was Trumland

House, island of Rousay, Orkney, and he was vice-lieutenant of Orkney and Shetland. He died at 61 St George's Road, London, on 9 April 1905 and was buried at Brompton cemetery.   H. M. VIBART, *rev.* JAMES LUNT

Sources *Army List* · *Hart's Army List* · Burke, *Gen. GB* · Walford, *County families* · *The Thin Red Line* [regimental journal of the 93rd Sutherland highlanders] (May 1905) · J. P. Groves, *History of the 93rd Sutherland highlanders* (1895) · W. Munro, *Reminiscences of service with the 93rd Sutherland highlanders* (1883) · J. W. Kaye and G. B. Malleson, *Kaye's and Malleson's History of the Indian mutiny of 1857–8*, 4 (1889), 129 · W. H. Paget, *A record of the expeditions against the north-west frontier tribes, since the annexation of the Punjab*, rev. A. H. Mason (1884) · M. Barthorp, *The north-west frontier: British India and Afghanistan, a pictorial history, 1839–1947* (1982) · A. W. Kinglake, *The invasion of the Crimea*, [new edn], 9 vols. (1877–88) · *WWW*

Archives Argyll and Sutherland Highlanders Regimental Museum, Stirling Castle, reminiscences, 1857; narrative of the relief of Lucknow · NL Scot., corresp.; Indian mutiny journal · Orkney Archives, family and estate papers

Wealth at death £1750 19s. 10d.: confirmation, 27 Sept 1905, CCI

Burroughs, George (d. 1692). *See under* Salem witches and their accusers (*act.* 1692).

Burroughs, Joseph (1685–1761), Baptist minister, was born in London on 1 January 1685, the son of Humphrey Burroughs, a weaver in Spitalfields. His father was a member of Virginia Street Particular Baptist Church, London, which in 1712 amalgamated with the non-aligned but closed-communion Baptist church in Paul's Alley, Barbican. Joseph was educated at the academy of the Presbyterian minister John Ker (1639–1723) at Highgate, Middlesex, and at the University of Leiden in the Netherlands, where he was admitted in 1708. In 1714 he received a call to become co-pastor with Richard Allen at the Barbican church. He declined the invitation on account of his age and lack of experience in the ministerial office, but agreed to be one of the church's regular preachers. On Allen's death in 1717 he was elected pastor and ordained on 1 May 1717.

During his long Barbican pastorate of forty-four years Burroughs was assisted first by Allen's assistants Nathaniel Foxwell (*fl.* 1700–1721) and John Gale (1680–1721), the renowned defender of believers' baptism contra William Wall; and second, from 1722 to 1724, by Isaac Kimber (1692–1753). For the next twenty years, from 1724 to 1744, James Foster (1697–1753), a celebrated preacher, was his co-pastor until Foster moved to the open-communion Baptist church at Pinners' Hall. After this the afternoon service at the Barbican was given up in favour of the White's Alley General Baptist Church. For the next fourteen years Burroughs shouldered the church duties alone until 1758 when, because of 'various bodily dispositions' (Noble, 36), the church elected Francis Webb first as co-pastor and then as successor. For a short while from 1724 his brother James Burroughs was also an assistant, until his untimely death in 1728.

Burroughs's views of believers' baptism were sufficiently strict to place him with the party of closed communion; but his general sentiments were liberal and progressive. Both he and Foster were non-subscribers at the Salters' Hall synod in 1719. They allowed the anti-Trinitarian

Thomas Emlyn (1663–1741) to occupy the Barbican pulpit, and they established an education fund (1726) (later known as the General Baptist Education Fund) when the Particular Baptist Fund declined to fund Barbican ministry because of the Socinianism of its pastors. Burroughs spoke fluent French and Latin and is known to have preached in both those languages. A number of his sermons were published, including funeral sermons for John Gale (1722), John Weatherly (1752), and Isaac Kimber (1755); two sermons against popery (both 1735); and a sermon 'occasioned by a total eclipse of the sun, 22 April' (1715). He also exchanged tracts concerning baptism with the paedobaptist Socinian Caleb Fleming (1742–3), and edited volumes of sermons by his brother James (1733) and by Joseph Morris (1753). He was a Salters' Hall lecturer, and 'in the general course of his life was so regularly and uniformly virtuous, as to render him an honour to his profession' (Noble, 30).

Burroughs seems to have been twice married; by April 1735 he was married to his second wife, Ann. He had three daughters, Judith (d. June 1739), June, and Mary, and one son, Joseph (1713/14–1799). Burroughs died in London on 23 November 1761.

ALEXANDER GORDON, rev. ANDREW M. HILL

Sources W. Wilson, *The history and antiquities of the dissenting churches and meeting houses in London, Westminster and Southwark*, 4 vols. (1808–14), vol. 3, pp. 228–60 · D. Noble, *Funeral sermon for Joseph Burroughs* (1761) · T. Crosby, *The history of the English Baptists, from the Reformation to the beginning of the reign of King George I*, 4 vols. (1738–40), vol. 4, pp. 183–9 · E. Peacock, *Index to English speaking students who have graduated at Leyden University* (1883), 16 · H. McLachlan, *English education under the Test Acts: being the history of the nonconformist academies, 1662–1820* (1931), 85–90 · *Paul's Alley church book, 1739–1768*, General Baptist Assembly Occasional Paper, 10 (July 1990)
Likenesses print, DWL

Burroughs, (Silas) Mainville (1846–1895), manufacturing chemist, was born on 24 December 1846, in Medina, New York state, United States of America. His family was influential and wealthy, his father, Silas Mainville Burroughs (1810–1860), being a lawyer and US congressman. His education was in his native state, and an uncle in Medina reportedly instilled business sense in him. After leaving school he worked in New York state, as an apprentice to the merchant store of E. T. Coann in Albion for two years and subsequently for the drug stores of T. J. Chadwick in Lockport and S. H. T. Champlin in Buffalo. About 1873 he was employed by Wyeth & Brother of Philadelphia, and evidently continued to work for them while he studied at the Philadelphia College of Pharmacy, from where he graduated in 1877. His thesis demonstrated his early interest in new methods of producing compressed medicines.

In 1878 Burroughs went to London as Wyeths' European agent, intending to stay for about six months. He soon saw that there was much potential in the pharmaceutical industry overseas, and employed his own capital to establish a company which he intended would become a world trader in supplying pharmaceuticals. In May 1878 S. M. Burroughs & Co. was established, first in Southampton Street, Strand, London, and soon after at 92–3 Great Russell Street and in the basement of 1 Cock Lane in the City. In 1879 the company moved to 8 Snow Hill, Holborn.

Initially Burroughs concentrated on introducing American pharmaceuticals to doctors and dentists in the UK by travelling and advertising and by making contacts with hospitals and pharmacists. He soon realized that he needed a reliable hand to manage the business while he was travelling, and in January 1879 invited Henry Solomon *Wellcome, also a pharmaceutical salesman and some seven years Burroughs's junior, to join him. They probably met in the mid-1870s, although the first existing correspondence dates from 1877. During 1879 Burroughs continued to invite Wellcome, currently working for McKesson and Robbins of New York, to England. 'I think that we can make big fortunes over here if we work things right and we ought to know how to do this with our combined experience' he wrote on 30 August 1879; and again 'You are the only man I want to pull with, and we have confidence in each other's ability and straightforwardness' (20 October 1879). Wellcome arrived in England in April 1880 with agency rights for McKesson and Robbins. Subsequent negotiations by Burroughs with that company led to mutually agreed terms for the articles of partnership between Burroughs and Wellcome to be signed on 27 September for the establishment of Burroughs, Wellcome & Co. Under that deed Burroughs put up £1200 and Wellcome £800 (of which he could contribute only £400, borrowing the rest from Burroughs at 10 per cent annual interest).

From October 1881 to March 1884, Burroughs, carrying quantities of samples, undertook a world tour of Europe, Egypt, India, Ceylon and Burma, Australia, New Zealand, and the US, promoting the firm, establishing new markets, and making valuable contacts which laid the foundation of the company's foreign markets. Early business was mostly derived from its agency sales, but the company started to manufacture certain products near Snow Hill, London, in 1882, and opened manufacturing works in Wandsworth the following year. The range of products expanded and sold well, largely because of the firm's high standard and excellent publicity; it produced medicine chests for prominent figures including W. E. Gladstone and Sir Henry Morton Stanley, the latter of whom was greatly admired by both men. Early in 1884 the firm moved into larger premises on a prominent site at Snow Hill Buildings, Holborn Viaduct, and the same year the company registered the trade mark 'tabloid'.

The first cracks in the friendship between Burroughs and his partner surfaced in 1882, when Burroughs, an impulsive and often imprudent man, requested Wellcome to postpone his rights to increase his capital holding as specified in the partnership agreement. Further differences emerged in correspondence over Burroughs's proposed engagement to Olive Augusta Chase of western New York state, when Burroughs asked if the business prospects were such that they would warrant his marriage and Wellcome advised against a hasty move. Burroughs, however, married Olive in the USA early in 1884, returning with her to London briefly before setting out for a tour of Europe. They had a son and two daughters. Relations between the partners became increasingly strained, but a new partnership was negotiated in May 1885 after which Burroughs returned to the United States for the rest of the year. Further disputes led to litigation in 1887, 1889, and 1891.

In spite of these strains, the company thrived: it ended the agreement with Wyeths and moved its own manufactory to Dartford in 1889. Burroughs purchased the Dartford mills and leased them to the company (the cause of legal wrangles after his death), and played a key part in introducing progressive working conditions. Strongly influenced by Henry George, the proponent of free trade and a single tax on land values, Burroughs publicized and implemented these views, introducing an eight-hour working day and a profit-sharing system, based on a fixed percentage of the profits, and encouraging social activities by the Dartford workers. Burroughs was a staunch Presbyterian, regularly attending lunchtime services at the City Temple, and believing in a society that approached socialist ideals. He wrote a short work called *A Strange Dream*, forecasting an ideal state where the principles of religion were the basis of contracts between capital and labour, and had 60,000 copies of George's *Protection of Free Trade* printed and sent throughout Europe. He was a strong supporter of the cause of international arbitration and peace and of socialist and labour clubs, chaired the Dartford Radical and Liberal Association, was a committee member of the Tenant Tradesmen's National Union, and a member of several political pressure groups including the City Liberal ('a bit stiff'), and the United Democratic clubs. He also believed in free travel and that free railways would be a means of untying the knot of town life. Burroughs's political interests may have been one reason for his taking British nationality in May 1890, it being reported that 'he has now lived so long in this country, is so completely identified with its interests, and takes so deep a concern in its social welfare, that his adoption of its nationality is not to be wondered at' (*Chemist and Druggist*, 17 May 1890).

Burroughs, who was a teetotaller, had a reputation for boundless energy and even his recreation pursuit of cycling made demands on him. His health suffered, possibly as a result of over-zealous work, and in December 1894 he caught a severe cold and was advised by doctors to winter abroad for his health. He travelled to the Riviera and soon recovered from his cold, but on 3 February 1895, while out cycling wearing a thin jacket, he caught a chill which resulted in pleurisy and rapidly developed into pneumonia. He died on 6 February at the Hotel Windsor in Monte Carlo with his sister Mrs Riggs beside him, but before his wife, travelling from London, could reach him. He was buried in Monte Carlo two days later. A service was held at Dartford parish church with a special train laid on to bring mourners from London.

Obituaries were unanimous in emphasizing the strong impression Burroughs made on those who met him. He had a handsome, well-dressed appearance, was of moderate height with piercing blue eyes, with an open and lively manner, considerable charm and humour; he was a good speaker, with boundless enthusiasm. He was without affectation or snobbishness and he delighted in mixing with all classes. He was generous to a fault (on his death promissory notes and IOUs in his possession amounted to more than £7000) and notoriously open-handed in supporting individuals and organizations of many different political and religious persuasions. He left one twenty-fourth of his estate to be equally divided among all employees of Burroughs, Wellcome & Co., and made many other charitable legacies. Although negotiations for a dissolution of the partnership were under way when Burroughs died, the agreement with Wellcome still stood and Olive Burroughs was obliged to sell Wellcome her interest in the company.   JULIA SHEPPARD

Sources *Pharmaceutical Era* (14 Feb 1895) · *Pharmaceutical Era* (6 June 1895) · *Chemist and Druggist* (9–16 Feb 1895) · *Chemist and Druggist* (28 Oct 1895) · *British and Colonial Druggist* (8–15 Feb 1895) · J. Davies, 'Silas Burroughs', *Wellcome Journal*, 6 (1991) · correspondence and legal records, Glaxo Wellcome archives, Greenford · A. W. J. Haggis, unpubd biography of Henry Wellcome, Wellcome L., Wellcome archives · R. Rhodes James, *Henry Wellcome* (1994) · G. MacDonald, *In Pursuit of excellence* (1980) · L. G. Matthews, 'Silas M. Burroughs—glimpses of the late partner', *Foundation News*, 30 (1980) · L. G. Matthews, 'Mr Burroughs' reports', *Foundation News*, 13 (1963) · S. M. Burroughs, 'An enlightened policy in Morocco', *Chemist and Druggist* (28 Jan 1893) · *Chemist and Druggist* (17 May 1890), 671

Archives Wellcome L., papers, incl. letter-books and business records

Likenesses photograph, *c.*1880, Wellcome L.; repro. in Rhodes James, *Henry Wellcome* · photographs, 1885–99, Wellcome L. · marble bust, after 1895, Livingstone Memorial Hospital, Dartford, Kent; repro. in MacDonald, *In pursuit of excellence*

Wealth at death £125,926 1s. 9d.: probate, 9 April 1895, CGPLA Eng. & Wales

Burrow, Edward John (1785–1861), Church of England clergyman and author, was born on 29 June 1785 at Sutton, Surrey, the son of Edward Broadley Burrow of Sutton. He was privately educated at Greenwich under Dr Charles Burney, and then went to Magdalene College, Cambridge, graduating BA in 1805 and MA in 1808; he was then incorporated a member of Trinity College, Oxford, and took the degrees of BD and DD in 1820. He was incumbent of Bempton, Yorkshire, 1810–16, and minister of the chapel of ease at Hampstead, 1816–23. From 1823 to 1835 he was domestic chaplain to Sir George Tomline, bishop of Winchester. In July 1827 he accepted the office of principal of Mount Radford College and School, Exeter, and entered on his duties on 29 September. Following a dispute with the owners he resigned or was dismissed from this office (the immediate cause of his leaving depends on the rights of the case) in the following January. In 1835 he went out to Gibraltar as civil chaplain, and was appointed archdeacon of Gibraltar in 1842. He remained there until his health declined, then returned to England and lived at Bath, Lyme Regis, and other places on the south coast.

Burrow was elected FRS in 1818 and was a member of

other learned societies. He published *Elements of Conchology* (1815), *The Elgin Marbles* (1817), with forty plates drawn and etched by himself, and *A letter ... to W. Marsh ... on the nature ... of certain principles ... falsely denominated evangelical* (1819, which reached a third edition in the same year). He followed these with *A Second Letter* (1819, 2 edns) and *A Summary of Christian Faith and Practice* (3 vols., 1822), and published several other works on theology and the Bible. He died at Honiton on 8 August 1861.

WILLIAM HUNT, *rev.* H. C. G. MATTHEW

Sources Venn, *Alum. Cant.* · *GM*, 3rd ser., 11 (1861), 332 · Mount Radford College and School, *A statement of the manner in which ... E. J. Burrow became connected with Mount Radford, and of ... his removal* (1828) · Foster, *Alum. Oxon.* · *CGPLA Eng. & Wales* (1861)
Wealth at death £4000: probate, 22 Aug 1861, *CGPLA Eng. & Wales*

Burrow, Sir James (1701–1782), law reporter, was born on 28 November 1701, the son of Thomas Burrow (*d.* 1724) of Clapham, Surrey. In 1733, at the age of thirty-two, he succeeded to the post of master of the crown office, the reversion to which had been granted to him in 1724, and retained it until his death. In 1724 he was called to the bar at the Inner Temple, was elected a bencher in 1754, became reader in 1763, and treasurer in 1764. He was elected FSA in April 1751, and FRS in April 1737, and was an honorary member of the Société des Antiquités at Kassel. For two short periods he discharged the duties of president of the Royal Society (the first lasting from September to November 1768, the second from July to November 1772), and when the society presented an address to the king on 10 August 1773 Burrow received the honour of knighthood.

Burrow won great renown on account of his merits as a law reporter. His collection, *Reports of cases argued and determined in the court of king's bench during the time of Lord Mansfield's presiding*, covering the years 1756–72, was published in five volumes between 1766 and 1780. In 1773 he turned aside at the request of his friends to publish separately, in anticipation of its inclusion in his general volume of *Reports*, his 'lucid and valuable' narrative, *The question concerning literary property determined by the court of king's bench, 20 April 1769, in the cause between Andrew Millar and Robert Taylor*, a question which dealt with the much-vexed point of the copyright of books. *The decisions of the court of king's bench upon settlement cases from the death of Lord Raymond, March 1732*, was published in three volumes between 1768 and 1776, to the second of which was added a tract entitled 'A few thoughts upon pointing'. This was struck off with a separate title-page in 1768, and was reprinted in an enlarged and improved form in 1771. Burrow was the author, under the thin disguise of A Member of the Royal Society and of the Society of Antiquaries, of a pamphlet called *A few anecdotes and observations relating to Oliver Cromwell and his family ... to rectify several errors ... by Nicolaus Commenus Papadopoli in his 'Historia gymnasii Patavini'* (1763). A tract entitled *Serious reflections on the present state of domestic and foreign affairs. With proposals for a new lottery* (1757) has also been attributed to him. Five papers

Sir James Burrow (1701–1782), by Jean Baptiste van Loo, *c.*1742

on earthquakes were contributed by him to the *Philosophical Transactions* of the Royal Society. Burrow was the owner of Starborough Castle in the parish of Lingfield, Surrey, and he died there on 5 November 1782; he was buried in the chancel of Lingfield church. His epitaph, with unusual frankness, sums up his virtues in the phrase: 'The convivial character was what he chiefly affected, and it was his constant wish to be easy and chearful himself and to see others in a like disposition.'

W. P. COURTNEY, *rev.* DAVID IBBETSON

Sources *GM*, 1st ser., 52 (1782), 551 · F. A. Inderwick and R. A. Roberts, eds., *A calendar of the Inner Temple records*, 4–5 (1933–6) · O. Manning and W. Bray, *The history and antiquities of the county of Surrey*, 2 (1809), 359 · will, PRO, PROB 11/1097, fol. 40 · father's will, PRO, PROB 11/601, fol. 15*v* · patent granting reversion of mastership of crown office, BL, Egerton Charter 8129 · abstract of descent of Starborough, BL, MS Egerton 1967, fol. 97 · sketch of family tree by Burrow, BL, Add. MS 5487, fol. 49*v* · Holdsworth, *Eng. law*, 12.110–112
Likenesses J. B. van Loo, oils, *c.*1742, RS [*see illus.*] · J. Basire, line engraving, 1780 (after J. Devis), BM, NPG · A. Devis, oils, Uppark, West Sussex · oils, law courts, London
Wealth at death see will, PRO, PROB 11/1097, fol. 40

Burrow, Reuben (1747–1792), mathematician and orientalist, was born on 30 December 1747 on a small farm at Hoberly, near Shadwell, 5 miles north-east of Leeds. When he was about twelve the family moved to a larger farm at Roundhay, nearer town. For some ten years from the age of five, Reuben was educated intermittently, between bouts of farm work. Then, interested in mathematics, he attended the Leeds mathematical school of John Crookes (*fl.* 1762–1779), who was, according to a Leeds writer, 'the most famous mathematician in this part of the country'

(J. N., 101). In July 1765 Burrow walked to London to work as a clerk to a timber merchant. A year later he became usher in the Bunhill Row School of Benjamin Webb (*fl.* 1751–1776), a well-known writing master, and soon afterward he left to establish a school of his own in Portsmouth.

This venture probably failed, as in March 1771 Burrow was appointed assistant to Nevil Maskelyne, astronomer royal, at Greenwich. In 1772 Burrow married Anne Purvis (*d. c.*1795), daughter of a poulterer in Leadenhall Street. Finding his pay inadequate, he opened an academy in Park Row, Greenwich, 'for Compting House, University, Army or Navy', but he nevertheless remained in post at the observatory until September 1773. In the following January he agreed to help Maskelyne on the Royal Society's expedition to Schiehallion, Perthshire, to measure the mountain's gravitational attraction, and from early summer to mid-November 1774 Burrow carried out the land surveying to calculate the volume of the mountain and the latitude difference between its two sides. While Maskelyne received the Copley medal for his astronomical observations on Schiehallion, Burrow felt undervalued and refused to hand over his observations. The two had already clashed, with what a later biographer described as a lack of empathy 'between the buckram of divinity, tinselled with F.R.S., and the unqualifying republican stiffness of conscious talent' (Swale, 268). The fact that Charles Hutton was to work out the results of the survey may have provoked Burrow's antipathy towards Hutton as well.

Soon afterwards Burrow was appointed mathematical master of the drawing-room in the Tower, a parallel establishment to Woolwich Academy, where Hutton held a better-paid post—further grounds for jealousy. In 1776, in association with Thomas Carnan, publisher, Burrow initiated the *Ladies' and Gentlemen's Diary, or, Royal Almanack* in opposition to the *Ladies' Diary* edited by Hutton. It challenged the Stationers' Company regulatory monopoly, but the company's claim against Carnan was disallowed in a celebrated court action. In 1780 the title became simply *Ladies' Diary*; three 'companion' volumes were issued in 1779–81. Burrow aimed to publish more substantial articles than Hutton, and maintained a high standard during his six-year editorship, with such as his patron, Colonel Henry Watson, and his friend Isaac Dalby among other well-known almanac contributors.

In 1779 Burrow issued his only separate publication, *A restitution of the geometrical treatise of Apollonius Pergaeus on inclinations; also the theory of gunnery*. A similar work had been published by Samuel Horsley in 1770: in his preface Burrow criticizes it as clumsy and employing quasi-algebraic methods, and justifiably claims much greater simplicity and directness for his own work. The ability and elegance of his investigations, both here and in the *Diary*, were admitted even by his critics.

Burrow's family was increasing, and in April 1782 he resigned from the Tower and accepted an appointment in India through Watson, many years chief engineer in Bengal. In Calcutta he met William Jones, the orientalist, who recommended him to Warren Hastings. In an interesting letter to Hastings, Burrow said that he wished to make money in order to have leisure for research, that he was interested in ancient geometry, as proved by his *Apollonius*, and wanted to investigate Hindu and other oriental literature. Already a competent linguist, he then learned Sanskrit and collected many Sanskrit and Persian manuscripts. He is credited with being the first European to appreciate Hindu algebra and knowledge of the binomial theorem. An early member of the Asiatic Society of Bengal, he contributed valuable papers to its *Researches* (vols. 1–3, 1788–92).

Through Hastings, Burrow became mathematical master to the corps of engineers and then chief surveyor to the East India Company. In anticipation of its trigonometrical survey he measured differences of latitude and longitude over distances of about 77 and 40 miles respectively. He died soon after, leaving his papers to Isaac Dalby, who published *A short account of the late Mr. Burrow's measurement of a degree of longitude and … latitude near the Tropic in Bengal* (1796). According to a later writer, Burrow's 'form was athletic, and countenance expressive, with a penetrating eye' (Taylor, 189). Much has been made of his quarrelsome disposition. It was apparently not unknown for him to use his fists once 'the rites of Bacchus had roused his energies' (Swale, 269). An exaggerated emphasis on his pugnacious nature and strong language has sadly overshadowed his merits as an honest and talented mathematician and distinguished geometer.

Burrow died at Buxar, Hindustan, on 7 June 1792. His wife, who with his son and three daughters had joined him in 1790, returned home; the son died as a lieutenant with the East India Company. Burrow's journals are in the library of the Royal Astronomical Society.

LESLIE STEPHEN, *rev.* RUTH WALLIS

Sources J. H. Swale, 'A short memoir of Reuben Burrow', *Mechanics' Magazine*, 52 (1850), 267–9 • 'Mr Reuben Burrow', *Supplement of the Biographia Leodiensis, or, Biographical sketches of the worthies of Leeds*, ed. R. V. Taylor (1867), 187–9 • *GM*, 1st ser., 63 (1793), 767 • D. Howse, *Nevil Maskelyne: the seaman's astronomer* (1989), 118, 132–41 • A. De Morgan, 'Fly-leaves of books', *N&Q*, 12 (1855), 142–3 • J. N., 'John Ryley', *Leeds Correspondent*, 2 (1816), 101 • Senex, 'Board of ordnance in other days', *Mechanics' Magazine*, 55 (1851), 324–9 • T. T. Wilkinson, 'Mathematics and mathematicians, the journals of the late Reuben Burrow [pts 1–2]', *London, Edinburgh, and Dublin Philosophical Magazine*, 4th ser., 5 (1853), 185–93, 514–22 • T. T. Wilkinson, 'Mathematics and mathematicians, the journals of the late Reuben Burrow [pt 3]', *London, Edinburgh, and Dublin Philosophical Magazine*, 4th ser., 6 (1853), 196–204 • T. T. Wilkinson, 'Mathematical periodicals … Burrow's Diary', *Mechanics' Magazine*, 51 (1849), 244–7, 293–7, 350–57 • J. Cockle, 'Mathematical bibliography', *N&Q*, 2nd ser., 10 (1860), 309–10
Archives RAS, MS journals, MSS Add. 7
Wealth at death Oriental MSS allegedly to son, when sufficiently learned: Cockle, 'Mathematical bibliography'

Burrow, Thomas (1909–1986), orientalist, was born on 29 June 1909 in Leck, north Lancashire, the eldest in the family of five sons and one daughter of Joshua Burrow, farmer, and his wife, Frances Eleanor Carter. He was educated at Queen Elizabeth's School, Kirkby Lonsdale, and won a scholarship to Christ's College, Cambridge. He first read classics, specializing in comparative philology, and obtained first classes in parts one and two of the tripos (1929 and 1930). He then went on to study oriental languages, in which he also got firsts in both parts of the tripos (1931 and 1932). He began research for a year at the School of Oriental Studies, London University, and continued in Cambridge, where after two more years he was awarded a PhD. He became a research fellow of Christ's College (1935–7).

Burrow's first book, *The Language of the Kharoṣṭhī, Documents from Chinese Turkestan* (1937), was based on his doctoral thesis. The language in question, sometimes known as Niya Prakrit, was an official language in central Asia after the Kushan dynasty; the documents had been discovered and brought to Europe by Sir Aurel Stein. Burrow published his translation of them in 1940.

Burrow was assistant keeper in the department of oriental printed books and manuscripts at the British Museum from 1937 to 1944. During this period he mainly devoted himself to studying Dravidian languages. In 1944 he was appointed Boden professor of Sanskrit at Oxford University and professorial fellow of Balliol College, positions which he held until his retirement in 1976. Until 1965 he was the university's sole teacher in classical Indology. Besides Sanskrit he had to teach Pali and Prakrit. His practice was to read a set Sanskrit text with a BA student (or students, on the rare occasions when there was more than one in a year) for three hours a week; those texts not covered in class the students read unaided in the vacations. He gave some extra classes in Pali or Prakrit and in Sanskrit composition, but he may never have set an essay.

Of Burrow's many publications on Sanskrit, the best known are *The Sanskrit Language* (1955, revised edn 1973) and *The Problem of Shwa in Sanskrit* (1979). His views on the development of the Sanskrit vowel system were at odds with those of most Indo-Europeanists, but otherwise his exposition of Sanskrit was orthodox in the mainstream of comparative philology. His early interest in Prakrit did not develop further.

Burrow was happiest as a Dravidologist and did his most important work in Dravidian linguistics. In 1949 he began to collaborate with Professor Murray B. Emeneau of Berkeley. Together they published *A Dravidian Etymological Dictionary* (1961) and *Dravidian Borrowings from Indo-Aryan* (1962). After retirement Burrow gave most of his energy to producing the second edition of the dictionary (1984); it was, as he intended, his last book. This work on comparative Dravidian linguistics was complemented by Burrow's research on hitherto unrecorded Dravidian languages which survive in small linguistic communities in central India. To record them, he undertook field trips with S. Bhattacharya of the anthropological survey of India; together they published *The Parji Language* (1953), *A Comparative Vocabulary of the Gondi Dialects* (1960), and *The Pengo Language* (1970). Further fruits of Burrow's research in this field are gathered in his *Collected Papers in Dravidian Linguistics* (1968).

Burrow was widely respected as a single-minded scholar of great learning. A Sanskrit panegyric was presented to him by the Sanskrit College, Calcutta. He was elected a fellow of the British Academy in 1970. In 1974 he became a fellow of the School of Oriental and African Studies of London University and in 1979 a number of the *Bulletin of the School of Oriental and African Studies* (vol. 42, no. 2) was devoted to articles in honour of his seventieth birthday.

In build Burrow was rather over middle size and his appearance, at least in later life, was somewhat lumbering, but he moved quietly. His habitual expression was mild, even vague. He had very short sight and blinked frequently. To his colleagues and students he was amiable but socially passive and taciturn. There were reports that of an evening he would visit his local pub in Kidlington, near Oxford, and entertain companions with lively conversation; but in Oxford he was reticent about his private life to the point of secrecy. In 1941 he married Inez Mary, daughter of Herbert John Haley; but when she died at their home in 1976 it came as a surprise to his Oxford acquaintances, who believed him to be living alone. He never brought his wife into college, and explained after her death that her health was poor. It may be that she suffered from depression after their only child died in early infancy. Burrow died of a heart attack in Oxford on 8 June 1986 and was buried in St Mary's churchyard, Kidlington.

RICHARD F. GOMBRICH, *rev.*

Sources private information (1996) · personal knowledge (1996) · *The Times* (18 June 1986) · *WW* (1986) · *CGPLA Eng. & Wales* (1986)
Likenesses photograph, repro. in *Bulletin of the School of Oriental and African Studies*, 42/2 (1979), frontispiece
Wealth at death £238,529: probate, 30 Sept 1986, *CGPLA Eng. & Wales*

Burrowes, John Freckleton (1787–1852), organist and composer, was born in London on 23 April 1787. He was a pupil of William Horsley, and for nearly forty years was organist of St James's, Piccadilly. His first published work was a set of six English ballads, 'Printed for the author, 5 Great Suffolk Street, Charing Cross', and in 1812 he published an overture (op. 8) which had been performed at the Vocal Concerts, Hanover Square. This was followed in 1817 by a similar work (op. 13) produced at the concerts of the Philharmonic Society, of which Burrowes was one of the original members. In 1818 appeared the first edition of *The Pianoforte Primer*, a little work which was very successful, and was still in use as an instruction book almost a century after its publication. In 1819 Burrowes brought out *The Thorough-Bass Primer*, which achieved a success equal to that of the earlier work and passed through many editions. In the course of his long career he also published *A Companion to the Pianoforte Primer* (1826), *A Companion to the Thorough-Bass Primer* (1832), *The Tutor's Assistant for the Pianoforte* (1834), a *Guide to Practice on the Pianoforte* (1841), collections of psalm tunes, preludes, dances, Scotch and Irish airs, sonatas, a trio for three flutes, op. 12 (1817), songs, and many arrangements of operas for the piano, which were very popular at the time. About 1834 Burrowes settled at 13 Nottingham Place, London, where he died, after a long and painful illness, on 31 March 1852.

W. B. SQUIRE, *rev.* DAVID J. GOLBY

Sources *Musical World* (24 April 1852), 269 · W. H. Husk, 'Burrowes, John Freckleton', *New Grove* · C. Ehrlich, *First philharmonic: a history of the Royal Philharmonic Society* (1995), 32 · *GM*, 2nd ser., 37 (1852), 534

Burrowes, Peter (1753–1841), barrister and politician, was born at Portarlington, Queen's county, in 1753. There are no clear details as to his parentage and close family relatives, but in a letter of 9 May 1822 Lawrence Parsons, second earl of Rosse, informed John Freeman-Mitford, first Baron Redesdale, that Burrowes's mother was a Roman Catholic, and that his brother was a Church of Ireland clergyman in co. Wicklow.

At Trinity College, Dublin, which he entered in 1774, Burrowes distinguished himself in the debates of the historical society, where he first became acquainted with Theobald Wolfe Tone. Burrowes also privately tutored a son of John Beresford, the first commissioner of the revenue, while attending university. Beresford offered him a seat in parliament, provided his politics coincided with those of his patron. However, he declined the offer, preferring to maintain his independence.

Burrowes was an early campaigner for Catholic emancipation, and while still a student at the Middle Temple, London, in 1784, he published a pamphlet on the subject, entitled *Plain arguments in defence of the people's absolute dominion over the constitution in which the question of Roman Catholic emancipation is fully considered*. The pamphlet brought him to the attention of Henry Flood and other leading patriot parliamentarians. A year later he was called to the bar, where he rapidly acquired a good practice.

In 1790 Burrowes was one of the first members of the United Irishmen. He was a zealous supporter of all the most important measures of constitutional and parliamentary reform, but opposed the overthrow of the crown. His continued friendship with Tone and the Emmets, long after others considered them traitors, exposed him to the ill favour of the authorities in the 1790s, and hampered considerably his progress in the legal profession. In fact, his career nearly came to a premature end in 1794, when he fought a duel with Somerset Butler at Kilkenny. His life was saved only by the ball's striking against some coppers which he happened to have in his waistcoat pocket.

The insurrection of 1798 had a major impact on Burrowes. His clergyman brother and his nephews were piked to death during its early stages. Moreover, he was unable to assist his lifelong friend, Tone, as he waited for execution in 1798. In a letter of 9 November 1798 to Thomas Russell he gave it as his opinion that Tone's case was 'totally hopeless', and that 'the nature of his [Tone's] departure from this country [1795] will not furnish any legal advantages … It is the most testing terrain I ever engaged in' (TCD, MS 868/2/279–80). Burrowes had likewise acted as legal counsel for Tone's younger brother, Matthew, who was executed only weeks earlier after the

Peter Burrowes (1753–1841), by unknown engraver, pubd 1849

defeat of General Humbert's forces at Ballinamuck, co. Mayo. In the aftermath of the rebellion he did what he could to protect and support his surviving friends and relatives, and it is testimony to his generous disposition that he gave an annuity to his niece and also to Tone's mother.

On 9 December 1798, along with thirteen other king's counsel, he protested against the proposals for a parliamentary union with Great Britain. After being elected as MP for Enniscorthy, co. Wexford, in 1800, he persisted in opposing the measure for as long as the Irish parliament existed. At one of the meetings of the opponents of the union, Burrowes proposed that an appeal should be made to the yeomanry to resist the measure by force of arms if necessary. He suggested that they circulate the appeal through the lawyers' corps to every corps in the kingdom. However, some of the key anti-unionists induced him to abandon his proposal, a decision he later regretted. His parliamentary career was short-lived, spanning only a few months, but before the borough of Enniscorthy was disfranchised, he procured and transacted its sale in 1800 to Cornelius O'Callaghan, second Baron Lismore.

In 1803 Burrowes acted as counsel for Robert Emmet along with Leonard MacNally, who, after his death, was identified as a political informer. His legal career received a boost in 1806, when he was appointed first counsel to the commissioners of the revenue under the Grenville administration. This was not a permanent post but at the time it was a lucrative one. In spite of his position within the administration, he corresponded with Thomas Addis Emmet, forgetting that the Banishment Acts of 1798, 1799, and 1800 punished with transportation any person who corresponded with the Irish exiles. However, Burrowes was notoriously absent-minded. Indeed, Emmet was aware of this character trait and, in a letter of 19 November 1806 published in Grattan's *Life*, he mildly rebuked Burrowes for asking him in a previous communication, 'Do you ever mean to visit us?', since his return to Ireland from America would condemn him to instant execution by law.

Burrowes continued to lend his support to the campaign for Catholic emancipation after the parliamentary union. He was counsel for the Roman Catholic delegates indicted under the Convention Act (1793) in 1811 and 1812, after the arrest of Lord Fingall, chairman of the Catholic board. In 1819 he was an active member of the committee of the Protestant Friends of Catholic Emancipation, and was in regular contact with Daniel O'Connell, the future 'liberator'. From 1821 to 1835 he was a commissioner of the insolvent debtors court.

Burrowes was described as 'ungainly in figure, awkward in action, and discordant in voice' but with a mind of the 'very highest order' (Phillips, 391). David Plunket thought him 'an honest but eccentric genius' (D. R. Plunket, *The Life, Letters, and Speeches of Lord Plunket*, 1, 1867, 36). It is not known when Burrowes married, but he was survived by his wife, Anne (who possessed property in Newport, Isle of Wight), and their two children, Mary and Peter. He died at his home in Henrietta Street, Cavendish Square, London, on 8 November 1841, in receipt of an income of £1600 per annum, that being the retiring pension of an insolvency commissioner in Ireland, and was buried in Kensal Green cemetery, Middlesex. DAVID LAMMEY

Sources Royal Irish Acad., Burrowes MS 23.K.53 · H. Grattan, *Memoirs of the life and times of the Rt Hon. Henry Grattan*, 5 vols. (1839–46) · M. Elliott, *Wolfe Tone: prophet of Irish independence* (1989) · W. O. Burrowes, ed., *Select speeches of the late Peter Burrowes, Esq. K.C., at the bar and in parliament* (1850) · *The correspondence of Daniel O'Connell*, ed. M. R. O'Connell, 1–3, IMC (1972–4) · *DNB* · constituency history, borough of Enniscorthy, co. Wexford, PRO NIre., ENV 5/HP/31/5 · C. Phillips, *Curran and his contemporaries*, [3rd edn] (1850) · [P. Burrowes], *Plain arguments in defence of the people's absolute dominion over the constitution in which the question of Roman Catholic emancipation is fully considered* (1784) · A. P. W. Malcomson, ed., *Eighteenth century Irish official papers in Great Britain*, 2 (1990), 132–3, 464–6 · O. Knox, *Rebels and informers: stirrings of Irish independence* (1997) · R. R. Madden, *The United Irishmen: their lives and times*, 2nd edn, 3rd ser. (1860), 440 · *Dublin Almanac* (1842) · *GM*, 2nd ser., 16 (1841), 662 · *GM*, 2nd ser., 17 (1842), 448

Archives Royal Irish Acad., Burrowes MSS, MS 23.K.53 | Birr Castle, letters to Lawrence Parsons · TCD, Sirr MSS, MSS 868–869

Likenesses S. Watts, engraving, c.1800, repro. in Malcomson, ed., *Eighteenth-century Irish official papers*, 2 · oils, c.1800, priv. coll. · T. Butler, effigy on monument, c.1841, Kensal Green cemetery, London · lithograph, pubd 1849, NPG [*see illus.*] · R. J. Lane, lithograph, NPG · J. Watts, line print, NPG

Wealth at death houses in Blessington Street, Nelson Street, and White's Lane, Dublin, as well as his normal residential property, 57 Lower Leeson Street, Dublin, valued at £60; properties divided between son and daughter; distributed well over £600 in cash and possessions (incl. piano) to relatives and friends: will, Burrowes MSS 23.K.53/28, Royal Irish Acad.; *Dublin Almanac*

Burrows, Arthur Richard (1882–1947), broadcaster, was born on 15 February 1882 at 21 Cambridge Street, St Ebbe's, Oxford, the younger son in the family of three children of Alfred Burrows (c.1844–1899), porter of Corpus Christi College, Oxford, and his wife, Jane Elizabeth Bourton (b. c.1853), daughter of a keeper of the university parks. His elder brother died in childhood. He was educated locally; having left school at the age of seventeen, after his father's death, he got a job teaching elementary science to evening classes at Oxford City Technical School. Among his many interests was cycling, and it was through the commanding officer of the Volunteer Cycle Unit that he was introduced to the editor of the *Oxford Times* in 1903 and taken on as an apprentice. After his five years' apprenticeship, during which he learned all aspects of newspaper production, he was kept on as a reporter. Having moved to London in 1911 he joined the staff of *The Standard*, specializing in scientific and technical subjects, and by the end of 1912 he was reporting the activities of amateur wireless enthusiasts. He also wrote for other journals, including articles on the application of wireless telegraphy to journalism for publications of Marconi's Wireless Telegraphy Company. On 25 April 1914 he married Nellie Gertrude (b. 1885/6), daughter of Thomas William Oxley, an upholsterer; they had three children.

When *The Standard* collapsed in 1914 Burrows became news editor of the new Wireless Press Service of the Marconi company, responsible for collecting and translating enemy propaganda broadcasts and for their distribution to government departments. He also prepared a nightly news bulletin for transmission by wireless telegraphy from the Marconi station at Poldhu, Cornwall, to naval and merchant ships at sea. As early as 1917 he was predicting the use of wireless telephony—the transmission of the human voice—as a means of mass communication, in an article later published in the Marconi yearbook for 1918. He envisaged broadcasting parliamentary debates to newspaper offices and concerts to private houses but warned of the danger of advertising agencies filling up the concert intervals with 'audible advertisements … on behalf of somebody's soap or tomato ketchup'. In 1918 he was called up into the Middlesex regiment and saw action in France before he was invalided out of the army.

After the war Burrows became publicity manager for the Marconi company. He worked with great enthusiasm to demonstrate the potential of wireless broadcasting, and was one of those responsible for Dame Nellie Melba's famous broadcast from the Marconi station at Writtle, near Chelmsford, in June 1920, which was heard as far away as Persia. He also had the idea of equipping the liner *Victoria* with a wireless telephone transmitter and receiver for her voyage to Quebec in August 1920, taking delegates to the imperial press conference in Ottawa. News transmitted from Poldhu and concerts from Writtle could be heard when the ship was over 2000 miles away. On board Burrows edited the material and produced a twice-daily newsheet, the *North Atlantic Times*, and, using a transmitter in Newfoundland, was able to arrange for the prime minister of Newfoundland to exchange greetings with Lord

Burnham, leader of the British delegation, while still 300 miles off the Canadian shore. This demonstration to the leading members of the British press of the possibilities of broadcasting gave maximum publicity to wireless telephony. Later in 1920 Burrows was asked to organize the transmission of reports from journalists to their newspapers from the first session of the League of Nations assembly in Geneva.

The first regular broadcast service in Britain began in February 1922, from Writtle, and a few months later Burrows was in charge of a new station, 2LO, broadcasting from London. This station was restricted to one hour's transmission a day, as the government was still worried about interference with official wireless services and each programme had to be approved by the Post Office in advance. The station opened on 11 May 1922 with a running commentary on the boxing match between Kid Lewis and Georges Carpentier. Burrows introduced most of the programmes himself, after ringing out the Westminster chimes on a set of tubular bells.

When the British Broadcasting Company was set up in October 1922 Burrows was chosen by Sir William Noble to introduce the first broadcast, on 14 November 1922, announcing the results of the general election. This was transmitted from the 2LO studio, temporary home of the BBC until the move to Savoy Hill in March 1923. In December he was appointed director of programmes, one of the first four members of the BBC staff. From the start he was determined that the programmes should be of high quality and should both entertain and educate, while he was also concerned with improving the quality of the sound. The first year's programmes included talks, concerts, plays, dance bands, news, weather forecasts, religious broadcasts, and variety shows, although he was anxious to keep these free of vulgarity. He was an early supporter of schools broadcasting, which began in 1924. He was also the first *Children's Hour* 'uncle', known to millions of listeners as Uncle Arthur. His voice was classless and devoid of any regional accent, and it set the standard for 'BBC English'. In 1924 he published *The Story of Broadcasting*.

In April 1925 Burrows was appointed first secretary-general of the Union Internationale de Radiophonie (UIR), set up in Geneva through the initiative of John Reith, general manager of the BBC. Burrows moved to Geneva with high hopes of helping the development of international understanding through broadcasting, but the immediate task was to deal with the problem of interference and to allocate wavelengths, and the Geneva plan was implemented in 1926. As the number and range of transmitters increased new agreements followed, drawn up at a series of international conferences and monitored by the control centre in Brussels. At the same time Burrows encouraged the international exchange of programmes. The spread of commercial broadcasting caused problems but he failed to prevent the very popular Radio Luxemburg, listened to in Britain by twice as many as tuned in to the BBC, from broadcasting to Britain. During his years in Geneva he was consulted by the League of Nations on many occasions on questions of international broadcasting, and from 1930 he was also League of Nations correspondent for *The Times*. He resigned from the UIR in April 1940 and the BBC suspended its membership in 1941.

Burrows rejoined the BBC, which appointed him temporary director of the northern region in May 1940. In April 1942 he was transferred to Broadcasting House in London, where he was asked to help with the co-ordination of ideas on the future of broadcasting after the war, and from September 1942 he was director of broadcasting at the Ministry of Information. He retired in 1945, and died on 26 November 1947 at 35 Highpoint, North Hill, Highgate, his London home. He was survived by his wife.   ANNE PIMLOTT BAKER

Sources BBC WAC, file 5236 [esp. memoir by his son, based on an unpubd autobiography] · A. Briggs, *The history of broadcasting in the United Kingdom*, rev. edn, 5 vols. (1995), vols. 1, 4 · A. R. Burrows, *The story of broadcasting* (1924) · W. J. Baker, *A history of the Marconi Company* (1970) · E. Pawley, *BBC engineering, 1922–1972* (1972) · J. Cain, *Seventy years of broadcasting* (1992) · *The Times* (27 Nov 1947) · b. cert. · m. cert. · d. cert.
Archives BBC WAC, MSS, file 5236
Likenesses eleven photographs, BBC WAC, file 5236 · photograph, repro. in Briggs, *History of broadcasting*, vol. 1, pl. 11
Wealth at death £5647 9s. 7d.: probate, 7 Feb 1948, *CGPLA Eng. & Wales*

Burrows, Christine Mary Elizabeth (1872–1959), educationist and university administrator, was born at New Street, Chipping Norton, Oxfordshire, on 4 January 1872. She was the only and posthumous child of Henry Parker Burrows (1833–1871), a partner in Langton Burrows Breweries, Maidenhead, and his wife, Esther Elizabeth *Burrows (1847–1935), daughter of William Bliss, a mill owner of Chipping Norton. Her childhood was spent in her grandfather's house among her Bliss relatives. After attending a small private school, she went in 1887 to Cheltenham Ladies' College, under Dorothea Beale, with a music scholarship. In 1891 she entered Lady Margaret Hall, Oxford, to read history but her studies were interrupted in 1893 when she was summoned to join and assist her mother who had just been appointed as principal of the newly founded St Hilda's Hall in Oxford.

Despite the demands of her own studies (which she continued as a registered home student), Christine Burrows took on heavy administrative and social duties while giving guidance to her mother (who had no knowledge of Oxford traditions) and to the small community of her fellow students. In 1894 she gained a second class in history and then remained at St Hilda's as history tutor in addition to her other responsibilities. In 1895 she became vice-principal. It was largely due to her ability, both as teacher and administrator, that St Hilda's was before long accepted on equal terms among the other women's foundations. In 1910 she succeeded her mother as principal, and directed the fortunes of St Hilda's through a period of steady growth and distinction—set back by the First World War but sharing in the general enfranchisement of women that followed. At school and college she had come under the influence of pioneers in women's education

Christine Mary Elizabeth Burrows (1872–1959), by unknown photographer

and notable men teachers who gave time to set the movement on its way; many of them remained her friends and she enlisted their support for St Hilda's, a hall she had helped create and shape.

In July 1919, however, Christine Burrows resigned from St Hilda's in order to live with her mother whose health was giving cause for concern. But in 1921 she resumed her career when she was appointed as principal of the Society of Oxford Home Students, a post which could be combined with residence in her own home with her mother. To this new and exacting work she gave the utmost of her mature powers. The Home Students was a non-resident society for women; students lived in their own homes or with hostesses in private houses. It was characteristic of her concern for detail and for good working relationships that she had visited all sixty hostesses before she took up office in 1921 and, as student numbers grew, she visited and interviewed every new hostess.

Perhaps the most striking features of Burrows's principalship were her clear interest in study and teaching and her pastoral care of students. The building of a strong tutorial staff at the Home Students owed much to her experience and initiative. With their admission to the university in 1920 (Burrows was made an MA by decree in 1921), women became subject to the disciplinary code of the university proctors. If this discipline was sometimes irksome to high-spirited post-war home students, its

acceptance was assured by the kindness and good sense with which she administered it. The eight years of her second principalship were not as creative as those at St Hilda's. It was not pioneer work which was needed but the capacity to adapt and consolidate. She did, however, steer the Home Students in a direction which would eventually lead to its becoming a residential college, incorporated as St Anne's College in 1952.

In 1929 Christine Burrows resigned from the Home Students to spend her time with her mother whose health was deteriorating. She continued to live in Oxford for the last thirty years of her life, quietly devoting herself to movements for developing women's powers and usefulness. She was a firm champion of women's rights. In 1908 she had joined a march in London supporting the suffrage movement; in the 1930s she was a member of the archbishops' committee on the place of women in the church and, although she signed its report, she did not alter her opinion that the ordination of women to the priesthood was right and would come in time.

Christine Burrows contributed an article on St Hilda's College to the Victoria county history of Oxfordshire (vol. 3, 1954). A longer history of the college remained as an early draft when her eyesight failed. She was a slight, wiry woman with dark hair. In some ways she always seemed older than her age because she had inherited many of her mother's Victorian manners. She died on 10 September 1959 at St Luke's Home, Linton Road, Oxford. After a funeral service at St Giles' Church, Oxford, on 14 September, her body was cremated.

R. F. BUTLER, rev. MARGARET E. RAYNER

Sources M. E. Rayner, *The centenary history of St Hilda's College, Oxford* (1993) · R. F. Butler, *History of St Anne's College* (1958) · *The Times* (11 Sept 1959) · *The Ship* [yearbook of St Anne's College] (1958) · *St Hilda's College Chronicle* (1959–60) · family MSS, priv. coll. · personal knowledge (1971) · b. cert. · d. cert. · *Reading Mercury, Oxford Gazette, Newbury Herald, and Berks County Paper* (28 Oct 1871), 5 · b. cert. [mother] · d. cert. [mother] · *The Times* (15 Sept 1959)
Archives St Hilda's College, Oxford, corresp.; draft history; notebooks; papers; etc.
Likenesses L. Brooke, chalk drawing, 1919, St Hilda's College, Oxford · C. Ouless, oils, *c*.1927, St Hilda's College, Oxford · J. De Glehn, chalk, 1929, St Anne's College, Oxford · photograph, St Hilda's College, Oxford [*see illus.*] · photographs (from childhood to old age), St Hilda's College, Oxford
Wealth at death £8334 9*s*. 9*d*.: probate, 19 Nov 1959, *CGPLA Eng. & Wales*

Burrows [*née* Bliss], **Esther Elizabeth** (1847–1935), college head, was born on 18 October 1847 at Chipping Norton, Oxfordshire, the third child and second daughter of William Bliss (1810–1883), a cloth manufacturer in the town, and his wife, Esther (1808–1882), daughter of Robert Cleaver of Saffron Walden. She was educated at schools for young ladies in Bristol (Mrs Glover's) and in Brighton (Miss Wilmshurst's) until, when she was sixteen, she was required to return home to take the place of her elder sister who was marrying. From then until her own marriage, Esther Bliss directed her father's large household and cared for her mother, who suffered from epilepsy. The Bliss mills prospered and William Bliss, who lived in the style of a country gentleman, expected his family to join in his philanthropic activities. Esther was given the management of the night school for the mill girls.

On 8 September 1870, Esther Bliss was married in Chipping Norton parish church to Henry Parker Burrows (*b.* 1833), partner in a firm of wine merchants and brewers in Maidenhead. In October 1871, Henry Burrows died unexpectedly, leaving a pregnant widow and very little money. Esther Burrows returned to live with her parents in Chipping Norton, where her daughter, Christine Mary Elizabeth *Burrows, was born. After 1872, the Bliss mills were less successful. Fashion in cloth changed and there was increased competition from other manufacturers. A fire destroyed one of the mills for which there was no insurance cover. When William Bliss died in 1883, there was insufficient money for his son to run the firm and the inheritance which his daughter could have expected had vanished.

Esther Burrows was determined that her daughter should have all the advantages which had by then been opened to women. To pay the fees for Christine to attend Cheltenham Ladies' College, she had by 1887 moved to Cheltenham and opened a house in which students of the college could board. Her earnings were sufficient to cover the expenses when Christine was awarded a place at Lady Margaret Hall, Oxford, in 1891.

In 1892, Dorothea Beale, principal of the Cheltenham Ladies' College, invited Esther Burrows to become principal of St Hilda's, a hall for women which she was establishing in Oxford; students at the hall would attend university lectures and prepare for university examinations. An essential part of the arrangement was that Christine should transfer from Lady Margaret Hall to help her mother prepare for the first students and to provide advice on Oxford procedure. The hall opened for Michaelmas term 1893 with six students and with Esther Burrows in sole charge. She continued her close collaboration with her daughter after 1894 when Christine remained at St Hilda's as tutor and, later, as vice-principal.

The survival of St Hilda's in its first few precarious years was largely the result of the wise and unobtrusive diplomacy of the first principal. Dorothea Beale was an outsider to Oxford and her motives for setting up a rival hall were deeply distrusted by other women's halls. Esther Burrows, however, won the confidence of the other women principals and of the Association for Promoting the Higher Education of Women in Oxford so that, after a three-year probationary period, St Hilda's achieved full status as a women's hall. Under Esther Burrows's management the number of students increased and extensions were added to the original building.

Despite the very tight budget Dorothea Beale imposed upon St Hilda's, Esther Burrows created an attractive and comfortable hall for her students. She was a gracious hostess and she welcomed visitors and new students as if St Hilda's were her own home. She was an elegant white-haired lady, generous and kind-hearted but insistent that rules and conventions be observed by students. She retired as principal in 1910 and was succeeded in that office by her daughter. She stayed in Oxford after her retirement and, after 1919, lived with Christine. She died in her home, 47 Woodstock Road, Oxford, from a stroke on 20 February 1935 after many years of ill health, and was buried at St Luke's, Maidenhead, after a funeral service at St Hilda's College.   MARGARET E. RAYNER

Sources M. E. Rayner, *The centenary history of St Hilda's College, Oxford* (1993) · H. M. Allen, *Chronicle of the Association of Senior Members* [St Hilda's College, Oxford] (1934–5) · *The Times* (21 Feb 1935) · b. cert. · m. cert. · d. cert. · *CGPLA Eng. & Wales* (1935)
Archives priv. coll. · St Hilda's College, Oxford, corresp., other MSS
Likenesses B. Maul, crayon drawing, 1900, St Hilda's College, Oxford · C. Ouless, oils, 1927, St Hilda's College, Oxford · photographs, St Hilda's College, Oxford · photographs, priv. coll.
Wealth at death £760 18s. 4d.: probate, 23 March 1935, *CGPLA Eng. & Wales*

Burrows, Sir Frederick John (1887–1973), trade unionist and governor of Bengal, was born at Bollow, Westbury-on-Severn, Gloucestershire, on 3 July 1887. He was fifth of five sons and the youngest of eleven children of John Burrows, a general labourer, and his wife, Ellen Abell. He was educated at Walmore Hill School and joined the Great Western Railway, becoming a goods checker at Backney near Ross-on-Wye. In 1912 he married Dora Beatrice (*d.* 1968), daughter of G. Hutchings, a Hereford railway guard. They had one son and one daughter. He served with the Grenadier Guards during the First World War, became a company sergeant-major, and won the meritorious service medal.

On his return to the Great Western Railway, Burrows worked initially at Grange Court and subsequently at Ross, where he became a well-known local figure. He was secretary of the small branch of the National Union of Railwaymen (NUR) and eventually became a justice of the peace. Until the mid-1930s Burrows seemed destined to remain a rural railwayman working assiduously to develop a labour movement in a Conservative community. However, thanks to his qualities, he became a member of his Great Western sectional council of the NUR and was elected to the NUR executive for the years 1937–9 as the representative for the union's goods section for south Wales and south-west England.

Burrows emerged quickly as a prominent member of the union's right-wing faction at a time when the left was increasing its strength among the NUR's activists. In July 1941 delegates to the annual general meeting elected him union president for 1942, a position he retained for the maximum three-year tenure. Although the presidency was a lay position, the volume of business meant that it was effectively a full-time post. Burrows worked closely with the union's new general secretary, John Benstead; their political and industrial views were similar. Burrows insisted that any wartime strike was 'unthinkable', but the industry's strategic importance, backed by state control, ensured wage advances. Under his presidency, the NUR's relationships with other railway unions became unusually cordial.

Burrows's wartime views articulated a progressive patriotism. 'There must be no two Englands when the peace is planned; no stately homes and insanitary cottages, no

Princes of Industry and men on the dole'. Soviet resistance to the German invasion appeared to demonstrate the value of meritocracy. 'There not only do the workers fight, but the workers also lead, and ability only is the password for promotion'. He welcomed the 1944 Education Act as a step towards the democratization of education, but felt that a Labour government should tackle 'the Public School question'. His advocacy of equality of opportunity included sexual equality. The exigencies of wartime mobilization should have destroyed any idea of women's inferiority (NUR presidential addresses, 1942, 1943, 1944, NUR collection).

Despite his widely shared enthusiasm for the Soviet war effort, Burrows remained a thorough opponent of the Communist Party. During his presidency he served on the Labour Party's national executive committee (NEC) as his union's nominee to the trade union section, and strongly opposed communist attempts to affiliate to the Labour Party. However, the NUR voted narrowly at its annual general meeting in 1943 to support communist affiliation. Nevertheless Burrows's reputation among the party's senior politicians increased. He was more active than many trade unionists within the NEC, not least on the party's international committee. His record as NUR president seems also to have attracted the positive approval of Winston Churchill.

This reputation as a capable representative of the Labour viewpoint led to Burrows's selection as a member of the three-man commission on constitutional reform for Ceylon under Lord Soulbury. The trio arrived on the island in late December 1945 and left early in the following April. Their task was essentially to assess and to amend an earlier constitutional draft produced by the Ceylon ministers. Burrows subsequently worked on the Colonial Advisory Board; in both roles he was regarded as successful. Attlee's verdict in August 1945 was 'first class abilities'. This assessment had particular significance since it was in a prime-ministerial memorandum to the secretary of state for India, Lord Pethick-Lawrence, concerning candidates for Indian governorships. In November 1945 Burrows's appointment as governor of Bengal was announced, a symbolic action in the early months of the Labour government.

Burrows arrived in India in February 1946. His rapport with the viceroy, Lord Wavell, was immediate. His solidity and imperturbability appealed to the viceroy, as did his pride in his own military experience: 'he is really a complete Conservative in his ideas and thinks the Grenadier Guards the finest body ever collected' (*Wavell: the Viceroy's Journal*, 329, 8 Aug 1946). The situation in Bengal was extremely difficult. One feature fitted easily with his established political sentiments, however: he detected communist influence in strikes and other agitations. More seriously, Bengal at this time saw escalating communal tensions between Muslims and Hindus. Burrows was painfully aware of his limited resources of police and army units, in both numbers and morale.

Within Bengal, Burrows had to bargain with a newly elected and Muslim-dominated provincial government

under H. S. Suhrawardy. His attempts to facilitate agreement on an inter-communal coalition were unsuccessful. Instead there were communal conflicts marked by heavy loss of life, first in Calcutta in August 1946, and later that year at Noakhali in East Bengal. The Calcutta killings provoked a sombre comparison by Burrows: 'I observed very great damage to property and streets littered with corpses. I can honestly say that parts of the city … were as bad as anything I saw when I was with the Guards on the Somme' (Burrows to Wavell, 22 Aug 1946, in Mansbergh and Moon, 8, doc. 197).

The Congress movement criticized Burrows's apparent failure to protect Hindus, but several other observers felt he had achieved as much as was feasible, given his limited resources. 'I realised that I was taking on an extremely difficult job, I did not realise that I was taking on a practically impossible one' was his assessment in November 1946 (*Wavell: the Viceroy's Journal*, 369, 3 Nov 1946). The 'impossibility' was the product not just of the situation in Bengal, where partition became increasingly likely, but also of shifts and obscurities within British government strategy. In such a situation Burrows's calmness was a particular strength, when 'holding the ring' seemed to be the only option until the transfer of power in August 1947.

Burrows's actions were underpinned by a thorough belief in the durability and desirability of the British empire. One episode during his governorship was revealing. In May 1946 he wrote to Attlee deprecating the report of the Anglo-American committee on Palestine. He feared that recommendations responsive to the Jewish case might inflame Muslim opinion in India, but there was a more fundamental concern that would have gladdened the more conservative elements in the Foreign Office: 'I earnestly hope that, at whatever cost, the recommendations of the Report, which endanger the life-line of the British Empire will be repudiated' (Burrows to Attlee, 6 May 1946, Mansbergh and Moon, 8, doc. 205).

Following his return to England, Burrows served as chairman of the Agricultural Land Commission from 1948 until 1963 and was a director of Lloyds Bank from 1950 to 1958. He was high sheriff of Herefordshire in 1955 and deputy lieutenant from 1950 until his death in 1973. He was appointed GCIE in 1945 and GCSI in 1947. During the 1959 general election he announced in a letter to *The Times* that he could no longer support the Labour Party. He gave two principal reasons: the party policies on steel nationalization and the municipalization of rented houses. He characterized the latter as 'so Gilbertian that it could well have appeared in Alice in Wonderland' (*The Times*, 1 Oct 1959).

Burrows was physically a commanding figure, 6 feet tall and 16 stone. He spoke in a west-country 'burr' and was thought friendly, a quality which, when allied to firmly held and often conventional views, made him a reassuring figure, not least to those distant from the labour movement. His working life was spent in uniform: the Great Western Railway, the British army, the Bengal governorship. These experiences were readily reconciled with his work within the NUR, given its rule-governed procedures and its strong sense of solidarity. His moderation was complemented by a sense of duty to both workmates and the wider society. 'I have always been prepared to do everything possible for England' was his response to the challenge of the Bengal governorship (*News Chronicle*, 7 Nov 1945). His wife, who was awarded the kaisar-i-Hind gold medal in 1947, died in 1968. Burrows died at Ross-on-Wye, Herefordshire, on 20 April 1973.

DAVID HOWELL

Sources *The Times* (24 April 1973) · *DNB* · N. Mansbergh and P. Moon, eds., *The transfer of power*, 6–12 (1976–80) · *Wavell: the viceroy's journal*, ed. P. Moon (1973) · D. Howell, *Respectable radicals: studies in the politics of railway trade unionism* (1999) · *The Second World War diary of Hugh Dalton, 1940–1945*, ed. B. Pimlott (1986) · C. R. Attlee, *As it happened* (1954) · press cuttings collection, People's History Museum, Manchester · U. Warwick Mod. RC, National Union of Railwaymen papers · *CGPLA Eng. & Wales* (1973)
Archives People's History Museum, Manchester, labour party national executive committee minutes, 1942–5 · U. Warwick Mod. RC, National Union of Railwaymen collection | FILM BFI NFTVA, current affairs footage · IWM FVA, actuality footage
Likenesses W. Stoneman, photograph, 1946, NPG
Wealth at death £43,697: probate, 18 July 1973, *CGPLA Eng. & Wales*

Burrows, Sir George, first baronet (1801–1887), physician, was born in Bloomsbury Square, London, on 28 November 1801, the eldest of the five sons and four daughters of George Man *Burrows (1771–1846), physician, of Bloomsbury Square, and his wife, Sophia (d. 1858), second daughter of Thomas Druce, a lawyer, of Chancery Lane, London. He was educated for six years at Ealing, under Dr Nicholas, where he had John Henry Newman for a schoolfellow. After leaving school, in 1819 he attended the lectures of John *Abernethy (1764–1831), his future father-in-law, at St Bartholomew's Hospital, London, and he took other courses, delivered by W. T. Brande and Michael Faraday, at the Royal Institution. He was admitted a scholar of Gonville and Caius College, Cambridge, on 7 October 1820, and graduated BA in 1825 (tenth wrangler), MB in 1826, and MD in 1831. He also won the Tancred medical studentship. While at Cambridge he was well known as both a cricketer and an oarsman. He was junior fellow and mathematical lecturer of Gonville and Caius College from 1825 to 1835.

After returning to St Bartholomew's Hospital from Cambridge, Burrows studied as a dresser under Sir William Lawrence, and as a clinical clerk under Peter Mere Latham. Soon afterwards he travelled with a patient on the continent, and studied at Pavia and in France and Germany. He spent six months in Paris in the anatomical schools under G. Breschet, and while in Italy he studied under A. Scarpa and B. Panizza.

In 1829 Cambridge University granted Burrows a licence to practise, and he was admitted in the same year as an inceptor candidate at the Royal College of Physicians. He had seen and studied cholera in Italy, and in 1832, during the cholera epidemic in London, the governors of St Bartholomew's Hospital put him in charge of an auxiliary establishment. At the end of 1832 he was appointed joint lecturer on medical jurisprudence at St Bartholomew's

Sir George Burrows, first baronet (1801–1887), by George Richmond, 1871

Hospital with George Leith Roupell, and in 1834 he became sole lecturer on this subject. His first lecture on forensic medicine, which was separately printed, was published in the *London Medical and Surgical Journal* for 4 February 1832. In 1836 he was made joint lecturer on medicine with Peter Mere Latham, and in 1841 he succeeded as sole lecturer. His lectures were plain, judicious, and comprehensive. On 18 September 1834 he married Elinor (d. 1882), youngest daughter of John Abernethy, with whom he had eight children; two children died in early life, and three sons who reached adulthood also predeceased him.

Burrows was appointed the first assistant physician to St Bartholomew's in 1834, and had the charge of medical out-patients. He was promoted full physician in 1841 and held this post until 1863, when he was placed on the consulting staff. On this occasion he was presented with a testimonial by his colleagues. He was for many years physician to Christ's Hospital, London. He joined the Royal College of Physicians as a member in 1829 and was elected a fellow in 1832. In that institution he subsequently delivered the Goulstonian lectures (1834), the Croonian lectures (1835–6), and the Lumleian lectures (1843–4). He held the office of censor in 1839, 1840, 1843, and 1846; of councillor for five periods of three years between 1838 and 1870; and of college representative at the General Medical Council from 1860 to 1869. He was a college treasurer from 1860 to 1863, and president from 1871 to 1875. In 1846 he was elected a fellow of the Royal Society. He received the degree of DCL from Oxford in 1872, and of LLD from Cambridge in 1881.

In 1862 Burrows was president of the British Medical Association and in 1869 he became president of the Royal Medical and Chirurgical Society. In 1870 he was made physician-extraordinary to Queen Victoria, and in 1873, on the death of Sir Henry Holland, he became physician-in-ordinary. In 1874 he was created a baronet. He was also a member of the senate of London University. On 11 December 1880 he was elected honorary fellow of Gonville and Caius College, Cambridge.

In person Burrows was tall and well formed, with handsome and expressive features; his voice was clear, and he always spoke briefly and to the point. He 'invariably inspired confidence in his patients ... although he rarely smiled, and still more rarely laughed' (*BMJ*, 1299). He continued to see patients at his residence, 18 Cavendish Square, until shortly before his death, when he became incapacitated by bronchitis and emphysema, of which he died at Cavendish Square on 12 December 1887. He was buried at Highgate cemetery on Saturday, 17 December 1887. He was succeeded as second baronet by his son, Sir Frederick Abernethy Burrows.

Burrows's Lumleian lectures *On disorders of the cerebral circulation and the connection between affections of the brain and diseases of the heart* were published in 1846. In them he explained and illustrated experimentally the condition of the circulation in the brain under varying conditions of pressure. In 1840 and 1841 he wrote the articles 'Rubeola and scarlet fever' and 'Haemorrhages' for Alexander Tweedie's *The Library of Medicine* (8 vols., 1840–42). He also published 'Clinical lectures on medicine' in the *Medical Times and Gazette*, and papers in the *Medico-Chirurgical Transactions* (vols. 27 and 30).

W. W. WEBB, rev. MICHAEL BEVAN

Sources *BMJ* (24 Dec 1887), 1298–9 · Munk, *Roll* · Burke, *Peerage* · private information (1901) · J. Paget, *St Bartholomew's Hospital Reports*, 23 (1887), xxxiii-xl · Venn, *Alum. Cant.*
Archives UCL, SDUK MSS
Likenesses J. P. Knight, oils, exh. RA 1865, St Bartholomew's Hospital, London · G. Richmond, oils, 1871, RCP Lond. [*see illus.*] · M. Wagmüller, marble bust, 1873, RCP Lond.; D. Sodini, replica, 1898 General Medical Council, London · Beynon & Co., lithograph (*The past surgeons and physicians of St Bartholomew's Hospital, London*; after F. Hager), Wellcome L. · W. Richmond, portrait, priv. coll.
Wealth at death £104,628 2s.: probate, 3 Feb 1888, *CGPLA Eng. & Wales*

Burrows, George Man (1771–1846), general practitioner and alienist, was born at Chalk, near Gravesend, Kent, the son of a medical practitioner who died when Burrows was still a child. After being educated at King's School in Canterbury, he was apprenticed to Richard Thompson, a surgeon-apothecary in Rochester, at the age of sixteen. In 1793 he went to London to complete his medical education at Guy's and St Thomas's hospitals. During the following year he qualified as a member of the Company of Surgeons and became a licentiate of the Society of Apothecaries. He then settled in London, where he built an extensive practice at Bloomsbury Square and Gower Street.

Burrows soon became interested in the question of

improving the legal and professional status of general practitioners. He became involved in the effort to reform the laws regulating medical practice through raising the standard of the medical education of apothecaries and the exclusion of irregular practitioners, who were a source of competition for general practitioners. In 1794 Burrows became a member of the short-lived General Pharmaceutical Association, the first of the numerous associations set up to try to reform medical practice. On 9 March 1797 Burrows married Sophia (d. 1858), daughter of Thomas Druce of Chancery Lane, London; they had four daughters and five sons, one of whom was Sir George *Burrows (1801–1887).

When the Association of Apothecaries and Surgeon-Apothecaries was formed in 1812 Burrows was appointed its chairman. The association quickly grew and agitated for an act to set up a body to regulate general practice independent of the three established medical corporations: the colleges of physicians and surgeons, and the Society of Apothecaries. Negotiating with the medical establishment and resolving conflicts within the association made Burrows's task extremely difficult. He later recalled that between 1812 and 1815 he had attended 130 committee meetings and had personally answered 1500 letters. In addition to this, with William Royston he started a monthly journal, *London Medical, Surgical, and Pharmaceutical Repository*, in 1814, and published *Observations on the Comparative Mortality of London and Paris* in 1815. Burrows's efforts finally bore fruit in the Apothecaries' Act 1815, which by and large regulated the licensing of apothecaries. The association expressed its gratitude to Burrows by making him a handsome present of 500 guineas. Even so, the act was not exactly what Burrows and his colleague wanted. Burrows became deeply disillusioned at the nepotistic way in which the act, especially its licensing procedure, was enforced by the Society of Apothecaries. In 1817 he published a *Statement of Circumstances Connected with the Apothecaries' Act* which detailed his disagreements with the society.

Burrows retired from general practice about 1816 and began the second phase of his career, this time as a specialist in the treatment of insanity. As such, he showed the same energy and industry as he did as a general practitioner, becoming engaged both in the scientific and the social-legislative sides of the subject. Two short tracts in 1819 and 1820 were followed by a comprehensive volume, *Commentaries on the Causes, Forms, Symptoms and Treatment, Moral and Medical, of Insanity* (1828), which received general approval and was translated into German. This work shows Burrows's wide-ranging clinical experience and his leaning towards somatic understanding of mental illness. He became MD at St Andrews in 1824, and a fellow of the Royal College of Physicians in 1839. He was also regularly called for as an expert alienist in medical-legal issues, in which he often gave a competent and forceful performance. Burrows's psychiatric practice flourished, too, no doubt thanks to his own industry and the extensive contacts he had cultivated within the medical profession. At first he kept a small asylum at Chelsea, but in 1823 he established a large and well-equipped retreat at Clapham, Surrey. His fortunes, however, suffered greatly and irrevocably towards the end of 1829 when he was involved in two successive cases of wrongful confinement involving Freeman Anderdon and Edward Davies. Although in neither case did Burrows act out of any ill intent he was painted as an unscrupulous mad-doctor in newspapers and journals. The *Quarterly Review* coined the phrase 'burrowsed', meaning wrongfully confined. Despite mounting a defence in *A Letter to Sir Henry Halford* (1830), Burrows's practice was badly damaged and he largely withdrew from work as an alienist. He died at his home, 18 Upper Gower Street, London, on 29 October 1846.

AKIHITO SUZUKI

Sources *London Medical Directory* (1847), 189–93 · I. Loudon, *Medical care and the general practitioner, 1750–1850* (1986) · *GM*, 1st ser., 67 (1797), 523 · d. cert. · *DNB* · Burke, *Peerage* (1879) [Sir George Burrows] · P. J. Wallis and R. V. Wallis, *Eighteenth century medics*, 2nd edn (1988)
Archives RCP Lond. | LUL, Brougham MSS
Likenesses J. G. Middleton, oils, Apothecaries Hall, London

Burrows, Herbert (1845–1922), socialist organizer, was born on 12 June 1845 in Redgrave, Suffolk, the son of Amos Burrows, tailor and Chartist leader, and his wife, Ann, formerly Thompson. He educated himself using Cassell's shilling handbooks, and became a pupil teacher at the age of thirteen. In 1872 he entered Cambridge University as a non-collegiate student but did not take a degree. Between school and Cambridge he worked as an excise officer in Norwich, Barnet, and Blackburn, and he continued in the Inland Revenue service until 1907, when he resigned to concentrate on voluntary activities.

Burrows moved to London in 1877, and by the early 1880s was active in the National Secular Society and the Social and Political Education League, for which he lectured regularly to radical and working men's clubs. He became vice-president of the Manhood Suffrage League, the most important of these clubs. In 1881 he joined H. M. Hyndman in forming the Democratic Federation, which in 1884 became the Social Democratic Federation, the first important socialist organization in Britain. He was appointed its treasurer in 1883, supported its overt commitment to socialism in 1884, and was one of its best-known propagandists. He wrote articles for its newspaper, *Justice*, often using the pseudonym C. V. He helped the federation to organize demonstrations against unemployment throughout the mid-1880s, and, when these climaxed in clashes with police during the riots of 1887, he represented it on the executive of the Law and Liberty League, formed to promote popular control of the police. There were moments of light relief. In December 1887 he wrote a sermon which socialists wanted the bishop of London to preach; as the sermon was reprinted in the labour and national press of America, so its origin was lost, and the impression given that the bishop really had resigned to commit himself to socialism. Burrows played a particularly important role within the federation because of his links with radicals and secularists, its main recruiting grounds. These links were especially notable in Tower

Hamlets, where he stood unsuccessfully as a candidate in the 1885 election to the London school board.

Throughout the 1880s Burrows complained about wage levels and working conditions for unskilled women. In July 1888 he and Annie Besant organized a successful strike of match girls at Bryant and May, which attracted much publicity and widespread sympathy. The strike led to the formation of the Union of Women Matchmakers, with Burrows as its treasurer. The union, with 800 members, was the largest women's trade union in England at the time. Furthermore, the success of the strike, and the emergence of the union, helped to inspire the new unionism of the 1890s. Here too Burrows was not idle; he promoted unionization among chain makers, mat makers, omnibusmen, silk weavers, and others. He remained active in the Women's Trade Union League and the Women's Industrial Council until 1917.

Within the federation Burrows stood out for the peculiarly ethical nature of his socialism. He came from a nonconformist family, and helped found a Unitarian church in Cambridge, before drifting towards secularism. His socialism incorporated aspects of his search for a spiritual and moral basis to life. He thought the weakness of most socialism lay in its crude materialism and consequent overemphasis on social conditions. He wanted to temper this crude materialism with an ethical revolt against individualism: a revolt to inspire a genuine, social democracy characterized by the abolition of class interests, and the recognition of the duties of individuals to the social whole. He pursued his spiritual and ethical concerns as an Appointed Lecturer for the South Place Ethical Society; as a member of the Rainbow Circle, a discussion group of social reformers concerned with the ethical basis of progressivism; and, from 1889 onwards, as an active member of the Theosophical Society, and later treasurer of its European section.

Burrows was a fairly tall man, who sported a moustache but was otherwise closely shaven. He usually dressed in a flannel shirt and a tweed suit. Most reports record him being gentle and sympathetic with a naturally graceful manner but a noticeably pessimistic streak. He was a teetotaller, non-smoker, vegetarian, and committed pacifist—a member of the committee of the International Arbitration and Peace Association and the International Arbitration League. He enjoyed travelling, and visited, among other places, France in 1879, America in 1893, south-eastern Europe in 1899, and Bosnia in 1901. Usually he was accompanied by William Clarke, radical journalist and Fabian socialist, a friend from his Cambridge days. He married an American woman whose health was poor, and who died in April 1899. His son and daughter survived him.

The federation was committed to electoral participation. In 1908, and again in 1910, Burrows contested the parliamentary seat of Haggerston, Shoreditch, but he was unsuccessful, polling respectively 986 and 701 votes, behind both the Conservative and Liberal candidates. In 1911 he resigned from the federation (by then the Social Democratic Party) in protest at its adopting resolutions supporting the maintenance of a navy and citizens' army. Besides, his experiences as a parliamentary candidate had convinced him the federation was becoming politically irrelevant because it refused to affiliate to the Labour Party. He intended to spend his last years writing a history of the federation but could not do so because he was stricken with paralysis in April 1917. He died at his home, 90 Sotheby Road, Highbury Park, London, on 14 December 1922.   MARK BEVIR

Sources *Justice* (21 Dec 1922) · *Monthly List* (Jan 1923) · *The Star* (9 Oct 1888) · *The Times* (20 Dec 1922) · M. Freeden, ed., *Minutes of the Rainbow Circle, 1894–1924* (1989) · b. cert. · *CGPLA Eng. & Wales* (1923) **Wealth at death** £662: probate, 8 June 1923, *CGPLA Eng. & Wales*

Burrows, Sir John Cordy (1813–1876), surgeon and local politician, eldest son of Robert Burrows, silversmith, of Ipswich, and his wife, Elizabeth, daughter of James Cordy of London, was born at Ipswich, Suffolk, on 5 August 1813. He was educated at Ipswich grammar school but left it at an early age and became an apprentice to William Jefferson, a surgeon in Framlingham. Burrows next studied at Guy's and St Thomas's hospitals in London. He qualified at the Society of Apothecaries in 1835 and became a member of the Royal College of Surgeons in 1836; he was admitted FRCS in 1852.

In 1837 Burrows moved to Brighton, and for two years he acted as assistant to Edward Dix, a surgeon and distant relative, after which he established a practice of his own and soon became involved with public life. In 1841, along with Dr Turrell, he projected the Royal Literary and Scientific Institution. He also took part in the establishment of the Brighton Mechanics' Institution, of which he was secretary from 1841 to 1857, and afterwards treasurer. He proposed the fountain on the Steine in 1846, raised the money for its erection, and laid out and planted the enclosures near it entirely at his own expense. He then became concerned with the sanitary condition of the town, and under his advice the Health of Towns Act was adopted. He became even better known in 1849 as one of the town committee who purchased the Royal Pavilion from the commissioners of woods and forests for the sum of £53,000.

When the charter for Brighton was obtained in 1854 Burrows was elected for the Pavilion ward. In 1857 he was elected mayor, an office he retained the following year. The high regard in which he was held by the inhabitants of Brighton was shown in 1871, when he was presented with a handsome carriage and a pair of horses, and other gifts. Following a petition to the crown, asking that his services to Brighton might receive public recognition, he was knighted by the queen at Osborne on 5 February 1873.

Burrows was a fellow of the Linnean, Zoological, Geographical, and other learned societies, brigade surgeon of the Brighton artillery corps, and chairman of the lifeboat committee. He was one of the promoters of the extramural cemetery, and at great expense to himself he obtained the order for discontinuing sepultures in the churches, chapels, and graveyards of the town. He

strongly disliked street organ players and itinerant hawkers, none of whom was allowed in his borough in the period during which his will was law.

Burrows married, on 19 October 1842, Jane, daughter of Arthur Dendy of Dorking; she died in 1877, leaving one son, William Seymour Burrows, who succeeded to his father's practice. Sir John Burrows died at his home, 62 Old Steine, Brighton, on 25 March 1876. His interment took place at the extramural cemetery on 1 April, the funeral procession containing 1500 mourners. His statue, erected in the grounds of the Royal Pavilion, was unveiled on 14 February 1878.

G. C. BOASE, *rev.* PATRICK WALLIS

Sources *Medical Times and Gazette* (1 April 1876), 375 · *The Lancet* (1 April 1876), 515 · *The Lancet* (8 April 1876), 548 · *BMJ* (18 March 1876), 426 · *Sussex Daily News* (27 March 1876), 5–6 · V. G. Plarr, *Plarr's Lives of the fellows of the Royal College of Surgeons of England*, rev. D'A. Power, 2 vols. (1930) · *CGPLA Eng. & Wales* (1876) **Archives** W. Sussex RO, letters to duke of Richmond **Likenesses** E. B. Stephens, marble statue, 1878, Royal Pavilion, Brighton, East Sussex · portrait, repro. in *ILN*, 68 (1876), 335 · portrait (after statue by E. B. Stevens), repro. in *ILN*, 72 (1878), 173 **Wealth at death** under £5000: probate, 9 May 1876, *CGPLA Eng. & Wales*

Burrows, Montagu (1819–1905), historian and university administrator, born at Hadley, Middlesex, on 27 October 1819, was the third son of Lieutenant-General Montagu Burrows (1775–1848) and his wife, Mary Anne Pafford, eldest daughter of Joseph Larcom, captain RN, and sister of Sir Thomas Aiskew *Larcom. After attending Kingsmills' Boys' School, Southampton, Burrows entered the Royal Naval College, Portsmouth, as a cadet in August 1832. Two years later, in October 1834, at the age of fifteen, he joined the *Andromache* as a midshipman, and in 1842 he passed through the college as a mate. During his period of active service (1834–46) he was decorated for his part in the bombardment of Acre, in November 1840, which brought Mehmet Ali, the rebellious pasha of Egypt, to terms, and he served under Henry Ducie Chads in suppressing piracy in the Straits Settlements and slave-trading on the west coast of Africa.

In November 1846 Burrows was appointed gunnery lieutenant on the training ship *Excellent*, and, in 1852, he became commander. Immediately on his promotion he decided to study at Oxford. On 13 September 1849, he had married Mary Anna, third daughter of Sir James Whalley Smythe Gardiner, third baronet, of Roche Court, Fareham, and he therefore entered Magdalen Hall, one of the few societies that admitted married men at that time, in 1853. In Michaelmas term 1856 he was placed in the first class of *literae humaniores*, and after little more than four months' further reading and extensive private tuition took a first class in the newly created honour school of law and modern history (Easter term 1857). After graduating Burrows engaged with much success in private teaching, mainly in law and modern history. In 1860 he published *Pass and Class*, a useful handbook to all the Oxford schools (3rd edn, 1866). In 1862 he became a retired post captain, and gave up the navy, believing that his short-sightedness

Montagu Burrows (1819–1905), by James Russell & Sons

and slight deafness would have interfered seriously with his effectiveness as a ship's captain.

At Oxford, Burrows was always active in both church and political affairs. A devout, though moderate, churchman, he was a member of the English Church Union, acting as chairman of the Oxford branch until 1866. He was secretary to the Oxford branch of the Universities' Mission to Central Africa on its foundation in 1859, and acted as joint secretary of the church congress, which held its second meeting at Oxford in 1862. During the same year he materially assisted in the building of the church of Sts Philip and James in north Oxford. Later he actively fought the cause of church denominational schools in Oxford, was for many years president of the Church Schools Managers and Teachers Association, and had much to do with the establishment of the Oxford diocesan conference. He was a member of the committee that founded Keble College in 1870. He wrote regularly for *The Guardian*, and founded two short-lived papers, the *Church and State Review* (1861) and *The Churchman* (1866), which he hoped would form a firmer platform for his views. Burrows's political affiliation was once described as 'militant conservative'. He was a perennially active campaigner for the tory cause in Oxford.

In 1862 Burrows was elected to the Chichele professorship of modern history, which had been founded by the royal commission of 1852. His election was a surprise to himself and others. Stubbs, Freeman, and A. J. Froude, all established historians, were among the candidates. But his candidature was warmly supported by Samuel Wilberforce, bishop of Oxford, and apparently by Gladstone, who was still burgess for the University of Oxford. The school of law and modern history, founded on 23 April 1850, was relatively new and still not firmly established. None of the other more formidable candidates had had any experience of teaching, and in the developing academic context Burrows's reputation as a teacher and as the author of *Pass and Class* carried weight. In his new role, he was effective in helping to develop a pragmatic reassessment of the role of history in higher education, and the basis upon which it should be taught and studied. In his inaugural lecture on 30 October 1862, he argued that the Oxford practice of studying history in the manner of Greats, through commentary on set texts, was rendered anachronistic by the great explosion of historical research. He suggested that the real value of studying history lay not in 'mere acquaintance with a multitude of facts', but in comparing, contrasting, and weighing evidence, which developed a critical habit of mind. Burrows's views were instrumental in generating support for the examination statute of 1864, which enabled students in Oxford to read for the final school of law and modern history directly after moderations without first having to read for the final school of *literae humaniores*, and also for the hebdomadal council revisions of 1869, which separated law from modern history. By 1900 the school of modern history, of which Burrows was chairman between 1889 and 1893, was the largest of the Oxford schools.

Elected a fellow of All Souls in 1870, Burrows wrote and edited fifteen books, published six sets of his lectures, and contributed to the *Dictionary of National Biography*. His published work falls into four main classes: first, general history, arising from his teaching and written predominantly for an undergraduate audience (*History of the Foreign Policy of Great Britain*, 1895); second, naval history (*Cinque Ports*, 1888); third, antiquarian studies (*The Worthies of All Souls*, 1874); and fourth, ecclesiastical polemic (*Parliament and the Church of England*, 1875). Although never regarded as an outstanding historian, Burrows did study original sources, and was created *officier de l'instruction publique* by the French government for his work on the Gascon rolls. Burrows served on the Oxford extension committee which led to the foundation of the society of non-collegiate students in 1868. Owing to increasing deafness, he transferred his professorial work to a deputy in the summer of 1900. He remained active in university, college, and city affairs until his death on 10 July 1905 at his home, 9 Norham Gardens, Oxford. His wife died soon after, on 3 June 1906. Of their six children, three sons survived their father: the eldest, Edward Henry Burrows (b. 1851), was inspector of schools until his death in 1910.

A. H. JOHNSON, *rev.* PETER R. H. SLEE

Sources *Autobiography of Montagu Burrows*, ed. S. M. Burrows (1908) • C. Oman, *On the writing of history* (1939), 233–4 • M. Burrows, *Inaugural lecture delivered October 30, 1862* (privately printed, Oxford, 1862) • M. Burrows, *History of the family of Burrows* (1877) • P. R. H.

Slee, *Learning and a liberal education: the study of modern history in the universities of Oxford, Cambridge and Manchester, 1800–1914* (1986), 86–9, 45–52, 95–6 · private information (2004) [J. S. G. Simmonds]
Archives All Souls Oxf., letters to Sir W. R. Anson · BL, letters to F. J. Baigent, Add. MS 39985
Likenesses J. Russell & Sons, photographs, repro. in *Autobiography of Montagu Burrows [see illus.]*
Wealth at death £42,707 12s. 7d.: probate, 18 Aug 1905, *CGPLA Eng. & Wales*

Burrows, Ronald Montagu (1867–1920), classical scholar and university principal, was born in Rugby, Warwickshire, on 16 August 1867, the youngest of the three sons of the Revd Leonard Francis Burrows, a master at Rugby School and later rector of Limington, Somerset, and his wife, Mary Vicars (d. 1886). He was educated at Charterhouse School and at Christ Church, Oxford, where he held a scholarship and took firsts in classical honour moderations (1888) and *literae humaniores* (1890). From 1891 to 1897 he was assistant to the professor of Greek at Glasgow University. In 1892 he married Una Geraldine, daughter of Charles John Ridgeway, later bishop of Chichester. They had no children.

In 1898 Burrows was appointed professor of Greek at University College, Cardiff, moving to Manchester University as Hulme professor of Greek in 1908. In 1907 he published *The Discoveries in Crete and their Bearing on the History of Ancient Civilization*, which was well received by contemporary scholars, including Arthur Evans. A Christian socialist (and lifelong speculator on the stock exchange), Burrows, during his travels and archaeological expeditions, acquired a fascination for the history and politics of modern Greece. He became an Oxford DLitt in 1910.

Like many of his contemporaries Burrows was bowled over by the charismatic personality of Eleutherios Venizelos, the Greek politician. His enthusiastic championing of the Greek, and more particularly the Venizelist, cause found its fullest expression during his energetic and popular principalship of King's College, London, between 1913 and 1920. A founder in 1913 of the Anglo-Hellenic League, he wrote numerous articles supporting Greek territorial claims and upholding Venizelos in his feud with King Constantine I. With R. W. Seton-Watson, a colleague at King's, Burrows formulated in the autumn of 1915 the unsuccessful scheme, which was taken up by the Foreign Office, to lure Greece into the First World War on the side of the entente through the offer of Cyprus. So closely did Burrows identify with Venizelos that the Greek statesman invited him in 1916 to act as the 'semi-official' representative in London of his breakaway provisional government in Salonika.

With Seton-Watson, Burrows was instrumental in the establishment in 1915 of the School of Slavonic Studies (subsequently the School of Slavonic and East European Studies of the University of London). This became a powerhouse of academic propaganda in favour of self-determination for the peoples of eastern Europe. Thomas Garrigue Masaryk (subsequently president of Czechoslovakia) was appointed a professor in the school and, in October 1915, delivered a highly influential lecture entitled 'The problem of small nations in the European crisis'.

Besides his pioneering support for Russian and east European studies, Burrows was also responsible for the establishment of the Cervantes chair of Spanish and the Camoens chair of Portuguese. His most cherished foundation, however, was the Koraes chair of modern Greek and Byzantine history, language, and literature which was endowed by well-to-do Anglo-Greeks, by Venizelos himself, and by the Greek government. Burrows lived long enough to secure the appointment of Arnold Toynbee to the chair in 1919. But his death in the principal's residence at King's College, Strand, London, on 14 May 1920, at the early age of fifty-two, spared him the furious controversy that arose when the donors sought Toynbee's removal on political grounds.

A romantic philhellene to the end, in a letter written on his deathbed Burrows expressed his 'boundless faith' in Venizelos ('my Pericles') and his love for Hellas. Burrows was one of the progenitors of 'area studies' in Britain. His enthusiastic and entrepreneurial promotion of these studies, however, was combined with a political naïvety that blinded him to the problems that can arise from reliance on external sources of funding in politically charged fields of study.   RICHARD CLOGG, rev.

Sources G. Glasgow, *Ronald Burrows: a memoir* (1924) · R. Clogg, *Politics and the academy: Arnold Toynbee and the Koraes chair* (1986)
Archives King's Lond., college archives
Likenesses Elliott & Fry, photograph, repro. in Glasgow, *Ronald Burrows*, frontispiece · photographs, repro. in Glasgow, *Ronald Burrows*, 8, 18, 66, 274
Wealth at death £12,868 8s. 9d.: probate, 8 July 1920, *CGPLA Eng. & Wales*

Burscough, Robert (1650/51–1709), Church of England clergyman, the son of Thomas Burscough, was born at Cartmel, Lancashire. No details of his parents are known, but in 1695 he asked of Anthony Wood only that he be remembered as one 'born of honest parents', a request he was induced to ask 'by the sense I have of their love and care for me' (Bodl. Oxf., MS Wood F40, fol. 329). He entered Queen's College, Oxford, in 1668 aged seventeen, graduated BA in 1672, and was created MA in 1682. In 1681 he was presented by Charles II to the vicarage of Totnes, Devon, in succession to John Prince, author of *The Worthies of Devon* (1701).

In 1692 Burscough wrote *A Treatise of Church Government*, in response to Richard Burthogge's *Nature of Church Government Freely Discussed* of the same year. Burscough refuted Burthogge's claim that episcopacy was a 'prudential' or 'alterable' thing, arguing instead that bishops were of a 'Divine original'. He later claimed that this work was forced out of his hand 'in a hurry by the importunity of my enemies' and that he was made to put his name to it 'by the importunity of my friends' (Bodl. Oxf., MS Wood F. 40, fol. 328). His work provides evidence of the survival of theories of *jure divino* episcopacy but, in spite of his belief that the spiritual jurisdiction of bishops 'came out of the hands of Christ and his apostles' (Burscough, *Treatise of*

Church Government, 5), Burscough had no apparent problem submitting to the temporal jurisdiction of William III. He respected the learning of some nonjurors but believed that the controversy over the new oaths of allegiance had damaged the church, and he sided with Humfrey Hody in supporting giving obedience to William's bishops.

Burscough also published *A Discourse of Schism* (1699) in which he accused nonconformists who had set up separate congregations after the Toleration Act of 1689 of departing from communion with the universal church. His attack was focused not on those dissenters who scrupled at the liturgy and ceremonies of the Church of England but on those who before 1689 had conformed with the church but had deserted it. He refuted John Owen's argument that only divisions within a particular church, not a separation from it, constituted schism by citing the Novatian and Donatist heresies of Constantine's time. This provoked replies from Humfrey Smith and Samuel Stodden, which in turn Burscough answered in two further pamphlets. He also wrote the preface for his friend Zachary Mayne's *Sanctification by Faith Vindicated* (1693). *A Vindication of the Twenty-Third Article of Religion* (1702) has also been ascribed to him but this seems to have been written by William Thornton, principal of Hart Hall, Oxford.

Burscough was made a prebendary of Exeter Cathedral in 1701 and archdeacon of Barnstaple in 1703. In 1705 he was appointed rector of Cheriton Bishop, Devon. On 18 June 1704 at Totnes he married Joane Tucker (it is not known whether this late marriage was his first). He was buried at Bath on 29 July 1709. Anthony Wood described him as 'one of the most truly ingenious, learned and pious of all the ministers in the world' (Bodl. Oxf., MS Rawl. D. 912, fol. 585b). His fine library, rich in medieval manuscripts, was made great use of by Prince in compiling his *Worthies of Devon* and is now part of the Harley collection in the British Library.   EDWARD VALLANCE

Sources Bodl. Oxf., MS Wood F. 40, fols. 328–9 · Foster, *Alum. Oxon.* · T. C. Hughes, 'Some notes on the vicars of Totnes', *Report and Transactions of the Devonshire Association*, 32 (1900), 455–6 · *DNB* · R. Burscough, *A treatise of church government* (1692) · R. Burscough, *A discourse of schism; addressed to those dissenters who conformed before the toleration* (1699) · *IGI*
Archives BL, HL MS 3778, fols. 161–2 · BL, HL MS 3780, fol. 12 | BL, Harley MSS · Bodl. Oxf., MS Rawlinson D. 912, fol. 585b · Bodl. Oxf., MS Rawlinson J. 42, fol. 65 · Bodl. Oxf., Wood MS F. 40, fols. 328–9
Wealth at death substantial library: *DNB*; J. Prince, *The worthies of Devon* (1701), 600; BL Harley MSS, catalogue

Burstall, Sara Annie (1859–1939), headmistress, was born in Aberdeen on 2 November 1859. She was the eldest child, and only daughter, of Henry Abraham Burstall and his wife, Annie Hepzibah King. Her father was the Aberdeen agent of a London firm, and was in charge of three granite quarries and the transport of the stone by sea to England. The family were members of the Church of England and attended what was called the English Chapel because the episcopal churches in Scotland were not then unified. In 1871 Henry Burstall was made redundant and returned with his family to London, where he tried to set himself up as a house builder; but he gave up the business in the late 1870s when he inherited a family legacy. His wife came from a Devon family, and was described by her daughter as an independent woman who had been involved with the Chartist movement, and had attended lectures on hygiene at one of the first mechanics' institutes to provide classes for women. Sara Burstall's two brothers were apprenticed to a firm of marine engineers in London and attended night school to gain engineering qualifications.

The family was relatively poor after 1871, and Sara Burstall's educational success was based on winning scholarships. In her early years she had a governess and then attended Dr Lyon's Union Street Scottish Academy in Aberdeen, a mixed school. In London she went to Camden School for Girls, the lower-middle-class school founded by Frances Mary Buss for families unable to pay the fees at the North London Collegiate School. At Camden, where Emma J. Elford was headmistress, she was taught divinity, arithmetic, English, history, geography, and French, and a limited amount of Latin in her final year. At fifteen she took the Cambridge junior local examinations, and did so well that she won a scholarship to the North London Collegiate School, which she entered in 1875; Miss Buss was the headmistress of the school she had founded. Here Sara Burstall specialized in mathematics (well taught by Sophie Bryant), and became the joint head girl with Charlotte Angas Scott. In 1878, she sat the London University's general examination for women, and won a scholarship to Girton College, Cambridge. There were only six students in her year, including Hertha Marks (later Ayrton). They were the generation who started the Girton College fire brigade, which was lampooned by *Punch* but which was an entirely sensible response to the college's geographical isolation. She read for the mathematical tripos although she wanted to change to history; the college insisted she continue with maths, and presented her for the last winter tripos in 1881–2. She reports that she had lost motivation, was stale, and 'just lost my First'; but she received a letter of commiseration from Emily Davies.

In 1882 Sara Burstall returned to the North London Collegiate School as an assistant mistress on a salary of £120 per annum, at the same time attending teacher-training classes under the auspices of the College of Preceptors. Miss Buss encouraged her staff to take the opportunity presented by the opening of London degrees to women in 1878, and Sara Burstall graduated BA in history in 1884 and obtained a London diploma in divinity in 1886. She began her long career as an activist in teachers' organizations in 1884 when she became involved with the Assistant Mistresses' Association and the Teachers' Guild. In 1888 she set up her own independent household, which she maintained until her retirement. She and a friend rented one of her father's properties and let rooms to other ladies active in education (as teachers or students). In 1893 she travelled to the USA, to attend the world fair in Chicago and to study female education, funded by a travel scholarship from the Gilchrist Education Trust. Her research led to her first book, *The Education of Girls in America*, published in 1894. In that same year Miss Buss died and Sophie Bryant became headmistress of North London Collegiate, with Sara Burstall as her deputy.

In 1898, at the age of thirty-eight, Sara Burstall became headmistress of the Manchester High School for Girls, on the retirement of Elizabeth Day who had held the position since the foundation of the school in 1874. Like others of her generation of headmistresses, Sara Burstall was faced with girls who were not academically brilliant, and not enthusiastic to learn classics and mathematics, alongside those who were the potential university entrants, and for whom the pioneer schools had been founded. Secondary education was becoming normal for upper-middle and middle-class girls, but not all of them were scholars. To meet their needs, she designed courses in domestic subjects (cookery, laundry, needlework) and in secretarial skills (bookkeeping, shorthand, and Spanish) to run parallel to the academic courses for the university aspirants. Her phrase for these two groups was 'express trains and slow trains'. Her introduction of home management and other domestic subjects into the curriculum for middle-class girls was a retreat from the insistence of the pioneer generation of headmistresses on a strictly academic curriculum. She believed this was necessary in order to attract a substantial number of fee-paying pupils aged over fifteen, and was better suited to many girls' abilities. But the policy was controversial in her own time, and remains so a century later. It was either a sensible adjustment to the interests of non-academic girls or a betrayal of everything feminist educators had spent fifty years campaigning to achieve.

Manchester high school grew and prospered during Sara Burstall's period of office. She was also prominent in other educational activities. In 1903, she became one of three women members of the newly formed education committee of Manchester city council, where she initiated the appointment of a woman inspector of infant schools, and the earmarking for girls of two of the four local-authority university scholarships. In 1907–8, she took sabbatical leave and again visited the USA to do the research for her book *Impressions of American Education in 1908*. In 1909, she was elected president of the Association of Headmistresses of Public Secondary Schools (AHM), serving until 1911. During this period of intense debate about the curriculum for girls, the AHM gave evidence to the government consultative committee which produced the *Report on Practical Work in Secondary Schools*, and stressed the importance of domestic subjects in the female curriculum.

Sara Burstall regarded the period from 1908 to 1914 as the peak of her career. Depressed by the miseries of the 1914–18 war, and the educational and social changes of the post-war period, she retired from Manchester high school in the school's jubilee year, 1924. In that year she became a magistrate in Manchester, but resigned in 1927, feeling, she said, that married women were better suited to the work. In 1925 she was the first woman to be appointed to a

Colonial Office advisory committee, that on native education in Africa. At this period she moved away from Manchester so that she would not impede her successor as headmistress; she lived in Derby before settling in London in 1931. She published her autobiography in 1933. The last of her seven books was a biography of Miss Buss, published in 1938. Sara Burstall died at her home, 46 Stevenage Road, Fulham, in London, on 26 March 1939.

SARA DELAMONT

Sources S. A. Burstall, *Retrospect and prospect: sixty years of women's education* (1933) · K. T. Butler and H. I. McMorran, eds., *Girton College register, 1869–1946* (1948) · d. cert. · *CGPLA Eng. & Wales* (1939) **Likenesses** G. Tydernan, portrait, Manchester High School for Girls **Wealth at death** £1286 3s. 1d.: probate, 5 June 1939, *CGPLA Eng. & Wales*

Bursted [Berstede], **Sir Walter of** (*fl.* 1253–1266), administrator and justice, was a small landholder in Kent, and appears to have taken his name from Bursted in the parish of Bishopsbourne, a few miles south-east of Canterbury. But he had estates elsewhere in the county, and is first recorded, in 1253, as holding half a knight's fee in Ewell of the bishop of Rochester. Nothing is known of his parentage or early career, but by 1255 he had entered the service of the locally important Cobham family, and represented Reginald of Cobham, who was then sheriff of Kent, at that year's eyre in the county. In May 1256 he answered for Cobham at the exchequer, and remained under-sheriff until Cobham's death in December 1257, when he was promoted to the shrievalty. When Nicholas de Molis was appointed sheriff in March 1258, Bursted reverted to being under-sheriff. Perhaps because he was still holding office in the county, Bursted came relatively unscathed through proceedings held in Kent by the justiciar, Hugh Bigod (d. 1266), in 1259, with only few and relatively trivial offences being alleged against him. But even in the inquiries recorded on the hundred rolls in the mid-1270s, long after he had left office, little was said to his discredit.

Administrative experience had clearly brought legal expertise. In February 1261 Bursted was one of four justices commissioned to deliver Maidstone gaol, and in the following year he was appointed a justice on eyre, one of the colleagues of Martin of Littlebury in the midlands and south-east, with a yearly salary of 40 marks. On 1 January 1263 he received a robe as one of the king's justices, and was appointed to accompany Littlebury on eyre in Lincolnshire. He may have owed his promotion in part to his perceived loyalty to the king at a time of political crisis, since on 12 July 1262 he was appointed keeper of Dover Castle, then under royal control. He was certainly regarded as a royalist by the king's opponents, who seized and devastated his lands at Wrotham and elsewhere in Kent. Accounts of these attacks refer to him as a knight, but it is not known when, or by whom, he was knighted. In the aftermath of the civil war, in February 1266, Bursted was appointed a justice of the bench, and received the customary robes. He is recorded as taking assizes in Kent, and as inquiring into killings allegedly committed in self-defence, during that year, but he was not appointed to any of the eyres held between 1268 and 1272, so his career may have come to an end by then. It is not known when he died.   HENRY SUMMERSON

Sources Justices Itinerant, Plea Rolls, PRO, JUST 1/361, 873 · Exchequer, Queen's Remembrancer, Memoranda Rolls, PRO, E 159/29 m. 27 · patent rolls, PRO, C 66/76, m. 19 · *Chancery records* · [W. Illingworth], ed., *Rotuli hundredorum temp. Hen. III et Edw. I*, RC, 2 (1818), 200, 219, 224 · A. Hughes, *List of sheriffs for England and Wales: from the earliest times to AD 1831*, PRO (1898), 67 · *Calendar of inquisitions miscellaneous (chancery)*, PRO, 1 (1916), 724, 763 · E. Hasted, *The history and topographical survey of the county of Kent*, 2nd edn, 9 (1800), 333 · I. J. Churchill, R. Griffin, F. W. Hardman, and F. W. Jessup, eds., *Calendar of Kent feet of fines to the end of Henry III's reign*, 5 vols., Kent Archaeological Society Records Branch, 15 (1939–56), 276 · J. Greenstreet, 'Holders of knight's fees in Kent at the knighting of the king's son, *anno* 38 Henry III (AD 1253–4)', *Archaeologia Cantiana*, 12 (1878), 197–237 · C. Johnson, 'A claim to "royal fish" stranded off Dungeness', *Archaeologia Cantiana*, 47 (1935), 103–16 · D. Crook, *Records of the general eyre*, Public Record Office Handbooks, 20 (1982)

Burstow, Henry (1826–1916), singer and bell-ringer, was born on 11 December 1826 at 34 The Bishopric, Horsham, Sussex, the second youngest of nine children. His father, William (*b.* 1781), and mother, Ellen (*d.* 1857) made clay tobacco pipes; their home, in the poorest and roughest part of Horsham, was also a factory and shop. A shoemaker all his working life, Burstow's fame rests principally upon his singing, his importance to the early twentieth-century folk-song revival, and his *Reminiscences of Horsham*, published in 1911. Although Burstow possessed exceptional qualities, it is largely by chance that we are relatively well-informed about his life. He attended a number of Horsham schools until apprenticed to a shoemaker in 1840. Following his apprenticeship he was employed making women's boots at 1*s.* 6*d.* a pair, earning on average 15*s.* a week and working 60–70 hours a week. He declared that he 'never made enough money to warp [his] political convictions' (Burstow, 23).

On 30 April 1855 Burstow married Elizabeth Pratt (1833–1909), the daughter of a Horsham gardener; they had no children. On his wedding day Burstow rang peals with seven other shoemakers, including Warnham musician Michael Turner. He had taken up bell-ringing soon after he was apprenticed, and this became one of his chief pursuits until very late in life. Disappointed that the Horsham ringers had neither the necessary skill nor the inclination to recreate the change-ringing feats of their eighteenth-century predecessors, Burstow developed his skills elsewhere, until the 1860s when, under his leadership, Horsham again became a place where change-ringing records were set. Burstow rang and taught in many Sussex churches, gaining some supplementary income. At one time he would walk 8 miles to Newdigate every Saturday evening, ring for three hours, then 'adjourn to the "Six Bells" Public House for a jollification, drinking and smoking and song singing in turn' (Burstow, 99)—although Burstow himself neither smoked nor drank—before walking home after midnight.

In an age when singing was part of everyday life, Burstow was a respected singer within his community. He

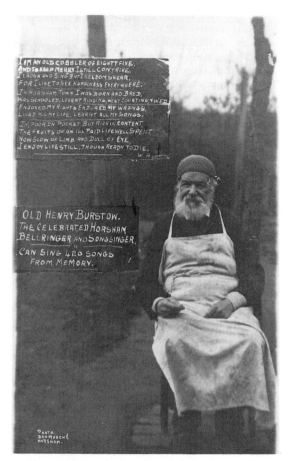

Henry Burstow (1826–1916), by Bonmarché, *c.*1911

knew 420 songs by heart; 84 came from his father, and others from his mother, fellow workers, and bellringers (some of whose names and occupations Burstow recorded in his *Reminiscences*). Some he learned in public houses; others from printed ballad sheets. In 1892–3 he lent his list of songs to Lucy Broadwood, who selected those she considered to be 'of the traditional ballad type' (Broadwood, xi). She noted forty-six at her home at Lyne (in practice Broadwood, or the Horsham organist Herbert Buttifant, took down the tunes, and Burstow wrote out the words later). More were collected by W. H. Gill (1911) and Ralph Vaughan Williams, who noted thirty-one songs between 1903 and 1907, including two which he recorded on the phonograph. Although these recordings were lost, Broadwood published a full transcription of one, which illustrates the traditional singer's ability to adapt a song's tune and phrasing verse by verse (Broadwood, 114–15). A number of Burstow's songs were published; he was 'perhaps the most important singer that the pre-First World War collectors discovered, both to them and to posterity' (Gammon, 184). Ironically the literate, town-dwelling Burstow, learning many of his songs from printed sources, did not readily fit with the collectors' romantic vision of a folk-singer.

By 1907 Burstow and his wife were faced with the prospect of the workhouse. The saddler William Albery organized a fund to provide a weekly pension, and was also responsible for bringing together and publishing the *Reminiscences*, though his name appeared nowhere in the work. Two impressions—of five and of four hundred—were printed, all profits going to Burstow. The book's title is apt. Neither a formal history of Horsham nor an autobiography, it presents a picture of small-town life through the eyes of a working man: the hardships of everyday life; political events (the passing of the 1832 Reform Bill, and the corruption and disorder surrounding elections), and the festivals of the traditional calendar (May day, St Crispin's day, Guy Fawkes's night). It is also an extremely rare example of a traditional singer's words preserved in print, providing details of how songs were transmitted and the social context of music-making.

A religious and political freethinker, convinced of the truth of Darwinism and not inclined to conceal his beliefs, Burstow encountered some prejudice—indeed his views deterred some from contributing to the funds set up to relieve his poverty. However, he seems to have become something of a local celebrity: articles on Burstow appeared in newspapers and magazines, focusing on his singing, bell-ringing, prodigious memory, fascination with figures, and even his atheism. Burstow died on 30 January 1916 at his home in Spencer's Road, Horsham, and was buried on 4 February at Hill's cemetery; several Sussex newspapers carried obituaries. He had lived all his life in Horsham—forty-two years at The Bishopric—spending only six nights away from home.

ANDREW R. TURNER

Sources H. Burstow, *Reminiscences of Horsham*, ed. A. E. Green and T. Wales (1975) · H. Burstow, *Reminiscences of Horsham* (1911) · V. Gammon, 'Popular Music in Rural Society: Sussex, 1815–1914', PhD diss., U. Sussex, 1985 · William Albery collection, Horsham Museum, MSS 875–884 · [W. Albery], 'Henry Burstow, by one who knew him', *West Sussex County Times* (5 Aug 1916) · L. E. Broadwood, ed., *English traditional songs and carols* (1908); repr. (1974) · 'A famous Horsham bellringer', *West Sussex County Times* (16 March 1907) · *West Sussex County Times & Standard* (5 Feb 1916) · *Journal of the Folk Song Society*, 1/4 (1899), 142–76 · Ralph Vaughan Williams MSS, Vaughan Williams Memorial Library, London · S. Godman, 'Henry Burstow: the Horsham singer and bellringer', *Sussex County Magazine*, 28/11 (Nov 1954), 519–22 · parish register, Horsham, W. Sussex RO [baptism], 14/12/1826

Archives Horsham Museum, William Albery collection · Vaughan Williams Memorial Library, London, Ralph Vaughan Williams and Lucy Broadwood MSS

Likenesses M. Salmon, photograph, 1909, repro. in Burstow, *Reminiscences* (1975) · Bonmarché, photograph, *c*.1911, Horsham Museum [*see illus.*] · Sprague & Co., photograph, Horsham Museum · photograph, repro. in R. Palmer, ed., *Folk songs collected by Ralph Vaughan Williams* (1983) · photograph (with his wife), repro. in *Country Life* (10 Feb 1912)

Wealth at death probably negligible; subsisting on state pension plus profits from *Reminiscences*: Burstow, *Reminiscences of Horsham* (1975)

PICTURE CREDITS

Brown, Alexander Crum (1838–1922)—Wellcome Library, London

Brown, Sir Arthur Whitten (1886–1948)—by courtesy of Felix Rosenstiel's Widow & Son Ltd., London, on behalf of the Estate of Sir John Lavery / courtesy of the Trustees of the Royal Air Force Museum

Brown, Christy (1932–1981)—Rex Features

Brown, Elizabeth (1830–1899)—© Royal Astronomical Society Library

Brown, Ford Madox (1821–1893)—courtesy of the Fogg Art Museum, Harvard University Art Museums. Bequest of Grenville L. Winthrop. Photograph: Katya Kallsen © President and Fellows of Harvard College

Brown, Sir George (1790–1865)—© National Portrait Gallery, London

Brown, George Alfred, Baron George-Brown (1914–1985)—© Paul Joyce / National Portrait Gallery, London

Brown, Sir (Ernest) Henry Phelps (1906–1994)—© reserved / News International Syndication; photograph National Portrait Gallery, London

Brown, Horatio Robert Forbes (1854–1926)—University of Bristol, Information Services, Special Collections

Brown, Ivor John Carnegie (1891–1974)—© reserved; collection National Portrait Gallery, London

Brown, John [of Haddington] (1722–1787)—© National Portrait Gallery, London

Brown, John (bap. 1735, d. 1788)—National Museums of Scotland; photograph courtesy the Scottish National Portrait Gallery

Brown, John [of Whitburn] (1754–1832)—The Trustees of the National Museums of Scotland; photograph courtesy the Scottish National Portrait Gallery

Brown, John (1810–1882)—Scottish National Portrait Gallery

Brown, John (1826–1883)—© National Portrait Gallery, London

Brown, Lancelot [Capability Brown] (bap. 1716, d. 1783)—© National Portrait Gallery, London

Brown, Sir (George) Lindor (1903–1971)—© National Portrait Gallery, London

Brown, Pamela Mary (1917–1975)—© Kenneth Hughes / National Portrait Gallery, London

Brown, Peter Hume (1849–1918)—© National Portrait Gallery, London

Brown, Rawdon Lubbock (1806–1883)—Archivio di Stato, Venice

Brown, Sir Robert, first baronet (d. 1760)—The Marquess of Salisbury. Photograph: Photographic Survey, Courtauld Institute of Art, London

Brown, Robert (1773–1858)—by permission of the Linnean Society of London; photograph National Portrait Gallery, London

Brown, Thomas (1778–1820)—© National Portrait Gallery, London

Brown, Sir William, first baronet (1784–1864)—Board of Trustees of the National Museums and Galleries on Merseyside (Walker Art Gallery, Liverpool)

Brown, William Francis (1862–1951)—© National Portrait Gallery, London

Brown, William John (1894–1960)—© National Portrait Gallery, London

Browne, Sir Anthony (c.1500–1548)—© National Portrait Gallery, London

Browne, Anthony, first Viscount Montagu (1528–1592)—© National Portrait Gallery, London

Browne, Arthur (1756?–1805)—by kind permission of the Board of Trinity College Dublin

Browne, Coral Edith (1913–1991)—© Kenneth Hughes / National Portrait Gallery, London

Browne, Edward Harold (1811–1891)—by permission of the Master, Fellows, and Scholars of Emmanuel College in the University of Cambridge

Browne, Hablot Knight (1815–1882)—courtesy Charles Dickens Museum

Browne, Sir Samuel James (1824–1901)—The British Library

Browne, Dame Sidney Jane (1850–1941)—© National Portrait Gallery, London

Browne, Stanley George (1907–1986)—© National Portrait Gallery, London

Browne, Sir Thomas (1605–1682)—© National Portrait Gallery, London

Browne, Thomas Arthur (1870–1910)—© Kay Robertson

Brownell, Sonia Mary [Sonia Orwell] (1918–1980)—UCL, MSSRB, Orwell Archive 3B18

Browning, Elizabeth Barrett (1806–1861)—© National Portrait Gallery, London

Browning, Sir Frederick Arthur Montague (1896–1965)—© reserved; private collection; © reserved in the photograph

Browning, Sir Montague Edward (1863–1947)—© National Portrait Gallery, London

Browning, Oscar (1837–1923)—by kind permission of the Provost and Fellows of King's College, Cambridge

Browning, Robert (1812–1889)—© National Portrait Gallery, London

Brownlow, Richard (1553–1638)—© National Portrait Gallery, London

Brownrigg, Sir Robert, first baronet (1759–1833)—courtesy of the Director, National Army Museum, London

Brownrigg, Thomas Marcus (1902–1967)—© reserved

Bruce, Alexander, second earl of Kincardine (c.1629–1680)—The Earl of Elgin and Kincardine, K.T.

Bruce, Charles Granville (1866–1939)—© National Portrait Gallery, London

Bruce, Sir David (1855–1931)—Wellcome Library, London

Bruce, (Josephine) Esther (1912–1994)—photograph © Sandra Knight / Collection Stephen Bourne

Bruce, George Wyndham Hamilton Knight- (1852–1896)—© National Portrait Gallery, London

Bruce, Henry Austin, first Baron Aberdare (1815–1895)—© National Portrait Gallery, London

Bruce, Sir Henry Harvey (1862–1948)—unknown collection; photograph Sotheby's Picture Library, London / National Portrait Gallery, London

Bruce, James, of Kinnaird (1730–1794)—© National Portrait Gallery, London

Bruce, James, eighth earl of Elgin and twelfth earl of Kincardine (1811–1863)—© National Portrait Gallery, London

Bruce, Stanley Melbourne, Viscount Bruce of Melbourne (1883–1967)—© National Portrait Gallery, London

Bruce, Thomas, seventh earl of Elgin and eleventh earl of Kincardine (1766–1841)—The Earl of Elgin and Kincardine, K.T.

Bruce, Victor Alexander, ninth earl of Elgin and thirteenth earl of Kincardine (1849–1917)—© National Portrait Gallery, London

Bruce, William (1757–1841)—© National Portrait Gallery, London

Bruce, William Speirs (1867–1921)—reproduced by permission of the Scott Polar Research Institute

Brudenell, James Thomas, seventh earl of Cardigan (1797–1868)—© National Portrait Gallery, London

Brudenell, Sir Robert (1461–1531)—© National Portrait Gallery, London

Bruges, William (c.1375–1450)—The British Library

Brummell, George Bryan [Beau Brummell] (1778–1840)—unknown collection; photograph © Christie's Images Ltd

Brunel, Sir (Marc) Isambard (1769–1849)—© National Portrait Gallery, London

Brunel, Isambard Kingdom (1806–1859)—© National Portrait Gallery, London

Brunner, Sir John Tomlinson, first baronet (1842–1919)—University of Liverpool Art Gallery and Collections

Bryan, Margaret (fl. 1795–1816)—© National Portrait Gallery, London

Bryant, Benjamin (1905–1994)—© National Portrait Gallery, London

Bryant, Sophie (1850–1922)—© National Portrait Gallery, London

Bryant, Wilberforce (1837–1906)—Christie's Images Ltd. (2004)

Bryce, David (1803–1876)—Scottish National Portrait Gallery

Bryce, James, Viscount Bryce (1838–1922)—© National Portrait Gallery, London

Bryden, Beryl Audrey (1920–1998)—photograph David Redfern / Redferns

Brydges, Sir Harford Jones, first baronet (1764–1847)—© reserved

Brydges, James, first duke of Chandos (1674–1744)—James Brydges, 1st Duke of Chandos, n.d., Michael Dahl / The Berger Collection at the Denver Art Museum, TL-17970 / © Denver Art Museum 2004

Brydon, William (c.1811–1873)—© National Portrait Gallery, London

Brzeska, Henri Alphonse Séraphin Marie Gaudier- (1891–1915)—© National Portrait Gallery, London

Bucer, Martin (1491–1551)—© National Portrait Gallery, London

Buchan, Charles Murray (1891–1960)—Getty Images – Hulton Archive

Buchan, John, first Baron Tweedsmuir (1875–1940)—Scottish National Portrait Gallery

Buchan, William (1728/9–1805)—© Copyright The British Museum

Buchanan, Claudius (1766–1815)—© National Portrait Gallery, London

Buchanan, George (1506–1582)—© National Portrait Gallery, London

Buchanan, George (1890–1955)—© National Portrait Gallery, London

Buchanan, Sir George William (1854–1924)—© National Portrait Gallery, London

Buchanan, Sir John Scoular (1883–1966)—© National Portrait Gallery, London

Buchanan, Robert (1813–1866)—© National Portrait Gallery, London

Buchanan, Robert Williams (1841–1901)—© National Portrait Gallery, London

Buchanan, Walter John (1890–1957)—courtesy Kobal

Buchman, Frank Nathan Daniel (1878–1961)—© National Portrait Gallery, London

Buck, Adam (1759–1833)—Yale Center for British Art, Paul Mellon Collection

Buck, Samuel (1696–1779)—© National Portrait Gallery, London

Buckeridge, John (d. 1631)—The President and Fellows of St John's College, Oxford

Buckingham, James Silk (1786–1855)—The Royal Geographical Society, London

Buckland, William (1784–1856)—unknown collection; photograph Library of Department of Geology and Mineralogy, Oxford / National Portrait Gallery, London

Buckland, William Warwick (1859–1946)—reproduced by kind permission of the Master and Fellows of Gonville and Caius College, Cambridge, and the Estate of the Artist / Photograph: Christopher Hurst

Buckle, George Earle (1854–1935)—© National Portrait Gallery, London

Buckle, Henry Thomas (1821–1862)—© National Portrait Gallery, London

Buckler, Benjamin (1716/17–1780)—All Souls College, Oxford

Buckmaster, Maurice James (1902–1992)—© News International Newspapers Ltd.

Buckmaster, Stanley Owen, first Viscount Buckmaster (1861–1934)—© National Portrait Gallery, London

Buckton, Raymond William (1922–1995)—Getty Images – Hulton Archive

Budgen, Nicholas William (1937–1998)—© News International Newspapers Ltd

Bufton, Eleanor (1842–1893)—© National Portrait Gallery, London

Bugg, Francis (1640–1727)—© National Portrait Gallery, London

Buhler, Robert (1916–1989)—© courtesy the Artist's Estate / Bridgeman Art Library; collection Austin Desmond Fine Art

Buissière, Paul (d. 1739)—© The Royal Society

Bülbring, Edith (1903–1990)—Godfrey Argent Studios / Royal Society

Bull, George (1634–1710)—© National Portrait Gallery, London

Bull, Joan (supp. fl. 1928–1946)—Evening Standard; collection University of Kent at Canterbury

Bull, John (1559x63–1628)—Faculty of Music, University of Oxford; photograph © National Portrait Gallery, London

Bull, John (supp. fl. 1712–2000)—© Copyright The British Museum

Bullar, John (1778–1864)—Sotheby's Picture Library, London; photograph National Portrait Gallery, London

Bullard, Sir Reader William (1885–1976)—© National Portrait Gallery, London

Bullein, William (c.1515–1576)—© National Portrait Gallery, London

Bullen, Arthur Henry (1857–1920)—© National Portrait Gallery, London

Buller, Charles (1806–1848)—© National Portrait Gallery, London

Buller, Sir Francis, first baronet (1746–1800)—© National Portrait Gallery, London

Buller, Sir Redvers Henry (1839–1908)—© National Portrait Gallery, London

Buller, Reginald Edward Manningham-, first Viscount Dilhorne (1905–1980)—© National Portrait Gallery, London

Buller, Sir Walter Lawry (1838–1906)—Collection of the Museum of New Zealand, Te Papa Tongarewa (B.041113)

Bullock, William (b. in or before 1667, d. 1742)—© Copyright The British Museum

Bulmer, (George Henry) Bertram (1902–1993)—© News International Newspapers Ltd

Bulwer, (William) Henry Lytton Earle, Baron Dalling and Bulwer (1801–1872)—© National Portrait Gallery, London

Bulwer, John (bap. 1606, d. 1656)—© National Portrait Gallery, London

Bunbury, Henry William (1750–1811)—© National Portrait Gallery, London

Bunbury, Selina (1802–1882)—National Gallery of Ireland

Bunn, Margaret Agnes (1799–1883)—© National Portrait Gallery, London

Bunsen, Sir Bernard de (1907–1990)—© National Portrait Gallery, London

Bunting, Jabez (1779–1858)—© National Portrait Gallery, London

Bunting, Sir Percy William (1836–1911)—© National Portrait Gallery, London

Bunyan, John (bap. 1628, d. 1688)—© National Portrait Gallery, London

Burchell, William John (1781–1863)—© National Portrait Gallery, London

Burckhardt, Johann Ludwig (1784–1817)—© National Portrait Gallery, London

Burder, George (1752–1832)—© National Portrait Gallery, London

Burdett, Sir Francis, fifth baronet (1770–1844)—© National Portrait Gallery, London

Burdett, Sir Henry Charles (1847–1920)—© National Portrait Gallery, London

Burdett, Jane, Lady Burdett (d. 1637)—unknown collection; photograph Sotheby's Picture Library, London / National Portrait Gallery, London

Burdett, Peter Perez (1734/5–1793)—National Gallery of Prague

Burge, Hubert Murray (1862–1925)—© National Portrait Gallery, London

Burgers, Thomas François (1834–1881)—© reserved

Burges, Sir James Bland, first baronet (1752–1824)—© National Portrait Gallery, London

Burges, William (1827–1881)—© National Portrait Gallery, London

Burgess, Daniel (1646–1713)—© National Portrait Gallery, London

Burgess, Guy Francis de Moncy (1911–1963)—© National Portrait Gallery, London

Burgess, Thomas (1756–1837)—by permission of the President and Scholars, Corpus Christi College, Oxford; photograph National Portrait Gallery, London

Burgess, Thomas (1791–1854)—© National Portrait Gallery, London

Burgh, Hubert de, earl of Kent (c.1170–1243)—The British Library

Burgh, Ulick John de, first marquess of Clanricarde (1802–1874)—© National Portrait Gallery, London

Burgh, Walter Hussey (1742–1783)—by courtesy of the National Gallery of Ireland

Burghersh, Bartholomew, the elder, second Lord Burghersh (d. 1355)—Lincoln Cathedral Library

Burgoyne, John (1723–1792)—© The Frick Collection, New York

Burgoyne, Sir John Fox, baronet (1782–1871)—© National Portrait Gallery, London

Burke, Sir (John) Bernard (1814–1892)—© National Portrait Gallery, London

Burke, Edmund (1729/30–1797)—private collection; photograph © National Portrait Gallery, London

Burke, Thomas Henry (1829–1882)—National Gallery of Ireland

Burke, Ulick, marquess of Clanricarde (1604–1658)—© National Portrait Gallery, London

Burke, William (1728x30–1798)—© reserved

Burke, William (1792–1829)—Scottish National Portrait Gallery

Burkitt, Denis Parsons (1911–1993)—Godfrey Argent Studios / Royal Society

Burnaby, Frederick Gustavus (1842–1885)—© National Portrait Gallery, London

Burnand, Sir Francis Cowley (1836–1917)—© National Portrait Gallery, London

Burnet, Elizabeth (1661–1709)—© National Portrait Gallery, London

Burnet, Sir Frank Macfarlane (1899–1985)—© National Portrait Gallery, London

Burnet, Gilbert (1643–1715)—Wimpole Hall, The Bambridge Collection (The National Trust). Photograph: Photographic Survey, Courtauld Institute of Art, London

Burnet, John (1863–1928)—© National Portrait Gallery, London

Burnet, Thomas (c.1635–1715)—© reserved

Burnett, Frances Eliza Hodgson (1849–1924)—© National Portrait Gallery, London

Burnett, Dame Ivy Compton- (1884–1969)—© National Portrait Gallery, London

Burnett, James, Lord Monboddo (bap. 1714, d. 1799)—Scottish National Portrait Gallery

Burnett, Sir Robert Lindsay (1887–1959)—© National Portrait Gallery, London

Burney, Charles (1726–1814)—© National Portrait Gallery, London

Burney, Charles (1757–1817)—private collection

Burney, Frances (1752–1840)—© National Portrait Gallery, London

Burnham, Frederick Russell (1861–1947)—© National Portrait Gallery, London

Burns, John Elliott (1858–1943)—© National Portrait Gallery, London

Burns, Robert (1759–1796)—Scottish National Portrait Gallery

Burns, William Chalmers (1815–1868)—© National Portrait Gallery, London

Burra, Edward John (1905–1976)—Maurice Ambler / Camera Press

Burrough, Sir James (1749–1837)—© National Portrait Gallery, London

Burroughes, Jeremiah (bap. 1601?, d. 1646)—© National Portrait Gallery, London

Burrow, Sir James (1701–1782)—© The Royal Society

Burrowes, Peter (1753–1841)—© National Portrait Gallery, London

Burrows, Christine Mary Elizabeth (1872–1959)—Principal and Fellows of St Hilda's College, Oxford

Burrows, Sir George, first baronet (1801–1887)—by permission of the Royal College of Physicians, London

Burrows, Montagu (1819–1905)—© National Portrait Gallery, London

Burstow, Henry (1826–1916)—Horsham Museum (Horsham District Council)